A Look at Tomorrow Today

Leonard Cataldo and Robert Pelletier

Whitford Press
1469 Morstein Road
West Chester, Pennsylvania 19380 U.S.A.

A Look at Tomorrow Today
by Leonard Cataldo and Robert Pelletier

Library of Congress Card Number: 89-50770
International Standard Book Number: 0-914918-94-X

Manufactured in the United States of America

Published by Whitford Press,
A division of
Schiffer Publishing, Ltd.
1469 Morstein Road
West Chester, Pennsylvania 19380
Please write for a free catalog.
This book may be purchased from the publisher.
Please include $2.00 postage.
Try your bookstore first.

Cover painting by Matthew Martelli

Dedication

Dedicated in memory of Albert Einstein, who said, "Long live impudence, it is my guardian angel in this world."

To all those who in search of truth realize that ignorance is the hallmark of tyranny.

Contents

NOTE: All Appendices are reproductions of *The American Ephemeris 1931 to 1980.*

Introduction

This book is about the most important person in the world: YOU. Hundreds of volumes have been written about human behavior throughout the ages by men and women of science in an attempt to unravel the mystery of why people behave as they do. The mystery of what urges behavior to occur as it does remains elusive to even the most careful investigator using the most up-to-date techniques for testing and experimentation.

We offer the suggestion that everyone has the necessary information at hand to solve the dilemma of how to understand oneself.

A mythical story may well help you better understand this problem. Resting in his quarters one day, Jesus was visited by a beggar in garments that were old and soiled as was his person. Jesus welcomed the visitor and listened to his pleas.

"Jesus," he said, "I am hungry and destitute with no place to sleep or rest. I am feverish and pray that my end will come soon to relieve me of this pain and suffering. Though proud, I am begging for help and guidance. I beg of you some miracle to restore dignity to my worthless life."

Jesus instructed his disciple to show the man where he could bathe and ordered the disciple to clean, repair and prepare the garments of this poor unfortunate soul.

Having prepared a table, he later invited the beggar to partake in some food and drink after which he could sleep and rest in peace.

When the beggar awoke Jesus said to him, "Upon the return of your garments you shall take your leave and return here in seven days. During this time you shall have searched yourself thoroughly, looking only to yourself for any assistance you may require in your endeavors. Take sound heed of this advice and instruction. Within seven days you should have found wealth, happiness and health."

Seven days passed, and the beggar returned as instructed. Clothed in the same garments and dirty as in his first visit, he said to Jesus, "You promised wealth, happiness and health for me should I restore my faith in myself. I have done all that is possible to help myself but all to no avail. I am no better for it than I was when last I was here."

"Ah!" said Jesus, "You had only to search yourself and have faith as I instructed and you would have found an abundance of wealth that would have brought happiness and health to you. Had you done this, you would have found this abundance of wealth."

Removing the beggar's outer garments, Jesus showed him where his disciple had hidden some precious gems in the seam of his outer garment during the first visit.

You too have an abundance of wealth hidden within the depths of your own being. With faith in yourself and a willingness to use your potential, you too can gain wealth, happiness and health.

Let's look at Albert Einstein's early years to help explain the foregoing in some detail. Albert never spoke until after his first year. He never laughed or played with toys, games or other children. Albert had a great dislike for soldiers, whom children generally admire. Those close to him as well as his parents thought he was intellectually slow or even retarded. One day an uncle brought Albert a toy compass. His parents and relatives alike were amazed at how such a simple toy could fascinate and capture the attention of this child. Albert's entire nature changed. He started asking many questions about how the compass operated and why.

During his school years he was a problem to his teachers. He disliked the way they forced discipline upon him and directed him on what was and wasn't permissible. They continuously informed him of what levels of authority there were and his place in observing the rules they established. As he became older he became the more of a problem for his teachers. He constantly questioned them and even contradicted their teachings and views. Because of his behavior he was dismissed, and serious consideration was given to sending him to a sanitarium for therapy. Financial losses forced his family to move from Germany, thus saving young Albert from being institutionalized.

It was learned later that Einstein's superior intellect caused his impatience with the learning level of his peers. His fascination with the fields of energy characteristic of the compass indicate that his level of intellectual functioning was far beyond that of his fellow students. The world of science was dazzled when Albert Einstein, at the age of twenty-six, submitted his "Theory of Relativity": E = MC2. This from an individual whose future was most doubtful given his seeming lack of intellectual prowess during his formative years. More detailed reasons for his behavior and his potentials are offered in Chapter 9: Aspect Delineations.

You can examine many more similar cases of this nature as presented in Frank Edwards's book entitled *Strange People*, published by Citadel Press. It is not uncommon for the world to regard those who don't follow expected paths to be strange, different and even of questionable character. The "follow-the-leader" category usually only includes those who believe they have little creative energy or show no self-determination to follow their own inner voices. Differences tend to divide and alienate people from one another, whereas sameness tends to gather them together. Those who are resourceful in their creativity hear the beat of a different drummer and thus plot a course that may be remarkably different from those of others. Yet we offer the view that every individual is a differentiated composite of all the same ingredients that go into every other individual on this planet.

As we progress you will be offered scientific evidence to discern the truth in these works. Though controversial, the subject matter is derived from extensive research that unfailingly supports the value of astrological symbolism in its human application. It is hardly the "belief system" many regard it to be, but a rich source of valuable information about human behavior and the forces urging action in directions that can be determined with a high degree of probability. We urge you to defer an opinion until you have gained sufficient information to form a substantive conclusion.

Within the scientific community absolute truths are comparatively rare but opinions rendered under that banner gain credibility from the masses. This is due to the absolute power structure of science that is intimidating to the person on the street. Yet change does occur and innovations force revisions from previous works and belief structures. An ever-widening field of useful accomplishments result that benefit the public at large. Vast sums of money for research are available to the laboratories found in most universities and institutions.

Whether you realize it or not, there is no one else in this world that is exactly like you, and that makes you very special.

Numerous experiments conducted on babies only minutes old have shown mental abilities that have baffled scientists. From the origin of life to this very moment, every detail of every function of life is stored in your memory bank. If it were possible to put on paper all that is stored in your memory, it would take a warehouse to store the text. It is through this memory and all that now is being programmed into it which makes you function as you do. It is through this memory that you can determine exactly who and what you are, why you are here, where you are going, and how you will accomplish your objectives.

Not even the most technologically advanced computers can match your mental abilities, function with greater speed, or surpass your memory bank. If you are compelled to challenge the validity of the foregoing and reject it without investigation, then this book is not for you. But if you truly care about yourself and your loved ones, then read on, for this book was written especially for you.

We realize that many of you will scoff and say this is absurd, but others with greater vision and understanding will realize the truth as it is presented here.

Someone once very aptly said, "The damned fool always does in the end that which the intelligent person does in the beginning."

The decision is yours to make. Continue reading and learn what you can now or stop and learn it in the end.

Our ends are joined by a common link:
With one we sit, with one we think.
Success depends on which we use.
Heads we win, tails we lose.

--Unknown

Chapter 1
A Moment of Truth

Let us turn for a moment to the world of computers. This may seem insignificant and irrelevant to you, but its relevance to the dynamics of behavior will become obvious as you read on. You may not realize it, but it is because of you that computers were invented. You probably are aware of how modern computers function. Whatever material is programmed into the memory bank of the computer remains there. When any part or all of this material is desired, you type in the correct code and the data programmed for that particular code is presented. There are many kinds of computers with many different programs in many varying categories. It is precisely what the word "program" means: "a plan for future procedure." In the more-advanced technical computers, it is possible to gain access to another person's computer system and retrieve all that is stored in that system. Legislation is to be enacted that will make it a crime to tap into another person's system.

Yale University's Artificial Intelligence Laboratory has in operation thinking computers with assigned names of SAM (Script Applier Mechanism) and PAM (Plan Applied Mechanism).

SAM can scan newspaper stories and reduce them to short summaries, then answer questions pertaining to the stories. This is accomplished by scripts which describe the detailed and appropriate sequence of actions of a particular event. It is all predetermined for well-known everyday situations. By processing large numbers of scripts, Sam now can draw conclusions, fill in inferences from details, and create a linked chain representing what took place in the story. This can be done for almost any situation that one may encounter in everyday life. PAM functions by the knowledge of goals to figure out the intentions of the characters and records the goals of each character. PAM is equipped with many rules about intentions and with words and all their possible uses. PAM then draws conclusions. When given a hypothetical situation, PAM can rewrite any story given and give the point of view of any participants. Inferences can then be drawn by PAM about things that are not mentioned in the original story because of the pre-programming of words and their uses, goals, and intentions.

Take a moment now and think about how your brain draws on and makes conclusions based on previous experiences which were recorded in your memory.

Massachusetts Institute of Technology has a computer named "Eliza" that is capable of conversing with a human operator on any subject from cooking to psychotherapy, including taking the role of the therapist. Eliza answers all questions asked by the patient as well as commenting on the patients' replies. Eliza functions, of course, by a predetermined script.

You shouldn't be too surprised to find these units available to doctors and hospitals. They then could treat more patients in an assembly line procedure. This shouldn't make much difference in the therapy and at the least should make therapy much cheaper. This also should serve as proof of their present predetermined theories employed in therapy.

Psychobiologists are now cooperating with computer specialists in an attempt to test various hypotheses about brain functioning. Computer specialists feel the best way to learn computer designing may come from learning about psychobiology.

We suggest that both fields should be studying this material. As you realize how, when, where, and why the brain was programmed with this infinite knowledge; what brings this knowledge forth; and who has the complete control; you also may realize how much there is to know about yourself that will now be accessible to you.

To paraphrase Dr. Restak in his book entitled *The Brain*, we don't know how the process works, but the fact that it does proves conclusively that what we have previously believed about the brain was wrong. Behavioral psychology as a legitimate explanation of human behavior is a failure and should be quietly buried at a small private funeral limited to B. F. Skinner and other members of the immediate family. In its place we must develop a psychology that is relevant to the everyday world we live in. We don't spend our lives in cages, and an explanation of the subtleties of human behavior based on such models is ludicrous.

With our present-day technology there is no question that a computerized robot can be created that would be indistinguishable from a human being. However perfect this creation may be, its capabilities would be limited to the extent of the programmer's knowledge. The programmer's memory from which he makes his own decisions never can be instituted because even the programmer himself doesn't know what his memory contains. No person truly can know what is stored in his or her memory. The only way to retrieve any of this from the memory is by the same way it was programmed: through his own five senses.

The brain and computers function by the same principle of programming. Recall that the word "program" means "a plan for future procedure." Though they both function through memory, that of the computer is only a minute fraction of the programmer's knowledge. The memory in an individual's brain comes from his own personal experiences and through the evolution in life itself from the beginning.

Necessity always was and still is the mother of invention. The needs were real and the technique for satisfying them was through nature's skillful application which eventually became a science. What once was thought impossible is now reality.

Lyall Watson, biologist and author of *Supernature*, says

> Science no longer holds any absolute truths. Even the discipline of physics, whose laws once went unchallenged, has had to submit to the indignity of an uncertainty principle. In this climate of disbelief, we have begun to doubt even fundamental propositions, and the old distinction between natural and supernatural has become meaningless.
>
> Fifty years ago naturalists were content with the observation that bats catch moths. Then came the discovery that bats produce sounds inaudible to the human ear and use echoes to locate their prey. Now it appears that not only do moths have soundproofing, but that they have ears specifically designed to listen into an approaching enemy transmitter. To counter this advance, bats developed an irregular flight path, which confused the moths until they in turn came up with an ultrasonic jamming device. But bats still catch moths, and it can only be a matter of time before research discovers the next development in this escalating drama of nature. [1]

A public television program describing the importance of our rain forests and what they can do for science gave another fine example of nature's skillful application of necessity.

In the rain forests of Costa Rica a particular species of tree was slowly dying off and would soon be extinct. Investigating, science learned that because of insects that were feeding off its leaves and sap, the trees couldn't keep up with the demand. To counter these killing attacks from all these insects, the trees developed a toxic sap that began killing off the insects. The insects developed an immunity system that protected them from the toxic sap. It has now been discovered that there are armies of killer ants residing within the confines of these trees that attack any and all insects regardless of size and devour them.

For this age period at least, the trees are safe.

Dr. George Gamow, a professor of physics and author of the book *Biography of the Earth* notes, "During the Paleozoic period (150,000,000 B.C.) only reptiles inhabited the earth. During this time, because of the necessity of feeding their babies, the smaller reptiles developed milk-producing organs." [2]

To paraphrase Dr. Richard M. Restak:

> The limbic system is a repository of ancient emotional responses that are pre-logical or unreasonable, if you prefer. These are inherited by us from our less "advanced" ancestors and expressed through the action of those parts of our brain which we share with the early reptiles and early mammals. This implies, in my opinion, that what has been referred to over the centuries as "human behavior" is to a large extent genetically programmed. [3]

The escalating developments of survival techniques between the bats and the moths and the trees of Costa Rica and their insect tenants are common phenomena among all living creatures whether they are vegetable, animal or human.

Some people believe that the lack of formal education must deny them the understanding of how life evolves or that it is too deep a subject to grasp. In fact, the subject matter itself is complex but absolutely fascinating. Viewing some of the nature programs presented by public television should make you aware of the great similarities between all creatures great and small who inhabit this planet. Examine some of these broadcasts and you will realize that the natural cycles of living permeate all living creatures and how these creatures depend on the environmental impulses for their energy. Our world is caught up in this electromagnetic force field.

We can name many personalities from the past who have distinguished themselves by their accomplishments without the seeming advantage of any formal education. Among these are Abraham Lincoln and Andrew Jackson (both U.S. presidents), Stephen Douglas (justice of the Supreme Court of Illinois), Patrick Henry, Daniel Webster, John Jay, Roger Taney, and Salmon Chase (all Supreme Court justices), and Clarence Darrow, the world-famous lawyer who brilliantly defended in the much-heralded Leopold and Loeb murder case in the 1920s. Native intelligence was promoted carefully and utilized to achieve the level of success these persons attained. Native intelligence is common to everyone in varying degrees, but it always is sufficient to allow a ready grasp of the essentials of behavior that is our subject. Scientist Robert Broom once stated that the average workman, quarryman or miner usually has as much mental ability as the average university professor--and often has more enthusiasm in searching for new scientific facts.

With our greatest respect and admiration for the majority of scientists who have devoted their lives to the improvement of mankind, we offer our apologies for the offense that may be taken.

We also feel the need to offer our findings, and for the very same reasons and purposes. Our intentions are not to criticize or condemn but to bring forth the truth. The many critics within the scientific community should be exposed, in the interest of a caring public, because of their arrogance and ignorance.

We do not mean to imply that we are more knowledgeable in any of the scientific fields. Neither do we wish to infer that we know anything whatever about any of them other than what we have learned through reading and studying their findings. We do not qualify ourselves as experts in their fields as they do in our field without the benefit of any studying or reading. We do know and can prove beyond any doubt that when correlating all of their findings we obtain all the necessary data to prove our study which they claim has no merit. We merely will correlate their combined findings as a whole, not in part only, and apply them to human behavior. We believe that to be simple common sense intelligence that we all possess (although not all of us use).

It is necessary that you understand the origin of life and the cycles governing its development. Because of this crucial aspect of our behavior, we will offer some of the scientific evidence supporting this process. We present brief summaries and the approximate dates of the relevant facts. To do this we must begin with the most commonly held opinion on how life itself began on planet Earth.

Approximately two billion B.C. the planet Earth was only a sphere of molten matter with a solid crust forming. Heavy downpours of rain from the then extremely dense atmosphere continuously fell, forming our oceans and cooling the surface of the Earth, which resulted in thicker layers of crust.

Life in the oceans originated because the water being introduced to the organic and inorganic particles formed various chemical compositions and organizations that then evolved into life forms. The form of life was dependent upon the specific chemical composition and organization.

In time the dense atmosphere cleared sufficiently to allow the Sun's energies to penetrate to Earth. Because of these newly supplied energies, chemical compositions and organizations also changed, resulting in yet newer forms of life.

During the Paleozoic period (250,000,000to 200,000,000 B.C.) only ocean life and reptiles inhabited the Earth. It was during this period that milk-producing organs were developed in the smaller reptiles so that they could feed their babies.

All future life evolved from these early reptiles on through to the Cretaceous period (136,000,000 to 65,000,000 B.C.). During this period various forms of life existed, from the smallest shrew to the giant dinosaurs. All present species of life evolved from them, with man himself having evolved from reptile to shrew to homo erectus to present.

Somewhere between the Miocene period (26,000,000 to 5,000,000 B.C.) and the Pliocene period (5,000,000 to 1,800,000 B.C.) man's development originated. From this period, man evolved up to his "knuckle-walking" stage (walking on all fours) to upright walking (homo erectus) of the Pliocene period. As man developed from stage to stage, the brain also was developing in size from a total capacity of 150 to 450 and then 600 cc.

Paleontologists have discovered fossils of jaw bones, skulls, pelvic bones, and other parts of skeletons that they determined (as accurately as possible) to range from one to four million years old. From the pelvic bones they could learn just when the knuckle walkers evolved to upright walking. From the skull cavities they learned of the progressive increase in brain size. From the Pliocene period (5,000,000 to 1,800,000 B.C.) to the Pleistocene period (1,800,000 to 10,000 B.C.) on through to modern man, total brain capacity developed to 2000-plus cc.

Questions arose as to the reasons for these changes. Identical findings were discovered hundreds of miles and even as far as 1000 miles apart. The creatures also varied in height from three and four feet to five and six feet to baffle scientists trying solve this puzzle. The mystery is largely one of one person's refutation of another's findings--and the unwillingness to make any conciliatory comments in the light of new evidence. This attitude reached a point where groups of researchers with differing opinions formed cliques in support of their positions. Some even went so far as to deceive others about the age of some of the more recently discovered fossils and even altered the recorded ages of some others. One scientist went so far as to create his own fossil remains from stolen relics in order to outperform his contemporaries. This fossil is known as the "Piltdown Man."

Richard Leakey gained recognition and fame for discovering a skull (#1470) determined to be between 3.5 and 4 million years old. Later finds by other teams created doubts about #1470--resulting in more specific tests that proved that #1470 could not be more that 1.5 to 2 million years old.

Sir Arthur Keith, premier paleontologist and anthropologist of the British Museum, most arrogantly and persistently insisted on the accuracy of his findings--although he miscalculated by nearly twenty million years!

With the foregoing arrogance, deceit, and egomania that prevailed among some of the most respected men and women in their fields, we therefore must conclude that other areas in which science offers "unimpeachable evidence" must be viewed with tongue in cheek. Such is the case in the subject matter of this book, where science repeatedly has challenged the value of astrology as a useful tool for understanding the dynamics of human behavior.

There should have been no reason for these mysteries, for there really were none. It was only because of all the jealousy, authoritative protocol with their meddling intellects and red tape that no one had the time or the enthusiasm to find the real answers. These attitudes resulted in feuds between the cliques, museums, and contributing organizations--including The National Geographic --who sponsors Richard Leakey, their supernova paleontologist with only a high school education. How could anyone have any enthusiasm in learning the real truth? They had to actually fight "City Hall" to present anything, then attempt to prove it to deaf ears, and at the same time figure out what they could do to acquire another grant for their next expedition.

Before we present our theory, which we have reason to believe was the actual sequence of escalations, we will quote one scientist to another during an experiment. Question: "How can you believe something you can't prove?" Answer: "You accept it as probable if it satisfies the data and if it seems logical. Like evolution, because the theory has been kicked around for so long, it withstood all that violent treatment and yet it is still logical."

We present three possible theories for the distribution of life on Earth.

Life had its origin when organic and inorganic particles were introduced to water and formed specific chemical compositions and organizations. First, we must conclude that life had its origin wherever on this planet these conditions existed, not in any one particular area. Should this be correct it would account for the same types of fossils being found hundreds of miles apart. But would they evolve in the same sequence and cycles? With similar conditions and age periods, why wouldn't they?

Second, should that not be the actual case, then the inundation of the Earth every four million years (as science says occurs) could account for the distribution of these life-giving particles to the various areas. When the waters recede after these periodic inundations, the particles remain, new life forms, and the cycles repeat themselves but in much more advanced states.

Third, the only other logical and probable cause is the migration instinct, which to this day exists in all living creatures, including man.

Any one of the three is logical and probable, with the most likely being the three theories combined, which would account for many of our present-day fears, natural instincts, migrating instincts, and so forth.

The question now arises: Why all the different species of living creatures? If life originated from these particles and water, etc., and only ocean life and reptiles existed, why all the different species from age period to age period? This is a most difficult question to answer in detailed sequence, and especially since there is no possible absolute proof, we only can state what we believe to be factual by sound and logical reasoning. We will be brief but to the point. Through your own intelligence you will be able to elaborate for yourself.

Similar to present-day scientifically proven and accepted facts, mothers who are drug addicts, alcoholics, and so forth change the chemical composition of the fetus and thereby endanger its life. Various infectious diseases cause abnormalities in fetuses as well as those who may contract the disease. Mongoloids all look similar, yet are of different parents. Albinos, though few, do not come from albino parents. There are many more examples with which you are familiar. It is that specific chemical composition and organization that is the deciding factor.

Reptiles, the only life roaming the earth during the Paleozoic period, undoubtedly fed on whatever nourishment was available and probably one another as well. The vegetation at the time and any available drinking water unquestionably was covered and/or saturated with sulphur, volcanic ash, plus various chemicals from all the marsh gasses and the contaminated atmosphere. With a diet consisting of all these combined elements, it was only natural for the babies to be born of different chemical compositions and organizations. This resulted in distorted species being produced. With generation following generation with the same conditions and diets, changes in the chemistry of each of the species continuously resulted in yet more changes of the species. With the undoubtedly extreme temperatures from the hot gases and very warm earth crust and all the sulphur included in their diet and drinking water, it should be no wonder whatever that the Cretaceous period arrived with monstrous creatures such as the dinosaurs. Over the generations and time periods, the atmosphere slowly cleared to allow the Sun's energy to penetrate fully. New vegetation, fruit- and berry-producing plant life, subsiding volcanic activity and marsh gasses, purer drinking water, and the general lessening of contaminants resulted in more stable all-around conditions. The more stable the environment became, the more stable life became. The Miocene period (26,000,000 to 5,000,000 B.C.) followed, bringing the beginning of man's development. The prehistoric elements vanished along with its inhabitants, with all future life being evolved from the now-purer conditioning of the Earth and all its life. During all those periods of time there were no apelike creatures, chimpanzees, monkeys or the like, but only the shrew from which man possibly evolved. It must be considered that up to and including the development of man to his knuckle-walking stage, the brain size of all creatures was at its lowest total capacity, approximately 150 cc.

At this stage in the evolution of man, the only concern was survival and this only to the extent of his search for nourishment and protection from predators. These survival necessities were the only concern and experiences of the brain's abilities. These limited necessities probably explain why the total brain capacity was at its smallest.

With nourishment dwindling and becoming increasingly scarce, knuckle-walking man wasn't very likely reaching the fruits and berries of the higher trees and shrubs. Standing on their hinds became a common factor in order to obtain these much-needed vitals. This is an exercise most animals perform to this day. Because of the scarcity of foodstuffs, the species had to go in search of other areas where they could feast and survive. Traveling to strange areas resulted in more brain programming and abilities due to the different experiences encountered --the routes taken, landscapes, and various obstacles. The creature now had to consider new predators, possibly a different species of man and/or beast, and also protection from them. All of this required standing on their hinds for the use of their forearms. With the senses constantly programming the brain with the slightest change or anything not previously experienced, the creature would react instantly by raising up on his hinds ready for battle. These new experiences necessary for survival became a constant factor in the memory and the abilities of the brain.

There should be no question as to their sexual activities, which resulted in the necessity of a den, cave, or similar covering for the care and protection of their young. While still at the knuckle-walking stage, the dwindling supply of nourishment necessitated the gathering of that which they couldn't reach along with the migrations with their offspring clinging to their backs and stomachs. This resulted in yet more serious difficulties because of the need to stand to pick food, climb trees, hold for balance, provide protection from predators, and so forth. There also should be no question of the numerous and varied obstacles that caused injuries and/or death to the offspring, mother or father, or all of them. The further they had to migrate, the more new experiences encountered for the brain to record and act upon. Combining all of these varied experiences, it shouldn't be difficult to realize that walking on their hinds for long periods of time became necessary for the care and welfare of the young, the carrying of foodstuffs in addition to their young and possibly a weapon for protection. Walking upright was unquestionably the greatest necessity next to survival itself; it was survival.

Because of all these new experiences recorded by the brain, it now had more memory from which to make more creative decisions for survival. The more memory that has to be stored, the larger the brain must grow, and grow it did.

Similar to the escalating dramas of the reptile developing milk-producing organs, the rain forest trees and insects, the bats and the moths and so forth, so it was with man. The necessity to walk upright with a larger and more-advanced brain was crucial to survival. Nature developed in man exactly what was necessary: homo erectus with a larger brain capacity.

New age periods brought new developments and experiences that resulted in greater mental abilities. Continuing on over periods of time, more new experiences resulted in a more-advanced and larger brain in which to store all this new information.

Survival now included not only nourishment and protection for personal survival but also the conservation of these necessities, communication, grouping together for security as well as protection from any intruding predators, companionship, work, and so on. Because of all the previous experiences, the brain now functions with greater capacity, which results in the reasonably civilized society of today.

Through the various evolutionary stages from reptile, shrew, knuckle walker, and upright walker, man became civilized to face the limitations imposed by the conditions of modern times. The sequence of evolutionary cycles remains in place, although the substance and conditions that provoke change are different. What we have become is the product of all that preceded this moment in time.

The cycles can be viewed in a condensed form as follows.

First Cycle: In the beginning man made the observation that he *was*--a living creature aware of the self. The most primitive urge was born and it was the desire to continue living. Survival was of immediate necessity and it had to be dealt with at once.

Second Cycle: The next step for man was to find ways to guarantee his survival. His primary urge was making sure there always was enough nourishment so that his survival was not threatened. The principle of selfish concern and greed eventually grew from this primitive necessity.

Third Cycle: Once survival was assured so that life was not longer in doubt, man's attention turned to matters in the immediate surroundings. The desire to learn about everything observed led to the development of a means of communicating with others. In time, a label was applied to everything so that a meaningful exchange was possible between people through the language that was devised.

Fourth Cycle:The key to promoting greater security for the individual was in establishing people in groups. This initially was done through families gathering in communities sometimes called tribes. The "herd" instinct was the result and it served to protect the individual within the group and made it possible for different groups to eventually merge to form a community, village, city, or nation. The close familiarity that prevailed within the family extended to other families through the realization that mutual survival was possible as long as a sincere concern for others was shown by everyone.

Fifth Cycle: In the continuing process of human development, there was a growing need to achieve greater personal fulfillment. This was accomplished by finding ways to exploit creative ability in tasks from which a great deal of personal satisfaction was derived. The initial impulse was directed toward one's closest relatives, especially one's children, in an emotional display of caring that went beyond that normally extended to offspring. A further step in this process was in utilizing energy to achieve certain objectives that did not necessarily relate to loved ones.

Sixth Cycle: Early man had to devise ways to develop greater yield in resources to keep pace with the increased responsibilities of family and community. The earth and the sea offered unlimited returns after the tools and techniques for working with them were devised. The realization that increasing one's skills enhanced the return from personal effort led to the development of a broader range of skills. There also was an awareness that conservation of personal and material resources was the only way to prevent physical depletion of self and nature. Discrimination in management was the result.

Seventh Cycle: The evolutionary process up to now has focused on personal issues of limited scope. Development was generally in matters affecting close relationships of the family or the immediate community of families. Expansion of consciousness and awareness made it necessary to show a concern for those beyond the immediate family or community. It was now apparent that no one could be excused from the growing responsibility resulting from the emerging social structure. The self-serving focus of the individual shifted from "I" consciousness to the mutually rewarding and satisfying focus of "We" consciousness.

Eighth Cycle: The parts made whole through the bonding commitment in personal and social responsibility also suddenly were aware of the fragility of life.

The matter of mortality and immortality was a constant and insistent preoccupation. Procreation and the soul that merged with the physical was a hint of the ongoing continuity of life in which everyone played and still plays a part. There grew the seed of genuine concern for necessities of life--for others. The realization that everyone benefitted when they shared with others set the stage for developing special skills with which to enhance the level and quality of that contribution. The pursuit of the unknown grew during this phase of human development.

Ninth Cycle: As a result of these deep mental excursions into the unknown, the search for immortality, it now became necessary to construct some sort of philosophy. The intellectual mind came into focus. A set of beliefs, whatever they may have been, was constructed. These served as guidelines for the particular activities of the group. Regardless of what a group consisted of or what their activities were, guidelines were and are a necessity, civilized or not. Religion, laws, and so forth became a necessity of life.

Tenth Cycle: Beyond the guidelines set forth for all to follow came the need to see to it that all members obeyed these guidelines. Thereby came the necessity for authorities and the execution of these guidelines by the authorities so that all obey in order to maintain unity and bond the group together as an organized group with organized discipline.

Eleventh Cycle: Having become reasonably secure by this assigned authority, it became most important for each member to join in the benefits which accrued from the results of this now tightly organized group. These mutual benefits made it possible for each member to become a master over the *things* of life--master over the Earth, making it possible for him to indulge himself in the more highly evolved socialistic kind of society. Freedom from the burdens of matter became possible so that each member benefitted from that which was produced by the other group members. However, this resulted in each individual feeling he was an authority unto himself--thus, he began thinking for himself.

Twelfth Cycle: Having reached what was believed to be man's development, with each member an authority unto himself, the group was on the path to ruin and decay. This resulted in the social obligation to keep the unit reasonably secure. Leaders then came forth in an attempt to prevent this decay of mankind, this being their social obligation. Regardless of the outcome, they made the sacrifice and accepted the burdens of society that all others refused.

The sequence of these cycles of life remain the same, no matter who, what, or where you are. You will have experienced each and every cycle in their order and witness them every day of your life. All that is needed is a look around you to see them functioning.

The programming of our memory from our reptilian ancestry to the present is a perpetually functioning process. It is forgotten completely until such time as survival is in jeopardy.

Let us examine this process today from birth to death and from generation to generation. The brain and nervous system of an approximately sixteen-to-seventeen-week-old fetus functions to a point where it has the mental ability to react to disturbances such as the probing of the attending physician. There is movement in the arms and legs. Development continues until the moment of birth. When ready, the birth process takes place, resulting in discomfort and pain for the mother. In a similar fashion, the baby chick cracks open its shell in order to emerge into the world when it is ready.

American and Soviet scientists have proven that immediately upon birth, a baby, when placed in a tank of water, instinctively will swim to the surface. Numerous scientific experiments have proven that babies only minutes old have remarkable mental abilities. When placed on specially constructed glass tables, the baby will not crawl over the edge. The moment the baby sees the drop to the floor below, it stops abruptly and changes its course. Yet, as we all know, a newly born baby doesn't have the strength to crawl or swim. That is, of course, when survival is not in jeopardy.

From generation to generation the beginning cycles of life are the same for all living creatures. It is only when the new experiences from the outside start programming the brain that the individualism of the species begins to project itself, resulting in the advancement from the old and established to the new.

A newborn seeks its nourishment immediately upon its entrance into this world. It enters into life with the full knowledge that nourishment is necessary for its survival.

Placed on its back when not awake and sometimes even in sleep, a baby continuously will attempt to turn over onto its stomach with its arms and legs spread apart. As the baby gets a bit older and develops a bit of strength in its arms and legs, it begins to push and pull in an attempt to crawl, a feat that soon is accomplished. Before long the baby is crawling around in the crib like an animal in a cage.

Parents usually attach some toy to the crib for the baby to amuse itself. The infant continuously tries to reach for whatever is placed there, and once successful, immediately puts it into the mouth. The infant's eyes take in everything around; the ears detect every sound.

Within months the child is allowed out of the playpen and an entire room is available for crawling about. Soon the additional freedom and exercise enables it to get into the standing position.

Much before this child is a year old, it has progressed from helpless infant to a standing and walking child. By age one, the child is running around the house knowing where it wants to go, what it wants, and why.

You must realize that up to this point in its life, the baby has employed its own instincts for all this activity and development. It hasn't been taught to follow this sequence of actions. If these instincts are not proof of our reptilian ancestry, then where did our instinctual mental abilities originate?

From this point in life, parents start their programming of the child while the child is using its own inherited instincts. This is the time when the child encounters the first real frustration to its desires, when the parent denies or has to scold it for misbehavior. It might well be necessary for the child's protection but the child doesn't know that. It only realizes that the reaction to some of its actions was not expected. But this too is recorded in the memory bank as a learning experience. Now the brain has to start recording a whole new area of learning bits and try to correlate them with previous experiences. Scolding, falling objects, broken toys, bruises in falls, etc. are all part of the growing process and are entered in the catalog of imprinted life activity. Even when something happens that would ordinarily result in a scolding but is avoided for one reason or another, that too is recorded.

The mental faculties now have vastly multiplied in only a year due to all the new experiences. The brain now has more to correlate before any attempted activity. Where was I when mother screamed? What was I doing? What did I taste, touch, or feel? Because the child is not too sure what this is all about, it repeats these actions one by one only to learn just exactly what took place, at times more than once, until it is clear in its own mind. Was what took place pleasurable enough to suffer the punishment, or was it the reverse? This time in the life is referred by most authorities as baby's testing of the parents. Not so of course; the baby merely is attempting to correct the little mistakes it feels it made so that it won't be punished again unless punishment was deserved.

The process continues on with more programming advancement as the child is taken from its home to that of relatives, friends, and neighbors. The new surroundings, people, and playmates it enjoys and dislikes all are programmed into the brain. Similar activities continue on through the school years, the grouping of the children for classes and games, the pleasant and unpleasant teachers and all the subjects of study, continuously programming the child. Programming throughout the teen years and into adulthood results in continuous new experiences and decisions. This procedure continues throughout the life to the point of old age, where activity diminishes--resulting in less brain activity to no activity and on to death. Because the body is merely the insulation for our massive electrical system, the only conclusion possible is that at death the insulation (the body) ceases to function but not the energies within. The first law of thermodynamics very clearly states that energy can be changed from one form to another but it cannot be created or destroyed. Thus, from the death and decay of the old, new life forms (a new body) with the cycles repeating themselves. Life creates death--death sustains life. Without life there would be no death. Without death there would be no life.

Generation follows generation with new natural developments and life follows life with each generation attempting to program the new life with the old standards.

Extinction is the result of predators, progress, or an act of God. As this also is true for man, we too must fear our predators and their progress: Science. "They murder in order to dissect," said William Wordsworth.

In keeping with the first law of nature--survival of the fittest--life itself is a process of "becoming." From its origin life's repetitive experiences and programming of the brain resulted in new developments of both brain and body. We "became" what we are today because of what we did yesterday. We will "become" tomorrow what we program or allow ourselves to become today.

To become well balanced and harmonious of body, spirit, and soul, we must correct our mistakes as we make them, for only then are we free to realize the peace and harmony for which we all strive. For example, an accomplished pianist programs himself through continuous study and repetitive practice, correcting every note, finger movement and any other error as often as he makes them. Thus he programs his memory with tens of thousands of musical notes from dozens of different musical scores which function simultaneously with the movement of his fingers, hands, feet, and body. When he later selects a medley from his vast repertoire and plays it for an audience, he doesn't think about where to place his fingers and hands and how much pressure to exert. The moment he strikes the first note of any score selected, his fingers, hands, and feet all instinctively and simultaneously move across the keyboard exactly where and when they were programmed to do so.

The trumpet player only has three valves to depress to exact depths for specific notes, in unison with the contraction or relaxing of his lip muscles, with both of these in unison with his eye movements for reading the music. Similar to the pianist and almost all musicians, he also studied and practiced continuously to correct all mistakes as they were made and for the same purpose, programming himself. He doesn't have to think, either, when playing a medley of tunes. His fingers instinctively depress the proper valve to the exact depth while his lips simultaneously contract or relax accordingly.

Science admits to "The Electric Phenomena" as the necessity for life. They also state that they don't know what causes it. Should that be true, then it should be dismissed as having "no merit" due to lack of proof, a requirement they themselves demand from all outside of their disciples. The real truth is they do know, but because of their arrogant and stubborn prejudice, they refuse to admit that they are the magnetic fields caused by the planets in their respective orbits around the Sun. These, in conjunction with other factors, all are the "units of matter" referred to by Albert Einstein as "mass" in his theory of relativity.

As Einstein said, God didn't play dice with the cosmos. Each planet has its part to play--its own specific magnetic field--a unit of electrical frequencies that reaches Earth in the same manner as the Sun's energy. Electrical energy travels via vibrating alternating currents.

It is only a matter of time before scientists find a name in the jargon of physics and apply it to these currents. They then will be credited with a new discovery, followed by the usual cash grants to further the same research that Albert Einstein proved many years ago.

An article from the *Boston Herald* stated that the $5-billion National Institute of Health soon would be proposing formal rules to help officials deal with scientific misconduct and fraud.

With the many reasons as to how and why, the article noted that the "capital crimes" of science--data forgery and manipulation--are well publicized once detected. But other "less outrageous" ethical problems tend to be ignored, even though their cumulative effect in distorting scientific research is probably greater."

There is no question that man is a massive electrical system complete with a main distribution panel (the brain) and complete wiring set up throughout the body (the nervous system) with receptors, relays, transmitters, and so forth. All of this is rendered useless unless an outside power source energizes it. This outside power source is "The Electric Phenomena."

Science has proven that nerve cells communicate via electrochemical impulses. The brain's 15 billion electrochemical impulses perpetually are functioning, and the nervous system receives these impulses from the environment. These impulses are sent to the brain for analysis after which the messages are returned to that particular area of the body for the action decided upon.

There also can be no question whatsoever that "The Electric Phenomena" has existed for as long as the Sun and the planets, for without it there would be no life. "When energy changes cease, life also ceases." Survival depends on these energy changes.

Considering these scientifically proven and accepted facts, one can only conclude, by sound logical reasoning, that only through perpetually functioning energies from external sources will the internal system function.

The theories offered were reduced to essentials for the sole purpose of simplification. We have no doubt whatever that science will, as we stated, find the proper jargon to exploit them. It then will be a new discovery and of course will mean more grants....

We will conclude this discussion with a quote by Dr. Richard Restak: "Though we cannot prove how the process works, the fact that it does work should be sufficient proof." [4]

For the sake of your life, take a moment to realize the truth in the statement "The pen is mightier than the sword."

Are you what you were meant to be, or are you what someone else wants you to be?

There are many ways to program the brain, the most damaging are those used by the power brokers of the world through written material.

Every day of our lives is controlled by what someone in authority has written, is writing, or will write, whether it is religion, politics, fashion, or health. It is reasonable to say that some in positions of authority use the power of words to maintain control. This is true with parents or guardians, elected officials at all levels of government, the media at large, industry and small businesses, educational institutions, and those delegated to enforce their rules. For the sake of your life, you must realize that the pen is indeed mightier than the sword. As these conditions and methods of programming are discussed, you will realize that only the will and opinions of these powerful individuals get results, while the masses are led and exploited from childhood to adulthood. Though many are offended by this process, it is difficult to know what can be done about it. There is something you can do and we will show you how.

All of us are well aware of the effects of parental influence, and we need not discuss that here. However, we will discuss in great detail the detrimental effects of parental and authoritarian influence in Chapter 11: Crucial Age Periods. Authorities do not realize the problems they cause because they always believe they know what is best. Teachers are even more guilty of this due to their purportedly superior knowledge of discipline as they deal with the young on a daily basis. It is possible that they do in fact possess superior knowledge in terms of their subjects, but discipline is an entirely different matter. This too will be discussed in later chapters.

We also have serious doubts about the teaching methods utilized in our schools. The crime, scandal, and turmoil in our secondary schools and universities is very sobering and disturbing. Len Katz wrote in the *Boston Globe* that thousands of radical professors in U.S. colleges, some of whom have authored textbooks, are teaching students that communism and the Soviet Union are admirable, while the American system is evil!

Do you realize how much money is spent in advertising in industry and small businesses? Hundreds of millions of dollars go to various advertising agencies, who themselves spend as much as $250,000 for a 30-second commercial. The celebrities acting in them are paid as much as $15 million a year.

Most all radio and television commercials are calculated to contain phrases that are used repetitively with greater volume (although the industry denies this) to ensure they are remembered. It seems that someone is constantly reminding us what to eat, wear, go and buy. We have been taken out of the world of reality and carried into the world of fantasy whether we know it or not--much as the children were when they followed the Pied Piper of Hamelin, another clever fantasy. They would have you believe they are experts on the subject of whatever it is that is being promoted. It is the repetitiveness of this kind of programming that instills the image of the product or service in the mind of the average individual. This creates minds filled with so much unrealistic debris that when a decision is made it is done through correlating all that was derived from these Pied Pipers of the media and not necessarily from truly meaningful input.

From childhood to our early teens, we are under the control of and programmed by our parents, teachers, and others in authority. Some of the rebelliousness observed during the growing years may be due to the deprivation of the due process of "becoming" according to the basic drive and potential of that age group. When adulthood arrives we have the privilege of being our own individual selves. Woe unto us, for we are the prey for the "privileged." They insult us as they appeal to our intelligence.

Political candidates and elected officials make statements that are assumed to be true, but often they are challenged by those opposing them for their veracity. The technique for gaining support of their constituency is to engage in what is truly "doublespeak," which usually says nothing but simply sounds as though it did. The public generally concedes to those in power and has reasonable respect for their greater knowledge or access to information that is relevant to the issue at hand.

The media must now interfere to inform us on the real truth. They too offer their facts and evidence from their reliable and official sources. Their facts can never be disputed because they do not have to reveal their sources--and of course they wouldn't lie or distort the truth--only other people do such things. When statements are made by politicians (even honest statements) the media feels it most important to rephrase what was said with their own word-twisting phrases that are virtually unintelligible. They also must tell you what was meant by what was said and the motives behind them. In order to make you believe whatever they want you to, they provide experts. They can locate more experts in any given field than anyone ever knew existed. It would make interesting reading to learn how these experts earned their titles. We may be wrong, but we believe that in order to qualify for the title of expert one should have considerable practical experience along with regular practice. Then again, who knows? They probably do have qualifications.

Can you imagine anyone becoming a star quarterback just by studying the game of football? or a home run slugger by reading about the all-time greats? or an expert marksman by studying weaponry? The media thinks that all you need is a political plum job or the title of doctor in front of your name to qualify as an expert.

All major networks and newspaper publishers claim to be reporting the news in the interest of the public. "The public has a right to know, it is our obligation to inform the public," they say. That possibly could be, but wouldn't it be decent to admit that 80 percent of their business is advertising? This is not in the public's interest, but in the interest of their paying clients. Could that account for the news items and garbage repeated all day and sometimes all week while their clients continue to pay for the advertising?

Wherever did they learn that all the public wants is sports and politics? In terms of sports, most people will have seen the game anyway. When they show a game it usually is cluttered with constant references to other games along with constant chattering about the game you are watching. They act as though we are blind as well as stupid. In terms of politics, how can these commentators believe that the public wants to listen to their political garbage every day of the year? The majority of adults won't even cast a vote when necessary.

Surveys have shown that when shown a blank world map, a very large percentage of teens didn't know the geographical location of the United States. How could these people possibly be interested in politics?

Considering that all the news correspondents have their own "reliable" and "official" sources as well as their own investigating teams, isn't it quite odd that they all have the same ones who say the same things? Every network has the same news at the same time every day. The only difference is that the commentaries are not in the same order although they all are just as repetitive.

Really now, isn't that telling you something? It is really through the news exchange that they get all their news.

That mighty pen also signs those mighty checks. Have you ever considered how much more money these would-be pied pipers earn than the president of the United States, the most powerful and important person in the world? It is an absolute disgrace.

Realize that these pen wielders and pied pipers never give you any credit whatsoever for having any intelligence of your own. We are human robots being psychologically programmed to do their bidding.

A comparatively recent front page headline of the *National Enquirer* read: "Why 32 million Americans are turning to astrology for answers to questions about life that modern technology, science and religion have failed to answer --according to six prominent psychiatrists."

These psychiatrists went on to give the major reasons why an amazing 22 percent of all Americans now believe in astrology as a useful source of information and guidance. The doctors were Dr. Allan Rosenberg, Dr. Edward Hornick, Dr. Edward Whitmont and Dr. Percy Ryberg, all of New York; Dr. Stephen Applebaum of the Menninger Foundation of Topeka, Kansas; and Dr. Henry E. Altenberg of West Hartford, Connecticut.

This was followed by a lengthy article under the large heading "Psychiatrists Using Astrology to Treat Mental Patients." The principle opinion they offered for its use was "astrology is an important tool in the treatment of the mentally disturbed, and a growing number of psychiatrists are using it in major U.S. cities." These doctors, however, refused to be quoted by name, fearing repercussions from the medical profession, which generally frowns on astrology.

The scientific community, greatly dissatisfied with this and other articles and surveys, decided to conduct its own survey in an attempt to discredit these articles. Their survey was conducted throughout schools in the U.S. and at the teenage level (ages 13-19). They believed this would best serve their purposes. It surely did. Their own survey showed a whopping 55 percent accepted astrology and the occult studies in general. Angered by the results, they immediately went forth contacting all publishing firms ordering them to insert

"For Entertainment Only" above all horoscope columns and articles on the subject if they could not eliminate them entirely.

Honestly, wouldn't it be interesting to learn why such highly intellectual men and women of such a prestigious society would spend so much money and time to exterminate a study that they claim is worthless superstitious nonsense? If astrology has no value, why are they so troubled by it? Why spend a small fortune attempting to eliminate a study that can't possibly hurt anyone? The study has been in existence for thousands of years and now is stronger than ever. Like evolution, "it has been kicked around for so long and it still is logical." Only the truth can survive all that hostility.

Isn't it ironic that the media never gave it any coverage--no investigating teams, no reliable sources? We dare Ted Koppel to invite us to debate this most-wanted study with any of his science experts.

We only can conclude then that all these doctors, millions of people, and the science community do not come under the category of "in the public's interest." The public spends $2 billion annually for astrology--without any advertising. Interested people seek it out on their own.

Except in the previously noted instance of provocation by the scientific community, the media rarely covers astrology for its accomplishments. Evidently this is because it is not considered to be "in the public's interest." Strange, but the public spends $2 billion annually for this subject matter and this without any meaningful media coverage.

Just as the Old Testament was revised to eliminate the truth by the leaders of the day, so is the truth being denied the public in its struggle for survival by the privileged few with their commentary. However, they all should realize that truth is truth and no matter how much it is distorted or hidden, it will always and in all ways survive. Only through truth can we remain free. We do understand, of course, that we never could be a controlled people if the truth was available to all--as the powerful individuals who try to suppress it understand this.

An article by Robert Cooke of the *Boston Globe* deserves mention here. The article related that decisions made by the scientific advisory panel appear to be facing increasing commercial influence because of strong links being forged between industry and doctors and biologists.

Increasing numbers of scientists tied to the burgeoning biotechnology industry may be distorting the process of setting public policy.

The scientific community becomes desensitized to the social impacts of science. It leads to a conservative shift in attitudes and behavior. Scientists and engineers with a stake in the commercial outcome of a particular enterprise cannot, at the same time, retain a public interest perspective that gives critical attention to the perversion of science in the interest of markets.

A study of 345 scientists affiliated with fifty different biotechnology firms found that sixty-two of them are members of the National Academy of Sciences.

In the December 1, 1985, *Boston Herald* Gary Nager wrote, "Radio Shrinks: Is It Therapy--or Theatre?" The December 11, 1985, ABC World News report with Peter Jennings quoted: "1 in 50 doctors are frauds--500,000 fraudulent medical practitioners?"

Numerous other articles could be cited, but we ask only that you make a sincere effort to understand the critical factor we want to bring to your attention: It is from the world of science that astrology faces its greatest adversary in presenting the value of its findings.

We offered the previously published items as a reminder of the serious and possibly dangerous implications that are indicated. We must constantly review our opinions about all those in whom we place our trust and question their motivation and sincerity.

It baffles the serious investigator to learn that scientists simply refuse to apply the same approach, methods, and techniques to astrology as is customarily the case with any other subject of study. This kind of scientific procedure has been used by astrologers and other interested researchers in the field to gain the kind of information that can withstand the most rigorous tests and meet the discipline and controls devised by the scientific community.

There have been tests of a sort that are patently ludicrous and embarrassing. Such tests involve the use of Sun signs, which are simply the signs of the zodiac, and offer almost nothing in the way of a useful and relevant frame of reference. After all, there are only twelve signs of the zodiac. This means dividing the world's population into twelve equal parts so that there literally are millions of people who are born "under" each of the signs. That anyone would expect to gain any meaningful information from this kind of investigation is amazing for its naivete. That would be no different than believing that everyone born of the same given name should have the same disposition and character traits. We wouldn't dare insult your intelligence.

Debates and/or interviews are presented frequently by our major networks, and many different people--friends and enemies, and even Charles Manson--are interviewed on a wide variety of subjects of general and special interests. Very rarely is a guest representing astrology as a special interest ever presented. Many years ago David Susskind had several astrologers as his guests, but he also invited two or three scientists. What resulted wasn't too far from utter chaos. The scientists were almost unrelenting in denying the astrologers the opportunity to present their opinions, and determined that the viewing public have a chance to witness a display of their intellectual superiority. It would be more appropriate to refer to that scenario as an example of their tasteless intellectual arrogance. Net yield from this kind of encounter: nothing.

Perhaps this kind of debate would be a more meaningful exchange of ideas today, but only if the protagonists are sincere in achieving that objective. We offer astrology as a topic of continued wide interest and suggest that authorities both pro and con debate the subject. Astronomer Carl Sagan comes to mind since among scientists he is the leading antagonist to astrology and its practitioners. There are a great many astrologers who have distinguished themselves in various professions and gained much respect from their colleagues who would welcome the chance to debate Carl Sagan.

Drs. Michel and Francoise Gauquelin of France have done exhaustive behavioral/planetary research for years with results that startled the scientific community. The media never reported these results--although tests were more rigid than even the scientific community would have thought necessary!

Why haven't these results been reported by the media? Because the science community hid all these tests that even went beyond their requirements. Why?

As did many critics of astrology before him, Malcolm Dean, a radio broadcast journalist in Toronto, decided to investigate the subject. He pursued his study diligently and with much enthusiasm and derived a great deal of information about astrology at the local and international level. He examined their tests, examinations, studies, and investigations to gain as complete a picture as possible of what was taking place. He gives names of investigators, the nature of their research and tests and the results so that a comprehensive view could emerge--and it did. He cites instances where the researchers' works were "dismissed" when the results were contrary to those expected by science. In other cases the results were completely distorted to produce the results the scientists wanted. In far too many cases of careful scientific effort, the recitation of the results was positively appalling! The results of Mr. Dean's investigations formed the nucleus for his most revealing book, *The Astrology Game*, published by Beaufort Books. We urge you to get a copy for a look at astrology as well as how far science will go to exterminate its study that never before has been presented. It seems appropriate at this time to recall the article "Capital Crimes of Science." None of the foregoing ever was mentioned by the media, let alone investigated. The public seeks truth, not bamboozlement.

With genuine interest and a sincere study of this book, you will learn to appreciate the dissimilarities between people and how that provides the excitement in the dynamics of human exchange.

You will be fascinated and intrigued as you learn how the dynamics of behavior are determined and how they work for you. You will have ample opportunity to test and examine all the principles of the zodiacal signs, houses, planets, aspects, and how they describe the way you are motivated and how you live in your personal and social affairs.

As you relate to these simple examinations and tests that you perform yourself, you will realize the value and importance of evaluating the character and motivation of all those in whom you place your trust, such as your babysitter, nursery attendant, teachers, neighbors, friends, and of course, the electorate. It is by the evidence before you that you will judge the validity of astrology and its relevance in your life.

In the following chapters you will learn that astrology today is the product resulting from using scientific facts, methods, and procedures without variations to derive information that is revised as the evidence indicates is necessary. It is most unfortunate that few scientists don't know even the rudiments of astrology and yet make the most blatant claims against it. Some would be severely admonished by members of their community if a similar procedure ever was used to sustain or disclaim a subject under examination in a research laboratory.

The media goes all out to interview psychiatrists, psychologists, sociologists, and all the other "-ists" who through their bungling theories and guesswork free homicidal criminals, rapists, child molesters, and so forth. Their justice for these supposed victims of circumstances is a crime in itself. These "doctors" are so talented they can rehabilitate the hardest of criminals in just two or three short years. Isn't it rather odd that they cannot tell who will or will not commit a crime before they do, or who will repeat their crimes?

We suggest you examine their repertoire of theories used for their usual misjudgment in attempts to learn of their problems. "Temporarily insane," "diminished capacity," "post-traumatic stress disorder," "post-partum psychosis," and so forth equal license to murder, and many more will be thought up as attorneys need them.

This is what should be termed "pseudoscience" instead of "astrology," as scientists claim it to be. These are the very same people who always insist on absolute proof--from others only of course, not from their immediate family of "-ists."

You will learn that the methods and procedures used by astrologers are the very same techniques advocated by scientists. Hence, scientists' criticisms of the methods used is without any foundation whatever.

All we ask is that you judge with a mind uncontaminated by the influence and programming of others.

Information brought back by the astronauts regarding outer space, for example, has confirmed astrology's claim that the Sun, Earth, planets, and fixed stars all are charged bodies possessing magnetic fields of differing intensities.

Albert Einstein's work with gravitational and electromagnetic fields as well as recent discoveries made by space scientists and others support many of the hypotheses of astrology.

These scientific facts, methods, and procedures, when applied to human behavior, will show you

1. How to determine how the dynamics of behavior work for you.
2. How others view you as opposed to how you think you appear to them.
3. How to discover what your potentials and weaknesses are and how to handle them, whether it be those of your children, loved ones, and/or strangers.
4. How to discover how to determine the causes and solutions to most of your stress problems, depressions, diseases, mental conflicts, and so on.
5. How to learn to detect the passionate from the frigid and liars and frauds from the honest and sincere.
6. How to learn what a unique individual you really are and what makes you so special.
7. How to look ahead to the developing cycles in your life for the coming days, weeks, months, or years. You will discover that you are not merely a constituent of one of the twelve zodiacal signs. You will learn far more than just what your Sun sign is. After all, there are other planets in the solar system and they too contribute to all that your potentials indicate.

This work is especially for the person who truly cares enough about himself to want to know about himself, his loved ones, his potentials, and how to develop and utilize them for a meaningful life. It is for a person who wants to learn of the character and traits of all those in whom he places his trust. The subject of astrology has been a controversial one for a long time, and yet it still fascinates and intrigues the public in spite of the critics who fervently question its scientific validity. Most of this criticism is due to misinformation on the subject or worse still, a complete lack of knowledge. We again point to the dedication which is appropriate in such instances.

The critics would have you believe that you merely are one of the twelve signs and that as such you all should behave in similar fashion. It is because you don't behave in similar fashion as those of the same sign that astrology is considered a farce. As we have previously stated, that sort of belief is as ludicrous as to believe that you should behave similar to all others bearing your given name. Though it is true that when hearing the name you all would react to the sound of it, all of you surely would react in different ways. Only the basic reaction of listening to the name would be similar--not the individuals themselves.

The commonly held belief that the stars rule the life is so much nonsense. The fact is that while the planets determine the nature and conditions upon which all life depends, it is the individual that has to make the decisions about how to handle himself within his environment. No two persons are ever exactly alike, though there may be similarities between them. Astrology defines these differences and how they tend to influence behavior, but the final decision in actualizing this energy is still up to the individual.

How to determine the foregoing is accomplished by specific methodical procedures that are without variation and are fairly universal to astrologers adhering to Western philosophy. There are many different ways of erecting a horoscope and varied approaches to an analysis, but the end result differs very little since the basic principles are the same.

Don't be dismayed by the many symbols or glyphs for the signs of the zodiac, planets, and aspects. They are simply the vocabulary of astrology and are necessary to expedite their use during a chart analysis. However, they too have significant meaning. Be assured that you will be given all the guidelines you require to assist you through this learning stage of this study.

A serious astrologer does not guess or employ a variety of theories in his analysis. An astrologer sets up a chart for the individual by true scientific techniques. When the chart is completed, he then studies the entire chart, giving consideration to every detail. Information such as the planetary locations and their relationships to one another, the locality, relocation from birthplace (if any), and many other factors that are crucial for a correct analysis are covered. This is astrology, not what the science community claims it to be.

This is what you are about to learn by your own intelligence. This cannot be done by Sun-sign method or any other method other than the proper procedures we present. A computer can set up a chart, give every detail, and a reading of every detail. However, it cannot delineate or give a complete analysis. Each detail in and by itself could be insignificant unless combined with other factors. Depending upon what particular factors are involved, the entire delineation could be revised. This is the astrology you are about to learn.

Historically, astrology was considered "The Forbidden Knowledge," accessible only to those in authority and leadership, whether in politics or religion. The same held true for any occult studies, so that a comparatively small number of people had absolute power over the masses. The material may be different today, but the name of the game remains the same as politicians and authorities wheel and deal to personal advantage by manipulating and exploiting the public with information that is not made available to the public. Astrology provides you with a distinct advantage over the average individual when making decisions on those running for public office, holding a public office, or anyone in authority for that matter, including all law enforcement officials and officers. Regardless of what the media or other sources say or print about any particular candidate or person seeking a position of authority, you will have the means for establishing that person's worthiness and credentials for the position he or she seeks. It should be apparent by now that the value of astrology has been greatly underestimated, especially where the power of the vote is concerned. Rather than arbitrarily selecting a candidate from a well-engineered campaign where the emphasis is on tactical programming and conditioning of the voter, you may draw a chart for the particular candidates to determine their character development, behavioral dynamics, emotional stability, and so forth. You also may learn of the real reason for seeking the position of choice. Astrology can and will cleanse the political and science arenas of all their debris. An informed public is the best way to assure a desirable official in a position of trust. The reverse is true in many of the Third World countries where totalitarian leaders thrive when the masses are ignorant or deliberately misinformed.

Since this is the Age of Aquarius, the planetary energy representing this era is Uranus, the planet of rebellion, permissiveness, nonconformism, political insurrection, and the unrelenting demand for the truth. "Freedom" is the byline of these times. Even those justifiably denied their freedom for having broken the law are challenging the institutions containing them on the premise that their rights are being denied. The people of both Communist Russia and China are now demanding and receiving more freedom than they have ever known. The young generation of Switzerland, the most peaceful and neutral country in the world, now is demanding a relaxation of all old traditions and replacing some of them with new ones. The extreme sexual permissiveness at every level and of any nature is now an open fact of life. Sexual behavior is openly and continuously discussed. Sexual activities now are common in most motion pictures and television presentations.

Ever-increasing sociological problems today are those of crime, child molestation, child abuse, rape, and so forth and those convicted of such crimes. There is mounting evidence that behavioral sciences are unable to determine if or when an individual is rehabilitated enough to return to society. Recidivism is high and probably indicates that science simply cannot accurately judge whether a convicted felon is benign in his social attitude to be safely returned to society. Recent attacks on prominent people, some of which ended tragically, are a reminder of how poorly science worked in these cases.

The increasing phenomenon of rebellion throughout the world suggests that world leaders would gain greater insight and understanding of these problems if they had a grasp of astrological principles. Through these principles, much of this could have been corrected and possibly avoided. These are times of continuing resistance to anything that even resembles an attempt to curtail anyone's personal freedom. The "might makes right" principle persists, especially among the countries where illiteracy is a major problem. And yet rebels are as prevalent in the more affluent countries as in the poorer ones, so that we must examine the reasons with more care to determine what truly causes and provokes rebellion. The struggles seem to focus on those conditions that deny the individual the means and opportunity to improve his general circumstances and overall quality of life. We have seen open confrontations between the masses and the leaders that govern them and between the young and their elders. We cannot ignore the increasing numbers of incidents that include people of all ages and in all countries of the world today. Is it any wonder that many gain enormous power by effectively representing those factions in society that express the greatest dissatisfaction with authority and order? While we can cite persons such as Billy Graham, Jimmy Swaggart, Richard Roberts, Pat Robertson, and others for the way they inspire others with their spiritual messages, can we ignore Sun Myung Moon, Jim Jones, Mararishi Mahesh Yogi, Moammar Quaddafi, or even the many cult groups in existence today? For many people these latter persons are the standard bearers, especially when they lack personal vision to establish their own goals. In such instances they submit their futures to these merchants of good and evil.

We hold the view that most people have the ability to direct their own futures once they have a better understanding of themselves and their potentials. We strongly support the idea that everyone should have their chart (horoscope) cast and read, either by themselves or by a competent astrologer. There is no better way to gain access to one's potentials and bring them into greater utilization. This is how greater fulfillment is achieved, which results in greater personal satisfaction for a job well done.

We feel confident that astrology could provide a more useful and accurate service in determining the proper methods of combatting all those conditions mentioned. Astrology even could help in determining whether or not a felon had achieved a level and degree of acceptable social attitude to be safely returned to society. We even could accurately determine those who possibly would commit acts of rape, child molestation and abuse, and so forth. It is indeed a very tragic commentary on the limitations science frequently imposes on society out of an obscene determination to retain its image and power. It is particularly sad when the effectiveness and value that astrology can provide is denied that opportunity. It is society's loss when rigid control is imposed on a matter that touches everyone directly or indirectly through personal involvement or taxes for a crisis condition that is an affront to the sensitivities of a caring public.

Science in general tries to insulate the public from examining astrology as a valid, interpretive technique for reasons that never have been made clear. In our opinion you must use whatever system, method, mode, technique, program, arrangement, plan or course of action necessary to get the job done! It is just unconscionable that any procedure and its protagonists dare to exclude any other--except to satisfy some subtle anxiety about their own ability to get the right answers and results to the problems we all face.

In the following chapters you will learn about astrology and what it can and cannot do. You will learn how to set up a chart with the kind of accuracy that is necessary for an accurate analysis and subsequent synthesis. The way to determine when critical periods will take place and how to deal with them also will be examined. You also will learn how to read charts for those who don't know their birth time. You will learn how to become aware of, when to act, or when to postpone for a better time and for better results. In the end you will get to know yourself better and be pleased with what you learn about your potentials, drives, anxieties, talents, frustrations, limitations and your reserves of creativity waiting to be tapped and utilized. Life is a process of becoming, and your chart is a guide for its fullest manifestation. You'll learn how to wield the mightiest pen of all.

In conclusion we offer the following quote from the *Encyclopedia of Astrology* by Nicholas Devore.

Rev. John Butler, rector of Litchborough, felt himself called upon to exterminate astrology in England. To do so effectively he began to read "moderately" on the subject-- with the result in his own words:

> "It begot in me a reverence for these gray hairs which as unjustly as ignorantly I had despised....I find that next to theology, nothing leads me more near unto sight of God than this sacred astrological study of the great works of nature." [5]

Footnotes

[1] Lyall Watson, *Supernature*. Garden City, N.Y.: Anchor Press/Doubleday, 1973.
[2] George Gamow, *Biography of the Earth*. New York: Mentor Books, 1948.
[3] Richard Restak, M.D., *The Brain--The Last Frontier*. New York: Warner Books, 1975.
[4] *Ibid*.
[5] Nicholas deVore, *Encyclopedia of Astrology*. New York: Philosophical Library, 1947.

Chapter 2
According to Science

How can anyone possibly determine the behavior of another simply by the time and place of the birth? How can planets billions of miles away affect man? How can the Moon govern man's emotions, moods, and behavior, as astrologers believe? Science claims that astrologers are superstitious, hit-or-miss dabblers. You may possibly agree--that is your choice to make. All we ask is that you do just that: judge. Judge through your own intelligence, not because of what we or the critics would have you believe, but by the evidence presented in these works.

The scientific evidence that has been and is to be presented is not what we believe to be scientific, but proven and accepted scientific facts based in approved college textbooks for students of biology. We offer this evidence in the order by which we believe it will offer proof of our claims.

Astrological Facts

1. No two charts are ever exactly alike, not even for twins born only minutes apart.

Science teaches that no two living things ever are exactly alike.

2. The time, date, and place of the birth are the crucial factors that inform the astrologer of what particular energy forces were focused in that particular environment at that exact time. This applies for both the Sun sign (the constellation the Sun was in and its degrees) and also the sign (constellation) that was on the eastern horizon(the ascending sign). Both of these are most crucial to a correctly cast chart.

Science teaches that life on Earth depends on the energy from the thermonuclear reactions taking place in the Sun. Solar energy in combination with other factors is responsible for the climate over the surface of the Earth. The amount of energy reaching the different parts of the Earth's surface is not uniform and changes hourly and seasonally. It is the energy flow that characterizes life. It always is associated with matter and changes in matter. Organisms change energy constantly, in fact if energy changes cease, life also ceases. The first law of thermodynamics clearly states that energy can be changed from one form to another but it cannot be created or destroyed.

3. Because the Moon governs the ebbs and flows of the tides, and the body is more than 60 percent water, its gravitational pull (along with the Sun's gravitational pull) also becomes a crucial factor in the behavioral dynamics of the individual.

Science agrees that the pull of the Moon causes the Earth to oscillate like a spinning top. Because it is relatively close, it has a strong gravitational pull on Earth.

Science also teaches that the total percentage of body water is 62 percent for males and 59 percent for females.

4. There is no end to astrological studies and research because the energy forces interact by their relationships with all other planetary energies that are constantly changing due to their movements, distances, locations, and so forth. The differing frequencies are infinite.

Science claims there is no end to scientific explorations; solving one problem results in the need for further investigation. The more they learn about life, the more they learn remains to be discovered. Science also agrees that life is chemical and involves matter and changes in matter. Life involves energy changes, and the forces that govern the changes on the matter of our Earth have a vital influence on all life.

5. True and sincere astrologers follow a standard and fairly universal procedure for casting a chart. They are the only means by which a chart can be cast correctly. It is by these very same methodical procedures that astrologers can achieve the same results every time for any person, and for anywhere in this world. There can be no variations of any kind of these procedures.

Science is made up of various procedures with technical methods to (a) carry out an outlined procedure without variation, (b) make accurate observations, and (c) record and report all findings.

6. We firmly believe that through the five senses, we perpetually receive impulses from "The Electric Phenomena" of the particular environment. These impulses are sent to the brain through the central nervous system. Upon receiving these impulses the brain relays them to the memory bank either for storage for future use, or for correlating all related experiences already stored. The impulses now are returned for the brain to make its decision. This is, of course, through the individual's own free will and choice of action--dependent on all previous experience. You must realize that the memory and mind, although they act independently, are part of the brain. The brain as a whole is one massive electrical system that is in perpetual activity and that when viewed using technical electronic medical apparatus would appear as the grand finale of a Fourth of July fireworks display.

Science agrees that the central nervous system receives impressions from your surroundings and stores them in the brain, originates activity, and carries impulses to all parts of the body. Science also claims that for almost 200 years they have known that nerve conduction is somehow associated with The Electric Phenomena.

7. Astrologers state that the planetary energies reaching Earth are electrical impulses that are picked up by the five senses. It is by these planetary energies (The Electric Phenomena) that the astrologer knows of the individual's emotional and intellectual abilities (among other matters) and can diagnose the mental conflicts taking place that result in his behavioral dynamics accordingly with the planets that created these impulses in the first place.

Science now claims that the brain's activities can be measured in voltage. Thus when there is a mental problem, it can be measured by the electrical activity of the disturbed individual's brain. This is done by comparing the individual's brain activity with that of a supposedly normal brain. This is supposed to tell them the nature of the problem. Apparently, they feel all brain activity is the same. If that is so, then we all would have the same problems, think alike, act alike, and so forth.

8. Astrologers state that the brain is programmed by various means by external forces: parents, teachers, authorities, and so on. When an individual does not have previous experience, is ignorant of any particular circumstances in life, or does not have control of his own life, this creates extreme stress and emotional problems with which the individual cannot cope.

Science claims that there must be an emotional and intellectual balance within the brain, and that emotional stress and panic attacks cause biological change, depressions, phobias, and so forth. Science also claims that early environment can cause changes in the individual's natural individuality. Circumstances in environment can change behavioral dynamics.

Astrology fails to see any differences in what it teaches and what science holds to be absolute fact. The only difference is that astrology teaches that planetary energies create the individual's natural individuality and problems generally arise when the individual cannot cope with the external forces (or external environment). As noted before, this results in stress, panic, depression, phobias, and so forth. As often as not, the individual is *born* with these problems *--that is his natural individuality.*

Science claims that for over 200 years they knew that The Electric Phenomena was crucial as the energy factor of all life.

Isn't it rather ironic that during that time (1600-1700 A.D.) astrology was the power source of all sciences, including medicine? When the power moguls realized what could be done with this knowledge, they began to exterminate its' study, renamed astrology "The Electric Phenomena" and began setting up their own power structure using the same procedures but with new words. Grants for further research have been flowing ever since.

Science says that in early times man was satisfied with answers unsupported by logic or fact but based on guesswork or superstitious beliefs. They then ask if anyone ever found an evidence for this belief or if anyone even tried.

Astrologers would like to learn how scientists possibly can make such statements when they haven't even tried. Better yet, where is there evidence for this so-called superstition? The ancients accomplished much more than science has, so much so that science still is baffled as to how it was accomplished. Can you truly say that the pyramids, Stonehenge, and all the other wonders were accomplished without logic or facts? Superstition or not, if it were not for the beliefs of the ancients, we would not have what we have today.

Science claims that it took centuries for them to throw off the yoke of superstition and prejudice and establish a new system of objective thinking and investigation. With their new system came scientific freedom to prove and disprove, freedom to investigate, freedom to base conclusions on observable facts.

Astrology says that if not for the ancient astrologers observed facts of the movements of the Sun, Moon, and other heavenly bodies; our present time; the calendar; and even the circumference of the Earth probably never would have been known for scientists to copy. Agriculture probably never would have been developed; Columbus may never have been able to sail to the Americas (he used astrological ephemerides to guide him). Then there are the pyramids, Stonehenge, Easter Island, and other examples. Nostradamus made hundreds of astrological predictions and never has been proven wrong. You may add more from your own knowledge of ancient history, from the Sumerian civilization to the birth of Jesus Christ and hundreds of years afterward. How could they possibly have survived without this so-called objective thinking? They all faired very well until these power-starved moguls took away their peace and harmony.

All of the ancient philosophers were astrologers, and that is why their philosophies still are recognized to this very day. Can you truly believe that only until our science community came into power that logic and reason became known? Not for a single moment do we believe this--and neither do 55 percent of the younger generation and 22 percent of the older generation (based on a survey done by the scientific community).

We only are waiting to learn how they plan to reword, rephrase, and invent new scientific words so that astrological principles will become science and scientists can capture the Nobel prize for *their discovery* of the dynamics of human behavior.

In our opinion, science and its scientists never really have examined the subject of astrology with any semblance of dedication to understanding its principles. Those that may have aren't willing to admit what the study must compel them to reveal to the public for fear of ridicule after steadfastly denying there was any validity to astrology for such a long period of time.

For Entertainment Only

In a February 1, 1987, article in *Boston Globe*'s *Parade* magazine entitled "The Fine Art of Baloney," the leading antagonist of astrology, Carl Sagan, said, "One of the saddest lessons of history is this: If we have been bamboozled long enough we tend to reject any evidence of the bamboozle. We're no longer interested in finding out truth, the bamboozle has captured us. It is too painful to acknowledge--even to ourselves--that we've been so credulous." [1]

In the same article but in heavy, dark print he also said, "**STOP THE LIES**."

A more honest and truthful statement never before has been made. If given the opportunity, that is exactly what we would have said word for word about the science community. We couldn't possibly agree more with Mr. Sagan: Neither could the media, the White House, and the general public.

As you are to be judge and jury of this entire material, you be the judge of just who bamboozles who.

In 1912 a newcomer into the world of science named Richard Dawson presented his new discovery: "The Piltdown Man" (the missing link) which he claimed to have discovered in a gravel pit only a few miles from London. This find turned the entire scientific community topsy-turvy because it went against all their previous beliefs. Though this discovery went unchecked, it nevertheless was backed and vouched for by two of the most renown men in British science, Sir Arthur Keith and Sir Arthur Smith Woodward, in addition to others. Who would dare--or better yet, who could dispute--these great men and their power structure?

This, of course, was a fraud that took almost fifty years to be discovered. The science world then took credit for the discovery, which undoubtedly brought with it more grants for more research. What Mr. Dawson and a few of his colleagues did was to steal some fossils to make up a complete skull. They then filed each piece to fit perfectly into place, after which the pieces were chemically treated and dyed to the proper coloring of the era which "insured" its authenticity.

Not only did these scientists bamboozle all other scientists, but they also bamboozled everyone else as well. So what? They keep collecting grant money no matter which way it turns out.

Should you disbelieve what you have just read, then you should read the Pulitzer Prize-winning book entitled *The Piltdown Men* by Ronald Millar.

The April 13, 1988, *Boston Herald* published an article about a Nobel Prize-winning study that was challenged as a fraud. After testifying before Congress Margot O'Toole, the "whistle blower," who was joined by another former M.I.T researcher, quit science completely disillusioned when she faced reprisals. Both M.I.T. and Tufts University senior officials said she was acting in a "socially unacceptable" manner. Why?

On October 30, 1988, public television station WENH presented a "Nova" program entitled "Do Scientists Cheat?" This program examined various case studies throughout the many schools of science that have proved bogus. All professors stated that whistle-blowing is an unacceptable manner, especially among the enthusiastic beginners.

These fraudulent activities shouldn't come to you as a surprise. They have been prevailing within the scientific community since they took over the thinking system of the world. Since 1912 to this present date, scientists have been bamboozling everyone including one another. How else could they earn their keep if not by the generous grants for their more often than not ridiculous research programs from which fraudulent activities arise?

Should there be any doubt as to these bamboozles as well as the arrogance and ego of these people of science, you may also wish to read the book entitled *Lucy* by Donald Johanson and Maitland Edey.

You, too, will become disillusioned similar to our heroine whistle-blower --we astrologers, 55 percent of the older teens and 22 percent of adults.

It would be most interesting to learn why billions of tax dollars are given away annually to these frauds. Five billion dollars annually for research under the well chosen, emotionally touching heading, "Department of Health and Human Services"? It should read, " Department of Welfare for Scientists."

Is it any wonder that Mr. Sagan finally spoke his mind, that he knows so well? Somewhere someone once said, "It is better to be quiet and thought a fool, than to speak and remove all doubt."

You be the judge: Would Mr. Sagan or we be better off to take heed of that saying?

More for Entertainment Only

Did you know that approximately 200 years ago, Dr. Edward Jenner, ignored by his colleagues, almost was stoned to death by his townspeople for vaccinating a boy against smallpox and thereby saving his life?

Did you know that roughly 100 years ago Louis Pasteur was ridiculed when he tried to convince world scientists that invisible microbes (bacteria) were the cause of infectious diseases?

Do you know that no one who has studied astrology has ever refuted it?

Did you know that astrologers, for thousands of years, have been teaching how the Moon affects human beings? Really now, what could be more ridiculous than to believe the Moon affects humans? It is no wonder science says we are superstitious. We astrologers foolishly believe that the Moon governs the ebbs and flows of the tides. Water always rises to its own level; water always follows the path of least resistance. Full Moon phases always cause the highest tides. How could we astrologers possibly believe that just because we humans are 59 to 62 percent water, that the Moon could possibly effect us?

> Fools we are, and fools we'll be,
> but it's only the fool that won't agree.

Now for the punch line to this joke.

The following article was taken from *People* weekly magazine in May 1982. The article appeared under the caption "Discovery" in very large lettering to insure that it caught your attention. "There is more to full-Moon mania than horror film monsters, warns researcher Ralph Morris."[2]

A picture at his home shows him floating on a mat in his large Jacuzzi with a great big smile on his face.

"Dr. Ralph Morris, author. Dr. Morris is a professor of pharmacology. He received a B.A. in psychology and Masters in zoology before completing his

Ph.D. in pharmacology.

"Dr. Ralph Morris says the fault is not in the stars: the Moon can cause woes."

The article then proceeds to report his findings of the increase in the various crimes committed during full-Moon phases. These increases are in every precinct in the U.S. Another special notice mentioned the Journal of the American Medical Association.

"The journal of the American Medical Association reported on the research of Morris showing the Moon's effect on human ailments. Sixty-four percent of angina pectoris attacks experienced by 88 patients at the University of Illinois Hospital occurred during the seven days between the full and last-quarter Moons. Bleeding ulcers were most severe just before a full Moon--according to nearly all 1000 patients with bleeding disorders in a recent survey of a New York Hospital."[3]

Many more cases involving the Moon's phases were mentioned, but we don't wish to bore you with such "superstitious" nonsense, as science claims astrology to be. This discriminating practice by these arrogant intellectuals leaves no doubt of their attempts to exterminate astrology. How and why are these ignorant "snobs" allowed the freedom to condemn and ridicule the true discoveries of a particular science while at the time praise some "hot dog" character for supposedly discovering the same thing? How can scientists do this when they "discover" things already known to astrologers for hundreds of years? It appears that when they speak about the freedom to prove, freedom to disprove, and freedom to investigate, it is for themselves only and for the sole purpose of allowing them to investigate what has been discovered and then rewrite it in their own jargon. We wonder what astrological book Morris stole that information from, for all astrologers make those very same statements. Then again, maybe he is one of the "science astrologers" who fears letting it be known.

We don't blame him one bit for laughing, we are too--at such blatant arrogance and ignorance. That was really quite an accomplishment for a scientist. That is what we term "For Entertainment Only."

Well, in any event, if we were you we would take some good honest advice from some superstitious believers. Should it ever become necessary to undergo surgery during a full-Moon phase, delay the surgery if at all possible. Do not let it matter who says what, for you will be best served to be considered a fool than to suffer any unnecessary disorders. Physicians and surgeons never consider the Moon's phases when surgery is to be scheduled.

Located in the main corridor of the School of Medicine at the University of California at San Diego, a large plaque stands. This plaque pays homage to a man referred to as "the Father Of Medicine." The plaque's message reads: " A man who stands out among physicians of antiquity, Hippocrates [who lived in Greece around 460 B.C.]. To be spoken of as the Hippocrates of your time is the highest distinction that can befall a medical practitioner. The doctor who [as the "Hippocratic" Oath declares] lived his life and practiced his art serenely and sacredly, who thus became a perpetual exhortation, a stimulus to conscience, a leader on the road to physicianship."

No person has ever received such a distinguished honor. Every doctor who ever has received his degrees has sworn to the "Hippocratic Oath." We do believe that at this point we could refer to their sworn oath as the"hypocritical" oath because every doctor swears an oath to honor a man whose profession they frown upon. Hippocrates was an astrologer. Astrology was his love and his art for which he left his mark by saying, "No man has the right to call himself a physician unless he has the knowledge of astrology." That should be most entertaining for the entire medical profession.

We could go on to offer a few more such examples in other scientific categories, but no doubt you have had enough entertainment for now. Let us now return to the truth and facts of life and nature

Like Hippocrates there also was Nostradamus, "The Man Who Saw Tomorrow." He also was a physician turned astrologer. He made hundreds of astrological predictions hundreds of years in advance and as yet never has been wrong.

Some of our most honored men of history and of our present times were and are astrologers. This never has been mentioned, of course, but they nonetheless were astrologers of great renown among their other achievements as physicians and scientists.

There was Sir Isaac Newton, physicist. When asked why he believed in astrology, he answered, "Sir, I have studied it."

Ralph Waldo Emerson said, "Astrology is astronomy brought to earth and applied to men."

Carl Jung, in his numerous volumes of writings, agrees with and makes several statements as to the validity of astrological concepts.

Johannes Kepler, who discovered laws of motions in orbits, said, "An unfailing experience of mundane events in harmony with the changes occurring in the heavens, has instructed and compelled my unwilling belief."

Tycho Brahe discovered the first nova. He said, "The stars rule the lot of man."

Mark Twain left his immortal quote: "I was born during the passing of Halley's comet and I will die upon its return. " He did.

Many more famous people can be cited and quoted, but to conclude we offer Theodore Roosevelt, former president of the United States. He was referred to as "The Brain" and "Brain Power." He was the youngest president ever and was said to be the most fascinating figure in American history. Next to George Washington, he is considered the greatest president ever. He had his horoscope mounted on a table in his room in the White House. Winning the Nobel Prize was the noblest of his accomplishments.

It is very difficult to believe that Carl Sagan ever would agree with astrologers. And there is no doubt Sagan would have the arrogance to call all of these great men superstitious fools and hit-or-miss dabblers. Would the rest of the scientific community be so arrogant?

It is so very true that the general public is no longer interested in learning the truth. It is too painful to acknowledge and it is the saddest lesson of history. Science has been bamboozling the world for so long with their mighty pens and limitless tax dollars that everyone else feels helpless. When will they be made to "stop the lies"?

Think about how often science has been wrong since they have taken control and the volume of fraudulent cases since their time began. Investigations of these are published continuously in the news, and we wonder how many more went undetected and how many more are necessary before they stop their lies and cheating. Is it any wonder that such a large percentage of the general public, both teens and adults, have no faith in science. Enrollment for the various science studies are at their lowest ebb ever throughout the country's schools. We say "stop the lies," the public no longer is bamboozled by and with their new scientific words and research programs that have been utilized to no end other than the purpose of covering up what already has been submitted or what some unknown layman may have discovered. After all, scientific research is conducted the world over and all of their submitted articles published. All this is known to most scientists, who are well aware of this as well as the millions of papers submitted. There is no way that the authorities can study each and every one or keep track of each to insure its originality and authenticity. It is a very simple task to rewrite any one of these already submitted articles with their newly discovered words and tests and again receive more grants to fill their already-bulging pockets. This, too, has been publicized in the news, and yet these power-starved moguls continue to flaunt their unchallenged power, ignorance, and arrogance only to keep the public and the benefactors bamboozled.

A great many of their research programs are not even conducted by scientific methods or procedures as they require of anyone else. On numerous occasions their "no merit" response is based solely on their own opinions, be it either just a verbal response or after a makeshift test to back up their response. That's what we call hit-or-miss dabbling.

The evolution of mankind and all related to it has been theorized to no end. Every belief and theory the science world could conjecture has been researched and investigated over and over again up to and including our present-day beliefs. All this has been done by scientific methods of outlined procedures without variation.

Through research, many ways have been discovered to utilize the energies of The Electric Phenomena. Because of these energies we now have numerous and varied remote control devices. Push a button and on goes the TV set, up goes the garage door and on go the lights. Model cars, planes, boats, trains and other devices can be made to go in just about any direction you may wish. Each unit has its own operating device with its own frequency by which it is activated or deactivated. One unit will not function for another. Communication systems relayed through and from space have been in existence for some time now, with the space vehicle Voyager sending back data from the planet Uranus billions of miles in space. There is no question whatever that these vibrating frequencies do exist and are of infinite count. One does not interfere with another except when one is more powerful than the other. The more powerful frequency does not eliminate the weaker one, it merely blocks it out temporarily. The Electric

Phenomena exists wherever on this planet life exists. These are the very same "forces that govern the changes in matter" measured in millivolts and having both positive and negative charges.

A recent television program presented by the scientific community over the public television stations called "Neuron Suite" showed and explained how the human body functioned through the nervous system. The nervous system is the electrical system of the body. Every minute detail of this massive electrical system was explained, including the details of the main line, branches, relays, outlets, and so forth, all of which are perpetually receiving and sending messages. This is a two-way system, so that when contacts are made (perpetually) with any section of this system, the entire system is affected in one way or another. The Electric Phenomena is what serious astrology is all about.

The brain of a fetus begins perpetual functioning at approximately 16 to 17 weeks, as the fetus begins moving its fingers and so forth. The fetus does not know what future life will bring or if there is to be any; it doesn't know where it is or where it is going, but it does realize that it is a living organism that somehow must survive. What makes this brain react in this way? Where could these mental abilities have originated if not from past experiences as stated in our theory?

We do possess what science refers to as the "past brain," located at the rear base of the brain.

Any one of us can change our personality at will if we so desire and "become" anyone we choose to be so long as we have seen and heard them. Actors do this for a living on a regular basis. We can also block out all that we do not wish to endure. Regardless of what it is, the brain retains all of it.

A single sound, sight, or thought can change the personality of an individual and aid in developing "schizophrenia." When this occurs against the desire and/or will of an individual, it only can be because the brain was tapped into bringing out personalities that we either have experienced previously or blocked out for one reason or another.

The human brain is very similar to the more technical computers. When the proper frequencies are tapped into, out comes all the data that is stored there under that frequency. Data you don't remember putting there comes out whether you want it to or not. The only difference is that you cannot permanently erase what was put into the brain unless you damage the past brain, then all memory is erased.

With all the research that has been conducted on the various animals, there never has been any evidence whatever that schizophrenic conditions existed. There is no evidence whatever that they ever existed in primitive man or in the earlier centuries either. Almost all of the mental disabilities of earlier centuries were due to the drinking and eating utensils that contained lead and caused lead poisoning. We base our conclusions of those cases cited on the fact that these conditions do not exist in our present-day animals in the lives of our present day Eskimo tribes, Hopi Indian tribes, and many existing African tribes from the small African villages, all of which still live by their old ancestral customs. The most crucial of these customs is a natural birth that allows the individual to "become" exactly what it is meant to become.

When one considers all these facts and conditions, one only can conclude (by sound logical reasoning and observed facts) that most serious mental disabilities are caused by the existing "freedoms" that allow for the research, investigations and primarily the altering of God's creations. This includes, in some cases, child abuse, although not necessarily in present lifetime experiences, for this form of cruelty existed in centuries past.

The Cause and Effect/The Action and Reaction

We would like to conclude with a bit more scientific data to verify our theories. The theories are the authors', the evidence belongs to the science community.

The distance from the planet Earth to the Sun and all the other planets varies during the Earth's orbit around the Sun. The varying distance combined with the oscillation of each heavenly body results in constant changes in the magnetic fields. These fields differing accordingly within specific areas between the degrees of arc traveled by the planet Earth. These specific areas we believe to be 0-7 1/2 degrees, 7 1/2-10 degrees, 10-15 degrees, 15-20 degrees, 20-22 1/2 degrees, 22 1/2-30 degrees of arc traveled, through each of the constellations.

We believe each of the constellations is of equal areas of 30 degrees of arc. It also is reasonable and logical to believe that the magnetic fields differ from constellation to constellation because they differ in distance from Earth, while they simultaneously differ in distance from all the planets as well. Therefore, as viewed from Earth, the Sun is in the area of each constellation for a period of 30 days or 30 degrees of arc, projecting the same magnetic field while in a particular constellation while differing only slightly in the theorized areas as stated. For example, in your bedroom you have a ceiling light, a table lamp by your bed, and possibly a nightlight. While the main light is on and shining brightly, you move by your bedside to turn on your table lamp. That bit of additional light does not change the power of the main light, but only adds to it. The same would be true should you now decide to turn on the nightlight. It also only would be adding light, not changing or blocking out the other lights.

The same would stand true for each of the other magnetic fields produced by each of the other planets, each field differing from the other.

The Moon, on the other hand, although also contributing its forces to these fields and for the very same reasons, results in more rapid changes because of its speed of approximately 14 degrees of arc every 24 hours along with its phases and oscillation against the Sun's speed of approximately 1 degree of arc every 24 hours. Mercury and Venus are a bit faster than the Sun and the slower remaining planets. It is because these slower moving planets remain in the magnetic fields longer and exert their forces over the faster-moving ones. They do not block out the other fields, but merely add their forces. (Astrologers refer to that phenomena as "Planetary Protocol.")

The planet Earth travels counterclockwise in its orbit around the Sun. As Earth revolves, it appears (as viewed from Earth) that the Sun is traveling through the constellations. Earth is rotating on its axis in four minutes less than 24 hours at a speed of 18 1/2 miles per second as it revolves on its 600-million-mile orbit around the Sun.

Though not noticeable the Earth's axis also has a motion, making one turn in approximately every 26,000 years.

North and south poles are not stationary but wander in rough circles about 40 feet in diameter.

There also is a solar motion of 12 miles per second. All this and more occurs while our galaxy whirls through space at 170 miles per second.

As Earth rotates on its axis from west to east every 24 hours, the Sun rises in the east and sets in the west. As viewed from any given point on Earth, the constellation that is ascending on the eastern horizon changes 1 degree of arc every four minutes. This also creates a change in the magnetic fields. The eastern horizon is the focal point because it is the Sun's rising point (as far as we here on Earth are concerned). This is most crucial because of the changes in the magnetic field at the Sun's rising point at the time of an individual's birth, as well as the constellation that the Sun is in, that is the determining factor for the Sun sign. These are two entirely separate fields. "The angle of the Sun's rays is still the most important factor in determining the plant and human life in a region."

In order to properly evaluate any individual astrologically, all conditions must be considered. The Sun sign is only a minute consideration in relation to the entire horoscope. The Sun sign is the main frequency by which the individual attempts to "become." He makes this attempt to become through and by all the other factors stated. What he is attempting to become is what the positive natures of his Sun sign represent.

No two charts are ever exactly alike because of all these factors and conditions. There also are many factors that will change the chemical composition and organization of a fetus that are unknown to an astrologer at the least. Factors such as use of illegal drugs, excessive alcohol use, excessive air pollution and even too many prescription medicines and drugs, as well as many other conditions to which the mother may have subjected herself. There also is the very strong factor of the various "tools of the trade" for examination during the pregnancy and delivery of the baby, and the now-common caesarian section birth method that has become popular with doctors. There are many other factors that interfere with and alter a natural birth. This does not occur in our animals, Eskimos, Hopi Indians and all the primitive peoples of the world today. All of which have plain natural births and do not interfere with God's creations.

Human life should not, under any circumstances other than extreme emergencies, be interfered with or altered in any way. The natural cycles of life should be allowed to proceed and become based on the individual's own potentials from fetus to death.The individual will learn to take control of his own life in his own way and time. Excluding the formal schooling from kindergarten through college, no one has the right to interfere, restrict, alter, and prevent that God-willed privilege. Like sending these tiny tots to nursery school it always is done for self-serving purposes under the guise of being "for its own good." No one is the wiser as to the damage they are causing.

There are many other forms of life that just cannot be interfered with, altered, rushed, put aside, or hampered in any other way--especially any one of the cycles of life as previously stated. These, too, must follow in their natural cycles as God has willed. Just as nature plants its own seeds, so does the farmer--and generally during the same periods of time. The seeds are planted based on their individual requirements. They are nourished, protected from any harm when at all possible, and allowed to grow in their own environment and in their own good time. Grow they do--and usually to become the healthy plants they were intended to be. The farmer never pulls up his plants to relocate them elsewhere for convenience, or to put them all in the same bed to save time and space, neither does he interfere with their natural growth.He just watches over them, gives the nourishments and waits patiently for a healthy crop. The same occurs with all our natural wild perennials and cultivated plants. You may move them if you wish to your own satisfaction or to suit your decor, but if it is not the proper environment you never will get a healthy plant. Neither can you change any plant to be the type you wish it to be because you love one type better than the other. You cannot turn one fruit-bearing tree into another because you wish. There is no possible way that anyone can accomplish these feats for any reason whatever other than to splice the seeds themselves, but when that is done you get an entirely different fruit.

Neither can anyone change an individual from what he was born to become to someone that someone else wants him to become. However, this is accomplished and is being done constantly, just like the splicing of seeds which brings about new plants different from the original genetic coding.

Authorities, doctors, and parents all claim they know what is best. When they are doubted or criticized for it, those who dare to question them are considered problem people that supposedly need professional help.

Recall what the authorities and all the "experts" said and wanted to do to Albert Einstein. They were the problem, not Albert. He knew exactly what he wanted to do and become--they didn't. The astrological chart and details of Einstein's behavior and genius are offered in Chapter 9: Aspect Delineations, when we make a brief analysis of his and other notables charts.

How many more Einsteins were confined? How many more will be before the so-called authorities are forced to understand? Remember the classic movie *One Flew Over The Cuckoo's Nest*. Remember the slogan from a TV commercial of the 1970s: "A mind is a terrible thing to waste."

"Science is operating on the wrong level of organization, bogging themselves down in category mistakes." [4]

Footnotes

[1] Carl Sagan, "The Fine Art of Baloney,"*Parade* magazine, Feb. 1, 1987, pp. 12-13.
[2] *People* weekly magazine, May 10, 1982.
[3] *Ibid*.
[4] Richard Restak, *The Brain--The Last Frontier*. New York: Warner Books, 1975.

Chapter 3

Introduction to Astrology: Signs of the Zodiac

"A teacher who hesitates to repeat shrinks from his most important duty, and a learner who dislikes to hear the same thing twice over lacks his most essential acquisition." [1]

--William Gowers

The critics will have you believe that astrology is a superstitious belief, fortune telling and whatever else may come to mind. The truth is they don't have any factual foundation for any of their derogatory statements. In Chapter 1 we explained all that astrology can do for you. We called the chapter "A Moment of Truth." In Chapter 2 you were offered some of science's own valid statements and evidence which should verify astrological principles.

Our intentions now are to present facts that you personally experience, live with, and see around you every day of your life. You then can use this evidence to help formulate your own opinion about the validity and value of astrology. Someone once said, "A man convinced against his will has his own opinion still." Therefore we have no intentions of attempting to convince you of the validity of this science. However, we will offer you the opportunity to look into this study by the correct procedures by which you can then form your own opinion through your own intelligence and investigations. You alone are judge and jury as you relate to the evidence presented.

Before going into any discussion, we first would like to explain what the words "astrology" and "zodiac" mean. Astrology is taken from the ancient Latin words "astra-logo," meaning "wisdom of life." Zodiac means "wheel of life." Combined they refer to the wisdom of the cycles of life. How this wisdom is utilized is entirely up to the individual.

For your benefit and for the sake of simplicity, we will first examine the cycles of life in terms and facts as you personally understand them. These facts are the realities of life which no one can deny, dispute, or ignore. As Albert Einstein said, "God doesn't play dice with the cosmos ." "There is a reason for everything and everything has a reason. All matter on this planet as well as the planet itself revolves in cycles." [2]

Life is a process of becoming where one cycle leads to the next. The cycle goes from birth to death. From death's decay new life forms. Death sustains life, with survival being the first law of nature. This law applies to all life--including we human beings and even to a single seed of grass that overcomes overwhelming odds in order to become a plant. As human beings we believe that we have become what we are today because of what we did yesterday. What we do today is because of what we wish to become tomorrow.

As we discuss and examine these facts, you must realize that all living things follow these same cycles. To make these cycles as simple as possible for you to follow and recall, we shall begin with a blank zodiac (wheel of life). The twelve segments, numbered from one through twelve, represent the twelve cycles of life that we are about to discuss. You need only to follow the number on the blank chart for these cycles as we present them and as you know them to be.

Spring brings new life for all vegetation, trees, shrubs, and other plant life of the perennial variety. For the annuals, farmers and the general public plant their seeds accordingly. Nature runs its course for its own wild variety of perennials while the farmers and the general public have to care for their own plants, but in similar fashion. In either case the same cycles of life follow in their order for all life if the plant is to become.

Figure 1: Blank Zodiac

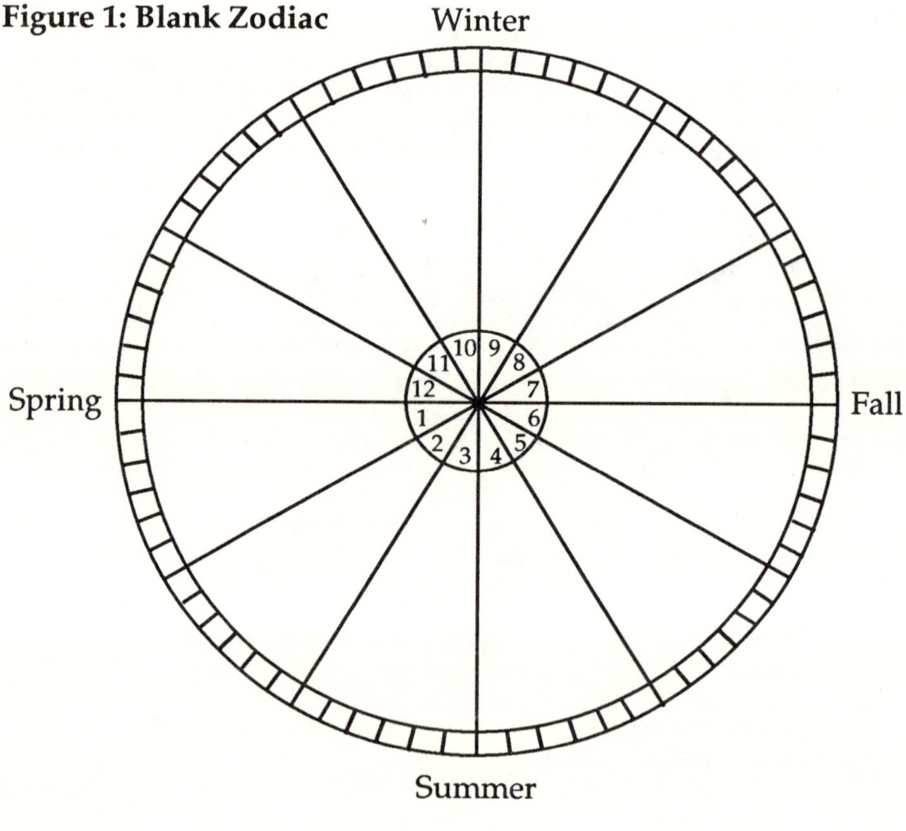

The Twelve Cycles of Life

End of Winter - Beginning of Spring

First Cycle Nature's wild seeds that have found their place in the earth and the manually planted seeds crack open their shells for their first burst into life. Fruit-bearing trees and shrubs awake to start running their sap, by which the fruits are nourished. The first law of nature is survival.

Second Cycle In order to survive, nourishment becomes necessary. The earth, which stabilizes the seeds, the roots of trees, shrubs, and so forth also serves as a container for this nourishment. All remain in fixed positions awaiting the vital life force.

Third Cycle Seeds start developing their roots, which travel in every direction in search for water, while trees and shrubs and the variety of vegetation that maintain their roots also begin their continuous search in similar fashion.

End of Spring - Beginning of Summer

Fourth Cycle Receiving the vital nourishment, normal care and protection from any adverse conditions, all is left to grow in its own good time and manner. There is no interference, alteration, or relocation from one area to another at this time.

Fifth Cycle Having received their nourishment, care and protection, all now begin to show their beauty. With continued nourishment, care, and protection, all is left to its own fixed positions and beauty to become the vegetable, fruit, flower, or plant that it was meant to be.

Sixth Cycle The well being and health of all these plants is now dependent upon extra considerations of care and work to ensure against damage of any nature or from any source such as insects, extra growths, exposed roots, solidifying earth, and so forth.

End of Summer - Beginning of Fall

Seventh Cycle Harvest time has arrived. Farmers and the general public alike can now enjoy the fruits of their labor for a job well done, for having left the plants to grow in their own good time and way. Nature continues on with her task of ensuring continued growth for all that yet has not been cultivated.

Eighth Cycle That which has not been harvested or that was spoiled or damaged in one way or another now is left to grow to its full maturity. Nature continues to supply the nourishment for all that remains by allowing these remaining plants to bear their seeds, thereby maintaining continuation of the species.

Ninth Cycle Having been more or less left on their own, the seed-bearing pods now open up, exposing seeds that are carried away by the winds with no purposeful direction. Their destiny obviously is unknown as the wind carries them from place to place until such time as they become secure on or in the ground. Intentionally cultivated seeds are taken carefully from their pods, prepared, and stored away to await their new life cycles.

End of Fall - Beginning of Winter

Tenth Cycle Having no further use for the pods that protected them, the winds having scattered these seeds in every direction, the naturally cultivated seeds now are on their own wherever they may have settled. The vines, stems, and branches that have supported these seeds are no longer necessary or helpful. Each and every seed is under its own control. Whether or not it is in its proper environment to ensure new life is unknown. For the present they are secure.

Eleventh Cycle Having become detached from any and all the ties that bound them, each seed is completely on its own as well as those that lie scattered in groups over the ground--such as the over-ripened fruits and so forth that were purposely left for seeds or those that just couldn't be reached. Neither really has any control over its destiny because it has been taken out of its natural environment.

Twelfth Cycle Having been secluded in some crevice in the earth, thus escaping the harsh winter season, those seeds that were not destroyed or consumed by insects or parasites are safe from any dangers while they lay in seclusion awaiting their destiny of new life or death.

End of Winter - Beginning of Spring

The cycles now repeat themselves; spring is here. Because survival is the first law of nature and all life must follow these very same natural cycles, we can only conclude that all life--including human life--must also follow these very same cycles and for the same reasons. You also will realize this fact as we examine life as applied to humans in these same cycles, as you personally know them to be. We will be as brief and as concise as possible. You may elaborate at will from your own experiences or knowledge.

First Cycle From fetus to actual birth, this living being doesn't know its mother or father or where it is or where it is going. All that this creature knows is that it is a living thing and as such must survive.

Second Cycle This infant is born knowing that nourishment is vital to its survival. The infant now eats constantly, consumes much more than is required for its survival, throws it up, and then cries for more. It doesn't know when it has had enough or how much is enough. Regardless of what this infant manages to grasp with its tiny hands, it instinctively will put it into its mouth. Its only thoughts are for nourishment for its survival. This infant, content with these conditions, remains settled for quite some time, living in a constant cycle of sleeping and resting.

Third Cycle In order to survive, communication, both verbal and otherwise, becomes necessary. This, of course, started at birth and continues on until all communication forms are learned. This communication then becomes its vital lifeline. Through the five senses the brain records in its memory bank every detail of all that transpires: every odor, sound, sight, feeling, and taste. Within a very short period of time, the infant learns how to inform you of every little discomfort and desire, from hunger to wet diapers or just wishing to be held and comforted. As time passes this communication extends to crawling around its crib, playpen, nursery, and household through to the walking stage. Soon the baby is talking, asking question after question and more or less placing mental labels on everything. As the child gets older, the communication extends outside of the home and around its own neighborhood.

Fourth Cycle During this time there were many hurts, bruises, scoldings from other children and neighbors, and so forth. When these incidents occurred, the child went scurrying to the safety zone: home, for the protection and comfort it knows so well. The scoldings and punishments from the family members always were followed (hopefully) by tender loving care, soothing words, and caresses from any one or all of the family members. The child was pampered for everything from the slightest discomfort to its greatest hurt. It now has been learned that in the home there is much loving, care, and protection and realizes its dependency on all those within.

Fifth Cycle Up to this point in time, the child has not learned any lessons whatever. All this child really learned is how to dramatize its feelings in order to have its wishes granted. The resulting feature is "A Star Is Born." With its dramatics and inflated ego, the child usually gets his wishes granted. The child just seems to draw you to himself with his magnetic charm. How often have you heard: "She/he knows just how to get around you." "That beautiful little brat." "How can you punish her/him?" "You know who the boss is around this house." There are many other similar praising statements.

Sixth Cycle This cycle continues until school age. Off to school they go, with their inflated egos and dramatics, ready to conquer the outside world. Into the classroom they go, all set to display their talents. They learn their very first lessons when their dramatics result only in reprimands or some sort of minor punishment. They now learn that discipline and obedience are required. Rules and regulations must be adhered to, along with organized procedures outside of the classroom. They now are told what to do and when and how to do it. They now are told when they may or may not go to the bathroom. This is the cycle of life in which they learn to analyze and discriminate, focus on work, and have less playtime. And learn they do. They learn reading, writing, arithmetic, and even the facts of life through fairy tales.

The most important lesson is that they learn for themselves and between themselves, that there is a distinct difference between boys and girls. This is learned when they realize that boys and girls use separate bathrooms. Why? They never learned this at home, where everyone used the same one. There is nothing in their memory about that sort of thing. Though this learning process is all important, these children don't realize that yet. When they return home with all their minor complaints, seeking that caring and comforting dialogue, it isn't there any longer. The parents, like the teacher, now also insist that discipline, obedience, and organization must be dealt with or punishment follows. Between the demands of parents and the teachers, all of their time is organized for them; their lives now are controlled for them. They can no longer do as they wish. Their egos are deflated; their charm "demagnetized." No one cares to listen to their gripes and problems; they now find fault with just about everyone and everything. This results in the birth of the "critic." This, of course, is only because they could not do as they wished and have their way as they have been so accustomed to. They still are becoming--learning all the necessary life skills.

Seventh Cycle The early teens have arrived: it's now harvest time. Twenty-five hundred years ago Socrates said, "These youngsters will ruin this world." These same statements are being made to this day.

No one ever cared enough to find out why these negative attitudes exist. We do, however, know they do not exist in all teenagers. Why? Brothers and sisters born of the same parents attend the same school and live in the same environment but are not of the same character. One may be a typical problem child while the other is an ideal one. Why? You will realize the answer before you finish reading this chapter. Having been all work and no play throughout the past few years and missing out on the opportunities to grow and become in their own good time, they now reap the fruits of their labors. It's harvest time. The brain's memory recalls the benefits of communication, the dramatics, the self-discipline and so forth. The brain especially recalls the tender love and care, the caresses, the pleasures and comfort that has all but disappeared. The brain's perpetual scanning of the memory recalls the most important discovery: the difference between boys and girls. The search for a partner of the opposite sex that will supply those much-desired needs is now the priority in the life. Excluding all adults and with no exceptions, these teenagers are at peace with everyone--especially members of the opposite sex. They recall that adults do not understand the minds of the young. Adults only see life through their own eyes. They block out their own teenage years with the excuse that they know best for having been through it. The young resent this, for they have their own minds and abilities and the God-given right to use them as they see fit. The result is the generation gap. This results only because adults and the authorities do not care to listen to these young minds. Adults always believe they know best; what they don't understand or are ignorant of is either useless or stupid. Remember that Albert Einstein was considered a problem child, too, and for the very same reasons. These teenagers now are going to do their own thing at their own pace in their own way and with whom they choose. They genuinely believe they have it all together. The balance of nature must take place. Any of the natural cycles of life they were forced to relinquish will now be taken up and experienced. That is, they now will think, act, and do all that they feel they must and should do and not what others think they should or must do.

Eighth Cycle Everyone knows why partners of the opposite sex are necessary and so do these young ones. Every attempt is now made to conceal their strong physical desires. As a thief believes that everyone is dishonest, a liar believes everyone tells lies, and so on, so do these youth believe that everyone feels just as they do and is after the same thing. This results in a deeply suspicious nature where barriers are set up between themselves and others. In an attempt to learn the sincerity of others, a sort of detective is born who probes, questions, pries, and analyzes every statement and movement. Similar to the seeds secluded by the barrier of the pod that bears them and allows them to mature in their own fashion, so does this cycle cause these teenagers to mature in their own way as they search for immortality through their seeds (offspring).

Ninth Cycle The cycle of life where, having been through it all and having learned all the skills of life (or so they believe), they become complete optimists in complete control of their lives. Everything they have ever learned and have been taught is put to use. Wheeling and dealing, scheming and planning seems to be their life. They have reached the late teens and they know exactly what and how to say whatever is needed to go and get whatever they are seeking. They usually succeed, not because of their intellectual capacity but because of their daring and independent attitude. Their refusal to listen to anyone or ask advice makes them seriously believe they have all the answers. There really is no need to elaborate on the reasons these older teenagers give for doing whatever it is they wish to do, but the most common of answers to any inquiry is: "I am old enough to know what I'm doing." But are they? Their elders typically respond, "They are old enough to know better " or "They are too old to punish." Are they? The real problem now is that neither the teenagers nor their elders know where these teens are heading. It is true they are going somewhere in order to become, but where and what are they trying to become?

Tenth Cycle Adulthood has been reached. The status the younger generation waits for now is attained since their manhood or womanhood now is recognized. They must prove themselves to be the authorities they believe themselves to be to all concerned (and especially themselves). They now are in control of their own futures and in order to maintain this control, this status, they use every scheme, trick, person, and opportunity available to them in any way possible. They just roll along with the punches with the ability to transform any negative situation into a positive one. Thus the "politician" is born. Undoubtedly you all know the definition of a politician. If by some chance you don't, a politician is everything you have read or will read from cycles one through twelve.

Eleventh Cycle Having now become authorities unto themselves (self-appointed) and having mastered all that came before them, they feel no obligation to anyone or to society in general. They feel no responsibility to obey any rules, regulations, or any of the accepted standards of society or nature. As far as they are concerned these are all restrictions to their freedom and will not be tolerated. They have detached themselves from all the ties that bound them and now are free to do and act for themselves. They bury themselves in their own little worlds as the individualists they believe themselves to be and associate, without discrimination, with all others who believe as they do. United they stand for whatever it is they believe is better for the common cause. Nothing that even resembles restriction will be tolerated.

Twelfth Cycle Having been immersed in their own selected environments, the time arrives when they must evaluate their accomplishments (28 to 29 years of age). This really is the true maturity age where they ready themselves for rebirth (new life). Woe be to them when this evaluation takes place and they realize they have accomplished nothing except developing resentments from all, including society. All they believed was merely a figment of their imagination. The acknowledgment of shattered dreams and dissolved hopes results in a deep, subconscious guilt for all the waste and debris left behind. The fear of ridicule, fear of starting over, and fear of failure again builds in the "escape mechanism," where one escapes from the realities of life. The harshness of all these realities become unbearable. It is because of all this that a new way of life begins. The life is either restructured on solid facts and standards as it should have been to begin with or a new way of life in seclusion, alienation, and escape results. Either way, there is a new way of life.

You must realize, of course, that there are many who do not fit into the cycles 8 through 12 in their entirety for logical and what may be obvious reasons. We refer here to all those children possessing special talents and abilities that were obvious to teachers and parents alike, such as music, art, and other forms of creativity and inventiveness. These children were allowed to develop their talents, for the teachers and parents alike understood them. Therefore, these children were becoming what they themselves wished to become and not what someone else attempted to make them become. Their natural cycles of life followed one another in an orderly fashion. These children did not have to relinquish any of their cycles and thereby didn't have to pick them up in their later years. Their personal survival and preservation was not jeopardized. These children more or less had control of their own destinies in their own way and time. This can only result in both mental and physical harmony. They only can excel when they can exploit and utilize their personal potentials, not when they are expected to become extensions of their mothers, fathers, sisters or brothers. "What is a man, what has he got, if not himself, then he has naught."

We have offered you the facts (cycles) of the realities of life as you personally know them to be. We now wish to offer you these very same facts (cycles) as we believe they applied to earliest man when he first realized that he was a living creature. You will find similarities in these cycles of modern and primitive man to be obvious. Only the basic necessities of life of modern man versus primitive man are on different levels.

The rise of mankind from the lower life forms and its subsequent integration as a species can be traced symbolically through the signs of the Zodiac. The process has been repeated constantly throughout the history of man's emergence in an endless continuum to this day, though much of it has been incorporated in the instinctual mechanism for survival. It especially is evident in the newborn, whose first cry is the statement of individual identity seeking to establish its claim to life, parallel to others who already have laid claim to theirs. A simplistic presentation of this process follows.

First Cycle Man first realized he was a living creature. He experienced the sudden awareness of one's self, the scarcity of others about. He realized he was alone, with no one to consider other than himself. He saw that something must be done for survival.

Second Cycle Survival requires nourishment and sufficient quantities of food to ensure against starvation. Should he become unable to acquire these vitals, survival would be in jeopardy. He therefore must consume all that he can to enable him to survive until he can obtain more. What cannot be consumed, he stores for future use. This must be done immediately--any delay may mean the difference between life and death. For as long as he has nourishment, his survival is secure.

Third Cycle The realization that he was a living being and the acquisition of nourishment makes him begin to think outside of himself. Communication manifests itself. He now searches his area and labels all he sees, hears, smells, touches, and tastes. He must learn to communicate with others he may find to allow for peace and understanding which will allow each to go his own way without fear. The search and struggle for survival is a constant and continuing task.

Fourth Cycle As man progressed to thinking beyond himself, he realized the importance of protecting himself and all he had from any intruding forces. He made a home for comfort, security, storage, a gathering place, and protection of self and others of his unit or group. Close affiliations of those close to him--a warm, emotional rapport with the group--developed.

Fifth Cycle Having acquired all the necessities for survival as well as the skills for acquiring his needs, man now found the need to dramatize to his counterparts this proud awareness of self and the necessity to reproduce himself through his offspring. The protection, comfort, and security he was nurtured by is now applied to his offspring, the product of his creativity and the extension of himself.

Sixth Cycle Life now seemed to be fairly well established with respect to personal fulfillment. Mankind now began to analyze conditions and situations and realized that should injury or illness occur, the survival dynamics would be jeopardized. Man became aware that he had to be concerned about his health, which resulted in his being most discriminating in respect to his work and activities. Something had to be done to secure the survival of his offspring; their security, comfort, and protection had to be considered. There was serious analysis of every activity and function of life.

Seventh Cycle Out of this resulted the necessity to inform others of these conditions. Offspring were taught how to relate to others and become members of the group. The more personal issues dealt with allowed for the development of a greater social structure that included various groups that formerly were contained in limited geographical environments. Societies grew out of a desire for greater human contact.

Eighth Cycle Consideration for the affairs of others who shared relationships helped assure the continuity of a social structure. A recognition of personal concern for others also included physical contact in procreation. The guarantee of immortality was assured to some degree through the birth of offspring. This resulted in deep excursions into the then-unknown concepts of death, immortality, and rebirth.

Ninth Cycle As a result of these deep excursions, it became necessary to construct some sort of philosophy. The intellectual mind came into focus, and a set of beliefs, whatever they may have been in the primitive past, were constructed. These served as guidelines for the particular activities of the group. Regardless of what a group consisted of or what or where their activities were, guidelines were a necessity, civilized or not. Religion, regulations, laws, and so forth became a necessity of life.

Tenth Cycle Beyond the guidelines set forth came the necessity to see to it that all members obeyed these guidelines. Authorities put the guidelines into practice to see to it that all obeyed in order to maintain group unity with organized discipline.

Eleventh Cycle Having become reasonably secure through this assigned authority, it then became most important for each member to join in the benefits accrued from the maintenance of this tightly organized group. These mutual benefits made it possible for each member to become a master over the "things" of life. Mastery over the Earth made it possible for him to indulge himself in the more highly evolved, socialistic kind of society. Freedom from the burdens of matter became possible so that each member benefitted from that which was produced by the other members of the group. However, this resulted in each individual's feeling that he was an authority unto himself. This started man thinking for himself.

Twelfth Cycle Having reached what was believed to be man's development, with each member an authority unto himself, the group was on the path to ruin and decay. "The escape mechanism" was born, where one refuses to accept the burdens of the society regardless of the outcome of this action. This resulted in a social obligation to keep the unit reasonably secure. Leaders then came forth in sacrifice in an attempt to prevent this ruin and decay of mankind.

Having presented the twelve cycles of life from plant to human, from their origin to the present, it should now be obvious that all of life responds to the natural order of these stages.

Figure 2 : The Natural Zodiac

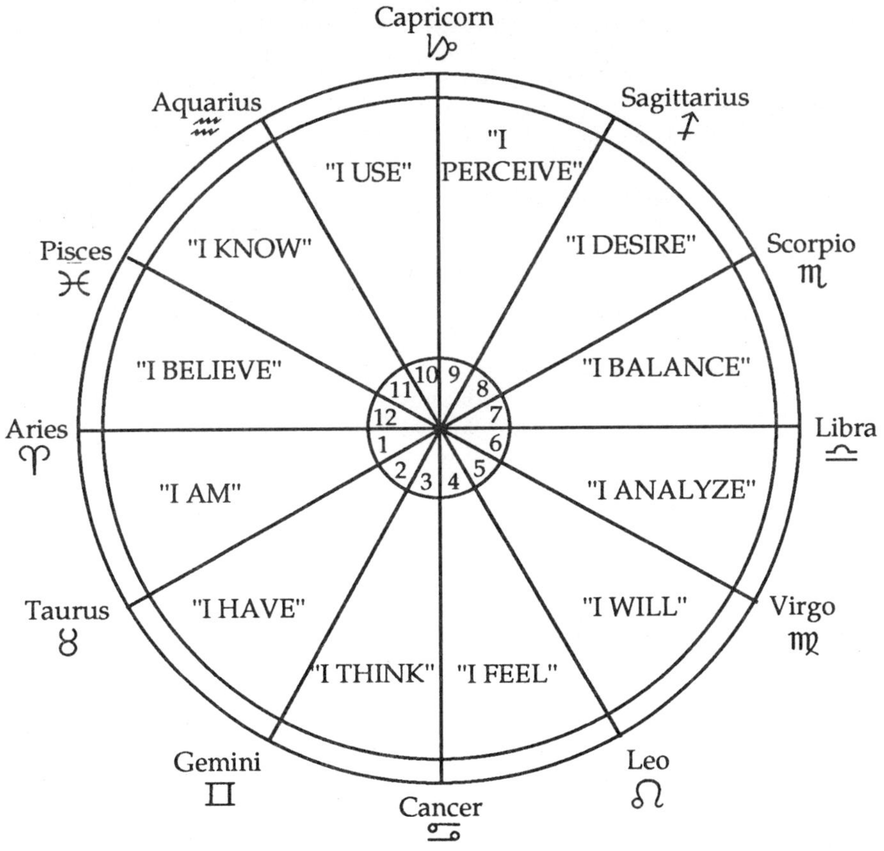

Let us look at the very same cycles in the terms of astrological principles, the signs of the Zodiac. Each of the signs represents one cycle of the life as well as one segment referred to as the house. Each house is one of the cycles of life's circumstances.

> "X-rays coming from the stars which abundantly emit these rays, exercise influence on the life organisms of each of us." [3]
>
> --Charles Nordmann

As we continue with the signs, please note that the circumstances of the corresponding houses are given. It is, of course, impossible to present every detail for every sign and house because of space limitations, but what is more important is that you grasp the basic significance indicated in each case. They are the characteristics that contribute to the evolutionary process of human consciousness. Although they originated during primitive times, they still are intact and can be discerned in the development of the child.

1. The newborn child has no knowledge of its parents as identifying entities, although it quickly forms an attachment to its mother for the support it needs. The will to live is probably an extension of the "I AM" consciousness and the development of a survival factor.
2. Survival depends on nourishment and crying is partly to satisfy that need. This clearly shows that survival depends on a proper reaction to the discomfort of hunger with a suitable action.
3. After dealing with the urgency of life sustenance, the attention is directed to the distractions that are everywhere. The mental faculties are aroused in wanting to become familiar with all things. All the senses are brought into play with increasing skill. Seeing, touching, feeling, hearing, and smelling soon became reliable guides in the learning process.
4. With increased familiarity with the immediate world, there is cautious interest in the broader world beyond. The child tests his learned information by reaching beyond the safety of the home, but a quick retreat to that security occurs when his safety is threatened in any way.

It is in this context that the signs should be examined on the personal level. We present each of the signs with this frame of reference, each representing an important stage or cycle in man's development. There is ample evidence that this process continues to this day and gives credence to its contribution to the survival dynamic.

ARIES "I AM" 1st Cycle

The key words "I AM" best describe the primitive burst of a vital life-force that gives notice of personal identity and self-actualization. The instinct here is of immediacy and continuity, just as a seed of grass endures overwhelming odds at times in its struggle to fulfill its destiny as a plant.

Personal survival is the top priority. This is the reason for their aggressiveness, daring, and disregard of the realities of life and the lack of feelings for others. Action here is constant, for here "survival of the fittest" is their credo.

TAURUS "I HAVE" 2nd Cycle

Once assured of its rightful claim to life according to nature's plan, it was urgent to assure survival, and the instinct for it was a necessary development. The expansion of this mechanism eventually included a wide diversity of ways to gain sustenance until today when "earning a living" means exactly that. "I HAVE" are the keywords for Taurus.

The values and necessities of life are top priorities here. They are most resourceful, acquisitive, demanding, stubborn, and most reluctant to adapt to change due to circumstances. Invariably others are judged by what they have and not what they really are. Sensuality is a very strong factor here, as it most assuredly is a necessity of life.

GEMINI "I THINK" 3rd Cycle

Once assured of survival, there was time to observe the immediate environment and the development of the initial phase of social contact, primitive as it was. In observing the surroundings, attention was given to understanding them and the way they differed from the self. Curiosity led to investigation and the search for answers. To this day, the Gemini principle is that of asking questions. The keywords "I THINK" characterize it.

Because of their insatiable curiosity, questions and more questions are a trait of the Gemini person. Their mind is so preoccupied with what to ask next that there never is any time allowed to get answers. They possess a variety of interests and a lack of discrimination with respect to these interests. They are unable to relax. They are much too concerned with talking about everything and anything that really doesn't matter much either to themselves or the others to whom they are talking. Whether the subject is true or false really doesn't matter much, either.

CANCER "I FEEL" 4th Cycle

The attention was now turned to establishing a system that would give protection to those in the immediate environment--especially the family. The "herd instinct" meant protection from predators. The closeness of family members and the caring for one another's welfare and safety grew out of a developing feeling nature for others like oneself. This basic drive is best identified by the keywords "I FEEL."

A very strong survival dynamic is inherent in this sign. The Cancerian person never says, "I think," or "I believe I should or I must do this, (that or whatever)," it is usually "I feel (like doing, having, and so forth)." Whatever activity they do is based on their feelings and not through any sound logical reasoning. A Cancer usually does not think, as such. Their thinking is controlled solely by the way they feel. Those born under this sign are most insecure and most tenacious and grasp for anything they can hold on to, and usually do. They lack the ability to face up to the realities of life and more often than not they are unaware of what these realities are other than food for nourishment and sleep for rest.

LEO "I WILL" 5th Cycle

Having asserted oneself (Aries), gained the means for survival (Taurus), appraised the environment (Gemini), and developed an enduring continuity through the "herding principle" (Cancer), the efforts now were directed to exploiting creativity to achieve greater personal fulfillment. Love extended beyond that which was formerly limited to offspring to include a wide spectrum of applications. The desire to produce creative works beyond that of biological reproduction required the exercise of aggression tempered with imagination and sensitivity in a display of personal will. "I WILL" symbolizes the extension of desire in creative exercises.

The "I WILL" refers to the determination to create, to succeed, and to accept the challenge of leadership--no task being too great or too small. The Leo ego presents a charming, affable, and magnetic personality. Time is allowed for fun, fancy, and pleasures, the proud and royal "star" who must dramatize their personal wills.

VIRGO "I ANALYZE" 6th Cycle

There developed the need to gain greater utilization of the resources of the Earth, so techniques were devised to accomplish this task. A growth in personal skills resulted from this need and increasing control over the environment improved the quality of life. The demanding efforts often resulted in physical deterioration necessitating more prudent examination of the methods used. "I ANALYZE" are the keywords describing the talent for the discrimination that followed.

"I ANALYZE" is most appropriate here in describing their talents, discriminating abilities (in terms of talents and interests), versatility, sense of perfection, and ability to perform their tasks (which could be many and varied). They possess the ability to teach and serve others to better enable them to be more self-sufficient.

Similar to the houses, the first six cycles brought out the spread of human emotions within one's self. Like all else in this world, the following six cycles are the opposite of the first six. Being on the opposite side of the Zodiac, the furthest point away, means that these signs are in opposition to those across from them.

According to ancient legend, only ten Zodiac signs prevailed long ago. Virgo and Scorpio were a single sign, with no Libra. During the time of this division, the species noted that they were separated by two counterparts (male and female). It appeared then that each was only half a gender and only could be "whole" when combined. Union between the two then was necessary to become reabsorbed into a "whole" (as one). It is believed that this is the reason for the term, "we are now one"--the main purpose of a marriage ceremony. Libra, the sign of marriage, unity, compromise, and balance, came into being. To restore the order of "wholeness," illness seriously was considered (Virgo) as this would cause death (Scorpio). Death could destroy the life-giving force. The signs were then divided: Virgo = illness; Scorpio = death; Libra was instituted as the sign of balance between the opposites.

LIBRA "I BALANCE" 7th Cycle

As Libra represents the other half of one's self where the "I," the self-consciousness, becomes manifested to "we" in terms of compromise; where one meets one half way. Unless compromise is considered, then it would remain "I" only. Marriage with persons outside the local limits became increasingly common and the original group became the community, then the village, then the city, and then the nation. Cooperation obviously was necessary to allow this process to succeed and grow. The keywords explain the nature of Librans, and explains why no gender is a "whole" in itself. It requires the other half to make it a "whole." "I" is only half a gender; "we" is the "whole." Marriage is the first stage of this conciliation and cooperation. "I BALANCE" are the keywords.

To acquire the other half, many adjustments and compromises must be made to insure this bond. Because of this necessity, a strong fear that they may be rejected sets in their nature. It is because of this fear of rejection and the need of the other's half that it becomes very difficult for Librans to reach any decisions. This is their assurance that they will not offend anyone. The resulting feature is that grace and charm become a natural feature that makes them very popular with many people. They enjoy people and express themselves best when among a group. Though this is all very enjoyable and gratifying, it does present a great liability. To face life's realities, there must be sensitivity to the feelings of others as well as fair and honest opinions. When this is done decisions can be reached without offense to others.

SCORPIO "I DESIRE" 8th Cycle

This, the sign of death, refers to death not only in terms of the human organism, but also death of a relationship, love, friendship, and so forth. This also is the sign of life and immortality; the sign of the extremes. These conditions resulted in the deep mental excursions of these unknown concepts: the deep secret search for immortality.

Only through wholeness can this be possible, for the wholeness is nourished by the assurance of immortality through their children. This also is the sign of sex, not so much for the sexual relationship but for the subconscious search for immortality. However, for whatever the reason, the "I DESIRE" nature is very strongly placed here.

Those born under this sign are deep, secretive, and often moody and withdrawn. Their thoughts and actions are kept secret. They are fascinated by mystery, with life having more meaning for them than for anyone else. Their suspicious nature results in a barrier between themselves and others. They truly lack belief in themselves as well as others. They are much too preoccupied with their "DESIRES."

SAGITTARIUS "I PERCEIVE" 9th Cycle

The experience of death expressed through Scorpio fostered the development of a belief system in which the burden for successful transfer to another reality was delegated. A philosophy was devised to provide answers to questions for which there were no rational explanations. Where possible, answers were found and it stimulated the pursuit of the vast unknown. Knowledge gained improved confidence and perception. "I PERCEIVE" describes this process and this sign to perfection.

It is because of this that Sagittarian people have great difficulty in consolidating their resources to a specific goal, regardless of its necessity for success. They are most hopeful, independent, and breezy without ever a thought of failure. They continuously wheel and deal and plan new schemes by which to reach the pinnacle of success. However, the thought of listening to other people's suggestions never occurs to them; they always believe they know best what to do and how to do it. They have traveled through the deep unknown and never really have stopped traveling. Their motto should have been "don't fence me in," although they just may be much better off if they were.

CAPRICORN "I USE" 1Oth Cycle

The interplay between internal and external forces was bridged by the development of worthwhile talents that produced visible results. The capacity to form accurate judgments was developed, and it improved the ability to gain greater control over the environment so it was better utilized. With control came increased responsibility for its application. "I UTILIZE" are the keywords.

Because of this cycle, those born under this sign come into life seeking "status." Material gains are most important to these individuals, who have the motto "I USE." Use they do--everything and everyone available to them in their constant struggle to reach the top, just like the mountain goat that depicts them. They are most efficient and organized, with the talent and ability to transform unfavorable conditions into favorable ones. However, it usually is so that they neglect all those who helped them reach their goals and achieve their gains. Their growing pains never cease.

AQUARIUS "I KNOW" 11th Cycle

From the inner motivation of Scorpio, the perception gained in Sagittarius, and the resourcefulness of Capricorn, it was evident that the future could be faced with greater optimism and expectation. Man had gained dominion over the forces in nature and was able to shape the future to allow for greater freedom and self-determination. The keywords "I KNOW" are the realization that knowledge offers freedom.

It is because of this cycle of life that those born under this sign feel they know what is best. Through these tendencies of having lost their individual identities, they become associated with causes that reject personal responsibilities. Their ability to think for themselves independently of others make them most permissive (in all ways), tolerant, and hopeful. These people pride themselves in their belief that their understanding of people--whether they be saints or sinners. Freedom from the burdens of matter and freedom from wants and authorities are the primary concerns here. They reject all authorities and accepted standards, for they are considered as restrictions to personal freedom and restrictions will not be tolerated. Thus is born the "Nonconformist."

PISCES "I BELIEVE" 12th Cycle

The vast resources gained throughout the developmental process of the first eleven signs revealed how intimate was the tie between the self and others with whom the Earth was shared. Social responsibility and obligation were necessary to assure mutual survival and the survival of the species. The bond of sharing was held together by an undying faith of the interdependence of one member of society with another. "I BELIEVE" are the keywords describing the mystical Piscean.

Years may be spent attempting to find the best way to express the talents of a Pisces, but there is never an excuse for inaction. The need to become organized is a must for them if they ever expect to get the most from their talents. The chaos in their mind in an attempt to escape their social obligations results in mental confusion. Though their mental abilities are very strong, versatile, artistic, and dreamy, they should realize that society needs them as much as they need society. The deep subconscious guilt of the past haunts the mind to create the sacrifice they believe will relieve them of this guilt.

You may have noticed that only positive attitudes have been commented on, with no negative traits mentioned. Liabilities, yes, but they are not negative traits. There are no negative traits within the signs or houses. These traits result from where they are placed in the individual's horoscope. It is the unfavorable aspects and placements that bring out the negative tendencies. These unfavorable aspects are made by the planets that rule the particular signs and houses by their location in relation to their natural house location. It is the planets that assess the positive and negative attitudes with respect to human behavior, not the signs.

You should now have a complete picture of the basic traits and tendencies of the signs. Keep in mind that all these traits are an integral part of your makeup, not just your Sun sign. This does not necessarily mean that they all are obvious, but that they are built into your behavioral tendencies. More often than not your Sun sign traits will be obvious to anyone caring to take notice, and at times they may be very subtle and not noticeable at all, but you will know that they are there. You will learn the reasons for these differences in later chapters. For now we only wish for you to make your comparisons from the evidence presented. You cannot judge an individual merely by the sign he was born under any more than you can judge another person because he has the same name as you.

We will conclude this chapter with a statement offered by Lyall Watson, Ph.D., in his book *Supernature.*

> There are some mystical things about astrology, but there is nothing supernatural about the way it works. Man is affected by his environment according to clearly defined physical forces, and his life, like all others, becomes organized by natural and universal laws. To believe otherwise is tantamount to assuming that the *Encyclopedia Britannica* was thrown together by an explosion in a printing press.[4]

Footnotes

[1] Richard Restak, *The Brain--The Last Frontier*. New York: Warner Books, 1975. Page 415.
[2] Nicholas deVore, *Encyclopedia of Astrology*. New York: Philosophical Library, 1947.
[3] *Ibid.*, p. 11.
[4] Lyall Watson, *Supernature*. Garden City, N.Y.: Anchor Books/Doubleday, 1973.

Chapter 4

Astrological Terminology

The language of astrology uses many words that are not generally found in common, everyday use. As with any special interest such as chemistry, physics, medicine, law, and so forth, astrology uses words peculiar to its own special requirements and particular relevant applications. We present the most commonly used words and their meanings because they may differ somewhat from the way they are usually applied.

Acceleration A factor of 9.86 seconds/hour is the difference between solar time and sidereal time. With each successive rotation of the Earth, the Sun has also moved 1 degree and the 9.86 seconds per hour equals the time it takes for the Earth to pass by the point relative to the Sun, amounting to nearly four minutes per day (3.945 minutes).

Air One of the four basic elements, included by many cultures in their philosophical, religious, or mythological traditions. As applied to astrology, air symbolizes one of man's four faculties, that of intellect and reason.

Apparent Motion The motion of the earth as it rotates on it axis makes it appear that the Sun, signs, and planets are rising in the east. It is the illusion resulting from the inability to detect the actual motion of the earth as it revolves.

Ascendant The ascendant or rising sign refers to the zodiacal sign that is coming into view on the eastern horizon at the moment and place of birth. Of course, the earth's rotation makes it appear that the sign is rising in the same way the Sun appears to rise.

Aspect The angular relationship between planets in the zodiac. It also applies to the angular distances that may occur between planets and the houses of the horoscope in their zodiacal positions.

Benefic Refers to aspects or other zodiacal factors considered favorable.

Cardinal The signs of the zodiac that mark the beginning of each of the seasons. They occupy the cardinal points of the compass and are descriptive of the persons born then as leading and initiating.

Chart This is another way to describe a horoscope or a map of the heavens. On it is drawn the symbols for the signs of the zodiac, the planets and their locations in the signs, and houses of that chart.

Compatible Those conditions, factors, and details of the planets, signs, and houses that are considered favorable.

Conjunction When two or more planets are in the same degree of the same sign of the zodiac (plus or minus 8 degrees).

Cusp The imaginary line that divides a sign or house from those adjacent to it.

Decanate A subdivision of a sign into 10-degree segments. There are three decanates in each sign of 30 degrees.

Degree One of the 360 units into which the circumference of a circle is divided. As used on the Earth's surface, a degree equals four minutes of time. A complete rotation of the Earth is 360 degrees multiplied by four minutes for a total of 1440 minutes; divided by 60 minutes (hour) equals a 24-hour day.

Earth As used symbolically in astrology, this is one of man's four basic elements, representing the physical and material resources.

Eastern Horizon This is the imaginary horizontal line that divides the lower from the upper halves of the chart and divides the 1st House from the 12th.

Ecliptic The elliptical band in which the constellations are located. It is the Sun's apparent path around the Earth or the orbit of the Earth as viewed from the Sun.

Element The symbolic subdivisions of matter that are the basic principles describing man's faculties. The four elements are fire, earth, air and water.

Ephemeris An almanac showing the exact locations of the planets each day. These planetary positions are recorded in precise hours, minutes, and seconds every day and include the sidereal time for that moment. Prior to 1925 these positions were recorded at 12:00 noon every day, although there are some ephemerides that still are publishing the information for the noon hour.

Fire One of the four basic symbolic elements that make up the faculties of man. Fire represents creativity and inspiration.

Fixed The signs that are at the midpoint of each season of the year are the fixed signs. They include Taurus, Leo, Scorpio, and Aquarius and tenacity and determination are descriptive of their natures.

Horoscope Means "view of the hour" and is the only accurate description for a chart drawn when the time of birth is known.

Inconjunct When two or more planets are separated by an angle of 150 degrees in the zodiac, plus or minus three degrees, this aspect prevails.

Interval The time difference between 0 hours (or 12 noon) Greenwich and Greenwich Mean Time (G.M.T.) at the time of birth or any event.

Key Cycle A forecasting technique devised by "Wynn," the pseudonym of astrologer Sidney K. Bennett. It is a variation of the solar return in which the difference between the sidereal times from two successive solar returns is divided by 12 and the result added each month to the sidereal time for the first year's return. This continues for each month for the entire year. This technique produces an ascendant in the return that is constantly changing throughout the year.

Latitude Geographical divisions of the earth in the vertical plane from the equator to the North Pole and from the equator to the South Pole. Each of these comprises 90 degrees of north and 90 degrees of south latitude.

Local Mean Time The precise time of day at a particular location suitably corrected for the Zone Standard Time and, if required, Daylight Saving Time.

Longitude Measure of distance on the surface of the earth east or west of Greenwich, England, which is the point of origin. They are designated in degrees (360 degrees in all), measured from 0 degrees to 180 degrees east and from 0 degrees to 180 degrees west at the International Date Line.

Malefic Refers to planetary relationships (aspects) that are considered unfavorable when applied to behavior. It indicates that there are flaws in how the individual handles certain energies.

Military Time A clock with 24-hour increments rather than the 12-hour clock with two revolutions per day. There is no designation of A.M. or P.M. since this is necessary only for the 12-hour clock. Thus, 1 P.M. is 1300 hours, and 1:30 is 1330 hours. If any seconds of time is indicated it is recorded as 13:30:15 hours.

Mutable Describes the signs that the Sun occupies in the final month of each of the seasons of the year. Persons born during this period are described as adaptable, changeable, mutable, and resilient.

Natural Aspects See Chapter 8: Aspects and Special Configurations.

Negative A behavioral condition of passivity that is or is not desirable. Describes one who is unsure or who is "laid-back."

Opposition See Chapter 8: Aspects and Special Configurations.

Orb The allowable range of disparity in degrees in aspects between planets. For example, two planets separated by 120 degrees are considered in a trine aspect, but if there is an orb of 6 degrees before and after 120 degrees that is the orb of influence permitted. Planets separated by 114 degrees to 126 degrees still are within the limits of a trine aspect.

Orbit The paths of the planets in their revolution around the Sun or a center.

Positive Converse to **negative** (previously mentioned), and therefore a behavioral attitude that is aggressive, assertive, leading, forward, and self-confident.

Quality Describes the basic temperament, outlook, and attitude of a sign.

Sextile See Chapter 8: Aspects and Special Configurations.

Sidereal Time A method of determining the time elapsed and between two successive passages of a particular star over a given point on the Earth. The time is recorded on a clock that registers the accumulated value of approximately four minutes per day throughout the year. The time is recorded in degrees of arc from 00 hours 00 minutes 00 seconds of the sign Aries to the meridian of a given place. Taken from a sidereal clock that is set to register when Aries is on the M.C. (zenith), it moves forward through 360 degrees (in 24 hours) by 1 degree of arc (equal to 4 minutes of time) each day. No A.M. or P.M. is recorded since this is a 24-hour device which equals 360 degrees and then repeats the procedure. It can be determined from this time precisely how far the Sun has traveled in its orbit at any given time of day.

Signature The sign that is the summary of the preponderance of the planets in the chart found in the various qualities and elements. For example, you may be an Aries Sun sign person, but if the positions of your planets are in the fixed, water signs, you will have a signature that is decidedly Scorpio since that is the only sign that is fixed and water.

Square See Chapter 8: Aspects and Special Configurations.

Stellium See Chapter 8: Aspects and Special Configurations.

Sun Sign This is the sign under which you are born and is determined by the position of the Sun in the zodiac on the date of birth. An ephemeris must be consulted to determine the Sun's exact location in the zodiac because the exact date and time of day vary from year to year.

"T"-Cross See Chapter 8: Aspects and Special Configurations.

Water One of the basic elements used for centuries to symbolically describe four principle behavioral techniques. Water symbolizes the feeling nature and the capacity to love, sustain, nourish, and have compassion for others.

Yod See Chapter 8: Aspects and Special Configurations.

Zenith The point directly overhead in the sky. Mathematically, it is the pole of the horizon. It often is used to describe the line of the tenth house of the horoscope that divides it from the ninth house.

Zodiac Name given to a broad belt in the heavens that is the path of the Sun each year and which has been divided into twelve equal spaces of 30 degrees each.

Zone Standard Time This is the division of the world into time-zone meridians spaced at 15 degrees of longitude east and west of Greenwich. All clocks within each zone are set with the same time of day at the center of the zone. The method simplified the "local" time (Sun time) that made it nearly impossible to conduct any business without extreme difficulty and made meeting train schedules a nightmare.

These are simple meanings and functions for the language common to astrology. They will be dealt with in greater detail when appropriate in the following material.

Chapter 5

The Zodiac

To ensure full knowledge of the intricacies of astrology, it is essential that the zodiac be completely understood. The intention here is to simplify the meanings, functions, and influences with respect to human behavior and not to offer all the minute details.

Within the houses of the zodiac lie the various circumstances of the life, the natural characteristics that make up the individual, and the various changes throughout the individual's life. We as astrologers use the zodiac for the specific purpose as defined in the words and terminology in Chapter 4: Astrological Terminology.

The zodiac is the broad belt of space in which the Sun and planets travel in their respective orbits. This 360-degree circle is divided into 12 equal spaces of 30 degrees which are the signs of the zodiac. The zodiac begins on or about March 21 and the first 30 degrees is called Aries. Every 30 days afterward is assigned to a different sign throughout the year for a total of 12 signs of the zodiac. Each of these spaces or segments also can be referred to as a solar house. When presented in a circular chart with twelve equal divisions, there is a division between the upper and lower halves of the circle called the horizon. The upper half is referred to as the northern hemisphere. The lower half is the southern hemisphere, where the first six houses are situated. The northern hemisphere houses the remaining six houses. Aries is located at the left side of the chart (eastern half), in the 30 degrees of space immediately below the horizon line. This also is the first house. In the next 30 degrees of space, the second house and the sign of Taurus are located. This continues around the chart with the remaining signs of the zodiac in a counterclockwise direction. Each of the twelve spaces is called a house and has characteristics similar to the sign with which it is identified. There also is a division line between the eastern half of the circle and the western half, thus offering the four points of the compass.

Each house takes on the characteristic nature of the planet that rules the sign that naturally belongs to that space. We earlier said that Aries is located on the left side of the chart (east) in the 30 degrees of space immediately below the division line. The planet Mars rules Aries and the space Aries occupies in the natural zodiac, the 1st House. If some other sign occupies that house because of the time of day you were born, Mars still refers to the action of that house even though that energy will work according to the sign that is there. If, for example, the sign Leo was rising because of the time of the birth, you will be aggressive (Mars) in displaying your authority (Leo). If the birth occurs two hours later, Virgo will be rising. You will be aggressive (Mars) in displaying your talents and skills (Virgo).

The signs show the natural characteristics of the person handling those circumstances, while the planet that naturally rules that house shows the

Figure 3

The Zodiacal Signs and Their Ruling Planets

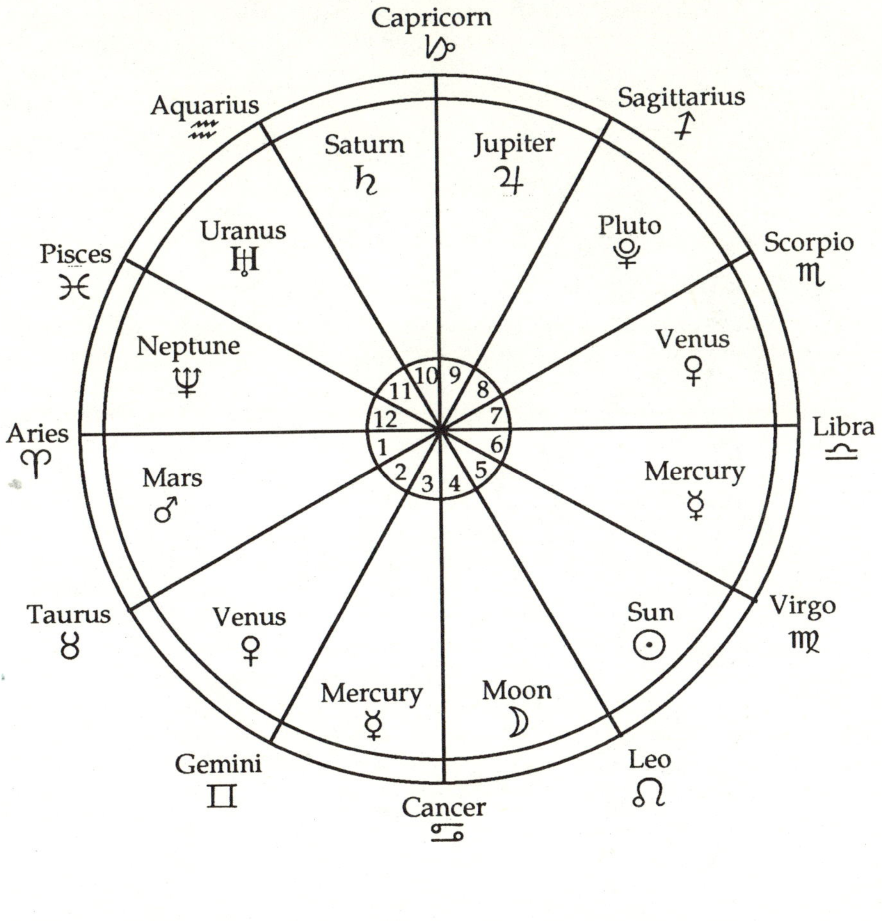

energies used. The affairs of the houses never change, but the nature of the energies with which to handle them depends on the sign that is found there. There are twelve signs and only ten planets, but Mercury and Venus each rule two signs (houses).

As each sign or solar house consists of 30 degrees, they also are equal to two hours of time. The signs rise above the horizon at the rate of one degree of arc for every four minutes of time. Since there are 30 degrees in a sign, it will take 120 minutes or two hours of time for each sign to pass over a given point, such as the horizon. At this rate it will take 24 hours for all 360 degrees (all signs) of the zodiac to pass over the eastern horizon. But at the same time each day the degree of the same sign will have advanced by one degree because the Sun moves one degree per day as viewed from the Earth. That one degree equals four minutes of time on the clock. At the same moment of each day, this delay of four minutes will allow an additional one degree of the sign rising at that time to reach the eastern point of the horizon. This is what the term "apparent motion" is all about (see Chapter 4: Astrological Terminology for a full definition). It is actually the position of the Earth in its axial rotation that accounts for this variance. While the Earth's rotation is approximately one degree of arc for every four minutes of time, the Sun's orbital travel is nearly one degree of arc for every 24 hours of time.

Figure 4: The Zodiac and the 24-Hour Clock

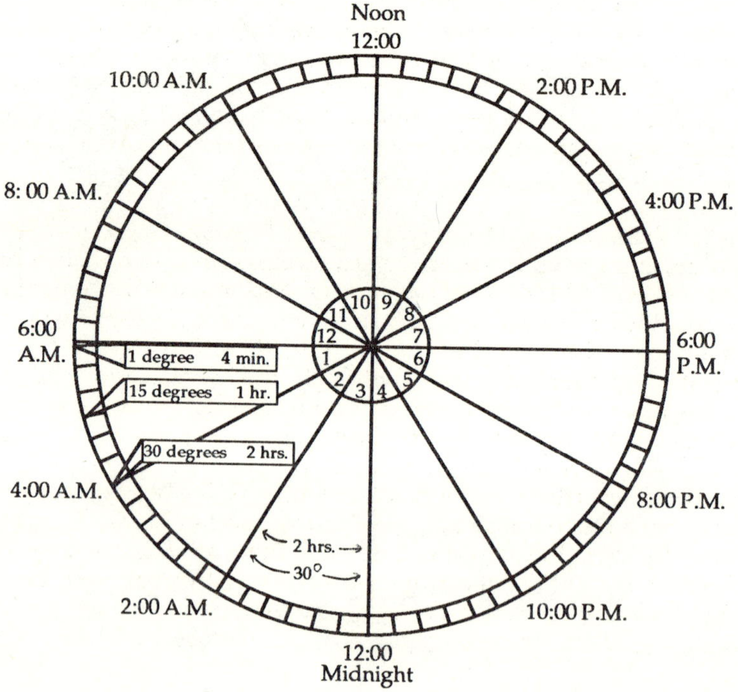

It may be difficult to grasp the significance of Figure 4 at this time, but its purpose is to familiarize you with the phenomenon of how the signs rise (as the Sun does) completely every day. From this illustration you should see that if the Sun currently is in the sign of Gemini, then the Sun and that sign will be on the eastern horizon at Sunrise, directly overhead at noon, and on the western horizon when the Sun is setting. If the Sun in Gemini is setting on the western horizon, then it should be obvious that the opposite sign of the zodiac must be rising on the eastern horizon! This is true of all the signs as the Sun passes through them, not just the sign of Gemini. We have spelled out the names of the signs of the zodiac and the planets and also their symbols or glyphs so that you may familiarize yourself with them. As we continue using these symbols, we will dispense with the words they represent as they become unnecessary and cumbersome.

We have presented the signs, planets, houses, and their respective motions briefly to acquaint you with the basic information that is essential to begin. We now must start fitting the pieces together in their proper places. There are twelve signs and only ten planets so that it is obvious that there will be signs without planets in them and the same applies to the houses of the horoscope. It then also becomes obvious that at least two (and more often than not) more signs and houses are without any planets in them. These vacant signs and houses have a much lower priority (if any at all) than those with planets in them. It may happen that the affairs of those empty locales only are brought into action when the planets that rule the signs located there are activated elsewhere.

The circumstances of each house are part of a major cycle of life and the entire process of living. This basic cycle (as we previously have stated) originated in primitive times as a necessary technique for survival. There have been changes, but only in the sense that man had to adapt to changing circumstances. When we speak of the substance of these cycles in human behavior as observed in the signs of the zodiac, we also must include the houses appropriate to each of those signs. For example, Aries, the first sign of the zodiac, has an intimate relationship to the 1st House of the horoscope and the planet Mars, which symbolically rules them both. Consequently, they all refer to aggression, belligerence, assertion, energy, violence, ardor, sexual drive, and so on. They relate to the principle of the "I AM" of consciousness where the self is the major priority. The first house describes the individuality, appearance, subjectivity, power, personal survival, and action. The same is true of Mars, the ruler of Aries and the 1st House. Although the sign Aries is the temperament and character, the house is the circumstance of environmental conditioning, and Mars is the energy principle of action, technically they all are the same.

The basic principles of the sign and house never change although there may be modifications according to the place and time in history. The principle of survival may have made it necessary to destroy another human being to gain access to food during primitive times, but today there would be a more civilized system of getting food without having to resort to that sort of violence. In each case, however, the principle of survival was served, only the method changed.

In examining charts there are modifications that occur when a sign or a planet occupies a house that is not its own natural location. What this does is increase the complexity of behavior. A simple example may be helpful in explaining how these modifications happen. Let's assume that the horoscope is an apartment complex with twelve houses as individual apartments. Aries owns this complex and he lives in one of them. He may have rules and regulations for the rest of the tenants to adhere to, but he reserves the privilege of accepting or rejecting them for himself. How different this would be if he lived elsewhere and someone else made him live by their rules. The same is true of the signs that occupy a house that is different from their own. Matters get complicated by the complex adjustments required.

The Meaning of the Houses

1st House: The self and all that affects it and the function of the ego. It is action based on impulse and not reason. It is a self-motivating opinion. It is becoming individualized through appearances, manners, personality, the habits, and desires. The physical appearance, body shape and size, and personal well-being are described by this house's influence.

2nd House: This is the house of personal and material values. Strong desires here are those for money, food, sex, property, and possessions. It is the capacity for earning and accumulating resources, and secret thoughts which are predominantly relative to survival needs.

3rd House: This house represents mental faculties, the way you think as an individual, memory, perception, speech, and communication in general. It is the ability to rationalize and adapt to social and environmental changes. Curiosity about everything and an insatiable desire for knowledge prevail here. It is writing, rumors, publicity, and the local media. It also is short journeys, the neighborhood, brothers, and sisters.

4th House: This is the house of home and domestic affairs. It represents where you establish your roots and the foundation for your accomplishments. It is the mother, offering emotion, compassion, moods, nostalgia, and the warmth and security of the family. It is overly protective of loved ones from life's abrasions. Emotional insecurity threatens the ability to face reality. It is the herding instinct.

5th House: The house of creative expression, love, pride, and affection. It also indicates one's children and the love given them, love, love affairs, and other activities that give pleasure and satisfaction. Creative potential and its development are found here, but so is gambling when pleasure is derived from it.

6th House: The ability to analyze and discriminate are found in this house. It is the mastery gained in the development of various skills. Personal health and hygiene and their concerns are found here. The rendering of service to those in need also is a product of this cycle. It is work and the laboring factor in society.

The first six houses primarily are focused on self-interests, and this is derived from Aries, which set the stage for that kind of urgent priority. The last six houses, however, are focused primarily on matters that relate to a more socially defined frame of reference where other than self-interests prevail. There is a kind of adversarial relationship between the 1st and 7th Houses, 2nd and 8th Houses, 3rd and 9th Houses, and so on for the remaining houses of the horoscope. Let us now examine the last six houses and see that they represent matters that are socially relevant to the continuing development of the individual.

7th House: This is the house of "others," social relationships in general but marital relationships in particular whether legal, common law, or simple cohabitation. It is compromise and conciliation, fairness and equality. It is peace, but it also is war.

8th House: This is the house of extremes where life or death, sacrifice or indulgence, wealth or poverty, courage or cowardice, give or take rule. It is the purging process that transforms degeneration into regeneration. What you owe here is compared to what you have in the 2nd House as resources. Insurance, legacies, and inheritances are found in this sector as well as investments and retirement funds.

9th House: Knowledge gained from institutions, philosophy of living, interest in spiritual matters, and understanding are products of this house. All professions and how they are learned, the wheeler and dealer, the media, libraries, and propaganda emerge from the influence of this house. Long journeys in the real as well as the abstract world are undertaken here. Religion and religious experiences occur from this influence.

10th House: This house represents the father and any other figure of authority in the outer world. It is the establishment; the laws that exercise control; the executive branch of government; the president; and all things political, business, and social that are related. Public visibility, reputation, fame, disgrace, social status, and credibility are found here.

11th House: This is the house of the future and the goals to be achieved. It is security from the success from the 10th House. It is shared rewards and universal brotherhood at the broadest social level, friends and social allies in causes that serve future generations. Freedom from want and poverty produce high hopes.

12th House: This is the house of self-undoing when hidden fears are not dealt with. Seclusion and secrecy, crime and punishment, social debt, imagination, fantasy, daydreaming, escape, retirement, inspiration, compassion, sympathy, solace, and sacrifice are represented here.

The foregoing is only part of what each of the houses signifies. What is important is that the basic principle of each house is understood. There are endless variations of the themes the houses represent. We have presented the concepts at work so that you can surmise what the result will be when a particular planet functions in that kind of environment. A capsule presentation of the basic meanings of the houses can be seen in Figure 5: The Houses and Their Affairs.

Note: House affairs represent the natural cycles of life. These cycles are exploited by the nature of the sign located on its cusp. The sign's ruling planet, and the planets or planets posited therein, will show the energies used. The house affairs never change, only the signs on the cusps and the planetary energies do.

"All life is organized by natural and universal laws."
--Lyall Watson, Ph.D.

Figure 5: The Houses and Their Affairs

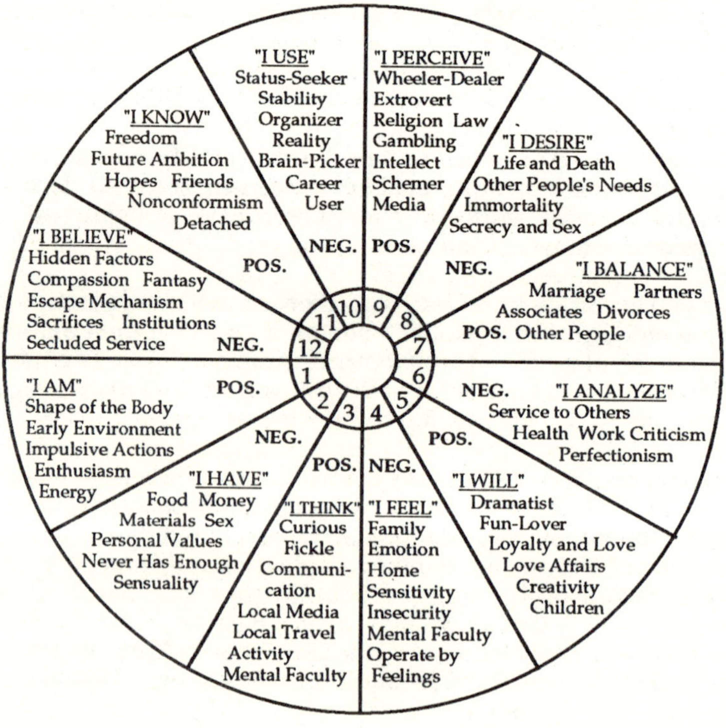

Chapter 6

Planetary Characteristics

For the sake of simplicity, astrologers customarily consider the Sun and Moon as planets, even though one is a star and the other a satellite of the Earth. In geocentric astrology, the Earth is not included as exerting an influence on behavior as do the remaining planets in our solar system. However, it is the gravitational effect of Earth that draws the cosmic rays from the other planets. Albert Einstein explained that "gravity is the weakest of the four forces, yet the most powerful, for it affects all matter."

In discussing the planets, we will present only the basic principles of their respective influence. For additional details about each of the planets we recommend *The Cosmic Informer.* We adhere to the principle of "planetary protocol" as we discuss the planets. This means that the slower a planet revolves in its orbit the greater its influence over those planets with faster orbits. The planets, listed in order from fastest to slowest orbiting speeds, are Moon, Mercury, Venus, Sun, Mars, Jupiter, Saturn, Uranus, Neptune, and Pluto. It is this principle that determines which planet exerts an influence when they are involved in an angular relationship called an aspect. The positive or negative (benefic or malefic) characteristic involved is based on the nature of that specific aspect. In general, the relatively benign aspects tend to bring the more favorable indications of a planet and thus the individual's behavior that it represents. Conversely, the unfavorable or malefic aspects tend to promote undesirable behavior in an individual along the lines defined by the symbolic natures of the planets involved. It is precisely because of the complex nature of human behavior that planetary protocol must be utilized to simplify the task of understanding why people behave as they do and what motivates them to act that way.

What follows is a tabulation of all the planets as they are used in astrology, including details on their orbital revolution, the length of stay in a zodiacal sign, and their average daily motion. The listing is in order by planetary protocol.

Figure 6
Planetary Motions

Planet	Average Daily Motion (approx.)	Stay in a Sign (approximate)	Time to Orbit (approximate)
☽ Moon	13° per day 1/2° per hour 1° per 2 hrs. of time	2 1/2 days	28 days
☿ Mercury	1° 23' per day 3 1/2' per hour	14-18 days	88 days
♀ Venus	1° 12' per day 3' per hour	23-24 days	255 days
☉ Sun	59' 08" per day 2 1/2' per hour	30 days	365 days
♂ Mars	31' 27" per day	45-47 days	1 year, 325 days
♃ Jupiter	4' 59" per day	1 year	12 years
♄ Saturn	2' 01" per day	2 1/2 years	29 1/2 years
♅ Uranus	42" per day	7 years	29 1/2 years
♆ Neptune	24 " per day	14 years avg.	165 years
♇ Pluto	15" per day	20 years avg.	248 years

(° = degrees, ' = minutes, " = seconds)

The listing in this planetary protocol table shows only the approximate daily motion, length of stay in a sign, and the time to orbit the Sun. Though orbital time is generally of no significance for the majority of the planets, it is important in the cases of Saturn , Neptune, Uranus, and Pluto for the important milestones in the life they represent. These will be discussed in a later chapter.

Moon The inability to concentrate; indecisive, with emotions that are easily influenced by suggestion. There is a strong protective sense with maternal instincts, psychic qualities, and extrasensory perception. The Moon is the unconscious side of the personality, habits, and instincts. It is the constantly changing personality that responds and reacts to external stimuli. The feelings and emotions interfere with creative thinking and self-expression. The Moon represents maternal--not romantic--love which often is confused with ownership toward loved ones out of a need to satisfy emotional insecurity.

Mercury This planet rules communication and the intellect. Because of this, there is an insatiable curiosity about everything. This results in the ability to interpret and solve problems with deductive logic and also is the door to impartial understanding. Mercury represents concrete mental faculties that sometimes are vacillating, argumentative, cunning, and crafty. Thoughts, reasoning, and rational judgment also are under this planet's influence.

Venus This is the planet that rules love, but it also rules "adjustment" as a process frequently necessary in situations in order to satisfy one's desires. Venus is the compromising and the gestures one makes in hopes that others will reciprocate. It is the desire for relationships, companionship, and affectionate ties that often result from social contacts. It is an acquisitive and sensuous nature that results from active participation in social affairs. This satisfies the need to be among people. It is because of this need that a strong fear of being rejected often is felt.

Sun The Sun is the will and the ego striving for significance. It is the solar energy that flows and enables life to exist and one's destiny to be pursued. It is the creative urge that is sustained by the will to live, indicative of the future in which the whole idea of the "self" can be fulfilled. The Sun is the primary indicator of what an individual is trying to achieve. The Sun gives initiative energy to the planets it aspects, including the ascendant.

Mars Action, aggressiveness, acquisitiveness, anger, violence, carelessness, sexual ardor, and intimidation all are qualities of this planet's influence. The vital faculties are not easily rebuffed and never are discouraged. Accomplishments usually are achieved through direct action with little planning. There is unsurpassed energy, which is used either constructively or destructively and with little feeling of guilt at the time if that action doesn't turn out as expected. It is the residual traces of man's animal nature; it is the desire, passion, and the assertion of the "self" rather than the "will" and eager for competition. It is the "survival of the fittest" and especially resistant to reason and logic.

Jupiter The planet of optimism, expansion, and growth as applied to the accumulation of wealth in any form. Jupiter is the high expectations that the future will reward one's greatest hopes. It is the higher mental faculties that search for meaning in the affairs of life beyond the physical dimension. There is a pronounced enthusiasm for a rich and fulfilling life, and it increases aspirations, but allows a tendency to bite off more than is necessary. Sometimes expectations exceed the willingness to contribute something in return. It often refers to an interest in gambling or schemes to satisfy the desires. It is the belief that failure is unlikely, and that any restraint is intolerable. It gives the ability to overcome any opposition with forceful but impersonal argument. It represents the confidence game and/or something for nothing.

Saturn This planet represents wisdom, judgment, responsibility, and personal credibility and self-worth. It is the realization that reward is the result of personal effort and responsibility. It is the reality and the acceptance of the burdens of duty. It is the practical ability to achieve, the well-organized mind, and the authority of experience. It is secretive, noncommittal and noncommunicative, reserved and extremely cautious; it is justice dealt with a strong and firm hand. Saturn is the policeman of the zodiac who insures that all debts owed are paid in full when due. Because of this it often is called "the cosmic boomerang": you reap what you sow. It also is the law of self-preservation and purposeful endeavors. Saturn places emphasis on the ego with a difficulty in expressing affection and an outlook on life that sometimes is morbidly serious. It is cold, slow, deliberate, and conservative, but it also exhibits fear, inhibition, and uncertainty that sometimes results in lack of confidence.

Uranus This is the higher octave of Mercury and is therefore the higher mental faculties where insight prevails. The battle cry here is freedom from responsibility, authority, and limitation. Its will is unbending when insisting on independence. It is the awareness to cope with the material so it doesn't restrict action. Uranus represents detachment from custom and tradition and conventional morality. It is the instigator of sudden upsets and reversals. It identifies with mass consciousness and cultivates the right to explore new dimensions and realities and urges free expression and individualism. It is the standard-bearer for knowledge as the key to freedom from the bonds of ignorance.

Neptune This planet represents the force that gives the tendencies toward fulfilling social obligations in response to deep-seated feelings of guilt. Because it is so difficult to define why society must be served, it sometimes causes aimless wandering in search of a purpose or an objective. It is sensitivity to social injustice and the motivation to do something to compensate for the decaying conditions afflicting society that one frequently observes. Those moved to action on these concerns somehow sense that their personal guilt will be relieved somewhat.

Neptune is imagination, psychism, sympathy, empathy, rhythm and illusion. It also is everything that is indefinable, false hopes, and being susceptible to the power of suggestion. Like the water it rules, Neptune dissolves, distorts, and dilutes reality and often replaces it with fantasy and illusion.

Pluto Pluto represents the systems that purge wastes and toxins of the body and the mind. It is the power that causes eruptions of all kinds, verbal and otherwise. Pluto is transformation, regeneration, and the sacrifices to an evolving social development. Pluto is the motivating force of destruction and resurrection. It is the dynamics that produce the foundations for advancement of human welfare and relations, professional associations, and better social conditions, but it also can produce organized crime and the gangsters to commit crimes against society. It is the "Godfather" who makes offers you can't refuse. Depending on the level of evolvement, there is power for good or evil, and the difference between someone who has lost the way and someone on the right path.

Though only a portion of the planetary influences have been given, these are the most important. We have cited mostly positive natures although we realize that the negative features are only a matter of personal motivation and evolvement in social responsibility.

Please note that the influences of the planets, signs, and the circumstances of the houses are quite alike in many respects. When a chart is completed, we can see how changes occur depending on the planet in a sign and house. For example, Pluto may be in the 1st House and in the sign of Pisces, and that would mean one thing. Pluto in the 6th House and in the sign of Scorpio would mean something else, while Pluto in Virgo in the 10th House would have still another meaning. There are many variations in these influences that also must include the aspects they make to other planets.

Before going into the explanations of the aspects, we want you to understand that these symbols representing the planets are not merely some sort of heiroglyphics but that they have meanings in themselves. These symbols, apparently well considered for their meanings by the ancients, are similar to the natures of the planets and the signs and houses they rule.

Meaning of the Planetary Symbols

Spirit - ☉	Soul - ☽	Body - †
(Life)	(Conscience)	(Matter)

☽ - Conscience past and present
☿ - Life trapped between matter and conscience
♀ - Matter supporting life
☉ - New life entrapped by conscience past, present, and future
♂ - Life supporting matter
♃ - Conscience and topsy-turvy matter ?
♄ - Conscience supporting matter
♅ - New life held down by part matter, conscience present and future
♆ - Conscience past, present, future, and topsy-turvy matter
♇ - Matter supporting conscience with new life coming forth

The following table of planetary characteristics, showing the positive and negative natures, will help you determine which forces are at work in the completed horoscope. This is done by computing the aspects between the planets. They either can be positive (benefic) or negative (malefic) by nature and influence. Benefic aspects tend to bring out the favorable natures of the planets involved while the malefic aspects bring out their undesirable natures. Recall that the benefic aspects are the sextile (60 degrees) and the trine (120 degrees). The malefic aspects are the conjunction (8 degrees), square (90 degrees), inconjunct (150 degrees), and the opposition (180 degrees).

To determine the positive or negative forces at work by the aspects involved, refer to the planetary characteristics following.

MOON

Positive	Negative
Maternal	Moody
Protective	Unreliable
Sensitive	Unstable
Acquisitive	Lax
Imaginative	Faulty reasoning
Good memory	Remembers slights
Instinctive mind	Procrastinating
Peace loving	Touchy

MERCURY

Positive	Negative
Understanding	Mental waywardness
Knowledgeable	Questionable
Intelligent	Slick
Clever	Nervous
Perceptive	Vacillating
Expressive	Nosy
Talkative	Critical
Practical	Gossipy

VENUS

Pacifistic	Dissatisfied
Tactful	Indecisive
Gracious	Vain
Loving	Sensual
Romantic	In love w/ love
Patronizing	Vain
Cheerful	Weak
Adaptable	Dissolute

SUN

Dignified	Arrogant
Faithful	Resistant
Loyal	Domineering
Powerful	Overbearing
Proud	Extravagant
Ambitious	Egotistical
Outspoken	Boastful
Grandeur	Pompous

MARS

Energetic	Restless
Fearless	Rude
Direct	Arrogant
Impulsive	Foolhardy
Courageous	Careless
Passionate	Thoughtless
Desiring	Cruel
Acquisitive	Destructive

JUPITER

Optimistic	Extremist
Generous	Wasteful
Jovial	Provocative
Fond of gambling	Trusting to luck
Organized	Scheming
Broad outlook	Nondetailed
Creative faculties	Boastful
Common sense	Hypocritical

SATURN

Prudent	Mean
Cautious	Fearful
Controlled	Limited
Serious	Dull
Practical	Pessimistic
Creative faculties	Uninspired
Organized	Fatalistic
Defensive	Tyrannical

URANUS

Reformative	Rebellious
Inventive	Nonconformist
Strong willed	Dangerous
Outspoken	Eccentric
Unconventional	Detached
Positive	Impulsive
Self-reliant	Inferiority complex
Organized	Anarchistic

NEPTUNE		PLUTO	
Imaginative	Deceptive	Evolving	Obsessive
Inspirational	Subversive	Elimination	Eruptive
Sensitive	Perverse	Revealing	Violent
Idealistic	Careless	Regenerative	Criminal
Subtle	Fantasy	Rebirth	Destructive
Emotional	Unstable	Organized	Racketeering
ESP	Scheming	Professional	Gang leader
Psychic	Neurotic	Powerful	Forceful

Because it involved hundreds of years of research and study to realize how these energies influence us, it is difficult to imagine that primitive man also was influenced by these same characteristics we have offered. We will therefore conclude this chapter with the basic characteristics as they applied to early man.

☽	☿	♀	☉
The compassion for others and their survival	The communication necessary for the survival	The peace and good will for all to survive	The will and ego to survive
♂	♃	♄	♅
The energy force to insure the survival	The daring to overcome the obstacles	The caution to insure the success	The ability to ignore the dangers
	♆	♇	
	The vision that all will go well	Revelations of their evolving	

Chapter 7

Qualities, Elements, and Other Factors

We have emphasized the fact that no one can make a correct analysis of an individual by their Sun sign. There are many variables and considerations that alter these individual Sun signs. This especially is true with an important phase of the study that serves as the foundation for understanding how the dynamics of behavior operate. The first of these separate considerations is the matter of the qualities and elements. The signs of the zodiac are divided into three groups of four signs called qualities and divided again into four groups of three signs called elements.

Qualities

Each of the three groups of four signs has a name. The first group is called **Cardinal** and represents the cardinal points of the compass: north, east, south, and west. The signs belonging to this group are Aries, Cancer, Libra, and Capricorn. The distinguishing feature of these signs is that they basically are hostile to one another. That incompatibility produces frustration, anxiety, fear, intimidation, inhibition, stress, and anger. While this might appear negative and defeating at first, it also has the positive effect of stimulating and energizing the individual to pursue a course of action that can result in success through careful planning, self-discipline, and application. The disharmony that exists between these signs largely is because they each belong to a different element. Aries is fire, Cancer is water, Libra is air and Capricorn is earth. In other words, they are elementarily different, not better or worse than one another. Their respective attitudes vary from one another. Just as you are comfortable with some people and not with others, so it is with the temperament of the signs. The fiery Aries usually is impatient with the emotional sentimentality of Cancer (water), the maddening rationale and logic of Libra (air) and the painfully arduous concern with reality of a Capricorn (earth). We can follow a similar route with each of the cardinal signs with respect to the others in that group and come up with similar anxieties for each of them. The most significant feature of this arrangement is that it produces a reaction/action effect which is the key for unlocking the door to change, opportunity, and growth. Not everyone succeeds in this endeavor, which probably is the reason why so many people find that their lives aren't more successful and rewarding. The characteristics of a cardinal sign are initiation, leadership, stimulation, eagerness, spontaneity, restlessness, and impatience. It is important to remember that each of the cardinal signs will have these characteristics, but they will display and use them for very different reasons determined by their individual element which establishes technique and style.

The second group of signs is called the **Fixed** group, which represents the halfway point in each of the seasons. The signs belonging to this group are Taurus, Leo, Scorpio, and Aquarius. They, too, basically are hostile to one another and it should be apparent that problems surely will result if each refuses to yield to the other so that compromise is difficult if not impossible. Taurus represent mid-spring of the year, Leo represents midsummer, Scorpio is mid-fall and Aquarius is midwinter. They pertain to the ingrained pattern of respective seasons when any significant change in those patterns is unlikely. So it is with those born under these particular signs. They stay in place until *they* decide otherwise. The characteristics of the fixed signs are steadfastness, firmness, determination, resistance, reliability, dependence, patience, stoicism, unyielding nature, uncompromising attitude, and loyalty. They will display evidence of some or all of these characteristics as they seem appropriate to their individual technique in taking any action.

The third group of signs is called **Mutable**. They represent the phase of completion for each of the seasons. They are Gemini, Virgo, Sagittarius, and Pisces. They basically are hostile to one another although the problems that result from this lack of accord are not as severe as those that occur between the signs of the cardinal or fixed groups because there is flexibility and adaptability in these signs that often helps when a solution is required to end friction or disagreement. Gemini occurs at the end of spring, Virgo is the harvest after the summer growing season, Sagittarius draws the curtain on fall, and Pisces bids winter farewell. Those belonging to these signs have difficulty yielding to the demands or expectations of other mutables. They are changeable, adaptable, resilient, reflective, fussy, resourceful, diffusive, unstable, irresolute, deliberative, and versatile.

Elements

Each of the four groups of three signs are quite different from one another. They are identified with the four basic elements in nature and their psychological correspondences, not their chemical properties. As has been said previously, the basic elements are fire, earth, air, and water. There is compatibility and harmony among the signs of the same element. In the circle of the zodiacal wheel, they occupy positions 120 degrees from one another, forming a triangle and, traditionally, a benign geometric configuration. There is a free flow of energy between the signs of the same element although the provocation for taking action may differ because they each belong to a different quality. For example, the fire signs are Aries, Leo, and Sagittarius. They share creative drive, enthusiasm, excitement, and responsiveness to stimuli. They will act according to their different temperaments; Aries quickly responds to stimuli, Leo deliberates before reacting so that the correct action prevails once initiated, but Sagittarius ponders until a variety of applications can be developed for simultaneous action. These differences occur because Aries belongs to the cardinal quality, Leo is from the fixed quality, and Sagittarius functions from the mutable quality.

The earth signs are Taurus, Virgo, and Capricorn, and they also share psychological similarities in that they all operate from the field of physical reality. They discern the value of their observations by the intrinsic properties that can be measured for their usefulness. They basically are utilitarian in the way they conduct their affairs so that some kind of substantive return for their efforts is derived. They are rational in their conclusions because they are discriminating analysts. They are factual, concrete, discerning, evidential, realistic, and resourceful. They differ in how they react to stimuli, however, because they each belong to a different quality. Taurus is a fixed sign and is slow to react to provocation due to its deliberation and thoroughness in assessing a situation. Virgo is a mutable sign that seeks as many alternative uses or solutions to the problems it faces and generally finds many applications for its skills. Capricorn also is a cardinal sign and therefore endeavors to make the most of any situation so that its status may be benefitted.

The air signs are Gemini, Libra, and Aquarius. Their expertise is in the transmission of ideas. Communication, education, teaching, writing, social enterprises, and the world of ideas are shared by these signs. How they are urged to perform is largely a matter of the particular quality to which they belong. Gemini is one of the mutable qualities and is therefore varied in the ways it applies the knowledge it possesses. Its insatiable curiosity enriches its ability to find a suitable application for its talents. Libra is part of the cardinal quality and is impatient with getting its plans under way. It is eager to display its talents and seeks a favorable social reaction for its efforts. Aquarius is methodical and painstaking in planning for the future because it belongs to the fixed quality. It never wants to waste time in redoing anything that needs to be done correctly the first time. It plans for the unexpected so that a solution can be reached quickly if it becomes necessary. Aquarians take pride in knowing people find them reliable and dependable. They rarely fail to respond as expected.

Those born under water signs enjoy a heightened ability to know things without the benefit of observation or evidence. Theirs is a talent for knowing through sensation and impression via the medium of psychic transmission. Knowledge is "felt" rather than known in the way others gain information, and the degree of accuracy sometimes is startling. They function largely on the astral plane where "matter" doesn't have the same characteristics as that found on the earth plane. As with the signs belonging to the other elements, each of the water signs is urged to behave according to their individual qualities. The water signs are Cancer, Scorpio, and Pisces. Cancer belongs to the cardinal quality and therefore is eager to respond to stimuli. The slightest impression arousing concern for a loved one causes them to react immediately to render whatever assistance may be required. This is the sign of the mothering principle and it is this factor that is quickly brought into play when a loved one is in jeopardy. Scorpio belongs to the fixed quality and therefore is slow to react when provoked. In its desire to succeed in every activity, Scorpio dwells and deliberates until every detail is examined before taking any action. Once under way however, there is little that can deter them from their objectives. Pisces is the last of the water signs and it belongs to the mutable quality. Delay, postponement, reflection, indecision, apathy, and anxiety are some of the tactics employed to avoid taking action. Fear of failing those depending on them is the main reason they check and recheck this--that and the other characteristics in the misguided idea that they may have overlooked something important. What usually results is that they are more qualified than necessary and often have wasted precious time. They generally have several alternatives to follow in the event that any of them fail to perform as expected.

It should be noted that the fire and air signs are positive and therefore assertive, leading, stimulating, and outgoing by nature. Starting with and including Aries, every other sign is positive. These are then Aries, Gemini, Leo, Libra, Sagittarius, and Aquarius. Contrasting with these are the earth and water signs: Taurus, Cancer, Virgo, Scorpio, Capricorn, and Pisces, and they are negative. This means they are passive, reactive followers who are withdrawn by nature.

ELEMENTS		SIGNS	
Fire Signs	Aries	Leo	Sagittarius
Earth Signs	Taurus	Virgo	Capricorn
Air Signs	Gemini	Libra	Aquarius
Water Signs	Cancer	Scorpio	Pisces

As previously indicated the qualities represent temperament and disposition. Notable are the cardinals' desire to initiate action, so they respond eagerly to opportunity when it occurs. This, however, has absolutely nothing to do with whether or not they are successful. It simply means that they are first in line to take action when a proposition is offered. **Aries** starts on the first day of spring, **Cancer** gets the summer started, **Libra** beckons the fall, and **Capricorn** brings winter around.

Fixed signs follow the same pattern as the cardinal signs. Each shares a common temperament and basic character identity. They occur during the middle of the four seasons and are therefore centered, resistant to change, and stable. **Taurus** starts in the middle of spring, **Leo** is in the middle of summer,

Scorpio is mid-fall, and **Aquarius** is midwinter.

The mutable signs are similar in their positions as the first two qualities. They represent factors that are coming to an end. The seasons are due to change --and dramatically so--for renewal is indicated going from mutable to cardinal. **Gemini** draws spring to a close, **Virgo** ends the summer growth, **Sagittarius** completes the harvest of fall, and **Pisces** closes the door on winter.

QUALITIES	SIGNS			
Cardinal Signs	Aries	Cancer	Libra	Capricorn
Fixed Signs	Taurus	Leo	Scorpio	Aquarius
Mutable Signs	Gemini	Virgo	Sagittarius	Pisces

As it is with these elements and qualities, so it is with people. It is the combination resulting from these distinctions that produces the differences between people. But even with this arrangement, you could say that all persons with the same Sun sign are alike. However, that would not consider another important factor or variation. This variation is called the "signature" of the chart and it is determined by the combined energies of all the planets' positions in the signs of the zodiac on the day you were born. This is accomplished by counting the number of planets in the four elements and the three qualities. What usually (but not always) results is a predominance of planets in a particular element and quality. If the majority of planets occupy a cardinal sign (any of them) and also are in a water sign (any of them), there only can be one sign to which this combination applies. The cardinal signs are Aries, Cancer, Libra, and Capricorn. Only one of these also is water and that is Cancer. The person may have an Aries Sun but will demonstrate the technique and methodology of behavior that is mainly that of a Cancer person. The planet ruling this signature sign will have an overriding influence on this individual and be motivated in performing like this sign.

A simple method for determining the signature is by using the Signature Table that follows. Select the proper quality indicated on the first column on the left. Read across to the column under the appropriate element that predominates among the planets. The sign at the intersection of these two predominating qualities and elements is the signature. Use the example given above with the cardinal prominence and the water prominence and you have Cancer where they intersect in the chart.

SIGNATURE TABLE

	FIRE	WATER	AIR	EARTH
CARDINAL	Aries	Cancer	Libra	Capricorn
FIXED	Leo	Scorpio	Aquarius	Taurus
MUTABLE	Sagittarius	Pisces	Gemini	Virgo

It sometimes happens that the distribution of the planets fails to indicate any significant prominence in both divisions. When that happens you cannot determine the signature with certainty. It may happen, however, that a prominence occurs in the qualities or the elements. You then can establish that the person's behavior is or is not consistent with the Sun sign. If an Aries has the majority of planets in the fixed signs, it is safe to regard that person as slow, deliberate, and painstaking--quite different from the expected ardor and quick response of an Aries Sun sign person. Because it was not possible to determine the prominence in the elements, we cannot tell how this person will approach and handle problems. We cannot tell what technique or methodology will be used to accomplish tasks. Conversely, there may be a prominence among the elements allowing you to determine the underlying procedure that will be used in handling problems, but you may not know the structure of the person's character and temperament that provokes taking action.

In addition to the signature or modifications for determining it, there also is the matter of the specific degree of the Sun's position in the signs. This allows you to know why persons with the same Sun sign are not the same. The Sun, Moon, and planets can be anywhere from 1 degree to 30 degrees in a sign and where they are makes a difference. The technique allows us to determine how the person effectively uses certain skills and what hazards have to be dealt with when taking any action. This procedure yields an understanding of human behavior that is basic to a successful analysis.

Each sign belongs to a particular element that is shared by two other signs. Let us take the fire signs for example. They are Aries, Leo, and Sagittarius. We know that each sign has 30 degrees. We divide the sign into three equal parts of 10 degrees each. If we use Aries, then the first 10 degrees specifically is Aries; the second 10 degrees (from 10 degrees to 20 degrees) comes under the sub-influence of Leo, the second of the fire signs. The last 10 degrees (from 20 degrees to 30 degrees) comes under the influence of Sagittarius, the last of the fire signs. What this means is that an Aries person with the Sun at 15 degrees of the sign will function as an Aries, but will use the dramatic flair and determined leadership that are Leo characteristics. This person will have more persistence and follow-through than is customary with an Aries nature. If the person has the Sun at 23 degrees of Aries, there will be considerable evidence of the grandiose approach to life with large-scale enterprises that are "sure to succeed." The drive of Aries is seen but it is enriched by a temperament that only is happy when handling matters that are substantial in their content and widespread in their influence. This is because the last 10 degrees (from 20 degrees to 30 degrees) has a sub-influence of Sagittarius where hope and high expectation prevail. This shows that there are favorable facets to every sign that enables them to achieve their objectives with skills that are beyond what the Sun sign itself allows. This division of the signs into 10-degree sectors is called a decanate. The first 10 degrees of Aries is the Aries decanate, from 10 degrees to 20 degrees is the Leo decanate and, from 20 degrees to 30 degrees is called the Sagittarius decanate.

Each sign also belongs to a particular quality that is shared by the three other signs of that group. For example, the cardinal signs are Aries, Cancer,

Libra, and Capricorn. We know that each sign has 30 degrees. We divide the signs into four equal parts of 7 1/2 degrees each. Again, if we use Aries, the first 7 1/2 degrees specifically is Aries; the second 7 1/2 degrees (from 7 1/2 degrees to 15 degrees) comes under the sub-influence of Cancer, the second of the cardinal signs. The third 7 1/2 degrees (from 15 degrees to 22 1/2 degrees) has a sub-influence of Libra, the third of the cardinal signs. The fourth 7 1/2 degrees (from 22 1/2 degrees to 30 degrees) has a sub-influence of Capricorn, the fourth of the cardinal signs. Remember, we said that the elements are favorable to one another but that the qualities are basically hostile and inharmonious to one another. The same holds true in dividing the signs into three decanates that are favorable to the Sun sign in question. By dividing the signs into equal quarters, the signs belonging to each of these is hostile to the Sun sign in question. They show flaws and stress factors that the person with that Sun sign has to cope with and resolve. The following decanate graph illustrates the division of a sign into its 10-degree element parts, using Leo's decanates.

0°	10°	20° 30°
Leo	Sagittarius	Aries

This same procedure is used to illustrate the division of each sign into the four quarters representing the qualities. We again use Leo to demonstrate.

0°	7 1/2°	15°	22 1/2° 30°
Leo	Scorpio	Aquarius	Taurus

When we combine these two illustrations in a single linear graph, it becomes readily apparent how the favorable (decanate/element) factors of a sign also include the unfavorable (quarter/quality) factors of that sign. The linear graph below illustrates this combination.

0°	10°	20° 30°
Leo	Sagittarius	Aries

Leo	Scorpio	Aquarius	Taurus
0°	7 1/2°	15°	22 1/2° 30°

The top section containing the sign of the same element is favorable to the sign in question and therefore helpful to the individual. The lower section represents the signs belonging to the same quality and these are unfavorable to the sign in question. They represent factors that are disruptive and stressful to the individual and show the need to learn how to handle the problems they indicate in the development of character and personality. This procedure shows why people with the same Sun sign often are quite different in their aspirations and conflicts. This becomes even more apparent when the technique is presented in a linear form as follows, using Leo as an example.

The Sun enters Leo on or about July 22 and is thus in the first decanate of

LEO

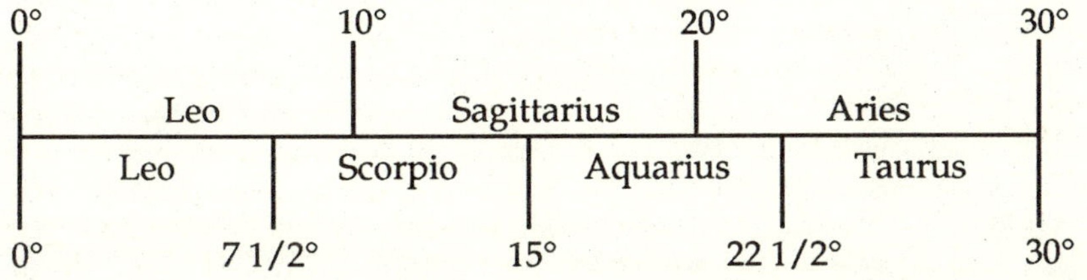

Leo of the element division, but it also is in the first quarter of the quality division. On or about July 30, the Sun has traveled to the 8-degrees location. It is still in the first decanate division of the element, but it is now in the second (Scorpio) quarter division of the qualities. On or about August 1, the Sun is at 10 degrees of Leo and has entered the second decanate (Sagittarius) division of the element, but it still is in the second (Scorpio) quarter division of the qualities. This procedure continues as the Sun moves approximately 1 degree per day and occupies various combinations of element/quality divisions of the sign in its progress through the 30 degrees of Leo. The same holds true for each of the signs according to their particular decanates and quarters. The date of birth determines the Sun's degree position in each sign. On the day the Sun enters Leo, the focus is exclusively Leo. The last 7 1/2 days of the Sun in Leo is remarkably different because the person under this influence is provoked to take action as if it were the first time, but the anxieties about any losses forces this person to make certain that something of value is derived from the effort. A short interpretation of this "trine and quartering" of a sign follows.

There are six distinct types belonging to each of the signs as you can see from the divisions in the linear display. Let's examine what this means for the Leo.

0 degrees to 7 1/2 degrees/Leo: The Sun occupying these degrees shows a pure Leo who is enthusiastic and determined to exploit his own creative talents. The disruptive quality (bottom section) shows an unwillingness to recognize anyone else's creative talents.

7 1/2 degrees to 10 degrees/Scorpio: Persistent effort makes gains and reaps rewards, but now the Scorpio (bottom section) shows a reluctance in motivating others to enjoy similar rewards. (This is the disruptive feature of this degree area of Leo.)

10 degrees to 15 degrees/Scorpio: The Sun now has moved into the next decanate, Sagittarius, but it is still in the Scorpio quarter and experiences the tension it indicates. The individual now gains the talent for promoting his enterprises that will gain attention (Sagittarius influence). When he learns to enrich others by these benefits, the best of both worlds will be realized.

15 degrees to 20 degrees/Aquarius: Although the decanate remains the same, the quarter where resistance occurs has changed from Scorpio to Aquarius. This individual must learn universal love and share with others as he would have them share with him.

20 degrees to 22 1/2 degrees/Aquarius: The decanate now has changed to Aries (ruled by Mars). Though this Aquarius individual will still be the persistent Leo, he will have acquired a renewed vitality in taking on new tasks, but must still maintain a loving attitude toward the world at large.

22 1/2 degrees to 30 degrees/Taurus: This individual is especially keen in developing imaginative enterprises that arouse the public's interest, but his lower quarter is now Taurus (Venus ruled) that will disrupt progress unless a way is found that will prove beneficial to the public as well as personal interests.

The Sun degrees must be examined in this fashion for each sign. This shows what the individual has in terms of talent potential and what lessons have to be learned before they can be translated easily into worthwhile results. The same procedure can be followed with all the planets and it gives you the kind of intimate detail about their influence that cannot be found elsewhere.

The Jones Patterns

Another useful technique to help understand how and why people are motivated as they are is the use of the Jones Patterns, named after the late Marc Jones, who devised them. They consist of the spatial distribution of the planets in the signs of the zodiac so that specific patterns are discerned. Jones devised seven patterns and gave them descriptive names, some of which are self-explanatory when observed. They are bundle, bowl, bucket, see-saw, locomotive, splay, and splash.

Bundle:The bundle is so obvious that it immediately catches the eye. It consists of a grouping of planets within 120 degrees of one another so that there is a vast area of 240 degrees that is completely unoccupied by any other planet. This shows an intense concentration of energy that oftentimes is directed in self-serving activity.

Bowl: When all the planets in a chart are dispersed within one-half of the signs, excluding the bundle, the resulting pattern is the bowl. It shows the individual is reasonably self-contained in a closely defined world. Where the hemisphere occurs is important, too. If it is largely in the eastern half of the chart, the life focus is mainly subjective while the western half bestows a more objective outlook. When the top of the chart (south) is principally occupied, the person tends to lose personal identity and often is focused by outer influences. Should the emphasis be in the lower (north) sector, the tendency is to become a loner.

The Bundle

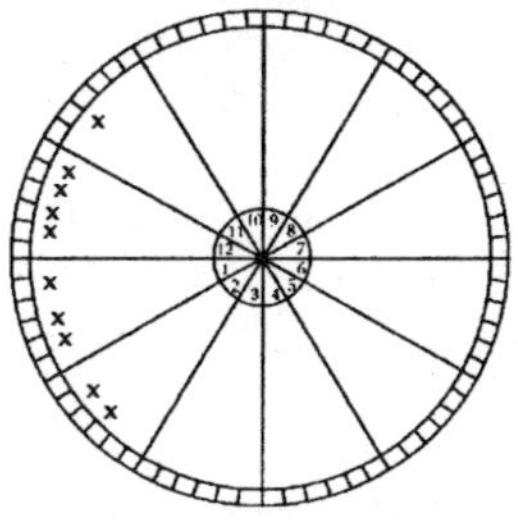

The Bowl

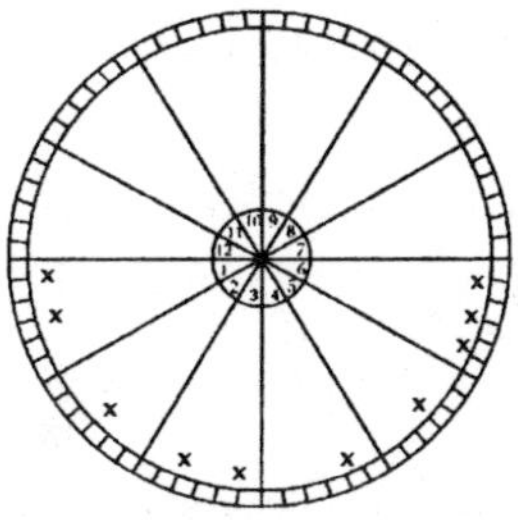

The Bucket

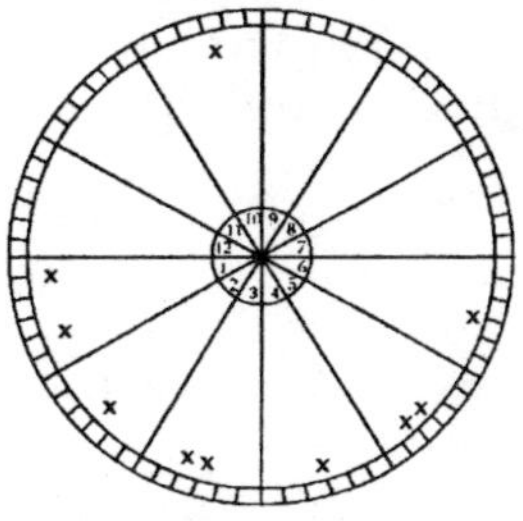

Bucket: This pattern is similar to the bowl, except that this has a handle. Usually one or two planets in a conjunction in the opposite hemisphere are the handle. The handle presents a focus through which much of the life will be expressed.

See-Saw: When planets are fairly evenly distributed within one or two signs opposing one another, the result is a see-saw. It creates ambivalence in the life and produces conditions and situations that are very difficult to integrate. The dichotomy may best be compared to the Jekyll-and-Hyde phenomenon.

The See-Saw

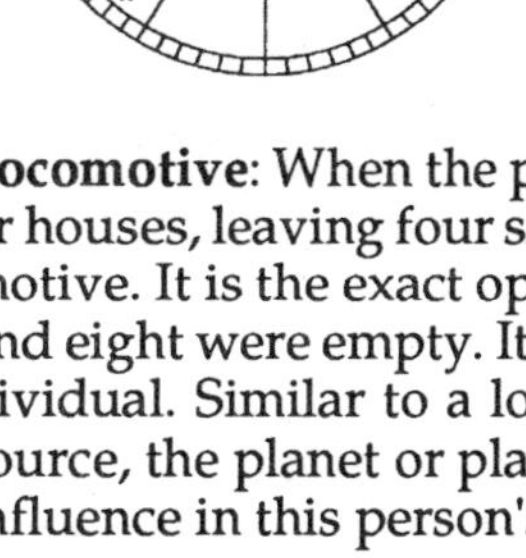

The Locomotive

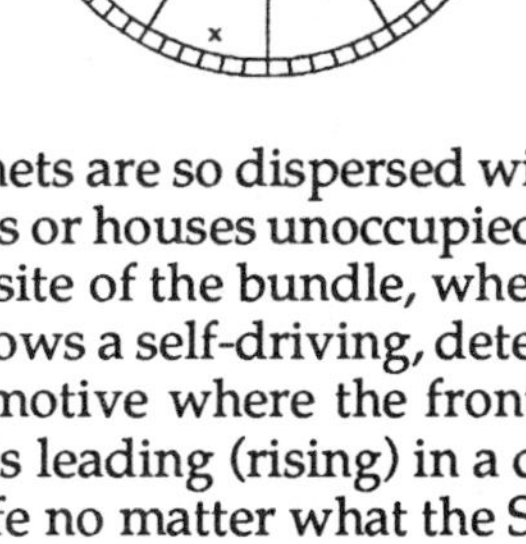

The Splay

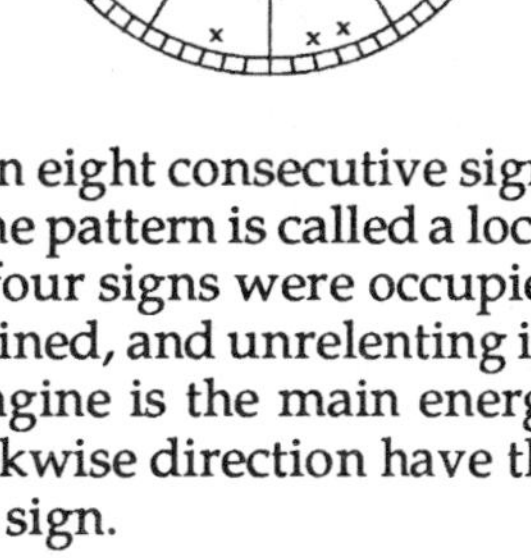

Locomotive: When the planets are so dispersed within eight consecutive signs or houses, leaving four signs or houses unoccupied, the pattern is called a locomotive. It is the exact opposite of the bundle, where four signs were occupied and eight were empty. It shows a self-driving, determined, and unrelenting individual. Similar to a locomotive where the front engine is the main energy source, the planet or planets leading (rising) in a clockwise direction have the influence in this person's life no matter what the Sun sign.

Splay: This occurs when the planets are distributed randomly around the signs and houses but with at least two pairs of planets involved in a conjunction aspect (preferably three pairs for emphasis). This individual's talents will be pronounced but difficult to develop and implement.

Splash: Although this is similar to the splay, the difference is that there are no pairs to give any kind of emphasis. It generally indicates diversity in the extreme so that developing a "handle" or focus is very difficult. It sometimes happens that the individual is unable to consolidate effort to maximize results, unless the chart contains an effective aspectual pattern to provide energetic focus.

The Splash

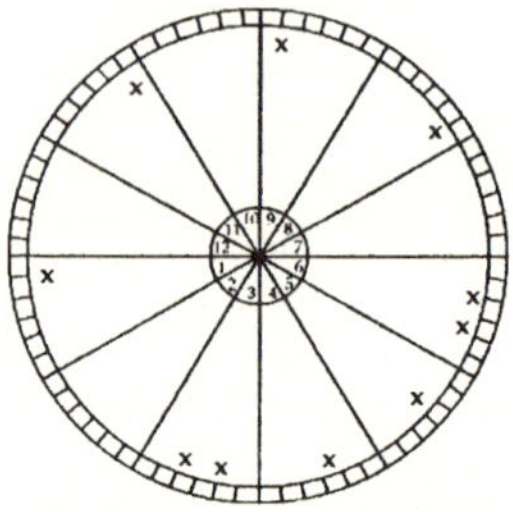

The Jones Patterns each have a very profound effect and should be given among the first (if not the first) considerations in the analysis of the chart.

Similar to the Jones Patterns, the hemispheric division of the planets is yet another astrological concept that must be given serious consideration in the analysis of a time chart. The distribution of the planets in their specific areas also offers valuable information in respect to the mental focus of the individual. A glance at Figure 7 will show the areas involved that are self-explanatory.

The qualities, elements, and other factors have great significance as well and should be given the consideration they justly deserve. When it is found that any of the qualities (cardinal, fixed, and mutable) are void of any planets, that particular quality will be lacking in life. Let's look at some brief examples.

Cardinal quality lacks planets. This person really would have what some psychiatrists refer to as "diminished capacity." This individual will neither see nor take advantage of the most noticeable and obvious opportunities.

Fixed quality is similar to the unoccupied cardinal signs. Here the person may see and realize an opportunity but just can't seem to set any direction or course of action for any particular objective.

Mutable: The ability to change within these signs does not seem to exist with those who have no planets here. When these signs are unoccupied the person seems unable to make even the slightest effort to any changing circumstances.

It now should be obvious that any of the quality signs that are void of any planets would result in the other quality signs having an abundance of planets, thus making the person's behavior more pronounced. This also stands true for the elements as follows.

With respect to the elements that lack any planets, we also offer some brief examples from which you will be able to elaborate.

Fire element is lacking any planets. This individual will be unable to get his act together or get too excited about anything. Their energy and enthusiasm seems to be dissipated, resulting in their being very depressed and pessimistic.

Earth is the stability, the realities of life, the everyday common sense which, when void of any planets, results in instability, lack of common sense, and inability to face the realities of life.

Air represents intellectual abilities and should thus make it obvious that without any planets here, intellectual abilities for these people will be lacking. Matters that require any thought or considerations readily will be dismissed.

Water, representing the emotions and compassion for others along with nourishment for all, will be washed away with no planets in these signs. Those with no planets here will be unable to express any feelings for anyone who truly may be in need of their comfort and sympathy.

It should be apparent at this point that to make an analysis and/or judge the validity of astrology by Sun signs, as the critics and some would-be astrologers do, is a grave error. It *simply cannot be done.*

Figure 7
Hemispheric Focus

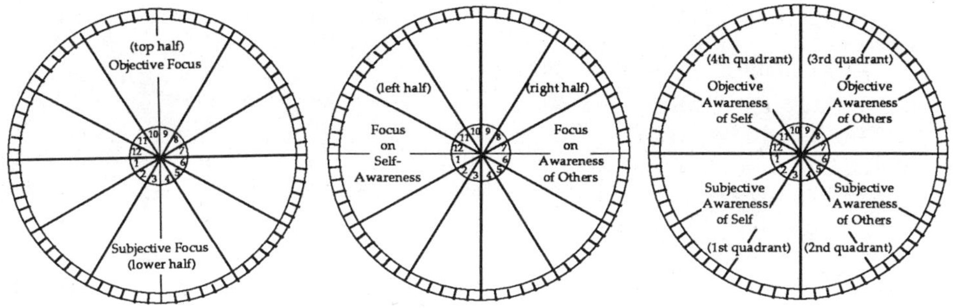

Chapter 8
Aspects and Special Configurations

Aspect means facing or fronting in a particular direction. Astrologers apply the term to the planets and zodiac signs within our solar system. At the moment of your birth, all the planets were facing and/or fronting a particular direction, which an astrologer would record in your natal chart (horoscope). As we intend to prove, the planets and their arrangements are a crucial factor in your dynamics of behavior. The continuing orbits of these planets around the Sun results in their continually facing and/or fronting the different planets and signs, which continually results in different aspects between the planets themselves as well as to their original positions as recorded in your natal chart. Excluding those aspects that existed at the moment of your birth which remain a factor in your behavior, all future aspects continue on in their regulated cycles, making regulated aspects to all planets in your natal chart as well as those aspects recorded therein. These regulated cycles of aspects continue on throughout life, and depending upon what aspects are being formed and/or parting, the behavior of the individual will be altered somewhat in one way or another. The altered behavior will remain manifested for as long as the planet or planets remain within the particular aspectual degrees. A complete orbit of any and all planets will include 10 individual type aspects. Although there may be more than one aspect of each of the different types, each of the regulated aspects to your natal chart will vary in the time it takes to form or separate as well as the length of time the aspect remains in effect. This is due to the varying speeds of the planets in completing their orbits. For example, the Moon moves at a rate of roughly 13 degrees per day and remains in the same zodiacal sign for 2-2 1/2 days. In 14 days it will have reached its opposite sign, or 180 degrees. During this time it will have moved through 60, 90, 120, and 150 aspectual degrees (all of which are crucial aspects) to its present 180 degrees. On its return to its natal position, it again will repeat these aspects but in a reverse manner. From its 180-

degree position it now will reach the 150-degree mark, followed by 120, then 90, and 60 to within 0 to 8 degrees of its original position. The Sun, on the other hand, moves at a rate of 1 degree per day. Thus, in 60 days it reaches its first aspectual position; then on to 90 days, followed by 120, 150, and eventually it reaches its opposite sign 180 days or 6 months later. The Sun also follows the same cycle in the reverse manner until it reaches within 0 to 8 degrees of its original position. When it reaches the same natal degree it has completed its orbit--and it's your birthday.

Few people realize how Einstein's theories of cause and effect and action and reaction make up their everyday activities. Serious astrologers refer to these particular activities as aspects.

Let's now apply these aspectual cycles to normal everyday activities and/or events that occur within everyone's life. You may follow these cycles by selecting any experience you may have had, be it a minor or major event in your life. We will number the cause and effect--action and reaction that occurs regularly in your daily life from 1 to 10 to represent the 10 individual type aspects. Depending upon the severity and importance of the incident, the complete sequence of cycles could last anywhere from minutes to days, weeks, months, and even years.

The Event

1 (0-8 degrees: the ☌) A minor or major incident occurs. It may have been verbal or physical, something you did or that was done to you, something you witnessed or was repeated to you, or whatever. Whatever the event, you either took the initial action or reacted to someone else's action. If it was considered beneficial, a favorable action or reaction resulted. If it was considered detrimental to your best interests, you would have exercised some sort of defensive action or reaction.

The Mental Process

2 (60 degrees: 3rd House ⚹) Following the action or reaction, the mind now begins making an analysis as to the justification for the action taken. It now considers all that was said and done as to the cause and circumstances surrounding the event. Should all these facts be known, they are taken into consideration, analyzed, and justified. In short, all that is pertinent to the incident and actions is thought about from the initial action, to the last word or act, what could have prevented it, what else could have been said or done, and so forth. This does not infer that all other daily activities are cast aside, but that the mind reacts upon the immediate impulse received regardless of who, what, where, when, or why.

The Uncertainty, Restrictions, Inhibitions

3 (90 degrees: 4th house □) Retracing all that was said and done, the mind now adds yet another dimension due to doubt, fear, and the uncertainty of being inadequately prepared to cope with the results of the action. The fear of reprisal, rejection, having erred, and so forth results in complete uncertainty, restrictions, and inhibitions of a sort from indulging in anything similar to or pertaining to that particular incident or event.

The Perceptions

4 (120 degrees: 5th House △) In the struggle to succeed, an individual weighs the pros and cons of all that has transpired and fills in all the possible oversights. Having perceived all avenues for favorable results, the person now decides that there is no difficulty in resolving the matter favorably and now stores away the issue until such time as it becomes necessary to act upon it.

The Search for Approval

5 (150 degrees: 6th House ⚻) Because there always is a certain amount of uncertainty attached to any forthcoming results, the mind now decides it is best to win approval for the actions from all concerned parties. In order to win this approval and acceptance, acts of service and favoritism are extended to all in the hope of verifying that one's actions were justified.

The Adjustments and Compromises

6 (180 degrees: the ☍) The adversaries return to rekindle the issues at hand. The mind now calls for another deposition with itself to decide what can and cannot be done to resolve this issue. Compromises must take place and adjustments must be made in order to achieve the harmony desired, where one meets one half way. As survival is the first law of nature, it should be obvious that any compromises and adjustments (if any) will be made for personal benefit. It is because of this self-preservation that making the proper decisions now becomes a difficult task.

Our lessons must be learned from our experiences, thus when there are no experiences there are no lessons learned. Maturity is the result of growth and growth is the reward of experience. When a mature nature is extended in resolving an issue, a lesson has been learned. However, when a mature nature is not extended in any issue it then should be obvious that no lessons have been learned, but will have to be sooner or later.

Having traveled through the first half of their orbit (180 degrees), the planets now are on their way to their original natal positions. Returning there, they repeat the same aspects but in a reverse order. From their halfway aspect at 180 degrees, the next aspectual degree would be 30 degrees further on, or 210 degrees. Counting in a clockwise direction (the shortest distance) from its original position would yield 150 degrees; 30 degrees more of travel would be 240 degrees (or 120 degrees in the clockwise direction); 270 degrees will be 90 degrees clockwise followed by 300 degrees, which then would be 60 degrees and on to its natal position. Aspects are determined from their closest point to their original position either counterclockwise or clockwise. Although all aspects made during the second half of the orbit are similar in nature to those of the first half, they do incur a significant change in effects of the behavior.

The Search for Approval

7 (150/210 degrees: 8th House ⚻) Similar to the first 150-degrees aspect, this aspect results in the mind having another deposition because of the uncertainty of the adjustments and compromises made. The mind now correlates all that was stored away and makes new decisions on the matter. It now decides that it *must win* approval from all concerned. This is accomplished by volunteering oneself for almost any task and for anyone. The mind now is so overburdened from all these volunteered tasks that there just never seems to be enough time left to take care of one's personal tasks.

The Perceptions

8 (120/240 degrees: 9th House △) Similar to the first 120-degrees aspect, the mind again stores away the issue, but with complete assurance that favorable results will terminate the incident once and for all when and if the occasion arises. There appears to be no further need to ponder any issues that are well under control.

The Uncertainty--Restriction--Inhibitions

9 (90/270 degrees: 10th House □) Having had its mental depositions from the initial impulse on through the entire text of the memory, the mind now begins retracing all that took place up to this point. It now realizes that it cannot perceive what the adversaries may or may not accept, resulting in more uncertainty of the results. Because of this uncertainty the entire incident again is considered but in a much more mature and cautious manner to ensure that nothing is overlooked. Failure to resolve the issue favorably would be unforgivable. Every detail must be taken into consideration to ensure success. The mind at this point puts all else aside in order to concentrate on the most favorable actions only. As success is the only result acceptable, life itself with all its pleasures is passed over.

The Mental Process

10 (60/300 degrees: 11th House ⚹) Every aspect, both favorable and unfavorable, now is considered because one is completely aware of what the consequence will bring regardless of the outcome. A much more mature attitude toward either result exists, which allows one to restore pleasures of life into one's activities and care less about other's opinions, thoughts, acts, or demands. You now realize that you do know exactly what to do: "be yourself."

The next aspectual degree is the return of the planets to their original positions in your natal chart. This is between the specified 0 degrees to 8 degrees referred to as a conjunction. Each and every planet follows the same cycle of aspects with differences in the time involved in forming or separating from the aspects and the effects of each, both of which depend upon the planet making the aspect and the planet being aspected.

Applying these aspects to any of your personal incidents or events requires that you seriously recall the incident and all your mental reactions.

Let us discuss the details of these cycles and each major aspect as they are applied in actual astrological practice. "Aspect" is a term describing the angular distance that separates planets in the zodiac. They are crucial to a proper analysis of the chart for they indicate how the energies of the planets function separately and in their relations with the other planets. They are the prime indicators of how a person behaves and what it is that motivates that behavior. Critical to an accurate judgment of how a planet operates is how it may be influenced by the aspectual contacts it makes to other planets in the chart, the signs they occupy, and the houses in which they are found. The combinations involving the particular planets, signs, and houses are infinite and therefore there are no precise duplications. It is best to examine the problem of aspects by carefully noting the natures of the behavioral mechanism the planets represent and arrive at a reasonably accurate judgment of what each of the planets means and how that meaning is altered by the aspect it makes to another planet. For example, the Sun is the ego and the striving for significance through the effective use of power and authority. How this will be done is shown by the element of the sign it occupies. If it is a fire sign (Aries, Leo, or Sagittarius), there will be a lot of creative talent and a flair for getting support from people who will help. If the Sun is in an Earth sign (Taurus, Virgo, or Capricorn), there will be a talent for mobilizing the right kind of people with the necessary resources with which to reach the objectives. If the Sun is in an air sign (Gemini, Libra, or Aquarius), the skill in communication is sufficient to arouse people so they grasp the rationale for success that is offered. If the Sun is in a water sign (Cancer, Scorpio, or Pisces), there is an ability to attract followers who are as sympathetic to the causes you present as you are. In each of these different mediums of utilization a different characteristic is emphasized and, while their methods might differ, they each can satisfy the striving for significance that is the Sun's dominant purpose. In citing how the Sun in the different signs is changed, we have had to alter the Sun's operating method in keeping with the natures of those signs. The same principle must be applied to any planet that forms an aspect to the Sun. There are two different planetary energies--the Sun and another planet--both of which have been modified by their respective sign positions, involved in a particular aspect that also imparts its own characteristic to the configuration. In addition, the indications of the slower planet in the aspect imposes its energy on the faster planet. You must keep these subtleties in mind when analyzing the planets if there are more than two of them since they represent conditions that are extremely complex.

It is because of the importance of all these factors that careful consideration must be given when synthesizing the meaning of planets in aspect. The basic concept of each of the six aspects used in delineating a chart will be explained in detail. The names for each of these six aspects are conjunction, sextile, square, trine, inconjunct,and opposition. The names, descriptions, and symbols (glyphs) for each aspect are

Conjunction (☌) This aspect occurs when two (or more) planets are within 8 degrees of each other in any zodiacal sign.

Sextile (⚹) When two or more planets are separated by 60 degrees plus or minus 6 degrees, they are in a sextile relationship.

Square (□) Two or more planets separated by 90 degrees, plus or minus 8 degrees, are in a square aspect.

Trine (△) Planets separated by a distance of 120 degrees, plus or minus 8 degrees, are considered to be in a trine aspect.

Inconjunct (⚻) This is the aspect in which 150 degrees, plus or minus 3 degrees, is the distance that separates two or more planets.

Opposition (☍) When two or more planets are on opposite sides of the zodiac and 180 degrees plus or minus 8 degrees separates them, they are in an opposition aspect.

The aspects bear an intimate relationship to the houses through the degrees that identify them. For instance, the zodiac begins with Aries, the first sign, and the house of the chart associated with Aries is located in the 30 degrees of space immediately following the left side of the horizontal line of the chart in a counterclockwise direction. In essence, the conjunction aspect has the same invigorating energy as that which characterizes Aries or the 1st House. The sextile (60 degrees) is associated with the sign and house that is 60 degrees from the first point of Aries, or the 1st House. In a counterclockwise direction we find Gemini or the 3rd House; in a clockwise direction we find Aquarius or the 11th House. Because of these associated references points, the sextile aspect greatly resembles the energies associated with Mercury and Uranus (the rulers of Gemini and Aquarius and of the 3rd and 11th Houses with which these signs correspond).

The illustrations that follow merely are to acquaint you with the identifying features of the different aspects. In actual practice, you may find aspects between planets located anywhere in the chart, but the aspects still will bear the natures of the signs, houses, and planetary energies that are revealed through the associations counting from the beginning of Aries. You may have a sextile between a planet in Leo and one in Libra. They will function through the fields provided by these two signs but they still will behave with the energy common to Mars and Mercury or Mars and Uranus. Communication is the primary principle at work in a sextile and its curiosity is parallel that of Mercury and Uranus.

You may have two planets conjunct in the sign Virgo, which is ruled by the planet Mercury, but the display of energy in a conjunction is not dissimilar from that found in Aries, the first house that is ruled by Mars. The ardor of planets conjunct in Virgo is not easily restrained or restricted (Mars, Aries, 1st house), only the method of their function will be focused through a medium that is a comfortable outlet for the Virgoan mode.

Figure 8

Aspect Illustrations

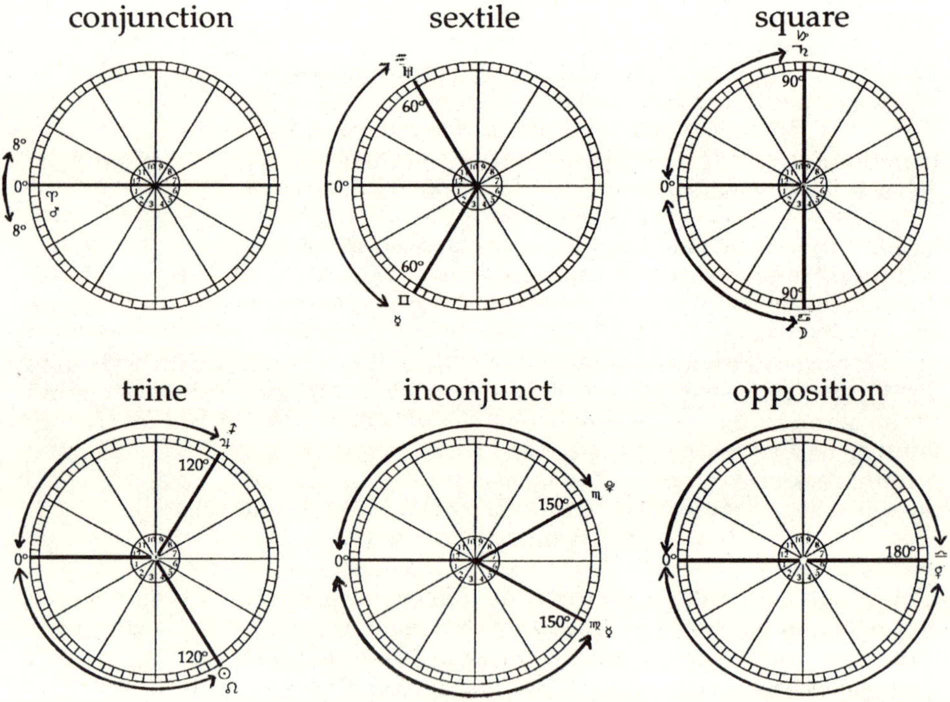

The Nature of Aspects

Aspects between planets either can be favorable or unfavorable and you also may find them referred to as benefic or malefic. Favorable aspects bring out the positive or benign natures of the planets involved. The favorable aspects are the sextiles which occur when planets are separated by 60 degrees, and the trines occur when planets are separated by 120 degrees. Unfavorable aspects bring out the undesirable or negative natures of the planets involved. The unfavorable aspects are the square at 90-degree angles, the inconjunct at 150-degree angles, and the opposition when planets are separated by 180 degrees. The conjunction requires special attention because everything depends on the natures of the planets involved. The result either can be favorable or unfavorable and the basic natures of the planets determine the effect. If both planets basically are benign, as with Venus and Jupiter, the result largely is favorable, but if either planet basically is malefic the result primarily is difficult. As a general rule the conjunction can be considered benign or favorable when the Sun, Moon, Mercury, Venus, and Jupiter are involved in the aspect. On the other hand if *one* of the planets involved is Mars, Saturn, Uranus, Neptune, or Pluto you must consider it an unfavorable influence.

Planetary Protocol

It is essential to understand the principle of planetary protocol in determining the effect of one planet in aspect with another. The rule is: *The slower planet always exerts a dominant force over the faster planet*. This especially is important when analyzing the planets involved in a conjunction, but it also is true with any aspect. As an example, suppose you have Jupiter conjunct Saturn. Saturn is the slower of the two, and its negative influence will dominate Jupiter. The result suggests that this person has high expectations for reaching his goals fairly early in life (Jupiter) but the harsh realities of life soon will impress on him that nothing is gained without a lot of study, hard work, and a willingness to accept full responsibility for the gains made (Saturn). All this will take a lot of time and effort suitably directed into well-focused areas of attention. This is not to say that Jupiter doesn't play an important part in the successes gained, for most certainly it is the undiminished enthusiasm and hope that guides that person throughout the arduous times that culminate with the eventual rewards. For this benign influence we must be grateful for Jupiter's share in the gains.

The Individual Aspects: Composition and Dynamics of Behavior

Conjunction (☌) 0 degrees to 8 degrees When two planets are within 8 degrees of each other in the zodiac they are in the aspect called the conjunction. There may be more than two planets within the 8-degree orb for this aspect and it sometimes happens that several planets form a group conjunction that is called a stellium. In such cases they only can be considered conjunct if no more than 8 degrees separates them from one another. Although a "spread" of this kind is not infrequent, if there are more than 8 degrees separating any of them, it dissolves the link that would otherwise combine all of them in a complex planetary dynamic. When this happens only those planets separated by no more than 8 degrees can be considered conjunct. It also is possible to have more than one conjunct aspect in the same sign.

Planets in a conjunction are strongly stimulated by the inferred energy of Aries, the 1st House, and their associated ruler, Mars. The energy in a conjunction is intense, direct, and unyielding. A thorough examination and guides detailing the procedure for analyzing aspects involving many different kinds of planetary energy will be presented elsewhere in the text.

Sextile (⚹) 60 degrees plus or minus 6 degrees (from 54 degrees to 66 degrees). This is the aspect of communication and understanding, which has the nature of Mercury and Uranus. We say Mercury because it rules Gemini and the 3rd House (60 degrees counting from the beginning [Aries or the 1st House] in a counterclockwise direction). It also has the nature of Uranus because counting clockwise from Aries or the 1st House for 60 degrees brings us to Aquarius (or the 11th House) which is ruled by Uranus. When any two or more planets are sextile there should be no difficulty in expressing their energy in communication and understanding. As the conjunction is like Aries or the 1st House and Mars, so the sextile bears a similarity with Gemini and Aquarius, the 3rd and 11th Houses and their rulers, Mercury and Uranus. Sextiles always are favorable because they unite frames of reference that are compatible as are their respective rulers.

Square (□) 90 degrees plus or minus 8 degrees (from 82 degrees to 98 degrees). The square is an aspect of conflict, fear, and inhibiting factors. It has the quality of the Moon or Saturn. The Moon is here because it rules the 4th House (or 90 degrees from the 1st counting counterclockwise), and Saturn because it rules the 10th House at 90 degrees from the 1st counting clockwise. Conflicts exist because this usually is where your accustomed behavior runs into opposition. Your habits run into sudden reversals and you become emotionally hurt by it. Squares always are considered unfavorable because they always will fall within a 1st and 4th or a 1st and 10th House nature--the signs and houses that will always be hostile to each other.

You should realize at this time that aspects become favorable or unfavorable depending upon the compatibility of the signs and houses of their locations and not because of some ancient, superstitious fool who just decided they were so. Aspects are no different than the human feelings they influence. When you are with friends and relatives or with others who have the same interests, you are at ease and pleasant. Should you by chance be forced by circumstances to be with people you dislike, with adversaries and others, or in places against your wishes, you naturally are ill at ease, irritable, and probably hostile.

Trine (△) 120 degrees plus or minus 8 degrees (from 112 degrees to 128 degrees). The trine is considered to be a lucky aspect and always is considered favorable though we may not do anything with it. It has the nature of the Sun or Jupiter. The Sun rules the 5th House, 120 degrees from the 1st counting counterclockwise. Jupiter rules the 9th House, 120 degrees from the 1st counting clockwise. It is creative and enables enthusiasm. It is sustaining and generates life because it is the Sun. It builds up hopes because it is Jupiter. But because it is built within us, we usually do nothing about it. We just take the gamble and believe that all will turn out favorably.

The trine is considered to be favorable at all times because it always must fall within signs of the same element and houses of the same element.

Inconjunct (⚻) 150 degrees plus or minus 3 degrees (from 147 degrees to 153 degrees). This aspect takes on the nature of Mercury or Pluto. Counting from the 1st House in either direction, Mercury rules the 6th House (150 degrees away) and Pluto rules the 8th House (150 degrees away). This is where we usually neglect ourselves. It involves a health or destructive aspect of our lives. This is where we usually volunteer ourselves to others in an attempt to prove ourselves and be accepted, where we work in service to others (6th House) and do ourselves in serving other peoples' needs (8th House). It almost always causes a dilemma because there is a tendency to feel powerless to do anything about it. It becomes very difficult to avert problems.

Opposition (☍) 180 degrees plus or minus 8 degrees (from 172 degrees to 188 degrees). This is a Venus quality aspect as Venus rules the 7th House (180 degrees from the 1st House), its opposite. The 1st House is the "I am" house (Aries), the 7th House is the "we" house: of partners, marriage, and so forth. This aspect almost always has to do with relationships and attempts to resolve differences. Venus is the gestures and adjustments you make hoping others will reciprocate and the compromise you hope will result: the opposition, the 1st House, the opposite, the partner, the 7th House, you, your partner. The solution always is there also, all that is needed is the compromise (Venus): the 7th House of balance, judge the facts.

No matter where this aspect may lie, it always will be in opposite signs and houses, the complete opposites and therefore always unfavorable.

In the study of astrology, as in any other study, there is never a problem or crisis that presents itself without an answer or solution to it also being present. The sextiles and the trines are the favorable aspects that should be employed in overcoming the unfavorable ones: the conjunctions, squares, inconjuncts, and oppositions. Here is a listing of the solutions to the stresses and anxieties that result from these aspects.

Conjunction: Use these energies for creative talents, not for your personal, physical, or biological indulgences.

Sextile: These mental abilities should be used in service to others in their search for freedom--thus helping you gain yours.

Square: You must learn to give in to the characteristics of the signs of the square.

Trine: The tendency to sit on your laurels and do nothing should be overcome. Your resources should be used and not lay idle until such time as you are up against the wall.

Inconjunct: You must learn to *judge the facts* and then assert yourself to a factual decision. Don't volunteer for anything only to prove yourself.

Opposition: You must learn to give in to the characteristics of the opposing signs and make the decision now, not later.

Because aspects are so crucial to our behavior, we feel it most important to explain them in detail. This will allow you every opportunity to interpret our explanations correctly as well as assist you in your synthesis. We have just illustrated why aspects possess the qualities they have. We now will explain how and why their influences vary accordingly to the signs and house of their locations. When all these conditions are considered, then and only then will the proper influence be determined.

For example, let us say that the chart shows Venus conjunct Mars. This is an aspect of two planetary forces concentrated into a single mass of energy. This particular energy will be modified according to the sign of its placement. Let us now assume that this aspect is located in the sign of Aries. Because Aries's ruler is Mars, and Venus is in its opposing sign, the Mars negative forces will run roughshod over Venus's positive forces. The animal instincts of crudeness and coarseness will prevail.

Let us now assume that this same aspect is in the sign of Libra. Because Venus rules Libra and Mars is in its opposing sign, Venus is the stronger of the two here. Venus's strength here will override that of Mars and will curtail the animal instincts, crudeness, and coarseness. However, because Mars is the slower planet, and the slower planet always exerts its negative forces over the positive forces of the faster planet, Mars's influence will prevail. Love will triumph but in a more refined manner. The sensuality, magnetism, and so forth is very strong by the aspect itself, but how it is used depends on the sign and house. Let us assume another change by house. The same aspect located in the 1st House would be more or less the same as when in the sign of Aries. The same would be true in the 7th House of Libra, but what if the aspect as originally stated was in Aries but located in the 4th House? This modifies the entire aspect's characteristics of sensuality, magnetism, and so forth. We still will have those characteristics, but how they will be utilized changes to the attitude and circumstances of the 4th House. The Moon rules the 4th House, so we now have to consider its nature. Saturn rules the 10th House and we also have to consider its fearsome and restrictive nature. Why Saturn? Because the 4th House happens to be Venus's 10th House (counting counterclockwise from Venus's natural 7th House). The 4th House squares both Venus's and Mars's natural locations.

This all may sound very complicated at first, but it really isn't after you are familiar with these dynamics, which we now are going to explain in very simple to understand terms. All that is required is a sincere desire to know and a genuine commitment to the task.

We will start with an illustration of the zodiac with the houses numbered 1 through 12 counting counterclockwise. The zodiacal signs will be placed in their natural locations shown by their glyphs, only on the cusp of their natural house

Figure 9

Natural Zodiac

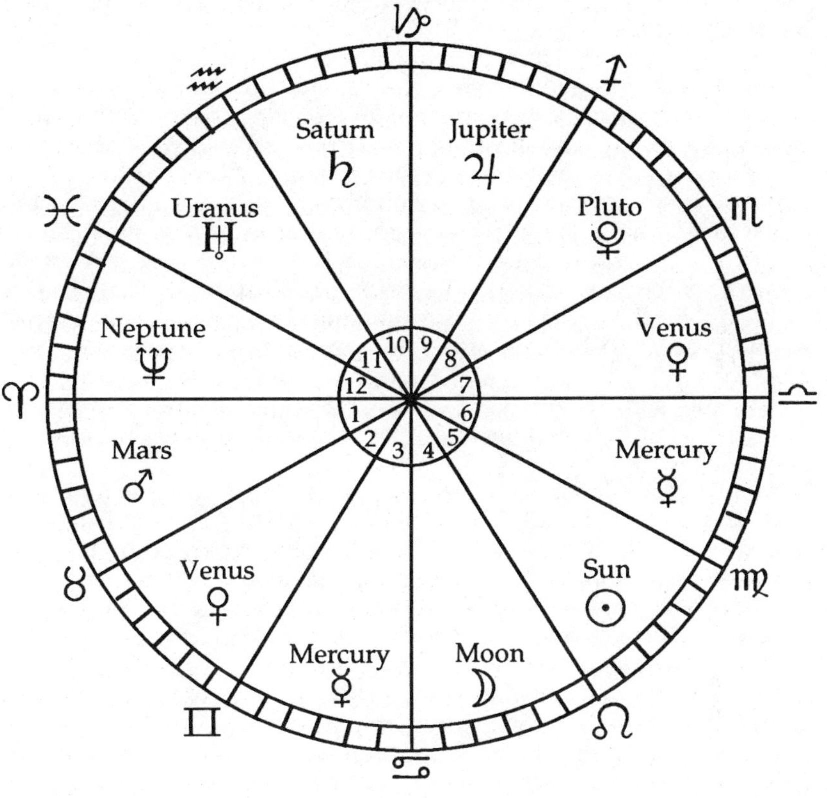

where and how they always should be displayed in the natural zodiac. The planets only will be spelled out at this time, with its symbol shown in parentheses.

When reading the following explanations, you will find it much easier to understand if you follow the explanations while simultaneously looking at the illustration of the natural zodiac in Figure 9.

When counting signs or planetary placements in the zodiac, you always must count in a counterclockwise direction. The natural order of the zodiac always must be followed. There are 12 Houses in the zodiac numbered 1 through 12. Now, counting counterclockwise and starting at the 1st House, the 2nd House becomes the second house from the 1st House, the 3rd House becomes the third house from the 1st, the 4th House becomes the fourth from the 1st and so on through the 12 Houses. Simple, isn't it? Now we are going to do the exact same thing again, except that we are going to start counting at the 2nd House instead of the 1st. Notice the changes that will take place. Starting at the

2nd House, the 3rd House now is the second house from the 2nd, the 4th House becomes the third house from the 2nd, the 5th is now the fourth counting from the 2nd, and so on through the 1st House which now becomes the twelfth house from the 2nd. Repeating this procedure with each house through the zodiac, you will find that each house is the twelfth house of the house that is immediately in front of it, while at the same time causing the house in front of another to become the second house of the one immediately in back of it. This means that every house in the zodiac can be any one of Houses 1 through 12 to the other houses, or every house consists of all the other houses with reference to their effects as shown in the illustrations of the aspects.

Another simple method of determining these house effects is by just glancing at the zodiac. Knowing there are only 12 Houses, you should realize at a glance at any one of the houses and see that it is the twelfth house from the one in front of it or the second house from the one back of it. Therefore, when delineating a chart this is the procedure that must be used for a correct analysis. Unless this procedure is understood and employed, the analysis could be incorrect.

Planets and signs, planets *in* signs, and signs *on* house cusps all are delineated in this procedure which results in the variations of the basic traits of a sign and planet.

For example, the planet Mars is in the sign of Aries. An astrologer would say Mars is in its own sign. Should Mars be in the sign of Aries but located in the 4th House, we would then say Mars is in the fourth square from its own.

With planets in the signs, Saturn in Sagittarius would be in its own 12th sign, and if in the 9th House it then would be in its own 12th House. Saturn in Aries then would be Saturn in its 4th sign square its own, and Saturn in Aries in the 4th House then would be Saturn in its own 4th sign opposing its own house.

Wherever a sign and/or planet is located in a time chart, and you wish to learn of its aspect to its natural location, you must start counting in a counter-clockwise direction from its *natural* location to its physical placement in the chart. That is the reason for our stating that Venus in the 10th House from its own when in Libra in the 4th. Counting counterclockwise from the 7th House, the natural house of Venus, the 4th House is the 10th House from the 7th. This yields a 10th House or Saturn effect with fears, restrictions, inhibitions, and so forth.

Special Configurations and/or Complexes

The planets frequently are arranged in complexes or configurations that have a special meaning. These have been identified and classified according to their observed effects. It is especially significant if the Sun in the chart is implicated in any of these complexes or configurations because of the impact on the ego, will, and identity and how striving for significance is influenced. These special planetary arrangements are Stellium, "T" Cross, Grand Cross, Grand Trine and the Yod. We offer an illustration and explanation for each of these.

Stellium When four or more planets are in or near the same degree of the same sign they form a stellium. This creates a strong, complex identity requiring the development of focus in the life. There are strong energy forces according to the nature of the particular sign in which it is located.

"T" Cross When two or more planets oppose each other at 180 degrees and a third planet is 90 degrees from them, a letter "T" configuration occurs and they occupy signs belonging to the same quality whether cardinal, fixed, or mutable. Since this is a "T" formation, one of the signs obviously is not occupied. (There are four signs in quality groups.) This missing sign invariably represents a problem because the individual often fails to include the factors indicated by that sign or house into the life. Much more often than not the problems will occur in their relationships.

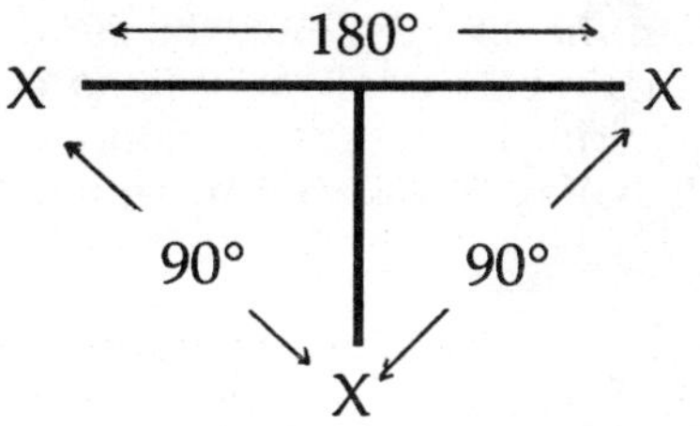

Grand Cross Similar to the "T" cross except that there is at least one planet in each sign belonging to the same quality so that a cross is formed. It represents deep-seated anxieties and unresolved tension difficult to deal with because of the basic hostility between all the signs involved.

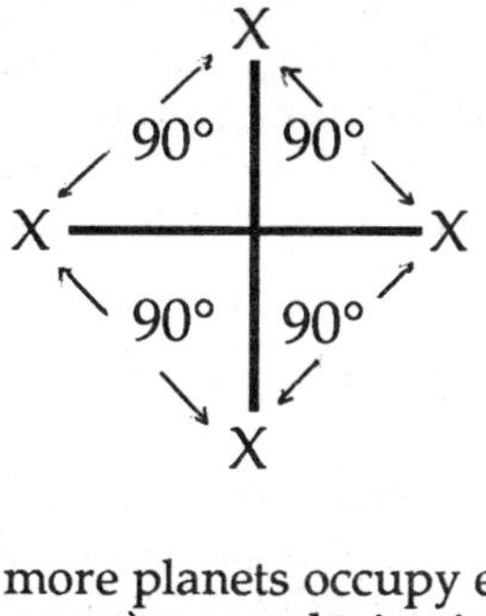

Grand Trine When one or more planets occupy each of the three signs of the same element (120 degrees apart) a grand trine is formed. Although basically harmonious by nature, it usually happens that the individual fails to take advantage of opportunities or live up to his ambitions. (See Grand Trine illustration on following page.)

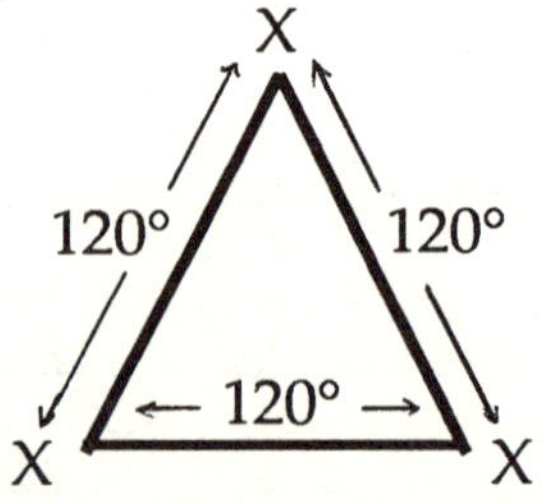

Yod occurs when one or more planets is 150 degrees from another planet in a clockwise direction and also is 150 degrees from another planet in a counter-clockwise direction, forming what is known as an inconjunct relationship to those planets. The two planets that are equally 150 degrees from the third planet must be within 60 degrees of each other. This forms what is called a sextile relationship. Viewed from the single planet the configuration looks like the letter "Y." The person with this pattern always seems to be in the midst of those persons and situations requiring his or her attention, and does in fact make some kind of commitment in behalf of those wanting or needing assistance.

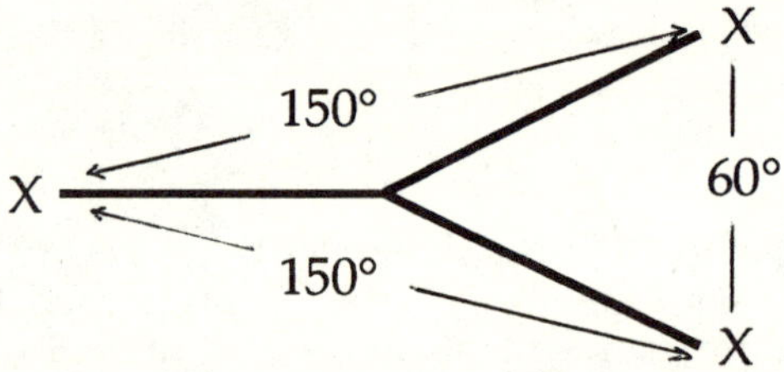

When counting the distances between planets to determine the aspects, it is the shortest distance that matters, either in a clockwise or counterclockwise direction. It is when counting the degrees between the planets that you must always count in a counterclockwise direction to determine the exact degrees separating them. As often as not a planet may be closer in the clockwise direction. (See Figure 10, after this discussion.) For example, the Sun is located at 14 degrees Aries, in the 1st House, with the Moon at 11 degrees Scorpio in the 8th House and Mercury at 14 degrees Virgo in the 6th. It is obvious that the Moon is closest to the Sun in the clockwise direction while Mercury is closest counter-clockwise. Therefore, when computing the Sun's aspect to the Moon, you must count counterclockwise starting with the Moon (which already has traveled 11 degrees into the sign of Scorpio and therefore has 19 degrees left to travel in that sign). Add this to the 30 degrees for each of the four signs between (Sagittarius, Capricorn, Aquarius, and Pisces, which equals 120 degrees), plus the 14 degrees that the Sun has traveled into Aries. The total is 19+120+14=153 degrees. This is an inconjunct aspect. With the Sun to Mercury, you would start counting counterclockwise with the Sun, which has 16 degrees left to travel in Aries. Then add 30 degrees for each of the four signs of Taurus, Gemini, Cancer, Leo (a sum

Figure 10: Aspect Illustration--The Yod

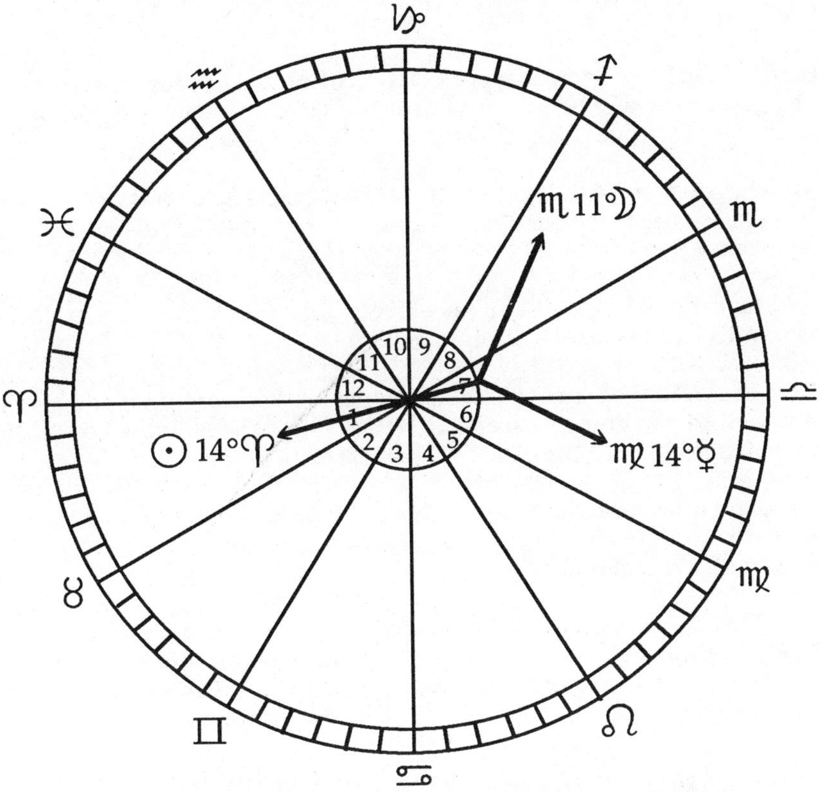

of 120 degrees total), plus the 14 degrees of travel of Mercury. This adds up to 16+120+14=150 degrees. This also is an inconjunct aspect. Counterclockwise from Mercury to the Moon would be 16 degrees (left in Virgo for Mercury to travel) plus the 30 degrees of Libra and the 11 degrees the Moon has traveled into Scorpio. The total here is 16+30+11=57 degrees, yielding a sextile aspect. Take notice that the three planets combined form a special configuration called the Yod. (Recall that we stated that all signs and houses are equal to 30 degrees each when counting). (See Figure 10.)

Although we refer to some of the aspects as special configurations and complexes, they all actually are aspects. They are special because of their distinct patterns and effects and complex because of the intricacies in their delineations.

We also have stated the importance and significance of the planets that do not make any aspects. For example:

Sun With no aspects to the Sun, there will be a lack of self-worth, a sense of inadequacy. This also would be true when there are no aspects to the ascendant.

Moon Though seldom found unaspected due to its speed, it does occur. When it does the individual will have a sort of uncaring, unemotional attitude towards *everyone.*

Mercury When Mercury is unaspected you will notice a shy or conceited person, but that judgment will be in error. No aspects to this planet of communication result in the individual lacking the desire for conversation.

Venus This unaspected planet will cause much stress for this person when it becomes necessary to make adjustments or compromises. They will not want to do the work.

Mars No aspects to Mars is like a car without gasoline. There is no energy to get going and the individual lacks enthusiasm.

Jupiter Similar to the Mars problem, this person has no aspects to Jupiter and seems to withdraw from any social activities. He or she will resist expansion or growth of any kind. It's a small world for these people.

Saturn Saturn is the planet that symbolizes status and ambitions. Through mobilized resources there is neither organization nor ambition; they simply can't get their act together.

Uranus This is the planet of the nonconformist, the rebel without a cause, freedom. It probably is best for the Aquarian people to have this planet unaspected because this will cause them to be most satisfied with living their lives out by tradition. There will be no rebellions, demonstrations, *no nothing.*

Neptune When this planet is unaspected, you will be like "Houdini"--a real escape artist. These people will not get involved with any social problems of any kind, and probably even will refuse to cast a vote at voting time.

Pluto This is the planet of the extremes. We refer to Pluto as the planet of "either/ or": either you make changes or else. When there are no aspects here the individuals can't seem to get motivated to make any changes that may become necessary for everyone's survival. Survival for all is achieved by contributions from all.

Ascendant We briefly have stated the importance of the sign rising at the moment of birth. The details and significance of this all-important sign intentionally were omitted and reserved for this chapter on aspects--which is exactly what it is all about. We said that the sign rising on the eastern horizon at the moment of birth is the manner by which you view life, the way you are viewed by others, and the way that you project yourself into life. These are the effects of that particular sign. It is because all effects must have a cause that the following details must be known and considered. At the time of birth, the sign that is rising also will be at a specific degree within that sign. In actual practice this sign and its degree is placed on the cusp of the 1st House (the eastern horizon). When computing the aspects between the planets, the ascendant also must be included for its aspects to the planets by its degrees. This is the same as for the planets and for the very same reasons, except that with the ascendant only 3 degrees is allowed for the orb. The planet that rules this ascendant is considered to be the ruling planet of the chart, and its aspects will have a sort of overriding effect over some others. The affairs of the house of its location will be a priority in the life. A most important factor of this rising sign is its location from its natural house placement (as we have explained for the signs and houses). The rising sign must be considered in the same fashion by aspects and house placement. For example, the sign of Taurus rising would place it in its own 12th House, which results in all the other signs also being in their own 12th House. (This is the house of your own undoing.) Should Cancer or Capricorn be rising, they would be square to their own natural locations, which automatically will place all the other signs square to their natural locations (fears, restrictions, inhibitors, and so forth). Virgo or Scorpio would result in all signs being inconjunct their own places. These people would tend to attempt to prove themselves, to be accepted, and so on. Libra rising would cause all signs to oppose their own locations, resulting in these people always seeming to meet opposition of a sort through no fault of their own. These many and varied conditions always must be considered if a correct analysis is desired.

We sincerely hope we have succeeded in our explanations, although they will require more serious, continued study. In the next chapter we will continue with an explanation of how to properly interpret the six basic aspects.

Chapter 9
Aspect Delineations

Interpreting the Aspects

The process by which you derive information from the horoscope consists of an accurate delineation of the many diverse factors it contains. Each of these different phases of the chart is complete and whole unto itself although incomplete in the sense that it cannot, by itself, define the behavior of the individual. Each of these factors is one of a number of complex building blocks upon which the structure of the individual depends for growth and development. This is the basic premise for each of the many factors that are part of the delineating procedure and which, when summarized, accurately describe behavior and what motivates it.

For this presentation, we will offer some of the guidelines to help you to analyze the aspects and how to arrive at a meaningful synthesis of the behavior they indicate.

Although it should be evident that you must have a fairly intimate understanding of what the planets mean in the dynamics of behavior, we must emphasize clearly that an accurate synthesis of the chart is impossible without this information. Although there are books that offer comprehensive delineations of all the aspects between the planets, it is far better that you grasp the technique by which these were derived. Once you understand the method of synthesis, you will be able to handle any and all complex factors in a chart and summarize them with comparative ease.

The basic principle in delineating aspects is the concept of planetary protocol. This means that in any planetary relationship (aspect) the planet that is the slower of the two (or more) has an overriding influence over the faster planet. Once you apply this principle you will realize how it greatly simplifies the process of analyzing the aspects.

The influence of the signs the planets occupy play an important role in how you delineate aspects. It should be obvious that Venus in Cancer is quite different from what Venus in Aquarius means. Although this kind of distinction will *not* be considered in this discussion, it is one you must include as you examine the aspects. We will pay particular attention to those relationships that may involve three or more planets in aspects that are dissimilar and indicate conditions that are complex enough to warrant a more painstaking analysis than when only two planets are involved. This is not to diminish the need for adequate attention in the case of an aspect between two planets. Even those two will be casting energy from a particular sign (or signs) and involve a house (or houses) of the chart, not to mention that either or both of these planets may be individually involved in aspects to other planets in the chart. It now should be obvious to you how important it is to have a procedure to follow so that nothing is left out that should be included in the analysis.

Let us examine the aspects involving Venus/Mars and how the initial meaning is altered when other factors are introduced.

In the classic zodiacal arrangement of the signs and their planetary rulers, Mars rules the first sign (Aries), and Venus rules the second sign (Taurus). This still prevails. Across the zodiac from Aries is Libra, ruled by Venus. Adjacent to Libra is Scorpio, and Mars was and still is ruler of this sign along with Pluto. In this assignment of signs and rulers, Venus follows Mars in ruling the first two

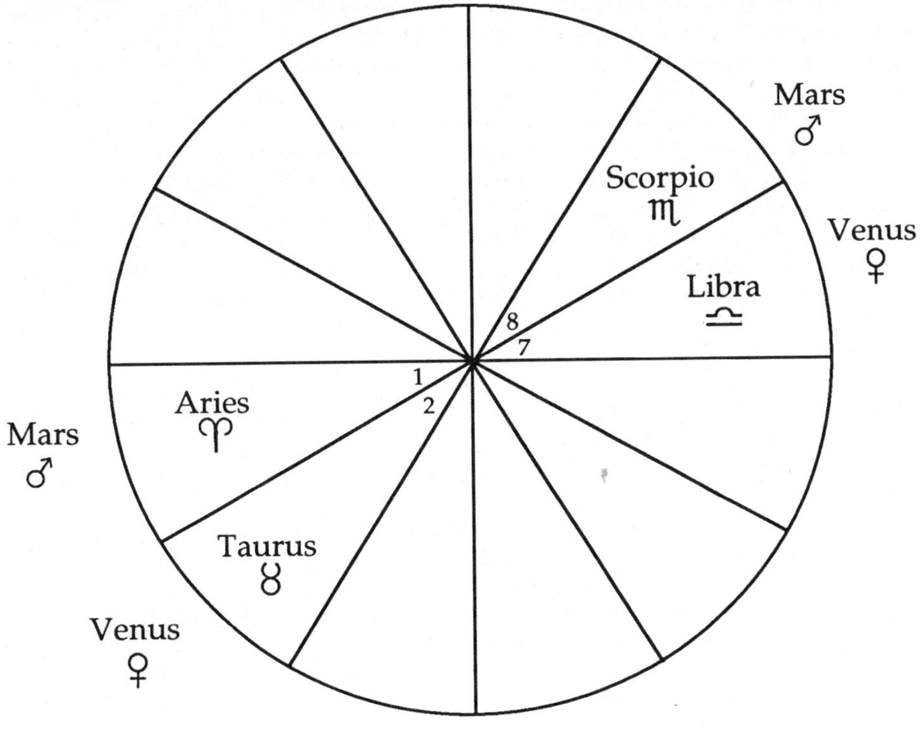

signs and Mars follows Venus in ruling the 7th and 8th signs. They oppose one another from Aries to Libra and from Taurus to Scorpio. It is noteworthy that Mars is male, aggression, hate, and war while Venus is female, conciliation, love, and peace. Mars is the animus and Venus is the anima as put forth by Carl Jung in his dynamics of human behavior. To illustrate this behavioral mechanism more clearly, we offer the appropriate signs and their rulers.

It should be apparent that Venus and Mars both would be out of their respective elements in the signs that oppose the ones they rule. Not only would the two planets be in foreign territory, but the dynamics of behavior they represent would be equally strained by that discomfort. This early experience of stress eventually would prove beneficial because these signs would provide the opportunity for resolving the need to establish a moderate position and utilization of the planetary energies of both these planets. Venus in Aries would eventually gain the ability to declare unhesitatingly that there is a fondness or even a love for someone. Mars in Libra eventually would learn to curtail the impulse for taking action in a particular situation and be willing to enter into a reciprocal agreement before making that decision. What happens after a time is a refinement of the basic principles the planets represent, resulting in a more mature and evolved use of those same urges.

With Venus in Scorpio and Mars in Taurus, a similar process takes place eventually, and that refining process mentioned above now is directed in urging the person with Venus in Scorpio to be willing to share personal and material resources with the valid expectation that this will enrich the relationship it serves. In a similar fashion Mars in Taurus learns the lesson of conservation of personal and material resources so that greater stability enters into the relationship the person with this planetary position hopes to preserve.

Initially, however, the persons with these planets in the signs opposing their own will display resentment and perhaps some bitterness that they have been dealt such a blow. The truth is that they have been blessed with the opportunity to derive many advantages from these planetary positions. What happens in planets occupying the signs opposing their own is the chance to polarize the basic urges represented and derive many benefits for the maturity that this kind of integration indicates.

The above shows how signs alone can alter the way a planet operates. This is true for every planet in every sign other than the one it rules. The word to remember is adjustment. Who could long tolerate someone with Mars in Aries who never missed a chance to strike the first blow, intimidate, and attack even presumed adversaries out of the misguided assumption that they would if he didn't? Similarly, can you imagine the boredom of someone with Venus in Libra who was so fragile in his own social competence that he always waited for someone else to express an opinion before indicating that he would go along with that opinion? It isn't difficult to detect a kind of primitive behavior in each of the foregoing, with ample room for growth that stress from sign position or aspects can stimulate.

The art of synthesis requires an intimate grasp of what the signs, houses, planets, aspects, elements, and qualities represent in the dynamics of human behavior. Just as the artist understands what will happen when he combines two different colors and knows what color will result from the mixture, so the astrologer must truly understand planetary energy so thoroughly that he immediately knows what behavior to expect when he observes two planets involved in an aspect between them. He knows that neither planet will function separately but with the principles of the other planet implicated in that function. Take Mars and Saturn, for instance. Mars is the "yes" planet and Saturn is the "no" planet. Let us suppose they are involved in a conjunction aspect and we know that planetary protocol will prevail. Saturn is the dominant planet in the aspect and will exercise restraint on the person's desire to take action. But we must understand what it is that produces this effect. Mars is the energy with which to take any kind of action and it often works spontaneously, taking many risks. Within the consciousness of that person are the faculties of reason, self-discipline, and planning that override the more primitive impulses of Mars. The person reflects long enough to reconsider if he should take action after all. While the better decision prevailed so that a more mature decision took place, there still is unrequited energy that was denied manifestation. Feelings of frustration and anger could torment him for some time. This person may act out his impulses in youth and even into his adult years--he may be an example of the person who has to learn the hard way. Some people never seem to learn. They spend a lifetime butting their heads against overwhelming odds or struggling with people who refuse to tolerate an individual who refuses to grow up. One unmistakable fact is that the force within that Saturn represents never will yield to the spoiled brat energy that Mars sets in motion. Self-control is the desirable course to take. This indicates inner growth and development, but lacks certainty that some form of control will take place from some external source.

Saturn is the exercise of law and order. There is an innate sense of right and wrong within us that guides our behavior so that we do not impose our wills on others through the use of our Mars energy, which then is mindless energy. We earlier discussed how Mars needed to learn compromise and conciliation before taking any action and that learning to think is an important part of the growth and the maturity he and the energy he represents need to acquire. While Saturn teaches Mars to behave properly, Saturn, too, must yield to the same principle of planetary protocol when faced with the force that Uranus presents.

From the foregoing dissertation on the effects of a Mars-Saturn conjunction, it should be clear that a great deal of painstaking analysis goes into a meaningful synthesis. Even in this short discussion of how Mars and Saturn function, we have not even considered the sign in which this conjunction takes place. That also would significantly alter the final meaning. Remember that we said that signs alter how a planet operates, especially if that sign position is one other than the one ruled by the planet in question. We said that the one word to remember is adjustment. That is exactly what happens to every planet in a horoscope by sign, house, and most significantly by the aspects to other planets.

While the problem of analyzing two planets in their respective sign positions and in aspects demands considerable skill, the problem is compounded enormously when three or more planets are involved by aspect to one another.

Horoscope of Sigmund Freud 5/6/1856

Sun	in Taurus	16°
Moon	in Gemini	14°
Mercury	in Taurus	27°
Venus	in Aries	26°
Mars	in Libra	3°
Jupiter	in Pisces	29°
Saturn	in Gemini	27°
Uranus	in Taurus	20°
Neptune	in Pisces	19°
Pluto	in Taurus	4°

Ascendant Sign

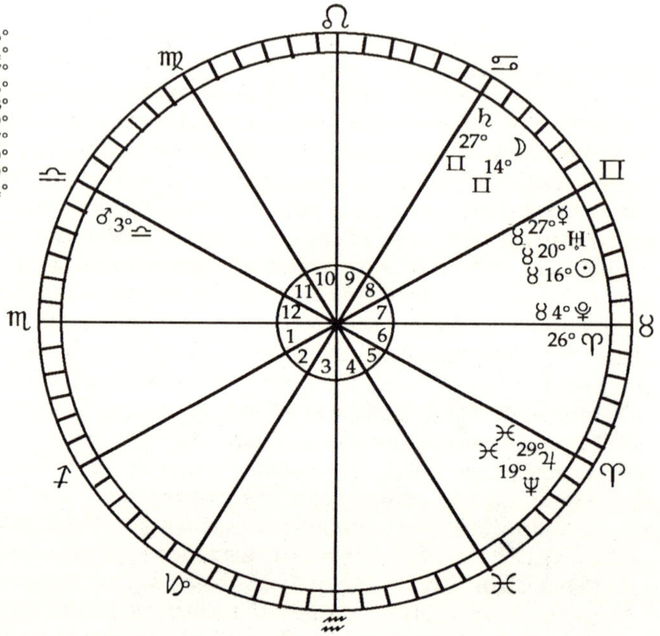

Natal Aspects

Fire: 1
Earth: 4
Air: 3
Water: 2
Cardinal: 2
Fixed: 4 + rising sign
Mutable: 4

Signature: Fixed - Earth = Taurus

Lacking: nil

Ruling planet: Mars - Pluto

Chart type (Jones Pattern): Bucket

Special Formations: none
and/or
Complexes: none

Unaspected planets: none

Special notes

	☉	☽	☿	♀	♂	♃	♄	♅	♆	♇
☉			☌					☌	⚹	
☽									□	
☿						⚹		☌	⚹	
♀							⚹			
♂										⚻
♃							□			
♄									□	
♅									⚹	
♆										
♇										

It is the kind of predicament that really can test your knowledge and skill in how to proceed. Again we must refer you to the matter of planetary protocol to guide you as you unravel the complex situation before you.

Since we have just discussed Venus, Mars, Saturn, and Uranus, we offer the evidence of how these function in actual practice. We submit the charts of three world famous individuals: Sigmund Freud, Carl Jung, and Albert Einstein. Their charts, though similar, nevertheless were quite different.

Sigmund Freud's chart contains revealing evidence of the most compelling and enduring feature of his psychoanalytic discoveries: the driving force of the sexual urge in human behavior. Did he truly discover this or was it really his own personal sexual urge that he made known? Not only was the sign generally associated with the function of sex rising in the east at the time he was born, but also Mars, the traditional planetary ruler of Scorpio, was by itself in one hemisphere of his chart and formed the handle of the "bucket" pattern, a most outstanding feature of prominence in his chart. Mars symbolizes sex, physical drive, aggression, and violence.

It also is significant that Mars represents the male and is in Libra, the sign ruled by Venus, its polar opposite representing the female. Venus is the ruler of his Sun sign, Taurus, which also happens to be his astrological signature--another factor of importance. Taurus is the sign of sensuality among other related factors.

In his chart we note that Aries, the other sign ruled by Mars, is located in the 6th House, the department of illness. Venus also is posited there in the sign of Aries. It must be considered that not only is Venus in its opposing sign, but it also is the 12th sign and 12th House of Venus. The thread of relevance continues as we observe that Mars also is in the 12th House, which also is its own 12th House and sign. The 12th House is the sector representing the subconscious and self-undoing! All of these factors relate in great detail how Freud fulfilled his chart's potentials and dared enter the domain of the unknown, developing a method of probing that area of the mind that gave him the answers he sought. What answers was he truly seeking?

How did he reach the conclusion that mental disturbances were due largely to childhood sexual fantasies? Indeed, because he possessed a wild and vivid sexual imagination that would surely produce such fantasies, it seemed only that it was a natural instinct to believe that of all of his patients.

His chart also indicates that he had difficulty in separating fact from fiction (Moon square Neptune). This aspect causes one to "adjust" reality (the square) to what would be emotionally tolerable (Moon) for themselves. When this is not possible, the individual may create an artificial environment to which he can escape (Neptune). Since Freud was a very sensual man (Taurus) with strong sexual desires (Scorpio) and both planets that rule sex (Mars and Pluto) most prominent and ruler of his chart, it should be obvious that all his energies were focused on sexual matters. This is especially true since Venus ruled both his Sun sign and astrological signature--two very significant factors. Venus in the sign of Aries and ruled by Mars is indicative of strong sexual needs as well. There appears to be no self-control because Saturn is not involved in any positive manner other than a sextile to Venus and its aspect as a square to Jupiter. (As stated earlier, Saturn is the "no" planet ruling control, responsibility, reality, caution, and know-how.) These aspects are detrimental to self-control.

Venus sextile Saturn This aspects indicates that you understand (sextile) what you want (Venus) and know how (Saturn) to get it.

Jupiter square Saturn This is indicative of problems in self-awareness (Jupiter) and tendencies to put yourself down (square) when comparing your capabilities to the skills of others. Actually, you are trying to avoid your responsibilities to yourself and others who may depend on you (Saturn).

These aspects most likely are the reasons for his daring to enter the domain of the unknown, an area no one else of his time even considered let alone dared to examine. This is the exact area of his very own problems.

The sign on the 3rd House (house of the personal mind) is the nature by which all the other energies are channeled.

Saturn is the ruler of this house because its rulership of Capricorn on its cusp adds to his "know-how." This is the ability to transform negative situations into beneficial ones (Capricorn), using everyone and everything available in order to take control (Saturn) and obtain "status" (Capricorn). Recall the key words of Saturn ("I use") and the glyph of Capricorn (the mountain goat that climbs to the highest peaks), both of which rule the natural 10th House (cycle of life)--the authority that maintains control.

In conclusion, with a brief summary we find that Freud's chart indicates a man who is sexually minded to the extremes (Venus-Mars-Pluto) and who because of his feelings of inferiority in comparison to his colleagues (Jupiter square Mars) sought other channels and means to acquire his control and status (Capricorn, 3rd House). Because he knew how to turn a negative situation into a beneficial one (Capricorn) and knew what he wanted and how to get it (Venus sextile Saturn), he selected an area he personally experienced and knew all about (sexuality) and thereby minimized any and all criticism. Since mental disturbances are more prevalent, what better area was there than one he experienced? Because sexual fantasies were a priority in his life, it was only natural for him to associate all he came in contact with to sexual fantasies. It is only sound logical reasoning, then, that all his theories of mental disturbances were due largely to sexual fantasies--in reality his own fantasies. It was Freud and not his patients who were troubled by these fantasies throughout his life (Venus-Mars-Pluto).

Additional concurring evidence of his most powerful libido may be found in Chapter 10: Sexual Behavior Patterns.

Should one desire to read more about Freud's personal life, studies, and works, you may find the information in the February 1984 issue of the *Atlantic Monthly* magazine. You also will learn of what he did and had done through surgery to "Emma Eckstein" one of his many patients, who more than likely was an example of how he satisfied some of his fantasies.

Horoscope of Carl Jung 7/26/1875

Sun	in Leo	3°
Moon	in Taurus	15°
Mercury	in Cancer	13°
Venus	in Cancer	17°
Mars	in Sagittarius	21°
Jupiter	in Libra	23°
Saturn	in Aquarius	24°
Uranus	in Leo	14°
Neptune	in Taurus	3°
Pluto	in Taurus	23°

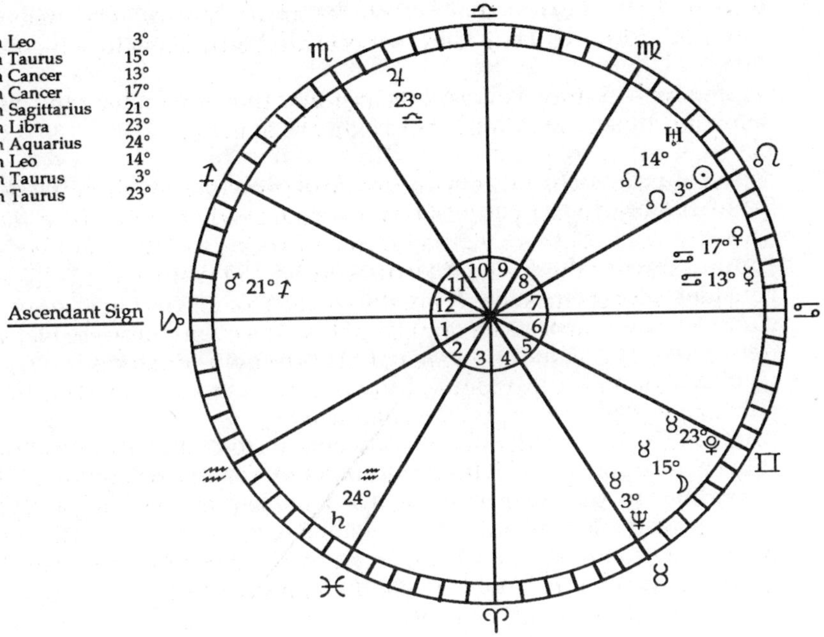

Natal Aspects

	☉	☽	☿	♀	♂	♃	♄	♅	♆	♇
☉									□	
☽			⚹	⚹				□		
☿				☌						
♀						□				⚹
♂						⚹	⚹	△		⚻
♃							△			⚻
♄										□
♅										
♆										
♇										

Fire: 3
Earth: 3 + rising sign
Air: 2
Water: 2
Cardinal: 3
Fixed: 6
Mutable: 1

Signature: Fixed - Earth= Taurus

Lacking: nil

Ruling planet: Saturn

Chart type (Jones Pattern): Splash

Special Formations: none
and/or
Complexes: none

Unaspected planets: none

Special notes

Carl Jung, a colleague of Freud, had a chart that was similar in some respects to Freud's. His chart had one hemisphere with three planets there while Freud's chart had only one. They both had Mars in that half of their charts and both in the 12th House (the subconscious) but Jung also had Jupiter, the planet representing the spiritual awareness that alters and sometimes even guides human behavior, in sextile to Mars (a benefic aspect) as well as Saturn as his ruling planet (Capricorn rising) also sextile to Mars. This results in yet another benefic aspect of a trine of Jupiter and Saturn. To make the meaning of these aspects clear we offer a brief summary of each.

Jupiter sextile Mars This aspect indicates that you can effectively use your considerable resources of mind and body to gain your objectives. You understand (sextile) how to assert yourself (Mars) under pressure, for you have developed your talent for effective communication with clever use of words (Jupiter).

Mars sextile Saturn This aspect indicates the blending of brain and brawn. You think before you act, which pays dividends in the results you achieve. Your self-discipline and patience enable you to accomplish more than your competitors because you take the time to understand every detail of a problem before attempting to solve it (Saturn). You understand (sextile) how to assert yourself (Mars) so you won't have to do something over again (Saturn).

Jupiter trine Saturn You integrate the lessons you have learned through past experiences with your designs for the future. Your goals are within the guidelines you've set for yourself. Success is not a surprise: you expect it because your proposals are within your capabilities. You have access to useful information and are skilled in evaluating the details on which you base your actions (trine). Having great faith in yourself, you project a wholesome expectation of success in all your endeavors (Jupiter). You don't waste precious time and effort on trivia, but are thoughtful and know how to apply yourself to the matters that you feel are important (Saturn).

While there were many specific areas of disagreement between Jung and Freud (why should now be obvious), the placement of Jupiter and Saturn in Jung's chart is at the root of their distinctive philosophies on human behavior. This produced a direction of thought that Jung chose that added a validating principle to that behavior.

Saturn was his ruling planet and Capricorn his rising sign. He had complete self-control in organizing his abilities to achieve status. These energies were channeled through the 3rd House of the mind with the sign of Pisces there. Pisces represents the subconscious, imagination, idealism, sacrifices, and social obligations among many other factors.

It is interesting that Jung wrote extensively. There is a 21-volume collection of his works in the Bollingen Series XX from the Princeton University Press. It isn't a coincidence that Jupiter represents writing and books, libraries, education, teaching, lecturing, religious symbolism, and vision. Jupiter rules Sagitta-

Horoscope of Albert Einstein 3/14/1879

Sun	in Pisces	3°
Moon	in Sagittarius	14°
Mercury	in Aries	3°
Venus	in Aries	16°
Mars	in Capricorn	26°
Jupiter	in Aquarius	27°
Saturn	in Aries	4°
Uranus	in Virgo	1°
Neptune	in Taurus	7°
Pluto	in Taurus	24°

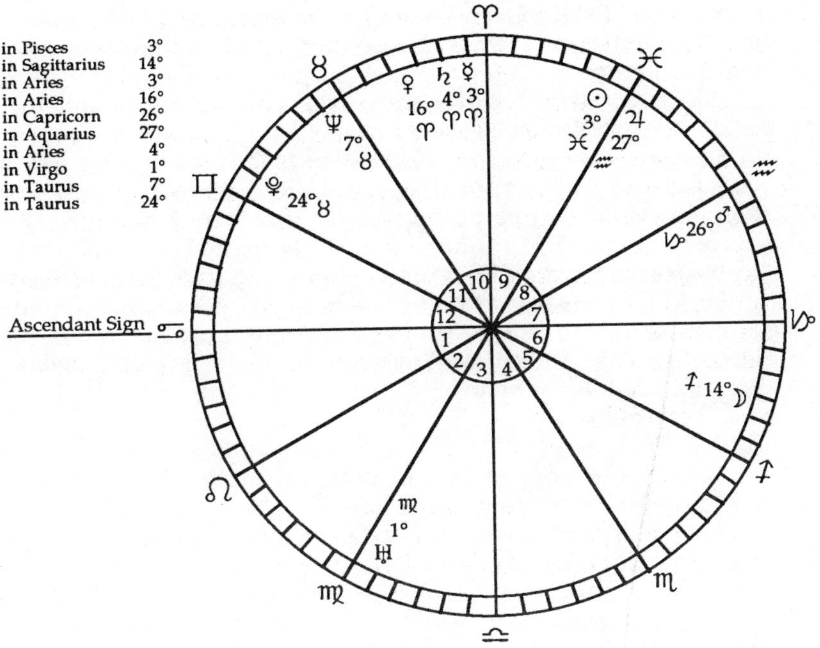

Natal Aspects

	☉	☽	☿	♀	♂	♃	♄	♅	♆	♇
☉								☍	□	
☽				△						
☿							☌	⚻		
♀										
♂										△
♃										□
♄								⚻		
♅									△	
♆										
♇										

Fire:	4 + Moon
Earth:	4
Air:	1
Water:	1
Cardinal:	4 = rising sign
Fixed:	3
Mutable:	3

Signature: Cardinal - Fire = Aries

Lacking: nil

Ruling planet: Moon - Uranus

Chart type (Jones Pattern): Bucket

Special Formations: none
and/or
Complexes: none

Unaspected planets: none

Special notes

rius (the 12th House of his chart) where Mars is located. This planet and its aspects added a dimension to Jung's understanding of why people behave as they do when it isn't provoked by strong sexual fantasies. Sexual fantasies were Freud's reference.

Albert Einstein's chart, similar to Freud's, also contains compelling evidence of his work and discoveries in the field of physics. Not only is Uranus most prominent in his chart, but it also serves as the handle to his "bucket" chart and is located in the 3rd House in the sign of Virgo the analyst. Uranus rules physics; represents the inventive mind, goals, ambitions, and the future; and is the higher octave of Mercury, the ruling planet of both the 3rd House and Virgo. Every facet of electrical energy is represented by these two planets--from the nervous system of the body to the infinite laws of physics. Both planets and sign are very compatible to each other's energies and characteristics, with the nature of Virgo significant in the utilization of these energies because of the detailing, questioning, and analytical mental process it provides. A brief summary of these conditions follows.

1 - Third House. The personal mental process outside of the self.
2 - Mercury. The curiosity, questions.
3 - Uranus. The awareness and ability to think for one's self.
4 - Virgo. The analyst and the perfectionist.

It also is significant to note that Uranus, the ruling planet of his chart, also rules the 8th House because Aquarius is there. The 8th House represents extremes, the unknown concepts, and the excursions there. The Uranian nature of the 11th House of freedom, adventure, and future expectations has both the planets Neptune (imagination) and Pluto (revelation, obsessions, and power). The principle of planetary protocol indicates that all of the overriding energies in his chart (Pluto, Neptune, Uranus, and Saturn) show that he had no thoughts about anything that did not concern understanding this world. All this very likely was the reasoning behind his famous quote, "The Poor Fish": The poor fish spend their entire lives in an ocean they know nothing about.

A close look at the chart shows that he only had a single aspect for his Moon, Venus, Mars, and Jupiter. Uranus, the overriding planetary energy in his chart, is involved in four of nine aspects in the chart, including a trine to Neptune and its overriding energy. However, because of the trine (benefic) aspect that positive nature prevails. Let's now learn what effects these aspects involving Uranus made on his behavior, character, and ambitions.

Sun opposition Uranus This represents a high-strung, irritable, and nervous disposition, indicating a need to relax. He fears competition yet seeks out people who will challenge him. Dealing with others is the best way to prove himself. He knows that he is exceptionally talented and can succeed if he really wants to. He can meet people at the highest level of authority and easily match them in performance. Science, social service, and education are some of the many meaningful fields in which he can excel.

His erratic behavior can alienate him from those who may mean most to him. Because of his impatience with anyone who seems dull and unexciting, he may lose friends and associates who will not tolerate his outbursts.

Mercury inconjunct Uranus This shows that he will endure severe punishment in attempting to serve the world at large. He is an intellectual workhorse, and his serenity constantly is disturbed by the problems of others. He will project himself toward the abstract future, which is secure, if he can look back without regret for what he didn't do years ago.

Uranus trine Neptune This indicates that he will resent being told what to believe. He prefers to decide for himself whether he will accept or reject the ideas that have satisfied previous generations of believers. His intellectual awareness requires that he logically evaluate all ideologies, dogmas, and theories whether they are political, philosophical, or religious. He will feel that he cannot support a particular belief until he understands thoroughly how and why it was established. Seeking truth rather than illusions, he will be suspicious of ideas that may seriously alter his life and destiny. He will observe how masses of humanity are dominated by individuals who forced their ideologies on their subjects, mesmerizing them to accept those ideas blindly and obediently. Uranus was in Virgo the analyst in the 3rd House of the mind. The guide to Einstein's behavior and achievements was Uranus, the planet of revelation and insight awareness. This was the handle and most prominent planet of his "bucket" chart, and characterizes his future and the freedom he sought since his childhood.

Let's continue to examine some of the other aspects in his chart to learn what, if anything, they contributed to his genius.

Moon trine Venus This trine is indicative of a gentle and harmonious disposition. You don't have to work hard at having good intentions because your motives rarely are less than honorable.

Jupiter square Pluto This aspect inclines you to rebel against existing codes of ethics. You may challenge authority in your efforts to find easier ways to realize your goals.

Mars trine Pluto Your aggressiveness is well aligned with your dedication to causes. You can be effective in solving awesome problems in society because you have a deep understanding of those problems and their origins. You offer your services out of a spiritual conviction that you are obliged to do something constructive about your surroundings. You aren't concerned with power as an instrument for gain but see it rather as a force for continued growth.

You are fearless in defending your rights and may surprise your friends with your ruthless courage in the face of overwhelming odds.

The genius of Albert Einstein caused his superiors and parents alike to believe he was a problem child, possibly retarded and in need of professional help. Had these authorities understood astrological principles, they would have realized they had a young genius in the making.

Aren't we all fortunate that he had the genius to match and surpass the mental abilities of these arrogant authorities, who certainly would have confined him if his family's bankruptcy had not forced them to move out of the country? Consider what a waste of a mind that would have been.

The same is true of Carl Jung. He also was a genius, as can be verified through his writings, but the problem was and still is his affiliations with astrological principles that science rejects.

Because Sigmund Freud was a scientist, his so-called discoveries still are referred to by those in related fields. Should science bother to sincerely investigate Freud's theories they would find that everyone has sexual fantasies from childhood to maturity and far beyond as many medical surveys have proven. A serious investigation of Freud's chart would show that he was somewhat perverted in his sexual ideologies. When you consider the accuracy of both Einstein's and Jung's charts, how can anyone possibly dispute the accuracy of Freud's? The same procedures were carried out for all three of them.

We will continue with a more detailed examination of what causes sexual drives, aggressiveness, the conditions that bring out these tendencies, and so forth in our next chapter.

Chapter 10

Sexual Behavior Patterns

It is justifiable and reasonable to assume that sex is one of the more important factors in everyone's life. From it are derived some of the more exquisite sensory responses of which the body is capable, but among these also are some of the more painful and arduous experiences resulting in nervousness, depression, despair, discomfort, and many other physical and emotional distresses. It is a biological necessity, however, and requires dealing with whatever positive or negative reactions are experienced that differ from a normal or average expectancy. One of the more significant reasons for any difficulty that may arise is the lack of any meaningful compromise between the parties involved. In a sense, the act of lovemaking between consenting individuals is the epitome of compromise and agreement. Zodiacally, it is represented by the "I am" of Aries put forth by each participant that creates a new dynamic from the "we" of Libra in a shared experience.

Venus is the planetary ruler of Libra, and compromise is her most important product. Adjustment is the required process that resolves conflict when there is disagreement between individuals. Love is the qualifying ingredient that urges adjustment for the sake of harmony so that a mutually satisfying solution is found. Compromise is used to acquire the things that one wants in life. Many of these acquisitions often are used expressly for the purpose of impressing the opposite sex. Sometimes these techniques are obvious but mostly they are subtle and sometimes even devious.

In one way or another, sex is for sale. Sex frequently is given with the expectation of getting something in return. It can be money and all the creature comforts it can buy, power, position, influence. In many instances it quite simply is the need to be loved in return that precipitates an encounter and that often results in a marriage commitment. But even then, sex plays an important role and when that fails to satisfy, problems often develop in the relationship. In most cases, sex is rarely the focus of the trouble and some other conflict is cited as the source of any difficulty. In reality, however, sex more often than not is a major source of the stress that has entered the marriage. When either or both parties revert to the "I am" concept of the Aries principle, there is deep trouble in the relationship. The "I am" attitude is an adversarial one that denies the single most basic requirement of a "we" concept in a marital commitment: compromise. This results when there is a lack of understanding, an unwillingness to discuss and clarify the points of conflict and/or to make any adjustment that may be necessary. The planets that rule Aries (I am) and Libra (We are) concepts are Mars and Venus respectively.

Mars is the pure animal instinct that drives the procreative functions. It shares this activity with Venus, which humanizes and imparts a qualifying principle of love to the process. Love is the byproduct of their combined energies. There are, of course, many other factors involved, some of which are recognition and reaction, desire and deliberation, and activity or passivity in approach mode.

Mars is the active force that is an integral factor necessary in the pursuit of a love object, humanized as the partner in a love and sex encounter.

Venus is the subjective energy that is utilized to enhance and entice the love object into a compromising posture that encourages both the pursuer and the pursued to fulfill their respective roles. This is not to suggest that males use Mars principles and females use Venus principles to the exclusion of the other. The principles of both planets are utilized simultaneously by both partners as they pursue their respective objectives. This scenario probably is why we often hear the comment, "He/she pursued me until I caught him/her." This accurately describes the mating game. If Mars is the physical drive to mate, then Venus is the talent for artful compromise.

Let us examine how Venus and Mars function in each of the zodiacal signs. Planets function well in some signs and even better in others, but they may be in signs where they don't work well at all. Signs have modes and substance of their own and these may alter the way a planet functions when located in them. Let's look at Venus in each of the signs.

Venus in Aries: The purpose of activity here is to entice and entrap, to satisfy the desires. The tendency is to be quickly aroused and to respond to stimuli without reservation. This sign precedes Taurus, which is ruled by Venus, and it is therefore a 12th House sign position for Venus. This in itself carries some liability since it inclines to activity that is self-undoing. The perfect slogan for Venus here is "'Won't you come into my parlor?' said the spider to the fly."

Venus in Taurus: The criteria for action here is one of personal gain. The pursuit of the desires, needs, and wants is very strong and not easily put off. True love often is rejected here in consideration of any personal gain that might result from a relationship. Romantic ties have just got to be "worth" it.

Venus in Gemini: The impulse is to fall in love with everyone and keep a mental diary of what has happened in all the affairs, if only in fantasy. Discussing romantic connections is important if only because it tends to keep them alive and active. There is difficulty in focusing on single objectives. Affairs vary from many to none at all and the attitude is one of permissiveness.

Venus in Cancer: The romantic nature is one of being in love with love. In most encounters the conversation is generally toward the subject of marriage. There is a strong mothering nature that is not easily dismissed. Control over loved ones often is a liability since it sometimes leads to rejection.

Venus in Leo: A true romantic seeking sincere and enduring love relationships. There is a strong desire to be at the center of attention. This person cannot cope gracefully when the other person terminates their affair.

Venus in Virgo:The desire for a perfect relationship sets the stage for disappointment. The urge to revise, redo, alter, and improve the love object assures the end of any spontaneity and romance. This person often fails to notice favorable qualities or denies their value in the face of the many shortcomings observed. The need here is for an honest and sincere appraisal of the self and the willingness to concede to any flaws that may be revealed.

Venus in Libra: There is an interest in manipulating people in a kind of "confidence" game. This person readily compromises out of an almost desperate desire for some kind of relationship. Sweet talk is used to promote support in personal endeavors and to gain social advantages. There often is an inability to face reality while maintaining emotional stability at the same time.

Venus in Scorpio: There is a complexity to the persons with this position. Theirs is a depth perception that pervades the most self-contained individuals so they become unsettled by it. Magnetic and enticing, they easily expose human failings to gain a measure of control over those who have them. This also can function as a positive and useful technique to stimulate someone to action who otherwise would remain doubtful of their talent. The desire is for long-lasting relationships with substance and value for all time.

Venus in Sagittarius: The urge here is to do what one wants with whomever and whenever they want. They reserve the freedom to act out their desires at will and without having to offer any explanation to anyone. Enjoying a multiplicity of interests makes it difficult to achieve focus in any direction so that much time and energy is wasted. This person is not especially dependable in love; theirs is largely an unconfined and unrestrained love nature.

Venus in Capricorn: The emotions are deep and the need to feel wanted is considerable. Although appearing to be romantic, what this person wants is someone of quality and with whom there would be a conservative but enduring relationship. It is difficult for this person to project warmth and emotion because they are realistic enough to seek only those kinds of contacts that have substance and value. Their low-key appearance must not be judged as an inability to love.

Venus in Aquarius: There is an intellectual feature in this person's love nature. This must not be construed as detachment or lack of emotion, but simply that there is a more universal quality to the feelings that also involves the other person's lifestyle and social attitude. Mere physical attraction is inadequate to arouse this person's interest in a continuing relationship, he or she needs to be attracted by the other person's social, spiritual, and political views as well. There is much permissiveness regarding the way people interact. Most rules are discarded as outmoded and unnecessary in today's unrestrained social behavior.

Venus in Pisces: This person has a talent for deciding that the world will benefit from his or her contribution and uses this to demonstrate a caring and loving nature. There is a need to prove how much love there is by how much they will do for the one they love. Because of this they often are victimized. There is an inability to face reality and accept responsibility for the predicaments in their relationships. They tend to placate themselves with an endless variety of excuses for their difficulties in making the kinds of contacts that result in meaningful relationships.

Mars in the Signs

Mars in Aries: This is pure sexuality. The mechanics of the biological function are very pronounced. Sensuality is not an important consideration in this instance, but rather the pure exercise of the animal instincts. This is survival of the fittest where aggressiveness counts and resistance to that aggression rarely succeeds. Mars is the power and energy that enables you to pursue your goals with unending desire and intensity.

Mars in Taurus: The major concern here is with the resources and the general pursuit of things to enrich the circumstances of life. This sign is "ruled" by Venus so that there is a combination of two divergent energies that are, nevertheless, necessary to their respective needs. Mars is the aggressor and Venus is the response to stimuli. The drive to satisfy the physical needs is somewhat tempered by the anxiety that some losses will be incurred in the process. Mars sexuality is infused here with sensuality so that the desires are increased with the prospect of gaining a willing partner in a mutually satisfying encounter.

Mars in Gemini: This tends to produce a mental faculty that is somewhat out of control. The energy of Mars infuses the mind with continual restlessness and provokes the search for something new to keep it occupied. Not one to ever make a long story short, this person can be distracting because they never get to the point. In many instances, what would have been a pleasant sexual experience is so delayed by endless conversation that the interest fails.

Mars in Cancer: This person is sensitive and easily offended. The person often feels that people are trying to use him or want to override his decisions. This position of Mars inclines him to lack the forcefulness to present himself as a self-confident individual. Instead, he resorts to emotionally charged behavior of self-defense that usually is unnecessary.

Mars in Leo: The power of Mars here is to disregard authority, because they don't feel they have to answer to anyone or give an account of their actions. In their arrogant manner they indulge in lovemaking encounters rather than love relationships. Theirs is an attitude of fun and games and they have the dramatic flair to succeed where others surely would fail. Self-gratification is their calling card.

Mars in Virgo: Because Virgo is the 12th sign of Libra and marriage, this Mars can be truly troublesome in a relationship. Fault-finding and cantankerous, they demand perfection, and this is the main reason that love and loving people elude them. They often are workaholics, and often are too tired for many of the amenities of a successful, ardent, loving relationship.

Mars in Libra: Although Libra opposes Mars's own sign (Aries), the conflict nevertheless is stimulating. Mars is the doer, whereas Libra thinks and is social. This results in personal anxiety because dialogue must occur before any action can take place and that simply irritates persons with the Mars position. They are impatient with the needless talk when more important matters await. They often turn people off.

Mars in Scorpio: The matter of self-gratification is very important to those with Mars here. The attitude and general frame of reference is one that they feel is appropriate for everyone, but this is mainly a decision derived from the feelings, not the intellect. The extremes of Scorpio also can produce a life of celibacy. This can be related to the painful struggle to contain the desires that sometimes run counter to the traditional code of behavior. Life and death jointly occupy this sign along with the tormenting decision of choosing a course that enriches the living process or one that will most certainly terminate it, figuratively or literally. For many the purging of contaminants assures continuity in the lifestyle selected. Others, who are unable to mobilize their resources, are swept by conditions around them with little or no control over their destinies.

Mars in Sagittarius: Because this is a fire sign, Mars is free to function with little or no controls. This is part of the problem, because it also signifies lack of direction, and a reckless abandonment of meaningful enterprises. Coupled with other factors in the chart, it can be a significant asset. When this happens, there is ardor, drive, and aggressive pursuit of the goals. More often there is impatience with determining the truth before making outrageous statements or allegations. While this may stimulate wide interest and many followers, it is difficult to sustain this kind of chicanery for very long. Never boring, these persons are lively in the pursuits and reasonably successful in winning. Ardent lovers, they may lack continuity in relationships and prefer to play the field.

Mars in Capricorn: The pure biological principle of Mars has to struggle to assert its drive in the limiting confines of earthly Capricorn, and frustration is fairly certain. The sexual drive is used with reasonable expectations and only when all extraneous distractions have been disposed of. There is a sense of social propriety in the advances made by those with this placement of Mars. They may seem distant and unfeeling, but this only means that they do not convey their desires freely or casually. They do not indulge in playing games in matters that deal with relationships and affairs.

Mars in Aquarius: This is the sign of freedom from restraint. The permissive sexual behavior of today is especially pertinent to the attitude of those with Mars here. Beyond the personal consideration, they also have a love that extends to the masses and a concern that others enjoy their privileges. They regard themselves as spokespersons for everyone, champions of the needy, and friends to all. They sometimes have to know and understand you before they show some kind of interest in forming a sexual connection. The free-love approach sometimes is used to veil the desires in a free-from-responsibility-or-ties relationship as well.

Mars in Pisces: This is Mars's own 12th sign and represents the danger of taking action that primarily would be self-defeating. This is because there is the chance that what provoked action was misunderstood or of little importance. Stop, look, and listen always must guide those with this Mars, for they tend to attract negative circumstances and situations into which they are drawn and often consumed. The water effect of this sign tends to dissipate and dissolve the Mars energy so that it is ineffective. This doesn't mean that nothing can be accomplished, but it does mean a great deal of careful examining and probing must take place to ascertain that the problem requiring attention is a real one. There is much that is beneath the surface of the personality of those with this Mars, some of it bordering on guilt and persecution for reasons that are obscure. It is difficult to convince them that analysis would prove helpful if only to uncover the buried debris that emerges periodically to clutter their lives. In matters of sex, they often feel unworthy to enjoy this pleasure and may have to be seduced into a relationship so they won't have to feel guilty for indulging in it willingly.

The conditions relating to the sensual and sexual behavior are based on the individual characteristics of Venus and Mars in the signs and houses of the chart. Other factors also must be considered to provide greater detail of how they work when they are influenced by the other planets in the chart. Venus in aspect to Mars stimulates a love nature that must find a suitable avenue for expression, but the aspects to other planets alter the nature, method, and intensity of this love principle.

Transiting Mars aspecting Venus or transiting Venus aspecting Mars tends to arouse the desire nature beyond that which is found in the natal chart and remains so for the duration of the transit effect. Another influence occurs when either Venus or Mars transits through each other's signs or houses, as when Venus is in Aries and Scorpio or in the 1st or 8th Houses. Similarly, this occurs when Mars is in Taurus or Libra or in the 2nd or 7th Houses. Either planet traveling though the 5th House also stimulates attention to matters of a love nature. Although Venus and Mars are the principle indicators of love and sex, the other planets also impart something to this matter. We offer some of the indications that occur when other planets are involved in negative aspects that produce tension and stress and how they influence the whole subject of love, sex, and their variables.

Sun and Moon: This is the classic indicator of problems with the opposite sex. The difficulty is due largely to an inability to make adjustments or concessions.

Sun and Mars: The difficulties in life are mainly due to a nature that is hostile and aggressive. With other factors concurring, there may be cruelty.

Sun and Saturn: The will combines with control. The fear of being rejected often inhibits the formation of any kind of meaningful relationship.

Sun and Neptune: The will is merged with the talent for illusion and delusion. The result frequently is a rearranging of factors so they agree with the wishes and expectations. These persons may be victimized through seductive suggestion into questionable practices or situations.

Sun and Pluto: This indicates one who is compulsive and obsessive in nature. Power and control over others sometimes entices this person to use people to satisfy personal desires.

Moon and Venus: The Moon represents the emotions, feelings, and the subconscious. Venus is adjustment, compromise, and social graces. Together they incline this person to have trouble expressing himself convincingly. People generally are suspicious of how this person is motivated.

Moon and Mars: Because the Moon is the emotions and Mars is the animal nature, there is a fear that the advances will be rejected as being too ardent or too demanding. Unrequited sexual needs provoke much personal discontent.

Moon and Saturn: The feelings as shown by the Moon are in conflict with the caution and self-discipline of Saturn. The result is a deep concern about maintaining the ability to perform in lovemaking. There are deep references to early parental influence.

Moon and Uranus: The enigma of this conflict is in the exact opposite direction to which they relate. The Moon is the past and Uranus is the future, and this person has great difficulty dealing with change as it relates to close relationships and the way permissiveness allows for indulging without commitment or obligation.

Moon and Neptune: There is a basic rapport between these two planetary principles, but when joined by stress aspect it is difficult to make them work easily. What happens is that dreams become disappointments, plans become bogged down, and expectations are shattered. There is a lack of prudent, careful planning to compensate for the inability to face reality, which is seen as harsh and abrasive. A degree of masochism is sometimes found with this combination.

Moon and Pluto: The intensity of physical desires tends to overwhelm the passive emotionalism of the Moon. The result is a demanding sexual nature that seeks to be fulfilled without proper guidelines in selecting a partner.

Venus and Saturn: The coldness and restraint of Saturn diminishes the ability to enter into warm, ardent, and meaningful relationships. This person tends to feel that whatever pleasures are enjoyed are costly in terms of what has to be done to gain them.

Venus and Uranus: The unconventional nature of Uranus inclines this person to seek persons who will engage in a wide spectrum of sexual activity, without any concern for what is traditionally acceptable behavior. In most cases, this enriches the sexual relationships.

Venus and Neptune: In some ways this is similar to the Uranus influence, except that there is a lack of awareness of the dangers of some sexual practices. Hygiene and greater discretion especially are important with this combination.

Venus and Pluto: A powerful combination that drives the person to pursue a love object with persistent determination. The level of desire is high and the disregard for personal safety in the partners selected needs greater consideration.

Mars and Uranus: This is an explosive kind of a sexual drive that rarely accepts no for an answer. The spontaneity of this influence is mainly a biological one and romance isn't generally included. There is an almost mechanistic engagement wherein the emotions play an extremely minor role.

Mars and Neptune: The distortions possible with Neptune offer suggestions of a sexual nature that borders on the bizarre and peculiar. Sadism and masochism are some of the outlets considered by this planetary combination. A person under this influence needs a good role model during the formative years and ample opportunity to develop sexually along lines that generally are compatible with most partners.

Mars and Pluto: Whereas Pluto influenced Venus to become the pursued, here Pluto urges Mars to be the ardent pursuer. Venus is the seductress and invites sexual contact by being available, but Mars is the hunter and seeks after the prey with wild abandon. The extremes in both instances need moderation, because they almost certainly invite tragedy when self-control is missing.

You are sure to find similar planetary combinations in your own chart, but you need not be concerned--for as long as you've become aware of the problem you already are on your way to a solution. *In most cases* the chart reveals concurring information elsewhere to support the direction indicated in the Venus/Mars and other negative planetary combinations. This information will more than likely include the planets Jupiter and Saturn or both. When either one or both of these planets is negatively involved (sign, house, aspect) to Venus, Mars, or the other combinations, the dynamics are altered somewhat. With Jupiter (the optimist) involved, you would feel completely justified that your actions could be pursued without hesitation. With Saturn (the pessimist) there would be restraint due to fears of the consequences. Should both planets be involved, the Saturn energies would prevail because it is the slower moving planet. Recall the effects both these planets had when sextile to Mars in Jung's chart as opposed to Freud's (who had no control). You also should recall that it is the slower moving planet that exerts its energy over the faster one. This does not mean that the energies of the faster planets are ignored or rendered useless. It only means that they are overruled and overpowered. This is similar to young people who have their own ideas and plans but are restricted by parents and/or authorities who prevent them from bringing them to fruition.

To assist you in your delineations of the various combinations we offer some simple procedures. Assume that you have Venus in Aries with Jupiter in conjunction (8 degrees). You now combine what was said for Venus in Aries with what Jupiter in Aries indicates. Because a conjunction bears a Mars force you would then combine this force to the actions indicated. Should any other planet or planets be located there you then would continue to combine those indications. Should the involvement of the additional planets be by aspects other than a conjunction, you then would refer to the negative planetary combinations for their indications.

The foregoing procedures would be employed when solar charts are being delineated. When the birth time is known and a birth chart is cast, the procedure, though similar, is a bit more complex although it provides more details of the matter.

Let's employ the same combination of Venus in Aries but assume that we now know that they are located in the 9th House. Combine the indications of Venus and Aries with what we stated about a Venus-Mars contact because Mars now is co-ruler of the 9th House due to Aries's location on the cusp (Mars rules Aries). Because this is the natural house of Sagittarius you also will consider the indications of Venus in Sagittarius and Mars in Sagittarius. You now also must consider that the 9th House is both the 3rd House (counting from the 7th) and the 8th House (counting from the 2nd), the 3rd House (the way you think) the 8th House (sex and the extremes), these because the 2nd and 7th Houses are both the natural houses of Venus.

When delineations are being considered for sexual behavior, it always is best and most assuring when every factor of the planets, signs, houses, and their rulers are taken into consideration. We very strongly suggest that you make an analysis of some of the combinations in groups of three, four, or more by random selection. From this you should realize the numerous forms of perversion and the like existing within our society. Becoming aware of these facts will help you realize the importance of being most particular and discriminating regarding those in whom you place your trust. You will learn that under no conditions should you ever think a person is not a certain type because you can't believe that he or she would do something perverted or evil. Realize that every single rapist, child molester, child abuser, and so on had a mother, father, and friends who didn't believe they could do such things either. Never under any circumstances judge a book by its jacket. Read it through first and then judge. Do it yourself and then you will know.

Consider that in today's permissive Aquarian society, sex criminals, child molesters, and others are dealt with leniently in the courts. Consider the professionals who free the so-called "sick" through their various theories and all the therapists who believe they have the answers. We cannot stress strongly enough the fact that you are a most unique individual--and so are your problems. Be most selective with whom you discuss your problems, ask advice, or take advice from, because there are those who from simple suggestions and conversations of the subject will become extremely aroused. Don't become a guinea pig and have your problems judged by others.

Sigmund Freud, known as the "Father of Psychoanalysis," has become immortal because of his theories, all of which are based on childhood sexual fantasies. These theories could very well be true, but they also could be very much in error. There is no way possible that his therapy for his patients could be proven proper or improper at this point in history. However, considering the fact that he had the planet Mars for the handle of his "bucket" chart, there is no question as to what motivated his thoughts. The concurring evidence of this was his cruel and unwarranted treatment to Emma Eckstein, his most-famous patient, who suffered needlessly because of his theories and whose only problem was a "frigid nature and nightmares." This sort of problem simply could have been a combination of Venus and Saturn, the Moon and Mars, the Moon and Saturn, or any combination of them. Some of our present day Hollywood starlets have a similar problem and they are under no treatment. Don't become another Emma Eckstein--do your own chart so that you can determine your own solution.

It would be in your best interest to carefully select the persons with whom you will share a close relationship by examining their individual charts to note if any of the conflicts and stresses stated prevail. Some of these stresses can be particularly troublesome or critical. To help you gather more detailed information about those you deal with, we offer Crucial Age Periods, our next chapter.

Chapter 11
Crucial Age Periods

The various concepts in astrology refer to the variations in the behavioral dynamics in man. We have discussed some of these in reasonable detail and offered examples to demonstrate their value in analysis. We now offer another variation that *must be* considered in examining a chart, and it is the crucial age periods at which significant changes from critical planetary contacts occur. They represent important phases of developmental adjustment that everyone must cope with as they grow and mature. We will examine them as critical ages. However, they actually are aspects made by the continuing motion of the planets as they form angular relationships to their own birth locations as well as to other planets in a person's birth chart. We celebrate birthdays representing the day every year when the Sun returns to the same position it was in on the day you were born. When there are 8 degrees separating them we call that a conjunction. The average person doesn't realize this any more than the fact that there are many other planetary contacts whose influence is even more significant than the Sun's return each year.

Over 2400 years ago Socrates stated, "The attitude of these young ones will ruin this world." Times haven't really changed that much, since this is a fairly common expression today. This probably is because the cycles of development are the same regardless of the time period in which they occur. Some of the more common expressions of dismay and concern are:

> "What do you expect? The child came from a broken family."
> "After all, the father/mother is an alcoholic!"
> "I just don't know what suddenly got into him/her."
> "I don't understand it. He/she was never like that before."
> "These kids today, they just don't care about anything."
> "This generation is just too much for me to understand."

Since this predicament seems eternal, we must locate what provokes this dilemma. There are distinct forces at work at different age levels that can be identified and studied. This understanding makes it possible to cope with the problem and not simply consign it to some mysterious category that cannot be dealt with. Let us examine the most crucial age periods and the planets whose cycles they represent.

The approximate age periods when crisis occurs are 14, 21, 28, 35, and 42. In actual practice, however, there is a span of about three years centered on these years given when these influences are taking place. This span of approximately three years for each of the critical ages is due to the apparent backward motion of the planets called retrograde. It is because of this we consider the age periods from 13 to 15, 20 to 22, 27 to 29, 34 to 36, and 41 to 43 as the critical periods. The time periods of Saturn and Uranus and their backward motions (retrograde) account for this extended time for each critical stage. A detailed explanation of these aspects will be offered later in the chapter discussing long-range trends. For now only the easy-to-understand motions and effects will be explained.

We realize, of course, that there are changes in behavior that occur between the ages of 5 and 7. We have not included these simply because few parents are ready to make the kinds of concessions to growing children that would allow them to develop in the way the cycles occurring then would indicate. What generally happens then is a kind of tacit acceptance of the "growing pains of youth" or acknowledgment that "they will grow out of it" and "all children behave that way." This "solution" to the problem of growing-up difficulties is little more than buying time to avoid the crisis head on. In an increasing number of families, the problem is compounded by the absence of both parents for a prolonged period of time every day so that some surrogate father/mother is left with that kind of intimate task. Not surprisingly, the truly significant tensions occur when major cycles of additional changes begin at age 13 and beyond.

Let us consider the cycles of Saturn and Uranus and how they form intersecting and interlocking connections in everyone's lives. It takes Saturn 29 years to make a complete orbit around the Sun, at which time it would be at the same location it occupied in the birth chart and a major cycle of life will have occurred. If 29 years is one complete cycle, then an important milestone is reached every seven years, because during that time Saturn has traveled through one quarter of the zodiac, or 90 degrees. This is a point of crisis and compares to coming to an intersection in the road, making it necessary to stop and look before continuing on. It is this 90 degrees (quarter cycle) of Saturn from which the phrase "seven-year itch" is derived. Other mementos of this cycle are the Seven Rays of Occult Philosophy, the seven notes of the music scale (the eighth note is the first note repeated at a higher octave), the seven days of the week, Seven Wonders of the World, Seven Virtues and Seven Deadly Sins, Seven Ages of Man, and the seven classical planets in the solar system. There also are the Seven against Thebes and the Book of Seven Seals.

This 29-year cycle and its 7-year phases means that at age seven, Saturn is 90 degrees further into the zodiac than it was at birth. This is called a square aspect (a Cancer or 4th-House square) to Saturn's position at birth. At 14, Saturn has traveled another 90 degrees and is now at the opposition aspect (180 degrees, a Libra or 7th House opposition) to Saturn's position at birth. At age 21, Saturn has traveled another 90 degrees and making another square (a Capricorn or 10th House square). At age 28 to 29, Saturn will have made one complete revolution around the Sun and returned to its position at birth called a conjunction (8 degrees). It is during this age period, after having traveled through the entire zodiac (the 12 stages of life), that the individual evaluates the years past. It is the time for reviewing the past and examining all that has taken place, where they have been, where they are going, what they have lost, and what they have gained. It is time for a complete review of the past and an examination of the prospects of the future. Throughout life the cycles of Saturn (the past) and Uranus (the future) play important roles in the struggle to deal effectively with responsibility (Saturn), whose goal is fulfillment and freedom without strings (Uranus). Saturn continues to move and at age 35, a more mature repeat of the age seven square takes place, as do all the other seven-year contacts as they occurred during the first orbit of Saturn. At age 42, however, something else takes place that dramatically alters the significance of this second opposition of Saturn to its natal position. It is the influence of the planet Uranus! Uranus takes 84 years to orbit the Sun. This means that Saturn has time to orbit the Sun three times during the time that Uranus makes one orbit. Because of this age 21 is considered adulthood, although complete maturity occurs at age 28. When Saturn is making the second opposition to its birth location, Uranus is making its first opposition to its birth location. This is one of the reasons why the age 42 period is truly the most climactic time in everyone's life. The other reason will be offered shortly.

We offer the preceding commentary because the stress points of the individual must be resolved and corrected during the 28-year period or age 42 will represent some harsh memories and painful regrets for things gone wrong. There still is time to take care of this old business. If it isn't taken care of, however, at about age 63 these two planets will once more form unfavorable aspects to their individual positions in the birth chart. Saturn will be making another 4th-House square while Uranus is making a 10th-House square. By the way, there is little to be anxious about if understanding the need to grow through accepting responsibility was not incorporated in the life during the years culminating at the 28-year period and again at the 42-year period. In many instances it is the unwillingness to change and grow that causes problems; only rarely is it the product of taking misguided action. Let us take a closer look at Saturn to see what it represents symbolically in the real world.

Saturn represents fears, restrictions, tradition, and inhibitions. Between the ages of 13 and 15, Saturn has traveled and reached a point that is 180 degrees (an opposition) from the point it occupied at birth. An opposition means the opposing factors where compromises and adjustments (Venus) must be made in many areas of the life. If there is no compromise or adjustment, then the "I am" concept of youth prevails to deny progress toward maturity. Accepting responsibility and compromise is a way of dealing with the natural fears, restrictions, and traditional expectations that are part of growing up in a modern society. At this young age level, the young adult now feels unwilling to deal with such things and indicates that "It doesn't bother me any more. I am going to do all the things I feel I must and always wanted to do." Compromise is rejected by some so that the "I am" attitude continues. Hostility is common among the young who feel intimidated by the demands of the adults.

This continues until age 17 or 18, when adults are forced to make compromises because there is little else that can be done. The young are reaching adulthood. However, the second square of Saturn is closing in rapidly at age 21 when matters of career (10th House), status, and reality are gaining increased attention. For the first time, in many cases, thinking in adult terms becomes necessary.

The scenario now becomes something like "I am" going to work (Aries) so that "I have" money (Taurus) to do what "I think" (Gemini) and that is to get my own apartment. "I feel" (Cancer) and "I will" (Leo) succeed for I have "analyzed" (Virgo) every detail of the conditions and "I know" (Uranus) I can make it. It is because he incorporated the principles of Uranus at this point when Uranus is making its first square (4th House) at the same time Saturn is making its second square (10th House). Every 21 years Uranus forms a hostile aspect with the position it occupied in the birth chart so that an arrogant display of freedom (Uranus) occurs. It isn't really freedom, but license. Freedom is something earned from having learned responsibility and maturity that sets the tone for the freedom it gives. There is an unmistakable process or sequence in learning and living that cannot be set aside. The urge to circumvent certain steps in the learning experience is Uranian since it represents the unconventional practices, freedom from obligations, permissiveness, rebellion, and anarchy. "Down with tradition and routines of the past." The young quite often fail to realize that everything that is repeated soon becomes routine as well. When they realize this, they already are 25 or 26 years old and may have wasted precious time looking for an easy way to get the results they desire. An important cycle is at its beginning phase: Saturn is approaching the position it occupied in the birth chart (a conjunction) and this occurs between the ages of 27 to 29.

Saturn's return to its natal position (the conjunction) has the energy and characteristics of Aries/Mars force and the "I am" concept is very strong once more. This complete cycle of Saturn through all 12 stages of the life indicates the time for reevaluating the life thus far to see what has or has not been accomplished. Based on this review, changes are implemented or improvements made in the course to follow.

By ages 34 to 36, the past has been reviewed, necessary changes have been made, and a revised plan for life has been put in place. When properly done, this plan can result in the most productive period of life. A kind of routine is established in which significant gains are made that are as satisfying as they are enriching in the success they indicate. This pattern continues until the most critical cycle period is reached between 41 to 43 years of age. This represents the highest or the lowest point in the life in terms of manageability. It is the culmination of the many years leading to this time and the effect produced is visible testimony of input in the developing years. The decisions from the crisis years of 27 to 29 years of age are reflected when the other half of the Saturn cycle is reached at the age 41 to 43 period. Heightened awareness also occurs during this period because this is the halfway point of the Uranus cycle and the last opportunity to put the life in sharp focus.

Between the ages of 55 to 57, Saturn makes the second return conjunction to its birth chart position. This is the final opportunity to review the results of the previous half cycle at the 41-to-43-year age period. The heightened awareness and enhanced focus that occurred then now is subject to review and adjustment, if necessary. This is the time for reaping rich rewards from a job well done when responsible decisions are made.

Although there are many other aspects and many other planetary cycles at work during and within the cycles of Saturn and Uranus, theirs are the most critical and significant aspects in the monumental tasks they describe in the lives of everyone. Bondage and freedom are conditions that belong to Saturn and Uranus respectively, but the decision in using them is everyone's.

Recall the 12 natural stages where you made comparisons of all life as you know it to be. You also must recall what problem child Albert Einstein said, "There is a reason for everything, everything has a reason." (The cause and effect, the action and reaction.) You surely have witnessed the actions and the reactions, as well as the effects, and at this point you now should be able to realize "the cause" (the planets).

We now offer a graphic illustration to show the advancing positions of both Saturn and Uranus and how they interact at these crucial dates. You also will note that both Neptune and Pluto also are included in the graphic chart, and they too play an important role during these crucial age periods. We intentionally refrained from any commentary on Neptune and Pluto to avoid confusing or complicating this discussion, but now we will bring these planets into the picture.

Similar to Saturn and Uranus, Neptune and Pluto also add their influence and also at their crucial periods which interlock with both Saturn and Uranus. Neptune makes one complete orbit in 165 years while Pluto takes 248 years. Neptune stays in a sign approximately 14 years while Pluto stays 20 years. Taking this into consideration you then will realize that at 28 years of age, Neptune only has moved two signs from its natal position or 60 degrees (a sextile) to its natal location. So what we have now at the 27-to-29- year age period is Neptune adding its influence. More detailed explanations of these combined aspects will follow the graphic illustration. Pluto doesn't come into the picture until the critical 41-to-43-year age period, and that, too, will be mentioned when we later discuss all the age periods individually from the 13-to-15, 20-to-22, 27-to-29 and the 41-to-42-year periods.

Although Saturn, Uranus, Neptune, and Pluto may be physically located anywhere in the chart, the sequence of their aspects to their natal positions will follow as shown. The 1st House is used as a reference point only.

Figure 11
Saturn-Uranus-Neptune-Pluto Cycles

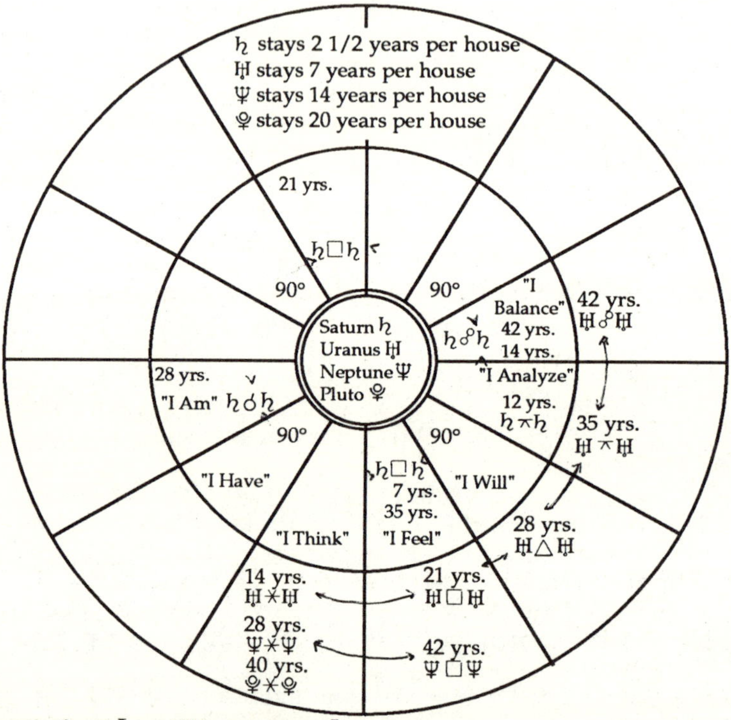

At 12 years of age ♄ will inconjunct ♄
At 14 years of age ♄ will oppose ♄ while ♅ sextiles ♅
At 21 years of age ♄ will square ♄ while ♅ squares ♅ and ♅ opposes ♄
At 28 years of age ♄ will conjunct ♄ while ♅ trines ♅ and ♆ sextiles ♆
At 35 years of age ♄ will square ♄ while ♅ inconjunct ♅
At 42 years of age ♄ will oppose ♄ while ♅ opposes ♅ and ♆ squares ♆ and ♇ sextiles ♇

Freedom is what Uranus demands and will always, in all ways, obtain.

As the Sun makes no dramatic changes in life on a monthly basis, neither does Saturn or Uranus on a yearly basis. their individual lengthy stays in each of the signs creates the changes.

For example, it takes the Sun one year to complete its orbit and return to its birth position. Saturn takes 29 years, Uranus 84 years, Neptune 165 years, and Pluto 248 years to complete theirs. Thus at seven years the Sun has made seven complete orbits while Saturn has advanced only 90 degrees (three signs).

Uranus at this point only has traveled 30 degrees (one sign), Neptune only 15 degrees (one-half of a sign), and Pluto hardly has moved.

Although nothing of great significance has taken place in life during this time, it does not mean that the mind has been idle. The mind has recorded every minute detail of life thus far. The life is under the control of the parents and/or guardians and further influenced by both the elementary school teachers and the parents between the ages of five to eight years. The child has had no opportunity to express his own will and ego (the Sun).

It has reached its first square aspect (90 degrees, 4th-House square) at the end of the seven-year period. It has no profound effect due to the Saturnian characteristics indicating fears, restrictions, inhibitions, and so forth as well as the lack of control over the life and activities. Uranus has no effect at this point because it does not contribute its energies until the 14-year period when it travels 60 degrees (two signs) to form its first sextile aspect. It is at this period that dramatic changes in the life commence: The cause and effect, the action and reaction. The will and ego strive for significance (the Sun). Fears, restrictions, and inhibitions (Saturn) no longer are applicable because at 14 years of age Saturn now opposes Saturn (180 degrees). Uranus in the meantime has moved two signs (60 degrees) to form its first sextile. This is the time for the demand for freedom, the time for detachment from all, the time to become authorities unto themselves and gain the ability to think and act for themselves (Uranus).

14-Year Period Aspects

Sun conjunct Sun The will and ego strive for individual significance.

Saturn opposes Saturn This indicates that because you were not allowed to handle your own life in your own way for the past 14 years, the time has arrived when you will. The "I am," "I have," "I think," "I feel," "I will," and "I analyze" no longer will be under the control of others, but will be under your own individual standards. "I use," the key words of Saturn, are quite applicable. Use they do--every conceivable scheme, excuse, person, or persons and so forth in order to obtain their individual status and individuality.

Uranus sextile Uranus This gives the awareness that the world around you is much greater than the home and family you have been accustomed to. You no longer believe in traditional beliefs and standards. This is the time when friends become more important than anything else. "I know" and freedom are the battle cry of Uranus.

The following brief and simple delineations summarize these aspects.

Following Planetary Protocol

Sun "I will" satisfy my own will and ego and thereby be recognized for the individual that "I am."

Saturn "I use" all that is available, excluding all the traditional beliefs and standards I have been taught to believe. These were set by others for me to follow.

Uranus "I know" how to obtain my freedom through my ability to think and act for myself, detaching myself from any and all ties that bind me.

21-Year Period and Its Aspects

Seven more years pass by. You now are 21 years of age, the age of adulthood in the world's eyes. This belief is truly not so, for you have not yet experienced the entire 12 stages of life. You have reached the stage of freedom from the ties that bound you. Freedom from these obligations is what you now demand and take. It is not freedom earned from responsible decisions and actions.

Let us now learn why.

By age 21 the Sun again has returned to its natal position. Saturn has traveled another 90 degrees and formed its second square (10th House) to its natal position while Uranus has advanced another 30 degrees to form its first square (4th House) to its natal position. At this point Uranus now also opposes Saturn. We now have both Saturn and Uranus squaring their birth locations while Uranus also opposes Saturn's present location. All these are malefic aspects and bring out the negative characteristics.

Let's look at what these malefic aspects indicate. At age seven, when Saturn made its first square (4th House), you were only a child. Although the effects of a square are the same, they differ only because of the experiences encountered in childhood as opposed to adulthood, localized environment as opposed to outside environment, and childhood experiences as opposed to mature experiences.

Recall Planetary Protocol

Saturn square Saturn in the 10th House is indicative of a great lack of self-confidence. You question yourself about what you are doing. This is the testing of your life experiences, the fear of having made mistakes and misjudgments, and so forth.

We realize that it seems a bit contradictory to the actual behavior of an average 21 year old. We agree but this nonetheless is fact. Reflect a bit on the age-old adage "action speaks louder than words" (or thoughts) and we will continue to offer the cause of this seeming contradiction.

Recall planetary protocol (the characteristics of Uranus overriding those of Saturn).

Uranus square Uranus (4th House) and **Uranus oppose Saturn** These cause the major changes in life. These changes occur at age 21 ("today I am a man") and age

63 when retirement age is closing in. It is the age of action and determination followed by the age of inaction and retirement. These are the periods where you demand and exert your own individuality against all odds inclusive of all the accepted and established standards. It signifies the rejection of anything and everything that even resembles the restriction of freedom (Uranus).

28-Year Period and Its Aspects

This behavioral attitude continues on for yet another seven years at which point you will reach your 28th birthday. The Sun again has returned to its birth position while Saturn at this point also has completed its first orbit and returned to its birth position (noting the true age of adulthood and having experienced all the natural stages of life). Uranus, in the meantime, only has advanced another 30 degrees. However, this advancement results in the benefic aspect of a trine (120 degrees; Uranus trine Uranus) while Saturn conjuncts Saturn and the Sun conjuncts the Sun. At this point Neptune influences life for it now has traveled 60 degrees (two signs) into the zodiac and formed its first and only sextile in the life.

Recall that the sextile and the trine are benefic aspects. The sextile, the mental abilities, and the trine are resources to progress.

Using the same planetary protocol, let's learn what these aspects indicate.

Sun conjunct Sun When the will and ego, because of complete adulthood and the responsibility of Saturn, help you begin to win significance in life but in a more responsible, mature, and realistic manner.

Saturn conjunct Saturn Having experienced all 12 stages of life, the re-evaluation of all these experiences now takes place. All the actions and/or inactions are closely examined, along with what has been gained and/or lost, why, the mistakes and their cost, and so forth. All these considerations through your own experiences bring about the changes that Uranus demands.

Uranus trine Uranus The awareness that you now have reached full adulthood and truly possess the ability to think and act for yourself as well as be authority unto yourself is indicated here. You now realize that rather than detaching yourself from the ties that bound you, you now detach yourself from all the factors that have limited your independence. Dramatic changes in the life start taking place, for now you start liberating yourself from any and all restrictions that limit your independence. Now it is "Down with the old, up with the new" be it habit, work, marriage, or whatever.

Neptune sextile Neptune On the positive side, Neptune gives the vision, the imagination, spiritual values, and makes you see the world as it really is and not what you previously believed. Before this period you have been establishing your own sense of who and what you are and believed you had the answers. At this point in your life, you now begin to re-evaluate what you have gained and the cost and what you have not gained and the sacrifices you made (Saturn). You become aware of and discover that all you have been doing with your life is not entirely appropriate, as there have been too many restrictions of one sort or another (Uranus). Neptune is the protocol ruler in this instance, exerting its positive influence and making you now realize what a large universe this really is and that you are a large part of it. This causes you to readjust your life in accordance with these new discoveries and visions. This period gives a sort of new beginning and a new life, in one form or another.

35-Year Period and Its Aspects

Because of the fears, restrictions, inhibitions, and so forth that Saturn implies, many mental deliberations take place during the next seven years. The pros and cons of all past experiences as previously explained keep pressing on the mind. During this time Uranus continues to trine its birth position. The trine is followed by the inconjunct (150 degrees) and both these aspects continue to dominate the life's actions and reactions. It is because of the characteristics of both Uranus and Neptune that, as statistics have shown, various upsets commence. Divorce and separations from marriage, cohabitation, home, work, and so forth occur. As we previously have mentioned, the dramatic changes take place in one way or another.

Uranus--rebellion, detachment, freedom, etc.
Neptune--vision, imagination, consciousness, etc.

An inconjunct aspect (150 degrees) indicates the search for approval, where you look to prove yourself to yourself.

Following the inconjunct aspect Uranus goes on to form its first opposition to its natal position. Saturn now also has advanced to its second opposition, with the Sun again at its birth position. Neptune at this time has advanced from its sextile aspect to its first (4th House) square aspect (3 signs or 90 degrees). During these periods of time Pluto finally has advanced two signs (60 degrees) and forms its first and only sextile in the life.

42-Year Period and Its Aspects (the most critical)

Upon attaining 42 years of age, many critical planetary aspects have formed and exert their pressure and influence in the life. Saturn is halfway through its second orbit and forms an opposition to its birth location. Uranus has reached the first half of its orbit and also forms an opposition to its natal position. Neptune meanwhile now has traveled 90 degrees, one quarter of its orbit, and formed its first square (4th House) to its birth position. Pluto finally has formed its first and only sextile aspect in the life, having advanced only two signs or 60 degrees. This is the only favorable aspect of this age period.

It is at this 42-year period that, because of all the planets involved and their aspects to their original locations as well as to each other, great changes usually take place. Moods, points of view, hidden concepts of your life, hidden secrets you have kept from others or that others have kept from you change. You constantly will be aware of these changes. You suddenly will become aware of new dimensions of reality that you have been afraid to acknowledge before. This will be a time of complete chaos and confusion wherein you won't know which direction to move, where to go, how to go, when to go, or whether or not you should go. You will feel like you've lost your grip on reality and feel completely disoriented. All the doubts and fears of Saturn and the squares will cause you to feel you no longer can handle your life. The subconscious mind ruled by Neptune will cause psychological problems, although those will be purely figments of your own mind. However, you can rest assured that there will be changes in one direction or another. Whether these changes are for better or worse depends on your own free will, which is the final decision maker. However, the changes generally are for the better when you can endure the grief.

Because all the aspects other than Pluto's are malefic (unfavorable), we offer only the negative characteristics of the planets involved. Recall that with malefic aspects it is the negative characteristics of the slower planet that exert its influence over the faster moving planet (planetary protocol).

To refresh your memory a little bit, the malefic characteristics of those planets involved are

Saturn--fears, restrictions, inhibitions, pessimism, and so forth.
Uranus--rebellion, nonconformism, freedom, sudden and unexpected changes, and so forth.
Neptune--chaos, confusion, illusion, seclusion, escape from reality, and so forth. The square and conjunction aspects offer more concurring evidence because their effects are also of a pessimistic nature indicating fears, doubts, inadequacies, and so forth.

Let's now learn what all these negative aspects mean. What effects do they create?

Sun conjunct Sun If not on your 28th birthday and not on your 35th birthday, you had better adhere to what all of the following aspects indicate. For only through responsible actions and decisions can your will and ego achieve the significance they deserve: freedom *earned* from wants and obligations *not taken*.

Saturn opposing Saturn Having experienced the 12 stages of life from your 14th birthday (first opposition), by your own standards you now begin to think about whether or not your actions were responsible as Saturn indicates you must. Although you took control of your own life at age 14, were all of your actions and decisions responsible or irresponsible? Similar to the first opposition, you now start contemplating taking control of your life again, but in a much greater and more responsible manner. The opposition as we stated suggests adjustments, sort of meeting the opposing factors halfway. This applies to Saturn as well.

Uranus opposing Uranus This indicates a major transition in the life, the awareness that you must come to terms with all the experiences in your life. All the good, bad, and indifferent things now must be considered. Am I happy with what I have gained or what I have lost? Have I accomplished anything? What have I got to show for all I have done? The opposition suggests that adjustments (Venus) must now be made if anything worthwhile is to become of the life.

Neptune square Neptune "All that glitters is not gold," then again it may well be. Neptune represents distortions, illusions, delusions, daydreaming, and so on. During the stay of this aspect, you most likely will be questioning your life, goals, and dreams. You may even go out in pursuit of some goal that is unattainable and probably not even worth attaining. The truth almost always is hidden with a negative Neptunian aspect so that you never really know whether it is real gold or fool's gold. Only time will tell which is which.

All these critical malefic aspects cause chaos, confusion, delusions, and so forth. Then how and why do we state that generally it all turns out for the better? Because Pluto has entered into its sextile position to its birth location as well as forming a trine to Saturn and Uranus. These all are benefic (favorable) aspects as well as planetary protocol overrides and that means Pluto, the power of the lot.

Let's now learn what Pluto and its aspects represent.

Pluto represents the purging system of the body and rules the bowels by which the body is cleansed of its wastes and contaminants. This also includes the cleansing of the mind by "blowing your top" to rid yourself of the contaminating mental pressures. Pluto rules life and also death along with resurrection. From destruction comes resurrection and from death new life forms. This is not necessarily life solely in the manner of the organism but also in the form of relationships, careers, habits, and so on. Pluto is the executioner who forces change. You are forced to make changes or suffer the consequences. Pluto is the outermost planet and makes offers "you can't refuse." The pressures exerted by Pluto start at approximately 40 years of age. These changes are constantly on your mind so that when Saturn, Uranus, and Neptune enter into the aspectual configurations at 42 years of age, chaos ensues. However, Pluto the power will eventually prevail and resurrection commences "or else." The "or else" results if and when you don't obey the rules of

> Saturn says, be responsible and face up to the realities of life.
>
> Uranus says, be aware and earn your freedom, don't just take it. You earn it by adhering to the Saturnian principles.
>
> Neptune says, obey the principles of Saturn by using the awareness and know-how of Uranus. You never will need to escape from the realities of life.
>
> Pluto says, if you haven't followed the rules of Saturn, Uranus, and Neptune, you will do so now, one way or another. The decision is yours.

Statistics show that it is during this age period that the largest majority of alcoholics, drug addicts, derelicts, and so forth seek out the appropriate rehabilitation centers for help, while others find solace in spiritual enterprises.

All the planets have their individual reasons for being. We have offered you the characteristics of all of them in their basic, brief form. We now will present our next chapter, "Chart Differences," by which complete and thorough accuracy may be reached in your learning of why we behave as we do.

I am not what I think I am.
I am not what you think I am.
I am what I think you think I am.

Chapter 12
Chart Differences

Before an honest judgment can be rendered on the validity of planetary influence (astrology), one first must be aware of the different methods and procedures employed in obtaining the data.

The types of methods used differ greatly, as well as the data they offer. Serious astrologers use only two methods, either a solar chart or a time chart, the difference to be explained as we discuss each.

As offered in Chapter 2, science says that cosmic rays, electrical phenomena, and other factors and environmental conditions all have a direct influence on all life. We believe that should be enough to prove the validity of planetary influence, especially because of the various types of phenomena that occur worldwide for which neither science nor religion has any explanation whatsoever.

"Horoscope" is the term used by the public in general, the media, and various publications when they have something to say about astrology. Although we can understand the use of it by the general public because they may not be aware of the meaning of the word itself, there is no excuse for others--for it is in complete error with respect to serious astrology. Horoscope means "view of the hour" and refers to the positions of the heavenly bodies as viewed from the place of birth at the time of birth. A horoscope is a map of the heavens as they relate to the individual born at that precise moment and place.

View of the hour legally may be used for almost any type of view of almost any place and for any reason and be correct. The general public is led to believe that it refers to you as an individual born under a particular zodiacal sign. Some even go so far as to give a span of birth dates of those born of the same sign. Because of the fascination with this belief, the general public is being exploited to no end. We only can offer you the truth--not because we see it that way but because that's the way it truly is.

The following explanations of the methods and procedures employed should give you some insight to assist you in your decision.

Sun Sign Astrology is used by every newspaper astrologer as well as many other publications. Serious, honest, and sincere astrologers *do not* use this method. Sun sign astrologers use the planetary positions of the day as they relate to each individual sign, meaning that predictions are made for the Sun's position in the individual signs by the decanates 0 degrees to 10 degrees, 10 degrees to 20 degrees, and 20 degrees to 30 degrees.

In most cases, the Sun sign only is used as the focal point to expedite matters. The predictions are made for the Sun's position *only*, nothing else. They cannot and do not consider the individual as a unique person. They do not and cannot take into account the aspects to the Sun, Moon, and other planets, nor do they nor can they consider that any individual can be the complete opposite of what his Sun sign may be. The fact of the matter is that they cannot and do not offer much of anything other than entertainment. To those of you who are fascinated by this subject, all that really is being offered is an educated guess. The extreme odds are that they are in complete error in their predictions.

Because of their interest the general public looks forward to reading these predictions of their lives. The psychological effect makes you then apply these predictions to yourself to fit your personality. It is not the predictions that fit the sign but the sign that applies itself to the prediction. Although these predictions do relate to the signs, and there are those that fit perfectly for a specific day or event, these are merely correct by the laws of chance. There have to be those that fit the predictions made, for there is no way that they can be in complete error in their entirety. Then again, Chinese fortune cookies are correct sometimes as well.

How anyone of normal intelligence possibly could believe that the world is made up of only 12 types of people is just too unimaginable. Just think for a moment, five billion people in this world and only of 12 types--can you possibly believe that? Noted astronomer and author Carl Sagan does. This is the method he uses in his attempts to discredit astrology. It is understandable that the public is unaware of this type of astrology because they are not aware of the true procedures and only can believe what the critics tell them. If Mr. Sagan really is the authority he is supposed to be, he really should know better. Then again, he probably hasn't been informed, either. Should that be the case, he should not attempt to discuss something he knows nothing about. Only fools make decisions on subjects of which they know nothing. As someone once very aptly said, "It is better to be quiet and thought a fool than to speak and clear all doubt."

Sun sign astrology has very little if any validity. It is solely for the purpose of commercial profit and the exploitation of a hungry public who is in search of answers to their problems that science, religion, and medicine cannot answer. Scientists and astrologers realize and both agree that no two living things are exactly alike. You also should keep in mind that life is a process of becoming for you the same as for any living thing. You are not a reflection of your Sun sign. That is what you are becoming.

Although the media as well as the critics use the term "horoscope" and exploit it to every extent, they do not and will not make any attempt at printing or stating the truth. They employ only the "hit-and-miss dabbling." Should you doubt or completely disbelieve this, then without doubt read *The Astrology Game*--that is, of course, if you want to hear the truth.

Solar Chart One of the two methods used by serious astrologers. It is the method used when the birth time is unknown. When this is the case, twelve o'clock noon is the time used to calculate the positions of the Sun, Moon, and remaining planets. This is because at the exact center of the day the Moon at most only would be 7 degrees off from its precise location which would allow for its aspects and sign location to be fairly accurate by estimation. The Sun, Mercury, and Venus then would be at most only one-half degree off from their actual positions and the remaining planetary locations wouldn't change significantly due to their slow speeds. It is the method used by the astrological computer concerns for those clients who can't obtain a birth time.

The solar chart is most valid in every respect. Although it does not offer as much detail about the person, what it does offer will not be contradicted by a "time chart." The characteristic tendencies, as indicated by a solar chart, although not contradicted may or may not be slightly altered by a time chart. This would be because of the ascendant (rising sign) which is learned from the birth time and the exact position of the Moon, both of which are most crucial in delineations.

When setting up a solar chart for noon, all the planetary positions are calculated for that time. The Sun's position (Sun sign) now is placed on the cusp of the 1st House (eastern horizon). Because the signs always must follow their natural order, you now must place the remaining 11 signs on their respective houses. The houses never change in any way any more than do the heavenly constellations, only the planets and the signs change their positions. For example, should the sign of Cancer be your Sun sign, then this sign would be placed on the 1st House with Leo on the cusp of the 2nd House, Virgo on the 3rd, and so on through the 12 signs. If your Sun sign is Virgo, then Virgo would be placed on the 1st House, followed by Libra on the 2nd, Scorpio on the 3rd, and so on. When this is done you then draw in the glyph of the planet or planets located in their respective locations by the degrees of their position. Starting with your Sun, check all the planets located in your Sun sign, then from the lowest degree draw in its glyph with its degree beside the glyph followed by the sign beside the degrees. This procedure is followed for all of the signs, ensuring that all ten planets are accounted for. Only the nearest degree need be recorded. The minutes and seconds have no significant value; their value was used when you calculated the planetary positions for noon. The uniform procedure for drawing in the planetary glyphs, degrees, and sign does have its value in conservation of time and errors as you will learn.

Aspects now must be calculated. This is accomplished by counting the degrees that separate the Sun from the other nine planets, followed by the Moon to the remaining eight planets, Mercury to the remaining seven and so on. We explained how this was done in the chapter discussing aspects. When considering the Moon's aspects, remember that its location only was estimated and therefore its aspects cannot be accurately depended upon. The closer the birth time can be determined, the more accurate the Moon's aspects can be. When there is any doubt about the Moon's aspects a close scrutiny of your moods, emotions, or whatever indications there are for its position or aspect will be noticed. Should the chart in question be for someone other than yourself, then a one-on-one conversation on the particular indications will bring out the facts.

We have next to count the number of planets located in the three fire signs and write in the total next to the word "fire" on the chart. Repeat this procedure for the total number of planets in the earth, air, and water signs.

Following this by the same procedure as for the elements, we now count the number of planets in the signs of the same quality of cardinal, fixed, and mutable and write in these totals in their proper places. A recheck on all phases up to this point should be made, ensuring that all ten planets are accounted for in each phase. If you have followed the uniform procedure we suggested (glyph-degrees-sign), the foregoing procedure would be a very simple matter as well as the one following.

Obtaining the astrological signature of the individual is the next step. This is achieved by checking which element has the majority of planets located there fire, earth, air or water. Follow this with whatever quality has the most planets cardinal, fixed or mutable. The element and quality that has the majority now is combined to determine which of the twelve zodiac signs possesses that particular combination. As no two signs possess the same quality and the same element, there only will be one sign of that combination and that sign will be the signature (see Signature Table in Chapter 7). Should there be a tie between any of the elements and or qualities, the ruling planet of the Sun sign then may be used to break the tie, this by the element and/or quality of the sign of its location.

If that is of no help in breaking the tie, the position of the Moon by the same method may be used. Should this be of no help, it then is best to ignore the individual signature but consider the combinations that exist as co-signatures that indicate a more complex individual. As the planet that rules the signature influences its priority in the life, then the co-signatures will exert their priorities as well.

SIGNATURE TABLE

	FIRE	WATER	AIR	EARTH
CARDINAL	Aries	Cancer	Libra	Capricorn
FIXED	Leo	Scorpio	Aquarius	Taurus
MUTABLE	Sagittarius	Pisces	Gemini	Virgo

The elements and qualities now must be checked to learn if any one of them is void of any planets. Voids in any element or quality presents liabilities (see Chapter 7).

The ruling planets of the Sun sign and the signature (can be the same as often as not) now must be considered for their positive or negative influences to learn of the directions they indicate.

Recall the Jones Patterns, the seven chart types we discussed. They, too, play a crucial role in the life and must not be overlooked. The chart should be very closely examined to determine the existence of any one of these types.

A very close examination of all the aspects should be made to ascertain if any planet or planets make no aspects. Planets that make no aspects present a most crucial liability and must be given serious attention. A planet that makes no aspects indicates that the individual would have no desires to exploit the energies that planet offers. For example, with an unaspected Sun (the Sun being the will and the ego), there would be no desire to exploit his will and ego. Should Mercury be unaspected, then there would be no desire to communicate, for Mercury represents communication.

The foregoing concepts were examined in great detail in Chapters 7 through 9 and their importance stressed at that time. There should be no question of their significance in a correct delineation of any type chart.

Time Chart As the solar chart indicates the characteristic tendencies of the individual, the time chart will indicate how these tendencies will be applied in relation to their locations within their assigned houses of the time chart. How the person will react to the various circumstances of life as well as how he views life will be shown by the ascendant sign, the sign rising at that moment of birth.

A time chart is the only true method by which the serious astrologer can offer a correct synthesis of the individual. The synthesis now is based on the exact time and place of birth with the exact positions of the planets for that time and place. Not only does it offer the ascendant sign for its significance (as we stated), but it also is another crucial factor of its aspects to its natural location. It follows that whatever aspect the ascending sign makes to its natural location, all the signs make the same aspect to their natural location. For example, should the sign Libra be the ascending sign (1st House), then Scorpio would fall on the 2nd, Sagittarius on the 3rd, and so on through the twelve signs. This results in all 12 signs being in opposition to its natural location. Libra's natural house is the 7th, Scorpio's the 8th, and Sagittarius the 9th, and so forth. Should the sign of Cancer or Capricorn be the ascending sign, then all signs would square (90 degrees) their natural location and present a most crucial negative attitude in almost all of their endeavors.

Because of the extreme importance of the ascending sign, we feel it necessary to elaborate a bit more on its movements (progression).

As the Sun rises and sets every 24 hours with a gain of one degree, so do the entire 12 signs of the zodiac. Following in their natural order, each sign progresses one degree of arc every four minutes of time, or 30 degrees of arc every two hours of time. Twelve signs, two hours each, equals the 24-hour day. At the exact same time each following day, the same sign will be rising on the horizon but will be one degree further into the sign. After completing 30 degrees (30 days), the next sign starts its travel on the horizon.

You must understand at this point that when we speak of time and rates of speed, they are the apparent motions with the exact time rounded off in keeping with the coordinated mean time.

The procedures that are employed by the serious astrologer in setting up a birth chart (time chart) are as methodical as possible. These procedures must be employed without any variations if any accuracy whatsoever is to be enjoyed. You now will have the opportunity to decide for yourself just who it is that dabbles in hit-and-miss tactics--serious astrologers or scientists. The procedures in themselves will help you decide that, whether or not you cast a chart. You will note that nothing whatsoever is left to chance or guess. However, casting a chart for yourself and getting the results we claim would be the valid proof of the planetary influence in our behavior that we claim to be fact.

Casting either a solar chart or time chart requires certain books in order to obtain the astrological data to carry out the various procedures necessary for erecting a correct chart.

For your convenience we offer Appendices, including one reproduction of the American Ephemeris for the years 1940 to 1994; Tables of Houses; Diurnal Motion of the Sun, Moon, and the Planets; and Longitudes and Latitudes of Major Cities in the World. These Appendices follow Chapter 14. We also offer all details and explanations of how, why, and what is to be done prior to the outlined procedures. We strongly believe that when one knows why and what he is doing, the task becomes much more simple and easier to understand. Although it may seem to be difficult and complicated, it really is not. Complex, yes; complicated, no. It shouldn't take more than an hour or so in its entirety, as you soon will learn.

A time chart may be purchased from an astrological computer concern that specializes in horoscopes and offers all the details, including a brief analysis of each plus the planetary aspects. However, although you receive these brief passages and analysis for each of the aspects and most of the other details, they do not and cannot give you a correct synthesis of the complete chart. This only can be done by a serious and competent astrologer. You also must realize that a computer service offers only a single chart for a specific fee. You are obligated to pay this fee for each chart.

The alternative is the purchase of the necessary books. Since there are many publications of the various books, the choice will be yours to make. We suggest the most convenient and least expensive choice, *The American Ephemeris 1931 to 1980*. This single volume gives all the necessary data for casting a chart for anyone born between the years 1931 to 1980. Under separate cover an additional volume of the same title covers the years 1900 through 2000, but only the ephemeris, not all of the other needed information. The purchase of these two volumes offers all the data required to cast charts from 1900 to 2000. The ephemeris for the years beyond the present year is a necessity. It is the only means by which you learn of the planetary location for the transiting planets for tomorrow, next month, next year, and so on. This also is the only means by which you locate the long-range trends that will take place in the coming years. The key cycle charts also are cast by this procedure for each month of the year and informs you of what to expect in your life on a month-to-month basis, your focal points, priorities, positive or negative attitudes, and so forth.

Following is an explanation of the astrological books required. The *American Ephemeris* gives the planetary locations as they are recorded for 0 hrs (midnight) by the Greenwich, England, observatory.

Although there are numerous encyclopedias that may offer the longitude and latitude for almost any place of your choice, we suggest *Longitudes and Latitudes in the United States*. This book also may be purchased for other countries should you so desire. This book is most necessary as it offers the exact time difference between Greenwich, England, and your particular longitude (not to be confused with Zone Standard Time).

By means of the sidereal time the tables of houses book gives the sign that is ascending on the horizon for every north latitude from 0 degrees to 60 degrees and for every four-minute interval from 0 hours 04 minutes through 23 hours 56 minutes. As the ascending sign moves one degree every four minutes of time, the table of houses records its position.

Diurnal Motions of the Planets offers the distance traveled by the planets for both minutes and hours, ranging from 1 to 59 minutes and from 1 to 24 hours. Because of the varying speeds of each planet, the Sun and Moon are recorded individually while the remaining planets are grouped by their speeds. This is recorded by each planet's motion for the day, which is obtained by subtracting the position of the planet of any given day from that of the following day. From this motion it is determined how far the planet will travel for any period of time during the day.

The American Ephemeris we suggested contains all this under a single cover while also giving the position of the Moon for both midnight and noon of each day. The precise time the Sun moves into a different sign also is an important factor that this volume offers. Although this may not be an important factor for most, it is important to those born on this day when the Sun changes signs. Greenwich time is used for this changeover, but to calculate the birth place time would be a very simple process.

Having presented the library necessary to cast a birth chart, we now will explain the procedures to learn the ascending sign. As there are 14 steps to these calculations, it follows that there should be 14 explanatory statements.

1. For obvious reasons the birth date of the individual must be noted.

2. The birthplace should be listed by city, state, and country. This aids in ascertaining the correct longitude and latitude of the birthplace.

3. Longitude is crucial, for it is this longitude time and latitude that gives the all-important ascendant sign.

4. Latitude is the means by which we learn exactly which eastern horizon is applicable.

5. Birth time is necessary or a birth chart cannot be possible.

6. The Zone Standard Time differs in various parts of the country and the world. It is necessary to coordinate the birth locality time with that of Greenwich, England. East of Greenwich, England, the Zone Standard Time is subtracted from the birth time while west of Greenwich it is added.

7. Daylight Savings Time must be subtracted from the result of line 5 and 6 should it have been in effect at the time of the birth. It is most significant to consider this one hour of time if any degree of accuracy is to be achieved.

8. The result of these calculations gives you the time in Greenwich.

9. Sidereal time is taken from the ephemeris on the same date and year of the birth. It will be the first column following the days of the month and shown as S.T. or time. This is not clock time, but the degrees of arc the Sun has traveled thus far into the zodiac (although it is recorded in hours [hrs], minutes ['], and seconds ["]).

10. The interval is in reference to the difference in time from 0 hours (midnight) to time of birth as it was in Greenwich, the result shown on line 8 is in Greenwich Mean Time. This time now must be added to the sidereal time taken from the ephemeris that was for 0 hours. By adding the interval time to the sidereal time, we get a very close approximation for sidereal time in Greenwich. See also the next step.

11. Acceleration on interval refers to the 9.86.16 seconds (rounded off to 10 seconds) per hour that is gained but not added to the time of day. This time, only amounting to minutes, must also be added to the result of lines 9 and 10 so that the precise Greenwich Sidereal Time at birth can be obtained.

12. Greenwich Sidereal Time at birth is the result of all the calculations thus far.

13. Longitude Equivalent Time is the precise time difference between Greenwich and the place of birth. It must now be subtracted from Greenwich Sidereal Time. This result gives the Local Sidereal Time for the moment of birth.

14. Local Sidereal Time is the time that indicates what sign is rising for that particular latitude.

Special Note: As we are calculating time and not ordinary digits, caution must be exercised at all times. When the final total reached exceeds 24 hours, you merely subtract 24:00:00 hours from that total. For example, should the final total be 28:42:51, you then subtract 24:00:00 (hours). The time really is the same at 4:42:51 as there are only 24 hours for the day. The same holds true should the occasion arise that you may have to subtract a larger period of time from a smaller one. You then would borrow 24:00:00 hours. The procedure then would be reversed.

When calculations are in progress and it becomes necessary to borrow a digit from the preceding column, you *always* must recall that it is "time" you are calculating. Therefore, when you borrow it is an hour (60 minutes) you borrow or one minute (60 seconds) and not elementary digits. Some simple examples for you to follow.

24:00:00 = 23:60:00 = 23:59:60 All are one and the same time.

We cannot subtract 23:14:47 from 23:07:32 unless we borrow 24 hours for the lesser time, which then amount to 47:07:32 (23:07:32 + 24:00:00 = 47:07:32).

47:07:32 (borrow 60 min.) = 46:67:32 (borrow 60 sec.) = 46:66:92 (all the same
-23:14:47 time)
23:52:45

23 hours, 52 minutes, and 45 seconds is the final total in time.

When adding time periods the same extreme caution must be exercised, because when a total of 60 seconds is reached it becomes one minute, and when 60 minutes is reached it becomes one hour. For example

Hence, 23:14:47
+ 2:53:27
26:08:14 We converted 60 seconds to 1 minute, 60 minutes to 1 hour.
- 24:00:00 We subtracted the necessary 24 hours.
2:08:14 = the final correct time.

We now offer the procedure employed in actual practice. Following each phase and explanation of the steps taken, we will offer a sample figure of each step. These figures are the actual duplicates taken from the American Ephemeris that we employed in casting the charts for Jane Doe. By following all these steps and figures, you will realize the simplicity of it all.

How to Set Up a Birth Chart

1 -- Birth date		6 / 26 / 1937 Mo./Day/Year
2 -- Birth place		Malden / Mass. / U.S.A. City / State / Country
3 -- Longitude	71 W 04	Longitude Time 4:44:16
4 -- Latitude	42 N 26	

	Hours / Min./ Sec.
5 -- Birth time (11:30 P.M.) A.M. __ P.M. x	23 / 30 / 00
6 -- Zone Standard Time East __ West x	+ 5 / 00 / 00
7 -- Daylight Saving Time	- 1 / 00 / 00
8 -- Greenwich Mean Time (6/27/37) A.M. x P.M. __ (3:30 A.M.)	27 / 30 / 00 - 24
9 -- Sidereal Time 0 Hrs. (midnight)	18 / 18 / 45
10 -- Interval from Midnight (0 hrs.) (line 8)	+ 3 / 30 / 00 = 21 / 48 / 45
11 -- Acceleration on Interval (10 seconds per hr.)	+ 00 / 00 / 35
12 -- Greenwich Sidereal Time at birth	21 / 49 / 20
13 -- Longitude Equivalent Time (line 3) East __ West x	- 4 / 44 / 16
14 -- Local Sidereal Time at birth	17 / 05 / 04
Subtract 24 hours (if necessary)	__ / __ / __

Figure 12: Longitude and Latitude of Major Cities

Kingston, NY	73W59	41N56	4:55:56	Mcallen, TX	98W14	26N12	6:32:56
Kingsville, TX	97W52	27N31	6:31:28	Mckeesport, PA	79W51	40N21	5:19:24
Kirkwood, MO	90W24	38N35	6:01:36	Macon, GA	83W38	32N51	5:34:32
Knoxville, TN	83W55	35N58	5:35:40	Madison, WI	89W24	43N04	5:57:36
Kokomo, IN	86W08	40N29	5:44:32	Madison Heights, MI	83W06	42N30	5:32:24
Lackaw'na, NY	78W50	42N50	5:15:20	Malden, MA	71W04	42N26	4:44:16
LaCrosse, WI	91W15	43N48	6:05:00	Manchester, CT	72W31	41N47	4:50:04
Lafayette, CA	122W07	37N53	8:08:28	Manchester, NH	71W28	43N00	4:45:52
Lafayette, IN	86W54	40N25	5:47:36	Manhattan, KS	96W35	39N11	6:26:20

Having completed the calculations for the sidereal time, we now refer to the Table of Houses to learn what sign was rising on the eastern horizon at that time. This volume lists its tables from 0 hours 4 minutes 0 seconds through 23 hours 56 minutes of sidereal time. Each group of tables also lists north latitudes from 0 degrees through 60 degrees. In the upper left corner, we now locate the column for that sidereal time of 17 hours 05 minutes 04 seconds. From the center column showing the latitudes we locate the latitude for the locality (42 degrees for Malden, Massachusetts). Where these two lines intersect shows the ascending sign, this being the first sign above the intersecting point of the degrees shown. As other houses also are included in these tables, we look under the center column showing "ASC" and its degrees. We now have the ascending sign and its degrees, but that is not the end but the beginning.

Figure 13: Table of Houses for Latitudes 0° to 60° North

Sidereal time Ascendant Latitude

17h 4m 0s 256° 0' 0" 17 ♐ 07

LAT.	11	12	ASC	2	3
0	14♑44	13♒32	14♓48	17♈21	18♉28
5	14 05	12 31	14 12	17 48	18 59
10	13 26	11 26	13 34	18 16	19 31
15	12 44	10 17	12 51	18 47	20 05
20	12 00	9 02	12 01	19 20	20 42
21	11 51	8 46	11 50	19 28	20 49
22	11 42	8 30	11 39	19 35	20 57
23	11 33	8 14	11 28	19 43	21 05
24	11 23	7 57	11 16	19 51	21 13
25	11 13	7 39	11 03	19 59	21 21
26	11 03	7 21	10 50	20 07	21 29
27	10 53	7 03	10 37	20 16	21 38
28	10 43	6 44	10 23	20 25	21 47
29	10 32	6 25	10 08	20 34	21 56
30	10 21	6 05	9 53	20 43	22 05
31	10 10	5 45	9 37	20 53	22 15
32	9 59	5 23	9 20	21 03	22 24
33	9 47	5 02	9 03	21 14	22 34
34	9 35	4 39	8 44	21 25	22 45
35	9 23	4 16	8 25	21 36	22 55
36	9 10	3 51	8 05	21 48	23 06
37	8 57	3 26	7 43	22 01	23 17
38	8 43	3 00	7 20	22 14	23 29
39	8 29	2 33	6 56	22 28	23 41
40	8 15	2 05	6 30	22 42	23 54
41	8 00	1 35	6 02	22 57	24 07
42	7 44	1 05	5 33	23 13	24 20
43	7 28	0 32	5 01	23 30	24 35
44	7 11	29♑58	4 27	23 48	24 49
45	6 54	29 23	3 50	24 06	25 05
46	6 36	28 45	3 10	24 27	25 21
47	6 16	28 06	2 26	24 48	25 38
48	5 56	27 24	1 39	25 11	25 56
49	5 35	26 40	0 47	25 35	26 15
50	5 13	25 53	29♒49	26 02	26 35
51	4 50	25 03	28 46	26 30	26 56
52	4 25	24 10	27 35	27 01	27 18
53	3 58	23 13	26 16	27 34	27 42
54	3 30	22 11	24 46	28 11	28 07
55	3 00	21 05	23 05	28 51	28 35
56	2 28	19 52	21 09	29 36	29 05
57	1 53	18 34	18 55	0♉25	29 37
58	1 15	17 08	16 20	1 20	0♊12
59	0 33	15 33	13 18	2 23	0 50
60	29♐47	13♑48	9♒44	3♉34	1♊33

17h 8m 0s 257° 0' 0" 18 ♐ 02

LAT.	11	12	ASC	2	3
0	15♑40	14♒32	15♓53	18♈26	19♉27
5	15 01	13 32	15 20	18 54	19 59
10	14 22	12 28	14 44	19 24	20 32
15	13 40	11 20	14 03	19 56	21 06
20	12 57	10 06	13 17	20 32	21 43
21	12 48	9 50	13 07	20 39	21 50
22	12 38	9 34	12 57	20 47	21 58
23	12 29	9 18	12 46	20 55	22 06
24	12 19	9 01	12 35	21 04	22 14
25	12 09	8 44	12 23	21 12	22 23
26	12 00	8 26	12 11	21 21	22 31
27	11 49	8 08	11 58	21 30	22 40
28	11 39	7 50	11 45	21 40	22 49
29	11 28	7 30	11 32	21 49	22 58
30	11 18	7 11	11 17	21 59	23 07
31	11 06	6 51	11 02	22 10	23 17
32	10 55	6 30	10 47	22 20	23 27
33	10 43	6 08	10 30	22 32	23 37
34	10 31	5 46	10 13	22 43	23 47
35	10 19	5 22	9 55	22 55	23 58
36	10 06	4 59	9 36	23 08	24 09
37	9 53	4 34	9 16	23 21	24 20
38	9 40	4 08	8 54	23 35	24 32
39	9 26	3 41	8 31	23 49	24 45
40	9 11	3 13	8 07	24 04	24 57
41	8 56	2 44	7 41	24 20	25 10
42	8 41	2 13	7 13	24 37	25 24
43	8 25	1 41	6 43	24 55	25 38
44	8 08	1 07	6 11	25 14	25 53
45	7 50	0 32	5 36	25 34	26 09
46	7 32	29♑55	4 59	25 55	26 25
47	7 13	29 15	4 18	26 17	26 43
48	6 53	28 34	3 33	26 41	27 01
49	6 32	27 50	2 43	27 07	27 20
50	6 09	27 03	1 49	27 35	27 40
51	5 46	26 13	0 48	28 05	28 01
52	5 21	25 20	29♒41	28 37	28 24
53	4 54	24 23	28 25	29 12	28 48
54	4 26	23 21	27 00	29 51	29 14
55	3 56	22 15	25 22	0♉33	29 42
56	3 23	21 03	23 30	1 20	0♊11
57	2 48	19 44	21 21	2 11	0 44
58	2 10	18 18	18 49	3 09	1 19
59	1 28	16 43	15 51	4 15	1 58
60	0♑42	14♑57	12♒19	5♉29	2♊42

17h 12m 0s 258° 0' 0" 18 ♐ 58

LAT.	11	12	ASC	2	3
0	16♑36	15♒32	16♓57	19♈30	20♉26
5	15 57	14 33	16 27	20 00	20 59
10	15 18	13 30	15 54	20 31	21 32
15	14 37	12 23	15 16	21 05	22 07
20	13 53	11 10	14 33	21 43	22 44
21	13 44	10 55	14 24	21 51	22 52
22	13 35	10 39	14 14	21 59	23 00
23	13 25	10 23	14 04	22 08	23 08
24	13 16	10 06	13 54	22 17	23 16
25	13 06	9 49	13 43	22 26	23 24
26	12 56	9 32	13 32	22 35	23 33
27	12 46	9 14	13 20	22 44	23 42
28	12 36	8 55	13 08	22 54	23 51
29	12 25	8 36	12 55	23 04	24 00
30	12 14	8 17	12 42	23 15	24 09
31	12 03	7 57	12 28	23 26	24 19
32	11 52	7 36	12 14	23 37	24 29
33	11 40	7 15	11 59	23 49	24 39
34	11 28	6 53	11 43	24 01	24 50
35	11 16	6 30	11 26	24 14	25 00
36	11 03	6 06	11 08	24 27	25 12
37	10 50	5 41	10 49	24 41	25 23
38	10 36	5 16	10 29	24 56	25 35
39	10 22	4 49	10 08	25 11	25 48
40	10 08	4 21	9 45	25 27	26 00
41	9 53	3 52	9 21	25 43	26 14
42	9 38	3 22	8 55	26 01	26 28
43	9 21	2 50	8 27	26 20	26 42
44	9 05	2 17	7 57	26 39	26 57
45	8 47	1 42	7 24	27 00	27 13
46	8 29	1 05	6 49	27 22	27 29
47	8 10	0 26	6 10	27 46	27 47
48	7 49	29♑44	5 28	28 11	28 05
49	7 28	29 01	4 42	28 38	28 24
50	7 06	28 14	3 50	29 07	28 45
51	6 42	27 24	2 53	29 38	29 06
52	6 17	26 31	1 49	0♉12	29 29
53	5 51	25 34	0 38	0 49	29 53
54	5 23	24 33	29♒16	1 29	0♊20
55	4 52	23 27	27 43	2 14	0 48
56	4 20	22 14	25 56	3 02	1 18
57	3 44	20 56	23 52	3 56	1 51
58	3 06	19 29	21 25	4 57	2 27
59	2 24	17 54	18 31	6 05	3 06
60	1♑38	16♑08	15♒03	7♉23	3♊50

17h 16m 0s 259° 19 ♐ 53

LAT.	11	12	ASC	2
0	17♑32	16♒33	18♓02	20♈3
5	16 53	15 34	17 34	21 0
10	16 14	14 32	17 04	21 3
15	15 33	13 26	16 29	22 1
20	14 49	12 14	15 50	22 5
21	14 40	11 59	15 41	23 0
22	14 31	11 44	15 32	23 1
23	14 22	11 28	15 23	23 2
24	14 12	11 11	15 13	23 2
25	14 03	10 54	15 04	23 3
26	13 53	10 37	14 53	23 4
27	13 43	10 20	14 42	23 5
28	13 32	10 01	14 31	24 0
29	13 22	9 43	14 20	24 1
30	13 11	9 24	14 07	24 3
31	13 00	9 04	13 55	24 4
32	12 48	8 43	13 41	24 5
33	12 37	8 22	13 27	25 0
34	12 25	8 00	13 12	25 1
35	12 12	7 38	12 57	25 3
36	12 00	7 14	12 40	25 4
37	11 47	6 50	12 23	26 0
38	11 33	6 24	12 04	26 1
39	11 19	5 58	11 45	26 3
40	11 05	5 30	11 24	26 4
41	10 50	5 02	11 01	27 0
42	10 34	4 31	10 37	27 2
43	10 18	4 00	10 11	27 4
44	10 01	3 27	9 43	28 0
45	9 44	2 52	9 13	28 2
46	9 26	2 15	8 40	28 4
47	9 06	1 37	8 04	29 1
48	8 46	0 55	7 25	29 4
49	8 25	0 12	6 41	0♉0
50	8 03	29♑26	5 54	0 3
51	7 39	28 36	5 00	1 1
52	7 14	27 43	4 00	1 4
53	6 48	26 47	2 53	2 2
54	6 19	25 45	1 36	3 0
55	5 49	24 39	0 08	3 5
56	5 16	23 27	28♒27	4 4
57	4 41	22 08	26 28	5 4
58	4 02	20 42	24 08	6 4
59	3 20	19 06	21 20	7 5
60	2♑34	17♑20	17♒56	9♉1

Figure 14: June 1937 Ephemeris

LONGITUDE

Sid. Time	☉	☽	☽ 12 Hour	Mean ☊	True ☊	☿	♀	♂	♃	♄	♅	♆	♇
h m s	° ′ ″	° ′ ″	° ′ ″	° ′	° ′	° ′	° ′	° ′	° ′	° ′	° ′	° ′	° ′
16 36 14	10♊ 4 37	25♒ 8 45	1♓ 39 13	15♐ 33	15♐ 7R	17♉ 31	27♈ 46	24♏ 8R	26♑ 54R	3♈ 24	11♉ 21	16♍ 11	27♋ 3
16 40 11	11 2 6	8♓ 15 7	14 56 38	15 29	15 7	18 7	28 26	23 49	26 51	3 28	11 24	16 11	27 4
16 44 7	11 59 34	21 44 4	28 37 33	15 26	15 7	18 47	29 7	23 31	26 47	3 32	11 27	16 11	27 5
16 48 4	12 57 1	5♈ 37 7	12♈ 42 43	15 23	15 7	19 31	29 48	23 13	26 44	3 36	11 30	16 11	27 7
16 52 0	13 54 28	19 54 7	27 10 57	15 20	15 6	20 18	0♉ 31	22 55	26 40	3 40	11 33	16 12	27 8
16 55 57	14 51 54	4♉ 32 43	11♉ 58 44	15 17	15 6D	21 10	1 15	22 38	26 36	3 44	11 36	16 12	27 9
16 59 53	15 49 19	19 28 10	27 0 4	15 13	15 6	22 5	1 59	22 22	26 32	3 48	11 39	16 12	27 10
17 3 50	16 46 44	4♊ 33 25	12♊ 7 3	15 10	15 6	23 3	2 44	22 6	26 28	3 52	11 42	16 12	27 12
17 7 47	17 44 9	19 39 51	27 10 42	15 7	15 7R	24 5	3 31	21 51	26 24	3 56	11 45	16 13	27 13
17 11 43	18 41 32	4♋ 38 31	12♋ 2 19	15 4	15 7	25 11	4 18	21 37	26 19	3 59	11 48	16 13	27 14
17 15 40	19 38 54	19 21 17	26 34 42	15 1	15 6	26 19	5 6	21 23	26 14	4 3	11 51	16 14	27 16
17 19 36	20 36 16	3♌ 42 2	10♌ 42 56	14 58	15 6	27 31	5 54	21 10	26 10	4 6	11 54	16 14	27 17
17 23 33	21 33 36	17 37 10	24 24 43	14 54	15 5	28 47	6 43	20 58	26 5	4 10	11 57	16 15	27 18
17 27 29	22 30 56	1♍ 5 38	7♍ 40 9	14 51	15 5	0♊ 5	7 33	20 46	26 0	4 13	12 0	16 15	27 20
17 31 26	23 28 14	14 8 34	20 31 17	14 48	15 4	1 27	8 24	20 36	25 54	4 16	12 2	16 16	27 21
17 35 22	24 25 32	26 48 45	3♎ 1 27	14 45	15 4D	2 51	9 15	20 26	25 49	4 19	12 5	16 16	27 23
17 39 19	25 22 49	9♎ 9 56	15 14 45	14 42	15 4	4 19	10 7	20 17	25 43	4 22	12 8	16 17	27 24
17 43 16	26 20 5	21 16 26	27 15 32	14 39	15 5	5 50	10 59	20 9	25 38	4 25	12 11	16 18	27 26
17 47 12	27 17 20	3♏ 12 36	9♏ 8 8	14 35	15 6	7 24	11 52	20 1	25 32	4 28	12 13	16 18	27 27
17 51 9	28 14 35	15 2 38	20 56 34	14 32	15 7	9 1	12 46	19 55	25 26	4 31	12 16	16 19	27 28
17 55 5	29 11 49	26 50 22	2♐ 44 28	14 29	15 8	10 41	13 40	19 49	25 20	4 33	12 18	16 20	27 30
17 59 2	0♋ 9 3	8♐ 39 13	14 34 58	14 26	15 9R	12 23	14 35	19 44	25 14	4 36	12 21	16 21	27 31
18 2 58	1 6 16	20 32 2	26 30 43	14 23	15 9	14 9	15 30	19 40	25 7	4 38	12 24	16 21	27 33
18 6 55	2 3 29	2♑ 31 17	8♑ 33 57	14 19	15 8	15 58	16 25	19 37	25 1	4 41	12 26	16 22	27 34
18 10 51	3 0 41	14 38 57	20 46 30	14 16	15 7	17 49	17 22	19 34	24 54	4 43	12 29	16 23	27 36
18 14 48	3 57 53	26 56 46	3♒ 9 56	14 13	15 5	19 43	18 18	19 33	24 48	4 45	12 31	16 24	27 37
18 18 45	4 55 5	9♒ 26 12	15 45 43	14 10	15 2	21 39	19 15	19 32D	24 41	4 47	12 34	16 25	27 39
18 22 41	5 52 17	22 8 40	28 35 13	14 7	14 59	23 38	20 12	19 32	24 34	4 49	12 36	16 26	27 41
18 26 38	6 49 29	5♓ 5 31	11♓ 39 45	14 4	14 56	25 40	21 10	19 33	24 27	4 51	12 38	16 27	27 42
18 30 34	7♋ 46 40	18♓ 18 4	25♓ 0 37	14♐ 0	14♐ 54	27♊ 43	22♉ 8	19♏ 35	24♑ 20	4♈ 53	12♉ 41	16♍ 28	27♋ 44

DAILY ASPECTARIAN

Day	Aspect	Time
	…∠♃	3am14
	…⊻♇	3 32
	…*♀	5 7
	…♆	10 10
	…∠♄	3pm16
	…☽	5am24
	…*♅	5 41
	…□♃	6 26
	…♇	6 53
	…∠♅	9 36
	…∠♀	9 47
	…♄	2pm 4
	…♆	2 12
	…∠♄	2 41
	…*☿	6 31
	…♃	7 7
	…♄	7 34
	…⊻♇	2am29
	…△♂	3 3
	…∠♅	8 16
	…*♃	8 47
	…△♇	9 21
	…⊻♀	1pm30
	…♄	8 33
	…∠☿	10 0
	…♆	10 23
	…♂	4am19
F	♀ ♉	6 41
	☽⊻♅	10 0
	☽‖♀	12pm55
	☉*☽	1 17
	☽⚻♆	5 50
5 S	☽⊻☿	0am42
	☽⚻♂	4 54
	☽□♃	11 6
	☽□♇	11 56
	☽‖☿	1pm26
	☉∠☽	3 51
	☽‖♅	4 14
	☽☌♀	6 21
	☽⚼♆	6 33
	♀⚼♆	10 31
	☽⊻♄	10 41
6 Su	☽☌♅	11am26
	☉⊻☽	5pm46
	☽△♆	6 46
	☽∠♄	10 56
7 M	☽#♂	1am58
	☽☌☿	4 27
	☽☍♂	4 32
	☿☍♂	5 37
	☿‖♅	8 12
	☉□♆	9 36
	☽△♃	11 13
	☽#♃	12pm 8
	☽*♇	12 17
	☽⊻♀	8 58
	☽*♄	10 54
8 T	☽⚼♃	10am55
	☽⊻♅	11 23
	☽∠♇	12pm 8
	☽□♆	6 30
	☉☌☽	8 43
	☽∠♀	10 4
9 W	☽⚻♂	3am26
	☽⊻☿	7 36
	☽⚻♃	10 42
	☽∠♅	11 21
	☽⊻♇	12pm 5
	♀⊻♄	1 56
	☽□♄	10 57
	☽*♀	11 25
10 Th	☽⚼♂	3am 8
	☽#♃	5 18
	☽∠☿	9 43
	☽*♅	11 39
	☽#♂	5pm 2
	☽*♆	6 51
	☿△♃	10 26
11	☉⊻☽	0am31
F	☽△♂	3 18
	☽☍♃	11 23
	☽*☿	12pm37
	☽☌♇	1 10
	☽‖☿	5 30
	☿*♇	7 13
	☽∠♆	7 50
12 S	☽△♄	0am42
	☽‖♅	2 36
	☉∠☽	3 28
	☽□♀	3 59
	☉⚻♂	11 36
	☽□♅	2pm 5
	☽⊻♆	9 36
	☽‖♀	11 23
13 Su	☽⚼♄	2am43
	☽□♂	5 48
	☉*☽	7 28
	☽⚻♃	2pm53
	☽⊻♇	5 12
	☽□☿	9 58
	☿ ♊	10 28
	☽‖♆	11 23
14 M	☽⚻♄	5am42
	☉∠♀	8 14
	☽△♀	12pm36
	☉‖♇	2 38
	☽⚼♃	6 1
	☽△♅	8 4
	☽∠♇	8 40
15 T	☽☌♆	3am58
	☽#♄	4 58
	☽‖♄	8 18
	☽*♂	11 59
	☽⚼♀	6pm44
	☉□☽	7 3
	☽△♃	10 6
16 W	☽⚼♅	0am31
	☽*♇	1 5
	☽△☿	1pm14
	☽☍♄	2 35
	☽#♆	3 1
	☽∠♂	4 29
17 Th	☿*♄	0am53
	☽⚻♀	2 1
	☽⚻♅	5 52
	☉⚻♃	7 49
	☽⊻♆	2pm 4
	☽⊻♂	9 46
	☽⚼☿	11 0
18 F	☽#♀	0am35
	☽□♃	8 39
	☉△☽	11 1
	☽□♇	12pm22
	☽#♅	6 23
	☽∠♆	8 9
	☉∠♅	10 11
19 S	☽⚻♄	2am33
	☉⊻♇	4 9
	☽⚻☿	9 48
	♀☌♅	9 50
	☿#♂	10 49
	☽☍♅	6pm20
	☽☍♀	6 59
	☉⚼☽	8 1
20 Su	☽*♆	2am36
	☽⚼♄	9 8
	☽‖♂	9 14
	☽☌♂	9 49
	☽#☿	2pm45
	☿⚼♃	7 19
	☽*♃	8 57
21 M	☽△♇	1am21
	☽‖♃	4 15
	☉⚻☽	5 13
	☽△♄	3pm45
	☉ ♋	8 12
	[illegible]	11 26
22	☿∠♇	1am51
T	☽∠♃	3 9
	☽⚻♅	7 31
	☽⚼♇	7 51
	☽☍☿	8 53
	☽⚻♀	1pm 0
	☽□♆	3 34
	☽⊻♂	10 16
23 W	☿#♃	5am11
	♂⚼♄	5 47
	☽⊻♃	9 8
	☽⚼♅	1pm49
	☽⚻♇	2 6
	☽⚼♀	9 38
	♀△♆	10 38
	☉☍☽	11 0
24 Th	☽#☿	1am45
	☽∠♂	4 9
	☽□♄	4 19
	☿□♆	5 24
	☽‖♃	6 50
	☿⊻♀	12pm10
	☽△♅	7 43
25 F	☽‖♂	1am59
	☽△♆	3 25
	☽△♀	5 46
	☽⚻☿	7 21
	☽*♂	9 38
	☽☌♃	7pm52
	☿⚻♂	9 53
26 S	☽☍♇	1am19
	☽⚼♆	8 37
	☉⚼♂	2pm23
	☉⚻☽	2 39
	☽#♅	2 52
	☽*♄	3 6
	☽⚼☿	5 43
	☽#♀	7 28
	☉□♄	8 39
27 Su	☽□♅	5am57
	♀☍♂	7 4
	♂SD	10 9
	☽⚻♆	1pm15
	♀∠♄	2 2
	☽□♂	7 6
	☽∠♄	7 38
	☽□♀	8 4
	☉⚼☽	9 25
28 M	☽△☿	3am19
	☽⊻♃	4 29
	☽⚻♇	10 20
	☿⚻♃	10 28
	☿‖♇	10 33
	☽#♆	4pm35
	☉‖☿	5 29
	☽⊻♄	11 34
29 T	☉△☽	3am25
	☽∠♃	7 54
	☽*♅	1pm49
	☽⚼♇	1 55
	☽☍♆	8 42
	♀‖♅	8 52
	☽‖♄	10 18
	☿∠♅	11 35
	☽#♄	11 50
30 W	☿⊻♇	0am12
	☽△♂	2 18
	☽*♀	7 25
	☉‖♇	8 45
	☽*♃	10 42
	☽∠♅	4pm47
	☽△♇	4 51
	☽□☿	7 50

NOTE: Sun enters Cancer at 8:12 P.M. G. M. T.

Figure 15: Diurnal Motion of the Sun

Motion of the Day

TIME	24 HOUR TRAVEL																			
	57 12	57 14	57 16	57 18	57 20	57 22	57 24	57 26	57 28	57 30	57 32	57 34	57 36	57 38	57 40	57 42	57 44	57 46	57 48	57 50
MINUTES																				
1	2	2	2	2	2	2	2	2	2	2	2	2	2	2	2	2	2	2	2	2
2	5	5	5	5	5	5	5	5	5	5	5	5	5	5	5	5	5	5	5	5
3	7	7	7	7	7	7	7	7	7	7	7	7	7	7	7	7	7	7	7	7
4	10	10	10	10	10	10	10	10	10	10	10	10	10	10	10	10	10	10	10	10
5	12	12	12	12	12	12	12	12	12	12	12	12	12	12	12	12	12	12	12	12
6	14	14	14	14	14	14	14	14	14	14	14	14	14	14	14	14	14	14	14	14
7	17	17	17	17	17	17	17	17	17	17	17	17	17	17	17	17	17	17	17	17
8	19	19	19	19	19	19	19	19	19	19	19	19	19	19	19	19	19	19	19	19
9	21	21	21	21	22	22	22	22	22	22	22	22	22	22	22	22	22	22	22	22
10	24	24	24	24	24	24	24	24	24	24	24	24	24	24	24	24	24	24	24	24
11	26	26	26	26	26	26	26	26	26	26	26	26	26	26	26	26	26	26	26	27
12	29	29	29	29	29	29	29	29	29	29	29	29	29	29	29	29	29	29	29	29
13	31	31	31	31	31	31	31	31	31	31	31	31	31	31	31	31	31	31	31	31
14	33	33	33	33	33	33	33	34	34	34	34	34	34	34	34	34	34	34	34	34
15	36	36	36	36	36	36	36	36	36	36	36	36	36	36	36	36	36	36	36	36
16	38	38	38	38	38	38	38	38	38	38	38	38	38	38	38	38	38	39	39	39
17	41	41	41	41	41	41	41	41	41	41	41	41	41	41	41	41	41	41	41	41
18	43	43	43	43	43	43	43	43	43	43	43	43	43	43	43	43	43	43	43	43
19	45	45	45	45	45	45	45	45	45	46	46	46	46	46	46	46	46	46	46	46
20	48	48	48	48	48	48	48	48	48	48	48	48	48	48	48	48	48	48	48	48
21	50	50	50	50	50	50	50	50	50	50	50	50	50	50	50	50	51	51	51	51
22	52	52	52	53	53	53	53	53	53	53	53	53	53	53	53	53	53	53	53	53
23	55	55	55	55	55	55	55	55	55	55	55	55	55	55	55	55	55	55	55	55
24	57	57	57	57	57	57	57	57	57	58	58	58	58	58	58	58	58	58	58	58
25	1 0	1 0	1 0	1 0	1 0	1 0	1 0	1 0	1 0	1 0	1 0	1 0	1 0	1 0	1 0	1 0	1 0	1 0	1 0	1 0
26	1 2	1 2	1 2	1 2	1 2	1 2	1 2	1 2	1 2	1 2	1 2	1 2	1 2	1 2	1 2	1 3	1 3	1 3	1 3	1 3
27	1 4	1 4	1 4	1 4	1 5	1 5	1 5	1 5	1 5	1 5	1 5	1 5	1 5	1 5	1 5	1 5	1 5	1 5	1 5	1 5
28	1 7	1 7	1 7	1 7	1 7	1 7	1 7	1 7	1 7	1 7	1 7	1 7	1 7	1 7	1 7	1 7	1 7	1 7	1 7	1 7
29	1 9	1 9	1 9	1 9	1 9	1 9	1 9	1 9	1 9	1 9	1 10	1 10	1 10	1 10	1 10	1 10	1 10	1 10	1 10	1 10
30	1 12	1 12	1 12	1 12	1 12	1 12	1 12	1 12	1 12	1 12	1 12	1 12	1 12	1 12	1 12	1 12	1 12	1 12	1 12	1 12
31	1 14	1 14	1 14	1 14	1 14	1 14	1 14	1 14	1 14	1 14	1 14	1 14	1 14	1 14	1 14	1 15	1 15	1 15	1 15	1 15
32	1 16	1 16	1 16	1 16	1 16	1 16	1 17	1 17	1 17	1 17	1 17	1 17	1 17	1 17	1 17	1 17	1 17	1 17	1 17	1 17
33	1 19	1 19	1 19	1 19	1 19	1 19	1 19	1 19	1 19	1 19	1 19	1 19	1 19	1 19	1 19	1 19	1 19	1 19	1 19	1 20
34	1 21	1 21	1 21	1 21	1 21	1 21	1 24	1 21	1 21	1 21	1 22	1 22	1 22	1 22	1 22	1 22	1 22	1 22	1 22	1 22
35	1 23	1 23	1 24	1 24	1 24	1 24	1 24	1 24	1 24	1 24	1 24	1 24	1 24	1 24	1 24	1 24	1 24	1 24	1 24	1 24
36	1 26	1 26	1 26	1 26	1 26	1 26	1 26	1 26	1 26	1 26	1 26	1 26	1 26	1 26	1 27	1 27	1 27	1 27	1 27	1 27
37	1 28	1 28	1 28	1 28	1 28	1 28	1 28	1 29	1 29	1 29	1 29	1 29	1 29	1 29	1 29	1 29	1 29	1 29	1 29	1 29
38	1 31	1 31	1 31	1 31	1 31	1 31	1 31	1 31	1 31	1 31	1 31	1 31	1 31	1 31	1 31	1 31	1 31	1 31	1 32	1 32
39	1 33	1 33	1 33	1 33	1 33	1 33	1 33	1 33	1 33	1 33	1 33	1 34	1 34	1 34	1 34	1 34	1 34	1 34	1 34	1 34
40	1 35	1 35	1 35	1 36	1 36	1 36	1 36	1 36	1 36	1 36	1 36	1 36	1 36	1 36	1 36	1 36	1 36	1 36	1 36	1 36
41	1 38	1 38	1 38	1 38	1 38	1 38	1 38	1 38	1 38	1 38	1 38	1 38	1 38	1 38	1 39	1 39	1 39	1 39	1 39	1 39
42	1 40	1 40	1 40	1 40	1 40	1 40	1 40	1 41	1 41	1 41	1 41	1 41	1 41	1 41	1 41	1 41	1 41	1 41	1 41	1 41
43	1 42	1 43	1 43	1 43	1 43	1 43	1 43	1 43	1 43	1 43	1 43	1 43	1 43	1 43	1 43	1 43	1 43	1 43	1 44	1 44
44	1 45	1 45	1 45	1 45	1 45	1 45	1 45	1 45	1 45	1 45	1 45	1 46	1 46	1 46	1 46	1 46	1 46	1 46	1 46	1 46
45	1 47	1 47	1 47	1 47	1 48	1 48	1 48	1 48	1 48	1 48	1 48	1 48	1 48	1 48	1 48	1 48	1 48	1 48	1 48	1 48
46	1 50	1 50	1 50	1 50	1 50	1 50	1 50	1 50	1 50	1 50	1 50	1 50	1 50	1 50	1 51	1 51	1 51	1 51	1 51	1 51
47	1 52	1 52	1 52	1 52	1 52	1 52	1 52	1 52	1 53	1 53	1 53	1 53	1 53	1 53	1 53	1 53	1 53	1 53	1 53	1 53
48	1 54	1 54	1 55	1 55	1 55	1 55	1 55	1 55	1 55	1 55	1 55	1 55	1 55	1 55	1 55	1 55	1 55	1 56	1 56	1 56
49	1 57	1 57	1 57	1 57	1 57	1 57	1 57	1 57	1 57	1 57	1 57	1 58	1 58	1 58	1 58	1 58	1 58	1 58	1 58	1 58
50	1 59	1 59	1 59	1 59	1 59	2 0	2 0	2 0	2 0	2 0	2 0	2 0	2 0	2 0	2 0	2 0	2 0	2 0	2 0	2 0
51	2 2	2 2	2 2	2 2	2 2	2 2	2 2	2 2	2 2	2 2	2 2	2 2	2 2	2 2	2 3	2 3	2 3	2 3	2 3	2 3
52	2 4	2 4	2 4	2 4	2 4	2 4	2 4	2 4	2 5	2 5	2 5	2 5	2 5	2 5	2 5	2 5	2 5	2 5	2 5	2 5
53	2 6	2 6	2 6	2 7	2 7	2 7	2 7	2 7	2 7	2 7	2 7	2 7	2 7	2 7	2 7	2 7	2 7	2 8	2 8	2 8
54	2 9	2 9	2 9	2 9	2 9	2 9	2 9	2 9	2 9	2 9	2 9	2 10	2 10	2 10	2 10	2 10	2 10	2 10	2 10	2 10
55	2 11	2 11	2 11	2 11	2 11	2 11	2 12	2 12	2 12	2 12	2 12	2 12	2 12	2 12	2 12	2 12	2 12	2 12	2 12	2 13
56	2 13	2 14	2 14	2 14	2 14	2 14	2 14	2 14	2 14	2 14	2 14	2 14	2 14	2 14	2 15	2 15	2 15	2 15	2 15	2 15
57	2 16	2 16	2 16	2 16	2 16	2 16	2 16	2 16	2 16	2 17	2 17	2 17	2 17	2 17	2 17	2 17	2 17	2 17	2 17	2 17
58	2 18	2 18	2 18	2 18	2 19	2 19	2 19	2 19	2 19	2 19	2 19	2 19	2 19	2 19	2 19	2 19	2 20	2 20	2 20	2 20
59	2 21	2 21	2 21	2 21	2 21	2 21	2 21	2 21	2 21	2 21	2 21	2 22	2 22	2 22	2 22	2 22	2 22	2 22	2 22	2 22
60	2 23	2 23	2 23	2 23	2 23	2 23	2 24	2 24	2 24	2 24	2 24	2 24	2 24	2 24	2 24	2 24	2 24	2 24	2 25	2 25
HOURS																				
1	2 23	2 23	2 23	2 23	2 23	2 23	2 24	2 24	2 24	2 24	2 24	2 24	2 24	2 24	2 24	2 24	2 24	2 24	2 25	2 25
2	4 46	4 46	4 46	4 47	4 47	4 47	4 47	4 47	4 47	4 48	4 48	4 48	4 48	4 48	4 48	4 49	4 49	4 49	4 49	4 49
3	7 9	7 9	7 10	7 10	7 10	7 10	7 11	7 11	7 11	7 11	7 12	7 12	7 12	7 12	7 13	7 13	7 13	7 13	7 14	7 14
4	9 32	9 32	9 33	9 33	9 33	9 34	9 34	9 34	9 35	9 35	9 35	9 36	9 36	9 36	9 37	9 37	9 37	9 38	9 38	9 38
5	11 55	11 55	11 56	11 56	11 57	11 57	11 58	11 58	11 58	11 59	11 59	12 0	12 0	12 0	12 1	12 1	12 2	12 2	12 3	12 3
6	14 18	14 19	14 19	14 20	14 20	14 21	14 21	14 22	14 22	14 23	14 23	14 24	14 24	14 25	14 25	14 26	14 26	14 27	14 27	14 28
7	16 41	16 42	16 42	16 43	16 43	16 44	16 45	16 45	16 46	16 46	16 47	16 47	16 48	16 49	16 49	16 50	16 50	16 51	16 52	16 52
8	19 4	19 5	19 5	19 6	19 7	19 7	19 8	19 9	19 9	19 10	19 11	19 11	19 12	19 13	19 13	19 14	19 15	19 15	19 16	19 17
9	21 27	21 28	21 29	21 29	21 30	21 31	21 32	21 32	21 33	21 34	21 35	21 35	21 36	21 37	21 38	21 38	21 39	21 40	21 41	21 41
10	23 50	23 51	23 52	23 53	23 53	23 54	23 55	23 56	23 57	23 58	23 58	23 59	24 0	24 1	24 2	24 3	24 3	24 4	24 5	24 6
11	26 13	26 14	26 15	26 16	26 17	26 18	26 19	26 19	26 20	26 21	26 22	26 23	26 24	26 25	26 26	26 27	26 28	26 29	26 30	26 30
12	28 36	28 37	28 38	28 39	28 40	28 41	28 42	28 43	28 44	28 45	28 46	28 47	28 48	28 49	28 50	28 51	28 52	28 53	28 54	28 55
13	30 59	31 0	31 1	31 2	31 3	31 4	31 6	31 7	31 8	31 9	31 10	31 11	31 12	31 13	31 14	31 15	31 16	31 17	31 19	31 20
14	33 22	33 23	33 24	33 26	33 27	33 28	33 29	33 30	33 31	33 33	33 34	33 35	33 36	33 37	33 38	33 40	33 41	33 42	33 43	33 44
15	35 45	35 46	35 48	35 49	35 50	35 51	35 53	35 54	35 55	35 56	35 58	35 59	36 0	36 1	36 3	36 4	36 5	36 6	36 8	36 9
16	38 8	38 9	38 11	38 12	38 13	38 15	38 16	38 17	38 19	38 20	38 21	38 23	38 24	38 25	38 27	38 28	38 29	38 31	38 32	38 33
17	40 31	40 32	40 34	40 35	40 37	40 38	40 40	40 41	40 42	40 44	40 45	40 47	40 48	40 49	40 51	40 52	40 54	40 55	40 57	40 58
18	42 54	42 56	42 57	42 59	43 0	43 2	43 3	43 5	43 6	43 8	43 9	43 11	43 12	43 14	43 15	43 17	43 18	43 20	43 21	43 23
19	45 17	45 19	45 20	45 22	45 23	45 25	45 27	45 28	45 30	45 31	45 33	45 34	45 36	45 38	45 39	45 41	45 42	45 44	45 46	45 47
20	47 40	47 42	47 43	47 45	47 47	47 48	47 50	47 52	47 53	47 55	47 57	47 58	48 0	48 2	48 3	48 5	48 7	48 8	48 10	48 12
21	50 3	50 5	50 7	50 8	50 10	50 12	50 14	50 15	50 17	50 19	50 21	50 22	50 24	50 26	50 28	50 29	50 31	50 33	50 35	50 36
22	52 26	52 28	52 30	52 32	52 33	52 35	52 37	52 39	52 41	52 43	52 44	52 46	52 48	52 50	52 52	52 54	52 55	52 57	52 59	53 1
23	54 49	54 51	54 53	54 55	54 57	54 59	55 1	55 2	55 4	55 6	55 8	55 10	55 12	55 14	55 16	55 18	55 20	55 22	55 24	55 25
24	57 12	57 14	57 16	57 18	57 20	57 22	57 24	57 26	57 28	57 30	57 32	57 34	57 36	57 38	57 40	57 42	57 44	57 46	57 48	57 50

Having learned the ascending sign, we now must calculate the exact positions of the Sun, Moon, Mercury, and Venus with respects to the locality of the birth. Because of their slow "motion," the position of the remaining planets need not be changed from their location as shown in the ephemeris for that day of the birth.

Don't be alarmed by these explanations and calculations, either, for they are as simple as learning Jane Doe's ascendant. We first subtract the position of the Sun for the day of birth from its position on the day following. The result of this is the motion of travel for that day. We now do the same thing for the Moon, Mercury, and Venus, for this is figured out in the same manner. After obtaining the motions for these planets, we then refer to diurnal motion of planets to learn how far these planets traveled during the interval from midnight to the time of birth. Referring to the Diurnal Motion of the Sun, we scan the top row for motion to the column that corresponds with the motion for that day of birth. This column is followed down to where it intersects with the *hours* of the interval (shown on both lower sides of the tables). The figures shown at this intersection will be the degrees of arc traveled for the *hours* selected. We now repeat this for the minutes of the interval and add both these figures for the hours and minutes as shown. From this we obtain the total distance traveled for the interval.

This final result is the precise position of the planets for Greenwich, England. However, as the birth occurred in Malden, Massachusetts, USA, we therefore must move these planets back 4 hours 44 minutes and 16 seconds, which is the Longitude Equivalent Time for this locality. All we do now is determine how far the planets moved during this time and subtract it from the Greenwich total and there we have it, the precise position of the planets for that birthplace and time. Simple, wasn't it?

To learn of the locality time of the Sun's entrance into the sign of Cancer, merely subtract the locality mean time (Zone Standard Time) from Greenwich Time.

Greenwich Time	8:12 P.M.
Zone Std. Malden	-5:00
Malden Mean Time	3:12 P.M.

Notice: Any Person born before 3:12 P.M. on June 21, 1937, would be born of the sign Gemini as shown on that ephemeris date. However, although the ephemeris date shows the midnight (0 hr.) position of the Sun for that date, it cannot show that anyone born after 3:12 P.M. on that date would therefore be of the Cancer sign.

Because the birth occurred at 11:30 P.M. when arriving at the Greenwich Time, we find that to be 3:30 A.M. of the 27th. We therefore use that date for both the sidereal time and planetary positions. Referring to the ephemeris (Figure 14), we find the data necessary for calculations.

June 27, 1937	Sidereal Time 18:18:45	Sun at 4° 55' 05" of Cancer
June 26, 1937		Sun at 3° 57' 53" of Cancer

27th Sun at 4° 55' 05" conversion to subtractable time	3° 114' 65"
26th Sun	- 3° 57' 53"
Motion of the day =	0° 57' 12"

We now refer to Diurnal Motion of the Sun (Figure 15) where we note in the column of 57 minutes 12 seconds that for the 3 hours (after midnight) the Sun has progressed 7 minutes 9 seconds with another 1 minute 12 seconds for the 30 minutes. Adding both these figures, we arrive at 8 minutes 21 seconds, which we add to the Sun's original midnight position of 4° 55' 05"

		4° 55' 05"
	+	8' 21"
Sun's position in Greenwich at 3:30 A.M.	=	5° 03' 26"

We now have to return the Sun's position to Malden, Massachusetts, where the birth occurred. This is done in the very same manner except that we now must use the Longitude Equivalent Time of the birthplace, Malden, which is 4 hours 44 minutes and 16 seconds. Under the same column of 57 minutes 12 seconds (daily motion), we find that the Sun has progressed 9 minutes 32 seconds in the 4 hours time and 1 minute 45 seconds for the 44 minutes. Adding these figures we get 11 minutes 17 seconds which must be subtracted from the Greenwich location of 5 hours 03 minutes 26 seconds.

		5° 03' 26"
		- 11' 17"
Exact location of the Sun in Malden	=	4° 52' 12"

Because of the speed of the Moon as opposed to the other planets and its crucial effects in behavior, we feel it most urgent to ensure its exact position. As often as not, a matter of only 2 or 3 degrees can change the personality from one extreme to another. Although this also is true of any planet, only the Moon travels fast enough during an A.M. or P.M. birth that can cause an extreme change in the behavior. This will be obvious to you when you examine either or both of the charts we present for Jane Doe, the solar chart or the time chart, as either one makes a complete change from the other. It is for these reasons that we stress the urgency of absolute accuracy when the Moon's position is being considered.

The Moon's position as well as that of both Mercury and Venus is obtained by the very same procedures as we have shown and explained for the Sun.

When the actual time and place of birth is used to learn of the exact position of the Moon, we learn that a most crucial change takes place. The exact position of 8 hours 16 minutes 13 seconds results in the Moon creating a "T" cross, a special configuration that now changes the behavior completely. You will learn about these changes in the next chapter.

Now the calculations for the Moon. As we stated the procedures are the same as for the Sun except that the Moon has its own table "Semidiurnal Motion of the Moon" (12 hours) while Mercury, Venus, and the remaining planets will be found under a separate table "Diurnal Motion of the Planets."

Recall that we are using June 27th positions because of the 3:30 A.M. G.M.T.

6/27/37	Moon's 0 hr. position	9° 26' 12" Aquarius
6/26/37	Moon's noon position	3° 9' 56" Aquarius
	Motion for the day	6° 16' 16"

At this rate of speed, the Moon in 3 hours travels	1° 02' 40"
In 30 minutes the Moon travels	+ 15' 40"
	= 1° 18' 20"
Moon's 0 hr. position	+ 9° 26' 12"
3:30 A.M. position Greenwich	= 10° 44' 32"

Longitude Equivalent Time in Malden Mass. is 4 hours, 44 minutes, and 16 seconds.

Moon in 4 hours' time travels	2° 05' 20"
Moon in 44 minutes' time travels	+ 22' 59"
Total movement in 4 hours 44 minutes	= 2° 28' 19"
Greenwich 3:30 A.M. position	10° 44' 32"
	- 2° 28' 19"
	8° 16' 13"

Exact Malden, Mass., position for the Moon is 8° 16' 13" Aquarius.

Having calculated the exact positions of the Sun, Moon, Mercury, and Venus, we now refer to the ephemeris for the locations of the remaining planets. These positions may be taken direct from that particular date and rounded off to the nearest degree.

Place the ascendant sign and its nearest degree on the cusp of the first house. In their natural order with the ascendant sign first, all the remaining signs should now be drawn on the cusp of the remaining houses with the same degree as the ascendant. For example, Pisces (the ascendant) is 6 degrees on the cusp of the 1st house, Aries is 6 degrees on the 2nd, Taurus is 6 degrees on the 3rd, Gemini is 6 degrees on the 4th, and so on. Upon completion of this phase, we have yet another phase to calculate. The calculations for all these procedures are nothing more than simple elementary arithmetic as you have seen. Just follow the procedures set forth and start counting by any method with which you feel comfortable. The charts of Jane Doe in our next chapter (Figures 16 "Solar Chart" and 17 "Birth Chart") should be of help to you.

If nothing else, you will have at least learned the truth about horoscopes and serious astrology. You also will have learned that it is anything but hit-or-miss dabbling and superstitious beliefs.

Let us now progress a bit further into the correct procedures for delineating a solar or time chart. The procedures are similar, only one is more complex than the other.

Chapter 13
Synthesis

Ascendant and Solar Charts

Both charts must be included in your delineations. Both are valid but simply are on different frames of reference. To illustrate, if you have Mars in your 12th House we can be reasonable sure that you will have serious problems dealing with the need to take action when it is indicated. Mars in the 12th House causes you to be considerably "watered down" by uncertainty, anxiety, fear, and self-doubt (all 12th House) in your ability to succeed and take action when necessary (Mars). The external affairs of your life have conditioned your action mechanism to be postponed until you have a chance to look things over more carefully. But a similar condition occurs when Mars occupies the sign preceding your Sun sign (12th sign from yours), because it's the one sign that is the "monkey on your back" of the Sun's striving to gain significance to satisfy the ego's needs. A large measure of satisfaction may be gained by demonstrating creative potential, but there will be much left undone because of the inability to get the show on the road. The birth chart Mars is a product of prevailing circumstances that disturb and distract the individual from taking action that clearly is appropriate. Over time there will develop a better understanding of how the motivation has been undermined--mainly through a lack of knowledge--that sustains the problem.

In the solar chart Mars, it is more a matter of doubting one's own degree of authority and adequacy that contains and restrains the taking of any action. The solar chart is a characterological one wherein all the planets and their solar house functions principally are in reference to character and its development. A planet in the solar 2nd House relates to those issues that help to give you personal enrichment and a feeling of adequacy that your survival factor is intact.

When using 12 noon for the position of the Moon with no knowledge whatsoever of the birth time, it is possible for you to figure out a fairly close estimate. From the noon position the Moon at most can only be 7 degrees off from its actual position. After calculating the aspects for the noon position, check to determine if these same aspects would apply if you were born at 10 A.M., 8 A.M., 6 A.M., 4 A.M., or 2 A.M. simply by subtracting 1 degree for every two hours of time. From these subtractions you will learn of the aspects during the A.M. period. Repeat this process for the P.M. periods except now you add 1 degree for every two hours after 12 noon to learn what aspects if any would apply for a P.M. birth. Record the aspects and their time period and then proceed to make a sincere study of both the positive and negative characteristics of the planets involved in order to determine what aspects apply to you. Recall that malefic aspects bring out the negative qualities of the planets. It would be wise to consult a close friend for an honest opinion on this procedure. Few people see themselves as others see them.

Delineating Procedure

The ascendant sign, its ruling planet, and all related to them intentionally are omitted in the guidelines as they are not applicable in a solar chart. However, upon conclusion of the solar chart delineation, we will proceed with the time chart where we will need only to add what the ascendant and related indications are to the solar chart synthesis and of course any changes that occur. A comparison of the charts will bring out the dramatic changes that are highly possible between them.

Before getting into the details of a chart, learn to make an at-a-glance survey of the chart. Don't get bogged down immediately in the endless details that in themselves don't contribute to your understanding of the general overview of the person in question. Because an at-a-glance survey may prove useless to the untrained person, we present some of the guides you will find useful.

Making notations from the following outline will ensure that no significant concept has been overlooked. Completion of the notations for each of the guidelines will enable you to elaborate on each one by referring to our brief discussion on them. With respect to hemisphere emphasis, you need only refer to Figure 5 in Chapter 5: The Houses and Their Affairs to realize the indications and their significance.

1. Jones Patterns
2. Signature
3. Unoccupied elements and/or qualities
4. Planets in their 12th sign
5. Aspects
6. Unaspected planets
7. Special configurations or complexes: stellium, T-cross, grand cross, yod, trine

Let us now take a glance at Jane's solar chart. Should an at-a-glance show nothing in particular, an extended view might prove otherwise.

To help simplify delineations try to imagine a picture puzzle in which you are trying to fit all the pieces, with the first glance being the first piece.

Figure 16

Solar Chart of Jane Doe 6/26/1937

Sun	in Cancer	5°
Moon	in Aquarius	3°
Mercury	in Gemini	20°
Venus	in Taurus	18°
Mars	in Scorpio	20°
Jupiter	in Capricorn	25°
Saturn	in Aries	5°
Uranus	in Taurus	13°
Neptune	in Virgo	16°
Pluto	in Cancer	28°

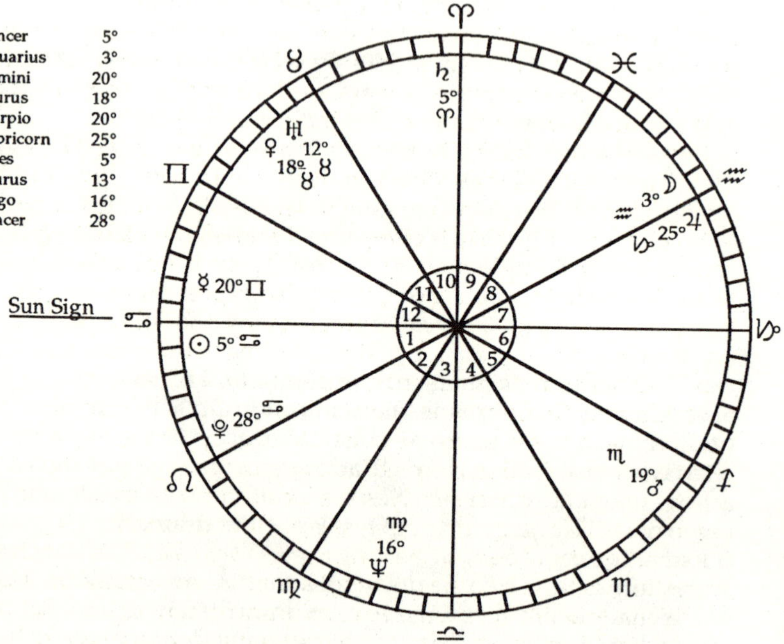

Natal Aspects

	☉	☽	☿	♀	♂	♃	♄	♅	♆	♇
☉							□			
☽										
☿					⚻				□	
♀					☍	△		☌	△	
♂						⚹		☍	⚹	△
♃										☍
♄										
♅									△	
♆										
♇										

Fire: 1
Earth: 4
Air: 2
Water: 3
Cardinal: 4
Fixed: 4 + ruling planet
Mutable: 2

Signature: Fixed - Earth = Taurus
Lacking: None
Ruling planet: Moon
Chart type (Jones Pattern): Splash
Special Formations: none
and/or
Complexes: none
Unaspected planets: none

Special notes

Only one aspect to Sun (square to Saturn)
Only one aspect to Saturn (square to Sun)

1. A glance at the chart shows no emphasis of planets or anything in particular that catches the eye other than the planets being randomly scattered in the chart.
2. With an extended view, however, we find that one of the Jones Patterns prevails, with the planets randomly scattered in the splash distribution. This indicates a well-diversified mental outlook with an eagerness to share the life and resources wherever a need is indicated.
3. Taurean people basically are conservative in every way, including their desire for conversation. Jane's chart indicates a Taurus signature to additionally confirm her reticence in engaging in small-talk or simple idle conversation.
4. No element or quality is completely void of any planets, but the fire element contains only a single planet (Saturn). There is not only a lack of enthusiasm from this planet's effect, but Saturn also represents fears, restrictions, inhibitions, and so forth. This is augmented by the additional factor of Saturn's position in Aries, its 4th House sign alluding to the effect of an inhibiting square aspect that also represents fear, uncertainty, and so forth.
5. Jane's Sun in Cancer is the Sun's own 12th House sign, which tends to undermine her sense of personal adequacy since the 12th House and all references to it in this or other arrangements give a sense of self-undoing in actions taken. It almost surely is the location of the anxiety factor than contains much creative energy that often simply lays dormant.
6. Excluding the Moon, all existing aspects are valid. We now learn that Jane has important aspects of a negative effect, more especially because these aspects nearly are exact in their degree relationships. Sun square Saturn and Mercury inconjunct Mars are in the exact degree with Mercury square Neptune. We also see Mars opposing Venus-Uranus conjunction and Jupiter opposing Pluto. Let's briefly break these down to individual indications, which we then add to Jane's general character indications.

Sun-Saturn: This notes a strong sense of personal authority that she is reluctant to implement and singular views that often alienate people with whom she disagrees.

Mercury-Mars: Represents a person who is argumentative and intolerant of others people's views who will let matters get out of hand from lack of tact and diplomacy.

Mercury-Neptune: This person will not accept reality when it imposes demands that are unbearable. Talents usually wasted in nonproductive enterprises. Escapism and inconsistency are major factors in the life.

Mars-Uranus: Represents a revolutionary spirit that is not easily restrained. The least provocation will cause her to get all worked up in a lather. Due to her argumentative nature, she may sometimes even delight in the contest.

Jupiter-Pluto: Jane sets her own codes in life and doesn't have too much regard for the consequences.

7. Although there are no unaspected planets, both the Sun and Saturn have only one aspect and that is to each other by an exact 90-degree square. Because of the various conditions of this aspect, Jane has to resolve many conflicts about her self-worth. She naturally is defensive and fears rejection by those she feels are superior to her. Because of this she underestimates her potential and does not assert herself when and where she should. However, her lack of confidence may develop into self-assurance in later life.
Note the following considerations that must be given this aspect: the Sun in Cancer is in its own 12th sign; Saturn in Aries is in its own 4th sign, which naturally is square to its own natural sign. These energies additionally are in square to each other! The Sun's energy is watered down in two ways through its location in a water sign and this sign its own 12th sign, also a water indicator. Saturn in Aries calms down the aggressiveness of Aries. Unaspected, the Sun shows Jane is unwilling to assert herself to satisfy her ego. The unaspected Saturn shows she lacks the mobilizing and organizing resources which will develop into a strong defense mechanism to justify her position.

8. Other than having a splash type of chart, there are no other special configurations or complexes.

Having completed our notations for the guidelines, let us now learn what the planets in the signs have to contribute to Jane's character.

Sun in Cancer: This indicates very strong family ties. Facts of hard reality are particularly foreign to a Cancerian person and this is the primary source of most of their problems. Being averse to the responsibility for taking action, they tend to withdraw rather than make decisions.

Moon in Aquarius: The Moon is the absolute past and Aquarius the absolute future. The Moon represents family and tradition and Aquarius represents freedom from both, plus. The Moon is emotions and moods and Aquarius is truth and detachment. With this combination the individual is attempting to travel in two opposite directions simultaneously.

Mercury in Gemini: This combination offers a sharp mental alertness with a great thirst for knowledge. Although money is not a major factor as it appears, it will help overcome their deep feelings of insecurity.

Venus in Taurus: This combination is most acquisitive here. Going without the comforts of life is especially painful, which makes money an important factor in life because it represents security. Even relationships are best served when the partner has the ability to earn a good living. Sex is also an important factor, but the pleasures of wining, dining, and dancing must precede that final experience.

Mars in Scorpio: This gives an intense and powerful sexual drive with considerable sexual needs. The likes and dislikes also are at an extreme here and possibly can lead to an obsession because the reactions to situations are emotional and sometimes very unrealistic.

Jupiter in Capricorn: Here is the ability to organize the knowledge, energy, and ambitions to realize your dreams, which results in very good judgment in making decisions.

Saturn in Aries: This gives a sort of double-standard way of life because the rules you establish for others are separate from those you adhere to yourself. This person is indifferent to the feelings of others on the one hand and totally unrealistic about taking on responsibilities on the other. These two factors can be a constant source of irritation.

Uranus in Taurus: With Uranus in Taurus you very easily are annoyed when people make demands on you. Although you maintain a low profile, you figuratively blow up when pushed a bit too far.

Neptune in Virgo: This combination indicates that difficulty is experienced when you try to do something that is right for you without hurting others.

Pluto in Cancer: Pluto represents change and Cancer the home and traditions. Pluto is the purging system with Cancer representing nostalgia. Combined, the chances are most favorable that changes will be made, albeit not voluntarily or willingly. This could be a divorce from the old to the new, the residence, traditions, marriage, and anything else that may need purging.

Having put all the pieces of the puzzle together, we now can take a good clear look at the picture in its entirety and offer a reasonably accurate synthesis.

Solar Chart Synthesis

As a Cancerian there is no doubt of Jane's insecurity and inability to face the realities of life. This feeling of insecurity is reinforced by Mercury in Gemini, Mercury-Neptune aspect, and the square aspect to Saturn.

The splash chart tells us that Jane has great mental diversification and a willingness to share her life and resources wherever there is a need. But the tenacity of a Cancerian along with the acquisitiveness of Taurus (her signature) and Venus in Taurus, makes Jane hold on to all that she can muster for herself. Mercury in Gemini adds more credence to the splash indications of mental diversification because this combination also gives sharp mental alertness as well as communicative abilities. When we combine these two factors, mental conflict results as to which is most beneficial to the life. Since a Cancerian basically reacts based on feelings and not facts, and Mars in Scorpio also reacts to situations through emotions, we are reasonably sure that Jane will be anything but a philanthropist sharing what is hers. This is more so because of the acquisitiveness we mentioned.

When we now add the conditions of the Moon in Aquarius, we really are adding more fuel to the already burning fire because the Moon is the tenacity and insecurity while Aquarius is the humanitarian. With what we stated about the Moon being the past and Aquarius being the future, Jane really doesn't know which end is up.

Jane does realize that she has a very alert mind (Mercury in Gemini) and is most capable of organizing her knowledge, energy, and ambitions (Jupiter in Capricorn), but she just can't get her act together (Sun in 12th sign and square to Saturn) to say the least. What this all means is that the Sun in its 12th sign, indicating fear, self-doubt, and uncertainty, makes facing reality very difficult. The square to Saturn also creates a similar condition. Mars in Scorpio doesn't help the cause. Add to this the fact that the Sun and Mars, the "energy" planets, both are in water signs, which diminishes the energy factor. The Sun is the will and ego and Mars is the drive to satisfy them. The Sun lacks any helpful aspects (energies) as well as Saturn, the planet of reality and organization. The only energy they offer is that of a square to each other and the square aspect is an aspect of conflict, fear, and inhibitions. Recall that in a malefic aspect it is the slower planet that exerts its negative force over the faster planet. That is Saturn overruling the Sun's will and ego. Although the will and ego always will be there, there also will be the uncertainty, self doubt, fear, and inhibitions.

Adding the effects of the Mercury to Mars and to Neptune aspects and the Mars-Uranus aspect is like adding more fuel to an already out-of-control inferno. Jane is not in the least interested in anyone else's views (Mercury-Mars). Should you attempt to discuss this situation you would receive nothing but an outburst and serious argument for your intrusion into her affairs. Mercury-Neptune suggests that she is most content with all her inconsistencies and her escape from reality, all of which is tolerated by her family and acquaintances to avoid the onslaught that Jane appears to delight in (Mars-Uranus). But of course, Jane does not realize this due to Neptune's distortion.

Sexual factors also contribute to the overburdened mental process, with her Venus in Taurus, Venus conjunct Uranus, Mars in Scorpio, and also the Moon in Aquarius. Why the Moon in Aquarius? Because if you recall, counting from the 4th House (the natural house of the Moon), to the 11th House (the natural house of Aquarius), we get 8th House effects and that is the house of sex. These sexual needs and drives also are restrained along with everything else, and this would cause serious problems in any relationship although it is seldom that anyone realizes that it is the root of most domestic problems.

It appears that there is no solution to Jane's condition. Jane will go along suffering with her (no doubt) constant mental fatigue and headaches. The only solution to this condition is that Jane will go along suffering by her uncaring self until the crucial age period comes along in her life that will force a change. This change may not be in her character traits, but they will at least be in the life in some way. Pluto in Cancer suggests this as well, for Pluto represents the purging system and with Pluto it is always "either/or" with no in-between. Either she changes her ways and/or conditions or continues suffering alone through life.

Having learned of Jane's character traits with all of their mental conflicts, we can be sure that there exists constant mental fatigue and constant severe headaches. This is because, if you can recall in Chapter 2, "The brain decides the priorities in life." Too great a load on the frontal cortex of the brain (the decision maker) causes serious mental stress. There must be a balance between the emotional and intellectual behavior or serious problems occur. With our Jane, there is just too much emotional stress not to cause some biological change.

Having completed the solar chart and its synthesis, let's continue now with the birth chart to learn what it offers (if anything) to help Jane out of this dilemma and how these traits effect the various circumstances of life.

For the sole purpose of showing the simplicity of setting up any type of chart by employing methodical procedures, we offered illustrations and all calculations for locating the ascendant sign, its degrees and exact position of both the Sun and Moon for the place of birth.

Although this data was available while offering the solar chart synthesis, we intentionally omitted any of the effects they may have contributed. Our intentions are to allow you to realize the extreme difference between them.

The synthesis of the solar chart stands as is, for the birth chart will not contradict this. There may or may not be some positive or negative altering effects to Jane's traits, but this will be due to the additional factors under consideration. These factors will inform us of just what altering effects take place and why and how Jane will react to the various circumstances of life and why.

Birth Chart: For the birth chart delineations (see chart on following page) we offer some additional outlines you might follow and Jane's time chart as it would be used in actual practice.

1. Hemisphere Emphasis--north or south, east or west, and the quadrants
2. Ascendant sign and its aspects
3. Ascendant's ruling planet and house location and its aspects
4. Moon's position and aspects
5. House positions for both signs and planets

The 2nd House is the house of values and holds the key to your survival. It is a learning/growing process where you benefit from all of your experiences. That is, of course, when you decide to take advantage of these opportunities, which then help you to evolve into a more positive individual. When the motivating factors are purely for selfish purposes, the results are generally of a negative nature.

The ascendant Pisces is on its own 2nd House and this automatically places all the remaining signs on their own 2nd-House positions. When the nature of the sign that follows yours is adopted, there always is a distinct advantage. For example, a Pisces may learn to be more aggressive and enthusiastic (Aries), an Aries may learn to be more stable and conservative (Taurus), Taurus may become more flexible and social (Gemini), and so forth.

1. Pisces on the 1st: The outlook on life will not be practical but emotional. Pisces is "the escape from reality" and with Jane, a Cancerian who has great difficulty

Figure 17
Birth Chart of Jane Doe 6/26/1937

Sun	in Cancer	5°
Moon	in Aquarius	3°
Mercury	in Gemini	20°
Venus	in Taurus	18°
Mars	in Scorpio	20°
Jupiter	in Capricorn	25°
Saturn	in Aries	5°
Uranus	in Taurus	13°
Neptune	in Virgo	16°
Pluto	in Cancer	28°

Asc. Sign

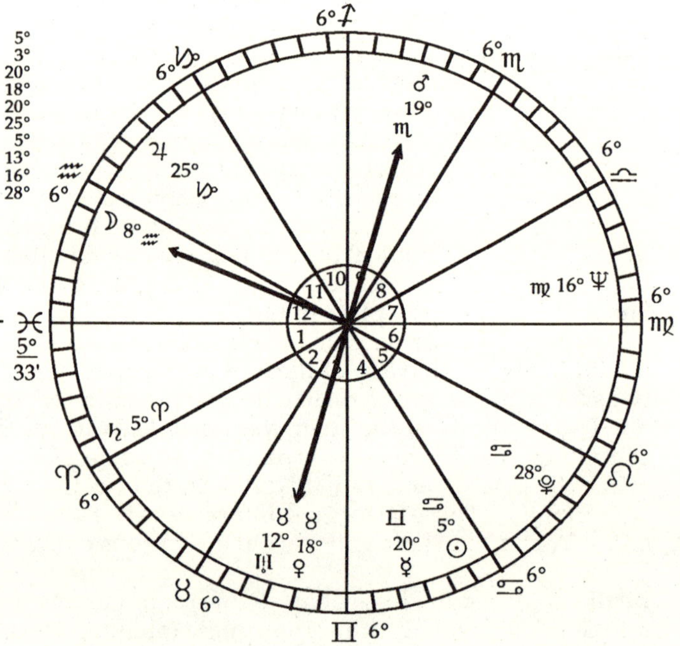

Natal Aspects

	☉	☽	☿	♀	♂	♃	♄	♅	♆	♇
Asc.	△									
☉		⚻					□			
☽				□	□		⚹	□		
☿					⚻				□	
♀					☍	△		☌	△	
♂						⚹		☍	⚹	
♃								△		☍
♄										
♅									△	
♆										
♇										

Fire:	1
Earth:	4
Air:	2
Water:	3
Cardinal:	4
Fixed:	4 + Moon in fix
Mutable:	2

Signature: Fixed - Earth = Taurus
Lacking: none (fire?)
Ruling planet: Neptune
Chart type (Jones Pattern): Splash
Special Formations: "T" Cross
and/or
Complexes: none
Unaspected planets: none (Sun and Saturn?)

<u>Special notes</u>
Only 2 aspects to Sun (square to Saturn, ⚻ to Moon)
Only 2 aspects to Saturn (square to Sun, ⚹ to Moon)
Only 1 aspect to Asc. (trine to Sun)
Only 1 aspect to Pluto (opposition to Jupiter)

in facing reality, we easily can see that Jane's life will be one of chaos and fantasy with little reality. However, since the ascendant is trine the Sun there is much benefit. This aspect is a resourceful one in that it gives an optimistic attitude and self- confidence in anything the individual decides to do. The problem is that it also tends toward laziness and putting off what needs to be done because there's plenty of time left to do it. This attitude doubtlessly will result in criticism from others, and Pisceans just cannot handle criticism since they already are preoccupied with their shortcomings and failures.

2. Neptune, ruler of Pisces and the 1st House is posited in the 7th House. Because Virgo is on this cusp, Mercury is its ruler along with the 4th House because of Gemini there. Mercury also is posited in the 4th House. Neptune's square aspect to Mercury results in the negative characteristics of Neptune exerting its forces on all circumstances involving the 1st House of the self, the 4th House of the home, and the 7th House of marriage. Neptune is the planet of "serve or suffer" and is located in the sign of "service to others" (Virgo). This certainly is no situation for someone who is selfish. Primarily, these three houses involved are the 1st, "I am" (the self); the 4th, "I feel" (the home); and the 7th, "I balance" (marriage). It should be abundantly clear where the problems will occur and why they do.

In order that you have a clear understanding of the problems to be encountered, imagine yourself as Jane's husband, lover, partner, associate, or other close relation. Cancer people do not even think about the realities of life for they are insecure, tenacious, and moody. Pisces also are insecure and uncertain and involve themselves in all sorts of trivial and nonproductive enterprises to escape from the harshness of reality. Pisces is "the escape from reality," hence the "mental chaos" of Pisceans.

When you now consider the negative characteristics of Neptune (her ruling planet) because of its malefic aspect to Mercury (ruler of the home and marriage) with both these planets posited in both these houses, and the nature of Virgo (the critic) on the house of marriage, there will be absolutely nothing but fault-finding and criticism of just about everything the husband says or does. When he is right, he will be wrong. When he speaks, he will say the wrong thing. When he doesn't speak, he will be considered arrogant. The aspect itself, the square, is one of fear, uncertainty, nonproductivity and inconsistency, and the co-ruling Moon (Cancer) is involved in three squares and to the most crucial of planets: Venus (the planet of compromise and adjustments), Mars (the planet of assertiveness and enthusiasm), and Uranus (the planet of awareness and freedom). Should you care to add more to what already has been said of Jane, you need only refer back to planetary characteristics and read the negative sides of these planets.

How long would any husband or partner tolerate someone who, to quote Billy Joel in his song "Innocent Man," continually says, "You don't want to hear what I say, you keep running away"? How long would someone stay with a person who is completely unorganized, inconsistent, critical of everything, suffers from mental waywardness, and has a vacillating mind? These attitudes warrant some criticism, but Jane will not tolerate criticism. Every indication is that of complete selfishness to every extent with no consideration whatsoever for anyone outside of her children, mother, and father--and they are safe only because Jane is a Cancer.

3. Placing the Moon in its actual location for the birth time, we find that it now has advanced to 8 degrees Aquarius (rounded off). This increase results in the forming of the "T" Cross formation. The Moon now forms a square aspect to Uranus, which is in conjunction to Venus, meaning that the Moon also squares Venus because of this connecting link to Uranus. Mars makes an exact opposition to Venus-Uranus conjunction. Because of the linkage of the Moon to Venus-Uranus, Mars also must be considered as aspecting the Moon. Combined they form the "T" cross.

In relationships a "T" cross invariably indicates problems because the individual does not have any desires in living that part of life's circumstances that is indicated by the unoccupied arm and house of this formation.

In Jane's case the Moon in Aquarius forms a fixed T cross (three of the four fixed signs in aspect to each other) with the fixed sign of Leo, unoccupied, as the missing arm of a cross.

Leo is the sign of life, love, and love affairs (the fun house sign). Consider all the circumstances that make up the pleasures and fun of life that are ignored completely by Jane. In so doing, we can conclude that there is no indulging in the gaieties of life such as social gatherings, partying, sports, and especially love. Jane just does not have any interests of any kind. With respects to the love nature, Jane probably doesn't even embrace or kiss her own children (Leo). Neither is there ever any consideration of others' feelings or any analysis given to these conditions and voids in the life (6th House affairs).

Recall that Jane is tenacious, acquisitive, selfish, and an escapist who will not face up to reality. She is not in the least interested in anyone else's viewpoints. The result is that there is no communication or conversation with anyone who dares to attempt to change her views and actions. This stubbornness, which is built in by the Taurus signature and the sign of Taurus on the 3rd House of the mind, now is reinforced doubly by the "T" cross, which is of the fixed quality. Fixed means steadfast, immovable, and stationary, which results in an individual who will prefer solitude and isolation to changing her nature.

4. Pisces is the sign of sacrifices. On the 1st House of "I am" is where this selfishness should be sacrificed. Neptune the ruler says, "serve or suffer" and because of the malefic aspect to Mercury there will be nothing but inconsistencies in life for the purpose of escaping these realities. For Jane, her values and resources are of the utmost importance, most especially so since Pisces also feels the same. It is only for what Jane considers of value that she might make adjustments in her behavior.

Aries 2nd House: With Aries on this house of values (material and spiritual), it gives a great ambition to achieve success in order to prove herself to herself. Here there is a deep subconscious inferiority complex that gives this drive. Mars ruling this house makes it very difficult to hold on to money. Aries (Mars) does not stop and think. The preference is to act first on the slightest impulse. Mars always needs control and on this house one can be most extravagant.

Taurus 3rd House: The most stubborn of all signs. On the house of the personal mind ("I think"), there will be nowhere to be found a more stubborn and fixed-thinking individual. This person may seem soft and easy-going, but that is a smoke screen. Anyone who has to deal with them knows their stubbornness. There is no way one can penetrate this mind, especially if you are trying to express viewpoints that are opposed to theirs. With Jane you would have to beware of her revolutionary spirit due to her Mars-Uranus aspect. Your slightest provocation will be rewarded with one of your greatest arguments, and you will lose even if you are right. She will delight in it.

With Taurus being so predominant in this life (especially on the 3rd House), you can wager your life that the number-one priority in the life is food. Money and material things are second and sex is a very strong third. In Jane's case in particular, we must exclude sex for the reasons explained. Regardless of the extreme passions built in, Pisceans are escapists who are experts at blocking out of their minds anything they wish--even within their dreams, which they never remember anyway.

Gemini 4th House: Mercury, ruler of this house, also is posited here. This can be a very beneficial placement for the mental process, but for the malefic aspect of Mercury and Neptune, its benefits are wasted. To attempt a description of all the indications here for our Jane would entail a complete volume in itself. We therefore offer a more simplistic alterative. Try to imagine a beautiful butterfly in a nursery hothouse flitting around in every direction but never in a straight path. It really doesn't know where it is going or on which flower to make its landing, for it doesn't know which flower has the nectar that it hasn't yet made up its mind on what it wants. Even when it does descend upon a flower it then realizes that it wasn't the one it wanted. Off it goes to another chance landing.

Living with a Pisces is not an easy thing to do. It is very interesting, indeed, but unless you understand their dual nature you will not believe their way of balancing friendship and solitude. This is depicted by the two fishes bound together swimming in opposite directions and going in circles.

Living with Jane at home is a clear illustration of the fishes swimming in opposite directions and going in circles. When she is not sleeping or lying down, she will be flitting all around the house either mentally or physically and chattering on the phone or with guests in between landings.

Cancer 5th House: The Sun and Pluto both posited in this house of life, love, and love affairs would be most beneficial were it not for the Moon ruler of this house and the malefic aspects in which each are involved. Here the planets of authority

(Sun) and power (Pluto) are taken over by a water nature. The indications here are that there will be very strong maternal and nurturing instincts, not only with her children but also with her husband as well. Cancer people don't really love as such, they own. Because of Leo missing on her "T" cross, there will be neither love nor love affairs. The mothering nature will care to every minute detail, but there will be no fondling, hugging, and kissing- not even with her children. As for Jane's husband or lover, he will be granted his biological needs when Jane feels he needs them, no sooner and no more often.

Leo 6th House: The sign of love here on this house of work and service to others is of great benefit to Jane. Work is most important to Jane (6th House), for she just loves it (Leo) and with such enthusiasm that she even will overwork herself. Her work will be of a sort where it is a "service to others." This will keep Jane happy and content, for this is what naturally is built into Jane and what she continually escapes from.

Virgo 7th House: When Mercury rules this house of marriage and balance where Neptune is posited in the sign of Virgo, it alters the analytic mind to the critical mind. The malefic Mercury-Neptune aspect indicates constant criticism to every extent from the ridiculous to the sublime for Jane's husband. In this house ruled by Mercury, the criticism will be of such trivial substance that should Jane somehow manage to keep a man, he surely would be most deserving of an Olympic gold medal for patience and endurance.

Libra 8th House: Venus is the ruler for this house of sex and other people's needs because Libra, the sign of balance, compromise, and socializing is on the cusp. We already have learned that none of these words are included in Jane's vocabulary and she does not care to learn their meanings.

Scorpio 9th House: With Mars the co-ruler of Scorpio here on and in this 9th House of the higher mind ("I perceive"), there is a great secrecy (Scorpio) about what goes on in this superconscious mind and how far it penetrates into the search for answers and truth. There is no way that one can find out either, for with her stubborn Taurean character she is most conservative in conversation among other things.

Sagittarius 1Oth House: With Jupiter ruling this house of reality, career, and power, there is the ability to be a leader in the profession of choice. Here the reality of what must be done to achieve success must be handled well. The all-important houses involved for a successful career are the 2nd (values), the 6th (the work place), and the 1Oth (organizational skill). Each of these houses has a fire sign on its cusp: Aries for assertiveness, Leo for the determination to achieve, and Sagittarius for the knowledge and basic know-how to proceed. With the three signs on the crucial earth houses sharing Jupiter (the optimist) as a ruler, there only can be a positive result in terms of accomplishments. There aren't any negative aspects to Jupiter and so only the positive effects will be manifested from the affairs of each of these houses. The sextile to Mars helps her to understand (sextile) where to focus her drives. The trine to Venus helps in the adjustments required to succeed. The trine to Uranus shows that she knows just what is necessary and is completely aware of all concepts related to her field. There isn't a problem Jane couldn't handle with superior skill and with the organized procedures to ensure success. This is the exact opposite of her home, where the opposite sign Gemini and Mercury have the opposite type aspects.

Capricorn 11th House: With Saturn as ruler of this house of friends and ambitions, there will be very few intimates, for a Pisces does not like crowds. Having Jupiter located in Capricorn will offer additional abilities to organize her knowledge and make decisions to achieve her ambitions.

Aquarius 12th House: The sign of freedom on this house of sacrifice is like being in prison for this Pisces. Here is the freedom from wants and from the burdens of society (Aquarius), ruling the sacrificial lambs (Pisces 12th House). *The result is escape from the world of reality and anything that will help in this escape is justified.*

Unless you are proficient in this study, do not attempt to achieve accuracy in your synthesis through memory alone. It always is wise to follow a guide enabling you to make notations to ensure that no significant details are overlooked. The guidelines we offered or similar ones always should be followed if accuracy is to be expected. For solar charts we offered guidelines 1 through 7; for time charts we offered an additional 1 through 5. However, when delineating a time chart, the latter five guidelines should precede the initial seven.

Time Chart Synthesis: Obviously Jane's behavior was very well known to herself and all who knew her. She is just one wonderful person and anyone who knows her will verify that--everyone, that is, except her husband, who lives with her. He will agree that she is one wonderful person, but he also will state that she is one most uncommon person (which no one would believe).

It is uncommon to not want to fondle, hug, and kiss your little children. It is uncommon to not want to make love with your own husband, especially when they are and appear to be the ideal couple who never are apart. Neither is it a common practice to have no conversations of any type--not even about domestic issues, which almost is a must in any marriage--other than to criticize your husband. The most successful marriages have issues and domestic differences that must be discussed. Communication is the most vital link to settle these differences no matter how minor or major they are. Yet Jane is a chatterbox with friends, neighbors, and on the phone.

It is not the least bit common to have no interest in anything whatsoever, even a newspaper, magazine, book, or other publication other than the celebrity gossip in weekly newspapers. Here she reads every word. Jane does not realize this is unusual because she believes the practice is so widespread.

This is the crucial difference between the two charts. The solar chart shows Jane to be the wonderful person that she truly is considering her character traits, mental conflicts, liabilities, and the resources and abilities she has to overcome them. The time chart makes the ascendant sign and its aspects visible. It reveals the Moon's actual position, its aspects, and the actual house positions of both the signs and planets, all of which show how and where the circumstances of life and their natures will function. Should the actual position of the Moon be unknown, we would never have known of the "T" cross and its missing arm of Leo and its effect on Jane's life. The ascendant sign and its effects and the chart positions of the signs and planets reveal a side to Jane's character only her husband would know about because of the proximity of the lives they share. Without the time chart we only would have delineated Jane a bit more accurately than her closest friends can through knowing her.

As previously stated, Jane realizes that she is not very easy to live with and that she is difficult to understand, with the often-repeated comment, "If you don't like it, there's the door." That generally is the extent of her discussion with her husband on any of these subjects. The reason for these outbursts is for the sole purpose of escaping from the realities that would be revealed in a honest discussion with her husband. Fantasies and idle talk may have their place, but when they serve to displace reality the matter deserves attention. Jane does not knowingly say or do anything malicious to anyone, so she doesn't really know that she sometimes torments her husband with her detached attitude. She feels she must be accepted just as she is to feel content about her life. Her husband loves her dearly in spite of this predicament of differing values. Recalling the indications of Saturn in Aries, and especially on the 2nd House of values, shows that she sets rules for others that vary greatly for those that she will live up to. Saturn's position in the chart indicates something painful that you mst discard in life. In Jane's case, it is the "I am" of Aries. Her Pisces ascendant (1st House of "I am") also is indicative of what she must be willing to sacrifice. Pisces is "serve or suffer"; Pluto says, "either/or," all of which says she must change her selfish, inconsiderate behavior or suffer the consequences.

Her husband really isn't to blame, as most therapists might conclude, for he is patient to a fault, giving into the extreme, considerate and understanding and has deeply loved Jane for many years. He is neither impotent nor cruel, neither addict nor foolhardy soul, but he is an honest, conscientious man who is attempting to be an ideal father and husband.

As there is a limit to everything and a turning point in every form of life, how long will it be until Jane's husband will stop tolerating her double standards? Jane already has been through one divorce and that occurred during a crucial age period (34 to 36 years of age). Call it coincidence if you will, but Pluto was in the sign of Libra at that time with Libra on the 8th House of death. It was the death of the marriage at that time, not of the self as it should have been.

Let's take a brief look at tomorrow for Jane and see what, if anything, is in store for her for the coming months or years. This is discovered by the use of the planets while in their transiting positions up to whatever time period is desired. This concept of the study is referred to as transits, our next concept for your scrutiny and judgment.

Chapter 14
Transits in Forecasting

Transits, the concluding concept to be examined in this enlightening discovery of the mysteries of human behavior, involves two separate techniques, long-range trends and the key cycle. Each are transits in themselves, yet they offer their own distinct value in forecasting.

The Basic Principles

The value of using transits in forecasting is in knowing that the technique is derived from the real world and not some symbolic abstraction that is difficult to translate and apply in real life situations. They are part of the ongoing and continuing developmental process that had its origin for you at birth. While this might appear to be an overly simplistic device from which to derive the many and varied intricacies of the living process, it is a rather complex tool that yields significant results once you understand how to use it properly.

Let's return for a moment to the basic principles and review what we learned early in our studies. We know that each of the planets represents principles of behavior and the dynamics of how they operate when they are involved in aspects to other planets. Your entire chart displays the panorama of this arrangement of planets, signs, and houses in a pattern that very rarely ever is duplicated. From this we realize how important it is to know the basics of the signs, planets, houses, aspects, and the many other special considerations that most charts present for examination. This initial observation reveals distinct levels of creative potential, developmental opportunity, character, personality, limitations, fears, anxieties, personal adequacy, degree of frustration, the ability to strive for significance in personal and social contexts, career goals, fulfillment of destiny, and the many intricate details that some or all of the foregoing mechanisms of unfolding development cause to manifest themselves. Whatever it is you become is the culmination of the potential that was evident in the birth chart. But make no mistake about the choices you have in this developing scenario so that you alone direct the course of your life to its ultimate plateau of achievement.

In the continuing travel through the zodiac after you were born, each of the planets not only will make aspects to their original positions in the signs, but also to every other planet in your chart as well. Think of the planets in your chart as receptors and transiting planets as instigators. The planetary arrangement in your chart inclines you in a particular direction of behavior and accompanying thought processes. A transiting planet focusing on any of the planets in your chart immediately provokes a response followed by some kind of reaction. The kind of action you take soon will let you know if you've acted properly or improperly. Chances are, if you suffered any pain or distress as a result of what you did, you won't repeat it and you have learned something of value. For example, if you were born with Sun conjunct Mars, sometime during your early life the transiting Sun squared that conjunction and probably provoked some kind of aggressive behavior that may well have antagonized the person to whom it was directed. A reaction of anger and defense could have produced an unpleasant situation with the other person who retaliated against this kind of "thoughtless arrogance." This is how you might learn a lesson in moderation and patience. You may realize that you overreacted to a comment you thought was meant for you when it really wasn't, so that your reaction would have been "much ado about nothing." This pattern of provocation by the transiting Sun will reoccur again and again every year, so it should not be difficult to see how urgent it is to get this matter resolved early. Even the so-called favorable aspects from the Sun or Mars or any of the other transiting planets can arouse this fighting potential and cause it to flare up because the transits can only stimulate and reinforce the program already in place. We aren't suggesting that this energy be denied or curtailed, but simply that it be applied more judiciously to yield positive results. It's really a matter of exercising control over impulse to action that frequently leads to mindless behavior and regrets.

Let us begin by acknowledging the fact that no forecasting technique will succeed if we fail to grasp the full significance of the chart in which it is applied. For example, when someone asks "What will happen when Mars transits over my Mercury?" the usual answer is "Probably nothing out of the ordinary." The person is taken by surprise that so little value is given to this kind of transit. But let's look at it realistically. Mars moves approximately one-half degree per day. Allowing a 3-degree orb, it would take Mars 12 days to make an applying orb and separating orb of a contact with Mercury. To expect a matter of meaningful significance to develop, mature, and be resolved in that time is to grasp at the most ephemeral straws. If something of importance does occur, it would not be the sole responsibility of this kind of agitating transit to have initiated it. Mars only could have served to "trigger" a process that already had reached what we call "critical mass" from the combined energies of other, more weighty transits.

Understanding human potential and the massive struggle often encountered in striving to gain a measure of personal significance is very important. A destiny is indicated in every person's horoscope and it requires the utilization of all the dynamics of the birth chart to see its fulfillment. All of the planets in their signs, houses, and aspects provide the complete blueprint with which to succeed in achieving the goals suggested by the chart.

The primary purpose of transits is to learn what aspects (if any) are applying to or separating from the natal planets. These show how and in what areas of life behavior will be affected. This is accomplished by learning what signs and houses are occupied by the transiting planets and how they relate to the natal chart. The results show the specific areas of life's circumstances requiring attention and how to apply or dismiss these influences when that decision is indicated.

Don't be dismayed at the explanations offered. Be assured that they are much more complex in the reading than in the actual doing, which is nothing more than simple elementary arithmetic and time. In all instances the required

Figure 18

Jane Doe Transits

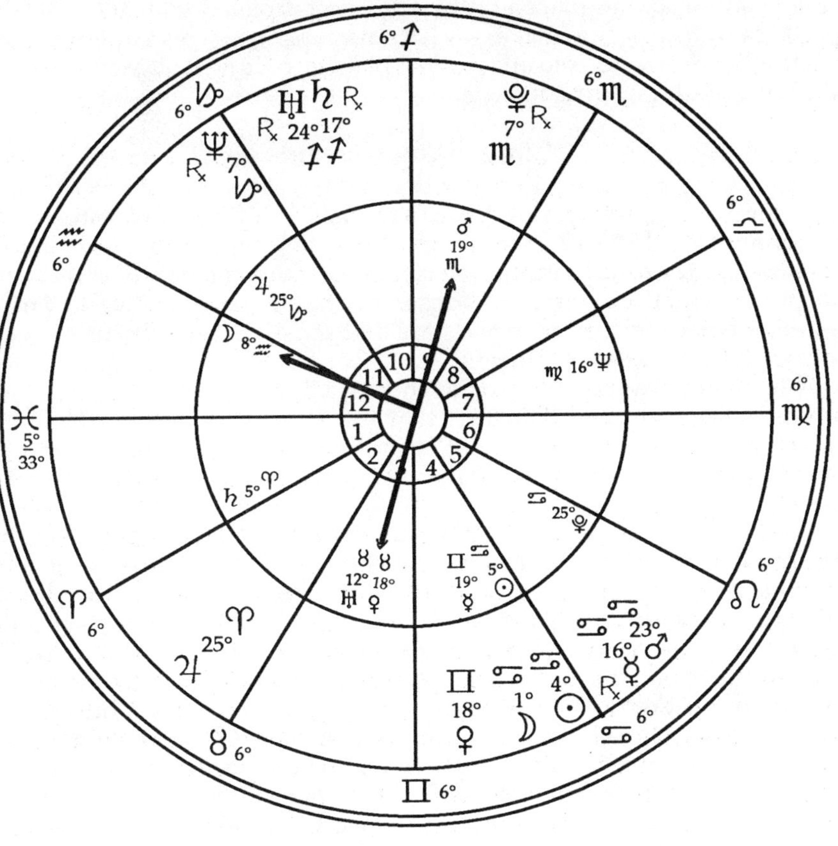

books on hand give all the data necessary. You merely need to calculate the differences.

All forecasting techniques actually are transits, even the daily horoscopes in the various newspapers. When considering transits, a double zodiac wheel is used, which is merely one wheel inside a larger one (see Figure 18).

The procedure in this technique for any period desired is to copy the natal chart in the inner circle with the ascendant sign on the extreme outer circle 1st House cusp. In the outer circle you enter the current locations of all the planets. It is best to do this with a colored pen for easier identification. For example, if you are a Cancer with the Sun at 5 degrees Cancer and the ephemeris shows the transiting Sun at 4 degrees Cancer, you enter the current Sun position in the outer circle next to the natal Sun at 5 degrees Cancer. Should the transiting Sun be at 4 degrees Libra, you then must enter it in the house with Libra on its cusp. In our example of Jane Doe (Figure 18), a Cancer with Pisces ascending at 6 degrees means that Pisces is located on the extreme outer circle 1st House cusp with Cancer on the 5th House cusp and Libra on the 8th House cusp, while a transiting Sun at 4 degrees Libra would be on the 8th cusp. This procedure must be followed for all ten planets. When this is completed you calculate all the aspects the transiting Sun makes to all ten natal planets. This is followed by the transiting Moon's aspects to all ten natal planets, followed by Mercury, Venus, and so on for all transiting planets.

Long-Range Trends

Long-range trends are nothing more than transits. There is a difference, however, for not only do we chart the current transiting aspects to the natal planets and houses, but we also indicate their future positions and how they relate to the natal positions of the planets and houses. As the title suggests, we now need to determine what the current aspects are and those that will occur to keep us informed for future developments.

We explained the transits and their house, along with what they signify, and many other factors involved. In this technique we will explain how these all will fit together and what they reveal. We indicated that transiting aspects were temporary in their effects--we now will determine what this means more precisely.

Jane Doe's chart (Figure 18) shows the transiting Sun at 4 degrees Cancer, with the natal Sun at 5 degrees Cancer. This is referred to as a "solar return" (returns to its natal position), another birthday when the Sun conjuncts the natal Sun. The tendencies during this aspect will be to assert the will and ego and the creative potentials. Had the transiting Sun been in Libra, it would have been square to the natal Sun. This aspect occurs twice a year, approximately three months before the birthday and three months after the birthday. With this aspect the person would be reluctant and uncertain to follow through with whatever he or she was occupied with or initiated during the period of the conjunction aspect. Of course, there may be many other alternatives depending on what other aspects may be involved or other planets involved in the same aspect. As there are many varying factors to consider it would be next to impossible to offer any delineations other than the individual aspect meaning which may have to be altered by other factors you have to consider.

Each and every aspect must be considered to include all other planets involved in each aspect and the houses involved. The delineations are made in the same way as we discussed previously according to planetary protocol. Careful delineation is required to include every special condition in the chart as they involve the nature of the planets, aspects, house positions, and various complex configurations. This requires a more serious study than generally is necessary in a simple solar chart. To offer more than already has been given may only confuse you at this time. We want to simplify matters through careful explanation and by offering procedures for you to follow as was done in the previous chapter on synthesis.

Allow an orb of 3 degrees for all transiting planets to natal or other transiting planets. This means an orb of 3 degrees approaching the aspect and 3 degrees as the aspect is leaving. Remember that when a transiting planet makes an aspect to a natal planet and then goes retrograde, the aspect remains in effect until it returns and passes the initial contact. The Moon remains in aspect for only a few hours and never retrogrades. The Sun, Mercury, and Venus remain in aspect six to seven days. Mars remains in aspect for up to 12 days, Uranus for as long as 7 years, and it is longer still for Neptune and Pluto (refer to planetary motions in Chapter 6).

In the order of their protocol, we will offer the approximate length of time the various aspects might last based on their speed (which determines their length of stay in a sign). We gave the approximate of the faster planets, which generally are referred to as the "personal planets," but we did offer that of the "outer planets" (the term used for Uranus, Neptune, and Pluto because they are so far out in relation to the others). It is these three outer planets that set the trend for this technique. By using any one or combination of these planets we will be able to determine what may be taking place at the present as well as any future time while they still are in aspect to the natal planet or planets.

As stated previously a transit aspect by itself does not cause any serious crises or events to occur. Crises and events occur when aspects start building up and involve other planets to make aspects to the same natal planet or configuration at the same time. When these conditions begin to occur, crises and events start taking place. This is the "trend" we now will discuss and explain. Don't be alarmed at the explanations, the doing is a simple task.

1. Using the same chart for Jane Doe (Figure 18), we are going to extend the transits a bit further into their orbits. In actual practice we set these charts up for one- year periods and year to year when requested. Should you wish to, you may extend them for as long a period as you feel necessary.

2. Check the transiting outer planets (Pluto, Neptune, and Uranus) to see if any one or combination of them makes any aspects to any natal planets or ascendant. As these planets remain in aspect for very long periods of time, they very well

could be showing a trend that is taking place and of which the individual is completely unaware. The individual aspect that now becomes visible will not create a crises or event by itself but it will show what could be taking shape.

Pluto, Neptune and Uranus are referred to as the "trend setters."

3. Searching the ephemeris for the current and coming years, locate the dates that Jupiter and/or Saturn will also aspect the same planet, planets, or ascendant while the outer planet aspect still is in effect. When this occurs the conditioning, identity, and form of this event or crisis now will be recognized. Having this knowledge the individual begins to contemplate a resolution to this matter.

Jupiter and Saturn are referred to as the "environmental conditioners."

4. Having located the date that Jupiter or Saturn also aspect the natal target, you continue searching the ephemeris for the date that the transiting Sun and/or Mars enters the picture with an aspect to this same target and at the same time as well.

The Sun and Mars are the "intensifiers."

What this means up to this point is that at least one trend-setting planet, one conditioning planet, and one intensifier must aspect the same natal planet or ascendant at the same time before anything really significant occurs. When either one or both of the intensifiers make their aspect, arguments, emotional outbursts, and such begin to take place. These types of outbursts could trigger the event or crisis because the Sun, (the will and ego) or Mars, (impulse to action) adds much intensity to a problem that was building up for some time, and now must be resolved one way or another. If the intensifiers don't trigger the event, which is quite possible, then the "triggers" undoubtedly will.

The "triggers" are the Moon (emotions), Mercury (nervous system), and Venus (desires).

The crisis or event that occurs depends on the natal planet that is being aspected. Its location by house and the house or houses it rules will be affected. The individual's natal chart must be considered before any prediction can be made as to whether or not the event or crisis will be beneficial or detrimental.

A significant event is one in which there is a planet from each of the groups involved in some kind of aspectual, sign, or house rulership connection with a receptor in the chart. Events occur when some of the participants are not involved, but the event lacks the significance of those that have full participation (see Figure 18, Jane Doe's Transits).

Procedure

The transiting planets are divided into groups that are an intimate part of the whole process of becoming and unfolding conscious awareness of personal potential.

Long-Range Trends

The Trend Setters

LONG-RANGE TRENDS

Pluto (♇) introduces change that can be in process for a long period of time.
Neptune (♆) suggests the dissolving or undermining of conditions (usually social).
Uranus (♅) notes the occasional cataclysm that uproots old conditions and attitudes.
(The individual is unaware that crises or events are forming.)

ENVIRONMENTAL CONDITIONERS

Saturn (♄) consolidates the subtle changes of Pluto, Neptune, or Uranus into form.
Jupiter (♃) enhances the growth factor potential of Pluto, Neptune, or Uranus changes.
(Gives form to the crises and allows the identify to surface.)

INTENSIFIERS

Mars (♂) the assertive energy for taking action in matters produced by Pluto, Neptune, or Uranus, and given form by Saturn or opportunity by Jupiter.
Sun (☉) is the desire to gain significance and notice from matters similar to Mars.
(Adds intensity to the crises and also may trigger crises.)

TRIGGERS

Venus (♀) is the attitude prevailing during the gathering energy of developing conditions.
Mercury (☿) is the concerns relative to the mounting evidence of events in process.
Moon (☽) is the principle "timer" of an event that is really the culmination of many conditions leading to some kind of conclusion involving the individual's participation in one way or another.
(When the event is not triggered by the intensifiers, the triggers will set it off.)

Explanations

Pluto rules obsessions, life and death, and is the executioner who will force action. Life begins and ends with Pluto, not only life itself, but circumstances as well. It rules the body wastes that could kill by contamination and the mental contaminations as well. Pluto is the purging system that causes irreversible changes. It is a rebirth from destruction to resurrection, a failure in order to succeed, a new life from the decay of the old.

Neptune causes erosion of the mental factors and stability through emotional disturbances that result in subconscious unrest. Because the problem is unknown, this is overlooked. It is like turning your back on the problem, which results in its corrosion. Deep spiritual feelings are set in motion where you give in to the human needs. Neptune is the capacity to be sensitized. It is necessary for contributing to human needs and to do whatever it takes to fulfill them. It is a need that must be fulfilled. Neptune is the certainty of the uncertainty.

Uranus is the awareness, the search for truth and the future. It eagerly seeks freedom from restrictions and wants never before known. It is the ability to intellectualize through the higher mental faculties. Uranus is sudden developments, detachment, the shock treatment that usually signifies divorce.

Saturn signifies the responsibilities that must be adhered to. When these responsibilities are ignored, serious problems result. Saturn is the "cosmic boomerang" that sooner or later always returns to you that which you threw out. Sooner or later, in one way or another, you will pay your dues. Saturn forces you to focus on the future.

Jupiter is anticipation, the tendencies to ignore the problems because of optimism and high hopes. However, when Jupiter makes the conditioner aspect, it tends to be beneficial--that is, if the problem is not ignored.

Mars is the impulsive energy that sort of forces action, the survival nature that you do something before something does something to you.

Sun is the will and the ego, the struggle for significance that adds intensity to the problem. Knowing the problem, emotional outbursts start taking place.

Venus is the rejection, weaknesses, and dissatisfaction.

Mercury is the nervous disorders, the concern, and the communication.

Moon is the severe emotional unrest and stress.

Trend and Crisis Time Table

Pluto
Neptune → The trends could last for as long as 7 years.
Uranus

Saturn
Jupiter — The conditioners could last for as long as 7 months.

Mars
Sun — The intensifiers usually last for one to two weeks.

Venus
Mercury
Moon — The triggers cause the event upon aspect.

Figure 18 shows the birth chart for Jane Doe 6/26/37 in the inner circle, with the transiting planets for 6/26/87 in the outer circle. You may make your transits for any year of your choice. It is from this type of chart that all focal points and calculations are determined. (Figure 20 shows Jane Doe's long-range trends and dates; see Figure 20 on page 205).

Procedures for Predictions

1. List all aspects made by transiting trend setters Pluto, Neptune, and Uranus to the personal natal planets from the Sun through and including Saturn (only 3 degrees).

2. The focal point will be the planet or planets that is/are being aspected by the transiting trend setters.

3. The ascendant and the sign on the 10th House cusp will also be involved whether or not they are included in the aspects. This is more especially true when the trend setter or conditioner planet rules the ascendant.

4. The affairs that will be affected are those pertaining to all the houses ruled by the trend setter planet or planets, their natural house, birth chart house, and the house of its natal position.

5. When Saturn and/or Jupiter, the conditioning planets, make their aspect, the houses they rule and their natural house also will be involved.

6. The affairs of the house ruled by the ascendant's ruling planet also is involved.

7. When an aspect is made by at least one of the trend setters, the date the aspect begins should be recorded the date it ends, inclusive of the retrograde period if any. Should it be that no current aspect is being formed by a trend setter to a personal natal planet, check to determine if one will be made in the coming year. You should not ignore a close aspect: check the date the aspect will be made.

8. When it is found that a trend setter does make an aspect to the natal planet, then a check is made to determine when a conditioner planet makes its aspect to the same natal planet and this date is recorded.

9. This same procedure now is carried out for the intensifiers, and then the triggers with these dates being recorded for the date that the event will occur.

This procedure in its entirety will show the trend that is taking place and when.

The following format should be followed when this technique is used. It will show only the planetary symbols and sign glyphs with their aspectual symbols. This format is being offered with intentions of showing the simplicity of this technique. However, they both will be spelled out with their symbols and glyphs in separate columns to allow you the ease by which to follow the explanations.

THE PLANETS AND SYMBOLS

Pluto	Neptune	Uranus	Saturn	Jupiter	Mars	Sun	Venus	Mercury	Moon
♇	♆	♅	♄	♃	♂	☉	♀	☿	☽

THE SIGNS AND GLYPHS

Aries	Taurus	Gemini	Cancer	Leo	Virgo	Libra	Scorpio	Sagittarius	Capricorn	Aquarius	Pisces
♈	♉	♊	♋	♌	♍	♎	♏	♐	♑	♒	♓

ASPECTS AND SYMBOLS

Conjunction	Sextile	Square	Trine	Inconjunct	Opposition
☌	⚹	□	△	⚻	☍
8°	60°	90°	120°	150°	180°

TRANSITING TRENDS FORMAT

Transit Locations 6/26/87		Transits to Natal Aspects
Pluto in Scorpio 7°	(♇-♏7°)	(♇△asc) Pluto trine Ascendant *
		(♇⚻☽) Pluto inconjunct Moon *
		(♇□☉) Pluto square Sun *
		(♇⚻♄) Pluto inconjunct Saturn *
Neptune in Capricorn 7°	(♆-♑7°)	(♆⚹asc) Neptune sextile Ascendant *
		(♆☍☉) Neptune opposition Sun *
		(♆□♄) Neptune square Saturn *
Uranus in Sagittarius 24°	(♅-♐24°)	(♅☍☿) Uranus opposition Mercury

****

<u>Transit Locations 6/26/87</u>		<u>Transits to Natal Aspects</u>
Saturn in Sagittarius 17°	(♄-♐ 17°)	(♄ ⚻ ♀) Saturn inconjunct Venus
Jupiter in Aries 25°	(♃-♈25°)	(♃ ⚹ ☿) Jupiter sextile Mercury
		(♃ □ ♃) Jupiter square Jupiter

****

Mars in Cancer 23°	(♂-♋23°)	(♂ ☍ ♃) Mars opposition Jupiter
Sun in Cancer 4°	(☉-♋ 4°)	(☉△asc.) Sun trine Ascendant *
		(☉☌☉) Sun conjunct Sun *
		(☉□♄) Sun square Saturn*

****

Venus in Gemini 18°	(♀-♊18°)	(♀ ⚻ ♂) Venus inconjunct Mars
Mercury in Cancer 15°	(☿-♋15°)	(☿ ⚹ ♀) Mercury trine Venus
		(☿ △ ♂) Mercury trine Mars
Moon in Cancer 1°	(☽-♋ 1°)	(nil) -------------

****

* *Denotes the natal planets in focus: Ascendant, Sun, Moon, and Saturn.*

Both trend setters Pluto and Neptune make the contact with neither of the conditioners getting involved. The Sun, an intensifier, makes three aspects, two of which are favorable and most importantly to the ascendant and the Sun. The square aspect to Saturn adds nothing to disturb Jane's tranquility at this point. On September 12, 1987, Pluto moved out ahead of this aspect. Neptune remained in aspect, but it too moved ahead and out of aspect on January 7, 1988, before any other aspects were made.

<u>Transit Locations 6/1988 Through 1989</u>

Uranus in Capricorn 4° <u>(Feb. through Sept. '89)</u>	(♅-♑4°)	(♅ ⚹ asc.) Uranus sextile Ascendant *
		(♅ ☍ ☉) Uranus opposition Sun*

****

Jupiter in Cancer 4° <u>(August 21, 1989)</u>	(♃-♋ 4°)	(♃△asc.) Jupiter trine Ascendant*
		(♃ ☌ ☉) Jupiter conjunct Sun

****

Mars inLibra 4° <u>(September 1989)</u>	(♂-♎ 4°)	(♂□☉) Mars square Sun*
Sun in Libra 4°	(☉-♎4°)	(☉□☉) Sun square Sun*

****

Moon in Libra 4° <u>(September 29, 1989)</u>	(☽-♎ 4°)	(☽□☉) Moon square Sun*

Because Uranus appeared to be closing in to make an aspect, we followed its motion for 1989. The following planetary motions were noted.

Just what does all this mean? Let's follow the procedures set forth and learn just what is going to take place, where, and why.

1. Transiting trend setter Uranus makes two aspects, one benefic to the ascendant and one malefic to the Sun.

2. As the ascendant and Sun both are aspected by the trend setter, both of them become the focal point of this transit.

3. Neptune, the ruler of the ascendant Pisces and Sagittarius on the 10th House cusp with Jupiter its ruling planet, are now involved in this trend.

4. The houses ruled by trend setter Uranus are the 11th (its natural house), 12th (in the birth chart), posited in the 3rd of the birth chart and transiting the 11th.

5. Jupiter the conditioner is ruler of the birth chart 10th, its natural 9th, positioned in the 11th and transiting the 4th.

6. Neptune rules the 1st but in the7th and is transiting the 11th adding to influences noted above (Uranus, Mars, Sun and Moon) in matters of the 8th and 9th Houses (Mars and the Moon in Libra).

The synthesis previously offered for Jane's charts informed us of her strong will and ego, her inconsiderate selfishness, and her determination to escape from the realities of life and responsibilities. In short, we have learned how Jane has taken control of her own life by her own personal standards.

There might be feelings that there isn't anything uncommon with Jane or any person that wishes to run their life in their own personal way. We previously have stated and sincerely agree that one *must* take control of his or her life and become what they were born to become. However, do we take the proper paths for this venture? Are we sufficiently responsible to realize where we are going and how to get there? Are we truly justified in our animalistic instincts for personal survival? Are we doing or serving justice to ourselves, or will justice make us pay the price for our errors and lack of responsibilities? Let's look at the answers to these questions, just as Jane will learn (should learn) when October of 1989 arrives.

Synthesis and Explanations of the Trend

Uranus is the planet of awareness, the higher octave of Mercury the communicator. It is the planet that represents freedom from wants and obligations, and the sudden changes in life. Aspecting the ascendant (the way you view life) by sextile, and by opposition to the Sun (will and ego), there will be some sudden changes in Jane's lifestyle and standards that are going to change (should change) her outlook on life. There also will be some changes in her strong will and ego (Sun). Jane will, of course, not be aware of what is taking place, for this is the very subtle trend that is building up starting in February of 1989 and continuing through August 1989.

On August 21,1989, Jupiter the conditioner made its aspects to both the ascendant and Sun. Both aspects of a benefic nature gave form to the crises. When this occurred the crises and the cause surfaced and were open for discussions by which both the crises and causes could be resolved.

Because Uranus sextiles the ascendant (understands her outlook on life) and the Jupiter trine ascendant (resources and ability to make corrections) Jane will be well aware of the problems and the causes.

Uranus transiting through Jane's 10th House indicates her social status and reputation. Her authority will be challenged. Changes (Uranus) from the old to the new will occur. Affairs of the 11th and 12th Houses ruled by Uranus will be brought into focus. The 11th House is the house of the future, ambitions, goals, and friends, all of which will be affected by Jane's problems unless she accepts the changes that Uranus signifies (truths) by which she "earns" freedom, and doesn't just take them. Either Jane makes these changes in life or the challenging forces will force a change one way or another in life.

The 12th House of hidden enemies, hidden thoughts, and the subconscious mind, where the conscious mind buries all the problems in order not to deal with them, now will surface and have to be dealt with. Because Jane merely blocked out all the normal problems of life, she now must deal with them as they merely were stored in her memory bank. All the problems she refused to face by turning her back now will come forth to be resolved. The time has arrived when Jane must accept her responsibilities and pay her debt to society.

Uranus sextile ascendant (♅⚹ asc) indicates the seeking of more freedom from friends and associates, including husband and family. They may suddenly seem boring and uninteresting.

Uranus opposition Sun (♅☍☉) indicates the attempt to get away from any restrictions encountered. As the opposition suggests, there will be challenges from the outside sources that may force change and more responsibilities into life. One sudden change could be that the marriage may end because Jane believes it is preventing her from being free. Uranus forces the release (freedom) of all that has been hidden and building up pressure. Jane will not realize that she is doing this to herself, but will believe that others are doing it to her.

Freedom is not for just the taking, *freedom must be earned.*

Jupiter transiting the 2nd House is associated with values. It is the material, spiritual, financial, and money-making values along with the standards and personal beliefs in life. Jupiter is the planet of expansion and optimism. The 2nd House is the natural house of Taurus with Uranus posited in the sign of Taurus in the birth chart, thereby involving these values in the changes suggested by Uranus as well. We know what Jane's values are, but Jupiter trine ascendant indicates that Jane may be intellectually eager at this time to learn more truths of life as well as become more tolerant of others' views. However, with Jupiter the hopes are high with never a thought of failure. Jane may ignore the threats of Uranus and turn her back on the crisis as she often does. The conjunction aspect similar to the trine aspect merely adds more energy to the indications stated.

Jupiter rules the 10th House in the birth chart as well as the natural 9th and is posited in the 11th. We already have explained the changes suggested by Uranus, which included these houses but not the 9th. The 9th House is the house of the higher mind, the answers to all questions of the inquisitive 3rd House, the planning and scheming, the house of the professionals who set the guidelines. With Jupiter the conditioner as ruler of this house, there should be no question as to who will decide the changes to be made (if any at all) as far as our Jane is concerned. But changes there will be, one way or another.

As the age-old saying states, "Be very careful of that for which you wish for, as it may be granted."

Both intensifiers (Mars and the Sun) make their aspects in September 1989. Mars square Mars (♂ □ ☉) gives high energy and strong self-confidence. There will be many arguments, disputes, and disagreements, and because of both Mars and/or the Sun, there will no chance of any compromise or backing down on any issues. She has a tendency to stand her ground for her beliefs.

Sun square Sun (☉ □ ☉) indicates crisis from others who are at odds with her efforts. In Jane's case she will feel that she is threatened for no reason other than to cause her problems. Jane will have no thoughts whatever that the other person will have their own efforts to enforce as well and that she may be threatening to them.

Both Mars and the Sun transiting through the sign of Libra (sign of marriage), the 7th House where Neptune (the ruling house of the ascendant) is located, will involve the 1st House (the self) Mars, the 2nd House of the birth chart with Aries there (her values), the 5th House of the Sun where the birth chart Sun is located (love and children), as well as the fun house, which Jane does not indulge in. The 7th House of her husband is most likely where the problems will arise (Neptune the ruling planet).

The Moon (the trigger), also transiting through the sign of Libra, made its aspect to the Sun on September 29, 1989. This resulted in severe emotional unrest and stress, either from the crises that already had been triggered by Mars and the Sun or the present contact of the Moon square Sun (☽ □ ☉).

The Moon square Sun aspect signifies a challenge to your daily routine of life, the home life relationships, relations, and so forth. Because we all have tensions we suppress and keep to ourselves, this aspect brings these tensions to the surface. The crises that are created by this type transit usually occur with people and situations that are taken for granted.

The Sun, Mars, and the Moon all are in the sign of Libra (a most social sign) transiting through Jane's 8th House (sex and other people's needs) with our Jane not in the least bit interested in any of those functions. This especially is true since the sign of Leo is the missing arm of her "T" cross. Is it any wonder that Jane has these kinds of problems?

Jane could have avoided these crises (which she created) had she taken heed of the suggestions of her birth chart. Recall her birth chart delineations.

Pisces Ascendant:

Neptune is the ruler in the 7th House and in the sign of Virgo, which suggests that Jane should "serve or suffer." Jane should have sacrificed the self (1st House-Aries) for the benefit of others in need.

Saturn in Aries:

Where Saturn is located is an indication of what you should rid yourself of. Jane should have outgrown that childish selfish nature (Aries, "I am"). This position of Saturn also indicates that Jane should have adhered to the same standards that she set for others. Saturn, if you recall, is the cosmic boomerang and debt collector: what you throw out there now comes back to you later. When it returns you either pay your debt or collect your reward. Jane will pay her debt.

Pluto in Cancer:

Pluto is the purging system as well as the executioner. It is the "either/or" planet, similar to Neptune"s "serve or suffer." Either you purge yourself of the contaminants or Pluto will do it for you. Jane purged herself of her first husband, and not the self as her entire chart suggested.

Leo the Missing Arm:

The "T" cross with Leo unoccupied suggested that Jane should have put more effort into her love nature and love of life with all its gaieties, and not only what the self enjoyed which was food (Taurus-Cancer), rest, and escape (Cancer-Pisces).

Although it might seem as though the foregoing is little more than pure chance or sheer coincidence, the truth is that this is a direct by-product of her character as shown in her birth chart. Its continuing development is the result of the pressure brought to bear by the experiences that are an extension of her need to grow.

Through astrological study Nostradamus made hundreds of predictions and never yet has been wrong. Was that coincidence or chance? It was long-range trends.

Mark Twain, also a known astrologer, said, "I was born with Halley's Comet, and I expect to die upon its return." He did. Coincidence? Hardly.

The Key Cycle:

There is a basic principle involved with delineating the key cycle as with any other analytical device an astrologer uses in his or her practice. The natal chart always has precedence over any forecasting technique, and it makes no difference what technique is used, they all are a transit system. Nothing ever occurs that somehow doesn't help fulfill what was established as potential in the natal chart. Astrology is, after all, a study of the process of being and becoming, and we always should maintain that philosophical position in our analyses. The struggle in our relationships, situations, and events affecting our careers and the varied incidents in our daily routines all serve to somehow urge us toward the greater utilization of our creative potential. Thus we may continue to grow throughout our lives. It is safe to assume that the key cycle chart offers a unique opportunity for utilizing every bit of creative ability as viewed through the portals of the ever-changing circumstances in our lives. Every four years the same conditions previously encountered are again revisited. However, their effects differ because we have grown (or should have) from the experiences of those intervening years. This refining process continues throughout our lives and we grow realizing how intimate are the ties that bind us to the destiny we have chosen.

Although the key cycle ascendant and the affairs of the house it occupies in the natal chart have the highest priority in your life during the time it is rising, the affairs of the remaining houses also are important as their complexion is altered by the nature of the sign now occupying those cusps. The key cycle ascendant provides a temporary overlay of attitude and outlook during the time it occupies that position. It does not replace the birth chart ascendant but merely superimposes its mode temporarily and we acquire a slightly altered attitude in the way we project ourselves. Any relocation, especially east-west moves, alters the key cycle chart as it does in the natal chart. North-south movement causes some changes, too, but they are slight. With a move to the east, the time difference between the locales must be *added* to the sidereal time of the key cycle and a new chart results. A move to the west requires that the time difference between the locales be *subtracted* from the sidereal time of the key cycle and the revised cusps determined from the Tables of Houses.

Because of these crucial changes in the attitudes of an individual, we offer the key cycle technique complete with all explanations, procedures, and illustrations.

Every year approximately 6 hours of time passes that is left to accumulate for four year periods, after which an extra day is added to the calendar, known as the leap year.

The key cycle is a technique whereby this annual accumulation of time is calculated and then utilized. When the exact amount of this time is known, it is divided equally into 12 monthly increments which then is added to the Local Sidereal Time (also on a monthly basis). Upon the completion of this technique, when correctly applied, then and then only do we have a true and accurate horoscope: the view of any and every hour of any and every year.

The technique and calculations are a simple matter, although the explanations are much more complex and time consuming. We ask only for your patience and indulgence.

During this four-year period all 12 of the zodiac signs will have risen on the horizon (the ascendant). This means that every year about three signs rise on the horizon while those six hours pass on and accumulate. As each sign's stay on the horizon varies due to the apparent motion of the Sun and Earth, we only can assume for the moment that three signs rise each year. The key cycle considers this and adds this time into the chart. This may appear as insignificant to the average layperson, but it does make a most significant change in the charts pertaining to accuracy in delineations. It takes any guessing out of forecasting and accounts for every second of time throughout the year. The inclusion of this time alters the Local Sidereal Time for each month by which the ascendant is determined. As the ascendant passes over the horizon, the remaining signs move ahead. The result is a running view of any given hour, day, month, or year for any individual chart cast. The key cycle ascendant has equal importance in the individual's life as does the natal ascendant. By this technique we can zero in, at any time, to determine exactly what attitude the person will be exercising, what is presently in focus, and what is coming into focus at the time. This is the true and accurate "view of the hour." Who or what else could be more accurate and detailed in this the study of human behavior?

The minute scientific details intentionally are omitted for these only would confuse and complicate the procedures that we wish to simplify. Be assured that nothing of any significant value to your understanding of this technique will be ignored.

It is imperative that you constantly remain aware that we are calculating both time and elementary arithmetic. *Do not confuse* the two.

Since all calculations are dependent on the *exact* position of the Sun, the exact time of birth must be known. Double check all calculations for accuracy.

Key Cycle Procedures

1. Calculate for the exact position of the Sun for the time and location of birth. Should you have completed this phase for your time chart, the Sun's position from that chart may be used. If not, refer to time chart in Chapter 12.

2. From the ephemeris for the same birth *day* but for the present year (not the year of the birth), record the position of the Sun for as close to, or up to the exact natal degree, *but not more than* the exact natal degree.

3. The position of the Sun from Step 2 now must be subtracted from Step 1 (the exact natal degree). The result will be the distance the Sun has yet to travel to reach it's exact natal degree (Step 1).

4. We must now determine how fast the Sun was traveling on this day (motion of the day). This is done by subtracting the position of the Sun for this day, from the position on the following day or the previous day's position from this present-day position. The result of this is the daily motion for the present year. It is from this motion that we must learn just how long it will take the Sun to reach its exact natal degree. Refer to Chapter 12 and the Diurnal Motion of the Sun. This is the book that gives all the motions of the day and the time involved. For this fourth step we use it in reverse order. Under the column for that particular

motion of the day, we locate the distance the Sun has to travel (minutes and second of arc) and then on either side of the columns look for the time it takes to travel that distance in hours and minutes of time. In the actual procedures it is referred to as "travel time."

5. From the ephemeris for the day the Sun returns to its natal position (Step 2) record the sidereal time as recorded in the ephemeris.

6. Add the travel time (from Step 5) to this sidereal time.

7. To the result of Step 6 we now add the *acceleration* time (10 seconds per hour) for the travel time *only* (Step 4).

8. The result of all this is Greenwich Sidereal Time.

9. From Greenwich Sidereal Time we now must *subtract* (for west) or *add* (for east) the Longitude Equivalent Time (the exact time difference between Greenwich and the place of birth, not the Zone Standard Time).

10. The result is Local Sidereal Time.

NOTE: Should there have been a change in residence, then the exact time difference between the place of birth and the locality of the present residence must be *subtracted* for west and *added* for east.

11. We now must repeat Steps 1 through 10 complete, but for the year following that one used in Step 2. This means that instead of using 1989 for Step 2, we now use 1990. These periods specifically were selected so that the long-range trend shown for Jane Doe would become obvious through her key cycle chart.

12. After completing Step 11 (sidereal time for the following year), *the result of Step 10 now must be subtracted* from Step 11. In other words, the Local Sidereal Time for 1989 must be subtracted from that for 1990.

13. The result from Step 12 is the yearly increment of time that would have been gained and left to accumulate.

What we have just completed is only half of this procedure. The explanations were only for learning how to obtain the amount of accumulated time. We now must show what to do with it and how to use that time. Confused? Don't be. A simple explanation and formula is following, along with all calculations worked out for the periods stated.

14. We now must convert that yearly increment of time into a total amount of seconds. These seconds are divided into 12 equal monthly increments which then are divided again by 60 in order to return to minutes and seconds again.

When this monthly amount of time is learned, we then add these monthly increments of time to the Local Sidereal Time for each month. The result of this is the *precise* Local Sidereal Time for each month of that year with no accumulation. The time is used as it passes on, as it actually happens throughout the world. Using the same format, we now will proceed with the actual calculations for Jane Doe's key cycle charts 1989 to 1990.

The American Ephemeris was used for all necessary data.

1--Sun's motion 57' 13" 6/26/37 Sun exact at 4° 52' 12" (♋)
2-- 6/26/89 Sun at 4° 22' 34" (♋)
3-- distance left to travel: 29' 38"
4--6/26/89 Sun at 4° 22' 34"
6/25/89 Sun at 3° 25' 20"
57' 14" motion for the day
Sun moves 28' 37" in 12 hours
Sun moves + 1' 01" in 25 min. 30 sec.
12 hrs, 25 mins., 30 secs. Sun moves 29' 38" ° of arc.

5-- 18:16:24 Sidereal Time 6/26/89
6-- + 12:25:30 Travel Time (result of 4)
30:41:54 (result of 5 and 6)
7-- + 2:05 Acceleration Time (10 secs. per hour)
8-- 30:43:59 Greenwich Sidereal Time
9-- - 4:44:16 Longitude Equivalent Time (not Zone Standard Time)
10-- 25:59:43
\- 24:00:00 hours
1:59:43 Local Sidereal Time 6/26/89

11-- *Repeat Steps 1 through 10 for 1990*

1--Sun's motion 57' 13" 6/26/37 Sun exact at 4° 52' 12"
2-- 6/26/90 Sun at 4° 9' 14"
3-- distance left to travel: 42' 58"
4--6/26/90 Sun at 4° 09' 14"
6/25/89 Sun at 3° 11' 59"
57' 15" motion of the Sun
Sun moves 42' 56" in 18 hours
Sun moves + 2" in 1 min.
18 hours, 01 min., 30 secs. Sun moves 42' 58" ° of arc.

18:15:27 Sidereal Time 6/26/90
\+ 18:01:00 Travel Time
36:16:27
\+ 3:00 Acceleration Time
36:19:27 Greenwich Sidereal Time
\- 4:44:16 Longitude Equivalent Time
31:35:11
\- 24:00:00 hours
7:35:11 Local Sidereal Time

12-- 6/26/90 Sidereal Time 7:35:11
6/26/89 Sidereal Time 1:59:43
Annual Increment 5:35:28

Formula for Conversion of Annual Increment

Using the actual figures for Jane Doe's key cycle increment, we now offer the simple mathematical formula. The accumulated increment of 5 hours, 35 minutes, and 28 seconds now must be converted into total number of seconds for the year, divided into 12 equal increments, and then converted back to minutes and seconds again for their monthly distribution.

$$\frac{5 \times 60 + 35 \times 60 + 28}{12} = \frac{20{,}128}{12} \text{ sec.} = \frac{1677}{60} \text{ sec. per month} = 27 \text{ min. } 57 \text{ sec.}$$

27 minutes and 57 seconds per month are to be added to the Local Sidereal Time with 4 seconds left over. These 4 seconds then are used up by adding 1 additional second to each of the first 4 months; thus 27 minutes and 58 seconds for 4 months.

Figure 19: Key Cycle Ascendants

	Date	Sidereal Time	Ascendant
Local Sidereal Time on	6/26/89	1:59:43	Leo 13 °
		27:58	
	7/26/89	2:27:41	Leo 18°
		27:58	
	8/26/89	2:55:39	Leo 23°
		27:58	
	9/26/89	3:23:37	Leo 29°
		27:58	
	10/26/89	3:51:35	Virgo 5°
		27:57	
	11/26/89	4:19:32	Virgo 10°
		27:57	
	12/26/89	4:47:29	Virgo 16°
		27:57	
	1/26/90	5:15:26	Virgo 21°
		27:57	
	2/26/90	5:43:23	Virgo 27°
		27:57	
	3/26/90	6:11:20	Libra 2°
		27:57	
	4/26/90	6:39:17	Libra 8°
		27:57	
	5/26/90	7:07:14	Libra 13°
		27:57	
Local Sidereal Time on	6/26/90	7:35:11	Libra 19°

Monthly Sidereal Time

Starting with the Local Sidereal Time for the year 1989 obtained in Step 10, we now add to that the monthly increment of 27 minutes 57 seconds along with that extra 1 minute for the first four months. The next month's Local Sidereal Time is obtained by adding the monthly increment to that total and so on through to the birthday of the following year.

When setting up a key cycle chart, you may start with any month you wish. However, we suggest that you keep an ongoing account from ascendant change to change. The value of this would have been realized from the synthesis for Jane Doe.

1. Local Sidereal Time for 6/26/89 is 01:59:43. The Table of Houses shows Leo at 13 degrees as the ascendant during this period.

2. On the extreme outside circle of the double circle chart, on the 1st House cusp, we draw the glyph of the sign Leo with the 13 degrees just below. This is followed by the glyph of Virgo on the 2nd House with 13 degrees also, Libra's glyph on the 3rd, and so on through the 12 signs and houses in their natural order. Completed correctly, Cancer should be on the 12th House cusp.

3. In the inner circle of this double circle chart, we draw in Jane's natal chart locations, but, in accordance with the key cycle houses, we do not add the natal houses. Starting with the natal ascendant that now is represented as a planet, draw its initials ("ASC") and its degrees into the proper key cycle house. For example, Jane has Pisces at 6 degrees for her natal ascendant. This is drawn into the 8th House area because that is where Pisces falls in the key cycle. Her Sun, which is 5 degrees of Cancer, would be placed in the 12th House key cycle area of Cancer. All the remaining planets are drawn into the inner circle by this same procedure.

The inner circle actually is Jane's natal chart. We only revolve the map, much the same as the Earth revolves and the signs rise quarterly. This is the means by which we realize when the changes in attitudes and actions take place.

4. Having completed drawing in the natal chart, we now must draw into the outer circle all of the planets in their transiting positions for the periods desired. In Jane's case we are using the 6/26/89 to 90 periods. Checking the ephemeris for that month, day, and year, we list all the transiting positions and then carefully draw them into their respective places in the double map.

5. After completing this phase we must return to our long- range trend and procedures to learn what is in store for Jane and when crises and events will occur.

through for all signs and house cusps. Frequently, it will be found that when drawing in the planetary symbol, degree, and sign in its proper location, it physically may be shown as being in the house before its own sign. For example, Jane's natal chart has a 6-degree cusp for all houses because she has Pisces at 6 degrees for her ascendant. Therefore, when drawing in the Sun at 5 degrees of Cancer, physically it will be in the 4th House just inside the imaginary line dividing the 4th from the 5th House. The same is true for Saturn at 5 degrees of Aries, which will be shown in the 1st House. You always must bear in mind that the lines that are dividing the houses are imaginary. Houses actually begin where the 0 degrees would be for that particular sign, and not the line that divides them. When the ascendant has a high degree, all the planets of a lesser degree in that sign will be shown in the house before it's own but, in every case the planet must be read as being in the house that bears its sign on the cusp. When drawing in the natal planets in the key cycle chart inner circle, the key cycle ascendant degree must be used on both inner and outer circles of the chart. It is by these means that all that is passing or arriving at the high priority level of consciousness becomes visible.

The following page shows Jane Doe's key cycle chart and also illustrates the long-range trend chart by which we keep track of the dates involved. These are the types of charts employed by serious astrologers in actual practice.

With three signs rising each year, it is safe to assume that Taurus (2nd House), Gemini (3rd House), and Cancer (4th House), all have risen during 1988. Those houses have arrived and passed with no serious crises developing. Leo, with its 6th House (affairs) rises as ascendant in approximately the middle of May 1989, but because Jane does not indulge in such affairs other than her work (which she loves), conditions remain very subtle although tension begins to build around her. Jane at least should have listened to other's views if not look at her chart. Had she done so she would have had ample time to accept the change demanded by Uranus. Indulging the self and as usual turning her back on her problems caused tensions to continue to build. On August 21, 1989, Jupiter joined Uranus, with its aspects to both ascendant and Sun giving form to the crises. This resulted in heated arguments, which Jane continued to ignore. Through most of September both the intensifiers join in the aspects resulting in serious outbursts and other manifestations of trouble. The crisis becomes very critical. Through most of September both the intensifiers join in the aspects, resulting in serious outbursts and other manifestations of trouble. The crisis becomes very critical.

It may be coincidence, chance, or whatever you may wish to believe, but look at what the key cycle chart shows. Just at the end of September the sign of Virgo and its 7th House affairs come into focus. Neptune, Jane's ruling planet, is located there and also is rising. This all occurs at the very same time that the Moon gets into the puzzle on September 29th and triggers an event: believe it or not--another divorce.

A chart for each month really isn't necessary. You need only revolve the chart in a clockwise direction accordingly with the key cycle ascendant (Figure 19) to observe the circumstances coming into focus and when. The transiting

NAME Jane Doe
CITY Revere
Relocated- Malden to Revere

BIRTH DATE 6/26/37
TIME 11:30 P.M.
6/26/89 to 6/26/90

Figure 20: Key Cycle Chart and Long Range Trends

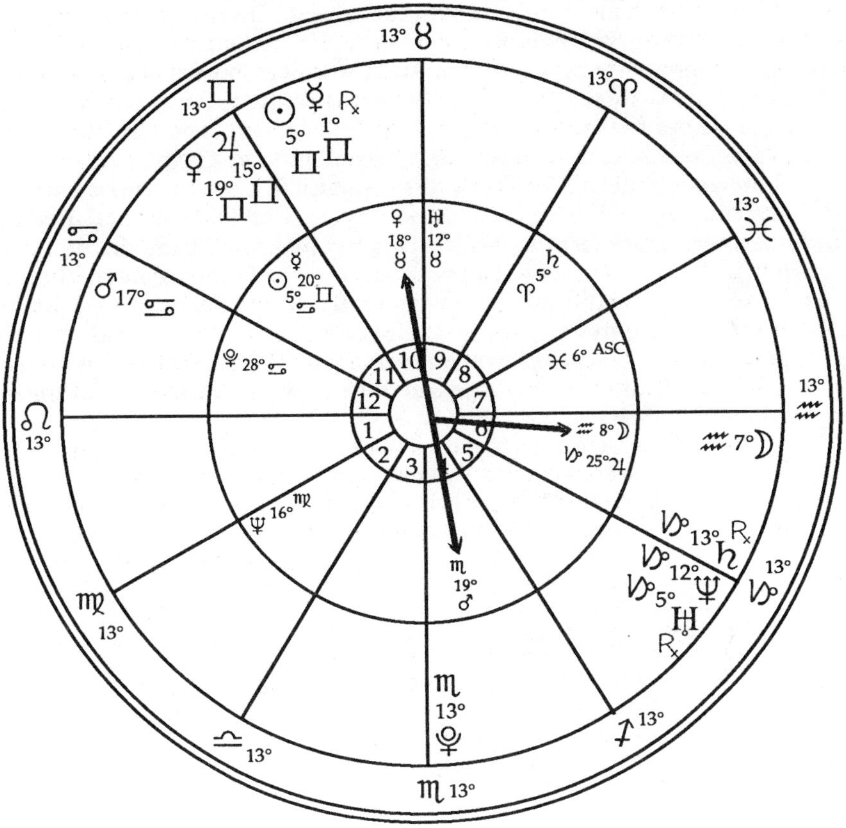

Long Range Trends

TREND SETTERS			CONDITIONERS		INTENSIFIERS		TRIGGERS		
PLUTO	NEPTUNE	URANUS	SATURN	JUPITER	MARS	SUN	MOON	MERCURY	VENUS
		♅ ✶ ASC ☍ ☉ 2/89 TO 9/89		♃ △ ASC ☌ ☉ 8/21/89	♂ □ ☉ 9/89	☉ □ ☉ 9/89	☽ □ ☉ 9/29/89		

planets, if not previously recorded in their progressed positions, will have to be rechecked for their positions for the period or periods desired.

To offer another complete and detailed synthesis of the key cycle chart only would be to reiterate what has been said. You need only refer to those already offered. The key cycle makes everything visible at a glance for whatever period of time you may wish and with complete accuracy with respects to the changes in behavioral dynamics. This is because of the ascending sign will be the temporary ascendant for the time it remains there with its own house affairs. The individual temporarily will behave in the nature of that sign and the characteristics of the planet that rules it and these, accordingly, with its influence by aspects, signs, and houses it rules in both natal and key cycle charts.

The house occupied by the key cycle ascendant in the natal chart has priority while it remains there. The house in the key cycle chart that the natal ascendant occupies also has a high priority with the planet that rules it, and in both charts.

Sufficient data complete with procedures, illustrations, calculations, and syntheses with the methodology for using them has been offered for your examination. You are free to explore their use in your own life and derive the greater meaning for living that it can reveal to you. What's it all about, you ask? You are what it's all about. Perhaps one of the following Einstein quotations will shed more light on the subject.

> "Everything has a reason, there's a reason for everything."
> "The cause and effect, the action and reaction."
> "God didn't play dice with the Cosmos."

> "We are born to search after truth;
> to possess it belongs to a greater power."
> --Montaigne

Bibliography

Helena Curtis, *Biology*. New York: Worth Publishers, Inc., 1979.
Nicholas deVore, *Encyclopedia of Astrology*. New York: Philosophical Library, 1947.
George Gamow, *Biography of the Earth*. New York: Mentor Books, 1948.
Donald C. Johanson and Edey A. Maitland, *Lucy: The Beginnings of Humankind*. New York: Simon and Schuster, 1981.
Robert M. Liebert and Michael D. Spiegler, *Personality, Strategies and Issues*. Homewood, Ill.: The Dorsey Press, 1978.
James H. Otto and Albert Towle, *Modern Biology*. New York: Holt, Rinehart, and Winston, 1965.
Richard M. Restak, M.D., *The Brain—The Last Frontier*. New York: Warner Books, 1975.
J. O. Thorne and T. C. Collocott, *Chambers Biographical Dictionary*. London, England: Butler and Tanner, Ltd.
Lyall Watson, *Supernature*. Garden City, N.Y.: Anchor Press/Doubleday, 1973.
Herbert S. Zim and Robert H. Baker, *Stars*. Racine: Western Publishing Co. Inc., 1975.

Dailies and Periodicals

The Boston Globe
The Boston Herald-American
The National Enquirer
Star
Atlantic Monthly
Time

Appendices

Appendix 1:

The American Ephemeris 1940 Through 1994

SIDEREAL . . . SUN . . . MOON . . . MERCURY . . . VENUS . . . MARS . . . JUPITER . . . SATURN . . . URANUS . . . NEPTUNE . . . PLUTO . . .

DAY	TIME	☉	☽	☿	♀	♂	♃	♄	♅	♆	♇
	h m s	° ' "	° '	° '	° '	° '	° '	° '	° '	° '	° '
J 1	6 38 2	9♑25 7	23♍40	22♐10	8♒18	27♓58	1♈ 9	24♈26	18♉16	25♍31	2♌15
A 2	6 41 58	10 26 16	7♎46	23 37	9 32	28 38	1 16	24 26	18R15	25R31	2R14
N 3	6 45 55	11 27 25	21 39	25 4	10 46	29 19	1 24	24 27	18 13	25 31	2 13
U 4	6 49 52	12 28 35	5♏20	26 33	12 1	0O 0	1 31	24 28	18 12	25 30	2 12
A 5	6 53 48	13 29 46	18 48	28 1	13 15	0♈41	1 39	24 28	18 11	25 30	2 10
R 6	6 57 45	14 30 56	2♐ 5	29 30	14 29	1 21	1 47	24 29	18 10	25 30	2 9
Y 7	7 1 41	15 32 7	15 12	1♑ 0	15 43	2 2	1 55	24 30	18 9	25 30	2 8
8	7 5 38	16 33 17	28 8	2 30	16 57	2 43	2 3	24 32	18 8	25 29	2 7
9	7 9 34	17 34 28	10♑53	4 1	18 12	3 24	2 11	24 33	18 7	25 29	2 5
10	7 13 31	18 35 38	23 26	5 32	19 26	4 4	2 19	24 34	18 6	25 28	2 4
11	7 17 28	19 36 48	5♒48	7 4	20 40	4 45	2 28	24 36	18 5	25 28	2 3
12	7 21 24	20 37 58	17 58	8 36	21 54	5 26	2 37	24 37	18 4	25 27	2 1
13	7 25 21	21 39 7	29 58	10 8	23 8	6 7	2 45	24 39	18 4	25 27	2 0
14	7 29 17	22 40 16	11♓51	11 41	24 22	6 48	2 54	24 41	18 3	25 26	1 59
15	7 33 14	23 41 24	23 39	13 14	25 36	7 29	3 3	24 43	18 2	25 26	1 57
16	7 37 10	24 42 31	5♈27	14 48	26 49	8 10	3 13	24 45	18 2	25 25	1 56
17	7 41 7	25 43 38	17 19	16 23	28 3	8 51	3 22	24 47	18 1	25 25	1 55
18	7 45 3	26 44 43	29 22	17 58	29 17	9 31	3 32	24 49	18 1	25 24	1 53
19	7 49 0	27 45 49	11♉40	19 33	0♓31	10 12	3 41	24 52	18 0	25 23	1 52
20	7 52 56	28 46 53	24 19	21 9	1 44	10 53	3 51	24 54	18 0	25 23	1 51
21	7 56 53	29 47 56	7♊23	22 46	2 58	11 34	4 1	24 57	18 0	25 22	1 49
22	8 0 50	0♒48 59	20 56	24 23	4 12	12 15	4 11	24 59	17 59	25 21	1 48
23	8 4 46	1 50 0	4♋58	26 0	5 25	12 56	4 21	25 2	17 59	25 20	1 47
24	8 8 43	2 51 1	19 26	27 39	6 39	13 37	4 31	25 5	17 59	25 19	1 45
25	8 12 39	3 52 1	4♌14	29 18	7 52	14 18	4 42	25 8	17 59	25 19	1 44
26	8 16 36	4 53 0	19 13	0♒57	9 5	14 59	4 52	25 11	17D59	25 18	1 43
27	8 20 32	5 53 59	4♍15	2 37	10 19	15 40	5 3	25 14	17 59	25 17	1 41
28	8 24 29	6 54 56	19 9	4 18	11 32	16 20	5 13	25 17	17 59	25 16	1 40
29	8 28 26	7 55 53	3♎48	5 59	12 45	17 1	5 24	25 21	17 59	25 15	1 38
30	8 32 22	8 56 49	18 9	7 42	13 58	17 42	5 35	25 24	17 59	25 14	1 37
31	8 36 19	9♒57 45	2♏ 8	9♒24	15♓11	18♈23	5♈46	25♈28	17♉59	25♍13	1♌36

THF SUN ENTERS THE SIGN OF AQUARIUS ON JAN 21 AT 04:44.

DAY	TIME	☉	☽	☿	♀	♂	♃	♄	♅	♆	♇
	h m s	° ' "	° '	° '	° '	° '	° '	° '	° '	° '	° '
F 1	8 40 15	10♒58 40	15♏47	11♒ 8	16♓24	19♈ 4	5♈57	25♈31	17♉59	25♍12	1♌34
E 2	8 44 12	11 59 34	29 7	12 52	17 37	19 45	6 8	25 35	18 0	25R11	1R33
B 3	8 48 8	13 0 27	12♐11	14 37	18 50	20 26	6 20	25 39	18 0	25 9	1 32
R 4	8 52 5	14 1 20	25 0	16 22	20 3	21 7	6 31	25 43	18 1	25 8	1 30
U 5	8 56 1	15 2 12	7♑38	18 8	21 15	21 47	6 43	25 47	18 1	25 7	1 29
A 6	8 59 58	16 3 3	20 4	19 55	22 28	22 28	6 54	25 51	18 1	25 6	1 28
R 7	9 3 55	17 3 52	2♒22	21 42	23 41	23 9	7 6	25 55	18 2	25 5	1 27
Y 8	9 7 51	18 4 41	14 31	23 30	24 53	23 50	7 18	25 59	18 3	25 3	1 25
9	9 11 48	19 5 28	26 32	25 19	26 6	24 31	7 30	26 4	18 3	25 2	1 24
10	9 15 44	20 6 14	8♓26	27 7	27 18	25 11	7 42	26 8	18 4	25 1	1 23
11	9 19 41	21 6 58	20 16	28 56	28 30	25 52	7 54	26 13	18 5	25 0	1 21
12	9 23 37	22 7 41	2♈ 3	0♓45	29 42	26 33	8 6	26 17	18 6	24 58	1 20
13	9 27 34	23 8 22	13 51	2 35	0♈55	27 14	8 18	26 22	18 7	24 57	1 19
14	9 31 30	24 9 2	25 43	4 24	2 7	27 55	8 31	26 27	18 7	24 56	1 18
15	9 35 27	25 9 40	7♉44	6 12	3 18	28 35	8 43	26 32	18 8	24 54	1 16
16	9 39 23	26 10 17	19 59	8 0	4 30	29 16	8 55	26 37	18 9	24 53	1 15
17	9 43 20	27 10 52	2♊34	9 47	5 42	29 57	9 8	26 42	18 11	24 51	1 14
18	9 47 17	28 11 25	15 32	11 33	6 54	0♉37	9 21	26 47	18 12	24 50	1 13
19	9 51 13	29 11 56	28 59	13 18	8 5	1 18	9 33	26 52	18 13	24 49	1 12
20	9 55 10	0♓12 25	12♋56	15 0	9 17	1 59	9 46	26 57	18 14	24 47	1 11
21	9 59 6	1 12 53	27 21	16 40	10 28	2 39	9 59	27 3	18 15	24 46	1 9
22	10 3 3	2 13 19	12♌12	18 16	11 39	3 20	10 12	27 8	18 17	24 44	1 8
23	10 6 59	3 13 43	27 20	19 49	12 50	4 1	10 25	27 13	18 18	24 43	1 7
24	10 10 56	4 14 5	12♍36	21 18	14 1	4 41	10 38	27 19	18 19	24 41	1 6
25	10 14 52	5 14 26	27 48	22 43	15 12	5 22	10 51	27 25	18 21	24 39	1 5
26	10 18 49	6 14 45	12♎48	24 1	16 23	6 2	11 4	27 30	18 22	24 38	1 4
27	10 22 46	7 15 2	27 27	25 14	17 33	6 43	11 17	27 36	18 24	24 36	1 3
28	10 26 42	8 15 19	11♏43	26 20	18 44	7 23	11 31	27 42	18 26	24 35	1 2
29	10 30 39	9♓15 33	25♏32	27♓19	19♈54	8♉ 4	11♈44	27♈48	18♉27	24♍33	1♌ 1

THE SUN ENTERS THE SIGN OF PISCES ON FEB 19 AT 19:04.

DAY	TIME	☉	☽	☿	♀	♂	♃	♄	♅	♆	♇
	h m s	° ' "	° '	° '	° '	° '	° '	° '	° '	° '	° '
M 1	10 34 35	10♓15 47	8♐57	28♓10	21♈ 5	8♉44	11♈57	27♈54	18♉29	24♍32	1♌ 0
A 2	10 38 32	11 15 59	21 59	28 53	22 15	9 25	12 11	28 0	18 31	24R30	0R59
R 3	10 42 28	12 16 9	4♑43	29 27	23 25	10 5	12 24	28 6	18 33	24 28	0 58
C 4	10 46 25	13 16 18	17 11	29 52	24 35	10 46	12 38	28 12	18 34	24 27	0 57
H 5	10 50 21	14 16 25	29 26	0♈ 8	25 44	11 26	12 52	28 18	18 36	24 25	0 56
6	10 54 18	15 16 30	11♒31	0R15	26 54	12 7	13 5	28 24	18 38	24 24	0 55
7	10 58 15	16 16 34	23 29	0 12	28 3	12 47	13 19	28 31	18 40	24 22	0 54
8	11 2 11	17 16 36	5♓23	0 1	29 13	13 27	13 33	28 37	18 42	24 20	0 53
9	11 6 8	18 16 36	17 12	29♓41	0♉22	14 8	13 46	28 43	18 44	24 19	0 52
10	11 10 4	19 16 34	29 0	29 13	1 31	14 48	14 0	28 50	18 46	24 17	0 51
11	11 14 1	20 16 30	10♈49	28 38	2 40	15 28	14 14	28 56	18 48	24 15	0 51
12	11 17 57	21 16 24	22 40	27 56	3 48	16 8	14 28	29 3	18 51	24 14	0 50
13	11 21 54	22 16 16	4♉37	27 9	4 57	16 49	14 42	29 10	18 53	24 12	0 49
14	11 25 50	23 16 6	16 43	26 18	6 5	17 29	14 56	29 16	18 55	24 10	0 48
15	11 29 47	24 15 54	29 1	25 23	7 13	18 9	15 10	29 23	18 57	24 9	0 48
16	11 33 43	25 15 40	11♊36	24 27	8 21	18 49	15 24	29 30	19 0	24 7	0 47
17	11 37 40	26 15 23	24 31	23 30	9 29	19 30	15 38	29 37	19 2	24 5	0 46
18	11 41 37	27 15 4	7♋51	22 34	10 37	20 10	15 52	29 43	19 5	24 4	0 46
19	11 45 33	28 14 43	21 37	21 40	11 44	20 50	16 7	29 50	19 7	24 2	0 45
20	11 49 30	29 14 19	5♌50	20 49	12 51	21 30	16 21	29 57	19 10	24 0	0 44
21	11 53 26	0♈13 53	20 27	20 1	13 58	22 10	16 35	0♉ 4	19 12	23 59	0 44
22	11 57 23	1 13 25	5♍26	19 18	15 5	22 50	16 49	0 11	19 15	23 57	0 43
23	12 1 19	2 12 55	20 36	18 40	16 12	23 30	17 3	0 18	19 17	23 55	0 43
24	12 5 16	3 12 22	5♎50	18 7	17 18	24 10	17 18	0 25	19 20	23 54	0 42
25	12 9 12	4 11 48	20 57	17 40	18 24	24 50	17 32	0 32	19 22	23 52	0 42
26	12 13 9	5 11 12	5♏48	17 19	19 30	25 30	17 46	0 40	19 25	23 50	0 41
27	12 17 6	6 10 33	20 17	17 3	20 36	26 10	18 1	0 47	19 28	23 49	0 41
28	12 21 2	7 9 53	4♐20	16 54	21 41	26 50	18 15	0 54	19 31	23 47	0 40
29	12 24 59	8 9 12	17 55	16D50	22 47	27 30	18 29	1 1	19 33	23 46	0 40
30	12 28 55	9 8 28	1♑ 5	16 52	23 51	28 9	18 44	1 8	19 36	23 44	0 39
31	12 32 52	10♈ 7 43	13♑51	17♓ 0	24♉56	28♉49	18♈58	1♉16	19♉39	23♍42	0♌39

THE SUN ENTERS THE SIGN OF ARIES ON MAR 20 AT 18:24.

♈	ARIES	♉	TAURUS	♊	GEMINI	♋	CANCER	♌	LEO	♍	VIRGO	♎	LIBRA

SIDEREAL . SUN . . MOON . . MERCURY . . VENUS . . MARS . . JUPITER . . SATURN . . URANUS . . NEPTUNE . . PLUTO .

DAY	TIME	☉	☽	☿	♀	♂	♃	♄	♅	♆	♇
	h m s	° ' "	° '	° '	° '	° '	° '	° '	° '	° '	° '
A 1	12 36 48	11♈ 6 56	26♑18	17♓13	26♉ 1	29♉29	19♈13	1♉23	19♉42	23♍41	0♌39
P 2	12 40 45	12 6 7	8♒30	17 31	27 5	0♊ 9	19 27	1 30	19 45	23R39	0R38
R 3	12 44 41	13 5 16	20 30	17 54	28 8	0 49	19 41	1 38	19 48	23 38	0 38
I 4	12 48 38	14 4 24	2♓22	18 21	29 12	1 28	19 56	1 45	19 51	23 36	0 38
L 5	12 52 35	15 3 29	14 11	18 53	0♊15	2 8	20 10	1 53	19 54	23 35	0 38
6	12 56 31	16 2 33	25 59	19 29	1 18	2 48	20 25	2 0	19 57	23 33	0 37
7	13 0 28	17 1 34	7♈48	20 9	2 21	3 27	20 39	2 8	20 0	23 32	0 37
8	13 4 24	18 0 34	19 41	20 53	3 23	4 7	20 54	2 15	20 3	23 30	0 37
9	13 8 21	18 59 32	1♉41	21 40	4 25	4 47	21 8	2 23	20 6	23 29	0 37
10	13 12 17	19 58 27	13 48	22 30	5 27	5 26	21 23	2 30	20 9	23 27	0 37
11	13 16 14	20 57 21	26 6	23 24	6 28	6 6	21 37	2 38	20 12	23 26	0 37
12	13 20 10	21 56 12	8♊35	24 21	7 29	6 45	21 52	2 45	20 15	23 24	0 37
13	13 24 7	22 55 2	21 19	25 20	8 30	7 25	22 6	2 53	20 18	23 23	0D37
14	13 28 3	23 53 49	4♋20	26 23	9 30	8 5	22 21	3 1	20 22	23 21	0 37
15	13 32 0	24 52 33	17 39	27 28	10 30	8 44	22 35	3 8	20 25	23 20	0 37
16	13 35 57	25 51 16	1♌18	28 35	11 29	9 23	22 50	3 16	20 28	23 19	0 37
17	13 39 53	26 49 56	15 18	29 45	12 28	10 3	23 4	3 23	20 31	23 17	0 37
18	13 43 50	27 48 34	29 39	0♈58	13 27	10 42	23 19	3 31	20 35	23 16	0 37
19	13 47 46	28 47 10	14♍17	2 12	14 25	11 22	23 33	3 39	20 38	23 15	0 37
20	13 51 43	29 45 43	29 8	3 29	15 22	12 1	23 47	3 46	20 41	23 14	0 37
21	13 55 39	0♉44 14	14♎ 6	4 48	16 19	12 40	24 2	3 54	20 44	23 12	0 38
22	13 59 36	1 42 44	29 2	6 9	17 16	13 20	24 16	4 2	20 48	23 11	0 38
23	14 3 32	2 41 11	13♏49	7 32	18 12	13 59	24 31	4 9	20 51	23 10	0 38
24	14 7 29	3 39 37	28 20	8 57	19 7	14 38	24 45	4 17	20 54	23 9	0 38
25	14 11 26	4 38 1	12♐28	10 24	20 2	15 18	24 59	4 25	20 58	23 7	0 39
26	14 15 22	5 36 24	26 11	11 52	20 56	15 57	25 14	4 32	21 1	23 6	0 39
27	14 19 19	6 34 44	9♑27	13 23	21 50	16 36	25 28	4 40	21 5	23 5	0 39
28	14 23 15	7 33 4	22 19	14 56	22 43	17 15	25 42	4 47	21 8	23 4	0 40
29	14 27 12	8 31 21	4♒50	16 30	23 36	17 54	25 57	4 55	21 11	23 3	0 40
30	14 31 8	9♉29 37	17♒ 3	18♈ 6	24♊28	18♊34	26♈11	5♉ 3	21♉15	23♍ 2	0♌40

THE SUN ENTERS THE SIGN OF TAURUS ON APR 20 AT 05:51.

DAY	TIME	☉	☽	☿	♀	♂	♃	♄	♅	♆	♇
	h m s	° ' "	° '	° '	° '	° '	° '	° '	° '	° '	° '
M 1	14 35 5	10♉27 52	29♒ 2	19♈45	25♊19	19♊13	26♈25	5♉10	21♉18	23♍ 1	0♌41
A 2	14 39 1	11 26 5	10♓54	21 25	26 9	19 52	26 39	5 18	21 22	23R 0	0 41
Y 3	14 42 58	12 24 16	22 41	23 7	26 59	20 31	26 54	5 26	21 25	22 59	0 42
4	14 46 55	13 22 26	4♈30	24 50	27 48	21 10	27 8	5 33	21 29	22 58	0 42
5	14 50 51	14 20 35	16 23	26 36	28 36	21 49	27 22	5 41	21 32	22 57	0 43
6	14 54 48	15 18 42	28 23	28 23	29 23	22 28	27 36	5 49	21 36	22 56	0 44
7	14 58 44	16 16 47	10♉33	0♉13	0♋10	23 7	27 50	5 56	21 39	22 55	0 44
8	15 2 41	17 14 51	22 55	2 4	0 56	23 46	28 4	6 4	21 43	22 55	0 45
9	15 6 37	18 12 53	5♊30	3 57	1 40	24 25	28 18	6 11	21 46	22 54	0 45
10	15 10 34	19 10 53	18 18	5 52	2 24	25 4	28 32	6 19	21 49	22 53	0 46
11	15 14 30	20 8 52	1♋20	7 49	3 7	25 43	28 46	6 26	21 53	22 52	0 47
12	15 18 27	21 6 49	14 36	9 47	3 49	26 22	29 0	6 34	21 56	22 52	0 47
13	15 22 24	22 4 44	28 5	11 47	4 30	27 1	29 14	6 41	22 0	22 51	0 48
14	15 26 20	23 2 38	11♌48	13 49	5 9	27 40	29 28	6 49	22 3	22 50	0 49
15	15 30 17	24 0 29	25 43	15 53	5 48	28 18	29 42	6 56	22 7	22 50	0 50
16	15 34 13	24 58 19	9♍51	17 58	6 25	28 57	29 55	7 4	22 10	22 49	0 51
17	15 38 10	25 56 7	24 11	20 5	7 1	29 36	0♉ 9	7 11	22 14	22 48	0 51
18	15 42 6	26 53 53	8♎39	22 13	7 36	0♋15	0 23	7 18	22 17	22 48	0 52
19	15 46 3	27 51 38	23 12	24 22	8 9	0 54	0 36	7 26	22 21	22 47	0 53
20	15 49 59	28 49 21	7♏46	26 33	8 41	1 32	0 50	7 33	22 24	22 47	0 54
21	15 53 56	29 47 3	22 14	28 43	9 12	2 11	1 4	7 40	22 28	22 46	0 55
22	15 57 53	0♊44 43	6♐31	0♊55	9 41	2 50	1 17	7 48	22 31	22 46	0 56
23	16 1 49	1 42 22	20 31	3 7	10 8	3 29	1 31	7 55	22 35	22 46	0 57
24	16 5 46	2 40 0	4♑11	5 18	10 34	4 7	1 44	8 2	22 38	22 45	0 58
25	16 9 42	3 37 37	17 28	7 30	10 58	4 46	1 57	8 9	22 42	22 45	0 59
26	16 13 39	4 35 13	0♒22	9 41	11 21	5 25	2 11	8 17	22 45	22 45	1 0
27	16 17 35	5 32 47	12 54	11 51	11 41	6 3	2 24	8 24	22 48	22 44	1 1
28	16 21 32	6 30 21	25 9	13 59	12 0	6 42	2 37	8 31	22 52	22 44	1 2
29	16 25 28	7 27 54	7♓ 9	16 7	12 17	7 20	2 50	8 38	22 55	22 44	1 3
30	16 29 25	8 25 26	19 1	18 13	12 32	7 59	3 3	8 45	22 59	22 44	1 4
31	16 33 22	9♊22 57	0♈50	20♊17	12♋45	8♋38	3♉16	8♉52	23♉ 2	22♍44	1♌ 5

THE SUN ENTERS THE SIGN OF GEMINI ON MAY 21 AT 05:23.

DAY	TIME	☉	☽	☿	♀	♂	♃	♄	♅	♆	♇
	h m s	° ' "	° '	° '	° '	° '	° '	° '	° '	° '	° '
J 1	16 37 18	10♊20 28	12♈40	22♊20	12♋56	9♋16	3♉29	8♉59	23♉ 5	22♍44	1♌ 5
U 2	16 41 15	11 17 57	24 36	24 20	13 5	9 55	3 42	9 6	23 9	22R44	1 8
N 3	16 45 11	12 15 26	6♉43	26 18	13 12	10 33	3 55	9 13	23 12	22D44	1 9
E 4	16 49 8	13 12 54	19 4	28 14	13 16	11 12	4 8	9 19	23 15	22 44	1 10
5	16 53 4	14 10 21	1♊41	0♋ 7	13R18	11 50	4 20	9 26	23 19	22 44	1 11
6	16 57 1	15 7 48	14 35	1 58	13 18	12 29	4 33	9 33	23 22	22 44	1 12
7	17 0 57	16 5 13	27 45	3 46	13 15	13 7	4 45	9 40	23 25	22 44	1 14
8	17 4 54	17 2 38	11♋11	5 32	13 10	13 46	4 58	9 46	23 29	22 44	1 15
9	17 8 51	18 0 2	24 50	7 15	13 3	14 24	5 10	9 53	23 32	22 44	1 16
10	17 12 47	18 57 24	8♌39	8 56	12 53	15 3	5 23	9 59	23 35	22 44	1 17
11	17 16 44	19 54 46	22 35	10 34	12 41	15 41	5 35	10 6	23 38	22 44	1 19
12	17 20 40	20 52 7	6♍38	12 10	12 27	16 19	5 47	10 12	23 42	22 45	1 20
13	17 24 37	21 49 26	20 44	13 42	12 10	16 58	5 59	10 19	23 45	22 45	1 21
14	17 28 33	22 46 45	4♎53	15 12	11 50	17 36	6 11	10 25	23 48	22 45	1 23
15	17 32 30	23 44 2	19 3	16 40	11 29	18 15	6 23	10 32	23 51	22 46	1 24
16	17 36 26	24 41 19	3♏14	18 4	11 5	18 53	6 35	10 38	23 54	22 46	1 26
17	17 40 23	25 38 35	17 22	19 26	10 39	19 31	6 47	10 44	23 57	22 47	1 27
18	17 44 20	26 35 50	1♐25	20 45	10 12	20 10	6 59	10 50	24 0	22 47	1 28
19	17 48 16	27 33 5	15 19	22 1	9 42	20 48	7 10	10 56	24 3	22 47	1 30
20	17 52 13	28 30 19	29 1	23 14	9 10	21 26	7 22	11 2	24 6	22 48	1 31
21	17 56 9	29 27 32	12♑26	24 24	8 38	22 4	7 33	11 8	24 9	22 49	1 33
22	18 0 6	0♋24 46	25 34	25 32	8 3	22 43	7 45	11 14	24 12	22 49	1 34
23	18 4 2	1 21 59	8♒22	26 36	7 28	23 21	7 56	11 20	24 15	22 50	1 36
24	18 7 59	2 19 11	20 51	27 37	6 52	23 59	8 7	11 26	24 18	22 50	1 37
25	18 11 55	3 16 24	3♓ 4	28 34	6 15	24 38	8 18	11 31	24 21	22 51	1 39
26	18 15 52	4 13 36	15 4	29 29	5 37	25 16	8 29	11 37	24 24	22 52	1 40
27	18 19 49	5 10 49	26 56	0♌20	5 0	25 54	8 40	11 43	24 27	22 52	1 42
28	18 23 45	6 8 1	8♈45	1 7	4 22	26 32	8 51	11 48	24 30	22 53	1 43
29	18 27 42	7 5 14	20 36	1 51	3 45	27 10	9 1	11 54	24 32	22 54	1 45
30	18 31 38	8♋ 2 26	2♉34	2♌30	3♋ 8	27♋49	9♉12	11♉59	24♉35	22♍55	1♌46

THE SUN ENTERS THE SIGN OF CANCER ON JUN 21 AT 13:37.

♏ SCORPIO ♐ SAGITTARIUS ♑ CAPRICORN ♒ AQUARIUS ♓ PISCES

SIDEREAL SUN MOON MERCURY VENUS MARS JUPITER SATURN URANUS NEPTUNE PLUTO

DAY	TIME	☉	☽	☿	♀	♂	♃	♄	♅	♆	♇
	h m s	° ' "	° '	° '	° '	° '	° '	° '	° '	° '	° '
J 1	18 35 35	8♋59 39	14♉45	3♌ 6	2♋32	28♋27	9♉22	12♉ 5	24♉38	22♍56	1♌48
U 2	18 39 31	9 56 52	27 13	3 38	1R57	29 5	9 33	12 10	24 41	22 57	1 50
L 3	18 43 28	10 54 5	10♊ 1	4 6	1 23	29 43	9 43	12 15	24 43	22 58	1 51
Y 4	18 47 24	11 51 18	23 11	4 29	0 51	0♌21	9 53	12 20	24 46	22 58	1 53
5	18 51 21	12 48 32	6♋42	4 48	0 20	1 0	10 3	12 25	24 49	22 59	1 54
6	18 55 18	13 45 45	20 31	5 3	29♊51	1 38	10 13	12 30	24 51	23 0	1 56
7	18 59 14	14 42 58	4♌35	5 12	29 23	2 16	10 23	12 35	24 54	23 2	1 58
8	19 3 11	15 40 12	18 49	5R18	28 58	2 54	10 33	12 40	24 56	23 3	1 59
9	19 7 7	16 37 25	3♍ 8	5 18	28 35	3 32	10 42	12 45	24 59	23 4	2 1
10	19 11 4	17 34 38	17 27	5 14	28 13	4 10	10 52	12 49	25 1	23 5	2 3
11	19 15 0	18 31 51	1♎42	5 5	27 54	4 49	11 1	12 54	25 3	23 6	2 4
12	19 18 57	19 29 4	15 52	4 51	27 38	5 27	11 10	12 58	25 6	23 7	2 6
13	19 22 53	20 26 17	29 56	4 33	27 23	6 5	11 19	13 3	25 8	23 8	2 7
14	19 26 50	21 23 30	13♏52	4 11	27 12	6 43	11 28	13 7	25 10	23 10	2 9
15	19 30 47	22 20 43	27 40	3 44	27 2	7 21	11 37	13 11	25 13	23 11	2 11
16	19 34 43	23 17 56	11♐20	3 14	26 55	7 59	11 46	13 16	25 15	23 12	2 12
17	19 38 40	24 15 9	24 49	2 40	26 50	8 37	11 55	13 20	25 17	23 13	2 14
18	19 42 36	25 12 23	8♑ 8	2 4	26D47	9 15	12 3	13 24	25 19	23 15	2 16
19	19 46 33	26 9 37	21 13	1 25	26 47	9 54	12 11	13 28	25 21	23 16	2 18
20	19 50 29	27 6 51	4♒ 3	0 44	26 50	10 32	12 20	13 32	25 23	23 18	2 19
21	19 54 26	28 4 6	16 39	0 3	26 54	11 10	12 28	13 35	25 25	23 19	2 21
22	19 58 23	29 1 21	29 0	29♋21	27 1	11 48	12 36	13 39	25 27	23 20	2 23
23	20 2 19	29 58 38	11♓ 7	28 40	27 10	12 26	12 43	13 43	25 29	23 22	2 24
24	20 6 16	0♌55 55	23 4	27 59	27 20	13 4	12 51	13 46	25 31	23 23	2 26
25	20 10 12	1 53 12	4♈54	27 21	27 33	13 42	12 58	13 49	25 33	23 25	2 28
26	20 14 9	2 50 31	16 42	26 46	27 49	14 20	13 6	13 53	25 35	23 26	2 29
27	20 18 5	3 47 50	28 32	26 13	28 6	14 58	13 13	13 56	25 36	23 28	2 31
28	20 22 2	4 45 11	10♉31	25 45	28 24	15 36	13 20	13 59	25 38	23 30	2 33
29	20 25 58	5 42 33	22 43	25 21	28 45	16 14	13 27	14 2	25 40	23 31	2 34
30	20 29 55	6 39 56	5♊13	25 2	29 7	16 52	13 34	14 5	25 42	23 33	2 36
31	20 33 51	7♌37 19	18♊ 5	24♋48	29♊32	17♌31	13♉40	14♉ 8	25♉43	23♍34	2♌38

THE SUN ENTERS THE SIGN OF LEO ON JUL 23 AT 00:35.

DAY	TIME	☉	☽	☿	♀	♂	♃	♄	♅	♆	♇
	h m s	° ' "	° '	° '	° '	° '	° '	° '	° '	° '	° '
A 1	20 37 48	8♌34 44	1♋23	24♋40	29♊57	18♌ 9	13♉47	14♉11	25♉45	23♍36	2♌40
U 2	20 41 45	9 32 10	15 6	24D39	0♋25	18 47	13 53	14 13	25 46	23 38	2 41
G 3	20 45 41	10 29 37	29 12	24 43	0 54	19 25	13 59	14 16	25 48	23 40	2 43
U 4	20 49 38	11 27 5	13♌37	24 54	1 24	20 3	14 5	14 18	25 49	23 41	2 45
S 5	20 53 34	12 24 34	28 15	25 12	1 56	20 41	14 11	14 21	25 50	23 43	2 46
T 6	20 57 31	13 22 4	12♍59	25 36	2 29	21 19	14 16	14 23	25 52	23 45	2 48
7	21 1 27	14 19 35	27 40	26 7	3 3	21 57	14 22	14 25	25 53	23 47	2 50
8	21 5 24	15 17 6	12♎13	26 44	3 39	22 35	14 27	14 27	25 54	23 48	2 51
9	21 9 20	16 14 38	26 35	27 28	4 16	23 13	14 32	14 29	25 55	23 50	2 53
10	21 13 17	17 12 11	10♏42	28 19	4 54	23 52	14 37	14 31	25 56	23 52	2 55
11	21 17 14	18 9 45	24 35	29 16	5 33	24 30	14 42	14 33	25 58	23 54	2 56
12	21 21 10	19 7 20	8♐13	0♌19	6 13	25 8	14 47	14 35	25 59	23 56	2 58
13	21 25 7	20 4 56	21 36	1 28	6 54	25 46	14 51	14 36	26 0	23 58	3 0
14	21 29 3	21 2 33	4♑46	2 43	7 37	26 24	14 55	14 38	26 0	24 0	3 1
15	21 33 0	22 0 10	17 43	4 3	8 20	27 2	14 59	14 39	26 1	24 2	3 3
16	21 36 56	22 57 49	0♒28	5 29	9 4	27 40	15 3	14 40	26 2	24 4	3 4
17	21 40 53	23 55 29	13 0	6 59	9 49	28 18	15 7	14 41	26 3	24 6	3 6
18	21 44 49	24 53 11	25 20	8 34	10 35	28 56	15 10	14 42	26 4	24 8	3 8
19	21 48 46	25 50 53	7♓29	10 14	11 22	29 35	15 14	14 43	26 4	24 10	3 9
20	21 52 43	26 48 37	19 29	11 57	12 10	0♍13	15 17	14 44	26 5	24 12	3 11
21	21 56 39	27 46 22	1♈22	13 43	12 58	0 51	15 20	14 45	26 6	24 14	3 12
22	22 0 36	28 44 9	13 10	15 32	13 47	1 29	15 22	14 45	26 6	24 16	3 14
23	22 4 32	29 41 58	24 56	17 24	14 37	2 7	15 25	14 46	26 7	24 18	3 15
24	22 8 29	0♍39 48	6♉46	19 18	15 28	2 45	15 27	14 46	26 7	24 20	3 17
25	22 12 25	1 37 41	18 44	21 14	16 19	3 24	15 30	14 47	26 8	24 22	3 19
26	22 16 22	2 35 35	0♊55	23 10	17 11	4 2	15 32	14 47	26 8	24 24	3 20
27	22 20 18	3 33 30	13 23	25 8	18 4	4 40	15 33	14R47	26 8	24 26	3 22
28	22 24 15	4 31 28	26 14	27 6	18 57	5 18	15 35	14 47	26 8	24 28	3 23
29	22 28 12	5 29 27	9♋30	29 5	19 51	5 56	15 36	14 47	26 9	24 30	3 25
30	22 32 8	6 27 29	23 14	1♍ 3	20 45	6 35	15 38	14 47	26 9	24 32	3 26
31	22 36 5	7♍25 32	7♌26	3♍ 2	21♋40	7♍13	15♉39	14♉46	26♉ 9	24♍35	3♌27

THE SUN ENTERS THE SIGN OF VIRGO ON AUG 23 AT 07:29.

DAY	TIME	☉	☽	☿	♀	♂	♃	♄	♅	♆	♇
	h m s	° ' "	° '	° '	° '	° '	° '	° '	° '	° '	° '
S 1	22 40 1	8♍23 37	22♌ 0	4♍59	22♋36	7♍51	15♉40	14♉46	26♉ 9	24♍37	3♌29
E 2	22 43 58	9 21 43	6♍52	6 57	23 32	8 29	15 40	14R45	26R 9	24 39	3 30
P 3	22 47 54	10 19 51	21 54	8 53	24 29	9 7	15 41	14 45	26 9	24 41	3 32
T 4	22 51 51	11 18 1	6♎57	10 49	25 26	9 46	15R41	14 44	26 9	24 43	3 33
E 5	22 55 47	12 16 13	21 51	12 44	26 23	10 24	15 41	14 43	26 8	24 45	3 35
M 6	22 59 44	13 14 26	6♏31	14 38	27 21	11 2	15 41	14 42	26 8	24 48	3 36
B 7	23 3 41	14 12 40	20 52	16 31	28 19	11 41	15 40	14 41	26 8	24 50	3 37
E 8	23 7 37	15 10 56	4♐51	18 22	29 18	12 19	15 40	14 40	26 8	24 52	3 39
R 9	23 11 34	16 9 14	18 29	20 13	0♌17	12 57	15 39	14 38	26 7	24 54	3 40
10	23 15 30	17 7 33	1♑46	22 3	1 17	13 35	15 38	14 37	26 7	24 56	3 41
11	23 19 27	18 5 54	14 45	23 51	2 17	14 14	15 37	14 35	26 6	24 59	3 43
12	23 23 23	19 4 16	27 27	25 38	3 17	14 52	15 35	14 34	26 6	25 1	3 44
13	23 27 20	20 2 40	9♒56	27 25	4 18	15 30	15 34	14 32	26 5	25 3	3 45
14	23 31 16	21 1 5	22 12	29 10	5 19	16 9	15 32	14 30	26 5	25 5	3 46
15	23 35 13	21 59 32	4♓19	0♎54	6 21	16 47	15 30	14 28	26 4	25 7	3 48
16	23 39 9	22 58 1	16 17	2 37	7 23	17 25	15 28	14 26	26 3	25 10	3 49
17	23 43 6	23 56 32	28 10	4 19	8 25	18 4	15 25	14 24	26 3	25 12	3 50
18	23 47 3	24 55 5	9♈59	5 59	9 27	18 42	15 23	14 22	26 2	25 14	3 51
19	23 50 59	25 53 40	21 46	7 39	10 30	19 21	15 20	14 20	26 1	25 16	3 52
20	23 54 56	26 52 16	3♉34	9 18	11 33	19 59	15 17	14 18	26 0	25 19	3 53
21	23 58 52	27 50 55	15 26	10 56	12 37	20 37	15 14	14 15	25 59	25 21	3 54
22	0 2 49	28 49 37	27 26	12 33	13 41	21 16	15 10	14 12	25 58	25 23	3 56
23	0 6 45	29 48 20	9♊37	14 8	14 45	21 54	15 7	14 10	25 57	25 25	3 57
24	0 10 42	0♎47 6	22 4	15 43	15 49	22 33	15 3	14 7	25 56	25 27	3 58
25	0 14 38	1 45 54	4♋51	17 17	16 54	23 11	14 59	14 4	25 55	25 30	3 59
26	0 18 35	2 44 44	18 2	18 50	17 58	23 50	14 55	14 1	25 54	25 32	4 0
27	0 22 32	3 43 36	1♌38	20 22	19 4	24 28	14 51	13 58	25 52	25 34	4 1
28	0 26 28	4 42 31	15 42	21 54	20 9	25 7	14 46	13 55	25 51	25 36	4 2
29	0 30 25	5 41 28	0♍11	23 24	21 15	25 45	14 42	13 52	25 50	25 39	4 3
30	0 34 21	6♎40 27	15♍ 2	24♎53	22♌21	26♍24	14♉37	13♉49	25♉48	25♍41	4♌ 4

THE SUN ENTERS THE SIGN OF LIBRA ON SEP 23 AT 04:47.

♈ ARIES ♉ TAURUS ♊ GEMINI ♋ CANCER ♌ LEO ♍ VIRGO ♎ LIBRA

1940

SIDEREAL · SUN. · MOON.. · MERCURY. · VENUS.. · MARS... · JUPITER. · SATURN. · URANUS. · NEPTUNE. · PLUTO..

DAY	TIME	☉	☽	☿	♀	♂	♃	♄	♅	♆	♇
	h m s	° ' "	° '	° '	° '	° '	° '	° '	° '	° '	° '
O 1	0 38 18	7♎39 28	0♎ 8	26♎22	23♌27	27♍ 2	14♉32	13♉45	25♉47	25♍43	4♌ 4
C 2	0 42 14	8 38 32	15 21	27 50	24 33	27 41	14R27	13R42	25R46	25 45	4 5
T 3	0 46 11	9 37 37	0♏30	29 16	25 40	28 20	14 21	13 38	25 44	25 47	4 6
O 4	0 50 7	10 36 45	15 26	0♏42	26 46	28 58	14 16	13 35	25 43	25 50	4 7
B 5	0 54 4	11 35 54	0♐ 3	2 7	27 53	29 37	14 10	13 31	25 41	25 52	4 8
E 6	0 58 1	12 35 5	14 16	3 30	29 1	0♎16	14 4	13 27	25 39	25 54	4 9
R 7	1 1 57	13 34 18	28 2	4 53	0♍ 8	0 54	13 58	13 24	25 38	25 56	4 9
8	1 5 54	14 33 33	11♑23	6 15	1 16	1 33	13 52	13 20	25 36	25 58	4 10
9	1 9 50	15 32 49	24 19	7 35	2 23	2 12	13 46	13 16	25 34	26 0	4 11
10	1 13 47	16 32 7	6♒56	8 55	3 31	2 50	13 40	13 12	25 33	26 2	4 11
11	1 17 43	17 31 27	19 15	10 13	4 39	3 29	13 33	13 8	25 31	26 4	4 12
12	1 21 40	18 30 49	1♓21	11 30	5 48	4 8	13 27	13 4	25 29	26 7	4 13
13	1 25 36	19 30 12	13 18	12 46	6 56	4 46	13 20	12 59	25 27	26 9	4 13
14	1 29 33	20 29 37	25 9	14 0	8 5	5 25	13 13	12 55	25 25	26 11	4 14
15	1 33 29	21 29 5	6♈58	15 12	9 14	6 4	13 6	12 51	25 23	26 13	4 15
16	1 37 26	22 28 34	18 45	16 23	10 23	6 43	12 59	12 47	25 21	26 15	4 15
17	1 41 23	23 28 5	0♉35	17 32	11 32	7 21	12 52	12 42	25 19	26 17	4 16
18	1 45 19	24 27 39	12 28	18 39	12 42	8 0	12 44	12 38	25 17	26 19	4 16
19	1 49 16	25 27 14	24 28	19 44	13 51	8 39	12 37	12 33	25 15	26 21	4 17
20	1 53 12	26 26 52	6♊35	20 47	15 1	9 18	12 29	12 29	25 13	26 23	4 17
21	1 57 9	27 26 32	18 54	21 46	16 11	9 57	12 22	12 24	25 11	26 25	4 17
22	2 1 5	28 26 14	1♋25	22 43	17 21	10 36	12 14	12 20	25 9	26 27	4 18
23	2 5 2	29 25 58	14 12	23 37	18 31	11 15	12 6	12 15	25 7	26 29	4 18
24	2 8 58	0♏25 45	27 19	24 27	19 41	11 54	11 58	12 10	25 5	26 31	4 18
25	2 12 55	1 25 34	10♌46	25 14	20 52	12 33	11 51	12 6	25 2	26 33	4 19
26	2 16 52	2 25 25	24 37	25 56	22 2	13 12	11 43	12 1	25 0	26 35	4 19
27	2 20 48	3 25 18	8♍51	26 33	23 13	13 51	11 35	11 56	24 58	26 36	4 19
28	2 24 45	4 25 14	23 26	27 5	24 24	14 30	11 27	11 51	24 56	26 38	4 20
29	2 28 41	5 25 11	8♎20	27 31	25 35	15 9	11 19	11 47	24 53	26 40	4 20
30	2 32 38	6 25 11	23 26	27 50	26 46	15 48	11 10	11 42	24 51	26 42	4 20
31	2 36 34	7♏25 13	8♏34	28♏ 3	27♍57	16♎27	11♉ 2	11♉37	24♉49	26♍44	4♌20

THE SUN ENTERS THE SIGN OF SCORPIO ON OCT 23 AT 13:40.

DAY	TIME	☉	☽	☿	♀	♂	♃	♄	♅	♆	♇
	h m s	° ' "	° '	° '	° '	° '	° '	° '	° '	° '	° '
N 1	2 40 31	8♏25 17	23♏35	28♏ 7	29♍ 8	17♎ 6	10♉54	11♉32	24♉46	26♍46	4♌20
O 2	2 44 27	9 25 22	8♐22	28R 3	0♎20	17 45	10R46	11R27	24R44	26 47	4 20
V 3	2 48 24	10 25 29	22 45	27 51	1 31	18 24	10 38	11 22	24 42	26 49	4 20
E 4	2 52 21	11 25 38	6♑42	27 29	2 43	19 3	10 30	11 18	24 39	26 51	4 20
M 5	2 56 17	12 25 48	20 10	26 57	3 55	19 42	10 21	11 13	24 37	26 52	4R20
B 6	3 0 14	13 26 0	3♒11	26 16	5 6	20 21	10 13	11 8	24 34	26 54	4 20
E 7	3 4 10	14 26 14	15 48	25 25	6 18	21 1	10 5	11 3	24 32	26 56	4 20
R 8	3 8 7	15 26 29	28 6	24 25	7 30	21 40	9 57	10 58	24 29	26 57	4 20
9	3 12 3	16 26 45	10♓ 8	23 17	8 43	22 19	9 49	10 53	24 27	26 59	4 20
10	3 16 0	17 27 3	22 1	22 3	9 55	22 58	9 41	10 49	24 24	27 1	4 20
11	3 19 56	18 27 22	3♈49	20 45	11 7	23 37	9 33	10 44	24 22	27 2	4 20
12	3 23 53	19 27 43	15 36	19 25	12 19	24 17	9 25	10 39	24 19	27 4	4 20
13	3 27 50	20 28 5	27 25	18 5	13 32	24 56	9 17	10 34	24 17	27 5	4 20
14	3 31 46	21 28 29	9♉20	16 49	14 45	25 35	9 9	10 30	24 14	27 7	4 19
15	3 35 43	22 28 54	21 22	15 38	15 57	26 15	9 2	10 25	24 12	27 8	4 19
16	3 39 39	23 29 21	3♊34	14 36	17 10	26 54	8 54	10 20	24 9	27 10	4 19
17	3 43 36	24 29 50	15 56	13 43	18 23	27 33	8 46	10 16	24 7	27 11	4 18
18	3 47 32	25 30 21	28 29	13 0	19 36	28 13	8 39	10 11	24 4	27 12	4 18
19	3 51 29	26 30 53	11♋14	12 30	20 49	28 52	8 32	10 6	24 2	27 14	4 18
20	3 55 25	27 31 26	24 11	12 11	22 2	29 32	8 24	10 2	23 59	27 15	4 17
21	3 59 22	28 32 2	7♌22	12D 3	23 15	0♏11	8 17	9 58	23 57	27 16	4 17
22	4 3 19	29 32 39	20 48	12 7	24 28	0 51	8 10	9 53	23 54	27 18	4 17
23	4 7 15	0♐33 18	4♍30	12 21	25 41	1 30	8 3	9 49	23 52	27 19	4 16
24	4 11 12	1 33 59	18 29	12 44	26 55	2 10	7 56	9 44	23 50	27 20	4 16
25	4 15 8	2 34 41	2♎45	13 16	28 8	2 49	7 49	9 40	23 47	27 21	4 15
26	4 19 5	3 35 25	17 16	13 56	29 22	3 29	7 43	9 36	23 45	27 22	4 15
27	4 23 1	4 36 10	2♏ 0	14 43	0♏35	4 8	7 36	9 32	23 42	27 23	4 14
28	4 26 58	5 36 57	16 50	15 36	1 49	4 48	7 30	9 28	23 40	27 24	4 14
29	4 30 54	6 37 46	1♐39	16 35	3 2	5 27	7 24	9 24	23 37	27 26	4 13
30	4 34 51	7♐38 35	16♐19	17♏38	4♏16	6♏ 7	7♉18	9♉20	23♉35	27♍27	4♌12

THE SUN ENTERS THE SIGN OF SAGITTARIUS ON NOV 22 AT 10:50.

DAY	TIME	☉	☽	☿	♀	♂	♃	♄	♅	♆	♇
	h m s	° ' "	° '	° '	° '	° '	° '	° '	° '	° '	° '
D 1	4 38 48	8♐39 26	0♑41	18♏45	5♏30	6♏47	7♉12	9♉16	23♉32	27♍28	4♌12
E 2	4 42 44	9 40 18	14 40	19 56	6 44	7 26	7R 6	9R12	23R30	27 28	4R11
C 3	4 46 41	10 41 11	28 13	21 9	7 58	8 6	7 0	9 8	23 28	27 29	4 10
E 4	4 50 37	11 42 5	11♒19	22 26	9 11	8 46	6 55	9 4	23 25	27 30	4 10
M 5	4 54 34	12 42 59	24 0	23 44	10 25	9 26	6 50	9 1	23 23	27 31	4 9
B 6	4 58 30	13 43 54	6♓20	25 4	11 39	10 5	6 45	8 57	23 21	27 32	4 8
E 7	5 2 27	14 44 50	18 24	26 27	12 53	10 45	6 40	8 54	23 18	27 33	4 7
R 8	5 6 23	15 45 47	0♈16	27 50	14 7	11 25	6 35	8 50	23 16	27 34	4 6
9	5 10 20	16 46 44	12 4	29 15	15 22	12 5	6 31	8 47	23 14	27 34	4 6
10	5 14 17	17 47 42	23 51	0♐40	16 36	12 45	6 26	8 44	23 12	27 35	4 5
11	5 18 13	18 48 41	5♉43	2 7	17 50	13 24	6 22	8 41	23 9	27 36	4 4
12	5 22 10	19 49 40	17 44	3 34	19 4	14 4	6 18	8 38	23 7	27 36	4 3
13	5 26 6	20 50 40	29 56	5 2	20 18	14 44	6 14	8 35	23 5	27 37	4 2
14	5 30 3	21 51 41	12♊21	6 31	21 33	15 24	6 11	8 32	23 3	27 37	4 1
15	5 33 59	22 52 42	25 1	8 0	22 47	16 4	6 7	8 29	23 1	27 38	4 0
16	5 37 56	23 53 44	7♋54	9 30	24 1	16 44	6 4	8 27	22 59	27 38	3 59
17	5 41 52	24 54 47	21 0	11 0	25 16	17 24	6 1	8 24	22 57	27 39	3 58
18	5 45 49	25 55 51	4♌18	12 30	26 30	18 4	5 58	8 22	22 55	27 39	3 57
19	5 49 46	26 56 55	17 46	14 1	27 45	18 44	5 56	8 19	22 53	27 40	3 56
20	5 53 42	27 58 0	1♍23	15 32	28 59	19 24	5 53	8 17	22 51	27 40	3 55
21	5 57 39	28 59 6	15 9	17 3	0♐14	20 4	5 51	8 15	22 49	27 40	3 54
22	6 1 35	0♑ 0 12	29 3	18 34	1 28	20 44	5 49	8 13	22 47	27 41	3 53
23	6 5 32	1 1 20	13♎ 7	20 6	2 43	21 24	5 47	8 11	22 45	27 41	3 52
24	6 9 28	2 2 28	27 19	21 38	3 57	22 4	5 46	8 9	22 44	27 41	3 51
25	6 13 25	3 3 36	11♏38	23 11	5 12	22 44	5 44	8 7	22 42	27 41	3 50
26	6 17 21	4 4 46	26 2	24 43	6 27	23 25	5 43	8 5	22 40	27 42	3 49
27	6 21 18	5 5 56	10♐25	26 16	7 41	24 5	5 42	8 4	22 39	27 42	3 47
28	6 25 15	6 7 6	24 42	27 49	8 56	24 45	5 42	8 2	22 37	27 42	3 46
29	6 29 11	7 8 17	8♑47	29 23	10 11	25 25	5 41	8 1	22 35	27 42	3 45
30	6 33 8	8 9 28	22 35	0♑56	11 25	26 5	5 41	8 0	22 34	27R42	3 44
31	6 37 4	9♑10 38	6♒ 2	2♑30	12♐40	26♏46	5♉41	7♉59	22♉32	27♍42	3♌43

THE SUN ENTERS THE SIGN OF CAPRICORN ON DEC 21 AT 23:55.

♏ SCORPIO ♐ SAGITTARIUS ♑ CAPRICORN ♒ AQUARIUS ♓ PISCES

1941

SIDEREAL SUN. MOON. MERCURY. VENUS. MARS. JUPITER. SATURN. URANUS. NEPTUNE. PLUTO.

DAY	TIME	☉	☽	☿	♀	♂	♃	♄	♅	♆	♇
	h m s	° ' "	° '	° '	° '	° '	° '	° '	° '	° '	° '
J 1	6 41 1	10♑11 49	19♒ 6	4♑ 5	13♐55	27♏26	5♉41	7♉58	22♉31	27♍42	3♌42
A 2	6 44 57	11 13 0	1♓47	5 39	15 10	28 6	5 41	7R57	22R29	27R42	3R40
N 3	6 48 54	12 14 10	14 8	7 14	16 25	28 47	5 41	7 56	22 28	27 42	3 39
U 4	6 52 50	13 15 20	26 14	8 49	17 39	29 27	5 42	7 55	22 27	27 41	3 38
A 5	6 56 47	14 16 30	8♈ 8	10 25	18 54	0♐ 7	5 43	7 55	22 25	27 41	3 37
R 6	7 0 44	15 17 39	19 56	12 1	20 9	0 48	5 44	7 54	22 24	27 41	3 35
Y 7	7 4 40	16 18 48	1♉44	13 37	21 24	1 28	5 46	7 54	22 23	27 41	3 34
8	7 8 37	17 19 57	13 38	15 14	22 39	2 8	5 47	7 54	22 22	27 40	3 33
9	7 12 33	18 21 5	25 42	16 51	23 53	2 49	5 49	7D54	22 21	27 40	3 31
10	7 16 30	19 22 13	8♊ 0	18 29	25 8	3 29	5 51	7 54	22 20	27 40	3 30
11	7 20 26	20 23 20	20 35	20 7	26 23	4 10	5 53	7 54	22 19	27 39	3 29
12	7 24 23	21 24 27	3♋30	21 46	27 38	4 50	5 55	7 54	22 18	27 39	3 27
13	7 28 20	22 25 33	16 42	23 25	28 53	5 31	5 58	7 54	22 17	27 39	3 26
14	7 32 16	23 26 39	0♌12	25 4	0♑ 8	6 11	6 1	7 55	22 16	27 38	3 25
15	7 36 13	24 27 45	13 55	26 44	1 23	6 52	6 4	7 55	22 15	27 38	3 23
16	7 40 9	25 28 50	27 49	28 25	2 38	7 32	6 7	7 56	22 14	27 37	3 22
17	7 44 6	26 29 54	11♍49	0♒ 6	3 53	8 13	6 10	7 57	22 14	27 36	3 21
18	7 48 2	27 30 59	25 53	1 47	5 7	8 53	6 14	7 58	22 13	27 36	3 19
19	7 51 59	28 32 3	9♎59	3 29	6 22	9 34	6 17	7 59	22 12	27 35	3 18
20	7 55 55	29 33 7	24 5	5 12	7 37	10 15	6 21	8 0	22 12	27 34	3 17
21	7 59 52	0♒34 10	8♏10	6 54	8 52	10 55	6 25	8 1	22 11	27 34	3 15
22	8 3 48	1 35 13	22 14	8 37	10 7	11 36	6 30	8 2	22 11	27 33	3 14
23	8 7 45	2 36 16	6♐15	10 21	11 22	12 17	6 34	8 4	22 10	27 32	3 13
24	8 11 42	3 37 19	20 11	12 5	12 37	12 57	6 39	8 5	22 10	27 31	3 11
25	8 15 38	4 38 20	4♑ 0	13 49	13 52	13 38	6 44	8 7	22 10	27 31	3 10
26	8 19 35	5 39 21	17 38	15 33	15 7	14 19	6 49	8 9	22 10	27 30	3 9
27	8 23 31	6 40 22	1♒ 3	17 17	16 22	15 0	6 54	8 11	22 9	27 29	3 7
28	8 27 28	7 41 21	14 12	19 0	17 37	15 41	6 59	8 13	22 9	27 28	3 6
29	8 31 24	8 42 19	27 3	20 44	18 52	16 21	7 5	8 15	22 9	27 27	3 5
30	8 35 21	9 43 17	9♓37	22 27	20 7	17 2	7 11	8 17	22D 9	27 26	3 3
31	8 39 18	10♒44 13	21♓55	24♒ 9	21♑22	17♐43	7♉17	8♉19	22♉ 9	27♍25	3♌ 2

THE SUN ENTERS THE SIGN OF AQUARIUS ON JAN 20 AT 10:34.

DAY	TIME	☉	☽	☿	♀	♂	♃	♄	♅	♆	♇
	h m s	° ' "	° '	° '	° '	° '	° '	° '	° '	° '	° '
F 1	8 43 14	11♒45 8	3♈59	25♒50	22♑37	18♐24	7♉23	8♉22	22♉ 9	27♍24	3♌ 0
E 2	8 47 11	12 46 1	15 53	27 30	23 52	19 5	7 29	8 24	22 9	27R23	2R59
B 3	8 51 7	13 46 53	27 42	29 7	25 7	19 46	7 36	8 27	22 9	27 22	2 58
R 4	8 55 4	14 47 44	9♉30	0♓43	26 22	20 26	7 42	8 30	22 10	27 21	2 56
U 5	8 59 0	15 48 34	21 24	2 16	27 37	21 7	7 49	8 32	22 10	27 20	2 55
A 6	9 2 57	16 49 22	3♊28	3 46	28 52	21 48	7 56	8 35	22 10	27 18	2 54
R 7	9 6 53	17 50 9	15 47	5 11	0♒ 7	22 29	8 3	8 38	22 11	27 17	2 52
Y 8	9 10 50	18 50 54	28 25	6 33	1 22	23 10	8 10	8 42	22 11	27 16	2 51
9	9 14 46	19 51 37	11♋25	7 49	2 37	23 51	8 18	8 45	22 12	27 15	2 50
10	9 18 43	20 52 20	24 49	8 59	3 52	24 32	8 25	8 48	22 12	27 14	2 49
11	9 22 40	21 53 0	8♌34	10 2	5 7	25 13	8 33	8 52	22 13	27 12	2 47
12	9 26 36	22 53 39	22 39	10 59	6 22	25 54	8 41	8 55	22 13	27 11	2 46
13	9 30 33	23 54 17	6♍58	11 47	7 36	26 35	8 49	8 59	22 14	27 10	2 45
14	9 34 29	24 54 54	21 27	12 26	8 51	27 16	8 57	9 2	22 15	27 8	2 44
15	9 38 26	25 55 29	5♎58	12 56	10 6	27 57	9 5	9 6	22 16	27 7	2 42
16	9 42 22	26 56 2	20 28	13 16	11 21	28 39	9 13	9 10	22 17	27 6	2 41
17	9 46 19	27 56 35	4♏51	13R26	12 36	29 20	9 22	9 14	22 17	27 4	2 40
18	9 50 15	28 57 7	19 5	13 25	13 51	0♑ 1	9 31	9 18	22 18	27 3	2 39
19	9 54 12	29 57 37	3♐ 8	13 15	15 6	0 42	9 40	9 22	22 19	27 1	2 37
20	9 58 9	0♓58 6	16 59	12 54	16 21	1 23	9 48	9 27	22 20	27 0	2 36
21	10 2 5	1 58 33	0♑37	12 24	17 36	2 4	9 58	9 31	22 22	26 59	2 35
22	10 6 2	2 59 0	14 3	11 45	18 51	2 45	10 7	9 36	22 23	26 57	2 34
23	10 9 58	3 59 25	27 15	10 58	20 6	3 27	10 16	9 40	22 24	26 56	2 33
24	10 13 55	4 59 48	10♒15	10 5	21 20	4 8	10 26	9 45	22 25	26 54	2 32
25	10 17 51	6 0 10	23 1	9 6	22 35	4 49	10 35	9 49	22 27	26 53	2 31
26	10 21 48	7 0 30	5♓34	8 4	23 50	5 30	10 45	9 54	22 28	26 51	2 30
27	10 25 44	8 0 48	17 54	7 1	25 5	6 12	10 55	9 59	22 29	26 49	2 28
28	10 29 41	9♓ 1 5	0♈ 3	5♓57	26♒20	6♑53	11♉ 5	10♉ 4	22♉31	26♍48	2♌27

THE SUN ENTERS THE SIGN OF PISCES ON FEB 19 AT 00:56.

DAY	TIME	☉	☽	☿	♀	♂	♃	♄	♅	♆	♇
	h m s	° ' "	° '	° '	° '	° '	° '	° '	° '	° '	° '
M 1	10 33 38	10♓ 1 20	12♈ 2	4♓54	27♒35	7♑34	11♉15	10♉ 9	22♉32	26♍46	2♌26
A 2	10 37 34	11 1 33	23 54	3R53	28 50	8 15	11 25	10 14	22 34	26R45	2R25
R 3	10 41 31	12 1 43	5♉42	2 56	0♓ 4	8 57	11 35	10 19	22 35	26 43	2 24
C 4	10 45 27	13 1 52	17 31	2 4	1 19	9 38	11 46	10 24	22 37	26 42	2 23
H 5	10 49 24	14 1 59	29 24	1 18	2 34	10 19	11 56	10 30	22 39	26 40	2 22
6	10 53 20	15 2 4	11♊26	0 37	3 49	11 1	12 7	10 35	22 40	26 38	2 21
7	10 57 17	16 2 6	23 43	0 3	5 4	11 42	12 18	10 41	22 42	26 37	2 20
8	11 1 13	17 2 7	6♋18	29♒36	6 18	12 23	12 28	10 46	22 44	26 35	2 20
9	11 5 10	18 2 5	19 16	29 15	7 33	13 5	12 39	10 52	22 46	26 33	2 19
10	11 9 7	19 2 1	2♌39	29 1	8 48	13 46	12 50	10 58	22 48	26 32	2 18
11	11 13 3	20 1 55	16 27	28D54	10 3	14 27	13 2	11 3	22 50	26 30	2 17
12	11 17 0	21 1 47	0♍41	28 53	11 17	15 9	13 13	11 9	22 52	26 29	2 16
13	11 20 56	22 1 37	15 16	28 58	12 32	15 50	13 24	11 15	22 54	26 27	2 15
14	11 24 53	23 1 24	0♎ 5	29 9	13 47	16 32	13 36	11 21	22 56	26 25	2 14
15	11 28 49	24 1 10	15 2	29 25	15 2	17 13	13 47	11 27	22 58	26 24	2 14
16	11 32 46	25 0 54	29 58	29 47	16 16	17 55	13 59	11 33	23 0	26 22	2 13
17	11 36 42	26 0 36	14♏46	0♓13	17 31	18 36	14 10	11 39	23 2	26 20	2 12
18	11 40 39	27 0 17	29 19	0 45	18 46	19 17	14 22	11 45	23 5	26 19	2 12
19	11 44 35	27 59 56	13♐34	1 20	20 0	19 59	14 34	11 52	23 7	26 17	2 11
20	11 48 32	28 59 33	27 29	2 0	21 15	20 40	14 46	11 58	23 9	26 15	2 10
21	11 52 29	29 59 8	11♑ 2	2 43	22 29	21 22	14 58	12 4	23 12	26 14	2 10
22	11 56 25	0♈58 42	24 16	3 30	23 44	22 3	15 10	12 11	23 14	26 12	2 9
23	12 0 22	1 58 14	7♒12	4 21	24 59	22 45	15 22	12 17	23 17	26 10	2 8
24	12 4 18	2 57 44	19 52	5 14	26 13	23 26	15 34	12 24	23 19	26 9	2 8
25	12 8 15	3 57 12	2♓19	6 11	27 28	24 8	15 47	12 30	23 22	26 7	2 7
26	12 12 11	4 56 39	14 34	7 11	28 42	24 49	15 59	12 37	23 24	26 5	2 7
27	12 16 8	5 56 3	26 40	8 13	29 57	25 31	16 11	12 44	23 27	26 4	2 6
28	12 20 4	6 55 25	8♈38	9 17	1♈12	26 12	16 24	12 50	23 29	26 2	2 6
29	12 24 1	7 54 45	20 31	10 24	2 26	26 54	16 36	12 57	23 32	26 0	2 5
30	12 27 58	8 54 4	2♉21	11 34	3 41	27 35	16 49	13 4	23 35	25 59	2 5
31	12 31 54	9♈53 20	14♉ 9	12♓45	4♈55	28♑17	17♉ 2	13♉11	23♉37	25♍57	2♌ 5

THE SUN ENTERS THE SIGN OF ARIES ON MAR 21 AT 00:20.

♈ ARIES ♉ TAURUS ♊ GEMINI ♋ CANCER ♌ LEO ♍ VIRGO ♎ LIBRA

SIDEREAL | SUN . | MOON . | MERCURY . | VENUS . | MARS . | JUPITER . | SATURN . | URANUS . | NEPTUNE . | PLUTO .

DAY	TIME h m s	☉ ° ' "	☽ ° '	☿ ° '	♀ ° '	♂ ° '	♃ ° '	♄ ° '	♅ ° '	♆ ° '	♇ ° '
A 1	12 35 51	10♈52 34	25♉59	13♓59	6♈10	28♑58	17♉15	13♉18	23♉40	25♍56	2♌ 4
P 2	12 39 47	11 51 45	7♊54	15 15	7 24	29 40	17 27	13 25	23 43	25R54	2R 4
R 3	12 43 44	12 50 55	19 57	16 32	8 39	0♒21	17 40	13 32	23 46	25 52	2 3
I 4	12 47 40	13 50 2	2♋12	17 52	9 53	1 3	17 53	13 39	23 48	25 51	2 3
L 5	12 51 37	14 49 7	14 43	19 13	11 7	1 44	18 6	13 46	23 51	25 49	2 3
6	12 55 33	15 48 9	27 35	20 37	12 22	2 26	18 19	13 53	23 54	25 48	2 3
7	12 59 30	16 47 10	10♌50	22 2	13 36	3 7	18 32	14 0	23 57	25 46	2 2
8	13 3 27	17 46 8	24 32	23 28	14 51	3 48	18 46	14 7	24 0	25 45	2 2
9	13 7 23	18 45 3	8♍41	24 56	16 5	4 30	18 59	14 14	24 3	25 43	2 2
10	13 11 20	19 43 56	23 15	26 26	17 19	5 11	19 12	14 22	24 6	25 42	2 2
11	13 15 16	20 42 48	8♎10	27 58	18 34	5 53	19 25	14 29	24 9	25 40	2 2
12	13 19 13	21 41 37	23 19	29 31	19 48	6 34	19 39	14 36	24 12	25 39	2 2
13	13 23 9	22 40 24	8♏33	1♈ 6	21 2	7 16	19 52	14 43	24 15	25 37	2 2
14	13 27 6	23 39 9	23 41	2 43	22 16	7 57	20 6	14 51	24 18	25 36	2D 2
15	13 31 2	24 37 53	8♐34	4 21	23 31	8 39	20 19	14 58	24 21	25 34	2 2
16	13 34 59	25 36 35	23 6	6 0	24 45	9 20	20 33	15 6	24 25	25 33	2 2
17	13 38 55	26 35 15	7♑12	7 42	25 59	10 1	20 46	15 13	24 28	25 32	2 2
18	13 42 52	27 33 53	20 51	9 24	27 13	10 43	21 0	15 21	24 31	25 30	2 2
19	13 46 49	28 32 30	4♒ 5	11 9	28 28	11 24	21 13	15 28	24 34	25 29	2 2
20	13 50 45	29 31 5	16 55	12 55	29 42	12 5	21 27	15 36	24 37	25 28	2 2
21	13 54 42	0♉29 39	29 25	14 43	0♉56	12 47	21 41	15 43	24 41	25 26	2 2
22	13 58 38	1 28 10	11♓40	16 32	2 10	13 28	21 55	15 51	24 44	25 25	2 2
23	14 2 35	2 26 41	23 44	18 23	3 24	14 9	22 8	15 58	24 47	25 24	2 3
24	14 6 31	3 25 9	5♈40	20 16	4 38	14 51	22 22	16 6	24 51	25 23	2 3
25	14 10 28	4 23 35	17 31	22 10	5 53	15 32	22 36	16 13	24 54	25 21	2 3
26	14 14 24	5 22 0	29 19	24 6	7 7	16 13	22 50	16 21	24 57	25 20	2 3
27	14 18 21	6 20 23	11♉ 8	26 4	8 21	16 54	23 4	16 29	25 0	25 19	2 4
28	14 22 18	7 18 45	22 58	28 3	9 35	17 36	23 18	16 36	25 4	25 18	2 4
29	14 26 14	8 17 4	4♊53	0♉ 4	10 49	18 17	23 32	16 44	25 7	25 17	2 4
30	14 30 11	9♉15 22	16♊53	2♉ 7	12♉ 3	18♒58	23♉46	16♉52	25♉11	25♍16	2♌ 5

THE SUN ENTERS THE SIGN OF TAURUS ON APR 20 AT 11:51.

DAY	TIME h m s	☉ ° ' "	☽ ° '	☿ ° '	♀ ° '	♂ ° '	♃ ° '	♄ ° '	♅ ° '	♆ ° '	♇ ° '
M 1	14 34 7	10♉13 37	29♊ 1	4♉10	13♉17	19♒39	24♉ 0	16♉59	25♉14	25♍14	2♌ 5
A 2	14 38 4	11 11 51	11♋19	6 16	14 31	20 20	24 14	17 7	25 17	25R13	2 6
Y 3	14 42 0	12 10 2	23 52	8 22	15 45	21 1	24 28	17 15	25 21	25 12	2 6
4	14 45 57	13 8 12	6♌41	10 30	16 59	21 42	24 42	17 22	25 24	25 11	2 6
5	14 49 53	14 6 20	19 50	12 38	18 13	22 23	24 56	17 30	25 28	25 10	2 7
6	14 53 50	15 4 25	3♍22	14 48	19 27	23 4	25 10	17 38	25 31	25 9	2 8
7	14 57 47	16 2 29	17 19	16 58	20 41	23 45	25 24	17 46	25 35	25 9	2 8
8	15 1 43	17 0 31	1♎42	19 8	21 55	24 26	25 38	17 53	25 38	25 8	2 9
9	15 5 40	17 58 31	16 28	21 18	23 9	25 7	25 52	18 1	25 42	25 7	2 9
10	15 9 36	18 56 29	1♏32	23 29	24 23	25 47	26 6	18 9	25 45	25 6	2 10
11	15 13 33	19 54 25	16 46	25 38	25 37	26 28	26 20	18 16	25 48	25 5	2 11
12	15 17 29	20 52 20	2♐ 0	27 47	26 50	27 9	26 34	18 24	25 52	25 4	2 11
13	15 21 26	21 50 14	17 3	29 56	28 4	27 50	26 49	18 32	25 55	25 4	2 12
14	15 25 22	22 48 6	1♑47	2♊ 2	29 18	28 30	27 3	18 40	25 59	25 3	2 13
15	15 29 19	23 45 57	16 4	4 7	0♊32	29 11	27 17	18 47	26 2	25 2	2 13
16	15 33 16	24 43 46	29 51	6 11	1 46	29 51	27 31	18 55	26 6	25 1	2 14
17	15 37 12	25 41 35	13♒10	8 12	3 0	0♓32	27 45	19 3	26 9	25 1	2 15
18	15 41 9	26 39 22	26 2	10 11	4 13	1 12	27 59	19 10	26 13	25 0	2 16
19	15 45 5	27 37 8	8♓31	12 8	5 27	1 53	28 13	19 18	26 16	25 0	2 17
20	15 49 2	28 34 53	20 43	14 2	6 41	2 33	28 28	19 26	26 20	24 59	2 18
21	15 52 58	29 32 37	2♈42	15 53	7 55	3 13	28 42	19 33	26 23	24 59	2 18
22	15 56 55	0♊30 20	14 33	17 42	9 8	3 53	28 56	19 41	26 27	24 58	2 19
23	16 0 51	1 28 1	26 21	19 27	10 22	4 34	29 10	19 49	26 30	24 58	2 20
24	16 4 48	2 25 42	8♉ 8	21 10	11 36	5 14	29 24	19 56	26 34	24 57	2 21
25	16 8 45	3 23 21	19 59	22 50	12 50	5 54	29 38	20 4	26 37	24 57	2 22
26	16 12 41	4 20 59	1♊55	24 27	14 3	6 34	29 52	20 11	26 41	24 56	2 23
27	16 16 38	5 18 36	13 57	26 0	15 17	7 13	0♊ 7	20 19	26 44	24 56	2 24
28	16 20 34	6 16 12	26 7	27 31	16 31	7 53	0 21	20 27	26 48	24 56	2 25
29	16 24 31	7 13 47	8♋25	28 58	17 44	8 33	0 35	20 34	26 51	24 55	2 26
30	16 28 27	8 11 21	20 54	0♋22	18 58	9 12	0 49	20 42	26 55	24 55	2 27
31	16 32 24	9♊ 8 53	3♌35	1♋43	20♊12	9♓52	1♊ 3	20♉49	26♉58	24♍55	2♌28

THE SUN ENTERS THE SIGN OF GEMINI ON MAY 21 AT 11:23.

DAY	TIME h m s	☉ ° ' "	☽ ° '	☿ ° '	♀ ° '	♂ ° '	♃ ° '	♄ ° '	♅ ° '	♆ ° '	♇ ° '
J 1	16 36 20	10♊ 6 23	16♌29	3♋ 1	21♊25	10♓31	1♊17	20♉56	27♉ 2	24♍55	2♌30
U 2	16 40 17	11 3 53	29 39	4 15	22 39	11 11	1 31	21 4	27 5	24R55	2 31
N 3	16 44 14	12 1 21	13♍ 6	5 26	23 53	11 50	1 45	21 11	27 8	24 55	2 32
E 4	16 48 10	12 58 48	26 55	6 33	25 6	12 29	1 59	21 19	27 12	24 55	2 33
5	16 52 7	13 56 14	11♎ 4	7 37	26 20	13 8	2 13	21 26	27 15	24D54	2 34
6	16 56 3	14 53 38	25 34	8 38	27 33	13 47	2 27	21 33	27 19	24 54	2 35
7	17 0 0	15 51 1	10♏22	9 34	28 47	14 26	2 41	21 41	27 22	24 55	2 37
8	17 3 56	16 48 24	25 22	10 27	0♋ 0	15 4	2 55	21 48	27 25	24 55	2 38
9	17 7 53	17 45 45	10♐25	11 16	1 14	15 43	3 9	21 55	27 29	24 55	2 39
10	17 11 49	18 43 6	25 21	12 1	2 27	16 22	3 23	22 2	27 32	24 55	2 40
11	17 15 46	19 40 26	10♑ 3	12 43	3 41	17 0	3 36	22 10	27 35	24 55	2 42
12	17 19 43	20 37 45	24 21	13 20	4 54	17 38	3 50	22 17	27 38	24 55	2 43
13	17 23 39	21 35 4	8♒12	13 53	6 8	18 16	4 4	22 24	27 42	24 55	2 44
14	17 27 36	22 32 22	21 34	14 22	7 21	18 54	4 18	22 31	27 45	24 56	2 46
15	17 31 32	23 29 40	4♓30	14 46	8 35	19 32	4 32	22 38	27 48	24 56	2 47
16	17 35 29	24 26 57	17 1	15 6	9 48	20 10	4 45	22 45	27 51	24 56	2 49
17	17 39 25	25 24 14	29 14	15 21	11 2	20 48	4 59	22 52	27 55	24 56	2 50
18	17 43 22	26 21 31	11♈14	15 32	12 15	21 25	5 13	22 59	27 58	24 57	2 51
19	17 47 18	27 18 47	23 5	15R38	13 28	22 3	5 26	23 6	28 1	24 57	2 53
20	17 51 15	28 16 3	4♉53	15 40	14 42	22 40	5 40	23 12	28 4	24 58	2 54
21	17 55 12	29 13 19	16 43	15 37	15 55	23 17	5 53	23 19	28 7	24 58	2 56
22	17 59 8	0♋10 35	28 38	15 30	17 9	23 54	6 7	23 26	28 10	24 59	2 57
23	18 3 5	1 7 51	10♊40	15 19	18 22	24 30	6 20	23 33	28 13	24 59	2 59
24	18 7 1	2 5 6	22 52	15 3	19 35	25 7	6 34	23 39	28 17	25 0	3 0
25	18 10 58	3 2 21	5♋15	14 43	20 49	25 43	6 47	23 46	28 20	25 0	3 2
26	18 14 54	3 59 36	17 49	14 20	22 2	26 19	7 0	23 52	28 23	25 1	3 3
27	18 18 51	4 56 50	0♌35	13 53	23 15	26 55	7 14	23 59	28 26	25 2	3 5
28	18 22 47	5 54 4	13 31	13 24	24 29	27 31	7 27	24 5	28 28	25 2	3 6
29	18 26 44	6 51 18	26 39	12 52	25 42	28 7	7 40	24 12	28 31	25 3	3 8
30	18 30 41	7♋48 31	10♍ 0	12♋18	26♋55	28♓42	7♊53	24♉18	28♉34	25♍ 4	3♌ 9

THE SUN ENTERS THE SIGN OF CANCER ON JUN 21 AT 19:34.

♏ SCORPIO ♐ SAGITTARIUS ♑ CAPRICORN ♒ AQUARIUS ♓ PISCES

SIDEREAL SUN. MOON. MERCURY. VENUS. MARS. JUPITER. SATURN. URANUS. NEPTUNE. PLUTO.

DAY	TIME	☉	☽	☿	♀	♂	♃	♄	♅	♆	♇
	h m s	° ' "	° '	° '	° '	° '	° '	° '	° '	° '	° '
J 1	18 34 37	8♋45 44	23♍33	11♋42	28♋ 8	29♓17	8♊ 6	24♉24	28♉37	25♍ 5	3♌11
U 2	18 38 34	9 42 56	7♎20	11R 6	29 22	29 52	8 19	24 31	28 40	25 5	3 12
L 3	18 42 30	10 40 8	21 22	10 29	0♌35	0♈27	8 32	24 37	28 43	25 6	3 14
Y 4	18 46 27	11 37 20	5♏38	9 53	1 48	1 2	8 45	24 43	28 46	25 7	3 16
5	18 50 23	12 34 31	20 7	9 18	3 1	1 36	8 58	24 49	28 48	25 8	3 17
6	18 54 20	13 31 42	4♐45	8 44	4 14	2 10	9 11	24 55	28 51	25 9	3 19
7	18 58 16	14 28 53	19 26	8 13	5 28	2 44	9 23	25 1	28 54	25 10	3 20
8	19 2 13	15 26 4	4♑ 2	7 45	6 41	3 17	9 36	25 7	28 56	25 11	3 22
9	19 6 10	16 23 15	18 27	7 19	7 54	3 51	9 49	25 13	28 59	25 12	3 24
10	19 10 6	17 20 26	2♒34	6 58	9 7	4 24	10 1	25 18	29 2	25 13	3 25
11	19 14 3	18 17 38	16 18	6 41	10 20	4 57	10 14	25 24	29 4	25 14	3 27
12	19 17 59	19 14 49	29 37	6 28	11 33	5 29	10 26	25 30	29 7	25 15	3 29
13	19 21 56	20 12 2	12♓32	6 20	12 46	6 2	10 39	25 35	29 9	25 16	3 30
14	19 25 52	21 9 14	25 5	6D17	13 59	6 34	10 51	25 41	29 12	25 17	3 32
15	19 29 49	22 6 27	7♈19	6 20	15 12	7 5	11 3	25 46	29 14	25 19	3 34
16	19 33 45	23 3 41	19 21	6 27	16 25	7 37	11 15	25 51	29 16	25 20	3 35
17	19 37 42	24 0 55	1♉14	6 41	17 38	8 8	11 28	25 57	29 19	25 21	3 37
18	19 41 39	24 58 10	13 4	6 59	18 51	8 39	11 40	26 2	29 21	25 22	3 39
19	19 45 35	25 55 26	24 57	7 24	20 4	9 9	11 52	26 7	29 23	25 24	3 40
20	19 49 32	26 52 43	6♊55	7 54	21 17	9 39	12 3	26 12	29 26	25 25	3 42
21	19 53 28	27 50 0	19 4	8 29	22 30	10 9	12 15	26 17	29 28	25 26	3 44
22	19 57 25	28 47 18	1♋25	9 11	23 43	10 39	12 27	26 22	29 30	25 28	3 45
23	20 1 21	29 44 37	14 1	9 57	24 56	11 8	12 39	26 27	29 32	25 29	3 47
24	20 5 18	0♌41 56	26 52	10 49	26 9	11 36	12 50	26 32	29 34	25 31	3 49
25	20 9 14	1 39 16	9♌56	11 47	27 22	12 5	13 2	26 36	29 36	25 32	3 51
26	20 13 11	2 36 36	23 14	12 50	28 34	12 33	13 13	26 41	29 38	25 34	3 52
27	20 17 8	3 33 58	6♍44	13 58	29 47	13 0	13 24	26 46	29 40	25 35	3 54
28	20 21 4	4 31 19	20 24	15 11	1♍ 0	13 27	13 36	26 50	29 42	25 37	3 56
29	20 25 1	5 28 41	4♎14	16 29	2 13	13 54	13 47	26 54	29 44	25 38	3 57
30	20 28 57	6 26 4	18 11	17 53	3 26	14 20	13 58	26 59	29 46	25 40	3 59
31	20 32 54	7♌23 27	2♏16	19♋20	4♍38	14♈46	14♊ 9	27♉ 3	29♉48	25♍41	4♌ 1

THE SUN ENTERS THE SIGN OF LEO ON JUL 23 AT 06:27.

DAY	TIME	☉	☽	☿	♀	♂	♃	♄	♅	♆	♇
	h m s	° ' "	° '	° '	° '	° '	° '	° '	° '	° '	° '
A 1	20 36 50	8♌20 51	16♏27	20♋52	5♍51	15♈11	14♊20	27♉ 7	29♉49	25♍43	4♌ 3
U 2	20 40 47	9 18 15	0♐42	22 29	7 4	15 36	14 30	27 11	29 51	25 45	4 4
G 3	20 44 43	10 15 40	14 59	24 9	8 16	16 1	14 41	27 15	29 53	25 46	4 6
U 4	20 48 40	11 13 6	29 14	25 54	9 29	16 25	14 52	27 19	29 54	25 48	4 8
S 5	20 52 37	12 10 32	13♑24	27 41	10 41	16 48	15 2	27 22	29 56	25 50	4 9
T 6	20 56 33	13 7 59	27 23	29 32	11 54	17 11	15 12	27 26	29 58	25 51	4 11
7	21 0 30	14 5 27	11♒ 7	1♌26	13 6	17 34	15 23	27 30	29 59	25 53	4 13
8	21 4 26	15 2 56	24 34	3 21	14 19	17 56	15 33	27 33	0♊ 1	25 55	4 14
9	21 8 23	16 0 27	7♓42	5 19	15 31	18 17	15 43	27 37	0 2	25 57	4 16
10	21 12 19	16 57 58	20 30	7 19	16 44	18 38	15 53	27 40	0 3	25 58	4 18
11	21 16 16	17 55 31	2♈59	9 20	17 56	18 58	16 3	27 43	0 5	26 0	4 19
12	21 20 12	18 53 4	15 13	11 22	19 9	19 18	16 12	27 46	0 6	26 2	4 21
13	21 24 9	19 50 40	27 15	13 24	20 21	19 37	16 22	27 49	0 7	26 4	4 23
14	21 28 6	20 48 17	9♉ 9	15 27	21 33	19 55	16 31	27 52	0 8	26 6	4 24
15	21 32 2	21 45 55	21 0	17 29	22 45	20 13	16 41	27 55	0 9	26 8	4 26
16	21 35 59	22 43 35	2♊54	19 32	23 58	20 31	16 50	27 58	0 10	26 10	4 28
17	21 39 55	23 41 16	14 55	21 34	25 10	20 47	16 59	28 0	0 11	26 12	4 29
18	21 43 52	24 38 59	27 6	23 35	26 22	21 3	17 8	28 3	0 12	26 14	4 31
19	21 47 48	25 36 44	9♋33	25 36	27 34	21 18	17 17	28 5	0 13	26 16	4 33
20	21 51 45	26 34 30	22 17	27 35	28 46	21 33	17 26	28 8	0 14	26 18	4 34
21	21 55 41	27 32 18	5♌20	29 34	29 59	21 47	17 35	28 10	0 15	26 20	4 36
22	21 59 38	28 30 7	18 42	1♍31	1♎11	22 0	17 43	28 12	0 16	26 22	4 37
23	22 3 35	29 27 58	2♍22	3 28	2 23	22 12	17 52	28 14	0 16	26 24	4 39
24	22 7 31	0♍25 50	16 16	5 23	3 35	22 24	18 0	28 16	0 17	26 26	4 41
25	22 11 28	1 23 43	0♎23	7 17	4 47	22 35	18 8	28 18	0 18	26 28	4 42
26	22 15 24	2 21 38	14 37	9 9	5 59	22 45	18 16	28 20	0 18	26 30	4 44
27	22 19 21	3 19 34	28 55	11 0	7 10	22 54	18 24	28 21	0 19	26 32	4 45
28	22 23 17	4 17 31	13♏14	12 50	8 22	23 3	18 31	28 23	0 19	26 34	4 47
29	22 27 14	5 15 30	27 30	14 39	9 34	23 11	18 39	28 24	0 20	26 36	4 48
30	22 31 10	6 13 30	11♐41	16 26	10 46	23 17	18 46	28 26	0 20	26 38	4 50
31	22 35 7	7♍11 32	25♐45	18♍12	11♎58	23♈24	18♊54	28♉27	0♊20	26♍40	4♌51

THE SUN ENTERS THE SIGN OF VIRGO ON AUG 23 AT 13:18.

DAY	TIME	☉	☽	☿	♀	♂	♃	♄	♅	♆	♇
	h m s	° ' "	° '	° '	° '	° '	° '	° '	° '	° '	° '
S 1	22 39 4	8♍ 9 34	9♑40	19♍57	13♎ 9	23♈29	19♊ 1	28♉28	0♊21	26♍42	4♌53
E 2	22 43 0	9 7 38	23 24	21 41	14 21	23 33	19 8	28 29	0 21	26 44	4 54
P 3	22 46 57	10 5 44	6♒56	23 23	15 33	23 37	19 15	28 30	0 21	26 47	4 56
T 4	22 50 53	11 3 51	20 15	25 4	16 44	23 40	19 21	28 31	0 21	26 49	4 57
E 5	22 54 50	12 1 59	3♓19	26 44	17 56	23 42	19 28	28 31	0R21	26 51	4 59
M 6	22 58 46	13 0 10	16 8	28 23	19 7	23R43	19 34	28 32	0 21	26 53	5 0
B 7	23 2 43	13 58 22	28 43	0♎ 0	20 18	23 43	19 40	28 32	0 21	26 55	5 1
E 8	23 6 39	14 56 35	11♈ 4	1 36	21 30	23 43	19 47	28 33	0 21	26 57	5 3
R 9	23 10 36	15 54 51	23 13	3 12	22 41	23 41	19 52	28 33	0 21	27 0	5 4
10	23 14 32	16 53 9	5♉13	4 46	23 52	23 39	19 58	28R33	0 21	27 2	5 5
11	23 18 29	17 51 29	17 6	6 18	25 4	23 35	20 4	28 33	0 21	27 4	5 7
12	23 22 26	18 49 50	28 58	7 50	26 15	23 31	20 9	28 33	0 20	27 6	5 8
13	23 26 22	19 48 14	10♊51	9 21	27 26	23 26	20 14	28 33	0 20	27 8	5 9
14	23 30 19	20 46 40	22 51	10 50	28 37	23 20	20 19	28 32	0 19	27 11	5 11
15	23 34 15	21 45 9	5♋ 1	12 19	29 48	23 14	20 24	28 32	0 19	27 13	5 12
16	23 38 12	22 43 39	17 27	13 46	0♏59	23 6	20 29	28 31	0 19	27 15	5 13
17	23 42 8	23 42 11	0♌13	15 12	2 10	22 58	20 34	28 31	0 18	27 17	5 14
18	23 46 5	24 40 46	13 20	16 37	3 21	22 49	20 38	28 30	0 17	27 20	5 16
19	23 50 1	25 39 23	26 51	18 0	4 32	22 39	20 42	28 29	0 17	27 22	5 17
20	23 53 58	26 38 1	10♍45	19 23	5 42	22 28	20 46	28 28	0 16	27 24	5 18
21	23 57 55	27 36 42	25 0	20 44	6 53	22 16	20 50	28 27	0 15	27 26	5 19
22	0 1 51	28 35 25	9♎32	22 4	8 4	22 4	20 54	28 26	0 15	27 28	5 20
23	0 5 48	29 34 10	24 13	23 22	9 15	21 51	20 57	28 25	0 14	27 31	5 21
24	0 9 44	0♎32 56	8♏58	24 40	10 25	21 37	21 0	28 23	0 13	27 33	5 22
25	0 13 41	1 31 44	23 40	25 55	11 36	21 23	21 4	28 22	0 12	27 35	5 24
26	0 17 37	2 30 35	8♐12	27 9	12 46	21 8	21 6	28 20	0 11	27 37	5 25
27	0 21 34	3 29 26	22 31	28 22	13 56	20 52	21 9	28 19	0 10	27 40	5 26
28	0 25 30	4 28 20	6♑33	29 33	15 7	20 36	21 12	28 17	0 9	27 42	5 27
29	0 29 27	5 27 15	20 17	0♏42	16 17	20 20	21 14	28 15	0 8	27 44	5 28
30	0 33 24	6♎26 12	3♒44	1♏49	17♏27	20♈ 3	21♊16	28♉13	0♊ 7	27♍46	5♌29

THE SUN ENTERS THE SIGN OF LIBRA ON SEP 23 AT 10:34.

♈ ARIES ♉ TAURUS ♊ GEMINI ♋ CANCER ♌ LEO ♍ VIRGO ♎ LIBRA

SIDEREAL SUN. MOON. MERCURY. VENUS. MARS. JUPITER. SATURN. URANUS. NEPTUNE. PLUTO.

DAY	TIME	☉	☽	☿	♀	♂	♃	♄	♅	♆	♇
	h m s	° ' "	° '	° '	° '	° '	° '	° '	° '	° '	° '
O 1	0 37 20	7♎25 11	16♒55	2♏54	18♏37	19♈46	21♊18	28♉11	0♊ 5	27♍48	5♌30
C 2	0 41 17	8 24 11	29 50	3 57	19 47	19R28	21 20	28R 9	0R 4	27 51	5 30
T 3	0 45 13	9 23 14	12♓32	4 57	20 57	19 10	21 21	28 7	0 3	27 53	5 31
O 4	0 49 10	10 22 18	25 2	5 54	22 7	18 52	21 23	28 4	0 2	27 55	5 32
B 5	0 53 6	11 21 24	7♈22	6 49	23 17	18 33	21 24	28 2	0 0	27 57	5 33
E 6	0 57 3	12 20 32	19 32	7 41	24 26	18 14	21 25	27 59	29♉59	27 59	5 34
R 7	1 0 59	13 19 43	1♉34	8 29	25 36	17 56	21 26	27 56	29 57	28 2	5 35
8	1 4 56	14 18 55	13 30	9 14	26 45	17 37	21 26	27 54	29 56	28 4	5 35
9	1 8 52	15 18 10	25 22	9 54	27 55	17 18	21 27	27 51	29 54	28 6	5 36
10	1 12 49	16 17 26	7♊13	10 30	29 4	16 59	21R27	27 48	29 53	28 8	5 37
11	1 16 46	17 16 46	19 6	11 2	0♐13	16 40	21 27	27 45	29 51	28 10	5 38
12	1 20 42	18 16 7	1♋ 4	11 28	1 23	16 22	21 26	27 42	29 49	28 12	5 38
13	1 24 39	19 15 31	13 11	11 48	2 32	16 3	21 26	27 39	29 48	28 14	5 39
14	1 28 35	20 14 57	25 33	12 2	3 41	15 45	21 25	27 35	29 46	28 17	5 40
15	1 32 32	21 14 25	8♌14	12R 9	4 49	15 27	21 25	27 32	29 44	28 19	5 40
16	1 36 28	22 13 56	21 17	12 9	5 58	15 9	21 24	27 28	29 42	28 21	5 41
17	1 40 25	23 13 29	4♍46	12 1	7 7	14 52	21 22	27 25	29 40	28 23	5 41
18	1 44 21	24 13 4	18 42	11 45	8 15	14 35	21 21	27 21	29 39	28 25	5 42
19	1 48 18	25 12 41	3♎ 5	11 20	9 24	14 18	21 19	27 18	29 37	28 27	5 43
20	1 52 15	26 12 21	17 51	10 46	10 32	14 2	21 17	27 14	29 35	28 29	5 43
21	1 56 11	27 12 2	2♏53	10 4	11 40	13 47	21 15	27 10	29 33	28 31	5 43
22	2 0 8	28 11 46	18 2	9 14	12 48	13 32	21 13	27 6	29 31	28 33	5 44
23	2 4 4	29 11 31	3♐ 8	8 15	13 56	13 17	21 11	27 2	29 29	28 35	5 44
24	2 8 1	0♏11 19	18 2	7 10	15 4	13 4	21 8	26 58	29 27	28 37	5 45
25	2 11 57	1 11 8	2♑36	5 59	16 12	12 51	21 5	26 54	29 24	28 39	5 45
26	2 15 54	2 10 59	16 47	4 44	17 20	12 38	21 2	26 50	29 22	28 41	5 45
27	2 19 50	3 10 51	0♒32	3 28	18 27	12 27	20 59	26 46	29 20	28 43	5 46
28	2 23 47	4 10 45	13 53	2 12	19 34	12 16	20 55	26 41	29 18	28 45	5 46
29	2 27 44	5 10 40	26 53	0 59	20 41	12 5	20 52	26 37	29 16	28 46	5 46
30	2 31 40	6 10 38	9♓34	29♎51	21 48	11 56	20 48	26 33	29 14	28 48	5 46
31	2 35 37	7♏10 36	22♓ 0	28♎50	22♐55	11♈47	20♊44	26♉28	29♉11	28♍50	5♌47

THE SUN ENTERS THE SIGN OF SCORPIO ON OCT 23 AT 19:28.

DAY	TIME	☉	☽	☿	♀	♂	♃	♄	♅	♆	♇
	h m s	° ' "	° '	° '	° '	° '	° '	° '	° '	° '	° '
N 1	2 39 33	8♏10 37	4♈15	27♎58	24♐ 2	11♈39	20♊40	26♉24	29♉ 9	28♍52	5♌47
O 2	2 43 30	9 10 39	16 21	27R17	25 8	11R32	20R35	26R19	29R 7	28 54	5 47
V 3	2 47 26	10 10 43	28 21	26 47	26 14	11 26	20 31	26 15	29 4	28 56	5 47
E 4	2 51 23	11 10 49	10♉16	26 28	27 20	11 21	20 26	26 10	29 2	28 57	5 47
M 5	2 55 19	12 10 57	22 9	26D21	28 26	11 16	20 21	26 5	29 0	28 59	5 47
B 6	2 59 16	13 11 6	4♊ 1	26 26	29 32	11 12	20 16	26 1	28 57	29 1	5R47
E 7	3 3 13	14 11 18	15 53	26 41	0♑37	11 9	20 11	25 56	28 55	29 3	5 47
R 8	3 7 9	15 11 31	27 48	27 6	1 43	11 7	20 6	25 51	28 52	29 4	5 47
9	3 11 6	16 11 47	9♋47	27 40	2 48	11 5	20 0	25 46	28 50	29 6	5 47
10	3 15 2	17 12 4	21 54	28 23	3 52	11D 5	19 54	25 42	28 48	29 8	5 47
11	3 18 59	18 12 23	4♌14	29 13	4 57	11 5	19 49	25 37	28 45	29 9	5 47
12	3 22 55	19 12 45	16 49	0♏ 9	6 1	11 6	19 42	25 32	28 43	29 11	5 47
13	3 26 52	20 13 8	29 44	1 12	7 5	11 7	19 36	25 27	28 40	29 12	5 47
14	3 30 48	21 13 33	13♍ 4	2 19	8 9	11 10	19 30	25 22	28 38	29 14	5 47
15	3 34 45	22 14 0	26 51	3 31	9 13	11 13	19 24	25 17	28 35	29 15	5 46
16	3 38 41	23 14 29	11♎ 7	4 46	10 16	11 17	19 17	25 13	28 33	29 17	5 46
17	3 42 38	24 14 59	25 50	6 4	11 19	11 22	19 10	25 8	28 30	29 18	5 46
18	3 46 35	25 15 32	10♏55	7 26	12 21	11 27	19 3	25 3	28 28	29 20	5 46
19	3 50 31	26 16 6	26 14	8 49	13 24	11 33	18 57	24 58	28 25	29 21	5 45
20	3 54 28	27 16 41	11♐34	10 14	14 26	11 40	18 49	24 53	28 23	29 23	5 45
21	3 58 24	28 17 19	26 45	11 41	15 28	11 48	18 42	24 48	28 20	29 24	5 45
22	4 2 21	29 17 57	11♑36	13 9	16 29	11 57	18 35	24 43	28 18	29 25	5 44
23	4 6 17	0♐18 37	26 1	14 38	17 30	12 6	18 28	24 38	28 15	29 27	5 44
24	4 10 14	1 19 17	9♒56	16 8	18 31	12 15	18 20	24 34	28 13	29 28	5 43
25	4 14 11	2 19 59	23 22	17 39	19 31	12 26	18 13	24 29	28 10	29 29	5 43
26	4 18 7	3 20 42	6♓22	19 11	20 31	12 37	18 5	24 24	28 8	29 30	5 42
27	4 22 4	4 21 26	18 59	20 42	21 30	12 49	17 57	24 19	28 5	29 31	5 42
28	4 26 0	5 22 10	1♈18	22 15	22 29	13 1	17 49	24 14	28 3	29 33	5 41
29	4 29 57	6 22 56	13 25	23 47	23 27	13 14	17 41	24 10	28 0	29 34	5 41
30	4 33 53	7♐23 43	25♈23	25♏20	24♑25	13♈28	17♊34	24♉ 5	27♉58	29♍35	5♌40

THE SUN ENTERS THE SIGN OF SAGITTARIUS ON NOV 22 AT 16:38.

DAY	TIME	☉	☽	☿	♀	♂	♃	♄	♅	♆	♇
	h m s	° ' "	° '	° '	° '	° '	° '	° '	° '	° '	° '
D 1	4 37 50	8♐24 31	7♉16	26♏53	25♑23	13♈42	17♊26	24♉ 0	27♉55	29♍36	5♌40
E 2	4 41 46	9 25 20	19 8	28 26	26 20	13 57	17R18	23R56	27R53	29 37	5R39
C 3	4 45 43	10 26 10	0♊59	29 59	27 16	14 12	17 10	23 51	27 50	29 38	5 38
E 4	4 49 40	11 27 1	12 53	1♐33	28 12	14 28	17 1	23 47	27 48	29 39	5 38
M 5	4 53 36	12 27 53	24 49	3 6	29 7	14 45	16 53	23 42	27 46	29 40	5 37
B 6	4 57 33	13 28 47	6♋50	4 39	0♒ 2	15 2	16 45	23 38	27 43	29 41	5 36
E 7	5 1 29	14 29 41	18 56	6 13	0 56	15 19	16 37	23 33	27 41	29 42	5 35
R 8	5 5 26	15 30 37	1♌10	7 46	1 50	15 37	16 29	23 29	27 38	29 43	5 35
9	5 9 22	16 31 34	13 34	9 20	2 42	15 55	16 21	23 24	27 36	29 43	5 34
10	5 13 19	17 32 31	26 10	10 54	3 34	16 14	16 12	23 20	27 34	29 44	5 33
11	5 17 15	18 33 30	9♍ 2	12 27	4 26	16 34	16 4	23 16	27 31	29 45	5 32
12	5 21 12	19 34 31	22 15	14 1	5 16	16 53	15 56	23 12	27 29	29 46	5 31
13	5 25 9	20 35 32	5♎51	15 35	6 6	17 14	15 48	23 8	27 27	29 46	5 30
14	5 29 5	21 36 34	19 53	17 9	6 55	17 34	15 40	23 4	27 25	29 47	5 30
15	5 33 2	22 37 37	4♏21	18 43	7 43	17 55	15 32	23 0	27 22	29 48	5 29
16	5 36 58	23 38 42	19 12	20 17	8 30	18 17	15 24	22 56	27 20	29 48	5 28
17	5 40 55	24 39 47	4♐19	21 51	9 16	18 39	15 16	22 52	27 18	29 49	5 27
18	5 44 51	25 40 53	19 35	23 25	10 2	19 1	15 8	22 49	27 16	29 49	5 26
19	5 48 48	26 42 0	4♑46	25 0	10 46	19 24	15 0	22 45	27 14	29 50	5 25
20	5 52 44	27 43 7	19 42	26 35	11 29	19 47	14 52	22 41	27 12	29 50	5 24
21	5 56 41	28 44 14	4♒16	28 10	12 11	20 10	14 44	22 38	27 10	29 51	5 23
22	6 0 38	29 45 22	18 21	29 45	12 52	20 34	14 37	22 35	27 8	29 51	5 22
23	6 4 34	0♑46 30	1♓55	1♑20	13 32	20 58	14 29	22 31	27 6	29 51	5 21
24	6 8 31	1 47 38	15 1	2 55	14 11	21 23	14 22	22 28	27 4	29 52	5 19
25	6 12 27	2 48 46	27 43	4 31	14 48	21 48	14 14	22 25	27 2	29 52	5 18
26	6 16 24	3 49 55	10♈ 4	6 7	15 24	22 13	14 7	22 22	27 0	29 52	5 17
27	6 20 20	4 51 3	22 10	7 43	15 59	22 38	14 0	22 19	26 58	29 52	5 16
28	6 24 17	5 52 11	4♉ 6	9 19	16 32	23 4	13 53	22 16	26 56	29 52	5 15
29	6 28 13	6 53 19	15 58	10 56	17 3	23 30	13 46	22 13	26 55	29 53	5 14
30	6 32 10	7 54 28	27 48	12 33	17 33	23 57	13 39	22 11	26 53	29 53	5 13
31	6 36 7	8♑55 36	9♊40	14♑10	18♒ 2	24♈23	13♊32	22♉ 8	26♉51	29♍53	5♌11

THE SUN ENTERS THE SIGN OF CAPRICORN ON DEC 22 AT 05:45.

♏ SCORPIO	♐ SAGITTARIUS	♑ CAPRICORN	♒ AQUARIUS	♓ PISCES

1942

SIDEREAL SUN. MOON. MERCURY. VENUS. MARS. JUPITER. SATURN. URANUS. NEPTUNE. PLUTO.

DAY	TIME	☉	☽	☿	♀	♂	♃	♄	♅	♆	♇
	h m s	° ' "	° '	° '	° '	° '	° '	° '	° '	° '	° '
J 1	6 40 3	9♑56 44	21♊37	15♑48	18♒28	24♈50	13♊26	22♉ 6	26♉50	29♍53	5♌10
A 2	6 44 0	10 57 53	3♋41	17 26	18 53	25 17	13R19	22R 3	26R48	29R53	5R 9
N 3	6 47 56	11 59 1	15 51	19 4	19 16	25 45	13 13	22 1	26 46	29 53	5 8
U 4	6 51 53	13 0 9	28 10	20 42	19 37	26 13	13 7	21 59	26 45	29 53	5 7
A 5	6 55 49	14 1 17	10♌38	22 21	19 56	26 40	13 1	21 57	26 43	29 53	5 5
R 6	6 59 46	15 2 26	23 15	24 0	20 13	27 9	12 55	21 55	26 42	29 52	5 4
Y 7	7 3 42	16 3 34	6♍ 3	25 38	20 28	27 37	12 49	21 53	26 41	29 52	5 3
8	7 7 39	17 4 42	19 4	27 17	20 41	28 6	12 44	21 51	26 39	29 52	5 2
9	7 11 36	18 5 51	2♎20	28 56	20 52	28 34	12 38	21 50	26 38	29 52	5 0
10	7 15 32	19 6 59	15 53	0♒35	21 0	29 3	12 33	21 48	26 37	29 51	4 59
11	7 19 29	20 8 8	29 46	2 14	21 6	29 33	12 28	21 47	26 35	29 51	4 58
12	7 23 25	21 9 16	13♏57	3 53	21 10	0♉ 2	12 23	21 45	26 34	29 51	4 56
13	7 27 22	22 10 25	28 27	5 31	21R11	0 32	12 18	21 44	26 33	29 50	4 55
14	7 31 18	23 11 33	13♐12	7 9	21 10	1 2	12 14	21 43	26 32	29 50	4 54
15	7 35 15	24 12 42	28 4	8 45	21 6	1 32	12 9	21 42	26 31	29 50	4 52
16	7 39 11	25 13 50	12♑56	10 21	21 0	2 2	12 5	21 41	26 30	29 49	4 51
17	7 43 8	26 14 57	27 39	11 56	20 52	2 32	12 1	21 40	26 29	29 49	4 50
18	7 47 5	27 16 4	12♒ 5	13 29	20 41	3 3	11 57	21 40	26 28	29 48	4 48
19	7 51 1	28 17 10	26 8	14 59	20 27	3 33	11 54	21 39	26 27	29 48	4 47
20	7 54 58	29 18 16	9♓46	16 28	20 11	4 4	11 50	21 39	26 27	29 47	4 46
21	7 58 54	0♒19 20	22 57	17 53	19 52	4 36	11 47	21 38	26 26	29 46	4 44
22	8 2 51	1 20 24	5♈44	19 15	19 31	5 7	11 44	21 38	26 25	29 46	4 43
23	8 6 47	2 21 27	18 11	20 33	19 8	5 38	11 41	21D38	26 24	29 45	4 41
24	8 10 44	3 22 28	0♉21	21 46	18 43	6 10	11 39	21 38	26 24	29 44	4 40
25	8 14 40	4 23 29	12 20	22 53	18 15	6 41	11 36	21 38	26 23	29 43	4 39
26	8 18 37	5 24 29	24 12	23 54	17 46	7 13	11 34	21 38	26 23	29 43	4 37
27	8 22 34	6 25 27	6♊ 4	24 48	17 15	7 45	11 32	21 39	26 22	29 42	4 36
28	8 26 30	7 26 25	17 58	25 34	16 42	8 17	11 30	21 39	26 22	29 41	4 35
29	8 30 27	8 27 21	29 58	26 11	16 8	8 50	11 29	21 40	26 22	29 40	4 33
30	8 34 23	9 28 16	12♋ 8	26 38	15 33	9 22	11 27	21 41	26 22	29 39	4 32
31	8 38 20	10♒29 10	24♋28	26♒55	14♒57	9♉54	11♊26	21♉41	26♉21	29♍38	4♌31

THE SUN ENTERS THE SIGN OF AQUARIUS ON JAN 20 AT 16:24.

DAY	TIME	☉	☽	☿	♀	♂	♃	♄	♅	♆	♇
	h m s	° ' "	° '	° '	° '	° '	° '	° '	° '	° '	° '
F 1	8 42 16	11♒30 3	7♌ 1	27♒ 1	14♒20	10♉27	11♊25	21♉42	26♉21	29♍37	4♌29
E 2	8 46 13	12 30 55	19 46	26R56	13R43	11 0	11R24	21 43	26R21	29R36	4R28
B 3	8 50 9	13 31 46	2♍44	26 40	13 5	11 33	11 24	21 45	26D21	29 35	4 26
R 4	8 54 6	14 32 35	15 54	26 12	12 28	12 5	11 23	21 46	26 21	29 34	4 25
U 5	8 58 3	15 33 24	29 16	25 35	11 51	12 38	11D23	21 47	26 21	29 33	4 24
A 6	9 1 59	16 34 12	12♎49	24 48	11 15	13 12	11 23	21 49	26 21	29 32	4 22
R 7	9 5 56	17 34 58	26 34	23 53	10 40	13 45	11 23	21 50	26 21	29 31	4 21
Y 8	9 9 52	18 35 44	10♏30	22 50	10 6	14 18	11 24	21 52	26 21	29 30	4 20
9	9 13 49	19 36 29	24 36	21 44	9 33	14 52	11 24	21 54	26 22	29 29	4 18
10	9 17 45	20 37 13	8♐51	20 34	9 2	15 25	11 25	21 56	26 22	29 27	4 17
11	9 21 42	21 37 56	23 13	19 23	8 32	15 59	11 26	21 58	26 22	29 26	4 16
12	9 25 38	22 38 38	7♑37	18 12	8 5	16 32	11 28	22 0	26 23	29 25	4 15
13	9 29 35	23 39 19	21 59	17 5	7 39	17 6	11 29	22 2	26 23	29 24	4 13
14	9 33 32	24 39 58	6♒14	16 2	7 16	17 40	11 31	22 4	26 24	29 23	4 12
15	9 37 28	25 40 36	20 18	15 4	6 54	18 14	11 32	22 7	26 24	29 21	4 11
16	9 41 25	26 41 13	4♓ 5	14 12	6 35	18 48	11 34	22 9	26 25	29 20	4 10
17	9 45 21	27 41 48	17 32	13 28	6 19	19 22	11 37	22 12	26 26	29 19	4 8
18	9 49 18	28 42 21	0♈40	12 50	6 5	19 57	11 39	22 15	26 26	29 17	4 7
19	9 53 14	29 42 53	13 27	12 21	5 53	20 31	11 42	22 18	26 27	29 16	4 6
20	9 57 11	0♓43 23	25 55	11 59	5 44	21 5	11 45	22 21	26 28	29 14	4 5
21	10 1 7	1 43 51	8♉ 8	11 45	5 37	21 40	11 48	22 24	26 29	29 13	4 3
22	10 5 4	2 44 18	20 10	11D38	5 33	22 14	11 51	22 27	26 30	29 12	4 2
23	10 9 1	3 44 42	2♊ 5	11 38	5D31	22 49	11 54	22 30	26 31	29 10	4 1
24	10 12 57	4 45 5	13 58	11 44	5 32	23 23	11 58	22 34	26 32	29 9	4 0
25	10 16 54	5 45 25	25 52	11 57	5 35	23 58	12 1	22 37	26 33	29 7	3 59
26	10 20 50	6 45 44	7♋54	12 16	5 40	24 33	12 5	22 41	26 34	29 6	3 58
27	10 24 47	7 46 1	20 7	12 40	5 48	25 8	12 10	22 44	26 35	29 4	3 57
28	10 28 43	8♓46 16	2♌34	13♒ 9	5♒58	25♉43	12♊14	22♉48	26♉37	29♍ 3	3♌55

THE SUN ENTERS THE SIGN OF PISCES ON FEB 19 AT 06:47.

DAY	TIME	☉	☽	☿	♀	♂	♃	♄	♅	♆	♇
	h m s	° ' "	° '	° '	° '	° '	° '	° '	° '	° '	° '
M 1	10 32 40	9♓46 29	15♌17	13♒43	6♒10	26♉17	12♊18	22♉52	26♉38	29♍ 1	3♌54
A 2	10 36 36	10 46 39	28 18	14 21	6 24	26 52	12 23	22 56	26 39	29R 0	3R53
R 3	10 40 33	11 46 49	11♍36	15 3	6 40	27 28	12 28	23 0	26 41	28 58	3 52
C 4	10 44 30	12 46 56	25 11	15 49	6 58	28 3	12 33	23 4	26 42	28 56	3 51
H 5	10 48 26	13 47 1	9♎ 1	16 39	7 18	28 38	12 38	23 8	26 44	28 55	3 50
6	10 52 23	14 47 5	23 2	17 32	7 40	29 13	12 43	23 13	26 45	28 53	3 49
7	10 56 19	15 47 7	7♏11	18 28	8 4	29 48	12 49	23 17	26 47	28 52	3 48
8	11 0 16	16 47 8	21 24	19 27	8 29	0♊23	12 54	23 21	26 48	28 50	3 47
9	11 4 12	17 47 6	5♐39	20 28	8 57	0 59	13 0	23 26	26 50	28 48	3 46
10	11 8 9	18 47 4	19 53	21 32	9 25	1 34	13 6	23 31	26 52	28 47	3 45
11	11 12 5	19 47 0	4♑ 2	22 38	9 56	2 9	13 13	23 35	26 54	28 45	3 45
12	11 16 2	20 46 54	18 5	23 47	10 28	2 45	13 19	23 40	26 55	28 43	3 44
13	11 19 58	21 46 47	2♒ 1	24 58	11 1	3 20	13 25	23 45	26 57	28 42	3 43
14	11 23 55	22 46 37	15 47	26 10	11 36	3 56	13 32	23 50	26 59	28 40	3 42
15	11 27 52	23 46 26	29 21	27 25	12 12	4 32	13 39	23 55	27 1	28 39	3 41
16	11 31 48	24 46 13	12♓43	28 41	12 49	5 7	13 46	24 0	27 3	28 37	3 40
17	11 35 45	25 45 59	25 51	29 59	13 28	5 43	13 53	24 5	27 5	28 35	3 40
18	11 39 41	26 45 42	8♈44	1♓19	14 7	6 19	14 0	24 11	27 7	28 34	3 39
19	11 43 38	27 45 23	21 22	2 41	14 48	6 54	14 7	24 16	27 9	28 32	3 38
20	11 47 34	28 45 2	3♉46	4 4	15 30	7 30	14 15	24 22	27 11	28 30	3 38
21	11 51 31	29 44 39	15 58	5 28	16 13	8 6	14 23	24 27	27 14	28 29	3 37
22	11 55 27	0♈44 13	28 0	6 54	16 56	8 42	14 30	24 33	27 16	28 27	3 36
23	11 59 24	1 43 46	9♊55	8 22	17 41	9 18	14 38	24 38	27 18	28 25	3 36
24	12 3 21	2 43 16	21 48	9 51	18 27	9 53	14 47	24 44	27 20	28 24	3 35
25	12 7 17	3 42 44	3♋42	11 21	19 13	10 29	14 55	24 50	27 23	28 22	3 34
26	12 11 14	4 42 10	15 43	12 53	20 1	11 5	15 3	24 56	27 25	28 20	3 34
27	12 15 10	5 41 33	27 54	14 26	20 49	11 41	15 12	25 2	27 28	28 19	3 33
28	12 19 7	6 40 54	10♌22	16 1	21 38	12 17	15 20	25 7	27 30	28 17	3 33
29	12 23 3	7 40 13	23 8	17 37	22 28	12 53	15 29	25 14	27 33	28 15	3 32
30	12 27 0	8 39 29	6♍17	19 15	23 18	13 29	15 38	25 20	27 35	28 14	3 32
31	12 30 56	9♈38 43	19♍49	20♓53	24♒ 9	14♊ 5	15♊47	25♉26	27♉38	28♍12	3♌31

THE SUN ENTERS THE SIGN OF ARIES ON MAR 21 AT 06:10.

♈ ARIES ♉ TAURUS ♊ GEMINI ♋ CANCER ♌ LEO ♍ VIRGO ♎ LIBRA

SIDEREAL | SUN. | MOON. | MERCURY | VENUS. | MARS. | JUPITER | SATURN. | URANUS. | NEPTUNE | PLUTO.

DAY	TIME h m s	☉ ° ' "	☽ ° '	☿ ° '	♀ ° '	♂ ° '	♃ ° '	♄ ° '	♅ ° '	♆ ° '	♇ ° '
A 1	12 34 53	10♈37 55	3♎44	22♓33	25♒ 1	14♊42	15♊56	25♉32	27♉40	28♍10	3♌31
P 2	12 38 50	11 37 5	17 59	24 15	25 54	15 18	16 5	25 38	27 43	28R 9	3R31
R 3	12 42 46	12 36 13	2♏29	25 58	26 47	15 54	16 14	25 45	27 46	28 7	3 30
I 4	12 46 43	13 35 20	17 7	27 43	27 40	16 30	16 24	25 51	27 48	28 6	3 30
L 5	12 50 39	14 34 24	1♐47	29 28	28 35	17 6	16 33	25 57	27 51	28 4	3 30
6	12 54 36	15 33 26	16 22	1♈16	29 30	17 42	16 43	26 4	27 54	28 3	3 29
7	12 58 32	16 32 27	0♑47	3 4	0♓25	18 19	16 53	26 11	27 57	28 1	3 29
8	13 2 29	17 31 26	14 57	4 55	1 21	18 55	17 3	26 17	27 59	27 59	3 29
9	13 6 25	18 30 24	28 53	6 46	2 17	19 31	17 13	26 24	28 2	27 58	3 29
10	13 10 22	19 29 20	12♒33	8 39	3 14	20 7	17 23	26 31	28 5	27 56	3 28
11	13 14 18	20 28 13	25 57	10 34	4 11	20 44	17 33	26 37	28 8	27 55	3 28
12	13 18 15	21 27 5	9♓ 8	12 30	5 9	21 20	17 43	26 44	28 11	27 53	3 28
13	13 22 12	22 25 56	22 6	14 28	6 7	21 56	17 54	26 51	28 14	27 52	3 28
14	13 26 8	23 24 44	4♈51	16 27	7 6	22 33	18 4	26 58	28 17	27 50	3 28
15	13 30 5	24 23 31	17 26	18 27	8 5	23 9	18 15	27 5	28 20	27 49	3 28
16	13 34 1	25 22 15	29 51	20 29	9 4	23 45	18 26	27 12	28 23	27 47	3D28
17	13 37 58	26 20 58	12♉ 5	22 32	10 4	24 22	18 37	27 19	28 26	27 46	3 28
18	13 41 54	27 19 39	24 11	24 36	11 4	24 58	18 47	27 26	28 29	27 45	3 28
19	13 45 51	28 18 17	6♊10	26 41	12 4	25 35	18 58	27 33	28 32	27 43	3 28
20	13 49 47	29 16 54	18 4	28 47	13 5	26 11	19 9	27 40	28 36	27 42	3 28
21	13 53 44	0♉15 28	29 55	0♉55	14 6	26 48	19 21	27 47	28 39	27 41	3 28
22	13 57 41	1 14 1	11♋48	3 2	15 7	27 24	19 32	27 54	28 42	27 39	3 28
23	14 1 37	2 12 31	23 46	5 10	16 9	28 1	19 43	28 2	28 45	27 38	3 28
24	14 5 34	3 10 59	5♌55	7 19	17 11	28 37	19 55	28 9	28 48	27 37	3 29
25	14 9 30	4 9 25	18 19	9 27	18 13	29 14	20 6	28 16	28 52	27 35	3 29
26	14 13 27	5 7 48	1♍ 3	11 34	19 16	29 50	20 18	28 24	28 55	27 34	3 29
27	14 17 23	6 6 10	14 11	13 42	20 18	0♋27	20 29	28 31	28 58	27 33	3 29
28	14 21 20	7 4 29	27 47	15 48	21 21	1 4	20 41	28 38	29 1	27 32	3 30
29	14 25 16	8 2 47	11♎50	17 53	22 25	1 40	20 53	28 46	29 5	27 30	3 30
30	14 29 13	9♉ 1 3	26♎19	19♉56	23♓28	2♋17	21♊ 5	28♉53	29♉ 8	27♍29	3♌30

THE SUN ENTERS THE SIGN OF TAURUS ON APR 20 AT 17:39.

DAY	TIME h m s	☉ ° ' "	☽ ° '	☿ ° '	♀ ° '	♂ ° '	♃ ° '	♄ ° '	♅ ° '	♆ ° '	♇ ° '
M 1	14 33 10	9♉59 16	11♏ 9	21♉57	24♓32	2♋53	21♊16	29♉ 1	29♉11	27♍28	3♌31
A 2	14 37 6	10 57 28	26 11	23 57	25 36	3 30	21 28	29 8	29 15	27R27	3 31
Y 3	14 41 3	11 55 39	11♐17	25 53	26 40	4 7	21 40	29 16	29 18	27 26	3 31
4	14 44 59	12 53 48	26 15	27 48	27 44	4 43	21 53	29 23	29 21	27 25	3 32
5	14 48 56	13 51 55	10♑58	29 39	28 49	5 20	22 5	29 31	29 25	27 24	3 32
6	14 52 52	14 50 1	25 20	1♊27	29 53	5 56	22 17	29 38	29 28	27 23	3 33
7	14 56 49	15 48 6	9♒19	3 12	0♈58	6 33	22 29	29 46	29 32	27 22	3 33
8	15 0 45	16 46 9	22 56	4 54	2 4	7 10	22 42	29 54	29 35	27 21	3 34
9	15 4 42	17 44 11	6♓11	6 32	3 9	7 46	22 54	0♊ 1	29 39	27 20	3 35
10	15 8 39	18 42 12	19 8	8 7	4 14	8 23	23 7	0 9	29 42	27 19	3 35
11	15 12 35	19 40 11	1♈49	9 38	5 20	9 0	23 19	0 17	29 45	27 18	3 36
12	15 16 32	20 38 9	14 18	11 5	6 26	9 37	23 32	0 24	29 49	27 17	3 36
13	15 20 28	21 36 5	26 38	12 29	7 32	10 13	23 44	0 32	29 52	27 16	3 37
14	15 24 25	22 34 0	8♉49	13 49	8 38	10 50	23 57	0 40	29 56	27 16	3 38
15	15 28 21	23 31 54	20 53	15 4	9 44	11 27	24 10	0 48	29 59	27 15	3 38
16	15 32 18	24 29 46	2♊52	16 16	10 51	12 4	24 22	0 55	0♊ 3	27 14	3 39
17	15 36 14	25 27 37	14 46	17 24	11 57	12 40	24 35	1 3	0 6	27 13	3 40
18	15 40 11	26 25 26	26 38	18 28	13 4	13 17	24 48	1 11	0 10	27 13	3 41
19	15 44 8	27 23 14	8♋29	19 28	14 11	13 54	25 1	1 19	0 13	27 12	3 42
20	15 48 4	28 21 0	20 22	20 23	15 18	14 31	25 14	1 26	0 17	27 12	3 42
21	15 52 1	29 18 45	2♌19	21 14	16 25	15 8	25 27	1 34	0 20	27 11	3 43
22	15 55 57	0♊16 28	14 27	22 1	17 32	15 44	25 40	1 42	0 24	27 10	3 44
23	15 59 54	1 14 9	26 48	22 43	18 39	16 21	25 53	1 50	0 27	27 10	3 45
24	16 3 50	2 11 49	9♍28	23 21	19 47	16 58	26 6	1 57	0 31	27 9	3 46
25	16 7 47	3 9 27	22 32	23 55	20 54	17 35	26 20	2 5	0 34	27 9	3 47
26	16 11 43	4 7 4	6♎ 3	24 24	22 2	18 12	26 33	2 13	0 38	27 8	3 48
27	16 15 40	5 4 40	20 4	24 48	23 10	18 49	26 46	2 21	0 41	27 8	3 49
28	16 19 37	6 2 13	4♏33	25 7	24 18	19 26	26 59	2 28	0 45	27 8	3 50
29	16 23 33	6 59 46	19 28	25 22	25 26	20 2	27 12	2 36	0 48	27 7	3 51
30	16 27 30	7 57 18	4♐40	25 32	26 34	20 39	27 26	2 44	0 52	27 7	3 52
31	16 31 26	8♊54 48	19♐59	25♊37	27♈42	21♋16	27♊39	2♊52	0♊55	27♍ 7	3♌53

THE SUN ENTERS THE SIGN OF GEMINI ON MAY 21 AT 17:09.

DAY	TIME h m s	☉ ° ' "	☽ ° '	☿ ° '	♀ ° '	♂ ° '	♃ ° '	♄ ° '	♅ ° '	♆ ° '	♇ ° '
J 1	16 35 23	9♊52 18	5♑14	25♊38	28♈50	21♋53	27♊53	2♊59	0♊59	27♍ 6	3♌54
U 2	16 39 19	10 49 46	20 13	25R34	29 59	22 30	28 6	3 7	1 2	27R 6	3 55
N 3	16 43 16	11 47 14	4♒49	25 26	1♉ 7	23 7	28 19	3 15	1 6	27 6	3 56
E 4	16 47 12	12 44 41	18 59	25 14	2 16	23 44	28 33	3 23	1 9	27 6	3 58
5	16 51 9	13 42 7	2♓41	24 58	3 24	24 21	28 46	3 30	1 13	27 6	3 59
6	16 55 6	14 39 33	15 57	24 38	4 33	24 58	29 0	3 38	1 16	27 6	4 0
7	16 59 2	15 36 58	28 51	24 14	5 42	25 35	29 13	3 46	1 20	27 6	4 1
8	17 2 59	16 34 22	11♈25	23 48	6 51	26 12	29 27	3 53	1 23	27D 6	4 2
9	17 6 55	17 31 46	23 46	23 19	8 0	26 49	29 40	4 1	1 26	27 6	4 4
10	17 10 52	18 29 9	5♉55	22 49	9 9	27 26	29 54	4 9	1 30	27 6	4 5
11	17 14 48	19 26 31	17 57	22 16	10 18	28 3	0♋ 8	4 16	1 33	27 6	4 6
12	17 18 45	20 23 54	29 54	21 43	11 28	28 40	0 21	4 24	1 37	27 6	4 7
13	17 22 41	21 21 15	11♊48	21 9	12 37	29 17	0 35	4 31	1 40	27 6	4 9
14	17 26 38	22 18 36	23 39	20 36	13 46	29 54	0 48	4 39	1 43	27 6	4 10
15	17 30 35	23 15 56	5♋31	20 3	14 56	0♌31	1 2	4 46	1 47	27 6	4 11
16	17 34 31	24 13 16	17 24	19 31	16 5	1 8	1 16	4 54	1 50	27 6	4 13
17	17 38 28	25 10 34	29 20	19 2	17 15	1 45	1 29	5 1	1 53	27 7	4 14
18	17 42 24	26 7 52	11♌22	18 34	18 25	2 22	1 43	5 9	1 56	27 7	4 16
19	17 46 21	27 5 10	23 33	18 10	19 34	2 59	1 57	5 16	2 0	27 7	4 17
20	17 50 17	28 2 26	5♍56	17 49	20 44	3 36	2 10	5 24	2 3	27 8	4 18
21	17 54 14	28 59 42	18 36	17 31	21 54	4 14	2 24	5 31	2 6	27 8	4 20
22	17 58 10	29 56 57	1♎36	17 17	23 4	4 51	2 38	5 38	2 9	27 8	4 21
23	18 2 7	0♋54 11	15 2	17 7	24 14	5 28	2 52	5 46	2 13	27 9	4 23
24	18 6 4	1 51 25	28 55	17D 2	25 24	6 5	3 5	5 53	2 16	27 9	4 24
25	18 10 0	2 48 38	13♏16	17 1	26 34	6 42	3 19	6 0	2 19	27 10	4 26
26	18 13 57	3 45 51	28 2	17 5	27 44	7 19	3 33	6 7	2 22	27 10	4 27
27	18 17 53	4 43 3	13♐ 8	17 14	28 55	7 57	3 46	6 15	2 25	27 11	4 29
28	18 21 50	5 40 15	28 24	17 27	0♊ 5	8 34	4 0	6 22	2 28	27 12	4 30
29	18 25 46	6 37 27	13♑40	17 46	1 15	9 11	4 14	6 29	2 31	27 12	4 32
30	18 29 43	7♋34 38	28♑45	18♊ 9	2♊26	9♌48	4♋27	6♊36	2♊34	27♍13	4♌33

THE SUN ENTERS THE SIGN OF CANCER ON JUN 22 AT 01:16.

♏ SCORPIO ♐ SAGITTARIUS ♑ CAPRICORN ♒ AQUARIUS ♓ PISCES

1942

SIDEREAL . . SUN . . MOON . . MERCURY . . VENUS . . MARS . . JUPITER . . SATURN . . URANUS . . NEPTUNE . . PLUTO .

DAY	TIME	☉	☽	☿	♀	♂	♃	♄	♅	♆	♇
	h m s	° ' "	° '	° '	° '	° '	° '	° '	° '	° '	° '
J 1	18 33 39	8♋31 49	13♒29	18♊37	3♊36	10♌25	4♋41	6♊43	2♊37	27♍14	4♌35
U 2	18 37 36	9 29 1	27 48	19 10	4 47	11 3	4 55	6 50	2 40	27 14	4 36
L 3	18 41 33	10 26 12	11♓38	19 47	5 57	11 40	5 8	6 57	2 43	27 15	4 38
Y 4	18 45 29	11 23 24	25 0	20 29	7 8	12 17	5 22	7 4	2 46	27 16	4 40
5	18 49 26	12 20 36	7♈57	21 16	8 19	12 54	5 36	7 11	2 49	27 17	4 41
6	18 53 22	13 17 48	20 33	22 8	9 30	13 32	5 49	7 17	2 52	27 18	4 43
7	18 57 19	14 15 1	2♉52	23 4	10 40	14 9	6 3	7 24	2 55	27 19	4 44
8	19 1 15	15 12 14	14 58	24 5	11 51	14 46	6 17	7 31	2 58	27 20	4 46
9	19 5 12	16 9 27	26 56	25 9	13 2	15 24	6 30	7 38	3 0	27 20	4 48
10	19 9 8	17 6 41	8♊49	26 19	14 13	16 1	6 44	7 44	3 3	27 21	4 49
11	19 13 5	18 3 55	20 41	27 33	15 25	16 38	6 57	7 51	3 6	27 22	4 51
12	19 17 2	19 1 9	2♋33	28 50	16 36	17 16	7 11	7 57	3 8	27 23	4 53
13	19 20 58	19 58 24	14 27	0♋13	17 47	17 53	7 24	8 4	3 11	27 25	4 54
14	19 24 55	20 55 38	26 25	1 39	18 58	18 31	7 38	8 10	3 14	27 26	4 56
15	19 28 51	21 52 54	8♌29	3 9	20 9	19 8	7 51	8 17	3 16	27 27	4 58
16	19 32 48	22 50 9	20 41	4 43	21 21	19 45	8 5	8 23	3 19	27 28	4 59
17	19 36 44	23 47 25	3♍ 2	6 21	22 32	20 23	8 18	8 29	3 21	27 29	5 1
18	19 40 41	24 44 40	15 34	8 3	23 44	21 0	8 31	8 35	3 24	27 30	5 3
19	19 44 37	25 41 56	28 22	9 48	24 55	21 38	8 45	8 42	3 26	27 32	5 5
20	19 48 34	26 39 13	11♎26	11 36	26 7	22 15	8 58	8 48	3 29	27 33	5 6
21	19 52 31	27 36 29	24 51	13 27	27 18	22 53	9 11	8 54	3 31	27 34	5 8
22	19 56 27	28 33 46	8♏38	15 22	28 30	23 30	9 25	9 0	3 34	27 35	5 10
23	20 0 24	29 31 3	22 48	17 19	29 42	24 8	9 38	9 6	3 36	27 37	5 11
24	20 4 20	0♌28 20	7♐19	19 18	0♋53	24 46	9 51	9 11	3 38	27 38	5 13
25	20 8 17	1 25 38	22 7	21 19	2 5	25 23	10 4	9 17	3 40	27 40	5 15
26	20 12 13	2 22 56	7♑ 6	23 22	3 17	26 1	10 18	9 23	3 43	27 41	5 17
27	20 16 10	3 20 14	22 8	25 26	4 29	26 38	10 31	9 28	3 45	27 42	5 18
28	20 20 6	4 17 34	7♒ 3	27 31	5 41	27 16	10 44	9 34	3 47	27 44	5 20
29	20 24 3	5 14 54	21 43	29 37	6 53	27 54	10 57	9 40	3 49	27 45	5 22
30	20 28 0	6 12 14	6♓ 1	1♌43	8 5	28 31	11 10	9 45	3 51	27 47	5 23
31	20 31 56	7♌ 9 36	19♓55	3♌49	9♋17	29♌ 9	11♋23	9♊50	3♊53	27♍48	5♌25

THE SUN ENTERS THE SIGN OF LEO ON JUL 23 AT 12:08.

DAY	TIME	☉	☽	☿	♀	♂	♃	♄	♅	♆	♇
	h m s	° ' "	° '	° '	° '	° '	° '	° '	° '	° '	° '
A 1	20 35 53	8♌ 6 59	3♈22	5♌55	10♋29	29♌47	11♋36	9♊56	3♊55	27♍50	5♌27
U 2	20 39 49	9 4 23	16 24	8 1	11 41	0♍24	11 48	10 1	3 57	27 52	5 29
G 3	20 43 46	10 1 48	29 4	10 6	12 54	1 2	12 1	10 6	3 59	27 53	5 30
U 4	20 47 42	10 59 14	11♉25	12 10	14 6	1 40	12 14	10 11	4 1	27 55	5 32
S 5	20 51 39	11 56 41	23 33	14 13	15 18	2 18	12 27	10 16	4 2	27 56	5 34
T 6	20 55 35	12 54 10	5♊31	16 15	16 31	2 56	12 39	10 21	4 4	27 58	5 35
7	20 59 32	13 51 40	17 24	18 16	17 43	3 33	12 52	10 26	4 6	28 0	5 37
8	21 3 29	14 49 11	29 15	20 15	18 56	4 11	13 5	10 31	4 7	28 2	5 39
9	21 7 25	15 46 43	11♋ 9	22 13	20 8	4 49	13 17	10 36	4 9	28 3	5 41
10	21 11 22	16 44 17	23 8	24 10	21 21	5 27	13 30	10 40	4 11	28 5	5 42
11	21 15 18	17 41 52	5♌14	26 5	22 34	6 5	13 42	10 45	4 12	28 7	5 44
12	21 19 15	18 39 28	17 29	27 59	23 46	6 43	13 54	10 49	4 14	28 9	5 46
13	21 23 11	19 37 5	29 55	29 52	24 59	7 21	14 7	10 54	4 15	28 10	5 47
14	21 27 8	20 34 43	12♍33	1♍43	26 12	7 59	14 19	10 58	4 16	28 12	5 49
15	21 31 4	21 32 23	25 23	3 32	27 25	8 37	14 31	11 2	4 18	28 14	5 51
16	21 35 1	22 30 3	8♎27	5 20	28 38	9 15	14 43	11 6	4 19	28 16	5 52
17	21 38 58	23 27 45	21 46	7 6	29 51	9 53	14 55	11 10	4 20	28 18	5 54
18	21 42 54	24 25 27	5♏19	8 51	1♌ 4	10 31	15 7	11 14	4 21	28 20	5 56
19	21 46 51	25 23 11	19 8	10 35	2 17	11 9	15 19	11 18	4 23	28 22	5 57
20	21 50 47	26 20 56	3♐12	12 17	3 30	11 47	15 31	11 22	4 24	28 24	5 59
21	21 54 44	27 18 42	17 29	13 58	4 43	12 25	15 43	11 25	4 25	28 26	6 1
22	21 58 40	28 16 29	1♑57	15 37	5 56	13 3	15 54	11 29	4 26	28 28	6 2
23	22 2 37	29 14 17	16 32	17 15	7 9	13 41	16 6	11 32	4 27	28 30	6 4
24	22 6 33	0♍12 6	1♒ 8	18 52	8 23	14 20	16 18	11 36	4 28	28 32	6 5
25	22 10 30	1 9 57	15 41	20 27	9 36	14 58	16 29	11 39	4 28	28 34	6 7
26	22 14 27	2 7 49	0♓ 3	22 1	10 49	15 36	16 40	11 42	4 29	28 36	6 9
27	22 18 23	3 5 42	14 9	23 33	12 3	16 14	16 52	11 46	4 30	28 38	6 10
28	22 22 20	4 3 37	27 56	25 5	13 16	16 52	17 3	11 49	4 31	28 40	6 12
29	22 26 16	5 1 34	11♈21	26 34	14 30	17 31	17 14	11 51	4 31	28 42	6 13
30	22 30 13	5 59 32	24 24	28 3	15 43	18 9	17 25	11 54	4 32	28 44	6 15
31	22 34 9	6♍57 32	7♉ 7	29♍30	16♌57	18♍47	17♋36	11♊57	4♊33	28♍46	6♌16

THE SUN ENTERS THE SIGN OF VIRGO ON AUG 23 AT 18:59.

DAY	TIME	☉	☽	☿	♀	♂	♃	♄	♅	♆	♇
	h m s	° ' "	° '	° '	° '	° '	° '	° '	° '	° '	° '
S 1	22 38 6	7♍55 35	19♉31	0♎55	18♌10	19♍26	17♋47	12♊ 0	4♊33	28♍48	6♌18
E 2	22 42 2	8 53 39	1♊40	2 19	19 24	20 4	17 58	12 2	4 33	28 50	6 19
P 3	22 45 59	9 51 45	13 39	3 42	20 38	20 43	18 9	12 5	4 34	28 52	6 21
T 4	22 49 56	10 49 53	25 33	5 4	21 51	21 21	18 19	12 7	4 34	28 54	6 22
E 5	22 53 52	11 48 3	7♋25	6 23	23 5	22 0	18 30	12 9	4 35	28 57	6 24
M 6	22 57 49	12 46 14	19 20	7 42	24 19	22 38	18 40	12 11	4 35	28 59	6 25
B 7	23 1 45	13 44 28	1♌23	8 58	25 33	23 17	18 51	12 13	4 35	29 1	6 27
E 8	23 5 42	14 42 44	13 36	10 13	26 47	23 55	19 1	12 15	4 35	29 3	6 28
R 9	23 9 38	15 41 2	26 3	11 26	28 1	24 34	19 11	12 17	4 35	29 5	6 29
10	23 13 35	16 39 21	8♍45	12 38	29 15	25 12	19 21	12 19	4R35	29 7	6 31
11	23 17 31	17 37 42	21 43	13 47	0♍29	25 51	19 31	12 20	4 35	29 10	6 32
12	23 21 28	18 36 5	4♎57	14 55	1 43	26 30	19 41	12 22	4 35	29 12	6 34
13	23 25 24	19 34 30	18 25	16 0	2 57	27 8	19 51	12 23	4 35	29 14	6 35
14	23 29 21	20 32 57	2♏ 7	17 4	4 11	27 47	20 0	12 25	4 35	29 16	6 36
15	23 33 18	21 31 25	16 0	18 5	5 25	28 26	20 10	12 26	4 35	29 18	6 38
16	23 37 14	22 29 55	0♐ 1	19 3	6 40	29 5	20 19	12 27	4 34	29 21	6 39
17	23 41 11	23 28 26	14 9	19 58	7 54	29 44	20 29	12 28	4 34	29 23	6 40
18	23 45 7	24 27 0	28 20	20 51	9 8	0♎22	20 38	12 29	4 34	29 25	6 41
19	23 49 4	25 25 34	12♑34	21 41	10 22	1 1	20 47	12 29	4 33	29 27	6 43
20	23 53 0	26 24 11	26 46	22 27	11 37	1 40	20 56	12 30	4 33	29 30	6 44
21	23 56 57	27 22 49	10♒56	23 10	12 51	2 19	21 5	12 30	4 32	29 32	6 45
22	0 0 53	28 21 29	25 1	23 48	14 6	2 58	21 13	12 31	4 32	29 34	6 46
23	0 4 50	29 20 10	8♓56	24 23	15 20	3 37	21 22	12 31	4 31	29 36	6 47
24	0 8 47	0♎18 53	22 41	24 52	16 35	4 16	21 30	12 31	4 31	29 38	6 48
25	0 12 43	1 17 38	6♈11	25 17	17 49	4 55	21 39	12R31	4 30	29 41	6 50
26	0 16 40	2 16 26	19 25	25 37	19 4	5 34	21 47	12 31	4 29	29 43	6 51
27	0 20 36	3 15 15	2♉22	25 51	20 18	6 13	21 55	12 31	4 28	29 45	6 52
28	0 24 33	4 14 6	15 1	25R59	21 33	6 52	22 3	12 31	4 27	29 47	6 53
29	0 28 29	5 13 0	27 24	26 0	22 47	7 31	22 11	12 31	4 26	29 50	6 54
30	0 32 26	6♎11 56	9♊34	25♎54	24♍ 2	8♎11	22♋18	12♊30	4♊26	29♍52	6♌55

THE SUN ENTERS THE SIGN OF LIBRA ON SEP 23 AT 16:17.

♈ ARIES ♉ TAURUS ♊ GEMINI ♋ CANCER ♌ LEO ♍ VIRGO ♎ LIBRA

SIDEREAL · SUN · MOON · MERCURY · VENUS · MARS · JUPITER · SATURN · URANUS · NEPTUNE · PLUTO

DAY	TIME h m s	☉ ° ' "	☽ ° '	☿ ° '	♀ ° '	♂ ° '	♃ ° '	♄ ° '	♅ ° '	♆ ° '	♇ ° '
O 1	Ø 36 22	7♎1Ø 54	21♊33	25♎41	25♍17	8♎5Ø	22♋26	12♊3Ø	4♊25	29♍54	6♌56
C 2	Ø 4Ø 19	8 9 55	3♋26	25R2Ø	26 31	9 29	22 33	12R29	4R23	29 56	6 57
T 3	Ø 44 16	9 8 58	15 17	24 52	27 46	1Ø 8	22 41	12 28	4 22	29 58	6 58
O 4	Ø 48 12	1Ø 8 3	27 12	24 16	29 1	1Ø 48	22 48	12 27	4 21	Ø♎ 1	6 59
B 5	Ø 52 9	11 7 1Ø	9♌16	23 32	Ø♎16	11 27	22 55	12 26	4 2Ø	Ø 3	7 Ø
E 6	Ø 56 5	12 6 2Ø	21 32	22 41	1 31	12 6	23 1	12 25	4 19	Ø 5	7 1
R 7	1 Ø 2	13 5 31	4♍ 6	21 44	2 45	12 46	23 8	12 24	4 18	Ø 7	7 1
8	1 3 58	14 4 45	17 Ø	2Ø 41	4 Ø	13 25	23 15	12 23	4 16	Ø 9	7 2
9	1 7 55	15 4 2	Ø♎15	19 33	5 15	14 5	23 21	12 21	4 15	Ø 12	7 3
1Ø	1 11 51	16 3 2Ø	13 52	18 23	6 3Ø	14 44	23 27	12 2Ø	4 13	Ø 14	7 4
11	1 15 48	17 2 4Ø	27 47	17 11	7 45	15 24	23 33	12 18	4 12	Ø 16	7 5
12	1 19 44	18 2 3	11♏57	16 Ø	9 Ø	16 3	23 39	12 16	4 11	Ø 18	7 5
13	1 23 41	19 1 27	26 18	14 52	1Ø 15	16 43	23 45	12 14	4 9	Ø 2Ø	7 6
14	1 27 38	2Ø Ø 53	1Ø♐42	13 49	11 3Ø	17 23	23 5Ø	12 12	4 7	Ø 22	7 7
15	1 31 34	21 Ø 21	25 5	12 53	12 45	18 2	23 56	12 1Ø	4 6	Ø 24	7 7
16	1 35 31	21 59 51	9♑23	12 5	14 Ø	18 42	24 1	12 8	4 4	Ø 27	7 8
17	1 39 27	22 59 23	23 33	11 27	15 15	19 22	24 6	12 6	4 2	Ø 29	7 9
18	1 43 24	23 58 56	7♒33	1Ø 59	16 3Ø	2Ø 2	24 11	12 3	4 1	Ø 31	7 9
19	1 47 2Ø	24 58 31	21 23	1Ø 42	17 45	2Ø 41	24 16	12 1	3 59	Ø 33	7 1Ø
2Ø	1 51 17	25 58 7	5♓ 3	1ØD36	19 Ø	21 21	24 2Ø	11 58	3 57	Ø 35	7 1Ø
21	1 55 13	26 57 46	18 33	1Ø 41	2Ø 15	22 1	24 25	11 56	3 55	Ø 37	7 11
22	1 59 1Ø	27 57 26	1♈52	1Ø 57	21 3Ø	22 41	24 29	11 53	3 53	Ø 39	7 11
23	2 3 7	28 57 8	15 Ø	11 24	22 46	23 21	24 33	11 5Ø	3 52	Ø 41	7 12
24	2 7 3	29 56 52	27 56	11 59	24 1	24 1	24 37	11 47	3 5Ø	Ø 43	7 12
25	2 11 Ø	Ø♏56 38	1Ø♉39	12 44	25 16	24 41	24 4Ø	11 44	3 48	Ø 45	7 13
26	2 14 56	1 56 26	23 9	13 36	26 31	25 21	24 44	11 41	3 46	Ø 47	7 13
27	2 18 53	2 56 16	5♊27	14 36	27 46	26 1	24 47	11 38	3 44	Ø 49	7 13
28	2 22 49	3 56 8	17 33	15 41	29 1	26 41	24 5Ø	11 35	3 42	Ø 51	7 14
29	2 26 46	4 56 2	29 3Ø	16 52	Ø♏17	27 21	24 53	11 31	3 39	Ø 53	7 14
3Ø	2 3Ø 42	5 55 58	11♋21	18 8	1 32	28 2	24 56	11 28	3 37	Ø 55	7 14
31	2 34 39	6♏55 57	23♋11	19♎27	2♏47	28♎42	24♋59	11♊24	3♊35	Ø♎57	7♌14

THE SUN ENTERS THE SIGN OF SCORPIO ON OCT 24 AT O1:16.

DAY	TIME h m s	☉ ° ' "	☽ ° '	☿ ° '	♀ ° '	♂ ° '	♃ ° '	♄ ° '	♅ ° '	♆ ° '	♇ ° '
N 1	2 38 36	7♏55 57	5♌ 3	2Ø♎5Ø	4♏ 2	29♎22	25♋ 1	11♊21	3♊33	Ø♎59	7♌15
O 2	2 42 32	8 56 Ø	17 4	22 16	5 18	Ø♏ 2	25 3	11R17	3R31	1 Ø	7 15
V 3	2 46 29	9 56 5	29 19	23 44	6 33	Ø 43	25 5	11 13	3 29	1 2	7 15
E 4	2 5Ø 25	1Ø 56 12	11♍53	25 14	7 48	1 23	25 7	11 9	3 26	1 4	7 15
M 5	2 54 22	11 56 21	24 5Ø	26 46	9 4	2 3	25 9	11 5	3 24	1 6	7 15
B 6	2 58 18	12 56 32	8♎13	28 19	1Ø 19	2 44	25 1Ø	11 1	3 22	1 8	7 15
E 7	3 2 15	13 56 45	22 3	29 53	11 34	3 24	25 11	1Ø 57	3 19	1 9	7 15
R 8	3 6 11	14 57 Ø	6♏19	1♏28	12 5Ø	4 5	25 12	1Ø 53	3 17	1 11	7R15
9	3 1Ø 8	15 57 17	2Ø 54	3 3	14 5	4 46	25 13	1Ø 49	3 15	1 13	7 15
1Ø	3 14 4	16 57 36	5♐42	4 39	15 2Ø	5 26	25 14	1Ø 45	3 12	1 15	7 15
11	3 18 1	17 57 56	2Ø 33	6 15	16 36	6 7	25 14	1Ø 41	3 1Ø	1 16	7 15
12	3 21 58	18 58 18	5♑21	7 52	17 51	6 47	25R14	1Ø 36	3 7	1 18	7 15
13	3 25 54	19 58 41	19 56	9 28	19 6	7 28	25 14	1Ø 32	3 5	1 19	7 15
14	3 29 51	2Ø 59 6	4♒16	11 5	2Ø 22	8 9	25 14	1Ø 27	3 3	1 21	7 15
15	3 33 47	21 59 31	18 17	12 41	21 37	8 5Ø	25 14	1Ø 23	3 Ø	1 23	7 15
16	3 37 44	22 59 59	2♓ Ø	14 18	22 52	9 3Ø	25 13	1Ø 18	2 58	1 24	7 15
17	3 41 4Ø	24 Ø 27	15 26	15 54	24 8	1Ø 11	25 12	1Ø 14	2 55	1 26	7 15
18	3 45 37	25 Ø 57	28 38	17 3Ø	25 23	1Ø 52	25 11	1Ø 9	2 53	1 27	7 14
19	3 49 34	26 1 28	11♈36	19 6	26 39	11 33	25 1Ø	1Ø 4	2 5Ø	1 29	7 14
2Ø	3 53 3Ø	27 2 Ø	24 24	2Ø 42	27 54	12 14	25 9	1Ø Ø	2 48	1 3Ø	7 14
21	3 57 27	28 2 34	7♉ Ø	22 18	29 9	12 55	25 7	9 55	2 45	1 32	7 13
22	4 1 23	29 3 9	19 27	23 54	Ø♐25	13 36	25 5	9 5Ø	2 43	1 33	7 13
23	4 5 2Ø	Ø♐ 3 45	1♊44	25 29	1 4Ø	14 17	25 4	9 45	2 4Ø	1 34	7 13
24	4 9 16	1 4 23	13 53	27 4	2 56	14 58	25 1	9 41	2 38	1 36	7 12
25	4 13 13	2 5 3	25 53	28 39	4 11	15 39	24 59	9 36	2 35	1 37	7 12
26	4 17 9	3 5 43	7♋47	Ø♐14	5 26	16 21	24 56	9 31	2 33	1 38	7 11
27	4 21 6	4 6 26	19 36	1 49	6 42	17 2	24 54	9 26	2 3Ø	1 4Ø	7 11
28	4 25 3	5 7 1Ø	1♌24	3 23	7 57	17 43	24 51	9 21	2 28	1 41	7 1Ø
29	4 28 59	6 7 55	13 14	4 58	9 13	18 24	24 48	9 16	2 25	1 42	7 1Ø
3Ø	4 32 56	7♐ 8 42	25♌13	6♐32	1Ø♐28	19♏ 6	24♋44	9♊11	2♊23	1♎43	7♌ 9

THE SUN ENTERS THE SIGN OF SAGITTARIUS ON NOV 22 AT 22:31.

DAY	TIME h m s	☉ ° ' "	☽ ° '	☿ ° '	♀ ° '	♂ ° '	♃ ° '	♄ ° '	♅ ° '	♆ ° '	♇ ° '
D 1	4 36 52	8♐ 9 3Ø	7♍24	8♐ 7	11♐43	19♏47	24♋41	9♊ 6	2♊2Ø	1♎44	7♌ 9
E 2	4 4Ø 49	9 1Ø 2Ø	19 53	9 41	12 59	2Ø 29	24R37	9R 1	2R18	1 45	7R 8
C 3	4 44 45	1Ø 11 11	2♎46	11 15	14 14	21 1Ø	24 33	8 56	2 15	1 46	7 8
E 4	4 48 42	11 12 4	16 6	12 49	15 3Ø	21 51	24 29	8 51	2 13	1 48	7 7
M 5	4 52 38	12 12 58	29 56	14 24	16 45	22 33	24 25	8 47	2 1Ø	1 49	7 6
B 6	4 56 35	13 13 53	14♏16	15 58	18 1	23 15	24 2Ø	8 42	2 8	1 5Ø	7 6
E 7	5 Ø 32	14 14 49	29 1	17 32	19 16	23 56	24 16	8 37	2 5	1 5Ø	7 5
R 8	5 4 28	15 15 47	14♐ 5	19 6	2Ø 31	24 38	24 11	8 32	2 3	1 51	7 4
9	5 8 25	16 16 45	29 17	2Ø 4Ø	21 47	25 2Ø	24 6	8 27	2 Ø	1 52	7 3
1Ø	5 12 21	17 17 45	14♑27	22 14	23 2	26 1	24 1	8 22	1 58	1 53	7 3
11	5 16 18	18 18 45	29 25	23 49	24 18	26 43	23 56	8 17	1 56	1 54	7 2
12	5 2Ø 14	19 19 46	14♒ 3	25 23	25 33	27 25	23 5Ø	8 13	1 53	1 55	7 1
13	5 24 11	2Ø 2Ø 47	28 17	26 57	26 49	28 7	23 45	8 8	1 51	1 56	7 Ø
14	5 28 7	21 21 49	12♓ 7	28 32	28 4	28 49	23 39	8 3	1 48	1 56	6 59
15	5 32 4	22 22 51	25 33	Ø♑ 6	29 2Ø	29 31	23 33	7 58	1 46	1 57	6 58
16	5 36 1	23 23 54	8♈39	1 41	Ø♑35	Ø♐12	23 27	7 54	1 44	1 58	6 57
17	5 39 57	24 24 57	21 27	3 16	1 5Ø	Ø 54	23 21	7 49	1 42	1 58	6 57
18	5 43 54	25 26 Ø	4♉ 1	4 5Ø	3 6	1 37	23 14	7 44	1 39	1 59	6 56
19	5 47 5Ø	26 27 4	16 23	6 25	4 21	2 19	23 8	7 4Ø	1 37	1 59	6 55
2Ø	5 51 47	27 28 8	28 36	8 Ø	5 37	3 1	23 1	7 35	1 35	2 Ø	6 54
21	5 55 43	28 29 13	1Ø♊41	9 35	6 52	3 43	22 55	7 31	1 33	2 Ø	6 53
22	5 59 4Ø	29 3Ø 18	22 4Ø	11 1Ø	8 7	4 25	22 48	7 27	1 31	2 1	6 52
23	6 3 36	Ø♑31 24	4♋34	12 44	9 23	5 7	22 41	7 22	1 28	2 1	6 51
24	6 7 33	1 32 3Ø	16 25	14 19	1Ø 38	5 49	22 34	7 18	1 26	2 2	6 49
25	6 11 3Ø	2 33 36	28 14	15 53	11 54	6 32	22 27	7 14	1 24	2 2	6 48
26	6 15 26	3 34 43	1Ø♌ 3	17 27	13 9	7 14	22 19	7 1Ø	1 22	2 2	6 47
27	6 19 23	4 35 51	21 56	19 1	14 24	7 56	22 12	7 6	1 2Ø	2 3	6 46
28	6 23 19	5 36 58	3♍56	2Ø 34	15 4Ø	8 39	22 5	7 2	1 18	2 3	6 45
29	6 27 16	6 38 7	16 7	22 6	16 55	9 21	21 57	6 58	1 16	2 3	6 44
3Ø	6 31 12	7 39 15	28 33	23 37	18 1Ø	1Ø 4	21 5Ø	6 54	1 14	2 3	6 43
31	6 35 9	8♑4Ø 25	11♎21	25♑ 8	19♑26	1Ø♐46	21♋42	6♊5Ø	1♊13	2♎ 3	6♌42

THE SUN ENTERS THE SIGN OF CAPRICORN ON DEC 22 AT 11:4O.

♏	SCORPIO	♐	SAGITTARIUS	♑	CAPRICORN	♒	AQUARIUS	♓	PISCES

SIDEREAL TIME · SUN · MOON · MERCURY · VENUS · MARS · JUPITER · SATURN · URANUS · NEPTUNE · PLUTO

DAY	TIME	☉	☽	☿	♀	♂	♃	♄	♅	♆	♇
	h m s	° ' "	° '	° '	° '	° '	° '	° '	° '	° '	° '
J 1	6 39 5	9♑41 34	24♎33	26♑37	2Ø♑41	11♐29	21♋34	6♊46	1♊11	2♎ 4	6♌4Ø
A 2	6 43 2	1Ø 42 44	8♏14	28 5	21 56	12 12	21R26	6R43	1R 9	2 4	6R39
N 3	6 46 59	11 43 55	22 24	29 3Ø	23 12	12 54	21 18	6 39	1 7	2R 4	6 38
U 4	6 5Ø 55	12 45 5	7♐ 1	Ø♒54	24 27	13 37	21 1Ø	6 35	1 5	2 4	6 37
A 5	6 54 52	13 46 16	22 2	2 14	25 42	14 2Ø	21 2	6 32	1 4	2 4	6 35
R 6	6 58 48	14 47 27	7♑16	3 32	26 58	15 2	2Ø 54	6 29	1 2	2 4	6 34
Y 7	7 2 45	15 48 38	22 34	4 45	28 13	15 45	2Ø 46	6 25	1 1	2 4	6 33
8	7 6 41	16 49 49	7♒45	5 54	29 28	16 28	2Ø 38	6 22	Ø 59	2 3	6 32
9	7 1Ø 38	17 5Ø 59	22 39	6 58	Ø♒44	17 11	2Ø 3Ø	6 19	Ø 58	2 3	6 3Ø
1Ø	7 14 35	18 52 9	7♓1Ø	7 56	1 59	17 54	2Ø 22	6 16	Ø 56	2 3	6 29
11	7 18 31	19 53 18	21 15	8 47	3 14	18 37	2Ø 14	6 13	Ø 55	2 3	6 28
12	7 22 28	2Ø 54 27	4♈51	9 31	4 3Ø	19 2Ø	2Ø 6	6 11	Ø 53	2 3	6 27
13	7 26 24	21 55 35	18 3	1Ø 6	5 45	2Ø 3	19 58	6 8	Ø 52	2 2	6 25
14	7 3Ø 21	22 56 43	Ø♉52	1Ø 31	7 Ø	2Ø 46	19 5Ø	6 5	Ø 51	2 2	6 24
15	7 34 17	23 57 5Ø	13 22	1ØR46	8 15	21 29	19 42	6 3	Ø 49	2 2	6 23
16	7 38 14	24 58 56	25 38	1Ø 5Ø	9 31	22 12	19 34	6 1	Ø 48	2 1	6 21
17	7 42 1Ø	26 Ø 1	7♊42	1Ø 43	1Ø 46	22 55	19 26	5 58	Ø 47	2 1	6 2Ø
18	7 46 7	27 1 6	19 39	1Ø 24	12 1	23 38	19 18	5 56	Ø 46	2 Ø	6 19
19	7 5Ø 3	28 2 1Ø	1♋32	9 53	13 16	24 22	19 1Ø	5 54	Ø 45	2 Ø	6 17
2Ø	7 54 Ø	29 3 13	13 22	9 11	14 31	25 5	19 2	5 52	Ø 44	1 59	6 16
21	7 57 57	Ø♒ 4 16	25 12	8 19	15 46	25 48	18 54	5 5Ø	Ø 43	1 59	6 14
22	8 1 53	1 5 18	7♌ 3	7 18	17 2	26 32	18 46	5 48	Ø 42	1 58	6 13
23	8 5 5Ø	2 6 19	18 58	6 1Ø	18 17	27 15	18 39	5 47	Ø 41	1 58	6 12
24	8 9 46	3 7 2Ø	Ø♍59	4 57	19 32	27 58	18 31	5 45	Ø 4Ø	1 57	6 1Ø
25	8 13 43	4 8 2Ø	13 7	3 41	2Ø 47	28 42	18 24	5 44	Ø 4Ø	1 56	6 9
26	8 17 39	5 9 19	25 26	2 25	22 2	29 25	18 16	5 42	Ø 39	1 55	6 8
27	8 21 36	6 1Ø 17	7♎59	1 1Ø	23 17	Ø♑ 9	18 9	5 41	Ø 38	1 55	6 6
28	8 25 32	7 11 15	2Ø 48	29♑59	24 32	Ø 52	18 1	5 4Ø	Ø 38	1 54	6 5
29	8 29 29	8 12 13	3♏57	28 54	25 47	1 36	17 54	5 39	Ø 37	1 53	6 3
3Ø	8 33 26	9 13 9	17 29	27 55	27 2	2 2Ø	17 47	5 38	Ø 37	1 52	6 2
31	8 37 22	1Ø♒14 6	1♐26	27♑ 4	28♒17	3♑ 3	17♋4Ø	5♊37	Ø♊36	1♎51	6♌ 1

THE SUN ENTERS THE SIGN OF AQUARIUS ON JAN 20 AT 22:19.

DAY	TIME	☉	☽	☿	♀	♂	♃	♄	♅	♆	♇
	h m s	° ' "	° '	° '	° '	° '	° '	° '	° '	° '	° '
F 1	8 41 19	11♒15 1	15♐46	26♑22	29♒32	3♑47	17♋33	5♊37	Ø♊36	1♎51	5♌59
E 2	8 45 15	12 15 56	Ø♑27	25R48	Ø♓47	4 31	17R26	5R36	ØR35	1R5Ø	5R58
B 3	8 49 12	13 16 5Ø	15 25	25 22	2 2	5 14	17 2Ø	5 36	Ø 35	1 49	5 57
R 4	8 53 8	14 17 42	Ø♒31	25 5	3 17	5 58	17 13	5 35	Ø 35	1 48	5 55
U 5	8 57 5	15 18 34	15 36	24D57	4 31	6 42	17 7	5 35	Ø 35	1 47	5 54
A 6	9 1 2	16 19 25	Ø♓32	24 56	5 46	7 26	17 1	5D35	Ø 35	1 46	5 53
R 7	9 4 58	17 2Ø 14	15 1Ø	25 2	7 1	8 1Ø	16 55	5 35	Ø 34	1 45	5 51
Y 8	9 8 55	18 21 2	29 25	25 15	8 16	8 54	16 49	5 35	ØD34	1 44	5 5Ø
9	9 12 51	19 21 48	13♈13	25 35	9 31	9 38	16 43	5 36	Ø 34	1 42	5 49
1Ø	9 16 48	2Ø 22 33	26 34	26 Ø	1Ø 45	1Ø 22	16 37	5 36	Ø 35	1 41	5 47
11	9 2Ø 44	21 23 16	9♉3Ø	26 31	12 Ø	11 6	16 32	5 36	Ø 35	1 4Ø	5 46
12	9 24 41	22 23 58	22 5	27 7	13 15	11 5Ø	16 26	5 37	Ø 35	1 39	5 45
13	9 28 37	23 24 38	4♊21	27 47	14 29	12 34	16 21	5 38	Ø 35	1 38	5 43
14	9 32 34	24 25 16	16 25	28 31	15 44	13 18	16 16	5 39	Ø 35	1 37	5 42
15	9 36 3Ø	25 25 53	28 19	29 19	16 59	14 2	16 11	5 39	Ø 36	1 35	5 41
16	9 4Ø 27	26 26 28	1Ø♋ 8	Ø♒11	18 13	14 46	16 7	5 41	Ø 36	1 34	5 39
17	9 44 24	27 27 1	21 57	1 6	19 28	15 31	16 2	5 42	Ø 37	1 33	5 38
18	9 48 2Ø	28 27 33	3♌48	2 4	2Ø 42	16 15	15 58	5 43	Ø 37	1 31	5 37
19	9 52 17	29 28 3	15 44	3 4	21 57	16 59	15 54	5 44	Ø 38	1 3Ø	5 36
2Ø	9 56 13	Ø♓28 31	27 48	4 8	23 11	17 43	15 5Ø	5 46	Ø 38	1 29	5 34
21	1Ø Ø 1Ø	1 28 58	1Ø♍ 1	5 13	24 25	18 28	15 46	5 47	Ø 39	1 27	5 33
22	1Ø 4 6	2 29 23	22 25	6 21	25 4Ø	19 12	15 42	5 49	Ø 4Ø	1 26	5 32
23	1Ø 8 3	3 29 47	5♎ 1	7 31	26 54	19 57	15 39	5 51	Ø 4Ø	1 25	5 31
24	1Ø 11 59	4 3Ø 9	17 49	8 43	28 8	2Ø 41	15 36	5 53	Ø 41	1 23	5 3Ø
25	1Ø 15 56	5 3Ø 3Ø	Ø♏52	9 56	29 23	21 25	15 33	5 55	Ø 42	1 22	5 28
26	1Ø 19 53	6 3Ø 49	14 1Ø	11 12	Ø♈37	22 1Ø	15 3Ø	5 57	Ø 43	1 2Ø	5 27
27	1Ø 23 49	7 31 7	27 43	12 28	1 51	22 54	15 27	5 59	Ø 44	1 19	5 26
28	1Ø 27 46	8♓31 23	11♐33	13♒47	3♈ 5	23♑39	15♋25	6♊ 2	Ø♊45	1♎17	5♌25

THE SUN ENTERS THE SIGN OF PISCES ON FEB 19 AT 12:40.

DAY	TIME	☉	☽	☿	♀	♂	♃	♄	♅	♆	♇
	h m s	° ' "	° '	° '	° '	° '	° '	° '	° '	° '	° '
M 1	1Ø 31 42	9♓31 38	25♐39	15♒ 7	4♈19	24♑24	15♋22	6♊ 4	Ø♊46	1♎16	5♌24
A 2	1Ø 35 39	1Ø 31 52	1Ø♑ Ø	16 29	5 33	25 8	15R2Ø	6 7	Ø 47	1R14	5R23
R 3	1Ø 39 35	11 32 4	24 32	17 51	6 47	25 53	15 18	6 9	Ø 48	1 13	5 22
C 4	1Ø 43 32	12 32 14	9♒13	19 16	8 1	26 37	15 17	6 12	Ø 5Ø	1 11	5 21
H 5	1Ø 47 28	13 32 23	23 56	2Ø 41	9 15	27 22	15 15	6 15	Ø 51	1 1Ø	5 2Ø
6	1Ø 51 25	14 32 3Ø	8♓35	22 8	1Ø 29	28 7	15 14	6 18	Ø 52	1 8	5 19
7	1Ø 55 22	15 32 35	23 3	23 36	11 43	28 52	15 13	6 21	Ø 54	1 7	5 18
8	1Ø 59 18	16 32 38	7♈14	25 5	12 57	29 36	15 12	6 24	Ø 55	1 5	5 17
9	11 3 15	17 32 39	21 4	26 36	14 11	Ø♒21	15 11	6 27	Ø 56	1 3	5 16
1Ø	11 7 11	18 32 39	4♉29	28 8	15 24	1 6	15 11	6 31	Ø 58	1 2	5 15
11	11 11 8	19 32 36	17 31	29 41	16 38	1 51	15 1Ø	6 34	1 Ø	1 Ø	5 14
12	11 15 4	2Ø 32 31	Ø♊11	1♓15	17 52	2 36	15D1Ø	6 38	1 1	Ø 59	5 13
13	11 19 1	21 32 23	12 31	2 5Ø	19 5	3 2Ø	15 1Ø	6 41	1 3	Ø 57	5 12
14	11 22 57	22 32 14	24 36	4 26	2Ø 19	4 5	15 11	6 45	1 5	Ø 55	5 11
15	11 26 54	23 32 2	6♋31	6 4	21 32	4 5Ø	15 11	6 49	1 6	Ø 54	5 1Ø
16	11 3Ø 51	24 31 48	18 2Ø	7 43	22 46	5 35	15 12	6 53	1 8	Ø 52	5 9
17	11 34 47	25 31 32	Ø♌ 9	9 23	23 59	6 2Ø	15 13	6 57	1 1Ø	Ø 5Ø	5 9
18	11 38 44	26 31 14	12 2	11 4	25 12	7 5	15 14	7 1	1 12	Ø 49	5 8
19	11 42 4Ø	27 3Ø 53	24 4	12 47	26 25	7 5Ø	15 15	7 5	1 14	Ø 47	5 7
2Ø	11 46 37	28 3Ø 31	6♍16	14 3Ø	27 39	8 35	15 16	7 1Ø	1 16	Ø 45	5 6
21	11 5Ø 33	29 3Ø 6	18 43	16 15	28 52	9 2Ø	15 18	7 14	1 18	Ø 44	5 6
22	11 54 3Ø	Ø♈29 39	1♎25	18 1	Ø♉ 5	1Ø 5	15 2Ø	7 19	1 2Ø	Ø 42	5 5
23	11 58 26	1 29 1Ø	14 22	19 49	1 18	1Ø 5Ø	15 22	7 23	1 22	Ø 4Ø	5 4
24	12 2 23	2 28 39	27 34	21 38	2 31	11 35	15 24	7 28	1 24	Ø 39	5 4
25	12 6 19	3 28 6	1Ø♏59	23 28	3 44	12 2Ø	15 26	7 32	1 26	Ø 37	5 3
26	12 1Ø 16	4 27 31	24 37	25 19	4 57	13 5	15 29	7 37	1 28	Ø 35	5 2
27	12 14 13	5 26 55	8♐25	27 12	6 9	13 5Ø	15 32	7 42	1 31	Ø 34	5 2
28	12 18 9	6 26 17	22 21	29 6	7 22	14 36	15 35	7 47	1 33	Ø 32	5 1
29	12 22 6	7 25 37	6♑24	1♈ 1	8 35	15 21	15 38	7 52	1 35	Ø 3Ø	5 1
3Ø	12 26 2	8 24 55	2Ø 33	2 58	9 47	16 6	15 41	7 57	1 38	Ø 29	5 Ø
31	12 29 59	9♈24 12	4♒46	4♈55	11♉ Ø	16♒51	15♋44	8♊ 3	1♊4Ø	Ø♎27	5♌ Ø

THE SUN ENTERS THE SIGN OF ARIES ON MAR 21 AT 12:03.

♈ ARIES ♉ TAURUS ♊ GEMINI ♋ CANCER ♌ LEO ♍ VIRGO ♎ LIBRA

SIDEREAL · SUN. · MOON. · MERCURY. · VENUS. · MARS. · JUPITER. · SATURN. · URANUS. · NEPTUNE. · PLUTO.

DAY	TIME	☉	☽	☿	♀	♂	♃	♄	♅	♆	♇
	h m s	° ' "	° '	° '	° '	° '	° '	° '	° '	° '	° '
A 1	12 33 55	10♈23 27	19♒ 2	6♈54	12♉12	17♒36	15♋48	8♊ 8	1♊43	0♎26	4♌59
P 2	12 37 52	11 22 40	3♓18	8 55	13 25	18 21	15 52	8 13	1 45	0R24	4R59
R 3	12 41 48	12 21 51	17 30	10 56	14 37	19 7	15 56	8 19	1 48	0 22	4 58
I 4	12 45 45	13 21 0	1♈35	12 58	15 49	19 52	16 0	8 24	1 50	0 21	4 58
L 5	12 49 42	14 20 8	15 28	15 1	17 2	20 37	16 4	8 30	1 53	0 19	4 58
6	12 53 38	15 19 13	29 5	17 5	18 14	21 22	16 9	8 35	1 55	0 17	4 57
7	12 57 35	16 18 16	12♉24	19 10	19 26	22 8	16 14	8 41	1 58	0 16	4 57
8	13 1 31	17 17 17	25 23	21 15	20 38	22 53	16 18	8 47	2 1	0 14	4 57
9	13 5 28	18 16 16	8♊ 2	23 20	21 50	23 38	16 23	8 53	2 3	0 13	4 56
10	13 9 24	19 15 12	20 23	25 25	23 2	24 23	16 29	8 59	2 6	0 11	4 56
11	13 13 21	20 14 7	2♋29	27 30	24 13	25 9	16 34	9 5	2 9	0 10	4 56
12	13 17 17	21 12 59	14 24	29 34	25 25	25 54	16 39	9 11	2 12	0 8	4 56
13	13 21 14	22 11 49	26 14	1♉38	26 37	26 39	16 45	9 17	2 15	0 7	4 56
14	13 25 11	23 10 36	8♌ 3	3 40	27 48	27 24	16 51	9 23	2 18	0 5	4 56
15	13 29 7	24 9 22	19 57	5 40	29 0	28 10	16 57	9 29	2 21	0 4	4 56
16	13 33 4	25 8 5	2♍ 2	7 39	0♊11	28 55	17 3	9 35	2 23	0 2	4 55
17	13 37 0	26 6 46	14 21	9 35	1 23	29 40	17 9	9 42	2 26	0 1	4 55
18	13 40 57	27 5 24	26 58	11 29	2 34	0♓26	17 16	9 48	2 29	29♍59	4D55
19	13 44 53	28 4 1	9♎55	13 19	3 45	1 11	17 22	9 55	2 32	29 58	4 55
20	13 48 50	29 2 36	23 12	15 7	4 56	1 56	17 29	10 1	2 35	29 56	4 55
21	13 52 46	0♉ 1 8	6♏48	16 51	6 7	2 41	17 36	10 8	2 39	29 55	4 55
22	13 56 43	0 59 39	20 40	18 31	7 18	3 27	17 43	10 14	2 42	29 54	4 56
23	14 0 39	1 58 8	4♐44	20 7	8 29	4 12	17 50	10 21	2 45	29 52	4 56
24	14 4 36	2 56 36	18 56	21 40	9 39	4 57	17 57	10 28	2 48	29 51	4 56
25	14 8 33	3 55 2	3♑10	23 8	10 50	5 43	18 4	10 34	2 51	29 50	4 56
26	14 12 29	4 53 26	17 23	24 31	12 0	6 28	18 12	10 41	2 54	29 48	4 56
27	14 16 26	5 51 48	1♒33	25 50	13 11	7 13	18 20	10 48	2 57	29 47	4 56
28	14 20 22	6 50 10	15 39	27 5	14 21	7 58	18 27	10 55	3 1	29 46	4 57
29	14 24 19	7 48 29	29 39	28 15	15 31	8 44	18 35	11 2	3 4	29 45	4 57
30	14 28 15	8♉46 47	13♓33	29♉20	16♊41	9♓29	18♋43	11♊ 9	3♊ 7	29♍43	4♌57

THE SUN ENTERS THE SIGN OF TAURUS ON APR 20 AT 23:32.

DAY	TIME	☉	☽	☿	♀	♂	♃	♄	♅	♆	♇
	h m s	° ' "	° '	° '	° '	° '	° '	° '	° '	° '	° '
M 1	14 32 12	9♉45 4	27♓20	0♊20	17♊51	10♓14	18♋52	11♊16	3♊10	29♍42	4♌58
A 2	14 36 8	10 43 19	10♈59	1 15	19 1	10 59	19 0	11 23	3 14	29R41	4 58
Y 3	14 40 5	11 41 32	24 28	2 5	20 11	11 44	19 8	11 30	3 17	29 40	4 58
4	14 44 2	12 39 44	7♉44	2 50	21 21	12 30	19 17	11 37	3 20	29 39	4 59
5	14 47 58	13 37 54	20 47	3 30	22 31	13 15	19 25	11 44	3 24	29 38	4 59
6	14 51 55	14 36 2	3♊33	4 5	23 40	14 0	19 34	11 52	3 27	29 37	5 0
7	14 55 51	15 34 9	16 4	4 34	24 49	14 45	19 43	11 59	3 30	29 35	5 0
8	14 59 48	16 32 13	28 20	4 58	25 59	15 30	19 52	12 6	3 34	29 34	5 1
9	15 3 44	17 30 16	10♋24	5 17	27 8	16 15	20 1	12 13	3 37	29 33	5 1
10	15 7 41	18 28 18	22 18	5 31	28 17	17 0	20 10	12 21	3 41	29 32	5 2
11	15 11 37	19 26 17	4♌ 6	5 40	29 26	17 45	20 20	12 28	3 44	29 32	5 2
12	15 15 34	20 24 14	15 55	5R43	0♋35	18 30	20 29	12 36	3 48	29 31	5 3
13	15 19 31	21 22 10	27 49	5 42	1 43	19 15	20 39	12 43	3 51	29 30	5 4
14	15 23 27	22 20 4	9♍54	5 36	2 52	20 0	20 48	12 50	3 54	29 29	5 4
15	15 27 24	23 17 56	22 15	5 25	4 0	20 45	20 58	12 58	3 58	29 28	5 5
16	15 31 20	24 15 46	4♎56	5 10	5 8	21 30	21 8	13 5	4 1	29 27	5 6
17	15 35 17	25 13 35	18 1	4 51	6 16	22 15	21 18	13 13	4 5	29 26	5 6
18	15 39 13	26 11 22	1♏31	4 28	7 24	23 0	21 28	13 21	4 8	29 26	5 7
19	15 43 10	27 9 8	15 25	4 2	8 32	23 45	21 38	13 28	4 12	29 25	5 8
20	15 47 6	28 6 52	29 40	3 33	9 40	24 30	21 48	13 36	4 15	29 24	5 9
21	15 51 3	29 4 35	14♐ 9	3 2	10 47	25 14	21 58	13 43	4 19	29 24	5 9
22	15 55 0	0♊ 2 16	28 47	2 30	11 55	25 59	22 9	13 51	4 22	29 23	5 10
23	15 58 56	0 59 57	13♑25	1 56	13 2	26 44	22 19	13 59	4 26	29 22	5 11
24	16 2 53	1 57 36	27 57	1 21	14 9	27 29	22 30	14 6	4 29	29 22	5 12
25	16 6 49	2 55 15	12♒20	0 47	15 16	28 13	22 41	14 14	4 33	29 21	5 13
26	16 10 46	3 52 52	26 31	0 14	16 22	28 58	22 51	14 22	4 36	29 21	5 14
27	16 14 42	4 50 28	10♓28	29♉41	17 29	29 42	23 2	14 29	4 40	29 20	5 15
28	16 18 39	5 48 4	24 11	29 11	18 35	0♈27	23 13	14 37	4 43	29 20	5 16
29	16 22 35	6 45 38	7♈42	28 43	19 41	1 12	23 24	14 45	4 47	29 19	5 17
30	16 26 32	7 43 12	21 1	28 17	20 47	1 56	23 35	14 53	4 50	29 19	5 18
31	16 30 29	8♊40 45	4♉ 7	27♉55	21♋53	2♈40	23♋46	15♊ 0	4♊54	29♍19	5♌19

THE SUN ENTERS THE SIGN OF GEMINI ON MAY 21 AT 23:03.

DAY	TIME	☉	☽	☿	♀	♂	♃	♄	♅	♆	♇
	h m s	° ' "	° '	° '	° '	° '	° '	° '	° '	° '	° '
J 1	16 34 25	9♊38 17	17♉ 2	27♉36	22♋58	3♈25	23♋57	15♊ 8	4♊57	29♍18	5♌20
U 2	16 38 22	10 35 48	29 44	27R21	24 4	4 9	24 9	15 16	5 1	29R18	5 21
N 3	16 42 18	11 33 19	12♊14	27 10	25 9	4 53	24 20	15 24	5 4	29 18	5 22
E 4	16 46 15	12 30 48	24 33	27 3	26 14	5 38	24 31	15 32	5 8	29 17	5 23
5	16 50 11	13 28 16	6♋40	27D 1	27 19	6 22	24 43	15 39	5 11	29 17	5 24
6	16 54 8	14 25 43	18 37	27 3	28 23	7 6	24 55	15 47	5 15	29 17	5 26
7	16 58 4	15 23 9	0♌28	27 9	29 28	7 50	25 6	15 55	5 18	29 17	5 27
8	17 2 1	16 20 34	12 15	27 20	0♌32	8 34	25 18	16 3	5 22	29 17	5 28
9	17 5 58	17 17 58	24 3	27 36	1 35	9 18	25 30	16 11	5 25	29 17	5 29
10	17 9 54	18 15 21	5♍56	27 56	2 39	10 2	25 41	16 18	5 29	29D17	5 31
11	17 13 51	19 12 43	18 0	28 20	3 42	10 46	25 53	16 26	5 32	29 17	5 32
12	17 17 47	20 10 3	0♎20	28 49	4 45	11 29	26 5	16 34	5 36	29 17	5 33
13	17 21 44	21 7 23	13 0	29 22	5 48	12 13	26 17	16 42	5 39	29 17	5 34
14	17 25 40	22 4 42	26 6	29 59	6 51	12 57	26 29	16 50	5 43	29 17	5 36
15	17 29 37	23 2 0	9♏39	0♊40	7 53	13 40	26 41	16 57	5 46	29 17	5 37
16	17 33 33	23 59 17	23 40	1 25	8 55	14 24	26 53	17 5	5 49	29 17	5 38
17	17 37 30	24 56 33	8♐ 6	2 15	9 56	15 7	27 6	17 13	5 53	29 17	5 40
18	17 41 27	25 53 49	22 51	3 8	10 58	15 51	27 18	17 21	5 56	29 17	5 41
19	17 45 23	26 51 5	7♑48	4 5	11 59	16 34	27 30	17 28	5 59	29 18	5 42
20	17 49 20	27 48 19	22 48	5 6	12 59	17 17	27 43	17 36	6 3	29 18	5 44
21	17 53 16	28 45 34	7♒42	6 11	13 59	18 0	27 55	17 44	6 6	29 18	5 45
22	17 57 13	29 42 48	22 24	7 19	14 59	18 43	28 7	17 51	6 9	29 19	5 47
23	18 1 9	0♋40 2	6♓48	8 31	15 59	19 26	28 20	17 59	6 13	29 19	5 48
24	18 5 6	1 37 16	20 52	9 47	16 58	20 9	28 32	18 7	6 16	29 19	5 50
25	18 9 2	2 34 29	4♈37	11 6	17 57	20 52	28 45	18 14	6 19	29 20	5 51
26	18 12 59	3 31 43	18 2	12 29	18 55	21 35	28 58	18 22	6 22	29 20	5 53
27	18 16 56	4 28 57	1♉ 9	13 55	19 53	22 18	29 10	18 30	6 26	29 21	5 54
28	18 20 52	5 26 11	14 1	15 24	20 51	23 0	29 23	18 37	6 29	29 21	5 56
29	18 24 49	6 23 25	26 38	16 57	21 48	23 43	29 36	18 45	6 32	29 22	5 57
30	18 28 45	7♋20 38	9♊ 4	18♊33	22♌45	24♈25	29♋48	18♊52	6♊35	29♍23	5♌59

THE SUN ENTERS THE SIGN OF CANCER ON JUN 22 AT 07:13.

♏ SCORPIO ♐ SAGITTARIUS ♑ CAPRICORN ♒ AQUARIUS ♓ PISCES

1943

SIDEREAL SUN MOON MERCURY VENUS MARS JUPITER SATURN URANUS NEPTUNE PLUTO

DAY	TIME	☉	☽	☿	♀	♂	♃	♄	♅	♆	♇
	h m s	° ' "	° '	° '	° '	° '	° '	° '	° '	° '	° '
J 1	18 32 42	8♋17 52	21♊19	20♊13	23♌41	25♈ 8	0♌ 1	19♊ 0	6♊38	29♍23	6♌ 0
U 2	18 36 38	9 15 6	3♋24	21 55	24 37	25 50	0 14	19 7	6 41	29 24	6 2
L 3	18 40 35	10 12 20	15 21	23 41	25 32	26 32	0 27	19 15	6 44	29 24	6 3
Y 4	18 44 32	11 9 33	27 13	25 30	26 27	27 14	0 40	19 22	6 47	29 25	6 5
5	18 48 28	12 6 47	9♌ 0	27 22	27 21	27 56	0 53	19 30	6 51	29 26	6 7
6	18 52 25	13 4 0	20 47	29 16	28 15	28 38	1 6	19 37	6 54	29 27	6 8
7	18 56 21	14 1 13	2♍35	1♋13	29 8	29 20	1 19	19 45	6 57	29 28	6 10
8	19 0 18	14 58 26	14 30	3 12	0♍ 0	0♉ 2	1 32	19 52	6 59	29 28	6 12
9	19 4 14	15 55 39	26 34	5 14	0 52	0 43	1 45	19 59	7 2	29 29	6 13
10	19 8 11	16 52 52	8♎53	7 17	1 43	1 25	1 58	20 6	7 5	29 30	6 15
11	19 12 7	17 50 5	21 32	9 23	2 34	2 6	2 11	20 14	7 8	29 31	6 16
12	19 16 4	18 47 17	4♏34	11 29	3 24	2 47	2 24	20 21	7 11	29 32	6 18
13	19 20 0	19 44 30	18 3	13 37	4 13	3 28	2 37	20 28	7 14	29 33	6 20
14	19 23 57	20 41 42	2♐ 0	15 45	5 1	4 9	2 50	20 35	7 17	29 34	6 21
15	19 27 54	21 38 55	16 23	17 54	5 49	4 50	3 3	20 42	7 19	29 35	6 23
16	19 31 50	22 36 8	1♑10	20 3	6 36	5 31	3 16	20 49	7 22	29 36	6 25
17	19 35 47	23 33 21	16 14	22 12	7 22	6 11	3 30	20 56	7 25	29 37	6 27
18	19 39 43	24 30 35	1♒25	24 20	8 7	6 52	3 43	21 3	7 27	29 38	6 28
19	19 43 40	25 27 48	16 34	26 28	8 51	7 32	3 56	21 10	7 30	29 40	6 30
20	19 47 36	26 25 3	1♓32	28 35	9 35	8 13	4 9	21 17	7 33	29 41	6 32
21	19 51 33	27 22 18	16 13	0♌41	10 17	8 53	4 22	21 24	7 35	29 42	6 33
22	19 55 30	28 19 34	0♈30	2 46	10 58	9 33	4 36	21 31	7 38	29 43	6 35
23	19 59 26	29 16 50	14 23	4 50	11 39	10 13	4 49	21 38	7 40	29 45	6 37
24	20 3 23	0♌14 8	27 51	6 52	12 18	10 53	5 2	21 44	7 43	29 46	6 39
25	20 7 19	1 11 26	10♉57	8 53	12 56	11 32	5 15	21 51	7 45	29 47	6 40
26	20 11 16	2 8 45	23 42	10 52	13 33	12 12	5 29	21 58	7 47	29 49	6 42
27	20 15 12	3 6 5	6♊10	12 50	14 9	12 51	5 42	22 4	7 50	29 50	6 44
28	20 19 9	4 3 27	18 24	14 46	14 44	13 30	5 55	22 11	7 52	29 51	6 45
29	20 23 5	5 0 49	0♋28	16 40	15 17	14 9	6 9	22 17	7 54	29 53	6 47
30	20 27 2	5 58 12	12 24	18 33	15 49	14 48	6 22	22 23	7 57	29 54	6 49
31	20 30 59	6♌55 36	24♋14	20♌24	16♍20	15♉27	6♌35	22♊30	7♊59	29♍56	6♌51

THE SUN ENTERS THE SIGN OF LEO ON JUL 23 AT 18:05.

DAY	TIME	☉	☽	☿	♀	♂	♃	♄	♅	♆	♇
	h m s	° ' "	° '	° '	° '	° '	° '	° '	° '	° '	° '
A 1	20 34 55	7♌53 1	6♌ 2	22♌14	16♍49	16♉ 5	6♌48	22♊36	8♊ 1	29♍57	6♌52
U 2	20 38 52	8 50 26	17 49	24 2	17 17	16 44	7 2	22 42	8 3	29 59	6 54
G 3	20 42 48	9 47 53	29 38	25 48	17 43	17 22	7 15	22 49	8 5	0♎ 0	6 56
U 4	20 46 45	10 45 20	11♍30	27 32	18 7	18 0	7 28	22 55	8 7	0 2	6 58
S 5	20 50 41	11 42 48	23 30	29 15	18 30	18 38	7 42	23 1	8 9	0 3	6 59
T 6	20 54 38	12 40 17	5♎40	0♍57	18 51	19 15	7 55	23 7	8 11	0 5	7 1
7	20 58 34	13 37 46	18 3	2 36	19 10	19 53	8 8	23 13	8 13	0 7	7 3
8	21 2 31	14 35 17	0♏43	4 14	19 28	20 30	8 21	23 18	8 15	0 8	7 5
9	21 6 27	15 32 48	13 42	5 51	19 43	21 7	8 35	23 24	8 17	0 10	7 6
10	21 10 24	16 30 20	27 5	7 26	19 57	21 44	8 48	23 30	8 18	0 12	7 8
11	21 14 21	17 27 53	10♐52	8 59	20 8	22 21	9 1	23 36	8 20	0 14	7 10
12	21 18 17	18 25 26	25 5	10 31	20 18	22 58	9 14	23 41	8 22	0 15	7 11
13	21 22 14	19 23 1	9♑41	12 1	20 25	23 34	9 27	23 47	8 24	0 17	7 13
14	21 26 10	20 20 37	24 35	13 29	20 30	24 10	9 40	23 52	8 25	0 19	7 15
15	21 30 7	21 18 13	9♒42	14 56	20R33	24 46	9 54	23 58	8 27	0 21	7 17
16	21 34 3	22 15 51	24 53	16 21	20 33	25 22	10 7	24 3	8 28	0 22	7 18
17	21 38 0	23 13 30	9♓58	17 45	20 31	25 57	10 20	24 8	8 30	0 24	7 20
18	21 41 57	24 11 11	24 48	19 7	20 27	26 33	10 33	24 13	8 31	0 26	7 22
19	21 45 53	25 8 52	9♈17	20 27	20 20	27 8	10 46	24 19	8 32	0 28	7 23
20	21 49 50	26 6 36	23 20	21 45	20 11	27 43	10 59	24 24	8 34	0 30	7 25
21	21 53 46	27 4 21	6♉56	23 1	20 0	28 17	11 12	24 28	8 35	0 32	7 27
22	21 57 43	28 2 8	20 5	24 16	19 46	28 52	11 25	24 33	8 36	0 34	7 28
23	22 1 39	28 59 56	2♊51	25 29	19 30	29 26	11 38	24 38	8 37	0 36	7 30
24	22 5 36	29 57 46	15 17	26 39	19 12	0♊ 0	11 51	24 43	8 39	0 38	7 31
25	22 9 32	0♍55 38	27 26	27 48	18 51	0 34	12 4	24 47	8 40	0 40	7 33
26	22 13 29	1 53 32	9♋24	28 54	18 28	1 7	12 17	24 52	8 41	0 42	7 35
27	22 17 25	2 51 27	21 15	29 58	18 4	1 40	12 30	24 57	8 42	0 44	7 36
28	22 21 22	3 49 24	3♌ 2	1♎ 0	17 37	2 13	12 42	25 1	8 43	0 46	7 38
29	22 25 19	4 47 23	14 49	1 59	17 8	2 46	12 55	25 5	8 44	0 48	7 40
30	22 29 15	5 45 24	26 38	2 56	16 38	3 18	13 8	25 9	8 44	0 50	7 41
31	22 33 12	6♍43 26	8♍33	3♎49	16♍ 6	3♊50	13♌21	25♊14	8♊45	0♎52	7♌43

THE SUN ENTERS THE SIGN OF VIRGO ON AUG 24 AT 00:56.

DAY	TIME	☉	☽	☿	♀	♂	♃	♄	♅	♆	♇
	h m s	° ' "	° '	° '	° '	° '	° '	° '	° '	° '	° '
S 1	22 37 8	7♍41 29	20♍36	4♎40	15♍33	4♊22	13♌33	25♊18	8♊46	0♎54	7♌44
E 2	22 41 5	8 39 34	2♎47	5 27	14R58	4 54	13 46	25 22	8 47	0 56	7 46
P 3	22 45 1	9 37 41	15 8	6 11	14 23	5 25	13 58	25 25	8 47	0 58	7 47
T 4	22 48 58	10 35 49	27 42	6 51	13 46	5 56	14 11	25 29	8 48	1 0	7 49
E 5	22 52 54	11 33 59	10♏30	7 28	13 10	6 26	14 23	25 33	8 48	1 2	7 50
M 6	22 56 51	12 32 10	23 34	8 0	12 32	6 57	14 36	25 36	8 49	1 5	7 52
B 7	23 0 48	13 30 23	6♐55	8 28	11 55	7 26	14 48	25 40	8 49	1 7	7 53
E 8	23 4 44	14 28 37	20 34	8 51	11 18	7 56	15 1	25 43	8 50	1 9	7 55
R 9	23 8 41	15 26 53	4♑34	9 9	10 42	8 25	15 13	25 47	8 50	1 11	7 56
10	23 12 37	16 25 10	18 53	9 21	10 6	8 54	15 25	25 50	8 50	1 13	7 58
11	23 16 34	17 23 29	3♒29	9R28	9 31	9 23	15 37	25 53	8 51	1 15	7 59
12	23 20 30	18 21 49	18 19	9 29	8 57	9 51	15 49	25 56	8 51	1 17	8 0
13	23 24 27	19 20 11	3♓15	9 24	8 24	10 19	16 2	25 59	8 51	1 20	8 2
14	23 28 23	20 18 35	18 11	9 12	7 53	10 46	16 14	26 2	8R51	1 22	8 3
15	23 32 20	21 17 0	2♈58	8 53	7 24	11 13	16 26	26 4	8 51	1 24	8 4
16	23 36 17	22 15 27	17 28	8 27	6 56	11 40	16 37	26 7	8 51	1 26	8 6
17	23 40 13	23 13 57	1♉36	7 55	6 31	12 7	16 49	26 9	8 51	1 28	8 7
18	23 44 10	24 12 28	15 18	7 16	6 7	12 32	17 1	26 12	8 51	1 31	8 8
19	23 48 6	25 11 2	28 32	6 30	5 46	12 58	17 13	26 14	8 50	1 33	8 10
20	23 52 3	26 9 38	11♊21	5 39	5 27	13 23	17 25	26 16	8 50	1 35	8 11
21	23 55 59	27 8 16	23 48	4 42	5 10	13 48	17 36	26 19	8 50	1 37	8 12
22	23 59 56	28 6 57	5♋57	3 42	4 56	14 12	17 48	26 20	8 50	1 40	8 13
23	0 3 52	29 5 39	17 54	2 38	4 44	14 36	17 59	26 22	8 49	1 42	8 15
24	0 7 49	0♎ 4 24	29 43	1 32	4 35	14 59	18 11	26 24	8 49	1 44	8 16
25	0 11 46	1 3 11	11♌30	0 27	4 28	15 22	18 22	26 26	8 48	1 46	8 17
26	0 15 42	2 2 0	23 19	29♍23	4 23	15 44	18 33	26 27	8 48	1 49	8 18
27	0 19 39	3 0 51	5♍13	28 22	4D21	16 6	18 44	26 29	8 47	1 51	8 19
28	0 23 35	3 59 45	17 16	27 26	4 22	16 27	18 55	26 30	8 47	1 53	8 20
29	0 27 32	4 58 40	29 31	26 36	4 24	16 48	19 6	26 31	8 46	1 55	8 21
30	0 31 28	5♎57 38	11♎58	25♍54	4♍29	17♊ 8	19♌17	26♊33	8♊45	1♎57	8♌22

THE SUN ENTERS THE SIGN OF LIBRA ON SEP 23 AT 22:12.

♈ ARIES ♉ TAURUS ♊ GEMINI ♋ CANCER ♌ LEO ♍ VIRGO ♎ LIBRA

SIDEREAL . SUN . MOON . MERCURY . VENUS . MARS . JUPITER . SATURN . URANUS . NEPTUNE . PLUTO .

DAY	TIME	☉	☽	☿	♀	♂	♃	♄	♅	♆	♇
	h m s	° ' "	° '	° '	° '	° '	° '	° '	° '	° '	° '
O 1	Ø 35 25	6♎56 37	24♎37	25♍21	4♍36	17♊28	19♌28	26♊34	8♊44	2♎ Ø	8♌24
C 2	Ø 39 21	7 55 39	7♏3Ø	24R58	4 46	17 47	19 39	26 35	8R44	2 2	8 25
T 3	Ø 43 18	8 54 42	2Ø 35	24D44	4 57	18 6	19 5Ø	26 35	8 43	2 4	8 26
O 4	Ø 47 14	9 53 47	3♐52	24 41	5 11	18 24	2Ø Ø	26 36	8 42	2 6	8 26
B 5	Ø 51 11	1Ø 52 54	17 21	24 49	5 26	18 41	2Ø 11	26 37	8 41	2 9	8 27
E 6	Ø 55 8	11 52 3	1♑ 2	25 7	5 44	18 58	2Ø 21	26 37	8 4Ø	2 11	8 28
R 7	Ø 59 4	12 51 14	14 56	25 35	6 4	19 15	2Ø 32	26 37	8 39	2 13	8 29
8	1 3 1	13 5Ø 26	29 1	26 12	6 25	19 3Ø	2Ø 42	26 38	8 38	2 15	8 3Ø
9	1 6 57	14 49 4Ø	13♒18	26 58	6 48	19 45	2Ø 52	26R38	8 36	2 17	8 31
1Ø	1 1Ø 54	15 48 56	27 44	27 52	7 13	2Ø Ø	21 2	26 38	8 35	2 2Ø	8 32
11	1 14 5Ø	16 48 14	12♓17	28 54	7 4Ø	2Ø 13	21 12	26 38	8 34	2 22	8 33
12	1 18 47	17 47 33	26 51	Ø♎ 2	8 8	2Ø 26	21 22	26 38	8 33	2 24	8 33
13	1 22 43	18 46 54	11♈2Ø	1 15	8 38	2Ø 39	21 32	26 37	8 31	2 26	8 34
14	1 26 4Ø	19 46 18	25 38	2 34	9 1Ø	2Ø 5Ø	21 41	26 37	8 3Ø	2 28	8 35
15	1 3Ø 37	2Ø 45 43	9♉38	3 58	9 43	21 1	21 51	26 36	8 28	2 3Ø	8 36
16	1 34 33	21 45 11	23 16	5 25	1Ø 17	21 12	22 Ø	26 36	8 27	2 32	8 36
17	1 38 3Ø	22 44 4Ø	6♊3Ø	6 55	1Ø 53	21 21	22 9	26 35	8 25	2 35	8 37
18	1 42 26	23 44 12	19 2Ø	8 28	11 3Ø	21 3Ø	22 19	26 34	8 24	2 37	8 38
19	1 46 23	24 43 47	1♋49	1Ø 3	12 8	21 38	22 28	26 33	8 22	2 39	8 38
2Ø	1 5Ø 19	25 43 23	13 59	11 39	12 48	21 45	22 37	26 32	8 21	2 41	8 39
21	1 54 16	26 43 2	25 57	13 17	13 28	21 52	22 46	26 31	8 19	2 43	8 39
22	1 58 12	27 42 43	7♌46	14 56	14 1Ø	21 57	22 54	26 3Ø	8 17	2 45	8 4Ø
23	2 2 9	28 42 27	19 34	16 36	14 53	22 2	23 3	26 28	8 16	2 47	8 4Ø
24	2 6 6	29 42 12	1♍24	18 16	15 37	22 6	23 12	26 27	8 14	2 49	8 41
25	2 1Ø 2	Ø♏42 Ø	13 23	19 57	16 22	22 9	23 2Ø	26 25	8 12	2 51	8 41
26	2 13 59	1 41 5Ø	25 33	21 38	17 8	22 12	23 28	26 23	8 1Ø	2 53	8 42
27	2 17 55	2 41 42	7♎59	23 19	17 55	22 13	23 36	26 22	8 8	2 55	8 42
28	2 21 52	3 41 36	2Ø 42	25 Ø	18 43	22R14	23 44	26 2Ø	8 6	2 57	8 43
29	2 25 48	4 41 32	3♏41	26 41	19 32	22 14	23 52	26 18	8 4	2 59	8 43
3Ø	2 29 45	5 41 3Ø	16 56	28 21	2Ø 21	22 13	24 Ø	26 15	8 2	3 1	8 43
31	2 33 41	6♏41 3Ø	Ø♐26	Ø♏ 2	21♍12	22♊11	24♌ 8	26♊13	8♊ Ø	3♎ 3	8♌44

THE SUN ENTERS THE SIGN OF SCORPIO ON OCT 24 AT 07:09.

DAY	TIME	☉	☽	☿	♀	♂	♃	♄	♅	♆	♇
	h m s	° ' "	° '	° '	° '	° '	° '	° '	° '	° '	° '
N 1	2 37 38	7♏41 31	14♐ 6	1♏42	22♍ 3	22♊ 8	24♌15	26♊11	7♊58	3♎ 5	8♌44
O 2	2 41 34	8 41 35	27 55	3 21	22 55	22R 4	24 22	26R 8	7R56	3 7	8 44
V 3	2 45 31	9 41 4Ø	11♑49	5 1	23 47	21 59	24 3Ø	26 6	7 54	3 9	8 44
E 4	2 49 28	1Ø 41 47	25 49	6 4Ø	24 4Ø	21 54	24 37	26 3	7 52	3 11	8 45
M 5	2 53 24	11 41 55	9♒52	8 18	25 34	21 47	24 44	26 1	7 5Ø	3 13	8 45
B 6	2 57 21	12 42 4	23 57	9 56	26 29	21 4Ø	24 5Ø	25 58	7 47	3 14	8 45
E 7	3 1 17	13 42 15	8♓ 5	11 34	27 24	21 32	24 57	25 55	7 45	3 16	8 45
R 8	3 5 14	14 42 28	22 14	13 11	28 2Ø	21 23	25 4	25 52	7 43	3 18	8 45
9	3 9 1Ø	15 42 42	6♈22	14 48	29 16	21 13	25 1Ø	25 49	7 41	3 2Ø	8 45
1Ø	3 13 7	16 42 58	2Ø 24	16 25	Ø♎13	21 2	25 16	25 45	7 38	3 21	8R45
11	3 17 3	17 43 15	4♉18	18 1	1 11	2Ø 5Ø	25 22	25 42	7 36	3 23	8 45
12	3 21 Ø	18 43 34	17 58	19 37	2 9	2Ø 38	25 28	25 39	7 34	3 25	8 45
13	3 24 57	19 43 54	1♊22	21 13	3 7	2Ø 25	25 34	25 35	7 31	3 27	8 45
14	3 28 53	2Ø 44 17	14 26	22 48	4 7	2Ø 11	25 39	25 32	7 29	3 28	8 45
15	3 32 5Ø	21 44 41	27 11	24 23	5 6	19 56	25 45	25 28	7 27	3 3Ø	8 45
16	3 36 46	22 45 7	9♋37	25 58	6 6	19 4Ø	25 5Ø	25 25	7 24	3 31	8 45
17	3 4Ø 43	23 45 35	21 47	27 32	7 7	19 24	25 55	25 21	7 22	3 33	8 44
18	3 44 39	24 46 4	3♌44	29 7	8 7	19 7	26 Ø	25 17	7 19	3 35	8 44
19	3 48 36	25 46 35	15 34	Ø♐4Ø	9 9	18 49	26 4	25 13	7 17	3 36	8 44
2Ø	3 52 32	26 47 8	27 22	2 14	1Ø 11	18 31	26 9	25 9	7 14	3 38	8 44
21	3 56 29	27 47 43	9♍13	3 48	11 13	18 12	26 13	25 5	7 12	3 39	8 44
22	4 Ø 26	28 48 2Ø	21 12	5 21	12 15	17 52	26 18	25 1	7 9	3 41	8 43
23	4 4 22	29 48 58	3♎26	6 54	13 18	17 32	26 22	24 57	7 7	3 42	8 43
24	4 8 19	Ø♐49 38	15 57	8 27	14 21	17 11	26 25	24 52	7 4	3 43	8 43
25	4 12 15	1 5Ø 19	28 5Ø	1Ø Ø	15 25	16 5Ø	26 29	24 48	7 2	3 45	8 42
26	4 16 12	2 51 2	12♏ 3	11 33	16 29	16 28	26 33	24 44	6 59	3 46	8 42
27	4 2Ø 8	3 51 47	25 38	13 6	17 33	16 6	26 36	24 39	6 57	3 48	8 41
28	4 24 5	4 52 33	9♐32	14 38	18 38	15 44	26 39	24 35	6 54	3 49	8 41
29	4 28 1	5 53 2Ø	23 38	16 1Ø	19 43	15 21	26 42	24 3Ø	6 52	3 5Ø	8 4Ø
3Ø	4 31 58	6♐54 9	7♑54	17♐43	2Ø♎48	14♊59	26♌45	24♊26	6♊49	3♎51	8♌4Ø

THE SUN ENTERS THE SIGN OF SAGITTARIUS ON NOV 23 AT 04:22.

DAY	TIME	☉	☽	☿	♀	♂	♃	♄	♅	♆	♇
	h m s	° ' "	° '	° '	° '	° '	° '	° '	° '	° '	° '
D 1	4 35 55	7♐54 58	22♑14	19♐15	21♎53	14♊36	26♌47	24♊21	6♊47	3♎53	8♌39
E 2	4 39 51	8 55 49	6♒32	2Ø 47	22 59	14R13	26 5Ø	24R17	6R44	3 54	8R39
C 3	4 43 48	9 56 4Ø	2Ø 47	22 18	24 5	13 49	26 52	24 12	6 42	3 55	8 38
E 4	4 47 44	1Ø 57 32	4♓56	23 5Ø	25 11	13 26	26 54	24 7	6 39	3 56	8 38
M 5	4 51 41	11 58 25	18 59	25 21	26 18	13 3	26 56	24 2	6 37	3 57	8 37
B 6	4 55 37	12 59 18	2♈53	26 52	27 24	12 4Ø	26 58	23 58	6 34	3 58	8 36
E 7	4 59 34	14 Ø 13	16 39	28 23	28 31	12 17	26 59	23 53	6 32	3 59	8 36
R 8	5 3 3Ø	15 1 8	Ø♉17	29 53	29 38	11 55	27 Ø	23 48	6 29	4 Ø	8 35
9	5 7 27	16 2 4	13 43	1♑23	Ø♏46	11 32	27 1	23 43	6 27	4 1	8 34
1Ø	5 11 24	17 3 Ø	26 58	2 53	1 53	11 1Ø	27 2	23 38	6 24	4 2	8 34
11	5 15 2Ø	18 3 58	1Ø♊ Ø	4 22	3 1	1Ø 48	27 3	23 33	6 22	4 3	8 33
12	5 19 17	19 4 56	22 46	5 5Ø	4 9	1Ø 27	27 3	23 28	6 19	4 4	8 32
13	5 23 13	2Ø 5 55	5♋18	7 17	5 17	1Ø 6	27R 4	23 23	6 17	4 5	8 31
14	5 27 1Ø	21 6 55	17 36	8 44	6 26	9 45	27 4	23 19	6 14	4 6	8 3Ø
15	5 31 6	22 7 56	29 41	1Ø 9	7 34	9 25	27 4	23 14	6 12	4 6	8 29
16	5 35 3	23 8 58	11♌37	11 33	8 43	9 5	27 3	23 9	6 1Ø	4 7	8 29
17	5 39 Ø	24 1Ø 1	23 26	12 55	9 52	8 46	27 3	23 4	6 7	4 8	8 28
18	5 42 56	25 11 4	5♍13	14 15	11 1	8 28	27 2	22 59	6 5	4 8	8 27
19	5 46 53	26 12 9	17 3	15 34	12 1Ø	8 1Ø	27 1	22 54	6 2	4 9	8 26
2Ø	5 5Ø 49	27 13 14	29 2	16 49	13 2Ø	7 53	27 Ø	22 49	6 Ø	4 1Ø	8 25
21	5 54 46	28 14 2Ø	11♎14	18 1	14 29	7 36	26 59	22 44	5 58	4 1Ø	8 24
22	5 58 42	29 15 27	23 44	19 1Ø	15 39	7 21	26 57	22 39	5 56	4 11	8 23
23	6 2 39	Ø♑16 35	6♏37	2Ø 15	16 49	7 6	26 56	22 34	5 53	4 11	8 22
24	6 6 35	1 17 43	19 54	21 15	17 59	6 51	26 54	22 29	5 51	4 12	8 21
25	6 1Ø 32	2 18 52	3♐37	22 9	19 9	6 38	26 52	22 24	5 49	4 12	8 2Ø
26	6 14 29	3 2Ø 1	17 44	22 57	2Ø 2Ø	6 25	26 5Ø	22 2Ø	5 47	4 13	8 19
27	6 18 25	4 21 11	2♑11	23 38	21 3Ø	6 13	26 47	22 15	5 45	4 13	8 18
28	6 22 22	5 22 22	16 51	24 1Ø	22 4Ø	6 2	26 44	22 1Ø	5 42	4 13	8 16
29	6 26 18	6 23 32	1♒38	24 34	23 51	5 51	26 42	22 5	5 4Ø	4 14	8 15
3Ø	6 3Ø 15	7 24 42	16 24	24R47	25 2	5 42	26 39	22 1	5 38	4 14	8 14
31	6 34 11	8♑25 53	1♓ 2	24♑5Ø	26♏13	5♊33	26♌35	21♊56	5♊36	4♎14	8♌13

THE SUN ENTERS THE SIGN OF CAPRICORN ON DEC 22 AT 17:30.

♏	SCORPIO	♐	SAGITTARIUS	♑	CAPRICORN	♒	AQUARIUS	♓	PISCES

SIDEREAL SUN . . . . . MOON . . . . MERCURY VENUS . . . MARS . . . JUPITER SATURN . . URANUS . . NEPTUNE . PLUTO .

DAY	TIME h m s	☉ ° ′ ″	☽ ° ′	☿ ° ′	♀ ° ′	♂ ° ′	♃ ° ′	♄ ° ′	♅ ° ′	♆ ° ′	♇ ° ′
J 1	6 38 8	9♑27 3	15♓29	24♑42	27♏24	5♊25	26♌32	21♊51	5♊34	4♎14	8♌12
A 2	6 42 4	10 28 13	29 40	24R22	28 35	5R18	26R28	21R47	5R32	4 15	8R11
N 3	6 46 1	11 29 23	13♈35	23 50	29 46	5 12	26 25	21 42	5 30	4 15	8 9
U 4	6 49 58	12 30 32	27 12	23 6	0♐57	5 7	26 21	21 38	5 29	4 15	8 8
A 5	6 53 54	13 31 41	10♉34	22 12	2 9	5 2	26 17	21 33	5 27	4 15	8 7
R 6	6 57 51	14 32 50	23 40	21 8	3 20	4 58	26 12	21 29	5 25	4R15	8 6
Y 7	7 1 47	15 33 59	6♊33	19 57	4 32	4 55	26 8	21 25	5 23	4 15	8 5
8	7 5 44	16 35 7	19 12	18 40	5 43	4 53	26 3	21 21	5 21	4 15	8 3
9	7 9 40	17 36 15	1♋39	17 20	6 55	4 52	25 58	21 16	5 20	4 15	8 2
10	7 13 37	18 37 23	13 55	16 0	8 7	4D51	25 53	21 12	5 18	4 15	8 1
11	7 17 33	19 38 30	26 1	14 42	9 19	4 52	25 48	21 8	5 16	4 14	7 59
12	7 21 30	20 39 37	7♌59	13 28	10 30	4 53	25 43	21 4	5 15	4 14	7 58
13	7 25 27	21 40 44	19 51	12 21	11 42	4 54	25 38	21 0	5 13	4 14	7 57
14	7 29 23	22 41 51	1♍39	11 21	12 55	4 57	25 32	20 56	5 12	4 14	7 56
15	7 33 20	23 42 57	13 27	10 30	14 7	5 0	25 26	20 53	5 10	4 14	7 54
16	7 37 16	24 44 3	25 17	9 49	15 19	5 4	25 20	20 49	5 9	4 13	7 53
17	7 41 13	25 45 9	7♎15	9 18	16 31	5 9	25 14	20 45	5 8	4 13	7 52
18	7 45 9	26 46 15	19 25	8 56	17 44	5 14	25 8	20 42	5 6	4 12	7 50
19	7 49 6	27 47 20	1♏51	8D43	18 56	5 20	25 2	20 39	5 5	4 12	7 49
20	7 53 2	28 48 25	14 38	8 39	20 9	5 27	24 56	20 35	5 4	4 12	7 47
21	7 56 59	29 49 30	27 49	8 43	21 21	5 34	24 49	20 32	5 3	4 11	7 46
22	8 0 56	0♒50 34	11♐27	8 55	22 34	5 42	24 42	20 29	5 2	4 11	7 45
23	8 4 52	1 51 38	25 32	9 14	23 46	5 51	24 36	20 26	5 0	4 10	7 43
24	8 8 49	2 52 42	10♑ 3	9 39	24 59	6 0	24 29	20 23	4 59	4 10	7 42
25	8 12 45	3 53 45	24 54	10 11	26 12	6 10	24 22	20 20	4 58	4 9	7 41
26	8 16 42	4 54 47	9♒57	10 47	27 25	6 21	24 15	20 17	4 58	4 8	7 39
27	8 20 38	5 55 48	25 6	11 29	28 37	6 32	24 8	20 14	4 57	4 8	7 38
28	8 24 35	6 56 48	10♓ 9	12 15	29 50	6 44	24 0	20 12	4 56	4 7	7 36
29	8 28 31	7 57 47	24 58	13 5	1♑ 3	6 56	23 53	20 9	4 55	4 6	7 35
30	8 32 28	8 58 45	9♈29	13 58	2 16	7 9	23 45	20 7	4 54	4 5	7 34
31	8 36 25	9♒59 42	23♈36	14♑55	3♑29	7♊22	23♌38	20♊ 4	4♊54	4♎ 5	7♌32

THE SUN ENTERS THE SIGN OF AQUARIUS ON JAN 21 AT 04:07.

DAY	TIME h m s	☉ ° ′ ″	☽ ° ′	☿ ° ′	♀ ° ′	♂ ° ′	♃ ° ′	♄ ° ′	♅ ° ′	♆ ° ′	♇ ° ′
F 1	8 40 21	11♒ 0 37	7♉19	15♑55	4♑42	7♊36	23♌30	20♊ 2	4♊53	4♎ 4	7♌31
E 2	8 44 18	12 1 31	20 38	16 57	5 55	7 50	23R23	20R 0	4R52	4R 3	7R30
B 3	8 48 14	13 2 23	3♊35	18 2	7 8	8 5	23 15	19 58	4 52	4 2	7 28
R 4	8 52 11	14 3 15	16 14	19 9	8 21	8 21	23 7	19 56	4 51	4 1	7 27
U 5	8 56 7	15 4 5	28 38	20 19	9 35	8 37	23 0	19 54	4 51	4 0	7 25
A 6	9 0 4	16 4 53	10♋50	21 30	10 48	8 53	22 52	19 53	4 51	3 59	7 24
R 7	9 4 0	17 5 41	22 52	22 43	12 1	9 10	22 44	19 51	4 50	3 58	7 23
Y 8	9 7 57	18 6 26	4♌47	23 58	13 14	9 27	22 36	19 50	4 50	3 57	7 21
9	9 11 54	19 7 11	16 39	25 14	14 28	9 45	22 28	19 48	4 50	3 56	7 20
10	9 15 50	20 7 54	28 27	26 32	15 41	10 3	22 20	19 47	4 50	3 55	7 19
11	9 19 47	21 8 36	10♍16	27 51	16 54	10 22	22 12	19 46	4 50	3 54	7 17
12	9 23 43	22 9 17	22 7	29 11	18 8	10 40	22 4	19 45	4D50	3 53	7 16
13	9 27 40	23 9 56	4♎ 1	0♒33	19 21	11 0	21 56	19 44	4 50	3 52	7 15
14	9 31 36	24 10 34	16 3	1 56	20 34	11 19	21 48	19 43	4 50	3 51	7 13
15	9 35 33	25 11 11	28 15	3 20	21 48	11 40	21 40	19 43	4 50	3 49	7 12
16	9 39 29	26 11 47	10♏40	4 46	23 1	12 0	21 32	19 42	4 50	3 48	7 11
17	9 43 26	27 12 21	23 23	6 12	24 15	12 21	21 25	19 42	4 50	3 47	7 9
18	9 47 23	28 12 55	6♐26	7 39	25 28	12 42	21 17	19 41	4 50	3 46	7 8
19	9 51 19	29 13 27	19 53	9 8	26 42	13 3	21 9	19 41	4 51	3 44	7 7
20	9 55 16	0♓13 58	3♑46	10 37	27 55	13 25	21 1	19D41	4 51	3 43	7 6
21	9 59 12	1 14 28	18 6	12 8	29 9	13 47	20 53	19 41	4 51	3 42	7 4
22	10 3 9	2 14 56	2♒49	13 39	0♒22	14 10	20 46	19 41	4 52	3 40	7 3
23	10 7 5	3 15 23	17 51	15 11	1 36	14 33	20 38	19 41	4 52	3 39	7 2
24	10 11 2	4 15 48	3♓ 5	16 45	2 50	14 56	20 30	19 42	4 53	3 38	7 1
25	10 14 58	5 16 11	18 20	18 19	4 3	15 19	20 23	19 42	4 54	3 36	6 59
26	10 18 55	6 16 33	3♈26	19 55	5 17	15 43	20 16	19 43	4 54	3 35	6 58
27	10 22 52	7 16 53	18 13	21 31	6 31	16 7	20 8	19 43	4 55	3 34	6 57
28	10 26 48	8 17 11	2♉36	23 8	7 44	16 31	20 1	19 44	4 56	3 32	6 56
29	10 30 45	9♓17 26	16♉31	24♒47	8♒58	16♊56	19♌54	19♊45	4♊57	3♎31	6♌55

THE SUN ENTERS THE SIGN OF PISCES ON FEB 19 AT 18:28.

DAY	TIME h m s	☉ ° ′ ″	☽ ° ′	☿ ° ′	♀ ° ′	♂ ° ′	♃ ° ′	♄ ° ′	♅ ° ′	♆ ° ′	♇ ° ′
M 1	10 34 41	10♓17 40	29♉57	26♒26	10♒12	17♊20	19♌47	19♊46	4♊58	3♎29	6♌54
A 2	10 38 38	11 17 52	12♊56	28 7	11 25	17 45	19R40	19 47	4 59	3R28	6R53
R 3	10 42 34	12 18 2	25 32	29 48	12 39	18 11	19 33	19 48	5 0	3 26	6 51
C 4	10 46 31	13 18 10	7♋50	1♓31	13 53	18 36	19 26	19 50	5 1	3 25	6 50
H 5	10 50 27	14 18 15	19 54	3 14	15 6	19 2	19 19	19 51	5 2	3 23	6 49
6	10 54 24	15 18 19	1♌49	4 59	16 20	19 28	19 13	19 53	5 3	3 21	6 48
7	10 58 21	16 18 20	13 38	6 45	17 34	19 54	19 7	19 54	5 4	3 20	6 47
8	11 2 17	17 18 19	25 25	8 32	18 48	20 21	19 0	19 56	5 5	3 18	6 46
9	11 6 14	18 18 16	7♍14	10 20	20 1	20 47	18 54	19 58	5 7	3 17	6 45
10	11 10 10	19 18 12	19 5	12 9	21 15	21 14	18 48	20 0	5 8	3 15	6 44
11	11 14 7	20 18 5	1♎ 2	13 59	22 29	21 41	18 42	20 2	5 9	3 14	6 43
12	11 18 3	21 17 57	13 6	15 51	23 43	22 8	18 37	20 4	5 11	3 12	6 42
13	11 22 0	22 17 46	25 17	17 44	24 56	22 36	18 31	20 7	5 12	3 10	6 41
14	11 25 56	23 17 34	7♏38	19 37	26 10	23 3	18 25	20 9	5 14	3 9	6 41
15	11 29 53	24 17 20	20 10	21 32	27 24	23 31	18 20	20 12	5 16	3 7	6 40
16	11 33 49	25 17 4	2♐56	23 28	28 38	23 59	18 15	20 14	5 17	3 5	6 39
17	11 37 46	26 16 47	15 58	25 25	29 51	24 27	18 10	20 17	5 19	3 4	6 38
18	11 41 43	27 16 28	29 19	27 23	1♓ 5	24 56	18 5	20 20	5 21	3 2	6 37
19	11 45 39	28 16 8	13♑ 0	29 22	2 19	25 24	18 1	20 23	5 22	3 1	6 36
20	11 49 36	29 15 45	27 4	1♈21	3 33	25 53	17 56	20 26	5 24	2 59	6 36
21	11 53 32	0♈15 21	11♒30	3 22	4 47	26 22	17 52	20 29	5 26	2 57	6 35
22	11 57 29	1 14 55	26 17	5 22	6 1	26 51	17 48	20 32	5 28	2 56	6 34
23	12 1 25	2 14 27	11♓17	7 24	7 14	27 20	17 44	20 35	5 30	2 54	6 34
24	12 5 22	3 13 57	26 24	9 25	8 28	27 49	17 40	20 39	5 32	2 52	6 33
25	12 9 18	4 13 25	11♈29	11 26	9 42	28 18	17 36	20 42	5 34	2 51	6 32
26	12 13 15	5 12 52	26 20	13 28	10 56	28 48	17 33	20 46	5 36	2 49	6 32
27	12 17 12	6 12 15	10♉49	15 28	12 10	29 18	17 29	20 50	5 38	2 47	6 31
28	12 21 8	7 11 37	24 52	17 28	13 23	29 48	17 26	20 54	5 40	2 46	6 30
29	12 25 5	8 10 57	8♊26	19 26	14 37	0♋18	17 23	20 57	5 43	2 44	6 30
30	12 29 1	9 10 14	21 31	21 23	15 51	0 48	17 21	21 1	5 45	2 42	6 29
31	12 32 58	10♈ 9 29	4♋11	23♈17	17♓ 5	1♋18	17♌18	21♊ 6	5♊47	2♎41	6♌29

THE SUN ENTERS THE SIGN OF ARIES ON MAR 20 AT 17:49.

♈ ARIES ♉ TAURUS ♊ GEMINI ♋ CANCER ♌ LEO ♍ VIRGO ♎ LIBRA

SIDEREAL TIME. SUN. MOON. MERCURY. VENUS. MARS. JUPITER. SATURN. URANUS. NEPTUNE. PLUTO.

DAY	TIME h m s	☉ ° ' "	☽ ° '	☿ ° '	♀ ° '	♂ ° '	♃ ° '	♄ ° '	♅ ° '	♆ ° '	♇ ° '
A 1	12 36 54	11♈ 8 42	16♋30	25♈ 9	18♓19	1♋48	17♌16	21♊10	5♊49	2♎39	6♌28
P 2	12 40 51	12 7 52	28 33	26 59	19 32	2 19	17R14	21 14	5 52	2R37	6R28
R 3	12 44 47	13 7 0	10♌26	28 45	20 46	2 50	17 12	21 18	5 54	2 36	6 28
I 4	12 48 44	14 6 5	22 14	0♉27	22 0	3 20	17 10	21 23	5 57	2 34	6 27
L 5	12 52 41	15 5 9	4♍ 1	2 6	23 14	3 51	17 8	21 27	5 59	2 33	6 27
6	12 56 37	16 4 10	15 52	3 40	24 28	4 22	17 7	21 32	6 2	2 31	6 26
7	13 0 34	17 3 9	27 49	5 10	25 41	4 53	17 6	21 37	6 4	2 29	6 26
8	13 4 30	18 2 6	9♎54	6 35	26 55	5 25	17 4	21 41	6 7	2 28	6 26
9	13 8 27	19 1 0	22 9	7 55	28 9	5 56	17 4	21 46	6 9	2 26	6 26
10	13 12 23	19 59 53	4♏35	9 9	29 23	6 27	17 3	21 51	6 12	2 25	6 25
11	13 16 20	20 58 44	17 11	10 19	0♈36	6 59	17 2	21 56	6 15	2 23	6 25
12	13 20 16	21 57 33	29 59	11 22	1 50	7 30	17 2	22 1	6 17	2 22	6 25
13	13 24 13	22 56 20	12♐58	12 19	3 4	8 2	17D 2	22 6	6 20	2 20	6 25
14	13 28 9	23 55 6	26 9	13 11	4 18	8 34	17 2	22 12	6 23	2 18	6 25
15	13 32 6	24 53 50	9♑33	13 57	5 31	9 6	17 2	22 17	6 26	2 17	6 24
16	13 36 3	25 52 32	23 13	14 36	6 45	9 38	17 3	22 22	6 29	2 15	6 24
17	13 39 59	26 51 12	7♒ 8	15 10	7 59	10 10	17 3	22 28	6 32	2 14	6 24
18	13 43 56	27 49 51	21 19	15 37	9 13	10 42	17 4	22 33	6 34	2 13	6D24
19	13 47 52	28 48 28	5♓46	15 58	10 26	11 14	17 5	22 39	6 37	2 11	6 24
20	13 51 49	29 47 3	20 25	16 13	11 40	11 47	17 6	22 45	6 40	2 10	6 24
21	13 55 45	0♉45 37	5♈11	16 22	12 54	12 19	17 8	22 50	6 43	2 8	6 24
22	13 59 42	1 44 9	19 56	16R25	14 8	12 52	17 9	22 56	6 46	2 7	6 24
23	14 3 38	2 42 39	4♉33	16 22	15 21	13 24	17 11	23 2	6 49	2 5	6 24
24	14 7 35	3 41 7	18 54	16 14	16 35	13 57	17 13	23 8	6 52	2 4	6 25
25	14 11 32	4 39 33	2♊53	16 1	17 49	14 30	17 15	23 14	6 55	2 3	6 25
26	14 15 28	5 37 58	16 27	15 42	19 3	15 3	17 17	23 20	6 59	2 1	6 25
27	14 19 25	6 36 20	29 34	15 19	20 16	15 35	17 20	23 26	7 2	2 0	6 25
28	14 23 21	7 34 40	12♋16	14 53	21 30	16 8	17 23	23 32	7 5	1 59	6 25
29	14 27 18	8 32 58	24 38	14 22	22 44	16 42	17 25	23 39	7 8	1 58	6 26
30	14 31 14	9♉31 15	6♌43	13♉49	23♈58	17♋15	17♌28	23♊45	7♊11	1♎56	6♌26

THE SUN ENTERS THE SIGN OF TAURUS ON APR 20 AT 05:18.

DAY	TIME h m s	☉ ° ' "	☽ ° '	☿ ° '	♀ ° '	♂ ° '	♃ ° '	♄ ° '	♅ ° '	♆ ° '	♇ ° '
M 1	14 35 11	10♉29 29	18♌38	13♉14	25♈11	17♋48	17♌32	23♊51	7♊15	1♎55	6♌26
A 2	14 39 7	11 27 41	0♍27	12R36	26 25	18 21	17 35	23 58	7 18	1R54	6 27
Y 3	14 43 4	12 25 51	12 16	11 58	27 39	18 55	17 38	24 4	7 21	1 53	6 27
4	14 47 1	13 23 59	24 10	11 20	28 52	19 28	17 42	24 11	7 24	1 52	6 27
5	14 50 57	14 22 5	6♎12	10 42	0♉ 6	20 1	17 46	24 17	7 28	1 50	6 28
6	14 54 54	15 20 9	18 26	10 6	1 20	20 35	17 50	24 24	7 31	1 49	6 28
7	14 58 50	16 18 12	0♏53	9 31	2 33	21 9	17 54	24 31	7 34	1 48	6 29
8	15 2 47	17 16 12	13 34	8 58	3 47	21 42	17 58	24 37	7 38	1 47	6 29
9	15 6 43	18 14 12	26 29	8 28	5 1	22 16	18 3	24 44	7 41	1 46	6 30
10	15 10 40	19 12 9	9♐37	8 2	6 14	22 50	18 8	24 51	7 44	1 45	6 30
11	15 14 36	20 10 6	22 57	7 39	7 28	23 24	18 12	24 58	7 48	1 44	6 31
12	15 18 33	21 8 1	6♑28	7 20	8 41	23 57	18 17	25 5	7 51	1 43	6 31
13	15 22 30	22 5 54	20 8	7 5	9 55	24 31	18 22	25 12	7 55	1 42	6 32
14	15 26 26	23 3 46	3♒57	6 54	11 9	25 5	18 28	25 19	7 58	1 41	6 33
15	15 30 23	24 1 38	17 55	6D48	12 22	25 39	18 33	25 26	8 1	1 40	6 33
16	15 34 19	24 59 27	2♓ 1	6 47	13 36	26 14	18 39	25 33	8 5	1 40	6 34
17	15 38 16	25 57 16	16 14	6 50	14 50	26 48	18 44	25 40	8 8	1 39	6 35
18	15 42 12	26 55 4	0♈34	6 58	16 3	27 22	18 50	25 47	8 12	1 38	6 35
19	15 46 9	27 52 50	14 55	7 10	17 17	27 56	18 56	25 54	8 15	1 37	6 36
20	15 50 5	28 50 35	29 15	7 27	18 31	28 31	19 3	26 2	8 19	1 36	6 37
21	15 54 2	29 48 19	13♉27	7 48	19 44	29 5	19 9	26 9	8 22	1 36	6 38
22	15 57 59	0♊46 2	27 26	8 13	20 58	29 39	19 15	26 16	8 26	1 35	6 39
23	16 1 55	1 43 44	11♊ 8	8 43	22 12	0♌14	19 22	26 23	8 29	1 34	6 40
24	16 5 52	2 41 24	24 30	9 17	23 25	0 49	19 29	26 31	8 33	1 34	6 40
25	16 9 48	3 39 4	7♋30	9 54	24 39	1 23	19 35	26 38	8 36	1 33	6 41
26	16 13 45	4 36 41	20 10	10 36	25 53	1 58	19 42	26 46	8 40	1 33	6 42
27	16 17 41	5 34 17	2♌31	11 21	27 6	2 33	19 50	26 53	8 43	1 32	6 43
28	16 21 38	6 31 52	14 37	12 10	28 20	3 7	19 57	27 1	8 47	1 32	6 44
29	16 25 34	7 29 26	26 33	13 3	29 33	3 42	20 4	27 8	8 50	1 31	6 45
30	16 29 31	8 26 58	8♍24	13 59	0♊47	4 17	20 12	27 16	8 54	1 31	6 46
31	16 33 28	9♊24 28	20♍15	14♉58	2♊ 1	4♌52	20♌19	27♊23	8♊57	1♎30	6♌47

THE SUN ENTERS THE SIGN OF GEMINI ON MAY 21 AT 04:51.

DAY	TIME h m s	☉ ° ' "	☽ ° '	☿ ° '	♀ ° '	♂ ° '	♃ ° '	♄ ° '	♅ ° '	♆ ° '	♇ ° '
J 1	16 37 24	10♊21 58	2♎11	16♉ 1	3♊14	5♌27	20♌27	27♊31	9♊ 1	1♎30	6♌48
U 2	16 41 21	11 19 26	14 17	17 6	4 28	6 2	20 35	27 38	9 4	1R30	6 49
N 3	16 45 17	12 16 53	26 36	18 15	5 42	6 37	20 43	27 46	9 8	1 29	6 50
E 4	16 49 14	13 14 18	9♏12	19 27	6 55	7 12	20 51	27 54	9 12	1 29	6 52
5	16 53 10	14 11 43	22 5	20 42	8 9	7 47	20 59	28 1	9 15	1 29	6 53
6	16 57 7	15 9 7	5♐17	22 0	9 22	8 22	21 8	28 9	9 19	1 28	6 54
7	17 1 3	16 6 29	18 45	23 21	10 36	8 57	21 16	28 17	9 22	1 28	6 55
8	17 5 0	17 3 51	2♑29	24 45	11 50	9 33	21 25	28 24	9 26	1 28	6 56
9	17 8 57	18 1 13	16 24	26 12	13 3	10 8	21 34	28 32	9 29	1 28	6 58
10	17 12 53	18 58 33	0♒28	27 41	14 17	10 43	21 42	28 40	9 33	1 28	6 59
11	17 16 50	19 55 53	14 37	29 14	15 31	11 19	21 51	28 47	9 36	1 28	7 0
12	17 20 46	20 53 13	28 50	0♊49	16 44	11 54	22 0	28 55	9 40	1D28	7 1
13	17 24 43	21 50 32	13♓ 3	2 27	17 58	12 30	22 9	29 3	9 43	1 28	7 3
14	17 28 39	22 47 50	27 14	4 8	19 12	13 5	22 19	29 11	9 46	1 28	7 4
15	17 32 36	23 45 9	11♈22	5 51	20 25	13 41	22 28	29 18	9 50	1 28	7 5
16	17 36 32	24 42 27	25 25	7 37	21 39	14 16	22 37	29 26	9 53	1 28	7 7
17	17 40 29	25 39 44	9♉20	9 26	22 53	14 52	22 47	29 34	9 57	1 28	7 8
18	17 44 26	26 37 2	23 6	11 18	24 6	15 27	22 57	29 42	10 0	1 28	7 9
19	17 48 22	27 34 19	6♊38	13 12	25 20	16 3	23 6	29 50	10 4	1 29	7 11
20	17 52 19	28 31 36	19 56	15 8	26 34	16 39	23 16	29 57	10 7	1 29	7 12
21	17 56 15	29 28 52	2♋59	17 7	27 47	17 15	23 26	0♋ 5	10 10	1 29	7 14
22	18 0 12	0♋26 8	15 44	19 8	29 1	17 51	23 36	0 13	10 14	1 29	7 15
23	18 4 8	1 23 24	28 14	21 12	0♋15	18 26	23 46	0 21	10 17	1 30	7 16
24	18 8 5	2 20 39	10♌29	23 16	1 28	19 2	23 56	0 29	10 21	1 30	7 18
25	18 12 2	3 17 53	22 33	25 23	2 42	19 38	24 7	0 37	10 24	1 30	7 19
26	18 15 58	4 15 7	4♍28	27 31	3 56	20 14	24 17	0 44	10 27	1 31	7 21
27	18 19 55	5 12 20	16 20	29 40	5 10	20 50	24 27	0 52	10 30	1 31	7 22
28	18 23 51	6 9 33	28 11	1♋50	6 23	21 26	24 38	1 0	10 34	1 32	7 24
29	18 27 48	7 6 46	10♎ 7	4 1	7 37	22 3	24 48	1 8	10 37	1 32	7 25
30	18 31 44	8♋ 3 58	22♎14	6♋12	8♋51	22♌39	24♌59	1♋15	10♊40	1♎33	7♌27

THE SUN ENTERS THE SIGN OF CANCER ON JUN 21 AT 13:03.

♏ SCORPIO ♐ SAGITTARIUS ♑ CAPRICORN ♒ AQUARIUS ♓ PISCES

1944

SIDEREAL · SUN · MOON. · MERCURY. · VENUS. · MARS. · JUPITER. · SATURN. · URANUS. · NEPTUNE. · PLUTO.

DAY	TIME h m s	☉ ° ' "	☽ ° '	☿ ° '	♀ ° '	♂ ° '	♃ ° '	♄ ° '	♅ ° '	♆ ° '	♇ ° '
J 1	18 35 41	9♋ 1 9	4♏34	8♋22	10♋ 5	23♌15	25♌10	1♋23	10♊43	1♎33	7♌29
U 2	18 39 37	9 58 21	17 13	10 33	11 18	23 51	25 21	1 31	10 47	1 34	7 30
L 3	18 43 34	10 55 32	0♐12	12 43	12 32	24 27	25 32	1 39	10 50	1 35	7 32
Y 4	18 47 31	11 52 43	13 33	14 52	13 46	25 4	25 42	1 46	10 53	1 35	7 33
5	18 51 27	12 49 54	27 16	17 1	15 0	25 40	25 54	1 54	10 56	1 36	7 35
6	18 55 24	13 47 4	11♑19	19 8	16 13	26 16	26 5	2 2	10 59	1 37	7 37
7	18 59 20	14 44 15	25 39	21 14	17 27	26 53	26 16	2 10	11 2	1 38	7 38
8	19 3 17	15 41 26	10♒ 9	23 18	18 41	27 29	26 27	2 17	11 5	1 38	7 40
9	19 7 13	16 38 37	24 44	25 21	19 55	28 6	26 38	2 25	11 8	1 39	7 41
10	19 11 10	17 35 49	9♓19	27 22	21 8	28 42	26 50	2 33	11 11	1 40	7 43
11	19 15 6	18 33 1	23 49	29 22	22 22	29 19	27 1	2 40	11 14	1 41	7 45
12	19 19 3	19 30 13	8♈ 9	1♌20	23 36	29 56	27 13	2 48	11 17	1 42	7 46
13	19 23 0	20 27 26	22 17	3 16	24 50	0♍32	27 24	2 55	11 20	1 43	7 48
14	19 26 56	21 24 40	6♉11	5 10	26 4	1 9	27 36	3 3	11 23	1 44	7 50
15	19 30 53	22 21 54	19 49	7 2	27 18	1 46	27 48	3 10	11 26	1 45	7 51
16	19 34 49	23 19 9	3♊13	8 53	28 31	2 22	27 59	3 18	11 29	1 46	7 53
17	19 38 46	24 16 24	16 22	10 41	29 45	2 59	28 11	3 25	11 32	1 47	7 55
18	19 42 42	25 13 40	29 16	12 28	0♌59	3 36	28 23	3 33	11 34	1 48	7 57
19	19 46 39	26 10 57	11♋57	14 13	2 13	4 13	28 35	3 40	11 37	1 49	7 58
20	19 50 35	27 8 14	24 25	15 56	3 27	4 50	28 47	3 48	11 40	1 50	8 0
21	19 54 32	28 5 32	6♌42	17 37	4 41	5 27	28 59	3 55	11 43	1 51	8 2
22	19 58 29	29 2 50	18 49	19 17	5 55	6 4	29 11	4 3	11 45	1 53	8 4
23	20 2 25	0♌ 0 9	0♍47	20 54	7 9	6 41	29 23	4 10	11 48	1 54	8 5
24	20 6 22	0 57 28	12 40	22 30	8 22	7 18	29 35	4 17	11 50	1 55	8 7
25	20 10 18	1 54 47	24 30	24 4	9 36	7 55	29 47	4 24	11 53	1 56	8 9
26	20 14 15	2 52 7	6♎21	25 36	10 50	8 32	29 59	4 32	11 56	1 58	8 10
27	20 18 11	3 49 28	18 17	27 6	12 4	9 9	0♍12	4 39	11 58	1 59	8 12
28	20 22 8	4 46 49	0♏22	28 35	13 18	9 47	0 24	4 46	12 0	2 0	8 14
29	20 26 4	5 44 10	12 40	0♍ 1	14 32	10 24	0 36	4 53	12 3	2 2	8 16
30	20 30 1	6 41 32	25 16	1 25	15 46	11 1	0 49	5 0	12 5	2 3	8 17
31	20 33 58	7♌38 55	8♐14	2♍48	17♌ 0	11♍39	1♍ 1	5♋ 7	12♊ 8	2♎ 5	8♌19

THE SUN ENTERS THE SIGN OF LEO ON JUL 22 AT 23:56.

DAY	TIME h m s	☉ ° ' "	☽ ° '	☿ ° '	♀ ° '	♂ ° '	♃ ° '	♄ ° '	♅ ° '	♆ ° '	♇ ° '
A 1	20 37 54	8♌36 18	21♐36	4♍ 9	18♌14	12♍16	1♍14	5♋14	12♊10	2♎ 6	8♌21
U 2	20 41 51	9 33 42	5♑23	5 27	19 28	12 54	1 26	5 21	12 12	2 8	8 23
G 3	20 45 47	10 31 7	19 36	6 44	20 42	13 31	1 39	5 28	12 14	2 9	8 24
U 4	20 49 44	11 28 32	4♒11	7 58	21 56	14 8	1 51	5 35	12 17	2 11	8 26
S 5	20 53 40	12 25 58	19 1	9 10	23 10	14 46	2 4	5 42	12 19	2 12	8 28
T 6	20 57 37	13 23 26	4♓ 1	10 20	24 23	15 24	2 17	5 48	12 21	2 14	8 30
7	21 1 33	14 20 54	19 0	11 28	25 37	16 1	2 29	5 55	12 23	2 16	8 31
8	21 5 30	15 18 24	3♈52	12 33	26 51	16 39	2 42	6 2	12 25	2 17	8 33
9	21 9 27	16 15 55	18 28	13 35	28 5	17 17	2 55	6 8	12 27	2 19	8 35
10	21 13 23	17 13 27	2♉45	14 35	29 19	17 54	3 7	6 15	12 29	2 20	8 37
11	21 17 20	18 11 1	16 40	15 33	0♍33	18 32	3 20	6 21	12 31	2 22	8 38
12	21 21 16	19 8 36	0♊12	16 27	1 47	19 10	3 33	6 28	12 33	2 24	8 40
13	21 25 13	20 6 13	13 23	17 18	3 1	19 48	3 46	6 34	12 34	2 26	8 42
14	21 29 9	21 3 51	26 16	18 6	4 15	20 26	3 59	6 41	12 36	2 27	8 44
15	21 33 6	22 1 31	8♋52	18 51	5 29	21 4	4 11	6 47	12 38	2 29	8 45
16	21 37 2	22 59 12	21 16	19 32	6 43	21 42	4 24	6 53	12 40	2 31	8 47
17	21 40 59	23 56 55	3♌28	20 10	7 57	22 20	4 37	6 59	12 41	2 33	8 49
18	21 44 56	24 54 39	15 33	20 43	9 11	22 58	4 50	7 5	12 43	2 35	8 50
19	21 48 52	25 52 24	27 31	21 13	10 25	23 36	5 3	7 12	12 44	2 36	8 52
20	21 52 49	26 50 11	9♍24	21 38	11 39	24 14	5 16	7 18	12 46	2 38	8 54
21	21 56 45	27 47 59	21 15	21 58	12 53	24 52	5 29	7 23	12 47	2 40	8 55
22	22 0 42	28 45 48	3♎ 5	22 13	14 7	25 30	5 42	7 29	12 49	2 42	8 57
23	22 4 38	29 43 39	14 57	22 23	15 21	26 9	5 55	7 35	12 50	2 44	8 59
24	22 8 35	0♍41 31	26 53	22R28	16 35	26 47	6 8	7 41	12 51	2 46	9 0
25	22 12 31	1 39 24	8♏57	22 27	17 49	27 25	6 21	7 47	12 53	2 48	9 2
26	22 16 28	2 37 19	21 13	22 20	19 3	28 4	6 34	7 52	12 54	2 50	9 4
27	22 20 25	3 35 14	3♐45	22 8	20 17	28 42	6 47	7 58	12 55	2 52	9 5
28	22 24 21	4 33 12	16 37	21 49	21 31	29 21	7 0	8 3	12 56	2 54	9 7
29	22 28 18	5 31 10	29 53	21 24	22 45	29 59	7 13	8 9	12 57	2 56	9 9
30	22 32 14	6 29 10	13♑35	20 54	23 59	0♎38	7 26	8 14	12 58	2 58	9 10
31	22 36 11	7♍27 11	27♑45	20♍17	25♍13	1♎17	7♍39	8♋19	12♊59	3♎ 0	9♌12

THE SUN ENTERS THE SIGN OF VIRGO ON AUG 23 AT 06:47.

DAY	TIME h m s	☉ ° ' "	☽ ° '	☿ ° '	♀ ° '	♂ ° '	♃ ° '	♄ ° '	♅ ° '	♆ ° '	♇ ° '
S 1	22 40 7	8♍25 13	12♒21	19♍35	26♍27	1♎55	7♍52	8♋24	13♊ 0	3♎ 2	9♌13
E 2	22 44 4	9 23 17	27 19	18R48	27 41	2 34	8 5	8 29	13 1	3 4	9 15
P 3	22 48 0	10 21 23	12♓32	17 57	28 54	3 13	8 18	8 34	13 2	3 6	9 16
T 4	22 51 57	11 19 30	27 48	17 2	0♎ 8	3 51	8 31	8 39	13 3	3 8	9 18
E 5	22 55 53	12 17 39	12♈58	16 5	1 22	4 30	8 44	8 44	13 3	3 10	9 20
M 6	22 59 50	13 15 50	27 52	15 6	2 36	5 9	8 57	8 49	13 4	3 13	9 21
B 7	23 3 47	14 14 3	12♉23	14 7	3 50	5 48	9 10	8 54	13 5	3 15	9 23
E 8	23 7 43	15 12 18	26 26	13 9	5 4	6 27	9 23	8 58	13 5	3 17	9 24
R 9	23 11 40	16 10 35	10♊ 1	12 13	6 18	7 6	9 36	9 3	13 6	3 19	9 25
10	23 15 36	17 8 54	23 9	11 21	7 32	7 45	9 49	9 7	13 6	3 21	9 27
11	23 19 33	18 7 16	5♋55	10 35	8 46	8 24	10 2	9 12	13 7	3 23	9 28
12	23 23 29	19 5 39	18 22	9 54	10 0	9 3	10 15	9 16	13 7	3 25	9 30
13	23 27 26	20 4 5	0♌35	9 21	11 13	9 42	10 28	9 20	13 7	3 28	9 31
14	23 31 22	21 2 32	12 37	8 55	12 27	10 22	10 41	9 24	13 8	3 30	9 33
15	23 35 19	22 1 2	24 33	8 39	13 41	11 1	10 54	9 28	13 8	3 32	9 34
16	23 39 16	22 59 33	6♍25	8D31	14 55	11 40	11 7	9 32	13 8	3 34	9 35
17	23 43 12	23 58 7	18 15	8 33	16 9	12 20	11 20	9 36	13 8	3 36	9 37
18	23 47 9	24 56 42	0♎ 6	8 45	17 23	12 59	11 33	9 40	13R 8	3 39	9 38
19	23 51 5	25 55 20	11 58	9 6	18 37	13 39	11 45	9 44	13 8	3 41	9 39
20	23 55 2	26 53 59	23 54	9 37	19 51	14 18	11 58	9 47	13 8	3 43	9 41
21	23 58 58	27 52 40	5♏56	10 16	21 4	14 58	12 11	9 51	13 8	3 45	9 42
22	0 2 55	28 51 23	18 4	11 4	22 18	15 37	12 24	9 54	13 8	3 47	9 43
23	0 6 51	29 50 7	0♐22	12 0	23 32	16 17	12 37	9 57	13 8	3 50	9 44
24	0 10 48	0♎48 54	12 54	13 3	24 46	16 57	12 49	10 0	13 7	3 52	9 46
25	0 14 45	1 47 42	25 42	14 13	26 0	17 36	13 2	10 4	13 7	3 54	9 47
26	0 18 41	2 46 32	8♑50	15 29	27 13	18 16	13 15	10 6	13 7	3 56	9 48
27	0 22 38	3 45 23	22 23	16 51	28 27	18 56	13 27	10 9	13 6	3 59	9 49
28	0 26 34	4 44 17	6♒22	18 17	29 41	19 36	13 40	10 12	13 6	4 1	9 50
29	0 30 31	5 43 12	20 47	19 48	0♏55	20 16	13 52	10 15	13 5	4 3	9 51
30	0 34 27	6♎42 9	5♓37	21♍22	2♏ 8	20♎56	14♍ 5	10♋17	13♊ 5	4♎ 5	9♌52

THE SUN ENTERS THE SIGN OF LIBRA ON SEP 23 AT 04:03.

♈ ARIES ♉ TAURUS ♊ GEMINI ♋ CANCER ♌ LEO ♍ VIRGO ♎ LIBRA

1944

SIDEREAL TIME · SUN. · MOON. · MERCURY. · VENUS. · MARS. · JUPITER. · SATURN. · URANUS. · NEPTUNE. · PLUTO.

DAY	TIME	☉	☽	☿	♀	♂	♃	♄	♅	♆	♇
	h m s	° ′ ″	° ′	° ′	° ′	° ′	° ′	° ′	° ′	° ′	° ′
O 1	0 38 24	7♎41 7	20♓46	22♍58	3♏22	21♎36	14♍17	10♋20	13♊ 4	4♎ 8	9♌53
C 2	0 42 20	8 40 8	6♈ 4	24 38	4 36	22 16	14 30	10 22	13R 4	4 10	9 54
T 3	0 46 17	9 39 10	21 20	26 19	5 50	22 56	14 42	10 25	13 3	4 12	9 55
O 4	0 50 13	10 38 15	6♉23	28 2	7 3	23 36	14 54	10 27	13 2	4 14	9 56
B 5	0 54 10	11 37 21	21 4	29 46	8 17	24 16	15 7	10 29	13 1	4 16	9 57
E 6	0 58 7	12 36 31	5♊16	1♎30	9 31	24 56	15 19	10 31	13 1	4 19	9 58
R 7	1 2 3	13 35 42	18 59	3 16	10 44	25 37	15 31	10 33	13 0	4 21	9 59
8	1 6 0	14 34 56	2♋12	5 2	11 58	26 17	15 43	10 34	12 59	4 23	10 0
9	1 9 56	15 34 12	14 59	6 48	13 11	26 57	15 56	10 36	12 58	4 25	10 1
10	1 13 53	16 33 30	27 25	8 33	14 25	27 38	16 8	10 38	12 57	4 28	10 2
11	1 17 49	17 32 51	9♌35	10 19	15 39	28 18	16 20	10 39	12 56	4 30	10 3
12	1 21 46	18 32 14	21 33	12 5	16 52	28 59	16 32	10 40	12 54	4 32	10 4
13	1 25 42	19 31 39	3♍25	13 50	18 6	29 39	16 44	10 41	12 53	4 34	10 4
14	1 29 39	20 31 7	15 14	15 34	19 19	0♏20	16 55	10 43	12 52	4 36	10 5
15	1 33 36	21 30 36	27 4	17 19	20 33	1 1	17 7	10 43	12 51	4 38	10 6
16	1 37 32	22 30 8	8♎58	19 2	21 47	1 41	17 19	10 44	12 49	4 41	10 7
17	1 41 29	23 29 42	20 56	20 45	23 0	2 22	17 31	10 45	12 48	4 43	10 7
18	1 45 25	24 29 18	3♏ 0	22 28	24 14	3 3	17 42	10 46	12 47	4 45	10 8
19	1 49 22	25 28 56	15 11	24 10	25 27	3 44	17 54	10 46	12 45	4 47	10 9
20	1 53 18	26 28 35	27 30	25 51	26 41	4 25	18 5	10 47	12 44	4 49	10 9
21	1 57 15	27 28 17	9♐58	27 32	27 54	5 6	18 17	10 47	12 42	4 51	10 10
22	2 1 11	28 28 1	22 37	29 12	29 8	5 47	18 28	10 47	12 41	4 53	10 10
23	2 5 8	29 27 46	5♑30	0♏52	0♐21	6 28	18 40	10R47	12 39	4 55	10 11
24	2 9 5	0♏27 33	18 38	2 30	1 34	7 9	18 51	10 47	12 37	4 57	10 12
25	2 13 1	1 27 22	2♒ 5	4 9	2 48	7 50	19 2	10 47	12 36	4 59	10 12
26	2 16 58	2 27 12	15 53	5 47	4 1	8 31	19 13	10 47	12 34	5 1	10 12
27	2 20 54	3 27 4	0♓ 4	7 24	5 15	9 13	19 24	10 46	12 32	5 4	10 13
28	2 24 51	4 26 58	14 36	9 1	6 28	9 54	19 35	10 46	12 30	5 6	10 13
29	2 28 47	5 26 53	29 26	10 37	7 41	10 35	19 46	10 45	12 28	5 8	10 14
30	2 32 44	6 26 50	14♈28	12 13	8 55	11 17	19 57	10 45	12 26	5 9	10 14
31	2 36 40	7♏26 48	29♈32	13♏48	10♐ 8	11♏58	20♍ 7	10♋44	12♊25	5♎11	10♌14

THE SUN ENTERS THE SIGN OF SCORPIO ON OCT 23 AT 12:57.

DAY	TIME	☉	☽	☿	♀	♂	♃	♄	♅	♆	♇
	h m s	° ′ ″	° ′	° ′	° ′	° ′	° ′	° ′	° ′	° ′	° ′
N 1	2 40 37	8♏26 49	14♉28	15♏23	11♐21	12♏40	20♍18	10♋43	12♊23	5♎13	10♌15
O 2	2 44 34	9 26 51	29 7	16 57	12 34	13 21	20 28	10R42	12R21	5 15	10 15
V 3	2 48 30	10 26 56	13♊22	18 31	13 48	14 3	20 39	10 41	12 19	5 17	10 15
E 4	2 52 27	11 27 3	27 9	20 5	15 1	14 45	20 49	10 40	12 17	5 19	10 15
M 5	2 56 23	12 27 11	10♋27	21 38	16 14	15 26	20 59	10 38	12 14	5 21	10 16
B 6	3 0 20	13 27 22	23 20	23 10	17 27	16 8	21 10	10 37	12 12	5 23	10 16
E 7	3 4 16	14 27 34	5♌49	24 43	18 40	16 50	21 20	10 35	12 10	5 25	10 16
R 8	3 8 13	15 27 49	18 1	26 15	19 53	17 32	21 30	10 33	12 8	5 27	10 16
9	3 12 9	16 28 6	0♍ 0	27 46	21 7	18 14	21 40	10 32	12 6	5 28	10 16
10	3 16 6	17 28 24	11 52	29 18	22 20	18 56	21 49	10 30	12 4	5 30	10 16
11	3 20 3	18 28 45	23 42	0♐49	23 33	19 38	21 59	10 28	12 1	5 32	10R16
12	3 23 59	19 29 7	5♎34	2 19	24 46	20 20	22 9	10 26	11 59	5 34	10 16
13	3 27 56	20 29 32	17 31	3 49	25 59	21 2	22 18	10 23	11 57	5 35	10 16
14	3 31 52	21 29 58	29 36	5 19	27 12	21 44	22 28	10 21	11 54	5 37	10 16
15	3 35 49	22 30 26	11♏50	6 49	28 25	22 26	22 37	10 19	11 52	5 39	10 16
16	3 39 45	23 30 55	24 14	8 18	29 37	23 9	22 46	10 16	11 50	5 40	10 16
17	3 43 42	24 31 26	6♐49	9 47	0♑50	23 51	22 55	10 14	11 47	5 42	10 16
18	3 47 38	25 31 59	19 35	11 15	2 3	24 33	23 4	10 11	11 45	5 44	10 15
19	3 51 35	26 32 33	2♑32	12 43	3 16	25 16	23 13	10 8	11 43	5 45	10 15
20	3 55 32	27 33 9	15 40	14 10	4 29	25 58	23 21	10 5	11 40	5 47	10 15
21	3 59 28	28 33 46	29 0	15 37	5 41	26 41	23 30	10 2	11 38	5 48	10 15
22	4 3 25	29 34 24	12♒33	17 3	6 54	27 23	23 38	9 59	11 35	5 50	10 14
23	4 7 21	0♐35 3	26 20	18 29	8 7	28 6	23 47	9 56	11 33	5 51	10 14
24	4 11 18	1 35 43	10♓22	19 53	9 19	28 48	23 55	9 53	11 30	5 53	10 14
25	4 15 14	2 36 24	24 37	21 17	10 32	29 31	24 3	9 49	11 28	5 54	10 13
26	4 19 11	3 37 6	9♈ 5	22 40	11 45	0♐14	24 11	9 46	11 25	5 55	10 13
27	4 23 7	4 37 49	23 40	24 1	12 57	0 57	24 19	9 42	11 23	5 57	10 13
28	4 27 4	5 38 33	8♉18	25 22	14 9	1 40	24 27	9 39	11 20	5 58	10 12
29	4 31 1	6 39 19	22 51	26 40	15 22	2 22	24 34	9 35	11 18	5 59	10 12
30	4 34 57	7♐40 5	7♊11	27♐58	16♑34	3♐ 5	24♍42	9♋31	11♊15	6♎ 1	10♌11

THE SUN ENTERS THE SIGN OF SAGITTARIUS ON NOV 22 AT 10:08.

DAY	TIME	☉	☽	☿	♀	♂	♃	♄	♅	♆	♇
	h m s	° ′ ″	° ′	° ′	° ′	° ′	° ′	° ′	° ′	° ′	° ′
D 1	4 38 54	8♐40 53	21♊14	29♐13	17♑46	3♐48	24♍49	9♋28	11♊13	6♎ 2	10♌11
E 2	4 42 50	9 41 42	4♋56	0♑25	18 59	4 31	24 56	9R24	11R10	6 3	10R10
C 3	4 46 47	10 42 33	18 13	1 36	20 11	5 15	25 3	9 20	11 8	6 4	10 10
E 4	4 50 43	11 43 24	1♌ 7	2 43	21 23	5 58	25 10	9 16	11 5	6 6	10 9
M 5	4 54 40	12 44 17	13 40	3 46	22 35	6 41	25 17	9 12	11 3	6 7	10 8
B 6	4 58 36	13 45 11	25 56	4 46	23 47	7 24	25 23	9 7	11 0	6 8	10 8
E 7	5 2 33	14 46 7	7♍58	5 41	24 59	8 7	25 30	9 3	10 57	6 9	10 7
R 8	5 6 30	15 47 3	19 53	6 31	26 11	8 51	25 36	8 59	10 55	6 10	10 6
9	5 10 26	16 48 1	1♎44	7 15	27 22	9 34	25 42	8 54	10 52	6 11	10 6
10	5 14 23	17 49 0	13 37	7 52	28 34	10 18	25 48	8 50	10 50	6 12	10 5
11	5 18 19	18 50 0	25 37	8 22	29 46	11 1	25 54	8 46	10 47	6 13	10 4
12	5 22 16	19 51 1	7♏46	8 43	0♒57	11 45	26 0	8 41	10 45	6 14	10 3
13	5 26 12	20 52 4	20 8	8R55	2 9	12 28	26 5	8 37	10 42	6 15	10 3
14	5 30 9	21 53 7	2♐44	8 57	3 20	13 12	26 10	8 32	10 40	6 16	10 2
15	5 34 5	22 54 11	15 35	8 48	4 32	13 56	26 16	8 27	10 37	6 16	10 1
16	5 38 2	23 55 16	28 42	8 28	5 43	14 39	26 21	8 23	10 35	6 17	10 0
17	5 41 59	24 56 21	12♑ 2	7 56	6 54	15 23	26 26	8 18	10 32	6 18	9 59
18	5 45 55	25 57 27	25 35	7 12	8 5	16 7	26 30	8 13	10 30	6 19	9 58
19	5 49 52	26 58 33	9♒19	6 17	9 16	16 51	26 35	8 8	10 28	6 19	9 57
20	5 53 48	27 59 40	23 12	5 13	10 27	17 35	26 39	8 3	10 25	6 20	9 56
21	5 57 45	29 0 47	7♓13	4 1	11 38	18 19	26 43	7 59	10 23	6 21	9 55
22	6 1 41	0♑ 1 54	21 19	2 42	12 48	19 3	26 47	7 54	10 21	6 21	9 54
23	6 5 38	1 3 1	5♈29	1 20	13 59	19 47	26 51	7 49	10 18	6 22	9 53
24	6 9 35	2 4 8	19 42	29♐58	15 10	20 31	26 55	7 44	10 16	6 22	9 52
25	6 13 31	3 5 16	3♉54	28 37	16 20	21 15	26 58	7 39	10 14	6 23	9 51
26	6 17 28	4 6 23	18 2	27 22	17 30	21 59	27 2	7 34	10 11	6 23	9 50
27	6 21 24	5 7 31	2♊ 4	26 13	18 40	22 44	27 5	7 29	10 9	6 24	9 49
28	6 25 21	6 8 38	15 56	25 12	19 50	23 28	27 8	7 24	10 7	6 24	9 48
29	6 29 17	7 9 46	29 35	24 21	21 0	24 12	27 11	7 19	10 5	6 24	9 47
30	6 33 14	8 10 54	12♋58	23 40	22 10	24 57	27 13	7 14	10 2	6 25	9 46
31	6 37 10	9♑12 2	26♋ 4	23♐10	23♒19	25♐41	27♍16	7♋ 9	10♊ 0	6♎25	9♌45

THE SUN ENTERS THE SIGN OF CAPRICORN ON DEC 21 AT 23:15.

♏ SCORPIO ♐ SAGITTARIUS ♑ CAPRICORN ♒ AQUARIUS ♓ PISCES

1945

SIDEREAL | SUN. | MOON. | MERCURY. | VENUS. | MARS. | JUPITER. | SATURN. | URANUS. | NEPTUNE. | PLUTO.

DAY	TIME	☉	☽	☿	♀	♂	♃	♄	♅	♆	♇
	h m s	° ' "	° '	° '	° '	° '	° '	° '	° '	° '	° '
J 1	6 41 7	10♑13 10	8♌52	22♐51	24♒29	26♐25	27♍18	7♋ 4	9♊58	6♎25	9♌44
A 2	6 45 4	11 14 19	21 23	22D41	25 38	27 10	27 20	6R59	9R56	6 25	9R42
N 3	6 49 0	12 15 27	3♍39	22 40	26 47	27 54	27 22	6 54	9 54	6 26	9 41
U 4	6 52 57	13 16 36	15 43	22 49	27 56	28 39	27 23	6 50	9 52	6 26	9 40
A 5	6 56 53	14 17 45	27 39	23 6	29 5	29 24	27 25	6 45	9 50	6 26	9 39
R 6	7 0 50	15 18 54	9♎32	23 29	0♓13	0♑ 8	27 26	6 40	9 48	6 26	9 38
Y 7	7 4 46	16 20 3	21 25	24 0	1 22	0 53	27 27	6 35	9 46	6R26	9 36
8	7 8 43	17 21 13	3♏24	24 37	2 30	1 38	27 28	6 30	9 44	6 26	9 35
9	7 12 39	18 22 22	15 33	25 19	3 38	2 23	27 29	6 25	9 43	6 26	9 34
10	7 16 36	19 23 31	27 57	26 6	4 46	3 8	27 29	6 21	9 41	6 26	9 32
11	7 20 33	20 24 41	10♐38	26 57	5 54	3 52	27 30	6 16	9 39	6 26	9 31
12	7 24 29	21 25 50	23 39	27 52	7 1	4 37	27R30	6 11	9 37	6 26	9 30
13	7 28 26	22 26 59	7♑ 1	28 50	8 9	5 22	27 30	6 6	9 36	6 26	9 29
14	7 32 22	23 28 8	20 43	29 52	9 16	6 7	27 30	6 2	9 34	6 25	9 27
15	7 36 19	24 29 17	4♒43	0♑56	10 23	6 52	27 29	5 57	9 32	6 25	9 26
16	7 40 15	25 30 25	18 57	2 3	11 29	7 38	27 28	5 53	9 31	6 25	9 25
17	7 44 12	26 31 32	3♓20	3 12	12 36	8 23	27 28	5 48	9 29	6 25	9 23
18	7 48 8	27 32 38	17 46	4 24	13 42	9 8	27 27	5 44	9 28	6 24	9 22
19	7 52 5	28 33 44	2♈11	5 37	14 48	9 53	27 25	5 39	9 26	6 24	9 21
20	7 56 2	29 34 48	16 31	6 51	15 54	10 38	27 24	5 35	9 25	6 23	9 19
21	7 59 58	0♒35 52	0♉42	8 8	16 59	11 24	27 22	5 31	9 24	6 23	9 18
22	8 3 55	1 36 55	14 43	9 26	18 4	12 9	27 21	5 27	9 22	6 23	9 16
23	8 7 51	2 37 57	28 32	10 45	19 9	12 54	27 19	5 23	9 21	6 22	9 15
24	8 11 48	3 38 57	12♊ 8	12 5	20 14	13 40	27 16	5 18	9 20	6 22	9 14
25	8 15 44	4 39 57	25 32	13 26	21 18	14 25	27 14	5 14	9 19	6 21	9 12
26	8 19 41	5 40 56	8♋43	14 49	22 22	15 11	27 11	5 11	9 18	6 20	9 11
27	8 23 37	6 41 54	21 42	16 12	23 25	15 56	27 9	5 7	9 17	6 20	9 10
28	8 27 34	7 42 50	4♌28	17 37	24 29	16 42	27 6	5 3	9 16	6 19	9 8
29	8 31 31	8 43 46	17 2	19 2	25 32	17 27	27 3	4 59	9 15	6 18	9 7
30	8 35 27	9 44 41	29 25	20 29	26 34	18 13	26 59	4 56	9 14	6 18	9 5
31	8 39 24	10♒45 35	11♍36	21♑56	27♓36	18♑58	26♍56	4♋52	9♊13	6♎17	9♌ 4

THE SUN ENTERS THE SIGN OF AQUARIUS ON JAN 20 AT 09:54.

DAY	TIME	☉	☽	☿	♀	♂	♃	♄	♅	♆	♇
	h m s	° ' "	° '	° '	° '	° '	° '	° '	° '	° '	° '
F 1	8 43 20	11♒46 28	23♍39	23♑24	28♓38	19♑44	26♍52	4♋49	9♊12	6♎16	9♌ 3
E 2	8 47 17	12 47 20	5♎34	24 53	29 39	20 30	26R49	4R45	9R11	6R15	9R 1
B 3	8 51 13	13 48 11	17 27	26 23	0♈40	21 16	26 45	4 42	9 11	6 15	9 0
R 4	8 55 10	14 49 1	29 19	27 53	1 41	22 1	26 40	4 39	9 10	6 14	8 58
U 5	8 59 6	15 49 51	11♏16	29 24	2 41	22 47	26 36	4 36	9 9	6 13	8 57
A 6	9 3 3	16 50 39	23 22	0♒56	3 41	23 33	26 32	4 33	9 9	6 12	8 56
R 7	9 7 0	17 51 27	5♐42	2 29	4 40	24 19	26 27	4 30	9 8	6 11	8 54
Y 8	9 10 56	18 52 14	18 21	4 3	5 38	25 5	26 22	4 27	9 8	6 10	8 53
9	9 14 53	19 52 59	1♑23	5 37	6 37	25 51	26 17	4 24	9 7	6 9	8 51
10	9 18 49	20 53 44	14 49	7 13	7 34	26 37	26 12	4 22	9 7	6 8	8 50
11	9 22 46	21 54 27	28 42	8 49	8 32	27 23	26 7	4 19	9 7	6 7	8 49
12	9 26 42	22 55 10	12♒59	10 25	9 28	28 9	26 1	4 17	9 7	6 6	8 47
13	9 30 39	23 55 50	27 37	12 3	10 24	28 55	25 56	4 14	9 6	6 5	8 46
14	9 34 35	24 56 30	12♓27	13 42	11 20	29 41	25 50	4 12	9 6	6 3	8 45
15	9 38 32	25 57 8	27 23	15 21	12 15	0♒27	25 44	4 10	9D 6	6 2	8 43
16	9 42 29	26 57 44	12♈15	17 1	13 9	1 13	25 38	4 8	9 6	6 1	8 42
17	9 46 25	27 58 18	26 55	18 43	14 2	1 59	25 32	4 6	9 6	6 0	8 41
18	9 50 22	28 58 51	11♉19	20 25	14 55	2 45	25 26	4 4	9 6	5 59	8 40
19	9 54 18	29 59 21	25 23	22 8	15 47	3 32	25 20	4 2	9 6	5 57	8 38
20	9 58 15	0♓59 50	9♊ 6	23 51	16 39	4 18	25 13	4 1	9 7	5 56	8 37
21	10 2 11	2 0 17	22 29	25 36	17 29	5 4	25 7	3 59	9 7	5 55	8 36
22	10 6 8	3 0 43	5♋35	27 22	18 19	5 50	25 0	3 58	9 7	5 54	8 34
23	10 10 4	4 1 6	18 25	29 9	19 8	6 37	24 53	3 57	9 8	5 52	8 33
24	10 14 1	5 1 27	1♌ 3	0♓57	19 56	7 23	24 46	3 55	9 8	5 51	8 32
25	10 17 58	6 1 47	13 31	2 45	20 43	8 9	24 39	3 54	9 8	5 50	8 31
26	10 21 54	7 2 4	25 49	4 35	21 29	8 56	24 32	3 53	9 9	5 48	8 30
27	10 25 51	8 2 20	7♍59	6 25	22 15	9 42	24 25	3 53	9 9	5 47	8 28
28	10 29 47	9♓ 2 34	20♍ 3	8♓17	22♈59	10♒28	24♍18	3♋52	9♊10	5♎45	8♌27

THE SUN ENTERS THE SIGN OF PISCES ON FEB 19 AT 00:15.

DAY	TIME	☉	☽	☿	♀	♂	♃	♄	♅	♆	♇
	h m s	° ' "	° '	° '	° '	° '	° '	° '	° '	° '	° '
M 1	10 33 44	10♓ 2 47	2♎ 1	10♓ 9	23♈42	11♒15	24♍10	3♋51	9♊11	5♎44	8♌26
A 2	10 37 40	11 2 57	13 55	12 3	24 24	12 1	24R 3	3R51	9 11	5R42	8R25
R 3	10 41 37	12 3 6	25 47	13 57	25 5	12 48	23 55	3 50	9 12	5 41	8 24
C 4	10 45 33	13 3 14	7♏39	15 52	25 45	13 34	23 48	3 50	9 13	5 39	8 23
H 5	10 49 30	14 3 20	19 35	17 47	26 23	14 21	23 40	3D50	9 14	5 38	8 22
6	10 53 27	15 3 24	1♐39	19 43	27 1	15 7	23 33	3 50	9 15	5 36	8 20
7	10 57 23	16 3 27	13 55	21 40	27 37	15 54	23 25	3 50	9 16	5 35	8 19
8	11 1 20	17 3 28	26 28	23 37	28 11	16 40	23 17	3 50	9 17	5 33	8 18
9	11 5 16	18 3 27	9♑24	25 34	28 44	17 27	23 10	3 50	9 18	5 32	8 17
10	11 9 13	19 3 25	22 45	27 31	29 16	18 13	23 2	3 51	9 19	5 30	8 16
11	11 13 9	20 3 21	6♒36	29 27	29 46	19 0	22 54	3 51	9 20	5 29	8 15
12	11 17 6	21 3 16	20 55	1♈23	0♉15	19 46	22 46	3 52	9 21	5 27	8 14
13	11 21 2	22 3 8	5♓41	3 18	0 42	20 33	22 38	3 53	9 23	5 26	8 13
14	11 24 59	23 2 59	20 46	5 12	1 7	21 20	22 31	3 54	9 24	5 24	8 12
15	11 28 55	24 2 48	6♈ 1	7 4	1 31	22 6	22 23	3 55	9 25	5 22	8 12
16	11 32 52	25 2 35	21 15	8 54	1 52	22 53	22 15	3 56	9 27	5 21	8 11
17	11 36 49	26 2 19	6♉17	10 41	2 12	23 40	22 7	3 57	9 28	5 19	8 10
18	11 40 45	27 2 2	20 59	12 25	2 30	24 26	22 0	3 58	9 30	5 17	8 9
19	11 44 42	28 1 42	5♊15	14 6	2 46	25 13	21 52	3 59	9 31	5 16	8 8
20	11 48 38	29 1 20	19 4	15 43	3 0	25 59	21 44	4 1	9 33	5 14	8 7
21	11 52 35	0♈ 0 55	2♋28	17 15	3 11	26 46	21 36	4 3	9 35	5 13	8 7
22	11 56 31	1 0 29	15 28	18 42	3 20	27 33	21 29	4 4	9 36	5 11	8 6
23	12 0 28	2 0 0	28 9	20 4	3 27	28 19	21 21	4 6	9 38	5 9	8 5
24	12 4 24	2 59 28	10♌35	21 21	3 32	29 6	21 14	4 8	9 40	5 8	8 4
25	12 8 21	3 58 55	22 50	22 31	3R35	29 53	21 6	4 10	9 42	5 6	8 4
26	12 12 18	4 58 19	4♍56	23 35	3 35	0♓39	20 59	4 12	9 44	5 4	8 3
27	12 16 14	5 57 41	16 56	24 33	3 32	1 26	20 51	4 15	9 46	5 3	8 2
28	12 20 11	6 57 1	28 53	25 23	3 27	2 13	20 44	4 17	9 48	5 1	8 2
29	12 24 7	7 56 18	10♎47	26 6	3 20	2 59	20 37	4 19	9 50	4 59	8 1
30	12 28 4	8 55 34	22 39	26 43	3 10	3 46	20 30	4 22	9 52	4 58	8 1
31	12 32 0	9♈54 48	4♏32	27♈12	2♉57	4♓33	20♍23	4♋25	9♊54	4♎56	8♌ 0

THE SUN ENTERS THE SIGN OF ARIES ON MAR 20 AT 23:38.

♈ ARIES ♉ TAURUS ♊ GEMINI ♋ CANCER ♌ LEO ♍ VIRGO ♎ LIBRA

1945

SIDEREAL | SUN | MOON | MERCURY | VENUS | MARS | JUPITER | SATURN | URANUS | NEPTUNE | PLUTO

DAY	TIME	☉	☽	☿	♀	♂	♃	♄	♅	♆	♇
	h m s	° ' "	° '	° '	° '	° '	° '	° '	° '	° '	° '
A 1	12 35 57	10♈53 59	16♏27	27♈33	2♉42	5♓19	20♍16	4♋27	9♊56	4♎54	7♌59
P 2	12 39 53	11 53 9	28 26	27 48	2R25	6 6	20R 9	4 30	9 58	4R53	7R59
R 3	12 43 50	12 52 17	10♐32	27R55	2 5	6 53	20 2	4 33	10 0	4 51	7 58
I 4	12 47 47	13 51 24	22 48	27 55	1 43	7 39	19 56	4 36	10 3	4 49	7 58
L 5	12 51 43	14 50 28	5♑19	27 48	1 19	8 26	19 49	4 40	10 5	4 48	7 58
6	12 55 40	15 49 31	18 10	27 35	0 52	9 13	19 43	4 43	10 7	4 46	7 57
7	12 59 36	16 48 32	1♒25	27 15	0 24	9 59	19 36	4 46	10 10	4 45	7 57
8	13 3 33	17 47 32	15 7	26 50	29♈54	10 46	19 30	4 50	10 12	4 43	7 57
9	13 7 29	18 46 29	29 18	26 20	29 22	11 33	19 24	4 53	10 15	4 41	7 56
10	13 11 26	19 45 25	13♓56	25 46	28 49	12 19	19 18	4 57	10 17	4 40	7 56
11	13 15 22	20 44 19	28 58	25 8	28 14	13 6	19 12	5 1	10 20	4 38	7 56
12	13 19 19	21 43 11	14♈14	24 27	27 38	13 52	19 7	5 4	10 22	4 37	7 55
13	13 23 15	22 42 1	29 34	23 44	27 2	14 39	19 1	5 8	10 25	4 35	7 55
14	13 27 12	23 40 49	14♉47	23 0	26 25	15 26	18 56	5 12	10 28	4 33	7 55
15	13 31 9	24 39 35	29 41	22 15	25 47	16 12	18 51	5 17	10 30	4 32	7 55
16	13 35 5	25 38 18	14♊ 9	21 31	25 9	16 59	18 46	5 21	10 33	4 30	7 55
17	13 39 2	26 37 0	28 9	20 49	24 31	17 45	18 41	5 25	10 36	4 29	7 55
18	13 42 58	27 35 40	11♋40	20 8	23 54	18 32	18 36	5 29	10 38	4 27	7 55
19	13 46 55	28 34 17	24 44	19 30	23 17	19 18	18 31	5 34	10 41	4 26	7 54
20	13 50 51	29 32 52	7♌26	18 55	22 41	20 5	18 27	5 38	10 44	4 24	7D54
21	13 54 48	0♉31 25	19 49	18 24	22 6	20 51	18 22	5 43	10 47	4 23	7 54
22	13 58 45	1 29 55	1♍59	17 56	21 33	21 38	18 18	5 48	10 50	4 22	7 54
23	14 2 41	2 28 23	14 0	17 34	21 0	22 24	18 14	5 53	10 53	4 20	7 55
24	14 6 38	3 26 50	25 55	17 16	20 30	23 10	18 11	5 57	10 56	4 19	7 55
25	14 10 34	4 25 14	7♎47	17 3	20 1	23 57	18 7	6 2	10 59	4 17	7 55
26	14 14 31	5 23 36	19 39	16 55	19 34	24 43	18 3	6 7	11 2	4 16	7 55
27	14 18 27	6 21 57	1♏33	16D51	19 10	25 29	18 0	6 13	11 5	4 15	7 55
28	14 22 24	7 20 15	13 29	16 53	18 47	26 16	17 57	6 18	11 8	4 13	7 55
29	14 26 20	8 18 32	25 30	17 0	18 27	27 2	17 54	6 23	11 11	4 12	7 55
30	14 30 17	9♉16 47	7♐37	17♈11	18♈ 9	27♓48	17♍51	6♋28	11♊14	4♎11	7♌56

THE SUN ENTERS THE SIGN OF TAURUS ON APR 20 AT 11:07.

DAY	TIME	☉	☽	☿	♀	♂	♃	♄	♅	♆	♇
	h m s	° ' "	° '	° '	° '	° '	° '	° '	° '	° '	° '
M 1	14 34 13	10♉15 1	19♐51	17♈27	17♈53	28♓34	17♍49	6♋34	11♊17	4♎ 9	7♌56
A 2	14 38 10	11 13 13	2♑15	17 48	17R40	29 21	17R46	6 39	11 20	4R 8	7 56
Y 3	14 42 7	12 11 23	14 52	18 13	17 30	0♈ 7	17 44	6 45	11 23	4 7	7 57
4	14 46 3	13 9 32	27 46	18 42	17 22	0 53	17 42	6 50	11 27	4 6	7 57
5	14 50 0	14 7 40	10♒59	19 15	17 16	1 39	17 40	6 56	11 30	4 5	7 57
6	14 53 56	15 5 46	24 35	19 53	17D13	2 25	17 39	7 2	11 33	4 3	7 58
7	14 57 53	16 3 51	8♓36	20 34	17 12	3 11	17 37	7 8	11 36	4 2	7 58
8	15 1 49	17 1 54	23 1	21 19	17 13	3 57	17 36	7 13	11 40	4 1	7 59
9	15 5 46	17 59 56	7♈47	22 7	17 17	4 43	17 35	7 19	11 43	4 0	7 59
10	15 9 42	18 57 56	22 48	22 59	17 23	5 29	17 34	7 25	11 46	3 59	8 0
11	15 13 39	19 55 56	7♉57	23 54	17 31	6 15	17 33	7 31	11 50	3 58	8 0
12	15 17 36	20 53 53	23 2	24 52	17 42	7 1	17 32	7 38	11 53	3 57	8 1
13	15 21 32	21 51 50	7♊53	25 53	17 54	7 47	17 32	7 44	11 56	3 56	8 1
14	15 25 29	22 49 44	22 24	26 57	18 9	8 33	17D32	7 50	12 0	3 55	8 2
15	15 29 25	23 47 37	6♋29	28 4	18 25	9 19	17 32	7 56	12 3	3 54	8 2
16	15 33 22	24 45 29	20 6	29 14	18 43	10 4	17 32	8 3	12 7	3 53	8 3
17	15 37 18	25 43 18	3♌17	0♉26	19 4	10 50	17 32	8 9	12 10	3 52	8 4
18	15 41 15	26 41 6	16 3	1 41	19 25	11 36	17 32	8 16	12 13	3 51	8 5
19	15 45 11	27 38 52	28 30	2 59	19 49	12 21	17 33	8 22	12 17	3 50	8 5
20	15 49 8	28 36 37	10♍41	4 19	20 15	13 7	17 34	8 29	12 20	3 50	8 6
21	15 53 5	29 34 20	22 41	5 42	20 41	13 52	17 35	8 35	12 24	3 49	8 7
22	15 57 1	0♊32 1	4♎36	7 7	21 10	14 38	17 36	8 42	12 27	3 48	8 8
23	16 0 58	1 29 41	16 27	8 34	21 40	15 23	17 38	8 49	12 31	3 47	8 8
24	16 4 54	2 27 19	28 20	10 4	22 11	16 9	17 39	8 55	12 34	3 47	8 9
25	16 8 51	3 24 56	10♏17	11 37	22 44	16 54	17 41	9 2	12 38	3 46	8 10
26	16 12 47	4 22 32	22 19	13 11	23 18	17 39	17 43	9 9	12 41	3 45	8 11
27	16 16 44	5 20 6	4♐29	14 48	23 53	18 25	17 45	9 16	12 45	3 45	8 12
28	16 20 40	6 17 39	16 47	16 28	24 30	19 10	17 47	9 23	12 48	3 44	8 13
29	16 24 37	7 15 12	29 16	18 9	25 8	19 55	17 50	9 30	12 52	3 44	8 14
30	16 28 34	8 12 43	11♑55	19 54	25 47	20 40	17 52	9 37	12 55	3 43	8 15
31	16 32 30	9♊10 13	24♑48	21♉40	26♈27	21♈25	17♍55	9♋44	12♊59	3♎43	8♌16

THE SUN ENTERS THE SIGN OF GEMINI ON MAY 21 AT 10:40.

DAY	TIME	☉	☽	☿	♀	♂	♃	♄	♅	♆	♇
	h m s	° ' "	° '	° '	° '	° '	° '	° '	° '	° '	° '
J 1	16 36 27	10♊ 7 43	7♒54	23♉29	27♈ 8	22♈10	17♍58	9♋51	13♊ 2	3♎42	8♌17
U 2	16 40 23	11 5 11	21 16	25 20	27 50	22 55	18 1	9 58	13 6	3R42	8 18
N 3	16 44 20	12 2 39	4♓55	27 13	28 33	23 40	18 5	10 5	13 9	3 41	8 19
E 4	16 48 16	13 0 6	18 51	29 9	29 17	24 25	18 8	10 13	13 13	3 41	8 20
5	16 52 13	13 57 33	3♈ 4	1♊ 6	0♉ 2	25 10	18 12	10 20	13 16	3 41	8 21
6	16 56 9	14 54 59	17 33	3 6	0 48	25 55	18 16	10 27	13 20	3 40	8 22
7	17 0 6	15 52 24	2♉13	5 8	1 34	26 40	18 19	10 34	13 24	3 40	8 24
8	17 4 3	16 49 49	16 58	7 12	2 22	27 24	18 24	10 42	13 27	3 40	8 25
9	17 7 59	17 47 13	1♊41	9 18	3 10	28 9	18 28	10 49	13 31	3 40	8 26
10	17 11 56	18 44 36	16 15	11 25	3 59	28 53	18 32	10 57	13 34	3 39	8 27
11	17 15 52	19 41 59	0♋34	13 33	4 48	29 38	18 37	11 4	13 38	3 39	8 28
12	17 19 49	20 39 21	14 33	15 43	5 38	0♉22	18 42	11 11	13 41	3 39	8 30
13	17 23 45	21 36 42	28 8	17 54	6 29	1 7	18 47	11 19	13 45	3 39	8 31
14	17 27 42	22 34 2	11♌20	20 5	7 21	1 51	18 52	11 26	13 48	3D39	8 32
15	17 31 39	23 31 21	24 10	22 17	8 13	2 35	18 57	11 34	13 52	3 39	8 33
16	17 35 35	24 28 40	6♍40	24 29	9 6	3 20	19 2	11 42	13 55	3 39	8 35
17	17 39 32	25 25 57	18 54	26 41	9 59	4 4	19 8	11 49	13 59	3 39	8 36
18	17 43 28	26 23 14	0♎57	28 52	10 53	4 48	19 13	11 57	14 2	3 39	8 37
19	17 47 25	27 20 30	12 52	1♋ 3	11 47	5 32	19 19	12 4	14 6	3 39	8 39
20	17 51 21	28 17 45	24 45	3 13	12 42	6 16	19 25	12 12	14 9	3 40	8 40
21	17 55 18	29 14 59	6♏39	5 21	13 37	7 0	19 31	12 20	14 13	3 40	8 42
22	17 59 14	0♋12 13	18 39	7 29	14 33	7 43	19 37	12 27	14 16	3 40	8 43
23	18 3 11	1 9 26	0♐47	9 35	15 29	8 27	19 44	12 35	14 20	3 40	8 45
24	18 7 8	2 6 39	13 6	11 39	16 26	9 11	19 50	12 43	14 23	3 40	8 46
25	18 11 4	3 3 52	25 38	13 42	17 23	9 54	19 57	12 50	14 26	3 41	8 47
26	18 15 1	4 1 4	8♑24	15 42	18 21	10 38	20 4	12 58	14 30	3 41	8 49
27	18 18 57	4 58 16	21 25	17 41	19 19	11 21	20 11	13 6	14 33	3 41	8 50
28	18 22 54	5 55 28	4♒39	19 38	20 17	12 5	20 18	13 14	14 36	3 42	8 52
29	18 26 50	6 52 39	18 7	21 33	21 16	12 48	20 25	13 21	14 40	3 42	8 53
30	18 30 47	7♋49 51	1♓48	23♋26	22♉15	13♉31	20♍32	13♋29	14♊43	3♎43	8♌55

THE SUN ENTERS THE SIGN OF CANCER ON JUN 21 AT 18:53.

♏ SCORPIO ♐ SAGITTARIUS ♑ CAPRICORN ♒ AQUARIUS ♓ PISCES

1945

SIDEREAL SUN MOON. MERCURY. VENUS. MARS. JUPITER. SATURN. URANUS. NEPTUNE. PLUTO.

DAY	TIME	☉	☽	☿	♀	♂	♃	♄	♅	♆	♇
	h m s	° ' "	° '	° '	° '	° '	° '	° '	° '	° '	° '
J 1	18 34 43	8♋47 3	15♓40	25♋16	23♉14	14♉15	20♍39	13♋37	14♊46	3♎43	8♌57
U 2	18 38 40	9 44 15	29 43	27 5	24 14	14 58	20 47	13 45	14 50	3 44	8 58
L 3	18 42 37	10 41 27	13♈53	28 52	25 14	15 41	20 55	13 53	14 53	3 44	9 0
Y 4	18 46 33	11 38 39	28 10	0♌36	26 15	16 24	21 2	14 0	14 56	3 45	9 1
5	18 50 30	12 35 52	12♉30	2 18	27 16	17 7	21 10	14 8	15 0	3 46	9 3
6	18 54 26	13 33 5	26 49	3 59	28 17	17 49	21 18	14 16	15 3	3 46	9 5
7	18 58 23	14 30 18	11♊ 5	5 37	29 18	18 32	21 26	14 24	15 6	3 47	9 6
8	19 2 19	15 27 32	25 13	7 13	0♊20	19 15	21 35	14 32	15 9	3 48	9 8
9	19 6 16	16 24 46	9♋10	8 47	1 22	19 57	21 43	14 39	15 12	3 48	9 9
10	19 10 12	17 22 0	22 51	10 19	2 24	20 40	21 51	14 47	15 15	3 49	9 11
11	19 14 9	18 19 14	6♌15	11 49	3 26	21 22	22 0	14 55	15 19	3 50	9 13
12	19 18 6	19 16 28	19 21	13 16	4 29	22 5	22 9	15 3	15 22	3 51	9 14
13	19 22 2	20 13 43	2♍ 8	14 41	5 32	22 47	22 18	15 10	15 25	3 52	9 16
14	19 25 59	21 10 57	14 37	16 5	6 35	23 29	22 26	15 18	15 28	3 53	9 18
15	19 29 55	22 8 12	26 52	17 25	7 39	24 11	22 35	15 26	15 31	3 54	9 19
16	19 33 52	23 5 26	8♎55	18 44	8 42	24 53	22 45	15 34	15 34	3 55	9 21
17	19 37 48	24 2 41	20 51	20 0	9 46	25 35	22 54	15 41	15 37	3 56	9 23
18	19 41 45	24 59 56	2♏44	21 14	10 50	26 17	23 3	15 49	15 40	3 57	9 25
19	19 45 41	25 57 11	14 39	22 26	11 55	26 59	23 13	15 57	15 43	3 58	9 26
20	19 49 38	26 54 26	26 40	23 35	12 59	27 40	23 22	16 5	15 45	3 59	9 28
21	19 53 35	27 51 42	8♐52	24 41	14 4	28 22	23 32	16 12	15 48	4 0	9 30
22	19 57 31	28 48 58	21 18	25 44	15 9	29 3	23 41	16 20	15 51	4 1	9 31
23	20 1 28	29 46 14	4♑ 1	26 45	16 14	29 45	23 51	16 28	15 54	4 2	9 33
24	20 5 24	0♌43 31	17 3	27 43	17 19	0♊26	24 1	16 35	15 57	4 3	9 35
25	20 9 21	1 40 49	0♒24	28 38	18 25	1 7	24 11	16 43	15 59	4 5	9 37
26	20 13 17	2 38 7	14 4	29 30	19 30	1 48	24 21	16 51	16 2	4 6	9 38
27	20 17 14	3 35 26	27 59	0♍18	20 36	2 29	24 31	16 58	16 5	4 7	9 40
28	20 21 11	4 32 45	12♓ 6	1 3	21 42	3 10	24 41	17 6	16 7	4 8	9 42
29	20 25 7	5 30 6	26 21	1 45	22 48	3 51	24 52	17 13	16 10	4 10	9 44
30	20 29 4	6 27 27	10♈39	2 22	23 55	4 31	25 2	17 21	16 12	4 11	9 46
31	20 33 0	7♌24 50	24♈57	2♍56	25♊ 1	5♊12	25♍13	17♋28	16♊15	4♎12	9♌47

THE SUN ENTERS THE SIGN OF LEO ON JUL 23 AT 05:46.

DAY	TIME	☉	☽	☿	♀	♂	♃	♄	♅	♆	♇
	h m s	° ' "	° '	° '	° '	° '	° '	° '	° '	° '	° '
A 1	20 36 57	8♌22 14	9♉12	3♍26	26♊ 8	5♊53	25♍23	17♋36	16♊17	4♎14	9♌49
U 2	20 40 53	9 19 39	23 20	3 51	27 15	6 33	25 34	17 43	16 20	4 15	9 51
G 3	20 44 50	10 17 5	7♊21	4 12	28 22	7 13	25 44	17 51	16 22	4 17	9 53
U 4	20 48 46	11 14 33	21 12	4 29	29 29	7 54	25 55	17 58	16 25	4 18	9 54
S 5	20 52 43	12 12 1	4♋54	4 40	0♋37	8 34	26 6	18 5	16 27	4 20	9 56
T 6	20 56 40	13 9 31	18 24	4R47	1 44	9 14	26 17	18 13	16 29	4 21	9 58
7	21 0 36	14 7 2	1♌43	4 48	2 52	9 54	26 28	18 20	16 32	4 23	10 0
8	21 4 33	15 4 34	14 48	4 44	3 59	10 33	26 39	18 27	16 34	4 24	10 1
9	21 8 29	16 2 7	27 40	4 35	5 7	11 13	26 50	18 35	16 36	4 26	10 3
10	21 12 26	16 59 42	10♍17	4 20	6 15	11 52	27 2	18 42	16 38	4 28	10 5
11	21 16 22	17 57 17	22 41	4 0	7 24	12 32	27 13	18 49	16 40	4 29	10 7
12	21 20 19	18 54 53	4♎53	3 35	8 32	13 11	27 24	18 56	16 42	4 31	10 8
13	21 24 15	19 52 30	16 54	3 4	9 40	13 50	27 36	19 3	16 44	4 33	10 10
14	21 28 12	20 50 8	28 48	2 29	10 49	14 30	27 47	19 10	16 46	4 34	10 12
15	21 32 8	21 47 47	10♏40	1 49	11 57	15 8	27 59	19 17	16 48	4 36	10 14
16	21 36 5	22 45 27	22 33	1 5	13 6	15 47	28 10	19 24	16 50	4 38	10 15
17	21 40 2	23 43 8	4♐33	0 18	14 15	16 26	28 22	19 31	16 52	4 40	10 17
18	21 43 58	24 40 50	16 44	29♌28	15 24	17 5	28 34	19 38	16 54	4 41	10 19
19	21 47 55	25 38 34	29 12	28 37	16 33	17 43	28 45	19 45	16 56	4 43	10 21
20	21 51 51	26 36 18	12♑ 0	27 45	17 43	18 21	28 57	19 52	16 57	4 45	10 22
21	21 55 48	27 34 4	25 12	26 53	18 52	19 0	29 9	19 58	16 59	4 47	10 24
22	21 59 44	28 31 51	8♒49	26 2	20 2	19 38	29 21	20 5	17 1	4 49	10 26
23	22 3 41	29 29 39	22 49	25 14	21 11	20 16	29 33	20 12	17 2	4 51	10 27
24	22 7 37	0♍27 29	7♓ 9	24 29	22 21	20 54	29 45	20 18	17 4	4 53	10 29
25	22 11 34	1 25 20	21 44	23 48	23 31	21 31	29 57	20 25	17 5	4 54	10 31
26	22 15 31	2 23 12	6♈26	23 13	24 41	22 9	0♎ 9	20 31	17 7	4 56	10 32
27	22 19 27	3 21 7	21 8	22 43	25 51	22 46	0 21	20 38	17 8	4 58	10 34
28	22 23 24	4 19 3	5♉43	22 21	27 1	23 24	0 33	20 44	17 10	5 0	10 36
29	22 27 20	5 17 1	20 5	22 6	28 11	24 1	0 46	20 51	17 11	5 2	10 37
30	22 31 17	6 15 1	4♊13	21D59	29 22	24 38	0 58	20 57	17 12	5 4	10 39
31	22 35 13	7♍13 3	18♊ 5	22♌ 0	0♌32	25♊15	1♎10	21♋ 3	17♊13	5♎ 6	10♌41

THE SUN ENTERS THE SIGN OF VIRGO ON AUG 23 AT 12:36.

DAY	TIME	☉	☽	☿	♀	♂	♃	♄	♅	♆	♇
	h m s	° ' "	° '	° '	° '	° '	° '	° '	° '	° '	° '
S 1	22 39 10	8♍11 7	1♋41	22♌ 9	1♌43	25♊52	1♎23	21♋ 9	17♊14	5♎ 8	10♌42
E 2	22 43 6	9 9 13	15 3	22 27	2 53	26 28	1 35	21 15	17 16	5 10	10 44
P 3	22 47 3	10 7 20	28 11	22 54	4 4	27 5	1 47	21 21	17 17	5 12	10 45
T 4	22 51 0	11 5 30	11♌ 8	23 28	5 15	27 41	2 0	21 27	17 18	5 14	10 47
E 5	22 54 56	12 3 41	23 53	24 11	6 26	28 17	2 12	21 33	17 19	5 17	10 49
M 6	22 58 53	13 1 55	6♍28	25 2	7 37	28 53	2 25	21 39	17 20	5 19	10 50
B 7	23 2 49	14 0 10	18 52	26 0	8 48	29 29	2 38	21 45	17 20	5 21	10 52
E 8	23 6 46	14 58 26	1♎ 7	27 5	10 0	0♋ 5	2 50	21 51	17 21	5 23	10 53
R 9	23 10 42	15 56 44	13 12	28 17	11 11	0 40	3 3	21 56	17 22	5 25	10 55
10	23 14 39	16 55 4	25 9	29 35	12 22	1 15	3 15	22 2	17 23	5 27	10 56
11	23 18 35	17 53 26	7♏ 1	0♍59	13 34	1 51	3 28	22 7	17 23	5 29	10 58
12	23 22 32	18 51 49	18 50	2 27	14 46	2 26	3 41	22 13	17 24	5 31	10 59
13	23 26 29	19 50 14	0♐41	4 0	15 57	3 0	3 54	22 18	17 24	5 34	11 1
14	23 30 25	20 48 41	12 38	5 37	17 9	3 35	4 6	22 24	17 25	5 36	11 2
15	23 34 22	21 47 9	24 46	7 17	18 21	4 9	4 19	22 29	17 25	5 38	11 3
16	23 38 18	22 45 39	7♑11	9 0	19 33	4 44	4 32	22 34	17 26	5 40	11 5
17	23 42 15	23 44 11	19 57	10 45	20 45	5 18	4 45	22 39	17 26	5 42	11 6
18	23 46 11	24 42 44	3♒10	12 32	21 57	5 52	4 58	22 44	17 27	5 44	11 8
19	23 50 8	25 41 19	16 51	14 21	23 9	6 25	5 11	22 49	17 27	5 47	11 9
20	23 54 4	26 39 55	1♓ 0	16 10	24 21	6 59	5 23	22 54	17 27	5 49	11 10
21	23 58 1	27 38 34	15 36	18 1	25 34	7 32	5 36	22 59	17 27	5 51	11 12
22	0 1 58	28 37 14	0♈31	19 52	26 46	8 5	5 49	23 3	17 27	5 53	11 13
23	0 5 54	29 35 56	15 36	21 43	27 59	8 38	6 2	23 8	17R27	5 55	11 14
24	0 9 51	0♎34 40	0♉42	23 33	29 11	9 11	6 15	23 12	17 27	5 58	11 15
25	0 13 47	1 33 26	15 38	25 24	0♍24	9 44	6 28	23 17	17 27	6 0	11 17
26	0 17 44	2 32 15	0♊17	27 15	1 37	10 16	6 41	23 21	17 27	6 2	11 18
27	0 21 40	3 31 6	14 35	29 5	2 49	10 48	6 54	23 25	17 27	6 4	11 19
28	0 25 37	4 29 59	28 29	0♎54	4 2	11 20	7 7	23 29	17 27	6 7	11 20
29	0 29 33	5 28 55	12♋ 2	2 43	5 15	11 52	7 20	23 34	17 26	6 9	11 21
30	0 33 30	6♎27 53	25♋14	4♎31	6♍28	12♋23	7♎33	23♋38	17♊26	6♎11	11♌22

THE SUN ENTERS THE SIGN OF LIBRA ON SEP 23 AT 09:51.

♈ ARIES ♉ TAURUS ♊ GEMINI ♋ CANCER ♌ LEO ♍ VIRGO ♎ LIBRA

1945

SIDEREAL . SUN . MOON . MERCURY . VENUS . MARS . JUPITER . SATURN . URANUS . NEPTUNE . PLUTO .

DAY	TIME	☉	☽	☿	♀	♂	♃	♄	♅	♆	♇
	h m s	° ' "	° '	° '	° '	° '	° '	° '	° '	° '	° '
O 1	0 37 26	7♎26 53	8♌10	6♎18	7♍41	12♋54	7♎46	23♋41	17♊26	6♎13	11♌24
C 2	0 41 23	8 25 55	20 50	8 5	8 55	13 25	7 59	23 45	17R25	6 16	11 25
T 3	0 45 20	9 25 0	3♍20	9 51	10 8	13 56	8 12	23 49	17 25	6 18	11 26
O 4	0 49 16	10 24 7	15 39	11 36	11 21	14 27	8 25	23 53	17 24	6 20	11 27
B 5	0 53 13	11 23 15	27 50	13 20	12 34	14 57	8 38	23 56	17 24	6 22	11 28
E 6	0 57 9	12 22 26	9♎54	15 3	13 48	15 27	8 51	23 59	17 23	6 24	11 29
R 7	1 1 6	13 21 39	21 52	16 46	15 1	15 57	9 4	24 3	17 22	6 27	11 30
8	1 5 2	14 20 54	3♏45	18 28	16 15	16 26	9 17	24 6	17 22	6 29	11 31
9	1 8 59	15 20 11	15 35	20 9	17 28	16 55	9 30	24 9	17 21	6 31	11 32
10	1 12 55	16 19 30	27 23	21 49	18 42	17 24	9 43	24 12	17 20	6 33	11 33
11	1 16 52	17 18 51	9♐14	23 28	19 56	17 53	9 56	24 15	17 19	6 36	11 34
12	1 20 49	18 18 14	21 10	25 7	21 9	18 21	10 8	24 18	17 18	6 38	11 34
13	1 24 45	19 17 39	3♑16	26 45	22 23	18 49	10 21	24 21	17 17	6 40	11 35
14	1 28 42	20 17 5	15 38	28 22	23 37	19 17	10 34	24 23	17 16	6 42	11 36
15	1 32 38	21 16 33	28 19	29 59	24 51	19 44	10 47	24 26	17 15	6 44	11 37
16	1 36 35	22 16 3	11♒26	1♏35	26 5	20 11	11 0	24 28	17 14	6 46	11 38
17	1 40 31	23 15 35	25 1	3 10	27 19	20 38	11 13	24 31	17 13	6 49	11 38
18	1 44 28	24 15 8	9♓ 7	4 45	28 33	21 5	11 26	24 33	17 12	6 51	11 39
19	1 48 24	25 14 43	23 42	6 19	29 47	21 31	11 39	24 35	17 10	6 53	11 40
20	1 52 21	26 14 19	8♈41	7 52	1♎ 1	21 57	11 51	24 37	17 9	6 55	11 40
21	1 56 18	27 13 58	23 56	9 25	2 15	22 22	12 4	24 39	17 8	6 57	11 41
22	2 0 14	28 13 39	9♉15	10 57	3 30	22 48	12 17	24 41	17 6	6 59	11 42
23	2 4 11	29 13 22	24 28	12 29	4 44	23 12	12 30	24 42	17 5	7 1	11 42
24	2 8 7	0♏13 7	9♊24	14 0	5 58	23 37	12 42	24 44	17 3	7 4	11 43
25	2 12 4	1 12 54	23 57	15 31	7 13	24 1	12 55	24 45	17 2	7 6	11 43
26	2 16 0	2 12 43	8♋ 4	17 0	8 27	24 25	13 8	24 47	17 0	7 8	11 44
27	2 19 57	3 12 35	21 43	18 30	9 42	24 48	13 20	24 48	16 59	7 10	11 44
28	2 23 53	4 12 29	4♌58	19 59	10 56	25 11	13 33	24 49	16 57	7 12	11 45
29	2 27 50	5 12 25	17 50	21 27	12 11	25 34	13 45	24 50	16 55	7 14	11 45
30	2 31 47	6 12 23	0♍25	22 55	13 25	25 56	13 58	24 51	16 54	7 16	11 46
31	2 35 43	7♏12 24	12♍45	24♏22	14♎40	26♋17	14♎10	24♋52	16♊52	7♎18	11♌46

THE SUN ENTERS THE SIGN OF SCORPIO ON OCT 23 AT 18:44.

DAY	TIME	☉	☽	☿	♀	♂	♃	♄	♅	♆	♇
	h m s	° ' "	° '	° '	° '	° '	° '	° '	° '	° '	° '
N 1	2 39 40	8♏12 26	24♍54	25♏48	15♎55	26♋39	14♎23	24♋52	16♊50	7♎20	11♌46
O 2	2 43 36	9 12 30	6♎56	27 14	17 9	27 0	14 35	24 53	16R48	7 22	11 47
V 3	2 47 33	10 12 37	18 52	28 39	18 24	27 20	14 47	24 53	16 46	7 24	11 47
E 4	2 51 29	11 12 45	0♏45	0♐ 3	19 39	27 40	15 0	24 54	16 45	7 26	11 47
M 5	2 55 26	12 12 55	12 35	1 27	20 54	27 59	15 12	24 54	16 43	7 28	11 48
B 6	2 59 22	13 13 7	24 25	2 49	22 8	28 18	15 24	24R54	16 41	7 30	11 48
E 7	3 3 19	14 13 21	6♐16	4 11	23 23	28 37	15 36	24 54	16 39	7 31	11 48
R 8	3 7 16	15 13 37	18 11	5 32	24 38	28 55	15 49	24 54	16 37	7 33	11 48
9	3 11 12	16 13 54	0♑12	6 52	25 53	29 13	16 1	24 54	16 35	7 35	11 48
10	3 15 9	17 14 13	12 23	8 10	27 8	29 30	16 13	24 53	16 32	7 37	11 48
11	3 19 5	18 14 33	24 46	9 27	28 23	29 46	16 25	24 53	16 30	7 39	11 48
12	3 23 2	19 14 55	7♒26	10 43	29 38	0♌ 2	16 37	24 52	16 28	7 41	11 48
13	3 26 58	20 15 18	20 28	11 57	0♏53	0 17	16 48	24 52	16 26	7 42	11R48
14	3 30 55	21 15 42	3♓55	13 9	2 8	0 32	17 0	24 51	16 24	7 44	11 48
15	3 34 51	22 16 8	17 49	14 19	3 23	0 46	17 12	24 50	16 21	7 46	11 48
16	3 38 48	23 16 35	2♈10	15 27	4 38	1 0	17 24	24 49	16 19	7 47	11 48
17	3 42 45	24 17 3	16 57	16 32	5 53	1 13	17 35	24 48	16 17	7 49	11 48
18	3 46 41	25 17 33	2♉ 1	17 33	7 8	1 26	17 47	24 47	16 15	7 51	11 48
19	3 50 38	26 18 4	17 16	18 32	8 23	1 37	17 58	24 45	16 12	7 52	11 48
20	3 54 34	27 18 36	2♊30	19 26	9 38	1 49	18 10	24 44	16 10	7 54	11 48
21	3 58 31	28 19 10	17 33	20 16	10 54	1 59	18 21	24 42	16 8	7 56	11 48
22	4 2 27	29 19 46	2♋17	21 1	12 9	2 9	18 33	24 41	16 5	7 57	11 47
23	4 6 24	0♐20 24	16 36	21 41	13 24	2 19	18 44	24 39	16 3	7 59	11 47
24	4 10 20	1 21 3	0♌27	22 14	14 39	2 27	18 55	24 37	16 0	8 0	11 47
25	4 14 17	2 21 43	13 51	22 40	15 54	2 35	19 6	24 35	15 58	8 2	11 46
26	4 18 14	3 22 25	26 49	22 58	17 10	2 42	19 17	24 33	15 55	8 3	11 46
27	4 22 10	4 23 9	9♍26	23R 7	18 25	2 49	19 28	24 31	15 53	8 5	11 46
28	4 26 7	5 23 54	21 45	23 7	19 40	2 55	19 39	24 29	15 50	8 6	11 45
29	4 30 3	6 24 41	3♎51	22 57	20 56	3 0	19 50	24 26	15 48	8 7	11 45
30	4 34 0	7♐25 29	15♎48	22♐36	22♏11	3♌ 4	20♎ 0	24♋24	15♊45	8♎ 9	11♌45

THE SUN ENTERS THE SIGN OF SAGITTARIUS ON NOV 22 AT 15:56.

DAY	TIME	☉	☽	☿	♀	♂	♃	♄	♅	♆	♇
	h m s	° ' "	° '	° '	° '	° '	° '	° '	° '	° '	° '
D 1	4 37 56	8♐26 19	27♎40	22♐ 4	23♏26	3♌ 8	20♎11	24♋21	15♊43	8♎10	11♌44
E 2	4 41 53	9 27 10	9♏30	21R21	24 42	3 10	20 21	24R18	15R40	8 11	11R44
C 3	4 45 49	10 28 2	21 20	20 28	25 57	3 12	20 32	24 16	15 38	8 13	11 43
E 4	4 49 46	11 28 56	3♐13	19 24	27 12	3R13	20 42	24 13	15 35	8 14	11 42
M 5	4 53 43	12 29 50	15 11	18 13	28 28	3 14	20 52	24 10	15 33	8 15	11 42
B 6	4 57 39	13 30 46	27 16	16 55	29 43	3 13	21 3	24 7	15 30	8 16	11 41
E 7	5 1 36	14 31 43	9♑29	15 33	0♐59	3 12	21 13	24 4	15 28	8 17	11 41
R 8	5 5 32	15 32 41	21 52	14 10	2 14	3 10	21 23	24 0	15 25	8 19	11 40
9	5 9 29	16 33 39	4♒27	12 49	3 29	3 7	21 33	23 57	15 23	8 20	11 39
10	5 13 25	17 34 38	17 16	11 32	4 45	3 3	21 42	23 54	15 20	8 21	11 39
11	5 17 22	18 35 38	0♓22	10 22	6 0	2 59	21 52	23 50	15 17	8 22	11 38
12	5 21 18	19 36 38	13 46	9 20	7 16	2 53	22 2	23 47	15 15	8 23	11 37
13	5 25 15	20 37 38	27 31	8 28	8 31	2 47	22 11	23 43	15 12	8 24	11 36
14	5 29 12	21 38 39	11♈37	7 48	9 46	2 40	22 20	23 39	15 10	8 25	11 36
15	5 33 8	22 39 41	26 3	7 18	11 2	2 32	22 30	23 35	15 7	8 26	11 35
16	5 37 5	23 40 43	10♉44	7 0	12 17	2 23	22 39	23 31	15 5	8 26	11 34
17	5 41 1	24 41 45	25 37	6D52	13 33	2 14	22 48	23 28	15 2	8 27	11 33
18	5 44 58	25 42 48	10♊33	6 54	14 48	2 3	22 57	23 23	15 0	8 28	11 32
19	5 48 54	26 43 52	25 25	7 6	16 4	1 52	23 5	23 19	14 57	8 29	11 31
20	5 52 51	27 44 56	10♋ 4	7 26	17 19	1 40	23 14	23 15	14 55	8 30	11 30
21	5 56 47	28 46 1	24 25	7 55	18 35	1 27	23 23	23 11	14 52	8 30	11 29
22	6 0 44	29 47 6	8♌22	8 30	19 50	1 13	23 31	23 7	14 50	8 31	11 29
23	6 4 41	0♑48 12	21 54	9 11	21 6	0 59	23 39	23 2	14 47	8 32	11 28
24	6 8 37	1 49 18	5♍ 1	9 58	22 21	0 44	23 48	22 58	14 45	8 32	11 27
25	6 12 34	2 50 25	17 44	10 50	23 36	0 28	23 56	22 54	14 43	8 33	11 26
26	6 16 30	3 51 33	0♎ 7	11 46	24 52	0 11	24 4	22 49	14 40	8 33	11 24
27	6 20 27	4 52 41	12 15	12 46	26 7	29♋53	24 11	22 44	14 38	8 34	11 23
28	6 24 23	5 53 50	24 12	13 49	27 23	29 35	24 19	22 40	14 36	8 34	11 22
29	6 28 20	6 54 59	6♏ 3	14 56	28 38	29 17	24 27	22 35	14 33	8 35	11 21
30	6 32 16	7 56 9	17 52	16 5	29 54	28 57	24 34	22 31	14 31	8 35	11 20
31	6 36 13	8♑57 19	29♏44	17♐16	1♑ 9	28♋37	24♎41	22♋26	14♊29	8♎35	11♌19

THE SUN ENTERS THE SIGN OF CAPRICORN ON DEC 22 AT 05:04.

♏ SCORPIO ♐ SAGITTARIUS ♑ CAPRICORN ♒ AQUARIUS ♓ PISCES

SIDEREAL SUN. MOON. MERCURY. VENUS. MARS. JUPITER. SATURN. URANUS. NEPTUNE. PLUTO.

DAY	TIME	☉	☽	☿	♀	♂	♃	♄	♅	♆	♇
	h m s	° ' "	° '	° '	° '	° '	° '	° '	° '	° '	° '
J 1	6 40 10	9♑58 30	11♐41	18♐30	2♑25	28♋17	24♎49	22♋21	14♊27	8♎36	11♌18
A 2	6 44 6	10 59 40	23 47	19 45	3 40	27R55	24 56	22R16	14R24	8 36	11R17
N 3	6 48 3	12 0 51	6♑ 4	21 2	4 56	27 34	25 2	22 12	14 22	8 36	11 16
U 4	6 51 59	13 2 2	18 33	22 20	6 11	27 12	25 9	22 7	14 20	8 37	11 14
A 5	6 55 56	14 3 12	1♒16	23 40	7 27	26 49	25 16	22 2	14 18	8 37	11 13
R 6	6 59 52	15 4 23	14 12	25 1	8 42	26 27	25 22	21 57	14 16	8 37	11 12
Y 7	7 3 49	16 5 33	27 21	26 23	9 58	26 3	25 28	21 52	14 14	8 37	11 11
8	7 7 46	17 6 43	10♓44	27 46	11 13	25 40	25 34	21 47	14 12	8 37	11 9
9	7 11 42	18 7 52	24 19	29 10	12 29	25 16	25 40	21 42	14 10	8 37	11 8
10	7 15 39	19 9 1	8♈ 7	0♑35	13 44	24 53	25 46	21 37	14 8	8R37	11 7
11	7 19 35	20 10 9	22 6	2 0	15 0	24 29	25 52	21 32	14 6	8 37	11 6
12	7 23 32	21 11 17	6♉16	3 27	16 15	24 5	25 57	21 27	14 4	8 37	11 4
13	7 27 28	22 12 24	20 34	4 54	17 31	23 41	26 3	21 22	14 2	8 37	11 3
14	7 31 25	23 13 31	4♊59	6 22	18 46	23 17	26 8	21 17	14 0	8 37	11 2
15	7 35 21	24 14 36	19 27	7 50	20 1	22 53	26 13	21 12	13 58	8 37	11 0
16	7 39 18	25 15 42	3♋52	9 19	21 17	22 29	26 18	21 8	13 57	8 37	10 59
17	7 43 15	26 16 46	18 11	10 48	22 32	22 5	26 22	21 3	13 55	8 36	10 58
18	7 47 11	27 17 50	2♌18	12 19	23 48	21 42	26 27	20 58	13 53	8 36	10 56
19	7 51 8	28 18 53	16 8	13 49	25 3	21 18	26 31	20 53	13 52	8 36	10 55
20	7 55 4	29 19 56	29 37	15 21	26 19	20 55	26 35	20 48	13 50	8 36	10 54
21	7 59 1	0♒20 59	12♍46	16 53	27 34	20 33	26 39	20 43	13 49	8 35	10 52
22	8 2 57	1 22 0	25 32	18 25	28 49	20 11	26 43	20 38	13 47	8 35	10 51
23	8 6 54	2 23 2	7♎59	19 58	0♒ 5	19 49	26 47	20 33	13 46	8 34	10 50
24	8 10 50	3 24 2	20 10	21 32	1 20	19 27	26 50	20 29	13 44	8 34	10 48
25	8 14 47	4 25 3	2♏ 9	23 6	2 36	19 7	26 54	20 24	13 43	8 33	10 47
26	8 18 44	5 26 2	14 0	24 41	3 51	18 46	26 57	20 19	13 41	8 33	10 45
27	8 22 40	6 27 2	25 50	26 17	5 6	18 26	27 0	20 15	13 40	8 32	10 44
28	8 26 37	7 28 0	7♐42	27 53	6 22	18 7	27 3	20 10	13 39	8 32	10 43
29	8 30 33	8 28 58	19 42	29 30	7 37	17 48	27 5	20 5	13 38	8 31	10 41
30	8 34 30	9 29 55	1♑54	1♒ 8	8 52	17 30	27 8	20 1	13 37	8 31	10 40
31	8 38 26	10♒30 52	14♑21	2♒46	10♒ 8	17♋13	27♎10	19♋56	13♊36	8♎30	10♌38

THE SUN ENTERS THE SIGN OF AQUARIUS ON JAN 20 AT 15:45.

DAY	TIME	☉	☽	☿	♀	♂	♃	♄	♅	♆	♇
	h m s	° ' "	° '	° '	° '	° '	° '	° '	° '	° '	° '
F 1	8 42 23	11♒31 47	27♑ 5	4♒25	11♒23	16♋56	27♎12	19♋52	13♊35	8♎29	10♌37
E 2	8 46 19	12 32 42	10♒ 8	6 4	12 39	16R41	27 14	19R48	13R34	8R28	10R36
B 3	8 50 16	13 33 35	23 29	7 45	13 54	16 25	27 15	19 43	13 33	8 28	10 34
R 4	8 54 13	14 34 27	7♓ 5	9 26	15 9	16 11	27 17	19 39	13 32	8 27	10 33
U 5	8 58 9	15 35 18	20 54	11 8	16 24	15 57	27 18	19 35	13 31	8 26	10 31
A 6	9 2 6	16 36 8	4♈53	12 50	17 40	15 44	27 19	19 31	13 30	8 25	10 30
R 7	9 6 2	17 36 56	18 57	14 33	18 55	15 32	27 20	19 27	13 29	8 24	10 29
Y 8	9 9 59	18 37 42	3♉ 4	16 18	20 10	15 21	27 21	19 23	13 29	8 23	10 27
9	9 13 55	19 38 27	17 12	18 2	21 26	15 11	27 21	19 19	13 28	8 23	10 26
10	9 17 52	20 39 11	1♊19	19 48	22 41	15 1	27 22	19 15	13 27	8 22	10 24
11	9 21 48	21 39 53	15 24	21 35	23 56	14 52	27R22	19 11	13 27	8 21	10 23
12	9 25 45	22 40 33	29 26	23 22	25 11	14 44	27 22	19 7	13 26	8 20	10 22
13	9 29 42	23 41 12	13♋23	25 10	26 26	14 37	27 22	19 4	13 26	8 18	10 20
14	9 33 38	24 41 49	27 13	26 59	27 42	14 30	27 21	19 0	13 26	8 17	10 19
15	9 37 35	25 42 24	10♌55	28 48	28 57	14 24	27 21	18 57	13 25	8 16	10 18
16	9 41 31	26 42 58	24 25	0♓38	0♓12	14 20	27 20	18 53	13 25	8 15	10 16
17	9 45 28	27 43 30	7♍40	2 29	1 27	14 15	27 19	18 50	13 25	8 14	10 15
18	9 49 24	28 44 1	20 39	4 20	2 42	14 12	27 18	18 47	13 25	8 13	10 14
19	9 53 21	29 44 30	3♎21	6 12	3 57	14 10	27 16	18 44	13 25	8 12	10 12
20	9 57 17	0♓44 58	15 46	8 3	5 12	14 8	27 15	18 41	13D25	8 10	10 11
21	10 1 14	1 45 25	27 57	9 56	6 27	14D 7	27 13	18 38	13 25	8 9	10 10
22	10 5 11	2 45 50	9♏56	11 48	7 43	14 6	27 11	18 35	13 25	8 8	10 8
23	10 9 7	3 46 13	21 47	13 39	8 58	14 7	27 9	18 32	13 25	8 7	10 7
24	10 13 4	4 46 36	3♐36	15 31	10 13	14 8	27 7	18 29	13 25	8 5	10 6
25	10 17 0	5 46 57	15 28	17 22	11 28	14 10	27 4	18 27	13 25	8 4	10 5
26	10 20 57	6 47 17	27 27	19 11	12 43	14 13	27 2	18 24	13 25	8 3	10 3
27	10 24 53	7 47 35	9♑41	20 59	13 58	14 16	26 59	18 22	13 26	8 1	10 2
28	10 28 50	8♓47 52	22♑13	22♓46	15♓13	14♋20	26♎56	18♋20	13♊26	8♎ 0	10♌ 1

THE SUN ENTERS THE SIGN OF PISCES ON FEB 19 AT 06:09.

DAY	TIME	☉	☽	☿	♀	♂	♃	♄	♅	♆	♇
	h m s	° ' "	° '	° '	° '	° '	° '	° '	° '	° '	° '
M 1	10 32 46	9♓48 7	5♒ 6	24♓30	16♓28	14♋25	26♎53	18♋18	13♊27	7♎59	10♌ 0
A 2	10 36 43	10 48 20	18 23	26 11	17 42	14 30	26R49	18R16	13 27	7R57	9R59
R 3	10 40 40	11 48 32	2♓ 4	27 50	18 57	14 36	26 46	18 14	13 28	7 56	9 57
C 4	10 44 36	12 48 42	16 5	29 24	20 12	14 43	26 42	18 12	13 28	7 54	9 56
H 5	10 48 33	13 48 50	0♈22	0♈54	21 27	14 50	26 38	18 10	13 29	7 53	9 55
6	10 52 29	14 48 56	14 49	2 19	22 42	14 58	26 34	18 8	13 29	7 51	9 54
7	10 56 26	15 49 0	29 19	3 39	23 57	15 7	26 30	18 7	13 30	7 50	9 53
8	11 0 22	16 49 3	13♉46	4 52	25 12	15 16	26 26	18 5	13 31	7 48	9 52
9	11 4 19	17 49 3	28 6	5 59	26 27	15 25	26 21	18 4	13 32	7 47	9 51
10	11 8 15	18 49 0	12♊16	6 59	27 41	15 36	26 16	18 3	13 33	7 45	9 50
11	11 12 12	19 48 56	26 15	7 51	28 56	15 47	26 12	18 2	13 34	7 44	9 49
12	11 16 9	20 48 50	10♋ 3	8 36	0♈11	15 58	26 7	18 1	13 35	7 42	9 48
13	11 20 5	21 48 41	23 41	9 12	1 25	16 10	26 1	18 0	13 36	7 41	9 47
14	11 24 2	22 48 30	7♌ 8	9 40	2 40	16 23	25 56	17 59	13 37	7 39	9 46
15	11 27 58	23 48 16	20 24	10 0	3 55	16 36	25 51	17 59	13 38	7 37	9 45
16	11 31 55	24 48 1	3♍30	10R11	5 9	16 49	25 45	17 58	13 39	7 36	9 44
17	11 35 51	25 47 43	16 25	10 13	6 24	17 3	25 39	17 58	13 41	7 34	9 43
18	11 39 48	26 47 24	29 7	10 7	7 39	17 18	25 33	17 57	13 42	7 33	9 42
19	11 43 44	27 47 2	11♎37	9 54	8 53	17 33	25 28	17 57	13 43	7 31	9 41
20	11 47 41	28 46 39	23 54	9 32	10 8	17 48	25 21	17D57	13 45	7 29	9 40
21	11 51 37	29 46 13	5♏59	9 4	11 22	18 4	25 15	17 57	13 46	7 28	9 40
22	11 55 34	0♈45 46	17 55	8 29	12 37	18 20	25 9	17 57	13 48	7 26	9 39
23	11 59 31	1 45 17	29 45	7 49	13 51	18 37	25 2	17 57	13 49	7 25	9 38
24	12 3 27	2 44 46	11♐33	7 4	15 6	18 54	24 56	17 58	13 51	7 23	9 37
25	12 7 24	3 44 14	23 23	6 16	16 20	19 12	24 49	17 58	13 52	7 21	9 36
26	12 11 20	4 43 39	5♑22	5 26	17 34	19 30	24 42	17 59	13 54	7 20	9 36
27	12 15 17	5 43 3	17 34	4 34	18 49	19 48	24 36	17 59	13 56	7 18	9 35
28	12 19 13	6 42 26	0♒ 5	3 42	20 3	20 7	24 29	18 0	13 58	7 16	9 34
29	12 23 10	7 41 46	12 59	2 50	21 17	20 26	24 22	18 1	13 59	7 15	9 34
30	12 27 6	8 41 4	26 20	2 1	22 32	20 45	24 14	18 2	14 1	7 13	9 33
31	12 31 3	9♈40 21	10♓ 9	1♈14	23♈46	21♋ 5	24♎ 7	18♋ 3	14♊ 3	7♎11	9♌33

THE SUN ENTERS THE SIGN OF ARIES ON MAR 21 AT 05:33.

♈ ARIES	♉ TAURUS	♊ GEMINI	♋ CANCER	♌ LEO	♍ VIRGO	♎ LIBRA

SIDEREAL · SUN · MOON · MERCURY · VENUS · MARS · JUPITER · SATURN · URANUS · NEPTUNE · PLUTO

DAY	TIME	☉	☽	☿	♀	♂	♃	♄	♅	♆	♇
	h m s	° ' "	° '	° '	° '	° '	° '	° '	° '	° '	° '
A 1	12 35 0	10♈39 36	24♓24	0♈30	25♈ 0	21♋25	24♎ 0	18♋ 4	14♊ 5	7♎10	9♌32
P 2	12 38 56	11 38 49	8♈59	29♓51	26 14	21 46	23R53	18 6	14 7	7R 8	9R31
R 3	12 42 53	12 37 59	23 49	29 16	27 29	22 7	23 45	18 7	14 9	7 6	9 31
I 4	12 46 49	13 37 8	8♉44	28 46	28 43	22 28	23 38	18 9	14 11	7 5	9 30
L 5	12 50 46	14 36 15	23 36	28 21	29 57	22 50	23 30	18 10	14 13	7 3	9 30
6	12 54 42	15 35 19	8♊17	28 2	1♉11	23 12	23 23	18 12	14 16	7 1	9 29
7	12 58 39	16 34 21	22 42	27 48	2 25	23 34	23 15	18 14	14 18	7 0	9 29
8	13 2 35	17 33 21	6♋49	27 40	3 39	23 56	23 8	18 16	14 20	6 58	9 29
9	13 6 32	18 32 18	20 37	27D37	4 53	24 19	23 0	18 18	14 22	6 57	9 28
10	13 10 29	19 31 13	4♌ 7	27 40	6 7	24 42	22 52	18 20	14 25	6 55	9 28
11	13 14 25	20 30 6	17 21	27 47	7 21	25 5	22 45	18 23	14 27	6 53	9 28
12	13 18 22	21 28 57	0♍21	28 0	8 35	25 29	22 37	18 25	14 29	6 52	9 27
13	13 22 18	22 27 45	13 8	28 18	9 49	25 53	22 29	18 28	14 32	6 50	9 27
14	13 26 15	23 26 31	25 44	28 40	11 3	26 17	22 22	18 30	14 34	6 49	9 27
15	13 30 11	24 25 15	8♎ 8	29 7	12 16	26 41	22 14	18 33	14 37	6 47	9 27
16	13 34 8	25 23 57	20 23	29 38	13 30	27 6	22 6	18 36	14 40	6 45	9 27
17	13 38 4	26 22 37	2♏29	0♈14	14 44	27 31	21 59	18 39	14 42	6 44	9 26
18	13 42 1	27 21 15	14 27	0 53	15 58	27 56	21 51	18 42	14 45	6 42	9 26
19	13 45 58	28 19 51	26 18	1 36	17 11	28 21	21 43	18 45	14 47	6 41	9 26
20	13 49 54	29 18 25	8♐ 6	2 23	18 25	28 47	21 36	18 48	14 50	6 39	9 26
21	13 53 51	0♉16 58	19 54	3 13	19 39	29 13	21 28	18 51	14 53	6 38	9 26
22	13 57 47	1 15 29	1♑45	4 6	20 52	29 39	21 21	18 55	14 56	6 36	9D26
23	14 1 44	2 13 58	13 43	5 2	22 6	0♌ 5	21 13	18 58	14 58	6 35	9 26
24	14 5 40	3 12 26	25 54	6 2	23 19	0 31	21 6	19 2	15 1	6 34	9 26
25	14 9 37	4 10 52	8♒23	7 4	24 33	0 58	20 58	19 5	15 4	6 32	9 26
26	14 13 33	5 9 17	21 14	8 9	25 46	1 25	20 51	19 9	15 7	6 31	9 26
27	14 17 30	6 7 39	4♓32	9 16	27 0	1 52	20 44	19 13	15 10	6 29	9 26
28	14 21 27	7 6 1	18 18	10 26	28 13	2 19	20 37	19 17	15 13	6 28	9 26
29	14 25 23	8 4 20	2♈33	11 39	29 26	2 47	20 30	19 21	15 16	6 27	9 27
30	14 29 20	9♉ 2 38	17♈13	12♈54	0♊40	3♌14	20♎23	19♋25	15♊19	6♎25	9♌27

THE SUN ENTERS THE SIGN OF TAURUS ON APR 20 AT 17:03.

DAY	TIME	☉	☽	☿	♀	♂	♃	♄	♅	♆	♇
	h m s	° ' "	° '	° '	° '	° '	° '	° '	° '	° '	° '
M 1	14 33 16	10♉ 0 55	2♉11	14♈11	1♊53	3♌42	20♎16	19♋29	15♊22	6♎24	9♌27
A 2	14 37 13	10 59 10	17 20	15 30	3 6	4 10	20R 9	19 33	15 25	6R23	9 27
Y 3	14 41 9	11 57 23	2♊29	16 52	4 20	4 38	20 2	19 38	15 28	6 21	9 28
4	14 45 6	12 55 34	17 29	18 16	5 33	5 7	19 56	19 42	15 31	6 20	9 28
5	14 49 2	13 53 44	2♋12	19 41	6 46	5 35	19 49	19 47	15 34	6 19	9 28
6	14 52 59	14 51 51	16 34	21 9	7 59	6 4	19 43	19 51	15 37	6 18	9 29
7	14 56 56	15 49 57	0♌32	22 39	9 12	6 33	19 36	19 56	15 40	6 16	9 29
8	15 0 52	16 48 0	14 6	24 12	10 25	7 2	19 30	20 1	15 44	6 15	9 29
9	15 4 49	17 46 2	27 19	25 46	11 38	7 31	19 24	20 6	15 47	6 14	9 30
10	15 8 45	18 44 1	10♍12	27 22	12 51	8 0	19 18	20 11	15 50	6 13	9 30
11	15 12 42	19 41 59	22 48	29 0	14 4	8 30	19 12	20 16	15 53	6 12	9 31
12	15 16 38	20 39 55	5♎11	0♉40	15 17	8 59	19 7	20 21	15 57	6 11	9 31
13	15 20 35	21 37 49	17 23	2 22	16 30	9 29	19 1	20 26	16 0	6 10	9 32
14	15 24 31	22 35 42	29 26	4 6	17 43	9 59	18 56	20 31	16 3	6 9	9 32
15	15 28 28	23 33 33	11♏22	5 52	18 56	10 29	18 50	20 37	16 7	6 8	9 33
16	15 32 24	24 31 22	23 13	7 41	20 8	10 59	18 45	20 42	16 10	6 7	9 34
17	15 36 21	25 29 10	5♐ 2	9 31	21 21	11 29	18 40	20 47	16 13	6 6	9 34
18	15 40 18	26 26 57	16 50	11 23	22 34	12 0	18 35	20 53	16 17	6 5	9 35
19	15 44 14	27 24 42	28 40	13 17	23 46	12 30	18 31	20 59	16 20	6 4	9 36
20	15 48 11	28 22 26	10♑34	15 13	24 59	13 1	18 26	21 4	16 23	6 3	9 36
21	15 52 7	29 20 9	22 37	17 11	26 12	13 32	18 22	21 10	16 27	6 2	9 37
22	15 56 4	0♊17 51	4♒51	19 11	27 24	14 3	18 17	21 16	16 30	6 1	9 38
23	16 0 0	1 15 32	17 22	21 13	28 37	14 34	18 13	21 22	16 34	6 0	9 39
24	16 3 57	2 13 12	0♓11	23 17	29 49	15 5	18 9	21 28	16 37	6 0	9 39
25	16 7 54	3 10 50	13 24	25 22	1♋ 1	15 37	18 6	21 34	16 41	5 59	9 40
26	16 11 50	4 8 28	27 3	27 29	2 14	16 8	18 2	21 40	16 44	5 58	9 41
27	16 15 47	5 6 5	11♈ 9	29 37	3 26	16 39	17 59	21 46	16 48	5 58	9 42
28	16 19 43	6 3 41	25 39	1♊47	4 38	17 11	17 55	21 52	16 51	5 57	9 43
29	16 23 40	7 1 16	10♉31	3 57	5 51	17 43	17 52	21 58	16 55	5 56	9 44
30	16 27 36	7 58 50	25 37	6 8	7 3	18 15	17 49	22 4	16 58	5 56	9 45
31	16 31 33	8♊56 23	10♊49	8♊20	8♋15	18♌47	17♎47	22♋11	17♊ 2	5♎55	9♌46

THE SUN ENTERS THE SIGN OF GEMINI ON MAY 21 AT 16:34.

DAY	TIME	☉	☽	☿	♀	♂	♃	♄	♅	♆	♇
	h m s	° ' "	° '	° '	° '	° '	° '	° '	° '	° '	° '
J 1	16 35 29	9♊53 55	25♊57	10♊32	9♋27	19♌19	17♎44	22♋17	17♊ 5	5♎55	9♌47
U 2	16 39 26	10 51 26	10♋51	12 44	10 39	19 51	17R42	22 24	17 9	5R54	9 48
N 3	16 43 23	11 48 56	25 26	14 56	11 51	20 24	17 40	22 30	17 12	5 54	9 49
E 4	16 47 19	12 46 24	9♌36	17 7	13 3	20 56	17 38	22 37	17 16	5 53	9 50
5	16 51 16	13 43 51	23 20	19 18	14 15	21 29	17 36	22 43	17 19	5 53	9 51
6	16 55 12	14 41 17	6♍37	21 27	15 27	22 1	17 34	22 50	17 23	5 52	9 52
7	16 59 9	15 38 42	19 32	23 35	16 39	22 34	17 33	22 56	17 27	5 52	9 53
8	17 3 5	16 36 6	2♎ 6	25 42	17 50	23 7	17 31	23 3	17 30	5 52	9 54
9	17 7 2	17 33 28	14 23	27 47	19 2	23 40	17 30	23 10	17 34	5 52	9 56
10	17 10 58	18 30 50	26 28	29 50	20 14	24 13	17 29	23 17	17 37	5 51	9 57
11	17 14 55	19 28 10	8♏24	1♋51	21 25	24 46	17 28	23 24	17 41	5 51	9 58
12	17 18 52	20 25 30	20 14	3 50	22 37	25 19	17 28	23 31	17 44	5 51	9 59
13	17 22 48	21 22 49	2♐ 2	5 47	23 48	25 52	17 27	23 38	17 48	5 51	10 0
14	17 26 45	22 20 7	13 51	7 41	25 0	26 26	17D27	23 45	17 51	5 51	10 2
15	17 30 41	23 17 24	25 42	9 34	26 11	26 59	17 27	23 52	17 55	5 50	10 3
16	17 34 38	24 14 41	7♑38	11 24	27 23	27 33	17 27	23 59	17 58	5 50	10 4
17	17 38 34	25 11 57	19 42	13 12	28 34	28 6	17 28	24 6	18 2	5D50	10 6
18	17 42 31	26 9 13	1♒55	14 57	29 45	28 40	17 28	24 13	18 6	5 50	10 7
19	17 46 27	27 6 29	14 19	16 40	0♌56	29 14	17 29	24 20	18 9	5 50	10 8
20	17 50 24	28 3 44	26 57	18 20	2 7	29 48	17 30	24 27	18 13	5 51	10 10
21	17 54 21	29 0 59	9♓51	19 58	3 18	0♍22	17 31	24 35	18 16	5 51	10 11
22	17 58 17	29 58 13	23 5	21 34	4 29	0 56	17 32	24 42	18 20	5 51	10 13
23	18 2 14	0♋55 28	6♈38	23 7	5 40	1 30	17 33	24 49	18 23	5 51	10 14
24	18 6 10	1 52 42	20 34	24 38	6 51	2 4	17 35	24 57	18 27	5 51	10 15
25	18 10 7	2 49 56	4♉50	26 6	8 2	2 39	17 36	25 4	18 30	5 51	10 17
26	18 14 3	3 47 11	19 26	27 32	9 13	3 13	17 38	25 11	18 33	5 52	10 18
27	18 18 0	4 44 25	4♊16	28 55	10 23	3 48	17 40	25 19	18 37	5 52	10 20
28	18 21 56	5 41 40	19 15	0♌16	11 34	4 22	17 43	25 26	18 40	5 52	10 21
29	18 25 53	6 38 54	4♋15	1 34	12 45	4 57	17 45	25 34	18 44	5 53	10 23
30	18 29 50	7♋36 8	19♋ 8	2♌50	13♌55	5♍32	17♎48	25♋41	18♊47	5♎53	10♌24

THE SUN ENTERS THE SIGN OF CANCER ON JUN 22 AT 00:45.

♏ SCORPIO ♐ SAGITTARIUS ♑ CAPRICORN ♒ AQUARIUS ♓ PISCES

1946

SIDEREAL SUN MOON MERCURY VENUS MARS JUPITER SATURN URANUS NEPTUNE PLUTO

DAY	TIME	☉	☽	☿	♀	♂	♃	♄	♅	♆	♇
	h m s	° ′ ″	° ′	° ′	° ′	° ′	° ′	° ′	° ′	° ′	° ′
J 1	18 33 46	8♋33 22	3♌45	4♌ 2	15♌ 5	6♍ 6	17♎50	25♋49	18♊51	5♎53	10♌26
U 2	18 37 43	9 30 36	18 0	5 12	16 16	6 41	17 53	25 56	18 54	5 54	10 27
L 3	18 41 39	10 27 49	1♍51	6 20	17 26	7 16	17 57	26 4	18 57	5 54	10 29
Y 4	18 45 36	11 25 2	15 15	7 24	18 36	7 51	18 0	26 11	19 1	5 55	10 31
5	18 49 32	12 22 15	28 13	8 25	19 46	8 26	18 3	26 19	19 4	5 55	10 32
6	18 53 29	13 19 27	10♎49	9 23	20 56	9 2	18 7	26 27	19 7	5 56	10 34
7	18 57 26	14 16 39	23 6	10 18	22 6	9 37	18 11	26 34	19 11	5 57	10 35
8	19 1 22	15 13 51	5♏ 9	11 9	23 16	10 12	18 15	26 42	19 14	5 57	10 37
9	19 5 19	16 11 3	17 2	11 58	24 26	10 48	18 19	26 50	19 17	5 58	10 39
10	19 9 15	17 8 15	28 51	12 42	25 36	11 23	18 23	26 57	19 21	5 59	10 40
11	19 13 12	18 5 27	10♐39	13 23	26 45	11 59	18 27	27 5	19 24	5 59	10 42
12	19 17 8	19 2 38	22 30	14 0	27 55	12 34	18 32	27 13	19 27	6 0	10 44
13	19 21 5	19 59 51	4♑27	14 33	29 4	13 10	18 37	27 20	19 30	6 1	10 45
14	19 25 1	20 57 3	16 33	15 2	0♍13	13 46	18 41	27 28	19 33	6 2	10 47
15	19 28 58	21 54 15	28 49	15 27	1 23	14 22	18 47	27 36	19 36	6 3	10 49
16	19 32 55	22 51 28	11♒17	15 47	2 32	14 57	18 52	27 44	19 40	6 4	10 50
17	19 36 51	23 48 41	23 58	16 3	3 41	15 33	18 57	27 51	19 43	6 4	10 52
18	19 40 48	24 45 55	6♓53	16 14	4 50	16 9	19 2	27 59	19 46	6 5	10 54
19	19 44 44	25 43 10	20 0	16R20	5 58	16 45	19 8	28 7	19 49	6 6	10 56
20	19 48 41	26 40 25	3♈22	16 21	7 7	17 22	19 14	28 15	19 52	6 7	10 57
21	19 52 37	27 37 40	16 58	16 18	8 16	17 58	19 20	28 22	19 55	6 8	10 59
22	19 56 34	28 34 57	0♉49	16 9	9 24	18 34	19 26	28 30	19 58	6 9	11 1
23	20 0 30	29 32 15	14 54	15 56	10 33	19 11	19 32	28 38	20 1	6 11	11 3
24	20 4 27	0♌29 33	29 13	15 38	11 41	19 47	19 38	28 46	20 4	6 12	11 4
25	20 8 24	1 26 53	13♊42	15 15	12 49	20 24	19 45	28 53	20 6	6 13	11 6
26	20 12 20	2 24 13	28 20	14 48	13 57	21 0	19 51	29 1	20 9	6 14	11 8
27	20 16 17	3 21 34	13♋ 0	14 17	15 5	21 37	19 58	29 9	20 12	6 15	11 10
28	20 20 13	4 18 56	27 36	13 41	16 13	22 13	20 5	29 17	20 15	6 16	11 11
29	20 24 10	5 16 19	12♌ 2	13 3	17 21	22 50	20 12	29 24	20 18	6 18	11 13
30	20 28 6	6 13 43	26 12	12 22	18 28	23 27	20 19	29 32	20 20	6 19	11 15
31	20 32 3	7♌11 7	10♍ 0	11♌39	19♍36	24♍ 4	20♎27	29♋40	20♊23	6♎20	11♌17

THE SUN ENTERS THE SIGN OF LEO ON JUL 23 AT 11:38.

DAY	TIME	☉	☽	☿	♀	♂	♃	♄	♅	♆	♇
	h m s	° ′ ″	° ′	° ′	° ′	° ′	° ′	° ′	° ′	° ′	° ′
A 1	20 35 59	8♌ 8 31	23♍24	10♌54	20♍43	24♍41	20♎34	29♋48	20♊26	6♎22	11♌18
U 2	20 39 56	9 5 57	6♎24	10R 9	21 50	25 18	20 41	29 55	20 28	6 23	11 20
G 3	20 43 53	10 3 23	19 2	9 23	22 57	25 55	20 49	0♌ 3	20 31	6 24	11 22
U 4	20 47 49	11 0 50	1♏20	8 39	24 4	26 32	20 57	0 11	20 34	6 26	11 24
S 5	20 51 46	11 58 17	13 23	7 57	25 11	27 10	21 5	0 18	20 36	6 27	11 26
T 6	20 55 42	12 55 45	25 16	7 17	26 18	27 47	21 13	0 26	20 39	6 29	11 27
7	20 59 39	13 53 14	7♐ 5	6 41	27 24	28 24	21 21	0 34	20 41	6 30	11 29
8	21 3 35	14 50 44	18 54	6 9	28 30	29 2	21 29	0 41	20 43	6 32	11 31
9	21 7 32	15 48 15	0♑48	5 42	29 36	29 39	21 38	0 49	20 46	6 33	11 33
10	21 11 28	16 45 46	12 52	5 20	0♎42	0♎17	21 46	0 56	20 48	6 35	11 34
11	21 15 25	17 43 19	25 8	5 5	1 48	0 54	21 55	1 4	20 50	6 36	11 36
12	21 19 22	18 40 52	7♒39	4D55	2 54	1 32	22 3	1 12	20 53	6 38	11 38
13	21 23 18	19 38 27	20 25	4 53	3 59	2 10	22 12	1 19	20 55	6 40	11 40
14	21 27 15	20 36 3	3♓27	4 57	5 4	2 48	22 21	1 27	20 57	6 41	11 42
15	21 31 11	21 33 40	16 44	5 9	6 9	3 25	22 30	1 34	20 59	6 43	11 43
16	21 35 8	22 31 18	0♈13	5 27	7 14	4 3	22 39	1 41	21 1	6 45	11 45
17	21 39 4	23 28 58	13 53	5 54	8 19	4 41	22 49	1 49	21 3	6 46	11 47
18	21 43 1	24 26 39	27 41	6 27	9 23	5 19	22 58	1 56	21 6	6 48	11 49
19	21 46 57	25 24 22	11♉37	7 8	10 27	5 58	23 7	2 4	21 7	6 50	11 50
20	21 50 54	26 22 7	25 40	7 55	11 31	6 36	23 17	2 11	21 9	6 52	11 52
21	21 54 51	27 19 53	9♊48	8 50	12 35	7 14	23 27	2 18	21 11	6 54	11 54
22	21 58 47	28 17 42	24 0	9 52	13 39	7 52	23 36	2 25	21 13	6 55	11 56
23	22 2 44	29 15 32	8♋15	10 59	14 42	8 31	23 46	2 33	21 15	6 57	11 57
24	22 6 40	0♍13 23	22 31	12 13	15 45	9 9	23 56	2 40	21 17	6 59	11 59
25	22 10 37	1 11 17	6♌43	13 33	16 48	9 48	24 6	2 47	21 18	7 1	12 1
26	22 14 33	2 9 12	20 47	14 58	17 51	10 26	24 16	2 54	21 20	7 3	12 2
27	22 18 30	3 7 8	4♍39	16 29	18 53	11 5	24 26	3 1	21 22	7 5	12 4
28	22 22 26	4 5 6	18 14	18 4	19 55	11 44	24 37	3 8	21 23	7 7	12 6
29	22 26 23	5 3 5	1♎30	19 42	20 57	12 22	24 47	3 15	21 25	7 9	12 7
30	22 30 20	6 1 6	14 25	21 25	21 59	13 1	24 58	3 22	21 26	7 11	12 9
31	22 34 16	6♍59 8	27♎ 0	23♌11	23♎ 0	13♎40	25♎ 8	3♌29	21♊28	7♎13	12♌11

THE SUN ENTERS THE SIGN OF VIRGO ON AUG 23 AT 18:27.

DAY	TIME	☉	☽	☿	♀	♂	♃	♄	♅	♆	♇
	h m s	° ′ ″	° ′	° ′	° ′	° ′	° ′	° ′	° ′	° ′	° ′
S 1	22 38 13	7♍57 12	9♏16	24♌59	24♎ 1	14♎19	25♎19	3♌36	21♊29	7♎15	12♌12
E 2	22 42 9	8 55 17	21 19	26 50	25 1	14 58	25 29	3 43	21 31	7 17	12 14
P 3	22 46 6	9 53 23	3♐12	28 42	26 2	15 37	25 40	3 50	21 32	7 19	12 16
T 4	22 50 2	10 51 32	15 0	0♍36	27 2	16 16	25 51	3 57	21 33	7 21	12 17
E 5	22 53 59	11 49 41	26 50	2 30	28 1	16 56	26 2	4 3	21 34	7 23	12 19
M 6	22 57 55	12 47 52	8♑46	4 26	29 0	17 35	26 13	4 10	21 35	7 25	12 20
B 7	23 1 52	13 46 4	20 54	6 22	29 59	18 14	26 24	4 17	21 37	7 27	12 22
E 8	23 5 49	14 44 18	3♒17	8 17	0♏58	18 53	26 35	4 23	21 38	7 29	12 24
R 9	23 9 45	15 42 34	15 59	10 13	1 56	19 33	26 46	4 30	21 39	7 31	12 25
10	23 13 42	16 40 51	29 1	12 9	2 54	20 12	26 58	4 36	21 40	7 33	12 27
11	23 17 38	17 39 10	12♓24	14 4	3 51	20 52	27 9	4 43	21 40	7 35	12 28
12	23 21 35	18 37 31	26 4	15 58	4 48	21 32	27 21	4 49	21 41	7 37	12 30
13	23 25 31	19 35 53	9♈59	17 52	5 44	22 11	27 32	4 55	21 42	7 39	12 31
14	23 29 28	20 34 17	24 4	19 44	6 40	22 51	27 44	5 1	21 43	7 42	12 33
15	23 33 24	21 32 44	8♉14	21 36	7 35	23 31	27 55	5 8	21 44	7 44	12 34
16	23 37 21	22 31 13	22 27	23 27	8 30	24 11	28 7	5 14	21 44	7 46	12 35
17	23 41 17	23 29 44	6♊38	25 18	9 24	24 51	28 19	5 20	21 45	7 48	12 37
18	23 45 14	24 28 17	20 47	27 7	10 18	25 31	28 31	5 26	21 45	7 50	12 38
19	23 49 11	25 26 52	4♋51	28 55	11 11	26 11	28 42	5 32	21 46	7 52	12 40
20	23 53 7	26 25 30	18 51	0♎42	12 4	26 51	28 54	5 38	21 46	7 55	12 41
21	23 57 4	27 24 10	2♌46	2 28	12 56	27 31	29 6	5 43	21 47	7 57	12 42
22	0 1 0	28 22 52	16 33	4 13	13 47	28 11	29 18	5 49	21 47	7 59	12 44
23	0 4 57	29 21 36	0♍12	5 57	14 38	28 52	29 30	5 55	21 47	8 1	12 45
24	0 8 53	0♎20 22	13 40	7 40	15 28	29 32	29 43	6 0	21 48	8 3	12 46
25	0 12 50	1 19 10	26 54	9 23	16 18	0♏13	29 55	6 6	21 48	8 6	12 48
26	0 16 46	2 18 0	9♎53	11 4	17 6	0 53	0♏ 7	6 11	21 48	8 8	12 49
27	0 20 43	3 16 52	22 36	12 44	17 54	1 34	0 19	6 17	21R48	8 10	12 50
28	0 24 40	4 15 47	5♏ 3	14 24	18 41	2 14	0 32	6 22	21 48	8 12	12 51
29	0 28 36	5 14 43	17 14	16 2	19 28	2 55	0 44	6 27	21 48	8 15	12 53
30	0 32 33	6♎13 41	29♏14	17♎40	20♏13	3♏36	0♏56	6♌32	21♊48	8♎17	12♌54

THE SUN ENTERS THE SIGN OF LIBRA ON SEP 23 AT 15:41.

♈ ARIES ♉ TAURUS ♊ GEMINI ♋ CANCER ♌ LEO ♍ VIRGO ♎ LIBRA

SIDEREAL. SUN. MOON. MERCURY. VENUS. MARS. JUPITER. SATURN. URANUS. NEPTUNE. PLUTO.

DAY	TIME	☉	☽	☿	♀	♂	♃	♄	♅	♆	♇
	h m s	° ' "	° '	° '	° '	° '	° '	° '	° '	° '	° '
O 1	0 36 29	7♎12 40	11♐ 5	19♎16	20♏58	4♏17	1♏ 9	6♌38	21♊48	8♎19	12♌55
C 2	0 40 26	8 11 42	22 52	20 52	21 41	4 57	1 21	6 43	21R48	8 21	12 56
T 3	0 44 22	9 10 45	4♑41	22 27	22 24	5 38	1 34	6 47	21 47	8 24	12 57
O 4	0 48 19	10 9 50	16 37	24 1	23 6	6 19	1 46	6 52	21 47	8 26	12 58
B 5	0 52 15	11 8 57	28 45	25 35	23 46	7 0	1 59	6 57	21 47	8 28	12 59
E 6	0 56 12	12 8 6	11♒10	27 7	24 26	7 42	2 12	7 2	21 46	8 30	13 0
R 7	1 0 9	13 7 16	23 56	28 39	25 4	8 23	2 24	7 6	21 46	8 32	13 2
8	1 4 5	14 6 28	7♓ 6	0♏10	25 41	9 4	2 37	7 11	21 45	8 35	13 3
9	1 8 2	15 5 42	20 41	1 40	26 17	9 45	2 50	7 15	21 45	8 37	13 4
10	1 11 58	16 4 58	4♈39	3 10	26 52	10 27	3 3	7 20	21 44	8 39	13 4
11	1 15 55	17 4 16	18 55	4 38	27 25	11 8	3 15	7 24	21 44	8 41	13 5
12	1 19 51	18 3 36	3♉26	6 6	27 57	11 50	3 28	7 28	21 43	8 44	13 6
13	1 23 48	19 2 58	18 3	7 33	28 27	12 31	3 41	7 32	21 42	8 46	13 7
14	1 27 44	20 2 23	2♊40	8 59	28 56	13 13	3 54	7 36	21 41	8 48	13 8
15	1 31 41	21 1 49	17 11	10 25	29 23	13 54	4 7	7 40	21 40	8 50	13 9
16	1 35 38	22 1 18	1♋33	11 49	29 49	14 36	4 20	7 44	21 40	8 52	13 10
17	1 39 34	23 0 50	15 43	13 13	0♐13	15 18	4 33	7 48	21 39	8 55	13 11
18	1 43 31	24 0 24	29 40	14 35	0 35	16 0	4 46	7 51	21 38	8 57	13 11
19	1 47 27	25 0 0	13♌23	15 57	0 56	16 42	4 59	7 55	21 37	8 59	13 12
20	1 51 24	25 59 38	26 53	17 18	1 15	17 24	5 12	7 58	21 35	9 1	13 13
21	1 55 20	26 59 18	10♍10	18 38	1 31	18 6	5 25	8 2	21 34	9 3	13 14
22	1 59 17	27 59 1	23 15	19 56	1 46	18 48	5 38	8 5	21 33	9 5	13 14
23	2 3 13	28 58 46	6♎ 6	21 13	1 59	19 30	5 51	8 8	21 32	9 7	13 15
24	2 7 10	29 58 32	18 45	22 29	2 9	20 12	6 4	8 11	21 31	9 10	13 15
25	2 11 6	0♏58 21	1♏11	23 44	2 18	20 55	6 17	8 14	21 29	9 12	13 16
26	2 15 3	1 58 12	13 26	24 57	2 24	21 37	6 30	8 17	21 28	9 14	13 17
27	2 19 0	2 58 5	25 29	26 8	2 28	22 19	6 43	8 20	21 27	9 16	13 17
28	2 22 56	3 58 0	7♐24	27 18	2R30	23 2	6 57	8 22	21 25	9 18	13 18
29	2 26 53	4 57 56	19 13	28 25	2 29	23 45	7 10	8 25	21 24	9 20	13 18
30	2 30 49	5 57 54	0♑59	29 30	2 26	24 27	7 23	8 27	21 22	9 22	13 19
31	2 34 46	6♏57 54	12♑47	0♐33	2♐20	25♏10	7♏36	8♌30	21♊20	9♎24	13♌19

THE SUN ENTERS THE SIGN OF SCORPIO ON OCT 24 AT 00:36.

DAY	TIME	☉	☽	☿	♀	♂	♃	♄	♅	♆	♇
	h m s	° ' "	° '	° '	° '	° '	° '	° '	° '	° '	° '
N 1	2 38 42	7♏57 56	24♑41	1♐32	2♐12	25♏53	7♏49	8♌32	21♊19	9♎26	13♌19
O 2	2 42 39	8 57 59	6♒46	2 29	2R 2	26 35	8 2	8 34	21R17	9 28	13 20
V 3	2 46 36	9 58 4	19 8	3 22	1 49	27 18	8 15	8 36	21 15	9 30	13 20
E 4	2 50 32	10 58 10	1♓51	4 11	1 34	28 1	8 29	8 38	21 14	9 32	13 20
M 5	2 54 29	11 58 18	14 59	4 55	1 16	28 44	8 42	8 40	21 12	9 34	13 21
B 6	2 58 25	12 58 27	28 34	5 35	0 56	29 27	8 55	8 41	21 10	9 36	13 21
E 7	3 2 22	13 58 38	12♈37	6 10	0 34	0♐10	9 8	8 43	21 8	9 38	13 21
R 8	3 6 18	14 58 51	27 3	6 38	0 10	0 53	9 21	8 44	21 6	9 40	13 21
9	3 10 15	15 59 5	11♉49	6 59	29♏43	1 36	9 34	8 46	21 4	9 42	13 22
10	3 14 11	16 59 21	26 47	7 13	29 15	2 20	9 47	8 47	21 2	9 44	13 22
11	3 18 8	17 59 39	11♊49	7R19	28 45	3 3	10 0	8 48	21 0	9 46	13 22
12	3 22 4	18 59 58	26 45	7 17	28 13	3 46	10 13	8 49	20 58	9 47	13 22
13	3 26 1	20 0 20	11♋29	7 5	27 40	4 30	10 26	8 50	20 56	9 49	13 22
14	3 29 58	21 0 44	25 55	6 42	27 6	5 13	10 40	8 51	20 54	9 51	13 22
15	3 33 54	22 1 9	10♌ 1	6 10	26 31	5 57	10 53	8 52	20 52	9 53	13R22
16	3 37 51	23 1 36	23 46	5 28	25 55	6 40	11 6	8 52	20 50	9 55	13 22
17	3 41 47	24 2 5	7♍10	4 35	25 19	7 24	11 19	8 53	20 48	9 56	13 22
18	3 45 44	25 2 36	20 16	3 33	24 43	8 8	11 32	8 53	20 46	9 58	13 22
19	3 49 40	26 3 9	3♎ 4	2 24	24 6	8 52	11 45	8 53	20 43	10 0	13 22
20	3 53 37	27 3 43	15 37	1 8	23 30	9 35	11 57	8R53	20 41	10 1	13 22
21	3 57 34	28 4 20	27 58	29♏47	22 54	10 19	12 10	8 53	20 39	10 3	13 22
22	4 1 30	29 4 57	10♏ 9	28 26	22 20	11 3	12 23	8 53	20 37	10 5	13 21
23	4 5 27	0♐ 5 37	22 11	27 5	21 46	11 47	12 36	8 53	20 34	10 6	13 21
24	4 9 23	1 6 18	4♐ 6	25 49	21 13	12 31	12 49	8 53	20 32	10 8	13 21
25	4 13 20	2 7 0	15 55	24 38	20 42	13 15	13 2	8 52	20 29	10 9	13 21
26	4 17 16	3 7 43	27 43	23 36	20 13	14 0	13 15	8 52	20 27	10 11	13 20
27	4 21 13	4 8 28	9♑29	22 44	19 45	14 44	13 27	8 51	20 25	10 12	13 20
28	4 25 9	5 9 14	21 19	22 3	19 19	15 28	13 40	8 50	20 22	10 14	13 20
29	4 29 6	6 10 1	3♒14	21 34	18 55	16 12	13 53	8 49	20 20	10 15	13 19
30	4 33 3	7♐10 49	15♒20	21♏16	18♏34	16♐57	14♏ 5	8♌48	20♊17	10♎17	13♌19

THE SUN ENTERS THE SIGN OF SAGITTARIUS ON NOV 22 AT 21:47.

DAY	TIME	☉	☽	☿	♀	♂	♃	♄	♅	♆	♇
	h m s	° ' "	° '	° '	° '	° '	° '	° '	° '	° '	° '
D 1	4 36 59	8♐11 38	27♒39	21♏ 9	18♏15	17♐41	14♏18	8♌47	20♊15	10♎18	13♌19
E 2	4 40 56	9 12 28	10♓17	21D14	17R58	18 26	14 31	8R46	20R12	10 19	13R18
C 3	4 44 52	10 13 19	23 17	21 28	17 43	19 10	14 43	8 45	20 10	10 21	13 18
E 4	4 48 49	11 14 10	6♈43	21 51	17 31	19 55	14 56	8 43	20 7	10 22	13 17
M 5	4 52 45	12 15 2	20 36	22 22	17 21	20 40	15 8	8 42	20 5	10 23	13 17
B 6	4 56 42	13 15 55	4♉56	23 1	17 14	21 24	15 20	8 40	20 2	10 25	13 16
E 7	5 0 38	14 16 49	19 41	23 47	17 9	22 9	15 33	8 38	20 0	10 26	13 15
R 8	5 4 35	15 17 44	4♊44	24 38	17D 7	22 54	15 45	8 37	19 57	10 27	13 15
9	5 8 32	16 18 40	19 57	25 35	17 7	23 39	15 57	8 35	19 55	10 28	13 14
10	5 12 28	17 19 37	5♋10	26 36	17 10	24 24	16 9	8 33	19 52	10 29	13 14
11	5 16 25	18 20 35	20 15	27 40	17 15	25 9	16 22	8 30	19 50	10 30	13 13
12	5 20 21	19 21 34	5♌ 1	28 49	17 23	25 54	16 34	8 28	19 47	10 31	13 12
13	5 24 18	20 22 34	19 25	0♐ 0	17 32	26 39	16 46	8 26	19 44	10 32	13 11
14	5 28 14	21 23 34	3♍21	1 14	17 44	27 24	16 58	8 23	19 42	10 34	13 11
15	5 32 11	22 24 36	16 51	2 30	17 58	28 9	17 10	8 21	19 39	10 34	13 10
16	5 36 7	23 25 39	29 56	3 48	18 15	28 54	17 21	8 18	19 37	10 35	13 9
17	5 40 4	24 26 43	12♎38	5 7	18 33	29 39	17 33	8 15	19 34	10 36	13 8
18	5 44 1	25 27 48	25 3	6 28	18 53	0♑25	17 45	8 12	19 32	10 37	13 7
19	5 47 57	26 28 53	7♏13	7 51	19 16	1 10	17 57	8 9	19 29	10 38	13 7
20	5 51 54	27 30 0	19 12	9 14	19 40	1 55	18 8	8 6	19 27	10 39	13 6
21	5 55 50	28 31 7	1♐ 5	10 39	20 6	2 41	18 20	8 3	19 24	10 40	13 5
22	5 59 47	29 32 15	12 53	12 4	20 33	3 26	18 31	8 0	19 22	10 40	13 4
23	6 3 43	0♑33 23	24 40	13 30	21 2	4 12	18 43	7 57	19 19	10 41	13 3
24	6 7 40	1 34 32	6♑28	14 57	21 33	4 58	18 54	7 53	19 17	10 42	13 2
25	6 11 37	2 35 41	18 19	16 24	22 6	5 43	19 5	7 50	19 14	10 42	13 1
26	6 15 33	3 36 50	0♒15	17 53	22 39	6 29	19 16	7 46	19 12	10 43	13 0
27	6 19 30	4 38 0	12 18	19 21	23 15	7 15	19 27	7 43	19 9	10 44	12 59
28	6 23 26	5 39 10	24 29	20 50	23 51	8 0	19 38	7 39	19 7	10 44	12 58
29	6 27 23	6 40 19	6♓53	22 20	24 29	8 46	19 49	7 35	19 4	10 45	12 57
30	6 31 19	7 41 29	19 31	23 50	25 8	9 32	20 0	7 31	19 2	10 45	12 56
31	6 35 16	8♑42 38	2♈26	25♐20	25♏49	10♑18	20♏11	7♌27	19♊ 0	10♎46	12♌55

THE SUN ENTERS THE SIGN OF CAPRICORN ON DEC 22 AT 10:54.

♏ SCORPIO ♐ SAGITTARIUS ♑ CAPRICORN ♒ AQUARIUS ♓ PISCES

SIDEREAL SUN. MOON. MERCURY. VENUS. MARS. JUPITER. SATURN. URANUS. NEPTUNE. PLUTO.

DAY	TIME	☉	☽	☿	♀	♂	♃	♄	♅	♆	♇
	h m s	° ' "	° '	° '	° '	° '	° '	° '	° '	° '	° '
J 1	6 39 12	9♑43 48	15♈42	26♐51	26♏30	11♑ 4	20♏22	7♌23	18♊57	10♎46	12♌53
A 2	6 43 9	10 44 57	29 22	28 22	27 13	11 50	20 32	7R19	18R55	10 46	12R52
N 3	6 47 6	11 46 6	13♉26	29 53	27 57	12 36	20 43	7 15	18 53	10 47	12 51
U 4	6 51 2	12 47 14	27 54	1♑25	28 42	13 22	20 53	7 11	18 50	10 47	12 50
A 5	6 54 59	13 48 23	12♊43	2 57	29 27	14 8	21 3	7 6	18 48	10 47	12 49
R 6	6 58 55	14 49 31	27 48	4 30	0♐14	14 54	21 14	7 2	18 46	10 48	12 48
Y 7	7 2 52	15 50 39	13♋ 1	6 3	1 2	15 40	21 24	6 58	18 44	10 48	12 46
8	7 6 48	16 51 47	28 11	7 36	1 50	16 26	21 34	6 53	18 41	10 48	12 45
9	7 10 45	17 52 55	13♌ 9	9 10	2 40	17 13	21 44	6 49	18 39	10 48	12 44
10	7 14 41	18 54 3	27 45	10 44	3 30	17 59	21 53	6 44	18 37	10 48	12 43
11	7 18 38	19 55 10	11♍55	12 19	4 21	18 45	22 3	6 40	18 35	10 48	12 41
12	7 22 35	20 56 17	25 36	13 54	5 13	19 32	22 13	6 35	18 33	10R48	12 40
13	7 26 31	21 57 25	8♎48	15 30	6 5	20 18	22 22	6 31	18 31	10 48	12 39
14	7 30 28	22 58 32	21 34	17 6	6 59	21 4	22 32	6 26	18 29	10 48	12 38
15	7 34 24	23 59 39	3♏58	18 42	7 53	21 51	22 41	6 21	18 27	10 48	12 36
16	7 38 21	25 0 46	16 5	20 19	8 47	22 37	22 50	6 16	18 25	10 48	12 35
17	7 42 17	26 1 53	28 0	21 56	9 42	23 24	22 59	6 12	18 23	10 48	12 34
18	7 46 14	27 2 59	9♐48	23 35	10 38	24 10	23 8	6 7	18 21	10 48	12 32
19	7 50 10	28 4 6	21 34	25 13	11 34	24 57	23 17	6 2	18 20	10 48	12 31
20	7 54 7	29 5 11	3♑21	26 52	12 31	25 44	23 26	5 57	18 18	10 47	12 30
21	7 58 4	0♒ 6 17	15 13	28 32	13 29	26 30	23 34	5 52	18 16	10 47	12 28
22	8 2 0	1 7 21	27 11	0♒12	14 27	27 17	23 43	5 47	18 14	10 47	12 27
23	8 5 57	2 8 25	9♒17	1 53	15 25	28 4	23 51	5 42	18 13	10 47	12 25
24	8 9 53	3 9 28	21 32	3 34	16 24	28 50	23 59	5 37	18 11	10 46	12 24
25	8 13 50	4 10 31	3♓58	5 16	17 23	29 37	24 7	5 32	18 10	10 46	12 23
26	8 17 46	5 11 32	16 34	6 59	18 23	0♒24	24 15	5 28	18 8	10 45	12 21
27	8 21 43	6 12 32	29 22	8 42	19 23	1 11	24 23	5 23	18 6	10 45	12 20
28	8 25 39	7 13 31	12♈23	10 26	20 24	1 58	24 31	5 18	18 5	10 44	12 18
29	8 29 36	8 14 29	25 39	12 10	21 25	2 44	24 38	5 13	18 4	10 44	12 17
30	8 33 33	9 15 26	9♉11	13 55	22 26	3 31	24 46	5 8	18 2	10 43	12 16
31	8 37 29	10♒16 21	23♉ 2	15♒41	23♐28	4♒18	24♏53	5♌ 3	18♊ 1	10♎43	12♌14

THE SUN ENTERS THE SIGN OF AQUARIUS ON JAN 20 AT 21:32.

DAY	TIME	☉	☽	☿	♀	♂	♃	♄	♅	♆	♇
	h m s	° ' "	° '	° '	° '	° '	° '	° '	° '	° '	° '
F 1	8 41 26	11♒17 15	7♊12	17♒27	24♐30	5♒ 5	25♏ 0	4♌58	18♊ 0	10♎42	12♌13
E 2	8 45 22	12 18 8	21 39	19 13	25 32	5 52	25 7	4R53	17R59	10R41	12R11
B 3	8 49 19	13 19 0	6♋23	20 59	26 35	6 39	25 14	4 48	17 57	10 41	12 10
R 4	8 53 15	14 19 50	21 16	22 46	27 38	7 26	25 21	4 44	17 56	10 40	12 9
U 5	8 57 12	15 20 39	6♌12	24 33	28 41	8 13	25 27	4 39	17 55	10 39	12 7
A 6	9 1 9	16 21 27	21 2	26 20	29 45	9 0	25 34	4 34	17 54	10 38	12 6
R 7	9 5 5	17 22 13	5♍37	28 7	0♑49	9 47	25 40	4 29	17 53	10 38	12 4
Y 8	9 9 2	18 22 59	19 49	29 53	1 53	10 34	25 46	4 24	17 52	10 37	12 3
9	9 12 58	19 23 43	3♎35	1♓39	2 57	11 21	25 52	4 20	17 51	10 36	12 2
10	9 16 55	20 24 26	16 54	3 24	4 2	12 8	25 58	4 15	17 51	10 35	12 0
11	9 20 51	21 25 8	29 45	5 8	5 7	12 55	26 4	4 11	17 50	10 34	11 59
12	9 24 48	22 25 49	12♏13	6 50	6 12	13 42	26 9	4 6	17 49	10 33	11 57
13	9 28 44	23 26 29	24 22	8 30	7 18	14 30	26 14	4 1	17 49	10 32	11 56
14	9 32 41	24 27 8	6♐19	10 8	8 24	15 17	26 20	3 57	17 48	10 31	11 55
15	9 36 37	25 27 45	18 7	11 43	9 29	16 4	26 25	3 53	17 47	10 30	11 53
16	9 40 34	26 28 22	29 54	13 14	10 36	16 51	26 29	3 48	17 47	10 29	11 52
17	9 44 31	27 28 57	11♑43	14 41	11 42	17 38	26 34	3 44	17 46	10 28	11 51
18	9 48 27	28 29 31	23 39	16 4	12 48	18 25	26 39	3 40	17 46	10 27	11 49
19	9 52 24	29 30 3	5♒45	17 21	13 55	19 13	26 43	3 36	17 46	10 26	11 48
20	9 56 20	0♓30 34	18 2	18 32	15 2	20 0	26 47	3 31	17 45	10 25	11 46
21	10 0 17	1 31 4	0♓33	19 36	16 9	20 47	26 51	3 27	17 45	10 23	11 45
22	10 4 13	2 31 32	13 16	20 33	17 16	21 34	26 55	3 23	17 45	10 22	11 44
23	10 8 10	3 31 58	26 13	21 21	18 24	22 22	26 59	3 19	17 45	10 21	11 43
24	10 12 6	4 32 22	9♈20	22 2	19 31	23 9	27 2	3 16	17 45	10 20	11 41
25	10 16 3	5 32 45	22 39	22 33	20 39	23 56	27 5	3 12	17D45	10 18	11 40
26	10 20 0	6 33 5	6♉ 7	22 54	21 47	24 43	27 9	3 8	17 45	10 17	11 39
27	10 23 56	7 33 24	19 46	23R 6	22 55	25 31	27 11	3 4	17 45	10 16	11 37
28	10 27 53	8♓33 41	3♊36	23♓ 9	24♑ 3	26♒18	27♏14	3♌ 1	17♊45	10♎15	11♌36

THE SUN ENTERS THE SIGN OF PISCES ON FEB 19 AT 11:52.

DAY	TIME	☉	☽	☿	♀	♂	♃	♄	♅	♆	♇
	h m s	° ' "	° '	° '	° '	° '	° '	° '	° '	° '	° '
M 1	10 31 49	9♓33 55	17♊36	23♓ 1	25♑11	27♒ 5	27♏17	2♌57	17♊45	10♎13	11♌35
A 2	10 35 46	10 34 8	1♋47	22R44	26 19	27 52	27 19	2R54	17 45	10R12	11R34
R 3	10 39 42	11 34 19	16 8	22 19	27 28	28 40	27 21	2 51	17 46	10 10	11 33
C 4	10 43 39	12 34 27	0♌36	21 45	28 36	29 27	27 24	2 48	17 46	10 9	11 31
H 5	10 47 35	13 34 33	15 6	21 3	29 45	0♓14	27 25	2 44	17 46	10 8	11 30
6	10 51 32	14 34 38	29 32	20 16	0♒54	1 1	27 27	2 41	17 47	10 6	11 29
7	10 55 29	15 34 40	13♍48	19 23	2 3	1 49	27 29	2 38	17 47	10 5	11 28
8	10 59 25	16 34 40	27 47	18 26	3 12	2 36	27 30	2 36	17 48	10 3	11 27
9	11 3 22	17 34 39	11♎26	17 28	4 21	3 23	27 31	2 33	17 49	10 2	11 26
10	11 7 18	18 34 36	24 40	16 28	5 31	4 10	27 32	2 30	17 49	10 0	11 25
11	11 11 15	19 34 31	7♏32	15 28	6 40	4 58	27 33	2 28	17 50	9 59	11 24
12	11 15 11	20 34 24	20 2	14 30	7 50	5 45	27 33	2 25	17 51	9 57	11 23
13	11 19 8	21 34 16	2♐14	13 35	8 59	6 32	27 34	2 23	17 52	9 56	11 22
14	11 23 4	22 34 6	14 13	12 43	10 9	7 19	27R34	2 20	17 52	9 54	11 20
15	11 27 1	23 33 54	26 4	11 57	11 19	8 7	27 34	2 18	17 53	9 53	11 20
16	11 30 58	24 33 41	7♑52	11 15	12 28	8 54	27 34	2 16	17 54	9 51	11 19
17	11 34 54	25 33 26	19 43	10 39	13 38	9 41	27 33	2 14	17 55	9 49	11 18
18	11 38 51	26 33 9	1♒43	10 9	14 48	10 28	27 33	2 12	17 56	9 48	11 17
19	11 42 47	27 32 51	13 54	9 46	15 59	11 15	27 32	2 11	17 58	9 46	11 16
20	11 46 44	28 32 31	26 20	9 28	17 9	12 2	27 31	2 9	17 59	9 45	11 15
21	11 50 40	29 32 8	9♓ 4	9 17	18 19	12 50	27 30	2 7	18 0	9 43	11 14
22	11 54 37	0♈31 44	22 4	9D12	19 29	13 37	27 28	2 6	18 1	9 41	11 13
23	11 58 33	1 31 18	5♈21	9 13	20 40	14 24	27 27	2 5	18 3	9 40	11 12
24	12 2 30	2 30 49	18 52	9 20	21 50	15 11	27 25	2 3	18 4	9 38	11 11
25	12 6 26	3 30 19	2♉35	9 32	23 1	15 58	27 23	2 2	18 5	9 36	11 11
26	12 10 23	4 29 46	16 27	9 50	24 11	16 45	27 21	2 1	18 7	9 35	11 10
27	12 14 20	5 29 12	0♊26	10 12	25 22	17 32	27 19	2 0	18 8	9 33	11 9
28	12 18 16	6 28 35	14 28	10 39	26 33	18 19	27 17	1 59	18 10	9 32	11 9
29	12 22 13	7 27 56	28 34	11 11	27 44	19 6	27 14	1 59	18 12	9 30	11 8
30	12 26 9	8 27 14	12♋42	11 46	28 54	19 53	27 11	1 58	18 13	9 28	11 7
31	12 30 6	9♈26 30	26♋50	12♓26	0♓ 5	20♓40	27♏ 8	1♌58	18♊15	9♎27	11♌ 7

THE SUN ENTERS THE SIGN OF ARIES ON MAR 21 AT 11:13.

♈ ARIES ♉ TAURUS ♊ GEMINI ♋ CANCER ♌ LEO ♍ VIRGO ♎ LIBRA

SIDEREAL SUN. MOON. MERCURY. VENUS. MARS. JUPITER. SATURN. URANUS. NEPTUNE. PLUTO.

DAY	TIME	☉	☽	☿	♀	♂	♃	♄	♅	♆	♇
	h m s	° ' "	° '	° '	° '	° '	° '	° '	° '	° '	° '
A 1	12 34 2	10♈25 44	10♌58	13♓10	1♓16	21♓27	27♏ 5	1♌57	18♊17	9♎25	11♌ 6
P 2	12 37 59	11 24 55	25 2	13 57	2 27	22 14	27R 2	1R57	18 19	9R23	11R 5
R 3	12 41 56	12 24 4	9♍ 0	14 47	3 38	23 1	26 58	1D57	18 20	9 22	11 5
I 4	12 45 52	13 23 10	22 48	15 41	4 49	23 48	26 55	1 57	18 22	9 20	11 4
L 5	12 49 49	14 22 15	6♎23	16 37	6 0	24 35	26 51	1 57	18 24	9 18	11 4
6	12 53 45	15 21 17	19 42	17 37	7 11	25 21	26 47	1 57	18 26	9 17	11 3
7	12 57 42	16 20 18	2♏43	18 39	8 23	26 8	26 43	1 58	18 28	9 15	11 3
8	13 1 38	17 19 16	15 25	19 44	9 34	26 55	26 38	1 58	18 30	9 13	11 2
9	13 5 35	18 18 13	27 51	20 51	10 45	27 42	26 34	1 58	18 32	9 12	11 2
10	13 9 31	19 17 8	10♐ 1	22 1	11 56	28 28	26 29	1 59	18 35	9 10	11 2
11	13 13 28	20 16 1	22 0	23 13	13 8	29 15	26 24	2 0	18 37	9 9	11 1
12	13 17 24	21 14 52	3♑52	24 27	14 19	0♈ 2	26 20	2 1	18 39	9 7	11 1
13	13 21 21	22 13 42	15 42	25 43	15 31	0 48	26 14	2 2	18 41	9 5	11 1
14	13 25 18	23 12 30	27 35	27 2	16 42	1 35	26 9	2 3	18 44	9 4	11 0
15	13 29 14	24 11 16	9♒35	28 22	17 54	2 22	26 4	2 4	18 46	9 2	11 0
16	13 33 11	25 10 0	21 49	29 44	19 5	3 8	25 58	2 5	18 48	9 1	11 0
17	13 37 7	26 8 43	4♓19	1♈ 8	20 17	3 55	25 53	2 6	18 51	8 59	11 0
18	13 41 4	27 7 24	17 8	2 34	21 29	4 41	25 47	2 8	18 53	8 57	10 59
19	13 45 0	28 6 3	0♈19	4 2	22 40	5 28	25 41	2 10	18 56	8 56	10 59
20	13 48 57	29 4 40	13 51	5 32	23 52	6 14	25 35	2 11	18 58	8 54	10 59
21	13 52 53	0♉ 3 16	27 42	7 3	25 4	7 1	25 29	2 13	19 1	8 53	10 59
22	13 56 50	1 1 49	11♉49	8 37	26 15	7 47	25 23	2 15	19 4	8 51	10 59
23	14 0 47	2 0 21	26 7	10 12	27 27	8 33	25 16	2 17	19 6	8 50	10D59
24	14 4 43	2 58 50	10♊32	11 48	28 39	9 19	25 10	2 19	19 9	8 48	10 59
25	14 8 40	3 57 18	24 58	13 27	29 51	10 6	25 3	2 21	19 12	8 47	10 59
26	14 12 36	4 55 44	9♋22	15 7	1♈ 3	10 52	24 56	2 24	19 14	8 45	10 59
27	14 16 33	5 54 7	23 39	16 49	2 15	11 38	24 50	2 26	19 17	8 44	10 59
28	14 20 29	6 52 28	7♌48	18 32	3 27	12 24	24 43	2 29	19 20	8 43	10 59
29	14 24 26	7 50 48	21 47	20 18	4 38	13 10	24 36	2 31	19 23	8 41	10 59
30	14 28 22	8♉49 4	5♍35	22♈ 5	5♈50	13♈56	24♏29	2♌34	19♊26	8♎40	10♌59

THE SUN ENTERS THE SIGN OF TAURUS ON APR 20 AT 22:40.

DAY	TIME	☉	☽	☿	♀	♂	♃	♄	♅	♆	♇
	h m s	° ' "	° '	° '	° '	° '	° '	° '	° '	° '	° '
M 1	14 32 19	9♉47 19	19♍10	23♈54	7♈ 2	14♈42	24♏22	2♌37	19♊29	8♎38	11♌ 0
A 2	14 36 16	10 45 32	2♎33	25 44	8 14	15 28	24R14	2 40	19 32	8R37	11 0
Y 3	14 40 12	11 43 43	15 42	27 37	9 26	16 14	24 7	2 43	19 34	8 36	11 0
4	14 44 9	12 41 52	28 37	29 31	10 38	17 0	24 0	2 46	19 37	8 34	11 0
5	14 48 5	13 39 59	11♏18	1♉27	11 50	17 46	23 53	2 49	19 40	8 33	11 1
6	14 52 2	14 38 5	23 46	3 25	13 2	18 32	23 45	2 52	19 44	8 32	11 1
7	14 55 58	15 36 9	6♐ 1	5 24	14 15	19 17	23 38	2 56	19 47	8 31	11 1
8	14 59 55	16 34 11	18 6	7 25	15 27	20 3	23 30	2 59	19 50	8 29	11 2
9	15 3 51	17 32 12	0♑ 2	9 28	16 39	20 49	23 23	3 3	19 53	8 28	11 2
10	15 7 48	18 30 12	11 54	11 32	17 51	21 34	23 15	3 6	19 56	8 27	11 2
11	15 11 45	19 28 10	23 44	13 38	19 3	22 20	23 7	3 10	19 59	8 26	11 3
12	15 15 41	20 26 7	5♒37	15 45	20 15	23 5	23 0	3 14	20 2	8 25	11 3
13	15 19 38	21 24 3	17 37	17 53	21 28	23 51	22 52	3 18	20 6	8 24	11 4
14	15 23 34	22 21 57	29 49	20 2	22 40	24 36	22 45	3 22	20 9	8 22	11 4
15	15 27 31	23 19 50	12♓18	22 13	23 52	25 22	22 37	3 26	20 12	8 21	11 5
16	15 31 27	24 17 41	25 7	24 23	25 4	26 7	22 29	3 30	20 15	8 20	11 5
17	15 35 24	25 15 32	8♈20	26 35	26 17	26 52	22 22	3 35	20 19	8 19	11 6
18	15 39 20	26 13 21	21 57	28 46	27 29	27 38	22 14	3 39	20 22	8 18	11 7
19	15 43 17	27 11 9	5♉58	0♊57	28 41	28 23	22 6	3 43	20 25	8 17	11 7
20	15 47 14	28 8 56	20 21	3 8	29 54	29 8	21 59	3 48	20 29	8 16	11 8
21	15 51 10	29 6 41	5♊ 0	5 18	1♉ 6	29 53	21 51	3 53	20 32	8 15	11 9
22	15 55 7	0♊ 4 26	19 49	7 27	2 18	0♉38	21 44	3 57	20 35	8 15	11 9
23	15 59 3	1 2 9	4♋40	9 35	3 31	1 23	21 36	4 2	20 39	8 14	11 10
24	16 3 0	1 59 50	19 27	11 41	4 43	2 8	21 29	4 7	20 42	8 13	11 11
25	16 6 56	2 57 30	4♌ 3	13 46	5 56	2 53	21 21	4 12	20 46	8 12	11 12
26	16 10 53	3 55 8	18 23	15 48	7 8	3 38	21 14	4 17	20 49	8 11	11 13
27	16 14 49	4 52 45	2♍25	17 49	8 21	4 23	21 7	4 22	20 52	8 11	11 13
28	16 18 46	5 50 20	16 7	19 47	9 33	5 7	21 0	4 27	20 56	8 10	11 14
29	16 22 43	6 47 53	29 30	21 43	10 45	5 52	20 52	4 32	20 59	8 9	11 15
30	16 26 39	7 45 26	12♎35	23 36	11 58	6 37	20 45	4 38	21 3	8 8	11 16
31	16 30 36	8♊42 56	25♎24	25♊27	13♉10	7♉21	20♏38	4♌43	21♊ 6	8♎ 8	11♌17

THE SUN ENTERS THE SIGN OF GEMINI ON MAY 21 AT 22:10.

DAY	TIME	☉	☽	☿	♀	♂	♃	♄	♅	♆	♇
	h m s	° ' "	° '	° '	° '	° '	° '	° '	° '	° '	° '
J 1	16 34 32	9♊40 26	7♏59	27♊16	14♉23	8♉ 6	20♏31	4♌48	21♊10	8♎ 7	11♌18
U 2	16 38 29	10 37 55	20 22	29 1	15 36	8 50	20R25	4 54	21 13	8R 7	11 19
N 3	16 42 25	11 35 22	2♐35	0♋44	16 48	9 34	20 18	4 59	21 17	8 6	11 20
E 4	16 46 22	12 32 48	14 39	2 24	18 1	10 19	20 11	5 5	21 20	8 6	11 21
5	16 50 18	13 30 14	26 36	4 1	19 13	11 3	20 5	5 11	21 24	8 5	11 22
6	16 54 15	14 27 39	8♑28	5 35	20 26	11 47	19 58	5 17	21 28	8 5	11 23
7	16 58 12	15 25 2	20 19	7 7	21 38	12 31	19 52	5 22	21 31	8 4	11 24
8	17 2 8	16 22 26	2♒ 9	8 36	22 51	13 16	19 46	5 28	21 35	8 4	11 26
9	17 6 5	17 19 48	14 3	10 1	24 4	14 0	19 40	5 34	21 38	8 4	11 27
10	17 10 1	18 17 10	26 4	11 24	25 16	14 44	19 34	5 40	21 42	8 3	11 28
11	17 13 58	19 14 31	8♓15	12 44	26 29	15 28	19 28	5 46	21 45	8 3	11 29
12	17 17 54	20 11 51	20 42	14 1	27 42	16 11	19 22	5 52	21 49	8 3	11 30
13	17 21 51	21 9 12	3♈27	15 15	28 55	16 55	19 17	5 59	21 52	8 2	11 31
14	17 25 48	22 6 31	16 35	16 25	0♊ 7	17 39	19 11	6 5	21 56	8 2	11 33
15	17 29 44	23 3 51	0♉ 8	17 33	1 20	18 23	19 6	6 11	22 0	8 2	11 34
16	17 33 41	24 1 10	14 8	18 37	2 33	19 6	19 1	6 17	22 3	8 2	11 35
17	17 37 37	24 58 28	28 33	19 38	3 46	19 50	18 56	6 24	22 7	8 2	11 37
18	17 41 34	25 55 47	13♊21	20 35	4 59	20 34	18 51	6 30	22 10	8 2	11 38
19	17 45 30	26 53 5	28 24	21 29	6 11	21 17	18 46	6 37	22 14	8D 2	11 39
20	17 49 27	27 50 22	13♋34	22 20	7 24	22 0	18 41	6 43	22 17	8 2	11 41
21	17 53 23	28 47 39	28 41	23 6	8 37	22 44	18 37	6 50	22 21	8 2	11 42
22	17 57 20	29 44 55	13♌36	23 49	9 50	23 27	18 33	6 57	22 24	8 2	11 43
23	18 1 17	0♋42 10	28 11	24 28	11 3	24 10	18 29	7 3	22 28	8 2	11 45
24	18 5 13	1 39 25	12♍23	25 3	12 16	24 53	18 25	7 10	22 32	8 2	11 46
25	18 9 10	2 36 39	26 9	25 34	13 29	25 36	18 21	7 17	22 35	8 2	11 48
26	18 13 6	3 33 53	9♎29	26 1	14 42	26 20	18 17	7 24	22 39	8 2	11 49
27	18 17 3	4 31 5	22 27	26 23	15 55	27 2	18 14	7 31	22 42	8 2	11 50
28	18 20 59	5 28 18	5♏ 5	26 41	17 8	27 45	18 11	7 37	22 46	8 3	11 52
29	18 24 56	6 25 30	17 27	26 54	18 21	28 28	18 7	7 44	22 49	8 3	11 53
30	18 28 52	7♋22 41	29♏37	27♋ 3	19♊34	29♉11	18♏ 5	7♌51	22♊53	8♎ 3	11♌55

THE SUN ENTERS THE SIGN OF CANCER ON JUN 22 AT 06:19.

♏ SCORPIO ♐ SAGITTARIUS ♑ CAPRICORN ♒ AQUARIUS ♓ PISCES

1947

SIDEREAL · SUN. · MOON. · MERCURY. · VENUS. · MARS. · JUPITER. · SATURN. · URANUS. · NEPTUNE. · PLUTO.

DAY	TIME	☉	☽	☿	♀	♂	♃	♄	♅	♆	♇
	h m s	° ' "	° '	° '	° '	° '	° '	° '	° '	° '	° '
J 1	18 32 49	8♋19 52	11♐38	27♋ 7	20♊47	29♉54	18♏ 2	7♌58	22♊56	8♎ 4	11♌57
U 2	18 36 46	9 17 3	23 33	27R 7	22 0	0♊36	17R59	8 6	23 0	8 4	11 58
L 3	18 40 42	10 14 14	5♑24	27 2	23 13	1 19	17 57	8 13	23 3	8 4	12 0
Y 4	18 44 39	11 11 25	17 15	26 52	24 26	2 1	17 55	8 20	23 6	8 5	12 1
5	18 48 35	12 8 36	29 6	26 38	25 39	2 44	17 52	8 27	23 10	8 5	12 3
6	18 52 32	13 5 47	10♒59	26 19	26 52	3 26	17 51	8 34	23 13	8 6	12 4
7	18 56 28	14 2 58	22 57	25 57	28 6	4 8	17 49	8 41	23 17	8 6	12 6
8	19 0 25	15 0 9	5♓ 1	25 30	29 19	4 51	17 47	8 49	23 20	8 7	12 8
9	19 4 21	15 57 20	17 15	25 1	0♋32	5 33	17 46	8 56	23 23	8 8	12 9
10	19 8 18	16 54 32	29 42	24 28	1 45	6 15	17 45	9 3	23 27	8 8	12 11
11	19 12 15	17 51 44	12♈25	23 53	2 59	6 57	17 44	9 11	23 30	8 9	12 13
12	19 16 11	18 48 57	25 27	23 16	4 12	7 39	17 43	9 18	23 33	8 9	12 14
13	19 20 8	19 46 10	8♉53	22 37	5 25	8 21	17 42	9 25	23 37	8 10	12 16
14	19 24 4	20 43 24	22 44	21 58	6 39	9 3	17 42	9 33	23 40	8 11	12 18
15	19 28 1	21 40 38	7♊ 2	21 19	7 52	9 45	17D42	9 40	23 43	8 12	12 19
16	19 31 57	22 37 53	21 44	20 40	9 5	10 26	17 42	9 48	23 46	8 13	12 21
17	19 35 54	23 35 9	6♋46	20 3	10 19	11 8	17 42	9 55	23 50	8 13	12 23
18	19 39 51	24 32 25	22 0	19 28	11 32	11 50	17 42	10 3	23 53	8 14	12 24
19	19 43 47	25 29 41	7♌15	18 55	12 46	12 31	17 42	10 10	23 56	8 15	12 26
20	19 47 44	26 26 58	22 21	18 26	13 59	13 12	17 43	10 18	23 59	8 16	12 28
21	19 51 40	27 24 15	7♍ 9	18 0	15 13	13 54	17 44	10 25	24 2	8 17	12 30
22	19 55 37	28 21 32	21 31	17 38	16 26	14 35	17 45	10 33	24 5	8 18	12 31
23	19 59 33	29 18 50	5♎24	17 22	17 40	15 16	17 46	10 41	24 8	8 19	12 33
24	20 3 30	0♌16 8	18 48	17 10	18 53	15 57	17 47	10 48	24 12	8 20	12 35
25	20 7 26	1 13 26	1♏46	17D 4	20 7	16 38	17 49	10 56	24 15	8 21	12 37
26	20 11 23	2 10 44	14 21	17 3	21 21	17 19	17 51	11 4	24 18	8 22	12 38
27	20 15 20	3 8 4	26 37	17 8	22 34	18 0	17 53	11 11	24 21	8 23	12 40
28	20 19 16	4 5 23	8♐41	17 20	23 48	18 41	17 55	11 19	24 23	8 25	12 42
29	20 23 13	5 2 43	20 36	17 37	25 2	19 22	17 57	11 27	24 26	8 26	12 44
30	20 27 9	6 0 4	2♑27	18 0	26 15	20 3	17 59	11 34	24 29	8 27	12 45
31	20 31 6	6♌57 25	14♑16	18♋30	27♋29	20♊43	18♏ 2	11♌42	24♊32	8♎28	12♌47

THE SUN ENTERS THE SIGN OF LEO ON JUL 23 AT 17:15.

DAY	TIME	☉	☽	☿	♀	♂	♃	♄	♅	♆	♇
	h m s	° ' "	° '	° '	° '	° '	° '	° '	° '	° '	° '
A 1	20 35 2	7♌54 47	26♑ 7	19♋ 6	28♋43	21♊24	18♏ 5	11♌50	24♊35	8♎30	12♌49
U 2	20 38 59	8 52 10	8♒ 2	19 48	29 57	22 4	18 8	11 57	24 38	8 31	12 51
G 3	20 42 55	9 49 34	20 1	20 36	1♌10	22 45	18 11	12 5	24 41	8 32	12 53
U 4	20 46 52	10 46 58	2♓ 7	21 30	2 24	23 25	18 14	12 13	24 43	8 34	12 54
S 5	20 50 49	11 44 24	14 20	22 30	3 38	24 5	18 18	12 20	24 46	8 35	12 56
T 6	20 54 45	12 41 50	26 42	23 36	4 52	24 45	18 21	12 28	24 49	8 36	12 58
7	20 58 42	13 39 18	9♈16	24 47	6 6	25 26	18 25	12 36	24 51	8 38	13 0
8	21 2 38	14 36 47	22 2	26 4	7 20	26 6	18 29	12 44	24 54	8 39	13 2
9	21 6 35	15 34 18	5♉ 4	27 26	8 34	26 46	18 33	12 51	24 56	8 41	13 3
10	21 10 31	16 31 49	18 26	28 53	9 48	27 25	18 37	12 59	24 59	8 42	13 5
11	21 14 28	17 29 23	2♊ 8	0♌25	11 2	28 5	18 42	13 7	25 1	8 44	13 7
12	21 18 24	18 26 57	16 14	2 1	12 16	28 45	18 46	13 14	25 4	8 45	13 9
13	21 22 21	19 24 34	0♋43	3 41	13 30	29 25	18 51	13 22	25 6	8 47	13 11
14	21 26 18	20 22 11	15 31	5 25	14 44	0♋ 4	18 56	13 30	25 9	8 48	13 12
15	21 30 14	21 19 51	0♌34	7 13	15 58	0 44	19 1	13 37	25 11	8 50	13 14
16	21 34 11	22 17 31	15 41	9 3	17 12	1 23	19 6	13 45	25 13	8 52	13 16
17	21 38 7	23 15 13	0♍44	10 56	18 26	2 2	19 12	13 53	25 16	8 53	13 18
18	21 42 4	24 12 56	15 32	12 51	19 40	2 42	19 17	14 0	25 18	8 55	13 20
19	21 46 0	25 10 40	29 57	14 48	20 55	3 21	19 23	14 8	25 20	8 57	13 21
20	21 49 57	26 8 25	13♎55	16 46	22 9	4 0	19 29	14 16	25 22	8 59	13 23
21	21 53 53	27 6 11	27 23	18 46	23 23	4 39	19 35	14 23	25 24	9 0	13 25
22	21 57 50	28 3 59	10♏24	20 45	24 37	5 18	19 41	14 31	25 26	9 2	13 27
23	22 1 47	29 1 47	23 1	22 46	25 51	5 57	19 47	14 38	25 28	9 4	13 28
24	22 5 43	29 59 37	5♐18	24 46	27 6	6 35	19 54	14 46	25 30	9 6	13 30
25	22 9 40	0♍57 28	17 21	26 46	28 20	7 14	20 0	14 53	25 32	9 8	13 32
26	22 13 36	1 55 21	29 15	28 46	29 34	7 52	20 7	15 1	25 34	9 9	13 34
27	22 17 33	2 53 14	11♑ 5	0♍45	0♍49	8 31	20 14	15 8	25 36	9 11	13 35
28	22 21 29	3 51 9	22 55	2 44	2 3	9 9	20 21	15 16	25 38	9 13	13 37
29	22 25 26	4 49 6	4♒49	4 42	3 17	9 48	20 28	15 23	25 40	9 15	13 39
30	22 29 22	5 47 4	16 49	6 38	4 32	10 26	20 35	15 31	25 41	9 17	13 40
31	22 33 19	6♍45 3	28♒57	8♍34	5♍46	11♋ 4	20♏43	15♌38	25♊43	9♎19	13♌42

THE SUN ENTERS THE SIGN OF VIRGO ON AUG 24 AT 00:10.

DAY	TIME	☉	☽	☿	♀	♂	♃	♄	♅	♆	♇
	h m s	° ' "	° '	° '	° '	° '	° '	° '	° '	° '	° '
S 1	22 37 16	7♍43 4	11♓14	10♍29	7♍ 1	11♋42	20♏50	15♌45	25♊45	9♎21	13♌44
E 2	22 41 12	8 41 6	23 41	12 22	8 15	12 20	20 58	15 53	25 46	9 23	13 45
P 3	22 45 9	9 39 10	6♈18	14 15	9 29	12 58	21 6	16 0	25 48	9 25	13 47
T 4	22 49 5	10 37 16	19 6	16 6	10 44	13 35	21 14	16 7	25 49	9 27	13 49
E 5	22 53 2	11 35 24	2♉ 5	17 56	11 58	14 13	21 22	16 15	25 51	9 29	13 50
M 6	22 56 58	12 33 34	15 16	19 45	13 13	14 51	21 30	16 22	25 52	9 31	13 52
B 7	23 0 55	13 31 46	28 42	21 32	14 27	15 28	21 38	16 29	25 53	9 33	13 54
E 8	23 4 51	14 30 0	12♊23	23 19	15 42	16 6	21 46	16 36	25 55	9 35	13 55
R 9	23 8 48	15 28 16	26 20	25 4	16 56	16 43	21 55	16 43	25 56	9 37	13 57
10	23 12 44	16 26 34	10♋35	26 48	18 11	17 20	22 4	16 50	25 57	9 39	13 58
11	23 16 41	17 24 55	25 5	28 31	19 26	17 57	22 12	16 57	25 58	9 41	14 0
12	23 20 38	18 23 17	9♌46	0♎13	20 40	18 34	22 21	17 4	25 59	9 43	14 1
13	23 24 34	19 21 41	24 33	1 54	21 55	19 11	22 30	17 11	26 0	9 45	14 3
14	23 28 31	20 20 8	9♍17	3 33	23 9	19 48	22 39	17 18	26 1	9 47	14 4
15	23 32 27	21 18 36	23 51	5 12	24 24	20 25	22 49	17 25	26 2	9 50	14 6
16	23 36 24	22 17 6	8♎ 7	6 49	25 39	21 1	22 58	17 32	26 3	9 52	14 7
17	23 40 20	23 15 38	22 0	8 26	26 53	21 38	23 7	17 39	26 4	9 54	14 9
18	23 44 17	24 14 11	5♏27	10 1	28 8	22 14	23 17	17 45	26 5	9 56	14 10
19	23 48 13	25 12 47	18 29	11 36	29 23	22 50	23 26	17 52	26 6	9 58	14 12
20	23 52 10	26 11 24	1♐ 8	13 9	0♎37	23 26	23 36	17 59	26 6	10 0	14 13
21	23 56 7	27 10 3	13 27	14 41	1 52	24 2	23 46	18 5	26 7	10 3	14 15
22	0 0 3	28 8 43	25 32	16 12	3 7	24 38	23 56	18 12	26 7	10 5	14 16
23	0 4 0	29 7 25	7♑27	17 43	4 21	25 14	24 6	18 18	26 8	10 7	14 17
24	0 7 56	0♎ 6 9	19 18	19 12	5 36	25 50	24 16	18 25	26 8	10 9	14 19
25	0 11 53	1 4 55	1♒10	20 40	6 51	26 25	24 26	18 31	26 9	10 11	14 20
26	0 15 49	2 3 42	13 7	22 8	8 6	27 1	24 37	18 38	26 9	10 14	14 21
27	0 19 46	3 2 32	25 13	23 34	9 20	27 36	24 47	18 44	26 10	10 16	14 23
28	0 23 42	4 1 23	7♓29	24 59	10 35	28 11	24 58	18 50	26 10	10 18	14 24
29	0 27 39	5 0 15	19 58	26 23	11 50	28 47	25 8	18 56	26 10	10 20	14 25
30	0 31 36	5♎59 10	2♈41	27♎46	13♎ 5	29♋21	25♏19	19♌ 2	26♊10	10♎22	14♌26

THE SUN ENTERS THE SIGN OF LIBRA ON SEP 23 AT 21:29.

♈ ARIES ♉ TAURUS ♊ GEMINI ♋ CANCER ♌ LEO ♍ VIRGO ♎ LIBRA

SIDEREAL SUN. MOON. MERCURY. VENUS. MARS. JUPITER. SATURN. URANUS. NEPTUNE. PLUTO.

DAY	TIME	☉	☽	☿	♀	♂	♃	♄	♅	♆	♇
	h m s	° ' "	° '	° '	° '	° '	° '	° '	° '	° '	° '
O 1	0 35 32	6♎58 7	15♈37	29♎ 8	14♎19	29♋56	25♏30	19♌ 8	26♊10	10♎25	14♌28
C 2	0 39 29	7 57 6	28 45	0♏29	15 34	0♌31	25 41	19 14	26R10	10 27	14 29
T 3	0 43 25	8 56 7	12♉ 5	1 48	16 49	1 6	25 52	19 20	26 10	10 29	14 30
O 4	0 47 22	9 55 10	25 36	3 6	18 4	1 40	26 3	19 26	26 10	10 31	14 31
B 5	0 51 18	10 54 16	9♊18	4 23	19 18	2 15	26 14	19 32	26 10	10 34	14 32
E 6	0 55 15	11 53 24	23 8	5 39	20 33	2 49	26 25	19 37	26 10	10 36	14 33
R 7	0 59 11	12 52 34	7♋ 8	6 53	21 48	3 23	26 36	19 43	26 10	10 38	14 34
8	1 3 8	13 51 47	21 17	8 6	23 3	3 57	26 48	19 49	26 10	10 40	14 36
9	1 7 5	14 51 2	5♌32	9 16	24 18	4 31	26 59	19 54	26 9	10 43	14 37
10	1 11 1	15 50 19	19 52	10 25	25 32	5 4	27 10	20 0	26 9	10 45	14 38
11	1 14 58	16 49 39	4♍12	11 32	26 47	5 38	27 22	20 5	26 9	10 47	14 39
12	1 18 54	17 49 1	18 29	12 37	28 2	6 11	27 34	20 10	26 8	10 49	14 40
13	1 22 51	18 48 25	2♎37	13 40	29 17	6 45	27 45	20 16	26 8	10 51	14 41
14	1 26 47	19 47 51	16 31	14 40	0♏32	7 18	27 57	20 21	26 7	10 54	14 41
15	1 30 44	20 47 19	0♏ 8	15 38	1 47	7 51	28 9	20 26	26 6	10 56	14 42
16	1 34 40	21 46 49	13 25	16 32	3 1	8 24	28 21	20 31	26 6	10 58	14 43
17	1 38 37	22 46 22	26 21	17 23	4 16	8 56	28 33	20 36	26 5	11 0	14 44
18	1 42 33	23 45 56	8♐58	18 11	5 31	9 29	28 45	20 41	26 4	11 3	14 45
19	1 46 30	24 45 32	21 17	18 54	6 46	10 1	28 57	20 45	26 4	11 5	14 46
20	1 50 27	25 45 9	3♑23	19 33	8 1	10 33	29 9	20 50	26 3	11 7	14 46
21	1 54 23	26 44 49	15 20	20 7	9 16	11 5	29 21	20 55	26 2	11 9	14 47
22	1 58 20	27 44 30	27 12	20 36	10 31	11 37	29 34	20 59	26 1	11 11	14 48
23	2 2 16	28 44 13	9♒ 5	20 59	11 45	12 9	29 46	21 3	26 0	11 13	14 49
24	2 6 13	29 43 58	21 3	21 15	13 0	12 40	29 58	21 8	25 59	11 16	14 49
25	2 10 9	0♏43 44	3♓10	21R25	14 15	13 11	0♐11	21 12	25 58	11 18	14 50
26	2 14 6	1 43 32	15 31	21 27	15 30	13 42	0 23	21 16	25 56	11 20	14 51
27	2 18 2	2 43 22	28 8	21 20	16 45	14 13	0 36	21 20	25 55	11 22	14 51
28	2 21 59	3 43 14	11♈ 2	21 5	18 0	14 44	0 48	21 24	25 54	11 24	14 52
29	2 25 56	4 43 7	24 15	20 41	19 15	15 15	1 1	21 28	25 53	11 26	14 52
30	2 29 52	5 43 3	7♉45	20 7	20 29	15 45	1 14	21 32	25 51	11 28	14 53
31	2 33 49	6♏43 0	21♉31	19♏25	21♏44	16♌15	1♐27	21♌36	25♊50	11♎30	14♌53

THE SUN ENTERS THE SIGN OF SCORPIO ON OCT 24 AT 06:27.

DAY	TIME	☉	☽	☿	♀	♂	♃	♄	♅	♆	♇
	h m s	° ' "	° '	° '	° '	° '	° '	° '	° '	° '	° '
N 1	2 37 45	7♏42 59	5♊30	18♏33	22♏59	16♌45	1♐39	21♌39	25♊49	11♎32	14♌54
O 2	2 41 42	8 43 1	19 37	17R33	24 14	17 15	1 52	21 43	25R47	11 34	14 54
V 3	2 45 38	9 43 4	3♋50	16 25	25 29	17 45	2 5	21 46	25 46	11 36	14 55
E 4	2 49 35	10 43 10	18 5	15 12	26 44	18 14	2 18	21 50	25 44	11 38	14 55
M 5	2 53 32	11 43 18	2♌20	13 55	27 58	18 43	2 31	21 53	25 42	11 40	14 55
B 6	2 57 28	12 43 28	16 32	12 36	29 13	19 12	2 44	21 56	25 41	11 42	14 56
E 7	3 1 25	13 43 40	0♍38	11 18	0♐28	19 41	2 57	21 59	25 39	11 44	14 56
R 8	3 5 21	14 43 54	14 37	10 3	1 43	20 9	3 10	22 2	25 37	11 46	14 56
9	3 9 18	15 44 10	28 27	8 54	2 58	20 37	3 23	22 5	25 36	11 48	14 56
10	3 13 14	16 44 28	12♎ 6	7 53	4 13	21 5	3 36	22 7	25 34	11 50	14 57
11	3 17 11	17 44 47	25 33	7 2	5 28	21 33	3 49	22 10	25 32	11 52	14 57
12	3 21 7	18 45 9	8♏45	6 21	6 42	22 1	4 2	22 13	25 30	11 54	14 57
13	3 25 4	19 45 33	21 43	5 52	7 57	22 28	4 15	22 15	25 28	11 56	14 57
14	3 29 0	20 45 58	4♐27	5 34	9 12	22 55	4 29	22 17	25 26	11 58	14 57
15	3 32 57	21 46 25	16 55	5D28	10 27	23 22	4 42	22 19	25 24	12 0	14 57
16	3 36 54	22 46 53	29 11	5 34	11 42	23 48	4 55	22 22	25 22	12 1	14R57
17	3 40 50	23 47 23	11♑15	5 49	12 57	24 14	5 9	22 24	25 20	12 3	14 57
18	3 44 47	24 47 54	23 12	6 15	14 11	24 40	5 22	22 25	25 18	12 5	14 57
19	3 48 43	25 48 27	5♒ 4	6 49	15 26	25 6	5 35	22 27	25 16	12 7	14 57
20	3 52 40	26 49 1	16 55	7 31	16 41	25 31	5 49	22 29	25 14	12 8	14 57
21	3 56 36	27 49 35	28 52	8 20	17 56	25 56	6 2	22 30	25 12	12 10	14 57
22	4 0 33	28 50 12	10♓57	9 15	19 11	26 21	6 15	22 32	25 9	12 12	14 57
23	4 4 30	29 50 49	23 16	10 16	20 26	26 46	6 29	22 33	25 7	12 13	14 57
24	4 8 26	0♐51 27	5♈53	11 21	21 40	27 10	6 42	22 34	25 5	12 15	14 57
25	4 12 23	1 52 7	18 51	12 31	22 55	27 34	6 56	22 36	25 3	12 17	14 56
26	4 16 19	2 52 48	2♉12	13 44	24 10	27 57	7 9	22 37	25 0	12 18	14 56
27	4 20 16	3 53 30	15 56	15 0	25 25	28 20	7 22	22 37	24 58	12 20	14 56
28	4 24 12	4 54 13	0♊ 3	16 18	26 39	28 43	7 36	22 38	24 56	12 21	14 56
29	4 28 9	5 54 58	14 27	17 39	27 54	29 6	7 49	22 39	24 53	12 23	14 55
30	4 32 5	6♐55 44	29♊ 4	19♏ 2	29♐ 9	29♌28	8♐ 3	22♌39	24♊51	12♎24	14♌55

THE SUN ENTERS THE SIGN OF SAGITTARIUS ON NOV 23 AT 03:38.

DAY	TIME	☉	☽	☿	♀	♂	♃	♄	♅	♆	♇
	h m s	° ' "	° '	° '	° '	° '	° '	° '	° '	° '	° '
D 1	4 36 2	7♐56 31	13♋47	20♏26	0♑24	29♌49	8♐16	22♌40	24♊48	12♎26	14♌55
E 2	4 39 59	8 57 20	28 28	21 51	1 38	0♍11	8 30	22 40	24R46	12 27	14R54
C 3	4 43 55	9 58 10	13♌ 2	23 18	2 53	0 32	8 43	22 40	24 44	12 29	14 54
E 4	4 47 52	10 59 2	27 24	24 46	4 8	0 53	8 57	22R41	24 41	12 30	14 53
M 5	4 51 48	11 59 54	11♍30	26 14	5 23	1 13	9 10	22 41	24 39	12 31	14 53
B 6	4 55 45	13 0 48	25 19	27 43	6 37	1 33	9 24	22 40	24 36	12 33	14 52
E 7	4 59 41	14 1 44	8♎52	29 13	7 52	1 52	9 37	22 40	24 34	12 34	14 52
R 8	5 3 38	15 2 41	22 9	0♐43	9 7	2 11	9 50	22 40	24 31	12 35	14 51
9	5 7 34	16 3 39	5♏11	2 14	10 21	2 30	10 4	22 39	24 29	12 36	14 51
10	5 11 31	17 4 38	18 0	3 45	11 36	2 48	10 17	22 39	24 26	12 38	14 50
11	5 15 28	18 5 38	0♐37	5 16	12 51	3 6	10 31	22 38	24 24	12 39	14 49
12	5 19 24	19 6 39	13 3	6 47	14 5	3 23	10 44	22 37	24 21	12 40	14 49
13	5 23 21	20 7 42	25 19	8 19	15 20	3 40	10 58	22 37	24 18	12 41	14 48
14	5 27 17	21 8 45	7♑26	9 51	16 35	3 56	11 11	22 35	24 16	12 42	14 47
15	5 31 14	22 9 48	19 27	11 23	17 49	4 12	11 24	22 34	24 13	12 43	14 46
16	5 35 10	23 10 52	1♒21	12 56	19 4	4 27	11 38	22 33	24 11	12 44	14 46
17	5 39 7	24 11 57	13 12	14 28	20 19	4 42	11 51	22 32	24 8	12 45	14 45
18	5 43 3	25 13 2	25 3	16 1	21 33	4 56	12 4	22 30	24 6	12 46	14 44
19	5 47 0	26 14 8	6♓58	17 34	22 48	5 10	12 18	22 29	24 3	12 47	14 43
20	5 50 57	27 15 13	18 59	19 7	24 2	5 23	12 31	22 27	24 0	12 48	14 42
21	5 54 53	28 16 19	1♈13	20 40	25 17	5 36	12 44	22 25	23 58	12 49	14 42
22	5 58 50	29 17 26	13 44	22 13	26 31	5 48	12 58	22 23	23 55	12 50	14 41
23	6 2 46	0♑18 32	26 37	23 47	27 46	5 59	13 11	22 21	23 53	12 50	14 40
24	6 6 43	1 19 39	9♉54	25 20	29 0	6 10	13 24	22 19	23 50	12 51	14 39
25	6 10 39	2 20 46	23 40	26 54	0♒15	6 20	13 37	22 17	23 48	12 52	14 38
26	6 14 36	3 21 53	7♊53	28 28	1 29	6 30	13 50	22 15	23 45	12 53	14 37
27	6 18 33	4 23 0	22 31	0♑ 3	2 44	6 39	14 3	22 13	23 43	12 53	14 36
28	6 22 29	5 24 8	7♋29	1 37	3 58	6 48	14 16	22 10	23 40	12 54	14 35
29	6 26 26	6 25 15	22 37	3 12	5 12	6 56	14 29	22 8	23 38	12 55	14 34
30	6 30 22	7 26 24	7♌45	4 48	6 27	7 3	14 42	22 5	23 35	12 55	14 33
31	6 34 19	8♑27 32	22♌44	6♑23	7♒41	7♍ 9	14♐55	22♌ 2	23♊33	12♎56	14♌32

THE SUN ENTERS THE SIGN OF CAPRICORN ON DEC 22 AT 16:43.

♏ SCORPIO ♐ SAGITTARIUS ♑ CAPRICORN ♒ AQUARIUS ♓ PISCES

SIDEREAL | SUN . | MOON . . | MERCURY | VENUS . . | MARS . . | JUPITER | SATURN . . | URANUS . . | NEPTUNE . | PLUTO . .

DAY	TIME	☉	☽	☿	♀	♂	♃	♄	♅	♆	♇
	h m s	° ' "	° '	° '	° '	° '	° '	° '	° '	° '	° '
J 1	6 38 15	9♑28 41	7♍26	7♑59	8♒55	7♍15	15♐ 8	21♌59	23♊30	12♎56	14♌31
A 2	6 42 12	10 29 50	21 45	9 35	10 9	7 20	15 21	21R56	23R28	12 57	14R29
N 3	6 46 8	11 30 59	5♎38	11 11	11 24	7 25	15 34	21 53	23 25	12 57	14 28
U 4	6 50 5	12 32 9	19 8	12 48	12 38	7 29	15 47	21 50	23 23	12 57	14 27
A 5	6 54 2	13 33 19	2♏14	14 25	13 52	7 32	15 59	21 47	23 21	12 58	14 26
R 6	6 57 58	14 34 29	15 2	16 3	15 6	7 34	16 12	21 44	23 18	12 58	14 25
Y 7	7 1 55	15 35 39	27 35	17 41	16 20	7 36	16 25	21 40	23 16	12 58	14 24
8	7 5 51	16 36 50	9♐55	19 19	17 34	7R36	16 37	21 37	23 14	12 59	14 22
9	7 9 48	17 38 0	22 6	20 58	18 48	7 37	16 50	21 33	23 11	12 59	14 21
10	7 13 44	18 39 11	4♑10	22 37	20 2	7 36	17 2	21 29	23 9	12 59	14 20
11	7 17 41	19 40 21	16 9	24 17	21 16	7 34	17 15	21 26	23 7	12 59	14 19
12	7 21 37	20 41 31	28 4	25 57	22 30	7 32	17 27	21 22	23 5	12 59	14 17
13	7 25 34	21 42 41	9♒56	27 37	23 44	7 29	17 40	21 18	23 3	12 59	14 16
14	7 29 31	22 43 50	21 48	29 17	24 58	7 25	17 52	21 14	23 0	13R 0	14 15
15	7 33 27	23 44 58	3♓40	0♒58	26 12	7 20	18 4	21 10	22 58	13 0	14 13
16	7 37 24	24 46 6	15 35	2 40	27 26	7 15	18 16	21 6	22 56	13 0	14 12
17	7 41 20	25 47 13	27 37	4 21	28 39	7 9	18 28	21 2	22 54	12 59	14 11
18	7 45 17	26 48 20	9♈48	6 3	29 53	7 2	18 40	20 58	22 52	12 59	14 10
19	7 49 13	27 49 25	22 14	7 45	1♓ 7	6 54	18 52	20 53	22 50	12 59	14 8
20	7 53 10	28 50 30	4♉58	9 27	2 20	6 45	19 4	20 49	22 48	12 59	14 7
21	7 57 6	29 51 34	18 7	11 8	3 34	6 36	19 16	20 45	22 46	12 59	14 5
22	8 1 3	0♒52 37	1♊43	12 50	4 47	6 25	19 28	20 40	22 44	12 59	14 4
23	8 5 0	1 53 39	15 48	14 31	6 1	6 14	19 39	20 36	22 43	12 58	14 3
24	8 8 56	2 54 40	0♋22	16 12	7 14	6 2	19 51	20 31	22 41	12 58	14 1
25	8 12 53	3 55 41	15 22	17 51	8 27	5 50	20 3	20 27	22 39	12 58	14 0
26	8 16 49	4 56 40	0♌38	19 30	9 41	5 36	20 14	20 22	22 37	12 57	13 59
27	8 20 46	5 57 38	16 1	21 7	10 54	5 22	20 25	20 18	22 36	12 57	13 57
28	8 24 42	6 58 36	1♍18	22 43	12 7	5 7	20 37	20 13	22 34	12 57	13 56
29	8 28 39	7 59 32	16 19	24 16	13 20	4 52	20 48	20 8	22 32	12 56	13 54
30	8 32 36	9 0 28	0♎54	25 47	14 33	4 36	20 59	20 4	22 31	12 56	13 53
31	8 36 32	10♒ 1 24	15♎ 1	27♒14	15♓46	4♍19	21♐10	19♌59	22♊29	12♎55	13♌52

THE SUN ENTERS THE SIGN OF AQUARIUS ON JAN 21 AT 03:19.

DAY	TIME	☉	☽	☿	♀	♂	♃	♄	♅	♆	♇
	h m s	° ' "	° '	° '	° '	° '	° '	° '	° '	° '	° '
F 1	8 40 29	11♒ 2 18	28♎38	28♒38	16♓59	4♍ 1	21♐21	19♌54	22♊28	12♎55	13♌50
E 2	8 44 25	12 3 12	11♏47	29 58	18 12	3R43	21 32	19R49	22R26	12R54	13R49
B 3	8 48 22	13 4 5	24 33	1♓12	19 24	3 24	21 43	19 44	22 25	12 53	13 47
R 4	8 52 18	14 4 57	7♐ 0	2 20	20 37	3 4	21 53	19 40	22 24	12 53	13 46
U 5	8 56 15	15 5 49	19 12	3 22	21 50	2 44	22 4	19 35	22 22	12 52	13 44
A 6	9 0 11	16 6 39	1♑15	4 16	23 2	2 23	22 15	19 30	22 21	12 51	13 43
R 7	9 4 8	17 7 29	13 11	5 2	24 14	2 2	22 25	19 25	22 20	12 51	13 42
Y 8	9 8 5	18 8 17	25 4	5 39	25 27	1 41	22 35	19 20	22 19	12 50	13 40
9	9 12 1	19 9 4	6♒55	6 7	26 39	1 18	22 45	19 15	22 18	12 49	13 39
10	9 15 58	20 9 50	18 47	6 24	27 51	0 56	22 56	19 10	22 17	12 48	13 37
11	9 19 54	21 10 35	0♓41	6R31	29 3	0 33	23 6	19 5	22 16	12 47	13 36
12	9 23 51	22 11 18	12 38	6 27	0♈15	0 10	23 15	19 0	22 15	12 47	13 35
13	9 27 47	23 11 59	24 39	6 13	1 27	29♌47	23 25	18 56	22 14	12 46	13 33
14	9 31 44	24 12 39	6♈46	5 48	2 39	29 23	23 35	18 51	22 13	12 45	13 32
15	9 35 40	25 13 18	19 2	5 13	3 51	29 0	23 44	18 46	22 12	12 44	13 30
16	9 39 37	26 13 55	1♉30	4 29	5 3	28 36	23 54	18 41	22 12	12 43	13 29
17	9 43 33	27 14 30	14 13	3 38	6 14	28 12	24 3	18 36	22 11	12 42	13 28
18	9 47 30	28 15 3	27 16	2 40	7 26	27 48	24 12	18 31	22 10	12 41	13 26
19	9 51 27	29 15 35	10♊43	1 37	8 37	27 24	24 22	18 27	22 10	12 40	13 25
20	9 55 23	0♓16 5	24 35	0 31	9 48	27 0	24 31	18 22	22 9	12 38	13 23
21	9 59 20	1 16 33	8♋55	29♒24	10 59	26 36	24 39	18 17	22 9	12 37	13 22
22	10 3 16	2 16 59	23 40	28 17	12 10	26 13	24 48	18 13	22 8	12 36	13 21
23	10 7 13	3 17 23	8♌45	27 12	13 21	25 49	24 57	18 8	22 8	12 35	13 19
24	10 11 9	4 17 45	24 1	26 11	14 32	25 26	25 5	18 3	22 7	12 34	13 18
25	10 15 6	5 18 6	9♍17	25 14	15 43	25 3	25 14	17 59	22 7	12 33	13 17
26	10 19 3	6 18 25	24 22	24 22	16 53	24 41	25 22	17 54	22 7	12 31	13 16
27	10 22 59	7 18 42	9♎ 6	23 37	18 3	24 19	25 30	17 50	22 7	12 30	13 14
28	10 26 56	8 18 58	23 23	22 59	19 14	23 57	25 38	17 45	22 7	12 29	13 13
29	10 30 52	9♓19 12	7♏10	22♒28	20♈24	23♌35	25♐46	17♌41	22♊ 7	12♎28	13♌12

THE SUN ENTERS THE SIGN OF PISCES ON FEB 19 AT 17:37.

DAY	TIME	☉	☽	☿	♀	♂	♃	♄	♅	♆	♇
	h m s	° ' "	° '	° '	° '	° '	° '	° '	° '	° '	° '
M 1	10 34 49	10♓19 25	20♏29	22♒ 4	21♈34	23♌15	25♐54	17♌37	22♊ 7	12♎26	13♌11
A 2	10 38 45	11 19 36	3♐21	21R47	22 44	22R54	26 1	17R32	22 7	12R25	13R 9
R 3	10 42 42	12 19 46	15 51	21 36	23 53	22 34	26 9	17 28	22 7	12 24	13 8
C 4	10 46 38	13 19 54	28 4	21D33	25 3	22 15	26 16	17 24	22 7	12 22	13 7
H 5	10 50 35	14 20 0	10♑ 5	21 36	26 12	21 56	26 23	17 20	22 7	12 21	13 6
6	10 54 31	15 20 5	21 59	21 45	27 22	21 38	26 30	17 16	22 7	12 19	13 4
7	10 58 28	16 20 9	3♒50	22 0	28 31	21 21	26 37	17 12	22 8	12 18	13 3
8	11 2 25	17 20 10	15 40	22 21	29 40	21 4	26 44	17 8	22 8	12 16	13 2
9	11 6 21	18 20 10	27 34	22 46	0♉49	20 48	26 50	17 4	22 9	12 15	13 1
10	11 10 18	19 20 8	9♓32	23 17	1 57	20 32	26 57	17 0	22 9	12 14	13 0
11	11 14 14	20 20 4	21 36	23 52	3 6	20 18	27 3	16 57	22 10	12 12	12 59
12	11 18 11	21 19 58	3♈48	24 31	4 14	20 4	27 9	16 53	22 10	12 11	12 58
13	11 22 7	22 19 50	16 7	25 14	5 22	19 51	27 15	16 50	22 11	12 9	12 57
14	11 26 4	23 19 40	28 36	26 0	6 30	19 38	27 21	16 46	22 11	12 7	12 56
15	11 30 0	24 19 28	11♉16	26 50	7 38	19 27	27 27	16 43	22 12	12 6	12 55
16	11 33 57	25 19 14	24 9	27 44	8 46	19 16	27 32	16 39	22 13	12 4	12 54
17	11 37 54	26 18 57	7♊17	28 40	9 53	19 6	27 37	16 36	22 14	12 3	12 53
18	11 41 50	27 18 39	20 43	29 39	11 1	18 57	27 43	16 33	22 15	12 1	12 52
19	11 45 47	28 18 18	4♋29	0♓41	12 8	18 48	27 48	16 30	22 16	12 0	12 51
20	11 49 43	29 17 55	18 36	1 45	13 14	18 40	27 52	16 27	22 17	11 58	12 50
21	11 53 40	0♈17 29	3♌ 3	2 52	14 21	18 34	27 57	16 24	22 18	11 56	12 49
22	11 57 36	1 17 1	17 46	4 1	15 27	18 27	28 2	16 22	22 19	11 55	12 48
23	12 1 33	2 16 31	2♍40	5 12	16 33	18 22	28 6	16 19	22 20	11 53	12 47
24	12 5 29	3 15 58	17 36	6 25	17 39	18 18	28 10	16 16	22 21	11 52	12 46
25	12 9 26	4 15 24	2♎26	7 40	18 45	18 14	28 14	16 14	22 22	11 50	12 46
26	12 13 23	5 14 47	17 2	8 57	19 50	18 11	28 18	16 12	22 24	11 48	12 45
27	12 17 19	6 14 8	1♏16	10 16	20 56	18 9	28 22	16 9	22 25	11 47	12 44
28	12 21 16	7 13 28	15 6	11 37	22 0	18 7	28 25	16 7	22 27	11 45	12 43
29	12 25 12	8 12 45	28 29	12 59	23 5	18D 6	28 28	16 5	22 28	11 43	12 43
30	12 29 9	9 12 1	11♐27	14 23	24 9	18 6	28 31	16 3	22 29	11 42	12 42
31	12 33 5	10♈11 15	24♐ 2	15♓49	25♉13	18♌ 7	28♐34	16♌ 1	22♊31	11♎40	12♌41

THE SUN ENTERS THE SIGN OF ARIES ON MAR 20 AT 16:57.

♈ ARIES ♉ TAURUS ♊ GEMINI ♋ CANCER ♌ LEO ♍ VIRGO ♎ LIBRA

1948

SIDEREAL . SUN . MOON . MERCURY . VENUS . MARS . JUPITER . SATURN . URANUS . NEPTUNE . PLUTO .

DAY	TIME	☉	☽	☿	♀	♂	♃	♄	♅	♆	♇
	h m s	° ' "	° '	° '	° '	° '	° '	° '	° '	° '	° '
A 1	12 37 2	11♈10 28	6♑20	17♓16	26♉17	18♌ 8	28♐37	15♌59	22♊33	11♎38	12♌41
P 2	12 40 58	12 9 38	18 25	18 45	27 21	18 11	28 40	15R58	22 34	11R37	12R40
R 3	12 44 55	13 8 47	0♒20	20 15	28 24	18 13	28 42	15 56	22 36	11 35	12 40
I 4	12 48 52	14 7 54	12 12	21 47	29 27	18 17	28 44	15 55	22 38	11 33	12 39
L 5	12 52 48	15 6 59	24 4	23 21	0♊29	18 21	28 46	15 53	22 40	11 32	12 38
6	12 56 45	16 6 2	6♓ 1	24 56	1 32	18 26	28 48	15 52	22 41	11 30	12 38
7	13 0 41	17 5 3	18 4	26 32	2 34	18 32	28 50	15 51	22 43	11 29	12 37
8	13 4 38	18 4 3	0♈16	28 10	3 35	18 38	28 51	15 50	22 45	11 27	12 37
9	13 8 34	19 3 0	12 39	29 50	4 37	18 45	28 53	15 49	22 47	11 25	12 37
10	13 12 31	20 1 55	25 14	1♈31	5 37	18 52	28 54	15 48	22 49	11 24	12 36
11	13 16 27	21 0 49	8♉ 2	3 13	6 38	19 0	28 55	15 47	22 51	11 22	12 36
12	13 20 24	21 59 40	21 2	4 58	7 38	19 9	28 55	15 47	22 53	11 20	12 35
13	13 24 20	22 58 30	4♊15	6 43	8 38	19 18	28 56	15 46	22 55	11 19	12 35
14	13 28 17	23 57 17	17 40	8 30	9 37	19 28	28 56	15 46	22 58	11 17	12 35
15	13 32 14	24 56 2	1♋19	10 19	10 36	19 39	28R56	15 46	23 0	11 16	12 34
16	13 36 10	25 54 45	15 11	12 9	11 34	19 50	28 56	15 45	23 2	11 14	12 34
17	13 40 7	26 53 25	29 15	14 1	12 32	20 1	28 56	15D45	23 4	11 12	12 34
18	13 44 3	27 52 3	13♌30	15 55	13 30	20 13	28 56	15 45	23 7	11 11	12 34
19	13 48 0	28 50 39	27 53	17 50	14 27	20 26	28 55	15 46	23 9	11 9	12 34
20	13 51 56	29 49 13	12♍21	19 46	15 23	20 39	28 54	15 46	23 11	11 8	12 33
21	13 55 53	0♉47 44	26 50	21 44	16 19	20 53	28 53	15 46	23 14	11 6	12 33
22	13 59 49	1 46 13	11♎13	23 44	17 14	21 7	28 52	15 47	23 16	11 5	12 33
23	14 3 46	2 44 41	25 25	25 45	18 9	21 22	28 51	15 47	23 19	11 3	12 33
24	14 7 43	3 43 6	9♏22	27 48	19 3	21 37	28 49	15 48	23 22	11 2	12D33
25	14 11 39	4 41 30	23 1	29 51	19 57	21 52	28 48	15 49	23 24	11 0	12 33
26	14 15 36	5 39 52	6♐19	1♉57	20 50	22 8	28 46	15 50	23 27	10 59	12 33
27	14 19 32	6 38 12	19 16	4 3	21 42	22 25	28 44	15 51	23 29	10 57	12 33
28	14 23 29	7 36 31	1♑54	6 10	22 34	22 42	28 42	15 52	23 32	10 56	12 33
29	14 27 25	8 34 48	14 14	8 19	23 25	22 59	28 39	15 53	23 35	10 54	12 33
30	14 31 22	9♉33 3	26♑22	10♉27	24♊15	23♌17	28♐37	15♌54	23♊38	10♎53	12♌34

THE SUN ENTERS THE SIGN OF TAURUS ON APR 20 AT 04:25.

DAY	TIME	☉	☽	☿	♀	♂	♃	♄	♅	♆	♇
	h m s	° ' "	° '	° '	° '	° '	° '	° '	° '	° '	° '
M 1	14 35 19	10♉31 18	8♒20	12♉37	25♊ 5	23♌35	28♐34	15♌56	23♊40	10♎52	12♌34
A 2	14 39 15	11 29 30	20 13	14 46	25 53	23 53	28R31	15 57	23 43	10R50	12 34
Y 3	14 43 12	12 27 41	2♓ 7	16 56	26 41	24 12	28 28	15 59	23 46	10 49	12 34
4	14 47 8	13 25 50	14 5	19 5	27 28	24 32	28 24	16 1	23 49	10 47	12 34
5	14 51 5	14 23 58	26 11	21 14	28 15	24 51	28 21	16 2	23 52	10 46	12 35
6	14 55 1	15 22 5	8♈30	23 22	29 0	25 11	28 17	16 4	23 55	10 45	12 35
7	14 58 58	16 20 10	21 3	25 28	29 45	25 32	28 13	16 6	23 58	10 44	12 35
8	15 2 54	17 18 13	3♉52	27 33	0♋28	25 53	28 9	16 9	24 1	10 42	12 36
9	15 6 51	18 16 15	16 59	29 36	1 11	26 14	28 5	16 11	24 4	10 41	12 36
10	15 10 47	19 14 16	0♊22	1♊38	1 52	26 35	28 1	16 13	24 7	10 40	12 36
11	15 14 44	20 12 15	14 1	3 37	2 33	26 57	27 56	16 16	24 10	10 39	12 37
12	15 18 41	21 10 12	27 53	5 33	3 12	27 19	27 52	16 18	24 13	10 37	12 37
13	15 22 37	22 8 7	11♋55	7 27	3 50	27 42	27 47	16 21	24 16	10 36	12 38
14	15 26 34	23 6 1	26 4	9 18	4 27	28 5	27 42	16 24	24 19	10 35	12 38
15	15 30 30	24 3 53	10♌17	11 6	5 3	28 28	27 37	16 26	24 23	10 34	12 39
16	15 34 27	25 1 43	24 31	12 52	5 37	28 51	27 31	16 29	24 26	10 33	12 39
17	15 38 23	25 59 31	8♍44	14 34	6 10	29 15	27 26	16 32	24 29	10 32	12 40
18	15 42 20	26 57 18	22 53	16 12	6 42	29 39	27 21	16 35	24 32	10 31	12 41
19	15 46 17	27 55 3	6♎56	17 48	7 12	0♍ 3	27 15	16 39	24 36	10 30	12 41
20	15 50 13	28 52 46	20 51	19 20	7 40	0 28	27 9	16 42	24 39	10 29	12 42
21	15 54 10	29 50 28	4♏36	20 49	8 7	0 53	27 3	16 45	24 42	10 28	12 43
22	15 58 6	0♊48 8	18 8	22 14	8 33	1 18	26 57	16 49	24 46	10 27	12 43
23	16 2 3	1 45 47	1♐27	23 36	8 56	1 43	26 51	16 52	24 49	10 26	12 44
24	16 5 59	2 43 25	14 30	24 55	9 18	2 8	26 45	16 56	24 52	10 25	12 45
25	16 9 56	3 41 1	27 18	26 10	9 39	2 34	26 38	17 0	24 56	10 24	12 46
26	16 13 52	4 38 37	9♑50	27 21	9 57	3 0	26 32	17 4	24 59	10 24	12 46
27	16 17 49	5 36 11	22 9	28 28	10 13	3 27	26 25	17 8	25 2	10 23	12 47
28	16 21 46	6 33 45	4♒16	29 32	10 28	3 53	26 19	17 12	25 6	10 22	12 48
29	16 25 42	7 31 17	16 14	0♋32	10 40	4 20	26 12	17 16	25 9	10 21	12 49
30	16 29 39	8 28 49	28 8	1 29	10 50	4 47	26 5	17 20	25 13	10 21	12 50
31	16 33 35	9♊26 20	10♓ 1	2♋21	10♋58	5♍14	25♐58	17♌24	25♊16	10♎20	12♌51

THE SUN ENTERS THE SIGN OF GEMINI ON MAY 21 AT 03:58.

DAY	TIME	☉	☽	☿	♀	♂	♃	♄	♅	♆	♇
	h m s	° ' "	° '	° '	° '	° '	° '	° '	° '	° '	° '
J 1	16 37 32	10♊23 50	21♓59	3♋ 9	11♋ 4	5♍42	25♐51	17♌29	25♊20	10♎19	12♌52
U 2	16 41 28	11 21 19	4♈ 6	3 54	11 8	6 9	25R44	17 33	25 23	10R19	12 53
N 3	16 45 25	12 18 47	16 26	4 34	11R 9	6 37	25 36	17 38	25 27	10 18	12 54
E 4	16 49 21	13 16 15	29 5	5 9	11 8	7 5	25 29	17 42	25 30	10 18	12 55
5	16 53 18	14 13 42	12♉ 3	5 41	11 5	7 34	25 22	17 47	25 34	10 17	12 56
6	16 57 15	15 11 8	25 24	6 8	10 59	8 2	25 14	17 52	25 37	10 16	12 57
7	17 1 11	16 8 34	9♊ 7	6 31	10 51	8 31	25 7	17 56	25 41	10 16	12 58
8	17 5 8	17 5 58	23 11	6 49	10 40	9 0	24 59	18 1	25 44	10 16	12 59
9	17 9 4	18 3 22	7♋30	7 2	10 28	9 29	24 52	18 6	25 48	10 15	13 0
10	17 13 1	19 0 45	22 0	7 11	10 12	9 58	24 44	18 11	25 51	10 15	13 1
11	17 16 57	19 58 7	6♌33	7R16	9 55	10 28	24 37	18 17	25 55	10 14	13 3
12	17 20 54	20 55 28	21 5	7 16	9 35	10 57	24 29	18 22	25 59	10 14	13 4
13	17 24 50	21 52 48	5♍30	7 11	9 12	11 27	24 22	18 27	26 2	10 14	13 5
14	17 28 47	22 50 7	19 43	7 2	8 48	11 57	24 14	18 32	26 6	10 14	13 6
15	17 32 44	23 47 25	3♎44	6 49	8 22	12 27	24 6	18 38	26 9	10 13	13 7
16	17 36 40	24 44 42	17 32	6 32	7 53	12 58	23 59	18 43	26 13	10 13	13 9
17	17 40 37	25 41 59	1♏ 5	6 11	7 23	13 28	23 51	18 49	26 16	10 13	13 10
18	17 44 33	26 39 14	14 26	5 47	6 51	13 59	23 43	18 54	26 20	10 13	13 11
19	17 48 30	27 36 29	27 34	5 19	6 18	14 30	23 36	19 0	26 24	10 13	13 13
20	17 52 26	28 33 43	10♐31	4 49	5 43	15 1	23 28	19 6	26 27	10 13	13 14
21	17 56 23	29 30 57	23 15	4 17	5 8	15 32	23 20	19 12	26 31	10D13	13 15
22	18 0 19	0♋28 10	5♑48	3 44	4 31	16 3	23 13	19 17	26 34	10 13	13 17
23	18 4 16	1 25 23	18 11	3 9	3 54	16 35	23 5	19 23	26 38	10 13	13 18
24	18 8 13	2 22 36	0♒22	2 34	3 16	17 7	22 58	19 29	26 41	10 13	13 20
25	18 12 9	3 19 48	12 25	1 59	2 39	17 38	22 50	19 35	26 45	10 13	13 21
26	18 16 6	4 17 0	24 22	1 25	2 1	18 10	22 43	19 41	26 49	10 13	13 23
27	18 20 2	5 14 12	6♓14	0 52	1 24	18 42	22 36	19 48	26 52	10 13	13 24
28	18 23 59	6 11 24	18 6	0 22	0 47	19 14	22 28	19 54	26 56	10 13	13 26
29	18 27 55	7 8 37	0♈ 2	29♊53	0 12	19 47	22 21	20 0	26 59	10 14	13 27
30	18 31 52	8♋ 5 49	12♈ 7	29♊28	29♊37	20♍19	22♐14	20♌ 6	27♊ 3	10♎14	13♌29

THE SUN ENTERS THE SIGN OF CANCER ON JUN 21 AT 12:11.

♏ SCORPIO ♐ SAGITTARIUS ♑ CAPRICORN ♒ AQUARIUS ♓ PISCES

SIDEREAL | SUN. | MOON. | MERCURY. | VENUS. | MARS. | JUPITER. | SATURN. | URANUS. | NEPTUNE. | PLUTO.

DAY	TIME	☉	☽	☿	♀	♂	♃	♄	♅	♆	♇
	h m s	° ' "	° '	° '	° '	° '	° '	° '	° '	° '	° '
J 1	18 35 49	9♋ 3 1	24♈26	29♊ 6	29♊ 3	20♍52	22♐ 7	20♌13	27♊ 6	10♎14	13♌30
U 2	18 39 45	10 0 14	7♉ 3	28R47	28R31	21 25	22R 0	20 19	27 10	10 15	13 32
L 3	18 43 42	10 57 26	20 4	28 33	28 1	21 58	21 53	20 26	27 13	10 15	13 33
Y 4	18 47 38	11 54 39	3♊31	28 23	27 32	22 31	21 46	20 32	27 17	10 15	13 35
5	18 51 35	12 51 53	17 25	28D18	27 6	23 4	21 39	20 39	27 20	10 16	13 36
6	18 55 31	13 49 6	1♋44	28 18	26 41	23 37	21 33	20 45	27 24	10 16	13 38
7	18 59 28	14 46 20	16 25	28 23	26 18	24 11	21 26	20 52	27 27	10 17	13 40
8	19 3 24	15 43 33	1♌19	28 33	25 58	24 44	21 20	20 59	27 31	10 17	13 41
9	19 7 21	16 40 47	16 18	28 48	25 40	25 18	21 14	21 5	27 34	10 18	13 43
10	19 11 18	17 38 1	1♍12	29 8	25 24	25 52	21 7	21 12	27 38	10 18	13 44
11	19 15 14	18 35 14	15 53	29 34	25 10	26 26	21 1	21 19	27 41	10 19	13 46
12	19 19 11	19 32 27	0♎17	0♋ 4	24 59	27 0	20 55	21 26	27 44	10 20	13 48
13	19 23 7	20 29 41	14 20	0 40	24 50	27 34	20 49	21 33	27 48	10 20	13 49
14	19 27 4	21 26 54	28 3	1 21	24 44	28 8	20 44	21 40	27 51	10 21	13 51
15	19 31 0	22 24 7	11♏26	2 7	24 40	28 43	20 38	21 47	27 54	10 22	13 53
16	19 34 57	23 21 21	24 31	2 59	24D38	29 17	20 33	21 54	27 58	10 22	13 55
17	19 38 53	24 18 35	7♐22	3 55	24 39	29 52	20 28	22 1	28 1	10 23	13 56
18	19 42 50	25 15 49	20 0	4 56	24 42	0♎27	20 22	22 8	28 4	10 24	13 58
19	19 46 47	26 13 3	2♑28	6 2	24 47	1 2	20 17	22 15	28 8	10 25	14 0
20	19 50 43	27 10 17	14 47	7 13	24 54	1 37	20 13	22 22	28 11	10 26	14 1
21	19 54 40	28 7 32	26 57	8 29	25 4	2 12	20 8	22 29	28 14	10 27	14 3
22	19 58 36	29 4 48	9♒ 1	9 49	25 15	2 47	20 3	22 37	28 17	10 28	14 5
23	20 2 33	0♌ 2 4	20 58	11 14	25 29	3 23	19 59	22 44	28 20	10 29	14 7
24	20 6 29	0 59 21	2♓51	12 43	25 45	3 58	19 55	22 51	28 24	10 30	14 9
25	20 10 26	1 56 38	14 42	14 17	26 2	4 34	19 51	22 58	28 27	10 31	14 10
26	20 14 22	2 53 57	26 33	15 54	26 22	5 9	19 47	23 6	28 30	10 32	14 12
27	20 18 19	3 51 16	8♈28	17 35	26 43	5 45	19 43	23 13	28 33	10 33	14 14
28	20 22 16	4 48 36	20 32	19 21	27 6	6 21	19 40	23 20	28 36	10 34	14 16
29	20 26 12	5 45 57	2♉48	21 9	27 30	6 57	19 36	23 28	28 39	10 35	14 17
30	20 30 9	6 43 19	15 22	23 0	27 57	7 33	19 33	23 35	28 42	10 36	14 19
31	20 34 5	7♌40 43	28♉20	24♋55	28♊25	8♎ 9	19♐30	23♌43	28♊45	10♎38	14♌21

THE SUN ENTERS THE SIGN OF LEO ON JUL 22 AT 23:08.

DAY	TIME	☉	☽	☿	♀	♂	♃	♄	♅	♆	♇
	h m s	° ' "	° '	° '	° '	° '	° '	° '	° '	° '	° '
A 1	20 38 2	8♌38 8	11♊45	26♋51	28♊54	8♎45	19♐27	23♌50	28♊48	10♎39	14♌23
U 2	20 41 58	9 35 33	25 39	28 50	29 25	9 22	19R24	23 58	28 51	10 40	14 25
G 3	20 45 55	10 33 0	10♋ 2	0♌51	29 57	9 58	19 22	24 5	28 54	10 41	14 26
U 4	20 49 51	11 30 28	24 51	2 53	0♋30	10 35	19 20	24 13	28 57	10 43	14 28
S 5	20 53 48	12 27 58	9♌57	4 56	1 5	11 12	19 17	24 20	29 0	10 44	14 30
T 6	20 57 45	13 25 28	25 12	7 0	1 41	11 48	19 15	24 28	29 2	10 45	14 32
7	21 1 41	14 22 58	10♍24	9 4	2 19	12 25	19 14	24 35	29 5	10 47	14 34
8	21 5 38	15 20 30	25 23	11 8	2 57	13 2	19 12	24 43	29 8	10 48	14 36
9	21 9 34	16 18 3	10♎ 1	13 12	3 37	13 39	19 11	24 50	29 11	10 50	14 37
10	21 13 31	17 15 36	24 14	15 16	4 17	14 17	19 9	24 58	29 13	10 51	14 39
11	21 17 27	18 13 11	8♏ 1	17 19	4 59	14 54	19 8	25 6	29 16	10 53	14 41
12	21 21 24	19 10 46	21 23	19 22	5 41	15 31	19 8	25 13	29 18	10 54	14 43
13	21 25 20	20 8 22	4♐24	21 23	6 25	16 9	19 7	25 21	29 21	10 56	14 45
14	21 29 17	21 5 59	17 6	23 24	7 9	16 46	19 6	25 29	29 24	10 57	14 46
15	21 33 14	22 3 37	29 33	25 23	7 55	17 24	19 6	25 36	29 26	10 59	14 48
16	21 37 10	23 1 16	11♑50	27 21	8 41	18 2	19D 6	25 44	29 28	11 0	14 50
17	21 41 7	23 58 57	23 57	29 18	9 28	18 40	19 6	25 51	29 31	11 2	14 52
18	21 45 3	24 56 38	5♒58	1♍13	10 16	19 18	19 6	25 59	29 33	11 4	14 54
19	21 49 0	25 54 21	17 55	3 7	11 4	19 56	19 7	26 7	29 36	11 5	14 55
20	21 52 56	26 52 5	29 48	5 0	11 54	20 34	19 7	26 14	29 38	11 7	14 57
21	21 56 53	27 49 50	11♓40	6 52	12 44	21 12	19 8	26 22	29 40	11 9	14 59
22	22 0 49	28 47 37	23 31	8 42	13 35	21 50	19 9	26 30	29 42	11 11	15 1
23	22 4 46	29 45 25	5♈24	10 30	14 26	22 29	19 11	26 37	29 45	11 12	15 2
24	22 8 43	0♍43 15	17 22	12 18	15 18	23 7	19 12	26 45	29 47	11 14	15 4
25	22 12 39	1 41 7	29 28	14 4	16 11	23 46	19 13	26 53	29 49	11 16	15 6
26	22 16 36	2 39 0	11♉45	15 48	17 4	24 25	19 15	27 0	29 51	11 18	15 8
27	22 20 32	3 36 56	24 18	17 31	17 58	25 3	19 17	27 8	29 53	11 20	15 9
28	22 24 29	4 34 53	7♊13	19 13	18 53	25 42	19 19	27 15	29 55	11 21	15 11
29	22 28 25	5 32 52	20 32	20 54	19 48	26 21	19 22	27 23	29 57	11 23	15 13
30	22 32 22	6 30 53	4♋19	22 34	20 44	27 0	19 24	27 31	29 59	11 25	15 15
31	22 36 18	7♍28 56	18♋35	24♍12	21♋40	27♎39	19♐27	27♌38	0♋ 1	11♎27	15♌16

THE SUN ENTERS THE SIGN OF VIRGO ON AUG 23 AT 06:04.

DAY	TIME	☉	☽	☿	♀	♂	♃	♄	♅	♆	♇
	h m s	° ' "	° '	° '	° '	° '	° '	° '	° '	° '	° '
S 1	22 40 15	8♍27 0	3♌17	25♍49	22♋37	28♎18	19♐30	27♌46	0♋ 2	11♎29	15♌18
E 2	22 44 12	9 25 7	18 21	27 24	23 34	28 58	19 33	27 53	0 4	11 31	15 20
P 3	22 48 8	10 23 15	3♍36	28 59	24 31	29 37	19 36	28 1	0 6	11 33	15 21
T 4	22 52 5	11 21 25	18 53	0♎32	25 29	0♏16	19 39	28 8	0 8	11 35	15 23
E 5	22 56 1	12 19 37	4♎ 1	2 4	26 28	0 56	19 43	28 16	0 9	11 37	15 25
M 6	22 59 58	13 17 50	18 49	3 34	27 27	1 36	19 46	28 23	0 11	11 39	15 26
B 7	23 3 54	14 16 5	3♏13	5 4	28 26	2 15	19 50	28 31	0 12	11 41	15 28
E 8	23 7 51	15 14 21	17 9	6 32	29 26	2 55	19 54	28 38	0 14	11 43	15 30
R 9	23 11 47	16 12 39	0♐38	7 59	0♌26	3 35	19 59	28 46	0 15	11 45	15 31
10	23 15 44	17 10 58	13 41	9 25	1 26	4 15	20 3	28 53	0 17	11 47	15 33
11	23 19 41	18 9 19	26 23	10 49	2 27	4 55	20 8	29 1	0 18	11 49	15 34
12	23 23 37	19 7 42	8♑47	12 12	3 28	5 35	20 12	29 8	0 19	11 51	15 36
13	23 27 34	20 6 6	20 59	13 34	4 30	6 15	20 17	29 15	0 20	11 53	15 38
14	23 31 30	21 4 32	3♒ 0	14 55	5 32	6 56	20 22	29 23	0 22	11 55	15 39
15	23 35 27	22 2 59	14 56	16 14	6 34	7 36	20 28	29 30	0 23	11 58	15 41
16	23 39 23	23 1 28	26 49	17 31	7 37	8 17	20 33	29 37	0 24	12 0	15 42
17	23 43 20	23 59 59	8♓40	18 47	8 39	8 57	20 39	29 44	0 25	12 2	15 44
18	23 47 16	24 58 32	20 33	20 2	9 43	9 38	20 44	29 51	0 26	12 4	15 45
19	23 51 13	25 57 6	2♈28	21 14	10 46	10 18	20 50	29 59	0 27	12 6	15 47
20	23 55 10	26 55 43	14 28	22 25	11 50	10 59	20 56	0♍ 6	0 28	12 8	15 48
21	23 59 6	27 54 22	26 34	23 35	12 54	11 40	21 2	0 13	0 29	12 10	15 50
22	0 3 3	28 53 2	8♉48	24 42	13 58	12 21	21 9	0 20	0 29	12 13	15 51
23	0 6 59	29 51 45	21 14	25 47	15 3	13 2	21 15	0 27	0 30	12 15	15 52
24	0 10 56	0♎50 30	3♊54	26 50	16 8	13 43	21 22	0 34	0 31	12 17	15 54
25	0 14 52	1 49 18	16 50	27 50	17 13	14 24	21 29	0 41	0 31	12 19	15 55
26	0 18 49	2 48 8	0♋ 8	28 48	18 18	15 6	21 36	0 48	0 32	12 21	15 56
27	0 22 45	3 47 0	13 48	29 44	19 24	15 47	21 43	0 55	0 32	12 24	15 58
28	0 26 42	4 45 54	27 52	0♏36	20 30	16 28	21 50	1 1	0 33	12 26	15 59
29	0 30 39	5 44 51	12♌19	1 25	21 36	17 10	21 57	1 8	0 33	12 28	16 0
30	0 34 35	6♎43 49	27♌ 5	2♏11	22♌42	17♏51	22♐ 5	1♍15	0♋34	12♎30	16♌ 2

THE SUN ENTERS THE SIGN OF LIBRA ON SEP 23 AT 03:23.

♈ ARIES ♉ TAURUS ♊ GEMINI ♋ CANCER ♌ LEO ♍ VIRGO ♎ LIBRA

1948

SIDEREAL TIME. SUN. MOON. MERCURY. VENUS. MARS. JUPITER. SATURN. URANUS. NEPTUNE. PLUTO.

DAY	TIME	☉	☽	☿	♀	♂	♃	♄	♅	♆	♇
	h m s	° ' "	° '	° '	° '	° '	° '	° '	° '	° '	° '
O 1	0 38 32	7♎42 51	12♍ 5	2♏52	23♌49	18♏33	22♐12	1♍22	0♋34	12♎33	16♌ 3
C 2	0 42 28	8 41 54	27 10	3 30	24 56	19 15	22 20	1 28	0 34	12 35	16 4
T 3	0 46 25	9 40 59	12♎11	4 3	26 3	19 57	22 28	1 35	0 35	12 37	16 5
O 4	0 50 21	10 40 6	26 58	4 31	27 10	20 38	22 36	1 41	0 35	12 39	16 6
B 5	0 54 18	11 39 16	11♏25	4 54	28 17	21 20	22 44	1 48	0 35	12 41	16 8
E 6	0 58 14	12 38 27	25 28	5 11	29 25	22 2	22 53	1 54	0R35	12 44	16 9
R 7	1 2 11	13 37 40	9♐ 4	5 21	0♍33	22 45	23 1	2 1	0 35	12 46	16 10
8	1 6 8	14 36 55	22 14	5R25	1 41	23 27	23 10	2 7	0 35	12 48	16 11
9	1 10 4	15 36 12	5♑ 0	5 22	2 49	24 9	23 18	2 13	0 35	12 50	16 12
10	1 14 1	16 35 30	17 27	5 11	3 57	24 51	23 27	2 19	0 34	12 53	16 13
11	1 17 57	17 34 51	29 39	4 52	5 6	25 34	23 36	2 26	0 34	12 55	16 14
12	1 21 54	18 34 13	11♒39	4 25	6 14	26 16	23 45	2 32	0 34	12 57	16 15
13	1 25 50	19 33 37	23 33	3 50	7 23	26 59	23 54	2 38	0 34	12 59	16 16
14	1 29 47	20 33 2	5♓24	3 6	8 32	27 41	24 4	2 44	0 33	13 2	16 17
15	1 33 43	21 32 30	17 16	2 14	9 41	28 24	24 13	2 50	0 33	13 4	16 18
16	1 37 40	22 31 59	29 12	1 15	10 51	29 7	24 23	2 56	0 32	13 6	16 19
17	1 41 36	23 31 30	11♈14	0 10	12 0	29 50	24 32	3 1	0 32	13 8	16 20
18	1 45 33	24 31 3	23 24	29♎ 0	13 10	0♐33	24 42	3 7	0 31	13 10	16 21
19	1 49 30	25 30 39	5♉43	27 47	14 20	1 16	24 52	3 13	0 31	13 13	16 21
20	1 53 26	26 30 16	18 14	26 32	15 30	1 59	25 2	3 18	0 30	13 15	16 22
21	1 57 23	27 29 55	0♊56	25 18	16 40	2 42	25 12	3 24	0 29	13 17	16 23
22	2 1 19	28 29 37	13 52	24 8	17 50	3 25	25 22	3 29	0 28	13 19	16 24
23	2 5 16	29 29 21	27 1	23 2	19 1	4 8	25 33	3 35	0 28	13 21	16 25
24	2 9 12	0♏29 7	10♋26	22 4	20 11	4 52	25 43	3 40	0 27	13 23	16 25
25	2 13 9	1 28 56	24 7	21 15	21 22	5 35	25 53	3 45	0 26	13 26	16 26
26	2 17 5	2 28 46	8♌ 4	20 36	22 33	6 18	26 4	3 50	0 25	13 28	16 27
27	2 21 2	3 28 39	22 16	20 8	23 44	7 2	26 15	3 56	0 24	13 30	16 27
28	2 24 59	4 28 34	6♍42	19D51	24 55	7 46	26 26	4 1	0 23	13 32	16 28
29	2 28 55	5 28 32	21 17	19 46	26 6	8 29	26 36	4 5	0 22	13 34	16 28
30	2 32 52	6 28 31	5♎57	19 52	27 17	9 13	26 47	4 10	0 20	13 36	16 29
31	2 36 48	7♏28 33	20♎35	20♎ 8	28♍28	9♐57	26♐58	4♍15	0♋19	13♎38	16♌29

THE SUN ENTERS THE SIGN OF SCORPIO ON OCT 23 AT 12:19.

DAY	TIME	☉	☽	☿	♀	♂	♃	♄	♅	♆	♇
	h m s	° ' "	° '	° '	° '	° '	° '	° '	° '	° '	° '
N 1	2 40 45	8♏28 36	5♏ 6	20♎35	29♍40	10♐41	27♐10	4♍20	0♋18	13♎40	16♌30
O 2	2 44 41	9 28 41	19 23	21 11	0♎52	11 25	27 21	4 24	0R17	13 42	16 30
V 3	2 48 38	10 28 49	3♐21	21 56	2 3	12 9	27 32	4 29	0 15	13 45	16 31
E 4	2 52 34	11 28 58	16 58	22 47	3 15	12 53	27 44	4 33	0 14	13 47	16 31
M 5	2 56 31	12 29 9	0♑11	23 46	4 27	13 37	27 55	4 38	0 12	13 49	16 32
B 6	3 0 28	13 29 21	13 2	24 50	5 39	14 21	28 7	4 42	0 11	13 51	16 32
E 7	3 4 24	14 29 35	25 32	26 0	6 51	15 6	28 18	4 46	0 9	13 53	16 32
R 8	3 8 21	15 29 50	7♒46	27 14	8 4	15 50	28 30	4 50	0 8	13 55	16 33
9	3 12 17	16 30 7	19 48	28 31	9 16	16 34	28 42	4 54	0 6	13 57	16 33
10	3 16 14	17 30 25	1♓42	29 52	10 28	17 19	28 54	4 58	0 4	13 59	16 33
11	3 20 10	18 30 45	13 33	1♏15	11 41	18 3	29 6	5 2	0 3	14 0	16 33
12	3 24 7	19 31 6	25 25	2 41	12 53	18 48	29 18	5 6	0 1	14 2	16 33
13	3 28 3	20 31 28	7♈24	4 9	14 6	19 33	29 30	5 9	29♊59	14 4	16 34
14	3 32 0	21 31 52	19 31	5 38	15 19	20 17	29 42	5 13	29 57	14 6	16 34
15	3 35 57	22 32 18	1♉52	7 8	16 31	21 2	29 55	5 16	29 56	14 8	16 34
16	3 39 53	23 32 45	14 26	8 39	17 44	21 47	0♑ 7	5 20	29 54	14 10	16 34
17	3 43 50	24 33 14	27 16	10 11	18 57	22 32	0 19	5 23	29 52	14 12	16R34
18	3 47 46	25 33 44	10♊22	11 44	20 10	23 17	0 32	5 26	29 50	14 13	16 34
19	3 51 43	26 34 16	23 42	13 17	21 23	24 2	0 44	5 29	29 48	14 15	16 34
20	3 55 39	27 34 49	7♋16	14 51	22 37	24 47	0 57	5 32	29 46	14 17	16 34
21	3 59 36	28 35 25	21 1	16 25	23 50	25 32	1 9	5 35	29 44	14 19	16 34
22	4 3 33	29 36 2	4♌55	17 59	25 3	26 17	1 22	5 38	29 42	14 20	16 34
23	4 7 29	0♐36 40	18 56	19 34	26 17	27 2	1 35	5 41	29 39	14 22	16 34
24	4 11 26	1 37 20	3♍ 3	21 8	27 30	27 48	1 48	5 43	29 37	14 24	16 33
25	4 15 22	2 38 2	17 14	22 42	28 44	28 33	2 1	5 46	29 35	14 25	16 33
26	4 19 19	3 38 46	1♎27	24 17	29 57	29 18	2 14	5 48	29 33	14 27	16 33
27	4 23 15	4 39 31	15 39	25 51	1♏11	0♑ 4	2 27	5 50	29 31	14 29	16 33
28	4 27 12	5 40 18	29 49	27 26	2 25	0 49	2 40	5 52	29 28	14 30	16 32
29	4 31 8	6 41 6	13♏52	29 0	3 38	1 35	2 53	5 54	29 26	14 32	16 32
30	4 35 5	7♐41 56	27♏47	0♐35	4♏52	2♑21	3♑ 6	5♍56	29♊24	14♎33	16♌32

THE SUN ENTERS THE SIGN OF SAGITTARIUS ON NOV 22 AT 09:30.

DAY	TIME	☉	☽	☿	♀	♂	♃	♄	♅	♆	♇
	h m s	° ' "	° '	° '	° '	° '	° '	° '	° '	° '	° '
D 1	4 39 2	8♐42 47	11♐28	2♐ 9	6♏ 6	3♑ 6	3♑19	5♍58	29♊21	14♎35	16♌31
E 2	4 42 58	9 43 39	24 53	3 43	7 20	3 52	3 32	6 0	29R19	14 36	16R31
C 3	4 46 55	10 44 32	8♑ 1	5 18	8 34	4 38	3 45	6 1	29 17	14 38	16 31
E 4	4 50 51	11 45 26	20 50	6 52	9 48	5 24	3 59	6 3	29 14	14 39	16 30
M 5	4 54 48	12 46 21	3♒20	8 26	11 2	6 9	4 12	6 4	29 12	14 40	16 30
B 6	4 58 44	13 47 17	15 35	10 0	12 16	6 55	4 25	6 6	29 9	14 42	16 29
E 7	5 2 41	14 48 14	27 38	11 34	13 30	7 41	4 39	6 7	29 7	14 43	16 29
R 8	5 6 37	15 49 11	9♓31	13 9	14 44	8 27	4 52	6 8	29 4	14 44	16 28
9	5 10 34	16 50 9	21 21	14 43	15 58	9 13	5 6	6 9	29 2	14 46	16 28
10	5 14 31	17 51 7	3♈13	16 17	17 13	10 0	5 19	6 10	28 59	14 47	16 27
11	5 18 27	18 52 6	15 11	17 51	18 27	10 46	5 33	6 10	28 57	14 48	16 26
12	5 22 24	19 53 6	27 21	19 26	19 41	11 32	5 46	6 11	28 54	14 49	16 26
13	5 26 20	20 54 6	9♉47	21 0	20 56	12 18	6 0	6 11	28 52	14 50	16 25
14	5 30 17	21 55 7	22 32	22 34	22 10	13 4	6 14	6 12	28 49	14 52	16 24
15	5 34 13	22 56 9	5♊39	24 9	23 24	13 51	6 27	6 12	28 47	14 53	16 24
16	5 38 10	23 57 11	19 6	25 44	24 39	14 37	6 41	6 12	28 44	14 54	16 23
17	5 42 6	24 58 14	2♋53	27 18	25 53	15 23	6 55	6R12	28 42	14 55	16 22
18	5 46 3	25 59 18	16 56	28 53	27 8	16 10	7 8	6 12	28 39	14 56	16 21
19	5 50 0	27 0 22	1♌ 9	0♑29	28 22	16 56	7 22	6 12	28 36	14 57	16 21
20	5 53 56	28 1 27	15 29	2 4	29 37	17 43	7 36	6 12	28 34	14 58	16 20
21	5 57 53	29 2 33	29 48	3 39	0♐51	18 29	7 50	6 11	28 31	14 59	16 19
22	6 1 49	0♑ 3 40	14♍ 5	5 15	2 6	19 16	8 4	6 11	28 29	15 0	16 18
23	6 5 46	1 4 47	28 15	6 51	3 21	20 3	8 17	6 10	28 26	15 0	16 17
24	6 9 42	2 5 55	12♎17	8 27	4 35	20 49	8 31	6 10	28 24	15 1	16 16
25	6 13 39	3 7 3	26 10	10 3	5 50	21 36	8 45	6 9	28 21	15 2	16 15
26	6 17 35	4 8 12	9♏56	11 40	7 5	22 23	8 59	6 8	28 18	15 3	16 14
27	6 21 32	5 9 22	23 32	13 16	8 19	23 10	9 13	6 7	28 16	15 3	16 13
28	6 25 29	6 10 32	7♐ 0	14 53	9 34	23 56	9 27	6 6	28 13	15 4	16 12
29	6 29 25	7 11 43	20 17	16 30	10 49	24 43	9 41	6 4	28 11	15 5	16 11
30	6 33 22	8 12 54	3♑22	18 7	12 4	25 30	9 55	6 3	28 8	15 5	16 10
31	6 37 18	9♑14 5	16♑15	19♑44	13♐18	26♑17	10♑ 8	6♍ 1	28♊ 6	15♎ 6	16♌ 9

THE SUN ENTERS THE SIGN OF CAPRICORN ON DEC 21 AT 22:34.

♏ SCORPIO ♐ SAGITTARIUS ♑ CAPRICORN ♒ AQUARIUS ♓ PISCES

1949

SIDEREAL · SUN. · MOON. · MERCURY. · VENUS. · MARS. · JUPITER. · SATURN. · URANUS. · NEPTUNE. · PLUTO.

DAY	TIME h m s	☉ ° ' "	☽ ° '	☿ ° '	♀ ° '	♂ ° '	♃ ° '	♄ ° '	♅ ° '	♆ ° '	♇ ° '
J 1	6 41 15	10♑15 17	28♑53	21♑22	14♐33	27♑ 4	10♑22	6♍ 0	28♊ 3	15♎ 6	16♌ 8
A 2	6 45 11	11 16 28	11♒18	22 59	15 48	27 51	10 36	5R58	28R 1	15 7	16R 7
N 3	6 49 8	12 17 39	23 29	24 36	17 3	28 38	10 50	5 56	27 58	15 7	16 6
U 4	6 53 5	13 18 49	5♓30	26 12	18 18	29 25	11 4	5 54	27 56	15 8	16 5
A 5	6 57 1	14 20 0	17 22	27 49	19 33	0♒12	11 18	5 52	27 53	15 8	16 3
R 6	7 0 58	15 21 10	29 10	29 25	20 48	0 59	11 32	5 50	27 51	15 9	16 2
Y 7	7 4 54	16 22 20	11♈ 0	1♒ 0	22 2	1 46	11 46	5 48	27 48	15 9	16 1
8	7 8 51	17 23 29	22 56	2 34	23 17	2 33	12 0	5 46	27 46	15 9	16 0
9	7 12 47	18 24 38	5♉ 3	4 8	24 32	3 21	12 14	5 43	27 44	15 10	15 59
10	7 16 44	19 25 46	17 28	5 40	25 47	4 8	12 27	5 41	27 41	15 10	15 57
11	7 20 40	20 26 54	0♊16	7 10	27 2	4 55	12 41	5 38	27 39	15 10	15 56
12	7 24 37	21 28 2	13 28	8 39	28 17	5 42	12 55	5 36	27 37	15 10	15 55
13	7 28 34	22 29 8	27 8	10 5	29 32	6 29	13 9	5 33	27 34	15 10	15 54
14	7 32 30	23 30 15	11♋13	11 28	0♑47	7 17	13 23	5 30	27 32	15 10	15 52
15	7 36 27	24 31 21	25 39	12 47	2 2	8 4	13 37	5 27	27 30	15 11	15 51
16	7 40 23	25 32 26	10♌21	14 3	3 17	8 51	13 50	5 24	27 28	15R11	15 50
17	7 44 20	26 33 31	25 9	15 14	4 32	9 38	14 4	5 21	27 26	15 11	15 48
18	7 48 16	27 34 35	9♍55	16 19	5 47	10 26	14 18	5 17	27 23	15 11	15 47
19	7 52 13	28 35 39	24 32	17 18	7 2	11 13	14 32	5 14	27 21	15 10	15 46
20	7 56 9	29 36 43	8♎56	18 10	8 17	12 0	14 45	5 11	27 19	15 10	15 44
21	8 0 6	0♒37 46	23 3	18 54	9 32	12 48	14 59	5 7	27 17	15 10	15 43
22	8 4 3	1 38 49	6♏53	19 29	10 46	13 35	15 13	5 4	27 15	15 10	15 42
23	8 7 59	2 39 52	20 27	19 54	12 1	14 23	15 26	5 0	27 13	15 10	15 40
24	8 11 56	3 40 54	3♐47	20R 9	13 16	15 10	15 40	4 56	27 11	15 10	15 39
25	8 15 52	4 41 56	16 53	20 13	14 32	15 57	15 53	4 53	27 9	15 9	15 37
26	8 19 49	5 42 57	29 48	20 5	15 47	16 45	16 7	4 49	27 8	15 9	15 36
27	8 23 45	6 43 58	12♑32	19 46	17 2	17 32	16 21	4 45	27 6	15 9	15 35
28	8 27 42	7 44 57	25 6	19 16	18 17	18 20	16 34	4 41	27 4	15 8	15 33
29	8 31 39	8 45 56	7♒30	18 35	19 32	19 7	16 47	4 37	27 2	15 8	15 32
30	8 35 35	9 46 54	19 43	17 45	20 47	19 55	17 1	4 33	27 1	15 7	15 30
31	8 39 32	10♒47 50	1♓47	16♒46	22♑ 2	20♒42	17♑14	4♍28	26♊59	15♎ 7	15♌29

THE SUN ENTERS THE SIGN OF AQUARIUS ON JAN 20 AT 09:09.

DAY	TIME h m s	☉ ° ' "	☽ ° '	☿ ° '	♀ ° '	♂ ° '	♃ ° '	♄ ° '	♅ ° '	♆ ° '	♇ ° '
F 1	8 43 28	11♒48 46	13♓43	15♒40	23♑17	21♒30	17♑28	4♍24	26♊57	15♎ 6	15♌27
E 2	8 47 25	12 49 40	25 32	14R30	24 32	22 17	17 41	4R20	26R56	15R 6	15R26
B 3	8 51 21	13 50 33	7♈19	13 17	25 47	23 4	17 54	4 16	26 54	15 5	15 25
R 4	8 55 18	14 51 24	19 7	12 4	27 2	23 52	18 7	4 11	26 53	15 5	15 23
U 5	8 59 14	15 52 15	1♉ 1	10 52	28 17	24 39	18 20	4 7	26 51	15 4	15 22
A 6	9 3 11	16 53 3	13 6	9 43	29 32	25 27	18 34	4 2	26 50	15 3	15 20
R 7	9 7 7	17 53 51	25 27	8 39	0♒47	26 14	18 47	3 58	26 48	15 3	15 19
Y 8	9 11 4	18 54 37	8♊10	7 42	2 2	27 2	19 0	3 53	26 47	15 2	15 17
9	9 15 1	19 55 21	21 19	6 51	3 17	27 49	19 13	3 48	26 46	15 1	15 16
10	9 18 57	20 56 4	4♋57	6 8	4 31	28 37	19 26	3 44	26 45	15 0	15 15
11	9 22 54	21 56 45	19 5	5 34	5 46	29 24	19 38	3 39	26 43	15 0	15 13
12	9 26 50	22 57 25	3♌40	5 7	7 1	0♓12	19 51	3 34	26 42	14 59	15 12
13	9 30 47	23 58 3	18 36	4 48	8 16	0 59	20 4	3 30	26 41	14 58	15 10
14	9 34 43	24 58 39	3♍44	4D37	9 31	1 47	20 17	3 25	26 40	14 57	15 9
15	9 38 40	25 59 14	18 53	4 33	10 46	2 34	20 29	3 20	26 39	14 56	15 8
16	9 42 37	26 59 48	3♎54	4 37	12 1	3 21	20 42	3 15	26 38	14 55	15 6
17	9 46 33	28 0 21	18 39	4 47	13 16	4 9	20 54	3 11	26 37	14 54	15 5
18	9 50 30	29 0 52	3♏ 2	5 4	14 31	4 56	21 7	3 6	26 37	14 53	15 3
19	9 54 26	0♓ 1 22	17 2	5 26	15 46	5 44	21 19	3 1	26 36	14 52	15 2
20	9 58 23	1 1 50	0♐39	5 53	17 1	6 31	21 32	2 56	26 35	14 51	15 1
21	10 2 19	2 2 18	13 55	6 26	18 16	7 18	21 44	2 51	26 34	14 50	14 59
22	10 6 16	3 2 44	26 53	7 3	19 31	8 6	21 56	2 46	26 34	14 49	14 58
23	10 10 12	4 3 9	9♑35	7 45	20 46	8 53	22 8	2 42	26 33	14 48	14 57
24	10 14 9	5 3 32	22 4	8 30	22 1	9 40	22 20	2 37	26 33	14 47	14 55
25	10 18 6	6 3 54	4♒22	9 19	23 16	10 28	22 32	2 32	26 32	14 45	14 54
26	10 22 2	7 4 14	16 31	10 11	24 30	11 15	22 44	2 27	26 32	14 44	14 53
27	10 25 59	8 4 33	28 33	11 7	25 45	12 2	22 56	2 22	26 31	14 43	14 51
28	10 29 55	9♓ 4 50	10♓29	12♒ 5	27♒ 0	12♓50	23♑ 7	2♍18	26♊31	14♎42	14♌50

THE SUN ENTERS THE SIGN OF PISCES ON FEB 18 AT 23:28.

DAY	TIME h m s	☉ ° ' "	☽ ° '	☿ ° '	♀ ° '	♂ ° '	♃ ° '	♄ ° '	♅ ° '	♆ ° '	♇ ° '
M 1	10 33 52	10♓ 5 5	22♓20	13♒ 6	28♒15	13♓37	23♑19	2♍13	26♊31	14♎40	14♌49
A 2	10 37 48	11 5 18	4♈ 8	14 10	29 30	14 24	23 31	2R 8	26R31	14R39	14R47
R 3	10 41 45	12 5 29	15 55	15 16	0♓45	15 11	23 42	2 3	26 31	14 38	14 46
C 4	10 45 41	13 5 38	27 45	16 24	2 0	15 59	23 54	1 58	26 30	14 36	14 45
H 5	10 49 38	14 5 46	9♉40	17 34	3 14	16 46	24 5	1 54	26D30	14 35	14 44
6	10 53 34	15 5 51	21 46	18 46	4 29	17 33	24 16	1 49	26 30	14 34	14 43
7	10 57 31	16 5 54	4♊ 6	20 0	5 44	18 20	24 27	1 45	26 31	14 32	14 41
8	11 1 28	17 5 55	16 45	21 16	6 59	19 7	24 38	1 40	26 31	14 31	14 40
9	11 5 24	18 5 54	29 48	22 34	8 14	19 54	24 49	1 35	26 31	14 30	14 39
10	11 9 21	19 5 51	13♋18	23 53	9 28	20 41	25 0	1 31	26 31	14 28	14 38
11	11 13 17	20 5 45	27 17	25 13	10 43	21 28	25 11	1 26	26 31	14 27	14 37
12	11 17 14	21 5 37	11♌45	26 36	11 58	22 15	25 21	1 22	26 32	14 25	14 36
13	11 21 10	22 5 28	26 36	27 59	13 13	23 2	25 32	1 18	26 32	14 24	14 35
14	11 25 7	23 5 15	11♍45	29 25	14 27	23 49	25 42	1 13	26 33	14 22	14 33
15	11 29 3	24 5 1	27 2	0♓51	15 42	24 36	25 53	1 9	26 33	14 21	14 32
16	11 33 0	25 4 45	12♎15	2 19	16 57	25 23	26 3	1 5	26 34	14 19	14 31
17	11 36 57	26 4 27	27 16	3 48	18 11	26 10	26 13	1 1	26 34	14 18	14 30
18	11 40 53	27 4 7	11♏57	5 19	19 26	26 57	26 23	0 57	26 35	14 16	14 29
19	11 44 50	28 3 46	26 12	6 51	20 41	27 44	26 33	0 52	26 36	14 14	14 28
20	11 48 46	29 3 22	10♐ 1	8 24	21 55	28 30	26 43	0 49	26 36	14 13	14 27
21	11 52 43	0♈ 2 57	23 25	9 59	23 10	29 17	26 53	0 45	26 37	14 11	14 26
22	11 56 39	1 2 31	6♑24	11 35	24 25	0♈ 4	27 2	0 41	26 38	14 10	14 26
23	12 0 36	2 2 2	19 4	13 12	25 39	0 50	27 12	0 37	26 39	14 8	14 25
24	12 4 32	3 1 32	1♒27	14 50	26 54	1 37	27 21	0 33	26 40	14 7	14 24
25	12 8 29	4 1 0	13 36	16 30	28 8	2 24	27 30	0 30	26 41	14 5	14 23
26	12 12 26	5 0 26	25 37	18 11	29 23	3 10	27 40	0 26	26 42	14 3	14 22
27	12 16 22	5 59 50	7♓30	19 54	0♈38	3 57	27 49	0 23	26 43	14 2	14 21
28	12 20 19	6 59 12	19 20	21 37	1 52	4 43	27 57	0 19	26 44	14 0	14 21
29	12 24 15	7 58 33	1♈ 8	23 23	3 7	5 30	28 6	0 16	26 46	13 58	14 20
30	12 28 12	8 57 51	12 57	25 9	4 21	6 16	28 15	0 13	26 47	13 57	14 19
31	12 32 8	9♈57 7	24♈48	26♓57	5♈36	7♈ 3	28♑23	0♍ 9	26♊48	13♎55	14♌18

THE SUN ENTERS THE SIGN OF ARIES ON MAR 20 AT 22:49.

♈ ARIES ♉ TAURUS ♊ GEMINI ♋ CANCER ♌ LEO ♍ VIRGO ♎ LIBRA

1949

SIDEREAL TIME. SUN. MOON. MERCURY. VENUS. MARS. JUPITER. SATURN. URANUS. NEPTUNE. PLUTO.

DAY	TIME	☉	☽	☿	♀	♂	♃	♄	♅	♆	♇
	h m s	° ' "	° '	° '	° '	° '	° '	° '	° '	° '	° '
A 1	12 36 5	10♈56 21	6♉44	28♓46	6♈50	7♈49	28♑32	0♍ 6	26♊50	13♎53	14♌18
P 2	12 40 1	11 55 33	18 47	0♈37	8 5	8 35	28 40	0R 3	26 51	13R52	14R17
R 3	12 43 58	12 54 43	1♊ 0	2 29	9 19	9 22	28 48	0 0	26 52	13 50	14 16
I 4	12 47 55	13 53 50	13 26	4 22	10 34	10 8	28 56	29♌58	26 54	13 49	14 16
L 5	12 51 51	14 52 55	26 8	6 17	11 48	10 54	29 4	29 55	26 56	13 47	14 15
6	12 55 48	15 51 58	9♋10	8 13	13 2	11 40	29 11	29 52	26 57	13 45	14 15
7	12 59 44	16 50 59	22 35	10 11	14 17	12 27	29 19	29 50	26 59	13 44	14 14
8	13 3 41	17 49 57	6♌23	12 10	15 31	13 13	29 26	29 47	27 1	13 42	14 14
9	13 7 37	18 48 53	20 36	14 10	16 46	13 59	29 34	29 45	27 2	13 40	14 13
10	13 11 34	19 47 47	5♍11	16 11	18 0	14 45	29 41	29 43	27 4	13 39	14 13
11	13 15 30	20 46 38	20 5	18 14	19 14	15 31	29 48	29 41	27 6	13 37	14 12
12	13 19 27	21 45 27	5♎10	20 18	20 29	16 16	29 55	29 38	27 8	13 35	14 12
13	13 23 24	22 44 14	20 18	22 23	21 43	17 2	0♒ 1	29 37	27 10	13 34	14 11
14	13 27 20	23 42 59	5♏19	24 28	22 57	17 48	0 8	29 35	27 12	13 32	14 11
15	13 31 17	24 41 43	20 6	26 34	24 11	18 34	0 14	29 33	27 14	13 31	14 11
16	13 35 13	25 40 24	4♐32	28 41	25 26	19 20	0 20	29 31	27 16	13 29	14 10
17	13 39 10	26 39 4	18 32	0♉48	26 40	20 5	0 26	29 30	27 18	13 27	14 10
18	13 43 6	27 37 42	2♑ 5	2 55	27 54	20 51	0 32	29 28	27 20	13 26	14 10
19	13 47 3	28 36 18	15 12	5 2	29 8	21 37	0 38	29 27	27 22	13 24	14 10
20	13 50 59	29 34 53	27 55	7 8	0♉22	22 22	0 44	29 26	27 25	13 23	14 9
21	13 54 56	0♉33 26	10♒19	9 13	1 37	23 8	0 49	29 24	27 27	13 21	14 9
22	13 58 53	1 31 57	22 27	11 18	2 51	23 53	0 54	29 23	27 29	13 19	14 9
23	14 2 49	2 30 26	4♓24	13 20	4 5	24 39	1 0	29 22	27 32	13 18	14 9
24	14 6 46	3 28 54	16 14	15 21	5 19	25 24	1 4	29 22	27 34	13 16	14 9
25	14 10 42	4 27 21	28 2	17 20	6 33	26 9	1 9	29 21	27 36	13 15	14 9
26	14 14 39	5 25 45	9♈50	19 17	7 47	26 55	1 14	29 20	27 39	13 13	14D 9
27	14 18 35	6 24 8	21 42	21 10	9 1	27 40	1 18	29 20	27 41	13 12	14 9
28	14 22 32	7 22 29	3♉40	23 1	10 16	28 25	1 22	29 19	27 44	13 10	14 9
29	14 26 28	8 20 48	15 46	24 49	11 30	29 10	1 27	29 19	27 46	13 9	14 9
30	14 30 25	9♉19 6	28♉ 2	26♉33	12♉44	29♈55	1♒30	29♌19	27♊49	13♎ 7	14♌ 9

THE SUN ENTERS THE SIGN OF TAURUS ON APR 20 AT 10:17.

DAY	TIME	☉	☽	☿	♀	♂	♃	♄	♅	♆	♇
	h m s	° ' "	° '	° '	° '	° '	° '	° '	° '	° '	° '
M 1	14 34 21	10♉17 21	10♊30	28♉14	13♉58	0♉40	1♒34	29♌19	27♊52	13♎ 6	14♌ 9
A 2	14 38 18	11 15 35	23 11	29 51	15 12	1 25	1 38	29D19	27 54	13R 5	14 9
Y 3	14 42 15	12 13 47	6♋ 6	1♊24	16 26	2 10	1 41	29 19	27 57	13 3	14 9
4	14 46 11	13 11 57	19 16	2 53	17 40	2 55	1 44	29 19	28 0	13 2	14 10
5	14 50 8	14 10 5	2♌43	4 19	18 54	3 40	1 47	29 19	28 3	13 0	14 10
6	14 54 4	15 8 11	16 27	5 40	20 8	4 25	1 50	29 20	28 6	12 59	14 10
7	14 58 1	16 6 15	0♍28	6 57	21 22	5 9	1 53	29 20	28 8	12 58	14 10
8	15 1 57	17 4 17	14 47	8 10	22 35	5 54	1 55	29 21	28 11	12 56	14 11
9	15 5 54	18 2 17	29 19	9 19	23 49	6 39	1 58	29 22	28 14	12 55	14 11
10	15 9 51	19 0 15	14♎ 2	10 23	25 3	7 23	2 0	29 23	28 17	12 54	14 11
11	15 13 47	19 58 11	28 50	11 22	26 17	8 8	2 2	29 24	28 20	12 53	14 12
12	15 17 44	20 56 6	13♏36	12 18	27 31	8 52	2 3	29 25	28 23	12 51	14 12
13	15 21 40	21 53 59	28 13	13 8	28 45	9 37	2 5	29 26	28 26	12 50	14 13
14	15 25 37	22 51 51	12♐34	13 54	29 59	10 21	2 6	29 27	28 29	12 49	14 13
15	15 29 33	23 49 42	26 35	14 36	1♊12	11 5	2 7	29 29	28 32	12 48	14 14
16	15 33 30	24 47 31	10♑12	15 12	2 26	11 49	2 8	29 30	28 35	12 47	14 14
17	15 37 26	25 45 19	23 23	15 44	3 40	12 34	2 9	29 32	28 38	12 46	14 15
18	15 41 23	26 43 5	6♒11	16 11	4 54	13 18	2 10	29 33	28 42	12 45	14 15
19	15 45 20	27 40 51	18 37	16 33	6 8	14 2	2 10	29 35	28 45	12 43	14 16
20	15 49 16	28 38 35	0♓47	16 50	7 21	14 46	2R10	29 37	28 48	12 42	14 16
21	15 53 13	29 36 19	12 44	17 3	8 35	15 30	2 10	29 39	28 51	12 41	14 17
22	15 57 9	0♊34 1	24 34	17 10	9 49	16 14	2 10	29 41	28 54	12 40	14 18
23	16 1 6	1 31 42	6♈22	17R13	11 3	16 58	2 10	29 43	28 58	12 39	14 18
24	16 5 2	2 29 22	18 12	17 11	12 16	17 42	2 9	29 46	29 1	12 39	14 19
25	16 8 59	3 27 1	0♉ 9	17 5	13 30	18 25	2 9	29 48	29 4	12 38	14 20
26	16 12 55	4 24 39	12 15	16 54	14 44	19 9	2 8	29 50	29 8	12 37	14 21
27	16 16 52	5 22 15	24 34	16 39	15 57	19 53	2 6	29 53	29 11	12 36	14 22
28	16 20 49	6 19 51	7♊ 6	16 20	17 11	20 36	2 5	29 56	29 14	12 35	14 22
29	16 24 45	7 17 26	19 54	15 58	18 25	21 20	2 4	29 58	29 18	12 34	14 23
30	16 28 42	8 15 0	2♋56	15 33	19 38	22 3	2 2	0♍ 1	29 21	12 33	14 24
31	16 32 38	9♊12 32	16♋11	15♊ 5	20♊52	22♉47	2♒ 0	0♍ 4	29♊25	12♎33	14♌25

THE SUN ENTERS THE SIGN OF GEMINI ON MAY 21 AT 09:51.

DAY	TIME	☉	☽	☿	♀	♂	♃	♄	♅	♆	♇
	h m s	° ' "	° '	° '	° '	° '	° '	° '	° '	° '	° '
J 1	16 36 35	10♊10 3	29♋39	14♊35	22♊ 6	23♉30	1♒58	0♍ 7	29♊28	12♎32	14♌26
U 2	16 40 31	11 7 33	13♌19	14R 3	23 19	24 14	1R56	0 11	29 31	12R31	14 27
N 3	16 44 28	12 5 1	27 9	13 30	24 33	24 57	1 53	0 14	29 35	12 31	14 28
E 4	16 48 24	13 2 28	11♍ 9	12 57	25 46	25 40	1 51	0 17	29 38	12 30	14 29
5	16 52 21	13 59 54	25 17	12 23	27 0	26 23	1 48	0 21	29 42	12 29	14 30
6	16 56 18	14 57 19	9♎32	11 50	28 13	27 6	1 45	0 24	29 45	12 29	14 31
7	17 0 14	15 54 42	23 52	11 19	29 27	27 49	1 42	0 28	29 49	12 28	14 32
8	17 4 11	16 52 5	8♏15	10 48	0♋40	28 32	1 39	0 31	29 52	12 28	14 33
9	17 8 7	17 49 26	22 37	10 21	1 54	29 15	1 35	0 35	29 56	12 27	14 34
10	17 12 4	18 46 47	6♐52	9 55	3 7	29 58	1 31	0 39	29 59	12 27	14 35
11	17 16 0	19 44 7	20 57	9 33	4 21	0♊41	1 28	0 43	0♋ 3	12 26	14 36
12	17 19 57	20 41 26	4♑46	9 15	5 34	1 24	1 24	0 47	0 6	12 26	14 38
13	17 23 54	21 38 44	18 15	9 0	6 48	2 7	1 19	0 51	0 10	12 26	14 39
14	17 27 50	22 36 2	1♒23	8 49	8 1	2 49	1 15	0 55	0 14	12 25	14 40
15	17 31 47	23 33 19	14 9	8 42	9 15	3 32	1 11	1 0	0 17	12 25	14 41
16	17 35 43	24 30 36	26 36	8D40	10 28	4 14	1 6	1 4	0 21	12 25	14 42
17	17 39 40	25 27 53	8♓46	8 42	11 41	4 57	1 1	1 8	0 24	12 24	14 44
18	17 43 36	26 25 9	20 44	8 49	12 55	5 39	0 56	1 13	0 28	12 24	14 45
19	17 47 33	27 22 25	2♈35	9 0	14 8	6 22	0 51	1 17	0 32	12 24	14 46
20	17 51 29	28 19 40	14 24	9 17	15 22	7 4	0 46	1 22	0 35	12 24	14 48
21	17 55 26	29 16 56	26 16	9 37	16 35	7 46	0 40	1 27	0 39	12 24	14 49
22	17 59 23	0♋14 11	8♉16	10 3	17 48	8 29	0 35	1 32	0 42	12 24	14 50
23	18 3 19	1 11 26	20 29	10 33	19 2	9 11	0 29	1 37	0 46	12D24	14 52
24	18 7 16	2 8 41	2♊58	11 7	20 15	9 53	0 23	1 42	0 49	12 24	14 53
25	18 11 12	3 5 56	15 46	11 46	21 28	10 35	0 17	1 47	0 53	12 24	14 55
26	18 15 9	4 3 11	28 53	12 29	22 41	11 17	0 11	1 52	0 57	12 24	14 56
27	18 19 5	5 0 25	12♋17	13 17	23 55	11 59	0 5	1 57	1 0	12 24	14 57
28	18 23 2	5 57 40	25 58	14 9	25 8	12 41	29♑59	2 2	1 4	12 24	14 59
29	18 26 58	6 54 53	9♌50	15 5	26 21	13 23	29 52	2 7	1 7	12 24	15 0
30	18 30 55	7♋52 7	23♌52	16♊ 6	27♋35	14♊ 5	29♑46	2♍13	1♋11	12♎24	15♌ 2

THE SUN ENTERS THE SIGN OF CANCER ON JUN 21 AT 18:03.

♏ SCORPIO ♐ SAGITTARIUS ♑ CAPRICORN ♒ AQUARIUS ♓ PISCES

SIDEREAL SUN . . MOON . . MERCURY . . VENUS . . MARS . . JUPITER . . SATURN . . URANUS . . NEPTUNE . . PLUTO .

DAY	TIME	☉	☽	☿	♀	♂	♃	♄	♅	♆	♇
	h m s	° ' "	° '	° '	° '	° '	° '	° '	° '	° '	° '
J 1	18 34 52	8♋49 20	7♍58	17♊10	28♋48	14♊46	29♑39	2♍18	1♋15	12♎25	15♌ 3
U 2	18 38 48	9 46 32	22 7	18 19	0♌ 1	15 28	29R32	2 24	1 18	12 25	15 5
L 3	18 42 45	10 43 45	6♎16	19 31	1 14	16 10	29 25	2 29	1 22	12 25	15 7
Y 4	18 46 41	11 40 57	20 23	20 47	2 27	16 51	29 18	2 35	1 25	12 25	15 8
5	18 50 38	12 38 8	4♏28	22 8	3 40	17 33	29 11	2 41	1 29	12 26	15 10
6	18 54 34	13 35 20	18 30	23 32	4 54	18 14	29 4	2 47	1 32	12 26	15 11
7	18 58 31	14 32 31	2♐28	25 0	6 7	18 55	28 57	2 52	1 36	12 27	15 13
8	19 2 27	15 29 42	16 18	26 32	7 20	19 37	28 50	2 58	1 39	12 27	15 14
9	19 6 24	16 26 53	29 58	28 7	8 33	20 18	28 42	3 4	1 43	12 27	15 16
10	19 10 21	17 24 4	13♑26	29 46	9 46	20 59	28 35	3 10	1 46	12 28	15 18
11	19 14 17	18 21 16	26 39	1♋28	10 59	21 40	28 27	3 16	1 50	12 28	15 19
12	19 18 14	19 18 27	9♒35	3 14	12 12	22 21	28 20	3 22	1 53	12 29	15 21
13	19 22 10	20 15 39	22 14	5 3	13 25	23 2	28 12	3 29	1 57	12 30	15 23
14	19 26 7	21 12 52	4♓35	6 55	14 38	23 43	28 5	3 35	2 0	12 30	15 24
15	19 30 3	22 10 4	16 43	8 50	15 51	24 24	27 57	3 41	2 4	12 31	15 26
16	19 34 0	23 7 18	28 39	10 47	17 4	25 5	27 49	3 47	2 7	12 32	15 28
17	19 37 56	24 4 31	10♈29	12 47	18 17	25 46	27 42	3 54	2 11	12 32	15 30
18	19 41 53	25 1 46	22 18	14 48	19 30	26 27	27 34	4 0	2 14	12 33	15 31
19	19 45 50	25 59 1	4♉10	16 52	20 43	27 8	27 26	4 7	2 17	12 34	15 33
20	19 49 46	26 56 17	16 12	18 57	21 55	27 48	27 18	4 13	2 21	12 35	15 35
21	19 53 43	27 53 34	28 28	21 3	23 8	28 29	27 11	4 20	2 24	12 36	15 36
22	19 57 39	28 50 52	11♊ 3	23 9	24 21	29 10	27 3	4 26	2 27	12 36	15 38
23	20 1 36	29 48 10	24 0	25 17	25 34	29 50	26 55	4 33	2 31	12 37	15 40
24	20 5 32	0♌45 29	7♋21	27 24	26 47	0♋30	26 47	4 40	2 34	12 38	15 42
25	20 9 29	1 42 49	21 4	29 32	28 0	1 11	26 40	4 46	2 37	12 39	15 44
26	20 13 26	2 40 10	5♌ 7	1♌39	29 12	1 51	26 32	4 53	2 40	12 40	15 45
27	20 17 22	3 37 31	19 25	3 45	0♍25	2 32	26 24	5 0	2 44	12 41	15 47
28	20 21 19	4 34 53	3♍51	5 51	1 38	3 12	26 17	5 7	2 47	12 42	15 49
29	20 25 15	5 32 16	18 21	7 56	2 50	3 52	26 9	5 14	2 50	12 43	15 51
30	20 29 12	6 29 39	2♎48	9 59	4 3	4 32	26 2	5 21	2 53	12 44	15 53
31	20 33 8	7♌27 2	17♎ 8	12♌ 2	5♍16	5♋12	25♑54	5♍28	2♋56	12♎46	15♌54

THE SUN ENTERS THE SIGN OF LEO ON JUL 23 AT 04:57.

DAY	TIME	☉	☽	☿	♀	♂	♃	♄	♅	♆	♇
	h m s	° ' "	° '	° '	° '	° '	° '	° '	° '	° '	° '
A 1	20 37 5	8♌24 26	1♏20	14♌ 3	6♍28	5♋52	25♑47	5♍35	2♋59	12♎47	15♌56
U 2	20 41 1	9 21 51	15 21	16 3	7 41	6 32	25R39	5 42	3 2	12 48	15 58
G 3	20 44 58	10 19 16	29 11	18 1	8 53	7 12	25 32	5 49	3 5	12 49	16 0
U 4	20 48 55	11 16 42	12♐51	19 58	10 6	7 52	25 25	5 56	3 8	12 50	16 2
S 5	20 52 51	12 14 9	26 19	21 53	11 18	8 32	25 18	6 3	3 11	12 52	16 3
T 6	20 56 48	13 11 37	9♑37	23 47	12 31	9 11	25 11	6 10	3 14	12 53	16 5
7	21 0 44	14 9 5	22 42	25 39	13 43	9 51	25 4	6 18	3 17	12 54	16 7
8	21 4 41	15 6 34	5♒34	27 30	14 56	10 30	24 57	6 25	3 20	12 56	16 9
9	21 8 37	16 4 4	18 13	29 19	16 8	11 10	24 50	6 32	3 23	12 57	16 11
10	21 12 34	17 1 36	0♓38	1♍ 7	17 20	11 50	24 43	6 39	3 26	12 58	16 13
11	21 16 30	17 59 8	12 51	2 53	18 33	12 29	24 37	6 47	3 29	13 0	16 14
12	21 20 27	18 56 42	24 52	4 37	19 45	13 8	24 30	6 54	3 31	13 1	16 16
13	21 24 24	19 54 17	6♈45	6 20	20 57	13 48	24 24	7 1	3 34	13 3	16 18
14	21 28 20	20 51 53	18 33	8 2	22 9	14 27	24 18	7 9	3 37	13 4	16 20
15	21 32 17	21 49 31	0♉20	9 42	23 22	15 6	24 12	7 16	3 40	13 6	16 22
16	21 36 13	22 47 10	12 12	11 20	24 34	15 45	24 6	7 23	3 42	13 7	16 24
17	21 40 10	23 44 51	24 13	12 57	25 46	16 24	24 0	7 31	3 45	13 9	16 25
18	21 44 6	24 42 34	6♊29	14 33	26 58	17 4	23 54	7 38	3 47	13 11	16 27
19	21 48 3	25 40 18	19 4	16 7	28 10	17 43	23 49	7 46	3 50	13 12	16 29
20	21 51 59	26 38 4	2♋ 3	17 40	29 22	18 21	23 43	7 53	3 52	13 14	16 31
21	21 55 56	27 35 52	15 28	19 11	0♎34	19 0	23 38	8 1	3 55	13 16	16 33
22	21 59 53	28 33 41	29 20	20 41	1 46	19 39	23 33	8 8	3 57	13 17	16 34
23	22 3 49	29 31 31	13♌36	22 9	2 58	20 18	23 28	8 16	4 0	13 19	16 36
24	22 7 46	0♍29 23	28 12	23 36	4 10	20 57	23 23	8 23	4 2	13 21	16 38
25	22 11 42	1 27 17	13♍ 0	25 1	5 22	21 35	23 18	8 31	4 4	13 22	16 40
26	22 15 39	2 25 12	27 53	26 25	6 33	22 14	23 14	8 38	4 7	13 24	16 42
27	22 19 35	3 23 8	12♎43	27 47	7 45	22 52	23 10	8 46	4 9	13 26	16 43
28	22 23 32	4 21 6	27 23	29 8	8 57	23 31	23 5	8 53	4 11	13 28	16 45
29	22 27 28	5 19 5	11♏48	0♎27	10 9	24 9	23 1	9 1	4 13	13 30	16 47
30	22 31 25	6 17 5	25 56	1 44	11 20	24 48	22 58	9 8	4 15	13 31	16 49
31	22 35 22	7♍15 7	9♐45	3♎ 0	12♎32	25♋26	22♑54	9♍16	4♋17	13♎33	16♌50

THE SUN ENTERS THE SIGN OF VIRGO ON AUG 23 AT 11:49.

DAY	TIME	☉	☽	☿	♀	♂	♃	♄	♅	♆	♇
	h m s	° ' "	° '	° '	° '	° '	° '	° '	° '	° '	° '
S 1	22 39 18	8♍13 10	23♐17	4♎14	13♎43	26♋ 4	22♑51	9♍24	4♋19	13♎35	16♌52
E 2	22 43 15	9 11 15	6♑33	5 26	14 55	26 42	22R47	9 31	4 21	13 37	16 54
P 3	22 47 11	10 9 21	19 33	6 36	16 6	27 20	22 44	9 39	4 23	13 39	16 56
T 4	22 51 8	11 7 28	2♒19	7 44	17 18	27 59	22 41	9 46	4 25	13 41	16 57
E 5	22 55 4	12 5 37	14 52	8 49	18 29	28 37	22 39	9 54	4 27	13 43	16 59
M 6	22 59 1	13 3 47	27 13	9 53	19 41	29 14	22 36	10 1	4 29	13 45	17 1
B 7	23 2 57	14 1 59	9♓24	10 54	20 52	29 52	22 34	10 9	4 31	13 47	17 2
E 8	23 6 54	15 0 13	21 26	11 53	22 3	0♌30	22 31	10 17	4 32	13 49	17 4
R 9	23 10 51	15 58 28	3♈21	12 49	23 14	1 8	22 29	10 24	4 34	13 51	17 6
10	23 14 47	16 56 46	15 10	13 42	24 25	1 46	22 28	10 32	4 36	13 53	17 7
11	23 18 44	17 55 5	26 57	14 32	25 36	2 23	22 26	10 39	4 37	13 55	17 9
12	23 22 40	18 53 26	8♉45	15 19	26 47	3 1	22 25	10 47	4 39	13 57	17 11
13	23 26 37	19 51 50	20 37	16 2	27 58	3 38	22 23	10 54	4 40	13 59	17 12
14	23 30 33	20 50 15	2♊38	16 42	29 9	4 16	22 22	11 2	4 42	14 1	17 14
15	23 34 30	21 48 43	14 52	17 17	0♏20	4 53	22 22	11 9	4 43	14 3	17 15
16	23 38 26	22 47 13	27 25	17 49	1 31	5 30	22 21	11 17	4 44	14 5	17 17
17	23 42 23	23 45 45	10♋20	18 15	2 42	6 8	22 21	11 24	4 46	14 8	17 18
18	23 46 19	24 44 19	23 41	18 37	3 52	6 45	22D20	11 32	4 47	14 10	17 20
19	23 50 16	25 42 56	7♌29	18 53	5 3	7 22	22 20	11 39	4 48	14 12	17 21
20	23 54 13	26 41 34	21 45	19 3	6 14	7 59	22 20	11 47	4 49	14 14	17 23
21	23 58 9	27 40 15	6♍25	19R 7	7 24	8 36	22 21	11 54	4 50	14 16	17 24
22	0 2 6	28 38 58	21 23	19 5	8 34	9 13	22 21	12 1	4 51	14 18	17 26
23	0 6 2	29 37 42	6♎30	18 56	9 45	9 50	22 22	12 9	4 52	14 20	17 27
24	0 9 59	0♎36 29	21 38	18 40	10 55	10 27	22 23	12 16	4 53	14 23	17 29
25	0 13 55	1 35 17	6♏38	18 16	12 6	11 3	22 24	12 23	4 54	14 25	17 30
26	0 17 52	2 34 8	21 21	17 45	13 16	11 40	22 25	12 31	4 55	14 27	17 32
27	0 21 48	3 33 0	5♐44	17 7	14 26	12 17	22 27	12 38	4 56	14 29	17 33
28	0 25 45	4 31 54	19 43	16 22	15 36	12 53	22 28	12 45	4 56	14 31	17 34
29	0 29 42	5 30 49	3♑17	15 30	16 46	13 30	22 30	12 52	4 57	14 34	17 36
30	0 33 38	6♎29 47	16♑29	14♎33	17♏56	14♌ 6	22♑32	12♍59	4♋58	14♎36	17♌37

THE SUN ENTERS THE SIGN OF LIBRA ON SEP 23 AT 09:07.

♈ ARIES ♉ TAURUS ♊ GEMINI ♋ CANCER ♌ LEO ♍ VIRGO ♎ LIBRA

SIDEREAL SUN. MOON. MERCURY. VENUS. MARS. JUPITER. SATURN. URANUS. NEPTUNE. PLUTO.

DAY	TIME	☉	☽	☿	♀	♂	♃	♄	♅	♆	♇
	h m s	° ' "	° '	° '	° '	° '	° '	° '	° '	° '	° '
O 1	0 37 35	7♎28 46	29♑21	13♎30	19♏ 6	14♌42	22♑35	13♍ 7	4♋58	14♎38	17♌38
C 2	0 41 31	8 27 47	11♒55	12R23	20 15	15 19	22 37	13 14	4 59	14 40	17 39
T 3	0 45 28	9 26 49	24 15	11 15	21 25	15 55	22 40	13 21	4 59	14 42	17 41
O 4	0 49 24	10 25 54	6♓23	10 6	22 35	16 31	22 43	13 28	5 0	14 45	17 42
B 5	0 53 21	11 25 0	18 23	8 58	23 44	17 7	22 46	13 35	5 0	14 47	17 43
E 6	0 57 17	12 24 8	0♈16	7 53	24 54	17 43	22 49	13 42	5 0	14 49	17 44
R 7	1 1 14	13 23 18	12 5	6 53	26 3	18 19	22 52	13 49	5 1	14 51	17 46
8	1 5 11	14 22 30	23 53	6 0	27 12	18 54	22 56	13 56	5 1	14 54	17 47
9	1 9 7	15 21 45	5♉41	5 15	28 21	19 30	23 0	14 3	5 1	14 56	17 48
10	1 13 4	16 21 1	17 32	4 40	29 30	20 6	23 4	14 9	5 1	14 58	17 49
11	1 17 0	17 20 20	29 29	4 15	0♐39	20 41	23 8	14 16	5R 1	15 0	17 50
12	1 20 57	18 19 41	11♊34	4D 0	1 48	21 17	23 12	14 23	5 1	15 3	17 51
13	1 24 53	19 19 4	23 51	3 57	2 57	21 52	23 17	14 30	5 1	15 5	17 52
14	1 28 50	20 18 29	6♋23	4 4	4 6	22 27	23 21	14 36	5 1	15 7	17 53
15	1 32 46	21 17 57	19 14	4 22	5 14	23 3	23 26	14 43	5 1	15 9	17 54
16	1 36 43	22 17 28	2♌28	4 50	6 22	23 38	23 31	14 49	5 0	15 11	17 55
17	1 40 40	23 17 0	16 6	5 28	7 31	24 13	23 36	14 56	5 0	15 14	17 56
18	1 44 36	24 16 35	0♍10	6 14	8 39	24 48	23 42	15 2	5 0	15 16	17 57
19	1 48 33	25 16 12	14 39	7 8	9 47	25 23	23 47	15 9	4 59	15 18	17 58
20	1 52 29	26 15 51	29 30	8 9	10 55	25 58	23 53	15 15	4 59	15 20	17 59
21	1 56 26	27 15 32	14♎36	9 16	12 3	26 32	23 59	15 21	4 59	15 23	17 59
22	2 0 22	28 15 15	29 48	10 29	13 11	27 7	24 5	15 28	4 58	15 25	18 0
23	2 4 19	29 15 1	14♏58	11 47	14 18	27 41	24 11	15 34	4 57	15 27	18 1
24	2 8 15	0♏14 48	29 55	13 9	15 26	28 16	24 17	15 40	4 57	15 29	18 2
25	2 12 12	1 14 38	14♐32	14 34	16 33	28 50	24 24	15 46	4 56	15 31	18 3
26	2 16 9	2 14 29	28 44	16 2	17 40	29 24	24 30	15 52	4 55	15 33	18 3
27	2 20 5	3 14 21	12♑28	17 32	18 47	29 59	24 37	15 58	4 55	15 36	18 4
28	2 24 2	4 14 16	25 45	19 5	19 54	0♍33	24 44	16 4	4 54	15 38	18 5
29	2 27 58	5 14 12	8♒37	20 39	21 0	1 7	24 51	16 10	4 53	15 40	18 5
30	2 31 55	6 14 9	21 8	22 14	22 7	1 40	24 59	16 16	4 52	15 42	18 6
31	2 35 51	7♏14 8	3♓21	23♎50	23♐13	2♍14	25♑ 6	16♍21	4♋51	15♎44	18♌ 6

THE SUN ENTERS THE SIGN OF SCORPIO ON OCT 23 AT 18:04.

DAY	TIME	☉	☽	☿	♀	♂	♃	♄	♅	♆	♇
	h m s	° ' "	° '	° '	° '	° '	° '	° '	° '	° '	° '
N 1	2 39 48	8♏14 9	15♓22	25♎27	24♐19	2♍48	25♑14	16♍27	4♋50	15♎46	18♌ 7
O 2	2 43 44	9 14 12	27 15	27 5	25 25	3 21	25 21	16 32	4R49	15 48	18 7
V 3	2 47 41	10 14 16	9♈ 3	28 42	26 31	3 55	25 29	16 38	4 48	15 50	18 8
E 4	2 51 38	11 14 21	20 50	0♏21	27 36	4 28	25 37	16 43	4 46	15 52	18 8
M 5	2 55 34	12 14 29	2♉39	1 59	28 42	5 1	25 45	16 49	4 45	15 55	18 9
B 6	2 59 31	13 14 38	14 32	3 37	29 47	5 34	25 54	16 54	4 44	15 57	18 9
E 7	3 3 27	14 14 50	26 31	5 15	0♑52	6 7	26 2	16 59	4 42	15 59	18 10
R 8	3 7 24	15 15 3	8♊38	6 54	1 56	6 40	26 11	17 4	4 41	16 1	18 10
9	3 11 20	16 15 18	20 54	8 32	3 1	7 13	26 19	17 10	4 40	16 3	18 10
10	3 15 17	17 15 35	3♋21	10 9	4 5	7 46	26 28	17 15	4 38	16 5	18 11
11	3 19 13	18 15 53	16 0	11 47	5 9	8 18	26 37	17 19	4 37	16 7	18 11
12	3 23 10	19 16 14	28 54	13 24	6 12	8 51	26 46	17 24	4 35	16 9	18 11
13	3 27 7	20 16 37	12♌ 5	15 1	7 15	9 23	26 56	17 29	4 34	16 10	18 11
14	3 31 3	21 17 1	25 35	16 38	8 18	9 55	27 5	17 34	4 32	16 12	18 12
15	3 35 0	22 17 28	9♍26	18 15	9 21	10 27	27 14	17 38	4 30	16 14	18 12
16	3 38 56	23 17 56	23 37	19 51	10 24	10 59	27 24	17 43	4 28	16 16	18 12
17	3 42 53	24 18 26	8♎ 9	21 27	11 26	11 31	27 34	17 47	4 27	16 18	18 12
18	3 46 49	25 18 58	22 57	23 3	12 28	12 3	27 44	17 52	4 25	16 20	18 12
19	3 50 46	26 19 32	7♏56	24 39	13 29	12 34	27 54	17 56	4 23	16 22	18R12
20	3 54 42	27 20 8	22 58	26 14	14 30	13 5	28 4	18 0	4 21	16 24	18 12
21	3 58 39	28 20 45	7♐54	27 49	15 31	13 37	28 14	18 4	4 19	16 25	18 12
22	4 2 36	29 21 23	22 35	29 24	16 31	14 8	28 24	18 8	4 17	16 27	18 12
23	4 6 32	0♐22 3	6♑55	0♐59	17 31	14 39	28 35	18 12	4 15	16 29	18 12
24	4 10 29	1 22 44	20 47	2 33	18 31	15 9	28 45	18 16	4 13	16 31	18 12
25	4 14 25	2 23 26	4♒11	4 8	19 30	15 40	28 56	18 20	4 11	16 32	18 12
26	4 18 22	3 24 10	17 8	5 42	20 29	16 10	29 7	18 23	4 9	16 34	18 11
27	4 22 18	4 24 54	29 42	7 16	21 27	16 41	29 17	18 27	4 7	16 36	18 11
28	4 26 15	5 25 39	11♓55	8 50	22 25	17 11	29 28	18 30	4 5	16 37	18 11
29	4 30 11	6 26 25	23 55	10 24	23 22	17 41	29 39	18 34	4 3	16 39	18 11
30	4 34 8	7♐27 12	5♈45	11♐58	24♑19	18♍11	29♑51	18♍37	4♋ 1	16♎40	18♌10

THE SUN ENTERS THE SIGN OF SAGITTARIUS ON NOV 22 AT 15:17.

DAY	TIME	☉	☽	☿	♀	♂	♃	♄	♅	♆	♇
	h m s	° ' "	° '	° '	° '	° '	° '	° '	° '	° '	° '
D 1	4 38 5	8♐28 1	17♈32	13♐31	25♑15	18♍40	0♒ 2	18♍40	3♋58	16♎42	18♌10
E 2	4 42 1	9 28 50	29 19	15 5	26 10	19 10	0 13	18 43	3R56	16 43	18R10
C 3	4 45 58	10 29 40	11♉12	16 39	27 5	19 39	0 25	18 46	3 54	16 45	18 9
E 4	4 49 54	11 30 31	23 11	18 12	28 0	20 8	0 36	18 49	3 51	16 46	18 9
M 5	4 53 51	12 31 23	5♊21	19 46	28 54	20 37	0 48	18 52	3 49	16 48	18 9
B 6	4 57 47	13 32 17	17 42	21 19	29 47	21 6	0 59	18 54	3 47	16 49	18 8
E 7	5 1 44	14 33 11	0♋15	22 53	0♒39	21 34	1 11	18 57	3 44	16 51	18 8
R 8	5 5 40	15 34 6	13 0	24 27	1 31	22 3	1 23	18 59	3 42	16 52	18 7
9	5 9 37	16 35 3	25 56	26 0	2 22	22 31	1 35	19 2	3 40	16 53	18 7
10	5 13 34	17 36 0	9♌ 4	27 34	3 12	22 59	1 47	19 4	3 37	16 55	18 6
11	5 17 30	18 36 59	22 24	29 7	4 1	23 26	1 59	19 6	3 35	16 56	18 6
12	5 21 27	19 37 59	5♍56	0♑40	4 50	23 54	2 12	19 8	3 32	16 57	18 5
13	5 25 23	20 38 59	19 41	2 14	5 37	24 21	2 24	19 10	3 30	16 59	18 4
14	5 29 20	21 40 1	3♎39	3 47	6 24	24 48	2 36	19 12	3 27	17 0	18 4
15	5 33 16	22 41 4	17 52	5 20	7 10	25 15	2 49	19 14	3 25	17 1	18 3
16	5 37 13	23 42 8	2♏17	6 53	7 55	25 42	3 1	19 15	3 22	17 2	18 2
17	5 41 10	24 43 13	16 51	8 26	8 38	26 8	3 14	19 17	3 20	17 3	18 2
18	5 45 6	25 44 19	1♐30	9 58	9 21	26 35	3 26	19 18	3 17	17 4	18 1
19	5 49 3	26 45 26	16 8	11 30	10 3	27 0	3 39	19 20	3 14	17 5	18 0
20	5 52 59	27 46 33	0♑36	13 2	10 43	27 26	3 52	19 21	3 12	17 6	17 59
21	5 56 56	28 47 41	14 48	14 32	11 22	27 52	4 5	19 22	3 9	17 7	17 58
22	6 0 52	29 48 49	28 38	16 3	12 0	28 17	4 18	19 23	3 7	17 8	17 58
23	6 4 49	0♑49 57	12♒ 3	17 32	12 37	28 42	4 31	19 24	3 4	17 9	17 57
24	6 8 45	1 51 6	25 3	19 0	13 12	29 6	4 44	19 24	3 2	17 10	17 56
25	6 12 42	2 52 15	7♓39	20 27	13 46	29 31	4 57	19 25	2 59	17 11	17 55
26	6 16 39	3 53 24	19 56	21 52	14 19	29 55	5 10	19 25	2 56	17 12	17 54
27	6 20 35	4 54 32	1♈57	23 15	14 50	0♎18	5 23	19 26	2 54	17 13	17 53
28	6 24 32	5 55 41	13 48	24 36	15 19	0 42	5 37	19 26	2 51	17 13	17 52
29	6 28 28	6 56 50	25 35	25 54	15 47	1 5	5 50	19 26	2 49	17 14	17 51
30	6 32 25	7 57 59	7♉24	27 9	16 12	1 28	6 3	19R26	2 46	17 15	17 50
31	6 36 21	8♑59 7	19♉19	28♑20	16♒37	1♎50	6♒17	19♍26	2♋44	17♎15	17♌49

THE SUN ENTERS THE SIGN OF CAPRICORN ON DEC 22 AT 04:23.

♏ SCORPIO ♐ SAGITTARIUS ♑ CAPRICORN ♒ AQUARIUS ♓ PISCES

SIDEREAL TIME, SUN, MOON, MERCURY, VENUS, MARS, JUPITER, SATURN, URANUS, NEPTUNE, PLUTO

DAY	TIME	☉	☽	☿	♀	♂	♃	♄	♅	♆	♇
	h m s	° ' "	° '	° '	° '	° '	° '	° '	° '	° '	° '
J 1	6 40 18	10♑ 0 16	1♊25	29♑27	16♒59	2♎13	6♒30	19♍26	2♋41	17♎16	17♌48
A 2	6 44 14	11 1 25	13 44	0♒28	17 19	2 35	6 44	19R26	2R38	17 17	17R47
N 3	6 48 11	12 2 33	26 19	1 24	17 37	2 56	6 57	19 26	2 36	17 17	17 46
U 4	6 52 8	13 3 42	9♋10	2 13	17 54	3 17	7 11	19 25	2 33	17 18	17 45
A 5	6 56 4	14 4 50	22 16	2 55	18 8	3 38	7 25	19 25	2 31	17 18	17 43
R 6	7 0 1	15 5 59	5♌36	3 27	18 19	3 59	7 38	19 24	2 28	17 19	17 42
Y 7	7 3 57	16 7 7	19 7	3 51	18 29	4 19	7 52	19 23	2 26	17 19	17 41
8	7 7 54	17 8 15	2♍48	4R 4	18 36	4 39	8 6	19 22	2 23	17 19	17 40
9	7 11 50	18 9 23	16 36	4 7	18 41	4 58	8 20	19 21	2 21	17 20	17 39
10	7 15 47	19 10 32	0♎30	3 57	18R44	5 17	8 34	19 20	2 18	17 20	17 38
11	7 19 44	20 11 40	14 29	3 36	18 44	5 36	8 48	19 19	2 16	17 20	17 36
12	7 23 40	21 12 48	28 33	3 4	18 42	5 54	9 1	19 17	2 14	17 21	17 35
13	7 27 37	22 13 57	12♏41	2 19	18 37	6 12	9 15	19 16	2 11	17 21	17 34
14	7 31 33	23 15 5	26 53	1 25	18 30	6 29	9 29	19 14	2 9	17 21	17 33
15	7 35 30	24 16 13	11♐ 5	0 22	18 20	6 46	9 43	19 13	2 6	17 21	17 31
16	7 39 26	25 17 21	25 14	29♑11	18 8	7 3	9 58	19 11	2 4	17 21	17 30
17	7 43 23	26 18 29	9♑16	27 56	17 53	7 19	10 12	19 9	2 2	17 21	17 29
18	7 47 19	27 19 36	23 7	26 38	17 36	7 34	10 26	19 7	2 0	17R21	17 27
19	7 51 16	28 20 43	6♒41	25 20	17 16	7 50	10 40	19 5	1 57	17 21	17 26
20	7 55 13	29 21 49	19 55	24 4	16 54	8 4	10 54	19 3	1 55	17 21	17 25
21	7 59 9	0♒22 54	2♓49	22 52	16 30	8 18	11 8	19 1	1 53	17 21	17 23
22	8 3 6	1 23 58	15 23	21 47	16 4	8 32	11 22	18 58	1 51	17 21	17 22
23	8 7 2	2 25 2	27 40	20 49	15 36	8 45	11 37	18 56	1 49	17 21	17 21
24	8 10 59	3 26 4	9♈42	19 59	15 6	8 58	11 51	18 53	1 47	17 21	17 19
25	8 14 55	4 27 5	21 34	19 18	14 34	9 10	12 5	18 51	1 44	17 21	17 18
26	8 18 52	5 28 6	3♉22	18 46	14 1	9 21	12 19	18 48	1 42	17 21	17 16
27	8 22 48	6 29 5	15 12	18 23	13 26	9 32	12 34	18 45	1 40	17 20	17 15
28	8 26 45	7 30 3	27 8	18 9	12 51	9 42	12 48	18 42	1 38	17 20	17 14
29	8 30 42	8 31 0	9♊15	18D 4	12 14	9 52	13 2	18 39	1 37	17 20	17 12
30	8 34 38	9 31 56	21 39	18 6	11 37	10 1	13 16	18 36	1 35	17 19	17 11
31	8 38 35	10♒32 51	4♋22	18♑15	11♒ 0	10♎10	13♒31	18♍33	1♋33	17♎19	17♌ 9

THE SUN ENTERS THE SIGN OF AQUARIUS ON JAN 20 AT 15:00.

DAY	TIME	☉	☽	☿	♀	♂	♃	♄	♅	♆	♇
	h m s	° ' "	° '	° '	° '	° '	° '	° '	° '	° '	° '
F 1	8 42 31	11♒33 44	17♋25	18♑32	10♒23	10♎18	13♒45	18♍30	1♋31	17♎18	17♌ 8
E 2	8 46 28	12 34 37	0♌49	18 55	9R46	10 25	13 59	18R26	1R29	17R18	17R 6
B 3	8 50 24	13 35 28	14 31	19 23	9 9	10 32	14 14	18 23	1 27	17 17	17 5
R 4	8 54 21	14 36 18	28 28	19 57	8 34	10 38	14 28	18 19	1 26	17 17	17 4
U 5	8 58 17	15 37 6	12♍36	20 36	7 59	10 44	14 42	18 16	1 24	17 16	17 2
A 6	9 2 14	16 37 54	26 50	21 19	7 25	10 48	14 57	18 12	1 23	17 16	17 1
R 7	9 6 11	17 38 41	11♎ 6	22 6	6 53	10 52	15 11	18 8	1 21	17 15	16 59
Y 8	9 10 7	18 39 27	25 21	22 57	6 23	10 56	15 25	18 5	1 19	17 15	16 58
9	9 14 4	19 40 11	9♏33	23 51	5 54	10 59	15 40	18 1	1 18	17 14	16 56
10	9 18 0	20 40 55	23 39	24 49	5 27	11 1	15 54	17 57	1 16	17 13	16 55
11	9 21 57	21 41 38	7♐39	25 49	5 2	11 2	16 8	17 53	1 15	17 12	16 53
12	9 25 53	22 42 20	21 32	26 52	4 40	11R 2	16 22	17 49	1 14	17 12	16 52
13	9 29 50	23 43 1	5♑17	27 57	4 20	11 2	16 37	17 45	1 12	17 11	16 51
14	9 33 46	24 43 41	18 51	29 4	4 2	11 1	16 51	17 40	1 11	17 10	16 49
15	9 37 43	25 44 19	2♒14	0♒14	3 47	11 0	17 5	17 36	1 10	17 9	16 48
16	9 41 40	26 44 56	15 24	1 26	3 34	10 57	17 19	17 32	1 9	17 8	16 46
17	9 45 36	27 45 32	28 18	2 39	3 23	10 54	17 34	17 28	1 8	17 7	16 45
18	9 49 33	28 46 6	10♓58	3 54	3 15	10 50	17 48	17 23	1 7	17 6	16 44
19	9 53 29	29 46 38	23 22	5 10	3 10	10 45	18 2	17 19	1 6	17 5	16 42
20	9 57 26	0♓47 9	5♈33	6 28	3D 7	10 39	18 16	17 14	1 5	17 4	16 41
21	10 1 22	1 47 37	17 33	7 48	3 6	10 33	18 30	17 10	1 4	17 3	16 39
22	10 5 19	2 48 5	29 24	9 9	3 8	10 26	18 45	17 5	1 3	17 2	16 38
23	10 9 15	3 48 30	11♉13	10 31	3 12	10 18	18 59	17 1	1 2	17 1	16 37
24	10 13 12	4 48 53	23 2	11 55	3 19	10 9	19 13	16 56	1 1	17 0	16 35
25	10 17 9	5 49 15	4♊58	13 20	3 27	10 0	19 27	16 51	1 1	16 59	16 34
26	10 21 5	6 49 34	17 4	14 46	3 38	9 50	19 41	16 47	1 0	16 58	16 33
27	10 25 2	7 49 52	29 27	16 13	3 51	9 39	19 55	16 42	0 59	16 57	16 31
28	10 28 58	8♓50 8	12♋10	17♒41	4♒ 6	9♎27	20♒ 9	16♍37	0♋59	16♎56	16♌30

THE SUN ENTERS THE SIGN OF PISCES ON FEB 19 AT 05:18.

DAY	TIME	☉	☽	☿	♀	♂	♃	♄	♅	♆	♇
	h m s	° ' "	° '	° '	° '	° '	° '	° '	° '	° '	° '
M 1	10 32 55	9♓50 21	25♋15	19♒11	4♒24	9♎14	20♒23	16♍33	0♋58	16♎54	16♌29
A 2	10 36 51	10 50 33	8♌46	20 41	4 43	9R 1	20 37	16R28	0R58	16R53	16R27
R 3	10 40 48	11 50 42	22 40	22 13	5 4	8 47	20 50	16 23	0 58	16 52	16 26
C 4	10 44 44	12 50 50	6♍55	23 46	5 27	8 32	21 4	16 18	0 57	16 51	16 25
H 5	10 48 41	13 50 56	21 26	25 19	5 51	8 17	21 18	16 14	0 57	16 49	16 23
6	10 52 38	14 51 0	6♎ 8	26 54	6 17	8 1	21 32	16 9	0 57	16 48	16 22
7	10 56 34	15 51 2	20 52	28 31	6 45	7 44	21 46	16 4	0 56	16 47	16 21
8	11 0 31	16 51 2	5♏32	0♓ 8	7 15	7 27	21 59	15 59	0 56	16 45	16 20
9	11 4 27	17 51 1	20 4	1 46	7 46	7 9	22 13	15 54	0D56	16 44	16 19
10	11 8 24	18 50 59	4♐22	3 26	8 19	6 50	22 26	15 50	0 56	16 42	16 17
11	11 12 20	19 50 54	18 26	5 6	8 53	6 31	22 40	15 45	0 56	16 41	16 16
12	11 16 17	20 50 49	2♑13	6 48	9 28	6 11	22 54	15 40	0 56	16 40	16 15
13	11 20 13	21 50 41	15 43	8 31	10 5	5 51	23 7	15 35	0 57	16 38	16 14
14	11 24 10	22 50 32	28 58	10 15	10 43	5 30	23 20	15 31	0 57	16 37	16 13
15	11 28 7	23 50 21	11♒59	12 0	11 22	5 9	23 34	15 26	0 57	16 35	16 12
16	11 32 3	24 50 8	24 45	13 47	12 2	4 47	23 47	15 21	0 57	16 34	16 11
17	11 36 0	25 49 54	7♓18	15 34	12 43	4 25	24 0	15 17	0 58	16 32	16 10
18	11 39 56	26 49 37	19 39	17 23	13 26	4 3	24 14	15 12	0 58	16 31	16 9
19	11 43 53	27 49 19	1♈50	19 13	14 9	3 40	24 27	15 7	0 59	16 29	16 8
20	11 47 49	28 48 58	13 52	21 5	14 53	3 17	24 40	15 3	0 59	16 28	16 7
21	11 51 46	29 48 35	25 47	22 57	15 39	2 54	24 53	14 58	1 0	16 26	16 6
22	11 55 42	0♈48 11	7♉37	24 51	16 25	2 31	25 6	14 54	1 0	16 24	16 5
23	11 59 39	1 47 44	19 25	26 46	17 12	2 8	25 19	14 49	1 1	16 23	16 4
24	12 3 36	2 47 15	1♊15	28 42	18 0	1 44	25 32	14 45	1 2	16 21	16 3
25	12 7 32	3 46 43	13 10	0♈40	18 48	1 21	25 44	14 40	1 2	16 20	16 2
26	12 11 29	4 46 10	25 16	2 38	19 38	0 57	25 57	14 36	1 3	16 18	16 1
27	12 15 25	5 45 34	7♋35	4 38	20 28	0 34	26 10	14 32	1 4	16 17	16 0
28	12 19 22	6 44 56	20 14	6 39	21 19	0 11	26 22	14 27	1 5	16 15	15 59
29	12 23 18	7 44 15	3♌15	8 40	22 10	29♍48	26 35	14 23	1 6	16 13	15 59
30	12 27 15	8 43 32	16 41	10 42	23 2	29 25	26 47	14 19	1 7	16 12	15 58
31	12 31 11	9♈42 47	0♍35	12♈45	23♒55	29♍ 2	27♒ 0	14♍15	1♋ 8	16♎10	15♌57

THE SUN ENTERS THE SIGN OF ARIES ON MAR 21 AT 04:35.

♈ ARIES ♉ TAURUS ♊ GEMINI ♋ CANCER ♌ LEO ♍ VIRGO ♎ LIBRA

1950

SIDEREAL | SUN. | MOON. | MERCURY. | VENUS. | MARS. | JUPITER. | SATURN. | URANUS. | NEPTUNE. | PLUTO.

DAY	TIME h	m	s	☉ ° ' "	☽ ° '	☿ ° '	♀ ° '	♂ ° '	♃ ° '	♄ ° '	♅ ° '	♆ ° '	♇ ° '
A 1	12	35	8	10♈42 0	14♍53	14♈49	24♒49	28♍40	27♒12	14♍11	1♋ 9	16♎ 8	15♌56
P 2	12	39	4	11 41 10	29 35	16 52	25 43	28R18	27 24	14R 7	1 11	16R 7	15R56
R 3	12	43	1	12 40 18	14♎32	18 56	26 37	27 56	27 36	14 3	1 12	16 5	15 55
I 4	12	46	58	13 39 24	29 37	20 59	27 32	27 35	27 49	13 59	1 13	16 3	15 54
L 5	12	50	54	14 38 28	14♏42	23 2	28 28	27 14	28 1	13 55	1 14	16 2	15 54
6	12	54	51	15 37 31	29 37	25 4	29 24	26 54	28 12	13 52	1 16	16 0	15 53
7	12	58	47	16 36 31	14♐15	27 5	0♓21	26 34	28 24	13 48	1 17	15 58	15 52
8	13	2	44	17 35 30	28 32	29 5	1 18	26 14	28 36	13 44	1 19	15 57	15 52
9	13	6	40	18 34 28	12♑25	1♉ 2	2 15	25 56	28 48	13 41	1 20	15 55	15 51
10	13	10	37	19 33 23	25 55	2 58	3 13	25 37	28 59	13 37	1 22	15 54	15 51
11	13	14	34	20 32 17	9♒ 2	4 51	4 12	25 20	29 11	13 34	1 24	15 52	15 50
12	13	18	30	21 31 9	21 49	6 40	5 11	25 3	29 22	13 31	1 25	15 50	15 50
13	13	22	27	22 29 59	4♓20	8 27	6 10	24 47	29 34	13 28	1 27	15 49	15 49
14	13	26	23	23 28 47	16 37	10 10	7 9	24 31	29 45	13 25	1 29	15 47	15 49
15	13	30	20	24 27 34	28 44	11 49	8 9	24 16	29 56	13 22	1 31	15 45	15 49
16	13	34	16	25 26 18	10♈43	13 24	9 10	24 2	0♓ 7	13 19	1 33	15 44	15 48
17	13	38	13	26 25 1	22 36	14 55	10 10	23 49	0 18	13 16	1 34	15 42	15 48
18	13	42	9	27 23 42	4♉26	16 21	11 11	23 36	0 29	13 13	1 36	15 40	15 48
19	13	46	6	28 22 21	16 15	17 43	12 13	23 24	0 39	13 10	1 38	15 39	15 47
20	13	50	2	29 20 57	28 4	18 59	13 14	23 13	0 50	13 8	1 40	15 37	15 47
21	13	53	59	0♉19 32	9♊57	20 11	14 16	23 3	1 1	13 5	1 43	15 36	15 47
22	13	57	56	1 18 5	21 55	21 17	15 18	22 53	1 11	13 3	1 45	15 34	15 47
23	14	1	52	2 16 36	4♋ 2	22 19	16 20	22 44	1 21	13 0	1 47	15 33	15 47
24	14	5	49	3 15 4	16 22	23 15	17 23	22 36	1 32	12 58	1 49	15 31	15 46
25	14	9	45	4 13 31	28 57	24 5	18 26	22 29	1 42	12 56	1 51	15 29	15 46
26	14	13	42	5 11 55	11♌53	24 50	19 29	22 23	1 52	12 54	1 54	15 28	15 46
27	14	17	38	6 10 17	25 11	25 30	20 33	22 17	2 1	12 52	1 56	15 26	15 46
28	14	21	35	7 8 37	8♍55	26 4	21 36	22 13	2 11	12 50	1 58	15 25	15D46
29	14	25	31	8 6 55	23 6	26 32	22 40	22 9	2 21	12 49	2 1	15 23	15 46
30	14	29	28	9♉ 5 11	7♎42	26♉55	23♓44	22♍ 5	2♓30	12♍47	2♋ 3	15♎22	15♌46

THE SUN ENTERS THE SIGN OF TAURUS ON APR 20 AT 15:59.

DAY	TIME h	m	s	☉ ° ' "	☽ ° '	☿ ° '	♀ ° '	♂ ° '	♃ ° '	♄ ° '	♅ ° '	♆ ° '	♇ ° '
M 1	14	33	25	10♉ 3 25	22♎39	27♉12	24♓48	22♍ 3	2♓40	12♍46	2♋ 6	15♎20	15♌46
A 2	14	37	21	11 1 37	7♏51	27 24	25 53	22R 1	2 49	12R44	2 8	15R19	15 46
Y 3	14	41	18	11 59 47	23 7	27R30	26 57	22D 1	2 58	12 43	2 11	15 18	15 46
4	14	45	14	12 57 56	8♐17	27 31	28 2	22 0	3 7	12 42	2 13	15 16	15 47
5	14	49	11	13 56 3	23 12	27 27	29 7	22 1	3 16	12 40	2 16	15 15	15 47
6	14	53	7	14 54 9	7♑44	27 18	0♈13	22 2	3 25	12 39	2 19	15 13	15 47
7	14	57	4	15 52 13	21 48	27 4	1 18	22 4	3 34	12 38	2 21	15 12	15 47
8	15	1	1	16 50 16	5♒24	26 45	2 24	22 7	3 42	12 38	2 24	15 11	15 47
9	15	4	57	17 48 17	18 32	26 23	3 30	22 11	3 51	12 37	2 27	15 9	15 48
10	15	8	54	18 46 17	1♓16	25 57	4 36	22 15	3 59	12 36	2 30	15 8	15 48
11	15	12	50	19 44 16	13 41	25 29	5 42	22 20	4 7	12 36	2 33	15 7	15 48
12	15	16	47	20 42 13	25 50	24 57	6 48	22 26	4 15	12 35	2 35	15 5	15 49
13	15	20	43	21 40 9	7♈49	24 24	7 54	22 32	4 23	12 35	2 38	15 4	15 49
14	15	24	40	22 38 4	19 40	23 49	9 1	22 39	4 30	12 35	2 41	15 3	15 50
15	15	28	36	23 35 58	1♉29	23 14	10 8	22 46	4 38	12D35	2 44	15 2	15 50
16	15	32	33	24 33 50	13 17	22 38	11 14	22 55	4 45	12 35	2 47	15 0	15 50
17	15	36	29	25 31 40	25 7	22 3	12 21	23 4	4 53	12 35	2 50	14 59	15 51
18	15	40	26	26 29 30	7♊ 0	21 29	13 28	23 13	5 0	12 35	2 53	14 58	15 51
19	15	44	23	27 27 17	18 59	20 57	14 36	23 23	5 7	12 35	2 56	14 57	15 52
20	15	48	19	28 25 4	1♋ 5	20 27	15 43	23 34	5 14	12 36	2 59	14 56	15 53
21	15	52	16	29 22 49	13 20	20 0	16 50	23 45	5 20	12 36	3 2	14 55	15 53
22	15	56	12	0♊20 32	25 45	19 35	17 58	23 57	5 27	12 37	3 6	14 54	15 54
23	16	0	9	1 18 14	8♌24	19 15	19 6	24 10	5 33	12 38	3 9	14 53	15 55
24	16	4	5	2 15 54	21 18	18 58	20 13	24 23	5 39	12 39	3 12	14 52	15 55
25	16	8	2	3 13 33	4♍32	18 45	21 21	24 36	5 45	12 40	3 15	14 51	15 56
26	16	11	59	4 11 10	18 7	18 36	22 29	24 51	5 51	12 41	3 18	14 50	15 57
27	16	15	55	5 8 45	2♎ 6	18D31	23 37	25 5	5 57	12 42	3 22	14 49	15 57
28	16	19	52	6 6 19	16 29	18 31	24 45	25 20	6 3	12 43	3 25	14 48	15 58
29	16	23	48	7 3 52	1♏14	18 35	25 54	25 36	6 8	12 44	3 28	14 47	15 59
30	16	27	45	8 1 23	16 15	18 44	27 2	25 52	6 13	12 46	3 32	14 46	16 0
31	16	31	41	8♊58 54	1♐26	18♉58	28♈10	26♍ 9	6♓18	12♍47	3♋35	14♎45	16♌ 1

THE SUN ENTERS THE SIGN OF GEMINI ON MAY 21 AT 15:28.

DAY	TIME h	m	s	☉ ° ' "	☽ ° '	☿ ° '	♀ ° '	♂ ° '	♃ ° '	♄ ° '	♅ ° '	♆ ° '	♇ ° '
J 1	16	35	38	9♊56 23	16♐36	19♉16	29♈19	26♍26	6♓23	12♍49	3♋38	14♎45	16♌ 2
U 2	16	39	34	10 53 51	1♑35	19 38	0♉28	26 44	6 28	12 51	3 42	14R44	16 3
N 3	16	43	31	11 51 18	16 13	20 4	1 36	27 2	6 32	12 53	3 45	14 43	16 3
E 4	16	47	28	12 48 45	0♒24	20 35	2 45	27 20	6 37	12 55	3 49	14 42	16 4
5	16	51	24	13 46 11	14 6	21 10	3 54	27 39	6 41	12 57	3 52	14 42	16 5
6	16	55	21	14 43 36	27 20	21 49	5 3	27 58	6 45	12 59	3 55	14 41	16 6
7	16	59	17	15 41 0	10♓ 6	22 32	6 12	28 18	6 49	13 1	3 59	14 41	16 7
8	17	3	14	16 38 24	22 31	23 19	7 21	28 38	6 53	13 4	4 2	14 40	16 8
9	17	7	10	17 35 47	4♈39	24 10	8 31	28 59	6 56	13 6	4 6	14 39	16 10
10	17	11	7	18 33 9	16 36	25 4	9 40	29 20	6 59	13 9	4 9	14 39	16 11
11	17	15	3	19 30 31	28 25	26 2	10 49	29 41	7 3	13 11	4 13	14 38	16 12
12	17	19	0	20 27 53	10♉13	27 3	11 59	0♎ 3	7 6	13 14	4 16	14 38	16 13
13	17	22	57	21 25 14	22 2	28 8	13 8	0 25	7 8	13 17	4 20	14 37	16 14
14	17	26	53	22 22 34	3♊56	29 17	14 18	0 48	7 11	13 20	4 23	14 37	16 15
15	17	30	50	23 19 54	15 56	0♊29	15 28	1 11	7 13	13 23	4 27	14 37	16 16
16	17	34	46	24 17 14	28 5	1 44	16 37	1 34	7 15	13 26	4 30	14 36	16 18
17	17	38	43	25 14 32	10♋23	3 2	17 47	1 58	7 18	13 29	4 34	14 36	16 19
18	17	42	39	26 11 51	22 51	4 24	18 57	2 22	7 19	13 32	4 38	14 36	16 20
19	17	46	36	27 9 8	5♌29	5 49	20 7	2 46	7 21	13 36	4 41	14 35	16 21
20	17	50	32	28 6 25	18 19	7 17	21 17	3 11	7 22	13 39	4 45	14 35	16 23
21	17	54	29	29 3 41	1♍21	8 48	22 27	3 36	7 24	13 43	4 48	14 35	16 24
22	17	58	26	0♋ 0 56	14 38	10 22	23 37	4 1	7 25	13 46	4 52	14 35	16 25
23	18	2	22	0 58 10	28 11	11 59	24 47	4 26	7 26	13 50	4 56	14 35	16 27
24	18	6	19	1 55 24	12♎ 3	13 40	25 57	4 52	7 26	13 54	4 59	14 35	16 28
25	18	10	15	2 52 38	26 13	15 23	27 8	5 18	7 27	13 58	5 3	14 35	16 30
26	18	14	12	3 49 50	10♏41	17 9	28 18	5 45	7 27	14 2	5 6	14D35	16 31
27	18	18	8	4 47 2	25 24	18 58	29 28	6 12	7R27	14 6	5 10	14 35	16 32
28	18	22	5	5 44 14	10♐16	20 50	0♊39	6 39	7 27	14 10	5 14	14 35	16 34
29	18	26	2	6 41 26	25 10	22 45	1 49	7 6	7 27	14 14	5 17	14 35	16 35
30	18	29	58	7♋38 37	9♑57	24♊42	3♊ 0	7♎34	7♓26	14♍18	5♋21	14♎35	16♌37

THE SUN ENTERS THE SIGN OF CANCER ON JUN 21 AT 23:37.

♏ SCORPIO ♐ SAGITTARIUS ♑ CAPRICORN ♒ AQUARIUS ♓ PISCES

1950

SIDEREAL · SUN. · MOON. · MERCURY. · VENUS. · MARS. · JUPITER. · SATURN. · URANUS. · NEPTUNE. · PLUTO.

DAY	TIME	☉	☽	☿	♀	♂	♃	♄	♅	♆	♇
	h m s	° ' "	° '	° '	° '	° '	° '	° '	° '	° '	° '
J 1	18 33 55	8♋35 48	24♑27	26♊41	4♊11	8♎ 2	7♓26	14♍23	5♋24	14♎35	16♌38
U 2	18 37 51	9 32 59	8♒36	28 43	5 21	8 3Ø	7R25	14 27	5 28	14 35	16 4Ø
L 3	18 41 48	1Ø 3Ø 1Ø	22 18	Ø♋47	6 32	8 58	7 24	14 32	5 32	14 35	16 41
Y 4	18 45 44	11 27 21	5♓32	2 52	7 43	9 27	7 22	14 36	5 35	14 36	16 43
5	18 49 41	12 24 33	18 22	4 59	8 54	9 56	7 21	14 41	5 39	14 36	16 45
6	18 53 37	13 21 44	Ø♈49	7 7	1Ø 5	1Ø 25	7 19	14 46	5 42	14 36	16 46
7	18 57 34	14 18 56	12 59	9 16	11 16	1Ø 54	7 17	14 51	5 46	14 36	16 48
8	19 1 31	15 16 8	24 56	11 26	12 27	11 24	7 15	14 56	5 5Ø	14 37	16 49
9	19 5 27	16 13 21	6♉47	13 35	13 38	11 54	7 13	15 1	5 53	14 37	16 51
1Ø	19 9 24	17 1Ø 34	18 37	15 45	14 49	12 24	7 11	15 6	5 57	14 38	16 53
11	19 13 2Ø	18 7 47	Ø♊29	17 55	16 Ø	12 54	7 8	15 11	6 Ø	14 38	16 54
12	19 17 17	19 5 1	12 28	2Ø 4	17 11	13 24	7 5	15 16	6 4	14 38	16 56
13	19 21 13	2Ø 2 15	24 36	22 12	18 23	13 55	7 3	15 21	6 7	14 39	16 58
14	19 25 1Ø	2Ø 59 3Ø	6♋55	24 2Ø	19 34	14 26	6 59	15 26	6 11	14 4Ø	16 59
15	19 29 6	21 56 45	19 28	26 26	2Ø 45	14 57	6 56	15 32	6 14	14 4Ø	17 1
16	19 33 3	22 54 1	2♌12	28 31	21 57	15 29	6 53	15 37	6 18	14 41	17 3
17	19 37 Ø	23 51 16	15 9	Ø♌35	23 8	16 Ø	6 49	15 43	6 21	14 41	17 4
18	19 4Ø 56	24 48 32	28 17	2 37	24 2Ø	16 32	6 45	15 48	6 25	14 42	17 6
19	19 44 53	25 45 48	11♍37	4 38	25 32	17 4	6 41	15 54	6 28	14 43	17 8
2Ø	19 48 49	26 43 5	25 8	6 37	26 43	17 37	6 37	16 Ø	6 32	14 44	17 1Ø
21	19 52 46	27 4Ø 21	8♎5Ø	8 35	27 55	18 9	6 32	16 5	6 35	14 44	17 11
22	19 56 42	28 37 38	22 43	1Ø 3Ø	29 7	18 42	6 28	16 11	6 39	14 45	17 13
23	2Ø Ø 39	29 34 55	6♏48	12 24	Ø♋18	19 14	6 23	16 17	6 42	14 46	17 15
24	2Ø 4 35	Ø♌32 13	21 3	14 17	1 3Ø	19 47	6 18	16 23	6 45	14 47	17 17
25	2Ø 8 32	1 29 3Ø	5♐27	16 7	2 42	2Ø 21	6 13	16 29	6 49	14 48	17 18
26	2Ø 12 29	2 26 49	19 56	17 56	3 54	2Ø 54	6 8	16 35	6 52	14 49	17 2Ø
27	2Ø 16 25	3 24 7	4♑25	19 43	5 6	21 28	6 3	16 41	6 55	14 5Ø	17 22
28	2Ø 2Ø 22	4 21 27	18 48	21 28	6 18	22 1	5 57	16 47	6 59	14 51	17 24
29	2Ø 24 18	5 18 47	2♒58	23 12	7 3Ø	22 35	5 51	16 54	7 2	14 52	17 26
3Ø	2Ø 28 15	6 16 7	16 51	24 54	8 42	23 9	5 46	17 Ø	7 5	14 53	17 27
31	2Ø 32 11	7♌13 29	Ø♓23	26♌34	9♋55	23♎43	5♓4Ø	17♍ 6	7♋ 9	14♎54	17♌29

THE SUN ENTERS THE SIGN OF LEO ON JUL 23 AT 10:31.

DAY	TIME	☉	☽	☿	♀	♂	♃	♄	♅	♆	♇
	h m s	° ' "	° '	° '	° '	° '	° '	° '	° '	° '	° '
A 1	2Ø 36 8	8♌1Ø 51	13♓32	28♌12	11♋ 7	24♎18	5♓34	17♍13	7♋12	14♎55	17♌31
U 2	2Ø 4Ø 4	9 8 14	26 19	29 49	12 19	24 52	5R28	17 19	7 15	14 56	17 33
G 3	2Ø 44 1	1Ø 5 39	8♈46	1♍24	13 31	25 27	5 21	17 25	7 18	14 57	17 35
U 4	2Ø 47 58	11 3 4	2Ø 57	2 58	14 44	26 2	5 15	17 32	7 21	14 58	17 36
S 5	2Ø 51 54	12 Ø 31	2♉56	4 29	15 56	26 37	5 8	17 38	7 24	14 59	17 38
T 6	2Ø 55 51	12 57 59	14 49	5 59	17 9	27 12	5 2	17 45	7 27	15 1	17 4Ø
7	2Ø 59 47	13 55 28	26 4Ø	7 27	18 21	27 48	4 55	17 52	7 31	15 2	17 42
8	21 3 44	14 52 59	8♊34	8 54	19 34	28 23	4 48	17 58	7 34	15 3	17 44
9	21 7 4Ø	15 5Ø 31	2Ø 37	1Ø 19	2Ø 47	28 59	4 41	18 5	7 37	15 4	17 46
1Ø	21 11 37	16 48 4	2♋51	11 42	21 59	29 35	4 34	18 12	7 4Ø	15 6	17 48
11	21 15 33	17 45 39	15 19	13 3	23 12	Ø♏11	4 27	18 18	7 43	15 7	17 49
12	21 19 3Ø	18 43 15	28 3	14 22	24 25	Ø 47	4 19	18 25	7 46	15 9	17 51
13	21 23 27	19 4Ø 52	11♌ 5	15 4Ø	25 38	1 23	4 12	18 32	7 48	15 1Ø	17 53
14	21 27 23	2Ø 38 3Ø	24 22	16 55	26 51	2 Ø	4 4	18 39	7 51	15 11	17 55
15	21 31 2Ø	21 36 9	7♍53	18 8	28 4	2 36	3 57	18 46	7 54	15 13	17 57
16	21 35 16	22 33 5Ø	21 37	19 2Ø	29 16	3 13	3 49	18 53	7 57	15 14	17 59
17	21 39 13	23 31 32	5♎3Ø	2Ø 29	Ø♌3Ø	3 5Ø	3 42	19 Ø	8 Ø	15 16	18 Ø
18	21 43 9	24 29 15	19 32	21 36	1 43	4 27	3 34	19 7	8 3	15 17	18 2
19	21 47 6	25 26 58	3♏38	22 41	2 56	5 4	3 26	19 14	8 5	15 19	18 4
2Ø	21 51 2	26 24 43	17 49	23 43	4 9	5 41	3 19	19 21	8 8	15 21	18 6
21	21 54 59	27 22 3Ø	2♐ 1	24 42	5 22	6 19	3 11	19 28	8 11	15 22	18 8
22	21 58 56	28 2Ø 17	16 12	25 39	6 35	6 57	3 3	19 35	8 13	15 24	18 1Ø
23	22 2 52	29 18 5	Ø♑22	26 33	7 49	7 34	2 55	19 43	8 16	15 26	18 11
24	22 6 49	Ø♍15 55	14 25	27 24	9 2	8 12	2 47	19 5Ø	8 18	15 27	18 13
25	22 1Ø 45	1 13 46	28 2Ø	28 12	1Ø 15	8 5Ø	2 39	19 57	8 21	15 29	18 15
26	22 14 42	2 11 38	12♒ 4	28 57	11 29	9 28	2 31	2Ø 4	8 23	15 31	18 17
27	22 18 38	3 9 31	25 33	29 37	12 42	1Ø 6	2 24	2Ø 12	8 26	15 32	18 19
28	22 22 35	4 7 26	8♓45	Ø♎15	13 56	1Ø 45	2 16	2Ø 19	8 28	15 34	18 21
29	22 26 31	5 5 23	21 41	Ø 47	15 9	11 23	2 8	2Ø 26	8 31	15 36	18 22
3Ø	22 3Ø 28	6 3 21	4♈19	1 16	16 23	12 2	2 Ø	2Ø 33	8 33	15 38	18 24
31	22 34 25	7♍ 1 21	16♈41	1♎4Ø	17♌36	12♏4Ø	1♓52	2Ø♍41	8♋35	15♎4Ø	18♌26

THE SUN ENTERS THE SIGN OF VIRGO ON AUG 23 AT 17:24.

DAY	TIME	☉	☽	☿	♀	♂	♃	♄	♅	♆	♇
	h m s	° ' "	° '	° '	° '	° '	° '	° '	° '	° '	° '
S 1	22 38 21	7♍59 22	28♈5Ø	1♎59	18♌5Ø	13♏19	1♓44	2Ø♍48	8♋37	15♎41	18♌28
E 2	22 42 18	8 57 26	1Ø♉49	2 14	2Ø 4	13 58	1R36	2Ø 56	8 4Ø	15 43	18 29
P 3	22 46 14	9 55 31	22 42	2 22	21 17	14 37	1 29	21 3	8 42	15 45	18 31
T 4	22 5Ø 11	1Ø 53 39	4♊34	2R25	22 31	15 16	1 21	21 1Ø	8 44	15 47	18 33
E 5	22 54 7	11 51 48	16 29	2 22	23 45	15 56	1 13	21 18	8 46	15 49	18 35
M 6	22 58 4	12 5Ø Ø	28 32	2 13	24 59	16 35	1 6	21 25	8 48	15 51	18 36
B 7	23 2 Ø	13 48 13	1Ø♋47	1 58	26 13	17 15	Ø 58	21 33	8 5Ø	15 53	18 38
E 8	23 5 57	14 46 28	23 19	1 36	27 27	17 54	Ø 51	21 4Ø	8 52	15 55	18 4Ø
R 9	23 9 54	15 44 46	6♌ 9	1 7	28 41	18 34	Ø 43	21 48	8 54	15 57	18 41
1Ø	23 13 5Ø	16 43 5	19 21	Ø 32	29 55	19 14	Ø 36	21 55	8 56	15 59	18 43
11	23 17 47	17 41 26	2♍54	29♍51	1♍ 9	19 54	Ø 29	22 3	8 57	16 1	18 45
12	23 21 43	18 39 49	16 46	29 5	2 23	2Ø 34	Ø 22	22 1Ø	8 59	16 3	18 46
13	23 25 4Ø	19 38 14	Ø♎55	28 13	3 37	21 14	Ø 14	22 18	9 1	16 5	18 48
14	23 29 36	2Ø 36 41	15 16	27 16	4 52	21 55	Ø 8	22 25	9 3	16 7	18 5Ø
15	23 33 33	21 35 9	29 44	26 17	6 6	22 35	Ø 1	22 32	9 4	16 9	18 51
16	23 37 29	22 33 4Ø	14♏13	25 15	7 2Ø	23 16	29♒54	22 4Ø	9 6	16 11	18 53
17	23 41 26	23 32 11	28 4Ø	24 12	8 34	23 57	29 47	22 47	9 7	16 13	18 54
18	23 45 23	24 3Ø 45	13♐ 1	23 9	9 49	24 37	29 41	22 55	9 9	16 15	18 56
19	23 49 19	25 29 2Ø	27 11	22 9	11 3	25 18	29 34	23 2	9 1Ø	16 17	18 58
2Ø	23 53 16	26 27 57	11♑ 9	21 12	12 17	25 59	29 28	23 1Ø	9 12	16 19	18 59
21	23 57 12	27 26 35	24 54	2Ø 2Ø	13 32	26 4Ø	29 22	23 17	9 13	16 22	19 1
22	Ø 1 9	28 25 15	8♒26	19 35	14 46	27 22	29 16	23 25	9 14	16 24	19 2
23	Ø 5 5	29 23 57	21 43	18 57	16 1	28 3	29 1Ø	23 32	9 15	16 26	19 4
24	Ø 9 2	Ø♎22 4Ø	4♓47	18 28	17 15	28 44	29 5	23 4Ø	9 17	16 28	19 5
25	Ø 12 58	1 21 26	17 37	18 8	18 3Ø	29 26	28 59	23 47	9 18	16 3Ø	19 7
26	Ø 16 55	2 2Ø 13	Ø♈15	17D58	19 44	Ø♐ 7	28 54	23 55	9 19	16 32	19 8
27	Ø 2Ø 52	3 19 2	12 39	17 58	2Ø 59	Ø 49	28 48	24 2	9 2Ø	16 35	19 9
28	Ø 24 48	4 17 53	24 53	18 8	22 13	1 31	28 43	24 1Ø	9 21	16 37	19 11
29	Ø 28 45	5 16 46	6♉57	18 28	23 28	2 13	28 38	24 17	9 22	16 39	19 12
3Ø	Ø 32 41	6♎15 42	18♉54	18♍58	24♍43	2♐55	28♒34	24♍24	9♋23	16♎41	19♌14

THE SUN ENTERS THE SIGN OF LIBRA ON SEP 23 AT 14:44.

♈ ARIES ♉ TAURUS ♊ GEMINI ♋ CANCER ♌ LEO ♍ VIRGO ♎ LIBRA

SIDEREAL . . SUN . . . MOON . . . MERCURY . . VENUS . . MARS . . JUPITER . . SATURN . . URANUS . . NEPTUNE . . PLUTO . .

DAY	TIME	☉	☽	☿	♀	♂	♃	♄	♅	♆	♇
	h m s	° ' "	° '	° '	° '	° '	° '	° '	° '	° '	° '
O 1	0 36 38	7♎14 40	0♊46	19♍37	25♍57	3♐37	28♒29	24♍32	9♋23	16♎43	19♌15
C 2	0 40 34	8 13 40	12 37	20 25	27 12	4 19	28R25	24 39	9 24	16 46	19 16
T 3	0 44 31	9 12 42	24 31	21 21	28 27	5 1	28 20	24 47	9 25	16 48	19 18
O 4	0 48 27	10 11 47	6♋32	22 24	29 42	5 43	28 16	24 54	9 26	16 50	19 19
B 5	0 52 24	11 10 54	18 45	23 33	0♎57	6 26	28 12	25 1	9 26	16 52	19 20
E 6	0 56 21	12 10 3	1♌13	24 49	2 11	7 8	28 9	25 8	9 27	16 54	19 21
R 7	1 0 17	13 9 14	14 2	26 10	3 26	7 51	28 5	25 16	9 27	16 57	19 23
8	1 4 14	14 8 28	27 15	27 35	4 41	8 34	28 2	25 23	9 28	16 59	19 24
9	1 8 10	15 7 44	10♍53	29 4	5 56	9 16	27 59	25 30	9 28	17 1	19 25
10	1 12 7	16 7 2	24 56	0♎36	7 11	9 59	27 56	25 37	9 28	17 3	19 26
11	1 16 3	17 6 22	9♎22	2 11	8 26	10 42	27 53	25 45	9 29	17 6	19 27
12	1 20 0	18 5 45	24 6	3 48	9 41	11 25	27 51	25 52	9 29	17 8	19 28
13	1 23 56	19 5 9	9♏ 0	5 27	10 56	12 9	27 48	25 59	9 29	17 10	19 29
14	1 27 53	20 4 35	23 57	7 7	12 11	12 52	27 46	26 6	9 29	17 12	19 31
15	1 31 49	21 4 4	8♐48	8 49	13 26	13 35	27 44	26 13	9 29	17 15	19 32
16	1 35 46	22 3 34	23 26	10 31	14 41	14 18	27 42	26 20	9R29	17 17	19 33
17	1 39 43	23 3 6	7♑46	12 13	15 56	15 2	27 41	26 27	9 29	17 19	19 34
18	1 43 39	24 2 40	21 45	13 56	17 11	15 46	27 39	26 34	9 29	17 21	19 35
19	1 47 36	25 2 15	5♒23	15 39	18 26	16 29	27 38	26 41	9 29	17 23	19 36
20	1 51 32	26 1 52	18 41	17 22	19 41	17 13	27 37	26 48	9 29	17 26	19 36
21	1 55 29	27 1 30	1♓40	19 5	20 56	17 57	27 36	26 55	9 29	17 28	19 37
22	1 59 25	28 1 11	14 24	20 47	22 12	18 41	27 36	27 1	9 28	17 30	19 38
23	2 3 22	29 0 53	26 55	22 30	23 27	19 25	27 35	27 8	9 28	17 32	19 39
24	2 7 19	0♏ 0 37	9♈14	24 12	24 42	20 9	27D35	27 15	9 28	17 35	19 40
25	2 11 15	1 0 23	21 25	25 54	25 57	20 53	27 35	27 22	9 27	17 37	19 41
26	2 15 12	2 0 10	3♉29	27 35	27 12	21 37	27 36	27 28	9 27	17 39	19 41
27	2 19 8	3 0 0	15 27	29 16	28 27	22 21	27 36	27 35	9 26	17 41	19 42
28	2 23 5	3 59 52	27 20	0♏56	29 43	23 5	27 37	27 41	9 26	17 43	19 43
29	2 27 1	4 59 46	9♊12	2 36	0♏58	23 50	27 38	27 48	9 25	17 45	19 44
30	2 30 58	5 59 42	21 3	4 15	2 13	24 34	27 39	27 54	9 24	17 48	19 44
31	2 34 54	6♏59 40	2♋57	5♏54	3♏28	25♐19	27♒40	28♍ 1	9♋23	17♎50	19♌45

THE SUN ENTERS THE SIGN OF SCORPIO ON OCT 23 AT 23:45.

DAY	TIME	☉	☽	☿	♀	♂	♃	♄	♅	♆	♇
	h m s	° ' "	° '	° '	° '	° '	° '	° '	° '	° '	° '
N 1	2 38 51	7♏59 40	14♋57	7♏32	4♏44	26♐ 3	27♒41	28♍ 7	9♋23	17♎52	19♌45
O 2	2 42 48	8 59 42	27 7	9 10	5 59	26 48	27 43	28 13	9R22	17 54	19 46
V 3	2 46 44	9 59 47	9♌30	10 48	7 14	27 33	27 45	28 20	9 21	17 56	19 47
E 4	2 50 41	10 59 53	22 13	12 25	8 29	28 18	27 47	28 26	9 20	17 58	19 47
M 5	2 54 37	12 0 2	5♍19	14 2	9 45	29 3	27 49	28 32	9 19	18 0	19 48
B 6	2 58 34	13 0 12	18 51	15 38	11 0	29 47	27 52	28 38	9 18	18 2	19 48
E 7	3 2 30	14 0 25	2♎51	17 14	12 15	0♑32	27 54	28 44	9 17	18 4	19 49
R 8	3 6 27	15 0 40	17 20	18 49	13 31	1 18	27 57	28 50	9 15	18 6	19 49
9	3 10 23	16 0 56	2♏12	20 24	14 46	2 3	28 0	28 56	9 14	18 9	19 49
10	3 14 20	17 1 15	17 21	21 59	16 1	2 48	28 3	29 2	9 13	18 11	19 50
11	3 18 16	18 1 35	2♐38	23 33	17 17	3 33	28 7	29 8	9 12	18 13	19 50
12	3 22 13	19 1 57	17 51	25 7	18 32	4 19	28 11	29 13	9 10	18 15	19 50
13	3 26 10	20 2 20	2♑50	26 41	19 47	5 4	28 14	29 19	9 9	18 17	19 51
14	3 30 6	21 2 45	17 26	28 14	21 3	5 49	28 18	29 25	9 8	18 18	19 51
15	3 34 3	22 3 12	1♒36	29 48	22 18	6 35	28 23	29 30	9 6	18 20	19 51
16	3 37 59	23 3 39	15 18	1♐21	23 34	7 21	28 27	29 36	9 4	18 22	19 51
17	3 41 56	24 4 8	28 34	2 53	24 49	8 6	28 32	29 41	9 3	18 24	19 51
18	3 45 52	25 4 38	11♓26	4 26	26 4	8 52	28 36	29 46	9 1	18 26	19 51
19	3 49 49	26 5 9	23 59	5 58	27 20	9 38	28 41	29 51	9 0	18 28	19 52
20	3 53 46	27 5 42	6♈18	7 30	28 35	10 23	28 46	29 57	8 58	18 30	19 52
21	3 57 42	28 6 15	18 26	9 1	29 50	11 9	28 52	0♎ 2	8 56	18 32	19R52
22	4 1 39	29 6 51	0♉26	10 33	1♐ 6	11 55	28 57	0 7	8 54	18 34	19 52
23	4 5 35	0♐ 7 27	12 21	12 4	2 21	12 41	29 3	0 12	8 53	18 35	19 52
24	4 9 32	1 8 5	24 14	13 35	3 37	13 27	29 9	0 17	8 51	18 37	19 52
25	4 13 28	2 8 44	6♊ 6	15 6	4 52	14 13	29 15	0 21	8 49	18 39	19 52
26	4 17 25	3 9 25	17 59	16 36	6 7	14 59	29 21	0 26	8 47	18 41	19 51
27	4 21 21	4 10 7	29 53	18 7	7 23	15 45	29 27	0 31	8 45	18 42	19 51
28	4 25 18	5 10 50	11♋51	19 37	8 38	16 31	29 34	0 35	8 43	18 44	19 51
29	4 29 15	6 11 35	23 54	21 6	9 54	17 18	29 40	0 40	8 41	18 46	19 51
30	4 33 11	7♐12 22	6♌ 6	22♐35	11♐ 9	18♑ 4	29♒47	0♎44	8♋39	18♎47	19♌51

THE SUN ENTERS THE SIGN OF SAGITTARIUS ON NOV 22 AT 21:03.

DAY	TIME	☉	☽	☿	♀	♂	♃	♄	♅	♆	♇
	h m s	° ' "	° '	° '	° '	° '	° '	° '	° '	° '	° '
D 1	4 37 8	8♐13 9	18♌29	24♐ 4	12♐24	18♑50	29♒54	0♎48	8♋37	18♎49	19♌50
E 2	4 41 4	9 13 59	1♍ 7	25 32	13 40	19 36	0♓ 1	0 53	8R35	18 50	19R50
C 3	4 45 1	10 14 49	14 5	27 0	14 55	20 23	0 9	0 57	8 32	18 52	19 50
E 4	4 48 57	11 15 41	27 27	28 27	16 11	21 9	0 16	1 1	8 30	18 54	19 50
M 5	4 52 54	12 16 35	11♎16	29 53	17 26	21 56	0 24	1 5	8 28	18 55	19 49
B 6	4 56 50	13 17 29	25 33	1♑18	18 41	22 42	0 31	1 9	8 26	18 57	19 49
E 7	5 0 47	14 18 25	10♏17	2 42	19 57	23 29	0 39	1 12	8 24	18 58	19 48
R 8	5 4 44	15 19 23	25 22	4 5	21 12	24 15	0 47	1 16	8 21	18 59	19 48
9	5 8 40	16 20 21	10♐40	5 27	22 28	25 2	0 56	1 20	8 19	19 1	19 47
10	5 12 37	17 21 21	26 1	6 47	23 43	25 49	1 4	1 23	8 17	19 2	19 47
11	5 16 33	18 22 21	11♑11	8 5	24 59	26 35	1 13	1 27	8 14	19 4	19 46
12	5 20 30	19 23 22	26 1	9 20	26 14	27 22	1 21	1 30	8 12	19 5	19 46
13	5 24 26	20 24 24	10♒23	10 33	27 29	28 9	1 30	1 33	8 9	19 6	19 45
14	5 28 23	21 25 26	24 16	11 43	28 45	28 56	1 39	1 36	8 7	19 7	19 45
15	5 32 20	22 26 29	7♓39	12 49	0♑ 0	29 42	1 48	1 39	8 4	19 9	19 44
16	5 36 16	23 27 32	20 34	13 52	1 16	0♒29	1 57	1 42	8 2	19 10	19 43
17	5 40 13	24 28 35	3♈ 7	14 49	2 31	1 16	2 7	1 45	8 0	19 11	19 43
18	5 44 9	25 29 39	15 23	15 41	3 47	2 3	2 16	1 48	7 57	19 12	19 42
19	5 48 6	26 30 43	27 26	16 26	5 2	2 50	2 26	1 50	7 54	19 13	19 41
20	5 52 2	27 31 47	9♉21	17 5	6 17	3 37	2 35	1 53	7 52	19 14	19 40
21	5 55 59	28 32 52	21 12	17 35	7 33	4 24	2 45	1 55	7 49	19 16	19 40
22	5 59 55	29 33 57	3♊ 3	17 57	8 48	5 11	2 55	1 58	7 47	19 17	19 39
23	6 3 52	0♑35 3	14 55	18R 9	10 3	5 58	3 5	2 0	7 44	19 18	19 38
24	6 7 49	1 36 9	26 51	18 10	11 19	6 45	3 16	2 2	7 42	19 19	19 37
25	6 11 45	2 37 16	8♋52	18 0	12 34	7 32	3 26	2 4	7 39	19 19	19 36
26	6 15 42	3 38 22	20 58	17 38	13 50	8 19	3 36	2 6	7 37	19 20	19 35
27	6 19 38	4 39 29	3♌11	17 5	15 5	9 6	3 47	2 8	7 34	19 21	19 34
28	6 23 35	5 40 37	15 32	16 20	16 20	9 53	3 58	2 9	7 31	19 22	19 33
29	6 27 31	6 41 45	28 3	15 24	17 36	10 40	4 8	2 11	7 29	19 23	19 33
30	6 31 28	7 42 53	10♍47	14 18	18 51	11 28	4 19	2 13	7 26	19 24	19 32
31	6 35 24	8♑44 2	23♍46	13♑ 5	20♑ 6	12♒15	4♓30	2♎14	7♋24	19♎24	19♌31

THE SUN ENTERS THE SIGN OF CAPRICORN ON DEC 22 AT 10:14.

♏ SCORPIO ♐ SAGITTARIUS ♑ CAPRICORN ♒ AQUARIUS ♓ PISCES

SIDEREAL SUN. MOON. MERCURY. VENUS. MARS. JUPITER. SATURN. URANUS. NEPTUNE. PLUTO.

DAY	TIME	☉	☽	☿	♀	♂	♃	♄	♅	♆	♇
	h m s	° ' "	° '	° '	° '	° '	° '	° '	° '	° '	° '
J 1	6 39 21	9♑45 11	7♎ 3	11♑47	21♑22	13♒ 2	4♓41	2♎15	7♋21	19♎25	19♌29
A 2	6 43 18	10 46 21	20 42	10R26	22 37	13 49	4 53	2 16	7R18	19 26	19R28
N 3	6 47 14	11 47 30	4♏44	9 5	23 52	14 36	5 4	2 17	7 16	19 26	19 27
U 4	6 51 11	12 48 41	19 10	7 46	25 8	15 24	5 15	2 18	7 13	19 27	19 26
A 5	6 55 7	13 49 51	3♐56	6 32	26 23	16 11	5 27	2 19	7 11	19 28	19 25
R 6	6 59 4	14 51 2	18 57	5 25	27 38	16 58	5 39	2 20	7 8	19 28	19 24
Y 7	7 3 0	15 52 13	4♑ 4	4 26	28 54	17 45	5 50	2 20	7 6	19 29	19 23
8	7 6 57	16 53 24	19 7	3 36	0♒ 9	18 32	6 2	2 21	7 3	19 29	19 22
9	7 10 54	17 54 35	3♒55	2 57	1 24	19 20	6 14	2 21	7 1	19 30	19 21
10	7 14 50	18 55 45	18 21	2 27	2 39	20 7	6 26	2 22	6 58	19 30	19 19
11	7 18 47	19 56 55	2♓20	2 7	3 55	20 54	6 38	2 22	6 56	19 30	19 18
12	7 22 43	20 58 4	15 50	1D57	5 10	21 42	6 50	2R22	6 53	19 31	19 17
13	7 26 40	21 59 12	28 53	1 56	6 25	22 29	7 3	2 22	6 51	19 31	19 16
14	7 30 36	23 0 20	11♈32	2 3	7 40	23 16	7 15	2 22	6 48	19 31	19 14
15	7 34 33	24 1 28	23 51	2 17	8 56	24 3	7 27	2 21	6 46	19 31	19 13
16	7 38 29	25 2 34	5♉55	2 39	10 11	24 51	7 40	2 21	6 43	19 32	19 12
17	7 42 26	26 3 40	17 51	3 8	11 26	25 38	7 52	2 21	6 41	19 32	19 11
18	7 46 22	27 4 46	29 42	3 42	12 41	26 25	8 5	2 20	6 38	19 32	19 9
19	7 50 19	28 5 50	11♊33	4 22	13 56	27 12	8 18	2 19	6 36	19 32	19 8
20	7 54 16	29 6 54	23 27	5 6	15 11	28 0	8 30	2 18	6 34	19 32	19 7
21	7 58 12	0♒ 7 57	5♋28	5 55	16 27	28 47	8 43	2 18	6 31	19R32	19 5
22	8 2 9	1 8 59	17 36	6 47	17 42	29 34	8 56	2 17	6 29	19 32	19 4
23	8 6 5	2 10 0	29 54	7 43	18 57	0♓21	9 9	2 15	6 27	19 32	19 3
24	8 10 2	3 11 1	12♌21	8 42	20 12	1 9	9 22	2 14	6 25	19 32	19 1
25	8 13 58	4 12 1	24 59	9 44	21 27	1 56	9 35	2 13	6 22	19 32	19 0
26	8 17 55	5 13 0	7♍48	10 49	22 42	2 43	9 49	2 11	6 20	19 32	18 58
27	8 21 52	6 13 58	20 48	11 56	23 57	3 30	10 2	2 10	6 18	19 32	18 57
28	8 25 48	7 14 56	4♎ 0	13 5	25 12	4 17	10 15	2 8	6 16	19 31	18 56
29	8 29 45	8 15 53	17 26	14 16	26 27	5 5	10 29	2 6	6 14	19 31	18 54
30	8 33 41	9 16 49	1♏ 7	15 29	27 42	5 52	10 42	2 5	6 12	19 31	18 53
31	8 37 38	10♒17 45	15♏ 3	16♑44	28♒57	6♓39	10♓56	2♎ 3	6♋10	19♎30	18♌51

THE SUN ENTERS THE SIGN OF AQUARIUS ON JAN 20 AT 20:53.

DAY	TIME	☉	☽	☿	♀	♂	♃	♄	♅	♆	♇
	h m s	° ' "	° '	° '	° '	° '	° '	° '	° '	° '	° '
F 1	8 41 34	11♒18 41	29♏14	18♑ 0	0♓12	7♓26	11♓ 9	2♎ 1	6♋ 8	19♎30	18♌50
E 2	8 45 31	12 19 35	13♐39	19 18	1 27	8 13	11 23	1R58	6R 6	19R30	18R48
B 3	8 49 27	13 20 29	28 14	20 37	2 41	9 0	11 36	1 56	6 4	19 29	18 47
R 4	8 53 24	14 21 22	12♑54	21 57	3 56	9 47	11 50	1 54	6 2	19 29	18 46
U 5	8 57 21	15 22 14	27 32	23 19	5 11	10 35	12 4	1 51	6 0	19 28	18 44
A 6	9 1 17	16 23 5	12♒ 0	24 41	6 26	11 22	12 18	1 49	5 58	19 28	18 43
R 7	9 5 14	17 23 54	26 13	26 5	7 41	12 9	12 31	1 46	5 57	19 27	18 41
Y 8	9 9 10	18 24 43	10♓ 5	27 30	8 56	12 56	12 45	1 44	5 55	19 27	18 40
9	9 13 7	19 25 29	23 34	28 56	10 10	13 43	12 59	1 41	5 53	19 26	18 38
10	9 17 3	20 26 15	6♈39	0♒22	11 25	14 30	13 13	1 38	5 51	19 26	18 37
11	9 21 0	21 26 59	19 22	1 50	12 40	15 17	13 27	1 35	5 50	19 25	18 35
12	9 24 56	22 27 41	1♉46	3 19	13 54	16 4	13 41	1 32	5 48	19 24	18 34
13	9 28 53	23 28 22	13 54	4 48	15 9	16 51	13 55	1 29	5 47	19 23	18 33
14	9 32 50	24 29 1	25 53	6 19	16 24	17 37	14 9	1 25	5 45	19 23	18 31
15	9 36 46	25 29 38	7♊46	7 50	17 38	18 24	14 23	1 22	5 44	19 22	18 30
16	9 40 43	26 30 14	19 38	9 23	18 53	19 11	14 38	1 19	5 43	19 21	18 28
17	9 44 39	27 30 48	1♋34	10 56	20 7	19 58	14 52	1 15	5 41	19 20	18 27
18	9 48 36	28 31 20	13 37	12 30	21 22	20 45	15 6	1 12	5 40	19 19	18 25
19	9 52 32	29 31 51	25 52	14 5	22 36	21 32	15 20	1 8	5 39	19 18	18 24
20	9 56 29	0♓32 20	8♌19	15 41	23 50	22 18	15 35	1 5	5 37	19 18	18 23
21	10 0 25	1 32 47	21 1	17 18	25 5	23 5	15 49	1 1	5 36	19 17	18 21
22	10 4 22	2 33 12	3♍57	18 56	26 19	23 52	16 3	0 57	5 35	19 16	18 20
23	10 8 19	3 33 36	17 8	20 35	27 33	24 38	16 18	0 53	5 34	19 15	18 18
24	10 12 15	4 33 58	0♎33	22 14	28 48	25 25	16 32	0 49	5 33	19 14	18 17
25	10 16 12	5 34 19	14 10	23 55	0♈ 2	26 11	16 46	0 45	5 32	19 12	18 16
26	10 20 8	6 34 38	27 58	25 37	1 16	26 58	17 1	0 41	5 31	19 11	18 14
27	10 24 5	7 34 56	11♏54	27 19	2 30	27 44	17 15	0 37	5 31	19 10	18 13
28	10 28 1	8♓35 12	25♏59	29♒ 3	3♈44	28♓31	17♓30	0♎33	5♋30	19♎ 9	18♌12

THE SUN ENTERS THE SIGN OF PISCES ON FEB 19 AT 11:10.

DAY	TIME	☉	☽	☿	♀	♂	♃	♄	♅	♆	♇
	h m s	° ' "	° '	° '	° '	° '	° '	° '	° '	° '	° '
M 1	10 31 58	9♓35 27	10♐ 8	0♓48	4♈58	29♓17	17♓44	0♎29	5♋29	19♎ 8	18♌10
A 2	10 35 54	10 35 41	24 22	2 34	6 12	0♈ 4	17 59	0R24	5R28	19R 7	18R 9
R 3	10 39 51	11 35 53	8♑36	4 20	7 26	0 50	18 13	0 20	5 28	19 6	18 8
C 4	10 43 48	12 36 3	22 49	6 8	8 40	1 36	18 28	0 16	5 27	19 4	18 6
H 5	10 47 44	13 36 12	6♒56	7 57	9 54	2 23	18 42	0 11	5 27	19 3	18 5
6	10 51 41	14 36 20	20 55	9 47	11 8	3 9	18 57	0 7	5 26	19 2	18 4
7	10 55 37	15 36 25	4♓42	11 38	12 21	3 55	19 11	0 2	5 26	19 1	18 2
8	10 59 34	16 36 29	18 14	13 30	13 35	4 42	19 26	29♍58	5 25	18 59	18 1
9	11 3 30	17 36 30	1♈29	15 23	14 49	5 28	19 40	29 53	5 25	18 58	18 0
10	11 7 27	18 36 30	14 27	17 18	16 3	6 14	19 55	29 49	5 25	18 57	17 59
11	11 11 23	19 36 28	27 7	19 13	17 16	7 0	20 9	29 44	5 24	18 55	17 57
12	11 15 20	20 36 23	9♉30	21 9	18 30	7 46	20 24	29 39	5 24	18 54	17 56
13	11 19 17	21 36 17	21 41	23 6	19 43	8 32	20 38	29 35	5 24	18 52	17 55
14	11 23 13	22 36 8	3♊41	25 4	20 57	9 18	20 53	29 30	5D24	18 51	17 54
15	11 27 10	23 35 57	15 35	27 2	22 10	10 4	21 8	29 25	5 24	18 49	17 53
16	11 31 6	24 35 44	27 28	29 1	23 23	10 50	21 22	29 21	5 24	18 48	17 52
17	11 35 3	25 35 29	9♋24	1♈ 0	24 37	11 36	21 37	29 16	5 24	18 47	17 51
18	11 38 59	26 35 12	21 28	3 0	25 50	12 21	21 51	29 11	5 24	18 45	17 50
19	11 42 56	27 34 52	3♌44	4 59	27 3	13 7	22 6	29 7	5 25	18 44	17 48
20	11 46 52	28 34 30	16 16	6 59	28 16	13 53	22 20	29 2	5 25	18 42	17 47
21	11 50 49	29 34 6	29 6	8 58	29 29	14 38	22 35	28 57	5 25	18 41	17 46
22	11 54 46	0♈33 39	12♍17	10 56	0♉42	15 24	22 49	28 52	5 26	18 39	17 45
23	11 58 42	1 33 11	25 48	12 52	1 55	16 10	23 4	28 48	5 26	18 37	17 44
24	12 2 39	2 32 40	9♎37	14 48	3 8	16 55	23 18	28 43	5 27	18 36	17 43
25	12 6 35	3 32 7	23 43	16 41	4 21	17 41	23 32	28 38	5 27	18 34	17 42
26	12 10 32	4 31 33	8♏ 0	18 32	5 34	18 26	23 47	28 33	5 28	18 33	17 42
27	12 14 28	5 30 56	22 23	20 20	6 46	19 11	24 1	28 29	5 28	18 31	17 41
28	12 18 25	6 30 18	6♐48	22 5	7 59	19 57	24 16	28 24	5 29	18 30	17 40
29	12 22 21	7 29 38	21 10	23 47	9 11	20 42	24 30	28 19	5 30	18 28	17 39
30	12 26 18	8 28 57	5♑25	25 24	10 24	21 27	24 44	28 15	5 31	18 26	17 38
31	12 30 14	9♈28 14	19♑31	26♈57	11♉36	22♈13	24♓59	28♍10	5♋31	18♎25	17♌37

THE SUN ENTERS THE SIGN OF ARIES ON MAR 21 AT 10:26.

♈ ARIES ♉ TAURUS ♊ GEMINI ♋ CANCER ♌ LEO ♍ VIRGO ♎ LIBRA

SIDEREAL TIME · SUN · MOON · MERCURY · VENUS · MARS · JUPITER · SATURN · URANUS · NEPTUNE · PLUTO

DAY	TIME	☉	☽	☿	♀	♂	♃	♄	♅	♆	♇
	h m s	° ' "	° '	° '	° '	° '	° '	° '	° '	° '	° '
A 1	12 34 11	10♈27 29	3♒26	28♈25	12♉49	22♈58	25♓13	28♍ 6	5♋32	18♎23	17♌37
P 2	12 38 8	11 26 42	17 10	29 48	14 1	23 43	25 27	28R 1	5 33	18R21	17R36
R 3	12 42 4	12 25 53	0♓42	1♉ 6	15 13	24 28	25 41	27 57	5 34	18 20	17 35
I 4	12 46 1	13 25 2	14 2	2 18	16 25	25 13	25 56	27 52	5 35	18 18	17 34
L 5	12 49 57	14 24 10	27 9	3 24	17 38	25 58	26 10	27 48	5 37	18 17	17 34
6	12 53 54	15 23 15	10♈ 3	4 24	18 50	26 43	26 24	27 43	5 38	18 15	17 33
7	12 57 50	16 22 19	22 45	5 18	20 2	27 28	26 38	27 39	5 39	18 13	17 32
8	13 1 47	17 21 20	5♉15	6 6	21 13	28 13	26 52	27 35	5 40	18 12	17 32
9	13 5 43	18 20 20	17 32	6 46	22 25	28 57	27 6	27 30	5 41	18 10	17 31
10	13 9 40	19 19 17	29 39	7 21	23 37	29 42	27 20	27 26	5 43	18 8	17 31
11	13 13 37	20 18 12	11♊38	7 48	24 49	0♉27	27 34	27 22	5 44	18 7	17 30
12	13 17 33	21 17 5	23 32	8 9	26 0	1 11	27 48	27 18	5 46	18 5	17 30
13	13 21 30	22 15 56	5♋24	8 24	27 12	1 56	28 2	27 14	5 47	18 3	17 29
14	13 25 26	23 14 44	17 19	8R32	28 23	2 41	28 16	27 10	5 49	18 2	17 29
15	13 29 23	24 13 30	29 20	8 33	29 35	3 25	28 30	27 6	5 50	18 0	17 28
16	13 33 19	25 12 14	11♌34	8 29	0♊46	4 9	28 43	27 2	5 52	17 58	17 28
17	13 37 16	26 10 56	24 5	8 18	1 57	4 54	28 57	26 58	5 54	17 57	17 27
18	13 41 12	27 9 35	6♍57	8 2	3 8	5 38	29 11	26 54	5 56	17 55	17 27
19	13 45 9	28 8 13	20 13	7 41	4 19	6 22	29 24	26 51	5 57	17 54	17 27
20	13 49 6	29 6 48	3♎54	7 15	5 30	7 7	29 38	26 47	5 59	17 52	17 26
21	13 53 2	0♉ 5 21	18 1	6 45	6 41	7 51	29 52	26 43	6 1	17 50	17 26
22	13 56 59	1 3 52	2♏29	6 11	7 51	8 35	0♈ 5	26 40	6 3	17 49	17 26
23	14 0 55	2 2 21	17 12	5 35	9 2	9 19	0 19	26 36	6 5	17 47	17 26
24	14 4 52	3 0 48	2♐ 4	4 56	10 13	10 3	0 32	26 33	6 7	17 46	17 25
25	14 8 48	3 59 14	16 55	4 16	11 23	10 47	0 45	26 30	6 9	17 44	17 25
26	14 12 45	4 57 38	1♑37	3 35	12 33	11 31	0 58	26 27	6 11	17 42	17 25
27	14 16 41	5 56 1	16 6	2 55	13 43	12 15	1 12	26 24	6 13	17 41	17 25
28	14 20 38	6 54 22	0♒16	2 15	14 54	12 59	1 25	26 21	6 15	17 39	17 25
29	14 24 35	7 52 41	14 7	1 37	16 4	13 42	1 38	26 18	6 18	17 38	17 25
30	14 28 31	8♉50 59	27♒39	1♉ 1	17♊13	14♉26	1♈51	26♍15	6♋20	17♎36	17♌25

THE SUN ENTERS THE SIGN OF TAURUS ON APR 20 AT 21:49.

DAY	TIME	☉	☽	☿	♀	♂	♃	♄	♅	♆	♇
	h m s	° ' "	° '	° '	° '	° '	° '	° '	° '	° '	° '
M 1	14 32 28	9♉49 16	10♓54	0♉27	18♊23	15♉10	2♈ 4	26♍12	6♋22	17♎35	17♌25
A 2	14 36 24	10 47 30	23 53	29♈57	19 33	15 53	2 17	26R 9	6 25	17R33	17 25
Y 3	14 40 21	11 45 44	6♈39	29 30	20 43	16 37	2 30	26 7	6 27	17 32	17 25
4	14 44 17	12 43 55	19 14	29 8	21 52	17 20	2 42	26 4	6 29	17 30	17 25
5	14 48 14	13 42 5	1♉39	28 49	23 1	18 4	2 55	26 2	6 32	17 29	17 25
6	14 52 10	14 40 14	13 55	28 35	24 11	18 47	3 8	25 59	6 34	17 27	17 25
7	14 56 7	15 38 21	26 3	28 26	25 20	19 31	3 20	25 57	6 37	17 26	17 26
8	15 0 4	16 36 26	8♊ 4	28D21	26 29	20 14	3 33	25 55	6 40	17 25	17 26
9	15 4 0	17 34 29	20 0	28 21	27 38	20 57	3 45	25 53	6 42	17 23	17 26
10	15 7 57	18 32 31	1♋52	28 26	28 47	21 41	3 58	25 51	6 45	17 22	17 26
11	15 11 53	19 30 31	13 43	28 36	29 55	22 24	4 10	25 49	6 48	17 21	17 27
12	15 15 50	20 28 29	25 36	28 49	1♋ 4	23 7	4 22	25 47	6 50	17 19	17 27
13	15 19 46	21 26 25	7♌36	29 8	2 12	23 50	4 34	25 46	6 53	17 18	17 27
14	15 23 43	22 24 20	19 47	29 31	3 20	24 33	4 46	25 44	6 56	17 17	17 28
15	15 27 39	23 22 13	2♍14	29 58	4 28	25 16	4 58	25 43	6 59	17 15	17 28
16	15 31 36	24 20 3	15 2	0♉29	5 36	25 59	5 10	25 41	7 1	17 14	17 28
17	15 35 33	25 17 53	28 16	1 5	6 44	26 42	5 22	25 40	7 4	17 13	17 29
18	15 39 29	26 15 40	11♎58	1 44	7 52	27 24	5 34	25 39	7 7	17 12	17 29
19	15 43 26	27 13 26	26 9	2 27	8 59	28 7	5 45	25 38	7 10	17 11	17 30
20	15 47 22	28 11 10	10♏46	3 13	10 6	28 50	5 57	25 37	7 13	17 9	17 30
21	15 51 19	29 8 53	25 45	4 3	11 14	29 32	6 8	25 36	7 16	17 8	17 31
22	15 55 15	0♊ 6 34	10♐56	4 57	12 21	0♊15	6 19	25 35	7 19	17 7	17 32
23	15 59 12	1 4 15	26 8	5 54	13 27	0 58	6 31	25 34	7 22	17 6	17 32
24	16 3 8	2 1 54	11♑11	6 54	14 34	1 40	6 42	25 34	7 25	17 5	17 33
25	16 7 5	2 59 32	25 57	7 57	15 40	2 22	6 53	25 33	7 28	17 4	17 34
26	16 11 2	3 57 9	10♒19	9 3	16 47	3 5	7 4	25 33	7 32	17 3	17 34
27	16 14 58	4 54 45	24 16	10 13	17 53	3 47	7 15	25 33	7 35	17 2	17 35
28	16 18 55	5 52 20	7♓47	11 25	18 59	4 29	7 25	25 32	7 38	17 1	17 36
29	16 22 51	6 49 55	20 56	12 40	20 4	5 12	7 36	25D32	7 41	17 0	17 36
30	16 26 48	7 47 28	3♈46	13 57	21 10	5 54	7 47	25 32	7 44	16 59	17 37
31	16 30 44	8♊45 1	16♈20	15♉18	22♋15	6♊36	7♈57	25♍33	7♋48	16♎58	17♌38

THE SUN ENTERS THE SIGN OF GEMINI ON MAY 21 AT 21:16.

DAY	TIME	☉	☽	☿	♀	♂	♃	♄	♅	♆	♇
	h m s	° ' "	° '	° '	° '	° '	° '	° '	° '	° '	° '
J 1	16 34 41	9♊42 32	28♈41	16♉41	23♋20	7♊18	8♈ 7	25♍33	7♋51	16♎57	17♌39
U 2	16 38 37	10 40 3	10♉54	18 7	24 25	8 0	8 18	25 33	7 54	16R57	17 40
N 3	16 42 34	11 37 33	22 58	19 35	25 30	8 42	8 28	25 34	7 58	16 56	17 41
E 4	16 46 31	12 35 2	4♊58	21 7	26 34	9 24	8 38	25 34	8 1	16 55	17 42
5	16 50 27	13 32 30	16 53	22 40	27 39	10 6	8 48	25 35	8 4	16 54	17 43
6	16 54 24	14 29 58	28 45	24 17	28 43	10 48	8 57	25 36	8 8	16 53	17 44
7	16 58 20	15 27 24	10♋36	25 56	29 46	11 30	9 7	25 36	8 11	16 53	17 45
8	17 2 17	16 24 49	22 28	27 37	0♌50	12 12	9 17	25 37	8 14	16 52	17 46
9	17 6 13	17 22 13	4♌23	29 21	1 53	12 53	9 26	25 38	8 18	16 51	17 47
10	17 10 10	18 19 37	16 23	1♊ 8	2 56	13 35	9 35	25 40	8 21	16 51	17 48
11	17 14 7	19 16 59	28 34	2 57	3 59	14 16	9 45	25 41	8 25	16 50	17 49
12	17 18 3	20 14 20	11♍ 0	4 49	5 1	14 58	9 54	25 42	8 28	16 50	17 50
13	17 22 0	21 11 40	23 45	6 43	6 3	15 40	10 2	25 44	8 32	16 49	17 51
14	17 25 56	22 8 59	6♎53	8 39	7 5	16 21	10 11	25 45	8 35	16 49	17 52
15	17 29 53	23 6 17	20 29	10 38	8 7	17 2	10 20	25 47	8 39	16 48	17 53
16	17 33 49	24 3 34	4♏35	12 39	9 8	17 44	10 28	25 49	8 42	16 48	17 55
17	17 37 46	25 0 51	19 9	14 42	10 9	18 25	10 37	25 51	8 46	16 48	17 56
18	17 41 42	25 58 6	4♐ 7	16 47	11 9	19 6	10 45	25 53	8 49	16 47	17 57
19	17 45 39	26 55 22	19 22	18 53	12 9	19 48	10 53	25 55	8 53	16 47	17 58
20	17 49 36	27 52 36	4♑42	21 1	13 9	20 29	11 1	25 57	8 56	16 47	18 0
21	17 53 32	28 49 50	19 56	23 10	14 9	21 10	11 9	25 59	9 0	16 46	18 1
22	17 57 29	29 47 4	4♒54	25 20	15 8	21 51	11 17	26 1	9 4	16 46	18 2
23	18 1 25	0♋44 18	19 29	27 31	16 6	22 32	11 24	26 4	9 7	16 46	18 3
24	18 5 22	1 41 31	3♓35	29 42	17 4	23 13	11 32	26 6	9 11	16 46	18 5
25	18 9 18	2 38 44	17 13	1♋54	18 2	23 54	11 39	26 9	9 14	16 46	18 6
26	18 13 15	3 35 57	0♈25	4 5	19 0	24 35	11 46	26 12	9 18	16 45	18 6
27	18 17 11	4 33 10	13 14	6 16	19 57	25 16	11 53	26 14	9 22	16 45	18 9
28	18 21 8	5 30 23	25 44	8 26	20 53	25 57	12 0	26 17	9 25	16D45	18 10
29	18 25 5	6 27 37	8♉ 0	10 36	21 49	26 37	12 6	26 20	9 29	16 45	18 12
30	18 29 1	7♋24 50	20♉ 5	12♋44	22♌45	27♊18	12♈13	26♍23	9♋32	16♎45	18♌13

THE SUN ENTERS THE SIGN OF CANCER ON JUN 22 AT 05:25.

♏ SCORPIO ♐ SAGITTARIUS ♑ CAPRICORN ♒ AQUARIUS ♓ PISCES

SIDEREAL SUN. MOON. MERCURY. VENUS. MARS. JUPITER. SATURN. URANUS. NEPTUNE. PLUTO.

DAY	TIME	☉	☽	☿	♀	♂	♃	♄	♅	♆	♇
	h m s	° ' "	° '	° '	° '	° '	° '	° '	° '	° '	° '
J 1	18 32 58	8♋22 3	2♊ 3	14♋51	23♌40	27♊59	12♈19	26♍27	9♋36	16♎45	18♌15
U 2	18 36 54	9 19 17	13 57	16 57	24 34	28 39	12 25	26 30	9 40	16 45	18 16
L 3	18 40 51	10 16 30	25 49	19 1	25 28	29 20	12 32	26 33	9 43	16 46	18 18
Y 4	18 44 47	11 13 43	7♋41	21 3	26 22	0♋ 0	12 37	26 37	9 47	16 46	18 19
5	18 48 44	12 10 57	19 33	23 4	27 15	0 41	12 43	26 40	9 51	16 46	18 21
6	18 52 41	13 8 10	1♌29	25 3	28 7	1 21	12 49	26 44	9 54	16 46	18 23
7	18 56 37	14 5 23	13 30	27 0	28 59	2 2	12 54	26 47	9 58	16 46	18 24
8	19 0 34	15 2 36	25 37	28 55	29 50	2 42	12 59	26 51	10 1	16 47	18 26
9	19 4 30	15 59 49	7♍54	0♌49	0♍40	3 23	13 4	26 55	10 5	16 47	18 27
10	19 8 27	16 57 2	20 24	2 40	1 30	4 3	13 9	26 59	10 9	16 47	18 29
11	19 12 23	17 54 15	3♎11	4 29	2 19	4 43	13 14	27 3	10 12	16 48	18 31
12	19 16 20	18 51 28	16 18	6 17	3 7	5 23	13 18	27 7	10 16	16 48	18 32
13	19 20 16	19 48 40	29 49	8 2	3 54	6 3	13 23	27 11	10 19	16 48	18 34
14	19 24 13	20 45 53	13♏46	9 46	4 41	6 44	13 27	27 16	10 23	16 49	18 36
15	19 28 10	21 43 6	28 8	11 27	5 26	7 24	13 31	27 20	10 27	16 49	18 37
16	19 32 6	22 40 19	12♐54	13 7	6 11	8 4	13 34	27 24	10 30	16 50	18 39
17	19 36 3	23 37 32	27 57	14 44	6 55	8 44	13 38	27 29	10 34	16 51	18 41
18	19 39 59	24 34 45	13♑ 9	16 20	7 38	9 24	13 41	27 33	10 37	16 51	18 42
19	19 43 56	25 31 59	28 18	17 54	8 20	10 4	13 45	27 38	10 41	16 52	18 44
20	19 47 52	26 29 13	13♒16	19 26	9 1	10 43	13 48	27 43	10 44	16 52	18 46
21	19 51 49	27 26 27	27 55	20 55	9 41	11 23	13 51	27 48	10 48	16 53	18 48
22	19 55 45	28 23 43	12♓ 7	22 23	10 20	12 3	13 53	27 52	10 51	16 54	18 49
23	19 59 42	29 20 58	25 52	23 49	10 58	12 43	13 56	27 57	10 55	16 55	18 51
24	20 3 39	0♌18 15	9♈10	25 13	11 34	13 22	13 58	28 2	10 58	16 55	18 53
25	20 7 35	1 15 33	22 4	26 34	12 10	14 2	14 0	28 7	11 2	16 56	18 55
26	20 11 32	2 12 51	4♉36	27 54	12 44	14 42	14 2	28 13	11 5	16 57	18 56
27	20 15 28	3 10 11	16 52	29 11	13 17	15 21	14 4	28 18	11 9	16 58	18 58
28	20 19 25	4 7 31	28 56	0♍27	13 48	16 1	14 5	28 23	11 12	16 59	19 0
29	20 23 21	5 4 53	10♊52	1 40	14 18	16 40	14 7	28 28	11 15	17 0	19 2
30	20 27 18	6 2 15	22 44	2 50	14 47	17 20	14 8	28 34	11 19	17 1	19 4
31	20 31 14	6♌59 39	4♋35	3♍59	15♍14	17♋59	14♈ 9	28♍39	11♋22	17♎ 2	19♌ 6

THE SUN ENTERS THE SIGN OF LEO ON JUL 23 AT 16:21.

DAY	TIME	☉	☽	☿	♀	♂	♃	♄	♅	♆	♇
	h m s	° ' "	° '	° '	° '	° '	° '	° '	° '	° '	° '
A 1	20 35 11	7♌57 3	16♋29	5♍ 4	15♍39	18♋39	14♈10	28♍45	11♋25	17♎ 3	19♌ 7
U 2	20 39 8	8 54 29	28 26	6 8	16 3	19 18	14 10	28 50	11 29	17 4	19 9
G 3	20 43 4	9 51 55	10♌29	7 8	16 25	19 57	14 11	28 56	11 32	17 5	19 11
U 4	20 47 1	10 49 22	22 40	8 6	16 45	20 37	14R11	29 2	11 35	17 6	19 13
S 5	20 50 57	11 46 50	5♍ 0	9 0	17 4	21 16	14 11	29 8	11 39	17 7	19 15
T 6	20 54 54	12 44 19	17 30	9 52	17 21	21 55	14 10	29 13	11 42	17 8	19 17
7	20 58 50	13 41 48	0♎14	10 41	17 35	22 34	14 10	29 19	11 45	17 9	19 18
8	21 2 47	14 39 19	13 11	11 26	17 48	23 13	14 9	29 25	11 48	17 11	19 20
9	21 6 43	15 36 50	26 25	12 7	17 59	23 52	14 9	29 31	11 51	17 12	19 22
10	21 10 40	16 34 22	9♏57	12 45	18 7	24 31	14 8	29 37	11 55	17 13	19 24
11	21 14 37	17 31 55	23 49	13 19	18 14	25 10	14 6	29 43	11 58	17 15	19 26
12	21 18 33	18 29 29	8♐ 0	13 49	18 18	25 49	14 5	29 49	12 1	17 16	19 28
13	21 22 30	19 27 4	22 29	14 14	18R20	26 28	14 3	29 56	12 4	17 17	19 30
14	21 26 26	20 24 39	7♑11	14 35	18 20	27 7	14 1	0♎ 2	12 7	17 19	19 31
15	21 30 23	21 22 16	22 1	14 51	18 17	27 46	13 59	0 8	12 10	17 20	19 33
16	21 34 19	22 19 54	6♒52	15 2	18 12	28 25	13 57	0 15	12 13	17 21	19 35
17	21 38 16	23 17 33	21 35	15R 8	18 4	29 4	13 55	0 21	12 16	17 23	19 37
18	21 42 12	24 15 13	6♓ 4	15 9	17 54	29 42	13 52	0 27	12 19	17 24	19 39
19	21 46 9	25 12 54	20 13	15 4	17 42	0♌21	13 49	0 34	12 22	17 26	19 41
20	21 50 6	26 10 37	3♈59	14 53	17 27	1 0	13 46	0 40	12 24	17 27	19 43
21	21 54 2	27 8 21	17 20	14 36	17 10	1 38	13 43	0 47	12 27	17 29	19 44
22	21 57 59	28 6 7	0♉18	14 14	16 51	2 17	13 40	0 54	12 30	17 31	19 46
23	22 1 55	29 3 55	12 54	13 46	16 29	2 56	13 36	1 0	12 33	17 32	19 48
24	22 5 52	0♍ 1 45	25 13	13 13	16 6	3 34	13 33	1 7	12 36	17 34	19 50
25	22 9 48	0 59 36	7♊18	12 34	15 40	4 13	13 29	1 14	12 38	17 35	19 52
26	22 13 45	1 57 29	19 15	11 51	15 12	4 51	13 25	1 20	12 41	17 37	19 54
27	22 17 41	2 55 24	1♋ 7	11 3	14 43	5 29	13 20	1 27	12 44	17 39	19 56
28	22 21 38	3 53 20	12 59	10 12	14 12	6 8	13 16	1 34	12 46	17 41	19 57
29	22 25 35	4 51 19	24 55	9 18	13 40	6 46	13 11	1 41	12 49	17 42	19 59
30	22 29 31	5 49 19	6♌57	8 22	13 6	7 24	13 7	1 48	12 51	17 44	20 1
31	22 33 28	6♍47 20	19♌10	7♍26	12♍31	8♌ 3	13♈ 2	1♎55	12♋54	17♎46	20♌ 3

THE SUN ENTERS THE SIGN OF VIRGO ON AUG 23 AT 23:17.

DAY	TIME	☉	☽	☿	♀	♂	♃	♄	♅	♆	♇
	h m s	° ' "	° '	° '	° '	° '	° '	° '	° '	° '	° '
S 1	22 37 24	7♍45 24	1♍34	6♍30	11♍55	8♌41	12♈56	2♎ 2	12♋56	17♎48	20♌ 5
E 2	22 41 21	8 43 29	14 10	5R37	11R19	9 19	12R51	2 9	12 59	17 49	20 6
P 3	22 45 17	9 41 36	27 0	4 46	10 42	9 57	12 46	2 16	13 1	17 51	20 8
T 4	22 49 14	10 39 44	10♎ 4	3 59	10 5	10 36	12 40	2 23	13 3	17 53	20 10
E 5	22 53 10	11 37 54	23 22	3 17	9 28	11 14	12 34	2 30	13 5	17 55	20 12
M 6	22 57 7	12 36 5	6♏53	2 42	8 51	11 52	12 28	2 37	13 8	17 57	20 13
B 7	23 1 4	13 34 18	20 37	2 14	8 14	12 30	12 22	2 44	13 10	17 59	20 15
E 8	23 5 0	14 32 32	4♐33	1 54	7 39	13 8	12 16	2 51	13 12	18 1	20 17
R 9	23 8 57	15 30 48	18 40	1D42	7 4	13 46	12 10	2 58	13 14	18 3	20 19
10	23 12 53	16 29 6	2♑55	1 39	6 31	14 24	12 3	3 6	13 16	18 5	20 20
11	23 16 50	17 27 25	17 16	1 45	5 59	15 1	11 57	3 13	13 18	18 7	20 22
12	23 20 46	18 25 45	1♒41	2 0	5 28	15 39	11 50	3 20	13 20	18 9	20 24
13	23 24 43	19 24 7	16 5	2 24	5 0	16 17	11 43	3 27	13 22	18 11	20 25
14	23 28 39	20 22 31	0♓23	2 57	4 33	16 55	11 36	3 35	13 24	18 13	20 27
15	23 32 36	21 20 56	14 30	3 38	4 8	17 32	11 29	3 42	13 26	18 15	20 29
16	23 36 33	22 19 24	28 24	4 28	3 45	18 10	11 22	3 49	13 28	18 17	20 30
17	23 40 29	23 17 53	12♈ 0	5 26	3 25	18 48	11 15	3 57	13 30	18 19	20 32
18	23 44 26	24 16 24	25 16	6 30	3 6	19 25	11 8	4 4	13 31	18 21	20 34
19	23 48 22	25 14 57	8♉13	7 42	2 50	20 3	11 0	4 11	13 33	18 23	20 35
20	23 52 19	26 13 32	20 50	9 0	2 37	20 41	10 53	4 19	13 35	18 25	20 37
21	23 56 15	27 12 10	3♊10	10 23	2 26	21 18	10 45	4 26	13 36	18 27	20 38
22	0 0 12	28 10 50	15 17	11 50	2 17	21 56	10 38	4 33	13 38	18 29	20 40
23	0 4 8	29 9 32	27 14	13 23	2 11	22 33	10 30	4 41	13 39	18 31	20 42
24	0 8 5	0♎ 8 16	9♋ 7	14 58	2 8	23 10	10 22	4 48	13 41	18 33	20 43
25	0 12 2	1 7 3	20 59	16 37	2D 6	23 48	10 14	4 56	13 42	18 36	20 45
26	0 15 58	2 5 51	2♌56	18 18	2 7	24 25	10 6	5 3	13 43	18 38	20 46
27	0 19 55	3 4 42	15 2	20 1	2 11	25 2	9 58	5 10	13 45	18 40	20 48
28	0 23 51	4 3 35	27 21	21 46	2 16	25 40	9 50	5 18	13 46	18 42	20 49
29	0 27 48	5 2 31	9♍56	23 32	2 24	26 17	9 42	5 25	13 47	18 44	20 50
30	0 31 44	6♎ 1 28	22♍49	25♍19	2♍35	26♌54	9♈34	5♎33	13♋48	18♎46	20♌52

THE SUN ENTERS THE SIGN OF LIBRA ON SEP 23 AT 20:37.

♈ ARIES ♉ TAURUS ♊ GEMINI ♋ CANCER ♌ LEO ♍ VIRGO ♎ LIBRA

SIDEREAL . SUN . MOON . MERCURY . VENUS . MARS . JUPITER . SATURN . URANUS . NEPTUNE . PLUTO .

DAY	TIME	☉	☽	☿	♀	♂	♃	♄	♅	♆	♇
	h m s	° ' "	° '	° '	° '	° '	° '	° '	° '	° '	° '
O 1	0 35 41	7♎ 0 27	6♎ 0	27♍ 7	2♍47	27♌31	9♈26	5♎40	13♋49	18♎49	20♌53
C 2	0 39 37	7 59 29	19 29	28 55	3 1	28 8	9R18	5 47	13 50	18 51	20 55
T 3	0 43 34	8 58 32	3♏14	0♎43	3 18	28 45	9 10	5 55	13 51	18 53	20 56
O 4	0 47 30	9 57 38	17 11	2 31	3 36	29 22	9 2	6 2	13 52	18 55	20 57
B 5	0 51 27	10 56 45	1♐17	4 19	3 56	29 59	8 54	6 10	13 53	18 57	20 59
E 6	0 55 24	11 55 54	15 29	6 6	4 18	0♍36	8 46	6 17	13 54	19 0	21 0
R 7	0 59 20	12 55 5	29 42	7 54	4 42	1 13	8 38	6 24	13 55	19 2	21 1
8	1 3 17	13 54 18	13♑54	9 40	5 8	1 50	8 30	6 32	13 55	19 4	21 2
9	1 7 13	14 53 33	28 3	11 26	5 35	2 27	8 22	6 39	13 56	19 6	21 4
10	1 11 10	15 52 49	12♒ 7	13 12	6 4	3 4	8 14	6 47	13 57	19 9	21 5
11	1 15 6	16 52 7	26 5	14 56	6 34	3 41	8 6	6 54	13 57	19 11	21 6
12	1 19 3	17 51 26	9♓55	16 40	7 6	4 17	7 58	7 1	13 58	19 13	21 7
13	1 22 59	18 50 48	23 36	18 24	7 40	4 54	7 50	7 9	13 58	19 15	21 8
14	1 26 56	19 50 11	7♈ 6	20 7	8 14	5 31	7 43	7 16	13 58	19 17	21 10
15	1 30 53	20 49 36	20 24	21 49	8 50	6 7	7 35	7 23	13 59	19 20	21 11
16	1 34 49	21 49 4	3♉27	23 30	9 28	6 44	7 27	7 30	13 59	19 22	21 12
17	1 38 46	22 48 33	16 14	25 11	10 6	7 20	7 20	7 38	13 59	19 24	21 13
18	1 42 42	23 48 5	28 46	26 51	10 46	7 57	7 13	7 45	13 59	19 26	21 14
19	1 46 39	24 47 39	11♊ 4	28 30	11 27	8 33	7 5	7 52	14 0	19 29	21 15
20	1 50 35	25 47 15	23 10	0♏ 9	12 10	9 9	6 58	7 59	14R 0	19 31	21 16
21	1 54 32	26 46 53	5♋ 6	1 47	12 53	9 46	6 51	8 7	14 0	19 33	21 17
22	1 58 28	27 46 34	16 57	3 24	13 37	10 22	6 44	8 14	14 0	19 35	21 18
23	2 2 25	28 46 17	28 48	5 1	14 22	10 58	6 37	8 21	14 0	19 38	21 19
24	2 6 22	29 46 2	10♌44	6 37	15 9	11 34	6 30	8 28	13 59	19 40	21 19
25	2 10 18	0♏45 49	22 49	8 13	15 56	12 11	6 23	8 35	13 59	19 42	21 20
26	2 14 15	1 45 39	5♍10	9 48	16 44	12 47	6 17	8 42	13 59	19 44	21 21
27	2 18 11	2 45 30	17 50	11 23	17 33	13 23	6 10	8 49	13 59	19 46	21 22
28	2 22 8	3 45 24	0♎52	12 57	18 23	13 59	6 4	8 56	13 58	19 49	21 23
29	2 26 4	4 45 20	14 19	14 31	19 13	14 35	5 58	9 3	13 58	19 51	21 23
30	2 30 1	5 45 18	28 9	16 4	20 5	15 11	5 52	9 10	13 57	19 53	21 24
31	2 33 57	6♏45 18	12♏20	17♏36	20♍57	15♍47	5♈46	9♎17	13♋57	19♎55	21♌25

THE SUN ENTERS THE SIGN OF SCORPIO ON OCT 24 AT 05:37.

DAY	TIME	☉	☽	☿	♀	♂	♃	♄	♅	♆	♇
	h m s	° ' "	° '	° '	° '	° '	° '	° '	° '	° '	° '
N 1	2 37 54	7♏45 20	26♏46	19♏ 9	21♍49	16♍22	5♈40	9♎24	13♋56	19♎57	21♌26
O 2	2 41 51	8 45 23	11♐21	20 40	22 43	16 58	5R35	9 30	13R56	19 59	21 26
V 3	2 45 47	9 45 29	25 57	22 12	23 37	17 34	5 29	9 37	13 55	20 2	21 27
E 4	2 49 44	10 45 36	10♑28	23 43	24 32	18 10	5 24	9 44	13 54	20 4	21 27
M 5	2 53 40	11 45 45	24 50	25 13	25 27	18 45	5 19	9 51	13 54	20 6	21 28
B 6	2 57 37	12 45 55	8♒59	26 43	26 23	19 21	5 14	9 57	13 53	20 8	21 28
E 7	3 1 33	13 46 6	22 54	28 12	27 20	19 56	5 10	10 4	13 52	20 10	21 29
R 8	3 5 30	14 46 19	6♓36	29 42	28 17	20 32	5 5	10 10	13 51	20 12	21 29
9	3 9 26	15 46 33	20 5	1♐10	29 14	21 7	5 1	10 17	13 50	20 14	21 30
10	3 13 23	16 46 49	3♈22	2 38	0♎13	21 42	4 57	10 23	13 49	20 16	21 30
11	3 17 20	17 47 7	16 28	4 6	1 11	22 18	4 53	10 30	13 48	20 18	21 31
12	3 21 16	18 47 26	29 24	5 33	2 10	22 53	4 49	10 36	13 47	20 20	21 31
13	3 25 13	19 47 46	12♉ 8	6 59	3 10	23 28	4 45	10 43	13 45	20 22	21 31
14	3 29 9	20 48 8	24 41	8 25	4 10	24 3	4 42	10 49	13 44	20 24	21 32
15	3 33 6	21 48 32	7♊ 3	9 51	5 11	24 38	4 39	10 55	13 43	20 26	21 32
16	3 37 2	22 48 58	19 14	11 15	6 12	25 13	4 36	11 1	13 42	20 28	21 32
17	3 40 59	23 49 26	1♋16	12 39	7 13	25 48	4 33	11 7	13 40	20 30	21 32
18	3 44 55	24 49 55	13 10	14 2	8 15	26 23	4 30	11 13	13 39	20 32	21 33
19	3 48 52	25 50 26	24 59	15 23	9 17	26 58	4 28	11 19	13 37	20 34	21 33
20	3 52 49	26 50 58	6♌47	16 44	10 20	27 33	4 26	11 25	13 36	20 36	21 33
21	3 56 45	27 51 33	18 40	18 4	11 23	28 7	4 24	11 31	13 34	20 38	21 33
22	4 0 42	28 52 9	0♍42	19 22	12 26	28 42	4 22	11 37	13 33	20 40	21 33
23	4 4 38	29 52 46	13 0	20 38	13 30	29 17	4 20	11 43	13 31	20 42	21R33
24	4 8 35	0♐53 26	25 37	21 53	14 34	29 51	4 19	11 49	13 30	20 43	21 33
25	4 12 31	1 54 7	8♎40	23 6	15 38	0♎26	4 18	11 54	13 28	20 45	21 33
26	4 16 28	2 54 50	22 10	24 16	16 43	1 0	4 17	12 0	13 26	20 47	21 33
27	4 20 24	3 55 34	6♏ 9	25 24	17 48	1 34	4 16	12 5	13 24	20 49	21 33
28	4 24 21	4 56 20	20 35	26 28	18 53	2 8	4 15	12 11	13 22	20 50	21 33
29	4 28 18	5 57 7	5♐22	27 29	19 58	2 43	4 15	12 16	13 21	20 52	21 33
30	4 32 14	6♐57 56	20♐21	28♐26	21♎ 4	3♎17	4♈15	12♎21	13♋19	20♎54	21♌32

THE SUN ENTERS THE SIGN OF SAGITTARIUS ON NOV 23 AT 02:52.

DAY	TIME	☉	☽	☿	♀	♂	♃	♄	♅	♆	♇
	h m s	° ' "	° '	° '	° '	° '	° '	° '	° '	° '	° '
D 1	4 36 11	7♐58 45	5♑24	29♐19	22♎10	3♎51	4♈15	12♎27	13♋17	20♎56	21♌32
E 2	4 40 7	8 59 36	20 20	0♑ 6	23 17	4 25	4 15	12 32	13R15	20 57	21R32
C 3	4 44 4	10 0 28	5♒ 1	0 48	24 23	4 58	4 16	12 37	13 13	20 59	21 32
E 4	4 48 0	11 1 20	19 23	1 22	25 30	5 32	4 16	12 42	13 11	21 0	21 32
M 5	4 51 57	12 2 14	3♓23	1 50	26 37	6 6	4 17	12 47	13 9	21 2	21 31
B 6	4 55 54	13 3 7	17 3	2 9	27 44	6 39	4 18	12 52	13 6	21 4	21 31
E 7	4 59 50	14 4 2	0♈23	2R19	28 51	7 13	4 20	12 57	13 4	21 5	21 30
R 8	5 3 47	15 4 57	13 26	2 19	29 59	7 46	4 21	13 1	13 2	21 7	21 30
9	5 7 43	16 5 53	26 15	2 8	1♏ 7	8 20	4 23	13 6	13 0	21 8	21 30
10	5 11 40	17 6 50	8♉53	1 46	2 15	8 53	4 25	13 11	12 58	21 9	21 29
11	5 15 36	18 7 48	21 19	1 13	3 23	9 26	4 27	13 15	12 55	21 11	21 29
12	5 19 33	19 8 46	3♊37	0 28	4 32	9 59	4 29	13 19	12 53	21 12	21 28
13	5 23 29	20 9 46	15 47	29♐33	5 40	10 32	4 32	13 24	12 51	21 14	21 28
14	5 27 26	21 10 46	27 49	28 27	6 49	11 5	4 35	13 28	12 48	21 15	21 27
15	5 31 23	22 11 46	9♋45	27 14	7 58	11 38	4 38	13 32	12 46	21 16	21 27
16	5 35 19	23 12 48	21 36	25 55	9 7	12 11	4 41	13 36	12 44	21 18	21 26
17	5 39 16	24 13 50	3♌24	24 33	10 17	12 43	4 44	13 40	12 41	21 19	21 25
18	5 43 12	25 14 53	15 12	23 10	11 26	13 16	4 48	13 44	12 39	21 20	21 25
19	5 47 9	26 15 57	27 5	21 49	12 36	13 48	4 51	13 48	12 36	21 21	21 24
20	5 51 5	27 17 2	9♍ 5	20 34	13 45	14 21	4 55	13 51	12 34	21 22	21 23
21	5 55 2	28 18 8	21 19	19 25	14 55	14 53	4 59	13 55	12 31	21 24	21 22
22	5 58 58	29 19 14	3♎52	18 25	16 5	15 25	5 4	13 59	12 29	21 25	21 22
23	6 2 55	0♑20 21	16 48	17 35	17 16	15 57	5 8	14 2	12 26	21 26	21 21
24	6 6 52	1 21 29	0♏12	16 56	18 26	16 29	5 13	14 5	12 24	21 27	21 20
25	6 10 48	2 22 37	14 6	16 27	19 36	17 1	5 18	14 9	12 21	21 28	21 19
26	6 14 45	3 23 47	28 30	16 9	20 47	17 32	5 23	14 12	12 19	21 29	21 18
27	6 18 41	4 24 56	13♐20	16D 2	21 58	18 4	5 28	14 15	12 16	21 30	21 18
28	6 22 38	5 26 7	28 28	16 4	23 9	18 35	5 33	14 18	12 14	21 31	21 17
29	6 26 34	6 27 17	13♑45	16 15	24 20	19 6	5 39	14 21	12 11	21 32	21 16
30	6 30 31	7 28 28	28 59	16 34	25 31	19 38	5 45	14 23	12 9	21 32	21 15
31	6 34 28	8♑29 39	14♒ 1	17♐ 1	26♏42	20♎ 9	5♈51	14♎26	12♋ 6	21♎33	21♌14

THE SUN ENTERS THE SIGN OF CAPRICORN ON DEC 22 AT 16:01.

♏ SCORPIO ♐ SAGITTARIUS ♑ CAPRICORN ♒ AQUARIUS ♓ PISCES

1952

SIDEREAL SUN. MOON.. MERCURY VENUS.. MARS... JUPITER. SATURN. URANUS.. NEPTUNE. PLUTO.

DAY	TIME	☉	☽	☿	♀	♂	♃	♄	♅	♆	♇
	h m s	° ' "	° '	° '	° '	° '	° '	° '	° '	° '	° '
J 1	6 38 24	9♑30 49	28♒41	17♐34	27♏53	20♎40	5♈57	14♎29	12♋ 3	21♎34	21♌13
A 2	6 42 21	10 31 59	12♓57	18 13	29 4	21 10	6 3	14 31	12R 1	21 35	21R12
N 3	6 46 17	11 33 9	26 47	18 58	0♐16	21 41	6 10	14 33	11 58	21 35	21 11
U 4	6 50 14	12 34 19	10♈11	19 48	1 27	22 11	6 16	14 36	11 56	21 36	21 10
A 5	6 54 10	13 35 29	23 13	20 41	2 39	22 42	6 23	14 38	11 53	21 37	21 9
R 6	6 58 7	14 36 38	5♉56	21 39	3 50	23 12	6 30	14 40	11 50	21 37	21 7
Y 7	7 2 3	15 37 47	18 24	22 40	5 2	23 42	6 37	14 42	11 48	21 38	21 6
8	7 6 0	16 38 55	0♊39	23 44	6 14	24 12	6 44	14 44	11 45	21 39	21 5
9	7 9 57	17 40 4	12 45	24 50	7 26	24 42	6 52	14 45	11 43	21 39	21 4
10	7 13 53	18 41 11	24 45	25 59	8 38	25 11	6 59	14 47	11 40	21 40	21 3
11	7 17 50	19 42 19	6♋39	27 11	9 50	25 41	7 7	14 49	11 38	21 40	21 2
12	7 21 46	20 43 26	18 30	28 24	11 2	26 10	7 15	14 50	11 35	21 40	21 0
13	7 25 43	21 44 33	0♌20	29 39	12 14	26 39	7 23	14 51	11 32	21 41	20 59
14	7 29 39	22 45 39	12 10	0♑55	13 27	27 8	7 31	14 52	11 30	21 41	20 58
15	7 33 36	23 46 46	24 2	2 13	14 39	27 37	7 40	14 54	11 27	21 41	20 57
16	7 37 32	24 47 51	5♍59	3 32	15 51	28 6	7 48	14 55	11 25	21 42	20 56
17	7 41 29	25 48 57	18 4	4 53	17 4	28 34	7 57	14 55	11 22	21 42	20 54
18	7 45 26	26 50 2	0♎21	6 14	18 16	29 2	8 6	14 56	11 20	21 42	20 53
19	7 49 22	27 51 7	12 53	7 37	19 29	29 30	8 15	14 57	11 17	21 42	20 52
20	7 53 19	28 52 11	25 46	9 0	20 41	29 58	8 24	14 58	11 15	21 42	20 50
21	7 57 15	29 53 16	9♏ 2	10 25	21 54	0♏26	8 33	14 58	11 13	21 43	20 49
22	8 1 12	0♒54 20	22 45	11 50	23 7	0 53	8 42	14 58	11 10	21 43	20 48
23	8 5 8	1 55 23	6♐55	13 17	24 20	1 21	8 52	14 59	11 8	21R43	20 46
24	8 9 5	2 56 27	21 32	14 44	25 33	1 48	9 1	14R59	11 5	21 43	20 45
25	8 13 1	3 57 29	6♑29	16 11	26 45	2 15	9 11	14 59	11 3	21 43	20 44
26	8 16 58	4 58 31	21 40	17 40	27 58	2 41	9 21	14 59	11 1	21 43	20 42
27	8 20 55	5 59 33	6♒55	19 9	29 11	3 8	9 31	14 58	10 58	21 43	20 41
28	8 24 51	7 0 33	22 3	20 39	0♑24	3 34	9 41	14 58	10 56	21 42	20 39
29	8 28 48	8 1 32	6♓55	22 10	1 37	4 0	9 51	14 58	10 54	21 42	20 38
30	8 32 44	9 2 31	21 25	23 41	2 51	4 26	10 1	14 57	10 52	21 42	20 37
31	8 36 41	10♒ 3 27	5♈29	25♑13	4♑ 4	4♏51	10♈12	14♎57	10♋50	21♎42	20♌35

THE SUN ENTERS THE SIGN OF AQUARIUS ON JAN 21 AT 02:39.

DAY	TIME	☉	☽	☿	♀	♂	♃	♄	♅	♆	♇
	h m s	° ' "	° '	° '	° '	° '	° '	° '	° '	° '	° '
F 1	8 40 37	11♒ 4 23	19♈ 5	26♑46	5♑17	5♏16	10♈22	14♎56	10♋47	21♎42	20♌34
E 2	8 44 34	12 5 18	2♉15	28 19	6 30	5 41	10 33	14R55	10R45	21R41	20R32
B 3	8 48 30	13 6 11	15 1	29 54	7 43	6 6	10 44	14 54	10 43	21 41	20 31
R 4	8 52 27	14 7 2	27 29	1♒28	8 56	6 31	10 55	14 53	10 41	21 41	20 29
U 5	8 56 24	15 7 53	9♊41	3 4	10 10	6 55	11 6	14 52	10 39	21 40	20 28
A 6	9 0 20	16 8 42	21 42	4 40	11 23	7 19	11 17	14 51	10 37	21 40	20 26
R 7	9 4 17	17 9 30	3♋35	6 18	12 36	7 42	11 28	14 49	10 35	21 39	20 25
Y 8	9 8 13	18 10 16	15 25	7 55	13 50	8 6	11 39	14 48	10 33	21 39	20 24
9	9 12 10	19 11 1	27 14	9 34	15 3	8 29	11 51	14 46	10 31	21 38	20 22
10	9 16 6	20 11 44	9♌ 5	11 13	16 17	8 52	12 2	14 45	10 30	21 38	20 21
11	9 20 3	21 12 26	20 59	12 54	17 30	9 14	12 14	14 43	10 28	21 37	20 19
12	9 24 0	22 13 7	3♍ 0	14 35	18 43	9 36	12 25	14 41	10 26	21 36	20 18
13	9 27 56	23 13 46	15 7	16 17	19 57	9 58	12 37	14 39	10 24	21 36	20 16
14	9 31 53	24 14 24	27 25	17 59	21 10	10 20	12 49	14 37	10 23	21 35	20 15
15	9 35 49	25 15 0	9♎54	19 43	22 24	10 41	13 1	14 35	10 21	21 34	20 13
16	9 39 46	26 15 36	22 36	21 27	23 37	11 2	13 13	14 33	10 19	21 34	20 12
17	9 43 42	27 16 10	5♏34	23 13	24 51	11 22	13 25	14 30	10 18	21 33	20 10
18	9 47 39	28 16 43	18 51	24 59	26 5	11 42	13 37	14 28	10 16	21 32	20 9
19	9 51 35	29 17 15	2♐27	26 46	27 18	12 2	13 50	14 25	10 15	21 31	20 8
20	9 55 32	0♓17 46	16 25	28 34	28 32	12 21	14 2	14 23	10 13	21 30	20 6
21	9 59 28	1 18 15	0♑42	0♓23	29 46	12 40	14 14	14 20	10 12	21 29	20 5
22	10 3 25	2 18 43	15 18	2 13	0♒59	12 59	14 27	14 17	10 11	21 29	20 3
23	10 7 22	3 19 10	0♒ 7	4 4	2 13	13 17	14 40	14 14	10 9	21 28	20 2
24	10 11 18	4 19 35	15 3	5 55	3 27	13 35	14 52	14 11	10 8	21 27	20 0
25	10 15 15	5 19 59	29 59	7 47	4 40	13 52	15 5	14 8	10 7	21 26	19 59
26	10 19 11	6 20 21	14♓46	9 40	5 54	14 9	15 18	14 5	10 6	21 25	19 58
27	10 23 8	7 20 41	29 17	11 34	7 8	14 26	15 31	14 2	10 5	21 24	19 56
28	10 27 4	8 20 59	13♈26	13 28	8 21	14 42	15 44	13 59	10 4	21 22	19 55
29	10 31 1	9♓21 16	27♈10	15♓22	9♒35	14♏58	15♈57	13♎55	10♋ 3	21♎21	19♌54

THE SUN ENTERS THE SIGN OF PISCES ON FEB 19 AT 16:57.

DAY	TIME	☉	☽	☿	♀	♂	♃	♄	♅	♆	♇
	h m s	° ' "	° '	° '	° '	° '	° '	° '	° '	° '	° '
M 1	10 34 57	10♓21 30	10♉29	17♓17	10♒49	15♏13	16♈10	13♎52	10♋ 2	21♎20	19♌52
A 2	10 38 54	11 21 43	23 22	19 12	12 3	15 27	16 23	13R48	10R 1	21R19	19R51
R 3	10 42 51	12 21 53	5♊54	21 7	13 17	15 41	16 36	13 45	10 0	21 18	19 49
C 4	10 46 47	13 22 1	18 9	23 2	14 30	15 55	16 49	13 41	9 59	21 17	19 48
H 5	10 50 44	14 22 8	0♋10	24 56	15 44	16 8	17 3	13 37	9 59	21 15	19 47
6	10 54 40	15 22 12	12 2	26 49	16 58	16 21	17 16	13 34	9 58	21 14	19 46
7	10 58 37	16 22 14	23 51	28 41	18 12	16 33	17 29	13 30	9 57	21 13	19 44
8	11 2 33	17 22 14	5♌40	0♈31	19 25	16 45	17 43	13 26	9 57	21 12	19 43
9	11 6 30	18 22 11	17 33	2 19	20 39	16 56	17 56	13 22	9 56	21 10	19 42
10	11 10 26	19 22 7	29 34	4 5	21 53	17 6	18 10	13 18	9 56	21 9	19 41
11	11 14 23	20 22 1	11♍44	5 48	23 7	17 16	18 24	13 14	9 55	21 8	19 39
12	11 18 20	21 21 52	24 7	7 27	24 21	17 25	18 37	13 10	9 55	21 6	19 38
13	11 22 16	22 21 42	6♎42	9 2	25 34	17 34	18 51	13 6	9 55	21 5	19 37
14	11 26 13	23 21 30	19 30	10 33	26 48	17 42	19 5	13 1	9 55	21 4	19 36
15	11 30 9	24 21 16	2♏33	11 59	28 2	17 50	19 19	12 57	9 54	21 2	19 35
16	11 34 6	25 21 0	15 48	13 19	29 16	17 57	19 32	12 53	9 54	21 1	19 33
17	11 38 2	26 20 43	29 17	14 34	0♓30	18 3	19 46	12 48	9 54	20 59	19 32
18	11 41 59	27 20 24	12♐59	15 42	1 44	18 8	20 0	12 44	9D54	20 58	19 31
19	11 45 55	28 20 3	26 53	16 43	2 58	18 13	20 14	12 40	9 54	20 56	19 30
20	11 49 52	29 19 40	10♑59	17 37	4 11	18 18	20 28	12 35	9 54	20 55	19 29
21	11 53 49	0♈19 16	25 15	18 24	5 25	18 21	20 42	12 31	9 54	20 53	19 28
22	11 57 45	1 18 50	9♒40	19 4	6 39	18 24	20 56	12 26	9 54	20 52	19 27
23	12 1 42	2 18 23	24 10	19 36	7 53	18 26	21 10	12 22	9 55	20 50	19 26
24	12 5 38	3 17 53	8♓40	19 59	9 7	18 28	21 24	12 17	9 55	20 49	19 25
25	12 9 35	4 17 21	23 6	20 15	10 21	18R28	21 39	12 12	9 55	20 47	19 24
26	12 13 31	5 16 48	7♈21	20R24	11 35	18 28	21 53	12 8	9 56	20 46	19 23
27	12 17 28	6 16 12	21 21	20 24	12 48	18 28	22 7	12 3	9 56	20 44	19 22
28	12 21 24	7 15 34	5♉ 2	20 18	14 2	18 26	22 21	11 58	9 57	20 42	19 21
29	12 25 21	8 14 54	18 21	20 4	15 16	18 24	22 35	11 54	9 57	20 41	19 20
30	12 29 18	9 14 12	1♊17	19 43	16 30	18 21	22 50	11 49	9 58	20 39	19 19
31	12 33 14	10♈13 28	13♊52	19♈16	17♓44	18♏17	23♈ 4	11♎44	9♋58	20♎38	19♌19

THE SUN ENTERS THE SIGN OF ARIES ON MAR 20 AT 16:14.

♈ ARIES ♉ TAURUS ♊ GEMINI ♋ CANCER ♌ LEO ♍ VIRGO ♎ LIBRA

SIDEREAL. SUN. MOON. MERCURY. VENUS. MARS. JUPITER. SATURN. URANUS. NEPTUNE. PLUTO.

DAY	TIME	☉	☽	☿	♀	♂	♃	♄	♅	♆	♇
	h m s	° ' "	° '	° '	° '	° '	° '	° '	° '	° '	° '
A 1	12 37 11	11♈12 42	26♊ 8	18♈44	18♓58	18♏12	23♈18	11♎40	9♋59	20♎36	19♌18
P 2	12 41 7	12 11 53	8♋11	18R 7	20 12	18R 7	23 33	11R35	10 0	20R34	19R17
R 3	12 45 4	13 11 2	20 4	17 26	21 25	18 1	23 47	11 30	10 1	20 33	19 16
I 4	12 49 0	14 10 8	1♌53	16 42	22 39	17 54	24 1	11 26	10 2	20 31	19 16
L 5	12 52 57	15 9 12	13 43	15 56	23 53	17 47	24 16	11 21	10 3	20 29	19 15
6	12 56 53	16 8 14	25 39	15 8	25 7	17 38	24 30	11 16	10 4	20 28	19 14
7	13 0 50	17 7 14	7♍45	14 21	26 21	17 29	24 44	11 12	10 5	20 26	19 13
8	13 4 47	18 6 11	20 5	13 34	27 35	17 19	24 59	11 7	10 6	20 25	19 13
9	13 8 43	19 5 6	2♎41	12 48	28 48	17 9	25 13	11 3	10 7	20 23	19 12
10	13 12 40	20 3 59	15 35	12 5	0♈ 2	16 57	25 28	10 58	10 8	20 21	19 12
11	13 16 36	21 2 50	28 46	11 24	1 16	16 45	25 42	10 53	10 9	20 20	19 11
12	13 20 33	22 1 39	12♏13	10 48	2 30	16 32	25 57	10 49	10 10	20 18	19 11
13	13 24 29	23 0 27	25 54	10 15	3 44	16 19	26 11	10 44	10 12	20 16	19 10
14	13 28 26	23 59 12	9♐45	9 47	4 57	16 5	26 26	10 40	10 13	20 15	19 10
15	13 32 22	24 57 56	23 44	9 23	6 11	15 50	26 40	10 35	10 15	20 13	19 9
16	13 36 19	25 56 38	7♑48	9 5	7 25	15 34	26 54	10 31	10 16	20 11	19 9
17	13 40 16	26 55 19	21 55	8 52	8 39	15 18	27 9	10 27	10 18	20 10	19 8
18	13 44 12	27 53 57	6♒ 3	8 44	9 53	15 1	27 23	10 22	10 19	20 8	19 8
19	13 48 9	28 52 35	20 11	8D41	11 6	14 44	27 38	10 18	10 21	20 7	19 8
20	13 52 5	29 51 10	4♓18	8 43	12 20	14 26	27 52	10 14	10 23	20 5	19 7
21	13 56 2	0♉49 44	18 22	8 50	13 34	14 7	28 7	10 9	10 24	20 3	19 7
22	13 59 58	1 48 16	2♈21	9 2	14 48	13 48	28 21	10 5	10 26	20 2	19 7
23	14 3 55	2 46 46	16 12	9 19	16 1	13 28	28 36	10 1	10 28	20 0	19 6
24	14 7 51	3 45 14	29 51	9 41	17 15	13 8	28 50	9 57	10 30	19 58	19 6
25	14 11 48	4 43 41	13♉16	10 7	18 29	12 48	29 4	9 53	10 32	19 57	19 6
26	14 15 44	5 42 6	26 24	10 37	19 43	12 27	29 19	9 49	10 34	19 55	19 6
27	14 19 41	6 40 29	9♊14	11 11	20 57	12 6	29 33	9 45	10 36	19 54	19 6
28	14 23 38	7 38 50	21 45	11 50	22 10	11 44	29 48	9 41	10 38	19 52	19 6
29	14 27 34	8 37 9	4♋ 0	12 32	23 24	11 23	0♉ 2	9 37	10 40	19 51	19 6
30	14 31 31	9♉35 26	16♋ 2	13♈17	24♈38	11♏ 1	0♉16	9♎34	10♋42	19♎49	19♌ 6

THE SUN ENTERS THE SIGN OF TAURUS ON APR 20 AT 03:37.

DAY	TIME	☉	☽	☿	♀	♂	♃	♄	♅	♆	♇
	h m s	° ' "	° '	° '	° '	° '	° '	° '	° '	° '	° '
M 1	14 35 27	10♉33 41	27♋55	14♈ 6	25♈51	10♏39	0♉31	9♎30	10♋44	19♎48	19♌ 6
A 2	14 39 24	11 31 54	9♌44	14 59	27 5	10R17	0 45	9R26	10 46	19R46	19 6
Y 3	14 43 20	12 30 4	21 34	15 54	28 19	9 54	0 59	9 23	10 48	19 45	19 6
4	14 47 17	13 28 13	3♍31	16 53	29 33	9 32	1 13	9 19	10 51	19 43	19 6
5	14 51 14	14 26 20	15 40	17 55	0♉46	9 10	1 28	9 16	10 53	19 42	19 6
6	14 55 10	15 24 25	28 5	18 59	2 0	8 48	1 42	9 13	10 55	19 40	19 6
7	14 59 7	16 22 28	10♎50	20 6	3 14	8 26	1 56	9 9	10 58	19 39	19 6
8	15 3 3	17 20 29	23 57	21 16	4 27	8 4	2 10	9 6	11 0	19 37	19 6
9	15 7 0	18 18 29	7♏27	22 28	5 41	7 43	2 24	9 3	11 3	19 36	19 6
10	15 10 56	19 16 27	21 18	23 43	6 55	7 21	2 39	9 0	11 5	19 35	19 7
11	15 14 53	20 14 23	5♐25	25 1	8 8	7 0	2 53	8 57	11 8	19 33	19 7
12	15 18 49	21 12 18	19 43	26 20	9 22	6 39	3 7	8 54	11 10	19 32	19 7
13	15 22 46	22 10 12	4♑ 7	27 43	10 36	6 19	3 21	8 52	11 13	19 30	19 8
14	15 26 43	23 8 4	18 30	29 7	11 49	5 59	3 35	8 49	11 16	19 29	19 8
15	15 30 39	24 5 55	2♒50	0♉34	13 3	5 40	3 49	8 46	11 18	19 28	19 8
16	15 34 36	25 3 45	17 2	2 3	14 17	5 20	4 3	8 44	11 21	19 27	19 9
17	15 38 32	26 1 34	1♓ 7	3 34	15 30	5 2	4 17	8 41	11 24	19 25	19 9
18	15 42 29	26 59 21	15 2	5 7	16 44	4 44	4 30	8 39	11 27	19 24	19 10
19	15 46 25	27 57 7	28 47	6 43	17 58	4 26	4 44	8 37	11 29	19 23	19 10
20	15 50 22	28 54 52	12♈24	8 21	19 11	4 10	4 58	8 35	11 32	19 22	19 11
21	15 54 18	29 52 37	25 50	10 1	20 25	3 53	5 12	8 33	11 35	19 21	19 11
22	15 58 15	0♊50 20	9♉ 6	11 43	21 39	3 38	5 26	8 31	11 38	19 19	19 12
23	16 2 12	1 48 1	22 9	13 28	22 52	3 23	5 39	8 29	11 41	19 18	19 12
24	16 6 8	2 45 42	4♊59	15 14	24 6	3 9	5 53	8 27	11 44	19 17	19 13
25	16 10 5	3 43 21	17 35	17 3	25 20	2 55	6 6	8 25	11 47	19 16	19 14
26	16 14 1	4 40 59	29 57	18 54	26 33	2 43	6 20	8 24	11 50	19 15	19 14
27	16 17 58	5 38 36	12♋ 6	20 47	27 47	2 31	6 33	8 22	11 53	19 14	19 15
28	16 21 54	6 36 12	24 4	22 43	29 1	2 20	6 47	8 21	11 56	19 13	19 16
29	16 25 51	7 33 46	5♌55	24 40	0♊14	2 10	7 0	8 19	11 59	19 12	19 16
30	16 29 47	8 31 19	17 42	26 40	1 28	2 0	7 14	8 18	12 3	19 11	19 17
31	16 33 44	9♊28 50	29♌32	28♉41	2♊42	1♏51	7♉27	8♎17	12♋ 6	19♎10	19♌18

THE SUN ENTERS THE SIGN OF GEMINI ON MAY 21 AT 03:04.

DAY	TIME	☉	☽	☿	♀	♂	♃	♄	♅	♆	♇
	h m s	° ' "	° '	° '	° '	° '	° '	° '	° '	° '	° '
J 1	16 37 41	10♊26 20	11♍28	0♊44	3♊55	1♏44	7♉40	8♎16	12♋ 9	19♎ 9	19♌19
U 2	16 41 37	11 23 48	23 36	2 49	5 9	1R37	7 53	8R15	12 12	19R 8	19 20
N 3	16 45 34	12 21 16	6♎ 2	4 56	6 23	1 30	8 6	8 14	12 15	19 8	19 21
E 4	16 49 30	13 18 42	18 50	7 4	7 36	1 25	8 19	8 14	12 19	19 7	19 21
5	16 53 27	14 16 7	2♏ 3	9 13	8 50	1 20	8 32	8 13	12 22	19 6	19 22
6	16 57 23	15 13 31	15 43	11 24	10 4	1 17	8 45	8 13	12 25	19 5	19 23
7	17 1 20	16 10 54	29 47	13 35	11 17	1 14	8 58	8 12	12 29	19 4	19 24
8	17 5 16	17 8 16	14♐13	15 47	12 31	1 12	9 11	8 12	12 32	19 4	19 25
9	17 9 13	18 5 37	28 54	17 59	13 44	1 10	9 24	8 12	12 35	19 3	19 26
10	17 13 10	19 2 58	13♑42	20 11	14 58	1D10	9 36	8D12	12 39	19 2	19 27
11	17 17 6	20 0 18	28 30	22 22	16 12	1 10	9 49	8 12	12 42	19 2	19 29
12	17 21 3	20 57 37	13♒ 9	24 34	17 25	1 11	10 2	8 12	12 46	19 1	19 30
13	17 24 59	21 54 56	27 36	26 44	18 39	1 13	10 14	8 12	12 49	19 1	19 31
14	17 28 56	22 52 14	11♓48	28 54	19 53	1 16	10 27	8 12	12 53	19 0	19 32
15	17 32 52	23 49 32	25 43	1♋ 2	21 6	1 19	10 39	8 13	12 56	19 0	19 33
16	17 36 49	24 46 50	9♈22	3 9	22 20	1 23	10 51	8 13	12 59	18 59	19 34
17	17 40 45	25 44 7	22 45	5 14	23 34	1 28	11 3	8 14	13 3	18 59	19 35
18	17 44 42	26 41 24	5♉54	7 17	24 47	1 34	11 15	8 14	13 6	18 58	19 37
19	17 48 39	27 38 41	18 50	9 19	26 1	1 40	11 28	8 15	13 10	18 58	19 38
20	17 52 35	28 35 58	1♊33	11 19	27 15	1 48	11 39	8 16	13 14	18 58	19 39
21	17 56 32	29 33 14	14 4	13 16	28 29	1 55	11 51	8 17	13 17	18 57	19 41
22	18 0 28	0♋30 30	26 24	15 12	29 42	2 4	12 3	8 18	13 21	18 57	19 42
23	18 4 25	1 27 45	8♋33	17 5	0♋56	2 13	12 15	8 19	13 24	18 57	19 43
24	18 8 21	2 25 1	20 34	18 57	2 10	2 23	12 27	8 21	13 28	18 57	19 45
25	18 12 18	3 22 15	2♌27	20 46	3 23	2 34	12 38	8 22	13 31	18 56	19 46
26	18 16 15	4 19 30	14 15	22 33	4 37	2 45	12 50	8 24	13 35	18 56	19 47
27	18 20 11	5 16 43	26 1	24 17	5 51	2 57	13 1	8 25	13 39	18 56	19 49
28	18 24 8	6 13 57	7♍50	26 0	7 5	3 10	13 12	8 27	13 42	18 56	19 50
29	18 28 4	7 11 9	19 45	27 40	8 18	3 23	13 23	8 29	13 46	18 56	19 52
30	18 32 1	8♋ 8 22	1♎53	29♋18	9♋32	3♏37	13♉34	8♎30	13♋49	18♎56	19♌53

THE SUN ENTERS THE SIGN OF CANCER ON JUN 21 AT 11:13.

♏	SCORPIO	♐	SAGITTARIUS	♑	CAPRICORN	♒	AQUARIUS	♓	PISCES

SIDEREAL TIME · SUN · MOON · MERCURY · VENUS · MARS · JUPITER · SATURN · URANUS · NEPTUNE · PLUTO

DAY	TIME	☉	☽	☿	♀	♂	♃	♄	♅	♆	♇
	h m s	° ' "	° '	° '	° '	° '	° '	° '	° '	° '	° '
J 1	18 35 57	9♋ 5 34	14♎17	0♌54	10♋46	3♏52	13♉45	8♎32	13♋53	18♎56	19♌55
U 2	18 39 54	10 2 46	27 3	2 27	12 0	4 7	13 56	8 35	13 57	18 56	19 56
L 3	18 43 50	10 59 57	10♏15	3 58	13 13	4 22	14 7	8 37	14 0	18 56	19 58
Y 4	18 47 47	11 57 8	23 54	5 27	14 27	4 39	14 18	8 39	14 4	18 56	19 59
5	18 51 44	12 54 19	8♐ 2	6 54	15 41	4 56	14 28	8 41	14 8	18 56	20 1
6	18 55 40	13 51 30	22 34	8 18	16 55	5 13	14 39	8 44	14 11	18 56	20 2
7	18 59 37	14 48 40	7♑26	9 40	18 8	5 31	14 49	8 46	14 15	18 57	20 4
8	19 3 33	15 45 51	22 30	11 0	19 22	5 49	15 0	8 49	14 18	18 57	20 5
9	19 7 30	16 43 2	7♒36	12 17	20 36	6 8	15 10	8 52	14 22	18 57	20 7
10	19 11 26	17 40 13	22 35	13 32	21 50	6 28	15 20	8 55	14 26	18 57	20 9
11	19 15 23	18 37 25	7♓21	14 44	23 4	6 48	15 30	8 57	14 29	18 58	20 10
12	19 19 19	19 34 37	21 47	15 53	24 17	7 8	15 40	9 0	14 33	18 58	20 12
13	19 23 16	20 31 49	5♈51	17 0	25 31	7 29	15 49	9 4	14 37	18 58	20 14
14	19 27 13	21 29 2	19 33	18 4	26 45	7 50	15 59	9 7	14 40	18 59	20 15
15	19 31 9	22 26 15	2♉53	19 5	27 59	8 12	16 8	9 10	14 44	18 59	20 17
16	19 35 6	23 23 30	15 54	20 3	29 13	8 35	16 18	9 13	14 47	19 0	20 19
17	19 39 2	24 20 45	28 37	20 58	0♌26	8 57	16 27	9 17	14 51	19 0	20 20
18	19 42 59	25 18 0	11♊ 6	21 50	1 40	9 21	16 36	9 20	14 55	19 1	20 22
19	19 46 55	26 15 17	23 23	22 39	2 54	9 44	16 45	9 24	14 58	19 1	20 24
20	19 50 52	27 12 33	5♋29	23 24	4 8	10 8	16 54	9 28	15 2	19 2	20 26
21	19 54 48	28 9 51	17 28	24 5	5 22	10 33	17 3	9 31	15 5	19 3	20 27
22	19 58 45	29 7 9	29 20	24 43	6 36	10 58	17 11	9 35	15 9	19 3	20 29
23	20 2 42	0♌ 4 27	11♌ 9	25 17	7 50	11 23	17 20	9 39	15 13	19 4	20 31
24	20 6 38	1 1 47	22 55	25 47	9 4	11 49	17 28	9 43	15 16	19 5	20 33
25	20 10 35	1 59 6	4♍43	26 12	10 18	12 15	17 36	9 47	15 20	19 6	20 34
26	20 14 31	2 56 26	16 34	26 33	11 31	12 41	17 45	9 51	15 23	19 6	20 36
27	20 18 28	3 53 47	28 32	26 50	12 45	13 8	17 52	9 56	15 27	19 7	20 38
28	20 22 24	4 51 8	10♎42	27 1	13 59	13 35	18 0	10 0	15 30	19 8	20 40
29	20 26 21	5 48 29	23 6	27R 8	15 13	14 3	18 8	10 4	15 34	19 9	20 42
30	20 30 17	6 45 51	5♏50	27 10	16 27	14 31	18 15	10 9	15 37	19 10	20 43
31	20 34 14	7♌43 14	18♏57	27♌ 7	17♌41	14♏59	18♉23	10♎13	15♋40	19♎11	20♌45

THE SUN ENTERS THE SIGN OF LEO ON JUL 22 AT 22:08.

DAY	TIME	☉	☽	☿	♀	♂	♃	♄	♅	♆	♇
	h m s	° ' "	° '	° '	° '	° '	° '	° '	° '	° '	° '
A 1	20 38 11	8♌40 37	2♐30	26♌58	18♌55	15♏28	18♉30	10♎18	15♋44	19♎12	20♌47
U 2	20 42 7	9 38 1	16 30	26R44	20 9	15 57	18 37	10 23	15 47	19 13	20 49
G 3	20 46 4	10 35 26	0♑56	26 26	21 23	16 26	18 44	10 28	15 51	19 14	20 51
U 4	20 50 0	11 32 52	15 45	26 2	22 37	16 56	18 51	10 32	15 54	19 15	20 53
S 5	20 53 57	12 30 18	0♒50	25 33	23 51	17 25	18 57	10 37	15 57	19 16	20 55
T 6	20 57 53	13 27 45	16 2	25 0	25 4	17 56	19 4	10 42	16 1	19 17	20 56
7	21 1 50	14 25 13	1♓12	24 22	26 18	18 26	19 10	10 47	16 4	19 18	20 58
8	21 5 47	15 22 42	16 12	23 41	27 32	18 57	19 16	10 52	16 7	19 20	21 0
9	21 9 43	16 20 12	0♈52	22 57	28 46	19 28	19 22	10 58	16 11	19 21	21 2
10	21 13 40	17 17 44	15 9	22 10	0♍ 0	19 59	19 28	11 3	16 14	19 22	21 4
11	21 17 36	18 15 17	29 0	21 22	1 14	20 31	19 34	11 8	16 17	19 23	21 6
12	21 21 33	19 12 51	12♉25	20 32	2 28	21 3	19 39	11 14	16 20	19 25	21 8
13	21 25 29	20 10 27	25 25	19 43	3 42	21 35	19 45	11 19	16 23	19 26	21 10
14	21 29 26	21 8 5	8♊ 5	18 55	4 56	22 7	19 50	11 25	16 27	19 27	21 11
15	21 33 22	22 5 44	20 26	18 9	6 10	22 40	19 55	11 30	16 30	19 29	21 13
16	21 37 19	23 3 24	2♋34	17 26	7 24	23 13	20 0	11 36	16 33	19 30	21 15
17	21 41 16	24 1 7	14 32	16 47	8 38	23 46	20 4	11 41	16 36	19 31	21 17
18	21 45 12	24 58 50	26 24	16 12	9 52	24 20	20 9	11 47	16 39	19 33	21 19
19	21 49 9	25 56 35	8♌12	15 43	11 6	24 54	20 13	11 53	16 42	19 34	21 21
20	21 53 5	26 54 21	19 59	15 20	12 20	25 28	20 17	11 59	16 45	19 36	21 23
21	21 57 2	27 52 9	1♍47	15 4	13 33	26 2	20 21	12 5	16 48	19 37	21 25
22	22 0 58	28 49 58	13 39	14D55	14 47	26 36	20 25	12 11	16 51	19 39	21 27
23	22 4 55	29 47 49	25 38	14 54	16 1	27 11	20 28	12 17	16 54	19 40	21 28
24	22 8 51	0♍45 41	7♎44	15 0	17 15	27 46	20 32	12 23	16 57	19 42	21 30
25	22 12 48	1 43 34	20 2	15 14	18 29	28 21	20 35	12 29	16 59	19 44	21 32
26	22 16 44	2 41 28	2♏32	15 36	19 43	28 56	20 38	12 35	17 2	19 45	21 34
27	22 20 41	3 39 24	15 19	16 6	20 57	29 32	20 41	12 41	17 5	19 47	21 36
28	22 24 38	4 37 21	28 24	16 44	22 11	0♐ 8	20 43	12 48	17 8	19 49	21 38
29	22 28 34	5 35 20	11♐50	17 29	23 25	0 44	20 46	12 54	17 10	19 50	21 40
30	22 32 31	6 33 20	25 40	18 22	24 39	1 20	20 48	13 0	17 13	19 52	21 41
31	22 36 27	7♍31 21	9♑52	19♌23	25♍53	1♐56	20♉50	13♎ 7	17♋16	19♎54	21♌43

THE SUN ENTERS THE SIGN OF VIRGO ON AUG 23 AT 05:04.

DAY	TIME	☉	☽	☿	♀	♂	♃	♄	♅	♆	♇
	h m s	° ' "	° '	° '	° '	° '	° '	° '	° '	° '	° '
S 1	22 40 24	8♍29 23	24♑26	20♌30	27♍ 7	2♐33	20♉52	13♎13	17♋18	19♎56	21♌45
E 2	22 44 20	9 27 27	9♒17	21 43	28 21	3 10	20 53	13 20	17 21	19 57	21 47
P 3	22 48 17	10 25 33	24 20	23 2	29 34	3 47	20 55	13 26	17 23	19 59	21 49
T 4	22 52 13	11 23 39	9♓26	24 27	0♎48	4 24	20 56	13 33	17 26	20 1	21 50
E 5	22 56 10	12 21 48	24 27	25 57	2 2	5 1	20 57	13 39	17 28	20 3	21 52
M 6	23 0 7	13 19 58	9♈14	27 31	3 16	5 39	20 58	13 46	17 31	20 5	21 54
B 7	23 4 3	14 18 11	23 39	29 9	4 30	6 16	20 59	13 53	17 33	20 7	21 56
E 8	23 8 0	15 16 25	7♉38	0♍51	5 44	6 54	20 59	13 59	17 36	20 8	21 58
R 9	23 11 56	16 14 41	21 10	2 36	6 58	7 32	20R59	14 6	17 38	20 10	21 59
10	23 15 53	17 13 0	4♊15	4 23	8 11	8 11	20 59	14 13	17 40	20 12	22 1
11	23 19 49	18 11 20	16 56	6 11	9 25	8 49	20 59	14 20	17 42	20 14	22 3
12	23 23 46	19 9 43	29 17	8 2	10 39	9 27	20 59	14 26	17 44	20 16	22 5
13	23 27 42	20 8 8	11♋22	9 53	11 53	10 6	20 58	14 33	17 47	20 18	22 6
14	23 31 39	21 6 35	23 17	11 46	13 7	10 45	20 58	14 40	17 49	20 20	22 8
15	23 35 36	22 5 4	5♌ 5	13 39	14 21	11 24	20 57	14 47	17 51	20 22	22 10
16	23 39 32	23 3 35	16 52	15 32	15 34	12 3	20 56	14 54	17 53	20 24	22 11
17	23 43 29	24 2 8	28 40	17 25	16 48	12 43	20 54	15 1	17 55	20 26	22 13
18	23 47 25	25 0 43	10♍33	19 18	18 2	13 22	20 53	15 8	17 57	20 28	22 15
19	23 51 22	25 59 20	22 34	21 10	19 16	14 2	20 51	15 15	17 58	20 30	22 16
20	23 55 18	26 57 59	4♎44	23 2	20 30	14 42	20 49	15 22	18 0	20 32	22 18
21	23 59 15	27 56 40	17 5	24 54	21 43	15 22	20 47	15 30	18 2	20 35	22 19
22	0 3 11	28 55 22	29 37	26 45	22 57	16 2	20 44	15 37	18 4	20 37	22 21
23	0 7 8	29 54 7	12♏22	28 35	24 11	16 42	20 42	15 44	18 5	20 39	22 23
24	0 11 5	0♎52 53	25 19	0♎24	25 25	17 23	20 39	15 51	18 7	20 41	22 24
25	0 15 1	1 51 42	8♐31	2 12	26 38	18 3	20 36	15 58	18 9	20 43	22 26
26	0 18 58	2 50 32	21 58	4 0	27 52	18 44	20 33	16 5	18 10	20 45	22 27
27	0 22 54	3 49 24	5♑41	5 46	29 6	19 25	20 30	16 13	18 12	20 47	22 29
28	0 26 51	4 48 17	19 41	7 32	0♏20	20 6	20 26	16 20	18 13	20 49	22 30
29	0 30 47	5 47 12	3♒56	9 17	1 33	20 47	20 23	16 27	18 14	20 52	22 32
30	0 34 44	6♎46 9	18♒27	11♎ 1	2♏47	21♐28	20♉19	16♎34	18♋16	20♎54	22♌33

THE SUN ENTERS THE SIGN OF LIBRA ON SEP 23 AT 02:25.

♈ ARIES ♉ TAURUS ♊ GEMINI ♋ CANCER ♌ LEO ♍ VIRGO ♎ LIBRA

SIDEREAL SUN MOON. MERCURY. VENUS. MARS. JUPITER. SATURN. URANUS. NEPTUNE. PLUTO.

DAY	TIME	☉	☽	☿	♀	♂	♃	♄	♅	♆	♇
	h m s	° ' "	° '	° '	° '	° '	° '	° '	° '	° '	° '
O 1	Ø 38 4Ø	7♎45 8	3♓ 9	12♎44	4♏ 1	22♐ 9	2Ø♉15	16♎42	18♋17	2Ø♎56	22♌35
C 2	Ø 42 37	8 44 8	17 56	14 26	5 14	22 51	2ØR1Ø	16 49	18 18	2Ø 58	22 36
T 3	Ø 46 34	9 43 1Ø	2♈43	16 7	6 28	23 32	2Ø 6	16 56	18 19	21 Ø	22 37
O 4	Ø 5Ø 3Ø	1Ø 42 15	17 21	17 48	7 42	24 14	2Ø 1	17 3	18 21	21 3	22 39
B 5	Ø 54 27	11 41 21	1♉43	19 27	8 55	24 56	19 56	17 11	18 22	21 5	22 4Ø
E 6	Ø 58 23	12 4Ø 3Ø	15 43	21 6	1Ø 9	25 38	19 52	17 18	18 23	21 7	22 41
R 7	1 2 2Ø	13 39 41	29 18	22 44	11 22	26 2Ø	19 46	17 25	18 24	21 9	22 43
8	1 6 16	14 38 54	12♊27	24 21	12 36	27 2	19 41	17 33	18 25	21 11	22 44
9	1 1Ø 13	15 38 9	25 11	25 58	13 49	27 44	19 36	17 4Ø	18 25	21 14	22 45
1Ø	1 14 9	16 37 27	7♋33	27 33	15 3	28 27	19 3Ø	17 47	18 26	21 16	22 47
11	1 18 6	17 36 47	19 39	29 8	16 17	29 9	19 24	17 55	18 27	21 18	22 48
12	1 22 3	18 36 1Ø	1♌34	Ø♏43	17 3Ø	29 52	19 18	18 2	18 28	21 2Ø	22 49
13	1 25 59	19 35 34	13 22	2 16	18 44	Ø♑34	19 12	18 9	18 28	21 23	22 5Ø
14	1 29 56	2Ø 35 1	25 9	3 49	19 57	1 17	19 6	18 17	18 29	21 25	22 51
15	1 33 52	21 34 3Ø	7♍ Ø	5 22	21 11	2 Ø	19 Ø	18 24	18 29	21 27	22 52
16	1 37 49	22 34 2	18 59	6 53	22 24	2 43	18 53	18 31	18 3Ø	21 29	22 54
17	1 41 45	23 33 35	1♎ 9	8 24	23 37	3 26	18 47	18 39	18 3Ø	21 32	22 55
18	1 45 42	24 33 11	13 33	9 54	24 51	4 9	18 4Ø	18 46	18 31	21 34	22 56
19	1 49 38	25 32 48	26 11	11 24	26 4	4 52	18 33	18 53	18 31	21 36	22 57
2Ø	1 53 35	26 32 28	9♏ 3	12 53	27 18	5 36	18 26	19 1	18 31	21 38	22 58
21	1 57 31	27 32 1Ø	22 9	14 21	28 31	6 19	18 19	19 8	18 32	21 4Ø	22 59
22	2 1 28	28 31 54	5♐27	15 49	29 45	7 3	18 12	19 15	18 32	21 43	23 Ø
23	2 5 25	29 31 39	18 56	17 16	Ø♐58	7 46	18 4	19 23	18 32	21 45	23 1
24	2 9 21	Ø♏31 27	2♑35	18 42	2 11	8 3Ø	17 57	19 3Ø	18R32	21 47	23 2
25	2 13 18	1 31 16	16 22	2Ø 7	3 25	9 14	17 49	19 37	18 32	21 49	23 2
26	2 17 14	2 31 7	Ø♒18	21 32	4 38	9 58	17 42	19 44	18 32	21 52	23 3
27	2 21 11	3 3Ø 59	14 23	22 56	5 51	1Ø 42	17 34	19 52	18 32	21 54	23 4
28	2 25 7	4 3Ø 53	28 35	24 19	7 5	11 26	17 26	19 59	18 32	21 56	23 5
29	2 29 4	5 3Ø 48	12♓53	25 41	8 18	12 1Ø	17 18	2Ø 6	18 32	21 58	23 6
3Ø	2 33 Ø	6 3Ø 45	27 15	27 2	9 31	12 54	17 11	2Ø 13	18 31	22 Ø	23 6
31	2 36 57	7♏3Ø 44	11♈37	28♏23	1Ø♐44	13♑39	17♉ 3	2Ø♎2Ø	18♋31	22♎ 3	23♌ 7

THE SUN ENTERS THE SIGN OF SCORPIO ON OCT 23 AT 11:23.

DAY	TIME	☉	☽	☿	♀	♂	♃	♄	♅	♆	♇
	h m s	° ' "	° '	° '	° '	° '	° '	° '	° '	° '	° '
N 1	2 4Ø 54	8♏3Ø 44	25♈53	29♏42	11♐57	14♑23	16♉55	2Ø♎27	18♋31	22♎ 5	23♌ 8
O 2	2 44 5Ø	9 3Ø 47	9♉58	1♐ Ø	13 11	15 7	16R47	2Ø 34	18R3Ø	22 7	23 9
V 3	2 48 47	1Ø 3Ø 51	23 46	2 16	14 24	15 52	16 39	2Ø 41	18 3Ø	22 9	23 9
E 4	2 52 43	11 3Ø 57	7♊13	3 31	15 37	16 36	16 3Ø	2Ø 49	18 29	22 11	23 1Ø
M 5	2 56 4Ø	12 31 6	2Ø 19	4 45	16 5Ø	17 21	16 22	2Ø 56	18 29	22 13	23 1Ø
B 6	3 Ø 36	13 31 16	3♋ 2	5 57	18 3	18 6	16 14	21 3	18 28	22 15	23 11
E 7	3 4 33	14 31 28	15 25	7 7	19 16	18 5Ø	16 6	21 9	18 27	22 18	23 12
R 8	3 8 3Ø	15 31 42	27 32	8 14	2Ø 29	19 35	15 58	21 16	18 27	22 2Ø	23 12
9	3 12 26	16 31 59	9♌27	9 19	21 42	2Ø 2Ø	15 5Ø	21 23	18 26	22 22	23 13
1Ø	3 16 23	17 32 17	21 15	1Ø 21	22 55	21 5	15 41	21 3Ø	18 25	22 24	23 13
11	3 2Ø 19	18 32 37	3♍ 3	11 21	24 8	21 5Ø	15 33	21 37	18 24	22 26	23 13
12	3 24 16	19 32 59	14 56	12 16	25 21	22 35	15 25	21 44	18 23	22 28	23 14
13	3 28 12	2Ø 33 23	26 59	13 8	26 34	23 2Ø	15 17	21 51	18 22	22 3Ø	23 14
14	3 32 9	21 33 49	9♎15	13 55	27 46	24 5	15 9	21 57	18 21	22 32	23 14
15	3 36 5	22 34 16	21 49	14 38	28 59	24 5Ø	15 1	22 4	18 2Ø	22 34	23 15
16	3 4Ø 2	23 34 46	4♏42	15 14	Ø♑12	25 36	14 53	22 11	18 19	22 36	23 15
17	3 43 58	24 35 17	17 54	15 45	1 25	26 21	14 45	22 17	18 18	22 38	23 15
18	3 47 55	25 35 5Ø	1♐23	16 8	2 37	27 6	14 37	22 24	18 16	22 4Ø	23 16
19	3 51 52	26 36 24	15 7	16 24	3 5Ø	27 52	14 29	22 3Ø	18 15	22 42	23 16
2Ø	3 55 48	27 37 Ø	29 1	16R31	5 3	28 37	14 21	22 37	18 14	22 44	23 16
21	3 59 45	28 37 37	13♑ 3	16 29	6 15	29 23	14 14	22 43	18 12	22 46	23 16
22	4 3 41	29 38 16	27 8	16 17	7 28	Ø♒ 8	14 6	22 5Ø	18 11	22 48	23 16
23	4 7 38	Ø♐38 55	11♒15	15 54	8 4Ø	Ø 54	13 59	22 56	18 9	22 49	23 16
24	4 11 34	1 39 36	25 21	15 21	9 53	1 39	13 51	23 2	18 8	22 51	23R16
25	4 15 31	2 4Ø 17	9♓26	14 37	11 5	2 25	13 44	23 8	18 6	22 53	23 16
26	4 19 28	3 41 Ø	23 29	13 43	12 18	3 11	13 37	23 15	18 5	22 55	23 16
27	4 23 24	4 41 43	7♈29	12 39	13 3Ø	3 57	13 3Ø	23 21	18 3	22 57	23 16
28	4 27 21	5 42 28	21 24	11 27	14 42	4 42	13 23	23 27	18 1	22 59	23 16
29	4 31 17	6 43 13	5♉13	1Ø 9	15 55	5 28	13 16	23 33	18 Ø	23 Ø	23 16
3Ø	4 35 14	7♐44 Ø	18♉51	8♐48	17♑ 7	6♒14	13♉ 9	23♎39	17♋58	23♎ 2	23♌16

THE SUN ENTERS THE SIGN OF SAGITTARIUS ON NOV 22 AT 08:36.

DAY	TIME	☉	☽	☿	♀	♂	♃	♄	♅	♆	♇
	h m s	° ' "	° '	° '	° '	° '	° '	° '	° '	° '	° '
D 1	4 39 1Ø	8♐44 48	2♊17	7♐25	18♑19	7♒ Ø	13♉ 2	23♎45	17♋56	23♎ 4	23♌16
E 2	4 43 7	9 45 37	15 27	6R 4	19 31	7 46	12R56	23 51	17R54	23 5	23R15
C 3	4 47 3	1Ø 46 27	28 2Ø	4 48	2Ø 43	8 32	12 49	23 56	17 52	23 7	23 15
E 4	4 51 Ø	11 47 19	1Ø♋55	3 38	21 55	9 18	12 43	24 2	17 51	23 9	23 15
M 5	4 54 57	12 48 12	23 14	2 37	23 7	1Ø 4	12 37	24 8	17 49	23 1Ø	23 15
B 6	4 58 53	13 49 6	5♌19	1 47	24 18	1Ø 5Ø	12 31	24 13	17 47	23 12	23 14
E 7	5 2 5Ø	14 5Ø 1	17 14	1 7	25 3Ø	11 36	12 25	24 19	17 45	23 13	23 14
R 8	5 6 46	15 5Ø 57	29 2	Ø 39	26 42	12 22	12 2Ø	24 24	17 42	23 15	23 14
9	5 1Ø 43	16 51 54	1Ø♍5Ø	Ø 22	27 53	13 8	12 14	24 3Ø	17 4Ø	23 16	23 13
1Ø	5 14 39	17 52 53	22 42	ØD16	29 5	13 54	12 9	24 35	17 38	23 18	23 13
11	5 18 36	18 53 52	4♎45	Ø 21	Ø♒16	14 4Ø	12 4	24 41	17 36	23 19	23 12
12	5 22 32	19 54 53	17 2	Ø 35	1 28	15 26	11 59	24 46	17 34	23 21	23 12
13	5 26 29	2Ø 55 55	29 39	Ø 57	2 39	16 12	11 54	24 51	17 32	23 22	23 11
14	5 3Ø 26	21 56 58	12♏38	1 28	3 5Ø	16 58	11 5Ø	24 56	17 29	23 24	23 11
15	5 34 22	22 58 2	26 1	2 5	5 1	17 45	11 45	25 1	17 27	23 25	23 1Ø
16	5 38 19	23 59 7	9♐47	2 49	6 12	18 31	11 41	25 6	17 25	23 26	23 1Ø
17	5 42 15	25 Ø 12	23 52	3 39	7 23	19 17	11 37	25 11	17 23	23 28	23 9
18	5 46 12	26 1 19	8♑13	4 33	8 34	2Ø 3	11 33	25 16	17 2Ø	23 29	23 8
19	5 5Ø 8	27 2 25	22 42	5 32	9 45	2Ø 49	11 3Ø	25 2Ø	17 18	23 3Ø	23 8
2Ø	5 54 5	28 3 32	7♒15	6 34	1Ø 55	21 36	11 26	25 25	17 15	23 31	23 7
21	5 58 2	29 4 4Ø	21 44	7 4Ø	12 6	22 22	11 23	25 29	17 13	23 32	23 6
22	6 1 58	Ø♑ 5 47	6♓ 7	8 49	13 16	23 8	11 2Ø	25 34	17 11	23 34	23 6
23	6 5 55	1 6 55	2Ø 2Ø	1Ø Ø	14 27	23 54	11 17	25 38	17 8	23 35	23 5
24	6 9 51	2 8 2	4♈22	11 14	15 37	24 41	11 14	25 43	17 6	23 36	23 4
25	6 13 48	3 9 1Ø	18 12	12 29	16 47	25 27	11 12	25 47	17 3	23 37	23 3
26	6 17 44	4 1Ø 18	1♉49	13 47	17 57	26 13	11 1Ø	25 51	17 1	23 38	23 2
27	6 21 41	5 11 26	15 15	15 6	19 7	27 Ø	11 8	25 55	16 58	23 39	23 1
28	6 25 37	6 12 34	28 28	16 26	2Ø 16	27 46	11 6	25 59	16 56	23 4Ø	23 1
29	6 29 34	7 13 42	11♊29	17 47	21 26	28 32	11 4	26 3	16 53	23 41	23 Ø
3Ø	6 33 31	8 14 5Ø	24 16	19 1Ø	22 35	29 18	11 3	26 6	16 5Ø	23 42	22 59
31	6 37 27	9♑15 58	6♋5Ø	2Ø♐33	23♒45	Ø♓ 5	11♉ 2	26♎1Ø	16♋48	23♎43	22♌58

THE SUN ENTERS THE SIGN OF CAPRICORN ON DEC 21 AT 21:44.

♏ SCORPIO ♐ SAGITTARIUS ♑ CAPRICORN ♒ AQUARIUS ♓ PISCES

SIDEREAL . SUN . MOON . MERCURY . VENUS . MARS . JUPITER . SATURN . URANUS . NEPTUNE . PLUTO .

DAY	TIME h m s	☉ ° ' "	☽ ° '	☿ ° '	♀ ° '	♂ ° '	♃ ° '	♄ ° '	♅ ° '	♆ ° '	♇ ° '
J 1	6 41 24	10♑17 7	19♋12	21♐58	24♒54	0♓51	11♉ 1	26♎14	16♋45	23♎43	22♌57
A 2	6 45 20	11 18 15	1♌22	23 23	26 2	1 37	11R 0	26 17	16R43	23 44	22R56
N 3	6 49 17	12 19 23	13 22	24 49	27 11	2 23	10 59	26 21	16 40	23 45	22 55
U 4	6 53 13	13 20 32	25 14	26 15	28 20	3 10	10 59	26 24	16 38	23 46	22 54
A 5	6 57 10	14 21 40	7♍ 2	27 43	29 28	3 56	10D59	26 27	16 35	23 46	22 53
R 6	7 1 6	15 22 49	18 49	29 11	0♓36	4 42	10 59	26 30	16 32	23 47	22 52
Y 7	7 5 3	16 23 58	0♎41	0♑39	1 44	5 28	10 59	26 33	16 30	23 48	22 50
8	7 9 0	17 25 7	12 42	2 8	2 52	6 14	10 59	26 36	16 27	23 48	22 49
9	7 12 56	18 26 16	24 57	3 38	4 0	7 1	11 0	26 39	16 25	23 49	22 48
10	7 16 53	19 27 25	7♏30	5 8	5 7	7 47	11 1	26 42	16 22	23 49	22 47
11	7 20 49	20 28 34	20 27	6 38	6 15	8 33	11 2	26 45	16 19	23 50	22 46
12	7 24 46	21 29 43	3♐48	8 10	7 22	9 19	11 3	26 47	16 17	23 50	22 45
13	7 28 42	22 30 52	17 37	9 41	8 29	10 5	11 5	26 50	16 14	23 51	22 43
14	7 32 39	23 32 1	1♑51	11 13	9 35	10 52	11 6	26 52	16 12	23 51	22 42
15	7 36 35	24 33 10	16 26	12 46	10 41	11 38	11 8	26 54	16 9	23 52	22 41
16	7 40 32	25 34 18	1♒16	14 19	11 48	12 24	11 10	26 57	16 6	23 52	22 40
17	7 44 29	26 35 25	16 13	15 53	12 53	13 10	11 13	26 59	16 4	23 52	22 38
18	7 48 25	27 36 32	1♓10	17 27	13 59	13 56	11 15	27 1	16 1	23 52	22 37
19	7 52 22	28 37 38	15 58	19 1	15 4	14 42	11 18	27 2	15 59	23 53	22 36
20	7 56 18	29 38 43	0♈31	20 37	16 10	15 28	11 21	27 4	15 56	23 53	22 35
21	8 0 15	0♒39 47	14 45	22 12	17 14	16 14	11 24	27 6	15 54	23 53	22 33
22	8 4 11	1 40 50	28 40	23 49	18 19	17 0	11 27	27 7	15 51	23 53	22 32
23	8 8 8	2 41 52	12♉13	25 26	19 23	17 46	11 31	27 9	15 49	23 53	22 30
24	8 12 4	3 42 54	25 28	27 3	20 27	18 32	11 34	27 10	15 46	23 53	22 29
25	8 16 1	4 43 54	8♊24	28 41	21 30	19 18	11 38	27 11	15 44	23R53	22 28
26	8 19 58	5 44 53	21 5	0♒20	22 34	20 4	11 42	27 12	15 42	23 53	22 26
27	8 23 54	6 45 51	3♋33	1 59	23 36	20 50	11 47	27 14	15 39	23 53	22 25
28	8 27 51	7 46 48	15 50	3 39	24 39	21 36	11 51	27 14	15 37	23 53	22 24
29	8 31 47	8 47 44	27 56	5 20	25 41	22 21	11 56	27 15	15 35	23 53	22 22
30	8 35 44	9 48 39	9♌56	7 1	26 43	23 7	12 0	27 16	15 32	23 53	22 21
31	8 39 40	10♒49 33	21♌49	8♒43	27♓44	23♓53	12♉ 5	27♎17	15♋30	23♎53	22♌19

THE SUN ENTERS THE SIGN OF AQUARIUS ON JAN 20 AT 08:22.

DAY	TIME h m s	☉ ° ' "	☽ ° '	☿ ° '	♀ ° '	♂ ° '	♃ ° '	♄ ° '	♅ ° '	♆ ° '	♇ ° '
F 1	8 43 37	11♒50 26	3♍39	10♒26	28♓45	24♓39	12♉11	27♎17	15♋28	23♎52	22♌18
E 2	8 47 34	12 51 17	15 27	12 9	29 45	25 24	12 16	27 17	15R25	23R52	22R16
B 3	8 51 30	13 52 8	27 16	13 54	0♈45	26 10	12 21	27 18	15 23	23 52	22 15
R 4	8 55 27	14 52 58	9♎10	15 38	1 45	26 56	12 27	27 18	15 21	23 52	22 14
U 5	8 59 23	15 53 47	21 11	17 24	2 44	27 41	12 33	27R18	15 19	23 51	22 12
A 6	9 3 20	16 54 35	3♏25	19 10	3 42	28 27	12 39	27 18	15 17	23 51	22 11
R 7	9 7 16	17 55 23	15 54	20 57	4 40	29 12	12 45	27 18	15 15	23 50	22 9
Y 8	9 11 13	18 56 9	28 44	22 45	5 38	29 58	12 52	27 17	15 13	23 50	22 8
9	9 15 9	19 56 54	11♐57	24 33	6 35	0♈43	12 58	27 17	15 11	23 49	22 6
10	9 19 6	20 57 39	25 37	26 22	7 31	1 29	13 5	27 17	15 9	23 49	22 5
11	9 23 3	21 58 22	9♑44	28 11	8 27	2 14	13 12	27 16	15 7	23 48	22 3
12	9 26 59	22 59 4	24 16	0♓ 0	9 23	3 0	13 19	27 15	15 5	23 48	22 2
13	9 30 56	23 59 45	9♒10	1 50	10 17	3 45	13 26	27 15	15 3	23 47	22 0
14	9 34 52	25 0 24	24 19	3 40	11 11	4 30	13 33	27 14	15 1	23 47	21 59
15	9 38 49	26 1 2	9♓32	5 30	12 5	5 16	13 41	27 13	14 59	23 46	21 57
16	9 42 45	27 1 39	24 41	7 20	12 57	6 1	13 48	27 12	14 58	23 45	21 56
17	9 46 42	28 2 13	9♈35	9 9	13 49	6 46	13 56	27 10	14 56	23 44	21 55
18	9 50 38	29 2 46	24 9	10 57	14 40	7 31	14 4	27 9	14 54	23 44	21 53
19	9 54 35	0♓ 3 18	8♉17	12 45	15 31	8 16	14 12	27 8	14 53	23 43	21 52
20	9 58 31	1 3 47	21 58	14 31	16 20	9 2	14 20	27 6	14 51	23 42	21 50
21	10 2 28	2 4 15	5♊13	16 16	17 9	9 47	14 29	27 5	14 49	23 41	21 49
22	10 6 25	3 4 40	18 5	17 58	17 57	10 32	14 37	27 3	14 48	23 40	21 47
23	10 10 21	4 5 4	0♋37	19 38	18 44	11 17	14 46	27 1	14 47	23 39	21 46
24	10 14 18	5 5 26	12 53	21 14	19 30	12 2	14 54	26 59	14 45	23 39	21 44
25	10 18 14	6 5 46	24 58	22 47	20 15	12 46	15 3	26 57	14 44	23 38	21 43
26	10 22 11	7 6 4	6♌54	24 15	20 59	13 31	15 12	26 55	14 42	23 37	21 42
27	10 26 7	8 6 20	18 45	25 39	21 42	14 16	15 22	26 53	14 41	23 36	21 40
28	10 30 4	9♓ 6 34	0♍34	26♓56	22♈23	15♈ 1	15♉31	26♎51	14♋40	23♎35	21♌39

THE SUN ENTERS THE SIGN OF PISCES ON FEB 18 AT 22:42.

DAY	TIME h m s	☉ ° ' "	☽ ° '	☿ ° '	♀ ° '	♂ ° '	♃ ° '	♄ ° '	♅ ° '	♆ ° '	♇ ° '
M 1	10 34 0	10♓ 6 47	12♍22	28♓ 8	23♈ 4	15♈46	15♉40	26♎48	14♋39	23♎33	21♌37
A 2	10 37 57	11 6 57	24 13	29 13	23 43	16 30	15 50	26R46	14R38	23R32	21R36
R 3	10 41 54	12 7 6	6♎ 7	0♈11	24 22	17 15	15 59	26 43	14 37	23 31	21 35
C 4	10 45 50	13 7 13	18 7	1 0	24 58	18 0	16 9	26 41	14 36	23 30	21 33
H 5	10 49 47	14 7 19	0♏15	1 42	25 34	18 44	16 19	26 38	14 35	23 29	21 32
6	10 53 43	15 7 23	12 33	2 15	26 8	19 29	16 29	26 35	14 34	23 28	21 31
7	10 57 40	16 7 25	25 4	2 39	26 41	20 13	16 39	26 32	14 33	23 27	21 29
8	11 1 36	17 7 26	7♐51	2 54	27 12	20 58	16 49	26 29	14 32	23 25	21 28
9	11 5 33	18 7 25	20 57	3R 0	27 42	21 42	17 0	26 26	14 31	23 24	21 27
10	11 9 29	19 7 23	4♑26	2 56	28 10	22 26	17 10	26 23	14 31	23 23	21 25
11	11 13 26	20 7 19	18 20	2 45	28 36	23 11	17 21	26 20	14 30	23 21	21 24
12	11 17 23	21 7 13	2♒38	2 25	29 1	23 55	17 31	26 17	14 29	23 20	21 23
13	11 21 19	22 7 6	17 20	1 57	29 24	24 39	17 42	26 13	14 29	23 19	21 22
14	11 25 16	23 6 57	2♓20	1 22	29 45	25 23	17 53	26 10	14 28	23 17	21 21
15	11 29 12	24 6 45	17 32	0 41	0♉ 4	26 7	18 4	26 7	14 28	23 16	21 19
16	11 33 9	25 6 32	2♈45	29♓55	0 21	26 51	18 15	26 3	14 27	23 15	21 18
17	11 37 5	26 6 17	17 49	29 4	0 36	27 35	18 26	25 59	14 27	23 13	21 17
18	11 41 2	27 6 0	2♉35	28 11	0 49	28 20	18 37	25 56	14 27	23 12	21 16
19	11 44 58	28 5 41	16 56	27 16	1 0	29 3	18 49	25 52	14 26	23 10	21 15
20	11 48 55	29 5 19	0♊48	26 20	1 9	29 47	19 0	25 48	14 26	23 9	21 14
21	11 52 52	0♈ 4 55	14 11	25 26	1 15	0♉31	19 12	25 44	14 26	23 8	21 12
22	11 56 48	1 4 29	27 6	24 33	1 19	1 15	19 23	25 40	14D26	23 6	21 11
23	12 0 45	2 4 1	9♋38	23 42	1R21	1 59	19 35	25 36	14 26	23 5	21 10
24	12 4 41	3 3 30	21 51	22 55	1 20	2 43	19 47	25 32	14 26	23 3	21 9
25	12 8 38	4 2 57	3♌52	22 13	1 16	3 26	19 59	25 28	14 26	23 2	21 8
26	12 12 34	5 2 22	15 43	21 35	1 11	4 10	20 10	25 24	14 26	23 0	21 7
27	12 16 31	6 1 44	27 31	21 3	1 2	4 53	20 22	25 20	14 26	22 58	21 6
28	12 20 27	7 1 5	9♍18	20 36	0 52	5 37	20 35	25 16	14 27	22 57	21 5
29	12 24 24	8 0 22	21 8	20 15	0 38	6 20	20 47	25 11	14 27	22 55	21 4
30	12 28 21	8 59 38	3♎ 4	20 0	0 23	7 4	20 59	25 7	14 27	22 54	21 4
31	12 32 17	9♈58 52	15♎ 6	19♓51	0♉ 4	7♉47	21♉11	25♎ 3	14♋28	22♎52	21♌ 3

THE SUN ENTERS THE SIGN OF ARIES ON MAR 20 AT 22:01.

♈ ARIES ♉ TAURUS ♊ GEMINI ♋ CANCER ♌ LEO ♍ VIRGO ♎ LIBRA

1953

SIDEREAL. SUN. MOON. MERCURY. VENUS. MARS. JUPITER. SATURN. URANUS. NEPTUNE. PLUTO.

DAY	TIME	☉	☽	☿	♀	♂	♃	♄	♅	♆	♇
	h m s	° ' "	° '	° '	° '	° '	° '	° '	° '	° '	° '
A 1	12 36 14	10♈58 4	27♎17	19♓47	29♈44	8♉31	21♉24	24♎58	14♋28	22♎51	21♌ 2
P 2	12 40 10	11 57 14	9♏36	19D49	29R21	9 14	21 36	24R54	14 29	22R49	21R 1
R 3	12 44 7	12 56 22	22 6	19 56	28 56	9 57	21 49	24 49	14 29	22 47	21 0
I 4	12 48 3	13 55 28	4♐47	20 9	28 29	10 40	22 1	24 45	14 30	22 46	20 59
L 5	12 52 0	14 54 32	17 41	20 27	28 0	11 23	22 14	24 40	14 31	22 44	20 59
6	12 55 56	15 53 35	0♑50	20 49	27 29	12 7	22 26	24 36	14 31	22 42	20 58
7	12 59 53	16 52 36	14 15	21 16	26 56	12 50	22 39	24 31	14 32	22 41	20 57
8	13 3 50	17 51 35	27 59	21 48	26 23	13 33	22 52	24 27	14 33	22 39	20 56
9	13 7 46	18 50 32	12♒ 4	22 23	25 47	14 16	23 5	24 22	14 34	22 38	20 56
10	13 11 43	19 49 28	26 27	23 3	25 11	14 59	23 18	24 18	14 35	22 36	20 55
11	13 15 39	20 48 22	11♓ 9	23 46	24 34	15 41	23 31	24 13	14 36	22 34	20 55
12	13 19 36	21 47 14	26 3	24 33	23 57	16 24	23 44	24 8	14 37	22 33	20 54
13	13 23 32	22 46 4	11♈ 3	25 23	23 19	17 7	23 57	24 4	14 38	22 31	20 53
14	13 27 29	23 44 52	25 58	26 17	22 42	17 50	24 10	23 59	14 39	22 29	20 53
15	13 31 25	24 43 39	10♉41	27 13	22 4	18 32	24 23	23 55	14 40	22 28	20 52
16	13 35 22	25 42 23	25 3	28 13	21 27	19 15	24 36	23 50	14 42	22 26	20 52
17	13 39 18	26 41 5	8♊58	29 15	20 50	19 58	24 50	23 45	14 43	22 24	20 51
18	13 43 15	27 39 45	22 26	0♈20	20 15	20 40	25 3	23 41	14 44	22 23	20 51
19	13 47 12	28 38 23	5♋25	1 27	19 40	21 23	25 16	23 36	14 46	22 21	20 51
20	13 51 8	29 36 59	18 1	2 37	19 7	22 5	25 30	23 32	14 47	22 19	20 50
21	13 55 5	0♉35 32	0♌17	3 49	18 36	22 48	25 43	23 27	14 48	22 18	20 50
22	13 59 1	1 34 4	12 17	5 4	18 6	23 30	25 57	23 22	14 50	22 16	20 50
23	14 2 58	2 32 33	24 9	6 20	17 38	24 12	26 10	23 18	14 52	22 15	20 49
24	14 6 54	3 31 0	5♍57	7 39	17 12	24 55	26 24	23 13	14 53	22 13	20 49
25	14 10 51	4 29 25	17 46	9 0	16 48	25 37	26 38	23 9	14 55	22 11	20 49
26	14 14 47	5 27 47	29 40	10 23	16 26	26 19	26 51	23 4	14 57	22 10	20 49
27	14 18 44	6 26 8	11♎42	11 48	16 7	27 1	27 5	23 0	14 58	22 8	20 48
28	14 22 41	7 24 27	23 54	13 15	15 50	27 43	27 19	22 56	15 0	22 7	20 48
29	14 26 37	8 22 44	6♏17	14 44	15 35	28 25	27 32	22 51	15 2	22 5	20 48
30	14 30 34	9♉20 59	18♏53	16♈15	15♈23	29♉ 7	27♉46	22♎47	15♋ 4	22♎ 3	20♌48

THE SUN ENTERS THE SIGN OF TAURUS ON APR 20 AT 09:25.

DAY	TIME	☉	☽	☿	♀	♂	♃	♄	♅	♆	♇
	h m s	° ' "	° '	° '	° '	° '	° '	° '	° '	° '	° '
M 1	14 34 30	10♉19 13	1♐41	17♈48	15♈13	29♉49	28♉ 0	22♎43	15♋ 6	22♎ 2	20♌48
A 2	14 38 27	11 17 25	14 40	19 23	15R 6	0♊31	28 14	22R38	15 8	22R 0	20D48
Y 3	14 42 23	12 15 36	27 50	21 0	15 1	1 13	28 27	22 34	15 10	21 59	20 48
4	14 46 20	13 13 45	11♑11	22 38	14D58	1 55	28 41	22 30	15 12	21 57	20 48
5	14 50 17	14 11 52	24 45	24 19	14 58	2 37	28 55	22 26	15 14	21 56	20 48
6	14 54 13	15 9 58	8♒30	26 1	15 1	3 18	29 9	22 22	15 16	21 54	20 48
7	14 58 10	16 8 3	22 28	27 45	15 5	4 0	29 23	22 18	15 19	21 53	20 48
8	15 2 6	17 6 6	6♓39	29 31	15 12	4 42	29 37	22 14	15 21	21 51	20 48
9	15 6 3	18 4 8	21 2	1♉19	15 21	5 23	29 51	22 10	15 23	21 50	20 48
10	15 9 59	19 2 9	5♈34	3 9	15 32	6 5	0♊ 5	22 6	15 26	21 49	20 49
11	15 13 56	20 0 8	20 10	5 1	15 46	6 46	0 19	22 2	15 28	21 47	20 49
12	15 17 52	20 58 6	4♉43	6 55	16 1	7 28	0 33	21 58	15 30	21 46	20 49
13	15 21 49	21 56 2	19 7	8 51	16 18	8 9	0 47	21 55	15 33	21 44	20 49
14	15 25 45	22 53 57	3♊14	10 48	16 37	8 51	1 1	21 51	15 35	21 43	20 50
15	15 29 42	23 51 51	17 1	12 47	16 58	9 32	1 15	21 47	15 38	21 42	20 50
16	15 33 39	24 49 43	0♋24	14 48	17 21	10 13	1 29	21 44	15 40	21 40	20 50
17	15 37 35	25 47 33	13 23	16 51	17 45	10 55	1 43	21 41	15 43	21 39	20 51
18	15 41 32	26 45 22	25 59	18 56	18 11	11 36	1 57	21 37	15 46	21 38	20 51
19	15 45 28	27 43 9	8♌16	21 2	18 39	12 17	2 11	21 34	15 48	21 37	20 52
20	15 49 25	28 40 54	20 19	23 9	19 8	12 58	2 25	21 31	15 51	21 35	20 52
21	15 53 21	29 38 38	2♍13	25 18	19 38	13 39	2 40	21 28	15 54	21 34	20 52
22	15 57 18	0♊36 20	14 3	27 28	20 10	14 20	2 54	21 25	15 57	21 33	20 53
23	16 1 15	1 34 0	25 54	29 38	20 44	15 1	3 8	21 22	15 59	21 32	20 54
24	16 5 11	2 31 39	7♎51	1♊50	21 18	15 42	3 22	21 19	16 2	21 31	20 54
25	16 9 8	3 29 16	19 58	4 1	21 54	16 23	3 36	21 16	16 5	21 29	20 55
26	16 13 4	4 26 53	2♏19	6 13	22 31	17 4	3 50	21 13	16 8	21 28	20 55
27	16 17 1	5 24 27	14 54	8 25	23 9	17 45	4 4	21 10	16 11	21 27	20 56
28	16 20 57	6 22 1	27 45	10 36	23 49	18 26	4 18	21 8	16 14	21 26	20 57
29	16 24 54	7 19 33	10♐52	12 47	24 29	19 6	4 32	21 5	16 17	21 25	20 57
30	16 28 50	8 17 5	24 13	14 56	25 11	19 47	4 46	21 3	16 20	21 24	20 58
31	16 32 47	9♊14 35	7♑46	17♊ 5	25♈53	20♊28	5♊ 0	21♎ 1	16♋23	21♎23	20♌59

THE SUN ENTERS THE SIGN OF GEMINI ON MAY 21 AT 08:53.

DAY	TIME	☉	☽	☿	♀	♂	♃	♄	♅	♆	♇
	h m s	° ' "	° '	° '	° '	° '	° '	° '	° '	° '	° '
J 1	16 36 44	10♊12 5	21♑29	19♊12	26♈37	21♊ 9	5♊14	20♎58	16♋26	21♎22	21♌ 0
U 2	16 40 40	11 9 33	5♒21	21 17	27 21	21 49	5 28	20R56	16 29	21R21	21 1
N 3	16 44 37	12 7 1	19 20	23 21	28 6	22 30	5 42	20 54	16 32	21 20	21 1
E 4	16 48 33	13 4 28	3♓24	25 23	28 52	23 10	5 56	20 52	16 36	21 19	21 2
5	16 52 30	14 1 54	17 33	27 22	29 39	23 51	6 10	20 50	16 39	21 19	21 3
6	16 56 26	14 59 20	1♈46	29 20	0♉27	24 31	6 24	20 49	16 42	21 18	21 4
7	17 0 23	15 56 45	15 59	1♋15	1 15	25 12	6 38	20 47	16 45	21 17	21 5
8	17 4 19	16 54 10	0♉11	3 7	2 4	25 52	6 52	20 45	16 48	21 16	21 6
9	17 8 16	17 51 34	14 17	4 57	2 54	26 32	7 6	20 44	16 52	21 15	21 7
10	17 12 13	18 48 57	28 14	6 45	3 45	27 13	7 20	20 42	16 55	21 15	21 8
11	17 16 9	19 46 20	11♊58	8 30	4 36	27 53	7 34	20 41	16 58	21 14	21 9
12	17 20 6	20 43 42	25 25	10 13	5 28	28 33	7 48	20 40	17 2	21 13	21 10
13	17 24 2	21 41 4	8♋34	11 53	6 20	29 13	8 2	20 39	17 5	21 13	21 11
14	17 27 59	22 38 25	21 23	13 31	7 13	29 54	8 16	20 38	17 8	21 12	21 12
15	17 31 55	23 35 44	3♌54	15 6	8 7	0♋34	8 30	20 37	17 12	21 12	21 13
16	17 35 52	24 33 3	16 9	16 38	9 1	1 14	8 43	20 36	17 15	21 11	21 15
17	17 39 48	25 30 22	28 12	18 8	9 55	1 54	8 57	20 35	17 19	21 10	21 16
18	17 43 45	26 27 39	10♍ 6	19 35	10 50	2 34	9 11	20 35	17 22	21 10	21 17
19	17 47 42	27 24 55	21 57	20 59	11 46	3 14	9 25	20 34	17 26	21 10	21 18
20	17 51 38	28 22 11	3♎50	22 21	12 42	3 54	9 38	20 34	17 29	21 9	21 19
21	17 55 35	29 19 26	15 48	23 40	13 38	4 34	9 52	20 33	17 33	21 9	21 21
22	17 59 31	0♋16 41	27 58	24 56	14 35	5 14	10 6	20 33	17 36	21 8	21 22
23	18 3 28	1 13 54	10♏23	26 9	15 33	5 54	10 19	20D33	17 40	21 8	21 23
24	18 7 24	2 11 8	23 5	27 20	16 30	6 33	10 33	20 33	17 43	21 8	21 25
25	18 11 21	3 8 20	6♐ 7	28 27	17 28	7 13	10 46	20 33	17 47	21 7	21 26
26	18 15 17	4 5 33	19 29	29 31	18 27	7 53	11 0	20 33	17 50	21 7	21 27
27	18 19 14	5 2 45	3♑10	0♌33	19 26	8 33	11 13	20 34	17 54	21 7	21 29
28	18 23 11	5 59 57	17 7	1 31	20 25	9 12	11 26	20 34	17 57	21 7	21 30
29	18 27 7	6 57 8	1♒16	2 25	21 25	9 52	11 40	20 34	18 1	21 7	21 32
30	18 31 4	7♋54 20	15♒33	3♌17	22♉24	10♋32	11♊53	20♎35	18♋ 5	21♎ 7	21♌33

THE SUN ENTERS THE SIGN OF CANCER ON JUN 21 AT 17:00.

♏ SCORPIO ♐ SAGITTARIUS ♑ CAPRICORN ♒ AQUARIUS ♓ PISCES

1953

SIDEREAL. SUN. MOON. MERCURY. VENUS. MARS. JUPITER. SATURN. URANUS. NEPTUNE. PLUTO.

DAY	TIME	☉	☽	☿	♀	♂	♃	♄	♅	♆	♇
	h m s	° ' "	° '	° '	° '	° '	° '	° '	° '	° '	° '
J 1	18 35 0	8♋51 31	29♒55	4♌ 4	23♉25	11♋11	12♊ 6	20♎36	18♋ 8	21♎ 7	21♌34
U 2	18 38 57	9 48 43	14♓16	4 49	24 25	11 51	12 20	20 36	18 12	21D 7	21 36
L 3	18 42 53	10 45 55	28 34	5 29	25 26	12 30	12 33	20 37	18 16	21 6	21 37
Y 4	18 46 50	11 43 7	12♈47	6 5	26 27	13 10	12 46	20 38	18 19	21 7	21 39
5	18 50 47	12 40 19	26 52	6 38	27 29	13 49	12 59	20 39	18 23	21 7	21 40
6	18 54 43	13 37 32	10♉46	7 6	28 31	14 29	13 12	20 41	18 26	21 7	21 42
7	18 58 40	14 34 45	24 30	7 30	29 33	15 8	13 25	20 42	18 30	21 7	21 44
8	19 2 36	15 31 58	8♊ 1	7 50	0♊35	15 48	13 38	20 43	18 34	21 7	21 45
9	19 6 33	16 29 12	21 19	8 5	1 38	16 27	13 51	20 45	18 37	21 7	21 47
10	19 10 29	17 26 26	4♋22	8 15	2 41	17 6	14 4	20 46	18 41	21 7	21 48
11	19 14 26	18 23 40	17 11	8R21	3 44	17 46	14 16	20 48	18 45	21 8	21 50
12	19 18 22	19 20 55	29 45	8 22	4 47	18 25	14 29	20 50	18 48	21 8	21 52
13	19 22 19	20 18 9	12♌ 6	8 19	5 50	19 4	14 42	20 51	18 52	21 8	21 53
14	19 26 16	21 15 24	24 15	8 10	6 54	19 43	14 54	20 53	18 56	21 8	21 55
15	19 30 12	22 12 39	6♍14	7 57	7 58	20 23	15 7	20 55	18 59	21 9	21 57
16	19 34 9	23 9 54	18 7	7 39	9 2	21 2	15 19	20 58	19 3	21 9	21 58
17	19 38 5	24 7 9	29 58	7 17	10 7	21 41	15 32	21 0	19 7	21 10	22 0
18	19 42 2	25 4 24	11♎50	6 51	11 11	22 20	15 44	21 2	19 10	21 10	22 2
19	19 45 58	26 1 40	23 48	6 20	12 16	22 59	15 56	21 4	19 14	21 11	22 3
20	19 49 55	26 58 56	5♏57	5 47	13 21	23 38	16 8	21 7	19 17	21 11	22 5
21	19 53 51	27 56 12	18 22	5 10	14 26	24 17	16 21	21 10	19 21	21 12	22 7
22	19 57 48	28 53 28	1♐ 5	4 31	15 32	24 56	16 33	21 12	19 25	21 12	22 9
23	20 1 45	29 50 45	14 10	3 50	16 37	25 35	16 45	21 15	19 28	21 13	22 10
24	20 5 41	0♌48 2	27 39	3 7	17 43	26 14	16 56	21 18	19 32	21 14	22 12
25	20 9 38	1 45 19	11♑31	2 25	18 49	26 53	17 8	21 21	19 35	21 14	22 14
26	20 13 34	2 42 37	25 45	1 42	19 55	27 32	17 20	21 24	19 39	21 15	22 16
27	20 17 31	3 39 56	10♒17	1 1	21 1	28 11	17 32	21 27	19 43	21 16	22 18
28	20 21 27	4 37 15	25 0	0 21	22 7	28 50	17 43	21 30	19 46	21 17	22 20
29	20 25 24	5 34 35	9♓47	29♋44	23 14	29 29	17 55	21 34	19 50	21 17	22 21
30	20 29 20	6 31 57	24 32	29 11	24 21	0♌ 7	18 6	21 37	19 53	21 18	22 23
31	20 33 17	7♌29 19	9♈ 9	28♋41	25♊28	0♌46	18♊18	21♎40	19♋57	21♎19	22♌25

THE SUN ENTERS THE SIGN OF LEO ON JUL 23 AT 03:53.

DAY	TIME	☉	☽	☿	♀	♂	♃	♄	♅	♆	♇
	h m s	° ' "	° '	° '	° '	° '	° '	° '	° '	° '	° '
A 1	20 37 14	8♌26 42	23♈32	28♋16	26♊35	1♌25	18♊29	21♎44	20♋ 0	21♎20	22♌27
U 2	20 41 10	9 24 6	7♉38	27R56	27 42	2 4	18 40	21 48	20 4	21 21	22 29
G 3	20 45 7	10 21 32	21 26	27 41	28 49	2 42	18 51	21 51	20 7	21 22	22 31
U 4	20 49 3	11 18 59	4♊55	27D33	29 57	3 21	19 2	21 55	20 11	21 23	22 32
S 5	20 53 0	12 16 27	18 8	27 30	1♋ 4	4 0	19 13	21 59	20 14	21 24	22 34
T 6	20 56 56	13 13 57	1♋ 4	27 34	2 12	4 38	19 24	22 3	20 18	21 25	22 36
7	21 0 53	14 11 27	13 46	27 45	3 20	5 17	19 35	22 7	20 21	21 26	22 38
8	21 4 49	15 8 59	26 15	28 2	4 28	5 56	19 45	22 11	20 25	21 27	22 40
9	21 8 46	16 6 32	8♌33	28 26	5 36	6 34	19 56	22 15	20 28	21 28	22 42
10	21 12 43	17 4 6	20 42	28 57	6 45	7 13	20 6	22 20	20 31	21 30	22 44
11	21 16 39	18 1 41	2♍43	29 35	7 53	7 52	20 17	22 24	20 35	21 31	22 46
12	21 20 36	18 59 17	14 38	0♌19	9 2	8 30	20 27	22 28	20 38	21 32	22 48
13	21 24 32	19 56 54	26 29	1 10	10 10	9 9	20 37	22 33	20 41	21 33	22 49
14	21 28 29	20 54 32	8♎19	2 8	11 19	9 47	20 47	22 37	20 45	21 34	22 51
15	21 32 25	21 52 11	20 11	3 12	12 28	10 26	20 57	22 42	20 48	21 36	22 53
16	21 36 22	22 49 52	2♏ 8	4 22	13 37	11 4	21 7	22 47	20 51	21 37	22 55
17	21 40 18	23 47 33	14 15	5 37	14 46	11 42	21 16	22 52	20 54	21 38	22 57
18	21 44 15	24 45 15	26 36	6 59	15 56	12 21	21 26	22 56	20 57	21 40	22 59
19	21 48 12	25 42 59	9♐15	8 25	17 5	12 59	21 35	23 1	21 1	21 41	23 1
20	21 52 8	26 40 44	22 16	9 56	18 14	13 38	21 45	23 6	21 4	21 43	23 3
21	21 56 5	27 38 29	5♑43	11 32	19 24	14 16	21 54	23 11	21 7	21 44	23 5
22	22 0 1	28 36 16	19 36	13 12	20 34	14 54	22 3	23 17	21 10	21 46	23 7
23	22 3 58	29 34 4	3♒56	14 56	21 44	15 33	22 12	23 22	21 13	21 47	23 8
24	22 7 54	0♍31 54	18 39	16 43	22 54	16 11	22 21	23 27	21 16	21 49	23 10
25	22 11 51	1 29 45	3♓38	18 32	24 4	16 49	22 30	23 32	21 19	21 50	23 12
26	22 15 47	2 27 37	18 47	20 24	25 14	17 27	22 38	23 38	21 22	21 52	23 14
27	22 19 44	3 25 30	3♈55	22 18	26 24	18 6	22 47	23 43	21 25	21 53	23 16
28	22 23 41	4 23 26	18 52	24 14	27 34	18 44	22 55	23 49	21 28	21 55	23 18
29	22 27 37	5 21 23	3♉31	26 10	28 45	19 22	23 3	23 54	21 31	21 57	23 20
30	22 31 34	6 19 22	17 48	28 7	29 55	20 0	23 11	24 0	21 34	21 58	23 22
31	22 35 30	7♍17 24	1♊38	0♍ 5	1♌ 6	20♌39	23♊19	24♎ 6	21♋36	22♎ 0	23♌23

THE SUN ENTERS THE SIGN OF VIRGO ON AUG 23 AT 10:46.

DAY	TIME	☉	☽	☿	♀	♂	♃	♄	♅	♆	♇
	h m s	° ' "	° '	° '	° '	° '	° '	° '	° '	° '	° '
S 1	22 39 27	8♍15 27	15♊ 4	2♍ 3	2♌17	21♌17	23♊27	24♎11	21♋39	22♎ 2	23♌25
E 2	22 43 23	9 13 32	28 7	4 1	3 28	21 55	23 35	24 17	21 42	22 4	23 27
P 3	22 47 20	10 11 39	10♋51	5 58	4 39	22 33	23 42	24 23	21 45	22 5	23 29
T 4	22 51 16	11 9 48	23 18	7 55	5 50	23 11	23 50	24 29	21 47	22 7	23 31
E 5	22 55 13	12 7 59	5♌33	9 52	7 1	23 49	23 57	24 35	21 50	22 9	23 33
M 6	22 59 10	13 6 11	17 38	11 47	8 12	24 27	24 4	24 41	21 53	22 11	23 34
B 7	23 3 6	14 4 26	29 36	13 42	9 23	25 5	24 11	24 47	21 55	22 13	23 36
E 8	23 7 3	15 2 42	11♍30	15 36	10 35	25 44	24 18	24 53	21 58	22 14	23 38
R 9	23 10 59	16 1 0	23 22	17 29	11 46	26 22	24 25	24 59	22 0	22 16	23 40
10	23 14 56	16 59 20	5♎12	19 21	12 58	27 0	24 31	25 5	22 3	22 18	23 42
11	23 18 52	17 57 41	17 3	21 12	14 10	27 38	24 37	25 12	22 5	22 20	23 43
12	23 22 49	18 56 5	28 57	23 2	15 21	28 16	24 44	25 18	22 7	22 22	23 45
13	23 26 45	19 54 29	10♏57	24 50	16 33	28 54	24 50	25 24	22 10	22 24	23 47
14	23 30 42	20 52 56	23 5	26 38	17 45	29 32	24 55	25 31	22 12	22 26	23 49
15	23 34 39	21 51 24	5♐24	28 24	18 57	0♍10	25 1	25 37	22 14	22 28	23 50
16	23 38 35	22 49 54	17 59	0♎10	20 9	0 47	25 7	25 43	22 17	22 30	23 52
17	23 42 32	23 48 26	0♑54	1 54	21 21	1 25	25 12	25 50	22 19	22 32	23 54
18	23 46 28	24 46 59	14 12	3 38	22 34	2 3	25 17	25 57	22 21	22 34	23 56
19	23 50 25	25 45 34	27 57	5 20	23 46	2 41	25 22	26 3	22 23	22 36	23 57
20	23 54 21	26 44 10	12♒10	7 1	24 58	3 19	25 27	26 10	22 25	22 38	23 59
21	23 58 18	27 42 49	26 49	8 41	26 11	3 57	25 32	26 16	22 27	22 40	24 1
22	0 2 14	28 41 28	11♓51	10 21	27 23	4 35	25 36	26 23	22 29	22 42	24 2
23	0 6 11	29 40 10	27 7	11 59	28 36	5 13	25 41	26 30	22 31	22 44	24 4
24	0 10 7	0♎38 54	12♈27	13 36	29 48	5 50	25 45	26 37	22 33	22 46	24 5
25	0 14 4	1 37 39	27 39	15 12	1♍ 1	6 28	25 49	26 43	22 34	22 48	24 7
26	0 18 1	2 36 27	12♉33	16 48	2 14	7 6	25 53	26 50	22 36	22 50	24 9
27	0 21 57	3 35 17	27 2	18 22	3 27	7 44	25 56	26 57	22 38	22 53	24 10
28	0 25 54	4 34 10	11♊ 2	19 56	4 40	8 22	26 0	27 4	22 40	22 55	24 12
29	0 29 50	5 33 5	24 32	21 29	5 53	8 59	26 3	27 11	22 41	22 57	24 13
30	0 33 47	6♎32 2	7♋35	23♎ 1	7♍ 6	9♍37	26♊ 6	27♎18	22♋43	22♎59	24♌15

THE SUN ENTERS THE SIGN OF LIBRA ON SEP 23 AT 08:07.

♈ ARIES	♉ TAURUS	♊ GEMINI	♋ CANCER	♌ LEO	♍ VIRGO	♎ LIBRA

1953

SIDEREAL SUN. MOON. MERCURY. VENUS. MARS. JUPITER. SATURN. URANUS. NEPTUNE. PLUTO.

DAY	TIME	☉	☽	☿	♀	♂	♃	♄	♅	♆	♇
	h m s	° ' "	° '	° '	° '	° '	° '	° '	° '	° '	° '
O 1	Ø 37 43	7♎31 1	2Ø♋15	24♎32	8♍19	1Ø♍15	26♊ 9	27♎25	22♋44	23♎ 1	24♌16
C 2	Ø 41 4Ø	8 3Ø 3	2♌36	26 2	9 32	1Ø 52	26 12	27 32	22 46	23 3	24 18
T 3	Ø 45 37	9 29 6	14 44	27 31	1Ø 46	11 3Ø	26 14	27 39	22 47	23 6	24 19
O 4	Ø 49 33	1Ø 28 13	26 41	28 59	11 59	12 8	26 16	27 46	22 49	23 8	24 2Ø
B 5	Ø 53 3Ø	11 27 21	8♍34	Ø♏27	13 13	12 46	26 18	27 53	22 5Ø	23 1Ø	24 22
E 6	Ø 57 26	12 26 31	2Ø 24	1 53	14 26	13 23	26 2Ø	28 Ø	22 51	23 12	24 23
R 7	1 1 23	13 25 44	2♎14	3 19	15 4Ø	14 1	26 22	28 7	22 53	23 14	24 25
8	1 5 19	14 24 58	14 6	4 43	16 53	14 39	26 24	28 14	22 54	23 17	24 26
9	1 9 16	15 24 15	26 2	6 7	18 7	15 16	26 25	28 21	22 55	23 19	24 27
1Ø	1 13 12	16 23 34	8♏ 3	7 3Ø	19 21	15 54	26 26	28 29	22 56	23 21	24 29
11	1 17 9	17 22 55	2Ø 9	8 52	2Ø 34	16 31	26 27	28 36	22 57	23 23	24 3Ø
12	1 21 5	18 22 17	2♐24	1Ø 12	21 48	17 9	26 28	28 43	22 58	23 25	24 31
13	1 25 2	19 21 42	14 48	11 32	23 2	17 47	26 28	28 5Ø	22 59	23 28	24 32
14	1 28 59	2Ø 21 8	27 25	12 5Ø	24 16	18 24	26 29	28 57	23 Ø	23 3Ø	24 34
15	1 32 55	21 2Ø 37	1Ø♑18	14 7	25 3Ø	19 2	26R29	29 5	23 1	23 32	24 35
16	1 36 52	22 2Ø 7	23 3Ø	15 23	26 44	19 39	26 29	29 12	23 1	23 34	24 36
17	1 4Ø 48	23 19 38	7♒ 5	16 38	27 58	2Ø 17	26 28	29 19	23 2	23 37	24 37
18	1 44 45	24 19 11	21 5	17 5Ø	29 12	2Ø 54	26 28	29 26	23 3	23 39	24 38
19	1 48 41	25 18 46	5♓3Ø	19 1	Ø♎26	21 32	26 27	29 33	23 3	23 41	24 39
2Ø	1 52 38	26 18 23	2Ø 18	2Ø 11	1 41	22 9	26 26	29 41	23 4	23 43	24 4Ø
21	1 56 34	27 18 2	5♈24	21 18	2 55	22 47	26 25	29 48	23 4	23 46	24 41
22	2 Ø 31	28 17 42	2Ø 38	22 23	4 9	23 24	26 24	29 55	23 5	23 48	24 42
23	2 4 28	29 17 24	5♉49	23 25	5 23	24 1	26 22	Ø♏ 3	23 5	23 5Ø	24 43
24	2 8 24	Ø♏17 9	2Ø 47	24 25	6 38	24 39	26 21	Ø 1Ø	23 5	23 52	24 44
25	2 12 21	1 16 55	5♊23	25 22	7 52	25 16	26 19	Ø 17	23 6	23 55	24 45
26	2 16 17	2 16 44	19 3Ø	26 16	9 7	25 54	26 17	Ø 24	23 6	23 57	24 46
27	2 2Ø 14	3 16 35	3♋ 8	27 6	1Ø 21	26 31	26 15	Ø 32	23 6	23 59	24 47
28	2 24 1Ø	4 16 28	16 17	27 53	11 36	27 8	26 12	Ø 39	23 6	24 1	24 48
29	2 28 7	5 16 24	29 Ø	28 34	12 5Ø	27 46	26 9	Ø 46	23R 6	24 3	24 49
3Ø	2 32 3	6 16 21	11♌22	29 11	14 5	28 23	26 6	Ø 53	23 6	24 6	24 5Ø
31	2 36 Ø	7♏16 21	23♌29	29♏43	15♎2Ø	29♍ Ø	26♊ 3	1♏ 1	23♋ 6	24♎ 8	24♌51

THE SUN ENTERS THE SIGN OF SCORPIO ON OCT 23 AT 17:07.

DAY	TIME	☉	☽	☿	♀	♂	♃	♄	♅	♆	♇
	h m s	° ' "	° '	° '	° '	° '	° '	° '	° '	° '	° '
N 1	2 39 57	8♏16 23	5♍25	Ø♐ 8	16♎34	29♍38	26♊ Ø	1♏ 8	23♋ 6	24♎1Ø	24♌51
O 2	2 43 53	9 16 26	17 16	Ø 27	17 49	Ø♎15	25R57	1 15	23R 6	24 12	24 52
V 3	2 47 5Ø	1Ø 16 32	29 5	ØR38	19 4	Ø 52	25 53	1 22	23 6	24 14	24 53
E 4	2 51 46	11 16 4Ø	1Ø♎57	Ø 41	2Ø 19	1 3Ø	25 49	1 3Ø	23 6	24 17	24 53
M 5	2 55 43	12 16 5Ø	22 53	Ø 36	21 34	2 7	25 45	1 37	23 5	24 19	24 54
B 6	2 59 39	13 17 2	4♏56	Ø 22	22 48	2 44	25 41	1 44	23 5	24 21	24 55
E 7	3 3 36	14 17 15	17 6	29♏58	24 3	3 21	25 37	1 51	23 4	24 23	24 55
R 8	3 7 32	15 17 31	29 25	29 24	25 18	3 59	25 32	1 58	23 4	24 25	24 56
9	3 11 29	16 17 48	11♐53	28 41	26 33	4 36	25 27	2 5	23 3	24 27	24 56
1Ø	3 15 26	17 18 7	24 31	27 47	27 48	5 13	25 22	2 13	23 3	24 29	24 57
11	3 19 22	18 18 27	7♑2Ø	26 46	29 3	5 5Ø	25 17	2 2Ø	23 2	24 31	24 57
12	3 23 19	19 18 49	2Ø 21	25 36	Ø♏18	6 27	25 12	2 27	23 1	24 34	24 58
13	3 27 15	2Ø 19 13	3♒36	24 2Ø	1 33	7 4	25 7	2 34	23 1	24 36	24 58
14	3 31 12	21 19 37	17 9	23 1	2 48	7 41	25 1	2 41	23 Ø	24 38	24 59
15	3 35 8	22 2Ø 3	1♓ Ø	21 4Ø	4 3	8 18	24 55	2 48	22 59	24 4Ø	24 59
16	3 39 5	23 2Ø 3Ø	15 1Ø	2Ø 21	5 18	8 55	24 49	2 55	22 58	24 42	24 59
17	3 43 1	24 2Ø 59	29 38	19 6	6 33	9 33	24 43	3 2	22 57	24 44	25 Ø
18	3 46 58	25 21 28	14♈21	17 56	7 49	1Ø 1Ø	24 37	3 9	22 56	24 46	25 Ø
19	3 5Ø 55	26 22 Ø	29 13	16 56	9 4	1Ø 47	24 31	3 16	22 55	24 48	25 Ø
2Ø	3 54 51	27 22 32	14♉ 6	16 5	1Ø 19	11 24	24 25	3 22	22 54	24 5Ø	25 Ø
21	3 58 48	28 23 6	28 5Ø	15 25	11 34	12 Ø	24 18	3 29	22 53	24 52	25 1
22	4 2 44	29 23 41	13♊18	14 57	12 49	12 37	24 11	3 36	22 52	24 54	25 1
23	4 6 41	Ø♐24 19	27 23	14D4Ø	14 5	13 14	24 4	3 43	22 5Ø	24 55	25 1
24	4 1Ø 37	1 24 57	11♋ 3	14 35	15 2Ø	13 51	23 57	3 5Ø	22 49	24 57	25 1
25	4 14 34	2 25 37	24 15	14 41	16 35	14 28	23 5Ø	3 56	22 48	24 59	25 1
26	4 18 3Ø	3 26 19	7♌ 3	14 57	17 5Ø	15 5	23 43	4 3	22 46	25 1	25R 1
27	4 22 27	4 27 2	19 3Ø	15 22	19 6	15 42	23 36	4 1Ø	22 45	25 3	25 1
28	4 26 24	5 27 47	1♍4Ø	15 56	2Ø 21	16 19	23 29	4 16	22 43	25 5	25 1
29	4 3Ø 2Ø	6 28 33	13 38	16 37	21 36	16 56	23 21	4 23	22 42	25 7	25 1
3Ø	4 34 17	7♐29 21	25♍31	17♏25	22♏52	17♎32	23♊13	4♏29	22♋4Ø	25♎ 8	25♌ 1

THE SUN ENTERS THE SIGN OF SAGITTARIUS ON NOV 22 AT 14:23.

DAY	TIME	☉	☽	☿	♀	♂	♃	♄	♅	♆	♇
	h m s	° ' "	° '	° '	° '	° '	° '	° '	° '	° '	° '
D 1	4 38 13	8♐3Ø 1Ø	7♎21	18♏19	24♏ 7	18♎ 9	23♊ 6	4♏36	22♋39	25♎1Ø	25♌ 1
E 2	4 42 1Ø	9 31 1	19 15	19 18	25 22	18 46	22R58	4 42	22R37	25 12	25R 1
C 3	4 46 6	1Ø 31 53	1♏15	2Ø 21	26 38	19 23	22 5Ø	4 49	22 35	25 14	25 1
E 4	4 5Ø 3	11 32 46	13 25	21 29	27 53	19 59	22 42	4 55	22 34	25 15	25 Ø
M 5	4 53 59	12 33 4Ø	25 46	22 39	29 8	2Ø 36	22 34	5 1	22 32	25 17	25 Ø
B 6	4 57 56	13 34 36	8♐19	23 53	Ø♐24	21 13	22 26	5 7	22 3Ø	25 19	25 Ø
E 7	5 1 53	14 35 33	21 5	25 9	1 39	21 49	22 18	5 14	22 28	25 2Ø	25 Ø
R 8	5 5 49	15 36 31	4♑ 3	26 27	2 55	22 26	22 1Ø	5 2Ø	22 26	25 22	24 59
9	5 9 46	16 37 3Ø	17 13	27 47	4 1Ø	23 2	22 2	5 26	22 24	25 23	24 59
1Ø	5 13 42	17 38 29	Ø♒34	29 9	5 26	23 39	21 54	5 32	22 22	25 25	24 59
11	5 17 39	18 39 29	14 6	Ø♐32	6 41	24 16	21 46	5 38	22 2Ø	25 26	24 58
12	5 21 35	19 4Ø 3Ø	27 49	1 56	7 56	24 52	21 38	5 44	22 18	25 28	24 58
13	5 25 32	2Ø 41 31	11♓44	3 22	9 12	25 28	21 3Ø	5 5Ø	22 16	25 29	24 57
14	5 29 29	21 42 32	25 48	4 48	1Ø 27	26 5	21 21	5 55	22 14	25 31	24 57
15	5 33 25	22 43 34	1Ø♈ 2	6 15	11 43	26 41	21 13	6 1	22 12	25 32	24 56
16	5 37 22	23 44 36	24 22	7 42	12 58	27 18	21 5	6 7	22 1Ø	25 34	24 56
17	5 41 18	24 45 39	8♉47	9 11	14 14	27 54	2Ø 57	6 12	22 8	25 35	24 55
18	5 45 15	25 46 42	23 1Ø	1Ø 39	15 29	28 3Ø	2Ø 49	6 18	22 5	25 36	24 55
19	5 49 11	26 47 46	7♊26	12 9	16 45	29 7	2Ø 41	6 24	22 3	25 38	24 54
2Ø	5 53 8	27 48 5Ø	21 31	13 38	18 Ø	29 43	2Ø 33	6 29	22 1	25 39	24 53
21	5 57 4	28 49 55	5♋2Ø	15 8	19 16	Ø♏19	2Ø 25	6 34	21 59	25 4Ø	24 53
22	6 1 1	29 51 Ø	18 49	16 39	2Ø 31	Ø 55	2Ø 17	6 4Ø	21 56	25 41	24 52
23	6 4 58	Ø♑52 6	1♌57	18 9	21 47	1 31	2Ø 9	6 45	21 54	25 43	24 51
24	6 8 54	1 53 12	14 45	19 41	23 2	2 8	2Ø 1	6 5Ø	21 51	25 44	24 51
25	6 12 51	2 54 19	27 14	21 12	24 17	2 44	19 53	6 55	21 49	25 45	24 5Ø
26	6 16 47	3 55 27	9♍27	22 44	25 33	3 2Ø	19 46	7 Ø	21 47	25 46	24 49
27	6 2Ø 44	4 56 34	21 28	24 16	26 48	3 56	19 38	7 5	21 44	25 47	24 48
28	6 24 4Ø	5 57 43	3♎22	25 48	28 4	4 32	19 3Ø	7 1Ø	21 42	25 48	24 47
29	6 28 37	6 58 52	15 14	27 2Ø	29 19	5 8	19 23	7 15	21 39	25 49	24 46
3Ø	6 32 33	8 Ø 1	27 9	28 53	Ø♑35	5 44	19 15	7 2Ø	21 37	25 5Ø	24 46
31	6 36 3Ø	9♑ 1 11	9♏1Ø	Ø♑26	1♑5Ø	6♏19	19♊ 8	7♏24	21♋34	25♎51	24♌45

THE SUN ENTERS THE SIGN OF CAPRICORN ON DEC 22 AT 03:32.

♏ SCORPIO ♐ SAGITTARIUS ♑ CAPRICORN ♒ AQUARIUS ♓ PISCES

SIDEREAL. SUN. MOON. MERCURY. VENUS. MARS. JUPITER. SATURN. URANUS. NEPTUNE. PLUTO.

DAY	TIME h m s	☉ ° ' "	☽ ° '	☿ ° '	♀ ° '	♂ ° '	♃ ° '	♄ ° '	♅ ° '	♆ ° '	♇ ° '
J 1	6 40 27	10♑ 2 21	21♏23	2♑ 0	3♑ 6	6♏55	19♊ 1	7♏29	21♋32	25♎52	24♌44
A 2	6 44 23	11 3 31	3♐50	3 33	4 21	7 31	18R54	7 33	21R29	25 53	24R43
N 3	6 48 20	12 4 42	16 34	5 8	5 37	8 7	18 47	7 38	21 27	25 54	24 42
U 4	6 52 16	13 5 53	29 35	6 42	6 52	8 43	18 40	7 42	21 24	25 54	24 41
A 5	6 56 13	14 7 4	12♑54	8 17	8 8	9 18	18 33	7 46	21 21	25 55	24 40
R 6	7 0 9	15 8 15	26 29	9 52	9 23	9 54	18 27	7 50	21 19	25 56	24 39
Y 7	7 4 6	16 9 26	10♒17	11 27	10 39	10 30	18 20	7 55	21 16	25 57	24 38
8	7 8 3	17 10 36	24 17	13 3	11 54	11 5	18 14	7 59	21 14	25 57	24 36
9	7 11 59	18 11 46	8♓25	14 40	13 10	11 41	18 8	8 3	21 11	25 58	24 35
10	7 15 56	19 12 55	22 37	16 17	14 25	12 16	18 2	8 6	21 8	25 59	24 34
11	7 19 52	20 14 4	6♈51	17 54	15 41	12 51	17 56	8 10	21 6	25 59	24 33
12	7 23 49	21 15 12	21 3	19 31	16 56	13 27	17 50	8 14	21 3	26 0	24 32
13	7 27 45	22 16 20	5♉12	21 10	18 12	14 2	17 45	8 17	21 1	26 0	24 31
14	7 31 42	23 17 26	19 15	22 48	19 27	14 37	17 40	8 21	20 58	26 1	24 29
15	7 35 38	24 18 33	3♊11	24 27	20 43	15 13	17 34	8 24	20 55	26 1	24 28
16	7 39 35	25 19 38	16 58	26 7	21 58	15 48	17 29	8 28	20 53	26 2	24 27
17	7 43 32	26 20 43	0♋33	27 47	23 14	16 23	17 24	8 31	20 50	26 2	24 26
18	7 47 28	27 21 48	13 56	29 27	24 29	16 58	17 20	8 34	20 48	26 2	24 25
19	7 51 25	28 22 51	27 4	1♒ 9	25 44	17 33	17 15	8 37	20 45	26 3	24 23
20	7 55 21	29 23 54	9♌58	2 50	27 0	18 8	17 11	8 40	20 43	26 3	24 22
21	7 59 18	0♒24 56	22 37	4 32	28 15	18 43	17 7	8 43	20 40	26 3	24 21
22	8 3 14	1 25 58	5♍ 1	6 15	29 31	19 17	17 3	8 45	20 37	26 3	24 19
23	8 7 11	2 26 59	17 13	7 58	0♒46	19 52	16 59	8 48	20 35	26 3	24 18
24	8 11 7	3 28 0	29 15	9 42	2 1	20 27	16 56	8 51	20 32	26 4	24 17
25	8 15 4	4 29 0	11♎10	11 25	3 17	21 2	16 52	8 53	20 30	26 4	24 15
26	8 19 1	5 29 59	23 2	13 10	4 32	21 36	16 49	8 55	20 27	26 4	24 14
27	8 22 57	6 30 58	4♏56	14 54	5 48	22 11	16 46	8 58	20 25	26R 4	24 12
28	8 26 54	7 31 56	16 56	16 39	7 3	22 45	16 43	9 0	20 22	26 4	24 11
29	8 30 50	8 32 54	29 7	18 24	8 18	23 20	16 40	9 2	20 20	26 4	24 10
30	8 34 47	9 33 51	11♐34	20 8	9 34	23 54	16 38	9 4	20 18	26 4	24 8
31	8 38 43	10♒34 47	24♐20	21♒53	10♒49	24♏28	16♊36	9♏ 6	20♋15	26♎ 4	24♌ 7

THE SUN ENTERS THE SIGN OF AQUARIUS ON JAN 20 AT 14:12.

DAY	TIME h m s	☉ ° ' "	☽ ° '	☿ ° '	♀ ° '	♂ ° '	♃ ° '	♄ ° '	♅ ° '	♆ ° '	♇ ° '
F 1	8 42 40	11♒35 43	7♑28	23♒37	12♒ 4	25♏ 2	16♊34	9♏ 7	20♋13	26♎ 3	24♌ 5
E 2	8 46 36	12 36 37	20 59	25 20	13 20	25 36	16R32	9 9	20R10	26R 3	24R 4
B 3	8 50 33	13 37 31	4♒53	27 3	14 35	26 11	16 30	9 11	20 8	26 3	24 3
R 4	8 54 30	14 38 24	19 7	28 45	15 50	26 45	16 29	9 12	20 6	26 3	24 1
U 5	8 58 26	15 39 15	3♓36	0♓25	17 6	27 18	16 28	9 13	20 3	26 3	24 0
A 6	9 2 23	16 40 5	18 14	2 3	18 21	27 52	16 27	9 15	20 1	26 2	23 58
R 7	9 6 19	17 40 53	2♈54	3 38	19 36	28 26	16 26	9 16	19 59	26 2	23 57
Y 8	9 10 16	18 41 40	17 30	5 11	20 52	29 0	16 25	9 17	19 57	26 2	23 55
9	9 14 12	19 42 26	1♉55	6 41	22 7	29 33	16 25	9 18	19 55	26 1	23 54
10	9 18 9	20 43 10	16 7	8 6	23 22	0♐ 7	16D25	9 18	19 52	26 1	23 52
11	9 22 5	21 43 52	0♊ 3	9 27	24 37	0 40	16 25	9 19	19 50	26 0	23 51
12	9 26 2	22 44 33	13 43	10 42	25 52	1 13	16 25	9 20	19 48	26 0	23 49
13	9 29 59	23 45 12	27 8	11 51	27 8	1 46	16 25	9 20	19 46	25 59	23 48
14	9 33 55	24 45 50	10♋19	12 53	28 23	2 20	16 26	9 21	19 44	25 59	23 46
15	9 37 52	25 46 26	23 17	13 48	29 38	2 53	16 27	9 21	19 42	25 58	23 45
16	9 41 48	26 47 0	6♌ 2	14 35	0♓53	3 25	16 28	9 21	19 40	25 57	23 43
17	9 45 45	27 47 32	18 37	15 12	2 8	3 58	16 29	9R21	19 38	25 57	23 42
18	9 49 41	28 48 3	1♍ 1	15 40	3 23	4 31	16 31	9 21	19 37	25 56	23 41
19	9 53 38	29 48 32	13 16	15 59	4 38	5 4	16 32	9 21	19 35	25 55	23 39
20	9 57 34	0♓49 0	25 22	16R 7	5 54	5 36	16 34	9 21	19 33	25 55	23 38
21	10 1 31	1 49 27	7♎21	16 5	7 9	6 9	16 36	9 20	19 31	25 54	23 36
22	10 5 28	2 49 52	19 16	15 53	8 24	6 41	16 38	9 20	19 29	25 53	23 35
23	10 9 24	3 50 15	1♏ 7	15 32	9 39	7 13	16 41	9 19	19 28	25 52	23 33
24	10 13 21	4 50 37	13 0	15 1	10 54	7 45	16 43	9 19	19 26	25 51	23 32
25	10 17 17	5 50 58	24 58	14 21	12 9	8 17	16 46	9 18	19 25	25 50	23 30
26	10 21 14	6 51 17	7♐ 6	13 34	13 24	8 49	16 49	9 17	19 23	25 50	23 29
27	10 25 10	7 51 35	19 28	12 41	14 39	9 21	16 52	9 16	19 22	25 49	23 27
28	10 29 7	8♓51 52	2♑ 9	11♓44	15♓54	9♐52	16♊56	9♏15	19♋20	25♎48	23♌26

THE SUN ENTERS THE SIGN OF PISCES ON FEB 19 AT 04:32.

DAY	TIME h m s	☉ ° ' "	☽ ° '	☿ ° '	♀ ° '	♂ ° '	♃ ° '	♄ ° '	♅ ° '	♆ ° '	♇ ° '
M 1	10 33 3	9♓52 7	15♑15	10♓42	17♓ 9	10♐24	16♊59	9♏14	19♋19	25♎47	23♌25
A 2	10 37 0	10 52 20	28 47	9R40	18 24	10·55	17 3	9R13	19R17	25R46	23R23
R 3	10 40 57	11 52 32	12♒47	8 37	19 38	11 27	17 7	9 11	19 16	25 45	23 22
C 4	10 44 53	12 52 42	27 13	7 35	20 53	11 58	17 11	9 10	19 15	25 43	23 20
H 5	10 48 50	13 52 50	12♓ 1	6 36	22 8	12 29	17 15	9 8	19 14	25 42	23 19
6	10 52 46	14 52 57	27 3	5 40	23 23	12 59	17 19	9 7	19 12	25 41	23 18
7	10 56 43	15 53 1	12♈10	4 49	24 38	13 30	17 24	9 5	19 11	25 40	23 16
8	11 0 39	16 53 4	27 11	4 4	25 53	14 1	17 29	9 3	19 10	25 39	23 15
9	11 4 36	17 53 4	11♉57	3 24	27 8	14 31	17 34	9 1	19 9	25 38	23 14
10	11 8 32	18 53 3	26 23	2 51	28 22	15 1	17 39	8 59	19 8	25 36	23 12
11	11 12 29	19 52 59	10♊26	2 24	29 37	15 31	17 44	8 57	19 7	25 35	23 11
12	11 16 25	20 52 53	24 5	2 4	0♈52	16 1	17 50	8 55	19 7	25 34	23 10
13	11 20 22	21 52 45	7♋21	1 51	2 6	16 31	17 55	8 53	19 6	25 33	23 9
14	11 24 19	22 52 34	20 19	1D44	3 21	17 0	18 1	8 50	19 5	25 31	23 7
15	11 28 15	23 52 21	3♌ 0	1 43	4 36	17 30	18 7	8 48	19 4	25 30	23 6
16	11 32 12	24 52 6	15 28	1 48	5 50	17 59	18 13	8 45	19 4	25 29	23 5
17	11 36 8	25 51 49	27 47	1 59	7 5	18 28	18 20	8 42	19 3	25 27	23 4
18	11 40 5	26 51 30	9♍57	2 15	8 20	18 57	18 26	8 40	19 3	25 26	23 2
19	11 44 1	27 51 8	22 1	2 37	9 34	19 26	18 33	8 37	19 2	25 25	23 1
20	11 47 58	28 50 45	4♎ 0	3 3	10 49	19 54	18 39	8 34	19 2	25 23	23 0
21	11 51 54	29 50 19	15 55	3 34	12 3	20 22	18 46	8 31	19 1	25 22	22 59
22	11 55 51	0♈49 52	27 48	4 10	13 18	20 51	18 53	8 28	19 1	25 20	22 58
23	11 59 48	1 49 23	9♏40	4 49	14 32	21 18	19 1	8 25	19 1	25 19	22 57
24	12 3 44	2 48 52	21 34	5 33	15 46	21 46	19 8	8 22	19 0	25 17	22 56
25	12 7 41	3 48 19	3♐32	6 19	17 1	22 14	19 15	8 18	19 0	25 16	22 55
26	12 11 37	4 47 44	15 38	7 10	18 15	22 41	19 23	8 15	19 0	25 14	22 54
27	12 15 34	5 47 8	27 58	8 3	19 29	23 8	19 31	8 12	19D 0	25 13	22 53
28	12 19 30	6 46 30	10♑34	9 0	20 44	23 35	19 39	8 8	19 0	25 11	22 52
29	12 23 27	7 45 50	23 33	9 59	21 58	24 1	19 47	8 5	19 0	25 10	22 51
30	12 27 23	8 45 8	6♒59	11 1	23 12	24 28	19 55	8 1	19 0	25 8	22 50
31	12 31 20	9♈44 25	20♒53	12♓ 6	24♈27	24♐54	20♊ 3	7♏57	19♋ 0	25♎ 7	22♌49

THE SUN ENTERS THE SIGN OF ARIES ON MAR 21 AT 03:53.

♈ ARIES ♉ TAURUS ♊ GEMINI ♋ CANCER ♌ LEO ♍ VIRGO ♎ LIBRA

1954

SIDEREAL SUN. MOON. MERCURY. VENUS. MARS. JUPITER. SATURN. URANUS. NEPTUNE. PLUTO.

DAY	TIME h m s	☉ ° ' "	☽ ° '	☿ ° '	♀ ° '	♂ ° '	♃ ° '	♄ ° '	♅ ° '	♆ ° '	♇ ° '
A 1	12 35 17	10♈43 40	5♓17	13♓13	25♈41	25♐20	20♊12	7♏53	19♋ 0	25♎ 5	22♌48
P 2	12 39 13	11 42 52	20 7	14 22	26 55	25 45	20 20	7R50	19 1	25R 3	22R47
R 3	12 43 10	12 42 3	5♈17	15 33	28 9	26 10	20 29	7 46	19 1	25 2	22 46
I 4	12 47 6	13 41 12	20 37	16 47	29 23	26 35	20 38	7 42	19 1	25 0	22 45
L 5	12 51 3	14 40 19	5♉54	18 3	0♉37	27 0	20 47	7 38	19 2	24 59	22 44
6	12 54 59	15 39 24	20 58	19 21	1 51	27 25	20 56	7 34	19 2	24 57	22 44
7	12 58 56	16 38 26	5♊40	20 40	3 5	27 49	21 5	7 30	19 3	24 55	22 43
8	13 2 52	17 37 27	19 55	22 2	4 19	28 12	21 14	7 26	19 3	24 54	22 42
9	13 6 49	18 36 25	3♋42	23 25	5 33	28 36	21 23	7 21	19 4	24 52	22 41
10	13 10 46	19 35 20	17 1	24 50	6 47	28 59	21 33	7 17	19 5	24 51	22 41
11	13 14 42	20 34 14	29 57	26 17	8 1	29 22	21 43	7 13	19 5	24 49	22 40
12	13 18 39	21 33 5	12♌33	27 46	9 15	29 45	21 52	7 9	19 6	24 47	22 39
13	13 22 35	22 31 54	24 53	29 16	10 29	0♑ 7	22 2	7 4	19 7	24 46	22 39
14	13 26 32	23 30 40	7♍ 3	0♈48	11 43	0 29	22 12	7 0	19 8	24 44	22 38
15	13 30 28	24 29 24	19 4	2 21	12 57	0 50	22 22	6 56	19 9	24 42	22 38
16	13 34 25	25 28 7	1♎ 1	3 57	14 10	1 12	22 32	6 51	19 10	24 41	22 37
17	13 38 21	26 26 47	12 54	5 33	15 24	1 32	22 43	6 47	19 11	24 39	22 37
18	13 42 18	27 25 25	24 47	7 12	16 38	1 53	22 53	6 42	19 12	24 37	22 36
19	13 46 14	28 24 1	6♏40	8 52	17 51	2 13	23 3	6 38	19 13	24 36	22 36
20	13 50 11	29 22 35	18 34	10 34	19 5	2 33	23 14	6 33	19 14	24 34	22 35
21	13 54 8	0♉21 8	0♐32	12 17	20 18	2 52	23 25	6 29	19 16	24 32	22 35
22	13 58 4	1 19 39	12 35	14 2	21 32	3 11	23 35	6 24	19 17	24 31	22 34
23	14 2 1	2 18 8	24 46	15 49	22 46	3 29	23 46	6 20	19 18	24 29	22 34
24	14 5 57	3 16 36	7♑ 9	17 37	23 59	3 47	23 57	6 15	19 20	24 28	22 34
25	14 9 54	4 15 1	19 46	19 27	25 12	4 5	24 8	6 11	19 21	24 26	22 33
26	14 13 50	5 13 26	2♒42	21 19	26 26	4 22	24 19	6 6	19 23	24 24	22 33
27	14 17 47	6 11 48	16 2	23 13	27 39	4 39	24 30	6 2	19 24	24 23	22 33
28	14 21 44	7 10 9	29 47	25 8	28 53	4 55	24 41	5 57	19 26	24 21	22 33
29	14 25 40	8 8 29	14♓ 1	27 5	0♊ 6	5 10	24 53	5 52	19 28	24 20	22 32
30	14 29 37	9♉ 6 47	28♓40	29♈ 3	1♊19	5♑26	25♊ 4	5♏48	19♋29	24♎18	22♌32

THE SUN ENTERS THE SIGN OF TAURUS ON APR 20 AT 15:20.

DAY	TIME h m s	☉ ° ' "	☽ ° '	☿ ° '	♀ ° '	♂ ° '	♃ ° '	♄ ° '	♅ ° '	♆ ° '	♇ ° '
M 1	14 33 33	10♉ 5 3	13♈41	1♉ 3	2♊32	5♑40	25♊16	5♏43	19♋31	24♎16	22♌32
A 2	14 37 30	11 3 18	28 54	3 5	3 46	5 54	25 27	5R39	19 33	24R15	22R32
Y 3	14 41 26	12 1 32	14♉11	5 8	4 59	6 8	25 39	5 34	19 35	24 13	22 32
4	14 45 23	12 59 43	29 18	7 12	6 12	6 21	25 51	5 30	19 36	24 12	22D32
5	14 49 19	13 57 53	14♊ 7	9 18	7 25	6 34	26 2	5 25	19 38	24 10	22 32
6	14 53 16	14 56 1	28 31	11 26	8 38	6 45	26 14	5 21	19 40	24 9	22 32
7	14 57 13	15 54 7	12♋27	13 34	9 51	6 57	26 26	5 16	19 42	24 7	22 32
8	15 1 9	16 52 11	25 54	15 43	11 4	7 8	26 38	5 12	19 44	24 6	22 32
9	15 5 6	17 50 14	8♌55	17 53	12 17	7 18	26 50	5 8	19 47	24 4	22 32
10	15 9 2	18 48 14	21 33	20 3	13 30	7 27	27 2	5 3	19 49	24 3	22 32
11	15 12 59	19 46 12	3♍53	22 14	14 43	7 36	27 14	4 59	19 51	24 1	22 33
12	15 16 55	20 44 9	16 1	24 25	15 56	7 45	27 27	4 55	19 53	24 0	22 33
13	15 20 52	21 42 3	27 59	26 35	17 9	7 52	27 39	4 50	19 55	23 58	22 33
14	15 24 48	22 39 56	9♎52	28 45	18 22	7 59	27 51	4 46	19 58	23 57	22 33
15	15 28 45	23 37 48	21 44	0♊54	19 34	8 6	28 4	4 42	20 0	23 56	22 33
16	15 32 41	24 35 38	3♏37	3 2	20 47	8 11	28 16	4 38	20 2	23 54	22 34
17	15 36 38	25 33 26	15 32	5 8	22 0	8 16	28 29	4 34	20 5	23 53	22 34
18	15 40 35	26 31 13	27 32	7 13	23 12	8 21	28 41	4 29	20 7	23 52	22 34
19	15 44 31	27 28 58	9♐38	9 15	24 25	8 24	28 54	4 25	20 10	23 50	22 35
20	15 48 28	28 26 42	21 52	11 16	25 37	8 27	29 6	4 21	20 12	23 49	22 35
21	15 52 24	29 24 25	4♑14	13 15	26 50	8 30	29 19	4 18	20 15	23 48	22 36
22	15 56 21	0♊22 7	16 47	15 11	28 2	8 31	29 32	4 14	20 18	23 47	22 36
23	16 0 17	1 19 48	29 34	17 4	29 15	8R32	29 45	4 10	20 20	23 45	22 37
24	16 4 14	2 17 27	12♒36	18 55	0♋27	8 32	29 57	4 6	20 23	23 44	22 37
25	16 8 11	3 15 6	25 57	20 43	1 39	8 31	0♋10	4 2	20 26	23 43	22 38
26	16 12 7	4 12 43	9♓39	22 28	2 51	8 30	0 23	3 59	20 28	23 42	22 38
27	16 16 4	5 10 20	23 43	24 10	4 4	8 27	0 36	3 55	20 31	23 41	22 39
28	16 20 0	6 7 56	8♈ 8	25 49	5 16	8 24	0 49	3 52	20 34	23 39	22 40
29	16 23 57	7 5 31	22 50	27 25	6 28	8 21	1 2	3 48	20 37	23 38	22 40
30	16 27 53	8 3 5	7♉45	28 59	7 40	8 16	1 15	3 45	20 40	23 37	22 41
31	16 31 50	9♊ 0 38	22♉44	0♋29	8♋52	8♑11	1♋29	3♏42	20♋43	23♎36	22♌42

THE SUN ENTERS THE SIGN OF GEMINI ON MAY 21 AT 14:48.

DAY	TIME h m s	☉ ° ' "	☽ ° '	☿ ° '	♀ ° '	♂ ° '	♃ ° '	♄ ° '	♅ ° '	♆ ° '	♇ ° '
J 1	16 35 46	9♊58 10	7♊38	1♋56	10♋ 4	8♑ 5	1♋42	3♏38	20♋46	23♎35	22♌42
U 2	16 39 43	10 55 41	22 19	3 20	11 16	7R58	1 55	3R35	20 49	23R34	22 43
N 3	16 43 40	11 53 12	6♋40	4 41	12 28	7 50	2 8	3 32	20 52	23 33	22 44
E 4	16 47 36	12 50 41	20 37	5 58	13 40	7 42	2 21	3 29	20 55	23 32	22 45
5	16 51 33	13 48 9	4♌ 8	7 13	14 52	7 33	2 35	3 26	20 58	23 31	22 46
6	16 55 29	14 45 35	17 14	8 24	16 4	7 23	2 48	3 23	21 1	23 30	22 47
7	16 59 26	15 43 1	29 57	9 31	17 15	7 13	3 1	3 21	21 4	23 30	22 48
8	17 3 22	16 40 25	12♍20	10 36	18 27	7 2	3 15	3 18	21 7	23 29	22 48
9	17 7 19	17 37 48	24 30	11 36	19 39	6 50	3 28	3 15	21 10	23 28	22 49
10	17 11 15	18 35 10	6♎29	12 33	20 50	6 38	3 41	3 13	21 14	23 27	22 50
11	17 15 12	19 32 31	18 23	13 27	22 2	6 24	3 55	3 10	21 17	23 26	22 51
12	17 19 9	20 29 52	0♏15	14 17	23 13	6 11	4 8	3 8	21 20	23 26	22 52
13	17 23 5	21 27 11	12 9	15 3	24 24	5 57	4 22	3 6	21 23	23 25	22 53
14	17 27 2	22 24 29	24 9	15 44	25 36	5 42	4 35	3 3	21 27	23 24	22 55
15	17 30 58	23 21 47	6♐16	16 22	26 47	5 27	4 49	3 1	21 30	23 24	22 56
16	17 34 55	24 19 4	18 32	16 56	27 58	5 11	5 2	2 59	21 33	23 23	22 57
17	17 38 51	25 16 21	1♑ 0	17 26	29 9	4 55	5 16	2 57	21 37	23 22	22 58
18	17 42 48	26 13 36	13 39	17 51	0♌20	4 38	5 29	2 56	21 40	23 22	22 59
19	17 46 44	27 10 52	26 31	18 12	1 32	4 21	5 43	2 54	21 43	23 21	23 0
20	17 50 41	28 8 7	9♒36	18 28	2 42	4 4	5 56	2 52	21 47	23 21	23 1
21	17 54 38	29 5 22	22 54	18 40	3 53	3 46	6 10	2 51	21 50	23 20	23 3
22	17 58 34	0♋ 2 36	6♓27	18 47	5 4	3 28	6 24	2 49	21 54	23 20	23 4
23	18 2 31	0 59 50	20 15	18R50	6 15	3 10	6 37	2 48	21 57	23 20	23 5
24	18 6 27	1 57 5	4♈16	18 48	7 26	2 52	6 51	2 46	22 1	23 19	23 7
25	18 10 24	2 54 19	18 30	18 42	8 36	2 33	7 4	2 45	22 4	23 19	23 8
26	18 14 20	3 51 33	2♉55	18 31	9 47	2 15	7 18	2 44	22 8	23 19	23 9
27	18 18 17	4 48 47	17 27	18 16	10 57	1 56	7 32	2 43	22 11	23 18	23 11
28	18 22 13	5 46 2	2♊ 0	17 57	12 8	1 37	7 45	2 42	22 15	23 18	23 12
29	18 26 10	6 43 16	16 30	17 34	13 18	1 19	7 59	2 41	22 18	23 18	23 13
30	18 30 7	7♋40 30	0♋50	17♋ 8	14♌28	1♑ 0	8♋13	2♏41	22♋22	23♎18	23♌15

THE SUN ENTERS THE SIGN OF CANCER ON JUN 21 AT 22:55.

♏ SCORPIO ♐ SAGITTARIUS ♑ CAPRICORN ♒ AQUARIUS ♓ PISCES

SIDEREAL · SUN. · MOON. · MERCURY. · VENUS. · MARS. · JUPITER. · SATURN. · URANUS. · NEPTUNE. · PLUTO.

DAY	TIME	☉	☽	☿	♀	♂	♃	♄	♅	♆	♇
	h m s	° ' "	° '	° '	° '	° '	° '	° '	° '	° '	° '
J 1	18 34 3	8♋37 44	14♋55	16♋39	15♌39	0♑42	8♋26	2♏40	22♋25	23♎17	23♌16
U 2	18 38 0	9 34 58	28 42	16R 7	16 49	0R23	8 40	2R40	22 29	23R17	23 18
L 3	18 41 56	10 32 12	12♌ 9	15 32	17 59	0 5	8 53	2 39	22 33	23 17	23 19
Y 4	18 45 53	11 29 26	25 13	14 57	19 9	29♐48	9 7	2 39	22 36	23 17	23 21
5	18 49 49	12 26 39	7♍57	14 20	20 19	29 30	9 21	2 39	22 40	23D17	23 22
6	18 53 46	13 23 52	20 23	13 43	21 29	29 13	9 34	2D39	22 43	23 17	23 24
7	18 57 43	14 21 5	2♎35	13 6	22 38	28 57	9 48	2 39	22 47	23 17	23 25
8	19 1 39	15 18 17	14 35	12 30	23 48	28 41	10 1	2 39	22 51	23 17	23 27
9	19 5 36	16 15 30	26 30	11 55	24 58	28 25	10 15	2 39	22 54	23 17	23 28
10	19 9 32	17 12 42	8♏23	11 23	26 7	28 10	10 29	2 39	22 58	23 17	23 30
11	19 13 29	18 9 54	20 19	10 53	27 16	27 55	10 42	2 40	23 2	23 18	23 32
12	19 17 25	19 7 7	2♐22	10 26	28 26	27 41	10 56	2 40	23 5	23 18	23 33
13	19 21 22	20 4 19	14 35	10 4	29 35	27 28	11 9	2 41	23 9	23 18	23 35
14	19 25 18	21 1 31	27 1	9 45	0♍44	27 15	11 23	2 41	23 13	23 18	23 36
15	19 29 15	21 58 44	9♑43	9 31	1 53	27 3	11 36	2 42	23 16	23 19	23 38
16	19 33 12	22 55 57	22 41	9 21	3 2	26 52	11 50	2 43	23 20	23 19	23 40
17	19 37 8	23 53 11	5♒55	9D17	4 11	26 42	12 3	2 44	23 24	23 19	23 41
18	19 41 5	24 50 24	19 25	9 18	5 19	26 32	12 17	2 45	23 27	23 20	23 43
19	19 45 1	25 47 38	3♓ 8	9 25	6 28	26 23	12 30	2 46	23 31	23 20	23 45
20	19 48 58	26 44 53	17 3	9 37	7 36	26 14	12 43	2 47	23 35	23 21	23 47
21	19 52 54	27 42 9	1♈ 6	9 55	8 45	26 7	12 57	2 49	23 38	23 21	23 48
22	19 56 51	28 39 25	15 16	10 19	9 53	26 0	13 10	2 50	23 42	23 22	23 50
23	20 0 47	29 36 42	29 29	10 48	11 1	25 54	13 23	2 52	23 45	23 22	23 52
24	20 4 44	0♌34 0	13♉43	11 24	12 9	25 49	13 37	2 53	23 49	23 23	23 54
25	20 8 41	1 31 20	27 56	12 5	13 17	25 44	13 50	2 55	23 53	23 23	23 55
26	20 12 37	2 28 40	12♊ 4	12 51	14 24	25 41	14 3	2 57	23 56	23 24	23 57
27	20 16 34	3 26 1	26 7	13 43	15 32	25 38	14 16	2 59	24 0	23 25	23 59
28	20 20 30	4 23 23	10♋ 0	14 41	16 40	25 37	14 30	3 1	24 4	23 25	24 1
29	20 24 27	5 20 45	23 42	15 44	17 47	25D36	14 43	3 3	24 7	23 26	24 3
30	20 28 23	6 18 9	7♌10	16 53	18 54	25 35	14 56	3 5	24 11	23 27	24 5
31	20 32 20	7♌15 33	20♌22	18♋ 7	20♍ 1	25♐36	15♋ 9	3♏ 7	24♋14	23♎28	24♌ 6

THE SUN ENTERS THE SIGN OF LEO ON JUL 23 AT 09:46.

DAY	TIME	☉	☽	☿	♀	♂	♃	♄	♅	♆	♇
	h m s	° ' "	° '	° '	° '	° '	° '	° '	° '	° '	° '
A 1	20 36 16	8♌12 58	3♍18	19♋25	21♍ 8	25♐38	15♋22	3♏10	24♋18	23♎29	24♌ 8
U 2	20 40 13	9 10 24	15 57	20 49	22 15	25 40	15 35	3 12	24 22	23 29	24 10
G 3	20 44 10	10 7 50	28 21	22 18	23 22	25 43	15 48	3 15	24 25	23 30	24 12
U 4	20 48 6	11 5 17	10♎31	23 51	24 28	25 48	16 1	3 18	24 29	23 31	24 14
S 5	20 52 3	12 2 45	22 32	25 28	25 35	25 52	16 14	3 20	24 32	23 32	24 16
T 6	20 55 59	13 0 14	4♏26	27 9	26 41	25 58	16 27	3 23	24 36	23 33	24 18
7	20 59 56	13 57 43	16 18	28 54	27 47	26 5	16 39	3 26	24 39	23 34	24 20
8	21 3 52	14 55 13	28 14	0♌42	28 53	26 12	16 52	3 29	24 43	23 35	24 21
9	21 7 49	15 52 44	10♐17	2 33	29 58	26 20	17 5	3 32	24 46	23 36	24 23
10	21 11 45	16 50 16	22 33	4 27	1♎ 4	26 29	17 17	3 35	24 50	23 37	24 25
11	21 15 42	17 47 49	5♑ 5	6 24	2 9	26 39	17 30	3 39	24 53	23 38	24 27
12	21 19 39	18 45 23	17 57	8 22	3 14	26 50	17 43	3 42	24 57	23 40	24 29
13	21 23 35	19 42 57	1♒10	10 21	4 19	27 1	17 55	3 46	25 0	23 41	24 31
14	21 27 32	20 40 33	14 45	12 22	5 24	27 13	18 8	3 49	25 4	23 42	24 33
15	21 31 28	21 38 10	28 39	14 23	6 29	27 25	18 20	3 53	25 7	23 43	24 35
16	21 35 25	22 35 48	12♓50	16 25	7 33	27 39	18 32	3 56	25 10	23 45	24 37
17	21 39 21	23 33 28	27 13	18 27	8 37	27 53	18 45	4 0	25 14	23 46	24 39
18	21 43 18	24 31 8	11♈40	20 29	9 41	28 7	18 57	4 4	25 17	23 47	24 41
19	21 47 14	25 28 51	26 8	22 31	10 44	28 23	19 9	4 8	25 20	23 48	24 42
20	21 51 11	26 26 35	10♉30	24 32	11 48	28 39	19 21	4 12	25 23	23 50	24 44
21	21 55 8	27 24 21	24 44	26 33	12 51	28 56	19 33	4 16	25 27	23 51	24 46
22	21 59 4	28 22 9	8♊48	28 32	13 54	29 13	19 45	4 20	25 30	23 53	24 48
23	22 3 1	29 19 58	22 40	0♍31	14 57	29 31	19 57	4 25	25 33	23 54	24 50
24	22 6 57	0♍17 49	6♋20	2 29	15 59	29 49	20 9	4 29	25 36	23 56	24 52
25	22 10 54	1 15 42	19 49	4 25	17 1	0♑ 9	20 21	4 33	25 40	23 57	24 54
26	22 14 50	2 13 37	3♌ 6	6 21	18 3	0 28	20 32	4 38	25 43	23 59	24 56
27	22 18 47	3 11 33	16 11	8 15	19 5	0 49	20 44	4 42	25 46	24 0	24 58
28	22 22 43	4 9 31	29 5	10 8	20 6	1 10	20 55	4 47	25 49	24 2	25 0
29	22 26 40	5 7 30	11♍46	11 59	21 7	1 31	21 7	4 52	25 52	24 3	25 2
30	22 30 37	6 5 30	24 14	13 50	22 8	1 53	21 18	4 56	25 55	24 5	25 4
31	22 34 33	7♍ 3 33	6♎31	15♍39	23♎ 8	2♑16	21♋30	5♏ 1	25♋58	24♎ 7	25♌ 5

THE SUN ENTERS THE SIGN OF VIRGO ON AUG 23 AT 16:37.

DAY	TIME	☉	☽	☿	♀	♂	♃	♄	♅	♆	♇
	h m s	° ' "	° '	° '	° '	° '	° '	° '	° '	° '	° '
S 1	22 38 30	8♍ 1 36	18♎38	17♍27	24♎ 8	2♑39	21♋41	5♏ 6	26♋ 1	24♎ 8	25♌ 7
E 2	22 42 26	8 59 42	0♏35	19 13	25 8	3 2	21 52	5 11	26 4	24 10	25 9
P 3	22 46 23	9 57 48	12 27	20 58	26 7	3 27	22 3	5 16	26 7	24 12	25 11
T 4	22 50 19	10 55 57	24 18	22 43	27 7	3 51	22 14	5 21	26 9	24 13	25 13
E 5	22 54 16	11 54 6	6♐11	24 25	28 5	4 16	22 25	5 26	26 12	24 15	25 15
M 6	22 58 12	12 52 17	18 12	26 7	29 3	4 42	22 36	5 32	26 15	24 17	25 17
B 7	23 2 9	13 50 30	0♑26	27 48	0♏ 1	5 8	22 47	5 37	26 18	24 19	25 18
E 8	23 6 6	14 48 44	12 57	29 27	0 59	5 34	22 57	5 42	26 21	24 20	25 20
R 9	23 10 2	15 47 0	25 52	1♎ 5	1 56	6 1	23 8	5 48	26 23	24 22	25 22
10	23 13 59	16 45 17	9♒12	2 42	2 52	6 29	23 18	5 53	26 26	24 24	25 24
11	23 17 55	17 43 36	22 59	4 18	3 48	6 56	23 29	5 59	26 29	24 26	25 26
12	23 21 52	18 41 56	7♓12	5 52	4 44	7 25	23 39	6 4	26 31	24 28	25 28
13	23 25 48	19 40 18	21 46	7 26	5 39	7 53	23 49	6 10	26 34	24 30	25 29
14	23 29 45	20 38 42	6♈35	8 58	6 33	8 22	23 59	6 16	26 36	24 32	25 31
15	23 33 41	21 37 8	21 29	10 30	7 27	8 51	24 9	6 21	26 39	24 34	25 33
16	23 37 38	22 35 36	6♉20	12 0	8 21	9 21	24 19	6 27	26 41	24 36	25 35
17	23 41 34	23 34 6	21 1	13 29	9 14	9 51	24 29	6 33	26 43	24 38	25 36
18	23 45 31	24 32 39	5♊25	14 57	10 6	10 22	24 39	6 39	26 46	24 40	25 38
19	23 49 28	25 31 13	19 31	16 24	10 58	10 52	24 48	6 45	26 48	24 42	25 40
20	23 53 24	26 29 50	3♋17	17 50	11 49	11 23	24 58	6 51	26 50	24 44	25 42
21	23 57 21	27 28 29	16 46	19 15	12 39	11 55	25 7	6 57	26 53	24 46	25 43
22	0 1 17	28 27 11	29 58	20 38	13 29	12 27	25 16	7 3	26 55	24 48	25 45
23	0 5 14	29 25 54	12♌56	22 1	14 18	12 59	25 25	7 9	26 57	24 50	25 47
24	0 9 10	0♎24 40	25 41	23 22	15 6	13 31	25 34	7 16	26 59	24 52	25 48
25	0 13 7	1 23 27	8♍16	24 42	15 53	14 4	25 43	7 22	27 1	24 54	25 50
26	0 17 3	2 22 17	20 41	26 0	16 40	14 37	25 52	7 28	27 3	24 56	25 52
27	0 21 0	3 21 9	2♎57	27 17	17 26	15 10	26 1	7 34	27 5	24 58	25 53
28	0 24 57	4 20 3	15 5	28 33	18 11	15 43	26 9	7 41	27 7	25 0	25 55
29	0 28 53	5 18 58	27 5	29 47	18 55	16 17	26 17	7 47	27 9	25 2	25 56
30	0 32 50	6♎17 56	8♏59	1♏ 0	19♏38	16♑51	26♋26	7♏54	27♋11	25♎ 4	25♌58

THE SUN ENTERS THE SIGN OF LIBRA ON SEP 23 AT 13:56.

♈ ARIES ♉ TAURUS ♊ GEMINI ♋ CANCER ♌ LEO ♍ VIRGO ♎ LIBRA

1954

SIDEREAL | SUN. | MOON. | MERCURY. | VENUS. | MARS. | JUPITER. | SATURN. | URANUS. | NEPTUNE. | PLUTO.

DAY	TIME	☉	☽	☿	♀	♂	♃	♄	♅	♆	♇
	h m s	° ' "	° '	° '	° '	° '	° '	° '	° '	° '	° '
O 1	0 36 46	7♎16 56	20♏48	2♏11	20♏20	17♑26	26♋34	8♏ 0	27♋12	25♎ 7	25♌59
C 2	0 40 43	8 15 57	2♐37	3 20	21 1	18 1	26 42	8 7	27 14	25 9	26 1
T 3	0 44 39	9 15 0	14 28	4 27	21 41	18 35	26 50	8 13	27 16	25 11	26 2
O 4	0 48 36	10 14 6	26 26	5 32	22 20	19 11	26 57	8 20	27 17	25 13	26 4
B 5	0 52 32	11 13 13	8♑36	6 35	22 57	19 46	27 5	8 27	27 19	25 15	26 5
E 6	0 56 29	12 12 21	21 4	7 36	23 34	20 22	27 12	8 33	27 21	25 17	26 7
R 7	1 0 26	13 11 32	3♒55	8 33	24 9	20 58	27 20	8 40	27 22	25 20	26 8
8	1 4 22	14 10 44	17 13	9 28	24 43	21 34	27 27	8 47	27 23	25 22	26 10
9	1 8 19	15 9 58	1♓ 0	10 20	25 16	22 10	27 34	8 54	27 25	25 24	26 11
10	1 12 15	16 9 13	15 17	11 8	25 47	22 47	27 41	9 0	27 26	25 26	26 12
11	1 16 12	17 8 31	0♈ 1	11 53	26 16	23 23	27 47	9 7	27 27	25 28	26 14
12	1 20 8	18 7 50	15 4	12 33	26 44	24 0	27 54	9 14	27 29	25 31	26 15
13	1 24 5	19 7 12	0♉18	13 9	27 11	24 37	28 0	9 21	27 30	25 33	26 16
14	1 28 1	20 6 36	15 30	13 40	27 36	25 15	28 7	9 28	27 31	25 35	26 18
15	1 31 58	21 6 2	0♊31	14 6	27 59	25 52	28 13	9 35	27 32	25 37	26 19
16	1 35 55	22 5 30	15 13	14 26	28 20	26 30	28 19	9 42	27 33	25 40	26 20
17	1 39 51	23 5 0	29 31	14 39	28 40	27 8	28 25	9 49	27 34	25 42	26 21
18	1 43 48	24 4 33	13♋23	14R45	28 57	27 46	28 30	9 56	27 35	25 44	26 22
19	1 47 44	25 4 8	26 52	14 44	29 13	28 24	28 36	10 3	27 36	25 46	26 24
20	1 51 41	26 3 46	9♌58	14 35	29 27	29 2	28 41	10 10	27 37	25 49	26 25
21	1 55 37	27 3 25	22 47	14 17	29 38	29 41	28 46	10 17	27 37	25 51	26 26
22	1 59 34	28 3 7	5♍20	13 51	29 48	0♒19	28 51	10 24	27 38	25 53	26 27
23	2 3 30	29 2 51	17 42	13 16	29 55	0 58	28 56	10 31	27 39	25 55	26 28
24	2 7 27	0♏ 2 37	29 54	12 32	0♐ 0	1 37	29 0	10 38	27 39	25 58	26 29
25	2 11 23	1 2 26	11♎58	11 39	0R 3	2 16	29 5	10 46	27 40	26 0	26 30
26	2 15 20	2 2 16	23 57	10 39	0 4	2 55	29 9	10 53	27 40	26 2	26 31
27	2 19 17	3 2 8	5♏51	9 32	0 2	3 35	29 13	11 0	27 41	26 4	26 32
28	2 23 13	4 2 3	17 42	8 19	29♏57	4 14	29 17	11 7	27 41	26 6	26 33
29	2 27 10	5 1 59	29 31	7 3	29 51	4 54	29 21	11 14	27 42	26 9	26 34
30	2 31 6	6 1 57	11♐20	5 46	29 41	5 34	29 25	11 21	27 42	26 11	26 35
31	2 35 3	7♏ 1 57	23♐13	4♏30	29♏30	6♒14	29♋28	11♏29	27♋42	26♎13	26♌36

THE SUN ENTERS THE SIGN OF SCORPIO ON OCT 23 AT 22:57.

DAY	TIME	☉	☽	☿	♀	♂	♃	♄	♅	♆	♇
	h m s	° ' "	° '	° '	° '	° '	° '	° '	° '	° '	° '
N 1	2 38 59	8♏ 1 58	5♑12	3♏18	29♏16	6♒54	29♋31	11♏36	27♋42	26♎15	26♌36
O 2	2 42 56	9 2 1	17 23	2R11	28R59	7 34	29 34	11 43	27 42	26 18	26 37
V 3	2 46 52	10 2 6	29 48	1 12	28 41	8 15	29 37	11 50	27R42	26 20	26 38
E 4	2 50 49	11 2 13	12♒34	0 22	28 20	8 55	29 40	11 57	27 42	26 22	26 39
M 5	2 54 46	12 2 20	25 45	29♎43	27 56	9 36	29 42	12 5	27 42	26 24	26 39
B 6	2 58 42	13 2 30	9♓23	29 15	27 31	10 16	29 44	12 12	27 42	26 26	26 40
E 7	3 2 39	14 2 41	23 32	28D59	27 4	10 57	29 46	12 19	27 42	26 28	26 41
R 8	3 6 35	15 2 53	8♈ 9	28 55	26 35	11 38	29 48	12 26	27 42	26 31	26 41
9	3 10 32	16 3 7	23 9	29 1	26 4	12 19	29 50	12 33	27 42	26 33	26 42
10	3 14 28	17 3 22	8♉24	29 18	25 32	13 0	29 52	12 41	27 41	26 35	26 43
11	3 18 25	18 3 40	23 44	29 45	24 58	13 41	29 53	12 48	27 41	26 37	26 43
12	3 22 21	19 3 59	8♊57	0♏21	24 23	14 22	29 54	12 55	27 40	26 39	26 44
13	3 26 18	20 4 20	23 53	1 5	23 48	15 3	29 55	13 2	27 40	26 41	26 44
14	3 30 15	21 4 43	8♋26	1 57	23 12	15 45	29 56	13 9	27 39	26 43	26 45
15	3 34 11	22 5 7	22 32	2 54	22 35	16 26	29 56	13 17	27 39	26 45	26 45
16	3 38 8	23 5 34	6♌10	3 57	21 59	17 8	29 56	13 24	27 38	26 47	26 46
17	3 42 4	24 6 2	19 21	5 5	21 22	17 49	29R57	13 31	27 37	26 49	26 46
18	3 46 1	25 6 32	2♍11	6 16	20 46	18 31	29 57	13 38	27 37	26 51	26 46
19	3 49 57	26 7 4	14 41	7 32	20 11	19 13	29 56	13 45	27 36	26 54	26 47
20	3 53 54	27 7 38	26 57	8 50	19 37	19 55	29 56	13 52	27 35	26 56	26 47
21	3 57 50	28 8 13	9♎ 1	10 11	19 3	20 36	29 55	13 59	27 34	26 58	26 47
22	4 1 47	29 8 51	20 59	11 34	18 31	21 18	29 54	14 6	27 33	26 59	26 47
23	4 5 44	0♐ 9 29	2♏51	12 59	18 1	22 0	29 53	14 13	27 32	27 1	26 48
24	4 9 40	1 10 10	14 42	14 25	17 32	22 42	29 52	14 20	27 31	27 3	26 48
25	4 13 37	2 10 52	26 32	15 53	17 6	23 25	29 50	14 27	27 30	27 5	26 48
26	4 17 33	3 11 35	8♐23	17 22	16 41	24 7	29 49	14 34	27 29	27 7	26 48
27	4 21 30	4 12 20	20 18	18 51	16 18	24 49	29 47	14 41	27 28	27 9	26 48
28	4 25 26	5 13 6	2♑18	20 22	15 57	25 31	29 45	14 48	27 26	27 11	26R48
29	4 29 23	6 13 53	14 26	21 53	15 39	26 14	29 42	14 55	27 25	27 13	26 48
30	4 33 20	7♐14 41	26♑44	23♏24	15♏23	26♒56	29♋40	15♏ 2	27♋24	27♎15	26♌48

THE SUN ENTERS THE SIGN OF SAGITTARIUS ON NOV 22 AT 20:15.

DAY	TIME	☉	☽	☿	♀	♂	♃	♄	♅	♆	♇
	h m s	° ' "	° '	° '	° '	° '	° '	° '	° '	° '	° '
D 1	4 37 16	8♐15 30	9♒14	24♏56	15♏10	27♒39	29♋37	15♏ 9	27♋22	27♎16	26♌48
E 2	4 41 13	9 16 20	22 2	26 28	14R59	28 21	29R35	15 16	27R21	27 18	26R48
C 3	4 45 9	10 17 11	5♓10	28 0	14 51	29 4	29 31	15 22	27 19	27 20	26 48
E 4	4 49 6	11 18 2	18 40	29 33	14 45	29 46	29 28	15 29	27 18	27 22	26 48
M 5	4 53 2	12 18 55	2♈35	1♐ 5	14D41	0♓29	29 25	15 36	27 16	27 23	26 47
B 6	4 56 59	13 19 48	16 55	2 38	14 40	1 12	29 21	15 43	27 15	27 25	26 47
E 7	5 0 55	14 20 42	1♉37	4 11	14 41	1 54	29 17	15 49	27 13	27 27	26 47
R 8	5 4 52	15 21 37	16 36	5 44	14 45	2 37	29 13	15 56	27 11	27 29	26 47
9	5 8 49	16 22 33	1♊43	7 17	14 51	3 20	29 9	16 2	27 9	27 30	26 47
10	5 12 45	17 23 29	16 50	8 51	15 0	4 3	29 5	16 9	27 8	27 32	26 46
11	5 16 42	18 24 27	1♋47	10 24	15 10	4 45	29 0	16 15	27 6	27 33	26 46
12	5 20 38	19 25 25	16 26	11 57	15 23	5 28	28 56	16 22	27 4	27 35	26 46
13	5 24 35	20 26 25	0♌42	13 31	15 38	6 11	28 51	16 28	27 2	27 36	26 45
14	5 28 31	21 27 25	14 30	15 4	15 56	6 54	28 46	16 35	27 0	27 38	26 45
15	5 32 28	22 28 26	27 52	16 38	16 15	7 37	28 41	16 41	26 58	27 39	26 44
16	5 36 24	23 29 29	10♍49	18 12	16 36	8 20	28 35	16 47	26 56	27 41	26 44
17	5 40 21	24 30 32	23 23	19 46	16 59	9 3	28 30	16 53	26 54	27 42	26 43
18	5 44 18	25 31 36	5♎40	21 20	17 24	9 46	28 24	17 0	26 52	27 44	26 43
19	5 48 14	26 32 41	17 44	22 54	17 50	10 29	28 18	17 6	26 50	27 45	26 42
20	5 52 11	27 33 47	29 38	24 28	18 19	11 12	28 13	17 12	26 48	27 46	26 42
21	5 56 7	28 34 54	11♏28	26 2	18 49	11 55	28 6	17 18	26 46	27 48	26 41
22	6 0 4	29 36 1	23 18	27 37	19 20	12 38	28 0	17 24	26 43	27 49	26 40
23	6 4 0	0♑37 9	5♐ 9	29 12	19 53	13 21	27 54	17 30	26 41	27 50	26 40
24	6 7 57	1 38 18	17 5	0♑47	20 28	14 4	27 47	17 36	26 39	27 52	26 39
25	6 11 53	2 39 27	29 9	2 22	21 4	14 47	27 41	17 41	26 37	27 53	26 38
26	6 15 50	3 40 37	11♑21	3 58	21 41	15 30	27 34	17 47	26 34	27 54	26 37
27	6 19 47	4 41 46	23 44	5 33	22 20	16 13	27 27	17 53	26 32	27 55	26 37
28	6 23 43	5 42 56	6♒18	7 9	23 0	16 56	27 20	17 59	26 29	27 56	26 36
29	6 27 40	6 44 7	19 5	8 46	23 41	17 39	27 13	18 4	26 27	27 57	26 35
30	6 31 36	7 45 17	2♓ 6	10 22	24 23	18 22	27 6	18 10	26 25	27 58	26 34
31	6 35 33	8♑46 26	15♓22	11♑59	25♏ 6	19♓ 6	26♋58	18♏15	26♋22	27♎59	26♌33

THE SUN ENTERS THE SIGN OF CAPRICORN ON DEC 22 AT 09:25.

♏ SCORPIO ♐ SAGITTARIUS ♑ CAPRICORN ♒ AQUARIUS ♓ PISCES

1955

SIDEREAL TIME · SUN · MOON · MERCURY · VENUS · MARS · JUPITER · SATURN · URANUS · NEPTUNE · PLUTO

JANUARY

DAY	TIME h m s	☉ ° ' "	☽ ° '	☿ ° '	♀ ° '	♂ ° '	♃ ° '	♄ ° '	♅ ° '	♆ ° '	♇ ° '
1	6 39 29	9♑47 36	28♓54	13♑36	25♏50	19♓49	26♋51	18♏20	26♋20	28♎ 0	26♌32
2	6 43 26	10 48 46	12♈42	15 14	26 35	20 32	26R44	18 26	26R17	28 1	26R31
3	6 47 22	11 49 55	26 47	16 52	27 22	21 15	26 36	18 31	26 15	28 2	26 30
4	6 51 19	12 51 4	11♉ 8	18 30	28 9	21 58	26 28	18 36	26 12	28 3	26 29
5	6 55 16	13 52 13	25 41	20 8	28 57	22 41	26 21	18 41	26 10	28 4	26 29
6	6 59 12	14 53 21	10♊22	21 47	29 46	23 24	26 13	18 46	26 7	28 5	26 27
7	7 3 9	15 54 30	25 6	23 26	0♐36	24 7	26 5	18 51	26 5	28 6	26 26
8	7 7 5	16 55 38	9♋45	25 5	1 26	24 50	25 57	18 56	26 2	28 6	26 25
9	7 11 2	17 56 46	24 14	26 45	2 18	25 34	25 49	19 1	26 0	28 7	26 24
10	7 14 58	18 57 53	8♌25	28 24	3 10	26 17	25 41	19 6	25 57	28 8	26 23
11	7 18 55	19 59 1	22 16	0♒ 4	4 3	27 0	25 33	19 10	25 54	28 8	26 22
12	7 22 52	21 0 8	5♍43	1 44	4 56	27 43	25 25	19 15	25 52	28 9	26 21
13	7 26 48	22 1 15	18 45	3 23	5 50	28 26	25 17	19 20	25 49	28 10	26 20
14	7 30 45	23 2 22	1♎26	5 3	6 45	29 9	25 9	19 24	25 47	28 10	26 19
15	7 34 41	24 3 29	13 47	6 42	7 41	29 52	25 1	19 28	25 44	28 11	26 17
16	7 38 38	25 4 35	25 53	8 21	8 37	0♈35	24 53	19 33	25 41	28 11	26 16
17	7 42 34	26 5 42	7♏49	9 59	9 33	1 18	24 45	19 37	25 39	28 12	26 15
18	7 46 31	27 6 48	19 39	11 36	10 31	2 1	24 37	19 41	25 36	28 12	26 14
19	7 50 27	28 7 54	1♐28	13 13	11 28	2 44	24 29	19 45	25 33	28 12	26 12
20	7 54 24	29 9 0	13 21	14 48	12 27	3 27	24 21	19 49	25 31	28 13	26 11
21	7 58 21	0♒10 5	25 22	16 21	13 25	4 10	24 13	19 53	25 28	28 13	26 10
22	8 2 17	1 11 9	7♑34	17 52	14 24	4 53	24 5	19 57	25 26	28 13	26 9
23	8 6 14	2 12 14	20 0	19 20	15 24	5 36	23 57	20 0	25 23	28 14	26 7
24	8 10 10	3 13 17	2♒40	20 46	16 24	6 19	23 49	20 4	25 21	28 14	26 6
25	8 14 7	4 14 20	15 36	22 7	17 24	7 1	23 41	20 8	25 18	28 14	26 5
26	8 18 3	5 15 21	28 47	23 25	18 25	7 44	23 33	20 11	25 15	28 14	26 3
27	8 22 0	6 16 22	12♓12	24 37	19 26	8 27	23 26	20 14	25 13	28 14	26 2
28	8 25 56	7 17 22	25 48	25 43	20 28	9 10	23 18	20 18	25 10	28 14	26 0
29	8 29 53	8 18 20	9♈35	26 43	21 30	9 53	23 10	20 21	25 8	28R14	25 59
30	8 33 50	9 19 17	23 31	27 36	22 32	10 36	23 3	20 24	25 5	28 14	25 58
31	8 37 46	10♒20 14	7♉33	28♒20	23♐35	11♈18	22♋56	20♏27	25♋ 3	28♎14	25♌56

THE SUN ENTERS THE SIGN OF AQUARIUS ON JAN 20 AT 20:02.

FEBRUARY

DAY	TIME h m s	☉ ° ' "	☽ ° '	☿ ° '	♀ ° '	♂ ° '	♃ ° '	♄ ° '	♅ ° '	♆ ° '	♇ ° '
1	8 41 43	11♒21 8	21♉41	28♒55	24♐38	12♈ 1	22♋48	20♏30	25♋ 0	28♎14	25♌55
2	8 45 39	12 22 2	5♊54	29 20	25 41	12 44	22R41	20 33	24R58	28R14	25R53
3	8 49 36	13 22 54	20 8	29R35	26 44	13 27	22 34	20 35	24 55	28 14	25 52
4	8 53 32	14 23 45	4♋23	29 39	27 48	14 9	22 27	20 38	24 53	28 14	25 51
5	8 57 29	15 24 34	18 34	29 32	28 52	14 52	22 20	20 40	24 50	28 14	25 49
6	9 1 25	16 25 23	2♌38	29 14	29 57	15 35	22 13	20 43	24 48	28 14	25 48
7	9 5 22	17 26 9	16 31	28 45	1♑ 1	16 17	22 6	20 45	24 46	28 13	25 46
8	9 9 19	18 26 55	0♍ 9	28 7	2 6	17 0	22 0	20 47	24 43	28 13	25 45
9	9 13 15	19 27 39	13 29	27 18	3 11	17 42	21 53	20 49	24 41	28 13	25 43
10	9 17 12	20 28 22	26 30	26 23	4 17	18 25	21 47	20 52	24 39	28 12	25 42
11	9 21 8	21 29 4	9♎11	25 20	5 22	19 7	21 41	20 53	24 37	28 12	25 40
12	9 25 5	22 29 45	21 34	24 14	6 28	19 50	21 35	20 55	24 34	28 12	25 39
13	9 29 1	23 30 24	3♏42	23 4	7 34	20 32	21 29	20 57	24 32	28 11	25 37
14	9 32 58	24 31 3	15 38	21 54	8 40	21 15	21 23	20 59	24 30	28 11	25 36
15	9 36 54	25 31 40	27 29	20 45	9 47	21 57	21 18	21 0	24 28	28 10	25 34
16	9 40 51	26 32 17	9♐18	19 39	10 53	22 40	21 12	21 2	24 26	28 10	25 33
17	9 44 48	27 32 52	21 12	18 37	12 0	23 22	21 7	21 3	24 24	28 9	25 31
18	9 48 44	28 33 26	3♑15	17 41	13 7	24 4	21 2	21 4	24 22	28 8	25 30
19	9 52 41	29 33 58	15 32	16 50	14 15	24 47	20 57	21 5	24 20	28 8	25 28
20	9 56 37	0♓34 29	28 6	16 7	15 22	25 29	20 52	21 6	24 18	28 7	25 27
21	10 0 34	1 34 59	11♒ 1	15 31	16 29	26 11	20 48	21 7	24 16	28 6	25 25
22	10 4 30	2 35 27	24 17	15 3	17 37	26 53	20 43	21 8	24 14	28 6	25 24
23	10 8 27	3 35 54	7♓52	14 42	18 45	27 35	20 39	21 9	24 12	28 5	25 22
24	10 12 23	4 36 18	21 45	14 28	19 53	28 18	20 35	21 9	24 10	28 4	25 21
25	10 16 20	5 36 41	5♈49	14D22	21 1	29 0	20 31	21 10	24 8	28 3	25 20
26	10 20 17	6 37 3	20 2	14 22	22 9	29 42	20 27	21 10	24 7	28 2	25 18
27	10 24 13	7 37 22	4♉17	14 29	23 18	0♉24	20 24	21 10	24 5	28 1	25 17
28	10 28 10	8♓37 39	18♉32	14♒43	24♑26	1♉ 6	20♋20	21♏11	24♋ 3	28♎ 1	25♌15

THE SUN ENTERS THE SIGN OF PISCES ON FEB 19 AT 10:19.

MARCH

DAY	TIME h m s	☉ ° ' "	☽ ° '	☿ ° '	♀ ° '	♂ ° '	♃ ° '	♄ ° '	♅ ° '	♆ ° '	♇ ° '
1	10 32 6	9♓37 55	2♊42	15♒ 1	25♑35	1♉48	20♋17	21♏11	24♋ 2	28♎ 0	25♌14
2	10 36 3	10 38 8	16 47	15 26	26 44	2 30	20R14	21R11	24R 0	27R59	25R12
3	10 39 59	11 38 19	0♋46	15 55	27 52	3 12	20 11	21 10	23 59	27 58	25 11
4	10 43 56	12 38 28	14 39	16 29	29 1	3 54	20 9	21 10	23 57	27 57	25 10
5	10 47 52	13 38 35	28 24	17 7	0♒10	4 36	20 7	21 10	23 56	27 56	25 8
6	10 51 49	14 38 40	12♌ 1	17 49	1 20	5 17	20 4	21 9	23 54	27 55	25 7
7	10 55 46	15 38 43	25 28	18 35	2 29	5 59	20 2	21 9	23 53	27 53	25 5
8	10 59 42	16 38 44	8♍44	19 25	3 38	6 41	20 0	21 8	23 52	27 52	25 4
9	11 3 39	17 38 42	21 47	20 17	4 48	7 23	19 59	21 8	23 50	27 51	25 3
10	11 7 35	18 38 39	4♎36	21 13	5 57	8 4	19 57	21 7	23 49	27 50	25 1
11	11 11 32	19 38 34	17 9	22 12	7 7	8 46	19 56	21 6	23 48	27 49	25 0
12	11 15 28	20 38 28	29 27	23 13	8 17	9 28	19 55	21 5	23 47	27 48	24 59
13	11 19 25	21 38 19	11♏33	24 17	9 27	10 9	19 54	21 4	23 46	27 46	24 57
14	11 23 21	22 38 9	23 28	25 24	10 37	10 51	19 54	21 2	23 45	27 45	24 56
15	11 27 18	23 37 57	5♐18	26 32	11 47	11 32	19 53	21 1	23 44	27 44	24 55
16	11 31 14	24 37 44	17 7	27 43	12 57	12 14	19D53	21 0	23 43	27 43	24 53
17	11 35 11	25 37 29	28 59	28 55	14 7	12 55	19 53	20 58	23 42	27 41	24 52
18	11 39 8	26 37 12	11♑ 2	0♓10	15 17	13 37	19 53	20 56	23 41	27 40	24 51
19	11 43 4	27 36 53	23 19	1 26	16 28	14 18	19 53	20 55	23 41	27 39	24 50
20	11 47 1	28 36 33	5♒57	2 45	17 38	15 0	19 54	20 53	23 40	27 37	24 49
21	11 50 57	29 36 10	18 58	4 5	18 49	15 41	19 54	20 51	23 39	27 36	24 47
22	11 54 54	0♈35 46	2♓24	5 26	19 59	16 22	19 55	20 49	23 39	27 34	24 46
23	11 58 50	1 35 20	16 16	6 49	21 10	17 4	19 56	20 47	23 38	27 33	24 45
24	12 2 47	2 34 52	0♈30	8 14	22 21	17 45	19 58	20 45	23 38	27 32	24 44
25	12 6 43	3 34 22	15 1	9 40	23 31	18 26	19 59	20 42	23 37	27 30	24 43
26	12 10 40	4 33 50	29 41	11 8	24 42	19 7	20 1	20 40	23 37	27 29	24 42
27	12 14 37	5 33 16	14♉22	12 38	25 53	19 48	20 3	20 38	23 36	27 27	24 41
28	12 18 33	6 32 39	28 58	14 8	27 4	20 29	20 5	20 35	23 36	27 26	24 40
29	12 22 30	7 32 1	13♊24	15 40	28 15	21 11	20 7	20 33	23 36	27 24	24 39
30	12 26 26	8 31 20	27 36	17 14	29 26	21 52	20 9	20 30	23 36	27 23	24 38
31	12 30 23	9♈30 36	11♋34	18♓49	0♒37	22♉33	20♋12	20♏27	23♋36	27♎21	24♌37

THE SUN ENTERS THE SIGN OF ARIES ON MAR 21 AT 09:35.

♈ ARIES ♉ TAURUS ♊ GEMINI ♋ CANCER ♌ LEO ♍ VIRGO ♎ LIBRA

1955

SIDEREAL SUN. MOON. MERCURY. VENUS. MARS. JUPITER. SATURN. URANUS. NEPTUNE. PLUTO.

DAY	TIME	☉	☽	☿	♀	♂	♃	♄	♅	♆	♇
	h m s	° ' "	° '	° '	° '	° '	° '	° '	° '	° '	° '
A 1	12 34 19	10♈29 51	25♋17	20♓26	1♓48	23♉14	20♋15	20♏24	23♋36	27♎20	24♌36
P 2	12 38 16	11 29 2	8♌46	22 3	2 59	23 55	20 18	20R21	23D36	27R18	24R35
R 3	12 42 12	12 28 12	22 3	23 43	4 10	24 35	20 21	20 18	23 36	27 16	24 34
I 4	12 46 9	13 27 19	5♍ 9	25 23	5 22	25 16	20 24	20 15	23 36	27 15	24 33
L 5	12 50 6	14 26 24	18 3	27 5	6 33	25 57	20 28	20 12	23 36	27 13	24 32
6	12 54 2	15 25 27	0♎45	28 49	7 44	26 38	20 31	20 9	23 36	27 12	24 31
7	12 57 59	16 24 27	13 16	0♈34	8 56	27 19	20 35	20 5	23 36	27 10	24 30
8	13 1 55	17 23 26	25 36	2 21	10 7	27 59	20 39	20 2	23 37	27 8	24 30
9	13 5 52	18 22 23	7♏46	4 9	11 18	28 40	20 43	19 59	23 37	27 7	24 29
10	13 9 48	19 21 18	19 45	5 58	12 30	29 21	20 48	19 55	23 38	27 5	24 28
11	13 13 45	20 20 11	1♐38	7 49	13 41	0♊ 1	20 52	19 52	23 38	27 4	24 27
12	13 17 41	21 19 2	13 26	9 41	14 53	0 42	20 57	19 48	23 39	27 2	24 27
13	13 21 38	22 17 51	25 14	11 35	16 5	1 23	21 2	19 44	23 39	27 0	24 26
14	13 25 35	23 16 39	7♑ 6	13 31	17 16	2 3	21 7	19 40	23 40	26 59	24 25
15	13 29 31	24 15 24	19 7	15 28	18 28	2 44	21 12	19 37	23 41	26 57	24 25
16	13 33 28	25 14 9	1♒22	17 26	19 40	3 24	21 17	19 33	23 41	26 55	24 24
17	13 37 24	26 12 51	13 58	19 26	20 51	4 5	21 23	19 29	23 42	26 54	24 24
18	13 41 21	27 11 32	26 58	21 27	22 3	4 45	21 28	19 25	23 43	26 52	24 23
19	13 45 17	28 10 11	10♓26	23 30	23 15	5 25	21 34	19 21	23 44	26 50	24 23
20	13 49 14	29 8 48	24 22	25 33	24 27	6 6	21 40	19 17	23 45	26 49	24 22
21	13 53 10	0♉ 7 23	8♈44	27 38	25 39	6 46	21 46	19 13	23 46	26 47	24 22
22	13 57 7	1 5 57	23 28	29 44	26 51	7 26	21 53	19 9	23 47	26 46	24 21
23	14 1 3	2 4 29	8♉27	1♉51	28 2	8 7	21 59	19 4	23 48	26 44	24 21
24	14 5 0	3 2 59	23 30	3 59	29 14	8 47	22 6	19 0	23 49	26 42	24 20
25	14 8 57	4 1 27	8♊28	6 7	0♈26	9 27	22 12	18 56	23 50	26 41	24 20
26	14 12 53	4 59 53	23 14	8 16	1 38	10 7	22 19	18 52	23 52	26 39	24 20
27	14 16 50	5 58 17	7♋42	10 24	2 50	10 47	22 26	18 47	23 53	26 37	24 19
28	14 20 46	6 56 39	21 50	12 33	4 2	11 27	22 33	18 43	23 54	26 36	24 19
29	14 24 43	7 54 59	5♌37	14 41	5 14	12 8	22 40	18 39	23 56	26 34	24 19
30	14 28 39	8♉53 16	19♌ 3	16♉48	6♈26	12♊48	22♋48	18♏34	23♋57	26♎33	24♌19

THE SUN ENTERS THE SIGN OF TAURUS ON APR 20 AT 20:58.

DAY	TIME	☉	☽	☿	♀	♂	♃	♄	♅	♆	♇
	h m s	° ' "	° '	° '	° '	° '	° '	° '	° '	° '	° '
M 1	14 32 36	9♉51 31	2♍11	18♉54	7♈38	13♊28	22♋55	18♏30	23♋59	26♎31	24♌19
A 2	14 36 33	10 49 45	15 3	20 59	8 51	14 8	23 3	18R25	24 0	26R29	24R18
Y 3	14 40 29	11 47 56	27 41	23 2	10 3	14 48	23 11	18 21	24 2	26 28	24 18
4	14 44 26	12 46 5	10♎ 7	25 3	11 15	15 27	23 19	18 16	24 4	26 26	24 18
5	14 48 22	13 44 13	22 23	27 1	12 27	16 7	23 27	18 12	24 5	26 25	24 18
6	14 52 19	14 42 19	4♏29	28 58	13 39	16 47	23 35	18 7	24 7	26 23	24D18
7	14 56 15	15 40 23	16 29	0♊51	14 51	17 27	23 43	18 3	24 9	26 22	24 18
8	15 0 12	16 38 25	28 22	2 42	16 3	18 7	23 52	17 58	24 11	26 20	24 18
9	15 4 8	17 36 26	10♐11	4 30	17 16	18 47	24 0	17 54	24 13	26 19	24 18
10	15 8 5	18 34 26	21 58	6 14	18 28	19 26	24 9	17 49	24 14	26 17	24 18
11	15 12 1	19 32 24	3♑47	7 55	19 40	20 6	24 17	17 45	24 16	26 16	24 18
12	15 15 58	20 30 20	15 41	9 33	20 52	20 46	24 26	17 40	24 18	26 14	24 18
13	15 19 55	21 28 16	27 43	11 7	22 5	21 25	24 35	17 36	24 21	26 13	24 19
14	15 23 51	22 26 10	9♒59	12 38	23 17	22 5	24 44	17 31	24 23	26 11	24 19
15	15 27 48	23 24 2	22 33	14 5	24 29	22 45	24 53	17 27	24 25	26 10	24 19
16	15 31 44	24 21 54	5♓30	15 28	25 42	23 24	25 3	17 22	24 27	26 8	24 19
17	15 35 41	25 19 44	18 53	16 48	26 54	24 4	25 12	17 18	24 29	26 7	24 20
18	15 39 37	26 17 33	2♈43	18 3	28 7	24 43	25 22	17 13	24 32	26 6	24 20
19	15 43 34	27 15 21	17 1	19 15	29 19	25 23	25 31	17 9	24 34	26 4	24 20
20	15 47 30	28 13 7	1♉44	20 23	0♉31	26 2	25 41	17 5	24 36	26 3	24 21
21	15 51 27	29 10 53	16 45	21 27	1 44	26 42	25 51	17 0	24 39	26 2	24 21
22	15 55 24	0♊ 8 37	1♊56	22 27	2 56	27 21	26 1	16 56	24 41	26 0	24 21
23	15 59 20	1 6 21	17 7	23 23	4 9	28 1	26 11	16 52	24 44	25 59	24 22
24	16 3 17	2 4 2	2♋ 9	24 15	5 21	28 40	26 21	16 47	24 46	25 58	24 22
25	16 7 13	3 1 43	16 53	25 3	6 34	29 19	26 31	16 43	24 49	25 57	24 23
26	16 11 10	3 59 21	1♌15	25 46	7 46	29 59	26 41	16 39	24 51	25 55	24 23
27	16 15 6	4 56 59	15 12	26 25	8 59	0♋38	26 52	16 35	24 54	25 54	24 24
28	16 19 3	5 54 34	28 44	26 59	10 11	1 17	27 2	16 31	24 56	25 53	24 24
29	16 23 0	6 52 8	11♍53	27 29	11 24	1 56	27 13	16 26	24 59	25 52	24 25
30	16 26 56	7 49 41	24 41	27 54	12 36	2 36	27 23	16 22	25 2	25 51	24 26
31	16 30 53	8♊47 13	7♎12	28♊15	13♉49	3♋15	27♋34	16♏18	25♋ 5	25♎50	24♌26

THE SUN ENTERS THE SIGN OF GEMINI ON MAY 21 AT 20:25.

DAY	TIME	☉	☽	☿	♀	♂	♃	♄	♅	♆	♇
	h m s	° ' "	° '	° '	° '	° '	° '	° '	° '	° '	° '
J 1	16 34 49	9♊44 43	19♎28	28♊31	15♉ 2	3♋54	27♋45	16♏14	25♋ 7	25♎48	24♌27
U 2	16 38 46	10 42 12	1♏33	28 42	16 14	4 33	27 56	16R10	25 10	25R47	24 28
N 3	16 42 42	11 39 39	13 30	28R49	17 27	5 12	28 7	16 7	25 13	25 46	24 29
E 4	16 46 39	12 37 6	25 22	28 51	18 39	5 51	28 18	16 3	25 16	25 45	24 29
5	16 50 35	13 34 32	7♐11	28 48	19 52	6 31	28 29	15 59	25 19	25 44	24 30
6	16 54 32	14 31 56	18 59	28 41	21 5	7 10	28 40	15 55	25 22	25 43	24 31
7	16 58 29	15 29 20	0♑49	28 30	22 17	7 49	28 51	15 52	25 25	25 43	24 32
8	17 2 25	16 26 43	12 42	28 15	23 30	8 28	29 2	15 48	25 28	25 42	24 33
9	17 6 22	17 24 5	24 42	27 56	24 43	9 7	29 14	15 45	25 31	25 41	24 34
10	17 10 18	18 21 27	6♒51	27 33	25 56	9 46	29 25	15 41	25 34	25 40	24 35
11	17 14 15	19 18 48	19 13	27 8	27 8	10 25	29 37	15 38	25 37	25 39	24 36
12	17 18 11	20 16 8	1♓50	26 40	28 21	11 3	29 48	15 35	25 40	25 38	24 37
13	17 22 8	21 13 28	14 47	26 9	29 34	11 42	0♌ 0	15 31	25 44	25 37	24 38
14	17 26 4	22 10 48	28 5	25 37	0♊47	12 21	0 12	15 28	25 47	25 37	24 39
15	17 30 1	23 8 7	11♈47	25 4	1 59	13 0	0 23	15 25	25 50	25 36	24 40
16	17 33 58	24 5 25	25 54	24 30	3 12	13 39	0 35	15 22	25 53	25 35	24 41
17	17 37 54	25 2 44	10♉25	23 56	4 25	14 18	0 47	15 19	25 56	25 35	24 42
18	17 41 51	26 0 2	25 14	23 23	5 38	14 57	0 59	15 16	26 0	25 34	24 43
19	17 45 47	26 57 20	10♊18	22 50	6 51	15 35	1 11	15 13	26 3	25 33	24 44
20	17 49 44	27 54 38	25 26	22 20	8 4	16 14	1 23	15 11	26 6	25 33	24 45
21	17 53 40	28 51 55	10♋30	21 52	9 17	16 53	1 35	15 8	26 10	25 32	24 47
22	17 57 37	29 49 11	25 21	21 26	10 30	17 32	1 47	15 5	26 13	25 32	24 48
23	18 1 33	0♋46 27	9♌53	21 3	11 43	18 11	2 0	15 3	26 16	25 31	24 49
24	18 5 30	1 43 42	24 0	20 44	12 56	18 49	2 12	15 1	26 20	25 31	24 50
25	18 9 27	2 40 57	7♍40	20 29	14 9	19 28	2 24	14 58	26 23	25 30	24 52
26	18 13 23	3 38 11	20 54	20 18	15 22	20 7	2 37	14 56	26 27	25 30	24 53
27	18 17 20	4 35 24	3♎45	20D11	16 35	20 45	2 49	14 54	26 30	25 30	24 54
28	18 21 16	5 32 37	16 14	20 9	17 48	21 24	3 1	14 52	26 34	25 29	24 56
29	18 25 13	6 29 50	28 27	20 12	19 1	22 3	3 14	14 50	26 37	25 29	24 57
30	18 29 9	7♋27 2	10♏27	20♊19	20♊14	22♋41	3♌26	14♏48	26♋41	25♎29	24♌58

THE SUN ENTERS THE SIGN OF CANCER ON JUN 22 AT 04:32.

♏ SCORPIO ♐ SAGITTARIUS ♑ CAPRICORN ♒ AQUARIUS ♓ PISCES

1955

SIDEREAL SUN. MOON. MERCURY. VENUS. MARS. JUPITER. SATURN. URANUS. NEPTUNE. PLUTO.

DAY	TIME h m s	☉ ° ' "	☽ ° '	☿ ° '	♀ ° '	♂ ° '	♃ ° '	♄ ° '	♅ ° '	♆ ° '	♇ ° '
J 1	18 33 6	8♋24 13	22♏20	20♊31	21♊27	23♋20	3♌39	14♏46	26♋44	25♎29	25♌ 0
U 2	18 37 2	9 21 25	4♐ 8	20 48	22 40	23 58	3 52	14R45	26 48	25R28	25 1
L 3	18 40 59	10 18 36	15 56	21 10	23 53	24 37	4 4	14 43	26 51	25 28	25 3
Y 4	18 44 56	11 15 47	27 46	21 37	25 6	25 16	4 17	14 41	26 55	25 28	25 4
5	18 48 52	12 12 58	9♑42	22 9	26 20	25 54	4 30	14 40	26 58	25 28	25 6
6	18 52 49	13 10 9	21 44	22 46	27 33	26 33	4 42	14 39	27 2	25 28	25 7
7	18 56 45	14 7 20	3♒55	23 27	28 46	27 11	4 55	14 37	27 6	25D28	25 9
8	19 0 42	15 4 31	16 17	24 14	29 59	27 50	5 8	14 36	27 9	25 28	25 10
9	19 4 38	16 1 42	28 52	25 5	1♋12	28 28	5 21	14 35	27 13	25 28	25 12
10	19 8 35	16 58 53	11♓40	26 1	2 26	29 7	5 34	14 34	27 16	25 28	25 13
11	19 12 31	17 56 5	24 43	27 1	3 39	29 45	5 46	14 33	27 20	25 28	25 15
12	19 16 28	18 53 18	8♈ 4	28 6	4 52	0♌23	5 59	14 33	27 24	25 28	25 16
13	19 20 25	19 50 30	21 42	29 15	6 6	1 2	6 12	14 32	27 27	25 28	25 18
14	19 24 21	20 47 44	5♉39	0♋29	7 19	1 40	6 25	14 31	27 31	25 28	25 20
15	19 28 18	21 44 58	19 54	1 47	8 33	2 19	6 38	14 31	27 35	25 29	25 21
16	19 32 14	22 42 13	4♊26	3 10	9 46	2 57	6 51	14 31	27 38	25 29	25 23
17	19 36 11	23 39 28	19 10	4 36	10 59	3 36	7 4	14 30	27 42	25 29	25 25
18	19 40 7	24 36 44	4♋ 2	6 7	12 13	4 14	7 17	14 30	27 46	25 30	25 26
19	19 44 4	25 34 1	18 53	7 42	13 26	4 52	7 31	14D30	27 49	25 30	25 28
20	19 48 1	26 31 18	3♌38	9 20	14 40	5 31	7 44	14 30	27 53	25 30	25 30
21	19 51 57	27 28 35	18 7	11 3	15 54	6 9	7 57	14 30	27 57	25 31	25 32
22	19 55 54	28 25 53	2♍16	12 48	17 7	6 47	8 10	14 30	28 0	25 31	25 33
23	19 59 50	29 23 11	16 0	14 37	18 21	7 26	8 23	14 31	28 4	25 32	25 35
24	20 3 47	0♌20 30	29 18	16 29	19 34	8 4	8 36	14 31	28 8	25 32	25 37
25	20 7 43	1 17 48	12♎12	18 24	20 48	8 42	8 49	14 32	28 11	25 33	25 39
26	20 11 40	2 15 7	24 43	20 22	22 2	9 21	9 3	14 32	28 15	25 33	25 40
27	20 15 36	3 12 27	6♏56	22 21	23 15	9 59	9 16	14 33	28 19	25 34	25 42
28	20 19 33	4 9 47	18 56	24 23	24 29	10 37	9 29	14 34	28 22	25 34	25 44
29	20 23 30	5 7 8	0♐47	26 25	25 43	11 16	9 42	14 35	28 26	25 35	25 46
30	20 27 26	6 4 29	12 35	28 30	26 56	11 54	9 55	14 36	28 30	25 36	25 48
31	20 31 23	7♌ 1 50	24♐24	0♌35	28♋10	12♌32	10♌ 9	14♏37	28♋33	25♎37	25♌50

THE SUN ENTERS THE SIGN OF LEO ON JUL 23 AT 15:25.

DAY	TIME h m s	☉ ° ' "	☽ ° '	☿ ° '	♀ ° '	♂ ° '	♃ ° '	♄ ° '	♅ ° '	♆ ° '	♇ ° '
A 1	20 35 19	7♌59 13	6♑18	2♌40	29♋24	13♌10	10♌22	14♏38	28♋37	25♎37	25♌51
U 2	20 39 16	8 56 36	18 21	4 46	0♌38	13 49	10 35	14 39	28 41	25 38	25 53
G 3	20 43 12	9 54 0	0♒35	6 51	1 52	14 27	10 48	14 41	28 44	25 39	25 55
U 4	20 47 9	10 51 24	13 1	8 57	3 5	15 5	11 2	14 42	28 48	25 40	25 57
S 5	20 51 5	11 48 50	25 41	11 2	4 19	15 43	11 15	14 44	28 52	25 41	25 59
T 6	20 55 2	12 46 16	8♓35	13 6	5 33	16 22	11 28	14 45	28 55	25 42	26 1
7	20 58 59	13 43 44	21 42	15 9	6 47	17 0	11 41	14 47	28 59	25 42	26 3
8	21 2 55	14 41 13	5♈ 1	17 11	8 1	17 38	11 54	14 49	29 2	25 43	26 5
9	21 6 52	15 38 43	18 33	19 12	9 15	18 16	12 8	14 51	29 6	25 44	26 7
10	21 10 48	16 36 14	2♉16	21 12	10 29	18 54	12 21	14 53	29 9	25 45	26 8
11	21 14 45	17 33 47	16 10	23 11	11 43	19 33	12 34	14 55	29 13	25 46	26 10
12	21 18 41	18 31 22	0♊15	25 8	12 57	20 11	12 47	14 57	29 16	25 48	26 12
13	21 22 38	19 28 57	14 30	27 4	14 11	20 49	13 0	15 0	29 20	25 49	26 14
14	21 26 34	20 26 35	28 53	28 58	15 25	21 27	13 14	15 2	29 24	25 50	26 16
15	21 30 31	21 24 14	13♋22	0♍51	16 39	22 5	13 27	15 4	29 27	25 51	26 18
16	21 34 28	22 21 54	27 51	2 42	17 53	22 44	13 40	15 7	29 30	25 52	26 20
17	21 38 24	23 19 36	12♌16	4 32	19 8	23 22	13 53	15 10	29 34	25 53	26 22
18	21 42 21	24 17 19	26 30	6 21	20 22	24 0	14 6	15 13	29 37	25 55	26 24
19	21 46 17	25 15 3	10♍28	8 8	21 36	24 38	14 19	15 15	29 41	25 56	26 26
20	21 50 14	26 12 48	24 7	9 54	22 50	25 16	14 32	15 18	29 44	25 57	26 28
21	21 54 10	27 10 35	7♎22	11 38	24 4	25 55	14 45	15 21	29 48	25 59	26 30
22	21 58 7	28 8 23	20 15	13 21	25 19	26 33	14 59	15 24	29 51	26 0	26 32
23	22 2 3	29 6 12	2♏46	15 3	26 33	27 11	15 12	15 28	29 54	26 1	26 34
24	22 6 0	0♍ 4 2	15 0	16 43	27 47	27 49	15 25	15 31	29 58	26 3	26 36
25	22 9 56	1 1 54	27 0	18 22	29 2	28 27	15 38	15 34	0♌ 1	26 4	26 38
26	22 13 53	1 59 47	8♐51	19 59	0♍16	29 6	15 50	15 38	0 4	26 6	26 39
27	22 17 50	2 57 41	20 39	21 35	1 30	29 44	16 3	15 41	0 7	26 7	26 41
28	22 21 46	3 55 36	2♑30	23 10	2 45	0♍22	16 16	15 45	0 11	26 9	26 43
29	22 25 43	4 53 33	14 28	24 43	3 59	1 0	16 29	15 49	0 14	26 10	26 45
30	22 29 39	5 51 31	26 37	26 15	5 13	1 38	16 42	15 53	0 17	26 12	26 47
31	22 33 36	6♍49 30	9♒ 1	27♍46	6♍28	2♍16	16♌55	15♏56	0♌20	26♎13	26♌49

THE SUN ENTERS THE SIGN OF VIRGO ON AUG 23 AT 22:19.

DAY	TIME h m s	☉ ° ' "	☽ ° '	☿ ° '	♀ ° '	♂ ° '	♃ ° '	♄ ° '	♅ ° '	♆ ° '	♇ ° '
S 1	22 37 32	7♍47 31	21♒43	29♍15	7♍42	2♍55	17♌ 8	16♏ 0	0♌23	26♎15	26♌51
E 2	22 41 29	8 45 34	4♓42	0♎43	8 57	3 33	17 20	16 4	0 26	26 17	26 53
P 3	22 45 25	9 43 38	17 57	2 10	10 11	4 11	17 33	16 8	0 29	26 18	26 55
T 4	22 49 22	10 41 43	1♈28	3 36	11 25	4 49	17 46	16 13	0 32	26 20	26 57
E 5	22 53 19	11 39 51	15 11	5 0	12 40	5 27	17 58	16 17	0 35	26 22	26 59
M 6	22 57 15	12 38 0	29 4	6 22	13 54	6 6	18 11	16 21	0 38	26 23	27 0
B 7	23 1 12	13 36 12	13♉ 2	7 43	15 9	6 44	18 23	16 26	0 41	26 25	27 2
E 8	23 5 8	14 34 25	27 5	9 3	16 23	7 22	18 36	16 30	0 44	26 27	27 4
R 9	23 9 5	15 32 41	11♊10	10 21	17 38	8 0	18 48	16 35	0 47	26 29	27 6
10	23 13 1	16 30 59	25 17	11 37	18 52	8 38	19 1	16 39	0 50	26 30	27 8
11	23 16 58	17 29 19	9♋24	12 52	20 7	9 17	19 13	16 44	0 53	26 32	27 10
12	23 20 54	18 27 40	23 31	14 6	21 22	9 55	19 26	16 49	0 55	26 34	27 12
13	23 24 51	19 26 4	7♌36	15 17	22 36	10 33	19 38	16 54	0 58	26 36	27 13
14	23 28 48	20 24 30	21 35	16 27	23 51	11 11	19 50	16 58	1 1	26 38	27 15
15	23 32 44	21 22 58	5♍25	17 34	25 5	11 49	20 2	17 3	1 3	26 40	27 17
16	23 36 41	22 21 28	19 4	18 40	26 20	12 28	20 14	17 8	1 6	26 42	27 19
17	23 40 37	23 20 0	2♎26	19 43	27 35	13 6	20 27	17 14	1 9	26 43	27 21
18	23 44 34	24 18 34	15 30	20 44	28 49	13 44	20 39	17 19	1 11	26 45	27 22
19	23 48 30	25 17 9	28 16	21 42	0♎ 4	14 22	20 51	17 24	1 14	26 47	27 24
20	23 52 27	26 15 46	10♏43	22 38	1 19	15 1	21 2	17 29	1 16	26 49	27 26
21	23 56 23	27 14 25	22 54	23 31	2 33	15 39	21 14	17 35	1 19	26 51	27 28
22	0 0 20	28 13 6	4♐52	24 20	3 48	16 17	21 26	17 40	1 21	26 53	27 29
23	0 4 17	29 11 49	16 43	25 7	5 3	16 55	21 38	17 45	1 23	26 55	27 31
24	0 8 13	0♎10 33	28 31	25 49	6 18	17 34	21 49	17 51	1 26	26 57	27 33
25	0 12 10	1 9 19	10♑21	26 28	7 32	18 12	22 1	17 57	1 28	26 59	27 35
26	0 16 6	2 8 7	22 20	27 2	8 47	18 50	22 13	18 2	1 30	27 2	27 36
27	0 20 3	3 6 56	4♒32	27 32	10 2	19 28	22 24	18 8	1 32	27 4	27 38
28	0 23 59	4 5 47	17 2	27 57	11 16	20 7	22 35	18 14	1 35	27 6	27 39
29	0 27 56	5 4 40	29 53	28 16	12 31	20 45	22 47	18 20	1 37	27 8	27 41
30	0 31 52	6♎ 3 35	13♓ 6	28♎30	13♎46	21♍23	22♌58	18♏25	1♌39	27♎10	27♌43

THE SUN ENTERS THE SIGN OF LIBRA ON SEP 23 AT 19:41.

♈ ARIES ♉ TAURUS ♊ GEMINI ♋ CANCER ♌ LEO ♍ VIRGO ♎ LIBRA

1955

SIDEREAL TIME. SUN. MOON. MERCURY. VENUS. MARS. JUPITER. SATURN. URANUS. NEPTUNE. PLUTO.

DAY	TIME	☉	☽	☿	♀	♂	♃	♄	♅	♆	♇
	h m s	° ′ ″	° ′	° ′	° ′	° ′	° ′	° ′	° ′	° ′	° ′
O 1	0 35 49	7♎ 2 31	26♓41	28♎37	15♎ 1	22♍ 2	23♌ 9	18♏31	1♌41	27♎12	27♌44
C 2	0 39 45	8 1 30	10♈35	28R38	16 15	22 40	23 20	18 37	1 43	27 14	27 46
T 3	0 43 42	9 0 30	24 44	28 31	17 30	23 18	23 31	18 43	1 45	27 16	27 47
O 4	0 47 39	9 59 33	9♉ 2	28 17	18 45	23 57	23 42	18 49	1 47	27 18	27 49
B 5	0 51 35	10 58 38	23 25	27 55	20 0	24 35	23 53	18 55	1 48	27 21	27 50
E 6	0 55 32	11 57 46	7♊47	27 26	21 14	25 13	24 4	19 2	1 50	27 23	27 52
R 7	0 59 28	12 56 55	22 4	26 48	22 29	25 52	24 14	19 8	1 52	27 25	27 53
8	1 3 25	13 56 7	6♋15	26 3	23 44	26 30	24 25	19 14	1 54	27 27	27 55
9	1 7 21	14 55 22	20 19	25 11	24 59	27 8	24 36	19 20	1 55	27 29	27 56
10	1 11 18	15 54 38	4♌13	24 12	26 14	27 47	24 46	19 27	1 57	27 32	27 58
11	1 15 14	16 53 57	17 59	23 7	27 28	28 25	24 56	19 33	1 58	27 34	27 59
12	1 19 11	17 53 19	1♍35	21 58	28 43	29 3	25 7	19 39	2 0	27 36	28 1
13	1 23 8	18 52 42	15 0	20 46	29 58	29 42	25 17	19 46	2 1	27 38	28 2
14	1 27 4	19 52 8	28 14	19 34	1♏13	0♎20	25 27	19 52	2 3	27 40	28 3
15	1 31 1	20 51 35	11♎15	18 23	2 28	0 59	25 37	19 59	2 4	27 43	28 5
16	1 34 57	21 51 5	24 1	17 15	3 42	1 37	25 47	20 6	2 5	27 45	28 6
17	1 38 54	22 50 37	6♏33	16 13	4 57	2 16	25 56	20 12	2 6	27 47	28 7
18	1 42 50	23 50 11	18 51	15 17	6 12	2 54	26 6	20 19	2 8	27 49	28 8
19	1 46 47	24 49 47	0♐56	14 31	7 27	3 32	26 16	20 25	2 9	27 52	28 10
20	1 50 43	25 49 25	12 51	13 54	8 42	4 11	26 25	20 32	2 10	27 54	28 11
21	1 54 40	26 49 5	24 40	13 28	9 57	4 49	26 34	20 39	2 11	27 56	28 12
22	1 58 37	27 48 46	6♑27	13D13	11 11	5 28	26 44	20 46	2 12	27 58	28 13
23	2 2 33	28 48 29	18 16	13 10	12 26	6 6	26 53	20 52	2 13	28 1	28 14
24	2 6 30	29 48 14	0♒13	13 18	13 41	6 45	27 2	20 59	2 14	28 3	28 15
25	2 10 26	0♏48 0	12 24	13 36	14 56	7 23	27 11	21 6	2 15	28 5	28 16
26	2 14 23	1 47 48	24 53	14 4	16 11	8 2	27 19	21 13	2 15	28 7	28 17
27	2 18 19	2 47 38	7♓45	14 42	17 26	8 40	27 28	21 20	2 16	28 9	28 18
28	2 22 16	3 47 30	21 2	15 28	18 40	9 19	27 37	21 27	2 17	28 12	28 19
29	2 26 12	4 47 23	4♈45	16 22	19 55	9 57	27 45	21 34	2 17	28 14	28 20
30	2 30 9	5 47 18	18 52	17 22	21 10	10 36	27 53	21 41	2 18	28 16	28 21
31	2 34 6	6♏47 15	3♉20	18♎28	22♏25	11♎15	28♌ 1	21♏48	2♌18	28♎18	28♌22

THE SUN ENTERS THE SIGN OF SCORPIO ON OCT 24 AT 04:44.

DAY	TIME	☉	☽	☿	♀	♂	♃	♄	♅	♆	♇
	h m s	° ′ ″	° ′	° ′	° ′	° ′	° ′	° ′	° ′	° ′	° ′
N 1	2 38 2	7♏47 14	18♉ 2	19♎40	23♏40	11♎53	28♌ 9	21♏55	2♌19	28♎21	28♌23
O 2	2 41 59	8 47 15	2♊51	20 56	24 54	12 32	28 17	22 2	2 19	28 23	28 24
V 3	2 45 55	9 47 17	17 39	22 16	26 9	13 10	28 25	22 9	2 19	28 25	28 25
E 4	2 49 52	10 47 22	2♋19	23 39	27 24	13 49	28 33	22 16	2 20	28 27	28 26
M 5	2 53 48	11 47 29	16 46	25 4	28 39	14 28	28 40	22 23	2 20	28 29	28 27
B 6	2 57 45	12 47 38	0♌59	26 32	29 54	15 6	28 48	22 30	2 20	28 32	28 27
E 7	3 1 41	13 47 50	14 54	28 2	1♐ 8	15 45	28 55	22 37	2 20	28 34	28 28
R 8	3 5 38	14 48 3	28 32	29 33	2 23	16 23	29 2	22 44	2R20	28 36	28 29
9	3 9 35	15 48 18	11♍54	1♏ 6	3 38	17 2	29 9	22 51	2 20	28 38	28 29
10	3 13 31	16 48 35	25 0	2 39	4 53	17 41	29 16	22 58	2 20	28 40	28 30
11	3 17 28	17 48 54	7♎53	4 14	6 8	18 19	29 22	23 6	2 20	28 42	28 31
12	3 21 24	18 49 16	20 32	5 48	7 23	18 58	29 29	23 13	2 20	28 45	28 31
13	3 25 21	19 49 38	2♏59	7 24	8 37	19 37	29 35	23 20	2 20	28 47	28 32
14	3 29 17	20 50 3	15 15	8 59	9 52	20 16	29 41	23 27	2 19	28 49	28 32
15	3 33 14	21 50 30	27 21	10 35	11 7	20 54	29 47	23 34	2 19	28 51	28 33
16	3 37 10	22 50 58	9♐19	12 11	12 22	21 33	29 53	23 41	2 19	28 53	28 33
17	3 41 7	23 51 27	21 10	13 47	13 37	22 12	29 59	23 48	2 18	28 55	28 34
18	3 45 4	24 51 58	2♑57	15 23	14 51	22 51	0♍ 5	23 56	2 18	28 57	28 34
19	3 49 0	25 52 31	14 43	16 59	16 6	23 29	0 10	24 3	2 17	28 59	28 35
20	3 52 57	26 53 5	26 32	18 35	17 21	24 8	0 15	24 10	2 17	29 1	28 35
21	3 56 53	27 53 40	8♒29	20 10	18 36	24 47	0 20	24 17	2 16	29 3	28 35
22	4 0 50	28 54 16	20 37	21 46	19 51	25 26	0 25	24 24	2 15	29 5	28 36
23	4 4 46	29 54 53	3♓ 2	23 21	21 5	26 4	0 30	24 31	2 14	29 7	28 36
24	4 8 43	0♐55 32	15 49	24 57	22 20	26 43	0 35	24 39	2 14	29 9	28 36
25	4 12 39	1 56 11	29 0	26 32	23 35	27 22	0 39	24 46	2 13	29 11	28 36
26	4 16 36	2 56 52	12♈38	28 7	24 50	28 1	0 43	24 53	2 12	29 13	28 36
27	4 20 33	3 57 34	26 44	29 42	26 4	28 40	0 47	25 0	2 11	29 15	28 37
28	4 24 29	4 58 17	11♉16	1♐17	27 19	29 19	0 51	25 7	2 10	29 17	28 37
29	4 28 26	5 59 1	26 8	2 51	28 34	29 57	0 55	25 14	2 9	29 19	28 37
30	4 32 22	6♐59 47	11♊13	4♐26	29♐48	0♏36	0♍59	25♏21	2♌ 8	29♎21	28♌37

THE SUN ENTERS THE SIGN OF SAGITTARIUS ON NOV 23 AT 02:02.

DAY	TIME	☉	☽	☿	♀	♂	♃	♄	♅	♆	♇
	h m s	° ′ ″	° ′	° ′	° ′	° ′	° ′	° ′	° ′	° ′	° ′
D 1	4 36 19	8♐ 0 33	26♊22	6♐ 0	1♑ 3	1♏15	1♍ 2	25♏28	2♌ 6	29♎23	28♌37
E 2	4 40 15	9 1 22	11♋25	7 35	2 18	1 54	1 5	25 35	2R 5	29 25	28R37
C 3	4 44 12	10 2 11	26 16	9 9	3 33	2 33	1 8	25 42	2 4	29 26	28 37
E 4	4 48 8	11 3 2	10♌46	10 43	4 47	3 12	1 11	25 49	2 3	29 28	28 37
M 5	4 52 5	12 3 54	24 54	12 18	6 2	3 51	1 14	25 56	2 1	29 30	28 37
B 6	4 56 2	13 4 47	8♍37	13 52	7 17	4 30	1 16	26 3	2 0	29 32	28 36
E 7	4 59 58	14 5 42	21 57	15 26	8 31	5 9	1 18	26 10	1 58	29 33	28 36
R 8	5 3 55	15 6 38	4♎56	17 0	9 46	5 48	1 20	26 17	1 57	29 35	28 36
9	5 7 51	16 7 35	17 36	18 34	11 1	6 27	1 22	26 24	1 55	29 37	28 36
10	5 11 48	17 8 33	0♏ 0	20 9	12 15	7 6	1 24	26 31	1 54	29 39	28 36
11	5 15 44	18 9 33	12 12	21 43	13 30	7 45	1 25	26 38	1 52	29 40	28 35
12	5 19 41	19 10 34	24 14	23 17	14 44	8 24	1 27	26 45	1 50	29 42	28 35
13	5 23 37	20 11 35	6♐10	24 52	15 59	9 3	1 28	26 51	1 49	29 43	28 35
14	5 27 34	21 12 38	18 0	26 26	17 14	9 42	1 29	26 58	1 47	29 45	28 34
15	5 31 31	22 13 41	29 48	28 1	18 28	10 21	1 29	27 5	1 45	29 46	28 34
16	5 35 27	23 14 45	11♑36	29 36	19 43	11 0	1 30	27 12	1 43	29 48	28 33
17	5 39 24	24 15 50	23 25	1♑11	20 57	11 39	1 30	27 18	1 41	29 50	28 33
18	5 43 20	25 16 55	5♒18	2 46	22 12	12 18	1R30	27 25	1 40	29 51	28 33
19	5 47 17	26 18 1	17 18	4 21	23 26	12 57	1 30	27 31	1 38	29 52	28 32
20	5 51 13	27 19 7	29 28	5 56	24 41	13 36	1 30	27 38	1 36	29 54	28 31
21	5 55 10	28 20 13	11♓52	7 31	25 55	14 15	1 30	27 44	1 34	29 55	28 31
22	5 59 6	29 21 19	24 33	9 6	27 10	14 54	1 29	27 51	1 31	29 57	28 30
23	6 3 3	0♑22 26	7♈36	10 42	28 24	15 33	1 28	27 57	1 29	29 58	28 30
24	6 7 0	1 23 33	21 3	12 17	29 39	16 13	1 27	28 4	1 27	29 59	28 29
25	6 10 56	2 24 40	4♉56	13 52	0♒53	16 52	1 26	28 10	1 25	0♏ 0	28 28
26	6 14 53	3 25 47	19 16	15 28	2 7	17 31	1 24	28 16	1 23	0 2	28 28
27	6 18 49	4 26 54	3♊59	17 3	3 22	18 10	1 23	28 23	1 21	0 3	28 27
28	6 22 46	5 28 1	19 2	18 38	4 36	18 49	1 21	28 29	1 18	0 4	28 26
29	6 26 42	6 29 9	4♋16	20 12	5 50	19 28	1 19	28 35	1 16	0 5	28 25
30	6 30 39	7 30 17	19 31	21 47	7 5	20 7	1 17	28 41	1 14	0 6	28 25
31	6 34 36	8♑31 25	4♌38	23♑20	8♒19	20♏47	1♍14	28♏47	1♌11	0♏ 7	28♌24

THE SUN ENTERS THE SIGN OF CAPRICORN ON DEC 22 AT 15:11.

♏ SCORPIO ♐ SAGITTARIUS ♑ CAPRICORN ♒ AQUARIUS ♓ PISCES

1956

SIDEREAL. SUN. MOON. MERCURY. VENUS. MARS. JUPITER. SATURN. URANUS. NEPTUNE. PLUTO.

DAY	TIME	☉	☽	☿	♀	♂	♃	♄	♅	♆	♇
	h m s	° ' "	° '	° '	° '	° '	° '	° '	° '	° '	° '
J 1	6 38 32	9♑32 33	19♌26	24♑53	9♒33	21♏26	1♍12	28♏53	1♌ 9	0♏ 9	28♌23
A 2	6 42 29	10 33 41	3♍51	26 25	10 47	22 5	1R 9	28 59	1R 7	0 10	28R22
N 3	6 46 25	11 34 50	17 47	27 56	12 1	22 44	1 6	29 5	1 4	0 11	28 21
U 4	6 50 22	12 35 59	1♎15	29 26	13 15	23 23	1 3	29 11	1 2	0 12	28 20
A 5	6 54 18	13 37 9	14 16	0♒54	14 30	24 3	1 0	29 17	0 59	0 12	28 19
R 6	6 58 15	14 38 18	26 54	2 20	15 44	24 42	0 56	29 23	0 57	0 13	28 18
Y 7	7 2 11	15 39 28	9♏12	3 43	16 58	25 21	0 52	29 28	0 55	0 14	28 17
8	7 6 8	16 40 38	21 17	5 4	18 12	26 0	0 49	29 34	0 52	0 15	28 16
9	7 10 5	17 41 48	3♐11	6 21	19 26	26 40	0 45	29 39	0 50	0 16	28 15
10	7 14 1	18 42 58	15 0	7 34	20 40	27 19	0 40	29 45	0 47	0 17	28 14
11	7 17 58	19 44 8	26 47	8 43	21 53	27 58	0 36	29 50	0 44	0 17	28 13
12	7 21 54	20 45 18	8♑34	9 46	23 7	28 37	0 31	29 56	0 42	0 18	28 12
13	7 25 51	21 46 27	20 24	10 43	24 21	29 17	0 27	0♐ 1	0 39	0 19	28 11
14	7 29 47	22 47 37	2♒20	11 33	25 35	29 56	0 22	0 6	0 37	0 19	28 10
15	7 33 44	23 48 45	14 22	12 15	26 49	0♐35	0 17	0 12	0 34	0 20	28 8
16	7 37 40	24 49 53	26 32	12 48	28 2	1 15	0 11	0 17	0 32	0 21	28 7
17	7 41 37	25 51 1	8♓51	13 11	29 16	1 54	0 6	0 22	0 29	0 21	28 6
18	7 45 34	26 52 8	21 22	13R24	0♓30	2 33	0 0	0 27	0 26	0 22	28 5
19	7 49 30	27 53 14	4♈ 7	13 26	1 43	3 12	29♌55	0 32	0 24	0 22	28 4
20	7 53 27	28 54 19	17 8	13 16	2 57	3 52	29 49	0 37	0 21	0 23	28 2
21	7 57 23	29 55 23	0♉27	12 55	4 10	4 31	29 43	0 41	0 18	0 23	28 1
22	8 1 20	0♒56 26	14 7	12 22	5 23	5 10	29 37	0 46	0 16	0 23	28 0
23	8 5 16	1 57 29	28 10	11 38	6 37	5 50	29 31	0 51	0 13	0 24	27 58
24	8 9 13	2 58 30	12♊34	10 45	7 50	6 29	29 24	0 55	0 11	0 24	27 57
25	8 13 9	3 59 31	27 18	9 43	9 3	7 8	29 18	1 0	0 8	0 24	27 56
26	8 17 6	5 0 30	12♋18	8 34	10 16	7 48	29 11	1 4	0 5	0 25	27 55
27	8 21 3	6 1 29	27 24	7 21	11 29	8 27	29 5	1 8	0 3	0 25	27 53
28	8 24 59	7 2 26	12♌29	6 5	12 42	9 6	28 58	1 13	0 0	0 25	27 52
29	8 28 56	8 3 23	27 22	4 50	13 55	9 46	28 51	1 17	29♋58	0 25	27 50
30	8 32 52	9 4 19	11♍55	3 36	15 8	10 25	28 44	1 21	29 55	0 25	27 49
31	8 36 49	10♒ 5 14	26♍ 1	2♒27	16♓21	11♐ 4	28♌37	1♐25	29♋52	0♏25	27♌48

THE SUN ENTERS THE SIGN OF AQUARIUS ON JAN 21 AT 01:49.

DAY	TIME	☉	☽	☿	♀	♂	♃	♄	♅	♆	♇
	h m s	° ' "	° '	° '	° '	° '	° '	° '	° '	° '	° '
F 1	8 40 45	11♒ 6 8	9♎38	1♒23	17♓34	11♐44	28♌29	1♐29	29♋50	0♏25	27♌46
E 2	8 44 42	12 7 1	22 46	0R26	18 46	12 23	28R22	1 33	29R47	0R25	27R45
B 3	8 48 38	13 7 54	5♏29	29♑37	19 59	13 3	28 15	1 36	29 45	0 25	27 43
R 4	8 52 35	14 8 46	17 49	28 56	21 11	13 42	28 7	1 40	29 42	0 25	27 42
U 5	8 56 32	15 9 37	29 53	28 23	22 24	14 21	28 0	1 43	29 40	0 25	27 40
A 6	9 0 28	16 10 27	11♐46	27 59	23 36	15 1	27 52	1 47	29 37	0 25	27 39
R 7	9 4 25	17 11 16	23 33	27 44	24 48	15 40	27 45	1 50	29 35	0 25	27 38
Y 8	9 8 21	18 12 4	5♑19	27D36	26 1	16 20	27 37	1 54	29 32	0 24	27 36
9	9 12 18	19 12 52	17 9	27 36	27 13	16 59	27 29	1 57	29 30	0 24	27 35
10	9 16 14	20 13 38	29 4	27 43	28 25	17 38	27 21	2 0	29 28	0 24	27 33
11	9 20 11	21 14 22	11♒ 8	27 57	29 37	18 18	27 13	2 3	29 25	0 24	27 32
12	9 24 7	22 15 6	23 22	28 17	0♈49	18 57	27 6	2 6	29 23	0 23	27 30
13	9 28 4	23 15 48	5♓47	28 43	2 0	19 37	26 58	2 9	29 20	0 23	27 29
14	9 32 1	24 16 28	18 23	29 14	3 12	20 16	26 50	2 12	29 18	0 22	27 27
15	9 35 57	25 17 7	1♈10	29 49	4 24	20 55	26 42	2 14	29 16	0 22	27 26
16	9 39 54	26 17 45	14 9	0♒30	5 35	21 35	26 34	2 17	29 14	0 22	27 24
17	9 43 50	27 18 20	27 20	1 14	6 46	22 14	26 26	2 19	29 11	0 21	27 23
18	9 47 47	28 18 54	10♉43	2 2	7 58	22 53	26 18	2 22	29 9	0 20	27 21
19	9 51 43	29 19 26	24 20	2 54	9 9	23 33	26 10	2 24	29 7	0 20	27 20
20	9 55 40	0♓19 57	8♊13	3 49	10 20	24 12	26 2	2 26	29 5	0 19	27 18
21	9 59 36	1 20 25	22 20	4 47	11 31	24 52	25 54	2 28	29 3	0 19	27 17
22	10 3 33	2 20 52	6♋43	5 47	12 41	25 31	25 46	2 30	29 1	0 18	27 15
23	10 7 30	3 21 17	21 19	6 50	13 52	26 10	25 39	2 32	28 59	0 17	27 14
24	10 11 26	4 21 40	6♌ 2	7 56	15 3	26 50	25 31	2 34	28 57	0 17	27 12
25	10 15 23	5 22 1	20 47	9 4	16 13	27 29	25 23	2 36	28 55	0 16	27 11
26	10 19 19	6 22 20	5♍25	10 13	17 23	28 8	25 15	2 37	28 53	0 15	27 9
27	10 23 16	7 22 37	19 48	11 25	18 34	28 48	25 8	2 39	28 51	0 14	27 8
28	10 27 12	8 22 53	3♎51	12 39	19 44	29 27	25 0	2 40	28 49	0 13	27 6
29	10 31 9	9♓23 7	17♎29	13♒54	20♈53	0♑ 6	24♌53	2♐41	28♋47	0♏13	27♌ 5

THE SUN ENTERS THE SIGN OF PISCES ON FEB 19 AT 16:05.

DAY	TIME	☉	☽	☿	♀	♂	♃	♄	♅	♆	♇
	h m s	° ' "	° '	° '	° '	° '	° '	° '	° '	° '	° '
M 1	10 35 5	10♓23 19	0♏40	15♒11	22♈ 3	0♑46	24♌45	2♐42	28♋45	0♏12	27♌ 3
A 2	10 39 2	11 23 30	13 27	16 30	23 13	1 25	24R38	2 44	28R44	0R11	27R 2
R 3	10 42 59	12 23 40	25 51	17 50	24 22	2 4	24 31	2 45	28 42	0 10	27 1
C 4	10 46 55	13 23 48	7♐58	19 11	25 31	2 44	24 24	2 45	28 40	0 9	26 59
H 5	10 50 52	14 23 54	19 53	20 34	26 41	3 23	24 16	2 46	28 39	0 8	26 58
6	10 54 48	15 23 59	1♑42	21 59	27 50	4 2	24 9	2 47	28 37	0 7	26 56
7	10 58 45	16 24 2	13 29	23 24	28 58	4 42	24 3	2 47	28 36	0 6	26 55
8	11 2 41	17 24 4	25 21	24 51	0♉ 7	5 21	23 56	2 48	28 34	0 5	26 54
9	11 6 38	18 24 4	7♒21	26 20	1 16	6 0	23 49	2 48	28 33	0 4	26 52
10	11 10 34	19 24 2	19 33	27 49	2 24	6 40	23 43	2 49	28 31	0 2	26 51
11	11 14 31	20 23 58	1♓59	29 20	3 32	7 19	23 36	2 49	28 30	0 1	26 49
12	11 18 28	21 23 53	14 40	0♓52	4 40	7 58	23 30	2R49	28 29	0 0	26 48
13	11 22 24	22 23 45	27 35	2 25	5 48	8 37	23 24	2 49	28 28	29♎59	26 47
14	11 26 21	23 23 35	10♈44	4 0	6 55	9 17	23 18	2 49	28 26	29 58	26 45
15	11 30 17	24 23 24	24 5	5 35	8 3	9 56	23 12	2 48	28 25	29 56	26 44
16	11 34 14	25 23 10	7♉36	7 12	9 10	10 35	23 6	2 48	28 24	29 55	26 43
17	11 38 10	26 22 54	21 16	8 50	10 17	11 14	23 0	2 48	28 23	29 54	26 42
18	11 42 7	27 22 36	5♊ 5	10 30	11 24	11 53	22 55	2 47	28 22	29 53	26 40
19	11 46 3	28 22 16	19 0	12 10	12 31	12 32	22 49	2 46	28 21	29 51	26 39
20	11 50 0	29 21 54	3♋ 3	13 52	13 37	13 12	22 44	2 46	28 20	29 50	26 38
21	11 53 56	0♈21 29	17 13	15 35	14 43	13 51	22 39	2 45	28 19	29 49	26 37
22	11 57 53	1 21 1	1♌29	17 20	15 49	14 30	22 34	2 44	28 19	29 47	26 35
23	12 1 50	2 20 32	15 47	19 5	16 55	15 9	22 30	2 43	28 18	29 46	26 34
24	12 5 46	3 20 0	0♍ 4	20 52	18 0	15 48	22 25	2 42	28 17	29 44	26 33
25	12 9 43	4 19 26	14 15	22 40	19 5	16 27	22 21	2 41	28 17	29 43	26 32
26	12 13 39	5 18 49	28 16	24 30	20 10	17 6	22 17	2 39	28 16	29 41	26 31
27	12 17 36	6 18 11	12♎ 1	26 21	21 15	17 45	22 12	2 38	28 15	29 40	26 30
28	12 21 32	7 17 30	25 26	28 13	22 19	18 24	22 9	2 36	28 15	29 39	26 29
29	12 25 29	8 16 48	8♏30	0♈ 6	23 23	19 3	22 5	2 35	28 14	29 37	26 28
30	12 29 25	9 16 4	21 13	2 1	24 27	19 42	22 1	2 33	28 14	29 36	26 27
31	12 33 22	10♈15 18	3♐37	3♈57	25♉30	20♑21	21♌58	2♐31	28♋14	29♎34	26♌26

THE SUN ENTERS THE SIGN OF ARIES ON MAR 20 AT 15:21.

♈ ARIES ♉ TAURUS ♊ GEMINI ♋ CANCER ♌ LEO ♍ VIRGO ♎ LIBRA

SIDEREAL SUN. MOON. MERCURY. VENUS. MARS. JUPITER. SATURN. URANUS. NEPTUNE. PLUTO.

DAY	TIME	☉	☽	☿	♀	♂	♃	♄	♅	♆	♇
	h m s	° ' "	° '	° '	° '	° '	° '	° '	° '	° '	° '
A 1	12 37 19	11♈14 30	15♐46	5♈55	26♉33	20♑59	21♌55	2♐29	28♋14	29♎33	26♌25
P 2	12 41 15	12 13 40	27 43	7 53	27 36	21 38	21R52	2R27	28R13	29R31	26R24
R 3	12 45 12	13 12 49	9♑33	9 53	28 39	22 17	21 49	2 25	28 13	29 29	26 23
I 4	12 49 8	14 11 55	21 23	11 54	29 41	22 56	21 46	2 23	28 13	29 28	26 22
L 5	12 53 5	15 11 0	3♒17	13 56	0♊43	23 35	21 44	2 21	28D13	29 26	26 21
6	12 57 1	16 10 3	15 20	15 59	1 44	24 14	21 42	2 19	28 13	29 25	26 20
7	13 0 58	17 9 5	27 36	18 3	2 45	24 52	21 40	2 16	28 13	29 23	26 19
8	13 4 54	18 8 4	10♓ 9	20 8	3 46	25 31	21 38	2 14	28 13	29 22	26 18
9	13 8 51	19 7 2	23 1	22 13	4 47	26 10	21 36	2 11	28 13	29 20	26 18
10	13 12 48	20 5 57	6♈12	24 19	5 47	26 48	21 35	2 8	28 14	29 18	26 17
11	13 16 44	21 4 51	19 41	26 25	6 46	27 27	21 33	2 6	28 14	29 17	26 16
12	13 20 41	22 3 43	3♉25	28 30	7 45	28 5	21 32	2 3	28 14	29 15	26 15
13	13 24 37	23 2 33	17 22	0♉36	8 44	28 44	21 31	2 0	28 15	29 13	26 15
14	13 28 34	24 1 20	1♊28	2 40	9 43	29 22	21 30	1 57	28 15	29 12	26 14
15	13 32 30	25 0 6	15 38	4 43	10 40	0♒ 1	21 30	1 54	28 15	29 10	26 13
16	13 36 27	25 58 49	29 51	6 45	11 38	0 39	21 29	1 51	28 16	29 9	26 13
17	13 40 23	26 57 30	14♋ 3	8 46	12 35	1 17	21D29	1 47	28 17	29 7	26 12
18	13 44 20	27 56 9	28 13	10 44	13 31	1 55	21 29	1 44	28 17	29 5	26 11
19	13 48 17	28 54 46	12♌20	12 40	14 27	2 34	21 29	1 41	28 18	29 4	26 11
20	13 52 13	29 53 20	26 21	14 33	15 22	3 12	21 30	1 37	28 19	29 2	26 10
21	13 56 10	0♉51 52	10♍15	16 23	16 17	3 50	21 30	1 34	28 20	29 0	26 10
22	14 0 6	1 50 22	23 59	18 10	17 11	4 28	21 31	1 30	28 20	28 59	26 9
23	14 4 3	2 48 49	7♎32	19 53	18 4	5 6	21 32	1 27	28 21	28 57	26 9
24	14 7 59	3 47 15	20 51	21 33	18 57	5 44	21 33	1 23	28 22	28 55	26 9
25	14 11 56	4 45 39	3♏55	23 8	19 49	6 22	21 34	1 20	28 23	28 54	26 8
26	14 15 52	5 44 1	16 43	24 40	20 41	7 0	21 36	1 16	28 24	28 52	26 8
27	14 19 49	6 42 21	29 16	26 8	21 32	7 37	21 37	1 12	28 25	28 51	26 8
28	14 23 45	7 40 40	11♐33	27 31	22 22	8 15	21 39	1 8	28 27	28 49	26 7
29	14 27 42	8 38 57	23 39	28 50	23 11	8 53	21 41	1 4	28 28	28 47	26 7
30	14 31 39	9♉37 12	5♑35	0♊ 4	24♊ 0	9♒30	21♌43	1♐ 0	28♋29	28♎46	26♌ 7

THE SUN ENTERS THE SIGN OF TAURUS ON APR 20 AT 02:43.

DAY	TIME	☉	☽	☿	♀	♂	♃	♄	♅	♆	♇
	h m s	° ' "	° '	° '	° '	° '	° '	° '	° '	° '	° '
M 1	14 35 35	10♉35 26	17♑26	1♊14	24♊47	10♒ 8	21♌46	0♐56	28♋30	28♎44	26♌ 7
A 2	14 39 32	11 33 38	29 17	2 19	25 34	10 45	21 48	0R52	28 32	28R43	26R 6
Y 3	14 43 28	12 31 49	11♒11	3 19	26 20	11 23	21 51	0 48	28 33	28 41	26 6
4	14 47 25	13 29 58	23 15	4 14	27 5	12 0	21 54	0 44	28 35	28 39	26 6
5	14 51 21	14 28 6	5♓32	5 5	27 50	12 37	21 57	0 40	28 36	28 38	26 6
6	14 55 18	15 26 12	18 7	5 50	28 33	13 14	22 0	0 35	28 38	28 36	26 6
7	14 59 14	16 24 17	1♈ 2	6 31	29 15	13 51	22 4	0 31	28 39	28 35	26D 6
8	15 3 11	17 22 21	14 21	7 6	29 56	14 28	22 7	0 27	28 41	28 33	26 6
9	15 7 8	18 20 23	28 2	7 36	0♋36	15 5	22 11	0 23	28 43	28 32	26 6
10	15 11 4	19 18 23	12♉ 4	8 2	1 15	15 42	22 15	0 18	28 45	28 30	26 6
11	15 15 1	20 16 22	26 23	8 22	1 53	16 19	22 19	0 14	28 46	28 29	26 6
12	15 18 57	21 14 20	10♊54	8 37	2 30	16 55	22 23	0 10	28 48	28 27	26 6
13	15 22 54	22 12 16	25 31	8 47	3 5	17 32	22 28	0 5	28 50	28 26	26 6
14	15 26 50	23 10 10	10♋ 8	8R52	3 39	18 8	22 32	0 1	28 52	28 24	26 6
15	15 30 47	24 8 2	24 40	8 52	4 12	18 44	22 37	29♏56	28 54	28 23	26 7
16	15 34 43	25 5 53	9♌ 2	8 47	4 43	19 20	22 42	29 52	28 56	28 21	26 7
17	15 38 40	26 3 42	23 12	8 38	5 12	19 57	22 47	29 47	28 58	28 20	26 7
18	15 42 37	27 1 29	7♍ 7	8 24	5 41	20 32	22 52	29 43	29 0	28 18	26 7
19	15 46 33	27 59 14	20 47	8 7	6 7	21 8	22 57	29 38	29 2	28 17	26 8
20	15 50 30	28 56 58	4♎12	7 45	6 32	21 44	23 3	29 34	29 5	28 16	26 8
21	15 54 26	29 54 40	17 22	7 20	6 55	22 19	23 8	29 29	29 7	28 14	26 8
22	15 58 23	0♊52 21	0♏18	6 53	7 17	22 55	23 14	29 25	29 9	28 13	26 9
23	16 2 19	1 50 0	13 0	6 23	7 36	23 30	23 20	29 21	29 12	28 12	26 9
24	16 6 16	2 47 38	25 29	5 51	7 54	24 5	23 26	29 16	29 14	28 10	26 10
25	16 10 12	3 45 14	7♐47	5 17	8 10	24 40	23 32	29 12	29 16	28 9	26 10
26	16 14 9	4 42 50	19 54	4 44	8 24	25 15	23 39	29 7	29 19	28 8	26 11
27	16 18 6	5 40 24	1♑54	4 10	8 35	25 50	23 45	29 3	29 21	28 7	26 11
28	16 22 2	6 37 57	13 47	3 36	8 45	26 25	23 52	28 58	29 24	28 6	26 12
29	16 25 59	7 35 30	25 38	3 3	8 52	26 59	23 59	28 54	29 26	28 4	26 12
30	16 29 55	8 33 1	7♒28	2 33	8 58	27 34	24 5	28 50	29 29	28 3	26 13
31	16 33 52	9♊30 31	19♒23	2♊ 4	9♋ 0	28♒ 8	24♌13	28♏45	29♋32	28♎ 2	26♌14

THE SUN ENTERS THE SIGN OF GEMINI ON MAY 21 AT 02:13.

DAY	TIME	☉	☽	☿	♀	♂	♃	♄	♅	♆	♇
	h m s	° ' "	° '	° '	° '	° '	° '	° '	° '	° '	° '
J 1	16 37 48	10♊28 1	1♓26	1♊38	9♋ 1	28♒42	24♌20	28♏41	29♋34	28♎ 1	26♌14
U 2	16 41 45	11 25 30	13 42	1R14	8R59	29 15	24 27	28R36	29 37	28R 0	26 15
N 3	16 45 41	12 22 58	26 14	0 55	8 55	29 49	24 34	28 32	29 40	27 59	26 16
E 4	16 49 38	13 20 25	9♈ 7	0 38	8 49	0♓22	24 42	28 28	29 42	27 58	26 17
5	16 53 35	14 17 52	22 25	0 26	8 40	0 56	24 50	28 24	29 45	27 57	26 17
6	16 57 31	15 15 18	6♉ 8	0 18	8 28	1 29	24 57	28 19	29 48	27 56	26 18
7	17 1 28	16 12 43	20 16	0D14	8 15	2 2	25 5	28 15	29 51	27 55	26 19
8	17 5 24	17 10 8	4♊47	0 15	7 59	2 34	25 13	28 11	29 54	27 54	26 20
9	17 9 21	18 7 32	19 35	0 20	7 40	3 7	25 22	28 7	29 57	27 53	26 21
10	17 13 17	19 4 55	4♋34	0 30	7 20	3 39	25 30	28 3	0♌ 0	27 52	26 22
11	17 17 14	20 2 18	19 35	0 44	6 57	4 11	25 38	27 59	0 3	27 51	26 23
12	17 21 11	20 59 39	4♌29	1 2	6 32	4 42	25 47	27 55	0 6	27 50	26 24
13	17 25 7	21 57 0	19 10	1 26	6 5	5 14	25 55	27 51	0 9	27 49	26 25
14	17 29 4	22 54 19	3♍31	1 53	5 36	5 45	26 4	27 47	0 12	27 49	26 26
15	17 33 0	23 51 38	17 31	2 25	5 5	6 16	26 13	27 44	0 15	27 48	26 27
16	17 36 57	24 48 55	1♎ 8	3 1	4 33	6 47	26 22	27 40	0 18	27 47	26 28
17	17 40 53	25 46 12	14 23	3 42	3 59	7 17	26 31	27 36	0 21	27 46	26 29
18	17 44 50	26 43 28	27 19	4 26	3 24	7 47	26 40	27 33	0 25	27 46	26 30
19	17 48 46	27 40 43	9♏58	5 15	2 48	8 17	26 49	27 29	0 28	27 45	26 31
20	17 52 43	28 37 58	22 23	6 8	2 12	8 47	26 59	27 26	0 31	27 45	26 32
21	17 56 40	29 35 11	4♐36	7 4	1 34	9 16	27 8	27 22	0 34	27 44	26 33
22	18 0 36	0♋32 25	16 41	8 5	0 57	9 45	27 18	27 19	0 38	27 43	26 35
23	18 4 33	1 29 38	28 39	9 9	0 19	10 14	27 27	27 15	0 41	27 43	26 36
24	18 8 29	2 26 50	10♑32	10 17	29♊42	10 42	27 37	27 12	0 44	27 42	26 37
25	18 12 26	3 24 3	22 23	11 29	29 4	11 10	27 47	27 9	0 48	27 42	26 38
26	18 16 22	4 21 15	4♒14	12 45	28 28	11 38	27 57	27 6	0 51	27 41	26 40
27	18 20 19	5 18 27	16 6	14 4	27 53	12 5	28 7	27 3	0 54	27 41	26 41
28	18 24 15	6 15 38	28 3	15 26	27 18	12 32	28 17	27 0	0 58	27 41	26 42
29	18 28 12	7 12 50	10♓ 7	16 53	26 45	12 59	28 27	26 57	1 1	27 40	26 44
30	18 32 9	8♋10 2	22♓22	18♊22	26♊13	13♓25	28♌37	26♏54	1♌ 5	27♎40	26♌45

THE SUN ENTERS THE SIGN OF CANCER ON JUN 21 AT 10:24.

♏ SCORPIO ♐ SAGITTARIUS ♑ CAPRICORN ♒ AQUARIUS ♓ PISCES

1956

SIDEREAL. SUN. MOON. MERCURY. VENUS. MARS. JUPITER. SATURN. URANUS. NEPTUNE. PLUTO.

DAY	TIME	☉	☽	☿	♀	♂	♃	♄	♅	♆	♇
	h m s	° ' "	° '	° '	° '	° '	° '	° '	° '	° '	° '
J 1	18 36 5	9♋ 7 14	4♈52	19♊56	25♊43	13♓51	28♌48	26♏51	1♌ 8	27♎40	26♌46
U 2	18 40 2	10 4 26	17 41	21 32	25R15	14 17	28 58	26R49	1 12	27R40	26 48
L 3	18 43 58	11 1 39	0♉52	23 12	24 49	14 42	29 9	26 46	1 15	27 39	26 49
Y 4	18 47 55	11 58 51	14 29	24 55	24 25	15 7	29 19	26 44	1 19	27 39	26 51
5	18 51 51	12 56 4	28 33	26 42	24 3	15 31	29 30	26 41	1 22	27 39	26 52
6	18 55 48	13 53 18	13♊ 2	28 31	23 43	15 55	29 41	26 39	1 26	27 39	26 54
7	18 59 44	14 50 31	27 54	0♋23	23 26	16 18	29 51	26 37	1 29	27 39	26 55
8	19 3 41	15 47 45	13♋ 2	2 18	23 11	16 41	0♍ 2	26 35	1 33	27 39	26 57
9	19 7 38	16 44 59	28 17	4 16	22 58	17 3	0 13	26 32	1 36	27D39	26 58
10	19 11 34	17 42 13	13♌28	6 16	22 48	17 25	0 24	26 30	1 40	27 39	27 0
11	19 15 31	18 39 26	28 25	8 18	22 40	17 47	0 35	26 29	1 44	27 39	27 2
12	19 19 27	19 36 40	13♍ 0	10 22	22 34	18 8	0 47	26 27	1 47	27 39	27 3
13	19 23 24	20 33 54	27 10	12 27	22D31	18 28	0 58	26 25	1 51	27 39	27 5
14	19 27 20	21 31 8	10♎51	14 34	22 30	18 48	1 9	26 23	1 55	27 39	27 6
15	19 31 17	22 28 22	24 6	16 42	22 32	19 7	1 21	26 22	1 58	27 39	27 8
16	19 35 13	23 25 36	6♏56	18 50	22 35	19 26	1 32	26 20	2 2	27 39	27 10
17	19 39 10	24 22 50	19 27	20 58	22 41	19 44	1 43	26 19	2 6	27 40	27 11
18	19 43 7	25 20 4	1♐42	23 7	22 49	20 2	1 55	26 18	2 9	27 40	27 13
19	19 47 3	26 17 19	13 46	25 15	22 59	20 19	2 7	26 17	2 13	27 40	27 15
20	19 51 0	27 14 34	25 42	27 23	23 12	20 35	2 18	26 16	2 17	27 41	27 17
21	19 54 56	28 11 49	7♑34	29 30	23 26	20 51	2 30	26 15	2 20	27 41	27 18
22	19 58 53	29 9 5	19 24	1♌37	23 42	21 6	2 42	26 14	2 24	27 41	27 20
23	20 2 49	0♌ 6 21	1♒15	3 42	24 0	21 21	2 54	26 13	2 28	27 42	27 22
24	20 6 46	1 3 37	13 8	5 46	24 20	21 35	3 6	26 12	2 31	27 42	27 24
25	20 10 42	2 0 55	25 4	7 49	24 42	21 48	3 18	26 12	2 35	27 43	27 25
26	20 14 39	2 58 13	7♓ 7	9 50	25 5	22 1	3 30	26 11	2 39	27 43	27 27
27	20 18 36	3 55 32	19 17	11 50	25 30	22 13	3 42	26 11	2 42	27 44	27 29
28	20 22 32	4 52 52	1♈36	13 48	25 57	22 24	3 54	26 10	2 46	27 44	27 31
29	20 26 29	5 50 13	14 8	15 45	26 25	22 34	4 6	26 10	2 50	27 45	27 33
30	20 30 25	6 47 35	26 56	17 40	26 55	22 44	4 18	26D10	2 53	27 46	27 35
31	20 34 22	7♌44 58	10♉ 2	19♌34	27♊26	22♓53	4♍30	26♏10	2♌57	27♎46	27♌36

THE SUN ENTERS THE SIGN OF LEO ON JUL 22 AT 21:20.

DAY	TIME	☉	☽	☿	♀	♂	♃	♄	♅	♆	♇
	h m s	° ' "	° '	° '	° '	° '	° '	° '	° '	° '	° '
A 1	20 38 18	8♌42 22	23♉32	21♌26	27♊59	23♓ 1	4♍42	26♏10	3♌ 1	27♎47	27♌38
U 2	20 42 15	9 39 48	7♊25	23 16	28 33	23 9	4 55	26 10	3 4	27 48	27 40
G 3	20 46 11	10 37 14	21 44	25 5	29 8	23 15	5 7	26 10	3 8	27 48	27 42
U 4	20 50 8	11 34 42	6♋27	26 52	29 45	23 21	5 20	26 11	3 12	27 49	27 44
S 5	20 54 5	12 32 11	21 29	28 37	0♋22	23 26	5 32	26 11	3 15	27 50	27 46
T 6	20 58 1	13 29 41	6♌42	0♍21	1 1	23 30	5 44	26 12	3 19	27 51	27 48
7	21 1 58	14 27 12	21 55	2 3	1 41	23 34	5 57	26 13	3 23	27 52	27 50
8	21 5 54	15 24 45	6♍58	3 44	2 22	23 36	6 9	26 13	3 26	27 53	27 52
9	21 9 51	16 22 17	21 42	5 23	3 4	23 38	6 22	26 14	3 30	27 54	27 53
10	21 13 47	17 19 51	5♎59	7 1	3 47	23R39	6 35	26 15	3 34	27 55	27 55
11	21 17 44	18 17 26	19 47	8 37	4 31	23 39	6 47	26 16	3 37	27 56	27 57
12	21 21 40	19 15 2	3♏ 6	10 11	5 15	23 39	7 0	26 17	3 41	27 57	27 59
13	21 25 37	20 12 39	15 58	11 44	6 1	23 37	7 13	26 18	3 44	27 58	28 1
14	21 29 34	21 10 16	28 27	13 15	6 48	23 35	7 25	26 20	3 48	27 59	28 3
15	21 33 30	22 7 55	10♐40	14 45	7 35	23 32	7 38	26 21	3 52	28 0	28 5
16	21 37 27	23 5 35	22 40	16 13	8 23	23 28	7 51	26 23	3 55	28 1	28 7
17	21 41 23	24 3 15	4♑33	17 39	9 12	23 23	8 4	26 24	3 59	28 2	28 9
18	21 45 20	25 0 57	16 22	19 4	10 1	23 18	8 16	26 26	4 2	28 4	28 11
19	21 49 16	25 58 40	28 12	20 28	10 52	23 12	8 29	26 28	4 6	28 5	28 13
20	21 53 13	26 56 24	10♒ 5	21 49	11 43	23 5	8 42	26 30	4 9	28 6	28 15
21	21 57 9	27 54 10	22 4	23 9	12 34	22 57	8 55	26 32	4 13	28 7	28 17
22	22 1 6	28 51 57	4♓ 9	24 27	13 26	22 48	9 8	26 34	4 16	28 9	28 19
23	22 5 3	29 49 45	16 21	25 44	14 19	22 39	9 21	26 36	4 19	28 10	28 21
24	22 8 59	0♍47 35	28 42	26 58	15 13	22 29	9 34	26 38	4 23	28 11	28 23
25	22 12 56	1 45 26	11♈13	28 11	16 7	22 19	9 47	26 41	4 26	28 13	28 25
26	22 16 52	2 43 19	23 54	29 21	17 2	22 7	9 59	26 43	4 30	28 14	28 27
27	22 20 49	3 41 14	6♉48	0♎30	17 57	21 56	10 12	26 46	4 33	28 16	28 29
28	22 24 45	4 39 11	19 57	1 36	18 53	21 43	10 25	26 48	4 36	28 17	28 30
29	22 28 42	5 37 9	3♊23	2 40	19 49	21 30	10 38	26 51	4 40	28 19	28 32
30	22 32 38	6 35 10	17 9	3 42	20 46	21 17	10 51	26 54	4 43	28 20	28 34
31	22 36 35	7♍33 13	1♋16	4♎41	21♋43	21♓ 3	11♍ 4	26♏57	4♌46	28♎22	28♌36

THE SUN ENTERS THE SIGN OF VIRGO ON AUG 23 AT 04:16.

DAY	TIME	☉	☽	☿	♀	♂	♃	♄	♅	♆	♇
	h m s	° ' "	° '	° '	° '	° '	° '	° '	° '	° '	° '
S 1	22 40 32	8♍31 17	15♋44	5♎37	22♋41	20♓48	11♍17	27♏ 0	4♌49	28♎23	28♌38
E 2	22 44 28	9 29 23	0♌28	6 31	23 39	20R33	11 30	27 3	4 53	28 25	28 40
P 3	22 48 25	10 27 32	15 25	7 22	24 37	20 18	11 43	27 6	4 56	28 27	28 42
T 4	22 52 21	11 25 42	0♍24	8 9	25 36	20 2	11 56	27 9	4 59	28 28	28 44
E 5	22 56 18	12 23 53	15 18	8 53	26 36	19 46	12 9	27 13	5 2	28 30	28 46
M 6	23 0 14	13 22 7	29 57	9 34	27 35	19 30	12 22	27 16	5 5	28 32	28 48
B 7	23 4 11	14 20 22	14♎13	10 10	28 36	19 14	12 35	27 19	5 8	28 33	28 50
E 8	23 8 7	15 18 38	28 3	10 42	29 36	18 57	12 48	27 23	5 11	28 35	28 52
R 9	23 12 4	16 16 57	11♏25	11 10	0♌37	18 41	13 1	27 27	5 14	28 37	28 54
10	23 16 0	17 15 17	24 20	11 33	1 38	18 24	13 14	27 30	5 17	28 39	28 55
11	23 19 57	18 13 38	6♐52	11 51	2 40	18 7	13 27	27 34	5 20	28 40	28 57
12	23 23 54	19 12 1	19 6	12 3	3 42	17 51	13 40	27 38	5 23	28 42	28 59
13	23 27 50	20 10 26	1♑ 7	12R10	4 44	17 34	13 53	27 42	5 26	28 44	29 1
14	23 31 47	21 8 52	13 0	12 11	5 47	17 18	14 6	27 46	5 29	28 46	29 3
15	23 35 43	22 7 20	24 50	12 5	6 50	17 2	14 19	27 50	5 32	28 48	29 5
16	23 39 40	23 5 49	6♒42	11 52	7 53	16 46	14 32	27 55	5 34	28 50	29 7
17	23 43 36	24 4 20	18 39	11 33	8 56	16 31	14 45	27 59	5 37	28 51	29 8
18	23 47 33	25 2 53	0♓44	11 6	10 0	16 16	14 58	28 3	5 40	28 53	29 10
19	23 51 29	26 1 28	12 58	10 33	11 4	16 1	15 11	28 8	5 43	28 55	29 12
20	23 55 26	27 0 5	25 24	9 53	12 8	15 46	15 24	28 12	5 45	28 57	29 14
21	23 59 23	27 58 43	8♈ 1	9 6	13 13	15 33	15 37	28 17	5 48	28 59	29 16
22	0 3 19	28 57 23	20 49	8 14	14 18	15 19	15 50	28 21	5 50	29 1	29 17
23	0 7 16	29 56 6	3♉48	7 16	15 23	15 6	16 2	28 26	5 53	29 3	29 19
24	0 11 12	0♎54 51	16 58	6 14	16 28	14 54	16 15	28 31	5 55	29 5	29 21
25	0 15 9	1 53 38	0♊19	5 9	17 34	14 42	16 28	28 36	5 58	29 7	29 23
26	0 19 5	2 52 27	13 54	4 2	18 40	14 31	16 41	28 41	6 0	29 9	29 24
27	0 23 2	3 51 19	27 41	2 56	19 46	14 20	16 53	28 46	6 3	29 11	29 26
28	0 26 58	4 50 13	11♋41	1 51	20 52	14 10	17 6	28 51	6 5	29 13	29 28
29	0 30 55	5 49 9	25 55	0 50	21 59	14 1	17 19	28 56	6 7	29 16	29 29
30	0 34 52	6♎48 7	10♌20	29♍54	23♌ 6	13♓53	17♍31	29♏ 1	6♌ 9	29♎18	29♌31

THE SUN ENTERS THE SIGN OF LIBRA ON SEP 23 AT 01:36.

♈ ARIES ♉ TAURUS ♊ GEMINI ♋ CANCER ♌ LEO ♍ VIRGO ♎ LIBRA

1956

SIDEREAL   SUN.   MOON.   MERCURY.   VENUS.   MARS.   JUPITER.   SATURN.   URANUS.   NEPTUNE.   PLUTO.

DAY	TIME	☉	☽	☿	♀	♂	♃	♄	♅	♆	♇
	h m s	° ' "	° '	° '	° '	° '	° '	° '	° '	° '	° '
O 1	Ø 38 48	7♎47 8	24♌53	29♍ 5	24♌13	13♓45	17♍44	29♏ 6	6♌12	29♎2Ø	29♌32
C 2	Ø 42 45	8 46 11	9♍28	28R24	25 2Ø	13R38	17 57	29 12	6 14	29 22	29 34
T 3	Ø 46 41	9 45 16	23 59	27 52	26 27	13 31	18 9	29 17	6 16	29 24	29 36
O 4	Ø 5Ø 38	1Ø 44 24	8♎19	27 3Ø	27 35	13 26	18 22	29 22	6 18	29 26	29 37
B 5	Ø 54 34	11 43 33	22 21	27D18	28 43	13 21	18 34	29 28	6 2Ø	29 28	29 39
E 6	Ø 58 31	12 42 44	6♏ 2	27 17	29 51	13 17	18 47	29 34	6 22	29 3Ø	29 4Ø
R 7	1 2 27	13 41 57	19 2Ø	27 27	Ø♍59	13 14	18 59	29 39	6 24	29 33	29 42
8	1 6 24	14 41 13	2♐15	27 47	2 7	13 11	19 11	29 45	6 26	29 35	29 43
9	1 1Ø 21	15 4Ø 3Ø	14 48	28 17	3 16	13 1Ø	19 24	29 51	6 28	29 37	29 45
1Ø	1 14 17	16 39 49	27 4	28 56	4 25	13D 9	19 36	29 56	6 29	29 39	29 46
11	1 18 14	17 39 9	9♑ 7	29 43	5 33	13 9	19 48	Ø♐ 2	6 31	29 41	29 48
12	1 22 1Ø	18 38 32	21 2	Ø♎39	6 42	13 1Ø	2Ø Ø	Ø 8	6 33	29 44	29 49
13	1 26 7	19 37 56	2♒53	1 42	7 52	13 12	2Ø 12	Ø 14	6 34	29 46	29 51
14	1 3Ø 3	2Ø 37 22	14 46	2 51	9 1	13 14	2Ø 24	Ø 2Ø	6 36	29 48	29 52
15	1 34 Ø	21 36 49	26 46	4 6	1Ø 1Ø	13 17	2Ø 37	Ø 26	6 38	29 5Ø	29 53
16	1 37 56	22 36 19	8♓56	5 25	11 2Ø	13 22	2Ø 48	Ø 32	6 39	29 52	29 55
17	1 41 53	23 35 5Ø	21 18	6 49	12 3Ø	13 26	21 Ø	Ø 38	6 4Ø	29 55	29 56
18	1 45 49	24 35 23	3♈55	8 16	13 4Ø	13 32	21 12	Ø 44	6 42	29 57	29 57
19	1 49 46	25 34 58	16 48	9 46	14 5Ø	13 38	21 24	Ø 51	6 43	29 59	29 58
2Ø	1 53 43	26 34 36	29 56	11 19	16 Ø	13 45	21 36	Ø 57	6 45	Ø♏ 1	Ø♍ Ø
21	1 57 39	27 34 15	13♉18	12 53	17 1Ø	13 53	21 48	1 3	6 46	Ø 4	Ø 1
22	2 1 36	28 33 56	26 52	14 3Ø	18 21	14 2	21 59	1 9	6 47	Ø 6	Ø 2
23	2 5 32	29 33 39	1Ø♊38	16 7	19 32	14 11	22 11	1 16	6 48	Ø 8	Ø 3
24	2 9 29	Ø♏33 25	24 31	17 46	2Ø 42	14 21	22 22	1 22	6 49	Ø 1Ø	Ø 4
25	2 13 25	1 33 13	8♋33	19 25	21 53	14 31	22 34	1 29	6 5Ø	Ø 13	Ø 6
26	2 17 22	2 33 3	22 39	21 5	23 4	14 43	22 45	1 35	6 51	Ø 15	Ø 7
27	2 21 18	3 32 55	6♌49	22 45	24 15	14 55	22 56	1 42	6 52	Ø 17	Ø 8
28	2 25 15	4 32 5Ø	21 2	24 25	25 27	15 7	23 8	1 48	6 53	Ø 19	Ø 9
29	2 29 12	5 32 47	5♍13	26 5	26 38	15 2Ø	23 19	1 55	6 54	Ø 22	Ø 1Ø
3Ø	2 33 8	6 32 45	19 22	27 45	27 5Ø	15 34	23 3Ø	2 2	6 55	Ø 24	Ø 11
31	2 37 5	7♏32 46	3♎24	29♎25	29♍ 1	15♓49	23♍41	2♐ 8	6♌55	Ø♏26	Ø♍12

THE SUN ENTERS THE SIGN OF SCORPIO ON OCT 23 AT 10:35.

DAY	TIME	☉	☽	☿	♀	♂	♃	♄	♅	♆	♇
	h m s	° ' "	° '	° '	° '	° '	° '	° '	° '	° '	° '
N 1	2 41 1	8♏32 49	17♎15	1♏ 5	Ø♎13	16♓ 4	23♍52	2♐15	6♌56	Ø♏28	Ø♍13
O 2	2 44 58	9 32 54	Ø♏54	2 45	1 25	16 19	24 3	2 22	6 56	Ø 3Ø	Ø 14
V 3	2 48 54	1Ø 33 1	14 16	4 24	2 37	16 36	24 13	2 28	6 57	Ø 33	Ø 14
E 4	2 52 51	11 33 1Ø	27 21	6 3	3 49	16 53	24 24	2 35	6 58	Ø 35	Ø 15
M 5	2 56 47	12 33 21	1Ø♐ 7	7 42	5 1	17 1Ø	24 35	2 42	6 58	Ø 37	Ø 16
B 6	3 Ø 44	13 33 33	22 37	9 2Ø	6 13	17 28	24 45	2 49	6 58	Ø 39	Ø 17
E 7	3 4 41	14 33 47	4♑52	1Ø 58	7 25	17 46	24 56	2 56	6 59	Ø 42	Ø 18
R 8	3 8 37	15 34 3	16 55	12 36	8 38	18 5	25 6	3 3	6 59	Ø 44	Ø 18
9	3 12 34	16 34 2Ø	28 51	14 13	9 5Ø	18 25	25 16	3 1Ø	6 59	Ø 46	Ø 19
1Ø	3 16 3Ø	17 34 38	1Ø♒43	15 5Ø	11 3	18 45	25 27	3 17	6 59	Ø 48	Ø 2Ø
11	3 2Ø 27	18 34 58	22 36	17 27	12 15	19 6	25 37	3 23	6 59	Ø 5Ø	Ø 2Ø
12	3 24 23	19 35 19	4♓35	19 3	13 28	19 27	25 47	3 3Ø	6R59	Ø 52	Ø 21
13	3 28 2Ø	2Ø 35 42	16 45	2Ø 39	14 41	19 48	25 57	3 37	6 59	Ø 55	Ø 22
14	3 32 16	21 36 6	29 9	22 15	15 54	2Ø 1Ø	26 6	3 44	6 59	Ø 57	Ø 22
15	3 36 13	22 36 31	11♈52	23 5Ø	17 7	2Ø 33	26 16	3 51	6 59	Ø 59	Ø 23
16	3 4Ø 1Ø	23 36 58	24 54	25 25	18 2Ø	2Ø 55	26 26	3 59	6 59	1 1	Ø 23
17	3 44 6	24 37 27	8♉17	27 Ø	19 33	21 19	26 35	4 6	6 59	1 3	Ø 24
18	3 48 3	25 37 56	22 Ø	28 35	2Ø 46	21 42	26 44	4 13	6 59	1 5	Ø 24
19	3 51 59	26 38 28	6♊ 1	Ø♐ 9	21 59	22 6	26 54	4 2Ø	6 58	1 7	Ø 25
2Ø	3 55 56	27 39 1	2Ø 15	1 43	23 12	22 31	27 3	4 27	6 58	1 9	Ø 25
21	3 59 52	28 39 35	4♋37	3 17	24 26	22 55	27 12	4 34	6 57	1 11	Ø 25
22	4 3 49	29 4Ø 12	19 4	4 51	25 39	23 2Ø	27 21	4 41	6 57	1 13	Ø 26
23	4 7 45	Ø♐4Ø 5Ø	3♌3Ø	6 24	26 53	23 46	27 3Ø	4 48	6 56	1 15	Ø 26
24	4 11 42	1 41 29	17 5Ø	7 58	28 6	24 12	27 38	4 55	6 56	1 17	Ø 26
25	4 15 39	2 42 1Ø	2♍ 2	9 31	29 2Ø	24 38	27 47	5 2	6 55	1 19	Ø 27
26	4 19 35	3 42 53	16 4	11 4	Ø♏34	25 4	27 56	5 9	6 54	1 21	Ø 27
27	4 23 32	4 43 38	29 53	12 37	1 47	25 31	28 4	5 17	6 54	1 23	Ø 27
28	4 27 28	5 44 24	13♎31	14 1Ø	3 1	25 58	28 12	5 24	6 53	1 25	Ø 27
29	4 31 25	6 45 11	26 55	15 43	4 15	26 26	28 2Ø	5 31	6 52	1 27	Ø 27
3Ø	4 35 21	7♐46 Ø	1Ø♏ 6	17♐16	5♏29	26♓53	28♍28	5♐38	6♌51	1♏29	Ø♍27

THE SUN ENTERS THE SIGN OF SAGITTARIUS ON NOV 22 AT 07:51.

DAY	TIME	☉	☽	☿	♀	♂	♃	♄	♅	♆	♇
	h m s	° ' "	° '	° '	° '	° '	° '	° '	° '	° '	° '
D 1	4 39 18	8♐46 51	23♏ 4	18♐48	6♏43	27♓22	28♍36	5♐45	6♌5Ø	1♏31	Ø♍27
E 2	4 43 14	9 47 42	5♐49	2Ø 21	7 57	27 5Ø	28 44	5 52	6R49	1 33	ØR27
C 3	4 47 11	1Ø 48 35	18 22	21 53	9 11	28 18	28 51	5 59	6 48	1 35	Ø 27
E 4	4 51 8	11 49 29	Ø♑43	23 25	1Ø 25	28 47	28 59	6 6	6 47	1 36	Ø 27
M 5	4 55 4	12 5Ø 24	12 53	24 57	11 39	29 17	29 6	6 13	6 46	1 38	Ø 27
B 6	4 59 1	13 51 2Ø	24 53	26 29	12 53	29 46	29 13	6 21	6 44	1 4Ø	Ø 27
E 7	5 2 57	14 52 16	6♒48	28 1	14 8	Ø♈16	29 2Ø	6 28	6 43	1 42	Ø 27
R 8	5 6 54	15 53 13	18 39	29 33	15 22	Ø 46	29 27	6 35	6 42	1 44	Ø 27
9	5 1Ø 5Ø	16 54 11	Ø♓31	1♑ 4	16 36	1 16	29 34	6 42	6 4Ø	1 45	Ø 27
1Ø	5 14 47	17 55 1Ø	12 28	2 35	17 5Ø	1 46	29 41	6 49	6 39	1 47	Ø 26
11	5 18 43	18 56 9	24 34	4 5	19 5	2 17	29 47	6 56	6 37	1 49	Ø 26
12	5 22 4Ø	19 57 9	6♈55	5 35	2Ø 19	2 47	29 53	7 3	6 36	1 5Ø	Ø 26
13	5 26 37	2Ø 58 9	19 34	7 5	21 34	3 19	29 59	7 1Ø	6 34	1 52	Ø 26
14	5 3Ø 33	21 59 1Ø	2♉36	8 34	22 48	3 5Ø	Ø♎ 5	7 17	6 33	1 53	Ø 25
15	5 34 3Ø	23 Ø 12	16 3	1Ø 1	24 2	4 21	Ø 11	7 24	6 31	1 55	Ø 25
16	5 38 26	24 1 14	29 56	11 28	25 17	4 53	Ø 17	7 31	6 29	1 57	Ø 24
17	5 42 23	25 2 16	14♊13	12 54	26 31	5 25	Ø 22	7 38	6 28	1 58	Ø 24
18	5 46 19	26 3 19	28 51	14 18	27 46	5 57	Ø 28	7 45	6 26	2 Ø	Ø 24
19	5 5Ø 16	27 4 23	13♋42	15 41	29 1	6 29	Ø 33	7 51	6 24	2 1	Ø 23
2Ø	5 54 13	28 5 27	28 38	17 2	Ø♐15	7 1	Ø 38	7 58	6 22	2 3	Ø 23
21	5 58 9	29 6 32	13♌31	18 2Ø	1 3Ø	7 34	Ø 43	8 5	6 2Ø	2 4	Ø 22
22	6 2 6	Ø♑ 7 38	28 13	19 36	2 44	8 6	Ø 48	8 12	6 18	2 5	Ø 21
23	6 6 2	1 8 45	12♍39	2Ø 48	3 59	8 39	Ø 52	8 19	6 16	2 7	Ø 21
24	6 9 59	2 9 52	26 44	21 57	5 14	9 12	Ø 57	8 25	6 14	2 8	Ø 2Ø
25	6 13 55	3 1Ø 59	1Ø♎28	23 1	6 29	9 45	1 1	8 32	6 12	2 9	Ø 2Ø
26	6 17 52	4 12 8	23 53	24 Ø	7 43	1Ø 18	1 5	8 39	6 1Ø	2 11	Ø 19
27	6 21 48	5 13 17	6♏59	24 54	8 58	1Ø 52	1 9	8 45	6 8	2 12	Ø 18
28	6 25 45	6 14 26	19 49	25 4Ø	1Ø 13	11 25	1 13	8 52	6 6	2 13	Ø 17
29	6 29 42	7 15 36	2♐26	26 2Ø	11 28	11 59	1 16	8 59	6 4	2 14	Ø 17
3Ø	6 33 38	8 16 47	14 52	26 51	12 43	12 33	1 19	9 5	6 2	2 16	Ø 16
31	6 37 35	9♑17 57	27♐ 9	27♑12	13♐57	13♈ 7	1♎23	9♐12	6♌ Ø	2♏17	Ø♍15

THE SUN ENTERS THE SIGN OF CAPRICORN ON DEC 21 AT 21:00.

♏ SCORPIO ♐ SAGITTARIUS ♑ CAPRICORN ♒ AQUARIUS ♓ PISCES

SIDEREAL SUN. MOON. MERCURY. VENUS. MARS. JUPITER. SATURN. URANUS. NEPTUNE. PLUTO.

DAY	TIME	☉	☽	☿	♀	♂	♃	♄	♅	♆	♇
	h m s	° ' "	° '	° '	° '	° '	° '	° '	° '	° '	° '
J 1	6 41 31	10♑19 8	9♑17	27♑24	15♐12	13♈41	1♎26	9♐18	5♌57	2♏18	0♍14
A 2	6 45 28	11 20 19	21 19	27R25	16 27	14 15	1 28	9 25	5R55	2 19	0R13
N 3	6 49 24	12 21 30	3♒16	27 14	17 42	14 50	1 31	9 31	5 53	2 20	0 13
U 4	6 53 21	13 22 41	15 9	26 51	18 57	15 24	1 33	9 37	5 50	2 21	0 12
A 5	6 57 17	14 23 51	27 0	26 16	20 12	15 59	1 36	9 44	5 48	2 22	0 11
R 6	7 1 14	15 25 1	8♓51	25 31	21 27	16 33	1 38	9 50	5 46	2 23	0 10
Y 7	7 5 11	16 26 11	20 47	24 34	22 42	17 8	1 40	9 56	5 43	2 24	0 9
8	7 9 7	17 27 20	2♈50	23 29	23 57	17 43	1 41	10 2	5 41	2 25	0 8
9	7 13 4	18 28 29	15 6	22 16	25 11	18 18	1 43	10 8	5 38	2 26	0 7
10	7 17 0	19 29 38	27 38	20 59	26 26	18 53	1 44	10 14	5 36	2 26	0 6
11	7 20 57	20 30 46	10♉33	19 39	27 41	19 28	1 45	10 20	5 33	2 27	0 5
12	7 24 53	21 31 53	23 53	18 20	28 56	20 4	1 46	10 26	5 31	2 28	0 4
13	7 28 50	22 33 0	7♊42	17 3	0♑11	20 39	1 47	10 32	5 28	2 29	0 2
14	7 32 46	23 34 6	22 0	15 51	1 26	21 14	1 47	10 38	5 26	2 29	0 1
15	7 36 43	24 35 12	6♋45	14 45	2 41	21 50	1 48	10 44	5 23	2 30	0 0
16	7 40 40	25 36 17	21 50	13 48	3 56	22 26	1R48	10 50	5 21	2 31	29♌59
17	7 44 36	26 37 22	7♌ 7	12 59	5 11	23 1	1 48	10 55	5 18	2 31	29 58
18	7 48 33	27 38 26	22 23	12 20	6 26	23 37	1 48	11 1	5 15	2 32	29 57
19	7 52 29	28 39 29	7♍28	11 50	7 41	24 13	1 47	11 7	5 13	2 32	29 55
20	7 56 26	29 40 32	22 14	11 30	8 56	24 49	1 47	11 12	5 10	2 33	29 54
21	8 0 22	0♒41 35	6♎33	11D18	10 11	25 25	1 46	11 17	5 8	2 33	29 53
22	8 4 19	1 42 37	20 25	11 16	11 26	26 1	1 45	11 23	5 5	2 34	29 52
23	8 8 15	2 43 39	3♏51	11 21	12 41	26 37	1 44	11 28	5 2	2 34	29 50
24	8 12 12	3 44 40	16 52	11 34	13 56	27 13	1 42	11 33	5 0	2 34	29 49
25	8 16 9	4 45 41	29 33	11 53	15 11	27 49	1 41	11 39	4 57	2 35	29 48
26	8 20 5	5 46 42	11♐58	12 19	16 26	28 25	1 39	11 44	4 55	2 35	29 46
27	8 24 2	6 47 42	24 11	12 51	17 41	29 2	1 37	11 49	4 52	2 35	29 45
28	8 27 58	7 48 41	6♑15	13 28	18 56	29 38	1 35	11 54	4 49	2 35	29 44
29	8 31 55	8 49 39	18 14	14 10	20 11	0♉15	1 33	11 59	4 47	2 36	29 42
30	8 35 51	9 50 37	0♒ 9	14 56	21 26	0 51	1 30	12 4	4 44	2 36	29 41
31	8 39 48	10♒51 33	12♒ 2	15♑46	22♑41	1♉28	1♎28	12♐ 8	4♌41	2♏36	29♌39

THE SUN ENTERS THE SIGN OF AQUARIUS ON JAN 20 AT 07:39.

DAY	TIME	☉	☽	☿	♀	♂	♃	♄	♅	♆	♇
	h m s	° ' "	° '	° '	° '	° '	° '	° '	° '	° '	° '
F 1	8 43 44	11♒52 29	23♒54	16♑39	23♑57	2♉ 4	1♎25	12♐13	4♌39	2♏36	29♌38
E 2	8 47 41	12 53 23	5♓46	17 36	25 12	2 41	1R22	12 18	4R36	2R36	29R37
B 3	8 51 38	13 54 16	17 40	18 36	26 27	3 18	1 18	12 22	4 34	2 36	29 35
R 4	8 55 34	14 55 8	29 39	19 38	27 42	3 55	1 15	12 27	4 31	2 36	29 34
U 5	8 59 31	15 55 58	11♈44	20 43	28 57	4 31	1 11	12 31	4 29	2 36	29 32
A 6	9 3 27	16 56 47	23 59	21 50	0♒12	5 8	1 8	12 36	4 26	2 36	29 31
R 7	9 7 24	17 57 35	6♉28	22 59	1 27	5 45	1 4	12 40	4 23	2 36	29 29
Y 8	9 11 20	18 58 21	19 16	24 11	2 42	6 22	1 0	12 44	4 21	2 35	29 28
9	9 15 17	19 59 6	2♊28	25 24	3 57	6 59	0 55	12 48	4 18	2 35	29 26
10	9 19 13	20 59 49	16 5	26 38	5 12	7 36	0 51	12 52	4 16	2 35	29 25
11	9 23 10	22 0 30	0♋12	27 55	6 27	8 13	0 46	12 56	4 13	2 35	29 23
12	9 27 7	23 1 10	14 48	29 12	7 42	8 50	0 41	13 0	4 11	2 35	29 22
13	9 31 3	24 1 48	29 48	0♒31	8 57	9 27	0 37	13 4	4 9	2 34	29 20
14	9 35 0	25 2 25	15♌ 5	1 52	10 12	10 5	0 31	13 7	4 6	2 34	29 19
15	9 38 56	26 3 0	0♍27	3 14	11 27	10 42	0 26	13 11	4 4	2 33	29 17
16	9 42 53	27 3 34	15 44	4 37	12 41	11 19	0 21	13 14	4 1	2 33	29 16
17	9 46 49	28 4 6	0♎43	6 1	13 56	11 56	0 15	13 18	3 59	2 33	29 14
18	9 50 46	29 4 37	15 17	7 26	15 11	12 33	0 10	13 21	3 57	2 32	29 13
19	9 54 42	0♓ 5 6	29 22	8 53	16 26	13 11	0 4	13 25	3 55	2 32	29 11
20	9 58 39	1 5 34	12♏56	10 20	17 41	13 48	29♍58	13 28	3 52	2 31	29 10
21	10 2 36	2 6 1	26 3	11 49	18 56	14 25	29 52	13 31	3 50	2 30	29 8
22	10 6 32	3 6 27	8♐45	13 18	20 11	15 2	29 46	13 34	3 48	2 30	29 7
23	10 10 29	4 6 52	21 9	14 49	21 26	15 40	29 39	13 37	3 46	2 29	29 5
24	10 14 25	5 7 15	3♑18	16 21	22 41	16 17	29 33	13 39	3 44	2 28	29 4
25	10 18 22	6 7 36	15 17	17 54	23 56	16 55	29 26	13 42	3 41	2 28	29 2
26	10 22 18	7 7 56	27 11	19 27	25 11	17 32	29 20	13 45	3 39	2 27	29 1
27	10 26 15	8 8 15	9♒ 2	21 2	26 26	18 10	29 13	13 47	3 37	2 26	28 59
28	10 30 11	9♓ 8 31	20♒53	22♒38	27♒41	18♉47	29♍ 6	13♐50	3♌35	2♏25	28♌58

THE SUN ENTERS THE SIGN OF PISCES ON FEB 18 AT 21:59.

DAY	TIME	☉	☽	☿	♀	♂	♃	♄	♅	♆	♇
	h m s	° ' "	° '	° '	° '	° '	° '	° '	° '	° '	° '
M 1	10 34 8	10♓ 8 46	2♓46	24♒15	28♒56	19♉24	28♍59	13♐52	3♌33	2♏25	28♌56
A 2	10 38 5	11 9 0	14 42	25 53	0♓10	20 2	28R52	13 54	3R31	2R24	28R55
R 3	10 42 1	12 9 11	26 43	27 31	1 25	20 40	28 45	13 56	3 30	2 23	28 54
C 4	10 45 58	13 9 21	8♈50	29 11	2 40	21 17	28 38	13 58	3 28	2 22	28 52
H 5	10 49 54	14 9 28	21 4	0♓52	3 55	21 55	28 30	14 0	3 26	2 21	28 51
6	10 53 51	15 9 34	3♉27	2 35	5 10	22 32	28 23	14 2	3 24	2 20	28 49
7	10 57 47	16 9 38	16 2	4 18	6 25	23 10	28 16	14 4	3 22	2 19	28 48
8	11 1 44	17 9 39	28 53	6 2	7 39	23 47	28 8	14 6	3 21	2 18	28 46
9	11 5 40	18 9 39	12♊ 2	7 47	8 54	24 25	28 1	14 7	3 19	2 17	28 45
10	11 9 37	19 9 36	25 33	9 34	10 9	25 3	27 53	14 9	3 17	2 16	28 44
11	11 13 33	20 9 31	9♋28	11 22	11 24	25 40	27 45	14 10	3 16	2 15	28 42
12	11 17 30	21 9 24	23 47	13 10	12 39	26 18	27 38	14 11	3 14	2 14	28 41
13	11 21 27	22 9 14	8♌30	15 0	13 53	26 56	27 30	14 12	3 13	2 13	28 39
14	11 25 23	23 9 3	23 29	16 51	15 8	27 33	27 22	14 13	3 12	2 11	28 38
15	11 29 20	24 8 49	8♍38	18 44	16 23	28 11	27 14	14 14	3 10	2 10	28 37
16	11 33 16	25 8 33	23 45	20 37	17 37	28 48	27 7	14 15	3 9	2 9	28 35
17	11 37 13	26 8 15	8♎41	22 32	18 52	29 26	26 59	14 16	3 8	2 8	28 34
18	11 41 9	27 7 55	23 18	24 27	20 7	0♊ 4	26 51	14 17	3 6	2 7	28 33
19	11 45 6	28 7 33	7♏28	26 24	21 21	0 41	26 43	14 17	3 5	2 5	28 31
20	11 49 2	29 7 10	21 11	28 22	22 36	1 19	26 36	14 18	3 4	2 4	28 30
21	11 52 59	0♈ 6 44	4♐25	0♈21	23 51	1 57	26 28	14 18	3 3	2 3	28 29
22	11 56 56	1 6 18	17 14	2 20	25 5	2 35	26 20	14 18	3 2	2 1	28 28
23	12 0 52	2 5 49	29 42	4 21	26 20	3 12	26 12	14 18	3 1	2 0	28 27
24	12 4 49	3 5 18	11♑54	6 22	27 35	3 50	26 5	14R18	3 0	1 59	28 25
25	12 8 45	4 4 46	23 54	8 24	28 49	4 28	25 57	14 18	2 59	1 57	28 24
26	12 12 42	5 4 12	5♒47	10 26	0♈ 4	5 5	25 49	14 18	2 58	1 56	28 23
27	12 16 38	6 3 36	17 38	12 28	1 18	5 43	25 42	14 18	2 57	1 54	28 22
28	12 20 35	7 2 59	29 30	14 30	2 33	6 21	25 34	14 18	2 57	1 53	28 21
29	12 24 31	8 2 19	11♓26	16 31	3 47	6 58	25 27	14 17	2 56	1 51	28 20
30	12 28 28	9 1 37	23 28	18 32	5 2	7 36	25 19	14 17	2 55	1 50	28 19
31	12 32 25	10♈ 0 54	5♈38	20♈32	6♈17	8♊14	25♍12	14♐16	2♌55	1♏49	28♌17

THE SUN ENTERS THE SIGN OF ARIES ON MAR 20 AT 21:17.

♈ ARIES ♉ TAURUS ♊ GEMINI ♋ CANCER ♌ LEO ♍ VIRGO ♎ LIBRA

SIDEREAL SUN. MOON. MERCURY. VENUS. MARS. JUPITER. SATURN. URANUS. NEPTUNE. PLUTO.

DAY	TIME	☉	☽	☿	♀	♂	♃	♄	♅	♆	♇
	h m s	° ' "	° '	° '	° '	° '	° '	° '	° '	° '	° '
A 1	12 36 21	11♈ 0 8	17♈57	22♈30	7♈31	8♊52	25♍ 5	14♐15	2♌54	1♏47	28♌16
P 2	12 40 18	11 59 20	0♉25	24 26	8 46	9 29	24R57	14R14	2R54	1R46	28R15
R 3	12 44 14	12 58 31	13 5	26 21	10 0	10 7	24 50	14 14	2 53	1 44	28 14
I 4	12 48 11	13 57 39	25 56	28 13	11 14	10 45	24 43	14 12	2 53	1 42	28 13
L 5	12 52 7	14 56 45	9♊ 0	0♉ 2	12 29	11 23	24 36	14 11	2 53	1 41	28 12
6	12 56 4	15 55 48	22 19	1 47	13 43	12 0	24 29	14 10	2 52	1 39	28 12
7	13 0 0	16 54 50	5♋54	3 29	14 58	12 38	24 23	14 9	2 52	1 38	28 11
8	13 3 57	17 53 49	19 46	5 7	16 12	13 16	24 16	14 7	2 52	1 36	28 10
9	13 7 53	18 52 45	3♌55	6 41	17 26	13 54	24 9	14 6	2 52	1 35	28 9
10	13 11 50	19 51 40	18 19	8 10	18 41	14 31	24 3	14 4	2D52	1 33	28 8
11	13 15 47	20 50 31	2♍55	9 34	19 55	15 9	23 57	14 3	2 52	1 31	28 7
12	13 19 43	21 49 21	17 38	10 53	21 9	15 47	23 51	14 1	2 52	1 30	28 6
13	13 23 40	22 48 9	2♎22	12 7	22 24	16 24	23 44	13 59	2 52	1 28	28 6
14	13 27 36	23 46 54	16 58	13 16	23 38	17 2	23 39	13 57	2 52	1 27	28 5
15	13 31 33	24 45 37	1♏20	14 19	24 52	17 40	23 33	13 55	2 52	1 25	28 4
16	13 35 29	25 44 19	15 22	15 16	26 7	18 18	23 27	13 53	2 53	1 23	28 4
17	13 39 26	26 42 58	29 2	16 8	27 21	18 55	23 22	13 50	2 53	1 22	28 3
18	13 43 22	27 41 36	12♐18	16 54	28 35	19 33	23 16	13 48	2 53	1 20	28 2
19	13 47 19	28 40 12	25 11	17 33	29 49	20 11	23 11	13 46	2 54	1 18	28 2
20	13 51 16	29 38 47	7♑44	18 7	1♉ 3	20 48	23 6	13 43	2 54	1 17	28 1
21	13 55 12	0♉37 20	20 0	18 35	2 18	21 26	23 1	13 41	2 55	1 15	28 1
22	13 59 9	1 35 51	2♒ 3	18 57	3 32	22 4	22 56	13 38	2 55	1 14	28 0
23	14 3 5	2 34 20	13 58	19 13	4 46	22 41	22 51	13 35	2 56	1 12	28 0
24	14 7 2	3 32 48	25 51	19 22	6 0	23 19	22 47	13 33	2 57	1 10	27 59
25	14 10 58	4 31 14	7♓45	19R27	7 14	23 57	22 42	13 30	2 58	1 9	27 59
26	14 14 55	5 29 39	19 43	19 25	8 28	24 34	22 38	13 27	2 58	1 7	27 58
27	14 18 51	6 28 2	1♈51	19 18	9 42	25 12	22 34	13 24	2 59	1 5	27 58
28	14 22 48	7 26 23	14 9	19 6	10 56	25 50	22 30	13 21	3 0	1 4	27 58
29	14 26 45	8 24 42	26 40	18 49	12 11	26 27	22 27	13 17	3 1	1 2	27 57
30	14 30 41	9♉23 0	9♉26	18♉28	13♉25	27♊ 5	22♍23	13♐14	3♌ 2	1♏ 1	27♌57

THE SUN ENTERS THE SIGN OF TAURUS ON APR 20 AT 08:41.

DAY	TIME	☉	☽	☿	♀	♂	♃	♄	♅	♆	♇
	h m s	° ' "	° '	° '	° '	° '	° '	° '	° '	° '	° '
M 1	14 34 38	10♉21 16	22♉26	18♉ 2	14♉39	27♊43	22♍20	13♐11	3♌ 3	0♏59	27♌57
A 2	14 38 34	11 19 30	5♊40	17R34	15 53	28 21	22R17	13R 7	3 4	0R57	27R56
Y 3	14 42 31	12 17 43	19 7	17 2	17 7	28 58	22 14	13 4	3 6	0 56	27 56
4	14 46 27	13 15 53	2♋47	16 27	18 21	29 36	22 11	13 0	3 7	0 54	27 56
5	14 50 24	14 14 2	16 38	15 51	19 35	0♋14	22 8	12 57	3 8	0 52	27 56
6	14 54 20	15 12 9	0♌39	15 14	20 49	0 51	22 6	12 53	3 9	0 51	27 56
7	14 58 17	16 10 13	14 47	14 37	22 2	1 29	22 3	12 50	3 11	0 49	27 56
8	15 2 14	17 8 16	29 2	14 0	23 16	2 7	22 1	12 46	3 12	0 48	27 56
9	15 6 10	18 6 17	13♍20	13 24	24 30	2 44	21 59	12 42	3 14	0 46	27D55
10	15 10 7	19 4 15	27 39	12 49	25 44	3 22	21 58	12 38	3 15	0 45	27 55
11	15 14 3	20 2 12	11♎54	12 16	26 58	3 59	21 56	12 34	3 17	0 43	27 56
12	15 18 0	21 0 7	26 1	11 46	28 12	4 37	21 55	12 30	3 18	0 42	27 56
13	15 21 56	21 58 1	9♏58	11 19	29 26	5 15	21 54	12 26	3 20	0 40	27 56
14	15 25 53	22 55 53	23 41	10 56	0♊40	5 52	21 53	12 22	3 22	0 39	27 56
15	15 29 49	23 53 43	7♐ 6	10 36	1 53	6 30	21 52	12 18	3 24	0 37	27 56
16	15 33 46	24 51 33	20 14	10 20	3 7	7 8	21 51	12 14	3 25	0 36	27 56
17	15 37 43	25 49 20	3♑ 3	10 9	4 21	7 45	21 51	12 10	3 27	0 34	27 56
18	15 41 39	26 47 7	15 35	10 2	5 35	8 23	21 50	12 6	3 29	0 33	27 56
19	15 45 36	27 44 52	27 52	9D59	6 48	9 0	21D50	12 2	3 31	0 31	27 57
20	15 49 32	28 42 37	9♒57	10 1	8 2	9 38	21 50	11 57	3 33	0 30	27 57
21	15 53 29	29 40 20	21 54	10 8	9 16	10 16	21 51	11 53	3 35	0 29	27 57
22	15 57 25	0♊38 1	3♓47	10 19	10 30	10 53	21 51	11 49	3 37	0 27	27 58
23	16 1 22	1 35 42	15 42	10 35	11 43	11 31	21 52	11 45	3 39	0 26	27 58
24	16 5 18	2 33 22	27 42	10 55	12 57	12 8	21 52	11 40	3 41	0 25	27 58
25	16 9 15	3 31 1	9♈52	11 19	14 11	12 46	21 53	11 36	3 44	0 23	27 59
26	16 13 12	4 28 39	22 15	11 48	15 24	13 24	21 55	11 31	3 46	0 22	27 59
27	16 17 8	5 26 16	4♉56	12 21	16 38	14 1	21 56	11 27	3 48	0 21	28 0
28	16 21 5	6 23 51	17 55	12 58	17 52	14 39	21 57	11 23	3 51	0 19	28 0
29	16 25 1	7 21 26	1♊14	13 38	19 5	15 16	21 59	11 18	3 53	0 18	28 1
30	16 28 58	8 19 0	14 52	14 23	20 19	15 54	22 1	11 14	3 55	0 17	28 1
31	16 32 54	9♊16 33	28♊46	15♉11	21♊33	16♋32	22♍ 3	11♐ 9	3♌58	0♏16	28♌ 2

THE SUN ENTERS THE SIGN OF GEMINI ON MAY 21 AT 08:11.

DAY	TIME	☉	☽	☿	♀	♂	♃	♄	♅	♆	♇
	h m s	° ' "	° '	° '	° '	° '	° '	° '	° '	° '	° '
J 1	16 36 51	10♊14 4	12♋54	16♉ 3	22♊46	17♋ 9	22♍ 5	11♐ 5	4♌ 0	0♏15	28♌ 3
U 2	16 40 47	11 11 35	27 10	16 58	24 0	17 47	22 8	11R 0	4 3	0R13	28 3
N 3	16 44 44	12 9 4	11♌30	17 57	25 13	18 24	22 10	10 56	4 5	0 12	28 4
E 4	16 48 41	13 6 31	25 50	18 59	26 27	19 2	22 13	10 52	4 8	0 11	28 5
5	16 52 37	14 3 58	10♍ 6	20 5	27 40	19 40	22 16	10 47	4 11	0 10	28 5
6	16 56 34	15 1 23	24 16	21 13	28 54	20 17	22 19	10 43	4 13	0 9	28 6
7	17 0 30	15 58 47	8♎18	22 25	0♋ 7	20 55	22 22	10 38	4 16	0 8	28 7
8	17 4 27	16 56 10	22 10	23 40	1 21	21 32	22 26	10 34	4 19	0 7	28 8
9	17 8 23	17 53 32	5♏52	24 58	2 34	22 10	22 29	10 29	4 22	0 6	28 9
10	17 12 20	18 50 52	19 22	26 19	3 48	22 47	22 33	10 25	4 24	0 5	28 10
11	17 16 16	19 48 12	2♐40	27 42	5 1	23 25	22 37	10 21	4 27	0 4	28 10
12	17 20 13	20 45 32	15 45	29 9	6 15	24 3	22 41	10 16	4 30	0 3	28 11
13	17 24 10	21 42 50	28 37	0♊39	7 28	24 40	22 45	10 12	4 33	0 2	28 12
14	17 28 6	22 40 8	11♑15	2 12	8 41	25 18	22 49	10 8	4 36	0 1	28 13
15	17 32 3	23 37 25	23 40	3 47	9 55	25 55	22 54	10 3	4 39	0 1	28 14
16	17 35 59	24 34 42	5♒53	5 26	11 8	26 33	22 59	9 59	4 42	0 0	28 15
17	17 39 56	25 31 58	17 56	7 7	12 22	27 10	23 3	9 55	4 45	29♎59	28 16
18	17 43 52	26 29 14	29 52	8 51	13 35	27 48	23 8	9 51	4 48	29 58	28 17
19	17 47 49	27 26 29	11♓45	10 38	14 48	28 26	23 14	9 47	4 51	29 58	28 19
20	17 51 45	28 23 45	23 39	12 27	16 2	29 3	23 19	9 43	4 54	29 57	28 20
21	17 55 42	29 21 0	5♈37	14 19	17 15	29 41	23 24	9 39	4 57	29 56	28 21
22	17 59 39	0♋18 15	17 47	16 14	18 28	0♌18	23 30	9 34	5 1	29 56	28 22
23	18 3 35	1 15 30	0♉11	18 11	19 41	0 56	23 36	9 31	5 4	29 55	28 23
24	18 7 32	2 12 44	12 55	20 11	20 55	1 33	23 41	9 27	5 7	29 55	28 24
25	18 11 28	3 9 59	26 2	22 12	22 8	2 11	23 47	9 23	5 10	29 54	28 26
26	18 15 25	4 7 14	9♊33	24 16	23 21	2 49	23 54	9 19	5 14	29 53	28 27
27	18 19 21	5 4 28	23 29	26 21	24 35	3 26	24 0	9 15	5 17	29 53	28 28
28	18 23 18	6 1 42	7♋46	28 28	25 48	4 4	24 6	9 11	5 20	29 53	28 30
29	18 27 14	6 58 56	22 20	0♋37	27 1	4 42	24 13	9 8	5 24	29 52	28 31
30	18 31 11	7♋56 10	7♌ 3	2♋46	28♋14	5♌19	24♍20	9♐ 4	5♌27	29♎52	28♌32

THE SUN ENTERS THE SIGN OF CANCER ON JUN 21 AT 16:21.

♏ SCORPIO ♐ SAGITTARIUS ♑ CAPRICORN ♒ AQUARIUS ♓ PISCES

SIDEREAL | SUN. | MOON.. | MERCURY | VENUS.. | MARS... | JUPITER | SATURN. | URANUS. | NEPTUNE | PLUTO.

DAY	TIME	☉	☽	☿	♀	♂	♃	♄	♅	♆	♇
	h m s	° ' "	° '	° '	° '	° '	° '	° '	° '	° '	° '
J 1	18 35 8	8♋53 24	21♌48	4♋56	29♋27	5♌57	24♍27	9♐0	5♌30	29♎51	28♌34
U 2	18 39 4	9 50 37	6♍27	7 7	0♌41	6 34	24 33	8R57	5 34	29R51	28 35
L 3	18 43 1	10 47 49	20 55	9 17	1 54	7 12	24 41	8 54	5 37	29 51	28 36
Y 4	18 46 57	11 45 2	5♎8	11 28	3 7	7 50	24 48	8 50	5 41	29 50	28 38
5	18 50 54	12 42 14	19 4	13 38	4 20	8 27	24 55	8 47	5 44	29 50	28 39
6	18 54 50	13 39 25	2♏43	15 48	5 33	9 5	25 3	8 44	5 47	29 50	28 41
7	18 58 47	14 36 37	16 7	17 56	6 46	9 43	25 10	8 40	5 51	29 50	28 42
8	19 2 43	15 33 48	29 16	20 4	7 59	10 20	25 18	8 37	5 55	29 50	28 44
9	19 6 40	16 31 0	12♐13	22 10	9 12	10 58	25 26	8 34	5 58	29 50	28 45
10	19 10 37	17 28 11	24 57	24 15	10 25	11 36	25 34	8 31	6 2	29 50	28 47
11	19 14 33	18 25 23	7♑32	26 19	11 38	12 13	25 42	8 28	6 5	29D50	28 48
12	19 18 30	19 22 34	19 56	28 21	12 51	12 51	25 50	8 26	6 9	29 50	28 50
13	19 22 26	20 19 46	2♒10	0♌21	14 4	13 29	25 58	8 23	6 12	29 50	28 52
14	19 26 23	21 16 58	14 16	2 20	15 17	14 6	26 7	8 20	6 16	29 50	28 53
15	19 30 19	22 14 11	26 15	4 17	16 30	14 44	26 15	8 18	6 20	29 50	28 55
16	19 34 16	23 11 24	8♓9	6 12	17 43	15 22	26 24	8 15	6 23	29 50	28 57
17	19 38 13	24 8 37	20 0	8 5	18 56	15 59	26 33	8 13	6 27	29 50	28 58
18	19 42 9	25 5 51	1♈52	9 57	20 8	16 37	26 42	8 10	6 30	29 50	29 0
19	19 46 6	26 3 6	13 49	11 47	21 21	17 15	26 51	8 8	6 34	29 50	29 2
20	19 50 2	27 0 22	25 56	13 34	22 34	17 53	27 0	8 6	6 38	29 51	29 3
21	19 53 59	27 57 38	8♉18	15 20	23 47	18 30	27 9	8 4	6 41	29 51	29 5
22	19 57 55	28 54 55	21 0	17 5	25 0	19 8	27 18	8 2	6 45	29 51	29 7
23	20 1 52	29 52 13	4♊6	18 47	26 12	19 46	27 27	8 0	6 49	29 52	29 9
24	20 5 48	0♌49 32	17 41	20 28	27 25	20 24	27 37	7 58	6 52	29 52	29 10
25	20 9 45	1 46 52	1♋44	22 7	28 38	21 1	27 47	7 56	6 56	29 52	29 12
26	20 13 42	2 44 13	16 13	23 44	29 50	21 39	27 56	7 55	7 0	29 53	29 14
27	20 17 38	3 41 34	1♌4	25 19	1♍3	22 17	28 6	7 53	7 3	29 53	29 16
28	20 21 35	4 38 56	16 8	26 52	2 16	22 55	28 16	7 52	7 7	29 54	29 18
29	20 25 31	5 36 19	1♍16	28 24	3 28	23 33	28 26	7 50	7 11	29 54	29 19
30	20 29 28	6 33 42	16 16	29 54	4 41	24 10	28 36	7 49	7 15	29 55	29 21
31	20 33 24	7♌31 6	1♎1	1♍22	5♍53	24♌48	28♍46	7♐48	7♌18	29♎55	29♌23

THE SUN ENTERS THE SIGN OF LEO ON JUL 23 AT 03:16.

DAY	TIME	☉	☽	☿	♀	♂	♃	♄	♅	♆	♇
	h m s	° ' "	° '	° '	° '	° '	° '	° '	° '	° '	° '
A 1	20 37 21	8♌28 31	15♎24	2♍48	7♍6	25♌26	28♍56	7♐47	7♌22	29♎56	29♌25
U 2	20 41 17	9 25 56	29 25	4 12	8 18	26 4	29 6	7R46	7 26	29 57	29 27
G 3	20 45 14	10 23 21	13♏2	5 34	9 31	26 42	29 17	7 45	7 29	29 57	29 29
U 4	20 49 11	11 20 48	26 18	6 54	10 43	27 20	29 27	7 44	7 33	29 58	29 31
S 5	20 53 7	12 18 15	9♐16	8 13	11 56	27 58	29 38	7 43	7 37	29 59	29 32
T 6	20 57 4	13 15 42	21 58	9 29	13 8	28 36	29 48	7 43	7 40	0♏0	29 34
7	21 1 0	14 13 11	4♑27	10 43	14 20	29 13	29 59	7 42	7 44	0 1	29 36
8	21 4 57	15 10 41	16 47	11 56	15 33	29 51	0♎10	7 42	7 48	0 1	29 38
9	21 8 53	16 8 11	28 58	13 5	16 45	0♍29	0 21	7 41	7 52	0 2	29 40
10	21 12 50	17 5 42	11♒3	14 13	17 57	1 7	0 32	7 41	7 55	0 3	29 42
11	21 16 46	18 3 15	23 2	15 18	19 9	1 45	0 43	7D41	7 59	0 4	29 44
12	21 20 43	19 0 48	4♓56	16 21	20 22	2 23	0 54	7 41	8 3	0 5	29 46
13	21 24 40	19 58 23	16 47	17 21	21 34	3 1	1 5	7 41	8 6	0 6	29 48
14	21 28 36	20 55 59	28 38	18 18	22 46	3 39	1 16	7 41	8 10	0 7	29 50
15	21 32 33	21 53 37	10♈30	19 13	23 58	4 17	1 27	7 41	8 13	0 8	29 52
16	21 36 29	22 51 16	22 27	20 4	25 10	4 55	1 38	7 42	8 17	0 9	29 54
17	21 40 26	23 48 56	4♉33	20 52	26 22	5 33	1 50	7 42	8 21	0 10	29 56
18	21 44 22	24 46 38	16 53	21 37	27 34	6 11	2 1	7 43	8 24	0 11	29 58
19	21 48 19	25 44 22	29 32	22 18	28 46	6 49	2 13	7 43	8 28	0 13	0♍0
20	21 52 15	26 42 7	12♊35	22 56	29 58	7 28	2 24	7 44	8 31	0 14	0 2
21	21 56 12	27 39 55	26 5	23 30	1♎10	8 6	2 36	7 45	8 35	0 15	0 4
22	22 0 8	28 37 43	10♋4	23 59	2 21	8 44	2 48	7 46	8 39	0 16	0 6
23	22 4 5	29 35 34	24 33	24 24	3 33	9 22	2 59	7 47	8 42	0 18	0 8
24	22 8 2	0♍33 26	9♌26	24 44	4 45	10 0	3 11	7 48	8 46	0 19	0 10
25	22 11 58	1 31 20	24 37	25 0	5 57	10 38	3 23	7 49	8 49	0 20	0 12
26	22 15 55	2 29 15	9♍56	25 10	7 8	11 17	3 35	7 50	8 53	0 22	0 13
27	22 19 51	3 27 11	25 10	25R15	8 20	11 55	3 47	7 52	8 56	0 23	0 15
28	22 23 48	4 25 9	10♎9	25 14	9 32	12 33	3 59	7 53	8 59	0 24	0 17
29	22 27 44	5 23 9	24 46	25 7	10 43	13 11	4 11	7 55	9 3	0 26	0 19
30	22 31 41	6 21 10	8♏57	24 54	11 55	13 50	4 23	7 57	9 6	0 27	0 21
31	22 35 37	7♍19 12	22♏41	24♍35	13♎6	14♍28	4♎35	7♐58	9♌10	0♏29	0♍23

THE SUN ENTERS THE SIGN OF VIRGO ON AUG 23 AT 10:08.

DAY	TIME	☉	☽	☿	♀	♂	♃	♄	♅	♆	♇
	h m s	° ' "	° '	° '	° '	° '	° '	° '	° '	° '	° '
S 1	22 39 34	8♍17 15	5♐59	24♍10	14♎18	15♍6	4♎47	8♐0	9♌13	0♏30	0♍25
E 2	22 43 31	9 15 20	18 54	23R39	15 29	15 44	5 0	8 2	9 16	0 32	0 27
P 3	22 47 27	10 13 26	1♑31	23 1	16 40	16 23	5 12	8 4	9 20	0 33	0 29
T 4	22 51 24	11 11 34	13 53	22 19	17 52	17 1	5 24	8 6	9 23	0 35	0 31
E 5	22 55 20	12 9 43	26 3	21 31	19 3	17 40	5 37	8 9	9 26	0 37	0 33
M 6	22 59 17	13 7 54	8♒6	20 38	20 14	18 18	5 49	8 11	9 29	0 38	0 35
B 7	23 3 13	14 6 6	20 3	19 42	21 25	18 56	6 1	8 14	9 33	0 40	0 37
E 8	23 7 10	15 4 20	1♓57	18 44	22 36	19 35	6 14	8 16	9 36	0 42	0 39
R 9	23 11 6	16 2 36	13 49	17 44	23 47	20 13	6 26	8 19	9 39	0 43	0 41
10	23 15 3	17 0 53	25 40	16 44	24 58	20 52	6 39	8 21	9 42	0 45	0 43
11	23 19 0	17 59 12	7♈33	15 45	26 9	21 30	6 52	8 24	9 45	0 47	0 45
12	23 22 56	18 57 33	19 30	14 49	27 20	22 9	7 4	8 27	9 48	0 49	0 47
13	23 26 53	19 55 57	1♉32	13 56	28 31	22 47	7 17	8 30	9 51	0 50	0 49
14	23 30 49	20 54 22	13 43	13 9	29 41	23 26	7 29	8 33	9 54	0 52	0 50
15	23 34 46	21 52 49	26 6	12 29	0♏52	24 4	7 42	8 36	9 57	0 54	0 52
16	23 38 42	22 51 19	8♊46	11 56	2 3	24 43	7 55	8 39	10 0	0 56	0 54
17	23 42 39	23 49 50	21 46	11 31	3 13	25 22	8 8	8 43	10 3	0 58	0 56
18	23 46 35	24 48 24	5♋10	11 15	4 24	26 0	8 20	8 46	10 6	1 0	0 58
19	23 50 32	25 47 0	19 1	11D 9	5 34	26 39	8 33	8 50	10 9	1 1	1 0
20	23 54 29	26 45 39	3♌18	11 13	6 44	27 18	8 46	8 53	10 12	1 3	1 2
21	23 58 25	27 44 19	18 0	11 26	7 55	27 56	8 59	8 57	10 15	1 5	1 3
22	0 2 22	28 43 2	3♍2	11 48	9 5	28 35	9 12	9 1	10 17	1 7	1 5
23	0 6 18	29 41 46	18 14	12 20	10 15	29 14	9 25	9 4	10 20	1 9	1 7
24	0 10 15	0♎40 33	3♎27	13 1	11 25	29 53	9 37	9 8	10 23	1 11	1 9
25	0 14 11	1 39 22	18 30	13 51	12 35	0♎32	9 50	9 12	10 25	1 13	1 10
26	0 18 8	2 38 12	3♏14	14 48	13 45	1 10	10 3	9 16	10 28	1 15	1 12
27	0 22 4	3 37 5	17 34	15 53	14 55	1 49	10 16	9 20	10 31	1 17	1 14
28	0 26 1	4 35 59	1♐27	17 4	16 5	2 28	10 29	9 25	10 33	1 19	1 16
29	0 29 57	5 34 55	14 52	18 21	17 15	3 7	10 42	9 29	10 36	1 21	1 17
30	0 33 54	6♎33 53	27♐52	19♍44	18♏25	3♎46	10♎55	9♐33	10♌38	1♏23	1♍19

THE SUN ENTERS THE SIGN OF LIBRA ON SEP 23 AT 07:27.

♈ ARIES ♉ TAURUS ♊ GEMINI ♋ CANCER ♌ LEO ♍ VIRGO ♎ LIBRA

1957

SIDEREAL TIME . SUN . MOON . MERCURY . VENUS . MARS . JUPITER . SATURN . URANUS . NEPTUNE . PLUTO .

DAY	TIME	☉	☽	☿	♀	♂	♃	♄	♅	♆	♇
	h m s	° ' "	° '	° '	° '	° '	° '	° '	° '	° '	° '
O 1	0 37 51	7♎32 53	10♑31	21♍11	19♏34	4♎25	11♎ 8	9♐38	10♌41	1♏25	1♍21
C 2	0 41 47	8 31 54	22 52	22 41	20 44	5 4	11 21	9 42	10 43	1 27	1 22
T 3	0 45 44	9 30 57	5♒ 0	24 16	21 53	5 43	11 34	9 47	10 45	1 30	1 24
O 4	0 49 40	10 30 2	16 58	25 52	23 2	6 22	11 47	9 51	10 48	1 32	1 26
B 5	0 53 37	11 29 9	28 52	27 32	24 12	7 1	12 0	9 56	10 50	1 34	1 27
E 6	0 57 33	12 28 17	10♓43	29 13	25 21	7 40	12 13	10 1	10 52	1 36	1 29
R 7	1 1 30	13 27 27	22 35	0♎55	26 30	8 19	12 26	10 6	10 54	1 38	1 30
8	1 5 26	14 26 40	4♈30	2 38	27 39	8 58	12 39	10 11	10 56	1 40	1 32
9	1 9 23	15 25 54	16 29	4 23	28 48	9 37	12 52	10 16	10 58	1 42	1 34
10	1 13 20	16 25 10	28 35	6 7	29 56	10 17	13 5	10 21	11 0	1 45	1 35
11	1 17 16	17 24 29	10♉48	7 52	1♐ 5	10 56	13 18	10 26	11 2	1 47	1 37
12	1 21 13	18 23 49	23 12	9 38	2 14	11 35	13 31	10 31	11 4	1 49	1 38
13	1 25 9	19 23 12	5♊47	11 23	3 22	12 14	13 44	10 36	11 6	1 51	1 39
14	1 29 6	20 22 38	18 36	13 8	4 30	12 54	13 57	10 41	11 8	1 53	1 41
15	1 33 2	21 22 5	1♋42	14 52	5 38	13 33	14 10	10 47	11 10	1 56	1 42
16	1 36 59	22 21 35	15 6	16 37	6 46	14 12	14 23	10 52	11 12	1 58	1 44
17	1 40 55	23 21 7	28 50	18 20	7 54	14 52	14 36	10 58	11 13	2 0	1 45
18	1 44 52	24 20 41	12♌55	20 4	9 2	15 31	14 48	11 3	11 15	2 2	1 46
19	1 48 49	25 20 18	27 20	21 47	10 10	16 10	15 1	11 9	11 17	2 4	1 48
20	1 52 45	26 19 57	12♍ 0	23 29	11 17	16 50	15 14	11 14	11 18	2 7	1 49
21	1 56 42	27 19 38	26 51	25 11	12 25	17 29	15 27	11 20	11 20	2 9	1 50
22	2 0 38	28 19 21	11♎46	26 52	13 32	18 9	15 40	11 26	11 21	2 11	1 52
23	2 4 35	29 19 7	26 37	28 33	14 39	18 48	15 53	11 32	11 22	2 13	1 53
24	2 8 31	0♏18 54	11♏15	0♏13	15 46	19 28	16 6	11 38	11 24	2 16	1 54
25	2 12 28	1 18 44	25 34	1 53	16 53	20 8	16 18	11 44	11 25	2 18	1 55
26	2 16 24	2 18 35	9♐30	3 32	18 0	20 47	16 31	11 49	11 26	2 20	1 56
27	2 20 21	3 18 28	23 1	5 10	19 6	21 27	16 44	11 56	11 28	2 22	1 58
28	2 24 17	4 18 23	6♑ 8	6 48	20 13	22 7	16 57	12 2	11 29	2 25	1 59
29	2 28 14	5 18 19	18 51	8 25	21 19	22 46	17 9	12 8	11 30	2 27	2 0
30	2 32 11	6 18 17	1♒15	10 2	22 25	23 26	17 22	12 14	11 31	2 29	2 1
31	2 36 7	7♏18 17	13♒25	11♏39	23♐31	24♎ 6	17♎35	12♐20	11♌32	2♏31	2♍ 2

THE SUN ENTERS THE SIGN OF SCORPIO ON OCT 23 AT 16:25.

DAY	TIME	☉	☽	☿	♀	♂	♃	♄	♅	♆	♇
	h m s	° ' "	° '	° '	° '	° '	° '	° '	° '	° '	° '
N 1	2 40 4	8♏18 18	25♒23	13♏15	24♐36	24♎46	17♎47	12♐26	11♌33	2♏34	2♍ 3
O 2	2 44 0	9 18 21	7♓16	14 50	25 41	25 25	18 0	12 33	11 34	2 36	2 4
V 3	2 47 57	10 18 26	19 6	16 25	26 47	26 5	18 12	12 39	11 34	2 38	2 5
E 4	2 51 53	11 18 32	0♈59	18 0	27 51	26 45	18 25	12 45	11 35	2 40	2 6
M 5	2 55 50	12 18 39	12 58	19 34	28 56	27 25	18 37	12 52	11 36	2 43	2 7
B 6	2 59 46	13 18 49	25 5	21 8	0♑ 1	28 5	18 50	12 58	11 36	2 45	2 7
E 7	3 3 43	14 19 0	7♉23	22 41	1 5	28 45	19 2	13 5	11 37	2 47	2 8
R 8	3 7 40	15 19 13	19 52	24 14	2 9	29 25	19 14	13 11	11 38	2 49	2 9
9	3 11 36	16 19 28	2♊35	25 47	3 12	0♏ 5	19 27	13 18	11 38	2 51	2 10
10	3 15 33	17 19 44	15 31	27 19	4 16	0 45	19 39	13 24	11 39	2 54	2 11
11	3 19 29	18 20 3	28 40	28 51	5 19	1 25	19 51	13 31	11 39	2 56	2 11
12	3 23 26	19 20 23	12♋ 3	0♐23	6 22	2 5	20 3	13 38	11 39	2 58	2 12
13	3 27 22	20 20 45	25 39	1 54	7 24	2 45	20 15	13 44	11 40	3 0	2 13
14	3 31 19	21 21 9	9♌27	3 25	8 27	3 25	20 27	13 51	11 40	3 2	2 13
15	3 35 15	22 21 35	23 27	4 56	9 28	4 6	20 39	13 58	11 40	3 4	2 14
16	3 39 12	23 22 3	7♍37	6 26	10 30	4 46	20 51	14 5	11 40	3 7	2 14
17	3 43 9	24 22 33	21 57	7 57	11 31	5 26	21 3	14 11	11R40	3 9	2 15
18	3 47 5	25 23 5	6♎21	9 26	12 32	6 7	21 15	14 18	11 40	3 11	2 16
19	3 51 2	26 23 38	20 48	10 56	13 33	6 47	21 27	14 25	11 40	3 13	2 16
20	3 54 58	27 24 13	5♏13	12 25	14 33	7 27	21 39	14 32	11 40	3 15	2 17
21	3 58 55	28 24 50	19 30	13 53	15 32	8 8	21 50	14 39	11 40	3 17	2 17
22	4 2 51	29 25 29	3♐34	15 21	16 32	8 48	22 2	14 46	11 39	3 19	2 17
23	4 6 48	0♐26 8	17 22	16 49	17 31	9 29	22 13	14 53	11 39	3 21	2 18
24	4 10 44	1 26 49	0♑50	18 16	18 29	10 9	22 25	15 0	11 39	3 23	2 18
25	4 14 41	2 27 32	13 57	19 43	19 27	10 50	22 36	15 7	11 38	3 25	2 18
26	4 18 38	3 28 15	26 43	21 9	20 24	11 30	22 48	15 14	11 38	3 27	2 19
27	4 22 34	4 29 0	9♒10	22 34	21 21	12 11	22 59	15 21	11 37	3 29	2 19
28	4 26 31	5 29 46	21 21	23 58	22 18	12 51	23 10	15 28	11 37	3 31	2 19
29	4 30 27	6 30 32	3♓21	25 21	23 14	13 32	23 21	15 35	11 36	3 33	2 19
30	4 34 24	7♐31 20	15♓13	26♐43	24♑ 9	14♏13	23♎32	15♐42	11♌36	3♏35	2♍19

THE SUN ENTERS THE SIGN OF SAGITTARIUS ON NOV 22 AT 13:40.

DAY	TIME	☉	☽	☿	♀	♂	♃	♄	♅	♆	♇
	h m s	° ' "	° '	° '	° '	° '	° '	° '	° '	° '	° '
D 1	4 38 20	8♐32 8	27♓ 4	28♐ 4	25♑ 4	14♏53	23♎43	15♐49	11♌35	3♏37	2♍20
E 2	4 42 17	9 32 57	8♈57	29 23	25 58	15 34	23 54	15 56	11R34	3 39	2 20
C 3	4 46 13	10 33 48	20 58	0♑41	26 51	16 15	24 5	16 3	11 33	3 41	2 20
E 4	4 50 10	11 34 39	3♉10	1 56	27 44	16 56	24 15	16 10	11 32	3 43	2R20
M 5	4 54 7	12 35 31	15 38	3 9	28 36	17 37	24 26	16 17	11 31	3 45	2 20
B 6	4 58 3	13 36 24	28 23	4 19	29 27	18 18	24 37	16 24	11 30	3 46	2 20
E 7	5 2 0	14 37 18	11♊26	5 27	0♒18	18 58	24 47	16 31	11 29	3 48	2 20
R 8	5 5 56	15 38 13	24 46	6 30	1 8	19 39	24 57	16 38	11 28	3 50	2 20
9	5 9 53	16 39 9	8♋23	7 30	1 57	20 20	25 8	16 45	11 27	3 52	2 19
10	5 13 49	17 40 7	22 12	8 24	2 45	21 1	25 18	16 52	11 26	3 54	2 19
11	5 17 46	18 41 5	6♌12	9 14	3 32	21 42	25 28	17 0	11 25	3 55	2 19
12	5 21 42	19 42 4	20 17	9 57	4 18	22 23	25 38	17 7	11 23	3 57	2 19
13	5 25 39	20 43 4	4♍26	10 33	5 3	23 5	25 48	17 14	11 22	3 59	2 19
14	5 29 36	21 44 5	18 35	11 1	5 48	23 46	25 58	17 21	11 21	4 0	2 18
15	5 33 32	22 45 8	2♎43	11 21	6 31	24 27	26 7	17 28	11 19	4 2	2 18
16	5 37 29	23 46 11	16 48	11R31	7 13	25 8	26 17	17 35	11 18	4 4	2 18
17	5 41 25	24 47 15	0♏49	11 30	7 54	25 49	26 27	17 42	11 16	4 5	2 17
18	5 45 22	25 48 21	14 45	11 19	8 34	26 31	26 36	17 49	11 15	4 7	2 17
19	5 49 18	26 49 27	28 34	10 56	9 13	27 12	26 45	17 56	11 13	4 8	2 17
20	5 53 15	27 50 34	12♐13	10 21	9 50	27 53	26 54	18 3	11 12	4 10	2 16
21	5 57 12	28 51 41	25 41	9 35	10 26	28 35	27 3	18 10	11 10	4 11	2 16
22	6 1 8	29 52 49	8♑54	8 38	11 1	29 16	27 12	18 17	11 8	4 13	2 15
23	6 5 5	0♑53 57	21 52	7 31	11 34	29 57	27 21	18 24	11 6	4 14	2 15
24	6 9 1	1 55 6	4♒33	6 17	12 6	0♐39	27 30	18 31	11 4	4 16	2 14
25	6 12 58	2 56 15	16 58	4 58	12 36	1 20	27 39	18 38	11 3	4 17	2 13
26	6 16 54	3 57 24	29 9	3 36	13 5	2 2	27 47	18 45	11 1	4 18	2 13
27	6 20 51	4 58 33	11♓ 8	2 14	13 31	2 43	27 55	18 52	10 59	4 20	2 12
28	6 24 47	5 59 42	23 0	0 55	13 57	3 25	28 4	18 59	10 57	4 21	2 11
29	6 28 44	7 0 51	4♈49	29♐41	14 20	4 7	28 12	19 6	10 55	4 22	2 11
30	6 32 41	8 2 0	16 41	28 34	14 41	4 48	28 20	19 13	10 53	4 23	2 10
31	6 36 37	9♑ 3 9	28♈41	27♐35	15♒ 1	5♐30	28♎27	19♐20	10♌51	4♏25	2♍ 9

THE SUN ENTERS THE SIGN OF CAPRICORN ON DEC 22 AT 02:49.

♏ SCORPIO ♐ SAGITTARIUS ♑ CAPRICORN ♒ AQUARIUS ♓ PISCES

SIDEREAL . SUN . MOON . MERCURY . VENUS . MARS . JUPITER . SATURN . URANUS . NEPTUNE . PLUTO .

DAY	TIME	☉	☽	☿	♀	♂	♃	♄	♅	♆	♇
	h m s	° ' "	° '	° '	° '	° '	° '	° '	° '	° '	° '
J 1	6 40 34	10♑ 4 17	10♉54	26♐47	15♒18	6♐12	28♎35	19♐26	10♌49	4♏26	2♍ 8
A 2	6 44 30	11 5 26	23 25	26R 8	15 33	6 53	28 43	19 33	10R46	4 27	2R 8
N 3	6 48 27	12 6 34	6♊18	25 40	15 47	7 35	28 50	19 40	10 44	4 28	2 7
U 4	6 52 23	13 7 43	19 34	25 23	15 58	8 17	28 58	19 47	10 42	4 29	2 6
A 5	6 56 20	14 8 51	3♋15	25D15	16 6	8 59	29 5	19 53	10 40	4 30	2 5
R 6	7 0 16	15 9 59	17 16	25 16	16 13	9 41	29 12	20 0	10 38	4 31	2 4
Y 7	7 4 13	16 11 7	1♌35	25 26	16 16	10 23	29 19	20 7	10 35	4 32	2 3
8	7 8 10	17 12 14	16 4	25 43	16R18	11 5	29 25	20 13	10 33	4 33	2 2
9	7 12 6	18 13 22	0♍37	26 8	16 17	11 47	29 32	20 20	10 31	4 34	2 1
10	7 16 3	19 14 30	15 7	26 39	16 14	12 29	29 38	20 26	10 28	4 35	2 0
11	7 19 59	20 15 37	29 29	27 17	16 8	13 11	29 45	20 33	10 26	4 36	1 59
12	7 23 56	21 16 45	13♎41	27 59	15 59	13 53	29 51	20 39	10 23	4 37	1 58
13	7 27 52	22 17 53	27 40	28 46	15 48	14 35	29 57	20 46	10 21	4 38	1 57
14	7 31 49	23 19 0	11♏27	29 37	15 35	15 17	0♏ 3	20 52	10 18	4 38	1 56
15	7 35 45	24 20 8	25 3	0♑32	15 19	15 59	0 8	20 58	10 16	4 39	1 55
16	7 39 42	25 21 15	8♐27	1 31	15 1	16 41	0 14	21 5	10 13	4 40	1 54
17	7 43 39	26 22 22	21 42	2 33	14 40	17 24	0 19	21 11	10 11	4 41	1 53
18	7 47 35	27 23 29	4♑46	3 37	14 17	18 6	0 25	21 17	10 8	4 41	1 51
19	7 51 32	28 24 35	17 38	4 44	13 52	18 48	0 30	21 23	10 6	4 42	1 50
20	7 55 28	29 25 41	0♒20	5 53	13 25	19 30	0 34	21 29	10 3	4 42	1 49
21	7 59 25	0♒26 46	12 49	7 4	12 56	20 13	0 39	21 36	10 1	4 43	1 48
22	8 3 21	1 27 50	25 5	8 17	12 25	20 55	0 44	21 42	9 58	4 43	1 46
23	8 7 18	2 28 53	7♓11	9 31	11 53	21 38	0 48	21 47	9 56	4 44	1 45
24	8 11 14	3 29 56	19 7	10 48	11 19	22 20	0 52	21 53	9 53	4 44	1 44
25	8 15 11	4 30 57	0♈57	12 5	10 44	23 3	0 56	21 59	9 50	4 45	1 43
26	8 19 8	5 31 58	12 45	13 24	10 8	23 45	1 0	22 5	9 48	4 45	1 41
27	8 23 4	6 32 57	24 34	14 44	9 32	24 28	1 4	22 11	9 45	4 45	1 40
28	8 27 1	7 33 56	6♉31	16 6	8 55	25 10	1 7	22 17	9 43	4 46	1 39
29	8 30 57	8 34 53	18 41	17 28	8 18	25 53	1 11	22 22	9 40	4 46	1 37
30	8 34 54	9 35 49	1♊10	18 52	7 41	26 35	1 14	22 28	9 37	4 46	1 36
31	8 38 50	10♒36 43	14♊ 2	20♑16	7♒ 4	27♐18	1♏17	22♐33	9♌35	4♏46	1♍34

THE SUN ENTERS THE SIGN OF AQUARIUS ON JAN 20 AT 13:29.

DAY	TIME	☉	☽	☿	♀	♂	♃	♄	♅	♆	♇
	h m s	° ' "	° '	° '	° '	° '	° '	° '	° '	° '	° '
F 1	8 42 47	11♒37 37	27♊21	21♑42	6♒28	28♐ 1	1♏20	22♐39	9♌32	4♏46	1♍33
E 2	8 46 43	12 38 29	11♋ 8	23 8	5R52	28 43	1 22	22 44	9R29	4 47	1R32
B 3	8 50 40	13 39 20	25 23	24 35	5 18	29 26	1 25	22 49	9 27	4 47	1 30
R 4	8 54 37	14 40 10	10♌ 1	26 3	4 45	0♑ 9	1 27	22 55	9 24	4 47	1 29
U 5	8 58 33	15 40 58	24 54	27 32	4 14	0 52	1 29	23 0	9 22	4R47	1 27
A 6	9 2 30	16 41 45	9♍53	29 2	3 44	1 35	1 31	23 5	9 19	4 47	1 26
R 7	9 6 26	17 42 32	24 49	0♒33	3 16	2 18	1 33	23 10	9 16	4 47	1 25
Y 8	9 10 23	18 43 17	9♎34	2 4	2 50	3 0	1 34	23 15	9 14	4 47	1 23
9	9 14 19	19 44 1	24 2	3 36	2 27	3 43	1 36	23 20	9 11	4 47	1 22
10	9 18 16	20 44 44	8♏11	5 10	2 5	4 26	1 37	23 25	9 9	4 46	1 20
11	9 22 12	21 45 26	21 59	6 44	1 46	5 9	1 38	23 30	9 6	4 46	1 19
12	9 26 9	22 46 8	5♐29	8 18	1 29	5 52	1 39	23 35	9 4	4 46	1 17
13	9 30 6	23 46 48	18 41	9 54	1 15	6 35	1 39	23 39	9 1	4 46	1 16
14	9 34 2	24 47 27	1♑39	11 30	1 3	7 19	1 40	23 44	8 59	4 45	1 14
15	9 37 59	25 48 5	14 24	13 8	0 54	8 2	1R40	23 48	8 56	4 45	1 13
16	9 41 55	26 48 41	26 57	14 46	0 47	8 45	1 40	23 53	8 54	4 45	1 11
17	9 45 52	27 49 17	9♒21	16 25	0 43	9 28	1 40	23 57	8 51	4 44	1 10
18	9 49 48	28 49 50	21 35	18 5	0D41	10 11	1 39	24 1	8 49	4 44	1 8
19	9 53 45	29 50 22	3♓41	19 45	0 42	10 54	1 39	24 6	8 46	4 44	1 7
20	9 57 41	0♓50 53	15 39	21 27	0 45	11 38	1 38	24 10	8 44	4 43	1 5
21	10 1 38	1 51 22	27 31	23 10	0 50	12 21	1 37	24 14	8 42	4 43	1 4
22	10 5 35	2 51 49	9♈19	24 53	0 58	13 4	1 36	24 18	8 39	4 42	1 2
23	10 9 31	3 52 15	21 6	26 38	1 7	13 48	1 35	24 22	8 37	4 41	1 0
24	10 13 28	4 52 38	2♉55	28 24	1 19	14 31	1 33	24 25	8 35	4 41	0 59
25	10 17 24	5 53 0	14 51	0♓10	1 33	15 14	1 32	24 29	8 32	4 40	0 57
26	10 21 21	6 53 20	26 59	1 58	1 49	15 58	1 30	24 33	8 30	4 40	0 56
27	10 25 17	7 53 38	9♊24	3 46	2 8	16 41	1 28	24 36	8 28	4 39	0 54
28	10 29 14	8♓53 54	22♊11	5♓36	2♒28	17♑25	1♏25	24♐40	8♌26	4♏38	0♍53

THE SUN ENTERS THE SIGN OF PISCES ON FEB 19 AT 03:49.

DAY	TIME	☉	☽	☿	♀	♂	♃	♄	♅	♆	♇
	h m s	° ' "	° '	° '	° '	° '	° '	° '	° '	° '	° '
M 1	10 33 10	9♓54 7	5♋24	7♓26	2♒50	18♑ 8	1♏23	24♐43	8♌24	4♏37	0♍51
A 2	10 37 7	10 54 19	19 7	9 17	3 13	18 51	1R20	24 46	8R22	4R37	0R50
R 3	10 41 4	11 54 29	3♌19	11 10	3 39	19 35	1 18	24 50	8 19	4 36	0 48
C 4	10 45 0	12 54 37	17 59	13 3	4 6	20 19	1 15	24 53	8 17	4 35	0 47
H 5	10 48 57	13 54 42	2♍59	14 57	4 34	21 2	1 11	24 56	8 15	4 34	0 45
6	10 52 53	14 54 46	18 12	16 52	5 5	21 46	1 8	24 59	8 13	4 33	0 44
7	10 56 50	15 54 48	3♎25	18 48	5 37	22 29	1 5	25 2	8 12	4 32	0 43
8	11 0 46	16 54 48	18 31	20 44	6 10	23 13	1 1	25 4	8 10	4 31	0 41
9	11 4 43	17 54 47	3♏19	22 41	6 44	23 57	0 57	25 7	8 8	4 30	0 40
10	11 8 39	18 54 44	17 45	24 39	7 20	24 40	0 53	25 10	8 6	4 29	0 38
11	11 12 36	19 54 39	1♐46	26 36	7 58	25 24	0 49	25 12	8 4	4 28	0 37
12	11 16 32	20 54 33	15 22	28 34	8 36	26 8	0 45	25 14	8 2	4 27	0 35
13	11 20 29	21 54 25	28 35	0♈32	9 16	26 52	0 40	25 17	8 1	4 26	0 34
14	11 24 26	22 54 15	11♑28	2 29	9 57	27 35	0 36	25 19	7 59	4 25	0 33
15	11 28 22	23 54 4	24 4	4 25	10 38	28 19	0 31	25 21	7 58	4 24	0 31
16	11 32 19	24 53 51	6♒26	6 20	11 21	29 3	0 26	25 23	7 56	4 23	0 30
17	11 36 15	25 53 36	18 37	8 14	12 5	29 47	0 21	25 25	7 54	4 22	0 29
18	11 40 12	26 53 19	0♓39	10 6	12 50	0♒31	0 15	25 27	7 53	4 20	0 27
19	11 44 8	27 53 0	12 35	11 56	13 36	1 15	0 10	25 28	7 52	4 19	0 26
20	11 48 5	28 52 40	24 26	13 43	14 23	1 59	0 5	25 30	7 50	4 18	0 25
21	11 52 1	29 52 17	6♈15	15 26	15 10	2 42	29♎59	25 32	7 49	4 17	0 23
22	11 55 58	0♈51 53	18 3	17 7	15 58	3 26	29 53	25 33	7 48	4 15	0 22
23	11 59 55	1 51 26	29 52	18 43	16 47	4 10	29 47	25 34	7 46	4 14	0 21
24	12 3 51	2 50 57	11♉45	20 14	17 37	4 54	29 41	25 36	7 45	4 13	0 19
25	12 7 48	3 50 26	23 46	21 41	18 28	5 38	29 35	25 37	7 44	4 11	0 18
26	12 11 44	4 49 53	5♊57	23 2	19 19	6 22	29 29	25 38	7 43	4 10	0 17
27	12 15 41	5 49 18	18 23	24 18	20 11	7 6	29 22	25 39	7 42	4 9	0 16
28	12 19 37	6 48 40	1♋ 8	25 27	21 4	7 50	29 16	25 39	7 41	4 7	0 15
29	12 23 34	7 48 0	14 16	26 31	21 57	8 34	29 9	25 40	7 40	4 6	0 14
30	12 27 30	8 47 17	27 50	27 27	22 50	9 18	29 2	25 41	7 39	4 4	0 12
31	12 31 27	9♈46 33	11♌51	28♈17	23♒45	10♒ 2	28♎55	25♐41	7♌38	4♏ 3	0♍11

THE SUN ENTERS THE SIGN OF ARIES ON MAR 21 AT 03:06.

♈ ARIES ♉ TAURUS ♊ GEMINI ♋ CANCER ♌ LEO ♍ VIRGO ♎ LIBRA

1958

SIDEREAL SUN . . MOON . . MERCURY . VENUS . . MARS . . JUPITER . SATURN . URANUS . NEPTUNE . PLUTO .

DAY	TIME	☉	☽	☿	♀	♂	♃	♄	♅	♆	♇
	h m s	° ′ ″	° ′	° ′	° ′	° ′	° ′	° ′	° ′	° ′	° ′
A 1	12 35 24	10♈45 46	26♌18	29♈ 0	24♒40	10♒47	28♎49	25♐42	7♌37	4♏ 2	0♍10
P 2	12 39 20	11 44 56	11♍ 9	29 36	25 35	11 31	28R42	25 42	7R37	4R 0	0R 9
R 3	12 43 17	12 44 4	26 15	0♉ 5	26 31	12 15	28 34	25 42	7 36	3 59	0 8
I 4	12 47 13	13 43 11	11♎29	0 27	27 27	12 59	28 27	25R42	7 35	3 57	0 7
L 5	12 51 10	14 42 15	26 41	0 41	28 24	13 43	28 20	25 42	7 35	3 56	0 6
6	12 55 6	15 41 17	11♏40	0R49	29 22	14 27	28 13	25 42	7 34	3 54	0 5
7	12 59 3	16 40 18	26 20	0 50	0♓19	15 11	28 5	25 42	7 34	3 52	0 4
8	13 2 59	17 39 16	10♐34	0 44	1 18	15 55	27 58	25 42	7 33	3 51	0 3
9	13 6 56	18 38 13	24 22	0 31	2 16	16 40	27 51	25 42	7 33	3 49	0 2
10	13 10 52	19 37 8	7♑44	0 13	3 15	17 24	27 43	25 41	7 33	3 48	0 1
11	13 14 49	20 36 2	20 41	29♈49	4 15	18 8	27 36	25 41	7 32	3 46	0 1
12	13 18 46	21 34 53	3♒17	29 21	5 14	18 52	27 28	25 40	7 32	3 45	0 0
13	13 22 42	22 33 43	15 35	28 48	6 15	19 36	27 20	25 39	7 32	3 43	29♌59
14	13 26 39	23 32 31	27 41	28 11	7 15	20 21	27 13	25 38	7 32	3 41	29 58
15	13 30 35	24 31 18	9♓37	27 31	8 16	21 5	27 5	25 37	7D32	3 40	29 57
16	13 34 32	25 30 2	21 27	26 49	9 17	21 49	26 57	25 36	7 32	3 38	29 57
17	13 38 28	26 28 45	3♈15	26 6	10 19	22 33	26 50	25 35	7 32	3 37	29 56
18	13 42 25	27 27 26	15 3	25 23	11 20	23 18	26 42	25 34	7 32	3 35	29 55
19	13 46 21	28 26 5	26 53	24 40	12 22	24 2	26 34	25 33	7 32	3 33	29 54
20	13 50 18	29 24 42	8♉49	23 58	13 25	24 46	26 27	25 31	7 33	3 32	29 54
21	13 54 15	0♉23 17	20 51	23 18	14 27	25 30	26 19	25 30	7 33	3 30	29 53
22	13 58 11	1 21 50	3♊ 2	22 40	15 30	26 14	26 11	25 28	7 33	3 28	29 53
23	14 2 8	2 20 22	15 24	22 5	16 33	26 59	26 4	25 26	7 34	3 27	29 52
24	14 6 4	3 18 51	28 0	21 34	17 37	27 43	25 56	25 25	7 34	3 25	29 52
25	14 10 1	4 17 18	10♋51	21 7	18 40	28 27	25 48	25 23	7 35	3 24	29 51
26	14 13 57	5 15 43	24 0	20 44	19 44	29 11	25 41	25 21	7 35	3 22	29 51
27	14 17 54	6 14 5	7♌30	20 26	20 48	29 55	25 33	25 19	7 36	3 20	29 50
28	14 21 50	7 12 26	21 21	20 13	21 52	0♓40	25 26	25 17	7 36	3 19	29 50
29	14 25 47	8 10 44	5♍33	20 4	22 57	1 24	25 19	25 14	7 37	3 17	29 49
30	14 29 44	9♉ 9 1	20♍ 5	20♈ 0	24♓ 1	2♓ 8	25♎11	25♐12	7♌38	3♏15	29♌49

THE SUN ENTERS THE SIGN OF TAURUS ON APR 20 AT 14:27.

DAY	TIME	☉	☽	☿	♀	♂	♃	♄	♅	♆	♇
	h m s	° ′ ″	° ′	° ′	° ′	° ′	° ′	° ′	° ′	° ′	° ′
M 1	14 33 40	10♉ 7 15	4♎53	20♈ 1	25♓ 6	2♓52	25♎ 4	25♐10	7♌39	3♏14	29♌49
A 2	14 37 37	11 5 27	19 51	20 7	26 11	3 36	24R57	25R 7	7 39	3R12	29R48
Y 3	14 41 33	12 3 38	4♏51	20 17	27 16	4 20	24 50	25 5	7 40	3 10	29 48
4	14 45 30	13 1 47	19 45	20 33	28 22	5 4	24 43	25 2	7 41	3 9	29 48
5	14 49 26	13 59 54	4♐25	20 53	29 27	5 48	24 36	24 59	7 42	3 7	29 48
6	14 53 23	14 58 0	18 44	21 17	0♈33	6 33	24 29	24 56	7 43	3 6	29 47
7	14 57 19	15 56 4	2♑40	21 45	1 39	7 17	24 22	24 54	7 45	3 4	29 47
8	15 1 16	16 54 6	16 9	22 18	2 45	8 1	24 16	24 51	7 46	3 3	29 47
9	15 5 13	17 52 8	29 12	22 55	3 51	8 45	24 9	24 48	7 47	3 1	29 47
10	15 9 9	18 50 8	11♒52	23 35	4 57	9 29	24 3	24 45	7 48	2 59	29 47
11	15 13 6	19 48 6	24 12	24 19	6 4	10 13	23 56	24 41	7 50	2 58	29D47
12	15 17 2	20 46 3	6♓17	25 7	7 11	10 57	23 50	24 38	7 51	2 56	29 47
13	15 20 59	21 43 59	18 12	25 58	8 17	11 41	23 44	24 35	7 52	2 55	29 47
14	15 24 55	22 41 54	0♈ 1	26 53	9 24	12 25	23 38	24 31	7 54	2 53	29 47
15	15 28 52	23 39 47	11 48	27 50	10 31	13 9	23 32	24 28	7 55	2 52	29 47
16	15 32 48	24 37 39	23 38	28 51	11 39	13 53	23 26	24 25	7 57	2 50	29 47
17	15 36 45	25 35 30	5♉34	29 55	12 46	14 36	23 21	24 21	7 59	2 49	29 47
18	15 40 41	26 33 19	17 38	1♉ 2	13 53	15 20	23 15	24 17	8 0	2 47	29 47
19	15 44 38	27 31 7	29 53	2 11	15 1	16 4	23 10	24 14	8 2	2 46	29 48
20	15 48 35	28 28 54	12♊19	3 23	16 9	16 48	23 5	24 10	8 4	2 44	29 48
21	15 52 31	29 26 39	24 59	4 38	17 16	17 32	23 0	24 6	8 6	2 43	29 48
22	15 56 28	0♊24 23	7♋52	5 56	18 24	18 15	22 55	24 2	8 7	2 41	29 48
23	16 0 24	1 22 6	20 59	7 16	19 32	18 59	22 50	23 59	8 9	2 40	29 49
24	16 4 21	2 19 46	4♌20	8 38	20 40	19 43	22 46	23 55	8 11	2 39	29 49
25	16 8 17	3 17 26	17 55	10 3	21 48	20 26	22 41	23 51	8 13	2 37	29 49
26	16 12 14	4 15 3	1♍44	11 31	22 57	21 10	22 37	23 47	8 15	2 36	29 50
27	16 16 11	5 12 40	15 47	13 1	24 5	21 53	22 33	23 43	8 17	2 35	29 50
28	16 20 7	6 10 14	0♎ 3	14 34	25 14	22 37	22 29	23 39	8 20	2 33	29 51
29	16 24 4	7 7 47	14 29	16 9	26 22	23 20	22 25	23 34	8 22	2 32	29 51
30	16 28 0	8 5 19	29 3	17 46	27 31	24 3	22 21	23 30	8 24	2 31	29 52
31	16 31 57	9♊ 2 50	13♏40	19♉26	28♈39	24♓47	22♎18	23♐26	8♌26	2♏30	29♌52

THE SUN ENTERS THE SIGN OF GEMINI ON MAY 21 AT 13:51.

DAY	TIME	☉	☽	☿	♀	♂	♃	♄	♅	♆	♇
	h m s	° ′ ″	° ′	° ′	° ′	° ′	° ′	° ′	° ′	° ′	° ′
J 1	16 35 53	10♊ 0 19	28♏15	21♉ 8	29♈48	25♓30	22♎15	23♐22	8♌29	2♏28	29♌53
U 2	16 39 50	10 57 48	12♐41	22 52	0♉57	26 13	22R12	23R18	8 31	2R27	29 54
N 3	16 43 46	11 55 15	26 52	24 39	2 6	26 56	22 9	23 13	8 33	2 26	29 54
E 4	16 47 43	12 52 41	10♑43	26 29	3 15	27 40	22 6	23 9	8 36	2 25	29 55
5	16 51 40	13 50 7	24 11	28 20	4 24	28 23	22 3	23 5	8 38	2 24	29 55
6	16 55 36	14 47 32	7♒16	0♊14	5 33	29 6	22 1	23 0	8 41	2 23	29 56
7	16 59 33	15 44 56	19 59	2 11	6 43	29 49	21 59	22 56	8 43	2 21	29 57
8	17 3 29	16 42 19	2♓21	4 9	7 52	0♈32	21 56	22 52	8 46	2 20	29 58
9	17 7 26	17 39 42	14 27	6 10	9 1	1 14	21 55	22 47	8 48	2 19	29 59
10	17 11 22	18 37 5	26 22	8 12	10 11	1 57	21 53	22 43	8 51	2 18	29 59
11	17 15 19	19 34 26	8♈12	10 17	11 21	2 40	21 51	22 38	8 54	2 17	0♍ 0
12	17 19 15	20 31 48	20 0	12 23	12 30	3 23	21 50	22 34	8 56	2 16	0 1
13	17 23 12	21 29 8	1♉53	14 30	13 40	4 5	21 49	22 30	8 59	2 15	0 2
14	17 27 9	22 26 29	13 54	16 39	14 50	4 48	21 48	22 25	9 2	2 15	0 3
15	17 31 5	23 23 49	26 7	18 50	16 0	5 30	21 47	22 21	9 5	2 14	0 4
16	17 35 2	24 21 8	8♊35	21 0	17 10	6 12	21 46	22 16	9 8	2 13	0 5
17	17 38 58	25 18 27	21 19	23 12	18 20	6 55	21 46	22 12	9 10	2 12	0 6
18	17 42 55	26 15 45	4♋20	25 24	19 30	7 37	21 45	22 7	9 13	2 11	0 7
19	17 46 51	27 13 3	17 36	27 36	20 40	8 19	21D45	22 3	9 16	2 10	0 8
20	17 50 48	28 10 20	1♌ 5	29 47	21 50	9 1	21 45	21 59	9 19	2 10	0 9
21	17 54 44	29 7 37	14 47	1♋58	23 0	9 43	21 46	21 54	9 22	2 9	0 10
22	17 58 41	0♋ 4 52	28 37	4 9	24 10	10 25	21 46	21 50	9 25	2 8	0 11
23	18 2 38	1 2 7	12♍35	6 18	25 21	11 7	21 47	21 46	9 28	2 7	0 12
24	18 6 34	1 59 22	26 39	8 26	26 31	11 48	21 48	21 41	9 32	2 7	0 14
25	18 10 31	2 56 36	10♎46	10 33	27 41	12 30	21 48	21 37	9 35	2 6	0 15
26	18 14 27	3 53 49	24 57	12 38	28 52	13 11	21 50	21 33	9 38	2 6	0 16
27	18 18 24	4 51 1	9♏10	14 41	0♊ 3	13 53	21 51	21 28	9 41	2 5	0 17
28	18 22 20	5 48 13	23 23	16 43	1 13	14 34	21 52	21 24	9 44	2 5	0 19
29	18 26 17	6 45 25	7♐32	18 43	2 24	15 15	21 54	21 20	9 47	2 4	0 20
30	18 30 13	7♋42 36	21♐35	20♋41	3♊34	15♈56	21♎56	21♐16	9♌51	2♏ 4	0♍21

THE SUN ENTERS THE SIGN OF CANCER ON JUN 21 AT 21:57.

♏ SCORPIO ♐ SAGITTARIUS ♑ CAPRICORN ♒ AQUARIUS ♓ PISCES

SIDEREAL . SUN . MOON . MERCURY . VENUS . MARS . JUPITER . SATURN . URANUS . NEPTUNE . PLUTO .

DAY	TIME	☉	☽	☿	♀	♂	♃	♄	♅	♆	♇
	h m s	° ' "	° '	° '	° '	° '	° '	° '	° '	° '	° '
J 1	18 34 10	8♋39 48	5♑26	22♋37	4♊45	16♈37	21♎58	21♐12	9♌54	2♏ 3	0♍23
U 2	18 38 7	9 36 59	19 2	24 31	5 56	17 18	22 0	21R 8	9 57	2R 3	0 24
L 3	18 42 3	10 34 10	2♒20	26 23	7 7	17 58	22 3	21 3	10 1	2 2	0 25
Y 4	18 46 0	11 31 20	15 18	28 13	8 18	18 39	22 5	20 59	10 4	2 2	0 27
5	18 49 56	12 28 31	27 57	0♌ 1	9 29	19 20	22 8	20 56	10 7	2 2	0 28
6	18 53 53	13 25 43	10♓17	1 47	10 40	20 0	22 11	20 52	10 11	2 1	0 30
7	18 57 49	14 22 54	22 23	3 31	11 51	20 40	22 14	20 48	10 14	2 1	0 31
8	19 1 46	15 20 6	4♈18	5 12	13 2	21 20	22 17	20 44	10 18	2 1	0 33
9	19 5 42	16 17 18	16 8	6 52	14 13	22 0	22 20	20 40	10 21	2 1	0 34
10	19 9 39	17 14 31	27 57	8 30	15 25	22 40	22 24	20 36	10 25	2 1	0 36
11	19 13 36	18 11 44	9♉51	10 5	16 36	23 20	22 28	20 33	10 28	2 1	0 37
12	19 17 32	19 8 57	21 56	11 39	17 47	24 0	22 32	20 29	10 32	2 0	0 39
13	19 21 29	20 6 11	4♊15	13 10	18 59	24 39	22 36	20 26	10 35	2 0	0 40
14	19 25 25	21 3 25	16 53	14 40	20 10	25 18	22 40	20 22	10 39	2D 0	0 42
15	19 29 22	22 0 40	29 51	16 7	21 22	25 57	22 44	20 19	10 42	2 0	0 43
16	19 33 18	22 57 56	13♋11	17 32	22 33	26 36	22 49	20 15	10 46	2 0	0 45
17	19 37 15	23 55 12	26 49	18 55	23 45	27 15	22 53	20 12	10 49	2 0	0 47
18	19 41 11	24 52 28	10♌44	20 16	24 57	27 54	22 58	20 9	10 53	2 1	0 48
19	19 45 8	25 49 44	24 51	21 34	26 8	28 32	23 3	20 5	10 57	2 1	0 50
20	19 49 5	26 47 1	9♍ 5	22 50	27 20	29 11	23 8	20 2	11 0	2 1	0 52
21	19 53 1	27 44 18	23 21	24 4	28 32	29 49	23 14	19 59	11 4	2 1	0 53
22	19 56 58	28 41 35	7♎36	25 15	29 44	0♉27	23 19	19 56	11 7	2 1	0 55
23	20 0 54	29 38 52	21 47	26 24	0♋56	1 5	23 25	19 53	11 11	2 2	0 57
24	20 4 51	0♌36 10	5♏53	27 31	2 8	1 42	23 30	19 51	11 15	2 2	0 59
25	20 8 47	1 33 28	19 54	28 34	3 20	2 20	23 36	19 48	11 18	2 2	1 0
26	20 12 44	2 30 47	3♐47	29 35	4 32	2 57	23 42	19 45	11 22	2 3	1 2
27	20 16 40	3 28 6	17 34	0♍33	5 44	3 34	23 49	19 43	11 26	2 3	1 4
28	20 20 37	4 25 25	1♑12	1 28	6 56	4 11	23 55	19 40	11 29	2 3	1 6
29	20 24 34	5 22 45	14 39	2 20	8 8	4 47	24 1	19 38	11 33	2 4	1 8
30	20 28 30	6 20 6	27 53	3 9	9 20	5 24	24 8	19 35	11 37	2 4	1 10
31	20 32 27	7♌17 27	10♒53	3♍54	10♋32	6♉ 0	24♎15	19♐33	11♌41	2♏ 5	1♍11

THE SUN ENTERS THE SIGN OF LEO ON JUL 23 AT 08:51.

DAY	TIME	☉	☽	☿	♀	♂	♃	♄	♅	♆	♇
	h m s	° ' "	° '	° '	° '	° '	° '	° '	° '	° '	° '
A 1	20 36 23	8♌14 49	23♒37	4♍36	11♋45	6♉36	24♎21	19♐31	11♌44	2♏ 5	1♍13
U 2	20 40 20	9 12 12	6♓ 6	5 14	12 57	7 12	24 28	19R29	11 48	2 6	1 15
G 3	20 44 16	10 9 36	18 21	5 48	14 10	7 47	24 36	19 27	11 52	2 7	1 17
U 4	20 48 13	11 7 1	0♈23	6 18	15 22	8 23	24 43	19 25	11 55	2 7	1 19
S 5	20 52 9	12 4 27	12 16	6 44	16 35	8 58	24 50	19 23	11 59	2 8	1 21
T 6	20 56 6	13 1 55	24 4	7 5	17 47	9 33	24 58	19 21	12 3	2 9	1 23
7	21 0 3	13 59 24	5♉52	7 22	19 0	10 7	25 5	19 20	12 7	2 9	1 25
8	21 3 59	14 56 54	17 46	7 33	20 12	10 42	25 13	19 18	12 10	2 10	1 27
9	21 7 56	15 54 25	29 51	7R40	21 25	11 16	25 21	19 17	12 14	2 11	1 28
10	21 11 52	16 51 58	12♊13	7 41	22 38	11 50	25 29	19 15	12 18	2 12	1 30
11	21 15 49	17 49 32	24 54	7 38	23 51	12 23	25 37	19 14	12 21	2 13	1 32
12	21 19 45	18 47 8	8♋ 0	7 28	25 4	12 57	25 45	19 13	12 25	2 14	1 34
13	21 23 42	19 44 44	21 30	7 14	26 16	13 30	25 54	19 12	12 29	2 14	1 36
14	21 27 38	20 42 23	5♌25	6 53	27 29	14 3	26 2	19 11	12 32	2 15	1 38
15	21 31 35	21 40 2	19 40	6 28	28 42	14 35	26 11	19 10	12 36	2 16	1 40
16	21 35 32	22 37 43	4♍11	5 57	29 55	15 7	26 19	19 9	12 40	2 17	1 42
17	21 39 28	23 35 25	18 49	5 21	1♌ 9	15 39	26 28	19 8	12 44	2 18	1 44
18	21 43 25	24 33 8	3♎29	4 41	2 22	16 10	26 37	19 8	12 47	2 20	1 46
19	21 47 21	25 30 52	18 4	3 56	3 35	16 42	26 46	19 7	12 51	2 21	1 48
20	21 51 18	26 28 37	2♏29	3 8	4 48	17 12	26 55	19 7	12 54	2 22	1 50
21	21 55 14	27 26 23	16 42	2 18	6 1	17 43	27 4	19 6	12 58	2 23	1 52
22	21 59 11	28 24 11	0♐41	1 25	7 15	18 13	27 14	19 6	13 2	2 24	1 54
23	22 3 7	29 22 0	14 27	0 32	8 28	18 43	27 23	19 6	13 5	2 25	1 56
24	22 7 4	0♍19 49	27 58	29♌39	9 41	19 13	27 33	19D 6	13 9	2 27	1 58
25	22 11 1	1 17 40	11♑16	28 47	10 55	19 42	27 42	19 6	13 13	2 28	2 0
26	22 14 57	2 15 33	24 21	27 58	12 8	20 10	27 52	19 6	13 16	2 29	2 2
27	22 18 54	3 13 26	7♒14	27 12	13 22	20 39	28 2	19 6	13 20	2 30	2 4
28	22 22 50	4 11 21	19 54	26 31	14 35	21 7	28 12	19 7	13 23	2 32	2 6
29	22 26 47	5 9 18	2♓22	25 55	15 49	21 34	28 22	19 7	13 27	2 33	2 8
30	22 30 43	6 7 16	14 37	25 25	17 3	22 2	28 32	19 7	13 30	2 35	2 10
31	22 34 40	7♍ 5 15	26♓42	25♌ 3	18♌16	22♉28	28♎42	19♐ 8	13♌34	2♏36	2♍12

THE SUN ENTERS THE SIGN OF VIRGO ON AUG 23 AT 15:47.

DAY	TIME	☉	☽	☿	♀	♂	♃	♄	♅	♆	♇
	h m s	° ' "	° '	° '	° '	° '	° '	° '	° '	° '	° '
S 1	22 38 36	8♍ 3 16	8♈39	24♌48	19♌30	22♉55	28♎53	19♐ 9	13♌37	2♏37	2♍14
E 2	22 42 33	9 1 20	20 28	24D41	20 44	23 21	29 3	19 10	13 41	2 39	2 16
P 3	22 46 29	9 59 24	2♉15	24 43	21 57	23 46	29 13	19 11	13 44	2 40	2 18
T 4	22 50 26	10 57 31	14 3	24 53	23 11	24 11	29 24	19 12	13 47	2 42	2 20
E 5	22 54 23	11 55 40	25 57	25 12	24 25	24 36	29 35	19 13	13 51	2 44	2 22
M 6	22 58 19	12 53 51	8♊ 0	25 39	25 39	25 0	29 45	19 14	13 54	2 45	2 24
B 7	23 2 16	13 52 4	20 20	26 15	26 53	25 24	29 56	19 15	13 58	2 47	2 26
E 8	23 6 12	14 50 19	3♋ 0	26 59	28 7	25 47	0♏ 7	19 17	14 1	2 48	2 28
R 9	23 10 9	15 48 36	16 5	27 51	29 21	26 9	0 18	19 18	14 4	2 50	2 30
10	23 14 5	16 46 55	29 36	28 50	0♍35	26 31	0 29	19 20	14 8	2 52	2 32
11	23 18 2	17 45 16	13♌35	29 57	1 49	26 53	0 40	19 21	14 11	2 53	2 34
12	23 21 58	18 43 39	27 58	1♍10	3 3	27 14	0 51	19 23	14 14	2 55	2 36
13	23 25 55	19 42 3	12♍42	2 29	4 18	27 35	1 2	19 25	14 17	2 57	2 38
14	23 29 52	20 40 30	27 39	3 53	5 32	27 54	1 14	19 27	14 20	2 59	2 40
15	23 33 48	21 38 59	12♎41	5 22	6 46	28 14	1 25	19 29	14 24	3 0	2 41
16	23 37 45	22 37 29	27 38	6 56	8 0	28 32	1 36	19 31	14 27	3 2	2 43
17	23 41 41	23 36 1	12♏23	8 33	9 15	28 50	1 48	19 33	14 30	3 4	2 45
18	23 45 38	24 34 35	26 52	10 14	10 29	29 8	2 0	19 36	14 33	3 6	2 47
19	23 49 34	25 33 10	11♐ 0	11 57	11 44	29 25	2 11	19 38	14 36	3 8	2 49
20	23 53 31	26 31 47	24 48	13 42	12 58	29 41	2 23	19 41	14 39	3 9	2 51
21	23 57 27	27 30 26	8♑15	15 29	14 12	29 57	2 35	19 43	14 42	3 11	2 53
22	0 1 24	28 29 6	21 22	17 17	15 27	0♊11	2 47	19 46	14 45	3 13	2 55
23	0 5 21	29 27 49	4♒13	19 6	16 41	0 26	2 58	19 49	14 48	3 15	2 56
24	0 9 17	0♎26 32	16 49	20 56	17 56	0 39	3 10	19 52	14 51	3 17	2 58
25	0 13 14	1 25 18	29 12	22 46	19 10	0 52	3 22	19 55	14 53	3 19	3 0
26	0 17 10	2 24 5	11♓24	24 36	20 25	1 4	3 34	19 58	14 56	3 21	3 2
27	0 21 7	3 22 54	23 27	26 26	21 40	1 16	3 46	20 1	14 59	3 23	3 4
28	0 25 3	4 21 45	5♈23	28 16	22 54	1 26	3 59	20 4	15 2	3 25	3 5
29	0 29 0	5 20 39	17 14	0♎ 6	24 9	1 36	4 11	20 7	15 4	3 27	3 7
30	0 32 56	6♎19 34	29♈ 2	1♎55	25♍24	1♊45	4♏23	20♐11	15♌ 7	3♏29	3♍ 9

THE SUN ENTERS THE SIGN OF LIBRA ON SEP 23 AT 13:10.

♈ ARIES ♉ TAURUS ♊ GEMINI ♋ CANCER ♌ LEO ♍ VIRGO ♎ LIBRA

1958

SIDEREAL SUN. MOON. MERCURY. VENUS. MARS. JUPITER. SATURN. URANUS. NEPTUNE. PLUTO.

DAY	TIME	☉	☽	☿	♀	♂	♃	♄	♅	♆	♇
	h m s	° ' "	° '	° '	° '	° '	° '	° '	° '	° '	° '
O 1	0 36 53	7♎18 31	10♉49	3♎43	26♍38	1♊54	4♏35	20♐14	15♌10	3♏31	3♍11
C 2	0 40 49	8 17 31	22 38	5 31	27 53	2 1	4 48	20 18	15 12	3 33	3 12
T 3	0 44 46	9 16 33	4♊34	7 18	29 8	2 8	5 0	20 22	15 15	3 35	3 14
O 4	0 48 43	10 15 37	16 39	9 5	0♎23	2 14	5 13	20 25	15 17	3 37	3 16
B 5	0 52 39	11 14 43	28 57	10 51	1 37	2 19	5 25	20 29	15 20	3 39	3 17
E 6	0 56 36	12 13 52	11♋34	12 36	2 52	2 24	5 38	20 33	15 22	3 42	3 19
R 7	1 0 32	13 13 3	24 33	14 20	4 7	2 27	5 50	20 37	15 25	3 44	3 21
8	1 4 29	14 12 17	7♌57	16 3	5 22	2 30	6 3	20 41	15 27	3 46	3 22
9	1 8 25	15 11 32	21 49	17 46	6 37	2 31	6 15	20 45	15 29	3 48	3 24
10	1 12 22	16 10 50	6♍ 7	19 28	7 52	2R32	6 28	20 49	15 31	3 50	3 25
11	1 16 18	17 10 10	20 49	21 9	9 7	2 32	6 41	20 54	15 34	3 52	3 27
12	1 20 15	18 9 33	5♎49	22 50	10 22	2 31	6 54	20 58	15 36	3 54	3 29
13	1 24 12	19 8 57	21 0	24 29	11 37	2 29	7 6	21 2	15 38	3 57	3 30
14	1 28 8	20 8 24	6♏12	26 8	12 52	2 26	7 19	21 7	15 40	3 59	3 32
15	1 32 5	21 7 52	21 15	27 47	14 7	2 23	7 32	21 11	15 42	4 1	3 33
16	1 36 1	22 7 23	6♐ 1	29 24	15 22	2 18	7 45	21 16	15 44	4 3	3 34
17	1 39 58	23 6 55	20 25	1♏ 1	16 37	2 13	7 58	21 21	15 46	4 5	3 36
18	1 43 54	24 6 29	4♑23	2 37	17 52	2 6	8 11	21 26	15 48	4 8	3 37
19	1 47 51	25 6 5	17 55	4 13	19 7	1 59	8 24	21 30	15 50	4 10	3 39
20	1 51 47	26 5 42	1♒ 2	5 48	20 22	1 51	8 37	21 35	15 52	4 12	3 40
21	1 55 44	27 5 21	13 48	7 22	21 38	1 42	8 50	21 40	15 53	4 14	3 41
22	1 59 41	28 5 2	26 15	8 56	22 53	1 32	9 3	21 45	15 55	4 17	3 43
23	2 3 37	29 4 45	8♓27	10 29	24 8	1 21	9 16	21 51	15 57	4 19	3 44
24	2 7 34	0♏ 4 29	20 29	12 2	25 23	1 10	9 29	21 56	15 58	4 21	3 45
25	2 11 30	1 4 15	2♈23	13 34	26 38	0 57	9 42	22 1	16 0	4 23	3 47
26	2 15 27	2 4 3	14 12	15 5	27 53	0 44	9 55	22 6	16 1	4 25	3 48
27	2 19 23	3 3 53	26 0	16 36	29 8	0 30	10 8	22 12	16 3	4 28	3 49
28	2 23 20	4 3 45	7♉48	18 7	0♏24	0 15	10 21	22 17	16 4	4 30	3 50
29	2 27 16	5 3 39	19 39	19 37	1 39	0 0	10 34	22 23	16 6	4 32	3 51
30	2 31 13	6 3 34	1♊35	21 6	2 54	29♉44	10 47	22 28	16 7	4 34	3 52
31	2 35 9	7♏ 3 32	13♊37	22♏35	4♏ 9	29♉27	11♏ 0	22♐34	16♌ 8	4♏37	3♍53

THE SUN ENTERS THE SIGN OF SCORPIO ON OCT 23 AT 22:12.

DAY	TIME	☉	☽	☿	♀	♂	♃	♄	♅	♆	♇
	h m s	° ' "	° '	° '	° '	° '	° '	° '	° '	° '	° '
N 1	2 39 6	8♏ 3 32	25♊49	24♏ 3	5♏25	29♉10	11♏14	22♐39	16♌ 9	4♏39	3♍55
O 2	2 43 3	9 3 34	8♋12	25 31	6 40	28R52	11 27	22 45	16 10	4 41	3 56
V 3	2 46 59	10 3 38	20 51	26 58	7 55	28 33	11 40	22 51	16 12	4 43	3 57
E 4	2 50 56	11 3 44	3♌47	28 25	9 10	28 14	11 53	22 57	16 13	4 46	3 58
M 5	2 54 52	12 3 53	17 3	29 51	10 26	27 54	12 6	23 3	16 14	4 48	3 59
B 6	2 58 49	13 4 3	0♍43	1♐16	11 41	27 34	12 19	23 9	16 14	4 50	4 0
E 7	3 2 45	14 4 15	14 46	2 41	12 56	27 13	12 33	23 15	16 15	4 52	4 0
R 8	3 6 42	15 4 30	29 13	4 4	14 12	26 52	12 46	23 21	16 16	4 55	4 1
9	3 10 38	16 4 46	14♎ 1	5 27	15 27	26 31	12 59	23 27	16 17	4 57	4 2
10	3 14 35	17 5 5	29 3	6 49	16 42	26 9	13 12	23 33	16 18	4 59	4 3
11	3 18 32	18 5 25	14♏13	8 11	17 58	25 48	13 25	23 39	16 18	5 1	4 4
12	3 22 28	19 5 47	29 20	9 31	19 13	25 26	13 39	23 45	16 19	5 3	4 5
13	3 26 25	20 6 11	14♐16	10 49	20 28	25 4	13 52	23 51	16 19	5 6	4 5
14	3 30 21	21 6 36	28 51	12 7	21 44	24 42	14 5	23 58	16 20	5 8	4 6
15	3 34 18	22 7 3	13♑ 1	13 23	22 59	24 19	14 18	24 4	16 20	5 10	4 7
16	3 38 14	23 7 31	26 43	14 37	24 15	23 57	14 31	24 10	16 21	5 12	4 7
17	3 42 11	24 8 1	9♒56	15 50	25 30	23 36	14 44	24 17	16 21	5 14	4 8
18	3 46 8	25 8 31	22 44	17 0	26 45	23 14	14 57	24 23	16 21	5 16	4 9
19	3 50 4	26 9 3	5♓10	18 8	28 1	22 52	15 10	24 30	16 22	5 19	4 9
20	3 54 1	27 9 36	17 19	19 13	29 16	22 31	15 23	24 36	16 22	5 21	4 10
21	3 57 57	28 10 10	29 16	20 15	0♐31	22 10	15 36	24 43	16 22	5 23	4 10
22	4 1 54	29 10 46	11♈ 6	21 13	1 47	21 49	15 50	24 49	16R22	5 25	4 11
23	4 5 50	0♐11 23	22 52	22 7	3 2	21 29	16 3	24 56	16 22	5 27	4 11
24	4 9 47	1 12 1	4♉40	22 57	4 18	21 9	16 15	25 3	16 22	5 29	4 11
25	4 13 43	2 12 40	16 31	23 42	5 33	20 50	16 28	25 9	16 22	5 31	4 12
26	4 17 40	3 13 21	28 29	24 20	6 48	20 31	16 41	25 16	16 21	5 33	4 12
27	4 21 36	4 14 3	10♊35	24 52	8 4	20 13	16 54	25 23	16 21	5 35	4 13
28	4 25 33	5 14 46	22 51	25 17	9 19	19 56	17 7	25 30	16 21	5 37	4 13
29	4 29 30	6 15 31	5♋16	25 34	10 35	19 39	17 20	25 37	16 21	5 39	4 13
30	4 33 26	7♐16 17	17♋53	25♐42	11♐50	19♉22	17♏33	25♐43	16♌20	5♏41	4♍13

THE SUN ENTERS THE SIGN OF SAGITTARIUS ON NOV 22 AT 19:30.

DAY	TIME	☉	☽	☿	♀	♂	♃	♄	♅	♆	♇
	h m s	° ' "	° '	° '	° '	° '	° '	° '	° '	° '	° '
D 1	4 37 23	8♐17 5	0♌42	25♐40	13♐ 5	19♉ 6	17♏46	25♐50	16♌20	5♏43	4♍13
E 2	4 41 19	9 17 54	13 45	25R27	14 21	18R51	17 58	25 57	16R19	5 45	4 14
C 3	4 45 16	10 18 44	27 2	25 4	15 36	18 37	18 11	26 4	16 19	5 47	4 14
E 4	4 49 12	11 19 36	10♍35	24 29	16 52	18 23	18 24	26 11	16 18	5 49	4 14
M 5	4 53 9	12 20 29	24 26	23 44	18 7	18 10	18 36	26 18	16 17	5 51	4 14
B 6	4 57 5	13 21 24	8♎34	22 48	19 22	17 58	18 49	26 25	16 17	5 53	4R14
E 7	5 1 2	14 22 19	23 0	21 42	20 38	17 47	19 2	26 32	16 16	5 55	4 14
R 8	5 4 59	15 23 16	7♏41	20 29	21 53	17 37	19 14	26 39	16 15	5 56	4 14
9	5 8 55	16 24 15	22 32	19 9	23 9	17 27	19 27	26 46	16 14	5 58	4 14
10	5 12 52	17 25 14	7♐25	17 47	24 24	17 18	19 39	26 53	16 13	6 0	4 14
11	5 16 48	18 26 15	22 13	16 24	25 39	17 10	19 52	27 0	16 12	6 2	4 14
12	5 20 45	19 27 16	6♑46	15 4	26 55	17 3	20 4	27 7	16 11	6 4	4 14
13	5 24 41	20 28 18	20 58	13 48	28 10	16 56	20 16	27 14	16 10	6 5	4 13
14	5 28 38	21 29 21	4♒45	12 40	29 26	16 51	20 28	27 21	16 9	6 7	4 13
15	5 32 35	22 30 24	18 4	11 41	0♑41	16 46	20 41	27 28	16 8	6 9	4 13
16	5 36 31	23 31 27	0♓57	10 52	1 56	16 42	20 53	27 35	16 6	6 10	4 13
17	5 40 28	24 32 31	13 26	10 14	3 12	16 39	21 5	27 42	16 5	6 12	4 12
18	5 44 24	25 33 35	25 37	9 46	4 27	16 37	21 17	27 49	16 4	6 14	4 12
19	5 48 21	26 34 40	7♈34	9 30	5 43	16 35	21 29	27 56	16 2	6 15	4 12
20	5 52 17	27 35 45	19 23	9D25	6 58	16D35	21 41	28 3	16 1	6 17	4 11
21	5 56 14	28 36 50	1♉10	9 29	8 13	16 35	21 53	28 10	15 59	6 18	4 11
22	6 0 10	29 37 56	12 59	9 42	9 29	16 36	22 4	28 18	15 58	6 20	4 10
23	6 4 7	0♑39 1	24 54	10 4	10 44	16 38	22 16	28 25	15 56	6 22	4 10
24	6 8 4	1 40 8	7♊ 0	10 33	12 0	16 40	22 28	28 32	15 55	6 23	4 9
25	6 12 0	2 41 14	19 18	11 9	13 15	16 43	22 39	28 39	15 53	6 24	4 9
26	6 15 57	3 42 21	1♋49	11 51	14 30	16 47	22 51	28 46	15 51	6 26	4 8
27	6 19 53	4 43 28	14 33	12 38	15 46	16 52	23 2	28 53	15 50	6 27	4 8
28	6 23 50	5 44 35	27 31	13 30	17 1	16 57	23 14	29 0	15 48	6 29	4 7
29	6 27 46	6 45 43	10♌40	14 27	18 16	17 4	23 25	29 7	15 46	6 30	4 6
30	6 31 43	7 46 51	24 1	15 27	19 32	17 10	23 36	29 14	15 44	6 31	4 6
31	6 35 39	8♑47 59	7♍31	16♐30	20♑47	17♉18	23♏47	29♐21	15♌42	6♏33	4♍ 5

THE SUN ENTERS THE SIGN OF CAPRICORN ON DEC 22 AT 08:40.

♏ SCORPIO ♐ SAGITTARIUS ♑ CAPRICORN ♒ AQUARIUS ♓ PISCES

1959

SIDEREAL. SUN. MOON. MERCURY. VENUS. MARS. JUPITER. SATURN. URANUS. NEPTUNE. PLUTO.

DAY	TIME	☉	☽	☿	♀	♂	♃	♄	♅	♆	♇
	h m s	° ' "	° '	° '	° '	° '	° '	° '	° '	° '	° '
J 1	6 39 36	9♑49 8	21♍10	17♐37	22♑ 2	17♉26	23♏58	29♐28	15♌40	6♏34	4♍ 4
A 2	6 43 33	10 50 17	5♎ 0	18 45	23 18	17 35	24 9	29 35	15R38	6 35	4R 3
N 3	6 47 29	11 51 27	18 59	19 57	24 33	17 44	24 20	29 42	15 36	6 36	4 3
U 4	6 51 26	12 52 36	3♏ 8	21 10	25 48	17 54	24 31	29 49	15 34	6 37	4 2
A 5	6 55 22	13 53 47	17 26	22 25	27 3	18 5	24 42	29 56	15 32	6 38	4 1
R 6	6 59 19	14 54 57	1♐51	23 42	28 19	18 16	24 52	0♑ 3	15 30	6 40	4 0
Y 7	7 3 15	15 56 8	16 18	25 0	29 34	18 28	25 3	0 10	15 28	6 41	3 59
8	7 7 12	16 57 18	0♑42	26 20	0♒49	18 41	25 13	0 17	15 26	6 42	3 58
9	7 11 8	17 58 29	14 56	27 40	2 5	18 54	25 24	0 24	15 24	6 43	3 57
10	7 15 5	18 59 39	28 55	29 2	3 20	19 8	25 34	0 31	15 21	6 44	3 56
11	7 19 2	20 0 49	12♒35	0♑25	4 35	19 22	25 44	0 37	15 19	6 45	3 55
12	7 22 58	21 1 58	25 51	1 49	5 50	19 36	25 54	0 44	15 17	6 46	3 54
13	7 26 55	22 3 7	8♓43	3 13	7 6	19 52	26 4	0 51	15 14	6 46	3 53
14	7 30 51	23 4 16	21 14	4 39	8 21	20 7	26 14	0 58	15 12	6 47	3 52
15	7 34 48	24 5 23	3♈27	6 5	9 36	20 24	26 24	1 5	15 10	6 48	3 51
16	7 38 44	25 6 30	15 26	7 32	10 51	20 40	26 34	1 11	15 7	6 49	3 50
17	7 42 41	26 7 36	27 16	9 0	12 6	20 58	26 43	1 18	15 5	6 50	3 49
18	7 46 37	27 8 42	9♉ 4	10 28	13 21	21 15	26 53	1 25	15 2	6 50	3 48
19	7 50 34	28 9 47	20 54	11 57	14 37	21 33	27 2	1 31	15 0	6 51	3 47
20	7 54 31	29 10 51	2♊52	13 27	15 52	21 52	27 11	1 38	14 57	6 52	3 46
21	7 58 27	0♒11 54	15 3	14 57	17 7	22 11	27 20	1 44	14 55	6 52	3 44
22	8 2 24	1 12 56	27 29	16 28	18 22	22 30	27 29	1 51	14 52	6 53	3 43
23	8 6 20	2 13 57	10♋13	17 59	19 37	22 50	27 38	1 57	14 50	6 53	3 42
24	8 10 17	3 14 58	23 15	19 31	20 52	23 10	27 47	2 4	14 47	6 54	3 41
25	8 14 13	4 15 58	6♌34	21 4	22 7	23 31	27 56	2 10	14 45	6 54	3 39
26	8 18 10	5 16 56	20 8	22 37	23 22	23 52	28 4	2 16	14 42	6 55	3 38
27	8 22 6	6 17 54	3♍54	24 11	24 37	24 13	28 13	2 23	14 40	6 55	3 37
28	8 26 3	7 18 52	17 48	25 46	25 52	24 35	28 21	2 29	14 37	6 56	3 35
29	8 30 0	8 19 48	1♎48	27 21	27 7	24 57	28 29	2 35	14 34	6 56	3 34
30	8 33 56	9 20 44	15 52	28 57	28 22	25 19	28 37	2 41	14 32	6 56	3 33
31	8 37 53	10♒21 39	29♎57	0♒33	29♒37	25♉42	28♏45	2♑47	14♌29	6♏57	3♍31

THE SUN ENTERS THE SIGN OF AQUARIUS ON JAN 20 AT 19:19.

DAY	TIME	☉	☽	☿	♀	♂	♃	♄	♅	♆	♇
	h m s	° ' "	° '	° '	° '	° '	° '	° '	° '	° '	° '
F 1	8 41 49	11♒22 34	14♏ 2	2♒11	0♓52	26♉ 5	28♏53	2♑53	14♌27	6♏57	3♍30
E 2	8 45 46	12 23 28	28 8	3 49	2 6	26 28	29 0	2 59	14R24	6 57	3R29
B 3	8 49 42	13 24 21	12♐12	5 27	3 21	26 52	29 8	3 5	14 21	6 57	3 27
R 4	8 53 39	14 25 14	26 13	7 7	4 36	27 16	29 15	3 11	14 19	6 57	3 26
U 5	8 57 35	15 26 5	10♑ 9	8 47	5 51	27 40	29 22	3 17	14 16	6 57	3 24
A 6	9 1 32	16 26 56	23 56	10 28	7 6	28 4	29 29	3 23	14 13	6 58	3 23
R 7	9 5 29	17 27 45	7♒30	12 9	8 20	28 29	29 36	3 29	14 11	6R58	3 22
Y 8	9 9 25	18 28 33	20 49	13 52	9 35	28 54	29 43	3 35	14 8	6 58	3 20
9	9 13 22	19 29 20	3♓51	15 35	10 50	29 19	29 50	3 40	14 6	6 58	3 19
10	9 17 18	20 30 5	16 35	17 19	12 5	29 45	29 56	3 46	14 3	6 57	3 17
11	9 21 15	21 30 49	29 1	19 4	13 19	0♊11	0♐ 3	3 51	14 0	6 57	3 16
12	9 25 11	22 31 32	11♈12	20 50	14 34	0 37	0 9	3 57	13 58	6 57	3 14
13	9 29 8	23 32 13	23 11	22 36	15 48	1 3	0 15	4 2	13 55	6 57	3 13
14	9 33 4	24 32 52	5♉ 2	24 23	17 3	1 30	0 21	4 8	13 53	6 57	3 11
15	9 37 1	25 33 29	16 50	26 11	18 17	1 57	0 27	4 13	13 50	6 57	3 10
16	9 40 58	26 34 5	28 41	28 0	19 32	2 24	0 32	4 18	13 47	6 56	3 8
17	9 44 54	27 34 40	10♊39	29 50	20 46	2 51	0 37	4 23	13 45	6 56	3 7
18	9 48 51	28 35 12	22 50	1♓40	22 1	3 18	0 43	4 28	13 42	6 56	3 5
19	9 52 47	29 35 43	5♋19	3 31	23 15	3 46	0 48	4 33	13 40	6 55	3 4
20	9 56 44	0♓36 12	18 8	5 22	24 29	4 14	0 53	4 38	13 37	6 55	3 2
21	10 0 40	1 36 39	1♌19	7 14	25 44	4 42	0 57	4 43	13 35	6 55	3 1
22	10 4 37	2 37 4	14 52	9 7	26 58	5 10	1 2	4 48	13 32	6 54	2 59
23	10 8 33	3 37 28	28 46	11 0	28 12	5 38	1 7	4 53	13 30	6 54	2 57
24	10 12 30	4 37 50	12♍56	12 52	29 26	6 7	1 11	4 58	13 28	6 53	2 56
25	10 16 27	5 38 10	27 18	14 45	0♈40	6 36	1 15	5 2	13 25	6 52	2 54
26	10 20 23	6 38 29	11♎46	16 38	1 55	7 5	1 19	5 7	13 23	6 52	2 53
27	10 24 20	7 38 46	26 14	18 30	3 9	7 34	1 23	5 11	13 21	6 51	2 51
28	10 28 16	8♓39 1	10♏39	20♓21	4♈23	8♊ 3	1♐26	5♑16	13♌18	6♏51	2♍50

THE SUN ENTERS THE SIGN OF PISCES ON FEB 19 AT 09:38.

DAY	TIME	☉	☽	☿	♀	♂	♃	♄	♅	♆	♇
	h m s	° ' "	° '	° '	° '	° '	° '	° '	° '	° '	° '
M 1	10 32 13	9♓39 16	24♏56	22♓11	5♈37	8♊33	1♐29	5♑20	13♌16	6♏50	2♍48
A 2	10 36 9	10 39 29	9♐ 5	23 59	6 51	9 2	1 33	5 24	13R14	6R49	2R47
R 3	10 40 6	11 39 40	23 2	25 46	8 4	9 32	1 36	5 28	13 11	6 49	2 45
C 4	10 44 2	12 39 50	6♑48	27 30	9 18	10 2	1 39	5 32	13 9	6 48	2 44
H 5	10 47 59	13 39 58	20 22	29 11	10 32	10 32	1 41	5 36	13 7	6 47	2 42
6	10 51 56	14 40 5	3♒43	0♈49	11 46	11 2	1 44	5 40	13 5	6 46	2 41
7	10 55 52	15 40 10	16 51	2 23	13 0	11 32	1 46	5 44	13 3	6 45	2 39
8	10 59 49	16 40 13	29 46	3 52	14 13	12 3	1 48	5 48	13 1	6 44	2 38
9	11 3 45	17 40 15	12♓27	5 16	15 27	12 33	1 50	5 52	12 59	6 43	2 36
10	11 7 42	18 40 15	24 55	6 35	16 40	13 4	1 52	5 55	12 57	6 43	2 35
11	11 11 38	19 40 12	7♈11	7 47	17 54	13 35	1 54	5 59	12 55	6 42	2 33
12	11 15 35	20 40 8	19 15	8 53	19 7	14 6	1 55	6 2	12 53	6 41	2 32
13	11 19 31	21 40 1	1♉11	9 52	20 21	14 37	1 56	6 6	12 51	6 40	2 31
14	11 23 28	22 39 53	13 1	10 43	21 34	15 8	1 57	6 9	12 49	6 38	2 29
15	11 27 24	23 39 42	24 49	11 27	22 48	15 39	1 58	6 12	12 47	6 37	2 28
16	11 31 21	24 39 29	6♊40	12 2	24 1	16 11	1 59	6 15	12 46	6 36	2 26
17	11 35 18	25 39 14	18 37	12 30	25 14	16 42	1 59	6 18	12 44	6 35	2 25
18	11 39 14	26 38 57	0♋47	12 49	26 27	17 14	1R59	6 21	12 42	6 34	2 24
19	11 43 11	27 38 38	13 13	12R59	27 40	17 46	1 59	6 24	12 40	6 33	2 22
20	11 47 7	28 38 16	25 59	13 1	28 53	18 18	1 59	6 26	12 39	6 32	2 21
21	11 51 4	29 37 52	9♌10	12 56	0♉ 6	18 50	1 59	6 29	12 37	6 31	2 20
22	11 55 0	0♈37 25	22 46	12 42	1 19	19 22	1 59	6 32	12 36	6 29	2 18
23	11 58 57	1 36 57	6♍47	12 21	2 32	19 54	1 58	6 34	12 34	6 28	2 17
24	12 2 53	2 36 26	21 11	11 53	3 45	20 26	1 57	6 36	12 33	6 27	2 16
25	12 6 50	3 35 53	5♎52	11 19	4 58	20 58	1 56	6 39	12 32	6 25	2 14
26	12 10 47	4 35 18	20 44	10 40	6 10	21 31	1 55	6 41	12 30	6 24	2 13
27	12 14 43	5 34 41	5♏39	9 57	7 23	22 3	1 53	6 43	12 29	6 23	2 12
28	12 18 40	6 34 3	20 30	9 10	8 35	22 36	1 52	6 45	12 28	6 21	2 11
29	12 22 36	7 33 22	5♐ 9	8 20	9 48	23 8	1 50	6 47	12 27	6 20	2 9
30	12 26 33	8 32 40	19 31	7 30	11 0	23 41	1 48	6 48	12 25	6 19	2 8
31	12 30 29	9♈31 56	3♑35	6♈39	12♉12	24♊14	1♐46	6♑50	12♌24	6♏17	2♍ 7

THE SUN ENTERS THE SIGN OF ARIES ON MAR 21 AT 08:55.

♈ ARIES ♉ TAURUS ♊ GEMINI ♋ CANCER ♌ LEO ♍ VIRGO ♎ LIBRA

SIDEREAL TIME · SUN · MOON · MERCURY · VENUS · MARS · JUPITER · SATURN · URANUS · NEPTUNE · PLUTO

DAY	TIME	☉	☽	☿	♀	♂	♃	♄	♅	♆	♇
	h m s	° ' "	° '	° '	° '	° '	° '	° '	° '	° '	° '
A 1	12 34 26	10♈31 11	17♑19	5♈49	13♉25	24♊47	1♐43	6♑52	12♌23	6♏16	2♍ 6
P 2	12 38 22	11 30 24	0♒43	5R 0	14 37	25 20	1R41	6 53	12R22	6R14	2R 5
R 3	12 42 19	12 29 34	13 49	4 14	15 49	25 53	1 38	6 55	12 21	6 13	2 4
I 4	12 46 16	13 28 43	26 38	3 31	17 1	26 26	1 35	6 56	12 20	6 12	2 3
L 5	12 50 12	14 27 50	9♓12	2 52	18 13	26 59	1 32	6 57	12 20	6 10	2 2
6	12 54 9	15 26 56	21 34	2 18	19 25	27 33	1 29	6 58	12 19	6 9	2 1
7	12 58 5	16 25 59	3♈46	1 48	20 37	28 6	1 26	6 59	12 18	6 7	2 0
8	13 2 2	17 25 0	15 49	1 23	21 48	28 39	1 22	7 0	12 17	6 6	1 59
9	13 5 58	18 24 0	27 45	1 4	23 0	29 13	1 18	7 1	12 17	6 4	1 58
10	13 9 55	19 22 57	9♉37	0 50	24 12	29 46	1 14	7 2	12 16	6 2	1 57
11	13 13 51	20 21 52	21 26	0 42	25 23	0♋20	1 10	7 2	12 16	6 1	1 56
12	13 17 48	21 20 45	3♊14	0D38	26 35	0 54	1 6	7 3	12 15	5 59	1 55
13	13 21 44	22 19 36	15 6	0 41	27 46	1 27	1 2	7 3	12 15	5 58	1 54
14	13 25 41	23 18 25	27 5	0 48	28 57	2 1	0 57	7 4	12 14	5 56	1 53
15	13 29 38	24 17 12	9♋14	1 1	0♊ 8	2 35	0 52	7 4	12 14	5 55	1 52
16	13 33 34	25 15 56	21 37	1 18	1 20	3 9	0 48	7R 4	12 14	5 53	1 51
17	13 37 31	26 14 38	4♌19	1 40	2 31	3 43	0 43	7 4	12 14	5 51	1 51
18	13 41 27	27 13 18	17 23	2 6	3 42	4 17	0 37	7 4	12 13	5 50	1 50
19	13 45 24	28 11 55	0♍52	2 37	4 52	4 51	0 32	7 4	12 13	5 48	1 49
20	13 49 20	29 10 31	14 49	3 12	6 3	5 25	0 27	7 3	12D13	5 47	1 49
21	13 53 17	0♉ 9 4	29 12	3 51	7 14	5 59	0 21	7 3	12 13	5 45	1 48
22	13 57 13	1 7 35	13♎58	4 33	8 24	6 34	0 15	7 2	12 13	5 43	1 47
23	14 1 10	2 6 4	29 1	5 19	9 35	7 8	0 10	7 2	12 14	5 42	1 47
24	14 5 7	3 4 31	14♏12	6 9	10 45	7 42	0 4	7 1	12 14	5 40	1 46
25	14 9 3	4 2 57	29 23	7 2	11 55	8 16	29♏57	7 0	12 14	5 38	1 45
26	14 13 0	5 1 20	14♐23	7 58	13 5	8 51	29 51	7 0	12 14	5 37	1 45
27	14 16 56	5 59 43	29 4	8 57	14 15	9 25	29 45	6 59	12 15	5 35	1 44
28	14 20 53	6 58 3	13♑21	9 59	15 25	10 0	29 39	6 58	12 15	5 33	1 44
29	14 24 49	7 56 22	27 12	11 3	16 35	10 34	29 32	6 56	12 15	5 32	1 43
30	14 28 46	8♉54 40	10♒37	12♈11	17♊45	11♋ 9	29♏25	6♑55	12♌16	5♏30	1♍43

THE SUN ENTERS THE SIGN OF TAURUS ON APR 20 AT 20:17.

DAY	TIME	☉	☽	☿	♀	♂	♃	♄	♅	♆	♇
	h m s	° ' "	° '	° '	° '	° '	° '	° '	° '	° '	° '
M 1	14 32 42	9♉52 56	23♒38	13♈21	18♊54	11♋44	29♏19	6♑54	12♌16	5♏29	1♍43
A 2	14 36 39	10 51 10	6♓18	14 33	20 4	12 18	29R12	6R52	12 17	5R27	1R42
Y 3	14 40 36	11 49 23	18 41	15 48	21 13	12 53	29 5	6 51	12 18	5 25	1 42
4	14 44 32	12 47 35	0♈51	17 5	22 22	13 28	28 58	6 49	12 18	5 24	1 42
5	14 48 29	13 45 45	12 51	18 24	23 31	14 3	28 51	6 48	12 19	5 22	1 41
6	14 52 25	14 43 53	24 44	19 46	24 40	14 37	28 44	6 46	12 20	5 20	1 41
7	14 56 22	15 42 0	6♉34	21 10	25 49	15 12	28 36	6 44	12 21	5 19	1 41
8	15 0 18	16 40 5	18 23	22 36	26 58	15 47	28 29	6 42	12 22	5 17	1 41
9	15 4 15	17 38 8	0♊12	24 4	28 7	16 22	28 22	6 40	12 23	5 16	1 41
10	15 8 11	18 36 10	12 4	25 34	29 15	16 57	28 14	6 38	12 24	5 14	1 40
11	15 12 8	19 34 11	24 1	27 6	0♋23	17 32	28 7	6 36	12 25	5 12	1 40
12	15 16 5	20 32 9	6♋ 4	28 41	1 32	18 7	27 59	6 33	12 26	5 11	1 40
13	15 20 1	21 30 6	18 17	0♉17	2 40	18 43	27 52	6 31	12 27	5 9	1D40
14	15 23 58	22 28 1	0♌41	1 55	3 48	19 18	27 44	6 28	12 28	5 8	1 40
15	15 27 54	23 25 54	13 22	3 36	4 55	19 53	27 37	6 26	12 30	5 6	1 40
16	15 31 51	24 23 46	26 21	5 19	6 3	20 28	27 29	6 23	12 31	5 5	1 40
17	15 35 47	25 21 35	9♍42	7 3	7 11	21 4	27 22	6 21	12 32	5 3	1 40
18	15 39 44	26 19 23	23 28	8 50	8 18	21 39	27 14	6 18	12 34	5 2	1 40
19	15 43 40	27 17 9	7♎41	10 39	9 25	22 14	27 6	6 15	12 35	5 0	1 41
20	15 47 37	28 14 54	22 18	12 30	10 32	22 50	26 59	6 12	12 37	4 59	1 41
21	15 51 33	29 12 37	7♏16	14 22	11 39	23 25	26 51	6 9	12 38	4 57	1 41
22	15 55 30	0♊10 18	22 27	16 17	12 45	24 0	26 43	6 6	12 40	4 56	1 41
23	15 59 27	1 7 59	7♐43	18 14	13 52	24 36	26 36	6 3	12 42	4 54	1 41
24	16 3 23	2 5 38	22 53	20 13	14 58	25 11	26 28	5 59	12 43	4 53	1 42
25	16 7 20	3 3 16	7♑46	22 14	16 4	25 47	26 21	5 56	12 45	4 52	1 42
26	16 11 16	4 0 53	22 15	24 16	17 10	26 22	26 13	5 53	12 47	4 50	1 42
27	16 15 13	4 58 28	6♒16	26 21	18 16	26 58	26 6	5 49	12 49	4 49	1 43
28	16 19 9	5 56 3	19 47	28 27	19 21	27 34	25 58	5 46	12 51	4 47	1 43
29	16 23 6	6 53 37	2♓50	0♊34	20 26	28 9	25 51	5 42	12 53	4 46	1 44
30	16 27 3	7 51 10	15 29	2 43	21 31	28 45	25 43	5 39	12 55	4 45	1 44
31	16 30 59	8♊48 43	27♓49	4♊53	22♋36	29♋21	25♏36	5♑35	12♌57	4♏44	1♍45

THE SUN ENTERS THE SIGN OF GEMINI ON MAY 21 AT 19:43.

DAY	TIME	☉	☽	☿	♀	♂	♃	♄	♅	♆	♇
	h m s	° ' "	° '	° '	° '	° '	° '	° '	° '	° '	° '
J 1	16 34 56	9♊46 14	9♈54	7♊ 4	23♋41	29♋56	25♏29	5♑31	12♌59	4♏42	1♍45
U 2	16 38 52	10 43 45	21 48	9 15	24 45	0♌32	25R22	5R28	13 1	4R41	1 46
N 3	16 42 49	11 41 14	3♉38	11 27	25 49	1 8	25 15	5 24	13 3	4 40	1 46
E 4	16 46 45	12 38 43	15 25	13 39	26 53	1 44	25 7	5 20	13 5	4 39	1 47
5	16 50 42	13 36 11	27 14	15 51	27 57	2 20	25 1	5 16	13 8	4 37	1 47
6	16 54 38	14 33 39	9♊ 7	18 3	29 0	2 56	24 54	5 12	13 10	4 36	1 48
7	16 58 35	15 31 5	21 5	20 14	0♌ 3	3 31	24 47	5 8	13 12	4 35	1 49
8	17 2 32	16 28 31	3♋10	22 24	1 6	4 7	24 40	5 4	13 15	4 34	1 49
9	17 6 28	17 25 55	15 23	24 33	2 9	4 43	24 34	5 0	13 17	4 33	1 50
10	17 10 25	18 23 19	27 45	26 40	3 11	5 19	24 27	4 56	13 20	4 32	1 51
11	17 14 21	19 20 42	10♌18	28 46	4 13	5 56	24 21	4 52	13 22	4 31	1 52
12	17 18 18	20 18 3	23 4	0♋51	5 15	6 32	24 15	4 48	13 25	4 30	1 53
13	17 22 14	21 15 24	6♍ 5	2 53	6 16	7 8	24 8	4 43	13 27	4 29	1 53
14	17 26 11	22 12 44	19 24	4 53	7 18	7 44	24 2	4 39	13 30	4 28	1 54
15	17 30 7	23 10 2	3♎ 2	6 52	8 18	8 20	23 56	4 35	13 32	4 27	1 55
16	17 34 4	24 7 20	17 3	8 48	9 19	8 56	23 51	4 31	13 35	4 26	1 56
17	17 38 1	25 4 37	1♏26	10 42	10 19	9 32	23 45	4 26	13 38	4 25	1 57
18	17 41 57	26 1 53	16 8	12 33	11 19	10 9	23 40	4 22	13 41	4 24	1 58
19	17 45 54	26 59 8	1♐ 6	14 23	12 18	10 45	23 34	4 18	13 43	4 23	1 59
20	17 49 50	27 56 23	16 11	16 10	13 17	11 21	23 29	4 13	13 46	4 22	2 0
21	17 53 47	28 53 37	1♑14	17 54	14 15	11 58	23 24	4 9	13 49	4 22	2 1
22	17 57 43	29 50 51	16 5	19 37	15 13	12 34	23 19	4 4	13 52	4 21	2 2
23	18 1 40	0♋48 4	0♒35	21 17	16 11	13 10	23 14	4 0	13 55	4 20	2 3
24	18 5 36	1 45 17	14 39	22 54	17 8	13 47	23 9	3 56	13 58	4 19	2 5
25	18 9 33	2 42 30	28 15	24 30	18 5	14 23	23 5	3 51	14 1	4 19	2 6
26	18 13 30	3 39 43	11♓22	26 2	19 2	14 59	23 1	3 47	14 4	4 18	2 7
27	18 17 26	4 36 56	24 4	27 33	19 57	15 36	22 56	3 42	14 7	4 17	2 8
28	18 21 23	5 34 8	6♈24	29 1	20 53	16 12	22 52	3 38	14 10	4 17	2 9
29	18 25 19	6 31 21	18 29	0♌26	21 48	16 49	22 49	3 34	14 13	4 16	2 11
30	18 29 16	7♋28 34	0♉24	1♌49	22♌42	17♌26	22♏45	3♑29	14♌16	4♏16	2♍12

THE SUN ENTERS THE SIGN OF CANCER ON JUN 22 AT 03:50.

♏ SCORPIO ♐ SAGITTARIUS ♑ CAPRICORN ♒ AQUARIUS ♓ PISCES

1959

SIDEREAL SUN. MOON. MERCURY. VENUS. MARS. JUPITER. SATURN. URANUS. NEPTUNE. PLUTO.

DAY	TIME	☉	☽	☿	♀	♂	♃	♄	♅	♆	♇
	h m s	° ' "	° '	° '	° '	° '	° '	° '	° '	° '	° '
J 1	18 33 12	8♋25 47	12♉13	3♌10	23♌36	18♌ 2	22♏41	3♑25	14♌19	4♏15	2♍13
U 2	18 37 9	9 23 0	24 2	4 28	24 29	18 39	22R38	3R20	14 23	4R15	2 15
L 3	18 41 5	10 20 13	5♊54	5 43	25 22	19 15	22 35	3 16	14 26	4 14	2 16
Y 4	18 45 2	11 17 27	17 52	6 56	26 14	19 52	22 32	3 12	14 29	4 14	2 17
5	18 48 59	12 14 40	29 58	8 6	27 5	20 29	22 29	3 7	14 32	4 13	2 19
6	18 52 55	13 11 54	12♋14	9 13	27 56	21 6	22 26	3 3	14 36	4 13	2 20
7	18 56 52	14 9 7	24 41	10 18	28 46	21 42	22 24	2 59	14 39	4 13	2 22
8	19 0 48	15 6 20	7♌19	11 19	29 35	22 19	22 21	2 54	14 42	4 12	2 23
9	19 4 45	16 3 34	20 8	12 17	0♍24	22 56	22 19	2 50	14 46	4 12	2 25
10	19 8 41	17 0 47	3♍ 8	13 13	1 12	23 33	22 17	2 46	14 49	4 12	2 26
11	19 12 38	17 58 0	16 20	14 5	1 59	24 10	22 15	2 42	14 52	4 12	2 28
12	19 16 34	18 55 14	29 45	14 53	2 45	24 47	22 14	2 38	14 56	4 12	2 29
13	19 20 31	19 52 27	13♎24	15 38	3 31	25 24	22 12	2 33	14 59	4 11	2 31
14	19 24 28	20 49 40	27 20	16 19	4 15	26 1	22 11	2 29	15 3	4 11	2 32
15	19 28 24	21 46 53	11♏30	16 57	4 59	26 38	22 10	2 25	15 6	4 11	2 34
16	19 32 21	22 44 6	25 56	17 30	5 42	27 15	22 9	2 21	15 10	4D11	2 35
17	19 36 17	23 41 19	10♐33	18 0	6 23	27 52	22 8	2 17	15 13	4 11	2 37
18	19 40 14	24 38 33	25 16	18 25	7 4	28 29	22 8	2 13	15 17	4 11	2 39
19	19 44 10	25 35 46	9♑59	18 46	7 44	29 6	22 8	2 10	15 20	4 11	2 40
20	19 48 7	26 33 1	24 33	19 2	8 22	29 43	22D 7	2 6	15 24	4 11	2 42
21	19 52 3	27 30 15	8♒51	19 13	8 59	0♍20	22 8	2 2	15 27	4 11	2 44
22	19 56 0	28 27 30	22 48	19R20	9 35	0 57	22 8	1 58	15 31	4 12	2 45
23	19 59 57	29 24 46	6♓19	19 22	10 10	1 34	22 8	1 55	15 35	4 12	2 47
24	20 3 53	0♌22 2	19 26	19 19	10 44	2 12	22 9	1 51	15 38	4 12	2 49
25	20 7 50	1 19 19	2♈ 9	19 11	11 16	2 49	22 9	1 47	15 42	4 12	2 51
26	20 11 46	2 16 37	14 31	18 58	11 47	3 26	22 10	1 44	15 46	4 13	2 52
27	20 15 43	3 13 56	26 38	18 40	12 16	4 4	22 11	1 40	15 49	4 13	2 54
28	20 19 39	4 11 16	8♉35	18 17	12 44	4 41	22 13	1 37	15 53	4 13	2 56
29	20 23 36	5 8 37	20 26	17 50	13 11	5 18	22 14	1 34	15 56	4 14	2 58
30	20 27 32	6 5 59	2♊16	17 18	13 35	5 56	22 16	1 30	16 0	4 14	3 0
31	20 31 29	7♌ 3 22	14♊12	16♌43	13♍59	6♍33	22♏18	1♑27	16♌ 4	4♏14	3♍ 1

THE SUN ENTERS THE SIGN OF LEO ON JUL 23 AT 14:46.

DAY	TIME	☉	☽	☿	♀	♂	♃	♄	♅	♆	♇
	h m s	° ' "	° '	° '	° '	° '	° '	° '	° '	° '	° '
A 1	20 35 26	8♌ 0 46	26♊15	16♌ 4	14♍20	7♍11	22♏20	1♑24	16♌ 8	4♏15	3♍ 3
U 2	20 39 22	8 58 12	8♋29	15R22	14 40	7 48	22 22	1R21	16 11	4 15	3 5
G 3	20 43 19	9 55 38	20 57	14 38	14 58	8 26	22 24	1 18	16 15	4 16	3 7
U 4	20 47 15	10 53 5	3♌39	13 53	15 14	9 3	22 27	1 15	16 19	4 17	3 9
S 5	20 51 12	11 50 33	16 34	13 6	15 28	9 41	22 30	1 12	16 22	4 17	3 11
T 6	20 55 8	12 48 2	29 43	12 20	15 40	10 19	22 32	1 10	16 26	4 18	3 13
7	20 59 5	13 45 32	13♍ 5	11 35	15 49	10 56	22 36	1 7	16 30	4 18	3 15
8	21 3 1	14 43 2	26 37	10 52	15 57	11 34	22 39	1 4	16 34	4 19	3 17
9	21 6 58	15 40 34	10♎19	10 11	16 3	12 12	22 42	1 2	16 37	4 20	3 19
10	21 10 55	16 38 6	24 11	9 34	16R 6	12 50	22 46	0 59	16 41	4 21	3 20
11	21 14 51	17 35 39	8♏11	9 1	16 7	13 27	22 49	0 57	16 45	4 21	3 22
12	21 18 48	18 33 13	22 19	8 33	16 6	14 5	22 53	0 55	16 48	4 22	3 24
13	21 22 44	19 30 48	6♐33	8 10	16 2	14 43	22 57	0 53	16 52	4 23	3 26
14	21 26 41	20 28 24	20 51	7 54	15 56	15 21	23 2	0 51	16 56	4 24	3 28
15	21 30 37	21 26 1	5♑11	7D44	15 48	15 59	23 6	0 49	17 0	4 25	3 30
16	21 34 34	22 23 39	19 27	7 41	15 37	16 37	23 11	0 47	17 3	4 26	3 32
17	21 38 30	23 21 18	3♒35	7 45	15 24	17 15	23 15	0 45	17 7	4 27	3 34
18	21 42 27	24 18 58	17 29	7 57	15 9	17 53	23 20	0 43	17 11	4 28	3 36
19	21 46 24	25 16 39	1♓ 8	8 16	14 51	18 31	23 25	0 41	17 14	4 29	3 38
20	21 50 20	26 14 22	14 26	8 42	14 31	19 9	23 31	0 40	17 18	4 30	3 40
21	21 54 17	27 12 6	27 25	9 16	14 8	19 47	23 36	0 38	17 22	4 31	3 42
22	21 58 13	28 9 51	10♈ 3	9 57	13 44	20 25	23 41	0 37	17 26	4 32	3 44
23	22 2 10	29 7 39	22 25	10 46	13 17	21 3	23 47	0 36	17 29	4 33	3 46
24	22 6 6	0♍ 5 27	4♉32	11 41	12 49	21 42	23 53	0 35	17 33	4 34	3 48
25	22 10 3	1 3 18	16 29	12 44	12 19	22 20	23 59	0 33	17 37	4 36	3 50
26	22 13 59	2 1 10	28 22	13 52	11 47	22 58	24 5	0 32	17 40	4 37	3 52
27	22 17 56	2 59 5	10♊14	15 7	11 14	23 37	24 11	0 31	17 44	4 38	3 54
28	22 21 53	3 57 1	22 11	16 28	10 40	24 15	24 18	0 31	17 47	4 39	3 56
29	22 25 49	4 54 58	4♋16	17 54	10 4	24 53	24 24	0 30	17 51	4 41	3 58
30	22 29 46	5 52 58	16 35	19 25	9 28	25 32	24 31	0 29	17 55	4 42	4 0
31	22 33 42	6♍50 59	29♋10	21♌ 1	8♍51	26♍10	24♏38	0♑29	17♌58	4♏43	4♍ 2

THE SUN ENTERS THE SIGN OF VIRGO ON AUG 23 AT 21:44.

DAY	TIME	☉	☽	☿	♀	♂	♃	♄	♅	♆	♇
	h m s	° ' "	° '	° '	° '	° '	° '	° '	° '	° '	° '
S 1	22 37 39	7♍49 3	12♌ 3	22♌40	8♍14	26♍49	24♏45	0♑28	18♌ 2	4♏45	4♍ 4
E 2	22 41 35	8 47 8	25 15	24 23	7R37	27 27	24 52	0R28	18 5	4 46	4 6
P 3	22 45 32	9 45 14	8♍44	26 9	7 0	28 6	24 59	0 28	18 9	4 48	4 8
T 4	22 49 28	10 43 22	22 29	27 58	6 24	28 45	25 6	0 28	18 12	4 49	4 10
E 5	22 53 25	11 41 32	6♎27	29 49	5 48	29 23	25 14	0D27	18 16	4 51	4 12
M 6	22 57 21	12 39 44	20 35	1♍41	5 12	0♎ 2	25 21	0 28	18 19	4 52	4 14
B 7	23 1 18	13 37 57	4♏49	3 34	4 38	0 41	25 29	0 28	18 23	4 54	4 16
E 8	23 5 15	14 36 11	19 5	5 28	4 5	1 19	25 37	0 28	18 26	4 55	4 18
R 9	23 9 11	15 34 28	3♐22	7 23	3 34	1 58	25 45	0 28	18 30	4 57	4 20
10	23 13 8	16 32 45	17 35	9 18	3 4	2 37	25 53	0 29	18 33	4 58	4 22
11	23 17 4	17 31 4	1♑43	11 14	2 36	3 16	26 2	0 29	18 37	5 0	4 24
12	23 21 1	18 29 25	15 43	13 9	2 10	3 55	26 10	0 30	18 40	5 2	4 26
13	23 24 57	19 27 47	29 35	15 3	1 46	4 34	26 18	0 31	18 43	5 3	4 28
14	23 28 54	20 26 11	13♒15	16 57	1 24	5 13	26 27	0 31	18 47	5 5	4 30
15	23 32 50	21 24 36	26 43	18 51	1 4	5 52	26 36	0 32	18 50	5 7	4 32
16	23 36 47	22 23 4	9♓57	20 43	0 47	6 31	26 45	0 33	18 53	5 8	4 34
17	23 40 44	23 21 33	22 56	22 35	0 32	7 10	26 54	0 35	18 56	5 10	4 36
18	23 44 40	24 20 3	5♈39	24 26	0 19	7 49	27 3	0 36	19 0	5 12	4 38
19	23 48 37	25 18 36	18 8	26 17	0 9	8 28	27 12	0 37	19 3	5 14	4 40
20	23 52 33	26 17 11	0♉24	28 6	0 1	9 8	27 21	0 38	19 6	5 16	4 42
21	23 56 30	27 15 48	12 29	29 54	29♌55	9 47	27 31	0 40	19 9	5 18	4 44
22	0 0 26	28 14 27	24 25	1♎41	29D53	10 26	27 40	0 42	19 12	5 19	4 46
23	0 4 23	29 13 9	6♊17	3 28	29 52	11 5	27 50	0 43	19 15	5 21	4 48
24	0 8 19	0♎11 52	18 9	5 13	29 54	11 45	28 0	0 45	19 18	5 23	4 49
25	0 12 16	1 10 38	0♋ 5	6 57	29 58	12 24	28 10	0 47	19 21	5 25	4 51
26	0 16 13	2 9 26	12 10	8 41	0♍ 4	13 4	28 19	0 49	19 24	5 27	4 53
27	0 20 9	3 8 17	24 28	10 23	0 13	13 43	28 30	0 51	19 27	5 29	4 55
28	0 24 6	4 7 9	7♌ 4	12 5	0 24	14 23	28 40	0 53	19 30	5 31	4 57
29	0 28 2	5 6 4	20 0	13 45	0 37	15 2	28 50	0 55	19 33	5 33	4 59
30	0 31 59	6♎ 5 1	3♍19	15♎25	0♍52	15♎42	29♏ 0	0♑58	19♌36	5♏35	5♍ 0

THE SUN ENTERS THE SIGN OF LIBRA ON SEP 23 AT 19:09.

♈ ARIES ♉ TAURUS ♊ GEMINI ♋ CANCER ♌ LEO ♍ VIRGO ♎ LIBRA

1959

SIDEREAL . SUN . . MOON . . MERCURY VENUS . . MARS . . JUPITER SATURN . URANUS . NEPTUNE PLUTO . .

DAY	TIME	☉	☽	☿	♀	♂	♃	♄	♅	♆	♇
	h m s	° ' "	° '	° '	° '	° '	° '	° '	° '	° '	° '
O 1	0 35 55	7♎ 4 0	17♍ 2	17♎ 4	1♍ 9	16♎22	29♏11	1♑ 0	19♌39	5♏37	5♍ 2
C 2	0 39 52	8 3 2	1♎ 6	18 42	1 28	17 1	29 21	1 3	19 41	5 39	5 4
T 3	0 43 48	9 2 5	15 28	20 19	1 49	17 41	29 32	1 5	19 44	5 41	5 6
O 4	0 47 45	10 1 11	0♏ 3	21 55	2 12	18 21	29 43	1 8	19 47	5 43	5 7
B 5	0 51 41	11 0 18	14 45	23 31	2 36	19 1	29 53	1 11	19 50	5 45	5 9
E 6	0 55 38	11 59 27	29 27	25 5	3 3	19 41	0♐ 4	1 14	19 52	5 47	5 11
R 7	0 59 35	12 58 38	14♐ 2	26 39	3 30	20 21	0 15	1 17	19 55	5 49	5 13
8	1 3 31	13 57 51	28 26	28 12	4 0	21 0	0 26	1 20	19 57	5 51	5 14
9	1 7 28	14 57 6	12♑35	29 45	4 31	21 40	0 37	1 23	20 0	5 54	5 16
10	1 11 24	15 56 23	26 27	1♏16	5 3	22 21	0 49	1 26	20 2	5 56	5 17
11	1 15 21	16 55 41	10♒ 3	2 47	5 37	23 1	1 0	1 30	20 5	5 58	5 19
12	1 19 17	17 55 1	23 23	4 17	6 12	23 41	1 11	1 33	20 7	6 0	5 21
13	1 23 14	18 54 22	6♓27	5 46	6 48	24 21	1 23	1 37	20 10	6 2	5 22
14	1 27 10	19 53 46	19 17	7 15	7 26	25 1	1 34	1 40	20 12	6 4	5 24
15	1 31 7	20 53 11	1♈55	8 43	8 5	25 41	1 46	1 44	20 14	6 6	5 25
16	1 35 4	21 52 38	14 21	10 9	8 45	26 22	1 58	1 48	20 16	6 9	5 27
17	1 39 0	22 52 8	26 37	11 36	9 27	27 2	2 9	1 51	20 19	6 11	5 28
18	1 42 57	23 51 39	8♉44	13 1	10 9	27 42	2 21	1 55	20 21	6 13	5 30
19	1 46 53	24 51 13	20 44	14 26	10 53	28 23	2 33	1 59	20 23	6 15	5 31
20	1 50 50	25 50 49	2♊38	15 49	11 37	29 3	2 45	2 3	20 25	6 17	5 33
21	1 54 46	26 50 26	14 29	17 12	12 23	29 44	2 57	2 8	20 27	6 20	5 34
22	1 58 43	27 50 7	26 21	18 34	13 9	0♏24	3 9	2 12	20 29	6 22	5 35
23	2 2 39	28 49 49	8♋16	19 55	13 57	1 5	3 21	2 16	20 31	6 24	5 37
24	2 6 36	29 49 34	20 18	21 15	14 45	1 45	3 33	2 20	20 32	6 26	5 38
25	2 10 33	0♏49 20	2♌32	22 34	15 34	2 26	3 46	2 25	20 34	6 29	5 39
26	2 14 29	1 49 9	15 3	23 51	16 24	3 7	3 58	2 29	20 36	6 31	5 41
27	2 18 26	2 49 1	27 55	25 7	17 15	3 48	4 10	2 34	20 38	6 33	5 42
28	2 22 22	3 48 54	11♍11	26 22	18 6	4 28	4 23	2 39	20 39	6 35	5 43
29	2 26 19	4 48 50	24 55	27 35	18 59	5 9	4 35	2 43	20 41	6 38	5 44
30	2 30 15	5 48 48	9♎ 5	28 47	19 52	5 50	4 48	2 48	20 43	6 40	5 46
31	2 34 12	6♏48 47	23♎40	29♏56	20♍45	6♏31	5♐ 0	2♑53	20♌44	6♏42	5♍47

THE SUN ENTERS THE SIGN OF SCORPIO ON OCT 24 AT 04:12.

DAY	TIME	☉	☽	☿	♀	♂	♃	♄	♅	♆	♇
	h m s	° ' "	° '	° '	° '	° '	° '	° '	° '	° '	° '
N 1	2 38 8	7♏48 49	8♏35	1♐ 4	21♍40	7♏12	5♐13	2♑58	20♌46	6♏44	5♍48
O 2	2 42 5	8 48 53	23 40	2 9	22 35	7 53	5 26	3 3	20 47	6 46	5 49
V 3	2 46 1	9 48 59	8♐47	3 12	23 30	8 34	5 38	3 8	20 48	6 49	5 50
E 4	2 49 58	10 49 6	23 47	4 12	24 26	9 15	5 51	3 13	20 50	6 51	5 51
M 5	2 53 55	11 49 15	8♑29	5 8	25 23	9 57	6 4	3 19	20 51	6 53	5 52
B 6	2 57 51	12 49 26	22 50	6 1	26 20	10 38	6 17	3 24	20 52	6 55	5 53
E 7	3 1 48	13 49 37	6♒47	6 50	27 18	11 19	6 30	3 29	20 53	6 58	5 54
R 8	3 5 44	14 49 51	20 19	7 34	28 16	12 0	6 43	3 35	20 54	7 0	5 55
9	3 9 41	15 50 6	3♓29	8 14	29 15	12 42	6 56	3 40	20 55	7 2	5 56
10	3 13 37	16 50 22	16 19	8 48	0♎14	13 23	7 9	3 46	20 56	7 4	5 57
11	3 17 34	17 50 40	28 52	9 15	1 14	14 5	7 22	3 51	20 57	7 7	5 58
12	3 21 30	18 50 59	11♈13	9 36	2 14	14 46	7 35	3 57	20 58	7 9	5 59
13	3 25 27	19 51 20	23 25	9 49	3 15	15 28	7 48	4 2	20 59	7 11	6 0
14	3 29 24	20 51 42	5♉29	9R53	4 16	16 9	8 1	4 8	21 0	7 13	6 0
15	3 33 20	21 52 6	17 27	9 49	5 18	16 51	8 14	4 14	21 0	7 15	6 1
16	3 37 17	22 52 32	29 22	9 35	6 19	17 32	8 27	4 20	21 1	7 18	6 2
17	3 41 13	23 52 59	11♊14	9 11	7 22	18 14	8 41	4 26	21 2	7 20	6 3
18	3 45 10	24 53 28	23 6	8 36	8 24	18 56	8 54	4 32	21 2	7 22	6 3
19	3 49 6	25 53 59	4♋59	7 51	9 27	19 38	9 7	4 38	21 3	7 24	6 4
20	3 53 3	26 54 32	16 55	6 56	10 31	20 20	9 20	4 44	21 3	7 26	6 4
21	3 56 59	27 55 6	28 57	5 52	11 34	21 1	9 34	4 50	21 4	7 28	6 5
22	4 0 56	28 55 41	11♌ 9	4 41	12 39	21 43	9 47	4 56	21 4	7 31	6 6
23	4 4 53	29 56 19	23 36	3 23	13 43	22 25	10 1	5 2	21 4	7 33	6 6
24	4 8 49	0♐56 58	6♍21	2 2	14 48	23 7	10 14	5 8	21 4	7 35	6 7
25	4 12 46	1 57 39	19 28	0 40	15 53	23 49	10 27	5 15	21 4	7 37	6 7
26	4 16 42	2 58 21	3♎ 2	29♏20	16 58	24 32	10 41	5 21	21 5	7 39	6 7
27	4 20 39	3 59 5	17 5	28 4	18 3	25 14	10 54	5 27	21R 5	7 41	6 8
28	4 24 35	4 59 51	1♏37	26 56	19 9	25 56	11 8	5 34	21 5	7 43	6 8
29	4 28 32	6 0 38	16 33	25 56	20 15	26 38	11 21	5 40	21 5	7 45	6 8
30	4 32 28	7♐ 1 27	1♐47	25♏ 7	21♎22	27♏21	11♐35	5♑47	21♌ 4	7♏47	6♍ 9

THE SUN ENTERS THE SIGN OF SAGITTARIUS ON NOV 23 AT 01:28.

DAY	TIME	☉	☽	☿	♀	♂	♃	♄	♅	♆	♇
	h m s	° ' "	° '	° '	° '	° '	° '	° '	° '	° '	° '
D 1	4 36 25	8♐ 2 17	17♐ 8	24♏28	22♎28	28♏ 3	11♐48	5♑53	21♌ 4	7♏49	6♍ 9
E 2	4 40 22	9 3 8	2♑25	24R 1	23 35	28 45	12 2	6 0	21R 4	7 51	6 9
C 3	4 44 18	10 4 0	17 26	23D46	24 42	29 28	12 15	6 6	21 4	7 53	6 9
E 4	4 48 15	11 4 53	2♒ 3	23 42	25 50	0♐10	12 29	6 13	21 3	7 55	6 10
M 5	4 52 11	12 5 47	16 12	23 48	26 57	0 53	12 42	6 20	21 3	7 57	6 10
B 6	4 56 8	13 6 42	29 51	24 4	28 5	1 35	12 56	6 26	21 2	7 59	6 10
E 7	5 0 4	14 7 37	13♓ 2	24 29	29 13	2 18	13 9	6 33	21 2	8 1	6 10
R 8	5 4 1	15 8 33	25 49	25 2	0♏21	3 1	13 23	6 40	21 1	8 3	6R10
9	5 7 57	16 9 30	8♈16	25 42	1 29	3 43	13 36	6 47	21 1	8 5	6 10
10	5 11 54	17 10 27	20 29	26 28	2 38	4 26	13 50	6 53	21 0	8 6	6 10
11	5 15 51	18 11 25	2♉32	27 20	3 46	5 9	14 4	7 0	20 59	8 8	6 10
12	5 19 47	19 12 24	14 28	28 17	4 55	5 52	14 17	7 7	20 59	8 10	6 10
13	5 23 44	20 13 24	26 20	29 18	6 4	6 35	14 31	7 14	20 58	8 12	6 10
14	5 27 40	21 14 24	8♊12	0♐23	7 13	7 18	14 44	7 21	20 57	8 14	6 10
15	5 31 37	22 15 25	20 4	1 31	8 23	8 1	14 58	7 28	20 56	8 15	6 9
16	5 35 33	23 16 27	1♋59	2 42	9 32	8 44	15 11	7 35	20 55	8 17	6 9
17	5 39 30	24 17 29	13 57	3 56	10 42	9 27	15 24	7 42	20 54	8 19	6 9
18	5 43 27	25 18 32	25 59	5 11	11 52	10 10	15 38	7 49	20 53	8 21	6 9
19	5 47 23	26 19 36	8♌ 7	6 29	13 2	10 53	15 51	7 56	20 52	8 22	6 8
20	5 51 20	27 20 41	20 24	7 48	14 12	11 36	16 5	8 3	20 50	8 24	6 8
21	5 55 16	28 21 46	2♍53	9 9	15 22	12 20	16 18	8 10	20 49	8 25	6 8
22	5 59 13	29 22 52	15 36	10 31	16 32	13 3	16 32	8 17	20 48	8 27	6 7
23	6 3 9	0♑23 59	28 38	11 54	17 43	13 46	16 45	8 24	20 46	8 29	6 7
24	6 7 6	1 25 7	12♎ 2	13 19	18 53	14 30	16 58	8 31	20 45	8 30	6 7
25	6 11 2	2 26 15	25 52	14 44	20 4	15 13	17 12	8 38	20 44	8 32	6 6
26	6 14 59	3 27 24	10♏ 9	16 9	21 15	15 57	17 25	8 45	20 42	8 33	6 6
27	6 18 56	4 28 34	24 51	17 36	22 26	16 40	17 38	8 52	20 41	8 35	6 5
28	6 22 52	5 29 44	9♐54	19 3	23 37	17 24	17 52	8 59	20 39	8 36	6 4
29	6 26 49	6 30 55	25 8	20 31	24 48	18 7	18 5	9 6	20 37	8 37	6 4
30	6 30 45	7 32 6	10♑24	21 59	26 0	18 51	18 18	9 13	20 36	8 39	6 3
31	6 34 42	8♑33 17	25♑30	23♐28	27♏11	19♐35	18♐31	9♑20	20♌34	8♏40	6♍ 3

THE SUN ENTERS THE SIGN OF CAPRICORN ON DEC 22 AT 14:35.

♏ SCORPIO ♐ SAGITTARIUS ♑ CAPRICORN ♒ AQUARIUS ♓ PISCES

1960

SIDEREAL SUN. MOON. MERCURY. VENUS. MARS. JUPITER. SATURN. URANUS. NEPTUNE. PLUTO.

DAY	TIME	☉	☽	☿	♀	♂	♃	♄	♅	♆	♇
	h m s	° ' "	° '	° '	° '	° '	° '	° '	° '	° '	° '
J 1	6 38 38	9♑34 28	10♒16	24♐58	28♏22	20♐18	18♐44	9♑27	20♌32	8♏41	6♍ 2
A 2	6 42 35	10 35 39	24 34	26 27	29 34	21 2	18 57	9 34	20R31	8 43	6R 1
N 3	6 46 31	11 36 50	8♓23	27 58	0♐46	21 46	19 10	9 42	20 29	8 44	6 0
U 4	6 50 28	12 38 0	21 43	29 28	1 57	22 30	19 23	9 49	20 27	8 45	6 0
A 5	6 54 25	13 39 10	4♈35	0♑59	3 9	23 14	19 36	9 56	20 25	8 46	5 59
R 6	6 58 21	14 40 20	17 5	2 31	4 21	23 58	19 49	10 3	20 23	8 48	5 58
Y 7	7 2 18	15 41 29	29 18	4 2	5 33	24 42	20 2	10 10	20 21	8 49	5 57
8	7 6 14	16 42 39	11♉19	5 35	6 45	25 26	20 15	10 17	20 19	8 50	5 56
9	7 10 11	17 43 47	23 12	7 7	7 57	26 10	20 28	10 24	20 17	8 51	5 55
10	7 14 7	18 44 56	5♊ 3	8 41	9 9	26 54	20 41	10 31	20 15	8 52	5 55
11	7 18 4	19 46 4	16 54	10 14	10 22	27 38	20 53	10 38	20 13	8 53	5 54
12	7 22 0	20 47 11	28 48	11 48	11 34	28 22	21 6	10 45	20 11	8 54	5 53
13	7 25 57	21 48 18	10♋48	13 22	12 46	29 7	21 19	10 52	20 8	8 55	5 52
14	7 29 54	22 49 25	22 54	14 57	13 59	29 51	21 31	10 59	20 6	8 56	5 51
15	7 33 50	23 50 31	5♌ 7	16 33	15 11	0♑35	21 44	11 6	20 4	8 57	5 50
16	7 37 47	24 51 37	17 28	18 8	16 24	1 19	21 56	11 13	20 2	8 58	5 49
17	7 41 43	25 52 42	29 58	19 45	17 36	2 4	22 9	11 20	19 59	8 58	5 47
18	7 45 40	26 53 47	12♍39	21 21	18 49	2 48	22 21	11 27	19 57	8 59	5 46
19	7 49 36	27 54 52	25 31	22 59	20 2	3 33	22 33	11 34	19 55	9 0	5 45
20	7 53 33	28 55 56	8♎39	24 37	21 15	4 17	22 46	11 41	19 52	9 1	5 44
21	7 57 29	29 57 0	22 3	26 15	22 27	5 2	22 58	11 48	19 50	9 1	5 43
22	8 1 26	0♒58 4	5♏46	27 54	23 40	5 46	23 10	11 54	19 47	9 2	5 42
23	8 5 23	1 59 7	19 49	29 34	24 53	6 31	23 22	12 1	19 45	9 3	5 41
24	8 9 19	3 0 10	4♐12	1♒14	26 6	7 16	23 34	12 8	19 42	9 3	5 39
25	8 13 16	4 1 13	18 52	2 55	27 19	8 0	23 46	12 15	19 40	9 4	5 38
26	8 17 12	5 2 15	3♑44	4 36	28 32	8 45	23 58	12 22	19 37	9 4	5 37
27	8 21 9	6 3 16	18 39	6 18	29 45	9 30	24 9	12 28	19 35	9 5	5 36
28	8 25 5	7 4 17	3♒30	8 1	0♑59	10 15	24 21	12 35	19 32	9 5	5 34
29	8 29 2	8 5 16	18 7	9 44	2 12	11 0	24 33	12 42	19 30	9 6	5 33
30	8 32 58	9 6 15	2♓23	11 28	3 25	11 45	24 44	12 48	19 27	9 6	5 32
31	8 36 55	10♒ 7 12	16♓14	13♒13	4♑38	12♑30	24♐56	12♑55	19♌25	9♏ 7	5♍30

THE SUN ENTERS THE SIGN OF AQUARIUS ON JAN 21 AT 01:10.

DAY	TIME	☉	☽	☿	♀	♂	♃	♄	♅	♆	♇
	h m s	° ' "	° '	° '	° '	° '	° '	° '	° '	° '	° '
F 1	8 40 52	11♒ 8 9	29♓38	14♒58	5♑52	13♑15	25♐ 7	13♑ 1	19♌22	9♏ 7	5♍29
E 2	8 44 48	12 9 4	12♈37	16 44	7 5	14 0	25 19	13 8	19R19	9 7	5R27
B 3	8 48 45	13 9 57	25 13	18 30	8 18	14 45	25 30	13 14	19 17	9 7	5 26
R 4	8 52 41	14 10 49	7♉31	20 17	9 32	15 30	25 41	13 21	19 14	9 8	5 25
U 5	8 56 38	15 11 40	19 34	22 4	10 45	16 15	25 52	13 27	19 12	9 8	5 23
A 6	9 0 34	16 12 30	1♊30	23 51	11 58	17 0	26 3	13 34	19 9	9 8	5 22
R 7	9 4 31	17 13 18	13 21	25 39	13 12	17 45	26 14	13 40	19 6	9 8	5 20
Y 8	9 8 27	18 14 5	25 13	27 26	14 25	18 30	26 25	13 46	19 4	9 8	5 19
9	9 12 24	19 14 50	7♋10	29 14	15 39	19 15	26 35	13 52	19 1	9 8	5 18
10	9 16 21	20 15 33	19 14	1♓ 2	16 52	20 1	26 46	13 59	18 58	9R 8	5 16
11	9 20 17	21 16 16	1♌28	2 49	18 6	20 46	26 56	14 5	18 56	9 8	5 15
12	9 24 14	22 16 56	13 53	4 35	19 19	21 31	27 7	14 11	18 53	9 8	5 13
13	9 28 10	23 17 36	26 30	6 20	20 33	22 17	27 17	14 17	18 51	9 8	5 12
14	9 32 7	24 18 14	9♍19	8 5	21 46	23 2	27 27	14 23	18 48	9 8	5 10
15	9 36 3	25 18 50	22 21	9 47	23 0	23 48	27 37	14 29	18 45	9 8	5 9
16	9 40 0	26 19 25	5♎34	11 27	24 14	24 33	27 47	14 35	18 43	9 8	5 7
17	9 43 56	27 19 59	19 0	13 5	25 27	25 18	27 57	14 41	18 40	9 7	5 6
18	9 47 53	28 20 32	2♏38	14 40	26 41	26 4	28 7	14 46	18 38	9 7	5 4
19	9 51 50	29 21 3	16 27	16 11	27 55	26 50	28 17	14 52	18 35	9 7	5 3
20	9 55 46	0♓21 33	0♐28	17 37	29 8	27 35	28 26	14 58	18 32	9 7	5 1
21	9 59 43	1 22 3	14 40	18 59	0♒22	28 21	28 36	15 3	18 30	9 6	4 59
22	10 3 39	2 22 30	29 0	20 15	1 36	29 6	28 45	15 9	18 27	9 6	4 58
23	10 7 36	3 22 57	13♑26	21 25	2 50	29 52	28 54	15 15	18 25	9 5	4 56
24	10 11 32	4 23 22	27 52	22 28	4 3	0♒38	29 3	15 20	18 22	9 5	4 55
25	10 15 29	5 23 45	12♒14	23 23	5 17	1 23	29 12	15 25	18 20	9 5	4 53
26	10 19 25	6 24 7	26 27	24 11	6 31	2 9	29 21	15 31	18 17	9 4	4 52
27	10 23 22	7 24 27	10♓24	24 49	7 45	2 55	29 30	15 36	18 15	9 3	4 50
28	10 27 19	8 24 46	24 4	25 19	8 59	3 41	29 39	15 41	18 12	9 3	4 49
29	10 31 15	9♓25 2	7♈22	25♓39	10♒12	4♒27	29♐47	15♑46	18♌10	9♏ 2	4♍47

THE SUN ENTERS THE SIGN OF PISCES ON FEB 19 AT 15:27.

DAY	TIME	☉	☽	☿	♀	♂	♃	♄	♅	♆	♇
	h m s	° ' "	° '	° '	° '	° '	° '	° '	° '	° '	° '
M 1	10 35 12	10♓25 17	20♈20	25♓50	11♒26	5♒12	29♐55	15♑51	18♌ 8	9♏ 2	4♍46
A 2	10 39 8	11 25 30	2♉58	25R51	12 40	5 58	0♑ 4	15 56	18R 5	9R 1	4R44
R 3	10 43 5	12 25 40	15 19	25 43	13 54	6 44	0 12	16 1	18 3	9 0	4 43
C 4	10 47 1	13 25 49	27 26	25 26	15 8	7 30	0 20	16 6	18 1	9 0	4 41
H 5	10 50 58	14 25 55	9♊24	25 0	16 22	8 16	0 28	16 11	17 58	8 59	4 40
6	10 54 54	15 26 0	21 17	24 26	17 35	9 2	0 35	16 16	17 56	8 58	4 38
7	10 58 51	16 26 2	3♋10	23 45	18 49	9 48	0 43	16 20	17 54	8 57	4 37
8	11 2 47	17 26 3	15 8	22 58	20 3	10 34	0 50	16 25	17 52	8 56	4 35
9	11 6 44	18 26 1	27 14	22 6	21 17	11 20	0 58	16 30	17 49	8 55	4 34
10	11 10 41	19 25 57	9♌33	21 10	22 31	12 6	1 5	16 34	17 47	8 55	4 32
11	11 14 37	20 25 50	22 7	20 12	23 45	12 52	1 12	16 38	17 45	8 54	4 31
12	11 18 34	21 25 42	4♍57	19 14	24 59	13 38	1 19	16 43	17 43	8 53	4 29
13	11 22 30	22 25 32	18 5	18 15	26 13	14 24	1 25	16 47	17 41	8 52	4 28
14	11 26 27	23 25 19	1♎30	17 18	27 26	15 10	1 32	16 51	17 39	8 51	4 26
15	11 30 23	24 25 5	15 10	16 24	28 40	15 56	1 38	16 55	17 37	8 50	4 25
16	11 34 20	25 24 49	29 3	15 34	29 54	16 42	1 44	16 59	17 35	8 49	4 23
17	11 38 16	26 24 31	13♏ 6	14 48	1♓ 8	17 28	1 51	17 3	17 33	8 48	4 22
18	11 42 13	27 24 11	27 16	14 7	2 22	18 14	1 57	17 7	17 32	8 46	4 21
19	11 46 10	28 23 50	11♐29	13 32	3 36	19 0	2 2	17 11	17 30	8 45	4 19
20	11 50 6	29 23 27	25 43	13 2	4 50	19 47	2 8	17 14	17 28	8 44	4 18
21	11 54 3	0♈23 2	9♑55	12 39	6 4	20 33	2 13	17 18	17 26	8 43	4 16
22	11 57 59	1 22 36	24 2	12 22	7 18	21 19	2 19	17 21	17 25	8 42	4 15
23	12 1 56	2 22 8	8♒ 4	12 11	8 31	22 5	2 24	17 25	17 23	8 41	4 14
24	12 5 52	3 21 38	21 57	12D 6	9 45	22 51	2 29	17 28	17 21	8 39	4 12
25	12 9 49	4 21 6	5♓40	12 7	10 59	23 38	2 34	17 31	17 20	8 38	4 11
26	12 13 45	5 20 32	19 11	12 14	12 13	24 24	2 38	17 34	17 18	8 37	4 10
27	12 17 42	6 19 56	2♈28	12 26	13 27	25 10	2 43	17 37	17 17	8 35	4 9
28	12 21 38	7 19 18	15 31	12 43	14 41	25 56	2 47	17 40	17 15	8 34	4 7
29	12 25 35	8 18 38	28 18	13 5	15 55	26 43	2 51	17 43	17 14	8 33	4 6
30	12 29 32	9 17 56	10♉50	13 32	17 9	27 29	2 55	17 46	17 13	8 31	4 5
31	12 33 28	10♈17 12	23♉ 9	14♓ 4	18♓23	28♒15	2♑59	17♑49	17♌11	8♏30	4♍ 4

THE SUN ENTERS THE SIGN OF ARIES ON MAR 20 AT 14:43.

♈ ARIES ♉ TAURUS ♊ GEMINI ♋ CANCER ♌ LEO ♍ VIRGO ♎ LIBRA

1960

SIDEREAL SUN.... MOON... MERCURY VENUS.. MARS... JUPITER SATURN. URANUS. NEPTUNE PLUTO..

DAY	TIME	☉	☽	☿	♀	♂	♃	♄	♅	♆	♇
	h m s	° ' "	° '	° '	° '	° '	° '	° '	° '	° '	° '
A 1	12 37 25	11♈16 26	5♊16	14♓39	19♓37	29♒ 1	3♑ 3	17♑51	17♌1Ø	8♏29	4♍ 3
P 2	12 41 21	12 15 37	17 14	15 19	2Ø 51	29 48	3 6	17 54	17R 9	8R27	4R 1
R 3	12 45 18	13 14 46	29 7	16 2	22 4	Ø♓34	3 9	17 56	17 8	8 26	4 Ø
I 4	12 49 14	14 13 53	11♋ Ø	16 49	23 18	1 2Ø	3 12	17 59	17 7	8 24	3 59
L 5	12 53 11	15 12 57	22 57	17 39	24 32	2 6	3 15	18 1	17 6	8 23	3 58
6	12 57 7	16 11 59	5♌ 3	18 32	25 46	2 53	3 18	18 3	17 5	8 21	3 57
7	13 1 4	17 1Ø 59	17 22	19 29	27 Ø	3 39	3 21	18 5	17 4	8 2Ø	3 56
8	13 5 1	18 9 57	29 59	2Ø 28	28 14	4 25	3 23	18 7	17 3	8 18	3 55
9	13 8 57	19 8 52	12♍56	21 3Ø	29 28	5 11	3 25	18 9	17 2	8 17	3 54
1Ø	13 12 54	2Ø 7 45	26 16	22 35	Ø♈41	5 58	3 27	18 11	17 1	8 15	3 53
11	13 16 5Ø	21 6 36	9♎59	23 42	1 55	6 44	3 29	18 12	17 1	8 14	3 52
12	13 2Ø 47	22 5 25	24 2	24 52	3 9	7 3Ø	3 31	18 14	17 Ø	8 12	3 51
13	13 24 43	23 4 12	8♏23	26 3	4 23	8 16	3 32	18 15	16 59	8 11	3 5Ø
14	13 28 4Ø	24 2 57	22 55	27 18	5 37	9 3	3 33	18 17	16 59	8 9	3 49
15	13 32 36	25 1 4Ø	7♐32	28 34	6 51	9 49	3 34	18 18	16 58	8 8	3 48
16	13 36 33	26 Ø 22	22 8	29 52	8 4	1Ø 35	3 35	18 19	16 58	8 6	3 48
17	13 4Ø 3Ø	26 59 2	6♑36	1♈13	9 18	11 21	3 36	18 2Ø	16 57	8 4	3 47
18	13 44 26	27 57 4Ø	2Ø 53	2 35	1Ø 32	12 8	3 36	18 21	16 57	8 3	3 46
19	13 48 23	28 56 16	4♒55	3 59	11 46	12 54	3 37	18 22	16 57	8 1	3 45
2Ø	13 52 19	29 54 51	18 44	5 25	13 Ø	13 4Ø	3R37	18 23	16 56	8 Ø	3 45
21	13 56 16	Ø♉53 25	2♓17	6 53	14 13	14 26	3 37	18 24	16 56	7 58	3 44
22	14 Ø 12	1 51 56	15 36	8 23	15 27	15 12	3 37	18 24	16 56	7 56	3 43
23	14 4 9	2 5Ø 26	28 42	9 55	16 41	15 58	3 36	18 25	16 56	7 55	3 42
24	14 8 5	3 48 54	11♈36	11 28	17 55	16 45	3 36	18 25	16D56	7 53	3 42
25	14 12 2	4 47 21	24 19	13 4	19 9	17 31	3 35	18 25	16 56	7 52	3 41
26	14 15 59	5 45 45	6♉5Ø	14 41	2Ø 22	18 17	3 34	18 26	16 56	7 5Ø	3 41
27	14 19 55	6 44 8	19 11	16 2Ø	21 36	19 3	3 33	18R26	16 56	7 48	3 4Ø
28	14 23 52	7 42 29	1♊22	18 Ø	22 5Ø	19 49	3 31	18 26	16 56	7 47	3 4Ø
29	14 27 48	8 4Ø 48	13 25	19 43	24 4	2Ø 35	3 3Ø	18 26	16 56	7 45	3 39
3Ø	14 31 45	9♉39 5	25♊21	21♈27	25♈18	21♓21	3♑28	18♑25	16♌57	7♏43	3♍39

THE SUN ENTERS THE SIGN OF TAURUS ON APR 20 AT 02:06.

DAY	TIME	☉	☽	☿	♀	♂	♃	♄	♅	♆	♇
	h m s	° ' "	° '	° '	° '	° '	° '	° '	° '	° '	° '
M 1	14 35 41	1Ø♉37 2Ø	7♋13	23♈13	26♈31	22♓ 7	3♑26	18♑25	16♌57	7♏42	3♍38
A 2	14 39 38	11 35 33	19 5	25 Ø	27 45	22 53	3R24	18R25	16 57	7R4Ø	3R38
Y 3	14 43 34	12 33 45	1♌ Ø	26 5Ø	28 59	23 39	3 22	18 24	16 58	7 38	3 37
4	14 47 31	13 31 54	13 4	28 41	Ø♉12	24 25	3 19	18 24	16 58	7 37	3 37
5	14 51 28	14 3Ø 1	25 2Ø	Ø♉34	1 26	25 11	3 16	18 23	16 59	7 35	3 37
6	14 55 24	15 28 6	7♍54	2 29	2 4Ø	25 57	3 14	18 22	17 Ø	7 34	3 37
7	14 59 21	16 26 1Ø	2Ø 51	4 26	3 54	26 43	3 11	18 21	17 Ø	7 32	3 36
8	15 3 17	17 24 11	4♎13	6 24	5 7	27 29	3 7	18 2Ø	17 1	7 3Ø	3 36
9	15 7 14	18 22 11	18 3	8 25	6 21	28 14	3 4	18 19	17 2	7 29	3 36
1Ø	15 11 1Ø	19 2Ø 8	2♏2Ø	1Ø 26	7 35	29 Ø	3 Ø	18 18	17 2	7 27	3 36
11	15 15 7	2Ø 18 5	17 Ø	12 3Ø	8 48	29 46	2 57	18 17	17 3	7 26	3 36
12	15 19 3	21 15 59	1♐55	14 35	1Ø 2	Ø♈32	2 53	18 16	17 4	7 24	3 35
13	15 23 Ø	22 13 52	16 58	16 41	11 16	1 17	2 49	18 14	17 5	7 22	3 35
14	15 26 56	23 11 44	1♑58	18 49	12 29	2 3	2 45	18 13	17 6	7 21	3 35
15	15 3Ø 53	24 9 35	16 46	2Ø 58	13 43	2 49	2 4Ø	18 11	17 7	7 19	3D35
16	15 34 5Ø	25 7 24	1♒17	23 8	14 57	3 34	2 36	18 9	17 8	7 18	3 35
17	15 38 46	26 5 12	15 26	25 18	16 11	4 2Ø	2 31	18 8	17 1Ø	7 16	3 35
18	15 42 43	27 2 59	29 12	27 3Ø	17 24	5 6	2 26	18 6	17 11	7 15	3 35
19	15 46 39	28 Ø 45	12♓38	29 41	18 38	5 51	2 21	18 4	17 12	7 13	3 36
2Ø	15 5Ø 36	28 58 3Ø	25 44	1♊53	19 52	6 37	2 16	18 2	17 13	7 12	3 36
21	15 54 32	29 56 14	8♈34	4 4	21 5	7 22	2 11	18 Ø	17 15	7 1Ø	3 36
22	15 58 29	Ø♊53 56	21 11	6 14	22 19	8 8	2 5	17 57	17 16	7 9	3 36
23	16 2 25	1 51 38	3♉36	8 24	23 33	8 53	2 Ø	17 55	17 18	7 7	3 36
24	16 6 22	2 49 18	15 53	1Ø 33	24 46	9 38	1 54	17 53	17 19	7 6	3 36
25	16 1Ø 19	3 46 57	28 2	12 4Ø	26 Ø	1Ø 24	1 48	17 5Ø	17 21	7 4	3 37
26	16 14 15	4 44 35	1Ø♊ 4	14 46	27 14	11 9	1 42	17 48	17 22	7 3	3 37
27	16 18 12	5 42 12	22 1	16 5Ø	28 27	11 54	1 36	17 45	17 24	7 2	3 37
28	16 22 8	6 39 48	3♋54	18 52	29 41	12 39	1 3Ø	17 42	17 26	7 Ø	3 38
29	16 26 5	7 37 22	15 45	2Ø 52	Ø♊55	13 24	1 24	17 4Ø	17 28	6 59	3 38
3Ø	16 3Ø 1	8 34 55	27 36	22 5Ø	2 8	14 9	1 17	17 37	17 29	6 58	3 39
31	16 33 58	9♊32 27	9♌31	24♊45	3♊22	14♈54	1♑11	17♑34	17♌31	6♏56	3♍39

THE SUN ENTERS THE SIGN OF GEMINI ON MAY 21 AT 01:34.

DAY	TIME	☉	☽	☿	♀	♂	♃	♄	♅	♆	♇
	h m s	° ' "	° '	° '	° '	° '	° '	° '	° '	° '	° '
J 1	16 37 54	1Ø♊29 57	21♌33	26♊38	4♊36	15♈39	1♑ 4	17♑31	17♌33	6♏55	3♍4Ø
U 2	16 41 51	11 27 26	3♍47	28 28	5 49	16 24	ØR57	17R28	17 35	6R54	3 4Ø
N 3	16 45 48	12 24 54	16 17	Ø♋15	7 3	17 9	Ø 51	17 25	17 37	6 52	3 41
E 4	16 49 44	13 22 21	29 1Ø	2 Ø	8 17	17 54	Ø 44	17 21	17 39	6 51	3 41
5	16 53 41	14 19 46	12♎29	3 43	9 3Ø	18 39	Ø 37	17 18	17 41	6 5Ø	3 42
6	16 57 37	15 17 1Ø	26 16	5 22	1Ø 44	19 23	Ø 3Ø	17 15	17 43	6 49	3 42
7	17 1 34	16 14 33	1Ø♏34	6 59	11 58	2Ø 8	Ø 22	17 11	17 46	6 47	3 43
8	17 5 3Ø	17 11 56	25 18	8 33	13 11	2Ø 53	Ø 15	17 8	17 48	6 46	3 44
9	17 9 27	18 9 17	1Ø♐23	1Ø 4	14 25	21 37	Ø 8	17 4	17 5Ø	6 45	3 45
1Ø	17 13 23	19 6 37	25 4Ø	11 33	15 39	22 22	Ø 1	17 1	17 52	6 44	3 45
11	17 17 2Ø	2Ø 3 57	1Ø♑56	12 58	16 52	23 6	29♐53	16 57	17 55	6 43	3 46
12	17 21 17	21 1 16	26 2	14 21	18 6	23 5Ø	29 46	16 53	17 57	6 42	3 47
13	17 25 13	21 58 34	1Ø♒48	15 41	19 2Ø	24 35	29 38	16 5Ø	18 Ø	6 41	3 48
14	17 29 1Ø	22 55 52	25 9	16 57	2Ø 33	25 19	29 31	16 46	18 2	6 4Ø	3 49
15	17 33 6	23 53 1Ø	9♓ 2	18 11	21 47	26 3	29 23	16 42	18 5	6 39	3 49
16	17 37 3	24 5Ø 27	22 3Ø	19 22	23 1	26 47	29 16	16 38	18 7	6 38	3 5Ø
17	17 4Ø 59	25 47 44	5♈33	2Ø 29	24 14	27 32	29 8	16 34	18 1Ø	6 37	3 51
18	17 44 56	26 45 1	18 17	21 34	25 28	28 16	29 Ø	16 3Ø	18 12	6 36	3 52
19	17 48 53	27 42 17	Ø♉44	22 35	26 42	28 59	28 53	16 26	18 15	6 35	3 53
2Ø	17 52 49	28 39 33	13 Ø	23 33	27 55	29 43	28 45	16 22	18 18	6 34	3 54
21	17 56 46	29 36 49	25 6	24 27	29 9	Ø♉27	28 37	16 18	18 2Ø	6 33	3 55
22	18 Ø 42	Ø♋34 5	7♊ 6	25 18	Ø♋23	1 11	28 3Ø	16 14	18 23	6 33	3 56
23	18 4 39	1 31 2Ø	19 2	26 6	1 37	1 55	28 22	16 1Ø	18 26	6 32	3 58
24	18 8 35	2 28 36	Ø♋54	26 49	2 5Ø	2 38	28 14	16 5	18 29	6 31	3 59
25	18 12 32	3 25 5Ø	12 46	27 29	4 4	3 22	28 7	16 1	18 32	6 3Ø	4 Ø
26	18 16 28	4 23 5	24 37	28 4	5 18	4 5	27 59	15 57	18 34	6 3Ø	4 1
27	18 2Ø 25	5 2Ø 19	6♌31	28 36	6 31	4 49	27 51	15 53	18 37	6 29	4 2
28	18 24 22	6 17 33	18 29	29 3	7 45	5 32	27 44	15 48	18 4Ø	6 28	4 3
29	18 28 18	7 14 46	Ø♍34	29 27	8 59	6 15	27 36	15 44	18 43	6 28	4 5
3Ø	18 32 15	8♋11 59	12♍5Ø	29♋45	1Ø♋13	6♉58	27♐29	15♑4Ø	18♌46	6♏27	4♍ 6

THE SUN ENTERS THE SIGN OF CANCER ON JUN 21 AT 09:43.

♏ SCORPIO ♐ SAGITTARIUS ♑ CAPRICORN ♒ AQUARIUS ♓ PISCES

SIDEREAL SUN MOON MERCURY VENUS MARS JUPITER SATURN URANUS NEPTUNE PLUTO

DAY	TIME h m s	☉ ° ' "	☽ ° '	☿ ° '	♀ ° '	♂ ° '	♃ ° '	♄ ° '	♅ ° '	♆ ° '	♇ ° '
J 1	18 36 11	9♋ 9 11	25♍21	29♋59	11♋26	7♉42	27♐22	15♑35	18♌49	6♏27	4♍ 7
U 2	18 40 8	10 6 23	8♎11	0♌ 9	12 40	8 25	27R14	15R31	18 53	6R26	4 8
L 3	18 44 4	11 3 35	21 25	0R14	13 54	9 7	27 7	15 26	18 56	6 26	4 10
Y 4	18 48 1	12 0 47	5♏ 6	0 14	15 8	9 50	27 0	15 22	18 59	6 25	4 11
5	18 51 57	12 57 58	19 15	0 10	16 22	10 33	26 53	15 18	19 2	6 25	4 13
6	18 55 54	13 55 9	3♐52	0 1	17 35	11 16	26 45	15 13	19 5	6 24	4 14
7	18 59 51	14 52 20	18 51	29♋47	18 49	11 58	26 39	15 9	19 8	6 24	4 15
8	19 3 47	15 49 30	4♑ 5	29 29	20 3	12 41	26 32	15 4	19 12	6 24	4 17
9	19 7 44	16 46 41	19 24	29 7	21 17	13 23	26 25	15 0	19 15	6 23	4 18
10	19 11 40	17 43 52	4♒35	28 41	22 30	14 6	26 18	14 56	19 18	6 23	4 20
11	19 15 37	18 41 4	19 29	28 11	23 44	14 48	26 12	14 51	19 21	6 23	4 21
12	19 19 33	19 38 15	3♓59	27 39	24 58	15 30	26 5	14 47	19 25	6 23	4 23
13	19 23 30	20 35 27	18 2	27 3	26 12	16 12	25 59	14 42	19 28	6 22	4 24
14	19 27 26	21 32 40	1♈36	26 26	27 26	16 54	25 52	14 38	19 32	6 22	4 26
15	19 31 23	22 29 53	14 44	25 47	28 39	17 36	25 46	14 34	19 35	6 22	4 28
16	19 35 20	23 27 7	27 29	25 7	29 53	18 18	25 40	14 29	19 38	6 22	4 29
17	19 39 16	24 24 21	9♉55	24 27	1♌ 7	18 59	25 34	14 25	19 42	6 22	4 31
18	19 43 13	25 21 36	22 7	23 47	2 21	19 41	25 28	14 21	19 45	6D22	4 32
19	19 47 9	26 18 52	4♊ 9	23 9	3 35	20 23	25 23	14 16	19 49	6 22	4 34
20	19 51 6	27 16 9	16 5	22 32	4 49	21 4	25 17	14 12	19 52	6 22	4 36
21	19 55 2	28 13 26	27 57	21 58	6 2	21 45	25 12	14 8	19 56	6 22	4 37
22	19 58 59	29 10 44	9♋48	21 27	7 16	22 27	25 7	14 4	19 59	6 22	4 39
23	20 2 55	0♌ 8 2	21 41	21 0	8 30	23 8	25 1	13 59	20 3	6 22	4 41
24	20 6 52	1 5 22	3♌36	20 38	9 44	23 49	24 56	13 55	20 6	6 22	4 43
25	20 10 49	2 2 41	15 36	20 20	10 58	24 29	24 52	13 51	20 10	6 23	4 44
26	20 14 45	3 0 2	27 42	20 7	12 12	25 10	24 47	13 47	20 14	6 23	4 46
27	20 18 42	3 57 22	9♍57	19D59	13 26	25 51	24 42	13 43	20 17	6 23	4 48
28	20 22 38	4 54 44	22 22	19 58	14 40	26 31	24 38	13 39	20 21	6 23	4 50
29	20 26 35	5 52 6	5♎ 0	20 2	15 54	27 12	24 34	13 35	20 25	6 24	4 52
30	20 30 31	6 49 28	17 55	20 13	17 7	27 52	24 30	13 31	20 28	6 24	4 53
31	20 34 28	7♌46 51	1♏10	20♋30	18♌21	28♉32	24♐26	13♑28	20♌32	6♏25	4♍55

THE SUN ENTERS THE SIGN OF LEO ON JUL 22 AT 20:38.

DAY	TIME h m s	☉ ° ' "	☽ ° '	☿ ° '	♀ ° '	♂ ° '	♃ ° '	♄ ° '	♅ ° '	♆ ° '	♇ ° '
A 1	20 38 24	8♌44 15	14♏46	20♋53	19♌35	29♉12	24♐22	13♑24	20♌36	6♏25	4♍57
U 2	20 42 21	9 41 39	28 46	21 22	20 49	29 52	24R19	13R20	20 39	6 25	4 59
G 3	20 46 18	10 39 4	13♐ 9	21 58	22 3	0♊32	24 16	13 16	20 43	6 26	5 1
U 4	20 50 14	11 36 30	27 52	22 40	23 17	1 12	24 12	13 13	20 47	6 26	5 3
S 5	20 54 11	12 33 56	12♑50	23 28	24 31	1 52	24 10	13 9	20 50	6 27	5 5
T 6	20 58 7	13 31 23	27 54	24 23	25 45	2 31	24 7	13 6	20 54	6 28	5 7
7	21 2 4	14 28 51	12♒55	25 23	26 59	3 10	24 4	13 2	20 58	6 28	5 8
8	21 6 0	15 26 20	27 44	26 29	28 13	3 50	24 2	12 59	21 1	6 29	5 10
9	21 9 57	16 23 50	12♓14	27 41	29 26	4 29	23 59	12 56	21 5	6 29	5 12
10	21 13 53	17 21 21	26 20	28 59	0♍40	5 8	23 57	12 52	21 9	6 30	5 14
11	21 17 50	18 18 54	10♈ 0	0♌22	1 54	5 47	23 55	12 49	21 13	6 31	5 16
12	21 21 47	19 16 28	23 13	1 50	3 8	6 25	23 54	12 46	21 16	6 32	5 18
13	21 25 43	20 14 3	6♉ 3	3 22	4 22	7 4	23 52	12 43	21 20	6 33	5 20
14	21 29 40	21 11 40	18 32	4 59	5 36	7 42	23 51	12 40	21 24	6 33	5 22
15	21 33 36	22 9 19	0♊46	6 40	6 50	8 21	23 50	12 37	21 28	6 34	5 24
16	21 37 33	23 6 59	12 47	8 25	8 4	8 59	23 49	12 34	21 31	6 35	5 26
17	21 41 29	24 4 41	24 42	10 13	9 18	9 37	23 48	12 31	21 35	6 36	5 28
18	21 45 26	25 2 24	6♋33	12 3	10 32	10 15	23 47	12 29	21 39	6 37	5 30
19	21 49 22	26 0 8	18 25	13 57	11 46	10 52	23 47	12 26	21 42	6 38	5 32
20	21 53 19	26 57 55	0♌21	15 52	12 59	11 30	23D47	12 24	21 46	6 39	5 34
21	21 57 16	27 55 42	12 22	17 49	14 13	12 7	23 47	12 21	21 50	6 40	5 36
22	22 1 12	28 53 31	24 32	19 47	15 27	12 45	23 47	12 19	21 54	6 41	5 38
23	22 5 9	29 51 22	6♍51	21 46	16 41	13 22	23 47	12 17	21 57	6 42	5 40
24	22 9 5	0♍49 14	19 21	23 45	17 55	13 59	23 48	12 14	22 1	6 43	5 42
25	22 13 2	1 47 7	2♎ 3	25 45	19 9	14 35	23 48	12 12	22 5	6 44	5 44
26	22 16 58	2 45 2	14 58	27 45	20 23	15 12	23 49	12 10	22 8	6 46	5 46
27	22 20 55	3 42 58	28 7	29 44	21 37	15 48	23 50	12 8	22 12	6 47	5 48
28	22 24 51	4 40 55	11♏31	1♍43	22 51	16 24	23 52	12 6	22 16	6 48	5 50
29	22 28 48	5 38 54	25 12	3 42	24 5	17 0	23 53	12 5	22 20	6 49	5 52
30	22 32 44	6 36 54	9♐ 8	5 39	25 18	17 36	23 55	12 3	22 23	6 51	5 54
31	22 36 41	7♍34 55	23♐20	7♍36	26♍32	18♊12	23♐57	12♑ 2	22♌27	6♏52	5♍56

THE SUN ENTERS THE SIGN OF VIRGO ON AUG 23 AT 03:35.

DAY	TIME h m s	☉ ° ' "	☽ ° '	☿ ° '	♀ ° '	♂ ° '	♃ ° '	♄ ° '	♅ ° '	♆ ° '	♇ ° '
S 1	22 40 38	8♍32 58	7♑44	9♍32	27♍46	18♊48	23♐59	12♑ 0	22♌30	6♏53	5♍59
E 2	22 44 34	9 31 2	22 19	11 27	29 0	19 23	24 1	11R59	22 34	6 55	6 1
P 3	22 48 31	10 29 8	6♒58	13 20	0♎14	19 58	24 3	11 57	22 38	6 56	6 3
T 4	22 52 27	11 27 14	21 36	15 13	1 28	20 33	24 6	11 56	22 41	6 58	6 5
E 5	22 56 24	12 25 23	6♓ 7	17 4	2 42	21 8	24 9	11 55	22 45	6 59	6 7
M 6	23 0 20	13 23 33	20 23	18 55	3 55	21 42	24 11	11 54	22 48	7 1	6 9
B 7	23 4 17	14 21 45	4♈22	20 44	5 9	22 17	24 15	11 53	22 52	7 2	6 11
E 8	23 8 13	15 19 59	17 59	22 32	6 23	22 51	24 18	11 52	22 56	7 4	6 13
R 9	23 12 10	16 18 15	1♉14	24 19	7 37	23 25	24 21	11 52	22 59	7 5	6 15
10	23 16 7	17 16 32	14 6	26 4	8 51	23 59	24 25	11 51	23 3	7 7	6 17
11	23 20 3	18 14 52	26 38	27 49	10 4	24 32	24 29	11 50	23 6	7 8	6 19
12	23 24 0	19 13 14	8♊54	29 32	11 18	25 5	24 33	11 50	23 9	7 10	6 21
13	23 27 56	20 11 38	20 58	1♎14	12 32	25 38	24 37	11 50	23 13	7 12	6 23
14	23 31 53	21 10 5	2♋53	2 56	13 46	26 11	24 41	11 49	23 16	7 13	6 25
15	23 35 49	22 8 33	14 45	4 36	14 59	26 44	24 46	11D49	23 20	7 15	6 27
16	23 39 46	23 7 4	26 38	6 15	16 13	27 16	24 50	11 49	23 23	7 17	6 29
17	23 43 42	24 5 36	8♌36	7 53	17 27	27 49	24 55	11 49	23 26	7 18	6 31
18	23 47 39	25 4 11	20 43	9 30	18 41	28 20	25 0	11 49	23 30	7 20	6 33
19	23 51 36	26 2 48	3♍ 2	11 6	19 54	28 52	25 5	11 50	23 33	7 22	6 35
20	23 55 32	27 1 26	15 35	12 41	21 8	29 24	25 11	11 50	23 36	7 24	6 37
21	23 59 29	28 0 7	28 24	14 15	22 22	29 55	25 16	11 50	23 40	7 26	6 38
22	0 3 25	28 58 50	11♎27	15 48	23 36	0♋26	25 22	11 51	23 43	7 27	6 40
23	0 7 22	29 57 35	24 46	17 20	24 49	0 56	25 28	11 52	23 46	7 29	6 42
24	0 11 18	0♎56 21	8♏19	18 51	26 3	1 26	25 34	11 52	23 49	7 31	6 44
25	0 15 15	1 55 9	22 4	20 21	27 17	1 57	25 40	11 53	23 52	7 33	6 46
26	0 19 11	2 54 0	5♐59	21 50	28 30	2 26	25 46	11 54	23 55	7 35	6 48
27	0 23 8	3 52 51	20 2	23 18	29 44	2 56	25 53	11 55	23 59	7 37	6 50
28	0 27 4	4 51 45	4♑11	24 45	0♏58	3 25	25 59	11 56	24 2	7 39	6 52
29	0 31 1	5 50 40	18 24	26 11	2 11	3 54	26 6	11 58	24 5	7 41	6 54
30	0 34 58	6♎49 38	2♒39	27♎36	3♏25	4♋22	26♐13	11♑59	24♌ 8	7♏43	6♍55

THE SUN ENTERS THE SIGN OF LIBRA ON SEP 23 AT 01:00.

♈ ARIES ♉ TAURUS ♊ GEMINI ♋ CANCER ♌ LEO ♍ VIRGO ♎ LIBRA

196Ø

SIDEREAL . . SUN . . MOON . . MERCURY . . VENUS . . MARS . . JUPITER . . SATURN . . URANUS . . NEPTUNE . . PLUTO .

DAY	TIME	☉	☽	☿	♀	♂	♃	♄	♅	♆	♇
	h m s	° ' "	° '	° '	° '	° '	° '	° '	° '	° '	° '
O 1	Ø 38 54	7♎48 36	16♒52	29♎ Ø	4♏38	4♋51	26♐2Ø	12♑ Ø	24♌11	7♏45	6♍57
C 2	Ø 42 51	8 47 37	1♓ 2	Ø♏23	5 52	5 19	26 27	12 2	24 14	7 47	6 59
T 3	Ø 46 47	9 46 39	15 5	1 45	7 6	5 46	26 34	12 4	24 16	7 49	7 1
O 4	Ø 5Ø 44	1Ø 45 43	28 59	3 6	8 19	6 13	26 42	12 5	24 19	7 51	7 3
B 5	Ø 54 4Ø	11 44 49	12♈39	4 25	9 33	6 4Ø	26 49	12 7	24 22	7 53	7 4
E 6	Ø 58 37	12 43 58	26 4	5 44	1Ø 46	7 7	26 57	12 9	24 25	7 55	7 6
R 7	1 2 33	13 43 8	9♉11	7 1	12 Ø	7 33	27 5	12 11	24 28	7 57	7 8
8	1 6 3Ø	14 42 21	22 Ø	8 16	13 13	7 59	27 13	12 13	24 3Ø	7 59	7 9
9	1 1Ø 27	15 41 35	4♊31	9 31	14 27	8 25	27 21	12 15	24 33	8 1	7 11
1Ø	1 14 23	16 4Ø 52	16 47	1Ø 43	15 4Ø	8 5Ø	27 29	12 18	24 36	8 3	7 13
11	1 18 2Ø	17 4Ø 12	28 51	11 54	16 54	9 15	27 38	12 2Ø	24 38	8 5	7 14
12	1 22 16	18 39 34	1Ø♋46	13 3	18 7	9 39	27 46	12 22	24 41	8 7	7 16
13	1 26 13	19 38 58	22 37	14 1Ø	19 2Ø	1Ø 3	27 55	12 25	24 43	8 1Ø	7 18
14	1 3Ø 9	2Ø 38 24	4♌3Ø	15 16	2Ø 34	1Ø 27	28 4	12 28	24 46	8 12	7 19
15	1 34 6	21 37 52	16 28	16 18	21 47	1Ø 5Ø	28 13	12 3Ø	24 48	8 14	7 21
16	1 38 2	22 37 23	28 38	17 19	23 1	11 13	28 22	12 33	24 51	8 16	7 22
17	1 41 59	23 36 56	11♍ 2	18 16	24 14	11 35	28 31	12 36	24 53	8 18	7 24
18	1 45 56	24 36 32	23 46	19 11	25 27	11 57	28 4Ø	12 39	24 55	8 2Ø	7 25
19	1 49 52	25 36 9	6♎49	2Ø 2	26 41	12 18	28 5Ø	12 42	24 58	8 23	7 27
2Ø	1 53 49	26 35 49	2Ø 14	2Ø 49	27 54	12 39	28 59	12 46	25 Ø	8 25	7 28
21	1 57 45	27 35 3Ø	3♏59	21 33	29 7	13 Ø	29 9	12 49	25 2	8 27	7 3Ø
22	2 1 42	28 35 14	18 Ø	22 11	Ø♐21	13 2Ø	29 19	12 52	25 4	8 29	7 31
23	2 5 38	29 34 59	2♐13	22 45	1 34	13 39	29 28	12 56	25 6	8 32	7 33
24	2 9 35	Ø♏34 47	16 33	23 14	2 47	13 58	29 38	12 59	25 8	8 34	7 34
25	2 13 31	1 34 36	Ø♑55	23 36	4 1	14 17	29 49	13 3	25 1Ø	8 36	7 35
26	2 17 28	2 34 27	15 13	23 52	5 14	14 35	29 59	13 7	25 12	8 38	7 37
27	2 21 25	3 34 2Ø	29 26	24R Ø	6 27	14 52	Ø♑ 9	13 1Ø	25 14	8 4Ø	7 38
28	2 25 21	4 34 14	13♒31	24 1	7 4Ø	15 9	Ø 19	13 14	25 16	8 43	7 39
29	2 29 18	5 34 9	27 26	23 53	8 53	15 25	Ø 3Ø	13 18	25 18	8 45	7 41
3Ø	2 33 14	6 34 7	11♓13	23 36	1Ø 6	15 41	Ø 41	13 22	25 2Ø	8 47	7 42
31	2 37 11	7♏34 6	24♓5Ø	23♏11	11♐2Ø	15♋56	Ø♑51	13♑26	25♌21	8♏49	7♍43

THE SUN ENTERS THE SIGN OF SCORPIO ON OCT 23 AT 10:03.

DAY	TIME	☉	☽	☿	♀	♂	♃	♄	♅	♆	♇
	h m s	° ' "	° '	° '	° '	° '	° '	° '	° '	° '	° '
N 1	2 41 7	8♏34 6	8♈17	22♏35	12♐33	16♋11	1♑ 2	13♑3Ø	25♌23	8♏52	7♍44
O 2	2 45 4	9 34 8	21 33	21R5Ø	13 46	16 25	1 13	13 35	25 25	8 54	7 45
V 3	2 49 Ø	1Ø 34 13	4♉38	2Ø 56	14 59	16 38	1 24	13 39	25 26	8 56	7 47
E 4	2 52 57	11 34 18	17 29	19 54	16 12	16 51	1 35	13 44	25 28	8 58	7 48
M 5	2 56 53	12 34 26	Ø♊ 8	18 45	17 25	17 3	1 46	13 48	25 29	9 1	7 49
B 6	3 Ø 5Ø	13 34 36	12 33	17 3Ø	18 38	17 14	1 57	13 53	25 31	9 3	7 5Ø
E 7	3 4 47	14 34 48	24 45	16 12	19 51	17 25	2 9	13 57	25 32	9 5	7 51
R 8	3 8 43	15 35 2	6♋46	14 52	21 3	17 35	2 2Ø	14 2	25 33	9 7	7 52
9	3 12 4Ø	16 35 17	18 4Ø	13 34	22 16	17 45	2 32	14 7	25 35	9 1Ø	7 53
1Ø	3 16 36	17 35 35	Ø♌3Ø	12 21	23 29	17 53	2 43	14 12	25 36	9 12	7 54
11	3 2Ø 33	18 35 54	12 2Ø	11 13	24 42	18 1	2 55	14 17	25 37	9 14	7 55
12	3 24 29	19 36 16	24 16	1Ø 14	25 55	18 9	3 7	14 22	25 38	9 16	7 56
13	3 28 26	2Ø 36 39	6♍23	9 24	27 7	18 15	3 19	14 27	25 39	9 19	7 56
14	3 32 22	21 37 5	18 47	8 46	28 2Ø	18 21	3 31	14 32	25 4Ø	9 21	7 57
15	3 36 19	22 37 32	1♎33	8 19	29 33	18 26	3 43	14 37	25 41	9 23	7 58
16	3 4Ø 16	23 38 1	14 43	8D 4	Ø♑46	18 3Ø	3 55	14 42	25 42	9 25	7 59
17	3 44 12	24 38 32	28 2Ø	8 1	1 58	18 34	4 7	14 47	25 43	9 27	8 Ø
18	3 48 9	25 39 5	12♏22	8 8	3 11	18 36	4 19	14 53	25 43	9 3Ø	8 Ø
19	3 52 5	26 39 39	26 47	8 26	4 23	18 38	4 31	14 58	25 44	9 32	8 1
2Ø	3 56 2	27 4Ø 15	11♐28	8 53	5 36	18R39	4 44	15 4	25 45	9 34	8 2
21	3 59 58	28 4Ø 52	26 16	9 29	6 48	18 39	4 56	15 9	25 45	9 36	8 2
22	4 3 55	29 41 31	11♑ 4	1Ø 12	8 1	18 39	5 9	15 15	25 46	9 38	8 3
23	4 7 51	Ø♐42 1Ø	25 43	11 2	9 13	18 37	5 21	15 21	25 46	9 4Ø	8 3
24	4 11 48	1 42 51	1Ø♒ 9	11 58	1Ø 25	18 35	5 34	15 26	25 47	9 42	8 4
25	4 15 45	2 43 33	24 17	13 Ø	11 38	18 31	5 46	15 32	25 47	9 45	8 4
26	4 19 41	3 44 16	8♓ 9	14 5	12 5Ø	18 27	5 59	15 38	25 48	9 47	8 5
27	4 23 38	4 45 Ø	21 43	15 15	14 2	18 23	6 12	15 44	25 48	9 49	8 5
28	4 27 34	5 45 45	5♈ 3	16 28	15 14	18 17	6 25	15 5Ø	25 48	9 51	8 6
29	4 31 31	6 46 31	18 9	17 44	16 26	18 1Ø	6 38	15 56	25 48	9 53	8 6
3Ø	4 35 27	7♐47 18	1♉ 4	19♏ 2	17♑38	18♋ 3	6♑51	16♑ 2	25♌48	9♏55	8♍ 6

THE SUN ENTERS THE SIGN OF SAGITTARIUS ON NOV 22 AT 07:19.

DAY	TIME	☉	☽	☿	♀	♂	♃	♄	♅	♆	♇
	h m s	° ' "	° '	° '	° '	° '	° '	° '	° '	° '	° '
D 1	4 39 24	8♐48 6	13♉48	2Ø♏23	18♑5Ø	17♋54	7♑ 4	16♑ 8	25♌48	9♏57	8♍ 7
E 2	4 43 2Ø	9 48 55	26 21	21 45	2Ø 2	17R45	7 17	16 14	25R48	9 59	8 7
C 3	4 47 17	1Ø 49 46	8♊45	23 9	21 14	17 35	7 3Ø	16 2Ø	25 48	1Ø 1	8 7
E 4	4 51 14	11 5Ø 37	2Ø 59	24 34	22 26	17 24	7 43	16 27	25 48	1Ø 3	8 7
M 5	4 55 1Ø	12 51 3Ø	3♋ 4	26 Ø	23 37	17 13	7 56	16 33	25 48	1Ø 5	8 8
B 6	4 59 7	13 52 23	15 1	27 27	24 49	17 Ø	8 9	16 39	25 48	1Ø 7	8 8
E 7	5 3 3	14 53 18	26 52	28 55	26 Ø	16 47	8 23	16 46	25 47	1Ø 9	8 8
R 8	5 7 Ø	15 54 14	8♌4Ø	Ø♐24	27 12	16 33	8 36	16 52	25 47	1Ø 11	8 8
9	5 1Ø 56	16 55 11	2Ø 29	1 53	28 23	16 18	8 49	16 58	25 47	1Ø 13	8 8
1Ø	5 14 53	17 56 9	2♍23	3 23	29 35	16 2	9 3	17 5	25 46	1Ø 15	8R 8
11	5 18 49	18 57 9	14 27	4 53	Ø♒46	15 46	9 16	17 11	25 46	1Ø 16	8 8
12	5 22 46	19 58 9	26 46	6 24	1 57	15 29	9 3Ø	17 18	25 45	1Ø 18	8 8
13	5 26 43	2Ø 59 11	9♎27	7 55	3 8	15 11	9 43	17 25	25 44	1Ø 2Ø	8 8
14	5 3Ø 39	22 Ø 13	22 34	9 26	4 19	14 52	9 57	17 31	25 44	1Ø 22	8 8
15	5 34 36	23 1 17	6♏1Ø	1Ø 57	5 3Ø	14 33	1Ø 11	17 38	25 43	1Ø 24	8 8
16	5 38 32	24 2 22	2Ø 16	12 29	6 41	14 13	1Ø 24	17 45	25 42	1Ø 25	8 7
17	5 42 29	25 3 27	4♐49	14 1	7 51	13 53	1Ø 38	17 51	25 41	1Ø 27	8 7
18	5 46 25	26 4 33	19 45	15 33	9 2	13 32	1Ø 52	17 58	25 41	1Ø 29	8 7
19	5 5Ø 22	27 5 4Ø	4♑53	17 5	1Ø 12	13 1Ø	11 5	18 5	25 4Ø	1Ø 31	8 7
2Ø	5 54 19	28 6 48	2Ø 4	18 38	11 23	12 48	11 19	18 12	25 39	1Ø 32	8 6
21	5 58 15	29 7 56	5♒ 6	2Ø 11	12 33	12 26	11 33	18 18	25 38	1Ø 34	8 6
22	6 2 12	Ø♑ 9 4	19 52	21 43	13 43	12 4	11 47	18 25	25 36	1Ø 35	8 6
23	6 6 8	1 1Ø 12	4♓17	23 17	14 53	11 41	12 Ø	18 32	25 35	1Ø 37	8 5
24	6 1Ø 5	2 11 2Ø	18 18	24 5Ø	16 3	11 17	12 14	18 39	25 34	1Ø 39	8 5
25	6 14 1	3 12 29	1♈55	26 23	17 13	1Ø 54	12 28	18 46	25 33	1Ø 4Ø	8 5
26	6 17 58	4 13 37	15 11	27 57	18 22	1Ø 3Ø	12 42	18 53	25 32	1Ø 42	8 4
27	6 21 54	5 14 46	28 8	29 31	19 32	1Ø 6	12 56	19 Ø	25 3Ø	1Ø 43	8 4
28	6 25 51	6 15 54	1Ø♉49	1♑ 5	2Ø 41	9 43	13 1Ø	19 7	25 29	1Ø 45	8 3
29	6 29 48	7 17 3	23 18	2 4Ø	21 5Ø	9 19	13 24	19 14	25 27	1Ø 46	8 2
3Ø	6 33 44	8 18 11	5♊36	4 15	22 59	8 55	13 38	19 21	25 26	1Ø 47	8 2
31	6 37 41	9♑19 2Ø	17♊46	5♑5Ø	24♒ 8	8♋31	13♑51	19♑28	25♌24	1Ø♏49	8♍ 1

THE SUN ENTERS THE SIGN OF CAPRICORN ON DEC 21 AT 20:27.

♏ SCORPIO ♐ SAGITTARIUS ♑ CAPRICORN ♒ AQUARIUS ♓ PISCES

SIDEREAL   SUN.   MOON.   MERCURY.   VENUS.   MARS.   JUPITER.   SATURN.   URANUS.   NEPTUNE.   PLUTO.

DAY	TIME	☉	☽	☿	♀	♂	♃	♄	♅	♆	♇
	h m s	° ' "	° '	° '	° '	° '	° '	° '	° '	° '	° '
J 1	6 41 37	10♑20 28	29♊49	7♑25	25♒17	8♋ 7	14♑ 5	19♑35	25♌23	10♏50	8♍ 1
A 2	6 45 34	11 21 37	11♋46	9 1	26 26	7R44	14 19	19 42	25R21	10 52	8R 0
N 3	6 49 30	12 22 45	23 38	10 37	27 34	7 21	14 33	19 49	25 19	10 53	7 59
U 4	6 53 27	13 23 54	5♌28	12 14	28 42	6 58	14 47	19 56	25 18	10 54	7 59
A 5	6 57 23	14 25 3	17 16	13 50	29 50	6 35	15 1	20 3	25 16	10 55	7 58
R 6	7 1 20	15 26 11	29 6	15 28	0♓58	6 12	15 15	20 10	25 14	10 57	7 57
Y 7	7 5 17	16 27 20	11♍ 2	17 5	2 5	5 50	15 29	20 17	25 12	10 58	7 56
8	7 9 13	17 28 29	23 6	18 43	3 13	5 29	15 43	20 24	25 10	10 59	7 55
9	7 13 10	18 29 38	5♎24	20 22	4 20	5 8	15 57	20 32	25 9	11 0	7 54
10	7 17 6	19 30 47	18 1	22 0	5 27	4 47	16 11	20 39	25 7	11 1	7 54
11	7 21 3	20 31 55	1♏ 1	23 40	6 34	4 27	16 25	20 46	25 5	11 2	7 53
12	7 24 59	21 33 4	14 28	25 19	7 40	4 7	16 39	20 53	25 3	11 3	7 52
13	7 28 56	22 34 13	28 25	27 0	8 47	3 49	16 53	21 0	25 0	11 4	7 51
14	7 32 52	23 35 22	12♐50	28 40	9 53	3 30	17 7	21 7	24 58	11 5	7 50
15	7 36 49	24 36 31	27 41	0♒21	10 58	3 13	17 21	21 14	24 56	11 6	7 49
16	7 40 46	25 37 39	12♑50	2 2	12 4	2 56	17 35	21 21	24 54	11 7	7 48
17	7 44 42	26 38 47	28 8	3 44	13 9	2 39	17 49	21 28	24 52	11 8	7 47
18	7 48 39	27 39 54	13♒23	5 26	14 14	2 24	18 3	21 36	24 50	11 9	7 46
19	7 52 35	28 41 1	28 26	7 8	15 19	2 9	18 17	21 43	24 47	11 10	7 44
20	7 56 32	29 42 7	13♓ 8	8 51	16 23	1 55	18 30	21 50	24 45	11 10	7 43
21	8 0 28	0♒43 12	27 24	10 34	17 27	1 42	18 44	21 57	24 43	11 11	7 42
22	8 4 25	1 44 15	11♈14	12 16	18 31	1 29	18 58	22 4	24 40	11 12	7 41
23	8 8 21	2 45 18	24 37	13 59	19 35	1 18	19 12	22 11	24 38	11 13	7 40
24	8 12 18	3 46 20	7♉36	15 41	20 38	1 7	19 26	22 18	24 36	11 13	7 39
25	8 16 15	4 47 21	20 16	17 23	21 41	0 57	19 39	22 25	24 33	11 14	7 37
26	8 20 11	5 48 21	2♊39	19 4	22 43	0 48	19 53	22 32	24 31	11 14	7 36
27	8 24 8	6 49 19	14 49	20 44	23 45	0 39	20 7	22 39	24 28	11 15	7 35
28	8 28 4	7 50 17	26 50	22 23	24 47	0 32	20 21	22 46	24 26	11 15	7 34
29	8 32 1	8 51 14	8♋44	24 1	25 48	0 25	20 34	22 53	24 23	11 16	7 32
30	8 35 57	9 52 9	20 36	25 37	26 49	0 19	20 48	23 0	24 21	11 16	7 31
31	8 39 54	10♒53 3	2♌25	27♒10	27♓49	0♋14	21♑ 1	23♑ 7	24♌18	11♏17	7♍30

THE SUN ENTERS THE SIGN OF AQUARIUS ON JAN 20 AT 07:01.

DAY	TIME	☉	☽	☿	♀	♂	♃	♄	♅	♆	♇
	h m s	° ' "	° '	° '	° '	° '	° '	° '	° '	° '	° '
F 1	8 43 50	11♒53 56	14♌15	28♒41	28♓49	0♋10	21♑15	23♑13	24♌16	11♏17	7♍28
E 2	8 47 47	12 54 49	26 7	0♓ 8	29 48	0R 6	21 29	23 20	24R13	11 17	7R27
B 3	8 51 44	13 55 40	8♍ 4	1 32	0♈47	0 3	21 42	23 27	24 11	11 18	7 25
R 4	8 55 40	14 56 30	20 7	2 50	1 46	0 1	21 55	23 34	24 8	11 18	7 24
U 5	8 59 37	15 57 19	2♎19	4 4	2 44	0 0	22 9	23 41	24 6	11 18	7 23
A 6	9 3 33	16 58 7	14 44	5 11	3 41	0D 0	22 22	23 47	24 3	11 18	7 21
R 7	9 7 30	17 58 54	27 24	6 12	4 38	0 0	22 36	23 54	24 0	11 19	7 20
Y 8	9 11 26	18 59 40	10♏23	7 4	5 34	0 1	22 49	24 1	23 58	11 19	7 18
9	9 15 23	20 0 25	23 44	7 49	6 30	0 3	23 2	24 7	23 55	11 19	7 17
10	9 19 19	21 1 9	7♐29	8 24	7 25	0 5	23 15	24 14	23 52	11 19	7 15
11	9 23 16	22 1 52	21 39	8 50	8 19	0 8	23 29	24 21	23 50	11R19	7 14
12	9 27 13	23 2 34	6♑12	9R 5	9 13	0 12	23 42	24 27	23 47	11 19	7 13
13	9 31 9	24 3 15	21 4	9 11	10 6	0 17	23 55	24 34	23 45	11 19	7 11
14	9 35 6	25 3 55	6♒ 8	9 5	10 59	0 22	24 8	24 40	23 42	11 19	7 10
15	9 39 2	26 4 33	21 16	8 49	11 50	0 28	24 21	24 47	23 39	11 19	7 8
16	9 42 59	27 5 10	6♓19	8 23	12 41	0 35	24 34	24 53	23 37	11 19	7 7
17	9 46 55	28 5 46	21 7	7 47	13 32	0 42	24 46	24 59	23 34	11 18	7 5
18	9 50 52	29 6 19	5♈33	7 3	14 21	0 50	24 59	25 6	23 31	11 18	7 3
19	9 54 48	0♓ 6 51	19 35	6 11	15 9	0 58	25 12	25 12	23 29	11 18	7 2
20	9 58 45	1 7 21	3♉ 9	5 13	15 57	1 8	25 25	25 18	23 26	11 18	7 0
21	10 2 42	2 7 49	16 17	4 11	16 44	1 17	25 37	25 24	23 24	11 17	6 59
22	10 6 38	3 8 15	29 1	3 6	17 29	1 28	25 50	25 31	23 21	11 17	6 57
23	10 10 35	4 8 40	11♊26	2 0	18 14	1 39	26 2	25 37	23 18	11 17	6 56
24	10 14 31	5 9 2	23 35	0 54	18 58	1 50	26 15	25 43	23 16	11 16	6 54
25	10 18 28	6 9 23	5♋33	29♒51	19 40	2 2	26 27	25 49	23 13	11 16	6 53
26	10 22 24	7 9 42	17 25	28 50	20 22	2 15	26 39	25 55	23 11	11 15	6 51
27	10 26 21	8 9 58	29 13	27 55	21 2	2 28	26 52	26 1	23 8	11 15	6 50
28	10 30 17	9♓10 13	11♌ 2	27♒ 5	21♈41	2♋41	27♑ 4	26♑ 6	23♌ 6	11♏14	6♍48

THE SUN ENTERS THE SIGN OF PISCES ON FEB 18 AT 21:17.

DAY	TIME	☉	☽	☿	♀	♂	♃	♄	♅	♆	♇
	h m s	° ' "	° '	° '	° '	° '	° '	° '	° '	° '	° '
M 1	10 34 14	10♓10 26	22♌55	26♒21	22♈19	2♋55	27♑16	26♑12	23♌ 3	11♏14	6♍46
A 2	10 38 11	11 10 37	4♍54	25R43	22 56	3 10	27 28	26 18	23R 1	11R13	6R45
R 3	10 42 7	12 10 46	17 1	25 13	23 31	3 25	27 40	26 24	22 58	11 13	6 43
C 4	10 46 4	13 10 53	29 18	24 49	24 4	3 40	27 52	26 29	22 56	11 12	6 42
H 5	10 50 0	14 10 59	11♎46	24 33	24 37	3 56	28 3	26 35	22 54	11 11	6 40
6	10 53 57	15 11 2	24 26	24D23	25 7	4 13	28 15	26 40	22 51	11 11	6 39
7	10 57 53	16 11 5	7♏20	24 20	25 36	4 29	28 27	26 46	22 49	11 10	6 37
8	11 1 50	17 11 5	20 29	24 24	26 4	4 47	28 38	26 51	22 46	11 9	6 36
9	11 5 46	18 11 4	3♐54	24 33	26 30	5 4	28 50	26 56	22 44	11 8	6 34
10	11 9 43	19 11 1	17 36	24 48	26 54	5 22	29 1	27 2	22 42	11 7	6 33
11	11 13 39	20 10 57	1♑34	25 9	27 16	5 41	29 12	27 7	22 40	11 7	6 31
12	11 17 36	21 10 51	15 49	25 34	27 37	6 0	29 23	27 12	22 37	11 6	6 30
13	11 21 33	22 10 44	0♒19	26 5	27 55	6 19	29 34	27 17	22 35	11 5	6 28
14	11 25 29	23 10 34	14 58	26 39	28 11	6 39	29 45	27 22	22 33	11 4	6 27
15	11 29 26	24 10 23	29 44	27 18	28 26	6 58	29 56	27 27	22 31	11 3	6 25
16	11 33 22	25 10 10	14♓28	28 1	28 38	7 19	0♒ 7	27 32	22 29	11 2	6 24
17	11 37 19	26 9 55	29 4	28 48	28 48	7 39	0 18	27 37	22 27	11 1	6 22
18	11 41 15	27 9 38	13♈26	29 38	28 56	8 0	0 28	27 41	22 25	11 0	6 21
19	11 45 12	28 9 19	27 27	0♓31	29 2	8 22	0 39	27 46	22 23	10 59	6 20
20	11 49 8	29 8 58	11♉ 5	1 27	29R 5	8 43	0 49	27 51	22 21	10 58	6 18
21	11 53 5	0♈ 8 35	24 19	2 26	29 6	9 5	1 0	27 55	22 19	10 56	6 17
22	11 57 2	1 8 9	7♊ 9	3 28	29 4	9 28	1 10	28 0	22 17	10 55	6 15
23	12 0 58	2 7 41	19 38	4 32	29 0	9 50	1 20	28 4	22 15	10 54	6 14
24	12 4 55	3 7 11	1♋49	5 38	28 53	10 13	1 30	28 8	22 13	10 53	6 13
25	12 8 51	4 6 39	13 48	6 47	28 44	10 36	1 40	28 12	22 11	10 52	6 11
26	12 12 48	5 6 4	25 40	7 58	28 33	11 0	1 49	28 17	22 10	10 51	6 10
27	12 16 44	6 5 27	7♌28	9 12	28 19	11 23	1 59	28 21	22 8	10 49	6 9
28	12 20 41	7 4 47	19 18	10 27	28 2	11 47	2 9	28 25	22 6	10 48	6 7
29	12 24 37	8 4 6	1♍15	11 44	27 43	12 12	2 18	28 28	22 5	10 47	6 6
30	12 28 34	9 3 22	13 21	13 3	27 22	12 36	2 27	28 32	22 3	10 45	6 5
31	12 32 30	10♈ 2 36	25♍40	14♓23	26♈58	13♋ 1	2♒36	28♑36	22♌ 2	10♏44	6♍ 4

THE SUN ENTERS THE SIGN OF ARIES ON MAR 20 AT 20:33.

♈ ARIES	♉ TAURUS	♊ GEMINI	♋ CANCER	♌ LEO	♍ VIRGO	♎ LIBRA

SIDEREAL · SUN. · MOON. · MERCURY. · VENUS. · MARS. · JUPITER. · SATURN. · URANUS. · NEPTUNE. · PLUTO.

DAY	TIME	☉	☽	☿	♀	♂	♃	♄	♅	♆	♇
	h m s	° ' "	° '	° '	° '	° '	° '	° '	° '	° '	° '
A 1	12 36 27	11♈ 1 48	8♎12	15♓46	26♈33	13♋26	2♒45	28♑40	22♌ 0	10♏43	6♍ 2
P 2	12 40 24	12 0 57	21 0	17 10	26R 5	13 51	2 54	28 43	21R59	10R41	6R 1
R 3	12 44 20	13 0 5	4♏ 2	18 36	25 35	14 17	3 3	28 47	21 57	10 40	6 0
I 4	12 48 17	13 59 11	17 19	20 4	25 4	14 42	3 12	28 50	21 56	10 39	5 59
L 5	12 52 13	14 58 15	0♐48	21 33	24 30	15 8	3 20	28 53	21 55	10 37	5 58
6	12 56 10	15 57 17	14 29	23 3	23 56	15 34	3 29	28 57	21 54	10 36	5 57
7	13 0 6	16 56 18	28 20	24 36	23 21	16 0	3 37	29 0	21 52	10 34	5 55
8	13 4 3	17 55 16	12♑19	26 9	22 44	16 27	3 45	29 3	21 51	10 33	5 54
9	13 7 59	18 54 13	26 26	27 45	22 7	16 54	3 53	29 6	21 50	10 31	5 53
10	13 11 56	19 53 9	10♒38	29 22	21 29	17 21	4 1	29 9	21 49	10 30	5 52
11	13 15 53	20 52 2	24 55	1♈ 0	20 51	17 48	4 9	29 11	21 48	10 28	5 51
12	13 19 49	21 50 54	9♓14	2 40	20 14	18 15	4 16	29 14	21 47	10 27	5 50
13	13 23 46	22 49 44	23 31	4 22	19 36	18 42	4 24	29 17	21 46	10 25	5 49
14	13 27 42	23 48 32	7♈43	6 5	18 59	19 10	4 31	29 19	21 46	10 24	5 48
15	13 31 39	24 47 18	21 45	7 50	18 23	19 38	4 38	29 22	21 45	10 22	5 47
16	13 35 35	25 46 2	5♉33	9 36	17 48	20 6	4 45	29 24	21 44	10 21	5 47
17	13 39 32	26 44 45	19 3	11 24	17 14	20 34	4 52	29 26	21 43	10 19	5 46
18	13 43 28	27 43 25	2♊13	13 13	16 42	21 3	4 59	29 28	21 43	10 17	5 45
19	13 47 25	28 42 3	15 2	15 4	16 11	21 31	5 5	29 30	21 42	10 16	5 44
20	13 51 22	29 40 39	27 31	16 57	15 42	22 0	5 12	29 32	21 42	10 14	5 43
21	13 55 18	0♉39 13	9♋44	18 51	15 14	22 29	5 18	29 34	21 41	10 13	5 42
22	13 59 15	1 37 45	21 43	20 47	14 49	22 58	5 24	29 36	21 41	10 11	5 42
23	14 3 11	2 36 14	3♌35	22 44	14 26	23 27	5 30	29 38	21 40	10 9	5 41
24	14 7 8	3 34 42	15 24	24 43	14 5	23 56	5 36	29 39	21 40	10 8	5 40
25	14 11 4	4 33 7	27 15	26 43	13 47	24 26	5 42	29 41	21 40	10 6	5 40
26	14 15 1	5 31 30	9♍14	28 45	13 30	24 55	5 47	29 42	21 40	10 5	5 39
27	14 18 57	6 29 51	21 26	0♉49	13 17	25 25	5 52	29 43	21 39	10 3	5 38
28	14 22 54	7 28 10	3♎53	2 53	13 5	25 55	5 57	29 45	21 39	10 1	5 38
29	14 26 50	8 26 27	16 39	4 59	12 56	26 25	6 2	29 46	21D39	10 0	5 37
30	14 30 47	9♉24 42	29♎45	7♉ 6	12♈50	26♋55	6♒ 7	29♑47	21♌39	9♏58	5♍37

THE SUN ENTERS THE SIGN OF TAURUS ON APR 20 AT 07:55.

DAY	TIME	☉	☽	☿	♀	♂	♃	♄	♅	♆	♇
	h m s	° ' "	° '	° '	° '	° '	° '	° '	° '	° '	° '
M 1	14 34 44	10♉22 56	13♏10	9♉14	12♈46	27♋25	6♒12	29♑48	21♌39	9♏56	5♍36
A 2	14 38 40	11 21 7	26 52	11 23	12D44	27 56	6 16	29 48	21 39	9R55	5R36
Y 3	14 42 37	12 19 17	10♐48	13 33	12 45	28 26	6 21	29 49	21 40	9 53	5 35
4	14 46 33	13 17 26	24 53	15 42	12 48	28 57	6 25	29 50	21 40	9 51	5 35
5	14 50 30	14 15 33	9♑ 4	17 52	12 54	29 28	6 29	29 50	21 40	9 50	5 35
6	14 54 26	15 13 38	23 15	20 2	13 1	29 58	6 32	29 51	21 40	9 48	5 34
7	14 58 23	16 11 43	7♒26	22 11	13 11	0♌29	6 36	29 51	21 41	9 47	5 34
8	15 2 20	17 9 45	21 34	24 20	13 23	1 0	6 39	29 51	21 41	9 45	5 34
9	15 6 16	18 7 47	5♓37	26 27	13 37	1 32	6 43	29R51	21 42	9 43	5 33
10	15 10 13	19 5 47	19 37	28 34	13 53	2 3	6 46	29 51	21 42	9 42	5 33
11	15 14 9	20 3 46	3♈30	0♊38	14 11	2 34	6 49	29 51	21 43	9 40	5 33
12	15 18 6	21 1 43	17 16	2 41	14 31	3 6	6 51	29 51	21 44	9 39	5 33
13	15 22 2	21 59 39	0♉53	4 42	14 52	3 38	6 54	29 51	21 44	9 37	5 33
14	15 25 59	22 57 34	14 19	6 40	15 16	4 9	6 56	29 50	21 45	9 35	5 32
15	15 29 55	23 55 27	27 31	8 36	15 41	4 41	6 58	29 50	21 46	9 34	5 32
16	15 33 52	24 53 19	10♊27	10 30	16 8	5 13	7 0	29 49	21 47	9 32	5 32
17	15 37 48	25 51 9	23 6	12 20	16 36	5 45	7 2	29 49	21 48	9 31	5D32
18	15 41 45	26 48 58	5♋30	14 8	17 5	6 17	7 3	29 48	21 49	9 29	5 32
19	15 45 42	27 46 45	17 39	15 52	17 37	6 50	7 5	29 47	21 50	9 28	5 32
20	15 49 38	28 44 31	29 38	17 34	18 9	7 22	7 6	29 46	21 51	9 26	5 32
21	15 53 35	29 42 15	11♌28	19 12	18 43	7 54	7 7	29 45	21 52	9 25	5 33
22	15 57 31	0♊39 57	23 16	20 47	19 18	8 27	7 8	29 44	21 53	9 23	5 33
23	16 1 28	1 37 38	5♍ 7	22 19	19 54	9 0	7 9	29 43	21 54	9 22	5 33
24	16 5 24	2 35 18	17 7	23 48	20 32	9 32	7 9	29 41	21 56	9 20	5 33
25	16 9 21	3 32 55	29 20	25 13	21 11	10 5	7R 9	29 40	21 57	9 19	5 33
26	16 13 17	4 30 31	11♎51	26 35	21 50	10 38	7 9	29 38	21 58	9 17	5 33
27	16 17 14	5 28 6	24 44	27 53	22 31	11 11	7 9	29 37	22 0	9 16	5 34
28	16 21 11	6 25 40	8♏ 2	29 8	23 13	11 44	7 9	29 35	22 1	9 14	5 34
29	16 25 7	7 23 12	21 44	0♋19	23 56	12 17	7 8	29 33	22 3	9 13	5 34
30	16 29 4	8 20 43	5♐47	1 27	24 40	12 50	7 8	29 32	22 4	9 12	5 35
31	16 33 0	9♊18 13	20♐ 8	2♋31	25♈24	13♌24	7♒ 7	29♑30	22♌ 6	9♏10	5♍35

THE SUN ENTERS THE SIGN OF GEMINI ON MAY 21 AT 07:22.

DAY	TIME	☉	☽	☿	♀	♂	♃	♄	♅	♆	♇
	h m s	° ' "	° '	° '	° '	° '	° '	° '	° '	° '	° '
J 1	16 36 57	10♊15 42	4♑39	3♋32	26♈10	13♌57	7♒ 6	29♑28	22♌ 8	9♏ 9	5♍36
U 2	16 40 53	11 13 11	19 14	4 28	26 56	14 30	7R 4	29R25	22 9	9R 7	5 36
N 3	16 44 50	12 10 38	3♒47	5 21	27 43	15 4	7 3	29 23	22 11	9 6	5 37
E 4	16 48 47	13 8 4	18 12	6 10	28 31	15 38	7 1	29 21	22 13	9 5	5 37
5	16 52 43	14 5 30	2♓27	6 55	29 20	16 11	6 59	29 19	22 15	9 4	5 38
6	16 56 40	15 2 56	16 30	7 36	0♉ 9	16 45	6 57	29 16	22 17	9 2	5 38
7	17 0 36	16 0 20	0♈21	8 13	1 0	17 19	6 55	29 14	22 19	9 1	5 39
8	17 4 33	16 57 44	13 59	8 45	1 50	17 53	6 53	29 11	22 21	9 0	5 39
9	17 8 29	17 55 8	27 26	9 13	2 42	18 27	6 50	29 8	22 23	8 59	5 40
10	17 12 26	18 52 31	10♉40	9 37	3 34	19 1	6 47	29 5	22 25	8 58	5 41
11	17 16 22	19 49 53	23 43	9 56	4 27	19 35	6 44	29 3	22 27	8 56	5 41
12	17 20 19	20 47 15	6♊34	10 11	5 20	20 9	6 41	29 0	22 29	8 55	5 42
13	17 24 16	21 44 36	19 12	10 21	6 14	20 43	6 38	28 57	22 31	8 54	5 43
14	17 28 12	22 41 57	1♋38	10R26	7 8	21 18	6 35	28 54	22 33	8 53	5 44
15	17 32 9	23 39 17	13 51	10 27	8 3	21 52	6 31	28 50	22 36	8 52	5 45
16	17 36 5	24 36 36	25 53	10 24	8 58	22 26	6 27	28 47	22 38	8 51	5 46
17	17 40 2	25 33 54	7♌47	10 16	9 54	23 1	6 23	28 44	22 41	8 50	5 46
18	17 43 58	26 31 12	19 35	10 3	10 50	23 36	6 19	28 41	22 43	8 49	5 47
19	17 47 55	27 28 29	1♍22	9 47	11 47	24 10	6 15	28 37	22 45	8 48	5 48
20	17 51 51	28 25 45	13 12	9 27	12 44	24 45	6 10	28 34	22 48	8 47	5 49
21	17 55 48	29 23 0	25 11	9 4	13 41	25 20	6 5	28 30	22 50	8 46	5 50
22	17 59 45	0♋20 15	7♎23	8 37	14 39	25 55	6 1	28 27	22 53	8 45	5 51
23	18 3 41	1 17 29	19 54	8 7	15 37	26 30	5 56	28 23	22 56	8 44	5 52
24	18 7 38	2 14 42	2♏48	7 35	16 36	27 4	5 50	28 19	22 58	8 44	5 53
25	18 11 34	3 11 55	16 9	7 2	17 35	27 40	5 45	28 16	23 1	8 43	5 55
26	18 15 31	4 9 7	29 56	6 27	18 34	28 15	5 40	28 12	23 4	8 42	5 56
27	18 19 27	5 6 19	14♐10	5 52	19 34	28 50	5 34	28 8	23 6	8 41	5 57
28	18 23 24	6 3 31	28 46	5 16	20 34	29 25	5 29	28 4	23 9	8 41	5 58
29	18 27 20	7 0 42	13♑37	4 41	21 34	0♍ 0	5 23	28 0	23 12	8 40	5 59
30	18 31 17	7♋57 54	28♑34	4♋ 7	22♉35	0♍36	5♒17	27♑56	23♌15	8♏39	6♍ 0

THE SUN ENTERS THE SIGN OF CANCER ON JUN 21 AT 15:31.

♏ SCORPIO ♐ SAGITTARIUS ♑ CAPRICORN ♒ AQUARIUS ♓ PISCES

SIDEREAL TIME · SUN · MOON · MERCURY · VENUS · MARS · JUPITER · SATURN · URANUS · NEPTUNE · PLUTO

DAY	TIME	☉	☽	☿	♀	♂	♃	♄	♅	♆	♇
	h m s	° ' "	° '	° '	° '	° '	° '	° '	° '	° '	° '
J 1	18 35 14	8♋55 5	13♒29	3♋35	23♉36	1♍11	5♒11	27♑52	23♌18	8♏39	6♍ 2
U 2	18 39 10	9 52 16	28 15	3R 6	24 37	1 46	5R 4	27R48	23 21	8R38	6 3
L 3	18 43 7	10 49 27	12♓45	2 39	25 39	2 22	4 58	27 44	23 24	8 38	6 4
Y 4	18 47 3	11 46 39	26 58	2 16	26 41	2 58	4 52	27 40	23 27	8 37	6 6
5	18 51 0	12 43 51	10♈51	1 56	27 43	3 33	4 45	27 36	23 30	8 36	6 7
6	18 54 56	13 41 3	24 25	1 40	28 45	4 9	4 38	27 31	23 33	8 36	6 8
7	18 58 53	14 38 16	7♉41	1 29	29 48	4 45	4 32	27 27	23 36	8 36	6 10
8	19 2 49	15 35 28	20 42	1D23	0♊51	5 20	4 25	27 23	23 39	8 35	6 11
9	19 6 46	16 32 42	3♊27	1 21	1 54	5 56	4 18	27 18	23 42	8 35	6 12
10	19 10 43	17 29 55	16 0	1 25	2 58	6 32	4 11	27 14	23 45	8 34	6 14
11	19 14 39	18 27 9	28 21	1 33	4 1	7 8	4 4	27 10	23 49	8 34	6 15
12	19 18 36	19 24 24	10♋32	1 47	5 5	7 44	3 56	27 5	23 52	8 34	6 17
13	19 22 32	20 21 38	22 34	2 6	6 9	8 20	3 49	27 1	23 55	8 33	6 18
14	19 26 29	21 18 53	4♌29	2 31	7 13	8 57	3 42	26 57	23 58	8 33	6 20
15	19 30 25	22 16 8	16 18	3 1	8 18	9 33	3 34	26 52	24 2	8 33	6 22
16	19 34 22	23 13 23	28 5	3 36	9 23	10 9	3 27	26 48	24 5	8 33	6 23
17	19 38 18	24 10 39	9♍52	4 17	10 27	10 45	3 19	26 43	24 8	8 33	6 25
18	19 42 15	25 7 54	21 42	5 3	11 32	11 22	3 12	26 39	24 12	8 33	6 26
19	19 46 12	26 5 10	3♎41	5 54	12 38	11 58	3 4	26 35	24 15	8 33	6 28
20	19 50 8	27 2 26	15 53	6 50	13 43	12 35	2 56	26 30	24 18	8D33	6 30
21	19 54 5	27 59 42	28 22	7 51	14 49	13 11	2 49	26 26	24 22	8 33	6 31
22	19 58 1	28 56 59	11♏13	8 57	15 54	13 48	2 41	26 21	24 25	8 33	6 33
23	20 1 58	29 54 16	24 30	10 9	17 0	14 25	2 33	26 17	24 29	8 33	6 35
24	20 5 54	0♌51 33	8♐14	11 25	18 7	15 1	2 25	26 12	24 32	8 33	6 36
25	20 9 51	1 48 51	22 26	12 46	19 13	15 38	2 18	26 8	24 36	8 33	6 38
26	20 13 47	2 46 9	7♑ 4	14 11	20 19	16 15	2 10	26 4	24 39	8 33	6 40
27	20 17 44	3 43 28	22 0	15 41	21 26	16 52	2 2	25 59	24 43	8 33	6 42
28	20 21 41	4 40 47	7♒ 9	17 15	22 33	17 29	1 54	25 55	24 46	8 33	6 43
29	20 25 37	5 38 7	22 19	18 53	23 39	18 6	1 47	25 50	24 50	8 34	6 45
30	20 29 34	6 35 28	7♓22	20 35	24 47	18 43	1 39	25 46	24 54	8 34	6 47
31	20 33 30	7♌32 49	22♓10	22♋21	25♊54	19♍20	1♒31	25♑42	24♌57	8♏34	6♍49

THE SUN ENTERS THE SIGN OF LEO ON JUL 23 AT 02:24.

DAY	TIME	☉	☽	☿	♀	♂	♃	♄	♅	♆	♇
	h m s	° ' "	° '	° '	° '	° '	° '	° '	° '	° '	° '
A 1	20 37 27	8♌30 12	6♈37	24♋10	27♊ 1	19♍57	1♒23	25♑38	25♌ 1	8♏35	6♍51
U 2	20 41 23	9 27 36	20 40	26 2	28 9	20 34	1R16	25R33	25 4	8 35	6 53
G 3	20 45 20	10 25 1	4♉19	27 57	29 16	21 11	1 8	25 29	25 8	8 35	6 54
U 4	20 49 16	11 22 28	17 35	29 54	0♋24	21 49	1 1	25 25	25 12	8 36	6 56
S 5	20 53 13	12 19 55	0♊30	1♌53	1 32	22 26	0 53	25 21	25 15	8 36	6 58
T 6	20 57 10	13 17 24	13 6	3 54	2 40	23 4	0 46	25 17	25 19	8 37	7 0
7	21 1 6	14 14 54	25 27	5 55	3 48	23 41	0 38	25 13	25 23	8 37	7 2
8	21 5 3	15 12 26	7♋36	7 58	4 57	24 19	0 31	25 9	25 26	8 38	7 4
9	21 8 59	16 9 58	19 36	10 2	6 5	24 56	0 24	25 5	25 30	8 38	7 6
10	21 12 56	17 7 32	1♌29	12 5	7 14	25 34	0 17	25 1	25 34	8 39	7 8
11	21 16 52	18 5 7	13 18	14 9	8 22	26 12	0 10	24 57	25 38	8 40	7 10
12	21 20 49	19 2 43	25 5	16 13	9 31	26 49	0 3	24 53	25 41	8 40	7 12
13	21 24 45	20 0 20	6♍52	18 16	10 40	27 27	29♑56	24 49	25 45	8 41	7 14
14	21 28 42	20 57 59	18 42	20 18	11 49	28 5	29 49	24 45	25 49	8 42	7 16
15	21 32 39	21 55 38	0♎38	22 20	12 58	28 43	29 42	24 42	25 53	8 43	7 18
16	21 36 35	22 53 19	12 42	24 20	14 8	29 21	29 36	24 38	25 56	8 44	7 20
17	21 40 32	23 51 0	24 57	26 20	15 17	29 59	29 29	24 34	26 0	8 44	7 22
18	21 44 28	24 48 43	7♏28	28 18	16 27	0♎37	29 23	24 31	26 4	8 45	7 24
19	21 48 25	25 46 27	20 17	0♍15	17 36	1 15	29 17	24 27	26 8	8 46	7 26
20	21 52 21	26 44 12	3♐29	2 11	18 46	1 53	29 10	24 24	26 11	8 47	7 28
21	21 56 18	27 41 58	17 5	4 6	19 56	2 32	29 4	24 21	26 15	8 48	7 30
22	22 0 14	28 39 45	1♑ 7	5 59	21 6	3 10	28 59	24 17	26 19	8 49	7 32
23	22 4 11	29 37 33	15 33	7 51	22 16	3 48	28 53	24 14	26 23	8 50	7 34
24	22 8 8	0♍35 23	0♒21	9 41	23 26	4 27	28 47	24 11	26 26	8 51	7 36
25	22 12 4	1 33 13	15 25	11 30	24 36	5 5	28 42	24 8	26 30	8 52	7 38
26	22 16 1	2 31 5	0♓36	13 18	25 46	5 43	28 37	24 5	26 34	8 53	7 40
27	22 19 57	3 28 59	15 46	15 5	26 57	6 22	28 32	24 2	26 37	8 55	7 42
28	22 23 54	4 26 54	0♈44	16 50	28 7	7 1	28 27	23 59	26 41	8 56	7 44
29	22 27 50	5 24 51	15 23	18 34	29 18	7 39	28 22	23 56	26 45	8 57	7 46
30	22 31 47	6 22 50	29 38	20 16	0♌29	8 18	28 17	23 54	26 49	8 58	7 48
31	22 35 43	7♍20 50	13♉26	21♍58	1♌39	8♎57	28♑13	23♑51	26♌52	8♏59	7♍50

THE SUN ENTERS THE SIGN OF VIRGO ON AUG 23 AT 09:19.

DAY	TIME	☉	☽	☿	♀	♂	♃	♄	♅	♆	♇
	h m s	° ' "	° '	° '	° '	° '	° '	° '	° '	° '	° '
S 1	22 39 40	8♍18 53	26♉48	23♍38	2♌50	9♎36	28♑ 8	23♑49	26♌56	9♏ 1	7♍52
E 2	22 43 36	9 16 57	9♊44	25 17	4 1	10 14	28R 4	23R46	27 0	9 2	7 54
P 3	22 47 33	10 15 4	22 18	26 54	5 12	10 53	28 0	23 44	27 3	9 3	7 56
T 4	22 51 30	11 13 12	4♋34	28 31	6 24	11 32	27 56	23 41	27 7	9 5	7 59
E 5	22 55 26	12 11 22	16 37	0♎ 6	7 35	12 11	27 53	23 39	27 11	9 6	8 1
M 6	22 59 23	13 9 35	28 31	1 40	8 46	12 51	27 49	23 37	27 14	9 8	8 3
B 7	23 3 19	14 7 49	10♌19	3 12	9 58	13 30	27 46	23 35	27 18	9 9	8 5
E 8	23 7 16	15 6 5	22 6	4 44	11 9	14 9	27 43	23 33	27 22	9 10	8 7
R 9	23 11 12	16 4 23	3♍54	6 14	12 21	14 48	27 40	23 31	27 25	9 12	8 9
10	23 15 9	17 2 42	15 45	7 43	13 33	15 28	27 37	23 30	27 29	9 13	8 11
11	23 19 5	18 1 4	27 43	9 11	14 45	16 7	27 35	23 28	27 32	9 15	8 13
12	23 23 2	18 59 27	9♎48	10 38	15 57	16 46	27 32	23 26	27 36	9 17	8 15
13	23 26 59	19 57 52	22 3	12 4	17 8	17 26	27 30	23 25	27 39	9 18	8 17
14	23 30 55	20 56 19	4♏29	13 28	18 21	18 5	27 28	23 23	27 43	9 20	8 19
15	23 34 52	21 54 47	17 8	14 51	19 33	18 45	27 26	23 22	27 47	9 21	8 21
16	23 38 48	22 53 17	0♐ 3	16 13	20 45	19 25	27 25	23 21	27 50	9 23	8 23
17	23 42 45	23 51 49	13 14	17 33	21 57	20 4	27 23	23 20	27 53	9 25	8 25
18	23 46 41	24 50 22	26 44	18 52	23 10	20 44	27 22	23 19	27 57	9 26	8 27
19	23 50 38	25 48 57	10♑35	20 9	24 22	21 24	27 21	23 18	28 0	9 28	8 29
20	23 54 34	26 47 34	24 46	21 25	25 34	22 4	27 20	23 17	28 4	9 30	8 31
21	23 58 31	27 46 12	9♒16	22 40	26 47	22 44	27 20	23 16	28 7	9 32	8 33
22	0 2 28	28 44 52	24 2	23 53	28 0	23 24	27 19	23 16	28 11	9 33	8 35
23	0 6 24	29 43 34	8♓59	25 4	29 12	24 4	27D19	23 15	28 14	9 35	8 37
24	0 10 21	0♎42 18	23 58	26 13	0♍25	24 44	27 19	23 15	28 17	9 37	8 39
25	0 14 17	1 41 3	8♈53	27 20	1 38	25 24	27 19	23 15	28 20	9 39	8 41
26	0 18 14	2 39 50	23 34	28 26	2 51	26 4	27 20	23 14	28 24	9 41	8 43
27	0 22 10	3 38 40	7♉53	29 29	4 4	26 45	27 20	23D14	28 27	9 43	8 45
28	0 26 7	4 37 32	21 48	0♏29	5 17	27 25	27 21	23 14	28 30	9 45	8 46
29	0 30 3	5 36 26	5♊15	1 27	6 30	28 5	27 22	23 14	28 33	9 47	8 48
30	0 34 0	6♎35 22	18♊16	2♏23	7♍43	28♎46	27♑23	23♑14	28♌37	9♏48	8♍50

THE SUN ENTERS THE SIGN OF LIBRA ON SEP 23 AT 06:44.

♈ ARIES ♉ TAURUS ♊ GEMINI ♋ CANCER ♌ LEO ♍ VIRGO ♎ LIBRA

SIDEREAL TIME . . SUN . . MOON . . MERCURY . . VENUS . . MARS . . JUPITER . . SATURN . . URANUS . . NEPTUNE . . PLUTO . .

DAY	TIME	☉	☽	☿	♀	♂	♃	♄	♅	♆	♇
	h m s	° ' "	° '	° '	° '	° '	° '	° '	° '	° '	° '
O 1	0 37 56	7♎34 21	0♋52	3♏15	8♍57	29♎26	27♑24	23♑15	28♌40	9♏50	8♍52
C 2	0 41 53	8 33 22	13 9	4 4	10 10	0♏ 7	27 26	23 15	28 43	9 52	8 54
T 3	0 45 50	9 32 25	25 10	4 50	11 23	0 47	27 28	23 15	28 46	9 54	8 56
O 4	0 49 46	10 31 31	7♌ 2	5 31	12 37	1 28	27 30	23 16	28 49	9 56	8 58
B 5	0 53 43	11 30 38	18 49	6 9	13 50	2 9	27 32	23 17	28 52	9 58	8 59
E 6	0 57 39	12 29 48	0♍36	6 42	15 4	2 49	27 34	23 17	28 55	10 0	9 1
R 7	1 1 36	13 29 0	12 27	7 9	16 17	3 30	27 36	23 18	28 58	10 2	9 3
8	1 5 32	14 28 15	24 26	7 32	17 31	4 11	27 39	23 19	29 1	10 4	9 5
9	1 9 29	15 27 31	6♎33	7 48	18 45	4 52	27 42	23 20	29 4	10 7	9 6
10	1 13 25	16 26 50	18 53	7R58	19 59	5 33	27 45	23 22	29 6	10 9	9 8
11	1 17 22	17 26 10	1♏24	8 2	21 13	6 14	27 48	23 23	29 9	10 11	9 10
12	1 21 19	18 25 33	14 8	7 57	22 26	6 55	27 52	23 24	29 12	10 13	9 12
13	1 25 15	19 24 58	27 5	7 45	23 40	7 36	27 55	23 26	29 15	10 15	9 13
14	1 29 12	20 24 24	10♐14	7 25	24 54	8 18	27 59	23 27	29 17	10 17	9 15
15	1 33 8	21 23 52	23 35	6 57	26 8	8 59	28 3	23 29	29 20	10 19	9 17
16	1 37 5	22 23 22	7♑ 9	6 20	27 22	9 40	28 7	23 31	29 23	10 21	9 18
17	1 41 1	23 22 54	20 55	5 35	28 37	10 22	28 12	23 32	29 25	10 24	9 20
18	1 44 58	24 22 28	4♒54	4 41	29 51	11 3	28 16	23 34	29 28	10 26	9 21
19	1 48 54	25 22 3	19 7	3 41	1♎ 5	11 45	28 21	23 36	29 30	10 28	9 23
20	1 52 51	26 21 40	3♓31	2 34	2 19	12 26	28 26	23 39	29 33	10 30	9 24
21	1 56 48	27 21 18	18 4	1 22	3 34	13 8	28 31	23 41	29 35	10 32	9 26
22	2 0 44	28 20 59	2♈41	0 8	4 48	13 50	28 36	23 43	29 37	10 35	9 27
23	2 4 41	29 20 41	17 16	28♎53	6 2	14 31	28 41	23 46	29 40	10 37	9 29
24	2 8 37	0♏20 25	1♉43	27 39	7 17	15 13	28 47	23 48	29 42	10 39	9 30
25	2 12 34	1 20 11	15 55	26 28	8 31	15 55	28 53	23 51	29 44	10 41	9 32
26	2 16 30	2 19 59	29 46	25 24	9 46	16 37	28 59	23 53	29 47	10 43	9 33
27	2 20 27	3 19 50	13♊13	24 27	11 0	17 19	29 5	23 56	29 49	10 46	9 35
28	2 24 23	4 19 42	26 15	23 39	12 15	18 1	29 11	23 59	29 51	10 48	9 36
29	2 28 20	5 19 37	8♋53	23 2	13 29	18 43	29 17	24 2	29 53	10 50	9 37
30	2 32 17	6 19 33	21 12	22 36	14 44	19 25	29 24	24 5	29 55	10 52	9 39
31	2 36 13	7♏19 32	3♌14	22♎22	15♎59	20♏ 7	29♑31	24♑ 8	29♌57	10♏55	9♍40

THE SUN ENTERS THE SIGN OF SCORPIO ON OCT 23 AT 15:48.

DAY	TIME	☉	☽	☿	♀	♂	♃	♄	♅	♆	♇
	h m s	° ' "	° '	° '	° '	° '	° '	° '	° '	° '	° '
N 1	2 40 10	8♏19 34	15♌ 7	22♎19	17♎14	20♏49	29♑38	24♑11	29♌59	10♏57	9♍41
O 2	2 44 6	9 19 37	26 54	22 27	18 28	21 32	29 45	24 15	0♍ 1	10 59	9 42
V 3	2 48 3	10 19 42	8♍43	22 46	19 43	22 14	29 52	24 18	0 2	11 1	9 44
E 4	2 51 59	11 19 49	20 36	23 15	20 58	22 57	29 59	24 22	0 4	11 4	9 45
M 5	2 55 56	12 19 59	2♎41	23 53	22 13	23 39	0♒ 7	24 25	0 6	11 6	9 46
B 6	2 59 52	13 20 10	14 58	24 39	23 28	24 22	0 14	24 29	0 8	11 8	9 47
E 7	3 3 49	14 20 23	27 31	25 32	24 43	25 4	0 22	24 33	0 9	11 10	9 48
R 8	3 7 45	15 20 38	10♏21	26 31	25 58	25 47	0 30	24 37	0 11	11 13	9 49
9	3 11 42	16 20 55	23 26	27 36	27 13	26 29	0 38	24 41	0 12	11 15	9 50
10	3 15 39	17 21 14	6♐47	28 46	28 28	27 12	0 46	24 45	0 14	11 17	9 51
11	3 19 35	18 21 35	20 19	0♏ 0	29 43	27 55	0 55	24 49	0 15	11 19	9 52
12	3 23 32	19 21 57	4♑ 1	1 18	0♏58	28 38	1 3	24 53	0 17	11 21	9 53
13	3 27 28	20 22 20	17 50	2 39	2 13	29 21	1 12	24 57	0 18	11 24	9 54
14	3 31 25	21 22 45	1♒45	4 2	3 28	0♐ 4	1 21	25 1	0 19	11 26	9 55
15	3 35 21	22 23 11	15 45	5 27	4 43	0 47	1 30	25 6	0 20	11 28	9 56
16	3 39 18	23 23 38	29 49	6 54	5 58	1 30	1 39	25 10	0 21	11 30	9 57
17	3 43 15	24 24 7	13♓57	8 23	7 13	2 13	1 48	25 15	0 23	11 33	9 58
18	3 47 11	25 24 37	28 7	9 53	8 28	2 56	1 57	25 19	0 24	11 35	9 58
19	3 51 8	26 25 8	12♈18	11 24	9 44	3 40	2 6	25 24	0 25	11 37	9 59
20	3 55 4	27 25 40	26 27	12 55	10 59	4 23	2 16	25 29	0 26	11 39	10 0
21	3 59 1	28 26 14	10♉28	14 27	12 14	5 6	2 26	25 34	0 26	11 41	10 0
22	4 2 57	29 26 49	24 19	16 0	13 29	5 50	2 35	25 39	0 27	11 44	10 1
23	4 6 54	0♐27 26	7♊53	17 33	14 44	6 33	2 45	25 44	0 28	11 46	10 2
24	4 10 50	1 28 4	21 9	19 7	16 0	7 17	2 55	25 49	0 29	11 48	10 2
25	4 14 47	2 28 44	4♋ 5	20 40	17 15	8 0	3 6	25 54	0 29	11 50	10 3
26	4 18 44	3 29 25	16 41	22 14	18 30	8 44	3 16	25 59	0 30	11 52	10 4
27	4 22 40	4 30 8	28 58	23 48	19 46	9 27	3 26	26 4	0 31	11 54	10 4
28	4 26 37	5 30 52	11♌ 1	25 22	21 1	10 11	3 37	26 9	0 31	11 56	10 4
29	4 30 33	6 31 38	22 54	26 56	22 16	10 55	3 47	26 15	0 31	11 58	10 5
30	4 34 30	7♐32 25	4♍42	28♏30	23♏32	11♐39	3♒58	26♑20	0♍32	12♏ 0	10♍ 5

THE SUN ENTERS THE SIGN OF SAGITTARIUS ON NOV 22 AT 13:08.

DAY	TIME	☉	☽	☿	♀	♂	♃	♄	♅	♆	♇
	h m s	° ' "	° '	° '	° '	° '	° '	° '	° '	° '	° '
D 1	4 38 26	8♐33 13	16♍31	0♐ 4	24♏47	12♐23	4♒ 9	26♑26	0♍32	12♏ 3	10♍ 6
E 2	4 42 23	9 34 3	28 26	1 38	26 2	13 7	4 20	26 31	0 32	12 5	10 6
C 3	4 46 19	10 34 55	10♎32	3 12	27 18	13 51	4 31	26 37	0 33	12 7	10 6
E 4	4 50 16	11 35 48	22 54	4 46	28 33	14 35	4 42	26 43	0 33	12 9	10 7
M 5	4 54 12	12 36 42	5♏35	6 20	29 48	15 19	4 53	26 48	0 33	12 11	10 7
B 6	4 58 9	13 37 37	18 38	7 55	1♐ 4	16 3	5 4	26 54	0R33	12 13	10 7
E 7	5 2 6	14 38 34	2♐ 1	9 29	2 19	16 47	5 16	27 0	0 33	12 15	10 7
R 8	5 6 2	15 39 31	15 44	11 3	3 35	17 32	5 27	27 6	0 33	12 17	10 8
9	5 9 59	16 40 30	29 42	12 37	4 50	18 16	5 39	27 12	0 33	12 19	10 8
10	5 13 55	17 41 30	13♑51	14 11	6 6	19 0	5 51	27 18	0 33	12 20	10 8
11	5 17 52	18 42 30	28 6	15 45	7 21	19 45	6 2	27 24	0 32	12 22	10 8
12	5 21 48	19 43 31	12♒23	17 19	8 37	20 29	6 14	27 30	0 32	12 24	10R 8
13	5 25 45	20 44 32	26 38	18 53	9 52	21 14	6 26	27 36	0 32	12 26	10 8
14	5 29 42	21 45 34	10♓48	20 27	11 7	21 58	6 38	27 42	0 31	12 28	10 8
15	5 33 38	22 46 36	24 54	22 2	12 23	22 43	6 50	27 49	0 31	12 30	10 8
16	5 37 35	23 47 39	8♈53	23 36	13 38	23 27	7 3	27 55	0 30	12 32	10 8
17	5 41 31	24 48 42	22 45	25 11	14 54	24 12	7 15	28 1	0 30	12 33	10 8
18	5 45 28	25 49 45	6♉28	26 46	16 9	24 57	7 27	28 8	0 29	12 35	10 7
19	5 49 24	26 50 49	20 3	28 21	17 25	25 42	7 40	28 14	0 28	12 37	10 7
20	5 53 21	27 51 54	3♊26	29 56	18 40	26 27	7 52	28 21	0 28	12 39	10 7
21	5 57 17	28 52 58	16 37	1♑31	19 56	27 12	8 5	28 27	0 27	12 40	10 7
22	6 1 14	29 54 4	29 33	3 6	21 11	27 56	8 17	28 34	0 26	12 42	10 6
23	6 5 11	0♑55 9	12♋14	4 42	22 27	28 41	8 30	28 40	0 25	12 44	10 6
24	6 9 7	1 56 15	24 40	6 18	23 42	29 26	8 43	28 47	0 24	12 45	10 6
25	6 13 4	2 57 22	6♌52	7 54	24 58	0♑12	8 56	28 53	0 23	12 47	10 5
26	6 17 0	3 58 29	18 52	9 30	26 13	0 57	9 9	29 0	0 22	12 49	10 5
27	6 20 57	4 59 36	0♍44	11 7	27 29	1 42	9 22	29 7	0 21	12 50	10 5
28	6 24 53	6 0 45	12 32	12 44	28 44	2 27	9 35	29 13	0 20	12 52	10 4
29	6 28 50	7 1 53	24 21	14 21	0♑ 0	3 12	9 48	29 20	0 19	12 53	10 4
30	6 32 46	8 3 2	6♎15	15 58	1 15	3 58	10 1	29 27	0 17	12 55	10 3
31	6 36 43	9♑ 4 11	18♎19	17♑35	2♑31	4♑43	10♒14	29♑34	0♍16	12♏56	10♍ 2

THE SUN ENTERS THE SIGN OF CAPRICORN ON DEC 22 AT 02:20.

♏ SCORPIO ♐ SAGITTARIUS ♑ CAPRICORN ♒ AQUARIUS ♓ PISCES

SIDEREAL TIME . SUN . MOON . MERCURY . VENUS . MARS . JUPITER . SATURN . URANUS . NEPTUNE . PLUTO .

DAY	TIME	☉	☽	☿	♀	♂	♃	♄	♅	♆	♇
	h m s	° ' "	° '	° '	° '	° '	° '	° '	° '	° '	° '
J 1	6 40 40	10♑ 5 21	0♏40	19♑13	3♑46	5♑28	10♒28	29♑41	0♍15	12♏57	10♍ 2
A 2	6 44 36	11 6 31	13 22	20 50	5 2	6 14	10 41	29 48	0R13	12 59	10R 1
N 3	6 48 33	12 7 42	26 27	22 28	6 17	6 59	10 54	29 55	0 12	13 0	10 1
U 4	6 52 29	13 8 52	9♐57	24 6	7 33	7 45	11 8	0♒ 1	0 10	13 2	10 0
A 5	6 56 26	14 10 3	23 51	25 44	8 48	8 31	11 21	0 8	0 9	13 3	9 59
R 6	7 0 22	15 11 14	8♑ 7	27 21	10 4	9 16	11 35	0 15	0 7	13 4	9 59
Y 7	7 4 19	16 12 25	22 39	28 59	11 19	10 2	11 48	0 22	0 6	13 5	9 58
8	7 8 15	17 13 36	7♒21	0♒36	12 35	10 48	12 2	0 29	0 4	13 7	9 57
9	7 12 12	18 14 46	22 6	2 12	13 50	11 33	12 16	0 36	0 2	13 8	9 56
10	7 16 9	19 15 56	6♓47	3 48	15 6	12 19	12 29	0 43	0 0	13 9	9 55
11	7 20 5	20 17 5	21 17	5 23	16 21	13 5	12 43	0 50	29♌59	13 10	9 54
12	7 24 2	21 18 14	5♈35	6 57	17 37	13 51	12 57	0 58	29 57	13 11	9 54
13	7 27 58	22 19 22	19 38	8 30	18 52	14 37	13 11	1 5	29 55	13 12	9 53
14	7 31 55	23 20 30	3♉24	10 1	20 7	15 23	13 25	1 12	29 53	13 13	9 52
15	7 35 51	24 21 36	16 54	11 29	21 23	16 9	13 39	1 19	29 51	13 14	9 51
16	7 39 48	25 22 42	0♊10	12 55	22 38	16 55	13 53	1 26	29 49	13 15	9 50
17	7 43 44	26 23 48	13 10	14 18	23 54	17 41	14 7	1 33	29 47	13 16	9 49
18	7 47 41	27 24 53	25 58	15 38	25 9	18 27	14 21	1 40	29 45	13 17	9 48
19	7 51 38	28 25 57	8♋32	16 53	26 25	19 13	14 35	1 47	29 43	13 18	9 47
20	7 55 34	29 27 0	20 55	18 3	27 40	19 59	14 49	1 54	29 41	13 19	9 46
21	7 59 31	0♒28 2	3♌ 7	19 7	28 56	20 45	15 3	2 2	29 39	13 20	9 44
22	8 3 27	1 29 4	15 10	20 5	0♒11	21 31	15 17	2 9	29 36	13 21	9 43
23	8 7 24	2 30 6	27 5	20 56	1 26	22 18	15 31	2 16	29 34	13 21	9 42
24	8 11 20	3 31 6	8♍55	21 38	2 42	23 4	15 45	2 23	29 32	13 22	9 41
25	8 15 17	4 32 6	20 43	22 11	3 57	23 50	16 0	2 30	29 30	13 23	9 40
26	8 19 13	5 33 5	2♎32	22 34	5 12	24 36	16 14	2 37	29 27	13 23	9 39
27	8 23 10	6 34 4	14 26	22R47	6 28	25 23	16 28	2 44	29 25	13 24	9 37
28	8 27 7	7 35 2	26 29	22 49	7 43	26 9	16 42	2 52	29 23	13 25	9 36
29	8 31 3	8 36 0	8♏47	22 39	8 59	26 56	16 57	2 59	29 20	13 25	9 35
30	8 35 0	9 36 56	21 23	22 18	10 14	27 42	17 11	3 6	29 18	13 26	9 34
31	8 38 56	10♒37 52	4♐23	21♒46	11♒29	28♑29	17♒25	3♒13	29♌15	13♏26	9♍32

THE SUN ENTERS THE SIGN OF AQUARIUS ON JAN 20 AT 12:58.

DAY	TIME	☉	☽	☿	♀	♂	♃	♄	♅	♆	♇
	h m s	° ' "	° '	° '	° '	° '	° '	° '	° '	° '	° '
F 1	8 42 53	11♒38 48	17♐48	21♒ 3	12♒45	29♑15	17♒39	3♒20	29♌13	13♏27	9♍31
E 2	8 46 49	12 39 43	1♑40	20R12	14 0	0♒ 2	17 54	3 27	29R10	13 27	9R30
B 3	8 50 46	13 40 36	15 58	19 12	15 15	0 48	18 8	3 34	29 8	13 28	9 28
R 4	8 54 42	14 41 29	0♒39	18 6	16 31	1 35	18 22	3 41	29 5	13 28	9 27
U 5	8 58 39	15 42 21	15 36	16 56	17 46	2 22	18 37	3 48	29 3	13 28	9 25
A 6	9 2 36	16 43 12	0♓42	15 44	19 1	3 8	18 51	3 55	29 0	13 28	9 24
R 7	9 6 32	17 44 1	15 47	14 31	20 17	3 55	19 6	4 2	28 58	13 29	9 23
Y 8	9 10 29	18 44 48	0♈43	13 21	21 32	4 42	19 20	4 9	28 55	13 29	9 21
9	9 14 25	19 45 35	15 22	12 14	22 47	5 28	19 34	4 16	28 53	13 29	9 20
10	9 18 22	20 46 19	29 39	11 11	24 2	6 15	19 49	4 23	28 50	13 29	9 18
11	9 22 18	21 47 3	13♉33	10 15	25 18	7 2	20 3	4 30	28 47	13 29	9 17
12	9 26 15	22 47 44	27 4	9 26	26 33	7 49	20 17	4 37	28 45	13 29	9 15
13	9 30 11	23 48 24	10♊12	8 45	27 48	8 35	20 32	4 44	28 42	13R29	9 14
14	9 34 8	24 49 2	23 0	8 11	29 3	9 22	20 46	4 51	28 40	13 30	9 12
15	9 38 5	25 49 39	5♋32	7 46	0♓18	10 9	21 0	4 58	28 37	13 29	9 11
16	9 42 1	26 50 14	17 50	7 28	1 33	10 56	21 15	5 5	28 34	13 29	9 9
17	9 45 58	27 50 47	29 58	7D18	2 49	11 43	21 29	5 11	28 32	13 29	9 8
18	9 49 54	28 51 18	11♌57	7 15	4 4	12 30	21 43	5 18	28 29	13 29	9 6
19	9 53 51	29 51 48	23 51	7 19	5 19	13 17	21 58	5 25	28 26	13 29	9 5
20	9 57 47	0♓52 16	5♍41	7 30	6 34	14 4	22 12	5 32	28 24	13 29	9 3
21	10 1 44	1 52 43	17 30	7 47	7 49	14 50	22 26	5 38	28 21	13 29	9 2
22	10 5 40	2 53 8	29 20	8 9	9 4	15 37	22 40	5 45	28 18	13 28	9 0
23	10 9 37	3 53 32	11♎12	8 37	10 19	16 24	22 55	5 52	28 16	13 28	8 59
24	10 13 34	4 53 54	23 9	9 9	11 34	17 11	23 9	5 58	28 13	13 28	8 57
25	10 17 30	5 54 15	5♏15	9 47	12 49	17 58	23 23	6 5	28 11	13 27	8 56
26	10 21 27	6 54 34	17 33	10 28	14 4	18 45	23 37	6 11	28 8	13 27	8 54
27	10 25 23	7 54 52	0♐ 7	11 13	15 19	19 32	23 52	6 18	28 5	13 27	8 52
28	10 29 20	8♓55 8	13♐ 0	12♒ 2	16♓34	20♒19	24♒ 6	6♒24	28♌ 3	13♏26	8♍51

THE SUN ENTERS THE SIGN OF PISCES ON FEB 19 AT 03:15.

DAY	TIME	☉	☽	☿	♀	♂	♃	♄	♅	♆	♇
	h m s	° ' "	° '	° '	° '	° '	° '	° '	° '	° '	° '
M 1	10 33 16	9♓55 23	26♐15	12♒55	17♓49	21♒ 6	24♒20	6♒30	28♌ 0	13♏26	8♍49
A 2	10 37 13	10 55 36	9♑56	13 50	19 4	21 54	24 34	6 37	27R58	13R25	8R48
R 3	10 41 9	11 55 48	24 4	14 48	20 19	22 41	24 48	6 43	27 55	13 25	8 46
C 4	10 45 6	12 55 59	8♒37	15 49	21 34	23 28	25 2	6 49	27 53	13 24	8 45
H 5	10 49 3	13 56 7	23 32	16 53	22 48	24 15	25 16	6 55	27 50	13 23	8 43
6	10 52 59	14 56 14	8♓41	17 59	24 3	25 2	25 30	7 2	27 48	13 23	8 42
7	10 56 56	15 56 19	23 57	19 7	25 18	25 49	25 44	7 8	27 45	13 22	8 40
8	11 0 52	16 56 23	9♈ 8	20 17	26 33	26 36	25 58	7 14	27 43	13 21	8 38
9	11 4 49	17 56 24	24 5	21 29	27 48	27 23	26 12	7 20	27 40	13 21	8 37
10	11 8 45	18 56 23	8♉39	22 43	29 2	28 10	26 26	7 26	27 38	13 20	8 35
11	11 12 42	19 56 20	22 47	23 59	0♈17	28 57	26 39	7 32	27 36	13 19	8 34
12	11 16 38	20 56 14	6♊26	25 17	1 32	29 44	26 53	7 38	27 33	13 18	8 32
13	11 20 35	21 56 7	19 37	26 36	2 47	0♓31	27 7	7 43	27 31	13 17	8 31
14	11 24 32	22 55 57	2♋24	27 57	4 1	1 19	27 21	7 49	27 29	13 17	8 29
15	11 28 28	23 55 45	14 51	29 19	5 16	2 6	27 34	7 55	27 26	13 16	8 28
16	11 32 25	24 55 31	27 1	0♓43	6 30	2 53	27 48	8 0	27 24	13 15	8 26
17	11 36 21	25 55 15	9♌ 0	2 8	7 45	3 40	28 1	8 6	27 22	13 14	8 25
18	11 40 18	26 54 56	20 52	3 35	9 0	4 27	28 15	8 12	27 20	13 13	8 23
19	11 44 14	27 54 35	2♍41	5 3	10 14	5 14	28 28	8 17	27 17	13 12	8 22
20	11 48 11	28 54 12	14 28	6 33	11 29	6 1	28 42	8 22	27 15	13 11	8 20
21	11 52 7	29 53 47	26 18	8 4	12 43	6 48	28 55	8 28	27 13	13 10	8 19
22	11 56 4	0♈53 20	8♎12	9 36	13 57	7 35	29 8	8 33	27 11	13 9	8 18
23	12 0 0	1 52 51	20 11	11 10	15 12	8 22	29 22	8 38	27 9	13 7	8 16
24	12 3 57	2 52 20	2♏17	12 45	16 26	9 9	29 35	8 43	27 7	13 6	8 15
25	12 7 54	3 51 47	14 32	14 21	17 41	9 56	29 48	8 48	27 5	13 5	8 13
26	12 11 50	4 51 13	26 57	15 59	18 55	10 43	0♓ 1	8 53	27 3	13 4	8 12
27	12 15 47	5 50 36	9♐35	17 38	20 9	11 30	0 14	8 58	27 1	13 3	8 11
28	12 19 43	6 49 58	22 29	19 18	21 24	12 17	0 27	9 3	26 59	13 2	8 9
29	12 23 40	7 49 18	5♑40	21 0	22 38	13 4	0 40	9 8	26 58	13 0	8 8
30	12 27 36	8 48 36	19 11	22 43	23 52	13 51	0 53	9 13	26 56	12 59	8 7
31	12 31 33	9♈47 53	3♒ 5	24♓27	25♈ 6	14♓38	1♓ 6	9♒17	26♌54	12♏58	8♍ 5

THE SUN ENTERS THE SIGN OF ARIES ON MAR 21 AT 02:29.

♈ ARIES ♉ TAURUS ♊ GEMINI ♋ CANCER ♌ LEO ♍ VIRGO ♎ LIBRA

SIDEREAL . SUN . MOON . MERCURY . VENUS . MARS . JUPITER . SATURN . URANUS . NEPTUNE . PLUTO .

DAY	TIME	☉	☽	☿	♀	♂	♃	♄	♅	♆	♇
	h m s	° ' "	° '	° '	° '	° '	° '	° '	° '	° '	° '
A 1	12 35 29	10♈47 8	17♒22	26♓13	26♈20	15♓25	1♓18	9♒22	26♌52	12♏57	8♍ 4
P 2	12 39 26	11 46 20	2♓ 2	28 0	27 35	16 12	1 31	9 27	26R51	12R55	8R 3
R 3	12 43 23	12 45 32	16 58	29 48	28 49	16 59	1 43	9 31	26 49	12 54	8 2
I 4	12 47 19	13 44 41	2♈ 5	1♈38	0♉ 3	17 46	1 56	9 35	26 48	12 52	8 1
L 5	12 51 16	14 43 48	17 14	3 30	1 17	18 33	2 8	9 40	26 46	12 51	7 59
6	12 55 12	15 42 53	2♉13	5 23	2 31	19 20	2 21	9 44	26 45	12 50	7 58
7	12 59 9	16 41 56	16 54	7 17	3 45	20 7	2 33	9 48	26 43	12 48	7 57
8	13 3 5	17 40 57	1♊10	9 13	4 59	20 53	2 45	9 52	26 42	12 47	7 56
9	13 7 2	18 39 55	14 57	11 10	6 13	21 40	2 57	9 56	26 41	12 45	7 55
10	13 10 58	19 38 52	28 15	13 8	7 27	22 27	3 9	10 0	26 39	12 44	7 54
11	13 14 55	20 37 46	11♋ 6	15 8	8 41	23 14	3 21	10 4	26 38	12 42	7 53
12	13 18 52	21 36 38	23 35	17 9	9 55	24 1	3 33	10 8	26 37	12 41	7 52
13	13 22 48	22 35 27	5♌45	19 11	11 8	24 47	3 45	10 11	26 36	12 39	7 51
14	13 26 45	23 34 14	17 42	21 15	12 22	25 34	3 57	10 15	26 35	12 38	7 50
15	13 30 41	24 32 59	29 32	23 19	13 36	26 21	4 8	10 18	26 34	12 36	7 49
16	13 34 38	25 31 42	11♍19	25 25	14 50	27 7	4 20	10 22	26 33	12 35	7 48
17	13 38 34	26 30 23	23 8	27 31	16 3	27 54	4 31	10 25	26 32	12 33	7 47
18	13 42 31	27 29 1	5♎ 1	29 38	17 17	28 41	4 43	10 28	26 31	12 32	7 46
19	13 46 27	28 27 38	17 1	1♉45	18 30	29 27	4 54	10 32	26 30	12 30	7 45
20	13 50 24	29 26 12	29 10	3 53	19 44	0♈14	5 5	10 35	26 29	12 29	7 44
21	13 54 20	0♉24 45	11♏29	6 0	20 58	1 0	5 16	10 38	26 28	12 27	7 43
22	13 58 17	1 23 15	23 59	8 7	22 11	1 47	5 27	10 41	26 28	12 25	7 42
23	14 2 14	2 21 44	6♐39	10 13	23 25	2 33	5 38	10 43	26 27	12 24	7 42
24	14 6 10	3 20 12	19 30	12 19	24 38	3 19	5 49	10 46	26 27	12 22	7 41
25	14 10 7	4 18 37	2♑33	14 23	25 51	4 6	6 0	10 49	26 26	12 21	7 40
26	14 14 3	5 17 1	15 50	16 25	27 5	4 52	6 10	10 51	26 26	12 19	7 39
27	14 18 0	6 15 24	29 21	18 26	28 18	5 39	6 21	10 54	26 25	12 17	7 39
28	14 21 56	7 13 45	13♒ 9	20 24	29 31	6 25	6 31	10 56	26 25	12 16	7 38
29	14 25 53	8 12 4	27 13	22 20	0♊45	7 11	6 41	10 58	26 24	12 14	7 37
30	14 29 49	9♉10 22	11♓35	24♉13	1♊58	7♈57	6♓51	11♒ 0	26♌24	12♏13	7♍37

THE SUN ENTERS THE SIGN OF TAURUS ON APR 20 AT 13:51.

DAY	TIME	☉	☽	☿	♀	♂	♃	♄	♅	♆	♇
	h m s	° ' "	° '	° '	° '	° '	° '	° '	° '	° '	° '
M 1	14 33 46	10♉ 8 38	26♓11	26♉ 4	3♊11	8♈44	7♓ 1	11♒ 3	26♌24	12♏11	7♍36
A 2	14 37 43	11 6 53	10♈58	27 51	4 24	9 30	7 11	11 5	26R24	12R 9	7R36
Y 3	14 41 39	12 5 6	25 48	29 34	5 37	10 16	7 21	11 6	26 24	12 8	7 35
4	14 45 36	13 3 17	10♉32	1♊14	6 50	11 2	7 31	11 8	26D24	12 6	7 35
5	14 49 32	14 1 27	25 4	2 51	8 3	11 48	7 41	11 10	26 24	12 4	7 34
6	14 53 29	14 59 36	9♊15	4 24	9 17	12 34	7 50	11 11	26 24	12 3	7 34
7	14 57 25	15 57 42	23 1	5 53	10 30	13 20	7 59	11 13	26 24	12 1	7 34
8	15 1 22	16 55 47	6♋21	7 18	11 42	14 6	8 9	11 14	26 24	11 59	7 33
9	15 5 18	17 53 49	19 14	8 39	12 55	14 52	8 18	11 16	26 24	11 58	7 33
10	15 9 15	18 51 50	1♌45	9 56	14 8	15 38	8 27	11 17	26 24	11 56	7 33
11	15 13 12	19 49 49	13 57	11 9	15 21	16 24	8 35	11 18	26 25	11 55	7 32
12	15 17 8	20 47 46	25 57	12 17	16 34	17 9	8 44	11 19	26 25	11 53	7 32
13	15 21 5	21 45 41	7♍48	13 22	17 47	17 55	8 53	11 20	26 26	11 51	7 32
14	15 25 1	22 43 35	19 37	14 22	18 59	18 41	9 1	11 21	26 26	11 50	7 32
15	15 28 58	23 41 27	1♎28	15 17	20 12	19 26	9 10	11 22	26 27	11 48	7 32
16	15 32 54	24 39 17	13 25	16 8	21 25	20 12	9 18	11 22	26 27	11 47	7 31
17	15 36 51	25 37 5	25 33	16 55	22 37	20 58	9 26	11 23	26 28	11 45	7 31
18	15 40 47	26 34 52	7♏52	17 37	23 50	21 43	9 34	11 23	26 29	11 43	7 31
19	15 44 44	27 32 37	20 25	18 15	25 2	22 28	9 41	11 23	26 29	11 42	7D31
20	15 48 41	28 30 21	3♐11	18 47	26 15	23 14	9 49	11 24	26 30	11 40	7 31
21	15 52 37	29 28 4	16 11	19 15	27 27	23 59	9 57	11R24	26 31	11 39	7 31
22	15 56 34	0♊25 45	29 22	19 39	28 39	24 45	10 4	11 24	26 32	11 37	7 31
23	16 0 30	1 23 26	12♑45	19 57	29 52	25 30	10 11	11 24	26 33	11 36	7 31
24	16 4 27	2 21 5	26 17	20 11	1♋ 4	26 15	10 18	11 24	26 34	11 34	7 32
25	16 8 23	3 18 43	10♒ 0	20 19	2 16	27 0	10 25	11 23	26 35	11 33	7 32
26	16 12 20	4 16 20	23 53	20R23	3 28	27 45	10 32	11 23	26 36	11 31	7 32
27	16 16 16	5 13 56	7♓55	20 23	4 40	28 30	10 38	11 23	26 37	11 30	7 32
28	16 20 13	6 11 32	22 6	20 18	5 52	29 15	10 45	11 22	26 39	11 28	7 32
29	16 24 10	7 9 6	6♈25	20 8	7 5	0♉ 0	10 51	11 21	26 40	11 27	7 33
30	16 28 6	8 6 40	20 49	19 55	8 17	0 45	10 57	11 21	26 41	11 25	7 33
31	16 32 3	9♊ 4 12	5♉14	19♊37	9♋28	1♉30	11♓ 3	11♒20	26♌43	11♏24	7♍33

THE SUN ENTERS THE SIGN OF GEMINI ON MAY 21 AT 13:17.

DAY	TIME	☉	☽	☿	♀	♂	♃	♄	♅	♆	♇
	h m s	° ' "	° '	° '	° '	° '	° '	° '	° '	° '	° '
J 1	16 35 59	10♊ 1 44	19♉33	19♊16	10♋40	2♉15	11♓ 9	11♒19	26♌44	11♏23	7♍34
U 2	16 39 56	10 59 15	3♊42	18R52	11 52	3 0	11 15	11R18	26 45	11R21	7 34
N 3	16 43 52	11 56 45	17 35	18 25	13 4	3 44	11 20	11 17	26 47	11 20	7 34
E 4	16 47 49	12 54 14	1♋ 9	17 56	14 16	4 29	11 25	11 16	26 49	11 19	7 35
5	16 51 45	13 51 42	14 20	17 24	15 28	5 14	11 31	11 14	26 50	11 17	7 35
6	16 55 42	14 49 9	27 10	16 52	16 39	5 58	11 35	11 13	26 52	11 16	7 36
7	16 59 39	15 46 35	9♌40	16 18	17 51	6 43	11 40	11 11	26 54	11 15	7 36
8	17 3 35	16 44 0	21 52	15 45	19 2	7 27	11 45	11 10	26 55	11 13	7 37
9	17 7 32	17 41 23	3♍53	15 12	20 14	8 11	11 49	11 8	26 57	11 12	7 38
10	17 11 28	18 38 46	15 46	14 39	21 25	8 56	11 54	11 6	26 59	11 11	7 38
11	17 15 25	19 36 7	27 36	14 9	22 37	9 40	11 58	11 5	27 1	11 10	7 39
12	17 19 21	20 33 28	9♎29	13 40	23 48	10 24	12 2	11 3	27 3	11 9	7 40
13	17 23 18	21 30 47	21 30	13 14	24 59	11 8	12 5	11 1	27 5	11 7	7 40
14	17 27 14	22 28 6	3♏42	12 51	26 10	11 52	12 9	10 59	27 7	11 6	7 41
15	17 31 11	23 25 23	16 10	12 31	27 22	12 36	12 12	10 56	27 9	11 5	7 42
16	17 35 8	24 22 40	28 53	12 15	28 33	13 20	12 16	10 54	27 11	11 4	7 43
17	17 39 4	25 19 56	11♐55	12 2	29 44	14 4	12 19	10 52	27 13	11 3	7 44
18	17 43 1	26 17 12	25 13	11 54	0♌55	14 48	12 21	10 49	27 15	11 2	7 44
19	17 46 57	27 14 27	8♑47	11D51	2 5	15 32	12 24	10 47	27 18	11 1	7 45
20	17 50 54	28 11 42	22 34	11 51	3 16	16 15	12 27	10 44	27 20	11 0	7 46
21	17 54 50	29 8 56	6♒31	11 57	4 27	16 59	12 29	10 41	27 22	10 59	7 47
22	17 58 47	0♋ 6 10	20 35	12 7	5 38	17 43	12 31	10 39	27 25	10 58	7 48
23	18 2 44	1 3 24	4♓44	12 22	6 48	18 26	12 33	10 36	27 27	10 57	7 49
24	18 6 40	2 0 38	18 55	12 41	7 59	19 10	12 35	10 33	27 30	10 56	7 50
25	18 10 37	2 57 51	3♈ 7	13 5	9 9	19 53	12 36	10 30	27 32	10 55	7 51
26	18 14 33	3 55 5	17 18	13 34	10 20	20 36	12 37	10 27	27 35	10 55	7 52
27	18 18 30	4 52 19	1♉25	14 8	11 30	21 20	12 39	10 24	27 37	10 54	7 53
28	18 22 26	5 49 32	15 27	14 46	12 40	22 3	12 40	10 21	27 40	10 53	7 55
29	18 26 23	6 46 46	29 20	15 28	13 50	22 46	12 40	10 17	27 43	10 52	7 56
30	18 30 19	7♋44 0	13♊ 2	16♊15	15♌ 1	23♉29	12♓41	10♒14	27♌45	10♏51	7♍57

THE SUN ENTERS THE SIGN OF CANCER ON JUN 21 AT 21:25.

♏ SCORPIO ♐ SAGITTARIUS ♑ CAPRICORN ♒ AQUARIUS ♓ PISCES

SIDEREAL SUN. MOON. MERCURY. VENUS. MARS. JUPITER. SATURN. URANUS. NEPTUNE. PLUTO.

DAY	TIME	☉	☽	☿	♀	♂	♃	♄	♅	♆	♇
	h m s	° ' "	° '	° '	° '	° '	° '	° '	° '	° '	° '
J 1	18 34 16	8♋41 14	26♊30	17♊ 7	16♌11	24♉12	12♓41	10♒11	27♌48	10♏51	7♍58
U 2	18 38 13	9 38 28	9♋42	18 3	17 21	24 55	12R41	10R 7	27 51	10R50	7 59
L 3	18 42 9	10 35 41	22 38	19 3	18 30	25 38	12 41	10 4	27 54	10 49	8 1
Y 4	18 46 6	11 32 55	5♌16	20 7	19 40	26 20	12 41	10 0	27 56	10 49	8 2
5	18 50 2	12 30 8	17 39	21 15	20 50	27 3	12 41	9 56	27 59	10 48	8 3
6	18 53 59	13 27 21	29 49	22 28	22 0	27 46	12 40	9 53	28 2	10 48	8 5
7	18 57 55	14 24 34	11♍48	23 44	23 9	28 28	12 39	9 49	28 5	10 47	8 6
8	19 1 52	15 21 47	23 41	25 5	24 18	29 11	12 38	9 45	28 8	10 47	8 7
9	19 5 48	16 19 0	5♎32	26 29	25 28	29 53	12 37	9 41	28 11	10 46	8 9
10	19 9 45	17 16 12	17 25	27 58	26 37	0♊36	12 36	9 37	28 14	10 46	8 10
11	19 13 42	18 13 25	29 27	29 30	27 46	1 18	12 34	9 33	28 17	10 45	8 12
12	19 17 38	19 10 37	11♏40	1♋ 6	28 55	2 0	12 32	9 29	28 20	10 45	8 13
13	19 21 35	20 7 50	24 10	2 45	0♍ 4	2 42	12 30	9 25	28 23	10 45	8 14
14	19 25 31	21 5 2	6♐59	4 28	1 13	3 24	12 28	9 21	28 26	10 44	8 16
15	19 29 28	22 2 15	20 9	6 15	2 22	4 6	12 26	9 17	28 30	10 44	8 17
16	19 33 24	22 59 28	3♑41	8 4	3 30	4 48	12 23	9 13	28 33	10 44	8 19
17	19 37 21	23 56 41	17 33	9 57	4 39	5 30	12 21	9 9	28 36	10 44	8 21
18	19 41 17	24 53 54	1♒42	11 52	5 47	6 12	12 18	9 4	28 39	10 43	8 22
19	19 45 14	25 51 8	16 5	13 50	6 56	6 53	12 15	9 0	28 43	10 43	8 24
20	19 49 11	26 48 23	0♓36	15 50	8 4	7 35	12 11	8 56	28 46	10 43	8 25
21	19 53 7	27 45 38	15 9	17 52	9 12	8 16	12 8	8 52	28 49	10 43	8 27
22	19 57 4	28 42 53	29 39	19 56	10 20	8 58	12 4	8 47	28 53	10 43	8 29
23	20 1 0	29 40 10	14♈ 3	22 1	11 27	9 39	12 1	8 43	28 56	10D43	8 30
24	20 4 57	0♌37 27	28 16	24 7	12 35	10 21	11 57	8 39	28 59	10 43	8 32
25	20 8 53	1 34 46	12♉16	26 13	13 43	11 2	11 52	8 34	29 3	10 43	8 34
26	20 12 50	2 32 5	26 3	28 20	14 50	11 43	11 48	8 30	29 6	10 43	8 36
27	20 16 46	3 29 26	9♊36	0♌27	15 57	12 24	11 44	8 25	29 10	10 43	8 37
28	20 20 43	4 26 47	22 53	2 34	17 4	13 5	11 39	8 21	29 13	10 43	8 39
29	20 24 40	5 24 10	5♋57	4 41	18 11	13 46	11 34	8 16	29 17	10 44	8 41
30	20 28 36	6 21 33	18 47	6 46	19 18	14 27	11 29	8 12	29 20	10 44	8 43
31	20 32 33	7♌18 57	1♌23	8♌51	20♍25	15♊ 7	11♓24	8♒ 8	29♌24	10♏44	8♍44

THE SUN ENTERS THE SIGN OF LEO ON JUL 23 AT 08:19.

DAY	TIME	☉	☽	☿	♀	♂	♃	♄	♅	♆	♇
	h m s	° ' "	° '	° '	° '	° '	° '	° '	° '	° '	° '
A 1	20 36 29	8♌16 22	13♌46	10♌55	21♍32	15♊48	11♓19	8♒ 3	29♌27	10♏44	8♍46
U 2	20 40 26	9 13 47	25 59	12 58	22 38	16 29	11R13	7R59	29 31	10 45	8 48
G 3	20 44 22	10 11 14	8♍ 2	15 0	23 44	17 9	11 7	7 54	29 34	10 45	8 50
U 4	20 48 19	11 8 41	19 58	17 0	24 50	17 50	11 2	7 50	29 38	10 45	8 52
S 5	20 52 15	12 6 9	1♎50	18 59	25 56	18 30	10 56	7 45	29 42	10 46	8 54
T 6	20 56 12	13 3 38	13 40	20 56	27 2	19 10	10 50	7 41	29 45	10 46	8 56
7	21 0 9	14 1 7	25 33	22 52	28 8	19 50	10 44	7 36	29 49	10 46	8 58
8	21 4 5	14 58 38	7♏33	24 46	29 13	20 30	10 37	7 32	29 52	10 47	8 59
9	21 8 2	15 56 9	19 44	26 39	0♎18	21 10	10 31	7 28	29 56	10 47	9 1
10	21 11 58	16 53 41	2♐12	28 31	1 23	21 50	10 24	7 23	0♍ 0	10 48	9 3
11	21 15 55	17 51 14	14 59	0♍21	2 28	22 30	10 18	7 19	0 3	10 49	9 5
12	21 19 51	18 48 48	28 9	2 9	3 33	23 9	10 11	7 14	0 7	10 49	9 7
13	21 23 48	19 46 23	11♑45	3 56	4 37	23 49	10 4	7 10	0 11	10 50	9 9
14	21 27 44	20 43 58	25 46	5 41	5 41	24 29	9 57	7 6	0 15	10 51	9 11
15	21 31 41	21 41 35	10♒10	7 25	6 45	25 8	9 50	7 2	0 18	10 51	9 13
16	21 35 38	22 39 13	24 52	9 7	7 49	25 47	9 43	6 57	0 22	10 52	9 15
17	21 39 34	23 36 52	9♓47	10 48	8 53	26 27	9 36	6 53	0 26	10 53	9 17
18	21 43 31	24 34 33	24 45	12 27	9 56	27 6	9 28	6 49	0 30	10 54	9 19
19	21 47 27	25 32 15	9♈39	14 5	10 59	27 45	9 21	6 45	0 33	10 54	9 21
20	21 51 24	26 29 59	24 21	15 42	12 2	28 24	9 13	6 41	0 37	10 55	9 23
21	21 55 20	27 27 44	8♉46	17 17	13 4	29 2	9 6	6 37	0 41	10 56	9 25
22	21 59 17	28 25 31	22 50	18 50	14 6	29 41	8 58	6 33	0 44	10 57	9 27
23	22 3 13	29 23 20	6♊32	20 23	15 8	0♋20	8 50	6 29	0 48	10 58	9 29
24	22 7 10	0♍21 10	19 53	21 53	16 10	0 58	8 43	6 25	0 52	10 59	9 31
25	22 11 6	1 19 3	2♋55	23 23	17 12	1 37	8 35	6 21	0 56	11 0	9 34
26	22 15 3	2 16 57	15 41	24 51	18 13	2 15	8 27	6 17	1 0	11 1	9 36
27	22 19 0	3 14 52	28 11	26 17	19 14	2 54	8 19	6 14	1 3	11 2	9 38
28	22 22 56	4 12 50	10♌30	27 42	20 14	3 32	8 11	6 10	1 7	11 3	9 40
29	22 26 53	5 10 49	22 40	29 6	21 14	4 10	8 3	6 6	1 11	11 4	9 42
30	22 30 49	6 8 49	4♍42	0♎28	22 14	4 48	7 56	6 3	1 15	11 6	9 44
31	22 34 46	7♍ 6 52	16♍38	1♎48	23♎14	5♋26	7♓48	5♒59	1♍18	11♏ 7	9♍46

THE SUN ENTERS THE SIGN OF VIRGO ON AUG 23 AT 15:13.

DAY	TIME	☉	☽	☿	♀	♂	♃	♄	♅	♆	♇
	h m s	° ' "	° '	° '	° '	° '	° '	° '	° '	° '	° '
S 1	22 38 42	8♍ 4 55	28♍30	3♎ 7	24♎13	6♋ 3	7♓40	5♒56	1♍22	11♏ 8	9♍48
E 2	22 42 39	9 3 1	10♎21	4 24	25 12	6 41	7R32	5R53	1 26	11 9	9 50
P 3	22 46 35	10 1 7	22 11	5 40	26 10	7 18	7 24	5 49	1 29	11 11	9 52
T 4	22 50 32	10 59 16	4♏ 5	6 54	27 8	7 56	7 16	5 46	1 33	11 12	9 54
E 5	22 54 29	11 57 26	16 5	8 6	28 6	8 33	7 8	5 43	1 37	11 13	9 56
M 6	22 58 25	12 55 37	28 14	9 16	29 3	9 10	7 0	5 40	1 41	11 15	9 58
B 7	23 2 22	13 53 50	10♐38	10 24	0♏ 0	9 47	6 52	5 37	1 44	11 16	10 1
E 8	23 6 18	14 52 4	23 20	11 30	0 56	10 24	6 45	5 34	1 48	11 17	10 3
R 9	23 10 15	15 50 20	6♑24	12 33	1 52	11 1	6 37	5 31	1 52	11 19	10 5
10	23 14 11	16 48 38	19 54	13 35	2 47	11 38	6 29	5 28	1 55	11 20	10 7
11	23 18 8	17 46 57	3♒52	14 33	3 42	12 14	6 21	5 25	1 59	11 22	10 9
12	23 22 4	18 45 17	18 16	15 29	4 36	12 51	6 14	5 23	2 3	11 23	10 11
13	23 26 1	19 43 39	3♓ 6	16 23	5 30	13 27	6 6	5 20	2 6	11 25	10 13
14	23 29 58	20 42 3	18 12	17 13	6 23	14 3	5 59	5 18	2 10	11 26	10 15
15	23 33 54	21 40 29	3♈28	18 0	7 15	14 39	5 52	5 15	2 14	11 28	10 17
16	23 37 51	22 38 56	18 42	18 43	8 7	15 15	5 44	5 13	2 17	11 29	10 19
17	23 41 47	23 37 26	3♉43	19 23	8 59	15 51	5 37	5 11	2 21	11 31	10 21
18	23 45 44	24 35 58	18 24	19 58	9 49	16 27	5 30	5 9	2 24	11 33	10 23
19	23 49 40	25 34 32	2♊39	20 29	10 39	17 3	5 23	5 7	2 28	11 34	10 25
20	23 53 37	26 33 8	16 26	20 56	11 28	17 38	5 16	5 5	2 31	11 36	10 27
21	23 57 33	27 31 46	29 46	21 17	12 17	18 13	5 9	5 3	2 35	11 38	10 29
22	0 1 30	28 30 27	12♋42	21 33	13 5	18 49	5 3	5 1	2 38	11 40	10 31
23	0 5 27	29 29 10	25 17	21 43	13 52	19 24	4 56	4 59	2 42	11 41	10 33
24	0 9 23	0♎27 55	7♌37	21R46	14 38	19 59	4 50	4 58	2 45	11 43	10 35
25	0 13 20	1 26 43	19 44	21 44	15 23	20 33	4 43	4 56	2 49	11 45	10 37
26	0 17 16	2 25 32	1♍44	21 34	16 7	21 8	4 37	4 55	2 52	11 47	10 39
27	0 21 13	3 24 23	13 38	21 17	16 51	21 42	4 31	4 54	2 55	11 49	10 41
28	0 25 9	4 23 17	25 29	20 52	17 33	22 17	4 25	4 52	2 59	11 50	10 43
29	0 29 6	5 22 13	7♎20	20 21	18 15	22 51	4 20	4 51	3 2	11 52	10 45
30	0 33 2	6♎21 10	19♎11	19♎41	18♏55	23♋25	4♓14	4♒50	3♍ 5	11♏54	10♍47

THE SUN ENTERS THE SIGN OF LIBRA ON SEP 23 AT 12:36.

♈ ARIES ♉ TAURUS ♊ GEMINI ♋ CANCER ♌ LEO ♍ VIRGO ♎ LIBRA

SIDEREAL TIME · SUN · MOON · MERCURY · VENUS · MARS · JUPITER · SATURN · URANUS · NEPTUNE · PLUTO

DAY	TIME	☉	☽	☿	♀	♂	♃	♄	♅	♆	♇
	h m s	° ' "	° '	° '	° '	° '	° '	° '	° '	° '	° '
O 1	0 36 59	7♎20 10	1♏ 5	18♎55	19♏35	23♋59	4♓ 9	4♒49	3♍ 9	11♏56	10♍49
C 2	0 40 55	8 19 11	13 3	18R 1	20 13	24 32	4R 3	4R49	3 12	11 58	10 51
T 3	0 44 52	9 18 15	25 6	17 2	20 50	25 6	3 58	4 48	3 15	12 0	10 53
O 4	0 48 49	10 17 20	7♐18	15 58	21 26	25 39	3 53	4 47	3 18	12 2	10 54
B 5	0 52 45	11 16 27	19 42	14 51	22 1	26 13	3 48	4 47	3 21	12 4	10 56
E 6	0 56 42	12 15 36	2♑21	13 41	22 34	26 46	3 44	4 46	3 25	12 6	10 58
R 7	1 0 38	13 14 47	15 19	12 31	23 6	27 18	3 39	4 46	3 28	12 8	11 0
8	1 4 35	14 13 59	28 40	11 23	23 36	27 51	3 35	4 46	3 31	12 10	11 2
9	1 8 31	15 13 14	12♒26	10 18	24 5	28 24	3 31	4D46	3 34	12 12	11 4
10	1 12 28	16 12 30	26 41	9 19	24 32	28 56	3 27	4 46	3 37	12 14	11 5
11	1 16 24	17 11 47	11♓21	8 26	24 58	29 28	3 23	4 46	3 40	12 16	11 7
12	1 20 21	18 11 7	26 24	7 43	25 22	0♌ 0	3 20	4 46	3 43	12 18	11 9
13	1 24 18	19 10 28	11♈40	7 9	25 44	0 32	3 16	4 46	3 46	12 20	11 11
14	1 28 14	20 9 51	27 0	6 46	26 5	1 4	3 13	4 47	3 49	12 22	11 12
15	1 32 11	21 9 17	12♉11	6D33	26 23	1 35	3 10	4 47	3 51	12 24	11 14
16	1 36 7	22 8 44	27 3	6 32	26 40	2 6	3 7	4 48	3 54	12 27	11 16
17	1 40 4	23 8 14	11♊29	6 41	26 54	2 37	3 5	4 48	3 57	12 29	11 17
18	1 44 0	24 7 46	25 25	7 1	27 7	3 8	3 2	4 49	4 0	12 31	11 19
19	1 47 57	25 7 21	8♋51	7 31	27 18	3 39	3 0	4 50	4 2	12 33	11 21
20	1 51 53	26 6 58	21 50	8 10	27 26	4 9	2 58	4 51	4 5	12 35	11 22
21	1 55 50	27 6 37	4♌25	8 58	27 32	4 39	2 56	4 52	4 8	12 37	11 24
22	1 59 47	28 6 18	16 41	9 54	27 36	5 9	2 55	4 53	4 10	12 40	11 25
23	2 3 43	29 6 2	28 44	10 56	27R38	5 39	2 53	4 55	4 13	12 42	11 27
24	2 7 40	0♏ 5 47	10♍39	12 4	27 37	6 8	2 52	4 56	4 15	12 44	11 28
25	2 11 36	1 5 35	22 30	13 18	27 34	6 38	2 51	4 57	4 18	12 46	11 30
26	2 15 33	2 5 25	4♎19	14 36	27 28	7 7	2 50	4 59	4 20	12 48	11 31
27	2 19 29	3 5 17	16 11	15 58	27 20	7 36	2 50	5 1	4 23	12 51	11 33
28	2 23 26	4 5 11	28 6	17 23	27 10	8 4	2 49	5 2	4 25	12 53	11 34
29	2 27 22	5 5 7	10♏ 6	18 51	26 57	8 32	2D49	5 4	4 27	12 55	11 36
30	2 31 19	6 5 5	22 12	20 21	26 42	9 1	2 49	5 6	4 30	12 57	11 37
31	2 35 15	7♏ 5 5	4♐26	21♎53	26♏24	9♌28	2♓49	5♒ 8	4♍32	13♏ 0	11♍38

THE SUN ENTERS THE SIGN OF SCORPIO ON OCT 23 AT 21:41.

DAY	TIME	☉	☽	☿	♀	♂	♃	♄	♅	♆	♇
	h m s	° ' "	° '	° '	° '	° '	° '	° '	° '	° '	° '
N 1	2 39 12	8♏ 5 6	16♐47	23♎27	26♏ 5	9♌56	2♓50	5♒11	4♍34	13♏ 2	11♍40
O 2	2 43 9	9 5 10	29 19	25 2	25R43	10 23	2 50	5 13	4 36	13 4	11 41
V 3	2 47 5	10 5 15	12♑ 3	26 37	25 18	10 50	2 51	5 15	4 38	13 6	11 42
E 4	2 51 2	11 5 21	25 2	28 14	24 52	11 17	2 52	5 18	4 40	13 9	11 44
M 5	2 54 58	12 5 29	8♒19	29 51	24 24	11 43	2 53	5 20	4 42	13 11	11 45
B 6	2 58 55	13 5 39	21 57	1♏28	23 54	12 9	2 55	5 23	4 44	13 13	11 46
E 7	3 2 51	14 5 50	5♓57	3 5	23 23	12 35	2 57	5 26	4 46	13 15	11 47
R 8	3 6 48	15 6 3	20 21	4 43	22 50	13 1	2 58	5 29	4 48	13 18	11 48
9	3 10 44	16 6 16	5♈ 5	6 21	22 16	13 26	3 0	5 31	4 49	13 20	11 49
10	3 14 41	17 6 32	20 5	7 58	21 41	13 51	3 3	5 34	4 51	13 22	11 50
11	3 18 38	18 6 49	5♉11	9 36	21 5	14 15	3 5	5 38	4 53	13 24	11 52
12	3 22 34	19 7 8	20 15	11 13	20 28	14 39	3 8	5 41	4 54	13 26	11 53
13	3 26 31	20 7 28	5♊ 4	12 50	19 52	15 3	3 11	5 44	4 56	13 29	11 54
14	3 30 27	21 7 51	19 33	14 27	19 15	15 27	3 14	5 47	4 58	13 31	11 55
15	3 34 24	22 8 15	3♋34	16 4	18 39	15 50	3 17	5 51	4 59	13 33	11 56
16	3 38 20	23 8 41	17 6	17 41	18 3	16 13	3 20	5 54	5 0	13 35	11 56
17	3 42 17	24 9 8	0♌11	19 17	17 28	16 36	3 24	5 58	5 2	13 38	11 57
18	3 46 14	25 9 38	12 50	20 53	16 54	16 58	3 28	6 2	5 3	13 40	11 58
19	3 50 10	26 10 9	25 10	22 29	16 21	17 20	3 32	6 6	5 4	13 42	11 59
20	3 54 7	27 10 42	7♍14	24 5	15 50	17 41	3 36	6 10	5 6	13 44	12 0
21	3 58 3	28 11 17	19 9	25 40	15 20	18 2	3 40	6 14	5 7	13 46	12 1
22	4 2 0	29 11 54	1♎ 0	27 16	14 53	18 22	3 45	6 18	5 8	13 49	12 1
23	4 5 56	0♐12 32	12 50	28 51	14 27	18 43	3 50	6 22	5 9	13 51	12 2
24	4 9 53	1 13 12	24 44	0♐26	14 3	19 2	3 54	6 26	5 10	13 53	12 3
25	4 13 49	2 13 53	6♏44	2 0	13 41	19 22	4 0	6 30	5 11	13 55	12 3
26	4 17 46	3 14 36	18 52	3 35	13 22	19 40	4 5	6 35	5 12	13 57	12 4
27	4 21 42	4 15 21	1♐10	5 9	13 4	19 59	4 10	6 39	5 13	13 59	12 5
28	4 25 39	5 16 6	13 38	6 44	12 50	20 17	4 16	6 44	5 13	14 2	12 5
29	4 29 36	6 16 53	26 16	8 18	12 38	20 34	4 22	6 48	5 14	14 4	12 6
30	4 33 32	7♐17 41	9♑ 5	9♐52	12♏28	20♌51	4♓28	6♒53	5♍15	14♏ 6	12♍ 6

THE SUN ENTERS THE SIGN OF SAGITTARIUS ON NOV 22 AT 19:03.

DAY	TIME	☉	☽	☿	♀	♂	♃	♄	♅	♆	♇
	h m s	° ' "	° '	° '	° '	° '	° '	° '	° '	° '	° '
D 1	4 37 29	8♐18 31	22♑ 5	11♐26	12♏20	21♌ 8	4♓34	6♒58	5♍15	14♏ 8	12♍ 7
E 2	4 41 25	9 19 21	5♒17	13 0	12R16	21 24	4 40	7 2	5 16	14 10	12 7
C 3	4 45 22	10 20 12	18 42	14 34	12D13	21 39	4 47	7 7	5 16	14 12	12 7
E 4	4 49 18	11 21 4	2♓21	16 8	12 13	21 54	4 53	7 12	5 17	14 14	12 8
M 5	4 53 15	12 21 57	16 15	17 42	12 16	22 8	5 0	7 17	5 17	14 16	12 8
B 6	4 57 12	13 22 50	0♈25	19 15	12 21	22 22	5 7	7 23	5 17	14 18	12 8
E 7	5 1 8	14 23 44	14 49	20 49	12 28	22 35	5 14	7 28	5 18	14 20	12 9
R 8	5 5 5	15 24 39	29 24	22 23	12 37	22 48	5 22	7 33	5 18	14 22	12 9
9	5 9 1	16 25 35	14♉ 4	23 57	12 49	23 0	5 29	7 38	5 18	14 24	12 9
10	5 12 58	17 26 31	28 42	25 31	13 3	23 12	5 37	7 44	5 18	14 26	12 9
11	5 16 54	18 27 29	13♊12	27 5	13 19	23 23	5 45	7 49	5R18	14 28	12 9
12	5 20 51	19 28 27	27 27	28 38	13 37	23 33	5 53	7 55	5 18	14 30	12 10
13	5 24 47	20 29 26	11♋21	0♑12	13 57	23 43	6 1	8 0	5 18	14 32	12 10
14	5 28 44	21 30 26	24 51	1 46	14 19	23 52	6 9	8 6	5 18	14 34	12R10
15	5 32 41	22 31 27	7♌57	3 20	14 42	24 1	6 17	8 11	5 18	14 36	12 10
16	5 36 37	23 32 28	20 41	4 54	15 8	24 8	6 26	8 17	5 18	14 38	12 10
17	5 40 34	24 33 31	3♍ 4	6 28	15 35	24 16	6 35	8 23	5 17	14 39	12 10
18	5 44 30	25 34 35	15 13	8 1	16 5	24 22	6 43	8 29	5 17	14 41	12 10
19	5 48 27	26 35 39	27 11	9 35	16 35	24 28	6 52	8 35	5 17	14 43	12 9
20	5 52 23	27 36 44	9♎ 3	11 8	17 7	24 33	7 1	8 41	5 16	14 45	12 9
21	5 56 20	28 37 50	20 55	12 41	17 41	24 37	7 11	8 47	5 16	14 47	12 9
22	6 0 16	29 38 57	2♏50	14 13	18 16	24 41	7 20	8 53	5 15	14 48	12 9
23	6 4 13	0♑40 5	14 54	15 46	18 53	24 44	7 29	8 59	5 14	14 50	12 9
24	6 8 10	1 41 13	27 8	17 17	19 31	24 46	7 39	9 5	5 14	14 52	12 8
25	6 12 6	2 42 22	9♐36	18 48	20 10	24 47	7 49	9 11	5 13	14 53	12 8
26	6 16 3	3 43 31	22 18	20 17	20 50	24R48	7 59	9 18	5 12	14 55	12 8
27	6 19 59	4 44 41	5♑15	21 46	21 32	24 48	8 9	9 24	5 11	14 57	12 7
28	6 23 56	5 45 51	18 26	23 13	22 15	24 47	8 19	9 30	5 10	14 58	12 7
29	6 27 52	6 47 1	1♒51	24 39	22 58	24 45	8 29	9 37	5 9	15 0	12 7
30	6 31 49	7 48 11	15 27	26 2	23 43	24 42	8 39	9 43	5 8	15 1	12 6
31	6 35 45	8♑49 22	29♒13	27♑23	24♏29	24♌39	8♓50	9♒50	5♍ 7	15♏ 3	12♍ 6

THE SUN ENTERS THE SIGN OF CAPRICORN ON DEC 22 AT 08:16.

♏ SCORPIO ♐ SAGITTARIUS ♑ CAPRICORN ♒ AQUARIUS ♓ PISCES

SIDEREAL . . SUN . . MOON . . MERCURY . . VENUS . . MARS . . JUPITER . . SATURN . . URANUS . . NEPTUNE . . PLUTO .

DAY	TIME	☉	☽	☿	♀	♂	♃	♄	♅	♆	♇
	h m s	° ' "	° '	° '	° '	° '	° '	° '	° '	° '	° '
J 1	6 39 42	9♑50 32	13♓ 8	28♑42	25♏16	24♌35	9♓ 0	9♒56	5♍ 6	15♏ 4	12♍ 5
A 2	6 43 39	10 51 42	27 11	29 56	26 3	24R30	9 11	10 3	5R 5	15 6	12R 5
N 3	6 47 35	11 52 51	11♈19	1♒ 7	26 52	24 24	9 22	10 9	5 4	15 7	12 4
U 4	6 51 32	12 54 0	25 31	2 14	27 41	24 17	9 33	10 16	5 3	15 9	12 3
A 5	6 55 28	13 55 9	9♉45	3 14	28 31	24 10	9 44	10 22	5 1	15 10	12 3
R 6	6 59 25	14 56 18	23 57	4 9	29 22	24 2	9 55	10 29	5 0	15 11	12 2
Y 7	7 3 21	15 57 27	8♊ 6	4 57	0♐14	23 53	10 6	10 36	4 59	15 13	12 1
8	7 7 18	16 58 35	22 6	5 37	1 6	23 43	10 18	10 43	4 57	15 14	12 1
9	7 11 14	17 59 43	5♋54	6 8	1 59	23 32	10 29	10 50	4 56	15 15	12 0
10	7 15 11	19 0 50	19 27	6 30	2 53	23 21	10 40	10 56	4 54	15 17	11 59
11	7 19 8	20 1 58	2♌44	6R41	3 48	23 8	10 52	11 3	4 52	15 18	11 58
12	7 23 4	21 3 5	15 42	6 41	4 43	22 55	11 4	11 10	4 51	15 19	11 57
13	7 27 1	22 4 11	28 22	6 29	5 39	22 41	11 16	11 17	4 49	15 20	11 57
14	7 30 57	23 5 18	10♍46	6 5	6 35	22 27	11 28	11 24	4 47	15 21	11 56
15	7 34 54	24 6 24	22 56	5 30	7 32	22 12	11 40	11 31	4 46	15 22	11 55
16	7 38 50	25 7 30	4♎56	4 44	8 29	21 55	11 52	11 38	4 44	15 23	11 54
17	7 42 47	26 8 36	16 50	3 48	9 27	21 39	12 4	11 45	4 42	15 24	11 53
18	7 46 43	27 9 42	28 43	2 43	10 26	21 21	12 16	11 52	4 40	15 25	11 52
19	7 50 40	28 10 48	10♏38	1 32	11 25	21 3	12 28	11 59	4 38	15 26	11 51
20	7 54 37	29 11 53	22 42	0 16	12 24	20 44	12 41	12 6	4 36	15 27	11 50
21	7 58 33	0♒12 58	4♐58	28♑58	13 24	20 25	12 53	12 13	4 34	15 28	11 49
22	8 2 30	1 14 2	17 29	27 41	14 24	20 5	13 6	12 20	4 32	15 29	11 48
23	8 6 26	2 15 6	0♑19	26 27	15 25	19 44	13 19	12 27	4 30	15 30	11 47
24	8 10 23	3 16 9	13 30	25 17	16 26	19 23	13 31	12 34	4 28	15 31	11 45
25	8 14 19	4 17 12	27 1	24 13	17 27	19 2	13 44	12 42	4 26	15 31	11 44
26	8 18 16	5 18 14	10♒50	23 17	18 29	18 40	13 57	12 49	4 24	15 32	11 43
27	8 22 13	6 19 15	24 55	22 29	19 31	18 17	14 10	12 56	4 22	15 33	11 42
28	8 26 9	7 20 15	9♓11	21 50	20 34	17 55	14 23	13 3	4 19	15 34	11 41
29	8 30 6	8 21 14	23 33	21 20	21 36	17 32	14 36	13 10	4 17	15 34	11 39
30	8 34 2	9 22 12	7♈57	20 58	22 40	17 8	14 49	13 17	4 15	15 35	11 38
31	8 37 59	10♒23 9	22♈19	20♑46	23♐43	16♌45	15♓ 2	13♒25	4♍13	15♏35	11♍37

THE SUN ENTERS THE SIGN OF AQUARIUS ON JAN 20 AT 18:54.

DAY	TIME	☉	☽	☿	♀	♂	♃	♄	♅	♆	♇
	h m s	° ' "	° '	° '	° '	° '	° '	° '	° '	° '	° '
F 1	8 41 55	11♒24 4	6♉34	20♑41	24♐47	16♌21	15♓16	13♒32	4♍10	15♏36	11♍36
E 2	8 45 52	12 24 58	20 40	20D44	25 51	15R57	15 29	13 39	4R 8	15 36	11R34
B 3	8 49 48	13 25 50	4♊35	20 55	26 55	15 33	15 42	13 46	4 5	15 37	11 33
R 4	8 53 45	14 26 42	18 19	21 12	27 59	15 9	15 56	13 53	4 3	15 37	11 32
U 5	8 57 42	15 27 32	1♋52	21 35	29 4	14 45	16 9	14 0	4 1	15 38	11 30
A 6	9 1 38	16 28 20	15 12	22 4	0♑ 9	14 21	16 23	14 8	3 58	15 38	11 29
R 7	9 5 35	17 29 7	28 19	22 38	1 15	13 57	16 36	14 15	3 56	15 38	11 28
Y 8	9 9 31	18 29 53	11♌14	23 17	2 20	13 33	16 50	14 22	3 53	15 39	11 26
9	9 13 28	19 30 38	23 56	24 0	3 26	13 10	17 4	14 29	3 51	15 39	11 25
10	9 17 24	20 31 21	6♍26	24 47	4 32	12 47	17 17	14 36	3 48	15 39	11 23
11	9 21 21	21 32 3	18 43	25 38	5 38	12 24	17 31	14 44	3 46	15 39	11 22
12	9 25 17	22 32 43	0♎51	26 33	6 44	12 1	17 45	14 51	3 43	15 40	11 20
13	9 29 14	23 33 23	12 50	27 30	7 51	11 38	17 59	14 58	3 40	15 40	11 19
14	9 33 10	24 34 1	24 44	28 30	8 58	11 16	18 13	15 5	3 38	15 40	11 17
15	9 37 7	25 34 38	6♏36	29 33	10 5	10 55	18 27	15 12	3 35	15 40	11 16
16	9 41 4	26 35 14	18 30	0♒38	11 12	10 34	18 41	15 19	3 33	15R40	11 14
17	9 45 0	27 35 49	0♐32	1 45	12 19	10 13	18 55	15 26	3 30	15 40	11 13
18	9 48 57	28 36 23	12 44	2 55	13 27	9 53	19 9	15 33	3 27	15 40	11 11
19	9 52 53	29 36 55	25 14	4 6	14 34	9 34	19 23	15 40	3 25	15 40	11 10
20	9 56 50	0♓37 26	8♑ 3	5 19	15 42	9 15	19 37	15 47	3 22	15 40	11 8
21	10 0 46	1 37 56	21 17	6 34	16 50	8 56	19 51	15 54	3 20	15 40	11 7
22	10 4 43	2 38 24	4♒57	7 51	17 58	8 39	20 6	16 2	3 17	15 39	11 5
23	10 8 39	3 38 51	19 1	9 9	19 6	8 22	20 20	16 8	3 14	15 39	11 4
24	10 12 36	4 39 16	3♓28	10 29	20 15	8 5	20 34	16 15	3 12	15 39	11 2
25	10 16 33	5 39 40	18 11	11 50	21 23	7 50	20 48	16 22	3 9	15 39	11 1
26	10 20 29	6 40 1	3♈ 3	13 12	22 32	7 35	21 3	16 29	3 6	15 38	10 59
27	10 24 26	7 40 21	17 55	14 36	23 41	7 21	21 17	16 36	3 4	15 38	10 57
28	10 28 22	8♓40 39	2♉40	16♒ 1	24♑50	7♌ 7	21♓31	16♒43	3♍ 1	15♏38	10♍56

THE SUN ENTERS THE SIGN OF PISCES ON FEB 19 AT 09:09.

DAY	TIME	☉	☽	☿	♀	♂	♃	♄	♅	♆	♇
	h m s	° ' "	° '	° '	° '	° '	° '	° '	° '	° '	° '
M 1	10 32 19	9♓40 55	17♉10	17♒27	25♑59	6♌55	21♓46	16♒50	2♍59	15♏37	10♍54
A 2	10 36 15	10 41 9	1♊23	18 54	27 8	6R43	22 0	16 57	2R56	15R37	10R53
R 3	10 40 12	11 41 21	15 15	20 23	28 17	6 32	22 15	17 3	2 53	15 36	10 51
C 4	10 44 8	12 41 31	28 48	21 53	29 26	6 22	22 29	17 10	2 51	15 36	10 50
H 5	10 48 5	13 41 39	12♋ 4	23 23	0♒36	6 12	22 43	17 17	2 48	15 35	10 48
6	10 52 2	14 41 44	25 3	24 55	1 45	6 4	22 58	17 24	2 46	15 35	10 46
7	10 55 58	15 41 48	7♌49	26 29	2 55	5 56	23 12	17 30	2 43	15 34	10 45
8	10 59 55	16 41 49	20 23	28 3	4 4	5 49	23 27	17 37	2 40	15 33	10 43
9	11 3 51	17 41 49	2♍48	29 38	5 14	5 43	23 41	17 43	2 38	15 33	10 42
10	11 7 48	18 41 46	15 3	1♓15	6 24	5 37	23 56	17 50	2 35	15 32	10 40
11	11 11 44	19 41 41	27 11	2 52	7 34	5 32	24 10	17 56	2 33	15 31	10 39
12	11 15 41	20 41 35	9♎13	4 31	8 44	5 28	24 25	18 3	2 30	15 31	10 37
13	11 19 37	21 41 27	21 9	6 11	9 54	5 25	24 39	18 9	2 28	15 30	10 36
14	11 23 34	22 41 16	3♏ 2	7 52	11 4	5 23	24 54	18 16	2 26	15 29	10 34
15	11 27 31	23 41 5	14 54	9 35	12 15	5 21	25 8	18 22	2 23	15 28	10 33
16	11 31 27	24 40 51	26 47	11 18	13 25	5D20	25 23	18 28	2 21	15 27	10 31
17	11 35 24	25 40 36	8♐47	13 3	14 36	5 20	25 38	18 35	2 18	15 26	10 30
18	11 39 20	26 40 19	20 56	14 49	15 46	5 21	25 52	18 41	2 16	15 26	10 28
19	11 43 17	27 40 0	3♑21	16 36	16 57	5 22	26 7	18 47	2 14	15 25	10 27
20	11 47 13	28 39 40	16 5	18 24	18 7	5 24	26 21	18 53	2 12	15 24	10 25
21	11 51 10	29 39 17	29 14	20 14	19 18	5 27	26 36	18 59	2 9	15 23	10 24
22	11 55 6	0♈38 53	12♒51	22 5	20 29	5 30	26 50	19 5	2 7	15 22	10 22
23	11 59 3	1 38 28	26 57	23 57	21 40	5 34	27 5	19 11	2 5	15 21	10 21
24	12 3 0	2 38 0	11♓31	25 51	22 51	5 39	27 19	19 17	2 3	15 19	10 19
25	12 6 56	3 37 30	26 27	27 45	24 2	5 44	27 34	19 23	2 1	15 18	10 18
26	12 10 53	4 36 59	11♈38	29 41	25 13	5 50	27 48	19 29	1 58	15 17	10 16
27	12 14 49	5 36 25	26 52	1♈38	26 24	5 57	28 3	19 34	1 56	15 16	10 15
28	12 18 46	6 35 49	11♉59	3 37	27 35	6 5	28 17	19 40	1 54	15 15	10 14
29	12 22 42	7 35 11	26 49	5 36	28 46	6 13	28 32	19 46	1 52	15 14	10 12
30	12 26 39	8 34 31	11♊16	7 36	29 57	6 21	28 46	19 51	1 50	15 13	10 11
31	12 30 35	9♈33 49	25♊18	9♈38	1♓ 8	6♌30	29♓ 1	19♒57	1♍48	15♏11	10♍10

THE SUN ENTERS THE SIGN OF ARIES ON MAR 21 AT 08:20.

♈ ARIES	♉ TAURUS	♊ GEMINI	♋ CANCER	♌ LEO	♍ VIRGO	♎ LIBRA

SIDEREAL SUN... MOON... MERCURY VENUS... MARS... JUPITER SATURN.. URANUS.. NEPTUNE. PLUTO.

DAY	TIME	☉	☽	☿	♀	♂	♃	♄	♅	♆	♇
	h m s	° ' "	° '	° '	° '	° '	° '	° '	° '	° '	° '
A 1	12 34 32	10♈33 4	8♋53	11♈40	2♓20	6♌40	29♓15	20♒ 2	1♍47	15♏10	10♍ 8
P 2	12 38 28	11 32 16	22 4	13 43	3 31	6 50	29 29	20 7	1R45	15R 9	10R 7
R 3	12 42 25	12 31 27	4♌54	15 47	4 42	7 1	29 44	20 13	1 43	15 7	10 6
I 4	12 46 22	13 30 35	17 28	17 51	5 54	7 13	29 58	20 18	1 41	15 6	10 4
L 5	12 50 18	14 29 41	29 49	19 55	7 5	7 25	0♈12	20 23	1 39	15 5	10 3
6	12 54 15	15 28 44	12♍ 1	21 59	8 17	7 37	0 27	20 28	1 38	15 3	10 2
7	12 58 11	16 27 45	24 5	24 3	9 28	7 50	0 41	20 33	1 36	15 2	10 1
8	13 2 8	17 26 44	6♎ 4	26 6	10 40	8 4	0 55	20 38	1 35	15 1	10 0
9	13 6 4	18 25 41	18 0	28 9	11 51	8 18	1 9	20 43	1 33	14 59	9 58
10	13 10 1	19 24 36	29 53	0♉10	13 3	8 32	1 23	20 48	1 31	14 58	9 57
11	13 13 57	20 23 29	11♏45	2 9	14 14	8 47	1 38	20 53	1 30	14 56	9 56
12	13 17 54	21 22 21	23 38	4 6	15 26	9 3	1 52	20 58	1 29	14 55	9 55
13	13 21 51	22 21 10	5♐34	6 1	16 38	9 19	2 6	21 2	1 27	14 54	9 54
14	13 25 47	23 19 58	17 36	7 54	17 50	9 35	2 20	21 7	1 26	14 52	9 53
15	13 29 44	24 18 43	29 46	9 43	19 1	9 52	2 34	21 11	1 25	14 51	9 52
16	13 33 40	25 17 28	12♑ 9	11 29	20 13	10 9	2 48	21 16	1 23	14 49	9 51
17	13 37 37	26 16 10	24 50	13 12	21 25	10 26	3 2	21 20	1 22	14 48	9 50
18	13 41 33	27 14 51	7♒54	14 50	22 37	10 44	3 16	21 24	1 21	14 46	9 49
19	13 45 30	28 13 30	21 23	16 24	23 49	11 3	3 30	21 29	1 20	14 44	9 48
20	13 49 26	29 12 7	5♓21	17 55	25 1	11 21	3 43	21 33	1 19	14 43	9 47
21	13 53 23	0♉10 43	19 48	19 20	26 13	11 40	3 57	21 37	1 18	14 41	9 46
22	13 57 20	1 9 16	4♈41	20 41	27 25	12 0	4 11	21 41	1 17	14 40	9 45
23	14 1 16	2 7 49	19 53	21 57	28 37	12 20	4 25	21 45	1 16	14 38	9 44
24	14 5 13	3 6 19	5♉12	23 9	29 49	12 40	4 38	21 48	1 15	14 37	9 44
25	14 9 9	4 4 47	20 29	24 15	1♈ 1	13 1	4 52	21 52	1 14	14 35	9 43
26	14 13 6	5 3 14	5♊32	25 16	2 13	13 22	5 5	21 56	1 14	14 33	9 42
27	14 17 2	6 1 39	20 12	26 12	3 25	13 43	5 19	21 59	1 13	14 32	9 41
28	14 20 59	7 0 1	4♋25	27 3	4 37	14 4	5 32	22 3	1 12	14 30	9 41
29	14 24 55	7 58 22	18 8	27 49	5 50	14 26	5 46	22 6	1 12	14 29	9 40
30	14 28 52	8♉56 40	1♌24	28♉29	7♈ 2	14♌49	5♈59	22♒ 9	1♍11	14♏27	9♍39

THE SUN ENTERS THE SIGN OF TAURUS ON APR 20 AT 19:37.

DAY	TIME	☉	☽	☿	♀	♂	♃	♄	♅	♆	♇
	h m s	° ' "	° '	° '	° '	° '	° '	° '	° '	° '	° '
M 1	14 32 49	9♉54 56	14♌16	29♉ 3	8♈14	15♌11	6♈12	22♒13	1♍11	14♏25	9♍39
A 2	14 36 45	10 53 10	26 48	29 33	9 26	15 34	6 26	22 16	1R10	14R24	9R38
Y 3	14 40 42	11 51 22	9♍ 4	29 56	10 38	15 57	6 39	22 19	1 10	14 22	9 37
4	14 44 38	12 49 32	21 10	0♊15	11 50	16 21	6 52	22 22	1 10	14 20	9 37
5	14 48 35	13 47 40	3♎ 8	0 27	13 3	16 44	7 5	22 25	1 9	14 19	9 36
6	14 52 31	14 45 47	15 2	0R35	14 15	17 8	7 18	22 27	1 9	14 17	9 36
7	14 56 28	15 43 51	26 54	0 37	15 27	17 33	7 31	22 30	1 9	14 16	9 35
8	15 0 24	16 41 54	8♏46	0 34	16 40	17 57	7 44	22 33	1 9	14 14	9 35
9	15 4 21	17 39 55	20 41	0 27	17 52	18 22	7 56	22 35	1D 9	14 12	9 35
10	15 8 17	18 37 54	2♐38	0 14	19 4	18 47	8 9	22 38	1 9	14 11	9 34
11	15 12 14	19 35 52	14 41	29♉57	20 16	19 12	8 22	22 40	1 9	14 9	9 34
12	15 16 11	20 33 49	26 49	29 37	21 29	19 38	8 34	22 42	1 9	14 7	9 34
13	15 20 7	21 31 44	9♑ 7	29 12	22 41	20 3	8 47	22 44	1 9	14 6	9 33
14	15 24 4	22 29 38	21 37	28 45	23 54	20 29	8 59	22 46	1 9	14 4	9 33
15	15 28 0	23 27 30	4♒21	28 14	25 6	20 55	9 12	22 48	1 10	14 3	9 33
16	15 31 57	24 25 22	17 24	27 42	26 18	21 22	9 24	22 50	1 10	14 1	9 33
17	15 35 53	25 23 12	0♓50	27 8	27 31	21 49	9 36	22 52	1 10	13 59	9 33
18	15 39 50	26 21 1	14 40	26 33	28 43	22 15	9 48	22 53	1 11	13 58	9 32
19	15 43 47	27 18 48	28 55	25 58	29 56	22 42	10 0	22 55	1 11	13 56	9 32
20	15 47 43	28 16 35	13♈33	25 24	1♉ 8	23 10	10 12	22 56	1 12	13 55	9 32
21	15 51 40	29 14 20	28 31	24 50	2 21	23 37	10 24	22 58	1 12	13 53	9D32
22	15 55 36	0♊12 5	13♉39	24 17	3 33	24 5	10 36	22 59	1 13	13 51	9 32
23	15 59 33	1 9 48	28 48	23 47	4 46	24 33	10 48	23 0	1 14	13 50	9 32
24	16 3 29	2 7 30	13♊48	23 19	5 59	25 1	11 0	23 1	1 15	13 48	9 32
25	16 7 26	3 5 10	28 30	22 54	7 11	25 29	11 11	23 2	1 15	13 47	9 32
26	16 11 22	4 2 50	12♋47	22 33	8 24	25 58	11 23	23 3	1 16	13 45	9 33
27	16 15 19	5 0 27	26 37	22 15	9 36	26 26	11 34	23 4	1 17	13 44	9 33
28	16 19 16	5 58 4	10♌ 0	22 1	10 49	26 55	11 45	23 5	1 18	13 42	9 33
29	16 23 12	6 55 39	22 57	21 51	12 2	27 24	11 56	23 5	1 19	13 41	9 33
30	16 27 9	7 53 12	5♍32	21D45	13 14	27 53	12 7	23 6	1 20	13 39	9 33
31	16 31 5	8♊50 44	17♍50	21♉44	14♉27	28♌23	12♈18	23♒ 6	1♍21	13♏38	9♍34

THE SUN ENTERS THE SIGN OF GEMINI ON MAY 21 AT 18:59.

DAY	TIME	☉	☽	☿	♀	♂	♃	♄	♅	♆	♇
	h m s	° ' "	° '	° '	° '	° '	° '	° '	° '	° '	° '
J 1	16 35 2	9♊48 14	29♍55	21♉47	15♉39	28♌52	12♈29	23♒ 6	1♍22	13♏37	9♍34
U 2	16 38 58	10 45 44	11♎52	21 55	16 52	29 22	12 40	23 7	1 24	13R35	9 34
N 3	16 42 55	11 43 12	23 45	22 7	18 5	29 52	12 51	23R 7	1 25	13 34	9 35
E 4	16 46 51	12 40 39	5♏37	22 24	19 17	0♍22	13 1	23 7	1 26	13 32	9 35
5	16 50 48	13 38 4	17 31	22 45	20 30	0 52	13 12	23 7	1 28	13 31	9 35
6	16 54 45	14 35 29	29 29	23 10	21 43	1 22	13 22	23 6	1 29	13 30	9 36
7	16 58 41	15 32 53	11♐34	23 40	22 56	1 53	13 32	23 6	1 31	13 28	9 36
8	17 2 38	16 30 16	23 47	24 14	24 8	2 23	13 43	23 6	1 32	13 27	9 37
9	17 6 34	17 27 38	6♑ 8	24 52	25 21	2 54	13 53	23 5	1 34	13 26	9 37
10	17 10 31	18 24 59	18 40	25 34	26 34	3 25	14 3	23 5	1 35	13 24	9 38
11	17 14 27	19 22 20	1♒24	26 20	27 47	3 56	14 12	23 4	1 37	13 23	9 39
12	17 18 24	20 19 40	14 22	27 10	28 59	4 27	14 22	23 3	1 39	13 22	9 39
13	17 22 20	21 17 0	27 34	28 3	0♊12	4 59	14 32	23 2	1 40	13 21	9 40
14	17 26 17	22 14 19	11♓ 4	29 1	1 25	5 30	14 41	23 1	1 42	13 20	9 41
15	17 30 14	23 11 37	24 52	0♊ 2	2 38	6 2	14 50	23 0	1 44	13 18	9 41
16	17 34 10	24 8 56	8♈59	1 6	3 51	6 34	15 0	22 59	1 46	13 17	9 42
17	17 38 7	25 6 14	23 22	2 14	5 4	7 5	15 9	22 58	1 48	13 16	9 43
18	17 42 3	26 3 31	8♉ 0	3 26	6 17	7 37	15 18	22 56	1 50	13 15	9 44
19	17 46 0	27 0 49	22 46	4 41	7 30	8 10	15 26	22 55	1 52	13 14	9 44
20	17 49 56	27 58 6	7♊33	5 59	8 43	8 42	15 35	22 53	1 54	13 13	9 45
21	17 53 53	28 55 23	22 15	7 21	9 56	9 14	15 44	22 52	1 56	13 12	9 46
22	17 57 49	29 52 39	6♋44	8 46	11 9	9 47	15 52	22 50	1 58	13 11	9 47
23	18 1 46	0♋49 55	20 54	10 14	12 22	10 19	16 1	22 48	2 1	13 10	9 48
24	18 5 43	1 47 11	4♌42	11 45	13 35	10 52	16 9	22 46	2 3	13 9	9 49
25	18 9 39	2 44 26	18 6	13 20	14 48	11 25	16 17	22 44	2 5	13 8	9 50
26	18 13 36	3 41 40	1♍ 6	14 58	16 1	11 58	16 25	22 42	2 7	13 7	9 51
27	18 17 32	4 38 54	13 45	16 39	17 14	12 31	16 32	22 40	2 10	13 6	9 52
28	18 21 29	5 36 7	26 6	18 23	18 27	13 5	16 40	22 38	2 12	13 5	9 53
29	18 25 25	6 33 20	8♎13	20 9	19 40	13 38	16 47	22 35	2 15	13 4	9 54
30	18 29 22	7♋30 32	20♎11	21♊59	20♊53	14♍11	16♈55	22♒33	2♍17	13♏ 4	9♍56

THE SUN ENTERS THE SIGN OF CANCER ON JUN 22 AT 03:04.

♏ SCORPIO ♐ SAGITTARIUS ♑ CAPRICORN ♒ AQUARIUS ♓ PISCES

1963

SIDEREAL SUN. MOON. MERCURY. VENUS. MARS. JUPITER. SATURN. URANUS. NEPTUNE. PLUTO.

DAY	TIME	☉	☽	☿	♀	♂	♃	♄	♅	♆	♇
	h m s	° ' "	° '	° '	° '	° '	° '	° '	° '	° '	° '
J 1	18 33 18	8♋27 44	2♏ 5	23♊52	22♊ 6	14♍45	17♈ 2	22♒31	2♍2Ø	13♏ 3	9♍57
U 2	18 37 15	9 24 55	13 58	25 47	23 19	15 19	17 9	22R28	2 22	13R 2	9 58
L 3	18 41 12	1Ø 22 7	25 54	27 45	24 33	15 52	17 16	22 25	2 25	13 1	9 59
Y 4	18 45 8	11 19 18	7♐57	29 45	25 46	16 26	17 22	22 23	2 28	13 1	1Ø Ø
5	18 49 5	12 16 28	2Ø 1Ø	1♋47	26 59	17 Ø	17 29	22 2Ø	2 3Ø	13 Ø	1Ø 2
6	18 53 1	13 13 39	2♑34	3 51	28 12	17 34	17 35	22 17	2 33	12 59	1Ø 3
7	18 56 58	14 1Ø 5Ø	15 12	5 57	29 25	18 9	17 42	22 14	2 36	12 59	1Ø 4
8	19 Ø 54	15 8 1	28 3	8 4	Ø♋39	18 43	17 48	22 11	2 39	12 58	1Ø 5
9	19 4 51	16 5 12	11♒ 8	1Ø 12	1 52	19 17	17 54	22 8	2 41	12 58	1Ø 7
1Ø	19 8 47	17 2 23	24 27	12 21	3 5	19 52	17 59	22 5	2 44	12 57	1Ø 8
11	19 12 44	17 59 34	7♓59	14 3Ø	4 19	2Ø 27	18 5	22 1	2 47	12 57	1Ø 1Ø
12	19 16 41	18 56 46	21 44	16 4Ø	5 32	21 1	18 1Ø	21 58	2 5Ø	12 56	1Ø 11
13	19 2Ø 37	19 53 58	5♈4Ø	18 49	6 45	21 36	18 16	21 55	2 53	12 56	1Ø 13
14	19 24 34	2Ø 51 11	19 46	2Ø 59	7 59	22 11	18 21	21 51	2 56	12 56	1Ø 14
15	19 28 3Ø	21 48 25	4♉ 1	23 7	9 12	22 46	18 26	21 48	2 59	12 55	1Ø 15
16	19 32 27	22 45 39	18 21	25 15	1Ø 26	23 21	18 3Ø	21 44	3 2	12 55	1Ø 17
17	19 36 23	23 42 53	2♊43	27 22	11 39	23 56	18 35	21 4Ø	3 5	12 55	1Ø 19
18	19 4Ø 2Ø	24 4Ø 9	17 4	29 27	12 53	24 32	18 39	21 37	3 8	12 54	1Ø 2Ø
19	19 44 16	25 37 25	1♋2Ø	1♌31	14 6	25 7	18 44	21 33	3 11	12 54	1Ø 22
2Ø	19 48 13	26 34 42	15 25	3 34	15 2Ø	25 42	18 48	21 29	3 15	12 54	1Ø 23
21	19 52 1Ø	27 31 59	29 17	5 36	16 33	26 18	18 51	21 25	3 18	12 54	1Ø 25
22	19 56 6	28 29 17	12♌52	7 35	17 47	26 54	18 55	21 21	3 21	12 54	1Ø 27
23	2Ø Ø 3	29 26 35	26 8	9 34	19 1	27 3Ø	18 59	21 17	3 24	12 53	1Ø 28
24	2Ø 3 59	Ø♌23 53	9♍ 4	11 3Ø	2Ø 14	28 5	19 2	21 13	3 28	12 53	1Ø 3Ø
25	2Ø 7 56	1 21 12	21 42	13 25	21 28	28 41	19 5	21 9	3 31	12D53	1Ø 32
26	2Ø 11 52	2 18 31	4♎ 4	15 18	22 42	29 17	19 8	21 5	3 34	12 53	1Ø 33
27	2Ø 15 49	3 15 51	16 12	17 9	23 55	29 54	19 11	21 1	3 38	12 53	1Ø 35
28	2Ø 19 45	4 13 11	28 11	18 59	25 9	Ø♎3Ø	19 13	2Ø 57	3 41	12 53	1Ø 37
29	2Ø 23 42	5 1Ø 32	1Ø♏ 5	2Ø 47	26 23	1 6	19 16	2Ø 53	3 44	12 54	1Ø 39
3Ø	2Ø 27 39	6 7 53	21 58	22 33	27 37	1 43	19 18	2Ø 48	3 48	12 54	1Ø 4Ø
31	2Ø 31 35	7♌ 5 15	3♐56	24♌18	28♋5Ø	2♎19	19♈2Ø	2Ø♒44	3♍51	12♏54	1Ø♍42

THE SUN ENTERS THE SIGN OF LEO ON JUL 23 AT 13:60.

DAY	TIME	☉	☽	☿	♀	♂	♃	♄	♅	♆	♇
	h m s	° ' "	° '	° '	° '	° '	° '	° '	° '	° '	° '
A 1	2Ø 35 32	8♌ 2 37	16♐ 2	26♌ 1	Ø♌ 4	2♎56	19♈22	2Ø♒4Ø	3♍55	12♏54	1Ø♍44
U 2	2Ø 39 28	9 Ø Ø	28 2Ø	27 42	1 18	3 32	19 23	2ØR35	3 58	12 54	1Ø 46
G 3	2Ø 43 25	9 57 24	1Ø♑54	29 22	2 32	4 9	19 25	2Ø 31	4 2	12 54	1Ø 48
U 4	2Ø 47 21	1Ø 54 48	23 46	1♍ Ø	3 46	4 46	19 26	2Ø 27	4 5	12 55	1Ø 49
S 5	2Ø 51 18	11 52 14	6♒56	2 36	5 Ø	5 23	19 27	2Ø 22	4 9	12 55	1Ø 51
T 6	2Ø 55 15	12 49 4Ø	2Ø 25	4 1Ø	6 13	6 Ø	19 28	2Ø 18	4 12	12 55	1Ø 53
7	2Ø 59 11	13 47 7	4♓1Ø	5 43	7 27	6 37	19 28	2Ø 13	4 16	12 56	1Ø 55
8	21 3 8	14 44 35	18 9	7 14	8 41	7 14	19 29	2Ø 9	4 19	12 56	1Ø 57
9	21 7 4	15 42 5	2♈18	8 44	9 55	7 51	19R29	2Ø 5	4 23	12 57	1Ø 59
1Ø	21 11 1	16 39 36	16 32	1Ø 12	11 9	8 28	19 29	2Ø Ø	4 27	12 57	11 1
11	21 14 57	17 37 8	Ø♉49	11 38	12 23	9 6	19 29	19 56	4 3Ø	12 58	11 3
12	21 18 54	18 34 41	15 4	13 2	13 37	9 43	19 28	19 51	4 34	12 58	11 5
13	21 22 5Ø	19 32 17	29 15	14 25	14 51	1Ø 21	19 28	19 47	4 38	12 59	11 7
14	21 26 47	2Ø 29 53	13♊2Ø	15 46	16 6	1Ø 59	19 27	19 42	4 41	12 59	11 9
15	21 3Ø 43	21 27 32	27 18	17 5	17 2Ø	11 36	19 26	19 38	4 45	13 Ø	11 11
16	21 34 4Ø	22 25 11	11♋ 7	18 22	18 34	12 14	19 25	19 33	4 49	13 1	11 13
17	21 38 37	23 22 53	24 46	19 38	19 48	12 52	19 24	19 29	4 52	13 1	11 15
18	21 42 33	24 2Ø 35	8♌14	2Ø 51	21 2	13 3Ø	19 22	19 24	4 56	13 2	11 17
19	21 46 3Ø	25 18 19	21 28	22 2	22 16	14 8	19 2Ø	19 2Ø	5 Ø	13 3	11 19
2Ø	21 5Ø 26	26 16 4	4♍29	23 12	23 31	14 46	19 18	19 15	5 3	13 4	11 21
21	21 54 23	27 13 51	17 15	24 18	24 45	15 24	19 16	19 11	5 7	13 4	11 23
22	21 58 19	28 11 39	29 47	25 23	25 59	16 3	19 14	19 6	5 11	13 5	11 25
23	22 2 16	29 9 28	12♎ 4	26 25	27 13	16 41	19 11	19 2	5 15	13 6	11 27
24	22 6 12	Ø♍ 7 18	24 11	27 25	28 28	17 2Ø	19 8	18 58	5 18	13 7	11 29
25	22 1Ø 9	1 5 1Ø	6♏ 8	28 22	29 42	17 58	19 6	18 53	5 22	13 8	11 31
26	22 14 6	2 3 3	18 1	29 16	Ø♍56	18 37	19 2	18 49	5 26	13 9	11 33
27	22 18 2	3 Ø 57	29 52	Ø♎ 7	2 11	19 15	18 59	18 45	5 3Ø	13 1Ø	11 35
28	22 21 59	3 58 53	11♐48	Ø 55	3 25	19 54	18 56	18 4Ø	5 33	13 11	11 37
29	22 25 55	4 56 5Ø	23 53	1 4Ø	4 39	2Ø 33	18 52	18 36	5 37	13 12	11 39
3Ø	22 29 52	5 54 48	6♑13	2 21	5 54	21 12	18 48	18 32	5 41	13 13	11 41
31	22 33 48	6♍52 47	18♑51	2♎58	7♍ 8	21♎51	18♈44	18♒28	5♍45	13♏14	11♍44

THE SUN ENTERS THE SIGN OF VIRGO ON AUG 23 AT 20:58.

DAY	TIME	☉	☽	☿	♀	♂	♃	♄	♅	♆	♇
	h m s	° ' "	° '	° '	° '	° '	° '	° '	° '	° '	° '
S 1	22 37 45	7♍5Ø 48	1♒51	3♎31	8♍23	22♎3Ø	18♈4Ø	18♒24	5♍49	13♏15	11♍46
E 2	22 41 41	8 48 51	15 15	4 Ø	9 37	23 9	18R35	18R2Ø	5 52	13 17	11 48
P 3	22 45 38	9 46 54	29 3	4 24	1Ø 51	23 48	18 31	18 16	5 56	13 18	11 5Ø
T 4	22 49 35	1Ø 45 Ø	13♓13	4 43	12 6	24 28	18 26	18 12	6 Ø	13 19	11 52
E 5	22 53 31	11 43 7	27 39	4 57	13 2Ø	25 7	18 21	18 8	6 4	13 2Ø	11 54
M 6	22 57 28	12 41 16	12♈16	5R 5	14 35	25 46	18 16	18 4	6 7	13 22	11 56
B 7	23 1 24	13 39 27	26 55	5 8	15 49	26 26	18 11	18 Ø	6 11	13 23	11 58
E 8	23 5 21	14 37 39	11♉31	5 5	17 4	27 6	18 5	17 56	6 15	13 24	12 Ø
R 9	23 9 17	15 35 54	25 58	4 55	18 18	27 45	18 Ø	17 52	6 19	13 26	12 2
1Ø	23 13 14	16 34 11	1Ø♊11	4 39	19 33	28 25	17 54	17 49	6 22	13 27	12 5
11	23 17 1Ø	17 32 31	24 1Ø	4 17	2Ø 47	29 5	17 48	17 45	6 26	13 28	12 7
12	23 21 7	18 3Ø 52	7♋54	3 48	22 2	29 45	17 42	17 42	6 3Ø	13 3Ø	12 9
13	23 25 4	19 29 15	21 24	3 12	23 17	Ø♏25	17 36	17 38	6 33	13 31	12 11
14	23 29 Ø	2Ø 27 41	4♌41	2 3Ø	24 31	1 5	17 3Ø	17 35	6 37	13 33	12 13
15	23 32 57	21 26 8	17 45	1 42	25 46	1 45	17 23	17 31	6 41	13 34	12 15
16	23 36 53	22 24 38	Ø♍38	Ø 49	27 Ø	2 25	17 17	17 28	6 44	13 36	12 17
17	23 4Ø 5Ø	23 23 9	13 21	29♍51	28 15	3 5	17 1Ø	17 25	6 48	13 37	12 19
18	23 44 46	24 21 43	25 52	28 5Ø	29 3Ø	3 46	17 3	17 22	6 52	13 39	12 21
19	23 48 43	25 2Ø 18	8♎12	27 47	Ø♎44	4 26	16 56	17 19	6 55	13 41	12 23
2Ø	23 52 39	26 18 55	2Ø 23	26 43	1 59	5 7	16 49	17 16	6 59	13 42	12 25
21	23 56 36	27 17 34	2♏24	25 4Ø	3 14	5 47	16 42	17 13	7 3	13 44	12 27
22	Ø Ø 32	28 16 15	14 18	24 39	4 28	6 28	16 35	17 1Ø	7 6	13 46	12 29
23	Ø 4 29	29 14 58	26 8	23 42	5 43	7 9	16 28	17 7	7 1Ø	13 47	12 31
24	Ø 8 26	Ø♎13 42	7♐58	22 51	6 58	7 49	16 2Ø	17 5	7 13	13 49	12 33
25	Ø 12 22	1 12 29	19 51	22 6	8 13	8 3Ø	16 13	17 2	7 17	13 51	12 35
26	Ø 16 19	2 11 16	1♑53	21 29	9 27	9 11	16 5	16 59	7 2Ø	13 53	12 37
27	Ø 2Ø 15	3 1Ø 6	14 1Ø	21 Ø	1Ø 42	9 52	15 58	16 57	7 24	13 54	12 39
28	Ø 24 12	4 8 58	26 45	2Ø 42	11 57	1Ø 33	15 5Ø	16 55	7 27	13 56	12 41
29	Ø 28 8	5 7 51	9♒45	2ØD33	13 11	11 14	15 42	16 52	7 31	13 58	12 43
3Ø	Ø 32 5	6♎ 6 46	23♒13	2Ø♍35	14♎26	11♏56	15♈34	16♒5Ø	7♍34	14♏ Ø	12♍45

THE SUN ENTERS THE SIGN OF LIBRA ON SEP 23 AT 18:24.

♈ ARIES ♉ TAURUS ♊ GEMINI ♋ CANCER ♌ LEO ♍ VIRGO ♎ LIBRA

1963

SIDEREAL . SUN . MOON . MERCURY . VENUS . MARS . JUPITER . SATURN . URANUS . NEPTUNE . PLUTO .

DAY	TIME	☉	☽	☿	♀	♂	♃	♄	♅	♆	♇
	h m s	° ' "	° '	° '	° '	° '	° '	° '	° '	° '	° '
O 1	0 36 1	7♎ 5 42	7♓ 9	20♍47	15♎41	12♏37	15♈26	16♒48	7♍38	14♏ 2	12♍47
C 2	0 39 58	8 4 41	21 33	21 9	16 56	13 18	15R18	16R46	7 41	14 4	12 49
T 3	0 43 55	9 3 41	6♈18	21 40	18 10	14 0	15 10	16 44	7 44	14 6	12 51
O 4	0 47 51	10 2 43	21 18	22 21	19 25	14 41	15 2	16 43	7 48	14 7	12 53
B 5	0 51 48	11 1 48	6♉23	23 11	20 40	15 23	14 54	16 41	7 51	14 9	12 55
E 6	0 55 44	12 0 55	21 22	24 8	21 55	16 4	14 46	16 39	7 54	14 11	12 57
R 7	0 59 41	13 0 4	6♊ 8	25 12	23 9	16 46	14 38	16 38	7 57	14 13	12 59
8	1 3 37	13 59 15	20 34	26 23	24 24	17 28	14 30	16 36	8 1	14 15	13 1
9	1 7 34	14 58 29	4♋38	27 39	25 39	18 10	14 22	16 35	8 4	14 17	13 3
10	1 11 30	15 57 45	18 20	29 1	26 54	18 51	14 14	16 34	8 7	14 19	13 4
11	1 15 27	16 57 4	1♌42	0♎26	28 8	19 33	14 6	16 33	8 10	14 21	13 6
12	1 19 24	17 56 24	14 46	1 56	29 23	20 16	13 58	16 32	8 13	14 23	13 8
13	1 23 20	18 55 47	27 35	3 28	0♏38	20 58	13 50	16 31	8 16	14 25	13 10
14	1 27 17	19 55 13	10♍11	5 3	1 53	21 40	13 42	16 30	8 20	14 28	13 12
15	1 31 13	20 54 40	22 37	6 40	3 7	22 22	13 34	16 29	8 23	14 30	13 13
16	1 35 10	21 54 10	4♎53	8 18	4 22	23 4	13 26	16 29	8 26	14 32	13 15
17	1 39 6	22 53 41	17 2	9 58	5 37	23 47	13 18	16 28	8 28	14 34	13 17
18	1 43 3	23 53 15	29 4	11 38	6 52	24 29	13 10	16 28	8 31	14 36	13 19
19	1 46 59	24 52 51	10♏59	13 20	8 7	25 12	13 2	16 27	8 34	14 38	13 20
20	1 50 56	25 52 29	22 50	15 2	9 21	25 54	12 55	16 27	8 37	14 40	13 22
21	1 54 53	26 52 8	4♐39	16 44	10 36	26 37	12 47	16D27	8 40	14 42	13 23
22	1 58 49	27 51 50	16 28	18 26	11 51	27 20	12 40	16 27	8 43	14 45	13 25
23	2 2 46	28 51 33	28 20	20 8	13 6	28 3	12 32	16 27	8 46	14 47	13 27
24	2 6 42	29 51 18	10♑20	21 51	14 21	28 46	12 25	16 27	8 48	14 49	13 28
25	2 10 39	0♏51 5	22 33	23 33	15 36	29 29	12 17	16 27	8 51	14 51	13 30
26	2 14 35	1 50 54	5♒ 5	25 14	16 50	0♐12	12 10	16 28	8 54	14 53	13 31
27	2 18 32	2 50 44	17 59	26 56	18 5	0 55	12 3	16 28	8 56	14 56	13 33
28	2 22 28	3 50 36	1♓21	28 37	19 20	1 38	11 56	16 29	8 59	14 58	13 34
29	2 26 25	4 50 29	15 13	0♏17	20 35	2 21	11 49	16 30	9 1	15 0	13 36
30	2 30 22	5 50 24	29 35	1 57	21 49	3 4	11 43	16 30	9 4	15 2	13 37
31	2 34 18	6♏50 21	14♈24	3♏37	23♏ 4	3♐48	11♈36	16♒31	9♍ 6	15♏ 4	13♍39

THE SUN ENTERS THE SIGN OF SCORPIO ON OCT 24 AT 03:30.

DAY	TIME	☉	☽	☿	♀	♂	♃	♄	♅	♆	♇
	h m s	° ' "	° '	° '	° '	° '	° '	° '	° '	° '	° '
N 1	2 38 15	7♏50 20	29♈33	5♏16	24♏19	4♐31	11♈30	16♒32	9♍ 8	15♏ 7	13♍40
O 2	2 42 11	8 50 20	14♉51	6 55	25 34	5 14	11R23	16 33	9 11	15 9	13 42
V 3	2 46 8	9 50 23	0♊ 7	8 33	26 49	5 58	11 17	16 35	9 13	15 11	13 43
E 4	2 50 4	10 50 27	15 11	10 11	28 3	6 42	11 11	16 36	9 15	15 13	13 44
M 5	2 54 1	11 50 34	29 55	11 49	29 18	7 25	11 5	16 37	9 18	15 16	13 45
B 6	2 57 57	12 50 42	14♋13	13 26	0♐33	8 9	10 59	16 39	9 20	15 18	13 47
E 7	3 1 54	13 50 53	28 4	15 3	1 48	8 53	10 54	16 40	9 22	15 20	13 48
R 8	3 5 51	14 51 6	11♌30	16 39	3 2	9 37	10 48	16 42	9 24	15 22	13 49
9	3 9 47	15 51 20	24 32	18 15	4 17	10 20	10 43	16 44	9 26	15 25	13 50
10	3 13 44	16 51 37	7♍15	19 50	5 32	11 4	10 38	16 46	9 28	15 27	13 52
11	3 17 40	17 51 56	19 43	21 25	6 47	11 48	10 33	16 48	9 30	15 29	13 53
12	3 21 37	18 52 16	1♎58	23 0	8 2	12 33	10 28	16 50	9 32	15 31	13 54
13	3 25 33	19 52 39	14 4	24 35	9 16	13 17	10 24	16 52	9 34	15 34	13 55
14	3 29 30	20 53 3	26 3	26 9	10 31	14 1	10 19	16 55	9 35	15 36	13 56
15	3 33 26	21 53 29	7♏57	27 43	11 46	14 45	10 15	16 57	9 37	15 38	13 57
16	3 37 23	22 53 57	19 49	29 17	13 1	15 30	10 11	16 59	9 39	15 40	13 58
17	3 41 19	23 54 27	1♐38	0♐50	14 15	16 14	10 7	17 2	9 40	15 43	13 59
18	3 45 16	24 54 58	13 28	2 23	15 30	16 58	10 4	17 5	9 42	15 45	14 0
19	3 49 13	25 55 30	25 20	3 56	16 45	17 43	10 0	17 7	9 44	15 47	14 1
20	3 53 9	26 56 4	7♑17	5 29	18 0	18 28	9 57	17 10	9 45	15 49	14 2
21	3 57 6	27 56 39	19 21	7 1	19 14	19 12	9 54	17 13	9 46	15 51	14 3
22	4 1 2	28 57 16	1♒37	8 34	20 29	19 57	9 51	17 16	9 48	15 54	14 3
23	4 4 59	29 57 54	14 8	10 6	21 44	20 42	9 48	17 20	9 49	15 56	14 4
24	4 8 55	0♐58 33	26 59	11 38	22 59	21 26	9 46	17 23	9 50	15 58	14 5
25	4 12 52	1 59 13	10♓13	13 10	24 13	22 11	9 44	17 26	9 52	16 0	14 6
26	4 16 49	2 59 54	23 54	14 41	25 28	22 56	9 41	17 30	9 53	16 2	14 6
27	4 20 45	4 0 36	8♈ 4	16 12	26 43	23 41	9 40	17 33	9 54	16 5	14 7
28	4 24 42	5 1 19	22 40	17 43	27 58	24 26	9 38	17 37	9 55	16 7	14 8
29	4 28 38	6 2 3	7♉38	19 14	29 12	25 11	9 37	17 40	9 56	16 9	14 8
30	4 32 35	7♐ 2 48	22♉50	20♐45	0♑27	25♐56	9♈35	17♒44	9♍57	16♏11	14♍ 9

THE SUN ENTERS THE SIGN OF SAGITTARIUS ON NOV 23 AT 00:50.

DAY	TIME	☉	☽	☿	♀	♂	♃	♄	♅	♆	♇
	h m s	° ' "	° '	° '	° '	° '	° '	° '	° '	° '	° '
D 1	4 36 31	8♐ 3 35	8♊ 7	22♐15	1♑42	26♐42	9♈34	17♒48	9♍58	16♏13	14♍ 9
E 2	4 40 28	9 4 22	23 17	23 45	2 56	27 27	9R33	17 52	9 59	16 15	14 10
C 3	4 44 24	10 5 11	8♋11	25 15	4 11	28 12	9 33	17 56	9 59	16 17	14 10
E 4	4 48 21	11 6 2	22 42	26 44	5 25	28 57	9 32	18 0	10 0	16 19	14 11
M 5	4 52 18	12 6 53	6♌47	28 13	6 40	29 43	9D32	18 4	10 1	16 22	14 11
B 6	4 56 14	13 7 46	20 23	29 41	7 55	0♑28	9 32	18 9	10 1	16 24	14 12
E 7	5 0 11	14 8 40	3♍33	1♑ 8	9 9	1 14	9 33	18 13	10 2	16 26	14 12
R 8	5 4 7	15 9 36	16 20	2 35	10 24	1 59	9 33	18 17	10 2	16 28	14 12
9	5 8 4	16 10 32	28 47	4 1	11 39	2 45	9 34	18 22	10 3	16 30	14 13
10	5 12 0	17 11 30	10♎59	5 25	12 53	3 31	9 34	18 27	10 3	16 32	14 13
11	5 15 57	18 12 29	23 0	6 49	14 8	4 16	9 35	18 31	10 3	16 34	14 13
12	5 19 53	19 13 29	4♏55	8 11	15 22	5 2	9 37	18 36	10 4	16 36	14 13
13	5 23 50	20 14 31	16 45	9 31	16 37	5 48	9 38	18 41	10 4	16 38	14 13
14	5 27 47	21 15 33	28 34	10 49	17 51	6 34	9 40	18 46	10 4	16 40	14 14
15	5 31 43	22 16 36	10♐25	12 5	19 6	7 20	9 42	18 51	10 4	16 42	14 14
16	5 35 40	23 17 40	22 20	13 18	20 20	8 6	9 44	18 56	10R 4	16 43	14 14
17	5 39 36	24 18 44	4♑20	14 28	21 35	8 52	9 46	19 1	10 4	16 45	14R14
18	5 43 33	25 19 50	16 27	15 34	22 49	9 38	9 49	19 6	10 4	16 47	14 14
19	5 47 29	26 20 55	28 43	16 36	24 4	10 24	9 51	19 11	10 4	16 49	14 14
20	5 51 26	27 22 1	11♒10	17 32	25 18	11 10	9 54	19 16	10 4	16 51	14 14
21	5 55 22	28 23 8	23 51	18 23	26 33	11 56	9 57	19 22	10 4	16 53	14 13
22	5 59 19	29 24 15	6♓47	19 8	27 47	12 42	10 1	19 27	10 3	16 54	14 13
23	6 3 16	0♑25 22	20 1	19 45	29 1	13 28	10 4	19 33	10 3	16 56	14 13
24	6 7 12	1 26 29	3♈36	20 14	0♒16	14 15	10 8	19 38	10 3	16 58	14 13
25	6 11 9	2 27 36	17 32	20 34	1 30	15 1	10 12	19 44	10 2	17 0	14 13
26	6 15 5	3 28 43	1♉49	20R44	2 44	15 47	10 16	19 50	10 2	17 1	14 12
27	6 19 2	4 29 50	16 25	20 42	3 59	16 34	10 20	19 55	10 1	17 3	14 12
28	6 22 58	5 30 58	1♊15	20 30	5 13	17 20	10 25	20 1	10 0	17 5	14 12
29	6 26 55	6 32 5	16 13	20 6	6 27	18 7	10 29	20 7	10 0	17 6	14 11
30	6 30 51	7 33 13	1♋10	19 29	7 41	18 53	10 34	20 13	9 59	17 8	14 11
31	6 34 48	8♑34 21	15♋58	18♑42	8♒56	19♑40	10♈39	20♒19	9♍58	17♏10	14♍11

THE SUN ENTERS THE SIGN OF CAPRICORN ON DEC 22 AT 14:02.

♏ SCORPIO ♐ SAGITTARIUS ♑ CAPRICORN ♒ AQUARIUS ♓ PISCES

1964

SIDEREAL · SUN. · MOON. · MERCURY · VENUS. · MARS. · JUPITER · SATURN. · URANUS. · NEPTUNE. · PLUTO.

DAY	TIME	☉	☽	☿	♀	♂	♃	♄	♅	♆	♇
	h m s	° ' "	° '	° '	° '	° '	° '	° '	° '	° '	° '
J 1	6 38 45	9♑35 29	0♌30	17♑44	10♒10	20♑26	10♈44	20♒25	9♍57	17♏11	14♍10
A 2	6 42 41	10 36 37	14 40	16R37	11 24	21 13	10 50	20 31	9R56	17 13	14R10
N 3	6 46 38	11 37 45	28 25	15 22	12 38	21 59	10 55	20 37	9 55	17 14	14 9
U 4	6 50 34	12 38 54	11♍44	14 4	13 52	22 46	11 1	20 43	9 54	17 16	14 9
A 5	6 54 31	13 40 2	24 39	12 42	15 6	23 33	11 7	20 50	9 53	17 17	14 8
R 6	6 58 27	14 41 11	7♎11	11 22	16 20	24 20	11 13	20 56	9 52	17 18	14 7
Y 7	7 2 24	15 42 21	19 26	10 4	17 34	25 6	11 19	21 2	9 51	17 20	14 7
8	7 6 21	16 43 30	1♏28	8 52	18 48	25 53	11 25	21 9	9 50	17 21	14 6
9	7 10 17	17 44 39	13 21	7 47	20 2	26 40	11 32	21 15	9 49	17 23	14 6
10	7 14 14	18 45 49	25 10	6 50	21 15	27 27	11 39	21 22	9 47	17 24	14 5
11	7 18 10	19 46 58	6♐59	6 3	22 29	28 14	11 46	21 28	9 46	17 25	14 4
12	7 22 7	20 48 8	18 53	5 25	23 43	29 1	11 53	21 35	9 45	17 26	14 3
13	7 26 3	21 49 17	0♑53	4 58	24 57	29 48	12 0	21 41	9 43	17 28	14 2
14	7 30 0	22 50 26	13 3	4 40	26 10	0♒35	12 7	21 48	9 42	17 29	14 2
15	7 33 56	23 51 35	25 25	4D31	27 24	1 22	12 15	21 54	9 40	17 30	14 1
16	7 37 53	24 52 43	7♒59	4 31	28 38	2 9	12 23	22 1	9 39	17 31	14 0
17	7 41 50	25 53 51	20 46	4 39	29 51	2 56	12 31	22 8	9 37	17 32	13 59
18	7 45 46	26 54 58	3♓47	4 55	1♓ 5	3 43	12 39	22 15	9 35	17 33	13 58
19	7 49 43	27 56 4	17 1	5 18	2 18	4 30	12 47	22 21	9 33	17 34	13 57
20	7 53 39	28 57 9	0♈28	5 47	3 31	5 17	12 55	22 28	9 32	17 35	13 56
21	7 57 36	29 58 14	14 8	6 21	4 45	6 4	13 4	22 35	9 30	17 36	13 55
22	8 1 32	0♒59 18	28 1	7 1	5 58	6 52	13 12	22 42	9 28	17 37	13 54
23	8 5 29	2 0 20	12♉ 6	7 46	7 11	7 39	13 21	22 49	9 26	17 38	13 53
24	8 9 25	3 1 22	26 22	8 35	8 24	8 26	13 30	22 56	9 24	17 39	13 52
25	8 13 22	4 2 23	10♊46	9 27	9 37	9 13	13 39	23 3	9 22	17 40	13 51
26	8 17 19	5 3 22	25 15	10 23	10 50	10 0	13 48	23 10	9 20	17 41	13 50
27	8 21 15	6 4 21	9♋45	11 22	12 3	10 48	13 57	23 17	9 18	17 41	13 48
28	8 25 12	7 5 19	24 11	12 24	13 16	11 35	14 7	23 24	9 16	17 42	13 47
29	8 29 8	8 6 15	8♌26	13 29	14 29	12 22	14 16	23 31	9 14	17 43	13 46
30	8 33 5	9 7 11	22 27	14 36	15 42	13 10	14 26	23 38	9 12	17 44	13 45
31	8 37 1	10♒ 8 6	6♍ 9	15♑45	16♓54	13♒57	14♈36	23♒45	9♍10	17♏44	13♍44

THE SUN ENTERS THE SIGN OF AQUARIUS ON JAN 21 AT 00:41.

DAY	TIME	☉	☽	☿	♀	♂	♃	♄	♅	♆	♇
	h m s	° ' "	° '	° '	° '	° '	° '	° '	° '	° '	° '
F 1	8 40 58	11♒ 9 0	19♍29	16♑56	18♓ 7	14♒44	14♈46	23♒52	9♍ 8	17♏45	13♍42
E 2	8 44 54	12 9 53	2♎26	18 9	19 20	15 32	14 56	23 59	9R 5	17 45	13R41
B 3	8 48 51	13 10 45	15 3	19 23	20 32	16 19	15 6	24 7	9 3	17 46	13 40
R 4	8 52 48	14 11 36	27 22	20 39	21 44	17 6	15 16	24 14	9 1	17 47	13 39
U 5	8 56 44	15 12 26	9♏25	21 57	22 57	17 54	15 27	24 21	8 59	17 47	13 37
A 6	9 0 41	16 13 16	21 20	23 16	24 9	18 41	15 37	24 28	8 56	17 47	13 36
R 7	9 4 37	17 14 5	3♐ 9	24 36	25 21	19 28	15 48	24 35	8 54	17 48	13 34
Y 8	9 8 34	18 14 52	14 59	25 58	26 33	20 16	15 58	24 43	8 51	17 48	13 33
9	9 12 30	19 15 39	26 54	27 20	27 45	21 3	16 9	24 50	8 49	17 49	13 32
10	9 16 27	20 16 25	8♑59	28 44	28 57	21 51	16 20	24 57	8 47	17 49	13 30
11	9 20 23	21 17 10	21 18	0♒ 9	0♈ 8	22 38	16 31	25 4	8 44	17 49	13 29
12	9 24 20	22 17 53	3♒53	1 35	1 20	23 26	16 42	25 12	8 42	17 49	13 27
13	9 28 17	23 18 35	16 45	3 2	2 32	24 13	16 54	25 19	8 39	17 49	13 26
14	9 32 13	24 19 16	29 55	4 30	3 43	25 0	17 5	25 26	8 37	17 50	13 25
15	9 36 10	25 19 55	13♓21	5 58	4 55	25 48	17 16	25 33	8 34	17 50	13 23
16	9 40 6	26 20 33	27 2	7 28	6 6	26 35	17 28	25 41	8 32	17 50	13 22
17	9 44 3	27 21 9	10♈53	8 59	7 17	27 23	17 40	25 48	8 29	17 50	13 20
18	9 47 59	28 21 43	24 52	10 31	8 28	28 10	17 51	25 55	8 26	17R50	13 19
19	9 51 56	29 22 16	8♉57	12 3	9 39	28 58	18 3	26 2	8 24	17 50	13 17
20	9 55 52	0♓22 47	23 3	13 37	10 50	29 45	18 15	26 10	8 21	17 50	13 16
21	9 59 49	1 23 16	7♊10	15 11	12 0	0♓32	18 27	26 17	8 19	17 50	13 14
22	10 3 46	2 23 43	21 17	16 47	13 11	1 20	18 39	26 24	8 16	17 50	13 12
23	10 7 42	3 24 8	5♋23	18 23	14 21	2 7	18 51	26 31	8 13	17 50	13 11
24	10 11 39	4 24 31	19 25	20 0	15 32	2 55	19 4	26 38	8 11	17 50	13 9
25	10 15 35	5 24 53	3♌22	21 39	16 42	3 42	19 16	26 46	8 8	17 50	13 8
26	10 19 32	6 25 12	17 12	23 18	17 52	4 30	19 28	26 53	8 6	17 49	13 6
27	10 23 28	7 25 30	0♍51	24 58	19 2	5 17	19 41	27 0	8 3	17 49	13 5
28	10 27 25	8 25 46	14 16	26 39	20 12	6 4	19 53	27 7	8 0	17 49	13 3
29	10 31 21	9♓26 0	27♍25	28♒22	21♈21	6♓52	20♈ 6	27♒14	7♍58	17♏48	13♍ 2

THE SUN ENTERS THE SIGN OF PISCES ON FEB 19 AT 14:58.

DAY	TIME	☉	☽	☿	♀	♂	♃	♄	♅	♆	♇
	h m s	° ' "	° '	° '	° '	° '	° '	° '	° '	° '	° '
M 1	10 35 18	10♓26 12	10♎17	0♓ 5	22♈31	7♓39	20♈19	27♒21	7♍55	17♏48	13♍ 0
A 2	10 39 14	11 26 23	22 51	1 49	23 40	8 26	20 31	27 29	7R52	17R48	12R58
R 3	10 43 11	12 26 32	5♏ 8	3 35	24 49	9 14	20 44	27 36	7 50	17 47	12 57
C 4	10 47 8	13 26 40	17 13	5 21	25 58	10 1	20 57	27 43	7 47	17 47	12 55
H 5	10 51 4	14 26 46	29 7	7 9	27 7	10 48	21 10	27 50	7 45	17 46	12 54
6	10 55 1	15 26 50	10♐56	8 57	28 15	11 36	21 23	27 57	7 42	17 46	12 52
7	10 58 57	16 26 53	22 46	10 47	29 24	12 23	21 36	28 4	7 39	17 45	12 51
8	11 2 54	17 26 55	4♑41	12 38	0♉32	13 10	21 49	28 11	7 37	17 45	12 49
9	11 6 50	18 26 54	16 48	14 30	1 40	13 57	22 2	28 18	7 34	17 44	12 47
10	11 10 47	19 26 52	29 10	16 23	2 48	14 45	22 16	28 25	7 32	17 43	12 46
11	11 14 43	20 26 49	11♒52	18 17	3 56	15 32	22 29	28 32	7 29	17 43	12 44
12	11 18 40	21 26 43	24 57	20 12	5 4	16 19	22 42	28 39	7 27	17 42	12 43
13	11 22 37	22 26 36	8♓24	22 8	6 11	17 6	22 56	28 46	7 24	17 41	12 41
14	11 26 33	23 26 27	22 14	24 5	7 18	17 53	23 9	28 52	7 22	17 40	12 40
15	11 30 30	24 26 15	6♈21	26 3	8 25	18 40	23 23	28 59	7 19	17 40	12 38
16	11 34 26	25 26 2	20 41	28 1	9 32	19 28	23 36	29 6	7 17	17 39	12 36
17	11 38 23	26 25 47	5♉ 7	0♈ 0	10 39	20 15	23 50	29 13	7 14	17 38	12 35
18	11 42 19	27 25 29	19 33	2 0	11 45	21 2	24 4	29 19	7 12	17 37	12 33
19	11 46 16	28 25 10	3♊55	4 0	12 51	21 49	24 17	29 26	7 9	17 36	12 32
20	11 50 12	29 24 48	18 9	6 1	13 57	22 36	24 31	29 33	7 7	17 35	12 30
21	11 54 9	0♈24 24	2♋13	8 1	15 3	23 23	24 45	29 39	7 5	17 34	12 29
22	11 58 6	1 23 57	16 7	10 1	16 8	24 10	24 59	29 46	7 2	17 33	12 27
23	12 2 2	2 23 28	29 51	12 0	17 13	24 57	25 13	29 52	7 0	17 32	12 26
24	12 5 59	3 22 57	13♌26	13 58	18 18	25 44	25 27	29 59	6 58	17 31	12 25
25	12 9 55	4 22 23	26 50	15 55	19 23	26 31	25 40	0♓ 5	6 55	17 30	12 23
26	12 13 52	5 21 48	10♍ 4	17 50	20 27	27 17	25 54	0 12	6 53	17 29	12 22
27	12 17 48	6 21 10	23 7	19 44	21 31	28 4	26 8	0 18	6 51	17 28	12 20
28	12 21 45	7 20 29	5♎58	21 34	22 35	28 51	26 22	0 24	6 49	17 27	12 19
29	12 25 41	8 19 47	18 35	23 22	23 38	29 38	26 37	0 31	6 47	17 26	12 17
30	12 29 38	9 19 3	0♏59	25 7	24 42	0♈24	26 51	0 37	6 45	17 25	12 16
31	12 33 35	10♈18 17	13♏11	26♈47	25♉44	1♈11	27♈ 5	0♓43	6♍43	17♏23	12♍15

THE SUN ENTERS THE SIGN OF ARIES ON MAR 20 AT 14:10.

♈ ARIES ♉ TAURUS ♊ GEMINI ♋ CANCER ♌ LEO ♍ VIRGO ♎ LIBRA

SIDEREAL SUN. MOON. MERCURY. VENUS. MARS. JUPITER. SATURN. URANUS. NEPTUNE. PLUTO.

DAY	TIME	☉	☽	☿	♀	♂	♃	♄	♅	♆	♇
	h m s	° ' "	° '	° '	° '	° '	° '	° '	° '	° '	° '
A 1	12 37 31	11♈17 29	25♏12	28♈24	26♉47	1♈58	27♈19	0♓49	6♍41	17♏22	12♍13
P 2	12 41 28	12 16 39	7♐ 4	29 56	27 49	2 45	27 33	0 55	6R39	17R21	12R12
R 3	12 45 24	13 15 48	18 53	1♉24	28 51	3 31	27 47	1 1	6 37	17 20	12 11
I 4	12 49 21	14 14 54	0♑41	2 46	29 52	4 18	28 1	1 7	6 35	17 18	12 9
L 5	12 53 17	15 13 59	12 35	4 3	0♊53	5 4	28 16	1 13	6 33	17 17	12 8
6	12 57 14	16 13 2	24 41	5 15	1 54	5 51	28 30	1 19	6 31	17 16	12 7
7	13 1 10	17 12 4	7♒ 2	6 20	2 54	6 37	28 44	1 25	6 29	17 14	12 6
8	13 5 7	18 11 3	19 45	7 20	3 54	7 24	28 59	1 30	6 27	17 13	12 4
9	13 9 4	19 10 1	2♓53	8 13	4 54	8 10	29 13	1 36	6 26	17 12	12 3
10	13 13 0	20 8 57	16 29	9 0	5 53	8 56	29 27	1 42	6 24	17 10	12 2
11	13 16 57	21 7 51	0♈30	9 41	6 52	9 43	29 42	1 47	6 22	17 9	12 1
12	13 20 53	22 6 43	14 55	10 16	7 50	10 29	29 56	1 53	6 21	17 7	12 0
13	13 24 50	23 5 33	29 37	10 43	8 47	11 15	0♉10	1 58	6 19	17 6	11 59
14	13 28 46	24 4 22	14♉28	11 5	9 45	12 2	0 25	2 4	6 18	17 4	11 57
15	13 32 43	25 3 8	29 19	11 20	10 42	12 48	0 39	2 9	6 16	17 3	11 56
16	13 36 39	26 1 52	14♊ 3	11R29	11 38	13 34	0 53	2 14	6 15	17 2	11 55
17	13 40 36	27 0 34	28 34	11 31	12 33	14 20	1 8	2 19	6 13	17 0	11 54
18	13 44 32	27 59 13	12♋48	11 28	13 29	15 6	1 22	2 25	6 12	16 59	11 53
19	13 48 29	28 57 51	26 45	11 18	14 23	15 52	1 37	2 30	6 11	16 57	11 52
20	13 52 26	29 56 26	10♌24	11 4	15 17	16 38	1 51	2 35	6 9	16 55	11 51
21	13 56 22	0♉54 59	23 47	10 44	16 11	17 24	2 5	2 40	6 8	16 54	11 50
22	14 0 19	1 53 29	6♍55	10 19	17 3	18 10	2 20	2 44	6 7	16 52	11 50
23	14 4 15	2 51 58	19 51	9 51	17 55	18 56	2 34	2 49	6 6	16 51	11 49
24	14 8 12	3 50 24	2♎34	9 18	18 47	19 41	2 49	2 54	6 5	16 49	11 48
25	14 12 8	4 48 49	15 5	8 43	19 37	20 27	3 3	2 59	6 4	16 48	11 47
26	14 16 5	5 47 11	27 26	8 6	20 27	21 13	3 17	3 3	6 3	16 46	11 46
27	14 20 1	6 45 32	9♏37	7 27	21 16	21 58	3 32	3 8	6 2	16 44	11 45
28	14 23 58	7 43 50	21 40	6 47	22 5	22 44	3 46	3 12	6 1	16 43	11 45
29	14 27 55	8 42 7	3♐35	6 8	22 52	23 30	4 1	3 16	6 1	16 41	11 44
30	14 31 51	9♉40 23	15♐24	5♉28	23♊39	24♈15	4♉15	3♓21	6♍ 0	16♏40	11♍43

THE SUN ENTERS THE SIGN OF TAURUS ON APR 20 AT 01:27.

DAY	TIME	☉	☽	☿	♀	♂	♃	♄	♅	♆	♇
	h m s	° ' "	° '	° '	° '	° '	° '	° '	° '	° '	° '
M 1	14 35 48	10♉38 37	27♐12	4♉51	24♊25	25♈ 1	4♉29	3♓25	5♍59	16♏38	11♍43
A 2	14 39 44	11 36 49	9♑ 0	4R15	25 10	25 46	4 44	3 29	5R58	16R36	11R42
Y 3	14 43 41	12 35 0	20 54	3 41	25 53	26 31	4 58	3 33	5 58	16 35	11 41
4	14 47 37	13 33 9	2♒59	3 11	26 36	27 17	5 12	3 37	5 57	16 33	11 41
5	14 51 34	14 31 17	15 19	2 44	27 18	28 2	5 27	3 41	5 57	16 31	11 40
6	14 55 30	15 29 23	28 0	2 21	27 59	28 47	5 41	3 45	5 56	16 30	11 40
7	14 59 27	16 27 28	11♓ 5	2 2	28 39	29 32	5 55	3 48	5 56	16 28	11 39
8	15 3 24	17 25 32	24 38	1 48	29 18	0♉18	6 9	3 52	5 56	16 27	11 39
9	15 7 20	18 23 34	8♈40	1 38	29 55	1 3	6 24	3 56	5 55	16 25	11 38
10	15 11 17	19 21 35	23 8	1D32	0♋31	1 48	6 38	3 59	5 55	16 23	11 38
11	15 15 13	20 19 34	7♉58	1 31	1 6	2 33	6 52	4 2	5 55	16 22	11 38
12	15 19 10	21 17 32	23 2	1 35	1 40	3 18	7 6	4 6	5 55	16 20	11 37
13	15 23 6	22 15 28	8♊11	1 44	2 12	4 2	7 20	4 9	5D55	16 18	11 37
14	15 27 3	23 13 23	23 14	1 57	2 43	4 47	7 34	4 12	5 55	16 17	11 37
15	15 30 59	24 11 16	8♋ 4	2 14	3 12	5 32	7 48	4 15	5 55	16 15	11 36
16	15 34 56	25 9 8	22 34	2 36	3 40	6 17	8 3	4 18	5 55	16 14	11 36
17	15 38 53	26 6 57	6♌43	3 3	4 6	7 1	8 17	4 21	5 55	16 12	11 36
18	15 42 49	27 4 45	20 28	3 33	4 30	7 46	8 31	4 24	5 55	16 10	11 36
19	15 46 46	28 2 32	3♍50	4 7	4 53	8 31	8 45	4 26	5 56	16 9	11 36
20	15 50 42	29 0 16	16 53	4 46	5 14	9 15	8 58	4 29	5 56	16 7	11 36
21	15 54 39	29 57 59	29 38	5 28	5 33	10 0	9 12	4 31	5 56	16 6	11 35
22	15 58 35	0♊55 40	12♎ 8	6 14	5 50	10 44	9 26	4 34	5 57	16 4	11D35
23	16 2 32	1 53 20	24 26	7 3	6 6	11 28	9 40	4 36	5 57	16 2	11 35
24	16 6 28	2 50 58	6♏34	7 56	6 19	12 13	9 54	4 38	5 58	16 1	11 35
25	16 10 25	3 48 35	18 34	8 53	6 30	12 57	10 8	4 40	5 58	15 59	11 35
26	16 14 22	4 46 11	0♐28	9 52	6 39	13 41	10 21	4 42	5 59	15 58	11 36
27	16 18 18	5 43 45	12 18	10 55	6 46	14 25	10 35	4 44	6 0	15 56	11 36
28	16 22 15	6 41 19	24 6	12 1	6 50	15 9	10 49	4 46	6 1	15 55	11 36
29	16 26 11	7 38 51	5♑54	13 9	6R52	15 53	11 2	4 48	6 1	15 53	11 36
30	16 30 8	8 36 23	17 46	14 21	6 52	16 37	11 16	4 49	6 2	15 52	11 36
31	16 34 4	9♊33 53	29♑43	15♉36	6♋50	17♉21	11♉29	4♓51	6♍ 3	15♏50	11♍36

THE SUN ENTERS THE SIGN OF GEMINI ON MAY 21 AT 00:50.

DAY	TIME	☉	☽	☿	♀	♂	♃	♄	♅	♆	♇
	h m s	° ' "	° '	° '	° '	° '	° '	° '	° '	° '	° '
J 1	16 38 1	10♊31 23	11♒51	16♉54	6♋45	18♉ 5	11♉43	4♓52	6♍ 4	15♏49	11♍37
U 2	16 41 57	11 28 51	24 13	18 14	6R37	18 49	11 56	4 54	6 5	15R48	11 37
N 3	16 45 54	12 26 19	6♓53	19 37	6 28	19 33	12 9	4 55	6 6	15 46	11 37
E 4	16 49 51	13 23 47	19 55	21 3	6 16	20 16	12 23	4 56	6 7	15 45	11 38
5	16 53 47	14 21 13	3♈22	22 32	6 1	21 0	12 36	4 57	6 8	15 43	11 38
6	16 57 44	15 18 39	17 16	24 3	5 44	21 43	12 49	4 58	6 10	15 42	11 38
7	17 1 40	16 16 4	1♉37	25 37	5 25	22 27	13 2	4 59	6 11	15 41	11 39
8	17 5 37	17 13 29	16 20	27 14	5 4	23 10	13 15	5 0	6 12	15 39	11 39
9	17 9 33	18 10 53	1♊22	28 53	4 40	23 54	13 28	5 0	6 14	15 38	11 40
10	17 13 30	19 8 17	16 32	0♊35	4 14	24 37	13 41	5 1	6 15	15 37	11 40
11	17 17 27	20 5 39	1♋43	2 20	3 47	25 21	13 54	5 1	6 16	15 35	11 41
12	17 21 23	21 3 1	16 44	4 7	3 17	26 4	14 7	5 2	6 18	15 34	11 42
13	17 25 20	22 0 22	1♌28	5 57	2 46	26 47	14 20	5 2	6 20	15 33	11 42
14	17 29 16	22 57 42	15 49	7 49	2 13	27 30	14 33	5 2	6 21	15 32	11 43
15	17 33 13	23 55 2	29 44	9 44	1 39	28 13	14 45	5R 2	6 23	15 30	11 44
16	17 37 9	24 52 20	13♍13	11 41	1 4	28 56	14 58	5 2	6 25	15 29	11 44
17	17 41 6	25 49 37	26 18	13 40	0 28	29 39	15 11	5 2	6 26	15 28	11 45
18	17 45 2	26 46 54	9♎ 1	15 42	29♊51	0♊22	15 23	5 2	6 28	15 27	11 46
19	17 48 59	27 44 9	21 26	17 45	29 14	1 5	15 35	5 2	6 30	15 26	11 47
20	17 52 56	28 41 24	3♏37	19 51	28 36	1 48	15 48	5 1	6 32	15 25	11 48
21	17 56 52	29 38 38	15 37	21 58	27 59	2 30	16 0	5 1	6 34	15 24	11 48
22	18 0 49	0♋35 52	27 30	24 6	27 21	3 13	16 12	5 0	6 36	15 23	11 49
23	18 4 45	1 33 5	9♐19	26 15	26 44	3 55	16 24	4 59	6 38	15 22	11 50
24	18 8 42	2 30 18	21 7	28 26	26 8	4 38	16 36	4 59	6 40	15 21	11 51
25	18 12 38	3 27 31	2♑56	0♋37	25 33	5 20	16 48	4 58	6 42	15 20	11 52
26	18 16 35	4 24 43	14 49	2 48	24 59	6 3	17 0	4 57	6 44	15 19	11 53
27	18 20 31	5 21 55	26 48	4 59	24 26	6 45	17 12	4 55	6 46	15 18	11 54
28	18 24 28	6 19 6	8♒55	7 10	23 55	7 27	17 23	4 54	6 49	15 17	11 55
29	18 28 25	7 16 18	21 12	9 21	23 25	8 10	17 35	4 53	6 51	15 16	11 56
30	18 32 21	8♋13 29	3♓42	11♋30	22♊58	8♊52	17♉47	4♓52	6♍53	15♏15	11♍57

THE SUN ENTERS THE SIGN OF CANCER ON JUN 21 AT 08:57.

♏ SCORPIO ♐ SAGITTARIUS ♑ CAPRICORN ♒ AQUARIUS ♓ PISCES

SIDEREAL SUN. MOON. MERCURY. VENUS. MARS. JUPITER. SATURN. URANUS. NEPTUNE. PLUTO.

DAY	TIME	☉	☽	☿	♀	♂	♃	♄	♅	♆	♇
	h m s	° ' "	° '	° '	° '	° '	° '	° '	° '	° '	° '
J 1	18 36 18	9♋10 41	16♓27	13♋39	22♊32	9♊34	17♉58	4♓50	6♍56	15♏14	11♍59
U 2	18 40 14	10 7 53	29 31	15 47	22R 9	10 16	18 9	4R49	6 58	15R14	12 0
L 3	18 44 11	11 5 5	12♈55	17 53	21 47	10 58	18 21	4 47	7 0	15 13	12 1
Y 4	18 48 7	12 2 17	26 40	19 58	21 28	11 40	18 32	4 45	7 3	15 12	12 2
5	18 52 4	12 59 30	10♉48	22 1	21 12	12 22	18 43	4 43	7 6	15 11	12 3
6	18 56 0	13 56 42	25 16	24 3	20 58	13 4	18 54	4 41	7 8	15 11	12 5
7	18 59 57	14 53 56	10♊ 3	26 3	20 46	13 45	19 5	4 39	7 11	15 10	12 6
8	19 3 54	15 51 9	25 1	28 1	20 36	14 27	19 16	4 37	7 13	15 9	12 7
9	19 7 50	16 48 23	10♋ 3	29 57	20 29	15 9	19 26	4 35	7 16	15 9	12 9
10	19 11 47	17 45 37	25 2	1♌51	20 24	15 50	19 37	4 33	7 19	15 8	12 10
11	19 15 43	18 42 51	9♌48	3 44	20D22	16 32	19 47	4 30	7 22	15 8	12 11
12	19 19 40	19 40 6	24 15	5 34	20 22	17 13	19 58	4 28	7 24	15 7	12 13
13	19 23 36	20 37 20	8♍17	7 23	20 24	17 55	20 8	4 25	7 27	15 7	12 14
14	19 27 33	21 34 34	21 53	9 9	20 28	18 36	20 18	4 23	7 30	15 6	12 16
15	19 31 29	22 31 48	5♎ 3	10 54	20 35	19 17	20 28	4 20	7 33	15 6	12 17
16	19 35 26	23 29 2	17 49	12 37	20 44	19 59	20 38	4 17	7 36	15 6	12 19
17	19 39 23	24 26 17	0♏14	14 18	20 54	20 40	20 48	4 14	7 39	15 5	12 20
18	19 43 19	25 23 31	12 23	15 57	21 7	21 21	20 58	4 11	7 42	15 5	12 22
19	19 47 16	26 20 46	24 20	17 34	21 22	22 2	21 7	4 8	7 45	15 5	12 23
20	19 51 12	27 18 1	6♐10	19 9	21 39	22 43	21 17	4 5	7 48	15 4	12 25
21	19 55 9	28 15 17	17 58	20 43	21 58	23 24	21 26	4 2	7 51	15 4	12 26
22	19 59 5	29 12 32	29 47	22 14	22 18	24 5	21 35	3 59	7 54	15 4	12 28
23	20 3 2	0♌ 9 49	11♑40	23 43	22 41	24 45	21 44	3 56	7 57	15 4	12 30
24	20 6 58	1 7 5	23 41	25 11	23 4	25 26	21 53	3 52	8 0	15 4	12 31
25	20 10 55	2 4 23	5♒51	26 36	23 30	26 7	22 2	3 49	8 4	15 4	12 33
26	20 14 52	3 1 41	18 11	28 0	23 57	26 47	22 11	3 45	8 7	15 4	12 35
27	20 18 48	3 58 59	0♓44	29 21	24 26	27 28	22 20	3 42	8 10	15D 4	12 36
28	20 22 45	4 56 19	13 30	0♍41	24 56	28 8	22 28	3 38	8 13	15 4	12 38
29	20 26 41	5 53 39	26 29	1 58	25 28	28 49	22 36	3 34	8 17	15 4	12 40
30	20 30 38	6 51 0	9♈42	3 13	26 1	29 29	22 45	3 31	8 20	15 4	12 42
31	20 34 34	7♌48 23	23♈10	4♍26	26♊35	0♋ 9	22♉53	3♓27	8♍23	15♏ 4	12♍44

THE SUN ENTERS THE SIGN OF LEO ON JUL 22 AT 19:53.

DAY	TIME	☉	☽	☿	♀	♂	♃	♄	♅	♆	♇
	h m s	° ' "	° '	° '	° '	° '	° '	° '	° '	° '	° '
A 1	20 38 31	8♌45 46	6♉53	5♍37	27♊11	0♋50	23♉ 1	3♓23	8♍27	15♏ 4	12♍45
U 2	20 42 27	9 43 11	20 51	6 45	27 48	1 30	23 8	3R19	8 30	15 4	12 47
G 3	20 46 24	10 40 37	5♊ 5	7 50	28 26	2 10	23 16	3 15	8 34	15 4	12 49
U 4	20 50 21	11 38 5	19 31	8 54	29 5	2 50	23 24	3 11	8 37	15 5	12 51
S 5	20 54 17	12 35 33	4♋ 8	9 54	29 45	3 30	23 31	3 7	8 40	15 5	12 53
T 6	20 58 14	13 33 3	18 51	10 52	0♋26	4 10	23 38	3 3	8 44	15 5	12 55
7	21 2 10	14 30 34	3♌33	11 47	1 8	4 50	23 45	2 59	8 47	15 5	12 57
8	21 6 7	15 28 6	18 8	12 39	1 52	5 30	23 52	2 54	8 51	15 6	12 58
9	21 10 3	16 25 39	2♍28	13 27	2 36	6 9	23 59	2 50	8 55	15 6	13 0
10	21 14 0	17 23 13	16 28	14 13	3 21	6 49	24 6	2 46	8 58	15 7	13 2
11	21 17 56	18 20 48	0♎ 4	14 54	4 7	7 29	24 12	2 42	9 2	15 7	13 4
12	21 21 53	19 18 23	13 16	15 33	4 53	8 8	24 18	2 37	9 5	15 8	13 6
13	21 25 50	20 16 0	26 4	16 7	5 41	8 48	24 25	2 33	9 9	15 8	13 8
14	21 29 46	21 13 38	8♏30	16 37	6 29	9 27	24 31	2 29	9 12	15 9	13 10
15	21 33 43	22 11 17	20 39	17 2	7 18	10 6	24 36	2 24	9 16	15 9	13 12
16	21 37 39	23 8 56	2♐36	17 23	8 8	10 46	24 42	2 20	9 20	15 10	13 14
17	21 41 36	24 6 37	14 26	17 40	8 59	11 25	24 47	2 15	9 23	15 11	13 16
18	21 45 32	25 4 19	26 14	17 51	9 50	12 4	24 53	2 11	9 27	15 11	13 18
19	21 49 29	26 2 2	8♑ 5	17R57	10 41	12 43	24 58	2 6	9 31	15 12	13 20
20	21 53 25	26 59 46	20 4	17 57	11 34	13 22	25 3	2 2	9 34	15 13	13 22
21	21 57 22	27 57 32	2♒13	17 52	12 27	14 1	25 8	1 57	9 38	15 13	13 24
22	22 1 19	28 55 19	14 35	17 41	13 21	14 40	25 12	1 53	9 42	15 14	13 26
23	22 5 15	29 53 7	27 13	17 25	14 15	15 18	25 17	1 48	9 46	15 15	13 28
24	22 9 12	0♍50 56	10♓ 5	17 2	15 10	15 57	25 21	1 44	9 49	15 16	13 31
25	22 13 8	1 48 47	23 13	16 34	16 5	16 36	25 25	1 39	9 53	15 17	13 33
26	22 17 5	2 46 39	6♈33	16 0	17 1	17 14	25 29	1 35	9 57	15 18	13 35
27	22 21 1	3 44 34	20 5	15 20	17 57	17 53	25 33	1 30	10 1	15 19	13 37
28	22 24 58	4 42 29	3♉47	14 36	18 54	18 31	25 36	1 26	10 4	15 20	13 39
29	22 28 54	5 40 27	17 37	13 47	19 51	19 10	25 40	1 21	10 8	15 21	13 41
30	22 32 51	6 38 27	1♊36	12 55	20 49	19 48	25 43	1 17	10 12	15 22	13 43
31	22 36 48	7♍36 29	15♊41	12♍ 0	21♋47	20♋26	25♉46	1♓12	10♍16	15♏23	13♍45

THE SUN ENTERS THE SIGN OF VIRGO ON AUG 23 AT 02:52.

DAY	TIME	☉	☽	☿	♀	♂	♃	♄	♅	♆	♇
	h m s	° ' "	° '	° '	° '	° '	° '	° '	° '	° '	° '
S 1	22 40 44	8♍34 33	29♊52	11♍ 4	22♋46	21♋ 5	25♉49	1♓ 8	10♍19	15♏24	13♍47
E 2	22 44 41	9 32 38	14♋ 8	10R 6	23 45	21 43	25 51	1R 3	10 23	15 25	13 49
P 3	22 48 37	10 30 46	28 26	9 10	24 44	22 21	25 54	0 59	10 27	15 26	13 52
T 4	22 52 34	11 28 56	12♌44	8 15	25 44	22 59	25 56	0 54	10 31	15 28	13 54
E 5	22 56 30	12 27 7	26 56	7 23	26 45	23 37	25 58	0 50	10 34	15 29	13 56
M 6	23 0 27	13 25 20	10♍58	6 36	27 45	24 15	26 0	0 45	10 38	15 30	13 58
B 7	23 4 23	14 23 35	24 44	5 54	28 46	24 52	26 2	0 41	10 42	15 31	14 0
E 8	23 8 20	15 21 51	8♎11	5 19	29 47	25 30	26 3	0 37	10 46	15 33	14 2
R 9	23 12 17	16 20 9	21 17	4 51	0♌49	26 8	26 4	0 32	10 50	15 34	14 4
10	23 16 13	17 18 29	4♏ 2	4 31	1 51	26 45	26 5	0 28	10 53	15 35	14 6
11	23 20 10	18 16 51	16 27	4D20	2 53	27 23	26 6	0 24	10 57	15 37	14 9
12	23 24 6	19 15 14	28 36	4 18	3 56	28 0	26 7	0 20	11 1	15 38	14 11
13	23 28 3	20 13 38	10♐33	4 25	4 59	28 37	26 7	0 16	11 5	15 39	14 13
14	23 31 59	21 12 5	22 22	4 41	6 2	29 15	26R 8	0 12	11 8	15 41	14 15
15	23 35 56	22 10 33	4♑11	5 7	7 6	29 52	26 8	0 7	11 12	15 42	14 17
16	23 39 52	23 9 2	16 3	5 41	8 10	0♌29	26 8	0 3	11 16	15 44	14 19
17	23 43 49	24 7 34	28 5	6 24	9 14	1 6	26 7	0 0	11 19	15 45	14 21
18	23 47 46	25 6 7	10♒20	7 15	10 18	1 43	26 7	29♒56	11 23	15 47	14 23
19	23 51 42	26 4 41	22 52	8 14	11 23	2 19	26 6	29 52	11 27	15 49	14 25
20	23 55 39	27 3 18	5♓44	9 20	12 27	2 56	26 5	29 48	11 30	15 50	14 27
21	23 59 35	28 1 56	18 55	10 33	13 33	3 33	26 4	29 44	11 34	15 52	14 30
22	0 3 32	29 0 36	2♈25	11 52	14 38	4 10	26 3	29 41	11 38	15 53	14 32
23	0 7 28	29 59 18	16 10	13 16	15 44	4 46	26 1	29 37	11 41	15 55	14 34
24	0 11 25	0♎58 2	0♉ 8	14 44	16 49	5 22	25 59	29 33	11 45	15 57	14 36
25	0 15 21	1 56 48	14 13	16 17	17 55	5 59	25 57	29 30	11 49	15 59	14 38
26	0 19 18	2 55 37	28 22	17 52	19 2	6 35	25 55	29 27	11 52	16 0	14 40
27	0 23 14	3 54 28	12♊31	19 31	20 8	7 11	25 53	29 23	11 56	16 2	14 42
28	0 27 11	4 53 21	26 40	21 12	21 15	7 47	25 50	29 20	11 59	16 4	14 44
29	0 31 8	5 52 16	10♋46	22 55	22 22	8 23	25 48	29 17	12 3	16 6	14 46
30	0 35 4	6♎51 14	24♋49	24♍40	23♌29	8♌59	25♉45	29♒14	12♍ 6	16♏ 7	14♍48

THE SUN ENTERS THE SIGN OF LIBRA ON SEP 23 AT 00:18.

♈ ARIES ♉ TAURUS ♊ GEMINI ♋ CANCER ♌ LEO ♍ VIRGO ♎ LIBRA

SIDEREAL TIME · SUN · MOON · MERCURY · VENUS · MARS · JUPITER · SATURN · URANUS · NEPTUNE · PLUTO

DAY	TIME h m s	☉ ° ' "	☽ ° '	☿ ° '	♀ ° '	♂ ° '	♃ ° '	♄ ° '	♅ ° '	♆ ° '	♇ ° '
O 1	Ø 39 1	7♎5Ø 14	8♌48	26♍26	24♌37	9♌35	25♉41	29♒11	12♍1Ø	16♏ 9	14♍5Ø
C 2	Ø 42 57	8 49 17	22 41	28 12	25 44	1Ø 11	25R38	29R 8	12 13	16 11	14 52
T 3	Ø 46 54	9 48 21	6♍28	29 59	26 52	1Ø 47	25 35	29 5	12 17	16 13	14 54
O 4	Ø 5Ø 5Ø	1Ø 47 28	2Ø 4	1♎46	28 Ø	11 22	25 31	29 2	12 2Ø	16 15	14 56
B 5	Ø 54 47	11 46 37	3♎28	3 34	29 8	11 58	25 27	28 59	12 24	16 17	14 58
E 6	Ø 58 43	12 45 48	16 37	5 21	Ø♍17	12 33	25 23	28 57	12 27	16 19	15 Ø
R 7	1 2 4Ø	13 45 1	29 3Ø	7 8	1 25	13 8	25 19	28 54	12 31	16 21	15 2
8	1 6 37	14 44 16	12♏ 5	8 55	2 34	13 43	25 14	28 52	12 34	16 23	15 3
9	1 1Ø 33	15 43 33	24 25	1Ø 41	3 43	14 19	25 1Ø	28 49	12 37	16 25	15 5
1Ø	1 14 3Ø	16 42 52	6♐3Ø	12 27	4 52	14 54	25 5	28 47	12 4Ø	16 27	15 7
11	1 18 26	17 42 13	18 25	14 12	6 1	15 28	25 Ø	28 45	12 44	16 29	15 9
12	1 22 23	18 41 36	Ø♑14	15 57	7 1Ø	16 3	24 55	28 43	12 47	16 31	15 11
13	1 26 19	19 41 Ø	12 1	17 41	8 2Ø	16 38	24 49	28 41	12 5Ø	16 33	15 13
14	1 3Ø 16	2Ø 4Ø 26	23 53	19 24	9 29	17 12	24 44	28 39	12 53	16 35	15 15
15	1 34 12	21 39 54	5♒54	21 7	1Ø 39	17 47	24 38	28 37	12 57	16 37	15 16
16	1 38 9	22 39 24	18 11	22 49	11 49	18 21	24 33	28 35	13 Ø	16 39	15 18
17	1 42 6	23 38 55	Ø♓46	24 3Ø	12 59	18 55	24 27	28 33	13 3	16 41	15 2Ø
18	1 46 2	24 38 29	13 44	26 11	14 9	19 3Ø	24 21	28 32	13 6	16 43	15 22
19	1 49 59	25 38 4	27 7	27 51	15 19	2Ø 4	24 14	28 3Ø	13 9	16 45	15 23
2Ø	1 53 55	26 37 4Ø	1Ø♈53	29 3Ø	16 3Ø	2Ø 38	24 8	28 29	13 12	16 47	15 25
21	1 57 52	27 37 19	24 59	1♏ 9	17 41	21 11	24 2	28 28	13 15	16 5Ø	15 27
22	2 1 48	28 37 Ø	9♉21	2 47	18 51	21 45	23 55	28 27	13 18	16 52	15 28
23	2 5 45	29 36 43	23 53	4 25	2Ø 2	22 19	23 48	28 26	13 21	16 54	15 3Ø
24	2 9 41	Ø♏36 28	8♊28	6 2	21 13	22 52	23 41	28 25	13 24	16 56	15 32
25	2 13 38	1 36 15	23 Ø	7 38	22 24	23 25	23 34	28 24	13 26	16 58	15 33
26	2 17 35	2 36 5	7♋24	9 14	23 35	23 59	23 27	28 23	13 29	17 Ø	15 35
27	2 21 31	3 35 57	21 39	1Ø 5Ø	24 47	24 32	23 2Ø	28 22	13 32	17 3	15 36
28	2 25 28	4 35 51	5♌41	12 25	25 58	25 5	23 13	28 22	13 35	17 5	15 38
29	2 29 24	5 35 47	19 31	13 59	27 1Ø	25 38	23 5	28 21	13 37	17 7	15 4Ø
3Ø	2 33 21	6 35 45	3♍ 9	15 33	28 22	26 1Ø	22 58	28 21	13 4Ø	17 9	15 41
31	2 37 17	7♏35 46	16♍34	17♏ 6	29♍33	26♌43	22♉5Ø	28♒21	13♍43	17♏12	15♍43

THE SUN ENTERS THE SIGN OF SCORPIO ON OCT 23 AT 09:22.

DAY	TIME h m s	☉ ° ' "	☽ ° '	☿ ° '	♀ ° '	♂ ° '	♃ ° '	♄ ° '	♅ ° '	♆ ° '	♇ ° '
N 1	2 41 14	8♏35 48	29♍46	18♏39	Ø♎45	27♌15	22♉42	28♒21	13♍45	17♏14	15♍44
O 2	2 45 1Ø	9 35 53	12♎47	2Ø 12	1 57	27 48	22R35	28D21	13 48	17 16	15 45
V 3	2 49 7	1Ø 35 59	25 34	21 44	3 9	28 2Ø	22 27	28 21	13 5Ø	17 18	15 47
E 4	2 53 4	11 36 8	8♏ 8	23 16	4 22	28 52	22 19	28 21	13 53	17 2Ø	15 48
M 5	2 57 Ø	12 36 19	2Ø 3Ø	24 47	5 34	29 24	22 11	28 21	13 55	17 23	15 49
B 6	3 Ø 57	13 36 31	2♐39	26 18	6 46	29 56	22 3	28 21	13 57	17 25	15 51
E 7	3 4 53	14 36 45	14 39	27 49	7 59	Ø♍27	21 55	28 22	14 Ø	17 27	15 52
R 8	3 8 5Ø	15 37 Ø	26 3Ø	29 19	9 11	Ø 59	21 47	28 23	14 2	17 29	15 53
9	3 12 46	16 37 18	8♑18	Ø♐48	1Ø 24	1 3Ø	21 39	28 23	14 4	17 32	15 55
1Ø	3 16 43	17 37 36	2Ø 4	2 18	11 37	2 1	21 31	28 24	14 6	17 34	15 56
11	3 2Ø 39	18 37 57	1♒55	3 46	12 49	2 32	21 22	28 25	14 8	17 36	15 57
12	3 24 36	19 38 18	13 54	5 15	14 2	3 3	21 14	28 26	14 1Ø	17 38	15 58
13	3 28 33	2Ø 38 41	26 8	6 43	15 15	3 33	21 6	28 27	14 12	17 41	15 59
14	3 32 29	21 39 6	8♓4Ø	8 1Ø	16 28	4 4	2Ø 58	28 28	14 14	17 43	16 Ø
15	3 36 26	22 39 31	21 36	9 37	17 41	4 34	2Ø 5Ø	28 3Ø	14 16	17 45	16 2
16	3 4Ø 22	23 39 59	4♈58	11 3	18 54	5 4	2Ø 42	28 31	14 18	17 47	16 3
17	3 44 19	24 4Ø 27	18 47	12 29	2Ø 8	5 34	2Ø 33	28 33	14 2Ø	17 5Ø	16 4
18	3 48 15	25 4Ø 57	3♉ 2	13 53	21 21	6 4	2Ø 25	28 34	14 22	17 52	16 5
19	3 52 12	26 41 28	17 38	15 18	22 34	6 34	2Ø 17	28 36	14 24	17 54	16 6
2Ø	3 56 8	27 42 1	2♊3Ø	16 41	23 48	7 3	2Ø 9	28 38	14 25	17 56	16 6
21	4 Ø 5	28 42 35	17 29	18 3	25 1	7 32	2Ø 1	28 4Ø	14 27	17 59	16 7
22	4 4 2	29 43 11	2♋26	19 24	26 15	8 1	19 53	28 42	14 29	18 1	16 8
23	4 7 58	Ø♐43 49	17 15	2Ø 44	27 28	8 3Ø	19 45	28 44	14 3Ø	18 3	16 9
24	4 11 55	1 44 28	1♌49	22 3	28 42	8 59	19 38	28 46	14 32	18 5	16 1Ø
25	4 15 51	2 45 9	16 4	23 19	29 56	9 27	19 3Ø	28 48	14 33	18 7	16 11
26	4 19 48	3 45 51	29 58	24 34	1♏ 9	9 56	19 22	28 51	14 34	18 1Ø	16 11
27	4 23 44	4 46 35	13♍32	25 47	2 23	1Ø 24	19 14	28 53	14 36	18 12	16 12
28	4 27 41	5 47 2Ø	26 47	26 58	3 37	1Ø 51	19 7	28 56	14 37	18 14	16 13
29	4 31 37	6 48 7	9♎44	28 6	4 51	11 19	18 59	28 59	14 38	18 16	16 14
3Ø	4 35 34	7♐48 56	22♎26	29♐1Ø	6♏ 5	11♍46	18♉52	29♒ 1	14♍39	18♏18	16♍14

THE SUN ENTERS THE SIGN OF SAGITTARIUS ON NOV 22 AT 06:40.

DAY	TIME h m s	☉ ° ' "	☽ ° '	☿ ° '	♀ ° '	♂ ° '	♃ ° '	♄ ° '	♅ ° '	♆ ° '	♇ ° '
D 1	4 39 31	8♐49 46	4♏54	Ø♑11	7♏19	12♍13	18♉45	29♒ 4	14♍4Ø	18♏2Ø	16♍15
E 2	4 43 27	9 5Ø 37	17 11	1 8	8 33	12 4Ø	18R38	29 7	14 41	18 23	16 15
C 3	4 47 24	1Ø 51 3Ø	29 18	2 Ø	9 47	13 7	18 31	29 11	14 42	18 25	16 16
E 4	4 51 2Ø	11 52 24	11♐17	2 47	11 2	13 33	18 24	29 14	14 43	18 27	16 16
M 5	4 55 17	12 53 19	23 9	3 27	12 16	14 Ø	18 17	29 17	14 44	18 29	16 17
B 6	4 59 13	13 54 14	4♑58	4 1	13 3Ø	14 25	18 1Ø	29 2Ø	14 45	18 31	16 17
E 7	5 3 1Ø	14 55 11	16 45	4 27	14 44	14 51	18 4	29 24	14 46	18 33	16 18
R 8	5 7 6	15 56 9	28 32	4 45	15 59	15 16	17 58	29 27	14 47	18 35	16 18
9	5 11 3	16 57 7	1Ø♒24	4R53	17 13	15 41	17 51	29 31	14 47	18 37	16 18
1Ø	5 15 Ø	17 58 6	22 24	4 5Ø	18 27	16 6	17 45	29 35	14 48	18 39	16 19
11	5 18 56	18 59 6	4♓36	4 37	19 42	16 31	17 39	29 39	14 48	18 41	16 19
12	5 22 53	2Ø Ø 6	17 4	4 13	2Ø 56	16 55	17 33	29 43	14 49	18 43	16 19
13	5 26 49	21 1 7	29 53	3 37	22 11	17 19	17 28	29 47	14 49	18 45	16 19
14	5 3Ø 46	22 2 8	13♈ 6	2 5Ø	23 25	17 43	17 22	29 51	14 5Ø	18 47	16 19
15	5 34 42	23 3 1Ø	26 46	1 52	24 4Ø	18 6	17 17	29 55	14 5Ø	18 49	16 2Ø
16	5 38 39	24 4 12	1Ø♉54	Ø 45	25 54	18 29	17 12	29 59	14 5Ø	18 51	16 2Ø
17	5 42 35	25 5 15	25 27	29♐3Ø	27 9	18 52	17 7	Ø♓ 3	14 51	18 53	16 2Ø
18	5 46 32	26 6 18	1Ø♊22	28 1Ø	28 23	19 14	17 2	Ø 8	14 51	18 55	16R2Ø
19	5 5Ø 29	27 7 21	25 32	26 47	29 38	19 36	16 58	Ø 12	14 51	18 57	16 2Ø
2Ø	5 54 25	28 8 26	1Ø♋46	25 24	Ø♐53	19 58	16 53	Ø 17	14R51	18 59	16 2Ø
21	5 58 22	29 9 31	25 55	24 5	2 7	2Ø 19	16 49	Ø 21	14 51	19 Ø	16 2Ø
22	6 2 18	Ø♑1Ø 36	1Ø♌5Ø	22 51	3 22	2Ø 4Ø	16 45	Ø 26	14 51	19 2	16 2Ø
23	6 6 15	1 11 42	25 25	21 44	4 37	21 1	16 41	Ø 31	14 51	19 4	16 2Ø
24	6 1Ø 11	2 12 49	9♍34	2Ø 47	5 52	21 21	16 38	Ø 36	14 5Ø	19 6	16 19
25	6 14 8	3 13 56	23 16	19 59	7 6	21 41	16 34	Ø 41	14 5Ø	19 8	16 19
26	6 18 5	4 15 4	6♎32	19 22	8 21	22 1	16 31	Ø 46	14 5Ø	19 9	16 19
27	6 22 1	5 16 12	19 25	18 56	9 36	22 2Ø	16 28	Ø 51	14 5Ø	19 11	16 19
28	6 25 58	6 17 21	1♏58	18 4Ø	1Ø 51	22 38	16 25	Ø 56	14 49	19 13	16 18
29	6 29 54	7 18 31	14 15	18D35	12 6	22 57	16 22	1 1	14 49	19 14	16 18
3Ø	6 33 51	8 19 41	26 2Ø	18 38	13 21	23 15	16 2Ø	1 7	14 48	19 16	16 18
31	6 37 47	9♑2Ø 51	8♐16	18♐51	14♐35	23♍32	16♉18	1♓12	14♍48	19♏18	16♍17

THE SUN ENTERS THE SIGN OF CAPRICORN ON DEC 21 AT 19:50.

♏ SCORPIO ♐ SAGITTARIUS ♑ CAPRICORN ♒ AQUARIUS ♓ PISCES

1965

SIDEREAL · SUN. · MOON. · MERCURY. · VENUS.. · MARS.. · JUPITER. · SATURN. · URANUS. · NEPTUNE. · PLUTO.

DAY	TIME h	m	s	☉ ° ' "	☽ ° '	☿ ° '	♀ ° '	♂ ° '	♃ ° '	♄ ° '	♅ ° '	♆ ° '	♇ ° '
J 1	6	41	44	10♑22 2	20♐ 7	19♐11	15♐50	23♍49	16♉15	1♓17	14♍47	19♏19	16♍17
A 2	6	45	40	11 23 13	1♑54	19 39	17 5	24 6	16R14	1 23	14R46	19 21	16R17
N 3	6	49	37	12 24 24	13 42	20 13	18 20	24 22	16 12	1 28	14 46	19 22	16 16
U 4	6	53	34	13 25 34	25 31	20 53	19 35	24 37	16 10	1 34	14 45	19 24	16 16
A 5	6	57	30	14 26 45	7♒24	21 38	20 50	24 52	16 9	1 40	14 44	19 25	16 15
R 6	7	1	27	15 27 56	19 22	22 27	22 5	25 7	16 8	1 46	14 43	19 27	16 14
Y 7	7	5	23	16 29 6	1♓28	23 21	23 20	25 21	16 7	1 51	14 42	19 28	16 14
8	7	9	20	17 30 16	13 44	24 19	24 35	25 35	16 7	1 57	14 41	19 30	16 13
9	7	13	16	18 31 25	26 14	25 20	25 50	25 48	16 6	2 3	14 40	19 31	16 13
10	7	17	13	19 32 34	9♈ 0	26 24	27 5	26 0	16D 6	2 9	14 39	19 32	16 12
11	7	21	9	20 33 42	22 5	27 30	28 20	26 12	16 6	2 15	14 38	19 34	16 11
12	7	25	6	21 34 50	5♉33	28 39	29 35	26 24	16 6	2 21	14 37	19 35	16 10
13	7	29	3	22 35 57	19 26	29 50	0♑50	26 34	16 7	2 27	14 35	19 36	16 10
14	7	32	59	23 37 3	3♊43	1♑ 3	2 5	26 45	16 8	2 34	14 34	19 37	16 9
15	7	36	56	24 38 9	18 24	2 18	3 20	26 54	16 8	2 40	14 33	19 39	16 8
16	7	40	52	25 39 14	3♋24	3 34	4 35	27 4	16 9	2 46	14 31	19 40	16 7
17	7	44	49	26 40 19	18 36	4 52	5 50	27 12	16 11	2 52	14 30	19 41	16 6
18	7	48	45	27 41 23	3♌49	6 11	7 5	27 20	16 12	2 59	14 28	19 42	16 5
19	7	52	42	28 42 27	18 55	7 31	8 20	27 27	16 14	3 5	14 27	19 43	16 4
20	7	56	38	29 43 29	3♍43	8 53	9 35	27 34	16 16	3 12	14 25	19 44	16 4
21	8	0	35	0♒44 32	18 6	10 15	10 50	27 40	16 18	3 18	14 24	19 45	16 3
22	8	4	32	1 45 34	2♎ 1	11 39	12 5	27 45	16 20	3 25	14 22	19 46	16 2
23	8	8	28	2 46 35	15 26	13 3	13 20	27 50	16 23	3 31	14 20	19 47	16 0
24	8	12	25	3 47 36	28 24	14 28	14 35	27 54	16 25	3 38	14 18	19 48	15 59
25	8	16	21	4 48 36	10♏58	15 54	15 50	27 57	16 28	3 45	14 17	19 49	15 58
26	8	20	18	5 49 36	23 12	17 21	17 5	28 0	16 31	3 52	14 15	19 50	15 57
27	8	24	14	6 50 36	5♐12	18 49	18 20	28 1	16 34	3 58	14 13	19 51	15 56
28	8	28	11	7 51 34	17 4	20 18	19 35	28R 2	16 38	4 5	14 11	19 51	15 55
29	8	32	7	8 52 33	28 50	21 47	20 51	28 3	16 42	4 12	14 9	19 52	15 54
30	8	36	4	9 53 30	10♑37	23 17	22 6	28 2	16 45	4 19	14 7	19 53	15 53
31	8	40	1	10♒54 26	22♑25	24♑48	23♑21	28♍ 1	16♉49	4♓26	14♍ 5	19♏54	15♍51

THE SUN ENTERS THE SIGN OF AQUARIUS ON JAN 20 AT 06:29.

DAY	TIME h	m	s	☉ ° ' "	☽ ° '	☿ ° '	♀ ° '	♂ ° '	♃ ° '	♄ ° '	♅ ° '	♆ ° '	♇ ° '
F 1	8	43	57	11♒55 22	4♒20	26♑20	24♑36	27♍59	16♉54	4♓33	14♍ 3	19♏54	15♍50
E 2	8	47	54	12 56 16	16 21	27 52	25 51	27R57	16 58	4 40	14R 1	19 55	15R49
B 3	8	51	50	13 57 9	28 30	29 25	27 6	27 53	17 3	4 47	13 59	19 56	15 48
R 4	8	55	47	14 58 1	10♓49	0♒59	28 21	27 49	17 7	4 54	13 57	19 56	15 46
U 5	8	59	43	15 58 52	23 18	2 33	29 36	27 44	17 12	5 1	13 54	19 57	15 45
A 6	9	3	40	16 59 42	5♈59	4 8	0♒51	27 38	17 17	5 8	13 52	19 57	15 44
R 7	9	7	36	18 0 30	18 52	5 44	2 6	27 31	17 23	5 15	13 50	19 58	15 42
Y 8	9	11	33	19 1 16	1♉59	7 21	3 21	27 24	17 28	5 22	13 48	19 58	15 41
9	9	15	30	20 2 1	15 22	8 58	4 36	27 15	17 34	5 29	13 45	19 58	15 40
10	9	19	26	21 2 44	29 4	10 37	5 51	27 6	17 40	5 36	13 43	19 59	15 38
11	9	23	23	22 3 26	13♊ 5	12 16	7 6	26 57	17 46	5 43	13 41	19 59	15 37
12	9	27	19	23 4 6	27 26	13 56	8 21	26 46	17 52	5 51	13 38	19 59	15 35
13	9	31	16	24 4 45	12♋ 4	15 37	9 36	26 35	17 58	5 58	13 36	20 0	15 34
14	9	35	12	25 5 22	26 56	17 18	10 51	26 23	18 5	6 5	13 33	20 0	15 32
15	9	39	9	26 5 57	11♌55	19 1	12 6	26 10	18 11	6 12	13 31	20 0	15 31
16	9	43	5	27 6 31	26 51	20 44	13 21	25 56	18 18	6 20	13 28	20 0	15 30
17	9	47	2	28 7 3	11♍36	22 28	14 36	25 42	18 25	6 27	13 26	20 0	15 28
18	9	50	59	29 7 33	26 1	24 13	15 51	25 27	18 32	6 34	13 23	20 0	15 27
19	9	54	55	0♓ 8 3	10♎ 1	25 59	17 6	25 11	18 39	6 41	13 21	20 0	15 25
20	9	58	52	1 8 31	23 32	27 46	18 21	24 55	18 47	6 49	13 18	20R 0	15 23
21	10	2	48	2 8 57	6♏36	29 34	19 36	24 38	18 54	6 56	13 16	20 0	15 22
22	10	6	45	3 9 22	19 15	1♓23	20 51	24 20	19 2	7 3	13 13	20 0	15 20
23	10	10	41	4 9 46	1♐32	3 13	22 6	24 2	19 10	7 11	13 11	20 0	15 19
24	10	14	38	5 10 9	13 34	5 4	23 21	23 43	19 18	7 18	13 8	20 0	15 17
25	10	18	34	6 10 30	25 26	6 55	24 36	23 23	19 26	7 25	13 5	20 0	15 16
26	10	22	31	7 10 50	7♑13	8 47	25 51	23 3	19 34	7 33	13 3	20 0	15 14
27	10	26	28	8 11 8	19 0	10 40	27 5	22 42	19 43	7 40	13 0	20 0	15 13
28	10	30	24	9♓11 24	0♒52	12♓34	28♒20	22♍21	19♉51	7♓47	12♍58	19♏59	15♍11

THE SUN ENTERS THE SIGN OF PISCES ON FEB 18 AT 20:48.

DAY	TIME h	m	s	☉ ° ' "	☽ ° '	☿ ° '	♀ ° '	♂ ° '	♃ ° '	♄ ° '	♅ ° '	♆ ° '	♇ ° '
M 1	10	34	21	10♓11 39	12♒52	14♓29	29♒35	22♍ 0	20♉ 0	7♓54	12♍55	19♏59	15♍ 9
A 2	10	38	17	11 11 53	25 3	16 24	0♓50	21R38	20 9	8 2	12R52	19R59	15R 8
R 3	10	42	14	12 12 4	7♓26	18 19	2 5	21 15	20 18	8 9	12 50	19 58	15 6
C 4	10	46	10	13 12 14	20 1	20 15	3 20	20 53	20 27	8 16	12 47	19 58	15 5
H 5	10	50	7	14 12 22	2♈49	22 10	4 35	20 30	20 36	8 24	12 44	19 58	15 3
6	10	54	3	15 12 28	15 48	24 6	5 50	20 7	20 46	8 31	12 42	19 57	15 2
7	10	58	0	16 12 32	28 59	26 1	7 4	19 43	20 55	8 38	12 39	19 57	15 0
8	11	1	57	17 12 34	12♉21	27 56	8 19	19 20	21 5	8 46	12 37	19 56	14 58
9	11	5	53	18 12 34	25 53	29 49	9 34	18 56	21 14	8 53	12 34	19 56	14 57
10	11	9	50	19 12 31	9♊36	1♈41	10 49	18 32	21 24	9 0	12 31	19 55	14 55
11	11	13	46	20 12 27	23 31	3 32	12 4	18 9	21 34	9 7	12 29	19 55	14 54
12	11	17	43	21 12 20	7♋38	5 20	13 18	17 45	21 44	9 15	12 26	19 54	14 52
13	11	21	39	22 12 11	21 57	7 5	14 33	17 22	21 54	9 22	12 24	19 53	14 50
14	11	25	36	23 12 0	6♌24	8 48	15 48	16 58	22 5	9 29	12 21	19 53	14 49
15	11	29	32	24 11 47	20 57	10 26	17 3	16 35	22 15	9 36	12 18	19 52	14 47
16	11	33	29	25 11 31	5♍29	12 1	18 17	16 12	22 26	9 43	12 16	19 51	14 46
17	11	37	26	26 11 13	19 53	13 31	19 32	15 49	22 36	9 50	12 13	19 50	14 44
18	11	41	22	27 10 53	4♎ 4	14 56	20 47	15 26	22 47	9 58	12 11	19 50	14 43
19	11	45	19	28 10 31	17 54	16 15	22 1	15 4	22 58	10 5	12 8	19 49	14 41
20	11	49	15	29 10 8	1♏22	17 29	23 16	14 42	23 9	10 12	12 6	19 48	14 40
21	11	53	12	0♈ 9 42	14 25	18 36	24 31	14 21	23 19	10 19	12 3	19 47	14 38
22	11	57	8	1 9 15	27 5	19 36	25 45	14 0	23 31	10 26	12 1	19 46	14 37
23	12	1	5	2 8 46	9♐25	20 30	27 0	13 40	23 42	10 33	11 59	19 45	14 35
24	12	5	1	3 8 15	21 30	21 16	28 15	13 20	23 53	10 40	11 56	19 44	14 34
25	12	8	58	4 7 43	3♑24	21 55	29 29	13 0	24 4	10 47	11 54	19 43	14 32
26	12	12	55	5 7 8	15 13	22 26	0♈44	12 41	24 16	10 54	11 51	19 42	14 31
27	12	16	51	6 6 32	27 2	22 50	1 58	12 23	24 27	11 1	11 49	19 41	14 29
28	12	20	48	7 5 55	8♒57	23 6	3 13	12 5	24 39	11 7	11 47	19 40	14 28
29	12	24	44	8 5 15	21 2	23R14	4 27	11 48	24 51	11 14	11 45	19 39	14 26
30	12	28	41	9 4 33	3♓20	23 15	5 42	11 32	25 2	11 21	11 42	19 38	14 25
31	12	32	37	10♈ 3 50	15♓54	23♈ 8	6♈57	11♍16	25♉14	11♓28	11♍40	19♏37	14♍23

THE SUN ENTERS THE SIGN OF ARIES ON MAR 20 AT 20:05.

♈ ARIES ♉ TAURUS ♊ GEMINI ♋ CANCER ♌ LEO ♍ VIRGO ♎ LIBRA

SIDEREAL SUN. MOON. MERCURY. VENUS. MARS. JUPITER. SATURN. URANUS. NEPTUNE. PLUTO.

DAY	TIME	☉	☽	☿	♀	♂	♃	♄	♅	♆	♇
	h m s	° ' "	° '	° '	° '	° '	° '	° '	° '	° '	° '
A 1	12 36 34	11♈ 3 4	28♓45	22♈55	8♈11	11♍ 1	25♉26	11♓34	11♍38	19♏35	14♍22
P 2	12 40 30	12 2 17	11♈51	22R36	9 26	10R47	25 38	11 41	11R36	19R34	14R21
R 3	12 44 27	13 1 27	25 13	22 10	10 40	10 33	25 50	11 48	11 34	19 33	14 19
I 4	12 48 23	14 0 36	8♉48	21 39	11 54	10 21	26 2	11 54	11 31	19 32	14 18
L 5	12 52 20	14 59 42	22 33	21 3	13 9	10 9	26 15	12 1	11 29	19 30	14 17
6	12 56 17	15 58 46	6♊25	20 23	14 23	9 57	26 27	12 7	11 27	19 29	14 15
7	13 0 13	16 57 48	20 24	19 41	15 38	9 47	26 39	12 14	11 25	19 28	14 14
8	13 4 10	17 56 48	4♋27	18 56	16 52	9 37	26 52	12 20	11 23	19 27	14 13
9	13 8 6	18 55 45	18 34	18 9	18 7	9 29	27 4	12 27	11 21	19 25	14 12
10	13 12 3	19 54 40	2♌43	17 23	19 21	9 21	27 17	12 33	11 20	19 24	14 10
11	13 15 59	20 53 33	16 53	16 37	20 35	9 13	27 29	12 39	11 18	19 23	14 9
12	13 19 56	21 52 23	1♍ 2	15 52	21 50	9 7	27 42	12 46	11 16	19 21	14 8
13	13 23 52	22 51 11	15 6	15 9	23 4	9 1	27 55	12 52	11 14	19 20	14 7
14	13 27 49	23 49 57	29 3	14 30	24 18	8 56	28 8	12 58	11 12	19 18	14 6
15	13 31 46	24 48 40	12♎48	13 53	25 32	8 52	28 21	13 4	11 11	19 17	14 4
16	13 35 42	25 47 22	26 17	13 21	26 47	8 49	28 33	13 10	11 9	19 15	14 3
17	13 39 39	26 46 2	9♏28	12 53	28 1	8 46	28 46	13 16	11 8	19 14	14 2
18	13 43 35	27 44 40	22 21	12 29	29 15	8 45	28 59	13 22	11 6	19 13	14 1
19	13 47 32	28 43 16	4♐56	12 11	0♉29	8D44	29 12	13 28	11 4	19 11	14 0
20	13 51 28	29 41 50	17 13	11 57	1 43	8 43	29 26	13 34	11 3	19 10	13 59
21	13 55 25	0♉40 23	29 18	11 48	2 58	8 44	29 39	13 40	11 2	19 8	13 58
22	13 59 21	1 38 54	11♑13	11D45	4 12	8 45	29 52	13 45	11 0	19 6	13 57
23	14 3 18	2 37 23	23 3	11 47	5 26	8 47	0♊ 5	13 51	10 59	19 5	13 56
24	14 7 15	3 35 51	4♒54	11 53	6 40	8 49	0 19	13 57	10 58	19 3	13 55
25	14 11 11	4 34 17	16 51	12 5	7 54	8 53	0 32	14 2	10 56	19 2	13 54
26	14 15 8	5 32 42	28 57	12 21	9 8	8 57	0 45	14 8	10 55	19 0	13 54
27	14 19 4	6 31 4	11♓19	12 42	10 22	9 1	0 59	14 13	10 54	18 59	13 53
28	14 23 1	7 29 26	23 58	13 7	11 36	9 7	1 12	14 18	10 53	18 57	13 52
29	14 26 57	8 27 45	6♈58	13 37	12 51	9 13	1 26	14 24	10 52	18 55	13 51
30	14 30 54	9♉26 3	20♈19	14♈11	14♉ 5	9♍19	1♊39	14♓29	10♍51	18♏54	13♍50

THE SUN ENTERS THE SIGN OF TAURUS ON APR 20 AT 07:26.

DAY	TIME	☉	☽	☿	♀	♂	♃	♄	♅	♆	♇
	h m s	° ' "	° '	° '	° '	° '	° '	° '	° '	° '	° '
M 1	14 34 50	10♉24 19	3♉59	14♈49	15♉19	9♍27	1♊53	14♓34	10♍50	18♏52	13♍50
A 2	14 38 47	11 22 34	17 56	15 30	16 33	9 35	2 6	14 39	10R49	18R51	13R49
Y 3	14 42 44	12 20 47	2♊ 6	16 15	17 47	9 43	2 20	14 44	10 48	18 49	13 48
4	14 46 40	13 18 58	16 25	17 4	19 1	9 52	2 34	14 49	10 47	18 47	13 48
5	14 50 37	14 17 7	0♋48	17 56	20 15	10 2	2 47	14 54	10 47	18 46	13 47
6	14 54 33	15 15 15	15 11	18 51	21 29	10 13	3 1	14 59	10 46	18 44	13 46
7	14 58 30	16 13 20	29 30	19 49	22 42	10 24	3 15	15 4	10 45	18 43	13 46
8	15 2 26	17 11 24	13♌43	20 50	23 56	10 35	3 29	15 8	10 45	18 41	13 45
9	15 6 23	18 9 25	27 47	21 54	25 10	10 47	3 42	15 13	10 44	18 39	13 45
10	15 10 19	19 7 25	11♍42	23 1	26 24	11 0	3 56	15 18	10 44	18 38	13 44
11	15 14 16	20 5 22	25 26	24 11	27 38	11 13	4 10	15 22	10 43	18 36	13 44
12	15 18 13	21 3 18	8♎57	25 23	28 52	11 27	4 24	15 26	10 43	18 34	13 43
13	15 22 9	22 1 12	22 15	26 38	0♊ 6	11 41	4 38	15 31	10 43	18 33	13 43
14	15 26 6	22 59 4	5♏20	27 55	1 20	11 56	4 52	15 35	10 42	18 31	13 43
15	15 30 2	23 56 55	18 10	29 15	2 33	12 11	5 5	15 39	10 42	18 30	13 42
16	15 33 59	24 54 45	0♐46	0♉37	3 47	12 27	5 19	15 43	10 42	18 28	13 42
17	15 37 55	25 52 33	13 8	2 1	5 1	12 43	5 33	15 47	10 42	18 26	13 42
18	15 41 52	26 50 19	25 19	3 28	6 15	13 0	5 47	15 51	10D42	18 25	13 42
19	15 45 48	27 48 5	7♑19	4 57	7 28	13 17	6 1	15 55	10 42	18 23	13 41
20	15 49 45	28 45 49	19 13	6 29	8 42	13 34	6 15	15 59	10 42	18 21	13 41
21	15 53 42	29 43 32	1♒ 4	8 2	9 56	13 52	6 29	16 2	10 42	18 20	13 41
22	15 57 38	0♊41 14	12 55	9 38	11 9	14 11	6 43	16 6	10 42	18 18	13 41
23	16 1 35	1 38 55	24 51	11 16	12 23	14 30	6 57	16 9	10 42	18 17	13 41
24	16 5 31	2 36 35	6♓58	12 57	13 37	14 49	7 11	16 13	10 42	18 15	13 41
25	16 9 28	3 34 13	19 18	14 40	14 51	15 8	7 25	16 16	10 43	18 14	13D41
26	16 13 24	4 31 51	1♈58	16 25	16 4	15 28	7 39	16 19	10 43	18 12	13 41
27	16 17 21	5 29 28	14 59	18 12	17 18	15 49	7 53	16 22	10 44	18 10	13 41
28	16 21 17	6 27 4	28 24	20 1	18 31	16 10	8 7	16 25	10 44	18 9	13 41
29	16 25 14	7 24 39	12♉13	21 53	19 45	16 31	8 21	16 28	10 45	18 7	13 41
30	16 29 11	8 22 13	26 25	23 47	20 59	16 52	8 35	16 31	10 45	18 6	13 41
31	16 33 7	9♊19 46	10♊55	25♉43	22♊12	17♍14	8♊49	16♓34	10♍46	18♏ 4	13♍41

THE SUN ENTERS THE SIGN OF GEMINI ON MAY 21 AT 06:51.

DAY	TIME	☉	☽	☿	♀	♂	♃	♄	♅	♆	♇
	h m s	° ' "	° '	° '	° '	° '	° '	° '	° '	° '	° '
J 1	16 37 4	10♊17 18	25♊38	27♉41	23♊26	17♍37	9♊ 3	16♓37	10♍46	18♏ 3	13♍41
U 2	16 41 0	11 14 49	10♋26	29 41	24 39	17 59	9 17	16 39	10 47	18R 1	13 42
N 3	16 44 57	12 12 19	25 14	1♊43	25 53	18 22	9 31	16 42	10 48	18 0	13 42
E 4	16 48 53	13 9 47	9♌53	3 47	27 6	18 45	9 45	16 44	10 49	17 59	13 42
5	16 52 50	14 7 15	24 19	5 53	28 20	19 9	9 59	16 47	10 50	17 57	13 43
6	16 56 46	15 4 41	8♍29	8 0	29 33	19 33	10 13	16 49	10 51	17 56	13 43
7	17 0 43	16 2 5	22 21	10 8	0♋47	19 57	10 27	16 51	10 52	17 54	13 43
8	17 4 40	16 59 29	5♎53	12 18	2 0	20 22	10 41	16 53	10 53	17 53	13 44
9	17 8 36	17 56 51	19 8	14 29	3 14	20 47	10 55	16 55	10 54	17 52	13 44
10	17 12 33	18 54 13	2♏ 6	16 40	4 27	21 12	11 9	16 57	10 55	17 50	13 45
11	17 16 29	19 51 33	14 50	18 52	5 41	21 37	11 23	16 59	10 56	17 49	13 45
12	17 20 26	20 48 53	27 20	21 4	6 54	22 3	11 37	17 0	10 58	17 48	13 46
13	17 24 22	21 46 12	9♐39	23 16	8 8	22 29	11 51	17 2	10 59	17 46	13 46
14	17 28 19	22 43 30	21 48	25 28	9 21	22 55	12 5	17 3	11 0	17 45	13 47
15	17 32 15	23 40 47	3♑49	27 39	10 34	23 22	12 19	17 5	11 2	17 44	13 48
16	17 36 12	24 38 4	15 45	29 49	11 48	23 48	12 32	17 6	11 3	17 42	13 48
17	17 40 9	25 35 20	27 36	1♋58	13 1	24 15	12 46	17 7	11 5	17 41	13 49
18	17 44 5	26 32 36	9♒26	4 5	14 14	24 43	13 0	17 8	11 6	17 40	13 50
19	17 48 2	27 29 52	21 18	6 11	15 28	25 10	13 14	17 9	11 8	17 39	13 50
20	17 51 58	28 27 7	3♓15	8 16	16 41	25 38	13 28	17 10	11 9	17 38	13 51
21	17 55 55	29 24 22	15 21	10 19	17 54	26 6	13 41	17 11	11 11	17 37	13 52
22	17 59 51	0♋21 37	27 40	12 19	19 7	26 34	13 55	17 11	11 13	17 36	13 53
23	18 3 48	1 18 51	10♈16	14 18	20 21	27 3	14 9	17 12	11 15	17 34	13 54
24	18 7 45	2 16 6	23 13	16 15	21 34	27 32	14 22	17 12	11 16	17 33	13 54
25	18 11 41	3 13 20	6♉35	18 10	22 47	28 0	14 36	17 13	11 18	17 32	13 55
26	18 15 38	4 10 35	20 22	20 3	24 0	28 30	14 49	17 13	11 20	17 31	13 56
27	18 19 34	5 7 49	4♊36	21 53	25 13	28 59	15 3	17 13	11 22	17 30	13 57
28	18 23 31	6 5 4	19 14	23 41	26 27	29 29	15 17	17R13	11 24	17 29	13 58
29	18 27 27	7 2 18	4♋10	25 28	27 40	29 58	15 30	17 13	11 26	17 29	13 59
30	18 31 24	7♋59 33	19♋17	27♋12	28♋53	0♎29	15♊43	17♓13	11♍28	17♏28	14♍ 0

THE SUN ENTERS THE SIGN OF CANCER ON JUN 21 AT 14:56.

♏ SCORPIO ♐ SAGITTARIUS ♑ CAPRICORN ♒ AQUARIUS ♓ PISCES

1965

SIDEREAL. SUN. MOON. MERCURY. VENUS. MARS. JUPITER. SATURN. URANUS. NEPTUNE. PLUTO.

DAY	TIME	☉	☽	☿	♀	♂	♃	♄	♅	♆	♇
	h m s	° ' "	° '	° '	° '	° '	° '	° '	° '	° '	° '
J 1	18 35 20	8♋56 47	4♌25	28♋54	0♌ 6	0♎59	15♊57	17♓13	11♍31	17♏27	14♍ 2
U 2	18 39 17	9 54 0	19 25	0♌33	1 19	1 29	16 10	17R13	11 33	17R26	14 3
L 3	18 43 14	10 51 14	4♍ 9	2 11	2 32	2 0	16 24	17 12	11 35	17 25	14 4
Y 4	18 47 10	11 48 27	18 30	3 46	3 45	2 31	16 37	17 12	11 37	17 24	14 5
5	18 51 7	12 45 39	2♎27	5 19	4 58	3 2	16 50	17 11	11 40	17 23	14 6
6	18 55 3	13 42 51	15 59	6 50	6 11	3 33	17 3	17 10	11 42	17 23	14 7
7	18 59 0	14 40 4	29 7	8 19	7 25	4 4	17 16	17 9	11 44	17 22	14 9
8	19 2 56	15 37 16	11♏54	9 45	8 38	4 36	17 30	17 8	11 47	17 21	14 10
9	19 6 53	16 34 27	24 24	11 9	9 50	5 8	17 43	17 7	11 49	17 21	14 11
10	19 10 49	17 31 39	6♐40	12 31	11 3	5 40	17 56	17 6	11 52	17 20	14 12
11	19 14 46	18 28 51	18 46	13 50	12 16	6 12	18 9	17 5	11 55	17 19	14 14
12	19 18 43	19 26 3	0♑45	15 7	13 29	6 44	18 21	17 4	11 57	17 19	14 15
13	19 22 39	20 23 15	12 39	16 22	14 42	7 17	18 34	17 2	12 0	17 18	14 17
14	19 26 36	21 20 27	24 30	17 34	15 55	7 49	18 47	17 1	12 2	17 18	14 18
15	19 30 32	22 17 40	6♒21	18 44	17 8	8 22	19 0	16 59	12 5	17 17	14 19
16	19 34 29	23 14 53	18 12	19 50	18 21	8 55	19 13	16 58	12 8	17 17	14 21
17	19 38 25	24 12 6	0♓ 7	20 54	19 33	9 28	19 25	16 56	12 11	17 17	14 22
18	19 42 22	25 9 20	12 8	21 56	20 46	10 2	19 38	16 54	12 14	17 16	14 24
19	19 46 18	26 6 35	24 16	22 54	21 59	10 35	19 50	16 52	12 16	17 16	14 25
20	19 50 15	27 3 50	6♈35	23 49	23 12	11 9	20 3	16 50	12 19	17 15	14 27
21	19 54 12	28 1 6	19 10	24 41	24 24	11 42	20 15	16 48	12 22	17 15	14 29
22	19 58 8	28 58 23	2♉ 2	25 30	25 37	12 16	20 28	16 46	12 25	17 15	14 30
23	20 2 5	29 55 40	15 17	26 16	26 50	12 50	20 40	16 43	12 28	17 15	14 32
24	20 6 1	0♌52 59	28 57	26 57	28 2	13 25	20 52	16 41	12 31	17 14	14 33
25	20 9 58	1 50 18	13♊ 4	27 35	29 15	13 59	21 4	16 38	12 34	17 14	14 35
26	20 13 54	2 47 39	27 36	28 10	0♍28	14 34	21 16	16 36	12 37	17 14	14 37
27	20 17 51	3 45 0	12♋31	28 40	1 40	15 8	21 28	16 33	12 40	17 14	14 38
28	20 21 47	4 42 22	27 42	29 6	2 53	15 43	21 40	16 30	12 44	17 14	14 40
29	20 25 44	5 39 45	12♌58	29 27	4 5	16 18	21 52	16 28	12 47	17D14	14 42
30	20 29 41	6 37 9	28 10	29 44	5 18	16 53	22 4	16 25	12 50	17 14	14 44
31	20 33 37	7♌34 33	13♍ 7	29♌56	6♍30	17♎28	22♊16	16♓22	12♍53	17♏14	14♍45

THE SUN ENTERS THE SIGN OF LEO ON JUL 23 AT 01:49.

DAY	TIME	☉	☽	☿	♀	♂	♃	♄	♅	♆	♇
	h m s	° ' "	° '	° '	° '	° '	° '	° '	° '	° '	° '
A 1	20 37 34	8♌31 58	27♍40	0♍ 3	7♍43	18♎ 4	22♊27	16♓19	12♍56	17♏14	14♍47
U 2	20 41 30	9 29 23	11♎46	0R 5	8 55	18 39	22 39	16R16	13 0	17 14	14 49
G 3	20 45 27	10 26 49	25 23	0 2	10 7	19 15	22 50	16 12	13 3	17 14	14 51
U 4	20 49 23	11 24 16	8♏32	29♌54	11 20	19 51	23 2	16 9	13 6	17 14	14 53
S 5	20 53 20	12 21 43	21 16	29 40	12 32	20 27	23 13	16 6	13 10	17 15	14 54
T 6	20 57 16	13 19 11	3♐41	29 22	13 44	21 3	23 24	16 2	13 13	17 15	14 56
7	21 1 13	14 16 40	15 50	28 58	14 57	21 39	23 35	15 59	13 17	17 15	14 58
8	21 5 10	15 14 10	27 50	28 29	16 9	22 15	23 46	15 55	13 20	17 15	15 0
9	21 9 6	16 11 41	9♑42	27 55	17 21	22 52	23 57	15 52	13 23	17 16	15 2
10	21 13 3	17 9 12	21 32	27 17	18 33	23 28	24 8	15 48	13 27	17 16	15 4
11	21 16 59	18 6 45	3♒23	26 36	19 45	24 5	24 19	15 44	13 30	17 16	15 6
12	21 20 56	19 4 18	15 15	25 51	20 57	24 42	24 29	15 40	13 34	17 17	15 8
13	21 24 52	20 1 53	27 11	25 3	22 9	25 19	24 40	15 37	13 37	17 17	15 10
14	21 28 49	20 59 29	9♓13	24 14	23 21	25 56	24 50	15 33	13 41	17 18	15 12
15	21 32 45	21 57 6	21 21	23 23	24 33	26 33	25 1	15 29	13 44	17 18	15 14
16	21 36 42	22 54 44	3♈37	22 33	25 45	27 10	25 11	15 25	13 48	17 19	15 16
17	21 40 39	23 52 24	16 3	21 44	26 57	27 48	25 21	15 21	13 52	17 19	15 18
18	21 44 35	24 50 6	28 41	20 57	28 9	28 25	25 31	15 17	13 55	17 20	15 20
19	21 48 32	25 47 49	11♉35	20 13	29 21	29 3	25 41	15 12	13 59	17 21	15 22
20	21 52 28	26 45 34	24 46	19 33	0♎33	29 41	25 51	15 8	14 2	17 21	15 24
21	21 56 25	27 43 20	8♊19	18 57	1 44	0♏19	26 1	15 4	14 6	17 22	15 26
22	22 0 21	28 41 8	22 14	18 28	2 56	0 57	26 10	15 0	14 10	17 23	15 28
23	22 4 18	29 38 58	6♋34	18 4	4 8	1 35	26 20	14 55	14 13	17 23	15 30
24	22 8 14	0♍36 50	21 16	17 48	5 19	2 13	26 29	14 51	14 17	17 24	15 32
25	22 12 11	1 34 44	6♌15	17D39	6 31	2 51	26 39	14 47	14 21	17 25	15 34
26	22 16 8	2 32 39	21 24	17 37	7 42	3 30	26 48	14 42	14 25	17 26	15 36
27	22 20 4	3 30 35	6♍32	17 44	8 54	4 8	26 57	14 38	14 28	17 27	15 38
28	22 24 1	4 28 33	21 30	17 58	10 5	4 47	27 6	14 33	14 32	17 28	15 41
29	22 27 57	5 26 32	6♎ 7	18 21	11 17	5 26	27 15	14 29	14 36	17 29	15 43
30	22 31 54	6 24 33	20 18	18 52	12 28	6 5	27 23	14 24	14 40	17 30	15 45
31	22 35 50	7♍22 35	4♏ 0	19♌31	13♎39	6♏44	27♊32	14♓20	14♍43	17♏31	15♍47

THE SUN ENTERS THE SIGN OF VIRGO ON AUG 23 AT 08:44.

DAY	TIME	☉	☽	☿	♀	♂	♃	♄	♅	♆	♇
	h m s	° ' "	° '	° '	° '	° '	° '	° '	° '	° '	° '
S 1	22 39 47	8♍20 39	17♏13	20♌17	14♎51	7♏23	27♊40	14♓15	14♍47	17♏32	15♍49
E 2	22 43 43	9 18 44	0♐ 0	21 12	16 2	8 2	27 49	14R11	14 51	17 33	15 51
P 3	22 47 40	10 16 50	12 25	22 13	17 13	8 41	27 57	14 6	14 55	17 34	15 53
T 4	22 51 37	11 14 58	24 34	23 21	18 24	9 21	28 5	14 1	14 58	17 35	15 55
E 5	22 55 33	12 13 8	6♑32	24 35	19 35	10 0	28 13	13 57	15 2	17 36	15 58
M 6	22 59 30	13 11 19	18 23	25 56	20 46	10 40	28 20	13 52	15 6	17 37	16 0
B 7	23 3 26	14 9 31	0♒13	27 22	21 57	11 19	28 28	13 48	15 10	17 38	16 2
E 8	23 7 23	15 7 45	12 4	28 52	23 8	11 59	28 35	13 43	15 13	17 40	16 4
R 9	23 11 19	16 6 0	24 1	0♍27	24 19	12 39	28 43	13 39	15 17	17 41	16 6
10	23 15 16	17 4 17	6♓ 4	2 6	25 30	13 19	28 50	13 34	15 21	17 42	16 8
11	23 19 12	18 2 36	18 16	3 48	26 40	13 59	28 57	13 29	15 25	17 44	16 10
12	23 23 9	19 0 57	0♈36	5 32	27 51	14 40	29 4	13 25	15 29	17 45	16 13
13	23 27 6	19 59 19	13 6	7 19	29 2	15 20	29 11	13 20	15 32	17 46	16 15
14	23 31 2	20 57 44	25 46	9 8	0♏12	16 0	29 17	13 16	15 36	17 48	16 17
15	23 34 59	21 56 11	8♉37	10 58	1 23	16 41	29 24	13 11	15 40	17 49	16 19
16	23 38 55	22 54 39	21 40	12 49	2 33	17 21	29 30	13 7	15 44	17 51	16 21
17	23 42 52	23 53 10	4♊57	14 41	3 43	18 2	29 36	13 2	15 47	17 52	16 23
18	23 46 48	24 51 43	18 29	16 33	4 54	18 43	29 42	12 58	15 51	17 54	16 25
19	23 50 45	25 50 19	2♋19	18 26	6 4	19 24	29 48	12 53	15 55	17 55	16 27
20	23 54 41	26 48 56	16 26	20 18	7 14	20 5	29 53	12 49	15 59	17 57	16 30
21	23 58 38	27 47 36	0♌51	22 10	8 24	20 46	29 59	12 45	16 2	17 58	16 32
22	0 2 35	28 46 18	15 30	24 2	9 34	21 27	0♋ 4	12 40	16 6	18 0	16 34
23	0 6 31	29 45 2	0♍18	25 53	10 44	22 8	0 9	12 36	16 10	18 1	16 36
24	0 10 28	0♎43 49	15 8	27 44	11 54	22 50	0 14	12 32	16 13	18 3	16 38
25	0 14 24	1 42 37	29 50	29 33	13 4	23 31	0 19	12 27	16 17	18 5	16 40
26	0 18 21	2 41 27	14♎18	1♎23	14 14	24 13	0 24	12 23	16 21	18 6	16 42
27	0 22 17	3 40 19	28 23	3 11	15 23	24 54	0 28	12 19	16 24	18 8	16 44
28	0 26 14	4 39 14	12♏ 4	4 58	16 33	25 36	0 32	12 15	16 28	18 10	16 46
29	0 30 10	5 38 10	25 18	6 45	17 42	26 18	0 37	12 11	16 32	18 12	16 48
30	0 34 7	6♎37 7	8♐ 8	8♎31	18♏52	27♏ 0	0♋40	12♓ 7	16♍35	18♏13	16♍50

THE SUN ENTERS THE SIGN OF LIBRA ON SEP 23 AT 06:07.

♈ ARIES ♉ TAURUS ♊ GEMINI ♋ CANCER ♌ LEO ♍ VIRGO ♎ LIBRA

SIDEREAL SUN. MOON. MERCURY. VENUS. MARS. JUPITER. SATURN. URANUS. NEPTUNE. PLUTO.

DAY	TIME	☉	☽	☿	♀	♂	♃	♄	♅	♆	♇
	h m s	° ' "	° '	° '	° '	° '	° '	° '	° '	° '	° '
O 1	0 38 3	7♎36 7	20♐36	10♎16	20♏ 1	27♏42	0♋44	12♓ 3	16♍39	18♏15	16♍52
C 2	0 42 0	8 35 9	2♑47	12 0	21 10	28 24	0 48	11R59	16 43	18 17	16 54
T 3	0 45 57	9 34 12	14 46	13 43	22 19	29 6	0 51	11 56	16 46	18 19	16 56
O 4	0 49 53	10 33 17	26 38	15 26	23 28	29 48	0 54	11 52	16 50	18 21	16 58
B 5	0 53 50	11 32 23	8♒29	17 7	24 37	0♐30	0 57	11 48	16 53	18 23	17 0
E 6	0 57 46	12 31 32	20 23	18 48	25 46	1 13	1 0	11 44	16 57	18 24	17 2
R 7	1 1 43	13 30 42	2♓24	20 28	26 55	1 55	1 3	11 41	17 0	18 26	17 4
8	1 5 39	14 29 54	14 34	22 7	28 4	2 38	1 5	11 37	17 4	18 28	17 6
9	1 9 36	15 29 8	26 55	23 45	29 12	3 21	1 7	11 34	17 7	18 30	17 8
10	1 13 32	16 28 24	9♈30	25 23	0♐21	4 3	1 9	11 31	17 10	18 32	17 10
11	1 17 29	17 27 42	22 17	26 59	1 29	4 46	1 11	11 27	17 14	18 34	17 12
12	1 21 26	18 27 2	5♉17	28 35	2 37	5 29	1 13	11 24	17 17	18 36	17 14
13	1 25 22	19 26 24	18 29	0♏11	3 45	6 12	1 14	11 21	17 21	18 38	17 16
14	1 29 19	20 25 49	1♊52	1 46	4 53	6 55	1 16	11 18	17 24	18 40	17 18
15	1 33 15	21 25 16	15 26	3 20	6 1	7 38	1 17	11 15	17 27	18 42	17 20
16	1 37 12	22 24 45	29 10	4 53	7 8	8 21	1 18	11 12	17 31	18 44	17 22
17	1 41 8	23 24 16	13♋ 4	6 26	8 16	9 5	1 18	11 9	17 34	18 46	17 23
18	1 45 5	24 23 50	27 8	7 58	9 23	9 48	1 19	11 7	17 37	18 48	17 25
19	1 49 1	25 23 26	11♌21	9 29	10 31	10 31	1R19	11 4	17 40	18 50	17 27
20	1 52 58	26 23 4	25 40	11 0	11 38	11 15	1 19	11 2	17 43	18 53	17 29
21	1 56 55	27 22 45	10♍ 3	12 30	12 45	11 59	1 19	10 59	17 47	18 55	17 30
22	2 0 51	28 22 27	24 25	14 0	13 52	12 42	1 18	10 57	17 50	18 57	17 32
23	2 4 48	29 22 12	8♎41	15 28	14 58	13 26	1 18	10 54	17 53	18 59	17 34
24	2 8 44	0♏21 59	22 45	16 57	16 5	14 10	1 17	10 52	17 56	19 1	17 36
25	2 12 41	1 21 48	6♏33	18 24	17 11	14 54	1 16	10 50	17 59	19 3	17 37
26	2 16 37	2 21 39	20 2	19 51	18 17	15 38	1 15	10 48	18 2	19 5	17 39
27	2 20 34	3 21 32	3♐10	21 18	19 23	16 22	1 14	10 46	18 5	19 8	17 41
28	2 24 30	4 21 27	15 57	22 43	20 29	17 6	1 12	10 44	18 8	19 10	17 42
29	2 28 27	5 21 23	28 25	24 8	21 35	17 50	1 10	10 43	18 10	19 12	17 44
30	2 32 24	6 21 21	10♑37	25 32	22 40	18 34	1 8	10 41	18 13	19 14	17 45
31	2 36 20	7♏21 21	22♑38	26♏56	23♐45	19♐19	1♋ 6	10♓40	18♍16	19♏16	17♍47

THE SUN ENTERS THE SIGN OF SCORPIO ON OCT 23 AT 15:11.

DAY	TIME	☉	☽	☿	♀	♂	♃	♄	♅	♆	♇
	h m s	° ' "	° '	° '	° '	° '	° '	° '	° '	° '	° '
N 1	2 40 17	8♏21 23	4♒32	28♏18	24♐50	20♐ 3	1♋ 4	10♓38	18♍19	19♏19	17♍48
O 2	2 44 13	9 21 26	16 24	29 40	25 55	20 48	1R 1	10R37	18 22	19 21	17 50
V 3	2 48 10	10 21 30	28 19	1♐ 0	27 0	21 32	0 59	10 36	18 24	19 23	17 51
E 4	2 52 6	11 21 36	10♓21	2 19	28 4	22 17	0 56	10 35	18 27	19 25	17 53
M 5	2 56 3	12 21 44	22 34	3 38	29 8	23 1	0 53	10 34	18 30	19 28	17 54
B 6	2 59 59	13 21 53	5♈ 2	4 55	0♑12	23 46	0 49	10 33	18 32	19 30	17 56
E 7	3 3 56	14 22 4	17 47	6 10	1 15	24 31	0 46	10 32	18 35	19 32	17 57
R 8	3 7 53	15 22 17	0♉49	7 24	2 18	25 16	0 42	10 31	18 37	19 34	17 58
9	3 11 49	16 22 31	14 9	8 36	3 21	26 1	0 38	10 31	18 40	19 37	18 0
10	3 15 46	17 22 47	27 45	9 46	4 24	26 46	0 34	10 30	18 42	19 39	18 1
11	3 19 42	18 23 5	11♊35	10 54	5 26	27 31	0 30	10 30	18 44	19 41	18 2
12	3 23 39	19 23 25	25 36	11 59	6 28	28 16	0 25	10 29	18 47	19 43	18 3
13	3 27 35	20 23 47	9♋44	13 1	7 30	29 1	0 21	10 29	18 49	19 46	18 5
14	3 31 32	21 24 10	23 56	14 0	8 31	29 46	0 16	10D29	18 51	19 48	18 6
15	3 35 28	22 24 36	8♌10	14 56	9 32	0♑31	0 11	10 29	18 53	19 50	18 7
16	3 39 25	23 25 3	22 22	15 48	10 33	1 17	0 6	10 29	18 55	19 52	18 8
17	3 43 22	24 25 32	6♍32	16 35	11 33	2 2	0 1	10 30	18 57	19 55	18 9
18	3 47 18	25 26 3	20 35	17 16	12 33	2 48	29♊55	10 30	18 59	19 57	18 10
19	3 51 15	26 26 36	4♎32	17 52	13 32	3 33	29 50	10 30	19 1	19 59	18 11
20	3 55 11	27 27 11	18 19	18 22	14 31	4 19	29 44	10 31	19 3	20 1	18 12
21	3 59 8	28 27 47	1♏54	18 44	15 30	5 4	29 38	10 32	19 5	20 4	18 13
22	4 3 4	29 28 25	15 16	18 59	16 28	5 50	29 32	10 32	19 7	20 6	18 14
23	4 7 1	0♐29 5	28 24	19R 4	17 26	6 36	29 26	10 33	19 9	20 8	18 15
24	4 10 57	1 29 46	11♐17	19 0	18 23	7 22	29 19	10 34	19 11	20 10	18 16
25	4 14 54	2 30 28	23 54	18 46	19 20	8 8	29 13	10 35	19 12	20 12	18 17
26	4 18 51	3 31 12	6♑17	18 21	20 16	8 53	29 6	10 37	19 14	20 15	18 18
27	4 22 47	4 31 56	18 27	17 46	21 11	9 39	28 59	10 38	19 16	20 17	18 19
28	4 26 44	5 32 42	0♒28	16 59	22 6	10 25	28 53	10 39	19 17	20 19	18 19
29	4 30 40	6 33 29	12 22	16 2	23 1	11 11	28 46	10 41	19 19	20 21	18 20
30	4 34 37	7♐34 17	24♒14	14♐56	23♑54	11♑58	28♊38	10♓43	19♍20	20♏23	18♍21

THE SUN ENTERS THE SIGN OF SAGITTARIUS ON NOV 22 AT 12:30.

DAY	TIME	☉	☽	☿	♀	♂	♃	♄	♅	♆	♇
	h m s	° ' "	° '	° '	° '	° '	° '	° '	° '	° '	° '
D 1	4 38 33	8♐35 6	6♓ 7	13♐43	24♑48	12♑44	28♊31	10♓44	19♍21	20♏26	18♍22
E 2	4 42 30	9 35 56	18 7	12R24	25 40	13 30	28R24	10 46	19 23	20 28	18 22
C 3	4 46 26	10 36 46	0♈19	11 1	26 32	14 16	28 16	10 48	19 24	20 30	18 23
E 4	4 50 23	11 37 37	12 46	9 39	27 23	15 2	28 9	10 50	19 25	20 32	18 23
M 5	4 54 20	12 38 30	25 33	8 18	28 13	15 49	28 1	10 52	19 26	20 34	18 24
B 6	4 58 16	13 39 23	8♉42	7 3	29 2	16 35	27 54	10 54	19 28	20 36	18 24
E 7	5 2 13	14 40 17	22 14	5 56	29 51	17 21	27 46	10 57	19 29	20 38	18 25
R 8	5 6 9	15 41 12	6♊ 9	4 57	0♒38	18 8	27 38	10 59	19 30	20 40	18 25
9	5 10 6	16 42 8	20 23	4 9	1 25	18 54	27 30	11 2	19 31	20 43	18 26
10	5 14 2	17 43 5	4♋53	3 32	2 11	19 41	27 22	11 4	19 31	20 45	18 26
11	5 17 59	18 44 2	19 31	3 7	2 56	20 27	27 14	11 7	19 32	20 47	18 27
12	5 21 56	19 45 1	4♌11	2D52	3 40	21 14	27 6	11 10	19 33	20 49	18 27
13	5 25 52	20 46 1	18 47	2 48	4 22	22 1	26 58	11 13	19 34	20 51	18 27
14	5 29 49	21 47 2	3♍14	2 55	5 4	22 47	26 50	11 16	19 34	20 53	18 27
15	5 33 45	22 48 4	17 27	3 10	5 44	23 34	26 42	11 19	19 35	20 55	18 28
16	5 37 42	23 49 7	1♎24	3 34	6 24	24 21	26 34	11 22	19 36	20 57	18 28
17	5 41 38	24 50 11	15 5	4 6	7 2	25 8	26 26	11 25	19 36	20 59	18 28
18	5 45 35	25 51 15	28 31	4 45	7 38	25 54	26 18	11 29	19 37	21 1	18 28
19	5 49 31	26 52 21	11♏42	5 29	8 14	26 41	26 9	11 32	19 37	21 2	18 28
20	5 53 28	27 53 27	24 39	6 19	8 48	27 28	26 1	11 36	19 37	21 4	18 28
21	5 57 25	28 54 35	7♐24	7 14	9 20	28 15	25 53	11 40	19 38	21 6	18R28
22	6 1 21	29 55 43	19 57	8 13	9 51	29 2	25 45	11 43	19 38	21 8	18 28
23	6 5 18	0♑56 51	2♑20	9 15	10 21	29 49	25 37	11 47	19 38	21 10	18 28
24	6 9 14	1 58 0	14 33	10 21	10 48	0♒36	25 29	11 51	19 38	21 12	18 28
25	6 13 11	2 59 9	26 38	11 30	11 15	1 23	25 21	11 55	19R38	21 14	18 28
26	6 17 7	4 0 18	8♒35	12 41	11 39	2 10	25 13	11 59	19 38	21 15	18 28
27	6 21 4	5 1 28	20 28	13 54	12 1	2 57	25 5	12 4	19 38	21 17	18 28
28	6 25 0	6 2 37	2♓19	15 10	12 22	3 44	24 57	12 8	19 38	21 19	18 27
29	6 28 57	7 3 47	14 11	16 27	12 40	4 31	24 49	12 12	19 37	21 21	18 27
30	6 32 54	8 4 56	26 9	17 45	12 57	5 19	24 41	12 17	19 37	21 22	18 27
31	6 36 50	9♑ 6 5	8♈16	19♐ 5	13♒11	6♒ 6	24♊34	12♓21	19♍37	21♏24	18♍27

THE SUN ENTERS THE SIGN OF CAPRICORN ON DEC 22 AT 01:41.

♏ SCORPIO ♐ SAGITTARIUS ♑ CAPRICORN ♒ AQUARIUS ♓ PISCES

1966

SIDEREAL TIME. SUN. MOON. MERCURY. VENUS. MARS. JUPITER. SATURN. URANUS. NEPTUNE. PLUTO.

DAY	TIME	☉	☽	☿	♀	♂	♃	♄	♅	♆	♇
	h m s	° ' "	° '	° '	° '	° '	° '	° '	° '	° '	° '
J 1	6 40 47	10♑ 7 14	20♈38	20♐26	13♒24	6♒53	24♊26	12♓26	19♍37	21♏26	18♍26
A 2	6 44 43	11 8 23	3♉20	21 49	13 33	7 40	24R19	12 30	19R36	21 27	18R26
N 3	6 48 40	12 9 32	16 25	23 12	13 41	8 27	24 11	12 35	19 36	21 29	18 26
U 4	6 52 36	13 10 40	29 56	24 36	13 46	9 15	24 4	12 40	19 35	21 30	18 25
A 5	6 56 33	14 11 49	13♊56	26 1	13R49	10 2	23 57	12 45	19 35	21 32	18 25
R 6	7 0 29	15 12 57	28 22	27 27	13 50	10 49	23 49	12 50	19 34	21 33	18 24
Y 7	7 4 26	16 14 5	13♋10	28 53	13 48	11 36	23 42	12 55	19 33	21 35	18 24
8	7 8 23	17 15 13	28 13	0♑20	13 43	12 24	23 36	13 0	19 33	21 36	18 23
9	7 12 19	18 16 20	13♌21	1 48	13 36	13 11	23 29	13 5	19 32	21 38	18 23
10	7 16 16	19 17 28	28 24	3 16	13 27	13 58	23 22	13 11	19 31	21 39	18 22
11	7 20 12	20 18 35	13♍13	4 45	13 14	14 46	23 16	13 16	19 30	21 41	18 21
12	7 24 9	21 19 42	27 41	6 15	13 0	15 33	23 9	13 21	19 29	21 42	18 21
13	7 28 5	22 20 49	11♎46	7 45	12 43	16 20	23 3	13 27	19 28	21 43	18 20
14	7 32 2	23 21 57	25 27	9 15	12 23	17 8	22 57	13 32	19 27	21 45	18 19
15	7 35 59	24 23 4	8♏44	10 47	12 2	17 55	22 51	13 38	19 26	21 46	18 18
16	7 39 55	25 24 11	21 42	12 18	11 38	18 42	22 45	13 44	19 25	21 47	18 18
17	7 43 52	26 25 17	4♐22	13 50	11 12	19 30	22 39	13 49	19 24	21 48	18 17
18	7 47 48	27 26 24	16 50	15 23	10 44	20 17	22 34	13 55	19 23	21 50	18 16
19	7 51 45	28 27 30	29 6	16 56	10 14	21 5	22 29	14 1	19 21	21 51	18 15
20	7 55 41	29 28 36	11♑15	18 30	9 42	21 52	22 23	14 7	19 20	21 52	18 14
21	7 59 38	0♒29 41	23 18	20 5	9 9	22 39	22 18	14 13	19 18	21 53	18 13
22	8 3 34	1 30 45	5♒15	21 40	8 35	23 27	22 14	14 19	19 17	21 54	18 12
23	8 7 31	2 31 49	17 9	23 15	8 0	24 14	22 9	14 25	19 16	21 55	18 11
24	8 11 28	3 32 52	29 1	24 51	7 24	25 2	22 5	14 31	19 14	21 56	18 10
25	8 15 24	4 33 54	10♓53	26 28	6 47	25 49	22 0	14 38	19 12	21 57	18 9
26	8 19 21	5 34 55	22 46	28 5	6 10	26 37	21 56	14 44	19 11	21 58	18 8
27	8 23 17	6 35 54	4♈43	29 43	5 33	27 24	21 52	14 50	19 9	21 59	18 7
28	8 27 14	7 36 53	16 49	1♒21	4 56	28 11	21 48	14 56	19 7	22 0	18 6
29	8 31 10	8 37 51	29 6	3 1	4 20	28 59	21 45	15 3	19 6	22 1	18 5
30	8 35 7	9 38 47	11♉41	4 41	3 44	29 46	21 42	15 9	19 4	22 1	18 4
31	8 39 3	10♒39 42	24♉38	6♒21	3♒10	0♓33	21♊38	15♓16	19♍ 2	22♏ 2	18♍ 3

THE SUN ENTERS THE SIGN OF AQUARIUS ON JAN 20 AT 12:20.

DAY	TIME	☉	☽	☿	♀	♂	♃	♄	♅	♆	♇
	h m s	° ' "	° '	° '	° '	° '	° '	° '	° '	° '	° '
F 1	8 43 0	11♒40 36	8♊ 0	8♒ 2	2♒36	1♓21	21♊35	15♓22	19♍ 0	22♏ 3	18♍ 1
E 2	8 46 57	12 41 29	21 52	9 44	2R 4	2 8	21R33	15 29	18R58	22 4	18R 0
B 3	8 50 53	13 42 20	6♋14	11 27	1 33	2 56	21 30	15 36	18 56	22 4	17 59
R 4	8 54 50	14 43 10	21 2	13 10	1 4	3 43	21 28	15 42	18 54	22 5	17 58
U 5	8 58 46	15 43 59	6♌12	14 55	0 37	4 30	21 26	15 49	18 52	22 6	17 56
A 6	9 2 43	16 44 46	21 33	16 39	0 12	5 18	21 24	15 56	18 50	22 6	17 55
R 7	9 6 39	17 45 33	6♍54	18 25	29♑50	6 5	21 22	16 2	18 48	22 7	17 54
Y 8	9 10 36	18 46 18	22 2	20 11	29 29	6 52	21 20	16 9	18 46	22 7	17 52
9	9 14 32	19 47 1	6♎49	21 58	29 11	7 39	21 19	16 16	18 44	22 8	17 51
10	9 18 29	20 47 44	21 9	23 46	28 56	8 27	21 18	16 23	18 42	22 8	17 50
11	9 22 26	21 48 26	4♏59	25 34	28 43	9 14	21 17	16 30	18 39	22 9	17 48
12	9 26 22	22 49 7	18 21	27 23	28 32	10 1	21 16	16 37	18 37	22 9	17 47
13	9 30 19	23 49 47	1♐18	29 13	28 24	10 48	21 15	16 44	18 35	22 9	17 46
14	9 34 15	24 50 25	13 54	1♓ 3	28 18	11 36	21 15	16 51	18 33	22 10	17 44
15	9 38 12	25 51 3	26 13	2 53	28D15	12 23	21D15	16 58	18 30	22 10	17 43
16	9 42 8	26 51 39	8♑21	4 44	28 14	13 10	21 15	17 5	18 28	22 10	17 41
17	9 46 5	27 52 14	20 21	6 34	28 16	13 57	21 15	17 12	18 25	22 10	17 40
18	9 50 1	28 52 48	2♒16	8 25	28 20	14 44	21 16	17 19	18 23	22 10	17 38
19	9 53 58	29 53 20	14 8	10 16	28 27	15 31	21 16	17 27	18 21	22 11	17 37
20	9 57 55	0♓53 51	26 0	12 5	28 35	16 18	21 17	17 34	18 18	22 11	17 35
21	10 1 51	1 54 20	7♓52	13 55	28 46	17 6	21 18	17 41	18 16	22 11	17 34
22	10 5 48	2 54 48	19 47	15 43	28 59	17 53	21 19	17 48	18 13	22R11	17 32
23	10 9 44	3 55 13	1♈45	17 29	29 14	18 40	21 21	17 55	18 11	22 11	17 31
24	10 13 41	4 55 37	13 47	19 14	29 32	19 27	21 23	18 3	18 8	22 11	17 29
25	10 17 37	5 56 0	25 58	20 56	29 51	20 14	21 24	18 10	18 6	22 11	17 28
26	10 21 34	6 56 20	8♉18	22 35	0♒12	21 1	21 26	18 17	18 3	22 11	17 26
27	10 25 30	7 56 38	20 53	24 12	0 35	21 47	21 29	18 25	18 1	22 10	17 24
28	10 29 27	8♓56 55	3♊46	25♓44	0♒59	22♓34	21♊31	18♓32	17♍58	22♏10	17♍23

THE SUN ENTERS THE SIGN OF PISCES ON FEB 19 AT 02:38.

DAY	TIME	☉	☽	☿	♀	♂	♃	♄	♅	♆	♇
	h m s	° ' "	° '	° '	° '	° '	° '	° '	° '	° '	° '
M 1	10 33 24	9♓57 9	17♊ 1	27♓12	1♒25	23♓21	21♊34	18♓39	17♍55	22♏10	17♍21
A 2	10 37 20	10 57 21	0♋41	28 34	1 53	24 8	21 36	18 47	17R53	22R10	17R20
R 3	10 41 17	11 57 32	14 50	29 51	2 23	24 55	21 39	18 54	17 50	22 10	17 18
C 4	10 45 13	12 57 40	29 25	1♈ 1	2 54	25 42	21 43	19 1	17 48	22 9	17 17
H 5	10 49 10	13 57 46	14♌23	2 5	3 26	26 28	21 46	19 9	17 45	22 9	17 15
6	10 53 6	14 57 50	29 36	3 2	4 0	27 15	21 50	19 16	17 42	22 9	17 13
7	10 57 3	15 57 52	14♍55	3 50	4 35	28 2	21 53	19 23	17 40	22 8	17 12
8	11 0 59	16 57 52	0♎ 7	4 30	5 12	28 48	21 57	19 31	17 37	22 8	17 10
9	11 4 56	17 57 50	15 2	5 2	5 50	29 35	22 1	19 38	17 35	22 7	17 9
10	11 8 53	18 57 47	29 32	5 25	6 29	0♈21	22 6	19 46	17 32	22 7	17 7
11	11 12 49	19 57 42	13♏33	5 39	7 9	1 8	22 10	19 53	17 29	22 6	17 5
12	11 16 46	20 57 35	27 4	5R44	7 50	1 54	22 15	20 0	17 27	22 6	17 4
13	11 20 42	21 57 27	10♐ 8	5 41	8 33	2 41	22 19	20 8	17 24	22 5	17 2
14	11 24 39	22 57 17	22 48	5 29	9 16	3 27	22 24	20 15	17 21	22 5	17 1
15	11 28 35	23 57 5	5♑ 9	5 9	10 1	4 14	22 30	20 23	17 19	22 4	16 59
16	11 32 32	24 56 52	17 15	4 41	10 46	5 0	22 35	20 30	17 16	22 3	16 57
17	11 36 28	25 56 37	29 13	4 7	11 32	5 46	22 40	20 37	17 14	22 3	16 56
18	11 40 25	26 56 20	11♒ 5	3 27	12 19	6 33	22 46	20 45	17 11	22 2	16 54
19	11 44 22	27 56 1	22 56	2 41	13 7	7 19	22 52	20 52	17 8	22 1	16 53
20	11 48 18	28 55 41	4♓47	1 52	13 56	8 5	22 58	20 59	17 6	22 0	16 51
21	11 52 15	29 55 18	16 43	1 0	14 46	8 51	23 4	21 7	17 3	21 59	16 50
22	11 56 11	0♈54 53	28 43	0 6	15 36	9 38	23 10	21 14	17 1	21 59	16 48
23	12 0 8	1 54 27	10♈49	29♓12	16 27	10 24	23 16	21 21	16 58	21 58	16 47
24	12 4 4	2 53 58	23 3	28 18	17 19	11 10	23 23	21 29	16 56	21 57	16 45
25	12 8 1	3 53 28	5♉25	27 26	18 11	11 56	23 30	21 36	16 53	21 56	16 43
26	12 11 57	4 52 55	17 57	26 37	19 4	12 42	23 37	21 43	16 51	21 55	16 42
27	12 15 54	5 52 20	0♊42	25 51	19 57	13 28	23 44	21 51	16 48	21 54	16 40
28	12 19 50	6 51 43	13 41	25 9	20 51	14 13	23 51	21 58	16 46	21 53	16 39
29	12 23 47	7 51 3	26 58	24 32	21 46	14 59	23 58	22 5	16 44	21 52	16 38
30	12 27 44	8 50 21	10♋35	24 0	22 41	15 45	24 6	22 12	16 41	21 51	16 36
31	12 31 40	9♈49 37	24♋33	23♓34	23♒37	16♈31	24♊13	22♓20	16♍39	21♏50	16♍35

THE SUN ENTERS THE SIGN OF ARIES ON MAR 21 AT 01:53.

♈ ARIES ♉ TAURUS ♊ GEMINI ♋ CANCER ♌ LEO ♍ VIRGO ♎ LIBRA

SIDEREAL. SUN. MOON. MERCURY. VENUS. MARS. JUPITER. SATURN. URANUS. NEPTUNE. PLUTO.

DAY	TIME	☉	☽	☿	♀	♂	♃	♄	♅	♆	♇
	h m s	° ' "	° '	° '	° '	° '	° '	° '	° '	° '	° '
A 1	12 35 37	10♈48 51	8♌52	23♓13	24♒33	17♈17	24♊21	22♓27	16♍37	21♏49	16♍33
P 2	12 39 33	11 48 2	23 30	22R58	25 30	18 2	24 29	22 34	16R34	21R47	16R32
R 3	12 43 30	12 47 11	8♍22	22 48	26 27	18 48	24 37	22 41	16 32	21 46	16 30
I 4	12 47 26	13 46 17	23 21	22D44	27 25	19 33	24 45	22 48	16 30	21 45	16 29
L 5	12 51 23	14 45 21	8♎17	22 46	28 23	20 19	24 53	22 55	16 28	21 44	16 28
6	12 55 19	15 44 24	23 2	22 53	29 21	21 4	25 2	23 2	16 25	21 43	16 26
7	12 59 16	16 43 24	7♏28	23 5	0♓20	21 50	25 10	23 9	16 23	21 41	16 25
8	13 3 13	17 42 22	21 30	23 23	1 19	22 35	25 19	23 16	16 21	21 40	16 24
9	13 7 9	18 41 19	5♐6	23 45	2 19	23 20	25 28	23 23	16 19	21 39	16 22
10	13 11 6	19 40 14	18 16	24 12	3 19	24 6	25 36	23 30	16 17	21 38	16 21
11	13 15 2	20 39 7	1♑2	24 43	4 19	24 51	25 45	23 37	16 15	21 36	16 20
12	13 18 59	21 37 58	13 28	25 18	5 20	25 36	25 55	23 44	16 13	21 35	16 19
13	13 22 55	22 36 48	25 38	25 57	6 21	26 21	26 4	23 51	16 11	21 34	16 17
14	13 26 52	23 35 36	7♒37	26 40	7 22	27 6	26 13	23 57	16 9	21 32	16 16
15	13 30 48	24 34 22	19 31	27 27	8 24	27 52	26 23	24 4	16 7	21 31	16 15
16	13 34 45	25 33 6	1♓22	28 17	9 26	28 37	26 32	24 11	16 5	21 29	16 14
17	13 38 42	26 31 49	13 16	29 10	10 28	29 21	26 42	24 17	16 3	21 28	16 13
18	13 42 38	27 30 30	25 15	0♈6	11 31	0♉6	26 52	24 24	16 2	21 26	16 11
19	13 46 35	28 29 9	7♈21	1 5	12 33	0 51	27 2	24 31	16 0	21 25	16 10
20	13 50 31	29 27 46	19 38	2 7	13 37	1 36	27 12	24 37	15 58	21 24	16 9
21	13 54 28	0♉26 21	2♉5	3 12	14 40	2 21	27 22	24 44	15 57	21 22	16 8
22	13 58 24	1 24 55	14 44	4 19	15 43	3 6	27 32	24 50	15 55	21 21	16 7
23	14 2 21	2 23 26	27 35	5 29	16 47	3 50	27 42	24 57	15 53	21 19	16 6
24	14 6 17	3 21 56	10♊39	6 41	17 51	4 35	27 53	25 3	15 52	21 18	16 5
25	14 10 14	4 20 23	23 57	7 55	18 55	5 19	28 3	25 9	15 50	21 16	16 4
26	14 14 11	5 18 49	7♋27	9 12	20 0	6 4	28 14	25 16	15 49	21 14	16 3
27	14 18 7	6 17 12	21 12	10 31	21 4	6 48	28 24	25 22	15 48	21 13	16 2
28	14 22 4	7 15 34	5♌10	11 52	22 9	7 33	28 35	25 28	15 46	21 11	16 2
29	14 26 0	8 13 53	19 21	13 15	23 14	8 17	28 46	25 34	15 45	21 10	16 1
30	14 29 57	9♉12 10	3♍42	14♈40	24♓19	9♉1	28♊57	25♓40	15♍44	21♏8	16♍0

THE SUN ENTERS THE SIGN OF TAURUS ON APR 20 AT 13:12.

DAY	TIME	☉	☽	☿	♀	♂	♃	♄	♅	♆	♇
	h m s	° ' "	° '	° '	° '	° '	° '	° '	° '	° '	° '
M 1	14 33 53	10♉10 24	18♍11	16♈8	25♓24	9♉46	29♊8	25♓46	15♍43	21♏7	15♍59
A 2	14 37 50	11 8 37	2♎43	17 37	26 30	10 30	29 19	25 52	15R41	21R5	15R58
Y 3	14 41 46	12 6 48	17 12	19 8	27 36	11 14	29 30	25 58	15 40	21 3	15 58
4	14 45 43	13 4 57	1♏33	20 41	28 41	11 58	29 42	26 4	15 39	21 2	15 57
5	14 49 40	14 3 4	15 40	22 16	29 47	12 42	29 53	26 10	15 38	21 0	15 56
6	14 53 36	15 1 10	29 30	23 53	0♈54	13 26	0♋4	26 15	15 37	20 59	15 55
7	14 57 33	15 59 14	12♐59	25 32	2 0	14 10	0 16	26 21	15 36	20 57	15 55
8	15 1 29	16 57 17	26 7	27 13	3 6	14 54	0 27	26 27	15 36	20 55	15 54
9	15 5 26	17 55 18	8♑54	28 56	4 13	15 38	0 39	26 32	15 35	20 54	15 54
10	15 9 22	18 53 18	21 23	0♉40	5 20	16 21	0 51	26 38	15 34	20 52	15 53
11	15 13 19	19 51 16	3♒36	2 27	6 27	17 5	1 3	26 43	15 33	20 50	15 53
12	15 17 15	20 49 13	15 39	4 16	7 34	17 49	1 14	26 48	15 33	20 49	15 52
13	15 21 12	21 47 9	27 34	6 6	8 41	18 32	1 26	26 54	15 32	20 47	15 52
14	15 25 9	22 45 3	9♓27	7 59	9 48	19 16	1 38	26 59	15 32	20 46	15 51
15	15 29 5	23 42 56	21 22	9 53	10 56	20 0	1 50	27 4	15 31	20 44	15 51
16	15 33 2	24 40 48	3♈23	11 49	12 3	20 43	2 2	27 9	15 31	20 42	15 50
17	15 36 58	25 38 39	15 35	13 48	13 11	21 26	2 15	27 14	15 30	20 41	15 50
18	15 40 55	26 36 28	28 0	15 48	14 19	22 10	2 27	27 19	15 30	20 39	15 50
19	15 44 51	27 34 17	10♉40	17 50	15 26	22 53	2 39	27 24	15 30	20 37	15 50
20	15 48 48	28 32 3	23 36	19 53	16 34	23 36	2 51	27 29	15 29	20 36	15 49
21	15 52 44	29 29 49	6♊49	21 58	17 42	24 20	3 4	27 34	15 29	20 34	15 49
22	15 56 41	0♊27 33	20 18	24 5	18 51	25 3	3 16	27 38	15 29	20 33	15 49
23	16 0 38	1 25 16	4♋1	26 13	19 59	25 46	3 29	27 43	15D29	20 31	15 49
24	16 4 34	2 22 58	17 55	28 22	21 7	26 29	3 41	27 47	15 29	20 29	15 49
25	16 8 31	3 20 38	1♌59	0♊33	22 16	27 12	3 54	27 52	15 29	20 28	15 48
26	16 12 27	4 18 16	16 9	2 44	23 24	27 55	4 7	27 56	15 29	20 26	15 48
27	16 16 24	5 15 53	0♍22	4 55	24 33	28 38	4 19	28 1	15 29	20 25	15D48
28	16 20 20	6 13 28	14 36	7 7	25 42	29 21	4 32	28 5	15 30	20 23	15 48
29	16 24 17	7 11 2	28 49	9 19	26 50	0♊3	4 45	28 9	15 30	20 22	15 48
30	16 28 13	8 8 35	12♎57	11 31	27 59	0 46	4 58	28 13	15 30	20 20	15 49
31	16 32 10	9♊6 6	26♎59	13♊42	29♈8	1♊29	5♋11	28♓17	15♍30	20♏18	15♍49

THE SUN ENTERS THE SIGN OF GEMINI ON MAY 21 AT 12:32.

DAY	TIME	☉	☽	☿	♀	♂	♃	♄	♅	♆	♇
	h m s	° ' "	° '	° '	° '	° '	° '	° '	° '	° '	° '
J 1	16 36 7	10♊3 35	10♏52	15♊52	0♉17	2♊11	5♋23	28♓21	15♍31	20♏17	15♍49
U 2	16 40 3	11 1 4	24 33	18 2	1 26	2 54	5 36	28 25	15 31	20R15	15 49
N 3	16 44 0	11 58 32	8♐1	20 10	2 36	3 36	5 49	28 28	15 32	20 14	15 49
E 4	16 47 56	12 55 58	21 14	22 16	3 45	4 19	6 2	28 32	15 32	20 12	15 49
5	16 51 53	13 53 24	4♑11	24 21	4 54	5 1	6 15	28 35	15 33	20 11	15 50
6	16 55 49	14 50 49	16 52	26 24	6 4	5 44	6 29	28 39	15 34	20 10	15 50
7	16 59 46	15 48 13	29 18	28 25	7 13	6 26	6 42	28 42	15 34	20 8	15 50
8	17 3 42	16 45 37	11♒31	0♋24	8 23	7 8	6 55	28 46	15 35	20 7	15 50
9	17 7 39	17 43 0	23 33	2 20	9 32	7 50	7 8	28 49	15 36	20 5	15 51
10	17 11 36	18 40 22	5♓29	4 14	10 42	8 33	7 21	28 52	15 37	20 4	15 51
11	17 15 32	19 37 43	17 22	6 6	11 52	9 15	7 34	28 55	15 38	20 3	15 52
12	17 19 29	20 35 4	29 17	7 56	13 2	9 57	7 48	28 58	15 39	20 1	15 52
13	17 23 25	21 32 25	11♈19	9 43	14 11	10 39	8 1	29 1	15 40	20 0	15 53
14	17 27 22	22 29 45	23 32	11 28	15 21	11 21	8 14	29 3	15 41	19 59	15 53
15	17 31 18	23 27 5	6♉1	13 10	16 31	12 3	8 28	29 6	15 42	19 57	15 54
16	17 35 15	24 24 24	18 49	14 49	17 42	12 44	8 41	29 9	15 43	19 56	15 54
17	17 39 11	25 21 43	1♊58	16 27	18 52	13 26	8 54	29 11	15 45	19 55	15 55
18	17 43 8	26 19 2	15 30	18 1	20 2	14 8	9 8	29 14	15 46	19 53	15 56
19	17 47 5	27 16 20	29 22	19 33	21 12	14 50	9 21	29 16	15 47	19 52	15 56
20	17 51 1	28 13 38	13♋31	21 3	22 23	15 31	9 35	29 18	15 49	19 51	15 57
21	17 54 58	29 10 55	27 54	22 29	23 33	16 13	9 48	29 20	15 50	19 50	15 58
22	17 58 54	0♋8 12	12♌23	23 54	24 43	16 55	10 2	29 22	15 52	19 49	15 59
23	18 2 51	1 5 27	26 54	25 15	25 54	17 36	10 15	29 24	15 53	19 48	15 59
24	18 6 47	2 2 42	11♍20	26 34	27 4	18 18	10 29	29 26	15 55	19 46	16 0
25	18 10 44	2 59 57	25 38	27 50	28 15	18 59	10 42	29 28	15 56	19 45	16 1
26	18 14 41	3 57 11	9♎45	29 4	29 26	19 40	10 56	29 29	15 58	19 44	16 2
27	18 18 37	4 54 24	23 39	0♌14	0♊36	20 22	11 9	29 31	16 0	19 43	16 3
28	18 22 34	5 51 36	7♏21	1 22	1 47	21 3	11 23	29 32	16 2	19 42	16 4
29	18 26 30	6 48 49	20 50	2 26	2 58	21 44	11 36	29 33	16 4	19 41	16 5
30	18 30 27	7♋46 1	4♐7	3♌28	4♊9	22♊25	11♋50	29♓35	16♍5	19♏40	16♍6

THE SUN ENTERS THE SIGN OF CANCER ON JUN 21 AT 20:34.

♏ SCORPIO ♐ SAGITTARIUS ♑ CAPRICORN ♒ AQUARIUS ♓ PISCES

1966

SIDEREAL TIME · SUN · MOON · MERCURY · VENUS · MARS · JUPITER · SATURN · URANUS · NEPTUNE · PLUTO

DAY	TIME			☉	☽	☿	♀	♂	♃	♄	♅	♆	♇
	h	m	s	° ' "	° '	° '	° '	° '	° '	° '	° '	° '	° '
J 1	18	34	23	8♋43 12	17♐12	4♌26	5♊20	23♊ 6	12♋ 3	29♓36	16♍ 7	19♏39	16♍ 7
U 2	18	38	20	9 40 24	0♑ 4	5 21	6 31	23 47	12 17	29 37	16 9	19R38	16 8
L 3	18	42	16	10 37 35	12 45	6 13	7 42	24 28	12 30	29 38	16 11	19 38	16 9
Y 4	18	46	13	11 34 46	25 14	7 1	8 53	25 9	12 44	29 38	16 13	19 37	16 10
5	18	50	10	12 31 57	7♒32	7 46	10 4	25 50	12 58	29 39	16 16	19 36	16 11
6	18	54	6	13 29 9	19 40	8 26	11 15	26 31	13 11	29 40	16 18	19 35	16 12
7	18	58	3	14 26 20	1♓40	9 3	12 26	27 12	13 25	29 40	16 20	19 34	16 14
8	19	1	59	15 23 32	13 33	9 37	13 37	27 53	13 38	29 41	16 22	19 34	16 15
9	19	5	56	16 20 44	25 25	10 5	14 49	28 33	13 52	29 41	16 24	19 33	16 16
10	19	9	52	17 17 56	7♈18	10 30	16 0	29 14	14 5	29 41	16 27	19 32	16 17
11	19	13	49	18 15 9	19 18	10 50	17 11	29 54	14 19	29R41	16 29	19 31	16 19
12	19	17	45	19 12 22	1♉30	11 6	18 23	0♋35	14 32	29 41	16 31	19 31	16 20
13	19	21	42	20 9 36	13 59	11 17	19 34	1 16	14 46	29 41	16 34	19 30	16 21
14	19	25	39	21 6 50	26 48	11R24	20 46	1 56	14 59	29 41	16 36	19 30	16 23
15	19	29	35	22 4 5	10♊ 3	11 25	21 58	2 37	15 13	29 41	16 39	19 29	16 24
16	19	33	32	23 1 20	23 44	11 22	23 9	3 17	15 26	29 40	16 41	19 28	16 25
17	19	37	28	23 58 36	7♋51	11 14	24 21	3 57	15 40	29 40	16 44	19 28	16 27
18	19	41	25	24 55 53	22 21	11 1	25 33	4 38	15 53	29 39	16 47	19 28	16 28
19	19	45	21	25 53 10	7♌ 8	10 44	26 45	5 18	16 7	29 38	16 49	19 27	16 30
20	19	49	18	26 50 27	22 3	10 22	27 57	5 58	16 20	29 38	16 52	19 27	16 31
21	19	53	14	27 47 45	6♍57	9 56	29 8	6 38	16 34	29 37	16 55	19 26	16 33
22	19	57	11	28 45 2	21 43	9 25	0♋20	7 18	16 47	29 36	16 58	19 26	16 35
23	20	1	8	29 42 20	6♎13	8 52	1 32	7 58	17 0	29 35	17 0	19 26	16 36
24	20	5	4	0♌39 39	20 25	8 15	2 44	8 38	17 14	29 33	17 3	19 25	16 38
25	20	9	1	1 36 57	4♏16	7 35	3 56	9 18	17 27	29 32	17 6	19 25	16 39
26	20	12	57	2 34 16	17 48	6 53	5 9	9 58	17 40	29 31	17 9	19 25	16 41
27	20	16	54	3 31 36	1♐ 3	6 10	6 21	10 38	17 54	29 29	17 12	19 25	16 43
28	20	20	50	4 28 56	14 2	5 27	7 33	11 18	18 7	29 28	17 15	19 25	16 44
29	20	24	47	5 26 16	26 48	4 43	8 45	11 58	18 20	29 26	17 18	19 25	16 46
30	20	28	44	6 23 37	9♑22	4 1	9 58	12 37	18 33	29 24	17 21	19 24	16 48
31	20	32	40	7♌20 59	21♑47	3♌20	11♋10	13♋17	18♋47	29♓22	17♍24	19♏24	16♍49

THE SUN ENTERS THE SIGN OF LEO ON JUL 23 AT 07:24.

DAY	TIME			☉	☽	☿	♀	♂	♃	♄	♅	♆	♇
	h	m	s	° ' "	° '	° '	° '	° '	° '	° '	° '	° '	° '
A 1	20	36	37	8♌18 21	4♒ 3	2♌42	12♋22	13♋57	19♋ 0	29♓20	17♍27	19♏24	16♍51
U 2	20	40	33	9 15 45	16 11	2R 7	13 35	14 36	19 13	29R18	17 31	19D24	16 53
G 3	20	44	30	10 13 9	28 12	1 36	14 47	15 16	19 26	29 16	17 34	19 24	16 55
U 4	20	48	26	11 10 34	10♓ 8	1 10	16 0	15 55	19 39	29 14	17 37	19 24	16 57
S 5	20	52	23	12 8 0	21 59	0 48	17 12	16 35	19 52	29 12	17 40	19 25	16 58
T 6	20	56	19	13 5 27	3♈49	0 33	18 25	17 14	20 5	29 9	17 43	19 25	17 0
7	21	0	16	14 2 55	15 42	0D23	19 38	17 53	20 18	29 7	17 47	19 25	17 2
8	21	4	12	15 0 25	27 40	0 20	20 51	18 33	20 31	29 4	17 50	19 25	17 4
9	21	8	9	15 57 56	9♉49	0 24	22 3	19 12	20 44	29 2	17 53	19 25	17 6
10	21	12	6	16 55 28	22 15	0 34	23 16	19 51	20 56	28 59	17 57	19 26	17 8
11	21	16	2	17 53 2	5♊ 1	0 51	24 29	20 30	21 9	28 56	18 0	19 26	17 10
12	21	19	59	18 50 37	18 14	1 15	25 42	21 10	21 22	28 53	18 3	19 26	17 12
13	21	23	55	19 48 14	1♋55	1 46	26 55	21 49	21 35	28 50	18 7	19 27	17 14
14	21	27	52	20 45 52	16 5	2 24	28 8	22 28	21 47	28 47	18 10	19 27	17 16
15	21	31	48	21 43 32	0♌43	3 9	29 21	23 7	22 0	28 44	18 14	19 27	17 18
16	21	35	45	22 41 13	15 42	4 1	0♌34	23 46	22 12	28 41	18 17	19 28	17 20
17	21	39	42	23 38 55	0♍54	4 59	1 47	24 25	22 25	28 37	18 21	19 28	17 22
18	21	43	38	24 36 38	16 7	6 4	3 0	25 4	22 37	28 34	18 24	19 29	17 24
19	21	47	35	25 34 22	1♎11	7 15	4 14	25 42	22 50	28 30	18 28	19 29	17 26
20	21	51	31	26 32 8	15 58	8 31	5 27	26 21	23 2	28 27	18 31	19 30	17 28
21	21	55	28	27 29 55	0♏21	9 53	6 40	27 0	23 14	28 23	18 35	19 31	17 30
22	21	59	24	28 27 43	14 19	11 21	7 54	27 39	23 26	28 20	18 39	19 31	17 32
23	22	3	21	29 25 32	27 52	12 53	9 7	28 17	23 39	28 16	18 42	19 32	17 34
24	22	7	17	0♍23 22	11♐ 2	14 30	10 21	28 56	23 51	28 12	18 46	19 33	17 36
25	22	11	14	1 21 13	23 53	16 10	11 34	29 35	24 3	28 8	18 49	19 33	17 38
26	22	15	10	2 19 6	6♑28	17 54	12 48	0♌13	24 15	28 4	18 53	19 34	17 40
27	22	19	7	3 17 0	18 50	19 42	14 1	0 52	24 26	28 1	18 57	19 35	17 42
28	22	23	4	4 14 55	1♒ 3	21 32	15 15	1 30	24 38	27 57	19 0	19 36	17 44
29	22	27	0	5 12 52	13 8	23 24	16 28	2 8	24 50	27 52	19 4	19 37	17 46
30	22	30	57	6 10 50	25 7	25 17	17 42	2 47	25 2	27 48	19 8	19 38	17 49
31	22	34	53	7♍ 8 49	7♓ 2	27♌12	18♌56	3♌25	25♋13	27♓44	19♍12	19♏39	17♍51

THE SUN ENTERS THE SIGN OF VIRGO ON AUG 23 AT 14:18.

DAY	TIME			☉	☽	☿	♀	♂	♃	♄	♅	♆	♇
	h	m	s	° ' "	° '	° '	° '	° '	° '	° '	° '	° '	° '
S 1	22	38	50	8♍ 6 50	18♓55	29♌ 9	20♌ 9	4♌ 3	25♋25	27♓40	19♍15	19♏40	17♍53
E 2	22	42	46	9 4 53	0♈45	1♍ 5	21 23	4 41	25 36	27R36	19 19	19 41	17 55
P 3	22	46	43	10 2 58	12 37	3 2	22 37	5 20	25 48	27 31	19 23	19 42	17 57
T 4	22	50	39	11 1 4	24 31	5 0	23 51	5 58	25 59	27 27	19 26	19 43	17 59
E 5	22	54	36	11 59 12	6♉31	6 57	25 5	6 36	26 10	27 23	19 30	19 44	18 1
M 6	22	58	33	12 57 23	18 42	8 53	26 19	7 14	26 22	27 18	19 34	19 45	18 3
B 7	23	2	29	13 55 35	1♊ 6	10 49	27 33	7 52	26 33	27 14	19 38	19 46	18 6
E 8	23	6	26	14 53 49	13 50	12 45	28 47	8 30	26 44	27 9	19 41	19 47	18 8
R 9	23	10	22	15 52 6	26 57	14 40	0♍ 1	9 8	26 55	27 5	19 45	19 48	18 10
10	23	14	19	16 50 24	10♋32	16 34	1 15	9 46	27 5	27 0	19 49	19 50	18 12
11	23	18	15	17 48 45	24 35	18 27	2 29	10 23	27 16	26 56	19 53	19 51	18 14
12	23	22	12	18 47 8	9♌ 7	20 19	3 43	11 1	27 27	26 51	19 57	19 52	18 16
13	23	26	8	19 45 32	24 3	22 10	4 58	11 39	27 37	26 47	20 0	19 53	18 19
14	23	30	5	20 43 59	9♍15	24 0	6 12	12 17	27 48	26 42	20 4	19 55	18 21
15	23	34	2	21 42 27	24 33	25 48	7 26	12 54	27 58	26 38	20 8	19 56	18 23
16	23	37	58	22 40 57	9♎46	27 36	8 41	13 32	28 9	26 33	20 12	19 57	18 25
17	23	41	55	23 39 29	24 44	29 23	9 55	14 9	28 19	26 28	20 16	19 59	18 27
18	23	45	51	24 38 3	9♏20	1♎ 9	11 9	14 47	28 29	26 24	20 19	20 0	18 29
19	23	49	48	25 36 39	23 28	2 54	12 24	15 24	28 39	26 19	20 23	20 2	18 32
20	23	53	44	26 35 16	7♐ 9	4 37	13 38	16 2	28 49	26 14	20 27	20 3	18 34
21	23	57	41	27 33 55	20 23	6 20	14 53	16 39	28 59	26 10	20 31	20 5	18 36
22	0	1	37	28 32 36	3♑15	8 2	16 7	17 16	29 8	26 5	20 34	20 6	18 38
23	0	5	34	29 31 18	15 47	9 42	17 22	17 53	29 18	26 0	20 38	20 8	18 40
24	0	9	31	0♎30 2	28 4	11 22	18 36	18 31	29 27	25 56	20 42	20 9	18 42
25	0	13	27	1 28 48	10♒10	13 1	19 51	19 8	29 37	25 51	20 46	20 11	18 44
26	0	17	24	2 27 35	22 9	14 38	21 5	19 45	29 46	25 47	20 49	20 13	18 47
27	0	21	20	3 26 24	4♓ 3	16 15	22 20	20 22	29 55	25 42	20 53	20 14	18 49
28	0	25	17	4 25 15	15 55	17 51	23 35	20 59	0♌ 4	25 37	20 57	20 16	18 51
29	0	29	13	5 24 8	27 46	19 26	24 49	21 36	0 13	25 33	21 0	20 18	18 53
30	0	33	10	6♎23 3	9♈40	21♎ 0	26♍ 4	22♌13	0♌22	25♓28	21♍ 4	20♏19	18♍55

THE SUN ENTERS THE SIGN OF LIBRA ON SEP 23 AT 11:44.

♈ ARIES ♉ TAURUS ♊ GEMINI ♋ CANCER ♌ LEO ♍ VIRGO ♎ LIBRA

1966

SIDEREAL SUN... MOON.... MERCURY VENUS... MARS... JUPITER SATURN. URANUS. NEPTUNE PLUTO..

DAY	TIME	☉	☽	☿	♀	♂	♃	♄	♅	♆	♇
	h m s	° ' "	° '	° '	° '	° '	° '	° '	° '	° '	° '
O 1	0 37 6	7♎22 0	21♈36	22♎34	27♍19	22♌50	0♌30	25♓24	21♍ 8	20♏21	18♍57
C 2	0 41 3	8 20 59	3♉37	24 6	28 34	23 26	0 39	25R19	21 12	20 23	18 59
T 3	0 45 0	9 20 0	15 46	25 38	29 48	24 3	0 47	25 15	21 15	20 25	19 1
O 4	0 48 56	10 19 3	28 4	27 8	1♎ 3	24 40	0 56	25 10	21 19	20 27	19 3
B 5	0 52 53	11 18 9	10♊35	28 38	2 18	25 17	1 4	25 6	21 22	20 28	19 5
E 6	0 56 49	12 17 17	23 22	0♏ 7	3 33	25 53	1 12	25 2	21 26	20 30	19 7
R 7	1 0 46	13 16 28	6♋29	1 35	4 48	26 30	1 20	24 57	21 30	20 32	19 9
8	1 4 42	14 15 40	19 58	3 3	6 3	27 6	1 27	24 53	21 33	20 34	19 11
9	1 8 39	15 14 55	3♌51	4 29	7 18	27 43	1 35	24 49	21 37	20 36	19 13
10	1 12 35	16 14 13	18 8	5 55	8 32	28 19	1 42	24 45	21 40	20 38	19 15
11	1 16 32	17 13 32	2♍48	7 19	9 47	28 56	1 50	24 41	21 44	20 40	19 17
12	1 20 29	18 12 54	17 44	8 43	11 2	29 32	1 57	24 37	21 47	20 42	19 19
13	1 24 25	19 12 18	2♎50	10 6	12 17	0♍ 8	2 4	24 33	21 51	20 44	19 21
14	1 28 22	20 11 44	17 56	11 28	13 32	0 44	2 11	24 29	21 54	20 46	19 23
15	1 32 18	21 11 12	2♏52	12 49	14 48	1 20	2 18	24 25	21 58	20 48	19 25
16	1 36 15	22 10 43	17 31	14 8	16 3	1 57	2 24	24 21	22 1	20 50	19 27
17	1 40 11	23 10 15	1♐46	15 27	17 18	2 33	2 31	24 17	22 4	20 52	19 29
18	1 44 8	24 9 49	15 34	16 44	18 33	3 8	2 37	24 13	22 8	20 54	19 31
19	1 48 4	25 9 25	28 57	18 0	19 48	3 44	2 43	24 10	22 11	20 56	19 32
20	1 52 1	26 9 2	11♑54	19 15	21 3	4 20	2 49	24 6	22 14	20 58	19 34
21	1 55 58	27 8 42	24 29	20 27	22 18	4 56	2 55	24 3	22 18	21 0	19 36
22	1 59 54	28 8 23	6♒48	21 39	23 33	5 32	3 1	23 59	22 21	21 2	19 38
23	2 3 51	29 8 5	18 53	22 48	24 48	6 7	3 6	23 56	22 24	21 4	19 40
24	2 7 47	0♏ 7 50	0♓49	23 56	26 4	6 43	3 12	23 52	22 27	21 6	19 41
25	2 11 44	1 7 36	12 41	25 1	27 19	7 18	3 17	23 49	22 31	21 8	19 43
26	2 15 40	2 7 23	24 32	26 4	28 34	7 54	3 22	23 46	22 34	21 11	19 45
27	2 19 37	3 7 13	6♈25	27 4	29 49	8 29	3 27	23 43	22 37	21 13	19 47
28	2 23 33	4 7 4	18 23	28 1	1♏ 4	9 5	3 31	23 40	22 40	21 15	19 48
29	2 27 30	5 6 58	0♉27	28 55	2 20	9 40	3 36	23 37	22 43	21 17	19 50
30	2 31 26	6 6 53	12 40	29 45	3 35	10 15	3 40	23 34	22 46	21 19	19 52
31	2 35 23	7♏ 6 50	25♉ 4	0♐31	4♏50	10♍50	3♌44	23♓32	22♍49	21♏21	19♍53

THE SUN ENTERS THE SIGN OF SCORPIO ON OCT 23 AT 20:51.

DAY	TIME	☉	☽	☿	♀	♂	♃	♄	♅	♆	♇
	h m s	° ' "	° '	° '	° '	° '	° '	° '	° '	° '	° '
N 1	2 39 20	8♏ 6 49	7♊38	1♐12	6♏ 5	11♍25	3♌48	23♓29	22♍52	21♏24	19♍55
O 2	2 43 16	9 6 51	20 25	1 49	7 20	12 0	3 52	23R26	22 55	21 26	19 56
V 3	2 47 13	10 6 54	3♋26	2 20	8 36	12 35	3 56	23 24	22 58	21 28	19 58
E 4	2 51 9	11 6 59	16 41	2 44	9 51	13 10	3 59	23 22	23 1	21 30	19 59
M 5	2 55 6	12 7 7	0♌13	3 2	11 6	13 45	4 3	23 19	23 3	21 33	20 1
B 6	2 59 2	13 7 17	14 2	3R12	12 22	14 20	4 6	23 17	23 6	21 35	20 2
E 7	3 2 59	14 7 28	28 7	3 14	13 37	14 55	4 8	23 15	23 9	21 37	20 4
R 8	3 6 55	15 7 42	12♍28	3 8	14 52	15 29	4 11	23 13	23 12	21 39	20 5
9	3 10 52	16 7 58	27 0	2 52	16 8	16 4	4 14	23 11	23 14	21 41	20 7
10	3 14 49	17 8 16	11♎41	2 26	17 23	16 38	4 16	23 9	23 17	21 44	20 8
11	3 18 45	18 8 35	26 24	1 50	18 38	17 12	4 18	23 8	23 19	21 46	20 9
12	3 22 42	19 8 57	11♏ 2	1 4	19 54	17 47	4 20	23 6	23 22	21 48	20 11
13	3 26 38	20 9 20	25 29	0 9	21 9	18 21	4 22	23 5	23 24	21 50	20 12
14	3 30 35	21 9 45	9♐38	29♏ 5	22 24	18 55	4 23	23 3	23 27	21 53	20 13
15	3 34 31	22 10 12	23 27	27 53	23 40	19 29	4 25	23 2	23 29	21 55	20 14
16	3 38 28	23 10 40	6♑53	26 36	24 55	20 3	4 26	23 1	23 32	21 57	20 16
17	3 42 25	24 11 9	19 55	25 16	26 10	20 37	4 27	23 0	23 34	22 0	20 17
18	3 46 21	25 11 40	2♒35	23 55	27 26	21 11	4 28	22 59	23 36	22 2	20 18
19	3 50 18	26 12 12	14 56	22 36	28 41	21 45	4 28	22 58	23 38	22 4	20 19
20	3 54 14	27 12 45	27 3	21 21	29 56	22 18	4 29	22 57	23 41	22 6	20 20
21	3 58 11	28 13 20	9♓ 0	20 14	1♐12	22 52	4R29	22 57	23 43	22 9	20 21
22	4 2 7	29 13 55	20 52	19 15	2 27	23 25	4 29	22 56	23 45	22 11	20 22
23	4 6 4	0♐14 32	2♈42	18 27	3 43	23 58	4 29	22 56	23 47	22 13	20 23
24	4 10 0	1 15 10	14 37	17 50	4 58	24 32	4 28	22 55	23 49	22 15	20 24
25	4 13 57	2 15 49	26 39	17 24	6 13	25 5	4 28	22 55	23 51	22 17	20 25
26	4 17 53	3 16 30	8♉52	17D10	7 29	25 38	4 27	22D55	23 53	22 20	20 26
27	4 21 50	4 17 11	21 18	17 8	8 44	26 11	4 26	22 55	23 55	22 22	20 27
28	4 25 47	5 17 54	3♊59	17 15	9 59	26 44	4 25	22 55	23 56	22 24	20 28
29	4 29 43	6 18 39	16 55	17 33	11 15	27 16	4 23	22 55	23 58	22 26	20 29
30	4 33 40	7♐19 25	0♋ 5	18♏ 0	12♐30	27♍49	4♌22	22♓55	24♍ 0	22♏29	20♍30

THE SUN ENTERS THE SIGN OF SAGITTARIUS ON NOV 22 AT 18:15.

DAY	TIME	☉	☽	☿	♀	♂	♃	♄	♅	♆	♇
	h m s	° ' "	° '	° '	° '	° '	° '	° '	° '	° '	° '
D 1	4 37 36	8♐20 12	13♋30	18♏35	13♐46	28♍22	4♌20	22♓56	24♍ 1	22♏31	20♍30
E 2	4 41 33	9 21 0	27 7	19 17	15 1	28 54	4R18	22 56	24 3	22 33	20 31
C 3	4 45 29	10 21 50	10♌55	20 6	16 16	29 27	4 16	22 57	24 5	22 35	20 32
E 4	4 49 26	11 22 41	24 51	21 1	17 32	29 59	4 13	22 58	24 6	22 37	20 32
M 5	4 53 23	12 23 33	8♍55	22 0	18 47	0♎31	4 11	22 59	24 8	22 39	20 33
B 6	4 57 19	13 24 27	23 4	23 3	20 3	1 3	4 8	23 0	24 9	22 42	20 34
E 7	5 1 16	14 25 22	7♎16	24 11	21 18	1 35	4 5	23 1	24 10	22 44	20 34
R 8	5 5 12	15 26 18	21 31	25 21	22 33	2 7	4 2	23 2	24 11	22 46	20 35
9	5 9 9	16 27 16	5♏45	26 35	23 49	2 38	3 59	23 3	24 13	22 48	20 35
10	5 13 5	17 28 15	19 54	27 51	25 4	3 10	3 55	23 4	24 14	22 50	20 36
11	5 17 2	18 29 15	3♐57	29 9	26 20	3 41	3 51	23 6	24 15	22 52	20 36
12	5 20 58	19 30 16	17 48	0♐29	27 35	4 13	3 47	23 7	24 16	22 54	20 37
13	5 24 55	20 31 18	1♑24	1 50	28 50	4 44	3 43	23 9	24 17	22 56	20 37
14	5 28 52	21 32 21	14 42	3 13	0♑ 6	5 15	3 39	23 11	24 18	22 58	20 37
15	5 32 48	22 33 24	27 42	4 37	1 21	5 46	3 35	23 13	24 19	23 0	20 38
16	5 36 45	23 34 27	10♒22	6 2	2 37	6 16	3 30	23 15	24 20	23 2	20 38
17	5 40 41	24 35 32	22 45	7 27	3 52	6 47	3 25	23 17	24 21	23 4	20 38
18	5 44 38	25 36 36	4♓53	8 54	5 7	7 17	3 20	23 19	24 21	23 6	20 38
19	5 48 34	26 37 41	16 50	10 21	6 23	7 48	3 15	23 22	24 22	23 8	20 39
20	5 52 31	27 38 46	28 41	11 49	7 38	8 18	3 10	23 24	24 23	23 10	20 39
21	5 56 27	28 39 52	10♈31	13 18	8 53	8 48	3 4	23 26	24 23	23 12	20 39
22	6 0 24	29 40 57	22 25	14 47	10 9	9 18	2 59	23 29	24 24	23 14	20 39
23	6 4 21	0♑42 3	4♉29	16 16	11 24	9 47	2 53	23 32	24 24	23 16	20R39
24	6 8 17	1 43 10	16 46	17 46	12 40	10 17	2 47	23 35	24 24	23 18	20 39
25	6 12 14	2 44 16	29 21	19 16	13 55	10 46	2 41	23 38	24 25	23 20	20 39
26	6 16 10	3 45 23	12♊15	20 46	15 10	11 15	2 35	23 41	24 25	23 21	20 39
27	6 20 7	4 46 30	25 31	22 17	16 26	11 44	2 29	23 44	24 25	23 23	20 39
28	6 24 3	5 47 37	9♋ 7	23 49	17 41	12 13	2 22	23 47	24 25	23 25	20 39
29	6 28 0	6 48 45	23 0	25 20	18 56	12 42	2 16	23 50	24 25	23 27	20 38
30	6 31 57	7 49 52	7♌ 6	26 52	20 12	13 11	2 9	23 54	24R26	23 29	20 38
31	6 35 53	8♑51 0	21♌20	28♐24	21♑27	13♎39	2♌ 2	23♓57	24♍26	23♏30	20♍38

THE SUN ENTERS THE SIGN OF CAPRICORN ON DEC 22 AT 07:29.

♏ SCORPIO ♐ SAGITTARIUS ♑ CAPRICORN ♒ AQUARIUS ♓ PISCES

SIDEREAL · SUN. · MOON. · MERCURY. · VENUS. · MARS. · JUPITER. · SATURN. · URANUS. · NEPTUNE. · PLUTO.

DAY	TIME	☉	☽	☿	♀	♂	♃	♄	♅	♆	♇
	h m s	° ' "	° '	° '	° '	° '	° '	° '	° '	° '	° '
J 1	6 39 50	9♑52 9	5♍37	29♐57	22♑42	14♎ 7	1♌55	24♓ 1	24♍25	23♏32	20♍38
A 2	6 43 46	10 53 17	19 54	1♑29	23 57	14 35	1R48	24 4	24R25	23 34	20R37
N 3	6 47 43	11 54 26	4♎ 5	3 3	25 13	15 3	1 41	24 8	24 25	23 35	20 37
U 4	6 51 39	12 55 36	18 11	4 36	26 28	15 30	1 34	24 12	24 25	23 37	20 37
A 5	6 55 36	13 56 45	2♏10	6 10	27 43	15 58	1 27	24 16	24 25	23 39	20 36
R 6	6 59 32	14 57 55	16 1	7 44	28 59	16 25	1 19	24 20	24 24	23 40	20 36
Y 7	7 3 29	15 59 5	29 44	9 19	0♒14	16 52	1 12	24 24	24 24	23 42	20 36
8	7 7 26	17 0 16	13♐19	10 54	1 29	17 19	1 4	24 28	24 23	23 43	20 35
9	7 11 22	18 1 26	26 44	12 29	2 44	17 45	0 56	24 33	24 23	23 45	20 35
10	7 15 19	19 2 36	9♑58	14 5	4 0	18 11	0 49	24 37	24 22	23 46	20 34
11	7 19 15	20 3 46	22 59	15 41	5 15	18 37	0 41	24 41	24 22	23 48	20 33
12	7 23 12	21 4 56	5♒47	17 18	6 30	19 3	0 33	24 46	24 21	23 49	20 33
13	7 27 8	22 6 5	18 20	18 55	7 45	19 29	0 25	24 51	24 20	23 51	20 32
14	7 31 5	23 7 14	0♓38	20 33	9 0	19 54	0 17	24 55	24 19	23 52	20 31
15	7 35 1	24 8 22	12 44	22 11	10 16	20 19	0 9	25 0	24 19	23 53	20 31
16	7 38 58	25 9 29	24 40	23 49	11 31	20 44	0 1	25 5	24 18	23 55	20 30
17	7 42 55	26 10 36	6♈30	25 29	12 46	21 8	29♋53	25 10	24 17	23 56	20 29
18	7 46 51	27 11 42	18 18	27 8	14 1	21 33	29 45	25 15	24 16	23 57	20 29
19	7 50 48	28 12 47	0♉10	28 48	15 16	21 57	29 37	25 20	24 15	23 58	20 28
20	7 54 44	29 13 51	12 11	0♒29	16 31	22 20	29 29	25 25	24 14	24 0	20 27
21	7 58 41	0♒14 55	24 27	2 10	17 46	22 44	29 21	25 30	24 12	24 1	20 26
22	8 2 37	1 15 58	7♊ 3	3 52	19 1	23 7	29 13	25 36	24 11	24 2	20 25
23	8 6 34	2 16 59	20 3	5 34	20 16	23 30	29 5	25 41	24 10	24 3	20 24
24	8 10 30	3 18 0	3♋29	7 17	21 31	23 52	28 57	25 47	24 9	24 4	20 23
25	8 14 27	4 19 0	17 20	9 1	22 46	24 14	28 49	25 52	24 7	24 5	20 22
26	8 18 24	5 19 59	1♌35	10 44	24 1	24 36	28 41	25 58	24 6	24 6	20 21
27	8 22 20	6 20 57	16 8	12 29	25 16	24 58	28 33	26 3	24 5	24 7	20 20
28	8 26 17	7 21 55	0♍51	14 13	26 31	25 19	28 25	26 9	24 3	24 8	20 19
29	8 30 13	8 22 51	15 36	15 58	27 46	25 40	28 17	26 15	24 2	24 9	20 18
30	8 34 10	9 23 47	0♎16	17 44	29 1	26 1	28 10	26 21	24 0	24 10	20 17
31	8 38 6	10♒24 42	14♎45	19♒29	0♓16	26♎21	28♋ 2	26♓27	23♍58	24♏11	20♍16

THE SUN ENTERS THE SIGN OF AQUARIUS ON JAN 20 AT 18:08.

DAY	TIME	☉	☽	☿	♀	♂	♃	♄	♅	♆	♇
	h m s	° ' "	° '	° '	° '	° '	° '	° '	° '	° '	° '
F 1	8 42 3	11♒25 36	28♎59	21♒15	1♓31	26♎41	27♋54	26♓32	23♍57	24♏12	20♍15
E 2	8 45 59	12 26 29	12♏57	23 0	2 46	27 0	27R47	26 38	23R55	24 12	20R14
B 3	8 49 56	13 27 22	26 39	24 45	4 0	27 19	27 39	26 45	23 53	24 13	20 12
R 4	8 53 53	14 28 14	10♐ 7	26 30	5 15	27 38	27 32	26 51	23 51	24 14	20 11
U 5	8 57 49	15 29 6	23 21	28 14	6 30	27 56	27 24	26 57	23 50	24 14	20 10
A 6	9 1 46	16 29 56	6♑24	29 57	7 45	28 14	27 17	27 3	23 48	24 15	20 9
R 7	9 5 42	17 30 45	19 16	1♓39	8 59	28 32	27 10	27 9	23 46	24 16	20 7
Y 8	9 9 39	18 31 34	1♒57	3 19	10 14	28 49	27 3	27 16	23 44	24 16	20 6
9	9 13 35	19 32 21	14 27	4 58	11 29	29 5	26 56	27 22	23 42	24 17	20 5
10	9 17 32	20 33 6	26 47	6 33	12 43	29 21	26 49	27 29	23 40	24 17	20 3
11	9 21 29	21 33 51	8♓56	8 6	13 58	29 37	26 42	27 35	23 38	24 18	20 2
12	9 25 25	22 34 34	20 56	9 35	15 13	29 52	26 36	27 42	23 36	24 18	20 1
13	9 29 22	23 35 15	2♈49	11 0	16 27	0♏ 7	26 29	27 48	23 34	24 19	19 59
14	9 33 18	24 35 55	14 37	12 20	17 42	0 21	26 23	27 55	23 31	24 19	19 58
15	9 37 15	25 36 33	26 24	13 34	18 56	0 35	26 17	28 2	23 29	24 20	19 57
16	9 41 11	26 37 9	8♉14	14 42	20 10	0 48	26 11	28 8	23 27	24 20	19 56
17	9 45 0	27 37 44	20 13	15 43	21 25	1 1	26 5	28 15	23 25	24 20	19 54
18	9 49 4	28 38 17	2♊26	16 37	22 39	1 13	25 59	28 22	23 22	24 20	19 52
19	9 53 1	29 38 49	14 58	17 22	23 54	1 25	25 53	28 29	23 20	24 21	19 51
20	9 56 57	0♓39 18	27 54	17 58	25 8	1 36	25 48	28 36	23 18	24 21	19 49
21	10 0 54	1 39 46	11♋19	18 24	26 22	1 47	25 42	28 43	23 15	24 21	19 48
22	10 4 51	2 40 12	25 13	18 41	27 36	1 57	25 37	28 50	23 13	24 21	19 46
23	10 8 47	3 40 36	9♌35	18R48	28 51	2 6	25 32	28 57	23 11	24 21	19 45
24	10 12 44	4 40 58	24 20	18 45	0♈ 5	2 15	25 27	29 4	23 8	24R21	19 43
25	10 16 40	5 41 18	9♍22	18 32	1 19	2 23	25 23	29 11	23 6	24 21	19 42
26	10 20 37	6 41 37	24 30	18 9	2 33	2 31	25 18	29 18	23 3	24 21	19 40
27	10 24 33	7 41 54	9♎33	17 38	3 47	2 38	25 14	29 25	23 1	24 21	19 39
28	10 28 30	8♓42 10	24♎24	16♓58	5♈ 1	2♏45	25♋10	29♓32	22♍58	24♏21	19♍37

THE SUN ENTERS THE SIGN OF PISCES ON FEB 19 AT 08:24.

DAY	TIME	☉	☽	☿	♀	♂	♃	♄	♅	♆	♇
	h m s	° ' "	° '	° '	° '	° '	° '	° '	° '	° '	° '
M 1	10 32 26	9♓42 24	8♏57	16♓12	6♈15	2♏50	25♋ 6	29♓39	22♍56	24♏21	19♍35
A 2	10 36 23	10 42 36	23 7	15R19	7 28	2 55	25R 2	29 46	22R53	24R21	19R34
R 3	10 40 20	11 42 47	6♐55	14 22	8 42	3 0	24 58	29 53	22 51	24 21	19 32
C 4	10 44 16	12 42 57	20 21	13 22	9 56	3 4	24 55	0♈ 1	22 48	24 20	19 31
H 5	10 48 13	13 43 5	3♑28	12 20	11 10	3 7	24 52	0 8	22 46	24 20	19 29
6	10 52 9	14 43 12	16 19	11 18	12 23	3 9	24 49	0 15	22 43	24 20	19 28
7	10 56 6	15 43 17	28 55	10 17	13 37	3 11	24 46	0 23	22 41	24 20	19 26
8	11 0 2	16 43 20	11♒20	9 19	14 51	3R12	24 43	0 30	22 38	24 19	19 24
9	11 3 59	17 43 22	23 35	8 25	16 4	3 12	24 40	0 37	22 35	24 19	19 23
10	11 7 55	18 43 22	5♓41	7 35	17 18	3 11	24 38	0 45	22 33	24 18	19 21
11	11 11 52	19 43 19	17 40	6 50	18 31	3 10	24 36	0 52	22 30	24 18	19 20
12	11 15 49	20 43 15	29 34	6 12	19 45	3 8	24 34	0 59	22 27	24 18	19 18
13	11 19 45	21 43 9	11♈23	5 39	20 58	3 5	24 32	1 7	22 25	24 17	19 16
14	11 23 42	22 43 1	23 10	5 13	22 11	3 1	24 31	1 14	22 22	24 16	19 15
15	11 27 38	23 42 51	4♉58	4 54	23 24	2 57	24 29	1 22	22 20	24 16	19 13
16	11 31 35	24 42 39	16 50	4 40	24 38	2 52	24 28	1 29	22 17	24 15	19 11
17	11 35 31	25 42 24	28 50	4D34	25 51	2 46	24 27	1 37	22 14	24 15	19 10
18	11 39 28	26 42 8	11♊ 2	4 33	27 4	2 39	24 27	1 44	22 12	24 14	19 8
19	11 43 24	27 41 49	23 32	4 38	28 17	2 32	24 26	1 52	22 9	24 13	19 7
20	11 47 21	28 41 28	6♋23	4 49	29 30	2 24	24 26	1 59	22 7	24 13	19 5
21	11 51 18	29 41 4	19 41	5 6	0♉43	2 15	24D26	2 6	22 4	24 12	19 4
22	11 55 14	0♈40 39	3♌27	5 27	1 55	2 5	24 26	2 14	22 1	24 11	19 2
23	11 59 11	1 40 11	17 42	5 54	3 8	1 54	24 26	2 21	21 59	24 10	19 0
24	12 3 7	2 39 40	2♍23	6 24	4 21	1 43	24 26	2 29	21 56	24 9	18 59
25	12 7 4	3 39 8	17 25	7 0	5 34	1 31	24 27	2 36	21 54	24 9	18 57
26	12 11 0	4 38 33	2♎39	7 39	6 46	1 18	24 28	2 44	21 51	24 8	18 56
27	12 14 57	5 37 56	17 54	8 22	7 59	1 5	24 29	2 51	21 49	24 7	18 54
28	12 18 53	6 37 17	3♏ 1	9 9	9 11	0 51	24 30	2 59	21 46	24 6	18 53
29	12 22 50	7 36 37	17 51	9 59	10 23	0 36	24 31	3 6	21 44	24 5	18 51
30	12 26 47	8 35 54	2♐18	10 52	11 36	0 20	24 33	3 14	21 41	24 4	18 50
31	12 30 43	9♈35 10	16♐19	11♓48	12♉48	0♏ 4	24♋34	3♈21	21♍39	24♏ 3	18♍48

THE SUN ENTERS THE SIGN OF ARIES ON MAR 21 AT 07:37.

♈ ARIES ♉ TAURUS ♊ GEMINI ♋ CANCER ♌ LEO ♍ VIRGO ♎ LIBRA

SIDEREAL . SUN . . MOON . . MERCURY . VENUS . . MARS . . JUPITER . SATURN . . URANUS . NEPTUNE . PLUTO .

DAY	TIME	☉	☽	☿	♀	♂	♃	♄	♅	♆	♇
	h m s	° ' "	° '	° '	° '	° '	° '	° '	° '	° '	° '
A 1	12 34 40	10♈34 24	29♐54	12♓47	14♉ 0	29♎47	24♋36	3♈29	21♍36	24♏ 2	18♍47
P 2	12 38 36	11 33 37	13♑ 4	13 49	15 12	29R30	24 38	3 36	21R34	24R 1	18R45
R 3	12 42 33	12 32 47	25 53	14 54	16 24	29 12	24 41	3 44	21 31	24 0	18 44
I 4	12 46 29	13 31 56	8♒24	16 1	17 36	28 53	24 43	3 51	21 29	23 58	18 42
L 5	12 50 26	14 31 3	20 41	17 10	18 48	28 34	24 46	3 58	21 27	23 57	18 41
6	12 54 22	15 30 8	2♓46	18 22	19 59	28 14	24 49	4 6	21 24	23 56	18 40
7	12 58 19	16 29 12	14 43	19 35	21 11	27 54	24 52	4 13	21 22	23 55	18 38
8	13 2 16	17 28 13	26 34	20 51	22 23	27 33	24 55	4 20	21 20	23 54	18 37
9	13 6 12	18 27 12	8♈23	22 9	23 34	27 12	24 58	4 28	21 18	23 52	18 36
10	13 10 9	19 26 10	20 11	23 29	24 46	26 51	25 2	4 35	21 15	23 51	18 34
11	13 14 5	20 25 5	2♉ 0	24 50	25 57	26 29	25 5	4 42	21 13	23 50	18 33
12	13 18 2	21 23 59	13 53	26 14	27 8	26 7	25 9	4 50	21 11	23 49	18 32
13	13 21 58	22 22 50	25 51	27 39	28 20	25 45	25 13	4 57	21 9	23 47	18 30
14	13 25 55	23 21 39	7♊58	29 6	29 31	25 22	25 18	5 4	21 7	23 46	18 29
15	13 29 51	24 20 26	20 17	0♈35	0♊42	25 0	25 22	5 12	21 5	23 45	18 28
16	13 33 48	25 19 11	2♋50	2 5	1 53	24 37	25 27	5 19	21 3	23 43	18 27
17	13 37 45	26 17 54	15 42	3 38	3 3	24 14	25 31	5 26	21 1	23 42	18 25
18	13 41 41	27 16 34	28 56	5 11	4 14	23 51	25 36	5 33	20 59	23 40	18 24
19	13 45 38	28 15 13	12♌33	6 47	5 25	23 28	25 41	5 40	20 57	23 39	18 23
20	13 49 34	29 13 49	26 36	8 24	6 35	23 6	25 46	5 47	20 55	23 38	18 22
21	13 53 31	0♉12 22	11♍ 2	10 3	7 46	22 43	25 52	5 54	20 53	23 36	18 21
22	13 57 27	1 10 54	25 49	11 44	8 56	22 20	25 57	6 1	20 51	23 35	18 20
23	14 1 24	2 9 23	10♎52	13 26	10 6	21 58	26 3	6 8	20 50	23 33	18 19
24	14 5 20	3 7 50	26 1	15 10	11 16	21 36	26 9	6 15	20 48	23 32	18 18
25	14 9 17	4 6 16	11♏ 7	16 56	12 27	21 14	26 15	6 22	20 46	23 30	18 17
26	14 13 13	5 4 39	26 2	18 43	13 36	20 53	26 21	6 29	20 44	23 29	18 16
27	14 17 10	6 3 1	10♐38	20 32	14 46	20 32	26 27	6 36	20 43	23 27	18 15
28	14 21 7	7 1 22	24 51	22 23	15 56	20 11	26 34	6 43	20 41	23 26	18 14
29	14 25 3	7 59 41	8♑36	24 15	17 5	19 51	26 40	6 50	20 40	23 24	18 13
30	14 29 0	8♉57 58	21♑55	26♈ 9	18♊15	19♎31	26♋47	6♈56	20♍38	23♏23	18♍12

THE SUN ENTERS THE SIGN OF TAURUS ON APR 20 AT 18:56.

DAY	TIME	☉	☽	☿	♀	♂	♃	♄	♅	♆	♇
	h m s	° ' "	° '	° '	° '	° '	° '	° '	° '	° '	° '
M 1	14 32 56	9♉56 14	4♒49	28♈ 5	19♊24	19♎12	26♋54	7♈ 3	20♍37	23♏21	18♍11
A 2	14 36 53	10 54 28	17 21	0♉ 3	20 33	18R53	27 1	7 10	20R35	23R19	18R10
Y 3	14 40 49	11 52 41	29 36	2 2	21 43	18 35	27 8	7 16	20 34	23 18	18 9
4	14 44 46	12 50 52	11♓38	4 3	22 52	18 18	27 15	7 23	20 33	23 16	18 8
5	14 48 43	13 49 2	23 31	6 5	24 0	18 1	27 23	7 30	20 32	23 15	18 8
6	14 52 39	14 47 10	5♈19	8 9	25 9	17 44	27 30	7 36	20 30	23 13	18 7
7	14 56 36	15 45 16	17 6	10 15	26 18	17 29	27 38	7 43	20 29	23 11	18 6
8	15 0 32	16 43 22	28 56	12 21	27 26	17 14	27 46	7 49	20 28	23 10	18 6
9	15 4 29	17 41 25	10♉50	14 29	28 35	17 0	27 54	7 55	20 27	23 8	18 5
10	15 8 25	18 39 27	22 51	16 38	29 43	16 46	28 2	8 2	20 26	23 7	18 4
11	15 12 22	19 37 28	5♊ 1	18 48	0♋51	16 34	28 10	8 8	20 25	23 5	18 4
12	15 16 18	20 35 27	17 21	20 58	1 59	16 22	28 18	8 14	20 24	23 3	18 3
13	15 20 15	21 33 24	29 54	23 9	3 6	16 11	28 26	8 20	20 23	23 2	18 3
14	15 24 12	22 31 19	12♋40	25 20	4 14	16 0	28 35	8 26	20 23	23 0	18 2
15	15 28 8	23 29 13	25 42	27 31	5 21	15 51	28 44	8 32	20 22	22 58	18 2
16	15 32 5	24 27 5	9♌ 0	29 41	6 29	15 42	28 52	8 38	20 21	22 57	18 1
17	15 36 1	25 24 56	22 35	1♊51	7 36	15 34	29 1	8 44	20 20	22 55	18 1
18	15 39 58	26 22 44	6♍29	4 0	8 43	15 27	29 10	8 50	20 20	22 54	18 0
19	15 43 54	27 20 31	20 40	6 7	9 50	15 21	29 19	8 56	20 19	22 52	18 0
20	15 47 51	28 18 16	5♎ 8	8 13	10 56	15 15	29 28	9 2	20 19	22 50	18 0
21	15 51 47	29 15 59	19 49	10 17	12 3	15 11	29 38	9 7	20 18	22 49	17 59
22	15 55 44	0♊13 41	4♏38	12 19	13 9	15 7	29 47	9 13	20 18	22 47	17 59
23	15 59 41	1 11 21	19 28	14 20	14 15	15 4	29 57	9 19	20 18	22 45	17 59
24	16 3 37	2 9 0	4♐13	16 17	15 21	15 1	0♌ 6	9 24	20 17	22 44	17 59
25	16 7 34	3 6 38	18 44	18 13	16 26	15 0	0 16	9 30	20 17	22 42	17 59
26	16 11 30	4 4 15	2♑57	20 5	17 32	14D59	0 26	9 35	20 17	22 41	17 59
27	16 15 27	5 1 51	16 45	21 55	18 37	14 59	0 36	9 40	20 17	22 39	17 58
28	16 19 23	5 59 26	0♒ 9	23 43	19 42	15 0	0 46	9 46	20D17	22 37	17 58
29	16 23 20	6 56 59	13 7	25 27	20 47	15 2	0 56	9 51	20 17	22 36	17D58
30	16 27 16	7 54 32	25 43	27 9	21 51	15 4	1 6	9 56	20 17	22 34	17 58
31	16 31 13	8♊52 4	8♓ 0	28♊48	22♋55	15♎ 7	1♌16	10♈ 1	20♍17	22♏33	17♍58

THE SUN ENTERS THE SIGN OF GEMINI ON MAY 21 AT 18:18.

DAY	TIME	☉	☽	☿	♀	♂	♃	♄	♅	♆	♇
	h m s	° ' "	° '	° '	° '	° '	° '	° '	° '	° '	° '
J 1	16 35 10	9♊49 35	20♓ 2	0♋24	24♋ 0	15♎11	1♌27	10♈ 6	20♍17	22♏31	17♍58
U 2	16 39 6	10 47 6	1♈55	1 56	25 3	15 16	1 37	10 11	20 17	22R30	17 58
N 3	16 43 3	11 44 35	13 43	3 26	26 7	15 21	1 47	10 16	20 17	22 28	17 59
E 4	16 46 59	12 42 4	25 31	4 53	27 10	15 27	1 58	10 20	20 18	22 27	17 59
5	16 50 56	13 39 32	7♉24	6 17	28 13	15 34	2 9	10 25	20 18	22 25	17 59
6	16 54 52	14 36 59	19 24	7 38	29 16	15 41	2 20	10 30	20 18	22 24	17 59
7	16 58 49	15 34 25	1♊36	8 55	0♌19	15 49	2 30	10 34	20 19	22 22	17 59
8	17 2 45	16 31 51	14 0	10 10	1 21	15 58	2 41	10 39	20 19	22 21	18 0
9	17 6 42	17 29 16	26 38	11 21	2 23	16 7	2 52	10 43	20 20	22 19	18 0
10	17 10 39	18 26 40	9♋31	12 29	3 25	16 18	3 3	10 47	20 21	22 18	18 0
11	17 14 35	19 24 3	22 38	13 33	4 26	16 28	3 15	10 52	20 21	22 17	18 1
12	17 18 32	20 21 26	5♌57	14 34	5 27	16 40	3 26	10 56	20 22	22 15	18 1
13	17 22 28	21 18 47	19 29	15 32	6 28	16 52	3 37	11 0	20 23	22 14	18 1
14	17 26 25	22 16 7	3♍13	16 26	7 28	17 4	3 48	11 4	20 24	22 12	18 2
15	17 30 21	23 13 26	17 7	17 16	8 28	17 18	4 0	11 8	20 25	22 11	18 2
16	17 34 18	24 10 45	1♎11	18 3	9 28	17 31	4 11	11 12	20 25	22 10	18 3
17	17 38 14	25 8 2	15 24	18 45	10 27	17 46	4 23	11 15	20 26	22 8	18 3
18	17 42 11	26 5 19	29 45	19 24	11 26	18 1	4 35	11 19	20 27	22 7	18 4
19	17 46 8	27 2 34	14♏10	19 59	12 24	18 16	4 46	11 22	20 29	22 6	18 5
20	17 50 4	27 59 49	28 36	20 29	13 22	18 32	4 58	11 26	20 30	22 5	18 5
21	17 54 1	28 57 4	12♐58	20 55	14 20	18 49	5 10	11 29	20 31	22 3	18 6
22	17 57 57	29 54 18	27 11	21 17	15 17	19 6	5 22	11 33	20 32	22 2	18 7
23	18 1 54	0♋51 31	11♑11	21 34	16 13	19 24	5 34	11 36	20 33	22 1	18 7
24	18 5 50	1 48 45	24 51	21 47	17 10	19 42	5 46	11 39	20 35	22 0	18 8
25	18 9 47	2 45 58	8♒11	21 55	18 5	20 0	5 58	11 42	20 36	21 59	18 9
26	18 13 44	3 43 10	21 8	21R59	19 1	20 19	6 10	11 45	20 38	21 58	18 10
27	18 17 40	4 40 23	3♓44	21 58	19 55	20 39	6 22	11 48	20 39	21 56	18 11
28	18 21 37	5 37 35	16 1	21 52	20 49	20 59	6 34	11 50	20 41	21 55	18 12
29	18 25 33	6 34 48	28 4	21 42	21 43	21 19	6 46	11 53	20 42	21 54	18 13
30	18 29 30	7♋32 0	9♈57	21♋28	22♌36	21♎40	6♌58	11♈56	20♍44	21♏53	18♍13

THE SUN ENTERS THE SIGN OF CANCER ON JUN 22 AT 02:23.

♏ SCORPIO · ♐ SAGITTARIUS ♑ CAPRICORN ♒ AQUARIUS ♓ PISCES

1967

SIDEREAL SUN. MOON. MERCURY. VENUS. MARS. JUPITER. SATURN. URANUS. NEPTUNE. PLUTO.

DAY	TIME	☉	☽	☿	♀	♂	♃	♄	♅	♆	♇
	h m s	° ' "	° '	° '	° '	° '	° '	° '	° '	° '	° '
J 1	18 33 26	8♋29 13	21♈46	21♋10	23♌28	22♎ 2	7♌11	11♈58	20♍46	21♏52	18♍14
U 2	18 37 23	9 26 26	3♉36	20R47	24 20	22 24	7 23	12 1	20 47	21R51	18 15
L 3	18 41 19	10 23 39	15 31	20 21	25 11	22 46	7 36	12 3	20 49	21 50	18 16
Y 4	18 45 16	11 20 52	27 38	19 52	26 2	23 8	7 48	12 5	20 51	21 49	18 18
5	18 49 13	12 18 6	9♊58	19 20	26 52	23 31	8 1	12 7	20 53	21 48	18 19
6	18 53 9	13 15 19	22 36	18 46	27 41	23 55	8 13	12 9	20 55	21 48	18 20
7	18 57 6	14 12 33	5♋32	18 10	28 29	24 19	8 26	12 11	20 57	21 47	18 21
8	19 1 2	15 9 47	18 46	17 33	29 17	24 43	8 38	12 13	20 59	21 46	18 22
9	19 4 59	16 7 1	2♌17	16 55	0♍ 3	25 7	8 51	12 14	21 1	21 45	18 23
10	19 8 55	17 4 14	16 1	16 17	0 49	25 32	9 4	12 16	21 3	21 44	18 24
11	19 12 52	18 1 28	29 55	15 40	1 35	25 58	9 16	12 18	21 5	21 44	18 26
12	19 16 48	18 58 42	13♍57	15 4	2 19	26 23	9 29	12 19	21 7	21 43	18 27
13	19 20 45	19 55 56	28 2	14 31	3 2	26 50	9 42	12 20	21 9	21 42	18 28
14	19 24 42	20 53 9	12♎10	14 0	3 45	27 16	9 55	12 21	21 12	21 42	18 30
15	19 28 38	21 50 23	26 17	13 32	4 26	27 43	10 8	12 22	21 14	21 41	18 31
16	19 32 35	22 47 37	10♏25	13 8	5 6	28 10	10 20	12 23	21 16	21 40	18 32
17	19 36 31	23 44 51	24 30	12 48	5 45	28 37	10 33	12 24	21 19	21 40	18 34
18	19 40 28	24 42 5	8♐33	12 32	6 23	29 5	10 46	12 25	21 21	21 39	18 35
19	19 44 24	25 39 19	22 30	12 21	7 0	29 33	10 59	12 26	21 24	21 39	18 37
20	19 48 21	26 36 33	6♑19	12D16	7 36	0♏ 1	11 12	12 26	21 26	21 38	18 38
21	19 52 17	27 33 48	19 56	12 16	8 11	0 30	11 25	12 27	21 29	21 38	18 40
22	19 56 14	28 31 3	3♒19	12 22	8 44	0 59	11 38	12 27	21 31	21 37	18 41
23	20 0 11	29 28 19	16 25	12 33	9 15	1 28	11 51	12 28	21 34	21 37	18 43
24	20 4 7	0♌25 36	29 13	12 50	9 46	1 58	12 4	12 28	21 37	21 37	18 44
25	20 8 4	1 22 53	11♓44	13 13	10 15	2 27	12 17	12R28	21 39	21 36	18 46
26	20 12 0	2 20 11	23 58	13 42	10 42	2 57	12 30	12 28	21 42	21 36	18 47
27	20 15 57	3 17 29	5♈59	14 17	11 8	3 28	12 43	12 28	21 45	21 36	18 49
28	20 19 53	4 14 49	17 51	14 58	11 32	3 58	12 57	12 27	21 48	21 36	18 51
29	20 23 50	5 12 10	29 40	15 44	11 54	4 29	13 10	12 27	21 51	21 35	18 52
30	20 27 46	6 9 32	11♉30	16 36	12 15	5 0	13 23	12 27	21 53	21 35	18 54
31	20 31 43	7♌ 6 54	23♉26	17♋34	12♍34	5♏32	13♌36	12♈26	21♍56	21♏35	18♍56

THE SUN ENTERS THE SIGN OF LEO ON JUL 23 AT 13:17.

DAY	TIME	☉	☽	☿	♀	♂	♃	♄	♅	♆	♇
	h m s	° ' "	° '	° '	° '	° '	° '	° '	° '	° '	° '
A 1	20 35 40	8♌ 4 18	5♊35	18♋38	12♍51	6♏ 3	13♌49	12♈25	21♍59	21♏35	18♍57
U 2	20 39 36	9 1 43	18 1	19 47	13 6	6 35	14 2	12R25	22 2	21R35	18 59
G 3	20 43 33	9 59 9	0♋47	21 1	13 19	7 7	14 15	12 24	22 5	21D35	19 1
U 4	20 47 29	10 56 37	13 56	22 21	13 31	7 39	14 29	12 23	22 8	21 35	19 3
S 5	20 51 26	11 54 5	27 27	23 45	13 40	8 12	14 42	12 22	22 11	21 35	19 5
T 6	20 55 22	12 51 34	11♌19	25 14	13 47	8 45	14 55	12 21	22 15	21 35	19 6
7	20 59 19	13 49 5	25 28	26 48	13 51	9 18	15 8	12 19	22 18	21 35	19 8
8	21 3 16	14 46 36	9♍48	28 26	13R54	9 51	15 21	12 18	22 21	21 35	19 10
9	21 7 12	15 44 8	24 14	0♌ 8	13 54	10 25	15 35	12 17	22 24	21 35	19 12
10	21 11 9	16 41 41	8♎40	1 53	13 52	10 58	15 48	12 15	22 27	21 36	19 14
11	21 15 5	17 39 14	23 1	3 42	13 48	11 32	16 1	12 13	22 31	21 36	19 16
12	21 19 2	18 36 49	7♏15	5 34	13 41	12 7	16 14	12 12	22 34	21 36	19 18
13	21 22 58	19 34 25	21 21	7 28	13 32	12 41	16 27	12 10	22 37	21 36	19 20
14	21 26 55	20 32 1	5♐17	9 25	13 20	13 16	16 40	12 8	22 40	21 37	19 22
15	21 30 51	21 29 38	19 3	11 23	13 6	13 50	16 54	12 6	22 44	21 37	19 23
16	21 34 48	22 27 17	2♑39	13 22	12 50	14 25	17 7	12 4	22 47	21 37	19 25
17	21 38 45	23 24 56	16 4	15 23	12 31	15 1	17 20	12 2	22 51	21 38	19 27
18	21 42 41	24 22 37	29 18	17 24	12 10	15 36	17 33	11 59	22 54	21 38	19 29
19	21 46 38	25 20 18	12♒19	19 25	11 47	16 11	17 46	11 57	22 57	21 39	19 31
20	21 50 34	26 18 1	25 6	21 27	11 22	16 47	17 59	11 54	23 1	21 39	19 34
21	21 54 31	27 15 45	7♓40	23 28	10 54	17 23	18 12	11 52	23 4	21 40	19 36
22	21 58 27	28 13 31	19 59	25 29	10 25	17 59	18 26	11 49	23 8	21 40	19 38
23	22 2 24	29 11 18	2♈ 6	27 29	9 54	18 35	18 39	11 46	23 11	21 41	19 40
24	22 6 20	0♍ 9 7	14 3	29 29	9 22	19 12	18 52	11 44	23 15	21 42	19 42
25	22 10 17	1 6 57	25 53	1♍27	8 48	19 49	19 5	11 41	23 18	21 42	19 44
26	22 14 13	2 4 49	7♉41	3 25	8 14	20 25	19 18	11 38	23 22	21 43	19 46
27	22 18 10	3 2 43	19 30	5 22	7 38	21 2	19 31	11 35	23 26	21 44	19 48
28	22 22 7	4 0 39	1♊26	7 18	7 1	21 40	19 44	11 31	23 29	21 44	19 50
29	22 26 3	4 58 36	13 34	9 12	6 25	22 17	19 57	11 28	23 33	21 45	19 52
30	22 30 0	5 56 35	26 0	11 5	5 47	22 54	20 10	11 25	23 37	21 46	19 54
31	22 33 56	6♍54 37	8♋48	12♍57	5♍10	23♏32	20♌22	11♈21	23♍40	21♏47	19♍56

THE SUN ENTERS THE SIGN OF VIRGO ON AUG 23 AT 20:13.

DAY	TIME	☉	☽	☿	♀	♂	♃	♄	♅	♆	♇
	h m s	° ' "	° '	° '	° '	° '	° '	° '	° '	° '	° '
S 1	22 37 53	7♍52 40	22♋ 0	14♍48	4♍33	24♏10	20♌35	11♈18	23♍44	21♏48	19♍59
E 2	22 41 49	8 50 45	5♌39	16 37	3R57	24 48	20 48	11R15	23 48	21 49	20 1
P 3	22 45 46	9 48 51	19 44	18 26	3 21	25 26	21 1	11 11	23 51	21 50	20 3
T 4	22 49 42	10 47 0	4♍10	20 13	2 46	26 4	21 14	11 7	23 55	21 51	20 5
E 5	22 53 39	11 45 10	18 51	21 58	2 13	26 43	21 27	11 4	23 59	21 52	20 7
M 6	22 57 36	12 43 22	3♎40	23 43	1 40	27 21	21 39	11 0	24 2	21 53	20 9
B 7	23 1 32	13 41 35	18 30	25 26	1 9	28 0	21 52	10 56	24 6	21 54	20 12
E 8	23 5 29	14 39 50	3♏12	27 9	0 40	28 39	22 5	10 52	24 10	21 55	20 14
R 9	23 9 25	15 38 7	17 43	28 50	0 13	29 18	22 17	10 48	24 14	21 56	20 16
10	23 13 22	16 36 25	1♐58	0♎29	29♌48	29 57	22 30	10 44	24 17	21 57	20 18
11	23 17 18	17 34 44	15 55	2 8	29 24	0♐36	22 42	10 40	24 21	21 58	20 20
12	23 21 15	18 33 6	29 36	3 46	29 3	1 16	22 55	10 36	24 25	22 0	20 22
13	23 25 11	19 31 28	13♑ 0	5 22	28 44	1 56	23 7	10 31	24 29	22 1	20 25
14	23 29 8	20 29 52	26 8	6 58	28 28	2 35	23 20	10 27	24 32	22 2	20 27
15	23 33 5	21 28 18	9♒ 2	8 32	28 13	3 15	23 32	10 23	24 36	22 3	20 29
16	23 37 1	22 26 46	21 43	10 5	28 1	3 55	23 44	10 19	24 40	22 5	20 31
17	23 40 58	23 25 15	4♓12	11 37	27 52	4 35	23 57	10 14	24 44	22 6	20 33
18	23 44 54	24 23 46	16 29	13 8	27 45	5 16	24 9	10 10	24 48	22 7	20 36
19	23 48 51	25 22 19	28 36	14 38	27 40	5 56	24 21	10 5	24 51	22 9	20 38
20	23 52 47	26 20 53	10♈35	16 7	27D38	6 37	24 33	10 1	24 55	22 10	20 40
21	23 56 44	27 19 30	22 27	17 35	27 39	7 17	24 45	9 56	24 59	22 12	20 42
22	0 0 40	28 18 9	4♉15	19 2	27 41	7 58	24 57	9 52	25 3	22 13	20 44
23	0 4 37	29 16 50	16 1	20 27	27 46	8 39	25 9	9 47	25 6	22 15	20 46
24	0 8 34	0♎15 33	27 51	21 52	27 53	9 20	25 21	9 43	25 10	22 16	20 49
25	0 12 30	1 14 19	9♊46	23 15	28 3	10 1	25 33	9 38	25 14	22 18	20 51
26	0 16 27	2 13 6	21 54	24 38	28 14	10 42	25 45	9 33	25 18	22 19	20 53
27	0 20 23	3 11 56	4♋17	25 59	28 28	11 24	25 56	9 29	25 22	22 21	20 55
28	0 24 20	4 10 48	17 1	27 19	28 44	12 5	26 8	9 24	25 25	22 22	20 57
29	0 28 16	5 9 43	0♌10	28 37	29 1	12 47	26 20	9 19	25 29	22 24	20 59
30	0 32 13	6♎ 8 40	13♌46	29♎54	29♌21	13♐28	26♌31	9♈15	25♍33	22♏26	21♍ 1

THE SUN ENTERS THE SIGN OF LIBRA ON SEP 23 AT 17:39.

♈ ARIES ♉ TAURUS ♊ GEMINI ♋ CANCER ♌ LEO ♍ VIRGO ♎ LIBRA

SIDEREAL . SUN . MOON . MERCURY . VENUS . MARS . JUPITER . SATURN . URANUS . NEPTUNE . PLUTO .

DAY	TIME	☉	☽	☿	♀	♂	♃	♄	♅	♆	♇
	h m s	° ' "	° '	° '	° '	° '	° '	° '	° '	° '	° '
O 1	0 36 9	7♎ 7 39	27♌49	1♏10	29♌43	14♐10	26♌43	9♈10	25♍37	22♏28	21♍ 4
C 2	0 40 6	8 6 40	12♍18	2 24	0♍ 6	14 52	26 54	9R 5	25 40	22 29	21 6
T 3	0 44 3	9 5 43	27 8	3 37	0 31	15 34	27 5	9 1	25 44	22 31	21 8
O 4	0 47 59	10 4 48	12♎12	4 48	0 58	16 16	27 17	8 56	25 48	22 33	21 10
B 5	0 51 56	11 3 56	27 20	5 57	1 26	16 59	27 28	8 51	25 51	22 34	21 12
E 6	0 55 52	12 3 5	12♏23	7 5	1 56	17 41	27 39	8 46	25 55	22 36	21 14
R 7	0 59 49	13 2 17	27 13	8 10	2 27	18 23	27 50	8 42	25 59	22 38	21 16
8	1 3 45	14 1 30	11♐45	9 13	3 0	19 6	28 1	8 37	26 2	22 40	21 18
9	1 7 42	15 0 45	25 54	10 13	3 34	19 49	28 12	8 32	26 6	22 42	21 20
10	1 11 38	16 0 2	9♑40	11 11	4 10	20 31	28 23	8 28	26 10	22 44	21 22
11	1 15 35	16 59 20	23 2	12 6	4 47	21 14	28 33	8 23	26 13	22 46	21 24
12	1 19 32	17 58 40	6♒ 3	12 58	5 25	21 57	28 44	8 18	26 17	22 48	21 26
13	1 23 28	18 58 2	18 46	13 47	6 4	22 40	28 54	8 14	26 20	22 49	21 28
14	1 27 25	19 57 26	1♓13	14 31	6 45	23 24	29 5	8 9	26 24	22 51	21 30
15	1 31 21	20 56 52	13 27	15 11	7 27	24 7	29 15	8 5	26 28	22 53	21 32
16	1 35 18	21 56 19	25 31	15 47	8 9	24 50	29 25	8 0	26 31	22 55	21 34
17	1 39 14	22 55 48	7♈28	16 18	8 53	25 34	29 36	7 56	26 35	22 57	21 36
18	1 43 11	23 55 19	19 20	16 43	9 38	26 17	29 46	7 51	26 38	22 59	21 38
19	1 47 7	24 54 53	1♉ 8	17 2	10 24	27 1	29 56	7 47	26 42	23 1	21 40
20	1 51 4	25 54 28	12 56	17 15	11 10	27 44	0♍ 5	7 43	26 45	23 3	21 42
21	1 55 0	26 54 5	24 44	17R20	11 58	28 28	0 15	7 38	26 48	23 5	21 44
22	1 58 57	27 53 45	6♊37	17 18	12 47	29 12	0 25	7 34	26 52	23 8	21 46
23	2 2 54	28 53 27	18 37	17 8	13 36	29 56	0 34	7 30	26 55	23 10	21 47
24	2 6 50	29 53 11	0♋47	16 49	14 26	0♑40	0 44	7 26	26 59	23 12	21 49
25	2 10 47	0♏52 57	13 11	16 21	15 17	1 24	0 53	7 21	27 2	23 14	21 51
26	2 14 43	1 52 45	25 52	15 44	16 9	2 8	1 2	7 17	27 5	23 16	21 53
27	2 18 40	2 52 36	8♌55	14 58	17 1	2 52	1 12	7 13	27 8	23 18	21 55
28	2 22 36	3 52 29	22 21	14 3	17 54	3 37	1 21	7 9	27 12	23 20	21 56
29	2 26 33	4 52 24	6♍13	13 1	18 48	4 21	1 29	7 5	27 15	23 22	21 58
30	2 30 29	5 52 21	20 32	11 52	19 43	5 6	1 38	7 2	27 18	23 25	22 0
31	2 34 26	6♏52 20	5♎14	10♏38	20♍38	5♑50	1♍47	6♈58	27♍21	23♏27	22♍ 1

THE SUN ENTERS THE SIGN OF SCORPIO ON OCT 24 AT 02:45.

DAY	TIME	☉	☽	☿	♀	♂	♃	♄	♅	♆	♇
	h m s	° ' "	° '	° '	° '	° '	° '	° '	° '	° '	° '
N 1	2 38 23	7♏52 22	20♎14	9♏21	21♍33	6♑35	1♍55	6♈54	27♍24	23♏29	22♍ 3
O 2	2 42 19	8 52 25	5♏26	8R 4	22 30	7 19	2 4	6R51	27 27	23 31	22 5
V 3	2 46 16	9 52 31	20 38	6 47	23 27	8 4	2 12	6 47	27 30	23 33	22 6
E 4	2 50 12	10 52 38	5♐43	5 35	24 24	8 49	2 20	6 43	27 33	23 35	22 8
M 5	2 54 9	11 52 47	20 30	4 30	25 22	9 34	2 28	6 40	27 36	23 38	22 9
B 6	2 58 5	12 52 57	4♑54	3 32	26 20	10 19	2 36	6 37	27 39	23 40	22 11
E 7	3 2 2	13 53 10	18 51	2 45	27 19	11 4	2 44	6 33	27 42	23 42	22 13
R 8	3 5 59	14 53 23	2♒21	2 8	28 19	11 49	2 52	6 30	27 45	23 44	22 14
9	3 9 55	15 53 38	15 24	1 43	29 18	12 34	2 59	6 27	27 48	23 47	22 16
10	3 13 52	16 53 55	28 4	1D29	0♎19	13 20	3 7	6 24	27 51	23 49	22 17
11	3 17 48	17 54 13	10♓25	1 27	1 19	14 5	3 14	6 21	27 54	23 51	22 18
12	3 21 45	18 54 32	22 32	1 36	2 21	14 50	3 21	6 18	27 56	23 53	22 20
13	3 25 41	19 54 53	4♈28	1 56	3 22	15 36	3 28	6 16	27 59	23 56	22 21
14	3 29 38	20 55 15	16 18	2 24	4 24	16 21	3 35	6 13	28 2	23 58	22 23
15	3 33 34	21 55 39	28 6	3 2	5 26	17 7	3 41	6 10	28 4	24 0	22 24
16	3 37 31	22 56 4	9♉53	3 47	6 29	17 52	3 48	6 8	28 7	24 2	22 25
17	3 41 27	23 56 31	21 44	4 39	7 32	18 38	3 54	6 6	28 9	24 5	22 26
18	3 45 24	24 57 0	3♊39	5 38	8 36	19 23	4 0	6 3	28 12	24 7	22 28
19	3 49 21	25 57 30	15 41	6 41	9 39	20 9	4 7	6 1	28 14	24 9	22 29
20	3 53 17	26 58 2	27 51	7 49	10 44	20 55	4 12	5 59	28 17	24 11	22 30
21	3 57 14	27 58 35	10♋10	9 1	11 48	21 41	4 18	5 57	28 19	24 14	22 31
22	4 1 10	28 59 10	22 42	10 17	12 53	22 26	4 24	5 55	28 21	24 16	22 32
23	4 5 7	29 59 47	5♌27	11 35	13 58	23 12	4 29	5 53	28 24	24 18	22 33
24	4 9 3	1♐ 0 25	18 29	12 56	15 3	23 58	4 35	5 52	28 26	24 20	22 34
25	4 13 0	2 1 6	1♍49	14 18	16 9	24 44	4 40	5 50	28 28	24 23	22 35
26	4 16 57	3 1 47	15 29	15 43	17 15	25 30	4 45	5 49	28 30	24 25	22 36
27	4 20 53	4 2 31	29 31	17 9	18 21	26 16	4 49	5 47	28 32	24 27	22 37
28	4 24 50	5 3 16	13♎55	18 36	19 27	27 2	4 54	5 46	28 34	24 29	22 38
29	4 28 46	6 4 2	28 37	20 4	20 34	27 49	4 58	5 45	28 36	24 32	22 39
30	4 32 43	7♐ 4 50	13♏34	21♏33	21♎41	28♑35	5♍ 3	5♈44	28♍38	24♏34	22♍40

THE SUN ENTERS THE SIGN OF SAGITTARIUS ON NOV 23 AT 00:06.

DAY	TIME	☉	☽	☿	♀	♂	♃	♄	♅	♆	♇
	h m s	° ' "	° '	° '	° '	° '	° '	° '	° '	° '	° '
D 1	4 36 39	8♐ 5 40	28♏38	23♏ 3	22♎48	29♑21	5♍ 7	5♈43	28♍40	24♏36	22♍41
E 2	4 40 36	9 6 30	13♐40	24 34	23 55	0♒ 7	5 11	5R42	28 42	24 38	22 42
C 3	4 44 32	10 7 22	28 31	26 5	25 3	0 54	5 14	5 41	28 44	24 40	22 43
E 4	4 48 29	11 8 15	13♑ 3	27 36	26 10	1 40	5 18	5 40	28 46	24 43	22 43
M 5	4 52 26	12 9 9	27 9	29 8	27 18	2 26	5 21	5 40	28 47	24 45	22 44
B 6	4 56 22	13 10 4	10♒47	0♐39	28 27	3 13	5 25	5 39	28 49	24 47	22 45
E 7	5 0 19	14 11 0	23 56	2 12	29 35	3 59	5 28	5 39	28 51	24 49	22 45
R 8	5 4 15	15 11 56	6♓40	3 44	0♏43	4 46	5 30	5 39	28 52	24 51	22 46
9	5 8 12	16 12 53	19 3	5 16	1 52	5 32	5 33	5D39	28 54	24 53	22 47
10	5 12 8	17 13 50	1♈ 8	6 49	3 1	6 19	5 36	5 39	28 55	24 55	22 47
11	5 16 5	18 14 48	13 2	8 22	4 10	7 5	5 38	5 39	28 56	24 58	22 48
12	5 20 1	19 15 47	24 50	9 55	5 19	7 52	5 40	5 39	28 58	25 0	22 48
13	5 23 58	20 16 46	6♉36	11 28	6 29	8 38	5 42	5 39	28 59	25 2	22 49
14	5 27 55	21 17 46	18 25	13 1	7 38	9 25	5 44	5 40	29 0	25 4	22 49
15	5 31 51	22 18 47	0♊21	14 34	8 48	10 12	5 45	5 40	29 1	25 6	22 50
16	5 35 48	23 19 48	12 25	16 7	9 58	10 58	5 46	5 41	29 3	25 8	22 50
17	5 39 44	24 20 50	24 39	17 41	11 8	11 45	5 48	5 42	29 4	25 10	22 50
18	5 43 41	25 21 53	7♋ 4	19 14	12 18	12 32	5 49	5 43	29 5	25 12	22 51
19	5 47 37	26 22 57	19 41	20 48	13 28	13 18	5 49	5 44	29 6	25 14	22 51
20	5 51 34	27 24 1	2♌30	22 22	14 38	14 5	5 50	5 45	29 6	25 16	22 51
21	5 55 31	28 25 6	15 30	23 56	15 49	14 52	5 50	5 46	29 7	25 18	22 51
22	5 59 27	29 26 11	28 41	25 30	17 0	15 38	5R50	5 47	29 8	25 20	22 51
23	6 3 24	0♑27 17	12♍ 6	27 4	18 10	16 25	5 50	5 49	29 9	25 22	22 52
24	6 7 20	1 28 24	25 43	28 39	19 21	17 12	5 50	5 50	29 9	25 24	22 52
25	6 11 17	2 29 32	9♎35	0♑14	20 32	17 59	5 50	5 52	29 10	25 26	22 52
26	6 15 13	3 30 40	23 41	1 49	21 43	18 45	5 49	5 54	29 11	25 28	22R52
27	6 19 10	4 31 49	8♏ 2	3 24	22 55	19 32	5 48	5 56	29 11	25 29	22 52
28	6 23 6	5 32 59	22 34	4 59	24 6	20 19	5 47	5 58	29 12	25 31	22 52
29	6 27 3	6 34 9	7♐15	6 35	25 17	21 6	5 46	6 0	29 12	25 33	22 52
30	6 31 0	7 35 19	21 57	8 11	26 29	21 53	5 45	6 2	29 12	25 35	22 51
31	6 34 56	8♑36 30	6♑34	9♑48	27♏41	22♒39	5♍43	6♈ 4	29♍13	25♏37	22♍51

THE SUN ENTERS THE SIGN OF CAPRICORN ON DEC 22 AT 13:17.

♏ SCORPIO ♐ SAGITTARIUS ♑ CAPRICORN ♒ AQUARIUS ♓ PISCES

SIDEREAL   SUN . . .   MOON . .   MERCURY   VENUS . .   MARS . .   JUPITER   SATURN .   URANUS .   NEPTUNE   PLUTO . .

DAY	TIME	☉	☽	☿	♀	♂	♃	♄	♅	♆	♇
	h m s	° ' "	° '	° '	° '	° '	° '	° '	° '	° '	° '
J 1	6 38 53	9♑37 41	20♑56	11♑24	28♏52	23♒26	5♍41	6♈ 6	29♍13	25♏38	22♍51
A 2	6 42 49	10 38 52	4♒59	13 1	0♐ 4	24 13	5R40	6 9	29 13	25 40	22R51
N 3	6 46 46	11 40 3	18 38	14 39	1 16	25 0	5 37	6 11	29 13	25 42	22 51
U 4	6 50 42	12 41 14	1♓51	16 16	2 28	25 47	5 35	6 14	29R13	25 44	22 50
A 5	6 54 39	13 42 24	14 38	17 54	3 40	26 34	5 32	6 17	29 13	25 45	22 50
R 6	6 58 35	14 43 34	27 4	19 33	4 52	27 20	5 30	6 20	29 13	25 47	22 50
Y 7	7 2 32	15 44 44	9♈11	21 11	6 4	28 7	5 27	6 23	29 13	25 49	22 49
8	7 6 29	16 45 53	21 7	22 50	7 16	28 54	5 24	6 26	29 13	25 50	22 49
9	7 10 25	17 47 2	2♉55	24 30	8 29	29 41	5 20	6 29	29 12	25 52	22 49
10	7 14 22	18 48 10	14 43	26 9	9 41	0♓28	5 17	6 32	29 12	25 53	22 48
11	7 18 18	19 49 19	26 34	27 49	10 53	1 14	5 13	6 36	29 12	25 55	22 48
12	7 22 15	20 50 26	8♊33	29 29	12 6	2 1	5 9	6 39	29 11	25 56	22 47
13	7 26 11	21 51 33	20 45	1♒10	13 18	2 48	5 5	6 43	29 11	25 58	22 46
14	7 30 8	22 52 40	3♋11	2 50	14 31	3 35	5 1	6 46	29 10	25 59	22 46
15	7 34 4	23 53 46	15 52	4 31	15 44	4 22	4 57	6 50	29 10	26 1	22 45
16	7 38 1	24 54 52	28 49	6 11	16 56	5 8	4 52	6 54	29 9	26 2	22 45
17	7 41 58	25 55 57	12♌ 0	7 51	18 9	5 55	4 48	6 58	29 9	26 3	22 44
18	7 45 54	26 57 2	25 23	9 31	19 22	6 42	4 43	7 2	29 8	26 5	22 43
19	7 49 51	27 58 6	8♍57	11 11	20 35	7 28	4 38	7 6	29 7	26 6	22 42
20	7 53 47	28 59 10	22 39	12 49	21 48	8 15	4 33	7 10	29 6	26 7	22 42
21	7 57 44	0♒ 0 13	6♎28	14 27	23 1	9 2	4 27	7 15	29 5	26 8	22 41
22	8 1 40	1 1 16	20 23	16 4	24 14	9 48	4 22	7 19	29 4	26 10	22 40
23	8 5 37	2 2 19	4♏24	17 40	25 27	10 35	4 16	7 23	29 3	26 11	22 39
24	8 9 33	3 3 22	18 32	19 13	26 40	11 22	4 10	7 28	29 2	26 12	22 38
25	8 13 30	4 4 24	2♐44	20 44	27 53	12 8	4 5	7 32	29 1	26 13	22 37
26	8 17 27	5 5 25	16 58	22 13	29 6	12 55	3 59	7 37	29 0	26 14	22 36
27	8 21 23	6 6 26	1♑13	23 38	0♑20	13 41	3 52	7 42	28 59	26 15	22 35
28	8 25 20	7 7 27	15 22	24 59	1 33	14 28	3 46	7 47	28 58	26 16	22 34
29	8 29 16	8 8 26	29 22	26 16	2 46	15 15	3 40	7 52	28 56	26 17	22 33
30	8 33 13	9 9 25	13♒ 6	27 27	3 59	16 1	3 33	7 57	28 55	26 18	22 32
31	8 37 9	10♒10 23	26♒33	28♒33	5♑13	16♓48	3♍26	8♈ 2	28♍54	26♏19	22♍31

THE SUN ENTERS THE SIGN OF AQUARIUS ON JAN 20 AT 23:55.

DAY	TIME	☉	☽	☿	♀	♂	♃	♄	♅	♆	♇
	h m s	° ' "	° '	° '	° '	° '	° '	° '	° '	° '	° '
F 1	8 41 6	11♒11 19	9♓38	29♒31	6♑26	17♓34	3♍20	8♈ 7	28♍52	26♏20	22♍30
E 2	8 45 3	12 12 14	22 23	0♓22	7 40	18 20	3R13	8 12	28R51	26 21	22R29
B 3	8 48 59	13 13 8	4♈48	1 5	8 53	19 7	3 6	8 18	28 49	26 22	22 28
R 4	8 52 56	14 14 1	16 56	1 38	10 7	19 53	2 59	8 23	28 48	26 23	22 27
U 5	8 56 52	15 14 52	28 53	2 2	11 20	20 40	2 51	8 28	28 46	26 23	22 26
A 6	9 0 49	16 15 42	10♉43	2R15	12 34	21 26	2 44	8 34	28 44	26 24	22 24
R 7	9 4 45	17 16 31	22 31	2 17	13 47	22 12	2 37	8 40	28 43	26 25	22 23
Y 8	9 8 42	18 17 18	4♊23	2 8	15 1	22 59	2 29	8 45	28 41	26 25	22 22
9	9 12 38	19 18 3	16 25	1 48	16 14	23 45	2 22	8 51	28 39	26 26	22 21
10	9 16 35	20 18 48	28 40	1 18	17 28	24 31	2 14	8 57	28 37	26 27	22 19
11	9 20 32	21 19 30	11♋13	0 38	18 41	25 17	2 7	9 3	28 35	26 27	22 18
12	9 24 28	22 20 11	24 5	29♒49	19 55	26 3	1 59	9 9	28 33	26 28	22 17
13	9 28 25	23 20 51	7♌17	28 53	21 9	26 50	1 51	9 15	28 31	26 28	22 15
14	9 32 21	24 21 29	20 48	27 51	22 22	27 36	1 43	9 21	28 30	26 29	22 14
15	9 36 18	25 22 5	4♍36	26 44	23 36	28 22	1 36	9 27	28 27	26 29	22 13
16	9 40 14	26 22 40	18 36	25 36	24 50	29 8	1 28	9 33	28 25	26 30	22 11
17	9 44 11	27 23 14	2♎44	24 26	26 4	29 54	1 20	9 39	28 23	26 30	22 10
18	9 48 7	28 23 46	16 57	23 19	27 17	0♈40	1 12	9 45	28 21	26 30	22 8
19	9 52 4	29 24 17	1♏11	22 14	28 31	1 26	1 4	9 52	28 19	26 31	22 7
20	9 56 1	0♓24 47	15 23	21 13	29 45	2 11	0 56	9 58	28 17	26 31	22 6
21	9 59 57	1 25 16	29 32	20 18	0♒59	2 57	0 48	10 4	28 15	26 31	22 4
22	10 3 54	2 25 44	13♐36	19 29	2 12	3 43	0 40	10 11	28 12	26 31	22 3
23	10 7 50	3 26 10	27 34	18 47	3 26	4 29	0 33	10 17	28 10	26 32	22 1
24	10 11 47	4 26 35	11♑25	18 12	4 40	5 15	0 25	10 24	28 8	26 32	22 0
25	10 15 43	5 26 58	25 7	17 45	5 54	6 0	0 17	10 31	28 6	26 32	21 58
26	10 19 40	6 27 20	8♒39	17 25	7 8	6 46	0 9	10 37	28 3	26 32	21 57
27	10 23 36	7 27 40	21 57	17 12	8 22	7 32	0 1	10 44	28 1	26R32	21 55
28	10 27 33	8 27 59	5♓ 2	17D 6	9 36	8 17	29♌53	10 51	27 58	26 32	21 53
29	10 31 30	9♓28 16	17♓50	17♒ 7	10♒50	9♈ 3	29♌46	10♈58	27♍56	26♏32	21♍52

THE SUN ENTERS THE SIGN OF PISCES ON FEB 19 AT 14:10.

DAY	TIME	☉	☽	☿	♀	♂	♃	♄	♅	♆	♇
	h m s	° ' "	° '	° '	° '	° '	° '	° '	° '	° '	° '
M 1	10 35 26	10♓28 31	0♈23	17♒14	12♒ 3	9♈48	29♌38	11♈ 4	27♍54	26♏32	21♍50
A 2	10 39 23	11 28 44	12 41	17 28	13 17	10 34	29R30	11 11	27R51	26R32	21R49
R 3	10 43 19	12 28 55	24 47	17 47	14 31	11 19	29 23	11 18	27 49	26 32	21 47
C 4	10 47 16	13 29 4	6♉43	18 11	15 45	12 5	29 15	11 25	27 46	26 31	21 46
H 5	10 51 12	14 29 11	18 32	18 40	16 59	12 50	29 8	11 32	27 44	26 31	21 44
6	10 55 9	15 29 16	0♊21	19 14	18 13	13 35	29 0	11 39	27 41	26 31	21 42
7	10 59 5	16 29 19	12 13	19 52	19 27	14 20	28 53	11 46	27 39	26 31	21 41
8	11 3 2	17 29 20	24 14	20 35	20 41	15 6	28 46	11 53	27 36	26 30	21 39
9	11 6 59	18 29 19	6♋29	21 21	21 55	15 51	28 39	12 1	27 33	26 30	21 38
10	11 10 55	19 29 15	19 1	22 10	23 9	16 36	28 32	12 8	27 31	26 30	21 36
11	11 14 52	20 29 10	1♌56	23 3	24 23	17 21	28 25	12 15	27 28	26 29	21 34
12	11 18 48	21 29 2	15 13	23 58	25 37	18 6	28 18	12 22	27 26	26 29	21 33
13	11 22 45	22 28 52	28 55	24 57	26 50	18 51	28 12	12 29	27 23	26 28	21 31
14	11 26 41	23 28 40	12♍59	25 58	28 4	19 36	28 5	12 37	27 21	26 28	21 29
15	11 30 38	24 28 26	27 21	27 2	29 18	20 21	27 59	12 44	27 18	26 27	21 28
16	11 34 34	25 28 9	11♎55	28 8	0♓32	21 6	27 52	12 51	27 15	26 27	21 26
17	11 38 31	26 27 51	26 36	29 17	1 46	21 51	27 46	12 59	27 13	26 26	21 25
18	11 42 27	27 27 32	11♏16	0♓27	3 0	22 35	27 40	13 6	27 10	26 26	21 23
19	11 46 24	28 27 10	25 50	1 40	4 14	23 20	27 34	13 13	27 7	26 25	21 21
20	11 50 21	29 26 47	10♐14	2 55	5 28	24 5	27 28	13 21	27 5	26 24	21 20
21	11 54 17	0♈26 22	24 25	4 11	6 42	24 49	27 23	13 28	27 2	26 23	21 18
22	11 58 14	1 25 56	8♑20	5 30	7 56	25 34	27 17	13 36	27 0	26 23	21 17
23	12 2 10	2 25 27	22 0	6 50	9 10	26 19	27 12	13 43	26 57	26 22	21 15
24	12 6 7	3 24 57	5♒24	8 11	10 24	27 3	27 6	13 51	26 54	26 21	21 13
25	12 10 3	4 24 25	18 33	9 35	11 38	27 47	27 1	13 58	26 52	26 20	21 12
26	12 14 0	5 23 51	1♓28	11 0	12 52	28 32	26 56	14 6	26 49	26 20	21 10
27	12 17 56	6 23 16	14 9	12 26	14 6	29 16	26 52	14 13	26 47	26 19	21 9
28	12 21 53	7 22 38	26 38	13 54	15 20	0♉ 0	26 47	14 21	26 44	26 18	21 7
29	12 25 50	8 21 58	8♈55	15 24	16 34	0 45	26 43	14 28	26 42	26 17	21 6
30	12 29 46	9 21 16	21 3	16 55	17 48	1 29	26 38	14 36	26 39	26 16	21 4
31	12 33 43	10♈20 32	3♉ 1	18♓27	19♓ 2	2♉13	26♌34	14♈43	26♍37	26♏15	21♍ 3

THE SUN ENTERS THE SIGN OF ARIES ON MAR 20 AT 13:22.

♈ ARIES ♉ TAURUS ♊ GEMINI ♋ CANCER ♌ LEO ♍ VIRGO ♎ LIBRA

SIDEREAL SUN. MOON. MERCURY. VENUS. MARS. JUPITER. SATURN. URANUS. NEPTUNE. PLUTO.

DAY	TIME	☉	☽	☿	♀	♂	♃	♄	♅	♆	♇
	h m s	° ' "	° '	° '	° '	° '	° '	° '	° '	° '	° '
A 1	12 37 39	11♈19 46	14♉54	20♓ 1	20♓15	2♉57	26♌30	14♈51	26♍34	26♏14	21♍ 1
P 2	12 41 36	12 18 58	26 43	21 37	21 29	3 41	26R27	14 58	26R32	26R13	21R 0
R 3	12 45 32	13 18 8	8♊32	23 14	22 43	4 25	26 23	15 6	26 29	26 12	20 58
I 4	12 49 29	14 17 15	20 24	24 52	23 57	5 9	26 20	15 13	26 27	26 11	20 57
L 5	12 53 25	15 16 21	2♋24	26 32	25 11	5 53	26 16	15 21	26 24	26 10	20 55
6	12 57 22	16 15 24	14 37	28 13	26 25	6 37	26 13	15 29	26 22	26 8	20 54
7	13 1 19	17 14 24	27 6	29 56	27 39	7 21	26 11	15 36	26 19	26 7	20 52
8	13 5 15	18 13 22	9♌56	1♈40	28 53	8 5	26 8	15 44	26 17	26 6	20 51
9	13 9 12	19 12 18	23 11	3 25	0♈ 7	8 48	26 5	15 51	26 15	26 5	20 50
10	13 13 8	20 11 12	6♍51	5 12	1 21	9 32	26 3	15 59	26 12	26 4	20 48
11	13 17 5	21 10 3	20 58	7 1	2 34	10 16	26 1	16 6	26 10	26 2	20 47
12	13 21 1	22 8 52	5♎28	8 51	3 48	10 59	25 59	16 14	26 8	26 1	20 46
13	13 24 58	23 7 39	20 17	10 43	5 2	11 43	25 57	16 21	26 6	26 0	20 44
14	13 28 54	24 6 24	5♏18	12 36	6 16	12 26	25 56	16 29	26 3	25 59	20 43
15	13 32 51	25 5 8	20 23	14 31	7 30	13 10	25 54	16 36	26 1	25 57	20 42
16	13 36 48	26 3 49	5♐21	16 27	8 44	13 53	25 53	16 44	25 59	25 56	20 41
17	13 40 44	27 2 29	20 6	18 25	9 58	14 36	25 52	16 51	25 57	25 55	20 39
18	13 44 41	28 1 7	4♑32	20 24	11 11	15 20	25 51	16 59	25 55	25 53	20 38
19	13 48 37	28 59 43	18 36	22 25	12 25	16 3	25 51	17 6	25 53	25 52	20 37
20	13 52 34	29 58 18	2♒17	24 27	13 39	16 46	25 50	17 14	25 51	25 50	20 36
21	13 56 30	0♉56 51	15 34	26 30	14 53	17 29	25D50	17 21	25 49	25 49	20 35
22	14 0 27	1 55 22	28 32	28 35	16 7	18 12	25 50	17 29	25 47	25 47	20 33
23	14 4 23	2 53 52	11♓11	0♉40	17 21	18 55	25 50	17 36	25 45	25 46	20 32
24	14 8 20	3 52 20	23 36	2 47	18 34	19 38	25 50	17 43	25 43	25 45	20 31
25	14 12 17	4 50 46	5♈48	4 55	19 48	20 21	25 51	17 51	25 41	25 43	20 30
26	14 16 13	5 49 11	17 52	7 3	21 2	21 4	25 51	17 58	25 39	25 42	20 29
27	14 20 10	6 47 34	29 49	9 12	22 16	21 47	25 52	18 5	25 37	25 40	20 28
28	14 24 6	7 45 55	11♉41	11 21	23 30	22 30	25 53	18 13	25 36	25 39	20 27
29	14 28 3	8 44 14	23 30	13 30	24 44	23 12	25 54	18 20	25 34	25 37	20 26
30	14 31 59	9♉42 32	5♊19	15♉38	25♈57	23♉55	25♌56	18♈27	25♍32	25♏35	20♍25

THE SUN ENTERS THE SIGN OF TAURUS ON APR 20 AT 00:41.

DAY	TIME	☉	☽	☿	♀	♂	♃	♄	♅	♆	♇
	h m s	° ' "	° '	° '	° '	° '	° '	° '	° '	° '	° '
M 1	14 35 56	10♉40 47	17♊10	17♉46	27♈11	24♉38	25♌57	18♈34	25♍31	25♏34	20♍24
A 2	14 39 52	11 39 1	29 5	19 54	28 25	25 20	25 59	18 42	25R29	25R32	20R23
Y 3	14 43 49	12 37 13	11♋ 7	21 59	29 39	26 3	26 1	18 49	25 28	25 31	20 23
4	14 47 46	13 35 23	23 20	24 4	0♉52	26 45	26 3	18 56	25 26	25 29	20 22
5	14 51 42	14 33 31	5♌47	26 6	2 6	27 28	26 5	19 3	25 25	25 28	20 21
6	14 55 39	15 31 36	18 33	28 7	3 20	28 10	26 8	19 10	25 23	25 26	20 20
7	14 59 35	16 29 40	1♍40	0♊ 5	4 34	28 53	26 11	19 17	25 22	25 24	20 19
8	15 3 32	17 27 42	15 13	2 1	5 47	29 35	26 13	19 24	25 21	25 23	20 19
9	15 7 28	18 25 42	29 12	3 54	7 1	0♊17	26 16	19 31	25 20	25 21	20 18
10	15 11 25	19 23 40	13♎37	5 44	8 15	0 59	26 19	19 38	25 18	25 20	20 17
11	15 15 21	20 21 37	28 26	7 31	9 29	1 42	26 23	19 45	25 17	25 18	20 17
12	15 19 18	21 19 31	13♏32	9 15	10 42	2 24	26 26	19 52	25 16	25 16	20 16
13	15 23 15	22 17 25	28 48	10 55	11 56	3 6	26 30	19 59	25 15	25 15	20 16
14	15 27 11	23 15 17	14♐ 1	12 32	13 10	3 48	26 34	20 5	25 14	25 13	20 15
15	15 31 8	24 13 7	29 3	14 6	14 23	4 30	26 38	20 12	25 13	25 11	20 14
16	15 35 4	25 10 56	13♑46	15 37	15 37	5 12	26 42	20 19	25 12	25 10	20 14
17	15 39 1	26 8 44	28 2	17 3	16 51	5 53	26 46	20 25	25 11	25 8	20 14
18	15 42 57	27 6 31	11♒50	18 26	18 4	6 35	26 51	20 32	25 10	25 7	20 13
19	15 46 54	28 4 17	25 10	19 46	19 18	7 17	26 55	20 39	25 10	25 5	20 13
20	15 50 50	29 2 1	8♓ 5	21 1	20 32	7 59	27 0	20 45	25 9	25 3	20 12
21	15 54 47	29 59 44	20 39	22 13	21 46	8 40	27 5	20 52	25 8	25 2	20 12
22	15 58 44	0♊57 27	2♈55	23 22	22 59	9 22	27 10	20 58	25 8	25 0	20 12
23	16 2 40	1 55 8	14 59	24 26	24 13	10 4	27 15	21 4	25 7	24 58	20 11
24	16 6 37	2 52 48	26 54	25 26	25 27	10 45	27 21	21 11	25 7	24 57	20 11
25	16 10 33	3 50 27	8♉44	26 23	26 40	11 27	27 26	21 17	25 6	24 55	20 11
26	16 14 30	4 48 5	20 33	27 15	27 54	12 8	27 32	21 23	25 6	24 54	20 11
27	16 18 26	5 45 42	2♊22	28 3	29 8	12 50	27 38	21 29	25 5	24 52	20 11
28	16 22 23	6 43 18	14 13	28 47	0♊21	13 31	27 44	21 35	25 5	24 50	20 10
29	16 26 19	7 40 52	26 9	29 26	1 35	14 12	27 50	21 41	25 5	24 49	20 10
30	16 30 16	8 38 26	8♋10	0♋ 2	2 49	14 54	27 56	21 47	25 5	24 47	20 10
31	16 34 13	9♊35 58	20♋19	0♋33	4♊ 2	15♊35	28♌ 3	21♈53	25♍ 5	24♏46	20♍10

THE SUN ENTERS THE SIGN OF GEMINI ON MAY 21 AT 00:06.

DAY	TIME	☉	☽	☿	♀	♂	♃	♄	♅	♆	♇
	h m s	° ' "	° '	° '	° '	° '	° '	° '	° '	° '	° '
J 1	16 38 9	10♊33 29	2♌38	0♋59	5♊16	16♊16	28♌ 9	21♈59	25♍ 5	24♏44	20♍10
U 2	16 42 6	11 30 58	15 9	1 21	6 30	16 57	28 16	22 5	25D 4	24R43	20 10
N 3	16 46 2	12 28 27	27 55	1 38	7 43	17 39	28 23	22 11	25 5	24 41	20 10
E 4	16 49 59	13 25 54	10♍59	1 50	8 57	18 20	28 30	22 17	25 5	24 40	20 11
5	16 53 55	14 23 20	24 24	1 58	10 11	19 1	28 37	22 22	25 5	24 38	20 11
6	16 57 52	15 20 44	8♎12	2R 1	11 24	19 42	28 44	22 28	25 5	24 37	20 11
7	17 1 48	16 18 8	22 25	2 0	12 38	20 23	28 52	22 33	25 5	24 35	20 11
8	17 5 45	17 15 30	7♏ 2	1 54	13 52	21 3	28 59	22 39	25 5	24 34	20 11
9	17 9 42	18 12 51	21 59	1 44	15 5	21 44	29 7	22 44	25 6	24 32	20 12
10	17 13 38	19 10 12	7♐ 9	1 30	16 19	22 25	29 14	22 49	25 6	24 31	20 12
11	17 17 35	20 7 32	22 22	1 12	17 33	23 6	29 22	22 55	25 7	24 29	20 12
12	17 21 31	21 4 51	7♑28	0 51	18 46	23 47	29 30	23 0	25 7	24 28	20 13
13	17 25 28	22 2 9	22 16	0 26	20 0	24 27	29 38	23 5	25 8	24 26	20 13
14	17 29 24	22 59 27	6♒41	29♊58	21 14	25 8	29 47	23 10	25 8	24 25	20 13
15	17 33 21	23 56 44	20 36	29 28	22 28	25 49	29 55	23 15	25 9	24 24	20 14
16	17 37 18	24 54 1	4♓ 2	28 56	23 41	26 29	0♍ 3	23 20	25 10	24 22	20 14
17	17 41 14	25 51 18	17 0	28 23	24 55	27 10	0 12	23 25	25 10	24 21	20 15
18	17 45 11	26 48 34	29 34	27 49	26 9	27 50	0 20	23 29	25 11	24 20	20 15
19	17 49 7	27 45 50	11♈49	27 15	27 22	28 31	0 29	23 34	25 12	24 18	20 16
20	17 53 4	28 43 6	23 50	26 41	28 36	29 11	0 38	23 39	25 13	24 17	20 17
21	17 57 0	29 40 22	5♉43	26 8	29 50	29 51	0 47	23 43	25 14	24 16	20 17
22	18 0 57	0♋37 37	17 31	25 36	1♋ 3	0♋32	0 56	23 47	25 15	24 15	20 18
23	18 4 53	1 34 52	29 19	25 7	2 17	1 12	1 5	23 52	25 16	24 13	20 19
24	18 8 50	2 32 7	11♊10	24 40	3 31	1 52	1 15	23 56	25 17	24 12	20 19
25	18 12 47	3 29 22	23 7	24 16	4 45	2 33	1 24	24 0	25 18	24 11	20 20
26	18 16 43	4 26 37	5♋11	23 56	5 58	3 13	1 33	24 4	25 20	24 10	20 21
27	18 20 40	5 23 51	17 23	23 39	7 12	3 53	1 43	24 8	25 21	24 9	20 22
28	18 24 36	6 21 5	29 44	23 27	8 26	4 33	1 53	24 12	25 22	24 8	20 22
29	18 28 33	7 18 19	12♌15	23 19	9 40	5 13	2 3	24 16	25 24	24 7	20 23
30	18 32 29	8♋15 32	24♌57	23♊15	10♋53	5♋53	2♍12	24♈20	25♍25	24♏ 5	20♍24

THE SUN ENTERS THE SIGN OF CANCER ON JUN 21 AT 08:14.

♏ SCORPIO ♐ SAGITTARIUS ♑ CAPRICORN ♒ AQUARIUS ♓ PISCES

1968

SIDEREAL SUN. MOON. MERCURY. VENUS. MARS. JUPITER. SATURN. URANUS. NEPTUNE. PLUTO.

DAY	TIME	☉	☽	☿	♀	♂	♃	♄	♅	♆	♇
	h m s	° ' "	° '	° '	° '	° '	° '	° '	° '	° '	° '
J 1	18 36 26	9♋12 45	7♍51	23♊16	12♋ 7	6♋33	2♍22	24♈24	25♍27	24♏ 4	20♍25
U 2	18 40 22	10 9 58	21 0	23 22	13 21	7 13	2 32	24 27	25 28	24R 3	20 26
L 3	18 44 19	11 7 10	4♎24	23 33	14 35	7 53	2 43	24 31	25 30	24 2	20 27
Y 4	18 48 16	12 4 22	18 7	23 49	15 48	8 33	2 53	24 34	25 31	24 1	20 28
5	18 52 12	13 1 34	2♏ 9	24 10	17 2	9 13	3 3	24 37	25 33	24 1	20 29
6	18 56 9	13 58 45	16 31	24 36	18 16	9 53	3 13	24 41	25 35	24 0	20 30
7	19 0 5	14 55 56	1♐11	25 7	19 30	10 33	3 24	24 44	25 37	23 59	20 31
8	19 4 2	15 53 7	16 2	25 43	20 43	11 12	3 34	24 47	25 38	23 58	20 33
9	19 7 58	16 50 19	1♑ 0	26 24	21 57	11 52	3 45	24 50	25 40	23 57	20 34
10	19 11 55	17 47 30	15 53	27 10	23 11	12 32	3 56	24 53	25 42	23 56	20 35
11	19 15 52	18 44 41	0♒34	28 0	24 25	13 11	4 7	24 56	25 44	23 55	20 36
12	19 19 48	19 41 53	14 55	28 56	25 39	13 51	4 17	24 58	25 46	23 55	20 37
13	19 23 45	20 39 5	28 50	29 56	26 52	14 31	4 28	25 1	25 48	23 54	20 39
14	19 27 41	21 36 17	12♓17	1♋ 1	28 6	15 10	4 39	25 3	25 50	23 53	20 40
15	19 31 38	22 33 30	25 18	2 10	29 20	15 50	4 50	25 6	25 52	23 53	20 41
16	19 35 34	23 30 43	7♈54	3 24	0♌34	16 29	5 1	25 8	25 55	23 52	20 43
17	19 39 31	24 27 57	20 12	4 43	1 48	17 8	5 13	25 10	25 57	23 51	20 44
18	19 43 27	25 25 12	2♉14	6 6	3 1	17 48	5 24	25 12	25 59	23 51	20 45
19	19 47 24	26 22 27	14 7	7 33	4 15	18 27	5 35	25 14	26 1	23 50	20 47
20	19 51 21	27 19 44	25 57	9 4	5 29	19 7	5 47	25 16	26 4	23 50	20 48
21	19 55 17	28 17 1	7♊47	10 40	6 43	19 46	5 58	25 18	26 6	23 49	20 50
22	19 59 14	29 14 19	19 42	12 19	7 57	20 25	6 10	25 20	26 9	23 49	20 51
23	20 3 10	0♌11 37	1♋45	14 2	9 11	21 5	6 21	25 21	26 11	23 48	20 53
24	20 7 7	1 8 56	13 58	15 48	10 25	21 44	6 33	25 23	26 13	23 48	20 54
25	20 11 3	2 6 16	26 23	17 38	11 38	22 23	6 45	25 24	26 16	23 48	20 56
26	20 15 0	3 3 37	9♌ 0	19 31	12 52	23 2	6 56	25 26	26 19	23 47	20 58
27	20 18 56	4 0 58	21 48	21 26	14 6	23 41	7 8	25 27	26 21	23 47	20 59
28	20 22 53	4 58 20	4♍48	23 24	15 20	24 20	7 20	25 28	26 24	23 47	21 1
29	20 26 50	5 55 43	18 0	25 24	16 34	25 0	7 32	25 29	26 27	23 46	21 2
30	20 30 46	6 53 6	1♎23	27 25	17 48	25 39	7 44	25 30	26 29	23 46	21 4
31	20 34 43	7♌50 29	14♎57	29♋28	19♌ 2	26♋18	7♍56	25♈31	26♍32	23♏46	21♍ 6

THE SUN ENTERS THE SIGN OF LEO ON JUL 22 AT 19:08.

DAY	TIME	☉	☽	☿	♀	♂	♃	♄	♅	♆	♇
	h m s	° ' "	° '	° '	° '	° '	° '	° '	° '	° '	° '
A 1	20 38 39	8♌47 53	28♎44	1♌32	20♌16	26♋57	8♍ 8	25♈31	26♍35	23♏46	21♍ 7
U 2	20 42 36	9 45 18	12♏43	3 37	21 30	27 36	8 20	25 32	26 38	23R46	21 9
G 3	20 46 32	10 42 43	26 54	5 42	22 43	28 15	8 32	25 32	26 41	23 46	21 11
U 4	20 50 29	11 40 10	11♐17	7 47	23 57	28 53	8 44	25 33	26 44	23 46	21 13
S 5	20 54 25	12 37 36	25 47	9 52	25 11	29 32	8 57	25 33	26 47	23D46	21 15
T 6	20 58 22	13 35 4	10♑20	11 57	26 25	0♌11	9 9	25 33	26 50	23 46	21 16
7	21 2 19	14 32 32	24 49	14 1	27 39	0 50	9 21	25R33	26 53	23 46	21 18
8	21 6 15	15 30 2	9♒ 9	16 4	28 53	1 29	9 34	25 33	26 56	23 46	21 20
9	21 10 12	16 27 32	23 13	18 7	0♍ 7	2 7	9 46	25 33	26 59	23 46	21 22
10	21 14 8	17 25 3	6♓57	20 8	1 21	2 46	9 58	25 33	27 2	23 46	21 24
11	21 18 5	18 22 36	20 18	22 8	2 34	3 25	10 11	25 32	27 5	23 46	21 26
12	21 22 1	19 20 10	3♈16	24 7	3 48	4 4	10 23	25 32	27 8	23 46	21 28
13	21 25 58	20 17 45	15 52	26 5	5 2	4 42	10 36	25 31	27 11	23 47	21 30
14	21 29 54	21 15 22	28 10	28 1	6 16	5 21	10 48	25 31	27 14	23 47	21 31
15	21 33 51	22 13 0	10♉15	29 56	7 30	5 59	11 1	25 30	27 18	23 47	21 33
16	21 37 48	23 10 39	22 10	1♍49	8 44	6 38	11 14	25 29	27 21	23 47	21 35
17	21 41 44	24 8 21	4♊ 1	3 41	9 50	7 17	11 26	25 28	27 24	23 48	21 37
18	21 45 41	25 6 4	15 53	5 32	11 12	7 55	11 39	25 27	27 28	23 48	21 39
19	21 49 37	26 3 48	27 51	7 21	12 25	8 34	11 52	25 26	27 31	23 49	21 41
20	21 53 34	27 1 34	9♋59	9 9	13 39	9 12	12 5	25 25	27 34	23 49	21 43
21	21 57 30	27 59 22	22 20	10 55	14 53	9 51	12 17	25 23	27 38	23 50	21 45
22	22 1 27	28 57 11	4♌56	12 40	16 7	10 29	12 30	25 22	27 41	23 50	21 48
23	22 5 23	29 55 2	17 47	14 24	17 21	11 7	12 43	25 20	27 45	23 51	21 50
24	22 9 20	0♍52 54	0♍54	16 6	18 35	11 46	12 56	25 18	27 48	23 51	21 52
25	22 13 17	1 50 48	14 16	17 47	19 49	12 24	13 9	25 17	27 52	23 52	21 54
26	22 17 13	2 48 43	27 51	19 26	21 3	13 2	13 21	25 15	27 55	23 53	21 56
27	22 21 10	3 46 40	11♎38	21 4	22 16	13 41	13 34	25 13	27 59	23 53	21 58
28	22 25 6	4 44 38	25 32	22 41	23 30	14 19	13 47	25 11	28 2	23 54	22 0
29	22 29 3	5 42 37	9♏34	24 17	24 44	14 57	14 0	25 9	28 6	23 55	22 2
30	22 32 59	6 40 37	23 42	25 51	25 58	15 36	14 13	25 6	28 9	23 56	22 4
31	22 36 56	7♍38 39	7♐52	27♍24	27♍12	16♌14	14♍26	25♈ 4	28♍13	23♏56	22♍ 6

THE SUN ENTERS THE SIGN OF VIRGO ON AUG 23 AT 02:04.

DAY	TIME	☉	☽	☿	♀	♂	♃	♄	♅	♆	♇
	h m s	° ' "	° '	° '	° '	° '	° '	° '	° '	° '	° '
S 1	22 40 52	8♍36 43	22♐ 5	28♍56	28♍26	16♌52	14♍39	25♈ 1	28♍16	23♏57	22♍ 9
E 2	22 44 49	9 34 47	6♑17	0♎26	29 40	17 30	14 52	24R59	28 20	23 58	22 11
P 3	22 48 46	10 32 54	20 26	1 55	0♎53	18 8	15 5	24 56	28 24	23 59	22 13
T 4	22 52 42	11 31 1	4♒28	3 23	2 7	18 46	15 18	24 54	28 27	24 0	22 15
E 5	22 56 39	12 29 10	18 21	4 50	3 21	19 24	15 31	24 51	28 31	24 1	22 17
M 6	23 0 35	13 27 21	2♓ 0	6 15	4 35	20 2	15 44	24 48	28 35	24 2	22 19
B 7	23 4 32	14 25 33	15 23	7 38	5 48	20 40	15 57	24 45	28 38	24 3	22 22
E 8	23 8 28	15 23 47	28 29	9 1	7 2	21 18	16 10	24 42	28 42	24 4	22 24
R 9	23 12 25	16 22 2	11♈16	10 22	8 16	21 56	16 23	24 39	28 46	24 5	22 26
10	23 16 21	17 20 20	23 47	11 41	9 30	22 34	16 36	24 36	28 50	24 6	22 28
11	23 20 18	18 18 40	6♉ 3	12 59	10 43	23 12	16 49	24 32	28 53	24 7	22 30
12	23 24 15	19 17 2	18 7	14 16	11 57	23 50	17 2	24 29	28 57	24 8	22 33
13	23 28 11	20 15 25	0♊ 2	15 31	13 11	24 28	17 15	24 25	29 1	24 10	22 35
14	23 32 8	21 13 51	11 54	16 44	14 25	25 6	17 28	24 22	29 4	24 11	22 37
15	23 36 4	22 12 20	23 47	17 55	15 38	25 44	17 41	24 18	29 8	24 12	22 39
16	23 40 1	23 10 50	5♋46	19 5	16 52	26 22	17 54	24 15	29 12	24 13	22 41
17	23 43 57	24 9 22	17 55	20 13	18 6	27 0	18 7	24 11	29 16	24 15	22 44
18	23 47 54	25 7 57	0♌18	21 18	19 19	27 37	18 20	24 7	29 20	24 16	22 46
19	23 51 50	26 6 34	12 59	22 21	20 33	28 15	18 33	24 3	29 23	24 17	22 48
20	23 55 47	27 5 13	25 59	23 22	21 47	28 53	18 46	23 59	29 27	24 19	22 50
21	23 59 44	28 3 53	9♍21	24 21	23 0	29 31	18 59	23 55	29 31	24 20	22 52
22	0 3 40	29 2 36	23 2	25 17	24 14	0♍ 8	19 11	23 51	29 35	24 22	22 55
23	0 7 37	0♎ 1 21	7♎ 1	26 10	25 28	0 46	19 24	23 47	29 39	24 23	22 57
24	0 11 33	1 0 8	21 14	26 59	26 41	1 24	19 37	23 43	29 42	24 25	22 59
25	0 15 30	1 58 57	5♏37	27 46	27 55	2 1	19 50	23 39	29 46	24 26	23 1
26	0 19 26	2 57 47	20 3	28 28	29 9	2 39	20 3	23 35	29 50	24 28	23 3
27	0 23 23	3 56 40	4♐30	29 7	0♏22	3 17	20 16	23 30	29 54	24 29	23 6
28	0 27 19	4 55 34	18 52	29 41	1 36	3 54	20 29	23 26	29 57	24 31	23 8
29	0 31 16	5 54 30	3♑ 6	0♏11	2 49	4 32	20 41	23 21	0♎ 1	24 32	23 10
30	0 35 13	6♎53 28	17♑10	0♏35	4♏ 3	5♍ 9	20♍54	23♈17	0♎ 5	24♏34	23♍12

THF SUN ENTERS THE SIGN OF LIBRA ON SEP 22 AT 23:27.

♈ ARIES ♉ TAURUS ♊ GEMINI ♋ CANCER ♌ LEO ♍ VIRGO ♎ LIBRA

SIDEREAL SUN. MOON. MERCURY. VENUS. MARS. JUPITER. SATURN. URANUS. NEPTUNE. PLUTO.

DAY	TIME	☉	☽	☿	♀	♂	♃	♄	♅	♆	♇
	h m s	° ' "	° '	° '	° '	° '	° '	° '	° '	° '	° '
O 1	0 39 9	7♎52 27	1♒ 2	0♏54	5♏16	5♍47	21♍ 7	23♈13	0♎ 9	24♏36	23♍14
C 2	0 43 6	8 51 28	14 42	1 8	6 30	6 24	21 20	23R 8	0 13	24 37	23 16
T 3	0 47 2	9 50 31	28 8	1R14	7 43	7 2	21 32	23 3	0 16	24 39	23 18
O 4	0 50 59	10 49 35	11♓21	1 14	8 57	7 39	21 45	22 59	0 20	24 41	23 21
B 5	0 54 55	11 48 42	24 20	1 7	10 10	8 16	21 57	22 54	0 24	24 43	23 23
E 6	0 58 52	12 47 50	7♈ 6	0 52	11 24	8 54	22 10	22 50	0 28	24 44	23 25
R 7	1 2 48	13 47 1	19 39	0 29	12 37	9 31	22 23	22 45	0 31	24 46	23 27
8	1 6 45	14 46 13	1♉59	29♎58	13 51	10 9	22 35	22 40	0 35	24 48	23 29
9	1 10 41	15 45 28	14 9	29 19	15 4	10 46	22 48	22 36	0 39	24 50	23 31
10	1 14 38	16 44 45	26 9	28 33	16 18	11 23	23 0	22 31	0 42	24 52	23 33
11	1 18 35	17 44 4	8♊ 4	27 38	17 31	12 0	23 12	22 26	0 46	24 54	23 35
12	1 22 31	18 43 25	19 55	26 38	18 44	12 38	23 25	22 21	0 50	24 55	23 37
13	1 26 28	19 42 49	1♋47	25 31	19 58	13 15	23 37	22 17	0 53	24 57	23 39
14	1 30 24	20 42 15	13 44	24 21	21 11	13 52	23 49	22 12	0 57	24 59	23 41
15	1 34 21	21 41 43	25 50	23 8	22 24	14 29	24 2	22 7	1 1	25 1	23 43
16	1 38 17	22 41 14	8♌11	21 55	23 38	15 6	24 14	22 2	1 4	25 3	23 45
17	1 42 14	23 40 46	20 50	20 44	24 51	15 44	24 26	21 57	1 8	25 5	23 47
18	1 46 10	24 40 21	3♍51	19 36	26 4	16 21	24 38	21 53	1 11	25 7	23 49
19	1 50 7	25 39 59	17 16	18 35	27 17	16 58	24 50	21 48	1 15	25 9	23 51
20	1 54 4	26 39 38	1♎ 7	17 40	28 31	17 35	25 2	21 43	1 18	25 11	23 53
21	1 58 0	27 39 20	15 22	16 55	29 44	18 12	25 14	21 38	1 22	25 13	23 55
22	2 1 57	28 39 3	29 56	16 21	0♐57	18 49	25 26	21 34	1 25	25 15	23 57
23	2 5 53	29 38 49	14♏45	15 57	2 10	19 26	25 38	21 29	1 29	25 17	23 59
24	2 9 50	0♏38 37	29 40	15D45	3 23	20 3	25 49	21 24	1 32	25 19	24 1
25	2 13 46	1 38 26	14♐32	15 43	4 37	20 40	26 1	21 20	1 36	25 21	24 3
26	2 17 43	2 38 18	29 15	15 53	5 50	21 17	26 13	21 15	1 39	25 24	24 4
27	2 21 39	3 38 11	13♑42	16 14	7 3	21 54	26 24	21 10	1 42	25 26	24 6
28	2 25 36	4 38 5	27 50	16 44	8 16	22 30	26 36	21 6	1 46	25 28	24 8
29	2 29 33	5 38 1	11♒38	17 24	9 29	23 7	26 47	21 1	1 49	25 30	24 10
30	2 33 29	6 37 59	25 5	18 11	10 42	23 44	26 59	20 57	1 52	25 32	24 12
31	2 37 26	7♏37 58	8♓14	19♎ 6	11♐55	24♍21	27♍10	20♈52	1♎56	25♏34	24♍13

THE SUN ENTERS THE SIGN OF SCORPIO ON OCT 23 AT 08:31.

DAY	TIME	☉	☽	☿	♀	♂	♃	♄	♅	♆	♇
	h m s	° ' "	° '	° '	° '	° '	° '	° '	° '	° '	° '
N 1	2 41 22	8♏37 59	21♓ 6	20♎ 8	13♐ 8	24♍58	27♍21	20♈48	1♎59	25♏36	24♍15
O 2	2 45 19	9 38 2	3♈44	21 15	14 21	25 34	27 32	20R43	2 2	25 39	24 17
V 3	2 49 15	10 38 6	16 11	22 27	15 34	26 11	27 44	20 39	2 5	25 41	24 18
E 4	2 53 12	11 38 12	28 28	23 43	16 47	26 48	27 55	20 35	2 8	25 43	24 20
M 5	2 57 8	12 38 19	10♉36	25 3	18 0	27 24	28 6	20 31	2 12	25 45	24 22
B 6	3 1 5	13 38 29	22 38	26 26	19 13	28 1	28 16	20 26	2 15	25 47	24 23
E 7	3 5 2	14 38 41	4♊34	27 52	20 25	28 38	28 27	20 22	2 18	25 50	24 25
R 8	3 8 58	15 38 54	16 27	29 19	21 38	29 14	28 38	20 18	2 21	25 52	24 26
9	3 12 55	16 39 9	28 18	0♏49	22 51	29 51	28 49	20 14	2 24	25 54	24 28
10	3 16 51	17 39 26	10♋10	2 19	24 4	0♎27	28 59	20 10	2 27	25 56	24 29
11	3 20 48	18 39 45	22 6	3 51	25 16	1 4	29 10	20 6	2 30	25 59	24 31
12	3 24 44	19 40 6	4♌10	5 24	26 29	1 40	29 20	20 2	2 33	26 1	24 32
13	3 28 41	20 40 29	16 26	6 58	27 42	2 16	29 30	19 59	2 35	26 3	24 34
14	3 32 37	21 40 54	28 59	8 32	28 54	2 53	29 40	19 55	2 38	26 5	24 35
15	3 36 34	22 41 21	11♍53	10 7	0♑ 7	3 29	29 51	19 51	2 41	26 8	24 36
16	3 40 31	23 41 49	25 12	11 42	1 19	4 6	0♎ 1	19 48	2 44	26 10	24 38
17	3 44 27	24 42 20	8♎59	13 17	2 32	4 42	0 10	19 44	2 46	26 12	24 39
18	3 48 24	25 42 52	23 15	14 53	3 44	5 18	0 20	19 41	2 49	26 14	24 40
19	3 52 20	26 43 26	7♏57	16 28	4 56	5 54	0 30	19 38	2 52	26 17	24 42
20	3 56 17	27 44 1	22 59	18 3	6 9	6 30	0 40	19 34	2 54	26 19	24 43
21	4 0 13	28 44 39	8♐13	19 39	7 21	7 7	0 49	19 31	2 57	26 21	24 44
22	4 4 10	29 45 17	23 28	21 14	8 33	7 43	0 58	19 28	2 59	26 23	24 45
23	4 8 6	0♐45 57	8♑34	22 49	9 46	8 19	1 8	19 25	3 2	26 26	24 46
24	4 12 3	1 46 39	23 20	24 25	10 58	8 55	1 17	19 22	3 4	26 28	24 48
25	4 16 0	2 47 21	7♒42	26 0	12 10	9 31	1 26	19 19	3 7	26 30	24 49
26	4 19 56	3 48 4	21 36	27 35	13 22	10 7	1 35	19 17	3 9	26 32	24 50
27	4 23 53	4 48 48	5♓ 4	29 9	14 34	10 43	1 44	19 14	3 11	26 35	24 51
28	4 27 49	5 49 33	18 7	0♐44	15 46	11 19	1 53	19 12	3 13	26 37	24 52
29	4 31 46	6 50 19	0♈49	2 19	16 58	11 54	2 1	19 9	3 16	26 39	24 53
30	4 35 42	7♐51 7	13♈15	3♐53	18♑10	12♎30	2♎10	19♈ 7	3♎18	26♏41	24♍54

THE SUN ENTERS THE SIGN OF SAGITTARIUS ON NOV 22 AT 05:50.

DAY	TIME	☉	☽	☿	♀	♂	♃	♄	♅	♆	♇
	h m s	° ' "	° '	° '	° '	° '	° '	° '	° '	° '	° '
D 1	4 39 39	8♐51 55	25♈28	5♐28	19♑21	13♎ 6	2♎18	19♈ 5	3♎20	26♏44	24♍55
E 2	4 43 35	9 52 44	7♉33	7 2	20 33	13 42	2 26	19R 2	3 22	26 46	24 55
C 3	4 47 32	10 53 34	19 31	8 37	21 45	14 17	2 34	19 0	3 24	26 48	24 56
E 4	4 51 29	11 54 25	1♊26	10 11	22 56	14 53	2 42	18 58	3 26	26 50	24 57
M 5	4 55 25	12 55 17	13 19	11 45	24 8	15 29	2 50	18 57	3 28	26 52	24 58
B 6	4 59 22	13 56 11	25 11	13 19	25 19	16 4	2 58	18 55	3 29	26 55	24 59
E 7	5 3 18	14 57 5	7♋ 4	14 54	26 30	16 40	3 6	18 53	3 31	26 57	24 59
R 8	5 7 15	15 58 0	18 59	16 28	27 42	17 15	3 13	18 52	3 33	26 59	25 0
9	5 11 11	16 58 57	0♌59	18 2	28 53	17 51	3 20	18 50	3 35	27 1	25 1
10	5 15 8	17 59 55	13 5	19 36	0♒ 4	18 26	3 28	18 49	3 36	27 3	25 1
11	5 19 5	19 0 53	25 21	21 11	1 15	19 1	3 35	18 48	3 38	27 5	25 2
12	5 23 1	20 1 53	7♍50	22 45	2 26	19 37	3 42	18 47	3 40	27 7	25 2
13	5 26 58	21 2 54	20 38	24 20	3 37	20 12	3 48	18 46	3 41	27 10	25 3
14	5 30 54	22 3 56	3♎48	25 54	4 47	20 47	3 55	18 45	3 42	27 12	25 3
15	5 34 51	23 4 59	17 24	27 29	5 58	21 22	4 1	18 44	3 44	27 14	25 4
16	5 38 47	24 6 2	1♏28	29 4	7 8	21 57	4 8	18 43	3 45	27 16	25 4
17	5 42 44	25 7 7	16 1	0♑39	8 19	22 32	4 14	18 43	3 46	27 18	25 5
18	5 46 40	26 8 13	0♐58	2 14	9 29	23 7	4 20	18 42	3 48	27 20	25 5
19	5 50 37	27 9 20	16 12	3 49	10 39	23 42	4 26	18 42	3 49	27 22	25 5
20	5 54 34	28 10 27	1♑34	5 25	11 49	24 17	4 32	18 42	3 50	27 24	25 6
21	5 58 30	29 11 35	16 51	7 0	12 59	24 52	4 37	18D42	3 51	27 26	25 6
22	6 2 27	0♑12 43	1♒51	8 36	14 9	25 27	4 42	18 42	3 52	27 28	25 6
23	6 6 23	1 13 51	16 27	10 12	15 19	26 2	4 48	18 42	3 53	27 30	25 6
24	6 10 20	2 15 0	0♓34	11 47	16 28	26 36	4 53	18 42	3 54	27 32	25 6
25	6 14 16	3 16 8	14 10	13 23	17 38	27 11	4 58	18 42	3 55	27 34	25 6
26	6 18 13	4 17 17	27 18	14 59	18 47	27 45	5 2	18 43	3 55	27 36	25 7
27	6 22 9	5 18 25	10♈ 1	16 35	19 56	28 20	5 7	18 43	3 56	27 38	25R 7
28	6 26 6	6 19 34	22 24	18 11	21 5	28 54	5 11	18 44	3 57	27 39	25 7
29	6 30 3	7 20 43	4♉33	19 47	22 14	29 28	5 16	18 45	3 57	27 41	25 7
30	6 33 59	8 21 51	16 32	21 22	23 23	0♏ 3	5 20	18 46	3 58	27 43	25 7
31	6 37 56	9♑22 59	28♉25	22♑58	24♒31	0♏37	5♎24	18♈47	3♎59	27♏45	25♍ 6

THE SUN ENTERS THE SIGN OF CAPRICORN ON DEC 21 AT 19:00.

♏ SCORPIO ♐ SAGITTARIUS ♑ CAPRICORN ♒ AQUARIUS ♓ PISCES

SIDEREAL . SUN . MOON . MERCURY . VENUS . MARS . JUPITER . SATURN . URANUS . NEPTUNE . PLUTO .

DAY	TIME	☉	☽	☿	♀	♂	♃	♄	♅	♆	♇
	h m s	° ' "	° '	° '	° '	° '	° '	° '	° '	° '	° '
J 1	6 41 52	10♑24 8	10♊16	24♑32	25♒40	1♏11	5♎27	18♈48	3♎59	27♏47	25♍ 6
A 2	6 45 49	11 25 16	22 8	26 7	26 48	1 45	5 31	18 49	3 59	27 48	25R 6
N 3	6 49 45	12 26 25	4♋ 2	27 40	27 56	2 19	5 34	18 50	4 0	27 50	25 6
U 4	6 53 42	13 27 33	15 59	29 13	29 3	2 53	5 37	18 52	4 0	27 52	25 6
A 5	6 57 39	14 28 41	28 2	0♒44	0♓11	3 27	5 40	18 53	4 0	27 54	25 5
R 6	7 1 35	15 29 50	10♌10	2 14	1 18	4 1	5 43	18 55	4 0	27 55	25 5
Y 7	7 5 32	16 30 58	22 25	3 43	2 25	4 34	5 46	18 57	4 0	27 57	25 5
8	7 9 28	17 32 6	4♍49	5 9	3 32	5 8	5 48	18 59	4R 1	27 59	25 5
9	7 13 25	18 33 14	17 25	6 33	4 39	5 41	5 51	19 1	4 1	28 0	25 4
10	7 17 21	19 34 22	0♎15	7 53	5 45	6 15	5 53	19 3	4 0	28 2	25 4
11	7 21 18	20 35 30	13 22	9 10	6 52	6 48	5 55	19 5	4 0	28 3	25 3
12	7 25 14	21 36 38	26 50	10 23	7 57	7 22	5 56	19 7	4 0	28 5	25 3
13	7 29 11	22 37 46	10♏42	11 31	9 3	7 55	5 58	19 10	4 0	28 6	25 2
14	7 33 8	23 38 55	24 58	12 33	10 9	8 28	5 59	19 12	4 0	28 8	25 2
15	7 37 4	24 40 3	9♐36	13 29	11 14	9 1	6 0	19 15	3 59	28 9	25 1
16	7 41 1	25 41 10	24 33	14 18	12 19	9 34	6 1	19 17	3 59	28 11	25 0
17	7 44 57	26 42 18	9♑41	14 58	13 23	10 7	6 2	19 20	3 58	28 12	25 0
18	7 48 54	27 43 25	24 48	15 29	14 28	10 40	6 3	19 23	3 58	28 13	24 59
19	7 52 50	28 44 32	9♒46	15 51	15 32	11 12	6 3	19 26	3 57	28 15	24 58
20	7 56 47	29 45 37	24 24	16R 1	16 35	11 45	6R 3	19 29	3 57	28 16	24 58
21	8 0 43	0♒46 42	8♓37	16 1	17 39	12 17	6 3	19 32	3 56	28 17	24 57
22	8 4 40	1 47 46	22 21	15 49	18 42	12 50	6 3	19 36	3 55	28 19	24 56
23	8 8 37	2 48 49	5♈37	15 25	19 44	13 22	6 3	19 39	3 55	28 20	24 55
24	8 12 33	3 49 51	18 27	14 50	20 47	13 54	6 2	19 43	3 54	28 21	24 55
25	8 16 30	4 50 52	0♉55	14 5	21 49	14 26	6 1	19 46	3 53	28 22	24 54
26	8 20 26	5 51 52	13 6	13 10	22 50	14 58	6 1	19 50	3 52	28 23	24 53
27	8 24 23	6 52 51	25 5	12 7	23 51	15 30	5 59	19 54	3 51	28 24	24 52
28	8 28 19	7 53 49	6♊58	10 58	24 52	16 2	5 58	19 58	3 50	28 26	24 51
29	8 32 16	8 54 46	18 49	9 45	25 52	16 33	5 57	20 2	3 49	28 27	24 50
30	8 36 12	9 55 41	0♋41	8 30	26 52	17 5	5 55	20 6	3 48	28 28	24 49
31	8 40 9	10♒56 35	12♋38	7♒15	27♓51	17♏36	5♎53	20♈10	3♎46	28♏29	24♍48

THE SUN ENTERS THE SIGN OF AQUARIUS ON JAN 20 AT 05:39.

DAY	TIME	☉	☽	☿	♀	♂	♃	♄	♅	♆	♇
	h m s	° ' "	° '	° '	° '	° '	° '	° '	° '	° '	° '
F 1	8 44 6	11♒57 29	24♋41	6♒ 3	28♓50	18♏ 7	5♎51	20♈14	3♎45	28♏30	24♍47
E 2	8 48 2	12 58 21	6♌53	4R55	29 49	18 39	5R49	20 18	3R44	28 30	24R46
B 3	8 51 59	13 59 11	19 14	3 53	0♈46	19 10	5 46	20 23	3 42	28 31	24 45
R 4	8 55 55	15 0 1	1♍44	2 58	1 44	19 40	5 43	20 27	3 41	28 32	24 43
U 5	8 59 52	16 0 50	14 25	2 10	2 40	20 11	5 41	20 32	3 40	28 33	24 42
A 6	9 3 48	17 1 37	27 17	1 31	3 36	20 42	5 38	20 36	3 38	28 34	24 41
R 7	9 7 45	18 2 24	10♎21	1 0	4 32	21 12	5 34	20 41	3 37	28 35	24 40
Y 8	9 11 41	19 3 9	23 39	0 37	5 27	21 43	5 31	20 46	3 35	28 35	24 39
9	9 15 38	20 3 54	7♏11	0 22	6 21	22 13	5 28	20 51	3 33	28 36	24 37
10	9 19 35	21 4 37	21 0	0D15	7 15	22 43	5 24	20 56	3 32	28 37	24 36
11	9 23 31	22 5 20	5♐ 5	0 16	8 8	23 13	5 20	21 1	3 30	28 37	24 35
12	9 27 28	23 6 2	19 25	0 24	9 0	23 42	5 16	21 6	3 28	28 38	24 34
13	9 31 24	24 6 42	3♑58	0 38	9 51	24 12	5 12	21 11	3 27	28 38	24 32
14	9 35 21	25 7 22	18 39	0 58	10 42	24 41	5 7	21 17	3 25	28 39	24 31
15	9 39 17	26 8 0	3♒21	1 24	11 32	25 11	5 3	21 22	3 23	28 39	24 30
16	9 43 14	27 8 37	17 57	1 56	12 21	25 40	4 58	21 27	3 21	28 40	24 28
17	9 47 11	28 9 12	2♓21	2 32	13 9	26 9	4 53	21 33	3 19	28 40	24 27
18	9 51 7	29 9 45	16 25	3 12	13 56	26 37	4 48	21 39	3 17	28 41	24 25
19	9 55 4	0♓10 17	0♈ 6	3 56	14 43	27 6	4 43	21 44	3 15	28 41	24 24
20	9 59 0	1 10 48	13 23	4 45	15 28	27 34	4 37	21 50	3 13	28 41	24 22
21	10 2 57	2 11 16	26 17	5 36	16 13	28 2	4 32	21 56	3 11	28 42	24 21
22	10 6 53	3 11 43	8♉50	6 31	16 56	28 30	4 26	22 1	3 9	28 42	24 20
23	10 10 50	4 12 8	21 6	7 29	17 38	28 58	4 20	22 7	3 7	28 42	24 18
24	10 14 46	5 12 30	3♊ 9	8 29	18 19	29 25	4 15	22 13	3 4	28 42	24 17
25	10 18 43	6 12 51	15 4	9 33	18 59	29 53	4 9	22 19	3 2	28 42	24 15
26	10 22 39	7 13 11	26 56	10 38	19 38	0♐20	4 2	22 25	3 0	28 42	24 13
27	10 26 36	8 13 28	8♋50	11 46	20 16	0 47	3 56	22 32	2 58	28 43	24 12
28	10 30 33	9♓13 43	20♋49	12♒55	20♈52	1♐14	3♎50	22♈38	2♎55	28♏43	24♍10

THE SUN ENTERS THE SIGN OF PISCES ON FEB 18 AT 19:55.

DAY	TIME	☉	☽	☿	♀	♂	♃	♄	♅	♆	♇
	h m s	° ' "	° '	° '	° '	° '	° '	° '	° '	° '	° '
M 1	10 34 29	10♓13 56	2♌57	14♒ 7	21♈26	1♐40	3♎43	22♈44	2♎53	28♏43	24♍ 9
A 2	10 38 26	11 14 7	15 16	15 21	22 0	2 6	3R37	22 50	2R51	28R43	24R 7
R 3	10 42 22	12 14 16	27 49	16 36	22 31	2 32	3 30	22 57	2 48	28 43	24 6
C 4	10 46 19	13 14 24	10♍36	17 53	23 2	2 58	3 23	23 3	2 46	28 42	24 4
H 5	10 50 15	14 14 29	23 38	19 12	23 30	3 24	3 16	23 10	2 44	28 42	24 3
6	10 54 12	15 14 33	6♎54	20 32	23 57	3 49	3 9	23 16	2 41	28 42	24 1
7	10 58 8	16 14 34	20 22	21 54	24 23	4 14	3 2	23 23	2 39	28 42	23 59
8	11 2 5	17 14 35	4♏ 2	23 17	24 46	4 39	2 55	23 29	2 36	28 42	23 58
9	11 6 2	18 14 33	17 53	24 41	25 8	5 3	2 48	23 36	2 34	28 41	23 56
10	11 9 58	19 14 30	1♐52	26 7	25 27	5 28	2 40	23 43	2 31	28 41	23 55
11	11 13 55	20 14 26	15 59	27 34	25 45	5 52	2 33	23 50	2 29	28 41	23 53
12	11 17 51	21 14 19	0♑11	29 3	26 1	6 15	2 25	23 56	2 26	28 41	23 51
13	11 21 48	22 14 12	14 27	0♓33	26 14	6 39	2 18	24 3	2 24	28 40	23 50
14	11 25 44	23 14 2	28 43	2 4	26 26	7 2	2 10	24 10	2 21	28 40	23 48
15	11 29 41	24 13 51	12♒56	3 36	26 35	7 24	2 3	24 17	2 19	28 39	23 46
16	11 33 37	25 13 38	27 2	5 10	26 42	7 47	1 55	24 24	2 16	28 39	23 45
17	11 37 34	26 13 23	10♓58	6 44	26 47	8 9	1 47	24 31	2 13	28 38	23 43
18	11 41 31	27 13 6	24 40	8 21	26R49	8 31	1 40	24 38	2 11	28 38	23 42
19	11 45 27	28 12 47	8♈ 6	9 58	26 49	8 52	1 32	24 45	2 8	28 37	23 40
20	11 49 24	29 12 26	21 14	11 37	26 47	9 13	1 24	24 52	2 6	28 37	23 38
21	11 53 20	0♈12 3	4♉ 3	13 16	26 42	9 34	1 16	25 0	2 3	28 36	23 37
22	11 57 17	1 11 38	16 36	14 57	26 35	9 55	1 9	25 7	2 0	28 35	23 35
23	12 1 13	2 11 11	28 53	16 40	26 25	10 15	1 1	25 14	1 58	28 35	23 33
24	12 5 10	3 10 41	10♊58	18 24	26 12	10 34	0 53	25 21	1 55	28 34	23 32
25	12 9 6	4 10 9	22 54	20 8	25 57	10 53	0 45	25 29	1 53	28 33	23 30
26	12 13 3	5 9 35	4♋48	21 55	25 40	11 12	0 38	25 36	1 50	28 32	23 29
27	12 17 0	6 8 59	16 41	23 42	25 20	11 31	0 30	25 43	1 47	28 31	23 27
28	12 20 56	7 8 20	28 41	25 31	24 58	11 49	0 22	25 51	1 45	28 31	23 26
29	12 24 53	8 7 39	10♌50	27 22	24 34	12 6	0 14	25 58	1 42	28 30	23 24
30	12 28 49	9 6 56	23 13	29 13	24 7	12 23	0 7	26 5	1 40	28 29	23 22
31	12 32 46	10♈ 6 10	5♍54	1♈ 6	23♈39	12♐40	29♍59	26♈13	1♎37	28♏28	23♍21

THE SUN ENTERS THE SIGN OF ARIES ON MAR 20 AT 19:09.

♈	ARIES	♉	TAURUS	♊	GEMINI	♋	CANCER	♌	LEO	♍	VIRGO	♎	LIBRA

SIDEREAL . SUN . MOON . MERCURY . VENUS . MARS . JUPITER . SATURN . URANUS . NEPTUNE . PLUTO .

DAY	TIME	☉	☽	☿	♀	♂	♃	♄	♅	♆	♇
	h m s	° ' "	° '	° '	° '	° '	° '	° '	° '	° '	° '
A 1	12 36 42	11♈ 5 22	18♍53	3♈ 0	23♈ 9	12♐56	29♍52	26♈20	1♎34	28♏27	23♍19
P 2	12 40 39	12 4 32	2♎13	4 56	22R37	13 12	29R44	26 28	1R32	28R26	23R18
R 3	12 44 35	13 3 40	15 51	6 53	22 3	13 28	29 37	26 35	1 29	28 25	23 16
I 4	12 48 32	14 2 45	29 47	8 51	21 28	13 43	29 29	26 43	1 27	28 24	23 15
L 5	12 52 29	15 1 49	13♏56	10 51	20 52	13 57	29 22	26 50	1 24	28 23	23 13
6	12 56 25	16 0 51	28 14	12 52	20 15	14 11	29 15	26 58	1 22	28 22	23 12
7	13 0 22	16 59 52	12♐36	14 54	19 38	14 24	29 8	27 5	1 19	28 21	23 10
8	13 4 18	17 58 50	26 58	16 57	19 0	14 37	29 1	27 13	1 17	28 20	23 9
9	13 8 15	18 57 47	11♑16	19 0	18 22	14 49	28 54	27 20	1 14	28 19	23 8
10	13 12 11	19 56 43	25 26	21 5	17 44	15 1	28 47	27 28	1 12	28 17	23 6
11	13 16 8	20 55 36	9♒28	23 11	17 7	15 12	28 40	27 36	1 10	28 16	23 5
12	13 20 4	21 54 28	23 19	25 17	16 30	15 23	28 34	27 43	1 7	28 15	23 3
13	13 24 1	22 53 17	6♓59	27 23	15 55	15 33	28 27	27 51	1 5	28 14	23 2
14	13 27 58	23 52 5	20 27	29 29	15 20	15 42	28 21	27 59	1 2	28 12	23 1
15	13 31 54	24 50 52	3♈43	1♉35	14 47	15 51	28 14	28 6	1 0	28 11	22 59
16	13 35 51	25 49 36	16 47	3 40	14 15	15 59	28 8	28 14	0 58	28 10	22 58
17	13 39 47	26 48 18	29 37	5 45	13 44	16 7	28 2	28 21	0 56	28 9	22 57
18	13 43 44	27 46 59	12♉14	7 48	13 16	16 14	27 56	28 29	0 53	28 7	22 55
19	13 47 40	28 45 37	24 39	9 50	12 50	16 20	27 50	28 37	0 51	28 6	22 54
20	13 51 37	29 44 14	6♊51	11 50	12 25	16 26	27 44	28 44	0 49	28 5	22 53
21	13 55 33	0♉42 48	18 55	13 48	12 3	16 31	27 39	28 52	0 47	28 3	22 52
22	13 59 30	1 41 21	0♋51	15 43	11 43	16 35	27 33	29 0	0 45	28 2	22 51
23	14 3 27	2 39 51	12 43	17 36	11 25	16 38	27 28	29 7	0 43	28 0	22 49
24	14 7 23	3 38 19	24 36	19 25	11 10	16 41	27 23	29 15	0 41	27 59	22 48
25	14 11 20	4 36 45	6♌34	21 11	10 57	16 43	27 18	29 23	0 38	27 57	22 47
26	14 15 16	5 35 9	18 42	22 54	10 47	16 45	27 13	29 30	0 37	27 56	22 46
27	14 19 13	6 33 31	1♍ 4	24 33	10 39	16R46	27 8	29 38	0 35	27 55	22 45
28	14 23 9	7 31 50	13 45	26 8	10 34	16 45	27 4	29 45	0 33	27 53	22 44
29	14 27 6	8 30 8	26 49	27 40	10D30	16 45	27 0	29 53	0 31	27 52	22 43
30	14 31 2	9♉28 23	10♎18	29♉ 7	10♈30	16♐43	26♍55	0♉ 1	0♎29	27♏50	22♍42

THE SUN ENTERS THE SIGN OF TAURUS ON APR 20 AT 06:27.

DAY	TIME	☉	☽	☿	♀	♂	♃	♄	♅	♆	♇
	h m s	° ' "	° '	° '	° '	° '	° '	° '	° '	° '	° '
M 1	14 34 59	10♉26 37	24♎11	0♊29	10♈31	16♐41	26♍51	0♉ 8	0♎27	27♏48	22♍41
A 2	14 38 55	11 24 48	8♏28	1 48	10 35	16R38	26R47	0 16	0R25	27R47	22R40
Y 3	14 42 52	12 22 59	23 3	3 2	10 41	16 34	26 44	0 23	0 24	27 45	22 39
4	14 46 49	13 21 7	7♐49	4 12	10 50	16 30	26 40	0 31	0 22	27 44	22 38
5	14 50 45	14 19 14	22 38	5 17	11 1	16 25	26 37	0 38	0 20	27 42	22 37
6	14 54 42	15 17 20	7♑23	6 17	11 13	16 19	26 34	0 46	0 19	27 41	22 36
7	14 58 38	16 15 24	21 56	7 13	11 28	16 12	26 31	0 53	0 17	27 39	22 36
8	15 2 35	17 13 26	6♒14	8 3	11 45	16 4	26 28	1 1	0 16	27 38	22 35
9	15 6 31	18 11 28	20 14	8 49	12 3	15 56	26 25	1 8	0 14	27 36	22 34
10	15 10 28	19 9 28	3♓55	9 31	12 24	15 47	26 22	1 15	0 13	27 34	22 33
11	15 14 25	20 7 26	17 19	10 7	12 46	15 37	26 20	1 23	0 11	27 33	22 33
12	15 18 21	21 5 23	0♈27	10 38	13 10	15 27	26 18	1 30	0 10	27 31	22 32
13	15 22 18	22 3 19	13 22	11 4	13 36	15 15	26 16	1 38	0 9	27 30	22 31
14	15 26 14	23 1 14	26 5	11 26	14 3	15 3	26 14	1 45	0 7	27 28	22 31
15	15 30 11	23 59 7	8♉36	11 42	14 32	14 51	26 13	1 52	0 6	27 26	22 30
16	15 34 7	24 56 59	20 58	11 53	15 3	14 37	26 11	1 59	0 5	27 25	22 29
17	15 38 4	25 54 50	3♊12	11R59	15 34	14 23	26 10	2 7	0 4	27 23	22 29
18	15 42 0	26 52 39	15 17	12 1	16 7	14 9	26 9	2 14	0 3	27 21	22 28
19	15 45 57	27 50 26	27 16	11 57	16 42	13 53	26 8	2 21	0 2	27 20	22 28
20	15 49 54	28 48 13	9♋ 9	11 50	17 17	13 37	26 7	2 28	0 1	27 18	22 27
21	15 53 50	29 45 57	21 0	11 37	17 54	13 21	26 7	2 35	0 0	27 17	22 27
22	15 57 47	0♊43 40	2♌52	11 21	18 32	13 4	26 6	2 42	29♍59	27 15	22 27
23	16 1 43	1 41 22	14 48	11 1	19 11	12 47	26D 6	2 49	29 58	27 13	22 26
24	16 5 40	2 39 2	26 53	10 37	19 52	12 29	26 6	2 56	29 57	27 12	22 26
25	16 9 36	3 36 40	9♍12	10 11	20 33	12 10	26 6	3 3	29 57	27 10	22 26
26	16 13 33	4 34 17	21 50	9 42	21 15	11 51	26 7	3 10	29 56	27 8	22 25
27	16 17 29	5 31 52	4♎52	9 11	21 58	11 32	26 7	3 17	29 55	27 7	22 25
28	16 21 26	6 29 26	18 21	8 38	22 43	11 13	26 8	3 24	29 55	27 5	22 25
29	16 25 23	7 26 58	2♏18	8 4	23 28	10 53	26 9	3 31	29 54	27 4	22 25
30	16 29 19	8 24 30	16 44	7 31	24 13	10 33	26 10	3 38	29 54	27 2	22 25
31	16 33 16	9♊22 0	1♐33	6♊57	25♈ 0	10♐13	26♍11	3♉44	29♍53	27♏ 0	22♍25

THE SUN ENTERS THE SIGN OF GEMINI ON MAY 21 AT 05:50.

DAY	TIME	☉	☽	☿	♀	♂	♃	♄	♅	♆	♇
	h m s	° ' "	° '	° '	° '	° '	° '	° '	° '	° '	° '
J 1	16 37 12	10♊19 29	16♐38	6♊24	25♈48	9♐53	26♍13	3♉51	29♍53	26♏59	22♍25
U 2	16 41 9	11 16 57	1♑49	5R53	26 36	9R33	26 15	3 58	29R53	26R57	22D24
N 3	16 45 5	12 14 24	16 56	5 24	27 25	9 12	26 16	4 4	29 53	26 56	22 24
E 4	16 49 2	13 11 51	1♒48	4 57	28 15	8 52	26 18	4 11	29 52	26 54	22 25
5	16 52 58	14 9 16	16 20	4 32	29 5	8 31	26 21	4 17	29 52	26 53	22 25
6	16 56 55	15 6 41	0♓27	4 12	29 56	8 11	26 23	4 24	29 52	26 51	22 25
7	17 0 52	16 4 6	14 9	3 54	0♉48	7 51	26 25	4 30	29D52	26 50	22 25
8	17 4 48	17 1 29	27 29	3 41	1 40	7 31	26 28	4 36	29 52	26 48	22 25
9	17 8 45	17 58 53	10♈28	3 32	2 33	7 11	26 31	4 43	29 52	26 47	22 25
10	17 12 41	18 56 15	23 10	3D26	3 26	6 51	26 34	4 49	29 52	26 45	22 25
11	17 16 38	19 53 37	5♉38	3 26	4 20	6 32	26 37	4 55	29 52	26 44	22 26
12	17 20 34	20 50 59	17 56	3 29	5 15	6 13	26 40	5 1	29 53	26 42	22 26
13	17 24 31	21 48 20	0♊ 6	3 38	6 10	5 54	26 44	5 7	29 53	26 41	22 26
14	17 28 27	22 45 41	12 8	3 51	7 6	5 36	26 48	5 13	29 53	26 39	22 27
15	17 32 24	23 43 1	24 6	4 8	8 2	5 18	26 51	5 19	29 54	26 38	22 27
16	17 36 21	24 40 20	6♋ 0	4 30	8 58	5 1	26 55	5 25	29 54	26 37	22 27
17	17 40 17	25 37 39	17 52	4 57	9 55	4 45	27 0	5 31	29 55	26 35	22 28
18	17 44 14	26 34 57	29 42	5 27	10 52	4 28	27 4	5 37	29 55	26 34	22 28
19	17 48 10	27 32 14	11♌35	6 3	11 50	4 13	27 8	5 42	29 56	26 32	22 29
20	17 52 7	28 29 30	23 31	6 42	12 48	3 58	27 13	5 48	29 56	26 31	22 29
21	17 56 3	29 26 46	5♍37	7 26	13 46	3 44	27 18	5 54	29 57	26 30	22 30
22	18 0 0	0♋24 1	17 54	8 14	14 45	3 31	27 23	5 59	29 58	26 29	22 30
23	18 3 57	1 21 16	0♎30	9 6	15 44	3 18	27 28	6 5	29 59	26 27	22 31
24	18 7 53	2 18 30	13 27	10 2	16 44	3 6	27 33	6 10	0♎ 0	26 26	22 32
25	18 11 50	3 15 43	26 51	11 2	17 44	2 55	27 39	6 15	0 1	26 25	22 32
26	18 15 46	4 12 56	10♏44	12 6	18 44	2 44	27 44	6 21	0 1	26 24	22 33
27	18 19 43	5 10 8	25 6	13 14	19 44	2 34	27 50	6 26	0 3	26 22	22 34
28	18 23 39	6 7 20	9♐55	14 26	20 45	2 26	27 56	6 31	0 4	26 21	22 35
29	18 27 36	7 4 31	25 4	15 41	21 46	2 18	28 2	6 36	0 5	26 20	22 36
30	18 31 32	8♋ 1 42	10♑23	17♊ 0	22♉48	2♐10	28♍ 8	6♉41	0♎ 6	26♏19	22♍36

THE SUN ENTERS THE SIGN OF CANCER ON JUN 21 AT 13:56.

♏ SCORPIO ♐ SAGITTARIUS ♑ CAPRICORN ♒ AQUARIUS ♓ PISCES

SIDEREAL SUN. MOON. MERCURY. VENUS. MARS. JUPITER. SATURN. URANUS. NEPTUNE. PLUTO.

DAY	TIME	☉	☽	☿	♀	♂	♃	♄	♅	♆	♇
	h m s	° ' "	° '	° '	° '	° '	° '	° '	° '	° '	° '
J 1	18 35 29	8♋58 54	25♑41	18♊23	23♉49	2♐ 4	28♍14	6♉46	0♎ 7	26♏18	22♍37
U 2	18 39 26	9 56 5	10♒46	19 50	24 51	1R58	28 20	6 51	0 8	26R17	22 38
L 3	18 43 22	10 53 16	25 31	21 20	25 54	1 53	28 27	6 55	0 10	26 16	22 39
Y 4	18 47 19	11 50 27	9♓49	22 54	26 56	1 49	28 34	7 0	0 11	26 15	22 40
5	18 51 15	12 47 38	23 39	24 31	27 59	1 46	28 40	7 4	0 12	26 14	22 41
6	18 55 12	13 44 50	7♈ 2	26 11	29 2	1 44	28 47	7 9	0 14	26 13	22 42
7	18 59 8	14 42 2	20 1	27 55	0♊ 5	1 43	28 54	7 13	0 15	26 12	22 43
8	19 3 5	15 39 15	2♉40	29 42	1 9	1D42	29 2	7 18	0 17	26 11	22 44
9	19 7 1	16 36 27	15 3	1♋32	2 12	1 42	29 9	7 22	0 19	26 10	22 45
10	19 10 58	17 33 41	27 13	3 25	3 16	1 43	29 16	7 26	0 20	26 9	22 46
11	19 14 55	18 30 54	9♊15	5 21	4 20	1 45	29 24	7 30	0 22	26 8	22 48
12	19 18 51	19 28 9	21 11	7 19	5 25	1 48	29 32	7 34	0 24	26 7	22 49
13	19 22 48	20 25 23	3♋ 4	9 19	6 29	1 51	29 39	7 38	0 26	26 7	22 50
14	19 26 44	21 22 38	14 56	11 22	7 34	1 56	29 47	7 42	0 27	26 6	22 51
15	19 30 41	22 19 53	26 47	13 26	8 39	2 1	29 55	7 46	0 29	26 5	22 52
16	19 34 37	23 17 8	8♌41	15 32	9 44	2 7	0♎ 4	7 49	0 31	26 4	22 54
17	19 38 34	24 14 24	20 37	17 38	10 49	2 13	0 12	7 53	0 33	26 4	22 55
18	19 42 31	25 11 40	2♍40	19 46	11 55	2 21	0 20	7 56	0 35	26 3	22 56
19	19 46 27	26 8 56	14 51	21 54	13 1	2 29	0 29	8 0	0 37	26 2	22 58
20	19 50 24	27 6 13	27 13	24 2	14 6	2 38	0 37	8 3	0 40	26 2	22 59
21	19 54 20	28 3 29	9♎51	26 10	15 12	2 48	0 46	8 6	0 42	26 1	23 1
22	19 58 17	29 0 46	22 47	28 18	16 19	2 58	0 55	8 9	0 44	26 1	23 2
23	20 2 13	29 58 3	6♏ 7	0♌25	17 25	3 10	1 4	8 12	0 46	26 0	23 4
24	20 6 10	0♌55 21	19 53	2 32	18 31	3 22	1 13	8 15	0 49	26 0	23 5
25	20 10 6	1 52 39	4♐ 5	4 37	19 38	3 34	1 22	8 18	0 51	25 59	23 7
26	20 14 3	2 49 57	18 42	6 42	20 45	3 48	1 31	8 21	0 53	25 59	23 8
27	20 18 0	3 47 16	3♑40	8 45	21 52	4 2	1 41	8 24	0 56	25 59	23 10
28	20 21 56	4 44 36	18 50	10 47	22 59	4 16	1 50	8 26	0 58	25 58	23 11
29	20 25 53	5 41 56	4♒ 4	12 47	24 6	4 32	2 0	8 29	1 1	25 58	23 13
30	20 29 49	6 39 17	19 9	14 46	25 13	4 48	2 9	8 31	1 3	25 58	23 15
31	20 33 46	7♌36 38	3♓58	16♌44	26♊21	5♐ 4	2♎19	8♉33	1♎ 6	25♏57	23♍16

THE SUN ENTERS THE SIGN OF LEO ON JUL 23 AT 00:49.

DAY	TIME	☉	☽	☿	♀	♂	♃	♄	♅	♆	♇
	h m s	° ' "	° '	° '	° '	° '	° '	° '	° '	° '	° '
A 1	20 37 42	8♌34 1	18♓23	18♌39	27♊29	5♐21	2♎29	8♉35	1♎ 8	25♏57	23♍18
U 2	20 41 39	9 31 24	2♈20	20 34	28 36	5 39	2 39	8 37	1 11	25R57	23 20
G 3	20 45 35	10 28 49	15 50	22 26	29 44	5 58	2 49	8 39	1 14	25 57	23 21
U 4	20 49 32	11 26 15	28 55	24 17	0♋52	6 17	2 59	8 41	1 16	25 57	23 23
S 5	20 53 29	12 23 42	11♉36	26 7	2 1	6 36	3 9	8 43	1 19	25 56	23 25
T 6	20 57 25	13 21 10	23 59	27 55	3 9	6 56	3 19	8 45	1 22	25 56	23 27
7	21 1 22	14 18 40	6♊ 8	29 41	4 17	7 17	3 30	8 46	1 25	25D56	23 28
8	21 5 18	15 16 11	18 7	1♍26	5 26	7 38	3 40	8 48	1 28	25 56	23 30
9	21 9 15	16 13 44	0♋ 1	3 9	6 35	8 0	3 51	8 49	1 31	25 56	23 32
10	21 13 11	17 11 17	11 52	4 50	7 44	8 22	4 1	8 50	1 34	25 56	23 34
11	21 17 8	18 8 52	23 44	6 30	8 53	8 45	4 12	8 51	1 37	25 57	23 36
12	21 21 4	19 6 28	5♌38	8 9	10 2	9 8	4 23	8 52	1 40	25 57	23 38
13	21 25 1	20 4 6	17 38	9 46	11 11	9 31	4 33	8 53	1 43	25 57	23 40
14	21 28 58	21 1 44	29 43	11 21	12 20	9 56	4 44	8 54	1 46	25 57	23 41
15	21 32 54	21 59 24	11♍57	12 55	13 30	10 20	4 55	8 55	1 49	25 57	23 43
16	21 36 51	22 57 5	24 20	14 27	14 39	10 46	5 6	8 55	1 52	25 58	23 45
17	21 40 47	23 54 40	6♎55	15 50	15 49	11 11	5 18	8 56	1 55	25 58	23 47
18	21 44 44	24 52 30	19 43	17 28	16 58	11 37	5 29	8 56	1 58	25 58	23 49
19	21 48 40	25 50 14	2♏48	18 55	18 8	12 4	5 40	8 57	2 1	25 58	23 51
20	21 52 37	26 47 59	16 10	20 22	19 18	12 31	5 51	8 57	2 5	25 59	23 53
21	21 56 33	27 45 45	29 53	21 46	20 28	12 58	6 3	8R57	2 8	25 59	23 55
22	22 0 30	28 43 33	13♐55	23 9	21 38	13 26	6 14	8 57	2 11	26 0	23 57
23	22 4 27	29 41 22	28 17	24 31	22 48	13 54	6 26	8 57	2 15	26 0	23 59
24	22 8 23	0♍39 12	12♑56	25 50	23 59	14 22	6 37	8 56	2 18	26 1	24 2
25	22 12 20	1 37 3	27 46	27 8	25 9	14 51	6 49	8 56	2 21	26 1	24 4
26	22 16 16	2 34 55	12♒40	28 25	26 20	15 20	7 0	8 56	2 25	26 2	24 6
27	22 20 13	3 32 49	27 30	29 39	27 30	15 50	7 12	8 55	2 28	26 2	24 8
28	22 24 9	4 30 44	12♓ 9	0♎52	28 41	16 20	7 24	8 54	2 32	26 3	24 10
29	22 28 6	5 28 41	26 29	2 2	29 52	16 50	7 36	8 54	2 35	26 4	24 12
30	22 32 2	6 26 40	10♈28	3 11	1♌ 3	17 21	7 48	8 53	2 38	26 4	24 14
31	22 35 59	7♍24 40	24♈ 1	4♎17	2♌14	17♐52	8♎ 0	8♉52	2♎42	26♏ 5	24♍16

THE SUN ENTERS THE SIGN OF VIRGO ON AUG 23 AT 07:44.

DAY	TIME	☉	☽	☿	♀	♂	♃	♄	♅	♆	♇
	h m s	° ' "	° '	° '	° '	° '	° '	° '	° '	° '	° '
S 1	22 39 56	8♍22 42	7♉ 9	5♎21	3♌25	18♐23	8♎12	8♉51	2♎45	26♏ 6	24♍18
E 2	22 43 52	9 20 46	19 55	6 23	4 36	18 55	8 24	8R50	2 49	26 7	24 21
P 3	22 47 49	10 18 52	2♊22	7 22	5 47	19 27	8 36	8 48	2 53	26 8	24 23
T 4	22 51 45	11 17 0	14 33	8 19	6 58	19 59	8 48	8 47	2 56	26 8	24 25
E 5	22 55 42	12 15 10	26 33	9 12	8 10	20 32	9 0	8 45	3 0	26 9	24 27
M 6	22 59 38	13 13 22	8♋26	10 3	9 21	21 5	9 12	8 44	3 3	26 10	24 29
B 7	23 3 35	14 11 36	20 18	10 50	10 33	21 38	9 25	8 42	3 7	26 11	24 31
E 8	23 7 31	15 9 52	2♌11	11 35	11 45	22 11	9 37	8 40	3 11	26 12	24 34
R 9	23 11 28	16 8 10	14 9	12 15	12 57	22 45	9 49	8 39	3 14	26 13	24 36
10	23 15 25	17 6 30	26 16	12 51	14 8	23 19	10 2	8 37	3 18	26 14	24 38
11	23 19 21	18 4 51	8♍32	13 24	15 20	23 53	10 14	8 34	3 22	26 15	24 40
12	23 23 18	19 3 15	21 1	13 51	16 32	24 28	10 27	8 32	3 25	26 16	24 42
13	23 27 14	20 1 40	3♎42	14 14	17 45	25 3	10 39	8 30	3 29	26 18	24 45
14	23 31 11	21 0 7	16 37	14 32	18 57	25 38	10 52	8 28	3 33	26 19	24 47
15	23 35 7	21 58 36	29 46	14 44	20 9	26 13	11 4	8 25	3 36	26 20	24 49
16	23 39 4	22 57 7	13♏ 8	14R51	21 21	26 48	11 17	8 23	3 40	26 21	24 51
17	23 43 0	23 55 39	26 44	14 51	22 34	27 24	11 30	8 20	3 44	26 22	24 54
18	23 46 57	24 54 13	10♐33	14 45	23 46	28 0	11 42	8 17	3 48	26 24	24 56
19	23 50 53	25 52 49	24 33	14 31	24 59	28 37	11 55	8 14	3 51	26 25	24 58
20	23 54 50	26 51 26	8♑45	14 11	26 11	29 13	12 8	8 11	3 55	26 26	25 0
21	23 58 47	27 50 5	23 5	13 44	27 24	29 50	12 21	8 8	3 59	26 28	25 2
22	0 2 43	28 48 45	7♒30	13 10	28 37	0♑27	12 33	8 5	4 3	26 29	25 5
23	0 6 40	29 47 27	21 57	12 28	29 50	1 4	12 46	8 2	4 7	26 30	25 7
24	0 10 36	0♎46 11	6♓22	11 41	1♍ 2	1 41	12 59	7 59	4 10	26 32	25 9
25	0 14 33	1 44 57	20 38	10 47	2 15	2 19	13 12	7 55	4 14	26 33	25 11
26	0 18 29	2 43 45	4♈42	9 47	3 28	2 57	13 25	7 52	4 18	26 35	25 14
27	0 22 26	3 42 34	18 29	8 44	4 41	3 35	13 38	7 49	4 22	26 36	25 16
28	0 26 22	4 41 26	1♉57	7 38	5 55	4 13	13 50	7 45	4 25	26 38	25 18
29	0 30 19	5 40 20	15 4	6 30	7 8	4 51	14 3	7 41	4 29	26 39	25 20
30	0 34 16	6♎39 16	27♉51	5♎23	8♍21	5♑29	14♎16	7♉38	4♎33	26♏41	25♍22

THE SUN ENTERS THE SIGN OF LIBRA ON SEP 23 AT 05:08.

♈ ARIES ♉ TAURUS ♊ GEMINI ♋ CANCER ♌ LEO ♍ VIRGO ♎ LIBRA

SIDEREAL SUN. MOON. MERCURY. VENUS. MARS. JUPITER. SATURN. URANUS. NEPTUNE. PLUTO.

DAY	TIME	☉	☽	☿	♀	♂	♃	♄	♅	♆	♇
	h m s	° ' "	° '	° '	° '	° '	° '	° '	° '	° '	° '
O 1	0 38 12	7♎38 14	10♊19	4♎18	9♍34	6♑ 8	14♎29	7♉34	4♎37	26♏43	25♍25
C 2	0 42 9	8 37 15	22 32	3R17	10 48	6 47	14 42	7R30	4 41	26 44	25 27
T 3	0 46 5	9 36 18	4♋33	2 21	12 1	7 26	14 55	7 26	4 44	26 46	25 29
O 4	0 50 2	10 35 24	16 27	1 33	13 15	8 5	15 8	7 22	4 48	26 47	25 31
B 5	0 53 58	11 34 31	28 18	0 53	14 28	8 44	15 21	7 18	4 52	26 49	25 33
E 6	0 57 55	12 33 41	10♌12	0 22	15 42	9 24	15 34	7 14	4 56	26 51	25 35
R 7	1 1 51	13 32 53	22 13	0 2	16 56	10 3	15 47	7 10	4 59	26 53	25 38
8	1 5 48	14 32 7	4♍25	29♍52	18 10	10 43	16 0	7 6	5 3	26 54	25 40
9	1 9 45	15 31 24	16 51	29D53	19 23	11 23	16 13	7 1	5 7	26 56	25 42
10	1 13 41	16 30 42	29 34	0♎ 4	20 37	12 3	16 26	6 57	5 11	26 58	25 44
11	1 17 38	17 30 3	12♎35	0 26	21 51	12 44	16 39	6 53	5 14	27 0	25 46
12	1 21 34	18 29 26	25 53	0 58	23 5	13 24	16 52	6 48	5 18	27 2	25 48
13	1 25 31	19 28 51	9♏28	1 39	24 19	14 5	17 5	6 44	5 22	27 4	25 50
14	1 29 27	20 28 18	23 17	2 28	25 33	14 45	17 18	6 39	5 26	27 5	25 52
15	1 33 24	21 27 47	7♐16	3 26	26 47	15 26	17 31	6 35	5 29	27 7	25 54
16	1 37 20	22 27 18	21 23	4 30	28 2	16 7	17 44	6 30	5 33	27 9	25 56
17	1 41 17	23 26 50	5♑33	5 40	29 16	16 48	17 57	6 25	5 37	27 11	25 58
18	1 45 14	24 26 24	19 45	6 55	0♎30	17 29	18 10	6 21	5 40	27 13	26 0
19	1 49 10	25 26 0	3♒55	8 15	1 44	18 11	18 23	6 16	5 44	27 15	26 2
20	1 53 7	26 25 38	18 2	9 39	2 59	18 52	18 36	6 11	5 48	27 17	26 4
21	1 57 3	27 25 17	2♓ 5	11 6	4 13	19 34	18 49	6 7	5 51	27 19	26 6
22	2 1 0	28 24 58	16 1	12 37	5 27	20 15	19 2	6 2	5 55	27 21	26 8
23	2 4 56	29 24 40	29 50	14 9	6 42	20 57	19 15	5 57	5 58	27 23	26 10
24	2 8 53	0♏24 25	13♈29	15 43	7 56	21 39	19 28	5 52	6 2	27 25	26 12
25	2 12 49	1 24 11	26 55	17 19	9 11	22 21	19 41	5 48	6 5	27 27	26 14
26	2 16 46	2 23 59	10♉ 8	18 56	10 25	23 3	19 54	5 43	6 9	27 29	26 16
27	2 20 43	3 23 49	23 5	20 34	11 40	23 45	20 7	5 38	6 12	27 31	26 18
28	2 24 39	4 23 42	5♊46	22 12	12 55	24 28	20 19	5 33	6 16	27 34	26 20
29	2 28 36	5 23 36	18 12	23 52	14 9	25 10	20 32	5 28	6 19	27 36	26 22
30	2 32 32	6 23 33	0♋24	25 31	15 24	25 53	20 45	5 23	6 23	27 38	26 23
31	2 36 29	7♏23 32	12♋24	27♎10	16♎39	26♑35	20♎58	5♉19	6♎26	27♏40	26♍25

THE SUN ENTERS THE SIGN OF SCORPIO ON OCT 23 AT 14:12.

DAY	TIME	☉	☽	☿	♀	♂	♃	♄	♅	♆	♇
	h m s	° ' "	° '	° '	° '	° '	° '	° '	° '	° '	° '
N 1	2 40 25	8♏23 33	24♋17	28♎50	17♎54	27♑18	21♎10	5♉14	6♎29	27♏42	26♍27
O 2	2 44 22	9 23 36	6♌ 7	0♏29	19 8	28 1	21 23	5R 9	6 33	27 44	26 29
V 3	2 48 18	10 23 41	18 0	2 9	20 23	28 43	21 36	5 4	6 36	27 46	26 30
E 4	2 52 15	11 23 48	0♍ 0	3 48	21 38	29 26	21 49	4 59	6 39	27 49	26 32
M 5	2 56 12	12 23 57	12 12	5 27	22 53	0♒ 9	22 1	4 55	6 43	27 51	26 34
B 6	3 0 8	13 24 8	24 42	7 6	24 8	0 52	22 14	4 50	6 46	27 53	26 36
E 7	3 4 5	14 24 21	7♎33	8 44	25 23	1 35	22 26	4 45	6 49	27 55	26 37
R 8	3 8 1	15 24 36	20 47	10 22	26 38	2 19	22 39	4 40	6 52	27 57	26 39
9	3 11 58	16 24 53	4♏25	12 0	27 53	3 2	22 51	4 36	6 55	28 0	26 40
10	3 15 54	17 25 12	18 24	13 38	29 8	3 45	23 4	4 31	6 59	28 2	26 42
11	3 19 51	18 25 33	2♐41	15 15	0♏23	4 29	23 16	4 26	7 2	28 4	26 44
12	3 23 47	19 25 55	17 10	16 52	1 38	5 12	23 29	4 22	7 5	28 6	26 45
13	3 27 44	20 26 19	1♑44	18 28	2 53	5 56	23 41	4 17	7 8	28 8	26 47
14	3 31 41	21 26 45	16 15	20 5	4 8	6 40	23 53	4 13	7 11	28 11	26 48
15	3 35 37	22 27 12	0♒40	21 41	5 23	7 23	24 5	4 8	7 14	28 13	26 50
16	3 39 34	23 27 40	14 53	23 16	6 39	8 7	24 18	4 4	7 17	28 15	26 51
17	3 43 30	24 28 9	28 55	24 52	7 54	8 51	24 30	3 59	7 20	28 17	26 52
18	3 47 27	25 28 39	12♓43	26 27	9 9	9 35	24 42	3 55	7 22	28 20	26 54
19	3 51 23	26 29 11	26 20	28 2	10 24	10 19	24 54	3 51	7 25	28 22	26 55
20	3 55 20	27 29 44	9♈44	29 36	11 39	11 3	25 6	3 47	7 28	28 24	26 56
21	3 59 16	28 30 18	22 58	1♐11	12 55	11 47	25 18	3 42	7 31	28 26	26 58
22	4 3 13	29 30 53	6♉ 2	2 45	14 10	12 31	25 30	3 38	7 33	28 29	26 59
23	4 7 10	0♐31 30	18 54	4 19	15 25	13 15	25 41	3 34	7 36	28 31	27 0
24	4 11 6	1 32 8	1♊35	5 53	16 40	13 59	25 53	3 30	7 39	28 33	27 1
25	4 15 3	2 32 48	14 4	7 27	17 56	14 43	26 5	3 26	7 41	28 35	27 3
26	4 18 59	3 33 29	26 22	9 0	19 11	15 27	26 16	3 23	7 44	28 38	27 4
27	4 22 56	4 34 11	8♋28	10 34	20 26	16 12	26 28	3 19	7 46	28 40	27 5
28	4 26 52	5 34 55	20 26	12 7	21 42	16 56	26 40	3 15	7 49	28 42	27 6
29	4 30 49	6 35 41	2♌17	13 40	22 57	17 40	26 51	3 11	7 51	28 44	27 7
30	4 34 45	7♐36 27	14♌ 5	15♐14	24♏12	18♒24	27♎ 2	3♉ 8	7♎54	28♏47	27♍ 8

THE SUN ENTERS THE SIGN OF SAGITTARIUS ON NOV 22 AT 11:32.

DAY	TIME	☉	☽	☿	♀	♂	♃	♄	♅	♆	♇
	h m s	° ' "	° '	° '	° '	° '	° '	° '	° '	° '	° '
D 1	4 38 42	8♐37 16	25♌55	16♐47	25♏28	19♒ 9	27♎14	3♉ 4	7♎56	28♏49	27♍ 9
E 2	4 42 39	9 38 5	7♍52	18 20	26 43	19 53	27 25	3R 1	7 58	28 51	27 10
C 3	4 46 35	10 38 56	20 1	19 53	27 58	20 38	27 36	2 58	8 0	28 53	27 11
E 4	4 50 32	11 39 49	2♎28	21 26	29 14	21 22	27 47	2 55	8 3	28 56	27 12
M 5	4 54 28	12 40 42	15 18	22 58	0♐29	22 7	27 58	2 51	8 5	28 58	27 13
B 6	4 58 25	13 41 37	28 35	24 31	1 45	22 51	28 9	2 48	8 7	29 0	27 13
E 7	5 2 21	14 42 34	12♏20	26 4	3 0	23 36	28 20	2 45	8 9	29 2	27 14
R 8	5 6 18	15 43 31	26 33	27 36	4 16	24 20	28 31	2 42	8 11	29 4	27 15
9	5 10 14	16 44 30	11♐ 9	29 9	5 31	25 5	28 41	2 40	8 13	29 7	27 16
10	5 14 11	17 45 30	26 2	0♑41	6 47	25 50	28 52	2 37	8 15	29 9	27 17
11	5 18 8	18 46 30	11♑ 2	2 13	8 2	26 34	29 2	2 34	8 17	29 11	27 17
12	5 22 4	19 47 31	26 0	3 45	9 17	27 19	29 13	2 32	8 18	29 13	27 18
13	5 26 1	20 48 33	10♒47	5 16	10 33	28 4	29 23	2 30	8 20	29 15	27 18
14	5 29 57	21 49 36	25 16	6 47	11 48	28 48	29 33	2 27	8 22	29 17	27 19
15	5 33 54	22 50 38	9♓26	8 18	13 4	29 33	29 43	2 25	8 23	29 19	27 20
16	5 37 50	23 51 41	23 15	9 48	14 19	0♓18	29 53	2 23	8 25	29 22	27 20
17	5 41 47	24 52 45	6♈44	11 17	15 35	1 3	0♏ 3	2 21	8 27	29 24	27 21
18	5 45 44	25 53 48	19 57	12 46	16 50	1 47	0 13	2 19	8 28	29 26	27 21
19	5 49 40	26 54 52	2♉54	14 13	18 6	2 32	0 23	2 17	8 29	29 28	27 21
20	5 53 37	27 55 57	15 38	15 39	19 21	3 17	0 33	2 16	8 31	29 30	27 22
21	5 57 33	28 57 2	28 12	17 4	20 37	4 2	0 42	2 14	8 32	29 32	27 22
22	6 1 30	29 58 7	10♊36	18 27	21 52	4 47	0 51	2 12	8 33	29 34	27 22
23	6 5 26	0♑59 13	22 50	19 48	23 8	5 31	1 1	2 11	8 35	29 36	27 23
24	6 9 23	2 0 19	4♋57	21 6	24 23	6 16	1 10	2 10	8 36	29 38	27 23
25	6 13 19	3 1 25	16 57	22 22	25 39	7 1	1 19	2 9	8 37	29 40	27 23
26	6 17 16	4 2 32	28 50	23 34	26 54	7 46	1 28	2 8	8 38	29 42	27 23
27	6 21 13	5 3 39	10♌39	24 43	28 10	8 30	1 37	2 7	8 39	29 44	27 23
28	6 25 9	6 4 47	22 27	25 47	29 25	9 15	1 46	2 6	8 40	29 46	27 23
29	6 29 6	7 5 55	4♍16	26 45	0♑41	10 0	1 54	2 5	8 41	29 48	27 24
30	6 33 2	8 7 3	16 12	27 38	1 56	10 45	2 3	2 5	8 42	29 49	27R24
31	6 36 59	9♑ 8 12	28♍19	28♑23	3♑12	11♓29	2♏11	2♉ 4	8♎43	29♏51	27♍24

THE SUN ENTERS THE SIGN OF CAPRICORN ON DEC 22 AT 00:45.

♏ SCORPIO ♐ SAGITTARIUS ♑ CAPRICORN ♒ AQUARIUS ♓ PISCES

1970

SIDEREAL SUN . . . MOON . . . MERCURY . VENUS . . MARS . . JUPITER . SATURN . URANUS . NEPTUNE . PLUTO .

DAY	TIME h m s	☉ ° ' "	☽ ° '	☿ ° '	♀ ° '	♂ ° '	♃ ° '	♄ ° '	♅ ° '	♆ ° '	♇ ° '
J 1	6 40 55	10♑ 9 21	10♎42	29♑ 1	4♑27	12♓14	2♏19	2♉ 4	8♎43	29♏53	27♍24
A 2	6 44 52	11 10 30	23 26	29 31	5 43	12 59	2 28	2R 3	8 44	29 55	27R23
N 3	6 48 48	12 11 40	6♏37	29 50	6 58	13 44	2 36	2D 3	8 45	29 57	27 23
U 4	6 52 45	13 12 50	20 17	29R59	8 14	14 28	2 44	2 3	8 45	29 59	27 23
A 5	6 56 42	14 14 1	4♐27	29 58	9 29	15 13	2 51	2 3	8 46	0♐ 0	27 23
R 6	7 0 38	15 15 12	19 5	29 44	10 45	15 58	2 59	2 4	8 46	0 2	27 23
Y 7	7 4 35	16 16 22	4♑ 5	29 19	12 0	16 43	3 6	2 4	8 46	0 4	27 23
8	7 8 31	17 17 33	19 19	28 42	13 16	17 27	3 14	2 4	8 47	0 5	27 22
9	7 12 28	18 18 44	4♒34	27 54	14 31	18 12	3 21	2 5	8 47	0 7	27 22
10	7 16 24	19 19 54	19 41	26 55	15 47	18 57	3 28	2 5	8 47	0 9	27 22
11	7 20 21	20 21 3	4♓31	25 48	17 2	19 41	3 35	2 6	8 47	0 10	27 21
12	7 24 18	21 22 12	18 58	24 35	18 18	20 26	3 42	2 7	8 48	0 12	27 21
13	7 28 14	22 23 20	3♈ 0	23 17	19 33	21 11	3 48	2 8	8R48	0 14	27 20
14	7 32 11	23 24 28	16 36	21 58	20 49	21 55	3 55	2 9	8 48	0 15	27 20
15	7 36 7	24 25 35	29 49	20 39	22 4	22 40	4 1	2 10	8 47	0 17	27 19
16	7 40 4	25 26 41	12♉41	19 24	23 19	23 24	4 7	2 12	8 47	0 18	27 19
17	7 44 0	26 27 47	25 16	18 14	24 35	24 9	4 13	2 13	8 47	0 20	27 18
18	7 47 57	27 28 52	7♊38	17 10	25 50	24 54	4 19	2 14	8 47	0 21	27 18
19	7 51 53	28 29 56	19 50	16 15	27 6	25 38	4 25	2 16	8 47	0 22	27 17
20	7 55 50	29 30 59	1♋53	15 28	28 21	26 23	4 31	2 18	8 46	0 24	27 16
21	7 59 47	0♒32 1	13 50	14 51	29 37	27 7	4 36	2 20	8 46	0 25	27 16
22	8 3 43	1 33 3	25 43	14 23	0♒52	27 51	4 41	2 22	8 45	0 26	27 15
23	8 7 40	2 34 4	7♌33	14 4	2 7	28 36	4 46	2 24	8 45	0 28	27 14
24	8 11 36	3 35 5	19 22	13D54	3 23	29 20	4 51	2 26	8 44	0 29	27 14
25	8 15 33	4 36 4	1♍12	13 52	4 38	0♈ 5	4 56	2 28	8 44	0 30	27 13
26	8 19 29	5 37 3	13 6	13 59	5 54	0 49	5 1	2 31	8 43	0 31	27 12
27	8 23 26	6 38 1	25 6	14 12	7 9	1 33	5 5	2 33	8 42	0 33	27 11
28	8 27 22	7 38 58	7♎16	14 32	8 24	2 18	5 9	2 36	8 42	0 34	27 10
29	8 31 19	8 39 55	19 40	14 59	9 40	3 2	5 14	2 38	8 41	0 35	27 9
30	8 35 16	9 40 51	2♏22	15 31	10 55	3 46	5 17	2 41	8 40	0 36	27 8
31	8 39 12	10♒41 47	15♏27	16♑ 8	12♒10	4♈30	5♏21	2♉44	8♎39	0♐37	27♍ 7

THE SUN ENTERS THE SIGN OF AQUARIUS ON JAN 20 AT 11:24.

DAY	TIME h m s	☉ ° ' "	☽ ° '	☿ ° '	♀ ° '	♂ ° '	♃ ° '	♄ ° '	♅ ° '	♆ ° '	♇ ° '
F 1	8 43 9	11♒42 41	28♏57	16♑50	13♒26	5♈14	5♏25	2♉47	8♎38	0♐38	27♍ 6
E 2	8 47 5	12 43 36	12♐55	17 36	14 41	5 59	5 28	2 50	8R37	0 39	27R 5
B 3	8 51 2	13 44 29	27 20	18 26	15 56	6 43	5 31	2 53	8 36	0 40	27 4
R 4	8 54 58	14 45 21	12♑ 9	19 20	17 12	7 27	5 35	2 57	8 35	0 41	27 3
U 5	8 58 55	15 46 13	27 15	20 17	18 27	8 11	5 37	3 0	8 33	0 42	27 2
A 6	9 2 51	16 47 3	12♒30	21 16	19 42	8 55	5 40	3 4	8 32	0 43	27 1
R 7	9 6 48	17 47 52	27 43	22 19	20 58	9 39	5 43	3 7	8 31	0 43	27 0
Y 8	9 10 45	18 48 40	12♓44	23 23	22 13	10 23	5 45	3 11	8 30	0 44	26 59
9	9 14 41	19 49 27	27 25	24 31	23 28	11 7	5 47	3 15	8 28	0 45	26 57
10	9 18 38	20 50 11	11♈41	25 40	24 43	11 51	5 49	3 18	8 27	0 46	26 56
11	9 22 34	21 50 55	25 30	26 51	25 59	12 35	5 51	3 22	8 25	0 46	26 55
12	9 26 31	22 51 36	8♉52	28 4	27 14	13 19	5 52	3 27	8 24	0 47	26 54
13	9 30 27	23 52 16	21 50	29 18	28 29	14 3	5 54	3 31	8 22	0 48	26 52
14	9 34 24	24 52 55	4♊26	0♒35	29 44	14 46	5 55	3 35	8 21	0 48	26 51
15	9 38 20	25 53 32	16 45	1 52	0♓59	15 30	5 56	3 39	8 19	0 49	26 50
16	9 42 17	26 54 7	28 51	3 12	2 14	16 14	5 57	3 44	8 17	0 50	26 48
17	9 46 14	27 54 40	10♋48	4 32	3 30	16 57	5 57	3 48	8 15	0 50	26 47
18	9 50 10	28 55 12	22 40	5 54	4 45	17 41	5 58	3 53	8 14	0 50	26 46
19	9 54 7	29 55 42	4♌29	7 17	6 0	18 25	5R58	3 57	8 12	0 51	26 44
20	9 58 3	0♓56 10	16 18	8 41	7 15	19 8	5 58	4 2	8 10	0 51	26 43
21	10 2 0	1 56 36	28 10	10 7	8 30	19 52	5 58	4 7	8 8	0 52	26 41
22	10 5 56	2 57 1	10♍ 6	11 33	9 45	20 35	5 58	4 12	8 6	0 52	26 40
23	10 9 53	3 57 25	22 9	13 1	11 0	21 19	5 57	4 17	8 4	0 52	26 39
24	10 13 49	4 57 46	4♎20	14 30	12 15	22 2	5 57	4 22	8 2	0 53	26 37
25	10 17 46	5 58 6	16 41	16 0	13 30	22 46	5 56	4 27	8 0	0 53	26 36
26	10 21 43	6 58 25	29 16	17 30	14 45	23 29	5 55	4 32	7 58	0 53	26 34
27	10 25 39	7 58 42	12♏ 5	19 2	16 0	24 12	5 53	4 38	7 56	0 53	26 33
28	10 29 36	8♓58 58	25♏12	20♒35	17♓15	24♈55	5♏52	4♉43	7♎54	0♐53	26♍31

THE SUN ENTERS THE SIGN OF PISCES ON FEB 19 AT 01:42.

DAY	TIME h m s	☉ ° ' "	☽ ° '	☿ ° '	♀ ° '	♂ ° '	♃ ° '	♄ ° '	♅ ° '	♆ ° '	♇ ° '
M 1	10 33 32	9♓59 12	8♐38	22♒10	18♓30	25♈39	5♏50	4♉48	7♎52	0♐53	26♍29
A 2	10 37 29	10 59 25	22 26	23 45	19 45	26 22	5R49	4 54	7R49	0 53	26R28
R 3	10 41 25	11 59 37	6♑35	25 21	20 59	27 5	5 47	5 0	7 47	0R53	26 26
C 4	10 45 22	12 59 47	21 4	26 58	22 14	27 48	5 44	5 5	7 45	0 53	26 25
H 5	10 49 18	13 59 55	5♒49	28 36	23 29	28 31	5 42	5 11	7 43	0 53	26 23
6	10 53 15	15 0 2	20 45	0♓16	24 44	29 14	5 40	5 17	7 40	0 53	26 22
7	10 57 12	16 0 7	5♓44	1 56	25 59	29 57	5 37	5 23	7 38	0 53	26 20
8	11 1 8	17 0 10	20 37	3 38	27 14	0♉40	5 34	5 29	7 36	0 53	26 18
9	11 5 5	18 0 11	5♈18	5 21	28 28	1 23	5 31	5 34	7 33	0 53	26 17
10	11 9 1	19 0 10	19 39	7 4	29 43	2 6	5 28	5 41	7 31	0 53	26 15
11	11 12 58	20 0 7	3♉36	8 49	0♈58	2 49	5 24	5 47	7 28	0 52	26 14
12	11 16 54	21 0 2	17 7	10 35	2 13	3 32	5 21	5 53	7 26	0 52	26 12
13	11 20 51	21 59 55	0♊12	12 23	3 27	4 15	5 17	5 59	7 23	0 52	26 10
14	11 24 47	22 59 46	12 54	14 11	4 42	4 57	5 13	6 5	7 21	0 52	26 9
15	11 28 44	23 59 35	25 16	16 1	5 56	5 40	5 9	6 12	7 19	0 51	26 7
16	11 32 41	24 59 21	7♋23	17 51	7 11	6 23	5 4	6 18	7 16	0 51	26 5
17	11 36 37	25 59 5	19 19	19 43	8 26	7 5	5 0	6 25	7 13	0 50	26 4
18	11 40 34	26 58 47	1♌ 9	21 37	9 40	7 48	4 55	6 31	7 11	0 50	26 2
19	11 44 30	27 58 26	12 57	23 31	10 55	8 30	4 51	6 38	7 8	0 49	26 1
20	11 48 27	28 58 3	24 47	25 26	12 9	9 13	4 46	6 44	7 6	0 49	25 59
21	11 52 23	29 57 38	6♍44	27 23	13 24	9 55	4 41	6 51	7 3	0 48	25 57
22	11 56 20	0♈57 11	18 48	29 21	14 38	10 38	4 36	6 58	7 1	0 48	25 56
23	12 0 16	1 56 42	1♎ 3	1♈19	15 52	11 20	4 30	7 4	6 58	0 47	25 54
24	12 4 13	2 56 11	13 30	3 19	17 7	12 2	4 25	7 11	6 56	0 46	25 52
25	12 8 10	3 55 38	26 10	5 19	18 21	12 45	4 19	7 18	6 53	0 46	25 51
26	12 12 6	4 55 3	9♏ 4	7 21	19 35	13 27	4 13	7 25	6 50	0 45	25 49
27	12 16 3	5 54 26	22 11	9 23	20 50	14 9	4 7	7 32	6 48	0 44	25 48
28	12 19 59	6 53 48	5♐31	11 25	22 4	14 51	4 1	7 39	6 45	0 44	25 46
29	12 23 56	7 53 7	19 5	13 27	23 18	15 33	3 55	7 46	6 43	0 43	25 44
30	12 27 52	8 52 25	2♑53	15 30	24 32	16 15	3 49	7 53	6 40	0 42	25 43
31	12 31 49	9♈51 41	16♑54	17♈32	25♈46	16♉57	3♏43	8♉ 0	6♎37	0♐41	25♍41

THE SUN ENTERS THE SIGN OF ARIES ON MAR 21 AT 00:56.

♈ ARIES ♉ TAURUS ♊ GEMINI ♋ CANCER ♌ LEO ♍ VIRGO ♎ LIBRA

1970

SIDEREAL SUN. MOON. MERCURY. VENUS. MARS. JUPITER. SATURN. URANUS. NEPTUNE. PLUTO.

DAY	TIME	☉	☽	☿	♀	♂	♃	♄	♅	♆	♇
	h m s	° ' "	° '	° '	° '	° '	° '	° '	° '	° '	° '
A 1	12 35 45	10♈50 56	1♒ 6	19♈34	27♈ 1	17♉39	3♏36	8♉ 7	6♎35	0♐40	25♍40
P 2	12 39 42	11 50 8	15 29	21 35	28 15	18 21	3R30	8 14	6R32	0R39	25R38
R 3	12 43 39	12 49 19	29 59	23 35	29 29	19 3	3 23	8 21	6 30	0 38	25 37
I 4	12 47 35	13 48 28	14♓33	25 34	0♉43	19 45	3 16	8 29	6 27	0 37	25 35
L 5	12 51 32	14 47 35	29 4	27 30	1 57	20 27	3 9	8 36	6 24	0 36	25 34
6	12 55 28	15 46 40	13♈28	29 24	3 11	21 9	3 2	8 43	6 22	0 35	25 32
7	12 59 25	16 45 43	27 38	1♉16	4 25	21 51	2 55	8 51	6 19	0 34	25 31
8	13 3 21	17 44 44	11♉30	3 4	5 39	22 32	2 48	8 58	6 17	0 33	25 29
9	13 7 18	18 43 43	25 1	4 49	6 53	23 14	2 41	9 5	6 14	0 32	25 28
10	13 11 14	19 42 40	8♊ 8	6 30	8 7	23 56	2 34	9 13	6 12	0 31	25 26
11	13 15 11	20 41 35	20 53	8 8	9 21	24 37	2 26	9 20	6 9	0 30	25 25
12	13 19 7	21 40 27	3♋18	9 41	10 34	25 19	2 19	9 28	6 7	0 29	25 23
13	13 23 4	22 39 17	15 27	11 9	11 48	26 0	2 11	9 35	6 4	0 28	25 22
14	13 27 1	23 38 5	27 24	12 33	13 2	26 42	2 4	9 43	6 2	0 26	25 20
15	13 30 57	24 36 51	9♌14	13 51	14 16	27 23	1 56	9 50	5 59	0 25	25 19
16	13 34 54	25 35 34	21 3	15 5	15 29	28 5	1 49	9 58	5 57	0 24	25 18
17	13 38 50	26 34 15	2♍55	16 13	16 43	28 46	1 41	10 5	5 55	0 23	25 16
18	13 42 47	27 32 54	14 55	17 16	17 56	29 27	1 34	10 13	5 52	0 21	25 15
19	13 46 43	28 31 31	27 7	18 13	19 10	0♊ 9	1 26	10 20	5 50	0 20	25 14
20	13 50 40	29 30 5	9♎34	19 5	20 24	0 50	1 18	10 28	5 48	0 19	25 12
21	13 54 36	0♉28 38	22 18	19 51	21 37	1 31	1 11	10 36	5 45	0 17	25 11
22	13 58 33	1 27 9	5♏19	20 31	22 51	2 12	1 3	10 43	5 43	0 16	25 10
23	14 2 30	2 25 38	18 36	21 5	24 4	2 53	0 55	10 51	5 41	0 15	25 9
24	14 6 26	3 24 5	2♐ 7	21 33	25 17	3 34	0 48	10 59	5 39	0 13	25 7
25	14 10 23	4 22 30	15 51	21 56	26 31	4 15	0 40	11 6	5 36	0 12	25 6
26	14 14 19	5 20 54	29 44	22 12	27 44	4 56	0 32	11 14	5 34	0 10	25 5
27	14 18 16	6 19 16	13♑44	22 23	28 57	5 37	0 25	11 22	5 32	0 9	25 4
28	14 22 12	7 17 37	27 49	22R29	0♊10	6 18	0 17	11 29	5 30	0 8	25 3
29	14 26 9	8 15 56	11♒56	22 28	1 24	6 59	0 10	11 37	5 28	0 6	25 2
30	14 30 5	9♉14 14	26♒ 5	22♉23	2♊37	7♊40	0♏ 2	11♉45	5♎26	0♐ 5	25♍ 1

THE SUN ENTERS THE SIGN OF TAURUS ON APR 20 AT 12:15.

DAY	TIME	☉	☽	☿	♀	♂	♃	♄	♅	♆	♇
	h m s	° ' "	° '	° '	° '	° '	° '	° '	° '	° '	° '
M 1	14 34 2	10♉12 30	10♓15	22♉12	3♊50	8♊21	29♎55	11♉52	5♎24	0♐ 3	25♍ 0
A 2	14 37 59	11 10 44	24 23	21R57	5 3	9 2	29R47	12 0	5R22	0R 2	24R59
Y 3	14 41 55	12 8 57	8♈28	21 37	6 16	9 42	29 40	12 8	5 20	0 0	24 58
4	14 45 52	13 7 9	22 27	21 13	7 29	10 23	29 32	12 15	5 18	29♏59	24 57
5	14 49 48	14 5 19	6♉15	20 45	8 42	11 4	29 25	12 23	5 16	29 57	24 56
6	14 53 45	15 3 27	19 50	20 15	9 55	11 44	29 18	12 31	5 15	29 55	24 55
7	14 57 41	16 1 34	3♊ 8	19 42	11 8	12 25	29 11	12 39	5 13	29 54	24 54
8	15 1 38	16 59 39	16 8	19 7	12 21	13 6	29 4	12 46	5 11	29 52	24 53
9	15 5 34	17 57 42	28 48	18 31	13 34	13 46	28 57	12 54	5 9	29 51	24 52
10	15 9 31	18 55 43	11♋11	17 54	14 47	14 27	28 50	13 2	5 8	29 49	24 51
11	15 13 28	19 53 43	23 19	17 17	15 59	15 7	28 43	13 9	5 6	29 48	24 51
12	15 17 24	20 51 41	5♌16	16 42	17 12	15 48	28 37	13 17	5 4	29 46	24 50
13	15 21 21	21 49 37	17 6	16 7	18 25	16 28	28 30	13 25	5 3	29 44	24 49
14	15 25 17	22 47 31	28 55	15 34	19 37	17 8	28 24	13 32	5 1	29 43	24 48
15	15 29 14	23 45 23	10♍48	15 4	20 50	17 49	28 17	13 40	5 0	29 41	24 48
16	15 33 10	24 43 13	22 51	14 37	22 3	18 29	28 11	13 48	4 59	29 40	24 47
17	15 37 7	25 41 2	5♎ 7	14 13	23 15	19 9	28 5	13 55	4 57	29 38	24 46
18	15 41 3	26 38 49	17 42	13 52	24 28	19 49	27 59	14 3	4 56	29 36	24 46
19	15 45 0	27 36 35	0♏38	13 36	25 40	20 30	27 53	14 10	4 55	29 35	24 45
20	15 48 57	28 34 19	13 56	13 24	26 52	21 10	27 47	14 18	4 54	29 33	24 45
21	15 52 53	29 32 2	27 35	13 16	28 5	21 50	27 41	14 25	4 52	29 31	24 44
22	15 56 50	0♊29 43	11♐32	13D12	29 17	22 30	27 36	14 33	4 51	29 30	24 44
23	16 0 46	1 27 24	25 42	13 13	0♋29	23 10	27 31	14 41	4 50	29 28	24 43
24	16 4 43	2 25 3	10♑ 1	13 19	1 41	23 50	27 25	14 48	4 49	29 27	24 43
25	16 8 39	3 22 41	24 22	13 29	2 53	24 30	27 20	14 55	4 48	29 25	24 43
26	16 12 36	4 20 18	8♒41	13 43	4 5	25 10	27 15	15 3	4 47	29 23	24 42
27	16 16 33	5 17 54	22 56	14 2	5 17	25 50	27 11	15 10	4 46	29 22	24 42
28	16 20 29	6 15 29	7♓ 3	14 26	6 29	26 30	27 6	15 18	4 46	29 20	24 42
29	16 24 26	7 13 3	21 3	14 53	7 41	27 10	27 1	15 25	4 45	29 19	24 41
30	16 28 22	8 10 36	4♈55	15 25	8 53	27 49	26 57	15 32	4 44	29 17	24 41
31	16 32 19	9♊ 8 9	18♈39	16♉ 1	10♋ 5	28♊29	26♎53	15♉40	4♎43	29♏15	24♍41

THE SUN ENTERS THE SIGN OF GEMINI ON MAY 21 AT 11:38.

DAY	TIME	☉	☽	☿	♀	♂	♃	♄	♅	♆	♇
	h m s	° ' "	° '	° '	° '	° '	° '	° '	° '	° '	° '
J 1	16 36 15	10♊ 5 40	2♉13	16♉41	11♋17	29♊ 9	26♎49	15♉47	4♎43	29♏14	24♍41
U 2	16 40 12	11 3 11	15 37	17 24	12 29	29 49	26R45	15 54	4R42	29R12	24R41
N 3	16 44 8	12 0 41	28 49	18 12	13 40	0♋28	26 41	16 1	4 42	29 11	24 41
E 4	16 48 5	12 58 11	11♊48	19 3	14 52	1 8	26 38	16 9	4 41	29 9	24 41
5	16 52 2	13 55 39	24 32	19 58	16 4	1 48	26 35	16 16	4 41	29 7	24D41
6	16 55 58	14 53 6	7♋ 2	20 56	17 15	2 27	26 31	16 23	4 40	29 6	24 41
7	16 59 55	15 50 32	19 18	21 58	18 27	3 7	26 28	16 30	4 40	29 4	24 41
8	17 3 51	16 47 57	1♌21	23 3	19 38	3 47	26 25	16 37	4 40	29 3	24 41
9	17 7 48	17 45 22	13 15	24 11	20 49	4 26	26 23	16 44	4 40	29 1	24 41
10	17 11 44	18 42 45	25 4	25 22	22 1	5 6	26 20	16 51	4 39	29 0	24 41
11	17 15 41	19 40 7	6♍52	26 37	23 12	5 45	26 18	16 58	4 39	28 58	24 41
12	17 19 37	20 37 27	18 44	27 55	24 23	6 25	26 16	17 5	4D39	28 57	24 41
13	17 23 34	21 34 47	0♎46	29 16	25 34	7 4	26 14	17 12	4 39	28 55	24 42
14	17 27 31	22 32 6	13 4	0♊40	26 45	7 43	26 12	17 19	4 39	28 54	24 42
15	17 31 27	23 29 24	25 41	2 7	27 56	8 23	26 11	17 25	4 40	28 52	24 42
16	17 35 24	24 26 42	8♏42	3 36	29 7	9 2	26 9	17 32	4 40	28 51	24 43
17	17 39 20	25 23 58	22 9	5 9	0♌18	9 41	26 8	17 39	4 40	28 50	24 43
18	17 43 17	26 21 14	6♐ 2	6 45	1 29	10 21	26 7	17 45	4 40	28 48	24 43
19	17 47 13	27 18 29	20 17	8 24	2 40	11 0	26 6	17 52	4 41	28 47	24 44
20	17 51 10	28 15 44	4♑49	10 6	3 50	11 39	26 5	17 58	4 41	28 45	24 44
21	17 55 6	29 12 58	19 32	11 50	5 1	12 18	26 5	18 5	4 41	28 44	24 45
22	17 59 3	0♋10 12	4♒17	13 38	6 11	12 58	26 4	18 11	4 42	28 43	24 45
23	18 3 0	1 7 26	18 58	15 28	7 22	13 37	26D 4	18 18	4 42	28 41	24 46
24	18 6 56	2 4 39	3♓29	17 21	8 32	14 16	26 4	18 24	4 43	28 40	24 46
25	18 10 53	3 1 52	17 47	19 16	9 43	14 55	26 4	18 30	4 44	28 39	24 47
26	18 14 49	3 59 5	1♈49	21 14	10 53	15 34	26 5	18 36	4 44	28 38	24 48
27	18 18 46	4 56 19	15 35	23 14	12 3	16 13	26 5	18 43	4 45	28 36	24 48
28	18 22 42	5 53 32	29 7	25 16	13 13	16 52	26 6	18 49	4 46	28 35	24 49
29	18 26 39	6 50 45	12♉24	27 20	14 23	17 31	26 7	18 55	4 47	28 34	24 50
30	18 30 35	7♋47 59	25♉28	29♊26	15♌33	18♋10	26♎ 8	19♉ 1	4♎48	28♏33	24♍51

THE SUN ENTERS THE SIGN OF CANCER ON JUN 21 AT 19:43.

♏ SCORPIO ♐ SAGITTARIUS ♑ CAPRICORN ♒ AQUARIUS ♓ PISCES

1970

SIDEREAL · SUN · MOON · MERCURY · VENUS · MARS · JUPITER · SATURN · URANUS · NEPTUNE · PLUTO

DAY	TIME	☉	☽	☿	♀	♂	♃	♄	♅	♆	♇
	h m s	° ′ ″	° ′	° ′	° ′	° ′	° ′	° ′	° ′	° ′	° ′
J 1	18 34 32	8♋45 12	8♊20	1♋34	16♌43	18♋49	26♎ 9	19♉ 7	4♎49	28♏32	24♍51
U 2	18 38 29	9 42 26	20 59	3 42	17 52	19 28	26 11	19 12	4 50	28R30	24 52
L 3	18 42 25	10 39 40	3♋26	5 52	19 2	20 7	26 12	19 18	4 51	28 29	24 53
Y 4	18 46 22	11 36 53	15 41	8 2	20 12	20 46	26 14	19 24	4 52	28 28	24 54
5	18 50 18	12 34 7	27 47	10 12	21 21	21 25	26 16	19 30	4 53	28 27	24 55
6	18 54 15	13 31 20	9♌43	12 22	22 31	22 4	26 18	19 35	4 54	28 26	24 56
7	18 58 11	14 28 34	21 34	14 33	23 40	22 43	26 21	19 41	4 55	28 25	24 57
8	19 2 8	15 25 47	3♍20	16 42	24 49	23 22	26 23	19 46	4 57	28 24	24 58
9	19 6 5	16 23 0	15 7	18 51	25 58	24 1	26 26	19 52	4 58	28 23	24 59
10	19 10 1	17 20 13	26 59	20 59	27 7	24 39	26 29	19 57	4 59	28 22	25 0
11	19 13 58	18 17 26	9♎ 1	23 6	28 16	25 18	26 32	20 2	5 1	28 21	25 1
12	19 17 54	19 14 38	21 17	25 12	29 25	25 57	26 35	20 7	5 2	28 20	25 2
13	19 21 51	20 11 51	3♏53	27 16	0♍34	26 36	26 38	20 13	5 4	28 20	25 3
14	19 25 47	21 9 4	16 52	29 19	1 42	27 14	26 42	20 18	5 6	28 19	25 5
15	19 29 44	22 6 17	0♐19	1♌20	2 51	27 53	26 45	20 23	5 7	28 18	25 6
16	19 33 40	23 3 30	14 14	3 19	3 59	28 32	26 49	20 27	5 9	28 17	25 7
17	19 37 37	24 0 43	28 35	5 17	5 7	29 11	26 53	20 32	5 11	28 16	25 8
18	19 41 34	24 57 57	13♑18	7 13	6 15	29 49	26 58	20 37	5 12	28 16	25 10
19	19 45 30	25 55 11	28 17	9 8	7 23	0♌28	27 2	20 42	5 14	28 15	25 11
20	19 49 27	26 52 25	13♒21	11 0	8 31	1 6	27 6	20 46	5 16	28 14	25 12
21	19 53 23	27 49 40	28 22	12 51	9 39	1 45	27 11	20 51	5 18	28 14	25 14
22	19 57 20	28 46 55	13♓13	14 40	10 46	2 24	27 16	20 55	5 20	28 13	25 15
23	20 1 16	29 44 11	27 46	16 27	11 54	3 2	27 21	21 0	5 22	28 12	25 16
24	20 5 13	0♌41 28	12♈ 0	18 12	13 1	3 41	27 26	21 4	5 24	28 12	25 18
25	20 9 9	1 38 46	25 51	19 55	14 8	4 19	27 31	21 8	5 26	28 11	25 19
26	20 13 6	2 36 5	9♉21	21 37	15 15	4 58	27 36	21 12	5 29	28 11	25 21
27	20 17 3	3 33 25	22 31	23 17	16 22	5 36	27 42	21 16	5 31	28 10	25 22
28	20 20 59	4 30 46	5♊23	24 55	17 29	6 15	27 48	21 20	5 33	28 10	25 24
29	20 24 56	5 28 8	18 0	26 32	18 36	6 53	27 54	21 24	5 35	28 10	25 25
30	20 28 52	6 25 31	0♋23	28 7	19 42	7 32	28 0	21 28	5 38	28 9	25 27
31	20 32 49	7♌22 55	12♋36	29♌39	20♍49	8♌10	28♎ 6	21♉31	5♎40	28♏ 9	25♍29

THE SUN ENTERS THE SIGN OF LEO ON JUL 23 AT 06:38.

DAY	TIME	☉	☽	☿	♀	♂	♃	♄	♅	♆	♇
	h m s	° ′ ″	° ′	° ′	° ′	° ′	° ′	° ′	° ′	° ′	° ′
A 1	20 36 45	8♌20 19	24♋39	1♍11	21♍55	8♌49	28♎12	21♉35	5♎42	28♏ 9	25♍30
U 2	20 40 42	9 17 45	6♌35	2 40	23 1	9 27	28 18	21 38	5 45	28R 8	25 32
G 3	20 44 38	10 15 11	18 25	4 8	24 7	10 6	28 25	21 42	5 47	28 8	25 34
U 4	20 48 35	11 12 39	0♍12	5 33	25 12	10 44	28 32	21 45	5 50	28 8	25 35
S 5	20 52 32	12 10 7	11 59	6 57	26 18	11 23	28 38	21 48	5 52	28 8	25 37
T 6	20 56 28	13 7 36	23 47	8 19	27 23	12 1	28 45	21 51	5 55	28 8	25 39
7	21 0 25	14 5 6	5♎41	9 40	28 28	12 39	28 52	21 54	5 58	28 7	25 41
8	21 4 21	15 2 36	17 45	10 58	29 33	13 18	29 0	21 57	6 0	28 7	25 42
9	21 8 18	16 0 8	0♏ 1	12 14	0♎38	13 56	29 7	22 0	6 3	28 7	25 44
10	21 12 14	16 57 40	12 36	13 28	1 42	14 34	29 15	22 3	6 6	28D 7	25 46
11	21 16 11	17 55 13	25 32	14 40	2 47	15 13	29 22	22 5	6 9	28 7	25 48
12	21 20 7	18 52 47	8♐53	15 50	3 51	15 51	29 30	22 8	6 11	28 7	25 50
13	21 24 4	19 50 22	22 41	16 57	4 54	16 29	29 38	22 10	6 14	28 7	25 52
14	21 28 1	20 47 58	6♑56	18 3	5 58	17 8	29 46	22 13	6 17	28 8	25 53
15	21 31 57	21 45 35	21 35	19 5	7 2	17 46	29 54	22 15	6 20	28 8	25 55
16	21 35 54	22 43 13	6♒34	20 5	8 5	18 24	0♏ 2	22 17	6 23	28 8	25 57
17	21 39 50	23 40 53	21 44	21 3	9 8	19 3	0 10	22 19	6 26	28 8	25 59
18	21 43 47	24 38 33	6♓57	21 57	10 10	19 41	0 19	22 21	6 29	28 8	26 1
19	21 47 43	25 36 15	22 2	22 49	11 13	20 19	0 27	22 23	6 32	28 9	26 3
20	21 51 40	26 33 58	6♈51	23 37	12 15	20 57	0 36	22 24	6 35	28 9	26 5
21	21 55 36	27 31 43	21 18	24 22	13 16	21 36	0 45	22 26	6 38	28 9	26 7
22	21 59 33	28 29 29	5♉21	25 4	14 18	22 14	0 54	22 27	6 42	28 10	26 9
23	22 3 30	29 27 17	18 57	25 41	15 19	22 52	1 3	22 29	6 45	28 10	26 11
24	22 7 26	0♍25 7	2♊ 8	26 15	16 20	23 30	1 12	22 30	6 48	28 10	26 13
25	22 11 23	1 22 59	14 57	26 45	17 21	24 8	1 21	22 31	6 51	28 11	26 15
26	22 15 19	2 20 53	27 27	27 10	18 21	24 47	1 30	22 32	6 54	28 11	26 17
27	22 19 16	3 18 48	9♋41	27 30	19 21	25 25	1 40	22 33	6 58	28 12	26 20
28	22 23 12	4 16 45	21 44	27 46	20 21	26 3	1 49	22 34	7 1	28 12	26 22
29	22 27 9	5 14 44	3♌38	27 56	21 20	26 41	1 59	22 35	7 4	28 13	26 24
30	22 31 5	6 12 44	15 28	28R 0	22 19	27 19	2 9	22 36	7 8	28 14	26 26
31	22 35 2	7♍10 46	27♌15	27♍59	23♎17	27♌58	2♏19	22♉36	7♎11	28♏14	26♍28

THE SUN ENTERS THE SIGN OF VIRGO ON AUG 23 AT 13:35.

DAY	TIME	☉	☽	☿	♀	♂	♃	♄	♅	♆	♇
	h m s	° ′ ″	° ′	° ′	° ′	° ′	° ′	° ′	° ′	° ′	° ′
S 1	22 38 59	8♍ 8 50	9♍ 2	27♍52	24♎16	28♌36	2♏29	22♉37	7♎15	28♏15	26♍30
E 2	22 42 55	9 6 55	20 52	27R39	25 13	29 14	2 39	22 37	7 18	28 16	26 32
P 3	22 46 52	10 5 2	2♎46	27 19	26 11	29 52	2 49	22 37	7 21	28 17	26 34
T 4	22 50 48	11 3 11	14 47	26 54	27 8	0♍30	2 59	22R37	7 25	28 17	26 37
E 5	22 54 45	12 1 21	26 58	26 22	28 4	1 8	3 9	22 37	7 28	28 18	26 39
M 6	22 58 41	12 59 33	9♏21	25 44	29 0	1 47	3 20	22 37	7 32	28 19	26 41
B 7	23 2 38	13 57 46	21 58	25 0	29 56	2 25	3 30	22 37	7 36	28 20	26 43
E 8	23 6 34	14 56 1	4♐54	24 11	0♏51	3 3	3 41	22 37	7 39	28 21	26 45
R 9	23 10 31	15 54 17	18 10	23 18	1 45	3 41	3 51	22 36	7 43	28 22	26 48
10	23 14 28	16 52 35	1♑48	22 21	2 39	4 19	4 2	22 36	7 46	28 23	26 50
11	23 18 24	17 50 54	15 50	21 21	3 33	4 57	4 13	22 35	7 50	28 24	26 52
12	23 22 21	18 49 15	0♒16	20 20	4 25	5 35	4 24	22 34	7 53	28 25	26 54
13	23 26 17	19 47 37	15 1	19 19	5 18	6 13	4 35	22 34	7 57	28 26	26 56
14	23 30 14	20 46 1	0♓ 2	18 20	6 9	6 52	4 46	22 33	8 1	28 27	26 59
15	23 34 10	21 44 27	15 9	17 23	7 0	7 30	4 57	22 32	8 4	28 28	27 1
16	23 38 7	22 42 54	0♈15	16 30	7 50	8 8	5 8	22 30	8 8	28 29	27 3
17	23 42 3	23 41 24	15 11	15 43	8 40	8 46	5 19	22 29	8 12	28 30	27 5
18	23 46 0	24 39 55	29 47	15 3	9 29	9 24	5 30	22 28	8 15	28 31	27 8
19	23 49 57	25 38 29	13♉59	14 30	10 17	10 2	5 42	22 26	8 19	28 33	27 10
20	23 53 53	26 37 5	27 44	14 6	11 4	10 40	5 53	22 25	8 23	28 34	27 12
21	23 57 50	27 35 43	11♊ 1	13 51	11 51	11 18	6 5	22 23	8 27	28 35	27 14
22	0 1 46	28 34 23	23 52	13D46	12 36	11 56	6 16	22 21	8 30	28 37	27 17
23	0 5 43	29 33 6	6♋22	13 51	13 21	12 34	6 28	22 19	8 34	28 38	27 19
24	0 9 39	0♎31 50	18 34	14 6	14 5	13 12	6 40	22 17	8 38	28 39	27 21
25	0 13 36	1 30 37	0♌32	14 30	14 48	13 51	6 52	22 15	8 42	28 41	27 23
26	0 17 32	2 29 27	12 23	15 4	15 30	14 29	7 3	22 13	8 45	28 42	27 26
27	0 21 29	3 28 18	24 10	15 47	16 11	15 7	7 15	22 11	8 49	28 44	27 28
28	0 25 26	4 27 11	5♍57	16 38	16 51	15 45	7 27	22 8	8 53	28 45	27 30
29	0 29 22	5 26 7	17 47	17 37	17 29	16 23	7 39	22 6	8 57	28 46	27 32
30	0 33 19	6♎25 4	29♍43	18♍43	18♏ 7	17♍ 1	7♏51	22♉ 3	9♎ 1	28♏48	27♍34

THE SUN ENTERS THE SIGN OF LIBRA ON SEP 23 AT 11:00.

♈ ARIES ♉ TAURUS ♊ GEMINI ♋ CANCER ♌ LEO ♍ VIRGO ♎ LIBRA

1970

SIDEREAL SUN. MOON. MERCURY. VENUS. MARS. JUPITER. SATURN. URANUS. NEPTUNE. PLUTO.

DAY	TIME	☉	☽	☿	♀	♂	♃	♄	♅	♆	♇
	h m s	° ' "	° '	° '	° '	° '	° '	° '	° '	° '	° '
O 1	0 37 15	7♎24 4	11♎48	19♍55	18♏43	17♍39	8♏ 4	22♉ 1	9♎ 4	28♏50	27♍37
C 2	0 41 12	8 23 6	24 1	21 13	19 19	18 17	8 16	21R58	9 8	28 51	27 39
T 3	0 45 8	9 22 10	6♏26	22 36	19 52	18 55	8 28	21 55	9 12	28 53	27 41
O 4	0 49 5	10 21 15	19 3	24 3	20 25	19 33	8 40	21 52	9 16	28 54	27 43
B 5	0 53 1	11 20 23	1♐52	25 35	20 56	20 11	8 53	21 49	9 19	28 56	27 46
E 6	0 56 58	12 19 32	14 55	27 9	21 26	20 50	9 5	21 46	9 23	28 58	27 48
R 7	1 0 55	13 18 44	28 13	28 46	21 54	21 28	9 17	21 43	9 27	28 59	27 50
8	1 4 51	14 17 57	11♑47	0♎25	22 20	22 6	9 30	21 40	9 31	29 1	27 52
9	1 8 48	15 17 11	25 39	2 5	22 45	22 44	9 42	21 36	9 35	29 3	27 54
10	1 12 44	16 16 28	9♒48	3 47	23 8	23 22	9 55	21 33	9 38	29 5	27 56
11	1 16 41	17 15 46	24 13	5 30	23 30	24 0	10 8	21 29	9 42	29 6	27 59
12	1 20 37	18 15 6	8♓52	7 14	23 49	24 38	10 20	21 26	9 46	29 8	28 1
13	1 24 34	19 14 28	23 41	8 58	24 7	25 16	10 33	21 22	9 50	29 10	28 3
14	1 28 30	20 13 51	8♈32	10 42	24 23	25 54	10 46	21 18	9 53	29 12	28 5
15	1 32 27	21 13 17	23 18	12 26	24 36	26 32	10 58	21 14	9 57	29 14	28 7
16	1 36 23	22 12 44	7♉50	14 11	24 48	27 10	11 11	21 10	10 1	29 15	28 9
17	1 40 20	23 12 14	22 3	15 55	24 57	27 48	11 24	21 7	10 5	29 17	28 11
18	1 44 17	24 11 46	5♊51	17 39	25 5	28 26	11 37	21 2	10 8	29 19	28 13
19	1 48 13	25 11 20	19 13	19 22	25 10	29 5	11 50	20 58	10 12	29 21	28 15
20	1 52 10	26 10 57	2♋ 8	21 5	25R12	29 43	12 2	20 54	10 16	29 23	28 17
21	1 56 6	27 10 36	14 40	22 48	25 13	0♎21	12 15	20 50	10 19	29 25	28 19
22	2 0 3	28 10 17	26 53	24 30	25 11	0 59	12 28	20 46	10 23	29 27	28 21
23	2 3 59	29 10 0	8♌52	26 12	25 6	1 37	12 41	20 41	10 27	29 29	28 23
24	2 7 56	0♏ 9 45	20 42	27 53	25 0	2 15	12 54	20 37	10 30	29 31	28 25
25	2 11 52	1 9 33	2♍28	29 34	24 50	2 53	13 7	20 33	10 34	29 33	28 27
26	2 15 49	2 9 23	14 17	1♏14	24 39	3 31	13 20	20 28	10 38	29 35	28 29
27	2 19 46	3 9 15	26 11	2 53	24 25	4 9	13 34	20 24	10 41	29 37	28 31
28	2 23 42	4 9 9	8♎15	4 32	24 9	4 47	13 47	20 19	10 45	29 39	28 33
29	2 27 39	5 9 5	20 31	6 11	23 50	5 25	14 0	20 15	10 48	29 41	28 35
30	2 31 35	6 9 3	3♏ 1	7 49	23 29	6 4	14 13	20 10	10 52	29 43	28 37
31	2 35 32	7♏ 9 3	15♏44	9♏26	23♏ 6	6♎42	14♏26	20♉ 5	10♎55	29♏46	28♍39

THE SUN ENTERS THE SIGN OF SCORPIO ON OCT 23 AT 20:05.

DAY	TIME	☉	☽	☿	♀	♂	♃	♄	♅	♆	♇
	h m s	° ' "	° '	° '	° '	° '	° '	° '	° '	° '	° '
N 1	2 39 28	8♏ 9 5	28♏41	11♏ 3	22♏41	7♎20	14♏39	20♉ 1	10♎59	29♏48	28♍41
O 2	2 43 25	9 9 9	11♐51	12 40	22R14	7 58	14 52	19R56	11 2	29 50	28 43
V 3	2 47 21	10 9 15	25 12	14 16	21 45	8 36	15 6	19 51	11 6	29 52	28 44
E 4	2 51 18	11 9 22	8♑44	15 52	21 14	9 14	15 19	19 46	11 9	29 54	28 46
M 5	2 55 15	12 9 31	22 25	17 27	20 42	9 52	15 32	19 41	11 13	29 56	28 48
B 6	2 59 11	13 9 41	6♒15	19 2	20 9	10 30	15 45	19 37	11 16	29 58	28 50
E 7	3 3 8	14 9 53	20 15	20 36	19 34	11 8	15 58	19 32	11 19	0♐ 1	28 51
R 8	3 7 4	15 10 6	4♓24	22 10	18 59	11 46	16 12	19 27	11 23	0 3	28 53
9	3 11 1	16 10 21	18 42	23 44	18 23	12 25	16 25	19 22	11 26	0 5	28 55
10	3 14 57	17 10 37	3♈ 5	25 17	17 46	13 3	16 38	19 17	11 29	0 7	28 56
11	3 18 54	18 10 54	17 30	26 50	17 10	13 41	16 51	19 12	11 32	0 9	28 58
12	3 22 50	19 11 13	1♉53	28 23	16 33	14 19	17 4	19 7	11 36	0 12	29 0
13	3 26 47	20 11 34	16 7	29 55	15 57	14 57	17 18	19 2	11 39	0 14	29 1
14	3 30 44	21 11 57	0♊ 6	1♐27	15 22	15 35	17 31	18 58	11 42	0 16	29 3
15	3 34 40	22 12 21	13 46	2 59	14 47	16 13	17 44	18 53	11 45	0 18	29 4
16	3 38 37	23 12 47	27 4	4 30	14 13	16 51	17 57	18 48	11 48	0 21	29 6
17	3 42 33	24 13 15	9♋58	6 2	13 41	17 29	18 10	18 43	11 51	0 23	29 7
18	3 46 30	25 13 44	22 31	7 32	13 11	18 8	18 24	18 38	11 54	0 25	29 9
19	3 50 26	26 14 15	4♌45	9 3	12 42	18 46	18 37	18 33	11 57	0 27	29 10
20	3 54 23	27 14 48	16 45	10 33	12 14	19 24	18 50	18 29	12 0	0 30	29 12
21	3 58 20	28 15 23	28 36	12 3	11 49	20 2	19 3	18 24	12 3	0 32	29 13
22	4 2 16	29 15 59	10♍24	13 33	11 26	20 40	19 16	18 19	12 6	0 34	29 14
23	4 6 13	0♐16 37	22 13	15 2	11 6	21 18	19 29	18 14	12 9	0 36	29 16
24	4 10 9	1 17 17	4♎10	16 31	10 47	21 56	19 43	18 10	12 12	0 39	29 17
25	4 14 6	2 17 59	16 19	18 0	10 31	22 34	19 56	18 5	12 14	0 41	29 18
26	4 18 2	3 18 42	28 44	19 28	10 18	23 13	20 9	18 0	12 17	0 43	29 19
27	4 21 59	4 19 26	11♏26	20 56	10 7	23 51	20 22	17 56	12 20	0 45	29 21
28	4 25 55	5 20 12	24 28	22 23	9 58	24 29	20 35	17 51	12 23	0 48	29 22
29	4 29 52	6 21 0	7♐46	23 49	9 52	25 7	20 48	17 47	12 25	0 50	29 23
30	4 33 49	7♐21 48	21♐21	25♐14	9♏48	25♎45	21♏ 1	17♉42	12♎28	0♐52	29♍24

THE SUN ENTERS THE SIGN OF SAGITTARIUS ON NOV 22 AT 17:25.

DAY	TIME	☉	☽	☿	♀	♂	♃	♄	♅	♆	♇
	h m s	° ' "	° '	° '	° '	° '	° '	° '	° '	° '	° '
D 1	4 37 45	8♐22 38	5♑ 8	26♐39	9♏47	26♎23	21♏14	17♉38	12♎30	0♐54	29♍25
E 2	4 41 42	9 23 29	19 3	28 3	9D48	27 1	21 27	17R33	12 33	0 57	29 26
C 3	4 45 38	10 24 21	3♒ 4	29 25	9 52	27 39	21 40	17 29	12 35	0 59	29 27
E 4	4 49 35	11 25 14	17 8	0♑46	9 58	28 17	21 53	17 25	12 38	1 1	29 28
M 5	4 53 31	12 26 7	1♓13	2 6	10 6	28 56	22 5	17 21	12 40	1 3	29 29
B 6	4 57 28	13 27 1	15 18	3 24	10 16	29 34	22 18	17 17	12 42	1 6	29 30
E 7	5 1 24	14 27 56	29 23	4 39	10 29	0♏12	22 31	17 12	12 45	1 8	29 31
R 8	5 5 21	15 28 51	13♈26	5 53	10 44	0 50	22 44	17 8	12 47	1 10	29 32
9	5 9 18	16 29 48	27 26	7 3	11 1	1 28	22 56	17 5	12 49	1 12	29 33
10	5 13 14	17 30 44	11♉21	8 10	11 19	2 6	23 9	17 1	12 51	1 14	29 33
11	5 17 11	18 31 42	25 8	9 14	11 40	2 44	23 22	16 57	12 53	1 17	29 34
12	5 21 7	19 32 41	8♊43	10 13	12 3	3 22	23 34	16 53	12 55	1 19	29 35
13	5 25 4	20 33 40	22 3	11 7	12 28	4 0	23 47	16 50	12 57	1 21	29 36
14	5 29 0	21 34 40	5♋ 7	11 56	12 54	4 38	23 59	16 46	12 59	1 23	29 36
15	5 32 57	22 35 41	17 52	12 38	13 22	5 17	24 12	16 42	13 1	1 25	29 37
16	5 36 53	23 36 43	0♌19	13 13	13 52	5 55	24 24	16 39	13 3	1 27	29 37
17	5 40 50	24 37 46	12 31	13 40	14 23	6 33	24 37	16 36	13 5	1 30	29 38
18	5 44 47	25 38 49	24 31	13 57	14 56	7 11	24 49	16 33	13 6	1 32	29 39
19	5 48 43	26 39 53	6♍22	14R 5	15 30	7 49	25 1	16 29	13 8	1 34	29 39
20	5 52 40	27 40 58	18 10	14 3	16 6	8 27	25 13	16 26	13 10	1 36	29 40
21	5 56 36	28 42 4	29 59	13 48	16 43	9 5	25 25	16 23	13 11	1 38	29 40
22	6 0 33	29 43 11	11♎56	13 23	17 22	9 43	25 38	16 20	13 13	1 40	29 40
23	6 4 29	0♑44 18	24 6	12 45	18 2	10 21	25 50	16 18	13 14	1 42	29 41
24	6 8 26	1 45 26	6♏33	11 57	18 42	10 59	26 2	16 15	13 16	1 44	29 41
25	6 12 22	2 46 35	19 20	10 57	19 25	11 37	26 13	16 12	13 17	1 46	29 41
26	6 16 19	3 47 44	2♐31	9 49	20 8	12 15	26 25	16 10	13 19	1 48	29 42
27	6 20 16	4 48 54	16 4	8 34	20 52	12 53	26 37	16 8	13 20	1 50	29 42
28	6 24 12	5 50 4	29 59	7 14	21 37	13 31	26 49	16 5	13 21	1 52	29 42
29	6 28 9	6 51 15	14♑10	5 52	22 23	14 9	27 0	16 3	13 22	1 54	29 42
30	6 32 5	7 52 26	28 33	4 30	23 11	14 48	27 12	16 1	13 23	1 56	29 42
31	6 36 2	8♑53 36	13♒ 2	3♑12	23♏59	15♏26	27♏24	15♉59	13♎24	1♐58	29♍42

THE SUN ENTERS THE SIGN OF CAPRICORN ON DEC 22 AT 06:37.

♏ SCORPIO ♐ SAGITTARIUS ♑ CAPRICORN ♒ AQUARIUS ♓ PISCES

SIDEREAL | SUN. | MOON. | MERCURY. | VENUS. | MARS. | JUPITER. | SATURN. | URANUS. | NEPTUNE. | PLUTO.

DAY	TIME h m s	☉ ° ' "	☽ ° '	☿ ° '	♀ ° '	♂ ° '	♃ ° '	♄ ° '	♅ ° '	♆ ° '	♇ ° '
J 1	6 39 58	9♑54 47	27♒31	2♑ 0	24♏48	16♏ 4	27♏35	15♉57	13♎25	2♐ 0	29♍42
A 2	6 43 55	10 55 57	11♓55	0R55	25 37	16 42	27 46	15R55	13 26	2 1	29R42
N 3	6 47 52	11 57 8	26 11	29♐59	26 28	17 20	27 58	15 54	13 27	2 3	29 42
U 4	6 51 48	12 58 17	10♈18	29 13	27 19	17 58	28 9	15 52	13 28	2 5	29 42
A 5	6 55 45	13 59 27	24 14	28 37	28 11	18 35	28 20	15 51	13 29	2 7	29 42
R 6	6 59 41	15 0 36	7♉59	28 11	29 4	19 13	28 31	15 49	13 30	2 9	29 42
Y 7	7 3 38	16 1 45	21 33	27 55	29 58	19 51	28 42	15 48	13 30	2 10	29 42
8	7 7 34	17 2 54	4♊54	27D49	0♐52	20 29	28 53	15 47	13 31	2 12	29 42
9	7 11 31	18 4 2	18 3	27 52	1 47	21 7	29 4	15 46	13 31	2 14	29 42
10	7 15 27	19 5 10	0♋59	28 2	2 42	21 45	29 14	15 45	13 32	2 16	29 41
11	7 19 24	20 6 17	13 42	28 21	3 38	22 23	29 25	15 44	13 32	2 17	29 41
12	7 23 21	21 7 24	26 11	28 47	4 35	23 1	29 35	15 44	13 33	2 19	29 41
13	7 27 17	22 8 31	8♌28	29 19	5 32	23 39	29 46	15 43	13 33	2 21	29 40
14	7 31 14	23 9 38	20 33	29 56	6 29	24 17	29 56	15 43	13 33	2 22	29 40
15	7 35 10	24 10 44	2♍30	0♑39	7 28	24 55	0♐ 6	15 42	13 34	2 24	29 40
16	7 39 7	25 11 50	14 20	1 26	8 26	25 33	0 17	15 42	13 34	2 25	29 39
17	7 43 3	26 12 55	26 7	2 18	9 25	26 11	0 27	15D42	13 34	2 27	29 39
18	7 47 0	27 14 1	7♎56	3 13	10 25	26 48	0 37	15 42	13R34	2 28	29 38
19	7 50 56	28 15 6	19 52	4 11	11 25	27 26	0 46	15 42	13 34	2 30	29 38
20	7 54 53	29 16 10	2♏ 0	5 13	12 25	28 4	0 56	15 42	13 34	2 31	29 37
21	7 58 50	0♒17 15	14 24	6 17	13 26	28 42	1 6	15 43	13 34	2 33	29 36
22	8 2 46	1 18 19	27 9	7 24	14 28	29 20	1 15	15 43	13 34	2 34	29 36
23	8 6 43	2 19 22	10♐18	8 33	15 29	29 58	1 25	15 44	13 33	2 35	29 35
24	8 10 39	3 20 26	23 53	9 44	16 31	0♐35	1 34	15 44	13 33	2 37	29 34
25	8 14 36	4 21 28	7♑54	10 56	17 34	1 13	1 43	15 45	13 33	2 38	29 34
26	8 18 32	5 22 30	22 18	12 11	18 36	1 51	1 52	15 46	13 32	2 39	29 33
27	8 22 29	6 23 32	7♒ 0	13 27	19 39	2 29	2 1	15 47	13 32	2 41	29 32
28	8 26 26	7 24 32	21 53	14 44	20 43	3 6	2 10	15 48	13 31	2 42	29 31
29	8 30 22	8 25 31	6♓49	16 3	21 46	3 44	2 19	15 49	13 31	2 43	29 30
30	8 34 19	9 26 29	21 40	17 23	22 50	4 22	2 28	15 51	13 30	2 44	29 29
31	8 38 15	10♒27 26	6♈19	18♑45	23♐54	4♐59	2♐36	15♉52	13♎29	2♐45	29♍29

THE SUN ENTERS THE SIGN OF AQUARIUS ON JAN 20 AT 17:13.

DAY	TIME h m s	☉ ° ' "	☽ ° '	☿ ° '	♀ ° '	♂ ° '	♃ ° '	♄ ° '	♅ ° '	♆ ° '	♇ ° '
F 1	8 42 12	11♒28 22	20♈42	20♑ 7	24♐59	5♐37	2♐44	15♉54	13♎29	2♐46	29♍28
E 2	8 46 8	12 29 16	4♉45	21 31	26 4	6 15	2 53	15 55	13R28	2 47	29R27
B 3	8 50 5	13 30 9	18 29	22 55	27 8	6 52	3 1	15 57	13 27	2 49	29 26
R 4	8 54 1	14 31 1	1♊53	24 21	28 14	7 30	3 9	15 59	13 26	2 50	29 25
U 5	8 57 58	15 31 51	14 59	25 47	29 19	8 7	3 16	16 1	13 25	2 50	29 24
A 6	9 1 55	16 32 40	27 49	27 14	0♑25	8 45	3 24	16 3	13 24	2 51	29 23
R 7	9 5 51	17 33 27	10♋25	28 43	1 31	9 22	3 32	16 5	13 23	2 52	29 21
Y 8	9 9 48	18 34 13	22 48	0♒12	2 37	10 0	3 39	16 8	13 22	2 53	29 20
9	9 13 44	19 34 58	5♌ 1	1 42	3 43	10 37	3 46	16 10	13 21	2 54	29 19
10	9 17 41	20 35 41	17 4	3 12	4 50	11 15	3 54	16 13	13 20	2 55	29 18
11	9 21 37	21 36 23	29 1	4 44	5 56	11 52	4 1	16 15	13 19	2 56	29 17
12	9 25 34	22 37 3	10♍53	6 17	7 3	12 30	4 7	16 18	13 17	2 56	29 16
13	9 29 30	23 37 42	22 42	7 50	8 10	13 7	4 14	16 21	13 16	2 57	29 14
14	9 33 27	24 38 20	4♎30	9 24	9 18	13 44	4 21	16 24	13 15	2 58	29 13
15	9 37 24	25 38 57	16 21	10 59	10 25	14 22	4 27	16 27	13 13	2 58	29 12
16	9 41 20	26 39 32	28 19	12 35	11 33	14 59	4 33	16 30	13 12	2 59	29 11
17	9 45 17	27 40 6	10♏26	14 12	12 40	15 36	4 40	16 33	13 10	3 0	29 9
18	9 49 13	28 40 39	22 47	15 50	13 48	16 14	4 46	16 37	13 9	3 0	29 8
19	9 53 10	29 41 11	5♐26	17 28	14 56	16 51	4 51	16 40	13 7	3 1	29 7
20	9 57 6	0♓41 42	18 28	19 8	16 5	17 28	4 57	16 44	13 5	3 1	29 5
21	10 1 3	1 42 11	1♑55	20 48	17 13	18 5	5 3	16 47	13 4	3 2	29 4
22	10 4 59	2 42 39	15 49	22 30	18 21	18 42	5 8	16 51	13 2	3 2	29 2
23	10 8 56	3 43 6	0♒10	24 12	19 30	19 20	5 13	16 55	13 0	3 2	29 1
24	10 12 53	4 43 31	14 54	25 55	20 39	19 57	5 18	16 59	12 58	3 3	28 59
25	10 16 49	5 43 54	29 56	27 40	21 48	20 34	5 23	17 3	12 56	3 3	28 58
26	10 20 46	6 44 16	15♓ 8	29 25	22 57	21 11	5 28	17 7	12 54	3 3	28 57
27	10 24 42	7 44 36	0♈19	1♓11	24 6	21 48	5 32	17 11	12 53	3 4	28 55
28	10 28 39	8♓44 54	15♈20	2♓58	25♑15	22♐25	5♐37	17♉16	12♎51	3♐ 4	28♍54

THE SUN ENTERS THE SIGN OF PISCES ON FEB 19 AT 07:27.

DAY	TIME h m s	☉ ° ' "	☽ ° '	☿ ° '	♀ ° '	♂ ° '	♃ ° '	♄ ° '	♅ ° '	♆ ° '	♇ ° '
M 1	10 32 35	9♓45 10	0♉ 3	4♓47	26♑24	23♐ 1	5♐41	17♉20	12♎49	3♐ 4	28♍52
A 2	10 36 32	10 45 24	14 23	6 36	27 34	23 38	5 45	17 24	12R47	3 4	28R51
R 3	10 40 28	11 45 36	28 17	8 26	28 43	24 15	5 49	17 29	12 44	3 4	28 49
C 4	10 44 25	12 45 46	11♊44	10 18	29 53	24 52	5 52	17 34	12 42	3 4	28 47
H 5	10 48 22	13 45 54	24 47	12 10	1♒ 3	25 29	5 56	17 38	12 40	3R 4	28 46
6	10 52 18	14 46 0	7♋28	14 3	2 12	26 5	5 59	17 43	12 38	3 4	28 44
7	10 56 15	15 46 4	19 52	15 57	3 22	26 42	6 2	17 48	12 36	3 4	28 43
8	11 0 11	16 46 6	2♌ 3	17 52	4 32	27 19	6 5	17 53	12 34	3 4	28 41
9	11 4 8	17 46 5	14 4	19 48	5 42	27 55	6 8	17 58	12 31	3 4	28 40
10	11 8 4	18 46 3	25 58	21 45	6 53	28 32	6 10	18 3	12 29	3 4	28 38
11	11 12 1	19 45 58	7♍48	23 42	8 3	29 8	6 13	18 8	12 27	3 4	28 36
12	11 15 57	20 45 51	19 36	25 40	9 13	29 45	6 15	18 14	12 24	3 4	28 35
13	11 19 54	21 45 43	1♎26	27 38	10 23	0♑21	6 17	18 19	12 22	3 4	28 33
14	11 23 50	22 45 32	13 18	29 36	11 34	0 57	6 19	18 24	12 20	3 3	28 31
15	11 27 47	23 45 20	25 14	1♈35	12 44	1 34	6 21	18 30	12 17	3 3	28 30
16	11 31 44	24 45 6	7♏17	3 33	13 55	2 10	6 22	18 35	12 15	3 3	28 28
17	11 35 40	25 44 50	19 29	5 30	15 6	2 46	6 23	18 41	12 12	3 2	28 27
18	11 39 37	26 44 32	1♐52	7 27	16 16	3 22	6 25	18 47	12 10	3 2	28 25
19	11 43 33	27 44 13	14 31	9 23	17 27	3 58	6 26	18 53	12 8	3 1	28 23
20	11 47 30	28 43 52	27 28	11 16	18 38	4 34	6 26	18 58	12 5	3 1	28 22
21	11 51 26	29 43 29	10♑46	13 8	19 49	5 10	6 27	19 4	12 3	3 1	28 20
22	11 55 23	0♈43 5	24 28	14 58	21 0	5 46	6 27	19 10	12 0	3 0	28 18
23	11 59 19	1 42 39	8♒36	16 44	22 11	6 22	6R27	19 16	11 58	2 59	28 17
24	12 3 16	2 42 11	23 8	18 28	23 22	6 58	6 27	19 22	11 55	2 59	28 15
25	12 7 13	3 41 41	8♓ 1	20 7	24 33	7 33	6 27	19 29	11 52	2 58	28 13
26	12 11 9	4 41 9	23 10	21 43	25 44	8 9	6 27	19 35	11 50	2 58	28 12
27	12 15 6	5 40 35	8♈24	23 13	26 56	8 45	6 26	19 41	11 47	2 57	28 10
28	12 19 2	6 39 59	23 34	24 39	28 7	9 20	6 25	19 47	11 45	2 56	28 9
29	12 22 59	7 39 22	8♉30	26 0	29 18	9 56	6 25	19 54	11 42	2 56	28 7
30	12 26 55	8 38 41	23 3	27 15	0♓30	10 31	6 23	20 0	11 40	2 55	28 5
31	12 30 52	9♈37 59	7♊ 8	28♈23	1♓41	11♑ 6	6♐22	20♉ 7	11♎37	2♐54	28♍ 4

THE SUN ENTERS THE SIGN OF ARIES ON MAR 21 AT 06:38.

♈ ARIES ♉ TAURUS ♊ GEMINI ♋ CANCER ♌ LEO ♍ VIRGO ♎ LIBRA

1971

SIDEREAL SUN. MOON. MERCURY. VENUS. MARS. JUPITER. SATURN. URANUS. NEPTUNE. PLUTO.

DAY	TIME	☉	☽	☿	♀	♂	♃	♄	♅	♆	♇
	h m s	° ' "	° '	° '	° '	° '	° '	° '	° '	° '	° '
A 1	12 34 48	10♈37 15	20♊44	29♈26	2♓52	11♑41	6♐21	20♉13	11♎34	2♐53	28♍ 2
P 2	12 38 45	11 36 28	3♋52	0♉22	4 4	12 16	6R19	20 20	11R32	2R52	28R 1
R 3	12 42 42	12 35 38	16 34	1 12	5 15	12 52	6 17	20 27	11 29	2 52	27 59
I 4	12 46 38	13 34 47	28 56	1 54	6 27	13 26	6 15	20 33	11 27	2 51	27 57
L 5	12 50 35	14 33 53	11♌ 2	2 30	7 39	14 1	6 13	20 40	11 24	2 50	27 56
6	12 54 31	15 32 57	22 57	2 59	8 50	14 36	6 10	20 47	11 21	2 49	27 54
7	12 58 28	16 31 58	4♍47	3 21	10 2	15 11	6 8	20 54	11 19	2 48	27 53
8	13 2 24	17 30 57	16 34	3 36	11 14	15 45	6 5	21 1	11 16	2 47	27 51
9	13 6 21	18 29 54	28 23	3R44	12 25	16 20	6 2	21 7	11 14	2 46	27 50
10	13 10 17	19 28 49	10♎15	3 46	13 37	16 54	5 59	21 14	11 11	2 45	27 48
11	13 14 14	20 27 42	22 13	3 41	14 49	17 29	5 55	21 21	11 9	2 44	27 47
12	13 18 11	21 26 33	4♏19	3 29	16 1	18 3	5 52	21 29	11 6	2 43	27 45
13	13 22 7	22 25 22	16 32	3 12	17 13	18 37	5 48	21 36	11 3	2 41	27 44
14	13 26 4	23 24 9	28 56	2 50	18 24	19 11	5 45	21 43	11 1	2 40	27 42
15	13 30 0	24 22 55	11♐30	2 22	19 36	19 45	5 41	21 50	10 58	2 39	27 41
16	13 33 57	25 21 38	24 16	1 51	20 48	20 19	5 36	21 57	10 56	2 38	27 39
17	13 37 53	26 20 20	7♑16	1 15	22 0	20 52	5 32	22 4	10 53	2 37	27 38
18	13 41 50	27 19 0	20 32	0 37	23 12	21 26	5 28	22 12	10 51	2 35	27 37
19	13 45 46	28 17 39	4♒ 8	29♈56	24 24	21 59	5 23	22 19	10 49	2 34	27 35
20	13 49 43	29 16 16	18 3	29 14	25 36	22 33	5 18	22 26	10 46	2 33	27 34
21	13 53 40	0♉14 51	2♓19	28 32	26 48	23 6	5 13	22 34	10 44	2 32	27 33
22	13 57 36	1 13 25	16 55	27 50	28 1	23 39	5 8	22 41	10 41	2 30	27 31
23	14 1 33	2 11 56	1♈47	27 9	29 13	24 12	5 3	22 48	10 39	2 29	27 30
24	14 5 29	3 10 26	16 47	26 29	0♈25	24 45	4 58	22 56	10 37	2 28	27 29
25	14 9 26	4 8 55	1♉48	25 52	1 37	25 17	4 52	23 3	10 34	2 26	27 28
26	14 13 22	5 7 21	16 39	25 17	2 49	25 50	4 46	23 11	10 32	2 25	27 26
27	14 17 19	6 5 46	1♊13	24 46	4 1	26 22	4 41	23 18	10 30	2 23	27 25
28	14 21 15	7 4 9	15 21	24 19	5 14	26 54	4 35	23 26	10 28	2 22	27 24
29	14 25 12	8 2 30	29 2	23 56	6 26	27 26	4 29	23 34	10 25	2 21	27 23
30	14 29 9	9♉ 0 48	12♋14	23♈37	7♈38	27♑58	4♐23	23♉41	10♎23	2♐19	27♍22

THE SUN ENTERS THE SIGN OF TAURUS ON APR 20 AT 17:55.

DAY	TIME	☉	☽	☿	♀	♂	♃	♄	♅	♆	♇
	h m s	° ' "	° '	° '	° '	° '	° '	° '	° '	° '	° '
M 1	14 33 5	9♉59 5	25♋ 0	23♈23	8♈50	28♑30	4♐16	23♉49	10♎21	2♐18	27♍21
A 2	14 37 2	10 57 20	7♌25	23R14	10 3	29 1	4R10	23 56	10R19	2R16	27R19
Y 3	14 40 58	11 55 32	19 32	23D 9	11 15	29 33	4 3	24 4	10 17	2 15	27 18
4	14 44 55	12 53 43	1♍27	23 10	12 27	0♒ 4	3 57	24 12	10 15	2 13	27 17
5	14 48 51	13 51 51	13 17	23 15	13 40	0 35	3 50	24 19	10 13	2 12	27 16
6	14 52 48	14 49 58	25 4	23 25	14 52	1 6	3 43	24 27	10 11	2 10	27 15
7	14 56 44	15 48 2	6♎55	23 39	16 4	1 36	3 37	24 35	10 9	2 9	27 14
8	15 0 41	16 46 5	18 53	23 58	17 17	2 7	3 30	24 42	10 7	2 7	27 13
9	15 4 37	17 44 6	0♏59	24 22	18 29	2 37	3 23	24 50	10 5	2 6	27 13
10	15 8 34	18 42 6	13 16	24 49	19 41	3 7	3 15	24 58	10 3	2 4	27 12
11	15 12 31	19 40 4	25 44	25 21	20 54	3 37	3 8	25 6	10 1	2 2	27 11
12	15 16 27	20 38 0	8♐23	25 57	22 6	4 7	3 1	25 13	10 0	2 1	27 10
13	15 20 24	21 35 55	21 14	26 37	23 19	4 36	2 54	25 21	9 58	1 59	27 9
14	15 24 20	22 33 48	4♑17	27 20	24 31	5 5	2 46	25 29	9 56	1 58	27 8
15	15 28 17	23 31 41	17 31	28 7	25 44	5 34	2 39	25 37	9 54	1 56	27 8
16	15 32 13	24 29 32	0♒56	28 58	26 56	6 3	2 32	25 44	9 53	1 55	27 7
17	15 36 10	25 27 21	14 35	29 52	28 9	6 31	2 24	25 52	9 51	1 53	27 6
18	15 40 7	26 25 10	28 27	0♉49	29 21	7 0	2 16	26 0	9 50	1 51	27 6
19	15 44 3	27 22 57	12♓33	1 49	0♉34	7 27	2 9	26 8	9 48	1 50	27 5
20	15 48 0	28 20 43	26 52	2 52	1 46	7 55	2 1	26 15	9 47	1 48	27 4
21	15 51 56	29 18 28	11♈23	3 59	2 59	8 23	1 54	26 23	9 45	1 46	27 4
22	15 55 53	0♊16 12	26 1	5 8	4 12	8 50	1 46	26 31	9 44	1 45	27 3
23	15 59 49	1 13 55	10♉39	6 20	5 24	9 16	1 38	26 39	9 43	1 43	27 3
24	16 3 46	2 11 37	25 11	7 35	6 37	9 43	1 31	26 46	9 41	1 42	27 2
25	16 7 42	3 9 18	9♊29	8 52	7 49	10 9	1 23	26 54	9 40	1 40	27 2
26	16 11 39	4 6 57	23 28	10 12	9 2	10 35	1 15	27 2	9 39	1 38	27 1
27	16 15 36	5 4 35	7♋ 4	11 35	10 15	11 1	1 8	27 10	9 38	1 37	27 1
28	16 19 32	6 2 12	20 14	13 0	11 27	11 26	1 0	27 17	9 37	1 35	27 1
29	16 23 29	6 59 47	3♌ 1	14 27	12 40	11 51	0 53	27 25	9 36	1 33	27 0
30	16 27 25	7 57 21	15 26	15 58	13 53	12 15	0 45	27 33	9 35	1 32	27 0
31	16 31 22	8♊54 54	27♌35	17♉30	15♉ 5	12♒39	0♐38	27♉40	9♎34	1♐30	27♍ 0

THE SUN ENTERS THE SIGN OF GEMINI ON MAY 21 AT 17:16.

DAY	TIME	☉	☽	☿	♀	♂	♃	♄	♅	♆	♇
	h m s	° ' "	° '	° '	° '	° '	° '	° '	° '	° '	° '
J 1	16 35 18	9♊52 25	9♍33	19♉ 6	16♉18	13♒ 3	0♐30	27♉48	9♎33	1♐29	26♍59
U 2	16 39 15	10 49 55	21 24	20 43	17 31	13 27	0R23	27 56	9R32	1R27	26R59
N 3	16 43 11	11 47 23	3♎14	22 24	18 44	13 50	0 15	28 3	9 31	1 25	26 59
E 4	16 47 8	12 44 50	15 8	24 6	19 56	14 13	0 8	28 11	9 31	1 24	26 59
5	16 51 5	13 42 16	27 10	25 51	21 9	14 35	0 1	28 19	9 30	1 22	26 59
6	16 55 1	14 39 41	9♏23	27 39	22 22	14 57	29♏53	28 26	9 29	1 21	26 59
7	16 58 58	15 37 5	21 50	29 29	23 35	15 18	29 46	28 34	9 29	1 19	26D59
8	17 2 54	16 34 28	4♐32	1♊21	24 47	15 39	29 39	28 41	9 28	1 18	26 59
9	17 6 51	17 31 50	17 30	3 16	26 0	16 0	29 32	28 49	9 28	1 16	26 59
10	17 10 47	18 29 11	0♑41	5 12	27 13	16 20	29 25	28 56	9 27	1 14	26 59
11	17 14 44	19 26 32	14 6	7 12	28 26	16 40	29 19	29 4	9 27	1 13	26 59
12	17 18 40	20 23 52	27 41	9 13	29 39	16 59	29 12	29 11	9 27	1 11	26 59
13	17 22 37	21 21 11	11♒26	11 16	0♊52	17 18	29 5	29 19	9 26	1 10	26 59
14	17 26 34	22 18 30	25 19	13 21	2 5	17 36	28 59	29 26	9 26	1 8	26 59
15	17 30 30	23 15 48	9♓20	15 28	3 18	17 54	28 52	29 33	9 26	1 7	27 0
16	17 34 27	24 13 6	23 26	17 36	4 30	18 11	28 46	29 41	9 26	1 5	27 0
17	17 38 23	25 10 24	7♈38	19 45	5 43	18 28	28 40	29 48	9D26	1 4	27 0
18	17 42 20	26 7 41	21 53	21 56	6 56	18 44	28 34	29 55	9 26	1 3	27 0
19	17 46 16	27 4 58	6♉ 9	24 7	8 9	18 59	28 28	0♊ 2	9 26	1 1	27 1
20	17 50 13	28 2 15	20 21	26 18	9 22	19 14	28 22	0 10	9 26	1 0	27 1
21	17 54 9	28 59 32	4♊26	28 30	10 35	19 29	28 16	0 17	9 26	0 58	27 2
22	17 58 6	29 56 48	18 20	0♋42	11 48	19 43	28 11	0 24	9 26	0 57	27 2
23	18 2 3	0♋54 4	1♋58	2 53	13 1	19 56	28 5	0 31	9 27	0 56	27 3
24	18 5 59	1 51 20	15 17	5 3	14 15	20 8	28 0	0 38	9 27	0 54	27 3
25	18 9 56	2 48 35	28 17	7 13	15 28	20 20	27 55	0 45	9 27	0 53	27 4
26	18 13 52	3 45 50	10♌58	9 22	16 41	20 32	27 50	0 52	9 28	0 52	27 4
27	18 17 49	4 43 4	23 20	11 29	17 54	20 42	27 45	0 59	9 28	0 50	27 5
28	18 21 45	5 40 18	5♍29	13 35	19 7	20 52	27 40	1 6	9 29	0 49	27 5
29	18 25 42	6 37 31	17 27	15 40	20 20	21 1	27 35	1 13	9 29	0 48	27 6
30	18 29 39	7♋34 44	29♍19	17♋42	21♊33	21♒10	27♏31	1♊19	9♎30	0♐47	27♍ 7

THE SUN ENTERS THE SIGN OF CANCER ON JUN 22 AT 01:20.

♏ SCORPIO ♐ SAGITTARIUS ♑ CAPRICORN ♒ AQUARIUS ♓ PISCES

SIDEREAL SUN. MOON. MERCURY. VENUS. MARS. JUPITER. SATURN. URANUS. NEPTUNE. PLUTO.

DAY	TIME	☉	☽	☿	♀	♂	♃	♄	♅	♆	♇
	h m s	° ' "	° '	° '	° '	° '	° '	° '	° '	° '	° '
J 1	18 33 35	8♋31 56	11♎10	19♋43	22♊47	21♒18	27♏27	1♊26	9♎31	0♐45	27♍ 8
U 2	18 37 32	9 29 8	23 6	21 42	24 0	21 25	27R23	1 33	9 31	0R44	27 8
L 3	18 41 28	10 26 19	5♏10	23 40	25 13	21 32	27 19	1 40	9 32	0 43	27 9
Y 4	18 45 25	11 23 30	17 27	25 35	26 26	21 37	27 15	1 46	9 33	0 42	27 10
5	18 49 21	12 20 42	0♐ 0	27 28	27 39	21 43	27 11	1 53	9 34	0 41	27 11
6	18 53 18	13 17 52	12 52	29 19	28 53	21 47	27 8	1 59	9 35	0 40	27 12
7	18 57 14	14 15 3	26 3	1♌ 8	0♋ 6	21 50	27 5	2 6	9 36	0 39	27 13
8	19 1 11	15 12 14	9♑34	2 56	1 19	21 53	27 1	2 12	9 37	0 38	27 14
9	19 5 8	16 9 25	23 20	4 41	2 33	21 55	26 59	2 18	9 38	0 37	27 15
10	19 9 4	17 6 36	7♒21	6 24	3 46	21 57	26 56	2 25	9 39	0 36	27 16
11	19 13 1	18 3 47	21 32	8 5	4 59	21R57	26 53	2 31	9 40	0 35	27 17
12	19 16 57	19 0 59	5♓49	9 44	6 13	21 57	26 51	2 37	9 42	0 34	27 18
13	19 20 54	19 58 10	20 8	11 21	7 26	21 56	26 49	2 43	9 43	0 33	27 19
14	19 24 50	20 55 23	4♈26	12 57	8 40	21 55	26 46	2 49	9 44	0 32	27 20
15	19 28 47	21 52 36	18 41	14 30	9 53	21 52	26 45	2 55	9 46	0 31	27 21
16	19 32 43	22 49 49	2♉50	16 1	11 7	21 49	26 43	3 1	9 47	0 30	27 22
17	19 36 40	23 47 4	16 51	17 30	12 20	21 45	26 41	3 7	9 49	0 29	27 23
18	19 40 37	24 44 19	0♊42	18 56	13 34	21 40	26 40	3 13	9 50	0 28	27 25
19	19 44 33	25 41 35	14 21	20 21	14 47	21 34	26 39	3 19	9 52	0 28	27 26
20	19 48 30	26 38 51	27 48	21 44	16 1	21 28	26 38	3 24	9 53	0 27	27 27
21	19 52 26	27 36 8	11♋ 1	23 4	17 14	21 21	26 37	3 30	9 55	0 26	27 28
22	19 56 23	28 33 26	23 59	24 23	18 28	21 13	26 37	3 36	9 57	0 26	27 30
23	20 0 19	29 30 44	6♌42	25 39	19 42	21 5	26 36	3 41	9 59	0 25	27 31
24	20 4 16	0♌28 2	19 11	26 52	20 55	20 56	26D36	3 47	10 1	0 24	27 33
25	20 8 13	1 25 21	1♍26	28 4	22 9	20 46	26 36	3 52	10 2	0 24	27 34
26	20 12 9	2 22 41	13 31	29 13	23 23	20 35	26 36	3 57	10 4	0 23	27 35
27	20 16 6	3 20 1	25 27	0♍19	24 36	20 24	26 36	4 2	10 6	0 23	27 37
28	20 20 2	4 17 21	7♎18	1 23	25 50	20 13	26 37	4 8	10 8	0 22	27 38
29	20 23 59	5 14 42	19 9	2 24	27 4	20 0	26 37	4 13	10 10	0 22	27 40
30	20 27 55	6 12 4	1♏ 4	3 22	28 18	19 48	26 38	4 18	10 12	0 21	27 41
31	20 31 52	7♌ 9 26	13♏ 8	4♍17	29♋32	19♒35	26♏39	4♊23	10♎15	0♐21	27♍43

THE SUN ENTERS THE SIGN OF LEO ON JUL 23 AT 12:16.

DAY	TIME	☉	☽	☿	♀	♂	♃	♄	♅	♆	♇
	h m s	° ' "	° '	° '	° '	° '	° '	° '	° '	° '	° '
A 1	20 35 48	8♌ 6 49	25♏25	5♍ 9	0♌45	19♒21	26♏41	4♊27	10♎17	0♐20	27♍45
U 2	20 39 45	9 4 12	7♐59	5 58	1 59	19R 7	26 42	4 32	10 19	0R20	27 46
G 3	20 43 41	10 1 36	20 53	6 44	3 13	18 53	26 44	4 37	10 21	0 20	27 48
U 4	20 47 38	10 59 0	4♑10	7 26	4 27	18 38	26 45	4 41	10 24	0 19	27 50
S 5	20 51 35	11 56 26	17 51	8 4	5 41	18 23	26 47	4 46	10 26	0 19	27 51
T 6	20 55 31	12 53 52	1♒54	8 38	6 55	18 8	26 49	4 50	10 28	0 19	27 53
7	20 59 28	13 51 19	16 16	9 9	8 9	17 52	26 52	4 55	10 31	0 19	27 55
8	21 3 24	14 48 47	0♓52	9 35	9 23	17 36	26 54	4 59	10 33	0 19	27 56
9	21 7 21	15 46 16	15 36	9 56	10 37	17 21	26 57	5 3	10 36	0 18	27 58
10	21 11 17	16 43 47	0♈20	10 13	11 51	17 5	27 0	5 7	10 38	0 18	28 0
11	21 15 14	17 41 18	14 59	10 25	13 5	16 49	27 3	5 11	10 41	0 18	28 2
12	21 19 10	18 38 51	29 27	10R32	14 19	16 33	27 6	5 15	10 44	0D18	28 4
13	21 23 7	19 36 26	13♉40	10 33	15 33	16 17	27 9	5 19	10 46	0 18	28 5
14	21 27 4	20 34 2	27 36	10 29	16 47	16 1	27 13	5 23	10 49	0 18	28 7
15	21 31 0	21 31 40	11♊15	10 20	18 1	15 46	27 16	5 26	10 52	0 18	28 9
16	21 34 57	22 29 19	24 36	10 5	19 15	15 30	27 20	5 30	10 55	0 18	28 11
17	21 38 53	23 27 0	7♋42	9 45	20 29	15 15	27 24	5 33	10 57	0 19	28 13
18	21 42 50	24 24 42	20 32	9 19	21 44	15 0	27 28	5 37	11 0	0 19	28 15
19	21 46 46	25 22 26	3♌ 9	8 48	22 58	14 45	27 33	5 40	11 3	0 19	28 17
20	21 50 43	26 20 11	15 34	8 11	24 12	14 31	27 37	5 43	11 6	0 19	28 19
21	21 54 40	27 17 57	27 49	7 30	25 26	14 17	27 42	5 46	11 9	0 19	28 21
22	21 58 36	28 15 45	9♍54	6 45	26 41	14 4	27 47	5 49	11 12	0 20	28 23
23	22 2 33	29 13 34	21 53	5 56	27 55	13 51	27 52	5 52	11 15	0 20	28 25
24	22 6 29	0♍11 25	3♎46	5 5	29 9	13 39	27 57	5 55	11 18	0 20	28 27
25	22 10 26	1 9 16	15 36	4 12	0♍23	13 27	28 2	5 58	11 21	0 21	28 29
26	22 14 22	2 7 9	27 27	3 17	1 38	13 16	28 8	6 0	11 24	0 21	28 31
27	22 18 19	3 5 4	9♏21	2 23	2 52	13 5	28 13	6 3	11 27	0 22	28 33
28	22 22 15	4 3 0	21 23	1 31	4 6	12 55	28 19	6 5	11 31	0 22	28 35
29	22 26 12	5 0 57	3♐37	0 40	5 21	12 46	28 25	6 8	11 34	0 23	28 37
30	22 30 8	5 58 55	16 7	29♌54	6 35	12 37	28 31	6 10	11 37	0 23	28 39
31	22 34 5	6♍56 55	28♐57	29♌12	7♍50	12♒30	28♏37	6♊12	11♎40	0♐24	28♍41

THE SUN ENTERS THE SIGN OF VIRGO ON AUG 23 AT 19:16.

DAY	TIME	☉	☽	☿	♀	♂	♃	♄	♅	♆	♇
	h m s	° ' "	° '	° '	° '	° '	° '	° '	° '	° '	° '
S 1	22 38 2	7♍54 56	12♑12	28♌36	9♍ 4	12♒22	28♏44	6♊14	11♎44	0♐24	28♍44
E 2	22 41 58	8 52 59	25 53	28R 6	10 18	12R16	28 50	6 16	11 47	0 25	28 46
P 3	22 45 55	9 51 3	10♒ 0	27 43	11 33	12 11	28 57	6 18	11 50	0 26	28 48
T 4	22 49 51	10 49 8	24 33	27 28	12 47	12 6	29 4	6 19	11 54	0 26	28 50
E 5	22 53 48	11 47 15	9♓25	27D22	14 2	12 2	29 10	6 21	11 57	0 27	28 52
M 6	22 57 44	12 45 23	24 30	27 24	15 16	11 59	29 18	6 22	12 0	0 28	28 54
B 7	23 1 41	13 43 34	9♈37	27 35	16 31	11 56	29 25	6 24	12 4	0 29	28 57
E 8	23 5 37	14 41 46	24 39	27 55	17 45	11 54	29 32	6 25	12 7	0 29	28 59
R 9	23 9 34	15 40 0	9♉26	28 23	19 0	11D54	29 40	6 26	12 11	0 30	29 1
10	23 13 31	16 38 17	23 51	29 0	20 14	11 53	29 47	6 27	12 14	0 31	29 3
11	23 17 27	17 36 35	7♊53	29 46	21 29	11 54	29 55	6 28	12 18	0 32	29 5
12	23 21 24	18 34 56	21 30	0♍39	22 43	11 56	0♐ 3	6 29	12 21	0 33	29 8
13	23 25 20	19 33 19	4♋43	1 40	23 58	11 58	0 11	6 30	12 25	0 34	29 10
14	23 29 17	20 31 44	17 36	2 48	25 13	12 1	0 19	6 30	12 28	0 35	29 12
15	23 33 13	21 30 11	0♌11	4 2	26 27	12 5	0 27	6 31	12 32	0 36	29 14
16	23 37 10	22 28 40	12 33	5 22	27 42	12 10	0 36	6 31	12 36	0 37	29 17
17	23 41 6	23 27 11	24 43	6 47	28 56	12 15	0 44	6 31	12 39	0 38	29 19
18	23 45 3	24 25 44	6♍46	8 17	0♎11	12 22	0 53	6 32	12 43	0 39	29 21
19	23 49 0	25 24 19	18 43	9 51	1 26	12 29	1 1	6R32	12 47	0 41	29 23
20	23 52 56	26 22 56	0♎36	11 29	2 40	12 37	1 10	6 32	12 50	0 42	29 26
21	23 56 53	27 21 35	12 27	13 9	3 55	12 45	1 19	6 32	12 54	0 43	29 28
22	0 0 49	28 20 16	24 17	14 52	5 10	12 55	1 28	6 31	12 58	0 44	29 30
23	0 4 46	29 18 59	6♏ 9	16 37	6 24	13 5	1 38	6 31	13 1	0 46	29 32
24	0 8 42	0♎17 43	18 5	18 24	7 39	13 16	1 47	6 30	13 5	0 47	29 35
25	0 12 39	1 16 30	0♐ 8	20 12	8 54	13 27	1 56	6 30	13 9	0 48	29 37
26	0 16 35	2 15 18	12 21	22 0	10 8	13 40	2 6	6 29	13 12	0 50	29 39
27	0 20 32	3 14 8	24 47	23 49	11 23	13 53	2 16	6 28	13 16	0 51	29 41
28	0 24 29	4 13 0	7♑32	25 39	12 38	14 6	2 25	6 27	13 20	0 52	29 44
29	0 28 25	5 11 53	20 39	27 28	13 53	14 21	2 35	6 26	13 24	0 54	29 46
30	0 32 22	6♎10 48	4♒12	29♍18	15♎ 7	14♒36	2♐45	6♊25	13♎27	0♐55	29♍48

THE SUN ENTERS THE SIGN OF LIBRA ON SEP 23 AT 16:46.

♈ ARIES ♉ TAURUS ♊ GEMINI ♋ CANCER ♌ LEO ♍ VIRGO ♎ LIBRA

1971

SIDEREAL TIME · SUN. · MOON. · MERCURY. · VENUS. · MARS. · JUPITER. · SATURN. · URANUS. · NEPTUNE. · PLUTO.

DAY	TIME	☉	☽	☿	♀	♂	♃	♄	♅	♆	♇
	h m s	° ' "	° '	° '	° '	° '	° '	° '	° '	° '	° '
O 1	Ø 36 18	7♎ 9 45	18♒12	1♎ 7	16♎22	14♒51	2♐55	6♊24	13♎31	Ø♐57	29♍5Ø
C 2	Ø 4Ø 15	8 8 44	2♓4Ø	2 55	17 37	15 8	3 5	6R23	13 35	Ø 58	29 53
T 3	Ø 44 11	9 7 44	17 34	4 44	18 51	15 25	3 16	6 21	13 39	1 Ø	29 55
O 4	Ø 48 8	1Ø 6 46	2♈45	6 31	2Ø 6	15 42	3 26	6 2Ø	13 42	1 1	29 57
B 5	Ø 52 4	11 5 51	18 4	8 18	21 21	16 Ø	3 36	6 18	13 46	1 3	29 59
E 6	Ø 56 1	12 4 57	3♉21	1Ø 5	22 36	16 19	3 47	6 16	13 5Ø	1 5	Ø♎ 2
R 7	Ø 59 58	13 4 6	18 25	11 5Ø	23 5Ø	16 38	3 57	6 14	13 54	1 6	Ø 4
8	1 3 54	14 3 17	3♊ 5	13 35	25 5	16 58	4 8	6 12	13 58	1 8	Ø 6
9	1 7 51	15 2 3Ø	17 18	15 2Ø	26 2Ø	17 18	4 19	6 1Ø	14 1	1 9	Ø 8
1Ø	1 11 47	16 1 46	1♋ 1	17 3	27 34	17 39	4 3Ø	6 8	14 5	1 11	Ø 1Ø
11	1 15 44	17 1 3	14 16	18 46	28 49	18 Ø	4 41	6 6	14 9	1 13	Ø 13
12	1 19 4Ø	18 Ø 24	27 6	2Ø 28	Ø♏ 4	18 22	4 52	6 4	14 13	1 15	Ø 15
13	1 23 37	18 59 46	9♌36	22 9	1 19	18 45	5 3	6 1	14 17	1 16	Ø 17
14	1 27 33	19 59 11	21 49	23 5Ø	2 34	19 7	5 14	5 59	14 2Ø	1 18	Ø 19
15	1 31 3Ø	2Ø 58 38	3♍51	25 3Ø	3 48	19 31	5 26	5 56	14 24	1 2Ø	Ø 21
16	1 35 27	21 58 7	15 47	27 9	5 3	19 54	5 37	5 53	14 28	1 22	Ø 24
17	1 39 23	22 57 39	27 38	28 47	6 18	2Ø 19	5 48	5 5Ø	14 32	1 24	Ø 26
18	1 43 2Ø	23 57 12	9♎28	Ø♏25	7 33	2Ø 43	6 Ø	5 47	14 35	1 26	Ø 28
19	1 47 16	24 56 48	21 19	2 2	8 47	21 8	6 12	5 44	14 39	1 27	Ø 3Ø
2Ø	1 51 13	25 56 26	3♏13	3 39	1Ø 2	21 34	6 23	5 41	14 43	1 29	Ø 32
21	1 55 9	26 56 6	15 1Ø	5 15	11 17	22 Ø	6 35	5 38	14 47	1 31	Ø 34
22	1 59 6	27 55 47	27 13	6 5Ø	12 32	22 26	6 47	5 35	14 5Ø	1 33	Ø 36
23	2 3 2	28 55 31	9♐21	8 25	13 46	22 53	6 59	5 31	14 54	1 35	Ø 38
24	2 6 59	29 55 16	21 39	9 59	15 1	23 2Ø	7 11	5 28	14 58	1 37	Ø 4Ø
25	2 1Ø 55	Ø♏55 4	4♑ 8	11 32	16 16	23 48	7 23	5 24	15 1	1 39	Ø 42
26	2 14 52	1 54 53	16 52	13 5	17 31	24 16	7 35	5 21	15 5	1 41	Ø 44
27	2 18 49	2 54 43	29 54	14 38	18 46	24 44	7 47	5 17	15 9	1 43	Ø 46
28	2 22 45	3 54 36	13♒17	16 1Ø	2Ø Ø	25 12	7 59	5 13	15 12	1 45	Ø 48
29	2 26 42	4 54 3Ø	27 6	17 41	21 15	25 41	8 12	5 9	15 16	1 47	Ø 5Ø
3Ø	2 3Ø 38	5 54 25	11♓2Ø	19 12	22 3Ø	26 11	8 24	5 5	15 2Ø	1 49	Ø 52
31	2 34 35	6♏54 22	26♓ Ø	2Ø♏43	23♏45	26♒4Ø	8♐36	5♊ 2	15♎23	1♐51	Ø♎54

THE SUN ENTERS THE SIGN OF SCORPIO ON OCT 24 AT 01:54.

DAY	TIME	☉	☽	☿	♀	♂	♃	♄	♅	♆	♇
	h m s	° ' "	° '	° '	° '	° '	° '	° '	° '	° '	° '
N 1	2 38 31	7♏54 21	11♈ Ø	22♏13	24♏59	27♒1Ø	8♐49	4♊57	15♎27	1♐54	Ø♎56
O 2	2 42 28	8 54 21	26 14	23 42	26 14	27 4Ø	9 1	4R53	15 3Ø	1 56	Ø 58
V 3	2 46 24	9 54 24	11♉29	25 11	27 29	28 11	9 14	4 49	15 34	1 58	1 Ø
E 4	2 5Ø 21	1Ø 54 28	26 36	26 39	28 44	28 41	9 26	4 45	15 38	2 Ø	1 2
M 5	2 54 18	11 54 34	11♊24	28 7	29 58	29 12	9 39	4 41	15 41	2 2	1 3
B 6	2 58 14	12 54 43	25 45	29 35	1♐13	29 44	9 52	4 36	15 45	2 4	1 5
E 7	3 2 11	13 54 53	9♋37	1♐ 1	2 28	Ø♓15	1Ø 5	4 32	15 48	2 6	1 7
R 8	3 6 7	14 55 6	22 59	2 28	3 43	Ø 47	1Ø 17	4 27	15 51	2 8	1 9
9	3 1Ø 4	15 55 2Ø	5♌53	3 53	4 57	1 19	1Ø 3Ø	4 23	15 55	2 11	1 11
1Ø	3 14 Ø	16 55 36	18 25	5 18	6 12	1 51	1Ø 43	4 18	15 58	2 13	1 12
11	3 17 57	17 55 55	Ø♍38	6 42	7 27	2 24	1Ø 56	4 14	16 2	2 15	1 14
12	3 21 53	18 56 15	12 39	8 5	8 42	2 56	11 9	4 9	16 5	2 17	1 16
13	3 25 5Ø	19 56 37	24 32	9 28	9 56	3 29	11 22	4 5	16 8	2 19	1 17
14	3 29 47	2Ø 57 1	6♎21	1Ø 49	11 11	4 2	11 35	4 Ø	16 12	2 22	1 19
15	3 33 43	21 57 27	18 11	12 1Ø	12 26	4 36	11 48	3 55	16 15	2 24	1 21
16	3 37 4Ø	22 57 55	Ø♏ 5	13 29	13 41	5 9	12 1	3 5Ø	16 18	2 26	1 22
17	3 41 36	23 58 25	12 4	14 47	14 55	5 43	12 15	3 45	16 21	2 28	1 24
18	3 45 33	24 58 56	24 9	16 3	16 1Ø	6 17	12 28	3 41	16 24	2 31	1 25
19	3 49 29	25 59 29	6♐23	17 17	17 25	6 51	12 41	3 36	16 28	2 33	1 27
2Ø	3 53 26	27 Ø 3	18 44	18 3Ø	18 39	7 26	12 54	3 31	16 31	2 35	1 28
21	3 57 22	28 Ø 39	1♑15	19 41	19 54	8 Ø	13 8	3 26	16 34	2 37	1 3Ø
22	4 1 19	29 1 16	13 56	2Ø 49	21 9	8 35	13 21	3 21	16 37	2 4Ø	1 31
23	4 5 16	Ø♐ 1 55	26 49	21 54	22 24	9 1Ø	13 34	3 16	16 4Ø	2 42	1 33
24	4 9 12	1 2 34	9♒55	22 56	23 38	9 45	13 48	3 11	16 43	2 44	1 34
25	4 13 9	2 3 15	23 18	23 54	24 53	1Ø 2Ø	14 1	3 6	16 46	2 46	1 35
26	4 17 5	3 3 56	7♓ Ø	24 48	26 8	1Ø 56	14 14	3 1	16 49	2 49	1 37
27	4 21 2	4 4 39	21 1	25 38	27 22	11 31	14 28	2 57	16 52	2 51	1 38
28	4 24 58	5 5 23	5♈23	26 22	28 37	12 7	14 41	2 52	16 55	2 53	1 39
29	4 28 55	6 6 7	2Ø 1	27 Ø	29 52	12 43	14 55	2 47	16 57	2 55	1 4Ø
3Ø	4 32 52	7♐ 6 53	4♉53	27♐31	1♑ 6	13♓19	15♐ 8	2♊42	17♎ Ø	2♐58	1♎42

THE SUN ENTERS THE SIGN OF SAGITTARIUS ON NOV 22 AT 23:15.

DAY	TIME	☉	☽	☿	♀	♂	♃	♄	♅	♆	♇
	h m s	° ' "	° '	° '	° '	° '	° '	° '	° '	° '	° '
D 1	4 36 48	8♐ 7 4Ø	19♉49	27♐54	2♑21	13♓55	15♐22	2♊37	17♎ 3	3♐ Ø	1♎43
E 2	4 4Ø 45	9 8 28	4♊4Ø	28 1Ø	3 35	14 31	15 35	2R32	17 6	3 2	1 44
C 3	4 44 41	1Ø 9 17	19 19	28R16	4 5Ø	15 7	15 49	2 27	17 8	3 4	1 45
E 4	4 48 38	11 1Ø 8	3♋37	28 11	6 5	15 44	16 2	2 22	17 11	3 7	1 46
M 5	4 52 34	12 1Ø 59	17 3Ø	27 57	7 19	16 2Ø	16 16	2 18	17 13	3 9	1 47
B 6	4 56 31	13 11 52	Ø♌57	27 31	8 34	16 57	16 3Ø	2 13	17 16	3 11	1 48
E 7	5 Ø 27	14 12 46	13 56	26 54	9 48	17 34	16 43	2 8	17 18	3 13	1 49
R 8	5 4 24	15 13 41	26 33	26 6	11 3	18 11	16 57	2 3	17 21	3 16	1 5Ø
9	5 8 21	16 14 38	8♍5Ø	25 7	12 18	18 48	17 1Ø	1 59	17 23	3 18	1 51
1Ø	5 12 17	17 15 36	2Ø 54	23 59	13 32	19 25	17 24	1 54	17 26	3 2Ø	1 52
11	5 16 14	18 16 34	2♎48	22 44	14 47	2Ø 2	17 37	1 49	17 28	3 22	1 53
12	5 2Ø 1Ø	19 17 34	14 39	21 24	16 1	2Ø 39	17 51	1 45	17 3Ø	3 24	1 54
13	5 24 7	2Ø 18 36	26 31	2Ø 1	17 16	21 17	18 5	1 4Ø	17 32	3 27	1 54
14	5 28 3	21 19 38	8♏27	18 38	18 3Ø	21 54	18 18	1 36	17 35	3 29	1 55
15	5 32 Ø	22 2Ø 41	2Ø 31	17 19	19 45	22 32	18 32	1 31	17 37	3 31	1 56
16	5 35 56	23 21 45	2♐45	16 5	2Ø 59	23 1Ø	18 45	1 27	17 39	3 33	1 57
17	5 39 53	24 22 5Ø	15 11	14 59	22 13	23 47	18 59	1 22	17 41	3 35	1 57
18	5 43 5Ø	25 23 56	27 48	14 2	23 28	24 25	19 13	1 18	17 43	3 37	1 58
19	5 47 46	26 25 2	1Ø♑38	13 16	24 42	25 3	19 26	1 14	17 45	3 4Ø	1 58
2Ø	5 51 43	27 26 9	23 4Ø	12 4Ø	25 57	25 41	19 4Ø	1 1Ø	17 47	3 42	1 59
21	5 55 39	28 27 16	6♒53	12 15	27 11	26 19	19 53	1 6	17 49	3 44	1 59
22	5 59 36	29 28 23	2Ø 17	12D 1	28 25	26 58	2Ø 7	1 2	17 5Ø	3 46	2 Ø
23	6 3 32	Ø♑29 31	3♓53	11 58	29 4Ø	27 36	2Ø 2Ø	Ø 58	17 52	3 48	2 Ø
24	6 7 29	1 3Ø 39	17 41	12 4	Ø♒54	28 14	2Ø 34	Ø 54	17 54	3 5Ø	2 1
25	6 11 25	2 31 47	1♈4Ø	12 19	2 8	28 53	2Ø 47	Ø 5Ø	17 55	3 52	2 1
26	6 15 22	3 32 55	15 5Ø	12 41	3 23	29 31	21 1	Ø 46	17 57	3 54	2 2
27	6 19 19	4 34 3	Ø♉ 9	13 12	4 37	Ø♈ 9	21 14	Ø 43	17 59	3 56	2 2
28	6 23 15	5 35 11	14 34	13 48	5 51	Ø 48	21 28	Ø 39	18 Ø	3 58	2 2
29	6 27 12	6 36 19	29 1	14 31	7 5	1 27	21 41	Ø 35	18 1	4 Ø	2 2
3Ø	6 31 8	7 37 27	13♊24	15 19	8 19	2 5	21 54	Ø 32	18 3	4 2	2 3
31	6 35 5	8♑38 35	27♊38	16♐11	9♒33	2♈44	22♐ 8	Ø♊29	18♎ 4	4♐ 4	2♎ 3

THE SUN ENTERS THE SIGN OF CAPRICORN ON DEC 22 AT 12:25.

♏ SCORPIO ♐ SAGITTARIUS ♑ CAPRICORN ♒ AQUARIUS ♓ PISCES

1972

SIDEREAL · SUN · MOON · MERCURY · VENUS · MARS · JUPITER · SATURN · URANUS · NEPTUNE · PLUTO

DAY	TIME	☉	☽	☿	♀	♂	♃	♄	♅	♆	♇
	h m s	° ' "	° '	° '	° '	° '	° '	° '	° '	° '	° '
J 1	6 39 1	9♑39 44	11♋37	17♐ 8	10♒47	3♈23	22♐21	0♊25	18♎ 5	4♐ 6	2♎ 3
A 2	6 42 58	10 40 52	25 18	18 8	12 1	4 2	22 34	0R22	18 7	4 8	2 3
N 3	6 46 55	11 42 1	8♌38	19 11	13 15	4 40	22 48	0 19	18 8	4 10	2 3
U 4	6 50 51	12 43 9	21 37	20 17	14 29	5 19	23 1	0 16	18 9	4 12	2R 3
A 5	6 54 48	13 44 18	4♍16	21 26	15 43	5 58	23 14	0 13	18 10	4 13	2 3
R 6	6 58 44	14 45 27	16 36	22 37	16 57	6 37	23 27	0 11	18 11	4 15	2 3
Y 7	7 2 41	15 46 36	28 43	23 50	18 11	7 16	23 40	0 8	18 12	4 17	2 3
8	7 6 37	16 47 45	10♎40	25 5	19 25	7 55	23 53	0 5	18 13	4 19	2 3
9	7 10 34	17 48 55	22 33	26 21	20 39	8 34	24 6	0 3	18 14	4 21	2 3
10	7 14 30	18 50 4	4♏26	27 39	21 52	9 13	24 19	0 0	18 14	4 22	2 3
11	7 18 27	19 51 14	16 23	28 59	23 6	9 53	24 32	29♉58	18 15	4 24	2 2
12	7 22 24	20 52 23	28 29	0♑19	24 20	10 32	24 45	29 56	18 16	4 26	2 2
13	7 26 20	21 53 32	10♐48	1 41	25 33	11 11	24 58	29 54	18 16	4 28	2 2
14	7 30 17	22 54 42	23 22	3 4	26 47	11 50	25 11	29 52	18 17	4 29	2 2
15	7 34 13	23 55 51	6♑13	4 27	28 1	12 29	25 24	29 50	18 17	4 31	2 1
16	7 38 10	24 56 59	19 22	5 52	29 14	13 9	25 37	29 48	18 18	4 32	2 1
17	7 42 6	25 58 8	2♒47	7 17	0♓27	13 48	25 49	29 46	18 18	4 34	2 1
18	7 46 3	26 59 15	16 26	8 43	1 41	14 27	26 2	29 45	18 19	4 36	2 0
19	7 49 59	28 0 22	0♓18	10 10	2 54	15 7	26 15	29 43	18 19	4 37	2 0
20	7 53 56	29 1 28	14 20	11 38	4 7	15 46	26 27	29 42	18 19	4 39	1 59
21	7 57 53	0♒ 2 33	28 28	13 6	5 21	16 26	26 40	29 41	18 19	4 40	1 59
22	8 1 49	1 3 38	12♈40	14 35	6 34	17 5	26 52	29 40	18 19	4 42	1 58
23	8 5 46	2 4 41	26 52	16 5	7 47	17 45	27 5	29 39	18R19	4 43	1 57
24	8 9 42	3 5 44	11♉ 3	17 35	9 0	18 24	27 17	29 38	18 19	4 44	1 57
25	8 13 39	4 6 45	25 10	19 6	10 13	19 4	27 29	29 37	18 19	4 46	1 56
26	8 17 35	5 7 45	9♊12	20 38	11 26	19 43	27 41	29 36	18 19	4 47	1 55
27	8 21 32	6 8 45	23 6	22 10	12 39	20 23	27 53	29 36	18 19	4 48	1 55
28	8 25 28	7 9 43	6♋49	23 43	13 51	21 2	28 5	29 35	18 19	4 50	1 54
29	8 29 25	8 10 40	20 21	25 16	15 4	21 42	28 17	29 35	18 18	4 51	1 53
30	8 33 22	9 11 36	3♌39	26 50	16 17	22 21	28 29	29 35	18 18	4 52	1 52
31	8 37 18	10♒12 31	16♌42	28♑25	17♓29	23♈ 1	28♐41	29♉35	18♎18	4♐53	1♎52

THE SUN ENTERS THE SIGN OF AQUARIUS ON JAN 20 AT 22:60.

DAY	TIME	☉	☽	☿	♀	♂	♃	♄	♅	♆	♇
	h m s	° ' "	° '	° '	° '	° '	° '	° '	° '	° '	° '
F 1	8 41 15	11♒13 25	29♌30	0♒ 1	18♓42	23♈40	28♐53	29♉35	18♎17	4♐55	1♎51
E 2	8 45 11	12 14 18	12♍ 3	1 37	19 54	24 20	29 5	29 35	18R17	4 56	1R50
B 3	8 49 8	13 15 10	24 22	3 14	21 6	25 0	29 16	29 35	18 16	4 57	1 49
R 4	8 53 4	14 16 1	6♎29	4 52	22 18	25 39	29 28	29 35	18 16	4 58	1 48
U 5	8 57 1	15 16 51	18 27	6 30	23 31	26 19	29 39	29 36	18 15	4 59	1 47
A 6	9 0 57	16 17 41	0♏21	8 9	24 43	26 58	29 51	29 36	18 14	5 0	1 46
R 7	9 4 54	17 18 29	12 13	9 49	25 54	27 38	0♑ 2	29 37	18 13	5 1	1 45
Y 8	9 8 51	18 19 17	24 10	11 30	27 6	28 18	0 13	29 38	18 13	5 2	1 44
9	9 12 47	19 20 3	6♐15	13 11	28 18	28 57	0 24	29 39	18 12	5 3	1 43
10	9 16 44	20 20 49	18 33	14 53	29 30	29 37	0 36	29 40	18 11	5 4	1 42
11	9 20 40	21 21 34	1♑ 9	16 36	0♈41	0♉16	0 46	29 41	18 10	5 5	1 41
12	9 24 37	22 22 17	14 5	18 20	1 53	0 56	0 57	29 42	18 9	5 5	1 39
13	9 28 33	23 22 59	27 24	20 5	3 4	1 36	1 8	29 44	18 8	5 6	1 38
14	9 32 30	24 23 40	11♒ 5	21 51	4 15	2 15	1 19	29 45	18 6	5 7	1 37
15	9 36 27	25 24 20	25 8	23 37	5 27	2 55	1 29	29 47	18 5	5 8	1 36
16	9 40 23	26 24 58	9♓28	25 24	6 38	3 34	1 40	29 48	18 4	5 8	1 34
17	9 44 20	27 25 34	24 0	27 12	7 49	4 14	1 50	29 50	18 3	5 9	1 33
18	9 48 16	28 26 9	8♈37	29 1	8 59	4 54	2 1	29 52	18 1	5 10	1 32
19	9 52 13	29 26 42	23 13	0♓51	10 10	5 33	2 11	29 54	18 0	5 10	1 31
20	9 56 9	0♓27 14	7♉42	2 41	11 21	6 13	2 21	29 56	17 59	5 11	1 29
21	10 0 6	1 27 43	22 0	4 32	12 31	6 53	2 31	29 59	17 57	5 11	1 28
22	10 4 2	2 28 11	6♊ 4	6 24	13 41	7 32	2 41	0♊ 1	17 56	5 12	1 27
23	10 7 59	3 28 37	19 52	8 17	14 52	8 12	2 51	0 3	17 54	5 12	1 25
24	10 11 55	4 29 0	3♋26	10 10	16 2	8 51	3 0	0 6	17 52	5 13	1 24
25	10 15 52	5 29 22	16 46	12 3	17 12	9 31	3 10	0 9	17 51	5 13	1 22
26	10 19 49	6 29 42	29 52	13 56	18 21	10 11	3 19	0 11	17 49	5 14	1 21
27	10 23 45	7 30 0	12♌45	15 50	19 31	10 50	3 29	0 14	17 47	5 14	1 19
28	10 27 42	8 30 16	25 28	17 43	20 40	11 30	3 38	0 17	17 46	5 14	1 18
29	10 31 38	9♓30 31	7♍59	19♓37	21♈50	12♉ 9	3♑47	0♊20	17♎44	5♐14	1♎16

THE SUN ENTERS THE SIGN OF PISCES ON FEB 19 AT 13:12.

DAY	TIME	☉	☽	☿	♀	♂	♃	♄	♅	♆	♇
	h m s	° ' "	° '	° '	° '	° '	° '	° '	° '	° '	° '
M 1	10 35 35	10♓30 43	20♍20	21♓29	22♈59	12♉49	3♑56	0♊23	17♎42	5♐15	1♎15
A 2	10 39 31	11 30 54	2♎31	23 21	24 8	13 28	4 5	0 27	17R40	5 15	1R13
R 3	10 43 28	12 31 3	14 35	25 11	25 17	14 8	4 14	0 30	17 38	5 15	1 12
C 4	10 47 24	13 31 10	26 31	27 0	26 25	14 47	4 22	0 34	17 36	5 15	1 10
H 5	10 51 21	14 31 16	8♏24	28 46	27 34	15 27	4 31	0 37	17 34	5 15	1 9
6	10 55 18	15 31 20	20 16	0♈30	28 42	16 6	4 39	0 41	17 32	5 15	1 7
7	10 59 14	16 31 22	2♐11	2 11	29 50	16 46	4 47	0 45	17 30	5R15	1 6
8	11 3 11	17 31 23	14 13	3 48	0♉58	17 25	4 55	0 48	17 28	5 15	1 4
9	11 7 7	18 31 23	26 28	5 21	2 6	18 5	5 3	0 52	17 26	5 15	1 3
10	11 11 4	19 31 20	9♑ 0	6 50	3 14	18 44	5 11	0 56	17 24	5 15	1 1
11	11 15 0	20 31 17	21 53	8 13	4 21	19 23	5 19	1 0	17 21	5 15	0 59
12	11 18 57	21 31 11	5♒12	9 31	5 28	20 3	5 26	1 5	17 19	5 15	0 58
13	11 22 53	22 31 3	18 58	10 42	6 35	20 42	5 34	1 9	17 17	5 15	0 56
14	11 26 50	23 30 54	3♓12	11 47	7 42	21 22	5 41	1 13	17 15	5 15	0 54
15	11 30 47	24 30 43	17 49	12 45	8 48	22 1	5 48	1 18	17 12	5 14	0 53
16	11 34 43	25 30 30	2♈44	13 35	9 55	22 40	5 55	1 22	17 10	5 14	0 51
17	11 38 40	26 30 15	17 47	14 18	11 1	23 20	6 2	1 27	17 8	5 14	0 50
18	11 42 36	27 29 58	2♉50	14 53	12 7	23 59	6 9	1 32	17 5	5 13	0 48
19	11 46 33	28 29 38	17 42	15 20	13 12	24 38	6 15	1 37	17 3	5 13	0 46
20	11 50 29	29 29 17	2♊16	15 38	14 18	25 18	6 22	1 41	17 1	5 13	0 45
21	11 54 26	0♈28 53	16 29	15R48	15 23	25 57	6 28	1 46	16 58	5 12	0 43
22	11 58 22	1 28 27	0♋19	15 51	16 28	26 36	6 34	1 52	16 56	5 12	0 41
23	12 2 19	2 27 58	13 46	15 45	17 32	27 16	6 40	1 57	16 53	5 11	0 40
24	12 6 16	3 27 27	26 53	15 32	18 37	27 55	6 46	2 2	16 51	5 11	0 38
25	12 10 12	4 26 54	9♌43	15 11	19 41	28 34	6 51	2 7	16 48	5 10	0 36
26	12 14 9	5 26 19	22 19	14 44	20 44	29 13	6 57	2 13	16 46	5 10	0 35
27	12 18 5	6 25 41	4♍44	14 11	21 48	29 53	7 2	2 18	16 43	5 9	0 33
28	12 22 2	7 25 1	17 0	13 33	22 51	0♊32	7 7	2 23	16 41	5 8	0 31
29	12 25 58	8 24 19	29 8	12 51	23 54	1 11	7 12	2 29	16 38	5 8	0 30
30	12 29 55	9 23 34	11♎11	12 5	24 56	1 50	7 17	2 35	16 36	5 7	0 28
31	12 33 51	10♈22 48	23♎ 9	11♈17	25♉58	2♊29	7♑21	2♊40	16♎33	5♐ 6	0♎27

THE SUN ENTERS THE SIGN OF ARIES ON MAR 20 AT 12:22.

♈ ARIES	♉ TAURUS	♊ GEMINI	♋ CANCER	♌ LEO	♍ VIRGO	♎ LIBRA

SIDEREAL SUN. MOON. MERCURY. VENUS. MARS. JUPITER. SATURN. URANUS. NEPTUNE. PLUTO.

DAY	TIME	☉	☽	☿	♀	♂	♃	♄	♅	♆	♇
	h m s	° ' "	° '	° '	° '	° '	° '	° '	° '	° '	° '
A 1	12 37 48	11♈22 0	5♏ 3	10♈28	27♉ 0	3♊ 8	7♑26	2♊46	16♎30	5♐ 5	0♎25
P 2	12 41 44	12 21 10	16 55	9R38	28 1	3 48	7 30	2 52	16R28	5R 5	0R23
R 3	12 45 41	13 20 18	28 47	8 48	29 2	4 27	7 34	2 58	16 25	5 4	0 22
I 4	12 49 38	14 19 24	10♐42	8 1	0♊ 3	5 6	7 38	3 4	16 23	5 3	0 20
L 5	12 53 34	15 18 28	22 44	7 15	1 3	5 45	7 42	3 10	16 20	5 2	0 19
6	12 57 31	16 17 31	4♑56	6 33	2 3	6 24	7 46	3 16	16 18	5 1	0 17
7	13 1 27	17 16 32	17 24	5 55	3 2	7 3	7 49	3 22	16 15	5 0	0 15
8	13 5 24	18 15 31	0♒12	5 21	4 1	7 42	7 52	3 28	16 12	4 59	0 14
9	13 9 20	19 14 28	13 25	4 51	5 0	8 21	7 55	3 35	16 10	4 58	0 12
10	13 13 17	20 13 24	27 6	4 27	5 58	9 0	7 58	3 41	16 7	4 57	0 11
11	13 17 13	21 12 17	11♓17	4 7	6 56	9 39	8 1	3 48	16 5	4 56	0 9
12	13 21 10	22 11 9	25 56	3 53	7 53	10 18	8 4	3 54	16 2	4 55	0 8
13	13 25 7	23 9 59	10♈58	3 44	8 50	10 57	8 6	4 0	15 59	4 54	0 6
14	13 29 3	24 8 47	26 13	3D41	9 46	11 36	8 8	4 7	15 57	4 53	0 5
15	13 33 0	25 7 34	11♉32	3 43	10 41	12 14	8 10	4 14	15 54	4 52	0 3
16	13 36 56	26 6 18	26 42	3 50	11 36	12 53	8 12	4 20	15 52	4 51	0 2
17	13 40 53	27 5 0	11♊33	4 2	12 31	13 32	8 13	4 27	15 49	4 49	0 0
18	13 44 49	28 3 40	26 0	4 19	13 25	14 11	8 15	4 34	15 47	4 48	29♍59
19	13 48 46	29 2 18	9♋59	4 40	14 18	14 50	8 16	4 41	15 44	4 47	29 58
20	13 52 42	0♉ 0 53	23 31	5 6	15 10	15 29	8 17	4 48	15 42	4 46	29 56
21	13 56 39	0 59 26	6♌37	5 36	16 2	16 8	8 18	4 54	15 39	4 44	29 55
22	14 0 36	1 57 57	19 23	6 11	16 54	16 46	8 19	5 1	15 37	4 43	29 54
23	14 4 32	2 56 26	1♍51	6 49	17 44	17 25	8 19	5 8	15 34	4 42	29 52
24	14 8 29	3 54 53	14 6	7 31	18 34	18 4	8 19	5 15	15 32	4 41	29 51
25	14 12 25	4 53 17	26 12	8 17	19 23	18 43	8R19	5 22	15 30	4 39	29 50
26	14 16 22	5 51 40	8♎12	9 6	20 11	19 21	8 19	5 30	15 27	4 38	29 48
27	14 20 18	6 50 0	20 7	9 58	20 58	20 0	8 19	5 37	15 25	4 36	29 47
28	14 24 15	7 48 19	2♏ 1	10 54	21 45	20 39	8 19	5 44	15 23	4 35	29 46
29	14 28 11	8 46 36	13 53	11 53	22 30	21 17	8 18	5 51	15 20	4 34	29 45
30	14 32 8	9♉44 51	25♏46	12♈54	23♊15	21♊56	8♑17	5♊58	15♎18	4♐32	29♍44

THE SUN ENTERS THE SIGN OF TAURUS ON APR 19 AT 23:38.

DAY	TIME	☉	☽	☿	♀	♂	♃	♄	♅	♆	♇
	h m s	° ' "	° '	° '	° '	° '	° '	° '	° '	° '	° '
M 1	14 36 5	10♉43 4	7♐42	13♈58	23♊58	22♊35	8♑16	6♊ 6	15♎16	4♐31	29♍42
A 2	14 40 1	11 41 16	19 41	15 5	24 41	23 13	8R15	6 13	15R13	4R29	29R41
Y 3	14 43 58	12 39 27	1♑47	16 15	25 23	23 52	8 13	6 20	15 11	4 28	29 40
4	14 47 54	13 37 35	14 2	17 27	26 3	24 31	8 12	6 28	15 9	4 26	29 39
5	14 51 51	14 35 43	26 31	18 42	26 43	25 9	8 10	6 35	15 7	4 25	29 38
6	14 55 47	15 33 49	9♒18	19 59	27 21	25 48	8 8	6 43	15 5	4 23	29 37
7	14 59 44	16 31 53	22 26	21 18	27 58	26 26	8 6	6 50	15 3	4 22	29 36
8	15 3 40	17 29 56	6♓ 0	22 40	28 34	27 5	8 4	6 58	15 1	4 20	29 35
9	15 7 37	18 27 58	20 2	24 4	29 8	27 43	8 1	7 5	14 59	4 19	29 34
10	15 11 34	19 25 58	4♈31	25 30	29 41	28 22	7 58	7 13	14 57	4 17	29 33
11	15 15 30	20 23 57	19 24	26 58	0♋13	29 0	7 56	7 20	14 55	4 16	29 32
12	15 19 27	21 21 55	4♉34	28 28	0 44	29 39	7 53	7 28	14 53	4 14	29 31
13	15 23 23	22 19 51	19 52	0♉ 1	1 12	0♋17	7 49	7 35	14 51	4 13	29 30
14	15 27 20	23 17 46	5♊ 5	1 36	1 40	0 56	7 46	7 43	14 49	4 11	29 30
15	15 31 16	24 15 39	20 3	3 12	2 5	1 34	7 42	7 51	14 47	4 9	29 29
16	15 35 13	25 13 31	4♋39	4 51	2 29	2 13	7 39	7 58	14 45	4 8	29 28
17	15 39 9	26 11 21	18 47	6 32	2 52	2 51	7 35	8 6	14 44	4 6	29 27
18	15 43 6	27 9 9	2♌27	8 15	3 12	3 29	7 31	8 14	14 42	4 5	29 27
19	15 47 3	28 6 56	15 39	10 0	3 31	4 8	7 26	8 21	14 40	4 3	29 26
20	15 50 59	29 4 41	28 27	11 48	3 47	4 46	7 22	8 29	14 39	4 1	29 25
21	15 54 56	0♊ 2 24	10♍56	13 37	4 2	5 25	7 17	8 37	14 37	4 0	29 25
22	15 58 52	1 0 5	23 9	15 28	4 14	6 3	7 13	8 45	14 36	3 58	29 24
23	16 2 49	1 57 45	5♎12	17 22	4 25	6 41	7 8	8 52	14 34	3 57	29 23
24	16 6 45	2 55 24	17 7	19 17	4 33	7 20	7 3	9 0	14 33	3 55	29 23
25	16 10 42	3 53 1	29 0	21 15	4 39	7 58	6 58	9 8	14 31	3 53	29 22
26	16 14 38	4 50 37	10♏52	23 15	4 43	8 36	6 52	9 16	14 30	3 52	29 22
27	16 18 35	5 48 11	22 45	25 16	4R45	9 14	6 47	9 24	14 29	3 50	29 22
28	16 22 32	6 45 45	4♐42	27 19	4 44	9 53	6 41	9 31	14 27	3 48	29 21
29	16 26 28	7 43 17	16 44	29 24	4 40	10 31	6 36	9 39	14 26	3 47	29 21
30	16 30 25	8 40 48	28 52	1♊31	4 35	11 9	6 30	9 47	14 25	3 45	29 20
31	16 34 21	9♊38 18	11♑ 8	3♊39	4♋27	11♋47	6♑24	9♊55	14♎24	3♐44	29♍20

THE SUN ENTERS THE SIGN OF GEMINI ON MAY 20 AT 23:00.

DAY	TIME	☉	☽	☿	♀	♂	♃	♄	♅	♆	♇
	h m s	° ' "	° '	° '	° '	° '	° '	° '	° '	° '	° '
J 1	16 38 18	10♊35 47	23♑34	5♊48	4♋16	12♋26	6♑18	10♊ 3	14♎23	3♐42	29♍20
U 2	16 42 14	11 33 15	6♒13	7 59	4R 3	13 4	6R11	10 10	14R22	3R40	29R20
N 3	16 46 11	12 30 43	19 6	10 10	3 48	13 42	6 5	10 18	14 21	3 39	29 19
E 4	16 50 8	13 28 10	2♓17	12 22	3 30	14 20	5 59	10 26	14 20	3 37	29 19
5	16 54 4	14 25 36	15 49	14 34	3 11	14 58	5 52	10 34	14 19	3 36	29 19
6	16 58 1	15 23 1	29 43	16 46	2 48	15 37	5 45	10 41	14 18	3 34	29 19
7	17 1 57	16 20 26	14♈ 0	18 58	2 24	16 15	5 39	10 49	14 17	3 32	29 19
8	17 5 54	17 17 50	28 37	21 9	1 58	16 53	5 32	10 57	14 17	3 31	29 19
9	17 9 50	18 15 14	13♉29	23 20	1 29	17 31	5 25	11 5	14 16	3 29	29D19
10	17 13 47	19 12 37	28 29	25 29	0 59	18 9	5 18	11 13	14 15	3 28	29 19
11	17 17 43	20 10 0	13♊29	27 38	0 28	18 47	5 11	11 20	14 15	3 26	29 19
12	17 21 40	21 7 22	28 19	29 45	29♊55	19 25	5 4	11 28	14 14	3 25	29 19
13	17 25 37	22 4 43	12♋51	1♋50	29 20	20 4	4 56	11 36	14 14	3 23	29 19
14	17 29 33	23 2 3	27 0	3 53	28 45	20 42	4 49	11 43	14 13	3 22	29 19
15	17 33 30	23 59 23	10♌44	5 55	28 8	21 20	4 42	11 51	14 13	3 20	29 19
16	17 37 26	24 56 41	24 1	7 55	27 31	21 58	4 34	11 59	14 12	3 19	29 19
17	17 41 23	25 53 59	6♍54	9 52	26 54	22 36	4 27	12 7	14 12	3 17	29 20
18	17 45 19	26 51 16	19 26	11 47	26 16	23 14	4 19	12 14	14 12	3 16	29 20
19	17 49 16	27 48 32	1♎42	13 41	25 39	23 52	4 12	12 22	14 12	3 14	29 20
20	17 53 12	28 45 47	13 45	15 32	25 2	24 30	4 4	12 29	14 12	3 13	29 21
21	17 57 9	29 43 2	25 41	17 20	24 25	25 8	3 56	12 37	14D12	3 11	29 21
22	18 1 6	0♋40 16	7♏33	19 7	23 49	25 46	3 49	12 45	14 12	3 10	29 21
23	18 5 2	1 37 29	19 26	20 51	23 14	26 24	3 41	12 52	14 12	3 9	29 22
24	18 8 59	2 34 42	1♐22	22 33	22 40	27 2	3 33	13 0	14 12	3 7	29 22
25	18 12 55	3 31 55	13 25	24 12	22 8	27 40	3 26	13 7	14 12	3 6	29 23
26	18 16 52	4 29 7	25 35	25 49	21 38	28 18	3 18	13 15	14 12	3 5	29 23
27	18 20 48	5 26 18	7♑56	27 24	21 9	28 56	3 10	13 22	14 12	3 3	29 24
28	18 24 45	6 23 30	20 27	28 56	20 42	29 34	3 3	13 29	14 13	3 2	29 24
29	18 28 41	7 20 41	3♒10	0♌26	20 17	0♌12	2 55	13 37	14 13	3 1	29 25
30	18 32 38	8♋17 53	16♒ 6	1♌54	19♊54	0♌50	2♑48	13♊44	14♎13	2♐59	29♍26

THE SUN ENTERS THE SIGN OF CANCER ON JUN 21 AT 07:07.

♏ SCORPIO ♐ SAGITTARIUS ♑ CAPRICORN ♒ AQUARIUS ♓ PISCES

SIDEREAL . SUN . MOON . MERCURY . VENUS . MARS . JUPITER . SATURN . URANUS . NEPTUNE . PLUTO .

DAY	TIME	☉	☽	☿	♀	♂	♃	♄	♅	♆	♇
	h m s	° ' "	° '	° '	° '	° '	° '	° '	° '	° '	° '
J 1	18 36 35	9♋15 4	29♒16	3♌20	19♊33	1♌28	2♑40	13♊52	14♎14	2♐58	29♍26
U 2	18 40 31	10 12 15	12♓40	4 42	19R15	2 6	2R32	13 59	14 14	2R57	29 27
L 3	18 44 28	11 9 27	26 20	6 3	18 59	2 44	2 25	14 6	14 15	2 56	29 28
Y 4	18 48 24	12 6 39	10♈14	7 21	18 45	3 22	2 17	14 13	14 16	2 55	29 29
5	18 52 21	13 3 51	24 23	8 36	18 34	4 0	2 10	14 20	14 16	2 53	29 29
6	18 56 17	14 1 3	8♉45	9 49	18 25	4 38	2 2	14 28	14 17	2 52	29 30
7	19 0 14	14 58 16	23 16	10 59	18 19	5 16	1 55	14 35	14 18	2 51	29 31
8	19 4 10	15 55 29	7♊52	12 6	18 15	5 54	1 48	14 42	14 19	2 50	29 32
9	19 8 7	16 52 43	22 27	13 11	18D13	6 32	1 41	14 49	14 19	2 49	29 33
10	19 12 4	17 49 57	6♋55	14 12	18 14	7 10	1 33	14 56	14 20	2 48	29 34
11	19 16 0	18 47 11	21 10	15 11	18 17	7 48	1 26	15 3	14 21	2 47	29 35
12	19 19 57	19 44 25	5♌ 9	16 6	18 22	8 26	1 19	15 10	14 22	2 46	29 36
13	19 23 53	20 41 39	18 46	16 58	18 29	9 4	1 13	15 17	14 24	2 45	29 37
14	19 27 50	21 38 54	2♍ 2	17 47	18 39	9 42	1 6	15 23	14 25	2 44	29 38
15	19 31 46	22 36 8	14 56	18 32	18 50	10 20	0 59	15 30	14 26	2 43	29 39
16	19 35 43	23 33 23	27 31	19 14	19 4	10 58	0 52	15 37	14 27	2 42	29 40
17	19 39 40	24 30 38	9♎48	19 52	19 20	11 36	0 46	15 44	14 28	2 41	29 42
18	19 43 36	25 27 53	21 54	20 26	19 37	12 14	0 40	15 50	14 30	2 41	29 43
19	19 47 33	26 25 8	3♏50	20 56	19 56	12 52	0 33	15 57	14 31	2 40	29 44
20	19 51 29	27 22 23	15 43	21 22	20 17	13 30	0 27	16 3	14 33	2 39	29 45
21	19 55 26	28 19 39	27 37	21 43	20 40	14 8	0 21	16 10	14 34	2 38	29 47
22	19 59 22	29 16 55	9♐36	22 0	21 5	14 46	0 15	16 16	14 36	2 38	29 48
23	20 3 19	0♌14 11	21 43	22 12	21 31	15 24	0 9	16 23	14 37	2 37	29 49
24	20 7 15	1 11 28	4♑ 2	22R19	21 58	16 2	0 4	16 29	14 39	2 36	29 51
25	20 11 12	2 8 46	16 35	22 21	22 28	16 40	29♐58	16 35	14 40	2 36	29 52
26	20 15 9	3 6 3	29 24	22 19	22 58	17 18	29 53	16 42	14 42	2 35	29 53
27	20 19 5	4 3 22	12♒28	22 11	23 30	17 56	29 48	16 48	14 44	2 34	29 55
28	20 23 2	5 0 41	25 47	21 58	24 4	18 34	29 43	16 54	14 46	2 34	29 56
29	20 26 58	5 58 1	9♓21	21 40	24 38	19 12	29 38	17 0	14 48	2 33	29 58
30	20 30 55	6 55 22	23 8	21 18	25 14	19 50	29 33	17 6	14 50	2 33	29 59
31	20 34 51	7♌52 44	7♈ 5	20♌50	25♊51	20♌28	29♐28	17♊12	14♎52	2♐32	0♎ 1

THE SUN ENTERS THE SIGN OF LEO ON JUL 22 AT 18:03.

DAY	TIME	☉	☽	☿	♀	♂	♃	♄	♅	♆	♇
	h m s	° ' "	° '	° '	° '	° '	° '	° '	° '	° '	° '
A 1	20 38 48	8♌50 7	21♈10	20♌18	26♊30	21♌ 6	29♐24	17♊18	14♎54	2♐32	0♎ 2
U 2	20 42 44	9 47 31	5♉21	19R43	27 9	21 44	29R20	17 23	14 56	2R32	0 4
G 3	20 46 41	10 44 57	19 34	19 3	27 50	22 22	29 15	17 29	14 58	2 31	0 6
U 4	20 50 38	11 42 24	3♊49	18 21	28 31	23 0	29 12	17 35	15 0	2 31	0 7
S 5	20 54 34	12 39 52	18 2	17 36	29 14	23 38	29 8	17 40	15 2	2 31	0 9
T 6	20 58 31	13 37 21	2♋10	16 50	29 57	24 16	29 4	17 46	15 4	2 30	0 11
7	21 2 27	14 34 52	16 11	16 2	0♋42	24 54	29 1	17 51	15 7	2 30	0 12
8	21 6 24	15 32 24	0♌ 2	15 15	1 27	25 32	28 57	17 57	15 9	2 30	0 14
9	21 10 20	16 29 56	13 40	14 29	2 13	26 10	28 54	18 2	15 11	2 30	0 16
10	21 14 17	17 27 30	27 2	13 44	3 0	26 48	28 51	18 7	15 14	2 29	0 17
11	21 18 13	18 25 5	10♍ 8	13 3	3 48	27 26	28 49	18 12	15 16	2 29	0 19
12	21 22 10	19 22 41	22 56	12 24	4 37	28 4	28 46	18 17	15 19	2 29	0 21
13	21 26 7	20 20 18	5♎28	11 50	5 26	28 42	28 44	18 22	15 21	2 29	0 23
14	21 30 3	21 17 56	17 45	11 21	6 16	29 20	28 41	18 27	15 24	2D29	0 25
15	21 34 0	22 15 35	29 50	10 58	7 7	29 58	28 39	18 32	15 26	2 29	0 27
16	21 37 56	23 13 15	11♏47	10 41	7 58	0♍37	28 37	18 37	15 29	2 29	0 29
17	21 41 53	24 10 56	23 39	10D31	8 50	1 15	28 36	18 42	15 31	2 29	0 30
18	21 45 49	25 8 38	5♐32	10 28	9 42	1 53	28 34	18 46	15 34	2 29	0 32
19	21 49 46	26 6 22	17 31	10 32	10 36	2 31	28 33	18 51	15 37	2 30	0 34
20	21 53 42	27 4 6	29 40	10 43	11 29	3 9	28 32	18 55	15 40	2 30	0 36
21	21 57 39	28 1 52	12♑ 4	11 3	12 24	3 47	28 31	19 0	15 43	2 30	0 38
22	22 1 36	28 59 38	24 46	11 30	13 19	4 25	28 30	19 4	15 45	2 30	0 40
23	22 5 32	29 57 26	7♒48	12 4	14 14	5 3	28 30	19 8	15 48	2 30	0 42
24	22 9 29	0♍55 16	21 11	12 46	15 10	5 42	28 29	19 12	15 51	2 31	0 44
25	22 13 25	1 53 6	4♓54	13 35	16 6	6 20	28D29	19 16	15 54	2 31	0 46
26	22 17 22	2 50 59	18 56	14 32	17 3	6 58	28 29	19 20	15 57	2 31	0 48
27	22 21 18	3 48 52	3♈10	15 35	18 1	7 36	28 30	19 24	16 0	2 32	0 50
28	22 25 15	4 46 48	17 33	16 45	18 59	8 14	28 30	19 28	16 3	2 32	0 52
29	22 29 11	5 44 45	1♉58	18 1	19 57	8 52	28 31	19 31	16 6	2 33	0 55
30	22 33 8	6 42 44	16 21	19 23	20 56	9 31	28 31	19 35	16 9	2 33	0 57
31	22 37 5	7♍40 45	0♊38	20♌50	21♋55	10♍ 9	28♐32	19♊38	16♎12	2♐34	0♎59

THE SUN ENTERS THE SIGN OF VIRGO ON AUG 23 AT 01:04.

DAY	TIME	☉	☽	☿	♀	♂	♃	♄	♅	♆	♇
	h m s	° ' "	° '	° '	° '	° '	° '	° '	° '	° '	° '
S 1	22 41 1	8♍38 49	14♊46	22♌22	22♋54	10♍47	28♐33	19♊42	16♎16	2♐34	1♎ 1
E 2	22 44 58	9 36 54	28 44	23 58	23 54	11 25	28 35	19 45	16 19	2 35	1 3
P 3	22 48 54	10 35 1	12♋31	25 38	24 54	12 4	28 36	19 48	16 22	2 36	1 5
T 4	22 52 51	11 33 10	26 7	27 22	25 55	12 42	28 38	19 51	16 25	2 36	1 7
E 5	22 56 47	12 31 21	9♌32	29 8	26 56	13 20	28 40	19 54	16 29	2 37	1 10
M 6	23 0 44	13 29 33	22 46	0♍56	27 58	13 59	28 42	19 57	16 32	2 38	1 12
B 7	23 4 40	14 27 48	5♍48	2 47	28 59	14 37	28 44	20 0	16 35	2 38	1 14
E 8	23 8 37	15 26 4	18 38	4 39	0♌ 1	15 15	28 47	20 3	16 39	2 39	1 16
R 9	23 12 34	16 24 22	1♎14	6 32	1 4	15 54	28 49	20 5	16 42	2 40	1 18
10	23 16 30	17 22 42	13 38	8 26	2 6	16 32	28 52	20 8	16 45	2 41	1 21
11	23 20 27	18 21 3	25 50	10 20	3 9	17 10	28 55	20 10	16 49	2 42	1 23
12	23 24 23	19 19 27	7♏52	12 14	4 13	17 49	28 58	20 12	16 52	2 43	1 25
13	23 28 20	20 17 52	19 47	14 9	5 16	18 27	29 2	20 15	16 56	2 44	1 27
14	23 32 16	21 16 18	1♐37	16 3	6 20	19 6	29 5	20 17	16 59	2 45	1 29
15	23 36 13	22 14 46	13 28	17 57	7 24	19 44	29 9	20 19	17 3	2 46	1 32
16	23 40 9	23 13 16	25 25	19 50	8 29	20 22	29 13	20 21	17 6	2 47	1 34
17	23 44 6	24 11 48	7♑32	21 42	9 33	21 1	29 17	20 22	17 10	2 48	1 36
18	23 48 2	25 10 21	19 55	23 34	10 38	21 39	29 21	20 24	17 13	2 49	1 39
19	23 51 59	26 8 55	2♒38	25 25	11 43	22 18	29 26	20 26	17 17	2 50	1 41
20	23 55 56	27 7 32	15 46	27 16	12 49	22 56	29 30	20 27	17 21	2 51	1 43
21	23 59 52	28 6 10	29 20	29 5	13 54	23 35	29 35	20 28	17 24	2 52	1 45
22	0 3 49	29 4 50	13♓20	0♎53	15 0	24 13	29 40	20 30	17 28	2 53	1 48
23	0 7 45	0♎ 3 32	27 43	2 41	16 6	24 52	29 45	20 31	17 31	2 55	1 50
24	0 11 42	1 2 15	12♈24	4 27	17 12	25 31	29 50	20 32	17 35	2 56	1 52
25	0 15 38	2 1 1	27 14	6 13	18 19	26 9	29 56	20 33	17 39	2 57	1 54
26	0 19 35	2 59 49	12♉ 5	7 57	19 26	26 48	0♑ 1	20 33	17 42	2 58	1 57
27	0 23 31	3 58 39	26 48	9 41	20 33	27 26	0 7	20 34	17 46	3 0	1 59
28	0 27 28	4 57 32	11♊19	11 23	21 40	28 5	0 13	20 35	17 50	3 1	2 1
29	0 31 25	5 56 27	25 32	13 5	22 47	28 44	0 19	20 35	17 54	3 3	2 4
30	0 35 21	6♎55 24	9♋27	14♎46	23♌55	29♍22	0♑25	20♊35	17♎57	3♐ 4	2♎ 6

THE SUN ENTERS THE SIGN OF LIBRA ON SEP 22 AT 22:34.

♈ ARIES ♉ TAURUS ♊ GEMINI ♋ CANCER ♌ LEO ♍ VIRGO ♎ LIBRA

1972

S I D E R E A L — SUN.... — MOON... — MERCURY — VENUS.. — MARS... — JUPITER — SATURN. — URANUS. — NEPTUNE — PLUTO..

DAY	TIME	☉	☽	☿	♀	♂	♃	♄	♅	♆	♇
	h m s	° ' "	° '	° '	° '	° '	° '	° '	° '	° '	° '
O 1	0 39 18	7♎54 24	23♋ 3	16♎26	25♌ 3	0♎ 1	0♑32	20♊36	18♎ 1	3♐ 5	2♎ 8
C 2	0 43 14	8 53 25	6♌24	18 5	26 11	0 40	0 38	20R36	18 5	3 7	2 10
T 3	0 47 11	9 52 29	19 30	19 44	27 19	1 18	0 45	20 36	18 8	3 8	2 13
O 4	0 51 7	10 51 36	2♍23	21 21	28 27	1 57	0 52	20 36	18 12	3 10	2 15
B 5	0 55 4	11 50 44	15 6	22 58	29 36	2 36	0 59	20 36	18 16	3 12	2 17
E 6	0 59 0	12 49 55	27 37	24 34	0♍44	3 15	1 6	20 35	18 20	3 13	2 19
R 7	1 2 57	13 49 8	10♎ 0	26 9	1 53	3 54	1 13	20 35	18 24	3 15	2 22
8	1 6 54	14 48 22	22 12	27 43	3 2	4 32	1 20	20 34	18 27	3 16	2 24
9	1 10 50	15 47 39	4♏17	29 17	4 11	5 11	1 28	20 34	18 31	3 18	2 26
10	1 14 47	16 46 58	16 14	0♏49	5 20	5 50	1 36	20 33	18 35	3 20	2 28
11	1 18 43	17 46 19	28 5	2 22	6 30	6 29	1 43	20 32	18 39	3 21	2 31
12	1 22 40	18 45 42	9♐54	3 53	7 40	7 8	1 51	20 31	18 42	3 23	2 33
13	1 26 36	19 45 6	21 43	5 24	8 49	7 47	2 0	20 30	18 46	3 25	2 35
14	1 30 33	20 44 33	3♑37	6 53	9 59	8 26	2 8	20 29	18 50	3 27	2 37
15	1 34 29	21 44 1	15 40	8 23	11 9	9 5	2 16	20 27	18 54	3 28	2 39
16	1 38 26	22 43 31	27 59	9 51	12 19	9 44	2 25	20 26	18 58	3 30	2 42
17	1 42 23	23 43 3	10♒39	11 19	13 30	10 23	2 33	20 25	19 1	3 32	2 44
18	1 46 19	24 42 36	23 43	12 46	14 40	11 2	2 42	20 23	19 5	3 34	2 46
19	1 50 16	25 42 11	7♓17	14 12	15 51	11 41	2 51	20 21	19 9	3 36	2 48
20	1 54 12	26 41 48	21 21	15 38	17 1	12 20	3 0	20 19	19 13	3 38	2 50
21	1 58 9	27 41 27	5♈52	17 2	18 12	12 59	3 9	20 17	19 16	3 39	2 52
22	2 2 5	28 41 7	20 47	18 26	19 23	13 38	3 18	20 15	19 20	3 41	2 54
23	2 6 2	29 40 50	5♉56	19 49	20 34	14 17	3 28	20 13	19 24	3 43	2 57
24	2 9 58	0♏40 34	21 9	21 11	21 45	14 56	3 37	20 11	19 28	3 45	2 59
25	2 13 55	1 40 21	6♊14	22 32	22 57	15 35	3 47	20 9	19 31	3 47	3 1
26	2 17 52	2 40 10	21 4	23 52	24 8	16 15	3 57	20 6	19 35	3 49	3 3
27	2 21 48	3 40 1	5♋32	25 11	25 20	16 54	4 6	20 4	19 39	3 51	3 5
28	2 25 45	4 39 55	19 35	26 29	26 31	17 33	4 16	20 1	19 43	3 53	3 7
29	2 29 41	5 39 50	3♌14	27 45	27 43	18 12	4 27	19 58	19 46	3 55	3 9
30	2 33 38	6 39 48	16 31	29 0	28 55	18 52	4 37	19 56	19 50	3 57	3 11
31	2 37 34	7♏39 48	29♌28	0♐14	0♎ 7	19♎31	4♑47	19♊53	19♎54	3♐59	3♎13

THE SUN ENTERS THE SIGN OF SCORPIO ON OCT 23 AT 07:43.

DAY	TIME	☉	☽	☿	♀	♂	♃	♄	♅	♆	♇
	h m s	° ' "	° '	° '	° '	° '	° '	° '	° '	° '	° '
N 1	2 41 31	8♏39 50	12♍ 9	1♐25	1♎19	20♎10	4♑57	19♊50	19♎57	4♐ 1	3♎15
O 2	2 45 27	9 39 54	24 37	2 35	2 31	20 50	5 8	19R46	20 1	4 4	3 17
V 3	2 49 24	10 40 0	6♎55	3 43	3 43	21 29	5 18	19 43	20 4	4 6	3 19
E 4	2 53 20	11 40 9	19 4	4 48	4 56	22 8	5 29	19 40	20 8	4 8	3 20
M 5	2 57 17	12 40 19	1♏ 7	5 51	6 8	22 48	5 40	19 37	20 12	4 10	3 22
B 6	3 1 14	13 40 31	13 3	6 51	7 21	23 27	5 51	19 33	20 15	4 12	3 24
E 7	3 5 10	14 40 45	24 56	7 48	8 33	24 7	6 2	19 30	20 19	4 14	3 26
R 8	3 9 7	15 41 1	6♐45	8 41	9 46	24 46	6 13	19 26	20 22	4 16	3 28
9	3 13 3	16 41 18	18 34	9 29	10 59	25 26	6 24	19 22	20 26	4 18	3 30
10	3 17 0	17 41 37	0♑24	10 14	12 12	26 5	6 35	19 19	20 29	4 21	3 31
11	3 20 56	18 41 57	12 19	10 53	13 25	26 45	6 47	19 15	20 33	4 23	3 33
12	3 24 53	19 42 19	24 23	11 26	14 38	27 24	6 58	19 11	20 36	4 25	3 35
13	3 28 50	20 42 43	6♒40	11 53	15 51	28 4	7 10	19 7	20 40	4 27	3 37
14	3 32 46	21 43 8	19 15	12 12	17 4	28 44	7 21	19 3	20 43	4 29	3 38
15	3 36 43	22 43 34	2♓13	12R24	18 17	29 23	7 33	18 59	20 46	4 32	3 40
16	3 40 39	23 44 1	15 39	12 27	19 30	0♏ 3	7 45	18 54	20 50	4 34	3 42
17	3 44 36	24 44 30	29 34	12 21	20 44	0 42	7 57	18 50	20 53	4 36	3 43
18	3 48 32	25 45 0	13♈58	12 5	21 57	1 22	8 9	18 46	20 56	4 38	3 45
19	3 52 29	26 45 31	28 49	11 39	23 11	2 2	8 21	18 42	21 0	4 41	3 46
20	3 56 25	27 46 4	13♉59	11 2	24 24	2 42	8 33	18 37	21 3	4 43	3 48
21	4 0 22	28 46 38	29 18	10 14	25 38	3 21	8 45	18 33	21 6	4 45	3 49
22	4 4 19	29 47 14	14♊36	9 17	26 51	4 1	8 57	18 28	21 9	4 47	3 51
23	4 8 15	0♐47 51	29 40	8 11	28 5	4 41	9 9	18 24	21 12	4 50	3 52
24	4 12 12	1 48 30	14♋24	6 57	29 19	5 21	9 22	18 19	21 15	4 52	3 54
25	4 16 8	2 49 10	28 43	5 38	0♏33	6 1	9 34	18 14	21 19	4 54	3 55
26	4 20 5	3 49 52	12♌33	4 17	1 46	6 41	9 47	18 10	21 22	4 56	3 57
27	4 24 1	4 50 36	25 57	2 54	3 0	7 21	9 59	18 5	21 25	4 59	3 58
28	4 27 58	5 51 21	8♍56	1 35	4 14	8 1	10 12	18 0	21 28	5 1	3 59
29	4 31 54	6 52 8	21 35	0 21	5 28	8 41	10 25	17 55	21 31	5 3	4 1
30	4 35 51	7♐52 56	3♎58	29♏14	6♏43	9♏21	10♑37	17♊51	21♎33	5♐ 5	4♎ 2

THE SUN ENTERS THE SIGN OF SAGITTARIUS ON NOV 22 AT 05:04.

DAY	TIME	☉	☽	☿	♀	♂	♃	♄	♅	♆	♇
	h m s	° ' "	° '	° '	° '	° '	° '	° '	° '	° '	° '
D 1	4 39 48	8♐53 45	16♎ 8	28♏16	7♏57	10♏ 1	10♑50	17♊46	21♎36	5♐ 8	4♎ 3
E 2	4 43 44	9 54 36	28 9	27R29	9 11	10 41	11 3	17R41	21 39	5 10	4 4
C 3	4 47 41	10 55 29	10♏ 4	26 54	10 25	11 21	11 16	17 36	21 42	5 12	4 5
E 4	4 51 37	11 56 23	21 55	26 30	11 39	12 1	11 29	17 31	21 45	5 14	4 7
M 5	4 55 34	12 57 17	3♐45	26D17	12 54	12 41	11 42	17 26	21 47	5 17	4 8
B 6	4 59 30	13 58 13	15 35	26 15	14 8	13 21	11 55	17 21	21 50	5 19	4 9
E 7	5 3 27	14 59 11	27 28	26 23	15 22	14 1	12 8	17 16	21 53	5 21	4 10
R 8	5 7 23	16 0 9	9♑24	26 41	16 37	14 42	12 21	17 11	21 55	5 23	4 11
9	5 11 20	17 1 7	21 26	27 7	17 51	15 22	12 35	17 6	21 58	5 26	4 12
10	5 15 17	18 2 7	3♒37	27 41	19 6	16 2	12 48	17 1	22 1	5 28	4 13
11	5 19 13	19 3 7	16 0	28 22	20 20	16 42	13 1	16 56	22 3	5 30	4 14
12	5 23 10	20 4 8	28 38	29 9	21 35	17 23	13 15	16 51	22 5	5 32	4 15
13	5 27 6	21 5 9	11♓35	0♐ 1	22 49	18 3	13 28	16 47	22 8	5 34	4 15
14	5 31 3	22 6 11	24 54	0 59	24 4	18 43	13 41	16 42	22 10	5 37	4 16
15	5 34 59	23 7 13	8♈38	2 0	25 18	19 24	13 55	16 37	22 13	5 39	4 17
16	5 38 56	24 8 16	22 47	3 5	26 33	20 4	14 9	16 32	22 15	5 41	4 18
17	5 42 52	25 9 19	7♉20	4 13	27 48	20 45	14 22	16 27	22 17	5 43	4 18
18	5 46 49	26 10 23	22 12	5 24	29 2	21 25	14 36	16 22	22 19	5 45	4 19
19	5 50 46	27 11 27	7♊18	6 38	0♐17	22 6	14 49	16 17	22 21	5 47	4 20
20	5 54 42	28 12 31	22 28	7 53	1 32	22 46	15 3	16 12	22 23	5 50	4 20
21	5 58 39	29 13 36	7♋33	9 10	2 46	23 27	15 17	16 8	22 25	5 52	4 21
22	6 2 35	0♑14 42	22 22	10 29	4 1	24 7	15 30	16 3	22 27	5 54	4 22
23	6 6 32	1 15 48	6♌50	11 50	5 16	24 48	15 44	15 58	22 29	5 56	4 22
24	6 10 28	2 16 54	20 52	13 12	6 31	25 28	15 58	15 54	22 31	5 58	4 23
25	6 14 25	3 18 2	4♍27	14 34	7 46	26 9	16 12	15 49	22 33	6 0	4 23
26	6 18 22	4 19 9	17 35	15 58	9 0	26 50	16 26	15 44	22 35	6 2	4 23
27	6 22 18	5 20 18	0♎20	17 23	10 15	27 30	16 39	15 40	22 37	6 4	4 24
28	6 26 15	6 21 26	12 45	18 48	11 30	28 11	16 53	15 35	22 38	6 6	4 24
29	6 30 11	7 22 36	24 54	20 15	12 45	28 52	17 7	15 31	22 40	6 8	4 24
30	6 34 8	8 23 46	6♏53	21 42	14 0	29 32	17 21	15 27	22 42	6 10	4 25
31	6 38 4	9♑24 56	18♏44	23♐ 9	15♐15	0♐13	17♑35	15♊22	22♎43	6♐12	4♎25

THE SUN ENTERS THE SIGN OF CAPRICORN ON DEC 21 AT 18:14.

♏	SCORPIO	♐	SAGITTARIUS	♑	CAPRICORN	♒	AQUARIUS	♓	PISCES

SIDEREAL SUN. MOON. MERCURY. VENUS. MARS. JUPITER. SATURN. URANUS. NEPTUNE. PLUTO.

DAY	TIME h m s	☉ ° ' "	☽ ° '	☿ ° '	♀ ° '	♂ ° '	♃ ° '	♄ ° '	♅ ° '	♆ ° '	♇ ° '
J 1	6 42 1	10♑26 7	0♐33	24♐37	16♐30	0♐54	17♑49	15♊18	22♎45	6♐14	4♎25
A 2	6 45 57	11 27 18	12 23	26 6	17 45	1 35	18 3	15R14	22 46	6 16	4 25
N 3	6 49 54	12 28 29	24 16	27 35	19 0	2 16	18 17	15 10	22 47	6 18	4 25
U 4	6 53 51	13 29 40	6♑15	29 5	20 15	2 57	18 31	15 6	22 49	6 20	4 26
A 5	6 57 47	14 30 51	18 21	0♑35	21 30	3 38	18 45	15 2	22 50	6 22	4 26
R 6	7 1 44	15 32 2	0♒37	2 6	22 45	4 18	18 59	14 58	22 51	6 24	4R26
Y 7	7 5 40	16 33 13	13 4	3 37	24 0	4 59	19 13	14 54	22 52	6 25	4 26
8	7 9 37	17 34 23	25 42	5 8	25 15	5 40	19 27	14 50	22 53	6 27	4 26
9	7 13 33	18 35 33	8♓34	6 40	26 30	6 21	19 41	14 46	22 54	6 29	4 25
10	7 17 30	19 36 43	21 41	8 12	27 45	7 2	19 55	14 43	22 55	6 31	4 25
11	7 21 26	20 37 52	5♈ 4	9 45	29 0	7 44	20 9	14 39	22 56	6 33	4 25
12	7 25 23	21 39 1	18 44	11 18	0♑15	8 25	20 23	14 36	22 57	6 34	4 25
13	7 29 20	22 40 8	2♉41	12 52	1 30	9 6	20 37	14 33	22 58	6 36	4 25
14	7 33 16	23 41 16	16 55	14 26	2 45	9 47	20 51	14 29	22 59	6 38	4 25
15	7 37 13	24 42 22	1♊24	16 1	4 0	10 28	21 5	14 26	23 0	6 39	4 24
16	7 41 9	25 43 28	16 4	17 36	5 15	11 9	21 19	14 23	23 0	6 41	4 24
17	7 45 6	26 44 33	0♋50	19 11	6 30	11 50	21 33	14 20	23 1	6 43	4 24
18	7 49 2	27 45 38	15 35	20 47	7 45	12 31	21 47	14 17	23 1	6 44	4 23
19	7 52 59	28 46 42	0♌12	22 24	9 0	13 13	22 1	14 14	23 2	6 46	4 23
20	7 56 55	29 47 45	14 34	24 1	10 15	13 54	22 15	14 12	23 2	6 47	4 22
21	8 0 52	0♒48 48	28 37	25 39	11 30	14 35	22 29	14 9	23 3	6 49	4 22
22	8 4 49	1 49 50	12♍16	27 17	12 45	15 17	22 43	14 6	23 3	6 50	4 21
23	8 8 45	2 50 51	25 31	28 56	14 0	15 58	22 57	14 4	23 3	6 52	4 21
24	8 12 42	3 51 52	8♎23	0♒36	15 15	16 39	23 11	14 2	23 3	6 53	4 20
25	8 16 38	4 52 52	20 53	2 16	16 31	17 21	23 25	13 59	23 4	6 55	4 20
26	8 20 35	5 53 52	3♏ 6	3 57	17 46	18 2	23 39	13 57	23 4	6 56	4 19
27	8 24 31	6 54 52	15 5	5 38	19 1	18 44	23 53	13 55	23R 4	6 58	4 18
28	8 28 28	7 55 50	26 57	7 20	20 16	19 25	24 7	13 53	23 4	6 59	4 18
29	8 32 24	8 56 49	8♐46	9 3	21 31	20 7	24 20	13 52	23 4	7 0	4 17
30	8 36 21	9 57 46	20 36	10 46	22 46	20 48	24 34	13 50	23 4	7 1	4 16
31	8 40 18	10♒58 43	2♑33	12♒30	24♑ 1	21♐30	24♑48	13♊48	23♎ 3	7♐ 3	4♎15

THE SUN ENTERS THE SIGN OF AQUARIUS ON JAN 20 AT 04:49.

DAY	TIME h m s	☉ ° ' "	☽ ° '	☿ ° '	♀ ° '	♂ ° '	♃ ° '	♄ ° '	♅ ° '	♆ ° '	♇ ° '
F 1	8 44 14	11♒59 38	14♑38	14♒15	25♑16	22♐11	25♑ 2	13♊47	23♎ 3	7♐ 4	4♎15
E 2	8 48 11	13 0 33	26 56	16 0	26 31	22 53	25 15	13R46	23R 3	7 5	4R14
B 3	8 52 7	14 1 27	9♒27	17 46	27 46	23 34	25 29	13 44	23 2	7 6	4 13
R 4	8 56 4	15 2 20	22 14	19 33	29 1	24 16	25 43	13 43	23 2	7 7	4 12
U 5	9 0 0	16 3 11	5♓15	21 20	0♒17	24 58	25 56	13 42	23 2	7 8	4 11
A 6	9 3 57	17 4 1	18 30	23 7	1 32	25 39	26 10	13 41	23 1	7 10	4 10
R 7	9 7 53	18 4 50	1♈59	24 55	2 47	26 21	26 24	13 40	23 1	7 11	4 9
Y 8	9 11 50	19 5 37	15 39	26 43	4 2	27 3	26 37	13 40	23 0	7 12	4 8
9	9 15 47	20 6 23	29 29	28 32	5 17	27 44	26 51	13 39	22 59	7 12	4 7
10	9 19 43	21 7 7	13♉27	0♓20	6 32	28 26	27 4	13 39	22 58	7 13	4 6
11	9 23 40	22 7 50	27 32	2 9	7 47	29 8	27 18	13 38	22 58	7 14	4 5
12	9 27 36	23 8 31	11♊44	3 57	9 2	29 50	27 31	13 38	22 57	7 15	4 4
13	9 31 33	24 9 10	25 59	5 45	10 17	0♑32	27 44	13D38	22 56	7 16	4 2
14	9 35 29	25 9 48	10♋16	7 32	11 32	1 13	27 58	13 38	22 55	7 17	4 1
15	9 39 26	26 10 24	24 33	9 17	12 47	1 55	28 11	13 38	22 54	7 18	4 0
16	9 43 22	27 10 58	8♌44	11 2	14 2	2 37	28 24	13 38	22 53	7 18	3 59
17	9 47 19	28 11 31	22 46	12 44	15 17	3 19	28 37	13 39	22 52	7 19	3 58
18	9 51 16	29 12 2	6♍34	14 25	16 32	4 1	28 50	13 39	22 51	7 20	3 56
19	9 55 12	0♓12 31	20 5	16 2	17 47	4 43	29 3	13 40	22 50	7 20	3 55
20	9 59 9	1 12 59	3♎17	17 37	19 2	5 25	29 16	13 40	22 48	7 21	3 54
21	10 3 5	2 13 26	16 8	19 7	20 17	6 7	29 29	13 41	22 47	7 22	3 52
22	10 7 2	3 13 51	28 40	20 33	21 32	6 49	29 42	13 42	22 46	7 22	3 51
23	10 10 58	4 14 15	10♏55	21 54	22 47	7 31	29 55	13 43	22 44	7 23	3 50
24	10 14 55	5 14 37	22 56	23 9	24 2	8 13	0♒ 8	13 44	22 43	7 23	3 48
25	10 18 51	6 14 58	4♐49	24 18	25 17	8 55	0 20	13 45	22 41	7 24	3 47
26	10 22 48	7 15 18	16 38	25 20	26 32	9 37	0 33	13 47	22 40	7 24	3 45
27	10 26 45	8 15 36	28 29	26 14	27 47	10 19	0 46	13 48	22 38	7 24	3 44
28	10 30 41	9♓15 53	10♑26	27♓ 0	29♒ 1	11♑ 2	0♒58	13♊50	22♎37	7♐25	3♎43

THE SUN ENTERS THE SIGN OF PISCES ON FEB 18 AT 19:02.

DAY	TIME h m s	☉ ° ' "	☽ ° '	☿ ° '	♀ ° '	♂ ° '	♃ ° '	♄ ° '	♅ ° '	♆ ° '	♇ ° '
M 1	10 34 38	10♓16 8	22♑36	27♓37	0♓16	11♑44	1♒11	13♊51	22♎35	7♐25	3♎41
A 2	10 38 34	11 16 22	5♒ 1	28 5	1 31	12 26	1 23	13 53	22R33	7 25	3R40
R 3	10 42 31	12 16 33	17 45	28 25	2 46	13 8	1 35	13 55	22 32	7 26	3 38
C 4	10 46 27	13 16 44	0♓49	28R34	4 1	13 50	1 48	13 57	22 30	7 26	3 37
H 5	10 50 24	14 16 52	14 13	28 35	5 16	14 33	2 0	13 59	22 28	7 26	3 35
6	10 54 20	15 16 58	27 54	28 26	6 31	15 15	2 12	14 1	22 26	7 26	3 34
7	10 58 17	16 17 3	11♈51	28 8	7 46	15 57	2 24	14 4	22 24	7 26	3 32
8	11 2 14	17 17 5	25 57	27 42	9 0	16 39	2 36	14 6	22 22	7 26	3 30
9	11 6 10	18 17 6	10♉ 9	27 8	10 15	17 22	2 48	14 9	22 21	7R26	3 29
10	11 10 7	19 17 4	24 22	26 28	11 30	18 4	3 0	14 11	22 19	7 26	3 27
11	11 14 3	20 17 1	8♊33	25 41	12 45	18 46	3 11	14 14	22 17	7 26	3 26
12	11 18 0	21 16 55	22 41	24 50	14 0	19 29	3 23	14 17	22 14	7 26	3 24
13	11 21 56	22 16 46	6♋43	23 55	15 15	20 11	3 34	14 20	22 12	7 26	3 22
14	11 25 53	23 16 36	20 41	22 58	16 29	20 53	3 46	14 23	22 10	7 26	3 21
15	11 29 49	24 16 23	4♌32	22 1	17 44	21 36	3 57	14 26	22 8	7 26	3 19
16	11 33 46	25 16 8	18 16	21 3	18 59	22 18	4 9	14 29	22 6	7 26	3 18
17	11 37 43	26 15 51	1♍51	20 8	20 13	23 0	4 20	14 33	22 4	7 25	3 16
18	11 41 39	27 15 31	15 16	19 15	21 28	23 43	4 31	14 36	22 1	7 25	3 14
19	11 45 36	28 15 10	28 28	18 25	22 43	24 25	4 42	14 40	21 59	7 25	3 13
20	11 49 32	29 14 46	11♎26	17 40	23 57	25 8	4 53	14 43	21 57	7 24	3 11
21	11 53 29	0♈14 21	24 8	17 0	25 12	25 50	5 4	14 47	21 55	7 24	3 9
22	11 57 25	1 13 53	6♏34	16 26	26 27	26 33	5 14	14 51	21 52	7 24	3 8
23	12 1 22	2 13 24	18 46	15 57	27 41	27 15	5 25	14 55	21 50	7 23	3 6
24	12 5 18	3 12 53	0♐46	15 34	28 56	27 58	5 36	14 59	21 47	7 23	3 4
25	12 9 15	4 12 20	12 38	15 17	0♈11	28 40	5 46	15 3	21 45	7 22	3 3
26	12 13 11	5 11 46	24 27	15 6	1 25	29 23	5 56	15 7	21 43	7 22	3 1
27	12 17 8	6 11 10	6♑17	15D 1	2 40	0♒ 5	6 6	15 11	21 40	7 21	2 59
28	12 21 5	7 10 32	18 14	15 2	3 54	0 48	6 17	15 16	21 38	7 21	2 58
29	12 25 1	8 9 52	0♒24	15 8	5 9	1 30	6 27	15 20	21 35	7 20	2 56
30	12 28 58	9 9 10	12 51	15 20	6 23	2 13	6 37	15 25	21 33	7 19	2 55
31	12 32 54	10♈ 8 26	25♒41	15♓37	7♈38	2♒56	6♒46	15♊29	21♎30	7♐19	2♎53

THE SUN ENTERS THE SIGN OF ARIES ON MAR 20 AT 18:13.

♈ ARIES ♉ TAURUS ♊ GEMINI ♋ CANCER ♌ LEO ♍ VIRGO ♎ LIBRA

SIDEREAL. SUN. MOON. MERCURY. VENUS. MARS. JUPITER. SATURN. URANUS. NEPTUNE. PLUTO.

DAY	TIME	☉	☽	☿	♀	♂	♃	♄	♅	♆	♇
	h m s	° ' "	° '	° '	° '	° '	° '	° '	° '	° '	° '
A 1	12 36 51	11♈ 7 41	8♓54	15♓59	8♈52	3♒38	6♒56	15♊34	21♎28	7♐18	2♎51
P 2	12 40 47	12 6 53	22 33	16 26	10 7	4 21	7 5	15 39	21R25	7R17	2R50
R 3	12 44 44	13 6 4	6♈35	16 57	11 21	5 3	7 15	15 44	21 23	7 17	2 48
I 4	12 48 40	14 5 13	20 56	17 32	12 36	5 46	7 24	15 49	21 20	7 16	2 46
L 5	12 52 37	15 4 19	5♉29	18 12	13 50	6 29	7 33	15 54	21 18	7 15	2 45
6	12 56 34	16 3 24	20 8	18 55	15 5	7 11	7 42	15 59	21 15	7 14	2 43
7	13 0 30	17 2 26	4♊44	19 41	16 19	7 54	7 51	16 4	21 12	7 13	2 42
8	13 4 27	18 1 27	19 13	20 31	17 34	8 36	8 0	16 9	21 10	7 12	2 40
9	13 8 23	19 0 24	3♋30	21 24	18 48	9 19	8 9	16 15	21 7	7 11	2 38
10	13 12 20	19 59 20	17 34	22 21	20 2	10 2	8 17	16 20	21 5	7 11	2 37
11	13 16 16	20 58 13	1♌25	23 20	21 17	10 44	8 26	16 26	21 2	7 10	2 35
12	13 20 13	21 57 4	15 2	24 22	22 31	11 27	8 34	16 31	21 0	7 9	2 34
13	13 24 9	22 55 52	28 27	25 26	23 45	12 10	8 42	16 37	20 57	7 8	2 32
14	13 28 6	23 54 39	11♍41	26 33	25 0	12 52	8 50	16 42	20 54	7 6	2 31
15	13 32 3	24 53 22	24 43	27 43	26 14	13 35	8 58	16 48	20 52	7 5	2 29
16	13 35 59	25 52 4	7♎33	28 54	27 28	14 17	9 6	16 54	20 49	7 4	2 28
17	13 39 56	26 50 44	20 12	0♈ 8	28 42	15 0	9 14	17 0	20 47	7 3	2 26
18	13 43 52	27 49 22	2♏39	1 25	29 57	15 43	9 21	17 6	20 44	7 2	2 25
19	13 47 49	28 47 58	14 54	2 43	1♉11	16 25	9 28	17 12	20 42	7 1	2 23
20	13 51 45	29 46 32	26 59	4 3	2 25	17 8	9 36	17 18	20 39	7 0	2 22
21	13 55 42	0♉45 5	8♐55	5 26	3 39	17 50	9 43	17 24	20 37	6 58	2 20
22	13 59 38	1 43 35	20 45	6 50	4 53	18 33	9 50	17 30	20 34	6 57	2 19
23	14 3 35	2 42 4	2♑32	8 17	6 7	19 16	9 56	17 37	20 31	6 56	2 18
24	14 7 32	3 40 32	14 22	9 45	7 22	19 58	10 3	17 43	20 29	6 55	2 16
25	14 11 28	4 38 57	26 18	11 15	8 36	20 41	10 9	17 49	20 27	6 53	2 15
26	14 15 25	5 37 21	8♒27	12 47	9 50	21 23	10 16	17 56	20 24	6 52	2 14
27	14 19 21	6 35 44	20 53	14 21	11 4	22 6	10 22	18 2	20 22	6 51	2 12
28	14 23 18	7 34 5	3♓41	15 56	12 18	22 48	10 28	18 9	20 19	6 49	2 11
29	14 27 14	8 32 24	16 56	17 34	13 32	23 31	10 34	18 15	20 17	6 48	2 10
30	14 31 11	9♉30 41	0♈38	19♈13	14♉46	24♒13	10♒39	18♊22	20♎14	6♐47	2♎ 8

THE SUN ENTERS THE SIGN OF TAURUS ON APR 20 AT 05:31.

DAY	TIME	☉	☽	☿	♀	♂	♃	♄	♅	♆	♇
	h m s	° ' "	° '	° '	° '	° '	° '	° '	° '	° '	° '
M 1	14 35 7	10♉28 58	14♈48	20♈54	16♉ 0	24♒56	10♒45	18♊29	20♎12	6♐45	2♎ 7
A 2	14 39 4	11 27 12	29 22	22 37	17 14	25 38	10 50	18 35	20R10	6R44	2R 6
Y 3	14 43 1	12 25 25	14♉13	24 21	18 28	26 21	10 55	18 42	20 7	6 42	2 5
4	14 46 57	13 23 36	29 12	26 8	19 42	27 3	11 0	18 49	20 5	6 41	2 4
5	14 50 54	14 21 46	14♊11	27 56	20 56	27 46	11 5	18 56	20 3	6 40	2 3
6	14 54 50	15 19 54	29 1	29 46	22 10	28 28	11 10	19 3	20 0	6 38	2 2
7	14 58 47	16 17 59	13♋37	1♉38	23 24	29 10	11 14	19 10	19 58	6 37	2 0
8	15 2 43	17 16 3	27 53	3 32	24 38	29 53	11 18	19 17	19 56	6 35	1 59
9	15 6 40	18 14 5	11♌49	5 28	25 52	0♓35	11 23	19 24	19 54	6 34	1 58
10	15 10 36	19 12 5	25 25	7 25	27 6	1 17	11 27	19 31	19 52	6 32	1 57
11	15 14 33	20 10 3	8♍42	9 25	28 19	1 59	11 30	19 38	19 50	6 31	1 56
12	15 18 30	21 7 59	21 43	11 26	29 33	2 42	11 34	19 45	19 47	6 29	1 55
13	15 22 26	22 5 53	4♎29	13 28	0♊47	3 24	11 37	19 53	19 45	6 27	1 54
14	15 26 23	23 3 45	17 2	15 33	2 1	4 6	11 41	20 0	19 43	6 26	1 54
15	15 30 19	24 1 36	29 24	17 38	3 15	4 48	11 44	20 7	19 41	6 24	1 53
16	15 34 16	24 59 26	11♏36	19 45	4 28	5 30	11 47	20 14	19 39	6 23	1 52
17	15 38 12	25 57 14	23 40	21 54	5 42	6 12	11 49	20 22	19 38	6 21	1 51
18	15 42 9	26 55 0	5♐36	24 3	6 56	6 54	11 52	20 29	19 36	6 20	1 50
19	15 46 5	27 52 45	17 28	26 14	8 10	7 36	11 54	20 37	19 34	6 18	1 49
20	15 50 2	28 50 29	29 15	28 25	9 23	8 18	11 56	20 44	19 32	6 16	1 49
21	15 53 59	29 48 12	11♑ 3	0♊36	10 37	9 0	11 58	20 51	19 30	6 15	1 48
22	15 57 55	0♊45 53	22 54	2 48	11 51	9 42	12 0	20 59	19 28	6 13	1 47
23	16 1 52	1 43 34	4♒51	4 59	13 4	10 24	12 2	21 6	19 27	6 11	1 47
24	16 5 48	2 41 13	17 0	7 10	14 18	11 5	12 3	21 14	19 25	6 10	1 46
25	16 9 45	3 38 51	29 25	9 21	15 32	11 47	12 4	21 22	19 23	6 8	1 46
26	16 13 41	4 36 28	12♓11	11 30	16 45	12 29	12 5	21 29	19 22	6 7	1 45
27	16 17 38	5 34 4	25 22	13 39	17 59	13 10	12 6	21 37	19 20	6 5	1 44
28	16 21 34	6 31 40	9♈ 0	15 46	19 12	13 52	12 7	21 44	19 19	6 3	1 44
29	16 25 31	7 29 14	23 6	17 51	20 26	14 33	12 7	21 52	19 17	6 2	1 44
30	16 29 28	8 26 48	7♉38	19 54	21 40	15 15	12R 8	22 0	19 16	6 0	1 43
31	16 33 24	9♊24 21	22♉32	21♊56	22♊53	15♓56	12♒ 8	22♊ 7	19♎15	5♐59	1♎43

THE SUN ENTERS THE SIGN OF GEMINI ON MAY 21 AT 04:54.

DAY	TIME	☉	☽	☿	♀	♂	♃	♄	♅	♆	♇
	h m s	° ' "	° '	° '	° '	° '	° '	° '	° '	° '	° '
J 1	16 37 21	10♊21 53	7♊39	23♊55	24♊ 7	16♓37	12♒ 8	22♊15	19♎13	5♐57	1♎42
U 2	16 41 17	11 19 24	22 50	25 52	25 20	17 18	12R 7	22 23	19R12	5R55	1R42
N 3	16 45 14	12 16 54	7♋56	27 46	26 34	18 0	12 7	22 31	19 11	5 54	1 42
E 4	16 49 10	13 14 22	22 48	29 38	27 47	18 41	12 6	22 38	19 10	5 52	1 41
5	16 53 7	14 11 50	7♌19	1♋28	29 1	19 22	12 5	22 46	19 9	5 50	1 41
6	16 57 3	15 9 16	21 27	3 15	0♋14	20 3	12 4	22 54	19 7	5 49	1 41
7	17 1 0	16 6 41	5♍10	4 59	1 28	20 43	12 3	23 2	19 6	5 47	1 41
8	17 4 57	17 4 5	18 30	6 41	2 41	21 24	12 2	23 9	19 5	5 46	1 41
9	17 8 53	18 1 28	1♎27	8 20	3 55	22 5	12 0	23 17	19 4	5 44	1 41
10	17 12 50	18 58 49	14 6	9 56	5 8	22 45	11 58	23 25	19 4	5 43	1 40
11	17 16 46	19 56 10	26 30	11 30	6 21	23 26	11 56	23 33	19 3	5 41	1D40
12	17 20 43	20 53 30	8♏40	13 1	7 35	24 6	11 54	23 41	19 2	5 39	1 40
13	17 24 39	21 50 48	20 42	14 29	8 48	24 46	11 51	23 48	19 1	5 38	1 40
14	17 28 36	22 48 6	2♐37	15 54	10 1	25 27	11 49	23 56	19 1	5 36	1 40
15	17 32 32	23 45 24	14 27	17 17	11 15	26 7	11 46	24 4	19 0	5 35	1 41
16	17 36 29	24 42 41	26 15	18 37	12 28	26 47	11 43	24 12	18 59	5 33	1 41
17	17 40 26	25 39 57	8♑ 3	19 54	13 41	27 27	11 40	24 20	18 59	5 32	1 41
18	17 44 22	26 37 12	19 54	21 7	14 55	28 6	11 37	24 27	18 58	5 30	1 41
19	17 48 19	27 34 27	1♒50	22 18	16 8	28 46	11 33	24 35	18 58	5 29	1 41
20	17 52 15	28 31 42	13 54	23 26	17 21	29 26	11 30	24 43	18 57	5 27	1 42
21	17 56 12	29 28 57	26 8	24 31	18 34	0♈ 5	11 26	24 51	18 57	5 26	1 42
22	18 0 8	0♋26 11	8♓37	25 32	19 48	0 44	11 22	24 59	18 57	5 24	1 42
23	18 4 5	1 23 25	21 23	26 30	21 1	1 24	11 18	25 6	18 57	5 23	1 42
24	18 8 2	2 20 39	4♈31	27 25	22 14	2 3	11 14	25 14	18 56	5 22	1 43
25	18 11 58	3 17 53	18 3	28 17	23 27	2 42	11 9	25 22	18 56	5 20	1 43
26	18 15 55	4 15 7	1♉59	29 4	24 40	3 21	11 4	25 30	18D56	5 19	1 44
27	18 19 51	5 12 21	16 20	29 48	25 53	3 59	11 0	25 38	18 56	5 17	1 44
28	18 23 48	6 9 35	1♊ 3	0♌29	27 7	4 38	10 55	25 45	18 56	5 16	1 45
29	18 27 44	7 6 49	16 2	1 5	28 20	5 16	10 49	25 53	18 56	5 15	1 45
30	18 31 41	8♋ 4 3	1♋10	1♌37	29♋33	5♈54	10♒44	26♊ 1	18♎56	5♐13	1♎46

THE SUN ENTERS THE SIGN OF CANCER ON JUN 21 AT 13:01.

♏ SCORPIO ♐ SAGITTARIUS ♑ CAPRICORN ♒ AQUARIUS ♓ PISCES

1973

SIDEREAL . . . SUN . . . MOON . . . MERCURY . . . VENUS . . . MARS . . . JUPITER . . . SATURN . . . URANUS . . . NEPTUNE . . . PLUTO .

DAY	TIME	☉	☽	☿	♀	♂	♃	♄	♅	♆	♇
	h m s	° ' "	° '	° '	° '	° '	° '	° '	° '	° '	° '
J 1	18 35 37	9♋ 1 17	16♋18	2♌ 5	0♌46	6♈32	10♒39	26♊ 8	18♎57	5♐12	1♎46
U 2	18 39 34	9 58 30	1♌17	2 29	1 59	7 10	10R33	26 16	18 57	5R11	1 47
L 3	18 43 31	10 55 44	15 58	2 49	3 12	7 48	10 28	26 24	18 57	5 10	1 48
Y 4	18 47 27	11 52 57	0♍17	3 4	4 25	8 26	10 22	26 31	18 58	5 8	1 48
5	18 51 24	12 50 10	14 9	3 14	5 38	9 3	10 16	26 39	18 58	5 7	1 49
6	18 55 20	13 47 23	27 35	3R20	6 51	9 40	10 10	26 47	18 58	5 6	1 50
7	18 59 17	14 44 35	10♎36	3 21	8 4	10 17	10 3	26 54	18 59	5 5	1 51
8	19 3 13	15 41 47	23 14	3 17	9 17	10 54	9 57	27 2	18 59	5 4	1 52
9	19 7 10	16 38 59	5♏34	3 8	10 30	11 31	9 51	27 9	19 0	5 3	1 52
10	19 11 6	17 36 11	17 40	2 55	11 43	12 7	9 44	27 17	19 1	5 2	1 53
11	19 15 3	18 33 23	29 36	2 38	12 56	12 44	9 37	27 24	19 1	5 0	1 54
12	19 19 0	19 30 35	11♐26	2 16	14 8	13 20	9 31	27 32	19 2	4 59	1 55
13	19 22 56	20 27 47	23 14	1 50	15 21	13 55	9 24	27 39	19 3	4 58	1 56
14	19 26 53	21 25 0	5♑ 2	1 21	16 34	14 31	9 17	27 47	19 4	4 57	1 57
15	19 30 49	22 22 12	16 54	0 48	17 47	15 7	9 10	27 54	19 5	4 56	1 58
16	19 34 46	23 19 25	28 52	0 13	19 0	15 42	9 3	28 1	19 6	4 55	1 59
17	19 38 42	24 16 38	10♒58	29♋35	20 12	16 17	8 55	28 9	19 7	4 55	2 0
18	19 42 39	25 13 51	23 13	28 55	21 25	16 52	8 48	28 16	19 8	4 54	2 2
19	19 46 35	26 11 6	5♓40	28 14	22 38	17 26	8 41	28 23	19 9	4 53	2 3
20	19 50 32	27 8 20	18 19	27 33	23 50	18 0	8 33	28 30	19 10	4 52	2 4
21	19 54 29	28 5 36	1♈14	26 53	25 3	18 34	8 26	28 38	19 11	4 51	2 5
22	19 58 25	29 2 52	14 25	26 13	26 16	19 8	8 18	28 45	19 13	4 50	2 6
23	20 2 22	0♌ 0 9	27 54	25 35	27 28	19 42	8 11	28 52	19 14	4 50	2 8
24	20 6 18	0 57 27	11♉42	25 0	28 41	20 15	8 3	28 59	19 15	4 49	2 9
25	20 10 15	1 54 46	25 50	24 28	29 53	20 48	7 55	29 6	19 17	4 48	2 10
26	20 14 11	2 52 6	10♊16	24 0	1♍ 6	21 21	7 48	29 13	19 18	4 47	2 12
27	20 18 8	3 49 27	24 57	23 36	2 18	21 53	7 40	29 20	19 20	4 47	2 13
28	20 22 4	4 46 49	9♋49	23 16	3 31	22 25	7 32	29 27	19 21	4 46	2 14
29	20 26 1	5 44 11	24 44	23 2	4 43	22 57	7 24	29 34	19 23	4 46	2 16
30	20 29 58	6 41 35	9♌35	22D54	5 56	23 28	7 16	29 40	19 25	4 45	2 17
31	20 33 54	7♌38 59	24♌14	22♋52	7♍ 8	23♈59	7♒ 9	29♊47	19♎26	4♐44	2♎19

THE SUN ENTERS THE SIGN OF LEO ON JUL 22 AT 23:56.

DAY	TIME	☉	☽	☿	♀	♂	♃	♄	♅	♆	♇
	h m s	° ' "	° '	° '	° '	° '	° '	° '	° '	° '	° '
A 1	20 37 51	8♌36 24	8♍34	22♋55	8♍20	24♈30	7♒ 1	29♊54	19♎28	4♐44	2♎20
U 2	20 41 47	9 33 49	22 31	23 5	9 33	25 0	6R53	0♋ 0	19 30	4R43	2 22
G 3	20 45 44	10 31 16	6♎ 1	23 22	10 45	25 30	6 45	0 7	19 32	4 43	2 23
U 4	20 49 40	11 28 42	19 6	23 44	11 57	26 0	6 38	0 14	19 34	4 43	2 25
S 5	20 53 37	12 26 10	1♏46	24 14	13 9	26 29	6 30	0 20	19 36	4 42	2 27
T 6	20 57 33	13 23 38	14 7	24 49	14 22	26 58	6 22	0 27	19 38	4 42	2 28
7	21 1 30	14 21 8	26 12	25 32	15 34	27 27	6 14	0 33	19 40	4 42	2 30
8	21 5 27	15 18 38	8♐ 7	26 20	16 46	27 55	6 7	0 39	19 42	4 41	2 32
9	21 9 23	16 16 8	19 55	27 15	17 58	28 23	5 59	0 46	19 44	4 41	2 33
10	21 13 20	17 13 40	1♑43	28 16	19 10	28 50	5 52	0 52	19 46	4 41	2 35
11	21 17 16	18 11 13	13 34	29 23	20 22	29 17	5 44	0 58	19 48	4 41	2 37
12	21 21 13	19 8 46	25 32	0♌36	21 34	29 44	5 37	1 4	19 51	4 40	2 38
13	21 25 9	20 6 21	7♒39	1 54	22 46	0♉10	5 30	1 10	19 53	4 40	2 40
14	21 29 6	21 3 57	19 58	3 18	23 58	0 35	5 22	1 16	19 55	4 40	2 42
15	21 33 2	22 1 33	2♓30	4 47	25 10	1 1	5 15	1 22	19 58	4 40	2 44
16	21 36 59	22 59 12	15 15	6 20	26 21	1 25	5 8	1 28	20 0	4D40	2 46
17	21 40 56	23 56 51	28 13	7 58	27 33	1 50	5 1	1 34	20 3	4 40	2 48
18	21 44 52	24 54 32	11♈24	9 39	28 45	2 13	4 54	1 39	20 5	4 40	2 50
19	21 48 49	25 52 14	24 47	11 25	29 56	2 37	4 47	1 45	20 8	4 40	2 51
20	21 52 45	26 49 59	8♉23	13 13	1♎ 8	2 59	4 41	1 51	20 10	4 40	2 53
21	21 56 42	27 47 45	22 11	15 4	2 20	3 22	4 34	1 56	20 13	4 40	2 55
22	22 0 38	28 45 32	6♊11	16 57	3 31	3 43	4 28	2 2	20 16	4 41	2 57
23	22 4 35	29 43 22	20 22	18 53	4 43	4 4	4 21	2 7	20 18	4 41	2 59
24	22 8 31	0♍41 13	4♋43	20 49	5 54	4 25	4 15	2 12	20 21	4 41	3 1
25	22 12 28	1 39 6	19 12	22 47	7 6	4 45	4 9	2 18	20 24	4 41	3 3
26	22 16 25	2 37 0	3♌45	24 46	8 17	5 4	4 3	2 23	20 27	4 41	3 5
27	22 20 21	3 34 57	18 16	26 45	9 28	5 23	3 57	2 28	20 29	4 42	3 7
28	22 24 18	4 32 54	2♍39	28 44	10 40	5 41	3 51	2 33	20 32	4 42	3 9
29	22 28 14	5 30 54	16 48	0♍43	11 51	5 58	3 46	2 38	20 35	4 43	3 11
30	22 32 11	6 28 54	0♎38	2 41	13 2	6 15	3 40	2 43	20 38	4 43	3 14
31	22 36 7	7♍26 57	14♎ 6	4♍40	14♎13	6♉31	3♒35	2♋47	20♎41	4♐43	3♎16

THE SUN ENTERS THE SIGN OF VIRGO ON AUG 23 AT 06:55.

DAY	TIME	☉	☽	☿	♀	♂	♃	♄	♅	♆	♇
	h m s	° ' "	° '	° '	° '	° '	° '	° '	° '	° '	° '
S 1	22 40 4	8♍25 0	27♎10	6♍37	15♎24	6♉47	3♒30	2♋52	20♎44	4♐44	3♎18
E 2	22 44 0	9 23 6	9♏51	8 34	16 36	7 1	3R25	2 57	20 47	4 44	3 20
P 3	22 47 57	10 21 12	22 13	10 30	17 47	7 15	3 20	3 1	20 50	4 45	3 22
T 4	22 51 54	11 19 20	4♐18	12 25	18 57	7 29	3 15	3 6	20 53	4 46	3 24
E 5	22 55 50	12 17 30	16 12	14 19	20 8	7 41	3 11	3 10	20 56	4 46	3 26
M 6	22 59 47	13 15 41	28 1	16 11	21 19	7 53	3 6	3 14	21 0	4 47	3 28
B 7	23 3 43	14 13 54	9♑50	18 3	22 30	8 4	3 2	3 19	21 3	4 47	3 31
E 8	23 7 40	15 12 8	21 44	19 54	23 41	8 15	2 58	3 23	21 6	4 48	3 33
R 9	23 11 36	16 10 23	3♒47	21 43	24 51	8 24	2 54	3 27	21 9	4 49	3 35
10	23 15 33	17 8 40	16 3	23 31	26 2	8 33	2 51	3 31	21 13	4 50	3 37
11	23 19 29	18 6 59	28 35	25 19	27 12	8 41	2 47	3 34	21 16	4 50	3 40
12	23 23 26	19 5 20	11♓24	27 5	28 23	8 49	2 44	3 38	21 19	4 51	3 42
13	23 27 23	20 3 42	24 30	28 49	29 33	8 55	2 41	3 42	21 22	4 52	3 44
14	23 31 19	21 2 6	7♈51	0♎33	0♏44	9 1	2 38	3 45	21 26	4 53	3 46
15	23 35 16	22 0 32	21 26	2 16	1 54	9 5	2 35	3 49	21 29	4 54	3 48
16	23 39 12	22 59 0	5♉11	3 58	3 4	9 9	2 33	3 52	21 33	4 55	3 51
17	23 43 9	23 57 30	19 3	5 38	4 14	9 12	2 30	3 55	21 36	4 56	3 53
18	23 47 5	24 56 3	3♊ 2	7 18	5 24	9 15	2 28	3 59	21 40	4 57	3 55
19	23 51 2	25 54 38	17 4	8 56	6 34	9R16	2 26	4 2	21 43	4 58	3 58
20	23 54 58	26 53 15	1♋10	10 34	7 44	9 16	2 25	4 5	21 47	4 59	4 0
21	23 58 55	27 51 54	15 17	12 10	8 54	9 16	2 23	4 8	21 50	5 0	4 2
22	0 2 52	28 50 35	29 26	13 46	10 4	9 14	2 22	4 10	21 54	5 1	4 4
23	0 6 48	29 49 19	13♌35	15 20	11 14	9 12	2 20	4 13	21 57	5 2	4 7
24	0 10 45	0♎48 5	27 40	16 54	12 23	9 9	2 19	4 16	22 1	5 4	4 9
25	0 14 41	1 46 53	11♍39	18 26	13 33	9 5	2 19	4 18	22 4	5 5	4 11
26	0 18 38	2 45 43	25 27	19 58	14 42	9 0	2 18	4 20	22 8	5 6	4 14
27	0 22 34	3 44 35	9♎ 0	21 29	15 52	8 54	2 18	4 23	22 12	5 7	4 16
28	0 26 31	4 43 29	22 15	22 59	17 1	8 47	2D17	4 25	22 15	5 9	4 18
29	0 30 27	5 42 24	5♏11	24 27	18 10	8 40	2 17	4 27	22 19	5 10	4 20
30	0 34 24	6♎41 22	17♏47	25♎55	19♏19	8♉31	2♒18	4♋29	22♎23	5♐11	4♎23

THE SUN ENTERS THE SIGN OF LIBRA ON SEP 23 AT 04:23.

♈ ARIES ♉ TAURUS ♊ GEMINI ♋ CANCER ♌ LEO ♍ VIRGO ♎ LIBRA

SIDEREAL SUN. MOON. MERCURY. VENUS. MARS. JUPITER. SATURN. URANUS. NEPTUNE. PLUTO.

DAY	TIME	☉	☽	☿	♀	♂	♃	♄	♅	♆	♇
	h m s	° ' "	° '	° '	° '	° '	° '	° '	° '	° '	° '
O 1	0 38 20	7♎40 22	0♐ 6	27♎22	20♏28	8♉22	2♒18	4♋31	22♎26	5♐13	4♎25
C 2	0 42 17	8 39 24	12 10	28 48	21 37	8R12	2 19	4 32	22 30	5 14	4 27
T 3	0 46 14	9 38 27	24 4	0♏13	22 46	8 1	2 19	4 34	22 34	5 16	4 30
O 4	0 50 10	10 37 32	5♑53	1 37	23 55	7 49	2 20	4 36	22 37	5 17	4 32
B 5	0 54 7	11 36 39	17 41	3 0	25 3	7 36	2 21	4 37	22 41	5 19	4 34
E 6	0 58 3	12 35 48	29 35	4 22	26 12	7 23	2 23	4 38	22 45	5 20	4 36
R 7	1 2 0	13 34 58	11♒41	5 43	27 20	7 9	2 24	4 39	22 49	5 22	4 39
8	1 5 56	14 34 10	24 1	7 3	28 29	6 55	2 26	4 40	22 52	5 23	4 41
9	1 9 53	15 33 24	6♓42	8 21	29 37	6 39	2 28	4 41	22 56	5 25	4 43
10	1 13 49	16 32 40	19 43	9 38	0♐45	6 23	2 30	4 42	23 0	5 26	4 46
11	1 17 46	17 31 58	3♈ 6	10 54	1 53	6 7	2 33	4 43	23 4	5 28	4 48
12	1 21 43	18 31 17	16 49	12 8	3 1	5 50	2 35	4 44	23 7	5 30	4 50
13	1 25 39	19 30 39	0♉49	13 21	4 8	5 32	2 38	4 44	23 11	5 31	4 52
14	1 29 36	20 30 3	15 1	14 32	5 16	5 14	2 41	4 45	23 15	5 33	4 55
15	1 33 32	21 29 29	29 19	15 42	6 23	4 56	2 44	4 45	23 19	5 35	4 57
16	1 37 29	22 28 58	13♊38	16 49	7 31	4 37	2 47	4 45	23 22	5 37	4 59
17	1 41 25	23 28 28	27 56	17 54	8 38	4 18	2 51	4R45	23 26	5 38	5 1
18	1 45 22	24 28 1	12♋ 8	18 57	9 45	3 58	2 54	4 45	23 30	5 40	5 3
19	1 49 18	25 27 37	26 15	19 58	10 51	3 39	2 58	4 45	23 34	5 42	5 6
20	1 53 15	26 27 14	10♌14	20 55	11 58	3 19	3 2	4 45	23 38	5 44	5 8
21	1 57 12	27 26 54	24 5	21 50	13 5	2 58	3 6	4 44	23 41	5 46	5 10
22	2 1 8	28 26 36	7♍48	22 41	14 11	2 38	3 11	4 44	23 45	5 48	5 12
23	2 5 5	29 26 21	21 21	23 28	15 17	2 18	3 15	4 43	23 49	5 49	5 14
24	2 9 1	0♏26 7	4♎43	24 11	16 23	1 58	3 20	4 43	23 53	5 51	5 16
25	2 12 58	1 25 56	17 53	24 50	17 29	1 37	3 25	4 42	23 56	5 53	5 19
26	2 16 54	2 25 46	0♏49	25 23	18 35	1 17	3 30	4 41	24 0	5 55	5 21
27	2 20 51	3 25 39	13 30	25 51	19 40	0 57	3 35	4 40	24 4	5 57	5 23
28	2 24 47	4 25 33	25 55	26 13	20 45	0 38	3 41	4 39	24 8	5 59	5 25
29	2 28 44	5 25 30	8♐ 7	26 28	21 50	0 18	3 46	4 37	24 11	6 1	5 27
30	2 32 41	6 25 28	20 8	26R35	22 55	29♈59	3 52	4 36	24 15	6 3	5 29
31	2 36 37	7♏25 28	1♑59	26♏35	24♐ 0	29♈40	3♒58	4♋35	24♎19	6♐ 5	5♎31

THE SUN ENTERS THE SIGN OF SCORPIO ON OCT 23 AT 13:31.

DAY	TIME	☉	☽	☿	♀	♂	♃	♄	♅	♆	♇
	h m s	° ' "	° '	° '	° '	° '	° '	° '	° '	° '	° '
N 1	2 40 34	8♏25 30	13♑47	26♏26	25♐ 4	29♈22	4♒ 4	4♋33	24♎23	6♐ 7	5♎33
O 2	2 44 30	9 25 33	25 34	26R 7	26 8	29R 4	4 11	4R31	24 26	6 9	5 35
V 3	2 48 27	10 25 38	7♒27	25 40	27 12	28 47	4 17	4 30	24 30	6 11	5 37
E 4	2 52 23	11 25 44	19 31	25 2	28 16	28 30	4 24	4 28	24 34	6 13	5 39
M 5	2 56 20	12 25 52	1♓51	24 15	29 19	28 14	4 30	4 26	24 37	6 16	5 41
B 6	3 0 16	13 26 1	14 31	23 19	0♑22	27 58	4 37	4 24	24 41	6 18	5 43
E 7	3 4 13	14 26 12	27 36	22 15	1 25	27 43	4 44	4 21	24 44	6 20	5 45
R 8	3 8 9	15 26 25	11♈ 6	21 4	2 27	27 28	4 52	4 19	24 48	6 22	5 47
9	3 12 6	16 26 39	25 1	19 48	3 29	27 15	4 59	4 17	24 52	6 24	5 48
10	3 16 3	17 26 55	9♉18	18 28	4 31	27 2	5 7	4 14	24 55	6 26	5 50
11	3 19 59	18 27 12	23 52	17 9	5 32	26 49	5 14	4 11	24 59	6 28	5 52
12	3 23 56	19 27 31	8♊36	15 51	6 33	26 38	5 22	4 9	25 2	6 31	5 54
13	3 27 52	20 27 53	23 23	14 38	7 34	26 27	5 30	4 6	25 6	6 33	5 56
14	3 31 49	21 28 16	8♋ 5	13 32	8 35	26 17	5 38	4 3	25 9	6 35	5 57
15	3 35 45	22 28 40	22 37	12 35	9 35	26 8	5 47	4 0	25 13	6 37	5 59
16	3 39 42	23 29 7	6♌55	11 48	10 34	25 59	5 55	3 57	25 16	6 39	6 1
17	3 43 39	24 29 36	20 58	11 12	11 33	25 51	6 4	3 54	25 20	6 42	6 3
18	3 47 35	25 30 6	4♍44	10 48	12 32	25 44	6 12	3 51	25 23	6 44	6 4
19	3 51 32	26 30 38	18 15	10D35	13 30	25 38	6 21	3 47	25 27	6 46	6 6
20	3 55 28	27 31 12	1♎30	10 34	14 28	25 33	6 30	3 44	25 30	6 48	6 8
21	3 59 25	28 31 48	14 31	10 44	15 25	25 28	6 39	3 40	25 33	6 50	6 9
22	4 3 21	29 32 25	27 18	11 4	16 22	25 25	6 48	3 37	25 37	6 53	6 11
23	4 7 18	0♐33 5	9♏53	11 32	17 19	25 22	6 58	3 33	25 40	6 55	6 12
24	4 11 14	1 33 45	22 16	12 10	18 14	25 20	7 7	3 29	25 43	6 57	6 14
25	4 15 11	2 34 27	4♐28	12 54	19 10	25 19	7 17	3 25	25 46	6 59	6 15
26	4 19 8	3 35 11	16 30	13 45	20 4	25D18	7 27	3 21	25 50	7 2	6 17
27	4 23 4	4 35 56	28 25	14 42	20 58	25 19	7 36	3 18	25 53	7 4	6 18
28	4 27 1	5 36 41	10♑14	15 43	21 52	25 20	7 46	3 13	25 56	7 6	6 20
29	4 30 57	6 37 29	22 0	16 50	22 45	25 22	7 57	3 9	25 59	7 8	6 21
30	4 34 54	7♐38 17	3♒47	17♏59	23♑37	25♈25	8♒ 7	3♋ 5	26♎ 2	7♐11	6♎22

THE SUN ENTERS THE SIGN OF SAGITTARIUS ON NOV 22 AT 10:55.

DAY	TIME	☉	☽	☿	♀	♂	♃	♄	♅	♆	♇
	h m s	° ' "	° '	° '	° '	° '	° '	° '	° '	° '	° '
D 1	4 38 50	8♐39 6	15♒40	19♏12	24♑28	25♈28	8♒17	3♋ 1	26♎ 5	7♐13	6♎24
E 2	4 42 47	9 39 56	27 42	20 28	25 19	25 32	8 27	2R57	26 8	7 15	6 25
C 3	4 46 43	10 40 46	9♓58	21 46	26 8	25 38	8 38	2 52	26 11	7 18	6 26
E 4	4 50 40	11 41 38	22 34	23 6	26 57	25 43	8 49	2 48	26 14	7 20	6 27
M 5	4 54 37	12 42 31	5♈33	24 28	27 46	25 50	8 59	2 43	26 17	7 22	6 29
B 6	4 58 33	13 43 24	18 58	25 52	28 33	25 57	9 10	2 39	26 20	7 24	6 30
E 7	5 2 30	14 44 18	2♉50	27 17	29 19	26 5	9 21	2 34	26 23	7 27	6 31
R 8	5 6 26	15 45 13	17 10	28 42	0♒ 4	26 14	9 32	2 30	26 25	7 29	6 32
9	5 10 23	16 46 9	1♊52	0♐ 9	0 49	26 23	9 44	2 25	26 28	7 31	6 33
10	5 14 19	17 47 5	16 51	1 37	1 32	26 33	9 55	2 20	26 31	7 33	6 34
11	5 18 16	18 48 3	1♋58	3 5	2 14	26 44	10 6	2 16	26 34	7 35	6 35
12	5 22 12	19 49 2	17 4	4 34	2 55	26 55	10 18	2 11	26 36	7 38	6 36
13	5 26 9	20 50 1	2♌ 1	6 3	3 35	27 7	10 29	2 6	26 39	7 40	6 37
14	5 30 6	21 51 1	16 40	7 33	4 14	27 19	10 41	2 1	26 41	7 42	6 38
15	5 34 2	22 52 3	0♍58	9 3	4 51	27 32	10 53	1 56	26 44	7 44	6 39
16	5 37 59	23 53 5	14 53	10 33	5 27	27 46	11 4	1 52	26 46	7 47	6 40
17	5 41 55	24 54 8	28 24	12 4	6 2	28 0	11 16	1 47	26 49	7 49	6 40
18	5 45 52	25 55 13	11♎32	13 35	6 35	28 15	11 28	1 42	26 51	7 51	6 41
19	5 49 48	26 56 18	24 21	15 7	7 7	28 30	11 41	1 37	26 54	7 53	6 42
20	5 53 45	27 57 24	6♏54	16 39	7 37	28 46	11 53	1 32	26 56	7 55	6 43
21	5 57 41	28 58 31	19 12	18 10	8 6	29 2	12 5	1 27	26 58	7 57	6 43
22	6 1 38	29 59 38	1♐20	19 43	8 33	29 19	12 17	1 22	27 0	8 0	6 44
23	6 5 35	1♑ 0 47	13 20	21 15	8 58	29 36	12 30	1 17	27 3	8 2	6 45
24	6 9 31	2 1 55	25 13	22 48	9 21	29 54	12 42	1 12	27 5	8 4	6 45
25	6 13 28	3 3 4	7♑ 2	24 20	9 43	0♉12	12 55	1 7	27 7	8 6	6 46
26	6 17 24	4 4 14	18 50	25 54	10 3	0 31	13 7	1 2	27 9	8 8	6 46
27	6 21 21	5 5 24	0♒38	27 27	10 20	0 50	13 20	0 57	27 11	8 10	6 47
28	6 25 17	6 6 33	12 28	29 0	10 36	1 10	13 33	0 52	27 13	8 12	6 47
29	6 29 14	7 7 43	24 24	0♑34	10 49	1 30	13 46	0 47	27 15	8 14	6 48
30	6 33 11	8 8 53	6♓28	2 8	11 1	1 50	13 59	0 42	27 16	8 16	6 48
31	6 37 7	9♑10 3	18♓45	3♑43	11♒10	2♉11	14♒12	0♋37	27♎18	8♐18	6♎48

THE SUN ENTERS THE SIGN OF CAPRICORN ON DEC 22 AT 00:09.

♏ SCORPIO ♐ SAGITTARIUS ♑ CAPRICORN ♒ AQUARIUS ♓ PISCES

1974

SIDEREAL SUN. MOON. MERCURY. VENUS. MARS. JUPITER. SATURN. URANUS. NEPTUNE. PLUTO.

DAY	TIME	☉	☽	☿	♀	♂	♃	♄	♅	♆	♇
	h m s	° ' "	° '	° '	° '	° '	° '	° '	° '	° '	° '
J 1	6 41 4	10♑11 12	1♈17	5♑17	11♒16	2♉33	14♒25	0♋33	27♎20	8♐20	6♎49
A 2	6 45 0	11 12 22	14 9	6 52	11 20	2 54	14 38	0R28	27 22	8 22	6 49
N 3	6 48 57	12 13 31	27 23	8 28	11R22	3 16	14 51	0 23	27 23	8 24	6 49
U 4	6 52 53	13 14 40	11♉ 4	10 3	11 22	3 39	15 4	0 18	27 25	8 26	6 49
A 5	6 56 50	14 15 49	25 11	11 39	11 19	4 2	15 17	0 13	27 26	8 28	6 49
R 6	7 0 46	15 16 57	9♊45	13 16	11 13	4 25	15 31	0 9	27 28	8 30	6 50
Y 7	7 4 43	16 18 5	24 40	14 53	11 5	4 48	15 44	0 4	27 29	8 32	6 50
8	7 8 40	17 19 13	9♋50	16 30	10 54	5 12	15 58	29♊59	27 31	8 34	6 50
9	7 12 36	18 20 21	25 6	18 8	10 41	5 36	16 11	29 55	27 32	8 36	6R50
10	7 16 33	19 21 28	10♌18	19 46	10 25	6 1	16 25	29 50	27 33	8 37	6 50
11	7 20 29	20 22 36	25 16	21 24	10 7	6 26	16 38	29 46	27 34	8 39	6 50
12	7 24 26	21 23 43	9♍52	23 3	9 47	6 51	16 52	29 41	27 35	8 41	6 50
13	7 28 22	22 24 50	24 2	24 42	9 24	7 16	17 6	29 37	27 37	8 43	6 49
14	7 32 19	23 25 57	7♎43	26 22	8 59	7 42	17 19	29 33	27 38	8 44	6 49
15	7 36 15	24 27 3	20 56	28 3	8 32	8 8	17 33	29 28	27 39	8 46	6 49
16	7 40 12	25 28 10	3♏45	29 43	8 3	8 34	17 47	29 24	27 40	8 48	6 49
17	7 44 9	26 29 17	16 12	1♒25	7 32	9 0	18 1	29 20	27 40	8 50	6 49
18	7 48 5	27 30 23	28 23	3 6	7 0	9 27	18 15	29 16	27 41	8 51	6 48
19	7 52 2	28 31 29	10♐22	4 48	6 26	9 54	18 29	29 12	27 42	8 53	6 48
20	7 55 58	29 32 35	22 14	6 31	5 52	10 21	18 43	29 8	27 43	8 54	6 48
21	7 59 55	0♒33 40	4♑ 2	8 13	5 16	10 48	18 57	29 4	27 43	8 56	6 47
22	8 3 51	1 34 44	15 48	9 56	4 40	11 16	19 11	29 0	27 44	8 58	6 47
23	8 7 48	2 35 48	27 37	11 40	4 3	11 44	19 25	28 57	27 45	8 59	6 46
24	8 11 44	3 36 52	9♒29	13 23	3 26	12 12	19 39	28 53	27 45	9 1	6 46
25	8 15 41	4 37 54	21 27	15 6	2 49	12 40	19 53	28 49	27 45	9 2	6 45
26	8 19 38	5 38 55	3♓32	16 50	2 13	13 9	20 7	28 46	27 46	9 4	6 45
27	8 23 34	6 39 56	15 45	18 33	1 37	13 38	20 21	28 42	27 46	9 5	6 44
28	8 27 31	7 40 55	28 9	20 15	1 1	14 7	20 35	28 39	27 46	9 6	6 44
29	8 31 27	8 41 54	10♈46	21 57	0 27	14 36	20 50	28 36	27 47	9 8	6 43
30	8 35 24	9 42 51	23 38	23 38	29♑54	15 5	21 4	28 33	27 47	9 9	6 42
31	8 39 20	10♒43 47	6♉47	25♒17	29♑23	15♉35	21♒18	28♊30	27♎47	9♐10	6♎41

THE SUN ENTERS THE SIGN OF AQUARIUS ON JAN 20 AT 10:46.

DAY	TIME	☉	☽	☿	♀	♂	♃	♄	♅	♆	♇
	h m s	° ' "	° '	° '	° '	° '	° '	° '	° '	° '	° '
F 1	8 43 17	11♒44 41	20♉17	26♒55	28♑53	16♉ 4	21♒32	28♊27	27♎47	9♐12	6♎41
E 2	8 47 13	12 45 35	4♊ 9	28 31	28R25	16 34	21 47	28R24	27R47	9 13	6R40
B 3	8 51 10	13 46 27	18 24	0♓ 5	27 59	17 4	22 1	28 21	27 47	9 14	6 39
R 4	8 55 7	14 47 17	3♋ 0	1 36	27 36	17 34	22 15	28 19	27 47	9 15	6 38
U 5	8 59 3	15 48 7	17 55	3 3	27 14	18 5	22 30	28 16	27 46	9 17	6 37
A 6	9 3 0	16 48 55	3♌ 2	4 26	26 55	18 35	22 44	28 14	27 46	9 18	6 37
R 7	9 6 56	17 49 41	18 10	5 44	26 38	19 6	22 58	28 11	27 46	9 19	6 36
Y 8	9 10 53	18 50 27	3♍11	6 56	26 23	19 37	23 13	28 9	27 46	9 20	6 35
9	9 14 49	19 51 11	17 55	8 2	26 11	20 8	23 27	28 7	27 45	9 21	6 34
10	9 18 46	20 51 54	2♎15	9 1	26 2	20 39	23 41	28 5	27 45	9 22	6 33
11	9 22 42	21 52 35	16 6	9 53	25 55	21 10	23 56	28 3	27 44	9 23	6 32
12	9 26 39	22 53 16	29 28	10 35	25 50	21 41	24 10	28 1	27 44	9 24	6 31
13	9 30 36	23 53 56	12♏22	11 9	25D48	22 13	24 25	28 0	27 43	9 25	6 29
14	9 34 32	24 54 35	24 52	11 33	25 49	22 45	24 39	27 58	27 42	9 26	6 28
15	9 38 29	25 55 12	7♐ 4	11R47	25 52	23 16	24 53	27 56	27 42	9 27	6 27
16	9 42 25	26 55 49	19 1	11 50	25 57	23 48	25 8	27 55	27 41	9 27	6 26
17	9 46 22	27 56 24	0♑51	11 43	26 4	24 20	25 22	27 54	27 40	9 28	6 25
18	9 50 18	28 56 58	12 37	11 26	26 14	24 52	25 37	27 53	27 39	9 29	6 24
19	9 54 15	29 57 30	24 24	10 58	26 26	25 24	25 51	27 51	27 38	9 30	6 22
20	9 58 11	0♓58 1	6♒16	10 22	26 40	25 57	26 5	27 51	27 37	9 30	6 21
21	10 2 8	1 58 31	18 15	9 37	26 57	26 29	26 20	27 50	27 36	9 31	6 20
22	10 6 5	2 58 59	0♓23	8 45	27 15	27 2	26 34	27 49	27 35	9 32	6 19
23	10 10 1	3 59 25	12 41	7 48	27 35	27 34	26 48	27 48	27 34	9 32	6 17
24	10 13 58	4 59 50	25 9	6 46	27 57	28 7	27 3	27 48	27 33	9 33	6 16
25	10 17 54	6 0 12	7♈49	5 42	28 21	28 40	27 17	27 47	27 31	9 33	6 15
26	10 21 51	7 0 34	20 40	4 37	28 46	29 13	27 31	27 47	27 30	9 34	6 13
27	10 25 47	8 0 53	3♉43	3 32	29 13	29 46	27 46	27D47	27 29	9 34	6 12
28	10 29 44	9♓ 1 10	16♉59	2♓30	29♑42	0♊19	28♒ 0	27♊47	27♎27	9♐35	6♎10

THE SUN ENTERS THE SIGN OF PISCES ON FEB 19 AT 00:59.

DAY	TIME	☉	☽	☿	♀	♂	♃	♄	♅	♆	♇
	h m s	° ' "	° '	° '	° '	° '	° '	° '	° '	° '	° '
M 1	10 33 40	10♓ 1 25	0♊28	1♓31	0♒12	0♊52	28♒14	27♊47	27♎26	9♐35	6♎ 9
A 2	10 37 37	11 1 38	14 13	0R37	0 44	1 26	28 28	27 47	27R25	9 35	6R 7
R 3	10 41 34	12 1 50	28 14	29♒48	1 17	1 59	28 43	27 48	27 23	9 36	6 6
C 4	10 45 30	13 1 59	12♋31	29 5	1 52	2 32	28 57	27 48	27 21	9 36	6 5
H 5	10 49 27	14 2 6	27 3	28 29	2 28	3 6	29 11	27 48	27 20	9 36	6 3
6	10 53 23	15 2 10	11♌46	27 59	3 5	3 40	29 25	27 49	27 18	9 36	6 2
7	10 57 20	16 2 13	26 34	27 36	3 43	4 13	29 39	27 50	27 17	9 37	6 0
8	11 1 16	17 2 14	11♍19	27 20	4 23	4 47	29 53	27 51	27 15	9 37	5 58
9	11 5 13	18 2 12	25 53	27D11	5 4	5 21	0♓ 7	27 52	27 13	9 37	5 57
10	11 9 9	19 2 9	10♎ 8	27 8	5 46	5 55	0 22	27 53	27 11	9 37	5 55
11	11 13 6	20 2 4	23 59	27 12	6 29	6 29	0 36	27 54	27 9	9 37	5 54
12	11 17 2	21 1 58	7♏23	27 21	7 13	7 3	0 50	27 55	27 7	9R37	5 52
13	11 20 59	22 1 50	20 22	27 37	7 57	7 37	1 3	27 57	27 6	9 37	5 51
14	11 24 56	23 1 40	2♐56	27 57	8 43	8 11	1 17	27 58	27 4	9 37	5 49
15	11 28 52	24 1 28	15 11	28 23	9 30	8 45	1 31	28 0	27 2	9 37	5 47
16	11 32 49	25 1 15	27 11	28 53	10 18	9 19	1 45	28 2	27 0	9 37	5 46
17	11 36 45	26 1 0	9♑ 2	29 28	11 6	9 54	1 59	28 3	26 58	9 37	5 44
18	11 40 42	27 0 43	20 49	0♓ 6	11 55	10 28	2 13	28 5	26 55	9 36	5 42
19	11 44 38	28 0 24	2♒39	0 49	12 45	11 3	2 26	28 7	26 53	9 36	5 41
20	11 48 35	29 0 4	14 34	1 36	13 36	11 37	2 40	28 10	26 51	9 36	5 39
21	11 52 31	29 59 42	26 39	2 25	14 27	12 12	2 54	28 12	26 49	9 36	5 38
22	11 56 28	0♈59 18	8♓57	3 18	15 19	12 46	3 7	28 14	26 47	9 35	5 36
23	12 0 25	1 58 51	21 29	4 14	16 12	13 21	3 21	28 17	26 45	9 35	5 34
24	12 4 21	2 58 23	4♈15	5 13	17 5	13 56	3 34	28 19	26 42	9 35	5 33
25	12 8 18	3 57 53	17 15	6 15	17 59	14 30	3 48	28 22	26 40	9 34	5 31
26	12 12 14	4 57 21	0♉28	7 19	18 53	15 5	4 1	28 25	26 38	9 34	5 29
27	12 16 11	5 56 47	13 51	8 26	19 48	15 40	4 14	28 28	26 35	9 33	5 28
28	12 20 7	6 56 10	27 24	9 35	20 44	16 15	4 28	28 31	26 33	9 33	5 26
29	12 24 4	7 55 32	11♊ 7	10 46	21 40	16 50	4 41	28 34	26 31	9 32	5 24
30	12 28 0	8 54 51	24 58	11 59	22 37	17 25	4 54	28 37	26 28	9 32	5 23
31	12 31 57	9♈54 7	8♋57	13♓14	23♒34	18♊ 0	5♓ 7	28♊40	26♎26	9♐31	5♎21

THE SUN ENTERS THE SIGN OF ARIES ON MAR 21 AT 00:07.

♈ ARIES ♉ TAURUS ♊ GEMINI ♋ CANCER ♌ LEO ♍ VIRGO ♎ LIBRA

SIDEREAL. SUN. MOON. MERCURY. VENUS. MARS. JUPITER. SATURN. URANUS. NEPTUNE. PLUTO.

DAY	TIME	☉	☽	☿	♀	♂	♃	♄	♅	♆	♇
	h m s	° ' "	° '	° '	° '	° '	° '	° '	° '	° '	° '
A 1	12 35 54	10♈53 22	23♋ 5	14♓31	24♒31	18♊35	5♓20	28♊44	26♎23	9♐31	5♎19
P 2	12 39 50	11 52 34	7♌19	15 50	25 29	19 10	5 33	28 47	26R21	9R30	5R18
R 3	12 43 47	12 51 43	21 39	17 11	26 27	19 45	5 46	28 51	26 18	9 29	5 16
I 4	12 47 43	13 50 50	6♍ 1	18 34	27 26	20 20	5 59	28 54	26 16	9 29	5 14
L 5	12 51 40	14 49 55	20 19	19 58	28 25	20 56	6 12	28 58	26 14	9 28	5 13
6	12 55 36	15 48 58	4♎28	21 24	29 24	21 31	6 25	29 2	26 11	9 27	5 11
7	12 59 33	16 47 59	18 24	22 52	0♓24	22 6	6 37	29 6	26 8	9 26	5 9
8	13 3 29	17 46 57	2♏ 0	24 21	1 24	22 41	6 50	29 10	26 6	9 25	5 8
9	13 7 26	18 45 54	15 16	25 52	2 25	23 17	7 2	29 14	26 3	9 25	5 6
10	13 11 23	19 44 49	28 10	27 25	3 26	23 52	7 15	29 18	26 1	9 24	5 5
11	13 15 19	20 43 42	10♐43	28 59	4 27	24 28	7 27	29 23	25 58	9 23	5 3
12	13 19 16	21 42 33	22 59	0♈35	5 29	25 3	7 39	29 27	25 56	9 22	5 1
13	13 23 12	22 41 23	5♑ 1	2 12	6 31	25 38	7 52	29 32	25 53	9 21	5 0
14	13 27 9	23 40 11	16 54	3 51	7 33	26 14	8 4	29 36	25 51	9 20	4 58
15	13 31 5	24 38 57	28 44	5 31	8 35	26 50	8 16	29 41	25 48	9 19	4 57
16	13 35 2	25 37 41	10♒35	7 14	9 38	27 25	8 28	29 46	25 45	9 18	4 55
17	13 38 58	26 36 24	22 33	8 57	10 41	28 1	8 40	29 50	25 43	9 17	4 54
18	13 42 55	27 35 4	4♓43	10 42	11 44	28 36	8 52	29 55	25 40	9 16	4 52
19	13 46 52	28 33 43	17 7	12 29	12 48	29 12	9 3	0♋ 0	25 38	9 15	4 51
20	13 50 48	29 32 21	29 49	14 18	13 51	29 48	9 15	0 5	25 35	9 13	4 49
21	13 54 45	0♉30 56	12♈49	16 8	14 55	0♋23	9 27	0 10	25 33	9 12	4 48
22	13 58 41	1 29 30	26 7	18 0	15 59	0 59	9 38	0 16	25 30	9 11	4 46
23	14 2 38	2 28 2	9♉42	19 53	17 4	1 35	9 50	0 21	25 28	9 10	4 45
24	14 6 34	3 26 32	23 30	21 48	18 8	2 11	10 1	0 26	25 25	9 9	4 43
25	14 10 31	4 25 0	7♊29	23 45	19 13	2 46	10 12	0 32	25 22	9 7	4 42
26	14 14 27	5 23 26	21 34	25 43	20 18	3 22	10 23	0 37	25 20	9 6	4 41
27	14 18 24	6 21 50	5♋44	27 42	21 23	3 58	10 34	0 43	25 17	9 5	4 39
28	14 22 21	7 20 12	19 55	29 44	22 28	4 34	10 45	0 48	25 15	9 4	4 38
29	14 26 17	8 18 31	4♌ 6	1♉47	23 34	5 10	10 56	0 54	25 12	9 2	4 37
30	14 30 14	9♉16 49	18♌15	3♉51	24♓39	5♋46	11♓ 7	1♋ 0	25♎10	9♐ 1	4♎35

THE SUN ENTERS THE SIGN OF TAURUS ON APR 20 AT 11:19.

DAY	TIME	☉	☽	☿	♀	♂	♃	♄	♅	♆	♇
	h m s	° ' "	° '	° '	° '	° '	° '	° '	° '	° '	° '
M 1	14 34 10	10♉15 4	2♍20	5♉56	25♓45	6♋22	11♓17	1♋ 6	25♎ 7	9♐ 0	4♎34
A 2	14 38 7	11 13 18	16 20	8 3	26 51	6 58	11 28	1 12	25R 5	8R58	4R33
Y 3	14 42 3	12 11 29	0♎12	10 11	27 57	7 34	11 38	1 18	25 3	8 57	4 32
4	14 46 0	13 9 38	13 53	12 19	29 4	8 10	11 49	1 24	25 0	8 55	4 30
5	14 49 56	14 7 46	27 22	14 29	0♈10	8 46	11 59	1 30	24 58	8 54	4 29
6	14 53 53	15 5 52	10♏36	16 39	1 17	9 22	12 9	1 36	24 55	8 52	4 28
7	14 57 49	16 3 56	23 34	18 49	2 23	9 58	12 19	1 42	24 53	8 51	4 27
8	15 1 46	17 1 58	6♐15	20 59	3 30	10 34	12 29	1 48	24 51	8 50	4 26
9	15 5 43	18 0 0	18 41	23 9	4 37	11 10	12 38	1 55	24 48	8 48	4 25
10	15 9 39	18 57 59	0♑53	25 18	5 44	11 46	12 48	2 1	24 46	8 47	4 24
11	15 13 36	19 55 57	12 53	27 27	6 52	12 23	12 58	2 8	24 44	8 45	4 22
12	15 17 32	20 53 54	24 47	29 34	7 59	12 59	13 7	2 14	24 42	8 44	4 21
13	15 21 29	21 51 49	6♒37	1♊40	9 7	13 35	13 16	2 21	24 39	8 42	4 20
14	15 25 25	22 49 44	18 29	3 44	10 14	14 11	13 25	2 27	24 37	8 40	4 19
15	15 29 22	23 47 36	0♓28	5 46	11 22	14 47	13 34	2 34	24 35	8 39	4 19
16	15 33 18	24 45 28	12 39	7 47	12 30	15 24	13 43	2 41	24 33	8 37	4 18
17	15 37 15	25 43 18	25 5	9 44	13 38	16 0	13 52	2 47	24 31	8 36	4 17
18	15 41 12	26 41 7	7♈50	11 40	14 46	16 36	14 1	2 54	24 29	8 34	4 16
19	15 45 8	27 38 55	20 57	13 32	15 54	17 12	14 9	3 1	24 27	8 33	4 15
20	15 49 5	28 36 42	4♉26	15 22	17 2	17 49	14 18	3 8	24 25	8 31	4 14
21	15 53 1	29 34 28	18 17	17 9	18 11	18 25	14 26	3 15	24 23	8 29	4 13
22	15 56 58	0♊32 12	2♊26	18 53	19 19	19 1	14 34	3 22	24 21	8 28	4 13
23	16 0 54	1 29 55	16 49	20 34	20 28	19 38	14 42	3 29	24 19	8 26	4 12
24	16 4 51	2 27 37	1♋21	22 12	21 36	20 14	14 50	3 36	24 17	8 25	4 11
25	16 8 48	3 25 17	15 56	23 47	22 45	20 51	14 57	3 43	24 15	8 23	4 11
26	16 12 44	4 22 56	0♌29	25 18	23 54	21 27	15 5	3 50	24 14	8 21	4 10
27	16 16 41	5 20 33	14 54	26 47	25 3	22 3	15 12	3 57	24 12	8 20	4 9
28	16 20 37	6 18 9	29 9	28 12	26 12	22 40	15 20	4 4	24 10	8 18	4 9
29	16 24 34	7 15 43	13♍12	29 33	27 21	23 16	15 27	4 12	24 9	8 17	4 8
30	16 28 30	8 13 16	27 0	0♋52	28 30	23 53	15 34	4 19	24 7	8 15	4 8
31	16 32 27	9♊10 47	10♎34	2♋ 7	29♈39	24♋29	15♓40	4♋26	24♎ 5	8♐13	4♎ 7

THE SUN ENTERS THE SIGN OF GEMINI ON MAY 21 AT 10:37.

DAY	TIME	☉	☽	☿	♀	♂	♃	♄	♅	♆	♇
	h m s	° ' "	° '	° '	° '	° '	° '	° '	° '	° '	° '
J 1	16 36 23	10♊ 8 17	23♎53	3♋18	0♉48	25♋ 6	15♓47	4♋34	24♎ 4	8♐12	4♎ 7
U 2	16 40 20	11 5 46	6♏57	4 26	1 57	25 42	15 53	4 41	24R 2	8R10	4R 6
N 3	16 44 16	12 3 14	19 48	5 31	3 7	26 19	16 0	4 48	24 1	8 8	4 6
E 4	16 48 13	13 0 41	2♐25	6 32	4 16	26 56	16 6	4 56	24 0	8 7	4 6
5	16 52 10	13 58 6	14 50	7 29	5 26	27 32	16 12	5 3	23 58	8 5	4 5
6	16 56 6	14 55 31	27 4	8 22	6 35	28 9	16 18	5 11	23 57	8 4	4 5
7	17 0 3	15 52 55	9♑ 8	9 12	7 45	28 45	16 24	5 18	23 56	8 2	4 5
8	17 3 59	16 50 18	21 4	9 57	8 55	29 22	16 29	5 26	23 54	8 0	4 4
9	17 7 56	17 47 40	2♒56	10 39	10 5	29 59	16 34	5 33	23 53	7 59	4 4
10	17 11 52	18 45 2	14 47	11 16	11 15	0♌35	16 40	5 41	23 52	7 57	4 4
11	17 15 49	19 42 23	26 39	11 50	12 25	1 12	16 45	5 49	23 51	7 56	4 4
12	17 19 46	20 39 44	8♓38	12 19	13 35	1 49	16 49	5 56	23 50	7 54	4 4
13	17 23 42	21 37 4	20 47	12 43	14 45	2 25	16 54	6 4	23 49	7 52	4 4
14	17 27 39	22 34 23	3♈11	13 3	15 55	3 2	16 59	6 11	23 48	7 51	4D 4
15	17 31 35	23 31 43	15 55	13 19	17 5	3 39	17 3	6 19	23 47	7 49	4 4
16	17 35 32	24 29 1	29 1	13 30	18 15	4 16	17 7	6 27	23 46	7 48	4 4
17	17 39 28	25 26 20	12♉31	13R37	19 26	4 52	17 11	6 35	23 45	7 46	4 4
18	17 43 25	26 23 38	26 27	13 39	20 36	5 29	17 15	6 42	23 45	7 45	4 4
19	17 47 21	27 20 56	10♊47	13 36	21 46	6 6	17 19	6 50	23 44	7 43	4 4
20	17 51 18	28 18 14	25 27	13 29	22 57	6 43	17 22	6 58	23 43	7 42	4 4
21	17 55 15	29 15 31	10♋20	13 18	24 7	7 20	17 25	7 6	23 43	7 40	4 5
22	17 59 11	0♋12 47	25 19	13 3	25 18	7 56	17 28	7 13	23 42	7 39	4 5
23	18 3 8	1 10 3	10♌15	12 43	26 29	8 33	17 31	7 21	23 42	7 37	4 5
24	18 7 4	2 7 19	25 1	12 20	27 39	9 10	17 34	7 29	23 41	7 36	4 5
25	18 11 1	3 4 33	9♍30	11 54	28 50	9 47	17 37	7 37	23 41	7 34	4 6
26	18 14 57	4 1 47	23 39	11 25	0♊ 1	10 24	17 39	7 44	23 40	7 33	4 6
27	18 18 54	4 59 1	7♎27	10 53	1 12	11 1	17 41	7 52	23 40	7 32	4 6
28	18 22 50	5 56 14	20 52	10 20	2 22	11 38	17 43	8 0	23 40	7 30	4 7
29	18 26 47	6 53 26	3♏58	9 45	3 33	12 15	17 45	8 8	23 40	7 29	4 7
30	18 30 44	7♋50 38	16♏45	9♋ 9	4♊44	12♌52	17♓46	8♋16	23♎40	7♐28	4♎ 8

THE SUN ENTERS THE SIGN OF CANCER ON JUN 21 AT 18:38.

♏ SCORPIO ♐ SAGITTARIUS ♑ CAPRICORN ♒ AQUARIUS ♓ PISCES

1974

SIDEREAL SUN. MOON. MERCURY. VENUS. MARS. JUPITER. SATURN. URANUS. NEPTUNE. PLUTO.

DAY	TIME	☉	☽	☿	♀	♂	♃	♄	♅	♆	♇
	h m s	° ' "	° '	° '	° '	° '	° '	° '	° '	° '	° '
J 1	18 34 40	8♋47 50	29♏18	8♋33	5♊55	13♌29	17♓48	8♋24	23♎40	7♐26	4♎ 8
U 2	18 38 37	9 45 1	11♐38	7R57	7 6	14 6	17 49	8 31	23D40	7R25	4 9
L 3	18 42 33	10 42 12	23 48	7 22	8 18	14 43	17 50	8 39	23 40	7 24	4 9
Y 4	18 46 30	11 39 23	5♑50	6 49	9 29	15 20	17 51	8 47	23 40	7 22	4 10
5	18 50 26	12 36 34	17 47	6 18	10 40	15 57	17 51	8 55	23 40	7 21	4 11
6	18 54 23	13 33 45	29 39	5 50	11 51	16 34	17 52	9 3	23 40	7 20	4 11
7	18 58 19	14 30 56	11♒30	5 25	13 3	17 11	17R52	9 10	23 40	7 19	4 12
8	19 2 16	15 28 7	23 21	5 4	14 14	17 49	17 52	9 18	23 40	7 17	4 13
9	19 6 13	16 25 19	5♓15	4 47	15 25	18 26	17 52	9 26	23 41	7 16	4 14
10	19 10 9	17 22 30	17 15	4 35	16 37	19 3	17 51	9 34	23 41	7 15	4 14
11	19 14 6	18 19 42	29 24	4 27	17 48	19 40	17 51	9 41	23 42	7 14	4 15
12	19 18 2	19 16 55	11♈46	4D24	19 0	20 17	17 50	9 49	23 42	7 13	4 16
13	19 21 59	20 14 8	24 26	4 26	20 12	20 55	17 49	9 57	23 43	7 12	4 17
14	19 25 55	21 11 22	7♉26	4 33	21 23	21 32	17 48	10 5	23 43	7 11	4 18
15	19 29 52	22 8 36	20 52	4 46	22 35	22 9	17 47	10 12	23 44	7 10	4 19
16	19 33 48	23 5 51	4♊43	5 4	23 47	22 46	17 45	10 20	23 45	7 9	4 20
17	19 37 45	24 3 6	19 2	5 28	24 59	23 24	17 44	10 28	23 45	7 8	4 21
18	19 41 42	25 0 23	3♋45	5 57	26 10	24 1	17 42	10 35	23 46	7 7	4 22
19	19 45 38	25 57 39	18 46	6 32	27 22	24 38	17 40	10 43	23 47	7 6	4 23
20	19 49 35	26 54 56	3♌59	7 12	28 34	25 16	17 37	10 51	23 48	7 5	4 24
21	19 53 31	27 52 14	19 12	7 58	29 46	25 53	17 35	10 58	23 49	7 4	4 25
22	19 57 28	28 49 32	4♍15	8 49	0♋58	26 31	17 32	11 6	23 50	7 3	4 27
23	20 1 24	29 46 50	19 1	9 45	2 10	27 8	17 29	11 13	23 51	7 2	4 28
24	20 5 21	0♌44 8	3♎21	10 47	3 23	27 45	17 26	11 21	23 52	7 1	4 29
25	20 9 17	1 41 27	17 15	11 53	4 35	28 23	17 23	11 28	23 53	7 1	4 30
26	20 13 14	2 38 46	0♏41	13 5	5 47	29 0	17 19	11 36	23 55	7 0	4 32
27	20 17 11	3 36 6	13 42	14 21	6 59	29 38	17 16	11 43	23 56	6 59	4 33
28	20 21 7	4 33 26	26 22	15 43	8 11	0♍16	17 12	11 51	23 57	6 58	4 34
29	20 25 4	5 30 46	8♐44	17 9	9 24	0 53	17 8	11 58	23 59	6 58	4 36
30	20 29 0	6 28 7	20 54	18 39	10 36	1 31	17 4	12 6	24 0	6 57	4 37
31	20 32 57	7♌25 29	2♑54	20♋14	11♋49	2♍ 8	17♓ 0	12♋13	24♎ 1	6♐57	4♎39

THE SUN ENTERS THE SIGN OF LEO ON JUL 23 AT 05:31.

DAY	TIME	☉	☽	☿	♀	♂	♃	♄	♅	♆	♇
	h m s	° ' "	° '	° '	° '	° '	° '	° '	° '	° '	° '
A 1	20 36 53	8♌22 51	14♑48	21♋53	13♋ 1	2♍46	16♓55	12♋20	24♎ 3	6♐56	4♎40
U 2	20 40 50	9 20 15	26 39	23 36	14 14	3 24	16R51	12 28	24 5	6R55	4 41
G 3	20 44 47	10 17 38	8♒30	25 22	15 26	4 1	16 46	12 35	24 6	6 55	4 43
U 4	20 48 43	11 15 3	20 21	27 12	16 39	4 39	16 41	12 42	24 8	6 54	4 44
S 5	20 52 40	12 12 29	2♓16	29 4	17 51	5 17	16 36	12 49	24 9	6 54	4 46
T 6	20 56 36	13 9 56	14 14	0♌59	19 4	5 54	16 30	12 56	24 11	6 54	4 48
7	21 0 33	14 7 23	26 19	2 57	20 17	6 32	16 25	13 3	24 13	6 53	4 49
8	21 4 29	15 4 52	8♈33	4 56	21 30	7 10	16 19	13 10	24 15	6 53	4 51
9	21 8 26	16 2 23	20 57	6 56	22 43	7 48	16 14	13 17	24 17	6 52	4 52
10	21 12 22	16 59 54	3♉36	8 58	23 55	8 26	16 8	13 24	24 19	6 52	4 54
11	21 16 19	17 57 27	16 33	11 1	25 8	9 3	16 2	13 31	24 21	6 52	4 56
12	21 20 15	18 55 2	29 51	13 4	26 21	9 41	15 56	13 38	24 23	6 52	4 58
13	21 24 12	19 52 38	13♊34	15 7	27 34	10 19	15 49	13 45	24 25	6 51	4 59
14	21 28 9	20 50 16	27 42	17 10	28 48	10 57	15 43	13 52	24 27	6 51	5 1
15	21 32 5	21 47 55	12♋16	19 13	0♌ 1	11 35	15 36	13 59	24 29	6 51	5 3
16	21 36 2	22 45 35	27 12	21 15	1 14	12 13	15 30	14 5	24 31	6 51	5 5
17	21 39 58	23 43 17	12♌23	23 17	2 27	12 51	15 23	14 12	24 34	6 51	5 7
18	21 43 55	24 41 0	27 38	25 17	3 40	13 29	15 16	14 19	24 36	6 51	5 8
19	21 47 51	25 38 44	12♍48	27 17	4 54	14 7	15 9	14 25	24 38	6D51	5 10
20	21 51 48	26 36 30	27 42	29 15	6 7	14 45	15 2	14 32	24 41	6 51	5 12
21	21 55 44	27 34 17	12♎12	1♍13	7 20	15 23	14 55	14 38	24 43	6 51	5 14
22	21 59 41	28 32 5	26 13	3 9	8 34	16 2	14 48	14 45	24 45	6 51	5 16
23	22 3 38	29 29 54	9♏44	5 4	9 47	16 40	14 40	14 51	24 48	6 51	5 18
24	22 7 34	0♍27 44	22 48	6 58	11 1	17 18	14 33	14 57	24 50	6 51	5 20
25	22 11 31	1 25 36	5♐27	8 50	12 14	17 56	14 25	15 3	24 53	6 51	5 22
26	22 15 27	2 23 29	17 47	10 41	13 28	18 34	14 18	15 10	24 56	6 52	5 24
27	22 19 24	3 21 23	29 52	12 31	14 41	19 13	14 10	15 16	24 58	6 52	5 26
28	22 23 20	4 19 18	11♑48	14 19	15 55	19 51	14 2	15 22	25 1	6 52	5 28
29	22 27 17	5 17 15	23 39	16 6	17 9	20 29	13 55	15 28	25 4	6 52	5 30
30	22 31 13	6 15 13	5♒29	17 52	18 22	21 8	13 47	15 34	25 7	6 53	5 32
31	22 35 10	7♍13 12	17♒20	19♍36	19♌36	21♍46	13♓39	15♋39	25♎ 9	6♐53	5♎34

THE SUN ENTERS THE SIGN OF VIRGO ON AUG 23 AT 12:30.

DAY	TIME	☉	☽	☿	♀	♂	♃	♄	♅	♆	♇
	h m s	° ' "	° '	° '	° '	° '	° '	° '	° '	° '	° '
S 1	22 39 7	8♍11 13	29♒15	21♍19	20♌50	22♍25	13♓31	15♋45	25♎12	6♐53	5♎36
E 2	22 43 3	9 9 16	11♓16	23 1	22 4	23 3	13R23	15 51	25 15	6 54	5 38
P 3	22 47 0	10 7 20	23 24	24 42	23 18	23 41	13 15	15 57	25 18	6 54	5 40
T 4	22 50 56	11 5 26	5♈39	26 21	24 32	24 20	13 7	16 2	25 21	6 55	5 43
E 5	22 54 53	12 3 34	18 3	28 0	25 46	24 58	13 0	16 8	25 24	6 55	5 45
M 6	22 58 49	13 1 43	0♉36	29 37	27 0	25 37	12 52	16 13	25 27	6 56	5 47
B 7	23 2 46	13 59 55	13 22	1♎12	28 14	26 16	12 44	16 19	25 30	6 57	5 49
E 8	23 6 42	14 58 9	26 22	2 47	29 28	26 54	12 36	16 24	25 33	6 57	5 51
R 9	23 10 39	15 56 24	9♊39	4 21	0♍42	27 33	12 28	16 29	25 36	6 58	5 53
10	23 14 36	16 54 42	23 15	5 53	1 56	28 12	12 20	16 34	25 39	6 59	5 56
11	23 18 32	17 53 2	7♋13	7 24	3 10	28 50	12 12	16 39	25 42	6 59	5 58
12	23 22 29	18 51 24	21 32	8 54	4 24	29 29	12 4	16 44	25 45	7 0	6 0
13	23 26 25	19 49 48	6♌12	10 23	5 39	0♎ 8	11 56	16 49	25 49	7 1	6 2
14	23 30 22	20 48 15	21 6	11 51	6 53	0 47	11 49	16 54	25 52	7 2	6 4
15	23 34 18	21 46 43	6♍ 8	13 17	8 7	1 26	11 41	16 59	25 55	7 2	6 7
16	23 38 15	22 45 13	21 9	14 43	9 22	2 4	11 33	17 3	25 58	7 3	6 9
17	23 42 11	23 43 45	5♎58	16 7	10 36	2 43	11 26	17 8	26 2	7 4	6 11
18	23 46 8	24 42 18	20 26	17 29	11 50	3 22	11 18	17 13	26 5	7 5	6 14
19	23 50 5	25 40 54	4♏30	18 51	13 5	4 1	11 10	17 17	26 9	7 6	6 16
20	23 54 1	26 39 31	18 4	20 11	14 19	4 40	11 3	17 21	26 12	7 7	6 18
21	23 57 58	27 38 10	1♐12	21 30	15 34	5 19	10 56	17 26	26 15	7 8	6 20
22	0 1 54	28 36 51	13 54	22 48	16 48	5 58	10 49	17 30	26 19	7 9	6 23
23	0 5 51	29 35 34	26 16	24 4	18 3	6 37	10 41	17 34	26 22	7 10	6 25
24	0 9 47	0♎34 18	8♑22	25 18	19 17	7 17	10 34	17 38	26 26	7 12	6 27
25	0 13 44	1 33 4	20 18	26 31	20 32	7 56	10 27	17 42	26 29	7 13	6 30
26	0 17 40	2 31 51	2♒ 9	27 42	21 47	8 35	10 21	17 45	26 33	7 14	6 32
27	0 21 37	3 30 41	13 59	28 52	23 1	9 14	10 14	17 49	26 36	7 15	6 34
28	0 25 33	4 29 32	25 53	29 59	24 16	9 53	10 7	17 53	26 40	7 16	6 37
29	0 29 30	5 28 25	7♓53	1♏ 4	25 31	10 33	10 1	17 56	26 43	7 18	6 39
30	0 33 27	6♎27 19	20♓ 2	2♏ 8	26♍45	11♎12	9♓55	18♋ 0	26♎47	7♐19	6♎41

THE SUN ENTERS THE SIGN OF LIBRA ON SEP 23 AT 09:60.

♈ ARIES ♉ TAURUS ♊ GEMINI ♋ CANCER ♌ LEO ♍ VIRGO ♎ LIBRA

1974

SIDEREAL SUN... MOON... MERCURY. VENUS... MARS... JUPITER. SATURN.. URANUS.. NEPTUNE. PLUTO.

DAY	TIME	☉	☽	☿	♀	♂	♃	♄	♅	♆	♇
	h m s	° ' "	° '	° '	° '	° '	° '	° '	° '	° '	° '
O 1	0 37 23	7♎26 16	2♈21	3♏ 8	28♍ 0	11♎51	9♓48	18♋ 3	26♎51	7♐20	6♎43
C 2	0 41 20	8 25 15	14 51	4 7	29 15	12 31	9R42	18 6	26 54	7 22	6 46
T 3	0 45 16	9 24 15	27 31	5 2	0♎30	13 10	9 36	18 9	26 58	7 23	6 48
O 4	0 49 13	10 23 18	10♉22	5 54	1 45	13 50	9 31	18 12	27 1	7 24	6 50
B 5	0 53 9	11 22 23	23 24	6 43	2 59	14 29	9 25	18 15	27 5	7 26	6 53
E 6	0 57 6	12 21 31	6♊38	7 29	4 14	15 9	9 19	18 18	27 9	7 27	6 55
R 7	1 1 2	13 20 41	20 4	8 10	5 29	15 48	9 14	18 21	27 12	7 29	6 57
8	1 4 59	14 19 53	3♋43	8 48	6 44	16 28	9 9	18 24	27 16	7 30	7 0
9	1 8 56	15 19 7	17 37	9 20	7 59	17 8	9 4	18 26	27 20	7 32	7 2
10	1 12 52	16 18 24	1♌45	9 48	9 14	17 47	8 59	18 29	27 24	7 33	7 4
11	1 16 49	17 17 43	16 6	10 10	10 29	18 27	8 55	18 31	27 27	7 35	7 6
12	1 20 45	18 17 4	0♍39	10 26	11 44	19 7	8 50	18 33	27 31	7 36	7 9
13	1 24 42	19 16 27	15 16	10R35	12 59	19 47	8 46	18 35	27 35	7 38	7 11
14	1 28 38	20 15 53	29 53	10 38	14 14	20 26	8 42	18 37	27 39	7 40	7 13
15	1 32 35	21 15 21	14♎22	10 33	15 29	21 6	8 38	18 39	27 42	7 41	7 16
16	1 36 31	22 14 51	28 36	10 19	16 44	21 46	8 34	18 41	27 46	7 43	7 18
17	1 40 28	23 14 23	12♏29	9 58	17 59	22 26	8 30	18 43	27 50	7 45	7 20
18	1 44 25	24 13 57	26 0	9 28	19 14	23 6	8 27	18 44	27 54	7 47	7 22
19	1 48 21	25 13 33	9♐ 6	8 49	20 29	23 46	8 24	18 46	27 57	7 48	7 25
20	1 52 18	26 13 11	21 50	8 2	21 45	24 26	8 21	18 47	28 1	7 50	7 27
21	1 56 14	27 12 50	4♑14	7 7	23 0	25 6	8 18	18 48	28 5	7 52	7 29
22	2 0 11	28 12 31	16 23	6 5	24 15	25 47	8 15	18 49	28 9	7 54	7 31
23	2 4 7	29 12 14	28 21	4 56	25 30	26 27	8 13	18 50	28 12	7 56	7 33
24	2 8 4	0♏11 59	10♒13	3 43	26 45	27 7	8 10	18 51	28 16	7 57	7 36
25	2 12 0	1 11 45	22 5	2 28	28 0	27 47	8 8	18 52	28 20	7 59	7 38
26	2 15 57	2 11 33	4♓ 1	1 12	29 15	28 27	8 7	18 53	28 24	8 1	7 40
27	2 19 54	3 11 22	16 5	29♎58	0♏31	29 8	8 5	18 53	28 28	8 3	7 42
28	2 23 50	4 11 14	28 20	28 48	1 46	29 48	8 4	18 54	28 31	8 5	7 44
29	2 27 47	5 11 7	10♈49	27 45	3 1	0♏28	8 2	18 54	28 35	8 7	7 46
30	2 31 43	6 11 2	23 32	26 49	4 16	1 9	8 1	18 54	28 39	8 9	7 48
31	2 35 40	7♏10 59	6♉31	26♎ 4	5♏32	1♏49	8♓ 0	18♋54	28♎43	8♐11	7♎51

THE SUN ENTERS THE SIGN OF SCORPIO ON OCT 23 AT 19:11.

DAY	TIME	☉	☽	☿	♀	♂	♃	♄	♅	♆	♇
	h m s	° ' "	° '	° '	° '	° '	° '	° '	° '	° '	° '
N 1	2 39 36	8♏10 57	19♉44	25♎29	6♏47	2♏30	8♓ 0	18♋54	28♎46	8♐13	7♎53
O 2	2 43 33	9 10 58	3♊ 9	25R 5	8 2	3 10	7R59	18R54	28 50	8 15	7 55
V 3	2 47 29	10 11 1	16 47	24D53	9 17	3 51	7D59	18 54	28 54	8 17	7 57
E 4	2 51 26	11 11 6	0♋34	24 53	10 33	4 32	7 59	18 54	28 58	8 19	7 59
M 5	2 55 23	12 11 13	14 29	25 4	11 48	5 12	7 59	18 53	29 1	8 21	8 1
B 6	2 59 19	13 11 22	28 32	25 25	13 3	5 53	8 0	18 53	29 5	8 23	8 3
E 7	3 3 16	14 11 33	12♌39	25 55	14 18	6 34	8 0	18 52	29 9	8 25	8 5
R 8	3 7 12	15 11 46	26 51	26 35	15 34	7 15	8 1	18 51	29 12	8 27	8 7
9	3 11 9	16 12 1	11♍ 5	27 22	16 49	7 55	8 2	18 51	29 16	8 30	8 9
10	3 15 5	17 12 18	25 17	28 16	18 4	8 36	8 4	18 50	29 20	8 32	8 10
11	3 19 2	18 12 37	9♎25	29 16	19 20	9 17	8 5	18 48	29 23	8 34	8 12
12	3 22 58	19 12 58	23 25	0♏22	20 35	9 58	8 7	18 47	29 27	8 36	8 14
13	3 26 55	20 13 21	7♏13	1 33	21 50	10 39	8 8	18 46	29 30	8 38	8 16
14	3 30 51	21 13 46	20 46	2 47	23 6	11 20	8 10	18 44	29 34	8 40	8 18
15	3 34 48	22 14 12	4♐ 1	4 5	24 21	12 1	8 13	18 43	29 38	8 42	8 20
16	3 38 45	23 14 40	16 59	5 25	25 36	12 42	8 15	18 41	29 41	8 45	8 22
17	3 42 41	24 15 9	29 38	6 48	26 52	13 24	8 18	18 40	29 45	8 47	8 23
18	3 46 38	25 15 40	12♑ 1	8 13	28 7	14 5	8 21	18 38	29 48	8 49	8 25
19	3 50 34	26 16 12	24 10	9 40	29 22	14 46	8 24	18 36	29 52	8 51	8 27
20	3 54 31	27 16 46	6♒ 9	11 8	0♐38	15 27	8 27	18 34	29 55	8 53	8 28
21	3 58 27	28 17 21	18 2	12 38	1 53	16 9	8 30	18 31	29 59	8 56	8 30
22	4 2 24	29 17 56	29 54	14 8	3 9	16 50	8 34	18 29	0♏ 2	8 58	8 32
23	4 6 21	0♐18 33	11♓50	15 39	4 24	17 31	8 38	18 27	0 5	9 0	8 33
24	4 10 17	1 19 12	23 54	17 11	5 39	18 13	8 42	18 24	0 9	9 2	8 35
25	4 14 14	2 19 51	6♈10	18 43	6 55	18 54	8 46	18 22	0 12	9 5	8 37
26	4 18 10	3 20 31	18 43	20 15	8 10	19 36	8 50	18 19	0 16	9 7	8 38
27	4 22 7	4 21 13	1♉35	21 48	9 25	20 17	8 55	18 16	0 19	9 9	8 40
28	4 26 3	5 21 56	14 46	23 21	10 41	20 59	9 0	18 13	0 22	9 11	8 41
29	4 30 0	6 22 40	28 18	24 55	11 56	21 40	9 5	18 10	0 25	9 14	8 43
30	4 33 56	7♐23 25	12♊ 8	26♏28	13♐11	22♏22	9♓10	18♋ 7	0♏29	9♐16	8♎44

THE SUN ENTERS THE SIGN OF SAGITTARIUS ON NOV 22 AT 16:39.

DAY	TIME	☉	☽	☿	♀	♂	♃	♄	♅	♆	♇
	h m s	° ' "	° '	° '	° '	° '	° '	° '	° '	° '	° '
D 1	4 37 53	8♐24 12	26♊13	28♏ 2	14♐27	23♏ 4	9♓15	18♋ 4	0♏32	9♐18	8♎45
E 2	4 41 50	9 24 59	10♋30	29 35	15 42	23 46	9 20	18R 1	0 35	9 20	8 47
C 3	4 45 46	10 25 49	24 53	1♐ 9	16 58	24 27	9 26	17 58	0 38	9 23	8 48
E 4	4 49 43	11 26 39	9♌17	2 43	18 13	25 9	9 32	17 54	0 41	9 25	8 49
M 5	4 53 39	12 27 31	23 39	4 17	19 28	25 51	9 38	17 51	0 44	9 27	8 51
B 6	4 57 36	13 28 24	7♍54	5 50	20 44	26 33	9 44	17 47	0 47	9 30	8 52
E 7	5 1 32	14 29 19	22 1	7 24	21 59	27 15	9 50	17 43	0 50	9 32	8 53
R 8	5 5 29	15 30 14	5♎57	8 58	23 14	27 57	9 57	17 40	0 53	9 34	8 54
9	5 9 25	16 31 11	19 42	10 32	24 30	28 39	10 4	17 36	0 56	9 36	8 56
10	5 13 22	17 32 10	3♏14	12 6	25 45	29 21	10 10	17 32	0 59	9 39	8 57
11	5 17 19	18 33 9	16 34	13 39	27 1	0♐ 3	10 17	17 28	1 2	9 41	8 58
12	5 21 15	19 34 10	29 41	15 13	28 16	0 46	10 25	17 24	1 5	9 43	8 59
13	5 25 12	20 35 11	12♐35	16 47	29 31	1 28	10 32	17 20	1 8	9 45	9 0
14	5 29 8	21 36 14	25 16	18 21	0♑47	2 10	10 39	17 16	1 10	9 47	9 1
15	5 33 5	22 37 17	7♑44	19 56	2 2	2 52	10 47	17 12	1 13	9 50	9 2
16	5 37 1	23 38 20	20 0	21 30	3 18	3 35	10 55	17 7	1 16	9 52	9 3
17	5 40 58	24 39 25	2♒ 6	23 4	4 33	4 17	11 3	17 3	1 18	9 54	9 4
18	5 44 54	25 40 29	14 4	24 39	5 48	4 59	11 11	16 59	1 21	9 56	9 5
19	5 48 51	26 41 35	25 57	26 13	7 4	5 42	11 19	16 54	1 23	9 59	9 6
20	5 52 48	27 42 40	7♓48	27 48	8 19	6 24	11 27	16 50	1 26	10 1	9 6
21	5 56 44	28 43 46	19 42	29 23	9 34	7 7	11 36	16 45	1 28	10 3	9 7
22	6 0 41	29 44 52	1♈43	0♑58	10 50	7 50	11 45	16 40	1 31	10 5	9 8
23	6 4 37	0♑45 58	13 56	2 34	12 5	8 32	11 53	16 36	1 33	10 7	9 9
24	6 8 34	1 47 4	26 25	4 9	13 20	9 15	12 2	16 31	1 36	10 9	9 9
25	6 12 30	2 48 11	9♉16	5 45	14 36	9 58	12 12	16 26	1 38	10 11	9 10
26	6 16 27	3 49 18	22 30	7 21	15 51	10 40	12 21	16 22	1 40	10 14	9 10
27	6 20 23	4 50 25	6♊10	8 57	17 6	11 23	12 30	16 17	1 42	10 16	9 11
28	6 24 20	5 51 32	20 14	10 34	18 22	12 6	12 40	16 12	1 45	10 18	9 12
29	6 28 17	6 52 39	4♋41	12 11	19 37	12 49	12 49	16 7	1 47	10 20	9 12
30	6 32 13	7 53 47	19 25	13 48	20 52	13 32	12 59	16 2	1 49	10 22	9 13
31	6 36 10	8♑54 54	4♌17	15♑25	22♑ 8	14♐15	13♓ 9	15♋57	1♏51	10♐24	9♎13

THE SUN ENTERS THE SIGN OF CAPRICORN ON DEC 22 AT 05:57.

♏ SCORPIO ♐ SAGITTARIUS ♑ CAPRICORN ♒ AQUARIUS ♓ PISCES

SIDEREAL SUN.. MOON.. MERCURY VENUS.. MARS.. JUPITER SATURN.. URANUS.. NEPTUNE PLUTO.

DAY	TIME	☉	☽	☿	♀	♂	♃	♄	♅	♆	♇
	h m s	° ' "	° '	° '	° '	° '	° '	° '	° '	° '	° '
J 1	6 40 6	9♑56 2	19♌11	17♑ 3	23♑23	14♐58	13♓19	15♋52	1♏53	10♐26	9♎13
A 2	6 44 3	10 57 11	3♍57	18 40	24 38	15 41	13 29	15R48	1 55	10 28	9 14
N 3	6 47 59	11 58 19	18 29	20 18	25 53	16 24	13 39	15 43	1 56	10 30	9 14
U 4	6 51 56	12 59 28	2♎43	21 56	27 9	17 7	13 50	15 38	1 58	10 32	9 14
A 5	6 55 52	14 0 37	16 37	23 35	28 24	17 50	14 0	15 33	2 0	10 34	9 15
R 6	6 59 49	15 1 46	0♏12	25 13	29 39	18 33	14 11	15 28	2 2	10 36	9 15
Y 7	7 3 46	16 2 56	13 27	26 52	0♒54	19 16	14 21	15 23	2 3	10 38	9 15
8	7 7 42	17 4 6	26 26	28 30	2 10	20 0	14 32	15 18	2 5	10 40	9 15
9	7 11 39	18 5 16	9♐11	0♒ 8	3 25	20 43	14 43	15 13	2 7	10 42	9 15
10	7 15 35	19 6 26	21 44	1 46	4 40	21 26	14 54	15 8	2 8	10 44	9 15
11	7 19 32	20 7 35	4♑ 7	3 24	5 55	22 10	15 5	15 3	2 10	10 45	9R15
12	7 23 28	21 8 45	16 21	5 1	7 10	22 53	15 17	14 58	2 11	10 47	9 15
13	7 27 25	22 9 54	28 28	6 38	8 26	23 37	15 28	14 53	2 12	10 49	9 15
14	7 31 22	23 11 3	10♒28	8 13	9 41	24 20	15 39	14 48	2 14	10 51	9 15
15	7 35 18	24 12 11	22 23	9 48	10 56	25 4	15 51	14 43	2 15	10 53	9 15
16	7 39 15	25 13 19	4♓15	11 21	12 11	25 47	16 2	14 39	2 16	10 54	9 15
17	7 43 11	26 14 26	16 6	12 52	13 26	26 31	16 14	14 34	2 17	10 56	9 15
18	7 47 8	27 15 33	27 59	14 21	14 41	27 14	16 26	14 29	2 18	10 58	9 15
19	7 51 4	28 16 38	9♈57	15 47	15 56	27 58	16 38	14 24	2 19	11 0	9 14
20	7 55 1	29 17 43	22 6	17 10	17 11	28 42	16 50	14 19	2 20	11 1	9 14
21	7 58 57	0♒18 47	4♉30	18 29	18 26	29 26	17 2	14 15	2 21	11 3	9 14
22	8 2 54	1 19 50	17 13	19 44	19 42	0♑ 9	17 14	14 10	2 22	11 4	9 14
23	8 6 51	2 20 52	0♊20	20 53	20 57	0 53	17 26	14 6	2 23	11 6	9 13
24	8 10 47	3 21 53	13 55	21 56	22 12	1 37	17 39	14 1	2 24	11 8	9 13
25	8 14 44	4 22 54	28 0	22 53	23 27	2 21	17 51	13 57	2 24	11 9	9 12
26	8 18 40	5 23 53	12♋32	23 42	24 41	3 5	18 4	13 52	2 25	11 11	9 12
27	8 22 37	6 24 51	27 28	24 22	25 56	3 49	18 16	13 48	2 26	11 12	9 11
28	8 26 33	7 25 48	12♌40	24 54	27 11	4 33	18 29	13 43	2 26	11 14	9 11
29	8 30 30	8 26 45	27 57	25 15	28 26	5 17	18 42	13 39	2 27	11 15	9 10
30	8 34 26	9 27 40	13♍ 7	25R25	29 41	6 1	18 55	13 35	2 27	11 16	9 10
31	8 38 23	10♒28 35	28♍ 1	25♒25	0♓56	6♑45	19♓ 7	13♋31	2♏27	11♐18	9♎ 9

THE SUN ENTERS THE SIGN OF AQUARIUS ON JAN 20 AT 16:37.

DAY	TIME	☉	☽	☿	♀	♂	♃	♄	♅	♆	♇
	h m s	° ' "	° '	° '	° '	° '	° '	° '	° '	° '	° '
F 1	8 42 20	11♒29 29	12♎32	25♒13	2♓11	7♑29	19♓20	13♋27	2♏28	11♐19	9♎ 8
E 2	8 46 16	12 30 22	26 37	24R50	3 25	8 14	19 33	13R23	2 28	11 21	9R 8
B 3	8 50 13	13 31 15	10♏14	24 16	4 40	8 58	19 46	13 19	2 28	11 22	9 7
R 4	8 54 9	14 32 7	23 26	23 32	5 55	9 42	20 0	13 15	2 28	11 23	9 6
U 5	8 58 6	15 32 58	6♐17	22 39	7 10	10 26	20 13	13 11	2 28	11 24	9 5
A 6	9 2 2	16 33 48	18 50	21 39	8 24	11 11	20 26	13 7	2R28	11 26	9 5
R 7	9 5 59	17 34 37	1♑10	20 33	9 39	11 55	20 39	13 4	2 28	11 27	9 4
Y 8	9 9 55	18 35 25	13 19	19 23	10 54	12 40	20 53	13 0	2 28	11 28	9 3
9	9 13 52	19 36 12	25 22	18 12	12 8	13 24	21 6	12 57	2 28	11 29	9 2
10	9 17 49	20 36 58	7♒19	17 0	13 23	14 9	21 20	12 53	2 28	11 30	9 1
11	9 21 45	21 37 43	19 14	15 51	14 37	14 53	21 33	12 50	2 28	11 31	9 0
12	9 25 42	22 38 26	1♓ 6	14 45	15 52	15 38	21 47	12 47	2 28	11 32	8 59
13	9 29 38	23 39 7	12 58	13 45	17 6	16 22	22 0	12 43	2 27	11 33	8 58
14	9 33 35	24 39 48	24 51	12 50	18 21	17 7	22 14	12 40	2 27	11 34	8 57
15	9 37 31	25 40 27	6♈46	12 3	19 35	17 51	22 28	12 37	2 26	11 35	8 56
16	9 41 28	26 41 4	18 47	11 23	20 50	18 36	22 42	12 35	2 26	11 36	8 55
17	9 45 24	27 41 39	0♉56	10 51	22 4	19 21	22 55	12 32	2 25	11 37	8 54
18	9 49 21	28 42 13	13 18	10 26	23 18	20 6	23 9	12 29	2 25	11 38	8 52
19	9 53 17	29 42 45	25 56	10 9	24 33	20 50	23 23	12 27	2 24	11 38	8 51
20	9 57 14	0♓43 15	8♊56	10D 0	25 47	21 35	23 37	12 24	2 23	11 39	8 50
21	10 1 11	1 43 44	22 21	9 58	27 1	22 20	23 51	12 22	2 22	11 40	8 49
22	10 5 7	2 44 10	6♋15	10 2	28 15	23 5	24 5	12 20	2 21	11 41	8 48
23	10 9 4	3 44 35	20 38	10 13	29 29	23 50	24 19	12 17	2 21	11 41	8 46
24	10 13 0	4 44 57	5♌28	10 30	0♈44	24 35	24 33	12 15	2 20	11 42	8 45
25	10 16 57	5 45 18	20 39	10 53	1 58	25 19	24 48	12 13	2 19	11 43	8 44
26	10 20 53	6 45 37	6♍ 1	11 21	3 12	26 4	25 2	12 11	2 18	11 43	8 42
27	10 24 50	7 45 55	21 21	11 54	4 25	26 49	25 16	12 10	2 17	11 44	8 41
28	10 28 46	8♓46 10	6♎29	12♒31	5♈39	27♑34	25♓30	12♋ 8	2♏15	11♐44	8♎40

THE SUN ENTERS THE SIGN OF PISCES ON FEB 19 AT 06:50.

DAY	TIME	☉	☽	☿	♀	♂	♃	♄	♅	♆	♇
	h m s	° ' "	° '	° '	° '	° '	° '	° '	° '	° '	° '
M 1	10 32 43	9♓46 24	21♎16	13♒12	6♈53	28♑19	25♓44	12♋ 7	2♏14	11♐45	8♎38
A 2	10 36 40	10 46 37	5♏34	13 58	8 7	29 4	25 59	12R 5	2R13	11 45	8R37
R 3	10 40 36	11 46 48	19 22	14 47	9 21	29 50	26 13	12 4	2 12	11 46	8 35
C 4	10 44 33	12 46 58	2♐41	15 39	10 34	0♒35	26 27	12 3	2 10	11 46	8 34
H 5	10 48 29	13 47 6	15 34	16 34	11 48	1 20	26 42	12 2	2 9	11 46	8 33
6	10 52 26	14 47 12	28 7	17 32	13 2	2 5	26 56	12 1	2 8	11 47	8 31
7	10 56 22	15 47 17	10♑22	18 33	14 15	2 50	27 11	12 0	2 6	11 47	8 30
8	11 0 19	16 47 21	22 26	19 37	15 29	3 35	27 25	11 59	2 5	11 47	8 28
9	11 4 15	17 47 22	4♒23	20 43	16 42	4 21	27 39	11 58	2 3	11 47	8 27
10	11 8 12	18 47 22	16 15	21 51	17 56	5 6	27 54	11 58	2 1	11 47	8 25
11	11 12 9	19 47 21	28 7	23 1	19 9	5 51	28 8	11 57	2 0	11 48	8 23
12	11 16 5	20 47 17	9♓58	24 13	20 22	6 37	28 23	11 57	1 58	11 48	8 22
13	11 20 2	21 47 11	21 53	25 27	21 36	7 22	28 37	11 57	1 56	11 48	8 20
14	11 23 58	22 47 4	3♈50	26 43	22 49	8 7	28 52	11D57	1 55	11R48	8 19
15	11 27 55	23 46 54	15 53	28 1	24 2	8 53	29 6	11 57	1 53	11 48	8 17
16	11 31 51	24 46 42	28 1	29 20	25 15	9 38	29 21	11 57	1 51	11 48	8 16
17	11 35 48	25 46 29	10♉18	0♓41	26 28	10 24	29 35	11 57	1 49	11 48	8 14
18	11 39 44	26 46 13	22 46	2 4	27 41	11 9	29 50	11 57	1 47	11 48	8 12
19	11 43 41	27 45 55	5♊28	3 28	28 54	11 54	0♈ 4	11 58	1 45	11 47	8 11
20	11 47 38	28 45 35	18 27	4 53	0♉ 7	12 40	0 19	11 58	1 43	11 47	8 9
21	11 51 34	29 45 12	1♋47	6 20	1 20	13 25	0 33	11 59	1 41	11 47	8 7
22	11 55 31	0♈44 47	15 32	7 49	2 32	14 11	0 48	12 0	1 39	11 47	8 6
23	11 59 27	1 44 20	29 41	9 19	3 45	14 56	1 3	12 1	1 37	11 47	8 4
24	12 3 24	2 43 51	14♌15	10 50	4 58	15 42	1 17	12 2	1 35	11 46	8 2
25	12 7 20	3 43 19	29 9	12 23	6 10	16 27	1 32	12 3	1 33	11 46	8 1
26	12 11 17	4 42 45	14♍16	13 57	7 23	17 13	1 46	12 4	1 31	11 46	7 59
27	12 15 13	5 42 9	29 27	15 32	8 35	17 58	2 1	12 6	1 29	11 45	7 57
28	12 19 10	6 41 30	14♎31	17 9	9 47	18 44	2 15	12 7	1 26	11 45	7 56
29	12 23 6	7 40 50	29 18	18 47	10 59	19 30	2 30	12 9	1 24	11 44	7 54
30	12 27 3	8 40 8	13♏42	20 26	12 12	20 15	2 44	12 10	1 22	11 44	7 52
31	12 31 0	9♈39 24	27♏38	22♓ 7	13♉24	21♒ 1	2♈59	12♋12	1♏19	11♐43	7♎51

THE SUN ENTERS THE SIGN OF ARIES ON MAR 21 AT 05:57.

♈ ARIES ♉ TAURUS ♊ GEMINI ♋ CANCER ♌ LEO ♍ VIRGO ♎ LIBRA

1975

SIDEREAL. SUN. MOON. MERCURY. VENUS. MARS. JUPITER. SATURN. URANUS. NEPTUNE. PLUTO.

DAY	TIME	☉	☽	☿	♀	♂	♃	♄	♅	♆	♇
	h m s	° ' "	° '	° '	° '	° '	° '	° '	° '	° '	° '
A 1	12 34 56	10♈38 38	11♐ 5	23♓49	14♉36	21♒46	3♈13	12♋14	1♏17	11♐43	7♎49
P 2	12 38 53	11 37 50	24 6	25 33	15 48	22 32	3 28	12 16	1R15	11R42	7R47
R 3	12 42 49	12 37 1	6♑43	27 18	16 59	23 18	3 42	12 18	1 12	11 42	7 46
I 4	12 46 46	13 36 10	19 2	29 4	18 11	24 3	3 56	12 20	1 10	11 41	7 44
L 5	12 50 42	14 35 17	1♒ 7	0♈52	19 23	24 49	4 11	12 23	1 8	11 40	7 42
6	12 54 39	15 34 22	13 3	2 41	20 35	25 35	4 25	12 25	1 5	11 40	7 41
7	12 58 35	16 33 26	24 55	4 32	21 46	26 21	4 40	12 28	1 3	11 39	7 39
8	13 2 32	17 32 27	6♓46	6 24	22 58	27 6	4 54	12 30	1 0	11 38	7 38
9	13 6 29	18 31 27	18 40	8 18	24 9	27 52	5 8	12 33	0 58	11 37	7 36
10	13 10 25	19 30 25	0♈38	10 13	25 20	28 38	5 23	12 36	0 55	11 36	7 34
11	13 14 22	20 29 21	12 42	12 9	26 31	29 23	5 37	12 39	0 53	11 36	7 33
12	13 18 18	21 28 15	24 55	14 7	27 43	0♓ 9	5 51	12 42	0 50	11 35	7 31
13	13 22 15	22 27 7	7♉17	16 6	28 54	0 55	6 5	12 45	0 48	11 34	7 29
14	13 26 11	23 25 56	19 49	18 7	0♊ 5	1 40	6 20	12 48	0 45	11 33	7 28
15	13 30 8	24 24 44	2♊32	20 9	1 15	2 26	6 34	12 51	0 43	11 32	7 26
16	13 34 4	25 23 30	15 28	22 12	2 26	3 12	6 48	12 55	0 40	11 31	7 25
17	13 38 1	26 22 14	28 38	24 17	3 37	3 58	7 2	12 58	0 38	11 30	7 23
18	13 41 58	27 20 55	12♋ 4	26 22	4 47	4 43	7 16	13 2	0 35	11 29	7 22
19	13 45 54	28 19 34	25 48	28 28	5 58	5 29	7 30	13 6	0 32	11 28	7 20
20	13 49 51	29 18 11	9♌49	0♉35	7 8	6 15	7 44	13 9	0 30	11 27	7 18
21	13 53 47	0♉16 45	24 8	2 43	8 19	7 0	7 58	13 13	0 27	11 26	7 17
22	13 57 44	1 15 18	8♍41	4 51	9 29	7 46	8 12	13 17	0 25	11 25	7 15
23	14 1 40	2 13 48	23 24	6 58	10 39	8 32	8 26	13 21	0 22	11 23	7 14
24	14 5 37	3 12 16	8♎11	9 6	11 49	9 17	8 40	13 25	0 20	11 22	7 13
25	14 9 33	4 10 41	22 54	11 13	12 58	10 3	8 54	13 30	0 17	11 21	7 11
26	14 13 30	5 9 6	7♏26	13 20	14 8	10 49	9 7	13 34	0 15	11 20	7 10
27	14 17 27	6 7 28	21 40	15 25	15 18	11 34	9 21	13 38	0 12	11 19	7 8
28	14 21 23	7 5 48	5♐32	17 29	16 27	12 20	9 35	13 43	0 9	11 17	7 7
29	14 25 20	8 4 7	19 0	19 31	17 37	13 5	9 49	13 47	0 7	11 16	7 5
30	14 29 16	9♉ 2 25	2♑ 4	21♉31	18♊46	13♓51	10♈ 2	13♋52	0♏ 4	11♐15	7♎ 4

THE SUN ENTERS THE SIGN OF TAURUS ON APR 20 AT 17:08.

DAY	TIME	☉	☽	☿	♀	♂	♃	♄	♅	♆	♇
	h m s	° ' "	° '	° '	° '	° '	° '	° '	° '	° '	° '
M 1	14 33 13	10♉ 0 40	14♑46	23♉29	19♊55	14♓37	10♈16	13♋57	0♏ 2	11♐13	7♎ 3
A 2	14 37 9	10 58 55	27 10	25 25	21 4	15 22	10 29	14 2	29♎59	11R12	7R 1
Y 3	14 41 6	11 57 7	9♒18	27 17	22 13	16 8	10 43	14 7	29 57	11 11	7 0
4	14 45 2	12 55 18	21 17	29 7	23 21	16 53	10 56	14 11	29 54	11 9	6 59
5	14 48 59	13 53 28	3♓10	0♊53	24 30	17 39	11 9	14 17	29 52	11 8	6 58
6	14 52 56	14 51 36	15 3	2 36	25 38	18 24	11 23	14 22	29 49	11 7	6 56
7	14 56 52	15 49 43	26 58	4 16	26 47	19 10	11 36	14 27	29 47	11 5	6 55
8	15 0 49	16 47 48	9♈ 1	5 52	27 55	19 55	11 49	14 32	29 45	11 4	6 54
9	15 4 45	17 45 52	21 13	7 24	29 3	20 41	12 2	14 37	29 42	11 2	6 53
10	15 8 42	18 43 54	3♉36	8 53	0♋11	21 26	12 15	14 43	29 40	11 1	6 52
11	15 12 38	19 41 55	16 13	10 17	1 18	22 12	12 28	14 48	29 37	10 59	6 50
12	15 16 35	20 39 55	29 3	11 38	2 26	22 57	12 41	14 54	29 35	10 58	6 49
13	15 20 31	21 37 52	12♊ 8	12 55	3 33	23 43	12 54	15 0	29 33	10 56	6 48
14	15 24 28	22 35 48	25 26	14 8	4 41	24 28	13 7	15 5	29 30	10 55	6 47
15	15 28 25	23 33 43	8♋58	15 17	5 48	25 13	13 20	15 11	29 28	10 53	6 46
16	15 32 21	24 31 36	22 41	16 21	6 55	25 59	13 32	15 17	29 26	10 52	6 45
17	15 36 18	25 29 27	6♌36	17 22	8 2	26 44	13 45	15 23	29 24	10 50	6 44
18	15 40 14	26 27 16	20 41	18 18	9 8	27 29	13 57	15 29	29 22	10 49	6 43
19	15 44 11	27 25 3	4♍53	19 9	10 14	28 14	14 10	15 35	29 19	10 47	6 42
20	15 48 7	28 22 49	19 11	19 57	11 21	28 59	14 22	15 41	29 17	10 46	6 42
21	15 52 4	29 20 33	3♎32	20 40	12 27	29 45	14 34	15 47	29 15	10 44	6 41
22	15 56 0	0♊18 15	17 52	21 18	13 32	0♈30	14 47	15 53	29 13	10 42	6 40
23	15 59 57	1 15 56	2♏ 6	21 52	14 38	1 15	14 59	15 59	29 11	10 41	6 39
24	16 3 54	2 13 35	16 12	22 21	15 43	2 0	15 11	16 6	29 9	10 39	6 38
25	16 7 50	3 11 14	0♐ 5	22 45	16 49	2 45	15 23	16 12	29 7	10 38	6 38
26	16 11 47	4 8 51	13 41	23 4	17 54	3 30	15 35	16 19	29 5	10 36	6 37
27	16 15 43	5 6 26	26 59	23 19	18 58	4 15	15 47	16 25	29 3	10 34	6 36
28	16 19 40	6 4 1	9♑58	23 29	20 3	4 59	15 58	16 32	29 1	10 33	6 35
29	16 23 36	7 1 35	22 39	23R35	21 7	5 44	16 10	16 38	28 59	10 31	6 35
30	16 27 33	7 59 7	5♒ 3	23 36	22 11	6 29	16 22	16 45	28 58	10 30	6 34
31	16 31 29	8♊56 39	17♒13	23♊32	23♋15	7♈14	16♈33	16♋51	28♎56	10♐28	6♎34

THE SUN ENTERS THE SIGN OF GEMINI ON MAY 21 AT 16:24.

DAY	TIME	☉	☽	☿	♀	♂	♃	♄	♅	♆	♇
	h m s	° ' "	° '	° '	° '	° '	° '	° '	° '	° '	° '
J 1	16 35 26	9♊54 10	29♒14	23♊24	24♋18	7♈59	16♈44	16♋58	28♎54	10♐26	6♎33
U 2	16 39 23	10 51 40	11♓ 8	23R11	25 22	8 43	16 56	17 5	28R52	10R25	6R33
N 3	16 43 19	11 49 9	23 2	22 55	26 25	9 28	17 7	17 12	28 51	10 23	6 32
E 4	16 47 16	12 46 37	4♈58	22 35	27 27	10 12	17 18	17 19	28 49	10 21	6 32
5	16 51 12	13 44 5	17 3	22 12	28 30	10 57	17 29	17 25	28 47	10 20	6 31
6	16 55 9	14 41 32	29 19	21 45	29 32	11 41	17 40	17 32	28 46	10 18	6 31
7	16 59 5	15 38 59	11♉50	21 17	0♌34	12 26	17 51	17 39	28 44	10 17	6 31
8	17 3 2	16 36 24	24 40	20 46	1 35	13 10	18 1	17 46	28 43	10 15	6 30
9	17 6 58	17 33 49	7♊47	20 14	2 36	13 55	18 12	17 54	28 42	10 13	6 30
10	17 10 55	18 31 14	21 14	19 40	3 37	14 39	18 23	18 1	28 40	10 12	6 30
11	17 14 52	19 28 37	4♋58	19 7	4 38	15 23	18 33	18 8	28 39	10 10	6 29
12	17 18 48	20 26 0	18 57	18 33	5 38	16 7	18 43	18 15	28 38	10 9	6 29
13	17 22 45	21 23 21	3♌ 6	18 1	6 38	16 51	18 53	18 22	28 36	10 7	6 29
14	17 26 41	22 20 42	17 22	17 29	7 38	17 35	19 4	18 29	28 35	10 5	6 29
15	17 30 38	23 18 2	1♍41	17 0	8 37	18 19	19 13	18 37	28 34	10 4	6 29
16	17 34 34	24 15 20	15 58	16 33	9 35	19 3	19 23	18 44	28 33	10 2	6 29
17	17 38 31	25 12 38	0♎11	16 9	10 34	19 47	19 33	18 51	28 32	10 1	6D29
18	17 42 27	26 9 55	14 18	15 47	11 32	20 31	19 43	18 59	28 31	9 59	6 29
19	17 46 24	27 7 11	28 16	15 30	12 29	21 14	19 52	19 6	28 30	9 58	6 29
20	17 50 21	28 4 26	12♏ 5	15 16	13 26	21 58	20 1	19 14	28 29	9 56	6 29
21	17 54 17	29 1 41	25 44	15 7	14 23	22 42	20 11	19 21	28 28	9 55	6 29
22	17 58 14	29 58 55	9♐11	15D 2	15 19	23 25	20 20	19 29	28 27	9 53	6 29
23	18 2 10	0♋56 9	22 25	15 1	16 14	24 8	20 29	19 36	28 27	9 52	6 29
24	18 6 7	1 53 22	5♑25	15 5	17 9	24 52	20 38	19 44	28 26	9 50	6 30
25	18 10 3	2 50 35	18 12	15 14	18 4	25 35	20 46	19 51	28 25	9 49	6 30
26	18 14 0	3 47 47	0♒45	15 27	18 58	26 18	20 55	19 59	28 25	9 47	6 30
27	18 17 56	4 44 59	13 4	15 46	19 51	27 1	21 3	20 6	28 24	9 46	6 30
28	18 21 53	5 42 11	25 13	16 9	20 44	27 44	21 12	20 14	28 24	9 44	6 31
29	18 25 50	6 39 23	7♓12	16 36	21 36	28 27	21 20	20 22	28 23	9 43	6 31
30	18 29 46	7♋36 36	19♓ 6	17♊ 9	22♌28	29♈10	21♈28	20♋29	28♎23	9♐42	6♎32

THE SUN ENTERS THE SIGN OF CANCER ON JUN 22 AT 00:27.

♏ SCORPIO ♐ SAGITTARIUS ♑ CAPRICORN ♒ AQUARIUS ♓ PISCES

1975

SIDEREAL SUN MOON MERCURY VENUS MARS JUPITER SATURN URANUS NEPTUNE PLUTO

DAY	TIME	☉	☽	☿	♀	♂	♃	♄	♅	♆	♇
	h m s	° ' "	° '	° '	° '	° '	° '	° '	° '	° '	° '
J 1	18 33 43	8♋33 48	0♈58	17♊46	23♌19	29♈53	21♈36	20♋37	28♎22	9♐40	6♎32
U 2	18 37 39	9 31 0	12 54	18 28	24 9	0♉36	21 44	20 45	28R22	9R39	6 33
L 3	18 41 36	10 28 12	24 58	19 14	24 58	1 18	21 51	20 52	28 22	9 37	6 33
Y 4	18 45 32	11 25 25	7♉14	20 5	25 47	2 1	21 59	21 0	28 22	9 36	6 34
5	18 49 29	12 22 38	19 48	21 0	26 35	2 43	22 6	21 8	28 22	9 35	6 34
6	18 53 25	13 19 51	2♊44	22 0	27 23	3 26	22 13	21 15	28 22	9 34	6 35
7	18 57 22	14 17 4	16 3	23 4	28 9	4 8	22 21	21 23	28D21	9 32	6 35
8	19 1 19	15 14 18	29 46	24 12	28 55	4 50	22 27	21 31	28 21	9 31	6 36
9	19 5 15	16 11 32	13♋52	25 25	29 40	5 32	22 34	21 39	28 22	9 30	6 37
10	19 9 12	17 8 46	28 16	26 42	0♍23	6 14	22 41	21 46	28 22	9 29	6 37
11	19 13 8	18 6 0	12♌53	28 2	1 6	6 56	22 47	21 54	28 22	9 27	6 38
12	19 17 5	19 3 13	27 35	29 27	1 48	7 38	22 53	22 2	28 22	9 26	6 39
13	19 21 1	20 0 27	12♍15	0♋56	2 29	8 20	23 0	22 10	28 22	9 25	6 40
14	19 24 58	20 57 41	26 47	2 29	3 9	9 1	23 6	22 18	28 23	9 24	6 41
15	19 28 54	21 54 55	11♎ 5	4 5	3 48	9 43	23 11	22 25	28 23	9 23	6 42
16	19 32 51	22 52 9	25 9	5 46	4 26	10 24	23 17	22 33	28 24	9 22	6 43
17	19 36 48	23 49 23	8♏56	7 29	5 2	11 5	23 22	22 41	28 24	9 21	6 44
18	19 40 44	24 46 37	22 28	9 16	5 38	11 46	23 28	22 49	28 25	9 20	6 45
19	19 44 41	25 43 51	5♐46	11 6	6 12	12 27	23 33	22 57	28 25	9 19	6 46
20	19 48 37	26 41 6	18 51	13 0	6 44	13 8	23 38	23 4	28 26	9 18	6 47
21	19 52 34	27 38 21	1♑43	14 55	7 16	13 49	23 43	23 12	28 27	9 17	6 48
22	19 56 30	28 35 36	14 25	16 54	7 45	14 30	23 47	23 20	28 27	9 16	6 49
23	20 0 27	29 32 51	26 56	18 54	8 14	15 10	23 52	23 28	28 28	9 15	6 50
24	20 4 24	0♌30 8	9♒16	20 56	8 40	15 51	23 56	23 35	28 29	9 14	6 51
25	20 8 20	1 27 24	21 28	23 0	9 6	16 31	24 0	23 43	28 30	9 13	6 52
26	20 12 17	2 24 42	3♓30	25 5	9 29	17 11	24 4	23 51	28 31	9 12	6 53
27	20 16 13	3 22 0	15 27	27 11	9 51	17 51	24 8	23 59	28 32	9 12	6 55
28	20 20 10	4 19 19	27 18	29 17	10 11	18 31	24 11	24 6	28 33	9 11	6 56
29	20 24 6	5 16 39	9♈ 9	1♌24	10 29	19 11	24 14	24 14	28 34	9 10	6 57
30	20 28 3	6 14 0	21 3	3 30	10 46	19 51	24 18	24 22	28 35	9 9	6 59
31	20 31 59	7♌11 22	3♉ 4	5♌37	11♍ 0	20♉30	24♈21	24♋29	28♎36	9♐ 9	7♎ 0

THE SUN ENTERS THE SIGN OF LEO ON JUL 23 AT 11:23.

DAY	TIME	☉	☽	☿	♀	♂	♃	♄	♅	♆	♇
	h m s	° ' "	° '	° '	° '	° '	° '	° '	° '	° '	° '
A 1	20 35 56	8♌ 8 45	15♉19	7♌42	11♍12	21♉10	24♈23	24♋37	28♎38	9♐ 8	7♎ 1
U 2	20 39 52	9 6 9	27 51	9 47	11 23	21 49	24 26	24 45	28 39	9R 7	7 3
G 3	20 43 49	10 3 35	10♊46	11 52	11 31	22 28	24 28	24 52	28 40	9 7	7 4
U 4	20 47 46	11 1 1	24 8	13 55	11 37	23 7	24 31	25 0	28 42	9 6	7 6
S 5	20 51 42	11 58 29	7♋57	15 57	11 41	23 46	24 33	25 7	28 43	9 6	7 7
T 6	20 55 39	12 55 58	22 15	17 57	11R43	24 24	24 35	25 15	28 45	9 5	7 9
7	20 59 35	13 53 28	6♌56	19 56	11 42	25 3	24 36	25 23	28 46	9 5	7 10
8	21 3 32	14 50 59	21 54	21 54	11 39	25 41	24 38	25 30	28 48	9 4	7 12
9	21 7 28	15 48 31	6♍59	23 51	11 34	26 19	24 39	25 38	28 49	9 4	7 13
10	21 11 25	16 46 4	22 1	25 46	11 26	26 57	24 40	25 45	28 51	9 3	7 15
11	21 15 21	17 43 38	6♎51	27 39	11 16	27 35	24 41	25 52	28 53	9 3	7 17
12	21 19 18	18 41 12	21 23	29 31	11 4	28 13	24 41	26 0	28 55	9 3	7 18
13	21 23 15	19 38 48	5♏33	1♍22	10 49	28 50	24 42	26 7	28 57	9 3	7 20
14	21 27 11	20 36 24	19 21	3 11	10 32	29 28	24R42	26 15	28 58	9 2	7 22
15	21 31 8	21 34 2	2♐46	4 58	10 12	0♊ 5	24 42	26 22	29 0	9 2	7 24
16	21 35 4	22 31 40	15 53	6 44	9 50	0 42	24 42	26 29	29 2	9 2	7 25
17	21 39 1	23 29 20	28 43	8 29	9 26	1 19	24 42	26 36	29 4	9 2	7 27
18	21 42 57	24 27 0	11♑20	10 12	9 0	1 55	24 41	26 44	29 6	9 2	7 29
19	21 46 54	25 24 42	23 46	11 54	8 33	2 32	24 40	26 51	29 9	9 1	7 31
20	21 50 51	26 22 24	6♒ 2	13 34	8 3	3 8	24 40	26 58	29 11	9 1	7 33
21	21 54 47	27 20 8	18 11	15 12	7 32	3 44	24 38	27 5	29 13	9D 1	7 34
22	21 58 44	28 17 54	0♓14	16 50	6 59	4 20	24 37	27 12	29 15	9 1	7 36
23	22 2 40	29 15 40	12 10	18 26	6 25	4 56	24 36	27 19	29 17	9 1	7 38
24	22 6 37	0♍13 28	24 3	20 0	5 49	5 31	24 34	27 26	29 20	9 1	7 40
25	22 10 33	1 11 18	5♈53	21 34	5 13	6 6	24 32	27 33	29 22	9 2	7 42
26	22 14 30	2 9 9	17 44	23 5	4 36	6 41	24 30	27 40	29 25	9 2	7 44
27	22 18 26	3 7 3	29 37	24 36	3 59	7 16	24 28	27 47	29 27	9 2	7 46
28	22 22 23	4 4 57	11♉38	26 5	3 22	7 51	24 25	27 54	29 29	9 2	7 48
29	22 26 19	5 2 54	23 51	27 32	2 45	8 25	24 22	28 0	29 32	9 2	7 50
30	22 30 16	6 0 53	6♊20	28 59	2 8	8 59	24 19	28 7	29 35	9 2	7 52
31	22 34 13	6♍58 53	19♊11	0♎23	1♍32	9♊33	24♈16	28♋14	29♎37	9♐ 3	7♎54

THE SUN ENTERS THE SIGN OF VIRGO ON AUG 23 AT 18:24.

DAY	TIME	☉	☽	☿	♀	♂	♃	♄	♅	♆	♇
	h m s	° ' "	° '	° '	° '	° '	° '	° '	° '	° '	° '
S 1	22 38 9	7♍56 55	2♋28	1♎47	0♍56	10♊ 7	24♈13	28♋20	29♎40	9♐ 3	7♎56
E 2	22 42 6	8 55 0	16 15	3 8	0R22	10 40	24R10	28 27	29 43	9 3	7 58
P 3	22 46 2	9 53 6	0♌31	4 29	29♌48	11 13	24 6	28 34	29 45	9 4	8 0
T 4	22 49 59	10 51 14	15 14	5 47	29 17	11 46	24 2	28 40	29 48	9 4	8 2
E 5	22 53 55	11 49 24	0♍19	7 5	28 46	12 19	23 58	28 46	29 51	9 5	8 5
M 6	22 57 52	12 47 35	15 35	8 20	28 18	12 51	23 54	28 53	29 54	9 5	8 7
B 7	23 1 48	13 45 48	0♎52	9 34	27 51	13 24	23 50	28 59	29 56	9 6	8 9
E 8	23 5 45	14 44 3	15 58	10 46	27 27	13 55	23 45	29 5	29 59	9 6	8 11
R 9	23 9 42	15 42 20	0♏45	11 56	27 4	14 27	23 40	29 12	0♏ 2	9 7	8 13
10	23 13 38	16 40 38	15 7	13 4	26 44	14 58	23 35	29 18	0 5	9 7	8 15
11	23 17 35	17 38 58	29 2	14 10	26 26	15 29	23 30	29 24	0 8	9 8	8 18
12	23 21 31	18 37 19	12♐31	15 13	26 10	16 0	23 25	29 30	0 11	9 9	8 20
13	23 25 28	19 35 42	25 37	16 15	25 57	16 31	23 20	29 36	0 14	9 10	8 22
14	23 29 24	20 34 6	8♑22	17 14	25 46	17 1	23 14	29 42	0 17	9 10	8 24
15	23 33 21	21 32 32	20 51	18 10	25 37	17 30	23 8	29 47	0 21	9 11	8 27
16	23 37 17	22 30 59	3♒ 7	19 3	25 31	18 0	23 3	29 53	0 24	9 12	8 29
17	23 41 14	23 29 29	15 14	19 53	25 27	18 29	22 57	29 59	0 27	9 13	8 31
18	23 45 11	24 27 59	27 14	20 40	25D26	18 58	22 50	0♌ 4	0 30	9 14	8 33
19	23 49 7	25 26 32	9♓10	21 24	25 27	19 26	22 44	0 10	0 33	9 14	8 36
20	23 53 4	26 25 7	21 3	22 3	25 30	19 55	22 38	0 15	0 37	9 15	8 38
21	23 57 0	27 23 43	2♈54	22 39	25 36	20 22	22 31	0 21	0 40	9 16	8 40
22	0 0 57	28 22 21	14 46	23 10	25 44	20 50	22 25	0 26	0 43	9 17	8 42
23	0 4 53	29 21 2	26 39	23 36	25 54	21 17	22 18	0 31	0 46	9 18	8 45
24	0 8 50	0♎19 44	8♉37	23 57	26 6	21 44	22 11	0 37	0 50	9 19	8 47
25	0 12 46	1 18 29	20 42	24 13	26 20	22 10	22 4	0 42	0 53	9 20	8 49
26	0 16 43	2 17 16	2♊58	24R22	26 36	22 36	21 57	0 47	0 57	9 22	8 52
27	0 20 39	3 16 5	15 29	24 25	26 55	23 2	21 49	0 52	1 0	9 23	8 54
28	0 24 36	4 14 57	28 18	24 22	27 15	23 27	21 42	0 57	1 3	9 24	8 56
29	0 28 33	5 13 50	11♋30	24 11	27 37	23 52	21 35	1 1	1 7	9 25	8 59
30	0 32 29	6♎12 46	25♋ 9	23♎54	28♌ 1	24♊16	21♈27	1♌ 6	1♏10	9♐26	9♎ 1

THE SUN ENTERS THE SIGN OF LIBRA ON SEP 23 AT 15:56.

♈ ARIES ♉ TAURUS ♊ GEMINI ♋ CANCER ♌ LEO ♍ VIRGO ♎ LIBRA

1975

SIDEREAL SUN. MOON. MERCURY. VENUS. MARS. JUPITER. SATURN. URANUS. NEPTUNE. PLUTO.

DAY	TIME	☉	☽	☿	♀	♂	♃	♄	♅	♆	♇
	h m s	° ' "	° '	° '	° '	° '	° '	° '	° '	° '	° '
O 1	0 36 26	7♎11 45	9♌15	23♎28	28♌27	24♊40	21♈20	1♌11	1♏14	9♐28	9♎ 3
C 2	0 40 22	8 10 45	23 47	22R55	28 54	25 3	21R12	1 15	1 18	9 29	9 6
T 3	0 44 19	9 9 48	8♍42	22 14	29 23	25 26	21 4	1 20	1 21	9 30	9 8
O 4	0 48 15	10 8 53	23 52	21 26	29 53	25 49	20 56	1 24	1 25	9 31	9 10
B 5	0 52 12	11 8 1	9♎ 7	20 32	0♍25	26 11	20 49	1 28	1 28	9 33	9 13
E 6	0 56 8	12 7 10	24 17	19 31	0 58	26 32	20 41	1 33	1 32	9 34	9 15
R 7	1 0 5	13 6 21	9♏11	18 25	1 33	26 53	20 33	1 37	1 35	9 36	9 17
8	1 4 2	14 5 34	23 43	17 17	2 9	27 14	20 25	1 41	1 39	9 37	9 20
9	1 7 58	15 4 49	7♐49	16 6	2 46	27 34	20 17	1 45	1 43	9 39	9 22
10	1 11 55	16 4 6	21 26	14 55	3 25	27 53	20 9	1 48	1 46	9 40	9 24
11	1 15 51	17 3 25	4♑38	13 47	4 5	28 12	20 0	1 52	1 50	9 42	9 27
12	1 19 48	18 2 45	17 26	12 42	4 45	28 31	19 52	1 56	1 54	9 43	9 29
13	1 23 44	19 2 7	29 55	11 43	5 27	28 49	19 44	1 59	1 57	9 45	9 31
14	1 27 41	20 1 31	12♒ 8	10 52	6 10	29 6	19 36	2 3	2 1	9 46	9 34
15	1 31 37	21 0 57	24 11	10 10	6 54	29 23	19 28	2 6	2 5	9 48	9 36
16	1 35 34	22 0 24	6♓ 7	9 38	7 39	29 39	19 20	2 9	2 9	9 50	9 38
17	1 39 31	22 59 54	17 59	9 17	8 26	29 54	19 12	2 13	2 12	9 51	9 40
18	1 43 27	23 59 25	29 50	9D 6	9 12	0♋ 9	19 4	2 16	2 16	9 53	9 43
19	1 47 24	24 58 58	11♈42	9 7	10 0	0 24	18 56	2 19	2 20	9 55	9 45
20	1 51 20	25 58 33	23 38	9 19	10 49	0 37	18 48	2 22	2 23	9 56	9 47
21	1 55 17	26 58 10	5♉39	9 41	11 39	0 50	18 40	2 24	2 27	9 58	9 49
22	1 59 13	27 57 49	17 47	10 13	12 29	1 3	18 32	2 27	2 31	10 0	9 52
23	2 3 10	28 57 30	0♊ 4	10 54	13 20	1 15	18 24	2 30	2 35	10 2	9 54
24	2 7 6	29 57 14	12 32	11 43	14 12	1 26	18 16	2 32	2 39	10 3	9 56
25	2 11 3	0♏56 59	25 12	12 40	15 4	1 36	18 9	2 34	2 42	10 5	9 58
26	2 14 59	1 56 47	8♋ 8	13 43	15 58	1 45	18 1	2 37	2 46	10 7	10 1
27	2 18 56	2 56 37	21 22	14 52	16 52	1 54	17 53	2 39	2 50	10 9	10 3
28	2 22 53	3 56 29	4♌56	16 6	17 46	2 2	17 46	2 41	2 54	10 11	10 5
29	2 26 49	4 56 24	18 51	17 25	18 42	2 10	17 39	2 43	2 57	10 13	10 7
30	2 30 46	5 56 20	3♍ 8	18 47	19 37	2 16	17 31	2 45	3 1	10 15	10 9
31	2 34 42	6♏56 19	17♍42	20♎12	20♍34	2♋22	17♈24	2♌46	3♏ 5	10♐17	10♎11

THE SUN ENTERS THE SIGN OF SCORPIO ON OCT 24 AT 01:08.

DAY	TIME	☉	☽	☿	♀	♂	♃	♄	♅	♆	♇
	h m s	° ' "	° '	° '	° '	° '	° '	° '	° '	° '	° '
N 1	2 38 39	7♏56 20	2♎31	21♎40	21♍31	2♋27	17♈17	2♌48	3♏ 9	10♐19	10♎14
O 2	2 42 35	8 56 23	17 28	23 10	22 28	2 31	17R10	2 49	3 12	10 21	10 16
V 3	2 46 32	9 56 28	2♏24	24 42	23 26	2 35	17 3	2 51	3 16	10 23	10 18
E 4	2 50 28	10 56 35	17 11	26 15	24 25	2 37	16 56	2 52	3 20	10 25	10 20
M 5	2 54 25	11 56 44	1♐41	27 49	25 24	2 39	16 50	2 53	3 24	10 27	10 22
B 6	2 58 22	12 56 55	15 50	29 24	26 23	2R40	16 43	2 54	3 27	10 29	10 24
E 7	3 2 18	13 57 7	29 34	1♏ 0	27 23	2 40	16 37	2 55	3 31	10 31	10 26
R 8	3 6 15	14 57 21	12♑53	2 36	28 24	2 39	16 31	2 56	3 35	10 33	10 28
9	3 10 11	15 57 36	25 47	4 13	29 25	2 37	16 25	2 57	3 39	10 35	10 30
10	3 14 8	16 57 53	8♒20	5 50	0♎26	2 35	16 19	2 57	3 42	10 37	10 32
11	3 18 4	17 58 11	20 36	7 27	1 28	2 31	16 13	2 58	3 46	10 39	10 34
12	3 22 1	18 58 31	2♓39	9 4	2 30	2 27	16 7	2 58	3 50	10 41	10 36
13	3 25 57	19 58 52	14 33	10 41	3 32	2 22	16 2	2 58	3 53	10 43	10 38
14	3 29 54	20 59 14	26 24	12 18	4 35	2 16	15 56	2R59	3 57	10 46	10 40
15	3 33 51	21 59 38	8♈15	13 55	5 38	2 9	15 51	2 59	4 1	10 48	10 42
16	3 37 47	23 0 3	20 10	15 31	6 41	2 1	15 46	2 58	4 4	10 50	10 43
17	3 41 44	24 0 30	2♉12	17 8	7 45	1 52	15 42	2 58	4 8	10 52	10 45
18	3 45 40	25 0 58	14 23	18 44	8 49	1 43	15 37	2 58	4 11	10 54	10 47
19	3 49 37	26 1 28	26 45	20 20	9 54	1 32	15 33	2 58	4 15	10 56	10 49
20	3 53 33	27 2 0	9♊19	21 56	10 58	1 21	15 28	2 57	4 19	10 59	10 51
21	3 57 30	28 2 33	22 6	23 32	12 3	1 9	15 24	2 56	4 22	11 1	10 52
22	4 1 26	29 3 7	5♋ 7	25 8	13 9	0 56	15 20	2 56	4 26	11 3	10 54
23	4 5 23	0♐ 3 44	18 21	26 43	14 14	0 42	15 17	2 55	4 29	11 5	10 56
24	4 9 20	1 4 21	1♌48	28 18	15 20	0 28	15 13	2 54	4 33	11 8	10 58
25	4 13 16	2 5 1	15 29	29 53	16 27	0 12	15 10	2 53	4 36	11 10	10 59
26	4 17 13	3 5 42	29 22	1♐28	17 33	29♊56	15 7	2 52	4 40	11 12	11 1
27	4 21 9	4 6 25	13♍27	3 3	18 40	29 39	15 4	2 50	4 43	11 14	11 2
28	4 25 6	5 7 9	27 43	4 37	19 47	29 22	15 1	2 49	4 46	11 17	11 4
29	4 29 2	6 7 55	12♎ 7	6 12	20 54	29 4	14 59	2 47	4 50	11 19	11 6
30	4 32 59	7♐ 8 43	26♎36	7♐46	22♎ 1	28♊45	14♈56	2♌46	4♏53	11♐21	11♎ 7

THE SUN ENTERS THE SIGN OF SAGITTARIUS ON NOV 22 AT 22:32.

DAY	TIME	☉	☽	☿	♀	♂	♃	♄	♅	♆	♇
	h m s	° ' "	° '	° '	° '	° '	° '	° '	° '	° '	° '
D 1	4 36 55	8♐ 9 32	11♏ 5	9♐20	23♎ 9	28♊25	14♈54	2♌44	4♏56	11♐23	11♎ 9
E 2	4 40 52	9 10 22	25 30	10 54	24 17	28R 5	14R52	2R42	5 0	11 26	11 10
C 3	4 44 49	10 11 14	9♐43	12 29	25 25	27 45	14 51	2 40	5 3	11 28	11 11
E 4	4 48 45	11 12 7	23 42	14 3	26 33	27 24	14 49	2 38	5 6	11 30	11 13
M 5	4 52 42	12 13 0	7♑22	15 37	27 41	27 2	14 48	2 36	5 9	11 32	11 14
B 6	4 56 38	13 13 55	20 41	17 11	28 50	26 40	14 47	2 34	5 13	11 35	11 16
E 7	5 0 35	14 14 51	3♒38	18 45	29 59	26 18	14 46	2 31	5 16	11 37	11 17
R 8	5 4 31	15 15 47	16 14	20 19	1♏ 8	25 55	14 45	2 29	5 19	11 39	11 18
9	5 8 28	16 16 44	28 33	21 53	2 17	25 32	14 45	2 26	5 22	11 41	11 19
10	5 12 25	17 17 42	10♓37	23 27	3 26	25 9	14D45	2 24	5 25	11 44	11 21
11	5 16 21	18 18 40	22 32	25 1	4 35	24 46	14 45	2 21	5 28	11 46	11 22
12	5 20 18	19 19 39	4♈23	26 35	5 45	24 22	14 45	2 18	5 31	11 48	11 23
13	5 24 14	20 20 39	16 14	28 9	6 55	23 59	14 45	2 15	5 34	11 50	11 24
14	5 28 11	21 21 39	28 10	29 44	8 4	23 35	14 46	2 12	5 37	11 53	11 25
15	5 32 7	22 22 40	10♉16	1♑18	9 14	23 12	14 47	2 9	5 40	11 55	11 26
16	5 36 4	23 23 41	22 35	2 52	10 25	22 48	14 48	2 6	5 43	11 57	11 27
17	5 40 0	24 24 43	5♊10	4 27	11 35	22 25	14 49	2 2	5 45	11 59	11 28
18	5 43 57	25 25 46	18 2	6 1	12 45	22 2	14 51	1 59	5 48	12 2	11 29
19	5 47 54	26 26 49	1♋12	7 35	13 56	21 39	14 52	1 55	5 51	12 4	11 30
20	5 51 50	27 27 53	14 39	9 10	15 7	21 17	14 54	1 52	5 54	12 6	11 31
21	5 55 47	28 28 57	28 20	10 44	16 17	20 55	14 56	1 48	5 56	12 8	11 32
22	5 59 43	29 30 2	12♌12	12 18	17 28	20 33	14 58	1 45	5 59	12 10	11 33
23	6 3 40	0♑31 8	26 12	13 52	18 39	20 11	15 1	1 41	6 2	12 13	11 34
24	6 7 36	1 32 14	10♍18	15 25	19 50	19 50	15 4	1 37	6 4	12 15	11 34
25	6 11 33	2 33 21	24 25	16 58	21 2	19 30	15 6	1 33	6 7	12 17	11 35
26	6 15 29	3 34 29	8♎34	18 31	22 13	19 10	15 10	1 29	6 9	12 19	11 36
27	6 19 26	4 35 37	22 41	20 3	23 25	18 50	15 13	1 25	6 11	12 21	11 37
28	6 23 23	5 36 46	6♏45	21 34	24 36	18 31	15 16	1 21	6 14	12 23	11 37
29	6 27 19	6 37 56	20 46	23 4	25 48	18 13	15 20	1 17	6 16	12 25	11 38
30	6 31 16	7 39 6	4♐41	24 34	27 0	17 55	15 24	1 12	6 18	12 27	11 38
31	6 35 12	8♑40 16	18♐29	26♑ 1	28♏11	17♊39	15♈28	1♌ 8	6♏21	12♐30	11♎39

THE SUN ENTERS THE SIGN OF CAPRICORN ON DEC 22 AT 11:46.

♏ SCORPIO ♐ SAGITTARIUS ♑ CAPRICORN ♒ AQUARIUS ♓ PISCES

1976

SIDEREAL SUN... MOON... MERCURY VENUS... MARS... JUPITER. SATURN.. URANUS. NEPTUNE. PLUTO.

DAY	TIME	☉	☽	☿	♀	♂	♃	♄	♅	♆	♇
	h m s	° ' "	° '	° '	° '	° '	° '	° '	° '	° '	° '
J 1	6 39 9	9♑41 27	2♑ 6	27♑27	29♏23	17♊22	15♈32	1♌ 4	6♏23	12♐32	11♎39
A 2	6 43 5	10 42 38	15 29	28 51	0♐35	17R 7	15 36	0R59	6 25	12 34	11 40
N 3	6 47 2	11 43 48	28 37	0♒12	1 47	16 52	15 41	0 55	6 27	12 36	11 40
U 4	6 50 58	12 44 59	11♒28	1 30	2 59	16 38	15 46	0 50	6 29	12 38	11 41
A 5	6 54 55	13 46 10	24 2	2 45	4 12	16 25	15 51	0 46	6 31	12 40	11 41
R 6	6 58 52	14 47 20	6♓20	3 56	5 24	16 12	15 56	0 41	6 33	12 42	11 41
Y 7	7 2 48	15 48 30	18 24	5 1	6 36	16 1	16 1	0 36	6 35	12 44	11 42
8	7 6 45	16 49 40	0♈19	6 1	7 49	15 50	16 7	0 32	6 37	12 46	11 42
9	7 10 41	17 50 49	12 9	6 55	9 1	15 40	16 13	0 27	6 39	12 48	11 42
10	7 14 38	18 51 58	23 58	7 42	10 14	15 31	16 19	0 22	6 41	12 50	11 42
11	7 18 34	19 53 6	5♉53	8 20	11 26	15 22	16 25	0 17	6 42	12 51	11 42
12	7 22 31	20 54 14	17 59	8 49	12 39	15 15	16 31	0 12	6 44	12 53	11 43
13	7 26 27	21 55 21	0♊21	9 9	13 52	15 8	16 37	0 8	6 45	12 55	11 43
14	7 30 24	22 56 28	13 2	9R18	15 4	15 2	16 44	0 3	6 47	12 57	11R43
15	7 34 21	23 57 34	26 6	9 15	16 17	14 57	16 51	29♋58	6 49	12 59	11 43
16	7 38 17	24 58 39	9♋34	9 1	17 30	14 53	16 57	29 53	6 50	13 1	11 43
17	7 42 14	25 59 44	23 24	8 35	18 43	14 50	17 4	29 48	6 51	13 3	11 43
18	7 46 10	27 0 49	7♌32	7 57	19 56	14 47	17 12	29 43	6 53	13 4	11 42
19	7 50 7	28 1 53	21 54	7 9	21 9	14 45	17 19	29 38	6 54	13 6	11 42
20	7 54 3	29 2 56	6♍23	6 11	22 22	14D44	17 27	29 33	6 55	13 8	11 42
21	7 58 0	0♒ 3 59	20 52	5 5	23 35	14 44	17 34	29 28	6 56	13 9	11 42
22	8 1 56	1 5 2	5♎16	3 54	24 48	14 44	17 42	29 23	6 58	13 11	11 42
23	8 5 53	2 6 4	19 32	2 38	26 1	14 46	17 50	29 18	6 59	13 13	11 41
24	8 9 50	3 7 6	3♏37	1 21	27 15	14 47	17 58	29 13	7 0	13 14	11 41
25	8 13 46	4 8 8	17 30	0 5	28 28	14 50	18 7	29 9	7 1	13 16	11 41
26	8 17 43	5 9 9	1♐13	28♑52	29 41	14 54	18 15	29 4	7 2	13 18	11 40
27	8 21 39	6 10 9	14 45	27 43	0♑55	14 58	18 24	28 59	7 2	13 19	11 40
28	8 25 36	7 11 9	28 7	26 41	2 8	15 3	18 32	28 54	7 3	13 21	11 39
29	8 29 32	8 12 8	11♑19	25 47	3 21	15 8	18 41	28 49	7 4	13 22	11 39
30	8 33 29	9 13 7	24 19	25 1	4 35	15 14	18 50	28 44	7 5	13 24	11 38
31	8 37 25	10♒14 4	7♒ 9	24♑24	5♑48	15♊21	18♈59	28♋39	7♏ 5	13♐25	11♎38

THE SUN ENTERS THE SIGN OF AQUARIUS ON JAN 20 AT 22:26.

DAY	TIME	☉	☽	☿	♀	♂	♃	♄	♅	♆	♇
	h m s	° ' "	° '	° '	° '	° '	° '	° '	° '	° '	° '
F 1	8 41 22	11♒15 1	19♒46	23♑55	7♑ 2	15♊29	19♈ 8	28♋35	7♏ 6	13♐26	11♎37
E 2	8 45 19	12 15 56	2♓10	23R35	8 15	15 37	19 18	28R30	7 6	13 28	11R37
B 3	8 49 15	13 16 50	14 22	23D23	9 29	15 46	19 27	28 25	7 7	13 29	11 36
R 4	8 53 12	14 17 43	26 23	23 20	10 42	15 55	19 37	28 21	7 7	13 31	11 35
U 5	8 57 8	15 18 35	8♈15	23 24	11 56	16 5	19 47	28 16	7 8	13 32	11 35
A 6	9 1 5	16 19 25	20 3	23 35	13 10	16 16	19 57	28 11	7 8	13 33	11 34
R 7	9 5 1	17 20 14	1♉51	23 53	14 23	16 27	20 7	28 7	7 8	13 34	11 33
Y 8	9 8 58	18 21 2	13 44	24 16	15 37	16 39	20 17	28 2	7 8	13 36	11 32
9	9 12 54	19 21 48	25 47	24 46	16 51	16 51	20 27	27 58	7 9	13 37	11 31
10	9 16 51	20 22 32	8♊ 6	25 20	18 4	17 4	20 37	27 53	7R 9	13 38	11 31
11	9 20 48	21 23 15	20 47	25 59	19 18	17 17	20 48	27 49	7 9	13 39	11 30
12	9 24 44	22 23 56	3♋52	26 42	20 32	17 31	20 58	27 45	7 9	13 40	11 29
13	9 28 41	23 24 36	17 26	27 30	21 45	17 46	21 9	27 41	7 9	13 41	11 28
14	9 32 37	24 25 14	1♌27	28 21	22 59	18 1	21 20	27 37	7 8	13 42	11 27
15	9 36 34	25 25 51	15 53	29 15	24 13	18 16	21 31	27 32	7 8	13 43	11 26
16	9 40 30	26 26 26	0♍37	0♒12	25 27	18 32	21 42	27 28	7 8	13 44	11 25
17	9 44 27	27 26 59	15 32	1 12	26 41	18 48	21 53	27 25	7 8	13 45	11 24
18	9 48 23	28 27 32	0♎28	2 15	27 54	19 5	22 4	27 21	7 7	13 46	11 23
19	9 52 20	29 28 2	15 17	3 20	29 8	19 22	22 16	27 17	7 7	13 47	11 22
20	9 56 17	0♓28 32	29 51	4 27	0♒22	19 40	22 27	27 13	7 6	13 48	11 20
21	10 0 13	1 29 0	14♏ 8	5 37	1 36	19 58	22 38	27 9	7 6	13 49	11 19
22	10 4 10	2 29 27	28 6	6 48	2 50	20 16	22 50	27 6	7 5	13 49	11 18
23	10 8 6	3 29 53	11♐45	8 1	4 4	20 35	23 2	27 2	7 5	13 50	11 17
24	10 12 3	4 30 18	25 6	9 16	5 18	20 54	23 14	26 59	7 4	13 51	11 16
25	10 15 59	5 30 41	8♑13	10 33	6 31	21 14	23 25	26 56	7 3	13 52	11 14
26	10 19 56	6 31 2	21 5	11 51	7 45	21 34	23 37	26 52	7 2	13 52	11 13
27	10 23 52	7 31 23	3♒47	13 11	8 59	21 54	23 49	26 49	7 2	13 53	11 12
28	10 27 49	8 31 41	16 17	14 32	10 13	22 15	24 2	26 46	7 1	13 53	11 11
29	10 31 46	9♓31 58	28♒37	15♒54	11♒27	22♊36	24♈14	26♋43	7♏ 0	13♐54	11♎ 9

THE SUN ENTERS THE SIGN OF PISCES ON FEB 19 AT 12:41.

DAY	TIME	☉	☽	☿	♀	♂	♃	♄	♅	♆	♇
	h m s	° ' "	° '	° '	° '	° '	° '	° '	° '	° '	° '
M 1	10 35 42	10♓32 13	10♓48	17♒18	12♒41	22♊57	24♈26	26♋40	6♏59	13♐55	11♎ 8
A 2	10 39 39	11 32 26	22 51	18 43	13 55	23 19	24 38	26R38	6R58	13 55	11R 6
R 3	10 43 35	12 32 38	4♈46	20 9	15 9	23 41	24 51	26 35	6 57	13 56	11 5
C 4	10 47 32	13 32 47	16 36	21 37	16 23	24 4	25 3	26 32	6 55	13 56	11 4
H 5	10 51 28	14 32 55	28 22	23 6	17 37	24 26	25 16	26 30	6 54	13 56	11 2
6	10 55 25	15 33 1	10♉10	24 36	18 51	24 49	25 29	26 27	6 53	13 57	11 1
7	10 59 21	16 33 4	22 2	26 7	20 5	25 12	25 41	26 25	6 52	13 57	10 59
8	11 3 18	17 33 6	4♊ 4	27 39	21 19	25 36	25 54	26 23	6 50	13 57	10 58
9	11 7 14	18 33 5	16 20	29 13	22 33	26 0	26 7	26 21	6 49	13 58	10 56
10	11 11 11	19 33 2	28 56	0♓47	23 47	26 24	26 20	26 19	6 48	13 58	10 55
11	11 15 8	20 32 57	11♋57	2 23	25 1	26 48	26 33	26 17	6 46	13 58	10 53
12	11 19 4	21 32 50	25 26	4 0	26 15	27 13	26 46	26 15	6 45	13 58	10 52
13	11 23 1	22 32 40	9♌25	5 38	27 29	27 38	26 59	26 14	6 43	13 58	10 50
14	11 26 57	23 32 29	23 52	7 18	28 43	28 3	27 12	26 12	6 42	13 58	10 49
15	11 30 54	24 32 15	8♍43	8 58	29 57	28 28	27 25	26 11	6 40	13R58	10 47
16	11 34 50	25 31 59	23 49	10 40	1♓11	28 54	27 39	26 9	6 38	13 58	10 45
17	11 38 47	26 31 41	9♎ 2	12 23	2 25	29 20	27 52	26 8	6 36	13 58	10 44
18	11 42 43	27 31 21	24 11	14 7	3 39	29 46	28 5	26 7	6 35	13 58	10 42
19	11 46 40	28 31 0	9♏ 6	15 52	4 53	0♋12	28 19	26 6	6 33	13 58	10 41
20	11 50 37	29 30 36	23 42	17 39	6 7	0 38	28 32	26 5	6 31	13 58	10 39
21	11 54 33	0♈30 11	7♐54	19 27	7 21	1 5	28 46	26 4	6 29	13 58	10 37
22	11 58 30	1 29 44	21 41	21 16	8 35	1 32	28 59	26 3	6 27	13 58	10 36
23	12 2 26	2 29 16	5♑ 5	23 6	9 49	1 59	29 13	26 3	6 25	13 57	10 34
24	12 6 23	3 28 46	18 8	24 58	11 3	2 26	29 27	26 2	6 23	13 57	10 32
25	12 10 19	4 28 14	0♒52	26 51	12 17	2 53	29 40	26 2	6 21	13 57	10 31
26	12 14 16	5 27 40	13 22	28 45	13 31	3 21	29 54	26 2	6 19	13 57	10 29
27	12 18 12	6 27 4	25 39	0♈41	14 45	3 49	0♉ 8	26D 2	6 17	13 56	10 27
28	12 22 9	7 26 26	7♓46	2 37	15 59	4 17	0 22	26 2	6 15	13 56	10 26
29	12 26 6	8 25 47	19 46	4 35	17 13	4 45	0 35	26 2	6 13	13 55	10 24
30	12 30 2	9 25 5	1♈40	6 34	18 27	5 13	0 49	26 2	6 11	13 55	10 22
31	12 33 59	10♈24 22	13♈30	8♈35	19♓41	5♋42	1♉ 3	26♋ 2	6♏ 9	13♐55	10♎21

THE SUN ENTERS THE SIGN OF ARIES ON MAR 20 AT 11:50.

♈ ARIES ♉ TAURUS ♊ GEMINI ♋ CANCER ♌ LEO ♍ VIRGO ♎ LIBRA

SIDEREAL . SUN . MOON . MERCURY . VENUS . MARS . JUPITER . SATURN . URANUS . NEPTUNE . PLUTO .

DAY	TIME	☉	☽	☿	♀	♂	♃	♄	♅	♆	♇
	h m s	° ' "	° '	° '	° '	° '	° '	° '	° '	° '	° '
A 1	12 37 55	11♈23 36	25♈18	10♈36	20♓55	6♋10	1♉17	26♋ 3	6♏ 6	13♐54	10♎19
P 2	12 41 52	12 22 49	7♉ 6	12 38	22 9	6 39	1 31	26 3	6R 4	13R54	10R17
R 3	12 45 48	13 21 59	18 56	14 42	23 23	7 8	1 45	26 4	6 2	13 53	10 16
I 4	12 49 45	14 21 7	0♊52	16 45	24 37	7 37	1 59	26 4	6 0	13 52	10 14
L 5	12 53 41	15 20 13	12 57	18 50	25 51	8 7	2 13	26 5	5 57	13 52	10 12
6	12 57 38	16 19 17	25 15	20 54	27 5	8 36	2 28	26 6	5 55	13 51	10 11
7	13 1 35	17 18 18	7♋51	22 59	28 19	9 6	2 42	26 7	5 53	13 50	10 9
8	13 5 31	18 17 17	20 48	25 4	29 32	9 35	2 56	26 8	5 50	13 50	10 7
9	13 9 28	19 16 14	4♌ 9	27 8	0♈46	10 5	3 10	26 10	5 48	13 49	10 6
10	13 13 24	20 15 8	17 58	29 11	2 0	10 35	3 24	26 11	5 45	13 48	10 4
11	13 17 21	21 14 0	2♍15	1♉14	3 14	11 5	3 38	26 13	5 43	13 47	10 2
12	13 21 17	22 12 50	16 56	3 15	4 28	11 36	3 53	26 14	5 41	13 46	10 1
13	13 25 14	23 11 38	1♎57	5 14	5 42	12 6	4 7	26 16	5 38	13 46	9 59
14	13 29 10	24 10 23	17 9	7 11	6 56	12 36	4 21	26 18	5 36	13 45	9 57
15	13 33 7	25 9 7	2♏22	9 6	8 10	13 7	4 35	26 20	5 33	13 44	9 56
16	13 37 3	26 7 48	17 28	10 57	9 24	13 38	4 50	26 22	5 31	13 43	9 54
17	13 41 0	27 6 28	2♐17	12 46	10 38	14 9	5 4	26 24	5 28	13 42	9 53
18	13 44 57	28 5 6	16 43	14 32	11 51	14 39	5 18	26 26	5 26	13 41	9 51
19	13 48 53	29 3 43	0♑44	16 13	13 5	15 10	5 33	26 28	5 23	13 40	9 50
20	13 52 50	0♉ 2 17	14 17	17 51	14 19	15 42	5 47	26 31	5 20	13 39	9 48
21	13 56 46	1 0 50	27 25	19 25	15 33	16 13	6 1	26 33	5 18	13 38	9 46
22	14 0 43	1 59 22	10♒11	20 54	16 47	16 44	6 16	26 36	5 15	13 37	9 45
23	14 4 39	2 57 52	22 37	22 20	18 1	17 16	6 30	26 39	5 13	13 36	9 43
24	14 8 36	3 56 20	4♓49	23 40	19 15	17 47	6 44	26 42	5 10	13 34	9 42
25	14 12 32	4 54 46	16 49	24 56	20 28	18 19	6 59	26 45	5 8	13 33	9 40
26	14 16 29	5 53 11	28 42	26 7	21 42	18 51	7 13	26 48	5 5	13 32	9 39
27	14 20 26	6 51 34	10♈31	27 13	22 56	19 23	7 27	26 51	5 3	13 31	9 38
28	14 24 22	7 49 55	22 19	28 14	24 10	19 55	7 42	26 54	5 0	13 30	9 36
29	14 28 19	8 48 15	4♉ 7	29 11	25 24	20 27	7 56	26 57	4 58	13 28	9 35
30	14 32 15	9♉46 33	15♉59	0♊ 2	26♈38	20♋59	8♉11	27♋ 1	4♏55	13♐27	9♎33

THE SUN ENTERS THE SIGN OF TAURUS ON APR 19 AT 23:04.

DAY	TIME	☉	☽	☿	♀	♂	♃	♄	♅	♆	♇
	h m s	° ' "	° '	° '	° '	° '	° '	° '	° '	° '	° '
M 1	14 36 12	10♉44 49	27♉57	0♊47	27♈51	21♋31	8♉25	27♋ 4	4♏52	13♐26	9♎32
A 2	14 40 8	11 43 3	10♊ 2	1 28	29 5	22 3	8 39	27 8	4R50	13R25	9R31
Y 3	14 44 5	12 41 16	22 17	2 3	0♉19	22 36	8 54	27 12	4 47	13 23	9 29
4	14 48 1	13 39 27	4♋45	2 33	1 33	23 8	9 8	27 15	4 45	13 22	9 28
5	14 51 58	14 37 35	17 28	2 58	2 47	23 41	9 22	27 19	4 42	13 21	9 27
6	14 55 55	15 35 42	0♌27	3 18	4 0	24 14	9 37	27 23	4 40	13 19	9 25
7	14 59 51	16 33 47	13 47	3 32	5 14	24 46	9 51	27 27	4 37	13 18	9 24
8	15 3 48	17 31 50	27 28	3 40	6 28	25 19	10 5	27 31	4 35	13 16	9 23
9	15 7 44	18 29 50	11♍32	3R44	7 42	25 52	10 19	27 36	4 32	13 15	9 22
10	15 11 41	19 27 49	25 56	3 43	8 55	26 25	10 34	27 40	4 30	13 14	9 20
11	15 15 37	20 25 46	10♎39	3 36	10 9	26 58	10 48	27 44	4 28	13 12	9 19
12	15 19 34	21 23 42	25 35	3 25	11 23	27 31	11 2	27 49	4 25	13 11	9 18
13	15 23 30	22 21 35	10♏37	3 10	12 37	28 4	11 16	27 53	4 23	13 9	9 17
14	15 27 27	23 19 28	25 36	2 50	13 50	28 38	11 31	27 58	4 20	13 8	9 16
15	15 31 24	24 17 18	10♐25	2 27	15 4	29 11	11 45	28 3	4 18	13 6	9 15
16	15 35 20	25 15 8	24 56	2 1	16 18	29 44	11 59	28 8	4 16	13 5	9 14
17	15 39 17	26 12 56	9♑ 3	1 32	17 31	0♌18	12 13	28 12	4 13	13 3	9 13
18	15 43 13	27 10 43	22 44	1 1	18 45	0 51	12 27	28 17	4 11	13 2	9 12
19	15 47 10	28 8 28	5♒59	0 27	19 59	1 25	12 41	28 22	4 9	13 0	9 11
20	15 51 6	29 6 13	18 50	29♉53	21 13	1 59	12 55	28 28	4 7	12 58	9 10
21	15 55 3	0♊ 3 56	1♓18	29 19	22 26	2 32	13 9	28 33	4 4	12 57	9 9
22	15 58 59	1 1 38	13 30	28 44	23 40	3 6	13 23	28 38	4 2	12 55	9 8
23	16 2 56	1 59 19	25 29	28 10	24 54	3 40	13 37	28 43	4 0	12 54	9 7
24	16 6 53	2 56 59	7♈20	27 38	26 7	4 14	13 51	28 49	3 58	12 52	9 6
25	16 10 49	3 54 39	19 7	27 7	27 21	4 48	14 5	28 54	3 56	12 51	9 6
26	16 14 46	4 52 17	0♉55	26 39	28 35	5 22	14 19	29 0	3 54	12 49	9 5
27	16 18 42	5 49 54	12 47	26 13	29 49	5 56	14 33	29 5	3 52	12 47	9 4
28	16 22 39	6 47 30	24 46	25 51	1♊ 2	6 30	14 47	29 11	3 50	12 46	9 3
29	16 26 35	7 45 5	6♊55	25 32	2 16	7 5	15 0	29 17	3 48	12 44	9 3
30	16 30 32	8 42 39	19 14	25 17	3 30	7 39	15 14	29 23	3 46	12 43	9 2
31	16 34 28	9♊40 11	1♋45	25♉ 6	4♊43	8♌13	15♉28	29♋28	3♏44	12♐41	9♎ 1

THE SUN ENTERS THE SIGN OF GEMINI ON MAY 20 AT 22:22.

DAY	TIME	☉	☽	☿	♀	♂	♃	♄	♅	♆	♇
	h m s	° ' "	° '	° '	° '	° '	° '	° '	° '	° '	° '
J 1	16 38 25	10♊37 43	14♋30	24♉59	5♊57	8♌48	15♉41	29♋34	3♏42	12♐39	9♎ 1
U 2	16 42 22	11 35 13	27 28	24D57	7 11	9 22	15 55	29 40	3R40	12R38	9R 0
N 3	16 46 18	12 32 43	10♌40	24 59	8 24	9 57	16 9	29 46	3 38	12 36	9 0
E 4	16 50 15	13 30 10	24 7	25 5	9 38	10 31	16 22	29 53	3 36	12 34	8 59
5	16 54 11	14 27 37	7♍49	25 16	10 52	11 6	16 35	29 59	3 35	12 33	8 59
6	16 58 8	15 25 2	21 45	25 32	12 6	11 41	16 49	0♌ 5	3 33	12 31	8 58
7	17 2 4	16 22 26	5♎56	25 52	13 19	12 15	17 2	0 11	3 31	12 30	8 58
8	17 6 1	17 19 49	20 19	26 16	14 33	12 50	17 16	0 18	3 30	12 28	8 58
9	17 9 57	18 17 11	4♏53	26 44	15 47	13 25	17 29	0 24	3 28	12 26	8 57
10	17 13 54	19 14 32	19 32	27 17	17 0	14 0	17 42	0 30	3 27	12 25	8 57
11	17 17 51	20 11 52	4♐12	27 54	18 14	14 35	17 55	0 37	3 25	12 23	8 57
12	17 21 47	21 9 12	18 45	28 36	19 28	15 10	18 8	0 43	3 24	12 21	8 56
13	17 25 44	22 6 30	3♑ 6	29 21	20 41	15 45	18 21	0 50	3 22	12 20	8 56
14	17 29 40	23 3 48	17 9	0♊10	21 55	16 20	18 34	0 57	3 21	12 18	8 56
15	17 33 37	24 1 5	0♒50	1 3	23 9	16 55	18 47	1 3	3 20	12 17	8 56
16	17 37 33	24 58 22	14 6	2 0	24 22	17 30	19 0	1 10	3 18	12 15	8 56
17	17 41 30	25 55 39	26 59	3 0	25 36	18 6	19 13	1 17	3 17	12 14	8 56
18	17 45 26	26 52 55	9♓30	4 4	26 50	18 41	19 26	1 24	3 16	12 12	8D56
19	17 49 23	27 50 11	21 43	5 12	28 3	19 16	19 39	1 30	3 15	12 10	8 56
20	17 53 20	28 47 26	3♈42	6 23	29 17	19 52	19 51	1 37	3 14	12 9	8 56
21	17 57 16	29 44 42	15 33	7 38	0♋31	20 27	20 4	1 44	3 13	12 7	8 56
22	18 1 13	0♋41 57	27 22	8 57	1 45	21 3	20 16	1 51	3 12	12 6	8 56
23	18 5 9	1 39 12	9♉11	10 18	2 58	21 38	20 29	1 58	3 11	12 4	8 56
24	18 9 6	2 36 27	21 8	11 43	4 12	22 14	20 41	2 5	3 10	12 3	8 56
25	18 13 2	3 33 42	3♊14	13 12	5 26	22 49	20 53	2 13	3 9	12 1	8 56
26	18 16 59	4 30 56	15 34	14 43	6 40	23 25	21 6	2 20	3 8	12 0	8 56
27	18 20 55	5 28 11	28 9	16 18	7 53	24 1	21 18	2 27	3 7	11 58	8 57
28	18 24 52	6 25 25	10♋59	17 57	9 7	24 37	21 30	2 34	3 7	11 57	8 57
29	18 28 49	7 22 39	24 6	19 38	10 21	25 12	21 42	2 41	3 6	11 56	8 57
30	18 32 45	8♋19 53	7♌26	21♊23	11♋35	25♌48	21♉54	2♌49	3♏ 5	11♐54	8♎58

THE SUN ENTERS THE SIGN OF CANCER ON JUN 21 AT 06:25.

♏ SCORPIO ♐ SAGITTARIUS ♑ CAPRICORN ♒ AQUARIUS ♓ PISCES

1976

SIDEREAL SUN.... MOON.... MERCURY.. VENUS.. MARS.... JUPITER.. SATURN... URANUS... NEPTUNE. PLUTO..

DAY	TIME	☉	☽	☿	♀	♂	♃	♄	♅	♆	♇
	h m s	° ' "	° '	° '	° '	° '	° '	° '	° '	° '	° '
J 1	18 36 42	9♋17 6	2Ø♌59	23♊1Ø	12♋48	26♌24	22♉ 6	2♌56	3♏ 5	11♐53	8♎58
U 2	18 4Ø 38	1Ø 14 19	4♍43	25 1	14 2	27 Ø	22 17	3 3	3R 4	11R51	8 58
L 3	18 44 35	11 11 32	18 35	26 54	15 16	27 36	22 29	3 11	3 4	11 5Ø	8 59
Y 4	18 48 31	12 8 44	2♎35	28 5Ø	16 3Ø	28 12	22 41	3 18	3 3	11 49	8 59
5	18 52 28	13 5 56	16 4Ø	Ø♋48	17 43	28 48	22 52	3 25	3 3	11 47	9 Ø
6	18 56 24	14 3 8	Ø♏51	2 49	18 57	29 25	23 3	3 33	3 3	11 46	9 Ø
7	19 Ø 21	15 Ø 2Ø	15 5	4 51	2Ø 11	Ø♍ 1	23 15	3 4Ø	3 3	11 45	9 1
8	19 4 18	15 57 31	29 21	6 56	21 25	Ø 37	23 26	3 48	3 2	11 43	9 2
9	19 8 14	16 54 43	13♐35	9 2	22 38	1 13	23 37	3 55	3 2	11 42	9 2
1Ø	19 12 11	17 51 54	27 45	11 9	23 52	1 5Ø	23 48	4 3	3 2	11 41	9 3
11	19 16 7	18 49 5	11♑45	13 17	25 6	2 26	23 59	4 1Ø	3D 2	11 4Ø	9 4
12	19 2Ø 4	19 46 17	25 32	15 26	26 2Ø	3 2	24 1Ø	4 18	3 2	11 38	9 4
13	19 24 Ø	2Ø 43 29	9♒ 1	17 35	27 34	3 39	24 21	4 26	3 2	11 37	9 5
14	19 27 57	21 4Ø 41	22 1Ø	19 45	28 47	4 15	24 31	4 33	3 2	11 36	9 6
15	19 31 54	22 37 53	4♓58	21 54	Ø♌ 1	4 52	24 42	4 41	3 2	11 35	9 7
16	19 35 5Ø	23 35 6	17 27	24 2	1 15	5 29	24 53	4 48	3 3	11 34	9 8
17	19 39 47	24 32 2Ø	29 4Ø	26 1Ø	2 29	6 5	25 3	4 56	3 3	11 33	9 9
18	19 43 43	25 29 34	11♈39	28 17	3 43	6 42	25 13	5 4	3 3	11 32	9 1Ø
19	19 47 4Ø	26 26 49	23 3Ø	Ø♌23	4 56	7 19	25 23	5 11	3 4	11 31	9 11
2Ø	19 51 36	27 24 5	5♉19	2 28	6 1Ø	7 55	25 33	5 19	3 4	11 3Ø	9 12
21	19 55 33	28 21 21	17 1Ø	4 31	7 24	8 32	25 43	5 27	3 5	11 29	9 13
22	19 59 29	29 18 39	29 9	6 33	8 38	9 9	25 53	5 34	3 5	11 28	9 14
23	2Ø 3 26	Ø♌15 57	11♊21	8 33	9 52	9 46	26 3	5 42	3 6	11 27	9 15
24	2Ø 7 23	1 13 16	23 49	1Ø 32	11 6	1Ø 23	26 12	5 5Ø	3 6	11 26	9 16
25	2Ø 11 19	2 1Ø 36	6♋37	12 3Ø	12 19	11 Ø	26 22	5 58	3 7	11 25	9 17
26	2Ø 15 16	3 7 56	19 45	14 25	13 33	11 37	26 31	6 5	3 8	11 24	9 18
27	2Ø 19 12	4 5 17	3♌13	16 19	14 47	12 14	26 4Ø	6 13	3 9	11 23	9 19
28	2Ø 23 9	5 2 39	16 58	18 11	16 1	12 51	26 5Ø	6 21	3 9	11 22	9 21
29	2Ø 27 5	6 Ø 2	Ø♍56	2Ø 2	17 15	13 28	26 59	6 29	3 1Ø	11 22	9 22
3Ø	2Ø 31 2	6 57 25	15 4	21 51	18 29	14 6	27 7	6 36	3 11	11 21	9 23
31	2Ø 34 58	7♌54 49	29♍16	23♌38	19♌43	14♍43	27♉16	6♌44	3♏12	11♐2Ø	9♎25

THE SUN ENTERS THE SIGN OF LEO ON JUL 22 AT 17:19.

DAY	TIME	☉	☽	☿	♀	♂	♃	♄	♅	♆	♇
	h m s	° ' "	° '	° '	° '	° '	° '	° '	° '	° '	° '
A 1	2Ø 38 55	8♌52 13	13♎29	25♌24	2Ø♌57	15♍2Ø	27♉25	6♌52	3♏13	11♐2Ø	9♎26
U 2	2Ø 42 51	9 49 38	27 41	27 8	22 1Ø	15 58	27 33	7 Ø	3 14	11R19	9 27
G 3	2Ø 46 48	1Ø 47 4	11♏49	28 5Ø	23 24	16 35	27 42	7 7	3 16	11 18	9 29
U 4	2Ø 5Ø 45	11 44 3Ø	25 53	Ø♍3Ø	24 38	17 12	27 5Ø	7 15	3 17	11 18	9 3Ø
S 5	2Ø 54 41	12 41 57	9♐51	2 9	25 52	17 5Ø	27 58	7 23	3 18	11 17	9 32
T 6	2Ø 58 38	13 39 24	23 44	3 47	27 6	18 27	28 6	7 3Ø	3 19	11 16	9 33
7	21 2 34	14 36 53	7♑29	5 22	28 2Ø	19 5	28 14	7 38	3 21	11 16	9 35
8	21 6 31	15 34 22	21 4	6 56	29 34	19 43	28 21	7 46	3 22	11 15	9 36
9	21 1Ø 27	16 31 52	4♒28	8 29	Ø♍47	2Ø 2Ø	28 29	7 54	3 24	11 15	9 38
1Ø	21 14 24	17 29 23	17 37	1Ø Ø	2 1	2Ø 58	28 36	8 1	3 25	11 15	9 39
11	21 18 21	18 26 56	Ø♓31	11 29	3 15	21 36	28 43	8 9	3 27	11 14	9 41
12	21 22 17	19 24 29	13 9	12 56	4 29	22 13	28 5Ø	8 17	3 28	11 14	9 43
13	21 26 14	2Ø 22 4	25 31	14 22	5 43	22 51	28 57	8 24	3 3Ø	11 13	9 44
14	21 3Ø 1Ø	21 19 4Ø	7♈39	15 46	6 57	23 29	29 4	8 32	3 31	11 13	9 46
15	21 34 7	22 17 17	19 36	17 9	8 1Ø	24 7	29 11	8 39	3 33	11 13	9 48
16	21 38 3	23 14 56	1♉26	18 3Ø	9 24	24 45	29 17	8 47	3 35	11 13	9 49
17	21 42 Ø	24 12 37	13 13	19 48	1Ø 38	25 23	29 23	8 55	3 37	11 12	9 51
18	21 45 56	25 1Ø 19	25 4	21 5	11 52	26 1	29 29	9 2	3 39	11 12	9 53
19	21 49 53	26 8 3	7♊ 4	22 21	13 6	26 39	29 35	9 1Ø	3 41	11 12	9 55
2Ø	21 53 49	27 5 48	19 17	23 34	14 2Ø	27 17	29 41	9 17	3 43	11 12	9 57
21	21 57 46	28 3 35	1♋49	24 45	15 33	27 56	29 47	9 25	3 45	11 12	9 58
22	22 1 43	29 1 24	14 43	25 54	16 47	28 34	29 52	9 32	3 47	11 12	1Ø Ø
23	22 5 39	29 59 14	28 1	27 1	18 1	29 12	29 58	9 4Ø	3 49	11D12	1Ø 2
24	22 9 36	Ø♍57 6	11♌43	28 6	19 15	29 51	Ø♊ 3	9 47	3 51	11 12	1Ø 4
25	22 13 32	1 54 59	25 48	29 8	2Ø 29	Ø♎29	Ø 8	9 54	3 53	11 12	1Ø 6
26	22 17 29	2 52 54	1Ø♍ 9	Ø♎ 8	21 43	1 7	Ø 13	1Ø 2	3 55	11 12	1Ø 8
27	22 21 25	3 5Ø 51	24 42	1 5	22 56	1 46	Ø 17	1Ø 9	3 58	11 12	1Ø 1Ø
28	22 25 22	4 48 48	9♎19	1 59	24 1Ø	2 24	Ø 22	1Ø 16	4 Ø	11 12	1Ø 12
29	22 29 18	5 46 48	23 54	2 5Ø	25 24	3 3	Ø 26	1Ø 24	4 2	11 12	1Ø 14
3Ø	22 33 15	6 44 48	8♏22	3 38	26 38	3 42	Ø 3Ø	1Ø 31	4 5	11 13	1Ø 16
31	22 37 12	7♍42 5Ø	22♏39	4♎23	27♍52	4♎2Ø	Ø♊34	1Ø♌38	4♏ 7	11♐13	1Ø♎18

THE SUN ENTERS THE SIGN OF VIRGO ON AUG 23 AT 00:20.

DAY	TIME	☉	☽	☿	♀	♂	♃	♄	♅	♆	♇
	h m s	° ' "	° '	° '	° '	° '	° '	° '	° '	° '	° '
S 1	22 41 8	8♍4Ø 54	6♐44	5♎ 4	29♍ 5	4♎59	Ø♊38	1Ø♌45	4♏1Ø	11♐13	1Ø♎2Ø
E 2	22 45 5	9 38 58	2Ø 36	5 41	Ø♎19	5 38	Ø 41	1Ø 52	4 12	11 13	1Ø 22
P 3	22 49 1	1Ø 37 4	4♑15	6 14	1 33	6 17	Ø 45	1Ø 59	4 15	11 14	1Ø 24
T 4	22 52 58	11 35 12	17 41	6 43	2 47	6 55	Ø 48	11 7	4 17	11 14	1Ø 26
E 5	22 56 54	12 33 21	Ø♒54	7 7	4 Ø	7 34	Ø 51	11 14	4 2Ø	11 15	1Ø 28
M 6	23 Ø 51	13 31 31	13 55	7 26	5 14	8 13	Ø 54	11 21	4 23	11 15	1Ø 3Ø
B 7	23 4 47	14 29 43	26 44	7 4Ø	6 28	8 52	Ø 56	11 27	4 25	11 15	1Ø 33
E 8	23 8 44	15 27 57	9♓19	7R49	7 42	9 31	Ø 59	11 34	4 28	11 16	1Ø 35
R 9	23 12 41	16 26 12	21 42	7 51	8 55	1Ø 1Ø	1 1	11 41	4 31	11 16	1Ø 37
1Ø	23 16 37	17 24 29	3♈53	7 48	1Ø 9	1Ø 5Ø	1 3	11 48	4 34	11 17	1Ø 39
11	23 2Ø 34	18 22 48	15 54	7 38	11 23	11 29	1 5	11 55	4 37	11 18	1Ø 41
12	23 24 3Ø	19 21 9	27 47	7 21	12 36	12 8	1 6	12 1	4 39	11 18	1Ø 43
13	23 28 27	2Ø 19 32	9♉35	6 58	13 5Ø	12 47	1 8	12 8	4 42	11 19	1Ø 46
14	23 32 23	21 17 57	21 21	6 28	15 4	13 27	1 9	12 15	4 45	11 2Ø	1Ø 48
15	23 36 2Ø	22 16 25	3♊11	5 51	16 17	14 6	1 1Ø	12 21	4 48	11 2Ø	1Ø 5Ø
16	23 4Ø 16	23 14 54	15 1Ø	5 8	17 31	14 45	1 11	12 28	4 51	11 21	1Ø 52
17	23 44 13	24 13 26	27 22	4 19	18 45	15 25	1 12	12 34	4 54	11 22	1Ø 55
18	23 48 9	25 11 59	9♋52	3 25	19 58	16 4	1 12	12 41	4 57	11 23	1Ø 57
19	23 52 6	26 1Ø 35	22 44	2 26	21 12	16 44	1R12	12 47	5 1	11 24	1Ø 59
2Ø	23 56 3	27 9 14	6♌ 3	1 24	22 25	17 24	1 12	12 53	5 4	11 24	11 1
21	23 59 59	28 7 54	19 49	Ø 2Ø	23 39	18 3	1 12	13 Ø	5 7	11 25	11 4
22	Ø 3 56	29 6 36	4♍ 1	29♍15	24 53	18 43	1 12	13 6	5 1Ø	11 26	11 6
23	Ø 7 52	Ø♎ 5 21	18 36	28 11	26 6	19 23	1 11	13 12	5 13	11 27	11 8
24	Ø 11 49	1 4 7	3♎26	27 9	27 2Ø	2Ø 3	1 11	13 18	5 17	11 28	11 11
25	Ø 15 45	2 2 56	18 25	26 12	28 33	2Ø 43	1 1Ø	13 24	5 2Ø	11 29	11 13
26	Ø 19 42	3 1 46	3♏23	25 21	29 47	21 22	1 9	13 3Ø	5 23	11 3Ø	11 15
27	Ø 23 38	4 Ø 38	18 12	24 36	1♏ Ø	22 2	1 7	13 36	5 26	11 31	11 18
28	Ø 27 35	4 59 33	2♐47	24 Ø	2 14	22 42	1 6	13 42	5 3Ø	11 33	11 2Ø
29	Ø 31 32	5 58 29	17 4	23 33	3 27	23 23	1 4	13 47	5 33	11 34	11 22
3Ø	Ø 35 28	6♎57 26	1♑ 1	23♍16	4♏41	24♎ 3	1♊ 2	13♌53	5♏37	11♐35	11♎25

THE SUN ENTERS THE SIGN OF LIBRA ON SEP 22 AT 21:49.

♈ ARIES ♉ TAURUS ♊ GEMINI ♋ CANCER ♌ LEO ♍ VIRGO ♎ LIBRA

SIDEREAL SUN MOON MERCURY VENUS MARS JUPITER SATURN URANUS NEPTUNE PLUTO

DAY	TIME	☉	☽	☿	♀	♂	♃	♄	♅	♆	♇
	h m s	° ' "	° '	° '	° '	° '	° '	° '	° '	° '	° '
O 1	Ø 39 25	7♎56 26	14♑37	23♍ 9	5♏54	24♎43	1♊ Ø	13♌59	5♏4Ø	11♐36	11♎27
C 2	Ø 43 21	8 55 27	27 54	23D12	7 8	25 23	ØR57	14 4	5 43	11 37	11 29
T 3	Ø 47 18	9 54 29	1Ø♒54	23 26	8 21	26 3	Ø 55	14 1Ø	5 47	11 39	11 32
O 4	Ø 51 14	1Ø 53 34	23 38	23 5Ø	9 35	26 44	Ø 52	14 15	5 5Ø	11 4Ø	11 34
B 5	Ø 55 11	11 52 4Ø	6♓ 8	24 24	1Ø 48	27 24	Ø 49	14 2Ø	5 54	11 41	11 36
E 6	Ø 59 7	12 51 48	18 27	25 6	12 1	28 5	Ø 46	14 26	5 57	11 43	11 39
R 7	1 3 4	13 5Ø 58	Ø♈35	25 57	13 15	28 45	Ø 43	14 31	6 1	11 44	11 41
8	1 7 1	14 5Ø 11	12 35	26 56	14 28	29 26	Ø 39	14 36	6 5	11 45	11 43
9	1 1Ø 57	15 49 25	24 29	28 1	15 41	Ø♏ 6	Ø 35	14 41	6 8	11 47	11 46
1Ø	1 14 54	16 48 41	6♉18	29 13	16 55	Ø 47	Ø 32	14 46	6 12	11 48	11 48
11	1 18 5Ø	17 47 59	18 5	Ø♎3Ø	18 8	1 27	Ø 27	14 51	6 15	11 5Ø	11 5Ø
12	1 22 47	18 47 2Ø	29 53	1 52	19 21	2 8	Ø 23	14 56	6 19	11 51	11 53
13	1 26 43	19 46 43	11♊44	3 18	2Ø 35	2 49	Ø 19	15 Ø	6 23	11 53	11 55
14	1 3Ø 4Ø	2Ø 46 8	23 44	4 48	21 48	3 3Ø	Ø 14	15 5	6 26	11 54	11 57
15	1 34 36	21 45 36	5♋55	6 2Ø	23 1	4 11	Ø 9	15 9	6 3Ø	11 56	12 Ø
16	1 38 33	22 45 5	18 22	7 54	24 14	4 52	Ø 4	15 14	6 34	11 58	12 2
17	1 42 3Ø	23 44 37	1♌1Ø	9 31	25 28	5 33	29♉59	15 18	6 37	11 59	12 4
18	1 46 26	24 44 12	14 22	11 9	26 41	6 14	29 54	15 23	6 41	12 1	12 7
19	1 5Ø 23	25 43 48	28 1	12 48	27 54	6 55	29 48	15 27	6 45	12 3	12 9
2Ø	1 54 19	26 43 27	12♍ 7	14 28	29 7	7 36	29 43	15 31	6 48	12 4	12 11
21	1 58 16	27 43 8	26 39	16 9	Ø♐2Ø	8 17	29 37	15 35	6 52	12 6	12 14
22	2 2 12	28 42 51	11♎32	17 5Ø	1 33	8 58	29 31	15 39	6 56	12 8	12 16
23	2 6 9	29 42 37	26 39	19 32	2 46	9 4Ø	29 25	15 43	7 Ø	12 9	12 18
24	2 1Ø 5	Ø♏42 24	11♏51	21 14	3 59	1Ø 21	29 19	15 46	7 3	12 11	12 2Ø
25	2 14 2	1 42 14	26 59	22 55	5 13	11 2	29 12	15 5Ø	7 7	12 13	12 23
26	2 17 58	2 42 5	11♐53	24 36	6 26	11 44	29 6	15 54	7 11	12 15	12 25
27	2 21 55	3 41 58	26 28	26 18	7 39	12 25	28 59	15 57	7 15	12 17	12 27
28	2 25 52	4 41 52	1Ø♑37	27 59	8 52	13 7	28 52	16 Ø	7 18	12 19	12 29
29	2 29 48	5 41 49	24 21	29 39	1Ø 5	13 49	28 46	16 4	7 22	12 21	12 31
3Ø	2 33 45	6 41 47	7♒39	1♏2Ø	11 17	14 3Ø	28 39	16 7	7 26	12 22	12 34
31	2 37 41	7♏41 46	2Ø♒35	3♏ Ø	12♐3Ø	15♏12	28♉31	16♌1Ø	7♏3Ø	12♐24	12♎36

THE SUN ENTERS THE SIGN OF SCORPIO ON OCT 23 AT 06:59.

DAY	TIME	☉	☽	☿	♀	♂	♃	♄	♅	♆	♇
	h m s	° ' "	° '	° '	° '	° '	° '	° '	° '	° '	° '
N 1	2 41 38	8♏41 47	3♓1Ø	4♏39	13♐43	15♏54	28♉24	16♌13	7♏33	12♐26	12♎38
O 2	2 45 34	9 41 5Ø	15 3Ø	6 18	14 56	16 36	28R17	16 16	7 37	12 28	12 4Ø
V 3	2 49 31	1Ø 41 54	27 37	7 57	16 9	17 17	28 9	16 18	7 41	12 3Ø	12 42
E 4	2 53 27	11 42 Ø	9♈34	9 35	17 22	17 59	28 2	16 21	7 45	12 32	12 44
M 5	2 57 24	12 42 7	21 26	11 13	18 34	18 41	27 54	16 24	7 48	12 34	12 47
B 6	3 1 21	13 42 17	3♉15	12 51	19 47	19 23	27 47	16 26	7 52	12 36	12 49
E 7	3 5 17	14 42 28	15 3	14 28	21 Ø	2Ø 5	27 39	16 28	7 56	12 38	12 51
R 8	3 9 14	15 42 41	26 52	16 4	22 13	2Ø 48	27 31	16 31	8 Ø	12 4Ø	12 53
9	3 13 1Ø	16 42 56	8♊44	17 41	23 25	21 3Ø	27 23	16 33	8 3	12 42	12 55
1Ø	3 17 7	17 43 12	2Ø 42	19 17	24 38	22 12	27 15	16 35	8 7	12 45	12 57
11	3 21 3	18 43 31	2♋48	2Ø 52	25 5Ø	22 54	27 7	16 37	8 11	12 47	12 59
12	3 25 Ø	19 43 51	15 4	22 27	27 3	23 37	26 59	16 39	8 15	12 49	13 1
13	3 28 56	2Ø 44 13	27 34	24 2	28 15	24 19	26 51	16 4Ø	8 18	12 51	13 3
14	3 32 53	21 44 38	1Ø♌2Ø	25 37	29 28	25 2	26 43	16 42	8 22	12 53	13 5
15	3 36 5Ø	22 45 4	23 26	27 11	Ø♑4Ø	25 44	26 35	16 43	8 26	12 55	13 7
16	3 4Ø 46	23 45 32	6♍54	28 46	1 52	26 27	26 27	16 45	8 29	12 57	13 9
17	3 44 43	24 46 1	2Ø 47	Ø♐19	3 5	27 9	26 18	16 46	8 33	12 59	13 1Ø
18	3 48 39	25 46 33	5♎ 3	1 53	4 17	27 52	26 1Ø	16 47	8 37	13 2	13 12
19	3 52 36	26 47 6	19 43	3 26	5 29	28 35	26 2	16 48	8 4Ø	13 4	13 14
2Ø	3 56 32	27 47 42	4♏41	5 Ø	6 41	29 17	25 54	16 49	8 44	13 6	13 16
21	4 Ø 29	28 48 19	19 5Ø	6 33	7 54	Ø♐ Ø	25 46	16 5Ø	8 47	13 8	13 18
22	4 4 25	29 48 57	5♐ 1	8 5	9 6	Ø 43	25 38	16 51	8 51	13 1Ø	13 2Ø
23	4 8 22	Ø♐49 37	2Ø 4	9 38	1Ø 18	1 26	25 29	16 51	8 55	13 13	13 21
24	4 12 19	1 5Ø 18	4♑51	11 11	11 3Ø	2 9	25 21	16 52	8 58	13 15	13 23
25	4 16 15	2 51 1	19 13	12 43	12 42	2 52	25 13	16 52	9 2	13 17	13 25
26	4 2Ø 12	3 51 44	3♒ 9	14 15	13 54	3 35	25 5	16 53	9 5	13 19	13 26
27	4 24 8	4 52 29	16 35	15 47	15 6	4 18	24 57	16R53	9 9	13 22	13 28
28	4 28 5	5 53 14	29 34	17 19	16 17	5 1	24 49	16 53	9 12	13 24	13 3Ø
29	4 32 1	6 54 Ø	12♓1Ø	18 5Ø	17 29	5 45	24 42	16 53	9 16	13 26	13 31
3Ø	4 35 58	7♐54 48	24♓26	2Ø♐22	18♑41	6♐28	24♉34	16♌52	9♏19	13♐28	13♎33

THE SUN ENTERS THE SIGN OF SAGITTARIUS ON NOV 22 AT 04:23.

DAY	TIME	☉	☽	☿	♀	♂	♃	♄	♅	♆	♇
	h m s	° ' "	° '	° '	° '	° '	° '	° '	° '	° '	° '
D 1	4 39 54	8♐55 36	6♈29	21♐53	19♑52	7♐11	24♉26	16♌52	9♏23	13♐31	13♎34
E 2	4 43 51	9 56 25	18 21	23 24	21 4	7 55	24R18	16R52	9 26	13 33	13 36
C 3	4 47 48	1Ø 57 16	Ø♉ 9	24 55	22 15	8 38	24 11	16 51	9 29	13 35	13 37
E 4	4 51 44	11 58 7	11 55	26 25	23 26	9 21	24 4	16 51	9 33	13 37	13 39
M 5	4 55 41	12 58 59	23 44	27 55	24 38	1Ø 5	23 56	16 5Ø	9 36	13 4Ø	13 4Ø
B 6	4 59 37	13 59 52	5♊38	29 25	25 49	1Ø 49	23 49	16 49	9 39	13 42	13 42
E 7	5 3 34	15 Ø 46	17 39	Ø♑54	27 Ø	11 32	23 42	16 48	9 42	13 44	13 43
R 8	5 7 3Ø	16 1 41	29 49	2 23	28 11	12 16	23 35	16 47	9 46	13 46	13 45
9	5 11 27	17 2 38	12♋ 8	3 51	29 22	13 Ø	23 28	16 46	9 49	13 49	13 46
1Ø	5 15 23	18 3 35	24 38	5 18	Ø♒33	13 43	23 21	16 44	9 52	13 51	13 47
11	5 19 2Ø	19 4 33	7♌19	6 44	1 43	14 27	23 15	16 43	9 55	13 53	13 48
12	5 23 17	2Ø 5 32	2Ø 13	8 9	2 54	15 11	23 8	16 41	9 58	13 55	13 5Ø
13	5 27 13	21 6 33	3♍21	9 33	4 5	15 55	23 2	16 4Ø	1Ø 1	13 58	13 51
14	5 31 1Ø	22 7 34	16 45	1Ø 55	5 15	16 39	22 55	16 38	1Ø 4	14 Ø	13 52
15	5 35 6	23 8 36	Ø♎27	12 16	6 25	17 23	22 49	16 36	1Ø 7	14 2	13 53
16	5 39 3	24 9 4Ø	14 27	13 34	7 36	18 7	22 43	16 34	1Ø 1Ø	14 4	13 54
17	5 42 59	25 1Ø 44	28 46	14 5Ø	8 46	18 51	22 38	16 32	1Ø 13	14 7	13 55
18	5 46 56	26 11 49	13♏22	16 4	9 56	19 35	22 32	16 3Ø	1Ø 16	14 9	13 56
19	5 5Ø 52	27 12 56	28 12	17 13	11 6	2Ø 2Ø	22 27	16 28	1Ø 19	14 11	13 57
2Ø	5 54 49	28 14 3	13♐ 7	18 19	12 15	21 4	22 21	16 25	1Ø 22	14 14	13 58
21	5 58 46	29 15 1Ø	28 1	19 21	13 25	21 48	22 16	16 23	1Ø 25	14 16	13 59
22	6 2 42	Ø♑16 18	12♑45	2Ø 17	14 35	22 33	22 11	16 2Ø	1Ø 28	14 18	14 Ø
23	6 6 39	1 17 27	27 9	21 7	15 44	23 17	22 6	16 18	1Ø 3Ø	14 2Ø	14 1
24	6 1Ø 35	2 18 36	11♒1Ø	21 51	16 53	24 1	22 2	16 15	1Ø 33	14 22	14 2
25	6 14 32	3 19 44	24 42	22 26	18 2	24 46	21 57	16 12	1Ø 36	14 24	14 3
26	6 18 28	4 2Ø 53	7♓48	22 54	19 11	25 3Ø	21 53	16 9	1Ø 38	14 26	14 3
27	6 22 25	5 22 2	2Ø 28	23 12	2Ø 2Ø	26 15	21 49	16 6	1Ø 41	14 29	14 4
28	6 26 22	6 23 11	2♈46	23R19	21 29	27 Ø	21 45	16 3	1Ø 43	14 31	14 5
29	6 3Ø 18	7 24 2Ø	14 49	23 16	22 37	27 44	21 42	16 Ø	1Ø 46	14 33	14 6
3Ø	6 34 15	8 25 29	26 41	23 Ø	23 45	28 29	21 38	15 57	1Ø 48	14 35	14 6
31	6 38 11	9♑26 37	8♉28	22♑33	24♒53	29♐14	21♉35	15♌53	1Ø♏51	14♐37	14♎ 7

THE SUN ENTERS THE SIGN OF CAPRICORN ON DEC 21 AT 17:36.

♏ SCORPIO ♐ SAGITTARIUS ♑ CAPRICORN ♒ AQUARIUS ♓ PISCES

1977

SIDEREAL SUN. MOON. MERCURY. VENUS. MARS. JUPITER. SATURN. URANUS. NEPTUNE. PLUTO.

DAY	TIME	☉	☽	☿	♀	♂	♃	♄	♅	♆	♇
	h m s	° ′ ″	° ′	° ′	° ′	° ′	° ′	° ′	° ′	° ′	° ′
J 1	6 42 8	10♑27 46	20♉16	21♑55	26♒ 1	29♐59	21♉32	15♌50	10♏53	14♐39	14♎ 7
A 2	6 46 4	11 28 55	2♊ 7	21R 5	27 9	0♑44	21R29	15R46	10 55	14 41	14 8
N 3	6 50 1	12 30 3	14 7	20 5	28 16	1 28	21 26	15 43	10 58	14 43	14 8
U 4	6 53 57	13 31 11	26 18	18 56	29 24	2 13	21 24	15 39	11 0	14 45	14 9
A 5	6 57 54	14 32 19	8♋41	17 41	0♓31	2 58	21 22	15 35	11 2	14 47	14 9
R 6	7 1 51	15 33 28	21 17	16 22	1 37	3 43	21 20	15 31	11 4	14 49	14 10
Y 7	7 5 47	16 34 35	4♌ 6	15 1	2 44	4 28	21 18	15 27	11 6	14 51	14 10
8	7 9 44	17 35 43	17 8	13 41	3 50	5 14	21 16	15 23	11 8	14 53	14 10
9	7 13 40	18 36 51	0♍20	12 25	4 57	5 59	21 15	15 19	11 10	14 55	14 10
10	7 17 37	19 37 59	13 43	11 14	6 2	6 44	21 14	15 15	11 12	14 57	14 11
11	7 21 33	20 39 6	27 16	10 11	7 8	7 29	21 12	15 11	11 14	14 59	14 11
12	7 25 30	21 40 14	10♎59	9 17	8 13	8 14	21 12	15 7	11 16	15 1	14 11
13	7 29 26	22 41 22	24 53	8 31	9 18	9 0	21 11	15 2	11 18	15 3	14 11
14	7 33 23	23 42 29	8♏58	7 56	10 23	9 45	21 11	14 58	11 19	15 5	14 11
15	7 37 20	24 43 37	23 14	7 30	11 28	10 30	21D10	14 54	11 21	15 7	14 11
16	7 41 16	25 44 44	7♐38	7 14	12 32	11 16	21 10	14 49	11 23	15 9	14R11
17	7 45 13	26 45 51	22 7	7D 6	13 36	12 1	21 11	14 45	11 24	15 10	14 11
18	7 49 9	27 46 58	6♑37	7 8	14 39	12 47	21 11	14 40	11 26	15 12	14 11
19	7 53 6	28 48 5	20 59	7 17	15 43	13 32	21 12	14 36	11 27	15 14	14 11
20	7 57 2	29 49 10	5♒ 9	7 34	16 46	14 18	21 13	14 31	11 29	15 16	14 11
21	8 0 59	0♒50 15	19 1	7 57	17 48	15 4	21 14	14 26	11 30	15 17	14 11
22	8 4 55	1 51 20	2♓29	8 27	18 50	15 49	21 15	14 22	11 32	15 19	14 11
23	8 8 52	2 52 23	15 34	9 2	19 52	16 35	21 16	14 17	11 33	15 21	14 11
24	8 12 49	3 53 25	28 16	9 42	20 54	17 21	21 18	14 12	11 34	15 23	14 10
25	8 16 45	4 54 27	10♈37	10 27	21 55	18 7	21 20	14 7	11 35	15 24	14 10
26	8 20 42	5 55 27	22 42	11 16	22 55	18 52	21 22	14 2	11 36	15 26	14 10
27	8 24 38	6 56 26	4♉36	12 8	23 55	19 38	21 24	13 58	11 37	15 27	14 9
28	8 28 35	7 57 24	16 24	13 4	24 55	20 24	21 27	13 53	11 38	15 29	14 9
29	8 32 31	8 58 21	28 13	14 3	25 54	21 10	21 29	13 48	11 39	15 30	14 9
30	8 36 28	9 59 17	10♊ 6	15 5	26 53	21 56	21 32	13 43	11 40	15 32	14 8
31	8 40 24	11♒ 0 11	22♊10	16♑10	27♓51	22♑42	21♉35	13♌38	11♏41	15♐33	14♎ 8

THE SUN ENTERS THE SIGN OF AQUARIUS ON JAN 20 AT 04:15.

DAY	TIME	☉	☽	☿	♀	♂	♃	♄	♅	♆	♇
	h m s	° ′ ″	° ′	° ′	° ′	° ′	° ′	° ′	° ′	° ′	° ′
F 1	8 44 21	12♒ 1 5	4♋28	17♑17	28♓49	23♑28	21♉38	13♌33	11♏42	15♐35	14♎ 7
E 2	8 48 18	13 1 57	17 2	18 25	29 46	24 14	21 42	13R28	11 43	15 36	14R 7
B 3	8 52 14	14 2 48	29 53	19 36	0♈43	25 0	21 46	13 23	11 43	15 38	14 6
R 4	8 56 11	15 3 37	13♌ 2	20 49	1 39	25 46	21 49	13 18	11 44	15 39	14 5
U 5	9 0 7	16 4 26	26 27	22 4	2 34	26 32	21 53	13 14	11 45	15 40	14 5
A 6	9 4 4	17 5 13	10♍ 4	23 20	3 29	27 18	21 58	13 9	11 45	15 42	14 4
R 7	9 8 0	18 5 59	23 52	24 37	4 23	28 5	22 2	13 4	11 46	15 43	14 3
Y 8	9 11 57	19 6 44	7♎46	25 56	5 16	28 51	22 6	12 59	11 46	15 44	14 2
9	9 15 53	20 7 28	21 46	27 16	6 9	29 37	22 11	12 54	11 46	15 46	14 2
10	9 19 50	21 8 12	5♏49	28 38	7 1	0♒23	22 16	12 49	11 47	15 47	14 1
11	9 23 47	22 8 54	19 54	0♒ 0	7 52	1 10	22 21	12 44	11 47	15 48	14 0
12	9 27 43	23 9 35	4♐ 0	1 24	8 42	1 56	22 26	12 40	11 47	15 49	13 59
13	9 31 40	24 10 15	18 7	2 49	9 32	2 42	22 32	12 35	11 47	15 50	13 58
14	9 35 36	25 10 54	2♑12	4 15	10 21	3 29	22 38	12 30	11R47	15 51	13 57
15	9 39 33	26 11 32	16 14	5 42	11 9	4 15	22 43	12 25	11 47	15 52	13 56
16	9 43 29	27 12 8	0♒ 8	7 10	11 56	5 1	22 49	12 21	11 47	15 53	13 55
17	9 47 26	28 12 43	13 52	8 39	12 42	5 48	22 55	12 16	11 47	15 54	13 54
18	9 51 22	29 13 17	27 22	10 9	13 27	6 34	23 2	12 12	11 47	15 55	13 53
19	9 55 19	0♓13 49	10♓34	11 40	14 11	7 21	23 8	12 7	11 47	15 56	13 52
20	9 59 16	1 14 19	23 28	13 12	14 54	8 7	23 15	12 2	11 47	15 57	13 51
21	10 3 12	2 14 48	6♈ 3	14 45	15 36	8 54	23 22	11 58	11 46	15 58	13 50
22	10 7 9	3 15 15	18 22	16 19	16 17	9 40	23 28	11 54	11 46	15 59	13 49
23	10 11 5	4 15 40	0♉27	17 54	16 56	10 27	23 36	11 49	11 45	16 0	13 48
24	10 15 2	5 16 4	12 21	19 30	17 35	11 14	23 43	11 45	11 45	16 0	13 47
25	10 18 58	6 16 25	24 10	21 6	18 12	12 0	23 50	11 41	11 44	16 1	13 45
26	10 22 55	7 16 44	6♊ 0	22 44	18 47	12 47	23 58	11 37	11 44	16 2	13 44
27	10 26 51	8 17 2	17 54	24 23	19 22	13 33	24 5	11 32	11 43	16 2	13 43
28	10 30 48	9♓17 17	29♊58	26♒ 3	19♈55	14♒20	24♉13	11♌28	11♏43	16♐ 3	13♎42

THE SUN ENTERS THE SIGN OF PISCES ON FEB 18 AT 18:31.

DAY	TIME	☉	☽	☿	♀	♂	♃	♄	♅	♆	♇
	h m s	° ′ ″	° ′	° ′	° ′	° ′	° ′	° ′	° ′	° ′	° ′
M 1	10 34 44	10♓17 31	12♋18	27♒43	20♈26	15♒ 7	24♉21	11♌24	11♏42	16♐ 4	13♎40
A 2	10 38 41	11 17 43	24 56	29 25	20 56	15 53	24 29	11R20	11R41	16 4	13R39
R 3	10 42 38	12 17 52	7♌56	1♓ 8	21 24	16 40	24 38	11 17	11 40	16 5	13 38
C 4	10 46 34	13 17 59	21 17	2 52	21 50	17 27	24 46	11 13	11 39	16 5	13 36
H 5	10 50 31	14 18 5	4♍59	4 37	22 15	18 13	24 55	11 9	11 38	16 6	13 35
6	10 54 27	15 18 8	19 0	6 23	22 38	19 0	25 3	11 6	11 37	16 6	13 33
7	10 58 24	16 18 10	3♎14	8 10	22 59	19 47	25 12	11 2	11 36	16 7	13 32
8	11 2 20	17 18 10	17 36	9 58	23 18	20 34	25 21	10 58	11 35	16 7	13 30
9	11 6 17	18 18 8	2♏ 2	11 48	23 35	21 20	25 30	10 55	11 34	16 7	13 29
10	11 10 13	19 18 5	16 26	13 38	23 50	22 7	25 39	10 52	11 33	16 8	13 28
11	11 14 10	20 18 0	0♐46	15 30	24 3	22 54	25 48	10 49	11 32	16 8	13 26
12	11 18 7	21 17 53	14 58	17 23	24 13	23 41	25 58	10 45	11 30	16 8	13 25
13	11 22 3	22 17 45	29 2	19 16	24 22	24 28	26 7	10 42	11 29	16 8	13 23
14	11 26 0	23 17 35	12♑54	21 11	24 28	25 14	26 17	10 39	11 28	16 8	13 21
15	11 29 56	24 17 24	26 36	23 7	24 32	26 1	26 27	10 37	11 26	16 9	13 20
16	11 33 53	25 17 11	10♒ 6	25 4	24R33	26 48	26 37	10 34	11 25	16 9	13 18
17	11 37 49	26 16 56	23 23	27 2	24 33	27 35	26 47	10 31	11 23	16 9	13 17
18	11 41 46	27 16 39	6♓27	29 1	24 29	28 22	26 57	10 28	11 22	16R 9	13 15
19	11 45 42	28 16 20	19 17	1♈ 0	24 23	29 9	27 7	10 26	11 20	16 9	13 14
20	11 49 39	29 15 59	1♈53	3 0	24 15	29 55	27 17	10 24	11 18	16 9	13 12
21	11 53 36	0♈15 36	14 15	5 1	24 4	0♓42	27 28	10 21	11 17	16 9	13 10
22	11 57 32	1 15 11	26 26	7 1	23 51	1 29	27 38	10 19	11 15	16 9	13 9
23	12 1 29	2 14 44	8♉26	9 2	23 35	2 16	27 49	10 17	11 13	16 8	13 7
24	12 5 25	3 14 15	20 19	11 3	23 17	3 3	28 0	10 15	11 12	16 8	13 5
25	12 9 22	4 13 44	2♊ 8	13 3	22 57	3 50	28 11	10 13	11 10	16 8	13 4
26	12 13 18	5 13 10	13 57	15 3	22 34	4 36	28 22	10 11	11 8	16 8	13 2
27	12 17 15	6 12 34	25 51	17 2	22 9	5 23	28 33	10 10	11 6	16 8	13 0
28	12 21 11	7 11 56	7♋55	18 59	21 42	6 10	28 44	10 8	11 4	16 7	12 59
29	12 25 8	8 11 16	20 13	20 54	21 12	6 57	28 55	10 7	11 2	16 7	12 57
30	12 29 4	9 10 33	2♌49	22 47	20 42	7 44	29 6	10 5	11 0	16 7	12 55
31	12 33 1	10♈ 9 48	15♌48	24♈37	20♈ 9	8♓31	29♉18	10♌ 4	10♏58	16♐ 6	12♎54

THE SUN ENTERS THE SIGN OF ARIES ON MAR 20 AT 17:43.

♈ ARIES ♉ TAURUS ♊ GEMINI ♋ CANCER ♌ LEO ♍ VIRGO ♎ LIBRA

1977

SIDEREAL TIME. SUN. MOON. MERCURY. VENUS. MARS. JUPITER. SATURN. URANUS. NEPTUNE. PLUTO.

DAY	TIME h m s	☉ ° ' "	☽ ° '	☿ ° '	♀ ° '	♂ ° '	♃ ° '	♄ ° '	♅ ° '	♆ ° '	♇ ° '
A 1	12 36 58	11♈ 9 0	29♌11	26♈25	19♈35	9♓17	29♉29	10♌ 3	10♏56	16♐ 6	12♎52
P 2	12 40 54	12 8 10	13♍ 0	28 9	19R 0	10 4	29 41	10R 2	10R54	16R 5	12R50
R 3	12 44 51	13 7 18	27 12	29 49	18 23	10 51	29 52	10 1	10 52	16 5	12 49
I 4	12 48 47	14 6 24	11♎44	1♉25	17 46	11 38	0♊ 4	10 0	10 50	16 4	12 47
L 5	12 52 44	15 5 28	26 29	2 56	17 9	12 24	0 16	9 59	10 47	16 4	12 45
6	12 56 40	16 4 30	11♏22	4 23	16 31	13 11	0 28	9 59	10 45	16 3	12 44
7	13 0 37	17 3 30	26 13	5 44	15 53	13 58	0 40	9 58	10 43	16 2	12 42
8	13 4 33	18 2 29	10♐56	7 1	15 15	14 45	0 52	9 58	10 41	16 2	12 40
9	13 8 30	19 1 26	25 25	8 12	14 38	15 31	1 4	9 57	10 38	16 1	12 39
10	13 12 27	20 0 20	9♑37	9 17	14 1	16 18	1 16	9 57	10 36	16 0	12 37
11	13 16 23	20 59 14	23 31	10 16	13 26	17 5	1 28	9D57	10 34	16 0	12 35
12	13 20 20	21 58 5	7♒ 5	11 9	12 52	17 52	1 41	9 57	10 31	15 59	12 34
13	13 24 16	22 56 55	20 20	11 56	12 19	18 38	1 53	9 57	10 29	15 58	12 32
14	13 28 13	23 55 43	3♓18	12 37	11 47	19 25	2 5	9 58	10 27	15 57	12 30
15	13 32 9	24 54 29	16 1	13 12	11 18	20 11	2 18	9 58	10 24	15 57	12 29
16	13 36 6	25 53 13	28 31	13 40	10 50	20 58	2 30	9 58	10 22	15 56	12 27
17	13 40 2	26 51 56	10♈49	14 2	10 25	21 45	2 43	9 59	10 19	15 55	12 26
18	13 43 59	27 50 37	22 57	14 18	10 1	22 31	2 56	10 0	10 17	15 54	12 24
19	13 47 56	28 49 15	4♉58	14 27	9 40	23 18	3 8	10 0	10 14	15 53	12 22
20	13 51 52	29 47 52	16 52	14R31	9 21	24 4	3 21	10 1	10 12	15 52	12 21
21	13 55 49	0♉46 27	28 42	14 28	9 4	24 51	3 34	10 2	10 9	15 51	12 19
22	13 59 45	1 45 0	10♊31	14 20	8 50	25 37	3 47	10 3	10 7	15 50	12 18
23	14 3 42	2 43 31	22 21	14 7	8 38	26 24	4 0	10 5	10 4	15 49	12 16
24	14 7 38	3 42 0	4♋16	13 48	8 29	27 10	4 13	10 6	10 2	15 48	12 15
25	14 11 35	4 40 27	16 19	13 25	8 22	27 57	4 26	10 7	9 59	15 47	12 13
26	14 15 31	5 38 51	28 35	12 58	8 17	28 43	4 39	10 9	9 57	15 45	12 12
27	14 19 28	6 37 14	11♌ 8	12 27	8D15	29 30	4 52	10 11	9 54	15 44	12 10
28	14 23 25	7 35 34	24 2	11 54	8 15	0♈16	5 5	10 12	9 52	15 43	12 9
29	14 27 21	8 33 52	7♍19	11 17	8 18	1 2	5 19	10 14	9 49	15 42	12 7
30	14 31 18	9♉32 8	21♍ 3	10♉40	8♈23	1♈48	5♊32	10♌16	9♏47	15♐41	12♎ 6

THE SUN ENTERS THE SIGN OF TAURUS ON APR 20 AT 04:57.

DAY	TIME h m s	☉ ° ' "	☽ ° '	☿ ° '	♀ ° '	♂ ° '	♃ ° '	♄ ° '	♅ ° '	♆ ° '	♇ ° '
M 1	14 35 14	10♉30 22	5♎14	10♉ 1	8♈30	2♈35	5♊45	10♌18	9♏44	15♐40	12♎ 4
A 2	14 39 11	11 28 35	19 50	9R22	8 39	3 21	5 59	10 20	9R42	15R38	12R 3
Y 3	14 43 7	12 26 45	4♏45	8 44	8 50	4 7	6 12	10 23	9 39	15 37	12 1
4	14 47 4	13 24 54	19 53	8 6	9 4	4 53	6 25	10 25	9 36	15 36	12 0
5	14 51 0	14 23 1	5♐ 4	7 31	9 19	5 39	6 39	10 27	9 34	15 34	11 59
6	14 54 57	15 21 6	20 8	6 57	9 37	6 25	6 52	10 30	9 31	15 33	11 57
7	14 58 53	16 19 10	4♑58	6 27	9 56	7 12	7 6	10 33	9 29	15 32	11 56
8	15 2 50	17 17 13	19 25	6 0	10 17	7 58	7 19	10 35	9 26	15 30	11 55
9	15 6 47	18 15 14	3♒28	5 36	10 40	8 44	7 33	10 38	9 24	15 29	11 53
10	15 10 43	19 13 14	17 5	5 17	11 5	9 30	7 47	10 41	9 21	15 28	11 52
11	15 14 40	20 11 13	0♓16	5 2	11 31	10 15	8 0	10 44	9 19	15 26	11 51
12	15 18 36	21 9 10	13 6	4 51	11 59	11 1	8 14	10 47	9 16	15 25	11 50
13	15 22 33	22 7 6	25 38	4D44	12 29	11 47	8 28	10 51	9 14	15 23	11 48
14	15 26 29	23 5 1	7♈54	4 43	13 0	12 33	8 41	10 54	9 11	15 22	11 47
15	15 30 26	24 2 54	19 59	4 46	13 32	13 19	8 55	10 57	9 9	15 20	11 46
16	15 34 22	25 0 46	1♉57	4 53	14 6	14 5	9 9	11 1	9 7	15 19	11 45
17	15 38 19	25 58 37	13 49	5 5	14 41	14 50	9 23	11 5	9 4	15 17	11 44
18	15 42 16	26 56 26	25 39	5 22	15 17	15 36	9 37	11 8	9 2	15 16	11 43
19	15 46 12	27 54 14	7♊28	5 43	15 54	16 22	9 50	11 12	8 59	15 14	11 42
20	15 50 9	28 52 1	19 18	6 8	16 33	17 7	10 4	11 16	8 57	15 13	11 41
21	15 54 5	29 49 46	1♋11	6 38	17 12	17 53	10 18	11 20	8 55	15 11	11 40
22	15 58 2	0♊47 30	13 11	7 11	17 53	18 38	10 32	11 24	8 52	15 10	11 39
23	16 1 58	1 45 12	25 18	7 49	18 35	19 24	10 46	11 28	8 50	15 8	11 38
24	16 5 55	2 42 53	7♌35	8 30	19 17	20 9	11 0	11 32	8 48	15 7	11 37
25	16 9 51	3 40 32	20 7	9 15	20 1	20 54	11 14	11 37	8 46	15 5	11 36
26	16 13 48	4 38 10	2♍57	10 4	20 46	21 40	11 28	11 41	8 43	15 3	11 35
27	16 17 45	5 35 46	16 8	10 56	21 31	22 25	11 42	11 45	8 41	15 2	11 35
28	16 21 41	6 33 21	29 43	11 52	22 17	23 10	11 56	11 50	8 39	15 0	11 34
29	16 25 38	7 30 54	13♎44	12 51	23 4	23 55	12 9	11 55	8 37	14 59	11 33
30	16 29 34	8 28 26	28 12	13 53	23 52	24 40	12 23	11 59	8 35	14 57	11 32
31	16 33 31	9♊25 56	13♏ 2	14♉59	24♈41	25♈25	12♊37	12♌ 4	8♏33	14♐55	11♎32

THE SUN ENTERS THE SIGN OF GEMINI ON MAY 21 AT 04:15.

DAY	TIME h m s	☉ ° ' "	☽ ° '	☿ ° '	♀ ° '	♂ ° '	♃ ° '	♄ ° '	♅ ° '	♆ ° '	♇ ° '
J 1	16 37 27	10♊23 26	28♏ 9	16♉ 7	25♈30	26♈10	12♊51	12♌ 9	8♏31	14♐54	11♎31
U 2	16 41 24	11 20 54	13♐25	17 19	26 20	26 55	13 5	12 14	8R29	14R52	11R30
N 3	16 45 20	12 18 22	28 39	18 33	27 11	27 40	13 19	12 19	8 27	14 51	11 30
E 4	16 49 17	13 15 48	13♑41	19 51	28 2	28 25	13 33	12 24	8 25	14 49	11 29
5	16 53 14	14 13 14	28 21	21 11	28 54	29 10	13 47	12 29	8 23	14 47	11 28
6	16 57 10	15 10 39	12♒34	22 34	29 46	29 54	14 1	12 34	8 21	14 46	11 28
7	17 1 7	16 8 3	26 18	24 0	0♉39	0♉39	14 15	12 40	8 19	14 44	11 27
8	17 5 3	17 5 27	9♓34	25 29	1 33	1 24	14 29	12 45	8 17	14 42	11 27
9	17 9 0	18 2 50	22 23	27 0	2 27	2 8	14 43	12 50	8 16	14 41	11 27
10	17 12 56	19 0 13	4♈51	28 35	3 22	2 53	14 57	12 56	8 14	14 39	11 26
11	17 16 53	19 57 35	17 2	0♊12	4 17	3 37	15 11	13 2	8 12	14 38	11 26
12	17 20 49	20 54 56	29 2	1 52	5 13	4 22	15 25	13 7	8 10	14 36	11 25
13	17 24 46	21 52 18	10♉54	3 34	6 9	5 6	15 39	13 13	8 9	14 34	11 25
14	17 28 43	22 49 38	22 42	5 19	7 6	5 50	15 53	13 19	8 7	14 33	11 25
15	17 32 39	23 46 58	4♊30	7 7	8 3	6 34	16 6	13 24	8 6	14 31	11 25
16	17 36 36	24 44 18	16 21	8 57	9 1	7 19	16 20	13 30	8 4	14 30	11 24
17	17 40 32	25 41 37	28 16	10 50	9 58	8 3	16 34	13 36	8 3	14 28	11 24
18	17 44 29	26 38 55	10♋16	12 46	10 57	8 47	16 48	13 42	8 1	14 26	11 24
19	17 48 25	27 36 13	22 24	14 44	11 55	9 31	17 2	13 48	8 0	14 25	11 24
20	17 52 22	28 33 31	4♌40	16 44	12 54	10 15	17 16	13 55	7 59	14 23	11 24
21	17 56 19	29 30 47	17 6	18 46	13 54	10 58	17 29	14 1	7 57	14 22	11D24
22	18 0 15	0♋28 3	29 44	20 50	14 53	11 42	17 43	14 7	7 56	14 20	11 24
23	18 4 12	1 25 18	12♍37	22 56	15 53	12 26	17 57	14 13	7 55	14 19	11 24
24	18 8 8	2 22 33	25 46	25 3	16 54	13 10	18 11	14 20	7 54	14 17	11 24
25	18 12 5	3 19 47	9♎15	27 12	17 54	13 53	18 24	14 26	7 53	14 16	11 24
26	18 16 1	4 17 0	23 6	29 21	18 55	14 37	18 38	14 32	7 52	14 14	11 24
27	18 19 58	5 14 13	7♏20	1♋32	19 57	15 20	18 52	14 39	7 51	14 13	11 24
28	18 23 54	6 11 25	21 56	3 43	20 58	16 3	19 5	14 45	7 50	14 11	11 25
29	18 27 51	7 8 37	6♐50	5 54	22 0	16 47	19 19	14 52	7 49	14 10	11 25
30	18 31 48	8♋ 5 49	21♐55	8♋ 5	23♉ 2	17♉30	19♊32	14♌59	7♏48	14♐ 8	11♎25

THE SUN ENTERS THE SIGN OF CANCER ON JUN 21 AT 12:14.

♏ SCORPIO ♐ SAGITTARIUS ♑ CAPRICORN ♒ AQUARIUS ♓ PISCES

SIDEREAL SUN. MOON. MERCURY. VENUS. MARS. JUPITER. SATURN. URANUS. NEPTUNE. PLUTO.

DAY	TIME	☉	☽	☿	♀	♂	♃	♄	♅	♆	♇
	h m s	° ' "	° '	° '	° '	° '	° '	° '	° '	° '	° '
J 1	18 35 44	9♋ 3 0	7♑ 3	10♋15	24♉ 4	18♉13	19♊46	15♌ 5	7♏47	14♐ 7	11♎25
U 2	18 39 41	10 0 12	22 2	12 25	25 7	18 56	19 59	15 12	7R47	14R 5	11 26
L 3	18 43 37	10 57 23	6♒43	14 34	26 10	19 39	20 13	15 19	7 46	14 4	11 26
Y 4	18 47 34	11 54 34	21 1	16 43	27 13	20 22	20 26	15 26	7 45	14 2	11 27
5	18 51 30	12 51 45	4♓49	18 49	28 16	21 5	20 40	15 33	7 45	14 1	11 27
6	18 55 27	13 48 57	18 9	20 55	29 20	21 48	20 53	15 40	7 44	14 0	11 27
7	18 59 23	14 46 9	1♈ 1	22 59	0♊24	22 30	21 6	15 46	7 43	13 58	11 28
8	19 3 20	15 43 21	13 31	25 1	1 28	23 13	21 20	15 53	7 43	13 57	11 28
9	19 7 17	16 40 34	25 42	27 2	2 32	23 56	21 33	16 0	7 43	13 56	11 29
10	19 11 13	17 37 47	7♉41	29 1	3 36	24 38	21 46	16 7	7 42	13 54	11 30
11	19 15 10	18 35 0	19 32	0♌58	4 41	25 21	21 59	16 15	7 42	13 53	11 30
12	19 19 6	19 32 14	1♊21	2 54	5 46	26 3	22 12	16 22	7 42	13 52	11 31
13	19 23 3	20 29 29	13 11	4 47	6 51	26 45	22 25	16 29	7 41	13 51	11 32
14	19 26 59	21 26 43	25 5	6 39	7 56	27 27	22 38	16 36	7 41	13 49	11 32
15	19 30 56	22 23 59	7♋ 7	8 29	9 1	28 9	22 51	16 43	7 41	13 48	11 33
16	19 34 52	23 21 14	19 17	10 16	10 7	28 52	23 4	16 51	7D41	13 47	11 34
17	19 38 49	24 18 30	1♌37	12 2	11 13	29 33	23 17	16 58	7 41	13 46	11 35
18	19 42 46	25 15 47	14 8	13 47	12 19	0♊15	23 30	17 5	7 41	13 45	11 36
19	19 46 42	26 13 3	26 49	15 29	13 25	0 57	23 43	17 12	7 41	13 44	11 36
20	19 50 39	27 10 20	9♍41	17 9	14 31	1 39	23 55	17 20	7 42	13 43	11 37
21	19 54 35	28 7 37	22 44	18 48	15 37	2 20	24 8	17 27	7 42	13 42	11 38
22	19 58 32	29 4 55	6♎ 1	20 24	16 44	3 2	24 21	17 35	7 42	13 41	11 39
23	20 2 28	0♌ 2 13	19 33	21 59	17 50	3 43	24 33	17 42	7 42	13 40	11 40
24	20 6 25	0 59 31	3♏20	23 32	18 57	4 25	24 46	17 50	7 43	13 39	11 41
25	20 10 21	1 56 49	17 25	25 3	20 4	5 6	24 58	17 57	7 43	13 38	11 42
26	20 14 18	2 54 8	1♐45	26 32	21 11	5 47	25 10	18 5	7 44	13 37	11 44
27	20 18 15	3 51 27	16 20	27 59	22 19	6 28	25 23	18 12	7 44	13 36	11 45
28	20 22 11	4 48 47	1♑ 4	29 24	23 26	7 9	25 35	18 20	7 45	13 35	11 46
29	20 26 8	5 46 7	15 51	0♍47	24 34	7 50	25 47	18 27	7 45	13 34	11 47
30	20 30 4	6 43 28	0♒33	2 9	25 41	8 31	25 59	18 35	7 46	13 33	11 48
31	20 34 1	7♌40 50	15♒ 2	3♍28	26♊49	9♊11	26♊11	18♌42	7♏47	13♐33	11♎50

THE SUN ENTERS THE SIGN OF LEO ON JUL 22 AT 23:04.

DAY	TIME	☉	☽	☿	♀	♂	♃	♄	♅	♆	♇
	h m s	° ' "	° '	° '	° '	° '	° '	° '	° '	° '	° '
A 1	20 37 57	8♌38 12	29♒11	4♍45	27♊57	9♊52	26♊23	18♌50	7♏48	13♐32	11♎51
U 2	20 41 54	9 35 35	12♓56	6 0	29 5	10 33	26 35	18 57	7 48	13R31	11 52
G 3	20 45 50	10 33 0	26 15	7 13	0♋13	11 13	26 47	19 5	7 49	13 30	11 53
U 4	20 49 47	11 30 25	9♈ 8	8 23	1 22	11 53	26 58	19 13	7 50	13 30	11 55
S 5	20 53 44	12 27 52	21 40	9 31	2 30	12 34	27 10	19 20	7 51	13 29	11 56
T 6	20 57 40	13 25 20	3♉53	10 37	3 39	13 14	27 22	19 28	7 52	13 28	11 58
7	21 1 37	14 22 49	15 54	11 40	4 47	13 54	27 33	19 36	7 53	13 28	11 59
8	21 5 33	15 20 20	27 47	12 41	5 56	14 34	27 44	19 43	7 55	13 27	12 1
9	21 9 30	16 17 52	9♊37	13 39	7 5	15 14	27 56	19 51	7 56	13 27	12 2
10	21 13 26	17 15 25	21 29	14 34	8 14	15 53	28 7	19 59	7 57	13 26	12 4
11	21 17 23	18 12 59	3♋28	15 26	9 23	16 33	28 18	20 6	7 58	13 26	12 5
12	21 21 19	19 10 35	15 36	16 15	10 33	17 12	28 29	20 14	8 0	13 25	12 7
13	21 25 16	20 8 12	27 57	17 0	11 42	17 52	28 40	20 22	8 1	13 25	12 8
14	21 29 13	21 5 51	10♌30	17 42	12 52	18 31	28 51	20 29	8 2	13 24	12 10
15	21 33 9	22 3 31	23 17	18 20	14 1	19 10	29 2	20 37	8 4	13 24	12 12
16	21 37 6	23 1 11	6♍17	18 55	15 11	19 50	29 13	20 45	8 6	13 24	12 13
17	21 41 2	23 58 54	19 30	19 25	16 21	20 29	29 23	20 52	8 7	13 23	12 15
18	21 44 59	24 56 37	2♎54	19 51	17 31	21 7	29 34	21 0	8 9	13 23	12 17
19	21 48 55	25 54 21	16 29	20 12	18 41	21 46	29 44	21 8	8 10	13 23	12 18
20	21 52 52	26 52 7	0♏14	20 28	19 51	22 25	29 55	21 15	8 12	13 23	12 20
21	21 56 48	27 49 53	14 8	20 40	21 1	23 3	0♋ 5	21 23	8 14	13 23	12 22
22	22 0 45	28 47 41	28 12	20R46	22 11	23 42	0 15	21 31	8 16	13 22	12 24
23	22 4 41	29 45 30	12♐24	20 46	23 22	24 20	0 25	21 38	8 18	13 22	12 26
24	22 8 38	0♍43 20	26 42	20 41	24 32	24 58	0 35	21 46	8 20	13 22	12 28
25	22 12 35	1 41 11	11♑ 4	20 30	25 43	25 36	0 45	21 54	8 22	13D22	12 29
26	22 16 31	2 39 4	25 25	20 13	26 54	26 14	0 54	22 1	8 24	13 22	12 31
27	22 20 28	3 36 58	9♒40	19 50	28 4	26 52	1 4	22 9	8 26	13 22	12 33
28	22 24 24	4 34 53	23 45	19 21	29 15	27 30	1 13	22 16	8 28	13 22	12 35
29	22 28 21	5 32 49	7♓34	18 47	0♌26	28 7	1 23	22 24	8 30	13 22	12 37
30	22 32 17	6 30 48	21 5	18 7	1 37	28 45	1 32	22 31	8 32	13 23	12 39
31	22 36 14	7♍28 47	4♈14	17♍22	2♌48	29♊22	1♋41	22♌39	8♏34	13♐23	12♎41

THE SUN ENTERS THE SIGN OF VIRGO ON AUG 23 AT 06:01.

DAY	TIME	☉	☽	☿	♀	♂	♃	♄	♅	♆	♇
	h m s	° ' "	° '	° '	° '	° '	° '	° '	° '	° '	° '
S 1	22 40 10	8♍26 49	17♈ 3	16♍32	4♌ 0	29♊59	1♋50	22♌46	8♏37	13♐23	12♎43
E 2	22 44 7	9 24 52	29 33	15R39	5 11	0♋37	1 59	22 54	8 39	13 23	12 45
P 3	22 48 4	10 22 58	11♉47	14 43	6 22	1 13	2 8	23 1	8 41	13 23	12 47
T 4	22 52 0	11 21 5	23 49	13 45	7 34	1 50	2 16	23 9	8 44	13 24	12 49
E 5	22 55 57	12 19 14	5♊43	12 47	8 45	2 27	2 25	23 16	8 46	13 24	12 51
M 6	22 59 53	13 17 25	17 34	11 49	9 57	3 4	2 33	23 24	8 49	13 24	12 53
B 7	23 3 50	14 15 39	29 28	10 54	11 9	3 40	2 41	23 31	8 51	13 25	12 56
E 8	23 7 46	15 13 54	11♋29	10 1	12 21	4 16	2 49	23 38	8 54	13 25	12 58
R 9	23 11 43	16 12 11	23 41	9 14	13 32	4 52	2 57	23 46	8 56	13 26	13 0
10	23 15 39	17 10 30	6♌ 8	8 32	14 44	5 28	3 5	23 53	8 59	13 26	13 2
11	23 19 36	18 8 52	18 51	7 56	15 57	6 4	3 13	24 0	9 1	13 27	13 4
12	23 23 33	19 7 15	1♍52	7 29	17 9	6 40	3 21	24 7	9 4	13 27	13 6
13	23 27 29	20 5 40	15 11	7 9	18 21	7 15	3 28	24 15	9 7	13 28	13 9
14	23 31 26	21 4 6	28 47	6D59	19 33	7 51	3 35	24 22	9 10	13 28	13 11
15	23 35 22	22 2 35	12♎36	6 58	20 46	8 26	3 42	24 29	9 13	13 29	13 13
16	23 39 19	23 1 6	26 37	7 6	21 58	9 1	3 49	24 36	9 15	13 30	13 15
17	23 43 15	23 59 38	10♏45	7 23	23 11	9 36	3 56	24 43	9 18	13 30	13 17
18	23 47 12	24 58 12	24 58	7 50	24 23	10 11	4 3	24 50	9 21	13 31	13 20
19	23 51 8	25 56 47	9♐13	8 26	25 36	10 45	4 9	24 57	9 24	13 32	13 22
20	23 55 5	26 55 25	23 27	9 11	26 49	11 20	4 16	25 4	9 27	13 33	13 24
21	23 59 2	27 54 3	7♑37	10 4	28 1	11 54	4 22	25 11	9 30	13 34	13 27
22	0 2 58	28 52 44	21 43	11 4	29 14	12 28	4 28	25 18	9 33	13 35	13 29
23	0 6 55	29 51 26	5♒41	12 11	0♍27	13 2	4 34	25 25	9 36	13 35	13 31
24	0 10 51	0♎50 10	19 29	13 25	1 40	13 35	4 40	25 31	9 39	13 36	13 33
25	0 14 48	1 48 55	3♓ 6	14 45	2 53	14 9	4 45	25 38	9 42	13 37	13 36
26	0 18 44	2 47 43	16 29	16 9	4 6	14 42	4 50	25 45	9 46	13 38	13 38
27	0 22 41	3 46 32	29 38	17 38	5 19	15 15	4 56	25 51	9 49	13 39	13 40
28	0 26 37	4 45 23	12♈31	19 11	6 33	15 48	5 1	25 58	9 52	13 40	13 43
29	0 30 34	5 44 17	25 8	20 47	7 46	16 21	5 6	26 4	9 55	13 41	13 45
30	0 34 30	6♎43 12	7♉31	22♍26	8♍59	16♋54	5♋10	26♌11	9♏59	13♐43	13♎47

THE SUN ENTERS THE SIGN OF LIBRA ON SEP 23 AT 03:31.

♈ ARIES ♉ TAURUS ♊ GEMINI ♋ CANCER ♌ LEO ♍ VIRGO ♎ LIBRA

1977

SIDEREAL. SUN. MOON. MERCURY. VENUS. MARS. JUPITER. SATURN. URANUS. NEPTUNE. PLUTO.

DAY	TIME	☉	☽	☿	♀	♂	♃	♄	♅	♆	♇
	h m s	° ' "	° '	° '	° '	° '	° '	° '	° '	° '	° '
O 1	0 38 27	7♎42 10	19♉42	24♍ 7	10♍13	17♋26	5♋15	26♌17	10♏ 2	13♐44	13♎50
C 2	0 42 24	8 41 9	1♊43	25 50	11 26	17 58	5 19	26 24	10 5	13 45	13 52
T 3	0 46 20	9 40 11	13 37	27 34	12 40	18 30	5 24	26 30	10 9	13 46	13 54
O 4	0 50 17	10 39 16	25 28	29 19	13 53	19 2	5 28	26 36	10 12	13 47	13 57
B 5	0 54 13	11 38 23	7♋22	1♎ 5	15 7	19 34	5 31	26 43	10 15	13 49	13 59
E 6	0 58 10	12 37 32	19 22	2 51	16 21	20 5	5 35	26 49	10 19	13 50	14 2
R 7	1 2 6	13 36 43	1♌33	4 38	17 34	20 36	5 39	26 55	10 22	13 51	14 4
8	1 6 3	14 35 56	14 0	6 24	18 48	21 7	5 42	27 1	10 26	13 52	14 6
9	1 9 59	15 35 12	26 46	8 11	20 2	21 38	5 45	27 7	10 29	13 54	14 9
10	1 13 56	16 34 30	9♍53	9 57	21 16	22 8	5 48	27 13	10 33	13 55	14 11
11	1 17 53	17 33 50	23 24	11 43	22 30	22 38	5 51	27 19	10 36	13 57	14 13
12	1 21 49	18 33 13	7♎16	13 28	23 44	23 8	5 53	27 24	10 40	13 58	14 16
13	1 25 46	19 32 37	21 28	15 13	24 58	23 38	5 56	27 30	10 43	14 0	14 18
14	1 29 42	20 32 4	5♏56	16 58	26 12	24 8	5 58	27 36	10 47	14 1	14 20
15	1 33 39	21 31 32	20 33	18 42	27 26	24 37	6 0	27 41	10 50	14 3	14 23
16	1 37 35	22 31 3	5♐13	20 25	28 41	25 6	6 1	27 47	10 54	14 4	14 25
17	1 41 32	23 30 35	19 49	22 8	29 55	25 34	6 3	27 52	10 58	14 6	14 27
18	1 45 28	24 30 9	4♑17	23 50	1♎ 9	26 3	6 4	27 58	11 1	14 7	14 30
19	1 49 25	25 29 45	18 32	25 31	2 24	26 31	6 6	28 3	11 5	14 9	14 32
20	1 53 22	26 29 22	2♒32	27 12	3 38	26 59	6 7	28 8	11 8	14 11	14 34
21	1 57 18	27 29 2	16 17	28 52	4 52	27 26	6 7	28 13	11 12	14 12	14 37
22	2 1 15	28 28 42	29 45	0♏31	6 7	27 54	6 8	28 18	11 16	14 14	14 39
23	2 5 11	29 28 25	12♓58	2 10	7 21	28 21	6 8	28 23	11 20	14 16	14 41
24	2 9 8	0♏28 9	25 57	3 49	8 36	28 47	6R 8	28 28	11 23	14 17	14 44
25	2 13 4	1 27 55	8♈43	5 26	9 50	29 14	6 8	28 33	11 27	14 19	14 46
26	2 17 1	2 27 43	21 16	7 4	11 5	29 40	6 8	28 38	11 31	14 21	14 48
27	2 20 57	3 27 33	3♉39	8 40	12 20	0♌ 5	6 8	28 42	11 34	14 23	14 51
28	2 24 54	4 27 25	15 52	10 16	13 34	0 31	6 7	28 47	11 38	14 25	14 53
29	2 28 50	5 27 18	27 56	11 52	14 49	0 56	6 6	28 51	11 42	14 26	14 55
30	2 32 47	6 27 14	9♊53	13 27	16 4	1 21	6 5	28 56	11 46	14 28	14 57
31	2 36 44	7♏27 12	21♊46	15♏ 2	17♎18	1♌45	6♋ 4	29♌ 0	11♏49	14♐30	14♎59

THE SUN ENTERS THE SIGN OF SCORPIO ON OCT 23 AT 12:42.

DAY	TIME	☉	☽	☿	♀	♂	♃	♄	♅	♆	♇
	h m s	° ' "	° '	° '	° '	° '	° '	° '	° '	° '	° '
N 1	2 40 40	8♏27 12	3♋37	16♏36	18♎33	2♌ 9	6♋ 3	29♌ 4	11♏53	14♐32	15♎ 2
O 2	2 44 37	9 27 14	15 29	18 10	19 48	2 33	6R 1	29 9	11 57	14 34	15 4
V 3	2 48 33	10 27 18	27 27	19 43	21 3	2 56	5 59	29 13	12 1	14 36	15 6
E 4	2 52 30	11 27 25	9♌35	21 16	22 18	3 19	5 57	29 17	12 4	14 38	15 8
M 5	2 56 26	12 27 33	21 58	22 48	23 33	3 42	5 55	29 21	12 8	14 40	15 10
B 6	3 0 23	13 27 43	4♍39	24 20	24 48	4 4	5 53	29 24	12 12	14 42	15 13
E 7	3 4 19	14 27 56	17 43	25 52	26 3	4 25	5 50	29 28	12 16	14 44	15 15
R 8	3 8 16	15 28 10	1♎13	27 24	27 18	4 47	5 47	29 32	12 19	14 46	15 17
9	3 12 13	16 28 27	15 11	28 54	28 33	5 8	5 44	29 35	12 23	14 48	15 19
10	3 16 9	17 28 45	29 34	0♐25	29 48	5 28	5 41	29 39	12 27	14 50	15 21
11	3 20 6	18 29 5	14♏19	1 55	1♏ 3	5 48	5 38	29 42	12 31	14 52	15 23
12	3 24 2	19 29 28	29 20	3 25	2 18	6 8	5 34	29 45	12 34	14 54	15 25
13	3 27 59	20 29 51	14♐26	4 55	3 33	6 27	5 30	29 48	12 38	14 56	15 27
14	3 31 55	21 30 17	29 28	6 24	4 48	6 45	5 26	29 51	12 42	14 58	15 29
15	3 35 52	22 30 43	14♑18	7 52	6 4	7 4	5 22	29 54	12 45	15 0	15 31
16	3 39 48	23 31 11	28 48	9 20	7 19	7 21	5 18	29 57	12 49	15 3	15 33
17	3 43 45	24 31 41	12♒55	10 48	8 34	7 38	5 13	0♍ 0	12 53	15 5	15 35
18	3 47 42	25 32 11	26 38	12 15	9 49	7 55	5 9	0 2	12 57	15 7	15 37
19	3 51 38	26 32 43	9♓58	13 42	11 4	8 11	5 4	0 5	13 0	15 9	15 39
20	3 55 35	27 33 16	22 58	15 8	12 20	8 27	4 59	0 7	13 4	15 11	15 41
21	3 59 31	28 33 50	5♈40	16 33	13 35	8 42	4 54	0 10	13 8	15 13	15 43
22	4 3 28	29 34 25	18 8	17 57	14 50	8 56	4 48	0 12	13 11	15 16	15 45
23	4 7 24	0♐35 2	0♉25	19 21	16 5	9 10	4 43	0 14	13 15	15 18	15 46
24	4 11 21	1 35 40	12 34	20 44	17 21	9 24	4 37	0 16	13 19	15 20	15 48
25	4 15 17	2 36 19	24 36	22 5	18 36	9 37	4 31	0 18	13 22	15 22	15 50
26	4 19 14	3 37 0	6♊33	23 25	19 51	9 49	4 25	0 19	13 26	15 24	15 52
27	4 23 11	4 37 42	18 27	24 44	21 7	10 0	4 19	0 21	13 29	15 27	15 53
28	4 27 7	5 38 25	0♋19	26 1	22 22	10 11	4 13	0 23	13 33	15 29	15 55
29	4 31 4	6 39 10	12 11	27 17	23 37	10 22	4 7	0 24	13 36	15 31	15 57
30	4 35 0	7♐39 56	24♋ 5	28♐30	24♏53	10♌31	4♋ 0	0♍26	13♏40	15♐33	15♎59

THE SUN ENTERS THE SIGN OF SAGITTARIUS ON NOV 22 AT 10:08.

DAY	TIME	☉	☽	☿	♀	♂	♃	♄	♅	♆	♇
	h m s	° ' "	° '	° '	° '	° '	° '	° '	° '	° '	° '
D 1	4 38 57	8♐40 44	6♌ 3	29♐41	26♏ 8	10♌41	3♋53	0♍27	13♏43	15♐36	16♎ 0
E 2	4 42 53	9 41 33	18 10	0♑48	27 23	10 49	3R47	0 28	13 47	15 38	16 2
C 3	4 46 50	10 42 23	0♍28	1 53	28 39	10 57	3 40	0 29	13 50	15 40	16 3
E 4	4 50 46	11 43 15	13 3	2 54	29 54	11 4	3 33	0 30	13 54	15 42	16 5
M 5	4 54 43	12 44 8	25 59	3 50	1♐10	11 10	3 26	0 31	13 57	15 45	16 6
B 6	4 58 40	13 45 2	9♎20	4 42	2 25	11 16	3 18	0 31	14 1	15 47	16 8
E 7	5 2 36	14 45 58	23 10	5 28	3 41	11 20	3 11	0 32	14 4	15 49	16 9
R 8	5 6 33	15 46 55	7♏29	6 8	4 56	11 25	3 4	0 32	14 7	15 51	16 11
9	5 10 29	16 47 53	22 14	6 40	6 11	11 28	2 56	0 33	14 11	15 54	16 12
10	5 14 26	17 48 52	7♐22	7 5	7 27	11 31	2 48	0 33	14 14	15 56	16 14
11	5 18 22	18 49 53	22 41	7 21	8 42	11 32	2 41	0R33	14 17	15 58	16 15
12	5 22 19	19 50 54	8♑ 1	7R27	9 58	11R33	2 33	0 33	14 21	16 0	16 16
13	5 26 15	20 51 56	23 10	7 23	11 13	11 34	2 25	0 33	14 24	16 3	16 18
14	5 30 12	21 52 58	7♒58	7 7	12 29	11 33	2 17	0 33	14 27	16 5	16 19
15	5 34 9	22 54 1	22 20	6 40	13 44	11 32	2 9	0 32	14 30	16 7	16 20
16	5 38 5	23 55 5	6♓12	6 1	15 0	11 30	2 1	0 32	14 33	16 9	16 21
17	5 42 2	24 56 8	19 36	5 12	16 15	11 27	1 53	0 31	14 36	16 12	16 22
18	5 45 58	25 57 12	2♈34	4 11	17 31	11 23	1 45	0 31	14 39	16 14	16 24
19	5 49 55	26 58 17	15 10	3 2	18 46	11 18	1 37	0 30	14 42	16 16	16 25
20	5 53 51	27 59 21	27 30	1 46	20 2	11 13	1 29	0 29	14 45	16 18	16 26
21	5 57 48	29 0 26	9♉38	0 25	21 17	11 6	1 21	0 28	14 48	16 21	16 27
22	6 1 44	0♑ 1 32	21 37	29♐ 2	22 33	10 59	1 13	0 27	14 51	16 23	16 28
23	6 5 41	1 2 37	3♊32	27 41	23 48	10 51	1 5	0 26	14 54	16 25	16 29
24	6 9 38	2 3 43	15 24	26 22	25 4	10 42	0 56	0 24	14 57	16 27	16 30
25	6 13 34	3 4 50	27 16	25 10	26 19	10 33	0 48	0 23	15 0	16 29	16 31
26	6 17 31	4 5 56	9♋10	24 5	27 35	10 22	0 40	0 21	15 3	16 32	16 31
27	6 21 27	5 7 3	21 5	23 10	28 50	10 11	0 32	0 20	15 5	16 34	16 32
28	6 25 24	6 8 10	3♌ 4	22 25	0♑ 6	9 59	0 24	0 18	15 8	16 36	16 33
29	6 29 20	7 9 18	15 8	21 50	1 21	9 46	0 16	0 16	15 11	16 38	16 34
30	6 33 17	8 10 26	27 19	21 26	2 37	9 33	0 8	0 14	15 13	16 40	16 35
31	6 37 14	9♑11 34	9♍40	21♐12	3♑52	9♌18	0♋ 0	0♍12	15♏16	16♐42	16♎35

THE SUN ENTERS THE SIGN OF CAPRICORN ON DEC 21 AT 23:24.

♏	SCORPIO	♐	SAGITTARIUS	♑	CAPRICORN	♒	AQUARIUS	♓	PISCES

SIDEREAL · SUN. · MOON. · MERCURY. · VENUS. · MARS. · JUPITER. · SATURN. · URANUS. · NEPTUNE. · PLUTO.

DAY	TIME	☉	☽	☿	♀	♂	♃	♄	♅	♆	♇
	h m s	° ' "	° '	° '	° '	° '	° '	° '	° '	° '	° '
J 1	6 41 10	10♑12 43	22♍15	21♐ 9	5♑ 8	9♌ 3	29♊52	0♍10	15♏19	16♐45	16♎36
A 2	6 45 7	11 13 52	5♎ 7	21 14	6 23	8R47	29R44	0R 7	15 21	16 47	16 37
N 3	6 49 3	12 15 1	18 20	21 27	7 39	8 31	29 36	0 5	15 24	16 49	16 37
U 4	6 53 0	13 16 11	1♏58	21 49	8 54	8 13	29 29	0 3	15 26	16 51	16 38
A 5	6 56 56	14 17 21	16 2	22 17	10 10	7 55	29 21	0 0	15 28	16 53	16 38
R 6	7 0 53	15 18 31	0♐34	22 52	11 25	7 36	29 13	29♌57	15 31	16 55	16 39
Y 7	7 4 49	16 19 42	15 29	23 32	12 41	7 17	29 6	29 55	15 33	16 57	16 39
8	7 8 46	17 20 52	0♑41	24 18	13 56	6 57	28 59	29 52	15 35	16 59	16 40
9	7 12 43	18 22 2	15 59	25 8	15 12	6 37	28 51	29 49	15 38	17 1	16 40
10	7 16 39	19 23 13	1♒12	26 2	16 27	6 16	28 44	29 46	15 40	17 3	16 40
11	7 20 36	20 24 22	16 9	27 0	17 43	5 54	28 37	29 43	15 42	17 5	16 41
12	7 24 32	21 25 32	0♓41	28 1	18 58	5 32	28 30	29 40	15 44	17 7	16 41
13	7 28 29	22 26 40	14 44	29 4	20 14	5 10	28 23	29 36	15 46	17 9	16 41
14	7 32 25	23 27 48	28 17	0♑11	21 29	4 47	28 16	29 33	15 48	17 11	16 41
15	7 36 22	24 28 56	11♈22	1 20	22 45	4 24	28 10	29 29	15 50	17 13	16 41
16	7 40 18	25 30 2	24 2	2 31	24 0	4 0	28 3	29 26	15 52	17 15	16 42
17	7 44 15	26 31 8	6♉23	3 43	25 16	3 37	27 57	29 22	15 54	17 16	16 42
18	7 48 12	27 32 14	18 29	4 58	26 31	3 13	27 51	29 19	15 55	17 18	16 42
19	7 52 8	28 33 18	0♊26	6 14	27 46	2 49	27 45	29 15	15 57	17 20	16R42
20	7 56 5	29 34 21	12 18	7 31	29 2	2 25	27 39	29 11	15 59	17 22	16 42
21	8 0 1	0♒35 24	24 9	8 50	0♒17	2 1	27 33	29 7	16 0	17 24	16 42
22	8 3 58	1 36 26	6♋ 1	10 10	1 33	1 37	27 27	29 3	16 2	17 25	16 42
23	8 7 54	2 37 27	17 57	11 32	2 48	1 13	27 22	28 59	16 3	17 27	16 41
24	8 11 51	3 38 28	29 59	12 54	4 3	0 49	27 17	28 55	16 5	17 29	16 41
25	8 15 47	4 39 27	12♌ 7	14 17	5 19	0 26	27 12	28 51	16 6	17 31	16 41
26	8 19 44	5 40 26	24 22	15 42	6 34	0 2	27 7	28 47	16 8	17 32	16 41
27	8 23 41	6 41 24	6♍46	17 7	7 50	29♋39	27 2	28 42	16 9	17 34	16 41
28	8 27 37	7 42 21	19 19	18 33	9 5	29 16	26 57	28 38	16 10	17 36	16 40
29	8 31 34	8 43 17	2♎ 4	20 0	10 20	28 53	26 53	28 34	16 12	17 37	16 40
30	8 35 30	9 44 13	15 2	21 28	11 36	28 30	26 49	28 29	16 13	17 39	16 40
31	8 39 27	10♒45 8	28♎17	22♑57	12♒51	28♋ 8	26♊45	28♌25	16♏14	17♐40	16♎39

THE SUN ENTERS THE SIGN OF AQUARIUS ON JAN 20 AT 10:05.

DAY	TIME	☉	☽	☿	♀	♂	♃	♄	♅	♆	♇
	h m s	° ' "	° '	° '	° '	° '	° '	° '	° '	° '	° '
F 1	8 43 23	11♒46 2	11♏50	24♑26	14♒ 6	27♋47	26♊41	28♌20	16♏15	17♐42	16♎39
E 2	8 47 20	12 46 56	25 44	25 56	15 22	27R26	26R37	28R16	16 16	17 43	16R38
B 3	8 51 16	13 47 49	9♐59	27 27	16 37	27 5	26 34	28 11	16 17	17 45	16 38
R 4	8 55 13	14 48 41	24 34	28 59	17 52	26 45	26 30	28 6	16 18	17 46	16 37
U 5	8 59 10	15 49 32	9♑23	0♒31	19 8	26 26	26 27	28 2	16 19	17 48	16 37
A 6	9 3 6	16 50 22	24 20	2 4	20 23	26 7	26 24	27 57	16 19	17 49	16 36
R 7	9 7 3	17 51 12	9♒16	3 38	21 38	25 49	26 22	27 52	16 20	17 50	16 35
Y 8	9 10 59	18 52 0	24 3	5 13	22 53	25 31	26 19	27 47	16 21	17 52	16 35
9	9 14 56	19 52 46	8♓31	6 49	24 9	25 14	26 17	27 43	16 21	17 53	16 34
10	9 18 52	20 53 31	22 35	8 25	25 24	24 58	26 15	27 38	16 22	17 54	16 33
11	9 22 49	21 54 15	6♈13	10 2	26 39	24 42	26 13	27 33	16 22	17 56	16 33
12	9 26 45	22 54 57	19 24	11 40	27 54	24 28	26 11	27 28	16 23	17 57	16 32
13	9 30 42	23 55 38	2♉11	13 19	29 9	24 14	26 9	27 23	16 23	17 58	16 31
14	9 34 39	24 56 16	14 37	14 59	0♓25	24 1	26 8	27 18	16 24	17 59	16 30
15	9 38 35	25 56 54	26 47	16 39	1 40	23 48	26 7	27 14	16 24	18 0	16 29
16	9 42 32	26 57 29	8♊46	18 20	2 55	23 36	26 6	27 9	16 24	18 1	16 28
17	9 46 28	27 58 3	20 39	20 3	4 10	23 26	26 5	27 4	16 24	18 2	16 27
18	9 50 25	28 58 35	2♋30	21 46	5 25	23 16	26 5	26 59	16 24	18 3	16 26
19	9 54 21	29 59 5	14 24	23 30	6 40	23 6	26 5	26 54	16R24	18 4	16 25
20	9 58 18	0♓59 34	26 23	25 15	7 55	22 58	26D 4	26 49	16 24	18 5	16 24
21	10 2 14	2 0 0	8♌31	27 1	9 10	22 50	26 4	26 45	16 24	18 6	16 23
22	10 6 11	3 0 25	20 49	28 47	10 25	22 43	26 5	26 40	16 24	18 7	16 22
23	10 10 8	4 0 49	3♍19	0♓35	11 40	22 37	26 5	26 35	16 24	18 8	16 21
24	10 14 4	5 1 10	16 0	2 24	12 55	22 32	26 6	26 30	16 24	18 9	16 20
25	10 18 1	6 1 30	28 53	4 13	14 10	22 28	26 7	26 25	16 24	18 10	16 19
26	10 21 57	7 1 49	11♎58	6 4	15 25	22 24	26 8	26 21	16 23	18 11	16 18
27	10 25 54	8 2 6	25 15	7 55	16 40	22 21	26 9	26 16	16 23	18 11	16 17
28	10 29 50	9♓ 2 21	8♏45	9♓48	17♓55	22♋19	26♊11	26♌11	16♏23	18♐12	16♎15

THE SUN ENTERS THE SIGN OF PISCES ON FEB 19 AT 00:21.

DAY	TIME	☉	☽	☿	♀	♂	♃	♄	♅	♆	♇
	h m s	° ' "	° '	° '	° '	° '	° '	° '	° '	° '	° '
M 1	10 33 47	10♓ 2 35	22♏28	11♓41	19♓10	22♋17	26♊12	26♌ 7	16♏22	18♐13	16♎14
A 2	10 37 43	11 2 47	6♐23	13 35	20 25	22D17	26 14	26R 2	16R22	18 13	16R13
R 3	10 41 40	12 2 59	20 30	15 30	21 40	22 17	26 16	25 57	16 21	18 14	16 11
C 4	10 45 36	13 3 8	4♑48	17 25	22 55	22 17	26 18	25 53	16 20	18 15	16 10
H 5	10 49 33	14 3 16	19 13	19 21	24 10	22 19	26 21	25 48	16 20	18 15	16 9
6	10 53 30	15 3 23	3♒43	21 17	25 24	22 21	26 24	25 44	16 19	18 16	16 7
7	10 57 26	16 3 28	18 10	23 13	26 39	22 24	26 26	25 39	16 18	18 16	16 6
8	11 1 23	17 3 31	2♓31	25 10	27 54	22 28	26 29	25 35	16 17	18 17	16 5
9	11 5 19	18 3 32	16 39	27 6	29 9	22 32	26 33	25 31	16 16	18 17	16 3
10	11 9 16	19 3 31	0♈29	29 2	0♈23	22 37	26 36	25 27	16 15	18 17	16 2
11	11 13 12	20 3 28	13 59	0♈56	1 38	22 43	26 39	25 22	16 14	18 18	16 0
12	11 17 9	21 3 24	27 8	2 50	2 53	22 49	26 43	25 18	16 13	18 18	15 59
13	11 21 5	22 3 17	9♉56	4 43	4 7	22 56	26 47	25 14	16 12	18 18	15 57
14	11 25 2	23 3 8	22 26	6 33	5 22	23 4	26 51	25 10	16 11	18 18	15 56
15	11 28 59	24 2 57	4♊39	8 21	6 37	23 12	26 56	25 6	16 10	18 19	15 54
16	11 32 55	25 2 44	16 41	10 6	7 51	23 21	27 0	25 2	16 9	18 19	15 53
17	11 36 52	26 2 28	28 36	11 48	9 6	23 30	27 5	24 58	16 7	18 19	15 51
18	11 40 48	27 2 10	10♋29	13 26	10 20	23 40	27 9	24 55	16 6	18 19	15 50
19	11 44 45	28 1 50	22 24	15 0	11 35	23 51	27 14	24 51	16 5	18 19	15 48
20	11 48 41	29 1 28	4♌25	16 30	12 49	24 2	27 20	24 47	16 3	18R19	15 47
21	11 52 38	0♈ 1 4	16 37	17 54	14 4	24 13	27 25	24 44	16 2	18 19	15 45
22	11 56 34	1 0 37	29 2	19 12	15 18	24 26	27 30	24 40	16 0	18 19	15 43
23	12 0 31	2 0 8	11♍43	20 25	16 32	24 38	27 36	24 37	15 59	18 19	15 42
24	12 4 28	2 59 37	24 41	21 31	17 47	24 52	27 42	24 34	15 57	18 19	15 40
25	12 8 24	3 59 4	7♎55	22 31	19 1	25 5	27 48	24 31	15 56	18 19	15 39
26	12 12 21	4 58 28	21 25	23 23	20 15	25 19	27 54	24 28	15 54	18 19	15 37
27	12 16 17	5 57 51	5♏ 9	24 9	21 30	25 34	28 0	24 25	15 52	18 19	15 35
28	12 20 14	6 57 12	19 5	24 47	22 44	25 49	28 6	24 22	15 50	18 18	15 34
29	12 24 10	7 56 32	3♐ 9	25 18	23 58	26 5	28 13	24 19	15 49	18 18	15 32
30	12 28 7	8 55 49	17 19	25 42	25 12	26 21	28 20	24 16	15 47	18 18	15 30
31	12 32 3	9♈55 5	1♑32	25♈57	26♈26	26♋37	28♊27	24♌13	15♏45	18♐18	15♎29

THE SUN ENTERS THE SIGN OF ARIES ON MAR 20 AT 23:34.

♈ ARIES ♉ TAURUS ♊ GEMINI ♋ CANCER ♌ LEO ♍ VIRGO ♎ LIBRA

SIDEREAL SUN. MOON. MERCURY. VENUS. MARS. JUPITER. SATURN. URANUS. NEPTUNE. PLUTO.

DAY	TIME	☉	☽	☿	♀	♂	♃	♄	♅	♆	♇
	h m s	° ' "	° '	° '	° '	° '	° '	° '	° '	° '	° '
A 1	12 36 0	10♈54 19	15♑46	26♈ 6	27♈40	26♋54	28♊34	24♌11	15♏43	18♐17	15♎27
P 2	12 39 56	11 53 32	29 57	26R 7	28 54	27 11	28 41	24R 8	15R41	18R17	15R25
R 3	12 43 53	12 52 42	14♒ 3	26 2	0♉ 9	27 29	28 48	24 6	15 39	18 16	15 24
I 4	12 47 50	13 51 51	28 3	25 49	1 23	27 47	28 56	24 4	15 37	18 16	15 22
L 5	12 51 46	14 50 58	11♓54	25 30	2 37	28 6	29 3	24 1	15 35	18 15	15 20
6	12 55 43	15 50 3	25 34	25 6	3 51	28 25	29 11	23 59	15 33	18 15	15 19
7	12 59 39	16 49 6	9♈ 1	24 36	5 4	28 44	29 19	23 57	15 31	18 14	15 17
8	13 3 36	17 48 7	22 13	24 1	6 18	29 3	29 27	23 55	15 29	18 14	15 15
9	13 7 32	18 47 6	5♉10	23 23	7 32	29 23	29 35	23 54	15 27	18 13	15 13
10	13 11 29	19 46 3	17 50	22 41	8 46	29 44	29 43	23 52	15 24	18 13	15 12
11	13 15 25	20 44 58	0♊16	21 58	10 0	0♌ 4	29 51	23 50	15 22	18 12	15 10
12	13 19 22	21 43 51	12 29	21 13	11 14	0 25	0♋ 0	23 49	15 20	18 11	15 8
13	13 23 19	22 42 41	24 32	20 27	12 27	0 47	0 9	23 47	15 18	18 11	15 7
14	13 27 15	23 41 30	6♋27	19 42	13 41	1 9	0 17	23 46	15 16	18 10	15 5
15	13 31 12	24 40 16	18 20	18 58	14 55	1 30	0 26	23 45	15 13	18 9	15 3
16	13 35 8	25 39 0	0♌14	18 16	16 8	1 53	0 35	23 44	15 11	18 8	15 2
17	13 39 5	26 37 42	12 15	17 37	17 22	2 15	0 44	23 43	15 9	18 7	15 0
18	13 43 1	27 36 21	24 27	17 1	18 36	2 38	0 53	23 42	15 6	18 7	14 59
19	13 46 58	28 34 58	6♍55	16 29	19 49	3 1	1 3	23 41	15 4	18 6	14 57
20	13 50 54	29 33 33	19 42	16 1	21 3	3 25	1 12	23 41	15 1	18 5	14 55
21	13 54 51	0♉32 6	2♎50	15 37	22 16	3 49	1 22	23 40	14 59	18 4	14 54
22	13 58 47	1 30 37	16 20	15 18	23 29	4 13	1 31	23 40	14 57	18 3	14 52
23	14 2 44	2 29 6	0♏12	15 4	24 43	4 37	1 41	23 39	14 54	18 2	14 50
24	14 6 41	3 27 33	14 22	14 55	25 56	5 1	1 51	23 39	14 52	18 1	14 49
25	14 10 37	4 25 58	28 47	14D52	27 9	5 26	2 1	23D39	14 49	18 0	14 47
26	14 14 34	5 24 22	13♐20	14 53	28 23	5 51	2 11	23 39	14 47	17 59	14 46
27	14 18 30	6 22 44	27 54	14 59	29 36	6 16	2 21	23 39	14 44	17 58	14 44
28	14 22 27	7 21 4	12♑24	15 9	0♊49	6 42	2 32	23 39	14 42	17 57	14 43
29	14 26 23	8 19 23	26 45	15 25	2 2	7 7	2 42	23 40	14 39	17 55	14 41
30	14 30 20	9♉17 41	10♒54	15♈45	3♊15	7♌33	2♋52	23♌40	14♏37	17♐54	14♎40

THE SUN ENTERS THE SIGN OF TAURUS ON APR 20 AT 10:50.

DAY	TIME	☉	☽	☿	♀	♂	♃	♄	♅	♆	♇
	h m s	° ' "	° '	° '	° '	° '	° '	° '	° '	° '	° '
M 1	14 34 17	10♉15 56	24♒50	16♈10	4♊28	7♌59	3♋ 3	23♌41	14♏34	17♐53	14♎38
A 2	14 38 13	11 14 11	8♓32	16 39	5 41	8 26	3 14	23 41	14R32	17R52	14R37
Y 3	14 42 10	12 12 24	22 0	17 12	6 54	8 52	3 24	23 42	14 29	17 51	14 35
4	14 46 6	13 10 35	5♈14	17 49	8 7	9 19	3 35	23 43	14 27	17 49	14 34
5	14 50 3	14 8 45	18 17	18 30	9 20	9 46	3 46	23 44	14 24	17 48	14 32
6	14 53 59	15 6 53	1♉ 7	19 14	10 33	10 13	3 57	23 45	14 21	17 47	14 31
7	14 57 56	16 5 0	13 46	20 2	11 46	10 40	4 8	23 46	14 19	17 46	14 30
8	15 1 52	17 3 5	26 14	20 54	12 59	11 8	4 19	23 47	14 16	17 44	14 28
9	15 5 49	18 1 9	8♊31	21 49	14 12	11 36	4 30	23 49	14 14	17 43	14 27
10	15 9 45	18 59 10	20 39	22 46	15 24	12 4	4 42	23 50	14 11	17 41	14 26
11	15 13 42	19 57 10	2♋38	23 47	16 37	12 32	4 53	23 52	14 9	17 40	14 24
12	15 17 39	20 55 9	14 32	24 51	17 50	13 0	5 5	23 54	14 6	17 39	14 23
13	15 21 35	21 53 5	26 24	25 58	19 2	13 29	5 16	23 55	14 4	17 37	14 22
14	15 25 32	22 51 0	8♌17	27 7	20 15	13 57	5 28	23 57	14 1	17 36	14 21
15	15 29 28	23 48 53	20 16	28 19	21 27	14 26	5 39	23 59	13 59	17 34	14 19
16	15 33 25	24 46 44	2♍25	29 33	22 40	14 55	5 51	24 1	13 56	17 33	14 18
17	15 37 21	25 44 34	14 51	0♉51	23 52	15 24	6 3	24 4	13 54	17 32	14 17
18	15 41 18	26 42 22	27 36	2 10	25 5	15 54	6 15	24 6	13 51	17 30	14 16
19	15 45 14	27 40 8	10♎47	3 32	26 17	16 23	6 27	24 8	13 49	17 29	14 15
20	15 49 11	28 37 52	24 24	4 57	27 29	16 53	6 39	24 11	13 47	17 27	14 14
21	15 53 8	29 35 35	8♏27	6 24	28 42	17 22	6 51	24 13	13 44	17 26	14 13
22	15 57 4	0♊33 17	22 56	7 53	29 54	17 52	7 3	24 16	13 42	17 24	14 12
23	16 1 1	1 30 57	7♐43	9 24	1♋ 6	18 22	7 15	24 19	13 39	17 22	14 11
24	16 4 57	2 28 36	22 41	10 58	2 18	18 53	7 27	24 22	13 37	17 21	14 10
25	16 8 54	3 26 14	7♑41	12 35	3 30	19 23	7 40	24 25	13 35	17 19	14 9
26	16 12 50	4 23 51	22 33	14 13	4 42	19 53	7 52	24 28	13 32	17 18	14 8
27	16 16 47	5 21 27	7♒10	15 54	5 54	20 24	8 4	24 31	13 30	17 16	14 7
28	16 20 43	6 19 2	21 28	17 37	7 6	20 55	8 17	24 34	13 28	17 15	14 6
29	16 24 40	7 16 36	5♓24	19 23	8 18	21 26	8 29	24 37	13 25	17 13	14 5
30	16 28 37	8 14 9	18 59	21 10	9 29	21 57	8 42	24 41	13 23	17 11	14 4
31	16 32 33	9♊11 42	2♈15	23♉ 0	10♋41	22♌28	8♋54	24♌44	13♏21	17♐10	14♎ 3

THE SUN ENTERS THE SIGN OF GEMINI ON MAY 21 AT 10:09.

DAY	TIME	☉	☽	☿	♀	♂	♃	♄	♅	♆	♇
	h m s	° ' "	° '	° '	° '	° '	° '	° '	° '	° '	° '
J 1	16 36 30	10♊ 9 13	15♈14	24♉53	11♋53	22♌59	9♋ 7	24♌48	13♏19	17♐ 8	14♎ 3
U 2	16 40 26	11 6 44	27 59	26 47	13 4	23 30	9 20	24 52	13R17	17R 7	14R 2
N 3	16 44 23	12 4 14	10♉31	28 44	14 16	24 2	9 32	24 55	13 15	17 5	14 1
E 4	16 48 19	13 1 43	22 54	0♊43	15 28	24 34	9 45	24 59	13 12	17 3	14 1
5	16 52 16	13 59 12	5♊ 8	2 43	16 39	25 5	9 58	25 3	13 10	17 2	14 0
6	16 56 12	14 56 39	17 14	4 46	17 50	25 37	10 11	25 7	13 8	17 0	13 59
7	17 0 9	15 54 6	29 15	6 51	19 2	26 9	10 24	25 12	13 6	16 59	13 59
8	17 4 6	16 51 31	11♋10	8 57	20 13	26 41	10 37	25 16	13 4	16 57	13 58
9	17 8 2	17 48 56	23 2	11 5	21 24	27 14	10 50	25 20	13 2	16 55	13 58
10	17 11 59	18 46 20	4♌52	13 14	22 36	27 46	11 3	25 24	13 1	16 54	13 57
11	17 15 55	19 43 42	16 44	15 24	23 47	28 18	11 16	25 29	12 59	16 52	13 57
12	17 19 52	20 41 4	28 42	17 35	24 58	28 51	11 29	25 33	12 57	16 50	13 56
13	17 23 48	21 38 25	10♍50	19 47	26 9	29 24	11 42	25 38	12 55	16 49	13 56
14	17 27 45	22 35 45	23 12	21 59	27 20	29 56	11 55	25 43	12 53	16 47	13 56
15	17 31 41	23 33 3	5♎54	24 11	28 31	0♍29	12 8	25 47	12 52	16 46	13 55
16	17 35 38	24 30 21	19 1	26 23	29 41	1 2	12 21	25 52	12 50	16 44	13 55
17	17 39 35	25 27 38	2♏35	28 34	0♌52	1 35	12 35	25 57	12 48	16 42	13 55
18	17 43 31	26 24 55	16 40	0♋44	2 3	2 9	12 48	26 2	12 47	16 41	13 55
19	17 47 28	27 22 10	1♐13	2 54	3 13	2 42	13 1	26 7	12 45	16 39	13 54
20	17 51 24	28 19 25	16 9	5 2	4 24	3 15	13 14	26 12	12 44	16 38	13 54
21	17 55 21	29 16 40	1♑21	7 9	5 34	3 49	13 28	26 18	12 42	16 36	13 54
22	17 59 17	0♋13 54	16 38	9 14	6 45	4 22	13 41	26 23	12 41	16 34	13 54
23	18 3 14	1 11 7	1♒48	11 18	7 55	4 56	13 54	26 28	12 39	16 33	13 54
24	18 7 11	2 8 21	16 42	13 20	9 5	5 30	14 8	26 34	12 38	16 31	13D54
25	18 11 7	3 5 34	1♓13	15 20	10 15	6 3	14 21	26 39	12 37	16 30	13 54
26	18 15 4	4 2 47	15 18	17 18	11 25	6 37	14 35	26 45	12 35	16 28	13 54
27	18 19 0	5 0 0	28 57	19 14	12 35	7 11	14 48	26 50	12 34	16 27	13 54
28	18 22 57	5 57 14	12♈11	21 8	13 45	7 46	15 1	26 56	12 33	16 25	13 54
29	18 26 53	6 54 27	25 3	23 0	14 55	8 20	15 15	27 2	12 32	16 24	13 54
30	18 30 50	7♋51 40	7♉39	24♋50	16♌ 4	8♍54	15♋28	27♌ 8	12♏31	16♐22	13♎54

THE SUN ENTERS THE SIGN OF CANCER ON JUN 21 AT 18:10.

♏ SCORPIO ♐ SAGITTARIUS ♑ CAPRICORN ♒ AQUARIUS ♓ PISCES

SIDEREAL . SUN . . . MOON . . . MERCURY . VENUS . . MARS . . . JUPITER . SATURN . URANUS . NEPTUNE . PLUTO .

DAY	TIME	☉	☽	☿	♀	♂	♃	♄	♅	♆	♇
	h m s	° ' "	° '	° '	° '	° '	° '	° '	° '	° '	° '
J 1	18 34 46	8♋48 54	2Ø♉ 1	26♋38	17♌14	9♍28	15♋42	27♌13	12♏3Ø	16♐21	13♎55
U 2	18 38 43	9 46 7	2♊12	28 23	18 24	1Ø 3	15 55	27 19	12R29	16R19	13 55
L 3	18 42 4Ø	1Ø 43 21	14 16	Ø♌ 6	19 33	1Ø 37	16 9	27 25	12 28	16 18	13 55
Y 4	18 46 36	11 4Ø 35	26 14	1 48	2Ø 42	11 12	16 22	27 31	12 27	16 16	13 55
5	18 5Ø 33	12 37 48	8♋ 9	3 27	21 52	11 47	16 36	27 37	12 26	16 15	13 56
6	18 54 29	13 35 2	2Ø 1	5 4	23 1	12 22	16 49	27 44	12 25	16 14	13 56
7	18 58 26	14 32 16	1♌52	6 39	24 1Ø	12 57	17 3	27 5Ø	12 24	16 12	13 57
8	19 2 22	15 29 3Ø	13 43	8 12	25 19	13 32	17 16	27 56	12 24	16 11	13 57
9	19 6 19	16 26 44	25 38	9 42	26 28	14 7	17 3Ø	28 2	12 23	16 1Ø	13 58
1Ø	19 1Ø 15	17 23 57	7♍38	11 1Ø	27 36	14 42	17 43	28 9	12 22	16 8	13 58
11	19 14 12	18 21 11	19 48	12 36	28 45	15 17	17 57	28 15	12 22	16 7	13 59
12	19 18 9	19 18 24	2♎11	14 Ø	29 54	15 52	18 1Ø	28 22	12 21	16 6	13 59
13	19 22 5	2Ø 15 38	14 51	15 22	1♍ 2	16 28	18 24	28 28	12 21	16 4	14 Ø
14	19 26 2	21 12 51	27 54	16 41	2 1Ø	17 3	18 37	28 35	12 2Ø	16 3	14 Ø
15	19 29 58	22 1Ø 5	11♏23	17 58	3 19	17 39	18 51	28 41	12 2Ø	16 2	14 1
16	19 33 55	23 7 18	25 2Ø	19 13	4 27	18 15	19 4	28 48	12 2Ø	16 1	14 2
17	19 37 51	24 4 32	9♐46	2Ø 25	5 35	18 5Ø	19 18	28 54	12 19	15 59	14 3
18	19 41 48	25 1 46	24 37	21 34	6 42	19 26	19 31	29 1	12 19	15 58	14 3
19	19 45 44	25 59 Ø	9♑47	22 41	7 5Ø	2Ø 2	19 45	29 8	12 19	15 57	14 4
2Ø	19 49 41	26 56 15	25 5	23 45	8 58	2Ø 38	19 58	29 15	12 19	15 56	14 5
21	19 53 38	27 53 3Ø	1Ø♒21	24 47	1Ø 5	21 14	2Ø 12	29 22	12D19	15 55	14 6
22	19 57 34	28 5Ø 45	25 24	25 45	11 12	21 5Ø	2Ø 25	29 29	12 19	15 54	14 7
23	2Ø 1 31	29 48 1	1Ø♓ 5	26 41	12 19	22 26	2Ø 38	29 35	12 19	15 53	14 8
24	2Ø 5 27	Ø♌45 18	24 2Ø	27 33	13 26	23 2	2Ø 52	29 42	12 19	15 52	14 9
25	2Ø 9 24	1 42 36	8♈ 6	28 22	14 33	23 39	21 5	29 49	12 19	15 51	14 1Ø
26	2Ø 13 2Ø	2 39 55	21 26	29 8	15 4Ø	24 15	21 19	29 56	12 19	15 5Ø	14 11
27	2Ø 17 17	3 37 14	4♉21	29 5Ø	16 46	24 51	21 32	Ø♍ 4	12 2Ø	15 49	14 12
28	2Ø 21 13	4 34 35	16 55	Ø♍28	17 53	25 28	21 45	Ø 11	12 2Ø	15 48	14 13
29	2Ø 25 1Ø	5 31 57	29 14	1 3	18 59	26 5	21 59	Ø 18	12 2Ø	15 47	14 14
3Ø	2Ø 29 7	6 29 19	11♊2Ø	1 33	2Ø 5	26 41	22 12	Ø 25	12 21	15 46	14 15
31	2Ø 33 3	7♌26 43	23♊19	1♍59	21♍11	27♍18	22♋25	Ø♍32	12♏21	15♐45	14♎16

THE SUN ENTERS THE SIGN OF LEO ON JUL 23 AT 05:01.

DAY	TIME	☉	☽	☿	♀	♂	♃	♄	♅	♆	♇
	h m s	° ' "	° '	° '	° '	° '	° '	° '	° '	° '	° '
A 1	2Ø 37 Ø	8♌24 8	5♋12	2♍21	22♍17	27♍55	22♋38	Ø♍39	12♏22	15♐44	14♎17
U 2	2Ø 4Ø 56	9 21 34	17 4	2 38	23 22	28 32	22 51	Ø 47	12 22	15R43	14 19
G 3	2Ø 44 53	1Ø 19 Ø	28 55	2 51	24 28	29 9	23 5	Ø 54	12 23	15 43	14 2Ø
U 4	2Ø 48 49	11 16 28	1Ø♌48	2R58	25 33	29 46	23 18	1 1	12 24	15 42	14 21
S 5	2Ø 52 46	12 13 56	22 45	3 1	26 38	Ø♎23	23 31	1 9	12 24	15 41	14 23
T 6	2Ø 56 42	13 11 26	4♍47	2 58	27 43	1 Ø	23 44	1 16	12 25	15 4Ø	14 24
7	21 Ø 39	14 8 56	16 55	2 5Ø	28 47	1 37	23 57	1 23	12 26	15 4Ø	14 25
8	21 4 36	15 6 27	29 13	2 36	29 52	2 15	24 1Ø	1 31	12 27	15 39	14 27
9	21 8 32	16 3 59	11♎44	2 18	Ø♎56	2 52	24 23	1 38	12 28	15 39	14 28
1Ø	21 12 29	17 1 32	24 29	1 53	2 Ø	3 3Ø	24 36	1 46	12 29	15 38	14 3Ø
11	21 16 25	17 59 6	7♏33	1 24	3 3	4 7	24 49	1 53	12 3Ø	15 37	14 31
12	21 2Ø 22	18 56 4Ø	2Ø 59	Ø 5Ø	4 7	4 45	25 2	2 Ø	12 31	15 37	14 33
13	21 24 18	19 54 16	4♐49	Ø 12	5 1Ø	5 23	25 15	2 8	12 32	15 36	14 34
14	21 28 15	2Ø 51 52	19 3	29♌3Ø	6 13	6 Ø	25 27	2 15	12 33	15 36	14 36
15	21 32 11	21 49 3Ø	3♑39	28 44	7 16	6 38	25 4Ø	2 23	12 35	15 35	14 37
16	21 36 8	22 47 8	18 32	27 56	8 19	7 16	25 53	2 3Ø	12 36	15 35	14 39
17	21 4Ø 5	23 44 47	3♒37	27 5	9 21	7 54	26 6	2 38	12 37	15 35	14 41
18	21 44 1	24 42 28	18 42	26 14	1Ø 23	8 32	26 18	2 46	12 39	15 34	14 42
19	21 47 58	25 4Ø 1Ø	3♓4Ø	25 23	11 24	9 1Ø	26 31	2 53	12 4Ø	15 34	14 44
2Ø	21 51 54	26 37 53	18 21	24 33	12 26	9 48	26 43	3 1	12 42	15 34	14 46
21	21 55 51	27 35 37	2♈39	23 45	13 27	1Ø 27	26 56	3 8	12 43	15 34	14 47
22	21 59 47	28 33 23	16 31	22 59	14 27	11 5	27 8	3 16	12 45	15 33	14 49
23	22 3 44	29 31 11	29 57	22 18	15 28	11 43	27 2Ø	3 23	12 46	15 33	14 51
24	22 7 4Ø	Ø♍29 1	12♉57	21 42	16 28	12 22	27 33	3 31	12 48	15 33	14 53
25	22 11 37	1 26 52	25 35	21 12	17 28	13 Ø	27 45	3 39	12 5Ø	15 33	14 55
26	22 15 33	2 24 45	7♊55	2Ø 48	18 27	13 39	27 57	3 46	12 52	15 33	14 56
27	22 19 3Ø	3 22 4Ø	2Ø 2	2Ø 31	19 26	14 17	28 9	3 54	12 53	15 33	14 58
28	22 23 27	4 2Ø 37	1♋59	2ØD22	2Ø 25	14 56	28 22	4 2	12 55	15D33	15 Ø
29	22 27 23	5 18 35	13 52	2Ø 21	21 23	15 35	28 34	4 9	12 57	15 33	15 2
3Ø	22 31 2Ø	6 16 35	25 43	2Ø 28	22 21	16 14	28 46	4 17	12 59	15 33	15 4
31	22 35 16	7♍14 37	7♌36	2Ø♌43	23♎19	16♎53	28♋57	4♍24	13♏ 1	15♐33	15♎ 6

THE SUN ENTERS THE SIGN OF VIRGO ON AUG 23 AT 11:58.

DAY	TIME	☉	☽	☿	♀	♂	♃	♄	♅	♆	♇
	h m s	° ' "	° '	° '	° '	° '	° '	° '	° '	° '	° '
S 1	22 39 13	8♍12 41	19♌33	21♌ 7	24♎16	17♎32	29♋ 9	4♍32	13♏ 3	15♐33	15♎ 8
E 2	22 43 9	9 1Ø 46	1♍38	21 39	25 12	18 11	29 21	4 4Ø	13 5	15 33	15 1Ø
P 3	22 47 6	1Ø 8 53	13 5Ø	22 18	26 9	18 5Ø	29 33	4 47	13 7	15 33	15 12
T 4	22 51 2	11 7 2	26 13	23 6	27 4	19 29	29 44	4 55	13 1Ø	15 34	15 14
E 5	22 54 59	12 5 12	8♎47	24 2	28 Ø	2Ø 8	29 56	5 2	13 12	15 34	15 16
M 6	22 58 56	13 3 24	21 33	25 4	28 54	2Ø 48	Ø♌ 7	5 1Ø	13 14	15 34	15 18
B 7	23 2 52	14 1 37	4♏33	26 13	29 48	21 27	Ø 19	5 17	13 16	15 34	15 2Ø
E 8	23 6 49	14 59 52	17 48	27 29	Ø♏42	22 6	Ø 3Ø	5 25	13 19	15 35	15 22
R 9	23 1Ø 45	15 58 9	1♐2Ø	28 5Ø	1 35	22 46	Ø 41	5 32	13 21	15 35	15 24
1Ø	23 14 42	16 56 27	15 8	Ø♍17	2 28	23 26	Ø 53	5 4Ø	13 24	15 35	15 27
11	23 18 38	17 54 46	29 12	1 48	3 2Ø	24 5	1 4	5 48	13 26	15 36	15 29
12	23 22 35	18 53 7	13♑32	3 24	4 11	24 45	1 15	5 55	13 29	15 36	15 31
13	23 26 31	19 51 3Ø	28 5	5 3	5 1	25 25	1 26	6 2	13 31	15 37	15 33
14	23 3Ø 28	2Ø 49 54	12♒45	6 45	5 51	26 5	1 36	6 1Ø	13 34	15 37	15 35
15	23 34 25	21 48 2Ø	27 27	8 3Ø	6 41	26 45	1 47	6 17	13 36	15 38	15 37
16	23 38 21	22 46 47	12♓ 5	1Ø 17	7 29	27 25	1 58	6 25	13 39	15 39	15 4Ø
17	23 42 18	23 45 16	26 31	12 5	8 17	28 5	2 9	6 32	13 42	15 39	15 42
18	23 46 14	24 43 47	1Ø♈41	13 55	9 3	28 45	2 19	6 4Ø	13 44	15 4Ø	15 44
19	23 5Ø 11	25 42 21	24 3Ø	15 45	9 5Ø	29 25	2 29	6 47	13 47	15 41	15 46
2Ø	23 54 7	26 4Ø 56	7♉57	17 37	1Ø 35	Ø♏ 5	2 4Ø	6 54	13 5Ø	15 41	15 49
21	23 58 4	27 39 33	21 Ø	19 28	11 19	Ø 45	2 5Ø	7 2	13 53	15 42	15 51
22	Ø 2 Ø	28 38 13	3♊42	21 2Ø	12 2	1 26	3 Ø	7 9	13 56	15 43	15 53
23	Ø 5 57	29 36 55	16 5	23 11	12 45	2 6	3 1Ø	7 16	13 59	15 44	15 55
24	Ø 9 53	Ø♎35 39	28 14	25 3	13 26	2 47	3 2Ø	7 23	14 2	15 45	15 58
25	Ø 13 5Ø	1 34 25	1Ø♋12	26 53	14 6	3 27	3 3Ø	7 3Ø	14 5	15 45	16 Ø
26	Ø 17 47	2 33 13	22 5	28 44	14 46	4 8	3 4Ø	7 38	14 8	15 46	16 2
27	Ø 21 43	3 32 4	3♌56	Ø♎33	15 24	4 49	3 49	7 45	14 11	15 47	16 5
28	Ø 25 4Ø	4 3Ø 57	15 51	2 22	16 1	5 29	3 59	7 52	14 14	15 48	16 7
29	Ø 29 36	5 29 52	27 53	4 11	16 36	6 1Ø	4 8	7 59	14 17	15 49	16 9
3Ø	Ø 33 33	6♎28 49	1Ø♍ 5	5♎58	17♏11	6♏51	4♌17	8♍ 6	14♏2Ø	15♐5Ø	16♎12

THE SUN ENTERS THE SIGN OF LIBRA ON SEP 23 AT 09:27.

♈ ARIES ♉ TAURUS ♊ GEMINI ♋ CANCER ♌ LEO ♍ VIRGO ♎ LIBRA

1978

SIDEREAL · SUN. · MOON. · MERCURY. · VENUS. · MARS. · JUPITER. · SATURN. · URANUS. · NEPTUNE. · PLUTO.

DAY	TIME	☉	☽	☿	♀	♂	♃	♄	♅	♆	♇
	h m s	° ' "	° '	° '	° '	° '	° '	° '	° '	° '	° '
O 1	0 37 29	7♎27 49	22♍30	7♎45	17♏44	7♏32	4♌26	8♍13	14♏23	15♐51	16♎14
C 2	0 41 26	8 26 50	5♎ 9	9 31	18 16	8 13	4 36	8 20	14 26	15 53	16 16
T 3	0 45 22	9 25 54	18 3	11 16	18 46	8 54	4 44	8 27	14 29	15 54	16 19
O 4	0 49 19	10 24 59	1♏13	13 0	19 15	9 36	4 53	8 34	14 33	15 55	16 21
B 5	0 53 16	11 24 6	14 36	14 43	19 42	10 17	5 2	8 40	14 36	15 56	16 23
E 6	0 57 12	12 23 16	28 13	16 26	20 8	10 58	5 10	8 47	14 39	15 57	16 26
R 7	1 1 9	13 22 27	12♐ 1	18 8	20 32	11 39	5 19	8 54	14 43	15 58	16 28
8	1 5 5	14 21 40	25 58	19 49	20 54	12 21	5 27	9 1	14 46	16 0	16 31
9	1 9 2	15 20 55	10♑ 3	21 29	21 15	13 2	5 35	9 7	14 49	16 1	16 33
10	1 12 58	16 20 11	24 14	23 8	21 34	13 44	5 43	9 14	14 53	16 2	16 35
11	1 16 55	17 19 30	8♒29	24 47	21 50	14 26	5 51	9 21	14 56	16 4	16 38
12	1 20 51	18 18 49	22 45	26 24	22 5	15 7	5 59	9 27	14 59	16 5	16 40
13	1 24 48	19 18 11	6♓59	28 2	22 18	15 49	6 7	9 34	15 3	16 7	16 42
14	1 28 45	20 17 34	21 9	29 38	22 28	16 31	6 14	9 40	15 6	16 8	16 45
15	1 32 41	21 17 0	5♈11	1♏14	22 37	17 13	6 22	9 46	15 10	16 9	16 47
16	1 36 38	22 16 27	19 1	2 49	22 43	17 55	6 29	9 53	15 13	16 11	16 50
17	1 40 34	23 15 56	2♉36	4 23	22 47	18 37	6 36	9 59	15 17	16 12	16 52
18	1 44 31	24 15 27	15 53	5 57	22R48	19 19	6 43	10 5	15 20	16 14	16 54
19	1 48 27	25 15 1	28 53	7 30	22 48	20 1	6 50	10 11	15 24	16 16	16 57
20	1 52 24	26 14 37	11♊33	9 2	22 44	20 43	6 57	10 17	15 28	16 17	16 59
21	1 56 20	27 14 15	23 57	10 34	22 39	21 25	7 3	10 23	15 31	16 19	17 1
22	2 0 17	28 13 55	6♋ 7	12 6	22 31	22 8	7 9	10 29	15 35	16 20	17 4
23	2 4 13	29 13 37	18 5	13 36	22 20	22 50	7 16	10 35	15 38	16 22	17 6
24	2 8 10	0♏13 22	29 58	15 6	22 8	23 33	7 22	10 41	15 42	16 24	17 8
25	2 12 7	1 13 9	11♌49	16 36	21 52	24 15	7 28	10 47	15 46	16 25	17 11
26	2 16 3	2 12 58	23 43	18 5	21 35	24 58	7 33	10 52	15 49	16 27	17 13
27	2 20 0	3 12 49	5♍47	19 33	21 15	25 40	7 39	10 58	15 53	16 29	17 15
28	2 23 56	4 12 42	18 3	21 1	20 53	26 23	7 44	11 4	15 57	16 31	17 18
29	2 27 53	5 12 38	0♎36	22 28	20 29	27 6	7 50	11 9	16 0	16 32	17 20
30	2 31 49	6 12 35	13 29	23 54	20 3	27 49	7 55	11 15	16 4	16 34	17 22
31	2 35 46	7♏12 35	26♎42	25♏20	19♏35	28♏32	8♌ 0	11♍20	16♏ 8	16♐36	17♎24

THE SUN ENTERS THE SIGN OF SCORPIO ON OCT 23 AT 18:38.

DAY	TIME	☉	☽	☿	♀	♂	♃	♄	♅	♆	♇
	h m s	° ' "	° '	° '	° '	° '	° '	° '	° '	° '	° '
N 1	2 39 42	8♏12 36	10♏16	26♏45	19♏ 5	29♏15	8♌ 4	11♍25	16♏12	16♐38	17♎27
O 2	2 43 39	9 12 40	24 7	28 9	18R34	29 58	8 9	11 30	16 15	16 40	17 29
V 3	2 47 36	10 12 45	8♐12	29 33	18 1	0♐41	8 13	11 36	16 19	16 42	17 31
E 4	2 51 32	11 12 52	22 26	0♐56	17 27	1 24	8 17	11 41	16 23	16 44	17 33
M 5	2 55 29	12 13 1	6♑45	2 17	16 52	2 7	8 22	11 46	16 26	16 46	17 36
B 6	2 59 25	13 13 11	21 3	3 38	16 17	2 50	8 25	11 51	16 30	16 48	17 38
E 7	3 3 22	14 13 23	5♒17	4 58	15 40	3 34	8 29	11 55	16 34	16 49	17 40
R 8	3 7 18	15 13 36	19 25	6 16	15 4	4 17	8 33	12 0	16 38	16 51	17 42
9	3 11 15	16 13 50	3♓25	7 34	14 27	5 1	8 36	12 5	16 41	16 53	17 44
10	3 15 11	17 14 6	17 18	8 49	13 51	5 44	8 39	12 9	16 45	16 55	17 46
11	3 19 8	18 14 24	1♈ 1	10 4	13 15	6 28	8 42	12 14	16 49	16 58	17 49
12	3 23 5	19 14 43	14 36	11 16	12 40	7 11	8 45	12 18	16 53	17 0	17 51
13	3 27 1	20 15 3	28 0	12 26	12 6	7 55	8 47	12 23	16 56	17 2	17 53
14	3 30 58	21 15 25	11♉14	13 34	11 33	8 39	8 50	12 27	17 0	17 4	17 55
15	3 34 54	22 15 49	24 14	14 40	11 1	9 22	8 52	12 31	17 4	17 6	17 57
16	3 38 51	23 16 14	7♊ 2	15 42	10 31	10 6	8 54	12 35	17 8	17 8	17 59
17	3 42 47	24 16 41	19 35	16 41	10 3	10 50	8 56	12 39	17 11	17 10	18 1
18	3 46 44	25 17 10	1♋54	17 37	9 37	11 34	8 57	12 43	17 15	17 12	18 3
19	3 50 40	26 17 40	14 1	18 28	9 12	12 18	8 59	12 47	17 19	17 14	18 5
20	3 54 37	27 18 12	25 58	19 15	8 50	13 2	9 0	12 50	17 22	17 16	18 7
21	3 58 34	28 18 46	7♌49	19 56	8 31	13 46	9 1	12 54	17 26	17 19	18 9
22	4 2 30	29 19 22	19 38	20 31	8 13	14 31	9 2	12 58	17 30	17 21	18 11
23	4 6 27	0♐19 59	1♍30	21 0	7 58	15 15	9 3	13 1	17 34	17 23	18 13
24	4 10 23	1 20 38	13 32	21 21	7 46	15 59	9 3	13 4	17 37	17 25	18 15
25	4 14 20	2 21 18	25 47	21R34	7 36	16 44	9R 4	13 8	17 41	17 27	18 16
26	4 18 16	3 22 0	8♎21	21 38	7 28	17 28	9 4	13 11	17 45	17 29	18 18
27	4 22 13	4 22 44	21 19	21 32	7 23	18 13	9 3	13 14	17 48	17 32	18 20
28	4 26 9	5 23 30	4♏42	21 16	7D21	18 57	9 3	13 17	17 52	17 34	18 22
29	4 30 6	6 24 16	18 32	20 48	7 20	19 42	9 3	13 20	17 55	17 36	18 24
30	4 34 3	7♐25 5	2♐45	20♐10	7♏23	20♐26	9♌ 2	13♍22	17♏59	17♐38	18♎25

THE SUN ENTERS THE SIGN OF SAGITTARIUS ON NOV 22 AT 16:06.

DAY	TIME	☉	☽	☿	♀	♂	♃	♄	♅	♆	♇
	h m s	° ' "	° '	° '	° '	° '	° '	° '	° '	° '	° '
D 1	4 37 59	8♐25 54	17♐17	19♐21	7♏27	21♐11	9♌ 1	13♍25	18♏ 3	17♐41	18♎27
E 2	4 41 56	9 26 45	2♑ 0	18R22	7 34	21 56	9R 0	13 28	18 6	17 43	18 29
C 3	4 45 52	10 27 36	16 46	17 14	7 44	22 41	8 58	13 30	18 10	17 45	18 30
E 4	4 49 49	11 28 29	1♒28	15 59	7 55	23 26	8 57	13 32	18 13	17 47	18 32
M 5	4 53 45	12 29 23	15 58	14 38	8 9	24 11	8 55	13 35	18 17	17 50	18 34
B 6	4 57 42	13 30 17	0♓14	13 16	8 25	24 56	8 53	13 37	18 20	17 52	18 35
E 7	5 1 38	14 31 12	14 13	11 53	8 42	25 41	8 51	13 39	18 24	17 54	18 37
R 8	5 5 35	15 32 7	27 55	10 34	9 2	26 26	8 49	13 41	18 27	17 56	18 38
9	5 9 32	16 33 3	11♈23	9 21	9 24	27 11	8 46	13 42	18 31	17 59	18 40
10	5 13 28	17 34 0	24 37	8 15	9 47	27 56	8 44	13 44	18 34	18 1	18 41
11	5 17 25	18 34 58	7♉40	7 19	10 13	28 41	8 41	13 46	18 37	18 3	18 43
12	5 21 21	19 35 56	20 31	6 33	10 40	29 27	8 38	13 47	18 41	18 5	18 44
13	5 25 18	20 36 55	3♊12	5 59	11 9	0♑12	8 35	13 48	18 44	18 8	18 45
14	5 29 14	21 37 55	15 42	5 36	11 39	0 57	8 31	13 50	18 47	18 10	18 47
15	5 33 11	22 38 56	28 2	5D24	12 11	1 43	8 27	13 51	18 51	18 12	18 48
16	5 37 7	23 39 57	10♋13	5 22	12 45	2 28	8 24	13 52	18 54	18 15	18 49
17	5 41 4	24 40 59	22 14	5 30	13 19	3 14	8 20	13 53	18 57	18 17	18 51
18	5 45 1	25 42 2	4♌ 8	5 47	13 56	3 59	8 15	13 54	19 0	18 19	18 52
19	5 48 57	26 43 5	15 57	6 12	14 33	4 45	8 11	13 54	19 4	18 21	18 53
20	5 52 54	27 44 10	27 45	6 45	15 12	5 31	8 7	13 55	19 7	18 24	18 54
21	5 56 50	28 45 15	9♍35	7 24	15 53	6 16	8 2	13 55	19 10	18 26	18 55
22	6 0 47	29 46 21	21 33	8 10	16 34	7 2	7 57	13 56	19 13	18 28	18 57
23	6 4 43	0♑47 27	3♎45	9 0	17 17	7 48	7 52	13 56	19 16	18 30	18 58
24	6 8 40	1 48 35	16 15	9 55	18 0	8 34	7 47	13R56	19 19	18 32	18 59
25	6 12 36	2 49 43	29 9	10 54	18 45	9 20	7 41	13 56	19 22	18 35	19 0
26	6 16 33	3 50 51	12♏31	11 57	19 31	10 6	7 36	13 56	19 25	18 37	19 1
27	6 20 30	4 52 1	26 23	13 2	20 17	10 52	7 30	13 56	19 28	18 39	19 2
28	6 24 26	5 53 11	10♐43	14 11	21 5	11 38	7 24	13 56	19 31	18 41	19 2
29	6 28 23	6 54 21	25 28	15 22	21 53	12 24	7 18	13 55	19 34	18 43	19 3
30	6 32 19	7 55 31	10♑30	16 35	22 43	13 10	7 12	13 55	19 36	18 46	19 4
31	6 36 16	8♑56 42	25♑39	17♐50	23♏33	13♑56	7♌ 6	13♍54	19♏39	18♐48	19♎ 5

THE SUN ENTERS THE SIGN OF CAPRICORN ON DEC 22 AT 05:22.

♏ SCORPIO ♐ SAGITTARIUS ♑ CAPRICORN ♒ AQUARIUS ♓ PISCES

1979

SIDEREAL | SUN. | MOON. | MERCURY. | VENUS. | MARS. | JUPITER. | SATURN. | URANUS. | NEPTUNE. | PLUTO.

DAY	TIME h m s	☉ ° ' "	☽ ° '	☿ ° '	♀ ° '	♂ ° '	♃ ° '	♄ ° '	♅ ° '	♆ ° '	♇ ° '
J 1	6 40 12	9♑57 53	10♒45	19♐ 7	24♏24	14♑42	7♌ 0	13♍54	19♏42	18♐50	19♎ 6
A 2	6 44 9	10 59 4	25 38	20 25	25 16	15 28	6R53	13R53	19 45	18 52	19 6
N 3	6 48 6	12 0 14	10♓11	21 45	26 8	16 15	6 47	13 52	19 47	18 54	19 7
U 4	6 52 2	13 1 24	24 23	23 6	27 1	17 1	6 40	13 51	19 50	18 56	19 8
A 5	6 55 59	14 2 34	8♈11	24 28	27 55	17 47	6 33	13 49	19 52	18 58	19 8
R 6	6 59 55	15 3 43	21 36	25 51	28 50	18 34	6 26	13 48	19 55	19 0	19 9
Y 7	7 3 52	16 4 52	4♉43	27 15	29 45	19 20	6 19	13 47	19 57	19 3	19 10
8	7 7 48	17 6 1	17 33	28 40	0♐40	20 7	6 12	13 45	20 0	19 5	19 10
9	7 11 45	18 7 9	0♊ 9	0♑ 5	1 37	20 53	6 4	13 44	20 2	19 7	19 11
10	7 15 41	19 8 17	12 33	1 31	2 33	21 40	5 57	13 42	20 5	19 9	19 11
11	7 19 38	20 9 25	24 49	2 58	3 31	22 26	5 50	13 40	20 7	19 11	19 11
12	7 23 35	21 10 32	6♋56	4 26	4 29	23 13	5 42	13 38	20 9	19 13	19 12
13	7 27 31	22 11 39	18 56	5 54	5 27	23 59	5 34	13 36	20 12	19 15	19 12
14	7 31 28	23 12 45	0♌51	7 23	6 26	24 46	5 27	13 34	20 14	19 17	19 12
15	7 35 24	24 13 51	12 42	8 53	7 25	25 33	5 19	13 32	20 16	19 19	19 13
16	7 39 21	25 14 57	24 30	10 23	8 25	26 19	5 11	13 30	20 18	19 21	19 13
17	7 43 17	26 16 2	6♍19	11 53	9 25	27 6	5 3	13 27	20 20	19 22	19 13
18	7 47 14	27 17 7	18 10	13 25	10 26	27 53	4 56	13 25	20 22	19 24	19 13
19	7 51 10	28 18 11	0♎ 9	14 56	11 27	28 40	4 48	13 22	20 24	19 26	19 13
20	7 55 7	29 19 15	12 20	16 29	12 29	29 27	4 40	13 19	20 26	19 28	19 13
21	7 59 4	0♒20 19	24 47	18 1	13 30	0♒13	4 32	13 17	20 28	19 30	19R13
22	8 3 0	1 21 23	7♏36	19 35	14 33	1 0	4 24	13 14	20 30	19 32	19 13
23	8 6 57	2 22 26	20 50	21 9	15 35	1 47	4 16	13 11	20 31	19 34	19 13
24	8 10 53	3 23 29	4♐33	22 43	16 38	2 34	4 8	13 8	20 33	19 35	19 13
25	8 14 50	4 24 31	18 45	24 19	17 41	3 21	4 0	13 5	20 35	19 37	19 13
26	8 18 46	5 25 33	3♑25	25 54	18 45	4 8	3 51	13 1	20 36	19 39	19 13
27	8 22 43	6 26 34	18 26	27 31	19 48	4 55	3 43	12 58	20 38	19 40	19 13
28	8 26 39	7 27 34	3♒41	29 8	20 53	5 42	3 35	12 55	20 39	19 42	19 13
29	8 30 36	8 28 34	18 58	0♒46	21 57	6 29	3 27	12 51	20 41	19 44	19 13
30	8 34 33	9 29 32	4♓ 7	2 24	23 2	7 16	3 19	12 48	20 42	19 45	19 12
31	8 38 29	10♒30 29	18♓59	4♒ 3	24♐ 6	8♒ 3	3♌12	12♍44	20♏44	19♐47	19♎12

THE SUN ENTERS THE SIGN OF AQUARIUS ON JAN 20 AT 16:01.

DAY	TIME h m s	☉ ° ' "	☽ ° '	☿ ° '	♀ ° '	♂ ° '	♃ ° '	♄ ° '	♅ ° '	♆ ° '	♇ ° '
F 1	8 42 26	11♒31 25	3♈27	5♒43	25♐12	8♒51	3♌ 4	12♍40	20♏45	19♐49	19♎12
E 2	8 46 22	12 32 20	17 29	7 23	26 17	9 38	2R56	12R37	20 46	19 50	19R11
B 3	8 50 19	13 33 13	1♉ 5	9 4	27 23	10 25	2 48	12 33	20 47	19 52	19 11
R 4	8 54 15	14 34 5	14 16	10 46	28 28	11 12	2 40	12 29	20 49	19 53	19 10
U 5	8 58 12	15 34 56	27 4	12 29	29 34	11 59	2 33	12 25	20 50	19 55	19 10
A 6	9 2 8	16 35 45	9♊35	14 12	0♑41	12 46	2 25	12 21	20 51	19 56	19 9
R 7	9 6 5	17 36 33	21 52	15 56	1 47	13 34	2 17	12 17	20 52	19 58	19 9
Y 8	9 10 2	18 37 19	3♋58	17 41	2 54	14 21	2 10	12 13	20 53	19 59	19 8
9	9 13 58	19 38 4	15 56	19 27	4 1	15 8	2 3	12 8	20 53	20 0	19 8
10	9 17 55	20 38 48	27 49	21 13	5 8	15 55	1 55	12 4	20 54	20 2	19 7
11	9 21 51	21 39 30	9♌39	23 0	6 15	16 42	1 48	12 0	20 55	20 3	19 6
12	9 25 48	22 40 10	21 28	24 48	7 22	17 30	1 41	11 56	20 56	20 4	19 6
13	9 29 44	23 40 50	3♍18	26 36	8 30	18 17	1 34	11 51	20 56	20 6	19 5
14	9 33 41	24 41 27	15 12	28 26	9 37	19 4	1 27	11 47	20 57	20 7	19 4
15	9 37 37	25 42 4	27 10	0♓15	10 45	19 52	1 20	11 42	20 58	20 8	19 3
16	9 41 34	26 42 39	9♎17	2 6	11 53	20 39	1 14	11 38	20 58	20 9	19 3
17	9 45 30	27 43 13	21 34	3 57	13 2	21 26	1 7	11 33	20 59	20 10	19 2
18	9 49 27	28 43 46	4♏ 6	5 48	14 10	22 14	1 1	11 28	20 59	20 11	19 1
19	9 53 24	29 44 17	16 55	7 39	15 18	23 1	0 55	11 24	20 59	20 12	19 0
20	9 57 20	0♓44 47	0♐ 5	9 31	16 27	23 48	0 48	11 19	21 0	20 14	18 59
21	10 1 17	1 45 16	13 38	11 22	17 36	24 36	0 42	11 14	21 0	20 15	18 58
22	10 5 13	2 45 44	27 37	13 13	18 45	25 23	0 37	11 10	21 0	20 16	18 57
23	10 9 10	3 46 10	12♑ 0	15 3	19 54	26 10	0 31	11 5	21 0	20 16	18 56
24	10 13 6	4 46 35	26 45	16 53	21 3	26 58	0 25	11 0	21R 0	20 17	18 55
25	10 17 3	5 46 58	11♒46	18 41	22 12	27 45	0 20	10 55	21 0	20 18	18 54
26	10 20 59	6 47 20	26 55	20 28	23 21	28 32	0 15	10 51	21 0	20 19	18 53
27	10 24 56	7 47 40	12♓ 2	22 13	24 31	29 20	0 10	10 46	21 0	20 20	18 52
28	10 28 53	8♓47 59	26♓59	23♓55	25♑40	0♓ 7	0♌ 5	10♍41	21♏ 0	20♐21	18♎50

THE SUN ENTERS THE SIGN OF PISCES ON FEB 19 AT 06:14.

DAY	TIME h m s	☉ ° ' "	☽ ° '	☿ ° '	♀ ° '	♂ ° '	♃ ° '	♄ ° '	♅ ° '	♆ ° '	♇ ° '
M 1	10 32 49	9♓48 15	11♈36	25♓34	26♑50	0♓54	0♌ 0	10♍36	21♏ 0	20♐22	18♎49
A 2	10 36 46	10 48 30	25 50	27 10	28 0	1 42	29♋55	10R31	20R59	20 22	18R48
R 3	10 40 42	11 48 42	9♉37	28 42	29 10	2 29	29 51	10 27	20 59	20 23	18 47
C 4	10 44 39	12 48 53	22 58	0♈ 9	0♒19	3 16	29 47	10 22	20 59	20 24	18 45
H 5	10 48 35	13 49 1	5♊53	1 30	1 29	4 4	29 43	10 17	20 58	20 24	18 44
6	10 52 32	14 49 8	18 27	2 46	2 40	4 51	29 39	10 12	20 58	20 25	18 43
7	10 56 28	15 49 12	0♋43	3 56	3 50	5 38	29 35	10 8	20 57	20 25	18 42
8	11 0 25	16 49 14	12 46	4 58	5 0	6 26	29 32	10 3	20 56	20 26	18 40
9	11 4 22	17 49 14	24 40	5 54	6 10	7 13	29 28	9 58	20 56	20 26	18 39
10	11 8 18	18 49 12	6♌30	6 41	7 21	8 0	29 25	9 53	20 55	20 27	18 37
11	11 12 15	19 49 8	18 18	7 20	8 31	8 48	29 22	9 49	20 54	20 27	18 36
12	11 16 11	20 49 2	0♍ 8	7 51	9 42	9 35	29 19	9 44	20 54	20 28	18 35
13	11 20 8	21 48 53	12 3	8 13	10 52	10 22	29 17	9 39	20 53	20 28	18 33
14	11 24 4	22 48 43	24 5	8 27	12 3	11 9	29 14	9 35	20 52	20 28	18 32
15	11 28 1	23 48 31	6♎15	8R31	13 14	11 57	29 12	9 30	20 51	20 29	18 30
16	11 31 57	24 48 16	18 36	8 28	14 24	12 44	29 10	9 25	20 50	20 29	18 29
17	11 35 54	25 48 0	1♏ 9	8 15	15 35	13 31	29 8	9 21	20 49	20 29	18 27
18	11 39 50	26 47 42	13 54	7 56	16 46	14 18	29 7	9 16	20 48	20 29	18 26
19	11 43 47	27 47 23	26 54	7 28	17 57	15 5	29 5	9 12	20 47	20 30	18 24
20	11 47 44	28 47 1	10♐10	6 55	19 8	15 52	29 4	9 8	20 45	20 30	18 23
21	11 51 40	29 46 38	23 43	6 15	20 19	16 40	29 3	9 3	20 44	20 30	18 21
22	11 55 37	0♈46 14	7♑34	5 30	21 31	17 27	29 2	8 59	20 43	20 30	18 20
23	11 59 33	1 45 47	21 42	4 42	22 42	18 14	29 1	8 55	20 42	20R30	18 18
24	12 3 30	2 45 19	6♒ 6	3 51	23 53	19 1	29 1	8 51	20 40	20 30	18 16
25	12 7 26	3 44 49	20 44	2 58	25 4	19 48	29 0	8 46	20 39	20 30	18 15
26	12 11 23	4 44 17	5♓30	2 5	26 16	20 35	29D 0	8 42	20 37	20 30	18 13
27	12 15 19	5 43 43	20 18	1 13	27 27	21 22	29 0	8 38	20 36	20 30	18 11
28	12 19 16	6 43 8	5♈ 1	0 22	28 39	22 9	29 1	8 34	20 34	20 29	18 10
29	12 23 13	7 42 30	19 32	29♓33	29 50	22 56	29 1	8 30	20 33	20 29	18 8
30	12 27 9	8 41 50	3♉45	28 48	1♓ 2	23 43	29 2	8 27	20 31	20 29	18 7
31	12 31 6	9♈41 8	17♉35	28♓ 7	2♓13	24♓30	29♋ 3	8♍23	20♏29	20♐29	18♎ 5

THE SUN ENTERS THE SIGN OF ARIES ON MAR 21 AT 05:22.

♈ ARIES ♉ TAURUS ♊ GEMINI ♋ CANCER ♌ LEO ♍ VIRGO ♎ LIBRA

SIDEREAL SUN. MOON. MERCURY. VENUS. MARS. JUPITER. SATURN. URANUS. NEPTUNE. PLUTO.

DAY	TIME	☉	☽	☿	♀	♂	♃	♄	♅	♆	♇
	h m s	° ' "	° '	° '	° '	° '	° '	° '	° '	° '	° '
A 1	12 35 2	10♈40 24	1♊ 1	27♓31	3♓25	25♓17	29♋ 4	8♍19	20♏28	20♐29	18♎ 3
P 2	12 38 59	11 39 37	14 2	26R59	4 36	26 4	29 5	8R16	20R26	20R28	18R 2
R 3	12 42 55	12 38 49	26 41	26 33	5 48	26 51	29 6	8 12	20 24	20 28	18 0
I 4	12 46 52	13 37 58	9♋ 0	26 13	7 0	27 37	29 8	8 9	20 22	20 28	17 58
L 5	12 50 48	14 37 4	21 4	25 57	8 12	28 24	29 10	8 5	20 20	20 27	17 57
6	12 54 45	15 36 9	2♌59	25 48	9 23	29 11	29 12	8 2	20 19	20 27	17 55
7	12 58 42	16 35 11	14 48	25D44	10 35	29 58	29 14	7 59	20 17	20 26	17 53
8	13 2 38	17 34 10	26 36	25 45	11 47	0♈44	29 16	7 55	20 15	20 26	17 51
9	13 6 35	18 33 8	8♍29	25 52	12 59	1 31	29 19	7 52	20 13	20 25	17 50
10	13 10 31	19 32 3	20 29	26 4	14 11	2 18	29 22	7 49	20 11	20 25	17 48
11	13 14 28	20 30 56	2♎41	26 21	15 23	3 4	29 25	7 47	20 9	20 24	17 46
12	13 18 24	21 29 47	15 5	26 43	16 35	3 51	29 28	7 44	20 7	20 23	17 45
13	13 22 21	22 28 36	27 43	27 9	17 47	4 38	29 31	7 41	20 4	20 23	17 43
14	13 26 17	23 27 23	10♏37	27 40	18 59	5 24	29 34	7 38	20 2	20 22	17 41
15	13 30 14	24 26 8	23 44	28 15	20 11	6 10	29 38	7 36	20 0	20 21	17 40
16	13 34 10	25 24 52	7♐ 5	28 53	21 23	6 57	29 42	7 33	19 58	20 21	17 38
17	13 38 7	26 23 33	20 38	29 36	22 35	7 43	29 46	7 31	19 56	20 20	17 36
18	13 42 4	27 22 13	4♑22	0♈22	23 47	8 30	29 50	7 29	19 53	20 19	17 35
19	13 46 0	28 20 51	18 16	1 11	24 59	9 16	29 54	7 27	19 51	20 18	17 33
20	13 49 57	29 19 28	2♒19	2 4	26 11	10 2	29 58	7 25	19 49	20 18	17 31
21	13 53 53	0♉18 3	16 30	3 0	27 23	10 49	0♌ 3	7 23	19 47	20 17	17 30
22	13 57 50	1 16 36	0♓47	3 59	28 36	11 35	0 8	7 21	19 44	20 16	17 28
23	14 1 46	2 15 8	15 7	5 1	29 48	12 21	0 13	7 19	19 42	20 15	17 27
24	14 5 43	3 13 38	29 29	6 5	1♈ 0	13 7	0 18	7 17	19 39	20 14	17 25
25	14 9 39	4 12 6	13♈48	7 12	2 12	13 53	0 23	7 16	19 37	20 13	17 23
26	14 13 36	5 10 33	27 58	8 22	3 25	14 39	0 28	7 14	19 35	20 12	17 22
27	14 17 33	6 8 57	11♉56	9 34	4 37	15 26	0 34	7 13	19 32	20 11	17 20
28	14 21 29	7 7 20	25 37	10 48	5 49	16 12	0 40	7 12	19 30	20 10	17 19
29	14 25 26	8 5 41	8♊58	12 5	7 2	16 57	0 46	7 10	19 27	20 9	17 17
30	14 29 22	9♉ 4 1	21♊57	13♈24	8♈14	17♈43	0♌52	7♍ 9	19♏25	20♐ 8	17♎15

THE SUN ENTERS THE SIGN OF TAURUS ON APR 20 AT 16:36.

DAY	TIME	☉	☽	☿	♀	♂	♃	♄	♅	♆	♇
	h m s	° ' "	° '	° '	° '	° '	° '	° '	° '	° '	° '
M 1	14 33 19	10♉ 2 18	4♋36	14♈45	9♈26	18♈29	0♌58	7♍ 8	19♏22	20♐ 6	17♎14
A 2	14 37 15	11 0 33	16 56	16 8	10 39	19 15	1 4	7R 8	19R20	20R 5	17R12
Y 3	14 41 12	11 58 46	29 1	17 34	11 51	20 1	1 11	7 7	19 17	20 4	17 11
4	14 45 8	12 56 57	10♌56	19 1	13 3	20 47	1 17	7 6	19 15	20 3	17 9
5	14 49 5	13 55 6	22 46	20 30	14 16	21 32	1 24	7 6	19 12	20 2	17 8
6	14 53 2	14 53 13	4♍35	22 2	15 28	22 18	1 31	7 5	19 10	20 1	17 7
7	14 56 58	15 51 18	16 30	23 35	16 41	23 3	1 38	7 5	19 7	19 59	17 5
8	15 0 55	16 49 22	28 34	25 10	17 53	23 49	1 45	7 5	19 5	19 58	17 4
9	15 4 51	17 47 23	10♎53	26 48	19 6	24 35	1 52	7D 5	19 2	19 57	17 2
10	15 8 48	18 45 23	23 29	28 27	20 18	25 20	2 0	7 5	19 0	19 55	17 1
11	15 12 44	19 43 21	6♏24	0♉ 8	21 31	26 5	2 7	7 5	18 57	19 54	17 0
12	15 16 41	20 41 17	19 38	1 51	22 43	26 51	2 15	7 5	18 55	19 53	16 58
13	15 20 37	21 39 12	3♐10	3 37	23 56	27 36	2 23	7 5	18 52	19 51	16 57
14	15 24 34	22 37 5	16 57	5 24	25 8	28 21	2 31	7 6	18 50	19 50	16 56
15	15 28 31	23 34 57	0♑55	7 13	26 21	29 7	2 39	7 6	18 47	19 49	16 54
16	15 32 27	24 32 48	15 0	9 4	27 33	29 52	2 47	7 7	18 45	19 47	16 53
17	15 36 24	25 30 37	29 9	10 57	28 46	0♉37	2 55	7 7	18 42	19 46	16 52
18	15 40 20	26 28 25	13♒19	12 53	29 59	1 22	3 4	7 8	18 40	19 44	16 51
19	15 44 17	27 26 13	27 27	14 50	1♉11	2 7	3 12	7 9	18 37	19 43	16 49
20	15 48 13	28 23 59	11♓34	16 49	2 24	2 52	3 21	7 10	18 35	19 41	16 48
21	15 52 10	29 21 43	25 37	18 49	3 36	3 37	3 29	7 11	18 32	19 40	16 47
22	15 56 6	0♊19 27	9♈36	20 52	4 49	4 22	3 38	7 13	18 30	19 38	16 46
23	16 0 3	1 17 10	23 29	22 56	6 2	5 6	3 47	7 14	18 27	19 37	16 45
24	16 4 0	2 14 52	7♉14	25 2	7 14	5 51	3 56	7 15	18 25	19 35	16 44
25	16 7 56	3 12 32	20 48	27 10	8 27	6 36	4 6	7 17	18 22	19 34	16 43
26	16 11 53	4 10 12	4♊10	29 18	9 40	7 21	4 15	7 19	18 20	19 32	16 42
27	16 15 49	5 7 50	17 15	1♊28	10 53	8 5	4 24	7 20	18 18	19 31	16 41
28	16 19 46	6 5 27	0♋ 5	3 39	12 5	8 50	4 34	7 22	18 15	19 29	16 40
29	16 23 42	7 3 2	12 37	5 50	13 18	9 34	4 43	7 24	18 13	19 28	16 39
30	16 27 39	8 0 37	24 53	8 2	14 31	10 19	4 53	7 26	18 11	19 26	16 38
31	16 31 35	8♊58 10	6♌56	10♊14	15♉44	11♉ 3	5♌ 3	7♍28	18♏ 8	19♐24	16♎37

THE SUN ENTERS THE SIGN OF GEMINI ON MAY 21 AT 15:55.

DAY	TIME	☉	☽	☿	♀	♂	♃	♄	♅	♆	♇
	h m s	° ' "	° '	° '	° '	° '	° '	° '	° '	° '	° '
J 1	16 35 32	9♊55 42	18♌50	12♊26	16♉56	11♉47	5♌13	7♍31	18♏ 6	19♐23	16♎36
U 2	16 39 29	10 53 12	0♍39	14 38	18 9	12 32	5 23	7 33	18R 4	19R21	16R36
N 3	16 43 25	11 50 41	12 28	16 48	19 22	13 16	5 33	7 35	18 2	19 20	16 35
E 4	16 47 22	12 48 9	24 23	18 58	20 35	14 0	5 43	7 38	17 59	19 18	16 34
5	16 51 18	13 45 35	6♎29	21 7	21 47	14 44	5 53	7 40	17 57	19 16	16 33
6	16 55 15	14 43 1	18 51	23 15	23 0	15 28	6 4	7 43	17 55	19 15	16 33
7	16 59 11	15 40 25	1♏34	25 21	24 13	16 12	6 14	7 46	17 53	19 13	16 32
8	17 3 8	16 37 48	14 39	27 25	25 26	16 56	6 25	7 49	17 51	19 12	16 31
9	17 7 4	17 35 11	28 8	29 27	26 39	17 40	6 35	7 52	17 49	19 10	16 31
10	17 11 1	18 32 32	12♐ 0	1♋27	27 52	18 24	6 46	7 55	17 47	19 8	16 30
11	17 14 58	19 29 52	26 11	3 25	29 5	19 7	6 57	7 58	17 45	19 7	16 30
12	17 18 54	20 27 12	10♑34	5 21	0♊18	19 51	7 7	8 2	17 43	19 5	16 29
13	17 22 51	21 24 32	25 5	7 15	1 30	20 35	7 18	8 5	17 41	19 3	16 29
14	17 26 47	22 21 50	9♒36	9 6	2 43	21 18	7 29	8 8	17 39	19 2	16 28
15	17 30 44	23 19 8	24 3	10 55	3 56	22 2	7 40	8 12	17 37	19 0	16 28
16	17 34 40	24 16 26	8♓21	12 41	5 9	22 45	7 52	8 16	17 35	18 59	16 27
17	17 38 37	25 13 44	22 29	14 25	6 22	23 29	8 3	8 19	17 33	18 57	16 27
18	17 42 33	26 11 1	6♈26	16 7	7 35	24 12	8 14	8 23	17 31	18 55	16 27
19	17 46 30	27 8 18	20 11	17 46	8 48	24 55	8 25	8 27	17 29	18 54	16 26
20	17 50 27	28 5 34	3♉46	19 22	10 1	25 38	8 37	8 31	17 28	18 52	16 26
21	17 54 23	29 2 51	17 9	20 57	11 14	26 22	8 48	8 35	17 26	18 51	16 26
22	17 58 20	0♋ 0 7	0♊20	22 28	12 28	27 5	9 0	8 39	17 24	18 49	16 26
23	18 2 16	0 57 23	13 19	23 57	13 41	27 48	9 11	8 43	17 23	18 47	16 26
24	18 6 13	1 54 39	26 6	25 24	14 54	28 31	9 23	8 48	17 21	18 46	16 25
25	18 10 9	2 51 54	8♋39	26 48	16 7	29 14	9 35	8 52	17 20	18 44	16 25
26	18 14 6	3 49 9	20 59	28 10	17 20	29 57	9 47	8 57	17 18	18 43	16 25
27	18 18 3	4 46 24	3♌ 7	29 28	18 33	0♊39	9 59	9 1	17 17	18 41	16D25
28	18 21 59	5 43 38	15 5	0♌44	19 46	1 22	10 10	9 6	17 15	18 40	16 25
29	18 25 56	6 40 52	26 56	1 58	21 0	2 5	10 22	9 10	17 14	18 38	16 25
30	18 29 52	7♋38 5	8♍43	3♌ 8	22♊13	2♊47	10♌34	9♍15	17♏13	18♐37	16♎25

THE SUN ENTERS THE SIGN OF CANCER ON JUN 21 AT 23:57.

♏ SCORPIO ♐ SAGITTARIUS ♑ CAPRICORN ♒ AQUARIUS ♓ PISCES

SIDEREAL · SUN. · MOON. · MERCURY. · VENUS. · MARS. · JUPITER. · SATURN. · URANUS. · NEPTUNE. · PLUTO.

DAY	TIME h m s	☉ ° ' "	☽ ° '	☿ ° '	♀ ° '	♂ ° '	♃ ° '	♄ ° '	♅ ° '	♆ ° '	♇ ° '
J 1	18 33 49	8♋35 18	20♍31	4♌16	23♊26	3♊30	10♌46	9♍20	17♏11	18♐35	16♎26
U 2	18 37 45	9 32 31	2♎25	5 21	24 39	4 12	10 59	9 25	17R10	18R34	16 26
L 3	18 41 42	10 29 43	14 31	6 23	25 52	4 55	11 11	9 30	17 9	18 32	16 26
Y 4	18 45 38	11 26 55	26 52	7 21	27 6	5 37	11 23	9 35	17 8	18 31	16 26
5	18 49 35	12 24 6	9♏36	8 17	28 19	6 19	11 35	9 40	17 7	18 29	16 26
6	18 53 31	13 21 18	22 44	9 9	29 32	7 2	11 47	9 45	17 6	18 28	16 27
7	18 57 28	14 18 29	6♐19	9 57	0♋46	7 44	12 0	9 51	17 5	18 26	16 27
8	19 1 25	15 15 40	20 21	10 42	1 59	8 26	12 12	9 56	17 4	18 25	16 27
9	19 5 21	16 12 51	4♑46	11 24	3 12	9 8	12 25	10 1	17 3	18 24	16 28
10	19 9 18	17 10 2	19 28	12 1	4 26	9 50	12 37	10 7	17 2	18 22	16 28
11	19 13 14	18 7 14	4♒21	12 35	5 39	10 32	12 50	10 12	17 1	18 21	16 29
12	19 17 11	19 4 25	19 15	13 4	6 53	11 13	13 2	10 18	17 1	18 19	16 29
13	19 21 7	20 1 37	4♓ 4	13 29	8 6	11 55	13 15	10 23	17 0	18 18	16 30
14	19 25 4	20 58 49	18 39	13 50	9 20	12 37	13 27	10 29	16 59	18 17	16 30
15	19 29 1	21 56 2	2♈59	14 7	10 33	13 19	13 40	10 35	16 59	18 16	16 31
16	19 32 57	22 53 16	17 0	14 18	11 47	14 0	13 53	10 41	16 58	18 14	16 31
17	19 36 54	23 50 30	0♉43	14R25	13 0	14 42	14 5	10 47	16 58	18 13	16 32
18	19 40 50	24 47 45	14 8	14 27	14 14	15 23	14 18	10 53	16 57	18 12	16 33
19	19 44 47	25 45 0	27 17	14 25	15 27	16 5	14 31	10 59	16 57	18 11	16 33
20	19 48 43	26 42 16	10♊11	14 17	16 41	16 46	14 44	11 5	16 56	18 9	16 34
21	19 52 40	27 39 33	22 52	14 5	17 54	17 27	14 57	11 11	16 56	18 8	16 35
22	19 56 36	28 36 51	5♋20	13 47	19 8	18 8	15 10	11 17	16 56	18 7	16 36
23	20 0 33	29 34 9	17 37	13 26	20 22	18 49	15 22	11 23	16 56	18 6	16 37
24	20 4 30	0♌31 28	29 45	13 0	21 35	19 30	15 35	11 29	16 55	18 5	16 37
25	20 8 26	1 28 48	11♌43	12 29	22 49	20 11	15 48	11 36	16 55	18 4	16 38
26	20 12 23	2 26 8	23 35	11 55	24 3	20 52	16 1	11 42	16D55	18 3	16 39
27	20 16 19	3 23 28	5♍23	11 18	25 17	21 33	16 14	11 49	16 55	18 2	16 40
28	20 20 16	4 20 49	17 9	10 38	26 30	22 14	16 27	11 55	16 55	18 1	16 41
29	20 24 12	5 18 11	28 57	9 55	27 44	22 55	16 40	12 2	16 55	18 0	16 42
30	20 28 9	6 15 33	10♎52	9 12	28 58	23 35	16 53	12 8	16 56	17 59	16 43
31	20 32 5	7♌12 56	22♎57	8♌27	0♌12	24♊16	17♌ 6	12♍15	16♏56	17♐58	16♎44

THE SUN ENTERS THE SIGN OF LEO ON JUL 23 AT 10:49.

DAY	TIME h m s	☉ ° ' "	☽ ° '	☿ ° '	♀ ° '	♂ ° '	♃ ° '	♄ ° '	♅ ° '	♆ ° '	♇ ° '
A 1	20 36 2	8♌10 19	5♏17	7♌43	1♌26	24♊56	17♌19	12♍21	16♏56	17♐57	16♎46
U 2	20 39 58	9 7 43	17 58	6R59	2 40	25 37	17 33	12 28	16 56	17R56	16 47
G 3	20 43 55	10 5 7	1♐ 3	6 17	3 54	26 17	17 46	12 35	16 57	17 55	16 48
U 4	20 47 52	11 2 32	14 35	5 38	5 7	26 57	17 59	12 42	16 57	17 54	16 49
S 5	20 51 48	11 59 58	28 35	5 2	6 21	27 37	18 12	12 48	16 58	17 54	16 50
T 6	20 55 45	12 57 25	13♑ 1	4 30	7 35	28 18	18 25	12 55	16 58	17 53	16 52
7	20 59 41	13 54 52	27 50	4 2	8 49	28 58	18 38	13 2	16 59	17 52	16 53
8	21 3 38	14 52 21	12♒53	3 40	10 3	29 38	18 51	13 9	16 59	17 51	16 54
9	21 7 34	15 49 50	28 2	3 24	11 17	0♋17	19 4	13 16	17 0	17 51	16 56
10	21 11 31	16 47 20	13♓ 9	3 13	12 31	0 57	19 18	13 23	17 1	17 50	16 57
11	21 15 28	17 44 52	28 3	3D10	13 45	1 37	19 31	13 30	17 1	17 49	16 59
12	21 19 24	18 42 25	12♈39	3 13	14 59	2 17	19 44	13 37	17 2	17 49	17 0
13	21 23 21	19 39 59	26 52	3 22	16 13	2 56	19 57	13 44	17 3	17 48	17 1
14	21 27 17	20 37 35	10♉42	3 40	17 28	3 36	20 10	13 51	17 4	17 48	17 3
15	21 31 14	21 35 13	24 8	4 4	18 42	4 15	20 23	13 58	17 5	17 47	17 4
16	21 35 10	22 32 52	7♊12	4 35	19 56	4 55	20 37	14 6	17 6	17 47	17 6
17	21 39 7	23 30 32	19 57	5 14	21 10	5 34	20 50	14 13	17 7	17 46	17 8
18	21 43 3	24 28 14	2♋26	5 59	22 24	6 13	21 3	14 20	17 8	17 46	17 9
19	21 47 0	25 25 58	14 41	6 52	23 38	6 53	21 16	14 27	17 10	17 46	17 11
20	21 50 56	26 23 43	26 46	7 51	24 53	7 32	21 29	14 35	17 11	17 45	17 13
21	21 54 53	27 21 30	8♌42	8 56	26 7	8 11	21 42	14 42	17 12	17 45	17 14
22	21 58 50	28 19 18	20 34	10 8	27 21	8 50	21 55	14 49	17 13	17 45	17 16
23	22 2 46	29 17 7	2♍21	11 25	28 36	9 29	22 8	14 56	17 15	17 44	17 18
24	22 6 43	0♍14 58	14 8	12 49	29 50	10 7	22 22	15 4	17 16	17 44	17 19
25	22 10 39	1 12 50	25 56	14 17	1♍ 4	10 46	22 35	15 11	17 18	17 44	17 21
26	22 14 36	2 10 44	7♎48	15 50	2 18	11 25	22 48	15 19	17 19	17 44	17 23
27	22 18 32	3 8 38	19 47	17 27	3 33	12 3	23 1	15 26	17 21	17 44	17 25
28	22 22 29	4 6 35	1♏56	19 9	4 47	12 42	23 14	15 33	17 23	17 43	17 27
29	22 26 25	5 4 32	14 18	20 53	6 2	13 20	23 27	15 41	17 24	17 43	17 29
30	22 30 22	6 2 31	26 58	22 41	7 16	13 58	23 40	15 48	17 26	17D43	17 30
31	22 34 19	7♍ 0 32	9♐58	24♌31	8♍30	14♋37	23♌53	15♍56	17♏28	17♐43	17♎32

THE SUN ENTERS THE SIGN OF VIRGO ON AUG 23 AT 17:48.

DAY	TIME h m s	☉ ° ' "	☽ ° '	☿ ° '	♀ ° '	♂ ° '	♃ ° '	♄ ° '	♅ ° '	♆ ° '	♇ ° '
S 1	22 38 15	7♍58 33	23♐23	26♌23	9♍45	15♋15	24♌ 6	16♍ 3	17♏30	17♐43	17♎34
E 2	22 42 12	8 56 36	7♑13	28 16	10 59	15 53	24 19	16 11	17 31	17 43	17 36
P 3	22 46 8	9 54 41	21 29	0♍11	12 14	16 31	24 32	16 18	17 33	17 44	17 38
T 4	22 50 5	10 52 46	6♒ 9	2 7	13 28	17 9	24 45	16 26	17 35	17 44	17 40
E 5	22 54 1	11 50 54	21 8	4 3	14 43	17 47	24 57	16 33	17 37	17 44	17 42
M 6	22 57 58	12 49 3	6♓18	6 0	15 57	18 24	25 10	16 41	17 39	17 44	17 44
B 7	23 1 54	13 47 13	21 30	7 56	17 12	19 2	25 23	16 48	17 41	17 44	17 46
E 8	23 5 51	14 45 25	6♈35	9 52	18 26	19 39	25 36	16 56	17 44	17 45	17 48
R 9	23 9 48	15 43 39	21 24	11 48	19 41	20 17	25 49	17 3	17 46	17 45	17 50
10	23 13 44	16 41 55	5♉50	13 43	20 55	20 54	26 1	17 11	17 48	17 45	17 52
11	23 17 41	17 40 14	19 51	15 38	22 10	21 32	26 14	17 18	17 50	17 46	17 55
12	23 21 37	18 38 34	3♊24	17 32	23 24	22 9	26 27	17 26	17 52	17 46	17 57
13	23 25 34	19 36 56	16 31	19 25	24 39	22 46	26 39	17 33	17 55	17 46	17 59
14	23 29 30	20 35 21	29 14	21 17	25 53	23 23	26 52	17 41	17 57	17 47	18 1
15	23 33 27	21 33 48	11♋38	23 8	27 8	24 0	27 4	17 48	18 0	17 47	18 3
16	23 37 23	22 32 16	23 47	24 58	28 22	24 37	27 17	17 56	18 2	17 48	18 5
17	23 41 20	23 30 47	5♌45	26 47	29 37	25 13	27 29	18 4	18 5	17 48	18 8
18	23 45 17	24 29 20	17 35	28 35	0♎52	25 50	27 42	18 11	18 7	17 49	18 10
19	23 49 13	25 27 55	29 23	0♎22	2 6	26 27	27 54	18 19	18 10	17 50	18 12
20	23 53 10	26 26 32	11♍ 9	2 8	3 21	27 3	28 6	18 26	18 12	17 50	18 14
21	23 57 6	27 25 11	22 59	3 53	4 36	27 40	28 19	18 33	18 15	17 51	18 16
22	0 1 3	28 23 52	4♎52	5 37	5 50	28 16	28 31	18 41	18 18	17 52	18 19
23	0 4 59	29 22 35	16 53	7 20	7 5	28 52	28 43	18 48	18 20	17 52	18 21
24	0 8 56	0♎21 20	29 2	9 2	8 20	29 28	28 55	18 56	18 23	17 53	18 23
25	0 12 52	1 20 6	11♏21	10 43	9 34	0♌ 4	29 7	19 3	18 26	17 54	18 26
26	0 16 49	2 18 55	23 52	12 23	10 49	0 40	29 19	19 11	18 29	17 55	18 28
27	0 20 45	3 17 45	6♐37	14 2	12 4	1 16	29 31	19 18	18 32	17 56	18 30
28	0 24 42	4 16 37	19 39	15 41	13 18	1 51	29 43	19 25	18 35	17 57	18 33
29	0 28 39	5 15 31	2♑59	17 18	14 33	2 27	29 55	19 33	18 38	17 58	18 35
30	0 32 35	6♎14 27	16♑40	18♎54	15♎48	3♌ 2	0♍ 7	19♍40	18♏41	17♐59	18♎37

THE SUN ENTERS THE SIGN OF LIBRA ON SEP 23 AT 15:17.

♈ ARIES ♉ TAURUS ♊ GEMINI ♋ CANCER ♌ LEO ♍ VIRGO ♎ LIBRA

SIDEREAL SUN. MOON. MERCURY. VENUS. MARS. JUPITER. SATURN. URANUS. NEPTUNE. PLUTO.

DAY	TIME	☉	☽	☿	♀	♂	♃	♄	♅	♆	♇
	h m s	° ' "	° '	° '	° '	° '	° '	° '	° '	° '	° '
O 1	0 36 32	7♎13 24	0♒42	20♎30	17♎ 2	3♌37	0♍18	19♍47	18♏44	18♐ 0	18♎40
C 2	0 40 28	8 12 23	15 4	22 4	18 17	4 13	0 30	19 55	18 47	18 1	18 42
T 3	0 44 25	9 11 23	29 45	23 38	19 32	4 48	0 42	20 2	18 50	18 2	18 44
O 4	0 48 21	10 10 26	14♓40	25 11	20 47	5 23	0 53	20 9	18 53	18 3	18 47
B 5	0 52 18	11 9 30	29 42	26 43	22 1	5 58	1 5	20 16	18 56	18 4	18 49
E 6	0 56 14	12 8 36	14♈42	28 15	23 16	6 32	1 16	20 24	18 59	18 5	18 51
R 7	1 0 11	13 7 45	29 32	29 45	24 31	7 7	1 27	20 31	19 2	18 6	18 54
8	1 4 8	14 6 55	14♉ 4	1♏15	25 45	7 41	1 39	20 38	19 5	18 7	18 56
9	1 8 4	15 6 8	28 11	2 44	27 0	8 16	1 50	20 45	19 9	18 9	18 58
10	1 12 1	16 5 23	11♊52	4 12	28 15	8 50	2 1	20 52	19 12	18 10	19 1
11	1 15 57	17 4 40	25 4	5 39	29 29	9 24	2 12	20 59	19 15	18 11	19 3
12	1 19 54	18 4 0	7♋51	7 6	0♏44	9 58	2 23	21 6	19 18	18 12	19 6
13	1 23 50	19 3 22	20 16	8 31	1 59	10 32	2 34	21 13	19 22	18 14	19 8
14	1 27 47	20 2 46	2♌24	9 56	3 14	11 6	2 44	21 20	19 25	18 15	19 10
15	1 31 43	21 2 13	14 20	11 20	4 28	11 40	2 55	21 27	19 29	18 17	19 13
16	1 35 40	22 1 41	26 8	12 43	5 43	12 13	3 6	21 34	19 32	18 18	19 15
17	1 39 37	23 1 12	7♍55	14 4	6 58	12 47	3 16	21 41	19 35	18 19	19 18
18	1 43 33	24 0 46	19 43	15 25	8 13	13 20	3 27	21 47	19 39	18 21	19 20
19	1 47 30	25 0 21	1♎37	16 45	9 27	13 53	3 37	21 54	19 42	18 22	19 22
20	1 51 26	25 59 58	13 39	18 4	10 42	14 26	3 47	22 1	19 46	18 24	19 25
21	1 55 23	26 59 38	25 52	19 21	11 57	14 59	3 58	22 8	19 49	18 25	19 27
22	1 59 19	27 59 20	8♏16	20 37	13 12	15 31	4 8	22 14	19 53	18 27	19 29
23	2 3 16	28 59 3	20 52	21 52	14 26	16 4	4 18	22 21	19 56	18 29	19 32
24	2 7 12	29 58 49	3♐40	23 5	15 41	16 36	4 28	22 27	20 0	18 30	19 34
25	2 11 9	0♏58 36	16 41	24 17	16 56	17 8	4 37	22 34	20 3	18 32	19 36
26	2 15 5	1 58 25	29 53	25 26	18 11	17 40	4 47	22 40	20 7	18 34	19 39
27	2 19 2	2 58 16	13♑19	26 34	19 25	18 12	4 57	22 46	20 11	18 35	19 41
28	2 22 59	3 58 8	26 58	27 40	20 40	18 44	5 6	22 53	20 14	18 37	19 44
29	2 26 55	4 58 2	10♒50	28 42	21 55	19 16	5 15	22 59	20 18	18 39	19 46
30	2 30 52	5 57 58	24 57	29 43	23 10	19 47	5 25	23 5	20 22	18 41	19 48
31	2 34 48	6♏57 55	9♓17	0♐40	24♏24	20♌18	5♍34	23♍11	20♏25	18♐42	19♎50

THE SUN ENTERS THE SIGN OF SCORPIO ON OCT 24 AT 00:29.

DAY	TIME	☉	☽	☿	♀	♂	♃	♄	♅	♆	♇
	h m s	° ' "	° '	° '	° '	° '	° '	° '	° '	° '	° '
N 1	2 38 45	7♏57 54	23♓49	1♐34	25♏39	20♌49	5♍43	23♍17	20♏29	18♐44	19♎53
O 2	2 42 41	8 57 55	8♈27	2 24	26 54	21 20	5 52	23 24	20 33	18 46	19 55
V 3	2 46 38	9 57 57	23 8	3 10	28 8	21 51	6 1	23 30	20 36	18 48	19 57
E 4	2 50 34	10 58 1	7♉43	3 51	29 23	22 21	6 9	23 35	20 40	18 50	20 0
M 5	2 54 31	11 58 6	22 5	4 27	0♐38	22 52	6 18	23 41	20 44	18 52	20 2
B 6	2 58 28	12 58 14	6♊ 8	4 57	1 53	23 22	6 26	23 47	20 47	18 53	20 4
E 7	3 2 24	13 58 24	19 48	5 21	3 7	23 52	6 35	23 53	20 51	18 55	20 6
R 8	3 6 21	14 58 36	3♋ 3	5 38	4 22	24 22	6 43	23 58	20 55	18 57	20 9
9	3 10 17	15 58 49	15 53	5R47	5 37	24 51	6 51	24 4	20 58	18 59	20 11
10	3 14 14	16 59 5	28 20	5 48	6 51	25 21	6 59	24 10	21 2	19 1	20 13
11	3 18 10	17 59 23	10♌30	5 39	8 6	25 50	7 7	24 15	21 6	19 3	20 15
12	3 22 7	18 59 42	22 26	5 21	9 21	26 19	7 14	24 20	21 10	19 5	20 17
13	3 26 3	20 0 4	4♍15	4 54	10 35	26 48	7 22	24 26	21 13	19 7	20 19
14	3 30 0	21 0 27	16 2	4 15	11 50	27 16	7 29	24 31	21 17	19 9	20 22
15	3 33 57	22 0 52	27 52	3 27	13 5	27 45	7 36	24 36	21 21	19 11	20 24
16	3 37 53	23 1 19	9♎51	2 30	14 19	28 13	7 44	24 41	21 25	19 13	20 26
17	3 41 50	24 1 48	22 1	1 23	15 34	28 41	7 51	24 46	21 28	19 16	20 28
18	3 45 46	25 2 19	4♏25	0 10	16 49	29 8	7 57	24 51	21 32	19 18	20 30
19	3 49 43	26 2 51	17 5	28♏52	18 4	29 36	8 4	24 56	21 36	19 20	20 32
20	3 53 39	27 3 25	0♐ 2	27 31	19 18	0♍ 3	8 11	25 1	21 40	19 22	20 34
21	3 57 36	28 4 1	13 12	26 10	20 33	0 30	8 17	25 6	21 43	19 24	20 36
22	4 1 32	29 4 38	26 36	24 51	21 48	0 56	8 23	25 10	21 47	19 26	20 38
23	4 5 29	0♐ 5 16	10♑10	23 38	23 2	1 23	8 29	25 15	21 51	19 28	20 40
24	4 9 26	1 5 56	23 53	22 32	24 17	1 49	8 35	25 19	21 54	19 30	20 42
25	4 13 22	2 6 36	7♒43	21 36	25 32	2 15	8 41	25 24	21 58	19 33	20 44
26	4 17 19	3 7 18	21 39	20 50	26 46	2 40	8 47	25 28	22 2	19 35	20 46
27	4 21 15	4 8 1	5♓41	20 15	28 1	3 5	8 52	25 32	22 5	19 37	20 48
28	4 25 12	5 8 44	19 47	19 52	29 15	3 30	8 58	25 36	22 9	19 39	20 50
29	4 29 8	6 9 29	3♈58	19D41	0♑30	3 55	9 3	25 40	22 13	19 41	20 51
30	4 33 5	7♐10 14	18♈12	19♏41	1♑45	4♍19	9♍ 8	25♍44	22♏16	19♐44	20♎53

THE SUN ENTERS THE SIGN OF SAGITTARIUS ON NOV 22 AT 21:55.

DAY	TIME	☉	☽	☿	♀	♂	♃	♄	♅	♆	♇
	h m s	° ' "	° '	° '	° '	° '	° '	° '	° '	° '	° '
D 1	4 37 1	8♐11 1	2♉25	19♏51	2♑59	4♍44	9♍12	25♍48	22♏20	19♐46	20♎55
E 2	4 40 58	9 11 49	16 34	20 10	4 14	5 7	9 17	25 52	22 24	19 48	20 57
C 3	4 44 55	10 12 38	0♊33	20 39	5 28	5 31	9 22	25 56	22 27	19 50	20 58
E 4	4 48 51	11 13 27	14 19	21 15	6 43	5 54	9 26	25 59	22 31	19 53	21 0
M 5	4 52 48	12 14 18	27 46	21 58	7 57	6 17	9 30	26 3	22 34	19 55	21 2
B 6	4 56 44	13 15 11	10♋53	22 48	9 12	6 39	9 34	26 6	22 38	19 57	21 4
E 7	5 0 41	14 16 4	23 39	23 43	10 26	7 2	9 38	26 10	22 42	19 59	21 5
R 8	5 4 37	15 16 59	6♌ 6	24 42	11 41	7 23	9 41	26 13	22 45	20 2	21 7
9	5 8 34	16 17 54	18 16	25 46	12 55	7 45	9 45	26 16	22 49	20 4	21 8
10	5 12 30	17 18 51	0♍13	26 54	14 10	8 6	9 48	26 19	22 52	20 6	21 10
11	5 16 27	18 19 49	12 3	28 4	15 24	8 27	9 51	26 22	22 56	20 8	21 11
12	5 20 24	19 20 48	23 50	29 17	16 39	8 47	9 54	26 25	22 59	20 11	21 13
13	5 24 20	20 21 49	5♎42	0♐33	17 53	9 7	9 57	26 27	23 3	20 13	21 14
14	5 28 17	21 22 50	17 42	1 51	19 8	9 26	9 59	26 30	23 6	20 15	21 16
15	5 32 13	22 23 52	29 56	3 10	20 22	9 46	10 2	26 33	23 9	20 17	21 17
16	5 36 10	23 24 56	12♏27	4 31	21 36	10 4	10 4	26 35	23 13	20 20	21 19
17	5 40 6	24 26 0	25 18	5 54	22 51	10 23	10 6	26 37	23 16	20 22	21 20
18	5 44 3	25 27 5	8♐30	7 17	24 5	10 40	10 7	26 39	23 19	20 24	21 21
19	5 47 59	26 28 11	22 1	8 42	25 20	10 58	10 9	26 42	23 23	20 26	21 23
20	5 51 56	27 29 17	5♑50	10 7	26 34	11 15	10 10	26 44	23 26	20 29	21 24
21	5 55 53	28 30 25	19 51	11 34	27 48	11 31	10 12	26 45	23 29	20 31	21 25
22	5 59 49	29 31 32	4♒ 0	13 1	29 2	11 47	10 13	26 47	23 32	20 33	21 26
23	6 3 46	0♑32 40	18 14	14 28	0♒17	12 3	10 13	26 49	23 36	20 35	21 27
24	6 7 42	1 33 48	2♓28	15 56	1 31	12 17	10 14	26 51	23 39	20 38	21 29
25	6 11 39	2 34 55	16 39	17 25	2 45	12 32	10 14	26 52	23 42	20 40	21 30
26	6 15 35	3 36 3	0♈46	18 54	3 59	12 46	10R15	26 53	23 45	20 42	21 31
27	6 19 32	4 37 11	14 49	20 24	5 14	12 59	10 15	26 55	23 48	20 44	21 32
28	6 23 28	5 38 19	28 46	21 54	6 28	13 12	10 14	26 56	23 51	20 47	21 33
29	6 27 25	6 39 27	12♉36	23 24	7 42	13 25	10 14	26 57	23 54	20 49	21 34
30	6 31 22	7 40 36	26 18	24 55	8 56	13 36	10 14	26 58	23 57	20 51	21 35
31	6 35 18	8♑41 44	9♊49	26♐26	10♒10	13♍48	10♍13	26♍59	24♏ 0	20♐53	21♎36

THE SUN ENTERS THE SIGN OF CAPRICORN ON DEC 22 AT 11:11.

♏ SCORPIO ♐ SAGITTARIUS ♑ CAPRICORN ♒ AQUARIUS ♓ PISCES

1980

SIDEREAL. SUN. MOON. MERCURY. VENUS. MARS. JUPITER. SATURN. URANUS. NEPTUNE. PLUTO.

DAY	TIME	☉	☽	☿	♀	♂	♃	♄	♅	♆	♇
	h m s	° ' "	° '	° '	° '	° '	° '	° '	° '	° '	° '
J 1	6 39 15	9♑42 52	23♊ 9	27♐57	11♒24	13♍58	1Ø♍12	26♍59	24♏ 3	2Ø♐55	21♎36
A 2	6 43 11	1Ø 44 Ø	6♋15	29 29	12 38	14 8	1ØR11	27 Ø	24 6	2Ø 58	21 37
N 3	6 47 8	11 45 8	19 5	1♑ 1	13 52	14 18	1Ø 9	27 Ø	24 9	21 Ø	21 38
U 4	6 51 4	12 46 16	1♌4Ø	2 34	15 6	14 27	1Ø 8	27 1	24 11	21 2	21 39
A 5	6 55 1	13 47 24	13 59	4 7	16 19	14 35	1Ø 6	27 1	24 14	21 4	21 4Ø
R 6	6 58 58	14 48 33	26 6	5 4Ø	17 33	14 42	1Ø 4	27R 1	24 17	21 6	21 4Ø
Y 7	7 2 54	15 49 41	8♍ 2	7 13	18 47	14 49	1Ø 2	27 1	24 19	21 8	21 41
8	7 6 51	16 5Ø 5Ø	19 51	8 47	2Ø 1	14 56	1Ø Ø	27 1	24 22	21 1Ø	21 42
9	7 1Ø 47	17 51 58	1♎39	1Ø 22	21 14	15 1	9 57	27 1	24 25	21 12	21 42
1Ø	7 14 44	18 53 7	13 3Ø	11 57	22 28	15 6	9 55	27 1	24 27	21 14	21 43
11	7 18 4Ø	19 54 15	25 29	13 32	23 42	15 1Ø	9 52	27 Ø	24 3Ø	21 16	21 43
12	7 22 37	2Ø 55 24	7♏42	15 7	24 55	15 14	9 49	27 Ø	24 32	21 19	21 44
13	7 26 33	21 56 33	2Ø 13	16 44	26 9	15 17	9 46	26 59	24 35	21 21	21 44
14	7 3Ø 3Ø	22 57 41	3♐ 6	18 2Ø	27 22	15 19	9 42	26 58	24 37	21 23	21 44
15	7 34 27	23 58 5Ø	16 23	19 57	28 36	15 2Ø	9 39	26 58	24 39	21 25	21 45
16	7 38 23	24 59 58	Ø♑ 5	21 35	29 49	15R21	9 35	26 57	24 42	21 27	21 45
17	7 42 2Ø	26 1 6	14 9	23 13	1♓ 2	15 21	9 31	26 56	24 44	21 28	21 45
18	7 46 16	27 2 14	28 32	24 51	2 16	15 2Ø	9 27	26 54	24 46	21 3Ø	21 46
19	7 5Ø 13	28 3 21	13♒ 8	26 3Ø	3 29	15 18	9 22	26 53	24 48	21 32	21 46
2Ø	7 54 9	29 4 27	27 49	28 1Ø	4 42	15 15	9 18	26 52	24 51	21 34	21 46
21	7 58 6	Ø♒ 5 32	12♓3Ø	29 5Ø	5 55	15 12	9 13	26 5Ø	24 53	21 36	21 46
22	8 2 2	1 6 37	27 4	1♒31	7 8	15 8	9 9	26 49	24 55	21 38	21 46
23	8 5 59	2 7 4Ø	11♈27	3 12	8 21	15 3	9 4	26 47	24 57	21 4Ø	21 46
24	8 9 56	3 8 43	25 36	4 54	9 34	14 57	8 58	26 45	24 59	21 42	21R47
25	8 13 52	4 9 44	9♉31	6 37	1Ø 47	14 51	8 53	26 44	25 1	21 43	21 47
26	8 17 49	5 1Ø 45	23 1Ø	8 2Ø	11 59	14 44	8 48	26 42	25 2	21 45	21 47
27	8 21 45	6 11 44	6♊34	1Ø 3	13 12	14 36	8 42	26 39	25 4	21 47	21 46
28	8 25 42	7 12 42	19 43	11 47	14 25	14 27	8 36	26 37	25 6	21 49	21 46
29	8 29 38	8 13 4Ø	2♋39	13 32	15 37	14 17	8 31	26 35	25 8	21 5Ø	21 46
3Ø	8 33 35	9 14 36	15 21	15 17	16 5Ø	14 7	8 25	26 33	25 9	21 52	21 46
31	8 37 31	1Ø♒15 31	27♋51	17♒ 3	18♓ 2	13♍56	8♍18	26♍3Ø	25♏11	21♐54	21♎46

THE SUN ENTERS THE SIGN OF AQUARIUS ON JAN 20 AT 21:49.

DAY	TIME	☉	☽	☿	♀	♂	♃	♄	♅	♆	♇
	h m s	° ' "	° '	° '	° '	° '	° '	° '	° '	° '	° '
F 1	8 41 28	11♒16 25	1Ø♌1Ø	18♒48	19♓14	13♍44	8♍12	26♍28	25♏12	21♐55	21♎46
E 2	8 45 25	12 17 18	22 18	2Ø 34	2Ø 27	13R31	8R 6	26R25	25 14	21 57	21R45
B 3	8 49 21	13 18 1Ø	4♍18	22 21	21 39	13 17	7 59	26 22	25 15	21 59	21 45
R 4	8 53 18	14 19 Ø	16 11	24 7	22 51	13 3	7 53	26 19	25 17	22 Ø	21 45
U 5	8 57 14	15 19 5Ø	28 Ø	25 53	24 3	12 48	7 46	26 16	25 18	22 2	21 44
A 6	9 1 11	16 2Ø 39	9♎48	27 39	25 15	12 33	7 39	26 13	25 19	22 3	21 44
R 7	9 5 7	17 21 27	21 39	29 24	26 26	12 16	7 32	26 1Ø	25 21	22 5	21 43
Y 8	9 9 4	18 22 14	3♏37	1♓ 9	27 38	11 59	7 25	26 7	25 22	22 6	21 43
9	9 13 Ø	19 23 Ø	15 48	2 53	28 5Ø	11 41	7 18	26 4	25 23	22 8	21 42
1Ø	9 16 57	2Ø 23 45	28 15	4 35	Ø♈ 1	11 23	7 11	26 1	25 24	22 9	21 42
11	9 2Ø 54	21 24 29	11♐ 3	6 16	1 12	11 4	7 3	25 57	25 25	22 1Ø	21 41
12	9 24 5Ø	22 25 12	24 15	7 54	2 24	1Ø 44	6 56	25 54	25 26	22 12	21 41
13	9 28 47	23 25 54	7♑54	9 3Ø	3 35	1Ø 24	6 49	25 5Ø	25 27	22 13	21 4Ø
14	9 32 43	24 26 35	21 59	11 2	4 46	1Ø 4	6 41	25 47	25 28	22 14	21 39
15	9 36 4Ø	25 27 14	6♒29	12 31	5 57	9 42	6 33	25 43	25 29	22 16	21 39
16	9 4Ø 36	26 27 53	21 18	13 55	7 8	9 21	6 26	25 39	25 29	22 17	21 38
17	9 44 33	27 28 29	6♓2Ø	15 14	8 18	8 59	6 18	25 35	25 3Ø	22 18	21 37
18	9 48 29	28 29 4	21 25	16 28	9 29	8 36	6 1Ø	25 31	25 31	22 19	21 36
19	9 52 26	29 29 38	6♈24	17 34	1Ø 39	8 13	6 3	25 27	25 31	22 21	21 35
2Ø	9 56 23	Ø♓3Ø 9	21 1Ø	18 34	11 5Ø	7 5Ø	5 55	25 23	25 32	22 22	21 35
21	1Ø Ø 19	1 3Ø 39	5♉37	19 26	13 Ø	7 27	5 47	25 19	25 32	22 23	21 34
22	1Ø 4 16	2 31 7	19 42	2Ø 1Ø	14 1Ø	7 4	5 39	25 15	25 33	22 24	21 33
23	1Ø 8 12	3 31 33	3♊24	2Ø 44	15 2Ø	6 4Ø	5 31	25 11	25 33	22 25	21 32
24	1Ø 12 9	4 31 57	16 43	21 9	16 3Ø	6 16	5 23	25 7	25 33	22 26	21 31
25	1Ø 16 5	5 32 2Ø	29 41	21 25	17 39	5 52	5 15	25 2	25 34	22 27	21 3Ø
26	1Ø 2Ø 2	6 32 4Ø	12♋22	21R3Ø	18 49	5 29	5 7	24 58	25 34	22 28	21 29
27	1Ø 23 58	7 32 58	24 47	21 26	19 58	5 5	5 Ø	24 54	25 34	22 29	21 28
28	1Ø 27 55	8 33 15	7♌ 1	21 12	21 7	4 41	4 52	24 49	25 34	22 29	21 27
29	1Ø 31 51	9♓33 3Ø	19♌ 5	2Ø♓49	22♈16	4♍17	4♍44	24♍45	25♏34	22♐3Ø	21♎26

THE SUN ENTERS THE SIGN OF PISCES ON FEB 19 AT 12:02.

DAY	TIME	☉	☽	☿	♀	♂	♃	♄	♅	♆	♇
	h m s	° ' "	° '	° '	° '	° '	° '	° '	° '	° '	° '
M 1	1Ø 35 48	1Ø♓33 42	1♍ 3	2Ø♓17	23♈25	3♍54	4♍36	24♍4Ø	25♏34	22♐31	21♎24
A 2	1Ø 39 45	11 33 53	12 55	19R37	24 34	3R31	4R28	24R36	25R34	22 32	21R23
R 3	1Ø 43 41	12 34 2	24 45	18 51	25 42	3 8	4 21	24 31	25 34	22 33	21 22
C 4	1Ø 47 38	13 34 9	6♎34	17 59	26 51	2 45	4 13	24 26	25 34	22 33	21 21
H 5	1Ø 51 34	14 34 15	18 24	17 2	27 59	2 22	4 5	24 22	25 34	22 34	21 2Ø
6	1Ø 55 31	15 34 19	Ø♏18	16 3	29 7	2 Ø	3 58	24 17	25 33	22 35	21 18
7	1Ø 59 27	16 34 21	12 2Ø	15 2	Ø♉14	1 39	3 5Ø	24 12	25 33	22 35	21 17
8	11 3 24	17 34 21	24 31	14 1	1 22	1 17	3 42	24 8	25 33	22 36	21 16
9	11 7 2Ø	18 34 2Ø	6♐56	13 2	2 29	Ø 57	3 35	24 3	25 32	22 36	21 14
1Ø	11 11 17	19 34 18	19 39	12 5	3 36	Ø 36	3 28	23 58	25 32	22 37	21 13
11	11 15 14	2Ø 34 13	2♑44	11 11	4 43	Ø 17	3 2Ø	23 54	25 31	22 37	21 12
12	11 19 1Ø	21 34 7	16 13	1Ø 23	5 5Ø	29♌57	3 13	23 49	25 31	22 38	21 1Ø
13	11 23 7	22 34 Ø	Ø♒ 8	9 39	6 57	29 39	3 6	23 44	25 3Ø	22 38	21 9
14	11 27 3	23 33 5Ø	14 3Ø	9 1	8 3	29 21	2 59	23 39	25 29	22 39	21 7
15	11 31 Ø	24 33 39	29 16	8 29	9 9	29 4	2 52	23 35	25 28	22 39	21 6
16	11 34 56	25 33 26	14♓19	8 4	1Ø 15	28 47	2 45	23 3Ø	25 28	22 39	21 4
17	11 38 53	26 33 11	29 33	7 45	11 2Ø	28 31	2 39	23 25	25 27	22 4Ø	21 3
18	11 42 49	27 32 54	14♈48	7 32	12 26	28 16	2 32	23 2Ø	25 26	22 4Ø	21 2
19	11 46 46	28 32 35	29 52	7D25	13 31	28 1	2 26	23 16	25 25	22 4Ø	21 Ø
2Ø	11 5Ø 43	29 32 14	14♉37	7 25	14 36	27 47	2 19	23 11	25 24	22 4Ø	2Ø 58
21	11 54 39	Ø♈31 51	28 57	7 3Ø	15 4Ø	27 34	2 13	23 6	25 23	22 4Ø	2Ø 57
22	11 58 36	1 31 25	12♊49	7 41	16 45	27 22	2 7	23 2	25 22	22 4Ø	2Ø 55
23	12 2 32	2 3Ø 57	26 13	7 58	17 49	27 11	2 1	22 57	25 21	22 41	2Ø 54
24	12 6 29	3 3Ø 27	9♋11	8 19	18 52	27 Ø	1 55	22 52	25 19	22R41	2Ø 52
25	12 1Ø 25	4 29 54	21 47	8 45	19 56	26 5Ø	1 49	22 48	25 18	22 41	2Ø 51
26	12 14 22	5 29 2Ø	4♌ 5	9 16	2Ø 59	26 41	1 44	22 43	25 17	22 41	2Ø 49
27	12 18 18	6 28 42	16 9	9 51	22 2	26 33	1 38	22 39	25 16	22 4Ø	2Ø 47
28	12 22 15	7 28 3	28 5	1Ø 3Ø	23 4	26 25	1 33	22 34	25 14	22 4Ø	2Ø 46
29	12 26 11	8 27 21	9♍55	11 13	24 6	26 18	1 28	22 3Ø	25 13	22 4Ø	2Ø 44
3Ø	12 3Ø 8	9 26 37	21 43	11 59	25 8	26 13	1 23	22 25	25 11	22 4Ø	2Ø 43
31	12 34 5	1Ø♈25 51	3♎32	12♓49	26♉ 9	26♌ 7	1♍18	22♍21	25♏1Ø	22♐4Ø	2Ø♎41

THE SUN ENTERS THE SIGN OF ARIES ON MAR 20 AT 11:10.

♈ ARIES ♉ TAURUS ♊ GEMINI ♋ CANCER ♌ LEO ♍ VIRGO ♎ LIBRA

1980

SIDEREAL SUN. MOON. MERCURY. VENUS. MARS. JUPITER. SATURN. URANUS. NEPTUNE. PLUTO.

DAY	TIME	☉	☽	☿	♀	♂	♃	♄	♅	♆	♇
	h m s	° ' "	° '	° '	° '	° '	° '	° '	° '	° '	° '
A 1	12 38 1	11♈25 3	15♎23	13♓42	27♉10	26♌ 3	1♍14	22♍16	25♏ 8	22♐40	20♎39
P 2	12 41 58	12 24 13	27 19	14 38	28 11	25R59	1R 9	22R12	25R 7	22R39	20R38
R 3	12 45 54	13 23 20	9♏21	15 37	29 11	25 56	1 5	22 8	25 5	22 39	20 36
I 4	12 49 51	14 22 26	21 30	16 39	0♊10	25 54	1 1	22 4	25 3	22 39	20 34
L 5	12 53 47	15 21 30	3♐49	17 43	1 10	25 53	0 57	21 59	25 2	22 38	20 33
6	12 57 44	16 20 33	16 20	18 50	2 9	25D52	0 53	21 55	25 0	22 38	20 31
7	13 1 40	17 19 33	29 4	19 59	3 7	25 52	0 49	21 51	24 58	22 38	20 29
8	13 5 37	18 18 32	12♑ 6	21 11	4 5	25 53	0 46	21 47	24 56	22 37	20 27
9	13 9 34	19 17 29	25 28	22 24	5 3	25 55	0 42	21 43	24 54	22 37	20 26
10	13 13 30	20 16 25	9♒12	23 40	6 0	25 57	0 39	21 39	24 53	22 36	20 24
11	13 17 27	21 15 18	23 19	24 58	6 56	26 0	0 36	21 36	24 51	22 36	20 22
12	13 21 23	22 14 10	7♓50	26 18	7 52	26 4	0 34	21 32	24 49	22 35	20 21
13	13 25 20	23 13 0	22 41	27 40	8 48	26 8	0 31	21 28	24 47	22 35	20 19
14	13 29 16	24 11 48	7♈46	29 3	9 42	26 13	0 29	21 24	24 45	22 34	20 17
15	13 33 13	25 10 34	22 56	0♈29	10 37	26 19	0 26	21 21	24 43	22 33	20 16
16	13 37 9	26 9 19	8♉ 2	1 56	11 30	26 25	0 24	21 17	24 41	22 33	20 14
17	13 41 6	27 8 1	22 54	3 25	12 24	26 32	0 23	21 14	24 38	22 32	20 12
18	13 45 3	28 6 41	7♊22	4 56	13 16	26 40	0 21	21 11	24 36	22 31	20 11
19	13 48 59	29 5 19	21 23	6 28	14 8	26 48	0 19	21 7	24 34	22 30	20 9
20	13 52 56	0♉ 3 55	4♋54	8 3	14 59	26 57	0 18	21 4	24 32	22 29	20 7
21	13 56 52	1 2 29	17 57	9 38	15 49	27 6	0 17	21 1	24 30	22 29	20 6
22	14 0 49	2 1 1	0♌35	11 16	16 39	27 16	0 16	20 58	24 28	22 28	20 4
23	14 4 45	2 59 30	12 53	12 55	17 27	27 27	0 16	20 55	24 25	22 27	20 2
24	14 8 42	3 57 57	24 56	14 37	18 15	27 38	0 15	20 52	24 23	22 26	20 1
25	14 12 38	4 56 22	6♍49	16 19	19 3	27 50	0 15	20 50	24 21	22 25	19 59
26	14 16 35	5 54 45	18 37	18 4	19 49	28 2	0D14	20 47	24 18	22 24	19 57
27	14 20 31	6 53 6	0♎25	19 50	20 34	28 15	0 15	20 45	24 16	22 23	19 56
28	14 24 28	7 51 25	12 15	21 38	21 18	28 28	0 15	20 42	24 14	22 22	19 54
29	14 28 25	8 49 42	24 11	23 28	22 2	28 42	0 15	20 40	24 11	22 21	19 53
30	14 32 21	9♉47 57	6♏15	25♈19	22♊44	28♌56	0♍16	20♍37	24♏ 9	22♐20	19♎51

THE SUN ENTERS THE SIGN OF TAURUS ON APR 19 AT 22:24.

DAY	TIME	☉	☽	☿	♀	♂	♃	♄	♅	♆	♇
	h m s	° ' "	° '	° '	° '	° '	° '	° '	° '	° '	° '
M 1	14 36 18	10♉46 11	18♏28	27♈12	23♊26	29♌11	0♍16	20♍35	24♏ 6	22♐19	19♎50
A 2	14 40 14	11 44 23	0♐51	29 7	24 6	29 26	0 17	20R33	24R 4	22R18	19R48
Y 3	14 44 11	12 42 33	13 23	1♉ 4	24 45	29 42	0 19	20 31	24 2	22 17	19 47
4	14 48 7	13 40 41	26 7	3 2	25 23	29 58	0 20	20 29	23 59	22 15	19 45
5	14 52 4	14 38 48	9♑ 2	5 2	26 0	0♍15	0 21	20 27	23 57	22 14	19 44
6	14 56 0	15 36 54	22 11	7 4	26 35	0 32	0 23	20 26	23 54	22 13	19 42
7	14 59 57	16 34 58	5♒34	9 7	27 9	0 50	0 25	20 24	23 52	22 12	19 41
8	15 3 54	17 33 1	19 14	11 12	27 42	1 7	0 27	20 22	23 49	22 11	19 39
9	15 7 50	18 31 2	3♓11	13 18	28 13	1 26	0 29	20 21	23 47	22 9	19 38
10	15 11 47	19 29 2	17 27	15 25	28 43	1 45	0 31	20 20	23 44	22 8	19 36
11	15 15 43	20 27 1	1♈59	17 34	29 11	2 4	0 34	20 18	23 42	22 7	19 35
12	15 19 40	21 24 58	16 44	19 43	29 38	2 23	0 37	20 17	23 39	22 5	19 33
13	15 23 36	22 22 54	1♉36	21 54	0♋ 3	2 43	0 40	20 16	23 37	22 4	19 32
14	15 27 33	23 20 49	16 27	24 4	0 27	3 3	0 43	20 15	23 34	22 3	19 31
15	15 31 29	24 18 43	1♊ 8	26 15	0 48	3 24	0 46	20 15	23 32	22 1	19 29
16	15 35 26	25 16 34	15 31	28 27	1 8	3 45	0 49	20 14	23 29	22 0	19 28
17	15 39 23	26 14 25	29 30	0♊37	1 26	4 6	0 53	20 13	23 27	21 59	19 27
18	15 43 19	27 12 13	13♋ 2	2 48	1 42	4 28	0 57	20 13	23 24	21 57	19 26
19	15 47 16	28 10 0	26 8	4 57	1 56	4 50	1 1	20 12	23 22	21 56	19 24
20	15 51 12	29 7 46	8♌49	7 6	2 8	5 13	1 5	20 12	23 19	21 54	19 23
21	15 55 9	0♊ 5 30	21 9	9 13	2 18	5 35	1 9	20 12	23 17	21 53	19 22
22	15 59 5	1 3 12	3♍13	11 18	2 26	5 58	1 13	20D12	23 14	21 51	19 21
23	16 3 2	2 0 52	15 8	13 22	2 31	6 22	1 18	20 12	23 12	21 50	19 20
24	16 6 58	2 58 31	26 57	15 24	2R34	6 45	1 23	20 12	23 9	21 48	19 19
25	16 10 55	3 56 9	8♎47	17 23	2 35	7 9	1 27	20 12	23 7	21 47	19 18
26	16 14 52	4 53 45	20 41	19 20	2 34	7 33	1 32	20 12	23 4	21 45	19 17
27	16 18 48	5 51 20	2♏43	21 15	2 30	7 58	1 38	20 13	23 2	21 44	19 15
28	16 22 45	6 48 53	14 55	23 7	2 23	8 23	1 43	20 13	22 59	21 42	19 14
29	16 26 41	7 46 25	27 20	24 56	2 14	8 48	1 48	20 14	22 57	21 41	19 13
30	16 30 38	8 43 56	9♐58	26 43	2 3	9 13	1 54	20 15	22 55	21 39	19 13
31	16 34 34	9♊41 26	22♐49	28♊27	1♋49	9♍39	2♍ 0	20♍15	22♏52	21♐38	19♎12

THE SUN ENTERS THE SIGN OF GEMINI ON MAY 20 AT 21:43.

DAY	TIME	☉	☽	☿	♀	♂	♃	♄	♅	♆	♇
	h m s	° ' "	° '	° '	° '	° '	° '	° '	° '	° '	° '
J 1	16 38 31	10♊38 55	5♑52	0♋ 8	1♋33	10♍ 5	2♍ 6	20♍16	22♏50	21♐36	19♎11
U 2	16 42 27	11 36 23	19 6	1 46	1R15	10 31	2 12	20 17	22R47	21R34	19R10
N 3	16 46 24	12 33 51	2♒32	3 22	0 54	10 57	2 18	20 18	22 45	21 33	19 9
E 4	16 50 21	13 31 17	16 7	4 54	0 31	11 24	2 24	20 20	22 43	21 31	19 8
5	16 54 17	14 28 43	29 54	6 24	0 6	11 50	2 31	20 21	22 41	21 30	19 7
6	16 58 14	15 26 8	13♓51	7 50	29♊39	12 18	2 37	20 22	22 38	21 28	19 7
7	17 2 10	16 23 32	27 59	9 14	29 10	12 45	2 44	20 24	22 36	21 26	19 6
8	17 6 7	17 20 56	12♈16	10 34	28 40	13 12	2 51	20 26	22 34	21 25	19 5
9	17 10 3	18 18 20	26 41	11 52	28 7	13 40	2 58	20 27	22 32	21 23	19 5
10	17 14 0	19 15 43	11♉ 9	13 6	27 34	14 8	3 5	20 29	22 30	21 22	19 4
11	17 17 56	20 13 5	25 35	14 18	26 59	14 36	3 12	20 31	22 27	21 20	19 3
12	17 21 53	21 10 27	9♊53	15 26	26 23	15 5	3 20	20 33	22 25	21 18	19 3
13	17 25 50	22 7 48	23 56	16 31	25 47	15 33	3 27	20 35	22 23	21 17	19 2
14	17 29 46	23 5 8	7♋42	17 32	25 9	16 2	3 35	20 37	22 21	21 15	19 2
15	17 33 43	24 2 28	21 5	18 30	24 32	16 31	3 43	20 40	22 19	21 13	19 1
16	17 37 39	24 59 47	4♌ 6	19 24	23 54	17 1	3 51	20 42	22 17	21 12	19 1
17	17 41 36	25 57 5	16 45	20 15	23 17	17 30	3 59	20 45	22 15	21 10	19 0
18	17 45 32	26 54 23	29 5	21 2	22 40	18 0	4 7	20 47	22 13	21 9	19 0
19	17 49 29	27 51 39	11♍11	21 46	22 4	18 29	4 15	20 50	22 11	21 7	19 0
20	17 53 26	28 48 55	23 7	22 25	21 28	18 59	4 23	20 53	22 9	21 5	18 59
21	17 57 22	29 46 10	4♎58	23 0	20 54	19 30	4 32	20 56	22 8	21 4	18 59
22	18 1 19	0♋43 25	16 50	23 32	20 20	20 0	4 41	20 59	22 6	21 2	18 59
23	18 5 15	1 40 38	28 46	23 59	19 49	20 31	4 49	21 2	22 4	21 1	18 59
24	18 9 12	2 37 52	10♏53	24 21	19 19	21 1	4 58	21 5	22 2	20 59	18 58
25	18 13 8	3 35 4	23 12	24 39	18 50	21 32	5 7	21 8	22 1	20 57	18 58
26	18 17 5	4 32 16	5♐47	24 53	18 24	22 3	5 16	21 11	21 59	20 56	18 58
27	18 21 1	5 29 28	18 38	25 2	18 0	22 35	5 25	21 15	21 58	20 54	18 58
28	18 24 58	6 26 40	1♑47	25R 7	17 37	23 6	5 34	21 18	21 56	20 53	18D58
29	18 28 55	7 23 51	15 11	25 6	17 17	23 38	5 44	21 22	21 54	20 51	18 58
30	18 32 51	8♋21 3	28♑49	25♋ 2	17♊ 0	24♍ 9	5♍53	21♍26	21♏53	20♐50	18♎58

THE SUN ENTERS THE SIGN OF CANCER ON JUN 21 AT 05:48.

♏ SCORPIO ♐ SAGITTARIUS ♑ CAPRICORN ♒ AQUARIUS ♓ PISCES

1980

SIDEREAL SUN. MOON. MERCURY. VENUS. MARS. JUPITER. SATURN. URANUS. NEPTUNE. PLUTO.

DAY	TIME	☉	☽	☿	♀	♂	♃	♄	♅	♆	♇
	h m s	° ' "	° '	° '	° '	° '	° '	° '	° '	° '	° '
J 1	18 36 48	9♋18 14	12♒38	24♋52	16♊45	24♍41	6♍ 3	21♍29	21♏52	20♐48	18♎58
U 2	18 40 44	10 15 25	26 36	24R39	16R32	25 13	6 12	21 33	21R50	20R47	18 58
L 3	18 44 41	11 12 36	10♓40	24 21	16 21	25 45	6 22	21 37	21 49	20 45	18 58
Y 4	18 48 37	12 9 48	24 49	23 59	16 13	26 18	6 32	21 41	21 47	20 44	18 59
5	18 52 34	13 6 59	9♈ 0	23 33	16 8	26 50	6 42	21 45	21 46	20 42	18 59
6	18 56 30	14 4 11	23 12	23 4	16D 4	27 23	6 52	21 49	21 45	20 41	18 59
7	19 0 27	15 1 24	7♉22	22 32	16 3	27 56	7 2	21 54	21 44	20 39	18 59
8	19 4 24	15 58 37	21 29	21 58	16 5	28 29	7 12	21 58	21 43	20 38	18 59
9	19 8 20	16 55 50	5♊29	21 21	16 8	29 2	7 22	22 2	21 42	20 36	19 0
10	19 12 17	17 53 4	19 20	20 44	16 14	29 35	7 32	22 7	21 41	20 35	19 0
11	19 16 13	18 50 18	2♋58	20 5	16 23	0♎ 8	7 43	22 11	21 40	20 34	19 1
12	19 20 10	19 47 32	16 20	19 27	16 33	0 42	7 53	22 16	21 39	20 32	19 1
13	19 24 6	20 44 47	29 26	18 49	16 45	1 16	8 4	22 21	21 38	20 31	19 1
14	19 28 3	21 42 2	12♌14	18 12	16 59	1 49	8 14	22 26	21 37	20 30	19 2
15	19 31 59	22 39 17	24 45	17 37	17 16	2 23	8 25	22 30	21 36	20 28	19 2
16	19 35 56	23 36 32	7♍ 2	17 5	17 34	2 57	8 36	22 35	21 35	20 27	19 3
17	19 39 53	24 33 47	19 6	16 36	17 54	3 32	8 47	22 40	21 35	20 26	19 4
18	19 43 49	25 31 2	1♎ 2	16 10	18 15	4 6	8 58	22 45	21 34	20 24	19 4
19	19 47 46	26 28 18	12 53	15 49	18 39	4 40	9 9	22 51	21 33	20 23	19 5
20	19 51 42	27 25 34	24 45	15 32	19 4	5 15	9 20	22 56	21 33	20 22	19 6
21	19 55 39	28 22 50	6♏43	15 20	19 30	5 50	9 31	23 1	21 32	20 21	19 6
22	19 59 35	29 20 7	18 50	15D14	19 58	6 24	9 42	23 6	21 32	20 20	19 7
23	20 3 32	0♌17 23	1♐11	15 12	20 28	6 59	9 54	23 12	21 31	20 18	19 8
24	20 7 28	1 14 41	13 51	15 17	20 59	7 35	10 5	23 17	21 31	20 17	19 9
25	20 11 25	2 11 58	26 50	15 28	21 32	8 10	10 16	23 23	21 31	20 16	19 10
26	20 15 22	3 9 16	10♑10	15 44	22 5	8 45	10 28	23 28	21 30	20 15	19 10
27	20 19 18	4 6 35	23 52	16 6	22 40	9 20	10 39	23 34	21 30	20 14	19 11
28	20 23 15	5 3 54	7♒51	16 35	23 17	9 56	10 51	23 40	21 30	20 13	19 12
29	20 27 11	6 1 15	22 6	17 10	23 54	10 32	11 3	23 46	21 30	20 12	19 13
30	20 31 8	6 58 35	6♓30	17 50	24 33	11 7	11 14	23 51	21D30	20 11	19 14
31	20 35 4	7♌55 57	21♓ 0	18♋37	25♊13	11♎43	11♍26	23♍57	21♏30	20♐10	19♎15

THE SUN ENTERS THE SIGN OF LEO ON JUL 22 AT 16:43.

DAY	TIME	☉	☽	☿	♀	♂	♃	♄	♅	♆	♇
	h m s	° ' "	° '	° '	° '	° '	° '	° '	° '	° '	° '
A 1	20 39 1	8♌53 20	5♈29	19♋29	25♊53	12♎19	11♍38	24♍ 3	21♏30	20♐ 9	19♎16
U 2	20 42 57	9 50 44	19 55	20 27	26 35	12 55	11 50	24 9	21 30	20R 8	19 18
G 3	20 46 54	10 48 9	4♉12	21 31	27 18	13 32	12 2	24 15	21 30	20 7	19 19
U 4	20 50 51	11 45 36	18 18	22 41	28 2	14 8	12 14	24 21	21 30	20 6	19 20
S 5	20 54 47	12 43 4	2♊12	23 56	28 47	14 44	12 26	24 27	21 31	20 6	19 21
T 6	20 58 44	13 40 33	15 53	25 16	29 32	15 21	12 38	24 34	21 31	20 5	19 22
7	21 2 40	14 38 3	29 20	26 41	0♋19	15 58	12 50	24 40	21 31	20 4	19 24
8	21 6 37	15 35 35	12♋32	28 11	1 6	16 34	13 2	24 46	21 32	20 3	19 25
9	21 10 33	16 33 8	25 31	29 46	1 54	17 11	13 14	24 53	21 32	20 3	19 26
10	21 14 30	17 30 42	8♌15	1♌25	2 43	17 48	13 27	24 59	21 33	20 2	19 27
11	21 18 26	18 28 17	20 47	3 7	3 32	18 25	13 39	25 5	21 33	20 1	19 29
12	21 22 23	19 25 53	3♍ 6	4 53	4 22	19 3	13 51	25 12	21 34	20 1	19 30
13	21 26 20	20 23 31	15 15	6 43	5 13	19 40	14 4	25 18	21 35	20 0	19 32
14	21 30 16	21 21 9	27 15	8 35	6 5	20 17	14 16	25 25	21 35	19 59	19 33
15	21 34 13	22 18 49	9♎ 8	10 29	6 57	20 55	14 28	25 32	21 36	19 59	19 35
16	21 38 9	23 16 29	20 59	12 26	7 50	21 32	14 41	25 38	21 37	19 58	19 36
17	21 42 6	24 14 11	2♏50	14 24	8 43	22 10	14 53	25 45	21 38	19 58	19 38
18	21 46 2	25 11 54	14 47	16 23	9 37	22 48	15 6	25 52	21 39	19 57	19 39
19	21 49 59	26 9 38	26 52	18 23	10 32	23 26	15 19	25 59	21 40	19 57	19 41
20	21 53 55	27 7 23	9♐12	20 24	11 27	24 4	15 31	26 5	21 41	19 56	19 42
21	21 57 52	28 5 9	21 49	22 25	12 22	24 42	15 44	26 12	21 42	19 56	19 44
22	22 1 49	29 2 56	4♑48	24 26	13 18	25 20	15 57	26 19	21 43	19 56	19 46
23	22 5 45	0♍ 0 45	18 12	26 26	14 15	25 59	16 9	26 26	21 44	19 55	19 47
24	22 9 42	0 58 34	2♒ 0	28 26	15 12	26 37	16 22	26 33	21 46	19 55	19 49
25	22 13 38	1 56 25	16 13	0♍26	16 9	27 16	16 35	26 40	21 47	19 55	19 51
26	22 17 35	2 54 18	0♓46	2 25	17 7	27 54	16 47	26 47	21 48	19 55	19 53
27	22 21 31	3 52 12	15 35	4 22	18 6	28 33	17 0	26 54	21 50	19 55	19 55
28	22 25 28	4 50 7	0♈30	6 19	19 4	29 12	17 13	27 1	21 51	19 54	19 56
29	22 29 24	5 48 4	15 25	8 15	20 3	29 51	17 26	27 8	21 52	19 54	19 58
30	22 33 21	6 46 3	0♉11	10 9	21 3	0♏29	17 39	27 15	21 54	19 54	20 0
31	22 37 17	7♍44 4	14♉43	12♍ 3	22♋ 3	1♏ 9	17♍52	27♍22	21♏56	19♐54	20♎ 2

THE SUN ENTERS THE SIGN OF VIRGO ON AUG 22 AT 23:42.

DAY	TIME	☉	☽	☿	♀	♂	♃	♄	♅	♆	♇
	h m s	° ' "	° '	° '	° '	° '	° '	° '	° '	° '	° '
S 1	22 41 14	8♍42 7	28♉55	13♍55	23♋ 3	1♏48	18♍ 4	27♍30	21♏57	19♐54	20♎ 4
E 2	22 45 11	9 40 12	12♊47	15 46	24 4	2 27	18 17	27 37	21 59	19 54	20 6
P 3	22 49 7	10 38 19	26 18	17 36	25 5	3 6	18 30	27 44	22 1	19 54	20 8
T 4	22 53 4	11 36 28	9♋30	19 25	26 7	3 46	18 43	27 51	22 2	19 54	20 10
E 5	22 57 0	12 34 38	22 24	21 12	27 9	4 25	18 56	27 59	22 4	19 54	20 12
M 6	23 0 57	13 32 51	5♌ 2	22 58	28 11	5 5	19 9	28 6	22 6	19 55	20 14
B 7	23 4 53	14 31 6	17 28	24 43	29 13	5 45	19 22	28 13	22 8	19 55	20 16
E 8	23 8 50	15 29 22	29 44	26 27	0♌16	6 24	19 35	28 20	22 10	19 55	20 18
R 9	23 12 46	16 27 40	11♍51	28 10	1 19	7 4	19 48	28 28	22 12	19 55	20 20
10	23 16 43	17 26 1	23 51	29 52	2 22	7 44	20 1	28 35	22 14	19 56	20 22
11	23 20 40	18 24 22	5♎45	1♎32	3 26	8 24	20 14	28 42	22 16	19 56	20 24
12	23 24 36	19 22 46	17 37	3 11	4 30	9 5	20 27	28 50	22 18	19 56	20 26
13	23 28 33	20 21 11	29 27	4 49	5 34	9 45	20 40	28 57	22 20	19 57	20 28
14	23 32 29	21 19 38	11♏19	6 26	6 38	10 25	20 53	29 5	22 23	19 57	20 30
15	23 36 26	22 18 7	23 15	8 2	7 43	11 6	21 6	29 12	22 25	19 57	20 32
16	23 40 22	23 16 37	5♐19	9 37	8 48	11 46	21 19	29 19	22 27	19 58	20 35
17	23 44 19	24 15 10	17 35	11 11	9 53	12 27	21 32	29 27	22 29	19 58	20 37
18	23 48 15	25 13 43	0♑ 8	12 44	10 58	13 7	21 45	29 34	22 32	19 59	20 39
19	23 52 12	26 12 19	13 1	14 16	12 4	13 48	21 58	29 42	22 34	20 0	20 41
20	23 56 9	27 10 56	26 19	15 47	13 10	14 29	22 11	29 49	22 37	20 0	20 43
21	0 0 5	28 9 34	10♒ 3	17 16	14 16	15 10	22 24	29 57	22 39	20 1	20 46
22	0 4 2	29 8 15	24 16	18 45	15 22	15 51	22 37	0♎ 4	22 42	20 1	20 48
23	0 7 58	0♎ 6 57	8♓55	20 13	16 29	16 32	22 50	0 12	22 44	20 2	20 50
24	0 11 55	1 5 41	23 55	21 39	17 35	17 13	23 3	0 19	22 47	20 3	20 52
25	0 15 51	2 4 27	9♈ 7	23 5	18 42	17 55	23 16	0 26	22 50	20 4	20 55
26	0 19 48	3 3 15	24 22	24 29	19 50	18 36	23 29	0 34	22 52	20 4	20 57
27	0 23 44	4 2 5	9♉29	25 53	20 57	19 17	23 41	0 41	22 55	20 5	20 59
28	0 27 41	5 0 57	24 19	27 15	22 4	19 59	23 54	0 49	22 58	20 6	21 2
29	0 31 37	5 59 52	8♊45	28 36	23 12	20 40	24 7	0 56	23 1	20 7	21 4
30	0 35 34	6♎58 48	22♊44	29♎56	24♌20	21♏22	24♍20	1♎ 4	23♏ 3	20♐ 8	21♎ 6

THE SUN ENTERS THE SIGN OF LIBRA ON SEP 22 AT 21:10.

♈ ARIES ♉ TAURUS ♊ GEMINI ♋ CANCER ♌ LEO ♍ VIRGO ♎ LIBRA

1980

SIDEREAL. | SUN. | MOON. | MERCURY. | VENUS. | MARS. | JUPITER. | SATURN. | URANUS. | NEPTUNE. | PLUTO.

DAY	TIME	☉	☽	☿	♀	♂	♃	♄	♅	♆	♇
	h m s	° ' "	° '	° '	° '	° '	° '	° '	° '	° '	° '
O 1	0 39 31	7♎57 48	6♋16	1♏14	25♌28	22♏ 4	24♍33	1♎11	23♏ 6	20♐ 9	21♎ 9
C 2	0 43 27	8 56 49	19 23	2 32	26 37	22 46	24 46	1 18	23 9	20 10	21 11
T 3	0 47 24	9 55 53	2♌ 7	3 47	27 45	23 28	24 58	1 26	23 12	20 11	21 13
O 4	0 51 20	10 54 59	14 35	5 2	28 54	24 10	25 11	1 33	23 15	20 12	21 16
B 5	0 55 17	11 54 8	26 48	6 15	0♍ 3	24 52	25 24	1 41	23 18	20 13	21 18
E 6	0 59 13	12 53 18	8♍52	7 26	1 11	25 34	25 37	1 48	23 21	20 14	21 20
R 7	1 3 10	13 52 31	20 49	8 35	2 21	26 16	25 49	1 55	23 24	20 15	21 23
8	1 7 6	14 51 46	2♎43	9 42	3 30	26 58	26 2	2 3	23 27	20 16	21 25
9	1 11 3	15 51 3	14 34	10 48	4 39	27 41	26 15	2 10	23 30	20 18	21 28
10	1 15 0	16 50 22	26 25	11 51	5 49	28 23	26 27	2 17	23 34	20 19	21 30
11	1 18 56	17 49 43	8♏17	12 52	6 59	29 6	26 40	2 25	23 37	20 20	21 32
12	1 22 53	18 49 6	20 12	13 50	8 9	29 49	26 52	2 32	23 40	20 21	21 35
13	1 26 49	19 48 31	2♐11	14 45	9 19	0♐31	27 5	2 39	23 43	20 23	21 37
14	1 30 46	20 47 58	14 18	15 37	10 29	1 14	27 17	2 46	23 46	20 24	21 40
15	1 34 42	21 47 26	26 34	16 25	11 39	1 57	27 30	2 54	23 50	20 25	21 42
16	1 38 39	22 46 57	9♑ 5	17 9	12 50	2 40	27 42	3 1	23 53	20 27	21 44
17	1 42 35	23 46 29	21 52	17 50	14 0	3 23	27 54	3 8	23 56	20 28	21 47
18	1 46 32	24 46 3	5♒ 2	18 25	15 11	4 6	28 7	3 15	24 0	20 30	21 49
19	1 50 29	25 45 39	18 37	18 56	16 22	4 49	28 19	3 22	24 3	20 31	21 51
20	1 54 25	26 45 16	2♓39	19 20	17 33	5 32	28 31	3 29	24 6	20 33	21 54
21	1 58 22	27 44 55	17 9	19 39	18 44	6 16	28 43	3 36	24 10	20 34	21 56
22	2 2 18	28 44 36	2♈ 3	19 51	19 55	6 59	28 55	3 43	24 13	20 36	21 59
23	2 6 15	29 44 18	17 16	19R55	21 6	7 42	29 7	3 50	24 17	20 37	22 1
24	2 10 11	0♏44 3	2♉36	19 52	22 17	8 26	29 19	3 57	24 20	20 39	22 3
25	2 14 8	1 43 49	17 53	19 40	23 29	9 9	29 31	4 4	24 24	20 40	22 6
26	2 18 4	2 43 38	2♊55	19 20	24 40	9 53	29 43	4 11	24 27	20 42	22 8
27	2 22 1	3 43 29	17 34	18 50	25 52	10 37	29 55	4 18	24 31	20 44	22 11
28	2 25 58	4 43 22	1♋44	18 11	27 4	11 21	0♎ 7	4 24	24 34	20 45	22 13
29	2 29 54	5 43 17	15 24	17 23	28 16	12 4	0 18	4 31	24 38	20 47	22 15
30	2 33 51	6 43 14	28 34	16 27	29 28	12 48	0 30	4 38	24 41	20 49	22 18
31	2 37 47	7♏43 14	11♌19	15♏22	0♎40	13♐32	0♎42	4♎45	24♏45	20♐51	22♎20

THE SUN ENTERS THE SIGN OF SCORPIO ON OCT 23 AT 06:19.

DAY	TIME	☉	☽	☿	♀	♂	♃	♄	♅	♆	♇
	h m s	° ' "	° '	° '	° '	° '	° '	° '	° '	° '	° '
N 1	2 41 44	8♏43 16	23♌44	14♏12	1♎52	14♐16	0♎53	4♎51	24♏49	20♐52	22♎22
O 2	2 45 40	9 43 19	5♍53	12R56	3 5	15 1	1 5	4 58	24 52	20 54	22 25
V 3	2 49 37	10 43 25	17 52	11 39	4 17	15 45	1 16	5 4	24 56	20 56	22 27
E 4	2 53 33	11 43 33	29 44	10 20	5 30	16 29	1 28	5 11	25 0	20 58	22 29
M 5	2 57 30	12 43 43	11♎34	9 5	6 42	17 13	1 39	5 17	25 3	21 0	22 31
B 6	3 1 26	13 43 55	23 24	7 53	7 55	17 58	1 50	5 24	25 7	21 2	22 34
E 7	3 5 23	14 44 8	5♏17	6 49	9 8	18 42	2 1	5 30	25 11	21 3	22 36
R 8	3 9 20	15 44 24	17 14	5 53	10 21	19 27	2 12	5 36	25 14	21 5	22 38
9	3 13 16	16 44 41	29 17	5 8	11 33	20 11	2 23	5 43	25 18	21 7	22 40
10	3 17 13	17 45 0	11♐25	4 34	12 46	20 56	2 34	5 49	25 22	21 9	22 43
11	3 21 9	18 45 21	23 41	4 11	14 0	21 41	2 45	5 55	25 [illegible]	21 11	22 45
12	3 25 6	19 45 43	6♑ 5	4D 0	15 13	22 26	2 56	6 1	25 29	21 13	22 47
13	3 29 2	20 46 7	18 41	4 1	16 26	23 10	3 6	6 7	25 33	21 15	22 49
14	3 32 59	21 46 32	1♒31	4 12	17 39	23 55	3 17	6 13	25 36	21 17	22 52
15	3 36 56	22 46 58	14 38	4 33	18 52	24 40	3 27	6 19	25 40	21 19	22 54
16	3 40 52	23 47 26	28 5	5 4	20 6	25 25	3 38	6 25	25 44	21 21	22 56
17	3 44 49	24 47 55	11♓55	5 43	21 19	26 10	3 48	6 31	25 48	21 23	22 58
18	3 48 45	25 48 25	26 9	6 30	22 33	26 56	3 58	6 36	25 51	21 25	23 0
19	3 52 42	26 48 57	10♈46	7 23	23 46	27 41	4 8	6 42	25 55	21 28	23 2
20	3 56 38	27 49 29	25 42	8 22	25 0	28 26	4 18	6 48	25 59	21 30	23 4
21	4 0 35	28 50 3	10♉48	9 26	26 14	29 11	4 28	6 53	26 3	21 32	23 6
22	4 4 31	29 50 39	25 57	10 34	27 27	29 57	4 38	6 59	26 6	21 34	23 8
23	4 8 28	0♐51 16	10♊56	11 46	28 41	0♑42	4 48	7 4	26 10	21 36	23 10
24	4 12 24	1 51 54	25 36	13 1	29 55	1 28	4 57	7 9	26 14	21 38	23 12
25	4 16 21	2 52 34	9♋51	14 20	1♏ 9	2 13	5 7	7 15	26 17	21 40	23 14
26	4 20 18	3 53 15	23 38	15 40	2 23	2 59	5 16	7 20	26 21	21 43	23 16
27	4 24 14	4 53 58	6♌55	17 3	3 37	3 44	5 26	7 25	26 25	21 45	23 18
28	4 28 11	5 54 43	19 46	18 27	4 51	4 30	5 35	7 30	26 29	21 47	23 20
29	4 32 7	6 55 29	2♍15	19 52	6 5	5 16	5 44	7 35	26 32	21 49	23 22
30	4 36 4	7♐56 16	14♍26	21♏19	7♏19	6♑ 2	5♎53	7♎40	26♏36	21♐51	23♎24

THE SUN ENTERS THE SIGN OF SAGITTARIUS ON NOV 22 AT 03:43.

DAY	TIME	☉	☽	☿	♀	♂	♃	♄	♅	♆	♇
	h m s	° ' "	° '	° '	° '	° '	° '	° '	° '	° '	° '
D 1	4 40 0	8♐57 5	26♍25	22♏47	8♏34	6♑47	6♎ 2	7♎45	26♏40	21♐54	23♎26
E 2	4 43 57	9 57 56	8♎17	24 15	9 48	7 33	6 11	7 49	26 43	21 56	23 27
C 3	4 47 54	10 58 47	20 7	25 45	11 2	8 19	6 19	7 54	26 47	21 58	23 29
E 4	4 51 50	11 59 40	1♏58	27 15	12 16	9 5	6 28	7 59	26 51	22 0	23 31
M 5	4 55 47	13 0 35	13 55	28 45	13 31	9 51	6 36	8 3	26 54	22 2	23 33
B 6	4 59 43	14 1 30	25 58	0♐16	14 45	10 37	6 44	8 7	26 58	22 5	23 34
E 7	5 3 40	15 2 27	8♐10	1 47	16 0	11 24	6 53	8 12	27 1	22 7	23 36
R 8	5 7 36	16 3 25	20 31	3 19	17 14	12 10	7 1	8 16	27 5	22 9	23 38
9	5 11 33	17 4 23	3♑ 2	4 51	18 29	12 56	7 8	8 20	27 9	22 11	23 39
10	5 15 29	18 5 23	15 43	6 23	19 43	13 42	7 16	8 24	27 12	22 14	23 41
11	5 19 26	19 6 23	28 35	7 55	20 58	14 29	7 24	8 28	27 16	22 16	23 43
12	5 23 23	20 7 24	11♒39	9 27	22 12	15 15	7 31	8 32	27 19	22 18	23 44
13	5 27 19	21 8 26	24 55	11 0	23 27	16 1	7 39	8 36	27 23	22 21	23 46
14	5 31 16	22 9 27	8♓26	12 32	24 41	16 48	7 46	8 40	27 26	22 23	23 47
15	5 35 12	23 10 30	22 13	14 5	25 56	17 34	7 53	8 43	27 30	22 25	23 49
16	5 39 9	24 11 32	6♈15	15 38	27 11	18 21	8 0	8 47	27 33	22 27	23 50
17	5 43 5	25 12 36	20 34	17 11	28 25	19 7	8 7	8 50	27 36	22 30	23 52
18	5 47 2	26 13 39	5♉ 6	18 44	29 40	19 54	8 13	8 54	27 40	22 32	23 53
19	5 50 58	27 14 43	19 46	20 17	0♐55	20 41	8 20	8 57	27 43	22 34	23 54
20	5 54 55	28 15 47	4♊29	21 51	2 10	21 27	8 26	9 0	27 47	22 36	23 56
21	5 58 52	29 16 52	19 7	23 25	3 24	22 14	8 32	9 3	27 50	22 39	23 57
22	6 2 48	0♑17 57	3♋32	24 58	4 39	23 1	8 39	9 6	27 53	22 41	23 58
23	6 6 45	1 19 2	17 39	26 32	5 54	23 48	8 44	9 9	27 56	22 43	23 59
24	6 10 41	2 20 8	1♌22	28 7	7 9	24 34	8 50	9 12	28 0	22 45	24 1
25	6 14 38	3 21 15	14 41	29 41	8 24	25 21	8 56	9 14	28 3	22 48	24 2
26	6 18 34	4 22 22	27 36	1♑16	9 39	26 8	9 1	9 17	28 6	22 50	24 3
27	6 22 31	5 23 30	10♍ 9	2 51	10 54	26 55	9 6	9 19	28 9	22 52	24 4
28	6 26 27	6 24 38	22 24	4 26	12 8	27 42	9 12	9 22	28 12	22 54	24 5
29	6 30 24	7 25 46	4♎27	6 1	13 23	28 29	9 17	9 24	28 16	22 57	24 6
30	6 34 21	8 26 55	16 21	7 37	14 38	29 16	9 21	9 26	28 19	22 59	24 7
31	6 38 17	9♑28 4	28♎13	9♑13	15♐53	0♒ 3	9♎26	9♎28	28♏22	23♐ 1	24♎ 8

THE SUN ENTERS THE SIGN OF CAPRICORN ON DEC 21 AT 16:57.

♏ SCORPIO ♐ SAGITTARIUS ♑ CAPRICORN ♒ AQUARIUS ♓ PISCES

SIDEREAL TIME. SUN. MOON. MERCURY. VENUS. MARS. JUPITER. SATURN. URANUS. NEPTUNE. PLUTO.

DAY	TIME	☉	☽	☿	♀	♂	♃	♄	♅	♆	♇
	h m s	° ' "	° '	° '	° '	° '	° '	° '	° '	° '	° '
J 1	6 42 14	10♑29 14	10♏ 6	10♑50	17♐ 8	0♒50	9♎30	9♎30	28♏25	23♐ 3	24♎ 9
A 2	6 46 10	11 30 24	22 5	12 26	18 23	1 37	9 35	9 32	28 28	23 5	24 10
N 3	6 50 7	12 31 35	4♐13	14 4	19 38	2 24	9 39	9 34	28 31	23 8	24 11
U 4	6 54 3	13 32 45	16 33	15 41	20 53	3 11	9 43	9 35	28 34	23 10	24 12
A 5	6 58 0	14 33 56	29 6	17 19	22 8	3 58	9 46	9 37	28 36	23 12	24 12
R 6	7 1 56	15 35 7	11♑54	18 57	23 23	4 46	9 50	9 38	28 39	23 14	24 13
Y 7	7 5 53	16 36 17	24 56	20 36	24 38	5 33	9 53	9 40	28 42	23 16	24 14
8	7 9 50	17 37 28	8♒11	22 15	25 53	6 20	9 57	9 41	28 45	23 18	24 15
9	7 13 46	18 38 38	21 39	23 54	27 9	7 7	10 0	9 42	28 48	23 20	24 15
10	7 17 43	19 39 48	5♓18	25 33	28 24	7 55	10 3	9 43	28 50	23 22	24 16
11	7 21 39	20 40 57	19 7	27 13	29 39	8 42	10 5	9 44	28 53	23 24	24 16
12	7 25 36	21 42 5	3♈ 4	28 54	0♑54	9 29	10 8	9 45	28 56	23 27	24 17
13	7 29 32	22 43 13	17 9	0♒34	2 9	10 17	10 10	9 45	28 58	23 29	24 17
14	7 33 29	23 44 20	1♉19	2 15	3 24	11 4	10 12	9 46	29 1	23 31	24 18
15	7 37 25	24 45 27	15 34	3 56	4 39	11 51	10 14	9 46	29 3	23 33	24 18
16	7 41 22	25 46 32	29 49	5 37	5 54	12 39	10 16	9 47	29 6	23 35	24 19
17	7 45 19	26 47 38	14♊ 3	7 19	7 9	13 26	10 18	9 47	29 8	23 37	24 19
18	7 49 15	27 48 42	28 10	9 0	8 24	14 13	10 19	9R47	29 10	23 39	24 19
19	7 53 12	28 49 46	12♋ 7	10 41	9 39	15 1	10 20	9 47	29 13	23 41	24 20
20	7 57 8	29 50 48	25 51	12 21	10 54	15 48	10 21	9 47	29 15	23 42	24 20
21	8 1 5	0♒51 51	9♌18	14 1	12 9	16 36	10 22	9 47	29 17	23 44	24 20
22	8 5 1	1 52 52	22 27	15 41	13 24	17 23	10 23	9 46	29 20	23 46	24 20
23	8 8 58	2 53 53	5♍17	17 19	14 40	18 10	10 23	9 46	29 22	23 48	24 21
24	8 12 55	3 54 53	17 50	18 57	15 55	18 58	10R23	9 46	29 24	23 50	24 21
25	8 16 51	4 55 53	0♎ 7	20 32	17 10	19 45	10 23	9 45	29 26	23 52	24 21
26	8 20 48	5 56 52	12 12	22 6	18 25	20 33	10 23	9 44	29 28	23 54	24R21
27	8 24 44	6 57 51	24 9	23 37	19 40	21 20	10 23	9 43	29 30	23 55	24 21
28	8 28 41	7 58 49	6♏ 1	25 6	20 55	22 8	10 22	9 42	29 32	23 57	24 21
29	8 32 37	8 59 46	17 55	26 31	22 10	22 55	10 22	9 41	29 34	23 59	24 21
30	8 36 34	10 0 43	29 54	27 52	23 25	23 43	10 21	9 40	29 35	24 1	24 21
31	8 40 30	11♒ 1 38	12♐ 3	29♒ 8	24♑40	24♒30	10♎20	9♎39	29♏37	24♐ 2	24♎20

THE SUN ENTERS THE SIGN OF AQUARIUS ON JAN 20 AT 03:37.

DAY	TIME	☉	☽	☿	♀	♂	♃	♄	♅	♆	♇
	h m s	° ' "	° '	° '	° '	° '	° '	° '	° '	° '	° '
F 1	8 44 27	12♒ 2 34	24♐26	0♓18	25♑55	25♒17	10♎18	9♎38	29♏39	24♐ 4	24♎20
E 2	8 48 23	13 3 28	7♑ 6	1 23	27 11	26 5	10R17	9R36	29 41	24 6	24R20
B 3	8 52 20	14 4 21	20 5	2 20	28 26	26 52	10 15	9 35	29 42	24 7	24 20
R 4	8 56 17	15 5 14	3♒24	3 9	29 41	27 40	10 13	9 33	29 44	24 9	24 19
U 5	9 0 13	16 6 5	17 2	3 50	0♒56	28 27	10 11	9 31	29 45	24 10	24 19
A 6	9 4 10	17 6 55	0♓57	4 21	2 11	29 15	10 9	9 29	29 47	24 12	24 19
R 7	9 8 6	18 7 44	15 6	4 43	3 26	0♓ 2	10 7	9 27	29 48	24 14	24 18
Y 8	9 12 3	19 8 31	29 23	4R54	4 41	0 50	10 4	9 25	29 50	24 15	24 18
9	9 15 59	20 9 17	13♈44	4 54	5 56	1 37	10 1	9 23	29 51	24 17	24 18
10	9 19 56	21 10 1	28 6	4 44	7 11	2 25	9 58	9 21	29 52	24 18	24 17
11	9 23 52	22 10 44	12♉23	4 22	8 26	3 12	9 55	9 18	29 53	24 19	24 17
12	9 27 49	23 11 25	26 34	3 51	9 41	4 0	9 52	9 16	29 55	24 21	24 16
13	9 31 46	24 12 5	10♊35	3 10	10 56	4 47	9 48	9 13	29 56	24 22	24 15
14	9 35 42	25 12 42	24 26	2 20	12 11	5 34	9 45	9 11	29 57	24 23	24 15
15	9 39 39	26 13 19	8♋ 6	1 24	13 26	6 22	9 41	9 8	29 58	24 25	24 14
16	9 43 35	27 13 53	21 35	0 22	14 42	7 9	9 37	9 5	29 59	24 26	24 13
17	9 47 32	28 14 26	4♌51	29♒16	15 57	7 57	9 33	9 2	0♐ 0	24 27	24 13
18	9 51 28	29 14 57	17 55	28 8	17 12	8 44	9 28	8 59	0 1	24 29	24 12
19	9 55 25	0♓15 26	0♍45	27 0	18 27	9 31	9 24	8 56	0 1	24 30	24 11
20	9 59 21	1 15 54	13 23	25 53	19 41	10 19	9 19	8 53	0 2	24 31	24 10
21	10 3 18	2 16 20	25 48	24 50	20 56	11 6	9 14	8 50	0 3	24 32	24 10
22	10 7 15	3 16 45	8♎ 1	23 51	22 11	11 53	9 9	8 47	0 3	24 33	24 9
23	10 11 11	4 17 8	20 5	22 57	23 26	12 40	9 4	8 43	0 4	24 34	24 8
24	10 15 8	5 17 30	2♏ 1	22 9	24 41	13 28	8 59	8 40	0 4	24 35	24 7
25	10 19 4	6 17 50	13 54	21 28	25 56	14 15	8 53	8 36	0 5	24 36	24 6
26	10 23 1	7 18 9	25 47	20 55	27 11	15 2	8 48	8 33	0 5	24 37	24 5
27	10 26 57	8 18 27	7♐44	20 28	28 26	15 49	8 42	8 29	0 6	24 38	24 4
28	10 30 54	9♓18 43	19♐51	20♒ 9	29♒41	16♓36	8♎36	8♎25	0♐ 6	24♐39	24♎ 3

THE SUN ENTERS THE SIGN OF PISCES ON FEB 18 AT 17:52.

DAY	TIME	☉	☽	☿	♀	♂	♃	♄	♅	♆	♇
	h m s	° ' "	° '	° '	° '	° '	° '	° '	° '	° '	° '
M 1	10 34 50	10♓18 58	2♑11	19♒56	0♓56	17♓24	8♎30	8♎21	0♐ 6	24♐40	24♎ 2
A 2	10 38 47	11 19 11	14 51	19D51	2 11	18 11	8R24	8R18	0 6	24 41	24R 1
R 3	10 42 44	12 19 22	27 52	19 52	3 26	18 58	8 18	8 14	0 7	24 42	24 0
C 4	10 46 40	13 19 32	11♒18	20 0	4 41	19 45	8 12	8 10	0 7	24 42	23 58
H 5	10 50 37	14 19 40	25 10	20 14	5 56	20 32	8 5	8 6	0R 7	24 43	23 57
6	10 54 33	15 19 47	9♓25	20 33	7 11	21 19	7 59	8 2	0 7	24 44	23 56
7	10 58 30	16 19 52	23 59	20 57	8 25	22 6	7 52	7 57	0 7	24 45	23 55
8	11 2 26	17 19 54	8♈45	21 26	9 40	22 53	7 45	7 53	0 6	24 45	23 54
9	11 6 23	18 19 55	23 35	22 0	10 55	23 40	7 38	7 49	0 6	24 46	23 52
10	11 10 19	19 19 53	8♉22	22 39	12 10	24 27	7 31	7 45	0 6	24 47	23 51
11	11 14 16	20 19 50	22 58	23 21	13 25	25 14	7 24	7 40	0 6	24 47	23 50
12	11 18 13	21 19 44	7♊18	24 7	14 40	26 1	7 17	7 36	0 5	24 48	23 48
13	11 22 9	22 19 36	21 20	24 56	15 54	26 48	7 10	7 32	0 5	24 48	23 47
14	11 26 6	23 19 26	5♋ 3	25 48	17 9	27 35	7 2	7 27	0 5	24 49	23 46
15	11 30 2	24 19 14	18 27	26 44	18 24	28 21	6 55	7 23	0 4	24 49	23 44
16	11 33 59	25 18 59	1♌36	27 43	19 39	29 8	6 48	7 18	0 4	24 49	23 43
17	11 37 55	26 18 42	14 30	28 44	20 53	29 55	6 40	7 14	0 3	24 50	23 41
18	11 41 52	27 18 23	27 12	29 48	22 8	0♈41	6 33	7 9	0 2	24 50	23 40
19	11 45 48	28 18 2	9♍43	0♓54	23 23	1 28	6 25	7 4	0 2	24 50	23 38
20	11 49 45	29 17 39	22 5	2 2	24 37	2 15	6 17	7 0	0 1	24 51	23 37
21	11 53 41	0♈17 13	4♎18	3 13	25 52	3 1	6 10	6 55	0 0	24 51	23 35
22	11 57 38	1 16 46	16 24	4 25	27 7	3 48	6 2	6 50	29♏59	24 51	23 34
23	12 1 35	2 16 16	28 23	5 40	28 21	4 34	5 54	6 46	29 58	24 51	23 32
24	12 5 31	3 15 45	10♏18	6 57	29 36	5 21	5 47	6 41	29 57	24 51	23 31
25	12 9 28	4 15 12	22 10	8 15	0♈51	6 7	5 39	6 36	29 56	24 51	23 29
26	12 13 24	5 14 37	4♐ 2	9 35	2 5	6 54	5 31	6 32	29 55	24 51	23 28
27	12 17 21	6 14 0	15 58	10 57	3 20	7 40	5 23	6 27	29 54	24R51	23 26
28	12 21 17	7 13 22	28 2	12 20	4 34	8 26	5 16	6 22	29 53	24 51	23 24
29	12 25 14	8 12 41	10♑19	13 46	5 49	9 13	5 8	6 18	29 52	24 51	23 23
30	12 29 10	9 11 59	22 53	15 12	7 3	9 59	5 0	6 13	29 51	24 51	23 21
31	12 33 7	10♈11 16	5♒50	16♓41	8♈18	10♈45	4♎52	6♎ 8	29♏49	24♐51	23♎20

THE SUN ENTERS THE SIGN OF ARIES ON MAR 20 AT 17:04.

♈ ARIES ♉ TAURUS ♊ GEMINI ♋ CANCER ♌ LEO ♍ VIRGO ♎ LIBRA

SIDEREAL TIME — SUN. — MOON. — MERCURY. — VENUS. — MARS. — JUPITER. — SATURN. — URANUS. — NEPTUNE. — PLUTO.

DAY	TIME	☉	☽	☿	♀	♂	♃	♄	♅	♆	♇
	h m s	° ' "	° '	° '	° '	° '	° '	° '	° '	° '	° '
A 1	12 37 4	11♈10 30	19♒14	18♓10	9♈32	11♈31	4♎45	6♎ 4	29♏48	24♐51	23♎18
P 2	12 41 0	12 9 43	3♓ 6	19 42	10 47	12 17	4R37	5R59	29R47	24R51	23R16
R 3	12 44 57	13 8 53	17 27	21 15	12 1	13 4	4 29	5 54	29 45	24 51	23 15
I 4	12 48 53	14 8 2	2♈13	22 49	13 16	13 50	4 22	5 50	29 44	24 50	23 13
L 5	12 52 50	15 7 9	17 17	24 25	14 30	14 36	4 14	5 45	29 42	24 50	23 11
6	12 56 46	16 6 13	2♉29	26 2	15 45	15 22	4 7	5 41	29 41	24 50	23 10
7	13 0 43	17 5 16	17 39	27 41	16 59	16 8	3 59	5 36	29 39	24 50	23 8
8	13 4 39	18 4 17	2♊36	29 21	18 14	16 53	3 52	5 31	29 37	24 49	23 6
9	13 8 36	19 3 15	17 13	1♈ 3	19 28	17 39	3 45	5 27	29 36	24 49	23 5
10	13 12 33	20 2 11	1♋25	2 46	20 42	18 25	3 38	5 22	29 34	24 48	23 3
11	13 16 29	21 1 5	15 12	4 31	21 57	19 11	3 30	5 18	29 32	24 48	23 1
12	13 20 26	21 59 56	28 34	6 17	23 11	19 57	3 23	5 14	29 31	24 47	23 0
13	13 24 22	22 58 45	11♌34	8 5	24 25	20 42	3 16	5 9	29 29	24 47	22 58
14	13 28 19	23 57 32	24 17	9 54	25 40	21 28	3 10	5 5	29 27	24 46	22 56
15	13 32 15	24 56 16	6♍45	11 45	26 54	22 13	3 3	5 1	29 25	24 46	22 55
16	13 36 12	25 54 59	19 2	13 38	28 8	22 59	2 56	4 56	29 23	24 45	22 53
17	13 40 8	26 53 39	1♎11	15 32	29 22	23 44	2 50	4 52	29 21	24 44	22 51
18	13 44 5	27 52 17	13 14	17 27	0♉37	24 30	2 43	4 48	29 19	24 44	22 49
19	13 48 1	28 50 53	25 12	19 24	1 51	25 15	2 37	4 44	29 17	24 43	22 48
20	13 51 58	29 49 27	7♏ 7	21 23	3 5	26 0	2 30	4 40	29 15	24 42	22 46
21	13 55 55	0♉47 59	18 59	23 23	4 19	26 46	2 24	4 36	29 13	24 42	22 44
22	13 59 51	1 46 30	0♐52	25 24	5 33	27 31	2 18	4 32	29 11	24 41	22 43
23	14 3 48	2 44 59	12 45	27 27	6 47	28 16	2 12	4 28	29 9	24 40	22 41
24	14 7 44	3 43 26	24 43	29 31	8 2	29 1	2 7	4 25	29 7	24 39	22 39
25	14 11 41	4 41 51	6♑48	1♉37	9 16	29 46	2 1	4 21	29 4	24 38	22 38
26	14 15 37	5 40 15	19 4	3 43	10 30	0♉31	1 56	4 17	29 2	24 37	22 36
27	14 19 34	6 38 37	1♒36	5 51	11 44	1 16	1 50	4 14	29 0	24 36	22 35
28	14 23 30	7 36 58	14 29	7 59	12 58	2 1	1 45	4 10	28 58	24 36	22 33
29	14 27 27	8 35 17	27 46	10 8	14 12	2 46	1 40	4 7	28 55	24 35	22 31
30	14 31 24	9♉33 34	11♓32	12♉17	15♉26	3♉31	1♎35	4♎ 3	28♏53	24♐34	22♎30

THE SUN ENTERS THE SIGN OF TAURUS ON APR 20 AT 04:19.

DAY	TIME	☉	☽	☿	♀	♂	♃	♄	♅	♆	♇
	h m s	° ' "	° '	° '	° '	° '	° '	° '	° '	° '	° '
M 1	14 35 20	10♉31 50	25♓46	14♉26	16♉40	4♉16	1♎30	4♎ 0	28♏51	24♐33	22♎28
A 2	14 39 17	11 30 5	10♈29	16 35	17 54	5 1	1R26	3R57	28R48	24R31	22R27
Y 3	14 43 13	12 28 18	25 33	18 44	19 8	5 45	1 21	3 53	28 46	24 30	22 25
4	14 47 10	13 26 29	10♉51	20 52	20 22	6 30	1 17	3 50	28 44	24 29	22 23
5	14 51 6	14 24 39	26 10	22 59	21 36	7 14	1 13	3 47	28 41	24 28	22 22
6	14 55 3	15 22 47	11♊20	25 5	22 50	7 59	1 9	3 44	28 39	24 27	22 20
7	14 58 59	16 20 53	26 10	27 9	24 4	8 44	1 5	3 42	28 37	24 26	22 19
8	15 2 56	17 18 57	10♋35	29 11	25 18	9 28	1 2	3 39	28 34	24 25	22 17
9	15 6 53	18 17 0	24 31	1♊11	26 32	10 12	0 58	3 36	28 32	24 23	22 16
10	15 10 49	19 15 0	7♌59	3 9	27 45	10 57	0 55	3 34	28 29	24 22	22 14
11	15 14 46	20 12 59	21 1	5 4	28 59	11 41	0 52	3 31	28 27	24 21	22 13
12	15 18 42	21 10 55	3♍42	6 56	0♊13	12 25	0 49	3 29	28 24	24 20	22 11
13	15 22 39	22 8 50	16 6	8 46	1 27	13 9	0 46	3 26	28 22	24 18	22 10
14	15 26 35	23 6 43	28 17	10 32	2 41	13 53	0 44	3 24	28 19	24 17	22 9
15	15 30 32	24 4 35	10♎19	12 15	3 54	14 37	0 41	3 22	28 17	24 16	22 7
16	15 34 28	25 2 24	22 15	13 55	5 8	15 21	0 39	3 20	28 14	24 14	22 6
17	15 38 25	26 0 12	4♏ 8	15 32	6 22	16 5	0 37	3 18	28 12	24 13	22 5
18	15 42 22	26 57 59	16 1	17 5	7 36	16 49	0 35	3 16	28 9	24 12	22 3
19	15 46 18	27 55 44	27 54	18 35	8 49	17 33	0 34	3 15	28 7	24 10	22 2
20	15 50 15	28 53 28	9♐49	20 2	10 3	18 17	0 32	3 13	28 4	24 9	22 1
21	15 54 11	29 51 10	21 48	21 25	11 17	19 1	0 31	3 11	28 2	24 7	21 59
22	15 58 8	0♊48 52	3♑52	22 44	12 30	19 44	0 30	3 10	27 59	24 6	21 58
23	16 2 4	1 46 32	16 3	24 0	13 44	20 28	0 29	3 8	27 57	24 5	21 57
24	16 6 1	2 44 11	28 26	25 12	14 58	21 11	0 28	3 7	27 54	24 3	21 56
25	16 9 57	3 41 49	11♒ 2	26 20	16 11	21 55	0 27	3 6	27 52	24 2	21 55
26	16 13 54	4 39 26	23 55	27 25	17 25	22 38	0 27	3 5	27 49	24 0	21 54
27	16 17 51	5 37 2	7♓10	28 25	18 38	23 22	0D27	3 4	27 47	23 59	21 52
28	16 21 47	6 34 37	20 49	29 22	19 52	24 5	0 27	3 3	27 44	23 57	21 51
29	16 25 44	7 32 11	4♈54	0♋15	21 6	24 49	0 27	3 2	27 42	23 56	21 50
30	16 29 40	8 29 45	19 24	1 4	22 19	25 32	0 27	3 2	27 39	23 54	21 49
31	16 33 37	9♊27 17	4♉15	1♋48	23♊33	26♉15	0♎28	3♎ 1	27♏37	23♐52	21♎48

THE SUN ENTERS THE SIGN OF GEMINI ON MAY 21 AT 03:40.

DAY	TIME	☉	☽	☿	♀	♂	♃	♄	♅	♆	♇
	h m s	° ' "	° '	° '	° '	° '	° '	° '	° '	° '	° '
J 1	16 37 33	10♊24 49	19♉21	2♋29	24♊46	26♉58	0♎28	3♎ 1	27♏35	23♐51	21♎47
U 2	16 41 30	11 22 20	4♊33	3 5	26 0	27 41	0 29	3R 0	27R32	23R49	21R46
N 3	16 45 26	12 19 50	19 39	3 36	27 13	28 24	0 30	3 0	27 30	23 48	21 45
E 4	16 49 23	13 17 19	4♋31	4 4	28 27	29 7	0 31	3 0	27 27	23 46	21 45
5	16 53 20	14 14 47	19 0	4 27	29 40	29 50	0 33	3D 0	27 25	23 45	21 44
6	16 57 16	15 12 13	3♌ 3	4 45	0♋54	0♊33	0 34	3 0	27 23	23 43	21 43
7	17 1 13	16 9 39	16 38	4 58	2 7	1 16	0 36	3 0	27 20	23 41	21 42
8	17 5 9	17 7 3	29 46	5 8	3 20	1 59	0 38	3 0	27 18	23 40	21 41
9	17 9 6	18 4 27	12♍31	5R12	4 34	2 41	0 40	3 1	27 16	23 38	21 41
10	17 13 2	19 1 49	24 56	5 12	5 47	3 24	0 42	3 1	27 13	23 37	21 40
11	17 16 59	19 59 10	7♎ 7	5 7	7 1	4 7	0 45	3 2	27 11	23 35	21 39
12	17 20 55	20 56 30	19 7	4 59	8 14	4 49	0 48	3 2	27 9	23 33	21 38
13	17 24 52	21 53 49	1♏ 2	4 45	9 27	5 32	0 50	3 3	27 7	23 32	21 38
14	17 28 49	22 51 7	12 54	4 28	10 41	6 14	0 53	3 4	27 5	23 30	21 37
15	17 32 45	23 48 25	24 46	4 8	11 54	6 56	0 56	3 5	27 2	23 28	21 37
16	17 36 42	24 45 42	6♐42	3 44	13 7	7 39	1 0	3 6	27 0	23 27	21 36
17	17 40 38	25 42 58	18 43	3 16	14 20	8 21	1 3	3 7	26 58	23 25	21 36
18	17 44 35	26 40 13	0♑50	2 47	15 34	9 3	1 7	3 8	26 56	23 24	21 35
19	17 48 31	27 37 29	13 5	2 15	16 47	9 45	1 11	3 10	26 54	23 22	21 35
20	17 52 28	28 34 43	25 30	1 42	18 0	10 28	1 14	3 11	26 52	23 20	21 34
21	17 56 25	29 31 57	8♒ 6	1 8	19 13	11 10	1 19	3 13	26 50	23 19	21 34
22	18 0 21	0♋29 11	20 55	0 33	20 26	11 52	1 23	3 14	26 48	23 17	21 34
23	18 4 18	1 26 25	3♓58	29♊58	21 39	12 34	1 27	3 16	26 46	23 16	21 33
24	18 8 14	2 23 39	17 19	29 25	22 53	13 15	1 32	3 18	26 44	23 14	21 33
25	18 12 11	3 20 52	0♈58	28 52	24 6	13 57	1 37	3 20	26 42	23 12	21 33
26	18 16 7	4 18 6	14 56	28 22	25 19	14 39	1 41	3 22	26 41	23 11	21 33
27	18 20 4	5 15 19	29 14	27 54	26 32	15 21	1 46	3 24	26 39	23 9	21 32
28	18 24 0	6 12 33	13♉47	27 29	27 45	16 3	1 52	3 26	26 37	23 8	21 32
29	18 27 57	7 9 47	28 32	27 7	28 58	16 44	1 57	3 28	26 35	23 6	21 32
30	18 31 54	8♋ 7 0	13♊23	26♊49	0♌11	17♊26	2♎ 2	3♎31	26♏34	23♐ 5	21♎32

THE SUN ENTERS THE SIGN OF CANCER ON JUN 21 AT 11:46.

♏ SCORPIO ♐ SAGITTARIUS ♑ CAPRICORN ♒ AQUARIUS ♓ PISCES

SIDEREAL SUN.... MOON... MERCURY VENUS.. MARS... JUPITER SATURN. URANUS. NEPTUNE PLUTO..

DAY	TIME	☉	☽	☿	♀	♂	♃	♄	♅	♆	♇
	h m s	° ' "	° '	° '	° '	° '	° '	° '	° '	° '	° '
J 1	18 35 50	9♋ 4 14	28♊11	26♊35	1♌24	18♊ 7	2♎ 8	3♎33	26♏32	23♐ 3	21♎32
U 2	18 39 47	10 1 28	12♋49	26R26	2 37	18 49	2 14	3 36	26R31	23R 1	21D32
L 3	18 43 43	10 58 42	27 10	26D21	3 50	19 30	2 20	3 39	26 29	23 0	21 32
Y 4	18 47 40	11 55 55	11♌10	26 21	5 3	20 12	2 26	3 41	26 27	22 58	21 32
5	18 51 36	12 53 9	24 46	26 25	6 16	20 53	2 32	3 44	26 26	22 57	21 32
6	18 55 33	13 50 22	7♍57	26 35	7 29	21 34	2 38	3 47	26 25	22 55	21 32
7	18 59 29	14 47 34	20 46	26 50	8 42	22 15	2 45	3 50	26 23	22 54	21 32
8	19 3 26	15 44 47	3♎14	27 10	9 55	22 56	2 51	3 53	26 22	22 52	21 33
9	19 7 23	16 42 0	15 28	27 35	11 8	23 38	2 58	3 57	26 21	22 51	21 33
10	19 11 19	17 39 12	27 29	28 5	12 21	24 19	3 5	4 0	26 19	22 50	21 33
11	19 15 16	18 36 24	9♏24	28 40	13 33	25 0	3 12	4 3	26 18	22 48	21 33
12	19 19 12	19 33 37	21 17	29 20	14 46	25 40	3 19	4 7	26 17	22 47	21 34
13	19 23 9	20 30 49	3♐11	0♋ 6	15 59	26 21	3 27	4 10	26 16	22 45	21 34
14	19 27 5	21 28 1	15 10	0 56	17 12	27 2	3 34	4 14	26 15	22 44	21 35
15	19 31 2	22 25 14	27 17	1 51	18 24	27 43	3 41	4 18	26 14	22 43	21 35
16	19 34 58	23 22 27	9♑34	2 51	19 37	28 24	3 49	4 22	26 13	22 41	21 35
17	19 38 55	24 19 40	22 4	3 56	20 50	29 4	3 57	4 26	26 12	22 40	21 36
18	19 42 52	25 16 53	4♒46	5 6	22 2	29 45	4 5	4 30	26 11	22 39	21 37
19	19 46 48	26 14 7	17 42	6 20	23 15	0♋25	4 13	4 34	26 10	22 37	21 37
20	19 50 45	27 11 22	0♓52	7 39	24 27	1 6	4 21	4 38	26 9	22 36	21 38
21	19 54 41	28 8 37	14 15	9 2	25 40	1 46	4 29	4 42	26 8	22 35	21 38
22	19 58 38	29 5 53	27 52	10 30	26 53	2 27	4 37	4 46	26 8	22 34	21 39
23	20 2 34	0♌ 3 10	11♈41	12 2	28 5	3 7	4 46	4 51	26 7	22 32	21 40
24	20 6 31	1 0 27	25 42	13 38	29 17	3 48	4 54	4 55	26 6	22 31	21 40
25	20 10 27	1 57 46	9♉52	15 18	0♍30	4 28	5 3	5 0	26 6	22 30	21 41
26	20 14 24	2 55 5	24 11	17 1	1 42	5 8	5 12	5 4	26 5	22 29	21 42
27	20 18 21	3 52 26	8♊35	18 49	2 55	5 48	5 21	5 9	26 5	22 28	21 43
28	20 22 17	4 49 47	23 0	20 39	4 7	6 28	5 30	5 14	26 5	22 27	21 44
29	20 26 14	5 47 10	7♋21	22 32	5 19	7 8	5 39	5 19	26 4	22 26	21 45
30	20 30 10	6 44 33	21 35	24 28	6 32	7 48	5 48	5 24	26 4	22 25	21 45
31	20 34 7	7♌41 57	5♌37	26♋26	7♍44	8♋28	5♎58	5♎29	26♏ 4	22♐23	21♎46

THE SUN ENTERS THE SIGN OF LEO ON JUL 22 AT 22:41.

DAY	TIME	☉	☽	☿	♀	♂	♃	♄	♅	♆	♇
	h m s	° ' "	° '	° '	° '	° '	° '	° '	° '	° '	° '
A 1	20 38 3	8♌39 22	19♌22	28♋26	8♍56	9♋ 8	6♎ 7	5♎34	26♏ 3	22♐22	21♎47
U 2	20 42 0	9 36 48	2♍49	0♌28	10 9	9 48	6 16	5 39	26R 3	22R22	21 48
G 3	20 45 56	10 34 15	15 56	2 31	11 21	10 28	6 26	5 44	26 3	22 21	21 50
U 4	20 49 53	11 31 42	28 44	4 35	12 33	11 8	6 36	5 49	26D 3	22 20	21 51
S 5	20 53 50	12 29 10	11♎13	6 39	13 45	11 47	6 46	5 54	26 3	22 19	21 52
T 6	20 57 46	13 26 39	23 28	8 44	14 57	12 27	6 55	6 0	26 3	22 18	21 53
7	21 1 43	14 24 8	5♏31	10 49	16 9	13 6	7 5	6 5	26 3	22 17	21 54
8	21 5 39	15 21 39	17 26	12 53	17 21	13 46	7 15	6 11	26 3	22 16	21 55
9	21 9 36	16 19 10	29 19	14 57	18 33	14 25	7 26	6 16	26 4	22 15	21 57
10	21 13 32	17 16 42	11♐13	17 0	19 45	15 5	7 36	6 22	26 4	22 15	21 58
11	21 17 29	18 14 15	23 15	19 3	20 57	15 44	7 46	6 27	26 4	22 14	21 59
12	21 21 25	19 11 49	5♑26	21 4	22 9	16 23	7 57	6 33	26 5	22 13	22 0
13	21 25 22	20 9 24	17 52	23 5	23 21	17 3	8 7	6 39	26 5	22 13	22 2
14	21 29 19	21 7 0	0♒34	25 4	24 32	17 42	8 18	6 45	26 5	22 12	22 3
15	21 33 15	22 4 37	13 34	27 2	25 44	18 21	8 28	6 51	26 6	22 11	22 5
16	21 37 12	23 2 15	26 52	28 58	26 56	19 0	8 39	6 57	26 7	22 11	22 6
17	21 41 8	23 59 54	10♓27	0♍54	28 7	19 39	8 50	7 3	26 7	22 10	22 7
18	21 45 5	24 57 35	24 17	2 48	29 19	20 18	9 1	7 9	26 8	22 10	22 9
19	21 49 1	25 55 17	8♈18	4 40	0♎31	20 57	9 12	7 15	26 9	22 9	22 10
20	21 52 58	26 53 1	22 27	6 31	1 42	21 36	9 23	7 21	26 9	22 9	22 12
21	21 56 54	27 50 47	6♉41	8 21	2 53	22 15	9 34	7 27	26 10	22 8	22 14
22	22 0 51	28 48 34	20 55	10 9	4 5	22 54	9 45	7 33	26 11	22 8	22 15
23	22 4 48	29 46 23	5♊ 8	11 56	5 16	23 32	9 56	7 40	26 12	22 7	22 17
24	22 8 44	0♍44 14	19 17	13 42	6 28	24 11	10 7	7 46	26 13	22 7	22 18
25	22 12 41	1 42 6	3♋20	15 26	7 39	24 50	10 19	7 53	26 14	22 7	22 20
26	22 16 37	2 40 1	17 16	17 9	8 50	25 28	10 30	7 59	26 15	22 6	22 22
27	22 20 34	3 37 57	1♌ 2	18 50	10 1	26 7	10 42	8 5	26 16	22 6	22 24
28	22 24 30	4 35 55	14 39	20 31	11 12	26 45	10 53	8 12	26 17	22 6	22 25
29	22 28 27	5 33 54	28 3	22 10	12 24	27 24	11 5	8 19	26 19	22 6	22 27
30	22 32 23	6 31 55	11♍13	23 47	13 35	28 2	11 17	8 25	26 20	22 6	22 29
31	22 36 20	7♍29 58	24♍ 8	25♍24	14♎46	28♋41	11♎28	8♎32	26♏21	22♐ 5	22♎31

THE SUN ENTERS THE SIGN OF VIRGO ON AUG 23 AT 05:40.

DAY	TIME	☉	☽	☿	♀	♂	♃	♄	♅	♆	♇
	h m s	° ' "	° '	° '	° '	° '	° '	° '	° '	° '	° '
S 1	22 40 17	8♍28 2	6♎48	26♍59	15♎57	29♋19	11♎40	8♎39	26♏23	22♐ 5	22♎33
E 2	22 44 13	9 26 7	19 13	28 32	17 7	29 57	11 52	8 45	26 24	22R 5	22 34
P 3	22 48 10	10 24 14	1♏25	0♎ 5	18 18	0♌35	12 4	8 52	26 26	22D 5	22 36
T 4	22 52 6	11 22 23	13 27	1 36	19 29	1 13	12 16	8 59	26 27	22 5	22 38
E 5	22 56 3	12 20 33	25 21	3 6	20 40	1 51	12 28	9 6	26 29	22 5	22 40
M 6	22 59 59	13 18 45	7♐12	4 35	21 51	2 29	12 40	9 13	26 30	22 5	22 42
B 7	23 3 56	14 16 58	19 6	6 3	23 1	3 7	12 52	9 19	26 32	22 5	22 44
E 8	23 7 52	15 15 12	1♑ 6	7 29	24 12	3 45	13 4	9 26	26 34	22 6	22 46
R 9	23 11 49	16 13 29	13 18	8 54	25 22	4 23	13 16	9 33	26 36	22 6	22 48
10	23 15 45	17 11 46	25 46	10 17	26 33	5 1	13 29	9 40	26 37	22 6	22 50
11	23 19 42	18 10 5	8♒35	11 40	27 43	5 38	13 41	9 47	26 39	22 6	22 52
12	23 23 39	19 8 26	21 47	13 0	28 53	6 16	13 53	9 54	26 41	22 6	22 54
13	23 27 35	20 6 49	5♓23	14 20	0♏ 3	6 54	14 6	10 1	26 43	22 7	22 56
14	23 31 32	21 5 13	19 21	15 38	1 13	7 31	14 18	10 8	26 45	22 7	22 58
15	23 35 28	22 3 39	3♈38	16 54	2 24	8 9	14 30	10 16	26 47	22 7	23 1
16	23 39 25	23 2 7	18 8	18 9	3 33	8 46	14 43	10 23	26 49	22 8	23 3
17	23 43 21	24 0 37	2♉44	19 22	4 43	9 23	14 55	10 30	26 51	22 8	23 5
18	23 47 18	24 59 10	17 19	20 34	5 53	10 1	15 8	10 37	26 53	22 9	23 7
19	23 51 14	25 57 44	1♊48	21 43	7 3	10 38	15 20	10 44	26 56	22 9	23 9
20	23 55 11	26 56 21	16 6	22 51	8 13	11 15	15 33	10 51	26 58	22 10	23 11
21	23 59 8	27 55 0	0♋11	23 57	9 22	11 52	15 46	10 59	27 0	22 10	23 14
22	0 3 4	28 53 41	14 2	25 0	10 32	12 30	15 58	11 6	27 3	22 11	23 16
23	0 7 1	29 52 25	27 40	26 1	11 41	13 7	16 11	11 13	27 5	22 11	23 18
24	0 10 57	0♎51 10	11♌ 4	27 0	12 51	13 44	16 24	11 21	27 7	22 12	23 20
25	0 14 54	1 49 58	24 17	27 55	14 0	14 20	16 37	11 28	27 10	22 13	23 23
26	0 18 50	2 48 48	7♍18	28 48	15 9	14 57	16 49	11 35	27 12	22 14	23 25
27	0 22 47	3 47 40	20 8	29 38	16 18	15 34	17 2	11 42	27 15	22 14	23 27
28	0 26 43	4 46 34	2♎47	0♏25	17 27	16 11	17 15	11 50	27 17	22 15	23 29
29	0 30 40	5 45 31	15 15	1 7	18 36	16 48	17 28	11 57	27 20	22 16	23 32
30	0 34 37	6♎44 29	27♎31	1♏46	19♏45	17♌24	17♎41	12♎ 4	27♏23	22♐17	23♎34

THE SUN ENTERS THE SIGN OF LIBRA ON SEP 23 AT 03:07.

♈ ARIES ♉ TAURUS ♊ GEMINI ♋ CANCER ♌ LEO ♍ VIRGO ♎ LIBRA

SIDEREAL | SUN. | MOON. | MERCURY. | VENUS. | MARS. | JUPITER. | SATURN. | URANUS. | NEPTUNE. | PLUTO.

DAY	TIME	☉	☽	☿	♀	♂	♃	♄	♅	♆	♇
	h m s	° ' "	° '	° '	° '	° '	° '	° '	° '	° '	° '
O 1	Ø 38 33	7♎43 29	9♏38	2♏2Ø	2Ø♏54	18♌ 1	17♎54	12♎12	27♏25	22♐18	23♎36
C 2	Ø 42 3Ø	8 42 31	21 35	2 5Ø	22 2	18 37	18 7	12 19	27 28	22 19	23 39
T 3	Ø 46 26	9 41 35	3♐27	3 14	23 11	19 14	18 2Ø	12 27	27 31	22 19	23 41
O 4	Ø 5Ø 23	1Ø 4Ø 4Ø	15 16	3 33	24 19	19 5Ø	18 33	12 34	27 34	22 2Ø	23 43
B 5	Ø 54 19	11 39 48	27 7	3 45	25 28	2Ø 26	18 45	12 41	27 36	22 21	23 46
E 6	Ø 58 16	12 38 57	9♑ 4	3R51	26 36	21 2	18 58	12 49	27 39	22 22	23 48
R 7	1 2 12	13 38 9	21 13	3 5Ø	27 44	21 38	19 11	12 56	27 42	22 24	23 51
8	1 6 9	14 37 21	3♒39	3 42	28 52	22 15	19 24	13 3	27 45	22 25	23 53
9	1 1Ø 5	15 36 36	16 27	3 26	Ø♐ Ø	22 51	19 37	13 11	27 48	22 26	23 55
1Ø	1 14 2	16 35 53	29 41	3 2	1 7	23 26	19 5Ø	13 18	27 51	22 27	23 58
11	1 17 59	17 35 11	13♓24	2 3Ø	2 15	24 2	2Ø 3	13 26	27 54	22 28	24 Ø
12	1 21 55	18 34 31	27 35	1 5Ø	3 22	24 38	2Ø 16	13 33	27 57	22 29	24 2
13	1 25 52	19 33 53	12♈1Ø	1 1	4 3Ø	25 14	2Ø 29	13 4Ø	28 Ø	22 31	24 5
14	1 29 48	2Ø 33 17	27 3	Ø 5	5 37	25 5Ø	2Ø 43	13 48	28 3	22 32	24 7
15	1 33 45	21 32 43	12♉ 4	29♎ 3	6 44	26 25	2Ø 56	13 55	28 7	22 33	24 1Ø
16	1 37 41	22 32 11	27 5	27 55	7 51	27 1	21 9	14 2	28 1Ø	22 34	24 12
17	1 41 38	23 31 41	11♊55	26 44	8 57	27 36	21 22	14 1Ø	28 13	22 36	24 14
18	1 45 34	24 31 14	26 29	25 3Ø	1Ø 4	28 11	21 35	14 17	28 16	22 37	24 17
19	1 49 31	25 3Ø 49	1Ø♋42	24 16	11 1Ø	28 47	21 48	14 24	28 19	22 39	24 19
2Ø	1 53 28	26 3Ø 27	24 34	23 5	12 16	29 22	22 1	14 31	28 23	22 4Ø	24 22
21	1 57 24	27 3Ø 7	8♌ 5	21 57	13 22	29 57	22 14	14 39	28 26	22 41	24 24
22	2 1 21	28 29 49	21 17	2Ø 56	14 28	Ø♍32	22 27	14 46	28 29	22 43	24 26
23	2 5 17	29 29 33	4♍14	2Ø 4	15 34	1 7	22 4Ø	14 53	28 33	22 44	24 29
24	2 9 14	Ø♏29 19	16 58	19 2Ø	16 39	1 42	22 53	15 Ø	28 36	22 46	24 31
25	2 13 1Ø	1 29 8	29 3Ø	18 48	17 44	2 17	23 6	15 8	28 39	22 47	24 34
26	2 17 7	2 28 58	11♎53	18 26	18 5Ø	2 52	23 19	15 15	28 43	22 49	24 36
27	2 21 3	3 28 51	24 7	18D16	19 54	3 26	23 32	15 22	28 46	22 51	24 38
28	2 25 Ø	4 28 46	6♏13	18 18	2Ø 59	4 1	23 45	15 29	28 5Ø	22 52	24 41
29	2 28 57	5 28 42	18 12	18 3Ø	22 3	4 35	23 57	15 36	28 53	22 54	24 43
3Ø	2 32 53	6 28 41	Ø♐ 5	18 52	23 8	5 1Ø	24 1Ø	15 43	28 57	22 56	24 46
31	2 36 5Ø	7♏28 41	11♐55	19♎25	24♐11	5♍44	24♎23	15♎5Ø	29♏ Ø	22♐57	24♎48

THE SUN ENTERS THE SIGN OF SCORPIO ON OCT 23 AT 12:14.

DAY	TIME	☉	☽	☿	♀	♂	♃	♄	♅	♆	♇
	h m s	° ' "	° '	° '	° '	° '	° '	° '	° '	° '	° '
N 1	2 4Ø 46	8♏28 43	23♐43	2Ø♎ 6	25♐15	6♍18	24♎36	15♎57	29♏ 4	22♐59	24♎5Ø
O 2	2 44 43	9 28 47	5♑32	2Ø 55	26 19	6 53	24 49	16 4	29 7	23 1	24 53
V 3	2 48 39	1Ø 28 53	17 28	21 51	27 22	7 27	25 2	16 11	29 11	23 3	24 55
E 4	2 52 36	11 29 Ø	29 34	22 53	28 25	8 1	25 15	16 18	29 14	23 4	24 57
M 5	2 56 32	12 29 8	11♒56	24 1	29 27	8 34	25 27	16 25	29 18	23 6	25 Ø
B 6	3 Ø 29	13 29 19	24 39	25 14	Ø♑29	9 8	25 4Ø	16 32	29 22	23 8	25 2
E 7	3 4 26	14 29 3Ø	7♓47	26 3Ø	1 31	9 42	25 53	16 39	29 25	23 1Ø	25 4
R 8	3 8 22	15 29 43	21 25	27 5Ø	2 33	1Ø 15	26 5	16 45	29 29	23 12	25 7
9	3 12 19	16 29 58	5♈34	29 13	3 34	1Ø 49	26 18	16 52	29 32	23 14	25 9
1Ø	3 16 15	17 3Ø 14	2Ø 11	Ø♏38	4 35	11 22	26 31	16 59	29 36	23 16	25 11
11	3 2Ø 12	18 3Ø 31	5♉11	2 6	5 36	11 55	26 43	17 6	29 4Ø	23 17	25 13
12	3 24 8	19 3Ø 51	2Ø 26	3 35	6 36	12 29	26 56	17 12	29 43	23 19	25 16
13	3 28 5	2Ø 31 12	5♊44	5 5	7 35	13 2	27 8	17 19	29 47	23 21	25 18
14	3 32 1	21 31 35	2Ø 54	6 37	8 35	13 35	27 21	17 25	29 51	23 23	25 2Ø
15	3 35 58	22 31 59	5♋46	8 9	9 34	14 7	27 33	17 32	29 54	23 25	25 22
16	3 39 55	23 32 26	2Ø 16	9 42	1Ø 32	14 4Ø	27 46	17 38	29 58	23 27	25 24
17	3 43 51	24 32 54	4♌19	11 16	11 3Ø	15 13	27 58	17 45	Ø♐ 2	23 29	25 27
18	3 47 48	25 33 24	17 56	12 5Ø	12 28	15 45	28 1Ø	17 51	Ø 6	23 31	25 29
19	3 51 44	26 33 56	1♍ 9	14 24	13 25	16 18	28 23	17 57	Ø 9	23 34	25 31
2Ø	3 55 41	27 34 3Ø	14 1	15 59	14 21	16 5Ø	28 35	18 4	Ø 13	23 36	25 33
21	3 59 37	28 35 5	26 36	17 34	15 17	17 22	28 47	18 1Ø	Ø 17	23 38	25 35
22	4 3 34	29 35 43	8♎58	19 9	16 13	17 54	28 59	18 16	Ø 2Ø	23 4Ø	25 37
23	4 7 3Ø	Ø♐36 21	21 8	2Ø 44	17 7	18 26	29 11	18 22	Ø 24	23 42	25 39
24	4 11 27	1 37 2	3♏11	22 18	18 2	18 58	29 23	18 28	Ø 28	23 44	25 41
25	4 15 24	2 37 44	15 9	23 53	18 55	19 3Ø	29 35	18 34	Ø 32	23 46	25 43
26	4 19 2Ø	3 38 27	27 2	25 28	19 49	2Ø 1	29 47	18 4Ø	Ø 35	23 48	25 45
27	4 23 17	4 39 12	8♐52	27 3	2Ø 41	2Ø 32	29 59	18 46	Ø 39	23 5Ø	25 47
28	4 27 13	5 39 58	2Ø 41	28 38	21 33	21 4	Ø♏11	18 52	Ø 43	23 53	25 49
29	4 31 1Ø	6 4Ø 45	2♑31	Ø♐12	22 24	21 35	Ø 22	18 58	Ø 46	23 55	25 51
3Ø	4 35 6	7♐41 34	14♑24	1♐47	23♑14	22♍ 6	Ø♏34	19♎ 3	Ø♐5Ø	23♐57	25♎53

THE SUN ENTERS THE SIGN OF SAGITTARIUS ON NOV 22 AT 09:37.

DAY	TIME	☉	☽	☿	♀	♂	♃	♄	♅	♆	♇
	h m s	° ' "	° '	° '	° '	° '	° '	° '	° '	° '	° '
D 1	4 39 3	8♐42 23	26♑24	3♐21	24♑ 3	22♍37	Ø♏46	19♎ 9	Ø♐54	23♐59	25♎55
E 2	4 42 59	9 43 14	8♒32	4 56	24 52	23 7	Ø 57	19 15	Ø 57	24 1	25 57
C 3	4 46 56	1Ø 44 5	2Ø 55	6 3Ø	25 39	23 38	1 9	19 2Ø	1 1	24 4	25 59
E 4	4 5Ø 53	11 44 57	3♓35	8 4	26 26	24 8	1 2Ø	19 26	1 5	24 6	26 1
M 5	4 54 49	12 45 5Ø	16 37	9 39	27 12	24 38	1 31	19 31	1 8	24 8	26 3
B 6	4 58 46	13 46 44	Ø♈ 6	11 13	27 57	25 8	1 43	19 36	1 12	24 1Ø	26 4
E 7	5 2 42	14 47 39	14 3	12 47	28 41	25 38	1 54	19 41	1 16	24 13	26 6
R 8	5 6 39	15 48 34	28 27	14 21	29 24	26 8	2 5	19 47	1 19	24 15	26 8
9	5 1Ø 35	16 49 3Ø	13♉16	15 55	Ø♒ 5	26 38	2 16	19 52	1 23	24 17	26 1Ø
1Ø	5 14 32	17 5Ø 26	28 24	17 3Ø	Ø 46	27 7	2 27	19 57	1 27	24 19	26 11
11	5 18 28	18 51 24	13♊41	19 4	1 25	27 36	2 38	2Ø 2	1 3Ø	24 22	26 13
12	5 22 25	19 52 22	28 56	2Ø 38	2 3	28 5	2 48	2Ø 7	1 34	24 24	26 15
13	5 26 22	2Ø 53 21	13♋59	22 13	2 4Ø	28 34	2 59	2Ø 11	1 37	24 26	26 16
14	5 3Ø 18	21 54 22	28 42	23 47	3 15	29 3	3 1Ø	2Ø 16	1 41	24 28	26 18
15	5 34 15	22 55 23	12♌59	25 22	3 49	29 31	3 2Ø	2Ø 21	1 44	24 31	26 19
16	5 38 11	23 56 25	26 49	26 57	4 22	Ø♎ Ø	3 31	2Ø 25	1 48	24 33	26 21
17	5 42 8	24 57 27	1Ø♍11	28 32	4 53	Ø 28	3 41	2Ø 3Ø	1 51	24 35	26 23
18	5 46 4	25 58 31	23 9	Ø♑ 7	5 22	Ø 56	3 51	2Ø 34	1 55	24 37	26 24
19	5 5Ø 1	26 59 36	5♎45	1 42	5 5Ø	1 24	4 2	2Ø 39	1 58	24 4Ø	26 25
2Ø	5 53 57	28 Ø 41	18 4	3 17	6 16	1 51	4 12	2Ø 43	2 2	24 42	26 27
21	5 57 54	29 1 48	Ø♏1Ø	4 52	6 41	2 18	4 22	2Ø 47	2 5	24 44	26 28
22	6 1 51	Ø♑ 2 55	12 7	6 28	7 3	2 45	4 31	2Ø 51	2 9	24 47	26 3Ø
23	6 5 47	1 4 2	23 59	8 4	7 24	3 12	4 41	2Ø 55	2 12	24 49	26 31
24	6 9 44	2 5 11	5♐49	9 4Ø	7 43	3 39	4 51	2Ø 59	2 15	24 51	26 32
25	6 13 4Ø	3 6 2Ø	17 38	11 16	7 59	4 5	5 Ø	21 3	2 19	24 53	26 33
26	6 17 37	4 7 29	29 3Ø	12 52	8 14	4 32	5 1Ø	21 6	2 22	24 56	26 35
27	6 21 33	5 8 39	11♑26	14 29	8 26	4 58	5 19	21 1Ø	2 25	24 58	26 36
28	6 25 3Ø	6 9 48	23 29	16 5	8 36	5 23	5 29	21 14	2 29	25 Ø	26 37
29	6 29 27	7 1Ø 59	5♒39	17 42	8 44	5 49	5 38	21 17	2 32	25 2	26 38
3Ø	6 33 23	8 12 9	17 59	19 18	8 5Ø	6 14	5 47	21 2Ø	2 35	25 4	26 39
31	6 37 2Ø	9♑13 19	Ø♓31	2Ø♑55	8♒53	6♎39	5♏56	21♎24	2♐38	25♐ 7	26♎4Ø

THE SUN ENTERS THE SIGN OF CAPRICORN ON DEC 21 AT 22:51.

♏ SCORPIO ♐ SAGITTARIUS ♑ CAPRICORN ♒ AQUARIUS ♓ PISCES

1982

SIDEREAL . . . SUN . . MOON . . MERCURY . VENUS . . MARS . . . JUPITER . SATURN . URANUS . NEPTUNE . PLUTO .

DAY	TIME	☉	☽	☿	♀	♂	♃	♄	♅	♆	♇
	h m s	° ' "	° '	° '	° '	° '	° '	° '	° '	° '	° '
J 1	6 41 16	10♑14 28	13♓18	22♑31	8♒54	7♎ 3	6♏ 4	21♎27	2♐41	25♐ 9	26♎41
A 2	6 45 13	11 15 38	26 22	24 8	8R52	7 28	6 13	21 30	2 45	25 11	26 42
N 3	6 49 9	12 16 48	9♈46	25 44	8 48	7 52	6 22	21 33	2 48	25 13	26 43
U 4	6 53 6	13 17 57	23 32	27 19	8 41	8 16	6 30	21 36	2 51	25 15	26 44
A 5	6 57 2	14 19 5	7♉40	28 54	8 32	8 39	6 38	21 39	2 54	25 18	26 45
R 6	7 0 59	15 20 14	22 9	0♒28	8 20	9 2	6 47	21 41	2 57	25 20	26 46
Y 7	7 4 56	16 21 22	6♊54	2 1	8 6	9 25	6 55	21 44	3 0	25 22	26 47
8	7 8 52	17 22 30	21 51	3 33	7 49	9 48	7 3	21 46	3 3	25 24	26 48
9	7 12 49	18 23 38	6♋51	5 4	7 30	10 10	7 10	21 49	3 5	25 26	26 48
10	7 16 45	19 24 45	21 47	6 32	7 9	10 32	7 18	21 51	3 8	25 28	26 49
11	7 20 42	20 25 52	6♌29	7 59	6 45	10 54	7 26	21 53	3 11	25 30	26 50
12	7 24 38	21 26 59	20 51	9 22	6 19	11 15	7 33	21 55	3 14	25 33	26 50
13	7 28 35	22 28 5	4♍49	10 43	5 51	11 36	7 40	21 57	3 17	25 35	26 51
14	7 32 31	23 29 11	18 21	12 0	5 21	11 57	7 47	21 59	3 19	25 37	26 52
15	7 36 28	24 30 18	1♎27	13 12	4 50	12 17	7 54	22 1	3 22	25 39	26 52
16	7 40 25	25 31 23	14 10	14 20	4 17	12 37	8 1	22 3	3 25	25 41	26 53
17	7 44 21	26 32 29	26 33	15 21	3 43	12 57	8 8	22 4	3 27	25 43	26 53
18	7 48 18	27 33 35	8♏40	16 16	3 8	13 16	8 14	22 6	3 30	25 45	26 54
19	7 52 14	28 34 40	20 37	17 3	2 32	13 35	8 21	22 7	3 32	25 47	26 54
20	7 56 11	29 35 45	2♐27	17 41	1 55	13 53	8 27	22 8	3 35	25 49	26 54
21	8 0 7	0♒36 49	14 16	18 11	1 18	14 11	8 33	22 9	3 37	25 51	26 55
22	8 4 4	1 37 54	26 6	18 30	0 41	14 29	8 39	22 10	3 40	25 53	26 55
23	8 8 0	2 38 57	8♑ 2	18R38	0 4	14 46	8 45	22 11	3 42	25 55	26 55
24	8 11 57	3 40 0	20 6	18 35	29♑28	15 3	8 50	22 12	3 44	25 57	26 55
25	8 15 54	4 41 2	2♒21	18 21	28 53	15 19	8 56	22 13	3 47	25 58	26 56
26	8 19 50	5 42 4	14 47	17 55	28 18	15 35	9 1	22 13	3 49	26 0	26 56
27	8 23 47	6 43 4	27 26	17 18	27 45	15 50	9 6	22 14	3 51	26 2	26 56
28	8 27 43	7 44 4	10♓17	16 31	27 12	16 5	9 11	22 14	3 53	26 4	26 56
29	8 31 40	8 45 2	23 23	15 35	26 42	16 19	9 16	22 15	3 55	26 6	26R56
30	8 35 36	9 45 59	6♈42	14 31	26 13	16 33	9 21	22 15	3 57	26 7	26 56
31	8 39 33	10♒46 55	20♈14	13♒22	25♑46	16♎46	9♏25	22♎15	3♐59	26♐ 9	26♎56

THE SUN ENTERS THE SIGN OF AQUARIUS ON JAN 20 AT 09:32.

DAY	TIME	☉	☽	☿	♀	♂	♃	♄	♅	♆	♇
	h m s	° ' "	° '	° '	° '	° '	° '	° '	° '	° '	° '
F 1	8 43 29	11♒47 50	4♉ 0	12♒ 9	25♑21	16♎59	9♏30	22♎15	4♐ 1	26♐11	26♎56
E 2	8 47 26	12 48 43	17 59	10R55	24R59	17 11	9 34	22R15	4 3	26 13	26R56
B 3	8 51 23	13 49 35	2♊10	9 42	24 38	17 23	9 38	22 14	4 5	26 14	26 55
R 4	8 55 19	14 50 26	16 32	8 31	24 20	17 34	9 42	22 14	4 7	26 16	26 55
U 5	8 59 16	15 51 16	1♋ 1	7 25	24 4	17 45	9 45	22 14	4 9	26 18	26 55
A 6	9 3 12	16 52 4	15 34	6 24	23 51	17 55	9 49	22 13	4 10	26 19	26 55
R 7	9 7 9	17 52 50	0♌ 6	5 30	23 40	18 5	9 52	22 12	4 12	26 21	26 55
Y 8	9 11 5	18 53 35	14 30	4 44	23 32	18 14	9 55	22 12	4 14	26 22	26 54
9	9 15 2	19 54 19	28 41	4 6	23 26	18 22	9 58	22 11	4 15	26 24	26 54
10	9 18 58	20 55 2	12♍34	3 37	23D23	18 30	10 1	22 10	4 17	26 26	26 53
11	9 22 55	21 55 43	26 6	3 15	23 22	18 37	10 3	22 9	4 18	26 27	26 53
12	9 26 52	22 56 23	9♎15	3 1	23 23	18 43	10 6	22 7	4 20	26 28	26 53
13	9 30 48	23 57 2	22 2	2D56	23 27	18 49	10 8	22 6	4 21	26 30	26 52
14	9 34 45	24 57 40	4♏29	2 57	23 33	18 54	10 10	22 5	4 22	26 31	26 52
15	9 38 41	25 58 17	16 40	3 5	23 42	18 59	10 12	22 3	4 23	26 33	26 51
16	9 42 38	26 58 52	28 38	3 20	23 53	19 2	10 13	22 2	4 25	26 34	26 50
17	9 46 34	27 59 27	10♐29	3 41	24 6	19 6	10 15	22 0	4 26	26 35	26 50
18	9 50 31	29 0 0	22 18	4 7	24 21	19 8	10 16	21 58	4 27	26 37	26 49
19	9 54 27	0♓ 0 32	4♑ 9	4 38	24 38	19 10	10 17	21 56	4 28	26 38	26 48
20	9 58 24	1 1 2	16 9	5 14	24 57	19R11	10 18	21 54	4 29	26 39	26 48
21	10 2 21	2 1 32	28 20	5 55	25 18	19 11	10 19	21 52	4 30	26 40	26 47
22	10 6 17	3 1 59	10♒45	6 39	25 41	19 10	10 19	21 50	4 31	26 42	26 46
23	10 10 14	4 2 25	23 27	7 27	26 6	19 9	10 20	21 48	4 32	26 43	26 45
24	10 14 10	5 2 50	6♓27	8 19	26 32	19 7	10R20	21 45	4 32	26 44	26 45
25	10 18 7	6 3 13	19 43	9 14	27 0	19 4	10 20	21 43	4 33	26 45	26 44
26	10 22 3	7 3 34	3♈14	10 11	27 30	19 1	10 19	21 40	4 34	26 46	26 43
27	10 26 0	8 3 53	16 58	11 12	28 1	18 56	10 19	21 38	4 34	26 47	26 42
28	10 29 56	9♓ 4 10	0♉51	12♒15	28♑33	18♎51	10♏18	21♎35	4♐35	26♐48	26♎41

THE SUN ENTERS THE SIGN OF PISCES ON FEB 18 AT 23:47.

DAY	TIME	☉	☽	☿	♀	♂	♃	♄	♅	♆	♇
	h m s	° ' "	° '	° '	° '	° '	° '	° '	° '	° '	° '
M 1	10 33 53	10♓ 4 26	14♉51	13♒20	29♑ 7	18♎45	10♏18	21♎32	4♐35	26♐49	26♎40
A 2	10 37 50	11 4 39	28 55	14 28	29 43	18R39	10R17	21R29	4 36	26 50	26R39
R 3	10 41 46	12 4 50	13♊ 2	15 38	0♒19	18 31	10 15	21 26	4 36	26 51	26 38
C 4	10 45 43	13 5 0	27 10	16 49	0 57	18 23	10 14	21 23	4 37	26 52	26 37
H 5	10 49 39	14 5 7	11♋17	18 3	1 36	18 14	10 13	21 20	4 37	26 52	26 36
6	10 53 36	15 5 12	25 24	19 18	2 16	18 4	10 11	21 17	4 37	26 53	26 34
7	10 57 32	16 5 14	9♌27	20 35	2 58	17 54	10 9	21 14	4 37	26 54	26 33
8	11 1 29	17 5 15	23 24	21 54	3 40	17 42	10 7	21 10	4 37	26 55	26 32
9	11 5 25	18 5 14	7♍11	23 14	4 24	17 30	10 4	21 7	4R38	26 55	26 31
10	11 9 22	19 5 11	20 46	24 36	5 8	17 18	10 2	21 3	4 38	26 56	26 30
11	11 13 18	20 5 5	4♎ 5	25 59	5 53	17 4	9 59	21 0	4 38	26 57	26 28
12	11 17 15	21 4 58	17 7	27 24	6 40	16 50	9 57	20 56	4 37	26 57	26 27
13	11 21 12	22 4 50	29 51	28 50	7 27	16 35	9 53	20 52	4 37	26 58	26 26
14	11 25 8	23 4 39	12♏17	0♓18	8 15	16 19	9 50	20 49	4 37	26 59	26 25
15	11 29 5	24 4 27	24 27	1 46	9 3	16 3	9 47	20 45	4 37	26 59	26 23
16	11 33 1	25 4 13	6♐26	3 16	9 53	15 46	9 43	20 41	4 37	26 59	26 22
17	11 36 58	26 3 57	18 17	4 48	10 43	15 29	9 40	20 37	4 36	27 0	26 20
18	11 40 54	27 3 40	0♑ 6	6 20	11 34	15 10	9 36	20 33	4 36	27 0	26 19
19	11 44 51	28 3 21	11 58	7 54	12 26	14 52	9 32	20 29	4 35	27 1	26 18
20	11 48 47	29 3 0	23 58	9 30	13 19	14 32	9 28	20 25	4 35	27 1	26 16
21	11 52 44	0♈ 2 37	6♒12	11 6	14 12	14 12	9 23	20 21	4 34	27 1	26 15
22	11 56 41	1 2 13	18 44	12 44	15 5	13 52	9 19	20 16	4 34	27 2	26 13
23	12 0 37	2 1 46	1♓37	14 23	15 59	13 31	9 14	20 12	4 33	27 2	26 12
24	12 4 34	3 1 18	14 52	16 3	16 54	13 10	9 9	20 8	4 32	27 2	26 10
25	12 8 30	4 0 48	28 29	17 45	17 50	12 48	9 4	20 4	4 31	27 2	26 9
26	12 12 27	5 0 16	12♈26	19 28	18 45	12 26	8 59	19 59	4 31	27 2	26 7
27	12 16 23	5 59 42	26 37	21 12	19 42	12 4	8 54	19 55	4 30	27 3	26 6
28	12 20 20	6 59 5	10♉58	22 58	20 39	11 41	8 48	19 50	4 29	27 3	26 4
29	12 24 16	7 58 27	25 22	24 45	21 36	11 18	8 43	19 46	4 28	27R 3	26 3
30	12 28 13	8 57 46	9♊43	26 33	22 34	10 55	8 37	19 41	4 27	27 3	26 1
31	12 32 10	9♈57 3	24♊ 0	28♓23	23♒32	10♎32	8♏31	19♎37	4♐26	27♐ 3	25♎59

THE SUN ENTERS THE SIGN OF ARIES ON MAR 20 AT 22:57.

♈ ARIES ♉ TAURUS ♊ GEMINI ♋ CANCER ♌ LEO ♍ VIRGO ♎ LIBRA

SIDEREAL SUN. MOON. MERCURY. VENUS. MARS. JUPITER. SATURN. URANUS. NEPTUNE. PLUTO.

DAY	TIME	☉	☽	☿	♀	♂	♃	♄	♅	♆	♇
	h m s	° ' "	° '	° '	° '	° '	° '	° '	° '	° '	° '
A 1	12 36 6	10♈56 18	8♋ 8	0♈14	24♒30	10♎ 9	8♏25	19♎32	4♐25	27♐ 3	25♎58
P 2	12 40 3	11 55 30	22 8	2 6	25 29	9R46	8R19	19R28	4R24	27R 2	25R56
R 3	12 43 59	12 54 40	5♌58	4 0	26 29	9 22	8 13	19 23	4 22	27 2	25 54
I 4	12 47 56	13 53 48	19 39	5 55	27 28	8 59	8 7	19 19	4 21	27 2	25 53
L 5	12 51 52	14 52 53	3♍11	7 52	28 28	8 36	8 0	19 14	4 20	27 2	25 51
6	12 55 49	15 51 56	16 34	9 50	29 29	8 13	7 54	19 9	4 19	27 2	25 50
7	12 59 45	16 50 56	29 45	11 49	0♓30	7 50	7 47	19 5	4 17	27 1	25 48
8	13 3 42	17 49 55	12♎44	13 49	1 31	7 28	7 40	19 0	4 16	27 1	25 46
9	13 7 38	18 48 52	25 30	15 51	2 32	7 6	7 33	18 56	4 14	27 1	25 45
10	13 11 35	19 47 46	8♏ 2	17 54	3 34	6 44	7 27	18 51	4 13	27 1	25 43
11	13 15 32	20 46 39	20 20	19 57	4 36	6 22	7 20	18 46	4 11	27 0	25 41
12	13 19 28	21 45 30	2♐27	22 2	5 38	6 1	7 12	18 42	4 10	27 0	25 39
13	13 23 25	22 44 19	14 23	24 8	6 41	5 40	7 5	18 37	4 8	26 59	25 38
14	13 27 21	23 43 7	26 13	26 14	7 44	5 19	6 58	18 32	4 6	26 59	25 36
15	13 31 18	24 41 52	8♑ 1	28 20	8 47	4 59	6 51	18 28	4 5	26 58	25 34
16	13 35 14	25 40 36	19 52	0♉27	9 50	4 40	6 43	18 23	4 3	26 58	25 33
17	13 39 11	26 39 18	1♒51	2 33	10 54	4 21	6 36	18 19	4 1	26 57	25 31
18	13 43 7	27 37 59	14 5	4 40	11 58	4 3	6 29	18 14	3 59	26 57	25 29
19	13 47 4	28 36 38	26 37	6 45	13 2	3 45	6 21	18 10	3 57	26 56	25 28
20	13 51 1	29 35 15	9♓33	8 50	14 6	3 28	6 13	18 5	3 56	26 55	25 26
21	13 54 57	0♉33 50	22 55	10 53	15 10	3 12	6 6	18 1	3 54	26 55	25 24
22	13 58 54	1 32 24	6♈44	12 55	16 15	2 56	5 58	17 56	3 52	26 54	25 23
23	14 2 50	2 30 55	20 57	14 54	17 20	2 41	5 51	17 52	3 50	26 53	25 21
24	14 6 47	3 29 25	5♉29	16 52	18 25	2 27	5 43	17 47	3 48	26 52	25 19
25	14 10 43	4 27 54	20 14	18 47	19 30	2 13	5 35	17 43	3 46	26 52	25 18
26	14 14 40	5 26 20	5♊ 3	20 39	20 36	2 0	5 28	17 39	3 44	26 51	25 16
27	14 18 36	6 24 44	19 48	22 28	21 42	1 48	5 20	17 34	3 42	26 50	25 14
28	14 22 33	7 23 7	4♋24	24 13	22 47	1 37	5 12	17 30	3 39	26 49	25 13
29	14 26 30	8 21 27	18 44	25 55	23 53	1 27	5 5	17 26	3 37	26 48	25 11
30	14 30 26	9♉19 45	2♌49	27♉34	24♓59	1♎17	4♏57	17♎22	3♐35	26♐47	25♎ 9

THE SUN ENTERS THE SIGN OF TAURUS ON APR 20 AT 10:08.

DAY	TIME	☉	☽	☿	♀	♂	♃	♄	♅	♆	♇
	h m s	° ' "	° '	° '	° '	° '	° '	° '	° '	° '	° '
M 1	14 34 23	10♉18 1	16♌36	29♉ 8	26♓ 6	1♎ 8	4♏49	17♎18	3♐33	26♐46	25♎ 8
A 2	14 38 19	11 16 15	0♍ 8	0♊39	27 12	1R 0	4R42	17R14	3R31	26R45	25R 6
Y 3	14 42 16	12 14 27	13 25	2 6	28 19	0 53	4 34	17 10	3 28	26 44	25 4
4	14 46 12	13 12 36	26 28	3 28	29 25	0 46	4 27	17 6	3 26	26 43	25 3
5	14 50 9	14 10 44	9♎19	4 47	0♈32	0 40	4 19	17 2	3 24	26 42	25 1
6	14 54 5	15 8 50	21 58	6 1	1 39	0 36	4 12	16 58	3 21	26 41	25 0
7	14 58 2	16 6 55	4♏26	7 10	2 46	0 32	4 4	16 54	3 19	26 40	24 58
8	15 1 59	17 4 57	16 44	8 15	3 53	0 28	3 57	16 51	3 17	26 39	24 57
9	15 5 55	18 2 58	28 51	9 16	5 1	0 26	3 50	16 47	3 14	26 38	24 55
10	15 9 52	19 0 57	10♐50	10 12	6 8	0 24	3 43	16 44	3 12	26 36	24 54
11	15 13 48	19 58 55	22 42	11 3	7 16	0D23	3 36	16 40	3 10	26 35	24 52
12	15 17 45	20 56 52	4♑30	11 50	8 24	0 23	3 28	16 37	3 7	26 34	24 51
13	15 21 41	21 54 47	16 17	12 32	9 31	0 23	3 21	16 33	3 5	26 33	24 49
14	15 25 38	22 52 41	28 8	13 9	10 39	0 25	3 15	16 30	3 2	26 31	24 48
15	15 29 34	23 50 34	10♒ 7	13 41	11 47	0 27	3 8	16 27	3 0	26 30	24 46
16	15 33 31	24 48 25	22 20	14 8	12 56	0 29	3 1	16 24	2 58	26 29	24 45
17	15 37 28	25 46 15	4♓51	14 30	14 4	0 33	2 54	16 21	2 55	26 28	24 43
18	15 41 24	26 44 4	17 45	14 48	15 12	0 37	2 48	16 18	2 53	26 26	24 42
19	15 45 21	27 41 52	1♈ 5	15 0	16 21	0 42	2 42	16 15	2 50	26 25	24 41
20	15 49 17	28 39 38	14 54	15 8	17 29	0 48	2 35	16 12	2 48	26 24	24 39
21	15 53 14	29 37 24	29 10	15R11	18 38	0 54	2 29	16 9	2 45	26 22	24 38
22	15 57 10	0♊35 8	13♉50	15 9	19 47	1 1	2 23	16 7	2 43	26 21	24 37
23	16 1 7	1 32 51	28 48	15 2	20 55	1 9	2 17	16 4	2 40	26 19	24 36
24	16 5 3	2 30 33	13♊53	14 51	22 4	1 17	2 11	16 2	2 38	26 18	24 34
25	16 9 0	3 28 14	28 58	14 36	23 13	1 26	2 6	15 59	2 35	26 16	24 33
26	16 12 57	4 25 53	13♋53	14 17	24 22	1 35	2 0	15 57	2 33	26 15	24 32
27	16 16 53	5 23 31	28 31	13 55	25 31	1 46	1 55	15 55	2 30	26 13	24 31
28	16 20 50	6 21 7	12♌49	13 30	26 41	1 57	1 49	15 52	2 28	26 12	24 30
29	16 24 46	7 18 42	26 44	13 2	27 50	2 8	1 44	15 50	2 25	26 10	24 28
30	16 28 43	8 16 15	10♍17	12 31	28 59	2 20	1 39	15 49	2 23	26 9	24 27
31	16 32 39	9♊13 47	23♍29	11♊59	0♉ 9	2♎33	1♏34	15♎47	2♐20	26♐ 7	24♎26

THE SUN ENTERS THE SIGN OF GEMINI ON MAY 21 AT 09:24.

DAY	TIME	☉	☽	☿	♀	♂	♃	♄	♅	♆	♇
	h m s	° ' "	° '	° '	° '	° '	° '	° '	° '	° '	° '
J 1	16 36 36	10♊11 17	6♎23	11♊26	1♉18	2♎46	1♏30	15♎45	2♐18	26♐ 6	24♎25
U 2	16 40 32	11 8 47	19 1	10R53	2 28	3 0	1R25	15R43	2R15	26R 4	24R24
N 3	16 44 29	12 6 15	1♏26	10 19	3 37	3 14	1 21	15 42	2 13	26 3	24 23
E 4	16 48 26	13 3 41	13 40	9 46	4 47	3 29	1 16	15 40	2 10	26 1	24 22
5	16 52 22	14 1 7	25 44	9 14	5 57	3 44	1 12	15 39	2 8	26 0	24 21
6	16 56 19	14 58 32	7♐42	8 44	7 6	4 0	1 9	15 38	2 6	25 58	24 20
7	17 0 15	15 55 56	19 34	8 17	8 16	4 16	1 5	15 36	2 3	25 57	24 19
8	17 4 12	16 53 19	1♑22	7 51	9 26	4 33	1 1	15 35	2 1	25 55	24 19
9	17 8 8	17 50 41	13 10	7 30	10 36	4 51	0 58	15 34	1 58	25 53	24 18
10	17 12 5	18 48 3	24 59	7 11	11 46	5 8	0 55	15 33	1 56	25 52	24 17
11	17 16 2	19 45 24	6♒53	6 56	12 56	5 27	0 51	15 33	1 54	25 50	24 16
12	17 19 58	20 42 44	18 55	6 46	14 6	5 45	0 49	15 32	1 51	25 49	24 15
13	17 23 55	21 40 4	1♓10	6D39	15 17	6 5	0 46	15 31	1 49	25 47	24 15
14	17 27 51	22 37 23	13 41	6 37	16 27	6 24	0 43	15 31	1 47	25 45	24 14
15	17 31 48	23 34 42	26 32	6 39	17 37	6 44	0 41	15 30	1 45	25 44	24 13
16	17 35 44	24 32 0	9♈48	6 46	18 48	7 5	0 39	15 30	1 42	25 42	24 13
17	17 39 41	25 29 19	23 30	6 58	19 58	7 26	0 37	15 30	1 40	25 40	24 12
18	17 43 37	26 26 36	7♉39	7 14	21 9	7 47	0 35	15D30	1 38	25 39	24 12
19	17 47 34	27 23 54	22 13	7 35	22 19	8 9	0 33	15 30	1 36	25 37	24 11
20	17 51 30	28 21 12	7♊ 8	8 0	23 30	8 31	0 32	15 30	1 34	25 36	24 10
21	17 55 27	29 18 29	22 16	8 30	24 41	8 53	0 30	15 30	1 31	25 34	24 10
22	17 59 24	0♋15 45	7♋27	9 4	25 51	9 16	0 29	15 30	1 29	25 32	24 10
23	18 3 20	1 13 2	22 33	9 43	27 2	9 39	0 28	15 31	1 27	25 31	24 9
24	18 7 17	2 10 17	7♌25	10 26	28 13	10 3	0 27	15 31	1 25	25 29	24 9
25	18 11 13	3 7 32	21 57	11 13	29 24	10 27	0 27	15 32	1 23	25 28	24 8
26	18 15 10	4 4 47	6♍ 3	12 4	0♊35	10 51	0 26	15 33	1 21	25 26	24 8
27	18 19 6	5 2 1	19 44	13 0	1 46	11 16	0D26	15 34	1 19	25 24	24 8
28	18 23 3	5 59 14	3♎ 0	14 0	2 57	11 41	0 26	15 34	1 17	25 23	24 8
29	18 27 0	6 56 27	15 52	15 3	4 8	12 6	0 26	15 35	1 16	25 21	24 7
30	18 30 56	7♋53 39	28♎26	16♊11	5♊19	12♎32	0♏27	15♎37	1♐14	25♐20	24♎ 7

THE SUN ENTERS THE SIGN OF CANCER ON JUN 21 AT 17:24.

♏ SCORPIO ♐ SAGITTARIUS ♑ CAPRICORN ♒ AQUARIUS ♓ PISCES

1982

SIDEREAL   SUN..   MOON..   MERCURY..   VENUS..   MARS..   JUPITER..   SATURN..   URANUS..   NEPTUNE..   PLUTO.

DAY	TIME	☉	☽	☿	♀	♂	♃	♄	♅	♆	♇
	h m s	° ' "	° '	° '	° '	° '	° '	° '	° '	° '	° '
J 1	18 34 53	8♋50 51	10♏43	17♊23	6♊30	12♎58	0♏27	15♎38	1♐12	25♐18	24♎ 7
U 2	18 38 49	9 48 3	22 48	18 38	7 41	13 24	0 28	15 39	1R10	25R16	24R 7
L 3	18 42 46	10 45 14	4♐45	19 57	8 52	13 51	0 29	15 40	1 8	25 15	24 7
Y 4	18 46 42	11 42 25	16 36	21 21	10 4	14 18	0 30	15 42	1 7	25 13	24D 7
5	18 50 39	12 39 36	28 24	22 47	11 15	14 45	0 31	15 44	1 5	25 12	24 7
6	18 54 35	13 36 47	10♑12	24 18	12 26	15 13	0 32	15 45	1 3	25 10	24 7
7	18 58 32	14 33 58	22 2	25 52	13 38	15 40	0 34	15 47	1 2	25 9	24 7
8	19 2 29	15 31 9	3♒57	27 30	14 49	16 8	0 36	15 49	1 0	25 7	24 7
9	19 6 25	16 28 21	15 59	29 11	16 1	16 37	0 38	15 51	0 59	25 6	24 7
10	19 10 22	17 25 32	28 9	0♋55	17 12	17 5	0 40	15 53	0 57	25 4	24 7
11	19 14 18	18 22 44	10♓32	2 43	18 24	17 34	0 42	15 55	0 56	25 3	24 8
12	19 18 15	19 19 56	23 9	4 33	19 36	18 3	0 44	15 57	0 55	25 1	24 8
13	19 22 11	20 17 8	6♈ 2	6 27	20 47	18 33	0 47	16 0	0 53	25 0	24 8
14	19 26 8	21 14 22	19 16	8 23	21 59	19 2	0 50	16 2	0 52	24 59	24 8
15	19 30 4	22 11 35	2♉51	10 22	23 11	19 32	0 53	16 5	0 51	24 57	24 9
16	19 34 1	23 8 50	16 50	12 23	24 23	20 2	0 56	16 7	0 49	24 56	24 9
17	19 37 58	24 6 5	1♊10	14 26	25 35	20 33	0 59	16 10	0 48	24 54	24 10
18	19 41 54	25 3 21	15 50	16 30	26 47	21 3	1 2	16 13	0 47	24 53	24 10
19	19 45 51	26 0 37	0♋46	18 36	27 59	21 34	1 6	16 16	0 46	24 52	24 10
20	19 49 47	26 57 54	15 49	20 42	29 11	22 5	1 10	16 19	0 45	24 50	24 11
21	19 53 44	27 55 12	0♌52	22 50	0♋23	22 37	1 14	16 22	0 44	24 49	24 12
22	19 57 40	28 52 30	15 46	24 58	1 35	23 8	1 18	16 25	0 43	24 48	24 12
23	20 1 37	29 49 48	0♍24	27 6	2 47	23 40	1 22	16 28	0 42	24 47	24 13
24	20 5 33	0♌47 7	14 38	29 13	3 59	24 12	1 27	16 32	0 41	24 45	24 13
25	20 9 30	1 44 26	28 26	1♌20	5 12	24 44	1 31	16 35	0 41	24 44	24 14
26	20 13 27	2 41 45	11♎48	3 27	6 24	25 17	1 36	16 39	0 40	24 43	24 15
27	20 17 23	3 39 5	24 44	5 33	7 36	25 49	1 41	16 42	0 39	24 42	24 15
28	20 21 20	4 36 26	7♏18	7 37	8 49	26 22	1 46	16 46	0 38	24 41	24 16
29	20 25 16	5 33 46	19 33	9 41	10 1	26 55	1 51	16 50	0 38	24 39	24 17
30	20 29 13	6 31 8	1♐35	11 43	11 14	27 28	1 56	16 53	0 37	24 38	24 18
31	20 33 9	7♌28 30	13♐28	13♌44	12♋26	28♎ 2	2♏ 2	16♎57	0♐37	24♐37	24♎19

THE SUN ENTERS THE SIGN OF LEO ON JUL 23 AT 04:16.

DAY	TIME	☉	☽	☿	♀	♂	♃	♄	♅	♆	♇
	h m s	° ' "	° '	° '	° '	° '	° '	° '	° '	° '	° '
A 1	20 37 6	8♌25 52	25♐17	15♌44	13♋39	28♎35	2♏ 8	17♎ 1	0♐36	24♐36	24♎20
U 2	20 41 2	9 23 15	7♑ 4	17 42	14 51	29 9	2 13	17 5	0R36	24R35	24 21
G 3	20 44 59	10 20 39	18 55	19 38	16 4	29 43	2 19	17 10	0 36	24 34	24 22
U 4	20 48 56	11 18 4	0♒51	21 33	17 17	0♏17	2 25	17 14	0 35	24 33	24 23
S 5	20 52 52	12 15 30	12 55	23 26	18 29	0 52	2 32	17 18	0 35	24 32	24 24
T 6	20 56 49	13 12 56	25 9	25 18	19 42	1 26	2 38	17 23	0 35	24 31	24 25
7	21 0 45	14 10 24	7♓35	27 8	20 55	2 1	2 45	17 27	0 35	24 30	24 26
8	21 4 42	15 7 53	20 12	28 57	22 8	2 36	2 51	17 32	0 35	24 29	24 27
9	21 8 38	16 5 23	3♈ 2	0♍44	23 21	3 11	2 58	17 36	0D35	24 29	24 28
10	21 12 35	17 2 54	16 7	2 29	24 34	3 46	3 5	17 41	0 35	24 28	24 29
11	21 16 31	18 0 26	29 26	4 13	25 47	4 22	3 12	17 46	0 35	24 27	24 30
12	21 20 28	18 58 0	13♉ 1	5 56	27 0	4 57	3 19	17 50	0 35	24 26	24 32
13	21 24 25	19 55 36	26 51	7 37	28 13	5 33	3 26	17 55	0 35	24 25	24 33
14	21 28 21	20 53 13	10♊59	9 16	29 26	6 9	3 34	18 0	0 35	24 25	24 34
15	21 32 18	21 50 51	25 21	10 54	0♌39	6 45	3 41	18 5	0 35	24 24	24 36
16	21 36 14	22 48 31	9♋56	12 30	1 52	7 21	3 49	18 10	0 36	24 23	24 37
17	21 40 11	23 46 13	24 39	14 5	3 6	7 57	3 57	18 16	0 36	24 23	24 38
18	21 44 7	24 43 56	9♌26	15 39	4 19	8 34	4 5	18 21	0 36	24 22	24 40
19	21 48 4	25 41 40	24 7	17 11	5 32	9 11	4 13	18 26	0 37	24 22	24 41
20	21 52 0	26 39 26	8♍38	18 41	6 46	9 48	4 21	18 31	0 37	24 21	24 43
21	21 55 57	27 37 13	22 49	20 10	7 59	10 25	4 29	18 37	0 38	24 20	24 44
22	21 59 54	28 35 1	6♎38	21 38	9 13	11 2	4 38	18 42	0 39	24 20	24 46
23	22 3 50	29 32 51	20 2	23 3	10 26	11 39	4 46	18 48	0 39	24 20	24 47
24	22 7 47	0♍30 41	3♏ 1	24 28	11 40	12 17	4 55	18 54	0 40	24 19	24 49
25	22 11 43	1 28 33	15 36	25 51	12 53	12 54	5 4	18 59	0 41	24 19	24 50
26	22 15 40	2 26 26	27 53	27 12	14 7	13 32	5 13	19 5	0 42	24 18	24 52
27	22 19 36	3 24 21	9♐55	28 31	15 21	14 10	5 22	19 11	0 43	24 18	24 54
28	22 23 33	4 22 16	21 47	29 49	16 34	14 48	5 31	19 17	0 44	24 18	24 55
29	22 27 29	5 20 13	3♑35	1♎ 5	17 48	15 26	5 40	19 22	0 44	24 17	24 57
30	22 31 26	6 18 12	15 24	2 20	19 2	16 4	5 49	19 28	0 46	24 17	24 59
31	22 35 23	7♍16 12	27♑18	3♎32	20♌16	16♏43	5♏59	19♎34	0♐47	24♐17	25♎ 1

THE SUN ENTERS THE SIGN OF VIRGO ON AUG 23 AT 11:16.

DAY	TIME	☉	☽	☿	♀	♂	♃	♄	♅	♆	♇
	h m s	° ' "	° '	° '	° '	° '	° '	° '	° '	° '	° '
S 1	22 39 19	8♍14 13	9♒21	4♎43	21♌29	17♏21	6♏ 8	19♎40	0♐48	24♐17	25♎ 2
E 2	22 43 16	9 12 15	21 36	5 51	22 43	18 0	6 18	19 46	0 49	24R17	25 4
P 3	22 47 12	10 10 20	4♓ 5	6 57	23 57	18 39	6 28	19 53	0 50	24 17	25 6
T 4	22 51 9	11 8 25	16 49	8 2	25 11	19 18	6 37	19 59	0 51	24 16	25 8
E 5	22 55 5	12 6 33	29 47	9 3	26 25	19 57	6 47	20 5	0 53	24D16	25 10
M 6	22 59 2	13 4 42	12♈58	10 3	27 39	20 36	6 57	20 11	0 54	24 16	25 12
B 7	23 2 58	14 2 53	26 22	10 59	28 53	21 15	7 7	20 18	0 56	24 16	25 14
E 8	23 6 55	15 1 6	9♉56	11 53	0♍ 7	21 55	7 18	20 24	0 57	24 16	25 16
R 9	23 10 51	15 59 22	23 40	12 44	1 21	22 34	7 28	20 30	0 59	24 17	25 18
10	23 14 48	16 57 39	7♊33	13 31	2 36	23 14	7 38	20 37	1 0	24 17	25 20
11	23 18 45	17 55 59	21 34	14 15	3 50	23 54	7 49	20 43	1 2	24 17	25 22
12	23 22 41	18 54 20	5♋43	14 56	5 4	24 34	7 59	20 50	1 4	24 17	25 24
13	23 26 38	19 52 44	19 59	15 32	6 18	25 14	8 10	20 57	1 5	24 17	25 26
14	23 30 34	20 51 10	4♌19	16 5	7 33	25 54	8 21	21 3	1 7	24 17	25 28
15	23 34 31	21 49 38	18 41	16 32	8 47	26 34	8 31	21 10	1 9	24 18	25 30
16	23 38 27	22 48 8	3♍ 0	16 55	10 1	27 15	8 42	21 16	1 11	24 18	25 32
17	23 42 24	23 46 40	17 10	17 13	11 16	27 55	8 53	21 23	1 13	24 18	25 34
18	23 46 20	24 45 14	1♎ 7	17 25	12 30	28 36	9 4	21 30	1 15	24 19	25 36
19	23 50 17	25 43 49	14 46	17R31	13 45	29 17	9 15	21 37	1 17	24 19	25 38
20	23 54 14	26 42 27	28 4	17 30	14 59	29 58	9 27	21 44	1 19	24 20	25 40
21	23 58 10	27 41 6	10♏59	17 23	16 14	0♐39	9 38	21 50	1 21	24 20	25 43
22	0 2 7	28 39 47	23 34	17 10	17 28	1 20	9 49	21 57	1 23	24 21	25 45
23	0 6 3	29 38 30	5♐50	16 49	18 43	2 1	10 1	22 4	1 25	24 21	25 47
24	0 10 0	0♎37 15	17 52	16 21	19 57	2 42	10 12	22 11	1 27	24 22	25 49
25	0 13 56	1 36 1	29 44	15 45	21 12	3 24	10 24	22 18	1 29	24 22	25 51
26	0 17 53	2 34 49	11♑32	15 3	22 27	4 5	10 35	22 25	1 32	24 23	25 54
27	0 21 49	3 33 39	23 22	14 13	23 41	4 47	10 47	22 32	1 34	24 24	25 56
28	0 25 46	4 32 31	5♒18	13 18	24 56	5 29	10 59	22 39	1 36	24 24	25 58
29	0 29 43	5 31 24	17 27	12 18	26 11	6 11	11 10	22 46	1 39	24 25	26 0
30	0 33 39	6♎30 19	29♒50	11♎13	27♍26	6♐52	11♏22	22♎53	1♐41	24♐26	26♎ 3

THE SUN ENTERS THE SIGN OF LIBRA ON SEP 23 AT 08:47.

♈ ARIES   ♉ TAURUS   ♊ GEMINI   ♋ CANCER   ♌ LEO   ♍ VIRGO   ♎ LIBRA

SIDEREAL SUN. MOON. MERCURY. VENUS. MARS. JUPITER. SATURN. URANUS. NEPTUNE. PLUTO.

DAY	TIME	☉	☽	☿	♀	♂	♃	♄	♅	♆	♇
	h m s	° ' "	° '	° '	° '	° '	° '	° '	° '	° '	° '
O 1	0 37 36	7♎29 16	12♓31	10♎ 6	28♍40	7♐34	11♏34	23♎ 1	1♐44	24♐27	26♎ 5
C 2	0 41 32	8 28 15	25 32	8R57	29 55	8 17	11 46	23 8	1 46	24 28	26 7
T 3	0 45 29	9 27 15	8♈51	7 49	1♎10	8 59	11 58	23 15	1 49	24 28	26 10
O 4	0 49 25	10 26 18	22 27	6 44	2 25	9 41	12 10	23 22	1 51	24 29	26 12
B 5	0 53 22	11 25 23	6♉16	5 43	3 40	10 24	12 22	23 29	1 54	24 30	26 14
E 6	0 57 18	12 24 30	20 14	4 48	4 55	11 6	12 34	23 36	1 57	24 31	26 17
R 7	1 1 15	13 23 40	4♊19	4 0	6 9	11 49	12 47	23 44	2 0	24 32	26 19
8	1 5 12	14 22 51	18 25	3 21	7 24	12 31	12 59	23 51	2 2	24 33	26 21
9	1 9 8	15 22 6	2♋33	2 52	8 39	13 14	13 11	23 58	2 5	24 34	26 24
10	1 13 5	16 21 22	16 39	2 33	9 54	13 57	13 24	24 5	2 8	24 35	26 26
11	1 17 1	17 20 41	0♌44	2D25	11 9	14 40	13 36	24 13	2 11	24 36	26 29
12	1 20 58	18 20 2	14 46	2 28	12 24	15 23	13 49	24 20	2 14	24 38	26 31
13	1 24 54	19 19 25	28 45	2 42	13 39	16 6	14 1	24 27	2 17	24 39	26 33
14	1 28 51	20 18 51	12♍38	3 6	14 54	16 49	14 14	24 34	2 20	24 40	26 36
15	1 32 47	21 18 19	26 22	3 40	16 9	17 33	14 26	24 42	2 23	24 41	26 38
16	1 36 44	22 17 49	9♎56	4 22	17 24	18 16	14 39	24 49	2 26	24 42	26 41
17	1 40 41	23 17 21	23 15	5 13	18 39	19 0	14 52	24 56	2 29	24 44	26 43
18	1 44 37	24 16 55	6♏18	6 12	19 55	19 43	15 4	25 4	2 32	24 45	26 45
19	1 48 34	25 16 31	19 3	7 17	21 10	20 27	15 17	25 11	2 35	24 46	26 48
20	1 52 30	26 16 9	1♐31	8 28	22 25	21 11	15 30	25 18	2 38	24 48	26 50
21	1 56 27	27 15 49	13 43	9 44	23 40	21 54	15 43	25 26	2 41	24 49	26 53
22	2 0 23	28 15 31	25 43	11 4	24 55	22 38	15 56	25 33	2 44	24 51	26 55
23	2 4 20	29 15 14	7♑34	12 29	26 10	23 22	16 9	25 40	2 48	24 52	26 57
24	2 8 16	0♏15 0	19 22	13 56	27 25	24 6	16 22	25 47	2 51	24 53	27 0
25	2 12 13	1 14 47	1♒11	15 26	28 41	24 51	16 35	25 55	2 54	24 55	27 2
26	2 16 10	2 14 35	13 7	16 58	29 56	25 35	16 48	26 2	2 57	24 56	27 5
27	2 20 6	3 14 26	25 16	18 32	1♏11	26 19	17 1	26 9	3 1	24 58	27 7
28	2 24 3	4 14 18	7♓42	20 8	2 26	27 4	17 14	26 16	3 4	25 0	27 9
29	2 27 59	5 14 11	20 28	21 44	3 41	27 48	17 27	26 24	3 7	25 1	27 12
30	2 31 56	6 14 7	3♈39	23 21	4 57	28 32	17 40	26 31	3 11	25 3	27 14
31	2 35 52	7♏14 4	17♈12	24♎59	6♏12	29♐17	17♏53	26♎38	3♐14	25♐ 4	27♎17

THE SUN ENTERS THE SIGN OF SCORPIO ON OCT 23 AT 17:59.

DAY	TIME	☉	☽	☿	♀	♂	♃	♄	♅	♆	♇
	h m s	° ' "	° '	° '	° '	° '	° '	° '	° '	° '	° '
N 1	2 39 49	8♏14 3	1♉ 8	26♎38	7♏27	0♑ 2	18♏ 6	26♎45	3♐18	25♐ 6	27♎19
O 2	2 43 45	9 14 4	15 21	28 16	8 42	0 46	18 19	26 53	3 21	25 8	27 21
V 3	2 47 42	10 14 6	29 46	29 55	9 58	1 31	18 32	27 0	3 25	25 10	27 24
E 4	2 51 38	11 14 11	14♊17	1♏34	11 13	2 16	18 45	27 7	3 28	25 11	27 26
M 5	2 55 35	12 14 18	28 48	3 13	12 28	3 1	18 59	27 14	3 31	25 13	27 29
B 6	2 59 32	13 14 27	13♋14	4 52	13 43	3 46	19 12	27 21	3 35	25 15	27 31
E 7	3 3 28	14 14 38	27 32	6 30	14 59	4 31	19 25	27 28	3 39	25 17	27 33
R 8	3 7 25	15 14 51	11♌39	8 8	16 14	5 16	19 38	27 35	3 42	25 18	27 36
9	3 11 21	16 15 6	25 35	9 47	17 29	6 1	19 51	27 42	3 46	25 20	27 38
10	3 15 18	17 15 23	9♍19	11 24	18 45	6 46	20 5	27 50	3 49	25 22	27 40
11	3 19 14	18 15 42	22 52	13 2	20 0	7 32	20 18	27 57	3 53	25 24	27 42
12	3 23 11	19 16 3	6♎13	14 39	21 15	8 17	20 31	28 4	3 56	25 26	27 45
13	3 27 7	20 16 26	19 22	16 16	22 31	9 3	20 44	28 10	4 0	25 28	27 47
14	3 31 4	21 16 51	2♏17	17 53	23 46	9 48	20 58	28 17	4 4	25 30	27 49
15	3 35 1	22 17 17	15 0	19 30	25 1	10 34	21 11	28 24	4 7	25 32	27 52
16	3 38 57	23 17 45	27 29	21 6	26 17	11 19	21 24	28 31	4 11	25 34	27 54
17	3 42 54	24 18 15	9♐46	22 42	27 32	12 5	21 37	28 38	4 15	25 36	27 56
18	3 46 50	25 18 46	21 51	24 17	28 47	12 51	21 51	28 45	4 18	25 38	27 58
19	3 50 47	26 19 19	3♑47	25 53	0♐ 3	13 36	22 4	28 52	4 22	25 40	28 0
20	3 54 43	27 19 53	15 36	27 28	1 18	14 22	22 17	28 58	4 26	25 42	28 3
21	3 58 40	28 20 29	27 22	29 3	2 33	15 8	22 30	29 5	4 29	25 44	28 5
22	4 2 36	29 21 5	9♒10	0♐38	3 49	15 54	22 44	29 12	4 33	25 46	28 7
23	4 6 33	0♐21 43	21 5	2 12	5 4	16 40	22 57	29 18	4 37	25 48	28 9
24	4 10 30	1 22 22	3♓11	3 46	6 20	17 26	23 10	29 25	4 40	25 50	28 11
25	4 14 26	2 23 2	15 34	5 21	7 35	18 12	23 23	29 32	4 44	25 52	28 13
26	4 18 23	3 23 43	28 19	6 55	8 50	18 58	23 37	29 38	4 48	25 54	28 15
27	4 22 19	4 24 25	11♈28	8 28	10 6	19 44	23 50	29 44	4 52	25 56	28 17
28	4 26 16	5 25 9	25 3	10 2	11 21	20 30	24 3	29 51	4 55	25 59	28 19
29	4 30 12	6 25 53	9♉ 5	11 36	12 36	21 17	24 16	29 57	4 59	26 1	28 21
30	4 34 9	7♐26 39	23♉31	13♐10	13♐52	22♑ 3	24♏29	0♏ 4	5♐ 3	26♐ 3	28♎23

THE SUN ENTERS THE SIGN OF SAGITTARIUS ON NOV 22 AT 15:24.

DAY	TIME	☉	☽	☿	♀	♂	♃	♄	♅	♆	♇
	h m s	° ' "	° '	° '	° '	° '	° '	° '	° '	° '	° '
D 1	4 38 5	8♐27 25	8♊15	14♐43	15♐ 7	22♑49	24♏42	0♏10	5♐ 6	26♐ 5	28♎25
E 2	4 42 2	9 28 13	23 10	16 16	16 22	23 36	24 55	0 16	5 10	26 7	28 27
C 3	4 45 59	10 29 3	8♋ 7	17 50	17 38	24 22	25 8	0 22	5 14	26 10	28 29
E 4	4 49 55	11 29 53	22 58	19 23	18 53	25 8	25 21	0 28	5 17	26 12	28 31
M 5	4 53 52	12 30 45	7♌38	20 56	20 9	25 55	25 34	0 34	5 21	26 14	28 33
B 6	4 57 48	13 31 38	22 1	22 30	21 24	26 41	25 47	0 40	5 25	26 16	28 35
E 7	5 1 45	14 32 33	6♍ 5	24 3	22 39	27 28	26 0	0 46	5 28	26 18	28 37
R 8	5 5 41	15 33 28	19 49	25 36	23 55	28 15	26 13	0 52	5 32	26 21	28 39
9	5 9 38	16 34 25	3♎13	27 9	25 10	29 1	26 26	0 58	5 36	26 23	28 41
10	5 13 35	17 35 23	16 19	28 42	26 25	29 48	26 39	1 4	5 39	26 25	28 42
11	5 17 31	18 36 23	29 10	0♑15	27 41	0♒34	26 52	1 10	5 43	26 27	28 44
12	5 21 28	19 37 23	11♏45	1 48	28 56	1 21	27 5	1 15	5 47	26 30	28 46
13	5 25 24	20 38 25	24 9	3 21	0♑11	2 8	27 17	1 21	5 50	26 32	28 47
14	5 29 21	21 39 27	6♐22	4 53	1 27	2 55	27 30	1 26	5 54	26 34	28 49
15	5 33 17	22 40 30	18 25	6 26	2 42	3 41	27 43	1 32	5 58	26 36	28 51
16	5 37 14	23 41 34	0♑22	7 58	3 58	4 28	27 55	1 37	6 1	26 39	28 52
17	5 41 10	24 42 39	12 13	9 29	5 13	5 15	28 8	1 43	6 5	26 41	28 54
18	5 45 7	25 43 44	24 0	11 0	6 28	6 2	28 20	1 48	6 8	26 43	28 56
19	5 49 4	26 44 50	5♒47	12 31	7 44	6 49	28 33	1 53	6 12	26 45	28 57
20	5 53 0	27 45 56	17 36	14 1	8 59	7 36	28 45	1 58	6 15	26 48	28 59
21	5 56 57	28 47 3	29 32	15 30	10 14	8 23	28 58	2 3	6 19	26 50	29 0
22	6 0 53	29 48 9	11♓37	16 58	11 30	9 10	29 10	2 8	6 22	26 52	29 1
23	6 4 50	0♑49 16	23 57	18 24	12 45	9 57	29 22	2 13	6 26	26 55	29 3
24	6 8 46	1 50 23	6♈35	19 50	14 0	10 44	29 35	2 18	6 29	26 57	29 4
25	6 12 43	2 51 31	19 36	21 13	15 16	11 31	29 47	2 23	6 33	26 59	29 6
26	6 16 39	3 52 38	3♉ 3	22 34	16 31	12 18	29 59	2 28	6 36	27 1	29 7
27	6 20 36	4 53 45	16 58	23 53	17 46	13 5	0♐11	2 32	6 39	27 4	29 8
28	6 24 33	5 54 53	1♊19	25 9	19 2	13 52	0 23	2 37	6 43	27 6	29 9
29	6 28 29	6 56 0	16 5	26 21	20 17	14 39	0 35	2 41	6 46	27 8	29 11
30	6 32 26	7 57 8	1♋ 8	27 29	21 32	15 26	0 47	2 46	6 49	27 10	29 12
31	6 36 22	8♑58 16	16♋20	28♑32	22♑47	16♒13	0♐59	2♏50	6♐53	27♐13	29♎13

THE SUN ENTERS THE SIGN OF CAPRICORN ON DEC 22 AT 04:39.

♏ SCORPIO ♐ SAGITTARIUS ♑ CAPRICORN ♒ AQUARIUS ♓ PISCES

SIDEREAL SUN. MOON. MERCURY VENUS. MARS. JUPITER SATURN. URANUS. NEPTUNE. PLUTO.

DAY	TIME	☉	☽	☿	♀	♂	♃	♄	♅	♆	♇
	h m s	° ' "	° '	° '	° '	° '	° '	° '	° '	° '	° '
J 1	6 40 19	9♑59 24	1♌32	29♑30	24♑ 3	17♒ 0	1♐11	2♏54	6♐56	27♐15	29♎14
A 2	6 44 15	11 0 32	16 35	0♒22	25 18	17 47	1 22	2 58	6 59	27 17	29 15
N 3	6 48 12	12 1 40	1♍19	1 6	26 33	18 34	1 34	3 2	7 2	27 19	29 16
U 4	6 52 9	13 2 49	15 40	1 42	27 48	19 21	1 45	3 6	7 6	27 21	29 17
A 5	6 56 5	14 3 58	29 34	2 10	29 4	20 8	1 57	3 10	7 9	27 24	29 18
R 6	7 0 2	15 5 7	13♎ 3	2 28	0♒19	20 56	2 8	3 14	7 12	27 26	29 19
Y 7	7 3 58	16 6 16	26 6	2R34	1 34	21 43	2 20	3 18	7 15	27 28	29 20
8	7 7 55	17 7 25	8♏49	2 30	2 49	22 30	2 31	3 21	7 18	27 30	29 21
9	7 11 51	18 8 35	21 14	2 14	4 4	23 17	2 42	3 25	7 21	27 32	29 22
10	7 15 48	19 9 45	3♐25	1 46	5 20	24 4	2 53	3 28	7 24	27 34	29 23
11	7 19 44	20 10 54	15 25	1 7	6 35	24 51	3 4	3 32	7 27	27 37	29 24
12	7 23 41	21 12 4	27 19	0 16	7 50	25 38	3 15	3 35	7 30	27 39	29 24
13	7 27 38	22 13 13	9♑ 8	29♑16	9 5	26 26	3 26	3 38	7 33	27 41	29 25
14	7 31 34	23 14 22	20 56	28 8	10 20	27 13	3 37	3 41	7 36	27 43	29 26
15	7 35 31	24 15 31	2♒44	26 54	11 35	28 0	3 47	3 44	7 39	27 45	29 26
16	7 39 27	25 16 39	14 34	25 37	12 51	28 47	3 58	3 47	7 41	27 47	29 27
17	7 43 24	26 17 46	26 29	24 18	14 6	29 34	4 8	3 50	7 44	27 49	29 28
18	7 47 20	27 18 53	8♓30	23 0	15 21	0♓21	4 19	3 52	7 47	27 51	29 28
19	7 51 17	28 19 59	20 40	21 46	16 36	1 8	4 29	3 55	7 50	27 53	29 29
20	7 55 13	29 21 4	3♈ 2	20 38	17 51	1 55	4 39	3 57	7 52	27 55	29 29
21	7 59 10	0♒22 9	15 39	19 36	19 6	2 43	4 49	4 0	7 55	27 57	29 29
22	8 3 7	1 23 12	28 34	18 43	20 21	3 30	4 59	4 2	7 57	27 59	29 30
23	8 7 3	2 24 15	11♉51	17 58	21 36	4 17	5 9	4 4	8 0	28 1	29 30
24	8 11 0	3 25 16	25 32	17 22	22 51	5 4	5 19	4 6	8 3	28 3	29 31
25	8 14 56	4 26 17	9♊38	16 56	24 6	5 51	5 29	4 8	8 5	28 5	29 31
26	8 18 53	5 27 16	24 9	16 39	25 21	6 38	5 38	4 10	8 7	28 7	29 31
27	8 22 49	6 28 15	9♋ 2	16D30	26 36	7 25	5 48	4 12	8 10	28 9	29 31
28	8 26 46	7 29 12	24 10	16 29	27 50	8 12	5 57	4 14	8 12	28 11	29 31
29	8 30 42	8 30 9	9♌25	16 37	29 5	8 59	6 7	4 15	8 14	28 13	29 32
30	8 34 39	9 31 4	24 37	16 51	0♓20	9 46	6 16	4 17	8 17	28 14	29 32
31	8 38 36	10♒31 59	9♍34	17♑12	1♓35	10♓33	6♐25	4♏18	8♐19	28♐16	29♎32

THE SUN ENTERS THE SIGN OF AQUARIUS ON JAN 20 AT 15:18.

DAY	TIME	☉	☽	☿	♀	♂	♃	♄	♅	♆	♇
	h m s	° ' "	° '	° '	° '	° '	° '	° '	° '	° '	° '
F 1	8 42 32	11♒32 52	24♍10	17♑39	2♓50	11♓20	6♐34	4♏19	8♐21	28♐18	29♎32
E 2	8 46 29	12 33 45	8♎19	18 11	4 4	12 7	6 42	4 20	8 23	28 20	29R32
B 3	8 50 25	13 34 37	21 58	18 49	5 19	12 54	6 51	4 21	8 25	28 22	29 32
R 4	8 54 22	14 35 28	5♏ 8	19 31	6 34	13 40	7 0	4 22	8 27	28 23	29 32
U 5	8 58 18	15 36 18	17 52	20 17	7 49	14 27	7 8	4 23	8 29	28 25	29 32
A 6	9 2 15	16 37 8	0♐16	21 7	9 3	15 14	7 16	4 24	8 31	28 27	29 31
R 7	9 6 11	17 37 57	12 22	22 0	10 18	16 1	7 25	4 25	8 33	28 28	29 31
Y 8	9 10 8	18 38 44	24 18	22 57	11 32	16 48	7 33	4 25	8 35	28 30	29 31
9	9 14 5	19 39 31	6♑ 6	23 57	12 47	17 35	7 40	4 26	8 37	28 31	29 31
10	9 18 1	20 40 17	17 53	24 59	14 2	18 21	7 48	4 26	8 38	28 33	29 30
11	9 21 58	21 41 1	29 40	26 4	15 16	19 8	7 56	4 26	8 40	28 35	29 30
12	9 25 54	22 41 44	11♒31	27 11	16 31	19 55	8 3	4R26	8 42	28 36	29 30
13	9 29 51	23 42 26	23 27	28 20	17 45	20 41	8 11	4 26	8 43	28 38	29 29
14	9 33 47	24 43 6	5♓32	29 31	18 59	21 28	8 18	4 26	8 45	28 39	29 29
15	9 37 44	25 43 45	17 45	0♒44	20 14	22 15	8 25	4 26	8 46	28 41	29 28
16	9 41 40	26 44 22	0♈ 7	1 59	21 28	23 1	8 32	4 26	8 48	28 42	29 28
17	9 45 37	27 44 58	12 40	3 15	22 42	23 48	8 39	4 25	8 49	28 43	29 27
18	9 49 34	28 45 32	25 25	4 32	23 57	24 34	8 45	4 25	8 50	28 45	29 27
19	9 53 30	29 46 4	8♉24	5 52	25 11	25 21	8 52	4 24	8 52	28 46	29 26
20	9 57 27	0♓46 35	21 39	7 12	26 25	26 7	8 58	4 23	8 53	28 47	29 26
21	10 1 23	1 47 3	5♊11	8 34	27 39	26 54	9 5	4 22	8 54	28 49	29 25
22	10 5 20	2 47 30	19 3	9 57	28 53	27 40	9 11	4 21	8 55	28 50	29 24
23	10 9 16	3 47 55	3♋16	11 22	0♈ 7	28 27	9 16	4 20	8 56	28 51	29 23
24	10 13 13	4 48 18	17 48	12 47	1 21	29 13	9 22	4 19	8 57	28 52	29 23
25	10 17 9	5 48 39	2♌37	14 14	2 35	29 59	9 28	4 18	8 58	28 53	29 22
26	10 21 6	6 48 58	17 35	15 42	3 49	0♈46	9 33	4 17	8 59	28 55	29 21
27	10 25 3	7 49 15	2♍36	17 11	5 3	1 32	9 38	4 15	9 0	28 56	29 20
28	10 28 59	8♓49 31	17♍29	18♒41	6♈17	2♈18	9♐44	4♏14	9♐ 1	28♐57	29♎19

THE SUN ENTERS THE SIGN OF PISCES ON FEB 19 AT 05:31.

DAY	TIME	☉	☽	☿	♀	♂	♃	♄	♅	♆	♇
	h m s	° ' "	° '	° '	° '	° '	° '	° '	° '	° '	° '
M 1	10 32 56	9♓49 44	2♎ 6	20♒12	7♈31	3♈ 4	9♐48	4♏12	9♐ 2	28♐58	29♎18
A 2	10 36 52	10 49 56	16 19	21 44	8 45	3 50	9 53	4R10	9 2	28 59	29R18
R 3	10 40 49	11 50 7	0♏ 5	23 18	9 58	4 36	9 58	4 8	9 3	29 0	29 17
C 4	10 44 45	12 50 16	13 22	24 52	11 12	5 22	10 2	4 7	9 4	29 1	29 16
H 5	10 48 42	13 50 23	26 12	26 28	12 25	6 8	10 7	4 5	9 4	29 2	29 15
6	10 52 38	14 50 29	8♐39	28 4	13 39	6 54	10 11	4 2	9 5	29 3	29 13
7	10 56 35	15 50 33	20 47	29 42	14 52	7 40	10 15	4 0	9 5	29 3	29 12
8	11 0 31	16 50 36	2♑43	1♓21	16 6	8 26	10 18	3 58	9 5	29 4	29 11
9	11 4 28	17 50 37	14 32	3 1	17 19	9 12	10 22	3 56	9 6	29 5	29 10
10	11 8 25	18 50 37	26 18	4 42	18 33	9 58	10 25	3 53	9 6	29 6	29 9
11	11 12 21	19 50 34	8♒ 8	6 24	19 46	10 44	10 29	3 50	9 6	29 6	29 8
12	11 16 18	20 50 30	20 3	8 7	20 59	11 29	10 32	3 48	9 6	29 7	29 7
13	11 20 14	21 50 24	2♓ 8	9 52	22 12	12 15	10 34	3 45	9 7	29 8	29 5
14	11 24 11	22 50 17	14 23	11 37	23 25	13 1	10 37	3 42	9R 7	29 8	29 4
15	11 28 7	23 50 7	26 51	13 24	24 38	13 46	10 40	3 39	9 7	29 9	29 3
16	11 32 4	24 49 55	9♈30	15 12	25 51	14 32	10 42	3 36	9 7	29 10	29 2
17	11 36 0	25 49 42	22 22	17 1	27 4	15 18	10 44	3 33	9 6	29 10	29 0
18	11 39 57	26 49 26	5♉25	18 51	28 17	16 3	10 46	3 30	9 6	29 11	28 59
19	11 43 54	27 49 8	18 38	20 43	29 30	16 48	10 48	3 27	9 6	29 11	28 58
20	11 47 50	28 48 48	2♊ 3	22 36	0♉43	17 34	10 49	3 24	9 6	29 11	28 56
21	11 51 47	29 48 25	15 40	24 30	1 56	18 19	10 51	3 20	9 6	29 12	28 55
22	11 55 43	0♈48 1	29 29	26 25	3 8	19 5	10 52	3 17	9 5	29 12	28 53
23	11 59 40	1 47 34	13♋31	28 21	4 21	19 50	10 53	3 13	9 5	29 13	28 52
24	12 3 36	2 47 5	27 46	0♈19	5 33	20 35	10 54	3 10	9 4	29 13	28 50
25	12 7 33	3 46 33	12♌12	2 17	6 46	21 20	10 55	3 6	9 4	29 13	28 49
26	12 11 29	4 45 59	26 46	4 17	7 58	22 5	10 55	3 2	9 3	29 13	28 47
27	12 15 26	5 45 23	11♍22	6 17	9 10	22 50	10R55	2 59	9 3	29 14	28 46
28	12 19 23	6 44 44	25 54	8 19	10 22	23 35	10 55	2 55	9 2	29 14	28 44
29	12 23 19	7 44 4	10♎14	10 21	11 34	24 20	10 55	2 51	9 1	29 14	28 43
30	12 27 16	8 43 21	24 17	12 24	12 46	25 5	10 55	2 47	9 0	29 14	28 41
31	12 31 12	9♈42 37	7♏57	14♈27	13♉58	25♈50	10♐55	2♏43	9♐ 0	29♐14	28♎40

THE SUN ENTERS THE SIGN OF ARIES ON MAR 21 AT 04:39.

♈ ARIES ♉ TAURUS ♊ GEMINI ♋ CANCER ♌ LEO ♍ VIRGO ♎ LIBRA

1983

SIDEREAL SUN.... MOON... MERCURY VENUS.. MARS... JUPITER SATURN. URANUS. NEPTUNE PLUTO..

DAY	TIME h m s	☉ ° ' "	☽ ° '	☿ ° '	♀ ° '	♂ ° '	♃ ° '	♄ ° '	♅ ° '	♆ ° '	♇ ° '
A 1	12 35 9	10♈41 50	21♏12	16♈30	15♉10	26♈35	10♐54	2♏39	8♐59	29♐14	28♎38
P 2	12 39 5	11 41 2	4♐ 4	18 33	16 22	27 20	10R53	2R35	8R58	29R14	28R37
R 3	12 43 2	12 40 12	16 33	20 36	17 34	28 5	10 52	2 31	8 57	29 14	28 35
I 4	12 46 58	13 39 20	28 44	22 38	18 45	28 49	10 51	2 27	8 56	29 14	28 33
L 5	12 50 55	14 38 27	10♑43	24 39	19 57	29 34	10 49	2 22	8 55	29 14	28 32
6	12 54 52	15 37 31	22 34	26 39	21 8	0♉18	10 48	2 18	8 54	29 14	28 30
7	12 58 48	16 36 34	4♒22	28 37	22 20	1 3	10 46	2 14	8 52	29 13	28 28
8	13 2 45	17 35 35	16 14	0♉33	23 31	1 48	10 44	2 10	8 51	29 13	28 27
9	13 6 41	18 34 35	28 14	2 27	24 42	2 32	10 42	2 5	8 50	29 13	28 25
10	13 10 38	19 33 32	10♓25	4 18	25 53	3 16	10 40	2 1	8 49	29 13	28 23
11	13 14 34	20 32 28	22 50	6 6	27 4	4 1	10 37	1 56	8 47	29 12	28 22
12	13 18 31	21 31 21	5♈31	7 50	28 15	4 45	10 34	1 52	8 46	29 12	28 20
13	13 22 27	22 30 13	18 28	9 31	29 26	5 29	10 32	1 47	8 45	29 12	28 18
14	13 26 24	23 29 3	1♉40	11 8	0♊37	6 13	10 29	1 43	8 43	29 11	28 17
15	13 30 20	24 27 51	15 6	12 40	1 48	6 58	10 25	1 38	8 42	29 11	28 15
16	13 34 17	25 26 37	28 43	14 8	2 58	7 42	10 22	1 34	8 40	29 10	28 13
17	13 38 14	26 25 20	12♊29	15 31	4 9	8 26	10 18	1 29	8 38	29 10	28 12
18	13 42 10	27 24 2	26 22	16 49	5 19	9 10	10 15	1 25	8 37	29 9	28 10
19	13 46 7	28 22 41	10♋22	18 2	6 29	9 54	10 11	1 20	8 35	29 9	28 8
20	13 50 3	29 21 18	24 26	19 10	7 40	10 38	10 7	1 16	8 33	29 8	28 7
21	13 54 0	0♉19 53	8♌35	20 13	8 50	11 22	10 2	1 11	8 32	29 8	28 5
22	13 57 56	1 18 26	22 46	21 10	10 0	12 5	9 58	1 6	8 30	29 7	28 3
23	14 1 53	2 16 56	6♍59	22 2	11 9	12 49	9 54	1 2	8 28	29 6	28 2
24	14 5 49	3 15 24	21 9	22 48	12 19	13 33	9 49	0 57	8 26	29 6	28 0
25	14 9 46	4 13 50	5♎13	23 28	13 29	14 16	9 44	0 53	8 24	29 5	27 58
26	14 13 43	5 12 14	19 7	24 3	14 38	15 0	9 39	0 48	8 22	29 4	27 56
27	14 17 39	6 10 36	2♏46	24 32	15 47	15 44	9 34	0 44	8 21	29 3	27 55
28	14 21 36	7 8 57	16 9	24 56	16 57	16 27	9 29	0 39	8 19	29 2	27 53
29	14 25 32	8 7 15	29 12	25 13	18 6	17 11	9 23	0 35	8 17	29 2	27 51
30	14 29 29	9♉ 5 32	11♐56	25♉25	19♊15	17♉54	9♐18	0♏30	8♐15	29♐ 1	27♎50

THE SUN ENTERS THE SIGN OF TAURUS ON APR 20 AT 15:51.

DAY	TIME h m s	☉ ° ' "	☽ ° '	☿ ° '	♀ ° '	♂ ° '	♃ ° '	♄ ° '	♅ ° '	♆ ° '	♇ ° '
M 1	14 33 25	10♉ 3 47	24♐22	25♉32	20♊24	18♉37	9♐12	0♏26	8♐12	29♐ 0	27♎48
A 2	14 37 22	11 2 1	6♑33	25R33	21 32	19 21	9R 6	0R21	8R10	28R59	27R47
Y 3	14 41 18	12 0 13	18 32	25 29	22 41	20 4	9 0	0 17	8 8	28 58	27 45
4	14 45 15	12 58 24	0♒25	25 19	23 49	20 47	8 54	0 12	8 6	28 57	27 43
5	14 49 12	13 56 33	12 15	25 5	24 57	21 30	8 48	0 8	8 4	28 56	27 42
6	14 53 8	14 54 41	24 8	24 47	26 6	22 13	8 42	0 4	8 2	28 55	27 40
7	14 57 5	15 52 47	6♓10	24 24	27 14	22 56	8 35	29♎59	8 0	28 54	27 38
8	15 1 1	16 50 52	18 24	23 58	28 21	23 39	8 29	29 55	7 57	28 53	27 37
9	15 4 58	17 48 56	0♈54	23 29	29 29	24 22	8 22	29 51	7 55	28 52	27 35
10	15 8 54	18 46 57	13 43	22 57	0♋37	25 5	8 15	29 46	7 53	28 51	27 34
11	15 12 51	19 44 58	26 53	22 23	1 44	25 48	8 8	29 42	7 50	28 49	27 32
12	15 16 47	20 42 57	10♉22	21 48	2 51	26 31	8 2	29 38	7 48	28 48	27 31
13	15 20 44	21 40 55	24 8	21 12	3 58	27 13	7 55	29 34	7 46	28 47	27 29
14	15 24 41	22 38 51	8♊10	20 36	5 5	27 56	7 47	29 30	7 43	28 46	27 28
15	15 28 37	23 36 46	22 22	20 1	6 12	28 39	7 40	29 26	7 41	28 45	27 26
16	15 32 34	24 34 39	6♋41	19 26	7 19	29 21	7 33	29 22	7 39	28 43	27 25
17	15 36 30	25 32 30	21 1	18 54	8 25	0♊ 4	7 26	29 18	7 36	28 42	27 23
18	15 40 27	26 30 20	5♌21	18 23	9 31	0 47	7 18	29 14	7 34	28 41	27 22
19	15 44 23	27 28 8	19 36	17 55	10 37	1 29	7 11	29 11	7 31	28 40	27 20
20	15 48 20	28 25 54	3♍45	17 31	11 43	2 11	7 4	29 7	7 29	28 38	27 19
21	15 52 16	29 23 38	17 45	17 10	12 48	2 54	6 56	29 3	7 26	28 37	27 18
22	15 56 13	0♊21 21	1♎36	16 53	13 54	3 36	6 49	29 0	7 24	28 36	27 16
23	16 0 10	1 19 2	15 16	16 39	14 59	4 18	6 41	28 56	7 22	28 34	27 15
24	16 4 6	2 16 41	28 43	16 30	16 4	5 0	6 34	28 53	7 19	28 33	27 14
25	16 8 3	3 14 20	11♏57	16D26	17 8	5 43	6 26	28 49	7 17	28 31	27 12
26	16 11 59	4 11 56	24 57	16 26	18 13	6 25	6 18	28 46	7 14	28 30	27 11
27	16 15 56	5 9 32	7♐41	16 30	19 17	7 7	6 11	28 43	7 12	28 28	27 10
28	16 19 52	6 7 7	20 12	16 39	20 21	7 49	6 3	28 40	7 9	28 27	27 9
29	16 23 49	7 4 40	2♑29	16 52	21 25	8 31	5 55	28 37	7 7	28 26	27 7
30	16 27 45	8 2 12	14 35	17 10	22 28	9 13	5 48	28 34	7 4	28 24	27 6
31	16 31 42	8♊59 44	26♑32	17♉32	23♋31	9♊54	5♐40	28♎31	7♐ 2	28♐23	27♎ 5

THE SUN ENTERS THE SIGN OF GEMINI ON MAY 21 AT 15:07.

DAY	TIME h m s	☉ ° ' "	☽ ° '	☿ ° '	♀ ° '	♂ ° '	♃ ° '	♄ ° '	♅ ° '	♆ ° '	♇ ° '
J 1	16 35 39	9♊57 14	8♒24	17♉59	24♋34	10♊36	5♐33	28♎28	6♐59	28♐21	27♎ 4
U 2	16 39 35	10 54 44	20 14	18 29	25 37	11 18	5R25	28R25	6R57	28R20	27R 3
N 3	16 43 32	11 52 13	2♓ 8	19 4	26 39	12 0	5 17	28 22	6 54	28 18	27 2
E 4	16 47 28	12 49 41	14 9	19 43	27 41	12 41	5 10	28 20	6 52	28 17	27 1
5	16 51 25	13 47 8	26 23	20 26	28 43	13 23	5 2	28 17	6 49	28 15	27 0
6	16 55 21	14 44 35	8♈53	21 13	29 44	14 5	4 55	28 15	6 47	28 13	26 59
7	16 59 18	15 42 1	21 44	22 3	0♌46	14 46	4 47	28 12	6 44	28 12	26 58
8	17 3 14	16 39 26	4♉57	22 57	1 46	15 28	4 40	28 10	6 42	28 10	26 57
9	17 7 11	17 36 51	18 34	23 55	2 47	16 9	4 33	28 8	6 40	28 9	26 56
10	17 11 8	18 34 15	2♊34	24 56	3 47	16 50	4 26	28 6	6 37	28 7	26 55
11	17 15 4	19 31 38	16 55	26 1	4 47	17 32	4 18	28 4	6 35	28 6	26 54
12	17 19 1	20 29 1	1♋30	27 8	5 46	18 13	4 11	28 2	6 32	28 4	26 53
13	17 22 57	21 26 23	16 14	28 20	6 45	18 54	4 4	28 0	6 30	28 2	26 52
14	17 26 54	22 23 44	1♌ 0	29 34	7 44	19 36	3 57	27 58	6 28	28 1	26 52
15	17 30 50	23 21 4	15 42	0♊52	8 42	20 17	3 50	27 57	6 25	27 59	26 51
16	17 34 47	24 18 24	0♍13	2 13	9 40	20 58	3 44	27 55	6 23	27 57	26 50
17	17 38 44	25 15 42	14 30	3 37	10 37	21 39	3 37	27 54	6 21	27 56	26 50
18	17 42 40	26 12 59	28 29	5 4	11 34	22 20	3 30	27 52	6 18	27 54	26 49
19	17 46 37	27 10 15	12♎11	6 34	12 30	23 1	3 24	27 51	6 16	27 53	26 48
20	17 50 33	28 7 31	25 36	8 7	13 26	23 42	3 17	27 50	6 14	27 51	26 48
21	17 54 30	29 4 46	8♏43	9 43	14 22	24 23	3 11	27 49	6 12	27 49	26 47
22	17 58 26	0♋ 2 0	21 35	11 23	15 17	25 4	3 5	27 48	6 9	27 48	26 47
23	18 2 23	0 59 14	4♐13	13 5	16 11	25 44	2 59	27 47	6 7	27 46	26 46
24	18 6 19	1 56 27	16 39	14 50	17 5	26 25	2 53	27 46	6 5	27 45	26 46
25	18 10 16	2 53 40	28 55	16 38	17 58	27 6	2 47	27 45	6 3	27 43	26 45
26	18 14 13	3 50 52	11♑ 1	18 28	18 50	27 47	2 42	27 45	6 1	27 41	26 45
27	18 18 9	4 48 5	23 0	20 22	19 42	28 27	2 36	27 44	5 59	27 40	26 44
28	18 22 6	5 45 17	4♒53	22 18	20 34	29 8	2 31	27 44	5 57	27 38	26 44
29	18 26 2	6 42 28	16 44	24 16	21 24	29 48	2 26	27 44	5 55	27 37	26 44
30	18 29 59	7♋39 40	28♒35	26♊17	22♌14	0♋29	2♐20	27♎43	5♐53	27♐35	26♎44

THE SUN ENTERS THE SIGN OF CANCER ON JUN 21 AT 23:10.

♏ SCORPIO ♐ SAGITTARIUS ♑ CAPRICORN ♒ AQUARIUS ♓ PISCES

1983

SIDEREAL SUN MOON. MERCURY. VENUS. MARS. JUPITER. SATURN. URANUS. NEPTUNE. PLUTO.

DAY	TIME h m s	☉ ° ' "	☽ ° '	☿ ° '	♀ ° '	♂ ° '	♃ ° '	♄ ° '	♅ ° '	♆ ° '	♇ ° '
J 1	18 33 55	8♋36 52	10♓29	28♊20	23♌ 4	1♋ 9	2♐15	27♎43	5♐51	27♐33	26♎43
U 2	18 37 52	9 34 4	22 30	0♋24	23 52	1 50	2R11	27D43	5R49	27R32	26R43
L 3	18 41 48	10 31 16	4♈42	2 31	24 40	2 30	2 6	27 43	5 47	27 30	26 43
Y 4	18 45 45	11 28 28	17 10	4 38	25 27	3 10	2 2	27 44	5 45	27 29	26 43
5	18 49 42	12 25 40	29 57	6 47	26 13	3 51	1 57	27 44	5 43	27 27	26 43
6	18 53 38	13 22 53	13♉ 7	8 56	26 59	4 31	1 53	27 44	5 41	27 26	26 43
7	18 57 35	14 20 6	26 42	11 6	27 43	5 11	1 49	27 45	5 40	27 24	26D43
8	19 1 31	15 17 19	10♊45	13 17	28 27	5 51	1 45	27 45	5 38	27 22	26 43
9	19 5 28	16 14 33	25 12	15 27	29 9	6 32	1 41	27 46	5 36	27 21	26 43
10	19 9 24	17 11 47	9♋59	17 36	29 51	7 12	1 38	27 47	5 34	27 19	26 43
11	19 13 21	18 9 1	25 1	19 46	0♍31	7 52	1 34	27 48	5 33	27 18	26 43
12	19 17 17	19 6 15	10♌ 8	21 54	1 11	8 32	1 31	27 49	5 31	27 16	26 43
13	19 21 14	20 3 29	25 12	24 1	1 49	9 12	1 28	27 50	5 30	27 15	26 43
14	19 25 11	21 0 44	10♍ 2	26 7	2 27	9 52	1 25	27 51	5 28	27 14	26 43
15	19 29 7	21 57 58	24 33	28 12	3 3	10 32	1 23	27 52	5 27	27 12	26 44
16	19 33 4	22 55 12	8♎40	0♌16	3 37	11 11	1 20	27 54	5 25	27 11	26 44
17	19 37 0	23 52 26	22 23	2 17	4 11	11 51	1 18	27 55	5 24	27 9	26 44
18	19 40 57	24 49 41	5♏42	4 18	4 43	12 31	1 16	27 57	5 23	27 8	26 45
19	19 44 53	25 46 55	18 39	6 16	5 14	13 11	1 14	27 58	5 21	27 6	26 45
20	19 48 50	26 44 10	1♐17	8 13	5 43	13 51	1 12	28 0	5 20	27 5	26 45
21	19 52 46	27 41 25	13 41	10 8	6 11	14 30	1 10	28 2	5 19	27 4	26 46
22	19 56 43	28 38 41	25 52	12 2	6 37	15 10	1 9	28 4	5 18	27 2	26 46
23	20 0 40	29 35 56	7♑55	13 53	7 2	15 49	1 8	28 6	5 17	27 1	26 47
24	20 4 36	0♌33 13	19 52	15 43	7 25	16 29	1 7	28 8	5 16	27 0	26 47
25	20 8 33	1 30 29	1♒45	17 31	7 46	17 8	1 6	28 10	5 15	26 59	26 48
26	20 12 29	2 27 47	13 36	19 18	8 5	17 48	1 5	28 13	5 14	26 57	26 48
27	20 16 26	3 25 5	25 27	21 2	8 23	18 27	1 5	28 15	5 13	26 56	26 49
28	20 20 22	4 22 23	7♓20	22 45	8 39	19 7	1 4	28 18	5 12	26 55	26 50
29	20 24 19	5 19 43	19 17	24 26	8 52	19 46	1D 4	28 20	5 11	26 54	26 50
30	20 28 15	6 17 4	1♈20	26 5	9 4	20 25	1 4	28 23	5 10	26 53	26 51
31	20 32 12	7♌14 25	13♈33	27♌43	9♍13	21♋ 5	1♐ 4	28♎26	5♐ 9	26♐51	26♎52

THE SUN ENTERS THE SIGN OF LEO ON JUL 23 AT 10:05.

DAY	TIME h m s	☉ ° ' "	☽ ° '	☿ ° '	♀ ° '	♂ ° '	♃ ° '	♄ ° '	♅ ° '	♆ ° '	♇ ° '
A 1	20 36 9	8♌11 48	25♈59	29♌19	9♍21	21♋44	1♐ 5	28♎29	5♐ 9	26♐50	26♎53
U 2	20 40 5	9 9 11	8♉43	0♍53	9 26	22 23	1 5	28 32	5R 8	26R49	26 54
G 3	20 44 2	10 6 36	21 47	2 26	9R29	23 2	1 6	28 35	5 7	26 48	26 55
U 4	20 47 58	11 4 2	5♊15	3 56	9 30	23 42	1 7	28 38	5 7	26 47	26 55
S 5	20 51 55	12 1 30	19 10	5 25	9 28	24 21	1 8	28 41	5 6	26 46	26 56
T 6	20 55 51	12 58 58	3♋32	6 53	9 24	25 0	1 10	28 44	5 6	26 45	26 57
7	20 59 48	13 56 28	18 18	8 18	9 18	25 39	1 11	28 48	5 6	26 44	26 58
8	21 3 45	14 53 59	3♌24	9 42	9 9	26 18	1 13	28 51	5 5	26 43	26 59
9	21 7 41	15 51 31	18 39	11 4	8 58	26 57	1 15	28 55	5 5	26 42	27 0
10	21 11 38	16 49 4	3♍55	12 23	8 45	27 36	1 17	28 58	5 5	26 41	27 2
11	21 15 34	17 46 38	18 59	13 41	8 29	28 15	1 19	29 2	5 4	26 40	27 3
12	21 19 31	18 44 13	3♎44	14 58	8 11	28 54	1 21	29 6	5 4	26 40	27 4
13	21 23 27	19 41 49	18 2	16 12	7 51	29 33	1 24	29 10	5 4	26 39	27 5
14	21 27 24	20 39 26	1♏51	17 24	7 29	0♌11	1 27	29 14	5D 4	26 38	27 6
15	21 31 20	21 37 3	15 12	18 33	7 4	0 50	1 30	29 18	5 4	26 37	27 8
16	21 35 17	22 34 42	28 7	19 41	6 37	1 29	1 33	29 22	5 4	26 36	27 9
17	21 39 13	23 32 22	10♐40	20 46	6 9	2 8	1 36	29 26	5 4	26 36	27 10
18	21 43 10	24 30 2	22 56	21 49	5 39	2 46	1 39	29 30	5 5	26 35	27 11
19	21 47 7	25 27 44	5♑ 0	22 49	5 7	3 25	1 43	29 35	5 5	26 34	27 13
20	21 51 3	26 25 27	16 56	23 46	4 33	4 4	1 47	29 39	5 5	26 34	27 14
21	21 55 0	27 23 11	28 48	24 41	3 59	4 42	1 51	29 44	5 5	26 33	27 16
22	21 58 56	28 20 57	10♒38	25 33	3 23	5 21	1 55	29 48	5 6	26 33	27 17
23	22 2 53	29 18 43	22 29	26 21	2 47	5 59	1 59	29 53	5 6	26 32	27 19
24	22 6 49	0♍16 31	4♓23	27 6	2 10	6 38	2 4	29 58	5 7	26 32	27 20
25	22 10 46	1 14 21	16 21	27 48	1 33	7 16	2 8	0♏ 2	5 7	26 31	27 22
26	22 14 42	2 12 12	28 25	28 26	0 55	7 55	2 13	0 7	5 8	26 31	27 23
27	22 18 39	3 10 5	10♈35	29 0	0 18	8 33	2 18	0 12	5 8	26 30	27 25
28	22 22 36	4 7 59	22 55	29 29	29♌41	9 11	2 23	0 17	5 9	26 30	27 26
29	22 26 32	5 5 55	5♉25	29 54	29 5	9 50	2 28	0 22	5 10	26 30	27 28
30	22 30 29	6 3 53	18 10	0♎15	28 30	10 28	2 34	0 27	5 11	26 29	27 30
31	22 34 25	7♍ 1 53	1♊12	0♎30	27♌56	11♌ 6	2♐39	0♏33	5♐11	26♐29	27♎31

THE SUN ENTERS THE SIGN OF VIRGO ON AUG 23 AT 17:09.

DAY	TIME h m s	☉ ° ' "	☽ ° '	☿ ° '	♀ ° '	♂ ° '	♃ ° '	♄ ° '	♅ ° '	♆ ° '	♇ ° '
S 1	22 38 22	7♍59 55	14♊34	0♎40	27♌23	11♌44	2♐45	0♏38	5♐12	26♐29	27♎33
E 2	22 42 18	8 57 58	28 19	0R45	26R52	12 23	2 51	0 43	5 13	26R28	27 35
P 3	22 46 15	9 56 4	12♋29	0 43	26 22	13 1	2 57	0 48	5 14	26 28	27 37
T 4	22 50 11	10 54 12	27 3	0 36	25 54	13 39	3 3	0 54	5 15	26 28	27 38
E 5	22 54 8	11 52 21	11♌57	0 22	25 28	14 17	3 9	0 59	5 16	26 28	27 40
M 6	22 58 5	12 50 33	27 5	0 2	25 4	14 55	3 16	1 5	5 17	26 28	27 42
B 7	23 2 1	13 48 46	12♍17	29♍36	24 42	15 33	3 22	1 11	5 19	26 28	27 44
E 8	23 5 58	14 47 1	27 22	29 3	24 23	16 11	3 29	1 16	5 20	26D28	27 46
R 9	23 9 54	15 45 17	12♎10	28 25	24 6	16 49	3 36	1 22	5 21	26 28	27 48
10	23 13 51	16 43 36	26 34	27 40	23 51	17 27	3 43	1 28	5 23	26 28	27 50
11	23 17 47	17 41 55	10♏30	26 50	23 38	18 5	3 50	1 34	5 24	26 28	27 52
12	23 21 44	18 40 17	23 55	25 56	23 28	18 43	3 57	1 40	5 25	26 28	27 54
13	23 25 40	19 38 40	6♐54	24 58	23 21	19 21	4 5	1 46	5 27	26 28	27 56
14	23 29 37	20 37 5	19 28	23 57	23 15	19 59	4 12	1 52	5 28	26 28	27 58
15	23 33 34	21 35 31	1♑44	22 55	23D12	20 37	4 20	1 58	5 30	26 28	28 0
16	23 37 30	22 33 59	13 46	21 53	23 12	21 14	4 28	2 4	5 32	26 29	28 2
17	23 41 27	23 32 28	25 40	20 53	23 14	21 52	4 36	2 10	5 33	26 29	28 4
18	23 45 23	24 30 59	7♒30	19 55	23 18	22 30	4 44	2 16	5 35	26 29	28 6
19	23 49 20	25 29 32	19 21	19 2	23 24	23 7	4 52	2 22	5 37	26 30	28 8
20	23 53 16	26 28 7	1♓14	18 15	23 33	23 45	5 1	2 29	5 39	26 30	28 10
21	23 57 13	27 26 43	13 13	17 35	23 44	24 23	5 9	2 35	5 40	26 30	28 12
22	0 1 9	28 25 21	25 20	17 3	23 56	25 0	5 18	2 41	5 42	26 31	28 14
23	0 5 6	29 24 2	7♈34	16 40	24 11	25 38	5 26	2 48	5 44	26 31	28 17
24	0 9 3	0♎22 44	19 58	16D27	24 28	26 15	5 35	2 54	5 46	26 32	28 19
25	0 12 59	1 21 28	2♉31	16 23	24 47	26 53	5 44	3 1	5 48	26 32	28 21
26	0 16 56	2 20 15	15 14	16 29	25 8	27 30	5 53	3 7	5 50	26 33	28 23
27	0 20 52	3 19 3	28 9	16 46	25 31	28 8	6 2	3 14	5 52	26 33	28 25
28	0 24 49	4 17 54	11♊17	17 12	25 55	28 45	6 12	3 20	5 55	26 34	28 28
29	0 28 45	5 16 47	24 40	17 47	26 21	29 22	6 21	3 27	5 57	26 35	28 30
30	0 32 42	6♎15 43	8♋21	18♍31	26♌49	0♍ 0	6♐31	3♏34	5♐59	26♐35	28♎32

THE SUN ENTERS THE SIGN OF LIBRA ON SEP 23 AT 14:43.

♈ ARIES ♉ TAURUS ♊ GEMINI ♋ CANCER ♌ LEO ♍ VIRGO ♎ LIBRA

1983

S I D E R E A L S U N . M O O N . M E R C U R Y . V E N U S . M A R S . J U P I T E R . S A T U R N . U R A N U S . N E P T U N E . P L U T O .

DAY	TIME	☉	☽	☿	♀	♂	♃	♄	♅	♆	♇
	h m s	° ' "	° '	° '	° '	° '	° '	° '	° '	° '	° '
O 1	0 36 38	7♎14 41	22♋20	19♍24	27♌18	0♍37	6♐40	3♏40	6♐ 1	26♐36	28♎34
C 2	0 40 35	8 13 41	6♌38	20 24	27 49	1 14	6 50	3 47	6 4	26 37	28 37
T 3	0 44 32	9 12 44	21 14	21 31	28 21	1 51	7 0	3 54	6 6	26 38	28 39
O 4	0 48 28	10 11 49	6♍ 1	22 45	28 55	2 29	7 10	4 1	6 9	26 39	28 41
B 5	0 52 25	11 10 56	20 54	24 4	29 30	3 6	7 20	4 8	6 11	26 39	28 44
E 6	0 56 21	12 10 5	5♎43	25 27	0♍ 7	3 43	7 30	4 14	6 14	26 40	28 46
R 7	1 0 18	13 9 16	20 21	26 55	0 44	4 20	7 40	4 21	6 16	26 41	28 48
8	1 4 14	14 8 29	4♏40	28 27	1 23	4 57	7 51	4 28	6 19	26 42	28 51
9	1 8 11	15 7 44	18 34	0♎ 1	2 4	5 34	8 1	4 35	6 21	26 43	28 53
10	1 12 7	16 7 1	2♐ 1	1 38	2 45	6 11	8 12	4 42	6 24	26 44	28 55
11	1 16 4	17 6 20	15 2	3 16	3 27	6 48	8 22	4 49	6 27	26 45	28 58
12	1 20 0	18 5 41	27 40	4 57	4 10	7 25	8 33	4 56	6 29	26 46	29 0
13	1 23 57	19 5 4	9♑58	6 38	4 55	8 2	8 44	5 3	6 32	26 47	29 2
14	1 27 54	20 4 28	22 2	8 21	5 40	8 39	8 55	5 10	6 35	26 48	29 5
15	1 31 50	21 3 54	3♒57	10 4	6 26	9 16	9 6	5 17	6 38	26 50	29 7
16	1 35 47	22 3 22	15 48	11 47	7 14	9 52	9 17	5 24	6 41	26 51	29 10
17	1 39 43	23 2 52	27 40	13 31	8 2	10 29	9 28	5 32	6 43	26 52	29 12
18	1 43 40	24 2 23	9♓37	15 14	8 51	11 6	9 39	5 39	6 46	26 53	29 15
19	1 47 36	25 1 57	21 41	16 58	9 40	11 43	9 50	5 46	6 49	26 54	29 17
20	1 51 33	26 1 32	3♈56	18 41	10 31	12 19	10 2	5 53	6 52	26 56	29 19
21	1 55 29	27 1 9	16 23	20 24	11 22	12 56	10 13	6 0	6 55	26 57	29 22
22	1 59 26	28 0 48	29 2	22 7	12 14	13 32	10 25	6 7	6 58	26 58	29 24
23	2 3 23	29 0 29	11♉54	23 49	13 7	14 9	10 36	6 15	7 1	27 0	29 27
24	2 7 19	0♏ 0 12	24 57	25 31	14 0	14 45	10 48	6 22	7 5	27 1	29 29
25	2 11 16	0 59 57	8♊12	27 13	14 54	15 22	11 0	6 29	7 8	27 3	29 31
26	2 15 12	1 59 45	21 38	28 54	15 49	15 58	11 12	6 36	7 11	27 4	29 34
27	2 19 9	2 59 35	5♋14	0♏34	16 44	16 35	11 24	6 43	7 14	27 6	29 36
28	2 23 5	3 59 26	19 2	2 14	17 40	17 11	11 36	6 51	7 17	27 7	29 39
29	2 27 2	4 59 21	3♌ 1	3 54	18 37	17 47	11 48	6 58	7 20	27 9	29 41
30	2 30 58	5 59 17	17 10	5 33	19 34	18 24	12 0	7 5	7 24	27 10	29 44
31	2 34 55	6♏59 16	1♍27	7♏11	20♍32	19♍ 0	12♐12	7♏12	7♐27	27♐12	29♎46

THE SUN ENTERS THE SIGN OF SCORPIO ON OCT 23 AT 23:55.

DAY	TIME	☉	☽	☿	♀	♂	♃	♄	♅	♆	♇
	h m s	° ' "	° '	° '	° '	° '	° '	° '	° '	° '	° '
N 1	2 38 52	7♏59 16	15♍51	8♏49	21♍30	19♍36	12♐24	7♏20	7♐30	27♐13	29♎48
O 2	2 42 48	8 59 19	0♎17	10 27	22 29	20 12	12 37	7 27	7 34	27 15	29 51
V 3	2 46 45	9 59 24	14 40	12 4	23 28	20 48	12 49	7 34	7 37	27 17	29 53
E 4	2 50 41	10 59 31	28 53	13 41	24 27	21 24	13 1	7 41	7 40	27 18	29 56
M 5	2 54 38	11 59 40	12♏52	15 17	25 27	22 0	13 14	7 49	7 44	27 20	29 58
B 6	2 58 34	12 59 51	26 33	16 52	26 28	22 36	13 26	7 56	7 47	27 22	0♏ 0
E 7	3 2 31	14 0 3	9♐52	18 28	27 29	23 12	13 39	8 3	7 51	27 24	0 3
R 8	3 6 27	15 0 17	22 50	20 3	28 30	23 48	13 52	8 10	7 54	27 25	0 5
9	3 10 24	16 0 33	5♑28	21 37	29 32	24 24	14 4	8 17	7 58	27 27	0 7
10	3 14 21	17 0 51	17 48	23 12	0♎34	25 0	14 17	8 25	8 1	27 29	0 10
11	3 18 17	18 1 9	29 54	24 46	1 36	25 36	14 30	8 32	8 5	27 31	0 12
12	3 22 14	19 1 30	11♒51	26 19	2 39	26 11	14 43	8 39	8 8	27 33	0 14
13	3 26 10	20 1 51	23 43	27 52	3 43	26 47	14 55	8 46	8 12	27 35	0 17
14	3 30 7	21 2 14	5♓36	29 25	4 46	27 23	15 8	8 53	8 15	27 37	0 19
15	3 34 3	22 2 39	17 34	0♐58	5 50	27 58	15 21	9 0	8 19	27 38	0 21
16	3 38 0	23 3 5	29 41	2 30	6 54	28 34	15 34	9 7	8 22	27 40	0 24
17	3 41 56	24 3 32	12♈ 1	4 3	7 59	29 9	15 47	9 15	8 26	27 42	0 26
18	3 45 53	25 4 0	24 36	5 35	9 3	29 45	16 1	9 22	8 30	27 44	0 28
19	3 49 50	26 4 30	7♉29	7 6	10 8	0♎20	16 14	9 29	8 33	27 46	0 30
20	3 53 46	27 5 2	20 39	8 37	11 14	0 55	16 27	9 36	8 37	27 48	0 33
21	3 57 43	28 5 35	4♊ 5	10 9	12 20	1 31	16 40	9 43	8 41	27 50	0 35
22	4 1 39	29 6 10	17 45	11 39	13 25	2 6	16 53	9 50	8 44	27 52	0 37
23	4 5 36	0♐ 6 46	1♋38	13 10	14 32	2 41	17 6	9 57	8 48	27 54	0 39
24	4 9 32	1 7 24	15 40	14 40	15 38	3 16	17 20	10 4	8 51	27 56	0 41
25	4 13 29	2 8 3	29 48	16 10	16 45	3 51	17 33	10 11	8 55	27 59	0 43
26	4 17 25	3 8 44	14♌ 0	17 40	17 52	4 26	17 46	10 17	8 59	28 1	0 46
27	4 21 22	4 9 27	28 12	19 9	18 59	5 1	18 0	10 24	9 2	28 3	0 48
28	4 25 19	5 10 11	12♍23	20 38	20 6	5 36	18 13	10 31	9 6	28 5	0 50
29	4 29 15	6 10 57	26 30	22 7	21 14	6 11	18 27	10 38	9 10	28 7	0 52
30	4 33 12	7♐11 45	10♎32	23♐35	22♎22	6♎46	18♐40	10♏45	9♐14	28♐ 9	0♏54

THE SUN ENTERS THE SIGN OF SAGITTARIUS ON NOV 22 AT 21:19.

DAY	TIME	☉	☽	☿	♀	♂	♃	♄	♅	♆	♇
	h m s	° ' "	° '	° '	° '	° '	° '	° '	° '	° '	° '
D 1	4 37 8	8♐12 33	24♎26	25♐ 2	23♎30	7♎20	18♐54	10♏51	9♐17	28♐11	0♏56
E 2	4 41 5	9 13 24	8♏10	26 29	24 38	7 55	19 7	10 58	9 21	28 13	0 58
C 3	4 45 1	10 14 15	21 41	27 55	25 47	8 29	19 21	11 5	9 25	28 16	1 0
E 4	4 48 58	11 15 8	4♐59	29 20	26 55	9 4	19 34	11 11	9 28	28 18	1 2
M 5	4 52 54	12 16 3	18 1	0♑44	28 4	9 38	19 48	11 18	9 32	28 20	1 4
B 6	4 56 51	13 16 58	0♑48	2 7	29 13	10 13	20 1	11 24	9 36	28 22	1 6
E 7	5 0 48	14 17 54	13 19	3 29	0♏22	10 47	20 15	11 31	9 39	28 24	1 8
R 8	5 4 44	15 18 51	25 37	4 49	1 32	11 21	20 28	11 37	9 43	28 27	1 10
9	5 8 41	16 19 49	7♒42	6 7	2 41	11 56	20 42	11 44	9 47	28 29	1 12
10	5 12 37	17 20 48	19 40	7 23	3 51	12 30	20 56	11 50	9 50	28 31	1 13
11	5 16 34	18 21 47	1♓32	8 36	5 1	13 4	21 9	11 56	9 54	28 33	1 15
12	5 20 30	19 22 47	13 24	9 47	6 10	13 38	21 23	12 3	9 58	28 36	1 17
13	5 24 27	20 23 47	25 20	10 54	7 20	14 12	21 36	12 9	10 1	28 38	1 19
14	5 28 24	21 24 48	7♈26	11 57	8 31	14 45	21 50	12 15	10 5	28 40	1 21
15	5 32 20	22 25 49	19 45	12 56	9 41	15 19	22 4	12 21	10 9	28 42	1 22
16	5 36 17	23 26 51	2♉21	13 50	10 51	15 53	22 17	12 27	10 12	28 45	1 24
17	5 40 13	24 27 54	15 19	14 38	12 2	16 26	22 31	12 33	10 16	28 47	1 26
18	5 44 10	25 28 57	28 39	15 19	13 13	17 0	22 45	12 39	10 19	28 49	1 27
19	5 48 6	26 30 0	12♊21	15 52	14 24	17 33	22 58	12 45	10 23	28 51	1 29
20	5 52 3	27 31 4	26 24	16 18	15 35	18 7	23 12	12 51	10 27	28 54	1 31
21	5 55 59	28 32 9	10♋45	16 33	16 46	18 40	23 26	12 57	10 30	28 56	1 32
22	5 59 56	29 33 14	25 17	16R39	17 57	19 13	23 39	13 3	10 34	28 58	1 34
23	6 3 53	0♑34 20	9♌55	16 34	19 8	19 46	23 53	13 8	10 37	29 0	1 35
24	6 7 49	1 35 26	24 31	16 17	20 19	20 19	24 6	13 14	10 41	29 3	1 37
25	6 11 46	2 36 33	9♍ 1	15 49	21 31	20 52	24 20	13 19	10 44	29 5	1 38
26	6 15 42	3 37 41	23 20	15 9	22 42	21 25	24 33	13 25	10 48	29 7	1 39
27	6 19 39	4 38 49	7♎24	14 18	23 54	21 58	24 47	13 30	10 51	29 10	1 41
28	6 23 35	5 39 58	21 14	13 16	25 6	22 30	25 1	13 36	10 55	29 12	1 42
29	6 27 32	6 41 8	4♏48	12 6	26 18	23 3	25 14	13 41	10 58	29 14	1 43
30	6 31 28	7 42 18	18 8	10 50	27 30	23 35	25 28	13 46	11 2	29 16	1 45
31	6 35 25	8♑43 28	1♐13	9♑29	28♏42	24♎ 7	25♐41	13♏51	11♐ 5	29♐19	1♏46

THE SUN ENTERS THE SIGN OF CAPRICORN ON DEC 22 AT 10:31.

♏ SCORPIO ♐ SAGITTARIUS ♑ CAPRICORN ♒ AQUARIUS ♓ PISCES

SIDEREAL. SUN. MOON. MERCURY. VENUS. MARS. JUPITER. SATURN. URANUS. NEPTUNE. PLUTO.

DAY	TIME	☉	☽	☿	♀	♂	♃	♄	♅	♆	♇
	h m s	° ' "	° '	° '	° '	° '	° '	° '	° '	° '	° '
J 1	6 39 22	9♑44 39	14♐ 6	8♑ 7	29♏54	24♎40	25♐55	13♏56	11♐ 8	29♐21	1♏47
A 2	6 43 18	10 45 50	26 47	6R47	1♐ 6	25 12	26 8	14 1	11 12	29 23	1 48
N 3	6 47 15	11 47 1	9♑17	5 30	2 18	25 44	26 21	14 6	11 15	29 25	1 50
U 4	6 51 11	12 48 12	21 36	4 20	3 31	26 16	26 35	14 11	11 18	29 27	1 51
A 5	6 55 8	13 49 24	3♒46	3 17	4 43	26 48	26 48	14 16	11 22	29 30	1 52
R 6	6 59 4	14 50 35	15 48	2 23	5 56	27 19	27 2	14 21	11 25	29 32	1 53
Y 7	7 3 1	15 51 45	27 44	1 39	7 8	27 51	27 15	14 25	11 28	29 34	1 54
8	7 6 57	16 52 56	9♓36	1 6	8 21	28 22	27 28	14 30	11 31	29 36	1 55
9	7 10 54	17 54 6	21 27	0 42	9 33	28 53	27 41	14 35	11 34	29 39	1 56
10	7 14 51	18 55 15	3♈21	0 28	10 46	29 25	27 55	14 39	11 38	29 41	1 57
11	7 18 47	19 56 24	15 23	0D23	11 59	29 56	28 8	14 43	11 41	29 43	1 58
12	7 22 44	20 57 33	27 37	0 27	13 12	0♏27	28 21	14 48	11 44	29 45	1 58
13	7 26 40	21 58 41	10♉ 8	0 39	14 24	0 57	28 34	14 52	11 47	29 47	1 59
14	7 30 37	22 59 48	23 1	0 59	15 37	1 28	28 47	14 56	11 50	29 49	2 0
15	7 34 33	24 0 55	6♊20	1 25	16 50	1 59	29 0	15 0	11 53	29 51	2 1
16	7 38 30	25 2 1	20 5	1 57	18 3	2 29	29 13	15 4	11 56	29 54	2 2
17	7 42 27	26 3 7	4♋18	2 35	19 16	2 59	29 26	15 8	11 59	29 56	2 2
18	7 46 23	27 4 12	18 56	3 18	20 29	3 29	29 39	15 11	12 1	29 58	2 3
19	7 50 20	28 5 16	3♌51	4 6	21 43	3 59	29 52	15 15	12 4	0♑ 0	2 3
20	7 54 16	29 6 20	18 56	4 57	22 56	4 29	0♑ 5	15 19	12 7	0 2	2 4
21	7 58 13	0♒ 7 23	4♍ 1	5 53	24 9	4 59	0 18	15 22	12 10	0 4	2 5
22	8 2 9	1 8 25	18 55	6 51	25 22	5 28	0 30	15 25	12 13	0 6	2 5
23	8 6 6	2 9 27	3♎33	7 53	26 36	5 58	0 43	15 29	12 15	0 8	2 5
24	8 10 2	3 10 29	17 48	8 57	27 49	6 27	0 55	15 32	12 18	0 10	2 6
25	8 13 59	4 11 31	1♏40	10 3	29 2	6 56	1 8	15 35	12 21	0 12	2 6
26	8 17 56	5 12 31	15 8	11 12	0♑16	7 25	1 21	15 38	12 23	0 14	2 7
27	8 21 52	6 13 32	28 16	12 23	1 29	7 53	1 33	15 41	12 26	0 16	2 7
28	8 25 49	7 14 32	11♐ 5	13 36	2 43	8 22	1 45	15 44	12 28	0 18	2 7
29	8 29 45	8 15 31	23 40	14 50	3 56	8 50	1 58	15 47	12 31	0 20	2 7
30	8 33 42	9 16 29	6♑ 3	16 6	5 10	9 18	2 10	15 49	12 33	0 21	2 8
31	8 37 38	10♒17 27	18♑17	17♑23	6♑23	9♏46	2♑22	15♏52	12♐36	0♑23	2♏ 8

THE SUN ENTERS THE SIGN OF AQUARIUS ON JAN 20 AT 21:06.

DAY	TIME	☉	☽	☿	♀	♂	♃	♄	♅	♆	♇
	h m s	° ' "	° '	° '	° '	° '	° '	° '	° '	° '	° '
F 1	8 41 35	11♒18 24	0♒24	18♑42	7♑37	10♏14	2♑34	15♏54	12♐38	0♑25	2♏ 8
E 2	8 45 31	12 19 19	12 25	20 2	8 51	10 42	2 46	15 57	12 40	0 27	2 8
B 3	8 49 28	13 20 14	24 22	21 23	10 4	11 9	2 58	15 59	12 43	0 29	2 8
R 4	8 53 25	14 21 7	6♓15	22 46	11 18	11 36	3 10	16 1	12 45	0 30	2R 8
U 5	8 57 21	15 22 0	18 6	24 9	12 32	12 3	3 22	16 3	12 47	0 32	2 8
A 6	9 1 18	16 22 50	29 58	25 34	13 45	12 30	3 34	16 5	12 49	0 34	2 8
R 7	9 5 14	17 23 40	11♈52	26 59	14 59	12 56	3 46	16 7	12 51	0 36	2 8
Y 8	9 9 11	18 24 28	23 53	28 26	16 13	13 22	3 57	16 9	12 53	0 37	2 8
9	9 13 7	19 25 14	6♉ 4	29 53	17 27	13 48	4 9	16 10	12 55	0 39	2 8
10	9 17 4	20 26 0	18 30	1♒22	18 40	14 14	4 20	16 12	12 57	0 41	2 8
11	9 21 0	21 26 43	1♊15	2 51	19 54	14 40	4 32	16 13	12 59	0 42	2 7
12	9 24 57	22 27 25	14 25	4 21	21 8	15 5	4 43	16 15	13 1	0 44	2 7
13	9 28 54	23 28 5	28 3	5 52	22 22	15 30	4 54	16 16	13 3	0 45	2 7
14	9 32 50	24 28 44	12♋11	7 24	23 36	15 55	5 5	16 17	13 5	0 47	2 6
15	9 36 47	25 29 21	26 48	8 57	24 49	16 19	5 16	16 18	13 6	0 48	2 6
16	9 40 43	26 29 57	11♌49	10 30	26 3	16 44	5 27	16 19	13 8	0 50	2 6
17	9 44 40	27 30 30	27 5	12 5	27 17	17 8	5 38	16 20	13 9	0 51	2 5
18	9 48 36	28 31 3	12♍27	13 40	28 31	17 31	5 49	16 21	13 11	0 53	2 5
19	9 52 33	29 31 33	27 42	15 17	29 45	17 55	6 0	16 21	13 13	0 54	2 4
20	9 56 29	0♓32 3	12♎38	16 54	0♒59	18 18	6 10	16 22	13 14	0 56	2 4
21	10 0 26	1 32 30	27 11	18 32	2 13	18 41	6 21	16 22	13 15	0 57	2 3
22	10 4 23	2 32 57	11♏14	20 11	3 27	19 4	6 31	16 23	13 17	0 58	2 3
23	10 8 19	3 33 23	24 49	21 51	4 41	19 26	6 41	16 23	13 18	1 0	2 2
24	10 12 16	4 33 47	7♐57	23 32	5 55	19 48	6 52	16R23	13 19	1 1	2 1
25	10 16 12	5 34 10	20 43	25 14	7 9	20 9	7 2	16 23	13 21	1 2	2 1
26	10 20 9	6 34 31	3♑10	26 57	8 23	20 31	7 12	16 23	13 22	1 3	2 0
27	10 24 5	7 34 51	15 24	28 41	9 37	20 52	7 21	16 23	13 23	1 4	1 59
28	10 28 2	8 35 9	27 29	0♓26	10 51	21 12	7 31	16 22	13 24	1 6	1 58
29	10 31 58	9♓35 26	9♒26	2♓12	12♒ 5	21♏32	7♑41	16♏22	13♐25	1♑ 7	1♏57

THE SUN ENTERS THE SIGN OF PISCES ON FEB 19 AT 11:17.

DAY	TIME	☉	☽	☿	♀	♂	♃	♄	♅	♆	♇
	h m s	° ' "	° '	° '	° '	° '	° '	° '	° '	° '	° '
M 1	10 35 55	10♓35 41	21♒20	3♓59	13♒19	21♏52	7♑50	16♏22	13♐26	1♑ 8	1♏57
A 2	10 39 52	11 35 54	3♓13	5 47	14 33	22 12	8 0	16R21	13 27	1 9	1R56
R 3	10 43 48	12 36 6	15 5	7 36	15 47	22 31	8 9	16 20	13 28	1 10	1 55
C 4	10 47 45	13 36 16	26 58	9 26	17 1	22 49	8 18	16 19	13 28	1 11	1 54
H 5	10 51 41	14 36 24	8♈53	11 17	18 15	23 8	8 27	16 18	13 29	1 12	1 53
6	10 55 38	15 36 29	20 52	13 9	19 29	23 26	8 36	16 17	13 30	1 13	1 52
7	10 59 34	16 36 33	2♉57	15 2	20 43	23 43	8 45	16 16	13 30	1 14	1 51
8	11 3 31	17 36 35	15 11	16 56	21 57	24 0	8 54	16 15	13 31	1 14	1 50
9	11 7 27	18 36 35	27 38	18 51	23 11	24 17	9 3	16 14	13 32	1 15	1 49
10	11 11 24	19 36 32	10♊21	20 47	24 25	24 33	9 11	16 12	13 32	1 16	1 48
11	11 15 20	20 36 28	23 25	22 44	25 39	24 48	9 19	16 11	13 32	1 17	1 46
12	11 19 17	21 36 21	6♋54	24 42	26 53	25 4	9 27	16 9	13 33	1 18	1 45
13	11 23 14	22 36 12	20 50	26 40	28 7	25 18	9 36	16 8	13 33	1 18	1 44
14	11 27 10	23 36 1	5♌14	28 38	29 21	25 32	9 43	16 6	13 33	1 19	1 43
15	11 31 7	24 35 47	20 4	0♈37	0♓35	25 46	9 51	16 4	13 34	1 20	1 42
16	11 35 3	25 35 31	5♍12	2 36	1 49	25 59	9 59	16 2	13 34	1 20	1 40
17	11 39 0	26 35 14	20 31	4 35	3 3	26 12	10 6	16 0	13 34	1 21	1 39
18	11 42 56	27 34 54	5♎48	6 34	4 17	26 24	10 14	15 58	13R34	1 21	1 38
19	11 46 53	28 34 32	20 52	8 32	5 31	26 36	10 21	15 55	13 34	1 22	1 36
20	11 50 49	29 34 8	5♏34	10 29	6 45	26 47	10 28	15 53	13 34	1 22	1 35
21	11 54 46	0♈33 42	19 49	12 24	7 59	26 58	10 35	15 51	13 34	1 23	1 34
22	11 58 43	1 33 15	3♐34	14 18	9 13	27 8	10 42	15 48	13 33	1 23	1 32
23	12 2 39	2 32 46	16 50	16 10	10 27	27 17	10 49	15 46	13 33	1 24	1 31
24	12 6 36	3 32 15	29 41	17 59	11 41	27 26	10 55	15 43	13 33	1 24	1 29
25	12 10 32	4 31 43	12♑10	19 45	12 55	27 34	11 1	15 40	13 33	1 24	1 28
26	12 14 29	5 31 8	24 23	21 28	14 10	27 42	11 8	15 37	13 32	1 24	1 27
27	12 18 25	6 30 32	6♒25	23 7	15 24	27 49	11 14	15 34	13 32	1 25	1 25
28	12 22 22	7 29 54	18 20	24 42	16 38	27 55	11 20	15 31	13 31	1 25	1 24
29	12 26 18	8 29 15	0♓11	26 12	17 52	28 1	11 25	15 28	13 31	1 25	1 22
30	12 30 15	9 28 33	12 2	27 37	19 6	28 6	11 31	15 25	13 30	1 25	1 21
31	12 34 12	10♈27 49	23♓55	28♈57	20♓20	28♏10	11♑36	15♏22	13♐30	1♑25	1♏19

THE SUN ENTERS THE SIGN OF ARIES ON MAR 20 AT 10:25.

♈ ARIES ♉ TAURUS ♊ GEMINI ♋ CANCER ♌ LEO ♍ VIRGO ♎ LIBRA

SIDEREAL. SUN. MOON. MERCURY. VENUS. MARS. JUPITER. SATURN. URANUS. NEPTUNE. PLUTO.

DAY	TIME	☉	☽	☿	♀	♂	♃	♄	♅	♆	♇
	h m s	° ' "	° '	° '	° '	° '	° '	° '	° '	° '	° '
A 1	12 38 8	11♈27 3	5♈52	0♉11	21♓34	28♏13	11♑42	15♏18	13♐29	1♑25	1♏17
P 2	12 42 5	12 26 16	17 54	1 19	22 48	28 16	11 47	15R15	13R28	1R25	1R16
R 3	12 46 1	13 25 26	0♉ 2	2 21	24 2	28 19	11 52	15 12	13 27	1 25	1 14
I 4	12 49 58	14 24 34	12 18	3 16	25 16	28 20	11 56	15 8	13 27	1 25	1 13
L 5	12 53 54	15 23 40	24 43	4 6	26 30	28R21	12 1	15 5	13 26	1 25	1 11
6	12 57 51	16 22 44	7♊20	4 48	27 44	28 21	12 5	15 1	13 25	1 25	1 9
7	13 1 47	17 21 45	20 11	5 24	28 58	28 20	12 10	14 57	13 24	1 25	1 8
8	13 5 44	18 20 45	3♋18	5 53	0♈12	28 19	12 14	14 53	13 23	1 25	1 6
9	13 9 41	19 19 42	16 45	6 15	1 26	28 16	12 18	14 50	13 22	1 25	1 5
10	13 13 37	20 18 37	0♌34	6 31	2 40	28 13	12 21	14 46	13 21	1 25	1 3
11	13 17 34	21 17 29	14 44	6R40	3 53	28 10	12 25	14 42	13 19	1 24	1 1
12	13 21 30	22 16 19	29 16	6 42	5 7	28 5	12 28	14 38	13 18	1 24	1 0
13	13 25 27	23 15 7	14♍ 5	6 38	6 21	28 0	12 31	14 34	13 17	1 24	0 58
14	13 29 23	24 13 52	29 4	6 28	7 35	27 54	12 34	14 30	13 16	1 23	0 56
15	13 33 20	25 12 36	14♎ 4	6 12	8 49	27 47	12 37	14 26	13 14	1 23	0 55
16	13 37 16	26 11 17	28 57	5 50	10 3	27 40	12 40	14 22	13 13	1 23	0 53
17	13 41 13	27 9 56	13♏34	5 24	11 17	27 31	12 42	14 17	13 12	1 22	0 51
18	13 45 9	28 8 34	27 49	4 54	12 31	27 22	12 45	14 13	13 10	1 22	0 50
19	13 49 6	29 7 10	11♐38	4 20	13 45	27 13	12 47	14 9	13 9	1 21	0 48
20	13 53 3	0♉ 5 44	25 0	3 43	14 59	27 2	12 49	14 5	13 7	1 21	0 46
21	13 56 59	1 4 17	7♑57	3 4	16 12	26 51	12 50	14 0	13 5	1 20	0 44
22	14 0 56	2 2 47	20 32	2 23	17 26	26 39	12 52	13 56	13 4	1 19	0 43
23	14 4 52	3 1 17	2♒49	1 41	18 40	26 26	12 53	13 51	13 2	1 19	0 41
24	14 8 49	3 59 44	14 53	1 0	19 54	26 13	12 55	13 47	13 0	1 18	0 39
25	14 12 45	4 58 10	26 48	0 19	21 8	25 59	12 56	13 43	12 59	1 17	0 38
26	14 16 42	5 56 34	8♓40	29♈40	22 22	25 44	12 56	13 38	12 57	1 17	0 36
27	14 20 38	6 54 57	20 32	29 3	23 36	25 28	12 57	13 34	12 55	1 16	0 34
28	14 24 35	7 53 18	2♈28	28 29	24 50	25 12	12 57	13 29	12 53	1 15	0 33
29	14 28 32	8 51 37	14 30	27 58	26 3	24 55	12R58	13 25	12 51	1 14	0 31
30	14 32 28	9♉49 55	26♈40	27♈31	27♈17	24♏38	12♑58	13♏20	12♐49	1♑14	0♏29

THE SUN ENTERS THE SIGN OF TAURUS ON APR 19 AT 21:39.

DAY	TIME	☉	☽	☿	♀	♂	♃	♄	♅	♆	♇
	h m s	° ' "	° '	° '	° '	° '	° '	° '	° '	° '	° '
M 1	14 36 25	10♉48 11	9♉ 0	27♈ 8	28♈31	24♏20	12♑58	13♏16	12♐47	1♑13	0♏28
A 2	14 40 21	11 46 25	21 31	26R49	29 45	24R 2	12R57	13R11	12R46	1R12	0R26
Y 3	14 44 18	12 44 37	4♊14	26 34	0♉59	23 43	12 57	13 7	12 43	1 11	0 24
4	14 48 14	13 42 48	17 10	26 24	2 13	23 24	12 56	13 2	12 41	1 10	0 23
5	14 52 11	14 40 57	0♋18	26D19	3 26	23 4	12 55	12 57	12 39	1 9	0 21
6	14 56 7	15 39 4	13 41	26 19	4 40	22 44	12 54	12 53	12 37	1 8	0 19
7	15 0 4	16 37 9	27 17	26 23	5 54	22 23	12 53	12 48	12 35	1 7	0 18
8	15 4 1	17 35 12	11♌ 8	26 32	7 8	22 2	12 51	12 44	12 33	1 6	0 16
9	15 7 57	18 33 13	25 14	26 45	8 22	21 41	12 50	12 39	12 31	1 5	0 15
10	15 11 54	19 31 13	9♍32	27 4	9 35	21 20	12 48	12 35	12 29	1 4	0 13
11	15 15 50	20 29 10	23 59	27 26	10 49	20 59	12 46	12 30	12 26	1 3	0 11
12	15 19 47	21 27 5	8♎33	27 53	12 3	20 37	12 44	12 26	12 24	1 2	0 10
13	15 23 43	22 24 59	23 7	28 24	13 17	20 15	12 41	12 22	12 22	1 0	0 8
14	15 27 40	23 22 51	7♏36	28 59	14 30	19 54	12 39	12 17	12 20	0 59	0 7
15	15 31 36	24 20 41	21 53	29 38	15 44	19 32	12 36	12 13	12 17	0 58	0 5
16	15 35 33	25 18 30	5♐54	0♉21	16 58	19 10	12 33	12 8	12 15	0 57	0 4
17	15 39 30	26 16 18	19 34	1 7	18 11	18 49	12 30	12 4	12 13	0 56	0 2
18	15 43 26	27 14 4	2♑53	1 57	19 25	18 27	12 27	12 0	12 10	0 54	0 1
19	15 47 23	28 11 50	15 51	2 50	20 39	18 6	12 23	11 55	12 8	0 53	29♎59
20	15 51 19	29 9 34	28 28	3 47	21 53	17 45	12 20	11 51	12 6	0 52	29 58
21	15 55 16	0♊ 7 16	10♒49	4 47	23 6	17 24	12 16	11 47	12 3	0 50	29 57
22	15 59 12	1 4 58	22 56	5 50	24 20	17 4	12 12	11 43	12 1	0 49	29 55
23	16 3 9	2 2 39	4♓54	6 55	25 34	16 44	12 8	11 39	11 58	0 48	29 54
24	16 7 6	3 0 18	16 47	8 4	26 47	16 24	12 4	11 35	11 56	0 46	29 52
25	16 11 2	3 57 57	28 40	9 16	28 1	16 5	11 59	11 31	11 54	0 45	29 51
26	16 14 59	4 55 34	10♈38	10 30	29 15	15 46	11 55	11 27	11 51	0 44	29 50
27	16 18 55	5 53 11	22 44	11 48	0♊29	15 28	11 50	11 23	11 49	0 42	29 49
28	16 22 52	6 50 47	5♉ 1	13 8	1 42	15 10	11 45	11 19	11 46	0 41	29 47
29	16 26 48	7 48 21	17 33	14 30	2 56	14 53	11 40	11 15	11 44	0 39	29 46
30	16 30 45	8 45 55	0♊19	15 55	4 10	14 36	11 35	11 11	11 41	0 38	29 45
31	16 34 41	9♊43 28	13♊22	17♉23	5♊23	14♏20	11♑29	11♏ 8	11♐39	0♑36	29♎44

THE SUN ENTERS THE SIGN OF GEMINI ON MAY 20 AT 20:58.

DAY	TIME	☉	☽	☿	♀	♂	♃	♄	♅	♆	♇
	h m s	° ' "	° '	° '	° '	° '	° '	° '	° '	° '	° '
J 1	16 38 38	10♊40 59	26♊41	18♉54	6♊37	14♏ 5	11♑24	11♏ 4	11♐36	0♑35	29♎42
U 2	16 42 35	11 38 30	10♋15	20 27	7 51	13R50	11R18	11R 0	11R34	0R33	29R41
N 3	16 46 31	12 35 59	24 1	22 2	9 5	13 37	11 12	10 57	11 31	0 32	29 40
E 4	16 50 28	13 33 27	7♌58	23 40	10 18	13 23	11 7	10 53	11 29	0 30	29 39
5	16 54 24	14 30 54	22 3	25 21	11 32	13 11	11 1	10 50	11 26	0 29	29 38
6	16 58 21	15 28 20	6♍14	27 4	12 46	12 59	10 54	10 47	11 24	0 27	29 37
7	17 2 17	16 25 44	20 28	28 49	13 59	12 49	10 48	10 43	11 21	0 26	29 36
8	17 6 14	17 23 7	4♎42	0♊37	15 13	12 39	10 42	10 40	11 19	0 24	29 35
9	17 10 10	18 20 30	18 55	2 28	16 27	12 29	10 35	10 37	11 16	0 23	29 34
10	17 14 7	19 17 51	3♏ 3	4 21	17 41	12 21	10 29	10 34	11 14	0 21	29 33
11	17 18 4	20 15 11	17 3	6 16	18 54	12 13	10 22	10 31	11 12	0 19	29 32
12	17 22 0	21 12 30	0♐53	8 14	20 8	12 7	10 15	10 28	11 9	0 18	29 31
13	17 25 57	22 9 48	14 31	10 13	21 22	12 1	10 8	10 25	11 7	0 16	29 30
14	17 29 53	23 7 6	27 54	12 15	22 35	11 55	10 1	10 23	11 4	0 15	29 29
15	17 33 50	24 4 23	11♑ 1	14 19	23 49	11 51	9 54	10 20	11 2	0 13	29 29
16	17 37 46	25 1 40	23 51	16 25	25 3	11 48	9 47	10 18	11 0	0 11	29 28
17	17 41 43	25 58 56	6♒24	18 32	26 16	11 45	9 40	10 15	10 57	0 10	29 27
18	17 45 39	26 56 12	18 44	20 40	27 30	11 43	9 33	10 13	10 55	0 8	29 26
19	17 49 36	27 53 27	0♓51	22 50	28 44	11D42	9 25	10 10	10 53	0 7	29 26
20	17 53 33	28 50 42	12 49	25 1	29 57	11 42	9 18	10 8	10 50	0 5	29 25
21	17 57 29	29 47 57	24 43	27 12	1♋11	11 43	9 11	10 6	10 48	0 3	29 25
22	18 1 26	0♋45 12	6♈36	29 23	2 25	11 44	9 3	10 4	10 46	0 2	29 24
23	18 5 22	1 42 26	18 34	1♋35	3 39	11 46	8 56	10 2	10 43	0 0	29 23
24	18 9 19	2 39 40	0♉41	3 46	4 52	11 49	8 48	10 0	10 41	29♐58	29 23
25	18 13 15	3 36 55	13 2	5 57	6 6	11 53	8 40	9 58	10 39	29 57	29 22
26	18 17 12	4 34 9	25 40	8 7	7 20	11 57	8 33	9 56	10 37	29 55	29 22
27	18 21 8	5 31 23	8♊39	10 17	8 34	12 3	8 25	9 55	10 34	29 54	29 21
28	18 25 5	6 28 37	21 58	12 25	9 47	12 9	8 17	9 53	10 32	29 52	29 21
29	18 29 2	7 25 51	5♋39	14 31	11 1	12 16	8 10	9 52	10 30	29 50	29 21
30	18 32 58	8♋23 5	19♋38	16♋36	12♋15	12♏23	8♑ 2	9♏51	10♐28	29♐49	29♎20

THE SUN ENTERS THE SIGN OF CANCER ON JUN 21 AT 05:03.

♏ SCORPIO ♐ SAGITTARIUS ♑ CAPRICORN ♒ AQUARIUS ♓ PISCES

SIDEREAL TIME · SUN · MOON · MERCURY · VENUS · MARS · JUPITER · SATURN · URANUS · NEPTUNE · PLUTO

DAY	TIME	☉	☽	☿	♀	♂	♃	♄	♅	♆	♇
	h m s	° ' "	° '	° '	° '	° '	° '	° '	° '	° '	° '
J 1	18 36 55	9♋20 19	3♌52	18♋40	13♋29	12♏32	7♑54	9♏49	10♐26	29♐47	29♎20
U 2	18 40 51	10 17 32	18 16	20 42	14 42	12 41	7R47	9R48	10R24	29R46	29R20
L 3	18 44 48	11 14 45	2♍44	22 42	15 56	12 51	7 39	9 47	10 22	29 44	29 20
Y 4	18 48 44	12 11 58	17 10	24 40	17 10	13 1	7 31	9 46	10 20	29 42	29 19
5	18 52 41	13 9 11	1♎31	26 37	18 24	13 12	7 24	9 45	10 18	29 41	29 19
6	18 56 38	14 6 23	15 42	28 31	19 37	13 24	7 16	9 45	10 16	29 39	29 19
7	19 0 34	15 3 34	29 43	0♌23	20 51	13 37	7 8	9 44	10 14	29 38	29 19
8	19 4 31	16 0 46	13♏32	2 14	22 5	13 50	7 1	9 43	10 12	29 36	29 19
9	19 8 27	16 57 58	27 9	4 2	23 19	14 4	6 53	9 43	10 11	29 35	29D19
10	19 12 24	17 55 9	10♐34	5 49	24 33	14 18	6 46	9 43	10 9	29 33	29 19
11	19 16 20	18 52 21	23 48	7 33	25 46	14 33	6 39	9 42	10 7	29 32	29 19
12	19 20 17	19 49 32	6♑49	9 16	27 0	14 49	6 31	9 42	10 5	29 30	29 19
13	19 24 13	20 46 44	19 38	10 57	28 14	15 5	6 24	9D42	10 4	29 29	29 19
14	19 28 10	21 43 56	2♒15	12 35	29 28	15 22	6 17	9 42	10 2	29 27	29 19
15	19 32 7	22 41 9	14 39	14 12	0♌41	15 39	6 10	9 42	10 0	29 26	29 19
16	19 36 3	23 38 21	26 53	15 46	1 55	15 57	6 3	9 42	9 59	29 24	29 20
17	19 40 0	24 35 35	8♓56	17 19	3 9	16 16	5 56	9 43	9 57	29 23	29 20
18	19 43 56	25 32 48	20 53	18 50	4 23	16 35	5 49	9 43	9 56	29 21	29 20
19	19 47 53	26 30 3	2♈45	20 18	5 37	16 54	5 42	9 44	9 54	29 20	29 20
20	19 51 49	27 27 18	14 37	21 45	6 50	17 14	5 35	9 44	9 53	29 19	29 21
21	19 55 46	28 24 34	26 33	23 9	8 4	17 35	5 29	9 45	9 52	29 17	29 21
22	19 59 42	29 21 50	8♉39	24 32	9 18	17 56	5 22	9 46	9 50	29 16	29 22
23	20 3 39	0♌19 8	20 59	25 52	10 32	18 18	5 16	9 47	9 49	29 15	29 22
24	20 7 36	1 16 26	3♊38	27 10	11 46	18 40	5 10	9 48	9 48	29 13	29 22
25	20 11 32	2 13 46	16 40	28 26	13 0	19 2	5 4	9 49	9 47	29 12	29 23
26	20 15 29	3 11 6	0♋ 9	29 39	14 13	19 25	4 58	9 50	9 45	29 11	29 24
27	20 19 25	4 8 27	14 3	0♍51	15 27	19 49	4 52	9 51	9 44	29 9	29 24
28	20 23 22	5 5 49	28 22	2 0	16 41	20 13	4 46	9 53	9 43	29 8	29 25
29	20 27 18	6 3 12	13♌ 0	3 6	17 55	20 37	4 40	9 54	9 42	29 7	29 25
30	20 31 15	7 0 35	27 50	4 10	19 9	21 2	4 35	9 56	9 41	29 6	29 26
31	20 35 11	7♌57 59	12♍43	5♍11	20♌23	21♏27	4♑30	9♏57	9♐40	29♐ 5	29♎27

THE SUN ENTERS THE SIGN OF LEO ON JUL 22 AT 15:59.

DAY	TIME	☉	☽	☿	♀	♂	♃	♄	♅	♆	♇
	h m s	° ' "	° '	° '	° '	° '	° '	° '	° '	° '	° '
A 1	20 39 8	8♌55 24	27♍31	6♍ 9	21♌36	21♏53	4♑24	9♏59	9♐39	29♐ 3	29♎28
U 2	20 43 5	9 52 49	12♎ 6	7 5	22 50	22 19	4R19	10 1	9R39	29R 2	29 28
G 3	20 47 1	10 50 15	26 25	7 57	24 4	22 46	4 15	10 3	9 38	29 1	29 29
U 4	20 50 58	11 47 41	10♏25	8 46	25 18	23 12	4 10	10 5	9 37	29 0	29 30
S 5	20 54 54	12 45 9	24 6	9 32	26 32	23 40	4 5	10 7	9 36	28 59	29 31
T 6	20 58 51	13 42 37	7♐29	10 14	27 46	24 7	4 1	10 9	9 36	28 58	29 32
7	21 2 47	14 40 5	20 37	10 52	28 59	24 35	3 57	10 12	9 35	28 57	29 33
8	21 6 44	15 37 35	3♑31	11 27	0♍13	25 4	3 52	10 14	9 35	28 56	29 34
9	21 10 40	16 35 5	16 13	11 58	1 27	25 32	3 49	10 17	9 34	28 55	29 35
10	21 14 37	17 32 36	28 44	12 24	2 41	26 1	3 45	10 19	9 34	28 54	29 36
11	21 18 34	18 30 9	11♒ 6	12 46	3 55	26 31	3 41	10 22	9 33	28 53	29 37
12	21 22 30	19 27 42	23 19	13 3	5 9	27 1	3 38	10 25	9 33	28 52	29 38
13	21 26 27	20 25 17	5♓25	13 15	6 22	27 31	3 35	10 28	9 33	28 51	29 39
14	21 30 23	21 22 52	17 23	13R22	7 36	28 1	3 32	10 31	9 32	28 51	29 40
15	21 34 20	22 20 29	29 16	13 24	8 50	28 32	3 29	10 34	9 32	28 50	29 41
16	21 38 16	23 18 8	11♈ 6	13 20	10 4	29 3	3 26	10 37	9 32	28 49	29 43
17	21 42 13	24 15 48	22 57	13 10	11 18	29 34	3 23	10 40	9 32	28 48	29 44
18	21 46 9	25 13 29	4♉52	12 55	12 31	0♐ 5	3 21	10 43	9D32	28 48	29 45
19	21 50 6	26 11 12	16 55	12 35	13 45	0 37	3 19	10 47	9 32	28 47	29 47
20	21 54 3	27 8 57	29 12	12 8	14 59	1 10	3 17	10 50	9 32	28 46	29 48
21	21 57 59	28 6 44	11♊48	11 37	16 13	1 42	3 15	10 54	9 32	28 46	29 49
22	22 1 56	29 4 32	24 49	11 0	17 27	2 15	3 14	10 57	9 32	28 45	29 51
23	22 5 52	0♍ 2 22	8♋16	10 18	18 40	2 48	3 12	11 1	9 33	28 44	29 52
24	22 9 49	1 0 14	22 14	9 32	19 54	3 21	3 11	11 5	9 33	28 44	29 54
25	22 13 45	1 58 7	6♌40	8 43	21 8	3 54	3 10	11 9	9 33	28 43	29 55
26	22 17 42	2 56 2	21 30	7 50	22 22	4 28	3 9	11 13	9 34	28 43	29 57
27	22 21 38	3 53 58	6♍36	6 56	23 35	5 2	3 8	11 17	9 34	28 42	29 58
28	22 25 35	4 51 56	21 48	6 1	24 49	5 37	3 8	11 21	9 34	28 42	0♏ 0
29	22 29 32	5 49 55	6♎56	5 6	26 3	6 11	3D 8	11 25	9 35	28 42	0 1
30	22 33 28	6 47 56	21 50	4 12	27 17	6 46	3 8	11 29	9 36	28 41	0 3
31	22 37 25	7♍45 58	6♏23	3♍21	28♍31	7♐21	3♑ 8	11♏34	9♐36	28♐41	0♏ 5

THE SUN ENTERS THE SIGN OF VIRGO ON AUG 22 AT 23:01.

DAY	TIME	☉	☽	☿	♀	♂	♃	♄	♅	♆	♇
	h m s	° ' "	° '	° '	° '	° '	° '	° '	° '	° '	° '
S 1	22 41 21	8♍44 2	20♏31	2♍34	29♍44	7♐56	3♑ 8	11♏38	9♐37	28♐41	0♏ 6
E 2	22 45 18	9 42 7	4♐14	1R51	0♎58	8 32	3 8	11 43	9 38	28R40	0 8
P 3	22 49 14	10 40 13	17 35	1 14	2 12	9 8	3 9	11 47	9 38	28 40	0 10
T 4	22 53 11	11 38 21	0♑35	0 45	3 25	9 44	3 10	11 52	9 39	28 40	0 11
E 5	22 57 7	12 36 30	13 17	0 22	4 39	10 20	3 11	11 56	9 40	28 40	0 13
M 6	23 1 4	13 34 41	25 46	0 8	5 53	10 56	3 12	12 1	9 41	28 40	0 15
B 7	23 5 1	14 32 53	8♒ 5	0D 2	7 6	11 33	3 14	12 6	9 42	28 39	0 17
E 8	23 8 57	15 31 7	20 15	0 5	8 20	12 10	3 15	12 11	9 43	28 39	0 19
R 9	23 12 54	16 29 22	2♓18	0 17	9 34	12 47	3 17	12 16	9 44	28D39	0 21
10	23 16 50	17 27 39	14 15	0 38	10 47	13 24	3 19	12 21	9 45	28 39	0 22
11	23 20 47	18 25 58	26 9	1 7	12 1	14 1	3 21	12 26	9 47	28 39	0 24
12	23 24 43	19 24 18	8♈ 0	1 46	13 15	14 39	3 24	12 31	9 48	28 39	0 26
13	23 28 40	20 22 41	19 50	2 32	14 28	15 17	3 26	12 37	9 49	28 39	0 28
14	23 32 36	21 21 6	1♉42	3 27	15 42	15 55	3 29	12 42	9 50	28 40	0 30
15	23 36 33	22 19 32	13 38	4 29	16 55	16 33	3 32	12 47	9 52	28 40	0 32
16	23 40 29	23 18 1	25 43	5 38	18 9	17 11	3 35	12 53	9 53	28 40	0 34
17	23 44 26	24 16 32	7♊59	6 53	19 23	17 49	3 38	12 58	9 55	28 40	0 36
18	23 48 23	25 15 5	20 33	8 14	20 36	18 28	3 42	13 4	9 56	28 40	0 38
19	23 52 19	26 13 41	3♋29	9 40	21 50	19 7	3 45	13 9	9 58	28 41	0 40
20	23 56 16	27 12 19	16 51	11 11	23 3	19 46	3 49	13 15	9 59	28 41	0 42
21	0 0 12	28 10 58	0♌41	12 46	24 17	20 25	3 53	13 21	10 1	28 41	0 45
22	0 4 9	29 9 41	15 1	14 23	25 30	21 4	3 57	13 26	10 3	28 42	0 47
23	0 8 5	0♎ 8 25	29 48	16 4	26 44	21 44	4 2	13 32	10 5	28 42	0 49
24	0 12 2	1 7 11	14♍54	17 47	27 57	22 24	4 6	13 38	10 6	28 43	0 51
25	0 15 58	2 5 59	0♎12	19 32	29 11	23 3	4 11	13 44	10 8	28 43	0 53
26	0 19 55	3 4 50	15 29	21 18	0♏24	23 43	4 16	13 50	10 10	28 44	0 55
27	0 23 52	4 3 42	0♏34	23 5	1 38	24 23	4 21	13 56	10 12	28 44	0 58
28	0 27 48	5 2 36	15 20	24 53	2 51	25 4	4 26	14 2	10 14	28 45	1 0
29	0 31 45	6 1 32	29 41	26 42	4 5	25 44	4 31	14 8	10 16	28 45	1 2
30	0 35 41	7♎ 0 30	13♐34	28♍31	5♏18	26♐25	4♑37	14♏14	10♐18	28♐46	1♏ 4

THE SUN ENTERS THE SIGN OF LIBRA ON SEP 22 AT 20:34.

♈ ARIES ♉ TAURUS ♊ GEMINI ♋ CANCER ♌ LEO ♍ VIRGO ♎ LIBRA

SIDEREAL · SUN. · MOON. · MERCURY. · VENUS. · MARS. · JUPITER. · SATURN. · URANUS. · NEPTUNE. · PLUTO.

DAY	TIME	☉	☽	☿	♀	♂	♃	♄	♅	♆	♇
	h m s	° ' "	° '	° '	° '	° '	° '	° '	° '	° '	° '
O 1	0 39 38	7≏59 30	27♐ 0	0≏19	6♏31	27♐ 5	4♑42	14♏21	10♐20	28♐47	1♏ 6
C 2	0 43 34	8 58 31	10♑ 1	2 8	7 45	27 46	4 48	14 27	10 23	28 47	1 9
T 3	0 47 31	9 57 34	22 42	3 56	8 58	28 27	4 54	14 33	10 25	28 48	1 11
O 4	0 51 27	10 56 39	5♒ 6	5 44	10 11	29 8	5 0	14 40	10 27	28 49	1 13
B 5	0 55 24	11 55 46	17 18	7 31	11 25	29 50	5 7	14 46	10 29	28 50	1 16
E 6	0 59 21	12 54 54	29 20	9 18	12 38	0♑31	5 13	14 52	10 32	28 50	1 18
R 7	1 3 17	13 54 4	11♓16	11 5	13 51	1 12	5 20	14 59	10 34	28 51	1 20
8	1 7 14	14 53 17	23 9	12 50	15 5	1 54	5 26	15 5	10 36	28 52	1 23
9	1 11 10	15 52 31	5♈ 1	14 35	16 18	2 36	5 33	15 12	10 39	28 53	1 25
10	1 15 7	16 51 47	16 52	16 19	17 31	3 18	5 40	15 18	10 41	28 54	1 27
11	1 19 3	17 51 5	28 46	18 3	18 44	4 0	5 48	15 25	10 44	28 55	1 30
12	1 23 0	18 50 25	10♉43	19 46	19 58	4 42	5 55	15 32	10 47	28 56	1 32
13	1 26 56	19 49 47	22 47	21 28	21 11	5 24	6 2	15 38	10 49	28 57	1 34
14	1 30 53	20 49 12	4♊59	23 9	22 24	6 6	6 10	15 45	10 52	28 58	1 37
15	1 34 50	21 48 39	17 22	24 50	23 37	6 48	6 18	15 52	10 54	28 59	1 39
16	1 38 46	22 48 8	29 59	26 30	24 50	7 31	6 26	15 59	10 57	29 1	1 42
17	1 42 43	23 47 40	12♋56	28 9	26 3	8 13	6 34	16 6	11 0	29 2	1 44
18	1 46 39	24 47 14	26 13	29 48	27 16	8 56	6 42	16 12	11 3	29 3	1 46
19	1 50 36	25 46 50	9♌55	1♏26	28 29	9 39	6 50	16 19	11 6	29 4	1 49
20	1 54 32	26 46 28	24 2	3 3	29 42	10 22	6 59	16 26	11 8	29 5	1 51
21	1 58 29	27 46 9	8♍33	4 40	0♐55	11 5	7 7	16 33	11 11	29 7	1 54
22	2 2 25	28 45 52	23 24	6 16	2 8	11 48	7 16	16 40	11 14	29 8	1 56
23	2 6 22	29 45 37	8≏28	7 51	3 21	12 31	7 25	16 47	11 17	29 9	1 59
24	2 10 19	0♏45 24	23 37	9 26	4 34	13 14	7 34	16 54	11 20	29 11	2 1
25	2 14 15	1 45 13	8♏40	11 1	5 47	13 58	7 43	17 1	11 23	29 12	2 3
26	2 18 12	2 45 4	23 29	12 35	7 0	14 41	7 52	17 8	11 26	29 14	2 6
27	2 22 8	3 44 58	7♐57	14 8	8 13	15 25	8 2	17 15	11 29	29 15	2 8
28	2 26 5	4 44 53	21 58	15 41	9 26	16 8	8 11	17 22	11 32	29 16	2 11
29	2 30 1	5 44 49	5♑33	17 13	10 39	16 52	8 21	17 29	11 36	29 18	2 13
30	2 33 58	6 44 47	18 42	18 45	11 52	17 36	8 30	17 36	11 39	29 20	2 16
31	2 37 54	7♏44 47	1♒27	20♏17	13♐ 5	18♑20	8♑40	17♏43	11♐42	29♐21	2♏18

THE SUN ENTERS THE SIGN OF SCORPIO ON OCT 23 AT 05:47.

DAY	TIME	☉	☽	☿	♀	♂	♃	♄	♅	♆	♇
	h m s	° ' "	° '	° '	° '	° '	° '	° '	° '	° '	° '
N 1	2 41 51	8♏44 49	13♒53	21♏48	14♐17	19♑ 4	8♑50	17♏50	11♐45	29♐23	2♏20
O 2	2 45 48	9 44 52	26 4	23 18	15 30	19 48	9 0	17 58	11 48	29 24	2 23
V 3	2 49 44	10 44 56	8♓ 4	24 48	16 43	20 32	9 10	18 5	11 52	29 26	2 25
E 4	2 53 41	11 45 3	19 57	26 18	17 56	21 16	9 21	18 12	11 55	29 28	2 28
M 5	2 57 37	12 45 10	1♈48	27 47	19 8	22 0	9 31	18 19	11 58	29 29	2 30
B 6	3 1 34	13 45 20	13 39	29 15	20 21	22 45	9 41	18 26	12 2	29 31	2 32
E 7	3 5 30	14 45 31	25 34	0♐43	21 33	23 29	9 52	18 33	12 5	29 33	2 35
R 8	3 9 27	15 45 44	7♉34	2 11	22 46	24 13	10 3	18 41	12 8	29 34	2 37
9	3 13 23	16 45 58	19 41	3 38	23 58	24 58	10 13	18 48	12 12	29 36	2 40
10	3 17 20	17 46 15	1♊58	5 4	25 11	25 42	10 24	18 55	12 15	29 38	2 42
11	3 21 17	18 46 33	14 25	6 30	26 23	26 27	10 35	19 2	12 19	29 40	2 44
12	3 25 13	19 46 53	27 3	7 55	27 36	27 12	10 46	19 9	12 22	29 42	2 47
13	3 29 10	20 47 15	9♋55	9 20	28 48	27 56	10 58	19 16	12 25	29 43	2 49
14	3 33 6	21 47 39	23 2	10 43	0♑ 0	28 41	11 9	19 24	12 29	29 45	2 51
15	3 37 3	22 48 5	6♌24	12 6	1 12	29 26	11 20	19 31	12 32	29 47	2 54
16	3 40 59	23 48 32	20 4	13 28	2 25	0♒11	11 32	19 38	12 36	29 49	2 56
17	3 44 56	24 49 2	4♍ 1	14 48	3 37	0 56	11 43	19 45	12 40	29 51	2 58
18	3 48 52	25 49 33	18 15	16 8	4 49	1 41	11 55	19 52	12 43	29 53	3 0
19	3 52 49	26 50 6	2≏44	17 26	6 1	2 26	12 6	20 0	12 47	29 55	3 3
20	3 56 46	27 50 41	17 23	18 43	7 13	3 11	12 18	20 7	12 50	29 57	3 5
21	4 0 42	28 51 18	2♏ 8	19 58	8 25	3 56	12 30	20 14	12 54	29 59	3 7
22	4 4 39	29 51 56	16 52	21 11	9 37	4 41	12 42	20 21	12 57	0♑ 1	3 9
23	4 8 35	0♐52 36	1♐28	22 21	10 49	5 26	12 54	20 28	13 1	0 3	3 12
24	4 12 32	1 53 17	15 49	23 30	12 1	6 12	13 6	20 35	13 5	0 5	3 14
25	4 16 28	2 54 0	29 50	24 35	13 13	6 57	13 18	20 42	13 8	0 7	3 16
26	4 20 25	3 54 44	13♑28	25 37	14 24	7 42	13 30	20 49	13 12	0 9	3 18
27	4 24 21	4 55 29	26 42	26 35	15 36	8 28	13 43	20 56	13 16	0 11	3 20
28	4 28 18	5 56 15	9♒32	27 29	16 48	9 13	13 55	21 3	13 19	0 13	3 23
29	4 32 15	6 57 2	22 3	28 18	17 59	9 59	14 8	21 10	13 23	0 15	3 25
30	4 36 11	7♐57 50	4♓16	29♐ 1	19♑10	10♒44	14♑20	21♏17	13♐27	0♑18	3♏27

THE SUN ENTERS THE SIGN OF SAGITTARIUS ON NOV 22 AT 03:12.

DAY	TIME	☉	☽	☿	♀	♂	♃	♄	♅	♆	♇
	h m s	° ' "	° '	° '	° '	° '	° '	° '	° '	° '	° '
D 1	4 40 8	8♐58 39	16♓17	29♐38	20♑22	11♒30	14♑33	21♏24	13♐30	0♑20	3♏29
E 2	4 44 4	9 59 29	28 10	0♑ 9	21 33	12 15	14 45	21 31	13 34	0 22	3 31
C 3	4 48 1	11 0 19	10♈ 0	0 31	22 44	13 1	14 58	21 38	13 38	0 24	3 33
E 4	4 51 57	12 1 11	21 52	0R44	23 56	13 46	15 11	21 45	13 41	0 26	3 35
M 5	4 55 54	13 2 3	3♉49	0 49	25 7	14 32	15 24	21 52	13 45	0 28	3 37
B 6	4 59 50	14 2 57	15 56	0 42	26 18	15 18	15 37	21 59	13 49	0 31	3 39
E 7	5 3 47	15 3 51	28 14	0 25	27 28	16 3	15 49	22 6	13 52	0 33	3 41
R 8	5 7 44	16 4 46	10♊46	29♐57	28 39	16 49	16 2	22 13	13 56	0 35	3 43
9	5 11 40	17 5 43	23 33	29 17	29 50	17 35	16 16	22 19	14 0	0 37	3 45
10	5 15 37	18 6 40	6♋34	28 26	1♒ 0	18 20	16 29	22 26	14 3	0 39	3 47
11	5 19 33	19 7 38	19 50	27 25	2 11	19 6	16 42	22 33	14 7	0 42	3 49
12	5 23 30	20 8 37	3♌18	26 15	3 21	19 52	16 55	22 39	14 11	0 44	3 50
13	5 27 26	21 9 38	16 58	24 59	4 32	20 37	17 8	22 46	14 14	0 46	3 52
14	5 31 23	22 10 39	0♍49	23 38	5 42	21 23	17 22	22 53	14 18	0 48	3 54
15	5 35 20	23 11 41	14 48	22 14	6 52	22 9	17 35	22 59	14 22	0 51	3 56
16	5 39 16	24 12 44	28 54	20 52	8 2	22 55	17 48	23 6	14 25	0 53	3 58
17	5 43 13	25 13 48	13≏ 5	19 34	9 11	23 41	18 2	23 12	14 29	0 55	3 59
18	5 47 9	26 14 53	27 20	18 22	10 21	24 26	18 15	23 19	14 32	0 57	4 1
19	5 51 6	27 15 59	11♏37	17 18	11 31	25 12	18 29	23 25	14 36	1 0	4 3
20	5 55 2	28 17 6	25 52	16 24	12 40	25 58	18 42	23 31	14 40	1 2	4 4
21	5 58 59	29 18 14	10♐ 2	15 40	13 49	26 44	18 56	23 38	14 43	1 4	4 6
22	6 2 55	0♑19 22	24 1	15 7	14 59	27 30	19 9	23 44	14 47	1 6	4 7
23	6 6 52	1 20 31	7♑48	14 44	16 8	28 16	19 23	23 50	14 50	1 9	4 9
24	6 10 49	2 21 40	21 17	14D33	17 16	29 1	19 37	23 56	14 54	1 11	4 11
25	6 14 45	3 22 50	4♒28	14 31	18 25	29 47	19 51	24 2	14 58	1 13	4 12
26	6 18 42	4 24 0	17 18	14 38	19 34	0♓33	20 4	24 9	15 1	1 16	4 13
27	6 22 38	5 25 9	29 50	14 55	20 42	1 19	20 18	24 15	15 5	1 18	4 15
28	6 26 35	6 26 19	12♓ 5	15 19	21 50	2 5	20 32	24 21	15 8	1 20	4 16
29	6 30 31	7 27 28	24 7	15 50	22 58	2 51	20 46	24 26	15 12	1 22	4 18
30	6 34 28	8 28 38	6♈ 1	16 27	24 6	3 37	21 0	24 32	15 15	1 25	4 19
31	6 38 24	9♑29 47	17♈50	17♐10	25♒14	4♓22	21♑14	24♏38	15♐19	1♑27	4♏20

THE SUN ENTERS THE SIGN OF CAPRICORN ON DEC 21 AT 16:24.

♏ SCORPIO ♐ SAGITTARIUS ♑ CAPRICORN ♒ AQUARIUS ♓ PISCES

1985

SIDEREAL SUN. MOON. MERCURY. VENUS. MARS. JUPITER. SATURN. URANUS. NEPTUNE. PLUTO.

DAY	TIME	☉	☽	☿	♀	♂	♃	♄	♅	♆	♇
	h m s	° ' "	° '	° '	° '	° '	° '	° '	° '	° '	° '
J 1	6 42 21	10♑30 57	29♈42	17♐58	26♒21	5♓ 8	21♑27	24♏44	15♐22	1♑29	4♏22
A 2	6 46 18	11 32 6	11♉40	18 51	27 28	5 54	21 41	24 50	15 25	1 31	4 23
N 3	6 50 14	12 33 15	23 49	19 48	28 35	6 40	21 55	24 55	15 29	1 34	4 24
U 4	6 54 11	13 34 24	6♊14	20 48	29 42	7 26	22 9	25 1	15 32	1 36	4 25
A 5	6 58 7	14 35 33	18 58	21 51	0♓49	8 12	22 23	25 6	15 35	1 38	4 26
R 6	7 2 4	15 36 41	2♋ 2	22 57	1 55	8 57	22 37	25 12	15 39	1 40	4 28
Y 7	7 6 0	16 37 49	15 26	24 6	3 1	9 43	22 51	25 17	15 42	1 43	4 29
8	7 9 57	17 38 58	29 9	25 17	4 7	10 29	23 5	25 22	15 45	1 45	4 30
9	7 13 53	18 40 6	13♌ 6	26 30	5 13	11 15	23 19	25 28	15 49	1 47	4 31
10	7 17 50	19 41 13	27 14	27 44	6 18	12 0	23 33	25 33	15 52	1 49	4 32
11	7 21 47	20 42 21	11♍28	29 0	7 23	12 46	23 47	25 38	15 55	1 51	4 33
12	7 25 43	21 43 29	25 43	0♑18	8 27	13 32	24 1	25 43	15 58	1 53	4 34
13	7 29 40	22 44 36	9♎55	1 37	9 32	14 18	24 15	25 48	16 1	1 56	4 34
14	7 33 36	23 45 44	24 3	2 58	10 36	15 3	24 30	25 53	16 4	1 58	4 35
15	7 37 33	24 46 51	8♏ 6	4 19	11 40	15 49	24 44	25 58	16 7	2 0	4 36
16	7 41 29	25 47 59	22 2	5 42	12 43	16 35	24 58	26 2	16 11	2 2	4 37
17	7 45 26	26 49 6	5♐51	7 5	13 46	17 20	25 12	26 7	16 14	2 4	4 38
18	7 49 22	27 50 13	19 33	8 29	14 49	18 6	25 26	26 12	16 17	2 6	4 38
19	7 53 19	28 51 20	3♑ 6	9 55	15 52	18 51	25 40	26 16	16 20	2 8	4 39
20	7 57 16	29 52 26	16 28	11 21	16 54	19 37	25 54	26 21	16 22	2 10	4 40
21	8 1 12	0♒53 31	29 39	12 48	17 55	20 23	26 8	26 25	16 25	2 12	4 40
22	8 5 9	1 54 36	12♒35	14 15	18 57	21 8	26 22	26 29	16 28	2 15	4 41
23	8 9 5	2 55 40	25 17	15 44	19 58	21 54	26 36	26 33	16 31	2 17	4 41
24	8 13 2	3 56 43	7♓43	17 13	20 58	22 39	26 50	26 38	16 34	2 19	4 42
25	8 16 58	4 57 45	19 56	18 42	21 58	23 25	27 4	26 42	16 37	2 21	4 42
26	8 20 55	5 58 46	1♈56	20 13	22 58	24 10	27 18	26 46	16 39	2 23	4 43
27	8 24 52	6 59 46	13 49	21 44	23 57	24 55	27 32	26 49	16 42	2 24	4 43
28	8 28 48	8 0 45	25 37	23 16	24 55	25 41	27 46	26 53	16 45	2 26	4 43
29	8 32 45	9 1 43	7♉27	24 48	25 54	26 26	28 0	26 57	16 47	2 28	4 44
30	8 36 41	10 2 40	19 23	26 21	26 51	27 12	28 14	27 1	16 50	2 30	4 44
31	8 40 38	11♒ 3 35	1♊31	27♑55	27♓48	27♓57	28♑28	27♏ 4	16♐52	2♑32	4♏44

THE SUN ENTERS THE SIGN OF AQUARIUS ON JAN 20 AT 02:58.

DAY	TIME	☉	☽	☿	♀	♂	♃	♄	♅	♆	♇
	h m s	° ' "	° '	° '	° '	° '	° '	° '	° '	° '	° '
F 1	8 44 34	12♒ 4 29	13♊57	29♑29	28♓45	28♓42	28♑42	27♏ 8	16♐55	2♑34	4♏44
E 2	8 48 31	13 5 22	26 44	1♒ 5	29 40	29 27	28 56	27 11	16 57	2 36	4 45
B 3	8 52 27	14 6 14	9♋57	2 40	0♈36	0♈13	29 10	27 14	17 0	2 38	4 45
R 4	8 56 24	15 7 4	23 35	4 17	1 30	0 58	29 23	27 17	17 2	2 39	4 45
U 5	9 0 21	16 7 53	7♌38	5 54	2 24	1 43	29 37	27 20	17 4	2 41	4R45
A 6	9 4 17	17 8 41	22 0	7 32	3 17	2 28	29 51	27 23	17 7	2 43	4 45
R 7	9 8 14	18 9 27	6♍37	9 11	4 10	3 13	0♒ 5	27 26	17 9	2 45	4 45
Y 8	9 12 10	19 10 12	21 19	10 51	5 2	3 58	0 19	27 29	17 11	2 46	4 45
9	9 16 7	20 10 57	5♎59	12 31	5 53	4 43	0 32	27 32	17 13	2 48	4 45
10	9 20 3	21 11 40	20 31	14 12	6 43	5 28	0 46	27 34	17 15	2 50	4 45
11	9 24 0	22 12 22	4♏51	15 54	7 32	6 13	1 0	27 37	17 17	2 51	4 44
12	9 27 56	23 13 3	18 56	17 37	8 21	6 58	1 13	27 39	17 19	2 53	4 44
13	9 31 53	24 13 43	2♐46	19 21	9 8	7 43	1 27	27 42	17 21	2 55	4 44
14	9 35 50	25 14 22	16 22	21 6	9 55	8 28	1 40	27 44	17 23	2 56	4 44
15	9 39 46	26 15 0	29 45	22 51	10 41	9 12	1 54	27 46	17 25	2 58	4 43
16	9 43 43	27 15 37	12♑55	24 37	11 25	9 57	2 7	27 48	17 27	2 59	4 43
17	9 47 39	28 16 12	25 55	26 24	12 9	10 42	2 21	27 50	17 29	3 1	4 43
18	9 51 36	29 16 46	8♒43	28 12	12 52	11 27	2 34	27 52	17 31	3 2	4 42
19	9 55 32	0♓17 18	21 21	0♓ 1	13 33	12 11	2 47	27 54	17 32	3 4	4 42
20	9 59 29	1 17 49	3♓48	1 51	14 14	12 56	3 0	27 55	17 34	3 5	4 41
21	10 3 25	2 18 19	16 3	3 42	14 53	13 40	3 14	27 57	17 35	3 7	4 41
22	10 7 22	3 18 46	28 8	5 33	15 31	14 25	3 27	27 58	17 37	3 8	4 40
23	10 11 19	4 19 12	10♈ 5	7 25	16 8	15 9	3 40	28 0	17 38	3 9	4 40
24	10 15 15	5 19 36	21 55	9 18	16 43	15 54	3 53	28 1	17 40	3 11	4 39
25	10 19 12	6 19 58	3♉42	11 11	17 17	16 38	4 6	28 2	17 41	3 12	4 39
26	10 23 8	7 20 18	15 30	13 5	17 49	17 23	4 19	28 3	17 43	3 13	4 38
27	10 27 5	8 20 36	27 24	14 59	18 20	18 7	4 32	28 4	17 44	3 14	4 37
28	10 31 1	9♓20 53	9♊30	16♓53	18♈49	18♈51	4♒45	28♏ 5	17♐45	3♑15	4♏36

THE SUN ENTERS THE SIGN OF PISCES ON FEB 18 AT 17:08.

DAY	TIME	☉	☽	☿	♀	♂	♃	♄	♅	♆	♇
	h m s	° ' "	° '	° '	° '	° '	° '	° '	° '	° '	° '
M 1	10 34 58	10♓21 7	21♊52	18♓47	19♈17	19♈36	4♒58	28♏ 5	17♐46	3♑17	4♏36
A 2	10 38 54	11 21 19	4♋37	20 42	19 43	20 20	5 10	28 6	17 47	3 18	4R35
R 3	10 42 51	12 21 30	17 48	22 35	20 7	21 4	5 23	28 7	17 49	3 19	4 34
C 4	10 46 48	13 21 38	1♌27	24 28	20 29	21 48	5 36	28 7	17 50	3 20	4 33
H 5	10 50 44	14 21 44	15 36	26 20	20 50	22 32	5 48	28 7	17 51	3 21	4 32
6	10 54 41	15 21 48	0♍10	28 11	21 8	23 16	6 1	28 7	17 52	3 22	4 31
7	10 58 37	16 21 50	15 4	29 59	21 25	24 0	6 13	28R 8	17 52	3 23	4 30
8	11 2 34	17 21 50	0♎ 7	1♈46	21 39	24 44	6 25	28 8	17 53	3 24	4 29
9	11 6 30	18 21 48	15 12	3 30	21 51	25 28	6 37	28 7	17 54	3 25	4 28
10	11 10 27	19 21 45	0♏ 7	5 10	22 1	26 12	6 50	28 7	17 55	3 26	4 27
11	11 14 23	20 21 40	14 47	6 47	22 9	26 56	7 2	28 7	17 55	3 27	4 26
12	11 18 20	21 21 33	29 7	8 19	22 14	27 40	7 14	28 7	17 56	3 27	4 25
13	11 22 16	22 21 25	13♐ 5	9 47	22R17	28 23	7 26	28 6	17 57	3 28	4 24
14	11 26 13	23 21 15	26 42	11 10	22 18	29 7	7 38	28 5	17 57	3 29	4 23
15	11 30 10	24 21 3	9♑58	12 26	22 16	29 51	7 49	28 5	17 57	3 30	4 22
16	11 34 6	25 20 50	22 58	13 37	22 12	0♉34	8 1	28 4	17 58	3 30	4 21
17	11 38 3	26 20 35	5♒42	14 41	22 5	1 18	8 13	28 3	17 58	3 31	4 19
18	11 41 59	27 20 18	18 14	15 37	21 56	2 1	8 24	28 2	17 59	3 32	4 18
19	11 45 56	28 19 59	0♓35	16 27	21 44	2 45	8 36	28 1	17 59	3 32	4 17
20	11 49 52	29 19 38	12 47	17 9	21 30	3 28	8 47	28 0	17 59	3 33	4 16
21	11 53 49	0♈19 16	24 50	17 43	21 13	4 12	8 59	27 58	17 59	3 33	4 14
22	11 57 45	1 18 51	6♈47	18 9	20 54	4 55	9 10	27 57	17R59	3 34	4 13
23	12 1 42	2 18 24	18 38	18 27	20 33	5 38	9 21	27 56	17 59	3 34	4 12
24	12 5 39	3 17 56	0♉26	18R37	20 9	6 22	9 32	27 54	17 59	3 35	4 10
25	12 9 35	4 17 25	12 13	18 39	19 44	7 5	9 43	27 52	17 59	3 35	4 9
26	12 13 32	5 16 52	24 2	18 34	19 16	7 48	9 54	27 50	17 59	3 35	4 7
27	12 17 28	6 16 16	5♊57	18 21	18 46	8 31	10 4	27 49	17 59	3 36	4 6
28	12 21 25	7 15 39	18 3	18 2	18 15	9 14	10 15	27 47	17 58	3 36	4 5
29	12 25 21	8 14 59	0♋24	17 35	17 42	9 57	10 26	27 45	17 58	3 36	4 3
30	12 29 18	9 14 17	13 5	17 4	17 7	10 40	10 36	27 42	17 58	3 36	4 2
31	12 33 14	10♈13 32	26♋10	16♈27	16♈32	11♉23	10♒46	27♏40	17♐57	3♑37	4♏ 0

THE SUN ENTERS THE SIGN OF ARIES ON MAR 20 AT 16:14.

♈ ARIES ♉ TAURUS ♊ GEMINI ♋ CANCER ♌ LEO ♍ VIRGO ♎ LIBRA

1985

SIDEREAL TIME | SUN. | MOON. | MERCURY. | VENUS. | MARS. | JUPITER. | SATURN. | URANUS. | NEPTUNE. | PLUTO.

DAY	TIME	☉	☽	☿	♀	♂	♃	♄	♅	♆	♇
	h m s	° ' "	° '	° '	° '	° '	° '	° '	° '	° '	° '
A 1	12 37 11	11♈12 45	9♌43	15♈45	15♈55	12♉ 6	10♒57	27♏38	17♐57	3♑37	3♏59
P 2	12 41 8	12 11 56	23 45	15R 1	15R18	12 49	11 7	27R36	17R57	3 37	3R57
R 3	12 45 4	13 11 5	8♍15	14 14	14 40	13 32	11 17	27 33	17 56	3 37	3 56
I 4	12 49 1	14 10 11	23 8	13 26	14 2	14 15	11 27	27 30	17 55	3 37	3 54
L 5	12 52 57	15 9 15	8♎17	12 37	13 24	14 57	11 36	27 28	17 55	3R37	3 52
6	12 56 54	16 8 17	23 32	11 49	12 47	15 40	11 46	27 25	17 54	3 37	3 51
7	13 0 50	17 7 17	8♏43	11 2	12 10	16 23	11 56	27 22	17 53	3 37	3 49
8	13 4 47	18 6 15	23 41	10 17	11 34	17 5	12 5	27 19	17 52	3 37	3 48
9	13 8 43	19 5 11	8♐18	9 36	10 58	17 48	12 14	27 16	17 52	3 37	3 46
10	13 12 40	20 4 6	22 30	8 58	10 24	18 30	12 23	27 13	17 51	3 37	3 44
11	13 16 37	21 2 59	6♑17	8 24	9 52	19 13	12 33	27 10	17 50	3 36	3 43
12	13 20 33	22 1 50	19 39	7 55	9 21	19 55	12 41	27 7	17 49	3 36	3 41
13	13 24 30	23 0 39	2♒38	7 30	8 52	20 37	12 50	27 4	17 48	3 36	3 39
14	13 28 26	23 59 27	15 18	7 11	8 25	21 20	12 59	27 0	17 47	3 36	3 38
15	13 32 23	24 58 13	27 41	6 56	8 0	22 2	13 8	26 57	17 46	3 35	3 36
16	13 36 19	25 56 57	9♓52	6 47	7 38	22 44	13 16	26 54	17 44	3 35	3 34
17	13 40 16	26 55 39	21 54	6D44	7 17	23 26	13 24	26 50	17 43	3 35	3 33
18	13 44 12	27 54 20	3♈48	6 45	6 59	24 8	13 32	26 46	17 42	3 34	3 31
19	13 48 9	28 52 59	15 38	6 51	6 43	24 50	13 41	26 43	17 41	3 34	3 29
20	13 52 6	29 51 35	27 26	7 3	6 30	25 33	13 48	26 39	17 39	3 33	3 28
21	13 56 2	0♉50 10	9♉14	7 19	6 19	26 15	13 56	26 35	17 38	3 33	3 26
22	13 59 59	1 48 43	21 4	7 40	6 11	26 57	14 4	26 31	17 36	3 32	3 24
23	14 3 55	2 47 14	2♊58	8 6	6 5	27 38	14 11	26 28	17 35	3 32	3 23
24	14 7 52	3 45 43	15 0	8 35	6 1	28 20	14 19	26 24	17 33	3 31	3 21
25	14 11 48	4 44 10	27 12	9 9	6D 0	29 2	14 26	26 20	17 32	3 31	3 19
26	14 15 45	5 42 35	9♋37	9 47	6 1	29 44	14 33	26 16	17 30	3 30	3 18
27	14 19 41	6 40 58	22 20	10 29	6 5	0♊26	14 40	26 12	17 29	3 29	3 16
28	14 23 38	7 39 19	5♌23	11 14	6 10	1 7	14 46	26 7	17 27	3 29	3 14
29	14 27 35	8 37 38	18 49	12 3	6 18	1 49	14 53	26 3	17 25	3 28	3 12
30	14 31 31	9♉35 54	2♍41	12♈55	6♈28	2♊31	14♒59	25♏59	17♐24	3♑27	3♏11

THE SUN ENTERS THE SIGN OF TAURUS ON APR 20 AT 03:26.

DAY	TIME	☉	☽	☿	♀	♂	♃	♄	♅	♆	♇
	h m s	° ' "	° '	° '	° '	° '	° '	° '	° '	° '	° '
M 1	14 35 28	10♉34 9	16♍57	13♈50	6♈41	3♊12	15♒ 6	25♏55	17♐22	3♑26	3♏ 9
A 2	14 39 24	11 32 21	1♎37	14 48	6 55	3 54	15 12	25R51	17R20	3R26	3R 7
Y 3	14 43 21	12 30 31	16 34	15 49	7 11	4 35	15 18	25 46	17 18	3 25	3 6
4	14 47 17	13 28 40	1♏42	16 53	7 29	5 17	15 24	25 42	17 16	3 24	3 4
5	14 51 14	14 26 47	16 52	18 0	7 49	5 58	15 29	25 38	17 14	3 23	3 2
6	14 55 10	15 24 52	1♐54	19 9	8 11	6 39	15 35	25 33	17 12	3 22	3 1
7	14 59 7	16 22 56	16 40	20 21	8 35	7 21	15 40	25 29	17 10	3 21	2 59
8	15 3 4	17 20 58	1♑ 4	21 36	9 0	8 2	15 45	25 25	17 8	3 20	2 58
9	15 7 0	18 18 59	15 1	22 53	9 27	8 43	15 50	25 20	17 6	3 19	2 56
10	15 10 57	19 16 58	28 32	24 12	9 56	9 24	15 55	25 16	17 4	3 18	2 54
11	15 14 53	20 14 56	11♒37	25 33	10 26	10 6	16 0	25 11	17 2	3 17	2 53
12	15 18 50	21 12 53	24 19	26 57	10 57	10 47	16 4	25 7	17 0	3 16	2 51
13	15 22 46	22 10 49	6♓42	28 24	11 30	11 28	16 9	25 2	16 58	3 15	2 50
14	15 26 43	23 8 43	18 50	29 52	12 4	12 9	16 13	24 58	16 56	3 14	2 48
15	15 30 39	24 6 36	0♈46	1♉22	12 40	12 50	16 17	24 53	16 54	3 13	2 46
16	15 34 36	25 4 27	12 37	2 55	13 16	13 31	16 21	24 49	16 51	3 11	2 45
17	15 38 33	26 2 17	24 24	4 30	13 54	14 12	16 24	24 44	16 49	3 10	2 43
18	15 42 29	27 0 6	6♉12	6 7	14 33	14 52	16 28	24 40	16 47	3 9	2 42
19	15 46 26	27 57 54	18 3	7 46	15 13	15 33	16 31	24 35	16 45	3 8	2 40
20	15 50 22	28 55 41	29 59	9 28	15 54	16 14	16 34	24 31	16 42	3 7	2 39
21	15 54 19	29 53 26	12♊ 3	11 11	16 37	16 55	16 37	24 26	16 40	3 5	2 37
22	15 58 15	0♊51 10	24 17	12 57	17 20	17 36	16 40	24 22	16 38	3 4	2 36
23	16 2 12	1 48 52	6♋42	14 45	18 4	18 16	16 42	24 17	16 35	3 3	2 34
24	16 6 8	2 46 33	19 20	16 35	18 49	18 57	16 44	24 13	16 33	3 1	2 33
25	16 10 5	3 44 12	2♌13	18 27	19 34	19 38	16 47	24 9	16 31	3 0	2 32
26	16 14 2	4 41 50	15 21	20 21	20 21	20 18	16 49	24 4	16 28	2 59	2 30
27	16 17 58	5 39 27	28 48	22 17	21 8	20 59	16 50	24 0	16 26	2 57	2 29
28	16 21 55	6 37 2	12♍33	24 16	21 57	21 39	16 52	23 56	16 23	2 56	2 28
29	16 25 51	7 34 35	26 37	26 16	22 45	22 20	16 53	23 51	16 21	2 54	2 26
30	16 29 48	8 32 7	10♎59	28 18	23 35	23 0	16 55	23 47	16 19	2 53	2 25
31	16 33 44	9♊29 38	25♎37	0♊22	24♈25	23♊40	16♒56	23♏43	16♐16	2♑52	2♏24

THE SUN ENTERS THE SIGN OF GEMINI ON MAY 21 AT 02:43.

DAY	TIME	☉	☽	☿	♀	♂	♃	♄	♅	♆	♇
	h m s	° ' "	° '	° '	° '	° '	° '	° '	° '	° '	° '
J 1	16 37 41	10♊27 7	10♏25	2♊28	25♈16	24♊21	16♒56	23♏38	16♐14	2♑50	2♏23
U 2	16 41 37	11 24 36	25 18	4 35	26 8	25 1	16 57	23R34	16R11	2R49	2R21
N 3	16 45 34	12 22 3	10♐ 9	6 44	27 0	25 41	16 57	23 30	16 9	2 47	2 20
E 4	16 49 31	13 19 29	24 49	8 53	27 53	26 22	16R58	23 26	16 6	2 46	2 19
5	16 53 27	14 16 54	9♑12	11 4	28 46	27 2	16 58	23 22	16 4	2 44	2 18
6	16 57 24	15 14 19	23 13	13 16	29 40	27 42	16 58	23 18	16 1	2 43	2 17
7	17 1 20	16 11 43	6♒49	15 28	0♉34	28 22	16 57	23 14	15 59	2 41	2 16
8	17 5 17	17 9 6	19 59	17 40	1 29	29 2	16 57	23 10	15 56	2 40	2 14
9	17 9 13	18 6 28	2♓44	19 52	2 25	29 42	16 56	23 6	15 54	2 38	2 13
10	17 13 10	19 3 50	15 9	22 3	3 21	0♋22	16 55	23 2	15 51	2 36	2 12
11	17 17 6	20 1 12	27 18	24 14	4 17	1 2	16 54	22 59	15 49	2 35	2 11
12	17 21 3	20 58 33	9♈14	26 25	5 14	1 42	16 53	22 55	15 47	2 33	2 10
13	17 25 0	21 55 53	21 3	28 34	6 11	2 22	16 52	22 51	15 44	2 32	2 9
14	17 28 56	22 53 13	2♉51	0♋41	7 9	3 2	16 50	22 48	15 42	2 30	2 9
15	17 32 53	23 50 33	14 41	2 48	8 7	3 42	16 48	22 44	15 39	2 29	2 8
16	17 36 49	24 47 52	26 37	4 52	9 5	4 22	16 46	22 41	15 37	2 27	2 7
17	17 40 46	25 45 11	8♊42	6 55	10 4	5 2	16 44	22 37	15 34	2 25	2 6
18	17 44 42	26 42 29	20 58	8 56	11 3	5 41	16 42	22 34	15 32	2 24	2 5
19	17 48 39	27 39 47	3♋28	10 55	12 3	6 21	16 39	22 31	15 30	2 22	2 4
20	17 52 36	28 37 4	16 12	12 51	13 3	7 1	16 36	22 28	15 27	2 21	2 4
21	17 56 32	29 34 21	29 9	14 46	14 3	7 40	16 33	22 24	15 25	2 19	2 3
22	18 0 29	0♋31 37	12♌20	16 38	15 3	8 20	16 30	22 21	15 22	2 17	2 2
23	18 4 25	1 28 52	25 44	18 29	16 4	9 0	16 27	22 18	15 20	2 16	2 2
24	18 8 22	2 26 7	9♍21	20 17	17 5	9 39	16 23	22 15	15 18	2 14	2 1
25	18 12 18	3 23 21	23 9	22 2	18 7	10 19	16 20	22 13	15 15	2 12	2 0
26	18 16 15	4 20 35	7♎ 8	23 46	19 8	10 58	16 16	22 10	15 13	2 11	2 0
27	18 20 11	5 17 48	21 17	25 27	20 10	11 38	16 12	22 7	15 11	2 9	1 59
28	18 24 8	6 15 0	5♏36	27 6	21 12	12 17	16 8	22 5	15 9	2 8	1 59
29	18 28 5	7 12 12	20 2	28 43	22 15	12 57	16 3	22 2	15 6	2 6	1 58
30	18 32 1	8♋ 9 24	4♐31	0♌17	23♉17	13♋36	15♒59	22♏ 0	15♐ 4	2♑ 4	1♏58

THE SUN ENTERS THE SIGN OF CANCER ON JUN 21 AT 10:45.

♏ SCORPIO ♐ SAGITTARIUS ♑ CAPRICORN ♒ AQUARIUS ♓ PISCES

1985

SIDEREAL SUN . . MOON . . MERCURY . VENUS . . MARS . . JUPITER . SATURN . . URANUS . . NEPTUNE . PLUTO .

DAY	TIME			☉	☽	☿	♀	♂	♃	♄	♅	♆	♇
	h	m	s	° ' "	° '	° '	° '	° '	° '	° '	° '	° '	° '
J 1	18	35	58	9♋ 6 35	18♐59	1♌49	24♉20	14♋16	15♒54	21♏57	15♐ 2	2♑ 3	1♏58
U 2	18	39	54	10 3 46	3♑21	3 19	25 24	14 55	15R49	21R55	15R 0	2R 1	1R57
L 3	18	43	51	11 0 57	17 30	4 46	26 27	15 34	15 44	21 53	14 58	2 0	1 57
Y 4	18	47	47	11 58 8	1♒22	6 12	27 31	16 14	15 39	21 51	14 56	1 58	1 57
5	18	51	44	12 55 19	14 53	7 34	28 34	16 53	15 34	21 49	14 53	1 56	1 56
6	18	55	40	13 52 30	28 1	8 55	29 38	17 32	15 29	21 47	14 51	1 55	1 56
7	18	59	37	14 49 42	10♓47	10 12	0♊43	18 11	15 23	21 45	14 49	1 53	1 56
8	19	3	34	15 46 53	23 13	11 28	1 47	18 51	15 17	21 43	14 47	1 52	1 56
9	19	7	30	16 44 5	5♈22	12 40	2 52	19 30	15 11	21 42	14 45	1 50	1 56
10	19	11	27	17 41 17	17 18	13 50	3 57	20 9	15 5	21 40	14 43	1 49	1 56
11	19	15	23	18 38 30	29 8	14 58	5 2	20 48	14 59	21 39	14 42	1 47	1 55
12	19	19	20	19 35 43	10♉57	16 2	6 7	21 27	14 53	21 37	14 40	1 46	1D55
13	19	23	16	20 32 57	22 49	17 4	7 13	22 6	14 47	21 36	14 38	1 44	1 55
14	19	27	13	21 30 11	4♊49	18 3	8 18	22 45	14 40	21 35	14 36	1 43	1 55
15	19	31	9	22 27 26	17 2	18 58	9 24	23 24	14 34	21 34	14 34	1 41	1 56
16	19	35	6	23 24 42	29 31	19 51	10 30	24 3	14 27	21 33	14 32	1 40	1 56
17	19	39	3	24 21 58	12♋17	20 40	11 36	24 42	14 20	21 32	14 31	1 38	1 56
18	19	42	59	25 19 14	25 21	21 26	12 43	25 21	14 13	21 31	14 29	1 37	1 56
19	19	46	56	26 16 31	8♌41	22 8	13 49	26 0	14 6	21 30	14 27	1 35	1 56
20	19	50	52	27 13 48	22 16	22 46	14 56	26 39	13 59	21 30	14 26	1 34	1 56
21	19	54	49	28 11 5	6♍ 3	23 21	16 2	27 18	13 52	21 29	14 24	1 32	1 57
22	19	58	45	29 8 23	19 58	23 51	17 9	27 57	13 45	21 29	14 23	1 31	1 57
23	20	2	42	0♌ 5 41	3♎59	24 17	18 16	28 36	13 37	21 28	14 21	1 30	1 57
24	20	6	38	1 2 59	18 4	24 39	19 23	29 15	13 30	21 28	14 20	1 28	1 58
25	20	10	35	2 0 17	2♏11	24 56	20 31	29 53	13 23	21D28	14 18	1 27	1 58
26	20	14	32	2 57 36	16 19	25 9	21 38	0♌32	13 15	21 28	14 17	1 26	1 59
27	20	18	28	3 54 56	0♐27	25 16	22 46	1 11	13 8	21 28	14 16	1 24	1 59
28	20	22	25	4 52 16	14 34	25R19	23 53	1 50	13 0	21 28	14 15	1 23	2 0
29	20	26	21	5 49 36	28 37	25 17	25 1	2 28	12 52	21 29	14 13	1 22	2 0
30	20	30	18	6 46 57	12♑34	25 9	26 9	3 7	12 45	21 29	14 12	1 20	2 1
31	20	34	14	7♌44 19	26♑20	24♌57	27♊17	3♌46	12♒37	21♏29	14♐11	1♑19	2♏ 1

THE SUN ENTERS THE SIGN OF LEO ON JUL 22 AT 21:37.

DAY	TIME			☉	☽	☿	♀	♂	♃	♄	♅	♆	♇
	h	m	s	° ' "	° '	° '	° '	° '	° '	° '	° '	° '	° '
A 1	20	38	11	8♌41 41	9♒54	24♌39	28♊25	4♌24	12♒29	21♏30	14♐10	1♑18	2♏ 2
U 2	20	42	8	9 39 4	23 10	24R16	29 34	5 3	12R21	21 31	14R 9	1R17	2 3
G 3	20	46	4	10 36 28	6♓ 8	23 49	0♋42	5 42	12 14	21 31	14 8	1 16	2 3
U 4	20	50	1	11 33 53	18 48	23 17	1 51	6 20	12 6	21 32	14 7	1 14	2 4
S 5	20	53	57	12 31 19	1♈10	22 41	3 0	6 59	11 58	21 33	14 6	1 13	2 5
T 6	20	57	54	13 28 47	13 17	22 1	4 8	7 37	11 50	21 34	14 5	1 12	2 6
7	21	1	50	14 26 15	25 13	21 18	5 17	8 16	11 42	21 35	14 4	1 11	2 7
8	21	5	47	15 23 45	7♉ 2	20 32	6 26	8 54	11 35	21 36	14 3	1 10	2 8
9	21	9	43	16 21 16	18 51	19 45	7 36	9 33	11 27	21 38	14 3	1 9	2 8
10	21	13	40	17 18 49	0♊44	18 57	8 45	10 12	11 19	21 39	14 2	1 8	2 9
11	21	17	36	18 16 23	12 46	18 8	9 54	10 50	11 11	21 41	14 1	1 7	2 10
12	21	21	33	19 13 58	25 4	17 21	11 4	11 28	11 4	21 42	14 1	1 6	2 11
13	21	25	30	20 11 35	7♋40	16 35	12 13	12 7	10 56	21 44	14 0	1 5	2 12
14	21	29	26	21 9 13	20 37	15 52	13 23	12 45	10 48	21 46	14 0	1 4	2 14
15	21	33	23	22 6 53	3♌57	15 13	14 33	13 24	10 41	21 48	13 59	1 3	2 15
16	21	37	19	23 4 34	17 38	14 38	15 43	14 2	10 33	21 50	13 59	1 3	2 16
17	21	41	16	24 2 16	1♍36	14 8	16 53	14 41	10 26	21 52	13 59	1 2	2 17
18	21	45	12	24 59 59	15 49	13 44	18 3	15 19	10 19	21 54	13 58	1 1	2 18
19	21	49	9	25 57 44	0♎ 9	13 27	19 13	15 57	10 11	21 56	13 58	1 0	2 19
20	21	53	5	26 55 30	14 32	13D16	20 24	16 36	10 4	21 59	13 58	0 59	2 21
21	21	57	2	27 53 16	28 53	13 13	21 34	17 14	9 57	22 1	13 58	0 59	2 22
22	22	0	59	28 51 4	13♏ 9	13 17	22 44	17 52	9 50	22 4	13 58	0 58	2 23
23	22	4	55	29 48 53	27 18	13 29	23 55	18 31	9 43	22 6	13D58	0 57	2 25
24	22	8	52	0♍46 44	11♐18	13 49	25 6	19 9	9 36	22 9	13 58	0 57	2 26
25	22	12	48	1 44 35	25 10	14 16	26 16	19 47	9 30	22 12	13 58	0 56	2 27
26	22	16	45	2 42 28	8♑53	14 51	27 27	20 25	9 23	22 15	13 58	0 56	2 29
27	22	20	41	3 40 22	22 26	15 34	28 38	21 4	9 17	22 18	13 58	0 55	2 30
28	22	24	38	4 38 17	5♒48	16 25	29 49	21 42	9 10	22 21	13 58	0 55	2 32
29	22	28	35	5 36 14	18 58	17 22	1♌ 0	22 20	9 4	22 24	13 59	0 54	2 33
30	22	32	31	6 34 12	1♓55	18 27	2 11	22 58	8 58	22 27	13 59	0 54	2 35
31	22	36	28	7♍32 12	14♓37	19♌38	3♌23	23♌36	8♒52	22♏31	13♐59	0♑53	2♏36

THE SUN ENTERS THE SIGN OF VIRGO ON AUG 23 AT 04:37.

DAY	TIME			☉	☽	☿	♀	♂	♃	♄	♅	♆	♇
	h	m	s	° ' "	° '	° '	° '	° '	° '	° '	° '	° '	° '
S 1	22	40	24	8♍30 13	27♓ 4	20♌55	4♌34	24♌15	8♒46	22♏34	14♐ 0	0♑53	2♏38
E 2	22	44	21	9 28 16	9♈18	22 17	5 46	24 53	8R40	22 37	14 0	0R53	2 40
P 3	22	48	17	10 26 21	21 20	23 45	6 57	25 31	8 35	22 41	14 1	0 52	2 41
T 4	22	52	14	11 24 28	3♉13	25 18	8 9	26 9	8 29	22 45	14 1	0 52	2 43
E 5	22	56	10	12 22 36	15 1	26 55	9 20	26 47	8 24	22 48	14 2	0 52	2 45
M 6	23	0	7	13 20 47	26 49	28 35	10 32	27 25	8 19	22 52	14 3	0 51	2 46
B 7	23	4	3	14 18 59	8♊41	0♍19	11 44	28 3	8 14	22 56	14 3	0 51	2 48
E 8	23	8	0	15 17 14	20 43	2 5	12 56	28 41	8 9	23 0	14 4	0 51	2 50
R 9	23	11	57	16 15 31	3♋ 0	3 54	14 8	29 19	8 4	23 4	14 5	0 51	2 52
10	23	15	53	17 13 50	15 37	5 44	15 20	29 58	8 0	23 8	14 6	0 51	2 54
11	23	19	50	18 12 11	28 38	7 36	16 32	0♍36	7 56	23 12	14 7	0 51	2 55
12	23	23	46	19 10 33	12♌ 5	9 28	17 45	1 14	7 51	23 17	14 8	0D51	2 57
13	23	27	43	20 8 58	25 57	11 22	18 57	1 52	7 47	23 21	14 9	0 51	2 59
14	23	31	39	21 7 25	10♍12	13 15	20 9	2 30	7 44	23 26	14 10	0 51	3 1
15	23	35	36	22 5 53	24 45	15 9	21 22	3 8	7 40	23 30	14 11	0 51	3 3
16	23	39	32	23 4 24	9♎29	17 3	22 34	3 46	7 37	23 35	14 12	0 51	3 5
17	23	43	29	24 2 56	24 17	18 56	23 47	4 24	7 33	23 39	14 14	0 51	3 7
18	23	47	26	25 1 30	9♏ 1	20 49	25 0	5 2	7 30	23 44	14 15	0 51	3 9
19	23	51	22	26 0 6	23 35	22 41	26 13	5 40	7 27	23 49	14 16	0 52	3 11
20	23	55	19	26 58 43	7♐56	24 33	27 25	6 18	7 25	23 54	14 18	0 52	3 13
21	23	59	15	27 57 23	22 0	26 24	28 38	6 56	7 22	23 59	14 19	0 52	3 15
22	0	3	12	28 56 3	5♑49	28 14	29 51	7 34	7 20	24 4	14 21	0 52	3 17
23	0	7	8	29 54 46	19 21	0♎ 3	1♍ 4	8 12	7 18	24 9	14 22	0 53	3 19
24	0	11	5	0♎53 30	2♒38	1 52	2 17	8 49	7 16	24 14	14 24	0 53	3 21
25	0	15	1	1 52 16	15 40	3 39	3 30	9 27	7 14	24 19	14 25	0 53	3 24
26	0	18	58	2 51 3	28 29	5 26	4 44	10 5	7 13	24 24	14 27	0 54	3 26
27	0	22	55	3 49 53	11♓ 6	7 12	5 57	10 43	7 11	24 30	14 29	0 54	3 28
28	0	26	51	4 48 44	23 30	8 56	7 10	11 21	7 10	24 35	14 31	0 55	3 30
29	0	30	48	5 47 37	5♈43	10 40	8 24	11 59	7 9	24 40	14 32	0 55	3 32
30	0	34	44	6♎46 32	17♈47	12♎23	9♍37	12♍37	7♒ 8	24♏46	14♐34	0♑56	3♏34

THE SUN ENTERS THE SIGN OF LIBRA ON SEP 23 AT 02:09.

♈ ARIES ♉ TAURUS ♊ GEMINI ♋ CANCER ♌ LEO ♍ VIRGO ♎ LIBRA

1985

SIDEREAL . SUN . MOON . MERCURY . VENUS . MARS . JUPITER . SATURN . URANUS . NEPTUNE . PLUTO .

DAY	TIME	☉	☽	☿	♀	♂	♃	♄	♅	♆	♇
	h m s	° ' "	° '	° '	° '	° '	° '	° '	° '	° '	° '
O 1	0 38 41	7♎45 29	29♈42	14♎ 5	10♍50	13♍15	7♒ 8	24♏51	14♐36	0♑57	3♏37
C 2	0 42 37	8 44 29	11♉32	15 46	12 4	13 52	7R 7	24 57	14 38	0 57	3 39
T 3	0 46 34	9 43 30	23 19	17 27	13 18	14 30	7D 7	25 3	14 40	0 58	3 41
O 4	0 50 30	10 42 34	5♊ 6	19 6	14 31	15 8	7 7	25 8	14 42	0 59	3 43
B 5	0 54 27	11 41 40	16 58	20 45	15 45	15 46	7 8	25 14	14 44	0 59	3 46
E 6	0 58 24	12 40 48	28 59	22 23	16 59	16 24	7 8	25 20	14 46	1 0	3 48
R 7	1 2 20	13 39 59	11♋15	24 0	18 13	17 2	7 9	25 26	14 49	1 1	3 50
8	1 6 17	14 39 12	23 48	25 36	19 27	17 39	7 9	25 32	14 51	1 2	3 53
9	1 10 13	15 38 28	6♌45	27 11	20 41	18 17	7 10	25 38	14 53	1 2	3 55
10	1 14 10	16 37 45	20 8	28 46	21 55	18 55	7 12	25 44	14 55	1 3	3 57
11	1 18 6	17 37 5	3♍59	0♏20	23 9	19 33	7 13	25 50	14 58	1 4	4 0
12	1 22 3	18 36 27	18 17	1 53	24 23	20 11	7 15	25 56	15 0	1 5	4 2
13	1 25 59	19 35 51	2♎57	3 26	25 37	20 48	7 16	26 2	15 3	1 6	4 4
14	1 29 56	20 35 18	17 54	4 58	26 51	21 26	7 18	26 9	15 5	1 7	4 7
15	1 33 52	21 34 46	3♏ 0	6 29	28 5	22 4	7 21	26 15	15 7	1 8	4 9
16	1 37 49	22 34 17	18 6	8 0	29 20	22 42	7 23	26 21	15 10	1 9	4 11
17	1 41 46	23 33 49	3♐ 2	9 29	0♎34	23 19	7 26	26 27	15 13	1 10	4 14
18	1 45 42	24 33 23	17 41	10 59	1 48	23 57	7 28	26 34	15 15	1 12	4 16
19	1 49 39	25 32 59	2♑ 0	12 27	3 3	24 35	7 31	26 40	15 18	1 13	4 19
20	1 53 35	26 32 37	15 56	13 55	4 17	25 12	7 35	26 47	15 21	1 14	4 21
21	1 57 32	27 32 17	29 29	15 22	5 31	25 50	7 38	26 53	15 23	1 15	4 23
22	2 1 28	28 31 58	12♒40	16 48	6 46	26 28	7 41	27 0	15 26	1 16	4 26
23	2 5 25	29 31 41	25 32	18 14	8 1	27 5	7 45	27 6	15 29	1 18	4 28
24	2 9 22	0♏31 25	8♓ 7	19 38	9 15	27 43	7 49	27 13	15 32	1 19	4 31
25	2 13 18	1 31 11	20 28	21 2	10 30	28 21	7 53	27 20	15 35	1 20	4 33
26	2 17 15	2 30 59	2♈37	22 25	11 44	28 58	7 57	27 26	15 37	1 22	4 36
27	2 21 11	3 30 49	14 38	23 48	12 59	29 36	8 2	27 33	15 40	1 23	4 38
28	2 25 8	4 30 41	26 32	25 9	14 14	0♎14	8 7	27 40	15 43	1 24	4 40
29	2 29 4	5 30 34	8♉23	26 29	15 28	0 51	8 11	27 47	15 46	1 26	4 43
30	2 33 1	6 30 30	20 10	27 48	16 43	1 29	8 16	27 53	15 49	1 27	4 45
31	2 36 57	7♏30 27	1♊58	29♏ 6	17♎58	2♎ 7	8♒21	28♏ 0	15♐52	1♑29	4♏48

THE SUN ENTERS THE SIGN OF SCORPIO ON OCT 23 AT 11:23.

DAY	TIME	☉	☽	☿	♀	♂	♃	♄	♅	♆	♇
	h m s	° ' "	° '	° '	° '	° '	° '	° '	° '	° '	° '
N 1	2 40 54	8♏30 27	13♊48	0♐23	19♎13	2♎44	8♒27	28♏ 7	15♐55	1♑30	4♏50
O 2	2 44 50	9 30 28	25 44	1 38	20 28	3 22	8 32	28 14	15 58	1 32	4 53
V 3	2 48 47	10 30 32	7♋48	2 52	21 43	3 59	8 38	28 21	16 2	1 33	4 55
E 4	2 52 44	11 30 38	20 4	4 4	22 58	4 37	8 44	28 28	16 5	1 35	4 57
M 5	2 56 40	12 30 46	2♌36	5 14	24 13	5 14	8 50	28 35	16 8	1 37	5 0
B 6	3 0 37	13 30 56	15 27	6 22	25 28	5 52	8 56	28 42	16 11	1 38	5 2
E 7	3 4 33	14 31 8	28 42	7 28	26 43	6 30	9 2	28 49	16 14	1 40	5 5
R 8	3 8 30	15 31 21	12♍22	8 30	27 58	7 7	9 9	28 56	16 18	1 42	5 7
9	3 12 26	16 31 37	26 29	9 30	29 13	7 45	9 16	29 3	16 21	1 43	5 9
10	3 16 23	17 31 55	11♎ 1	10 27	0♏28	8 22	9 22	29 10	16 24	1 45	5 12
11	3 20 19	18 32 15	25 54	11 20	1 43	9 0	9 29	29 17	16 28	1 47	5 14
12	3 24 16	19 32 37	11♏ 2	12 8	2 58	9 37	9 37	29 24	16 31	1 49	5 17
13	3 28 13	20 33 1	26 16	12 52	4 13	10 15	9 44	29 31	16 34	1 50	5 19
14	3 32 9	21 33 26	11♐26	13 31	5 28	10 52	9 51	29 38	16 38	1 52	5 21
15	3 36 6	22 33 53	26 23	14 3	6 43	11 30	9 59	29 45	16 41	1 54	5 24
16	3 40 2	23 34 21	10♑58	14 29	7 59	12 7	10 7	29 52	16 45	1 56	5 26
17	3 43 59	24 34 51	25 8	14 48	9 14	12 45	10 15	29 59	16 48	1 58	5 28
18	3 47 55	25 35 22	8♒50	14R58	10 29	13 22	10 23	0♐ 6	16 51	2 0	5 31
19	3 51 52	26 35 54	22 5	15 0	11 44	13 59	10 31	0 14	16 55	2 2	5 33
20	3 55 49	27 36 27	4♓55	14 52	13 0	14 37	10 39	0 21	16 58	2 4	5 35
21	3 59 45	28 37 2	17 25	14 34	14 15	15 14	10 48	0 28	17 2	2 6	5 38
22	4 3 42	29 37 37	29 38	14 5	15 30	15 52	10 56	0 35	17 5	2 8	5 40
23	4 7 38	0♐38 14	11♈39	13 26	16 45	16 29	11 5	0 42	17 9	2 10	5 42
24	4 11 35	1 38 52	23 32	12 36	18 1	17 6	11 14	0 49	17 13	2 12	5 44
25	4 15 31	2 39 32	5♉21	11 36	19 16	17 44	11 23	0 56	17 16	2 14	5 47
26	4 19 28	3 40 12	17 8	10 28	20 31	18 21	11 32	1 4	17 20	2 16	5 49
27	4 23 24	4 40 54	28 56	9 13	21 47	18 58	11 42	1 11	17 23	2 18	5 51
28	4 27 21	5 41 37	10♊49	7 53	23 2	19 36	11 51	1 18	17 27	2 20	5 53
29	4 31 18	6 42 22	22 46	6 30	24 18	20 13	12 0	1 25	17 31	2 22	5 55
30	4 35 14	7♐43 8	4♋51	5♐ 8	25♏33	20♎50	12♒10	1♐32	17♐34	2♑24	5♏58

THE SUN ENTERS THE SIGN OF SAGITTARIUS ON NOV 22 AT 08:52.

DAY	TIME	☉	☽	☿	♀	♂	♃	♄	♅	♆	♇
	h m s	° ' "	° '	° '	° '	° '	° '	° '	° '	° '	° '
D 1	4 39 11	8♐43 55	17♋ 4	3♐50	26♏48	21♎27	12♒20	1♐39	17♐38	2♑26	6♏ 0
E 2	4 43 7	9 44 44	29 29	2R37	28 4	22 5	12 30	1 46	17 41	2 28	6 2
C 3	4 47 4	10 45 34	12♌ 6	1 32	29 19	22 42	12 40	1 53	17 45	2 30	6 4
E 4	4 51 0	11 46 25	24 58	0 37	0♐35	23 19	12 50	2 1	17 49	2 32	6 6
M 5	4 54 57	12 47 18	8♍ 8	29♏52	1 50	23 56	13 0	2 8	17 52	2 35	6 8
B 6	4 58 53	13 48 12	21 38	29 19	3 5	24 34	13 11	2 15	17 56	2 37	6 10
E 7	5 2 50	14 49 7	5♎29	28 58	4 21	25 11	13 21	2 22	18 0	2 39	6 12
R 8	5 6 47	15 50 3	19 44	28D47	5 36	25 48	13 32	2 29	18 3	2 41	6 14
9	5 10 43	16 51 1	4♏19	28 47	6 52	26 25	13 43	2 36	18 7	2 43	6 16
10	5 14 40	17 52 0	19 12	28 58	8 7	27 2	13 53	2 43	18 11	2 46	6 18
11	5 18 36	18 53 1	4♐15	29 17	9 23	27 39	14 4	2 50	18 14	2 48	6 20
12	5 22 33	19 54 2	19 22	29 45	10 38	28 16	14 15	2 57	18 18	2 50	6 22
13	5 26 29	20 55 4	4♑21	0♐20	11 54	28 54	14 26	3 4	18 22	2 52	6 24
14	5 30 26	21 56 7	19 4	1 2	13 9	29 31	14 38	3 11	18 25	2 54	6 26
15	5 34 22	22 57 10	3♒23	1 49	14 25	0♏ 8	14 49	3 17	18 29	2 57	6 27
16	5 38 19	23 58 14	17 15	2 42	15 40	0 45	15 0	3 24	18 33	2 59	6 29
17	5 42 16	24 59 18	0♓38	3 40	16 56	1 22	15 12	3 31	18 36	3 1	6 31
18	5 46 12	26 0 23	13 34	4 41	18 11	1 59	15 24	3 38	18 40	3 3	6 33
19	5 50 9	27 1 27	26 5	5 46	19 27	2 36	15 35	3 45	18 44	3 6	6 35
20	5 54 5	28 2 33	8♈18	6 54	20 42	3 13	15 47	3 51	18 47	3 8	6 36
21	5 58 2	29 3 38	20 17	8 5	21 58	3 50	15 59	3 58	18 51	3 10	6 38
22	6 1 58	0♑ 4 44	2♉ 7	9 18	23 13	4 26	16 11	4 5	18 54	3 12	6 40
23	6 5 55	1 5 50	13 54	10 34	24 29	5 3	16 23	4 11	18 58	3 15	6 41
24	6 9 51	2 6 56	25 41	11 51	25 44	5 40	16 35	4 18	19 2	3 17	6 43
25	6 13 48	3 8 2	7♊32	13 10	27 0	6 17	16 48	4 25	19 5	3 19	6 44
26	6 17 45	4 9 9	19 31	14 30	28 15	6 54	17 0	4 31	19 9	3 22	6 46
27	6 21 41	5 10 16	1♋39	15 51	29 31	7 31	17 12	4 38	19 12	3 24	6 48
28	6 25 38	6 11 24	13 58	17 14	0♑46	8 7	17 25	4 44	19 16	3 26	6 49
29	6 29 34	7 12 31	26 27	18 37	2 2	8 44	17 37	4 51	19 19	3 28	6 51
30	6 33 31	8 13 39	9♌ 8	20 2	3 17	9 21	17 50	4 57	19 23	3 31	6 52
31	6 37 27	9♑14 47	22♌ 0	21♐27	4♑33	9♏58	18♒ 3	5♐ 3	19♐27	3♑33	6♏53

THE SUN ENTERS THE SIGN OF CAPRICORN ON DEC 21 AT 22:09.

♏ SCORPIO ♐ SAGITTARIUS ♑ CAPRICORN ♒ AQUARIUS ♓ PISCES

1986

SIDEREAL . SUN . MOON . MERCURY . VENUS . MARS . JUPITER . SATURN . URANUS . NEPTUNE . PLUTO .

DAY	TIME	☉	☽	☿	♀	♂	♃	♄	♅	♆	♇
	h m s	° ' "	° '	° '	° '	° '	° '	° '	° '	° '	° '
J 1	6 41 24	10♑15 56	5♍ 4	22♐53	5♑48	10♏34	18♒15	5♐10	19♐30	3♑35	6♏55
A 2	6 45 21	11 17 4	18 20	24 19	7 4	11 11	18 28	5 16	19 33	3 37	6 56
N 3	6 49 17	12 18 13	1♎50	25 47	8 19	11 48	18 41	5 22	19 37	3 40	6 57
U 4	6 53 14	13 19 23	15 34	27 15	9 35	12 24	18 54	5 28	19 40	3 42	6 59
A 5	6 57 10	14 20 32	29 34	28 43	10 50	13 1	19 7	5 34	19 44	3 44	7 0
R 6	7 1 7	15 21 42	13♏49	0♑12	12 6	13 37	19 20	5 40	19 47	3 46	7 1
Y 7	7 5 3	16 22 53	28 18	1 42	13 21	14 14	19 33	5 46	19 51	3 49	7 2
8	7 9 0	17 24 3	12♐58	3 12	14 37	14 50	19 46	5 52	19 54	3 51	7 3
9	7 12 56	18 25 14	27 43	4 42	15 52	15 27	20 0	5 58	19 57	3 53	7 5
10	7 16 53	19 26 24	12♑26	6 13	17 8	16 3	20 13	6 4	20 1	3 55	7 6
11	7 20 50	20 27 34	26 59	7 45	18 23	16 40	20 26	6 10	20 4	3 58	7 7
12	7 24 46	21 28 44	11♒14	9 17	19 39	17 16	20 40	6 16	20 7	4 0	7 8
13	7 28 43	22 29 53	25 6	10 49	20 54	17 52	20 53	6 21	20 10	4 2	7 9
14	7 32 39	23 31 2	8♓32	12 22	22 10	18 28	21 7	6 27	20 14	4 4	7 10
15	7 36 36	24 32 10	21 32	13 55	23 25	19 5	21 20	6 33	20 17	4 6	7 11
16	7 40 32	25 33 17	4♈ 7	15 29	24 41	19 41	21 34	6 38	20 20	4 8	7 11
17	7 44 29	26 34 24	16 23	17 4	25 56	20 17	21 48	6 43	20 23	4 11	7 12
18	7 48 25	27 35 30	28 24	18 38	27 12	20 53	22 2	6 49	20 26	4 13	7 13
19	7 52 22	28 36 35	10♉15	20 14	28 27	21 29	22 15	6 54	20 29	4 15	7 14
20	7 56 19	29 37 39	22 2	21 50	29 42	22 5	22 29	6 59	20 32	4 17	7 15
21	8 0 15	0♒38 42	3♊50	23 26	0♒58	22 41	22 43	7 5	20 35	4 19	7 15
22	8 4 12	1 39 45	15 45	25 3	2 13	23 17	22 57	7 10	20 38	4 21	7 16
23	8 8 8	2 40 47	27 50	26 41	3 29	23 53	23 11	7 15	20 41	4 23	7 17
24	8 12 5	3 41 47	10♋ 8	28 19	4 44	24 29	23 25	7 20	20 44	4 25	7 17
25	8 16 1	4 42 47	22 40	29 58	5 59	25 5	23 39	7 25	20 47	4 27	7 18
26	8 19 58	5 43 46	5♌28	1♒37	7 15	25 41	23 53	7 30	20 50	4 29	7 18
27	8 23 55	6 44 45	18 30	3 17	8 30	26 17	24 7	7 34	20 53	4 31	7 19
28	8 27 51	7 45 42	1♍44	4 58	9 45	26 52	24 21	7 39	20 56	4 33	7 19
29	8 31 48	8 46 38	15 10	6 39	11 1	27 28	24 35	7 44	20 59	4 35	7 20
30	8 35 44	9 47 34	28 46	8 21	12 16	28 4	24 49	7 48	21 1	4 37	7 20
31	8 39 41	10♒48 29	12♎29	10♒ 4	13♒32	28♏39	25♒ 3	7♐53	21♐ 4	4♑39	7♏20

THE SUN ENTERS THE SIGN OF AQUARIUS ON JAN 20 AT 08:47.

DAY	TIME	☉	☽	☿	♀	♂	♃	♄	♅	♆	♇
	h m s	° ' "	° '	° '	° '	° '	° '	° '	° '	° '	° '
F 1	8 43 37	11♒49 23	26♎20	11♒47	14♒47	29♏15	25♒18	7♐57	21♐ 7	4♑41	7♏21
E 2	8 47 34	12 50 17	10♏17	13 31	16 2	29 50	25 32	8 1	21 9	4 43	7 21
B 3	8 51 30	13 51 10	24 22	15 16	17 17	0♐26	25 46	8 6	21 12	4 45	7 21
R 4	8 55 27	14 52 2	8♐34	17 2	18 33	1 1	26 0	8 10	21 14	4 47	7 21
U 5	8 59 24	15 52 53	22 50	18 48	19 48	1 37	26 15	8 14	21 17	4 48	7 21
A 6	9 3 20	16 53 43	7♑ 7	20 34	21 3	2 12	26 29	8 18	21 19	4 50	7 22
R 7	9 7 17	17 54 33	21 23	22 22	22 19	2 47	26 43	8 22	21 22	4 52	7 22
Y 8	9 11 13	18 55 21	5♒31	24 9	23 34	3 22	26 58	8 26	21 24	4 54	7R22
9	9 15 10	19 56 8	19 26	25 58	24 49	3 58	27 12	8 29	21 26	4 56	7 22
10	9 19 6	20 56 54	3♓ 4	27 47	26 4	4 33	27 26	8 33	21 29	4 57	7 22
11	9 23 3	21 57 38	16 21	29 36	27 20	5 8	27 41	8 36	21 31	4 59	7 22
12	9 26 59	22 58 21	29 17	1♓25	28 35	5 43	27 55	8 40	21 33	5 1	7 22
13	9 30 56	23 59 2	11♈51	3 14	29 50	6 17	28 9	8 43	21 35	5 2	7 21
14	9 34 53	24 59 42	24 8	5 3	1♓ 5	6 52	28 24	8 47	21 38	5 4	7 21
15	9 38 49	26 0 20	6♉10	6 52	2 20	7 27	28 38	8 50	21 40	5 6	7 21
16	9 42 46	27 0 56	18 3	8 40	3 35	8 2	28 53	8 53	21 42	5 7	7 21
17	9 46 42	28 1 31	29 51	10 28	4 51	8 36	29 7	8 56	21 44	5 9	7 21
18	9 50 39	29 2 4	11♊41	12 14	6 6	9 11	29 21	8 59	21 46	5 10	7 20
19	9 54 35	0♓ 2 35	23 38	13 59	7 21	9 45	29 36	9 2	21 47	5 12	7 20
20	9 58 32	1 3 5	5♋46	15 42	8 36	10 20	29 50	9 5	21 49	5 13	7 20
21	10 2 28	2 3 32	18 9	17 22	9 51	10 54	0♓ 5	9 7	21 51	5 15	7 19
22	10 6 25	3 3 58	0♌51	18 59	11 6	11 28	0 19	9 10	21 53	5 16	7 19
23	10 10 22	4 4 22	13 52	20 33	12 21	12 3	0 34	9 12	21 55	5 18	7 18
24	10 14 18	5 4 44	27 12	22 3	13 36	12 37	0 48	9 15	21 56	5 19	7 18
25	10 18 15	6 5 4	10♍49	23 29	14 51	13 11	1 2	9 17	21 58	5 20	7 17
26	10 22 11	7 5 23	24 41	24 49	16 6	13 45	1 17	9 19	21 59	5 22	7 17
27	10 26 8	8 5 40	8♎42	26 3	17 21	14 18	1 31	9 21	22 1	5 23	7 16
28	10 30 4	9♓ 5 56	22♎51	27♓10	18♓36	14♐52	1♓45	9♐23	22♐ 2	5♑24	7♏15

THE SUN ENTERS THE SIGN OF PISCES ON FEB 18 AT 22:58.

DAY	TIME	☉	☽	☿	♀	♂	♃	♄	♅	♆	♇
	h m s	° ' "	° '	° '	° '	° '	° '	° '	° '	° '	° '
M 1	10 34 1	10♓ 6 10	7♏ 2	28♓11	19♓51	15♐26	2♓ 0	9♐25	22♐ 4	5♑25	7♏15
A 2	10 37 57	11 6 22	21 13	29 3	21 5	16 0	2 14	9 27	22 5	5 27	7R14
R 3	10 41 54	12 6 33	5♐23	29 48	22 20	16 33	2 29	9 29	22 7	5 28	7 13
C 4	10 45 50	13 6 43	19 30	0♈24	23 35	17 7	2 43	9 30	22 8	5 29	7 12
H 5	10 49 47	14 6 51	3♑32	0 51	24 50	17 40	2 57	9 32	22 9	5 30	7 12
6	10 53 44	15 6 58	17 29	1 9	26 5	18 13	3 11	9 33	22 10	5 31	7 11
7	10 57 40	16 7 3	1♒18	1R18	27 19	18 46	3 26	9 34	22 11	5 32	7 10
8	11 1 37	17 7 6	14 58	1 18	28 34	19 19	3 40	9 36	22 12	5 33	7 9
9	11 5 33	18 7 8	28 26	1 8	29 49	19 52	3 54	9 37	22 13	5 34	7 8
10	11 9 30	19 7 8	11♓40	0 50	1♈ 4	20 25	4 8	9 38	22 14	5 35	7 7
11	11 13 26	20 7 6	24 38	0 24	2 18	20 58	4 22	9 39	22 15	5 36	7 6
12	11 17 23	21 7 1	7♈20	29♓50	3 33	21 31	4 37	9 39	22 16	5 37	7 5
13	11 21 19	22 6 55	19 47	29 10	4 48	22 3	4 51	9 40	22 17	5 38	7 4
14	11 25 16	23 6 47	1♉59	28 24	6 2	22 35	5 5	9 41	22 18	5 39	7 3
15	11 29 13	24 6 37	13 59	27 34	7 17	23 8	5 19	9 41	22 18	5 39	7 2
16	11 33 9	25 6 24	25 52	26 40	8 31	23 40	5 33	9 42	22 19	5 40	7 1
17	11 37 6	26 6 10	7♊41	25 45	9 46	24 12	5 47	9 42	22 19	5 41	7 0
18	11 41 2	27 5 53	19 31	24 48	11 0	24 44	6 1	9 42	22 20	5 42	6 58
19	11 44 59	28 5 34	1♋27	23 52	12 15	25 16	6 15	9R42	22 21	5 42	6 57
20	11 48 55	29 5 13	13 35	22 58	13 29	25 47	6 29	9 42	22 21	5 43	6 56
21	11 52 52	0♈ 4 49	25 59	22 6	14 44	26 19	6 43	9 42	22 21	5 43	6 55
22	11 56 48	1 4 23	8♌42	21 17	15 58	26 50	6 56	9 42	22 22	5 44	6 54
23	12 0 45	2 3 55	21 48	20 33	17 12	27 21	7 10	9 42	22 22	5 45	6 52
24	12 4 42	3 3 24	5♍17	19 54	18 27	27 52	7 24	9 41	22 22	5 45	6 51
25	12 8 38	4 2 52	19 9	19 20	19 41	28 23	7 37	9 41	22 22	5 46	6 50
26	12 12 35	5 2 17	3♎21	18 51	20 55	28 54	7 51	9 40	22 22	5 46	6 48
27	12 16 31	6 1 40	17 47	18 29	22 10	29 25	8 5	9 39	22R22	5 46	6 47
28	12 20 28	7 1 1	2♏23	18 12	23 24	29 55	8 18	9 39	22 22	5 47	6 46
29	12 24 24	8 0 21	17 1	18 1	24 38	0♑26	8 32	9 38	22 22	5 47	6 44
30	12 28 21	8 59 38	1♐36	17D56	25 52	0 56	8 45	9 37	22 22	5 47	6 43
31	12 32 17	9♈58 54	16♐ 4	17♓57	27♈ 6	1♑26	8♓59	9♐36	22♐22	5♑48	6♏41

THE SUN ENTERS THE SIGN OF ARIES ON MAR 20 AT 22:04.

♈ ARIES	♉ TAURUS	♊ GEMINI	♋ CANCER	♌ LEO	♍ VIRGO	♎ LIBRA

SIDEREAL . SUN . MOON . MERCURY . VENUS . MARS . JUPITER . SATURN . URANUS . NEPTUNE . PLUTO .

DAY	TIME (h m s)	☉ (° ' ")	☽ (° ')	☿ (° ')	♀ (° ')	♂ (° ')	♃ (° ')	♄ (° ')	♅ (° ')	♆ (° ')	♇ (° ')
A 1	12 36 14	10♈58 8	0♑20	18♓ 3	28♈20	1♑56	9♓12	9♐34	22♐22	5♑48	6♏40
P 2	12 40 11	11 57 21	14 23	18 15	29 34	2 25	9 25	9R33	22R22	5 48	6R38
R 3	12 44 7	12 56 31	28 11	18 32	0♉48	2 55	9 38	9 32	22 21	5 48	6 37
I 4	12 48 4	13 55 40	11♒44	18 53	2 2	3 24	9 52	9 30	22 21	5 48	6 35
L 5	12 52 0	14 54 47	25 2	19 20	3 16	3 53	10 5	9 29	22 21	5 49	6 34
6	12 55 57	15 53 52	8♓ 6	19 50	4 30	4 22	10 18	9 27	22 20	5 49	6 32
7	12 59 53	16 52 56	20 56	20 25	5 44	4 51	10 31	9 25	22 20	5R49	6 31
8	13 3 50	17 51 57	3♈33	21 4	6 58	5 19	10 44	9 23	22 19	5 49	6 29
9	13 7 46	18 50 56	15 57	21 47	8 12	5 48	10 57	9 21	22 18	5 49	6 27
10	13 11 43	19 49 54	28 10	22 33	9 26	6 16	11 9	9 19	22 18	5 49	6 26
11	13 15 40	20 48 49	10♉14	23 23	10 39	6 43	11 22	9 17	22 17	5 48	6 24
12	13 19 36	21 47 42	22 10	24 16	11 53	7 11	11 35	9 15	22 16	5 48	6 23
13	13 23 33	22 46 33	4♊ 1	25 12	13 7	7 38	11 48	9 13	22 16	5 48	6 21
14	13 27 29	23 45 22	15 49	26 11	14 20	8 6	12 0	9 10	22 15	5 48	6 19
15	13 31 26	24 44 9	27 40	27 13	15 34	8 32	12 13	9 8	22 14	5 48	6 18
16	13 35 22	25 42 54	9♋36	28 17	16 48	8 59	12 25	9 5	22 13	5 47	6 16
17	13 39 19	26 41 36	21 42	29 24	18 1	9 26	12 37	9 3	22 12	5 47	6 14
18	13 43 15	27 40 17	4♌ 3	0♈33	19 15	9 52	12 49	9 0	22 11	5 47	6 13
19	13 47 12	28 38 55	16 44	1 45	20 28	10 18	13 2	8 57	22 10	5 46	6 11
20	13 51 9	29 37 30	29 46	2 59	21 42	10 43	13 14	8 54	22 9	5 46	6 9
21	13 55 5	0♉36 4	13♍14	4 15	22 55	11 9	13 26	8 51	22 7	5 46	6 8
22	13 59 2	1 34 35	27 8	5 34	24 8	11 34	13 38	8 48	22 6	5 45	6 6
23	14 2 58	2 33 4	11♎27	6 54	25 22	11 58	13 50	8 45	22 5	5 45	6 4
24	14 6 55	3 31 31	26 7	8 17	26 35	12 23	14 1	8 42	22 4	5 44	6 3
25	14 10 51	4 29 57	11♏ 2	9 41	27 48	12 47	14 13	8 39	22 2	5 44	6 1
26	14 14 48	5 28 20	26 4	11 8	29 2	13 11	14 25	8 35	22 1	5 43	5 59
27	14 18 44	6 26 42	11♐ 4	12 36	0♊15	13 34	14 36	8 32	21 59	5 43	5 58
28	14 22 41	7 25 3	25 54	14 6	1 28	13 58	14 47	8 29	21 58	5 42	5 56
29	14 26 38	8 23 22	10♑28	15 39	2 41	14 21	14 59	8 25	21 56	5 41	5 54
30	14 30 34	9♉21 39	24♑42	17♈13	3♊54	14♑43	15♓10	8♐22	21♐55	5♑41	5♏52

THE SUN ENTERS THE SIGN OF TAURUS ON APR 20 AT 09:13.

DAY	TIME (h m s)	☉ (° ' ")	☽ (° ')	☿ (° ')	♀ (° ')	♂ (° ')	♃ (° ')	♄ (° ')	♅ (° ')	♆ (° ')	♇ (° ')
M 1	14 34 31	10♉19 54	8♒33	18♈49	5♊ 7	15♑ 5	15♓21	8♐18	21♐53	5♑40	5♏51
A 2	14 38 27	11 18 9	22 1	20 26	6 20	15 27	15 32	8R14	21R52	5R39	5R49
Y 3	14 42 24	12 16 21	5♓ 9	22 6	7 33	15 49	15 43	8 11	21 50	5 38	5 47
4	14 46 20	13 14 32	17 57	23 47	8 46	16 10	15 54	8 7	21 48	5 38	5 46
5	14 50 17	14 12 42	0♈30	25 31	9 59	16 30	16 5	8 3	21 46	5 37	5 44
6	14 54 13	15 10 50	12 50	27 16	11 11	16 51	16 15	7 59	21 45	5 36	5 42
7	14 58 10	16 8 57	24 59	29 3	12 24	17 11	16 26	7 55	21 43	5 35	5 41
8	15 2 7	17 7 2	7♉ 0	0♉52	13 37	17 30	16 36	7 51	21 41	5 34	5 39
9	15 6 3	18 5 5	18 55	2 43	14 50	17 49	16 47	7 47	21 39	5 33	5 37
10	15 10 0	19 3 7	0♊46	4 36	16 2	18 8	16 57	7 43	21 37	5 32	5 36
11	15 13 56	20 1 8	12 35	6 30	17 15	18 26	17 7	7 39	21 35	5 31	5 34
12	15 17 53	20 59 6	24 25	8 27	18 28	18 43	17 17	7 35	21 33	5 30	5 33
13	15 21 49	21 57 3	6♋17	10 25	19 40	19 0	17 27	7 31	21 31	5 29	5 31
14	15 25 46	22 54 59	18 15	12 25	20 53	19 17	17 37	7 26	21 29	5 28	5 29
15	15 29 42	23 52 52	0♌22	14 27	22 5	19 33	17 46	7 22	21 27	5 27	5 28
16	15 33 39	24 50 44	12 42	16 30	23 17	19 49	17 56	7 18	21 25	5 26	5 26
17	15 37 36	25 48 34	25 19	18 35	24 30	20 4	18 5	7 13	21 23	5 25	5 25
18	15 41 32	26 46 22	8♍16	20 42	25 42	20 19	18 14	7 9	21 21	5 24	5 23
19	15 45 29	27 44 9	21 37	22 49	26 54	20 33	18 24	7 5	21 19	5 22	5 21
20	15 49 25	28 41 53	5♎24	24 58	28 6	20 47	18 33	7 0	21 16	5 21	5 20
21	15 53 22	29 39 37	19 38	27 8	29 19	21 0	18 42	6 56	21 14	5 20	5 18
22	15 57 18	0♊37 18	4♏17	29 19	0♋31	21 12	18 50	6 52	21 12	5 19	5 17
23	16 1 15	1 34 59	19 16	1♊31	1 43	21 24	18 59	6 47	21 10	5 17	5 15
24	16 5 11	2 32 38	4♐28	3 42	2 55	21 35	19 7	6 43	21 7	5 16	5 14
25	16 9 8	3 30 15	19 43	5 54	4 7	21 46	19 16	6 38	21 5	5 15	5 13
26	16 13 5	4 27 52	4♑51	8 6	5 19	21 56	19 24	6 34	21 3	5 14	5 11
27	16 17 1	5 25 28	19 42	10 16	6 30	22 6	19 32	6 29	21 1	5 12	5 10
28	16 20 58	6 23 2	4♒10	12 27	7 42	22 14	19 40	6 25	20 58	5 11	5 8
29	16 24 54	7 20 36	18 10	14 36	8 54	22 23	19 48	6 20	20 56	5 10	5 7
30	16 28 51	8 18 9	1♓43	16 44	10 6	22 30	19 56	6 16	20 54	5 8	5 6
31	16 32 47	9♊15 40	14♓49	18♊50	11♋17	22♑37	20♓ 3	6♐12	20♐51	5♑ 7	5♏ 4

THE SUN ENTERS THE SIGN OF GEMINI ON MAY 21 AT 08:29.

DAY	TIME (h m s)	☉ (° ' ")	☽ (° ')	☿ (° ')	♀ (° ')	♂ (° ')	♃ (° ')	♄ (° ')	♅ (° ')	♆ (° ')	♇ (° ')
J 1	16 36 44	10♊13 12	27♓32	20♊55	12♋29	22♑43	20♓11	6♐ 7	20♐49	5♑ 5	5♏ 3
U 2	16 40 40	11 10 42	9♈56	22 57	13 40	22 49	20 18	6R 3	20R46	5R 4	5R 2
N 3	16 44 37	12 8 11	22 6	24 58	14 52	22 53	20 25	5 58	20 44	5 2	5 0
E 4	16 48 34	13 5 40	4♉ 6	26 57	16 3	22 57	20 32	5 54	20 41	5 1	4 59
5	16 52 30	14 3 8	15 59	28 53	17 14	23 1	20 39	5 49	20 39	4 59	4 58
6	16 56 27	15 0 35	27 48	0♋47	18 26	23 3	20 46	5 45	20 37	4 58	4 57
7	17 0 23	15 58 2	9♊37	2 38	19 37	23 5	20 52	5 41	20 34	4 57	4 56
8	17 4 20	16 55 27	21 27	4 27	20 48	23R 6	20 58	5 36	20 32	4 55	4 54
9	17 8 16	17 52 52	3♋20	6 13	21 59	23 7	21 5	5 32	20 29	4 53	4 53
10	17 12 13	18 50 16	15 18	7 57	23 10	23 6	21 11	5 28	20 27	4 52	4 52
11	17 16 9	19 47 39	27 22	9 38	24 21	23 5	21 17	5 23	20 24	4 50	4 51
12	17 20 6	20 45 1	9♌35	11 17	25 32	23 3	21 22	5 19	20 22	4 49	4 50
13	17 24 3	21 42 22	21 58	12 53	26 43	23 1	21 28	5 15	20 19	4 47	4 49
14	17 27 59	22 39 42	4♍36	14 26	27 54	22 57	21 33	5 11	20 17	4 46	4 48
15	17 31 56	23 37 1	17 31	15 57	29 4	22 53	21 38	5 7	20 14	4 44	4 47
16	17 35 52	24 34 19	0♎45	17 25	0♌15	22 48	21 43	5 3	20 12	4 43	4 46
17	17 39 49	25 31 36	14 23	18 50	1 26	22 43	21 48	4 59	20 10	4 41	4 45
18	17 43 45	26 28 52	28 26	20 12	2 36	22 36	21 53	4 55	20 7	4 39	4 44
19	17 47 42	27 26 8	12♏54	21 32	3 47	22 29	21 58	4 51	20 5	4 38	4 44
20	17 51 38	28 23 23	27 45	22 49	4 57	22 21	22 2	4 47	20 2	4 36	4 43
21	17 55 35	29 20 37	12♐51	24 3	6 7	22 13	22 6	4 43	20 0	4 35	4 42
22	17 59 32	0♋17 51	28 5	25 14	7 17	22 4	22 10	4 39	19 57	4 33	4 41
23	18 3 28	1 15 4	13♑17	26 22	8 27	21 54	22 14	4 35	19 55	4 31	4 40
24	18 7 25	2 12 17	28 15	27 27	9 37	21 43	22 18	4 32	19 53	4 30	4 40
25	18 11 21	3 9 30	12♒51	28 28	10 47	21 32	22 21	4 28	19 50	4 28	4 39
26	18 15 18	4 6 43	26 59	29 27	11 57	21 20	22 24	4 24	19 48	4 26	4 38
27	18 19 14	5 3 55	10♓38	0♌22	13 7	21 8	22 27	4 21	19 46	4 25	4 38
28	18 23 11	6 1 8	23 48	1 14	14 16	20 55	22 30	4 17	19 43	4 23	4 37
29	18 27 8	6 58 20	6♈32	2 2	15 26	20 41	22 33	4 14	19 41	4 22	4 37
30	18 31 4	7♋55 33	18♈55	2♌47	16♌35	20♑27	22♓36	4♐11	19♐39	4♑20	4♏36

THE SUN ENTERS THE SIGN OF CANCER ON JUN 21 AT 16:31.

♏ SCORPIO ♐ SAGITTARIUS ♑ CAPRICORN ♒ AQUARIUS, ♓ PISCES

SIDEREAL . SUN . MOON . MERCURY . VENUS . MARS . JUPITER . SATURN . URANUS . NEPTUNE . PLUTO .

DAY	TIME	☉	☽	☿	♀	♂	♃	♄	♅	♆	♇
	h m s	° ' "	° '	° '	° '	° '	° '	° '	° '	° '	° '
J 1	18 35 1	8♋52 46	1♉ 3	3♌27	17♌45	20♑13	22♓38	4♐ 7	19♐36	4♑18	4♏36
U 2	18 38 57	9 49 59	12 59	4 4	18 54	19R58	22 40	4R 4	19R34	4R17	4R35
L 3	18 42 54	10 47 12	24 49	4 37	20 3	19 42	22 42	4 1	19 32	4 15	4 35
Y 4	18 46 50	11 44 25	6♊37	5 6	21 12	19 26	22 44	3 58	19 30	4 14	4 34
5	18 50 47	12 41 38	18 26	5 30	22 21	19 10	22 46	3 55	19 27	4 12	4 34
6	18 54 43	13 38 52	0♋20	5 51	23 30	18 53	22 47	3 52	19 25	4 10	4 34
7	18 58 40	14 36 5	12 19	6 6	24 39	18 37	22 48	3 49	19 23	4 9	4 33
8	19 2 37	15 33 19	24 26	6 17	25 48	18 19	22 49	3 46	19 21	4 7	4 33
9	19 6 33	16 30 33	6♌41	6R24	26 56	18 2	22 50	3 44	19 19	4 6	4 33
10	19 10 30	17 27 46	19 5	6 25	28 5	17 45	22 51	3 41	19 17	4 4	4 33
11	19 14 26	18 25 0	1♍40	6 22	29 13	17 27	22 51	3 39	19 15	4 2	4 32
12	19 18 23	19 22 14	14 26	6 14	0♍22	17 10	22R51	3 36	19 13	4 1	4 32
13	19 22 19	20 19 27	27 26	6 2	1 30	16 52	22 51	3 34	19 11	3 59	4 32
14	19 26 16	21 16 41	10♎42	5 45	2 38	16 35	22 51	3 32	19 9	3 58	4 32
15	19 30 12	22 13 54	24 16	5 24	3 46	16 17	22 51	3 29	19 7	3 56	4D32
16	19 34 9	23 11 8	8♏ 9	4 58	4 53	16 0	22 50	3 27	19 5	3 55	4 32
17	19 38 6	24 8 22	22 24	4 29	6 1	15 43	22 50	3 25	19 3	3 53	4 32
18	19 42 2	25 5 36	6♐58	3 56	7 9	15 27	22 49	3 23	19 1	3 52	4 32
19	19 45 59	26 2 50	21 47	3 20	8 16	15 10	22 48	3 21	18 59	3 50	4 32
20	19 49 55	27 0 4	6♑46	2 42	9 23	14 54	22 46	3 20	18 58	3 49	4 33
21	19 53 52	27 57 19	21 45	2 1	10 30	14 38	22 45	3 18	18 56	3 47	4 33
22	19 57 48	28 54 34	6♒35	1 20	11 37	14 23	22 43	3 16	18 54	3 46	4 33
23	20 1 45	29 51 50	21 7	0 38	12 44	14 8	22 41	3 15	18 52	3 45	4 33
24	20 5 42	0♌49 6	5♓15	29♋56	13 50	13 53	22 39	3 14	18 51	3 43	4 33
25	20 9 38	1 46 24	18 56	29 16	14 57	13 39	22 37	3 12	18 49	3 42	4 34
26	20 13 35	2 43 41	2♈ 9	28 37	16 3	13 26	22 34	3 11	18 48	3 40	4 34
27	20 17 31	3 41 0	14 56	28 0	17 9	13 13	22 32	3 10	18 46	3 39	4 35
28	20 21 28	4 38 20	27 21	27 27	18 15	13 1	22 29	3 9	18 45	3 38	4 35
29	20 25 24	5 35 41	9♉29	26 57	19 21	12 49	22 26	3 8	18 43	3 36	4 35
30	20 29 21	6 33 3	21 26	26 32	20 27	12 38	22 23	3 7	18 42	3 35	4 36
31	20 33 17	7♌30 26	3♊17	26♋11	21♍32	12♑28	22♓19	3♐ 6	18♐41	3♑34	4♏36

THE SUN ENTERS THE SIGN OF LEO ON JUL 23 AT 03:26.

DAY	TIME	☉	☽	☿	♀	♂	♃	♄	♅	♆	♇
	h m s	° ' "	° '	° '	° '	° '	° '	° '	° '	° '	° '
A 1	20 37 14	8♌27 50	15♊ 6	25♋56	22♍37	12♑18	22♓16	3♐ 6	18♐39	3♑33	4♏37
U 2	20 41 11	9 25 15	26 59	25R47	23 42	12R10	22R12	3R 5	18R38	3R31	4 38
G 3	20 45 7	10 22 41	8♋57	25D44	24 47	12 2	22 8	3 5	18 37	3 30	4 38
U 4	20 49 4	11 20 9	21 5	25 47	25 52	11 54	22 4	3 4	18 36	3 29	4 39
S 5	20 53 0	12 17 37	3♌22	25 56	26 56	11 48	21 59	3 4	18 34	3 28	4 40
T 6	20 56 57	13 15 6	15 51	26 12	28 1	11 42	21 55	3 4	18 33	3 27	4 40
7	21 0 53	14 12 36	28 32	26 35	29 5	11 37	21 50	3D 4	18 32	3 25	4 41
8	21 4 50	15 10 7	11♍24	27 4	0♎ 9	11 33	21 45	3 4	18 31	3 24	4 42
9	21 8 46	16 7 39	24 27	27 40	1 12	11 30	21 41	3 4	18 30	3 23	4 43
10	21 12 43	17 5 12	7♎42	28 22	2 16	11 27	21 35	3 4	18 29	3 22	4 43
11	21 16 40	18 2 46	21 9	29 11	3 19	11 26	21 30	3 5	18 29	3 21	4 44
12	21 20 36	19 0 21	4♏48	0♌ 7	4 22	11D25	21 25	3 5	18 28	3 20	4 45
13	21 24 33	19 57 56	18 41	1 9	5 24	11 25	21 19	3 5	18 27	3 19	4 46
14	21 28 29	20 55 33	2♐47	2 16	6 27	11 26	21 13	3 6	18 26	3 18	4 47
15	21 32 26	21 53 10	17 6	3 30	7 29	11 28	21 7	3 7	18 26	3 17	4 48
16	21 36 22	22 50 49	1♑35	4 49	8 30	11 31	21 1	3 8	18 25	3 16	4 49
17	21 40 19	23 48 28	16 10	6 14	9 32	11 34	20 55	3 8	18 24	3 15	4 50
18	21 44 15	24 46 9	0♒46	7 43	10 33	11 39	20 49	3 10	18 24	3 15	4 51
19	21 48 12	25 43 51	15 14	9 17	11 34	11 44	20 43	3 11	18 23	3 14	4 53
20	21 52 9	26 41 33	29 29	10 56	12 35	11 50	20 36	3 12	18 23	3 13	4 54
21	21 56 5	27 39 18	13♓25	12 38	13 35	11 56	20 29	3 13	18 23	3 12	4 55
22	22 0 2	28 37 3	26 58	14 24	14 35	12 4	20 23	3 14	18 22	3 11	4 56
23	22 3 58	29 34 50	10♈ 8	16 13	15 34	12 12	20 16	3 16	18 22	3 11	4 57
24	22 7 55	0♍32 39	22 54	18 4	16 34	12 21	20 9	3 18	18 22	3 10	4 59
25	22 11 51	1 30 30	5♉21	19 57	17 32	12 31	20 2	3 19	18 22	3 9	5 0
26	22 15 48	2 28 22	17 31	21 52	18 31	12 42	19 54	3 21	18 22	3 9	5 1
27	22 19 44	3 26 16	29 30	23 49	19 29	12 53	19 47	3 23	18D21	3 8	5 3
28	22 23 41	4 24 12	11♊22	25 46	20 27	13 5	19 40	3 25	18 21	3 7	5 4
29	22 27 38	5 22 10	23 13	27 44	21 24	13 18	19 32	3 27	18 21	3 7	5 6
30	22 31 34	6 20 10	5♋ 8	29 43	22 21	13 31	19 25	3 29	18 22	3 6	5 7
31	22 35 31	7♍18 11	17♋11	1♍41	23♎17	13♑45	19♓17	3♐31	18♐22	3♑ 6	5♏ 9

THE SUN ENTERS THE SIGN OF VIRGO ON AUG 23 AT 10:27.

DAY	TIME	☉	☽	☿	♀	♂	♃	♄	♅	♆	♇
	h m s	° ' "	° '	° '	° '	° '	° '	° '	° '	° '	° '
S 1	22 39 27	8♍16 14	29♋24	3♍40	24♎13	14♑ 0	19♓10	3♐34	18♐22	3♑ 5	5♏10
E 2	22 43 24	9 14 19	11♌52	5 37	25 8	14 16	19R 2	3 36	18 22	3R 5	5 12
P 3	22 47 20	10 12 26	24 34	7 35	26 3	14 32	18 54	3 38	18 22	3 5	5 13
T 4	22 51 17	11 10 35	7♍32	9 31	26 58	14 49	18 46	3 41	18 23	3 4	5 15
E 5	22 55 13	12 8 45	20 45	11 27	27 51	15 6	18 38	3 44	18 23	3 4	5 17
M 6	22 59 10	13 6 57	4♎11	13 22	28 45	15 24	18 31	3 46	18 24	3 4	5 18
B 7	23 3 6	14 5 10	17 49	15 16	29 38	15 43	18 23	3 49	18 24	3 3	5 20
E 8	23 7 3	15 3 25	1♏37	17 9	0♏30	16 2	18 15	3 52	18 25	3 3	5 22
R 9	23 11 0	16 1 42	15 33	19 1	1 21	16 22	18 7	3 55	18 25	3 3	5 23
10	23 14 56	17 0 0	29 36	20 52	2 12	16 43	17 59	3 58	18 26	3 3	5 25
11	23 18 53	17 58 20	13♐44	22 41	3 2	17 4	17 51	4 2	18 27	3 3	5 27
12	23 22 49	18 56 41	27 56	24 30	3 52	17 26	17 43	4 5	18 27	3 2	5 29
13	23 26 46	19 55 4	12♑10	26 18	4 41	17 48	17 35	4 8	18 28	3 2	5 31
14	23 30 42	20 53 28	26 23	28 4	5 29	18 11	17 27	4 12	18 29	3D 2	5 32
15	23 34 39	21 51 54	10♒31	29 49	6 16	18 34	17 19	4 15	18 30	3 2	5 34
16	23 38 36	22 50 21	24 32	1♎33	7 3	18 58	17 11	4 19	18 31	3 2	5 36
17	23 42 32	23 48 51	8♓20	3 16	7 48	19 22	17 3	4 23	18 32	3 2	5 38
18	23 46 29	24 47 22	21 54	4 58	8 33	19 46	16 55	4 27	18 33	3 3	5 40
19	23 50 25	25 45 54	5♈11	6 39	9 17	20 12	16 48	4 30	18 34	3 3	5 42
20	23 54 22	26 44 29	18 9	8 19	9 59	20 37	16 40	4 34	18 35	3 3	5 44
21	23 58 18	27 43 6	0♉49	9 58	10 41	21 3	16 32	4 38	18 36	3 3	5 46
22	0 2 15	28 41 45	13 12	11 36	11 22	21 30	16 25	4 42	18 38	3 3	5 48
23	0 6 11	29 40 26	25 22	13 13	12 2	21 57	16 17	4 47	18 39	3 3	5 50
24	0 10 8	0♎39 10	7♊21	14 49	12 40	22 24	16 10	4 51	18 40	3 4	5 52
25	0 14 4	1 37 55	19 15	16 24	13 18	22 52	16 2	4 55	18 42	3 4	5 54
26	0 18 1	2 36 43	1♋ 7	17 59	13 54	23 20	15 55	5 0	18 43	3 4	5 56
27	0 21 58	3 35 33	13 2	19 32	14 29	23 49	15 48	5 4	18 45	3 5	5 58
28	0 25 54	4 34 26	25 5	21 4	15 3	24 17	15 40	5 9	18 46	3 5	6 1
29	0 29 51	5 33 20	7♌21	22 35	15 35	24 47	15 33	5 13	18 48	3 6	6 3
30	0 33 47	6♎32 17	19♌53	24♎ 6	16♏ 6	25♑16	15♓26	5♐18	18♐49	3♑ 6	6♏ 5

THE SUN ENTERS THE SIGN OF LIBRA ON SEP 23 AT 08:00.

♈ ARIES ♉ TAURUS ♊ GEMINI ♋ CANCER ♌ LEO ♍ VIRGO ♎ LIBRA

SIDEREAL TIME · SUN · MOON · MERCURY · VENUS · MARS · JUPITER · SATURN · URANUS · NEPTUNE · PLUTO

DAY	TIME	☉	☽	☿	♀	♂	♃	♄	♅	♆	♇
	h m s	° ' "	° '	° '	° '	° '	° '	° '	° '	° '	° '
O 1	0 37 44	7♎31 16	2♍43	25♎36	16♏36	25♑46	15♓20	5♐23	18♐51	3♑ 7	6♏ 7
C 2	0 41 40	8 30 17	15 53	27 4	17 4	26 17	15R13	5 28	18 53	3 7	6 9
T 3	0 45 37	9 29 21	29 24	28 32	17 30	26 48	15 6	5 33	18 55	3 8	6 11
O 4	0 49 33	10 28 26	13♎12	29 59	17 55	27 19	15 0	5 37	18 56	3 8	6 14
B 5	0 53 30	11 27 33	27 17	1♏25	18 19	27 50	14 53	5 43	18 58	3 9	6 16
E 6	0 57 27	12 26 43	11♏32	2 50	18 40	28 22	14 47	5 48	19 0	3 10	6 18
R 7	1 1 23	13 25 54	25 55	4 14	19 0	28 54	14 41	5 53	19 2	3 10	6 20
8	1 5 20	14 25 7	10♐19	5 37	19 17	29 26	14 35	5 58	19 4	3 11	6 23
9	1 9 16	15 24 23	24 42	6 59	19 33	29 59	14 29	6 3	19 6	3 12	6 25
10	1 13 13	16 23 39	8♑59	8 19	19 47	0♒31	14 24	6 9	19 8	3 13	6 27
11	1 17 9	17 22 58	23 8	9 39	19 58	1 5	14 18	6 14	19 10	3 14	6 30
12	1 21 6	18 22 18	7♒ 6	10 58	20 8	1 38	14 13	6 20	19 13	3 14	6 32
13	1 25 2	19 21 40	20 53	12 15	20 15	2 12	14 8	6 25	19 15	3 15	6 34
14	1 28 59	20 21 4	4♓28	13 31	20 20	2 46	14 3	6 31	19 17	3 16	6 37
15	1 32 56	21 20 29	17 49	14 45	20R23	3 20	13 58	6 36	19 19	3 17	6 39
16	1 36 52	22 19 56	0♈58	15 58	20 24	3 55	13 53	6 42	19 22	3 18	6 41
17	1 40 49	23 19 25	13 52	17 10	20 22	4 29	13 49	6 48	19 24	3 19	6 44
18	1 44 45	24 18 56	26 33	18 19	20 17	5 4	13 44	6 54	19 27	3 20	6 46
19	1 48 42	25 18 30	9♉ 1	19 27	20 11	5 39	13 40	6 59	19 29	3 21	6 48
20	1 52 38	26 18 5	21 17	20 32	20 2	6 15	13 36	7 5	19 32	3 23	6 51
21	1 56 35	27 17 42	3♊23	21 35	19 50	6 50	13 33	7 11	19 34	3 24	6 53
22	2 0 31	28 17 22	15 20	22 36	19 36	7 26	13 29	7 17	19 37	3 25	6 56
23	2 4 28	29 17 4	27 13	23 33	19 20	8 2	13 26	7 23	19 39	3 26	6 58
24	2 8 25	0♏16 48	9♋ 4	24 28	19 1	8 38	13 22	7 30	19 42	3 27	7 1
25	2 12 21	1 16 34	20 58	25 19	18 40	9 15	13 19	7 36	19 45	3 29	7 3
26	2 16 18	2 16 23	3♌ 0	26 6	18 17	9 51	13 17	7 42	19 47	3 30	7 5
27	2 20 14	3 16 13	15 13	26 49	17 52	10 28	13 14	7 48	19 50	3 31	7 8
28	2 24 11	4 16 6	27 42	27 28	17 25	11 5	13 11	7 54	19 53	3 33	7 10
29	2 28 7	5 16 1	10♍32	28 1	16 56	11 42	13 9	8 1	19 56	3 34	7 13
30	2 32 4	6 15 58	23 45	28 28	16 25	12 19	13 7	8 7	19 59	3 35	7 15
31	2 36 0	7♏15 58	7♎23	28♏49	15♏53	12♒56	13♓ 5	8♐14	20♐ 1	3♑37	7♏17

THE SUN ENTERS THE SIGN OF SCORPIO ON OCT 23 AT 17:15.

DAY	TIME	☉	☽	☿	♀	♂	♃	♄	♅	♆	♇
	h m s	° ' "	° '	° '	° '	° '	° '	° '	° '	° '	° '
N 1	2 39 57	8♏15 59	21♎26	29♏ 3	15♏20	13♒34	13♓ 4	8♐20	20♐ 4	3♑38	7♏20
O 2	2 43 54	9 16 2	5♏50	29R 9	14R45	14 12	13R 2	8 26	20 7	3 40	7 22
V 3	2 47 50	10 16 7	20 31	29 8	14 10	14 50	13 1	8 33	20 10	3 41	7 25
E 4	2 51 47	11 16 15	5♐22	28 57	13 34	15 28	13 0	8 40	20 13	3 43	7 27
M 5	2 55 43	12 16 23	20 15	28 37	12 58	16 6	12 59	8 46	20 16	3 44	7 30
B 6	2 59 40	13 16 34	5♑ 1	28 7	12 21	16 44	12 59	8 53	20 19	3 46	7 32
E 7	3 3 36	14 16 46	19 34	27 28	11 45	17 23	12 58	8 59	20 23	3 47	7 34
R 8	3 7 33	15 17 0	3♒50	26 39	11 9	18 2	12D58	9 6	20 26	3 49	7 37
9	3 11 29	16 17 14	17 47	25 41	10 33	18 40	12 58	9 13	20 29	3 51	7 39
10	3 15 26	17 17 31	1♓24	24 34	9 59	19 19	12 58	9 20	20 32	3 52	7 42
11	3 19 23	18 17 48	14 42	23 22	9 25	19 58	12 59	9 26	20 35	3 54	7 44
12	3 23 19	19 18 7	27 43	22 4	8 53	20 37	12 59	9 33	20 38	3 56	7 47
13	3 27 16	20 18 28	10♈30	20 44	8 22	21 17	13 0	9 40	20 42	3 58	7 49
14	3 31 12	21 18 50	23 3	19 24	7 53	21 56	13 1	9 47	20 45	3 59	7 51
15	3 35 9	22 19 14	5♉26	18 7	7 25	22 36	13 3	9 54	20 48	4 1	7 54
16	3 39 5	23 19 39	17 40	16 55	7 0	23 15	13 4	10 1	20 52	4 3	7 56
17	3 43 2	24 20 6	29 46	15 50	6 36	23 55	13 6	10 8	20 55	4 5	7 58
18	3 46 58	25 20 34	11♊46	14 55	6 15	24 34	13 8	10 15	20 58	4 7	8 1
19	3 50 55	26 21 4	23 41	14 10	5 57	25 14	13 10	10 22	21 2	4 9	8 3
20	3 54 52	27 21 36	5♋33	13 37	5 40	25 54	13 12	10 29	21 5	4 10	8 5
21	3 58 48	28 22 9	17 24	13 16	5 26	26 34	13 14	10 36	21 9	4 12	8 8
22	4 2 45	29 22 44	29 17	13D 6	5 15	27 14	13 17	10 43	21 12	4 14	8 10
23	4 6 41	0♐23 21	11♌17	13 7	5 6	27 55	13 20	10 50	21 15	4 16	8 12
24	4 10 38	1 24 0	23 26	13 19	4 59	28 35	13 23	10 57	21 19	4 18	8 15
25	4 14 34	2 24 40	5♍50	13 41	4 55	29 15	13 26	11 4	21 22	4 20	8 17
26	4 18 31	3 25 21	18 33	14 11	4D54	29 56	13 30	11 11	21 26	4 22	8 19
27	4 22 27	4 26 4	1♎40	14 50	4 55	0♓36	13 33	11 18	21 29	4 24	8 21
28	4 26 24	5 26 49	15 14	15 35	4 58	1 17	13 37	11 25	21 33	4 26	8 24
29	4 30 21	6 27 36	29 16	16 27	5 4	1 57	13 41	11 32	21 37	4 28	8 26
30	4 34 17	7♐28 24	13♏46	17♏24	5♏12	2♓38	13♓45	11♐39	21♐40	4♑30	8♏28

THE SUN ENTERS THE SIGN OF SAGITTARIUS ON NOV 22 AT 14:45.

DAY	TIME	☉	☽	☿	♀	♂	♃	♄	♅	♆	♇
	h m s	° ' "	° '	° '	° '	° '	° '	° '	° '	° '	° '
D 1	4 38 14	8♐29 13	28♏39	18♏26	5♏22	3♓19	13♓50	11♐46	21♐44	4♑32	8♏30
E 2	4 42 10	9 30 4	13♐48	19 33	5 34	4 0	13 54	11 53	21 47	4 35	8 32
C 3	4 46 7	10 30 55	29 3	20 42	5 49	4 41	13 59	12 0	21 51	4 37	8 35
E 4	4 50 3	11 31 48	14♑14	21 55	6 6	5 22	14 4	12 8	21 54	4 39	8 37
M 5	4 54 0	12 32 42	29 9	23 11	6 25	6 3	14 9	12 15	21 58	4 41	8 39
B 6	4 57 57	13 33 37	13♒41	24 29	6 45	6 44	14 15	12 22	22 2	4 43	8 41
E 7	5 1 53	14 34 32	27 48	25 49	7 8	7 25	14 20	12 29	22 5	4 45	8 43
R 8	5 5 50	15 35 28	11♓27	27 11	7 32	8 6	14 26	12 36	22 9	4 47	8 45
9	5 9 46	16 36 24	24 41	28 34	7 58	8 47	14 32	12 43	22 13	4 50	8 47
10	5 13 43	17 37 22	7♈33	29 58	8 26	9 29	14 38	12 50	22 16	4 52	8 49
11	5 17 39	18 38 20	20 7	1♐23	8 56	10 10	14 44	12 57	22 20	4 54	8 51
12	5 21 36	19 39 18	2♉27	2 50	9 27	10 51	14 50	13 4	22 24	4 56	8 53
13	5 25 32	20 40 17	14 37	4 17	9 59	11 33	14 57	13 11	22 27	4 58	8 55
14	5 29 29	21 41 17	26 39	5 45	10 34	12 14	15 3	13 19	22 31	5 1	8 57
15	5 33 26	22 42 18	8♊36	7 13	11 9	12 56	15 10	13 26	22 34	5 3	8 59
16	5 37 22	23 43 19	20 31	8 42	11 46	13 37	15 17	13 33	22 38	5 5	9 1
17	5 41 19	24 44 21	2♋23	10 11	12 24	14 19	15 25	13 40	22 42	5 7	9 3
18	5 45 15	25 45 24	14 16	11 41	13 4	15 0	15 32	13 47	22 45	5 9	9 5
19	5 49 12	26 46 27	26 9	13 11	13 44	15 42	15 39	13 54	22 49	5 12	9 6
20	5 53 8	27 47 31	8♌ 6	14 42	14 26	16 24	15 47	14 1	22 53	5 14	9 8
21	5 57 5	28 48 36	20 7	16 13	15 9	17 5	15 55	14 8	22 56	5 16	9 10
22	6 1 1	29 49 41	2♍17	17 44	15 53	17 47	16 3	14 15	23 0	5 19	9 12
23	6 4 58	0♑50 47	14 39	19 16	16 38	18 29	16 11	14 22	23 4	5 21	9 13
24	6 8 55	1 51 54	27 17	20 47	17 25	19 10	16 19	14 29	23 7	5 23	9 15
25	6 12 51	2 53 2	10♎15	22 19	18 12	19 52	16 28	14 35	23 11	5 25	9 17
26	6 16 48	3 54 10	23 38	23 52	19 0	20 34	16 36	14 42	23 14	5 28	9 18
27	6 20 44	4 55 19	7♏30	25 24	19 49	21 16	16 45	14 49	23 18	5 30	9 20
28	6 24 41	5 56 28	21 50	26 57	20 38	21 57	16 54	14 56	23 22	5 32	9 21
29	6 28 37	6 57 38	6♐37	28 30	21 29	22 39	17 3	15 3	23 25	5 34	9 23
30	6 32 34	7 58 49	21 45	0♑ 3	22 20	23 21	17 12	15 9	23 29	5 37	9 25
31	6 36 30	9♑ 0 0	7♑ 6	1♑37	23♏12	24♓ 3	17♓21	15♐16	23♐32	5♑39	9♏26

THE SUN ENTERS THE SIGN OF CAPRICORN ON DEC 22 AT 04:03.

♏ SCORPIO ♐ SAGITTARIUS ♑ CAPRICORN ♒ AQUARIUS ♓ PISCES

SIDEREAL . . . SUN . . MOON . . MERCURY . . VENUS . . MARS . . JUPITER . . SATURN . . URANUS . . NEPTUNE . . PLUTO .

DAY	TIME	☉	☽	☿	♀	♂	♃	♄	♅	♆	♇
	h m s	° ' "	° '	° '	° '	° '	° '	° '	° '	° '	° '
J 1	6 40 27	10♑ 1 11	22♑27	3♑11	24♏ 5	24♓45	17♓31	15♐23	23♐36	5♑41	9♏28
A 2	6 44 24	11 2 22	7♒36	4 45	24 59	25 27	17 40	15 30	23 39	5 43	9 29
N 3	6 48 20	12 3 33	22 24	6 20	25 53	26 9	17 50	15 36	23 43	5 46	9 30
U 4	6 52 17	13 4 43	6♓45	7 54	26 48	26 51	18 0	15 43	23 47	5 48	9 32
A 5	6 56 13	14 5 53	20 35	9 30	27 43	27 33	18 9	15 49	23 50	5 50	9 33
R 6	7 0 10	15 7 3	3♈55	11 5	28 39	28 15	18 19	15 56	23 53	5 53	9 34
Y 7	7 4 6	16 8 13	16 49	12 41	29 35	28 56	18 30	16 2	23 57	5 55	9 36
8	7 8 3	17 9 22	29 22	14 18	0♐33	29 38	18 40	16 9	24 0	5 57	9 37
9	7 11 59	18 10 31	11♉38	15 54	1 30	0♈20	18 50	16 15	24 4	5 59	9 38
10	7 15 56	19 11 39	23 41	17 32	2 28	1 2	19 1	16 22	24 7	6 1	9 39
11	7 19 53	20 12 47	5♊37	19 9	3 27	1 44	19 11	16 28	24 11	6 4	9 40
12	7 23 49	21 13 54	17 30	20 47	4 26	2 26	19 22	16 34	24 14	6 6	9 41
13	7 27 46	22 15 1	29 21	22 26	5 26	3 8	19 33	16 41	24 17	6 8	9 43
14	7 31 42	23 16 8	11♋13	24 5	6 26	3 50	19 44	16 47	24 21	6 10	9 44
15	7 35 39	24 17 14	23 8	25 44	7 26	4 32	19 55	16 53	24 24	6 13	9 45
16	7 39 35	25 18 20	5♌ 7	27 24	8 27	5 14	20 6	16 59	24 27	6 15	9 46
17	7 43 32	26 19 25	17 11	29 5	9 28	5 56	20 17	17 5	24 30	6 17	9 47
18	7 47 29	27 20 30	29 21	0♒46	10 30	6 38	20 29	17 11	24 34	6 19	9 47
19	7 51 25	28 21 34	11♍39	2 27	11 32	7 20	20 40	17 17	24 37	6 21	9 48
20	7 55 22	29 22 38	24 8	4 9	12 34	8 2	20 52	17 23	24 40	6 23	9 49
21	7 59 18	0♒23 41	6♎49	5 51	13 37	8 43	21 3	17 29	24 43	6 25	9 50
22	8 3 15	1 24 44	19 46	7 34	14 40	9 25	21 15	17 35	24 46	6 28	9 51
23	8 7 11	2 25 47	3♏ 4	9 17	15 43	10 7	21 27	17 40	24 49	6 30	9 51
24	8 11 8	3 26 50	16 45	11 1	16 47	10 49	21 39	17 46	24 52	6 32	9 52
25	8 15 4	4 27 52	0♐50	12 45	17 51	11 31	21 51	17 52	24 55	6 34	9 53
26	8 19 1	5 28 53	15 20	14 29	18 55	12 13	22 3	17 57	24 58	6 36	9 53
27	8 22 58	6 29 55	0♑11	16 13	20 0	12 55	22 15	18 3	25 1	6 38	9 54
28	8 26 54	7 30 55	15 16	17 57	21 5	13 37	22 28	18 8	25 4	6 40	9 55
29	8 30 51	8 31 55	0♒27	19 41	22 10	14 18	22 40	18 14	25 7	6 42	9 55
30	8 34 47	9 32 53	15 32	21 24	23 15	15 0	22 52	18 19	25 10	6 44	9 56
31	8 38 44	10♒33 51	0♓21	23♒ 8	24♐21	15♈42	23♓ 5	18♐24	25♐13	6♑46	9♏56

THE SUN ENTERS THE SIGN OF AQUARIUS ON JAN 20 AT 14:41.

DAY	TIME	☉	☽	☿	♀	♂	♃	♄	♅	♆	♇
	h m s	° ' "	° '	° '	° '	° '	° '	° '	° '	° '	° '
F 1	8 42 40	11♒34 48	14♓47	24♒50	25♐26	16♈24	23♓17	18♐29	25♐16	6♑48	9♏56
E 2	8 46 37	12 35 43	28 46	26 31	26 32	17 6	23 30	18 35	25 19	6 50	9 57
B 3	8 50 33	13 36 37	12♈15	28 11	27 38	17 47	23 43	18 40	25 21	6 52	9 57
R 4	8 54 30	14 37 29	25 16	29 50	28 45	18 29	23 56	18 45	25 24	6 54	9 57
U 5	8 58 27	15 38 21	7♉54	1♓26	29 51	19 11	24 9	18 50	25 27	6 56	9 58
A 6	9 2 23	16 39 11	20 13	3 0	0♑58	19 53	24 22	18 54	25 29	6 57	9 58
R 7	9 6 20	17 39 59	2♊18	4 30	2 5	20 34	24 35	18 59	25 32	6 59	9 58
Y 8	9 10 16	18 40 46	14 14	5 57	3 12	21 16	24 48	19 4	25 34	7 1	9 58
9	9 14 13	19 41 32	26 5	7 19	4 20	21 58	25 1	19 9	25 37	7 3	9 58
10	9 18 9	20 42 16	7♋56	8 36	5 27	22 39	25 14	19 13	25 39	7 5	9 58
11	9 22 6	21 42 58	19 50	9 48	6 35	23 21	25 27	19 18	25 42	7 6	9R58
12	9 26 2	22 43 39	1♌49	10 53	7 43	24 3	25 41	19 22	25 44	7 8	9 58
13	9 29 59	23 44 19	13 56	11 51	8 51	24 44	25 54	19 26	25 47	7 10	9 58
14	9 33 56	24 44 57	26 10	12 40	9 59	25 26	26 7	19 31	25 49	7 12	9 58
15	9 37 52	25 45 34	8♍34	13 22	11 7	26 7	26 21	19 35	25 51	7 13	9 58
16	9 41 49	26 46 9	21 8	13 54	12 16	26 49	26 34	19 39	25 53	7 15	9 58
17	9 45 45	27 46 43	3♎52	14 16	13 24	27 30	26 48	19 43	25 56	7 16	9 58
18	9 49 42	28 47 15	16 48	14R28	14 33	28 12	27 2	19 47	25 58	7 18	9 58
19	9 53 38	29 47 47	29 57	14 30	15 42	28 53	27 15	19 51	26 0	7 20	9 58
20	9 57 35	0♓48 17	13♏21	14 21	16 51	29 35	27 29	19 54	26 2	7 21	9 57
21	10 1 31	1 48 46	27 1	14 2	18 0	0♉16	27 43	19 58	26 4	7 23	9 57
22	10 5 28	2 49 13	10♐59	13 34	19 9	0 57	27 57	20 2	26 6	7 24	9 57
23	10 9 25	3 49 40	25 13	12 57	20 18	1 39	28 11	20 5	26 8	7 26	9 56
24	10 13 21	4 50 5	9♑42	12 12	21 28	2 20	28 25	20 9	26 10	7 27	9 56
25	10 17 18	5 50 28	24 23	11 20	22 37	3 1	28 39	20 12	26 11	7 28	9 55
26	10 21 14	6 50 50	9♒ 8	10 23	23 47	3 43	28 53	20 15	26 13	7 30	9 55
27	10 25 11	7 51 11	23 50	9 22	24 57	4 24	29 7	20 19	26 15	7 31	9 54
28	10 29 7	8♓51 30	8♓23	8♓19	26♑ 7	5♉ 5	29♓21	20♐22	26♐17	7♑33	9♏54

THE SUN ENTERS THE SIGN OF PISCES ON FEB 19 AT 04:51.

DAY	TIME	☉	☽	☿	♀	♂	♃	♄	♅	♆	♇
	h m s	° ' "	° '	° '	° '	° '	° '	° '	° '	° '	° '
M 1	10 33 4	9♓51 47	22♓38	7♓15	27♑17	5♉46	29♓35	20♐25	26♐18	7♑34	9♏53
A 2	10 37 0	10 52 2	6♈32	6R12	28 27	6 28	29 49	20 27	26 20	7 35	9R53
R 3	10 40 57	11 52 15	20 2	5 10	29 37	7 9	0♈ 3	20 30	26 21	7 36	9 52
C 4	10 44 54	12 52 26	3♉ 8	4 13	0♒47	7 50	0 17	20 33	26 23	7 38	9 51
H 5	10 48 50	13 52 36	15 51	3 20	1 57	8 31	0 32	20 36	26 24	7 39	9 51
6	10 52 47	14 52 43	28 14	2 32	3 8	9 12	0 46	20 38	26 26	7 40	9 50
7	10 56 43	15 52 48	10♊23	1 50	4 18	9 53	1 0	20 41	26 27	7 41	9 49
8	11 0 40	16 52 51	22 22	1 15	5 29	10 34	1 14	20 43	26 28	7 42	9 48
9	11 4 36	17 52 52	4♋15	0 46	6 39	11 15	1 29	20 45	26 30	7 43	9 47
10	11 8 33	18 52 51	16 7	0 24	7 50	11 56	1 43	20 47	26 31	7 44	9 46
11	11 12 29	19 52 48	28 3	0 8	9 0	12 37	1 57	20 49	26 32	7 45	9 46
12	11 16 26	20 52 42	10♌ 5	29♒59	10 11	13 18	2 12	20 51	26 33	7 46	9 45
13	11 20 23	21 52 34	22 18	29D57	11 22	13 59	2 26	20 53	26 34	7 47	9 44
14	11 24 19	22 52 25	4♍43	0♓ 1	12 33	14 40	2 41	20 55	26 35	7 48	9 43
15	11 28 16	23 52 13	17 21	0 10	13 44	15 21	2 55	20 57	26 36	7 49	9 42
16	11 32 12	24 51 59	0♎14	0 26	14 55	16 2	3 10	20 58	26 37	7 50	9 41
17	11 36 9	25 51 43	13 20	0 46	16 6	16 42	3 24	21 0	26 38	7 51	9 40
18	11 40 5	26 51 25	26 39	1 11	17 17	17 23	3 39	21 1	26 38	7 51	9 39
19	11 44 2	27 51 6	10♏11	1 42	18 28	18 4	3 53	21 2	26 39	7 52	9 37
20	11 47 58	28 50 45	23 55	2 16	19 39	18 45	4 8	21 3	26 40	7 53	9 36
21	11 51 55	29 50 22	7♐49	2 55	20 51	19 25	4 22	21 5	26 40	7 53	9 35
22	11 55 52	0♈49 57	21 51	3 37	22 2	20 6	4 37	21 6	26 41	7 54	9 34
23	11 59 48	1 49 31	6♑ 1	4 24	23 14	20 46	4 51	21 6	26 41	7 55	9 33
24	12 3 45	2 49 3	20 17	5 13	24 25	21 27	5 6	21 7	26 42	7 55	9 31
25	12 7 41	3 48 33	4♒35	6 6	25 36	22 8	5 20	21 8	26 42	7 56	9 30
26	12 11 38	4 48 1	18 52	7 2	26 48	22 48	5 35	21 8	26 43	7 56	9 29
27	12 15 34	5 47 28	3♓ 5	8 1	28 0	23 29	5 49	21 9	26 43	7 57	9 28
28	12 19 31	6 46 52	17 9	9 2	29 11	24 9	6 4	21 9	26 43	7 57	9 26
29	12 23 27	7 46 15	1♈ 1	10 6	0♓23	24 50	6 18	21 10	26 43	7 58	9 25
30	12 27 24	8 45 36	14 37	11 13	1 35	25 30	6 33	21 10	26 44	7 58	9 23
31	12 31 20	9♈44 54	27♈56	12♓22	2♓46	26♉10	6♈47	21♐10	26♐44	7♑58	9♏22

THE SUN ENTERS THE SIGN OF ARIES ON MAR 21 AT 03:52.

♈ ARIES ♉ TAURUS ♊ GEMINI ♋ CANCER ♌ LEO ♍ VIRGO ♎ LIBRA

1987

SIDEREAL SUN. MOON. MERCURY. VENUS. MARS. JUPITER. SATURN. URANUS. NEPTUNE. PLUTO.

DAY	TIME	☉	☽	☿	♀	♂	♃	♄	♅	♆	♇
	h m s	° ' "	° '	° '	° '	° '	° '	° '	° '	° '	° '
A 1	12 35 17	10♈44 11	10♉56	13♓33	3♓58	26♉51	7♈ 2	21♐10	26♐44	7♑59	9♏21
P 2	12 39 14	11 43 25	23 37	14 46	5 10	27 31	7 16	21R10	26R44	7 59	9R19
R 3	12 43 10	12 42 37	6♊ 1	16 1	6 22	28 12	7 31	21 9	26 44	7 59	9 18
I 4	12 47 7	13 41 47	18 12	17 19	7 34	28 52	7 45	21 9	26 43	8 0	9 16
L 5	12 51 3	14 40 55	0♋13	18 38	8 45	29 32	8 0	21 9	26 43	8 0	9 15
6	12 55 0	15 40 0	12 7	19 59	9 57	0♊12	8 14	21 8	26 43	8 0	9 13
7	12 58 56	16 39 3	24 0	21 22	11 9	0 53	8 29	21 7	26 43	8 0	9 12
8	13 2 53	17 38 4	5♌56	22 46	12 21	1 33	8 43	21 7	26 42	8 0	9 10
9	13 6 49	18 37 2	18 0	24 12	13 33	2 13	8 58	21 6	26 42	8 0	9 9
10	13 10 46	19 35 58	0♍16	25 40	14 45	2 53	9 12	21 5	26 42	8R 0	9 7
11	13 14 43	20 34 52	12 47	27 10	15 57	3 33	9 26	21 4	26 41	8 0	9 6
12	13 18 39	21 33 44	25 36	28 41	17 9	4 13	9 41	21 3	26 41	8 0	9 4
13	13 22 36	22 32 33	8♎44	0♈14	18 21	4 53	9 55	21 2	26 40	8 0	9 2
14	13 26 32	23 31 21	22 11	1 49	19 34	5 33	10 9	21 0	26 39	8 0	9 1
15	13 30 29	24 30 6	5♏56	3 25	20 46	6 13	10 24	20 59	26 39	8 0	8 59
16	13 34 25	25 28 50	19 56	5 2	21 58	6 53	10 38	20 58	26 38	8 0	8 58
17	13 38 22	26 27 31	4♐ 8	6 42	23 10	7 33	10 52	20 56	26 37	7 59	8 56
18	13 42 18	27 26 11	18 26	8 23	24 22	8 13	11 6	20 54	26 36	7 59	8 54
19	13 46 15	28 24 50	2♑46	10 5	25 34	8 53	11 21	20 53	26 36	7 59	8 53
20	13 50 12	29 23 27	17 5	11 50	26 47	9 33	11 35	20 51	26 35	7 59	8 51
21	13 54 8	0♉22 2	1♒19	13 35	27 59	10 12	11 49	20 49	26 34	7 58	8 49
22	13 58 5	1 20 35	15 26	15 23	29 11	10 52	12 3	20 47	26 33	7 58	8 48
23	14 2 1	2 19 7	29 24	17 12	0♈24	11 32	12 17	20 45	26 32	7 57	8 46
24	14 5 58	3 17 37	13♓11	19 3	1 36	12 12	12 31	20 42	26 31	7 57	8 44
25	14 9 54	4 16 5	26 48	20 55	2 48	12 51	12 45	20 40	26 29	7 57	8 43
26	14 13 51	5 14 32	10♈13	22 49	4 1	13 31	12 59	20 38	26 28	7 56	8 41
27	14 17 47	6 12 57	23 25	24 45	5 13	14 11	13 13	20 35	26 27	7 56	8 39
28	14 21 44	7 11 20	6♉24	26 42	6 26	14 50	13 27	20 33	26 26	7 55	8 38
29	14 25 41	8 9 42	19 10	28 41	7 38	15 30	13 41	20 30	26 24	7 54	8 36
30	14 29 37	9♉ 8 1	1♊42	0♉42	8♈51	16♊10	13♈55	20♐27	26♐23	7♑54	8♏34

THE SUN ENTERS THE SIGN OF TAURUS ON APR 20 AT 14:58.

DAY	TIME	☉	☽	☿	♀	♂	♃	♄	♅	♆	♇
	h m s	° ' "	° '	° '	° '	° '	° '	° '	° '	° '	° '
M 1	14 33 34	10♉ 6 19	14♊ 1	2♉44	10♈ 3	16♊49	14♈ 8	20♐25	26♐22	7♑53	8♏32
A 2	14 37 30	11 4 35	26 9	4 48	11 15	17 29	14 22	20R22	26R20	7R52	8R31
Y 3	14 41 27	12 2 49	8♋ 9	6 53	12 28	18 8	14 36	20 19	26 19	7 52	8 29
4	14 45 23	13 1 1	20 3	8 59	13 40	18 48	14 50	20 16	26 17	7 51	8 27
5	14 49 20	13 59 11	1♌55	11 7	14 53	19 27	15 3	20 13	26 16	7 50	8 26
6	14 53 16	14 57 19	13 50	13 15	16 5	20 7	15 17	20 10	26 14	7 49	8 24
7	14 57 13	15 55 25	25 53	15 24	17 18	20 46	15 30	20 6	26 12	7 49	8 22
8	15 1 10	16 53 29	8♍ 7	17 34	18 30	21 25	15 44	20 3	26 11	7 48	8 21
9	15 5 6	17 51 31	20 39	19 45	19 43	22 5	15 57	20 0	26 9	7 47	8 19
10	15 9 3	18 49 31	3♎32	21 55	20 56	22 44	16 10	19 56	26 7	7 46	8 17
11	15 12 59	19 47 30	16 48	24 5	22 8	23 23	16 24	19 53	26 5	7 45	8 16
12	15 16 56	20 45 26	0♏29	26 15	23 21	24 3	16 37	19 49	26 4	7 44	8 14
13	15 20 52	21 43 21	14 33	28 25	24 33	24 42	16 50	19 46	26 2	7 43	8 12
14	15 24 49	22 41 15	28 58	0♊33	25 46	25 21	17 3	19 42	26 0	7 42	8 11
15	15 28 45	23 39 7	13♐37	2 40	26 59	26 0	17 16	19 38	25 58	7 41	8 9
16	15 32 42	24 36 58	28 23	4 45	28 11	26 39	17 29	19 35	25 56	7 40	8 8
17	15 36 39	25 34 47	13♑ 8	6 49	29 24	27 19	17 42	19 31	25 54	7 39	8 6
18	15 40 35	26 32 35	27 45	8 51	0♉37	27 58	17 55	19 27	25 52	7 38	8 4
19	15 44 32	27 30 22	12♒ 9	10 50	1 49	28 37	18 8	19 23	25 50	7 37	8 3
20	15 48 28	28 28 8	26 16	12 47	3 2	29 16	18 20	19 19	25 48	7 36	8 1
21	15 52 25	29 25 53	10♓ 6	14 42	4 15	29 55	18 33	19 15	25 46	7 35	8 0
22	15 56 21	0♊23 37	23 40	16 34	5 27	0♋34	18 46	19 11	25 44	7 33	7 58
23	16 0 18	1 21 19	6♈57	18 23	6 40	1 13	18 58	19 7	25 42	7 32	7 57
24	16 4 14	2 19 1	20 0	20 10	7 53	1 52	19 11	19 3	25 39	7 31	7 55
25	16 8 11	3 16 41	2♉50	21 53	9 6	2 31	19 23	18 59	25 37	7 30	7 54
26	16 12 8	4 14 21	15 29	23 33	10 18	3 10	19 35	18 54	25 35	7 28	7 52
27	16 16 4	5 11 59	27 58	25 11	11 31	3 49	19 48	18 50	25 33	7 27	7 51
28	16 20 1	6 9 36	10♊17	26 45	12 44	4 28	20 0	18 46	25 30	7 26	7 49
29	16 23 57	7 7 12	22 28	28 16	13 57	5 7	20 12	18 42	25 28	7 24	7 48
30	16 27 54	8 4 47	4♋30	29 44	15 9	5 46	20 24	18 37	25 26	7 23	7 46
31	16 31 50	9♊ 2 20	16♋26	1♋ 9	16♉22	6♋25	20♈36	18♐33	25♐24	7♑22	7♏45

THE SUN ENTERS THE SIGN OF GEMINI ON MAY 21 AT 14:11.

DAY	TIME	☉	☽	☿	♀	♂	♃	♄	♅	♆	♇
	h m s	° ' "	° '	° '	° '	° '	° '	° '	° '	° '	° '
J 1	16 35 47	9♊59 53	28♋18	2♋31	17♉35	7♋ 4	20♈48	18♐29	25♐21	7♑20	7♏44
U 2	16 39 44	10 57 24	10♌ 9	3 49	18 48	7 42	20 59	18R24	25R19	7R19	7R42
N 3	16 43 40	11 54 53	22 2	5 4	20 1	8 21	21 11	18 20	25 17	7 18	7 41
E 4	16 47 37	12 52 22	4♍ 3	6 16	21 14	9 0	21 23	18 15	25 14	7 16	7 40
5	16 51 33	13 49 49	16 15	7 24	22 27	9 39	21 34	18 11	25 12	7 15	7 38
6	16 55 30	14 47 15	28 43	8 29	23 39	10 18	21 45	18 7	25 9	7 13	7 37
7	16 59 26	15 44 39	11♎34	9 30	24 52	10 56	21 57	18 2	25 7	7 12	7 36
8	17 3 23	16 42 3	24 50	10 28	26 5	11 35	22 8	17 58	25 5	7 10	7 35
9	17 7 19	17 39 25	8♏35	11 22	27 18	12 14	22 19	17 53	25 2	7 9	7 33
10	17 11 16	18 36 47	22 47	12 12	28 31	12 52	22 30	17 49	25 0	7 7	7 32
11	17 15 13	19 34 7	7♐26	12 58	29 44	13 31	22 41	17 44	24 57	7 6	7 31
12	17 19 9	20 31 27	22 23	13 41	0♊57	14 10	22 52	17 40	24 55	7 4	7 30
13	17 23 6	21 28 46	7♑31	14 19	2 10	14 48	23 2	17 35	24 52	7 3	7 29
14	17 27 2	22 26 5	22 39	14 53	3 23	15 27	23 13	17 31	24 50	7 1	7 28
15	17 30 59	23 23 23	7♒36	15 23	4 36	16 6	23 24	17 27	24 48	7 0	7 27
16	17 34 55	24 20 40	22 16	15 48	5 49	16 44	23 34	17 22	24 45	6 58	7 26
17	17 38 52	25 17 57	6♓33	16 9	7 2	17 23	23 44	17 18	24 43	6 56	7 25
18	17 42 48	26 15 14	20 26	16 26	8 15	18 1	23 54	17 13	24 40	6 55	7 24
19	17 46 45	27 12 30	3♈55	16 38	9 28	18 40	24 4	17 9	24 38	6 53	7 23
20	17 50 42	28 9 47	17 4	16 46	10 41	19 18	24 14	17 5	24 35	6 52	7 22
21	17 54 38	29 7 3	29 55	16R49	11 54	19 57	24 24	17 0	24 33	6 50	7 21
22	17 58 35	0♋ 4 18	12♉31	16 47	13 7	20 35	24 34	16 56	24 30	6 48	7 20
23	18 2 31	1 1 34	24 55	16 41	14 20	21 14	24 44	16 52	24 28	6 47	7 19
24	18 6 28	1 58 49	7♊10	16 31	15 34	21 52	24 53	16 48	24 26	6 45	7 19
25	18 10 24	2 56 5	19 17	16 16	16 47	22 31	25 2	16 44	24 23	6 44	7 18
26	18 14 21	3 53 20	1♋18	15 57	18 0	23 9	25 12	16 39	24 21	6 42	7 17
27	18 18 18	4 50 34	13 15	15 35	19 13	23 48	25 21	16 35	24 18	6 40	7 16
28	18 22 14	5 47 49	25 7	15 9	20 26	24 26	25 30	16 31	24 16	6 39	7 16
29	18 26 11	6 45 2	6♌58	14 40	21 40	25 5	25 39	16 27	24 14	6 37	7 15
30	18 30 7	7♋42 16	18♌49	14♋ 9	22♊53	25♋43	25♈47	16♐23	24♐11	6♑36	7♏14

THE SUN ENTERS THE SIGN OF CANCER ON JUN 21 AT 22:12.

♏ SCORPIO ♐ SAGITTARIUS ♑ CAPRICORN ♒ AQUARIUS ♓ PISCES

SIDEREAL SUN. MOON. MERCURY. VENUS. MARS. JUPITER. SATURN. URANUS. NEPTUNE. PLUTO.

DAY	TIME	☉	☽	☿	♀	♂	♃	♄	♅	♆	♇
	h m s	° ′ ″	° ′	° ′	° ′	° ′	° ′	° ′	° ′	° ′	° ′
J 1	18 34 4	8♋39 29	0♍42	13♋35	24♊ 6	26♋21	25♈56	16♐19	24♐ 9	6♑34	7♏14
U 2	18 38 0	9 36 42	12 43	13R 0	25 19	27 0	26 5	16R15	24R 6	6R32	7R13
L 3	18 41 57	10 33 54	24 53	12 24	26 33	27 38	26 13	16 11	24 4	6 31	7 13
Y 4	18 45 53	11 31 7	7♎20	11 47	27 46	28 17	26 21	16 8	24 2	6 29	7 12
5	18 49 50	12 28 18	20 7	11 11	28 59	28 55	26 29	16 4	24 0	6 27	7 12
6	18 53 47	13 25 30	3♏18	10 35	0♋13	29 33	26 37	16 0	23 57	6 26	7 11
7	18 57 43	14 22 41	16 58	10 1	1 26	0♌12	26 45	15 57	23 55	6 24	7 11
8	19 1 40	15 19 52	1♐ 8	9 29	2 39	0 50	26 53	15 53	23 53	6 23	7 11
9	19 5 36	16 17 3	15 47	8 59	3 53	1 28	27 0	15 49	23 51	6 21	7 10
10	19 9 33	17 14 14	0♑48	8 33	5 6	2 6	27 7	15 46	23 48	6 20	7 10
11	19 13 29	18 11 26	16 4	8 11	6 20	2 45	27 15	15 43	23 46	6 18	7 10
12	19 17 26	19 8 37	1♒23	7 52	7 33	3 23	27 22	15 39	23 44	6 16	7 10
13	19 21 22	20 5 48	16 34	7 38	8 47	4 1	27 29	15 36	23 42	6 15	7 9
14	19 25 19	21 3 0	1♓28	7 29	10 0	4 39	27 35	15 33	23 40	6 13	7 9
15	19 29 16	22 0 12	15 57	7D24	11 14	5 18	27 42	15 30	23 38	6 12	7 9
16	19 33 12	22 57 25	29 59	7 25	12 27	5 56	27 48	15 27	23 36	6 10	7 9
17	19 37 9	23 54 38	13♈34	7 32	13 41	6 34	27 55	15 24	23 34	6 9	7 9
18	19 41 5	24 51 52	26 43	7 43	14 54	7 12	28 1	15 21	23 32	6 7	7D 9
19	19 45 2	25 49 7	9♉31	8 1	16 8	7 51	28 7	15 18	23 30	6 6	7 9
20	19 48 58	26 46 23	22 1	8 24	17 22	8 29	28 13	15 15	23 28	6 4	7 9
21	19 52 55	27 43 39	4♊18	8 52	18 35	9 7	28 18	15 12	23 26	6 3	7 9
22	19 56 51	28 40 56	16 24	9 27	19 49	9 45	28 24	15 10	23 24	6 1	7 9
23	20 0 48	29 38 14	28 24	10 6	21 3	10 24	28 29	15 7	23 22	6 0	7 9
24	20 4 45	0♌35 32	10♋18	10 52	22 16	11 2	28 34	15 5	23 20	5 58	7 9
25	20 8 41	1 32 52	22 11	11 43	23 30	11 40	28 39	15 2	23 19	5 57	7 10
26	20 12 38	2 30 11	4♌ 2	12 39	24 44	12 18	28 44	15 0	23 17	5 55	7 10
27	20 16 34	3 27 32	15 53	13 41	25 58	12 56	28 49	14 58	23 15	5 54	7 10
28	20 20 31	4 24 53	27 47	14 47	27 11	13 35	28 53	14 56	23 14	5 53	7 11
29	20 24 27	5 22 14	9♍46	15 59	28 25	14 13	28 57	14 54	23 12	5 51	7 11
30	20 28 24	6 19 36	21 51	17 17	29 39	14 51	29 1	14 52	23 10	5 50	7 11
31	20 32 20	7♌16 59	4♎ 6	18♋39	0♌53	15♌29	29♈ 5	14♐50	23♐ 9	5♑49	7♏12

THE SUN ENTERS THE SIGN OF LEO ON JUL 23 AT 09:07.

DAY	TIME	☉	☽	☿	♀	♂	♃	♄	♅	♆	♇
	h m s	° ′ ″	° ′	° ′	° ′	° ′	° ′	° ′	° ′	° ′	° ′
A 1	20 36 17	8♌14 22	16♎35	20♋ 5	2♌ 7	16♌ 7	29♈ 9	14♐48	23♐ 7	5♑47	7♏12
U 2	20 40 14	9 11 46	29 22	21 37	3 21	16 45	29 13	14R46	23R 6	5R46	7 13
G 3	20 44 10	10 9 11	12♏31	23 12	4 34	17 24	29 16	14 45	23 5	5 45	7 13
U 4	20 48 7	11 6 36	26 5	24 52	5 48	18 2	29 19	14 43	23 3	5 43	7 14
S 5	20 52 3	12 4 2	10♐ 5	26 35	7 2	18 40	29 22	14 42	23 2	5 42	7 14
T 6	20 56 0	13 1 28	24 33	28 22	8 16	19 18	29 25	14 41	23 1	5 41	7 15
7	20 59 56	13 58 56	9♑24	0♌12	9 30	19 56	29 27	14 39	22 59	5 40	7 16
8	21 3 53	14 56 24	24 31	2 5	10 44	20 34	29 30	14 38	22 58	5 39	7 16
9	21 7 50	15 53 53	9♒46	4 1	11 58	21 12	29 32	14 37	22 57	5 38	7 17
10	21 11 46	16 51 23	24 58	5 58	13 12	21 51	29 34	14 36	22 56	5 36	7 18
11	21 15 43	17 48 54	9♓55	7 57	14 26	22 29	29 36	14 35	22 55	5 35	7 19
12	21 19 39	18 46 26	24 32	9 58	15 40	23 7	29 38	14 35	22 54	5 34	7 19
13	21 23 36	19 44 0	8♈42	12 0	16 55	23 45	29 39	14 34	22 53	5 33	7 20
14	21 27 32	20 41 35	22 24	14 2	18 9	24 23	29 40	14 33	22 52	5 32	7 21
15	21 31 29	21 39 12	5♉40	16 4	19 23	25 1	29 41	14 33	22 51	5 31	7 22
16	21 35 25	22 36 50	18 31	18 7	20 37	25 39	29 42	14 33	22 50	5 30	7 23
17	21 39 22	23 34 29	1♊ 2	20 9	21 51	26 18	29 43	14 32	22 49	5 29	7 24
18	21 43 18	24 32 11	13 17	22 11	23 5	26 56	29 43	14 32	22 48	5 28	7 25
19	21 47 15	25 29 54	25 21	24 13	24 20	27 34	29R44	14D32	22 48	5 27	7 26
20	21 51 12	26 27 38	7♋17	26 13	25 34	28 12	29 44	14 32	22 47	5 26	7 27
21	21 55 8	27 25 24	19 9	28 13	26 48	28 50	29 44	14 32	22 47	5 26	7 28
22	21 59 5	28 23 12	1♌ 0	0♍12	28 2	29 28	29 43	14 32	22 46	5 25	7 29
23	22 3 1	29 21 1	12 52	2 9	29 17	0♍ 7	29 43	14 33	22 45	5 24	7 31
24	22 6 58	0♍18 51	24 48	4 6	0♍31	0 45	29 42	14 33	22 45	5 23	7 32
25	22 10 54	1 16 43	6♍49	6 1	1 45	1 23	29 41	14 34	22 45	5 22	7 33
26	22 14 51	2 14 36	18 57	7 55	3 0	2 1	29 40	14 34	22 44	5 22	7 34
27	22 18 47	3 12 31	1♎14	9 48	4 14	2 39	29 39	14 35	22 44	5 21	7 36
28	22 22 44	4 10 27	13 41	11 39	5 28	3 17	29 37	14 36	22 44	5 20	7 37
29	22 26 41	5 8 25	26 21	13 29	6 43	3 56	29 35	14 37	22 43	5 20	7 38
30	22 30 37	6 6 24	9♏16	15 18	7 57	4 34	29 34	14 38	22 43	5 19	7 40
31	22 34 34	7♍ 4 24	22♏28	17♍ 6	9♍11	5♍12	29♈31	14♐39	22♐43	5♑19	7♏41

THE SUN ENTERS THE SIGN OF VIRGO ON AUG 23 AT 16:11.

DAY	TIME	☉	☽	☿	♀	♂	♃	♄	♅	♆	♇
	h m s	° ′ ″	° ′	° ′	° ′	° ′	° ′	° ′	° ′	° ′	° ′
S 1	22 38 30	8♍ 2 26	6♐ 1	18♍52	10♍26	5♍50	29♈29	14♐40	22♐43	5♑18	7♏43
E 2	22 42 27	9 0 29	19 54	20 37	11 40	6 28	29R27	14 41	22D43	5R18	7 44
P 3	22 46 23	9 58 33	4♑ 8	22 21	12 55	7 7	29 24	14 42	22 43	5 17	7 45
T 4	22 50 20	10 56 39	18 41	24 3	14 9	7 45	29 21	14 44	22 43	5 17	7 47
E 5	22 54 16	11 54 46	3♒29	25 44	15 24	8 23	29 18	14 45	22 43	5 16	7 49
M 6	22 58 13	12 52 55	18 25	27 25	16 38	9 1	29 15	14 47	22 44	5 16	7 50
B 7	23 2 10	13 51 5	3♓20	29 3	17 53	9 40	29 11	14 49	22 44	5 16	7 52
E 8	23 6 6	14 49 17	18 7	0♎41	19 7	10 18	29 8	14 51	22 44	5 15	7 53
R 9	23 10 3	15 47 31	2♈39	2 18	20 22	10 56	29 4	14 53	22 44	5 15	7 55
10	23 13 59	16 45 46	16 49	3 53	21 36	11 34	29 0	14 55	22 45	5 15	7 57
11	23 17 56	17 44 4	0♉35	5 27	22 51	12 12	28 55	14 57	22 45	5 14	7 58
12	23 21 52	18 42 23	13 55	7 0	24 5	12 51	28 51	14 59	22 46	5 14	8 0
13	23 25 49	19 40 45	26 52	8 32	25 20	13 29	28 47	15 1	22 46	5 14	8 2
14	23 29 45	20 39 9	9♊27	10 3	26 34	14 7	28 42	15 4	22 47	5 14	8 4
15	23 33 42	21 37 35	21 44	11 33	27 49	14 46	28 37	15 6	22 48	5 14	8 6
16	23 37 39	22 36 3	3♋49	13 1	29 3	15 24	28 32	15 9	22 48	5 14	8 7
17	23 41 35	23 34 33	15 45	14 29	0♎18	16 2	28 27	15 12	22 49	5D14	8 9
18	23 45 32	24 33 5	27 36	15 55	1 33	16 40	28 21	15 14	22 50	5 14	8 11
19	23 49 28	25 31 40	9♌28	17 20	2 47	17 19	28 16	15 17	22 51	5 14	8 13
20	23 53 25	26 30 16	21 23	18 44	4 2	17 57	28 10	15 20	22 52	5 14	8 15
21	23 57 21	27 28 55	3♍24	20 7	5 16	18 35	28 4	15 23	22 53	5 14	8 17
22	0 1 18	28 27 35	15 35	21 28	6 31	19 14	27 58	15 26	22 54	5 14	8 19
23	0 5 14	29 26 18	27 56	22 48	7 46	19 52	27 52	15 29	22 55	5 14	8 21
24	0 9 11	0♎25 3	10♎29	24 7	9 0	20 31	27 46	15 33	22 56	5 15	8 23
25	0 13 8	1 23 49	23 15	25 25	10 15	21 9	27 39	15 36	22 57	5 15	8 25
26	0 17 4	2 22 38	6♏15	26 41	11 30	21 47	27 33	15 40	22 58	5 15	8 27
27	0 21 1	3 21 28	19 28	27 55	12 44	22 26	27 26	15 43	22 59	5 15	8 29
28	0 24 57	4 20 20	2♐55	29 8	13 59	23 4	27 19	15 47	23 1	5 16	8 31
29	0 28 54	5 19 14	16 36	0♏20	15 14	23 43	27 12	15 50	23 2	5 16	8 33
30	0 32 50	6♎18 10	0♑30	1♏29	16♎28	24♍21	27♈ 5	15♐54	23♐ 4	5♑16	8♏35

THE SUN ENTERS THE SIGN OF LIBRA ON SEP 23 AT 13:46.

♈ ARIES ♉ TAURUS ♊ GEMINI ♋ CANCER ♌ LEO ♍ VIRGO ♎ LIBRA

SIDEREAL SUN. MOON. MERCURY. VENUS. MARS. JUPITER. SATURN. URANUS. NEPTUNE. PLUTO.

DAY	TIME	☉	☽	☿	♀	♂	♃	♄	♅	♆	♇
	h m s	° ' "	° '	° '	° '	° '	° '	° '	° '	° '	° '
O 1	0 36 47	7♎17 7	14♑36	2♏37	17♎43	24♍59	26♈58	15♐58	23♐ 5	5♑17	8♏37
C 2	0 40 43	8 16 6	28 53	3 42	18 58	25 38	26R51	16 2	23 7	5 17	8 40
T 3	0 44 40	9 15 7	13♒18	4 45	20 12	26 16	26 43	16 6	23 8	5 18	8 42
O 4	0 48 37	10 14 10	27 47	5 46	21 27	26 55	26 36	16 10	23 10	5 18	8 44
B 5	0 52 33	11 13 14	12♓16	6 45	22 42	27 33	26 28	16 14	23 11	5 19	8 46
E 6	0 56 30	12 12 20	26 40	7 40	23 56	28 12	26 21	16 19	23 13	5 20	8 48
R 7	1 0 26	13 11 28	10♈53	8 32	25 11	28 50	26 13	16 23	23 15	5 20	8 51
8	1 4 23	14 10 38	24 51	9 22	26 26	29 29	26 5	16 27	23 17	5 21	8 53
9	1 8 19	15 9 51	8♉31	10 7	27 41	0♎ 7	25 58	16 32	23 18	5 22	8 55
10	1 12 16	16 9 5	21 49	10 49	28 55	0 46	25 50	16 36	23 20	5 22	8 57
11	1 16 12	17 8 22	4♊47	11 26	0♏10	1 24	25 42	16 41	23 22	5 23	9 0
12	1 20 9	18 7 41	17 24	11 58	1 25	2 3	25 34	16 46	23 24	5 24	9 2
13	1 24 6	19 7 2	29 44	12 25	2 39	2 42	25 26	16 50	23 26	5 25	9 4
14	1 28 2	20 6 26	11♋50	12 47	3 54	3 20	25 18	16 55	23 28	5 26	9 7
15	1 31 59	21 5 52	23 47	13 2	5 9	3 59	25 10	17 0	23 30	5 26	9 9
16	1 35 55	22 5 20	5♌38	13R11	6 23	4 37	25 2	17 5	23 32	5 27	9 11
17	1 39 52	23 4 51	17 30	13 12	7 38	5 16	24 54	17 10	23 35	5 28	9 14
18	1 43 48	24 4 23	29 27	13 6	8 53	5 55	24 45	17 15	23 37	5 29	9 16
19	1 47 45	25 3 58	11♍32	12 52	10 8	6 33	24 37	17 20	23 39	5 30	9 18
20	1 51 41	26 3 35	23 50	12 29	11 22	7 12	24 29	17 26	23 41	5 31	9 21
21	1 55 38	27 3 15	6♎24	11 57	12 37	7 51	24 21	17 31	23 44	5 32	9 23
22	1 59 34	28 2 56	19 14	11 17	13 52	8 29	24 13	17 36	23 46	5 33	9 25
23	2 3 31	29 2 39	2♏22	10 28	15 6	9 8	24 5	17 42	23 49	5 35	9 28
24	2 7 28	0♏ 2 25	15 47	9 31	16 21	9 47	23 57	17 47	23 51	5 36	9 30
25	2 11 24	1 2 12	29 27	8 27	17 36	10 26	23 49	17 53	23 54	5 37	9 33
26	2 15 21	2 2 2	13♐19	7 17	18 51	11 4	23 41	17 58	23 56	5 38	9 35
27	2 19 17	3 1 53	27 19	6 3	20 5	11 43	23 33	18 4	23 59	5 39	9 37
28	2 23 14	4 1 46	11♑26	4 46	21 20	12 22	23 25	18 10	24 1	5 41	9 40
29	2 27 10	5 1 40	25 36	3 30	22 35	13 1	23 17	18 15	24 4	5 42	9 42
30	2 31 7	6 1 36	9♒46	2 16	23 49	13 39	23 10	18 21	24 7	5 43	9 45
31	2 35 4	7♏ 1 34	23♒55	1♏ 7	25♏ 4	14♎18	23♈ 2	18♐27	24♐ 9	5♑45	9♏47

THE SUN ENTERS THE SIGN OF SCORPIO ON OCT 23 AT 23:02.

DAY	TIME	☉	☽	☿	♀	♂	♃	♄	♅	♆	♇
	h m s	° ' "	° '	° '	° '	° '	° '	° '	° '	° '	° '
N 1	2 39 0	8♏ 1 33	8♓ 1	0♏ 5	26♏19	14♎57	22♈54	18♐33	24♐12	5♑46	9♏50
O 2	2 42 57	9 1 33	22 3	29♎11	27 33	15 36	22R47	18 39	24 15	5 48	9 52
V 3	2 46 53	10 1 36	5♈58	28 28	28 48	16 15	22 39	18 45	24 18	5 49	9 54
E 4	2 50 50	11 1 40	19 45	27 55	0♐ 3	16 54	22 32	18 51	24 21	5 50	9 57
M 5	2 54 46	12 1 45	3♉21	27 34	1 18	17 33	22 25	18 57	24 24	5 52	9 59
B 6	2 58 43	13 1 53	16 44	27D25	2 32	18 11	22 18	19 3	24 27	5 53	10 2
E 7	3 2 39	14 2 3	29 51	27 27	3 47	18 50	22 11	19 10	24 29	5 55	10 4
R 8	3 6 36	15 2 14	12♊42	27 39	5 2	19 29	22 4	19 16	24 32	5 57	10 7
9	3 10 32	16 2 27	25 16	28 3	6 16	20 8	21 57	19 22	24 35	5 58	10 9
10	3 14 29	17 2 42	7♋34	28 35	7 31	20 47	21 51	19 28	24 39	6 0	10 11
11	3 18 26	18 3 0	19 40	29 16	8 46	21 26	21 44	19 35	24 42	6 1	10 14
12	3 22 22	19 3 19	1♌36	0♏ 4	10 0	22 5	21 38	19 41	24 45	6 3	10 16
13	3 26 19	20 3 40	13 27	1 0	11 15	22 44	21 31	19 48	24 48	6 5	10 19
14	3 30 15	21 4 3	25 18	2 1	12 29	23 23	21 25	19 54	24 51	6 7	10 21
15	3 34 12	22 4 27	7♍13	3 7	13 44	24 2	21 19	20 1	24 54	6 8	10 24
16	3 38 8	23 4 54	19 19	4 18	14 59	24 41	21 14	20 7	24 57	6 10	10 26
17	3 42 5	24 5 23	1♎39	5 32	16 13	25 20	21 8	20 14	25 1	6 12	10 28
18	3 46 1	25 5 53	14 19	6 50	17 28	26 0	21 3	20 20	25 4	6 14	10 31
19	3 49 58	26 6 25	27 21	8 10	18 43	26 39	20 57	20 27	25 7	6 15	10 33
20	3 53 55	27 6 59	10♏46	9 33	19 57	27 18	20 52	20 34	25 10	6 17	10 35
21	3 57 51	28 7 34	24 34	10 58	21 12	27 57	20 47	20 41	25 14	6 19	10 38
22	4 1 48	29 8 11	8♐41	12 24	22 27	28 36	20 42	20 47	25 17	6 21	10 40
23	4 5 44	0♐ 8 50	23 3	13 52	23 41	29 15	20 38	20 54	25 20	6 23	10 42
24	4 9 41	1 9 30	7♑32	15 21	24 56	29 55	20 33	21 1	25 24	6 25	10 45
25	4 13 37	2 10 11	22 2	16 51	26 10	0♏34	20 29	21 8	25 27	6 27	10 47
26	4 17 34	3 10 53	6♒28	18 21	27 25	1 13	20 25	21 15	25 31	6 29	10 49
27	4 21 31	4 11 36	20 45	19 53	28 40	1 52	20 21	21 21	25 34	6 31	10 52
28	4 25 27	5 12 20	4♓52	21 24	29 54	2 31	20 18	21 28	25 38	6 33	10 54
29	4 29 24	6 13 5	18 47	22 56	1♑ 9	3 11	20 14	21 35	25 41	6 35	10 56
30	4 33 20	7♐13 51	2♈30	24♏29	2♑23	3♏50	20♈11	21♐42	25♐45	6♑37	10♏58

THE SUN ENTERS THE SIGN OF SAGITTARIUS ON NOV 22 AT 20:30.

DAY	TIME	☉	☽	☿	♀	♂	♃	♄	♅	♆	♇
	h m s	° ' "	° '	° '	° '	° '	° '	° '	° '	° '	° '
D 1	4 37 17	8♐14 38	16♈ 2	26♏ 1	3♑38	4♏29	20♈ 8	21♐49	25♐48	6♑39	11♏ 1
E 2	4 41 13	9 15 26	29 23	27 34	4 52	5 9	20R 5	21 56	25 52	6 41	11 3
C 3	4 45 10	10 16 15	12♉34	29 7	6 7	5 48	20 2	22 3	25 55	6 43	11 5
E 4	4 49 6	11 17 5	25 35	0♐41	7 21	6 27	20 0	22 10	25 59	6 45	11 7
M 5	4 53 3	12 17 56	8♊24	2 14	8 36	7 7	19 57	22 17	26 2	6 47	11 9
B 6	4 57 0	13 18 48	21 1	3 47	9 50	7 46	19 55	22 24	26 6	6 49	11 12
E 7	5 0 56	14 19 41	3♋25	5 20	11 5	8 25	19 53	22 31	26 9	6 51	11 14
R 8	5 4 53	15 20 36	15 38	6 54	12 19	9 5	19 52	22 38	26 13	6 54	11 16
9	5 8 49	16 21 31	27 40	8 27	13 34	9 44	19 50	22 45	26 16	6 56	11 18
10	5 12 46	17 22 28	9♌34	10 1	14 48	10 24	19 49	22 52	26 20	6 58	11 20
11	5 16 42	18 23 25	21 23	11 35	16 3	11 3	19 48	23 0	26 24	7 0	11 22
12	5 20 39	19 24 24	3♍12	13 8	17 17	11 43	19 47	23 7	26 27	7 2	11 24
13	5 24 35	20 25 24	15 4	14 42	18 31	12 22	19 46	23 14	26 31	7 4	11 26
14	5 28 32	21 26 24	27 7	16 16	19 46	13 2	19 46	23 21	26 35	7 7	11 28
15	5 32 29	22 27 26	9♎25	17 50	21 0	13 41	19D46	23 28	26 38	7 9	11 30
16	5 36 25	23 28 29	22 3	19 23	22 14	14 21	19 46	23 35	26 42	7 11	11 32
17	5 40 22	24 29 33	5♏ 7	20 58	23 29	15 0	19 46	23 42	26 45	7 13	11 34
18	5 44 18	25 30 38	18 38	22 32	24 43	15 40	19 46	23 49	26 49	7 15	11 36
19	5 48 15	26 31 44	2♐37	24 6	25 57	16 19	19 47	23 56	26 53	7 18	11 38
20	5 52 11	27 32 50	17 2	25 41	27 11	16 59	19 48	24 3	26 56	7 20	11 40
21	5 56 8	28 33 58	1♑46	27 15	28 26	17 39	19 49	24 11	27 0	7 22	11 41
22	6 0 5	29 35 5	16 42	28 50	29 40	18 18	19 50	24 18	27 4	7 24	11 43
23	6 4 1	0♑36 13	1♒39	0♑25	0♒54	18 58	19 52	24 25	27 7	7 27	11 45
24	6 7 58	1 37 22	16 29	2 0	2 8	19 38	19 53	24 32	27 11	7 29	11 47
25	6 11 54	2 38 30	1♓ 6	3 36	3 22	20 17	19 55	24 39	27 15	7 31	11 49
26	6 15 51	3 39 38	15 24	5 11	4 37	20 57	19 57	24 46	27 18	7 34	11 50
27	6 19 47	4 40 47	29 22	6 47	5 51	21 37	20 0	24 53	27 22	7 36	11 52
28	6 23 44	5 41 55	13♈ 1	8 23	7 5	22 16	20 2	25 0	27 25	7 38	11 54
29	6 27 40	6 43 4	26 22	10 0	8 19	22 56	20 5	25 7	27 29	7 40	11 55
30	6 31 37	7 44 12	9♉27	11 37	9 33	23 36	20 8	25 14	27 33	7 43	11 57
31	6 35 34	8♑45 20	22♉19	13♑14	10♒47	24♏16	20♈11	25♐21	27♐36	7♑45	11♏58

THE SUN ENTERS THE SIGN OF CAPRICORN ON DEC 22 AT 09:47.

♏ SCORPIO ♐ SAGITTARIUS ♑ CAPRICORN ♒ AQUARIUS ♓ PISCES

SIDEREAL. SUN. MOON. MERCURY. VENUS. MARS. JUPITER. SATURN. URANUS. NEPTUNE. PLUTO.

DAY	TIME	☉	☽	☿	♀	♂	♃	♄	♅	♆	♇
	h m s	° ′ ″	° ′	° ′	° ′	° ′	° ′	° ′	° ′	° ′	° ′
J 1	6 39 30	9♑46 29	5♊ 0	14♑51	12♒ 1	24♏55	20♈14	25♐28	27♐40	7♑47	12♏ 0
A 2	6 43 27	10 47 37	17 30	16 28	13 14	25 35	20 18	25 35	27 43	7 49	12 1
N 3	6 47 23	11 48 45	29 51	18 6	14 28	26 15	20 21	25 42	27 47	7 52	12 3
U 4	6 51 20	12 49 54	12♋ 3	19 44	15 42	26 55	20 25	25 49	27 50	7 54	12 4
A 5	6 55 16	13 51 2	24 7	21 23	16 56	27 35	20 29	25 56	27 54	7 56	12 6
R 6	6 59 13	14 52 10	6♌ 3	23 1	18 10	28 15	20 33	26 2	27 58	7 59	12 7
Y 7	7 3 9	15 53 18	17 54	24 40	19 23	28 54	20 38	26 9	28 1	8 1	12 9
8	7 7 6	16 54 27	29 42	26 19	20 37	29 34	20 42	26 16	28 5	8 3	12 10
9	7 11 3	17 55 35	11♍30	27 58	21 50	0♐14	20 47	26 23	28 8	8 5	12 11
10	7 14 59	18 56 43	23 22	29 37	23 4	0 54	20 52	26 30	28 11	8 8	12 12
11	7 18 56	19 57 51	5♎23	1♒16	24 17	1 34	20 57	26 36	28 15	8 10	12 14
12	7 22 52	20 58 59	17 37	2 55	25 31	2 14	21 3	26 43	28 18	8 12	12 15
13	7 26 49	22 0 7	0♏11	4 34	26 44	2 54	21 8	26 50	28 22	8 14	12 16
14	7 30 45	23 1 16	13 8	6 13	27 58	3 34	21 14	26 56	28 25	8 16	12 17
15	7 34 42	24 2 24	26 34	7 50	29 11	4 14	21 20	27 3	28 29	8 19	12 18
16	7 38 38	25 3 32	10♐30	9 28	0♓24	4 54	21 26	27 10	28 32	8 21	12 19
17	7 42 35	26 4 40	24 56	11 4	1 37	5 34	21 32	27 16	28 35	8 23	12 20
18	7 46 32	27 5 47	9♑46	12 39	2 51	6 14	21 39	27 23	28 39	8 25	12 21
19	7 50 28	28 6 54	24 54	14 12	4 4	6 54	21 45	27 29	28 42	8 27	12 22
20	7 54 25	29 8 1	10♒ 8	15 43	5 17	7 34	21 52	27 35	28 45	8 30	12 23
21	7 58 21	0♒ 9 7	25 19	17 12	6 30	8 14	21 59	27 42	28 48	8 32	12 24
22	8 2 18	1 10 12	10♓17	18 38	7 43	8 54	22 6	27 48	28 52	8 34	12 25
23	8 6 14	2 11 16	24 54	20 1	8 55	9 34	22 13	27 54	28 55	8 36	12 26
24	8 10 11	3 12 19	9♈ 7	21 20	10 8	10 15	22 20	28 1	28 58	8 38	12 27
25	8 14 8	4 13 21	22 55	22 34	11 21	10 55	22 28	28 7	29 1	8 40	12 27
26	8 18 4	5 14 21	6♉18	23 43	12 33	11 35	22 36	28 13	29 4	8 42	12 28
27	8 22 1	6 15 21	19 20	24 45	13 46	12 15	22 44	28 19	29 7	8 44	12 29
28	8 25 57	7 16 20	2♊ 5	25 40	14 58	12 55	22 52	28 25	29 10	8 46	12 29
29	8 29 54	8 17 18	14 34	26 28	16 11	13 35	23 0	28 31	29 13	8 48	12 30
30	8 33 50	9 18 14	26 51	27 7	17 23	14 15	23 8	28 37	29 16	8 51	12 31
31	8 37 47	10♒19 10	8♋59	27♒36	18♓35	14♐56	23♈16	28♐43	29♐19	8♑53	12♏31

THE SUN ENTERS THE SIGN OF AQUARIUS ON JAN 20 AT 20:25.

DAY	TIME	☉	☽	☿	♀	♂	♃	♄	♅	♆	♇
	h m s	° ′ ″	° ′	° ′	° ′	° ′	° ′	° ′	° ′	° ′	° ′
F 1	8 41 43	11♒20 4	21♋ 0	27♒55	19♓48	15♐36	23♈25	28♐49	29♐22	8♑55	12♏32
E 2	8 45 40	12 20 57	2♌55	28R 4	21 0	16 16	23 34	28 55	29 25	8 57	12 32
B 3	8 49 37	13 21 49	14 46	28 1	22 12	16 56	23 43	29 1	29 28	8 58	12 33
R 4	8 53 33	14 22 40	26 36	27 47	23 23	17 37	23 52	29 6	29 31	9 0	12 33
U 5	8 57 30	15 23 30	8♍25	27 22	24 35	18 17	24 1	29 12	29 34	9 2	12 33
A 6	9 1 26	16 24 18	20 16	26 47	25 47	18 57	24 10	29 18	29 37	9 4	12 34
R 7	9 5 23	17 25 6	2♎11	26 2	26 58	19 37	24 19	29 23	29 39	9 6	12 34
Y 8	9 9 19	18 25 53	14 15	25 8	28 10	20 18	24 29	29 29	29 42	9 8	12 34
9	9 13 16	19 26 38	26 31	24 7	29 21	20 58	24 38	29 34	29 45	9 10	12 35
10	9 17 12	20 27 23	9♏ 4	23 2	0♈32	21 38	24 48	29 39	29 47	9 12	12 35
11	9 21 9	21 28 7	21 57	21 52	1 44	22 19	24 58	29 45	29 50	9 14	12 35
12	9 25 6	22 28 49	5♐15	20 41	2 55	22 59	25 8	29 50	29 53	9 15	12 35
13	9 29 2	23 29 31	19 1	19 31	4 6	23 39	25 18	29 55	29 55	9 17	12 35
14	9 32 59	24 30 12	3♑14	18 23	5 16	24 20	25 28	0♑ 0	29 58	9 19	12R35
15	9 36 55	25 30 51	17 53	17 19	6 27	25 0	25 39	0 5	0♑ 0	9 21	12 35
16	9 40 52	26 31 30	2♒52	16 20	7 38	25 40	25 49	0 10	0 2	9 22	12 35
17	9 44 48	27 32 6	18 5	15 27	8 48	26 21	26 0	0 15	0 5	9 24	12 35
18	9 48 45	28 32 42	3♓20	14 41	9 58	27 1	26 11	0 20	0 7	9 26	12 35
19	9 52 41	29 33 15	18 28	14 2	11 9	27 42	26 21	0 24	0 9	9 27	12 35
20	9 56 38	0♓33 48	3♈19	13 31	12 19	28 22	26 32	0 29	0 12	9 29	12 35
21	10 0 35	1 34 18	17 47	13 7	13 29	29 2	26 43	0 34	0 14	9 30	12 34
22	10 4 31	2 34 46	1♉49	12 51	14 38	29 43	26 54	0 38	0 16	9 32	12 34
23	10 8 28	3 35 13	15 23	12D43	15 48	0♑23	27 6	0 43	0 18	9 33	12 34
24	10 12 24	4 35 38	28 32	12 41	16 58	1 4	27 17	0 47	0 20	9 35	12 33
25	10 16 21	5 36 1	11♊18	12 46	18 7	1 44	27 28	0 51	0 22	9 36	12 33
26	10 20 17	6 36 22	23 46	12 58	19 16	2 24	27 40	0 56	0 24	9 38	12 33
27	10 24 14	7 36 41	5♋58	13 15	20 25	3 5	27 51	1 0	0 26	9 39	12 32
28	10 28 10	8 36 58	17 59	13 38	21 34	3 45	28 3	1 4	0 28	9 41	12 32
29	10 32 7	9♓37 13	29♋54	14♒ 6	22♈43	4♑26	28♈15	1♑ 8	0♑30	9♑42	12♏31

THE SUN ENTERS THE SIGN OF PISCES ON FEB 19 AT 10:36.

DAY	TIME	☉	☽	☿	♀	♂	♃	♄	♅	♆	♇
	h m s	° ′ ″	° ′	° ′	° ′	° ′	° ′	° ′	° ′	° ′	° ′
M 1	10 36 4	10♓37 26	11♌44	14♒39	23♈51	5♑ 6	28♈27	1♑12	0♑32	9♑43	12♏31
A 2	10 40 0	11 37 37	23 32	15 16	25 0	5 47	28 39	1 15	0 33	9 45	12R30
R 3	10 43 57	12 37 47	5♍22	15 57	26 8	6 27	28 51	1 19	0 35	9 46	12 30
C 4	10 47 53	13 37 54	17 15	16 42	27 16	7 8	29 3	1 23	0 37	9 47	12 29
H 5	10 51 50	14 38 0	29 13	17 31	28 23	7 48	29 15	1 26	0 38	9 48	12 28
6	10 55 46	15 38 3	11♎19	18 23	29 31	8 29	29 27	1 30	0 40	9 50	12 28
7	10 59 43	16 38 6	23 34	19 19	0♉38	9 9	29 39	1 33	0 41	9 51	12 27
8	11 3 39	17 38 6	6♏ 0	20 17	1 45	9 50	29 52	1 37	0 43	9 52	12 26
9	11 7 36	18 38 5	18 41	21 18	2 52	10 30	0♉ 4	1 40	0 44	9 53	12 25
10	11 11 32	19 38 2	1♐38	22 21	3 59	11 11	0 17	1 43	0 46	9 54	12 25
11	11 15 29	20 37 58	14 55	23 27	5 6	11 51	0 29	1 46	0 47	9 55	12 24
12	11 19 26	21 37 52	28 32	24 35	6 12	12 32	0 42	1 49	0 48	9 56	12 23
13	11 23 22	22 37 44	12♑32	25 45	7 18	13 12	0 55	1 52	0 49	9 57	12 22
14	11 27 19	23 37 35	26 53	26 57	8 24	13 53	1 8	1 55	0 50	9 58	12 21
15	11 31 15	24 37 24	11♒33	28 11	9 29	14 33	1 21	1 57	0 52	9 59	12 20
16	11 35 12	25 37 11	26 26	29 27	10 35	15 14	1 34	2 0	0 53	10 0	12 19
17	11 39 8	26 36 56	11♓26	0♓45	11 40	15 54	1 47	2 2	0 54	10 1	12 18
18	11 43 5	27 36 39	26 25	2 4	12 44	16 35	2 0	2 5	0 55	10 2	12 17
19	11 47 1	28 36 21	11♈14	3 26	13 49	17 15	2 13	2 7	0 55	10 2	12 16
20	11 50 58	29 36 0	25 46	4 48	14 53	17 56	2 26	2 9	0 56	10 3	12 15
21	11 54 55	0♈35 37	9♉56	6 13	15 57	18 36	2 39	2 11	0 57	10 4	12 14
22	11 58 51	1 35 12	23 39	7 38	17 1	19 17	2 53	2 13	0 58	10 5	12 13
23	12 2 48	2 34 45	6♊57	9 6	18 4	19 57	3 6	2 15	0 59	10 5	12 11
24	12 6 44	3 34 16	19 49	10 34	19 7	20 38	3 19	2 17	0 59	10 6	12 10
25	12 10 41	4 33 44	2♋20	12 4	20 10	21 18	3 33	2 19	1 0	10 7	12 9
26	12 14 37	5 33 10	14 34	13 36	21 12	21 59	3 46	2 20	1 0	10 7	12 8
27	12 18 34	6 32 33	26 34	15 9	22 14	22 39	4 0	2 22	1 1	10 8	12 7
28	12 22 30	7 31 55	8♌26	16 43	23 16	23 20	4 13	2 23	1 1	10 8	12 5
29	12 26 27	8 31 14	20 15	18 19	24 17	24 0	4 27	2 25	1 2	10 9	12 4
30	12 30 24	9 30 30	2♍ 3	19 56	25 18	24 41	4 41	2 26	1 2	10 9	12 3
31	12 34 20	10♈29 45	13♍56	21♓35	26♉19	25♑21	4♉54	2♑27	1♑ 2	10♑ 9	12♏ 1

THE SUN ENTERS THE SIGN OF ARIES ON MAR 20 AT 09:39.

♈ ARIES ♉ TAURUS ♊ GEMINI ♋ CANCER ♌ LEO ♍ VIRGO ♎ LIBRA

SIDEREAL . . SUN . . MOON . . MERCURY . . VENUS . . MARS . . JUPITER . . SATURN . . URANUS . . NEPTUNE . . PLUTO .

DAY	TIME	☉	☽	☿	♀	♂	♃	♄	♅	♆	♇
	h m s	° ' "	° '	° '	° '	° '	° '	° '	° '	° '	° '
A 1	12 38 17	11♈28 57	25♍55	23♓15	27♉19	26♑ 1	5♉ 8	2♑28	1♑ 2	10♑10	12♏ 0
P 2	12 42 13	12 28 7	8♎ 4	24 56	28 19	26 42	5 22	2 29	1 3	10 10	11R59
R 3	12 46 10	13 27 15	20 23	26 39	29 18	27 22	5 36	2 30	1 3	10 10	11 57
I 4	12 50 6	14 26 21	2♏55	28 23	0♊17	28 3	5 50	2 31	1R 3	10 11	11 56
L 5	12 54 3	15 25 26	15 40	0♈ 9	1 15	28 43	6 4	2 31	1 3	10 11	11 54
6	12 57 59	16 24 28	28 38	1 56	2 13	29 23	6 18	2 32	1 3	10 11	11 53
7	13 1 56	17 23 29	11♐50	3 44	3 10	0♒ 4	6 31	2 32	1 3	10 11	11 51
8	13 5 53	18 22 28	25 17	5 34	4 7	0 44	6 45	2 33	1 3	10 11	11 50
9	13 9 49	19 21 25	8♑57	7 25	5 4	1 24	6 59	2 33	1 2	10 12	11 48
10	13 13 46	20 20 20	22 51	9 18	6 0	2 5	7 14	2 33	1 2	10 12	11 47
11	13 17 42	21 19 14	6♒59	11 13	6 55	2 45	7 28	2R33	1 2	10R12	11 45
12	13 21 39	22 18 6	21 19	13 9	7 50	3 25	7 42	2 33	1 2	10 12	11 44
13	13 25 35	23 16 56	5♓48	15 6	8 44	4 6	7 56	2 33	1 1	10 12	11 42
14	13 29 32	24 15 44	20 23	17 5	9 37	4 46	8 10	2 33	1 1	10 12	11 40
15	13 33 28	25 14 30	4♈59	19 5	10 30	5 26	8 24	2 32	1 0	10 11	11 39
16	13 37 25	26 13 15	19 30	21 6	11 22	6 6	8 38	2 32	1 0	10 11	11 37
17	13 41 22	27 11 58	3♉50	23 9	12 14	6 47	8 53	2 31	0 59	10 11	11 36
18	13 45 18	28 10 39	17 53	25 13	13 5	7 27	9 7	2 31	0 58	10 11	11 34
19	13 49 15	29 9 18	1♊35	27 18	13 55	8 7	9 21	2 30	0 58	10 11	11 32
20	13 53 11	0♉ 7 54	14 54	29 25	14 44	8 47	9 35	2 29	0 57	10 10	11 31
21	13 57 8	1 6 29	27 50	1♉32	15 33	9 27	9 49	2 28	0 56	10 10	11 29
22	14 1 4	2 5 2	10♋24	3 39	16 21	10 7	10 4	2 27	0 55	10 10	11 27
23	14 5 1	3 3 32	22 40	5 47	17 8	10 47	10 18	2 26	0 54	10 10	11 26
24	14 8 57	4 2 0	4♌42	7 56	17 54	11 27	10 32	2 25	0 54	10 9	11 24
25	14 12 54	5 0 26	16 34	10 4	18 39	12 7	10 47	2 24	0 53	10 9	11 22
26	14 16 51	5 58 50	28 23	12 12	19 23	12 47	11 1	2 22	0 52	10 8	11 21
27	14 20 47	6 57 12	10♍13	14 19	20 6	13 27	11 15	2 21	0 50	10 8	11 19
28	14 24 44	7 55 31	22 9	16 25	20 48	14 7	11 30	2 19	0 49	10 7	11 17
29	14 28 40	8 53 49	4♎14	18 31	21 30	14 46	11 44	2 18	0 48	10 7	11 16
30	14 32 37	9♉52 4	16♎33	20♉34	22♊ 9	15♒26	11♉58	2♑16	0♑47	10♑ 6	11♏14

THE SUN ENTERS THE SIGN OF TAURUS ON APR 19 AT 20:46.

DAY	TIME	☉	☽	☿	♀	♂	♃	♄	♅	♆	♇
	h m s	° ' "	° '	° '	° '	° '	° '	° '	° '	° '	° '
M 1	14 36 33	10♉50 18	29♎ 7	22♉36	22♊48	16♒ 6	12♉13	2♑14	0♑46	10♑ 6	11♏12
A 2	14 40 30	11 48 30	11♏58	24 36	23 26	16 46	12 27	2R12	0R44	10R 5	11R11
Y 3	14 44 26	12 46 41	25 5	26 33	24 2	17 25	12 41	2 10	0 43	10 4	11 9
4	14 48 23	13 44 49	8♐27	28 28	24 37	18 5	12 56	2 8	0 42	10 4	11 7
5	14 52 20	14 42 57	22 2	0♊20	25 11	18 44	13 10	2 6	0 40	10 3	11 6
6	14 56 16	15 41 2	5♑48	2 9	25 43	19 24	13 24	2 3	0 39	10 2	11 4
7	15 0 13	16 39 7	19 43	3 55	26 14	20 3	13 38	2 1	0 37	10 1	11 2
8	15 4 9	17 37 10	3♒44	5 37	26 44	20 43	13 53	1 59	0 36	10 1	11 0
9	15 8 6	18 35 11	17 49	7 16	27 12	21 22	14 7	1 56	0 34	10 0	10 59
10	15 12 2	19 33 11	1♓58	8 52	27 38	22 1	14 21	1 53	0 33	9 59	10 57
11	15 15 59	20 31 10	16 9	10 23	28 2	22 41	14 36	1 51	0 31	9 58	10 55
12	15 19 55	21 29 7	0♈21	11 52	28 25	23 20	14 50	1 48	0 29	9 57	10 54
13	15 23 52	22 27 4	14 31	13 16	28 46	23 59	15 4	1 45	0 28	9 56	10 52
14	15 27 49	23 24 59	28 37	14 37	29 6	24 38	15 18	1 42	0 26	9 55	10 50
15	15 31 45	24 22 52	12♉33	15 53	29 23	25 17	15 33	1 39	0 24	9 54	10 49
16	15 35 42	25 20 44	26 18	17 6	29 39	25 56	15 47	1 36	0 22	9 53	10 47
17	15 39 38	26 18 35	9♊47	18 15	29 52	26 35	16 1	1 33	0 20	9 52	10 46
18	15 43 35	27 16 24	22 57	19 20	0♋ 3	27 14	16 15	1 30	0 18	9 51	10 44
19	15 47 31	28 14 12	5♋47	20 21	0 13	27 52	16 29	1 27	0 17	9 50	10 42
20	15 51 28	29 11 58	18 19	21 17	0 20	28 31	16 44	1 23	0 15	9 49	10 41
21	15 55 24	0♊ 9 43	0♌34	22 9	0 24	29 9	16 58	1 20	0 13	9 48	10 39
22	15 59 21	1 7 26	12 36	22 57	0R27	29 48	17 12	1 16	0 11	9 47	10 38
23	16 3 18	2 5 7	24 28	23 41	0 27	0♓26	17 26	1 13	0 9	9 45	10 36
24	16 7 14	3 2 47	6♍17	24 20	0 25	1 4	17 40	1 9	0 6	9 44	10 35
25	16 11 11	4 0 26	18 8	24 55	0 20	1 42	17 54	1 6	0 4	9 43	10 33
26	16 15 7	4 58 2	0♎ 5	25 25	0 13	2 20	18 8	1 2	0 2	9 42	10 32
27	16 19 4	5 55 38	12 14	25 50	0 4	2 58	18 22	0 58	0 0	9 40	10 30
28	16 23 0	6 53 12	24 40	26 11	29♊52	3 36	18 36	0 54	29♐58	9 39	10 29
29	16 26 57	7 50 44	7♏25	26 27	29 37	4 14	18 50	0 50	29 56	9 38	10 27
30	16 30 53	8 48 16	20 31	26 38	29 20	4 52	19 4	0 46	29 54	9 37	10 26
31	16 34 50	9♊45 46	3♐59	26♊45	29♊ 1	5♓29	19♉17	0♑43	29♐51	9♑35	10♏24

THE SUN ENTERS THE SIGN OF GEMINI ON MAY 20 AT 19:58.

DAY	TIME	☉	☽	☿	♀	♂	♃	♄	♅	♆	♇
	h m s	° ' "	° '	° '	° '	° '	° '	° '	° '	° '	° '
J 1	16 38 47	10♊43 15	17♐45	26♊47	28♊40	6♓ 7	19♉31	0♑39	29♐49	9♑34	10♏23
U 2	16 42 43	11 40 43	1♑46	26R45	28R16	6 44	19 45	0R35	29R47	9R33	10R21
N 3	16 46 40	12 38 11	15 58	26 38	27 51	7 21	19 59	0 30	29 45	9 31	10 20
E 4	16 50 36	13 35 37	0♒15	26 26	27 23	7 58	20 12	0 26	29 42	9 30	10 19
5	16 54 33	14 33 3	14 33	26 11	26 53	8 35	20 26	0 22	29 40	9 28	10 17
6	16 58 29	15 30 28	28 48	25 52	26 22	9 12	20 40	0 18	29 38	9 27	10 16
7	17 2 26	16 27 52	12♓58	25 30	25 49	9 49	20 53	0 14	29 35	9 25	10 15
8	17 6 23	17 25 16	27 2	25 4	25 15	10 25	21 7	0 10	29 33	9 24	10 14
9	17 10 19	18 22 39	10♈59	24 36	24 40	11 2	21 20	0 5	29 30	9 22	10 12
10	17 14 16	19 20 2	24 49	24 6	24 4	11 38	21 34	0 1	29 28	9 21	10 11
11	17 18 12	20 17 24	8♉31	23 34	23 27	12 14	21 47	29♐57	29 26	9 19	10 10
12	17 22 9	21 14 46	22 3	23 1	22 50	12 50	22 0	29 52	29 23	9 18	10 9
13	17 26 5	22 12 7	5♊24	22 27	22 12	13 26	22 14	29 48	29 21	9 16	10 8
14	17 30 2	23 9 28	18 32	21 53	21 35	14 1	22 27	29 44	29 18	9 15	10 7
15	17 33 58	24 6 48	1♋25	21 20	20 57	14 37	22 40	29 39	29 16	9 13	10 5
16	17 37 55	25 4 8	14 4	20 48	20 21	15 12	22 53	29 35	29 14	9 12	10 4
17	17 41 52	26 1 26	26 27	20 18	19 44	15 47	23 6	29 30	29 11	9 10	10 3
18	17 45 48	26 58 44	8♌36	19 50	19 9	16 22	23 19	29 26	29 9	9 9	10 2
19	17 49 45	27 56 1	20 35	19 25	18 35	16 57	23 32	29 21	29 6	9 7	10 1
20	17 53 41	28 53 18	2♍26	19 2	18 3	17 31	23 45	29 17	29 4	9 6	10 0
21	17 57 38	29 50 33	14 13	18 44	17 31	18 6	23 58	29 13	29 1	9 4	9 59
22	18 1 34	0♋47 48	26 3	18 29	17 2	18 40	24 11	29 8	28 59	9 2	9 58
23	18 5 31	1 45 3	8♎ 0	18 18	16 34	19 14	24 24	29 4	28 56	9 1	9 58
24	18 9 27	2 42 16	20 10	18D11	16 9	19 47	24 36	28 59	28 54	8 59	9 57
25	18 13 24	3 39 30	2♏38	18 9	15 45	20 21	24 49	28 55	28 52	8 58	9 56
26	18 17 21	4 36 42	15 28	18 12	15 23	20 54	25 1	28 50	28 49	8 56	9 55
27	18 21 17	5 33 54	28 42	18 19	15 4	21 27	25 14	28 46	28 47	8 54	9 54
28	18 25 14	6 31 6	12♐22	18 31	14 47	22 0	25 26	28 42	28 44	8 53	9 54
29	18 29 10	7 28 18	26 25	18 48	14 33	22 32	25 39	28 37	28 42	8 51	9 53
30	18 33 7	8♋25 29	10♑48	19♊10	14♊21	23♓ 4	25♉51	28♐33	28♐39	8♑49	9♏52

THE SUN ENTERS THE SIGN OF CANCER ON JUN 21 AT 03:57.

♏ SCORPIO ♐ SAGITTARIUS ♑ CAPRICORN ♒ AQUARIUS ♓ PISCES

SIDEREAL TIME . SUN . . MOON . . MERCURY . . VENUS . . MARS . . JUPITER . . SATURN . . URANUS . . NEPTUNE . . PLUTO .

DAY	TIME	☉	☽	☿	♀	♂	♃	♄	♅	♆	♇
	h m s	° ' "	° '	° '	° '	° '	° '	° '	° '	° '	° '
J 1	18 37 3	9♋22 40	25♑24	19♊37	14♊11	23♓36	26♉ 3	28♐29	28♐37	8♑48	9♏52
U 2	18 41 0	10 19 51	10♒ 6	20 8	14R 3	24 8	26 15	28R24	28R35	8R46	9R51
L 3	18 44 57	11 17 2	24 47	20 44	13 59	24 39	26 27	28 20	28 32	8 45	9 50
Y 4	18 48 53	12 14 13	9♓20	21 25	13D56	25 11	26 39	28 16	28 30	8 43	9 50
5	18 52 50	13 11 25	23 42	22 11	13 56	25 41	26 51	28 12	28 28	8 41	9 49
6	18 56 46	14 8 36	7♈51	23 2	13 58	26 12	27 3	28 8	28 25	8 40	9 49
7	19 0 43	15 5 48	21 45	23 56	14 2	26 42	27 15	28 3	28 23	8 38	9 48
8	19 4 39	16 3 1	5♉24	24 56	14 9	27 12	27 26	27 59	28 21	8 37	9 48
9	19 8 36	17 0 14	18 50	26 0	14 18	27 42	27 38	27 55	28 18	8 35	9 48
10	19 12 32	17 57 27	2♊ 2	27 8	14 28	28 11	27 49	27 51	28 16	8 33	9 47
11	19 16 29	18 54 41	15 1	28 21	14 41	28 40	28 1	27 47	28 14	8 32	9 47
12	19 20 26	19 51 55	27 49	29 38	14 56	29 9	28 12	27 43	28 12	8 30	9 47
13	19 24 22	20 49 9	10♋23	0♋59	15 13	29 37	28 23	27 39	28 9	8 29	9 46
14	19 28 19	21 46 24	22 46	2 24	15 32	0♈ 5	28 34	27 35	28 7	8 27	9 46
15	19 32 15	22 43 39	4♌57	3 53	15 52	0 32	28 46	27 32	28 5	8 25	9 46
16	19 36 12	23 40 54	16 59	5 27	16 15	0 59	28 56	27 28	28 3	8 24	9 46
17	19 40 8	24 38 10	28 52	7 4	16 39	1 26	29 7	27 24	28 1	8 22	9 46
18	19 44 5	25 35 26	10♍40	8 45	17 4	1 52	29 18	27 21	27 59	8 21	9 46
19	19 48 1	26 32 42	22 26	10 29	17 31	2 18	29 29	27 17	27 57	8 19	9 46
20	19 51 58	27 29 58	4♎15	12 17	18 0	2 43	29 39	27 13	27 55	8 18	9D46
21	19 55 55	28 27 14	16 12	14 8	18 30	3 8	29 50	27 10	27 53	8 16	9 46
22	19 59 51	29 24 31	28 21	16 1	19 2	3 32	0♊ 0	27 7	27 51	8 15	9 46
23	20 3 48	0♌21 48	10♏47	17 58	19 35	3 56	0 10	27 3	27 49	8 13	9 46
24	20 7 44	1 19 5	23 36	19 56	20 9	4 20	0 20	27 0	27 47	8 12	9 46
25	20 11 41	2 16 23	6♐50	21 57	20 44	4 43	0 30	26 57	27 45	8 10	9 46
26	20 15 37	3 13 41	20 32	24 0	21 21	5 5	0 40	26 54	27 43	8 9	9 46
27	20 19 34	4 11 0	4♑41	26 3	21 59	5 27	0 50	26 51	27 41	8 8	9 46
28	20 23 30	5 8 19	19 14	28 8	22 38	5 49	1 0	26 48	27 40	8 6	9 47
29	20 27 27	6 5 39	4♒ 5	0♌14	23 18	6 10	1 9	26 45	27 38	8 5	9 47
30	20 31 24	7 3 0	19 6	2 20	23 59	6 30	1 19	26 42	27 36	8 3	9 47
31	20 35 20	8♌ 0 21	4♓ 8	4♌26	24♊41	6♈50	1♊28	26♐39	27♐34	8♑ 2	9♏48

THE SUN ENTERS THE SIGN OF LEO ON JUL 22 AT 14:52.

DAY	TIME	☉	☽	☿	♀	♂	♃	♄	♅	♆	♇
	h m s	° ' "	° '	° '	° '	° '	° '	° '	° '	° '	° '
A 1	20 39 17	8♌57 44	19♓ 2	6♌32	25♊24	7♈10	1♊37	26♐36	27♐33	8♑ 1	9♏48
U 2	20 43 13	9 55 7	3♈42	8 38	26 8	7 28	1 46	26R34	27R31	7R59	9 48
G 3	20 47 10	10 52 32	18 4	10 43	26 53	7 47	1 55	26 31	27 30	7 58	9 49
U 4	20 51 6	11 49 57	2♉ 4	12 47	27 39	8 4	2 4	26 29	27 28	7 57	9 49
S 5	20 55 3	12 47 25	15 44	14 50	28 25	8 21	2 13	26 26	27 27	7 55	9 50
T 6	20 58 59	13 44 53	29 3	16 52	29 13	8 37	2 21	26 24	27 25	7 54	9 50
7	21 2 56	14 42 23	12♊ 4	18 53	0♋ 1	8 53	2 30	26 22	27 24	7 53	9 51
8	21 6 53	15 39 54	24 49	20 53	0 50	9 8	2 38	26 20	27 22	7 52	9 52
9	21 10 49	16 37 26	7♋20	22 51	1 40	9 22	2 46	26 18	27 21	7 51	9 52
10	21 14 46	17 35 0	19 39	24 48	2 30	9 36	2 54	26 16	27 20	7 49	9 53
11	21 18 42	18 32 35	1♌47	26 44	3 21	9 48	3 2	26 14	27 19	7 48	9 54
12	21 22 39	19 30 10	13 47	28 38	4 13	10 0	3 10	26 12	27 17	7 47	9 54
13	21 26 35	20 27 48	25 40	0♍30	5 6	10 12	3 18	26 10	27 16	7 46	9 55
14	21 30 32	21 25 26	7♍29	2 21	5 58	10 22	3 25	26 9	27 15	7 45	9 56
15	21 34 28	22 23 5	19 16	4 11	6 52	10 32	3 33	26 7	27 14	7 44	9 57
16	21 38 25	23 20 46	1♎ 3	5 59	7 46	10 41	3 40	26 6	27 13	7 43	9 58
17	21 42 22	24 18 27	12 53	7 46	8 41	10 50	3 47	26 4	27 12	7 42	9 59
18	21 46 18	25 16 10	24 51	9 31	9 36	10 57	3 54	26 3	27 11	7 41	10 0
19	21 50 15	26 13 54	7♏ 1	11 15	10 32	11 4	4 0	26 2	27 10	7 40	10 1
20	21 54 11	27 11 39	19 26	12 58	11 28	11 10	4 7	26 1	27 9	7 39	10 2
21	21 58 8	28 9 25	2♐12	14 39	12 24	11 15	4 13	26 0	27 9	7 38	10 3
22	22 2 4	29 7 13	15 21	16 18	13 22	11 19	4 20	25 59	27 8	7 37	10 4
23	22 6 1	0♍ 5 1	28 57	17 56	14 19	11 22	4 26	25 58	27 7	7 37	10 5
24	22 9 57	1 2 51	13♑ 0	19 33	15 17	11 25	4 32	25 58	27 7	7 36	10 6
25	22 13 54	2 0 42	27 29	21 9	16 16	11 27	4 38	25 57	27 6	7 35	10 7
26	22 17 51	2 58 34	12♒21	22 43	17 14	11R28	4 43	25 57	27 5	7 34	10 9
27	22 21 47	3 56 28	27 27	24 16	18 14	11 28	4 49	25 56	27 5	7 34	10 10
28	22 25 44	4 54 23	12♓39	25 47	19 13	11 27	4 54	25 56	27 4	7 33	10 11
29	22 29 40	5 52 19	27 48	27 17	20 13	11 25	4 59	25 56	27 4	7 32	10 12
30	22 33 37	6 50 17	12♈45	28 46	21 14	11 23	5 4	25D56	27 4	7 32	10 14
31	22 37 33	7♍48 17	27♈22	0♎13	22♋14	11♈20	5♊ 9	25♐56	27♐ 3	7♑31	10♏15

THE SUN ENTERS THE SIGN OF VIRGO ON AUG 22 AT 21:55.

DAY	TIME	☉	☽	☿	♀	♂	♃	♄	♅	♆	♇
	h m s	° ' "	° '	° '	° '	° '	° '	° '	° '	° '	° '
S 1	22 41 30	8♍46 20	11♉36	1♎39	23♋16	11♈16	5♊13	25♐56	27♐ 3	7♑30	10♏16
E 2	22 45 26	9 44 24	25 23	3 3	24 17	11R11	5 18	25 56	27R 3	7R30	10 18
P 3	22 49 23	10 42 30	8♊45	4 26	25 19	11 5	5 22	25 56	27 3	7 29	10 19
T 4	22 53 20	11 40 38	21 44	5 48	26 21	10 58	5 26	25 57	27 3	7 29	10 21
E 5	22 57 16	12 38 48	4♋22	7 8	27 23	10 51	5 30	25 57	27D 3	7 28	10 22
M 6	23 1 13	13 36 59	16 44	8 27	28 26	10 42	5 34	25 58	27 3	7 28	10 24
B 7	23 5 9	14 35 13	28 52	9 44	29 29	10 33	5 37	25 59	27 3	7 27	10 25
E 8	23 9 6	15 33 29	10♌51	10 59	0♌33	10 23	5 41	25 59	27 3	7 27	10 27
R 9	23 13 2	16 31 47	22 43	12 13	1 36	10 13	5 44	26 0	27 3	7 27	10 28
10	23 16 59	17 30 6	4♍31	13 25	2 40	10 2	5 47	26 1	27 3	7 26	10 30
11	23 20 55	18 28 28	16 18	14 35	3 44	9 50	5 49	26 2	27 3	7 26	10 32
12	23 24 52	19 26 51	28 6	15 43	4 49	9 37	5 52	26 3	27 4	7 26	10 33
13	23 28 49	20 25 16	9♎57	16 49	5 54	9 24	5 54	26 5	27 4	7 26	10 35
14	23 32 45	21 23 43	21 54	17 52	6 58	9 10	5 57	26 6	27 5	7 26	10 37
15	23 36 42	22 22 11	3♏59	18 54	8 4	8 55	5 59	26 8	27 5	7 25	10 39
16	23 40 38	23 20 42	16 14	19 53	9 9	8 40	6 0	26 9	27 6	7 25	10 40
17	23 44 35	24 19 14	28 43	20 49	10 15	8 25	6 2	26 11	27 6	7 25	10 42
18	23 48 31	25 17 47	11♐29	21 43	11 21	8 9	6 3	26 13	27 7	7D25	10 44
19	23 52 28	26 16 23	24 34	22 33	12 27	7 53	6 5	26 14	27 7	7 25	10 46
20	23 56 24	27 15 0	8♑ 2	23 20	13 33	7 36	6 6	26 16	27 8	7 25	10 48
21	0 0 21	28 13 39	21 53	24 3	14 39	7 19	6 7	26 18	27 9	7 25	10 50
22	0 4 18	29 12 19	6♒ 9	24 43	15 46	7 2	6 7	26 21	27 10	7 25	10 52
23	0 8 14	0♎11 1	20 47	25 19	16 53	6 45	6 8	26 23	27 11	7 25	10 54
24	0 12 11	1 9 45	5♓43	25 49	18 0	6 27	6R 8	26 25	27 12	7 26	10 56
25	0 16 7	2 8 30	20 50	26 16	19 8	6 9	6 8	26 28	27 12	7 26	10 58
26	0 20 4	3 7 18	6♈ 0	26 36	20 15	5 52	6 8	26 30	27 14	7 26	11 0
27	0 24 0	4 6 7	21 2	26 52	21 23	5 34	6 7	26 33	27 15	7 26	11 2
28	0 27 57	5 4 58	5♉49	27R 1	22 31	5 16	6 7	26 35	27 16	7 27	11 4
29	0 31 53	6 3 52	20 13	27 3	23 39	4 59	6 6	26 38	27 17	7 27	11 6
30	0 35 50	7♎ 2 48	4♊11	26♎59	24♌47	4♈41	6♊ 5	26♐41	27♐18	7♑27	11♏ 8

THE SUN ENTERS THE SIGN OF LIBRA ON SEP 22 AT 19:30.

♈ ARIES ♉ TAURUS ♊ GEMINI ♋ CANCER ♌ LEO ♍ VIRGO ♎ LIBRA

1988

SIDEREAL — SUN. MOON. MERCURY. VENUS. MARS. JUPITER. SATURN. URANUS. NEPTUNE. PLUTO.

DAY	TIME h m s	☉ ° ' "	☽ ° '	☿ ° '	♀ ° '	♂ ° '	♃ ° '	♄ ° '	♅ ° '	♆ ° '	♇ ° '
O 1	0 39 46	8♎ 1 47	17♊40	26♎48	25♌55	4♈24	6♊ 4	26♐44	27♐19	7♑28	11♏10
C 2	0 43 43	9 0 48	0♋43	26R29	27 4	4R 7	6R 2	26 47	27 21	7 28	11 12
T 3	0 47 40	9 59 51	13 22	26 2	28 13	3 50	6 1	26 50	27 22	7 29	11 14
O 4	0 51 36	10 58 56	25 41	25 28	29 22	3 33	5 59	26 53	27 24	7 29	11 16
B 5	0 55 33	11 58 4	7♌45	24 46	0♍31	3 17	5 57	26 57	27 25	7 30	11 19
E 6	0 59 29	12 57 13	19 39	23 56	1 40	3 1	5 55	27 0	27 26	7 30	11 21
R 7	1 3 26	13 56 25	1♍27	23 0	2 50	2 45	5 52	27 3	27 28	7 31	11 23
8	1 7 22	14 55 40	13 14	21 58	3 59	2 30	5 50	27 7	27 30	7 31	11 25
9	1 11 19	15 54 56	25 2	20 51	5 9	2 16	5 47	27 11	27 31	7 32	11 27
10	1 15 15	16 54 15	6♎54	19 41	6 19	2 2	5 44	27 14	27 33	7 33	11 30
11	1 19 12	17 53 35	18 54	18 29	7 29	1 49	5 41	27 18	27 35	7 33	11 32
12	1 23 9	18 52 58	1♏ 2	17 18	8 39	1 36	5 37	27 22	27 37	7 34	11 34
13	1 27 5	19 52 23	13 20	16 10	9 49	1 24	5 34	27 26	27 38	7 35	11 36
14	1 31 2	20 51 49	25 48	15 5	11 0	1 13	5 30	27 30	27 40	7 36	11 39
15	1 34 58	21 51 18	8♐29	14 7	12 10	1 2	5 26	27 34	27 42	7 36	11 41
16	1 38 55	22 50 49	21 24	13 17	13 21	0 52	5 22	27 38	27 44	7 37	11 43
17	1 42 51	23 50 21	4♑33	12 37	14 32	0 43	5 18	27 43	27 46	7 38	11 46
18	1 46 48	24 49 55	17 58	12 7	15 43	0 34	5 13	27 47	27 48	7 39	11 48
19	1 50 44	25 49 31	1♒41	11 47	16 54	0 26	5 9	27 51	27 50	7 40	11 50
20	1 54 41	26 49 8	15 41	11D39	18 5	0 20	5 4	27 56	27 53	7 41	11 53
21	1 58 38	27 48 47	0♓ 0	11 42	19 16	0 13	4 59	28 1	27 55	7 42	11 55
22	2 2 34	28 48 28	14 36	11 56	20 27	0 8	4 54	28 5	27 57	7 43	11 57
23	2 6 31	29 48 11	29 23	12 20	21 39	0 3	4 48	28 10	27 59	7 44	12 0
24	2 10 27	0♏47 55	14♈17	12 54	22 50	0♈ 0	4 43	28 15	28 2	7 45	12 2
25	2 14 24	1 47 41	29 9	13 37	24 2	29♓57	4 37	28 20	28 4	7 47	12 5
26	2 18 20	2 47 29	13♉51	14 28	25 14	29 55	4 31	28 24	28 6	7 48	12 7
27	2 22 17	3 47 20	28 16	15 26	26 26	29 53	4 25	28 29	28 9	7 49	12 9
28	2 26 13	4 47 12	12♊17	16 30	27 38	29D53	4 19	28 34	28 11	7 50	12 12
29	2 30 10	5 47 7	25 52	17 40	28 50	29 53	4 13	28 40	28 14	7 52	12 14
30	2 34 7	6 47 3	8♋59	18 54	0♎ 2	29 54	4 6	28 45	28 16	7 53	12 17
31	2 38 3	7♏47 2	21♋42	20♎13	1♎14	29♓56	4♊ 0	28♐50	28♐19	7♑54	12♏19

THE SUN ENTERS THE SIGN OF SCORPIO ON OCT 23 AT 04:46.

DAY	TIME h m s	☉ ° ' "	☽ ° '	☿ ° '	♀ ° '	♂ ° '	♃ ° '	♄ ° '	♅ ° '	♆ ° '	♇ ° '
N 1	2 42 0	8♏47 3	4♌ 3	21♎35	2♎27	29♓58	3♊53	28♐55	28♐22	7♑56	12♏22
O 2	2 45 56	9 47 6	16 7	23 0	3 39	0♈ 2	3R46	29 1	28 24	7 57	12 24
V 3	2 49 53	10 47 11	28 1	24 28	4 52	0 6	3 40	29 6	28 27	7 58	12 26
E 4	2 53 49	11 47 19	9♍48	25 58	6 4	0 11	3 33	29 12	28 30	8 0	12 29
M 5	2 57 46	12 47 28	21 35	27 29	7 17	0 16	3 25	29 17	28 32	8 1	12 31
B 6	3 1 42	13 47 39	3♎26	29 2	8 30	0 23	3 18	29 23	28 35	8 3	12 34
E 7	3 5 39	14 47 52	15 24	0♏35	9 43	0 30	3 11	29 28	28 38	8 4	12 36
R 8	3 9 36	15 48 8	27 33	2 10	10 56	0 37	3 3	29 34	28 41	8 6	12 39
9	3 13 32	16 48 25	9♏55	3 45	12 9	0 46	2 56	29 40	28 44	8 7	12 41
10	3 17 29	17 48 44	22 30	5 21	13 22	0 55	2 48	29 46	28 47	8 9	12 43
11	3 21 25	18 49 4	5♐18	6 57	14 35	1 5	2 40	29 52	28 50	8 10	12 46
12	3 25 22	19 49 27	18 19	8 33	15 48	1 16	2 33	29 58	28 53	8 12	12 48
13	3 29 18	20 49 51	1♑32	10 10	17 2	1 27	2 25	0♑ 4	28 56	8 14	12 51
14	3 33 15	21 50 16	14 56	11 46	18 15	1 39	2 17	0 10	28 59	8 15	12 53
15	3 37 11	22 50 43	28 30	13 22	19 29	1 52	2 9	0 16	29 2	8 17	12 55
16	3 41 8	23 51 11	12♒15	14 59	20 42	2 5	2 1	0 22	29 5	8 19	12 58
17	3 45 5	24 51 40	26 9	16 35	21 56	2 19	1 53	0 28	29 8	8 21	13 0
18	3 49 1	25 52 10	10♓14	18 11	23 9	2 33	1 45	0 34	29 11	8 22	13 3
19	3 52 58	26 52 42	24 29	19 47	24 23	2 48	1 37	0 41	29 14	8 24	13 5
20	3 56 54	27 53 15	8♈52	21 23	25 37	3 4	1 28	0 47	29 18	8 26	13 7
21	4 0 51	28 53 49	23 20	22 59	26 50	3 20	1 20	0 53	29 21	8 28	13 10
22	4 4 47	29 54 24	7♉48	24 34	28 4	3 37	1 12	1 0	29 24	8 30	13 12
23	4 8 44	0♐55 1	22 10	26 10	29 18	3 54	1 4	1 6	29 27	8 32	13 14
24	4 12 40	1 55 39	6♊20	27 45	0♏32	4 12	0 56	1 13	29 31	8 34	13 17
25	4 16 37	2 56 19	20 12	29 20	1 46	4 30	0 48	1 19	29 34	8 35	13 19
26	4 20 34	3 57 0	3♋42	0♐55	3 0	4 49	0 39	1 26	29 37	8 37	13 21
27	4 24 30	4 57 43	16 49	2 30	4 14	5 8	0 31	1 32	29 41	8 39	13 24
28	4 28 27	5 58 27	29 32	4 4	5 28	5 28	0 23	1 39	29 44	8 41	13 26
29	4 32 23	6 59 13	11♌55	5 39	6 43	5 48	0 15	1 45	29 47	8 43	13 28
30	4 36 20	7♐59 59	24♌ 1	7♐13	7♏57	6♈ 8	0♊ 7	1♑52	29♐51	8♑45	13♏31

THE SUN ENTERS THE SIGN OF SAGITTARIUS ON NOV 22 AT 02:13.

DAY	TIME h m s	☉ ° ' "	☽ ° '	☿ ° '	♀ ° '	♂ ° '	♃ ° '	♄ ° '	♅ ° '	♆ ° '	♇ ° '
D 1	4 40 16	9♐ 0 48	5♍56	8♐48	9♏11	6♈29	29♉59	1♑59	29♐54	8♑47	13♏33
E 2	4 44 13	10 1 38	17 44	10 22	10 25	6 51	29R51	2 5	29 58	8 49	13 35
C 3	4 48 10	11 2 29	29 32	11 56	11 40	7 13	29 43	2 12	0♑ 1	8 51	13 37
E 4	4 52 6	12 3 22	11♎25	13 30	12 54	7 35	29 35	2 19	0 5	8 53	13 40
M 5	4 56 3	13 4 15	23 27	15 5	14 9	7 58	29 28	2 26	0 8	8 56	13 42
B 6	4 59 59	14 5 11	5♏43	16 39	15 23	8 21	29 20	2 33	0 12	8 58	13 44
E 7	5 3 56	15 6 7	18 16	18 13	16 38	8 45	29 12	2 40	0 15	9 0	13 46
R 8	5 7 52	16 7 5	1♐ 7	19 47	17 52	9 8	29 5	2 46	0 19	9 2	13 48
9	5 11 49	17 8 4	14 15	21 21	19 7	9 33	28 57	2 53	0 22	9 4	13 50
10	5 15 45	18 9 3	27 40	22 55	20 21	9 57	28 50	3 0	0 26	9 6	13 52
11	5 19 42	19 10 4	11♑18	24 30	21 36	10 22	28 43	3 7	0 29	9 8	13 55
12	5 23 39	20 11 5	25 7	26 4	22 51	10 48	28 36	3 14	0 33	9 10	13 57
13	5 27 35	21 12 7	9♒ 2	27 39	24 5	11 13	28 29	3 21	0 37	9 13	13 59
14	5 31 32	22 13 9	23 3	29 13	25 20	11 39	28 22	3 28	0 40	9 15	14 1
15	5 35 28	23 14 12	7♓ 5	0♑48	26 35	12 5	28 15	3 35	0 44	9 17	14 3
16	5 39 25	24 15 15	21 9	2 22	27 49	12 32	28 8	3 42	0 47	9 19	14 5
17	5 43 21	25 16 19	5♈15	3 57	29 4	12 59	28 2	3 49	0 51	9 21	14 7
18	5 47 18	26 17 22	19 20	5 32	0♐19	13 26	27 56	3 56	0 55	9 24	14 9
19	5 51 14	27 18 26	3♉24	7 7	1 34	13 54	27 49	4 3	0 58	9 26	14 11
20	5 55 11	28 19 31	17 24	8 42	2 48	14 21	27 43	4 10	1 2	9 28	14 12
21	5 59 8	29 20 36	1♊19	10 16	4 3	14 49	27 37	4 18	1 5	9 30	14 14
22	6 3 4	0♑21 41	15 3	11 51	5 18	15 17	27 32	4 25	1 9	9 33	14 16
23	6 7 1	1 22 47	28 33	13 26	6 33	15 46	27 26	4 32	1 13	9 35	14 18
24	6 10 57	2 23 53	11♋47	15 1	7 48	16 15	27 21	4 39	1 16	9 37	14 20
25	6 14 54	3 24 59	24 43	16 35	9 3	16 44	27 15	4 46	1 20	9 39	14 22
26	6 18 50	4 26 6	7♌20	18 9	10 18	17 13	27 10	4 53	1 24	9 42	14 23
27	6 22 47	5 27 14	19 40	19 43	11 33	17 42	27 5	5 0	1 27	9 44	14 25
28	6 26 44	6 28 21	1♍46	21 16	12 48	18 12	27 1	5 7	1 31	9 46	14 27
29	6 30 40	7 29 29	13 41	22 49	14 3	18 42	26 56	5 14	1 34	9 48	14 28
30	6 34 37	8 30 38	25 30	24 21	15 18	19 12	26 52	5 21	1 38	9 51	14 30
31	6 38 33	9♑31 47	7♎18	25♑51	16♐33	19♈42	26♉48	5♑29	1♑42	9♑53	14♏32

THE SUN ENTERS THE SIGN OF CAPRICORN ON DEC 21 AT 15:29.

♏ SCORPIO ♐ SAGITTARIUS ♑ CAPRICORN ♒ AQUARIUS ♓ PISCES

1989

SIDEREAL TIME. SUN. MOON. MERCURY. VENUS. MARS. JUPITER. SATURN. URANUS. NEPTUNE. PLUTO.

DAY	TIME	☉	☽	☿	♀	♂	♃	♄	♅	♆	♇
	h m s	° ' "	° '	° '	° '	° '	° '	° '	° '	° '	° '
J 1	6 42 30	10♑32 56	19♎11	27♑21	17♐48	20♈12	26♉44	5♑36	1♑45	9♑55	14♏33
A 2	6 46 26	11 34 6	1♏14	28 49	19 3	20 43	26R40	5 43	1 49	9 58	14 35
N 3	6 50 23	12 35 16	13 32	0♒15	20 18	21 14	26 36	5 50	1 52	10 0	14 36
U 4	6 54 19	13 36 26	26 8	1 39	21 33	21 45	26 33	5 57	1 56	10 2	14 38
A 5	6 58 16	14 37 37	9♐ 7	3 1	22 48	22 16	26 30	6 4	2 0	10 4	14 39
R 6	7 2 13	15 38 48	22 28	4 19	24 3	22 47	26 26	6 11	2 3	10 7	14 41
Y 7	7 6 9	16 39 58	6♑11	5 33	25 18	23 19	26 24	6 18	2 7	10 9	14 42
8	7 10 6	17 41 9	20 12	6 43	26 33	23 50	26 21	6 25	2 10	10 11	14 44
9	7 14 2	18 42 19	4♒28	7 49	27 48	24 22	26 19	6 32	2 14	10 13	14 45
10	7 17 59	19 43 29	18 51	8 48	29 3	24 54	26 16	6 39	2 17	10 16	14 46
11	7 21 55	20 44 39	3♓17	9 41	0♑18	25 26	26 14	6 46	2 21	10 18	14 48
12	7 25 52	21 45 48	17 42	10 26	1 33	25 59	26 13	6 53	2 24	10 20	14 49
13	7 29 48	22 46 56	2♈ 1	11 2	2 49	26 31	26 11	7 0	2 28	10 22	14 50
14	7 33 45	23 48 4	16 12	11 30	4 4	27 4	26 10	7 7	2 31	10 25	14 51
15	7 37 42	24 49 11	0♉14	11 47	5 19	27 36	26 8	7 14	2 35	10 27	14 52
16	7 41 38	25 50 17	14 5	11R54	6 34	28 9	26 7	7 21	2 38	10 29	14 54
17	7 45 35	26 51 23	27 46	11 49	7 49	28 42	26 7	7 27	2 41	10 31	14 55
18	7 49 31	27 52 27	11♊15	11 32	9 4	29 15	26 6	7 34	2 45	10 34	14 56
19	7 53 28	28 53 31	24 33	11 4	10 19	29 49	26 6	7 41	2 48	10 36	14 57
20	7 57 24	29 54 35	7♋37	10 24	11 34	0♉22	26D 5	7 48	2 51	10 38	14 58
21	8 1 21	0♒55 37	20 29	9 34	12 49	0 55	26 6	7 54	2 55	10 40	14 59
22	8 5 17	1 56 39	3♌ 6	8 35	14 5	1 29	26 6	8 1	2 58	10 42	15 0
23	8 9 14	2 57 40	15 31	7 28	15 20	2 3	26 6	8 8	3 1	10 44	15 1
24	8 13 11	3 58 40	27 42	6 16	16 35	2 36	26 7	8 15	3 5	10 46	15 1
25	8 17 7	4 59 39	9♍44	5 1	17 50	3 10	26 8	8 21	3 8	10 49	15 2
26	8 21 4	6 0 38	21 37	3 44	19 5	3 44	26 9	8 28	3 11	10 51	15 3
27	8 25 0	7 1 37	3♎25	2 29	20 20	4 18	26 10	8 34	3 14	10 53	15 4
28	8 28 57	8 2 34	15 13	1 17	21 35	4 53	26 12	8 41	3 17	10 55	15 5
29	8 32 53	9 3 31	27 6	0 11	22 50	5 27	26 13	8 47	3 20	10 57	15 5
30	8 36 50	10 4 27	9♏ 7	29♑11	24 5	6 1	26 15	8 54	3 23	10 59	15 6
31	8 40 46	11♒ 5 23	21♏23	28♑18	25♑21	6♉36	26♉17	9♑ 0	3♑27	11♑ 1	15♏ 6

THE SUN ENTERS THE SIGN OF AQUARIUS ON JAN 20 AT 02:08.

DAY	TIME	☉	☽	☿	♀	♂	♃	♄	♅	♆	♇
	h m s	° ' "	° '	° '	° '	° '	° '	° '	° '	° '	° '
F 1	8 44 43	12♒ 6 18	3♐57	27♑34	26♑36	7♉10	26♉20	9♑ 6	3♑30	11♑ 3	15♏ 7
E 2	8 48 40	13 7 12	16 54	26R58	27 51	7 45	26 22	9 13	3 33	11 5	15 8
B 3	8 52 36	14 8 5	0♑17	26 31	29 6	8 19	26 25	9 19	3 36	11 7	15 8
R 4	8 56 33	15 8 57	14 5	26 12	0♒21	8 54	26 28	9 25	3 39	11 9	15 9
U 5	9 0 29	16 9 49	28 17	26D 2	1 36	9 29	26 31	9 31	3 41	11 11	15 9
A 6	9 4 26	17 10 39	12♒49	25 59	2 51	10 4	26 34	9 38	3 44	11 13	15 9
R 7	9 8 22	18 11 28	27 36	26 4	4 6	10 39	26 37	9 44	3 47	11 15	15 10
Y 8	9 12 19	19 12 16	12♓29	26 16	5 22	11 14	26 41	9 50	3 50	11 17	15 10
9	9 16 16	20 13 2	27 21	26 34	6 37	11 49	26 45	9 56	3 53	11 19	15 10
10	9 20 12	21 13 47	12♈ 4	26 58	7 52	12 24	26 49	10 2	3 55	11 20	15 11
11	9 24 9	22 14 30	26 34	27 27	9 7	13 0	26 53	10 8	3 58	11 22	15 11
12	9 28 5	23 15 12	10♉46	28 2	10 22	13 35	26 57	10 13	4 1	11 24	15 11
13	9 32 2	24 15 52	24 39	28 41	11 37	14 10	27 2	10 19	4 4	11 26	15 11
14	9 35 58	25 16 30	8♊13	29 24	12 52	14 46	27 7	10 25	4 6	11 28	15 11
15	9 39 55	26 17 6	21 29	0♒12	14 7	15 21	27 12	10 31	4 9	11 29	15 11
16	9 43 51	27 17 41	4♋28	1 3	15 22	15 57	27 17	10 36	4 11	11 31	15R11
17	9 47 48	28 18 14	17 12	1 57	16 37	16 32	27 22	10 42	4 14	11 33	15 11
18	9 51 45	29 18 46	29 43	2 54	17 52	17 8	27 28	10 47	4 16	11 35	15 11
19	9 55 41	0♓19 16	12♌ 2	3 54	19 7	17 44	27 33	10 53	4 19	11 36	15 11
20	9 59 38	1 19 44	24 11	4 57	20 22	18 20	27 39	10 58	4 21	11 38	15 11
21	10 3 34	2 20 10	6♍12	6 2	21 37	18 55	27 45	11 3	4 23	11 40	15 11
22	10 7 31	3 20 35	18 7	7 9	22 52	19 31	27 51	11 9	4 26	11 41	15 11
23	10 11 27	4 20 58	29 57	8 18	24 7	20 7	27 57	11 14	4 28	11 43	15 11
24	10 15 24	5 21 20	11♎46	9 29	25 22	20 43	28 4	11 19	4 30	11 44	15 10
25	10 19 20	6 21 40	23 35	10 43	26 37	21 19	28 10	11 24	4 32	11 46	15 10
26	10 23 17	7 21 58	5♏29	11 58	27 52	21 55	28 17	11 29	4 34	11 47	15 10
27	10 27 13	8 22 16	17 31	13 14	29 7	22 31	28 24	11 34	4 36	11 49	15 9
28	10 31 10	9♓22 31	29♏45	14♒32	0♓22	23♉ 7	28♉31	11♑39	4♑38	11♑50	15♏ 9

THE SUN ENTERS THE SIGN OF PISCES ON FEB 18 AT 16:21.

DAY	TIME	☉	☽	☿	♀	♂	♃	♄	♅	♆	♇
	h m s	° ' "	° '	° '	° '	° '	° '	° '	° '	° '	° '
M 1	10 35 7	10♓22 46	12♐15	15♒52	1♓37	23♉43	28♉38	11♑43	4♑40	11♑52	15♏ 9
A 2	10 39 3	11 22 59	25 6	17 13	2 52	24 19	28 46	11 48	4 42	11 53	15R 8
R 3	10 43 0	12 23 10	8♑20	18 36	4 7	24 56	28 53	11 53	4 44	11 54	15 8
C 4	10 46 56	13 23 20	22 2	20 0	5 22	25 32	29 1	11 57	4 46	11 56	15 7
H 5	10 50 53	14 23 28	6♒10	21 25	6 36	26 8	29 9	12 2	4 48	11 57	15 6
6	10 54 49	15 23 35	20 44	22 52	7 51	26 44	29 17	12 6	4 50	11 58	15 6
7	10 58 46	16 23 39	5♓37	24 19	9 6	27 21	29 25	12 11	4 51	11 59	15 5
8	11 2 42	17 23 42	20 45	25 48	10 21	27 57	29 33	12 15	4 53	12 1	15 5
9	11 6 39	18 23 43	5♈56	27 19	11 36	28 34	29 42	12 19	4 55	12 2	15 4
10	11 10 36	19 23 42	21 2	28 50	12 51	29 10	29 50	12 23	4 56	12 3	15 3
11	11 14 32	20 23 39	5♉53	0♓23	14 6	29 47	29 59	12 27	4 58	12 4	15 2
12	11 18 29	21 23 34	20 24	1 57	15 20	0♊23	0♊ 8	12 31	4 59	12 5	15 2
13	11 22 25	22 23 27	4♊29	3 32	16 35	1 0	0 16	12 35	5 1	12 6	15 1
14	11 26 22	23 23 17	18 8	5 8	17 50	1 36	0 25	12 39	5 2	12 7	15 0
15	11 30 18	24 23 6	1♋23	6 45	19 5	2 13	0 35	12 42	5 3	12 8	14 59
16	11 34 15	25 22 52	14 14	8 24	20 20	2 49	0 44	12 46	5 5	12 9	14 58
17	11 38 11	26 22 35	26 47	10 4	21 34	3 26	0 53	12 50	5 6	12 10	14 57
18	11 42 8	27 22 17	9♌ 5	11 45	22 49	4 2	1 3	12 53	5 7	12 11	14 56
19	11 46 5	28 21 56	21 11	13 27	24 4	4 39	1 13	12 56	5 8	12 12	14 55
20	11 50 1	29 21 33	3♍ 9	15 10	25 18	5 16	1 22	13 0	5 9	12 13	14 54
21	11 53 58	0♈21 8	15 1	16 55	26 33	5 52	1 32	13 3	5 10	12 14	14 53
22	11 57 54	1 20 41	26 51	18 41	27 48	6 29	1 42	13 6	5 11	12 14	14 52
23	12 1 51	2 20 11	8♎40	20 28	29 2	7 6	1 52	13 9	5 12	12 15	14 51
24	12 5 47	3 19 40	20 30	22 17	0♈17	7 43	2 2	13 12	5 13	12 16	14 50
25	12 9 44	4 19 7	2♏23	24 7	1 32	8 19	2 13	13 15	5 14	12 16	14 49
26	12 13 40	5 18 32	14 22	25 58	2 46	8 56	2 23	13 17	5 15	12 17	14 48
27	12 17 37	6 17 55	26 29	27 51	4 1	9 33	2 34	13 20	5 15	12 18	14 46
28	12 21 34	7 17 16	8♐46	29 44	5 15	10 10	2 44	13 23	5 16	12 18	14 45
29	12 25 30	8 16 36	21 16	1♈39	6 30	10 46	2 55	13 25	5 17	12 19	14 44
30	12 29 27	9 15 54	4♑ 4	3 36	7 44	11 23	3 6	13 28	5 17	12 19	14 43
31	12 33 23	10♈15 10	17♑11	5♈33	8♈59	12♊ 0	3♊17	13♑30	5♑18	12♑20	14♏41

THE SUN ENTERS THE SIGN OF ARIES ON MAR 20 AT 15:29.

♈ ARIES ♉ TAURUS ♊ GEMINI ♋ CANCER ♌ LEO ♍ VIRGO ♎ LIBRA

SIDEREAL TIME . SUN . MOON . MERCURY . VENUS . MARS . JUPITER . SATURN . URANUS . NEPTUNE . PLUTO .

DAY	TIME	☉	☽	☿	♀	♂	♃	♄	♅	♆	♇
	h m s	° ' "	° '	° '	° '	° '	° '	° '	° '	° '	° '
A 1	12 37 20	11♈14 24	0♒42	7♈32	10♈13	12♊37	3♊28	13♑32	5♑18	12♑20	14♏40
P 2	12 41 16	12 13 36	14 39	9 32	11 28	13 14	3 39	13 34	5 19	12 21	14R39
R 3	12 45 13	13 12 47	29 1	11 34	12 42	13 51	3 50	13 36	5 19	12 21	14 37
I 4	12 49 9	14 11 56	13♓46	13 36	13 57	14 28	4 1	13 38	5 19	12 21	14 36
L 5	12 53 6	15 11 3	28 49	15 39	15 11	15 5	4 13	13 40	5 20	12 22	14 35
6	12 57 3	16 10 8	14♈ 3	17 43	16 26	15 41	4 24	13 42	5 20	12 22	14 33
7	13 0 59	17 9 11	29 17	19 47	17 40	16 18	4 36	13 43	5 20	12 22	14 32
8	13 4 56	18 8 12	14♉20	21 52	18 55	16 55	4 47	13 45	5 20	12 22	14 30
9	13 8 52	19 7 11	29 4	23 58	20 9	17 32	4 59	13 46	5R20	12 23	14 29
10	13 12 49	20 6 7	13♊23	26 3	21 23	18 9	5 11	13 47	5 20	12 23	14 27
11	13 16 45	21 5 2	27 12	28 8	22 38	18 46	5 22	13 49	5 20	12 23	14 26
12	13 20 42	22 3 54	10♋32	0♉12	23 52	19 23	5 34	13 50	5 20	12 23	14 24
13	13 24 38	23 2 44	23 25	2 16	25 6	20 0	5 46	13 51	5 20	12R23	14 23
14	13 28 35	24 1 31	5♌56	4 18	26 21	20 37	5 58	13 52	5 19	12 23	14 21
15	13 32 32	25 0 17	18 10	6 19	27 35	21 14	6 11	13 53	5 19	12 23	14 20
16	13 36 28	25 59 0	0♍10	8 18	28 49	21 51	6 23	13 53	5 19	12 23	14 18
17	13 40 25	26 57 40	12 2	10 15	0♉ 3	22 28	6 35	13 54	5 19	12 23	14 17
18	13 44 21	27 56 19	23 50	12 9	1 18	23 5	6 47	13 54	5 18	12 23	14 15
19	13 48 18	28 54 55	5♎38	14 0	2 32	23 42	7 0	13 55	5 18	12 23	14 13
20	13 52 14	29 53 30	17 28	15 49	3 46	24 19	7 12	13 55	5 17	12 22	14 12
21	13 56 11	0♉52 2	29 23	17 33	5 0	24 56	7 25	13 55	5 17	12 22	14 10
22	14 0 7	1 50 33	11♏24	19 14	6 14	25 33	7 37	13R56	5 16	12 22	14 9
23	14 4 4	2 49 2	23 33	20 52	7 28	26 10	7 50	13 56	5 15	12 22	14 7
24	14 8 0	3 47 29	5♐50	22 25	8 43	26 47	8 3	13 56	5 15	12 21	14 5
25	14 11 57	4 45 55	18 17	23 54	9 57	27 25	8 15	13 55	5 14	12 21	14 4
26	14 15 54	5 44 18	0♑55	25 18	11 11	28 2	8 28	13 55	5 13	12 21	14 2
27	14 19 50	6 42 41	13 47	26 38	12 25	28 39	8 41	13 55	5 12	12 20	14 0
28	14 23 47	7 41 1	26 55	27 54	13 39	29 16	8 54	13 54	5 11	12 20	13 59
29	14 27 43	8 39 20	10♒21	29 5	14 53	29 53	9 7	13 54	5 10	12 19	13 57
30	14 31 40	9♉37 38	24♒ 7	0♊11	16♉ 7	0♋30	9♊20	13♑53	5♑ 9	12♑19	13♏55

THE SUN ENTERS THE SIGN OF TAURUS ON APR 20 AT 02:39.

DAY	TIME	☉	☽	☿	♀	♂	♃	♄	♅	♆	♇
	h m s	° ' "	° '	° '	° '	° '	° '	° '	° '	° '	° '
M 1	14 35 36	10♉35 54	8♓15	1♊12	17♉21	1♋ 7	9♊33	13♑53	5♑ 8	12♑18	13♏54
A 2	14 39 33	11 34 8	22 44	2 9	18 35	1 44	9 46	13R52	5R 7	12R18	13R52
Y 3	14 43 29	12 32 21	7♈31	3 0	19 49	2 21	9 59	13 51	5 6	12 17	13 50
4	14 47 26	13 30 33	22 31	3 46	21 3	2 58	10 12	13 50	5 5	12 17	13 48
5	14 51 23	14 28 43	7♉35	4 27	22 17	3 35	10 26	13 49	5 4	12 16	13 47
6	14 55 19	15 26 51	22 33	5 3	23 31	4 13	10 39	13 47	5 2	12 15	13 45
7	14 59 16	16 24 58	7♊17	5 34	24 45	4 50	10 52	13 46	5 1	12 15	13 43
8	15 3 12	17 23 3	21 38	6 0	25 58	5 27	11 6	13 45	5 0	12 14	13 42
9	15 7 9	18 21 6	5♋32	6 20	27 12	6 4	11 19	13 43	4 58	12 13	13 40
10	15 11 5	19 19 7	18 58	6 36	28 26	6 41	11 32	13 42	4 57	12 12	13 38
11	15 15 2	20 17 7	1♌55	6 46	29 40	7 18	11 46	13 40	4 56	12 12	13 37
12	15 18 59	21 15 4	14 29	6R51	0♊54	7 55	11 59	13 38	4 54	12 11	13 35
13	15 22 55	22 13 0	26 43	6 51	2 8	8 33	12 13	13 36	4 52	12 10	13 33
14	15 26 52	23 10 54	8♍44	6 46	3 21	9 10	12 26	13 34	4 51	12 9	13 32
15	15 30 48	24 8 46	20 35	6 36	4 35	9 47	12 40	13 32	4 49	12 8	13 30
16	15 34 45	25 6 36	2♎24	6 22	5 49	10 24	12 54	13 30	4 48	12 7	13 28
17	15 38 41	26 4 25	14 13	6 4	7 3	11 1	13 7	13 28	4 46	12 6	13 27
18	15 42 38	27 2 12	26 6	5 43	8 16	11 38	13 21	13 26	4 44	12 5	13 25
19	15 46 34	27 59 58	8♏ 7	5 18	9 30	12 16	13 35	13 23	4 42	12 4	13 23
20	15 50 31	28 57 42	20 18	4 50	10 44	12 53	13 48	13 21	4 41	12 3	13 22
21	15 54 28	29 55 25	2♐39	4 19	11 57	13 30	14 2	13 18	4 39	12 2	13 20
22	15 58 24	0♊53 6	15 11	3 47	13 11	14 7	14 16	13 16	4 37	12 1	13 19
23	16 2 21	1 50 47	27 54	3 13	14 25	14 44	14 30	13 13	4 35	12 0	13 17
24	16 6 17	2 48 26	10♑49	2 39	15 38	15 21	14 43	13 10	4 33	11 59	13 15
25	16 10 14	3 46 4	23 55	2 5	16 52	15 59	14 57	13 8	4 31	11 57	13 14
26	16 14 10	4 43 41	7♒13	1 31	18 5	16 36	15 11	13 5	4 29	11 56	13 12
27	16 18 7	5 41 17	20 44	0 59	19 19	17 13	15 25	13 2	4 27	11 55	13 11
28	16 22 3	6 38 52	4♓29	0 28	20 33	17 50	15 39	12 59	4 25	11 54	13 9
29	16 26 0	7 36 26	18 29	29♉59	21 46	18 27	15 52	12 55	4 23	11 52	13 8
30	16 29 57	8 34 0	2♈44	29 32	23 0	19 5	16 6	12 52	4 21	11 51	13 6
31	16 33 53	9♊31 32	17♈12	29♉ 9	24♊13	19♋42	16♊20	12♑49	4♑19	11♑50	13♏ 5

THE SUN ENTERS THE SIGN OF GEMINI ON MAY 21 AT 01:54.

DAY	TIME	☉	☽	☿	♀	♂	♃	♄	♅	♆	♇
	h m s	° ' "	° '	° '	° '	° '	° '	° '	° '	° '	° '
J 1	16 37 50	10♊29 4	1♉50	28♉50	25♊27	20♋19	16♊34	12♑46	4♑17	11♑49	13♏ 3
U 2	16 41 46	11 26 35	16 32	28R33	26 40	20 56	16 48	12R42	4R15	11R47	13R 2
N 3	16 45 43	12 24 5	1♊11	28 21	27 54	21 33	17 2	12 39	4 12	11 46	13 1
E 4	16 49 39	13 21 35	15 39	28 13	29 7	22 11	17 16	12 35	4 10	11 45	12 59
5	16 53 36	14 19 3	29 50	28D10	0♋20	22 48	17 30	12 32	4 8	11 43	12 58
6	16 57 32	15 16 31	13♋37	28 10	1 34	23 25	17 44	12 28	4 6	11 42	12 56
7	17 1 29	16 13 57	27 0	28 16	2 47	24 2	17 58	12 24	4 3	11 40	12 55
8	17 5 26	17 11 22	9♌58	28 25	4 1	24 40	18 11	12 21	4 1	11 39	12 54
9	17 9 22	18 8 46	22 33	28 39	5 14	25 17	18 25	12 17	3 59	11 38	12 52
10	17 13 19	19 6 9	4♍49	28 58	6 27	25 54	18 39	12 13	3 56	11 36	12 51
11	17 17 15	20 3 31	16 52	29 21	7 41	26 32	18 53	12 9	3 54	11 35	12 50
12	17 21 12	21 0 52	28 45	29 49	8 54	27 9	19 7	12 5	3 52	11 33	12 49
13	17 25 8	21 58 12	10♎35	0♊20	10 7	27 46	19 21	12 1	3 49	11 32	12 47
14	17 29 5	22 55 31	22 27	0 57	11 21	28 23	19 35	11 57	3 47	11 30	12 46
15	17 33 1	23 52 49	4♏24	1 37	12 34	29 1	19 49	11 53	3 45	11 29	12 45
16	17 36 58	24 50 6	16 31	2 21	13 47	29 38	20 3	11 49	3 42	11 27	12 44
17	17 40 55	25 47 23	28 51	3 9	15 0	0♌15	20 17	11 45	3 40	11 26	12 43
18	17 44 51	26 44 39	11♐25	4 2	16 14	0 53	20 30	11 41	3 37	11 24	12 42
19	17 48 48	27 41 54	24 13	4 58	17 27	1 30	20 44	11 36	3 35	11 22	12 41
20	17 52 44	28 39 9	7♑15	5 58	18 40	2 7	20 58	11 32	3 33	11 21	12 40
21	17 56 41	29 36 23	20 31	7 2	19 53	2 45	21 12	11 28	3 30	11 19	12 39
22	18 0 37	0♋33 38	3♒58	8 9	21 6	3 22	21 26	11 24	3 28	11 18	12 38
23	18 4 34	1 30 51	17 36	9 20	22 19	3 59	21 39	11 19	3 25	11 16	12 37
24	18 8 31	2 28 5	1♓22	10 35	23 32	4 37	21 53	11 15	3 23	11 15	12 36
25	18 12 27	3 25 18	15 18	11 53	24 45	5 14	22 7	11 11	3 20	11 13	12 35
26	18 16 24	4 22 32	29 21	13 15	25 59	5 51	22 21	11 6	3 18	11 11	12 34
27	18 20 20	5 19 45	13♈30	14 40	27 12	6 29	22 34	11 2	3 16	11 10	12 33
28	18 24 17	6 16 59	27 45	16 9	28 25	7 6	22 48	10 57	3 13	11 8	12 32
29	18 28 13	7 14 12	12♉ 3	17 41	29 38	7 43	23 2	10 53	3 11	11 7	12 32
30	18 32 10	8♋11 26	26♉21	19♊17	0♌51	8♌21	23♊15	10♑49	3♑ 8	11♑ 5	12♏31

THE SUN ENTERS THE SIGN OF CANCER ON JUN 21 AT 09:54.

♏ SCORPIO ♐ SAGITTARIUS ♑ CAPRICORN ♒ AQUARIUS ♓ PISCES

SIDEREAL TIME · SUN · MOON · MERCURY · VENUS · MARS · JUPITER · SATURN · URANUS · NEPTUNE · PLUTO

DAY	TIME h m s	⊙ ° ' "	☽ ° '	☿ ° '	♀ ° '	♂ ° '	♃ ° '	♄ ° '	♅ ° '	♆ ° '	♇ ° '
J 1	18 36 6	9♋ 8 40	10♊33	20♊55	2♌ 4	8♌58	23♊29	10♑44	3♑ 6	11♑ 3	12♏30
U 2	18 40 3	10 5 54	24 36	22 37	3 17	9 36	23 43	10R40	3R 3	11R 2	12R29
L 3	18 44 0	11 3 8	8♋25	24 22	4 29	10 13	23 56	10 35	3 1	11 0	12 29
Y 4	18 47 56	12 0 22	21 55	26 11	5 42	10 50	24 10	10 31	2 59	10 58	12 28
5	18 51 53	12 57 35	5♌ 6	28 2	6 55	11 28	24 23	10 26	2 56	10 57	12 27
6	18 55 49	13 54 49	17 57	29 56	8 8	12 5	24 37	10 22	2 54	10 55	12 27
7	18 59 46	14 52 2	0♍28	1♋52	9 21	12 43	24 50	10 18	2 51	10 54	12 26
8	19 3 42	15 49 15	12 43	3 51	10 34	13 20	25 4	10 13	2 49	10 52	12 26
9	19 7 39	16 46 29	24 46	5 52	11 47	13 58	25 17	10 9	2 47	10 50	12 25
10	19 11 35	17 43 41	6♎41	7 55	12 59	14 35	25 30	10 4	2 44	10 49	12 25
11	19 15 32	18 40 54	18 32	10 0	14 12	15 13	25 44	10 0	2 42	10 47	12 24
12	19 19 29	19 38 7	0♏25	12 6	15 25	15 50	25 57	9 56	2 40	10 45	12 24
13	19 23 25	20 35 20	12 24	14 14	16 38	16 28	26 10	9 51	2 37	10 44	12 24
14	19 27 22	21 32 33	24 35	16 22	17 50	17 5	26 23	9 47	2 35	10 42	12 23
15	19 31 18	22 29 46	7♐ 0	18 31	19 3	17 43	26 36	9 43	2 33	10 41	12 23
16	19 35 15	23 26 59	19 42	20 40	20 15	18 20	26 50	9 38	2 31	10 39	12 23
17	19 39 11	24 24 13	2♑43	22 48	21 28	18 58	27 3	9 34	2 28	10 38	12 23
18	19 43 8	25 21 26	16 3	24 57	22 41	19 36	27 16	9 30	2 26	10 36	12 22
19	19 47 4	26 18 41	29 39	27 5	23 53	20 13	27 29	9 26	2 24	10 34	12 22
20	19 51 1	27 15 55	13♒31	29 12	25 6	20 51	27 42	9 22	2 22	10 33	12 22
21	19 54 58	28 13 10	27 34	1♌18	26 18	21 28	27 54	9 18	2 20	10 31	12 22
22	19 58 54	29 10 26	11♓45	3 23	27 31	22 6	28 7	9 14	2 18	10 30	12 22
23	20 2 51	0♌ 7 42	26 1	5 27	28 43	22 44	28 20	9 10	2 16	10 28	12D22
24	20 6 47	1 4 59	10♈18	7 30	29 55	23 21	28 33	9 6	2 14	10 27	12 22
25	20 10 44	2 2 17	24 34	9 31	1♍ 8	23 59	28 45	9 2	2 12	10 25	12 22
26	20 14 40	2 59 36	8♉45	11 30	2 20	24 37	28 58	8 58	2 10	10 24	12 22
27	20 18 37	3 56 56	22 51	13 28	3 32	25 14	29 10	8 54	2 8	10 22	12 22
28	20 22 33	4 54 18	6♊49	15 24	4 45	25 52	29 23	8 50	2 6	10 21	12 22
29	20 26 30	5 51 40	20 36	17 19	5 57	26 30	29 35	8 47	2 4	10 20	12 23
30	20 30 27	6 49 3	4♋12	19 12	7 9	27 7	29 48	8 43	2 2	10 18	12 23
31	20 34 23	7♌46 27	17♋35	21♌ 4	8♍21	27♌45	0♋ 0	8♑39	2♑ 0	10♑17	12♏23

THE SUN ENTERS THE SIGN OF LEO ON JUL 22 AT 20:46.

DAY	TIME h m s	⊙ ° ' "	☽ ° '	☿ ° '	♀ ° '	♂ ° '	♃ ° '	♄ ° '	♅ ° '	♆ ° '	♇ ° '
A 1	20 38 20	8♌43 52	0♌42	22♌53	9♍33	28♌23	0♋12	8♑36	1♑58	10♑15	12♏23
U 2	20 42 16	9 41 18	13 35	24 42	10 46	29 1	0 25	8R32	1R57	10R14	12 24
G 3	20 46 13	10 38 45	26 12	26 28	11 58	29 39	0 37	8 29	1 55	10 13	12 24
U 4	20 50 9	11 36 12	8♍34	28 13	13 10	0♍16	0 49	8 26	1 53	10 11	12 24
S 5	20 54 6	12 33 40	20 45	29 56	14 22	0 54	1 1	8 22	1 51	10 10	12 25
T 6	20 58 3	13 31 10	2♎45	1♍38	15 34	1 32	1 13	8 19	1 50	10 9	12 25
7	21 1 59	14 28 39	14 39	3 18	16 46	2 10	1 24	8 16	1 48	10 7	12 26
8	21 5 56	15 26 10	26 30	4 56	17 57	2 48	1 36	8 13	1 47	10 6	12 26
9	21 9 52	16 23 42	8♏22	6 33	19 9	3 26	1 48	8 10	1 45	10 5	12 27
10	21 13 49	17 21 14	20 22	8 8	20 21	4 4	1 59	8 7	1 44	10 4	12 27
11	21 17 45	18 18 47	2♐32	9 42	21 33	4 42	2 11	8 4	1 42	10 3	12 28
12	21 21 42	19 16 21	14 57	11 14	22 45	5 19	2 22	8 1	1 41	10 1	12 29
13	21 25 38	20 13 56	27 41	12 44	23 56	5 57	2 34	7 59	1 40	10 0	12 29
14	21 29 35	21 11 33	10♑47	14 13	25 8	6 35	2 45	7 56	1 38	9 59	12 30
15	21 33 32	22 9 10	24 16	15 40	26 20	7 13	2 56	7 53	1 37	9 58	12 31
16	21 37 28	23 6 48	8♒ 8	17 6	27 31	7 51	3 7	7 51	1 36	9 57	12 32
17	21 41 25	24 4 27	22 20	18 29	28 43	8 29	3 18	7 49	1 35	9 56	12 33
18	21 45 21	25 2 8	6♓48	19 52	29 54	9 7	3 29	7 46	1 33	9 55	12 33
19	21 49 18	25 59 49	21 26	21 12	1♎ 6	9 46	3 40	7 44	1 32	9 54	12 34
20	21 53 14	26 57 33	6♈ 8	22 31	2 17	10 24	3 51	7 42	1 31	9 53	12 35
21	21 57 11	27 55 18	20 47	23 48	3 28	11 2	4 1	7 40	1 30	9 52	12 36
22	22 1 7	28 53 4	5♉19	25 3	4 39	11 40	4 12	7 38	1 29	9 51	12 37
23	22 5 4	29 50 53	19 38	26 16	5 51	12 18	4 22	7 36	1 28	9 50	12 38
24	22 9 0	0♍48 43	3♊41	27 27	7 2	12 56	4 33	7 34	1 28	9 49	12 39
25	22 12 57	1 46 35	17 29	28 36	8 13	13 34	4 43	7 33	1 27	9 48	12 40
26	22 16 54	2 44 29	0♋59	29 43	9 24	14 13	4 53	7 31	1 26	9 48	12 41
27	22 20 50	3 42 24	14 13	0♎48	10 35	14 51	5 3	7 29	1 25	9 47	12 43
28	22 24 47	4 40 22	27 13	1 50	11 46	15 29	5 13	7 28	1 25	9 46	12 44
29	22 28 43	5 38 20	9♌58	2 50	12 57	16 7	5 23	7 27	1 24	9 45	12 45
30	22 32 40	6 36 21	22 31	3 47	14 8	16 46	5 33	7 25	1 23	9 45	12 46
31	22 36 36	7♍34 23	4♍52	4♎41	15♎19	17♍24	5♋43	7♑24	1♑23	9♑44	12♏47

THE SUN ENTERS THE SIGN OF VIRGO ON AUG 23 AT 03:48.

DAY	TIME h m s	⊙ ° ' "	☽ ° '	☿ ° '	♀ ° '	♂ ° '	♃ ° '	♄ ° '	♅ ° '	♆ ° '	♇ ° '
S 1	22 40 33	8♍32 27	17♍ 3	5♎32	16♎29	18♍ 2	5♋52	7♑23	1♑22	9♑43	12♏49
E 2	22 44 29	9 30 32	29 6	6 20	17 40	18 41	6 2	7R22	1R22	9R43	12 50
P 3	22 48 26	10 28 39	11♎ 2	7 5	18 51	19 19	6 11	7 21	1 22	9 42	12 51
T 4	22 52 23	11 26 48	22 54	7 46	20 1	19 57	6 20	7 21	1 21	9 41	12 53
E 5	22 56 19	12 24 58	4♏44	8 24	21 12	20 36	6 29	7 20	1 21	9 41	12 54
M 6	23 0 16	13 23 10	16 36	8 57	22 22	21 14	6 38	7 19	1 21	9 40	12 56
B 7	23 4 12	14 21 23	28 34	9 26	23 33	21 53	6 47	7 19	1 20	9 40	12 57
E 8	23 8 9	15 19 38	10♐41	9 50	24 43	22 31	6 55	7 19	1 20	9 39	12 59
R 9	23 12 5	16 17 54	23 3	10 9	25 53	23 10	7 4	7 18	1 20	9 39	13 0
10	23 16 2	17 16 12	5♑44	10 23	27 4	23 48	7 12	7 18	1D20	9 39	13 2
11	23 19 58	18 14 31	18 47	10R31	28 14	24 27	7 21	7D18	1 20	9 38	13 3
12	23 23 55	19 12 52	2♒15	10 34	29 24	25 6	7 29	7 18	1 20	9 38	13 5
13	23 27 52	20 11 14	16 10	10 30	0♏34	25 44	7 37	7 18	1 20	9 38	13 7
14	23 31 48	21 9 38	0♓31	10 19	1 44	26 23	7 45	7 18	1 21	9 37	13 8
15	23 35 45	22 8 4	15 14	10 2	2 54	27 1	7 53	7 19	1 21	9 37	13 10
16	23 39 41	23 6 31	0♈13	9 38	4 3	27 40	8 0	7 19	1 21	9 37	13 12
17	23 43 38	24 5 1	15 19	9 7	5 13	28 19	8 8	7 20	1 21	9 37	13 13
18	23 47 34	25 3 32	0♉23	8 29	6 23	28 58	8 15	7 20	1 22	9 37	13 15
19	23 51 31	26 2 6	15 16	7 45	7 32	29 36	8 22	7 21	1 22	9 37	13 17
20	23 55 27	27 0 42	29 50	6 55	8 41	0♎15	8 29	7 22	1 23	9 37	13 19
21	23 59 24	27 59 20	14♊ 2	5 59	9 51	0 54	8 36	7 23	1 23	9D37	13 21
22	0 3 21	28 58 0	27 49	4 59	11 0	1 33	8 43	7 24	1 24	9 37	13 23
23	0 7 17	29 56 43	11♋13	3 56	12 9	2 12	8 50	7 25	1 25	9 37	13 24
24	0 11 14	0♎55 28	24 16	2 51	13 18	2 51	8 56	7 26	1 25	9 37	13 26
25	0 15 10	1 54 15	7♌ 0	1 45	14 27	3 30	9 2	7 27	1 26	9 37	13 28
26	0 19 7	2 53 4	19 28	0 40	15 36	4 8	9 9	7 29	1 27	9 37	13 30
27	0 23 3	3 51 56	1♍45	29♍38	16 45	4 47	9 15	7 30	1 28	9 37	13 32
28	0 27 0	4 50 49	13 53	28 41	17 54	5 26	9 20	7 32	1 28	9 37	13 34
29	0 30 56	5 49 45	25 53	27 50	19 2	6 6	9 26	7 33	1 29	9 37	13 36
30	0 34 53	6♎48 42	7♎49	27♍ 6	20♏11	6♎45	9♋32	7♑35	1♑30	9♑38	13♏38

THE SUN ENTERS THE SIGN OF LIBRA ON SEP 23 AT 01:21.

♈ ARIES ♉ TAURUS ♊ GEMINI ♋ CANCER ♌ LEO ♍ VIRGO ♎ LIBRA

SIDEREAL SUN. MOON. MERCURY. VENUS. MARS. JUPITER. SATURN. URANUS. NEPTUNE. PLUTO.

DAY	TIME	☉	☽	☿	♀	♂	♃	♄	♅	♆	♇
	h m s	° ' "	° '	° '	° '	° '	° '	° '	° '	° '	° '
O 1	0 38 50	7♎47 42	19♎41	26♍31	21♏19	7♎24	9♋37	7♑37	1♑31	9♑38	13♏40
C 2	0 42 46	8 46 44	1♏32	26R 5	22 28	8 3	9 42	7 39	1 33	9 38	13 42
T 3	0 46 43	9 45 47	13 23	25D50	23 36	8 42	9 47	7 41	1 34	9 39	13 44
O 4	0 50 39	10 44 53	25 16	25 44	24 44	9 21	9 52	7 43	1 35	9 39	13 46
B 5	0 54 36	11 44 0	7♐15	25 50	25 52	10 0	9 56	7 45	1 36	9 40	13 49
E 6	0 58 32	12 43 10	19 22	26 6	27 0	10 40	10 1	7 48	1 37	9 40	13 51
R 7	1 2 29	13 42 21	1♑40	26 31	28 7	11 19	10 5	7 50	1 39	9 41	13 53
8	1 6 25	14 41 34	14 16	27 7	29 15	11 58	10 9	7 53	1 40	9 41	13 55
9	1 10 22	15 40 48	27 11	27 51	0♐22	12 37	10 13	7 55	1 42	9 42	13 57
10	1 14 19	16 40 5	10♒32	28 43	1 30	13 17	10 17	7 58	1 43	9 42	13 59
11	1 18 15	17 39 23	24 19	29 43	2 37	13 56	10 21	8 1	1 45	9 43	14 2
12	1 22 12	18 38 42	8♓36	0♎50	3 44	14 36	10 24	8 4	1 46	9 44	14 4
13	1 26 8	19 38 4	23 19	2 3	4 51	15 15	10 27	8 7	1 48	9 44	14 6
14	1 30 5	20 37 27	8♈23	3 21	5 57	15 55	10 30	8 10	1 49	9 45	14 8
15	1 34 1	21 36 53	23 41	4 43	7 4	16 34	10 33	8 13	1 51	9 46	14 11
16	1 37 58	22 36 20	9♉0	6 9	8 10	17 14	10 36	8 16	1 53	9 47	14 13
17	1 41 54	23 35 50	24 11	7 39	9 16	17 53	10 38	8 20	1 55	9 47	14 15
18	1 45 51	24 35 22	9♊2	9 11	10 23	18 33	10 41	8 23	1 57	9 48	14 18
19	1 49 48	25 34 57	23 27	10 45	11 28	19 12	10 43	8 27	1 58	9 49	14 20
20	1 53 44	26 34 33	7♋23	12 22	12 34	19 52	10 45	8 30	2 0	9 50	14 22
21	1 57 41	27 34 12	20 51	13 59	13 39	20 32	10 46	8 34	2 2	9 51	14 25
22	2 1 37	28 33 53	3♌52	15 38	14 45	21 11	10 48	8 38	2 4	9 52	14 27
23	2 5 34	29 33 36	16 30	17 17	15 50	21 51	10 49	8 41	2 7	9 53	14 29
24	2 9 30	0♏33 22	28 51	18 58	16 55	22 31	10 50	8 45	2 9	9 54	14 32
25	2 13 27	1 33 10	10♍59	20 38	17 59	23 11	10 51	8 49	2 11	9 55	14 34
26	2 17 23	2 33 0	22 57	22 19	19 4	23 51	10 52	8 53	2 13	9 56	14 36
27	2 21 20	3 32 51	4♎51	24 0	20 8	24 30	10 52	8 57	2 15	9 57	14 39
28	2 25 16	4 32 46	16 42	25 41	21 12	25 10	10 53	9 2	2 18	9 59	14 41
29	2 29 13	5 32 42	28 33	27 21	22 15	25 50	10R53	9 6	2 20	10 0	14 44
30	2 33 10	6 32 40	10♏25	29 2	23 19	26 30	10 53	9 10	2 22	10 1	14 46
31	2 37 6	7♏32 40	22♏20	0♏42	24♐22	27♎10	10♋52	9♑15	2♑25	10♑2	14♏48

THE SUN ENTERS THE SIGN OF SCORPIO ON OCT 23 AT 10:36.

DAY	TIME	☉	☽	☿	♀	♂	♃	♄	♅	♆	♇
	h m s	° ' "	° '	° '	° '	° '	° '	° '	° '	° '	° '
N 1	2 41 3	8♏32 42	4♐18	2♏22	25♐25	27♎50	10♋52	9♑19	2♑27	10♑4	14♏51
O 2	2 44 59	9 32 45	16 23	4 2	26 28	28 31	10R51	9 24	2 30	10 5	14 53
V 3	2 48 56	10 32 51	28 34	5 41	27 30	29 11	10 50	9 29	2 32	10 6	14 56
E 4	2 52 52	11 32 58	10♑56	7 20	28 32	29 51	10 49	9 33	2 35	10 8	14 58
M 5	2 56 49	12 33 6	23 31	8 59	29 34	0♏31	10 48	9 38	2 37	10 9	15 0
B 6	3 0 46	13 33 17	6♒23	10 37	0♑35	1 11	10 46	9 43	2 40	10 10	15 3
E 7	3 4 42	14 33 28	19 35	12 15	1 36	1 51	10 44	9 48	2 43	10 12	15 5
R 8	3 8 39	15 33 41	3♓12	13 52	2 37	2 32	10 43	9 53	2 45	10 13	15 8
9	3 12 35	16 33 56	17 15	15 29	3 37	3 12	10 40	9 58	2 48	10 15	15 10
10	3 16 32	17 34 12	1♈45	17 6	4 37	3 52	10 38	10 3	2 51	10 16	15 13
11	3 20 28	18 34 29	16 38	18 42	5 37	4 33	10 36	10 9	2 54	10 18	15 15
12	3 24 25	19 34 48	1♉48	20 18	6 36	5 13	10 33	10 14	2 56	10 19	15 17
13	3 28 21	20 35 9	17 6	21 54	7 34	5 54	10 30	10 19	2 59	10 21	15 20
14	3 32 18	21 35 31	2♊19	23 29	8 32	6 34	10 27	10 25	3 2	10 23	15 22
15	3 36 15	22 35 55	17 18	25 4	9 30	7 15	10 24	10 30	3 5	10 24	15 25
16	3 40 11	23 36 21	1♋53	26 39	10 27	7 55	10 20	10 36	3 8	10 26	15 27
17	3 44 8	24 36 49	15 59	28 13	11 24	8 36	10 17	10 41	3 11	10 28	15 30
18	3 48 4	25 37 18	29 34	29 48	12 20	9 16	10 13	10 47	3 14	10 29	15 32
19	3 52 1	26 37 49	12♌41	1♐22	13 16	9 57	10 9	10 53	3 17	10 31	15 34
20	3 55 57	27 38 22	25 22	2 55	14 11	10 38	10 5	10 58	3 20	10 33	15 37
21	3 59 54	28 38 57	7♍44	4 29	15 6	11 18	10 0	11 4	3 23	10 35	15 39
22	4 3 50	29 39 33	19 50	6 2	16 0	11 59	9 56	11 10	3 26	10 37	15 42
23	4 7 47	0♐40 12	1♎46	7 36	16 53	12 40	9 51	11 16	3 30	10 38	15 44
24	4 11 44	1 40 51	13 37	9 9	17 45	13 21	9 46	11 22	3 33	10 40	15 46
25	4 15 40	2 41 33	25 27	10 42	18 37	14 2	9 41	11 28	3 36	10 42	15 49
26	4 19 37	3 42 16	7♏18	12 14	19 29	14 43	9 36	11 34	3 39	10 44	15 51
27	4 23 33	4 43 0	19 14	13 47	20 19	15 24	9 30	11 40	3 42	10 46	15 53
28	4 27 30	5 43 46	1♐15	15 20	21 9	16 4	9 25	11 46	3 46	10 48	15 56
29	4 31 26	6 44 33	13 23	16 52	21 58	16 46	9 19	11 53	3 49	10 50	15 58
30	4 35 23	7♐45 21	25♐39	18♐24	22♑46	17♏27	9♋13	11♑59	3♑52	10♑52	16♏0

THE SUN ENTERS THE SIGN OF SAGITTARIUS ON NOV 22 AT 08:06.

DAY	TIME	☉	☽	☿	♀	♂	♃	♄	♅	♆	♇
	h m s	° ' "	° '	° '	° '	° '	° '	° '	° '	° '	° '
D 1	4 39 19	8♐46 11	8♑3	19♐56	23♑33	18♏8	9♋7	12♑5	3♑56	10♑54	16♏3
E 2	4 43 16	9 47 2	20 37	21 28	24 20	18 49	9R 1	12 11	3 59	10 56	16 5
C 3	4 47 13	10 47 53	3♒21	23 0	25 5	19 30	8 54	12 18	4 2	10 58	16 7
E 4	4 51 9	11 48 46	16 19	24 32	25 49	20 11	8 48	12 24	4 6	11 0	16 9
M 5	4 55 6	12 49 39	29 33	26 3	26 33	20 52	8 41	12 31	4 9	11 2	16 12
B 6	4 59 2	13 50 33	13♓5	27 34	27 15	21 34	8 35	12 37	4 13	11 4	16 14
E 7	5 2 59	14 51 27	26 57	29 5	27 56	22 15	8 28	12 44	4 16	11 6	16 16
R 8	5 6 55	15 52 23	11♈10	0♑36	28 36	22 56	8 21	12 50	4 20	11 8	16 18
9	5 10 52	16 53 19	25 42	2 6	29 15	23 38	8 14	12 57	4 23	11 10	16 20
10	5 14 48	17 54 16	10♉31	3 36	29 52	24 19	8 7	13 4	4 27	11 12	16 22
11	5 18 45	18 55 13	25 28	5 5	0♒29	25 0	7 59	13 10	4 30	11 14	16 25
12	5 22 42	19 56 11	10♊25	6 33	1 3	25 42	7 52	13 17	4 34	11 17	16 27
13	5 26 38	20 57 10	25 14	8 1	1 37	26 23	7 45	13 24	4 37	11 19	16 29
14	5 30 35	21 58 10	9♋44	9 28	2 9	27 5	7 37	13 30	4 41	11 21	16 31
15	5 34 31	22 59 11	23 51	10 53	2 39	27 46	7 29	13 37	4 44	11 23	16 33
16	5 38 28	24 0 13	7♌31	12 18	3 7	28 28	7 22	13 44	4 48	11 25	16 35
17	5 42 24	25 1 15	20 43	13 40	3 34	29 10	7 14	13 51	4 51	11 27	16 37
18	5 46 21	26 2 18	3♍31	15 1	4 0	29 51	7 6	13 58	4 55	11 30	16 39
19	5 50 18	27 3 23	15 57	16 20	4 23	0♐33	6 58	14 5	4 58	11 32	16 41
20	5 54 14	28 4 28	28 7	17 36	4 45	1 15	6 50	14 12	5 2	11 34	16 43
21	5 58 11	29 5 33	10♎5	18 49	5 4	1 57	6 42	14 19	5 6	11 36	16 45
22	6 2 7	0♑6 40	21 57	19 59	5 22	2 38	6 34	14 25	5 9	11 39	16 47
23	6 6 4	1 7 47	3♏47	21 4	5 38	3 20	6 26	14 32	5 13	11 41	16 49
24	6 10 0	2 8 55	15 41	22 5	5 51	4 2	6 18	14 39	5 16	11 43	16 51
25	6 13 57	3 10 4	27 40	23 1	6 3	4 44	6 10	14 46	5 20	11 45	16 52
26	6 17 53	4 11 13	9♐48	23 50	6 12	5 26	6 2	14 53	5 24	11 48	16 54
27	6 21 50	5 12 23	22 7	24 33	6 19	6 8	5 54	15 1	5 27	11 50	16 56
28	6 25 47	6 13 33	4♑37	25 7	6 23	6 50	5 45	15 8	5 31	11 52	16 58
29	6 29 43	7 14 43	17 18	25 33	6R25	7 32	5 37	15 15	5 35	11 54	17 0
30	6 33 40	8 15 53	0♒12	25R48	6 25	8 15	5 29	15 22	5 38	11 57	17 1
31	6 37 36	9♑17 4	13♒16	25♑54	6♒22	8♐57	5♋21	15♑29	5♑42	11♑59	17♏3

THE SUN ENTERS THE SIGN OF CAPRICORN ON DEC 21 AT 21:23.

♏ SCORPIO ♐ SAGITTARIUS ♑ CAPRICORN ♒ AQUARIUS ♓ PISCES

1990

SIDEREAL SUN.... MON.... MERCURY VENUS.. MARS... JUPITER SATURN. URANUS. NEPTUNE PLUTO..

DAY	TIME	☉	☽	☿	♀	♂	♃	♄	♅	♆	♇
	h m s	° ' "	° '	° '	° '	° '	° '	° '	° '	° '	° '
J 1	6 41 33	10♑18 14	26♒33	25♑48	6♒17	9♐39	5♋13	15♑36	5♑45	12♑ 1	17♏ 5
A 2	6 45 29	11 19 24	10♓ 1	25R30	6R 9	10 21	5R 5	15 43	5 49	12 3	17 6
N 3	6 49 26	12 20 34	23 41	25 0	5 59	11 3	4 57	15 50	5 53	12 6	17 8
U 4	6 53 22	13 21 43	7♈34	24 19	5 46	11 46	4 49	15 57	5 56	12 8	17 10
A 5	6 57 19	14 22 53	21 39	23 27	5 31	12 28	4 41	16 4	6 0	12 10	17 11
R 6	7 1 16	15 24 2	5♉55	22 25	5 13	13 10	4 33	16 11	6 3	12 13	17 13
Y 7	7 5 12	16 25 10	20 19	21 15	4 53	13 53	4 25	16 19	6 7	12 15	17 14
8	7 9 9	17 26 18	4♊48	19 59	4 30	14 35	4 17	16 26	6 10	12 17	17 16
9	7 13 5	18 27 26	19 17	18 40	4 5	15 18	4 10	16 33	6 14	12 19	17 17
10	7 17 2	19 28 34	3♋39	17 19	3 39	16 0	4 2	16 40	6 18	12 22	17 18
11	7 20 58	20 29 41	17 49	16 1	3 10	16 43	3 55	16 47	6 21	12 24	17 20
12	7 24 55	21 30 48	1♌41	14 46	2 39	17 25	3 47	16 54	6 25	12 26	17 21
13	7 28 52	22 31 54	15 13	13 37	2 7	18 8	3 40	17 1	6 28	12 28	17 23
14	7 32 48	23 33 0	28 24	12 36	1 34	18 50	3 33	17 8	6 32	12 31	17 24
15	7 36 45	24 34 6	11♍13	11 43	0 59	19 33	3 26	17 15	6 35	12 33	17 25
16	7 40 41	25 35 12	23 42	11 0	0 23	20 16	3 18	17 22	6 39	12 35	17 26
17	7 44 38	26 36 17	5♎56	10 27	29♑47	20 59	3 12	17 29	6 42	12 37	17 27
18	7 48 34	27 37 23	17 57	10 3	29 10	21 41	3 5	17 37	6 45	12 40	17 29
19	7 52 31	28 38 28	29 52	9 48	28 33	22 24	2 58	17 44	6 49	12 42	17 30
20	7 56 27	29 39 32	11♏44	9D42	27 56	23 7	2 52	17 51	6 52	12 44	17 31
21	8 0 24	0♒40 36	23 38	9 44	27 20	23 50	2 45	17 58	6 56	12 46	17 32
22	8 4 20	1 41 40	5♐39	9 55	26 44	24 33	2 39	18 5	6 59	12 48	17 33
23	8 8 17	2 42 44	17 51	10 12	26 9	25 16	2 33	18 12	7 2	12 50	17 34
24	8 12 14	3 43 47	0♑17	10 36	25 35	25 59	2 27	18 19	7 6	12 53	17 35
25	8 16 10	4 44 49	12 58	11 6	25 2	26 42	2 21	18 25	7 9	12 55	17 36
26	8 20 7	5 45 51	25 56	11 42	24 30	27 25	2 15	18 32	7 12	12 57	17 37
27	8 24 3	6 46 52	9♒10	12 22	24 1	28 8	2 10	18 39	7 16	12 59	17 38
28	8 28 0	7 47 51	22 40	13 7	23 33	28 51	2 4	18 46	7 19	13 1	17 38
29	8 31 56	8 48 50	6♓24	13 56	23 7	29 34	1 59	18 53	7 22	13 3	17 39
30	8 35 53	9 49 48	20 18	14 49	22 43	0♑18	1 54	19 0	7 25	13 5	17 40
31	8 39 50	10♒50 45	4♈21	15♑45	22♑22	1♑ 1	1♋49	19♑ 7	7♑28	13♑ 7	17♏41

THE SUN ENTERS THE SIGN OF AQUARIUS ON JAN 20 AT 08:02.

DAY	TIME	☉	☽	☿	♀	♂	♃	♄	♅	♆	♇
	h m s	° ' "	° '	° '	° '	° '	° '	° '	° '	° '	° '
F 1	8 43 46	11♒51 40	18♈30	16♑44	22♑ 2	1♑44	1♋44	19♑13	7♑32	13♑ 9	17♏41
E 2	8 47 43	12 52 34	2♉41	17 46	21R46	2 27	1R40	19 20	7 35	13 12	17 42
B 3	8 51 39	13 53 27	16 53	18 50	21 31	3 11	1 36	19 27	7 38	13 14	17 42
R 4	8 55 36	14 54 18	1♊ 3	19 57	21 19	3 54	1 31	19 33	7 41	13 16	17 43
U 5	8 59 32	15 55 8	15 9	21 6	21 9	4 38	1 27	19 40	7 44	13 18	17 44
A 6	9 3 29	16 55 56	29 9	22 17	21 2	5 21	1 24	19 47	7 47	13 20	17 44
R 7	9 7 25	17 56 43	13♋ 1	23 29	20 58	6 4	1 20	19 53	7 50	13 22	17 45
Y 8	9 11 22	18 57 29	26 41	24 44	20D55	6 48	1 17	20 0	7 53	13 23	17 45
9	9 15 19	19 58 13	10♌ 9	25 59	20 56	7 31	1 13	20 6	7 56	13 25	17 45
10	9 19 15	20 58 56	23 22	27 17	20 58	8 15	1 10	20 13	7 59	13 27	17 46
11	9 23 12	21 59 37	6♍19	28 36	21 3	8 58	1 8	20 19	8 1	13 29	17 46
12	9 27 8	23 0 18	19 1	29 56	21 11	9 42	1 5	20 26	8 4	13 31	17 46
13	9 31 5	24 0 57	1♎27	1♒17	21 20	10 26	1 2	20 32	8 7	13 33	17 47
14	9 35 1	25 1 34	13 41	2 40	21 32	11 9	1 0	20 38	8 10	13 35	17 47
15	9 38 58	26 2 11	25 43	4 4	21 46	11 53	0 58	20 45	8 13	13 37	17 47
16	9 42 54	27 2 46	7♏39	5 29	22 2	12 37	0 56	20 51	8 15	13 38	17 47
17	9 46 51	28 3 20	19 32	6 55	22 21	13 21	0 55	20 57	8 18	13 40	17 47
18	9 50 48	29 3 53	1♐26	8 22	22 41	14 4	0 53	21 3	8 20	13 42	17 47
19	9 54 44	0♓ 4 25	13 26	9 50	23 3	14 48	0 52	21 9	8 23	13 44	17R47
20	9 58 41	1 4 55	25 37	11 20	23 26	15 32	0 51	21 15	8 26	13 45	17 47
21	10 2 37	2 5 24	8♑ 3	12 50	23 52	16 16	0 50	21 21	8 28	13 47	17 47
22	10 6 34	3 5 52	20 49	14 21	24 19	17 0	0 49	21 27	8 31	13 49	17 47
23	10 10 30	4 6 18	3♒56	15 53	24 48	17 44	0 49	21 33	8 33	13 50	17 47
24	10 14 27	5 6 43	17 25	17 27	25 18	18 28	0D49	21 39	8 35	13 52	17 47
25	10 18 23	6 7 6	1♓16	19 1	25 50	19 12	0 48	21 45	8 38	13 53	17 47
26	10 22 20	7 7 28	15 25	20 36	26 23	19 56	0 49	21 50	8 40	13 55	17 46
27	10 26 17	8 7 47	29 50	22 12	26 58	20 40	0 49	21 56	8 42	13 56	17 46
28	10 30 13	9♓ 8 5	14♈22	23♒49	27♑34	21♑24	0♋50	22♑ 1	8♑44	13♑58	17♏46

THE SUN ENTERS THE SIGN OF PISCES ON FEB 18 AT 22:15.

DAY	TIME	☉	☽	☿	♀	♂	♃	♄	♅	♆	♇
	h m s	° ' "	° '	° '	° '	° '	° '	° '	° '	° '	° '
M 1	10 34 10	10♓ 8 21	28♈57	25♒28	28♑12	22♑ 8	0♋50	22♑ 7	8♑47	13♑59	17♏46
A 2	10 38 6	11 8 35	13♉28	27 7	28 50	22 52	0 51	22 12	8 49	14 1	17R45
R 3	10 42 3	12 8 47	27 50	28 47	29 30	23 36	0 52	22 18	8 51	14 2	17 45
C 4	10 45 59	13 8 57	12♊ 0	0♓29	0♒11	24 21	0 54	22 23	8 53	14 4	17 44
H 5	10 49 56	14 9 4	25 57	2 11	0 52	25 5	0 55	22 29	8 55	14 5	17 44
6	10 53 52	15 9 10	9♋39	3 54	1 35	25 49	0 57	22 34	8 57	14 6	17 43
7	10 57 49	16 9 14	23 7	5 39	2 19	26 33	0 59	22 39	8 59	14 8	17 43
8	11 1 46	17 9 15	6♌22	7 25	3 4	27 18	1 1	22 44	9 1	14 9	17 42
9	11 5 42	18 9 14	19 24	9 11	3 50	28 2	1 3	22 49	9 2	14 10	17 42
10	11 9 39	19 9 11	2♍14	10 59	4 37	28 46	1 6	22 54	9 4	14 11	17 41
11	11 13 35	20 9 6	14 53	12 48	5 24	29 31	1 8	22 59	9 6	14 13	17 40
12	11 17 32	21 8 59	27 21	14 38	6 13	0♒15	1 11	23 4	9 8	14 14	17 40
13	11 21 28	22 8 51	9♎38	16 30	7 2	0 59	1 14	23 9	9 9	14 15	17 39
14	11 25 25	23 8 40	21 46	18 22	7 52	1 44	1 18	23 13	9 11	14 16	17 38
15	11 29 21	24 8 28	3♏46	20 16	8 43	2 28	1 21	23 18	9 12	14 17	17 37
16	11 33 18	25 8 13	15 41	22 10	9 34	3 13	1 25	23 22	9 14	14 18	17 37
17	11 37 14	26 7 58	27 33	24 6	10 26	3 57	1 28	23 27	9 15	14 19	17 36
18	11 41 11	27 7 40	9♐26	26 3	11 19	4 42	1 32	23 31	9 17	14 20	17 35
19	11 45 8	28 7 21	21 24	28 1	12 12	5 26	1 36	23 36	9 18	14 21	17 34
20	11 49 4	29 7 0	3♑32	0☉ 0	13 6	6 11	1 41	23 40	9 19	14 22	17 33
21	11 53 1	0♈ 6 37	15 56	1♈59	14 1	6 55	1 45	23 44	9 21	14 23	17 32
22	11 56 57	1 6 12	28 38	3 59	14 56	7 40	1 50	23 48	9 22	14 24	17 31
23	12 0 54	2 5 46	11♒45	6 0	15 51	8 25	1 55	23 52	9 23	14 25	17 30
24	12 4 50	3 5 18	25 17	8 1	16 48	9 9	2 0	23 56	9 24	14 25	17 29
25	12 8 47	4 4 48	9♓18	10 3	17 44	9 54	2 5	24 0	9 25	14 26	17 28
26	12 12 43	5 4 16	23 43	12 4	18 41	10 39	2 10	24 4	9 26	14 27	17 27
27	12 16 40	6 3 42	8♈29	14 6	19 39	11 23	2 16	24 7	9 27	14 28	17 26
28	12 20 37	7 3 6	23 27	16 6	20 37	12 8	2 21	24 11	9 28	14 28	17 25
29	12 24 33	8 2 28	8♉29	18 6	21 35	12 53	2 27	24 14	9 29	14 29	17 23
30	12 28 30	9 1 48	23 24	20 5	22 34	13 37	2 33	24 18	9 30	14 29	17 22
31	12 32 26	10♈ 1 5	8♊ 6	22♈ 2	23♒34	14♒22	2♋39	24♑21	9♑30	14♑30	17♏21

THE SUN ENTERS THE SIGN OF ARIES ON MAR 20 AT 21:20.

♈ ARIES ♉ TAURUS ♊ GEMINI ♋ CANCER ♌ LEO ♍ VIRGO ♎ LIBRA

1990

SIDEREAL / SUN. / MOON. / MERCURY. / VENUS. / MARS. / JUPITER. / SATURN. / URANUS. / NEPTUNE. / PLUTO.

DAY	TIME	☉	☽	☿	♀	♂	♃	♄	♅	♆	♇
	h m s	° ' "	° '	° '	° '	° '	° '	° '	° '	° '	° '
A 1	12 36 23	11♈ 0 20	22♊28	23♈57	24♒33	15♒ 7	2♋46	24♑25	9♑31	14♑30	17♏20
P 2	12 40 19	11 59 33	6♋28	25 50	25 33	15 52	2 52	24 28	9 32	14 31	17R18
R 3	12 44 16	12 58 44	20 5	27 40	26 33	16 36	2 59	24 31	9 32	14 31	17 17
I 4	12 48 12	13 57 52	3♌23	29 27	27 34	17 21	3 5	24 34	9 33	14 32	17 16
L 5	12 52 9	14 56 58	16 22	1♉10	28 35	18 6	3 12	24 37	9 33	14 32	17 15
6	12 56 6	15 56 2	29 6	2 50	29 36	18 51	3 19	24 40	9 34	14 33	17 13
7	13 0 2	16 55 3	11♍38	4 25	0♓38	19 35	3 26	24 42	9 34	14 33	17 12
8	13 3 59	17 54 2	24 0	5 56	1 40	20 20	3 34	24 45	9 34	14 33	17 10
9	13 7 55	18 52 59	6♎13	7 22	2 42	21 5	3 41	24 47	9 35	14 34	17 9
10	13 11 52	19 51 54	18 20	8 43	3 45	21 50	3 49	24 50	9 35	14 34	17 8
11	13 15 48	20 50 47	0♏21	9 59	4 47	22 35	3 56	24 52	9 35	14 34	17 6
12	13 19 45	21 49 37	12 17	11 9	5 50	23 20	4 4	24 55	9 35	14 34	17 5
13	13 23 41	22 48 27	24 10	12 13	6 54	24 4	4 12	24 57	9R35	14 34	17 3
14	13 27 38	23 47 14	6♐ 1	13 12	7 57	24 49	4 20	24 59	9 35	14 34	17 2
15	13 31 35	24 45 59	17 54	14 5	9 1	25 34	4 29	25 1	9 35	14 34	17 0
16	13 35 31	25 44 43	29 52	14 52	10 5	26 19	4 37	25 3	9 35	14R34	16 59
17	13 39 28	26 43 25	11♑59	15 33	11 9	27 4	4 45	25 5	9 35	14 34	16 57
18	13 43 24	27 42 5	24 18	16 8	12 14	27 49	4 54	25 6	9 35	14 34	16 56
19	13 47 21	28 40 44	6♒57	16 37	13 18	28 34	5 3	25 8	9 35	14 34	16 54
20	13 51 17	29 39 21	19 58	17 0	14 23	29 19	5 12	25 9	9 34	14 34	16 52
21	13 55 14	0♉37 56	3♓26	17 16	15 28	0♓ 3	5 21	25 11	9 34	14 34	16 51
22	13 59 10	1 36 30	17 24	17 27	16 33	0 48	5 30	25 12	9 34	14 34	16 49
23	14 3 7	2 35 2	1♈50	17R31	17 39	1 33	5 39	25 13	9 33	14 34	16 48
24	14 7 4	3 33 32	16 42	17 30	18 45	2 18	5 48	25 14	9 33	14 34	16 46
25	14 11 0	4 32 0	1♉52	17 23	19 50	3 3	5 58	25 15	9 32	14 33	16 44
26	14 14 57	5 30 27	17 10	17 11	20 56	3 48	6 7	25 16	9 32	14 33	16 43
27	14 18 53	6 28 52	2♊23	16 54	22 2	4 33	6 17	25 17	9 31	14 33	16 41
28	14 22 50	7 27 14	17 23	16 33	23 9	5 17	6 27	25 18	9 30	14 32	16 39
29	14 26 46	8 25 35	2♋ 0	16 7	24 15	6 2	6 37	25 19	9 30	14 32	16 38
30	14 30 43	9♉23 54	16♋11	15♉38	25♓22	6♓47	6♋46	25♑19	9♑29	14♑32	16♏36

THE SUN ENTERS THE SIGN OF TAURUS ON APR 20 AT 08:27.

DAY	TIME	☉	☽	☿	♀	♂	♃	♄	♅	♆	♇
	h m s	° ' "	° '	° '	° '	° '	° '	° '	° '	° '	° '
M 1	14 34 39	10♉22 11	29♋55	15♉ 5	26♓28	7♓32	6♋57	25♑20	9♑28	14♑31	16♏34
A 2	14 38 36	11 20 25	13♌12	14R30	27 35	8 17	7 7	25 20	9R27	14R31	16R33
Y 3	14 42 33	12 18 38	26 8	13 54	28 42	9 2	7 17	25 20	9 26	14 30	16 31
4	14 46 29	13 16 48	8♍44	13 16	29 49	9 46	7 27	25R20	9 25	14 30	16 29
5	14 50 26	14 14 57	21 6	12 38	0♈56	10 31	7 38	25 20	9 24	14 29	16 28
6	14 54 22	15 13 3	3♎18	12 0	2 4	11 16	7 48	25 20	9 23	14 28	16 26
7	14 58 19	16 11 8	15 21	11 23	3 11	12 1	7 59	25 20	9 22	14 28	16 24
8	15 2 15	17 9 11	27 19	10 48	4 19	12 45	8 10	25 20	9 21	14 27	16 23
9	15 6 12	18 7 12	9♏14	10 15	5 26	13 30	8 20	25 20	9 20	14 26	16 21
10	15 10 8	19 5 12	21 7	9 44	6 34	14 15	8 31	25 19	9 19	14 26	16 19
11	15 14 5	20 3 10	3♐ 0	9 17	7 42	14 59	8 42	25 19	9 17	14 25	16 18
12	15 18 2	21 1 6	14 53	8 53	8 50	15 44	8 53	25 18	9 16	14 24	16 16
13	15 21 58	21 59 2	26 49	8 33	9 58	16 29	9 4	25 17	9 15	14 23	16 14
14	15 25 55	22 56 55	8♑51	8 17	11 7	17 13	9 16	25 16	9 13	14 22	16 13
15	15 29 51	23 54 48	21 0	8 5	12 15	17 58	9 27	25 15	9 12	14 22	16 11
16	15 33 48	24 52 39	3♒22	7 58	13 23	18 42	9 38	25 14	9 10	14 21	16 9
17	15 37 44	25 50 29	15 59	7D55	14 32	19 27	9 50	25 13	9 9	14 20	16 8
18	15 41 41	26 48 18	28 57	7 57	15 40	20 11	10 1	25 12	9 7	14 19	16 6
19	15 45 37	27 46 5	12♓19	8 3	16 49	20 56	10 13	25 11	9 6	14 18	16 4
20	15 49 34	28 43 52	26 9	8 14	17 58	21 40	10 24	25 9	9 4	14 17	16 3
21	15 53 31	29 41 37	10♈27	8 30	19 7	22 25	10 36	25 8	9 2	14 16	16 1
22	15 57 27	0♊39 21	25 11	8 50	20 16	23 9	10 48	25 6	9 1	14 15	15 59
23	16 1 24	1 37 5	10♉16	9 14	21 25	23 53	11 0	25 5	8 59	14 14	15 58
24	16 5 20	2 34 47	25 32	9 43	22 34	24 38	11 12	25 3	8 57	14 13	15 56
25	16 9 17	3 32 28	10♊49	10 16	23 43	25 22	11 24	25 1	8 55	14 12	15 55
26	16 13 13	4 30 8	25 55	10 52	24 53	26 6	11 36	24 59	8 53	14 10	15 53
27	16 17 10	5 27 46	10♋41	11 33	26 2	26 50	11 48	24 57	8 52	14 9	15 51
28	16 21 6	6 25 23	25 2	12 17	27 11	27 35	12 0	24 55	8 50	14 8	15 50
29	16 25 3	7 22 59	8♌54	13 5	28 21	28 19	12 12	24 53	8 48	14 7	15 48
30	16 29 0	8 20 33	22 18	13 57	29 30	29 3	12 24	24 51	8 46	14 6	15 47
31	16 32 56	9♊18 5	5♍17	14♉52	0♉40	29♓47	12♋37	24♑48	8♑44	14♑ 5	15♏45

THE SUN ENTERS THE SIGN OF GEMINI ON MAY 21 AT 07:38.

DAY	TIME	☉	☽	☿	♀	♂	♃	♄	♅	♆	♇
	h m s	° ' "	° '	° '	° '	° '	° '	° '	° '	° '	° '
J 1	16 36 53	10♊15 36	17♍54	15♉50	1♉50	0♈31	12♋49	24♑46	8♑42	14♑ 3	15♏44
U 2	16 40 49	11 13 6	0♎14	16 52	2 59	1 15	13 1	24R43	8R40	14R 2	15R42
N 3	16 44 46	12 10 35	12 22	17 57	4 9	1 59	13 14	24 41	8 38	14 1	15 41
E 4	16 48 42	13 8 2	24 21	19 5	5 19	2 42	13 26	24 38	8 36	13 59	15 39
5	16 52 39	14 5 29	6♏15	20 16	6 29	3 26	13 39	24 35	8 33	13 58	15 38
6	16 56 35	15 2 54	18 7	21 31	7 39	4 10	13 52	24 32	8 31	13 57	15 37
7	17 0 32	16 0 18	0♐ 0	22 48	8 49	4 54	14 4	24 29	8 29	13 55	15 35
8	17 4 29	16 57 42	11 54	24 8	9 59	5 37	14 17	24 26	8 27	13 54	15 34
9	17 8 25	17 55 4	23 53	25 31	11 9	6 21	14 30	24 23	8 25	13 53	15 32
10	17 12 22	18 52 26	5♑56	26 57	12 19	7 4	14 42	24 20	8 23	13 51	15 31
11	17 16 18	19 49 47	18 7	28 26	13 30	7 48	14 55	24 17	8 20	13 50	15 30
12	17 20 15	20 47 7	0♒26	29 58	14 40	8 31	15 8	24 14	8 18	13 48	15 28
13	17 24 11	21 44 27	12 56	1♊33	15 50	9 14	15 21	24 11	8 16	13 47	15 27
14	17 28 8	22 41 46	25 41	3 10	17 1	9 58	15 34	24 7	8 13	13 45	15 26
15	17 32 4	23 39 5	8♓43	4 50	18 11	10 41	15 47	24 4	8 11	13 44	15 25
16	17 36 1	24 36 23	22 5	6 33	19 22	11 24	16 0	24 0	8 9	13 42	15 23
17	17 39 58	25 33 41	5♈49	8 19	20 33	12 7	16 13	23 57	8 6	13 41	15 22
18	17 43 54	26 30 59	19 56	10 7	21 43	12 50	16 26	23 53	8 4	13 39	15 21
19	17 47 51	27 28 17	4♉26	11 58	22 54	13 33	16 39	23 49	8 2	13 38	15 20
20	17 51 47	28 25 34	19 14	13 52	24 5	14 16	16 52	23 46	7 59	13 36	15 19
21	17 55 44	29 22 51	4♊14	15 48	25 15	14 59	17 5	23 42	7 57	13 35	15 18
22	17 59 40	0♋20 8	19 17	17 46	26 26	15 41	17 19	23 38	7 54	13 33	15 17
23	18 3 37	1 17 25	4♋14	19 47	27 37	16 24	17 32	23 34	7 52	13 31	15 16
24	18 7 34	2 14 41	18 57	21 50	28 48	17 6	17 45	23 30	7 50	13 30	15 15
25	18 11 30	3 11 57	3♌18	23 54	29 59	17 49	17 58	23 26	7 47	13 28	15 14
26	18 15 27	4 9 12	17 13	26 1	1♊10	18 31	18 11	23 22	7 45	13 27	15 13
27	18 19 23	5 6 26	0♍43	28 8	2 21	19 13	18 25	23 18	7 42	13 25	15 12
28	18 23 20	6 3 40	13 47	0♋17	3 33	19 56	18 38	23 14	7 40	13 24	15 11
29	18 27 16	7 0 54	26 28	2 27	4 44	20 38	18 51	23 10	7 38	13 22	15 10
30	18 31 13	7♋58 7	8♎51	4♋38	5♊55	21♈20	19♋ 5	23♑ 5	7♑35	13♑20	15♏ 9

THE SUN ENTERS THE SIGN OF CANCER ON JUN 21 AT 15:34.

♏ SCORPIO ♐ SAGITTARIUS ♑ CAPRICORN ♒ AQUARIUS ♓ PISCES

1990

SIDEREAL · SUN · MOON · MERCURY · VENUS · MARS · JUPITER · SATURN · URANUS · NEPTUNE · PLUTO

DAY	TIME	☉	☽	☿	♀	♂	♃	♄	♅	♆	♇
	h m s	° ' "	° '	° '	° '	° '	° '	° '	° '	° '	° '
J 1	18 35 9	8♋55 20	20♎59	6♋48	7♊ 6	22♈ 1	19♋18	23♑ 1	7♑33	13♑19	15♏ 8
U 2	18 39 6	9 52 32	2♏58	8 59	8 18	22 43	19 32	22R57	7R30	13R17	15R 8
L 3	18 43 3	10 49 44	14 52	11 10	9 29	23 25	19 45	22 53	7 28	13 15	15 7
Y 4	18 46 59	11 46 56	26 44	13 20	10 40	24 6	19 58	22 48	7 25	13 14	15 6
5	18 50 56	12 44 7	8♐38	15 30	11 52	24 48	20 12	22 44	7 23	13 12	15 5
6	18 54 52	13 41 18	20 36	17 38	13 3	25 29	20 25	22 40	7 21	13 11	15 5
7	18 58 49	14 38 30	2♑42	19 46	14 15	26 10	20 39	22 35	7 18	13 9	15 4
8	19 2 45	15 35 41	14 56	21 52	15 26	26 52	20 52	22 31	7 16	13 7	15 3
9	19 6 42	16 32 53	27 20	23 56	16 38	27 33	21 5	22 27	7 13	13 6	15 3
10	19 10 38	17 30 4	9♒55	25 59	17 50	28 14	21 19	22 22	7 11	13 4	15 2
11	19 14 35	18 27 16	22 42	28 1	19 1	28 54	21 32	22 18	7 9	13 3	15 2
12	19 18 32	19 24 28	5♓43	0♌ 1	20 13	29 35	21 46	22 13	7 6	13 1	15 1
13	19 22 28	20 21 40	18 58	1 59	21 25	0♉16	21 59	22 9	7 4	12 59	15 1
14	19 26 25	21 18 53	2♈29	3 55	22 37	0 56	22 13	22 4	7 1	12 58	15 1
15	19 30 21	22 16 7	16 16	5 50	23 49	1 36	22 26	22 0	6 59	12 56	15 0
16	19 34 18	23 13 21	0♉18	7 42	25 1	2 17	22 40	21 56	6 57	12 54	15 0
17	19 38 14	24 10 36	14 35	9 33	26 13	2 57	22 53	21 51	6 55	12 53	14 59
18	19 42 11	25 7 52	29 4	11 22	27 25	3 37	23 7	21 47	6 52	12 51	14 59
19	19 46 7	26 5 8	13♊41	13 9	28 37	4 16	23 20	21 42	6 50	12 50	14 59
20	19 50 4	27 2 25	28 20	14 55	29 49	4 56	23 34	21 38	6 48	12 48	14 59
21	19 54 1	27 59 43	12♋55	16 38	1♋ 1	5 35	23 47	21 33	6 46	12 47	14 59
22	19 57 57	28 57 1	27 20	18 20	2 13	6 15	24 0	21 29	6 43	12 45	14 58
23	20 1 54	29 54 20	11♌29	19 59	3 26	6 54	24 14	21 25	6 41	12 44	14 58
24	20 5 50	0♌51 39	25 18	21 37	4 38	7 33	24 27	21 20	6 39	12 42	14 58
25	20 9 47	1 48 58	8♍45	23 13	5 50	8 12	24 41	21 16	6 37	12 41	14 58
26	20 13 43	2 46 18	21 50	24 48	7 3	8 51	24 54	21 12	6 35	12 39	14D58
27	20 17 40	3 43 39	4♎34	26 20	8 15	9 29	25 7	21 7	6 33	12 38	14 58
28	20 21 36	4 41 0	16 59	27 51	9 27	10 7	25 21	21 3	6 31	12 36	14 58
29	20 25 33	5 38 21	29 10	29 19	10 40	10 46	25 34	20 59	6 29	12 35	14 58
30	20 29 30	6 35 43	11♏10	0♍46	11 53	11 24	25 47	20 55	6 27	12 33	14 58
31	20 33 26	7♌33 6	23♏ 4	2♍11	13♋ 5	12♉ 1	26♋ 1	20♑51	6♑25	12♑32	14♏59

THE SUN ENTERS THE SIGN OF LEO ON JUL 23 AT 02:23.

DAY	TIME	☉	☽	☿	♀	♂	♃	♄	♅	♆	♇
	h m s	° ' "	° '	° '	° '	° '	° '	° '	° '	° '	° '
A 1	20 37 23	8♌30 29	4♐57	3♍34	14♋18	12♉39	26♋14	20♑46	6♑23	12♑30	14♏59
U 2	20 41 19	9 27 52	16 52	4 55	15 30	13 17	26 27	20R42	6R21	12R29	14 59
G 3	20 45 16	10 25 17	28 55	6 14	16 43	13 54	26 41	20 38	6 19	12 27	14 59
U 4	20 49 12	11 22 42	11♑ 7	7 31	17 56	14 31	26 54	20 34	6 17	12 26	14 59
S 5	20 53 9	12 20 8	23 32	8 46	19 9	15 8	27 7	20 30	6 15	12 25	15 0
T 6	20 57 6	13 17 35	6♒11	9 59	20 22	15 45	27 20	20 26	6 13	12 23	15 0
7	21 1 2	14 15 2	19 6	11 9	21 34	16 21	27 33	20 22	6 12	12 22	15 1
8	21 4 59	15 12 31	2♓15	12 17	22 47	16 58	27 47	20 19	6 10	12 21	15 1
9	21 8 55	16 10 1	15 40	13 23	24 0	17 34	28 0	20 15	6 8	12 19	15 1
10	21 12 52	17 7 32	29 18	14 26	25 13	18 10	28 13	20 11	6 7	12 18	15 2
11	21 16 48	18 5 4	13♈ 7	15 27	26 26	18 45	28 26	20 7	6 5	12 17	15 2
12	21 20 45	19 2 37	27 7	16 25	27 39	19 21	28 39	20 4	6 3	12 16	15 3
13	21 24 41	20 0 12	11♉14	17 20	28 53	19 56	28 52	20 0	6 2	12 15	15 4
14	21 28 38	20 57 49	25 26	18 12	0♌ 6	20 31	29 5	19 57	6 0	12 13	15 4
15	21 32 34	21 55 27	9♊41	19 1	1 19	21 6	29 18	19 53	5 59	12 12	15 5
16	21 36 31	22 53 7	23 56	19 46	2 32	21 40	29 30	19 50	5 58	12 11	15 6
17	21 40 28	23 50 49	8♋ 9	20 28	3 46	22 15	29 43	19 47	5 56	12 10	15 6
18	21 44 24	24 48 31	22 17	21 7	4 59	22 49	29 56	19 43	5 55	12 9	15 7
19	21 48 21	25 46 16	6♌16	21 41	6 12	23 22	0♌ 9	19 40	5 54	12 8	15 8
20	21 52 17	26 44 1	20 4	22 12	7 26	23 56	0 21	19 37	5 52	12 7	15 9
21	21 56 14	27 41 48	3♍36	22 38	8 39	24 29	0 34	19 34	5 51	12 6	15 10
22	22 0 10	28 39 36	16 52	22 59	9 53	25 2	0 47	19 31	5 50	12 5	15 10
23	22 4 7	29 37 26	29 51	23 16	11 6	25 35	0 59	19 28	5 49	12 4	15 11
24	22 8 3	0♍35 17	12♎31	23 27	12 20	26 7	1 12	19 26	5 48	12 3	15 12
25	22 12 0	1 33 9	24 56	23R33	13 34	26 39	1 24	19 23	5 47	12 2	15 13
26	22 15 57	2 31 3	7♏ 6	23 34	14 47	27 11	1 37	19 20	5 46	12 1	15 14
27	22 19 53	3 28 57	19 6	23 28	16 1	27 43	1 49	19 18	5 45	12 0	15 15
28	22 23 50	4 26 53	1♐ 0	23 17	17 15	28 14	2 1	19 15	5 44	11 59	15 17
29	22 27 46	5 24 51	12 52	23 0	18 29	28 45	2 14	19 13	5 43	11 58	15 18
30	22 31 43	6 22 49	24 48	22 37	19 42	29 15	2 26	19 10	5 42	11 58	15 19
31	22 35 39	7♍20 50	6♑51	22♍ 7	20♌56	29♉45	2♌38	19♑ 8	5♑41	11♑57	15♏20

THE SUN ENTERS THE SIGN OF VIRGO ON AUG 23 AT 09:22.

DAY	TIME	☉	☽	☿	♀	♂	♃	♄	♅	♆	♇
	h m s	° ' "	° '	° '	° '	° '	° '	° '	° '	° '	° '
S 1	22 39 36	8♍18 51	19♑ 7	21♍32	22♌10	0♊15	2♌50	19♑ 6	5♑41	11♑56	15♏21
E 2	22 43 32	9 16 54	1♒39	20R51	23 24	0 45	3 2	19R 4	5R40	11R55	15 22
P 3	22 47 29	10 14 58	14 31	20 5	24 38	1 14	3 14	19 2	5 40	11 55	15 24
T 4	22 51 26	11 13 4	27 42	19 15	25 52	1 43	3 26	19 0	5 39	11 54	15 25
E 5	22 55 22	12 11 11	11♓15	18 21	27 6	2 11	3 38	18 58	5 38	11 54	15 26
M 6	22 59 19	13 9 20	25 5	17 23	28 20	2 40	3 50	18 57	5 38	11 53	15 28
B 7	23 3 15	14 7 31	9♈11	16 25	29 34	3 7	4 1	18 55	5 38	11 52	15 29
E 8	23 7 12	15 5 43	23 28	15 25	0♍48	3 35	4 13	18 54	5 37	11 52	15 30
R 9	23 11 8	16 3 58	7♉49	14 27	2 2	4 2	4 24	18 52	5 37	11 51	15 32
10	23 15 5	17 2 15	22 11	13 30	3 17	4 28	4 36	18 51	5 37	11 51	15 33
11	23 19 1	18 0 34	6♊29	12 37	4 31	4 54	4 47	18 50	5 36	11 51	15 35
12	23 22 58	18 58 55	20 41	11 49	5 45	5 20	4 59	18 48	5 36	11 50	15 36
13	23 26 55	19 57 18	4♋44	11 7	7 0	5 45	5 10	18 47	5 36	11 50	15 38
14	23 30 51	20 55 43	18 37	10 32	8 14	6 10	5 21	18 46	5D36	11 49	15 40
15	23 34 48	21 54 11	2♌21	10 5	9 28	6 35	5 32	18 46	5 36	11 49	15 41
16	23 38 44	22 52 40	15 54	9 46	10 43	6 59	5 43	18 45	5 36	11 49	15 43
17	23 42 41	23 51 12	29 16	9D37	11 57	7 22	5 54	18 44	5 36	11 49	15 44
18	23 46 37	24 49 45	12♍27	9 37	13 12	7 45	6 5	18 44	5 36	11 48	15 46
19	23 50 34	25 48 20	25 25	9 46	14 26	8 7	6 16	18 43	5 36	11 48	15 48
20	23 54 30	26 46 58	8♎10	10 5	15 41	8 29	6 27	18 43	5 37	11 48	15 50
21	23 58 27	27 45 37	20 42	10 34	16 55	8 51	6 37	18 42	5 37	11 48	15 51
22	0 2 24	28 44 18	3♏ 0	11 11	18 10	9 12	6 48	18 42	5 37	11 48	15 53
23	0 6 20	29 43 1	15 7	11 57	19 24	9 32	6 58	18D42	5 38	11D48	15 55
24	0 10 17	0♎41 45	27 5	12 52	20 39	9 52	7 9	18 42	5 38	11 48	15 57
25	0 14 13	1 40 32	8♐57	13 53	21 54	10 11	7 19	18 42	5 39	11 48	15 59
26	0 18 10	2 39 20	20 47	15 2	23 8	10 30	7 29	18 43	5 39	11 48	16 1
27	0 22 6	3 38 10	2♑40	16 17	24 23	10 48	7 39	18 43	5 40	11 48	16 2
28	0 26 3	4 37 2	14 42	17 37	25 38	11 5	7 49	18 43	5 41	11 48	16 4
29	0 29 59	5 35 55	26 56	19 3	26 52	11 22	7 59	18 44	5 41	11 48	16 6
30	0 33 56	6♎34 50	9♒29	20♍32	28♍ 7	11♊38	8♌ 9	18♑45	5♑42	11♑49	16♏ 8

THE SUN ENTERS THE SIGN OF LIBRA ON SEP 23 AT 06:57.

♈ ARIES ♉ TAURUS ♊ GEMINI ♋ CANCER ♌ LEO ♍ VIRGO ♎ LIBRA

199Ø

SIDEREAL. SUN. MOON. MERCURY. VENUS. MARS. JUPITER. SATURN. URANUS. NEPTUNE. PLUTO.

DAY	TIME	☉	☽	☿	♀	♂	♃	♄	♅	♆	♇
	h m s	° ' "	° '	° '	° '	° '	° '	° '	° '	° '	° '
O 1	Ø 37 53	7♎33 47	22♒25	22♍ 5	29♍22	11♊54	8♌18	18♑45	5♑43	11♑49	16♏1Ø
C 2	Ø 41 49	8 32 46	5♓46	23 42	Ø♎37	12 9	8 28	18 46	5 44	11 49	16 12
T 3	Ø 45 46	9 31 46	19 34	25 2Ø	1 52	12 23	8 37	18 47	5 45	11 49	16 14
O 4	Ø 49 42	1Ø 3Ø 49	3♈45	27 1	3 6	12 37	8 46	18 48	5 45	11 5Ø	16 16
B 5	Ø 53 39	11 29 53	18 17	28 43	4 21	12 5Ø	8 56	18 49	5 47	11 5Ø	16 18
E 6	Ø 57 35	12 28 59	3♉ 1	Ø♎27	5 36	13 2	9 5	18 5Ø	5 48	11 5Ø	16 21
R 7	1 1 32	13 28 8	17 49	2 12	6 51	13 14	9 14	18 52	5 49	11 51	16 23
8	1 5 28	14 27 19	2♊34	3 57	8 6	13 25	9 23	18 53	5 5Ø	11 51	16 25
9	1 9 25	15 26 32	17 9	5 42	9 21	13 35	9 31	18 55	5 51	11 52	16 27
1Ø	1 13 22	16 25 48	1♋29	7 28	1Ø 36	13 44	9 4Ø	18 56	5 52	11 52	16 29
11	1 17 18	17 25 6	15 31	9 14	11 51	13 53	9 48	18 58	5 54	11 53	16 31
12	1 21 15	18 24 26	29 16	11 Ø	13 6	14 Ø	9 57	19 Ø	5 55	11 53	16 33
13	1 25 11	19 23 49	12♌45	12 45	14 21	14 8	1Ø 5	19 2	5 56	11 54	16 36
14	1 29 8	2Ø 23 14	25 59	14 3Ø	15 36	14 14	1Ø 13	19 4	5 58	11 55	16 38
15	1 33 4	21 22 41	9♍ Ø	16 15	16 51	14 19	1Ø 21	19 6	5 59	11 55	16 4Ø
16	1 37 1	22 22 1Ø	21 5Ø	17 59	18 6	14 24	1Ø 29	19 8	6 1	11 56	16 42
17	1 4Ø 57	23 21 42	4♎29	19 43	19 21	14 27	1Ø 37	19 1Ø	6 2	11 57	16 45
18	1 44 54	24 21 15	16 58	21 26	2Ø 36	14 3Ø	1Ø 44	19 13	6 4	11 58	16 47
19	1 48 5Ø	25 2Ø 51	29 17	23 8	21 51	14 32	1Ø 52	19 15	6 6	11 58	16 49
2Ø	1 52 47	26 2Ø 28	11♏26	24 5Ø	23 6	14R33	1Ø 59	19 18	6 7	11 59	16 51
21	1 56 44	27 2Ø 8	23 27	26 32	24 22	14 34	11 6	19 2Ø	6 9	12 Ø	16 54
22	2 Ø 4Ø	28 19 49	5♐22	28 12	25 37	14 33	11 13	19 23	6 11	12 1	16 56
23	2 4 37	29 19 33	17 11	29 53	26 52	14 32	11 2Ø	19 26	6 13	12 2	16 58
24	2 8 33	Ø♏19 18	28 59	1♏32	28 7	14 29	11 27	19 29	6 15	12 3	17 1
25	2 12 3Ø	1 19 5	1Ø♑5Ø	3 11	29 22	14 26	11 33	19 32	6 17	12 4	17 3
26	2 16 26	2 18 54	22 48	4 5Ø	Ø♏37	14 22	11 39	19 35	6 19	12 5	17 5
27	2 2Ø 23	3 18 44	4♒59	6 28	1 53	14 17	11 46	19 38	6 21	12 6	17 8
28	2 24 19	4 18 36	17 28	8 5	3 8	14 11	11 52	19 41	6 23	12 7	17 1Ø
29	2 28 16	5 18 3Ø	Ø♓2Ø	9 42	4 23	14 4	11 58	19 45	6 25	12 8	17 13
3Ø	2 32 13	6 18 25	13 4Ø	11 18	5 38	13 56	12 4	19 48	6 27	12 9	17 15
31	2 36 9	7♏18 22	27♓3Ø	12♏54	6♏53	13♊48	12♌ 9	19♑52	6♑29	12♑11	17♏17

THE SUN ENTERS THE SIGN OF SCORPIO ON OCT 23 AT 16:15.

DAY	TIME	☉	☽	☿	♀	♂	♃	♄	♅	♆	♇
	h m s	° ' "	° '	° '	° '	° '	° '	° '	° '	° '	° '
N 1	2 4Ø 6	8♏18 2Ø	11♈49	14♏29	8♏ 9	13♊38	12♌15	19♑55	6♑32	12♑12	17♏2Ø
O 2	2 44 2	9 18 2Ø	26 33	16 4	9 24	13R28	12 2Ø	19 59	6 34	12 13	17 22
V 3	2 47 59	1Ø 18 22	11♉35	17 38	1Ø 39	13 17	12 25	2Ø 3	6 36	12 14	17 25
E 4	2 51 55	11 18 27	26 46	19 12	11 54	13 5	12 3Ø	2Ø 7	6 39	12 16	17 27
M 5	2 55 52	12 18 33	11♊54	2Ø 46	13 1Ø	12 52	12 35	2Ø 11	6 41	12 17	17 29
B 6	2 59 48	13 18 41	26 5Ø	22 19	14 25	12 39	12 39	2Ø 15	6 44	12 18	17 32
E 7	3 3 45	14 18 51	11♋27	23 52	15 4Ø	12 24	12 44	2Ø 19	6 46	12 2Ø	17 34
R 8	3 7 42	15 19 3	25 41	25 24	16 55	12 9	12 48	2Ø 23	6 49	12 21	17 37
9	3 11 38	16 19 17	9♌31	26 56	18 11	11 53	12 52	2Ø 27	6 51	12 23	17 39
1Ø	3 15 35	17 19 33	22 58	28 28	19 26	11 36	12 56	2Ø 32	6 54	12 24	17 41
11	3 19 31	18 19 51	6♍ 4	Ø♐ Ø	2Ø 41	11 19	13 Ø	2Ø 36	6 56	12 26	17 44
12	3 23 28	19 2Ø 11	18 54	1 31	21 57	11 1	13 4	2Ø 41	6 59	12 27	17 46
13	3 27 24	2Ø 2Ø 33	1♎29	3 1	23 12	1Ø 42	13 7	2Ø 45	7 2	12 29	17 49
14	3 31 21	21 2Ø 57	13 53	4 32	24 27	1Ø 23	13 1Ø	2Ø 5Ø	7 5	12 3Ø	17 51
15	3 35 17	22 21 23	26 7	6 2	25 43	1Ø 3	13 13	2Ø 55	7 7	12 32	17 54
16	3 39 14	23 21 5Ø	8♏14	7 31	26 58	9 43	13 16	2Ø 59	7 1Ø	12 33	17 56
17	3 43 11	24 22 2Ø	2Ø 14	9 Ø	28 13	9 22	13 19	21 4	7 13	12 35	17 58
18	3 47 7	25 22 51	2♐ 9	1Ø 29	29 29	9 1	13 21	21 9	7 16	12 37	18 1
19	3 51 4	26 23 23	14 Ø	11 58	Ø♐44	8 4Ø	13 23	21 14	7 19	12 38	18 3
2Ø	3 55 Ø	27 23 57	25 48	13 26	1 59	8 18	13 26	21 19	7 22	12 4Ø	18 6
21	3 58 57	28 24 32	7♑37	14 53	3 15	7 56	13 27	21 24	7 25	12 42	18 8
22	4 2 53	29 25 9	19 28	16 2Ø	4 3Ø	7 33	13 29	21 3Ø	7 28	12 44	18 1Ø
23	4 6 5Ø	Ø♐25 46	1♒26	17 47	5 45	7 11	13 31	21 35	7 31	12 45	18 13
24	4 1Ø 47	1 26 25	13 36	19 12	7 1	6 48	13 32	21 4Ø	7 34	12 47	18 15
25	4 14 43	2 27 5	26 1	2Ø 37	8 16	6 25	13 33	21 46	7 37	12 49	18 18
26	4 18 4Ø	3 27 47	8♓48	22 1	9 31	6 3	13 34	21 51	7 4Ø	12 51	18 2Ø
27	4 22 36	4 28 29	22 Ø	23 24	1Ø 47	5 4Ø	13 35	21 57	7 43	12 53	18 22
28	4 26 33	5 29 12	5♈42	24 46	12 2	5 17	13 35	22 2	7 46	12 55	18 25
29	4 3Ø 29	6 29 56	19 53	26 7	13 18	4 55	13 36	22 8	7 49	12 56	18 27
3Ø	4 34 26	7♐3Ø 41	4♉33	27♐26	14♐33	4♊33	13♌36	22♑14	7♑53	12♑58	18♏29

THE SUN ENTERS THE SIGN OF SAGITTARIUS ON NOV 22 AT 13:48.

DAY	TIME	☉	☽	☿	♀	♂	♃	♄	♅	♆	♇
	h m s	° ' "	° '	° '	° '	° '	° '	° '	° '	° '	° '
D 1	4 38 22	8♐31 28	19♉35	28♐44	15♐48	4♊11	13♌36	22♑19	7♑56	13♑ Ø	18♏32
E 2	4 42 19	9 32 15	4♊51	29 59	17 4	3R49	13R35	22 25	7 59	13 2	18 34
C 3	4 46 16	1Ø 33 4	2Ø 11	1♑13	18 19	3 27	13 35	22 31	8 2	13 4	18 36
E 4	4 5Ø 12	11 33 54	5♋22	2 24	19 34	3 6	13 34	22 37	8 6	13 6	18 39
M 5	4 54 9	12 34 45	2Ø 16	3 31	2Ø 5Ø	2 46	13 34	22 43	8 9	13 8	18 41
B 6	4 58 5	13 35 38	4♌47	4 36	22 5	2 26	13 32	22 49	8 12	13 1Ø	18 43
E 7	5 2 2	14 36 31	18 5Ø	5 37	23 2Ø	2 6	13 31	22 55	8 16	13 12	18 45
R 8	5 5 58	15 37 26	2♍26	6 33	24 36	1 47	13 3Ø	23 1	8 19	13 14	18 48
9	5 9 55	16 38 22	15 36	7 24	25 51	1 28	13 28	23 7	8 23	13 16	18 5Ø
1Ø	5 13 51	17 39 19	28 25	8 9	27 6	1 1Ø	13 26	23 14	8 26	13 19	18 52
11	5 17 48	18 4Ø 18	1Ø♎55	8 48	28 22	Ø 53	13 24	23 2Ø	8 29	13 21	18 54
12	5 21 45	19 41 18	23 12	9 19	29 37	Ø 36	13 22	23 26	8 33	13 23	18 56
13	5 25 41	2Ø 42 18	5♏17	9 43	Ø♑52	Ø 2Ø	13 2Ø	23 32	8 36	13 25	18 58
14	5 29 38	21 43 2Ø	17 15	9R56	2 8	Ø 5	13 17	23 39	8 4Ø	13 27	19 1
15	5 33 34	22 44 23	29 8	1Ø Ø	3 23	29♉5Ø	13 14	23 45	8 43	13 29	19 3
16	5 37 31	23 45 27	1Ø♐59	9 54	4 38	29 36	13 11	23 52	8 47	13 31	19 5
17	5 41 27	24 46 31	22 48	9 36	5 54	29 23	13 8	23 58	8 5Ø	13 34	19 7
18	5 45 24	25 47 36	4♑39	9 6	7 9	29 11	13 5	24 5	8 54	13 36	19 9
19	5 49 2Ø	26 48 42	16 32	8 25	8 24	29 Ø	13 1	24 11	8 57	13 38	19 11
2Ø	5 53 17	27 49 48	28 3Ø	7 32	9 4Ø	28 49	12 57	24 18	9 1	13 4Ø	19 13
21	5 57 14	28 5Ø 55	1Ø♒35	6 3Ø	1Ø 55	28 39	12 53	24 25	9 4	13 42	19 15
22	6 1 1Ø	29 52 1	22 51	5 19	12 1Ø	28 3Ø	12 49	24 31	9 8	13 45	19 17
23	6 5 7	Ø♑53 8	5♓2Ø	4 2	13 26	28 22	12 45	24 38	9 11	13 47	19 19
24	6 9 3	1 54 16	18 7	2 4Ø	14 41	28 14	12 41	24 45	9 15	13 49	19 21
25	6 13 Ø	2 55 23	1♈14	1 18	15 56	28 8	12 36	24 52	9 19	13 51	19 23
26	6 16 56	3 56 3Ø	14 46	29♐57	17 12	28 2	12 31	24 58	9 22	13 53	19 25
27	6 2Ø 53	4 57 38	28 43	28 4Ø	18 27	27 57	12 26	25 5	9 26	13 56	19 26
28	6 24 49	5 58 45	13♉ 6	27 29	19 42	27 53	12 21	25 12	9 29	13 58	19 28
29	6 28 46	6 59 53	27 51	26 27	2Ø 58	27 5Ø	12 16	25 19	9 33	14 Ø	19 3Ø
3Ø	6 32 43	8 1 1	12♊53	25 34	22 13	27 48	12 1Ø	25 26	9 37	14 2	19 32
31	6 36 39	9♑ 2 9	28♊ 4	24♐51	23♑28	27♉46	12♌ 5	25♑33	9♑4Ø	14♑ 5	19♏34

THE SUN ENTERS THE SIGN OF CAPRICORN ON DEC 22 AT 03:08.

♏ SCORPIO ♐ SAGITTARIUS ♑ CAPRICORN ♒ AQUARIUS ♓ PISCES

1991

SIDEREAL SUN.... MOON... MERCURY VENUS.. MARS... JUPITER SATURN. URANUS. NEPTUNE PLUTO..

DAY	TIME	☉	☽	☿	♀	♂	♃	♄	♅	♆	♇
	h m s	° ' "	° '	° '	° '	° '	° '	° '	° '	° '	° '
J 1	6 40 36	10♑ 3 16	13♋13	24♐19	24♑43	27♉45	11♌59	25♑40	9♑44	14♑ 7	19♏35
A 2	6 44 32	11 4 24	28 12	23R57	25 58	27D45	11R53	25 47	9 47	14 9	19 37
N 3	6 48 29	12 5 32	12♌51	23D45	27 14	27 46	11 47	25 54	9 51	14 12	19 39
U 4	6 52 25	13 6 40	27 7	23 43	28 29	27 48	11 41	26 1	9 55	14 14	19 41
A 5	6 56 22	14 7 49	10♍55	23 49	29 44	27 50	11 35	26 8	9 58	14 16	19 42
R 6	7 0 19	15 8 57	24 15	24 4	0♒59	27 53	11 28	26 15	10 2	14 18	19 44
Y 7	7 4 15	16 10 6	7♎11	24 27	2 15	27 56	11 22	26 22	10 5	14 21	19 45
8	7 8 12	17 11 15	19 45	24 56	3 30	28 1	11 15	26 29	10 9	14 23	19 47
9	7 12 8	18 12 24	2♏ 2	25 31	4 45	28 6	11 8	26 36	10 12	14 25	19 48
10	7 16 5	19 13 33	14 5	26 12	6 0	28 12	11 1	26 43	10 16	14 27	19 50
11	7 20 1	20 14 42	26 0	26 58	7 15	28 19	10 54	26 50	10 20	14 30	19 51
12	7 23 58	21 15 51	7♐49	27 48	8 30	28 26	10 47	26 57	10 23	14 32	19 53
13	7 27 54	22 17 0	19 38	28 42	9 45	28 34	10 40	27 4	10 27	14 34	19 54
14	7 31 51	23 18 9	1♑28	29 40	11 1	28 42	10 32	27 12	10 30	14 37	19 56
15	7 35 48	24 19 18	13 23	0♑41	12 16	28 51	10 25	27 19	10 34	14 39	19 57
16	7 39 44	25 20 26	25 25	1 45	13 31	29 1	10 17	27 26	10 37	14 41	19 58
17	7 43 41	26 21 33	7♒34	2 51	14 46	29 12	10 10	27 33	10 41	14 43	19 59
18	7 47 37	27 22 41	19 54	4 0	16 1	29 23	10 2	27 40	10 44	14 46	20 1
19	7 51 34	28 23 47	2♓25	5 10	17 16	29 34	9 55	27 47	10 48	14 48	20 2
20	7 55 30	29 24 52	15 8	6 23	18 31	29 47	9 47	27 54	10 51	14 50	20 3
21	7 59 27	0♒25 57	28 6	7 37	19 46	29 59	9 39	28 2	10 55	14 52	20 4
22	8 3 23	1 27 1	11♈20	8 53	21 1	0♊13	9 31	28 9	10 58	14 54	20 5
23	8 7 20	2 28 4	24 50	10 11	22 16	0 27	9 23	28 16	11 2	14 57	20 6
24	8 11 17	3 29 6	8♉39	11 29	23 31	0 41	9 15	28 23	11 5	14 59	20 7
25	8 15 13	4 30 7	22 46	12 49	24 46	0 56	9 7	28 30	11 8	15 1	20 8
26	8 19 10	5 31 7	7♊ 9	14 11	26 1	1 11	8 59	28 37	11 12	15 3	20 9
27	8 23 6	6 32 6	21 46	15 33	27 16	1 27	8 51	28 44	11 15	15 5	20 10
28	8 27 3	7 33 4	6♋32	16 56	28 30	1 44	8 43	28 51	11 18	15 7	20 11
29	8 30 59	8 34 0	21 21	18 20	29 45	2 0	8 35	28 58	11 22	15 10	20 12
30	8 34 56	9 34 56	6♌ 5	19 46	1♓ 0	2 18	8 27	29 6	11 25	15 12	20 13
31	8 38 52	10♒35 51	20♌37	21♑12	2♓15	2♊35	8♌19	29♑13	11♑28	15♑14	20♏14

THE SUN ENTERS THE SIGN OF AQUARIUS ON JAN 20 AT 13:48.

DAY	TIME	☉	☽	☿	♀	♂	♃	♄	♅	♆	♇
	h m s	° ' "	° '	° '	° '	° '	° '	° '	° '	° '	° '
F 1	8 42 49	11♒36 44	4♍51	22♑39	3♓29	2♊54	8♌11	29♑20	11♑31	15♑16	20♏15
E 2	8 46 46	12 37 37	18 44	24 7	4 44	3 12	8R 3	29 27	11 35	15 18	20 15
B 3	8 50 42	13 38 29	2♎11	25 35	5 59	3 31	7 55	29 34	11 38	15 20	20 16
R 4	8 54 39	14 39 19	15 14	27 5	7 14	3 51	7 47	29 41	11 41	15 22	20 17
U 5	8 58 35	15 40 9	27 54	28 35	8 28	4 10	7 40	29 48	11 44	15 24	20 17
A 6	9 2 32	16 40 59	10♏15	0♒ 6	9 43	4 31	7 32	29 55	11 47	15 26	20 18
R 7	9 6 28	17 41 47	22 20	1 38	10 57	4 51	7 24	0♒ 1	11 50	15 28	20 19
Y 8	9 10 25	18 42 34	4♐15	3 11	12 12	5 12	7 16	0 8	11 53	15 30	20 19
9	9 14 21	19 43 21	16 5	4 44	13 26	5 33	7 8	0 15	11 56	15 32	20 20
10	9 18 18	20 44 6	27 53	6 19	14 41	5 55	7 1	0 22	11 59	15 34	20 20
11	9 22 15	21 44 51	9♑46	7 54	15 55	6 17	6 53	0 29	12 2	15 36	20 20
12	9 26 11	22 45 34	21 46	9 30	17 10	6 39	6 46	0 36	12 5	15 38	20 21
13	9 30 8	23 46 16	3♒56	11 6	18 24	7 2	6 38	0 43	12 8	15 40	20 21
14	9 34 4	24 46 56	16 19	12 44	19 39	7 24	6 31	0 49	12 11	15 42	20 21
15	9 38 1	25 47 35	28 56	14 22	20 53	7 48	6 24	0 56	12 14	15 44	20 22
16	9 41 57	26 48 13	11♓48	16 2	22 7	8 11	6 17	1 3	12 17	15 45	20 22
17	9 45 54	27 48 49	24 55	17 42	23 21	8 35	6 10	1 9	12 20	15 47	20 22
18	9 49 50	28 49 24	8♈15	19 23	24 36	8 59	6 3	1 16	12 22	15 49	20 22
19	9 53 47	29 49 56	21 47	21 5	25 50	9 24	5 56	1 23	12 25	15 51	20 22
20	9 57 44	0♓50 28	5♉30	22 48	27 4	9 48	5 49	1 29	12 28	15 52	20 23
21	10 1 40	1 50 57	19 23	24 31	28 18	10 13	5 43	1 36	12 31	15 54	20 23
22	10 5 37	2 51 24	3♊25	26 16	29 32	10 38	5 36	1 42	12 33	15 56	20R23
23	10 9 33	3 51 50	17 34	28 2	0♈46	11 4	5 30	1 49	12 36	15 58	20 23
24	10 13 30	4 52 13	1♋49	29 48	2 0	11 29	5 24	1 55	12 38	15 59	20 23
25	10 17 26	5 52 35	16 8	1♓36	3 14	11 55	5 18	2 1	12 41	16 1	20 22
26	10 21 23	6 52 55	0♌28	3 24	4 28	12 22	5 12	2 8	12 43	16 3	20 22
27	10 25 19	7 53 12	14 45	5 14	5 42	12 48	5 6	2 14	12 46	16 4	20 22
28	10 29 16	8♓53 28	28♌55	7♓ 4	6♈55	13♊14	5♌ 0	2♒20	12♑48	16♑ 6	20♏22

THE SUN ENTERS THE SIGN OF PISCES ON FEB 19 AT 03:59.

DAY	TIME	☉	☽	☿	♀	♂	♃	♄	♅	♆	♇
	h m s	° ' "	° '	° '	° '	° '	° '	° '	° '	° '	° '
M 1	10 33 13	9♓53 42	12♍53	8♓56	8♈ 9	13♊41	4♌55	2♒26	12♑50	16♑ 7	20♏22
A 2	10 37 9	10 53 54	26 35	10 48	9 23	14 8	4R50	2 32	12 53	16 9	20R21
R 3	10 41 6	11 54 5	9♎58	12 41	10 36	14 35	4 45	2 38	12 55	16 10	20 21
C 4	10 45 2	12 54 14	23 0	14 35	11 50	15 3	4 40	2 45	12 57	16 12	20 21
H 5	10 48 59	13 54 21	5♏42	16 30	13 3	15 30	4 35	2 50	12 59	16 13	20 20
6	10 52 55	14 54 26	18 5	18 26	14 17	15 58	4 30	2 56	13 2	16 14	20 20
7	10 56 52	15 54 31	0♐12	20 22	15 30	16 26	4 26	3 2	13 4	16 16	20 20
8	11 0 48	16 54 33	12 8	22 19	16 44	16 54	4 21	3 8	13 6	16 17	20 19
9	11 4 45	17 54 34	23 58	24 16	17 57	17 23	4 17	3 14	13 8	16 19	20 19
10	11 8 42	18 54 33	5♑48	26 13	19 10	17 51	4 13	3 20	13 10	16 20	20 18
11	11 12 38	19 54 31	17 41	28 10	20 23	18 20	4 9	3 25	13 12	16 21	20 18
12	11 16 35	20 54 27	29 44	0♈ 6	21 36	18 49	4 6	3 31	13 13	16 22	20 17
13	11 20 31	21 54 21	12♒ 0	2 3	22 50	19 18	4 2	3 36	13 15	16 24	20 16
14	11 24 28	22 54 14	24 34	3 58	24 3	19 47	3 59	3 42	13 17	16 25	20 16
15	11 28 24	23 54 4	7♓27	5 52	25 16	20 16	3 56	3 47	13 19	16 26	20 15
16	11 32 21	24 53 53	20 39	7 44	26 28	20 46	3 53	3 53	13 21	16 27	20 14
17	11 36 17	25 53 40	4♈11	9 35	27 41	21 15	3 51	3 58	13 22	16 28	20 13
18	11 40 14	26 53 24	17 57	11 23	28 54	21 45	3 48	4 3	13 24	16 29	20 13
19	11 44 10	27 53 7	1♉56	13 7	0♉ 7	22 15	3 46	4 8	13 25	16 30	20 12
20	11 48 7	28 52 47	16 3	14 49	1 19	22 45	3 44	4 14	13 27	16 31	20 11
21	11 52 4	29 52 26	0♊13	16 27	2 32	23 15	3 42	4 19	13 28	16 32	20 10
22	11 56 0	0♈52 2	14 24	18 0	3 45	23 46	3 40	4 24	13 30	16 33	20 9
23	11 59 57	1 51 36	28 33	19 28	4 57	24 16	3 38	4 28	13 31	16 34	20 8
24	12 3 53	2 51 7	12♋38	20 52	6 9	24 47	3 37	4 33	13 32	16 35	20 7
25	12 7 50	3 50 36	26 40	22 9	7 22	25 18	3 36	4 38	13 34	16 36	20 6
26	12 11 46	4 50 3	10♌36	23 21	8 34	25 48	3 35	4 43	13 35	16 36	20 5
27	12 15 43	5 49 27	24 27	24 27	9 46	26 19	3 34	4 47	13 36	16 37	20 4
28	12 19 40	6 48 49	8♍10	25 25	10 58	26 50	3 34	4 52	13 37	16 38	20 3
29	12 23 36	7 48 9	21 43	26 17	12 10	27 22	3 33	4 56	13 38	16 39	20 2
30	12 27 33	8 47 27	5♎ 4	27 3	13 22	27 53	3D33	5 1	13 39	16 39	20 1
31	12 31 29	9♈46 42	18♎11	27♈40	14♉34	28♊24	3♌33	5♒ 5	13♑40	16♑40	20♏ 0

THE SUN ENTERS THE SIGN OF ARIES ON MAR 21 AT 03:02.

♈ ARIES ♉ TAURUS ♊ GEMINI ♋ CANCER ♌ LEO ♍ VIRGO ♎ LIBRA

SIDEREAL SUN . . MOON . . MERCURY VENUS . . MARS . . JUPITER SATURN . . URANUS . . NEPTUNE PLUTO .

DAY	TIME	☉	☽	☿	♀	♂	♃	♄	♅	♆	♇
	h m s	° ' "	° '	° '	° '	° '	° '	° '	° '	° '	° '
A 1	12 35 26	10♈45 56	1♏ 3	28♈11	15♉45	28♊56	3♌33	5♒ 9	13♑41	16♑41	19♏59
P 2	12 39 22	11 45 8	13 38	28 34	16 57	29 27	3 34	5 14	13 42	16 41	19R57
R 3	12 43 19	12 44 18	25 57	28 51	18 9	29 59	3 34	5 18	13 43	16 42	19 56
I 4	12 47 15	13 43 26	8♐ 3	28R59	19 20	0♋31	3 35	5 22	13 44	16 42	19 55
L 5	12 51 12	14 42 32	19 58	29 1	20 31	1 3	3 36	5 26	13 44	16 43	19 54
6	12 55 8	15 41 37	1♑48	28 56	21 43	1 35	3 37	5 29	13 45	16 43	19 52
7	12 59 5	16 40 39	13 37	28 44	22 54	2 7	3 38	5 33	13 46	16 44	19 51
8	13 3 2	17 39 40	25 30	28 27	24 5	2 39	3 40	5 37	13 46	16 44	19 50
9	13 6 58	18 38 39	7♒33	28 3	25 16	3 11	3 41	5 41	13 47	16 44	19 48
10	13 10 55	19 37 37	19 52	27 34	26 27	3 43	3 43	5 44	13 47	16 45	19 47
11	13 14 51	20 36 32	2♓30	27 1	27 38	4 16	3 45	5 48	13 48	16 45	19 46
12	13 18 48	21 35 26	15 31	26 24	28 49	4 48	3 48	5 51	13 48	16 45	19 44
13	13 22 44	22 34 18	28 57	25 44	29 59	5 21	3 50	5 54	13 48	16 45	19 43
14	13 26 41	23 33 8	12♈47	25 2	1♊10	5 53	3 53	5 57	13 48	16 46	19 41
15	13 30 37	24 31 56	26 57	24 18	2 21	6 26	3 55	6 0	13 49	16 46	19 40
16	13 34 34	25 30 42	11♉22	23 33	3 31	6 59	3 58	6 3	13 49	16 46	19 38
17	13 38 31	26 29 26	25 56	22 49	4 41	7 32	4 1	6 6	13 49	16 46	19 37
18	13 42 27	27 28 8	10♊31	22 6	5 51	8 5	4 5	6 9	13R49	16 46	19 35
19	13 46 24	28 26 48	25 1	21 25	7 1	8 38	4 8	6 12	13 49	16R46	19 34
20	13 50 20	29 25 26	9♋22	20 46	8 11	9 11	4 12	6 15	13 49	16 46	19 32
21	13 54 17	0♉24 2	23 32	20 11	9 21	9 44	4 16	6 17	13 49	16 46	19 31
22	13 58 13	1 22 35	7♌29	19 39	10 31	10 18	4 20	6 20	13 49	16 46	19 29
23	14 2 10	2 21 6	21 14	19 11	11 41	10 51	4 24	6 22	13 48	16 46	19 28
24	14 6 6	3 19 35	4♍46	18 47	12 50	11 24	4 28	6 24	13 48	16 46	19 26
25	14 10 3	4 18 1	18 8	18 28	13 59	11 58	4 33	6 27	13 48	16 45	19 24
26	14 14 0	5 16 26	1♎18	18 13	15 9	12 31	4 37	6 29	13 47	16 45	19 23
27	14 17 56	6 14 48	14 17	18 4	16 18	13 5	4 42	6 31	13 47	16 45	19 21
28	14 21 53	7 13 9	27 4	17D59	17 27	13 39	4 47	6 33	13 47	16 45	19 20
29	14 25 49	8 11 27	9♏38	18 0	18 35	14 12	4 52	6 34	13 46	16 44	19 18
30	14 29 46	9♉ 9 44	22♏ 0	18♈ 5	19♊44	14♋46	4♌58	6♒36	13♑46	16♑44	19♏16

THE SUN ENTERS THE SIGN OF TAURUS ON APR 20 AT 14:09.

DAY	TIME	☉	☽	☿	♀	♂	♃	♄	♅	♆	♇
	h m s	° ' "	° '	° '	° '	° '	° '	° '	° '	° '	° '
M 1	14 33 42	10♉ 8 0	4♐11	18♈15	20♊53	15♋20	5♌ 3	6♒38	13♑45	16♑44	19♏15
A 2	14 37 39	11 6 13	16 11	18 30	22 1	15 54	5 9	6 39	13R44	16R43	19R13
Y 3	14 41 35	12 4 25	28 4	18 50	23 9	16 28	5 14	6 41	13 44	16 43	19 11
4	14 45 32	13 2 36	9♑52	19 14	24 17	17 2	5 20	6 42	13 43	16 42	19 10
5	14 49 29	14 0 45	21 40	19 42	25 25	17 36	5 26	6 43	13 42	16 42	19 8
6	14 53 25	14 58 53	3♒33	20 14	26 33	18 10	5 33	6 44	13 41	16 41	19 6
7	14 57 22	15 56 59	15 35	20 50	27 41	18 44	5 39	6 45	13 40	16 41	19 5
8	15 1 18	16 55 3	27 53	21 31	28 48	19 18	5 45	6 46	13 39	16 40	19 3
9	15 5 15	17 53 6	10♓30	22 15	29 56	19 52	5 52	6 47	13 38	16 39	19 1
10	15 9 11	18 51 8	23 33	23 2	1♋ 3	20 27	5 59	6 48	13 37	16 39	19 0
11	15 13 8	19 49 9	7♈ 2	23 53	2 10	21 1	6 6	6 49	13 36	16 38	18 58
12	15 17 4	20 47 8	20 59	24 47	3 17	21 35	6 13	6 49	13 35	16 37	18 56
13	15 21 1	21 45 6	5♉21	25 44	4 24	22 10	6 20	6 50	13 34	16 37	18 55
14	15 24 58	22 43 2	20 3	26 45	5 30	22 44	6 27	6 50	13 33	16 36	18 53
15	15 28 54	23 40 57	4♊57	27 48	6 36	23 19	6 35	6 50	13 32	16 35	18 51
16	15 32 51	24 38 51	19 55	28 55	7 43	23 53	6 42	6 50	13 30	16 34	18 50
17	15 36 47	25 36 42	4♋47	0♉ 4	8 49	24 28	6 50	6R51	13 29	16 33	18 48
18	15 40 44	26 34 33	19 28	1 15	9 54	25 3	6 58	6 50	13 28	16 33	18 46
19	15 44 40	27 32 21	3♌52	2 30	11 0	25 38	7 6	6 50	13 26	16 32	18 45
20	15 48 37	28 30 8	17 56	3 47	12 5	26 12	7 14	6 50	13 25	16 31	18 43
21	15 52 33	29 27 53	1♍41	5 6	13 10	26 47	7 22	6 50	13 23	16 30	18 41
22	15 56 30	0♊25 36	15 8	6 28	14 15	27 22	7 30	6 49	13 22	16 29	18 40
23	16 0 27	1 23 18	28 18	7 53	15 20	27 57	7 39	6 49	13 20	16 28	18 38
24	16 4 23	2 20 58	11♎12	9 20	16 24	28 32	7 47	6 48	13 19	16 27	18 36
25	16 8 20	3 18 36	23 53	10 49	17 28	29 7	7 56	6 48	13 17	16 26	18 35
26	16 12 16	4 16 14	6♏22	12 21	18 32	29 42	8 5	6 47	13 15	16 25	18 33
27	16 16 13	5 13 50	18 41	13 55	19 36	0♌17	8 14	6 46	13 14	16 24	18 32
28	16 20 9	6 11 24	0♐49	15 32	20 39	0 52	8 23	6 45	13 12	16 23	18 30
29	16 24 6	7 8 58	12 50	17 11	21 42	1 27	8 32	6 44	13 10	16 21	18 28
30	16 28 2	8 6 30	24 44	18 52	22 45	2 3	8 41	6 43	13 8	16 20	18 27
31	16 31 59	9♊ 4 2	6♑33	20♉35	23♋48	2♌38	8♌50	6♒41	13♑ 6	16♑19	18♏25

THE SUN ENTERS THE SIGN OF GEMINI ON MAY 21 AT 13:21.

DAY	TIME	☉	☽	☿	♀	♂	♃	♄	♅	♆	♇
	h m s	° ' "	° '	° '	° '	° '	° '	° '	° '	° '	° '
J 1	16 35 56	10♊ 1 32	18♑20	22♉21	24♋50	3♌13	9♌ 0	6♒40	13♑ 5	16♑18	18♏24
U 2	16 39 52	10 59 2	0♒ 9	24 10	25 52	3 48	9 9	6R38	13R 3	16R17	18R22
N 3	16 43 49	11 56 30	12 2	26 0	26 54	4 24	9 19	6 37	13 1	16 15	18 21
E 4	16 47 45	12 53 58	24 5	27 53	27 55	4 59	9 29	6 35	12 59	16 14	18 19
5	16 51 42	13 51 25	6♓22	29 48	28 56	5 34	9 38	6 33	12 57	16 13	18 18
6	16 55 38	14 48 52	18 58	1♊46	29 57	6 10	9 48	6 32	12 55	16 11	18 16
7	16 59 35	15 46 17	1♈57	3 45	0♌57	6 45	9 58	6 30	12 53	16 10	18 15
8	17 3 31	16 43 43	15 23	5 47	1 57	7 21	10 8	6 28	12 51	16 9	18 13
9	17 7 28	17 41 7	29 17	7 50	2 57	7 57	10 19	6 26	12 48	16 7	18 12
10	17 11 25	18 38 31	13♉38	9 55	3 56	8 32	10 29	6 23	12 46	16 6	18 11
11	17 15 21	19 35 55	28 22	12 2	4 55	9 8	10 39	6 21	12 44	16 5	18 9
12	17 19 18	20 33 18	13♊24	14 11	5 53	9 43	10 50	6 19	12 42	16 3	18 8
13	17 23 14	21 30 40	28 33	16 20	6 51	10 19	11 0	6 16	12 40	16 2	18 7
14	17 27 11	22 28 1	13♋41	18 31	7 49	10 55	11 11	6 14	12 38	16 0	18 5
15	17 31 7	23 25 22	28 39	20 42	8 46	11 31	11 21	6 11	12 35	15 59	18 4
16	17 35 4	24 22 42	13♌19	22 54	9 43	12 7	11 32	6 9	12 33	15 57	18 3
17	17 39 1	25 20 1	27 37	25 6	10 39	12 43	11 43	6 6	12 31	15 56	18 1
18	17 42 57	26 17 19	11♍31	27 17	11 35	13 18	11 54	6 3	12 29	15 54	18 0
19	17 46 54	27 14 36	25 1	29 29	12 30	13 54	12 5	6 0	12 26	15 53	17 59
20	17 50 50	28 11 52	8♎ 9	1♋40	13 25	14 30	12 16	5 57	12 24	15 51	17 58
21	17 54 47	29 9 7	20 56	3 50	14 19	15 6	12 27	5 54	12 22	15 50	17 57
22	17 58 43	0♋ 6 22	3♏27	5 59	15 13	15 42	12 38	5 51	12 19	15 48	17 56
23	18 2 40	1 3 36	15 45	8 6	16 6	16 18	12 50	5 48	12 17	15 47	17 54
24	18 6 36	2 0 50	27 51	10 13	16 58	16 55	13 1	5 45	12 15	15 45	17 53
25	18 10 33	2 58 3	9♐50	12 17	17 50	17 31	13 12	5 41	12 12	15 44	17 52
26	18 14 30	3 55 16	21 42	14 20	18 41	18 7	13 24	5 38	12 10	15 42	17 51
27	18 18 26	4 52 28	3♑31	16 21	19 32	18 43	13 35	5 34	12 7	15 41	17 50
28	18 22 23	5 49 40	15 19	18 20	20 21	19 19	13 47	5 31	12 5	15 39	17 49
29	18 26 19	6 46 52	27 8	20 18	21 11	19 56	13 59	5 27	12 3	15 37	17 48
30	18 30 16	7♋44 4	9♒ 0	22♋13	21♌59	20♌32	14♌10	5♒24	12♑ 0	15♑36	17♏47

THE SUN ENTERS THE SIGN OF CANCER ON JUN 21 AT 21:20.

♏ SCORPIO ♐ SAGITTARIUS ♑ CAPRICORN ♒ AQUARIUS ♓ PISCES

SIDEREAL · SUN. · MOON. · MERCURY. · VENUS. · MARS. · JUPITER. · SATURN. · URANUS. · NEPTUNE. · PLUTO.

DAY	TIME h m s	☉ ° ' "	☽ ° '	☿ ° '	♀ ° '	♂ ° '	♃ ° '	♄ ° '	♅ ° '	♆ ° '	♇ ° '
J 1	18 34 12	8♋41 16	20♒59	24♋ 6	22♌46	21♌ 8	14♌22	5♒20	11♑58	15♑34	17♏46
U 2	18 38 9	9 38 28	3♓ 7	25 57	23 33	21 45	14 34	5R16	11R55	15R33	17R46
L 3	18 42 5	10 35 39	15 28	27 46	24 19	22 21	14 46	5 12	11 53	15 31	17 45
Y 4	18 46 2	11 32 51	28 6	29 33	25 4	22 57	14 58	5 9	11 50	15 29	17 44
5	18 49 59	12 30 3	11♈ 3	1♌18	25 48	23 34	15 10	5 5	11 48	15 28	17 43
6	18 53 55	13 27 16	24 23	3 1	26 31	24 10	15 22	5 1	11 46	15 26	17 42
7	18 57 52	14 24 29	8♉ 9	4 41	27 13	24 47	15 34	4 57	11 43	15 24	17 42
8	19 1 48	15 21 42	22 20	6 20	27 55	25 24	15 46	4 53	11 41	15 23	17 41
9	19 5 45	16 18 55	6♊54	7 57	28 35	26 0	15 58	4 49	11 38	15 21	17 40
10	19 9 41	17 16 9	21 48	9 31	29 14	26 37	16 11	4 45	11 36	15 20	17 40
11	19 13 38	18 13 24	6♋54	11 3	29 52	27 14	16 23	4 40	11 34	15 18	17 39
12	19 17 34	19 10 38	22 4	12 33	0♍29	27 50	16 35	4 36	11 31	15 16	17 39
13	19 21 31	20 7 53	7♌ 8	14 1	1 5	28 27	16 48	4 32	11 29	15 15	17 38
14	19 25 28	21 5 8	21 59	15 27	1 39	29 4	17 0	4 28	11 26	15 13	17 37
15	19 29 24	22 2 22	6♍28	16 51	2 12	29 41	17 12	4 23	11 24	15 12	17 37
16	19 33 21	22 59 37	20 32	18 12	2 44	0♍17	17 25	4 19	11 22	15 10	17 37
17	19 37 17	23 56 52	4♎10	19 31	3 14	0 54	17 37	4 15	11 19	15 8	17 36
18	19 41 14	24 54 7	17 22	20 48	3 43	1 31	17 50	4 10	11 17	15 7	17 36
19	19 45 10	25 51 22	0♏10	22 3	4 10	2 8	18 3	4 6	11 15	15 5	17 35
20	19 49 7	26 48 38	12 38	23 15	4 36	2 45	18 15	4 2	11 12	15 4	17 35
21	19 53 3	27 45 53	24 50	24 24	5 0	3 22	18 28	3 57	11 10	15 2	17 35
22	19 57 0	28 43 9	6♐50	25 31	5 22	3 59	18 41	3 53	11 8	15 0	17 35
23	20 0 57	29 40 26	18 43	26 35	5 43	4 36	18 53	3 48	11 5	14 59	17 34
24	20 4 53	0♌37 42	0♑31	27 37	6 2	5 14	19 6	3 44	11 3	14 57	17 34
25	20 8 50	1 34 59	12 19	28 35	6 18	5 51	19 19	3 39	11 1	14 56	17 34
26	20 12 46	2 32 17	24 9	29 31	6 33	6 28	19 32	3 35	10 59	14 54	17 34
27	20 16 43	3 29 35	6♒ 3	0♍24	6 46	7 5	19 45	3 31	10 57	14 53	17 34
28	20 20 39	4 26 54	18 3	1 13	6 57	7 42	19 58	3 26	10 54	14 51	17D34
29	20 24 36	5 24 14	0♓12	1 59	7 6	8 20	20 10	3 22	10 52	14 50	17 34
30	20 28 32	6 21 34	12 32	2 41	7 13	8 57	20 23	3 17	10 50	14 48	17 34
31	20 32 29	7♌18 56	25♓ 3	3♍20	7♍17	9♍34	20♌36	3♒13	10♑48	14♑47	17♏34

THE SUN ENTERS THE SIGN OF LEO ON JUL 23 AT 08:12.

DAY	TIME h m s	☉ ° ' "	☽ ° '	☿ ° '	♀ ° '	♂ ° '	♃ ° '	♄ ° '	♅ ° '	♆ ° '	♇ ° '
A 1	20 36 26	8♌16 18	7♈49	3♍55	7♍19	10♍12	20♌49	3♒ 8	10♑46	14♑45	17♏34
U 2	20 40 22	9 13 41	20 51	4 25	7R19	10 49	21 2	3R 4	10R44	14R44	17 34
G 3	20 44 19	10 11 6	4♉11	4 52	7 17	11 27	21 15	2 59	10 42	14 42	17 34
U 4	20 48 15	11 8 32	17 50	5 14	7 12	12 4	21 28	2 55	10 40	14 41	17 34
S 5	20 52 12	12 5 59	1♊49	5 32	7 5	12 42	21 41	2 51	10 38	14 40	17 35
T 6	20 56 8	13 3 28	16 8	5 44	6 55	13 19	21 54	2 46	10 36	14 38	17 35
7	21 0 5	14 0 57	0♋44	5R52	6 43	13 57	22 7	2 42	10 34	14 37	17 35
8	21 4 2	14 58 28	15 34	5 55	6 29	14 35	22 20	2 38	10 32	14 35	17 35
9	21 7 58	15 56 0	0♌31	5 52	6 12	15 12	22 34	2 33	10 30	14 34	17 36
10	21 11 55	16 53 34	15 27	5 44	5 54	15 50	22 47	2 29	10 29	14 33	17 36
11	21 15 51	17 51 8	0♍15	5 30	5 33	16 28	23 0	2 25	10 27	14 32	17 37
12	21 19 48	18 48 43	14 46	5 12	5 9	17 6	23 13	2 21	10 25	14 30	17 37
13	21 23 44	19 46 20	28 55	4 47	4 44	17 43	23 26	2 16	10 23	14 29	17 38
14	21 27 41	20 43 57	12♎38	4 18	4 17	18 21	23 39	2 12	10 22	14 28	17 38
15	21 31 37	21 41 35	25 54	3 44	3 48	18 59	23 52	2 8	10 20	14 27	17 39
16	21 35 34	22 39 14	8♏45	3 5	3 17	19 37	24 5	2 4	10 18	14 25	17 39
17	21 39 30	23 36 55	21 14	2 22	2 44	20 15	24 19	2 0	10 17	14 24	17 40
18	21 43 27	24 34 36	3♐26	1 35	2 11	20 53	24 32	1 56	10 15	14 23	17 41
19	21 47 24	25 32 18	15 24	0 46	1 36	21 31	24 45	1 52	10 14	14 22	17 41
20	21 51 20	26 30 2	27 15	29♌55	1 0	22 9	24 58	1 49	10 13	14 21	17 42
21	21 55 17	27 27 46	9♑ 3	29 3	0 23	22 47	25 11	1 45	10 11	14 20	17 43
22	21 59 13	28 25 32	20 52	28 10	29♌46	23 26	25 24	1 41	10 10	14 19	17 44
23	22 3 10	29 23 19	2♒45	27 19	29 9	24 4	25 37	1 37	10 8	14 18	17 44
24	22 7 6	0♍21 7	14 47	26 30	28 32	24 42	25 50	1 34	10 7	14 17	17 45
25	22 11 3	1 18 57	26 59	25 44	27 54	25 20	26 4	1 30	10 6	14 16	17 46
26	22 14 59	2 16 48	9♓23	25 2	27 18	25 59	26 17	1 27	10 5	14 15	17 47
27	22 18 56	3 14 41	22 0	24 25	26 42	26 37	26 30	1 23	10 4	14 14	17 48
28	22 22 53	4 12 35	4♈49	23 55	26 7	27 15	26 43	1 20	10 3	14 13	17 49
29	22 26 49	5 10 31	17 51	23 30	25 33	27 54	26 56	1 16	10 1	14 12	17 50
30	22 30 46	6 8 28	1♉ 6	23 14	25 1	28 32	27 9	1 13	10 0	14 11	17 51
31	22 34 42	7♍ 6 28	14♉34	23♌ 5	24♌30	29♍11	27♌22	1♒10	9♑59	14♑10	17♏52

THE SUN ENTERS THE SIGN OF VIRGO ON AUG 23 AT 15:14.

DAY	TIME h m s	☉ ° ' "	☽ ° '	☿ ° '	♀ ° '	♂ ° '	♃ ° '	♄ ° '	♅ ° '	♆ ° '	♇ ° '
S 1	22 38 39	8♍ 4 29	28♉15	23♌ 4	24♌ 1	29♍49	27♌35	1♒ 7	9♑59	14♑ 9	17♏53
E 2	22 42 35	9 2 33	12♊ 8	23 11	23R33	0♎28	27 48	1R 4	9R58	14R 9	17 55
P 3	22 46 32	10 0 38	26 14	23 27	23 8	1 7	28 1	1 1	9 57	14 8	17 56
T 4	22 50 28	10 58 46	10♋33	23 52	22 45	1 45	28 14	0 58	9 56	14 7	17 57
E 5	22 54 25	11 56 55	25 1	24 25	22 24	2 24	28 27	0 55	9 55	14 7	17 58
M 6	22 58 22	12 55 6	9♌35	25 6	22 5	3 3	28 40	0 52	9 55	14 6	17 59
B 7	23 2 18	13 53 19	24 11	25 55	21 49	3 42	28 53	0 50	9 54	14 5	18 1
E 8	23 6 15	14 51 34	8♍42	26 51	21 35	4 20	29 6	0 47	9 53	14 5	18 2
R 9	23 10 11	15 49 51	23 1	27 55	21 23	4 59	29 18	0 45	9 53	14 4	18 3
10	23 14 8	16 48 9	7♎ 3	29 5	21 14	5 38	29 31	0 42	9 52	14 4	18 5
11	23 18 4	17 46 29	20 43	0♍22	21 7	6 17	29 44	0 40	9 52	14 3	18 6
12	23 22 1	18 44 51	3♏59	1 45	21 3	6 56	29 57	0 38	9 52	14 3	18 8
13	23 25 57	19 43 15	16 51	3 12	21D 1	7 35	0♍10	0 35	9 51	14 2	18 9
14	23 29 54	20 41 40	29 21	4 44	21 1	8 14	0 22	0 33	9 51	14 2	18 11
15	23 33 51	21 40 6	11♐33	6 20	21 3	8 53	0 35	0 31	9 51	14 1	18 12
16	23 37 47	22 38 35	23 32	8 0	21 8	9 33	0 48	0 30	9 50	14 1	18 14
17	23 41 44	23 37 5	5♑23	9 42	21 16	10 12	1 0	0 28	9 50	14 1	18 15
18	23 45 40	24 35 36	17 11	11 27	21 25	10 51	1 13	0 26	9 50	14 0	18 17
19	23 49 37	25 34 9	29 1	13 13	21 36	11 30	1 25	0 24	9D50	14 0	18 19
20	23 53 33	26 32 44	10♒59	15 2	21 50	12 10	1 38	0 23	9 50	14 0	18 20
21	23 57 30	27 31 21	23 8	16 51	22 5	12 49	1 50	0 21	9 50	14 0	18 22
22	0 1 26	28 29 59	5♓32	18 41	22 23	13 28	2 3	0 20	9 50	14 0	18 24
23	0 5 23	29 28 39	18 11	20 32	22 42	14 8	2 15	0 19	9 50	13 59	18 25
24	0 9 20	0♎27 21	1♈ 7	22 22	23 4	14 47	2 27	0 18	9 51	13 59	18 27
25	0 13 16	1 26 5	14 19	24 13	23 27	15 27	2 40	0 17	9 51	13 59	18 29
26	0 17 13	2 24 51	27 44	26 4	23 52	16 7	2 52	0 16	9 51	13D59	18 31
27	0 21 9	3 23 40	11♉22	27 54	24 18	16 46	3 4	0 15	9 52	13 59	18 33
28	0 25 6	4 22 30	25 8	29 44	24 47	17 26	3 16	0 14	9 52	13 59	18 34
29	0 29 2	5 21 23	9♊ 1	1♎34	25 16	18 6	3 28	0 13	9 52	13 59	18 36
30	0 32 59	6♎20 18	23♊ 0	3♎22	25♌48	18♎45	3♍40	0♒13	9♑53	14♑ 0	18♏38

THE SUN ENTERS THE SIGN OF LIBRA ON SEP 23 AT 12:49.

♈ ARIES ♉ TAURUS ♊ GEMINI ♋ CANCER ♌ LEO ♍ VIRGO ♎ LIBRA

SIDEREAL. SUN. MOON. MERCURY. VENUS. MARS. JUPITER. SATURN. URANUS. NEPTUNE. PLUTO.

DAY	TIME	☉	☽	☿	♀	♂	♃	♄	♅	♆	♇
	h m s	° ' "	° '	° '	° '	° '	° '	° '	° '	° '	° '
O 1	0 36 55	7♎19 15	7♋ 3	5♎11	26♌20	19♎25	3♍52	0♒12	9♑54	14♑ 0	18♏40
C 2	0 40 52	8 18 15	21 9	6 58	26 55	20 5	4 4	0R12	9 54	14 0	18 42
T 3	0 44 49	9 17 17	5♌19	8 45	27 30	20 45	4 16	0 12	9 55	14 0	18 44
O 4	0 48 45	10 16 21	19 31	10 31	28 7	21 25	4 28	0 12	9 56	14 0	18 46
B 5	0 52 42	11 15 28	3♍41	12 16	28 45	22 5	4 39	0D12	9 56	14 1	18 48
E 6	0 56 38	12 14 37	17 46	14 0	29 24	22 45	4 51	0 12	9 57	14 1	18 50
R 7	1 0 35	13 13 48	1♎43	15 43	0♍ 5	23 25	5 3	0 12	9 58	14 1	18 52
8	1 4 31	14 13 1	15 27	17 26	0 46	24 5	5 14	0 12	9 59	14 2	18 54
9	1 8 28	15 12 16	28 53	19 8	1 29	24 45	5 26	0 12	10 0	14 2	18 56
10	1 12 24	16 11 33	12♏ 0	20 49	2 13	25 25	5 37	0 13	10 1	14 2	18 58
11	1 16 21	17 10 52	24 47	22 29	2 57	26 6	5 48	0 13	10 2	14 3	19 0
12	1 20 17	18 10 13	7♐15	24 9	3 43	26 46	6 0	0 14	10 3	14 3	19 3
13	1 24 14	19 9 35	19 25	25 48	4 29	27 26	6 11	0 15	10 4	14 4	19 5
14	1 28 11	20 9 0	1♑24	27 26	5 17	28 7	6 22	0 16	10 6	14 5	19 7
15	1 32 7	21 8 26	13 14	29 3	6 5	28 47	6 33	0 16	10 7	14 5	19 9
16	1 36 4	22 7 55	25 2	0♏40	6 54	29 28	6 44	0 18	10 8	14 6	19 11
17	1 40 0	23 7 24	6♒53	2 16	7 44	0♏ 8	6 55	0 19	10 10	14 6	19 14
18	1 43 57	24 6 56	18 52	3 52	8 35	0 49	7 6	0 20	10 11	14 7	19 16
19	1 47 53	25 6 29	1♓ 5	5 26	9 26	1 29	7 16	0 21	10 12	14 8	19 18
20	1 51 50	26 6 4	13 35	7 0	10 18	2 10	7 27	0 23	10 14	14 9	19 20
21	1 55 46	27 5 41	26 26	8 34	11 11	2 51	7 37	0 24	10 16	14 9	19 23
22	1 59 43	28 5 20	9♈37	10 7	12 5	3 32	7 48	0 26	10 17	14 10	19 25
23	2 3 40	29 5 1	23 9	11 39	12 59	4 12	7 58	0 28	10 19	14 11	19 27
24	2 7 36	0♏ 4 43	6♉59	13 11	13 54	4 53	8 9	0 29	10 20	14 12	19 29
25	2 11 33	1 4 28	21 2	14 42	14 49	5 34	8 19	0 31	10 22	14 13	19 32
26	2 15 29	2 4 15	5♊15	16 13	15 45	6 15	8 29	0 33	10 24	14 14	19 34
27	2 19 26	3 4 4	19 31	17 43	16 42	6 56	8 39	0 36	10 26	14 15	19 36
28	2 23 22	4 3 55	3♋47	19 12	17 39	7 37	8 49	0 38	10 28	14 16	19 39
29	2 27 19	5 3 49	18 0	20 41	18 37	8 18	8 58	0 40	10 30	14 17	19 41
30	2 31 15	6 3 44	2♌ 9	22 9	19 35	8 59	9 8	0 43	10 32	14 18	19 43
31	2 35 12	7♏ 3 42	16♌11	23♏37	20♍34	9♏41	9♍18	0♒45	10♑34	14♑19	19♏46

THE SUN ENTERS THE SIGN OF SCORPIO ON OCT 23 AT 22:06.

DAY	TIME	☉	☽	☿	♀	♂	♃	♄	♅	♆	♇
	h m s	° ' "	° '	° '	° '	° '	° '	° '	° '	° '	° '
N 1	2 39 9	8♏ 3 42	0♍ 7	25♏ 4	21♍33	10♏22	9♍27	0♒48	10♑36	14♑20	19♏48
O 2	2 43 5	9 3 44	13 56	26 31	22 33	11 3	9 37	0 50	10 38	14 22	19 51
V 3	2 47 2	10 3 48	27 37	27 57	23 33	11 44	9 46	0 53	10 40	14 23	19 53
E 4	2 50 58	11 3 55	11♎ 7	29 22	24 34	12 26	9 55	0 56	10 42	14 24	19 55
M 5	2 54 55	12 4 3	24 26	0♐47	25 35	13 7	10 4	0 59	10 44	14 25	19 58
B 6	2 58 51	13 4 13	7♏31	2 11	26 36	13 49	10 13	1 2	10 47	14 26	20 0
E 7	3 2 48	14 4 25	20 21	3 33	27 38	14 30	10 22	1 5	10 49	14 28	20 3
R 8	3 6 44	15 4 39	2♐56	4 56	28 40	15 12	10 31	1 8	10 51	14 29	20 5
9	3 10 41	16 4 55	15 15	6 17	29 43	15 53	10 39	1 12	10 54	14 31	20 7
10	3 14 38	17 5 12	27 22	7 37	0♎46	16 35	10 48	1 15	10 56	14 32	20 10
11	3 18 34	18 5 31	9♑17	8 56	1 49	17 17	10 56	1 19	10 59	14 33	20 12
12	3 22 31	19 5 51	21 6	10 13	2 52	17 59	11 4	1 22	11 1	14 35	20 15
13	3 26 27	20 6 13	2♒53	11 29	3 56	18 40	11 12	1 26	11 4	14 36	20 17
14	3 30 24	21 6 36	14 43	12 44	5 1	19 22	11 20	1 30	11 6	14 38	20 20
15	3 34 20	22 7 0	26 41	13 56	6 5	20 4	11 28	1 34	11 9	14 39	20 22
16	3 38 17	23 7 26	8♓53	15 7	7 10	20 46	11 36	1 37	11 11	14 41	20 24
17	3 42 13	24 7 53	21 23	16 15	8 15	21 28	11 43	1 41	11 14	14 42	20 27
18	3 46 10	25 8 22	4♈16	17 21	9 21	22 10	11 51	1 46	11 17	14 44	20 29
19	3 50 7	26 8 51	17 33	18 23	10 26	22 52	11 58	1 50	11 20	14 46	20 32
20	3 54 3	27 9 23	1♉15	19 22	11 32	23 34	12 5	1 54	11 22	14 47	20 34
21	3 58 0	28 9 55	15 21	20 18	12 38	24 17	12 12	1 58	11 25	14 49	20 36
22	4 1 56	29 10 29	29 46	21 9	13 45	24 59	12 19	2 3	11 28	14 51	20 39
23	4 5 53	0♐11 5	14♊24	21 55	14 52	25 41	12 26	2 7	11 31	14 53	20 41
24	4 9 49	1 11 42	29 7	22 36	15 59	26 23	12 32	2 12	11 34	14 54	20 44
25	4 13 46	2 12 21	13♋49	23 10	17 6	27 6	12 39	2 16	11 37	14 56	20 46
26	4 17 42	3 13 1	28 24	23 38	18 13	27 48	12 45	2 21	11 40	14 58	20 48
27	4 21 39	4 13 43	12♌48	23 58	19 21	28 31	12 51	2 26	11 43	15 0	20 51
28	4 25 36	5 14 26	26 57	24R 9	20 29	29 13	12 57	2 31	11 46	15 1	20 53
29	4 29 32	6 15 11	10♍52	24 11	21 37	29 56	13 3	2 36	11 49	15 3	20 55
30	4 33 29	7♐15 57	24♍30	24♐ 3	22♎45	0♐38	13♍ 9	2♒41	11♑52	15♑ 5	20♏58

THE SUN ENTERS THE SIGN OF SAGITTARIUS ON NOV 22 AT 19:37.

DAY	TIME	☉	☽	☿	♀	♂	♃	♄	♅	♆	♇
	h m s	° ' "	° '	° '	° '	° '	° '	° '	° '	° '	° '
D 1	4 37 25	8♐16 45	7♎54	23♐44	23♎54	1♐21	13♍14	2♒46	11♑55	15♑ 7	21♏ 0
E 2	4 41 22	9 17 35	21 3	23R15	25 2	2 4	13 20	2 51	11 58	15 9	21 2
C 3	4 45 18	10 18 26	3♏59	22 34	26 11	2 47	13 25	2 56	12 1	15 11	21 5
E 4	4 49 15	11 19 18	16 42	21 43	27 20	3 30	13 30	3 1	12 5	15 13	21 7
M 5	4 53 11	12 20 12	29 12	20 41	28 29	4 12	13 35	3 7	12 8	15 15	21 9
B 6	4 57 8	13 21 6	11♐30	19 31	29 39	4 55	13 39	3 12	12 11	15 17	21 12
E 7	5 1 5	14 22 2	23 39	18 14	0♏48	5 38	13 44	3 18	12 14	15 19	21 14
R 8	5 5 1	15 22 59	5♑38	16 53	1 58	6 21	13 48	3 23	12 18	15 21	21 16
9	5 8 58	16 23 57	17 30	15 30	3 8	7 4	13 52	3 29	12 21	15 23	21 19
10	5 12 54	17 24 55	29 17	14 8	4 18	7 47	13 56	3 34	12 24	15 25	21 21
11	5 16 51	18 25 54	11♒ 4	12 50	5 28	8 31	14 0	3 40	12 28	15 27	21 23
12	5 20 47	19 26 54	22 53	11 38	6 38	9 14	14 4	3 46	12 31	15 29	21 25
13	5 24 44	20 27 54	4♓50	10 35	7 48	9 57	14 7	3 52	12 34	15 31	21 27
14	5 28 41	21 28 55	16 59	9 41	8 59	10 40	14 10	3 57	12 38	15 33	21 30
15	5 32 37	22 29 57	29 25	8 58	10 9	11 24	14 14	4 3	12 41	15 35	21 32
16	5 36 34	23 30 58	12♈12	8 26	11 20	12 7	14 16	4 9	12 45	15 38	21 34
17	5 40 30	24 32 1	25 24	8 6	12 31	12 50	14 19	4 15	12 48	15 40	21 36
18	5 44 27	25 33 3	9♉ 3	7D56	13 42	13 34	14 22	4 21	12 51	15 42	21 38
19	5 48 23	26 34 7	23 10	7 56	14 53	14 17	14 24	4 28	12 55	15 44	21 40
20	5 52 20	27 35 10	7♊41	8 6	16 4	15 1	14 26	4 34	12 58	15 46	21 42
21	5 56 16	28 36 15	22 32	8 24	17 16	15 45	14 28	4 40	13 2	15 48	21 44
22	6 0 13	29 37 19	7♋35	8 51	18 27	16 28	14 30	4 46	13 5	15 51	21 46
23	6 4 10	0♑38 24	22 41	9 24	19 38	17 12	14 32	4 53	13 9	15 53	21 48
24	6 8 6	1 39 30	7♌42	10 4	20 50	17 56	14 33	4 59	13 12	15 55	21 50
25	6 12 3	2 40 36	22 29	10 50	22 2	18 40	14 34	5 5	13 16	15 57	21 52
26	6 15 59	3 41 43	6♍56	11 41	23 14	19 23	14 35	5 12	13 19	15 59	21 54
27	6 19 56	4 42 51	21 2	12 36	24 25	20 7	14 36	5 18	13 23	16 2	21 56
28	6 23 52	5 43 59	4♎44	13 35	25 37	20 51	14 37	5 25	13 27	16 4	21 58
29	6 27 49	6 45 7	18 3	14 38	26 49	21 35	14 37	5 31	13 30	16 6	22 0
30	6 31 45	7 46 17	1♏ 2	15 44	28 2	22 19	14R38	5 38	13 34	16 8	22 2
31	6 35 42	8♑47 26	13♏43	16♐52	29♏14	23♐ 3	14♍38	5♒45	13♑37	16♑11	22♏ 4

THE SUN ENTERS THE SIGN OF CAPRICORN ON DEC 22 AT 08:55.

♏ SCORPIO ♐ SAGITTARIUS ♑ CAPRICORN ♒ AQUARIUS ♓ PISCES

SIDEREAL. SUN. MOON. MERCURY. VENUS. MARS. JUPITER. SATURN. URANUS. NEPTUNE. PLUTO.

DAY	TIME	☉	☽	☿	♀	♂	♃	♄	♅	♆	♇
	h m s	° ' "	° '	° '	° '	° '	° '	° '	° '	° '	° '
J 1	6 39 39	9♑48 36	26♏ 9	18♐ 3	0♐26	23♐47	14♍38	5♒51	13♑41	16♑13	22♏ 5
A 2	6 43 35	10 49 47	8♐23	19 16	1 38	24 32	14R37	5 58	13 44	16 15	22 7
N 3	6 47 32	11 50 57	20 27	20 31	2 51	25 16	14 37	6 5	13 48	16 18	22 9
U 4	6 51 28	12 52 8	2♑24	21 47	4 3	26 0	14 36	6 12	13 52	16 20	22 11
A 5	6 55 25	13 53 19	14 16	23 5	5 16	26 44	14 35	6 18	13 55	16 22	22 12
R 6	6 59 21	14 54 30	26 4	24 25	6 29	27 29	14 34	6 25	13 59	16 24	22 14
Y 7	7 3 18	15 55 41	7♒52	25 45	7 41	28 13	14 33	6 32	14 2	16 27	22 16
8	7 7 14	16 56 51	19 40	27 7	8 54	28 57	14 31	6 39	14 6	16 29	22 17
9	7 11 11	17 58 1	1♓33	28 30	10 7	29 42	14 30	6 46	14 10	16 31	22 19
10	7 15 8	18 59 11	13 32	29 54	11 20	0♑26	14 28	6 53	14 13	16 33	22 20
11	7 19 4	20 0 20	25 42	1♑18	12 33	1 11	14 26	7 0	14 17	16 36	22 22
12	7 23 1	21 1 28	8♈ 5	2 44	13 46	1 55	14 23	7 7	14 20	16 38	22 24
13	7 26 57	22 2 36	20 47	4 10	14 59	2 40	14 21	7 14	14 24	16 40	22 25
14	7 30 54	23 3 44	3♉50	5 37	16 12	3 25	14 18	7 21	14 27	16 43	22 26
15	7 34 50	24 4 51	17 18	7 4	17 25	4 9	14 16	7 28	14 31	16 45	22 28
16	7 38 47	25 5 57	1♊13	8 33	18 38	4 54	14 13	7 35	14 34	16 47	22 29
17	7 42 43	26 7 2	15 35	10 1	19 51	5 39	14 9	7 42	14 38	16 49	22 31
18	7 46 40	27 8 7	0♋21	11 31	21 4	6 24	14 6	7 49	14 41	16 52	22 32
19	7 50 37	28 9 12	15 25	13 1	22 17	7 9	14 3	7 56	14 45	16 54	22 33
20	7 54 33	29 10 15	0♌40	14 32	23 31	7 54	13 59	8 3	14 49	16 56	22 35
21	7 58 30	0♒11 18	15 55	16 3	24 44	8 38	13 55	8 10	14 52	16 58	22 36
22	8 2 26	1 12 20	1♍ 1	17 35	25 57	9 23	13 51	8 18	14 55	17 0	22 37
23	8 6 23	2 13 22	15 48	19 7	27 11	10 8	13 47	8 25	14 59	17 3	22 38
24	8 10 19	3 14 23	0♎10	20 40	28 24	10 53	13 42	8 32	15 2	17 5	22 39
25	8 14 16	4 15 24	14 4	22 14	29 38	11 39	13 38	8 39	15 6	17 7	22 40
26	8 18 13	5 16 24	27 30	23 48	0♑51	12 24	13 33	8 46	15 9	17 9	22 41
27	8 22 9	6 17 24	10♏30	25 23	2 5	13 9	13 28	8 53	15 13	17 11	22 42
28	8 26 6	7 18 23	23 7	26 58	3 18	13 54	13 23	9 0	15 16	17 14	22 43
29	8 30 2	8 19 21	5♐26	28 34	4 32	14 39	13 18	9 8	15 19	17 16	22 44
30	8 33 59	9 20 19	17 31	0♒11	5 46	15 25	13 12	9 15	15 23	17 18	22 45
31	8 37 55	10♒21 17	29♐26	1♒49	6♑59	16♑10	13♍ 7	9♒22	15♑26	17♑20	22♏46

THE SUN ENTERS THE SIGN OF AQUARIUS ON JAN 20 AT 19:33.

DAY	TIME	☉	☽	☿	♀	♂	♃	♄	♅	♆	♇
	h m s	° ' "	° '	° '	° '	° '	° '	° '	° '	° '	° '
F 1	8 41 52	11♒22 13	11♑16	3♒27	8♑13	16♑55	13♍ 1	9♒29	15♑29	17♑22	22♏47
E 2	8 45 48	12 23 9	23 3	5 5	9 27	17 41	12R55	9 36	15 33	17 24	22 48
B 3	8 49 45	13 24 3	4♒50	6 45	10 41	18 26	12 49	9 44	15 36	17 26	22 49
R 4	8 53 42	14 24 57	16 40	8 25	11 54	19 12	12 43	9 51	15 39	17 29	22 50
U 5	8 57 38	15 25 49	28 35	10 6	13 8	19 57	12 37	9 58	15 43	17 31	22 50
A 6	9 1 35	16 26 40	10♓35	11 48	14 22	20 43	12 31	10 5	15 46	17 33	22 51
R 7	9 5 31	17 27 30	22 43	13 30	15 36	21 28	12 24	10 12	15 49	17 35	22 52
Y 8	9 9 28	18 28 18	5♈ 0	15 14	16 50	22 14	12 18	10 19	15 52	17 37	22 52
9	9 13 24	19 29 5	17 29	16 58	18 3	22 59	12 11	10 26	15 55	17 39	22 53
10	9 17 21	20 29 50	0♉13	18 42	19 17	23 45	12 4	10 34	15 58	17 41	22 53
11	9 21 17	21 30 34	13 12	20 28	20 31	24 31	11 57	10 41	16 1	17 43	22 54
12	9 25 14	22 31 17	26 32	22 14	21 45	25 16	11 50	10 48	16 5	17 45	22 54
13	9 29 11	23 31 57	10♊13	24 2	22 59	26 2	11 43	10 55	16 8	17 47	22 55
14	9 33 7	24 32 37	24 18	25 50	24 13	26 48	11 36	11 2	16 11	17 49	22 55
15	9 37 4	25 33 14	8♋46	27 38	25 27	27 34	11 29	11 9	16 14	17 50	22 56
16	9 41 0	26 33 50	23 35	29 28	26 41	28 19	11 21	11 16	16 17	17 52	22 56
17	9 44 57	27 34 24	8♌38	1♓18	27 55	29 5	11 14	11 23	16 19	17 54	22 56
18	9 48 53	28 34 56	23 49	3 8	29 9	29 51	11 6	11 30	16 22	17 56	22 57
19	9 52 50	29 35 27	8♍56	4 59	0♒23	0♒37	10 59	11 37	16 25	17 58	22 57
20	9 56 46	0♓35 56	23 50	6 51	1 37	1 23	10 51	11 44	16 28	18 0	22 57
21	10 0 43	1 36 24	8♎23	8 43	2 51	2 9	10 44	11 51	16 31	18 1	22 57
22	10 4 40	2 36 50	22 28	10 35	4 5	2 55	10 36	11 58	16 34	18 3	22 57
23	10 8 36	3 37 15	6♏ 3	12 27	5 19	3 41	10 28	12 5	16 36	18 5	22 57
24	10 12 33	4 37 39	19 10	14 19	6 33	4 27	10 20	12 11	16 39	18 7	22R57
25	10 16 29	5 38 1	1♐51	16 11	7 47	5 13	10 12	12 18	16 42	18 8	22 57
26	10 20 26	6 38 22	14 11	18 2	9 1	5 59	10 5	12 25	16 44	18 10	22 57
27	10 24 22	7 38 42	26 14	19 52	10 15	6 45	9 57	12 32	16 47	18 12	22 57
28	10 28 19	8 39 0	8♑ 7	21 41	11 29	7 31	9 49	12 38	16 49	18 13	22 57
29	10 32 15	9♓39 17	19♑54	23♓28	12♒43	8♒17	9♍41	12♒45	16♑52	18♑15	22♏57

THE SUN ENTERS THE SIGN OF PISCES ON FEB 19 AT 09:44.

DAY	TIME	☉	☽	☿	♀	♂	♃	♄	♅	♆	♇
	h m s	° ' "	° '	° '	° '	° '	° '	° '	° '	° '	° '
M 1	10 36 12	10♓39 32	1♒41	25♓12	13♒57	9♒ 4	9♍33	12♒52	16♑54	18♑16	22♏57
A 2	10 40 9	11 39 45	13 30	26 55	15 11	9 50	9R25	12 58	16 57	18 18	22R57
R 3	10 44 5	12 39 57	25 24	28 33	16 25	10 36	9 17	13 5	16 59	18 20	22 56
C 4	10 48 2	13 40 7	7♓27	0♈ 9	17 39	11 22	9 10	13 12	17 2	18 21	22 56
H 5	10 51 58	14 40 15	19 39	1 40	18 53	12 9	9 2	13 18	17 4	18 23	22 56
6	10 55 55	15 40 21	2♈ 0	3 6	20 7	12 55	8 54	13 25	17 6	18 24	22 56
7	10 59 51	16 40 25	14 33	4 27	21 21	13 41	8 46	13 31	17 8	18 25	22 55
8	11 3 48	17 40 28	27 16	5 42	22 36	14 27	8 39	13 37	17 11	18 27	22 55
9	11 7 44	18 40 28	10♉11	6 50	23 50	15 14	8 31	13 44	17 13	18 28	22 54
10	11 11 41	19 40 26	23 19	7 51	25 4	16 0	8 23	13 50	17 15	18 29	22 54
11	11 15 37	20 40 22	6♊40	8 46	26 18	16 46	8 16	13 56	17 17	18 31	22 53
12	11 19 34	21 40 16	20 17	9 32	27 32	17 33	8 8	14 2	17 19	18 32	22 53
13	11 23 31	22 40 8	4♋10	10 10	28 46	18 19	8 1	14 9	17 21	18 33	22 52
14	11 27 27	23 39 57	18 21	10 40	0♓ 0	19 6	7 53	14 15	17 23	18 34	22 52
15	11 31 24	24 39 44	2♌49	11 1	1 14	19 52	7 46	14 21	17 25	18 36	22 51
16	11 35 20	25 39 29	17 30	11 14	2 28	20 38	7 39	14 27	17 27	18 37	22 50
17	11 39 17	26 39 12	2♍20	11R19	3 42	21 25	7 32	14 33	17 28	18 38	22 50
18	11 43 13	27 38 52	17 10	11 15	4 56	22 11	7 25	14 39	17 30	18 39	22 49
19	11 47 10	28 38 30	1♎52	11 3	6 10	22 58	7 18	14 44	17 32	18 40	22 48
20	11 51 6	29 38 7	16 19	10 43	7 25	23 44	7 11	14 50	17 34	18 41	22 47
21	11 55 3	0♈37 41	0♏23	10 16	8 39	24 30	7 4	14 56	17 35	18 42	22 47
22	11 59 0	1 37 14	14 0	9 43	9 53	25 17	6 58	15 2	17 37	18 43	22 46
23	12 2 56	2 36 44	27 11	9 5	11 7	26 3	6 51	15 7	17 38	18 44	22 45
24	12 6 53	3 36 14	9♐56	8 21	12 21	26 50	6 45	15 13	17 40	18 45	22 44
25	12 10 49	4 35 41	22 20	7 34	13 35	27 36	6 38	15 18	17 41	18 46	22 43
26	12 14 46	5 35 6	4♑26	6 44	14 49	28 23	6 32	15 24	17 43	18 47	22 42
27	12 18 42	6 34 30	16 21	5 53	16 3	29 9	6 26	15 29	17 44	18 48	22 41
28	12 22 39	7 33 52	28 9	5 1	17 17	29 56	6 20	15 35	17 45	18 48	22 40
29	12 26 35	8 33 12	9♒57	4 9	18 31	0♓42	6 15	15 40	17 46	18 49	22 39
30	12 30 32	9 32 30	21 49	3 19	19 45	1 29	6 9	15 45	17 48	18 50	22 38
31	12 34 29	10♈31 47	3♓49	2♈32	20♓59	2♓16	6♍ 4	15♒50	17♑49	18♑51	22♏37

THE SUN ENTERS THE SIGN OF ARIES ON MAR 20 AT 08:49.

♈ ARIES ♉ TAURUS ♊ GEMINI ♋ CANCER ♌ LEO ♍ VIRGO ♎ LIBRA

SIDEREAL TIME · SUN · MOON · MERCURY · VENUS · MARS · JUPITER · SATURN · URANUS · NEPTUNE · PLUTO

DAY	TIME h m s	☉ ° ' "	☽ ° '	☿ ° '	♀ ° '	♂ ° '	♃ ° '	♄ ° '	♅ ° '	♆ ° '	♇ ° '
A 1	12 38 25	11♈31 1	16♓ 0	1♈47	22♓13	3♓ 2	5♍58	15♒55	17♑50	18♑51	22♏36
P 2	12 42 22	12 30 14	28 24	1R 7	23 27	3 49	5R53	16 0	17 51	18 52	22R34
R 3	12 46 18	13 29 24	11♈ 1	0 31	24 41	4 35	5 48	16 5	17 52	18 52	22 33
I 4	12 50 15	14 28 33	23 52	0O 0	25 55	5 22	5 43	16 10	17 53	18 53	22 32
L 5	12 54 11	15 27 39	6♉56	29♓34	27 10	6 8	5 39	16 15	17 54	18 54	22 31
6	12 58 8	16 26 44	20 11	29 13	28 24	6 55	5 34	16 20	17 55	18 54	22 30
7	13 2 4	17 25 46	3♊37	28 58	29 38	7 41	5 30	16 24	17 55	18 54	22 28
8	13 6 1	18 24 46	17 13	28 49	0♈52	8 28	5 26	16 29	17 56	18 55	22 27
9	13 9 57	19 23 44	0♋58	28D44	2 6	9 14	5 22	16 33	17 57	18 55	22 26
10	13 13 54	20 22 39	14 53	28 46	3 20	10 1	5 18	16 38	17 57	18 56	22 24
11	13 17 51	21 21 32	28 57	28 52	4 34	10 47	5 14	16 42	17 58	18 56	22 23
12	13 21 47	22 20 23	13♌10	29 4	5 47	11 34	5 10	16 46	17 58	18 56	22 22
13	13 25 44	23 19 12	27 30	29 20	7 1	12 20	5 7	16 51	17 59	18 57	22 20
14	13 29 40	24 17 58	11♍54	29 41	8 15	13 6	5 4	16 55	17 59	18 57	22 19
15	13 33 37	25 16 41	26 18	0♈ 7	9 29	13 53	5 1	16 59	18 0	18 57	22 17
16	13 37 33	26 15 23	10♎36	0 37	10 43	14 39	4 58	17 3	18 0	18 57	22 16
17	13 41 30	27 14 3	24 41	1 12	11 57	15 26	4 56	17 7	18 0	18 57	22 15
18	13 45 26	28 12 41	8♏29	1 50	13 11	16 12	4 53	17 11	18 1	18 57	22 13
19	13 49 23	29 11 17	21 57	2 32	14 25	16 58	4 51	17 14	18 1	18 57	22 12
20	13 53 20	0♉ 9 51	5♐ 2	3 18	15 39	17 45	4 49	17 18	18 1	18R57	22 10
21	13 57 16	1 8 23	17 46	4 7	16 53	18 31	4 47	17 21	18R 1	18 57	22 9
22	14 1 13	2 6 54	0♑ 9	5 0	18 7	19 18	4 45	17 25	18 1	18 57	22 7
23	14 5 9	3 5 23	12 18	5 55	19 21	20 4	4 44	17 28	18 1	18 57	22 5
24	14 9 6	4 3 50	24 14	6 54	20 35	20 50	4 42	17 32	18 1	18 57	22 4
25	14 13 2	5 2 16	6♒ 5	7 55	21 48	21 37	4 41	17 35	18 1	18 57	22 2
26	14 16 59	6 0 40	17 55	8 59	23 2	22 23	4 40	17 38	18 1	18 57	22 1
27	14 20 55	6 59 3	29 50	10 6	24 16	23 9	4 39	17 41	18 0	18 57	21 59
28	14 24 52	7 57 24	11♓53	11 16	25 30	23 55	4 39	17 44	18 0	18 57	21 58
29	14 28 49	8 55 43	24 10	12 28	26 44	24 42	4 38	17 47	18 0	18 56	21 56
30	14 32 45	9♉54 1	6♈42	13♈42	27♈58	25♓28	4♍38	17♒50	17♑59	18♑56	21♏54

THE SUN ENTERS THE SIGN OF TAURUS ON APR 19 AT 19:58.

DAY	TIME h m s	☉ ° ' "	☽ ° '	☿ ° '	♀ ° '	♂ ° '	♃ ° '	♄ ° '	♅ ° '	♆ ° '	♇ ° '
M 1	14 36 42	10♉52 17	19♈32	14♈58	29♈12	26♓14	4♍38	17♒52	17♑59	18♑56	21♏53
A 2	14 40 38	11 50 31	2♉40	16 17	0♉26	27 0	4 38	17 55	17R58	18R55	21R51
Y 3	14 44 35	12 48 44	16 4	17 38	1 39	27 46	4 38	17 57	17 58	18 55	21 49
4	14 48 31	13 46 55	29 43	19 2	2 53	28 32	4 39	18 0	17 57	18 54	21 48
5	14 52 28	14 45 5	13♊34	20 27	4 7	29 19	4 40	18 2	17 57	18 54	21 46
6	14 56 24	15 43 12	27 33	21 55	5 21	0♈ 5	4 40	18 4	17 56	18 54	21 44
7	15 0 21	16 41 18	11♋39	23 24	6 35	0 51	4 41	18 7	17 55	18 53	21 43
8	15 4 18	17 39 22	25 47	24 56	7 48	1 37	4 43	18 9	17 55	18 53	21 41
9	15 8 14	18 37 23	9♌58	26 29	9 2	2 23	4 44	18 11	17 54	18 52	21 39
10	15 12 11	19 35 23	24 8	28 5	10 16	3 8	4 46	18 12	17 53	18 51	21 38
11	15 16 7	20 33 21	8♍16	29 43	11 30	3 54	4 47	18 14	17 52	18 51	21 36
12	15 20 4	21 31 17	22 21	1♉22	12 44	4 40	4 49	18 16	17 51	18 50	21 34
13	15 24 0	22 29 11	6♎20	3 4	13 57	5 26	4 52	18 17	17 50	18 49	21 33
14	15 27 57	23 27 4	20 10	4 48	15 11	6 12	4 54	18 19	17 49	18 49	21 31
15	15 31 53	24 24 54	3♏48	6 34	16 25	6 58	4 56	18 20	17 48	18 48	21 29
16	15 35 50	25 22 44	17 12	8 21	17 39	7 43	4 59	18 22	17 47	18 47	21 28
17	15 39 47	26 20 32	0♐20	10 11	18 52	8 29	5 2	18 23	17 46	18 46	21 26
18	15 43 43	27 18 18	13 11	12 3	20 6	9 15	5 5	18 24	17 44	18 45	21 24
19	15 47 40	28 16 3	25 45	13 57	21 20	10 0	5 8	18 25	17 43	18 45	21 23
20	15 51 36	29 13 47	8♑ 4	15 53	22 34	10 46	5 11	18 26	17 42	18 44	21 21
21	15 55 33	0♊11 30	20 10	17 50	23 47	11 31	5 15	18 27	17 40	18 43	21 19
22	15 59 29	1 9 11	2♒ 7	19 50	25 1	12 17	5 18	18 27	17 39	18 42	21 18
23	16 3 26	2 6 52	13 58	21 52	26 15	13 2	5 22	18 28	17 38	18 41	21 16
24	16 7 22	3 4 31	25 49	23 55	27 29	13 48	5 26	18 28	17 36	18 40	21 14
25	16 11 19	4 2 9	7♓45	26 0	28 42	14 33	5 30	18 29	17 35	18 39	21 13
26	16 15 16	4 59 47	19 49	28 7	29 56	15 19	5 35	18 29	17 33	18 38	21 11
27	16 19 12	5 57 23	2♈ 8	0♊15	1♊10	16 4	5 39	18 29	17 32	18 37	21 10
28	16 23 9	6 54 58	14 43	2 24	2 23	16 49	5 44	18R29	17 30	18 36	21 8
29	16 27 5	7 52 33	27 39	4 34	3 37	17 34	5 49	18 29	17 28	18 35	21 6
30	16 31 2	8 50 7	10♉57	6 45	4 51	18 20	5 53	18 29	17 27	18 34	21 5
31	16 34 58	9♊47 39	24♉36	8♊57	6♊ 5	19♈ 5	5♍59	18♒29	17♑25	18♑32	21♏ 3

THE SUN ENTERS THE SIGN OF GEMINI ON MAY 20 AT 19:13.

DAY	TIME h m s	☉ ° ' "	☽ ° '	☿ ° '	♀ ° '	♂ ° '	♃ ° '	♄ ° '	♅ ° '	♆ ° '	♇ ° '
J 1	16 38 55	10♊45 11	8♊35	11♊ 9	7♊18	19♈50	6♍ 4	18♒29	17♑23	18♑31	21♏ 2
U 2	16 42 51	11 42 42	22 49	13 21	8 32	20 35	6 9	18R28	17R21	18R30	21R 0
N 3	16 46 48	12 40 12	7♋15	15 33	9 46	21 20	6 15	18 28	17 20	18 29	20 59
E 4	16 50 45	13 37 41	21 46	17 44	10 59	22 5	6 20	18 27	17 18	18 28	20 57
5	16 54 41	14 35 8	6♌18	19 55	12 13	22 49	6 26	18 27	17 16	18 26	20 56
6	16 58 38	15 32 34	20 45	22 4	13 27	23 34	6 32	18 26	17 14	18 25	20 54
7	17 2 34	16 29 59	5♍ 4	24 13	14 41	24 19	6 38	18 25	17 12	18 24	20 53
8	17 6 31	17 27 23	19 12	26 20	15 54	25 4	6 45	18 24	17 10	18 22	20 51
9	17 10 27	18 24 46	3♎ 8	28 25	17 8	25 48	6 51	18 23	17 8	18 21	20 50
10	17 14 24	19 22 7	16 50	0♋28	18 22	26 33	6 58	18 22	17 6	18 20	20 48
11	17 18 20	20 19 28	0♏18	2 30	19 35	27 17	7 4	18 21	17 4	18 18	20 47
12	17 22 17	21 16 47	13 32	4 29	20 49	28 2	7 11	18 19	17 2	18 17	20 46
13	17 26 14	22 14 6	26 31	6 27	22 3	28 46	7 18	18 18	17 0	18 16	20 44
14	17 30 10	23 11 24	9♐17	8 22	23 17	29 31	7 25	18 16	16 58	18 14	20 43
15	17 34 7	24 8 42	21 50	10 14	24 30	0♉15	7 32	18 15	16 55	18 13	20 41
16	17 38 3	25 5 58	4♑10	12 5	25 44	0 59	7 40	18 13	16 53	18 11	20 40
17	17 42 0	26 3 14	16 20	13 53	26 58	1 43	7 47	18 11	16 51	18 10	20 39
18	17 45 56	27 0 30	28 21	15 39	28 11	2 27	7 55	18 9	16 49	18 8	20 38
19	17 49 53	27 57 45	10♒15	17 22	29 25	3 11	8 2	18 7	16 47	18 7	20 36
20	17 53 50	28 55 0	22 6	19 3	0♋39	3 55	8 10	18 5	16 44	18 5	20 35
21	17 57 46	29 52 15	3♓57	20 42	1 52	4 39	8 18	18 3	16 42	18 4	20 34
22	18 1 43	0♋49 29	15 52	22 18	3 6	5 23	8 26	18 1	16 40	18 2	20 33
23	18 5 39	1 46 43	27 56	23 52	4 20	6 7	8 34	17 58	16 38	18 1	20 32
24	18 9 36	2 43 57	10♈13	25 23	5 34	6 51	8 43	17 56	16 35	17 59	20 30
25	18 13 32	3 41 11	22 47	26 52	6 47	7 34	8 51	17 54	16 33	17 58	20 29
26	18 17 29	4 38 25	5♉42	28 18	8 1	8 18	9 0	17 51	16 31	17 56	20 28
27	18 21 25	5 35 39	19 1	29 42	9 15	9 1	9 8	17 48	16 28	17 55	20 27
28	18 25 22	6 32 53	2♊45	1♌ 3	10 29	9 45	9 17	17 46	16 26	17 53	20 26
29	18 29 19	7 30 7	16 54	2 22	11 42	10 28	9 26	17 43	16 23	17 51	20 25
30	18 33 15	8♋27 21	1♋24	3♌38	12♋56	11♉11	9♍35	17♒40	16♑21	17♑50	20♏24

THE SUN ENTERS THE SIGN OF CANCER ON JUN 21 AT 03:15.

♏ SCORPIO ♐ SAGITTARIUS ♑ CAPRICORN ♒ AQUARIUS ♓ PISCES

SIDEREAL SUN MOON MERCURY VENUS MARS JUPITER SATURN URANUS NEPTUNE PLUTO

DAY	TIME	☉	☽	☿	♀	♂	♃	♄	♅	♆	♇
	h m s	° ' "	° '	° '	° '	° '	° '	° '	° '	° '	° '
J 1	18 37 12	9♋24 35	16♋10	4♌52	14♋10	11♉55	9♍44	17♒37	16♑19	17♑48	20♏23
U 2	18 41 8	10 21 49	1♌ 5	6 2	15 24	12 38	9 53	17R34	16R16	17R47	20R22
L 3	18 45 5	11 19 3	16 1	7 10	16 37	13 21	10 2	17 31	16 14	17 45	20 21
Y 4	18 49 1	12 16 16	0♍50	8 15	17 51	14 4	10 12	17 28	16 11	17 43	20 21
5	18 52 58	13 13 29	15 26	9 17	19 5	14 47	10 21	17 24	16 9	17 42	20 20
6	18 56 54	14 10 41	29 43	10 16	20 19	15 29	10 31	17 21	16 7	17 40	20 19
7	19 0 51	15 7 54	13♎40	11 11	21 32	16 12	10 40	17 18	16 4	17 38	20 18
8	19 4 48	16 5 6	27 16	12 4	22 46	16 55	10 50	17 14	16 2	17 37	20 17
9	19 8 44	17 2 18	10♏31	12 53	24 0	17 37	11 0	17 11	15 59	17 35	20 17
10	19 12 41	17 59 30	23 28	13 38	25 14	18 20	11 10	17 7	15 57	17 34	20 16
11	19 16 37	18 56 42	6♐ 9	14 20	26 28	19 2	11 20	17 4	15 54	17 32	20 15
12	19 20 34	19 53 54	18 36	14 58	27 41	19 45	11 30	17 0	15 52	17 30	20 15
13	19 24 30	20 51 6	0♑53	15 32	28 55	20 27	11 40	16 56	15 50	17 29	20 14
14	19 28 27	21 48 18	13 0	16 2	0♌ 9	21 9	11 50	16 52	15 47	17 27	20 14
15	19 32 23	22 45 31	25 0	16 28	1 23	21 51	12 1	16 48	15 45	17 26	20 13
16	19 36 20	23 42 44	6♒55	16 49	2 36	22 33	12 11	16 45	15 42	17 24	20 13
17	19 40 17	24 39 57	18 46	17 6	3 50	23 15	12 22	16 41	15 40	17 22	20 12
18	19 44 13	25 37 10	0♓37	17 18	5 4	23 57	12 32	16 37	15 38	17 21	20 12
19	19 48 10	26 34 25	12 29	17 26	6 18	24 38	12 43	16 33	15 35	17 19	20 11
20	19 52 6	27 31 40	24 25	17R29	7 32	25 20	12 54	16 29	15 33	17 18	20 11
21	19 56 3	28 28 55	6♈29	17 26	8 45	26 1	13 5	16 24	15 31	17 16	20 11
22	19 59 59	29 26 12	18 45	17 19	9 59	26 43	13 16	16 20	15 28	17 14	20 10
23	20 3 56	0♌23 29	1♉16	17 7	11 13	27 24	13 26	16 16	15 26	17 13	20 10
24	20 7 52	1 20 47	14 6	16 50	12 27	28 5	13 38	16 12	15 24	17 11	20 10
25	20 11 49	2 18 6	27 20	16 28	13 41	28 47	13 49	16 8	15 21	17 10	20 9
26	20 15 46	3 15 26	10♊59	16 2	14 54	29 28	14 0	16 3	15 19	17 8	20 9
27	20 19 42	4 12 47	25 6	15 32	16 8	0♊ 9	14 11	15 59	15 17	17 7	20 9
28	20 23 39	5 10 9	9♋39	14 57	17 22	0 49	14 22	15 55	15 15	17 5	20 9
29	20 27 35	6 7 32	24 33	14 20	18 36	1 30	14 34	15 50	15 12	17 4	20 9
30	20 31 32	7 4 56	9♌42	13 39	19 50	2 11	14 45	15 46	15 10	17 2	20D 9
31	20 35 28	8♌ 2 20	24♌55	12♌56	21♌ 3	2♊51	14♍57	15♒41	15♑ 8	17♑ 1	20♏ 9

THE SUN ENTERS THE SIGN OF LEO ON JUL 22 AT 14:10.

DAY	TIME	☉	☽	☿	♀	♂	♃	♄	♅	♆	♇
	h m s	° ' "	° '	° '	° '	° '	° '	° '	° '	° '	° '
A 1	20 39 25	8♌59 45	10♍ 3	12♌11	22♌17	3♊32	15♍ 8	15♒37	15♑ 6	16♑59	20♏ 9
U 2	20 43 21	9 57 11	24 56	11R26	23 31	4 12	15 20	15R32	15R 4	16R58	20 9
G 3	20 47 18	10 54 37	9♎27	10 41	24 45	4 52	15 32	15 28	15 2	16 56	20 9
U 4	20 51 15	11 52 4	23 32	9 56	25 59	5 32	15 43	15 24	15 0	16 55	20 9
S 5	20 55 11	12 49 32	7♏10	9 13	27 13	6 12	15 55	15 19	14 58	16 53	20 9
T 6	20 59 8	13 47 0	20 22	8 33	28 26	6 52	16 7	15 15	14 56	16 52	20 9
7	21 3 4	14 44 30	3♐12	7 55	29 40	7 32	16 19	15 10	14 54	16 50	20 10
8	21 7 1	15 42 0	15 42	7 22	0♍54	8 11	16 31	15 6	14 52	16 49	20 10
9	21 10 57	16 39 30	27 58	6 54	2 8	8 51	16 43	15 1	14 50	16 48	20 10
10	21 14 54	17 37 2	10♑ 3	6 31	3 22	9 30	16 55	14 57	14 48	16 46	20 11
11	21 18 51	18 34 35	22 1	6 13	4 35	10 9	17 7	14 52	14 46	16 45	20 11
12	21 22 47	19 32 9	3♒54	6 2	5 49	10 48	17 19	14 48	14 44	16 44	20 11
13	21 26 44	20 29 43	15 45	5D58	7 3	11 27	17 31	14 43	14 42	16 42	20 12
14	21 30 40	21 27 19	27 36	6 1	8 17	12 6	17 43	14 39	14 40	16 41	20 12
15	21 34 37	22 24 56	9♓28	6 11	9 30	12 45	17 56	14 34	14 39	16 40	20 13
16	21 38 33	23 22 35	21 24	6 28	10 44	13 24	18 8	14 30	14 37	16 39	20 13
17	21 42 30	24 20 15	3♈25	6 52	11 58	14 2	18 20	14 25	14 35	16 38	20 14
18	21 46 26	25 17 56	15 33	7 24	13 12	14 41	18 33	14 21	14 34	16 36	20 14
19	21 50 23	26 15 39	27 50	8 3	14 26	15 19	18 45	14 17	14 32	16 35	20 15
20	21 54 19	27 13 23	10♉21	8 49	15 39	15 57	18 58	14 12	14 30	16 34	20 16
21	21 58 16	28 11 9	23 9	9 42	16 53	16 35	19 10	14 8	14 29	16 33	20 16
22	22 2 13	29 8 57	6♊16	10 42	18 7	17 13	19 23	14 4	14 27	16 32	20 17
23	22 6 9	0♍ 6 47	19 48	11 49	19 21	17 50	19 35	14 0	14 26	16 31	20 18
24	22 10 6	1 4 39	3♋45	13 1	20 34	18 28	19 48	13 55	14 24	16 30	20 19
25	22 14 2	2 2 32	18 9	14 20	21 48	19 5	20 0	13 51	14 23	16 29	20 20
26	22 17 59	3 0 27	2♌57	15 44	23 2	19 43	20 13	13 47	14 22	16 28	20 20
27	22 21 55	3 58 23	18 3	17 13	24 16	20 20	20 26	13 43	14 20	16 27	20 21
28	22 25 52	4 56 21	3♍19	18 47	25 29	20 57	20 38	13 39	14 19	16 26	20 22
29	22 29 48	5 54 21	18 34	20 25	26 43	21 34	20 51	13 35	14 18	16 25	20 23
30	22 33 45	6 52 22	3♎37	22 7	27 57	22 10	21 4	13 31	14 17	16 24	20 24
31	22 37 42	7♍50 24	18♎18	23♌52	29♍10	22♊47	21♍17	13♒27	14♑16	16♑23	20♏25

THE SUN ENTERS THE SIGN OF VIRGO ON AUG 22 AT 21:11.

DAY	TIME	☉	☽	☿	♀	♂	♃	♄	♅	♆	♇
	h m s	° ' "	° '	° '	° '	° '	° '	° '	° '	° '	° '
S 1	22 41 38	8♍48 29	2♏32	25♌40	0♎24	23♊23	21♍29	13♒23	14♑15	16♑22	20♏26
E 2	22 45 35	9 46 34	16 17	27 30	1 38	23 59	21 42	13R20	14R14	16R21	20 27
P 3	22 49 31	10 44 41	29 32	29 22	2 51	24 35	21 55	13 16	14 13	16 21	20 28
T 4	22 53 28	11 42 49	12♐22	1♍15	4 5	25 11	22 8	13 12	14 12	16 20	20 30
E 5	22 57 24	12 40 59	24 50	3 10	5 19	25 47	22 21	13 9	14 11	16 19	20 31
M 6	23 1 21	13 39 10	7♑ 2	5 5	6 32	26 22	22 34	13 5	14 10	16 18	20 32
B 7	23 5 17	14 37 23	19 2	7 1	7 46	26 57	22 47	13 2	14 9	16 18	20 33
E 8	23 9 14	15 35 37	0♒55	8 57	9 0	27 33	23 0	12 58	14 8	16 17	20 35
R 9	23 13 11	16 33 53	12 45	10 52	10 13	28 8	23 13	12 55	14 8	16 17	20 36
10	23 17 7	17 32 10	24 35	12 48	11 27	28 42	23 25	12 51	14 7	16 16	20 37
11	23 21 4	18 30 29	6♓28	14 43	12 40	29 17	23 38	12 48	14 6	16 15	20 39
12	23 25 0	19 28 50	18 26	16 37	13 54	29 51	23 51	12 45	14 6	16 15	20 40
13	23 28 57	20 27 13	0♈29	18 31	15 7	0♋25	24 4	12 42	14 5	16 14	20 41
14	23 32 53	21 25 37	12 39	20 24	16 21	1 0	24 17	12 39	14 5	16 14	20 43
15	23 36 50	22 24 4	24 56	22 16	17 35	1 33	24 30	12 36	14 4	16 14	20 44
16	23 40 46	23 22 32	7♉23	24 7	18 48	2 7	24 43	12 33	14 4	16 13	20 46
17	23 44 43	24 21 3	20 1	25 57	20 2	2 40	24 56	12 30	14 4	16 13	20 47
18	23 48 40	25 19 36	2♊52	27 46	21 15	3 14	25 9	12 28	14 3	16 12	20 49
19	23 52 36	26 18 11	16 0	29 34	22 29	3 47	25 22	12 25	14 3	16 12	20 50
20	23 56 33	27 16 49	29 26	1♎22	23 42	4 19	25 35	12 23	14 3	16 12	20 52
21	0 0 29	28 15 28	13♋14	3 8	24 55	4 52	25 48	12 20	14 3	16 12	20 54
22	0 4 26	29 14 10	27 24	4 53	26 9	5 24	26 1	12 18	14D 3	16 11	20 55
23	0 8 22	0♎12 54	11♌56	6 37	27 22	5 57	26 14	12 16	14 3	16 11	20 57
24	0 12 19	1 11 40	26 47	8 21	28 36	6 28	26 27	12 13	14 3	16 11	20 59
25	0 16 15	2 10 29	11♍49	10 3	29 49	7 0	26 40	12 11	14 3	16 11	21 0
26	0 20 12	3 9 19	26 54	11 44	1♏ 3	7 32	26 53	12 9	14 3	16 11	21 2
27	0 24 8	4 8 11	11♎52	13 25	2 16	8 3	27 6	12 7	14 3	16D11	21 4
28	0 28 5	5 7 6	26 32	15 4	3 29	8 34	27 19	12 5	14 3	16 11	21 6
29	0 32 2	6 6 2	10♏49	16 43	4 43	9 4	27 32	12 4	14 4	16 11	21 8
30	0 35 58	7♎ 5 1	24♏38	18♎21	5♏56	9♋35	27♍45	12♒ 2	14♑ 4	16♑11	21♏10

THE SUN ENTERS THE SIGN OF LIBRA ON SEP 22 AT 18:44.

♈ ARIES ♉ TAURUS ♊ GEMINI ♋ CANCER ♌ LEO ♍ VIRGO ♎ LIBRA

SIDEREAL TIME · SUN · MOON · MERCURY · VENUS · MARS · JUPITER · SATURN · URANUS · NEPTUNE · PLUTO

DAY	TIME	☉	☽	☿	♀	♂	♃	♄	♅	♆	♇
	h m s	° ' "	° '	° '	° '	° '	° '	° '	° '	° '	° '
O 1	0 39 55	8♎ 4 1	7♐57	19♎57	7♏ 9	10♋ 5	27♍58	12♒ 1	14♑ 4	16♑11	21♏11
C 2	0 43 51	9 3 2	20 51	21 33	8 23	10 35	28 11	11R59	14 5	16 11	21 13
T 3	0 47 48	10 2 6	3♑21	23 9	9 36	11 4	28 23	11 58	14 5	16 11	21 15
O 4	0 51 44	11 1 12	15 34	24 43	10 49	11 34	28 36	11 57	14 6	16 12	21 17
B 5	0 55 41	12 0 19	27 34	26 16	12 3	12 3	28 49	11 55	14 6	16 12	21 19
E 6	0 59 37	12 59 27	9♒27	27 49	13 16	12 31	29 2	11 54	14 7	16 12	21 21
R 7	1 3 34	13 58 38	21 17	29 21	14 29	13 0	29 15	11 53	14 8	16 12	21 23
8	1 7 31	14 57 51	3♓ 9	0♏52	15 42	13 28	29 27	11 53	14 8	16 13	21 25
9	1 11 27	15 57 5	15 5	2 23	16 55	13 56	29 40	11 52	14 9	16 13	21 27
10	1 15 24	16 56 21	27 9	3 52	18 8	14 23	29 53	11 51	14 10	16 13	21 29
11	1 19 20	17 55 39	9♈22	5 21	19 22	14 50	0♎ 6	11 51	14 11	16 14	21 31
12	1 23 17	18 54 59	21 45	6 49	20 35	15 17	0 18	11 50	14 12	16 14	21 33
13	1 27 13	19 54 22	4♉18	8 -16	21 48	15 44	0 31	11 50	14 13	16 15	21 36
14	1 31 10	20 53 46	17 1	9 42	23 1	16 10	0 43	11 49	14 14	16 15	21 38
15	1 35 6	21 53 13	29 55	11 8	24 14	16 36	0 56	11 49	14 15	16 16	21 40
16	1 39 3	22 52 41	13♊ 0	12 33	25 27	17 2	1 9	11D49	14 16	16 16	21 42
17	1 43 0	23 52 12	26 18	13 57	26 40	17 27	1 21	11 49	14 17	16 17	21 44
18	1 46 56	24 51 46	9♋49	15 20	27 53	17 52	1 33	11 49	14 19	16 18	21 46
19	1 50 53	25 51 22	23 35	16 42	29 6	18 16	1 46	11 50	14 20	16 18	21 49
20	1 54 49	26 51 0	7♌37	18 3	0♐19	18 40	1 58	11 50	14 21	16 19	21 51
21	1 58 46	27 50 40	21 53	19 23	1 32	19 4	2 11	11 50	14 23	16 20	21 53
22	2 2 42	28 50 22	6♍23	20 41	2 45	19 27	2 23	11 51	14 24	16 21	21 55
23	2 6 39	29 50 7	21 1	21 59	3 58	19 50	2 35	11 52	14 26	16 21	21 58
24	2 10 35	0♏49 54	5♎42	23 15	5 10	20 13	2 47	11 52	14 27	16 22	22 0
25	2 14 32	1 49 43	20 19	24 30	6 23	20 35	3 0	11 53	14 29	16 23	22 2
26	2 18 29	2 49 34	4♏43	25 44	7 36	20 56	3 12	11 54	14 30	16 24	22 4
27	2 22 25	3 49 27	18 49	26 55	8 49	21 17	3 24	11 55	14 32	16 25	22 7
28	2 26 22	4 49 22	2♐33	28 5	10 2	21 38	3 36	11 56	14 34	16 26	22 9
29	2 30 18	5 49 19	15 52	29 13	11 14	21 58	3 48	11 58	14 35	16 27	22 11
30	2 34 15	6 49 17	28 46	0♐19	12 27	22 18	4 0	11 59	14 37	16 28	22 14
31	2 38 11	7♏49 18	11♑20	1♐22	13♐40	22♋37	4♎11	12♒ 1	14♑39	16♑29	22♏16

THE SUN ENTERS THE SIGN OF SCORPIO ON OCT 23 AT 03:59.

DAY	TIME	☉	☽	☿	♀	♂	♃	♄	♅	♆	♇
	h m s	° ' "	° '	° '	° '	° '	° '	° '	° '	° '	° '
N 1	2 42 8	8♏49 19	23♑35	2♐22	14♐53	22♋56	4♎23	12♒ 2	14♑41	16♑30	22♏18
O 2	2 46 4	9 49 23	5♒38	3 20	16 5	23 14	4 35	12 4	14 43	16 31	22 21
V 3	2 50 1	10 49 28	17 32	4 13	17 18	23 32	4 47	12 6	14 45	16 33	22 23
E 4	2 53 58	11 49 34	29 24	5 3	18 30	23 49	4 58	12 7	14 47	16 34	22 26
M 5	2 57 54	12 49 42	11♓17	5 49	19 43	24 6	5 10	12 9	14 49	16 35	22 28
B 6	3 1 51	13 49 52	23 16	6 30	20 55	24 22	5 21	12 11	14 51	16 36	22 30
E 7	3 5 47	14 50 3	5♈25	7 6	22 8	24 38	5 33	12 14	14 53	16 37	22 33
R 8	3 9 44	15 50 16	17 46	7 35	23 20	24 53	5 44	12 16	14 56	16 39	22 35
9	3 13 40	16 50 30	0♉21	7 58	24 32	25 7	5 55	12 18	14 58	16 40	22 38
10	3 17 37	17 50 46	13 11	8 14	25 45	25 21	6 6	12 21	15 0	16 41	22 40
11	3 21 33	18 51 4	26 14	8R22	26 57	25 35	6 18	12 23	15 2	16 43	22 42
12	3 25 30	19 51 24	9♊31	8 21	28 9	25 47	6 29	12 26	15 5	16 44	22 45
13	3 29 27	20 51 45	23 0	8 11	29 21	25 59	6 40	12 29	15 7	16 46	22 47
14	3 33 23	21 52 9	6♋40	7 51	0♑34	26 11	6 51	12 31	15 10	16 47	22 50
15	3 37 20	22 52 34	20 29	7 21	1 46	26 22	7 1	12 34	15 12	16 49	22 52
16	3 41 16	23 53 1	4♌26	6 41	2 58	26 32	7 12	12 37	15 15	16 50	22 54
17	3 45 13	24 53 29	18 30	5 50	4 10	26 41	7 23	12 40	15 17	16 52	22 57
18	3 49 9	25 54 0	2♍40	4 50	5 22	26 50	7 33	12 44	15 20	16 53	22 59
19	3 53 6	26 54 33	16 54	3 42	6 34	26 58	7 44	12 47	15 22	16 55	23 2
20	3 57 2	27 55 7	1♎ 9	2 27	7 45	27 5	7 54	12 50	15 25	16 57	23 4
21	4 0 59	28 55 43	15 22	1 7	8 57	27 12	8 5	12 54	15 28	16 58	23 6
22	4 4 56	29 56 21	29 29	29♏45	10 9	27 18	8 15	12 57	15 30	17 0	23 9
23	4 8 52	0♐57 0	13♏26	28 24	11 21	27 23	8 25	13 1	15 33	17 2	23 11
24	4 12 49	1 57 41	27 10	27 7	12 32	27 27	8 35	13 5	15 36	17 3	23 14
25	4 16 45	2 58 23	10♐36	25 55	13 44	27 31	8 45	13 8	15 39	17 5	23 16
26	4 20 42	3 59 7	23 44	24 51	14 55	27 34	8 55	13 12	15 42	17 7	23 18
27	4 24 38	4 59 52	6♑34	23 57	16 7	27 36	9 5	13 16	15 45	17 9	23 21
28	4 28 35	6 0 38	19 5	23 14	17 18	27R37	9 14	13 20	15 48	17 10	23 23
29	4 32 31	7 1 25	1♒21	22 42	18 30	27 37	9 24	13 25	15 50	17 12	23 26
30	4 36 28	8♐ 2 13	13♒25	22♏22	19♑41	27♋37	9♎33	13♒29	15♑53	17♑14	23♏28

THE SUN ENTERS THE SIGN OF SAGITTARIUS ON NOV 22 AT 01:27.

DAY	TIME	☉	☽	☿	♀	♂	♃	♄	♅	♆	♇
	h m s	° ' "	° '	° '	° '	° '	° '	° '	° '	° '	° '
D 1	4 40 25	9♐ 3 2	25♒21	22♏13	20♑52	27♋36	9♎42	13♒33	15♑56	17♑16	23♏30
E 2	4 44 21	10 3 52	7♓13	22D15	22 3	27R34	9 52	13 38	16 0	17 18	23 33
C 3	4 48 18	11 4 43	19 6	22 27	23 14	27 31	10 1	13 42	16 3	17 20	23 35
E 4	4 52 14	12 5 34	1♈ 6	22 48	24 25	27 27	10 10	13 47	16 6	17 22	23 37
M 5	4 56 11	13 6 27	13 15	23 18	25 36	27 22	10 19	13 51	16 9	17 24	23 40
B 6	5 0 7	14 7 20	25 39	23 55	26 47	27 17	10 27	13 56	16 12	17 26	23 42
E 7	5 4 4	15 8 14	8♉20	24 40	27 57	27 11	10 36	14 1	16 15	17 28	23 44
R 8	5 8 0	16 9 9	21 21	25 30	29 8	27 4	10 45	14 5	16 18	17 30	23 46
9	5 11 57	17 10 5	4♊41	26 25	0♒18	26 56	10 53	14 10	16 21	17 32	23 49
10	5 15 54	18 11 2	18 21	27 25	1 28	26 47	11 1	14 15	16 25	17 34	23 51
11	5 19 50	19 12 0	2♋17	28 29	2 39	26 37	11 10	14 20	16 28	17 36	23 53
12	5 23 47	20 12 58	16 25	29 37	3 49	26 27	11 18	14 26	16 31	17 38	23 55
13	5 27 43	21 13 58	0♌43	0♐47	4 59	26 15	11 25	14 31	16 35	17 40	23 58
14	5 31 40	22 14 58	15 5	2 0	6 8	26 3	11 33	14 36	16 38	17 42	24 0
15	5 35 36	23 16 0	29 26	3 16	7 18	25 50	11 41	14 41	16 41	17 44	24 2
16	5 39 33	24 17 2	13♍44	4 33	8 28	25 36	11 48	14 47	16 45	17 46	24 4
17	5 43 29	25 18 5	27 54	5 52	9 37	25 22	11 56	14 52	16 48	17 48	24 6
18	5 47 26	26 19 10	11♎56	7 13	10 47	25 7	12 3	14 58	16 51	17 50	24 9
19	5 51 23	27 20 15	25 48	8 35	11 56	24 50	12 10	15 3	16 55	17 53	24 11
20	5 55 19	28 21 21	9♏28	9 58	13 5	24 34	12 17	15 9	16 58	17 55	24 13
21	5 59 16	29 22 28	22 57	11 22	14 14	24 16	12 24	15 15	17 2	17 57	24 15
22	6 3 12	0♑23 36	6♐12	12 48	15 23	23 58	12 31	15 20	17 5	17 59	24 17
23	6 7 9	1 24 44	19 15	14 14	16 31	23 39	12 37	15 26	17 9	18 1	24 19
24	6 11 5	2 25 53	2♑ 5	15 40	17 40	23 19	12 44	15 32	17 12	18 3	24 21
25	6 15 2	3 27 2	14 41	17 7	18 48	22 59	12 50	15 38	17 15	18 6	24 23
26	6 18 59	4 28 11	27 4	18 35	19 56	22 39	12 56	15 44	17 19	18 8	24 25
27	6 22 55	5 29 21	9♒16	20 4	21 4	22 17	13 2	15 50	17 22	18 10	24 27
28	6 26 52	6 30 30	21 18	21 33	22 12	21 56	13 8	15 56	17 26	18 12	24 29
29	6 30 48	7 31 40	3♓14	23 2	23 19	21 34	13 13	16 2	17 30	18 15	24 31
30	6 34 45	8 32 49	15 6	24 32	24 27	21 11	13 19	16 9	17 33	18 17	24 33
31	6 38 41	9♑33 59	26♓58	26♐ 2	25♒34	20♋48	13♎24	16♒15	17♑37	18♑19	24♏34

THE SUN ENTERS THE SIGN OF CAPRICORN ON DEC 21 AT 14:44.

♏ SCORPIO ♐ SAGITTARIUS ♑ CAPRICORN ♒ AQUARIUS ♓ PISCES

1993

SIDEREAL · SUN. · MOON. · MERCURY. · VENUS. · MARS. · JUPITER. · SATURN. · URANUS. · NEPTUNE. · PLUTO.

DAY	TIME h	m	s	☉ ° ' "	☽ ° '	☿ ° '	♀ ° '	♂ ° '	♃ ° '	♄ ° '	♅ ° '	♆ ° '	♇ ° '
J 1	6	42	38	10♑35 8	8♈55	27♐33	26♒41	20♋25	13♎29	16♒21	17♑40	18♑21	24♏36
A 2	6	46	34	11 36 17	21 1	29 4	27 48	20R 2	13 34	16 27	17 44	18 24	24 38
N 3	6	50	31	12 37 26	3♉22	0♑35	28 54	19 38	13 39	16 34	17 47	18 26	24 40
U 4	6	54	28	13 38 35	16 1	2 7	0♓ 0	19 14	13 43	16 40	17 51	18 28	24 42
A 5	6	58	24	14 39 44	29 3	3 39	1 6	18 50	13 48	16 47	17 54	18 30	24 43
R 6	7	2	21	15 40 52	12♊30	5 11	2 12	18 27	13 52	16 53	17 58	18 33	24 45
Y 7	7	6	17	16 42 0	26 22	6 44	3 17	18 3	13 56	17 0	18 2	18 35	24 47
8	7	10	14	17 43 8	10♋37	8 18	4 23	17 39	14 0	17 6	18 5	18 37	24 49
9	7	14	10	18 44 15	25 11	9 51	5 28	17 15	14 4	17 13	18 9	18 40	24 50
10	7	18	7	19 45 22	9♌58	11 26	6 32	16 51	14 8	17 20	18 12	18 42	24 52
11	7	22	3	20 46 29	24 50	13 0	7 36	16 27	14 11	17 26	18 16	18 44	24 53
12	7	26	0	21 47 36	9♍38	14 35	8 41	16 4	14 14	17 33	18 19	18 46	24 55
13	7	29	57	22 48 43	24 16	16 11	9 44	15 41	14 18	17 40	18 23	18 49	24 56
14	7	33	53	23 49 50	8♎38	17 46	10 48	15 18	14 20	17 47	18 27	18 51	24 58
15	7	37	50	24 50 56	22 41	19 23	11 51	14 56	14 23	17 53	18 30	18 53	24 59
16	7	41	46	25 52 3	6♏25	21 0	12 53	14 34	14 26	18 0	18 34	18 55	25 1
17	7	45	43	26 53 9	19 50	22 37	13 56	14 12	14 28	18 7	18 37	18 58	25 2
18	7	49	39	27 54 15	2♐58	24 15	14 58	13 51	14 30	18 14	18 41	19 0	25 4
19	7	53	36	28 55 21	15 52	25 54	15 59	13 30	14 32	18 21	18 44	19 2	25 5
20	7	57	32	29 56 27	28 32	27 33	17 0	13 10	14 34	18 28	18 48	19 4	25 6
21	8	1	29	0♒57 32	11♑ 2	29 12	18 1	12 50	14 36	18 35	18 51	19 7	25 8
22	8	5	26	1 58 36	23 22	0♒53	19 1	12 31	14 37	18 42	18 55	19 9	25 9
23	8	9	22	2 59 40	5♒34	2 33	20 1	12 13	14 38	18 49	18 58	19 11	25 10
24	8	13	19	4 0 43	17 38	4 15	21 1	11 55	14 39	18 56	19 2	19 13	25 11
25	8	17	15	5 1 45	29 36	5 57	22 0	11 38	14 40	19 3	19 5	19 16	25 12
26	8	21	12	6 2 46	11♓30	7 39	22 58	11 22	14 41	19 10	19 9	19 18	25 14
27	8	25	8	7 3 46	23 21	9 22	23 56	11 7	14 41	19 17	19 12	19 20	25 15
28	8	29	5	8 4 45	5♈12	11 6	24 53	10 52	14R42	19 25	19 16	19 22	25 16
29	8	33	1	9 5 42	17 7	12 51	25 50	10 38	14 42	19 32	19 19	19 24	25 17
30	8	36	58	10 6 39	29 10	14 35	26 47	10 24	14 42	19 39	19 22	19 27	25 18
31	8	40	55	11♒ 7 35	11♉26	16♒21	27♓42	10♋12	14♎41	19♒46	19♑26	19♑29	25♏19

THE SUN ENTERS THE SIGN OF AQUARIUS ON JAN 20 AT 01:24.

DAY	TIME h	m	s	☉ ° ' "	☽ ° '	☿ ° '	♀ ° '	♂ ° '	♃ ° '	♄ ° '	♅ ° '	♆ ° '	♇ ° '
F 1	8	44	51	12♒ 8 29	23♉59	18♒ 7	28♓37	10♋ 0	14♎41	19♒53	19♑29	19♑31	25♏20
E 2	8	48	48	13 9 22	6♊55	19 53	29 32	9R49	14R40	20 0	19 33	19 33	25 20
B 3	8	52	44	14 10 13	20 16	21 40	0♈25	9 39	14 39	20 8	19 36	19 35	25 21
R 4	8	56	41	15 11 4	4♋ 7	23 26	1 18	9 30	14 38	20 15	19 39	19 37	25 22
U 5	9	0	37	16 11 53	18 26	25 13	2 11	9 22	14 37	20 22	19 42	19 39	25 23
A 6	9	4	34	17 12 40	3♌11	27 0	3 2	9 14	14 36	20 29	19 46	19 41	25 24
R 7	9	8	30	18 13 26	18 16	28 47	3 53	9 7	14 34	20 37	19 49	19 43	25 24
Y 8	9	12	27	19 14 11	3♍30	0♓34	4 43	9 1	14 32	20 44	19 52	19 45	25 25
9	9	16	24	20 14 55	18 43	2 20	5 32	8 56	14 30	20 51	19 55	19 47	25 26
10	9	20	20	21 15 37	3♎44	4 5	6 20	8 51	14 28	20 58	19 59	19 50	25 26
11	9	24	17	22 16 19	18 26	5 49	7 8	8 48	14 26	21 5	20 2	19 52	25 27
12	9	28	13	23 16 59	2♏42	7 32	7 54	8 45	14 23	21 13	20 5	19 53	25 27
13	9	32	10	24 17 39	16 31	9 13	8 39	8 43	14 20	21 20	20 8	19 55	25 28
14	9	36	6	25 18 17	29 55	10 51	9 24	8 41	14 17	21 27	20 11	19 57	25 28
15	9	40	3	26 18 54	12♐56	12 27	10 7	8D41	14 14	21 34	20 14	19 59	25 29
16	9	43	59	27 19 30	25 39	13 59	10 50	8 41	14 11	21 42	20 17	20 1	25 29
17	9	47	56	28 20 5	8♑ 5	15 27	11 31	8 42	14 8	21 49	20 20	20 3	25 30
18	9	51	53	29 20 39	20 21	16 50	12 11	8 43	14 4	21 56	20 23	20 5	25 30
19	9	55	49	0♓21 11	2♒28	18 9	12 49	8 46	14 0	22 3	20 26	20 7	25 30
20	9	59	46	1 21 41	14 29	19 21	13 27	8 49	13 56	22 10	20 29	20 9	25 31
21	10	3	42	2 22 10	26 25	20 27	14 3	8 52	13 52	22 18	20 32	20 11	25 31
22	10	7	39	3 22 38	8♓19	21 25	14 38	8 57	13 48	22 25	20 35	20 12	25 31
23	10	11	35	4 23 4	20 11	22 16	15 11	9 2	13 43	22 32	20 38	20 14	25 31
24	10	15	32	5 23 28	2♈ 3	22 58	15 43	9 8	13 39	22 39	20 40	20 16	25 31
25	10	19	28	6 23 50	13 56	23 31	16 14	9 14	13 34	22 46	20 43	20 18	25 31
26	10	23	25	7 24 10	25 53	23 54	16 42	9 21	13 29	22 53	20 46	20 19	25R31
27	10	27	22	8 24 29	7♉57	24R 9	17 9	9 29	13 24	23 0	20 49	20 21	25 31
28	10	31	18	9♓24 46	20♉12	24♓13	17♈35	9♋37	13♎19	23♒ 7	20♑51	20♑23	25♏31

THE SUN ENTERS THE SIGN OF PISCES ON FEB 18 AT 15:36.

DAY	TIME h	m	s	☉ ° ' "	☽ ° '	☿ ° '	♀ ° '	♂ ° '	♃ ° '	♄ ° '	♅ ° '	♆ ° '	♇ ° '
M 1	10	35	15	10♓25 0	2♊41	24♓ 8	17♈58	9♋46	13♎13	23♒14	20♑54	20♑24	25♏31
A 2	10	39	11	11 25 13	15 30	23R53	18 20	9 56	13R 8	23 21	20 57	20 26	25R31
R 3	10	43	8	12 25 24	28 43	23 29	18 40	10 6	13 2	23 28	20 59	20 27	25 31
C 4	10	47	4	13 25 32	12♋24	22 57	18 58	10 17	12 56	23 35	21 2	20 29	25 31
H 5	10	51	1	14 25 38	26 34	22 18	19 13	10 28	12 50	23 42	21 4	20 31	25 31
6	10	54	57	15 25 43	11♌13	21 31	19 27	10 40	12 44	23 49	21 7	20 32	25 30
7	10	58	54	16 25 45	26 16	20 40	19 38	10 52	12 38	23 56	21 9	20 34	25 30
8	11	2	51	17 25 45	11♍34	19 44	19 48	11 5	12 32	24 3	21 11	20 35	25 30
9	11	6	47	18 25 43	26 57	18 46	19 54	11 18	12 25	24 10	21 14	20 36	25 29
10	11	10	44	19 25 39	12♎12	17 46	19 59	11 32	12 19	24 17	21 16	20 38	25 29
11	11	14	40	20 25 34	27 8	16 46	20R 1	11 47	12 12	24 23	21 18	20 39	25 29
12	11	18	37	21 25 27	11♏39	15 48	20 1	12 1	12 5	24 30	21 20	20 40	25 28
13	11	22	33	22 25 18	25 41	14 52	19 58	12 17	11 58	24 37	21 22	20 42	25 28
14	11	26	30	23 25 8	9♐13	14 0	19 53	12 32	11 51	24 43	21 25	20 43	25 27
15	11	30	26	24 24 56	22 18	13 12	19 45	12 49	11 44	24 50	21 27	20 44	25 27
16	11	34	23	25 24 42	5♑ 0	12 30	19 35	13 5	11 37	24 57	21 29	20 46	25 26
17	11	38	19	26 24 27	17 23	11 52	19 23	13 22	11 30	25 3	21 31	20 47	25 26
18	11	42	16	27 24 9	29 33	11 21	19 8	13 40	11 23	25 10	21 33	20 48	25 25
19	11	46	13	28 23 50	11♒34	10 56	18 50	13 58	11 16	25 16	21 35	20 49	25 24
20	11	50	9	29 23 30	23 28	10 37	18 30	14 16	11 8	25 23	21 36	20 50	25 23
21	11	54	6	0♈23 7	5♓20	10 25	18 8	14 35	11 1	25 29	21 38	20 51	25 23
22	11	58	2	1 22 42	17 12	10D18	17 44	14 54	10 53	25 35	21 40	20 52	25 22
23	12	1	59	2 22 16	29 4	10 18	17 17	15 13	10 46	25 42	21 42	20 53	25 21
24	12	5	55	3 21 47	10♈59	10 23	16 49	15 33	10 38	25 48	21 43	20 54	25 20
25	12	9	52	4 21 16	22 58	10 34	16 18	15 53	10 30	25 54	21 45	20 55	25 20
26	12	13	48	5 20 44	5♉ 2	10 50	15 46	16 13	10 23	26 0	21 47	20 56	25 19
27	12	17	45	6 20 9	17 14	11 12	15 13	16 34	10 15	26 6	21 48	20 57	25 18
28	12	21	42	7 19 32	29 35	11 38	14 38	16 55	10 7	26 12	21 50	20 58	25 17
29	12	25	38	8 18 52	12♊ 8	12 8	14 2	17 17	10 0	26 18	21 51	20 59	25 16
30	12	29	35	9 18 11	24 58	12 43	13 25	17 39	9 52	26 24	21 53	21 0	25 15
31	12	33	31	10♈17 27	8♋ 8	13♓22	12♈48	18♋ 1	9♎44	26♒30	21♑54	21♑ 0	25♏14

THE SUN ENTERS THE SIGN OF ARIES ON MAR 20 AT 14:41.

♈ ARIES ♉ TAURUS ♊ GEMINI ♋ CANCER ♌ LEO ♍ VIRGO ♎ LIBRA

SIDEREAL . SUN . MOON . MERCURY . VENUS . MARS . JUPITER . SATURN . URANUS . NEPTUNE . PLUTO .

DAY	TIME	☉	☽	☿	♀	♂	♃	♄	♅	♆	♇
	h m s	° ′ ″	° ′	° ′	° ′	° ′	° ′	° ′	° ′	° ′	° ′
A 1	12 37 28	11♈16 41	21♋41	14♓ 4	12♈10	18♋23	9♎36	26♒36	21♑55	21♑ 1	25♏13
P 2	12 41 24	12 15 52	5♌40	14 51	11R32	18 46	9R29	26 42	21 56	21 2	25R12
R 3	12 45 21	13 15 1	20 4	15 40	10 54	19 9	9 21	26 48	21 58	21 3	25 11
I 4	12 49 17	14 14 8	4♍51	16 33	10 17	19 32	9 13	26 53	21 59	21 3	25 9
L 5	12 53 14	15 13 12	19 55	17 29	9 40	19 56	9 5	26 59	22 0	21 4	25 8
6	12 57 11	16 12 14	5♎ 7	18 28	9 5	20 19	8 58	27 5	22 1	21 4	25 7
7	13 1 7	17 11 14	20 17	19 29	8 30	20 44	8 50	27 10	22 2	21 5	25 6
8	13 5 4	18 10 12	5♏14	20 34	7 56	21 8	8 43	27 16	22 3	21 5	25 5
9	13 9 0	19 9 9	19 50	21 40	7 25	21 32	8 35	27 21	22 4	21 6	25 3
10	13 12 57	20 8 3	3♐59	22 49	6 54	21 57	8 28	27 26	22 5	21 6	25 2
11	13 16 53	21 6 56	17 39	24 1	6 26	22 22	8 20	27 32	22 5	21 7	25 1
12	13 20 50	22 5 47	0♑52	25 14	6 0	22 48	8 13	27 37	22 6	21 7	25 0
13	13 24 46	23 4 36	13 39	26 30	5 36	23 13	8 6	27 42	22 7	21 8	24 58
14	13 28 43	24 3 23	26 7	27 48	5 14	23 39	7 58	27 47	22 8	21 8	24 57
15	13 32 40	25 2 9	8♒18	29 8	4 54	24 5	7 51	27 52	22 8	21 8	24 56
16	13 36 36	26 0 53	20 18	0♈30	4 37	24 31	7 44	27 57	22 9	21 8	24 54
17	13 40 33	26 59 35	2♓12	1 54	4 22	24 57	7 37	28 2	22 9	21 9	24 53
18	13 44 29	27 58 16	14 3	3 19	4 10	25 24	7 30	28 6	22 10	21 9	24 51
19	13 48 26	28 56 55	25 55	4 47	4 0	25 51	7 23	28 11	22 10	21 9	24 50
20	13 52 22	29 55 31	7♈50	6 16	3 52	26 18	7 17	28 16	22 10	21 9	24 48
21	13 56 19	0♉54 7	19 50	7 47	3 47	26 45	7 10	28 20	22 11	21 9	24 47
22	14 0 15	1 52 40	1♉57	9 20	3D45	27 12	7 4	28 25	22 11	21R 9	24 45
23	14 4 12	2 51 11	14 13	10 54	3 45	27 40	6 57	28 29	22 11	21 9	24 44
24	14 8 8	3 49 41	26 38	12 31	3 47	28 8	6 51	28 34	22 11	21 9	24 42
25	14 12 5	4 48 8	9♊13	14 9	3 51	28 36	6 45	28 38	22 11	21 9	24 41
26	14 16 2	5 46 34	22 1	15 48	3 58	29 4	6 39	28 42	22R11	21 9	24 39
27	14 19 58	6 44 57	5♋ 2	17 30	4 7	29 32	6 33	28 46	22 11	21 9	24 38
28	14 23 55	7 43 19	18 19	19 13	4 18	0♌ 0	6 27	28 50	22 11	21 9	24 36
29	14 27 51	8 41 38	1♌54	20 58	4 31	0 29	6 21	28 54	22 11	21 9	24 35
30	14 31 48	9♉39 55	15♌48	22♈45	4♈46	0♌58	6♎16	28♒58	22♑11	21♑ 8	24♏33

THE SUN ENTERS THE SIGN OF TAURUS ON APR 20 AT 01:49.

DAY	TIME	☉	☽	☿	♀	♂	♃	♄	♅	♆	♇
	h m s	° ′ ″	° ′	° ′	° ′	° ′	° ′	° ′	° ′	° ′	° ′
M 1	14 35 44	10♉38 10	0♍ 0	24♈34	5♈ 3	1♌27	6♎11	29♒ 2	22♑11	21♑ 8	24♏31
A 2	14 39 41	11 36 23	14 28	26 24	5 22	1 56	6R 5	29 6	22R11	21R 8	24R30
Y 3	14 43 37	12 34 34	29 10	28 16	5 43	2 25	6 0	29 9	22 10	21 8	24 28
4	14 47 34	13 32 43	13♎59	0♉10	6 5	2 54	5 55	29 13	22 10	21 7	24 27
5	14 51 31	14 30 51	28 47	2 6	6 29	3 24	5 51	29 16	22 10	21 7	24 25
6	14 55 27	15 28 56	13♏28	4 3	6 55	3 54	5 46	29 20	22 9	21 6	24 23
7	14 59 24	16 27 0	27 52	6 2	7 23	4 23	5 42	29 23	22 9	21 6	24 22
8	15 3 20	17 25 2	11♐56	8 3	7 52	4 53	5 37	29 26	22 8	21 5	24 20
9	15 7 17	18 23 3	25 37	10 5	8 23	5 23	5 33	29 29	22 8	21 5	24 18
10	15 11 13	19 21 2	8♑52	12 9	8 55	5 54	5 29	29 32	22 7	21 4	24 17
11	15 15 10	20 19 0	21 45	14 15	9 28	6 24	5 25	29 35	22 6	21 4	24 15
12	15 19 6	21 16 57	4♒16	16 22	10 3	6 55	5 22	29 38	22 5	21 3	24 13
13	15 23 3	22 14 52	16 32	18 30	10 39	7 25	5 18	29 41	22 5	21 3	24 12
14	15 27 0	23 12 46	28 35	20 39	11 16	7 56	5 15	29 43	22 4	21 2	24 10
15	15 30 56	24 10 39	10♓30	22 49	11 54	8 27	5 12	29 46	22 3	21 1	24 8
16	15 34 53	25 8 30	22 22	25 0	12 34	8 58	5 9	29 49	22 2	21 1	24 7
17	15 38 49	26 6 20	4♈15	27 11	13 14	9 29	5 6	29 51	22 1	21 0	24 5
18	15 42 46	27 4 9	16 14	29 22	13 56	10 0	5 3	29 53	22 0	20 59	24 3
19	15 46 42	28 1 57	28 20	1♊33	14 38	10 31	5 1	29 55	21 59	20 58	24 2
20	15 50 39	28 59 44	10♉36	3 44	15 22	11 3	4 59	29 58	21 58	20 58	24 0
21	15 54 35	29 57 29	23 5	5 55	16 6	11 34	4 57	0♓ 0	21 57	20 57	23 58
22	15 58 32	0♊55 13	5♊47	8 4	16 52	12 6	4 55	0 2	21 56	20 56	23 57
23	16 2 29	1 52 56	18 42	10 12	17 38	12 38	4 53	0 3	21 54	20 55	23 55
24	16 6 25	2 50 37	1♋51	12 19	18 25	13 10	4 51	0 5	21 53	20 54	23 53
25	16 10 22	3 48 17	15 14	14 23	19 13	13 42	4 50	0 7	21 52	20 53	23 52
26	16 14 18	4 45 56	28 49	16 27	20 1	14 14	4 49	0 8	21 50	20 52	23 50
27	16 18 15	5 43 33	12♌37	18 28	20 50	14 46	4 48	0 10	21 49	20 51	23 48
28	16 22 11	6 41 9	26 36	20 26	21 40	15 18	4 47	0 11	21 48	20 50	23 47
29	16 26 8	7 38 43	10♍45	22 23	22 31	15 51	4 46	0 12	21 46	20 49	23 45
30	16 30 4	8 36 15	25 2	24 17	23 22	16 23	4 46	0 13	21 45	20 48	23 44
31	16 34 1	9♊33 47	9♎24	26♊ 8	24♈14	16♌56	4♎46	0♓15	21♑43	20♑47	23♏42

THE SUN ENTERS THE SIGN OF GEMINI ON MAY 21 AT 01:02.

DAY	TIME	☉	☽	☿	♀	♂	♃	♄	♅	♆	♇
	h m s	° ′ ″	° ′	° ′	° ′	° ′	° ′	° ′	° ′	° ′	° ′
J 1	16 37 58	10♊31 16	23♎47	27♊57	25♈ 6	17♌28	4♎45	0♓15	21♑41	20♑46	23♏40
U 2	16 41 54	11 28 45	8♏ 7	29 43	25 59	18 1	4D46	0 16	21R40	20R45	23R39
N 3	16 45 51	12 26 13	22 21	1♋26	26 53	18 34	4 46	0 17	21 38	20 43	23 37
E 4	16 49 47	13 23 39	6♐23	3 7	27 47	19 7	4 46	0 18	21 36	20 42	23 36
5	16 53 44	14 21 5	20 10	4 45	28 42	19 40	4 47	0 18	21 35	20 41	23 34
6	16 57 40	15 18 29	3♑39	6 20	29 37	20 13	4 48	0 19	21 33	20 40	23 33
7	17 1 37	16 15 53	16 48	7 52	0♉32	20 46	4 49	0 19	21 31	20 39	23 31
8	17 5 34	17 13 16	29 39	9 21	1 28	21 20	4 50	0 19	21 29	20 37	23 30
9	17 9 30	18 10 38	12♒11	10 48	2 25	21 53	4 51	0 20	21 27	20 36	23 28
10	17 13 27	19 8 0	24 28	12 11	3 22	22 26	4 53	0R20	21 26	20 35	23 27
11	17 17 23	20 5 21	6♓32	13 32	4 19	23 0	4 54	0 20	21 24	20 33	23 25
12	17 21 20	21 2 42	18 29	14 49	5 17	23 34	4 56	0 20	21 22	20 32	23 24
13	17 25 16	22 0 2	0♈22	16 4	6 16	24 7	4 58	0 19	21 20	20 31	23 22
14	17 29 13	22 57 22	12 17	17 15	7 14	24 41	5 0	0 19	21 18	20 29	23 21
15	17 33 9	23 54 41	24 17	18 23	8 13	25 15	5 3	0 19	21 16	20 28	23 20
16	17 37 6	24 52 0	6♉26	19 28	9 13	25 49	5 5	0 18	21 14	20 27	23 18
17	17 41 2	25 49 19	18 50	20 30	10 12	26 23	5 8	0 17	21 12	20 25	23 17
18	17 44 59	26 46 37	1♊29	21 28	11 12	26 57	5 11	0 17	21 9	20 24	23 16
19	17 48 56	27 43 55	14 26	22 23	12 13	27 31	5 14	0 16	21 7	20 22	23 14
20	17 52 52	28 41 12	27 42	23 15	13 13	28 6	5 17	0 15	21 5	20 21	23 13
21	17 56 49	29 38 29	11♋16	24 2	14 14	28 40	5 21	0 14	21 3	20 19	23 12
22	18 0 45	0♋35 46	25 5	24 46	15 15	29 14	5 24	0 13	21 1	20 18	23 11
23	18 4 42	1 33 2	9♌ 6	25 26	16 17	29 49	5 28	0 12	20 59	20 16	23 9
24	18 8 38	2 30 17	23 17	26 2	17 19	0♍23	5 32	0 10	20 56	20 15	23 8
25	18 12 35	3 27 32	7♍32	26 34	18 21	0 58	5 36	0 9	20 54	20 13	23 7
26	18 16 32	4 24 46	21 49	27 2	19 23	1 33	5 40	0 8	20 52	20 12	23 6
27	18 20 28	5 21 59	6♎ 4	27 26	20 26	2 8	5 44	0 6	20 50	20 10	23 5
28	18 24 25	6 19 12	20 14	27 45	21 28	2 42	5 49	0 4	20 47	20 9	23 4
29	18 28 21	7 16 25	4♏18	27 59	22 32	3 17	5 54	0 3	20 45	20 7	23 3
30	18 32 18	8♋13 37	18♏14	28♋ 9	23♉35	3♍52	5♎58	0♓ 1	20♑43	20♑ 5	23♏ 1

THE SUN ENTERS THE SIGN OF CANCER ON JUN 21 AT 09:01.

♏ SCORPIO ♐ SAGITTARIUS ♑ CAPRICORN ♒ AQUARIUS ♓ PISCES

SIDEREAL. SUN. MOON. MERCURY. VENUS. MARS. JUPITER. SATURN. URANUS. NEPTUNE. PLUTO.

DAY	TIME	☉	☽	☿	♀	♂	♃	♄	♅	♆	♇
	h m s	° ' "	° '	° '	° '	° '	° '	° '	° '	° '	° '
J 1	18 36 14	9♋10 48	2♐ 0	28♋14	24♉38	4♍27	6♎ 3	29♒59	20♑40	20♑ 4	23♏ 0
U 2	18 40 11	10 8 0	15 36	28R15	25 42	5 3	6 9	29R57	20R38	20R 2	22R59
L 3	18 44 7	11 5 11	28 59	28 11	26 46	5 38	6 14	29 55	20 35	20 1	22 58
Y 4	18 48 4	12 2 22	12♑ 9	28 3	27 50	6 13	6 19	29 52	20 33	19 59	22 58
5	18 52 1	12 59 33	25 5	27 50	28 54	6 48	6 25	29 50	20 31	19 57	22 57
6	18 55 57	13 56 44	7♒46	27 32	29 59	7 24	6 31	29 48	20 28	19 56	22 56
7	18 59 54	14 53 55	20 13	27 11	1♊ 4	7 59	6 36	29 45	20 26	19 54	22 55
8	19 3 50	15 51 7	2♓27	26 45	2 9	8 35	6 42	29 43	20 24	19 53	22 54
9	19 7 47	16 48 18	14 30	26 17	3 14	9 10	6 49	29 40	20 21	19 51	22 53
10	19 11 43	17 45 30	26 26	25 45	4 19	9 46	6 55	29 37	20 19	19 49	22 52
11	19 15 40	18 42 43	8♈19	25 10	5 25	10 22	7 1	29 35	20 16	19 48	22 52
12	19 19 36	19 39 55	20 12	24 33	6 30	10 58	7 8	29 32	20 14	19 46	22 51
13	19 23 33	20 37 9	2♉11	23 55	7 36	11 33	7 15	29 29	20 11	19 45	22 50
14	19 27 30	21 34 23	14 21	23 16	8 42	12 9	7 21	29 26	20 9	19 43	22 50
15	19 31 26	22 31 37	26 47	22 36	9 48	12 45	7 28	29 23	20 7	19 41	22 49
16	19 35 23	23 28 52	9♊32	21 57	10 55	13 21	7 35	29 20	20 4	19 40	22 48
17	19 39 19	24 26 8	22 39	21 19	12 1	13 57	7 43	29 16	20 2	19 38	22 48
18	19 43 16	25 23 24	6♋10	20 43	13 8	14 34	7 50	29 13	19 59	19 36	22 47
19	19 47 12	26 20 41	20 4	20 10	14 15	15 10	7 57	29 10	19 57	19 35	22 47
20	19 51 9	27 17 59	4♌18	19 39	15 22	15 46	8 5	29 6	19 55	19 33	22 46
21	19 55 5	28 15 16	18 47	19 13	16 29	16 23	8 13	29 3	19 52	19 32	22 46
22	19 59 2	29 12 34	3♍25	18 50	17 36	16 59	8 21	28 59	19 50	19 30	22 46
23	20 2 59	0♌ 9 53	18 3	18 32	18 43	17 36	8 29	28 56	19 48	19 28	22 45
24	20 6 55	1 7 11	2♎37	18 19	19 51	18 12	8 37	28 52	19 45	19 27	22 45
25	20 10 52	2 4 30	17 0	18D11	20 58	18 49	8 45	28 48	19 43	19 25	22 45
26	20 14 48	3 1 50	1♏10	18 9	22 6	19 25	8 53	28 44	19 40	19 24	22 44
27	20 18 45	3 59 9	15 5	18 13	23 14	20 2	9 2	28 41	19 38	19 22	22 44
28	20 22 41	4 56 30	28 45	18 22	24 22	20 39	9 10	28 37	19 36	19 21	22 44
29	20 26 38	5 53 50	12♐11	18 38	25 30	21 16	9 19	28 33	19 34	19 19	22 44
30	20 30 34	6 51 12	25 23	19 0	26 38	21 53	9 28	28 29	19 31	19 18	22 43
31	20 34 31	7♌48 34	8♑24	19♋28	27♊47	22♍30	9♎36	28♒25	19♑29	19♑16	22♏43

THE SUN ENTERS THE SIGN OF LEO ON JUL 22 AT 19:52.

DAY	TIME	☉	☽	☿	♀	♂	♃	♄	♅	♆	♇
	h m s	° ' "	° '	° '	° '	° '	° '	° '	° '	° '	° '
A 1	20 38 28	8♌45 56	21♑14	20♋ 3	28♊55	23♍ 7	9♎45	28♒21	19♑27	19♑14	22♏43
U 2	20 42 24	9 43 20	3♒52	20 43	0♋ 4	23 44	9 55	28R16	19R25	19R13	22D43
G 3	20 46 21	10 40 44	16 19	21 30	1 13	24 21	10 4	28 12	19 22	19 11	22 43
U 4	20 50 17	11 38 9	28 36	22 22	2 21	24 58	10 13	28 8	19 20	19 10	22 43
S 5	20 54 14	12 35 35	10♓44	23 21	3 30	25 36	10 22	28 4	19 18	19 9	22 43
T 6	20 58 10	13 33 2	22 43	24 26	4 39	26 13	10 32	28 0	19 16	19 7	22 43
7	21 2 7	14 30 30	4♈37	25 36	5 49	26 50	10 41	27 55	19 14	19 6	22 44
8	21 6 3	15 27 59	16 28	26 51	6 58	27 28	10 51	27 51	19 12	19 4	22 44
9	21 10 0	16 25 30	28 19	28 12	8 7	28 5	11 1	27 46	19 10	19 3	22 44
10	21 13 57	17 23 2	10♉16	29 38	9 17	28 43	11 11	27 42	19 8	19 1	22 44
11	21 17 53	18 20 36	22 24	1♌ 9	10 26	29 20	11 21	27 38	19 6	19 0	22 44
12	21 21 50	19 18 11	4♊47	2 44	11 36	29 58	11 31	27 33	19 4	18 59	22 45
13	21 25 46	20 15 47	17 31	4 24	12 46	0♎36	11 41	27 29	19 2	18 57	22 45
14	21 29 43	21 13 25	0♋40	6 7	13 56	1 14	11 51	27 24	19 0	18 56	22 45
15	21 33 39	22 11 5	14 17	7 54	15 6	1 52	12 1	27 20	18 58	18 55	22 46
16	21 37 36	23 8 46	28 22	9 44	16 16	2 30	12 12	27 15	18 56	18 54	22 46
17	21 41 32	24 6 28	12♌52	11 36	17 26	3 8	12 22	27 11	18 54	18 52	22 47
18	21 45 29	25 4 11	27 42	13 31	18 36	3 46	12 33	27 6	18 52	18 51	22 47
19	21 49 26	26 1 56	12♍43	15 27	19 47	4 24	12 43	27 2	18 51	18 50	22 48
20	21 53 22	26 59 42	27 45	17 25	20 57	5 2	12 54	26 57	18 49	18 49	22 48
21	21 57 19	27 57 29	12♎39	19 24	22 8	5 40	13 5	26 53	18 47	18 47	22 49
22	22 1 15	28 55 18	27 18	21 24	23 19	6 18	13 16	26 48	18 45	18 46	22 49
23	22 5 12	29 53 7	11♏37	23 24	24 29	6 57	13 27	26 44	18 44	18 45	22 50
24	22 9 8	0♍50 58	25 34	25 25	25 40	7 35	13 38	26 39	18 42	18 44	22 51
25	22 13 5	1 48 50	9♐ 9	27 25	26 51	8 14	13 49	26 35	18 41	18 43	22 52
26	22 17 1	2 46 43	22 25	29 25	28 2	8 52	14 0	26 30	18 39	18 42	22 52
27	22 20 58	3 44 38	5♑23	1♍24	29 13	9 31	14 11	26 26	18 38	18 41	22 53
28	22 24 55	4 42 33	18 8	3 22	0♌24	10 9	14 22	26 21	18 36	18 40	22 54
29	22 28 51	5 40 30	0♒40	5 20	1 36	10 48	14 34	26 17	18 35	18 39	22 55
30	22 32 48	6 38 29	13 3	7 17	2 47	11 27	14 45	26 12	18 33	18 38	22 56
31	22 36 44	7♍36 29	25♒17	9♍13	3♌58	12♎ 6	14♎57	26♒ 8	18♑32	18♑37	22♏57

THE SUN ENTERS THE SIGN OF VIRGO ON AUG 23 AT 02:52.

DAY	TIME	☉	☽	☿	♀	♂	♃	♄	♅	♆	♇
	h m s	° ' "	° '	° '	° '	° '	° '	° '	° '	° '	° '
S 1	22 40 41	8♍34 30	7♓23	11♍ 8	5♌10	12♎45	15♎ 8	26♒ 3	18♑31	18♑36	22♏58
E 2	22 44 37	9 32 33	19 24	13 1	6 21	13 24	15 20	25R59	18R30	18R35	22 59
P 3	22 48 34	10 30 38	1♈18	14 54	7 33	14 2	15 31	25 55	18 28	18 34	23 0
T 4	22 52 30	11 28 44	13 9	16 45	8 45	14 42	15 43	25 51	18 27	18 34	23 1
E 5	22 56 27	12 26 52	24 59	18 35	9 57	15 21	15 55	25 46	18 26	18 33	23 2
M 6	23 0 24	13 25 3	6♉50	20 24	11 9	16 0	16 7	25 42	18 25	18 32	23 3
B 7	23 4 20	14 23 15	18 46	22 12	12 21	16 39	16 19	25 38	18 24	18 31	23 4
E 8	23 8 17	15 21 29	0♊52	23 59	13 33	17 18	16 31	25 34	18 23	18 31	23 5
R 9	23 12 13	16 19 46	13 13	25 44	14 45	17 58	16 43	25 30	18 22	18 30	23 6
10	23 16 10	17 18 4	25 53	27 29	15 57	18 37	16 55	25 26	18 21	18 29	23 8
11	23 20 6	18 16 25	8♋58	29 12	17 9	19 17	17 7	25 22	18 20	18 29	23 9
12	23 24 3	19 14 47	22 31	0♎54	18 22	19 56	17 19	25 18	18 20	18 28	23 10
13	23 27 59	20 13 12	6♌35	2 35	19 34	20 36	17 31	25 14	18 19	18 27	23 12
14	23 31 56	21 11 38	21 7	4 14	20 47	21 15	17 43	25 10	18 18	18 27	23 13
15	23 35 52	22 10 7	6♍ 3	5 53	21 59	21 55	17 56	25 6	18 18	18 26	23 14
16	23 39 49	23 8 38	21 15	7 31	23 12	22 35	18 8	25 2	18 17	18 26	23 16
17	23 43 46	24 7 10	6♎32	9 7	24 25	23 15	18 20	24 59	18 16	18 25	23 17
18	23 47 42	25 5 45	21 43	10 43	25 37	23 55	18 33	24 55	18 16	18 25	23 19
19	23 51 39	26 4 21	6♏38	12 17	26 50	24 34	18 45	24 52	18 16	18 25	23 20
20	23 55 35	27 2 59	21 11	13 51	28 3	25 14	18 58	24 48	18 15	18 24	23 22
21	23 59 32	28 1 38	5♐18	15 24	29 16	25 55	19 10	24 45	18 15	18 24	23 23
22	0 3 28	29 0 20	18 58	16 55	0♍29	26 35	19 23	24 41	18 14	18 24	23 25
23	0 7 25	29 59 3	2♑14	18 26	1 42	27 15	19 35	24 38	18 14	18 23	23 26
24	0 11 21	0♎57 47	15 8	19 55	2 56	27 55	19 48	24 35	18 14	18 23	23 28
25	0 15 18	1 56 33	27 45	21 23	4 9	28 35	20 1	24 32	18 14	18 23	23 30
26	0 19 15	2 55 21	10♒ 8	22 51	5 22	29 16	20 13	24 29	18 14	18 23	23 31
27	0 23 11	3 54 11	22 20	24 17	6 35	29 56	20 26	24 26	18D14	18 23	23 33
28	0 27 8	4 53 3	4♓24	25 43	7 49	0♏37	20 39	24 23	18 14	18 23	23 35
29	0 31 4	5 51 56	16 22	27 7	9 2	1 17	20 52	24 20	18 14	18 23	23 37
30	0 35 1	6♎50 51	28♓16	28♎30	10♍16	1♏58	21♎ 4	24♒17	18♑14	18♑23	23♏38

THE SUN ENTERS THE SIGN OF LIBRA ON SEP 23 AT 00:24.

♈ ARIES ♉ TAURUS ♊ GEMINI ♋ CANCER ♌ LEO ♍ VIRGO ♎ LIBRA

1993

SIDEREAL TIME. SUN. MOON. MERCURY. VENUS. MARS. JUPITER. SATURN. URANUS. NEPTUNE. PLUTO.

DAY	TIME	☉	☽	☿	♀	♂	♃	♄	♅	♆	♇
	h m s	° ' "	° '	° '	° '	° '	° '	° '	° '	° '	° '
O 1	0 38 57	7♎49 49	10♈ 8	29♎53	11♍29	2♏38	21♎17	24♒15	18♑14	18♑23	23♏40
C 2	0 42 54	8 48 48	21 59	1♏14	12 43	3 19	21 30	24R12	18 14	18 23	23 42
T 3	0 46 50	9 47 49	3♉50	2 33	13 57	4 0	21 43	24 10	18 14	18 23	23 44
O 4	0 50 47	10 46 53	15 45	3 52	15 10	4 41	21 56	24 7	18 15	18 23	23 46
B 5	0 54 44	11 45 59	27 45	5 9	16 24	5 22	22 9	24 5	18 15	18 23	23 48
E 6	0 58 40	12 45 7	9♊54	6 25	17 38	6 3	22 22	24 3	18 16	18 23	23 50
R 7	1 2 37	13 44 17	22 17	7 40	18 52	6 44	22 34	24 1	18 16	18 23	23 52
8	1 6 33	14 43 30	4♋56	8 53	20 6	7 25	22 47	23 59	18 16	18 24	23 54
9	1 10 30	15 42 45	17 57	10 4	21 20	8 6	23 0	23 57	18 17	18 24	23 55
10	1 14 26	16 42 3	1♌23	11 13	22 34	8 47	23 13	23 55	18 18	18 24	23 57
11	1 18 23	17 41 22	15 16	12 21	23 48	9 28	23 26	23 53	18 18	18 25	24 0
12	1 22 19	18 40 44	29 38	13 26	25 2	10 9	23 39	23 51	18 19	18 25	24 2
13	1 26 16	19 40 8	14♍24	14 30	26 16	10 51	23 52	23 50	18 20	18 25	24 4
14	1 30 12	20 39 35	29 29	15 30	27 31	11 32	24 5	23 48	18 21	18 26	24 6
15	1 34 9	21 39 3	14♎45	16 29	28 45	12 14	24 18	23 47	18 21	18 26	24 8
16	1 38 6	22 38 34	29 59	17 24	29 59	12 55	24 32	23 46	18 22	18 27	24 10
17	1 42 2	23 38 6	15♏ 2	18 16	1♎14	13 37	24 45	23 44	18 23	18 27	24 12
18	1 45 59	24 37 41	29 45	19 4	2 28	14 19	24 58	23 43	18 24	18 28	24 14
19	1 49 55	25 37 18	14♐ 3	19 48	3 43	15 0	25 11	23 42	18 25	18 28	24 16
20	1 53 52	26 36 56	27 54	20 29	4 57	15 42	25 24	23 41	18 27	18 29	24 19
21	1 57 48	27 36 36	11♑17	21 4	6 12	16 24	25 37	23 41	18 28	18 30	24 21
22	2 1 45	28 36 18	24 16	21 34	7 26	17 6	25 50	23 40	18 29	18 30	24 23
23	2 5 41	29 36 1	6♒53	21 58	8 41	17 48	26 3	23 39	18 30	18 31	24 25
24	2 9 38	0♏35 46	19 14	22 16	9 55	18 30	26 16	23 39	18 32	18 32	24 27
25	2 13 35	1 35 33	1♓21	22R27	11 10	19 12	26 29	23 39	18 33	18 33	24 30
26	2 17 31	2 35 21	13 20	22 31	12 25	19 54	26 42	23 38	18 34	18 34	24 32
27	2 21 28	3 35 11	25 13	22 26	13 39	20 36	26 55	23 38	18 36	18 35	24 34
28	2 25 24	4 35 3	7♈ 5	22 13	14 54	21 19	27 8	23D38	18 37	18 35	24 36
29	2 29 21	5 34 57	18 56	21 51	16 9	22 1	27 21	23 38	18 39	18 36	24 39
30	2 33 17	6 34 52	0♉49	21 19	17 24	22 43	27 34	23 38	18 40	18 37	24 41
31	2 37 14	7♏34 50	12♉47	20♏38	18♎39	23♏26	27♎47	23♒38	18♑42	18♑38	24♏43

THE SUN ENTERS THE SIGN OF SCORPIO ON OCT 23 AT 09:38.

DAY	TIME	☉	☽	☿	♀	♂	♃	♄	♅	♆	♇
	h m s	° ' "	° '	° '	° '	° '	° '	° '	° '	° '	° '
N 1	2 41 10	8♏34 49	24♉50	19♏48	19♎53	24♏ 8	28♎ 0	23♒39	18♑44	18♑39	24♏46
O 2	2 45 7	9 34 51	7♊ 0	18R50	21 8	24 51	28 13	23 39	18 45	18 40	24 48
V 3	2 49 4	10 34 54	19 21	17 44	22 23	25 33	28 26	23 40	18 47	18 41	24 50
E 4	2 53 0	11 35 0	1♋53	16 31	23 38	26 16	28 39	23 40	18 49	18 43	24 53
M 5	2 56 57	12 35 7	14 40	15 15	24 53	26 59	28 52	23 41	18 51	18 44	24 55
B 6	3 0 53	13 35 17	27 43	13 56	26 8	27 41	29 4	23 42	18 53	18 45	24 57
E 7	3 4 50	14 35 28	11♌ 7	12 38	27 23	28 24	29 17	23 43	18 55	18 46	25 0
R 8	3 8 46	15 35 42	24 52	11 22	28 38	29 7	29 30	23 44	18 57	18 47	25 2
9	3 12 43	16 35 58	8♍59	10 12	29 53	29 50	29 43	23 45	18 59	18 49	25 5
10	3 16 39	17 36 15	23 27	9 9	1♏ 8	0♐33	29 56	23 47	19 1	18 50	25 7
11	3 20 36	18 36 35	8♎11	8 15	2 24	1 16	0♏ 8	23 48	19 3	18 51	25 9
12	3 24 33	19 36 57	23 7	7 32	3 39	1 59	0 21	23 49	19 5	18 53	25 12
13	3 28 29	20 37 20	8♏ 7	7 1	4 54	2 43	0 34	23 51	19 8	18 54	25 14
14	3 32 26	21 37 45	23 1	6 41	6 9	3 26	0 46	23 53	19 10	18 55	25 17
15	3 36 22	22 38 12	7♐42	6D32	7 24	4 9	0 59	23 54	19 12	18 57	25 19
16	3 40 19	23 38 41	22 3	6 35	8 40	4 53	1 12	23 56	19 14	18 58	25 21
17	3 44 15	24 39 11	6♑ 0	6 49	9 55	5 36	1 24	23 58	19 17	19 0	25 24
18	3 48 12	25 39 42	19 31	7 12	11 10	6 19	1 37	24 0	19 19	19 1	25 26
19	3 52 8	26 40 15	2♒37	7 44	12 25	7 3	1 49	24 3	19 22	19 3	25 29
20	3 56 5	27 40 48	15 20	8 25	13 41	7 47	2 1	24 5	19 24	19 4	25 31
21	4 0 2	28 41 23	27 43	9 12	14 56	8 30	2 14	24 7	19 27	19 6	25 33
22	4 3 58	29 41 59	9♓52	10 6	16 11	9 14	2 26	24 10	19 29	19 8	25 36
23	4 7 55	0♐42 37	21 49	11 6	17 27	9 58	2 38	24 12	19 32	19 9	25 38
24	4 11 51	1 43 15	3♈41	12 10	18 42	10 41	2 51	24 15	19 35	19 11	25 41
25	4 15 48	2 43 55	15 31	13 19	19 57	11 25	3 3	24 18	19 37	19 13	25 43
26	4 19 44	3 44 36	27 24	14 31	21 13	12 9	3 15	24 21	19 40	19 14	25 45
27	4 23 41	4 45 18	9♉21	15 46	22 28	12 53	3 27	24 24	19 43	19 16	25 48
28	4 27 37	5 46 1	21 26	17 4	23 43	13 37	3 39	24 27	19 45	19 18	25 50
29	4 31 34	6 46 45	3♊41	18 25	24 59	14 21	3 51	24 30	19 48	19 20	25 53
30	4 35 31	7♐47 31	16♊ 8	19♏47	26♏14	15♐ 5	4♏ 3	24♒33	19♑51	19♑21	25♏55

THE SUN ENTERS THE SIGN OF SAGITTARIUS ON NOV 22 AT 07:08.

DAY	TIME	☉	☽	☿	♀	♂	♃	♄	♅	♆	♇
	h m s	° ' "	° '	° '	° '	° '	° '	° '	° '	° '	° '
D 1	4 39 27	8♐48 18	28♊47	21♏11	27♏29	15♐50	4♏15	24♒36	19♑54	19♑23	25♏57
E 2	4 43 24	9 49 6	11♋38	22 36	28 45	16 34	4 27	24 40	19 57	19 25	26 0
C 3	4 47 20	10 49 56	24 43	24 2	0♐ 0	17 18	4 38	24 43	20 0	19 27	26 2
E 4	4 51 17	11 50 47	8♌ 2	25 29	1 16	18 2	4 50	24 47	20 3	19 29	26 4
M 5	4 55 13	12 51 39	21 34	26 58	2 31	18 47	5 2	24 51	20 6	19 31	26 7
B 6	4 59 10	13 52 32	5♍21	28 26	3 47	19 31	5 13	24 54	20 9	19 33	26 9
E 7	5 3 6	14 53 27	19 20	29 56	5 2	20 16	5 25	24 58	20 12	19 35	26 11
R 8	5 7 3	15 54 23	3♎31	1♐26	6 18	21 0	5 36	25 2	20 15	19 36	26 14
9	5 11 0	16 55 20	17 53	2 56	7 33	21 45	5 48	25 6	20 18	19 38	26 16
10	5 14 56	17 56 19	2♏22	4 27	8 48	22 30	5 59	25 10	20 21	19 40	26 18
11	5 18 53	18 57 19	16 54	5 58	10 4	23 14	6 10	25 14	20 24	19 42	26 20
12	5 22 49	19 58 20	1♐24	7 30	11 19	23 59	6 21	25 19	20 27	19 44	26 23
13	5 26 46	20 59 21	15 47	9 1	12 35	24 44	6 32	25 23	20 31	19 47	26 25
14	5 30 42	22 0 24	29 56	10 33	13 50	25 29	6 43	25 28	20 34	19 49	26 27
15	5 34 39	23 1 27	13♑47	12 5	15 6	26 14	6 54	25 32	20 37	19 51	26 29
16	5 38 36	24 2 31	27 18	13 38	16 21	26 59	7 5	25 37	20 40	19 53	26 32
17	5 42 32	25 3 36	10♒27	15 10	17 37	27 44	7 16	25 41	20 44	19 55	26 34
18	5 46 29	26 4 41	23 13	16 43	18 53	28 29	7 26	25 46	20 47	19 57	26 36
19	5 50 25	27 5 46	5♓40	18 15	20 8	29 14	7 37	25 51	20 50	19 59	26 38
20	5 54 22	28 6 51	17 51	19 48	21 24	29 59	7 47	25 56	20 54	20 1	26 40
21	5 58 18	29 7 57	29 50	21 21	22 39	0♑44	7 58	26 1	20 57	20 3	26 42
22	6 2 15	0♑ 9 3	11♈42	22 55	23 55	1 29	8 8	26 6	21 0	20 6	26 44
23	6 6 11	1 10 9	23 32	24 28	25 10	2 15	8 18	26 11	21 4	20 8	26 47
24	6 10 8	2 11 15	5♉25	26 2	26 26	3 0	8 28	26 16	21 7	20 10	26 49
25	6 14 5	3 12 22	17 25	27 36	27 41	3 45	8 38	26 21	21 10	20 12	26 51
26	6 18 1	4 13 29	29 36	29 10	28 57	4 31	8 48	26 27	21 14	20 14	26 53
27	6 21 58	5 14 36	12♊ 2	0♑44	0♑12	5 16	8 58	26 32	21 17	20 16	26 55
28	6 25 54	6 15 43	24 44	2 19	1 28	6 2	9 8	26 38	21 21	20 19	26 57
29	6 29 51	7 16 50	7♋44	3 54	2 43	6 47	9 17	26 43	21 24	20 21	26 59
30	6 33 47	8 17 58	21 0	5 29	3 59	7 33	9 27	26 49	21 28	20 23	27 1
31	6 37 44	9♑19 5	4♌32	7♑ 4	5♑14	8♑19	9♏36	26♒54	21♑31	20♑25	27♏ 3

THE SUN ENTERS THE SIGN OF CAPRICORN ON DEC 21 AT 20:27.

♏ SCORPIO ♐ SAGITTARIUS ♑ CAPRICORN ♒ AQUARIUS ♓ PISCES

1994

SIDEREAL — SUN. — MOON. — MERCURY. — VENUS. — MARS. — JUPITER. — SATURN. — URANUS. — NEPTUNE. — PLUTO.

DAY	TIME	☉	☽	☿	♀	♂	♃	♄	♅	♆	♇
	h m s	° ' "	° '	° '	° '	° '	° '	° '	° '	° '	° '
J 1	6 41 40	10♑20 13	18♌16	8♑40	6♑30	9♑ 4	9♏46	27♒ 0	21♑35	20♑28	27♏ 4
A 2	6 45 37	11 21 21	2♍10	10 16	7 45	9 50	9 55	27 6	21 38	20 30	27 6
N 3	6 49 34	12 22 30	16 11	11 52	9 1	10 36	10 4	27 12	21 42	20 32	27 8
U 4	6 53 30	13 23 38	0♎17	13 29	10 16	11 21	10 13	27 18	21 45	20 34	27 10
A 5	6 57 27	14 24 47	14 24	15 6	11 32	12 7	10 22	27 23	21 49	20 37	27 12
R 6	7 1 23	15 25 57	28 32	16 44	12 47	12 53	10 30	27 29	21 52	20 39	27 14
Y 7	7 5 20	16 27 6	12♏39	18 22	14 3	13 39	10 39	27 35	21 56	20 41	27 15
8	7 9 16	17 28 16	26 44	20 0	15 18	14 25	10 47	27 42	21 59	20 43	27 17
9	7 13 13	18 29 26	10♐45	21 39	16 34	15 11	10 56	27 48	22 3	20 46	27 19
10	7 17 9	19 30 36	24 40	23 18	17 49	15 57	11 4	27 54	22 7	20 48	27 20
11	7 21 6	20 31 45	8♑25	24 57	19 5	16 43	11 12	28 0	22 10	20 50	27 22
12	7 25 3	21 32 55	21 58	26 37	20 20	17 29	11 20	28 7	22 14	20 53	27 24
13	7 28 59	22 34 4	5♒16	28 18	21 35	18 16	11 28	28 13	22 17	20 55	27 25
14	7 32 56	23 35 12	18 17	29 58	22 51	19 2	11 35	28 19	22 21	20 57	27 27
15	7 36 52	24 36 20	1♓ 1	1♒39	24 6	19 48	11 43	28 26	22 24	20 59	27 28
16	7 40 49	25 37 28	13 27	3 21	25 22	20 34	11 50	28 32	22 28	21 2	27 30
17	7 44 45	26 38 35	25 38	5 2	26 37	21 21	11 58	28 39	22 31	21 4	27 31
18	7 48 42	27 39 40	7♈37	6 44	27 53	22 7	12 5	28 45	22 35	21 6	27 33
19	7 52 38	28 40 46	19 28	8 26	29 8	22 53	12 12	28 52	22 39	21 8	27 34
20	7 56 35	29 41 50	1♉17	10 8	0♒24	23 40	12 19	28 59	22 42	21 11	27 36
21	8 0 32	0♒42 53	13 9	11 50	1 39	24 26	12 26	29 5	22 46	21 13	27 37
22	8 4 28	1 43 56	25 9	13 31	2 54	25 13	12 32	29 12	22 49	21 15	27 38
23	8 8 25	2 44 58	7♊22	15 13	4 10	25 59	12 39	29 19	22 53	21 17	27 40
24	8 12 21	3 45 58	19 53	16 53	5 25	26 46	12 45	29 26	22 56	21 20	27 41
25	8 16 18	4 46 58	2♋45	18 33	6 41	27 32	12 51	29 32	23 0	21 22	27 42
26	8 20 14	5 47 57	16 0	20 12	7 56	28 19	12 57	29 39	23 3	21 24	27 43
27	8 24 11	6 48 55	29 38	21 50	9 11	29 5	13 3	29 46	23 7	21 26	27 45
28	8 28 7	7 49 52	13♌35	23 26	10 27	29 52	13 8	29 53	23 10	21 29	27 46
29	8 32 4	8 50 48	27 49	25 0	11 42	0♒39	13 14	0♓ 0	23 14	21 31	27 47
30	8 36 1	9 51 43	12♍12	26 31	12 57	1 25	13 19	0 7	23 17	21 33	27 48
31	8 39 57	10♒52 37	26♍39	28♒ 0	14♒13	2♒12	13♏24	0♓14	23♑21	21♑35	27♏49

THE SUN ENTERS THE SIGN OF AQUARIUS ON JAN 20 AT 07:08.

DAY	TIME	☉	☽	☿	♀	♂	♃	♄	♅	♆	♇
	h m s	° ' "	° '	° '	° '	° '	° '	° '	° '	° '	° '
F 1	8 43 54	11♒53 31	11♎ 3	29♒24	15♒28	2♒59	13♏30	0♓21	23♑24	21♑37	27♏50
E 2	8 47 50	12 54 24	25 22	0♓45	16 43	3 46	13 34	0 28	23 27	21 40	27 51
B 3	8 51 47	13 55 16	9♏31	2 0	17 59	4 32	13 39	0 35	23 31	21 42	27 52
R 4	8 55 43	14 56 7	23 30	3 10	19 14	5 19	13 44	0 42	23 34	21 44	27 53
U 5	8 59 40	15 56 57	7♐19	4 13	20 29	6 6	13 48	0 49	23 38	21 46	27 54
A 6	9 3 36	16 57 47	20 58	5 9	21 44	6 53	13 52	0 57	23 41	21 48	27 55
R 7	9 7 33	17 58 36	4♑27	5 57	23 0	7 40	13 56	1 4	23 44	21 50	27 55
Y 8	9 11 30	18 59 24	17 47	6 36	24 15	8 27	14 0	1 11	23 48	21 52	27 56
9	9 15 26	20 0 10	0♒56	7 5	25 30	9 14	14 4	1 18	23 51	21 54	27 57
10	9 19 23	21 0 56	13 53	7 25	26 45	10 1	14 7	1 25	23 54	21 56	27 58
11	9 23 19	22 1 40	26 38	7R34	28 1	10 48	14 11	1 33	23 57	21 58	27 58
12	9 27 16	23 2 22	9♓10	7 32	29 16	11 35	14 14	1 40	24 1	22 0	27 59
13	9 31 12	24 3 3	21 29	7 20	0♓31	12 22	14 17	1 47	24 4	22 2	28 0
14	9 35 9	25 3 43	3♈36	6 57	1 46	13 9	14 20	1 54	24 7	22 4	28 0
15	9 39 5	26 4 21	15 32	6 25	3 1	13 56	14 22	2 2	24 10	22 6	28 1
16	9 43 2	27 4 58	27 22	5 43	4 16	14 43	14 25	2 9	24 13	22 8	28 1
17	9 46 59	28 5 32	9♉10	4 53	5 32	15 30	14 27	2 16	24 16	22 10	28 2
18	9 50 55	29 6 5	21 0	3 57	6 47	16 17	14 29	2 23	24 19	22 12	28 2
19	9 54 52	0♓ 6 37	2♊57	2 55	8 2	17 4	14 31	2 31	24 23	22 14	28 2
20	9 58 48	1 7 6	15 8	1 50	9 17	17 51	14 32	2 38	24 26	22 16	28 3
21	10 2 45	2 7 34	27 38	0 43	10 32	18 38	14 34	2 45	24 29	22 18	28 3
22	10 6 41	3 8 0	10♋31	29♒36	11 47	19 25	14 35	2 53	24 32	22 20	28 3
23	10 10 38	4 8 24	23 51	28 30	13 2	20 12	14 36	3 0	24 34	22 22	28 4
24	10 14 34	5 8 46	7♌38	27 28	14 17	20 59	14 37	3 7	24 37	22 23	28 4
25	10 18 31	6 9 6	21 51	26 30	15 32	21 47	14 38	3 15	24 40	22 25	28 4
26	10 22 28	7 9 24	6♍26	25 38	16 47	22 34	14 39	3 22	24 43	22 27	28 4
27	10 26 24	8 9 41	21 14	24 51	18 2	23 21	14 39	3 29	24 46	22 29	28 4
28	10 30 21	9♓ 9 56	6♎ 8	24♒11	19♓17	24♒ 8	14♏39	3♓36	24♑49	22♑30	28♏ 4

THE SUN ENTERS THE SIGN OF PISCES ON FEB 18 AT 21:23.

DAY	TIME	☉	☽	☿	♀	♂	♃	♄	♅	♆	♇
	h m s	° ' "	° '	° '	° '	° '	° '	° '	° '	° '	° '
M 1	10 34 17	10♓10 9	20♎58	23♒39	20♓31	24♒55	14♏39	3♓44	24♑52	22♑32	28♏ 4
A 2	10 38 14	11 10 21	5♏38	23R13	21 46	25 42	14R39	3 51	24 54	22 34	28R 4
R 3	10 42 10	12 10 32	20 2	22 54	23 1	26 30	14 39	3 58	24 57	22 35	28 4
C 4	10 46 7	13 10 41	4♐ 8	22 43	24 16	27 17	14 38	4 5	25 0	22 37	28 4
H 5	10 50 3	14 10 48	17 56	22D38	25 31	28 4	14 38	4 13	25 2	22 39	28 4
6	10 54 0	15 10 54	1♑26	22 39	26 45	28 51	14 37	4 20	25 5	22 40	28 4
7	10 57 57	16 10 59	14 41	22 47	28 0	29 38	14 35	4 27	25 7	22 42	28 4
8	11 1 53	17 11 2	27 43	23 1	29 15	0♓25	14 34	4 34	25 10	22 43	28 4
9	11 5 50	18 11 3	10♒31	23 20	0♈30	1 13	14 33	4 41	25 12	22 45	28 3
10	11 9 46	19 11 2	23 9	23 45	1 44	2 0	14 31	4 49	25 15	22 46	28 3
11	11 13 43	20 10 59	5♓36	24 14	2 59	2 47	14 29	4 56	25 17	22 48	28 3
12	11 17 39	21 10 55	17 53	24 48	4 14	3 34	14 27	5 3	25 20	22 49	28 2
13	11 21 36	22 10 49	0♈ 0	25 26	5 28	4 21	14 25	5 10	25 22	22 50	28 2
14	11 25 32	23 10 41	11 59	26 8	6 43	5 9	14 22	5 17	25 24	22 52	28 2
15	11 29 29	24 10 30	23 52	26 54	7 57	5 56	14 20	5 24	25 27	22 53	28 1
16	11 33 25	25 10 18	5♉40	27 43	9 12	6 43	14 17	5 31	25 29	22 54	28 1
17	11 37 22	26 10 4	17 26	28 35	10 26	7 30	14 14	5 38	25 31	22 56	28 0
18	11 41 19	27 9 47	29 16	29 31	11 41	8 17	14 11	5 45	25 33	22 57	28 0
19	11 45 15	28 9 28	11♊12	0♓29	12 55	9 4	14 8	5 52	25 35	22 58	27 59
20	11 49 12	29 9 7	23 21	1 31	14 10	9 52	14 4	5 59	25 37	22 59	27 58
21	11 53 8	0♈ 8 44	5♋47	2 34	15 24	10 39	14 1	6 6	25 39	23 0	27 58
22	11 57 5	1 8 18	18 36	3 40	16 39	11 26	13 57	6 13	25 41	23 2	27 57
23	12 1 1	2 7 50	1♌52	4 49	17 53	12 13	13 53	6 20	25 43	23 3	27 56
24	12 4 58	3 7 20	15 37	5 59	19 7	13 0	13 49	6 26	25 45	23 4	27 56
25	12 8 54	4 6 48	29 51	7 12	20 21	13 47	13 44	6 33	25 47	23 5	27 55
26	12 12 51	5 6 13	14♍31	8 27	21 36	14 34	13 40	6 40	25 49	23 6	27 54
27	12 16 48	6 5 36	29 30	9 43	22 50	15 21	13 35	6 47	25 50	23 7	27 53
28	12 20 44	7 4 57	14♎40	11 2	24 4	16 8	13 30	6 53	25 52	23 8	27 52
29	12 24 41	8 4 16	29 50	12 22	25 18	16 55	13 25	7 0	25 54	23 9	27 51
30	12 28 37	9 3 33	14♏51	13 44	26 32	17 42	13 20	7 6	25 55	23 9	27 51
31	12 32 34	10♈ 2 49	29♏35	15♓ 7	27♈46	18♓29	13♏15	7♓13	25♑57	23♑10	27♏50

THE SUN ENTERS THE SIGN OF ARIES ON MAR 20 AT 20:29.

♈ ARIES ♉ TAURUS ♊ GEMINI ♋ CANCER ♌ LEO ♍ VIRGO ♎ LIBRA

SIDEREAL. SUN... MOON... MERCURY VENUS.. MARS... JUPITER SATURN. URANUS. NEPTUNE PLUTO..

DAY	TIME	☉	☽	☿	♀	♂	♃	♄	♅	♆	♇
	h m s	° ' "	° '	° '	° '	° '	° '	° '	° '	° '	° '
A 1	12 36 30	11♈ 2 2	13♐57	16♓33	29♈ 0	19♓16	13♏10	7♓20	25♑58	23♑11	27♏49
P 2	12 40 27	12 1 14	27 55	18 0	0♉14	20 3	13R 4	7 26	26 0	23 12	27R48
R 3	12 44 23	13 0 24	11♑30	19 28	1 28	20 50	12 59	7 32	26 1	23 13	27 47
I 4	12 48 20	13 59 33	24 43	20 58	2 42	21 37	12 53	7 39	26 2	23 13	27 46
L 5	12 52 17	14 58 39	7♒37	22 30	3 56	22 24	12 47	7 45	26 4	23 14	27 45
6	12 56 13	15 57 44	20 14	24 3	5 10	23 11	12 41	7 51	26 5	23 15	27 43
7	13 0 10	16 56 47	2♓38	25 38	6 24	23 58	12 35	7 58	26 6	23 15	27 42
8	13 4 6	17 55 48	14 51	27 14	7 38	24 44	12 28	8 4	26 7	23 16	27 41
9	13 8 3	18 54 47	26 55	28 52	8 52	25 31	12 22	8 10	26 9	23 17	27 40
10	13 11 59	19 53 45	8♈52	0♈31	10 5	26 18	12 16	8 16	26 10	23 17	27 39
11	13 15 56	20 52 40	20 44	2 12	11 19	27 5	12 9	8 22	26 11	23 18	27 38
12	13 19 52	21 51 33	2♉33	3 54	12 33	27 52	12 2	8 28	26 12	23 18	27 36
13	13 23 49	22 50 25	14 20	5 38	13 46	28 38	11 55	8 34	26 13	23 18	27 35
14	13 27 45	23 49 14	26 9	7 23	15 0	29 25	11 49	8 40	26 13	23 19	27 34
15	13 31 42	24 48 1	8♊ 1	9 10	16 14	0♈12	11 42	8 46	26 14	23 19	27 32
16	13 35 39	25 46 46	20 1	10 59	17 27	0 58	11 34	8 52	26 15	23 20	27 31
17	13 39 35	26 45 29	2♋12	12 49	18 41	1 45	11 27	8 57	26 16	23 20	27 30
18	13 43 32	27 44 10	14 39	14 40	19 54	2 31	11 20	9 3	26 16	23 20	27 28
19	13 47 28	28 42 48	27 25	16 33	21 8	3 18	11 13	9 8	26 17	23 20	27 27
20	13 51 25	29 41 25	10♌35	18 28	22 21	4 4	11 6	9 14	26 18	23 21	27 26
21	13 55 21	0♉39 58	24 12	20 25	23 34	4 51	10 58	9 19	26 18	23 21	27 24
22	13 59 18	1 38 30	8♍17	22 22	24 48	5 37	10 51	9 25	26 19	23 21	27 23
23	14 3 14	2 37 0	22 48	24 22	26 1	6 24	10 43	9 30	26 19	23 21	27 21
24	14 7 11	3 35 27	7♎41	26 23	27 14	7 10	10 36	9 35	26 19	23 21	27 20
25	14 11 8	4 33 53	22 49	28 25	28 27	7 56	10 28	9 41	26 20	23R21	27 18
26	14 15 4	5 32 16	8♏ 3	0♉29	29 40	8 43	10 21	9 46	26 20	23 21	27 17
27	14 19 1	6 30 38	23 14	2 34	0♊54	9 29	10 13	9 51	26 20	23 21	27 15
28	14 22 57	7 28 58	8♐11	4 40	2 7	10 15	10 5	9 56	26 20	23 21	27 14
29	14 26 54	8 27 17	22 47	6 47	3 20	11 1	9 58	10 1	26 21	23 21	27 12
30	14 30 50	9♉25 34	6♑59	8♉55	4♊33	11♈47	9♏50	10♓ 6	26♑21	23♑21	27♏11

THE SUN ENTERS THE SIGN OF TAURUS ON APR 20 AT 07:36.

DAY	TIME	☉	☽	☿	♀	♂	♃	♄	♅	♆	♇
	h m s	° ' "	° '	° '	° '	° '	° '	° '	° '	° '	° '
M 1	14 34 47	10♉23 49	20♑45	11♉ 4	5♊46	12♈34	9♏42	10♓11	26♑21	23♑21	27♏ 9
A 2	14 38 43	11 22 3	4♒ 4	13 13	6 59	13 20	9R35	10 15	26R21	23R20	27R 8
Y 3	14 42 40	12 20 15	17 0	15 23	8 11	14 6	9 27	10 20	26 21	23 20	27 6
4	14 46 37	13 18 26	29 35	17 33	9 24	14 52	9 19	10 25	26 20	23 20	27 4
5	14 50 33	14 16 36	11♓54	19 42	10 37	15 38	9 12	10 29	26 20	23 20	27 3
6	14 54 30	15 14 44	24 0	21 51	11 50	16 24	9 4	10 34	26 20	23 19	27 1
7	14 58 26	16 12 50	5♈56	23 59	13 2	17 10	8 57	10 38	26 20	23 19	26 59
8	15 2 23	17 10 55	17 47	26 6	14 15	17 55	8 49	10 42	26 19	23 18	26 58
9	15 6 19	18 8 59	29 35	28 11	15 28	18 41	8 42	10 46	26 19	23 18	26 56
10	15 10 16	19 7 1	11♉22	0♊15	16 40	19 27	8 34	10 51	26 19	23 18	26 55
11	15 14 12	20 5 1	23 12	2 16	17 53	20 13	8 27	10 55	26 18	23 17	26 53
12	15 18 9	21 3 0	5♊ 6	4 16	19 5	20 58	8 19	10 59	26 18	23 17	26 51
13	15 22 6	22 0 57	17 6	6 13	20 18	21 44	8 12	11 2	26 17	23 16	26 50
14	15 26 2	22 58 53	29 15	8 7	21 30	22 30	8 5	11 6	26 16	23 15	26 48
15	15 29 59	23 56 47	11♋35	9 59	22 43	23 15	7 58	11 10	26 16	23 15	26 46
16	15 33 55	24 54 40	24 9	11 48	23 55	24 1	7 51	11 14	26 15	23 14	26 45
17	15 37 52	25 52 30	7♌ 0	13 34	25 7	24 46	7 44	11 17	26 14	23 14	26 43
18	15 41 48	26 50 19	20 10	15 16	26 19	25 31	7 37	11 21	26 13	23 13	26 41
19	15 45 45	27 48 6	3♍41	16 56	27 31	26 17	7 30	11 24	26 13	23 12	26 40
20	15 49 41	28 45 52	17 35	18 32	28 44	27 2	7 23	11 27	26 12	23 11	26 38
21	15 53 38	29 43 35	1♎51	20 5	29 56	27 47	7 17	11 31	26 11	23 11	26 36
22	15 57 35	0♊41 17	16 27	21 35	1♋ 8	28 32	7 10	11 34	26 10	23 10	26 35
23	16 1 31	1 38 58	1♏20	23 1	2 20	29 17	7 4	11 37	26 9	23 9	26 33
24	16 5 28	2 36 37	16 22	24 24	3 31	0♉ 3	6 57	11 40	26 8	23 8	26 31
25	16 9 24	3 34 15	1♐25	25 43	4 43	0 48	6 51	11 43	26 7	23 7	26 30
26	16 13 21	4 31 52	16 21	26 59	5 55	1 33	6 45	11 45	26 5	23 6	26 28
27	16 17 17	5 29 27	1♑ 2	28 11	7 7	2 18	6 39	11 48	26 4	23 5	26 26
28	16 21 14	6 27 2	15 21	29 19	8 18	3 2	6 33	11 51	26 3	23 5	26 25
29	16 25 10	7 24 35	29 15	0♋24	9 30	3 47	6 27	11 53	26 2	23 4	26 23
30	16 29 7	8 22 8	12♒41	1 25	10 42	4 32	6 22	11 55	26 0	23 3	26 22
31	16 33 4	9♊19 40	25♒43	2♋22	11♋53	5♉17	6♏16	11♓58	25♑59	23♑ 1	26♏20

THE SUN ENTERS THE SIGN OF GEMINI ON MAY 21 AT 06:49.

DAY	TIME	☉	☽	☿	♀	♂	♃	♄	♅	♆	♇
	h m s	° ' "	° '	° '	° '	° '	° '	° '	° '	° '	° '
J 1	16 37 0	10♊17 10	8♓21	3♋16	13♋ 5	6♉ 1	6♏11	12♓ 0	25♑58	23♑ 0	26♏18
U 2	16 40 57	11 14 41	20 40	4 5	14 16	6 46	6R 6	12 2	25R56	22R59	26R17
N 3	16 44 53	12 12 10	2♈44	4 50	15 27	7 31	6 1	12 4	25 55	22 58	26 15
E 4	16 48 50	13 9 38	14 38	5 32	16 38	8 15	5 56	12 6	25 53	22 57	26 14
5	16 52 46	14 7 6	26 26	6 9	17 50	9 0	5 51	12 8	25 51	22 56	26 12
6	16 56 43	15 4 33	8♉14	6 41	19 1	9 44	5 47	12 10	25 50	22 55	26 10
7	17 0 39	16 2 0	20 3	7 10	20 12	10 28	5 42	12 11	25 48	22 54	26 9
8	17 4 36	16 59 25	1♊58	7 33	21 23	11 13	5 38	12 13	25 47	22 52	26 7
9	17 8 33	17 56 50	14 0	7 53	22 34	11 57	5 34	12 14	25 45	22 51	26 6
10	17 12 29	18 54 14	26 13	8 8	23 45	12 41	5 30	12 16	25 43	22 50	26 4
11	17 16 26	19 51 37	8♋36	8 18	24 56	13 25	5 26	12 17	25 41	22 49	26 3
12	17 20 22	20 49 0	21 13	8R23	26 6	14 9	5 22	12 18	25 40	22 47	26 1
13	17 24 19	21 46 21	4♌ 2	8 25	27 17	14 53	5 19	12 19	25 38	22 46	26 0
14	17 28 15	22 43 42	17 6	8 21	28 28	15 37	5 16	12 20	25 36	22 45	25 58
15	17 32 12	23 41 1	0♍24	8 13	29 38	16 21	5 12	12 21	25 34	22 43	25 57
16	17 36 8	24 38 20	13 58	8 1	0♌49	17 5	5 9	12 22	25 32	22 42	25 56
17	17 40 5	25 35 38	27 47	7 45	1 59	17 49	5 7	12 22	25 30	22 41	25 54
18	17 44 2	26 32 55	11♎51	7 25	3 9	18 32	5 4	12 23	25 28	22 39	25 53
19	17 47 58	27 30 11	26 11	7 2	4 20	19 16	5 2	12 23	25 26	22 38	25 51
20	17 51 55	28 27 26	10♏42	6 35	5 30	19 59	4 59	12 24	25 24	22 36	25 50
21	17 55 51	29 24 41	25 22	6 6	6 40	20 43	4 57	12 24	25 22	22 35	25 49
22	17 59 48	0♋21 55	10♐ 5	5 35	7 50	21 26	4 55	12 24	25 20	22 33	25 48
23	18 3 44	1 19 9	24 46	5 1	9 0	22 10	4 54	12R24	25 18	22 32	25 46
24	18 7 41	2 16 22	9♑16	4 27	10 10	22 53	4 52	12 24	25 16	22 30	25 45
25	18 11 38	3 13 35	23 30	3 52	11 19	23 36	4 51	12 24	25 13	22 29	25 44
26	18 15 34	4 10 47	7♒22	3 17	12 29	24 19	4 49	12 24	25 11	22 27	25 43
27	18 19 31	5 7 59	20 50	2 42	13 38	25 3	4 48	12 23	25 9	22 26	25 41
28	18 23 27	6 5 12	3♓54	2 9	14 48	25 46	4 48	12 23	25 7	22 24	25 40
29	18 27 24	7 2 24	16 35	1 38	15 57	26 29	4 47	12 22	25 5	22 23	25 39
30	18 31 20	7♋59 36	28♓55	1♋ 8	17♌ 6	27♉12	4♏47	12♓22	25♑ 2	22♑21	25♏38

THE SUN ENTERS THE SIGN OF CANCER ON JUN 21 AT 14:49.

♏ SCORPIO ♐ SAGITTARIUS ♑ CAPRICORN ♒ AQUARIUS ♓ PISCES

1994

SIDEREAL SUN. MOON. MERCURY. VENUS. MARS. JUPITER. SATURN. URANUS. NEPTUNE. PLUTO.

DAY	TIME h m s	☉ ° ' "	☽ ° '	☿ ° '	♀ ° '	♂ ° '	♃ ° '	♄ ° '	♅ ° '	♆ ° '	♇ ° '
J 1	18 35 17	8♋56 49	11♈ 0	0♋42	18♌16	27♉54	4♏46	12♓21	25♑ 0	22♑20	25♏37
U 2	18 39 13	9 54 1	22 54	0R19	19 25	28 37	4D46	12R20	24R58	22R18	25R36
L 3	18 43 10	10 51 14	4♉43	29♊59	20 34	29 20	4 46	12 19	24 55	22 17	25 35
Y 4	18 47 7	11 48 27	16 31	29 44	21 42	0♊ 3	4 46	12 18	24 53	22 15	25 34
5	18 51 3	12 45 40	28 24	29 33	22 51	0 45	4 47	12 17	24 51	22 13	25 33
6	18 55 0	13 42 53	10♊25	29D27	24 0	1 28	4 47	12 16	24 48	22 12	25 32
7	18 58 56	14 40 7	22 37	29 25	25 8	2 10	4 48	12 15	24 46	22 10	25 31
8	19 2 53	15 37 21	5♋ 3	29 29	26 17	2 53	4 49	12 13	24 44	22 9	25 30
9	19 6 49	16 34 34	17 45	29 37	27 25	3 35	4 50	12 12	24 41	22 7	25 29
10	19 10 46	17 31 48	0♌41	29 51	28 33	4 17	4 52	12 10	24 39	22 5	25 28
11	19 14 42	18 29 2	13 53	0♋10	29 41	4 59	4 53	12 9	24 37	22 4	25 27
12	19 18 39	19 26 16	27 17	0 34	0♍49	5 42	4 55	12 7	24 34	22 2	25 27
13	19 22 36	20 23 30	10♍53	1 3	1 57	6 24	4 57	12 5	24 32	22 0	25 26
14	19 26 32	21 20 45	24 39	1 38	3 5	7 6	4 59	12 3	24 29	21 59	25 25
15	19 30 29	22 17 59	8♎33	2 17	4 12	7 47	5 1	12 1	24 27	21 57	25 24
16	19 34 25	23 15 13	22 35	3 2	5 20	8 29	5 3	11 59	24 25	21 56	25 24
17	19 38 22	24 12 27	6♏44	3 52	6 27	9 11	5 6	11 57	24 22	21 54	25 23
18	19 42 18	25 9 41	20 58	4 47	7 34	9 53	5 9	11 54	24 20	21 52	25 22
19	19 46 15	26 6 56	5♐16	5 47	8 41	10 34	5 11	11 52	24 17	21 51	25 22
20	19 50 11	27 4 10	19 35	6 52	9 48	11 16	5 15	11 49	24 15	21 49	25 21
21	19 54 8	28 1 25	3♑51	8 2	10 55	11 57	5 18	11 47	24 13	21 48	25 21
22	19 58 5	28 58 41	17 59	9 17	12 1	12 39	5 21	11 44	24 10	21 46	25 20
23	20 2 1	29 55 57	1♒56	10 36	13 8	13 20	5 25	11 41	24 8	21 44	25 20
24	20 5 58	0♌53 13	15 36	12 0	14 14	14 1	5 28	11 39	24 5	21 43	25 19
25	20 9 54	1 50 30	28 56	13 28	15 20	14 42	5 32	11 36	24 3	21 41	25 19
26	20 13 51	2 47 48	11♓55	15 1	16 26	15 23	5 36	11 33	24 1	21 40	25 19
27	20 17 47	3 45 6	24 33	16 37	17 32	16 5	5 41	11 30	23 58	21 38	25 18
28	20 21 44	4 42 26	6♈53	18 18	18 37	16 45	5 45	11 27	23 56	21 36	25 18
29	20 25 40	5 39 46	18 58	20 2	19 42	17 26	5 50	11 23	23 54	21 35	25 18
30	20 29 37	6 37 7	0♉52	21 50	20 48	18 7	5 54	11 20	23 51	21 33	25 17
31	20 33 34	7♌34 30	12♉41	23♋41	21♍53	18♊48	5♏59	11♓17	23♑49	21♑32	25♏17

THE SUN ENTERS THE SIGN OF LEO ON JUL 23 AT 01:42.

DAY	TIME h m s	☉ ° ' "	☽ ° '	☿ ° '	♀ ° '	♂ ° '	♃ ° '	♄ ° '	♅ ° '	♆ ° '	♇ ° '
A 1	20 37 30	8♌31 54	24♉31	25♋35	22♍57	19♊28	6♏ 4	11♓13	23♑47	21♑30	25♏17
U 2	20 41 27	9 29 18	6♊25	27 31	24 2	20 9	6 9	11R10	23R44	21R29	25R17
G 3	20 45 23	10 26 44	18 30	29 29	25 6	20 50	6 15	11 6	23 42	21 27	25 17
U 4	20 49 20	11 24 11	0♋50	1♌29	26 10	21 30	6 20	11 3	23 40	21 26	25 17
S 5	20 53 16	12 21 39	13 28	3 31	27 14	22 10	6 26	10 59	23 37	21 24	25D17
T 6	20 57 13	13 19 9	26 25	5 34	28 18	22 51	6 31	10 55	23 35	21 23	25 17
7	21 1 9	14 16 39	9♌42	7 38	29 21	23 31	6 37	10 52	23 33	21 21	25 17
8	21 5 6	15 14 10	23 17	9 42	0♎25	24 11	6 43	10 48	23 31	21 20	25 17
9	21 9 3	16 11 42	7♍ 6	11 46	1 28	24 51	6 50	10 44	23 29	21 18	25 17
10	21 12 59	17 9 15	21 7	13 50	2 30	25 31	6 56	10 40	23 27	21 17	25 17
11	21 16 56	18 6 50	5♎14	15 54	3 33	26 11	7 2	10 36	23 24	21 15	25 17
12	21 20 52	19 4 25	19 24	17 57	4 35	26 50	7 9	10 32	23 22	21 14	25 17
13	21 24 49	20 2 0	3♏34	20 0	5 37	27 30	7 16	10 28	23 20	21 13	25 18
14	21 28 45	20 59 37	17 43	22 1	6 39	28 10	7 23	10 24	23 18	21 11	25 18
15	21 32 42	21 57 15	1♐49	24 2	7 40	28 49	7 30	10 19	23 16	21 10	25 18
16	21 36 38	22 54 54	15 51	26 1	8 41	29 28	7 37	10 15	23 14	21 9	25 18
17	21 40 35	23 52 34	29 49	27 59	9 42	0♋ 8	7 44	10 11	23 12	21 7	25 19
18	21 44 32	24 50 14	13♑41	29 56	10 42	0 47	7 52	10 7	23 10	21 6	25 19
19	21 48 28	25 47 56	27 24	1♍52	11 42	1 26	7 59	10 2	23 8	21 5	25 20
20	21 52 25	26 45 39	10♒57	3 46	12 42	2 5	8 7	9 58	23 6	21 4	25 20
21	21 56 21	27 43 24	24 16	5 39	13 42	2 44	8 15	9 53	23 5	21 2	25 21
22	22 0 18	28 41 9	7♓20	7 31	14 41	3 23	8 23	9 49	23 3	21 1	25 21
23	22 4 14	29 38 56	20 7	9 21	15 39	4 2	8 31	9 45	23 1	21 0	25 22
24	22 8 11	0♍36 45	2♈37	11 10	16 37	4 40	8 39	9 40	22 59	20 59	25 22
25	22 12 7	1 34 35	14 52	12 58	17 35	5 19	8 47	9 36	22 58	20 58	25 23
26	22 16 4	2 32 27	26 54	14 44	18 33	5 58	8 55	9 31	22 56	20 56	25 24
27	22 20 0	3 30 20	8♉47	16 29	19 30	6 36	9 4	9 27	22 54	20 55	25 24
28	22 23 57	4 28 16	20 35	18 12	20 26	7 14	9 13	9 22	22 53	20 54	25 25
29	22 27 54	5 26 13	2♊24	19 54	21 22	7 53	9 21	9 18	22 51	20 53	25 26
30	22 31 50	6 24 12	14 19	21 35	22 18	8 31	9 30	9 13	22 50	20 52	25 27
31	22 35 47	7♍22 13	26♊25	23♍15	23♎13	9♋ 9	9♏39	9♓ 8	22♑48	20♑51	25♏27

THE SUN ENTERS THE SIGN OF VIRGO ON AUG 23 AT 08:45.

DAY	TIME h m s	☉ ° ' "	☽ ° '	☿ ° '	♀ ° '	♂ ° '	♃ ° '	♄ ° '	♅ ° '	♆ ° '	♇ ° '
S 1	22 39 43	8♍20 16	8♋47	24♍53	24♎ 8	9♋47	9♏48	9♓ 4	22♑47	20♑50	25♏2S
E 2	22 43 40	9 18 21	21 31	26 30	25 2	10 25	9 57	8R59	22R45	20R49	25 29
P 3	22 47 36	10 16 27	4♌37	28 6	25 55	11 2	10 7	8 55	22 44	20 48	25 30
T 4	22 51 33	11 14 36	18 7	29 41	26 48	11 40	10 16	8 50	22 42	20 48	25 31
E 5	22 55 29	12 12 46	2♍ 0	1♎14	27 41	12 18	10 26	8 46	22 41	20 47	25 32
M 6	22 59 26	13 10 58	16 12	2 46	28 32	12 55	10 35	8 41	22 40	20 46	25 33
B 7	23 3 23	14 9 11	0♎38	4 17	29 24	13 32	10 45	8 36	22 39	20 45	25 34
E 8	23 7 19	15 7 26	15 10	5 47	0♏14	14 10	10 55	8 32	22 37	20 44	25 35
R 9	23 11 16	16 5 43	29 44	7 15	1 4	14 47	11 5	8 27	22 36	20 43	25 36
10	23 15 12	17 4 2	14♏13	8 43	1 53	15 24	11 15	8 23	22 35	20 43	25 37
11	23 19 9	18 2 22	28 33	10 9	2 42	16 1	11 25	8 18	22 34	20 42	25 39
12	23 23 5	19 0 43	12♐43	11 33	3 29	16 38	11 35	8 14	22 33	20 41	25 40
13	23 27 2	19 59 7	26 41	12 57	4 16	17 14	11 45	8 9	22 32	20 41	25 41
14	23 30 58	20 57 31	10♑27	14 19	5 2	17 51	11 56	8 5	22 31	20 40	25 42
15	23 34 55	21 55 58	24 0	15 40	5 47	18 27	12 6	8 1	22 31	20 40	25 44
16	23 38 52	22 54 25	7♒22	16 59	6 32	19 4	12 17	7 56	22 30	20 39	25 45
17	23 42 48	23 52 55	20 31	18 17	7 15	19 40	12 27	7 52	22 29	20 38	25 46
18	23 46 45	24 51 26	3♓28	19 33	7 57	20 16	12 38	7 48	22 28	20 38	25 48
19	23 50 41	25 49 59	16 12	20 48	8 39	20 52	12 49	7 44	22 28	20 38	25 49
20	23 54 38	26 48 34	28 42	22 1	9 19	21 28	13 0	7 39	22 27	20 37	25 51
21	23 58 34	27 47 10	11♈ 0	23 13	9 58	22 4	13 11	7 35	22 26	20 37	25 52
22	0 2 31	28 45 49	23 7	24 22	10 36	22 39	13 22	7 31	22 26	20 36	25 54
23	0 6 27	29 44 30	5♉ 3	25 30	11 13	23 15	13 33	7 27	22 25	20 36	25 55
24	0 10 24	0♎43 13	16 54	26 36	11 49	23 50	13 44	7 23	22 25	20 36	25 57
25	0 14 20	1 41 58	28 40	27 39	12 23	24 26	13 55	7 19	22 25	20 35	25 58
26	0 18 17	2 40 46	10♊28	28 40	12 56	25 1	14 7	7 15	22 24	20 35	26 0
27	0 22 14	3 39 35	22 22	29 39	13 28	25 36	14 18	7 11	22 24	20 35	26 1
28	0 26 10	4 38 27	4♋27	0♏35	13 58	26 11	14 29	7 7	22 24	20 35	26 3
29	0 30 7	5 37 21	16 48	1 28	14 27	26 46	14 41	7 4	22 24	20 35	26 5
30	0 34 3	6♎36 18	29♋30	2♏18	14♏54	27♋20	14♏53	7♓ 0	22♑23	20♑35	26♏ 7

THE SUN ENTERS THE SIGN OF LIBRA ON SEP 23 AT 06:21.

♈ ARIES ♉ TAURUS ♊ GEMINI ♋ CANCER ♌ LEO ♍ VIRGO ♎ LIBRA

SIDEREAL TIME. SUN. MOON. MERCURY. VENUS. MARS. JUPITER. SATURN. URANUS. NEPTUNE. PLUTO.

DAY	TIME	☉	☽	☿	♀	♂	♃	♄	♅	♆	♇
	h m s	° ' "	° '	° '	° '	° '	° '	° '	° '	° '	° '
O 1	0 38 0	7♎35 17	12♌36	3♏ 4	15♏19	27♋55	15♏ 4	6♓56	22♑23	20♑34	26♏ 8
C 2	0 41 56	8 34 18	26 9	3 47	15 43	28 29	15 16	6R53	22D23	20D34	26 10
T 3	0 45 53	9 33 21	10♍ 9	4 25	16 6	29 4	15 28	6 49	22 23	20 34	26 12
O 4	0 49 49	10 32 26	24 33	4 59	16 26	29 38	15 40	6 46	22 23	20 34	26 14
B 5	0 53 46	11 31 34	9♎15	5 29	16 45	0♌12	15 52	6 43	22 24	20 35	26 15
E 6	0 57 43	12 30 43	24 9	5 53	17 2	0 45	16 4	6 39	22 24	20 35	26 17
R 7	1 1 39	13 29 55	9♏ 6	6 11	17 16	1 19	16 16	6 36	22 24	20 35	26 19
8	1 5 36	14 29 8	23 59	6 23	17 29	1 53	16 28	6 33	22 24	20 35	26 21
9	1 9 32	15 28 24	8♐39	6R29	17 40	2 26	16 40	6 30	22 25	20 35	26 23
10	1 13 29	16 27 41	23 4	6 27	17 48	2 59	16 52	6 27	22 25	20 35	26 25
11	1 17 25	17 27 0	7♑ 9	6 18	17 55	3 32	17 4	6 24	22 25	20 36	26 27
12	1 21 22	18 26 20	20 55	6 1	17 59	4 5	17 17	6 21	22 26	20 36	26 29
13	1 25 18	19 25 43	4♒21	5 35	18R 1	4 38	17 29	6 19	22 26	20 36	26 31
14	1 29 15	20 25 7	17 29	5 2	18 0	5 10	17 41	6 16	22 27	20 37	26 33
15	1 33 12	21 24 33	0♓22	4 20	17 57	5 43	17 54	6 13	22 28	20 37	26 35
16	1 37 8	22 24 0	13 0	3 30	17 52	6 15	18 6	6 11	22 28	20 37	26 37
17	1 41 5	23 23 30	25 25	2 32	17 44	6 47	18 19	6 9	22 29	20 38	26 39
18	1 45 1	24 23 1	7♈39	1 28	17 33	7 19	18 32	6 6	22 30	20 38	26 41
19	1 48 58	25 22 34	19 44	0 19	17 21	7 50	18 44	6 4	22 31	20 39	26 43
20	1 52 54	26 22 10	1♉42	29♎ 6	17 6	8 22	18 57	6 2	22 32	20 39	26 45
21	1 56 51	27 21 47	13 33	27 51	16 48	8 53	19 10	6 0	22 32	20 40	26 48
22	2 0 47	28 21 27	25 21	26 37	16 28	9 24	19 22	5 58	22 33	20 41	26 50
23	2 4 44	29 21 8	7♊ 8	25 26	16 6	9 55	19 35	5 56	22 34	20 41	26 52
24	2 8 41	0♏20 52	18 57	24 19	15 42	10 26	19 48	5 55	22 36	20 42	26 54
25	2 12 37	1 20 38	0♋52	23 19	15 16	10 56	20 1	5 53	22 37	20 43	26 56
26	2 16 34	2 20 26	12 56	22 28	14 48	11 27	20 14	5 51	22 38	20 44	26 58
27	2 20 30	3 20 16	25 15	21 46	14 18	11 57	20 27	5 50	22 39	20 44	27 1
28	2 24 27	4 20 9	7♌53	21 16	13 47	12 27	20 40	5 49	22 40	20 45	27 3
29	2 28 23	5 20 4	20 53	20 57	13 14	12 57	20 53	5 48	22 42	20 46	27 5
30	2 32 20	6 20 1	4♍19	20D49	12 40	13 26	21 6	5 46	22 43	20 47	27 7
31	2 36 16	7♏20 0	18♍13	20♎53	12♏ 5	13♌55	21♏19	5♓45	22♑45	20♑48	27♏10

THE SUN ENTERS THE SIGN OF SCORPIO ON OCT 23 AT 15:37.

DAY	TIME	☉	☽	☿	♀	♂	♃	♄	♅	♆	♇
	h m s	° ' "	° '	° '	° '	° '	° '	° '	° '	° '	° '
N 1	2 40 13	8♏20 1	2♎33	21♎ 7	11♏30	14♌24	21♏32	5♓44	22♑46	20♑49	27♏12
O 2	2 44 9	9 20 4	17 17	21 32	10R53	14 53	21 45	5R44	22 48	20 50	27 14
V 3	2 48 6	10 20 10	2♏18	22 6	10 17	15 22	21 58	5 43	22 49	20 51	27 17
E 4	2 52 3	11 20 17	17 29	22 49	9 41	15 50	22 11	5 42	22 51	20 52	27 19
M 5	2 55 59	12 20 26	2♐40	23 39	9 4	16 18	22 24	5 42	22 52	20 53	27 21
B 6	2 59 56	13 20 37	17 41	24 36	8 29	16 46	22 37	5 41	22 54	20 54	27 24
E 7	3 3 52	14 20 49	2♑24	25 40	7 53	17 14	22 51	5 41	22 56	20 55	27 26
R 8	3 7 49	15 21 4	16 45	26 48	7 19	17 41	23 4	5 41	22 58	20 56	27 28
9	3 11 45	16 21 19	0♒41	28 1	6 46	18 8	23 17	5D41	23 0	20 57	27 31
10	3 15 42	17 21 36	14 10	29 18	6 15	18 35	23 30	5 41	23 1	20 59	27 33
11	3 19 39	18 21 54	27 16	0♏38	5 44	19 2	23 44	5 41	23 3	21 0	27 35
12	3 23 35	19 22 14	10♓ 1	2 1	5 16	19 28	23 57	5 41	23 5	21 1	27 38
13	3 27 32	20 22 35	22 28	3 26	4 49	19 54	24 10	5 41	23 7	21 3	27 40
14	3 31 28	21 22 58	4♈41	4 53	4 25	20 20	24 23	5 42	23 10	21 4	27 43
15	3 35 25	22 23 22	16 44	6 21	4 3	20 45	24 37	5 42	23 12	21 5	27 45
16	3 39 21	23 23 47	28 39	7 51	3 42	21 10	24 50	5 43	23 14	21 7	27 47
17	3 43 18	24 24 14	10♉29	9 22	3 25	21 35	25 3	5 44	23 16	21 8	27 50
18	3 47 14	25 24 43	22 17	10 54	3 9	21 59	25 16	5 45	23 18	21 10	27 52
19	3 51 11	26 25 13	4♊ 5	12 27	2 56	22 23	25 30	5 46	23 20	21 11	27 55
20	3 55 7	27 25 44	15 55	14 0	2 46	22 47	25 43	5 47	23 23	21 12	27 57
21	3 59 4	28 26 18	27 49	15 33	2 38	23 11	25 56	5 48	23 25	21 14	27 59
22	4 3 1	29 26 53	9♋50	17 7	2 32	23 34	26 10	5 49	23 28	21 16	28 2
23	4 6 57	0♐27 29	22 0	18 41	2D29	23 57	26 23	5 51	23 30	21 17	28 4
24	4 10 54	1 28 7	4♌22	20 15	2 29	24 19	26 36	5 52	23 32	21 19	28 6
25	4 14 50	2 28 47	16 59	21 50	2 31	24 41	26 50	5 54	23 35	21 20	28 9
26	4 18 47	3 29 29	29 55	23 24	2 35	25 3	27 3	5 55	23 37	21 22	28 11
27	4 22 43	4 30 12	13♍12	24 58	2 42	25 25	27 16	5 57	23 40	21 24	28 14
28	4 26 40	5 30 56	26 52	26 33	2 51	25 46	27 29	5 59	23 43	21 25	28 16
29	4 30 36	6 31 42	10♎58	28 7	3 2	26 6	27 43	6 1	23 45	21 27	28 18
30	4 34 33	7♐32 30	25♎28	29♏42	3♏16	26♌26	27♏56	6♓ 3	23♑48	21♑29	28♏21

THE SUN ENTERS THE SIGN OF SAGITTARIUS ON NOV 22 AT 13:07.

DAY	TIME	☉	☽	☿	♀	♂	♃	♄	♅	♆	♇
	h m s	° ' "	° '	° '	° '	° '	° '	° '	° '	° '	° '
D 1	4 38 30	8♐33 20	10♏19	1♐16	3♏31	26♌46	28♏ 9	6♓ 5	23♑51	21♑31	28♏23
E 2	4 42 26	9 34 10	25 25	2 50	3 49	27 5	28 22	6 8	23 53	21 32	28 26
C 3	4 46 23	10 35 2	10♐38	4 25	4 8	27 24	28 35	6 10	23 56	21 34	28 28
E 4	4 50 19	11 35 55	25 47	5 59	4 30	27 43	28 49	6 12	23 59	21 36	28 30
M 5	4 54 16	12 36 50	10♑43	7 33	4 53	28 1	29 2	6 15	24 2	21 38	28 33
B 6	4 58 12	13 37 45	25 19	9 7	5 18	28 18	29 15	6 18	24 5	21 40	28 35
E 7	5 2 9	14 38 40	9♒27	10 41	5 45	28 35	29 28	6 20	24 8	21 42	28 37
R 8	5 6 6	15 39 37	23 7	12 16	6 14	28 52	29 41	6 23	24 11	21 44	28 40
9	5 10 2	16 40 34	6♓19	13 50	6 44	29 8	29 54	6 26	24 14	21 46	28 42
10	5 13 59	17 41 32	19 5	15 24	7 16	29 24	0♐ 7	6 29	24 17	21 48	28 44
11	5 17 55	18 42 30	1♈30	16 58	7 49	29 39	0 20	6 33	24 20	21 49	28 47
12	5 21 52	19 43 30	13 38	18 32	8 24	29 53	0 33	6 36	24 23	21 51	28 49
13	5 25 48	20 44 29	25 35	20 7	9 0	0♍ 7	0 46	6 39	24 26	21 53	28 51
14	5 29 45	21 45 29	7♉25	21 41	9 38	0 21	0 59	6 43	24 29	21 55	28 53
15	5 33 41	22 46 30	19 11	23 15	10 16	0 34	1 12	6 46	24 32	21 58	28 56
16	5 37 38	23 47 32	0♊59	24 50	10 56	0 46	1 25	6 50	24 35	22 0	28 58
17	5 41 35	24 48 34	12 50	26 25	11 37	0 58	1 37	6 54	24 38	22 2	29 0
18	5 45 31	25 49 37	24 46	27 59	12 20	1 9	1 50	6 57	24 42	22 4	29 2
19	5 49 28	26 50 40	6♋51	29 34	13 3	1 20	2 3	7 1	24 45	22 6	29 4
20	5 53 24	27 51 44	19 4	1♑10	13 48	1 30	2 16	7 5	24 48	22 8	29 7
21	5 57 21	28 52 49	1♌26	2 45	14 33	1 39	2 28	7 9	24 51	22 10	29 9
22	6 1 17	29 53 54	14 0	4 20	15 20	1 48	2 41	7 13	24 55	22 12	29 11
23	6 5 14	0♑55 0	26 46	5 56	16 7	1 56	2 53	7 18	24 58	22 14	29 13
24	6 9 10	1 56 7	9♍45	7 32	16 56	2 4	3 6	7 22	25 1	22 16	29 15
25	6 13 7	2 57 14	23 0	9 8	17 45	2 11	3 18	7 26	25 5	22 19	29 17
26	6 17 4	3 58 22	6♎33	10 44	18 35	2 17	3 31	7 31	25 8	22 21	29 19
27	6 21 0	4 59 30	20 24	12 21	19 26	2 22	3 43	7 35	25 11	22 23	29 21
28	6 24 57	6 0 39	4♏35	13 58	20 18	2 27	3 55	7 40	25 15	22 25	29 23
29	6 28 53	7 1 49	19 5	15 34	21 10	2 31	4 8	7 45	25 18	22 27	29 25
30	6 32 50	8 2 59	3♐51	17 11	22 3	2 34	4 20	7 50	25 21	22 30	29 27
31	6 36 46	9♑ 4 10	18♐47	18♑49	22♏57	2♍37	4♐32	7♓54	25♑25	22♑32	29♏29

THE SUN ENTERS THE SIGN OF CAPRICORN ON DEC 22 AT 02:24.

♏ SCORPIO ♐ SAGITTARIUS ♑ CAPRICORN ♒ AQUARIUS ♓ PISCES

Appendix 3:
Diurnal Motion of the Sun

TIME	57'	6"	57'	8"	57'	10"	57'	12"	57'	14"	57'	16"	57'	18"	57'	20"	57'	22"	57'	24"	57'	26"	57'	28"	57'	30"	TIME
	'	"	'	"	'	"	'	"	'	"	'	"	'	"	'	"	'	"	'	"	'	"	'	"	'	"	
M 1		2		2		2		2		2		2		2		2		2		2		2		2		2	1 M
I 2		5		5		5		5		5		5		5		5		5		5		5		5		5	2 I
N 3		7		7		7		7		7		7		7		7		7		7		7		7		7	3 N
U 4		10		10		10		10		10		10		10		10		10		10		10		10		10	4 U
T 5		12		12		12		12		12		12		12		12		12		12		12		12		12	5 T
E 6		14		14		14		14		14		14		14		14		14		14		14		14		14	6 E
S 7		17		17		17		17		17		17		17		17		17		17		17		17		17	7 S
8		19		19		19		19		19		19		19		19		19		19		19		19		19	8
9		21		21		21		21		21		21		21		22		22		22		22		22		22	9
10		24		24		24		24		24		24		24		24		24		24		24		24		24	10
11		26		26		26		26		26		26		26		26		26		26		26		26		26	11
12		29		29		29		29		29		29		29		29		29		29		29		29		29	12
13		31		31		31		31		31		31		31		31		31		31		31		31		31	13
14		33		33		33		33		33		33		33		33		33		33		34		34		34	14
15		36		36		36		36		36		36		36		36		36		36		36		36		36	15
16		38		38		38		38		38		38		38		38		38		38		38		38		38	16
17		40		40		40		41		41		41		41		41		41		41		41		41		41	17
18		43		43		43		43		43		43		43		43		43		43		43		43		43	18
19		45		45		45		45		45		45		45		45		45		45		45		45		46	19
20		48		48		48		48		48		48		48		48		48		48		48		48		48	20
21		50		50		50		50		50		50		50		50		50		50		50		50		50	21
22		52		52		52		52		52		52		53		53		53		53		53		53		53	22
23		55		55		55		55		55		55		55		55		55		55		55		55		55	23
24		57		57		57		57		57		57		57		57		57		57		57		57		58	24
25		59	1	0	1	0	1	0	1	0	1	0	1	0	1	0	1	0	1	0	1	0	1	0	1	0	25
26	1	2	1	2	1	2	1	2	1	2	1	2	1	2	1	2	1	2	1	2	1	2	1	2	1	2	26
27	1	4	1	4	1	4	1	4	1	4	1	4	1	4	1	5	1	5	1	5	1	5	1	5	1	5	27
28	1	7	1	7	1	7	1	7	1	7	1	7	1	7	1	7	1	7	1	7	1	7	1	7	1	7	28
29	1	9	1	9	1	9	1	9	1	9	1	9	1	9	1	9	1	9	1	9	1	9	1	9	1	9	29
30	1	11	1	11	1	11	1	12	1	12	1	12	1	12	1	12	1	12	1	12	1	12	1	12	1	12	30
31	1	14	1	14	1	14	1	14	1	14	1	14	1	14	1	14	1	14	1	14	1	14	1	14	1	14	31
32	1	16	1	16	1	16	1	16	1	16	1	16	1	16	1	16	1	16	1	17	1	17	1	17	1	17	32
33	1	19	1	19	1	19	1	19	1	19	1	19	1	19	1	19	1	19	1	19	1	19	1	19	1	19	33
34	1	21	1	21	1	21	1	21	1	21	1	21	1	21	1	21	1	21	1	21	1	21	1	21	1	21	34
35	1	23	1	23	1	23	1	23	1	23	1	24	1	24	1	24	1	24	1	24	1	24	1	24	1	24	35
36	1	26	1	26	1	26	1	26	1	26	1	26	1	26	1	26	1	26	1	26	1	26	1	26	1	26	36
37	1	28	1	28	1	28	1	28	1	28	1	28	1	28	1	28	1	28	1	28	1	29	1	29	1	29	37
38	1	30	1	30	1	31	1	31	1	31	1	31	1	31	1	31	1	31	1	31	1	31	1	31	1	31	38
39	1	33	1	33	1	33	1	33	1	33	1	33	1	33	1	33	1	33	1	33	1	33	1	33	1	33	39
40	1	35	1	35	1	35	1	35	1	35	1	35	1	36	1	36	1	36	1	36	1	36	1	36	1	36	40
41	1	38	1	38	1	38	1	38	1	38	1	38	1	38	1	38	1	38	1	38	1	38	1	38	1	38	41
42	1	40	1	40	1	40	1	40	1	40	1	40	1	40	1	40	1	40	1	40	1	41	1	41	1	41	42
43	1	42	1	42	1	42	1	42	1	43	1	43	1	43	1	43	1	43	1	43	1	43	1	43	1	43	43
44	1	45	1	45	1	45	1	45	1	45	1	45	1	45	1	45	1	45	1	45	1	45	1	45	1	45	44
45	1	47	1	47	1	47	1	47	1	47	1	47	1	47	1	48	1	48	1	48	1	48	1	48	1	48	45
46	1	49	1	50	1	50	1	50	1	50	1	50	1	50	1	50	1	50	1	50	1	50	1	50	1	50	46
47	1	52	1	52	1	52	1	52	1	52	1	52	1	52	1	52	1	52	1	52	1	52	1	53	1	53	47
48	1	54	1	54	1	54	1	54	1	54	1	55	1	55	1	55	1	55	1	55	1	55	1	55	1	55	48
49	1	57	1	57	1	57	1	57	1	57	1	57	1	57	1	57	1	57	1	57	1	57	1	57	1	57	49
50	1	59	1	59	1	59	1	59	1	59	1	59	1	59	1	59	2	0	2	0	2	0	2	0	2	0	50
51	2	1	2	1	2	1	2	2	2	2	2	2	2	2	2	2	2	2	2	2	2	2	2	2	2	2	51
52	2	4	2	4	2	4	2	4	2	4	2	4	2	4	2	4	2	4	2	4	2	4	2	5	2	5	52
53	2	6	2	6	2	6	2	6	2	6	2	6	2	7	2	7	2	7	2	7	2	7	2	7	2	7	53
54	2	8	2	9	2	9	2	9	2	9	2	9	2	9	2	9	2	9	2	9	2	9	2	9	2	9	54
55	2	11	2	11	2	11	2	11	2	11	2	11	2	11	2	11	2	11	2	12	2	12	2	12	2	12	55
56	2	13	2	13	2	13	2	13	2	14	2	14	2	14	2	14	2	14	2	14	2	14	2	14	2	14	56
57	2	16	2	16	2	16	2	16	2	16	2	16	2	16	2	16	2	16	2	16	2	16	2	16	2	17	57
58	2	18	2	18	2	18	2	18	2	18	2	18	2	18	2	19	2	19	2	19	2	19	2	19	2	19	58
59	2	20	2	20	2	21	2	21	2	21	2	21	2	21	2	21	2	21	2	21	2	21	2	21	2	21	59
60	2	23	2	23	2	23	2	23	2	23	2	23	2	23	2	23	2	23	2	24	2	24	2	24	2	24	60
H 1	2	23	2	23	2	23	2	23	2	23	2	23	2	23	2	23	2	23	2	24	2	24	2	24	2	24	1 H
O 2	4	46	4	46	4	46	4	46	4	46	4	46	4	47	4	47	4	47	4	47	4	47	4	47	4	48	2 O
U 3	7	8	7	9	7	9	7	9	7	9	7	10	7	10	7	10	7	10	7	11	7	11	7	11	7	11	3 U
R 4	9	31	9	31	9	32	9	32	9	32	9	33	9	33	9	33	9	34	9	34	9	34	9	35	9	35	4 R
S 5	11	54	11	54	11	55	11	55	11	55	11	56	11	56	11	57	11	57	11	58	11	58	11	58	11	59	5 S
6	14	17	14	17	14	18	14	18	14	19	14	19	14	20	14	20	14	21	14	21	14	22	14	22	14	23	6
7	16	39	16	40	16	40	16	41	16	42	16	42	16	43	16	43	16	44	16	45	16	45	16	46	16	46	7
8	19	2	19	3	19	3	19	4	19	5	19	5	19	6	19	7	19	7	19	8	19	9	19	9	19	10	8
9	21	25	21	26	21	26	21	27	21	28	21	29	21	29	21	30	21	31	21	32	21	32	21	33	21	34	9
10	23	48	23	48	23	49	23	50	23	51	23	52	23	53	23	53	23	54	23	55	23	56	23	57	23	58	10
11	26	10	26	11	26	12	26	13	26	14	26	15	26	16	26	17	26	18	26	19	26	19	26	20	26	21	11
12	28	33	28	34	28	35	28	36	28	37	28	38	28	39	28	40	28	41	28	42	28	43	28	44	28	45	12
13	30	56	30	57	30	58	30	59	31	0	31	1	31	2	31	3	31	4	31	6	31	7	31	8	31	9	13
14	33	19	33	20	33	21	33	22	33	23	33	24	33	26	33	27	33	28	33	29	33	30	33	31	33	33	14
15	35	41	35	43	35	44	35	45	35	46	35	48	35	49	35	50	35	51	35	53	35	54	35	55	35	56	15
16	38	4	38	5	38	7	38	8	38	9	38	11	38	12	38	13	38	15	38	16	38	17	38	19	38	20	16
17	40	27	40	28	40	30	40	31	40	32	40	34	40	35	40	37	40	38	40	40	40	41	40	42	40	44	17
18	42	50	42	51	42	53	42	54	42	56	42	57	42	59	43	0	43	2	43	3	43	5	43	6	43	8	18
19	45	12	45	14	45	15	45	17	45	19	45	20	45	22	45	23	45	25	45	27	45	28	45	30	45	31	19
20	47	35	47	37	47	38	47	40	47	42	47	43	47	45	47	47	47	48	47	50	47	52	47	53	47	55	20
21	49	58	50	0	50	1	50	3	50	5	50	7	50	8	50	10	50	12	50	14	50	15	50	17	50	19	21
22	52	21	52	22	52	24	52	26	52	28	52	30	52	32	52	33	52	35	52	37	52	39	52	41	52	43	22
23	54	43	54	45	54	47	54	49	54	51	54	53	54	55	54	57	54	59	55	1	55	2	55	4	55	6	23
24	57	6	57	8	57	10	57	12	57	14	57	16	57	18	57	20	57	22	57	24	57	26	57	28	57	30	24

TIME	57' 32"	57' 34"	57' 36"	57' 38"	57' 40"	57' 42"	57' 44"	57' 46"	57' 48"	57' 50"	57' 52"	57' 54"	57' 56"	TIME
	' "	' "	' "	' "	' "	' "	' "	' "	' "	' "	' "	' "	' "	
MINUTES														MINUTES
1	2	2	2	2	2	2	2	2	2	2	2	2	2	1
2	5	5	5	5	5	5	5	5	5	5	5	5	5	2
3	7	7	7	7	7	7	7	7	7	7	7	7	7	3
4	10	10	10	10	10	10	10	10	10	10	10	10	10	4
5	12	12	12	12	12	12	12	12	12	12	12	12	12	5
6	14	14	14	14	14	14	14	14	14	14	14	14	14	6
7	17	17	17	17	17	17	17	17	17	17	17	17	17	7
8	19	19	19	19	19	19	19	19	19	19	19	19	19	8
9	22	22	22	22	22	22	22	22	22	22	22	22	22	9
10	24	24	24	24	24	24	24	24	24	24	24	24	24	10
11	26	26	26	26	26	26	26	26	26	27	27	27	27	11
12	29	29	29	29	29	29	29	29	29	29	29	29	29	12
13	31	31	31	31	31	31	31	31	31	31	31	31	31	13
14	34	34	34	34	34	34	34	34	34	34	34	34	34	14
15	36	36	36	36	36	36	36	36	36	36	36	36	36	15
16	38	38	38	38	38	38	38	39	39	39	39	39	39	16
17	41	41	41	41	41	41	41	41	41	41	41	41	41	17
18	43	43	43	43	43	43	43	43	43	43	43	43	43	18
19	46	46	46	46	46	46	46	46	46	46	46	46	46	19
20	48	48	48	48	48	48	48	48	48	48	48	48	48	20
21	50	50	50	50	50	50	51	51	51	51	51	51	51	21
22	53	53	53	53	53	53	53	53	53	53	53	53	53	22
23	55	55	55	55	55	55	55	55	55	55	55	55	56	23
24	58	58	58	58	58	58	58	58	58	58	58	58	58	24
25	1 0	1 0	1 0	1 0	1 0	1 0	1 0	1 0	1 0	1 0	1 0	1 0	1 0	25
26	1 2	1 2	1 2	1 2	1 2	1 3	1 3	1 3	1 3	1 3	1 3	1 3	1 3	26
27	1 5	1 5	1 5	1 5	1 5	1 5	1 5	1 5	1 5	1 5	1 5	1 5	1 5	27
28	1 7	1 7	1 7	1 7	1 7	1 7	1 7	1 7	1 7	1 7	1 8	1 8	1 8	28
29	1 10	1 10	1 10	1 10	1 10	1 10	1 10	1 10	1 10	1 10	1 10	1 10	1 10	29
30	1 12	1 12	1 12	1 12	1 12	1 12	1 12	1 12	1 12	1 12	1 12	1 12	1 12	30
31	1 14	1 14	1 14	1 14	1 14	1 15	1 15	1 15	1 15	1 15	1 15	1 15	1 15	31
32	1 17	1 17	1 17	1 17	1 17	1 17	1 17	1 17	1 17	1 17	1 17	1 17	1 17	32
33	1 19	1 19	1 19	1 19	1 19	1 19	1 19	1 19	1 19	1 20	1 20	1 20	1 20	33
34	1 22	1 22	1 22	1 22	1 22	1 22	1 22	1 22	1 22	1 22	1 22	1 22	1 22	34
35	1 24	1 24	1 24	1 24	1 24	1 24	1 24	1 24	1 24	1 24	1 24	1 24	1 24	35
36	1 26	1 26	1 26	1 26	1 27	1 27	1 27	1 27	1 27	1 27	1 27	1 27	1 27	36
37	1 29	1 29	1 29	1 29	1 29	1 29	1 29	1 29	1 29	1 29	1 29	1 29	1 29	37
38	1 31	1 31	1 31	1 31	1 31	1 31	1 31	1 31	1 32	1 32	1 32	1 32	1 32	38
39	1 33	1 34	1 34	1 34	1 34	1 34	1 34	1 34	1 34	1 34	1 34	1 34	1 34	39
40	1 36	1 36	1 36	1 36	1 36	1 36	1 36	1 36	1 36	1 36	1 36	1 37	1 37	40
41	1 38	1 38	1 38	1 38	1 39	1 39	1 39	1 39	1 39	1 39	1 39	1 39	1 39	41
42	1 41	1 41	1 41	1 41	1 41	1 41	1 41	1 41	1 41	1 41	1 41	1 41	1 41	42
43	1 43	1 43	1 43	1 43	1 43	1 43	1 43	1 43	1 44	1 44	1 44	1 44	1 44	43
44	1 45	1 46	1 46	1 46	1 46	1 46	1 46	1 46	1 46	1 46	1 46	1 46	1 46	44
45	1 48	1 48	1 48	1 48	1 48	1 48	1 48	1 48	1 48	1 48	1 49	1 49	1 49	45
46	1 50	1 50	1 50	1 50	1 51	1 51	1 51	1 51	1 51	1 51	1 51	1 51	1 51	46
47	1 53	1 53	1 53	1 53	1 53	1 53	1 53	1 53	1 53	1 53	1 53	1 53	1 53	47
48	1 55	1 55	1 55	1 55	1 55	1 55	1 55	1 56	1 56	1 56	1 56	1 56	1 56	48
49	1 57	1 58	1 58	1 58	1 58	1 58	1 58	1 58	1 58	1 58	1 58	1 58	1 58	49
50	2 0	2 0	2 0	2 0	2 0	2 0	2 0	2 0	2 0	2 0	2 1	2 1	2 1	50
51	2 2	2 2	2 2	2 2	2 3	2 3	2 3	2 3	2 3	2 3	2 3	2 3	2 3	51
52	2 5	2 5	2 5	2 5	2 5	2 5	2 5	2 5	2 5	2 5	2 5	2 5	2 6	52
53	2 7	2 7	2 7	2 7	2 7	2 7	2 7	2 8	2 8	2 8	2 8	2 8	2 8	53
54	2 9	2 10	2 10	2 10	2 10	2 10	2 10	2 10	2 10	2 10	2 10	2 10	2 10	54
55	2 12	2 12	2 12	2 12	2 12	2 12	2 12	2 12	2 12	2 13	2 13	2 13	2 13	55
56	2 14	2 14	2 14	2 14	2 15	2 15	2 15	2 15	2 15	2 15	2 15	2 15	2 15	56
57	2 17	2 17	2 17	2 17	2 17	2 17	2 17	2 17	2 17	2 17	2 17	2 18	2 18	57
58	2 19	2 19	2 19	2 19	2 19	2 19	2 20	2 20	2 20	2 20	2 20	2 20	2 20	58
59	2 21	2 22	2 22	2 22	2 22	2 22	2 22	2 22	2 22	2 22	2 22	2 22	2 22	59
60	2 24	2 24	2 24	2 24	2 24	2 24	2 24	2 24	2 25	2 25	2 25	2 25	2 25	60
HOURS														HOURS
1	2 24	2 24	2 24	2 24	2 24	2 24	2 24	2 24	2 25	2 25	2 25	2 25	2 25	1
2	4 48	4 48	4 48	4 48	4 48	4 49	4 49	4 49	4 49	4 49	4 49	4 50	4 50	2
3	7 12	7 12	7 12	7 12	7 13	7 13	7 13	7 13	7 14	7 14	7 14	7 14	7 15	3
4	9 35	9 36	9 36	9 36	9 37	9 37	9 37	9 38	9 38	9 38	9 39	9 39	9 39	4
5	11 59	12 0	12 0	12 0	12 1	12 1	12 2	12 2	12 3	12 3	12 3	12 4	12 4	5
6	14 23	14 24	14 24	14 25	14 25	14 26	14 26	14 27	14 27	14 28	14 28	14 29	14 29	6
7	16 47	16 47	16 48	16 49	16 49	16 50	16 50	16 51	16 52	16 52	16 53	16 53	16 54	7
8	19 11	19 11	19 12	19 13	19 13	19 14	19 15	19 15	19 16	19 17	19 17	19 18	19 19	8
9	21 35	21 35	21 36	21 37	21 38	21 38	21 39	21 40	21 41	21 41	21 42	21 43	21 44	9
10	23 58	23 59	24 0	24 1	24 2	24 3	24 3	24 4	24 5	24 6	24 7	24 8	24 8	10
11	26 22	26 23	26 24	26 25	26 26	26 27	26 28	26 29	26 30	26 30	26 31	26 32	26 33	11
12	28 46	28 47	28 48	28 49	28 50	28 51	28 52	28 53	28 54	28 55	28 56	28 57	28 58	12
13	31 10	31 11	31 12	31 13	31 14	31 15	31 16	31 17	31 19	31 20	31 21	31 22	31 23	13
14	33 34	33 35	33 36	33 37	33 38	33 40	33 41	33 42	33 43	33 44	33 45	33 47	33 48	14
15	35 58	35 59	36 0	36 1	36 3	36 4	36 5	36 6	36 8	36 9	36 10	36 11	36 13	15
16	38 21	38 23	38 24	38 25	38 27	38 28	38 29	38 31	38 32	38 33	38 35	38 36	38 37	16
17	40 45	40 47	40 48	40 49	40 51	40 52	40 54	40 55	40 57	40 58	40 59	41 1	41 2	17
18	43 9	43 11	43 12	43 14	43 15	43 17	43 18	43 20	43 21	43 23	43 24	43 26	43 27	18
19	45 33	45 34	45 36	45 38	45 39	45 41	45 42	45 44	45 46	45 47	45 49	45 50	45 52	19
20	47 57	47 58	48 0	48 2	48 3	48 5	48 7	48 8	48 10	48 12	48 13	48 15	48 17	20
21	50 21	50 22	50 24	50 26	50 28	50 29	50 31	50 33	50 35	50 36	50 38	50 40	50 42	21
22	52 44	52 46	52 48	52 50	52 52	52 54	52 55	52 57	52 59	53 1	53 3	53 5	53 6	22
23	55 8	55 10	55 12	55 14	55 16	55 18	55 20	55 22	55 24	55 25	55 27	55 29	55 31	23
24	57 32	57 34	57 36	57 38	57 40	57 42	57 44	57 46	57 48	57 50	57 52	57 54	57 56	24

24 HOUR TRAVEL

24 HOUR TRAVEL

TIME	57' 58"	58' 0"	58' 2"	58' 4"	58' 6"	58' 8"	58' 10"	58' 12"	58' 14"	58' 16"	58' 18"	58' 20"	58' 22"	TIME
MINUTES	' "	' "	' "	' "	' "	' "	' "	' "	' "	' "	' "	' "	' "	MINUTES
1	2	2	2	2	2	2	2	2	2	2	2	2	2	1
2	5	5	5	5	5	5	5	5	5	5	5	5	5	2
3	7	7	7	7	7	7	7	7	7	7	7	7	7	3
4	10	10	10	10	10	10	10	10	10	10	10	10	10	4
5	12	12	12	12	12	12	12	12	12	12	12	12	12	5
6	14	15	15	15	15	15	15	15	15	15	15	15	15	6
7	17	17	17	17	17	17	17	17	17	17	17	17	17	7
8	19	19	19	19	19	19	19	19	19	19	19	19	19	8
9	22	22	22	22	22	22	22	22	22	22	22	22	22	9
10	24	24	24	24	24	24	24	24	24	24	24	24	24	10
11	27	27	27	27	27	27	27	27	27	27	27	27	27	11
12	29	29	29	29	29	29	29	29	29	29	29	29	29	12
13	31	31	31	31	31	31	32	32	32	32	32	32	32	13
14	34	34	34	34	34	34	34	34	34	34	34	34	34	14
15	36	36	36	36	36	36	36	36	36	36	36	36	36	15
16	39	39	39	39	39	39	39	39	39	39	39	39	39	16
17	41	41	41	41	41	41	41	41	41	41	41	41	41	17
18	43	44	44	44	44	44	44	44	44	44	44	44	44	18
19	46	46	46	46	46	46	46	46	46	46	46	46	46	19
20	48	48	48	48	48	48	48	49	49	49	49	49	49	20
21	51	51	51	51	51	51	51	51	51	51	51	51	51	21
22	53	53	53	53	53	53	53	53	53	53	53	53	54	22
23	56	56	56	56	56	56	56	56	56	56	56	56	56	23
24	58	58	58	58	58	58	58	58	58	58	58	58	58	24
25	1 0	1 0	1 0	1 0	1 1	1 1	1 1	1 1	1 1	1 1	1 1	1 1	1 1	25
26	1 3	1 3	1 3	1 3	1 3	1 3	1 3	1 3	1 3	1 3	1 3	1 3	1 3	26
27	1 5	1 5	1 5	1 5	1 5	1 5	1 5	1 5	1 6	1 6	1 6	1 6	1 6	27
28	1 8	1 8	1 8	1 8	1 8	1 8	1 8	1 8	1 8	1 8	1 8	1 8	1 8	28
29	1 10	1 10	1 10	1 10	1 10	1 10	1 10	1 10	1 10	1 10	1 10	1 10	1 11	29
30	1 12	1 13	1 13	1 13	1 13	1 13	1 13	1 13	1 13	1 13	1 13	1 13	1 13	30
31	1 15	1 15	1 15	1 15	1 15	1 15	1 15	1 15	1 15	1 15	1 15	1 15	1 15	31
32	1 17	1 17	1 17	1 17	1 17	1 18	1 18	1 18	1 18	1 18	1 18	1 18	1 18	32
33	1 20	1 20	1 20	1 20	1 20	1 20	1 20	1 20	1 20	1 20	1 20	1 20	1 20	33
34	1 22	1 22	1 22	1 22	1 22	1 22	1 22	1 22	1 22	1 23	1 23	1 23	1 23	34
35	1 25	1 25	1 25	1 25	1 25	1 25	1 25	1 25	1 25	1 25	1 25	1 25	1 25	35
36	1 27	1 27	1 27	1 27	1 27	1 27	1 27	1 27	1 27	1 27	1 27	1 28	1 28	36
37	1 29	1 29	1 29	1 30	1 30	1 30	1 30	1 30	1 30	1 30	1 30	1 30	1 30	37
38	1 32	1 32	1 32	1 32	1 32	1 32	1 32	1 32	1 32	1 32	1 32	1 32	1 32	38
39	1 34	1 34	1 34	1 34	1 34	1 34	1 35	1 35	1 35	1 35	1 35	1 35	1 35	39
40	1 37	1 37	1 37	1 37	1 37	1 37	1 37	1 37	1 37	1 37	1 37	1 37	1 37	40
41	1 39	1 39	1 39	1 39	1 39	1 39	1 39	1 39	1 39	1 40	1 40	1 40	1 40	41
42	1 41	1 42	1 42	1 42	1 42	1 42	1 42	1 42	1 42	1 42	1 42	1 42	1 42	42
43	1 44	1 44	1 44	1 44	1 44	1 44	1 44	1 44	1 44	1 44	1 44	1 45	1 45	43
44	1 46	1 46	1 46	1 46	1 47	1 47	1 47	1 47	1 47	1 47	1 47	1 47	1 47	44
45	1 49	1 49	1 49	1 49	1 49	1 49	1 49	1 49	1 49	1 49	1 49	1 49	1 49	45
46	1 51	1 51	1 51	1 51	1 51	1 51	1 51	1 52	1 52	1 52	1 52	1 52	1 52	46
47	1 54	1 54	1 54	1 54	1 54	1 54	1 54	1 54	1 54	1 54	1 54	1 54	1 54	47
48	1 56	1 56	1 56	1 56	1 56	1 56	1 56	1 56	1 56	1 57	1 57	1 57	1 57	48
49	1 58	1 58	1 58	1 59	1 59	1 59	1 59	1 59	1 59	1 59	1 59	1 59	1 59	49
50	2 1	2 1	2 1	2 1	2 1	2 1	2 1	2 1	2 1	2 1	2 1	2 2	2 2	50
51	2 3	2 3	2 3	2 3	2 3	2 4	2 4	2 4	2 4	2 4	2 4	2 4	2 4	51
52	2 6	2 6	2 6	2 6	2 6	2 6	2 6	2 6	2 6	2 6	2 6	2 6	2 6	52
53	2 8	2 8	2 8	2 8	2 8	2 8	2 8	2 9	2 9	2 9	2 9	2 9	2 9	53
54	2 10	2 11	2 11	2 11	2 11	2 11	2 11	2 11	2 11	2 11	2 11	2 11	2 11	54
55	2 13	2 13	2 13	2 13	2 13	2 13	2 13	2 13	2 13	2 14	2 14	2 14	2 14	55
56	2 15	2 15	2 15	2 15	2 16	2 16	2 16	2 16	2 16	2 16	2 16	2 16	2 16	56
57	2 18	2 18	2 18	2 18	2 18	2 18	2 18	2 18	2 18	2 18	2 18	2 19	2 19	57
58	2 20	2 20	2 20	2 20	2 20	2 20	2 21	2 21	2 21	2 21	2 21	2 21	2 21	58
59	2 23	2 23	2 23	2 23	2 23	2 23	2 23	2 23	2 23	2 23	2 23	2 23	2 23	59
60	2 25	2 25	2 25	2 25	2 25	2 25	2 25	2 26	2 26	2 26	2 26	2 26	2 26	60
HOURS														HOURS
1	2 25	2 25	2 25	2 25	2 25	2 25	2 25	2 26	2 26	2 26	2 26	2 26	2 26	1
2	4 50	4 50	4 50	4 50	4 51	4 51	4 51	4 51	4 51	4 51	4 52	4 52	4 52	2
3	7 15	7 15	7 15	7 16	7 16	7 16	7 16	7 17	7 17	7 17	7 17	7 18	7 18	3
4	9 40	9 40	9 40	9 41	9 41	9 41	9 42	9 42	9 42	9 43	9 43	9 43	9 44	4
5	12 5	12 5	12 5	12 6	12 6	12 7	12 7	12 8	12 8	12 8	12 9	12 9	12 10	5
6	14 30	14 30	14 31	14 31	14 32	14 32	14 33	14 33	14 34	14 34	14 35	14 35	14 36	6
7	16 54	16 55	16 56	16 56	16 57	16 57	16 58	16 59	16 59	17 0	17 0	17 1	17 1	7
8	19 19	19 20	19 21	19 21	19 22	19 23	19 23	19 24	19 25	19 25	19 26	19 27	19 27	8
9	21 44	21 45	21 46	21 47	21 47	21 48	21 49	21 50	21 50	21 51	21 52	21 53	21 53	9
10	24 9	24 10	24 11	24 12	24 13	24 13	24 14	24 15	24 16	24 17	24 18	24 18	24 19	10
11	26 34	26 35	26 36	26 37	26 38	26 39	26 40	26 41	26 41	26 42	26 43	26 44	26 45	11
12	28 59	29 0	29 1	29 2	29 3	29 4	29 5	29 6	29 7	29 8	29 9	29 10	29 11	12
13	31 24	31 25	31 26	31 27	31 28	31 29	31 30	31 32	31 33	31 34	31 35	31 36	31 37	13
14	33 49	33 50	33 51	33 52	33 54	33 55	33 56	33 57	33 58	33 59	34 1	34 2	34 3	14
15	36 14	36 15	36 16	36 18	36 19	36 20	36 21	36 23	36 24	36 25	36 26	36 28	36 29	15
16	38 39	38 40	38 41	38 43	38 44	38 45	38 47	38 48	38 49	38 51	38 52	38 53	38 55	16
17	41 4	41 5	41 6	41 8	41 9	41 11	41 12	41 14	41 15	41 16	41 18	41 19	41 21	17
18	43 29	43 30	43 32	43 33	43 35	43 36	43 38	43 39	43 41	43 42	43 44	43 45	43 47	18
19	45 53	45 55	45 57	45 58	46 0	46 1	46 3	46 5	46 6	46 8	46 9	46 11	46 12	19
20	48 18	48 20	48 22	48 23	48 25	48 27	48 28	48 30	48 32	48 33	48 35	48 37	48 38	20
21	50 43	50 45	50 47	50 49	50 50	50 52	50 54	50 56	50 57	50 59	51 1	51 3	51 4	21
22	53 8	53 10	53 12	53 14	53 16	53 17	53 19	53 21	53 23	53 25	53 27	53 28	53 30	22
23	55 33	55 35	55 37	55 39	55 41	55 43	55 45	55 47	55 48	55 50	55 52	55 54	55 56	23
24	57 58	58 0	58 2	58 4	58 6	58 8	58 10	58 12	58 14	58 16	58 18	58 20	58 22	24

24 HOUR TRAVEL

	TIME	58 '	24 "	58 '	26 "	58 '	28 "	58 '	30 "	58 '	32 "	58 '	34 "	58 '	36 "	58 '	38 "	58 '	40 "	58 '	42 "	58 '	44 "	58 '	46 "	58 '	48 "
MINUTES	1		2		2		2		2		2		2		2		2		2		2		2		2		2
	2		5		5		5		5		5		5		5		5		5		5		5		5		5
	3		7		7		7		7		7		7		7		7		7		7		7		7		7
	4		10		10		10		10		10		10		10		10		10		10		10		10		10
	5		12		12		12		12		12		12		12		12		12		12		12		12		12
	6		15		15		15		15		15		15		15		15		15		15		15		15		15
	7		17		17		17		17		17		17		17		17		17		17		17		17		17
	8		19		19		19		20		20		20		20		20		20		20		20		20		20
	9		22		22		22		22		22		22		22		22		22		22		22		22		22
	10		24		24		24		24		24		24		24		24		24		24		24		24		25
	11		27		27		27		27		27		27		27		27		27		27		27		27		27
	12		29		29		29		29		29		29		29		29		29		29		29		29		29
	13		32		32		32		32		32		32		32		32		32		32		32		32		32
	14		34		34		34		34		34		34		34		34		34		34		34		34		34
	15		37		37		37		37		37		37		37		37		37		37		37		37		37
	16		39		39		39		39		39		39		39		39		39		39		39		39		39
	17		41		41		41		41		41		41		42		42		42		42		42		42		42
	18		44		44		44		44		44		44		44		44		44		44		44		44		44
	19		46		46		46		46		46		46		46		46		46		46		46		47		47
	20		49		49		49		49		49		49		49		49		49		49		49		49		49
	21		51		51		51		51		51		51		51		51		51		51		51		51		51
	22		54		54		54		54		54		54		54		54		54		54		54		54		54
	23		56		56		56		56		56		56		56		56		56		56		56		56		56
	24		58		58		58		59		59		59		59		59		59		59		59		59		59
	25	1	1	1	1	1	1	1	1	1	1	1	1	1	1	1	1	1	1	1	1	1	1	1	1	1	1
	26	1	3	1	3	1	3	1	3	1	3	1	3	1	3	1	4	1	4	1	4	1	4	1	4	1	4
	27	1	6	1	6	1	6	1	6	1	6	1	6	1	6	1	6	1	6	1	6	1	6	1	6	1	6
	28	1	8	1	8	1	8	1	8	1	8	1	8	1	8	1	8	1	8	1	8	1	9	1	9	1	9
	29	1	11	1	11	1	11	1	11	1	11	1	11	1	11	1	11	1	11	1	11	1	11	1	11	1	11
	30	1	13	1	13	1	13	1	13	1	13	1	13	1	13	1	13	1	13	1	13	1	13	1	13	1	14
	31	1	15	1	15	1	16	1	16	1	16	1	16	1	16	1	16	1	16	1	16	1	16	1	16	1	16
	32	1	18	1	18	1	18	1	18	1	18	1	18	1	18	1	18	1	18	1	18	1	18	1	18	1	18
	33	1	20	1	20	1	20	1	20	1	20	1	21	1	21	1	21	1	21	1	21	1	21	1	21	1	21
	34	1	23	1	23	1	23	1	23	1	23	1	23	1	23	1	23	1	23	1	23	1	23	1	23	1	23
	35	1	25	1	25	1	25	1	25	1	25	1	25	1	25	1	26	1	26	1	26	1	26	1	26	1	26
	36	1	28	1	28	1	28	1	28	1	28	1	28	1	28	1	28	1	28	1	28	1	28	1	28	1	28
	37	1	30	1	30	1	30	1	30	1	30	1	30	1	30	1	30	1	30	1	30	1	31	1	31	1	31
	38	1	32	1	33	1	33	1	33	1	33	1	33	1	33	1	33	1	33	1	33	1	33	1	33	1	33
	39	1	35	1	35	1	35	1	35	1	35	1	35	1	35	1	35	1	35	1	35	1	35	1	35	1	36
	40	1	37	1	37	1	37	1	38	1	38	1	38	1	38	1	38	1	38	1	38	1	38	1	38	1	38
	41	1	40	1	40	1	40	1	40	1	40	1	40	1	40	1	40	1	40	1	40	1	40	1	40	1	40
	42	1	42	1	42	1	42	1	42	1	42	1	42	1	43	1	43	1	43	1	43	1	43	1	43	1	43
	43	1	45	1	45	1	45	1	45	1	45	1	45	1	45	1	45	1	45	1	45	1	45	1	45	1	45
	44	1	47	1	47	1	47	1	47	1	47	1	47	1	47	1	47	1	48	1	48	1	48	1	48	1	48
	45	1	50	1	50	1	50	1	50	1	50	1	50	1	50	1	50	1	50	1	50	1	50	1	50	1	50
	46	1	52	1	52	1	52	1	52	1	52	1	52	1	52	1	52	1	52	1	53	1	53	1	53	1	53
	47	1	54	1	54	1	54	1	55	1	55	1	55	1	55	1	55	1	55	1	55	1	55	1	55	1	55
	48	1	57	1	57	1	57	1	57	1	57	1	57	1	57	1	57	1	57	1	57	1	57	1	58	1	58
	49	1	59	1	59	1	59	1	59	2	0	2	0	2	0	2	0	2	0	2	0	2	0	2	0	2	0
	50	2	2	2	2	2	2	2	2	2	2	2	2	2	2	2	2	2	2	2	2	2	2	2	2	2	3
	51	2	4	2	4	2	4	2	4	2	4	2	4	2	5	2	5	2	5	2	5	2	5	2	5	2	5
	52	2	7	2	7	2	7	2	7	2	7	2	7	2	7	2	7	2	7	2	7	2	7	2	7	2	7
	53	2	9	2	9	2	9	2	9	2	9	2	9	2	9	2	9	2	10	2	10	2	10	2	10	2	10
	54	2	11	2	11	2	12	2	12	2	12	2	12	2	12	2	12	2	12	2	12	2	12	2	12	2	12
	55	2	14	2	14	2	14	2	14	2	14	2	14	2	14	2	14	2	14	2	15	2	15	2	15	2	15
	56	2	16	2	16	2	16	2	17	2	17	2	17	2	17	2	17	2	17	2	17	2	17	2	17	2	17
	57	2	19	2	19	2	19	2	19	2	19	2	19	2	19	2	19	2	19	2	19	2	19	2	20	2	20
	58	2	21	2	21	2	21	2	21	2	21	2	22	2	22	2	22	2	22	2	22	2	22	2	22	2	22
	59	2	24	2	24	2	24	2	24	2	24	2	24	2	24	2	24	2	24	2	24	2	24	2	24	2	25
	60	2	26	2	26	2	26	2	26	2	26	2	26	2	27	2	27	2	27	2	27	2	27	2	27	2	27
HOURS	1	2	26	2	26	2	26	2	26	2	26	2	26	2	27	2	27	2	27	2	27	2	27	2	27	2	27
	2	4	52	4	52	4	52	4	53	4	53	4	53	4	53	4	53	4	53	4	54	4	54	4	54	4	54
	3	7	18	7	18	7	19	7	19	7	19	7	19	7	20	7	20	7	20	7	20	7	21	7	21	7	21
	4	9	44	9	44	9	45	9	45	9	45	9	46	9	46	9	46	9	47	9	47	9	47	9	48	9	48
	5	12	10	12	10	12	11	12	11	12	12	12	12	12	13	12	13	12	13	12	14	12	14	12	15	12	15
	6	14	36	14	37	14	37	14	38	14	38	14	39	14	39	14	40	14	40	14	41	14	41	14	42	14	42
	7	17	2	17	3	17	3	17	4	17	4	17	5	17	6	17	6	17	7	17	7	17	8	17	8	17	9
	8	19	28	19	29	19	29	19	30	19	31	19	31	19	32	19	33	19	33	19	34	19	35	19	35	19	36
	9	21	54	21	55	21	56	21	56	21	57	21	58	21	59	21	59	22	0	22	1	22	2	22	2	22	3
	10	24	20	24	21	24	22	24	23	24	23	24	24	24	25	24	26	24	27	24	28	24	28	24	29	24	30
	11	26	46	26	47	26	48	26	49	26	50	26	51	26	52	26	52	26	53	26	54	26	55	26	56	26	57
	12	29	12	29	13	29	14	29	15	29	16	29	17	29	18	29	19	29	20	29	21	29	22	29	23	29	24
	13	31	38	31	39	31	40	31	41	31	42	31	43	31	45	31	46	31	47	31	48	31	49	31	50	31	51
	14	34	4	34	5	34	6	34	8	34	9	34	10	34	11	34	12	34	13	34	15	34	16	34	17	34	18
	15	36	30	36	31	36	33	36	34	36	35	36	36	36	38	36	39	36	40	36	41	36	43	36	44	36	45
	16	38	56	38	57	38	59	39	0	39	1	39	3	39	4	39	5	39	7	39	8	39	9	39	11	39	12
	17	41	22	41	23	41	25	41	26	41	28	41	29	41	31	41	32	41	33	41	35	41	36	41	38	41	39
	18	43	48	43	50	43	51	43	53	43	54	43	56	43	57	43	59	44	0	44	2	44	3	44	5	44	6
	19	46	14	46	16	46	17	46	19	46	20	46	22	46	24	46	25	46	27	46	28	46	30	46	31	46	33
	20	48	40	48	42	48	43	48	45	48	47	48	48	48	50	48	52	48	53	48	55	48	57	48	58	49	0
	21	51	6	51	8	51	10	51	11	51	13	51	15	51	17	51	18	51	20	51	22	51	24	51	25	51	27
	22	53	32	53	34	53	36	53	38	53	39	53	41	53	43	53	45	53	47	53	49	53	50	53	52	53	54
	23	55	58	56	0	56	2	56	4	56	6	56	8	56	10	56	11	56	13	56	15	56	17	56	19	56	21
	24	58	24	58	26	58	28	58	30	58	32	58	34	58	36	58	38	58	40	58	42	58	44	58	46	58	48

24 HOUR TRAVEL

TIME	58′ 50″	58′ 52″	58′ 54″	58′ 56″	58′ 58″	59′ 0″	59′ 2″	59′ 4″	59′ 6″	59′ 8″	59′ 10″	59′ 12″	59′ 14″	TIME
	′ ″	′ ″	′ ″	′ ″	′ ″	′ ″	′ ″	′ ″	′ ″	′ ″	′ ″	′ ″	′ ″	
MINUTES 1	2	2	2	2	2	2	2	2	2	2	2	2	2	1 MINUTES
2	5	5	5	5	5	5	5	5	5	5	5	5	5	2
3	7	7	7	7	7	7	7	7	7	7	7	7	7	3
4	10	10	10	10	10	10	10	10	10	10	10	10	10	4
5	12	12	12	12	12	12	12	12	12	12	12	12	12	5
6	15	15	15	15	15	15	15	15	15	15	15	15	15	6
7	17	17	17	17	17	17	17	17	17	17	17	17	17	7
8	20	20	20	20	20	20	20	20	20	20	20	20	20	8
9	22	22	22	22	22	22	22	22	22	22	22	22	22	9
10	25	25	25	25	25	25	25	25	25	25	25	25	25	10
11	27	27	27	27	27	27	27	27	27	27	27	27	27	11
12	29	29	29	29	29	30	30	30	30	30	30	30	30	12
13	32	32	32	32	32	32	32	32	32	32	32	32	32	13
14	34	34	34	34	34	34	34	34	34	34	35	35	35	14
15	37	37	37	37	37	37	37	37	37	37	37	37	37	15
16	39	39	39	39	39	39	39	39	39	39	39	39	39	16
17	42	42	42	42	42	42	42	42	42	42	42	42	42	17
18	44	44	44	44	44	44	44	44	44	44	44	44	44	18
19	47	47	47	47	47	47	47	47	47	47	47	47	47	19
20	49	49	49	49	49	49	49	49	49	49	49	49	49	20
21	51	52	52	52	52	52	52	52	52	52	52	52	52	21
22	54	54	54	54	54	54	54	54	54	54	54	54	54	22
23	56	56	56	56	57	57	57	57	57	57	57	57	57	23
24	59	59	59	59	59	59	59	59	59	59	59	59	59	24
25	1 1	1 1	1 1	1 1	1 1	1 1	1 1	1 2	1 2	1 2	1 2	1 2	1 2	25
26	1 4	1 4	1 4	1 4	1 4	1 4	1 4	1 4	1 4	1 4	1 4	1 4	1 4	26
27	1 6	1 6	1 6	1 6	1 6	1 6	1 6	1 6	1 6	1 7	1 7	1 7	1 7	27
28	1 9	1 9	1 9	1 9	1 9	1 9	1 9	1 9	1 9	1 9	1 9	1 9	1 9	28
29	1 11	1 11	1 11	1 11	1 11	1 11	1 11	1 11	1 11	1 11	1 11	1 12	1 12	29
30	1 14	1 14	1 14	1 14	1 14	1 14	1 14	1 14	1 14	1 14	1 14	1 14	1 14	30
31	1 16	1 16	1 16	1 16	1 16	1 16	1 16	1 16	1 16	1 16	1 16	1 16	1 17	31
32	1 18	1 18	1 19	1 19	1 19	1 19	1 19	1 19	1 19	1 19	1 19	1 19	1 19	32
33	1 21	1 21	1 21	1 21	1 21	1 21	1 21	1 21	1 21	1 21	1 21	1 21	1 21	33
34	1 23	1 23	1 23	1 23	1 24	1 24	1 24	1 24	1 24	1 24	1 24	1 24	1 24	34
35	1 26	1 26	1 26	1 26	1 26	1 26	1 26	1 26	1 26	1 26	1 26	1 26	1 26	35
36	1 28	1 28	1 28	1 28	1 28	1 29	1 29	1 29	1 29	1 29	1 29	1 29	1 29	36
37	1 31	1 31	1 31	1 31	1 31	1 31	1 31	1 31	1 31	1 31	1 31	1 31	1 31	37
38	1 33	1 33	1 33	1 33	1 33	1 33	1 33	1 34	1 34	1 34	1 34	1 34	1 34	38
39	1 36	1 36	1 36	1 36	1 36	1 36	1 36	1 36	1 36	1 36	1 36	1 36	1 36	39
40	1 38	1 38	1 38	1 38	1 38	1 38	1 38	1 38	1 39	1 39	1 39	1 39	1 39	40
41	1 41	1 41	1 41	1 41	1 41	1 41	1 41	1 41	1 41	1 41	1 41	1 41	1 41	41
42	1 43	1 43	1 43	1 43	1 43	1 43	1 43	1 43	1 43	1 43	1 44	1 44	1 44	42
43	1 45	1 45	1 46	1 46	1 46	1 46	1 46	1 46	1 46	1 46	1 46	1 46	1 46	43
44	1 48	1 48	1 48	1 48	1 48	1 48	1 48	1 48	1 48	1 48	1 48	1 49	1 49	44
45	1 50	1 50	1 50	1 51	1 51	1 51	1 51	1 51	1 51	1 51	1 51	1 51	1 51	45
46	1 53	1 53	1 53	1 53	1 53	1 53	1 53	1 53	1 53	1 53	1 53	1 53	1 54	46
47	1 55	1 55	1 55	1 55	1 55	1 56	1 56	1 56	1 56	1 56	1 56	1 56	1 56	47
48	1 58	1 58	1 58	1 58	1 58	1 58	1 58	1 58	1 58	1 58	1 58	1 58	1 58	48
49	2 0	2 0	2 0	2 0	2 0	2 0	2 1	2 1	2 1	2 1	2 1	2 1	2 1	49
50	2 3	2 3	2 3	2 3	2 3	2 3	2 3	2 3	2 3	2 3	2 3	2 3	2 3	50
51	2 5	2 5	2 5	2 5	2 5	2 5	2 5	2 5	2 6	2 6	2 6	2 6	2 6	51
52	2 7	2 8	2 8	2 8	2 8	2 8	2 8	2 8	2 8	2 8	2 8	2 8	2 8	52
53	2 10	2 10	2 10	2 10	2 10	2 10	2 10	2 10	2 11	2 11	2 11	2 11	2 11	53
54	2 12	2 12	2 13	2 13	2 13	2 13	2 13	2 13	2 13	2 13	2 13	2 13	2 13	54
55	2 15	2 15	2 15	2 15	2 15	2 15	2 15	2 15	2 15	2 16	2 16	2 16	2 16	55
56	2 17	2 17	2 17	2 18	2 18	2 18	2 18	2 18	2 18	2 18	2 18	2 18	2 18	56
57	2 20	2 20	2 20	2 20	2 20	2 20	2 20	2 20	2 20	2 20	2 21	2 21	2 21	57
58	2 22	2 22	2 22	2 22	2 23	2 23	2 23	2 23	2 23	2 23	2 23	2 23	2 23	58
59	2 25	2 25	2 25	2 25	2 25	2 25	2 25	2 25	2 25	2 25	2 25	2 26	2 26	59
60	2 27	2 27	2 27	2 27	2 27	2 28	2 28	2 28	2 28	2 28	2 28	2 28	2 28	60
HOURS 1	2 27	2 27	2 27	2 27	2 27	2 28	2 28	2 28	2 28	2 28	2 28	2 28	2 28	1 HOURS
2	4 54	4 54	4 55	4 55	4 55	4 55	4 55	4 55	4 56	4 56	4 56	4 56	4 56	2
3	7 21	7 22	7 22	7 22	7 22	7 23	7 23	7 23	7 23	7 24	7 24	7 24	7 24	3
4	9 48	9 49	9 49	9 49	9 50	9 50	9 50	9 51	9 51	9 51	9 52	9 52	9 52	4
5	12 15	12 16	12 16	12 17	12 17	12 18	12 18	12 18	12 19	12 19	12 20	12 20	12 20	5
6	14 43	14 43	14 44	14 44	14 45	14 45	14 46	14 46	14 47	14 47	14 48	14 48	14 49	6
7	17 10	17 10	17 11	17 11	17 12	17 13	17 13	17 14	17 14	17 15	17 15	17 16	17 17	7
8	19 37	19 37	19 38	19 39	19 39	19 40	19 41	19 41	19 42	19 43	19 43	19 44	19 45	8
9	22 4	22 5	22 5	22 6	22 7	22 8	22 8	22 9	22 10	22 11	22 11	22 12	22 13	9
10	24 31	24 32	24 33	24 33	24 34	24 35	24 36	24 37	24 38	24 38	24 39	24 40	24 41	10
11	26 58	26 59	27 0	27 1	27 2	27 3	27 3	27 4	27 5	27 6	27 7	27 8	27 9	11
12	29 25	29 26	29 27	29 28	29 29	29 30	29 31	29 32	29 33	29 34	29 35	29 36	29 37	12
13	31 52	31 53	31 54	31 55	31 56	31 58	31 59	32 0	32 1	32 2	32 3	32 4	32 5	13
14	34 19	34 20	34 22	34 23	34 24	34 25	34 26	34 27	34 29	34 30	34 31	34 32	34 33	14
15	36 46	36 48	36 49	36 50	36 51	36 53	36 54	36 55	36 56	36 58	36 59	37 0	37 1	15
16	39 13	39 15	39 16	39 17	39 19	39 20	39 21	39 23	39 24	39 25	39 27	39 28	39 29	16
17	41 40	41 42	41 43	41 45	41 46	41 48	41 49	41 50	41 52	41 53	41 55	41 56	41 57	17
18	44 8	44 9	44 11	44 12	44 14	44 15	44 17	44 18	44 20	44 21	44 23	44 24	44 26	18
19	46 35	46 36	46 38	46 39	46 41	46 43	46 44	46 46	46 47	46 49	46 50	46 52	46 54	19
20	49 2	49 3	49 5	49 7	49 8	49 10	49 12	49 13	49 15	49 17	49 18	49 20	49 22	20
21	51 29	51 31	51 32	51 34	51 36	51 38	51 39	51 41	51 43	51 45	51 46	51 48	51 50	21
22	53 56	53 58	54 0	54 1	54 3	54 5	54 7	54 9	54 11	54 12	54 14	54 16	54 18	22
23	56 23	56 25	56 27	56 29	56 31	56 33	56 34	56 36	56 38	56 40	56 42	56 44	56 46	23
24	58 50	58 52	58 54	58 56	58 58	59 0	59 2	59 4	59 6	59 8	59 10	59 12	59 14	24

TIME	59' 16"	59' 18"	59' 20"	59' 22"	59' 24"	59' 26"	59' 28"	59' 30"	59' 32"	59' 34"	59' 36"	59' 38"	59' 40"	TIME
	' "	' "	' "	' "	' "	' "	' "	' "	' "	' "	' "	' "	' "	
MINUTES 1	2	2	2	2	2	2	2	2	2	2	2	2	2	1 MINUTES
2	5	5	5	5	5	5	5	5	5	5	5	5	5	2
3	7	7	7	7	7	7	7	7	7	7	7	7	7	3
4	10	10	10	10	10	10	10	10	10	10	10	10	10	4
5	12	12	12	12	12	12	12	12	12	12	12	12	12	5
6	15	15	15	15	15	15	15	15	15	15	15	15	15	6
7	17	17	17	17	17	17	17	17	17	17	17	17	17	7
8	20	20	20	20	20	20	20	20	20	20	20	20	20	8
9	22	22	22	22	22	22	22	22	22	22	22	22	22	9
10	25	25	25	25	25	25	25	25	25	25	25	25	25	10
11	27	27	27	27	27	27	27	27	27	27	27	27	27	11
12	30	30	30	30	30	30	30	30	30	30	30	30	30	12
13	32	32	32	32	32	32	32	32	32	32	32	32	32	13
14	35	35	35	35	35	35	35	35	35	35	35	35	35	14
15	37	37	37	37	37	37	37	37	37	37	37	37	37	15
16	40	40	40	40	40	40	40	40	40	40	40	40	40	16
17	42	42	42	42	42	42	42	42	42	42	42	42	42	17
18	44	44	45	45	45	45	45	45	45	45	45	45	45	18
19	47	47	47	47	47	47	47	47	47	47	47	47	47	19
20	49	49	49	49	50	50	50	50	50	50	50	50	50	20
21	52	52	52	52	52	52	52	52	52	52	52	52	52	21
22	54	54	54	54	54	54	55	55	55	55	55	55	55	22
23	57	57	57	57	57	57	57	57	57	57	57	57	57	23
24	59	59	59	59	59	59	59	1 0	1 0	1 0	1 0	1 0	1 0	24
25	1 2	1 2	1 2	1 2	1 2	1 2	1 2	1 2	1 2	1 2	1 2	1 2	1 2	25
26	1 4	1 4	1 4	1 4	1 4	1 4	1 4	1 4	1 4	1 5	1 5	1 5	1 5	26
27	1 7	1 7	1 7	1 7	1 7	1 7	1 7	1 7	1 7	1 7	1 7	1 7	1 7	27
28	1 9	1 9	1 9	1 9	1 9	1 9	1 9	1 9	1 9	1 9	1 10	1 10	1 10	28
29	1 12	1 12	1 12	1 12	1 12	1 12	1 12	1 12	1 12	1 12	1 12	1 12	1 12	29
30	1 14	1 14	1 14	1 14	1 14	1 14	1 14	1 14	1 14	1 14	1 15	1 15	1 15	30
31	1 17	1 17	1 17	1 17	1 17	1 17	1 17	1 17	1 17	1 17	1 17	1 17	1 17	31
32	1 19	1 19	1 19	1 19	1 19	1 19	1 19	1 19	1 19	1 19	1 19	1 20	1 20	32
33	1 21	1 22	1 22	1 22	1 22	1 22	1 22	1 22	1 22	1 22	1 22	1 22	1 22	33
34	1 24	1 24	1 24	1 24	1 24	1 24	1 24	1 24	1 24	1 24	1 24	1 24	1 25	34
35	1 26	1 26	1 27	1 27	1 27	1 27	1 27	1 27	1 27	1 27	1 27	1 27	1 27	35
36	1 29	1 29	1 29	1 29	1 29	1 29	1 29	1 29	1 29	1 29	1 29	1 29	1 30	36
37	1 31	1 31	1 31	1 32	1 32	1 32	1 32	1 32	1 32	1 32	1 32	1 32	1 32	37
38	1 34	1 34	1 34	1 34	1 34	1 34	1 34	1 34	1 34	1 34	1 34	1 34	1 34	38
39	1 36	1 36	1 36	1 36	1 37	1 37	1 37	1 37	1 37	1 37	1 37	1 37	1 37	39
40	1 39	1 39	1 39	1 39	1 39	1 39	1 39	1 39	1 39	1 39	1 39	1 39	1 39	40
41	1 41	1 41	1 41	1 41	1 41	1 42	1 42	1 42	1 42	1 42	1 42	1 42	1 42	41
42	1 44	1 44	1 44	1 44	1 44	1 44	1 44	1 44	1 44	1 44	1 44	1 44	1 44	42
43	1 46	1 46	1 46	1 46	1 46	1 46	1 47	1 47	1 47	1 47	1 47	1 47	1 47	43
44	1 49	1 49	1 49	1 49	1 49	1 49	1 49	1 49	1 49	1 49	1 49	1 49	1 49	44
45	1 51	1 51	1 51	1 51	1 51	1 51	1 52	1 52	1 52	1 52	1 52	1 52	1 52	45
46	1 54	1 54	1 54	1 54	1 54	1 54	1 54	1 54	1 54	1 54	1 54	1 54	1 54	46
47	1 56	1 56	1 56	1 56	1 56	1 56	1 56	1 57	1 57	1 57	1 57	1 57	1 57	47
48	1 59	1 59	1 59	1 59	1 59	1 59	1 59	1 59	1 59	1 59	1 59	1 59	1 59	48
49	2 1	2 1	2 1	2 1	2 1	2 1	2 1	2 1	2 2	2 2	2 2	2 2	2 2	49
50	2 3	2 4	2 4	2 4	2 4	2 4	2 4	2 4	2 4	2 4	2 4	2 4	2 4	50
51	2 6	2 6	2 6	2 6	2 6	2 6	2 6	2 6	2 7	2 7	2 7	2 7	2 7	51
52	2 8	2 8	2 9	2 9	2 9	2 9	2 9	2 9	2 9	2 9	2 9	2 9	2 9	52
53	2 11	2 11	2 11	2 11	2 11	2 11	2 11	2 11	2 11	2 12	2 12	2 12	2 12	53
54	2 13	2 13	2 14	2 14	2 14	2 14	2 14	2 14	2 14	2 14	2 14	2 14	2 14	54
55	2 16	2 16	2 16	2 16	2 16	2 16	2 16	2 16	2 16	2 17	2 17	2 17	2 17	55
56	2 18	2 18	2 18	2 19	2 19	2 19	2 19	2 19	2 19	2 19	2 19	2 19	2 19	56
57	2 21	2 21	2 21	2 21	2 21	2 21	2 21	2 21	2 21	2 21	2 22	2 22	2 22	57
58	2 23	2 23	2 23	2 23	2 24	2 24	2 24	2 24	2 24	2 24	2 24	2 24	2 24	58
59	2 26	2 26	2 26	2 26	2 26	2 26	2 26	2 26	2 26	2 26	2 27	2 27	2 27	59
60	2 28	2 28	2 28	2 28	2 29	2 29	2 29	2 29	2 29	2 29	2 29	2 29	2 29	60
HOURS 1	2 28	2 28	2 28	2 28	2 29	2 29	2 29	2 29	2 29	2 29	2 29	2 29	2 29	1 HOURS
2	4 56	4 57	4 57	4 57	4 57	4 57	4 57	4 58	4 58	4 58	4 58	4 58	4 58	2
3	7 25	7 25	7 25	7 25	7 26	7 26	7 26	7 26	7 27	7 27	7 27	7 27	7 28	3
4	9 53	9 53	9 53	9 54	9 54	9 54	9 55	9 55	9 55	9 56	9 56	9 56	9 57	4
5	12 21	12 21	12 22	12 22	12 23	12 23	12 23	12 24	12 24	12 25	12 25	12 25	12 26	5
6	14 49	14 50	14 50	14 51	14 51	14 52	14 52	14 53	14 53	14 54	14 54	14 55	14 55	6
7	17 17	17 18	17 18	17 19	17 20	17 20	17 21	17 21	17 22	17 22	17 23	17 24	17 24	7
8	19 45	19 46	19 47	19 47	19 48	19 49	19 49	19 50	19 51	19 51	19 52	19 53	19 53	8
9	22 14	22 14	22 15	22 16	22 17	22 17	22 18	22 19	22 20	22 20	22 21	22 22	22 23	9
10	24 42	24 43	24 43	24 44	24 45	24 46	24 47	24 48	24 48	24 49	24 50	24 51	24 52	10
11	27 10	27 11	27 12	27 13	27 14	27 14	27 15	27 16	27 17	27 18	27 19	27 20	27 21	11
12	29 38	29 39	29 40	29 41	29 42	29 43	29 44	29 45	29 46	29 47	29 48	29 49	29 50	12
13	32 6	32 7	32 8	32 9	32 11	32 12	32 13	32 14	32 15	32 16	32 17	32 18	32 19	13
14	34 34	34 36	34 37	34 38	34 39	34 40	34 41	34 43	34 44	34 45	34 46	34 47	34 48	14
15	37 3	37 4	37 5	37 6	37 8	37 9	37 10	37 11	37 13	37 14	37 15	37 16	37 18	15
16	39 31	39 32	39 33	39 35	39 36	39 37	39 39	39 40	39 41	39 43	39 44	39 45	39 47	16
17	41 59	42 0	42 2	42 3	42 5	42 6	42 7	42 9	42 10	42 12	42 13	42 14	42 16	17
18	44 27	44 29	44 30	44 32	44 33	44 35	44 36	44 38	44 39	44 41	44 42	44 44	44 45	18
19	46 55	46 57	46 58	47 0	47 2	47 3	47 5	47 6	47 8	47 9	47 11	47 13	47 14	19
20	49 23	49 25	49 27	49 28	49 30	49 32	49 33	49 35	49 37	49 38	49 40	49 42	49 43	20
21	51 52	51 53	51 55	51 57	51 59	52 0	52 2	52 4	52 6	52 7	52 9	52 11	52 13	21
22	54 20	54 22	54 23	54 25	54 27	54 29	54 31	54 33	54 34	54 36	54 38	54 40	54 42	22
23	56 48	56 50	56 52	56 54	56 56	56 57	56 59	57 1	57 3	57 5	57 7	57 9	57 11	23
24	59 16	59 18	59 20	59 22	59 24	59 26	59 28	59 30	59 32	59 34	59 36	59 38	59 40	24

24 HOUR TRAVEL

TIME	59' 42"	59' 44"	59' 46"	59' 48"	59' 50"	59' 52"	59' 54"	59' 56"	59' 58"	60' 0"	60' 2"	60' 4"	60' 6"	TIME
	24 HOUR TRAVEL													
	' "	' "	' "	' "	' "	' "	' "	' "	' "	' "	' "	' "	' "	
M 1	2	2	2	2	2	2	2	2	2	3	3	3	3	1 M
I 2	5	5	5	5	5	5	5	5	5	5	5	5	5	2 I
N 3	7	7	7	7	7	7	7	7	7	8	8	8	8	3 N
U 4	10	10	10	10	10	10	10	10	10	10	10	10	10	4 U
T 5	12	12	12	12	12	12	12	12	12	13	13	13	13	5 T
E 6	15	15	15	15	15	15	15	15	15	15	15	15	15	6 E
S 7	17	17	17	17	17	17	17	17	17	18	18	18	18	7 S
8	20	20	20	20	20	20	20	20	20	20	20	20	20	8
9	22	22	22	22	22	22	22	22	22	23	23	23	23	9
10	25	25	25	25	25	25	25	25	25	25	25	25	25	10
11	27	27	27	27	27	27	27	27	27	28	28	28	28	11
12	30	30	30	30	30	30	30	30	30	30	30	30	30	12
13	32	32	32	32	32	32	32	32	32	33	33	33	33	13
14	35	35	35	35	35	35	35	35	35	35	35	35	35	14
15	37	37	37	37	37	37	37	37	37	38	38	38	38	15
16	40	40	40	40	40	40	40	40	40	40	40	40	40	16
17	42	42	42	42	42	42	42	42	42	43	43	43	43	17
18	45	45	45	45	45	45	45	45	45	45	45	45	45	18
19	47	47	47	47	47	47	47	47	47	48	48	48	48	19
20	50	50	50	50	50	50	50	50	50	50	50	50	50	20
21	52	52	52	52	52	52	52	52	52	53	53	53	53	21
22	55	55	55	55	55	55	55	55	55	55	55	55	55	22
23	57	57	57	57	57	57	57	57	57	58	58	58	58	23
24	1 0	1 0	1 0	1 0	1 0	1 0	1 0	1 0	1 0	1 0	1 0	1 0	1 0	24
25	1 2	1 2	1 2	1 2	1 2	1 2	1 2	1 2	1 2	1 3	1 3	1 3	1 3	25
26	1 5	1 5	1 5	1 5	1 5	1 5	1 5	1 5	1 5	1 5	1 5	1 5	1 5	26
27	1 7	1 7	1 7	1 7	1 7	1 7	1 7	1 7	1 7	1 8	1 8	1 8	1 8	27
28	1 10	1 10	1 10	1 10	1 10	1 10	1 10	1 10	1 10	1 10	1 10	1 10	1 10	28
29	1 12	1 12	1 12	1 12	1 12	1 12	1 12	1 12	1 12	1 13	1 13	1 13	1 13	29
30	1 15	1 15	1 15	1 15	1 15	1 15	1 15	1 15	1 15	1 15	1 15	1 15	1 15	30
31	1 17	1 17	1 17	1 17	1 17	1 17	1 17	1 17	1 17	1 18	1 18	1 18	1 18	31
32	1 20	1 20	1 20	1 20	1 20	1 20	1 20	1 20	1 20	1 20	1 20	1 20	1 20	32
33	1 22	1 22	1 22	1 22	1 22	1 22	1 22	1 22	1 22	1 23	1 23	1 23	1 23	33
34	1 25	1 25	1 25	1 25	1 25	1 25	1 25	1 25	1 25	1 25	1 25	1 25	1 25	34
35	1 27	1 27	1 27	1 27	1 27	1 27	1 27	1 27	1 27	1 28	1 28	1 28	1 28	35
36	1 30	1 30	1 30	1 30	1 30	1 30	1 30	1 30	1 30	1 30	1 30	1 30	1 30	36
37	1 32	1 32	1 32	1 32	1 32	1 32	1 32	1 32	1 32	1 33	1 33	1 33	1 33	37
38	1 35	1 35	1 35	1 35	1 35	1 35	1 35	1 35	1 35	1 35	1 35	1 35	1 35	38
39	1 37	1 37	1 37	1 37	1 37	1 37	1 37	1 37	1 37	1 38	1 38	1 38	1 38	39
40	1 40	1 40	1 40	1 40	1 40	1 40	1 40	1 40	1 40	1 40	1 40	1 40	1 40	40
41	1 42	1 42	1 42	1 42	1 42	1 42	1 42	1 42	1 42	1 43	1 43	1 43	1 43	41
42	1 44	1 45	1 45	1 45	1 45	1 45	1 45	1 45	1 45	1 45	1 45	1 45	1 45	42
43	1 47	1 47	1 47	1 47	1 47	1 47	1 47	1 47	1 47	1 48	1 48	1 48	1 48	43
44	1 49	1 50	1 50	1 50	1 50	1 50	1 50	1 50	1 50	1 50	1 50	1 50	1 50	44
45	1 52	1 52	1 52	1 52	1 52	1 52	1 52	1 52	1 52	1 53	1 53	1 53	1 53	45
46	1 54	1 54	1 55	1 55	1 55	1 55	1 55	1 55	1 55	1 55	1 55	1 55	1 55	46
47	1 57	1 57	1 57	1 57	1 57	1 57	1 57	1 57	1 57	1 58	1 58	1 58	1 58	47
48	1 59	1 59	2 0	2 0	2 0	2 0	2 0	2 0	2 0	2 0	2 0	2 0	2 0	48
49	2 2	2 2	2 2	2 2	2 2	2 2	2 2	2 2	2 2	2 3	2 3	2 3	2 3	49
50	2 4	2 4	2 5	2 5	2 5	2 5	2 5	2 5	2 5	2 5	2 5	2 5	2 5	50
51	2 7	2 7	2 7	2 7	2 7	2 7	2 7	2 7	2 7	2 8	2 8	2 8	2 8	51
52	2 9	2 9	2 9	2 10	2 10	2 10	2 10	2 10	2 10	2 10	2 10	2 10	2 10	52
53	2 12	2 12	2 12	2 12	2 12	2 12	2 12	2 12	2 12	2 13	2 13	2 13	2 13	53
54	2 14	2 14	2 14	2 15	2 15	2 15	2 15	2 15	2 15	2 15	2 15	2 15	2 15	54
55	2 17	2 17	2 17	2 17	2 17	2 17	2 17	2 17	2 17	2 18	2 18	2 18	2 18	55
56	2 19	2 19	2 19	2 20	2 20	2 20	2 20	2 20	2 20	2 20	2 20	2 20	2 20	56
57	2 22	2 22	2 22	2 22	2 22	2 22	2 22	2 22	2 22	2 23	2 23	2 23	2 23	57
58	2 24	2 24	2 24	2 25	2 25	2 25	2 25	2 25	2 25	2 25	2 25	2 25	2 25	58
59	2 27	2 27	2 27	2 27	2 27	2 27	2 27	2 27	2 27	2 28	2 28	2 28	2 28	59
60	2 29	2 29	2 29	2 30	2 30	2 30	2 30	2 30	2 30	2 30	2 30	2 30	2 30	60
H 1	2 29	2 29	2 29	2 30	2 30	2 30	2 30	2 30	2 30	2 30	2 30	2 30	2 30	1 H
O 2	4 59	4 59	4 59	4 59	4 59	4 59	5 0	5 0	5 0	5 0	5 0	5 0	5 1	2 O
U 3	7 28	7 28	7 28	7 29	7 29	7 29	7 29	7 30	7 30	7 30	7 30	7 31	7 31	3 U
R 4	9 57	9 57	9 58	9 58	9 58	9 59	9 59	9 59	10 0	10 0	10 0	10 1	10 1	4 R
S 5	12 26	12 27	12 27	12 28	12 28	12 28	12 29	12 29	12 30	12 30	12 30	12 31	12 31	5 S
6	14 56	14 56	14 57	14 57	14 58	14 58	14 59	14 59	15 0	15 0	15 1	15 1	15 2	6
7	17 25	17 25	17 26	17 27	17 27	17 28	17 28	17 29	17 29	17 30	17 31	17 31	17 32	7
8	19 54	19 55	19 55	19 56	19 57	19 57	19 58	19 59	19 59	20 0	20 1	20 1	20 2	8
9	22 23	22 24	22 25	22 26	22 26	22 27	22 28	22 29	22 29	22 30	22 31	22 32	22 32	9
10	24 53	24 53	24 54	24 55	24 56	24 57	24 58	24 58	24 59	25 0	25 1	25 2	25 3	10
11	27 22	27 23	27 24	27 25	27 25	27 26	27 27	27 28	27 29	27 30	27 31	27 32	27 33	11
12	29 51	29 52	29 53	29 54	29 55	29 56	29 57	29 58	29 59	30 0	30 1	30 2	30 3	12
13	32 20	32 21	32 22	32 24	32 25	32 26	32 27	32 28	32 29	32 30	32 31	32 32	32 33	13
14	34 50	34 51	34 52	34 53	34 54	34 55	34 57	34 58	34 59	35 0	35 1	35 2	35 4	14
15	37 19	37 20	37 21	37 23	37 24	37 25	37 26	37 28	37 29	37 30	37 31	37 33	37 34	15
16	39 48	39 49	39 51	39 52	39 53	39 55	39 56	39 57	39 59	40 0	40 1	40 3	40 4	16
17	42 17	42 19	42 20	42 22	42 23	42 24	42 26	42 27	42 29	42 30	42 31	42 33	42 34	17
18	44 47	44 48	44 50	44 51	44 53	44 54	44 56	44 57	44 59	45 0	45 2	45 3	45 5	18
19	47 16	47 17	47 19	47 21	47 22	47 24	47 25	47 27	47 28	47 30	47 32	47 33	47 35	19
20	49 45	49 47	49 48	49 50	49 52	49 53	49 55	49 57	49 58	50 0	50 2	50 3	50 5	20
21	52 14	52 16	52 18	52 20	52 21	52 23	52 25	52 27	52 28	52 30	52 32	52 34	52 35	21
22	54 44	54 45	54 47	54 49	54 51	54 53	54 55	54 56	54 58	55 0	55 2	55 4	55 6	22
23	57 13	57 15	57 17	57 19	57 20	57 22	57 24	57 26	57 28	57 30	57 32	57 34	57 36	23
24	59 42	59 44	59 46	59 48	59 50	59 52	59 54	59 56	59 58	60 0	60 2	60 4	60 6	24

TIME	'	"	'	"	'	"	'	"	'	"	'	"	'	"	'	"	'	"	'	"	'	"	'	"	'	"	TIME
	60	8	60	10	60	12	60	14	60	16	60	18	60	20	60	22	60	24	60	26	60	28	60	30	60	32	
	'	"	'	"	'	"	'	"	'	"	'	"	'	"	'	"	'	"	'	"	'	"	'	"	'	"	
M 1		3		3		3		3		3		3		3		3		3		3		3		3		3	1 M
I 2		5		5		5		5		5		5		5		5		5		5		5		5		5	2 I
N 3		8		8		8		8		8		8		8		8		8		8		8		8		8	3 N
U 4		10		10		10		10		10		10		10		10		10		10		10		10		10	4 U
T 5		13		13		13		13		13		13		13		13		13		13		13		13		13	5 T
E 6		15		15		15		15		15		15		15		15		15		15		15		15		15	6 E
S 7		18		18		18		18		18		18		18		18		18		18		18		18		18	7 S
8		20		20		20		20		20		20		20		20		20		20		20		20		20	8
9		23		23		23		23		23		23		23		23		23		23		23		23		23	9
10		25		25		25		25		25		25		25		25		25		25		25		25		25	10
11		28		28		28		28		28		28		28		28		28		28		28		28		28	11
12		30		30		30		30		30		30		30		30		30		30		30		30		30	12
13		33		33		33		33		33		33		33		33		33		33		33		33		33	13
14		35		35		35		35		35		35		35		35		35		35		35		35		35	14
15		38		38		38		38		38		38		38		38		38		38		38		38		38	15
16		40		40		40		40		40		40		40		40		40		40		40		40		40	16
17		43		43		43		43		43		43		43		43		43		43		43		43		43	17
18		45		45		45		45		45		45		45		45		45		45		45		45		45	18
19		48		48		48		48		48		48		48		48		48		48		48		48		48	19
20		50		50		50		50		50		50		50		50		50		50		50		50		50	20
21		53		53		53		53		53		53		53		53		53		53		53		53		53	21
22		55		55		55		55		55		55		55		55		55		55		55		55		55	22
23		58		58		58		58		58		58		58		58		58		58		58		58		58	23
24	1	0	1	0	1	0	1	0	1	0	1	0	1	0	1	0	1	0	1	0	1	0	1	1	1	1	24
25	1	3	1	3	1	3	1	3	1	3	1	3	1	3	1	3	1	3	1	3	1	3	1	3	1	3	25
26	1	5	1	5	1	5	1	5	1	5	1	5	1	5	1	5	1	5	1	5	1	6	1	6	1	6	26
27	1	8	1	8	1	8	1	8	1	8	1	8	1	8	1	8	1	8	1	8	1	8	1	8	1	8	27
28	1	10	1	10	1	10	1	10	1	10	1	10	1	10	1	10	1	10	1	11	1	11	1	11	1	11	28
29	1	13	1	13	1	13	1	13	1	13	1	13	1	13	1	13	1	13	1	13	1	13	1	13	1	13	29
30	1	15	1	15	1	15	1	15	1	15	1	15	1	15	1	15	1	16	1	16	1	16	1	16	1	16	30
31	1	18	1	18	1	18	1	18	1	18	1	18	1	18	1	18	1	18	1	18	1	18	1	18	1	18	31
32	1	20	1	20	1	20	1	20	1	20	1	20	1	20	1	20	1	21	1	21	1	21	1	21	1	21	32
33	1	23	1	23	1	23	1	23	1	23	1	23	1	23	1	23	1	23	1	23	1	23	1	23	1	23	33
34	1	25	1	25	1	25	1	25	1	25	1	25	1	25	1	26	1	26	1	26	1	26	1	26	1	26	34
35	1	28	1	28	1	28	1	28	1	28	1	28	1	28	1	28	1	28	1	28	1	28	1	28	1	28	35
36	1	30	1	30	1	30	1	30	1	30	1	30	1	31	1	31	1	31	1	31	1	31	1	31	1	31	36
37	1	33	1	33	1	33	1	33	1	33	1	33	1	33	1	33	1	33	1	33	1	33	1	33	1	33	37
38	1	35	1	35	1	35	1	35	1	35	1	35	1	36	1	36	1	36	1	36	1	36	1	36	1	36	38
39	1	38	1	38	1	38	1	38	1	38	1	38	1	38	1	38	1	38	1	38	1	38	1	38	1	38	39
40	1	40	1	40	1	40	1	40	1	40	1	41	1	41	1	41	1	41	1	41	1	41	1	41	1	41	40
41	1	43	1	43	1	43	1	43	1	43	1	43	1	43	1	43	1	43	1	43	1	43	1	43	1	43	41
42	1	45	1	45	1	45	1	45	1	45	1	46	1	46	1	46	1	46	1	46	1	46	1	46	1	46	42
43	1	48	1	48	1	48	1	48	1	48	1	48	1	48	1	48	1	48	1	48	1	48	1	48	1	48	43
44	1	50	1	50	1	50	1	50	1	50	1	51	1	51	1	51	1	51	1	51	1	51	1	51	1	51	44
45	1	53	1	53	1	53	1	53	1	53	1	53	1	53	1	53	1	53	1	53	1	53	1	53	1	54	45
46	1	55	1	55	1	55	1	55	1	56	1	56	1	56	1	56	1	56	1	56	1	56	1	56	1	56	46
47	1	58	1	58	1	58	1	58	1	58	1	58	1	58	1	58	1	58	1	58	1	58	1	58	1	59	47
48	2	0	2	0	2	0	2	0	2	1	2	1	2	1	2	1	2	1	2	1	2	1	2	1	2	1	48
49	2	3	2	3	2	3	2	3	2	3	2	3	2	3	2	3	2	3	2	3	2	3	2	4	2	4	49
50	2	5	2	5	2	5	2	5	2	6	2	6	2	6	2	6	2	6	2	6	2	6	2	6	2	6	50
51	2	8	2	8	2	8	2	8	2	8	2	8	2	8	2	8	2	8	2	8	2	8	2	9	2	9	51
52	2	10	2	10	2	10	2	11	2	11	2	11	2	11	2	11	2	11	2	11	2	11	2	11	2	11	52
53	2	13	2	13	2	13	2	13	2	13	2	13	2	13	2	13	2	13	2	13	2	14	2	14	2	14	53
54	2	15	2	15	2	15	2	16	2	16	2	16	2	16	2	16	2	16	2	16	2	16	2	16	2	16	54
55	2	18	2	18	2	18	2	18	2	18	2	18	2	18	2	18	2	18	2	18	2	19	2	19	2	19	55
56	2	20	2	20	2	20	2	21	2	21	2	21	2	21	2	21	2	21	2	21	2	21	2	21	2	21	56
57	2	23	2	23	2	23	2	23	2	23	2	23	2	23	2	23	2	23	2	24	2	24	2	24	2	24	57
58	2	25	2	25	2	25	2	26	2	26	2	26	2	26	2	26	2	26	2	26	2	26	2	26	2	26	58
59	2	28	2	28	2	28	2	28	2	28	2	28	2	28	2	28	2	28	2	29	2	29	2	29	2	29	59
60	2	30	2	30	2	31	2	31	2	31	2	31	2	31	2	31	2	31	2	31	2	31	2	31	2	31	60
H 1	2	30	2	30	2	31	2	31	2	31	2	31	2	31	2	31	2	31	2	31	2	31	2	31	2	31	1 H
O 2	5	1	5	1	5	1	5	1	5	1	5	2	5	2	5	2	5	2	5	2	5	2	5	3	5	3	2 O
U 3	7	31	7	31	7	32	7	32	7	32	7	32	7	33	7	33	7	33	7	33	7	34	7	34	7	34	3 U
R 4	10	1	10	2	10	2	10	2	10	3	10	3	10	3	10	4	10	4	10	4	10	5	10	5	10	5	4 R
S 5	12	32	12	32	12	33	12	33	12	33	12	34	12	34	12	35	12	35	12	35	12	36	12	36	12	37	5 S
6	15	2	15	3	15	3	15	4	15	4	15	5	15	5	15	6	15	6	15	7	15	7	15	8	15	8	6
7	17	32	17	33	17	34	17	34	17	35	17	35	17	36	17	36	17	37	17	38	17	38	17	39	17	39	7
8	20	3	20	3	20	4	20	5	20	5	20	6	20	7	20	7	20	8	20	9	20	9	20	10	20	11	8
9	22	33	22	34	22	35	22	35	22	36	22	37	22	38	22	38	22	39	22	40	22	41	22	41	22	42	9
10	25	3	25	4	25	5	25	6	25	7	25	8	25	8	25	9	25	10	25	11	25	12	25	13	25	13	10
11	27	34	27	35	27	36	27	36	27	37	27	38	27	39	27	40	27	41	27	42	27	43	27	44	27	45	11
12	30	4	30	5	30	6	30	7	30	8	30	9	30	10	30	11	30	12	30	13	30	14	30	15	30	16	12
13	32	34	32	35	32	37	32	38	32	39	32	40	32	41	32	42	32	43	32	44	32	45	32	46	32	47	13
14	35	5	35	6	35	7	35	8	35	9	35	11	35	12	35	13	35	14	35	15	35	16	35	18	35	19	14
15	37	35	37	36	37	38	37	39	37	40	37	41	37	43	37	44	37	45	37	46	37	48	37	49	37	50	15
16	40	5	40	7	40	8	40	9	40	11	40	12	40	13	40	15	40	16	40	17	40	19	40	20	40	21	16
17	42	36	42	37	42	39	42	40	42	41	42	43	42	44	42	46	42	47	42	48	42	50	42	51	42	53	17
18	45	6	45	8	45	9	45	11	45	12	45	14	45	15	45	17	45	18	45	20	45	21	45	23	45	24	18
19	47	36	47	38	47	40	47	41	47	43	47	44	47	46	47	47	47	49	47	51	47	52	47	54	47	55	19
20	50	7	50	8	50	10	50	12	50	13	50	15	50	17	50	18	50	20	50	22	50	23	50	25	50	27	20
21	52	37	52	39	52	41	52	42	52	44	52	46	52	48	52	49	52	51	52	53	52	55	52	56	52	58	21
22	55	7	55	9	55	11	55	13	55	15	55	17	55	18	55	20	55	22	55	24	55	26	55	28	55	29	22
23	57	38	57	40	57	42	57	43	57	45	57	47	57	49	57	51	57	53	57	55	57	57	57	59	58	1	23
24	60	8	60	10	60	12	60	14	60	16	60	18	60	20	60	22	60	24	60	26	60	28	60	30	60	32	24

24 HOUR TRAVEL

TIME	60'	34"	60'	36"	60'	38"	60'	40"	60'	42"	60'	44"	60'	46"	60'	48"	60'	50"	60'	52"	60'	54"	60'	56"	60'	58"	TIME
	'	"	'	"	'	"	'	"	'	"	'	"	'	"	'	"	'	"	'	"	'	"	'	"	'	"	
MINUTES																											MINUTES
1		3		3		3		3		3		3		3		3		3		3		3		3		3	1
2		5		5		5		5		5		5		5		5		5		5		5		5		5	2
3		8		8		8		8		8		8		8		8		8		8		8		8		8	3
4		10		10		10		10		10		10		10		10		10		10		10		10		10	4
5		13		13		13		13		13		13		13		13		13		13		13		13		13	5
6		15		15		15		15		15		15		15		15		15		15		15		15		15	6
7		18		18		18		18		18		18		18		18		18		18		18		18		18	7
8		20		20		20		20		20		20		20		20		20		20		20		20		20	8
9		23		23		23		23		23		23		23		23		23		23		23		23		23	9
10		25		25		25		25		25		25		25		25		25		25		25		25		25	10
11		28		28		28		28		28		28		28		28		28		28		28		28		28	11
12		30		30		30		30		30		30		30		30		30		30		30		30		30	12
13		33		33		33		33		33		33		33		33		33		33		33		33		33	13
14		35		35		35		35		35		35		35		35		35		36		36		36		36	14
15		38		38		38		38		38		38		38		38		38		38		38		38		38	15
16		40		40		40		40		40		40		41		41		41		41		41		41		41	16
17		43		43		43		43		43		43		43		43		43		43		43		43		43	17
18		45		45		45		46		46		46		46		46		46		46		46		46		46	18
19		48		48		48		48		48		48		48		48		48		48		48		48		48	19
20		50		51		51		51		51		51		51		51		51		51		51		51		51	20
21		53		53		53		53		53		53		53		53		53		53		53		53		53	21
22		56		56		56		56		56		56		56		56		56		56		56		56		56	22
23		58		58		58		58		58		58		58		58		58		58		58		58		58	23
24	1	1	1	1	1	1	1	1	1	1	1	1	1	1	1	1	1	1	1	1	1	1	1	1	1	1	24
25	1	3	1	3	1	3	1	3	1	3	1	3	1	3	1	3	1	3	1	3	1	3	1	3	1	4	25
26	1	6	1	6	1	6	1	6	1	6	1	6	1	6	1	6	1	6	1	6	1	6	1	6	1	6	26
27	1	8	1	8	1	8	1	8	1	8	1	8	1	8	1	8	1	8	1	8	1	9	1	9	1	9	27
28	1	11	1	11	1	11	1	11	1	11	1	11	1	11	1	11	1	11	1	11	1	11	1	11	1	11	28
29	1	13	1	13	1	13	1	13	1	13	1	13	1	13	1	13	1	14	1	14	1	14	1	14	1	14	29
30	1	16	1	16	1	16	1	16	1	16	1	16	1	16	1	16	1	16	1	16	1	16	1	16	1	16	30
31	1	18	1	18	1	18	1	18	1	18	1	18	1	18	1	19	1	19	1	19	1	19	1	19	1	19	31
32	1	21	1	21	1	21	1	21	1	21	1	21	1	21	1	21	1	21	1	21	1	21	1	21	1	21	32
33	1	23	1	23	1	23	1	23	1	23	1	24	1	24	1	24	1	24	1	24	1	24	1	24	1	24	33
34	1	26	1	26	1	26	1	26	1	26	1	26	1	26	1	26	1	26	1	26	1	26	1	26	1	26	34
35	1	28	1	28	1	28	1	28	1	29	1	29	1	29	1	29	1	29	1	29	1	29	1	29	1	29	35
36	1	31	1	31	1	31	1	31	1	31	1	31	1	31	1	31	1	31	1	31	1	31	1	31	1	31	36
37	1	33	1	33	1	33	1	34	1	34	1	34	1	34	1	34	1	34	1	34	1	34	1	34	1	34	37
38	1	36	1	36	1	36	1	36	1	36	1	36	1	36	1	36	1	36	1	36	1	36	1	36	1	37	38
39	1	38	1	38	1	39	1	39	1	39	1	39	1	39	1	39	1	39	1	39	1	39	1	39	1	39	39
40	1	41	1	41	1	41	1	41	1	41	1	41	1	41	1	41	1	41	1	41	1	42	1	42	1	42	40
41	1	43	1	44	1	44	1	44	1	44	1	44	1	44	1	44	1	44	1	44	1	44	1	44	1	44	41
42	1	46	1	46	1	46	1	46	1	46	1	46	1	46	1	46	1	46	1	47	1	47	1	47	1	47	42
43	1	49	1	49	1	49	1	49	1	49	1	49	1	49	1	49	1	49	1	49	1	49	1	49	1	49	43
44	1	51	1	51	1	51	1	51	1	51	1	51	1	51	1	51	1	52	1	52	1	52	1	52	1	52	44
45	1	54	1	54	1	54	1	54	1	54	1	54	1	54	1	54	1	54	1	54	1	54	1	54	1	54	45
46	1	56	1	56	1	56	1	56	1	56	1	56	1	56	1	57	1	57	1	57	1	57	1	57	1	57	46
47	1	59	1	59	1	59	1	59	1	59	1	59	1	59	1	59	1	59	1	59	1	59	1	59	1	59	47
48	2	1	2	1	2	1	2	1	2	1	2	1	2	2	2	2	2	2	2	2	2	2	2	2	2	2	48
49	2	4	2	4	2	4	2	4	2	4	2	4	2	4	2	4	2	4	2	4	2	4	2	4	2	4	49
50	2	6	2	6	2	6	2	6	2	6	2	7	2	7	2	7	2	7	2	7	2	7	2	7	2	7	50
51	2	9	2	9	2	9	2	9	2	9	2	9	2	9	2	9	2	9	2	9	2	9	2	9	2	10	51
52	2	11	2	11	2	11	2	11	2	12	2	12	2	12	2	12	2	12	2	12	2	12	2	12	2	12	52
53	2	14	2	14	2	14	2	14	2	14	2	14	2	14	2	14	2	14	2	14	2	14	2	15	2	15	53
54	2	16	2	16	2	16	2	17	2	17	2	17	2	17	2	17	2	17	2	17	2	17	2	17	2	17	54
55	2	19	2	19	2	19	2	19	2	19	2	19	2	19	2	19	2	19	2	19	2	20	2	20	2	20	55
56	2	21	2	21	2	21	2	22	2	22	2	22	2	22	2	22	2	22	2	22	2	22	2	22	2	22	56
57	2	24	2	24	2	24	2	24	2	24	2	24	2	24	2	24	2	24	2	25	2	25	2	25	2	25	57
58	2	26	2	26	2	27	2	27	2	27	2	27	2	27	2	27	2	27	2	27	2	27	2	27	2	27	58
59	2	29	2	29	2	29	2	29	2	29	2	29	2	29	2	29	2	30	2	30	2	30	2	30	2	30	59
60	2	31	2	32	2	32	2	32	2	32	2	32	2	32	2	32	2	32	2	32	2	32	2	32	2	32	60
HOURS																											HOURS
1	2	31	2	32	2	32	2	32	2	32	2	32	2	32	2	32	2	32	2	32	2	32	2	32	2	32	1
2	5	3	5	3	5	3	5	3	5	4	5	4	5	4	5	4	5	4	5	4	5	5	5	5	5	5	2
3	7	34	7	35	7	35	7	35	7	35	7	36	7	36	7	36	7	36	7	37	7	37	7	37	7	37	3
4	10	6	10	6	10	6	10	7	10	7	10	7	10	8	10	8	10	8	10	9	10	9	10	9	10	10	4
5	12	37	12	38	12	38	12	38	12	39	12	39	12	40	12	40	12	40	12	41	12	41	12	42	12	42	5
6	15	9	15	9	15	10	15	10	15	11	15	11	15	12	15	12	15	13	15	13	15	14	15	14	15	15	6
7	17	40	17	41	17	41	17	42	17	42	17	43	17	43	17	44	17	45	17	45	17	46	17	46	17	47	7
8	20	11	20	12	20	13	20	13	20	14	20	15	20	15	20	16	20	17	20	17	20	18	20	19	20	19	8
9	22	43	22	44	22	44	22	45	22	46	22	47	22	47	22	48	22	49	22	50	22	50	22	51	22	52	9
10	25	14	25	15	25	16	25	17	25	18	25	18	25	19	25	20	25	21	25	22	25	23	25	23	25	24	10
11	27	46	27	47	27	47	27	48	27	49	27	50	27	51	27	52	27	53	27	54	27	55	27	56	27	57	11
12	30	17	30	18	30	19	30	20	30	21	30	22	30	23	30	24	30	25	30	26	30	27	30	28	30	29	12
13	32	48	32	50	32	51	32	52	32	53	32	54	32	55	32	56	32	57	32	58	32	59	33	0	33	1	13
14	35	20	35	21	35	22	35	23	35	25	35	26	35	27	35	28	35	29	35	30	35	32	35	33	35	34	14
15	37	51	37	53	37	54	37	55	37	56	37	58	37	59	38	0	38	1	38	3	38	4	38	5	38	6	15
16	40	23	40	24	40	25	40	27	40	28	40	29	40	31	40	32	40	33	40	35	40	36	40	37	40	39	16
17	42	54	42	56	42	57	42	58	43	0	43	1	43	3	43	4	43	5	43	7	43	8	43	10	43	11	17
18	45	26	45	27	45	29	45	30	45	32	45	33	45	35	45	36	45	38	45	39	45	41	45	42	45	44	18
19	47	57	47	59	48	0	48	2	48	3	48	5	48	6	48	8	48	10	48	11	48	13	48	14	48	16	19
20	50	28	50	30	50	32	50	33	50	35	50	37	50	38	50	40	50	42	50	43	50	45	50	47	50	48	20
21	53	0	53	2	53	3	53	5	53	7	53	9	53	10	53	12	53	14	53	16	53	17	53	19	53	21	21
22	55	31	55	33	55	35	55	37	55	39	55	40	55	42	55	44	55	46	55	48	55	50	55	51	55	53	22
23	58	3	58	5	58	6	58	8	58	10	58	12	58	14	58	16	58	18	58	20	58	22	58	24	58	26	23
24	60	34	60	36	60	38	60	40	60	42	60	44	60	46	60	48	60	50	60	52	60	54	60	56	60	58	24

TIME	61' 0"	61' 2"	61' 4"	61' 6"	61' 8"	61' 10"	61' 12"	61' 14"	61' 16"	61' 18"	61' 20"	61' 22"	61' 24"	TIME
MINUTES	' "	' "	' "	' "	' "	' "	' "	' "	' "	' "	' "	' "	' "	MINUTES
1	3	3	3	3	3	3	3	3	3	3	3	3	3	1
2	5	5	5	5	5	5	5	5	5	5	5	5	5	2
3	8	8	8	8	8	8	8	8	8	8	8	8	8	3
4	10	10	10	10	10	10	10	10	10	10	10	10	10	4
5	13	13	13	13	13	13	13	13	13	13	13	13	13	5
6	15	15	15	15	15	15	15	15	15	15	15	15	15	6
7	18	18	18	18	18	18	18	18	18	18	18	18	18	7
8	20	20	20	20	20	20	20	20	20	20	20	20	20	8
9	23	23	23	23	23	23	23	23	23	23	23	23	23	9
10	25	25	25	25	25	25	26	26	26	26	26	26	26	10
11	28	28	28	28	28	28	28	28	28	28	28	28	28	11
12	31	31	31	31	31	31	31	31	31	31	31	31	31	12
13	33	33	33	33	33	33	33	33	33	33	33	33	33	13
14	36	36	36	36	36	36	36	36	36	36	36	36	36	14
15	38	38	38	38	38	38	38	38	38	38	38	38	38	15
16	41	41	41	41	41	41	41	41	41	41	41	41	41	16
17	43	43	43	43	43	43	43	43	43	43	43	43	43	17
18	46	46	46	46	46	46	46	46	46	46	46	46	46	18
19	48	48	48	48	48	48	48	48	49	49	49	49	49	19
20	51	51	51	51	51	51	51	51	51	51	51	51	51	20
21	53	53	53	53	53	54	54	54	54	54	54	54	54	21
22	56	56	56	56	56	56	56	56	56	56	56	56	56	22
23	58	58	59	59	59	59	59	59	59	59	59	59	59	23
24	1 1	1 1	1 1	1 1	1 1	1 1	1 1	1 1	1 1	1 1	1 1	1 1	1 1	24
25	1 4	1 4	1 4	1 4	1 4	1 4	1 4	1 4	1 4	1 4	1 4	1 4	1 4	25
26	1 6	1 6	1 6	1 6	1 6	1 6	1 6	1 6	1 6	1 6	1 6	1 6	1 7	26
27	1 9	1 9	1 9	1 9	1 9	1 9	1 9	1 9	1 9	1 9	1 9	1 9	1 9	27
28	1 11	1 11	1 11	1 11	1 11	1 11	1 11	1 11	1 11	1 12	1 12	1 12	1 12	28
29	1 14	1 14	1 14	1 14	1 14	1 14	1 14	1 14	1 14	1 14	1 14	1 14	1 14	29
30	1 16	1 16	1 16	1 16	1 16	1 16	1 17	1 17	1 17	1 17	1 17	1 17	1 17	30
31	1 19	1 19	1 19	1 19	1 19	1 19	1 19	1 19	1 19	1 19	1 19	1 19	1 19	31
32	1 21	1 21	1 21	1 21	1 22	1 22	1 22	1 22	1 22	1 22	1 22	1 22	1 22	32
33	1 24	1 24	1 24	1 24	1 24	1 24	1 24	1 24	1 24	1 24	1 24	1 24	1 24	33
34	1 26	1 26	1 27	1 27	1 27	1 27	1 27	1 27	1 27	1 27	1 27	1 27	1 27	34
35	1 29	1 29	1 29	1 29	1 29	1 29	1 29	1 29	1 29	1 29	1 29	1 29	1 30	35
36	1 32	1 32	1 32	1 32	1 32	1 32	1 32	1 32	1 32	1 32	1 32	1 32	1 32	36
37	1 34	1 34	1 34	1 34	1 34	1 34	1 34	1 34	1 34	1 35	1 35	1 35	1 35	37
38	1 37	1 37	1 37	1 37	1 37	1 37	1 37	1 37	1 37	1 37	1 37	1 37	1 37	38
39	1 39	1 39	1 39	1 39	1 39	1 39	1 39	1 40	1 40	1 40	1 40	1 40	1 40	39
40	1 42	1 42	1 42	1 42	1 42	1 42	1 42	1 42	1 42	1 42	1 42	1 42	1 42	40
41	1 44	1 44	1 44	1 44	1 44	1 44	1 45	1 45	1 45	1 45	1 45	1 45	1 45	41
42	1 47	1 47	1 47	1 47	1 47	1 47	1 47	1 47	1 47	1 47	1 47	1 47	1 47	42
43	1 49	1 49	1 49	1 49	1 50	1 50	1 50	1 50	1 50	1 50	1 50	1 50	1 50	43
44	1 52	1 52	1 52	1 52	1 52	1 52	1 52	1 52	1 52	1 52	1 52	1 53	1 53	44
45	1 54	1 54	1 55	1 55	1 55	1 55	1 55	1 55	1 55	1 55	1 55	1 55	1 55	45
46	1 57	1 57	1 57	1 57	1 57	1 57	1 57	1 57	1 57	1 57	1 58	1 58	1 58	46
47	1 59	2 0	2 0	2 0	2 0	2 0	2 0	2 0	2 0	2 0	2 0	2 0	2 0	47
48	2 2	2 2	2 2	2 2	2 2	2 2	2 2	2 2	2 3	2 3	2 3	2 3	2 3	48
49	2 5	2 5	2 5	2 5	2 5	2 5	2 5	2 5	2 5	2 5	2 5	2 5	2 5	49
50	2 7	2 7	2 7	2 7	2 7	2 7	2 8	2 8	2 8	2 8	2 8	2 8	2 8	50
51	2 10	2 10	2 10	2 10	2 10	2 10	2 10	2 10	2 10	2 10	2 10	2 10	2 10	51
52	2 12	2 12	2 12	2 12	2 12	2 13	2 13	2 13	2 13	2 13	2 13	2 13	2 13	52
53	2 15	2 15	2 15	2 15	2 15	2 15	2 15	2 15	2 15	2 15	2 15	2 16	2 16	53
54	2 17	2 17	2 17	2 17	2 18	2 18	2 18	2 18	2 18	2 18	2 18	2 18	2 18	54
55	2 20	2 20	2 20	2 20	2 20	2 20	2 20	2 20	2 20	2 20	2 21	2 21	2 21	55
56	2 22	2 22	2 22	2 23	2 23	2 23	2 23	2 23	2 23	2 23	2 23	2 23	2 23	56
57	2 25	2 25	2 25	2 25	2 25	2 25	2 25	2 25	2 26	2 26	2 26	2 26	2 26	57
58	2 27	2 27	2 28	2 28	2 28	2 28	2 28	2 28	2 28	2 28	2 28	2 28	2 28	58
59	2 30	2 30	2 30	2 30	2 30	2 30	2 30	2 31	2 31	2 31	2 31	2 31	2 31	59
60	2 33	2 33	2 33	2 33	2 33	2 33	2 33	2 33	2 33	2 33	2 33	2 33	2 34	60
HOURS														HOURS
1	2 33	2 33	2 33	2 33	2 33	2 33	2 33	2 33	2 33	2 33	2 33	2 33	2 34	1
2	5 5	5 5	5 5	5 6	5 6	5 6	5 6	5 6	5 6	5 7	5 7	5 7	5 7	2
3	7 38	7 38	7 38	7 38	7 39	7 39	7 39	7 39	7 40	7 40	7 40	7 40	7 41	3
4	10 10	10 10	10 11	10 11	10 11	10 12	10 12	10 12	10 13	10 13	10 13	10 14	10 14	4
5	12 43	12 43	12 43	12 44	12 44	12 45	12 45	12 45	12 46	12 46	12 47	12 47	12 48	5
6	15 15	15 16	15 16	15 17	15 17	15 18	15 18	15 19	15 19	15 20	15 20	15 21	15 21	6
7	17 48	17 48	17 49	17 49	17 50	17 50	17 51	17 52	17 52	17 53	17 53	17 54	17 55	7
8	20 20	20 21	20 21	20 22	20 23	20 23	20 24	20 25	20 25	20 26	20 27	20 27	20 28	8
9	22 53	22 53	22 54	22 55	22 56	22 56	22 57	22 58	22 59	22 59	23 0	23 1	23 2	9
10	25 25	25 26	25 27	25 28	25 28	25 29	25 30	25 31	25 32	25 33	25 33	25 34	25 35	10
11	27 58	27 58	27 59	28 0	28 1	28 2	28 3	28 4	28 5	28 6	28 7	28 8	28 9	11
12	30 30	30 31	30 32	30 33	30 34	30 35	30 36	30 37	30 38	30 39	30 40	30 41	30 42	12
13	33 3	33 4	33 5	33 6	33 7	33 8	33 9	33 10	33 11	33 12	33 13	33 14	33 16	13
14	35 35	35 36	35 37	35 39	35 40	35 41	35 42	35 43	35 44	35 46	35 47	35 48	35 49	14
15	38 8	38 9	38 10	38 11	38 13	38 14	38 15	38 16	38 18	38 19	38 20	38 21	38 23	15
16	40 40	40 41	40 43	40 44	40 45	40 47	40 48	40 49	40 51	40 52	40 53	40 55	40 56	16
17	43 13	43 14	43 15	43 17	43 18	43 20	43 21	43 22	43 24	43 25	43 27	43 28	43 30	17
18	45 45	45 47	45 48	45 50	45 51	45 53	45 54	45 56	45 57	45 59	46 0	46 2	46 3	18
19	48 18	48 19	48 21	48 22	48 24	48 25	48 27	48 29	48 30	48 32	48 33	48 35	48 37	19
20	50 50	50 52	50 53	50 55	50 57	50 58	51 0	51 2	51 3	51 5	51 7	51 8	51 10	20
21	53 23	53 24	53 26	53 28	53 30	53 31	53 33	53 35	53 37	53 38	53 40	53 42	53 44	21
22	55 55	55 57	55 59	56 1	56 2	56 4	56 6	56 8	56 10	56 12	56 13	56 15	56 17	22
23	58 28	58 29	58 31	58 33	58 35	58 37	58 39	58 41	58 43	58 45	58 47	58 49	58 51	23
24	61 0	61 2	61 4	61 6	61 8	61 10	61 12	61 14	61 16	61 18	61 20	61 22	61 24	24

24 HOUR TRAVEL

Appendix 4:

Longitude and Latitude of Major Cities

Aberdeen, SD	98W29	45N28	6:33:56
Abilene, TX	99W43	32N28	6:38:52
Akron, OH	81W31	41N05	5:26:04
Alameda, CA	122W15	37N46	8:09:00
Albany, GA	84W10	31N35	5:36:40
Albany, NY	73W45	42N39	4:55:00
Albuquerque, NM	106W39	35N05	7:06:36
Alexandria, LA	92W27	31N18	6:09:48
Alexandria, VA	77W03	38N48	5:08:12
Alhambra, CA	118W06	34N08	7:52:24
Allen Park, MI	83W13	42N16	5:32:52
Allentown, PA	75W29	40N37	5:01:56
Alliance, OH	81W06	40N55	5:24:24
Altadena, CA	118W08	34N11	7:52:32
Alton, IL	90W10	38N53	6:00:40
Altoona, PA	78W24	40N31	5:13:36
Amarillo, TX	101W50	35N13	6:47:20
Ames, IA	93W37	42N02	6:14:28
Amherst, NY	78W48	42N59	5:15:12
Amsterdam, NY	74W11	42N56	4:56:44
Anaheim, CA	117W55	33N50	7:51:40
Anchorage, AK	149W54	61N13	9:59:36
Anderson, IN	85W41	40N10	5:42:44
Anderson, SC	82W39	34N31	5:30:36
Annandale, VA	77W12	38N50	5:08:48
Annapolis, MD	76W30	38N59	5:06:00
Ann Arbor, MI	83W45	42N17	5:35:00
Anniston, AL	85W50	33N39	5:43:20
Antioch, CA	121W48	38N01	8:07:12
Appleton, WI	88W25	44N16	5:53:40
Arcade, CA	121W26	38N37	8:05:44
Arcadia, CA	118W02	34N08	7:52:08
Arden, CA	121W23	38N36	8:05:32
Arlington, MA	71W09	42N25	4:44:36
Arlington, TX	97W07	32N44	6:28:28
Arlington, VA	77W07	38N53	5:08:28
Arlington Heights, IL	87W59	42N05	5:51:56
Arvada, CO	105W05	39N50	7:00:20
Asheville, NC	82W33	35N36	5:30:12
Ashland, KY	82W38	38N28	5:30:32
Astoria, NY	73W55	40N46	4:55:40
Athens, GA	83W23	33N57	5:33:32
Atlanta, GA	84W23	33N45	5:37:32
Atlantic City, NJ	74W27	39N21	4:57:48
Attleboro, MA	71W17	41N57	4:45:08
Auburn, NY	76W34	42N56	5:06:16
Augusta, GA	81W58	33N28	5:27:52
Augusta, ME	69W47	44N19	4:39:08
Aurora, CO	104W51	39N44	6:59:24
Aurora, IL	88W19	41N45	5:53:16
Austin, MN	92W58	43N40	6:11:52
Austin, TX	97W45	30N17	6:31:00
Azusa, CA	117W52	34N08	7:51:28
Bakersfield, CA	119W01	35N23	7:56:04
Baldwin, NY	73W36	40N39	4:54:24
Baldwin, PA	79W59	40N23	5:19:56
Baldwin Park, CA	117W58	34N04	7:51:52
Baltimore, MD	76W37	39N17	5:06:28
Bangor, ME	68W46	44N48	4:35:04
Barberton, OH	81W39	41N00	5:26:36
Bartlesville, OK	95W59	36N45	6:23:56
Baton Rouge, LA	91W11	30N27	6:04:44
Battle Creek, MI	85W11	42N19	5:40:44
Bay City, MI	83W54	43N36	5:35:36
Bayonne, NJ	74W07	40N40	4:56:28
Bay Shore, NY	73W15	40N43	4:53:00
Bayside, NY	73W46	40N46	4:55:04
Baytown, TX	94W59	29N43	6:19:56
Beaumont, TX	94W06	30N05	6:16:24
Bell, CA	118W11	33N59	7:52:44
Belleville, IL	89W59	38N31	5:59:56
Belleville, NJ	74W09	40N47	4:56:36
Bellevue, WA	122W12	47N37	8:08:48
Bellflower, CA	118W09	33N53	7:52:36
Bell Gardens, CA	118W10	33N58	7:52:40
Bellingham, WA	122W29	48N46	8:09:56
Belmont, CA	122W17	37N31	8:09:08
Belmont, MA	71W11	42N24	4:44:44
Beloit, WI	89W02	42N31	5:56:08
Bergenfield, NJ	74W00	40N56	4:56:00
Berkeley, CA	122W16	37N52	8:09:04
Berwyn, IL	87W47	41N51	5:51:08
Bessemer, AL	86W58	33N24	5:47:52
Bethel Park, PA	80W01	40N20	5:20:04
Bethesda, MD	77W06	38N59	5:08:24
Bethlehem, PA	75W23	40N37	5:01:32
Bethpage, NY	73W30	40N44	4:54:00
Beverly, MA	70W53	42N33	4:43:32
Beverly Hills, CA	118W25	34N04	7:53:40
Big Spring, TX	101W28	32N15	6:45:52
Billings, MT	108W30	45N47	7:14:00
Biloxi, MS	88W53	30N24	5:55:32
Binghamton, NY	75W55	42N06	5:03:40
Birmingham, AL	86W48	33N31	5:47:12
Birmingham, MI	83W13	42N33	5:32:52
Bismarck, ND	100W47	46N48	6:43:08
Bloomfield, NJ	74W12	40N48	4:56:48
Bloomington, IL	89W00	40N29	5:56:00
Bloomington, IN	86W32	39N10	5:46:08
Bloomington, MN	93W17	44N50	6:13:08
Boardman, OH	80W39	41N02	5:22:36
Boca Raton, FL	80W05	26N21	5:20:20
Boise, ID	116W13	43N37	7:44:52
Bossier City, LA	93W44	32N31	6:14:56
Boston, MA	71W04	42N22	4:44:16
Boulder, CO	105W17	40N01	7:01:08
Bountiful, UT	111W53	40N53	7:27:32
Bowie, MD	76W47	39N00	5:07:08
Bowling Green, KY	86W27	36N59	5:45:48
Braintree, MA	71W00	42N13	4:44:00
Bremerton, WA	122W38	47N34	8:10:32
Brentwood, NY	73W15	40N47	4:53:00
Bridgeport, CT	73W12	41N11	4:52:48
Brighton, NY	77W34	43N08	5:10:16
Bristol, CT	72W57	41N40	4:51:48
Brockton, MA	71W01	42N05	4:44:04
Bronx, NY	73W54	40N51	4:55:36
Brookfield, WI	88W09	43N04	5:52:36
Brookline, MA	71W07	42N20	4:44:28
Brooklyn, NY	73W56	40N38	4:55:44
Brooklyn Center, MN	93W20	45N05	6:13:20
Brooklyn Park, MN	93W23	45N06	6:13:32
Brook Park, OH	80W51	41N24	5:23:24
Broomall, PA	75W22	39N59	5:01:28
Brownsville, TX	97W30	25N54	6:30:00
Bryan, TX	96W22	30N40	6:25:28
Buena Park, CA	118W00	33N52	7:52:00
Buffalo, NY	78W53	42N53	5:15:32
Burbank, CA	118W19	34N11	7:53:16
Burbank, IL	87W45	41N44	5:51:00
Burlingame, CA	122W21	37N35	8:09:24
Burlington, IA	91W14	40N49	6:04:56
Burlington, NC	79W26	36N06	5:17:44
Burlington, VT	73W12	44N29	4:52:48
Calumet City, IL	87W32	41N37	5:50:08
Cambridge, MA	71W06	42N22	4:44:24
Camden, NJ	75W07	39N56	5:00:28
Campbell, CA	121W57	37N17	8:07:48
Canton, OH	81W23	40N48	5:25:32
Cape Girardeau, MO	89W32	37N19	5:58:08
Carmichael, CA	121W19	38N38	8:05:16
Carol City, FL	80W16	25N56	5:21:04
Carson, CA	118W17	33N48	7:53:08
Carson City, NV	119W46	39N10	7:59:04
Casper, WY	106W19	42N51	7:05:16
Castro Valley, CA	122W04	37N42	8:08:16
Catonsville, MD	76W44	39N17	5:06:56
Cedar Falls, IA	92W27	42N32	6:09:48
Cedar Rapids, IA	91W40	41N59	6:06:40
Central Islip, NY	73W12	40N47	4:52:48

Champaign, IL	88W15	40N07	5:53:00
Chapel Hill, NC	79W04	35N55	5:16:16
Charleston, SC	79W56	32N46	5:19:44
Charleston, WV	81W38	38N21	5:26:32
Charleston Heights, SC	80W00	32N51	5:20:00
Charlotte, NC	80W51	35N13	5:23:24
Charlottesville, VA	78W30	38N02	5:14:00
Chattanooga, TN	85W19	35N03	5:41:16
Cheektowaga, NY	78W45	42N54	5:15:00
Chelsea, MA	71W02	42N23	4:44:08
Cherry Hill, NJ	75W02	39N56	5:00:08
Chesapeake, VA	76W17	36N50	5:05:08
Chester, PA	75W22	39N51	5:01:28
Cheyenne, WY	104W49	41N08	6:59:16
Chicago, IL	87W39	41N52	5:50:36
Chicago Heights, IL	87W38	41N31	5:50:32
Chicopee, MA	72W37	42N09	4:50:28
Chino, CA	117W41	34N01	7:50:44
Chula Vista, CA	117W05	32N39	7:48:20
Cicero, IL	87W45	41N51	5:51:00
Cincinnati, OH	84W31	39N06	5:38:04
Citrus Heights, CA	121W17	38N42	8:05:08
Claremont, CA	117W43	34N06	7:50:52
Clarksville, TN	87W21	36N32	5:49:24
Clearwater, FL	82W48	27N58	5:31:12
Cleveland, OH	81W42	41N30	5:26:48
Cleveland Heights, OH	81W34	41N30	5:26:16
Clifton, NJ	74W09	40N52	4:56:36
Clinton, IA	90W12	41N51	6:00:48
Clinton Township, MI	83W58	42N04	5:35:52
Clovis, NM	103W12	34N24	6:52:48
College Park, MD	76W56	38N59	5:07:44
Colorado Springs, CO	104W49	38N50	6:59:16
Colton, CA	117W20	34N04	7:49:20
Columbia, MO	92W20	38N57	6:09:20
Columbia, SC	81W03	34N00	5:24:12
Columbus, GA	84W59	32N28	5:39:56
Columbus, IN	85W55	39N13	5:43:40
Columbus, MS	88W25	33N30	5:53:40
Columbus, OH	83W00	39N58	5:32:00
Compton, CA	118W13	33N54	7:52:52
Concord, CA	122W02	37N59	8:08:08
Concord, NH	71W32	43N12	4:46:08
Coon Rapids, MN	93W19	45N09	6:13:16
Coral Gables, FL	80W16	25N45	5:21:04
Corona, CA	117W34	33N53	7:50:16
Corona, NY	73W52	40N45	4:55:28
Coronado, CA	117W11	32N41	7:48:44
Corpus Christi, TX	97W24	27N47	6:29:36
Corvallis, OR	123W16	44N34	8:13:04
Costa Mesa, CA	117W55	33N38	7:51:40
Council Bluffs, IA	95W52	41N16	6:23:28
Covina, CA	117W52	34N05	7:51:28
Covington, KY	84W31	39N05	5:38:04
Cranford, NJ	74W18	40N40	4:57:12
Cranston, RI	71W26	41N47	4:45:44
Crystal, MN	93W22	45N03	6:13:28
Culver City, CA	118W25	34N01	7:53:40
Cumberland, MD	78W46	39N39	5:15:04
Cuyahoga Falls, OH	81W29	41N08	5:25:56
Cypress, CA	118W02	33N50	7:52:08
Dallas, TX	96W49	32N47	6:27:16
Daly City, CA	122W28	37N42	8:09:52
Danbury, CT	73W28	41N24	4:53:52
Danvers, MA	70W56	42N34	4:43:44
Danville, IL	87W37	40N08	5:50:28
Danville, VA	79W23	36N36	5:17:32
Davenport, IA	90W35	41N32	6:02:20
Davis, CA	121W44	38N33	8:06:56
Dayton, OH	84W12	39N45	5:36:48
Daytona Beach, FL	81W01	29N13	5:24:04
Dearborn, MI	83W11	42N19	5:32:44
Dearborn Heights, MI	83W18	42N20	5:33:12
Decatur, AL	86W59	34N36	5:47:56
Decatur, IL	88W57	39N51	5:55:48
Dedham, MA	71W10	42N15	4:44:40
Deer Park, NY	73W20	40N46	4:53:20
De Kalb, IL	88W46	41N56	5:55:04
Del City, OK	97W26	35N26	6:29:44
Denton, TX	97W08	33N13	6:28:32
Denver, CO	104W59	39N44	6:59:56
Des Moines, IA	93W37	41N35	6:14:28
Des Plaines, IL	87W52	42N03	5:51:28
Detroit, MI	83W03	42N20	5:32:12
Dolton, IL	87W36	41N38	5:50:24
Dothan, AL	85W24	31N13	5:41:36
Dover, DE	75W32	39N10	5:02:08
Downers Grove, IL	88W01	41N49	5:52:04
Downey, CA	118W08	33N56	7:52:32
Drexel Hill, PA	75W18	39N57	5:01:12
Dubuque, IA	90W41	42N30	6:02:44
Duluth, MN	92W07	46N47	6:08:28
Dundalk, MD	76W32	39N16	5:06:08
Durham, NC	78W54	36N00	5:15:36
East Brunswick, NJ	74W25	40N26	4:57:40
East Chicago, IN	87W29	41N38	5:49:56
East Cleveland, OH	81W33	41N33	5:26:12
East Detroit, MI	82W57	42N28	5:31:48
East Hartford, CT	72W37	41N46	4:50:28
East Haven, CT	72W52	41N17	4:51:28
East Lansing, MI	84W29	42N44	5:37:56
East Los Angeles, CA	118W09	34N01	7:52:36
East Meadow, NY	73W34	40N43	4:54:16
Easton, PA	75W13	40N41	5:00:52
East Orange, NJ	74W13	40N46	4:56:52
Eastpoint, GA	84W27	33N41	5:37:48
East Providence, RI	71W22	41N48	4:45:28
East Saint Louis, IL	90W09	38N37	6:00:36
Eau Claire, WI	91W30	44N49	6:06:00
Edina, MN	93W21	44N53	6:13:24
Edison, NJ	74W25	40N31	4:57:40
El Cajon, CA	116W58	32N48	7:47:52
El Cerrito, CA	122W19	37N55	8:09:16
El Dorado, AR	92W40	33N12	6:10:40
Elgin, IL	88W17	42N02	5:53:08
Elizabeth, NJ	74W13	40N40	4:56:52
Elkhart, IN	85W58	41N41	5:43:52
Elmhurst, IL	87W56	41N53	5:51:44
Elmira, NY	76W48	42N06	5:07:12
Elmont, NY	73W43	40N43	4:54:52
El Monte, CA	118W02	34N04	7:52:08
Elmwood Park, IL	87W49	41N56	5:51:16
El Paso, TX	106W29	31N45	7:05:56
Elyria, OH	82W07	41N22	5:28:28
Englewood, CO	104W59	39N39	6:59:56
Enid, OK	97W53	36N24	6:31:32
Erie, PA	80W05	42N08	5:20:20
Escondido, CA	117W05	33N07	7:48:20
Essex, MD	76W29	39N19	5:05:56
Euclid, OH	81W32	41N34	5:26:08
Eugene, OR	123W04	44N05	8:12:16
Eureka, CA	124W09	40N47	8:16:36
Evanston, IL	87W41	42N03	5:50:44
Evansville, IN	87W35	37N58	5:50:20
Everett, MA	71W04	42N24	4:44:16
Everett, WA	122W12	47N59	8:08:48
Evergreen Park, IL	87W41	41N43	5:50:44
Fairborn, OH	84W02	39N49	5:36:08
Fairfield, CA	122W03	38N15	8:08:12
Fairfield, CT	73W16	41N09	4:53:04

Fair Lawn, NJ	74W08	40N56	4:56:32
Fairmont, WV	80W09	39N29	5:20:36
Fall River, MA	71W10	41N43	4:44:40
Fargo, ND	96W48	46N53	6:27:12
Farmers Branch, TX	96W54	32N56	6:27:36
Fayetteville, AR	96W94	36N04	6:30:16
Fayetteville, NC	78W53	35N03	5:15:32
Ferguson, MO	90W18	38N45	6:01:12
Ferndale, MI	83W08	42N28	5:32:32
Findlay, OH	83W39	41N02	5:34:36
Fitchburg, MA	71W48	42N35	4:47:12
Flagstaff, AZ	111W39	35N12	7:26:36
Flint, MI	83W41	43N01	5:34:44
Florence, AL	87W41	34N48	5:50:44
Florence, CA	118W15	33N58	7:53:00
Florence, SC	79W46	34N12	5:19:04
Florissant, MO	90W20	38N48	6:01:20
Flushing, NY	73W49	40N45	4:55:16
Fond Du Lac, WI	88W27	43N47	5:53:48
Fontana, CA	117W26	34N06	7:49:44
Forest Hills, NY	73W51	40N42	4:55:24
Fort Collins, CO	105W05	40N35	7:00:20
Fort Dodge, IA	94W11	42N30	6:16:44
Fort Lauderdale, FL	80W08	26N07	5:20:32
Fort Lee, NJ	73W58	40N51	4:55:52
Fort Myers, FL	81W52	26N39	5:27:28
Fort Pierce, FL	80W20	27N27	5:21:20
Fort Smith, AR	94W25	35N23	6:17:40
Fort Wayne, IN	85W09	41N04	5:40:36
Fort Worth, TX	97W18	32N45	6:29:12
Fountain Valley, CA	117W58	33N42	7:51:52
Framingham, MA	71W25	42N17	4:45:40
Frankfort, KY	84W52	38N12	5:39:28
Franklin Square, NY	73W41	40N43	4:54:44
Freeport, IL	89W36	42N17	5:58:24
Freeport, NY	73W35	40N39	4:54:20
Fremont, CA	121W57	37N32	8:07:48
Fresno, CA	119W47	36N44	7:59:08
Fridley, MN	93W16	45N05	6:13:04
Fullerton, CA	117W56	33N53	7:51:44
Gadsden, AL	86W01	34N01	5:44:04
Gainesville, FL	82W20	29N40	5:29:20
Galesburg, IL	90W22	40N57	6:01:28
Galveston, TX	94W48	29N18	6:19:12
Gardena, CA	118W18	33N53	7:53:12
Garden City, MI	83W21	42N20	5:33:24
Garden City, NY	73W38	40N44	4:54:32
Garden Grove, CA	117W55	33N47	7:51:40
Garfield, NJ	74W06	40N52	4:56:24
Garfield Heights, OH	81W37	41N26	5:26:28
Garland, TX	96W38	32N55	6:26:32
Gary, IN	87W20	41N36	5:49:20
Gastonia, NC	81W11	35N16	5:24:44
Gates, NY	77W41	43N09	5:10:44
Glen Burnie, MD	76W37	39N10	5:06:28
Glen Cove, NY	73W38	40N52	4:54:32
Glendale, AZ	112W11	33N32	7:28:44
Glendale, CA	118W15	34N09	7:53:00
Glendora, CA	117W52	34N08	7:51:28
Gloucester, MA	70W40	42N37	4:42:40
Goldsboro, NC	77W59	35N23	5:11:56
Grand Forks, ND	97W03	47N55	6:28:12
Grand Island, NE	98W21	40N55	6:33:24
Grand Prairie, TX	97W00	32N45	6:28:00
Grand Rapids, MI	85W40	42N58	5:42:40
Granite City, IL	90W09	38N42	6:00:36
Great Falls, MT	111W17	47N30	7:25:08
Greece, NY	77W40	43N14	5:10:40
Greeley, CO	104W42	40N25	6:58:48
Green Bay, WI	88W00	44N31	5:52:00
Greensboro, NC	79W48	36N04	5:19:12
Greenville, MS	91W04	33N24	6:04:16
Greenville, NC	77W23	35N37	5:09:32
Greenville, SC	82W24	34N51	5:29:36
Greenwich, CT	73W38	41N02	4:54:32
Gulfport, MS	89W06	30N22	5:56:24
Hacienda Heights, CA	117W58	34N00	7:51:52
Hackensack, NJ	74W03	40N53	4:56:12
Hagerstown, MD	77W43	39N39	5:10:52
Haltom City, TX	97W16	32N48	6:29:04
Hamden, CT	72W54	41N23	4:51:36
Hamilton, OH	84W34	39N24	5:38:16
Hammond, IN	87W30	41N38	5:50:00
Hampton, VA	76W21	37N02	5:05:24
Hamtramck, MI	83W03	42N24	5:32:12
Harlingen, TX	97W42	26N12	6:30:48
Harrisburg, PA	76W53	40N16	5:07:32
Hartford, CT	72W41	41N46	4:50:44
Harvey, IL	87W50	41N36	5:51:20
Hattiesburg, MS	89W17	31N20	5:57:08
Haverhill, MA	71W05	42N47	4:44:20
Havertown, PA	75W18	39N58	5:01:12
Hawthorne, CA	118W21	33N55	7:53:24
Hayward, CA	122W05	37N40	8:08:20
Hazleton, PA	75W59	40N57	5:03:56
Helena, MT	112W02	46N36	7:28:08
Hempstead, NY	73W38	40N43	4:54:32
Hialeah, FL	80W17	25N50	5:21:08
Hicksville, NY	73W32	40N46	4:54:08
Highland Park, IL	87W48	42N11	5:51:12
Highland Park, MI	83W06	42N24	5:32:24
High Point, NC	80W00	35N57	5:20:00
Hillcrest Center, CA	118W57	35N23	7:55:48
Hilo, HI	155W05	19N44	10:20:20
Hobbs, NM	103W08	32N42	6:52:32
Hoboken, NJ	74W02	40N44	4:56:08
Holland, MI	86W07	42N47	5:44:28
Hollywood, FL	80W09	26N01	5:20:36
Holyoke, MA	72W37	42N12	4:50:28
Honolulu, HI	157W52	21N19	10:31:28
Hot Springs Nat Park, AR	93W03	34N30	6:12:12
Houma, LA	90W43	29N36	6:02:52
Houston, TX	95W22	29N46	6:21:28
Huntington, WV	82W27	38N25	5:29:48
Huntington Beach, CA	118W05	33N40	7:52:20
Huntington Park, CA	118W14	33N58	7:52:56
Huntington Station, NY	73W25	40N51	4:53:40
Huntsville, AL	86W35	34N44	5:46:20
Hurst, TX	97W09	32N49	6:28:36
Hutchinson, KS	97W56	38N05	6:31:44
Idaho Falls, ID	112W02	43N30	7:28:08
Imperial Beach, CA	117W08	32N35	7:48:32
Independence, MO	94W25	39N06	6:17:40
Indianapolis, IN	86W09	39N46	5:44:36
Inglewood, CA	118W21	33N58	7:53:24
Inkster, MI	83W19	42N18	5:33:16
Iowa City, IA	91W32	41N40	6:06:08
Irondequoit, NY	77W35	43N13	5:10:20
Irving, TX	96W56	32N49	6:27:44
Irvington, NJ	74W14	40N44	4:56:56
Ithaca, NY	76W30	42N27	5:06:00
Jackson, MI	84W24	42N15	5:37:36
Jackson, MS	90W12	32N18	6:00:48
Jackson, TN	88W49	35N37	5:55:16
Jacksonville, FL	81W39	30N20	5:26:36
Jamaica, NY	73W47	40N43	4:55:08
Jamestown, NY	79W14	42N06	5:16:56
Janesville, WI	89W01	42N41	5:56:04
Jefferson City, MO	92W10	38N34	6:08:40

Jersey City, NJ	74W04	40N44	4:56:16
Johnson City, TN	82W21	36N19	5:29:24
Joliet, IL	88W05	41N32	5:52:20
Johnstown, PA	78W55	40N19	5:15:40
Jonesboro, AR	90W42	35N50	6:02:48
Joplin, MO	94W31	37N06	6:18:04
Juneau, AK	134W25	58N18	8:57:40
Kailua, HI	157W47	21N24	10:31:08
Kalamazoo, MI	85W35	42N17	5:42:20
Kaneohe, HI	157W48	21N25	10:31:12
Kankakee, IL	87W52	41N07	5:51:28
Kannapolis, NC	80W37	35N30	5:22:28
Kansas City, KS	94W38	39N07	6:18:32
Kansas City, MO	94W35	39N06	6:18:20
Kearny, NJ	74W09	40N46	4:56:36
Kendall, FL	80W19	25N41	5:21:16
Kenner, LA	90W15	29N59	6:01:00
Kenosha, WI	87W49	42N35	5:51:16
Kent, OH	81W22	41N09	5:25:28
Kettering, OH	84W10	39N41	5:36:40
Kew Gardens, NY	73W50	40N42	4:55:20
Key West, FL	81W47	24N33	5:27:08
Killeen, TX	97W44	31N07	6:30:56
Kingsport, TN	82W33	36N33	5:30:12
Kingston, NY	73W59	41N56	4:55:56
Kingsville, TX	97W52	27N31	6:31:28
Kirkwood, MO	90W24	38N35	6:01:36
Knoxville, TN	83W55	35N58	5:35:40
Kokomo, IN	86W08	40N29	5:44:32
Lackawanna, NY	78W50	42N50	5:15:20
La Crosse, WI	91W15	43N48	6:05:00
Lafayette, CA	122W07	37N53	8:08:28
Lafayette, IN	86W54	40N25	5:47:36
Lafayette, LA	92W01	30N14	6:08:04
La Habra, CA	117W57	33N56	7:51:48
Lake Charles, LA	93W13	30N14	6:12:52
Lakeland, FL	81W57	28N03	5:27:48
Lakewood, CA	118W08	33N51	7:52:32
Lakewood, CO	105W05	39N44	7:00:20
Lakewood, NJ	74W13	40N06	4:56:52
Lakewood, OH	81W48	41N29	5:27:12
Lakewood Center, WA	122W32	47N11	8:10:08
La Mesa, CA	117W03	32N46	7:48:12
La Mirada, CA	118W02	33N51	7:52:08
Lancaster, CA	118W08	34N42	7:52:32
Lancaster, OH	82W36	39N43	5:30:24
Lancaster, PA	76W19	40N02	5:05:16
Lansing, IL	87W32	41N33	5:50:08
Lansing, MI	84W33	42N44	5:38:12
La Puente, CA	117W57	34N02	7:51:48
Laredo, TX	99W30	27N30	6:38:00
Las Cruces, NM	106W47	32N19	7:07:08
Las Vegas, NV	115W09	36N10	7:40:36
Lawndale, CA	118W21	33N54	7:53:24
Lawrence, KS	95W14	38N58	6:20:56
Lawrence, MA	71W10	42N43	4:44:40
Lawton, OK	98W25	34N37	6:33:40
Leavenworth, KS	94W55	39N19	6:19:40
Lebanon, PA	76W26	40N20	5:05:44
Lemay, MO	90W16	38N32	6:01:04
Lemon Grove, CA	117W02	32N45	7:48:08
Leominster, MA	71W46	42N32	4:47:04
Levittown, NY	73W31	40N44	4:54:04
Levittown, PA	74W51	40N09	4:59:24
Lewiston, ID	117W01	46N25	7:48:04
Lewiston, ME	70W13	44N06	4:40:52
Lexington, KY	84W30	38N03	5:38:00
Lexington, MA	71W14	42N27	4:44:56
Lima, OH	84W06	40N44	5:36:24
Lincoln, NE	96W41	40N49	6:26:44
Lincoln Park, MI	83W11	42N15	5:32:44
Linden, NJ	74W15	40N38	4:57:00
Lindenhurst, NY	73W23	40N41	4:53:32
Little Rock, AR	92W17	34N45	6:09:08

Littleton, CO	105W01	39N37	7:00:04
Livermore, CA	121W47	37N41	8:07:08
Livingston, NJ	74W19	40N48	4:57:16
Livonia, MI	83W23	42N23	5:33:32
Lockport, NY	78W42	43N10	5:14:48
Lodi, CA	121W16	38N08	8:05:04
Lodi, NJ	74W05	40N53	4:56:20
Lombard, IL	88W01	41N53	5:52:04
Lompoc, CA	120W28	34N38	8:01:52
Long Beach, CA	118W11	33N47	7:52:44
Long Beach, NY	73W39	40N35	4:54:36
Long Branch, NJ	74W00	40N18	4:56:00
Longview, TX	94W44	32N30	6:18:56
Longview, WA	122W57	46N08	8:11:48
Lorain, OH	82W11	41N28	5:28:44
Los Altos, CA	122W07	37N23	8:08:28
Los Angeles, CA	118W15	34N04	7:53:00
Los Gatos, CA	121W59	37N14	8:07:56
Louisville, KY	85W46	38N15	5:43:04
Lowell, MA	71W19	42N38	4:45:16
Lubbock, TX	101W51	33N35	6:47:24
Lynchburg, VA	79W09	37N25	5:16:36
Lynn, MA	70W57	42N28	4:43:48
Lynwood, CA	118W13	33N56	7:52:52
Mcallen, TX	98W14	26N12	6:32:56
Mckeesport, PA	79W51	40N21	5:19:24
Macon, GA	83W38	32N51	5:34:32
Madison, WI	89W24	43N04	5:57:36
Madison Heights, MI	83W06	42N30	5:32:24
Malden, MA	71W04	42N26	4:44:16
Manchester, CT	72W31	41N47	4:50:04
Manchester, NH	71W28	43N00	4:45:52
Manhattan, KS	96W35	39N11	6:26:20
Manhattan Beach, CA	118W25	33N54	7:53:40
Manitowoc, WI	87W41	44N05	5:50:44
Mankato, MN	94W00	44N10	6:16:00
Mansfield, OH	82W31	40N45	5:30:04
Maple Heights, OH	81W34	41N25	5:26:16
Maplewood, MN	93W03	45N00	6:12:12
Marietta, GA	84W33	33N57	5:38:12
Marion, IN	85W40	40N32	5:42:40
Marion, OH	83W08	40N35	5:32:32
Marlboro, MA	71W05	42N47	4:44:20
Marrero, LA	90W06	29N54	6:00:24
Marshalltown, IA	92W55	42N03	6:11:40
Mason City, IA	93W12	43N09	6:12:48
Massapequa, NY	73W29	40N41	4:53:56
Massillon, OH	81W32	40N48	5:26:08
Maywood, IL	87W51	41N53	5:51:24
Mckeesport, PA	79W51	40N21	5:19:24
Medford, MA	71W07	42N25	4:44:28
Medford, OR	122W52	42N19	8:11:28
Melbourne, FL	80W37	28N05	5:22:28
Melrose, MA	71W04	42N27	4:44:16
Memphis, TN	90W03	35N08	6:00:12
Menlo Park, CA	122W12	37N27	8:08:48
Menomonee Falls, WI	88W07	43N11	5:52:28
Mentor, OH	81W21	41N40	5:25:24
Merced, CA	120W29	37N18	8:01:56
Meriden, CT	72W48	41N32	4:51:12
Meridian, MS	88W42	32N22	5:54:48
Merrick, NY	73W33	40N40	4:54:12
Merritt Island, FL	80W42	28N21	5:22:48
Mesa, AZ	111W50	33N25	7:27:20
Mesquite, TX	96W36	32N46	6:26:24
Metairie, LA	90W10	29N58	6:00:40
Methuen, MA	71W11	42N44	4:44:44
Miami, FL	80W11	25N47	5:20:44
Miami Beach, FL	80W08	25N47	5:20:32
Michigan City, IN	86W54	41N43	5:47:36
Middletown, CT	72W39	41N34	4:50:36
Middletown, OH	84W24	39N31	5:37:36
Middletown, RI	71W18	41N32	4:45:12

Midland, MI	84W14	43N37	5:36:56
Midland, TX	102W05	32N00	6:48:20
Midwest City, OK	97W24	35N27	6:29:36
Milford, CT	73W04	41N14	4:52:16
Millbrae, CA	122W24	37N36	8:09:36
Millcreek, UT	111W51	40N43	7:27:24
Milpitas, CA	121W55	37N26	8:07:40
Milton, MA	71W05	42N15	4:44:20
Milwaukee, WI	87W55	43N02	5:51:40
Minneapolis, MN	93W16	44N59	6:13:04
Minnetonka, MN	93W27	44N56	6:13:48
Minot, ND	101W18	48N14	6:45:12
Mishawaka, IN	86W11	41N40	5:44:44
Missoula, MT	114W01	46N52	7:36:04
Mobile, AL	88W03	30N41	5:52:12
Modesto, CA	121W00	37N39	8:04:00
Moline, IL	90W31	41N30	6:02:04
Monroe, LA	92W07	32N30	6:08:28
Monroeville, PA	79W45	40N26	5:19:00
Monrovia, CA	118W00	34N09	7:52:00
Montclair, CA	117W42	34N03	7:50:48
Montclair, NJ	74W13	40N49	4:56:52
Montebello, CA	118W07	34N00	7:52:28
Monterey, CA	121W55	36N37	8:07:40
Monterey Park, CA	118W08	34N04	7:52:32
Montgomery, AL	86W19	32N23	5:45:16
Montpelier, VT	72W35	44N16	4:50:20
Moorhead, MN	96W45	46N53	6:27:00
Morgantown, WV	79W57	39N38	5:19:48
Morton Grove, IL	87W46	42N02	5:51:04
Mountain View, CA	122W05	37N23	8:08:20
Mount Lebanon, PA	80W03	40N23	5:20:12
Mount Prospect, IL	87W56	42N04	5:51:44
Mount Vernon, NY	73W50	40N55	4:55:20
Muncie, IN	85W23	40N12	5:41:32
Murfreesboro, TN	86W24	35N51	5:45:36
Muskegon, MI	86W16	43N14	5:45:04
Muskogee, OK	95W22	35N45	6:21:28
Nansemond, VA	76W35	36N44	5:06:20
Napa, CA	122W17	38N18	8:09:08
Nashua, NH	71W28	42N45	4:45:52
Nashville, TN	86W47	36N10	5:47:08
Natick, MA	71W21	42N17	4:45:24
National City, CA	117W06	32N41	7:48:24
Needham, MA	71W14	42N17	4:44:56
New Albany, IN	85W49	38N18	5:43:16
Newark, CA	122W02	37N32	8:08:08
Newark, NJ	74W10	40N44	4:56:40
Newark, OH	82W24	40N03	5:29:36
New Bedford, MA	70W56	41N38	4:43:44
New Berlin, WI	88W06	42N59	5:52:24
New Britain, CT	72W47	41N40	4:51:08
New Brunswick, NJ	74W27	40N30	4:57:48
Newburgh, NY	74W01	41N30	4:56:04
New Castle, PA	80W21	41N00	5:21:24
New City, NY	73W59	41N09	4:55:56
New Haven, CT	72W55	41N18	4:51:40
New Iberia, LA	91W49	30N01	6:07:16
New London, CT	72W06	41N22	4:48:24
New Orleans, LA	90W04	29N58	6:00:16
Newington, CT	72W44	41N41	4:50:56
Newport, KY	84W30	39N05	5:38:00
Newport, RI	71W19	41N29	4:45:16
Newport Beach, CA	117W56	33N37	7:51:44
Newport News, VA	76W25	36N59	5:05:40
New Rochelle, NY	73W47	40N55	4:55:08
Newton, MA	71W12	42N21	4:44:48
New York, NY	73W57	40N45	4:55:48
Niagara Falls, NY	79W03	43N06	5:16:12
Niles, IL	87W48	42N02	5:51:12
Norfolk, VA	76W17	36N51	5:05:08
Normal, IL	88W59	40N31	5:55:56
Norman, OK	97W26	35N13	6:29:44
Norristown, PA	75W21	40N07	5:01:24
Northampton, MA	72W38	42N19	4:50:32
North Babylon, NY	73W19	40N44	4:53:16

North Bergen, NJ	74W01	40N48	4:56:04
Northbrook, IL	87W50	42N08	5:51:20
North Chicago, IL	87W51	42N19	5:51:24
Northglenn, CO	104W58	39N53	6:59:52
North Highlands, CA	121W22	38N42	8:05:28
North Las Vegas, NV	115W07	36N12	7:40:28
North Little Rock, AR	92W16	34N45	6:09:04
North Miami, FL	80W11	25N54	5:20:44
North Miami Beach, FL	80W10	25N56	5:20:40
North Olmsted, OH	81W56	41N25	5:27:44
North Tonawanda, NY	78W53	43N02	5:15:32
Norwalk, CA	118W05	33N54	7:52:20
Norwalk, CT	73W22	41N07	4:53:28
Norwich, CT	72W05	41N31	4:48:20
Norwood, MA	71W12	42N12	4:44:48
Norwood, OH	84W27	39N10	5:37:48
Novato, CA	122W35	38N06	8:10:20
Nutley, NJ	74W09	40N49	4:56:36
Oakland, CA	122W16	37N49	8:09:04
Oak Lawn, IL	87W44	41N43	5:50:56
Oak Park, IL	87W47	41N53	5:51:08
Oak Park, MI	83W11	42N28	5:32:44
Oak Ridge, TN	84W16	36N01	5:37:04
Oceanside, CA	117W23	33N12	7:49:32
Oceanside, NY	73W38	40N38	4:54:32
Odessa, TX	102W23	31N52	6:49:32
Ogden, UT	111W58	41N13	7:27:52
Oildale, CA	119W01	35N25	7:56:04
Oklahoma City, OK	97W30	35N30	6:30:00
Olympia, WA	122W53	47N03	8:11:32
Omaha, NE	96W01	41N17	6:24:04
Ontario, CA	117W39	34N04	7:50:36
Orange, CA	117W51	33N47	7:51:24
Orange, NJ	74W14	40N46	4:56:56
Orem, UT	111W42	40N19	7:26:48
Orlando, FL	81W23	28N33	5:25:32
Oshkosh, WI	88W33	44N01	5:54:12
Ottumwa, IA	92W25	41N01	6:09:40
Overland Park, KS	94W40	38N58	6:18:40
Owensboro, KY	87W07	37N46	5:48:28
Oxnard, CA	119W10	34N12	7:56:40
Pacifica, CA	122W30	37N36	8:10:00
Paducah, KY	88W37	37N05	5:54:28
Palatine, IL	88W03	42N07	5:52:12
Palm Springs, CA	116W32	33N49	7:46:08
Palo Alto, CA	122W10	37N27	8:08:40
Panama City, FL	85W40	30N10	5:42:40
Paramount, CA	118W10	33N53	7:52:40
Paramus, NJ	74W04	40N55	4:56:16
Parkersburg, WV	81W34	39N16	5:26:16
Park Forest, IL	87W40	41N29	5:50:40
Park Ridge, IL	87W51	42N02	5:51:24
Parkville, MD	76W33	39N23	5:06:12
Parma, OH	81W43	41N23	5:26:52
Parma Heights, OH	81W46	41N23	5:27:04
Pasadena, CA	118W09	34N09	7:52:36
Pasadena, TX	95W13	29N43	6:20:52
Pascagoula, MS	88W33	30N21	5:54:12
Passaic, NJ	74W07	40N51	4:56:28
Paterson, NJ	74W11	40N55	4:56:44
Pawtucket, RI	71W23	41N53	4:45:32
Peabody, MA	70W56	42N31	4:43:44
Pekin, IL	89W40	40N35	5:58:40
Penn Hills, PA	79W52	40N28	5:19:28
Pennsauken, NJ	75W03	39N57	5:00:12
Pensacola, FL	87W13	30N25	5:48:52
Peoria, IL	89W36	40N42	5:58:24
Perth Amboy, NJ	74W16	40N31	4:57:04
Petaluma, CA	122W39	38N14	8:10:36
Petersburg, VA	77W24	37N14	5:09:36

Phenix City, AL	85W00	32N28	5:40:00
Philadelphia, PA	75W10	39N57	5:00:40
Phoenix, AZ	112W04	33N27	7:28:16
Pico Rivera, CA	118W05	33N59	7:52:20
Pierre, SD	100W21	44N22	6:41:24
Pine Bluff, AR	92W01	34N13	6:08:04
Piscataway, NJ	74W28	40N34	4:57:52
Pittsburg, CA	121W53	38N02	8:07:32
Pittsburgh, PA	80W01	40N26	5:20:04
Pittsfield, MA	73W15	42N27	4:53:00
Placentia, CA	117W52	33N53	7:51:28
Plainfield, NJ	74W25	40N37	4:57:40
Plainview, NY	73W29	40N46	4:53:56
Pleasant Hill, CA	122W04	37N57	8:08:16
Pocatello, ID	112W27	42N52	7:29:48
Pomona, CA	117W45	34N04	7:51:00
Pompano Beach, FL	80W08	26N14	5:20:32
Ponca City, OK	97W05	36N42	6:28:20
Pontiac, MI	83W18	42N38	5:33:12
Portage, MI	85W35	42N12	5:42:20
Port Arthur, TX	93W56	29N54	6:15:44
Port Chester, NY	73W40	41N00	4:54:40
Port Huron, MI	82W26	42N58	5:29:44
Portland, ME	70W16	43N39	4:41:04
Portland, OR	122W37	45N32	8:10:28
Portsmouth, NH	70W45	43N05	4:43:00
Portsmouth, OH	83W00	38N44	5:32:00
Portsmouth, VA	76W18	36N50	5:05:12
Pottstown, PA	75W39	40N15	5:02:36
Poughkeepsie, NY	73W56	41N42	4:55:44
Prairie Village, KS	94W38	39N00	6:18:32
Prichard, AL	88W05	30N44	5:52:20
Providence, RI	71W24	41N49	4:45:36
Provo, UT	111W39	40N14	7:26:36
Pueblo, CO	104W36	38N14	6:58:24
Queens, NY	73W52	40N43	4:55:28
Quincy, IL	91W23	39N56	6:05:32
Quincy, MA	71W00	42N15	4:44:00
Racine, WI	87W48	42N44	5:51:12
Rahway, NJ	74W16	40N37	4:57:04
Raleigh, NC	78W38	35N46	5:14:32
Rancho Cordova, CA	121W18	38N36	8:05:12
Randolph, MA	71W02	42N10	4:44:08
Rantoul, IL	88W09	40N19	5:52:36
Rapid City, SD	103W14	44N05	6:52:56
Raytown, MO	94W28	39N01	6:17:52
Reading, PA	75W56	40N20	5:03:44
Redford, MI	83W18	42N23	5:33:12
Redlands, CA	117W11	34N04	7:48:44
Redondo Beach, CA	118W23	33N50	7:53:32
Redwood City, CA	122W15	37N30	8:09:00
Rego Park, NY	73W52	40N44	4:55:28
Reno, NV	119W48	39N31	7:59:12
Renton, WA	122W12	47N29	8:08:48
Revere, MA	71W01	42N25	4:44:04
Rialto, CA	117W22	34N06	7:49:28
Richardson, TX	96W44	32N57	6:26:56
Richfield, MN	93W17	44N53	6:13:08
Richland, WA	119W18	46N17	7:57:12
Richmond, CA	122W21	37N56	8:09:24
Richmond, IN	84W54	39N50	5:39:36
Richmond, VA	77W27	37N33	5:09:48
Ridgewood, NJ	74W07	40N59	4:56:28
Riverside, CA	117W22	33N59	7:49:28
Riverton Heights, WA	122W17	47N28	8:09:08
Roanoke, VA	79W56	37N16	5:19:44
Rochester, MN	92W28	44N01	6:09:52
Rochester, NY	77W37	43N10	5:10:28
Rockford, IL	89W06	42N16	5:56:24
Rock Hill, SC	81W01	34N56	5:24:04
Rock Island, IL	90W34	41N30	6:02:16
Rockville, MD	77W09	39N05	5:08:36
Rockville Centre, NY	73W39	40N40	4:54:36
Rocky Mount, NC	77W46	35N55	5:11:04
Rome, GA	85W10	34N15	5:40:40
Rome, NY	75W27	43N13	5:01:48
Rosemead, CA	118W04	34N05	7:52:16
Roseville, MI	82W56	42N30	5:31:44
Roseville, MN	93W10	45N01	6:12:40
Roswell, NM	104W32	33N24	6:58:08
Rotterdam, NY	74W01	42N49	4:56:04
Royal Oak, MI	83W09	42N30	5:32:36
Sacramento, CA	121W29	38N35	8:05:56
Saginaw, MI	83W57	43N25	5:35:48
Saint Charles, MO	90W29	38N47	6:01:56
Saint Clair Shores, MI	82W54	42N30	5:31:36
Saint Cloud, MN	94W10	45N34	6:16:40
Saint Joseph, MO	94W50	39N46	6:19:20
Saint Louis, MO	90W12	38N37	6:00:48
Saint Louis Park, MN	93W21	44N57	6:13:24
Saint Paul, MN	93W06	44N57	6:12:24
Saint Petersburg, FL	82W39	27N46	5:30:36
Salem, MA	70W53	42N31	4:43:32
Salem, OR	123W02	44N56	8:12:08
Salina, KS	97W37	38N50	6:30:28
Salinas, CA	121W39	36N40	8:06:36
Salt Lake City, UT	111W53	40N45	7:27:32
San Angelo, TX	100W26	31N28	6:41:44
San Antonio, TX	98W30	29N25	6:34:00
San Bernardino, CA	117W19	34N07	7:49:16
San Bruno, CA	122W25	37N38	8:09:40
San Carlos, CA	122W16	37N31	8:09:04
San Diego, CA	117W09	32N43	7:48:36
Sandusky, OH	82W42	41N27	5:30:48
San Francisco, CA	122W25	37N47	8:09:40
San Gabriel, CA	118W06	34N06	7:52:24
San Jose, CA	121W53	37N20	8:07:32
San Leandro, CA	122W09	37N44	8:08:36
San Lorenzo, CA	122W08	37N41	8:08:32
San Luis Obispo, CA	120W40	35N17	8:02:40
San Mateo, CA	122W19	37N34	8:09:16
San Rafael, CA	122W32	37N58	8:10:08
Santa Ana, CA	117W52	33N46	7:51:28
Santa Barbara, CA	119W42	34N25	7:58:48
Santa Clara, CA	121W57	37N21	8:07:48
Santa Cruz, CA	122W01	36N58	8:08:04
Santa Fe, NM	105W57	35N41	7:03:48
Santa Maria, CA	120W26	34N57	8:01:44
Santa Monica, CA	118W29	34N01	7:53:56
Santa Rosa, CA	122W43	38N26	8:10:52
Sarasota, FL	82W32	27N20	5:30:08
Saratoga, CA	122W02	37N16	8:08:08
Saugus, MA	71W01	42N28	4:44:04
Savannah, GA	81W06	32N05	5:24:24
Sayreville, NJ	74W22	40N28	4:57:28
Schenectady, NY	73W57	42N49	4:55:48
Scottsdale, AZ	111W56	33N29	7:27:44
Scranton, PA	75W40	41N25	5:02:40
Seal Beach, CA	118W06	33N44	7:52:24
Seaside, CA	121W50	36N37	8:07:20
Seattle, WA	122W20	47N36	8:09:20
Selma, AL	87W01	32N25	5:48:04
Shaker Heights, OH	81W32	41N29	5:26:08
Shawnee, OK	96W55	35N20	6:27:40
Sheboygan, WI	87W45	43N46	5:51:00
Shelton, CT	73W05	41N19	4:52:20
Sherman, TX	96W36	33N38	6:26:24
Shreveport, LA	93W45	32N31	6:15:00
Silver Spring, MD	77W02	39N01	5:08:08
Simi, CA	118W47	34N16	7:55:08
Sioux City, IA	96W24	42N30	6:25:36

Sioux Falls, SD	96W44	43N33	6:26:56
Skokie, IL	87W45	42N03	5:51:00
Somerville, MA	71W06	42N23	4:44:24
South Bend, IN	86W15	41N41	5:45:00
South Euclid, OH	81W32	41N31	5:26:08
Southfield, MI	83W17	42N29	5:33:08
South Gate, CA	118W12	33N57	7:52:48
Southgate, MI	83W12	42N12	5:32:48
South Lake Tahoe, CA	119W59	38N57	7:59:56
South Pasadena, CA	118W09	34N07	7:52:36
South Saint Paul, MN	93W02	44N53	6:12:08
South San Francisco, CA	122W24	37N39	8:09:36
South Whittier, CA	118W02	33N56	7:52:08
Spartanburg, SC	81W57	34N56	5:27:48
Spokane, WA	117W24	47N40	7:49:36
Springfield, MA	72W35	42N06	4:50:20
Springfield, MO	93W17	37N13	6:13:08
Springfield, OH	83W49	39N55	5:35:16
Springfield, OR	123W01	44N03	8:12:04
Spring Valley, CA	116W58	32N45	7:47:52
Stamford, CT	73W32	41N03	4:54:08
State College, PA	77W52	40N48	5:11:28
Staten Island, NY	74W09	40N35	4:56:36
Sterling Heights, MI	83W01	42N35	5:32:04
Steubenville, OH	80W37	40N22	5:22:28
Stillwater, OK	97W04	36N07	6:28:16
Stockton, CA	121W17	37N58	8:05:08
Stratford, CT	73W08	41N12	4:52:32
Suitland, MD	76W56	38N51	5:07:44
Sunnyvale, CA	122W02	37N23	8:08:08
Superior, WI	92W06	46N44	6:08:24
Syracuse, NY	76W09	43N03	5:04:36
Tacoma, WA	122W26	47N14	8:09:44
Tallahassee, FL	84W17	30N27	5:37:08
Tampa, FL	82W27	27N57	5:29:48
Taunton, MA	71W06	41N54	4:44:24
Taylor, MI	83W16	42N14	5:33:04
Teaneck, NJ	74W01	40N53	4:56:04
Tempe, AZ	111W56	33N25	7:27:44
Temple, TX	97W21	31N06	6:29:24
Temple City, CA	118W01	34N07	7:52:04
Terre Haute, IN	87W25	39N28	5:49:40
Texarkana, TX	94W06	33N26	6:16:24
Texas City, TX	94W54	29N24	6:19:36
Thousand Oaks, CA	118W50	34N10	7:55:20
Titusville, FL	80W49	28N37	5:23:16
Toledo, OH	83W33	41N39	5:34:12
Topeka, KS	95W40	39N03	6:22:40
Torrance, CA	118W19	33N50	7:53:16
Torrington, CT	73W07	41N48	4:52:28
Town Of Tonawanda, NY	78W52	42N59	5:15:28
Towson, MD	76W36	39N24	5:06:24
Trenton, NJ	74W46	40N14	4:59:04
Troy, MI	83W09	42N37	5:32:36
Troy, NY	73W41	42N44	4:54:44
Trumbull, CT	73W12	41N15	4:52:48
Tucson, AZ	110W58	32N13	7:23:52
Tulsa, OK	95W55	36N10	6:23:40
Tuscaloosa, AL	87W34	33N12	5:50:16
Tustin, CA	117W49	33N44	7:51:16
Tyler, TX	95W18	32N21	6:21:12
Union, NJ	74W17	40N42	4:57:08
Union City, NJ	74W02	40N45	4:56:08
University City, MO	90W20	38N40	6:01:20
Upland, CA	117W39	34N06	7:50:36
Upper Arlington, OH	83W04	40N00	5:32:16
Upper Darby, PA	75W16	39N58	5:01:04
Urbana, IL	88W12	40N07	5:52:48
Utica, NY	75W14	43N06	5:00:56
Vacaville, CA	121W59	38N21	8:07:56
Valdosta, GA	83W17	30N50	5:33:08
Vallejo, CA	122W15	38N07	8:09:00
Valley Stream, NY	73W42	40N40	4:54:48
Vancouver, WA	122W40	45N38	8:10:40
Van Nuys, CA	118W26	34N11	7:53:44
Ventura, CA	119W18	34N17	7:57:12
Vernon, CT	72W28	41N51	4:49:52
Vicksburg, MS	90W53	32N21	6:03:32
Victoria, TX	97W00	28N48	6:28:00
Villa Park, IL	87W59	41N53	5:51:56
Vineland, NJ	75W02	39N29	5:00:08
Virginia Beach, VA	75W59	36N51	5:03:56
Visalia, CA	119W18	36N20	7:57:12
Vista, CA	117W14	33N12	7:48:56
Waco, TX	97W09	31N33	6:28:36
Wakefield, MA	71W04	42N30	4:44:16
Wallingford, CT	72W50	41N27	4:51:20
Walnut Creek, CA	122W04	37N54	8:08:16
Waltham, MA	71W14	42N23	4:44:56
Warminster, PA	75W06	40N12	5:00:24
Warner Robins, GA	83W36	32N37	5:34:24
Warren, MI	83W02	42N31	5:32:08
Warren, OH	80W49	41N14	5:23:16
Warwick, RI	71W28	41N42	4:45:52
Washington, DC	77W02	38N54	5:08:08
Waterbury, CT	73W03	41N33	4:52:12
Waterloo, IA	92W21	42N30	6:09:24
Watertown, MA	71W11	42N22	4:44:44
Watertown, NY	75W55	43N59	5:03:40
Waukegan, IL	87W50	42N22	5:51:20
Waukesha, WI	88W14	43N01	5:52:56
Wausau, WI	89W38	44N58	5:58:32
Wauwatosa, WI	88W00	43N03	5:52:00
Wayne, NJ	74W15	40N57	4:57:00
Webster Groves, MO	90W22	38N35	6:01:28
Weirton, WV	80W35	40N24	5:22:20
Wellesley, MA	71W18	42N18	4:45:12
West Allis, WI	88W00	43N01	5:52:00
West Babylon, NY	73W21	40N42	4:53:24
West Covina, CA	117W54	34N04	7:51:36
Westfield, MA	72W45	42N07	4:51:00
Westfield, NJ	74W21	40N39	4:57:24
West Hartford, CT	72W44	41N45	4:50:56
West Haven, CT	72W57	41N17	4:51:48
West Hempstead, NY	73W38	40N42	4:54:32
West Hollywood, CA	118W22	34N05	7:53:28
West Islip, NY	73W18	40N42	4:53:12
Westland, MI	83W23	42N18	5:33:32
West Memphis, AR	90W11	35N09	6:00:44
West Mifflin, PA	79W54	40N22	5:19:36
Westminster, CA	118W00	33N47	7:52:00
West New York, NJ	74W01	40N47	4:56:04
West Orange, NJ	74W14	40N47	4:56:56
West Palm Beach, FL	80W03	26N43	5:20:12
Westport, CT	73W22	41N09	4:53:28
West Seneca, NY	78W48	42N51	5:15:12
West Springfield, MA	72W38	42N06	4:50:32
Wethersfield, CT	72W40	41N42	4:50:40
Weymouth, MA	70W58	42N13	4:43:52
Wheaton, IL	88W06	41N52	5:52:24
Wheaton, MD	77W03	39N03	5:08:12
Wheat Ridge, CO	105W07	39N46	7:00:28
Wheeling, WV	80W43	40N04	5:22:52
Whitehall, OH	82W53	39N58	5:31:32
White Plains, NY	73W46	41N02	4:55:04
Whittier, CA	118W03	33N58	7:52:12
Wichita, KS	97W20	37N42	6:29:20
Wichita Falls, TX	98W30	33N54	6:34:00

Wilkes-barre, PA	75W53	41N15	5:03:32
Wilkinsburg, PA	79W53	40N26	5:19:32
Williamsport, PA	77W00	41N15	5:08:00
Willingboro, NJ	74W54	40N03	4:59:36
Willow Brook, CA	118W15	33N56	7:53:00
Wilmette, IL	87W42	42N05	5:50:48
Wilmington, DE	75W33	39N45	5:02:12
Wilmington, NC	77W55	34N14	5:11:40
Wilson, NC	77W55	35N44	5:11:40
Winona, MN	91W39	44N03	6:06:36
Winston-salem, NC	80W15	36N06	5:21:00
Woburn, MA	71W09	42N29	4:44:36
Woodbridge, VA	77W15	38N40	5:09:00
Woodland, CA	121W46	38N41	8:07:04
Woodside, NY	73W55	40N45	4:55:40
Woonsocket, RI	71W31	42N00	4:46:04
Worcester, MA	71W48	42N16	4:47:12
Wyandotte, MI	83W09	42N12	5:32:36
Wyoming, MI	85W42	42N54	5:42:48
Xenia, OH	83W56	39N41	5:35:44
Yakima, WA	120W30	46N37	8:02:00
Yonkers, NY	73W54	40N56	4:55:36
York, PA	76W44	39N58	5:06:56
Youngstown, OH	80W39	41N06	5:22:36
Ypsilanti, MI	83W37	42N14	5:34:28
Yuma, AZ	114W37	32N43	7:38:28
Zanesville, OH	82W01	39N56	5:28:04
Adelaide, Australia	138E35	34S55	-9:14:20
Agra, India	78E01	27N11	-5:12:04
Agram, Yugoslavia	15E58	45N48	-1:03:52
Ahmadabad, India	72E37	23N02	-4:50:28
Aleppo, Syria	37E10	36N12	-2:28:40
Alexandria, Egypt	29E54	31N12	-1:59:36
Algiers, Algeria	3E03	36N47	-0:12:12
Allahabad, India	81E51	25N57	-5:27:24
Amritsar, India	74E53	31N35	-4:59:32
Amsterdam, Netherlands	4E54	52N22	-0:19:36
Ankara, Turkey	32E52	39N56	-2:11:28
Antwerp, Belgium	4E25	51N13	-0:17:40
Athens, Greece	23E44	37N58	-1:34:56
Auckland, New Zealand	174E46	36S52	-11:39:04
Baghdad, Iraq	44E25	33N21	-2:57:40
Baku, USSR	49E51	40N23	-3:19:24
Bangalore, India	77E35	12N59	-5:10:20
Bangkok, Thailand	100E31	13N45	-6:42:04
Barcelona, Spain	2E11	41N23	-0:08:44
Beijing, China	116E25	39N55	-7:45:40
Belem, Brazil	48W29	01S27	3:13:56
Belfast, N Ireland	5W55	54N35	0:23:40
Benares, India	83E00	25N20	-5:32:00
Beograd, Yugoslavia	20E30	44N50	-1:22:00
Berlin, Germany	13E24	52N31	-0:53:36
Birmingham, England	1W50	52N30	0:07:20
Bogota, Colombia	74W05	04N36	4:56:20
Bologna, Italy	11E20	44N29	-0:45:20
Bombay, India	72E50	18N58	-4:51:20
Bonn, Germany	7E05	50N44	-0:28:20
Bordeaux, France	0W34	44N50	0:02:16
Bremen, Germany	8E49	53N04	-0:35:16
Breslau, Poland	17E00	51N06	-1:08:00
Brisbane, Australia	153E02	27S28	-10:12:08
Bristol, England	2W35	51N27	0:10:20
Brno, Czechoslovakia	16E37	49N12	-1:06:28
Bruxelles, Belgium	4E20	50N50	-0:17:20
Bucharest, Rumania	26E06	44N26	-1:44:24
Budapest, Hungary	19E05	47N30	-1:16:20
Buenos Aires, Argentina	58W27	34S36	3:53:48
Cairo, Egypt	31E15	30N03	-2:05:00
Calcutta, India	88E22	22N32	-5:53:28
Canton, China	113E16	23N06	-7:33:04
Capetown, S Africa	18E22	33S55	-1:13:28
Casablanca, Morocco	7W35	33N39	0:30:20
Catania, Italy	15E06	37N30	-1:00:24
Cawnpore, India	80E21	26N28	-5:21:24
Changsha, China	112E58	28N12	-7:31:52
Charkov, USSR	36E15	50N00	-2:25:00
Chemnitz, Germany	12E55	50N50	-0:51:40
Chittagong, Bangladesh	91E50	22N20	-6:07:20
Chungking, China	106E35	29N34	-7:06:20
Cologne, W Germany	6E59	50N56	-0:27:56
Colombo, Sri Lanka	79E51	06N56	-5:19:24
Cordoba, Argentina	64W11	31S24	4:16:44
Dacca, Bangladesh	90E25	23N43	-6:01:40
Damascus, Syria	36E18	33N30	-2:25:12
Danzig, Poland	18E40	54N23	-1:14:40
Delhi, India	77E13	28N40	-5:08:52
Dnepropetrovsk, USSR	34E59	48N27	-2:19:56
Dortmund, Germany	7E28	51N31	-0:29:52
Dresden, Germany	13E44	51N03	-0:54:56
Dublin, Ireland	6W15	53N20	0:25:00
Duisburg, Germany	6E46	51N25	-0:27:04
Durban, S Africa	30E56	29S55	-2:03:44
Dusseldorf, Germany	6E47	51N12	-0:27:08
Edinburgh, Scotland	3W13	55N57	0:12:52
Edmonton, Canada	113W28	53N33	7:33:52
Essen, W Germany	7E01	51N28	-0:28:04
Firenze, Italy	11E15	43N46	-0:45:00
Foochow, China	119E17	26N06	-7:57:08
Frankfurt, Germany	8E40	50N07	-0:34:40
Fukuoka, Japan	130E24	33N35	-8:41:36
Geneva, Switzerland	6E09	46N12	-0:24:36
Genoa, Italy	8E57	44N25	-0:35:48
Glasgow, Scotland	4W15	55N53	0:17:00
Gorki, USSR	44E00	56N20	-2:56:00
Goteborg, Sweden	11E58	57N43	-0:47:52
Greenwich, England	0W00	51N29	0:00:00
Guatemala, Guatemala	90W31	14N38	6:02:04
The Hague, Netherlands	4E18	52N06	-0:17:12
Hamburg, Germany	9E59	53N33	-0:39:56
Hamilton, Canada	79W51	43N15	5:19:24
Hangchow, China	120E07	30N15	-8:00:28
Hanover, Germany	9E44	52N24	-0:38:56
Harbin, China	126E41	45N45	-8:26:44
Havana, Cuba	82W22	23N08	5:29:28
Helsinki, Finland	24E58	60N10	-1:39:52
Hiroshima, Japan	132E27	34N24	-8:49:48
Hong Kong	114E12	22N17	-7:36:48
Hyderabad, India	78E29	17N23	-5:13:56
Hyderabad, Pakistan	68E22	25N22	-4:33:28
Ibadan, Nigeria	3E30	07N17	-0:14:00
Indore, India	75E50	22N43	-5:03:20
Istanbul, Turkey	28E58	41N01	-1:55:52
Jakarta, Indonesia	106E48	06S10	-7:07:12
Jerusalem, Israel	35E14	31N46	-2:20:56
Johannesburg, S Africa	28E00	26S15	-1:52:00

Karachi, Pakistan	67E03	24N51	-4:28:12
Kazan, USSR	49E08	55N45	-3:16:32
Kiel, Germany	10E08	54N20	-0:40:32
Kiev, USSR	30E31	50N26	-2:02:04
Kjobenhavn, Denmark	12E35	55N40	-0:50:20
Koln, Germany	6E59	50N56	-0:27:56
Konigsberg, USSR	20E30	54N43	-1:22:00
Krakow, Poland	19E58	50N03	-1:19:52
Kuybyshev, USSR	50E09	53N12	-3:20:36
Kyoto, Japan	135E45	35N00	-9:03:00
Lahore, Pakistan	74E18	31N35	-4:57:12
Lanchow, China	103E41	36N03	-6:54:44
La Paz, Bolivia	68W09	16S30	4:32:36
Leeds, England	1W35	53N50	0:06:20
Leipzig, Germany	12E20	51N19	-0:49:20
Leningrad, USSR	30E15	59N55	-2:01:00
Liege, Belgium	5E34	50N38	-0:22:16
Lille, France	3E04	50N38	-0:12:16
Lima, Peru	77W03	12S03	5:08:12
Liverpool, England	2W55	53N25	0:11:40
Lisbon, Portugal	9W08	38N43	0:36:32
Lodz, Poland	19E30	51N46	-1:18:00
London, England	0W10	51P30	0:00:40
Lucknow, India	80E55	26N51	-5:23:40
Lwow, USSR	24E00	49N50	-1:36:00
Lyon, France	4E51	45N45	-0:19:24
Madras, India	80E17	13N05	-5:21:08
Madrid, Spain	3W41	40N24	0:14:44
Madurai, India	78E07	09N56	-5:12:28
Magdeburg, Germany	11E38	52N07	-0:46:32
Manchester, England	2W15	53N30	0:09:00
Manila, Philippines	121E00	14N35	-8:04:00
Mannheim, Germany	8E29	49N29	-0:33:56
Marseille, France	5E24	43N18	-0:21:36
Mecca, Saudi Arabia	39E49	21N27	-2:39:16
Melbourne, Australia	144E58	37S49	-9:39:52
Mexico City, Mexico	99W09	19N24	6:36:36
Milano, Italy	9E12	45N28	-0:36:48
Monterrey, Mexico	100W19	25N40	6:41:16
Montevideo, Uruguay	56W11	34S53	3:44:44
Montreal, Canada	73W34	45N31	4:54:16
Moscow, USSR	37E35	55N45	-2:30:20
Mukden, China	123E27	41N48	-8:13:48
Munchen, Germany	11E34	48N08	-0:46:16
Nagoya, Japan	136E55	35N10	-9:07:40
Nagpur, India	79E06	21N09	-5:16:24
Nanking, China	118E47	32N03	-7:55:08
Naples, Italy	14E17	40N51	-0:57:08
Newcastle, England	3W06	52N26	0:12:24
Nice, France	7E15	43N42	-0:29:00
Nottingham, England	1W10	52N58	0:04:40
Novosibirsk, USSR	82E55	55N02	-5:31:40
Nurnberg, Germany	11E04	49N27	-0:44:16
Odessa, USSR	30E44	46N28	-2:02:56
Osaka, Japan	135E30	34N40	-9:02:00
Oslo, Norway	10E45	59N55	-0:43:00
Ottawa, Canada	75W42	45N25	5:02:48
Palermo, Italy	13E22	38N07	-0:53:28
Paris, France	2E20	48N52	-0:09:20
Patna, India	85E07	25N36	-5:40:28
Perth, Australia	115E50	31S56	-7:43:20
Poona, India	73E52	18N32	-4:55:28
Porto, Portugal	8W36	41N11	0:34:24
Porto Alegre, Brazil	51W13	30S04	3:24:52
Portsmouth, England	1W05	50N48	0:04:20
Posen, Poland	16E55	52N25	-1:07:40
Praha, Czechoslovakia	14E26	50N05	-0:57:44
Rangoon, Burma	96E10	16N47	-6:24:40
Recife, Brazil	34W54	08S03	2:19:36
Riga, USSR	24E06	56N57	-1:36:24
Rio De Janeiro, Brazil	43W14	22S54	2:52:56
Rome, Italy	12E29	41N54	-0:49:56
Rosario, Argentina	60W40	32S57	4:02:40
Rostovnadonu, USSR	39E42	47N14	-2:38:48
Rotterdam, Netherlands	4E28	51N55	-0:17:52
Saigon, Vietnam	106E40	10N45	-7:06:40
Salvador, Brazil	38W31	12S59	2:34:04
Santiago, Chile	70W40	33S27	4:42:40
Sao Paulo, Brazil	46W37	23S32	3:06:28
Saratov, USSR	46E02	51N34	-3:04:08
Seoul, Korea	126E58	37N33	-8:27:52
Shanghai, China	121E22	31N07	-8:05:28
Sheffield, England	1W30	53N23	0:06:00
Sian, China	108E52	34N15	-7:15:28
Singapore, Singapore	103E50	01N17	-6:55:20
Sofia, Bulgaria	23E19	42N40	-1:33:16
Stalino, USSR	37E48	48N00	-2:31:12
Stettin, Poland	14E32	53N24	-0:58:08
Stockholm, Sweden	18E03	59N20	-1:12:12
Stoke On Trent, England	2W10	53N00	0:08:40
Stuttgart, Germany	9E11	48N46	-0:36:44
Surabaya, Indonesia	112E45	07S15	-7:31:00
Sverdlovsk, USSR	60E36	56N51	-4:02:24
Sydney, Australia	151E13	33S52	-10:04:52
Taipei, Taiwan	121E30	25N03	-8:06:00
Talien, China	121E35	38N53	-8:06:20
Tashkent, USSR	69E18	41N20	-4:37:12
Tbilisi, USSR	44E49	41N43	-2:59:16
Teheran, Iran	51E26	35N40	-3:25:44
Tel Aviv-yafo, Israel	34E46	32N04	-2:19:04
Thessaloniki, Greece	22E56	40N38	-1:31:44
Tientsin, China	117E12	39N08	-7:48:48
Tokyo, Japan	139E45	35N40	-9:19:00
Toronto, Canada	79W23	43N39	5:17:32
Trieste, Italy	13E46	45N40	-0:55:04
Tsinan, China	116E57	36N40	-7:47:48
Tsingtao, China	120E19	36N06	-8:01:16
Turin, Italy	7E40	45N03	-0:30:40
Valencia, Spain	0W22	39N28	0:01:28
Vancouver, Canada	123W07	49N16	8:12:28
Venice, Italy	12E21	45N27	-0:49:24
Vienna, Austria	16E20	48N13	-1:05:20
Volgograd, USSR	44E25	48N44	-2:57:40
Voronezh, USSR	39E10	51N40	-2:36:40
Warsaw, Poland	21E00	52N15	-1:24:00
Wuhan, China	114E17	30N36	-7:37:08
Winnipeg, Canada	97W09	49N53	6:28:36
Wuppertal, Germany	7E11	51N16	-0:28:44
Yokohama, Japan	139E39	35N27	-9:18:36
Zurich, Switzerland	8E32	47N23	-0:34:08

Appendix 2:
Tables of Houses

0h 0m 0s — 0 ♈ 00 — 0° 0' 0"

11	12	ASC	2	3
2♉11	2♊05	0♋00	27♋55	27♌49
2 34	3 18	2 00	29 06	28 11
2 58	4 34	4 01	0♌16	28 34
3 23	5 53	6 05	1 28	28 56
3 49	7 19	8 14	2 40	29 19
3 55	7 37	8 41	2 55	29 24
4 01	7 55	9 08	3 10	29 29
4 07	8 14	9 35	3 25	29 34
4 13	8 33	10 03	3 41	29 38
4 19	8 52	10 31	3 56	29 43
4 25	9 12	10 59	4 12	29 48
4 32	9 33	11 28	4 27	29 53
4 38	9 53	11 57	4 43	29 59
4 45	10 15	12 26	5 00	0♍04
4 52	10 37	12 56	5 16	0 09
4 59	10 59	13 27	5 33	0 14
5 06	11 22	13 58	5 50	0 20
5 14	11 46	14 29	6 07	0 25
5 21	12 10	15 01	6 24	0 31
5 29	12 36	15 34	6 42	0 37
5 38	13 02	16 07	7 00	0 42
5 46	13 28	16 41	7 18	0 48
5 55	13 56	17 16	7 37	0 54
6 04	14 25	17 52	7 56	1 00
6 13	14 55	18 28	8 15	1 07
6 23	15 26	19 05	8 35	1 13
6 34	15 58	19 43	8 56	1 20
6 44	16 31	20 21	9 17	1 27
6 55	17 06	21 01	9 38	1 34
7 07	17 42	21 42	10 00	1 41
7 19	18 20	22 24	10 22	1 48
7 32	19 00	23 06	10 45	1 56
7 46	19 42	23 50	11 09	2 04
8 00	20 26	24 36	11 33	2 12
8 15	21 12	25 22	11 58	2 20
8 31	22 01	26 10	12 24	2 29
8 48	22 53	26 59	12 51	2 38
9 06	23 47	27 50	13 19	2 47
9 25	24 46	28 42	13 47	2 57
9 46	25 48	29 36	14 17	3 07
10 08	26 54	0♌32	14 47	3 17
10 32	28 05	1 30	15 19	3 28
10 58	29 21	2 29	15 52	3 39
11 26	0♋44	3 31	16 26	3 51
11♉58	2♋13	4♌34	17♌01	4♍03

0h 4m 0s — 1 ♈ 05 — 1° 0' 0"

11	12	ASC	2	3	LAT.
3♉13	3♊03	0♋55	28♋52	28♌52	0
3 37	4 16	2 55	0♌03	29 13	5
4 01	5 32	4 56	1 13	29 35	10
4 27	6 52	7 00	2 23	29 57	15
4 54	8 18	9 08	3 35	0♍19	20
5 00	8 36	9 35	3 50	0 24	21
5 06	8 54	10 02	4 05	0 29	22
5 12	9 13	10 29	4 20	0 33	23
5 18	9 32	10 56	4 35	0 38	24
5 25	9 52	11 24	4 50	0 43	25
5 31	10 12	11 52	5 05	0 48	26
5 38	10 32	12 20	5 21	0 52	27
5 44	10 53	12 49	5 37	0 57	28
5 51	11 14	13 19	5 53	1 02	29
5 58	11 36	13 48	6 09	1 07	30
6 06	11 59	14 19	6 25	1 13	31
6 13	12 22	14 49	6 42	1 18	32
6 21	12 46	15 21	6 59	1 23	33
6 29	13 10	15 53	7 16	1 29	34
6 37	13 35	16 25	7 34	1 34	35
6 45	14 01	16 58	7 52	1 40	36
6 54	14 28	17 32	8 10	1 46	37
7 03	14 56	18 06	8 28	1 51	38
7 12	15 25	18 41	8 47	1 57	39
7 22	15 55	19 17	9 06	2 04	40
7 32	16 26	19 54	9 26	2 10	41
7 43	16 58	20 31	9 46	2 16	42
7 54	17 31	21 10	10 06	2 23	43
8 05	18 06	21 49	10 27	2 30	44
8 17	18 42	22 29	10 49	2 37	45
8 30	19 20	23 11	11 11	2 44	46
8 43	20 00	23 53	11 34	2 51	47
8 57	20 41	24 36	11 57	2 59	48
9 11	21 25	25 21	12 21	3 07	49
9 27	22 11	26 07	12 46	3 15	50
9 43	23 00	26 54	13 11	3 23	51
10 01	23 51	27 43	13 38	3 32	52
10 19	24 46	28 33	14 05	3 41	53
10 39	25 43	29 25	14 33	3 50	54
11 00	26 45	0♌18	15 02	4 00	55
11 23	27 51	1 13	15 32	4 10	56
11 47	29 01	2 10	16 03	4 20	57
12 14	0♋17	3 08	16 35	4 31	58
12 43	1 38	4 09	17 09	4 42	59
13♉15	3♋06	5♌12	17♌44	4♍54	60

0h 8m 0s — 2 ♈ 11 — 2° 0' 0"

11	12	ASC	2	3
4♉16	4♊00	1♋50	29♋49	29♌54
4 40	5 14	3 50	0♌59	0♍15
5 05	6 30	5 50	2 09	0 36
5 31	7 51	7 54	3 19	0 58
5 59	9 17	10 02	4 30	1 19
6 05	9 35	10 28	4 45	1 24
6 11	9 53	10 55	4 59	1 28
6 17	10 12	11 22	5 14	1 33
6 24	10 31	11 49	5 29	1 37
6 30	10 51	12 17	5 44	1 42
6 37	11 11	12 45	5 59	1 47
6 43	11 31	13 13	6 15	1 52
6 50	11 52	13 42	6 30	1 56
6 57	12 14	14 11	6 46	2 01
7 05	12 36	14 41	7 02	2 06
7 12	12 58	15 11	7 18	2 11
7 20	13 22	15 41	7 35	2 16
7 28	13 45	16 12	7 51	2 21
7 36	14 10	16 44	8 08	2 27
7 44	14 35	17 16	8 26	2 32
7 53	15 01	17 49	8 43	2 38
8 02	15 28	18 22	9 01	2 43
8 11	15 56	18 56	9 19	2 49
8 21	16 24	19 31	9 38	2 55
8 31	16 54	20 06	9 57	3 01
8 41	17 25	20 43	10 16	3 07
8 52	17 57	21 20	10 36	3 13
9 03	18 30	21 58	10 56	3 19
9 15	19 05	22 37	11 17	3 26
9 27	19 41	23 17	11 38	3 32
9 40	20 19	23 57	12 00	3 39
9 53	20 59	24 39	12 22	3 47
10 07	21 40	25 22	12 45	3 54
10 22	22 24	26 06	13 09	4 01
10 38	23 10	26 52	13 33	4 09
10 55	23 58	27 38	13 58	4 17
11 13	24 49	28 26	14 24	4 26
11 32	25 43	29 16	14 51	4 34
11 52	26 40	0♌07	15 18	4 43
12 14	27 42	0 59	15 47	4 53
12 37	28 47	1 54	16 16	5 02
13 02	29 56	2 50	16 47	5 12
13 30	1♋11	3 47	17 19	5 23
13 59	2 32	4 47	17 52	5 34
14♉32	3♋59	5♌49	18♌26	5♍46

0h 12m 0s — 3 ♈ 16 — 3° 0' 0"

11	12	ASC	2	3
5♉18	4♊57	2♋45	0♌47	0♍57
5 42	6 11	4 44	1 57	1 18
6 08	7 28	6 45	3 05	1 38
6 35	8 49	8 48	4 14	1 59
7 04	10 15	10 56	5 25	2 20
7 10	10 34	11 22	5 39	2 24
7 16	10 52	11 48	5 54	2 28
7 22	11 11	12 15	6 08	2 33
7 29	11 30	12 42	6 23	2 37
7 35	11 50	13 10	6 38	2 42
7 42	12 10	13 38	6 53	2 46
7 49	12 30	14 06	7 08	2 51
7 56	12 51	14 34	7 24	2 55
8 03	13 13	15 03	7 39	3 00
8 11	13 35	15 33	7 55	3 05
8 18	13 58	16 02	8 11	3 10
8 26	14 21	16 33	8 27	3 15
8 34	14 45	17 03	8 44	3 20
8 43	15 09	17 35	9 01	3 25
8 51	15 34	18 07	9 18	3 30
9 00	16 00	18 39	9 35	3 35
9 09	16 27	19 12	9 53	3 41
9 19	16 55	19 46	10 11	3 46
9 28	17 24	20 20	10 29	3 52
9 39	17 53	20 56	10 48	3 57
9 49	18 24	21 32	11 07	4 03
10 00	18 56	22 08	11 26	4 09
10 12	19 29	22 46	11 46	4 16
10 24	20 04	23 24	12 07	4 22
10 36	20 40	24 04	12 27	4 28
10 49	21 18	24 44	12 49	4 35
11 03	21 57	25 25	13 11	4 42
11 18	22 39	26 08	13 33	4 49
11 33	23 22	26 52	13 57	4 56
11 49	24 08	27 36	14 21	5 04
12 06	24 56	28 22	14 45	5 12
12 25	25 46	29 10	15 11	5 20
12 44	26 40	29 59	15 37	5 28
13 05	27 37	0♌49	16 04	5 37
13 27	28 38	1 41	16 32	5 46
13 51	29 42	2 34	17 01	5 55
14 16	0♋51	3 29	17 31	6 05
14 45	2 05	4 26	18 02	6 15
15 15	3 25	5 25	18 34	6 26
15♉49	4♋51	6♌26	19♌08	6♍37

0h 16m 0s — 4 ♈ 22 — 4° 0' 0"

11	12	ASC	2	3
6♉19	5♊54	3♋40	1♌45	2♍00
6 45	7 08	5 39	2 54	2 20
7 11	8 26	7 40	4 02	2 40
7 39	9 47	9 42	5 10	3 00
8 08	11 14	11 49	6 20	3 20
8 14	11 32	12 15	6 34	3 24
8 21	11 51	12 42	6 48	3 28
8 27	12 10	13 08	7 03	3 33
8 34	12 29	13 35	7 17	3 37
8 40	12 49	14 03	7 32	3 41
8 47	13 09	14 30	7 47	3 46
8 54	13 29	14 58	8 02	3 50
9 02	13 50	15 26	8 17	3 55
9 09	14 12	15 55	8 33	3 59
9 17	14 34	16 24	8 48	4 04
9 24	14 56	16 54	9 04	4 08
9 32	15 20	17 24	9 20	4 13
9 41	15 43	17 55	9 36	4 18
9 49	16 08	18 26	9 53	4 23
9 58	16 33	18 57	10 10	4 28
10 07	16 59	19 29	10 27	4 33
10 16	17 26	20 02	10 44	4 38
10 26	17 54	20 36	11 02	4 44
10 36	18 22	21 10	11 20	4 49
10 46	18 52	21 45	11 38	4 55
10 57	19 23	22 20	11 57	5 00
11 08	19 55	22 57	12 16	5 06
11 20	20 28	23 34	12 36	5 12
11 32	21 03	24 12	12 56	5 18
11 45	21 39	24 51	13 17	5 24
11 59	22 16	25 31	13 38	5 31
12 13	22 56	26 11	13 59	5 37
12 28	23 37	26 53	14 22	5 44
12 43	24 20	27 37	14 44	5 51
13 00	25 05	28 21	15 08	5 59
13 17	25 53	29 06	15 32	6 06
13 36	26 43	29 53	15 57	6 14
13 56	27 37	0♌41	16 23	6 22
14 17	28 33	1 31	16 50	6 30
14 39	29 33	2 22	17 17	6 39
15 04	0♋37	3 15	17 45	6 48
15 30	1 45	4 09	18 15	6 57
15 59	2 58	5 05	18 46	7 07
16 30	4 17	6 03	19 17	7 18
17♉05	5♋42	7♌03	19♌50	7♍28

0h 20m 0s — 5 ♈ 27 — 5° 0' 0"

11	12	ASC	2	3	LAT.
7♉21	6♊50	4♋35	2♌43	3♍03	0
7 47	8 05	6 34	3 51	3 23	5
8 14	9 23	8 34	4 58	3 42	10
8 42	10 45	10 36	6 06	4 01	15
9 12	12 12	12 43	7 15	4 21	20
9 19	12 30	13 09	7 29	4 25	21
9 25	12 49	13 35	7 43	4 29	22
9 32	13 08	14 02	7 57	4 33	23
9 38	13 27	14 28	8 12	4 37	24
9 45	13 47	14 55	8 26	4 41	25
9 52	14 07	15 23	8 41	4 45	26
10 00	14 28	15 51	8 56	4 50	27
10 07	14 49	16 19	9 11	4 54	28
10 14	15 10	16 47	9 26	4 58	29
10 22	15 32	17 16	9 41	5 03	30
10 30	15 55	17 45	9 57	5 07	31
10 38	16 18	18 15	10 13	5 12	32
10 47	16 42	18 46	10 29	5 16	33
10 55	17 07	19 16	10 45	5 21	34
11 04	17 32	19 48	11 02	5 26	35
11 14	17 58	20 20	11 19	5 31	36
11 23	18 25	20 52	11 36	5 36	37
11 33	18 52	21 25	11 53	5 41	38
11 43	19 21	21 59	12 11	5 46	39
11 54	19 51	22 33	12 29	5 52	40
12 05	20 21	23 09	12 48	5 57	41
12 16	20 53	23 45	13 06	6 03	42
12 28	21 26	24 21	13 26	6 09	43
12 41	22 01	24 59	13 46	6 14	44
12 54	22 37	25 38	14 06	6 20	45
13 08	23 14	26 17	14 27	6 27	46
13 22	23 53	26 57	14 48	6 33	47
13 37	24 34	27 39	15 10	6 40	48
13 53	25 17	28 21	15 32	6 46	49
14 10	26 02	29 05	15 55	6 53	50
14 28	26 50	29 50	16 19	7 01	51
14 47	27 40	0♌36	16 44	7 08	52
15 07	28 33	1 24	17 09	7 16	53
15 29	29 29	2 13	17 35	7 24	54
15 52	0♋28	3 03	18 02	7 32	55
16 17	1 32	3 55	18 30	7 41	56
16 44	2 39	4 49	18 59	7 50	57
17 13	3 51	5 44	19 29	8 00	58
17 45	5 09	6 41	20 00	8 09	59
18♉20	6♋33	7♌40	20♌33	8♍20	60

0h 24m 0s — 6 ♈ 32 — 6° 0' 0"

11	12	ASC	2	3
8♉23	7♊47	5♋30	3♌41	4♍07
8 49	9 02	7 29	4 49	4 25
9 16	10 20	9 29	5 55	4 44
9 45	11 42	11 31	7 02	5 02
10 16	13 10	13 36	8 10	5 21
10 23	13 28	14 02	8 24	5 25
10 29	13 47	14 28	8 38	5 29
10 36	14 06	14 55	8 52	5 33
10 43	14 25	15 21	9 06	5 37
10 50	14 45	15 48	9 21	5 41
10 57	15 05	16 15	9 35	5 45
11 04	15 26	16 43	9 50	5 49
11 12	15 47	17 11	10 05	5 53
11 20	16 09	17 39	10 20	5 57
11 27	16 31	18 08	10 35	6 02
11 36	16 53	18 37	10 50	6 06
11 44	17 16	19 06	11 06	6 11
11 52	17 40	19 36	11 21	6 15
12 01	18 05	20 07	11 38	6 20
12 10	18 30	20 38	11 54	6 24
12 20	18 56	21 10	12 10	6 29
12 30	19 23	21 42	12 27	6 34
12 40	19 51	22 15	12 44	6 39
12 50	20 19	22 48	13 02	6 44
13 01	20 49	23 22	13 20	6 49
13 12	21 19	23 57	13 38	6 54
13 24	21 51	24 33	13 57	7 00
13 36	22 24	25 09	14 16	7 05
13 49	22 58	25 46	14 35	7 11
14 02	23 34	26 24	14 55	7 17
14 16	24 12	27 03	15 16	7 23
14 31	24 50	27 43	15 36	7 29
14 46	25 31	28 24	15 58	7 35
15 02	26 14	29 06	16 20	7 42
15 20	26 59	29 49	16 43	7 48
15 38	27 46	0♌34	17 06	7 55
15 57	28 36	1 19	17 30	8 03
16 18	29 28	2 06	17 55	8 10
16 40	0♋24	2 54	18 21	8 18
17 03	1 23	3 44	18 47	8 26
17 29	2 25	4 35	19 15	8 34
17 56	3 32	5 28	19 43	8 43
18 26	4 44	6 23	20 13	8 52
18 59	6 00	7 19	20 43	9 01
19♉35	7♋23	8♌17	21♌15	9♍11

0h 28m 0s — 7 ♈ 37 — 7° 0' 0"

11	12	ASC	2	3
9♉24	8♊43	6♋26	4♌39	5♍10
9 51	9 59	8 24	5 46	5 28
10 19	11 18	10 23	6 52	5 46
10 48	12 40	12 25	7 58	6 04
11 20	14 08	14 30	9 05	6 22
11 26	14 26	14 55	9 19	6 26
11 33	14 45	15 21	9 33	6 29
11 40	15 04	15 47	9 47	6 33
11 47	15 23	16 14	10 01	6 37
11 54	15 43	16 41	10 15	6 41
12 01	16 03	17 08	10 29	6 45
12 09	16 24	17 35	10 44	6 49
12 17	16 45	18 03	10 58	6 53
12 24	17 07	18 31	11 13	6 57
12 32	17 29	18 59	11 28	7 01
12 41	17 51	19 28	11 43	7 05
12 49	18 14	19 57	11 58	7 09
12 58	18 38	20 27	12 14	7 14
13 07	19 03	20 58	12 30	7 18
13 16	19 28	21 28	12 46	7 23
13 26	19 54	22 00	13 02	7 27
13 36	20 21	22 31	13 19	7 32
13 46	20 48	23 04	13 36	7 36
13 57	21 17	23 37	13 53	7 41
14 08	21 46	24 11	14 11	7 46
14 19	22 17	24 45	14 29	7 51
14 31	22 49	25 21	14 47	7 56
14 44	23 22	25 56	15 06	8 02
14 56	23 56	26 33	15 25	8 07
15 10	24 31	27 11	15 44	8 13
15 24	25 09	27 49	16 04	8 19
15 39	25 47	28 29	16 25	8 24
15 55	26 28	29 09	16 46	8 31
16 12	27 10	29 51	17 08	8 37
16 29	27 55	0♌33	17 30	8 43
16 48	28 42	1 17	17 53	8 50
17 07	29 31	2 02	18 17	8 57
17 28	0♋23	2 48	18 41	9 04
17 51	1 18	3 36	19 06	9 11
18 15	2 17	4 25	19 32	9 19
18 41	3 19	5 16	19 59	9 27
19 09	4 25	6 08	20 27	9 35
19 39	5 36	7 01	20 56	9 44
20 13	6 51	7 57	21 26	9 53
20♉50	8♋13	8♌54	21♌57	10♍03

0h 32m 0s — 8° 0' 0" — 8 ♈ 43

LAT.	11	12	ASC	2	3
0	10♉25	9♊40	7♋21	5♌38	6♍14
5	10 53	10 56	9 19	6 44	6 31
10	11 21	12 15	11 18	7 49	6 48
15	11 51	13 37	13 19	8 54	7 05
20	12 23	15 05	15 23	10 01	7 23
21	12 30	15 24	15 49	10 14	7 26
22	12 37	15 42	16 14	10 28	7 30
23	12 44	16 01	16 40	10 42	7 33
24	12 51	16 21	17 07	10 55	7 37
25	12 58	16 41	17 33	11 09	7 41
26	13 06	17 01	18 00	11 23	7 45
27	13 13	17 22	18 27	11 38	7 48
28	13 21	17 43	18 55	11 52	7 52
29	13 29	18 04	19 22	12 07	7 56
30	13 37	18 26	19 51	12 21	8 00
31	13 46	18 49	20 19	12 36	8 04
32	13 54	19 12	20 48	12 51	8 08
33	14 03	19 36	21 18	13 07	8 12
34	14 12	20 01	21 48	13 22	8 17
35	14 22	20 26	22 18	13 38	8 21
36	14 32	20 52	22 49	13 54	8 25
37	14 42	21 18	23 21	14 11	8 30
38	14 52	21 46	23 53	14 27	8 34
39	15 03	22 14	24 26	14 44	8 39
40	15 14	22 44	24 59	15 01	8 44
41	15 26	23 14	25 33	15 19	8 48
42	15 38	23 46	26 08	15 37	8 53
43	15 51	24 19	26 44	15 56	8 59
44	16 04	24 53	27 20	16 14	9 04
45	16 18	25 28	27 57	16 34	9 09
46	16 32	26 05	28 35	16 53	9 15
47	16 47	26 44	29 14	17 14	9 20
48	17 03	27 24	29 54	17 34	9 26
49	17 20	28 06	0♌35	17 56	9 32
50	17 38	28 51	1 17	18 18	9 38
51	17 57	29 37	2 01	18 40	9 45
52	18 17	0♋26	2 45	19 03	9 51
53	18 38	1 18	3 31	19 27	9 58
54	19 01	2 13	4 18	19 52	10 05
55	19 26	3 10	5 06	20 18	10 13
56	19 52	4 12	5 56	20 44	10 20
57	20 21	5 17	6 47	21 11	10 28
58	20 52	6 27	7 40	21 40	10 37
59	21 26	7 42	8 35	22 09	10 45
60	22♉03	9♋02	9♌31	22♌40	10♍54

0h 36m 0s — 9° 0' 0" — 9 ♈ 48

LAT.	11	12	ASC	2	3
0	11♉26	10♊36	8♋16	6♌37	7♍18
5	11 54	11 53	10 14	7 42	7 34
10	12 23	13 12	12 12	8 46	7 50
15	12 54	14 34	14 13	9 51	8 07
20	13 26	16 03	16 16	10 56	8 24
21	13 33	16 21	16 42	11 09	8 27
22	13 40	16 40	17 07	11 23	8 30
23	13 47	16 59	17 33	11 36	8 34
24	13 54	17 18	17 59	11 50	8 37
25	14 02	17 38	18 26	12 04	8 41
26	14 09	17 58	18 52	12 18	8 45
27	14 17	18 19	19 19	12 32	8 48
28	14 25	18 40	19 46	12 46	8 52
29	14 33	19 02	20 14	13 00	8 56
30	14 42	19 24	20 42	13 15	8 59
31	14 50	19 46	21 10	13 29	9 03
32	14 59	20 10	21 39	13 44	9 07
33	15 08	20 33	22 09	13 59	9 11
34	15 17	20 58	22 38	14 15	9 15
35	15 27	21 23	23 08	14 30	9 19
36	15 37	21 49	23 39	14 46	9 24
37	15 47	22 16	24 10	15 02	9 28
38	15 58	22 43	24 42	15 19	9 32
39	16 09	23 12	25 15	15 35	9 37
40	16 20	23 41	25 48	15 52	9 41
41	16 32	24 11	26 21	16 10	9 46
42	16 44	24 43	26 56	16 27	9 50
43	16 57	25 16	27 31	16 45	9 55
44	17 11	25 49	28 07	17 04	10 00
45	17 25	26 25	28 44	17 23	10 05
46	17 39	27 02	29 21	17 42	10 11
47	17 55	27 40	0♌00	18 02	10 16
48	18 11	28 20	0 39	18 23	10 22
49	18 28	29 02	1 20	18 44	10 27
50	18 46	29 46	2 01	19 05	10 33
51	19 06	0♋32	2 44	19 27	10 39
52	19 26	1 21	3 28	19 50	10 46
53	19 48	2 12	4 13	20 13	10 52
54	20 11	3 06	4 59	20 38	10 59
55	20 36	4 04	5 47	21 03	11 06
56	21 03	5 04	6 36	21 29	11 14
57	21 32	6 09	7 26	21 55	11 21
58	22 04	7 18	8 19	22 23	11 29
59	22 38	8 32	9 12	22 52	11 37
60	23♉17	9♋51	10♌08	23♌22	11♍46

0h 40m 0s — 10° 0' 0" — 10 ♈ 53

LAT.	11	12	ASC	2	3
0	12♉27	11♊32	9♋11	7♌35	8♍22
5	12 55	12 49	11 09	8 40	8 37
10	13 25	14 08	13 07	9 43	8 53
15	13 56	15 31	15 07	10 47	9 09
20	14 29	17 00	17 10	11 52	9 25
21	14 36	17 18	17 35	12 05	9 28
22	14 43	17 37	18 00	12 18	9 31
23	14 50	17 56	18 26	12 31	9 34
24	14 58	18 16	18 52	12 45	9 38
25	15 05	18 35	19 18	12 58	9 41
26	15 13	18 56	19 44	13 12	9 45
27	15 21	19 16	20 11	13 26	9 48
28	15 29	19 37	20 38	13 40	9 52
29	15 37	19 59	21 06	13 54	9 55
30	15 46	20 21	21 33	14 08	9 59
31	15 55	20 44	22 01	14 23	10 03
32	16 03	21 07	22 30	14 37	10 06
33	16 13	21 31	22 59	14 52	10 10
34	16 22	21 55	23 28	15 07	10 14
35	16 32	22 20	23 58	15 23	10 18
36	16 42	22 46	24 29	15 38	10 22
37	16 52	23 13	25 00	15 54	10 26
38	17 03	23 40	25 31	16 10	10 30
39	17 14	24 08	26 03	16 27	10 34
40	17 26	24 38	26 36	16 43	10 39
41	17 38	25 08	27 09	17 00	10 43
42	17 51	25 39	27 43	17 18	10 48
43	18 04	26 12	28 18	17 35	10 52
44	18 17	26 46	28 54	17 54	10 57
45	18 32	27 21	29 30	18 12	11 02
46	18 47	27 58	0♌07	18 31	11 07
47	19 02	28 36	0 45	18 51	11 12
48	19 19	29 16	1 24	19 11	11 17
49	19 36	29 57	2 04	19 31	11 23
50	19 55	0♋41	2 45	19 52	11 29
51	20 14	1 27	3 27	20 14	11 34
52	20 35	2 15	4 10	20 37	11 40
53	20 57	3 06	4 55	21 00	11 47
54	21 20	4 00	5 40	21 23	11 53
55	21 46	4 56	6 27	21 48	12 00
56	22 13	5 56	7 16	22 13	12 07
57	22 43	7 00	8 06	22 40	12 14
58	23 15	8 09	8 57	23 07	12 22
59	23 50	9 21	9 50	23 35	12 29
60	24♉29	10♋39	10♌45	24♌04	12♍38

0h 44m 0s — 11° 0' 0" — 11 ♈ 58

LAT.	11	12	ASC	2	3
0	13♉27	12♊28	10♋07	8♌34	9♍26
5	13 56	13 45	12 04	9 38	9 41
10	14 26	15 05	14 02	10 41	9 55
15	14 58	16 28	16 01	11 44	10 10
20	15 32	17 57	18 03	12 47	10 26
21	15 39	18 15	18 28	13 00	10 29
22	15 46	18 34	18 53	13 13	10 32
23	15 53	18 53	19 19	13 26	10 35
24	16 01	19 13	19 44	13 40	10 38
25	16 09	19 32	20 10	13 53	10 42
26	16 16	19 53	20 36	14 06	10 45
27	16 24	20 13	21 03	14 20	10 48
28	16 33	20 34	21 30	14 34	10 52
29	16 41	20 56	21 57	14 48	10 55
30	16 50	21 18	22 25	15 02	10 58
31	16 59	21 41	22 52	15 16	11 02
32	17 08	22 04	23 21	15 30	11 05
33	17 17	22 28	23 49	15 45	11 09
34	17 27	22 52	24 19	16 00	11 13
35	17 37	23 17	24 48	16 15	11 16
36	17 47	23 43	25 18	16 30	11 20
37	17 57	24 09	25 49	16 46	11 24
38	18 08	24 37	26 20	17 02	11 28
39	18 20	25 05	26 52	17 18	11 32
40	18 31	25 34	27 24	17 34	11 36
41	18 44	26 04	27 57	17 51	11 40
42	18 56	26 36	28 31	18 08	11 45
43	19 10	27 08	29 05	18 25	11 49
44	19 24	27 42	29 40	18 43	11 54
45	19 38	28 17	0♌16	19 02	11 58
46	19 53	28 53	0 53	19 20	12 03
47	20 09	29 31	1 30	19 39	12 08
48	20 26	0♋11	2 09	19 59	12 13
49	20 44	0 52	2 48	20 19	12 18
50	21 02	1 36	3 29	20 40	12 24
51	21 22	2 21	4 10	21 01	12 29
52	21 43	3 09	4 53	21 23	12 35
53	22 05	3 59	5 37	21 46	12 41
54	22 29	4 52	6 22	22 09	12 47
55	22 55	5 49	7 08	22 33	12 53
56	23 23	6 48	7 56	22 58	13 00
57	23 53	7 51	8 45	23 24	13 07
58	24 26	8 59	9 35	23 50	13 14
59	25 02	10 10	10 28	24 18	13 22
60	25♉41	11♋27	11♌22	24♌47	13♍30

0h 48m 0s — 12° 0' 0" — 13 ♈ 03

LAT.	11	12	ASC	2	3
0	14♉28	13♊24	11♋02	9♌34	10♍30
5	14 57	14 42	12 59	10 36	10 44
10	15 28	16 01	14 56	11 38	10 58
15	16 00	17 25	16 55	12 40	11 12
20	16 34	18 53	18 56	13 43	11 27
21	16 41	19 12	19 21	13 56	11 30
22	16 49	19 31	19 46	14 08	11 33
23	16 56	19 50	20 11	14 21	11 36
24	17 04	20 09	20 37	14 34	11 39
25	17 12	20 29	21 02	14 48	11 42
26	17 20	20 50	21 28	15 01	11 45
27	17 28	21 10	21 55	15 14	11 48
28	17 36	21 31	22 21	15 28	11 51
29	17 45	21 53	22 48	15 41	11 55
30	17 53	22 15	23 16	15 55	11 58
31	18 02	22 37	23 43	16 09	12 01
32	18 12	23 01	24 11	16 23	12 05
33	18 21	23 24	24 40	16 38	12 08
34	18 31	23 49	25 09	16 52	12 12
35	18 41	24 14	25 38	17 07	12 15
36	18 51	24 39	26 08	17 22	12 19
37	19 02	25 06	26 38	17 38	12 22
38	19 13	25 33	27 09	17 53	12 26
39	19 25	26 01	27 40	18 09	12 30
40	19 37	26 30	28 12	18 25	12 34
41	19 49	27 01	28 45	18 42	12 38
42	20 02	27 32	29 18	18 58	12 42
43	20 15	28 04	29 52	19 16	12 46
44	20 29	28 37	0♌27	19 33	12 51
45	20 44	29 12	1 02	19 51	12 55
46	20 59	29 48	1 39	20 09	12 59
47	21 16	0♋26	2 16	20 28	13 04
48	21 33	1 06	2 54	20 47	13 09
49	21 51	1 47	3 33	21 07	13 14
50	22 10	2 30	4 12	21 27	13 19
51	22 30	3 15	4 53	21 48	13 24
52	22 51	4 02	5 35	22 10	13 30
53	23 14	4 52	6 19	22 32	13 35
54	23 38	5 45	7 03	22 55	13 41
55	24 04	6 41	7 49	23 18	13 47
56	24 32	7 39	8 36	23 43	13 53
57	25 03	8 42	9 24	24 08	14 00
58	25 36	9 48	10 14	24 34	14 07
59	26 12	10 59	11 05	25 01	14 14
60	26♉53	12♋15	11♌58	25♌29	14♍21

0h 52m 0s — 13° 0' 0" — 14 ♈ 07

LAT.	11	12	ASC	2	3
0	15♉28	14♊20	11♋58	10♌33	11♍34
5	15 58	15 38	13 54	11 35	11 48
10	16 29	16 58	15 51	12 36	12 01
15	17 02	18 21	17 48	13 37	12 14
20	17 36	19 50	19 49	14 39	12 28
21	17 44	20 09	20 14	14 51	12 31
22	17 51	20 27	20 39	15 04	12 34
23	17 59	20 47	21 04	15 17	12 37
24	18 06	21 06	21 29	15 29	12 40
25	18 14	21 26	21 55	15 42	12 43
26	18 22	21 46	22 20	15 55	12 45
27	18 31	22 07	22 47	16 09	12 48
28	18 39	22 28	23 13	16 22	12 51
29	18 48	22 49	23 40	16 35	12 55
30	18 57	23 11	24 07	16 49	12 58
31	19 06	23 34	24 34	17 03	13 01
32	19 15	23 57	25 02	17 17	13 04
33	19 25	24 21	25 30	17 31	13 07
34	19 35	24 45	25 59	17 45	13 11
35	19 45	25 10	26 28	18 00	13 14
36	19 55	25 36	26 57	18 14	13 17
37	20 06	26 02	27 27	18 29	13 21
38	20 18	26 29	27 58	18 45	13 24
39	20 29	26 57	28 29	19 00	13 28
40	20 41	27 26	29 00	19 16	13 32
41	20 54	27 56	29 33	19 32	13 35
42	21 07	28 27	0♌05	19 49	13 39
43	21 21	28 59	0 39	20 06	13 43
44	21 35	29 33	1 13	20 23	13 47
45	21 50	0♋07	1 48	20 40	13 52
46	22 05	0 43	2 24	20 58	13 56
47	22 22	1 21	3 01	21 17	14 00
48	22 39	2 00	3 38	21 36	14 05
49	22 57	2 41	4 17	21 55	14 09
50	23 16	3 24	4 56	22 15	14 14
51	23 37	4 08	5 36	22 35	14 19
52	23 58	4 56	6 18	22 56	14 24
53	24 21	5 45	7 00	23 18	14 30
54	24 46	6 37	7 44	23 41	14 35
55	25 13	7 32	8 29	24 04	14 41
56	25 41	8 30	9 15	24 27	14 47
57	26 12	9 32	10 03	24 52	14 53
58	26 46	10 38	10 52	25 18	14 59
59	27 23	11 48	11 43	25 44	15 06
60	28♉04	13♋02	12♌35	26♌12	15♍13

0h 56m 0s — 14° 0' 0" — 15 ♈ 12

LAT.	11	12	ASC	2	3
0	16♉28	15♊16	12♋53	11♌32	12♍39
5	16 59	16 34	14 49	12 34	12 51
10	17 30	17 54	16 45	13 34	13 04
15	18 03	19 18	18 42	14 34	13 17
20	18 38	20 47	20 42	15 35	13 30
21	18 46	21 05	21 07	15 47	13 32
22	18 53	21 24	21 32	15 59	13 35
23	19 01	21 43	21 56	16 12	13 38
24	19 09	22 03	22 21	16 24	13 40
25	19 17	22 22	22 47	16 37	13 43
26	19 25	22 43	23 12	16 50	13 46
27	19 33	23 03	23 38	17 03	13 49
28	19 42	23 24	24 04	17 16	13 52
29	19 51	23 46	24 31	17 29	13 54
30	20 00	24 08	24 58	17 43	13 57
31	20 09	24 30	25 25	17 56	14 00
32	20 18	24 53	25 52	18 10	14 03
33	20 28	25 17	26 20	18 24	14 06
34	20 38	25 41	26 49	18 38	14 10
35	20 49	26 06	27 17	18 52	14 13
36	20 59	26 32	27 46	19 07	14 16
37	21 10	26 58	28 16	19 21	14 19
38	21 22	27 25	28 46	19 36	14 23
39	21 34	27 53	29 17	19 52	14 26
40	21 46	28 22	29 48	20 07	14 29
41	21 59	28 52	0♌20	20 23	14 33
42	22 12	29 23	0 53	20 39	14 37
43	22 26	29 55	1 26	20 56	14 40
44	22 40	0♋28	2 00	21 13	14 44
45	22 55	1 02	2 34	21 30	14 48
46	23 11	1 38	3 10	21 47	14 52
47	23 28	2 15	3 46	22 05	14 56
48	23 45	2 54	4 23	22 24	15 01
49	24 03	3 35	5 01	22 43	15 05
50	24 23	4 17	5 39	23 03	15 10
51	24 43	5 02	6 19	23 23	15 14
52	25 05	5 48	7 00	23 43	15 19
53	25 29	6 37	7 42	24 04	15 24
54	25 54	7 29	8 25	24 26	15 29
55	26 20	8 23	9 10	24 49	15 35
56	26 49	9 21	9 55	25 12	15 40
57	27 21	10 22	10 42	25 36	15 46
58	27 55	11 27	11 30	26 01	15 52
59	28 32	12 36	12 20	26 27	15 59
60	29♉14	13♋49	13♌12	26♌54	16♍05

1h 0m 0s — 15° 0' 0" — 16 ♈ 17

LAT.	11	12	ASC	2	3
0	17♉28	16♊11	13♋49	12♌32	13♍43
5	17 59	17 30	15 44	13 32	13 55
10	18 31	18 50	17 40	14 32	14 07
15	19 04	20 14	19 36	15 31	14 19
20	19 40	21 43	21 35	16 31	14 31
21	19 48	22 01	22 00	16 43	14 34
22	19 55	22 20	22 24	16 55	14 36
23	20 03	22 39	22 49	17 07	14 39
24	20 11	22 59	23 14	17 20	14 41
25	20 19	23 19	23 39	17 32	14 44
26	20 27	23 39	24 04	17 45	14 46
27	20 36	23 59	24 30	17 57	14 49
28	20 45	24 20	24 56	18 10	14 52
29	20 53	24 42	25 22	18 23	14 54
30	21 03	25 04	25 49	18 36	14 57
31	21 12	25 26	26 16	18 50	15 00
32	21 21	25 49	26 43	19 03	15 03
33	21 31	26 13	27 10	19 17	15 06
34	21 42	26 37	27 38	19 31	15 09
35	21 52	27 02	28 07	19 45	15 12
36	22 03	27 27	28 36	19 59	15 15
37	22 14	27 54	29 05	20 13	15 18
38	22 26	28 21	29 35	20 28	15 21
39	22 38	28 49	0♌05	20 43	15 24
40	22 50	29 17	0 36	20 58	15 27
41	23 03	29 47	1 08	21 14	15 31
42	23 16	0♋18	1 40	21 30	15 34
43	23 30	0 50	2 13	21 46	15 38
44	23 45	1 23	2 46	22 02	15 41
45	24 00	1 57	3 20	22 19	15 45
46	24 16	2 32	3 55	22 37	15 49
47	24 33	3 09	4 31	22 54	15 53
48	24 51	3 48	5 07	23 12	15 57
49	25 09	4 28	5 45	23 31	16 01
50	25 29	5 10	6 23	23 50	16 05
51	25 50	5 54	7 02	24 10	16 09
52	26 12	6 41	7 42	24 30	16 14
53	26 36	7 29	8 24	24 51	16 19
54	27 01	8 20	9 06	25 12	16 24
55	27 28	9 14	9 50	25 34	16 29
56	27 57	10 11	10 35	25 57	16 34
57	28 29	11 11	11 21	26 21	16 39
58	29 04	12 15	12 09	26 45	16 45
59	29 42	13 23	12 58	27 10	16 51
60	0♊24	14♋36	13♌49	27♌37	16♍57

1h 4m 0s 16° 0' 0"
17 ♈ 21

LAT.	11	12	ASC	2	3
0	18♉28	17♊07	14♋44	13♌32	14♍48
5	18 59	18 25	16 40	14 31	14 59
10	19 31	19 46	18 35	15 30	15 10
15	20 05	21 10	20 30	16 28	15 21
20	20 42	22 39	22 29	17 27	15 33
21	20 49	22 57	22 53	17 39	15 35
22	20 57	23 16	23 17	17 51	15 37
23	21 05	23 35	23 41	18 03	15 40
24	21 13	23 55	24 06	18 15	15 42
25	21 21	24 15	24 31	18 27	15 45
26	21 29	24 35	24 56	18 39	15 47
27	21 38	24 55	25 22	18 52	15 49
28	21 47	25 16	25 47	19 05	15 52
29	21 56	25 38	26 13	19 17	15 55
30	22 05	26 00	26 40	19 30	15 57
31	22 15	26 22	27 06	19 43	16 00
32	22 24	26 45	27 33	19 56	16 02
33	22 34	27 09	28 00	20 10	16 05
34	22 45	27 33	28 28	20 23	16 08
35	22 55	27 58	28 56	20 37	16 11
36	23 06	28 23	29 25	20 51	16 13
37	23 17	28 49	29 54	21 05	16 16
38	23 29	29 16	0♌23	21 20	16 19
39	23 41	29 44	0 53	21 34	16 22
40	23 54	0♋12	1 24	21 49	16 25
41	24 07	0 42	1 55	22 05	16 28
42	24 20	1 13	2 27	22 20	16 32
43	24 35	1 44	2 59	22 36	16 35
44	24 49	2 17	3 32	22 52	16 38
45	25 05	2 51	4 06	23 09	16 42
46	25 21	3 26	4 40	23 26	16 45
47	25 38	4 03	5 15	23 43	16 49
48	25 56	4 42	5 51	24 01	16 53
49	26 15	5 22	6 28	24 19	16 56
50	26 35	6 03	7 06	24 38	17 00
51	26 56	6 47	7 45	24 57	17 05
52	27 18	7 33	8 25	25 17	17 09
53	27 42	8 21	9 05	25 37	17 13
54	28 07	9 12	9 47	25 58	17 18
55	28 35	10 05	10 30	26 20	17 22
56	29 05	11 01	11 15	26 42	17 27
57	29 37	12 01	12 00	27 05	17 32
58	0♊12	13 04	12 47	27 29	17 38
59	0 50	14 11	13 35	27 54	17 43
60	1♊33	15♋22	14♌25	28♌19	17♍49

1h 8m 0s 17° 0' 0"
18 ♈ 26

LAT.	11	12	ASC	2	3
0	19♉27	18♊02	15♋40	14♌32	15♍53
5	19 59	19 21	17 35	15 30	16 03
10	20 32	20 42	19 29	16 28	16 13
15	21 06	22 06	21 24	17 25	16 24
20	21 43	23 35	23 22	18 23	16 34
21	21 50	23 53	23 46	18 35	16 36
22	21 58	24 12	24 10	18 46	16 39
23	22 06	24 31	24 34	18 58	16 41
24	22 14	24 51	24 58	19 10	16 43
25	22 23	25 11	25 23	19 22	16 45
26	22 31	25 31	25 48	19 34	16 48
27	22 40	25 51	26 13	19 47	16 50
28	22 49	26 12	26 39	19 59	16 52
29	22 58	26 34	27 04	20 11	16 55
30	23 07	26 56	27 30	20 24	16 57
31	23 17	27 18	27 57	20 37	16 59
32	23 27	27 41	28 23	20 50	17 02
33	23 37	28 04	28 50	21 03	17 04
34	23 47	28 28	29 18	21 16	17 07
35	23 58	28 53	29 46	21 30	17 10
36	24 09	29 18	0♌14	21 43	17 12
37	24 20	29 44	0 43	21 57	17 15
38	24 32	0♋11	1 12	22 12	17 18
39	24 45	0 39	1 41	22 26	17 20
40	24 57	1 07	2 12	22 41	17 23
41	25 10	1 37	2 42	22 55	17 26
42	25 24	2 07	3 14	23 11	17 29
43	25 38	2 39	3 46	23 26	17 32
44	25 53	3 11	4 18	23 42	17 35
45	26 09	3 45	4 52	23 58	17 38
46	26 25	4 20	5 26	24 15	17 42
47	26 43	4 57	6 00	24 32	17 45
48	27 01	5 35	6 36	24 49	17 49
49	27 20	6 14	7 12	25 07	17 52
50	27 40	6 56	7 49	25 25	17 56
51	28 01	7 39	8 28	25 44	18 00
52	28 24	8 25	9 07	26 03	18 04
53	28 48	9 12	9 47	26 23	18 08
54	29 14	10 02	10 28	26 44	18 12
55	29 42	10 55	11 11	27 05	18 16
56	0♊11	11 51	11 54	27 27	18 21
57	0 44	12 49	12 39	27 49	18 26
58	1 19	13 52	13 25	28 13	18 31
59	1 58	14 58	14 13	28 37	18 36
60	2♊42	16♋08	15♌02	29♌02	18♍41

1h 12m 0s 18° 0' 0"
19 ♈ 30

LAT.	11	12	ASC	2	3
0	20♉26	18♊58	16♋36	15♌32	16♍57
5	20 59	20 17	18 30	16 30	17 07
10	21 32	21 38	20 24	17 26	17 17
15	22 07	23 02	22 18	18 22	17 26
20	22 44	24 31	24 15	19 19	17 36
21	22 52	24 49	24 38	19 31	17 38
22	23 00	25 08	25 02	19 42	17 40
23	23 08	25 27	25 26	19 54	17 42
24	23 16	25 47	25 51	20 06	17 44
25	23 24	26 06	26 15	20 17	17 46
26	23 33	26 26	26 40	20 29	17 48
27	23 42	26 47	27 05	20 41	17 50
28	23 51	27 08	27 30	20 53	17 53
29	24 00	27 29	27 55	21 06	17 55
30	24 09	27 51	28 21	21 18	17 57
31	24 19	28 13	28 47	21 31	17 59
32	24 29	28 36	29 14	21 43	18 02
33	24 39	29 00	29 40	21 56	18 04
34	24 50	29 24	0♌08	22 09	18 06
35	25 00	29 48	0 35	22 22	18 09
36	25 12	0♋13	1 03	22 36	18 11
37	25 23	0 39	1 31	22 49	18 13
38	25 35	1 06	2 00	23 03	18 16
39	25 48	1 34	2 30	23 17	18 19
40	26 00	2 02	2 59	23 32	18 21
41	26 14	2 31	3 30	23 46	18 24
42	26 28	3 02	4 01	24 01	18 27
43	26 42	3 33	4 32	24 16	18 30
44	26 57	4 05	5 04	24 32	18 32
45	27 13	4 39	5 37	24 48	18 35
46	27 29	5 14	6 11	25 04	18 38
47	27 47	5 50	6 45	25 21	18 42
48	28 05	6 28	7 20	25 38	18 45
49	28 24	7 07	7 56	25 55	18 48
50	28 45	7 48	8 33	26 13	18 51
51	29 06	8 31	9 10	26 31	18 55
52	29 29	9 16	9 49	26 50	18 59
53	29 53	10 03	10 28	27 10	19 02
54	0♊20	10 53	11 09	27 30	19 06
55	0 48	11 45	11 51	27 50	19 10
56	1 18	12 40	12 34	28 12	19 15
57	1 51	13 38	13 18	28 34	19 19
58	2 27	14 40	14 03	28 56	19 24
59	3 06	15 45	14 50	29 20	19 28
60	3♊50	16♋54	15♌39	29♌44	19♍33

1h 16m 0s 19° 0' 0"
20 ♈ 34

LAT.	11	12	ASC	2	3
0	21♉26	19♊53	17♋32	16♌33	18♍02
5	21 58	21 12	19 26	17 29	18 11
10	22 32	22 33	21 19	18 25	18 20
15	23 07	23 58	23 12	19 20	18 29
20	23 45	25 26	25 08	20 15	18 38
21	23 52	25 45	25 31	20 27	18 40
22	24 01	26 04	25 55	20 38	18 41
23	24 09	26 23	26 19	20 49	18 43
24	24 17	26 42	26 43	21 01	18 45
25	24 26	27 02	27 07	21 13	18 47
26	24 34	27 22	27 32	21 24	18 49
27	24 43	27 43	27 56	21 36	18 51
28	24 52	28 03	28 21	21 48	18 53
29	25 01	28 25	28 46	22 00	18 55
30	25 11	28 46	29 12	22 12	18 57
31	25 21	29 09	29 38	22 24	18 59
32	25 31	29 31	0♌04	22 37	19 01
33	25 41	29 55	0 30	22 49	19 03
34	25 52	0♋19	0 57	23 02	19 05
35	26 03	0 43	1 24	23 15	19 08
36	26 14	1 08	1 52	23 28	19 10
37	26 26	1 34	2 20	23 42	19 12
38	26 38	2 01	2 49	23 55	19 15
39	26 50	2 28	3 17	24 09	19 17
40	27 03	2 56	3 47	24 23	19 19
41	27 17	3 25	4 17	24 37	19 22
42	27 31	3 56	4 47	24 52	19 24
43	27 45	4 27	5 19	25 07	19 27
44	28 01	4 59	5 50	25 22	19 30
45	28 17	5 32	6 23	25 37	19 32
46	28 33	6 07	6 56	25 53	19 35
47	28 51	6 43	7 30	26 09	19 38
48	29 09	7 20	8 04	26 26	19 41
49	29 29	7 59	8 40	26 43	19 44
50	29 49	8 40	9 16	27 01	19 47
51	0♊11	9 23	9 53	27 19	19 50
52	0 34	10 07	10 31	27 37	19 54
53	0 59	10 54	11 10	27 56	19 57
54	1 25	11 43	11 50	28 16	20 01
55	1 53	12 35	12 31	28 36	20 04
56	2 24	13 29	13 13	28 56	20 08
57	2 57	14 26	13 57	29 18	20 12
58	3 33	15 27	14 42	29 40	20 16
59	4 13	16 31	15 28	0♍03	20 21
60	4♊57	17♋40	16♌15	0♍27	20♍25

1h 20m 0s 20° 0' 0"
21 ♈ 38

LAT.	11	12	ASC	2	3
0	22♉25	20♊49	18♋28	17♌33	19♍07
5	22 58	22 08	20 21	18 29	19 15
10	23 32	23 29	22 13	19 23	19 23
15	24 07	24 53	24 06	20 17	19 31
20	24 45	26 22	26 01	21 12	19 40
21	24 53	26 40	26 24	21 23	19 41
22	25 01	26 59	26 48	21 34	19 43
23	25 10	27 18	27 11	21 45	19 45
24	25 18	27 38	27 35	21 57	19 46
25	25 27	27 57	27 59	22 08	19 48
26	25 35	28 17	28 23	22 19	19 50
27	25 44	28 38	28 48	22 31	19 52
28	25 53	28 59	29 12	22 43	19 53
29	26 03	29 20	29 37	22 54	19 55
30	26 12	29 42	0♌03	23 06	19 57
31	26 22	0♋04	0 28	23 18	19 59
32	26 32	0 27	0 54	23 30	20 01
33	26 43	0 50	1 20	23 43	20 03
34	26 54	1 14	1 47	23 55	20 05
35	27 05	1 38	2 14	24 08	20 07
36	27 16	2 03	2 41	24 21	20 09
37	27 28	2 29	3 09	24 34	20 11
38	27 40	2 55	3 37	24 47	20 13
39	27 53	3 22	4 05	25 01	20 15
40	28 06	3 51	4 34	25 14	20 17
41	28 19	4 20	5 04	25 28	20 20
42	28 34	4 49	5 34	25 43	20 22
43	28 48	5 20	6 05	25 57	20 24
44	29 04	5 52	6 36	26 12	20 27
45	29 20	6 26	7 08	26 27	20 29
46	29 37	7 00	7 41	26 43	20 32
47	29 54	7 36	8 14	26 58	20 34
48	0♊13	8 13	8 48	27 15	20 37
49	0 32	8 52	9 23	27 31	20 40
50	0 53	9 32	9 59	27 48	20 43
51	1 15	10 14	10 35	28 06	20 46
52	1 38	10 58	11 13	28 24	20 49
53	2 03	11 44	11 51	28 42	20 52
54	2 30	12 33	12 31	29 01	20 55
55	2 58	13 24	13 11	29 21	20 58
56	3 29	14 18	13 53	29 41	21 02
57	4 03	15 14	14 36	0♍02	21 06
58	4 39	16 14	15 20	0 24	21 09
59	5 19	17 18	16 05	0 46	21 13
60	6♊04	18♋25	16♌52	1♍10	21♍17

1h 24m 0s 21° 0' 0"
22 ♈ 42

LAT.	11	12	ASC	2	3
0	23♉23	21♊44	19♋24	18♌34	20♍12
5	23 57	23 03	21 17	19 29	20 20
10	24 31	24 24	23 08	20 22	20 27
15	25 07	25 49	25 00	21 15	20 34
20	25 46	27 17	26 54	22 08	20 42
21	25 54	27 36	27 17	22 19	20 43
22	26 02	27 55	27 40	22 30	20 45
23	26 10	28 14	28 04	22 41	20 46
24	26 19	28 33	28 27	22 52	20 48
25	26 27	28 53	28 51	23 03	20 49
26	26 36	29 13	29 15	23 15	20 51
27	26 45	29 33	29 39	23 26	20 52
28	26 54	29 54	0♌04	23 37	20 54
29	27 04	0♋15	0 28	23 49	20 56
30	27 14	0 37	0 53	24 00	20 57
31	27 24	0 59	1 19	24 12	20 59
32	27 34	1 21	1 44	24 24	21 01
33	27 44	1 45	2 10	24 36	21 02
34	27 55	2 08	2 36	24 48	21 04
35	28 06	2 33	3 03	25 01	21 06
36	28 18	2 58	3 30	25 13	21 08
37	28 30	3 23	3 57	25 26	21 10
38	28 42	3 49	4 25	25 39	21 12
39	28 55	4 17	4 53	25 52	21 14
40	29 08	4 45	5 22	26 06	21 16
41	29 22	5 13	5 51	26 19	21 18
42	29 36	5 43	6 21	26 33	21 20
43	29 51	6 14	6 51	26 47	21 22
44	0♊06	6 46	7 22	27 02	21 24
45	0 23	7 18	7 54	27 17	21 26
46	0 40	7 53	8 26	27 32	21 28
47	0 57	8 28	8 59	27 47	21 31
48	1 16	9 05	9 32	28 03	21 33
49	1 36	9 43	10 07	28 19	21 36
50	1 57	10 23	10 42	28 36	21 38
51	2 19	11 05	11 18	28 53	21 41
52	2 42	11 49	11 55	29 11	21 44
53	3 07	12 35	12 33	29 29	21 47
54	3 34	13 23	13 11	29 47	21 49
55	4 03	14 13	13 51	0♍07	21 52
56	4 34	15 06	14 32	0 26	21 56
57	5 08	16 02	15 14	0 47	21 59
58	5 45	17 01	15 58	1 08	22 02
59	6 25	18 04	16 42	1 30	22 06
60	7♊10	19♋10	17♌28	1♍52	22♍10

1h 28m 0s 22° 0' 0"
23 ♈ 46

LAT.	11	12	ASC	2	3
0	24♉22	22♊39	20♋20	19♌35	21♍17
5	24 56	23 59	22 12	20 28	21 24
10	25 30	25 20	24 03	21 21	21 30
15	26 07	26 44	25 54	22 13	21 37
20	26 46	28 13	27 47	23 05	21 43
21	26 54	28 31	28 10	23 16	21 45
22	27 02	28 50	28 33	23 26	21 46
23	27 10	29 09	28 56	23 37	21 48
24	27 19	29 28	29 19	23 48	21 49
25	27 28	29 48	29 43	23 59	21 50
26	27 37	0♋08	0♌07	24 10	21 52
27	27 46	0 28	0 31	24 21	21 53
28	27 55	0 49	0 55	24 32	21 55
29	28 05	1 10	1 19	24 43	21 56
30	28 15	1 32	1 44	24 55	21 58
31	28 25	1 54	2 09	25 06	21 59
32	28 35	2 16	2 34	25 18	22 01
33	28 46	2 39	3 00	25 30	22 02
34	28 57	3 03	3 26	25 42	22 04
35	29 08	3 27	3 52	25 54	22 05
36	29 19	3 52	4 19	26 06	22 07
37	29 31	4 17	4 46	26 18	22 09
38	29 44	4 44	5 13	26 31	22 10
39	29 57	5 10	5 41	26 44	22 12
40	0♊10	5 38	6 09	26 57	22 14
41	0 24	6 07	6 38	27 10	22 16
42	0 38	6 36	7 08	27 24	22 17
43	0 53	7 07	7 38	27 38	22 19
44	1 09	7 39	8 08	27 52	22 21
45	1 25	8 11	8 39	28 06	22 23
46	1 42	8 45	9 11	28 21	22 25
47	2 00	9 20	9 43	28 36	22 27
48	2 19	9 57	10 16	28 52	22 29
49	2 39	10 35	10 50	29 08	22 32
50	3 00	11 15	11 25	29 24	22 34
51	3 22	11 56	12 00	29 40	22 36
52	3 46	12 39	12 37	29 58	22 39
53	4 11	13 25	13 14	0♍15	22 41
54	4 38	14 12	13 52	0 33	22 44
55	5 07	15 02	14 31	0 52	22 47
56	5 39	15 54	15 12	1 11	22 49
57	6 13	16 50	15 53	1 31	22 52
58	6 50	17 48	16 36	1 52	22 55
59	7 31	18 49	17 20	2 13	22 59
60	8♊16	19♋55	18♌05	2♍35	23♍02

1h 32m 0s 23° 0' 0"
24 ♈ 50

LAT.	11	12	ASC	2	3
0	25♉21	23♊34	21♋17	20♌36	22♍23
5	25 55	24 54	23 08	21 28	22 28
10	26 30	26 15	24 58	22 20	22 34
15	27 06	27 39	26 48	23 11	22 40
20	27 46	29 08	28 40	24 02	22 45
21	27 54	29 26	29 03	24 12	22 47
22	28 02	29 45	29 26	24 23	22 48
23	28 11	0♋04	29 49	24 33	22 49
24	28 19	0 23	0♌12	24 44	22 50
25	28 28	0 43	0 35	24 54	22 51
26	28 37	1 03	0 58	25 05	22 53
27	28 46	1 23	1 22	25 16	22 54
28	28 56	1 44	1 46	25 27	22 55
29	29 05	2 05	2 10	25 38	22 56
30	29 15	2 26	2 35	25 49	22 58
31	29 25	2 48	2 59	26 00	22 59
32	29 36	3 11	3 24	26 12	23 00
33	29 47	3 34	3 50	26 23	23 02
34	29 58	3 57	4 15	26 35	23 03
35	0♊09	4 21	4 41	26 47	23 05
36	0 21	4 46	5 08	26 59	23 06
37	0 33	5 11	5 34	27 11	23 07
38	0 45	5 37	6 01	27 23	23 09
39	0 58	6 04	6 29	27 36	23 10
40	1 12	6 32	6 57	27 48	23 12
41	1 26	7 00	7 25	28 01	23 14
42	1 40	7 30	7 54	28 15	23 15
43	1 55	8 00	8 24	28 28	23 17
44	2 11	8 31	8 54	28 42	23 18
45	2 27	9 04	9 25	28 56	23 20
46	2 45	9 37	9 56	29 11	23 22
47	3 03	10 12	10 28	29 25	23 24
48	3 22	10 49	11 00	29 40	23 26
49	3 42	11 26	11 34	29 56	23 28
50	4 03	12 06	12 08	0♍12	23 30
51	4 25	12 47	12 43	0 28	23 32
52	4 49	13 29	13 19	0 45	23 34
53	5 15	14 14	13 55	1 02	23 36
54	5 42	15 01	14 33	1 19	23 38
55	6 11	15 50	15 12	1 38	23 41
56	6 43	16 42	15 51	1 56	23 43
57	7 17	17 37	16 32	2 16	23 46
58	7 54	18 34	17 14	2 36	23 48
59	8 36	19 35	17 57	2 56	23 51
60	9♊21	20♋39	18♌42	3♍18	23♍54

1h 36m 0s — 24° 0' 0" — 25 ♈ 53

LAT.	11	12	ASC	2	3
0	26♉19	24♊30	22♋13	21♌37	23♍28
5	26 53	25 49	24 04	22 29	23 33
10	27 29	27 10	25 53	23 19	23 38
15	28 06	28 35	27 42	24 09	23 42
20	28 45	0♋03	29 33	24 59	23 47
21	28 53	0 21	29 56	25 09	23 48
22	29 02	0 40	0♌18	25 19	23 49
23	29 10	0 59	0 41	25 29	23 50
24	29 19	1 18	1 04	25 40	23 52
25	29 28	1 38	1 27	25 50	23 53
26	29 37	1 58	1 50	26 01	23 54
27	29 47	2 18	2 14	26 11	23 55
28	29 56	2 38	2 37	26 22	23 56
29	0♊06	2 59	3 01	26 33	23 57
30	0 16	3 21	3 25	26 43	23 58
31	0 26	3 43	3 50	26 54	23 59
32	0 36	4 05	4 14	27 05	24 00
33	0 47	4 28	4 39	27 17	24 01
34	0 58	4 51	5 05	27 28	24 03
35	1 10	5 15	5 30	27 40	24 04
36	1 22	5 40	5 56	27 51	24 05
37	1 34	6 05	6 23	28 03	24 06
38	1 46	6 31	6 49	28 15	24 08
39	1 59	6 58	7 17	28 28	24 09
40	2 13	7 25	7 44	28 40	24 10
41	2 27	7 53	8 12	28 53	24 12
42	2 42	8 23	8 41	29 06	24 13
43	2 57	8 53	9 10	29 19	24 14
44	3 13	9 24	9 40	29 32	24 16
45	3 29	9 56	10 10	29 46	24 17
46	3 47	10 29	10 41	0♍00	24 19
47	4 05	11 04	11 12	0 14	24 20
48	4 24	11 40	11 44	0 29	24 22
49	4 44	12 17	12 17	0 44	24 24
50	5 05	12 56	12 51	0 59	24 25
51	5 28	13 37	13 25	1 15	24 27
52	5 52	14 19	14 00	1 32	24 29
53	6 18	15 04	14 37	1 48	24 31
54	6 45	15 50	15 14	2 05	24 33
55	7 15	16 39	15 52	2 23	24 35
56	7 46	17 30	16 31	2 41	24 37
57	8 21	18 24	17 11	3 00	24 39
58	8 58	19 21	17 52	3 20	24 41
59	9 40	20 21	18 35	3 40	24 44
60	10♊26	21♋24	19♌18	4♍01	24♍46

1h 40m 0s — 25° 0' 0" — 26 ♈ 57

LAT.	11	12	ASC	2	3
0	27♉17	25♊25	23♋10	22♌39	24♍33
5	27 52	26 44	25 00	23 29	24 37
10	28 27	28 06	26 48	24 18	24 41
15	29 05	29 30	28 37	25 07	24 45
20	29 45	0♋58	0♌26	25 56	24 49
21	29 53	1 16	0 49	26 06	24 50
22	0♊02	1 35	1 11	26 16	24 51
23	0 10	1 54	1 33	26 26	24 52
24	0 19	2 13	1 56	26 36	24 53
25	0 28	2 32	2 19	26 46	24 54
26	0 37	2 52	2 42	26 56	24 55
27	0 46	3 12	3 05	27 06	24 56
28	0 56	3 33	3 28	27 17	24 56
29	1 06	3 54	3 52	27 27	24 57
30	1 16	4 15	4 16	27 38	24 58
31	1 26	4 37	4 40	27 49	24 59
32	1 37	4 59	5 04	27 59	25 00
33	1 48	5 22	5 29	28 10	25 01
34	1 59	5 45	5 54	28 21	25 02
35	2 10	6 09	6 19	28 33	25 03
36	2 22	6 34	6 45	28 44	25 04
37	2 35	6 59	7 11	28 56	25 05
38	2 47	7 25	7 38	29 07	25 06
39	3 00	7 51	8 04	29 19	25 07
40	3 14	8 18	8 32	29 32	25 08
41	3 28	8 46	8 59	29 44	25 10
42	3 43	9 15	9 27	29 56	25 11
43	3 58	9 45	9 56	0♍09	25 12
44	4 14	10 16	10 25	0 22	25 13
45	4 31	10 48	10 55	0 36	25 14
46	4 48	11 21	11 26	0 49	25 16
47	5 07	11 56	11 57	1 03	25 17
48	5 26	12 31	12 28	1 18	25 18
49	5 46	13 08	13 01	1 32	25 20
50	6 08	13 47	13 34	1 47	25 21
51	6 30	14 27	14 08	2 03	25 23
52	6 55	15 09	14 42	2 19	25 24
53	7 20	15 53	15 18	2 35	25 26
54	7 48	16 39	15 54	2 51	25 27
55	8 17	17 27	16 32	3 09	25 29
56	8 49	18 18	17 10	3 26	25 31
57	9 24	19 11	17 50	3 45	25 33
58	10 02	20 07	18 30	4 04	25 35
59	10 44	21 06	19 12	4 23	25 36
60	11♊30	22♋08	19♌55	4♍44	25♍39

1h 44m 0s — 26° 0' 0" — 28 ♈ 00

LAT.	11	12	ASC	2	3
0	28♉15	26♊20	24♋06	23♌41	25♍38
5	28 50	27 40	25 56	24 30	25 42
10	29 26	29 01	27 43	25 18	25 45
15	0♊04	0♋25	29 31	26 05	25 48
20	0 44	1 53	1♌19	26 53	25 52
21	0 52	2 11	1 41	27 03	25 52
22	1 01	2 30	2 04	27 12	25 53
23	1 10	2 49	2 26	27 22	25 54
24	1 18	3 08	2 48	27 32	25 54
25	1 28	3 27	3 11	27 42	25 55
26	1 37	3 47	3 34	27 52	25 56
27	1 46	4 07	3 56	28 02	25 56
28	1 56	4 27	4 20	28 12	25 57
29	2 06	4 48	4 43	28 22	25 58
30	2 16	5 09	5 07	28 32	25 59
31	2 26	5 31	5 30	28 43	25 59
32	2 37	5 53	5 54	28 53	26 00
33	2 48	6 16	6 19	29 04	26 01
34	2 59	6 39	6 44	29 15	26 02
35	3 11	7 03	7 08	29 26	26 02
36	3 23	7 27	7 34	29 37	26 03
37	3 35	7 52	7 59	29 48	26 04
38	3 48	8 18	8 26	0♍00	26 05
39	4 01	8 44	8 52	0 11	26 06
40	4 15	9 11	9 19	0 23	26 07
41	4 29	9 39	9 46	0 35	26 08
42	4 44	10 08	10 14	0 47	26 09
43	4 59	10 38	10 42	1 00	26 10
44	5 15	11 08	11 11	1 13	26 10
45	5 32	11 40	11 40	1 26	26 11
46	5 50	12 13	12 10	1 39	26 13
47	6 08	12 47	12 41	1 52	26 14
48	6 27	13 22	13 12	2 06	26 15
49	6 48	13 59	13 44	2 21	26 16
50	7 09	14 37	14 17	2 35	26 17
51	7 32	15 17	14 50	2 50	26 18
52	7 57	15 59	15 24	3 06	26 19
53	8 23	16 42	15 59	3 21	26 21
54	8 50	17 27	16 35	3 38	26 22
55	9 20	18 15	17 12	3 54	26 23
56	9 52	19 05	17 49	4 12	26 25
57	10 27	19 57	18 28	4 29	26 26
58	11 05	20 52	19 08	4 48	26 28
59	11 47	21 51	19 49	5 07	26 29
60	12♊34	22♋52	20♌32	5♍27	26♍31

1h 48m 0s — 27° 0' 0" — 29 ♈ 03

LAT.	11	12	ASC	2	3
0	29♉13	27♊15	25♋03	24♌42	26♍44
5	29 48	28 35	26 52	25 30	26 46
10	0♊24	29 56	28 39	26 17	26 49
15	1 03	1♋20	0♌25	27 03	26 51
20	1 43	2 48	2 13	27 50	26 54
21	1 51	3 06	2 34	27 59	26 54
22	2 00	3 24	2 56	28 09	26 55
23	2 09	3 43	3 18	28 18	26 55
24	2 18	4 02	3 40	28 28	26 56
25	2 27	4 22	4 03	28 38	26 56
26	2 36	4 41	4 25	28 47	26 57
27	2 46	5 01	4 48	28 57	26 57
28	2 55	5 22	5 11	29 07	26 58
29	3 05	5 42	5 34	29 17	26 58
30	3 16	6 04	5 57	29 27	26 59
31	3 26	6 25	6 21	29 37	27 00
32	3 37	6 47	6 44	29 47	27 00
33	3 48	7 10	7 09	29 58	27 01
34	3 59	7 33	7 33	0♍08	27 01
35	4 11	7 57	7 58	0 19	27 02
36	4 23	8 21	8 23	0 30	27 02
37	4 35	8 46	8 48	0 41	27 03
38	4 48	9 11	9 14	0 52	27 04
39	5 01	9 37	9 40	1 03	27 04
40	5 15	10 04	10 06	1 15	27 05
41	5 30	10 32	10 33	1 26	27 06
42	5 44	11 01	11 00	1 38	27 06
43	6 00	11 30	11 28	1 50	27 07
44	6 16	12 00	11 57	2 03	27 08
45	6 33	12 32	12 26	2 16	27 09
46	6 51	13 04	12 55	2 28	27 09
47	7 09	13 38	13 25	2 42	27 10
48	7 29	14 13	13 56	2 55	27 11
49	7 49	14 50	14 27	3 09	27 12
50	8 11	15 27	14 59	3 23	27 13
51	8 34	16 07	15 32	3 38	27 14
52	8 58	16 48	16 06	3 53	27 14
53	9 24	17 31	16 40	4 08	27 15
54	9 52	18 16	17 15	4 24	27 16
55	10 22	19 03	17 52	4 40	27 17
56	10 54	19 52	18 29	4 57	27 18
57	11 29	20 44	19 07	5 14	27 20
58	12 08	21 38	19 46	5 32	27 21
59	12 50	22 36	20 27	5 50	27 22
60	13♊37	23♋36	21♌08	6♍09	27♍23

1h 52m 0s — 28° 0' 0" — 0 ♉ 06

LAT.	11	12	ASC	2	3
0	0♊11	28♊10	26♋00	25♌44	27♍49
5	0 46	29 30	27 48	26 31	27 51
10	1 23	0♋51	29 34	27 17	27 52
15	2 01	2 15	1♌19	28 02	27 54
20	2 42	3 42	3 06	28 47	27 56
21	2 50	4 01	3 27	28 57	27 56
22	2 59	4 19	3 49	29 06	27 56
23	3 08	4 38	4 11	29 15	27 57
24	3 17	4 57	4 33	29 24	27 57
25	3 26	5 16	4 55	29 34	27 57
26	3 35	5 36	5 17	29 43	27 58
27	3 45	5 56	5 39	29 53	27 58
28	3 55	6 16	6 02	0♍02	27 59
29	4 05	6 37	6 25	0 12	27 59
30	4 15	6 58	6 48	0 22	27 59
31	4 26	7 19	7 11	0 32	28 00
32	4 36	7 41	7 34	0 42	28 00
33	4 47	8 04	7 58	0 52	28 00
34	4 59	8 27	8 22	1 02	28 01
35	5 11	8 50	8 47	1 12	28 01
36	5 23	9 14	9 11	1 23	28 02
37	5 35	9 39	9 36	1 33	28 02
38	5 48	10 04	10 02	1 44	28 02
39	6 02	10 30	10 27	1 55	28 03
40	6 15	10 57	10 53	2 06	28 03
41	6 30	11 24	11 20	2 18	28 04
42	6 45	11 53	11 47	2 29	28 04
43	7 00	12 22	12 14	2 41	28 05
44	7 17	12 52	12 42	2 53	28 05
45	7 34	13 23	13 11	3 05	28 06
46	7 51	13 56	13 40	3 18	28 06
47	8 10	14 29	14 10	3 31	28 07
48	8 30	15 04	14 40	3 44	28 07
49	8 50	15 40	15 11	3 57	28 08
50	9 12	16 17	15 42	4 11	28 08
51	9 35	16 56	16 14	4 25	28 09
52	10 00	17 37	16 48	4 40	28 10
53	10 26	18 19	17 21	4 55	28 10
54	10 54	19 04	17 56	5 10	28 11
55	11 24	19 50	18 32	5 26	28 12
56	11 56	20 39	19 08	5 42	28 12
57	12 31	21 30	19 46	5 59	28 13
58	13 10	22 24	20 24	6 16	28 14
59	13 52	23 20	21 04	6 34	28 15
60	14♊39	24♋20	21♌45	6♍52	28♍15

1h 56m 0s — 29° 0' 0" — 1 ♉ 08

LAT.	11	12	ASC	2	3
0	1♊08	29♊05	26♋57	26♌47	28♍55
5	1 44	0♋25	28 44	27 32	28 55
10	2 21	1 46	0♌29	28 17	28 56
15	2 59	3 09	2 14	29 01	28 57
20	3 41	4 37	3 59	29 45	28 58
21	3 49	4 55	4 20	29 54	28 58
22	3 58	5 14	4 42	0♍03	28 58
23	4 07	5 32	5 03	0 12	28 58
24	4 16	5 51	5 25	0 21	28 59
25	4 25	6 10	5 47	0 30	28 59
26	4 34	6 30	6 09	0 39	28 59
27	4 44	6 50	6 31	0 48	28 59
28	4 54	7 10	6 53	0 58	28 59
29	5 04	7 31	7 16	1 07	28 59
30	5 14	7 52	7 38	1 16	29 00
31	5 25	8 13	8 01	1 26	29 00
32	5 36	8 35	8 24	1 36	29 00
33	5 47	8 57	8 48	1 46	29 00
34	5 58	9 20	9 12	1 55	29 00
35	6 10	9 43	9 36	2 06	29 01
36	6 22	10 07	10 00	2 16	29 01
37	6 35	10 32	10 25	2 26	29 01
38	6 48	10 57	10 50	2 37	29 01
39	7 01	11 23	11 15	2 47	29 01
40	7 15	11 49	11 41	2 58	29 02
41	7 30	12 17	12 07	3 09	29 02
42	7 45	12 45	12 33	3 20	29 02
43	8 01	13 14	13 00	3 32	29 02
44	8 17	13 44	13 28	3 44	29 03
45	8 34	14 15	13 56	3 55	29 03
46	8 52	14 47	14 25	4 08	29 03
47	9 10	15 20	14 54	4 20	29 03
48	9 30	15 54	15 24	4 33	29 04
49	9 51	16 30	15 54	4 46	29 04
50	10 13	17 07	16 25	4 59	29 04
51	10 36	17 46	16 57	5 13	29 05
52	11 01	18 26	17 29	5 27	29 05
53	11 27	19 08	18 03	5 41	29 05
54	11 55	19 52	18 37	5 56	29 05
55	12 25	20 38	19 12	6 11	29 06
56	12 58	21 26	19 47	6 27	29 06
57	13 33	22 16	20 24	6 43	29 07
58	14 11	23 09	21 02	7 00	29 07
59	14 54	24 05	21 41	7 17	29 07
60	15♊41	25♋04	22♌21	7♍35	29♍08

2h 0m 0s — 30° 0' 0" — 2 ♉ 11

LAT.	11	12	ASC	2	3
0	2♊05	0♋00	27♋55	27♌49	0♎00
5	2 42	1 20	29 41	28 33	0 00
10	3 19	2 41	1♌25	29 17	0 00
15	3 58	4 04	3 08	29 59	0 00
20	4 39	5 32	4 52	0♍42	0 00
21	4 48	5 50	5 13	0 51	0 00
22	4 56	6 08	5 35	1 00	0 00
23	5 05	6 27	5 56	1 08	0 00
24	5 14	6 46	6 17	1 17	0 00
25	5 24	7 05	6 39	1 26	0 00
26	5 33	7 24	7 00	1 35	0 00
27	5 43	7 44	7 22	1 44	0 00
28	5 53	8 04	7 44	1 53	0 00
29	6 03	8 25	8 07	2 02	0 00
30	6 13	8 45	8 29	2 11	0 00
31	6 24	9 07	8 52	2 21	0 00
32	6 35	9 28	9 14	2 30	0 00
33	6 46	9 51	9 38	2 40	0 00
34	6 58	10 13	10 01	2 49	0 00
35	7 10	10 37	10 25	2 59	0 00
36	7 22	11 00	10 49	3 09	0 00
37	7 34	11 25	11 13	3 19	0 00
38	7 48	11 50	11 38	3 29	0 00
39	8 01	12 15	12 03	3 39	0 00
40	8 15	12 42	12 28	3 50	0 00
41	8 30	13 09	12 54	4 01	0 00
42	8 45	13 37	13 20	4 12	0 00
43	9 00	14 06	13 46	4 23	0 00
44	9 17	14 35	14 14	4 34	0 00
45	9 34	15 06	14 41	4 45	0 00
46	9 52	15 38	15 09	4 57	0 00
47	10 11	16 11	15 38	5 09	0 00
48	10 30	16 45	16 07	5 22	0 00
49	10 51	17 20	16 37	5 34	0 00
50	11 13	17 57	17 08	5 47	0 00
51	11 36	18 35	17 39	6 00	0 00
52	12 01	19 15	18 11	6 14	0 00
53	12 27	19 56	18 44	6 28	0 00
54	12 56	20 40	19 17	6 42	0 00
55	13 26	21 25	19 52	6 57	0 00
56	13 59	22 12	20 27	7 12	0 00
57	14 34	23 02	21 03	7 28	0 00
58	15 13	23 54	21 40	7 44	0 00
59	15 55	24 49	22 19	8 01	0 00
60	16♊42	25♋47	22♌58	8♍18	0♎00

2h 4m 0s — 31° 0' 0" — 3 ♉ 13

LAT.	11	12	ASC	2	3
0	3♊03	0♋55	28♋52	28♌52	1♎05
5	3 39	2 15	0♌37	29 35	1 05
10	4 17	3 36	2 20	0♍17	1 04
15	4 56	4 59	4 03	0 58	1 03
20	5 37	6 26	5 46	1 40	1 02
21	5 46	6 44	6 06	1 48	1 02
22	5 55	7 02	6 27	1 57	1 02
23	6 04	7 21	6 48	2 05	1 02
24	6 13	7 40	7 10	2 14	1 01
25	6 22	7 59	7 31	2 22	1 01
26	6 32	8 18	7 52	2 31	1 01
27	6 42	8 38	8 14	2 40	1 01
28	6 52	8 58	8 36	2 48	1 01
29	7 02	9 18	8 57	2 57	1 01
30	7 12	9 39	9 20	3 06	1 00
31	7 23	10 00	9 42	3 15	1 00
32	7 34	10 22	10 04	3 24	1 00
33	7 45	10 44	10 27	3 34	1 00
34	7 57	11 07	10 50	3 43	1 00
35	8 09	11 30	11 14	3 52	0 59
36	8 21	11 53	11 37	4 02	0 59
37	8 34	12 18	12 01	4 12	0 59
38	8 47	12 42	12 25	4 22	0 59
39	9 00	13 08	12 50	4 32	0 59
40	9 14	13 34	13 15	4 42	0 58
41	9 29	14 01	13 40	4 52	0 58
42	9 44	14 29	14 06	5 03	0 58
43	10 00	14 57	14 32	5 13	0 58
44	10 16	15 27	14 59	5 24	0 57
45	10 34	15 57	15 26	5 36	0 57
46	10 52	16 29	15 54	5 47	0 57
47	11 11	17 01	16 22	5 59	0 57
48	11 30	17 35	16 51	6 10	0 56
49	11 51	18 10	17 20	6 23	0 56
50	12 13	18 46	17 50	6 35	0 56
51	12 37	19 24	18 21	6 48	0 55
52	13 01	20 03	18 53	7 01	0 55
53	13 28	20 44	19 25	7 15	0 55
54	13 56	21 27	19 58	7 29	0 55
55	14 26	22 12	20 31	7 43	0 54
56	14 59	22 59	21 06	7 58	0 54
57	15 35	23 48	21 42	8 13	0 53
58	16 13	24 39	22 18	8 28	0 53
59	16 56	25 33	22 56	8 45	0 53
60	17♊43	26♋31	23♌35	9♍01	0♎52

2h 8m 0s 32° 0' 0"
4 ♉ 16

LAT.	11	12	ASC	2	3
0	4♊00	1♋50	29♋49	29♌54	2♎11
5	4 36	3 10	1♌34	0♍36	2 09
10	5 14	4 31	3 16	1 17	2 08
15	5 54	5 54	4 57	1 57	2 06
20	6 35	7 21	6 39	2 37	2 04
21	6 44	7 39	7 00	2 46	2 04
22	6 53	7 57	7 20	2 54	2 04
23	7 02	8 15	7 41	3 02	2 03
24	7 11	8 34	8 02	3 10	2 03
25	7 21	8 53	8 23	3 19	2 03
26	7 30	9 12	8 44	3 27	2 02
27	7 40	9 32	9 05	3 35	2 02
28	7 50	9 52	9 27	3 44	2 01
29	8 00	10 12	9 48	3 52	2 01
30	8 11	10 33	10 10	4 01	2 01
31	8 21	10 54	10 32	4 10	2 00
32	8 33	11 15	10 54	4 19	2 00
33	8 44	11 37	11 17	4 28	2 00
34	8 56	12 00	11 40	4 37	1 59
35	9 08	12 23	12 03	4 46	1 59
36	9 20	12 46	12 26	4 55	1 58
37	9 33	13 10	12 50	5 05	1 58
38	9 46	13 35	13 13	5 14	1 58
39	9 59	14 00	13 38	5 24	1 57
40	10 14	14 26	14 02	5 34	1 57
41	10 28	14 53	14 27	5 44	1 56
42	10 43	15 20	14 53	5 54	1 56
43	10 59	15 49	15 18	6 04	1 55
44	11 16	16 18	15 45	6 15	1 55
45	11 33	16 48	16 11	6 26	1 54
46	11 51	17 19	16 39	6 37	1 54
47	12 10	17 52	17 06	6 48	1 53
48	12 30	18 25	17 35	6 59	1 53
49	12 51	19 00	18 04	7 11	1 52
50	13 13	19 36	18 33	7 23	1 52
51	13 36	20 13	19 03	7 36	1 51
52	14 01	20 52	19 34	7 48	1 50
53	14 28	21 32	20 06	8 01	1 50
54	14 56	22 15	20 38	8 15	1 49
55	15 26	22 59	21 11	8 29	1 48
56	15 59	23 45	21 45	8 43	1 48
57	16 35	24 33	22 20	8 58	1 47
58	17 14	25 24	22 56	9 13	1 46
59	17 56	26 18	23 33	9 28	1 45
60	18♊44	27♋14	24♌11	9♍45	1♎45

2h 12m 0s 33° 0' 0"
5 ♉ 18

LAT.	11	12	ASC	2	3
0	4♊57	2♋45	0♌47	0♍57	3♎16
5	5 34	4 05	2 31	1 38	3 14
10	6 12	5 25	4 12	2 17	3 11
15	6 51	6 48	5 52	2 56	3 09
20	7 33	8 15	7 32	3 35	3 06
21	7 42	8 33	7 53	3 43	3 06
22	7 51	8 51	8 13	3 51	3 05
23	8 00	9 09	8 34	3 59	3 05
24	8 09	9 28	8 54	4 07	3 04
25	8 19	9 47	9 15	4 15	3 04
26	8 28	10 06	9 36	4 23	3 03
27	8 38	10 26	9 57	4 31	3 03
28	8 48	10 45	10 18	4 39	3 02
29	8 59	11 06	10 39	4 48	3 02
30	9 09	11 26	11 01	4 56	3 01
31	9 20	11 47	11 23	5 05	3 00
32	9 31	12 09	11 44	5 13	3 00
33	9 42	12 30	12 07	5 22	2 59
34	9 54	12 53	12 29	5 30	2 59
35	10 06	13 15	12 52	5 39	2 58
36	10 19	13 39	13 15	5 48	2 58
37	10 31	14 03	13 38	5 57	2 57
38	10 45	14 27	14 01	6 07	2 56
39	10 58	14 52	14 25	6 16	2 56
40	11 12	15 18	14 49	6 26	2 55
41	11 27	15 45	15 14	6 35	2 54
42	11 42	16 12	15 39	6 45	2 54
43	11 58	16 40	16 04	6 55	2 53
44	12 15	17 09	16 30	7 05	2 52
45	12 32	17 39	16 57	7 16	2 51
46	12 50	18 10	17 23	7 26	2 51
47	13 09	18 42	17 51	7 37	2 50
48	13 29	19 15	18 18	7 48	2 49
49	13 50	19 49	18 47	8 00	2 48
50	14 12	20 25	19 16	8 11	2 47
51	14 36	21 02	19 46	8 23	2 46
52	15 01	21 40	20 16	8 36	2 46
53	15 27	22 20	20 47	8 48	2 45
54	15 56	23 02	21 19	9 01	2 44
55	16 26	23 45	21 51	9 14	2 43
56	16 59	24 31	22 25	9 28	2 42
57	17 35	25 19	22 59	9 42	2 40
58	18 13	26 09	23 34	9 57	2 39
59	18 56	27 02	24 11	10 12	2 38
60	19♊44	27♋57	24♌48	10♍28	2♎37

2h 16m 0s 34° 0' 0"
6 ♉ 19

LAT.	11	12	ASC	2	3
0	5♊54	3♋40	1♌45	2♍00	4♎22
5	6 31	5 00	3 27	2 39	4 18
10	7 09	6 20	5 07	3 18	4 15
15	7 49	7 43	6 47	3 55	4 12
20	8 31	9 09	8 26	4 33	4 08
21	8 40	9 27	8 46	4 41	4 08
22	8 49	9 45	9 06	4 48	4 07
23	8 58	10 03	9 26	4 56	4 06
24	9 07	10 22	9 47	5 04	4 06
25	9 17	10 41	10 07	5 11	4 05
26	9 26	11 00	10 28	5 19	4 04
27	9 36	11 19	10 48	5 27	4 04
28	9 46	11 39	11 09	5 35	4 03
29	9 57	11 59	11 30	5 43	4 02
30	10 07	12 20	11 51	5 51	4 01
31	10 18	12 40	12 13	5 59	4 01
32	10 29	13 02	12 34	6 08	4 00
33	10 41	13 23	12 56	6 16	3 59
34	10 52	13 46	13 18	6 24	3 58
35	11 05	14 08	13 41	6 33	3 58
36	11 17	14 31	14 03	6 42	3 57
37	11 30	14 55	14 26	6 50	3 56
38	11 43	15 19	14 49	6 59	3 55
39	11 57	15 44	15 13	7 08	3 54
40	12 11	16 10	15 37	7 17	3 53
41	12 26	16 36	16 01	7 27	3 52
42	12 41	17 03	16 25	7 36	3 51
43	12 57	17 31	16 50	7 46	3 50
44	13 14	18 00	17 16	7 56	3 50
45	13 31	18 30	17 42	8 06	3 49
46	13 49	19 00	18 08	8 16	3 47
47	14 08	19 32	18 35	8 27	3 46
48	14 28	20 05	19 02	8 37	3 45
49	14 49	20 38	19 30	8 48	3 44
50	15 12	21 14	19 59	9 00	3 43
51	15 35	21 50	20 28	9 11	3 42
52	16 00	22 28	20 58	9 23	3 41
53	16 27	23 08	21 28	9 35	3 39
54	16 55	23 49	21 59	9 48	3 38
55	17 25	24 32	22 31	10 00	3 37
56	17 58	25 17	23 04	10 14	3 35
57	18 34	26 04	23 38	10 27	3 34
58	19 13	26 54	24 12	10 41	3 32
59	19 56	27 45	24 48	10 56	3 31
60	20♊43	28♋40	25♌25	11♍11	3♎29

2h 20m 0s 35° 0' 0"
7 ♉ 21

LAT.	11	12	ASC	2	3
0	6♊50	4♋35	2♌43	3♍03	5♎27
5	7 28	5 55	4 24	3 41	5 23
10	8 06	7 15	6 03	4 18	5 19
15	8 46	8 38	7 41	4 55	5 15
20	9 29	10 04	9 19	5 31	5 11
21	9 37	10 21	9 39	5 38	5 10
22	9 46	10 39	9 59	5 46	5 09
23	9 56	10 58	10 19	5 53	5 08
24	10 05	11 16	10 39	6 01	5 07
25	10 14	11 35	10 59	6 08	5 06
26	10 24	11 54	11 20	6 16	5 05
27	10 34	12 13	11 40	6 23	5 04
28	10 44	12 33	12 00	6 31	5 04
29	10 55	12 53	12 21	6 39	5 03
30	11 05	13 13	12 42	6 46	5 02
31	11 16	13 34	13 03	6 54	5 01
32	11 27	13 55	13 24	7 02	5 00
33	11 39	14 16	13 46	7 10	4 59
34	11 51	14 38	14 08	7 18	4 58
35	12 03	15 01	14 30	7 27	4 57
36	12 15	15 24	14 52	7 35	4 56
37	12 28	15 47	15 14	7 43	4 55
38	12 41	16 12	15 37	7 52	4 54
39	12 55	16 36	16 00	8 01	4 53
40	13 09	17 02	16 24	8 09	4 52
41	13 24	17 28	16 48	8 18	4 50
42	13 40	17 55	17 12	8 28	4 49
43	13 56	18 22	17 36	8 37	4 48
44	14 12	18 51	18 01	8 46	4 47
45	14 30	19 20	18 27	8 56	4 46
46	14 48	19 50	18 53	9 06	4 44
47	15 07	20 22	19 19	9 16	4 43
48	15 27	20 54	19 46	9 26	4 42
49	15 48	21 28	20 13	9 37	4 40
50	16 10	22 03	20 41	9 48	4 39
51	16 34	22 39	21 10	9 59	4 37
52	16 59	23 16	21 39	10 10	4 36
53	17 26	23 55	22 09	10 22	4 34
54	17 54	24 36	22 40	10 34	4 33
55	18 24	25 19	23 11	10 46	4 31
56	18 57	26 03	23 43	10 59	4 29
57	19 33	26 49	24 16	11 12	4 27
58	20 12	27 38	24 50	11 26	4 25
59	20 55	28 29	25 25	11 40	4 24
60	21♊42	29♋23	26♌01	11♍54	4♎21

2h 24m 0s 36° 0' 0"
8 ♉ 23

LAT.	11	12	ASC	2	3
0	7♊47	5♋30	3♌41	4♍07	6♎32
5	8 24	6 50	5 22	4 43	6 27
10	9 03	8 10	6 59	5 19	6 22
15	9 43	9 32	8 36	5 54	6 18
20	10 26	10 58	10 13	6 29	6 13
21	10 35	11 15	10 33	6 36	6 12
22	10 44	11 33	10 52	6 43	6 11
23	10 53	11 52	11 12	6 50	6 10
24	11 03	12 10	11 32	6 57	6 08
25	11 12	12 29	11 51	7 05	6 07
26	11 22	12 47	12 11	7 12	6 06
27	11 32	13 07	12 32	7 19	6 05
28	11 42	13 26	12 52	7 27	6 04
29	11 52	13 46	13 12	7 34	6 03
30	12 03	14 06	13 33	7 42	6 02
31	12 14	14 27	13 54	7 49	6 01
32	12 25	14 48	14 14	7 57	6 00
33	12 37	15 09	14 36	8 05	5 59
34	12 49	15 31	14 57	8 12	5 57
35	13 01	15 53	15 19	8 20	5 56
36	13 13	16 16	15 41	8 28	5 55
37	13 26	16 40	16 03	8 36	5 54
38	13 40	17 04	16 25	8 45	5 52
39	13 53	17 28	16 48	8 53	5 51
40	14 08	17 53	17 11	9 02	5 50
41	14 22	18 19	17 34	9 10	5 48
42	14 38	18 46	17 58	9 19	5 47
43	14 54	19 13	18 22	9 28	5 46
44	15 11	19 41	18 47	9 37	5 44
45	15 28	20 11	19 12	9 46	5 43
46	15 46	20 41	19 37	9 56	5 41
47	16 05	21 12	20 03	10 06	5 40
48	16 25	21 44	20 30	10 15	5 38
49	16 47	22 17	20 56	10 26	5 36
50	17 09	22 51	21 24	10 36	5 35
51	17 32	23 27	21 52	10 47	5 33
52	17 57	24 04	22 21	10 58	5 31
53	18 24	24 43	22 50	11 09	5 29
54	18 53	25 23	23 20	11 20	5 27
55	19 23	26 05	23 51	11 32	5 25
56	19 56	26 49	24 23	11 44	5 23
57	20 32	27 35	24 55	11 57	5 21
58	21 10	28 23	25 28	12 10	5 19
59	21 53	29 13	26 03	12 23	5 16
60	22♊40	0♌06	26♌38	12♍37	5♎14

2h 28m 0s 37° 0' 0"
9 ♉ 24

LAT.	11	12	ASC	2	3
0	8♊43	6♋26	4♌39	5♍10	7♎37
5	9 21	7 45	6 19	5 45	7 32
10	10 00	9 05	7 56	6 20	7 26
15	10 40	10 27	9 31	6 53	7 20
20	11 23	11 52	11 07	7 27	7 15
21	11 32	12 10	11 26	7 34	7 13
22	11 41	12 27	11 45	7 41	7 12
23	11 50	12 45	12 05	7 48	7 11
24	12 00	13 04	12 24	7 54	7 10
25	12 09	13 22	12 44	8 01	7 09
26	12 19	13 41	13 03	8 08	7 07
27	12 29	14 00	13 23	8 15	7 06
28	12 39	14 20	13 43	8 23	7 05
29	12 50	14 39	14 03	8 30	7 04
30	13 01	14 59	14 23	8 37	7 02
31	13 12	15 20	14 44	8 44	7 01
32	13 23	15 41	15 05	8 51	7 00
33	13 34	16 02	15 25	8 59	6 58
34	13 46	16 24	15 46	9 06	6 57
35	13 58	16 46	16 08	9 14	6 55
36	14 11	17 09	16 29	9 22	6 54
37	14 24	17 32	16 51	9 30	6 53
38	14 37	17 56	17 13	9 37	6 51
39	14 51	18 20	17 35	9 45	6 50
40	15 06	18 45	17 58	9 54	6 48
41	15 20	19 11	18 21	10 02	6 46
42	15 36	19 37	18 44	10 10	6 45
43	15 52	20 04	19 08	10 19	6 43
44	16 09	20 32	19 32	10 28	6 42
45	16 26	21 01	19 57	10 37	6 40
46	16 44	21 31	20 22	10 46	6 38
47	17 04	22 01	20 47	10 55	6 36
48	17 24	22 33	21 13	11 05	6 34
49	17 45	23 06	21 40	11 14	6 32
50	18 07	23 40	22 07	11 24	6 30
51	18 31	24 15	22 34	11 34	6 28
52	18 56	24 52	23 02	11 45	6 26
53	19 22	25 30	23 31	11 56	6 24
54	19 51	26 10	24 01	12 07	6 22
55	20 21	26 51	24 31	12 18	6 19
56	20 54	27 34	25 02	12 30	6 17
57	21 30	28 20	25 34	12 42	6 14
58	22 09	29 07	26 07	12 54	6 12
59	22 51	29 57	26 40	13 07	6 09
60	23♊38	0♌49	27♌15	13♍20	6♎06

2h 32m 0s 38° 0' 0"
10 ♉ 25

LAT.	11	12	ASC	2	3
0	9♊40	7♋21	5♌38	6♍14	8♎43
5	10 18	8 40	7 16	6 48	8 36
10	10 57	10 00	8 52	7 21	8 30
15	11 37	11 21	10 26	7 53	8 23
20	12 20	12 46	12 00	8 25	8 17
21	12 29	13 04	12 19	8 32	8 15
22	12 38	13 21	12 38	8 38	8 14
23	12 48	13 39	12 57	8 45	8 12
24	12 57	13 58	13 17	8 52	8 11
25	13 07	14 16	13 36	8 58	8 10
26	13 17	14 35	13 55	9 05	8 08
27	13 27	14 54	14 15	9 12	8 07
28	13 37	15 13	14 34	9 18	8 05
29	13 47	15 33	14 54	9 25	8 04
30	13 58	15 53	15 14	9 32	8 02
31	14 09	16 13	15 34	9 39	8 01
32	14 20	16 34	15 55	9 46	7 59
33	14 32	16 55	16 15	9 53	7 58
34	14 44	17 16	16 36	10 01	7 56
35	14 56	17 38	16 57	10 08	7 55
36	15 09	18 01	17 18	10 15	7 53
37	15 22	18 24	17 39	10 23	7 51
38	15 35	18 47	18 01	10 30	7 50
39	15 49	19 12	18 23	10 38	7 48
40	16 03	19 36	18 45	10 46	7 46
41	16 18	20 02	19 08	10 54	7 44
42	16 34	20 28	19 31	11 02	7 43
43	16 50	20 55	19 54	11 10	7 41
44	17 06	21 23	20 18	11 18	7 39
45	17 24	21 51	20 42	11 27	7 37
46	17 42	22 20	21 06	11 36	7 35
47	18 01	22 51	21 31	11 45	7 33
48	18 22	23 22	21 57	11 54	7 31
49	18 43	23 55	22 23	12 03	7 28
50	19 05	24 28	22 49	12 13	7 26
51	19 29	25 03	23 16	12 22	7 24
52	19 54	25 40	23 44	12 32	7 21
53	20 20	26 17	24 12	12 43	7 19
54	20 49	26 56	24 41	12 53	7 16
55	21 19	27 37	25 11	13 04	7 13
56	21 52	28 20	25 41	13 15	7 11
57	22 28	29 05	26 13	13 27	7 08
58	23 06	29 51	26 45	13 39	7 05
59	23 49	0♌40	27 17	13 51	7 01
60	24♊36	1♌31	27♌51	14♍04	6♎58

2h 36m 0s 39° 0' 0"
11 ♉ 26

LAT.	11	12	ASC	2	3
0	10♊36	8♋16	6♌37	7♍18	9♎48
5	11 14	9 35	8 14	7 50	9 40
10	11 53	10 54	9 48	8 22	9 33
15	12 34	12 16	11 21	8 53	9 26
20	13 17	13 40	12 54	9 24	9 18
21	13 26	13 58	13 13	9 30	9 17
22	13 35	14 15	13 31	9 36	9 15
23	13 45	14 33	13 50	9 42	9 14
24	13 54	14 51	14 09	9 49	9 12
25	14 04	15 10	14 28	9 55	9 11
26	14 14	15 28	14 47	10 01	9 09
27	14 24	15 47	15 07	10 08	9 08
28	14 34	16 06	15 26	10 14	9 06
29	14 44	16 26	15 45	10 21	9 04
30	14 55	16 46	16 05	10 28	9 03
31	15 06	17 06	16 25	10 34	9 01
32	15 18	17 26	16 45	10 41	8 59
33	15 29	17 47	17 05	10 48	8 58
34	15 41	18 09	17 25	10 55	8 56
35	15 53	18 31	17 46	11 02	8 54
36	16 06	18 53	18 07	11 09	8 52
37	16 19	19 16	18 28	11 16	8 50
38	16 32	19 39	18 49	11 23	8 48
39	16 46	20 03	19 11	11 30	8 46
40	17 01	20 28	19 32	11 38	8 44
41	17 16	20 53	19 55	11 46	8 42
42	17 31	21 19	20 17	11 53	8 40
43	17 47	21 46	20 40	12 01	8 38
44	18 04	22 13	21 03	12 09	8 36
45	18 22	22 41	21 27	12 17	8 34
46	18 40	23 10	21 51	12 26	8 32
47	18 59	23 40	22 16	12 34	8 29
48	19 19	24 11	22 41	12 43	8 27
49	19 40	24 44	23 06	12 52	8 24
50	20 03	25 17	23 32	13 01	8 22
51	20 26	25 51	23 59	13 10	8 19
52	20 51	26 27	24 26	13 20	8 16
53	21 18	27 04	24 53	13 30	8 13
54	21 46	27 43	25 22	13 40	8 11
55	22 17	28 23	25 51	13 50	8 08
56	22 50	29 05	26 21	14 01	8 04
57	23 25	29 49	26 51	14 12	8 01
58	24 04	0♌35	27 23	14 23	7 58
59	24 46	1 23	27 55	14 35	7 54
60	25♊33	2♌14	28♌28	14♍47	7♎50

2h 40m 0s — 12 ♉ 27 — 40° 0' 0"

LAT.	11	12	ASC	2	3
0	11♊32	9♋11	7♌35	8♍22	10♎53
5	12 10	10 30	9 11	8 53	10 45
10	12 50	11 49	10 45	9 23	10 37
15	13 31	13 10	12 16	9 52	10 29
20	14 14	14 34	13 48	10 22	10 20
21	14 23	14 52	14 06	10 28	10 19
22	14 32	15 09	14 25	10 34	10 17
23	14 41	15 27	14 43	10 40	10 15
24	14 51	15 45	15 02	10 46	10 14
25	15 01	16 03	15 21	10 52	10 12
26	15 11	16 22	15 39	10 58	10 10
27	15 21	16 41	15 58	11 04	10 08
28	15 31	17 00	16 17	11 10	10 07
29	15 42	17 19	16 36	11 17	10 05
30	15 52	17 39	16 56	11 23	10 03
31	16 03	17 59	17 15	11 29	10 01
32	16 15	18 19	17 35	11 36	9 59
33	16 26	18 40	17 55	11 42	9 57
34	16 38	19 01	18 15	11 49	9 55
35	16 51	19 23	18 35	11 56	9 53
36	17 03	19 45	18 55	12 02	9 51
37	17 16	20 08	19 16	12 09	9 49
38	17 30	20 31	19 37	12 16	9 47
39	17 44	20 55	19 58	12 23	9 45
40	17 58	21 19	20 20	12 30	9 43
41	18 13	21 44	20 41	12 37	9 40
42	18 28	22 10	21 04	12 45	9 38
43	18 45	22 36	21 26	12 52	9 36
44	19 01	23 03	21 49	13 00	9 33
45	19 19	23 31	22 12	13 08	9 31
46	19 37	24 00	22 36	13 16	9 28
47	19 56	24 30	23 00	13 24	9 26
48	20 17	25 00	23 24	13 32	9 23
49	20 38	25 32	23 49	13 41	9 20
50	21 00	26 05	24 15	13 49	9 17
51	21 24	26 39	24 41	13 58	9 14
52	21 49	27 15	25 07	14 07	9 11
53	22 15	27 51	25 34	14 17	9 08
54	22 44	28 30	26 02	14 26	9 05
55	23 14	29 09	26 31	14 36	9 02
56	23 47	29 51	27 00	14 46	8 58
57	24 22	0♌34	27 30	14 57	8 54
58	25 01	1 19	28 01	15 08	8 51
59	25 43	2 07	28 32	15 19	8 47
60	26♊30	2♌56	29♌05	15♍30	8♎43

2h 44m 0s — 13 ♉ 27 — 41° 0' 0"

LAT.	11	12	ASC	2	3
0	12♊28	10♋07	8♌34	9♍26	11♎58
5	13 07	11 25	10 09	9 55	11 49
10	13 46	12 44	11 41	10 24	11 40
15	14 27	14 05	13 11	10 52	11 31
20	15 11	15 29	14 42	11 20	11 22
21	15 20	15 46	15 00	11 26	11 20
22	15 29	16 03	15 18	11 32	11 19
23	15 38	16 21	15 36	11 37	11 17
24	15 48	16 39	15 55	11 43	11 15
25	15 57	16 57	16 13	11 49	11 13
26	16 07	17 15	16 31	11 55	11 11
27	16 17	17 34	16 50	12 01	11 09
28	16 28	17 53	17 09	12 07	11 07
29	16 38	18 12	17 28	12 13	11 05
30	16 49	18 32	17 47	12 19	11 03
31	17 00	18 52	18 06	12 25	11 01
32	17 12	19 12	18 25	12 31	10 59
33	17 23	19 33	18 44	12 37	10 57
34	17 35	19 54	19 04	12 43	10 55
35	17 48	20 15	19 24	12 49	10 52
36	18 00	20 37	19 44	12 56	10 50
37	18 13	21 00	20 04	13 02	10 48
38	18 27	21 23	20 25	13 09	10 45
39	18 41	21 46	20 46	13 16	10 43
40	18 55	22 10	21 07	13 22	10 41
41	19 10	22 35	21 28	13 29	10 38
42	19 26	23 00	21 50	13 36	10 36
43	19 42	23 27	22 12	13 43	10 33
44	19 59	23 53	22 34	13 51	10 30
45	20 16	24 21	22 57	13 58	10 28
46	20 34	24 50	23 20	14 06	10 25
47	20 54	25 19	23 44	14 13	10 22
48	21 14	25 49	24 08	14 21	10 19
49	21 35	26 21	24 32	14 29	10 16
50	21 57	26 53	24 57	14 38	10 13
51	22 21	27 27	25 23	14 46	10 10
52	22 46	28 02	25 49	14 55	10 06
53	23 12	28 38	26 16	15 04	10 03
54	23 41	29 16	26 43	15 13	9 59
55	24 11	29 55	27 11	15 22	9 56
56	24 44	0♌36	27 39	15 32	9 52
57	25 19	1 19	28 09	15 42	9 48
58	25 58	2 03	28 39	15 52	9 44
59	26 40	2 50	29 10	16 03	9 39
60	27♊26	3♌39	29♌41	16♍14	9♎35

2h 48m 0s — 14 ♉ 28 — 42° 0' 0"

LAT.	11	12	ASC	2	3
0	13♊24	11♋02	9♌34	10♍30	13♎03
5	14 03	12 20	11 07	10 58	12 53
10	14 42	13 39	12 38	11 25	12 43
15	15 23	14 59	14 07	11 52	12 34
20	16 07	16 23	15 36	12 19	12 24
21	16 16	16 40	15 53	12 24	12 22
22	16 25	16 57	16 11	12 30	12 20
23	16 35	17 15	16 29	12 35	12 18
24	16 44	17 33	16 47	12 41	12 16
25	16 54	17 51	17 05	12 46	12 14
26	17 04	18 09	17 24	12 52	12 12
27	17 14	18 27	17 42	12 57	12 10
28	17 24	18 46	18 00	13 03	12 07
29	17 35	19 05	18 19	13 08	12 05
30	17 46	19 25	18 37	13 14	12 03
31	17 57	19 44	18 56	13 20	12 01
32	18 08	20 05	19 15	13 26	11 58
33	18 20	20 25	19 34	13 31	11 56
34	18 32	20 46	19 54	13 37	11 54
35	18 44	21 07	20 13	13 43	11 51
36	18 57	21 29	20 33	13 49	11 49
37	19 10	21 51	20 53	13 56	11 47
38	19 24	22 14	21 13	14 02	11 44
39	19 38	22 38	21 33	14 08	11 41
40	19 52	23 01	21 54	14 15	11 39
41	20 07	23 26	22 15	14 21	11 36
42	20 22	23 51	22 36	14 28	11 33
43	20 39	24 17	22 58	14 35	11 30
44	20 55	24 44	23 20	14 42	11 28
45	21 13	25 11	23 42	14 49	11 25
46	21 31	25 39	24 05	14 56	11 22
47	21 50	26 08	24 28	15 03	11 18
48	22 11	26 38	24 52	15 10	11 15
49	22 32	27 09	25 16	15 18	11 12
50	22 54	27 41	25 40	15 26	11 09
51	23 18	28 15	26 05	15 34	11 05
52	23 43	28 49	26 31	15 42	11 01
53	24 09	29 25	26 57	15 51	10 58
54	24 37	0♌02	27 23	15 59	10 54
55	25 08	0 41	27 51	16 08	10 50
56	25 40	1 21	28 19	16 17	10 45
57	26 16	2 03	28 47	16 27	10 41
58	26 54	2 47	29 17	16 36	10 37
59	27 36	3 33	29 47	16 47	10 32
60	28♊22	4♌21	0♍18	16♍57	10♎27

2h 52m 0s — 15 ♉ 28 — 43° 0' 0"

LAT.	11	12	ASC	2	3
0	14♊20	11♋58	10♌33	11♍34	14♎07
5	14 59	13 16	12 05	12 01	13 57
10	15 38	14 34	13 34	12 27	13 47
15	16 20	15 54	15 02	12 52	13 36
20	17 03	17 17	16 30	13 17	13 26
21	17 12	17 34	16 47	13 23	13 24
22	17 22	17 51	17 05	13 28	13 21
23	17 31	18 09	17 22	13 33	13 19
24	17 41	18 26	17 40	13 38	13 17
25	17 51	18 44	17 58	13 43	13 15
26	18 00	19 02	18 16	13 48	13 12
27	18 11	19 21	18 34	13 54	13 10
28	18 21	19 39	18 52	13 59	13 08
29	18 32	19 58	19 10	14 04	13 05
30	18 42	20 18	19 28	14 10	13 03
31	18 54	20 37	19 47	14 15	13 01
32	19 05	20 57	20 05	14 21	12 58
33	19 17	21 18	20 24	14 26	12 56
34	19 29	21 38	20 43	14 32	12 53
35	19 41	21 59	21 02	14 37	12 50
36	19 54	22 21	21 21	14 43	12 48
37	20 07	22 43	21 41	14 49	12 45
38	20 20	23 06	22 01	14 55	12 42
39	20 34	23 29	22 21	15 01	12 40
40	20 49	23 53	22 41	15 07	12 37
41	21 04	24 17	23 02	15 13	12 34
42	21 19	24 42	23 23	15 19	12 31
43	21 35	25 07	23 44	15 26	12 28
44	21 52	25 34	24 05	15 32	12 25
45	22 10	26 01	24 27	15 39	12 22
46	22 28	26 29	24 49	15 46	12 18
47	22 47	26 57	25 12	15 53	12 15
48	23 07	27 27	25 35	16 00	12 11
49	23 28	27 58	25 59	16 07	12 08
50	23 51	28 29	26 23	16 14	12 04
51	24 14	29 02	26 47	16 22	12 00
52	24 39	29 36	27 12	16 30	11 56
53	25 06	0♌12	27 38	16 38	11 52
54	25 34	0 48	28 04	16 46	11 48
55	26 04	1 27	28 31	16 54	11 44
56	26 37	2 06	28 58	17 03	11 39
57	27 12	2 48	29 26	17 12	11 34
58	27 50	3 31	29 55	17 21	11 29
59	28 32	4 16	0♍25	17 30	11 24
60	29♊18	5♌04	0♍55	17♍40	11♎19

2h 56m 0s — 16 ♉ 28 — 44° 0' 0"

LAT.	11	12	ASC	2	3
0	15♊16	12♋53	11♌32	12♍39	15♎12
5	15 55	14 11	13 03	13 04	15 01
10	16 34	15 29	14 31	13 28	14 50
15	17 16	16 48	15 58	13 52	14 39
20	18 00	18 11	17 24	14 16	14 27
21	18 09	18 28	17 41	14 21	14 25
22	18 18	18 45	17 58	14 26	14 23
23	18 27	19 02	18 16	14 31	14 20
24	18 37	19 20	18 33	14 35	14 18
25	18 47	19 38	18 50	14 40	14 15
26	18 57	19 56	19 08	14 45	14 13
27	19 07	20 14	19 26	14 50	14 11
28	19 17	20 33	19 43	14 55	14 08
29	19 28	20 51	20 01	15 00	14 05
30	19 39	21 10	20 19	15 05	14 03
31	19 50	21 30	20 37	15 10	14 00
32	20 01	21 50	20 55	15 16	13 58
33	20 13	22 10	21 14	15 21	13 55
34	20 25	22 31	21 32	15 26	13 52
35	20 37	22 51	21 51	15 31	13 49
36	20 50	23 13	22 10	15 37	13 47
37	21 03	23 35	22 29	15 42	13 44
38	21 17	23 57	22 49	15 48	13 41
39	21 31	24 20	23 08	15 54	13 38
40	21 45	24 44	23 28	15 59	13 35
41	22 00	25 08	23 49	16 05	13 32
42	22 16	25 32	24 09	16 11	13 28
43	22 32	25 58	24 30	16 17	13 25
44	22 49	26 24	24 51	16 23	13 22
45	23 06	26 50	25 12	16 29	13 18
46	23 24	27 18	25 34	16 36	13 15
47	23 44	27 46	25 56	16 42	13 11
48	24 04	28 16	26 19	16 49	13 07
49	24 25	28 46	26 42	16 56	13 04
50	24 47	29 17	27 05	17 03	13 00
51	25 10	29 50	27 29	17 10	12 55
52	25 35	0♌23	27 54	17 17	12 51
53	26 02	0 58	28 19	17 25	12 47
54	26 30	1 35	28 44	17 32	12 42
55	27 00	2 12	29 11	17 40	12 38
56	27 32	2 51	29 37	17 48	12 33
57	28 07	3 32	0♍05	17 57	12 28
58	28 45	4 15	0 33	18 06	12 22
59	29 27	5 00	1 02	18 14	12 17
60	0♋13	5♌46	1♍32	18♍24	12♎11

3h 0m 0s — 17 ♉ 28 — 45° 0' 0"

LAT.	11	12	ASC	2	3
0	16♊11	13♋49	12♌32	13♍43	16♎17
5	16 50	15 06	14 02	14 07	16 05
10	17 30	16 24	15 28	14 30	15 53
15	18 12	17 43	16 53	14 52	15 41
20	18 56	19 05	18 18	15 15	15 29
21	19 05	19 22	18 35	15 19	15 26
22	19 14	19 39	18 52	15 24	15 24
23	19 24	19 56	19 09	15 28	15 21
24	19 33	20 14	19 26	15 33	15 19
25	19 43	20 31	19 43	15 38	15 16
26	19 53	20 49	20 00	15 42	15 14
27	20 03	21 07	20 17	15 47	15 11
28	20 14	21 26	20 35	15 52	15 08
29	20 24	21 44	20 52	15 56	15 06
30	20 35	22 03	21 10	16 01	15 03
31	20 46	22 23	21 28	16 06	15 00
32	20 58	22 42	21 46	16 11	14 57
33	21 09	23 02	22 04	16 16	14 54
34	21 21	23 23	22 22	16 21	14 51
35	21 34	23 44	22 40	16 26	14 48
36	21 46	24 05	22 59	16 31	14 45
37	22 00	24 26	23 18	16 36	14 42
38	22 13	24 49	23 37	16 41	14 39
39	22 27	25 11	23 56	16 46	14 36
40	22 41	25 34	24 16	16 52	14 33
41	22 56	25 58	24 35	16 57	14 29
42	23 12	26 23	24 55	17 03	14 26
43	23 28	26 48	25 16	17 08	14 22
44	23 45	27 14	25 36	17 14	14 19
45	24 02	27 40	25 57	17 20	14 15
46	24 21	28 07	26 19	17 26	14 11
47	24 40	28 35	26 40	17 32	14 07
48	25 00	29 04	27 03	17 38	14 03
49	25 21	29 34	27 25	17 45	13 59
50	25 43	0♌05	27 48	17 51	13 55
51	26 07	0 37	28 11	17 58	13 51
52	26 31	1 11	28 35	18 05	13 46
53	26 58	1 45	29 00	18 12	13 41
54	27 26	2 21	29 25	18 19	13 36
55	27 56	2 58	29 50	18 26	13 31
56	28 28	3 36	0♍17	18 34	13 26
57	29 03	4 17	0 44	18 42	13 21
58	29 41	4 59	1 11	18 50	13 15
59	0♋22	5 43	1 39	18 58	13 09
60	1♋07	6♌29	2♍09	19♍07	13♎03

3h 4m 0s — 18 ♉ 28 — 46° 0' 0"

LAT.	11	12	ASC	2	3
0	17♊07	14♋44	13♌32	14♍48	17♎21
5	17 46	16 01	15 00	15 10	17 09
10	18 26	17 19	16 26	15 31	16 56
15	19 08	18 38	17 49	15 52	16 43
20	19 52	19 59	19 12	16 13	16 30
21	20 01	20 16	19 29	16 18	16 28
22	20 10	20 33	19 45	16 22	16 25
23	20 20	20 50	20 02	16 26	16 22
24	20 29	21 07	20 19	16 30	16 20
25	20 39	21 25	20 36	16 35	16 17
26	20 49	21 43	20 52	16 39	16 14
27	20 59	22 01	21 09	16 43	16 11
28	21 10	22 19	21 27	16 48	16 08
29	21 20	22 37	21 44	16 52	16 06
30	21 31	22 56	22 01	16 57	16 03
31	21 42	23 15	22 18	17 01	16 00
32	21 54	23 35	22 36	17 06	15 57
33	22 05	23 55	22 54	17 10	15 54
34	22 17	24 15	23 12	17 15	15 50
35	22 30	24 35	23 30	17 20	15 47
36	22 43	24 57	23 48	17 24	15 44
37	22 56	25 18	24 06	17 29	15 41
38	23 09	25 40	24 25	17 34	15 37
39	23 23	26 02	24 44	17 39	15 34
40	23 38	26 25	25 03	17 44	15 31
41	23 53	26 49	25 22	17 49	15 27
42	24 08	27 13	25 42	17 54	15 23
43	24 24	27 38	26 02	18 00	15 20
44	24 41	28 03	26 22	18 05	15 16
45	24 58	28 30	26 42	18 11	15 12
46	25 17	28 57	27 03	18 16	15 08
47	25 36	29 24	27 25	18 22	15 04
48	25 56	29 53	27 46	18 28	14 59
49	26 17	0♌23	28 08	18 34	14 55
50	26 39	0 53	28 31	18 40	14 50
51	27 02	1 25	28 54	18 46	14 46
52	27 27	1 58	29 17	18 52	14 41
53	27 53	2 31	29 41	18 59	14 36
54	28 21	3 07	0♍05	19 06	14 31
55	28 51	3 43	0 30	19 13	14 25
56	29 23	4 21	0 56	19 20	14 20
57	29 58	5 01	1 22	19 27	14 14
58	0♋36	5 42	1 49	19 35	14 08
59	1 17	6 26	2 17	19 42	14 01
60	2♋02	7♌11	2♍45	19♍51	13♎55

3h 8m 0s — 19 ♉ 27 — 47° 0' 0"

LAT.	11	12	ASC	2	3
0	18♊02	15♋40	14♌32	15♍53	18♎26
5	18 42	16 57	15 59	16 13	18 12
10	19 22	18 14	17 23	16 33	17 59
15	20 04	19 32	18 45	16 53	17 46
20	20 48	20 53	20 06	17 12	17 32
21	20 57	21 10	20 23	17 16	17 29
22	21 06	21 27	20 39	17 20	17 26
23	21 16	21 44	20 55	17 24	17 23
24	21 25	22 01	21 12	17 28	17 20
25	21 35	22 18	21 28	17 32	17 17
26	21 45	22 36	21 45	17 36	17 15
27	21 55	22 54	22 01	17 40	17 12
28	22 06	23 12	22 18	17 44	17 09
29	22 16	23 30	22 35	17 48	17 05
30	22 27	23 49	22 52	17 53	17 02
31	22 38	24 08	23 09	17 57	16 59
32	22 50	24 27	23 26	18 01	16 56
33	23 01	24 47	23 44	18 05	16 53
34	23 13	25 07	24 01	18 10	16 49
35	23 26	25 27	24 19	18 14	16 46
36	23 39	25 48	24 37	18 18	16 43
37	23 52	26 10	24 55	18 23	16 39
38	24 05	26 31	25 13	18 27	16 36
39	24 19	26 54	25 31	18 32	16 32
40	24 34	27 16	25 50	18 37	16 28
41	24 49	27 40	26 09	18 41	16 25
42	25 04	28 03	26 28	18 46	16 21
43	25 20	28 28	26 48	18 51	16 17
44	25 37	28 53	27 07	18 56	16 13
45	25 54	29 19	27 28	19 01	16 08
46	26 13	29 46	27 48	19 06	16 04
47	26 32	0♌13	28 09	19 12	16 00
48	26 52	0 42	28 30	19 17	15 55
49	27 13	1 11	28 51	19 23	15 51
50	27 35	1 41	29 13	19 28	15 46
51	27 58	2 12	29 36	19 34	15 41
52	28 23	2 44	29 59	19 40	15 36
53	28 49	3 18	0♍22	19 46	15 30
54	29 17	3 53	0 46	19 52	15 25
55	29 47	4 29	1 10	19 59	15 19
56	0♋19	5 06	1 35	20 05	15 13
57	0 53	5 45	2 01	20 12	15 07
58	1 30	6 26	2 27	20 19	15 01
59	2 11	7 09	2 54	20 26	14 54
60	2♋56	7♌53	3♍22	20♍34	14♎47

3h 12m 0s 48° 0' 0" 20 ♉ 26					3h 16m 0s 49° 0' 0" 21 ♉ 26						3h 20m 0s 50° 0' 0" 22 ♉ 25					3h 24m 0s 51° 0' 0" 23 ♉ 23				
11	12	ASC	2	3	11	12	ASC	2	3	LAT.	11	12	ASC	2	3	11	12	ASC	2	3
18♊58	16♋36	15♌32	16♍57	19♎30	19♊53	17♋32	16♌33	18♍02	20♎34	0	20♊49	18♋28	17♌33	19♍07	21♎38	21♊44	19♋24	18♌34	20♍12	22♎42
19 37	17 52	16 58	17 16	19 16	20 33	18 48	17 57	18 20	20 19	5	21 28	19 44	18 56	19 23	21 23	22 24	20 39	19 55	20 27	22 26
20 18	19 09	18 20	17 35	19 02	21 13	20 04	19 18	18 37	20 05	10	22 09	21 00	20 15	19 39	21 07	23 04	21 55	21 13	20 41	22 10
20 59	20 27	19 41	17 53	18 48	21 55	21 22	20 37	18 53	19 50	15	22 50	22 17	21 33	19 54	20 51	23 46	23 11	22 29	20 54	21 53
21 43	21 48	21 01	18 11	18 33	22 39	22 42	21 55	19 10	19 34	20	23 35	23 36	22 50	20 09	20 35	24 30	24 30	23 44	21 08	21 36
21 53	22 04	21 17	18 15	18 30	22 48	22 58	22 11	19 13	19 31	21	23 44	23 52	23 05	20 12	20 32	24 39	24 46	23 59	21 11	21 33
22 02	22 21	21 33	18 18	18 27	22 58	23 15	22 26	19 17	19 28	22	23 53	24 09	23 20	20 15	20 29	24 49	25 03	24 14	21 13	21 30
22 11	22 38	21 49	18 22	18 24	23 07	23 31	22 42	19 20	19 25	23	24 03	24 25	23 36	20 18	20 26	24 58	25 19	24 29	21 16	21 26
22 21	22 55	22 05	18 26	18 21	23 17	23 48	22 58	19 23	19 22	24	24 12	24 42	23 51	20 21	20 22	25 08	25 36	24 44	21 19	21 23
22 31	23 12	22 21	18 29	18 18	23 27	24 05	23 14	19 27	19 18	25	24 22	24 59	24 07	20 24	20 19	25 18	25 53	25 00	21 22	21 19
22 41	23 29	22 37	18 33	18 15	23 37	24 23	23 30	19 30	19 15	26	24 32	25 16	24 22	20 27	20 15	25 28	26 10	25 15	21 25	21 15
22 51	23 47	22 54	18 37	18 12	23 47	24 40	23 46	19 34	19 12	27	24 42	25 34	24 38	20 31	20 12	25 38	26 27	25 30	21 27	21 12
23 02	24 05	23 10	18 41	18 09	23 57	24 58	24 02	19 37	19 08	28	24 53	25 51	24 54	20 34	20 08	25 48	26 44	25 45	21 30	21 08
23 12	24 23	23 26	18 44	18 05	24 08	25 16	24 18	19 41	19 05	29	25 03	26 09	25 09	20 37	20 05	25 59	27 02	26 01	21 33	21 04
23 23	24 42	23 43	18 48	18 02	24 19	25 35	24 34	19 44	19 02	30	25 14	26 27	25 25	20 40	20 01	26 10	27 20	26 16	21 36	21 01
23 34	25 01	24 00	18 52	17 59	24 30	25 53	24 51	19 48	18 58	31	25 26	26 46	25 41	20 43	19 57	26 21	27 39	26 32	21 39	20 57
23 46	25 20	24 17	18 56	17 55	24 41	26 12	25 07	19 51	18 55	32	25 37	27 05	25 57	20 47	19 54	26 32	27 57	26 48	21 42	20 53
23 57	25 39	24 34	19 00	17 52	24 53	26 32	25 24	19 55	18 51	33	25 49	27 24	26 14	20 50	19 50	26 44	28 16	27 04	21 45	20 49
24 09	25 59	24 51	19 04	17 48	25 05	26 51	25 40	19 59	18 47	34	26 01	27 43	26 30	20 53	19 46	26 56	28 35	27 20	21 48	20 45
24 22	26 19	25 08	19 08	17 45	25 17	27 11	25 57	20 02	18 44	35	26 13	28 03	26 47	20 57	19 42	27 08	28 55	27 36	21 51	20 41
24 34	26 40	25 26	19 12	17 41	25 30	27 32	26 14	20 06	18 40	36	26 26	28 23	27 03	21 00	19 38	27 21	29 15	27 52	21 54	20 36
24 48	27 01	25 43	19 16	17 38	25 43	27 53	26 32	20 10	18 36	37	26 39	28 44	27 20	21 03	19 34	27 34	29 35	28 09	21 57	20 32
25 01	27 23	26 01	19 20	17 34	25 57	28 14	26 49	20 14	18 32	38	26 52	29 05	27 37	21 07	19 30	27 48	29 56	28 25	22 00	20 28
25 15	27 45	26 19	19 25	17 30	26 11	28 36	27 07	20 18	18 28	39	27 06	29 27	27 54	21 10	19 26	28 02	0♌18	28 42	22 03	20 23
25 29	28 07	26 37	19 29	17 26	26 25	28 58	27 25	20 22	18 24	40	27 21	29 49	28 12	21 14	19 21	28 16	0 39	28 59	22 07	20 19
25 44	28 30	26 56	19 33	17 22	26 40	29 21	27 43	20 26	18 20	41	27 35	0♌11	28 30	21 18	19 17	28 31	1 02	29 17	22 10	20 14
26 00	28 54	27 15	19 38	17 18	26 55	29 44	28 01	20 30	18 15	42	27 51	0 34	28 48	21 21	19 12	28 46	1 25	29 34	22 13	20 10
26 16	29 18	27 34	19 42	17 14	27 12	0♌08	28 20	20 34	18 11	43	28 07	0 58	29 06	21 25	19 08	29 02	1 48	29 52	22 17	20 05
26 33	29 43	27 53	19 47	17 09	27 28	0 33	28 39	20 38	18 06	44	28 24	1 22	29 24	21 29	19 03	29 19	2 12	0♍10	22 20	20 00
26 50	0♌09	28 13	19 52	17 05	27 46	0 58	28 58	20 42	18 02	45	28 41	1 47	29 43	21 33	18 58	29 36	2 37	0 28	22 24	19 55
27 08	0 35	28 33	19 57	17 01	28 04	1 24	29 17	20 47	17 57	46	28 59	2 13	0♍02	21 37	18 53	29 54	3 02	0 47	22 27	19 49
27 27	1 02	28 53	20 01	16 56	28 23	1 51	29 37	20 51	17 52	47	29 18	2 40	0 21	21 41	18 48	0♋13	3 28	1 06	22 31	19 44
27 47	1 30	29 14	20 06	16 51	28 43	2 18	29 57	20 56	17 47	48	29 38	3 07	0 41	21 45	18 43	0 33	3 55	1 25	22 35	19 38
28 08	1 59	29 35	20 12	16 46	29 04	2 47	0♍18	21 01	17 42	49	29 59	3 35	1 01	21 49	18 37	0 54	4 23	1 44	22 39	19 33
28 30	2 29	29 56	20 17	16 41	29 25	3 16	0 39	21 05	17 36	50	0♋21	4 04	1 22	21 54	18 31	1 15	4 51	2 04	22 42	19 27
28 53	2 59	0♍18	20 22	16 36	29 49	3 47	1 00	21 10	17 31	51	0 44	4 34	1 42	21 58	18 26	1 38	5 21	2 25	22 46	19 21
29 18	3 31	0 40	20 28	16 30	0♋13	4 18	1 22	21 15	17 25	52	1 08	5 05	2 04	22 03	18 20	2 03	5 52	2 45	22 51	19 14
29 44	4 04	1 03	20 33	16 25	0 39	4 51	1 44	21 20	17 19	53	1 34	5 37	2 25	22 08	18 13	2 28	6 23	3 07	22 55	19 08
0♋12	4 39	1 27	20 39	16 19	1 07	5 24	2 07	21 26	17 13	54	2 01	6 10	2 48	22 12	18 07	2 56	6 56	3 28	22 59	19 01
0 42	5 14	1 50	20 45	16 13	1 36	6 00	2 30	21 31	17 07	55	2 31	6 45	3 10	22 17	18 00	3 25	7 30	3 50	23 04	18 54
1 13	5 51	2 15	20 51	16 07	2 08	6 36	2 54	21 37	17 00	56	3 02	7 21	3 34	22 22	17 53	3 56	8 05	4 13	23 08	18 46
1 48	6 30	2 40	20 57	16 00	2 42	7 14	3 19	21 43	16 53	57	3 36	7 58	3 58	22 28	17 46	4 30	8 42	4 36	23 13	18 39
2 25	7 10	3 06	21 04	15 53	3 19	7 53	3 44	21 48	16 46	58	4 13	8 37	4 22	22 33	17 38	5 06	9 20	5 00	23 18	18 31
3 05	7 52	3 32	21 11	15 46	3 59	8 35	4 09	21 55	16 38	59	4 53	9 17	4 47	22 39	17 31	5 46	10 00	5 25	23 23	18 23
3♋50	8♌35	3♍59	21♍17	15♎39	4♋43	9♌18	4♍36	22♍01	16♎30	60	5♋36	10♌00	5♍13	22♍44	17♎22	6♋29	10♌42	5♍50	23♍28	18♎14

3h 28m 0s 52° 0' 0" 24 ♉ 22					3h 32m 0s 53° 0' 0" 25 ♉ 21						3h 36m 0s 54° 0' 0" 26 ♉ 19					3h 40m 0s 55° 0' 0" 27 ♉ 17				
11	12	ASC	2	3	11	12	ASC	2	3	LAT.	11	12	ASC	2	3	11	12	ASC	2	3
22♊39	20♋20	19♌35	21♍17	23♎46	23♊34	21♋17	20♌36	22♍23	24♎50	0	24♊30	22♋13	21♌37	23♍28	25♎53	25♊25	23♋10	22♌39	24♍33	26♎57
23 19	21 35	20 54	21 30	23 29	24 14	22 31	21 54	22 34	24 32	5	25 09	23 27	22 54	23 38	25 35	26 04	24 23	23 54	24 41	26 37
23 59	22 50	22 11	21 43	23 12	24 55	23 46	23 09	22 45	24 14	10	25 50	24 41	24 07	23 47	25 16	26 45	25 37	25 05	24 49	26 18
24 41	24 06	23 25	21 55	22 55	25 37	25 01	24 21	22 55	23 56	15	26 32	25 56	25 18	23 56	24 58	27 27	26 51	26 14	24 57	25 59
25 26	25 24	24 39	22 07	22 37	26 21	26 19	25 33	23 06	23 38	20	27 16	27 13	26 28	24 05	24 39	28 11	28 08	27 23	25 04	25 39
25 35	25 40	24 53	22 09	22 34	26 30	26 35	25 48	23 08	23 34	21	27 25	27 29	26 42	24 07	24 35	28 21	28 23	27 37	25 06	25 35
25 44	25 57	25 08	22 12	22 30	26 39	26 51	26 02	23 10	23 31	22	27 35	27 45	26 56	24 09	24 31	28 30	28 39	27 50	25 07	25 31
25 54	26 13	25 23	22 14	22 27	26 49	27 07	26 17	23 12	23 27	23	27 44	28 01	27 10	24 11	24 27	28 39	28 55	28 04	25 09	25 27
26 03	26 29	25 38	22 17	22 23	26 59	27 23	26 31	23 15	23 23	24	27 54	28 17	27 24	24 12	24 23	28 49	29 11	28 18	25 10	25 23
26 13	26 46	25 53	22 19	22 19	27 08	27 40	26 46	23 17	23 19	25	28 04	28 33	27 39	24 14	24 19	28 59	29 27	28 32	25 12	25 19
26 23	27 03	26 07	22 22	22 15	27 18	27 57	27 00	23 19	23 15	26	28 14	28 50	27 53	24 16	24 15	29 09	29 44	28 46	25 13	25 15
26 33	27 20	26 22	22 24	22 12	27 29	28 13	27 15	23 21	23 11	27	28 24	29 07	28 07	24 18	24 11	29 19	0♌00	28 59	25 15	25 10
26 44	27 38	26 37	22 27	22 08	27 39	28 31	27 29	23 23	23 07	28	28 34	29 24	28 21	24 20	24 07	29 29	0 17	29 13	25 17	25 06
26 54	27 55	26 52	22 29	22 04	27 50	28 48	27 44	23 26	23 03	29	28 45	29 41	28 36	24 22	24 03	29 40	0 34	29 27	25 18	25 02
27 05	28 13	27 08	22 32	22 00	28 01	29 06	27 59	23 28	22 59	30	28 56	29 59	28 50	24 24	23 58	29 51	0 51	29 42	25 20	24 57
27 16	28 31	27 23	22 34	21 56	28 12	29 24	28 14	23 30	22 55	31	29 07	0♌16	29 05	24 26	23 54	0♋02	1 09	29 56	25 21	24 53
27 28	28 50	27 38	22 37	21 52	28 23	29 42	28 29	23 32	22 51	32	29 18	0 34	29 19	24 28	23 49	0 13	1 27	0♍10	25 23	24 48
27 39	29 08	27 54	22 40	21 48	28 35	0♌01	28 44	23 35	22 46	33	29 30	0 53	29 34	24 30	23 45	0 25	1 45	0 24	25 25	24 44
27 51	29 27	28 09	22 42	21 43	28 47	0 19	28 59	23 37	22 42	34	29 42	1 12	29 49	24 32	23 40	0 37	2 04	0 39	25 26	24 39
28 04	29 47	28 25	22 45	21 39	28 59	0 39	29 15	23 39	22 37	35	29 54	1 31	0♍04	24 34	23 36	0 49	2 22	0 53	25 28	24 34
28 16	0♌07	28 41	22 48	21 35	29 12	0 58	29 30	23 42	22 33	36	0♋07	1 50	0 19	24 36	23 31	1 02	2 42	1 08	25 30	24 29
28 29	0 27	28 57	22 51	21 30	29 25	1 18	29 46	23 44	22 28	37	0 20	2 10	0 34	24 38	23 26	1 15	3 01	1 23	25 32	24 24
28 43	0 47	29 14	22 53	21 26	29 38	1 39	0♍02	23 47	22 24	38	0 33	2 30	0 50	24 40	23 21	1 28	3 21	1 38	25 33	24 19
28 57	1 09	29 30	22 56	21 21	29 52	2 00	0 18	23 49	22 19	39	0 47	2 50	1 06	24 42	23 16	1 42	3 41	1 53	25 35	24 14
29 11	1 30	29 47	22 59	21 16	0♋06	2 21	0 34	23 52	22 14	40	1 01	3 11	1 21	24 44	23 11	1 56	4 02	2 09	25 37	24 08
29 26	1 52	0♍03	23 02	21 12	0 21	2 43	0 50	23 54	22 09	41	1 16	3 33	1 37	24 46	23 06	2 11	4 23	2 24	25 39	24 03
29 41	2 15	0 21	23 05	21 07	0 36	3 05	1 07	23 57	22 04	42	1 31	3 55	1 54	24 49	23 00	2 26	4 45	2 40	25 41	23 57
29 57	2 38	0 38	23 08	21 01	0 52	3 28	1 24	24 00	21 58	43	1 47	4 18	2 10	24 51	22 55	2 42	5 07	2 56	25 42	23 51
0♋14	3 02	0 55	23 11	20 56	1 09	3 51	1 41	24 02	21 53	44	2 04	4 41	2 27	24 53	22 49	2 58	5 30	3 12	25 44	23 46
0 31	3 26	1 13	23 14	20 51	1 26	4 15	1 58	24 05	21 47	45	2 21	5 05	2 44	24 56	22 43	3 15	5 54	3 29	25 46	23 40
0 49	3 51	1 31	23 18	20 45	1 44	4 40	2 16	24 08	21 41	46	2 39	5 29	3 01	24 58	22 37	3 33	6 18	3 46	25 48	23 33
1 08	4 17	1 50	23 21	20 40	2 03	5 05	2 34	24 11	21 36	47	2 57	5 54	3 18	25 01	22 31	3 52	6 43	4 03	25 50	23 27
1 28	4 43	2 09	23 24	20 34	2 22	5 32	2 52	24 14	21 29	48	3 17	6 20	3 36	25 03	22 25	4 11	7 08	4 20	25 53	23 20
1 48	5 11	2 28	23 28	20 28	2 43	5 59	3 11	24 17	21 23	49	3 37	6 47	3 54	25 06	22 18	4 32	7 34	4 37	25 55	23 14
2 10	5 39	2 47	23 31	20 22	3 05	6 27	3 30	24 20	21 17	50	3 59	7 14	4 13	25 08	22 12	4 53	8 01	4 55	25 57	23 07
2 33	6 08	3 07	23 35	20 15	3 27	6 55	3 49	24 23	21 10	51	4 22	7 42	4 31	25 11	22 05	5 16	8 29	5 14	25 59	22 59
2 57	6 38	3 27	23 38	20 09	3 52	7 25	4 09	24 26	21 03	52	4 46	8 12	4 51	25 14	21 57	5 40	8 58	5 32	26 01	22 52
3 23	7 10	3 48	23 42	20 02	4 17	7 56	4 29	24 29	20 56	53	5 11	8 42	5 10	25 16	21 50	6 05	9 28	5 51	26 04	22 44
3 50	7 42	4 09	23 46	19 55	4 44	8 28	4 49	24 33	20 49	54	5 38	9 13	5 30	25 19	21 42	6 32	9 59	6 11	26 06	22 36
4 19	8 15	4 30	23 50	19 47	5 13	9 01	5 10	24 36	20 41	55	6 07	9 46	5 51	25 22	21 34	7 00	10 31	6 31	26 09	22 28
4 50	8 50	4 53	23 54	19 40	5 44	9 35	5 32	24 40	20 33	56	6 37	10 19	6 11	25 25	21 26	7 31	11 04	6 51	26 11	22 19
5 24	9 26	5 15	23 58	19 32	6 17	10 10	5 54	24 43	20 25	57	7 10	10 55	6 33	25 29	21 17	8 03	11 39	7 12	26 14	22 10
6 00	10 04	5 38	24 02	19 23	6 53	10 47	6 17	24 47	20 16	58	7 46	11 31	6 55	25 32	21 08	8 38	12 14	7 33	26 16	22 00
6 39	10 43	6 02	24 07	19 15	7 32	11 26	6 40	24 51	20 07	59	8 24	12 09	7 17	25 35	20 59	9 17	12 52	7 55	26 19	21 51
7♋22	11♌24	6♍27	24♍11	19♎06	8♋14	12♌06	7♍04	24♍55	19♎57	60	9♋06	12♌48	7♍40	25♍39	20♎49	9♋58	13♌31	8♍17	26♍22	21♎40

3h 44m 0s — 56° 0' 0" — 28 ♉ 15

LAT.	11	12	ASC	2	3
0	26♊20	24♋06	23♌41	25♍38	28♎00
5	27 00	25 20	24 53	25 45	27 40
10	27 40	26 33	26 03	25 51	27 20
15	28 22	27 46	27 11	25 57	27 00
20	29 06	29 02	28 18	26 03	26 40
21	29 16	29 17	28 31	26 05	26 36
22	29 25	29 33	28 45	26 06	26 32
23	29 34	29 49	28 58	26 07	26 27
24	29 44	0♌05	29 11	26 08	26 23
25	29 54	0 21	29 25	26 10	26 19
26	0♋04	0 37	29 38	26 11	26 14
27	0 14	0 54	29 52	26 12	26 10
28	0 24	1 10	0♍06	26 13	26 05
29	0 35	1 27	0 19	26 15	26 01
30	0 46	1 44	0 33	26 16	25 56
31	0 57	2 02	0 47	26 17	25 52
32	1 08	2 19	1 01	26 18	25 47
33	1 20	2 37	1 15	26 20	25 42
34	1 32	2 56	1 29	26 21	25 37
35	1 44	3 14	1 43	26 22	25 32
36	1 57	3 33	1 57	26 24	25 27
37	2 10	3 52	2 12	26 25	25 22
38	2 23	4 12	2 26	26 27	25 16
39	2 37	4 32	2 41	26 28	25 11
40	2 51	4 53	2 56	26 29	25 05
41	3 05	5 14	3 11	26 31	25 00
42	3 21	5 35	3 27	26 32	24 54
43	3 36	5 57	3 42	26 34	24 48
44	3 53	6 20	3 58	26 36	24 42
45	4 10	6 43	4 14	26 37	24 36
46	4 28	7 07	4 30	26 39	24 29
47	4 46	7 31	4 47	26 40	24 23
48	5 06	7 56	5 04	26 42	24 16
49	5 26	8 22	5 21	26 44	24 09
50	5 47	8 49	5 38	26 45	24 01
51	6 10	9 16	5 56	26 47	23 54
52	6 33	9 45	6 14	26 49	23 46
53	6 58	10 14	6 32	26 51	23 38
54	7 25	10 45	6 51	26 53	23 30
55	7 53	11 16	7 11	26 55	23 21
56	8 24	11 49	7 30	26 57	23 12
57	8 56	12 23	7 51	26 59	23 03
58	9 31	12 58	8 11	27 01	22 53
59	10 09	13 35	8 33	27 03	22 42
60	10♋50	14♌13	8♍54	27♍06	22♎32

3h 48m 0s — 57° 0' 0" — 29 ♉ 13

LAT.	11	12	ASC	2	3
0	27♊15	25♋03	24♌42	26♍44	29♎03
5	27 55	26 16	25 54	26 49	28 42
10	28 35	27 28	27 02	26 53	28 22
15	29 17	28 42	28 08	26 58	28 01
20	0♋02	29 56	29 13	27 03	27 40
21	0 11	0♌12	29 26	27 03	27 36
22	0 20	0 27	29 39	27 04	27 32
23	0 29	0 43	29 52	27 05	27 27
24	0 39	0 59	0♍05	27 06	27 23
25	0 49	1 15	0 18	27 07	27 18
26	0 59	1 31	0 31	27 08	27 14
27	1 09	1 47	0 44	27 09	27 09
28	1 19	2 04	0 58	27 10	27 05
29	1 30	2 20	1 11	27 11	27 00
30	1 41	2 37	1 24	27 12	26 55
31	1 52	2 54	1 38	27 13	26 50
32	2 03	3 12	1 51	27 14	26 45
33	2 15	3 30	2 05	27 15	26 40
34	2 27	3 48	2 19	27 16	26 35
35	2 39	4 06	2 32	27 17	26 30
36	2 51	4 25	2 46	27 18	26 25
37	3 04	4 44	3 00	27 19	26 19
38	3 18	5 03	3 15	27 20	26 14
39	3 31	5 23	3 29	27 21	26 08
40	3 45	5 43	3 44	27 22	26 03
41	4 00	6 04	3 58	27 23	25 57
42	4 15	6 25	4 13	27 24	25 51
43	4 31	6 47	4 28	27 25	25 44
44	4 47	7 09	4 44	27 27	25 38
45	5 04	7 32	4 59	27 28	25 32
46	5 22	7 56	5 15	27 29	25 25
47	5 40	8 20	5 31	27 30	25 18
48	6 00	8 45	5 47	27 31	25 11
49	6 20	9 10	6 04	27 33	25 04
50	6 41	9 36	6 21	27 34	24 56
51	7 03	10 03	6 38	27 35	24 48
52	7 27	10 31	6 56	27 37	24 40
53	7 52	11 00	7 14	27 38	24 32
54	8 18	11 30	7 32	27 40	24 23
55	8 46	12 01	7 51	27 41	24 14
56	9 16	12 33	8 10	27 43	24 05
57	9 49	13 07	8 30	27 44	23 55
58	10 23	13 41	8 50	27 46	23 45
59	11 01	14 17	9 10	27 48	23 34
60	11♋41	14♌55	9♍31	27♍49	23♎23

3h 52m 0s — 58° 0' 0" — 0 ♊ 11

LAT.	11	12	ASC	2	3
0	28♊10	26♋00	25♌44	27♍49	0♏06
5	28 50	27 12	26 54	27 52	29♎45
10	29 30	28 24	28 00	27 56	29 24
15	0♋12	29 37	29 05	27 59	29 02
20	0 57	0♌51	0♍08	28 02	28 41
21	1 06	1 06	0 21	28 02	28 36
22	1 15	1 22	0 33	28 03	28 32
23	1 24	1 37	0 46	28 04	28 27
24	1 34	1 53	0 59	28 04	28 23
25	1 44	2 08	1 11	28 05	28 18
26	1 54	2 24	1 24	28 05	28 13
27	2 04	2 40	1 37	28 06	28 08
28	2 14	2 57	1 50	28 07	28 04
29	2 25	3 13	2 03	28 07	27 59
30	2 36	3 30	2 16	28 08	27 54
31	2 47	3 47	2 29	28 09	27 49
32	2 58	4 04	2 42	28 09	27 44
33	3 10	4 22	2 55	28 10	27 39
34	3 21	4 40	3 08	28 11	27 33
35	3 34	4 58	3 22	28 11	27 28
36	3 46	5 16	3 35	28 12	27 22
37	3 59	5 35	3 49	28 13	27 17
38	4 12	5 55	4 03	28 13	27 11
39	4 26	6 14	4 17	28 14	27 05
40	4 40	6 34	4 31	28 15	26 59
41	4 55	6 55	4 45	28 15	26 53
42	5 10	7 16	5 00	28 16	26 47
43	5 25	7 37	5 15	28 17	26 41
44	5 42	7 59	5 29	28 18	26 34
45	5 58	8 21	5 44	28 19	26 28
46	6 16	8 45	6 00	28 19	26 21
47	6 34	9 08	6 15	28 20	26 13
48	6 54	9 33	6 31	28 21	26 06
49	7 14	9 58	6 47	28 22	25 59
50	7 35	10 24	7 04	28 23	25 51
51	7 57	10 50	7 20	28 24	25 43
52	8 20	11 18	7 38	28 25	25 34
53	8 45	11 46	7 55	28 25	25 26
54	9 11	12 16	8 13	28 26	25 17
55	9 39	12 46	8 31	28 27	25 07
56	10 09	13 18	8 49	28 28	24 58
57	10 41	13 51	9 08	28 29	24 48
58	11 15	14 25	9 28	28 31	24 37
59	11 52	15 00	9 48	28 32	24 26
60	12♋32	15♌37	10♍08	28♍33	24♎14

3h 56m 0s — 59° 0' 0" — 1 ♊ 08

LAT.	11	12	ASC	2	3
0	29♊05	26♋57	26♌47	28♍55	1♏08
5	29 45	28 09	27 54	28 56	0 47
10	0♋25	29 20	28 59	28 58	0 25
15	1 07	0♌32	0♍02	28 59	0 03
20	1 52	1 46	1 03	29 01	29♎41
21	2 01	2 01	1 16	29 01	29 36
22	2 10	2 16	1 28	29 01	29 31
23	2 19	2 31	1 40	29 02	29 27
24	2 29	2 47	1 52	29 02	29 22
25	2 39	3 02	2 05	29 02	29 17
26	2 49	3 18	2 17	29 03	29 12
27	2 59	3 34	2 30	29 03	29 08
28	3 09	3 50	2 42	29 03	29 03
29	3 20	4 06	2 55	29 04	28 58
30	3 30	4 23	3 07	29 04	28 53
31	3 41	4 40	3 20	29 04	28 47
32	3 53	4 57	3 33	29 05	28 42
33	4 04	5 14	3 46	29 05	28 37
34	4 16	5 32	3 58	29 05	28 31
35	4 28	5 50	4 11	29 06	28 26
36	4 41	6 08	4 25	29 06	28 20
37	4 54	6 27	4 38	29 06	28 14
38	5 07	6 46	4 51	29 07	28 09
39	5 20	7 05	5 05	29 07	28 03
40	5 34	7 25	5 19	29 07	27 56
41	5 49	7 45	5 32	29 08	27 50
42	6 04	8 06	5 46	29 08	27 44
43	6 20	8 27	6 01	29 08	27 37
44	6 36	8 48	6 15	29 09	27 30
45	6 53	9 11	6 30	29 09	27 23
46	7 10	9 33	6 45	29 10	27 16
47	7 28	9 57	7 00	29 10	27 09
48	7 48	10 21	7 15	29 10	27 01
49	8 08	10 46	7 31	29 11	26 53
50	8 28	11 11	7 47	29 11	26 45
51	8 51	11 37	8 03	29 12	26 37
52	9 14	12 04	8 19	29 12	26 28
53	9 38	12 32	8 36	29 13	26 19
54	10 04	13 01	8 53	29 13	26 10
55	10 32	13 31	9 11	29 14	26 00
56	11 02	14 03	9 29	29 14	25 50
57	11 33	14 35	9 47	29 15	25 40
58	12 07	15 08	10 06	29 15	25 29
59	12 44	15 43	10 26	29 16	25 18
60	13♋23	16♌19	10♍46	29♍16	25♎06

4h 0m 0s — 60° 0' 0" — 2 ♊ 05

LAT.	11	12	ASC	2	3
0	0♋00	27♋55	27♌49	0♎00	2♏11
5	0 40	29 06	28 55	0 00	1 49
10	1 20	0♌16	29 58	0 00	1 26
15	2 02	1 28	0♍59	0 00	1 04
20	2 46	2 40	1 58	0 00	0 41
21	2 56	2 55	2 10	0 00	0 36
22	3 05	3 10	2 22	0 00	0 31
23	3 14	3 25	2 34	0 00	0 26
24	3 24	3 41	2 46	0 00	0 22
25	3 34	3 56	2 58	0 00	0 17
26	3 44	4 12	3 10	0 00	0 12
27	3 54	4 27	3 22	0 00	0 07
28	4 04	4 43	3 34	0 00	0 01
29	4 14	5 00	3 47	0 00	29♎56
30	4 25	5 16	3 59	0 00	29 51
31	4 36	5 33	4 11	0 00	29 46
32	4 47	5 50	4 23	0 00	29 40
33	4 59	6 07	4 36	0 00	29 35
34	5 11	6 24	4 48	0 00	29 29
35	5 23	6 42	5 01	0 00	29 23
36	5 35	7 00	5 14	0 00	29 18
37	5 48	7 18	5 27	0 00	29 12
38	6 01	7 37	5 40	0 00	29 06
39	6 15	7 56	5 53	0 00	29 00
40	6 29	8 15	6 06	0 00	28 53
41	6 43	8 35	6 20	0 00	28 47
42	6 58	8 56	6 33	0 00	28 40
43	7 14	9 17	6 47	0 00	28 33
44	7 30	9 38	7 01	0 00	28 26
45	7 47	10 00	7 15	0 00	28 19
46	8 04	10 22	7 29	0 00	28 12
47	8 22	10 45	7 44	0 00	28 04
48	8 41	11 09	7 59	0 00	27 56
49	9 01	11 33	8 14	0 00	27 48
50	9 22	11 58	8 29	0 00	27 40
51	9 44	12 24	8 45	0 00	27 31
52	10 07	12 51	9 01	0 00	27 22
53	10 31	13 19	9 17	0 00	27 13
54	10 57	13 47	9 34	0 00	27 03
55	11 25	14 17	9 51	0 00	26 53
56	11 54	14 47	10 09	0 00	26 43
57	12 25	15 19	10 26	0 00	26 32
58	12 59	15 52	10 45	0 00	26 21
59	13 35	16 26	11 03	0 00	26 09
60	14♋14	17♌01	11♍23	0♎00	25♎57

4h 4m 0s — 61° 0' 0" — 3 ♊ 03

LAT.	11	12	ASC	2	3
0	0♋55	28♋52	28♌52	1♎05	3♏13
5	1 35	0♌03	29 56	1 04	2 50
10	2 15	1 13	0♍57	1 02	2 27
15	2 57	2 23	1 56	1 01	2 04
20	3 41	3 35	2 54	0 59	1 41
21	3 50	3 50	3 05	0 59	1 36
22	4 00	4 05	3 17	0 59	1 31
23	4 09	4 20	3 28	0 58	1 26
24	4 19	4 35	3 40	0 58	1 21
25	4 28	4 50	3 52	0 58	1 16
26	4 38	5 05	4 03	0 57	1 11
27	4 48	5 21	4 15	0 57	1 05
28	4 59	5 37	4 27	0 57	1 00
29	5 09	5 53	4 39	0 56	0 55
30	5 20	6 09	4 50	0 56	0 49
31	5 31	6 25	5 02	0 56	0 44
32	5 42	6 42	5 14	0 55	0 38
33	5 53	6 59	5 26	0 55	0 33
34	6 05	7 16	5 38	0 55	0 27
35	6 17	7 34	5 51	0 54	0 21
36	6 30	7 52	6 03	0 54	0 15
37	6 42	8 10	6 15	0 54	0 09
38	6 56	8 28	6 28	0 53	0 03
39	7 09	8 47	6 41	0 53	29♎56
40	7 23	9 06	6 54	0 53	29 50
41	7 37	9 26	7 07	0 52	29 43
42	7 52	9 46	7 20	0 52	29 36
43	8 08	10 06	7 33	0 52	29 29
44	8 24	10 27	7 47	0 51	29 22
45	8 41	10 49	8 00	0 51	29 15
46	8 58	11 11	8 14	0 50	29 07
47	9 16	11 34	8 28	0 50	28 59
48	9 35	11 57	8 43	0 50	28 51
49	9 55	12 21	8 57	0 49	28 43
50	10 15	12 46	9 12	0 49	28 34
51	10 37	13 11	9 27	0 48	28 25
52	11 00	13 38	9 43	0 48	28 16
53	11 24	14 05	9 59	0 47	28 07
54	11 50	14 33	10 15	0 47	27 57
55	12 17	15 02	10 31	0 46	27 46
56	12 46	15 32	10 48	0 46	27 36
57	13 17	16 03	11 05	0 45	27 25
58	13 50	16 35	11 23	0 45	27 13
59	14 26	17 09	11 41	0 44	27 01
60	15♋05	17♌44	12♍00	0♎44	26♎48

4h 8m 0s — 62° 0' 0" — 4 ♊ 00

LAT.	11	12	ASC	2	3
0	1♋50	29♋49	29♌54	2♎11	4♏16
5	2 30	0♌59	0♍56	2 08	3 52
10	3 10	2 09	1 56	2 04	3 28
15	3 52	3 19	2 53	2 01	3 05
20	4 36	4 30	3 49	1 58	2 40
21	4 45	4 45	4 00	1 58	2 35
22	4 55	4 59	4 12	1 57	2 30
23	5 04	5 14	4 23	1 56	2 25
24	5 14	5 29	4 34	1 56	2 20
25	5 23	5 44	4 45	1 55	2 15
26	5 33	5 59	4 56	1 55	2 10
27	5 43	6 15	5 08	1 54	2 04
28	5 53	6 30	5 19	1 53	1 59
29	6 04	6 46	5 31	1 53	1 53
30	6 15	7 02	5 42	1 52	1 48
31	6 25	7 18	5 54	1 51	1 42
32	6 37	7 35	6 05	1 51	1 36
33	6 48	7 51	6 17	1 50	1 31
34	7 00	8 08	6 28	1 49	1 25
35	7 12	8 26	6 40	1 49	1 19
36	7 24	8 43	6 52	1 48	1 12
37	7 37	9 01	7 04	1 47	1 06
38	7 50	9 19	7 16	1 47	1 00
39	8 03	9 38	7 29	1 46	0 53
40	8 17	9 57	7 41	1 45	0 47
41	8 32	10 16	7 54	1 45	0 40
42	8 46	10 36	8 06	1 44	0 33
43	9 02	10 56	8 19	1 43	0 25
44	9 18	11 17	8 32	1 42	0 18
45	9 34	11 38	8 46	1 41	0 10
46	9 52	12 00	8 59	1 41	0 03
47	10 10	12 22	9 13	1 40	29♎54
48	10 28	12 45	9 27	1 39	29 46
49	10 48	13 09	9 41	1 38	29 38
50	11 09	13 33	9 55	1 37	29 29
51	11 30	13 58	10 10	1 36	29 20
52	11 53	14 24	10 25	1 35	29 10
53	12 17	14 51	10 40	1 35	29 00
54	12 42	15 18	10 56	1 34	28 50
55	13 09	15 47	11 11	1 33	28 39
56	13 38	16 16	11 28	1 32	28 28
57	14 09	16 47	11 44	1 31	28 17
58	14 42	17 19	12 01	1 29	28 05
59	15 17	17 52	12 19	1 28	27 52
60	15♋56	18♌26	12♍37	1♎27	27♎39

4h 12m 0s — 63° 0' 0" — 4 ♊ 57

LAT.	11	12	ASC	2	3
0	2♋45	0♌47	0♍57	3♎16	5♏18
5	3 25	1 57	1 57	3 11	4 53
10	4 05	3 05	2 55	3 07	4 29
15	4 47	4 14	3 50	3 02	4 05
20	5 31	5 25	4 45	2 57	3 40
21	5 40	5 39	4 55	2 57	3 35
22	5 49	5 54	5 06	2 56	3 30
23	5 59	6 08	5 17	2 55	3 24
24	6 08	6 23	5 28	2 54	3 19
25	6 18	6 38	5 39	2 53	3 14
26	6 28	6 53	5 50	2 52	3 08
27	6 38	7 08	6 01	2 51	3 03
28	6 48	7 24	6 12	2 50	2 57
29	6 58	7 39	6 23	2 49	2 52
30	7 09	7 55	6 34	2 48	2 46
31	7 20	8 11	6 45	2 47	2 40
32	7 31	8 27	6 56	2 46	2 34
33	7 43	8 44	7 07	2 45	2 28
34	7 54	9 01	7 19	2 44	2 22
35	8 06	9 18	7 30	2 43	2 16
36	8 18	9 35	7 42	2 42	2 10
37	8 31	9 53	7 53	2 41	2 03
38	8 44	10 11	8 05	2 40	1 57
39	8 58	10 29	8 17	2 39	1 50
40	9 11	10 48	8 29	2 38	1 43
41	9 26	11 07	8 41	2 37	1 36
42	9 40	11 26	8 53	2 36	1 29
43	9 56	11 46	9 06	2 35	1 21
44	10 12	12 07	9 18	2 33	1 14
45	10 28	12 27	9 31	2 32	1 06
46	10 45	12 49	9 44	2 31	0 58
47	11 03	13 11	9 57	2 30	0 50
48	11 22	13 33	10 11	2 29	0 41
49	11 41	13 57	10 24	2 27	0 32
50	12 02	14 21	10 38	2 26	0 23
51	12 23	14 45	10 52	2 25	0 14
52	12 46	15 11	11 07	2 23	0 04
53	13 10	15 37	11 21	2 22	29♎54
54	13 35	16 04	11 36	2 20	29 43
55	14 02	16 32	11 52	2 19	29 32
56	14 30	17 01	12 07	2 17	29 21
57	15 00	17 31	12 23	2 16	29 09
58	15 33	18 02	12 40	2 14	28 56
59	16 08	18 34	12 57	2 12	28 44
60	16♋46	19♌08	13♍14	2♎11	28♎30

4h 16m 0s 5 ♊ 54 64° 0' 0"

LAT.	11	12	ASC	2	3
0	3♋40	1♌45	2♍00	4♎22	6♏19
5	4 20	2 54	2 58	4 15	5 55
10	5 00	4 02	3 54	4 09	5 30
15	5 42	5 10	4 47	4 03	5 05
20	6 26	6 20	5 40	3 57	4 39
21	6 35	6 34	5 50	3 55	4 34
22	6 44	6 48	6 01	3 54	4 29
23	6 54	7 03	6 11	3 53	4 23
24	7 03	7 17	6 22	3 52	4 18
25	7 13	7 32	6 32	3 50	4 13
26	7 22	7 47	6 43	3 49	4 07
27	7 32	8 02	6 53	3 48	4 01
28	7 43	8 17	7 04	3 47	3 56
29	7 53	8 33	7 15	3 45	3 50
30	8 04	8 48	7 25	3 44	3 44
31	8 15	9 04	7 36	3 43	3 38
32	8 26	9 20	7 47	3 42	3 32
33	8 37	9 36	7 58	3 40	3 26
34	8 49	9 53	8 09	3 39	3 20
35	9 01	10 10	8 20	3 38	3 13
36	9 13	10 27	8 31	3 36	3 07
37	9 25	10 44	8 42	3 35	3 00
38	9 38	11 02	8 53	3 33	2 53
39	9 52	11 20	9 05	3 32	2 47
40	10 05	11 38	9 16	3 31	2 39
41	10 20	11 57	9 28	3 29	2 32
42	10 34	12 16	9 40	3 28	2 25
43	10 50	12 36	9 52	3 26	2 17
44	11 05	12 56	10 04	3 24	2 09
45	11 22	13 17	10 16	3 23	2 01
46	11 39	13 38	10 29	3 21	1 53
47	11 57	13 59	10 42	3 20	1 44
48	12 15	14 22	10 54	3 18	1 36
49	12 35	14 44	11 08	3 16	1 27
50	12 55	15 08	11 21	3 15	1 17
51	13 16	15 32	11 35	3 13	1 08
52	13 39	15 57	11 48	3 11	0 57
53	14 02	16 23	12 03	3 09	0 47
54	14 27	16 50	12 17	3 07	0 36
55	14 54	17 17	12 32	3 05	0 25
56	15 22	17 45	12 47	3 03	0 13
57	15 52	18 15	13 02	3 01	0 01
58	16 24	18 46	13 18	2 59	29♎48
59	16 59	19 17	13 34	2 57	29 35
60	17♋36	19♌50	13♍51	2♎54	29♎21

4h 20m 0s 6 ♊ 50 65° 0' 0"

LAT.	11	12	ASC	2	3
0	4♋35	2♌43	3♍03	5♎27	7♏21
5	5 15	3 51	4 00	5 19	6 56
10	5 55	4 58	4 53	5 11	6 30
15	6 37	6 06	5 45	5 03	6 05
20	7 21	7 15	6 36	4 56	5 39
21	7 30	7 29	6 46	4 54	5 33
22	7 39	7 43	6 56	4 53	5 28
23	7 48	7 57	7 06	4 51	5 22
24	7 58	8 12	7 16	4 50	5 17
25	8 07	8 26	7 26	4 48	5 11
26	8 17	8 41	7 36	4 47	5 06
27	8 27	8 56	7 46	4 45	5 00
28	8 37	9 11	7 57	4 43	4 54
29	8 48	9 26	8 07	4 42	4 48
30	8 58	9 41	8 17	4 40	4 42
31	9 09	9 57	8 27	4 39	4 36
32	9 20	10 13	8 38	4 37	4 30
33	9 31	10 29	8 48	4 35	4 24
34	9 43	10 45	8 59	4 34	4 17
35	9 55	11 02	9 09	4 32	4 11
36	10 07	11 19	9 20	4 30	4 04
37	10 20	11 36	9 31	4 28	3 57
38	10 32	11 53	9 42	4 27	3 50
39	10 46	12 11	9 53	4 25	3 43
40	10 59	12 29	10 04	4 23	3 36
41	11 14	12 48	10 15	4 21	3 28
42	11 28	13 06	10 27	4 19	3 21
43	11 43	13 26	10 38	4 18	3 13
44	11 59	13 46	10 50	4 16	3 05
45	12 15	14 06	11 02	4 14	2 57
46	12 32	14 27	11 14	4 12	2 48
47	12 50	14 48	11 26	4 10	2 39
48	13 08	15 10	11 38	4 07	2 30
49	13 28	15 32	11 51	4 05	2 21
50	13 48	15 55	12 04	4 03	2 11
51	14 09	16 19	12 17	4 01	2 01
52	14 31	16 44	12 30	3 59	1 51
53	14 55	17 09	12 44	3 56	1 40
54	15 19	17 35	12 58	3 54	1 29
55	15 46	18 02	13 12	3 51	1 18
56	16 14	18 30	13 26	3 49	1 06
57	16 43	18 59	13 41	3 46	0 53
58	17 15	19 29	13 57	3 44	0 40
59	17 49	20 00	14 12	3 41	0 26
60	18♋26	20♌33	14♍28	3♎38	0♏12

4h 24m 0s 7 ♊ 47 66° 0' 0"

LAT.	11	12	ASC	2	3
0	5♋30	3♌41	4♍07	6♎32	8♏23
5	6 10	4 49	5 01	6 22	7 57
10	6 50	5 55	5 53	6 13	7 31
15	7 32	7 02	6 42	6 04	7 05
20	8 15	8 10	7 31	5 55	6 38
21	8 25	8 24	7 41	5 53	6 32
22	8 34	8 38	7 51	5 51	6 27
23	8 43	8 52	8 00	5 49	6 21
24	8 52	9 06	8 10	5 48	6 16
25	9 02	9 21	8 20	5 46	6 10
26	9 12	9 35	8 30	5 44	6 04
27	9 22	9 50	8 39	5 42	5 58
28	9 32	10 05	8 49	5 40	5 52
29	9 42	10 20	8 59	5 38	5 46
30	9 53	10 35	9 09	5 36	5 40
31	10 03	10 50	9 19	5 34	5 34
32	10 14	11 06	9 29	5 32	5 27
33	10 26	11 21	9 39	5 30	5 21
34	10 37	11 38	9 49	5 28	5 14
35	10 49	11 54	9 59	5 26	5 08
36	11 01	12 10	10 10	5 24	5 01
37	11 14	12 27	10 20	5 22	4 54
38	11 27	12 44	10 30	5 20	4 47
39	11 40	13 02	10 41	5 18	4 39
40	11 53	13 20	10 52	5 16	4 32
41	12 07	13 38	11 02	5 14	4 24
42	12 22	13 57	11 13	5 11	4 17
43	12 37	14 16	11 24	5 09	4 09
44	12 53	14 35	11 36	5 07	4 00
45	13 09	14 55	11 47	5 04	3 52
46	13 26	15 16	11 59	5 02	3 43
47	13 43	15 36	12 10	4 59	3 34
48	14 02	15 58	12 22	4 57	3 25
49	14 21	16 20	12 34	4 54	3 15
50	14 41	16 43	12 47	4 52	3 05
51	15 02	17 06	12 59	4 49	2 55
52	15 24	17 30	13 12	4 46	2 45
53	15 47	17 55	13 25	4 44	2 34
54	16 11	18 21	13 39	4 41	2 22
55	16 37	18 47	13 52	4 38	2 10
56	17 05	19 15	14 06	4 35	1 58
57	17 35	19 43	14 20	4 31	1 45
58	18 06	20 13	14 35	4 28	1 31
59	18 40	20 43	14 50	4 25	1 17
60	19♋16	21♌15	15♍05	4♎21	1♏02

4h 28m 0s 8 ♊ 43 67° 0' 0"

LAT.	11	12	ASC	2	3
0	6♋26	4♌39	5♍10	7♎37	9♏24
5	7 05	5 46	6 02	7 26	8 57
10	7 45	6 52	6 52	7 15	8 31
15	8 27	7 58	7 40	7 05	8 04
20	9 10	9 05	8 27	6 54	7 37
21	9 19	9 19	8 36	6 52	7 31
22	9 28	9 33	8 46	6 50	7 26
23	9 38	9 47	8 55	6 48	7 20
24	9 47	10 01	9 04	6 45	7 14
25	9 57	10 15	9 14	6 43	7 08
26	10 06	10 29	9 23	6 41	7 02
27	10 16	10 44	9 32	6 39	6 56
28	10 26	10 58	9 42	6 37	6 50
29	10 37	11 13	9 51	6 34	6 44
30	10 47	11 28	10 01	6 32	6 38
31	10 58	11 43	10 10	6 30	6 31
32	11 09	11 58	10 20	6 28	6 25
33	11 20	12 14	10 30	6 25	6 18
34	11 32	12 30	10 39	6 23	6 12
35	11 43	12 46	10 49	6 21	6 05
36	11 55	13 02	10 59	6 18	5 58
37	12 08	13 19	11 09	6 16	5 51
38	12 21	13 36	11 19	6 13	5 43
39	12 34	13 53	11 29	6 11	5 36
40	12 47	14 11	11 39	6 08	5 28
41	13 01	14 29	11 50	6 06	5 20
42	13 16	14 47	12 00	6 03	5 12
43	13 31	15 06	12 11	6 00	5 04
44	13 46	15 25	12 22	5 58	4 56
45	14 02	15 44	12 32	5 55	4 47
46	14 19	16 04	12 44	5 52	4 38
47	14 36	16 25	12 55	5 49	4 29
48	14 55	16 46	13 06	5 46	4 19
49	15 14	17 08	13 18	5 43	4 10
50	15 33	17 30	13 30	5 40	3 59
51	15 54	17 53	13 42	5 37	3 49
52	16 16	18 17	13 54	5 34	3 38
53	16 39	18 41	14 07	5 31	3 27
54	17 03	19 06	14 19	5 27	3 15
55	17 29	19 32	14 32	5 24	3 03
56	17 57	19 59	14 46	5 20	2 50
57	18 26	20 27	14 59	5 17	2 37
58	18 57	20 56	15 13	5 13	2 23
59	19 30	21 26	15 28	5 09	2 08
60	20♋06	21♌57	15♍42	5♎05	1♏53

4h 32m 0s 9 ♊ 40 68° 0' 0"

LAT.	11	12	ASC	2	3
0	7♋21	5♌38	6♍14	8♎43	10♏25
5	8 00	6 44	7 04	8 30	9 58
10	8 40	7 49	7 52	8 17	9 31
15	9 22	8 54	8 38	8 05	9 04
20	10 05	10 01	9 23	7 53	8 36
21	10 14	10 14	9 32	7 51	8 30
22	10 23	10 28	9 41	7 48	8 24
23	10 32	10 42	9 50	7 46	8 18
24	10 42	10 55	9 58	7 43	8 13
25	10 51	11 09	10 07	7 41	8 07
26	11 01	11 23	10 16	7 38	8 00
27	11 11	11 38	10 25	7 36	7 54
28	11 21	11 52	10 34	7 33	7 48
29	11 31	12 07	10 43	7 31	7 42
30	11 42	12 21	10 53	7 28	7 35
31	11 52	12 36	11 02	7 26	7 29
32	12 03	12 51	11 11	7 23	7 22
33	12 14	13 07	11 20	7 20	7 15
34	12 26	13 22	11 29	7 18	7 09
35	12 37	13 38	11 39	7 15	7 02
36	12 49	13 54	11 48	7 12	6 54
37	13 02	14 11	11 58	7 09	6 47
38	13 15	14 27	12 07	7 07	6 40
39	13 28	14 44	12 17	7 04	6 32
40	13 41	15 01	12 27	7 01	6 24
41	13 55	15 19	12 37	6 58	6 16
42	14 09	15 37	12 47	6 55	6 08
43	14 24	15 56	12 57	6 52	6 00
44	14 40	16 14	13 07	6 49	5 51
45	14 56	16 34	13 18	6 46	5 42
46	15 12	16 53	13 29	6 42	5 33
47	15 30	17 14	13 39	6 39	5 24
48	15 48	17 34	13 50	6 36	5 14
49	16 06	17 56	14 01	6 32	5 04
50	16 26	18 18	14 13	6 29	4 53
51	16 47	18 40	14 24	6 25	4 43
52	17 08	19 03	14 36	6 22	4 31
53	17 31	19 27	14 48	6 18	4 20
54	17 55	19 52	15 00	6 14	4 08
55	18 21	20 18	15 13	6 10	3 55
56	18 48	20 44	15 25	6 06	3 42
57	19 17	21 11	15 38	6 02	3 29
58	19 47	21 40	15 52	5 58	3 14
59	20 20	22 09	16 06	5 53	2 59
60	20♋56	22♌40	16♍20	5♎49	2♏44

4h 36m 0s 10 ♊ 36 69° 0' 0"

LAT.	11	12	ASC	2	3
0	8♋16	6♌37	7♍18	9♎48	11♏26
5	8 56	7 42	8 06	9 33	10 59
10	9 36	8 46	8 51	9 19	10 31
15	10 17	9 51	9 35	9 06	10 03
20	11 00	10 56	10 18	8 52	9 35
21	11 09	11 09	10 27	8 49	9 29
22	11 18	11 23	10 36	8 47	9 23
23	11 27	11 36	10 44	8 44	9 17
24	11 36	11 50	10 53	8 41	9 11
25	11 46	12 04	11 01	8 38	9 05
26	11 56	12 18	11 10	8 35	8 59
27	12 05	12 32	11 18	8 33	8 52
28	12 15	12 46	11 27	8 30	8 46
29	12 26	13 00	11 36	8 27	8 39
30	12 36	13 15	11 44	8 24	8 33
31	12 47	13 29	11 53	8 21	8 26
32	12 57	13 44	12 02	8 18	8 19
33	13 09	13 59	12 11	8 15	8 13
34	13 20	14 15	12 20	8 12	8 06
35	13 32	14 30	12 29	8 09	7 58
36	13 44	14 46	12 38	8 06	7 51
37	13 56	15 02	12 47	8 03	7 44
38	14 09	15 19	12 56	8 00	7 36
39	14 22	15 35	13 05	7 57	7 28
40	14 35	15 52	13 15	7 53	7 20
41	14 49	16 10	13 24	7 50	7 12
42	15 03	16 27	13 34	7 47	7 04
43	15 18	16 45	13 44	7 43	6 55
44	15 33	17 04	13 53	7 40	6 46
45	15 49	17 23	14 03	7 36	6 37
46	16 06	17 42	14 13	7 33	6 28
47	16 23	18 02	14 24	7 29	6 18
48	16 41	18 23	14 34	7 25	6 08
49	16 59	18 44	14 45	7 21	5 58
50	17 19	19 05	14 56	7 18	5 47
51	17 39	19 27	15 07	7 14	5 36
52	18 01	19 50	15 18	7 09	5 25
53	18 23	20 13	15 29	7 05	5 13
54	18 47	20 38	15 41	7 01	5 01
55	19 12	21 03	15 53	6 56	4 48
56	19 39	21 29	16 05	6 52	4 34
57	20 08	21 55	16 18	6 47	4 20
58	20 38	22 23	16 30	6 42	4 06
59	21 11	22 52	16 43	6 37	3 50
60	21♋46	23♌22	16♍57	6♎32	3♏34

4h 40m 0s 11 ♊ 32 70° 0' 0"

LAT.	11	12	ASC	2	3
0	9♋11	7♌35	8♍22	10♎53	12♏27
5	9 51	8 40	9 08	10 37	11 59
10	10 31	9 43	9 51	10 21	11 31
15	11 12	10 47	10 33	10 06	11 02
20	11 55	11 52	11 14	9 51	10 33
21	12 04	12 05	11 23	9 48	10 27
22	12 13	12 18	11 31	9 45	10 21
23	12 22	12 31	11 39	9 42	10 15
24	12 31	12 45	11 47	9 39	10 09
25	12 41	12 58	11 55	9 36	10 03
26	12 50	13 12	12 03	9 33	9 56
27	13 00	13 26	12 12	9 29	9 50
28	13 10	13 40	12 20	9 26	9 44
29	13 20	13 54	12 28	9 23	9 37
30	13 30	14 08	12 36	9 20	9 30
31	13 41	14 23	12 45	9 17	9 23
32	13 52	14 37	12 53	9 13	9 17
33	14 03	14 52	13 02	9 10	9 10
34	14 14	15 07	13 10	9 07	9 02
35	14 26	15 23	13 19	9 03	8 55
36	14 38	15 38	13 27	9 00	8 48
37	14 50	15 54	13 36	8 57	8 40
38	15 02	16 10	13 45	8 53	8 32
39	15 15	16 27	13 53	8 50	8 24
40	15 29	16 43	14 02	8 46	8 16
41	15 42	17 00	14 11	8 42	8 08
42	15 57	17 18	14 21	8 39	7 59
43	16 11	17 35	14 30	8 35	7 50
44	16 27	17 54	14 39	8 31	7 41
45	16 42	18 12	14 49	8 27	7 32
46	16 59	18 31	14 58	8 23	7 22
47	17 16	18 51	15 08	8 19	7 13
48	17 33	19 11	15 18	8 15	7 02
49	17 52	19 31	15 28	8 11	6 52
50	18 11	19 52	15 39	8 06	6 41
51	18 32	20 14	15 49	8 02	6 30
52	18 53	20 37	16 00	7 57	6 18
53	19 15	21 00	16 11	7 52	6 06
54	19 39	21 23	16 22	7 48	5 53
55	20 04	21 48	16 33	7 43	5 40
56	20 30	22 13	16 45	7 38	5 26
57	20 59	22 40	16 57	7 32	5 12
58	21 29	23 07	17 09	7 27	4 57
59	22 01	23 35	17 21	7 21	4 41
60	22♋35	24♌04	17♍34	7♎16	4♏25

4h 44m 0s 12 ♊ 28 71° 0' 0"

LAT.	11	12	ASC	2	3
0	10♋07	8♌34	9♍26	11♎58	13♏27
5	10 46	9 38	10 10	11 40	12 59
10	11 26	10 41	10 51	11 23	12 30
15	12 07	11 44	11 31	11 07	12 02
20	12 50	12 47	12 10	10 50	11 32
21	12 58	13 00	12 18	10 47	11 26
22	13 07	13 13	12 26	10 43	11 20
23	13 17	13 26	12 34	10 40	11 13
24	13 26	13 40	12 41	10 37	11 07
25	13 35	13 53	12 49	10 33	11 01
26	13 45	14 06	12 57	10 30	10 54
27	13 55	14 20	13 05	10 26	10 48
28	14 04	14 34	13 13	10 23	10 41
29	14 15	14 48	13 20	10 19	10 34
30	14 25	15 02	13 28	10 16	10 28
31	14 35	15 16	13 36	10 12	10 21
32	14 46	15 30	13 44	10 09	10 14
33	14 57	15 45	13 52	10 05	10 06
34	15 08	16 00	14 00	10 01	9 59
35	15 20	16 15	14 08	9 58	9 52
36	15 32	16 30	14 17	9 54	9 44
37	15 44	16 46	14 25	9 50	9 36
38	15 56	17 02	14 33	9 46	9 28
39	16 09	17 18	14 42	9 42	9 20
40	16 22	17 34	14 50	9 38	9 12
41	16 36	17 51	14 59	9 34	9 03
42	16 50	18 08	15 07	9 30	8 55
43	17 05	18 25	15 16	9 26	8 46
44	17 20	18 43	15 25	9 22	8 36
45	17 36	19 02	15 34	9 18	8 27
46	17 52	19 20	15 43	9 13	8 17
47	18 09	19 39	15 53	9 09	8 07
48	18 26	19 59	16 02	9 04	7 57
49	18 45	20 19	16 12	8 59	7 46
50	19 04	20 40	16 22	8 55	7 35
51	19 24	21 01	16 32	8 50	7 23
52	19 45	21 23	16 42	8 45	7 11
53	20 07	21 46	16 52	8 40	6 59
54	20 31	22 09	17 03	8 34	6 46
55	20 55	22 33	17 13	8 29	6 32
56	21 22	22 58	17 24	8 23	6 18
57	21 49	23 24	17 36	8 17	6 03
58	22 19	23 50	17 47	8 12	5 48
59	22 51	24 18	17 59	8 05	5 32
60	23♋25	24♌47	18♍11	7♎59	5♏15

4h 48m 0s — 72° 0' 0" — 13 ♊ 24

LAT.	11	12	ASC	2	3
0	11♋02	9♌34	10♍30	13♎03	14♏28
5	11 41	10 36	11 12	12 44	13 59
10	12 21	11 38	11 51	12 25	13 30
15	13 02	12 40	12 29	12 07	13 00
20	13 44	13 43	13 06	11 49	12 30
21	13 53	13 56	13 14	11 45	12 24
22	14 02	14 08	13 21	11 42	12 18
23	14 11	14 21	13 28	11 38	12 11
24	14 21	14 34	13 36	11 34	12 05
25	14 30	14 48	13 43	11 31	11 59
26	14 39	15 01	13 51	11 27	11 52
27	14 49	15 14	13 58	11 23	11 45
28	14 59	15 28	14 05	11 19	11 39
29	15 09	15 41	14 13	11 16	11 32
30	15 19	15 55	14 20	11 12	11 25
31	15 30	16 09	14 28	11 08	11 18
32	15 40	16 23	14 35	11 04	11 10
33	15 51	16 38	14 43	11 00	11 03
34	16 03	16 52	14 51	10 56	10 56
35	16 14	17 07	14 58	10 52	10 48
36	16 26	17 22	15 06	10 48	10 40
37	16 38	17 38	15 14	10 44	10 32
38	16 50	17 53	15 22	10 40	10 24
39	17 03	18 09	15 30	10 35	10 16
40	17 16	18 25	15 38	10 31	10 08
41	17 30	18 42	15 46	10 27	9 59
42	17 44	18 58	15 54	10 22	9 50
43	17 58	19 16	16 03	10 18	9 41
44	18 13	19 33	16 11	10 13	9 31
45	18 29	19 51	16 20	10 08	9 22
46	18 45	20 09	16 28	10 03	9 12
47	19 02	20 28	16 37	9 59	9 01
48	19 19	20 47	16 46	9 54	8 51
49	19 37	21 07	16 55	9 48	8 40
50	19 56	21 27	17 05	9 43	8 28
51	20 16	21 48	17 14	9 38	8 16
52	20 37	22 10	17 24	9 32	8 04
53	20 59	22 32	17 33	9 27	7 51
54	21 22	22 55	17 43	9 21	7 38
55	21 47	23 18	17 54	9 15	7 24
56	22 13	23 43	18 04	9 09	7 10
57	22 40	24 08	18 15	9 03	6 55
58	23 09	24 34	18 26	8 56	6 39
59	23 41	25 01	18 37	8 49	6 23
60	24♋14	25♌29	18♍48	8♎43	6♏05

4h 52m 0s — 73° 0' 0" — 14 ♊ 20

LAT.	11	12	ASC	2	3
0	11♋58	10♌33	11♍34	14♎07	15♏28
5	12 37	11 35	12 14	13 47	14 59
10	13 16	12 36	12 51	13 27	14 29
15	13 57	13 37	13 27	13 07	13 59
20	14 39	14 39	14 02	12 48	13 28
21	14 48	14 51	14 09	12 44	13 22
22	14 57	15 04	14 16	12 40	13 16
23	15 06	15 17	14 23	12 36	13 09
24	15 15	15 29	14 30	12 32	13 03
25	15 25	15 42	14 37	12 28	12 56
26	15 34	15 55	14 44	12 24	12 50
27	15 44	16 09	14 51	12 20	12 43
28	15 54	16 22	14 58	12 16	12 36
29	16 04	16 35	15 05	12 12	12 29
30	16 14	16 49	15 12	12 07	12 22
31	16 24	17 03	15 19	12 03	12 15
32	16 35	17 17	15 27	11 59	12 07
33	16 46	17 31	15 34	11 55	12 00
34	16 57	17 45	15 41	11 50	11 52
35	17 08	18 00	15 48	11 46	11 44
36	17 20	18 14	15 56	11 42	11 37
37	17 32	18 29	16 03	11 37	11 28
38	17 44	18 45	16 11	11 33	11 20
39	17 57	19 00	16 18	11 28	11 12
40	18 10	19 16	16 26	11 23	11 03
41	18 23	19 32	16 33	11 19	10 54
42	18 37	19 49	16 41	11 14	10 45
43	18 52	20 06	16 49	11 09	10 36
44	19 07	20 23	16 57	11 04	10 26
45	19 22	20 40	17 05	10 59	10 16
46	19 38	20 58	17 13	10 54	10 06
47	19 55	21 17	17 22	10 48	9 55
48	20 12	21 36	17 30	10 43	9 45
49	20 30	21 55	17 39	10 37	9 33
50	20 49	22 15	17 48	10 32	9 22
51	21 09	22 35	17 57	10 26	9 10
52	21 29	22 56	18 06	10 20	8 57
53	21 51	23 18	18 15	10 14	8 44
54	22 14	23 41	18 24	10 08	8 31
55	22 38	24 04	18 34	10 01	8 17
56	23 04	24 27	18 44	9 55	8 02
57	23 31	24 52	18 54	9 48	7 46
58	24 00	25 18	19 04	9 41	7 30
59	24 30	25 44	19 15	9 34	7 13
60	25♋03	26♌12	19♍26	9♎26	6♏56

4h 56m 0s — 74° 0' 0" — 15 ♊ 16

LAT.	11	12	ASC	2	3
0	12♋53	11♌32	12♍39	15♎12	16♏28
5	13 32	12 34	13 16	14 50	15 58
10	14 11	13 34	13 51	14 29	15 28
15	14 52	14 34	14 25	14 08	14 58
20	15 34	15 35	14 58	13 47	14 27
21	15 43	15 47	15 05	13 42	14 20
22	15 52	15 59	15 12	13 38	14 14
23	16 01	16 12	15 18	13 34	14 07
24	16 10	16 24	15 25	13 30	14 00
25	16 19	16 37	15 31	13 25	13 54
26	16 29	16 50	15 38	13 21	13 47
27	16 38	17 03	15 44	13 17	13 40
28	16 48	17 16	15 51	13 12	13 33
29	16 58	17 29	15 58	13 08	13 26
30	17 08	17 43	16 04	13 03	13 19
31	17 19	17 56	16 11	12 59	13 11
32	17 29	18 10	16 18	12 54	13 04
33	17 40	18 24	16 25	12 50	12 56
34	17 51	18 38	16 31	12 45	12 49
35	18 02	18 52	16 38	12 40	12 41
36	18 14	19 07	16 45	12 36	12 33
37	18 26	19 21	16 52	12 31	12 24
38	18 38	19 36	16 59	12 26	12 16
39	18 51	19 52	17 06	12 21	12 07
40	19 04	20 07	17 14	12 16	11 59
41	19 17	20 23	17 21	12 11	11 50
42	19 31	20 39	17 28	12 06	11 40
43	19 45	20 56	17 36	12 00	11 31
44	20 00	21 13	17 43	11 55	11 21
45	20 15	21 30	17 51	11 49	11 11
46	20 31	21 47	17 58	11 44	11 00
47	20 48	22 05	18 06	11 38	10 50
48	21 05	22 24	18 14	11 32	10 39
49	21 23	22 43	18 22	11 26	10 27
50	21 41	23 03	18 31	11 20	10 15
51	22 01	23 23	18 39	11 14	10 03
52	22 21	23 43	18 48	11 08	9 50
53	22 43	24 04	18 56	11 01	9 37
54	23 05	24 26	19 05	10 54	9 23
55	23 29	24 49	19 14	10 47	9 09
56	23 55	25 12	19 24	10 40	8 54
57	24 21	25 36	19 33	10 33	8 38
58	24 50	26 01	19 43	10 25	8 21
59	25 20	26 27	19 53	10 18	8 04
60	25♋53	26♌54	20♍03	10♎09	7♏46

5h 0m 0s — 75° 0' 0" — 16 ♊ 11

LAT.	11	12	ASC	2	3
0	13♋49	12♌32	13♍43	16♎17	17♏28
5	14 27	13 32	14 18	15 53	16 58
10	15 07	14 32	14 51	15 30	16 27
15	15 47	15 31	15 23	15 08	15 56
20	16 29	16 31	15 54	14 45	15 25
21	16 38	16 43	16 01	14 41	15 18
22	16 47	16 55	16 07	14 36	15 11
23	16 56	17 07	16 13	14 32	15 05
24	17 05	17 20	16 19	14 27	14 58
25	17 14	17 32	16 25	14 22	14 51
26	17 23	17 45	16 32	14 18	14 44
27	17 33	17 57	16 38	14 13	14 37
28	17 43	18 10	16 44	14 08	14 30
29	17 53	18 23	16 50	14 04	14 23
30	18 03	18 36	16 57	13 59	14 16
31	18 13	18 50	17 03	13 54	14 08
32	18 23	19 03	17 09	13 49	14 01
33	18 34	19 17	17 15	13 44	13 53
34	18 45	19 31	17 22	13 39	13 45
35	18 56	19 45	17 28	13 34	13 37
36	19 08	19 59	17 35	13 29	13 29
37	19 20	20 13	17 41	13 24	13 20
38	19 32	20 28	17 48	13 19	13 12
39	19 44	20 43	17 55	13 14	13 03
40	19 57	20 58	18 01	13 08	12 54
41	20 11	21 14	18 08	13 03	12 45
42	20 24	21 30	18 15	12 57	12 35
43	20 38	21 46	18 22	12 52	12 26
44	20 53	22 02	18 29	12 46	12 16
45	21 08	22 19	18 36	12 40	12 05
46	21 24	22 37	18 43	12 34	11 55
47	21 40	22 54	18 51	12 28	11 44
48	21 57	23 12	18 58	12 22	11 32
49	22 15	23 31	19 06	12 15	11 21
50	22 34	23 50	19 14	12 09	11 09
51	22 53	24 10	19 22	12 02	10 56
52	23 13	24 30	19 30	11 55	10 43
53	23 35	24 51	19 38	11 48	10 29
54	23 57	25 12	19 46	11 41	10 15
55	24 21	25 34	19 55	11 34	10 01
56	24 45	25 57	20 03	11 26	9 45
57	25 12	26 21	20 12	11 18	9 29
58	25 40	26 45	20 21	11 10	9 12
59	26 10	27 10	20 31	11 02	8 55
60	26♋42	27♌37	20♍40	10♎53	8♏36

5h 4m 0s — 76° 0' 0" — 17 ♊ 07

LAT.	11	12	ASC	2	3
0	14♋44	13♌32	14♍48	17♎21	18♏28
5	15 23	14 31	15 21	16 56	17 57
10	16 02	15 30	15 52	16 32	17 26
15	16 42	16 28	16 21	16 08	16 55
20	17 24	17 27	16 51	15 44	16 22
21	17 33	17 39	16 56	15 39	16 16
22	17 42	17 51	17 02	15 34	16 09
23	17 51	18 03	17 08	15 29	16 02
24	18 00	18 15	17 14	15 25	15 55
25	18 09	18 27	17 20	15 20	15 48
26	18 18	18 39	17 25	15 15	15 41
27	18 28	18 52	17 31	15 10	15 34
28	18 37	19 05	17 37	15 05	15 27
29	18 47	19 17	17 43	15 00	15 20
30	18 57	19 30	17 49	14 55	15 12
31	19 07	19 43	17 54	14 50	15 05
32	19 18	19 56	18 00	14 44	14 57
33	19 28	20 10	18 06	14 39	14 49
34	19 39	20 23	18 12	14 34	14 41
35	19 51	20 37	18 18	14 29	14 33
36	20 02	20 51	18 24	14 23	14 25
37	20 14	21 05	18 31	14 18	14 16
38	20 26	21 20	18 37	14 12	14 07
39	20 38	21 34	18 43	14 06	13 58
40	20 51	21 49	18 49	14 01	13 49
41	21 04	22 05	18 56	13 55	13 40
42	21 18	22 20	19 02	13 49	13 30
43	21 32	22 36	19 08	13 43	13 20
44	21 46	22 52	19 15	13 37	13 10
45	22 01	23 09	19 22	13 31	13 00
46	22 17	23 26	19 29	13 24	12 49
47	22 33	23 43	19 35	13 18	12 38
48	22 50	24 01	19 42	13 11	12 26
49	23 08	24 19	19 49	13 04	12 14
50	23 26	24 38	19 57	12 57	12 02
51	23 45	24 57	20 04	12 50	11 49
52	24 05	25 17	20 12	12 43	11 36
53	24 26	25 37	20 19	12 35	11 22
54	24 48	25 58	20 27	12 28	11 07
55	25 12	26 20	20 35	12 20	10 52
56	25 36	26 42	20 43	12 12	10 37
57	26 02	27 05	20 51	12 03	10 20
58	26 30	27 29	21 00	11 54	10 03
59	27 00	27 54	21 09	11 46	9 45
60	27♋31	28♌19	21♍17	11♎36	9♏26

5h 8m 0s — 77° 0' 0" — 18 ♊ 02

LAT.	11	12	ASC	2	3
0	15♋40	14♌32	15♍53	18♎26	19♏27
5	16 19	15 30	16 23	17 59	18 56
10	16 58	16 28	16 52	17 33	18 25
15	17 38	17 25	17 20	17 08	17 53
20	18 19	18 23	17 47	16 43	17 20
21	18 28	18 35	17 52	16 37	17 13
22	18 37	18 46	17 58	16 32	17 07
23	18 46	18 58	18 03	16 27	17 00
24	18 55	19 10	18 08	16 22	16 53
25	19 04	19 22	18 14	16 17	16 46
26	19 13	19 34	18 19	16 12	16 39
27	19 22	19 47	18 24	16 06	16 31
28	19 32	19 59	18 30	16 01	16 24
29	19 42	20 11	18 35	15 56	16 16
30	19 52	20 24	18 41	15 50	16 09
31	20 02	20 37	18 46	15 45	16 01
32	20 12	20 50	18 52	15 39	15 53
33	20 23	21 03	18 57	15 34	15 45
34	20 34	21 16	19 03	15 28	15 37
35	20 45	21 30	19 08	15 23	15 29
36	20 56	21 43	19 14	15 17	15 20
37	21 08	21 57	19 20	15 11	15 12
38	21 20	22 12	19 25	15 05	15 03
39	21 32	22 26	19 31	14 59	14 54
40	21 45	22 41	19 37	14 53	14 44
41	21 58	22 55	19 43	14 47	14 35
42	22 11	23 11	19 49	14 41	14 25
43	22 25	23 26	19 55	14 34	14 15
44	22 40	23 42	20 01	14 28	14 05
45	22 55	23 58	20 07	14 21	13 54
46	23 10	24 15	20 14	14 14	13 43
47	23 26	24 32	20 20	14 07	13 32
48	23 43	24 49	20 26	14 00	13 20
49	24 00	25 07	20 33	13 53	13 08
50	24 18	25 25	20 40	13 46	12 55
51	24 37	25 44	20 47	13 38	12 42
52	24 57	26 03	20 54	13 30	12 28
53	25 18	26 23	21 01	13 22	12 14
54	25 40	26 44	21 08	13 14	12 00
55	26 03	27 05	21 15	13 06	11 44
56	26 27	27 27	21 23	12 57	11 28
57	26 53	27 49	21 30	12 48	11 11
58	27 20	28 13	21 38	12 39	10 54
59	27 49	28 37	21 46	12 30	10 35
60	28♋21	29♌02	21♍55	12♎20	10♏16

5h 12m 0s — 78° 0' 0" — 18 ♊ 58

LAT.	11	12	ASC	2	3
0	16♋36	15♌32	16♍57	19♎30	20♏26
5	17 14	16 30	17 26	19 02	19 55
10	17 53	17 26	17 52	18 35	19 23
15	18 33	18 22	18 18	18 08	18 51
20	19 14	19 19	18 43	17 41	18 18
21	19 23	19 31	18 48	17 36	18 11
22	19 32	19 42	18 53	17 30	18 04
23	19 40	19 54	18 58	17 25	17 57
24	19 49	20 06	19 03	17 19	17 50
25	19 58	20 17	19 08	17 14	17 43
26	20 08	20 29	19 13	17 08	17 35
27	20 17	20 41	19 18	17 03	17 28
28	20 27	20 53	19 23	16 57	17 21
29	20 36	21 06	19 28	16 52	17 13
30	20 46	21 18	19 33	16 46	17 05
31	20 56	21 31	19 38	16 40	16 58
32	21 07	21 43	19 43	16 34	16 50
33	21 17	21 56	19 48	16 29	16 41
34	21 28	22 09	19 53	16 23	16 33
35	21 39	22 22	19 58	16 17	16 25
36	21 50	22 36	20 04	16 11	16 16
37	22 02	22 49	20 09	16 04	16 07
38	22 14	23 03	20 14	15 58	15 58
39	22 26	23 17	20 20	15 52	15 49
40	22 38	23 32	20 25	15 45	15 40
41	22 51	23 46	20 30	15 39	15 30
42	23 05	24 01	20 36	15 32	15 20
43	23 19	24 16	20 41	15 25	15 10
44	23 33	24 32	20 47	15 18	14 59
45	23 48	24 48	20 53	15 11	14 48
46	24 03	25 04	20 59	15 04	14 37
47	24 19	25 21	21 05	14 57	14 25
48	24 35	25 38	21 11	14 50	14 13
49	24 53	25 55	21 17	14 42	14 01
50	25 11	26 13	21 23	14 34	13 48
51	25 29	26 31	21 29	14 26	13 35
52	25 49	26 50	21 36	14 18	13 21
53	26 10	27 10	21 42	14 09	13 07
54	26 31	27 30	21 49	14 01	12 52
55	26 54	27 50	21 56	13 52	12 36
56	27 18	28 12	22 03	13 43	12 20
57	27 43	28 34	22 10	13 33	12 03
58	28 10	28 56	22 17	13 24	11 45
59	28 39	29 20	22 24	13 13	11 26
60	29♋10	29♌44	22♍32	13♎03	11♏06

5h 16m 0s — 79° 0' 0" — 19 ♊ 53

LAT.	11	12	ASC	2	3
0	17♋32	16♌33	18♍02	20♎34	21♏26
5	18 10	17 29	18 28	20 05	20 54
10	18 49	18 25	18 53	19 36	20 21
15	19 28	19 20	19 16	19 08	19 49
20	20 10	20 15	19 39	18 40	19 15
21	20 18	20 27	19 44	18 34	19 08
22	20 27	20 38	19 48	18 28	19 01
23	20 35	20 49	19 53	18 23	18 54
24	20 44	21 01	19 58	18 17	18 47
25	20 53	21 13	20 02	18 11	18 40
26	21 03	21 24	20 07	18 05	18 32
27	21 12	21 36	20 11	17 59	18 25
28	21 21	21 48	20 16	17 53	18 17
29	21 31	22 00	20 20	17 47	18 10
30	21 41	22 12	20 25	17 41	18 02
31	21 51	22 24	20 30	17 35	17 54
32	22 01	22 37	20 34	17 29	17 46
33	22 11	22 49	20 39	17 23	17 38
34	22 22	23 02	20 44	17 17	17 29
35	22 33	23 15	20 49	17 11	17 21
36	22 44	23 28	20 53	17 04	17 12
37	22 56	23 42	20 58	16 58	17 03
38	23 08	23 55	21 03	16 51	16 54
39	23 20	24 09	21 08	16 44	16 44
40	23 32	24 23	21 13	16 38	16 35
41	23 45	24 37	21 18	16 31	16 25
42	23 58	24 52	21 23	16 24	16 15
43	24 12	25 07	21 28	16 17	16 04
44	24 26	25 22	21 33	16 09	15 53
45	24 41	25 37	21 38	16 02	15 42
46	24 56	25 53	21 44	15 54	15 31
47	25 12	26 09	21 49	15 47	15 19
48	25 28	26 26	21 55	15 39	15 07
49	25 45	26 43	22 00	15 31	14 54
50	26 03	27 01	22 06	15 22	14 41
51	26 21	27 19	22 12	15 14	14 28
52	26 41	27 37	22 18	15 05	14 14
53	27 01	27 56	22 24	14 56	13 59
54	27 23	28 16	22 30	14 47	13 44
55	27 45	28 36	22 36	14 38	13 28
56	28 09	28 56	22 42	14 28	13 11
57	28 34	29 18	22 49	14 18	12 54
58	29 00	29 40	22 55	14 08	12 35
59	29 29	0♍03	23 02	13 57	12 16
60	29♋59	0♍27	23♍09	13♎46	11♏56

5h 20m 0s — 80° 0' 0" — 20 ♊ 49

LAT.	11	12	ASC	2	3
0	18♋28	17♌33	19♍07	21♎38	22♏25
5	19 06	18 29	19 31	21 07	21 52
10	19 44	19 23	19 53	20 37	21 20
15	20 24	20 17	20 15	20 08	20 47
20	21 05	21 12	20 36	19 38	20 12
21	21 13	21 23	20 40	19 32	20 05
22	21 22	21 34	20 44	19 26	19 58
23	21 31	21 45	20 48	19 20	19 51
24	21 39	21 57	20 52	19 14	19 44
25	21 48	22 08	20 56	19 08	19 36
26	21 57	22 19	21 01	19 02	19 29
27	22 07	22 31	21 05	18 56	19 21
28	22 16	22 43	21 09	18 50	19 14
29	22 26	22 54	21 13	18 43	19 06
30	22 35	23 06	21 17	18 37	18 58
31	22 45	23 18	21 21	18 31	18 50
32	22 55	23 30	21 26	18 24	18 42
33	23 06	23 43	21 30	18 18	18 33
34	23 16	23 55	21 34	18 11	18 25
35	23 27	24 08	21 39	18 04	18 16
36	23 38	24 21	21 43	17 58	18 07
37	23 50	24 34	21 47	17 51	17 58
38	24 02	24 47	21 52	17 44	17 49
39	24 14	25 01	21 56	17 37	17 39
40	24 26	25 14	22 01	17 30	17 30
41	24 39	25 28	22 05	17 23	17 20
42	24 52	25 43	22 10	17 15	17 09
43	25 05	25 57	22 14	17 08	16 59
44	25 19	26 12	22 19	17 00	16 48
45	25 34	26 27	22 24	16 52	16 36
46	25 49	26 43	22 29	16 44	16 25
47	26 05	26 58	22 34	16 36	16 13
48	26 21	27 15	22 39	16 28	16 01
49	26 38	27 31	22 44	16 19	15 48
50	26 55	27 48	22 49	16 11	15 34
51	27 13	28 06	22 54	16 02	15 21
52	27 33	28 24	23 00	15 53	15 06
53	27 53	28 42	23 05	15 43	14 51
54	28 14	29 01	23 11	15 34	14 36
55	28 36	29 21	23 16	15 24	14 19
56	28 59	29 41	23 22	15 14	14 02
57	29 24	0♍02	23 28	15 03	13 45
58	29 50	0 24	23 34	14 52	13 26
59	0♌18	0 46	23 40	14 41	13 06
60	0♌48	1♍10	23♍47	14♎30	12♏46

5h 24m 0s — 81° 0' 0" — 21 ♊ 44

LAT.	11	12	ASC	2	3
0	19♋24	18♌34	20♍12	22♎42	23♏23
5	20 02	19 29	20 34	22 10	22 51
10	20 40	20 22	20 54	21 38	22 18
15	21 19	21 15	21 13	21 07	21 44
20	22 00	22 08	21 32	20 36	21 10
21	22 08	22 19	21 36	20 30	21 02
22	22 17	22 30	21 40	20 24	20 55
23	22 26	22 41	21 43	20 18	20 48
24	22 34	22 52	21 47	20 11	20 41
25	22 43	23 03	21 51	20 05	20 33
26	22 52	23 15	21 54	19 59	20 26
27	23 02	23 26	21 58	19 52	20 18
28	23 11	23 37	22 02	19 46	20 10
29	23 20	23 49	22 06	19 39	20 02
30	23 30	24 00	22 10	19 32	19 54
31	23 40	24 12	22 13	19 26	19 46
32	23 50	24 24	22 17	19 19	19 38
33	24 00	24 36	22 21	19 12	19 29
34	24 11	24 48	22 25	19 05	19 21
35	24 22	25 01	22 29	18 58	19 12
36	24 33	25 13	22 33	18 51	19 03
37	24 44	25 26	22 37	18 44	18 53
38	24 56	25 39	22 41	18 37	18 44
39	25 07	25 52	22 45	18 30	18 34
40	25 20	26 06	22 49	18 22	18 24
41	25 32	26 19	22 53	18 14	18 14
42	25 45	26 33	22 57	18 07	18 04
43	25 59	26 47	23 01	17 59	17 53
44	26 13	27 02	23 05	17 51	17 42
45	26 27	27 17	23 10	17 43	17 30
46	26 42	27 32	23 14	17 34	17 19
47	26 57	27 47	23 18	17 26	17 07
48	27 13	28 03	23 23	17 17	16 54
49	27 30	28 19	23 27	17 08	16 41
50	27 47	28 36	23 32	16 59	16 27
51	28 06	28 53	23 37	16 50	16 13
52	28 25	29 11	23 42	16 40	15 59
53	28 44	29 29	23 46	16 30	15 43
54	29 05	29 47	23 51	16 20	15 28
55	29 27	0♍07	23 57	16 10	15 11
56	29 50	0 26	24 02	15 59	14 54
57	0♌15	0 47	24 07	15 48	14 36
58	0 40	1 08	24 13	15 37	14 16
59	1 08	1 30	24 18	15 25	13 56
60	1♌37	1♍52	24♍24	15♎13	13♏35

5h 28m 0s — 82° 0' 0" — 22 ♊ 39

LAT.	11	12	ASC	2	3
0	20♋20	19♌35	21♍17	23♎46	24♏22
5	20 58	20 28	21 36	23 12	23 49
10	21 36	21 21	21 54	22 39	23 16
15	22 15	22 13	22 12	22 07	22 42
20	22 55	23 05	22 28	21 35	22 07
21	23 04	23 16	22 32	21 28	21 59
22	23 12	23 26	22 35	21 22	21 52
23	23 21	23 37	22 38	21 15	21 45
24	23 30	23 48	22 42	21 08	21 37
25	23 38	23 59	22 45	21 02	21 30
26	23 47	24 10	22 48	20 55	21 22
27	23 56	24 21	22 52	20 48	21 14
28	24 06	24 32	22 55	20 42	21 06
29	24 15	24 43	22 58	20 35	20 58
30	24 25	24 55	23 02	20 28	20 50
31	24 35	25 06	23 05	20 21	20 42
32	24 45	25 18	23 09	20 14	20 34
33	24 55	25 30	23 12	20 07	20 25
34	25 05	25 42	23 15	19 59	20 16
35	25 16	25 54	23 19	19 52	20 07
36	25 27	26 06	23 22	19 45	19 58
37	25 38	26 18	23 26	19 37	19 49
38	25 50	26 31	23 29	19 30	19 39
39	26 01	26 44	23 33	19 22	19 29
40	26 14	26 57	23 36	19 14	19 19
41	26 26	27 10	23 40	19 06	19 09
42	26 39	27 24	23 44	18 58	18 58
43	26 52	27 38	23 48	18 50	18 47
44	27 06	27 52	23 51	18 42	18 36
45	27 20	28 06	23 55	18 33	18 24
46	27 35	28 21	23 59	18 24	18 12
47	27 50	28 36	24 03	18 15	18 00
48	28 06	28 52	24 07	18 06	17 47
49	28 23	29 08	24 11	17 57	17 34
50	28 40	29 24	24 15	17 47	17 20
51	28 58	29 40	24 19	17 38	17 06
52	29 16	29 58	24 24	17 28	16 51
53	29 36	0♍15	24 28	17 17	16 36
54	29 57	0 33	24 32	17 07	16 19
55	0♌18	0 52	24 37	16 56	16 03
56	0 41	1 11	24 42	16 45	15 45
57	1 05	1 31	24 46	16 33	15 26
58	1 30	1 52	24 51	16 21	15 07
59	1 57	2 13	24 56	16 09	14 47
60	2♌26	2♍35	25♍01	15♎56	14♏25

5h 32m 0s — 83° 0' 0" — 23 ♊ 34

LAT.	11	12	ASC	2	3
0	21♋17	20♌36	22♍23	24♎50	25♏21
5	21 54	21 28	22 39	24 15	24 47
10	22 32	22 20	22 55	23 40	24 13
15	23 11	23 11	23 10	23 07	23 39
20	23 51	24 02	23 25	22 33	23 04
21	23 59	24 12	23 28	22 26	22 56
22	24 08	24 23	23 31	22 19	22 49
23	24 16	24 33	23 34	22 12	22 41
24	24 25	24 44	23 36	22 06	22 34
25	24 33	24 54	23 39	21 59	22 26
26	24 42	25 05	23 42	21 52	22 19
27	24 51	25 16	23 45	21 45	22 11
28	25 01	25 27	23 48	21 37	22 03
29	25 10	25 38	23 51	21 30	21 55
30	25 20	25 49	23 54	21 23	21 46
31	25 29	26 00	23 57	21 16	21 38
32	25 39	26 12	24 00	21 09	21 29
33	25 49	26 23	24 03	21 01	21 21
34	26 00	26 35	24 06	20 54	21 12
35	26 10	26 47	24 09	20 46	21 03
36	26 21	26 59	24 12	20 38	20 53
37	26 32	27 11	24 15	20 30	20 44
38	26 44	27 23	24 18	20 23	20 34
39	26 55	27 36	24 21	20 15	20 24
40	27 07	27 48	24 24	20 06	20 14
41	27 20	28 02	24 28	19 58	20 03
42	27 33	28 15	24 31	19 50	19 53
43	27 46	28 28	24 34	19 41	19 42
44	27 59	28 42	24 37	19 32	19 30
45	28 13	28 56	24 41	19 23	19 18
46	28 28	29 11	24 44	19 14	19 06
47	28 43	29 25	24 48	19 05	18 54
48	28 59	29 40	24 51	18 55	18 41
49	29 15	29 56	24 55	18 46	18 27
50	29 32	0♍12	24 58	18 36	18 13
51	29 50	0 28	25 02	18 26	17 59
52	0♌08	0 45	25 06	18 15	17 43
53	0 28	1 02	25 09	18 04	17 28
54	0 48	1 19	25 13	17 53	17 11
55	1 09	1 38	25 17	17 42	16 54
56	1 32	1 56	25 21	17 30	16 36
57	1 55	2 16	25 26	17 18	16 17
58	2 20	2 36	25 30	17 06	15 57
59	2 47	2 56	25 34	16 53	15 37
60	3♌15	3♍18	25♍39	16♎40	15♏15

5h 36m 0s — 84° 0' 0" — 24 ♊ 30

LAT.	11	12	ASC	2	3
0	22♋13	21♌37	23♍28	25♎53	26♏19
5	22 50	22 29	23 42	25 17	25 45
10	23 28	23 19	23 56	24 41	25 11
15	24 06	24 09	24 09	24 06	24 36
20	24 46	24 59	24 21	23 31	24 00
21	24 55	25 09	24 24	23 24	23 53
22	25 03	25 19	24 26	23 17	23 46
23	25 11	25 29	24 29	23 10	23 38
24	25 20	25 40	24 31	23 03	23 30
25	25 29	25 50	24 34	22 55	23 23
26	25 37	26 01	24 36	22 48	23 15
27	25 46	26 11	24 39	22 41	23 07
28	25 56	26 22	24 41	22 33	22 59
29	26 05	26 33	24 44	22 26	22 50
30	26 14	26 43	24 46	22 18	22 42
31	26 24	26 54	24 49	22 11	22 34
32	26 34	27 05	24 51	22 03	22 25
33	26 44	27 17	24 54	21 55	22 16
34	26 54	27 28	24 56	21 48	22 07
35	27 05	27 40	24 59	21 40	21 58
36	27 15	27 51	25 02	21 32	21 48
37	27 26	28 03	25 04	21 24	21 39
38	27 38	28 15	25 07	21 15	21 29
39	27 49	28 28	25 10	21 07	21 19
40	28 01	28 40	25 12	20 58	21 09
41	28 13	28 53	25 15	20 50	20 58
42	28 26	29 06	25 18	20 41	20 47
43	28 39	29 19	25 21	20 32	20 36
44	28 53	29 32	25 23	20 23	20 24
45	29 07	29 46	25 26	20 14	20 12
46	29 21	0♍00	25 29	20 04	20 00
47	29 36	0 14	25 32	19 54	19 47
48	29 51	0 29	25 35	19 45	19 34
49	0♌08	0 44	25 38	19 34	19 20
50	0 24	0 59	25 41	19 24	19 06
51	0 42	1 15	25 44	19 13	18 51
52	1 00	1 32	25 48	19 02	18 36
53	1 19	1 48	25 51	18 51	18 20
54	1 39	2 05	25 54	18 40	18 03
55	2 00	2 23	25 58	18 28	17 46
56	2 22	2 41	26 01	18 16	17 27
57	2 46	3 00	26 05	18 03	17 08
58	3 10	3 20	26 08	17 50	16 48
59	3 37	3 40	26 12	17 37	16 27
60	4♌04	4♍01	26♍16	17♎23	16♏04

5h 40m 0s — 85° 0' 0" — 25 ♊ 25

LAT.	11	12	ASC	2	3
0	23♋10	22♌39	24♍33	26♎57	27♏17
5	23 47	23 29	24 45	26 19	26 43
10	24 24	24 18	24 56	25 42	26 08
15	25 02	25 07	25 07	25 05	25 33
20	25 42	25 56	25 18	24 29	24 57
21	25 50	26 06	25 20	24 22	24 50
22	25 58	26 16	25 22	24 14	24 42
23	26 07	26 26	25 24	24 07	24 34
24	26 15	26 36	25 26	23 59	24 27
25	26 24	26 46	25 28	23 52	24 19
26	26 33	26 56	25 30	23 44	24 11
27	26 42	27 06	25 32	23 37	24 03
28	26 51	27 17	25 34	23 29	23 55
29	27 00	27 27	25 36	23 21	23 46
30	27 09	27 38	25 39	23 14	23 38
31	27 19	27 49	25 41	23 06	23 29
32	27 29	27 59	25 43	22 58	23 21
33	27 38	28 10	25 45	22 50	23 12
34	27 49	28 21	25 47	22 42	23 02
35	27 59	28 33	25 49	22 33	22 53
36	28 10	28 44	25 51	22 25	22 44
37	28 21	28 56	25 54	22 17	22 34
38	28 32	29 07	25 56	22 08	22 24
39	28 43	29 19	25 58	21 59	22 14
40	28 55	29 32	26 00	21 51	22 03
41	29 07	29 44	26 03	21 42	21 52
42	29 20	29 56	26 05	21 32	21 41
43	29 33	0♍09	26 07	21 23	21 30
44	29 46	0 22	26 10	21 14	21 18
45	0♌00	0 36	26 12	21 04	21 06
46	0 14	0 49	26 14	20 54	20 53
47	0 29	1 03	26 17	20 44	20 40
48	0 44	1 18	26 19	20 34	20 27
49	1 00	1 32	26 22	20 23	20 13
50	1 17	1 47	26 24	20 12	19 59
51	1 34	2 03	26 27	20 01	19 44
52	1 52	2 19	26 30	19 50	19 28
53	2 11	2 35	26 32	19 38	19 12
54	2 31	2 51	26 35	19 26	18 55
55	2 51	3 09	26 38	19 14	18 37
56	3 13	3 26	26 41	19 01	18 18
57	3 36	3 45	26 44	18 48	17 59
58	4 00	4 04	26 47	18 34	17 38
59	4 26	4 23	26 50	18 20	17 16
60	4♌54	4♍44	26♍53	18♎06	16♏54

5h 44m 0s — 86° 0' 0" — 26 ♊ 20

LAT.	11	12	ASC	2	3
0	24♋06	23♌41	25♍38	28♎00	28♏15
5	24 43	24 30	25 48	27 21	27 40
10	25 20	25 18	25 57	26 42	27 06
15	25 58	26 05	26 06	26 05	26 30
20	26 38	26 53	26 14	25 27	25 54
21	26 46	27 03	26 16	25 19	25 46
22	26 54	27 12	26 17	25 12	25 39
23	27 02	27 22	26 19	25 04	25 31
24	27 11	27 32	26 21	24 56	25 23
25	27 19	27 42	26 22	24 49	25 15
26	27 28	27 52	26 24	24 41	25 07
27	27 37	28 02	26 26	24 33	24 59
28	27 46	28 12	26 27	24 25	24 51
29	27 55	28 22	26 29	24 17	24 42
30	28 04	28 32	26 31	24 09	24 34
31	28 14	28 43	26 32	24 01	24 25
32	28 23	28 53	26 34	23 52	24 16
33	28 33	29 04	26 36	23 44	24 07
34	28 43	29 15	26 38	23 36	23 58
35	28 54	29 26	26 39	23 27	23 48
36	29 04	29 37	26 41	23 18	23 39
37	29 15	29 48	26 43	23 10	23 29
38	29 26	0♍00	26 45	23 01	23 19
39	29 37	0 11	26 46	22 52	23 08
40	29 49	0 23	26 48	22 43	22 58
41	0♌01	0 35	26 50	22 33	22 47
42	0 13	0 47	26 52	22 24	22 35
43	0 26	1 00	26 54	22 14	22 24
44	0 39	1 13	26 56	22 04	22 12
45	0 53	1 26	26 58	21 54	22 00
46	1 07	1 39	26 59	21 44	21 47
47	1 22	1 52	27 01	21 33	21 34
48	1 37	2 06	27 03	21 23	21 20
49	1 53	2 21	27 05	21 12	21 06
50	2 09	2 35	27 08	21 00	20 51
51	2 26	2 50	27 10	20 49	20 36
52	2 44	3 06	27 12	20 37	20 20
53	3 02	3 21	27 14	20 25	20 04
54	3 22	3 38	27 16	20 12	19 46
55	3 42	3 54	27 18	20 00	19 28
56	4 04	4 12	27 21	19 46	19 09
57	4 27	4 29	27 23	19 33	18 49
58	4 50	4 48	27 26	19 19	18 28
59	5 16	5 07	27 28	19 04	18 06
60	5♌43	5♍27	27♍31	18♎49	17♏43

5h 48m 0s — 87° 0' 0" — 27 ♊ 15

LAT.	11	12	ASC	2	3
0	25♋03	24♌42	26♍44	29♎03	29♏13
5	25 40	25 30	26 51	28 22	28 38
10	26 17	26 17	26 58	27 43	28 03
15	26 54	27 03	27 04	27 04	27 27
20	27 33	27 50	27 11	26 25	26 50
21	27 41	27 59	27 12	26 17	26 43
22	27 50	28 09	27 13	26 09	26 35
23	27 58	28 18	27 14	26 01	26 27
24	28 06	28 28	27 16	25 53	26 19
25	28 15	28 38	27 17	25 45	26 11
26	28 23	28 47	27 18	25 37	26 03
27	28 32	28 57	27 19	25 29	25 55
28	28 41	29 07	27 21	25 21	25 46
29	28 50	29 17	27 22	25 12	25 38
30	28 59	29 27	27 23	25 04	25 29
31	29 09	29 37	27 24	24 55	25 20
32	29 18	29 47	27 26	24 47	25 11
33	29 28	29 58	27 27	24 38	25 02
34	29 38	0♍08	27 28	24 30	24 53
35	29 48	0 19	27 30	24 21	24 43
36	29 59	0 30	27 31	24 12	24 33
37	0♌09	0 41	27 32	24 03	24 23
38	0 20	0 52	27 33	23 53	24 13
39	0 31	1 03	27 35	23 44	24 03
40	0 43	1 15	27 36	23 34	23 52
41	0 55	1 26	27 38	23 25	23 41
42	1 07	1 38	27 39	23 15	23 29
43	1 20	1 50	27 40	23 05	23 18
44	1 33	2 03	27 42	22 55	23 06
45	1 46	2 16	27 43	22 44	22 53
46	2 00	2 28	27 45	22 34	22 40
47	2 15	2 42	27 46	22 23	22 27
48	2 30	2 55	27 48	22 12	22 13
49	2 45	3 09	27 49	22 00	21 59
50	3 01	3 23	27 51	21 49	21 44
51	3 18	3 38	27 52	21 37	21 28
52	3 36	3 53	27 54	21 24	21 12
53	3 54	4 08	27 55	21 12	20 55
54	4 13	4 24	27 57	20 59	20 38
55	4 33	4 40	27 59	20 46	20 20
56	4 55	4 57	28 01	20 32	20 00
57	5 17	5 14	28 02	20 18	19 40
58	5 41	5 32	28 04	20 03	19 19
59	6 05	5 50	28 06	19 48	18 56
60	6♌32	6♍09	28♍08	19♎32	18♏32

5h 52m 0s 28 ♊ 10 88° 0' 0"					5h 56m 0s 29 ♊ 05 89° 0' 0"						6h 0m 0s 0 ♋ 00 90° 0' 0"					6h 4m 0s 0 ♋ 55 91° 0' 0"				
11	12	ASC	2	3	11	12	ASC	2	3	LAT.	11	12	ASC	2	3	11	12	ASC	2	3
26♋00	25♌44	27♍49	0♏06	0♐11	26♋57	26♌47	28♍55	1♏08	1♐08	0	27♋55	27♌49	0♎00	2♏11	2♐05	28♋52	28♌52	1♎05	3♏13	3♐03
26 37	26 31	27 54	29♎24	29♏35	27 33	27 32	28 57	0 25	0 33	5	28 30	28 33	0 00	1 27	1 30	29 27	29 35	1 03	2 28	2 27
27 13	27 17	27 58	28 43	29 00	28 10	28 17	28 59	29♎43	29♏57	10	29 06	29 17	0 00	0 43	0 54	0♌03	0♍17	1 01	1 43	1 50
27 50	28 02	28 03	28 03	28 24	28 47	29 01	29 01	29 02	29 21	15	29 43	29 59	0 00	0 01	0 17	0 39	0 58	0 59	0 59	1 13
28 29	28 47	28 07	27 23	27 46	29 25	29 45	29 04	28 20	28 43	20	0♌21	0♍42	0 00	29♎18	29♏39	1 17	1 40	0 56	0 15	0 35
28 37	28 57	28 08	27 14	27 39	29 33	29 54	29 04	28 12	28 35	21	0 29	0 51	0 00	29 09	29 31	1 25	1 48	0 56	0 06	0 27
28 45	29 06	28 09	27 06	27 31	29 41	0♍03	29 04	28 03	28 27	22	0 37	1 00	0 00	29 00	29 23	1 33	1 57	0 56	29♎57	0 19
28 53	29 15	28 10	26 58	27 23	29 49	0 12	29 05	27 55	28 19	23	0 45	1 08	0 00	28 52	29 15	1 41	2 05	0 55	29 48	0 11
29 02	29 24	28 10	26 50	27 15	29 57	0 21	29 05	27 46	28 11	24	0 53	1 17	0 00	28 43	29 07	1 49	2 14	0 55	29 39	0 03
29 10	29 34	28 11	26 41	27 07	0♌06	0 30	29 06	27 38	28 03	25	1 01	1 26	0 00	28 34	28 59	1 57	2 22	0 54	29 30	29♏54
29 19	29 43	28 12	26 33	26 59	0 14	0 39	29 06	27 29	27 55	26	1 10	1 35	0 00	28 25	28 50	2 05	2 31	0 54	29 21	29 46
29 27	29 53	28 13	26 25	26 50	0 23	0 48	29 06	27 20	27 46	27	1 18	1 44	0 00	28 16	28 42	2 14	2 40	0 54	29 12	29 37
29 36	0♍02	28 14	26 16	26 42	0 31	0 58	29 07	27 12	27 38	28	1 27	1 53	0 00	28 07	28 33	2 22	2 48	0 53	29 02	29 29
29 45	0 12	28 15	26 08	26 33	0 40	1 07	29 07	27 03	27 29	29	1 36	2 02	0 00	27 58	28 24	2 31	2 57	0 53	28 53	29 20
29 54	0 22	28 15	25 59	26 25	0 49	1 16	29 08	26 54	27 20	30	1 45	2 11	0 00	27 49	28 15	2 40	3 06	0 52	28 44	29 11
0♌04	0 32	28 16	25 50	26 16	0 59	1 26	29 08	26 45	27 11	31	1 54	2 21	0 00	27 39	28 06	2 49	3 15	0 52	28 34	29 01
0 13	0 42	28 17	25 41	26 07	1 08	1 36	29 09	26 36	27 02	32	2 03	2 30	0 00	27 30	27 57	2 58	3 24	0 51	28 24	28 52
0 23	0 52	28 18	25 32	25 57	1 18	1 46	29 09	26 26	26 52	33	2 13	2 40	0 00	27 20	27 47	3 08	3 34	0 51	28 14	28 42
0 33	1 02	28 19	25 23	25 48	1 27	1 55	29 09	26 17	26 43	34	2 22	2 49	0 00	27 11	27 38	3 17	3 43	0 51	28 05	28 33
0 43	1 12	28 20	25 14	25 38	1 37	2 06	29 10	26 08	26 33	35	2 32	2 59	0 00	27 01	27 28	3 27	3 52	0 50	27 54	28 23
0 53	1 23	28 21	25 05	25 28	1 48	2 16	29 10	25 58	26 23	36	2 42	3 09	0 00	26 51	27 18	3 37	4 02	0 50	27 44	28 12
1 04	1 33	28 21	24 55	25 18	1 58	2 26	29 11	25 48	26 13	37	2 53	3 19	0 00	26 41	27 07	3 47	4 12	0 49	27 34	28 02
1 14	1 44	28 22	24 46	25 08	2 09	2 37	29 11	25 38	26 02	38	3 03	3 29	0 00	26 31	26 57	3 58	4 22	0 49	27 23	27 51
1 26	1 55	28 23	24 36	24 57	2 20	2 47	29 12	25 28	25 52	39	3 14	3 39	0 00	26 21	26 46	4 08	4 32	0 48	27 13	27 40
1 37	2 06	28 24	24 26	24 46	2 31	2 58	29 12	25 18	25 41	40	3 25	3 50	0 00	26 10	26 35	4 19	4 42	0 48	27 02	27 29
1 49	2 18	28 25	24 16	24 35	2 43	3 09	29 13	25 08	25 29	41	3 37	4 01	0 00	25 59	26 23	4 31	4 52	0 47	26 51	27 17
2 01	2 29	28 26	24 06	24 23	2 55	3 20	29 13	24 57	25 17	42	3 49	4 12	0 00	25 48	26 11	4 43	5 03	0 47	26 40	27 05
2 13	2 41	28 27	23 56	24 12	3 07	3 32	29 13	24 47	25 05	43	4 01	4 23	0 00	25 37	25 59	4 55	5 13	0 47	26 28	26 53
2 26	2 53	28 28	23 45	23 59	3 20	3 44	29 14	24 36	24 53	44	4 13	4 34	0 00	25 26	25 47	5 07	5 24	0 46	26 16	26 40
2 40	3 05	28 29	23 34	23 47	3 33	3 55	29 14	24 24	24 40	45	4 26	4 45	0 00	25 15	25 34	5 20	5 36	0 46	26 05	26 27
2 53	3 18	28 30	23 23	23 34	3 47	4 08	29 15	24 13	24 27	46	4 40	4 57	0 00	25 03	25 20	5 33	5 47	0 45	25 52	26 13
3 08	3 31	28 31	23 12	23 20	4 01	4 20	29 15	24 01	24 13	47	4 54	5 09	0 00	24 51	25 06	5 47	5 59	0 45	25 40	25 59
3 22	3 44	28 32	23 01	23 06	4 15	4 33	29 16	23 50	23 59	48	5 08	5 22	0 00	24 38	24 52	6 01	6 10	0 44	25 27	25 45
3 38	3 57	28 33	22 49	22 52	4 30	4 46	29 16	23 37	23 44	49	5 23	5 34	0 00	24 26	24 37	6 16	6 23	0 44	25 14	25 30
3 54	4 11	28 34	22 37	22 36	4 46	4 59	29 17	23 25	23 29	50	5 39	5 47	0 00	24 13	24 21	6 31	6 35	0 43	25 01	25 14
4 10	4 25	28 35	22 24	22 21	5 02	5 13	29 17	23 12	23 13	51	5 55	6 00	0 00	24 00	24 05	6 47	6 48	0 43	24 47	24 58
4 28	4 40	28 36	22 12	22 04	5 20	5 27	29 18	22 59	22 56	52	6 12	6 14	0 00	23 46	23 48	7 04	7 01	0 42	24 33	24 40
4 46	4 55	28 37	21 59	21 47	5 37	5 41	29 18	22 45	22 39	53	6 29	6 28	0 00	23 32	23 31	7 21	7 15	0 42	24 19	24 23
5 05	5 10	28 38	21 45	21 29	5 56	5 56	29 19	22 31	22 21	54	6 48	6 42	0 00	23 18	23 12	7 39	7 29	0 41	24 04	24 04
5 25	5 26	28 39	21 31	21 11	6 16	6 11	29 20	22 17	22 02	55	7 07	6 57	0 00	23 03	22 53	7 58	7 43	0 40	23 49	23 44
5 45	5 42	28 40	21 17	20 51	6 36	6 27	29 20	22 02	21 42	56	7 27	7 12	0 00	22 48	22 33	8 18	7 58	0 40	23 33	23 24
6 07	5 59	28 42	21 02	20 31	6 58	6 43	29 21	21 47	21 21	57	7 48	7 28	0 00	22 32	22 12	8 39	8 13	0 39	23 17	23 02
6 31	6 16	28 43	20 47	20 09	7 21	7 00	29 21	21 32	20 59	58	8 11	7 44	0 00	22 16	21 49	9 01	8 28	0 39	23 00	22 39
6 55	6 34	28 44	20 32	19 46	7 45	7 17	29 22	21 15	20 36	59	8 34	8 01	0 00	21 59	21 26	9 24	8 45	0 38	22 43	22 15
7♌21	6♍52	28♍45	20♎15	19♏22	8♌10	7♍35	29♍23	20♎59	20♏11	60	9♌00	8♍18	0♎00	21♎42	21♏00	9♌49	9♍01	0♎37	22♎25	21♏50

6h 8m 0s 1 ♋ 50 92° 0' 0"					6h 12m 0s 2 ♋ 45 93° 0' 0"						6h 16m 0s 3 ♋ 40 94° 0' 0"					6h 20m 0s 4 ♋ 35 95° 0' 0"				
11	12	ASC	2	3	11	12	ASC	2	3	LAT.	11	12	ASC	2	3	11	12	ASC	2	3
29♋49	29♌54	2♎11	4♏16	4♐00	0♌47	0♍57	3♎16	5♏18	4♐57	0	1♌45	2♍00	4♎22	6♏19	5♐54	2♌43	3♍03	5♎27	7♏21	6♐50
0♌25	0♍36	2 06	3 29	3 23	1 22	1 38	3 09	4 30	4 20	5	2 20	2 39	4 12	5 30	5 17	3 17	3 41	5 15	6 31	6 13
1 00	1 17	2 02	2 43	2 47	1 57	2 17	3 02	3 43	3 43	10	2 54	3 18	4 03	4 42	4 40	3 52	4 18	5 04	5 42	5 36
1 36	1 57	1 57	1 58	2 10	2 33	2 56	2 56	2 57	3 06	15	3 30	3 55	3 54	3 55	4 02	4 27	4 55	4 53	4 53	4 58
2 14	2 37	1 53	1 13	1 31	3 10	3 35	2 49	2 10	2 27	20	4 06	4 33	3 46	3 07	3 22	5 03	5 31	4 42	4 04	4 18
2 21	2 46	1 52	1 03	1 23	3 17	3 43	2 48	2 01	2 19	21	4 14	4 41	3 44	2 57	3 14	5 10	5 38	4 40	3 54	4 10
2 29	2 54	1 51	0 54	1 15	3 25	3 51	2 47	1 51	2 10	22	4 21	4 48	3 43	2 48	3 06	5 18	5 46	4 38	3 44	4 02
2 37	3 02	1 50	0 45	1 07	3 33	3 59	2 46	1 42	2 02	23	4 29	4 56	3 41	2 38	2 58	5 26	5 53	4 36	3 34	3 53
2 45	3 10	1 50	0 36	0 58	3 41	4 07	2 44	1 32	1 54	24	4 37	5 04	3 39	2 28	2 49	5 33	6 01	4 34	3 24	3 45
2 53	3 19	1 49	0 26	0 50	3 49	4 15	2 43	1 22	1 45	25	4 45	5 11	3 38	2 18	2 41	5 41	6 08	4 32	3 14	3 36
3 01	3 27	1 48	0 17	0 41	3 57	4 23	2 42	1 13	1 37	26	4 53	5 19	3 36	2 08	2 32	5 49	6 16	4 30	3 04	3 27
3 10	3 35	1 47	0 07	0 33	4 05	4 31	2 41	1 03	1 28	27	5 01	5 27	3 34	1 58	2 23	5 57	6 23	4 28	2 54	3 18
3 18	3 44	1 46	29♎58	0 24	4 14	4 39	2 39	0 53	1 19	28	5 09	5 35	3 33	1 48	2 14	6 05	6 31	4 26	2 43	3 09
3 27	3 52	1 45	29 48	0 15	4 22	4 48	2 38	0 43	1 10	29	5 18	5 43	3 31	1 38	2 05	6 14	6 39	4 24	2 33	3 00
3 35	4 01	1 45	29 38	0 06	4 31	4 56	2 37	0 33	1 01	30	5 26	5 51	3 29	1 28	1 56	6 22	6 46	4 21	2 22	2 51
3 44	4 10	1 44	29 28	29♏56	4 40	5 05	2 36	0 23	0 51	31	5 35	5 59	3 28	1 17	1 46	6 31	6 54	4 19	2 11	2 41
3 53	4 19	1 43	29 18	29 47	4 49	5 13	2 34	0 13	0 42	32	5 44	6 08	3 26	1 07	1 37	6 39	7 02	4 17	2 01	2 31
4 03	4 28	1 42	29 08	29 37	4 58	5 22	2 33	0 02	0 32	33	5 53	6 16	3 24	0 56	1 27	6 48	7 10	4 15	1 50	2 22
4 12	4 37	1 41	28 58	29 27	5 07	5 30	2 32	29♎52	0 22	34	6 02	6 24	3 22	0 45	1 17	6 58	7 18	4 13	1 39	2 11
4 22	4 46	1 40	28 48	29 17	5 17	5 39	2 30	29 41	0 12	35	6 12	6 33	3 21	0 34	1 06	7 07	7 27	4 11	1 27	2 01
4 32	4 55	1 39	28 37	29 07	5 27	5 48	2 29	29 30	0 01	36	6 21	6 42	3 19	0 23	0 56	7 16	7 35	4 09	1 16	1 50
4 42	5 05	1 39	28 27	28 56	5 37	5 57	2 28	29 19	29♏51	37	6 31	6 50	3 17	0 12	0 45	7 26	7 43	4 06	1 04	1 39
4 52	5 14	1 38	28 16	28 46	5 47	6 07	2 27	29 08	29 40	38	6 41	6 59	3 15	0 00	0 34	7 36	7 52	4 04	0 53	1 28
5 03	5 24	1 37	28 05	28 34	5 57	6 16	2 25	28 57	29 29	39	6 52	7 08	3 14	29♎49	0 23	7 46	8 01	4 02	0 41	1 17
5 14	5 34	1 36	27 54	28 23	6 08	6 26	2 24	28 45	29 17	40	7 02	7 17	3 12	29 37	0 11	7 57	8 09	4 00	0 28	1 05
5 25	5 44	1 35	27 42	28 11	6 19	6 35	2 22	28 34	29 05	41	7 13	7 27	3 10	29 25	29♏59	8 08	8 18	3 57	0 16	0 53
5 37	5 54	1 34	27 31	27 59	6 31	6 45	2 21	28 22	28 53	42	7 25	7 36	3 08	29 13	29 47	8 19	8 28	3 55	0 04	0 40
5 48	6 04	1 33	27 19	27 47	6 42	6 55	2 20	28 10	28 40	43	7 36	7 46	3 06	29 00	29 34	8 30	8 37	3 53	29♎51	0 27
6 01	6 15	1 32	27 07	27 34	6 54	7 05	2 18	27 57	28 27	44	7 48	7 56	3 04	28 47	29 21	8 42	8 46	3 50	29 38	0 14
6 13	6 26	1 31	26 55	27 20	7 07	7 16	2 17	27 44	28 14	45	8 00	8 06	3 02	28 34	29 07	8 54	8 56	3 48	29 24	0 00
6 26	6 37	1 30	26 42	27 07	7 20	7 26	2 15	27 32	28 00	46	8 13	8 16	3 01	28 21	28 53	9 07	9 06	3 46	29 11	29♏46
6 40	6 48	1 29	26 29	26 52	7 33	7 37	2 14	27 18	27 45	47	8 26	8 27	2 59	28 08	28 38	9 20	9 16	3 43	28 57	29 31
6 54	6 59	1 28	26 16	26 38	7 47	7 48	2 12	27 05	27 30	48	8 40	8 37	2 57	27 54	28 23	9 33	9 26	3 41	28 42	29 16
7 08	7 11	1 27	26 03	26 22	8 01	8 00	2 11	26 51	27 15	49	8 54	8 48	2 55	27 39	28 07	9 47	9 37	3 38	28 28	29 00
7 24	7 23	1 26	25 49	26 06	8 16	8 11	2 09	26 37	26 59	50	9 09	9 00	2 52	27 25	27 51	10 01	9 48	3 36	28 13	28 43
7 39	7 36	1 25	25 35	25 50	8 32	8 23	2 08	26 22	26 42	51	9 24	9 11	2 50	27 10	27 34	10 16	9 59	3 33	27 57	28 26
7 56	7 48	1 24	25 20	25 32	8 48	8 36	2 06	26 07	26 24	52	9 40	9 23	2 48	26 54	27 16	10 32	10 10	3 30	27 41	28 08
8 13	8 01	1 23	25 05	25 14	9 05	8 48	2 05	25 52	26 06	53	9 56	9 35	2 46	26 39	26 58	10 48	10 22	3 28	27 25	27 49
8 31	8 15	1 22	24 50	24 55	9 22	9 01	2 03	25 36	25 47	54	10 14	9 48	2 44	26 22	26 38	11 05	10 34	3 25	27 09	27 29
8 49	8 29	1 21	24 34	24 35	9 40	9 14	2 01	25 20	25 27	55	10 32	10 00	2 42	26 06	26 18	11 23	10 46	3 22	26 51	27 09
9 09	8 43	1 20	24 18	24 15	10 00	9 28	1 59	25 03	25 05	56	10 51	10 14	2 39	25 48	25 56	11 42	10 59	3 19	26 34	26 47
9 29	8 58	1 18	24 01	23 53	10 20	9 42	1 58	24 46	24 43	57	11 11	10 27	2 37	25 31	25 33	12 01	11 12	3 16	26 15	26 24
9 51	9 13	1 17	23 44	23 29	10 41	9 57	1 56	24 28	24 19	58	11 32	10 41	2 34	25 12	25 10	12 22	11 26	3 13	25 56	26 00
10 14	9 28	1 16	23 26	23 05	11 04	10 12	1 54	24 10	23 55	59	11 54	10 56	2 32	24 53	24 44	12 44	11 40	3 10	25 37	25 34
10♌38	9♍45	1♎15	23♎08	22♏39	11♌28	10♍28	1♎52	23♎51	23♏28	60	12♌17	11♍11	2♎29	24♎33	24♏17	13♌06	11♍54	3♎07	25♎16	25♏06

6h 24m 0s 96° 0' 0" 5 ♋ 30					6h 28m 0s 97° 0' 0" 6 ♋ 26						6h 32m 0s 98° 0' 0" 7 ♋ 21					6h 36m 0s 99° 0' 0" 8 ♋ 16				
11	12	ASC	2	3	11	12	ASC	2	3	LAT.	11	12	ASC	2	3	11	12	ASC	2	3
3♌41	4♍07	6♎32	8♏23	7♐47	4♌39	5♍10	7♎37	9♏24	8♐43	0	5♌38	6♍14	8♎43	10♏25	9♐40	6♌37	7♍18	9♎48	11♏26	10♐36
4 15	4 43	6 18	7 31	7 10	5 13	5 45	7 21	8 32	8 06	5	6 11	6 48	8 24	9 32	9 02	7 09	7 50	9 26	10 31	9 58
4 49	5 19	6 04	6 41	6 32	5 47	6 20	7 05	7 40	7 28	10	6 44	7 21	8 06	8 39	8 24	7 42	8 22	9 06	9 38	9 20
5 24	5 54	5 51	5 51	5 54	6 21	6 53	6 50	6 49	6 49	15	7 18	7 53	7 48	7 47	7 45	8 16	8 53	8 47	8 45	8 41
6 00	6 29	5 39	5 01	5 14	6 56	7 27	6 35	5 58	6 09	20	7 53	8 25	7 32	6 55	7 05	8 50	9 24	8 28	7 52	8 00
6 07	6 36	5 36	4 51	5 05	7 04	7 34	6 32	5 48	6 01	21	8 01	8 32	7 28	6 44	6 56	8 58	9 30	8 24	7 41	7 52
6 14	6 43	5 34	4 41	4 57	7 11	7 41	6 29	5 37	5 52	22	8 08	8 38	7 25	6 34	6 48	9 05	9 36	8 20	7 30	7 43
6 22	6 50	5 31	4 31	4 49	7 19	7 48	6 26	5 27	5 44	23	8 15	8 45	7 22	6 23	6 39	9 12	9 42	8 17	7 19	7 34
6 30	6 57	5 29	4 20	4 40	7 26	7 54	6 24	5 16	5 35	24	8 23	8 52	7 18	6 12	6 30	9 19	9 49	8 13	7 08	7 26
6 37	7 05	5 26	4 10	4 31	7 34	8 01	6 21	5 06	5 27	25	8 30	8 58	7 15	6 01	6 22	9 27	9 55	8 09	6 57	7 17
6 45	7 12	5 24	3 59	4 23	7 41	8 08	6 18	4 55	5 18	26	8 38	9 05	7 12	5 50	6 13	9 34	10 01	8 06	6 45	7 08
6 53	7 19	5 21	3 49	4 14	7 49	8 15	6 15	4 44	5 09	27	8 46	9 12	7 08	5 39	6 04	9 42	10 08	8 02	6 34	6 58
7 01	7 27	5 19	3 38	4 04	7 57	8 23	6 12	4 33	4 59	28	8 54	9 18	7 05	5 28	5 54	9 50	10 14	7 58	6 23	6 49
7 10	7 34	5 16	3 27	3 55	8 05	8 30	6 09	4 22	4 50	29	9 02	9 25	7 02	5 17	5 45	9 58	10 21	7 54	6 11	6 40
7 18	7 42	5 14	3 17	3 46	8 14	8 37	6 06	4 11	4 40	30	9 10	9 32	6 58	5 05	5 35	10 06	10 28	7 50	6 00	6 30
7 26	7 49	5 11	3 06	3 36	8 22	8 44	6 03	4 00	4 31	31	9 18	9 39	6 55	4 54	5 25	10 14	10 34	7 47	5 48	6 20
7 35	7 57	5 09	2 55	3 26	8 31	8 51	6 00	3 48	4 21	32	9 26	9 46	6 51	4 42	5 15	10 22	10 41	7 43	5 36	6 10
7 44	8 05	5 06	2 43	3 16	8 39	8 59	5 57	3 37	4 11	33	9 35	9 53	6 48	4 30	5 05	10 31	10 48	7 39	5 24	6 00
7 53	8 12	5 04	2 32	3 06	8 48	9 06	5 54	3 25	4 00	34	9 44	10 01	6 45	4 18	4 55	10 39	10 55	7 35	5 12	5 49
8 02	8 20	5 01	2 20	2 55	8 57	9 14	5 51	3 13	3 50	35	9 53	10 08	6 41	4 06	4 44	10 48	11 02	7 31	4 59	5 38
8 12	8 28	4 58	2 09	2 45	9 07	9 22	5 48	3 01	3 39	36	10 02	10 15	6 38	3 54	4 33	10 57	11 09	7 27	4 47	5 27
8 21	8 36	4 56	1 57	2 34	9 16	9 30	5 45	2 49	3 28	37	10 11	10 23	6 34	3 42	4 22	11 07	11 16	7 23	4 34	5 16
8 31	8 45	4 53	1 45	2 22	9 26	9 37	5 42	2 37	3 16	38	10 21	10 30	6 31	3 29	4 10	11 16	11 23	7 19	4 21	5 04
8 41	8 53	4 50	1 32	2 11	9 36	9 45	5 39	2 24	3 05	39	10 31	10 38	6 27	3 16	3 59	11 26	11 30	7 15	4 08	4 53
8 51	9 02	4 48	1 20	1 59	9 46	9 54	5 36	2 12	2 53	40	10 41	10 46	6 24	3 03	3 46	11 36	11 38	7 11	3 54	4 40
9 02	9 10	4 45	1 07	1 47	9 57	10 02	5 32	1 59	2 40	41	10 51	10 54	6 20	2 50	3 34	11 46	11 46	7 07	3 41	4 28
9 13	9 19	4 42	0 54	1 34	10 07	10 10	5 29	1 45	2 27	42	11 02	11 02	6 16	2 36	3 21	11 56	11 53	7 03	3 27	4 15
9 24	9 28	4 39	0 41	1 21	10 18	10 19	5 26	1 32	2 14	43	11 13	11 10	6 12	2 22	3 08	12 07	12 01	6 59	3 13	4 01
9 36	9 37	4 37	0 28	1 07	10 30	10 28	5 23	1 18	2 01	44	11 24	11 18	6 09	2 08	2 54	12 18	12 09	6 55	2 58	3 47
9 48	9 46	4 34	0 14	0 53	10 42	10 37	5 19	1 04	1 47	45	11 36	11 27	6 05	1 54	2 40	12 30	12 17	6 50	2 43	3 33
10 00	9 56	4 31	0 00	0 39	10 54	10 46	5 16	0 49	1 32	46	11 48	11 36	6 01	1 39	2 25	12 41	12 26	6 46	2 28	3 18
10 13	10 06	4 28	29♎46	0 24	11 06	10 55	5 12	0 35	1 17	47	12 00	11 45	5 57	1 24	2 10	12 53	12 34	6 42	2 13	3 03
10 26	10 15	4 25	29 31	0 09	11 19	11 05	5 09	0 20	1 01	48	12 13	11 54	5 53	1 08	1 54	13 06	12 43	6 37	1 57	2 47
10 40	10 26	4 22	29 16	29♏52	11 33	11 14	5 05	0 04	0 45	49	12 26	12 03	5 49	0 52	1 37	13 19	12 52	6 33	1 41	2 30
10 54	10 36	4 19	29 01	29 36	11 47	11 24	5 02	29♎48	0 28	50	12 40	12 13	5 45	0 36	1 20	13 33	13 01	6 28	1 24	2 13
11 09	10 47	4 16	28 45	29 18	12 01	11 34	4 58	29 32	0 10	51	12 54	12 22	5 41	0 20	1 02	13 47	13 10	6 23	1 07	1 54
11 24	10 58	4 12	28 28	29 00	12 17	11 45	4 54	29 15	29♏52	52	13 09	12 32	5 36	0 02	0 44	14 01	13 20	6 18	0 49	1 35
11 40	11 09	4 09	28 12	28 41	12 32	11 56	4 51	28 58	29 32	53	13 24	12 43	5 32	29♎45	0 24	14 17	13 30	6 14	0 31	1 16
11 57	11 20	4 06	27 55	28 21	12 49	12 07	4 47	28 41	29 12	54	13 41	12 53	5 28	29 27	0 03	14 32	13 40	6 09	0 13	0 55
12 14	11 32	4 02	27 37	28 00	13 06	12 18	4 43	28 22	28 51	55	13 57	13 04	5 23	29 08	29♏42	14 49	13 50	6 03	29♎53	0 33
12 33	11 44	3 59	27 19	27 38	13 24	12 30	4 39	28 04	28 28	56	14 15	13 15	5 18	28 49	29 19	15 06	14 01	5 58	29 34	0 10
12 52	11 57	3 55	27 00	27 14	13 43	12 42	4 34	27 44	28 05	57	14 34	13 27	5 14	28 29	28 55	15 24	14 12	5 53	29 13	29♏45
13 12	12 10	3 52	26 40	26 50	14 03	12 54	4 30	27 24	27 40	58	14 53	13 39	5 09	28 08	28 30	15 44	14 23	5 47	28 52	29 20
13 33	12 23	3 48	26 20	26 23	14 23	13 07	4 26	27 04	27 13	59	15 13	13 51	5 04	27 47	28 03	16 04	14 35	5 42	28 30	28 52
13♌56	12♍37	3♎44	25♎59	25♏56	14♌45	13♍20	4♎21	26♎42	26♏45	60	15♌35	14♍04	4♎59	27♎25	27♏34	16♌25	14♍47	5♎36	28♎08	28♏23

6h 40m 0s 100° 0' 0" 9 ♋ 11					6h 44m 0s 101° 0' 0" 10 ♋ 07						6h 48m 0s 102° 0' 0" 11 ♋ 02					6h 52m 0s 103° 0' 0" 11 ♋ 58				
11	12	ASC	2	3	11	12	ASC	2	3	LAT.	11	12	ASC	2	3	11	12	ASC	2	3
7♌35	8♍22	10♎53	12♏27	11♐32	8♌34	9♍26	11♎58	13♏27	12♐28	0	9♌34	10♍30	13♎03	14♏28	13♐24	10♌33	11♍34	14♎07	15♏28	14♐20
8 08	8 53	10 29	11 31	10 54	9 06	9 55	11 32	12 31	11 50	5	10 05	10 58	12 34	13 30	12 46	11 04	12 01	13 37	14 30	13 41
8 40	9 23	10 07	10 37	10 16	9 39	10 24	11 07	11 35	11 11	10	10 37	11 25	12 08	12 34	12 07	11 35	12 27	13 08	13 32	13 02
9 13	9 52	9 45	9 43	9 36	10 11	10 52	10 44	10 40	10 32	15	11 09	11 52	11 42	11 38	11 27	12 07	12 52	12 40	12 35	12 22
9 48	10 22	9 24	8 48	8 55	10 45	11 20	10 21	9 45	9 50	20	11 42	12 19	11 17	10 41	10 46	12 40	13 17	12 13	11 37	11 41
9 55	10 28	9 20	8 37	8 47	10 52	11 26	10 16	9 33	9 42	21	11 49	12 24	11 12	10 29	10 37	12 47	13 23	12 08	11 25	11 32
10 02	10 34	9 16	8 26	8 38	10 59	11 32	10 12	9 22	9 33	22	11 56	12 30	11 07	10 18	10 28	12 53	13 28	12 02	11 14	11 23
10 09	10 40	9 12	8 15	8 29	11 06	11 37	10 07	9 11	9 25	23	12 03	12 35	11 02	10 06	10 20	13 00	13 33	11 57	11 02	11 14
10 16	10 46	9 08	8 03	8 21	11 13	11 43	10 02	8 59	9 16	24	12 10	12 41	10 57	9 54	10 11	13 07	13 38	11 52	10 50	11 05
10 24	10 52	9 04	7 52	8 12	11 20	11 49	9 58	8 47	9 07	25	12 17	12 46	10 52	9 43	10 02	13 14	13 43	11 46	10 38	10 56
10 31	10 58	8 59	7 41	8 03	11 28	11 55	9 53	8 36	8 57	26	12 25	12 52	10 47	9 31	9 52	13 21	13 48	11 41	10 26	10 47
10 39	11 04	8 55	7 29	7 53	11 35	12 01	9 49	8 24	8 48	27	12 32	12 57	10 42	9 19	9 43	13 29	13 54	11 36	10 13	10 38
10 46	11 10	8 51	7 17	7 44	11 43	12 07	9 44	8 12	8 39	28	12 39	13 03	10 37	9 07	9 33	13 36	13 59	11 30	10 01	10 28
10 54	11 17	8 47	7 06	7 34	11 50	12 13	9 40	8 00	8 29	29	12 47	13 08	10 32	8 54	9 24	13 44	14 04	11 25	9 49	10 18
11 02	11 23	8 43	6 54	7 25	11 58	12 19	9 35	7 48	8 19	30	12 55	13 14	10 27	8 42	9 14	13 51	14 10	11 19	9 36	10 08
11 10	11 29	8 39	6 42	7 15	12 06	12 25	9 30	7 36	8 09	31	13 02	13 20	10 22	8 29	9 04	13 59	14 15	11 14	9 23	9 58
11 18	11 36	8 34	6 30	7 05	12 14	12 31	9 26	7 23	7 59	32	13 10	13 26	10 17	8 17	8 53	14 07	14 21	11 08	9 10	9 48
11 27	11 42	8 30	6 17	6 54	12 22	12 37	9 21	7 11	7 49	33	13 19	13 31	10 12	8 04	8 43	14 15	14 26	11 03	8 57	9 37
11 35	11 49	8 26	6 05	6 44	12 31	12 43	9 16	6 58	7 38	34	13 27	13 37	10 07	7 51	8 32	14 23	14 32	10 57	8 44	9 26
11 44	11 56	8 21	5 52	6 33	12 39	12 49	9 11	6 45	7 27	35	13 35	13 43	10 02	7 38	8 21	14 31	14 37	10 52	8 30	9 15
11 53	12 02	8 17	5 39	6 22	12 48	12 56	9 07	6 32	7 16	36	13 44	13 49	9 56	7 24	8 10	14 40	14 43	10 46	8 17	9 04
12 02	12 09	8 13	5 26	6 10	12 57	13 02	9 02	6 18	7 04	37	13 53	13 56	9 51	7 11	7 58	14 48	14 49	10 40	8 03	8 52
12 11	12 16	8 08	5 13	5 58	13 06	13 09	8 57	6 05	6 52	38	14 02	14 02	9 46	6 57	7 46	14 57	14 55	10 35	7 48	8 40
12 21	12 23	8 04	4 59	5 46	13 16	13 16	8 52	5 51	6 40	39	14 11	14 08	9 40	6 43	7 34	15 06	15 01	10 29	7 34	8 28
12 30	12 30	7 59	4 46	5 34	13 25	13 22	8 47	5 37	6 28	40	14 20	14 15	9 35	6 28	7 22	15 16	15 07	10 23	7 19	8 15
12 40	12 37	7 55	4 32	5 21	13 35	13 29	8 42	5 23	6 15	41	14 30	14 21	9 30	6 14	7 09	15 25	15 13	10 17	7 05	8 02
12 51	12 45	7 50	4 17	5 08	13 45	13 36	8 37	5 08	6 02	42	14 40	14 28	9 24	5 59	6 55	15 35	15 19	10 11	6 49	7 49
13 01	12 52	7 46	4 03	4 55	13 56	13 43	8 32	4 53	5 48	43	14 50	14 35	9 19	5 44	6 41	15 45	15 26	10 05	6 34	7 35
13 12	13 00	7 41	3 48	4 41	14 07	13 51	8 27	4 38	5 34	44	15 01	14 42	9 13	5 28	6 27	15 55	15 32	9 59	6 18	7 20
13 24	13 08	7 36	3 33	4 26	14 18	13 58	8 22	4 23	5 19	45	15 12	14 49	9 07	5 12	6 12	16 06	15 39	9 53	6 02	7 05
13 35	13 16	7 31	3 17	4 11	14 29	14 06	8 16	4 07	5 04	46	15 23	14 56	9 01	4 56	5 57	16 17	15 46	9 46	5 45	6 50
13 47	13 24	7 26	3 02	3 55	14 41	14 13	8 11	3 51	4 48	47	15 35	15 03	8 55	4 39	5 41	16 28	15 53	9 40	5 28	6 34
13 59	13 32	7 21	2 45	3 39	14 53	14 21	8 05	3 34	4 32	48	15 47	15 10	8 49	4 22	5 25	16 40	16 00	9 34	5 11	6 17
14 12	13 40	7 16	2 29	3 22	15 06	14 29	8 00	3 17	4 15	49	15 59	15 18	8 43	4 05	5 07	16 52	16 07	9 27	4 53	6 00
14 26	13 49	7 11	2 12	3 05	15 19	14 38	7 54	2 59	3 57	50	16 12	15 26	8 37	3 47	4 49	17 05	16 14	9 20	4 35	5 42
14 39	13 58	7 06	1 54	2 47	15 32	14 46	7 48	2 41	3 39	51	16 25	15 34	8 31	3 29	4 31	17 18	16 22	9 13	4 16	5 23
14 54	14 07	7 00	1 36	2 27	15 46	14 55	7 42	2 23	3 19	52	16 39	15 42	8 24	3 10	4 11	17 32	16 30	9 06	3 57	5 03
15 09	14 17	6 55	1 18	2 07	16 01	15 04	7 36	2 04	2 59	53	16 53	15 51	8 18	2 50	3 50	17 46	16 38	8 59	3 37	4 42
15 24	14 26	6 49	0 59	1 46	16 16	15 13	7 30	1 44	2 37	54	17 08	15 59	8 11	2 30	3 29	18 00	16 46	8 52	3 16	4 20
15 41	14 36	6 44	0 39	1 24	16 32	15 22	7 24	1 24	2 15	55	17 24	16 08	8 04	2 10	3 06	18 16	16 54	8 45	2 55	3 57
15 58	14 46	6 38	0 19	1 01	16 49	15 32	7 18	1 04	1 51	56	17 40	16 17	7 57	1 48	2 42	18 32	17 03	8 37	2 33	3 33
16 15	14 57	6 32	29♎58	0 36	17 06	15 42	7 11	0 42	1 26	57	17 57	16 27	7 50	1 26	2 17	18 49	17 12	8 30	2 11	3 07
16 34	15 08	6 26	29 36	0 10	17 25	15 52	7 05	0 20	1 00	58	18 15	16 36	7 43	1 04	1 50	19 06	17 21	8 22	1 47	2 40
16 54	15 19	6 20	29 14	29♏42	17 44	16 03	6 58	29♎57	0 31	59	18 34	16 47	7 36	0 40	1 21	19 25	17 30	8 14	1 23	2 11
17♌14	15♍30	6♎13	28♎50	29♏12	18♌04	16♍14	6♎51	29♎33	0♐01	60	18♌54	16♍57	7♎28	0♏16	0♐50	19♌44	17♍40	8♎05	0♏58	1♐39

6h 56m 0s — 104° 0' 0" — 12 ♋ 53

LAT.	11	12	ASC	2	3
0	11♌32	12♍39	15♎12	16♏28	15♐16
5	12 03	13 04	14 39	15 29	14 37
10	12 34	13 28	14 08	14 30	13 58
15	13 05	13 52	13 39	13 32	13 18
20	13 38	14 16	13 09	12 33	12 36
21	13 44	14 21	13 04	12 21	12 27
22	13 51	14 26	12 58	12 09	12 18
23	13 58	14 31	12 52	11 57	12 09
24	14 05	14 35	12 46	11 45	12 00
25	14 12	14 40	12 40	11 33	11 51
26	14 19	14 45	12 35	11 21	11 42
27	14 26	14 50	12 29	11 08	11 32
28	14 33	14 55	12 23	10 55	11 23
29	14 40	15 00	12 17	10 43	11 13
30	14 48	15 05	12 11	10 30	11 03
31	14 55	15 10	12 06	10 17	10 53
32	15 03	15 16	12 00	10 04	10 42
33	15 11	15 21	11 54	9 50	10 32
34	15 19	15 26	11 48	9 37	10 21
35	15 27	15 31	11 42	9 23	10 09
36	15 35	15 37	11 36	9 09	9 58
37	15 44	15 42	11 29	8 55	9 46
38	15 53	15 48	11 23	8 40	9 34
39	16 02	15 54	11 17	8 26	9 22
40	16 11	15 59	11 11	8 11	9 09
41	16 20	16 05	11 04	7 55	8 56
42	16 30	16 11	10 58	7 40	8 42
43	16 40	16 17	10 52	7 24	8 28
44	16 50	16 23	10 45	7 08	8 14
45	17 00	16 29	10 38	6 51	7 59
46	17 11	16 36	10 31	6 34	7 43
47	17 22	16 42	10 25	6 17	7 27
48	17 34	16 49	10 18	5 59	7 10
49	17 46	16 56	10 11	5 41	6 52
50	17 58	17 03	10 03	5 22	6 34
51	18 11	17 10	9 56	5 03	6 15
52	18 24	17 17	9 48	4 43	5 55
53	18 38	17 25	9 41	4 23	5 34
54	18 53	17 32	9 33	4 02	5 12
55	19 08	17 40	9 25	3 40	4 48
56	19 23	17 48	9 17	3 18	4 24
57	19 40	17 57	9 09	2 55	3 58
58	19 57	18 06	9 00	2 31	3 30
59	20 15	18 14	8 51	2 06	3 00
60	20♌34	18♍24	8♎43	1♏41	2♐29

7h 0m 0s — 105° 0' 0" — 13 ♋ 49

LAT.	11	12	ASC	2	3
0	12♌32	13♍43	16♎17	17♏28	16♐11
5	13 02	14 07	15 42	16 28	15 33
10	13 33	14 30	15 09	15 28	14 53
15	14 04	14 52	14 37	14 29	14 13
20	14 35	15 15	14 06	13 29	13 31
21	14 42	15 19	13 59	13 17	13 22
22	14 49	15 24	13 53	13 05	13 13
23	14 55	15 28	13 47	12 53	13 04
24	15 02	15 33	13 41	12 40	12 55
25	15 09	15 38	13 35	12 28	12 46
26	15 16	15 42	13 28	12 15	12 37
27	15 23	15 47	13 22	12 03	12 27
28	15 30	15 52	13 16	11 50	12 17
29	15 37	15 56	13 10	11 37	12 07
30	15 44	16 01	13 03	11 24	11 57
31	15 52	16 06	12 57	11 10	11 47
32	15 59	16 11	12 51	10 57	11 37
33	16 07	16 16	12 45	10 43	11 26
34	16 15	16 21	12 38	10 29	11 15
35	16 23	16 26	12 32	10 15	11 04
36	16 31	16 31	12 25	10 01	10 52
37	16 40	16 36	12 19	9 47	10 40
38	16 48	16 41	12 12	9 32	10 28
39	16 57	16 46	12 05	9 17	10 16
40	17 06	16 52	11 59	9 02	10 03
41	17 15	16 57	11 52	8 46	9 49
42	17 25	17 03	11 45	8 30	9 36
43	17 34	17 08	11 38	8 14	9 22
44	17 44	17 14	11 31	7 58	9 07
45	17 55	17 20	11 24	7 41	8 52
46	18 05	17 26	11 17	7 23	8 36
47	18 16	17 32	11 09	7 06	8 20
48	18 28	17 38	11 02	6 48	8 03
49	18 39	17 45	10 54	6 29	7 45
50	18 51	17 51	10 46	6 10	7 26
51	19 04	17 58	10 38	5 50	7 07
52	19 17	18 05	10 30	5 30	6 47
53	19 31	18 12	10 22	5 09	6 25
54	19 45	18 19	10 14	4 48	6 03
55	19 59	18 26	10 05	4 26	5 39
56	20 15	18 34	9 57	4 03	5 15
57	20 31	18 42	9 48	3 39	4 48
58	20 48	18 50	9 39	3 15	4 20
59	21 05	18 58	9 29	2 50	3 50
60	21♌24	19♍07	9♎20	2♏23	3♐18

7h 4m 0s — 106° 0' 0" — 14 ♋ 44

LAT.	11	12	ASC	2	3
0	13♌32	14♍48	17♎21	18♏28	17♐07
5	14 02	15 10	16 44	17 26	16 28
10	14 32	15 31	16 09	16 26	15 49
15	15 02	15 52	15 35	15 26	15 08
20	15 33	16 13	15 02	14 25	14 26
21	15 40	16 18	14 55	14 13	14 17
22	15 46	16 22	14 48	14 01	14 08
23	15 53	16 26	14 42	13 48	13 59
24	16 00	16 30	14 35	13 36	13 50
25	16 06	16 35	14 29	13 23	13 41
26	16 13	16 39	14 22	13 10	13 31
27	16 20	16 43	14 16	12 57	13 22
28	16 27	16 48	14 09	12 44	13 12
29	16 34	16 52	14 02	12 31	13 02
30	16 41	16 57	13 56	12 17	12 52
31	16 49	17 01	13 49	12 04	12 41
32	16 56	17 06	13 42	11 50	12 31
33	17 04	17 10	13 35	11 36	12 20
34	17 11	17 15	13 29	11 22	12 09
35	17 19	17 20	13 22	11 08	11 58
36	17 27	17 24	13 15	10 53	11 46
37	17 36	17 29	13 08	10 39	11 34
38	17 44	17 34	13 01	10 24	11 22
39	17 53	17 39	12 54	10 08	11 09
40	18 01	17 44	12 46	9 53	10 56
41	18 10	17 49	12 39	9 37	10 43
42	18 20	17 54	12 32	9 21	10 29
43	18 29	18 00	12 24	9 04	10 15
44	18 39	18 05	12 17	8 47	10 00
45	18 49	18 11	12 09	8 30	9 45
46	19 00	18 16	12 02	8 13	9 29
47	19 10	18 22	11 54	7 55	9 12
48	19 21	18 28	11 46	7 36	8 55
49	19 33	18 34	11 38	7 17	8 37
50	19 45	18 40	11 29	6 57	8 19
51	19 57	18 46	11 21	6 37	7 59
52	20 10	18 52	11 12	6 17	7 39
53	20 23	18 59	11 04	5 56	7 17
54	20 37	19 06	10 55	5 34	6 55
55	20 51	19 13	10 46	5 11	6 31
56	21 06	19 20	10 36	4 48	6 05
57	21 22	19 27	10 27	4 24	5 39
58	21 39	19 35	10 17	3 59	5 10
59	21 56	19 42	10 07	3 33	4 40
60	22♌14	19♍51	9♎57	3♏06	4♐07

7h 8m 0s — 107° 0' 0" — 15 ♋ 40

LAT.	11	12	ASC	2	3
0	14♌32	15♍53	18♎26	19♏27	18♐02
5	15 01	16 13	17 46	18 25	17 23
10	15 31	16 33	17 09	17 24	16 44
15	16 01	16 53	16 33	16 23	16 03
20	16 32	17 12	15 58	15 21	15 21
21	16 38	17 16	15 51	15 09	15 12
22	16 44	17 20	15 44	14 56	15 03
23	16 51	17 24	15 37	14 43	14 54
24	16 57	17 28	15 30	14 31	14 45
25	17 04	17 32	15 23	14 18	14 35
26	17 10	17 36	15 16	14 05	14 26
27	17 17	17 40	15 09	13 51	14 16
28	17 24	17 44	15 02	13 38	14 06
29	17 31	17 48	14 55	13 25	13 56
30	17 38	17 53	14 48	13 11	13 46
31	17 45	17 57	14 41	12 57	13 36
32	17 53	18 01	14 33	12 43	13 25
33	18 00	18 05	14 26	12 29	13 14
34	18 08	18 10	14 19	12 15	13 03
35	18 16	18 14	14 12	12 00	12 52
36	18 23	18 18	14 04	11 46	12 40
37	18 32	18 23	13 57	11 31	12 28
38	18 40	18 27	13 49	11 15	12 16
39	18 48	18 32	13 42	11 00	12 03
40	18 57	18 37	13 34	10 44	11 50
41	19 06	18 41	13 27	10 28	11 37
42	19 15	18 46	13 19	10 11	11 23
43	19 24	18 51	13 11	9 54	11 08
44	19 34	18 56	13 03	9 37	10 53
45	19 44	19 01	12 55	9 20	10 38
46	19 54	19 06	12 47	9 02	10 22
47	20 05	19 12	12 38	8 43	10 05
48	20 15	19 17	12 30	8 24	9 48
49	20 27	19 23	12 21	8 05	9 30
50	20 38	19 28	12 12	7 45	9 11
51	20 50	19 34	12 03	7 25	8 51
52	21 03	19 40	11 54	7 04	8 31
53	21 16	19 46	11 45	6 42	8 09
54	21 29	19 52	11 36	6 19	7 46
55	21 43	19 59	11 26	5 56	7 22
56	21 58	20 05	11 16	5 33	6 56
57	22 14	20 12	11 06	5 08	6 29
58	22 30	20 19	10 56	4 42	6 00
59	22 47	20 26	10 45	4 16	5 30
60	23♌04	20♍34	10♎34	3♏48	4♐57

7h 12m 0s — 108° 0' 0" — 16 ♋ 36

LAT.	11	12	ASC	2	3
0	15♌32	16♍57	19♎30	20♏26	18♐58
5	16 01	17 16	18 48	19 24	18 19
10	16 30	17 35	18 09	18 22	17 39
15	17 00	17 53	17 31	17 20	16 58
20	17 30	18 11	16 54	16 17	16 16
21	17 36	18 15	16 46	16 04	16 07
22	17 42	18 18	16 39	15 52	15 58
23	17 49	18 22	16 32	15 39	15 49
24	17 55	18 26	16 24	15 26	15 39
25	18 01	18 29	16 17	15 12	15 30
26	18 08	18 33	16 09	14 59	15 21
27	18 15	18 37	16 02	14 46	15 11
28	18 21	18 41	15 55	14 32	15 01
29	18 28	18 44	15 47	14 19	14 51
30	18 35	18 48	15 40	14 05	14 41
31	18 42	18 52	15 32	13 51	14 30
32	18 50	18 56	15 25	13 37	14 20
33	18 57	19 00	15 17	13 22	14 09
34	19 04	19 04	15 09	13 08	13 57
35	19 12	19 08	15 02	12 53	13 46
36	19 20	19 12	14 54	12 38	13 34
37	19 28	19 16	14 46	12 22	13 22
38	19 36	19 20	14 38	12 07	13 10
39	19 44	19 25	14 30	11 51	12 57
40	19 52	19 29	14 22	11 35	12 44
41	20 01	19 33	14 14	11 18	12 30
42	20 10	19 38	14 06	11 02	12 16
43	20 19	19 42	13 57	10 44	12 02
44	20 29	19 47	13 49	10 27	11 47
45	20 38	19 52	13 40	10 09	11 31
46	20 48	19 57	13 32	9 51	11 15
47	20 59	20 01	13 23	9 32	10 58
48	21 09	20 06	13 14	9 13	10 41
49	21 20	20 12	13 05	8 53	10 23
50	21 32	20 17	12 55	8 33	10 04
51	21 44	20 22	12 46	8 12	9 44
52	21 56	20 28	12 36	7 50	9 23
53	22 09	20 33	12 27	7 28	9 01
54	22 22	20 39	12 17	7 05	8 38
55	22 36	20 45	12 06	6 42	8 13
56	22 50	20 51	11 56	6 17	7 47
57	23 05	20 57	11 45	5 52	7 20
58	23 21	21 04	11 34	5 26	6 51
59	23 37	21 11	11 23	4 59	6 19
60	23♌55	21♍17	11♎12	4♏31	5♐46

7h 16m 0s — 109° 0' 0" — 17 ♋ 32

LAT.	11	12	ASC	2	3
0	16♌33	18♍02	20♎34	21♏26	19♐53
5	17 01	18 20	19 50	20 22	19 14
10	17 30	18 37	19 09	19 19	18 34
15	17 58	18 53	18 29	18 16	17 53
20	18 28	19 10	17 50	17 13	17 10
21	18 34	19 13	17 42	17 00	17 02
22	18 40	19 17	17 34	16 47	16 53
23	18 47	19 20	17 26	16 34	16 43
24	18 53	19 23	17 19	16 20	16 34
25	18 59	19 27	17 11	16 07	16 25
26	19 06	19 30	17 03	15 54	16 15
27	19 12	19 34	16 55	15 40	16 05
28	19 19	19 37	16 47	15 26	15 56
29	19 26	19 41	16 40	15 12	15 45
30	19 32	19 44	16 32	14 58	15 35
31	19 39	19 48	16 24	14 44	15 25
32	19 46	19 51	16 16	14 30	15 14
33	19 54	19 55	16 08	14 15	15 03
34	20 01	19 59	16 00	14 00	14 52
35	20 08	20 02	15 52	13 45	14 40
36	20 16	20 06	15 43	13 30	14 28
37	20 24	20 10	15 35	13 14	14 16
38	20 32	20 14	15 27	12 58	14 04
39	20 40	20 18	15 18	12 42	13 51
40	20 48	20 22	15 10	12 26	13 38
41	20 57	20 26	15 01	12 09	13 24
42	21 05	20 30	14 53	11 52	13 10
43	21 14	20 34	14 44	11 35	12 55
44	21 24	20 38	14 35	11 17	12 40
45	21 33	20 42	14 26	10 58	12 24
46	21 43	20 47	14 17	10 40	12 08
47	21 53	20 51	14 07	10 21	11 51
48	22 03	20 56	13 58	10 01	11 34
49	22 14	21 01	13 48	9 41	11 15
50	22 25	21 05	13 38	9 20	10 56
51	22 37	21 10	13 28	8 59	10 36
52	22 49	21 15	13 18	8 37	10 15
53	23 01	21 20	13 08	8 14	9 53
54	23 14	21 26	12 57	7 51	9 29
55	23 28	21 31	12 47	7 27	9 05
56	23 42	21 37	12 36	7 02	8 38
57	23 57	21 43	12 24	6 36	8 11
58	24 12	21 48	12 13	6 10	7 41
59	24 28	21 55	12 01	5 42	7 09
60	24♌45	22♍01	11♎49	5♏13	6♐35

7h 20m 0s — 110° 0' 0" — 18 ♋ 28

LAT.	11	12	ASC	2	3
0	17♌33	19♍07	21♎38	22♏25	20♐49
5	18 01	19 23	20 52	21 20	20 09
10	18 29	19 39	20 09	20 17	19 29
15	18 58	19 54	19 27	19 13	18 48
20	19 27	20 09	18 46	18 08	18 05
21	19 33	20 12	18 37	17 55	17 56
22	19 39	20 15	18 29	17 42	17 47
23	19 45	20 18	18 21	17 29	17 38
24	19 51	20 21	18 13	17 15	17 29
25	19 57	20 24	18 05	17 02	17 19
26	20 04	20 27	17 57	16 48	17 10
27	20 10	20 31	17 48	16 34	17 00
28	20 16	20 34	17 40	16 20	16 50
29	20 23	20 37	17 32	16 06	16 40
30	20 30	20 40	17 24	15 52	16 30
31	20 37	20 43	17 15	15 37	16 19
32	20 43	20 47	17 07	15 23	16 08
33	20 50	20 50	16 58	15 08	15 57
34	20 58	20 53	16 50	14 53	15 46
35	21 05	20 57	16 41	14 37	15 34
36	21 12	21 00	16 33	14 22	15 22
37	21 20	21 03	16 24	14 06	15 10
38	21 28	21 07	16 15	13 50	14 58
39	21 36	21 10	16 07	13 33	14 45
40	21 44	21 14	15 58	13 17	14 31
41	21 52	21 18	15 49	13 00	14 18
42	22 01	21 21	15 39	12 42	14 03
43	22 10	21 25	15 30	12 25	13 49
44	22 19	21 29	15 21	12 06	13 33
45	22 28	21 33	15 11	11 48	13 18
46	22 38	21 37	15 02	11 29	13 01
47	22 47	21 41	14 52	11 09	12 44
48	22 58	21 45	14 42	10 49	12 27
49	23 08	21 49	14 32	10 29	12 08
50	23 19	21 54	14 21	10 08	11 49
51	23 30	21 58	14 11	9 46	11 28
52	23 42	22 03	14 00	9 23	11 07
53	23 54	22 08	13 49	9 00	10 45
54	24 07	22 12	13 38	8 37	10 21
55	24 20	22 17	13 27	8 12	9 56
56	24 34	22 22	13 15	7 47	9 30
57	24 48	22 28	13 03	7 20	9 01
58	25 03	22 33	12 51	6 53	8 31
59	25 19	22 39	12 39	6 25	7 59
60	25♌35	22♍44	12♎26	5♏56	7♐25

7h 24m 0s — 111° 0' 0" — 19 ♋ 24

LAT.	11	12	ASC	2	3
0	18♌34	20♍12	22♎42	23♏23	21♐44
5	19 01	20 27	21 54	22 18	21 04
10	19 29	20 41	21 09	21 14	20 24
15	19 57	20 54	20 25	20 09	19 43
20	20 25	21 08	19 42	19 04	19 00
21	20 31	21 11	19 33	18 51	18 51
22	20 37	21 13	19 24	18 37	18 42
23	20 43	21 16	19 16	18 24	18 33
24	20 49	21 19	19 07	18 10	18 24
25	20 55	21 22	18 59	17 56	18 14
26	21 01	21 25	18 50	17 42	18 04
27	21 08	21 27	18 42	17 28	17 55
28	21 14	21 30	18 33	17 14	17 45
29	21 21	21 33	18 24	17 00	17 34
30	21 27	21 36	18 16	16 45	17 24
31	21 34	21 39	18 07	16 31	17 13
32	21 41	21 42	17 58	16 16	17 03
33	21 47	21 45	17 49	16 01	16 51
34	21 54	21 48	17 40	15 45	16 40
35	22 02	21 51	17 31	15 30	16 28
36	22 09	21 54	17 22	15 14	16 16
37	22 16	21 57	17 13	14 58	16 04
38	22 24	22 00	17 04	14 41	15 51
39	22 32	22 03	16 55	14 25	15 38
40	22 40	22 07	16 45	14 08	15 25
41	22 48	22 10	16 36	13 50	15 11
42	22 56	22 13	16 26	13 33	14 57
43	23 05	22 17	16 16	13 15	14 42
44	23 14	22 20	16 07	12 56	14 27
45	23 23	22 24	15 57	12 37	14 11
46	23 32	22 27	15 47	12 18	13 54
47	23 42	22 31	15 36	11 58	13 37
48	23 52	22 35	15 26	11 37	13 19
49	24 02	22 39	15 15	11 16	13 01
50	24 13	22 42	15 04	10 55	12 41
51	24 24	22 46	14 53	10 33	12 21
52	24 35	22 51	14 42	10 10	11 59
53	24 47	22 55	14 31	9 47	11 37
54	24 59	22 59	14 19	9 22	11 13
55	25 12	23 04	14 07	8 57	10 48
56	25 26	23 08	13 55	8 31	10 21
57	25 40	23 13	13 42	8 05	9 52
58	25 54	23 18	13 30	7 37	9 22
59	26 10	23 23	13 17	7 08	8 49
60	26♌26	23♍28	13♎03	6♏38	8♐14

7h 28m 0s — 112° 0' 0" — 20 ♋ 20

LAT.	11	12	ASC	2	3
0	19♌35	21♍17	23♎46	24♏22	22♐39
5	20 02	21 30	22 56	23 16	22 00
10	20 29	21 43	22 08	22 11	21 20
15	20 56	21 55	21 22	21 06	20 38
20	21 24	22 07	20 37	19 59	19 55
21	21 30	22 09	20 28	19 46	19 46
22	21 36	22 12	20 19	19 32	19 37
23	21 42	22 14	20 10	19 18	19 28
24	21 47	22 17	20 02	19 05	19 18
25	21 53	22 19	19 53	18 51	19 09
26	22 00	22 22	19 44	18 37	18 59
27	22 06	22 24	19 35	18 22	18 49
28	22 12	22 27	19 26	18 08	18 39
29	22 18	22 29	19 17	17 53	18 29
30	22 25	22 32	19 07	17 39	18 18
31	22 31	22 34	18 58	17 24	18 08
32	22 38	22 37	18 49	17 09	17 57
33	22 45	22 40	18 40	16 53	17 46
34	22 51	22 42	18 31	16 38	17 34
35	22 58	22 45	18 21	16 22	17 23
36	23 06	22 48	18 12	16 06	17 11
37	23 13	22 51	18 02	15 49	16 58
38	23 20	22 53	17 53	15 33	16 45
39	23 28	22 56	17 43	15 16	16 32
40	23 36	22 59	17 33	14 59	16 19
41	23 44	23 02	17 23	14 41	16 05
42	23 52	23 05	17 13	14 23	15 51
43	24 00	23 08	17 03	14 04	15 36
44	24 09	23 11	16 53	13 46	15 20
45	24 18	23 14	16 42	13 26	15 04
46	24 27	23 18	16 31	13 07	14 48
47	24 36	23 21	16 21	12 46	14 30
48	24 46	23 24	16 10	12 26	14 12
49	24 56	23 28	15 59	12 04	13 54
50	25 07	23 31	15 47	11 42	13 34
51	25 17	23 35	15 36	11 20	13 13
52	25 29	23 38	15 24	10 57	12 52
53	25 40	23 42	15 12	10 33	12 29
54	25 52	23 46	15 00	10 08	12 05
55	26 05	23 50	14 47	9 42	11 39
56	26 18	23 54	14 35	9 16	11 12
57	26 31	23 58	14 22	8 49	10 43
58	26 46	24 02	14 08	8 20	10 13
59	27 01	24 07	13 54	7 51	9 40
60	27♌16	24♍11	13♎40	7♏20	9♐04

7h 32m 0s — 113° 0' 0" — 21 ♋ 17

LAT.	11	12	ASC	2	3
0	20♌36	22♍23	24♎50	25♏21	23♐34
5	21 03	22 34	23 58	24 14	22 55
10	21 29	22 45	23 08	23 08	22 15
15	21 56	22 55	22 20	22 02	21 33
20	22 23	23 06	21 33	20 55	20 50
21	22 29	23 08	21 24	20 41	20 41
22	22 34	23 10	21 14	20 27	20 32
23	22 40	23 12	21 05	20 13	20 22
24	22 46	23 15	20 56	19 59	20 13
25	22 52	23 17	20 46	19 45	20 03
26	22 58	23 19	20 37	19 31	19 54
27	23 04	23 21	20 28	19 16	19 44
28	23 10	23 23	20 18	19 02	19 34
29	23 16	23 26	20 09	18 47	19 23
30	23 22	23 28	19 59	18 32	19 13
31	23 29	23 30	19 50	18 17	19 02
32	23 35	23 32	19 40	18 02	18 51
33	23 42	23 35	19 30	17 46	18 40
34	23 48	23 37	19 21	17 30	18 28
35	23 55	23 39	19 11	17 14	18 17
36	24 02	23 42	19 01	16 58	18 05
37	24 09	23 44	18 51	16 41	17 52
38	24 17	23 47	18 41	16 24	17 39
39	24 24	23 49	18 31	16 07	17 26
40	24 32	23 52	18 21	15 49	17 13
41	24 40	23 54	18 10	15 31	16 59
42	24 48	23 57	18 00	15 13	16 44
43	24 56	24 00	17 49	14 54	16 29
44	25 04	24 02	17 38	14 35	16 14
45	25 13	24 05	17 28	14 16	15 58
46	25 22	24 08	17 16	13 56	15 41
47	25 31	24 11	17 05	13 35	15 24
48	25 41	24 14	16 54	13 14	15 05
49	25 50	24 17	16 42	12 52	14 46
50	26 01	24 20	16 30	12 30	14 27
51	26 11	24 23	16 18	12 07	14 06
52	26 22	24 26	16 06	11 43	13 44
53	26 33	24 29	15 53	11 19	13 21
54	26 45	24 33	15 41	10 54	12 57
55	26 57	24 36	15 28	10 28	12 31
56	27 10	24 40	15 14	10 01	12 03
57	27 23	24 43	15 01	9 33	11 34
58	27 37	24 47	14 47	9 04	11 03
59	27 52	24 51	14 32	8 34	10 30
60	28♌07	24♍55	14♎18	8♏03	9♐54

7h 36m 0s — 114° 0' 0" — 22 ♋ 13

LAT.	11	12	ASC	2	3
0	21♌37	23♍28	25♎53	26♏19	24♐30
5	22 03	23 38	24 59	25 11	23 50
10	22 29	23 47	24 07	24 05	23 10
15	22 55	23 56	23 18	22 58	22 28
20	23 22	24 05	22 29	21 50	21 45
21	23 28	24 07	22 19	21 36	21 35
22	23 33	24 09	22 09	21 22	21 26
23	23 39	24 11	22 00	21 08	21 17
24	23 44	24 12	21 50	20 54	21 08
25	23 50	24 14	21 40	20 39	20 58
26	23 56	24 16	21 30	20 25	20 48
27	24 02	24 18	21 21	20 10	20 38
28	24 08	24 20	21 11	19 55	20 28
29	24 14	24 22	21 01	19 40	20 18
30	24 20	24 24	20 51	19 25	20 07
31	24 26	24 26	20 41	19 10	19 57
32	24 33	24 28	20 31	18 54	19 46
33	24 39	24 30	20 21	18 39	19 34
34	24 46	24 32	20 11	18 22	19 23
35	24 52	24 34	20 01	18 06	19 11
36	24 59	24 36	19 50	17 50	18 59
37	25 06	24 38	19 40	17 33	18 46
38	25 13	24 40	19 30	17 16	18 33
39	25 21	24 42	19 19	16 58	18 20
40	25 28	24 44	19 08	16 40	18 07
41	25 36	24 46	18 58	16 22	17 53
42	25 43	24 49	18 47	16 03	17 38
43	25 51	24 51	18 36	15 44	17 23
44	26 00	24 53	18 24	15 25	17 07
45	26 08	24 56	18 13	15 05	16 51
46	26 17	24 58	18 01	14 44	16 34
47	26 26	25 01	17 50	14 24	16 17
48	26 35	25 03	17 38	14 02	15 58
49	26 45	25 06	17 26	13 40	15 39
50	26 55	25 08	17 13	13 17	15 19
51	27 05	25 11	17 01	12 54	14 58
52	27 15	25 14	16 48	12 30	14 36
53	27 26	25 16	16 35	12 05	14 13
54	27 38	25 19	16 21	11 39	13 49
55	27 50	25 22	16 08	11 13	13 23
56	28 02	25 25	15 54	10 45	12 55
57	28 15	25 29	15 40	10 17	12 25
58	28 29	25 32	15 25	9 47	11 54
59	28 43	25 35	15 10	9 17	11 20
60	28♌58	25♍39	14♎55	8♏45	10♐44

7h 40m 0s — 115° 0' 0" — 23 ♋ 10

LAT.	11	12	ASC	2	3
0	22♌39	24♍33	26♎57	27♏17	25♐25
5	23 04	24 41	26 00	26 09	24 45
10	23 30	24 49	25 07	25 02	24 05
15	23 55	24 57	24 15	23 54	23 23
20	24 21	25 04	23 24	22 45	22 39
21	24 27	25 06	23 14	22 31	22 30
22	24 32	25 07	23 04	22 17	22 21
23	24 38	25 09	22 54	22 03	22 12
24	24 43	25 10	22 44	21 48	22 02
25	24 49	25 12	22 34	21 34	21 53
26	24 54	25 13	22 24	21 19	21 43
27	25 00	25 15	22 14	21 04	21 33
28	25 06	25 17	22 03	20 49	21 23
29	25 12	25 18	21 53	20 34	21 12
30	25 18	25 20	21 43	20 19	21 02
31	25 24	25 21	21 33	20 03	20 51
32	25 30	25 23	21 22	19 47	20 40
33	25 36	25 25	21 12	19 31	20 29
34	25 43	25 26	21 01	19 15	20 17
35	25 49	25 28	20 51	18 58	20 05
36	25 56	25 30	20 40	18 41	19 53
37	26 03	25 32	20 29	18 24	19 40
38	26 10	25 33	20 18	18 07	19 28
39	26 17	25 35	20 07	17 49	19 14
40	26 24	25 37	19 56	17 31	19 01
41	26 32	25 39	19 45	17 12	18 46
42	26 39	25 41	19 33	16 54	18 32
43	26 47	25 42	19 22	16 34	18 17
44	26 55	25 44	19 10	16 14	18 01
45	27 03	25 46	18 58	15 54	17 45
46	27 12	25 48	18 46	15 33	17 28
47	27 21	25 50	18 34	15 12	17 10
48	27 30	25 53	18 22	14 50	16 52
49	27 39	25 55	18 09	14 28	16 32
50	27 49	25 57	17 56	14 05	16 12
51	27 59	25 59	17 43	13 41	15 51
52	28 09	26 01	17 30	13 16	15 29
53	28 20	26 04	17 16	12 51	15 05
54	28 31	26 06	17 02	12 25	14 41
55	28 42	26 09	16 48	11 58	14 14
56	28 54	26 11	16 34	11 30	13 46
57	29 07	26 14	16 19	11 01	13 17
58	29 20	26 16	16 03	10 31	12 45
59	29 34	26 19	15 48	10 00	12 11
60	29♌48	26♍22	15♎32	9♏27	11♐34

7h 44m 0s — 116° 0' 0" — 24 ♋ 06

LAT.	11	12	ASC	2	3
0	23♌41	25♍38	28♎00	28♏15	26♐20
5	24 05	25 45	27 02	27 06	25 40
10	24 30	25 51	26 06	25 58	25 00
15	24 55	25 57	25 13	24 50	24 18
20	25 21	26 03	24 20	23 40	23 34
21	25 26	26 05	24 10	23 26	23 25
22	25 31	26 06	23 59	23 12	23 16
23	25 37	26 07	23 49	22 57	23 06
24	25 42	26 08	23 38	22 43	22 57
25	25 47	26 10	23 28	22 28	22 47
26	25 53	26 11	23 17	22 13	22 38
27	25 59	26 12	23 07	21 58	22 28
28	26 04	26 13	22 56	21 43	22 17
29	26 10	26 15	22 45	21 27	22 07
30	26 16	26 16	22 35	21 12	21 56
31	26 22	26 17	22 24	20 56	21 45
32	26 28	26 18	22 13	20 40	21 34
33	26 34	26 20	22 02	20 24	21 23
34	26 40	26 21	21 51	20 07	21 11
35	26 47	26 22	21 40	19 50	20 59
36	26 53	26 24	21 29	19 33	20 47
37	27 00	26 25	21 18	19 16	20 35
38	27 07	26 27	21 07	18 58	20 22
39	27 13	26 28	20 55	18 40	20 08
40	27 21	26 29	20 44	18 22	19 55
41	27 28	26 31	20 32	18 03	19 40
42	27 35	26 32	20 20	17 44	19 26
43	27 43	26 34	20 08	17 24	19 10
44	27 51	26 36	19 56	17 04	18 55
45	27 59	26 37	19 44	16 43	18 38
46	28 07	26 39	19 31	16 22	18 21
47	28 16	26 40	19 18	16 01	18 03
48	28 24	26 42	19 06	15 38	17 45
49	28 33	26 44	18 52	15 16	17 25
50	28 43	26 45	18 39	14 52	17 05
51	28 52	26 47	18 25	14 28	16 44
52	29 03	26 49	18 12	14 03	16 21
53	29 13	26 51	17 57	13 37	15 58
54	29 24	26 53	17 43	13 10	15 33
55	29 35	26 55	17 28	12 43	15 06
56	29 47	26 57	17 13	12 15	14 38
57	29 59	26 59	16 58	11 45	14 08
58	0♍12	27 01	16 42	11 14	13 36
59	0 25	27 03	16 26	10 43	13 01
60	0♍39	27♍06	16♎09	10♏10	12♐24

7h 48m 0s — 117° 0' 0" — 25 ♋ 03

LAT.	11	12	ASC	2	3
0	24♌42	26♍44	29♎03	29♏13	27♐15
5	25 07	26 49	28 03	28 03	26 35
10	25 31	26 53	27 05	26 55	25 55
15	25 55	26 58	26 10	25 46	25 13
20	26 20	27 03	25 15	24 35	24 29
21	26 25	27 03	25 05	24 21	24 20
22	26 30	27 04	24 54	24 06	24 11
23	26 36	27 05	24 43	23 52	24 01
24	26 41	27 06	24 32	23 37	23 52
25	26 46	27 07	24 21	23 22	23 42
26	26 52	27 08	24 10	23 07	23 32
27	26 57	27 09	23 59	22 52	23 22
28	27 03	27 10	23 48	22 36	23 12
29	27 08	27 11	23 37	22 21	23 02
30	27 14	27 12	23 26	22 05	22 51
31	27 20	27 13	23 15	21 49	22 40
32	27 26	27 14	23 04	21 33	22 29
33	27 32	27 15	22 53	21 16	22 17
34	27 38	27 16	22 41	20 59	22 06
35	27 44	27 17	22 30	20 42	21 54
36	27 50	27 18	22 18	20 25	21 42
37	27 57	27 19	22 07	20 07	21 29
38	28 03	27 20	21 55	19 49	21 16
39	28 10	27 21	21 43	19 31	21 02
40	28 17	27 22	21 31	19 12	20 49
41	28 24	27 23	21 19	18 53	20 34
42	28 31	27 24	21 07	18 34	20 20
43	28 39	27 25	20 54	18 14	20 04
44	28 46	27 27	20 42	17 53	19 48
45	28 54	27 28	20 29	17 33	19 32
46	29 02	27 29	20 16	17 11	19 15
47	29 10	27 30	20 03	16 49	18 57
48	29 19	27 31	19 49	16 27	18 38
49	29 28	27 33	19 36	16 03	18 19
50	29 37	27 34	19 22	15 39	17 58
51	29 46	27 35	19 08	15 15	17 37
52	29 56	27 37	18 53	14 49	17 14
53	0♍06	27 38	18 39	14 23	16 50
54	0 17	27 40	18 24	13 56	16 25
55	0 28	27 41	18 08	13 28	15 58
56	0 39	27 43	17 53	12 59	15 30
57	0 51	27 44	17 37	12 29	15 00
58	1 04	27 46	17 20	11 58	14 27
59	1 16	27 48	17 03	11 26	13 52
60	1♍30	27♍49	16♎46	10♏52	13♐14

7h 52m 0s — 118° 0' 0" — 26 ♋ 00

LAT.	11	12	ASC	2	3
0	25♌44	27♍49	0♏06	0♐11	28♐10
5	26 08	27 52	29♎04	29♏01	27 30
10	26 32	27 56	28 04	27 51	26 50
15	26 55	27 59	27 07	26 41	26 08
20	27 20	28 02	26 11	25 30	25 24
21	27 25	28 02	26 00	25 15	25 15
22	27 30	28 03	25 48	25 01	25 05
23	27 35	28 04	25 37	24 46	24 56
24	27 40	28 04	25 26	24 31	24 46
25	27 45	28 05	25 15	24 16	24 37
26	27 50	28 05	25 04	24 01	24 27
27	27 56	28 06	24 52	23 45	24 17
28	28 01	28 07	24 41	23 30	24 07
29	28 07	28 07	24 29	23 14	23 56
30	28 12	28 08	24 18	22 58	23 45
31	28 18	28 09	24 06	22 42	23 35
32	28 24	28 09	23 55	22 25	23 23
33	28 29	28 10	23 43	22 09	23 12
34	28 35	28 11	23 32	21 52	23 00
35	28 41	28 11	23 20	21 34	22 48
36	28 48	28 12	23 08	21 17	22 36
37	28 54	28 13	22 56	20 59	22 23
38	29 00	28 13	22 44	20 41	22 10
39	29 07	28 14	22 31	20 22	21 57
40	29 13	28 15	22 19	20 03	21 43
41	29 20	28 15	22 06	19 44	21 28
42	29 27	28 16	21 54	19 24	21 14
43	29 35	28 17	21 41	19 04	20 58
44	29 42	28 18	21 28	18 43	20 42
45	29 50	28 19	21 14	18 22	20 26
46	29 57	28 19	21 01	18 00	20 08
47	0♍06	28 20	20 47	17 38	19 50
48	0 14	28 21	20 33	17 15	19 32
49	0 22	28 22	20 19	16 51	19 12
50	0 31	28 23	20 05	16 27	18 51
51	0 40	28 24	19 50	16 02	18 30
52	0 50	28 25	19 35	15 36	18 07
53	1 00	28 25	19 20	15 09	17 43
54	1 10	28 26	19 04	14 42	17 18
55	1 21	28 27	18 49	14 13	16 51
56	1 32	28 28	18 32	13 44	16 22
57	1 43	28 29	18 16	13 13	15 51
58	1 55	28 31	17 59	12 41	15 18
59	2 08	28 32	17 41	12 08	14 43
60	2♍21	28♍33	17♎23	11♏34	14♐04

7h 56m 0s — 119° 0' 0" — 26 ♋ 57

LAT.	11	12	ASC	2	3
0	26♌47	28♍55	1♏08	1♐08	29♐05
5	27 10	28 56	0 04	29♏57	28 25
10	27 33	28 58	29♎03	28 47	27 45
15	27 56	28 59	28 04	27 37	27 03
20	28 19	29 01	27 06	26 25	26 19
21	28 24	29 01	26 55	26 10	26 10
22	28 29	29 01	26 43	25 55	26 00
23	28 34	29 02	26 32	25 40	25 51
24	28 39	29 02	26 20	25 25	25 41
25	28 44	29 02	26 08	25 10	25 32
26	28 49	29 03	25 57	24 55	25 22
27	28 55	29 03	25 45	24 39	25 12
28	29 00	29 03	25 33	24 23	25 01
29	29 05	29 04	25 21	24 07	24 51
30	29 11	29 04	25 10	23 51	24 40
31	29 16	29 04	24 58	23 35	24 29
32	29 22	29 05	24 46	23 18	24 18
33	29 27	29 05	24 34	23 01	24 07
34	29 33	29 05	24 22	22 44	23 55
35	29 39	29 06	24 09	22 26	23 43
36	29 45	29 06	23 57	22 08	23 30
37	29 51	29 06	23 45	21 50	23 18
38	29 57	29 07	23 32	21 32	23 04
39	0♍04	29 07	23 19	21 13	22 51
40	0 10	29 07	23 06	20 54	22 37
41	0 17	29 08	22 53	20 34	22 23
42	0 24	29 08	22 40	20 14	22 08
43	0 31	29 08	22 27	19 54	21 52
44	0 38	29 09	22 13	19 33	21 36
45	0 45	29 09	22 00	19 11	21 19
46	0 53	29 10	21 46	18 49	21 02
47	1 01	29 10	21 32	18 26	20 44
48	1 09	29 10	21 17	18 03	20 25
49	1 17	29 11	21 03	17 39	20 05
50	1 26	29 11	20 48	17 14	19 45
51	1 35	29 12	20 33	16 49	19 23
52	1 44	29 12	20 17	16 22	19 00
53	1 53	29 13	20 01	15 55	18 36
54	2 03	29 13	19 45	15 27	18 10
55	2 14	29 14	19 29	14 58	17 43
56	2 24	29 14	19 12	14 28	17 14
57	2 35	29 15	18 55	13 57	16 43
58	2 47	29 15	18 37	13 25	16 10
59	2 59	29 16	18 19	12 51	15 34
60	3♍12	29♍16	18♎00	12♏16	14♐55

8h 0m 0s 120° 0' 0"
27 ♋ 55

LAT.	11	12	ASC	2	3
0	27♌49	0♎00	2♏11	2♐05	0♑00
5	28 11	0 00	1 05	0 54	29♐20
10	28 34	0 00	0 02	29♏44	28 40
15	28 56	0 00	29♎01	28 32	27 58
20	29 19	0 00	28 02	27 20	27 14
21	29 24	0 00	27 50	27 05	27 04
22	29 29	0 00	27 38	26 50	26 55
23	29 34	0 00	27 26	26 35	26 46
24	29 38	0 00	27 14	26 19	26 36
25	29 43	0 00	27 02	26 04	26 26
26	29 48	0 00	26 50	25 48	26 16
27	29 53	0 00	26 38	25 33	26 06
28	29 59	0 00	26 26	25 17	25 56
29	0♍04	0 00	26 13	25 00	25 46
30	0 09	0 00	26 01	24 44	25 35
31	0 14	0 00	25 49	24 27	25 24
32	0 20	0 00	25 37	24 10	25 13
33	0 25	0 00	25 24	23 53	25 01
34	0 31	0 00	25 12	23 36	24 49
35	0 37	0 00	24 59	23 18	24 37
36	0 42	0 00	24 46	23 00	24 25
37	0 48	0 00	24 33	22 42	24 12
38	0 54	0 00	24 20	22 23	23 59
39	1 00	0 00	24 07	22 04	23 45
40	1 07	0 00	23 54	21 45	23 31
41	1 13	0 00	23 40	21 25	23 17
42	1 20	0 00	23 27	21 04	23 02
43	1 27	0 00	23 13	20 43	22 46
44	1 34	0 00	22 59	20 22	22 30
45	1 41	0 00	22 45	20 00	22 13
46	1 48	0 00	22 31	19 38	21 56
47	1 56	0 00	22 16	19 15	21 38
48	2 04	0 00	22 01	18 51	21 19
49	2 12	0 00	21 46	18 27	20 59
50	2 20	0 00	21 31	18 02	20 38
51	2 29	0 00	21 15	17 36	20 16
52	2 38	0 00	20 59	17 09	19 53
53	2 47	0 00	20 43	16 41	19 29
54	2 57	0 00	20 26	16 13	19 03
55	3 07	0 00	20 09	15 43	18 35
56	3 17	0 00	19 51	15 13	18 06
57	3 28	0 00	19 34	14 41	17 35
58	3 39	0 00	19 15	14 08	17 01
59	3 51	0 00	18 57	13 34	16 25
60	4♍03	0♎00	18♎37	12♏59	15♐46

8h 4m 0s 121° 0' 0"
28 ♋ 52

LAT.	11	12	ASC	2	3
0	28♌52	1♎05	3♏13	3♐03	0♑55
5	29 13	1 04	2 06	1 51	0 15
10	29 35	1 02	1 01	0 40	29♐35
15	29 57	1 01	29♎58	29♏28	28 53
20	0♍19	0 59	28 57	28 14	28 08
21	0 24	0 59	28 44	27 59	27 59
22	0 29	0 59	28 32	27 44	27 50
23	0 33	0 58	28 20	27 29	27 41
24	0 38	0 58	28 08	27 13	27 31
25	0 43	0 58	27 55	26 58	27 21
26	0 48	0 57	27 43	26 42	27 11
27	0 52	0 57	27 30	26 26	27 01
28	0 57	0 57	27 18	26 10	26 51
29	1 02	0 56	27 05	25 54	26 40
30	1 07	0 56	26 53	25 37	26 30
31	1 13	0 56	26 40	25 20	26 19
32	1 18	0 55	26 27	25 03	26 07
33	1 23	0 55	26 14	24 46	25 56
34	1 29	0 55	26 02	24 28	25 44
35	1 34	0 54	25 49	24 10	25 32
36	1 40	0 54	25 35	23 52	25 19
37	1 46	0 54	25 22	23 33	25 06
38	1 51	0 53	25 09	23 14	24 53
39	1 57	0 53	24 55	22 55	24 40
40	2 04	0 53	24 41	22 35	24 26
41	2 10	0 52	24 28	22 15	24 11
42	2 16	0 52	24 14	21 54	23 56
43	2 23	0 52	23 59	21 33	23 40
44	2 30	0 51	23 45	21 12	23 24
45	2 37	0 51	23 30	20 49	23 07
46	2 44	0 50	23 15	20 27	22 50
47	2 51	0 50	23 00	20 03	22 32
48	2 59	0 50	22 45	19 39	22 12
49	3 07	0 49	22 29	19 14	21 52
50	3 15	0 49	22 13	18 49	21 32
51	3 23	0 48	21 57	18 23	21 09
52	3 32	0 48	21 41	17 56	20 46
53	3 41	0 47	21 24	17 28	20 22
54	3 50	0 47	21 07	16 59	19 56
55	4 00	0 46	20 49	16 29	19 28
56	4 10	0 46	20 31	15 57	18 58
57	4 20	0 45	20 13	15 25	18 27
58	4 31	0 45	19 54	14 52	17 53
59	4 42	0 44	19 34	14 17	17 16
60	4♍54	0♎44	19♎14	13♏41	16♐37

8h 8m 0s 122° 0' 0"
29 ♋ 49

LAT.	11	12	ASC	2	3
0	29♌54	2♎11	4♏16	4♐00	1♑50
5	0♍15	2 08	3 06	2 48	1 10
10	0 36	2 04	2 00	1 36	0 30
15	0 58	2 01	0 55	0 23	29♐48
20	1 19	1 58	29♎52	29♏09	29 03
21	1 24	1 58	29 39	28 54	28 54
22	1 28	1 57	29 27	28 38	28 45
23	1 33	1 56	29 14	28 23	28 36
24	1 37	1 56	29 01	28 07	28 26
25	1 42	1 55	28 49	27 52	28 16
26	1 47	1 55	28 36	27 36	28 06
27	1 52	1 54	28 23	27 20	27 56
28	1 56	1 53	28 10	27 03	27 46
29	2 01	1 53	27 57	26 47	27 35
30	2 06	1 52	27 44	26 30	27 24
31	2 11	1 51	27 31	26 13	27 13
32	2 16	1 51	27 18	25 56	27 02
33	2 21	1 50	27 05	25 38	26 50
34	2 27	1 49	26 52	25 20	26 39
35	2 32	1 49	26 38	25 02	26 26
36	2 38	1 48	26 25	24 44	26 14
37	2 43	1 47	26 11	24 25	26 01
38	2 49	1 47	25 57	24 05	25 48
39	2 55	1 46	25 43	23 46	25 34
40	3 01	1 45	25 29	23 26	25 20
41	3 07	1 45	25 15	23 05	25 05
42	3 13	1 44	25 00	22 44	24 50
43	3 19	1 43	24 45	22 23	24 35
44	3 26	1 42	24 31	22 01	24 18
45	3 32	1 41	24 16	21 39	24 02
46	3 39	1 41	24 00	21 15	23 44
47	3 47	1 40	23 45	20 52	23 26
48	3 54	1 39	23 29	20 27	23 06
49	4 01	1 38	23 13	20 02	22 46
50	4 09	1 37	22 56	19 36	22 25
51	4 17	1 36	22 40	19 10	22 03
52	4 26	1 35	22 22	18 42	21 40
53	4 34	1 35	22 05	18 14	21 15
54	4 43	1 34	21 47	17 44	20 49
55	4 53	1 33	21 29	17 14	20 21
56	5 02	1 32	21 11	16 42	19 51
57	5 12	1 31	20 52	16 09	19 19
58	5 23	1 29	20 32	15 35	18 45
59	5 34	1 28	20 12	15 00	18 08
60	5♍46	1♎27	19♎52	14♏23	17♐28

8h 12m 0s 123° 0' 0"
0 ♌ 47

LAT.	11	12	ASC	2	3
0	0♍57	3♎16	5♏18	4♐57	2♑45
5	1 18	3 11	4 06	3 44	2 05
10	1 38	3 07	2 58	2 32	1 25
15	1 59	3 02	1 52	1 18	0 43
20	2 20	2 57	0 47	0 04	29♐58
21	2 24	2 57	0 34	29♏48	29 49
22	2 28	2 56	0 21	29 33	29 40
23	2 33	2 55	0 08	29 17	29 31
24	2 37	2 54	29♎55	29 01	29 21
25	2 42	2 53	29 42	28 45	29 11
26	2 46	2 52	29 29	28 29	29 01
27	2 51	2 51	29 16	28 13	28 51
28	2 55	2 50	29 02	27 56	28 41
29	3 00	2 49	28 49	27 40	28 30
30	3 05	2 48	28 36	27 23	28 19
31	3 10	2 47	28 22	27 06	28 08
32	3 15	2 46	28 09	26 48	27 57
33	3 20	2 45	27 55	26 30	27 45
34	3 25	2 44	27 41	26 12	27 33
35	3 30	2 43	27 28	25 54	27 21
36	3 35	2 42	27 14	25 35	27 09
37	3 41	2 41	27 00	25 16	26 56
38	3 46	2 40	26 45	24 57	26 42
39	3 52	2 39	26 31	24 37	26 29
40	3 57	2 38	26 16	24 17	26 15
41	4 03	2 37	26 02	23 56	26 00
42	4 09	2 36	25 47	23 35	25 45
43	4 16	2 35	25 32	23 13	25 29
44	4 22	2 33	25 16	22 51	25 13
45	4 28	2 32	25 01	22 28	24 56
46	4 35	2 31	24 45	22 04	24 38
47	4 42	2 30	24 29	21 40	24 20
48	4 49	2 29	24 13	21 15	24 00
49	4 56	2 27	23 56	20 50	23 40
50	5 04	2 26	23 39	20 24	23 19
51	5 12	2 25	23 22	19 57	22 57
52	5 20	2 23	23 04	19 29	22 33
53	5 28	2 22	22 46	19 00	22 08
54	5 37	2 20	22 28	18 30	21 42
55	5 46	2 19	22 09	17 59	21 14
56	5 55	2 17	21 50	17 27	20 44
57	6 05	2 16	21 30	16 53	20 11
58	6 15	2 14	21 10	16 19	19 37
59	6 26	2 12	20 50	15 43	18 59
60	6♍37	2♎11	20♎29	15♏05	18♐19

8h 16m 0s 124° 0' 0"
1 ♌ 45

LAT.	11	12	ASC	2	3
0	2♍00	4♎22	6♏19	5♐54	3♑40
5	2 20	4 15	5 07	4 40	3 00
10	2 40	4 09	3 57	3 27	2 20
15	3 00	4 03	2 49	2 14	1 38
20	3 20	3 57	1 42	0 58	0 54
21	3 24	3 55	1 29	0 43	0 44
22	3 28	3 54	1 15	0 27	0 35
23	3 33	3 53	1 02	0 11	0 26
24	3 37	3 52	0 49	29♏55	0 16
25	3 41	3 50	0 35	29 39	0 06
26	3 46	3 49	0 22	29 23	29♐56
27	3 50	3 48	0 08	29 06	29 46
28	3 55	3 47	29♎54	28 50	29 36
29	3 59	3 45	29 41	28 33	29 25
30	4 04	3 44	29 27	28 16	29 14
31	4 08	3 43	29 13	27 58	29 03
32	4 13	3 42	28 59	27 41	28 52
33	4 18	3 40	28 45	27 23	28 40
34	4 23	3 39	28 31	27 04	28 28
35	4 28	3 38	28 17	26 46	28 16
36	4 33	3 36	28 03	26 27	28 03
37	4 38	3 35	27 48	26 08	27 50
38	4 44	3 33	27 34	25 48	27 37
39	4 49	3 32	27 19	25 28	27 23
40	4 55	3 31	27 04	25 07	27 09
41	5 00	3 29	26 49	24 46	26 55
42	5 06	3 28	26 33	24 25	26 39
43	5 12	3 26	26 18	24 03	26 24
44	5 18	3 24	26 02	23 40	26 07
45	5 24	3 23	25 46	23 17	25 50
46	5 31	3 21	25 30	22 53	25 32
47	5 37	3 20	25 13	22 29	25 14
48	5 44	3 18	24 56	22 04	24 54
49	5 51	3 16	24 39	21 38	24 34
50	5 59	3 15	24 22	21 11	24 13
51	6 06	3 13	24 04	20 44	23 50
52	6 14	3 11	23 46	20 15	23 27
53	6 22	3 09	23 28	19 46	23 02
54	6 30	3 07	23 09	19 15	22 35
55	6 39	3 05	22 49	18 44	22 07
56	6 48	3 03	22 30	18 11	21 36
57	6 57	3 01	22 09	17 37	21 04
58	7 07	2 59	21 49	17 02	20 29
59	7 18	2 57	21 27	16 25	19 51
60	7♍28	2♎54	21♎06	15♏47	19♐10

8h 20m 0s 125° 0' 0"
2 ♌ 43

LAT.	11	12	ASC	2	3
0	3♍03	5♎27	7♏21	6♐50	4♑35
5	3 23	5 19	6 06	5 37	3 56
10	3 42	5 11	4 55	4 23	3 15
15	4 01	5 03	3 46	3 09	2 33
20	4 21	4 56	2 37	1 52	1 49
21	4 25	4 54	2 23	1 37	1 39
22	4 29	4 53	2 10	1 21	1 30
23	4 33	4 51	1 56	1 05	1 21
24	4 37	4 50	1 42	0 49	1 11
25	4 41	4 48	1 28	0 33	1 01
26	4 45	4 47	1 14	0 16	0 51
27	4 50	4 45	1 01	0 00	0 41
28	4 54	4 43	0 47	29♏43	0 31
29	4 58	4 42	0 33	29 26	0 20
30	5 03	4 40	0 18	29 09	0 09
31	5 07	4 39	0 04	28 51	29♐58
32	5 12	4 37	29♎50	28 33	29 47
33	5 16	4 35	29 36	28 15	29 35
34	5 21	4 34	29 21	27 56	29 23
35	5 26	4 32	29 07	27 38	29 11
36	5 31	4 30	28 52	27 18	28 58
37	5 36	4 28	28 37	26 59	28 45
38	5 41	4 27	28 22	26 39	28 32
39	5 46	4 25	28 07	26 19	28 18
40	5 52	4 23	27 51	25 58	28 04
41	5 57	4 21	27 36	25 37	27 49
42	6 03	4 19	27 20	25 15	27 34
43	6 09	4 18	27 04	24 53	27 18
44	6 14	4 16	26 48	24 30	27 02
45	6 20	4 14	26 31	24 06	26 45
46	6 27	4 12	26 14	23 42	26 27
47	6 33	4 10	25 57	23 17	26 08
48	6 40	4 07	25 40	22 52	25 49
49	6 46	4 05	25 23	22 26	25 28
50	6 53	4 03	25 05	21 59	25 07
51	7 01	4 01	24 46	21 31	24 44
52	7 08	3 59	24 28	21 02	24 20
53	7 16	3 56	24 09	20 32	23 55
54	7 24	3 54	23 49	20 01	23 28
55	7 32	3 51	23 29	19 29	23 00
56	7 41	3 49	23 09	18 56	22 29
57	7 50	3 46	22 48	18 21	21 57
58	8 00	3 44	22 27	17 46	21 22
59	8 09	3 41	22 05	17 08	20 43
60	8♍20	3♎38	21♎43	16♏29	20♐02

8h 24m 0s 126° 0' 0"
3 ♌ 41

LAT.	11	12	ASC	2	3
0	4♍07	6♎32	8♏23	7♐47	5♑30
5	4 25	6 22	7 06	6 33	4 51
10	4 44	6 13	5 53	5 19	4 10
15	5 02	6 04	4 42	4 04	3 28
20	5 21	5 55	3 32	2 47	2 44
21	5 25	5 53	3 18	2 31	2 35
22	5 29	5 51	3 04	2 15	2 25
23	5 33	5 49	2 50	1 59	2 16
24	5 37	5 48	2 36	1 43	2 06
25	5 41	5 46	2 21	1 27	1 56
26	5 45	5 44	2 07	1 10	1 46
27	5 49	5 42	1 53	0 53	1 36
28	5 53	5 40	1 39	0 36	1 26
29	5 57	5 38	1 24	0 19	1 15
30	6 02	5 36	1 10	0 01	1 04
31	6 06	5 34	0 55	29♏44	0 53
32	6 11	5 32	0 41	29 26	0 42
33	6 15	5 30	0 26	29 07	0 30
34	6 20	5 28	0 11	28 48	0 18
35	6 24	5 26	29♎56	28 29	0 06
36	6 29	5 24	29 41	28 10	29♐53
37	6 34	5 22	29 26	27 50	29 40
38	6 39	5 20	29 10	27 30	29 27
39	6 44	5 18	28 54	27 10	29 13
40	6 49	5 16	28 39	26 49	28 59
41	6 54	5 14	28 23	26 27	28 44
42	7 00	5 11	28 06	26 05	28 29
43	7 05	5 09	27 50	25 42	28 13
44	7 11	5 07	27 33	25 19	27 56
45	7 17	5 04	27 16	24 55	27 39
46	7 23	5 02	26 59	24 31	27 21
47	7 29	4 59	26 42	24 06	27 03
48	7 35	4 57	26 24	23 40	26 43
49	7 42	4 54	26 06	23 13	26 23
50	7 48	4 52	25 47	22 46	26 01
51	7 55	4 49	25 29	22 18	25 38
52	8 03	4 46	25 09	21 48	25 14
53	8 10	4 44	24 50	21 18	24 49
54	8 18	4 41	24 30	20 47	24 22
55	8 26	4 38	24 09	20 14	23 53
56	8 34	4 35	23 49	19 41	23 23
57	8 43	4 31	23 27	19 05	22 50
58	8 52	4 28	23 05	18 29	22 14
59	9 01	4 25	22 43	17 51	21 36
60	9♍11	4♎21	22♎20	17♏12	20♐54

8h 28m 0s 127° 0' 0"
4 ♌ 39

LAT.	11	12	ASC	2	3
0	5♍10	7♎37	9♏24	8♐43	6♑26
5	5 28	7 26	8 06	7 29	5 46
10	5 46	7 15	6 51	6 14	5 05
15	6 04	7 05	5 39	4 59	4 23
20	6 22	6 54	4 27	3 41	3 39
21	6 26	6 52	4 12	3 25	3 30
22	6 29	6 50	3 58	3 09	3 21
23	6 33	6 48	3 43	2 53	3 11
24	6 37	6 45	3 29	2 37	3 01
25	6 41	6 43	3 14	2 20	2 52
26	6 45	6 41	3 00	2 03	2 42
27	6 49	6 39	2 45	1 47	2 31
28	6 53	6 37	2 31	1 29	2 21
29	6 57	6 34	2 16	1 12	2 10
30	7 01	6 32	2 01	0 54	1 59
31	7 05	6 30	1 46	0 36	1 48
32	7 09	6 28	1 31	0 18	1 37
33	7 14	6 25	1 16	29♏59	1 25
34	7 18	6 23	1 01	29 41	1 13
35	7 23	6 21	0 45	29 21	1 01
36	7 27	6 18	0 30	29 02	0 48
37	7 32	6 16	0 14	28 42	0 35
38	7 36	6 13	29♎58	28 21	0 22
39	7 41	6 11	29 42	28 00	0 08
40	7 46	6 08	29 26	27 39	29♐54
41	7 51	6 06	29 10	27 17	29 39
42	7 56	6 03	28 53	26 55	29 24
43	8 02	6 00	28 36	26 32	29 08
44	8 07	5 58	28 19	26 09	28 51
45	8 13	5 55	28 02	25 45	28 34
46	8 19	5 52	27 44	25 20	28 16
47	8 24	5 49	27 26	24 55	27 57
48	8 31	5 46	27 08	24 28	27 38
49	8 37	5 43	26 49	24 01	27 17
50	8 43	5 40	26 30	23 33	26 55
51	8 50	5 37	26 11	23 05	26 33
52	8 57	5 34	25 51	22 35	26 08
53	9 04	5 31	25 31	22 04	25 43
54	9 11	5 27	25 11	21 32	25 16
55	9 19	5 24	24 50	20 59	24 47
56	9 27	5 20	24 28	20 25	24 16
57	9 35	5 17	24 06	19 50	23 43
58	9 44	5 13	23 43	19 13	23 07
59	9 53	5 09	23 20	18 34	22 28
60	10♍03	5♎05	22♎56	17♏54	21♐46

8h 32m 0s — 128° 0' 0" — 5 ♌ 38

LAT.	11	12	ASC	2	3
0	6♍14	8♎43	10♏25	9♐40	7♑21
5	6 31	8 30	9 06	8 25	6 41
10	6 48	8 17	7 49	7 10	6 01
15	7 05	8 05	6 35	5 54	5 19
20	7 23	7 53	5 21	4 36	4 34
21	7 26	7 51	5 07	4 20	4 25
22	7 30	7 48	4 52	4 03	4 16
23	7 33	7 46	4 37	3 47	4 06
24	7 37	7 43	4 22	3 31	3 57
25	7 41	7 41	4 07	3 14	3 47
26	7 45	7 38	3 53	2 57	3 37
27	7 48	7 36	3 38	2 40	3 27
28	7 52	7 33	3 23	2 22	3 16
29	7 56	7 31	3 08	2 05	3 06
30	8 00	7 28	2 52	1 47	2 55
31	8 04	7 26	2 37	1 29	2 44
32	8 08	7 23	2 22	1 10	2 32
33	8 12	7 20	2 06	0 52	2 21
34	8 17	7 18	1 51	0 33	2 09
35	8 21	7 15	1 35	0 13	1 56
36	8 25	7 12	1 19	29♏53	1 44
37	8 30	7 09	1 03	29 33	1 31
38	8 34	7 07	0 46	29 13	1 17
39	8 39	7 04	0 30	28 51	1 03
40	8 44	7 01	0 13	28 30	0 49
41	8 48	6 58	29♎57	28 08	0 34
42	8 53	6 55	29 39	27 45	0 19
43	8 59	6 52	29 22	27 22	0 03
44	9 04	6 49	29 05	26 58	29♐46
45	9 09	6 46	28 47	26 34	29 29
46	9 15	6 42	28 29	26 09	29 11
47	9 20	6 39	28 10	25 43	28 52
48	9 26	6 36	27 51	25 17	28 32
49	9 32	6 32	27 32	24 49	28 12
50	9 38	6 29	27 13	24 21	27 50
51	9 45	6 25	26 53	23 52	27 27
52	9 51	6 22	26 33	23 22	27 03
53	9 58	6 18	26 12	22 50	26 37
54	10 05	6 14	25 51	22 18	26 10
55	10 13	6 10	25 30	21 45	25 41
56	10 20	6 06	25 07	21 10	25 10
57	10 28	6 02	24 45	20 34	24 36
58	10 37	5 58	24 22	19 56	24 00
59	10 45	5 53	23 58	19 17	23 21
60	10♍54	5♎49	23♎33	18♏36	22♐38

8h 36m 0s — 129° 0' 0" — 6 ♌ 37

LAT.	11	12	ASC	2	3
0	7♍18	9♎48	11♏26	10♐36	8♑16
5	7 34	9 33	10 05	9 21	7 36
10	7 50	9 19	8 47	8 05	6 56
15	8 07	9 06	7 31	6 49	6 14
20	8 24	8 52	6 16	5 30	5 30
21	8 27	8 49	6 01	5 14	5 21
22	8 30	8 47	5 46	4 57	5 11
23	8 34	8 44	5 31	4 41	5 02
24	8 37	8 41	5 16	4 24	4 52
25	8 41	8 38	5 00	4 07	4 42
26	8 45	8 35	4 45	3 50	4 32
27	8 48	8 33	4 30	3 33	4 22
28	8 52	8 30	4 15	3 16	4 12
29	8 56	8 27	3 59	2 58	4 01
30	8 59	8 24	3 44	2 40	3 50
31	9 03	8 21	3 28	2 21	3 39
32	9 07	8 18	3 12	2 03	3 28
33	9 11	8 15	2 56	1 44	3 16
34	9 15	8 12	2 40	1 25	3 04
35	9 19	8 09	2 24	1 05	2 52
36	9 24	8 06	2 08	0 45	2 39
37	9 28	8 03	1 51	0 25	2 26
38	9 32	8 00	1 35	0 04	2 12
39	9 37	7 57	1 18	29♏42	1 58
40	9 41	7 53	1 01	29 21	1 44
41	9 46	7 50	0 43	28 58	1 29
42	9 50	7 47	0 26	28 35	1 14
43	9 55	7 43	0 08	28 12	0 58
44	10 00	7 40	29♎50	27 48	0 41
45	10 05	7 36	29 32	27 23	0 24
46	10 11	7 33	29 13	26 58	0 06
47	10 16	7 29	28 54	26 32	29♐47
48	10 22	7 25	28 35	26 05	29 27
49	10 27	7 21	28 16	25 37	29 06
50	10 33	7 18	27 56	25 09	28 45
51	10 39	7 14	27 35	24 39	28 22
52	10 46	7 09	27 15	24 08	27 57
53	10 52	7 05	26 53	23 37	27 32
54	10 59	7 01	26 32	23 04	27 04
55	11 06	6 56	26 10	22 30	26 35
56	11 14	6 52	25 47	21 55	26 04
57	11 21	6 47	25 24	21 18	25 30
58	11 29	6 42	25 00	20 40	24 54
59	11 37	6 37	24 35	20 00	24 14
60	11♍46	6♎32	24♎10	19♏18	23♐31

8h 40m 0s — 130° 0' 0" — 7 ♌ 35

LAT.	11	12	ASC	2	3
0	8♍22	10♎53	12♏27	11♐32	9♑11
5	8 37	10 37	11 04	10 16	8 32
10	8 53	10 21	9 45	9 00	7 51
15	9 09	10 06	8 27	7 43	7 10
20	9 25	9 51	7 10	6 24	6 25
21	9 28	9 48	6 55	6 08	6 16
22	9 31	9 45	6 40	5 51	6 07
23	9 34	9 42	6 24	5 35	5 57
24	9 38	9 39	6 09	5 18	5 48
25	9 41	9 36	5 53	5 01	5 38
26	9 45	9 33	5 38	4 44	5 28
27	9 48	9 29	5 22	4 26	5 18
28	9 52	9 26	5 06	4 09	5 07
29	9 55	9 23	4 51	3 51	4 57
30	9 59	9 20	4 35	3 33	4 46
31	10 03	9 17	4 19	3 14	4 34
32	10 06	9 13	4 03	2 55	4 23
33	10 10	9 10	3 46	2 36	4 11
34	10 14	9 07	3 30	2 17	3 59
35	10 18	9 03	3 13	1 57	3 47
36	10 22	9 00	2 57	1 37	3 34
37	10 26	8 57	2 40	1 16	3 21
38	10 30	8 53	2 23	0 55	3 08
39	10 34	8 50	2 06	0 33	2 54
40	10 39	8 46	1 48	0 11	2 39
41	10 43	8 42	1 30	29♏49	2 25
42	10 48	8 39	1 12	29 26	2 09
43	10 52	8 35	0 54	29 02	1 53
44	10 57	8 31	0 36	28 38	1 36
45	11 02	8 27	0 17	28 13	1 19
46	11 07	8 23	29♎58	27 47	1 01
47	11 12	8 19	29 39	27 20	0 42
48	11 17	8 15	29 19	26 53	0 22
49	11 23	8 11	28 59	26 25	0 01
50	11 29	8 06	28 38	25 56	29♐39
51	11 34	8 02	28 18	25 26	29 16
52	11 40	7 57	27 56	24 55	28 52
53	11 47	7 52	27 35	24 23	28 26
54	11 53	7 48	27 12	23 50	27 59
55	12 00	7 43	26 50	23 15	27 29
56	12 07	7 38	26 26	22 39	26 58
57	12 14	7 32	26 02	22 02	26 24
58	12 22	7 27	25 38	21 23	25 47
59	12 29	7 21	25 13	20 43	25 07
60	12♍38	7♎16	24♎47	20♏00	24♐24

8h 44m 0s — 131° 0' 0" — 8 ♌ 34

LAT.	11	12	ASC	2	3
0	9♍26	11♎58	13♏27	12♐28	10♑07
5	9 41	11 40	12 03	11 12	9 27
10	9 55	11 23	10 42	9 56	8 47
15	10 10	11 07	9 23	8 38	8 05
20	10 26	10 50	8 05	7 18	7 21
21	10 29	10 47	7 49	7 02	7 12
22	10 32	10 43	7 34	6 45	7 02
23	10 35	10 40	7 18	6 29	6 53
24	10 38	10 37	7 02	6 12	6 43
25	10 42	10 33	6 46	5 55	6 33
26	10 45	10 30	6 30	5 37	6 23
27	10 48	10 26	6 14	5 20	6 13
28	10 52	10 23	5 58	5 02	6 03
29	10 55	10 19	5 42	4 44	5 52
30	10 58	10 16	5 26	4 25	5 41
31	11 02	10 12	5 09	4 07	5 30
32	11 05	10 09	4 53	3 48	5 19
33	11 09	10 05	4 36	3 28	5 07
34	11 13	10 01	4 20	3 09	4 55
35	11 16	9 58	4 03	2 49	4 43
36	11 20	9 54	3 46	2 28	4 30
37	11 24	9 50	3 28	2 07	4 17
38	11 28	9 46	3 11	1 46	4 03
39	11 32	9 42	2 53	1 24	3 49
40	11 36	9 38	2 35	1 02	3 35
41	11 40	9 34	2 17	0 39	3 20
42	11 45	9 30	1 59	0 16	3 05
43	11 49	9 26	1 40	29♏52	2 48
44	11 54	9 22	1 21	29 27	2 32
45	11 58	9 18	1 02	29 02	2 14
46	12 03	9 13	0 43	28 36	1 56
47	12 08	9 09	0 23	28 09	1 37
48	12 13	9 04	0 03	27 42	1 17
49	12 18	8 59	29♎42	27 13	0 56
50	12 24	8 55	29 21	26 44	0 35
51	12 29	8 50	29 00	26 13	0 11
52	12 35	8 45	28 38	25 42	29♐47
53	12 41	8 40	28 16	25 09	29 21
54	12 47	8 34	27 53	24 36	28 53
55	12 53	8 29	27 30	24 00	28 24
56	13 00	8 23	27 06	23 24	27 52
57	13 07	8 17	26 41	22 46	27 18
58	13 14	8 12	26 16	22 07	26 41
59	13 22	8 05	25 51	21 25	26 01
60	13♍30	7♎59	25♎24	20♏42	25♐17

8h 48m 0s — 132° 0' 0" — 9 ♌ 34

LAT.	11	12	ASC	2	3
0	10♍30	13♎03	14♏28	13♐24	11♑02
5	10 44	12 44	13 02	12 08	10 23
10	10 58	12 25	11 40	10 51	9 42
15	11 12	12 07	10 19	9 33	9 01
20	11 27	11 49	8 59	8 12	8 17
21	11 30	11 45	8 43	7 56	8 07
22	11 33	11 42	8 27	7 39	7 58
23	11 36	11 38	8 11	7 22	7 49
24	11 39	11 34	7 55	7 05	7 39
25	11 42	11 31	7 39	6 48	7 29
26	11 45	11 27	7 23	6 31	7 19
27	11 48	11 23	7 06	6 13	7 09
28	11 51	11 19	6 50	5 55	6 58
29	11 55	11 16	6 34	5 37	6 48
30	11 58	11 12	6 17	5 18	6 37
31	12 01	11 08	6 00	4 59	6 26
32	12 05	11 04	5 43	4 40	6 14
33	12 08	11 00	5 26	4 21	6 03
34	12 12	10 56	5 09	4 01	5 51
35	12 15	10 52	4 52	3 41	5 38
36	12 19	10 48	4 34	3 20	5 26
37	12 22	10 44	4 17	2 59	5 12
38	12 26	10 40	3 59	2 37	4 59
39	12 30	10 35	3 41	2 15	4 45
40	12 34	10 31	3 23	1 53	4 31
41	12 38	10 27	3 04	1 30	4 16
42	12 42	10 22	2 45	1 06	4 00
43	12 46	10 18	2 26	0 42	3 44
44	12 51	10 13	2 07	0 17	3 27
45	12 55	10 08	1 47	29♏51	3 10
46	12 59	10 03	1 27	29 25	2 52
47	13 04	9 59	1 07	28 58	2 33
48	13 09	9 54	0 46	28 30	2 13
49	13 14	9 48	0 25	28 01	1 52
50	13 19	9 43	0 04	27 31	1 30
51	13 24	9 38	29♎42	27 01	1 07
52	13 30	9 32	29 20	26 29	0 42
53	13 35	9 27	28 57	25 56	0 16
54	13 41	9 21	28 33	25 21	29♐48
55	13 47	9 15	28 10	24 46	29 18
56	13 53	9 09	27 45	24 09	28 47
57	14 00	9 03	27 20	23 30	28 12
58	14 07	8 56	26 54	22 50	27 35
59	14 14	8 49	26 28	22 08	26 55
60	14♍21	8♎43	26♎01	21♏25	26♐10

8h 52m 0s — 133° 0' 0" — 10 ♌ 33

LAT.	11	12	ASC	2	3
0	11♍34	14♎07	15♏28	14♐20	11♑58
5	11 48	13 47	14 01	13 03	11 18
10	12 01	13 27	12 37	11 46	10 38
15	12 14	13 07	11 15	10 28	9 56
20	12 28	12 48	9 54	9 07	9 12
21	12 31	12 44	9 37	8 50	9 03
22	12 34	12 40	9 21	8 33	8 54
23	12 37	12 36	9 05	8 16	8 44
24	12 40	12 32	8 48	7 59	8 35
25	12 43	12 28	8 32	7 42	8 25
26	12 45	12 24	8 15	7 24	8 15
27	12 48	12 20	7 59	7 06	8 05
28	12 51	12 16	7 42	6 48	7 54
29	12 55	12 12	7 25	6 30	7 44
30	12 58	12 07	7 08	6 11	7 33
31	13 01	12 03	6 51	5 52	7 22
32	13 04	11 59	6 34	5 33	7 10
33	13 07	11 55	6 16	5 13	6 59
34	13 11	11 50	5 59	4 53	6 47
35	13 14	11 46	5 41	4 33	6 34
36	13 17	11 42	5 23	4 12	6 21
37	13 21	11 37	5 05	3 50	6 08
38	13 24	11 33	4 47	3 29	5 55
39	13 28	11 28	4 29	3 06	5 41
40	13 32	11 23	4 10	2 44	5 26
41	13 35	11 19	3 51	2 20	5 11
42	13 39	11 14	3 32	1 57	4 56
43	13 43	11 09	3 12	1 32	4 40
44	13 47	11 04	2 53	1 07	4 23
45	13 52	10 59	2 32	0 41	4 06
46	13 56	10 54	2 12	0 14	3 47
47	14 00	10 48	1 51	29♏47	3 28
48	14 05	10 43	1 30	29 18	3 08
49	14 09	10 37	1 09	28 49	2 47
50	14 14	10 32	0 47	28 19	2 25
51	14 19	10 26	0 24	27 48	2 02
52	14 24	10 20	0 01	27 16	1 37
53	14 30	10 14	29♎38	26 42	1 11
54	14 35	10 08	29 14	26 07	0 43
55	14 41	10 01	28 50	25 31	0 13
56	14 47	9 55	28 25	24 54	29♐41
57	14 53	9 48	27 59	24 15	29 07
58	14 59	9 41	27 33	23 34	28 30
59	15 06	9 34	27 06	22 51	27 49
60	15♍13	9♎26	26♎38	22♏07	27♐04

8h 56m 0s — 134° 0' 0" — 11 ♌ 32

LAT.	11	12	ASC	2	3
0	12♍39	15♎12	16♏28	15♐16	12♑53
5	12 51	14 50	15 00	13 59	12 14
10	13 04	14 29	13 34	12 41	11 34
15	13 17	14 08	12 11	11 22	10 52
20	13 30	13 47	10 48	10 01	10 08
21	13 32	13 42	10 31	9 44	9 59
22	13 35	13 38	10 15	9 27	9 50
23	13 38	13 34	9 58	9 10	9 40
24	13 40	13 30	9 41	8 53	9 31
25	13 43	13 25	9 24	8 35	9 21
26	13 46	13 21	9 08	8 17	9 11
27	13 49	13 17	8 51	7 59	9 01
28	13 52	13 12	8 33	7 41	8 50
29	13 54	13 08	8 16	7 23	8 40
30	13 57	13 03	7 59	7 04	8 29
31	14 00	12 59	7 42	6 45	8 18
32	14 03	12 54	7 24	6 25	8 06
33	14 06	12 50	7 06	6 05	7 55
34	14 10	12 45	6 48	5 45	7 43
35	14 13	12 40	6 30	5 25	7 30
36	14 16	12 36	6 12	5 03	7 17
37	14 19	12 31	5 54	4 42	7 04
38	14 23	12 26	5 35	4 20	6 51
39	14 26	12 21	5 16	3 58	6 37
40	14 29	12 16	4 57	3 35	6 22
41	14 33	12 11	4 38	3 11	6 07
42	14 37	12 06	4 18	2 47	5 52
43	14 40	12 00	3 58	2 22	5 36
44	14 44	11 55	3 38	1 57	5 19
45	14 48	11 49	3 18	1 30	5 02
46	14 52	11 44	2 57	1 03	4 43
47	14 56	11 38	2 35	0 36	4 24
48	15 01	11 32	2 14	0 07	4 04
49	15 05	11 26	1 52	29♏37	3 43
50	15 10	11 20	1 29	29 07	3 21
51	15 14	11 14	1 06	28 35	2 58
52	15 19	11 08	0 43	28 02	2 33
53	15 24	11 01	0 19	27 29	2 07
54	15 29	10 54	29♎55	26 53	1 39
55	15 35	10 47	29 30	26 17	1 09
56	15 40	10 40	29 04	25 39	0 37
57	15 46	10 33	28 38	24 59	0 02
58	15 52	10 25	28 11	24 18	29♐24
59	15 59	10 18	27 43	23 34	28 43
60	16♍05	10♎09	27♎15	22♏49	27♐58

9h 0m 0s — 135° 0' 0" — 12 ♌ 32

LAT.	11	12	ASC	2	3
0	13♍43	16♎17	17♏28	16♐11	13♑49
5	13 55	15 53	15 58	14 54	13 10
10	14 07	15 30	14 32	13 36	12 30
15	14 19	15 08	13 07	12 17	11 48
20	14 31	14 45	11 42	10 55	11 04
21	14 34	14 41	11 25	10 38	10 55
22	14 36	14 36	11 08	10 21	10 46
23	14 39	14 32	10 51	10 04	10 36
24	14 41	14 27	10 34	9 46	10 27
25	14 44	14 22	10 17	9 29	10 17
26	14 46	14 18	10 00	9 11	10 07
27	14 49	14 13	9 43	8 53	9 57
28	14 52	14 08	9 25	8 34	9 46
29	14 54	14 04	9 08	8 16	9 36
30	14 57	13 59	8 50	7 57	9 25
31	15 00	13 54	8 32	7 37	9 14
32	15 03	13 49	8 14	7 18	9 02
33	15 06	13 44	7 56	6 58	8 51
34	15 09	13 39	7 38	6 37	8 39
35	15 12	13 34	7 20	6 16	8 26
36	15 15	13 29	7 01	5 55	8 14
37	15 18	13 24	6 42	5 34	8 00
38	15 21	13 19	6 23	5 11	7 47
39	15 24	13 14	6 04	4 49	7 33
40	15 27	13 08	5 44	4 26	7 19
41	15 31	13 03	5 25	4 02	7 04
42	15 34	12 57	5 05	3 37	6 48
43	15 38	12 52	4 44	3 12	6 32
44	15 41	12 46	4 24	2 46	6 15
45	15 45	12 40	4 03	2 20	5 58
46	15 49	12 34	3 41	1 53	5 39
47	15 53	12 28	3 20	1 25	5 20
48	15 57	12 22	2 57	0 56	5 00
49	16 01	12 15	2 35	0 26	4 39
50	16 05	12 09	2 12	29♏55	4 17
51	16 09	12 02	1 49	29 23	3 53
52	16 14	11 55	1 25	28 49	3 29
53	16 19	11 48	1 00	28 15	3 02
54	16 24	11 41	0 35	27 39	2 34
55	16 29	11 34	0 10	27 02	2 04
56	16 34	11 26	29♎43	26 24	1 32
57	16 39	11 18	29 16	25 43	0 57
58	16 45	11 10	28 49	25 01	0 19
59	16 51	11 02	28 21	24 17	29♐38
60	16♍57	10♎53	27♎51	23♏31	28♐53

9h 4m 0s — 136° 0' 0" — 13 ♌ 32

LAT.	11	12	ASC	2	3
0	14♍48	17♎21	18♏28	17♐07	14♑44
5	14 59	16 56	16 57	15 49	14 05
10	15 10	16 32	15 29	14 31	13 26
15	15 21	16 08	14 02	13 12	12 44
20	15 33	15 44	12 36	11 49	12 00
21	15 35	15 39	12 19	11 32	11 51
22	15 37	15 34	12 02	11 15	11 42
23	15 40	15 29	11 44	10 58	11 33
24	15 42	15 25	11 27	10 40	11 23
25	15 45	15 20	11 10	10 22	11 13
26	15 47	15 15	10 52	10 04	11 03
27	15 49	15 10	10 34	9 46	10 53
28	15 52	15 05	10 17	9 27	10 43
29	15 55	15 00	9 59	9 09	10 32
30	15 57	14 55	9 41	8 50	10 21
31	16 00	14 50	9 23	8 30	10 10
32	16 02	14 44	9 05	8 10	9 59
33	16 05	14 39	8 46	7 50	9 47
34	16 08	14 34	8 28	7 29	9 35
35	16 11	14 29	8 09	7 09	9 23
36	16 13	14 23	7 50	6 47	9 10
37	16 16	14 18	7 31	6 25	8 57
38	16 19	14 12	7 11	6 03	8 43
39	16 22	14 06	6 52	5 40	8 29
40	16 25	14 01	6 32	5 16	8 15
41	16 28	13 55	6 11	4 52	8 00
42	16 32	13 49	5 51	4 28	7 44
43	16 35	13 43	5 30	4 02	7 28
44	16 38	13 37	5 09	3 36	7 11
45	16 42	13 31	4 48	3 10	6 54
46	16 45	13 24	4 26	2 42	6 36
47	16 49	13 18	4 04	2 14	6 16
48	16 53	13 11	3 41	1 44	5 56
49	16 56	13 04	3 18	1 14	5 35
50	17 00	12 57	2 55	0 43	5 13
51	17 05	12 50	2 31	0 10	4 50
52	17 09	12 43	2 06	29♏37	4 25
53	17 13	12 35	1 41	29 02	3 58
54	17 18	12 28	1 16	28 25	3 30
55	17 22	12 20	0 49	27 48	3 00
56	17 27	12 12	0 23	27 09	2 28
57	17 32	12 03	29♎55	26 28	1 53
58	17 38	11 54	29 27	25 45	1 15
59	17 43	11 46	28 58	25 00	0 33
60	17♍49	11♎36	28♎28	24♏14	29♐47

9h 8m 0s — 137° 0' 0" — 14 ♌ 32

LAT.	11	12	ASC	2	3
0	15♍53	18♎26	19♏27	18♐02	15♑40
5	16 03	17 59	17 55	16 44	15 01
10	16 13	17 33	16 26	15 26	14 22
15	16 24	17 08	14 58	14 06	13 40
20	16 34	16 43	13 30	12 43	12 57
21	16 36	16 37	13 13	12 26	12 48
22	16 39	16 32	12 55	12 09	12 38
23	16 41	16 27	12 38	11 51	12 29
24	16 43	16 22	12 20	11 34	12 19
25	16 45	16 17	12 02	11 16	12 09
26	16 48	16 12	11 44	10 58	12 00
27	16 50	16 06	11 26	10 39	11 49
28	16 52	16 01	11 08	10 21	11 39
29	16 55	15 56	10 50	10 02	11 28
30	16 57	15 50	10 32	9 42	11 18
31	16 59	15 45	10 13	9 23	11 06
32	17 02	15 39	9 55	9 03	10 55
33	17 04	15 34	9 36	8 42	10 43
34	17 07	15 28	9 17	8 22	10 31
35	17 10	15 23	8 58	8 01	10 19
36	17 12	15 17	8 39	7 39	10 06
37	17 15	15 11	8 19	7 17	9 53
38	17 18	15 05	7 59	6 54	9 40
39	17 20	14 59	7 39	6 31	9 26
40	17 23	14 53	7 19	6 07	9 11
41	17 26	14 47	6 58	5 43	8 56
42	17 29	14 41	6 37	5 18	8 41
43	17 32	14 34	6 16	4 53	8 25
44	17 35	14 28	5 55	4 26	8 08
45	17 38	14 21	5 33	3 59	7 50
46	17 42	14 14	5 11	3 31	7 32
47	17 45	14 07	4 48	3 03	7 13
48	17 49	14 00	4 25	2 33	6 53
49	17 52	13 53	4 01	2 02	6 32
50	17 56	13 46	3 37	1 31	6 09
51	18 00	13 38	3 13	0 58	5 46
52	18 04	13 30	2 48	0 24	5 21
53	18 08	13 22	2 22	29♏48	4 54
54	18 12	13 14	1 56	29 12	4 26
55	18 16	13 06	1 29	28 33	3 56
56	18 21	12 57	1 02	27 54	3 23
57	18 26	12 48	0 34	27 12	2 48
58	18 31	12 39	0 05	26 29	2 10
59	18 36	12 30	29♎35	25 44	1 28
60	18♍41	12♎20	29♎05	24♏56	0♑42

9h 12m 0s — 138° 0' 0" — 15 ♌ 32

LAT.	11	12	ASC	2	3
0	16♍57	19♎30	20♏26	18♐58	16♑36
5	17 07	19 02	18 53	17 40	15 57
10	17 17	18 35	17 22	16 21	15 18
15	17 26	18 08	15 53	15 01	14 37
20	17 36	17 41	14 24	13 37	13 53
21	17 38	17 36	14 07	13 20	13 44
22	17 40	17 30	13 49	13 03	13 35
23	17 42	17 25	13 31	12 45	13 25
24	17 44	17 19	13 13	12 27	13 16
25	17 46	17 14	12 55	12 09	13 06
26	17 48	17 08	12 36	11 51	12 56
27	17 50	17 03	12 18	11 33	12 46
28	17 53	16 57	12 00	11 14	12 36
29	17 55	16 52	11 41	10 55	12 25
30	17 57	16 46	11 23	10 35	12 14
31	17 59	16 40	11 04	10 16	12 03
32	18 02	16 34	10 45	9 55	11 52
33	18 04	16 29	10 26	9 35	11 40
34	18 06	16 23	10 06	9 14	11 28
35	18 09	16 17	9 47	8 53	11 16
36	18 11	16 11	9 27	8 31	11 03
37	18 13	16 04	9 07	8 09	10 50
38	18 16	15 58	8 47	7 46	10 36
39	18 19	15 52	8 27	7 22	10 22
40	18 21	15 45	8 06	6 59	10 08
41	18 24	15 39	7 45	6 34	9 53
42	18 27	15 32	7 24	6 09	9 38
43	18 30	15 25	7 02	5 43	9 21
44	18 32	15 18	6 40	5 16	9 05
45	18 35	15 11	6 18	4 49	8 47
46	18 38	15 04	5 55	4 21	8 29
47	18 42	14 57	5 32	3 52	8 10
48	18 45	14 50	5 08	3 22	7 49
49	18 48	14 42	4 44	2 51	7 28
50	18 51	14 34	4 20	2 19	7 06
51	18 55	14 26	3 55	1 45	6 42
52	18 59	14 18	3 29	1 11	6 17
53	19 02	14 09	3 03	0 35	5 51
54	19 06	14 01	2 37	29♏58	5 23
55	19 10	13 52	2 09	29 19	4 52
56	19 15	13 43	1 41	28 39	4 20
57	19 19	13 33	1 13	27 57	3 44
58	19 24	13 24	0 43	27 13	3 06
59	19 28	13 13	0 13	26 27	2 24
60	19♍33	13♎03	29♎42	25♏39	1♑38

9h 16m 0s — 139° 0' 0" — 16 ♌ 33

LAT.	11	12	ASC	2	3
0	18♍02	20♎34	21♏26	19♐53	17♑32
5	18 11	20 05	19 51	18 35	16 53
10	18 20	19 36	18 19	17 16	16 14
15	18 29	19 08	16 49	15 55	15 33
20	18 38	18 40	15 18	14 31	14 49
21	18 40	18 34	15 00	14 14	14 40
22	18 41	18 28	14 42	13 57	14 31
23	18 43	18 23	14 24	13 39	14 22
24	18 45	18 17	14 05	13 21	14 12
25	18 47	18 11	13 47	13 03	14 03
26	18 49	18 05	13 29	12 45	13 53
27	18 51	17 59	13 10	12 26	13 43
28	18 53	17 53	12 51	12 07	13 32
29	18 55	17 47	12 32	11 48	13 22
30	18 57	17 41	12 13	11 28	13 11
31	18 59	17 35	11 54	11 08	13 00
32	19 01	17 29	11 35	10 48	12 48
33	19 03	17 23	11 16	10 27	12 37
34	19 05	17 17	10 56	10 06	12 25
35	19 08	17 11	10 36	9 45	12 12
36	19 10	17 04	10 16	9 23	12 00
37	19 12	16 58	9 56	9 00	11 47
38	19 15	16 51	9 35	8 37	11 33
39	19 17	16 44	9 14	8 14	11 19
40	19 19	16 38	8 53	7 50	11 05
41	19 22	16 31	8 32	7 25	10 50
42	19 24	16 24	8 10	7 00	10 34
43	19 27	16 17	7 48	6 33	10 18
44	19 30	16 09	7 26	6 07	10 01
45	19 32	16 02	7 03	5 39	9 44
46	19 35	15 54	6 40	5 10	9 26
47	19 38	15 47	6 16	4 41	9 06
48	19 41	15 39	5 52	4 11	8 46
49	19 44	15 31	5 28	3 39	8 25
50	19 47	15 22	5 03	3 07	8 03
51	19 50	15 14	4 37	2 33	7 39
52	19 54	15 05	4 11	1 58	7 14
53	19 57	14 56	3 44	1 22	6 48
54	20 01	14 47	3 17	0 44	6 19
55	20 04	14 38	2 49	0 05	5 49
56	20 08	14 28	2 21	29♏24	5 16
57	20 12	14 18	1 51	28 41	4 41
58	20 16	14 08	1 21	27 57	4 02
59	20 21	13 57	0 50	27 10	3 20
60	20♍25	13♎46	0♏19	26♏21	2♑34

9h 20m 0s — 140° 0' 0" — 17 ♌ 33

LAT.	11	12	ASC	2	3
0	19♍07	21♎38	22♏25	20♐49	18♑28
5	19 15	21 07	20 49	19 30	17 50
10	19 23	20 37	19 15	18 11	17 10
15	19 31	20 08	17 44	16 50	16 29
20	19 40	19 38	16 12	15 26	15 46
21	19 41	19 32	15 54	15 08	15 37
22	19 43	19 26	15 35	14 51	15 28
23	19 45	19 20	15 17	14 33	15 19
24	19 46	19 14	14 58	14 15	15 09
25	19 48	19 08	14 39	13 57	14 59
26	19 50	19 02	14 21	13 38	14 49
27	19 52	18 56	14 02	13 19	14 39
28	19 53	18 50	13 43	13 00	14 29
29	19 55	18 43	13 24	12 41	14 18
30	19 57	18 37	13 04	12 21	14 08
31	19 59	18 31	12 45	12 01	13 57
32	20 01	18 24	12 25	11 41	13 45
33	20 03	18 18	12 05	11 20	13 34
34	20 05	18 11	11 45	10 59	13 22
35	20 07	18 04	11 25	10 37	13 09
36	20 09	17 58	11 05	10 15	12 57
37	20 11	17 51	10 44	9 52	12 44
38	20 13	17 44	10 23	9 29	12 30
39	20 15	17 37	10 02	9 05	12 16
40	20 17	17 30	9 40	8 41	12 02
41	20 20	17 23	9 19	8 16	11 47
42	20 22	17 15	8 56	7 50	11 32
43	20 24	17 08	8 34	7 24	11 15
44	20 27	17 00	8 11	6 57	10 59
45	20 29	16 52	7 48	6 29	10 41
46	20 32	16 44	7 24	6 00	10 23
47	20 34	16 36	7 00	5 30	10 04
48	20 37	16 28	6 36	5 00	9 43
49	20 40	16 20	6 11	4 28	9 22
50	20 43	16 11	5 45	3 55	9 00
51	20 46	16 02	5 19	3 21	8 36
52	20 49	15 53	4 53	2 45	8 11
53	20 52	15 43	4 26	2 09	7 45
54	20 55	15 34	3 58	1 30	7 16
55	20 58	15 24	3 29	0 51	6 46
56	21 02	15 14	3 00	0 09	6 13
57	21 06	15 03	2 30	29♏26	5 38
58	21 09	14 52	1 59	28 41	4 59
59	21 13	14 41	1 28	27 53	4 17
60	21♍17	14♎30	0♏55	27♏04	3♑30

9h 24m 0s — 141° 0' 0" — 18 ♌ 34

LAT.	11	12	ASC	2	3
0	20♍12	22♎42	23♏23	21♐44	19♑24
5	20 20	22 10	21 46	20 25	18 46
10	20 27	21 38	20 12	19 06	18 07
15	20 34	21 07	18 39	17 44	17 26
20	20 42	20 36	17 06	16 20	16 43
21	20 43	20 30	16 47	16 02	16 34
22	20 45	20 24	16 29	15 45	16 25
23	20 46	20 18	16 10	15 27	16 15
24	20 48	20 11	15 51	15 09	16 06
25	20 49	20 05	15 32	14 50	15 56
26	20 51	19 59	15 13	14 32	15 46
27	20 52	19 52	14 53	14 13	15 36
28	20 54	19 46	14 34	13 54	15 26
29	20 56	19 39	14 15	13 34	15 16
30	20 57	19 32	13 55	13 14	15 05
31	20 59	19 26	13 35	12 54	14 54
32	21 01	19 19	13 15	12 34	14 42
33	21 02	19 12	12 55	12 13	14 31
34	21 04	19 05	12 35	11 51	14 19
35	21 06	18 58	12 14	11 29	14 07
36	21 08	18 51	11 53	11 07	13 54
37	21 10	18 44	11 32	10 44	13 41
38	21 12	18 37	11 11	10 21	13 28
39	21 14	18 30	10 49	9 57	13 14
40	21 16	18 22	10 28	9 32	12 59
41	21 18	18 14	10 05	9 07	12 44
42	21 20	18 07	9 43	8 41	12 29
43	21 22	17 59	9 20	8 14	12 13
44	21 24	17 51	8 57	7 47	11 56
45	21 26	17 43	8 33	7 19	11 38
46	21 28	17 34	8 09	6 50	11 20
47	21 31	17 26	7 44	6 20	11 01
48	21 33	17 17	7 19	5 49	10 41
49	21 36	17 08	6 54	5 16	10 20
50	21 38	16 59	6 28	4 43	9 57
51	21 41	16 50	6 01	4 09	9 34
52	21 44	16 40	5 34	3 33	9 09
53	21 47	16 30	5 07	2 56	8 42
54	21 49	16 20	4 38	2 17	8 14
55	21 52	16 10	4 09	1 37	7 43
56	21 56	15 59	3 39	0 55	7 10
57	21 59	15 48	3 09	0 11	6 35
58	22 02	15 37	2 37	29♏25	5 56
59	22 06	15 25	2 05	28 37	5 14
60	22♍10	15♎13	1♏32	27♏46	4♑27

9h 28m 0s — 142° 0' 0" — 19 ♌ 35

LAT.	11	12	ASC	2	3
0	21♍17	23♎46	24♏22	22♐39	20♑20
5	21 24	23 12	22 44	21 20	19 42
10	21 30	22 39	21 08	20 00	19 03
15	21 37	22 07	19 34	18 39	18 23
20	21 43	21 35	18 00	17 14	17 40
21	21 45	21 28	17 41	16 56	17 31
22	21 46	21 22	17 22	16 39	17 22
23	21 48	21 15	17 03	16 21	17 12
24	21 49	21 08	16 43	16 02	17 03
25	21 50	21 02	16 24	15 44	16 53
26	21 52	20 55	16 05	15 25	16 43
27	21 53	20 48	15 45	15 06	16 33
28	21 55	20 42	15 26	14 47	16 23
29	21 56	20 35	15 06	14 27	16 13
30	21 58	20 28	14 46	14 07	16 02
31	21 59	20 21	14 26	13 47	15 51
32	22 01	20 14	14 05	13 26	15 40
33	22 02	20 07	13 45	13 05	15 28
34	22 04	19 59	13 24	12 44	15 16
35	22 05	19 52	13 03	12 22	15 04
36	22 07	19 45	12 42	11 59	14 51
37	22 09	19 37	12 21	11 36	14 38
38	22 10	19 30	11 59	11 13	14 25
39	22 12	19 22	11 37	10 48	14 11
40	22 14	19 14	11 15	10 24	13 57
41	22 16	19 06	10 52	9 58	13 42
42	22 17	18 58	10 29	9 32	13 26
43	22 19	18 50	10 06	9 05	13 10
44	22 21	18 42	9 42	8 37	12 54
45	22 23	18 33	9 18	8 09	12 36
46	22 25	18 24	8 54	7 40	12 18
47	22 27	18 15	8 29	7 09	11 59
48	22 29	18 06	8 03	6 38	11 38
49	22 32	17 57	7 37	6 05	11 17
50	22 34	17 47	7 11	5 32	10 55
51	22 36	17 38	6 44	4 57	10 31
52	22 39	17 28	6 16	4 20	10 06
53	22 41	17 17	5 48	3 43	9 40
54	22 44	17 07	5 19	3 04	9 11
55	22 47	16 56	4 49	2 23	8 41
56	22 49	16 45	4 19	1 40	8 08
57	22 52	16 33	3 47	0 55	7 32
58	22 55	16 21	3 15	0 09	6 54
59	22 59	16 09	2 43	29♏20	6 11
60	23♍02	15♎56	2♏09	28♏29	5♑24

9h 32m 0s — 143° 0' 0" — 20 ♌ 36

LAT.	11	12	ASC	2	3
0	22♍23	24♎50	25♏21	23♐34	21♑17
5	22 28	24 15	23 41	22 15	20 39
10	22 34	23 40	22 04	20 55	20 00
15	22 40	23 07	20 29	19 33	19 20
20	22 45	22 33	18 53	18 08	18 37
21	22 47	22 26	18 34	17 50	18 28
22	22 48	22 19	18 15	17 33	18 19
23	22 49	22 12	17 55	17 15	18 10
24	22 50	22 06	17 36	16 56	18 00
25	22 51	21 59	17 16	16 38	17 51
26	22 53	21 52	16 57	16 19	17 41
27	22 54	21 45	16 37	16 00	17 31
28	22 55	21 37	16 17	15 40	17 21
29	22 56	21 30	15 57	15 21	17 10
30	22 58	21 23	15 37	15 01	16 59
31	22 59	21 16	15 16	14 40	16 48
32	23 00	21 09	14 55	14 19	16 37
33	23 02	21 01	14 35	13 58	16 26
34	23 03	20 54	14 14	13 36	16 14
35	23 05	20 46	13 52	13 14	16 02
36	23 06	20 38	13 31	12 51	15 49
37	23 07	20 30	13 09	12 28	15 36
38	23 09	20 23	12 47	12 04	15 23
39	23 10	20 15	12 25	11 40	15 09
40	23 12	20 06	12 02	11 15	14 54
41	23 14	19 58	11 39	10 49	14 40
42	23 15	19 50	11 16	10 23	14 24
43	23 17	19 41	10 52	9 56	14 08
44	23 18	19 32	10 28	9 28	13 51
45	23 20	19 23	10 03	8 59	13 34
46	23 22	19 14	9 38	8 29	13 16
47	23 24	19 05	9 13	7 59	12 56
48	23 26	18 55	8 47	7 27	12 36
49	23 28	18 46	8 20	6 54	12 15
50	23 30	18 36	7 53	6 20	11 53
51	23 32	18 26	7 26	5 45	11 29
52	23 34	18 15	6 58	5 08	11 04
53	23 36	18 04	6 29	4 30	10 38
54	23 38	17 53	5 59	3 50	10 09
55	23 41	17 42	5 29	3 09	9 39
56	23 43	17 30	4 58	2 26	9 06
57	23 46	17 18	4 26	1 40	8 30
58	23 48	17 06	3 53	0 53	7 51
59	23 51	16 53	3 20	0 03	7 09
60	23♍54	16♎40	2♏45	29♏11	6♑22

9h 36m 0s — 144° 0' 0" — 21 ♌ 37

LAT.	11	12	ASC	2	3
0	23♍28	25♎53	26♏19	24♐30	22♑13
5	23 33	25 17	24 38	23 10	21 36
10	23 38	24 41	23 01	21 50	20 57
15	23 42	24 06	21 24	20 28	20 17
20	23 47	23 31	19 47	19 02	19 34
21	23 48	23 24	19 27	18 45	19 25
22	23 49	23 17	19 08	18 27	19 16
23	23 50	23 10	18 48	18 08	19 07
24	23 52	23 03	18 28	17 50	18 57
25	23 53	22 55	18 09	17 31	18 48
26	23 54	22 48	17 49	17 13	18 38
27	23 55	22 41	17 28	16 53	18 28
28	23 56	22 33	17 08	16 34	18 18
29	23 57	22 26	16 48	16 14	18 08
30	23 58	22 18	16 27	15 54	17 57
31	23 59	22 11	16 06	15 33	17 46
32	24 00	22 03	15 46	15 12	17 35
33	24 01	21 55	15 24	14 51	17 23
34	24 03	21 48	15 03	14 29	17 11
35	24 04	21 40	14 41	14 07	16 59
36	24 05	21 32	14 19	13 44	16 47
37	24 06	21 24	13 57	13 20	16 34
38	24 08	21 15	13 35	12 56	16 20
39	24 09	21 07	13 12	12 32	16 07
40	24 10	20 58	12 49	12 07	15 52
41	24 12	20 50	12 26	11 41	15 38
42	24 13	20 41	12 02	11 14	15 22
43	24 14	20 32	11 38	10 47	15 06
44	24 16	20 23	11 13	10 19	14 49
45	24 17	20 14	10 48	9 49	14 32
46	24 19	20 04	10 23	9 19	14 14
47	24 20	19 54	9 57	8 48	13 55
48	24 22	19 45	9 30	8 16	13 35
49	24 24	19 34	9 04	7 43	13 13
50	24 25	19 24	8 36	7 09	12 51
51	24 27	19 13	8 08	6 33	12 28
52	24 29	19 02	7 39	5 56	12 03
53	24 31	18 51	7 10	5 17	11 36
54	24 33	18 40	6 40	4 37	11 07
55	24 35	18 28	6 09	3 55	10 37
56	24 37	18 16	5 37	3 11	10 04
57	24 39	18 03	5 05	2 25	9 28
58	24 41	17 50	4 32	1 37	8 50
59	24 44	17 37	3 57	0 47	8 07
60	24♍46	17♎23	3♏22	29♏54	7♑20

9h 40m 0s — 145° 0' 0" — 22 ♌ 39

LAT.	11	12	ASC	2	3
0	24♍33	26♎57	27♏17	25♐25	23♑10
5	24 37	26 19	25 36	24 05	22 32
10	24 41	25 42	23 57	22 45	21 54
15	24 45	25 05	22 19	21 22	21 14
20	24 49	24 29	20 41	19 56	20 31
21	24 50	24 22	20 21	19 39	20 23
22	24 51	24 14	20 01	19 21	20 14
23	24 52	24 07	19 41	19 02	20 04
24	24 53	23 59	19 21	18 44	19 55
25	24 54	23 52	19 01	18 25	19 46
26	24 55	23 44	18 40	18 06	19 36
27	24 56	23 37	18 20	17 47	19 26
28	24 56	23 29	18 00	17 27	19 16
29	24 57	23 21	17 39	17 07	19 05
30	24 58	23 14	17 18	16 47	18 55
31	24 59	23 06	16 57	16 26	18 44
32	25 00	22 58	16 36	16 05	18 33
33	25 01	22 50	16 14	15 44	18 21
34	25 02	22 42	15 52	15 22	18 09
35	25 03	22 33	15 30	14 59	17 57
36	25 04	22 25	15 08	14 36	17 45
37	25 05	22 17	14 46	14 13	17 32
38	25 06	22 08	14 23	13 48	17 19
39	25 07	21 59	14 00	13 24	17 05
40	25 08	21 51	13 36	12 58	16 51
41	25 10	21 42	13 12	12 32	16 36
42	25 11	21 32	12 48	12 05	16 20
43	25 12	21 23	12 24	11 38	16 04
44	25 13	21 14	11 59	11 09	15 48
45	25 14	21 04	11 33	10 40	15 30
46	25 16	20 54	11 07	10 10	15 12
47	25 17	20 44	10 41	9 38	14 53
48	25 18	20 34	10 14	9 06	14 33
49	25 20	20 23	9 47	8 32	14 12
50	25 21	20 12	9 19	7 57	13 50
51	25 23	20 01	8 50	7 21	13 26
52	25 24	19 50	8 21	6 44	13 01
53	25 26	19 38	7 51	6 05	12 34
54	25 27	19 26	7 20	5 24	12 06
55	25 29	19 14	6 49	4 41	11 36
56	25 31	19 01	6 17	3 57	11 03
57	25 33	18 48	5 44	3 11	10 27
58	25 35	18 34	5 10	2 22	9 48
59	25 36	18 20	4 35	1 31	9 05
60	25♍39	18♎06	3♏59	0♐37	8♑18

9h 44m 0s — 146° 0' 0" — 23 ♌ 41

LAT.	11	12	ASC	2	3
0	25♍38	28♎00	28♏15	26♐20	24♑06
5	25 42	27 21	26 33	25 00	23 29
10	25 45	26 42	24 53	23 40	22 51
15	25 48	26 05	23 13	22 17	22 11
20	25 52	25 27	21 34	20 51	21 29
21	25 52	25 19	21 14	20 33	21 20
22	25 53	25 12	20 54	20 15	21 11
23	25 54	25 04	20 34	19 57	21 02
24	25 54	24 56	20 13	19 38	20 53
25	25 55	24 49	19 53	19 19	20 43
26	25 56	24 41	19 32	19 00	20 34
27	25 56	24 33	19 12	18 41	20 24
28	25 57	24 25	18 51	18 21	20 14
29	25 58	24 17	18 30	18 01	20 03
30	25 59	24 09	18 09	17 40	19 53
31	25 59	24 01	17 47	17 20	19 42
32	26 00	23 52	17 26	16 58	19 31
33	26 01	23 44	17 04	16 37	19 19
34	26 02	23 36	16 42	16 14	19 08
35	26 02	23 27	16 19	15 52	18 55
36	26 03	23 18	15 57	15 29	18 43
37	26 04	23 10	15 34	15 05	18 30
38	26 05	23 01	15 11	14 41	18 17
39	26 06	22 52	14 47	14 16	18 03
40	26 07	22 43	14 23	13 50	17 49
41	26 08	22 33	13 59	13 24	17 34
42	26 09	22 24	13 35	12 57	17 19
43	26 10	22 14	13 10	12 29	17 03
44	26 10	22 04	12 44	12 00	16 46
45	26 11	21 54	12 18	11 30	16 29
46	26 13	21 44	11 52	11 00	16 11
47	26 14	21 33	11 25	10 28	15 52
48	26 15	21 23	10 58	9 55	15 32
49	26 16	21 12	10 30	9 22	15 11
50	26 17	21 00	10 01	8 46	14 48
51	26 18	20 49	9 32	8 10	14 25
52	26 19	20 37	9 02	7 32	14 00
53	26 21	20 25	8 32	6 52	13 33
54	26 22	20 12	8 01	6 11	13 05
55	26 23	20 00	7 29	5 28	12 35
56	26 25	19 46	6 56	4 43	12 02
57	26 26	19 33	6 22	3 56	11 26
58	26 28	19 19	5 48	3 06	10 47
59	26 29	19 04	5 12	2 15	10 04
60	26♍31	18♎49	4♏35	1♐20	9♑17

9h 48m 0s — 147° 0' 0" — 24 ♌ 42

LAT.	11	12	ASC	2	3
0	26♍44	29♎03	29♏13	27♐15	25♑03
5	26 46	28 22	27 29	25 55	24 26
10	26 49	27 43	25 48	24 35	23 48
15	26 51	27 04	24 08	23 12	23 09
20	26 54	26 25	22 28	21 45	22 27
21	26 54	26 17	22 07	21 27	22 18
22	26 55	26 09	21 47	21 09	22 09
23	26 55	26 01	21 26	20 51	22 00
24	26 56	25 53	21 06	20 32	21 51
25	26 56	25 45	20 45	20 13	21 41
26	26 57	25 37	20 24	19 54	21 32
27	26 57	25 29	20 03	19 34	21 22
28	26 58	25 21	19 42	19 15	21 12
29	26 58	25 12	19 21	18 54	21 01
30	26 59	25 04	18 59	18 34	20 51
31	27 00	24 55	18 37	18 13	20 40
32	27 00	24 47	18 16	17 51	20 29
33	27 01	24 38	17 53	17 30	20 18
34	27 01	24 30	17 31	17 07	20 06
35	27 02	24 21	17 08	16 45	19 54
36	27 02	24 12	16 45	16 21	19 41
37	27 03	24 03	16 22	15 57	19 29
38	27 04	23 53	15 59	15 33	19 15
39	27 04	23 44	15 35	15 08	19 02
40	27 05	23 34	15 11	14 42	18 48
41	27 06	23 25	14 46	14 15	18 33
42	27 06	23 15	14 21	13 48	18 18
43	27 07	23 05	13 56	13 20	18 02
44	27 08	22 55	13 30	12 51	17 45
45	27 09	22 44	13 03	12 21	17 28
46	27 09	22 34	12 37	11 50	17 10
47	27 10	22 23	12 09	11 18	16 51
48	27 11	22 12	11 42	10 45	16 31
49	27 12	22 00	11 13	10 11	16 10
50	27 13	21 49	10 44	9 35	15 48
51	27 14	21 37	10 14	8 58	15 24
52	27 14	21 24	9 44	8 20	14 59
53	27 15	21 12	9 13	7 40	14 33
54	27 16	20 59	8 41	6 58	14 04
55	27 17	20 46	8 09	6 15	13 34
56	27 18	20 32	7 35	5 29	13 01
57	27 20	20 18	7 01	4 41	12 25
58	27 21	20 03	6 26	3 51	11 47
59	27 22	19 48	5 49	2 58	11 04
60	27♍23	19♎32	5♏12	2♐03	10♑16

9h 52m 0s — 148° 0' 0" — 25 ♌ 44

LAT.	11	12	ASC	2	3
0	27♍49	0♏06	0♐11	28♐10	26♑00
5	27 51	29♎24	28♏26	26 50	25 24
10	27 52	28 43	26 44	25 29	24 46
15	27 54	28 03	25 03	24 06	24 06
20	27 56	27 23	23 21	22 39	23 25
21	27 56	27 14	23 00	22 21	23 16
22	27 56	27 06	22 40	22 03	23 07
23	27 57	26 58	22 19	21 45	22 58
24	27 57	26 50	21 58	21 26	22 49
25	27 57	26 41	21 37	21 07	22 39
26	27 58	26 33	21 16	20 48	22 30
27	27 58	26 25	20 55	20 28	22 20
28	27 59	26 16	20 33	20 08	22 10
29	27 59	26 08	20 12	19 48	22 00
30	27 59	25 59	19 50	19 27	21 49
31	28 00	25 50	19 28	19 06	21 39
32	28 00	25 41	19 06	18 45	21 27
33	28 00	25 32	18 43	18 23	21 16
34	28 01	25 23	18 20	18 00	21 04
35	28 01	25 14	17 57	17 37	20 52
36	28 02	25 05	17 34	17 14	20 40
37	28 02	24 55	17 10	16 50	20 27
38	28 02	24 46	16 47	16 25	20 14
39	28 03	24 36	16 22	16 00	20 01
40	28 03	24 26	15 58	15 34	19 46
41	28 04	24 16	15 33	15 07	19 32
42	28 04	24 06	15 07	14 40	19 17
43	28 05	23 56	14 42	14 11	19 01
44	28 05	23 45	14 15	13 42	18 44
45	28 06	23 34	13 49	13 12	18 27
46	28 06	23 23	13 21	12 41	18 09
47	28 07	23 12	12 54	12 08	17 50
48	28 07	23 01	12 25	11 35	17 30
49	28 08	22 49	11 56	11 00	17 09
50	28 08	22 37	11 27	10 24	16 47
51	28 09	22 24	10 57	9 47	16 24
52	28 10	22 12	10 26	9 08	15 59
53	28 10	21 59	9 54	8 28	15 32
54	28 11	21 45	9 22	7 45	15 04
55	28 12	21 31	8 49	7 01	14 34
56	28 12	21 17	8 15	6 15	14 01
57	28 13	21 02	7 40	5 27	13 25
58	28 14	20 47	7 04	4 36	12 46
59	28 15	20 32	6 27	3 42	12 04
60	28♍15	20♎15	5♏49	2♐46	11♑16

9h 56m 0s — 149° 0' 0" — 26 ♌ 47

LAT.	11	12	ASC	2	3
0	28♍55	1♏08	1♐08	29♐05	26♑57
5	28 55	0 25	29♏23	27 45	26 21
10	28 56	29♎43	27 40	26 24	25 43
15	28 57	29 02	25 57	25 01	25 04
20	28 58	28 20	24 14	23 34	24 23
21	28 58	28 12	23 54	23 16	24 14
22	28 58	28 03	23 33	22 58	24 05
23	28 58	27 55	23 12	22 39	23 56
24	28 59	27 46	22 50	22 20	23 47
25	28 59	27 38	22 29	22 01	23 38
26	28 59	27 29	22 08	21 42	23 28
27	28 59	27 20	21 46	21 22	23 18
28	28 59	27 12	21 24	21 02	23 08
29	28 59	27 03	21 03	20 42	22 58
30	29 00	26 54	20 40	20 21	22 48
31	29 00	26 45	20 18	20 00	22 37
32	29 00	26 36	19 56	19 38	22 26
33	29 00	26 26	19 33	19 16	22 15
34	29 00	26 17	19 10	18 53	22 03
35	29 01	26 08	18 46	18 30	21 51
36	29 01	25 58	18 23	18 07	21 39
37	29 01	25 48	17 59	17 42	21 26
38	29 01	25 38	17 35	17 18	21 13
39	29 01	25 28	17 10	16 52	21 00
40	29 02	25 18	16 45	16 26	20 46
41	29 02	25 08	16 20	15 59	20 31
42	29 02	24 57	15 54	15 31	20 16
43	29 02	24 47	15 28	15 03	20 00
44	29 03	24 36	15 01	14 33	19 44
45	29 03	24 24	14 34	14 03	19 26
46	29 03	24 13	14 06	13 31	19 08
47	29 03	24 01	13 38	12 59	18 49
48	29 04	23 50	13 09	12 25	18 30
49	29 04	23 37	12 40	11 50	18 09
50	29 04	23 25	12 10	11 14	17 47
51	29 05	23 12	11 39	10 36	17 23
52	29 05	22 59	11 07	9 57	16 59
53	29 05	22 45	10 35	9 16	16 32
54	29 05	22 31	10 02	8 33	16 04
55	29 06	22 17	9 29	7 48	15 34
56	29 06	22 02	8 54	7 01	15 01
57	29 07	21 47	8 18	6 12	14 25
58	29 07	21 32	7 42	5 21	13 47
59	29 07	21 15	7 04	4 27	13 04
60	29♍08	20♎59	6♏25	3♐29	12♑17

10h 0m 0s — 150° 0' 0" — 27 ♌ 49

LAT.	11	12	ASC	2	3
0	0♎00	2♏11	2♐05	0♑00	27♑55
5	0 00	1 27	0 19	28♐40	27 18
10	0 00	0 43	28♏35	27 19	26 41
15	0 00	0 01	26 52	25 56	26 02
20	0 00	29♎18	25 08	24 28	25 21
21	0 00	29 09	24 47	24 10	25 12
22	0 00	29 00	24 25	23 52	25 04
23	0 00	28 52	24 04	23 33	24 55
24	0 00	28 43	23 43	23 14	24 46
25	0 00	28 34	23 21	22 55	24 36
26	0 00	28 25	23 00	22 36	24 27
27	0 00	28 16	22 38	22 16	24 17
28	0 00	28 07	22 16	21 56	24 07
29	0 00	27 58	21 53	21 35	23 57
30	0 00	27 49	21 31	21 15	23 47
31	0 00	27 39	21 08	20 53	23 36
32	0 00	27 30	20 46	20 32	23 25
33	0 00	27 20	20 22	20 09	23 14
34	0 00	27 11	19 59	19 47	23 02
35	0 00	27 01	19 35	19 23	22 50
36	0 00	26 51	19 11	19 00	22 38
37	0 00	26 41	18 47	18 35	22 26
38	0 00	26 31	18 22	18 10	22 12
39	0 00	26 21	17 57	17 45	21 59
40	0 00	26 10	17 32	17 18	21 45
41	0 00	25 59	17 06	16 51	21 30
42	0 00	25 48	16 40	16 23	21 15
43	0 00	25 37	16 14	15 54	21 00
44	0 00	25 26	15 46	15 25	20 43
45	0 00	25 15	15 19	14 54	20 26
46	0 00	25 03	14 51	14 22	20 08
47	0 00	24 51	14 22	13 49	19 49
48	0 00	24 38	13 53	13 15	19 30
49	0 00	24 26	13 23	12 40	19 09
50	0 00	24 13	12 52	12 03	18 47
51	0 00	24 00	12 21	11 25	18 24
52	0 00	23 46	11 49	10 45	17 59
53	0 00	23 32	11 16	10 04	17 33
54	0 00	23 18	10 43	9 20	17 04
55	0 00	23 03	10 08	8 35	16 34
56	0 00	22 48	9 33	7 48	16 01
57	0 00	22 32	8 57	6 58	15 26
58	0 00	22 16	8 20	6 06	14 47
59	0 00	21 59	7 41	5 11	14 05
60	0♎00	21♎42	7♏02	4♐13	13♑18

10h 4m 0s — 151° 0' 0" — 28 ♌ 52

LAT.	11	12	ASC	2	3
0	1♎05	3♏13	3♐03	0♑55	28♑52
5	1 05	2 28	1 16	29♐35	28 16
10	1 04	1 43	29♏31	28 14	27 39
15	1 03	0 59	27 46	26 51	27 01
20	1 02	0 15	26 01	25 23	26 19
21	1 02	0 06	25 40	25 05	26 11
22	1 02	29♎57	25 18	24 46	26 02
23	1 02	29 48	24 57	24 28	25 53
24	1 01	29 39	24 35	24 09	25 44
25	1 01	29 30	24 13	23 50	25 35
26	1 01	29 21	23 51	23 30	25 26
27	1 01	29 12	23 29	23 10	25 16
28	1 01	29 02	23 07	22 50	25 06
29	1 01	28 53	22 44	22 29	24 56
30	1 00	28 44	22 22	22 08	24 46
31	1 00	28 34	21 59	21 47	24 35
32	1 00	28 24	21 36	21 25	24 24
33	1 00	28 14	21 12	21 03	24 13
34	1 00	28 05	20 48	20 40	24 02
35	0 59	27 54	20 24	20 17	23 50
36	0 59	27 44	20 00	19 53	23 38
37	0 59	27 34	19 35	19 28	23 25
38	0 59	27 23	19 10	19 03	23 12
39	0 59	27 13	18 45	18 37	22 59
40	0 58	27 02	18 19	18 11	22 45
41	0 58	26 51	17 53	17 43	22 30
42	0 58	26 40	17 27	17 15	22 15
43	0 58	26 28	17 00	16 46	21 59
44	0 57	26 16	16 32	16 16	21 43
45	0 57	26 05	16 04	15 45	21 26
46	0 57	25 52	15 35	15 13	21 08
47	0 57	25 40	15 06	14 40	20 50
48	0 56	25 27	14 36	14 06	20 30
49	0 56	25 14	14 06	13 30	20 09
50	0 56	25 01	13 35	12 53	19 47
51	0 55	24 47	13 03	12 14	19 24
52	0 55	24 33	12 31	11 34	18 59
53	0 55	24 19	11 57	10 52	18 33
54	0 55	24 04	11 23	10 08	18 05
55	0 54	23 49	10 48	9 22	17 35
56	0 54	23 33	10 13	8 34	17 02
57	0 53	23 17	9 36	7 44	16 27
58	0 53	23 00	8 58	6 51	15 49
59	0 53	22 43	8 19	5 55	15 06
60	0♎52	22♎25	7♏39	4♐56	14♑19

10h 8m 0s	152° 0' 0"	29 ♌ 54			
LAT.	11	12	ASC	2	3
0	2♎11	4♏16	4♐00	1♑50	29♑49
5	2 09	3 29	2 12	0 30	29 14
10	2 08	2 43	0 26	29♐09	28 37
15	2 06	1 58	28♏41	27 45	27 59
20	2 04	1 13	26 54	26 18	27 18
21	2 04	1 03	26 33	25 59	27 10
22	2 04	0 54	26 11	25 41	27 01
23	2 03	0 45	25 49	25 22	26 52
24	2 03	0 36	25 27	25 03	26 43
25	2 03	0 26	25 05	24 44	26 34
26	2 02	0 17	24 43	24 24	26 25
27	2 02	0 07	24 21	24 04	26 15
28	2 01	29♎58	23 58	23 44	26 05
29	2 01	29 48	23 35	23 23	25 55
30	2 01	29 38	23 12	23 02	25 45
31	2 00	29 28	22 49	22 41	25 34
32	2 00	29 18	22 26	22 19	25 24
33	2 00	29 08	22 02	21 56	25 13
34	1 59	28 58	21 38	21 33	25 01
35	1 59	28 48	21 13	21 10	24 49
36	1 58	28 37	20 49	20 46	24 37
37	1 58	28 27	20 24	20 21	24 25
38	1 58	28 16	19 58	19 56	24 12
39	1 57	28 05	19 33	19 30	23 58
40	1 57	27 54	19 07	19 03	23 45
41	1 56	27 42	18 40	18 36	23 30
42	1 56	27 31	18 13	18 07	23 15
43	1 55	27 19	17 46	17 38	23 00
44	1 55	27 07	17 18	17 08	22 43
45	1 54	26 55	16 49	16 37	22 26
46	1 54	26 42	16 20	16 04	22 09
47	1 53	26 29	15 50	15 31	21 50
48	1 53	26 16	15 20	14 56	21 30
49	1 52	26 03	14 49	14 20	21 10
50	1 52	25 49	14 18	13 43	20 48
51	1 51	25 35	13 46	13 04	20 25
52	1 50	25 20	13 12	12 23	20 00
53	1 50	25 05	12 39	11 41	19 34
54	1 49	24 50	12 04	10 56	19 06
55	1 48	24 34	11 28	10 10	18 36
56	1 48	24 18	10 52	9 21	18 04
57	1 47	24 01	10 14	8 30	17 29
58	1 46	23 44	9 36	7 36	16 50
59	1 45	23 26	8 56	6 40	16 08
60	1♎45	23♎08	8♏15	5♐40	15♑21

10h 12m 0s	153° 0' 0"	0 ♍ 57			
LAT.	11	12	ASC	2	3
0	3♎16	5♏18	4♐57	2♑45	0♒47
5	3 14	4 30	3 08	1 25	0 12
10	3 11	3 43	1 21	0 04	29♑36
15	3 09	2 57	29♏35	28♐40	28 57
20	3 06	2 10	27 47	27 12	28 17
21	3 06	2 01	27 26	26 54	28 09
22	3 05	1 51	27 04	26 36	28 00
23	3 05	1 42	26 42	26 17	27 51
24	3 04	1 32	26 20	25 58	27 42
25	3 04	1 22	25 57	25 38	27 33
26	3 03	1 13	25 35	25 19	27 24
27	3 03	1 03	25 12	24 59	27 14
28	3 02	0 53	24 49	24 38	27 05
29	3 02	0 43	24 26	24 18	26 55
30	3 01	0 33	24 03	23 56	26 44
31	3 00	0 23	23 39	23 35	26 34
32	3 00	0 13	23 16	23 13	26 23
33	2 59	0 02	22 51	22 50	26 12
34	2 59	29♎52	22 27	22 27	26 01
35	2 58	29 41	22 02	22 03	25 49
36	2 58	29 30	21 37	21 39	25 37
37	2 57	29 19	21 12	21 14	25 25
38	2 56	29 08	20 46	20 49	25 12
39	2 56	28 57	20 20	20 23	24 59
40	2 55	28 45	19 54	19 56	24 45
41	2 54	28 34	19 27	19 28	24 30
42	2 54	28 22	19 00	18 59	24 16
43	2 53	28 10	18 32	18 30	24 00
44	2 52	27 57	18 03	18 00	23 44
45	2 51	27 44	17 34	17 28	23 27
46	2 51	27 32	17 05	16 56	23 09
47	2 50	27 18	16 35	16 22	22 51
48	2 49	27 05	16 04	15 47	22 31
49	2 48	26 51	15 33	15 10	22 11
50	2 47	26 37	15 01	14 33	21 49
51	2 46	26 22	14 28	13 53	21 26
52	2 46	26 07	13 54	13 12	21 02
53	2 45	25 52	13 20	12 29	20 36
54	2 44	25 36	12 45	11 44	20 08
55	2 43	25 20	12 08	10 57	19 38
56	2 42	25 03	11 31	10 08	19 06
57	2 40	24 46	10 53	9 16	18 31
58	2 39	24 28	10 14	8 22	17 52
59	2 38	24 10	9 33	7 24	17 10
60	2♎37	23♎51	8♏52	6♐24	16♑23

10h 16m 0s	154° 0' 0"	2 ♍ 00			
LAT.	11	12	ASC	2	3
0	4♎22	6♏19	5♐54	3♑40	1♒45
5	4 18	5 30	4 04	2 20	1 10
10	4 15	4 42	2 17	0 59	0 34
15	4 12	3 55	0 29	29♐35	29♑56
20	4 08	3 07	28♏41	28 07	29 16
21	4 08	2 57	28 19	27 49	29 08
22	4 07	2 48	27 56	27 30	28 59
23	4 06	2 38	27 34	27 11	28 50
24	4 06	2 28	27 12	26 52	28 42
25	4 05	2 18	26 49	26 33	28 32
26	4 04	2 08	26 26	26 13	28 23
27	4 04	1 58	26 04	25 53	28 14
28	4 03	1 48	25 40	25 33	28 04
29	4 02	1 38	25 17	25 12	27 54
30	4 01	1 28	24 53	24 51	27 44
31	4 01	1 17	24 30	24 29	27 34
32	4 00	1 07	24 06	24 07	27 23
33	3 59	0 56	23 41	23 44	27 12
34	3 58	0 45	23 16	23 21	27 01
35	3 58	0 34	22 52	22 57	26 49
36	3 57	0 23	22 26	22 33	26 37
37	3 56	0 12	22 01	22 08	26 25
38	3 55	0 00	21 34	21 42	26 12
39	3 54	29♎49	21 08	21 16	25 59
40	3 53	29 37	20 41	20 49	25 45
41	3 52	29 25	20 14	20 21	25 31
42	3 51	29 13	19 46	19 52	25 16
43	3 50	29 00	19 18	19 22	25 01
44	3 50	28 47	18 49	18 52	24 45
45	3 49	28 34	18 20	18 20	24 28
46	3 47	28 21	17 50	17 47	24 10
47	3 46	28 08	17 19	17 13	23 52
48	3 45	27 54	16 48	16 38	23 33
49	3 44	27 39	16 16	16 01	23 12
50	3 43	27 25	15 43	15 23	22 51
51	3 42	27 10	15 10	14 43	22 28
52	3 41	26 54	14 36	14 01	22 03
53	3 39	26 39	14 01	13 18	21 37
54	3 38	26 22	13 25	12 33	21 10
55	3 37	26 06	12 48	11 45	20 40
56	3 35	25 48	12 11	10 55	20 08
57	3 34	25 31	11 32	10 03	19 33
58	3 32	25 12	10 52	9 08	18 55
59	3 31	24 53	10 11	8 09	18 13
60	3♎29	24♎33	9♏28	7♐08	17♑26

10h 20m 0s	155° 0' 0"	3 ♍ 03			
LAT.	11	12	ASC	2	3
0	5♎27	7♏21	6♐50	4♑35	2♒43
5	5 23	6 31	5 00	3 16	2 08
10	5 19	5 42	3 12	1 54	1 33
15	5 15	4 53	1 23	0 30	0 55
20	5 11	4 04	29♏34	29♐02	0 15
21	5 10	3 54	29 11	28 44	0 07
22	5 09	3 44	28 49	28 25	29♑58
23	5 08	3 34	28 27	28 06	29 50
24	5 07	3 24	28 04	27 47	29 41
25	5 06	3 14	27 41	27 28	29 32
26	5 05	3 04	27 18	27 08	29 23
27	5 04	2 54	26 55	26 48	29 14
28	5 04	2 43	26 32	26 27	29 04
29	5 03	2 33	26 08	26 06	28 54
30	5 02	2 22	25 44	25 45	28 44
31	5 01	2 11	25 20	25 23	28 34
32	5 00	2 01	24 56	25 01	28 23
33	4 59	1 50	24 31	24 38	28 12
34	4 58	1 39	24 06	24 15	28 01
35	4 57	1 27	23 41	23 51	27 50
36	4 56	1 16	23 15	23 26	27 38
37	4 55	1 04	22 49	23 01	27 25
38	4 54	0 53	22 22	22 35	27 13
39	4 53	0 41	21 56	22 09	27 00
40	4 52	0 28	21 28	21 42	26 46
41	4 50	0 16	21 01	21 14	26 32
42	4 49	0 04	20 33	20 45	26 17
43	4 48	29♎51	20 04	20 15	26 02
44	4 47	29 38	19 35	19 44	25 46
45	4 46	29 24	19 05	19 12	25 29
46	4 44	29 11	18 34	18 39	25 12
47	4 43	28 57	18 03	18 04	24 53
48	4 42	28 42	17 32	17 29	24 34
49	4 40	28 28	16 59	16 52	24 14
50	4 39	28 13	16 26	16 13	23 52
51	4 37	27 57	15 52	15 33	23 30
52	4 36	27 41	15 18	14 51	23 05
53	4 34	27 25	14 42	14 07	22 40
54	4 33	27 09	14 06	13 21	22 12
55	4 31	26 51	13 28	12 33	21 43
56	4 29	26 34	12 50	11 42	21 11
57	4 27	26 15	12 10	10 49	20 36
58	4 25	25 56	11 30	9 53	19 58
59	4 24	25 37	10 48	8 54	19 16
60	4♎21	25♎16	10♏05	7♐52	18♑30

10h 24m 0s	156° 0' 0"	4 ♍ 07			
LAT.	11	12	ASC	2	3
0	6♎32	8♏23	7♐47	5♑30	3♒41
5	6 27	7 31	5 56	4 11	3 07
10	6 22	6 41	4 07	2 50	2 31
15	6 18	5 51	2 18	1 25	1 54
20	6 13	5 01	0 27	29♐57	1 15
21	6 12	4 51	0 04	29 39	1 07
22	6 11	4 41	29♏42	29 20	0 58
23	6 10	4 31	29 19	29 01	0 50
24	6 08	4 20	28 56	28 42	0 41
25	6 07	4 10	28 33	28 22	0 32
26	6 06	3 59	28 10	28 02	0 23
27	6 05	3 49	27 46	27 42	0 13
28	6 04	3 38	27 23	27 22	0 04
29	6 03	3 27	26 59	27 01	29♑54
30	6 02	3 17	26 35	26 39	29 44
31	6 01	3 06	26 10	26 17	29 34
32	6 00	2 55	25 46	25 55	29 24
33	5 59	2 43	25 21	25 32	29 13
34	5 57	2 32	24 55	25 09	29 02
35	5 56	2 20	24 30	24 45	28 50
36	5 55	2 09	24 04	24 20	28 38
37	5 54	1 57	23 37	23 55	28 26
38	5 52	1 45	23 11	23 29	28 14
39	5 51	1 32	22 43	23 02	28 01
40	5 50	1 20	22 16	22 35	27 47
41	5 48	1 07	21 48	22 07	27 33
42	5 47	0 54	21 19	21 37	27 18
43	5 46	0 41	20 50	21 07	27 03
44	5 44	0 28	20 20	20 36	26 47
45	5 43	0 14	19 50	20 04	26 31
46	5 41	0 00	19 19	19 31	26 13
47	5 40	29♎46	18 48	18 56	25 55
48	5 38	29 31	18 16	18 20	25 36
49	5 36	29 16	17 43	17 43	25 16
50	5 35	29 01	17 09	17 04	24 55
51	5 33	28 45	16 35	16 23	24 32
52	5 31	28 28	16 00	15 41	24 08
53	5 29	28 12	15 23	14 56	23 42
54	5 27	27 55	14 46	14 10	23 15
55	5 25	27 37	14 08	13 21	22 45
56	5 23	27 19	13 29	12 30	22 14
57	5 21	27 00	12 49	11 36	21 39
58	5 19	26 40	12 08	10 39	21 02
59	5 16	26 20	11 25	9 39	20 20
60	5♎14	25♎59	10♏42	8♐36	19♑34

10h 28m 0s	157° 0' 0"	5 ♍ 10			
LAT.	11	12	ASC	2	3
0	7♎37	9♏24	8♐43	6♑26	4♒39
5	7 32	8 32	6 52	5 06	4 05
10	7 26	7 40	5 02	3 45	3 30
15	7 20	6 49	3 12	2 21	2 54
20	7 15	5 58	1 20	0 52	2 14
21	7 13	5 48	0 57	0 34	2 06
22	7 12	5 37	0 34	0 15	1 58
23	7 11	5 27	0 11	29♐56	1 49
24	7 10	5 16	29♏48	29 37	1 41
25	7 09	5 06	29 25	29 17	1 32
26	7 07	4 55	29 02	28 57	1 23
27	7 06	4 44	28 38	28 37	1 14
28	7 05	4 33	28 14	28 16	1 04
29	7 04	4 22	27 50	27 55	0 55
30	7 02	4 11	27 25	27 34	0 45
31	7 01	4 00	27 01	27 12	0 35
32	7 00	3 48	26 36	26 49	0 24
33	6 58	3 37	26 10	26 26	0 13
34	6 57	3 25	25 45	26 03	0 02
35	6 55	3 13	25 19	25 39	29♑51
36	6 54	3 01	24 52	25 14	29 39
37	6 53	2 49	24 26	24 49	29 27
38	6 51	2 37	23 59	24 23	29 15
39	6 50	2 24	23 31	23 56	29 02
40	6 48	2 12	23 03	23 28	28 48
41	6 46	1 58	22 35	23 00	28 34
42	6 45	1 45	22 06	22 30	28 20
43	6 43	1 32	21 36	22 00	28 05
44	6 42	1 18	21 06	21 29	27 49
45	6 40	1 04	20 35	20 56	27 33
46	6 38	0 49	20 04	20 23	27 15
47	6 36	0 35	19 32	19 48	26 57
48	6 34	0 20	19 00	19 11	26 38
49	6 32	0 04	18 26	18 34	26 18
50	6 30	29♎48	17 52	17 54	25 57
51	6 28	29 32	17 17	17 13	25 35
52	6 26	29 15	16 41	16 31	25 11
53	6 24	28 58	16 05	15 46	24 45
54	6 22	28 41	15 27	14 59	24 18
55	6 19	28 22	14 48	14 10	23 49
56	6 17	28 04	14 09	13 18	23 17
57	6 14	27 44	13 28	12 23	22 43
58	6 12	27 24	12 46	11 26	22 06
59	6 09	27 04	12 03	10 25	21 24
60	6♎06	26♎42	11♏18	9♐21	20♑39

10h 32m 0s	158° 0' 0"	6 ♍ 14			
LAT.	11	12	ASC	2	3
0	8♎43	10♏25	9♐40	7♑21	5♒38
5	8 36	9 32	7 48	6 01	5 04
10	8 30	8 39	5 57	4 40	4 30
15	8 23	7 47	4 06	3 16	3 53
20	8 17	6 55	2 13	1 47	3 14
21	8 15	6 44	1 50	1 29	3 06
22	8 14	6 34	1 27	1 10	2 58
23	8 12	6 23	1 04	0 51	2 50
24	8 11	6 12	0 41	0 32	2 41
25	8 10	6 01	0 17	0 12	2 32
26	8 08	5 50	29♏53	29♐52	2 23
27	8 07	5 39	29 29	29 32	2 14
28	8 05	5 28	29 05	29 11	2 05
29	8 04	5 17	28 41	28 50	1 55
30	8 02	5 05	28 16	28 28	1 45
31	8 01	4 54	27 51	28 06	1 35
32	7 59	4 42	27 26	27 44	1 25
33	7 58	4 30	27 00	27 21	1 14
34	7 56	4 18	26 34	26 57	1 03
35	7 55	4 06	26 08	26 33	0 52
36	7 53	3 54	25 41	26 08	0 41
37	7 51	3 42	25 14	25 43	0 29
38	7 50	3 29	24 47	25 16	0 16
39	7 48	3 16	24 19	24 50	0 03
40	7 46	3 03	23 51	24 22	29♑50
41	7 44	2 50	23 22	23 53	29 36
42	7 43	2 36	22 52	23 24	29 22
43	7 41	2 22	22 22	22 53	29 07
44	7 39	2 08	21 52	22 21	28 51
45	7 37	1 54	21 21	21 49	28 35
46	7 35	1 39	20 49	21 15	28 18
47	7 33	1 24	20 17	20 40	28 00
48	7 31	1 08	19 44	20 03	27 41
49	7 28	0 52	19 10	19 25	27 21
50	7 26	0 36	18 35	18 45	27 00
51	7 24	0 20	18 00	18 04	26 38
52	7 21	0 02	17 23	17 21	26 14
53	7 19	29♎45	16 46	16 35	25 49
54	7 16	29 27	16 08	15 48	25 22
55	7 13	29 08	15 29	14 58	24 53
56	7 11	28 49	14 48	14 06	24 21
57	7 08	28 29	14 07	13 10	23 47
58	7 05	28 08	13 24	12 12	23 10
59	7 01	27 47	12 40	11 11	22 29
60	6♎58	27♎25	11♏55	10♐05	21♑44

10h 36m 0s	159° 0' 0"	7 ♍ 18			
LAT.	11	12	ASC	2	3
0	9♎48	11♏26	10♐36	8♑16	6♒37
5	9 40	10 31	8 43	6 57	6 03
10	9 33	9 38	6 52	5 36	5 29
15	9 26	8 45	5 00	4 11	4 53
20	9 18	7 52	3 06	2 43	4 14
21	9 17	7 41	2 43	2 24	4 06
22	9 15	7 30	2 20	2 05	3 58
23	9 14	7 19	1 56	1 46	3 50
24	9 12	7 08	1 33	1 27	3 41
25	9 11	6 57	1 09	1 07	3 33
26	9 09	6 45	0 45	0 47	3 24
27	9 08	6 34	0 21	0 27	3 15
28	9 06	6 23	29♏56	0 06	3 06
29	9 04	6 11	29 32	29♐45	2 56
30	9 03	6 00	29 07	29 23	2 46
31	9 01	5 48	28 41	29 01	2 36
32	8 59	5 36	28 16	28 39	2 26
33	8 58	5 24	27 50	28 15	2 16
34	8 56	5 12	27 24	27 52	2 05
35	8 54	4 59	26 57	27 27	1 54
36	8 52	4 47	26 30	27 02	1 42
37	8 50	4 34	26 03	26 37	1 30
38	8 48	4 21	25 35	26 11	1 18
39	8 46	4 08	25 07	25 43	1 05
40	8 44	3 54	24 38	25 15	0 52
41	8 42	3 41	24 09	24 47	0 38
42	8 40	3 27	23 39	24 17	0 24
43	8 38	3 13	23 09	23 46	0 09
44	8 36	2 58	22 38	23 14	29♑54
45	8 34	2 43	22 06	22 42	29 37
46	8 32	2 28	21 34	22 07	29 20
47	8 29	2 13	21 01	21 32	29 03
48	8 27	1 57	20 28	20 55	28 44
49	8 24	1 41	19 53	20 17	28 24
50	8 22	1 24	19 18	19 37	28 03
51	8 19	1 07	18 42	18 55	27 41
52	8 16	0 49	18 05	18 11	27 18
53	8 13	0 31	17 27	17 25	26 53
54	8 11	0 13	16 49	16 37	26 26
55	8 08	29♎53	16 09	15 47	25 57
56	8 04	29 34	15 28	14 54	25 26
57	8 01	29 13	14 46	13 58	24 52
58	7 58	28 52	14 02	12 59	24 15
59	7 54	28 30	13 18	11 56	23 35
60	7♎50	28♎08	12♏32	10♐50	22♑50

10h 40m 0s 160° 0' 0"
8 ♍ 22

LAT.	11	12	ASC	2	3
0	10♎53	12♏27	11♐32	9♑11	7♒35
5	10 45	11 31	9 39	7 52	7 02
10	10 37	10 37	7 47	6 31	6 28
15	10 29	9 43	5 54	5 07	5 53
20	10 20	8 48	3 59	3 38	5 15
21	10 19	8 37	3 36	3 20	5 07
22	10 17	8 26	3 12	3 01	4 59
23	10 15	8 15	2 49	2 42	4 50
24	10 14	8 03	2 25	2 22	4 42
25	10 12	7 52	2 01	2 03	4 33
26	10 10	7 41	1 37	1 43	4 25
27	10 08	7 29	1 12	1 22	4 16
28	10 07	7 17	0 48	1 01	4 07
29	10 05	7 06	0 23	0 40	3 57
30	10 03	6 54	29♏57	0 18	3 48
31	10 01	6 42	29 32	29♐56	3 38
32	9 59	6 30	29 06	29 33	3 28
33	9 57	6 17	28 40	29 10	3 17
34	9 55	6 05	28 13	28 46	3 06
35	9 53	5 52	27 46	28 22	2 55
36	9 51	5 39	27 19	27 57	2 44
37	9 49	5 26	26 51	27 31	2 32
38	9 47	5 13	26 23	27 05	2 20
39	9 45	4 59	25 55	26 38	2 07
40	9 43	4 46	25 26	26 09	1 54
41	9 40	4 32	24 56	25 40	1 41
42	9 38	4 17	24 26	25 11	1 26
43	9 36	4 03	23 55	24 40	1 12
44	9 33	3 48	23 24	24 08	0 56
45	9 31	3 33	22 52	23 34	0 40
46	9 28	3 17	22 19	23 00	0 23
47	9 26	3 02	21 46	22 24	0 06
48	9 23	2 45	21 12	21 47	29♑47
49	9 20	2 29	20 37	21 08	29 28
50	9 17	2 12	20 01	20 28	29 07
51	9 14	1 54	19 25	19 46	28 45
52	9 11	1 36	18 47	19 02	28 22
53	9 08	1 18	18 09	18 16	27 57
54	9 05	0 59	17 29	17 27	27 30
55	9 02	0 39	16 49	16 36	27 02
56	8 58	0 19	16 07	15 42	26 31
57	8 54	29♎58	15 24	14 46	25 57
58	8 51	29 36	14 40	13 46	25 21
59	8 47	29 14	13 55	12 42	24 41
60	8♎43	28♎50	13♏08	11♐35	23♑56

10h 44m 0s 161° 0' 0"
9 ♍ 26

LAT.	11	12	ASC	2	3
0	11♎58	13♏27	12♐28	10♑07	8♒34
5	11 49	12 31	10 34	8 48	8 02
10	11 40	11 35	8 41	7 27	7 28
15	11 31	10 40	6 48	6 02	6 53
20	11 22	9 45	4 52	4 34	6 15
21	11 20	9 33	4 29	4 15	6 08
22	11 19	9 22	4 05	3 56	5 59
23	11 17	9 11	3 41	3 37	5 51
24	11 15	8 59	3 17	3 18	5 43
25	11 13	8 47	2 53	2 58	5 34
26	11 11	8 36	2 28	2 38	5 26
27	11 09	8 24	2 04	2 17	5 17
28	11 07	8 12	1 39	1 57	5 08
29	11 05	8 00	1 14	1 35	4 59
30	11 03	7 48	0 48	1 14	4 49
31	11 01	7 36	0 22	0 51	4 39
32	10 59	7 23	29♏56	0 29	4 29
33	10 57	7 11	29 30	0 05	4 19
34	10 55	6 58	29 03	29♐41	4 08
35	10 52	6 45	28 36	29 17	3 57
36	10 50	6 32	28 08	28 52	3 46
37	10 48	6 18	27 40	28 26	3 34
38	10 45	6 05	27 11	27 59	3 22
39	10 43	5 51	26 43	27 32	3 10
40	10 41	5 37	26 13	27 04	2 57
41	10 38	5 23	25 43	26 35	2 43
42	10 36	5 08	25 13	26 04	2 29
43	10 33	4 53	24 41	25 33	2 15
44	10 30	4 38	24 10	25 01	1 59
45	10 28	4 23	23 37	24 28	1 43
46	10 25	4 07	23 04	23 53	1 27
47	10 22	3 51	22 30	23 17	1 09
48	10 19	3 34	21 56	22 40	0 51
49	10 16	3 17	21 20	22 01	0 31
50	10 13	2 59	20 44	21 20	0 11
51	10 10	2 41	20 07	20 37	29♑49
52	10 06	2 23	19 29	19 53	29 26
53	10 03	2 04	18 50	19 06	29 01
54	9 59	1 44	18 10	18 17	28 35
55	9 56	1 24	17 29	17 25	28 07
56	9 52	1 04	16 47	16 31	27 36
57	9 48	0 42	16 03	15 34	27 03
58	9 44	0 20	15 18	14 33	26 27
59	9 39	29♎57	14 32	13 29	25 47
60	9♎35	29♎33	13♏45	12♐20	25♑03

10h 48m 0s 162° 0' 0"
10 ♍ 30

LAT.	11	12	ASC	2	3
0	13♎03	14♏28	13♐24	11♑02	9♒34
5	12 53	13 30	11 30	9 43	9 01
10	12 43	12 34	9 36	8 22	8 28
15	12 34	11 38	7 42	6 58	7 53
20	12 24	10 41	5 45	5 29	7 16
21	12 22	10 29	5 22	5 11	7 08
22	12 20	10 18	4 58	4 52	7 00
23	12 18	10 06	4 34	4 33	6 52
24	12 16	9 54	4 09	4 13	6 44
25	12 14	9 43	3 45	3 54	6 36
26	12 12	9 31	3 20	3 34	6 27
27	12 10	9 19	2 55	3 13	6 18
28	12 07	9 07	2 30	2 52	6 09
29	12 05	8 54	2 05	2 31	6 00
30	12 03	8 42	1 39	2 09	5 51
31	12 01	8 29	1 13	1 47	5 41
32	11 58	8 17	0 46	1 24	5 31
33	11 56	8 04	0 20	1 00	5 21
34	11 54	7 51	29♏52	0 36	5 10
35	11 51	7 38	29 25	0 12	5 00
36	11 49	7 24	28 57	29♐47	4 48
37	11 47	7 11	28 29	29 21	4 37
38	11 44	6 57	28 00	28 54	4 25
39	11 41	6 43	27 30	28 26	4 12
40	11 39	6 28	27 01	27 58	4 00
41	11 36	6 14	26 30	27 29	3 46
42	11 33	5 59	25 59	26 58	3 32
43	11 30	5 44	25 28	26 27	3 18
44	11 28	5 28	24 56	25 55	3 03
45	11 25	5 12	24 23	25 21	2 47
46	11 22	4 56	23 49	24 46	2 31
47	11 18	4 39	23 15	24 10	2 13
48	11 15	4 22	22 40	23 32	1 55
49	11 12	4 05	22 04	22 53	1 36
50	11 09	3 47	21 27	22 12	1 15
51	11 05	3 29	20 50	21 29	0 54
52	11 01	3 10	20 11	20 44	0 31
53	10 58	2 50	19 32	19 57	0 07
54	10 54	2 30	18 51	19 07	29♑40
55	10 50	2 10	18 09	18 15	29 12
56	10 45	1 48	17 26	17 20	28 42
57	10 41	1 26	16 42	16 22	28 09
58	10 36	1 04	15 57	15 20	27 33
59	10 32	0 40	15 10	14 15	26 54
60	10♎27	0♏16	14♏21	13♐06	26♑10

10h 52m 0s 163° 0' 0"
11 ♍ 34

LAT.	11	12	ASC	2	3
0	14♎07	15♏28	14♐20	11♑58	10♒33
5	13 57	14 30	12 25	10 39	10 01
10	13 47	13 32	10 31	9 18	9 28
15	13 36	12 35	8 36	7 54	8 54
20	13 26	11 37	6 38	6 25	8 17
21	13 24	11 25	6 14	6 07	8 10
22	13 21	11 14	5 50	5 48	8 02
23	13 19	11 02	5 26	5 29	7 54
24	13 17	10 50	5 02	5 09	7 46
25	13 15	10 38	4 37	4 49	7 37
26	13 12	10 26	4 12	4 29	7 29
27	13 10	10 13	3 47	4 09	7 20
28	13 08	10 01	3 21	3 48	7 11
29	13 05	9 49	2 56	3 26	7 02
30	13 03	9 36	2 30	3 04	6 53
31	13 01	9 23	2 03	2 42	6 43
32	12 58	9 10	1 37	2 19	6 33
33	12 56	8 57	1 10	1 56	6 23
34	12 53	8 44	0 42	1 32	6 13
35	12 50	8 30	0 14	1 07	6 02
36	12 48	8 17	29♏46	0 42	5 51
37	12 45	8 03	29 17	0 16	5 40
38	12 42	7 48	28 48	29♐49	5 28
39	12 40	7 34	28 19	29 21	5 15
40	12 37	7 19	27 48	28 53	5 03
41	12 34	7 05	27 18	28 23	4 50
42	12 31	6 49	26 46	27 53	4 36
43	12 28	6 34	26 14	27 21	4 22
44	12 25	6 18	25 42	26 49	4 07
45	12 22	6 02	25 08	26 15	3 51
46	12 18	5 45	24 34	25 40	3 35
47	12 15	5 28	24 00	25 03	3 17
48	12 11	5 11	23 24	24 25	2 59
49	12 08	4 53	22 48	23 46	2 40
50	12 04	4 35	22 11	23 04	2 20
51	12 00	4 16	21 32	22 21	1 59
52	11 56	3 57	20 53	21 35	1 36
53	11 52	3 37	20 13	20 48	1 12
54	11 48	3 16	19 32	19 58	0 46
55	11 44	2 55	18 49	19 05	0 18
56	11 39	2 33	18 06	18 09	29♑49
57	11 34	2 11	17 21	17 11	29 16
58	11 29	1 47	16 35	16 08	28 41
59	11 24	1 23	15 47	15 02	28 02
60	11♎19	0♏58	14♏58	13♐52	27♑18

10h 56m 0s 164° 0' 0"
12 ♍ 39

LAT.	11	12	ASC	2	3
0	15♎12	16♏28	15♐16	12♑53	11♒32
5	15 01	15 29	13 20	11 35	11 01
10	14 50	14 30	11 25	10 14	10 29
15	14 39	13 32	9 30	8 50	9 55
20	14 27	12 33	7 31	7 21	9 18
21	14 25	12 21	7 07	7 03	9 11
22	14 23	12 09	6 43	6 44	9 03
23	14 20	11 57	6 19	6 25	8 55
24	14 18	11 45	5 54	6 05	8 47
25	14 15	11 33	5 29	5 45	8 39
26	14 13	11 21	5 04	5 25	8 31
27	14 11	11 08	4 38	5 05	8 22
28	14 08	10 55	4 13	4 44	8 13
29	14 05	10 43	3 47	4 22	8 04
30	14 03	10 30	3 20	4 00	7 55
31	14 00	10 17	2 54	3 38	7 45
32	13 58	10 04	2 27	3 15	7 36
33	13 55	9 50	2 00	2 51	7 26
34	13 52	9 37	1 32	2 27	7 15
35	13 49	9 23	1 04	2 02	7 05
36	13 47	9 09	0 35	1 37	6 54
37	13 44	8 55	0 06	1 11	6 43
38	13 41	8 40	29♏37	0 44	6 31
39	13 38	8 26	29 07	0 16	6 19
40	13 35	8 11	28 36	29♐48	6 06
41	13 32	7 55	28 05	29 18	5 53
42	13 28	7 40	27 33	28 47	5 40
43	13 25	7 24	27 01	28 16	5 25
44	13 22	7 08	26 28	27 43	5 11
45	13 18	6 51	25 54	27 09	4 55
46	13 15	6 34	25 20	26 34	4 39
47	13 11	6 17	24 45	25 57	4 22
48	13 07	5 59	24 09	25 18	4 04
49	13 04	5 41	23 32	24 38	3 45
50	13 00	5 22	22 54	23 57	3 25
51	12 55	5 03	22 15	23 13	3 04
52	12 51	4 43	21 35	22 27	2 42
53	12 47	4 23	20 55	21 39	2 18
54	12 42	4 02	20 13	20 48	1 53
55	12 38	3 40	19 30	19 55	1 25
56	12 33	3 18	18 45	18 59	0 55
57	12 28	2 55	18 00	17 59	0 23
58	12 22	2 31	17 13	16 56	29♑48
59	12 17	2 06	16 25	15 49	29 10
60	12♎11	1♏41	15♏35	14♐38	28♑27

11h 0m 0s 165° 0' 0"
13 ♍ 43

LAT.	11	12	ASC	2	3
0	16♎17	17♏28	16♐11	13♑49	12♒32
5	16 05	16 28	14 16	12 30	12 01
10	15 53	15 28	12 20	11 10	11 29
15	15 41	14 29	10 24	9 46	10 56
20	15 29	13 29	8 25	8 17	10 20
21	15 26	13 17	8 00	7 59	10 12
22	15 24	13 05	7 36	7 40	10 05
23	15 21	12 53	7 11	7 21	9 57
24	15 19	12 40	6 46	7 01	9 49
25	15 16	12 28	6 21	6 41	9 41
26	15 14	12 15	5 56	6 21	9 33
27	15 11	12 03	5 30	6 01	9 24
28	15 08	11 50	5 04	5 40	9 15
29	15 06	11 37	4 38	5 18	9 07
30	15 03	11 24	4 11	4 56	8 57
31	15 00	11 10	3 44	4 34	8 48
32	14 57	10 57	3 17	4 11	8 39
33	14 54	10 43	2 50	3 47	8 29
34	14 51	10 29	2 22	3 23	8 18
35	14 48	10 15	1 53	2 58	8 08
36	14 45	10 01	1 24	2 33	7 57
37	14 42	9 47	0 55	2 06	7 46
38	14 39	9 32	0 25	1 39	7 34
39	14 36	9 17	29♏55	1 11	7 22
40	14 33	9 02	29 24	0 43	7 10
41	14 29	8 46	28 52	0 13	6 57
42	14 26	8 30	28 20	29♐42	6 44
43	14 22	8 14	27 47	29 10	6 30
44	14 19	7 58	27 14	28 37	6 15
45	14 15	7 41	26 40	28 03	6 00
46	14 11	7 23	26 05	27 28	5 44
47	14 07	7 06	25 29	26 51	5 27
48	14 03	6 48	24 53	26 12	5 09
49	13 59	6 29	24 15	25 32	4 51
50	13 55	6 10	23 37	24 50	4 31
51	13 51	5 50	22 58	24 06	4 10
52	13 46	5 30	22 18	23 19	3 48
53	13 41	5 09	21 36	22 31	3 24
54	13 36	4 48	20 54	21 40	2 59
55	13 31	4 26	20 10	20 46	2 32
56	13 26	4 03	19 25	19 49	2 03
57	13 21	3 39	18 39	18 49	1 31
58	13 15	3 15	17 51	17 45	0 56
59	13 09	2 50	17 02	16 37	0 18
60	13♎03	2♏23	16♏11	15♐24	29♑36

11h 4m 0s 166° 0' 0"
14 ♍ 48

LAT.	11	12	ASC	2	3
0	17♎21	18♏28	17♐07	14♑44	13♒32
5	17 09	17 26	15 11	13 26	13 01
10	16 56	16 26	13 15	12 06	12 30
15	16 43	15 26	11 18	10 42	11 57
20	16 30	14 25	9 18	9 13	11 22
21	16 28	14 13	8 53	8 55	11 14
22	16 25	14 01	8 28	8 36	11 07
23	16 22	13 48	8 04	8 17	10 59
24	16 20	13 36	7 39	7 57	10 51
25	16 17	13 23	7 13	7 38	10 43
26	16 14	13 10	6 48	7 17	10 35
27	16 11	12 57	6 22	6 57	10 27
28	16 08	12 44	5 56	6 36	10 18
29	16 06	12 31	5 29	6 14	10 09
30	16 03	12 17	5 02	5 52	10 00
31	16 00	12 04	4 35	5 30	9 51
32	15 57	11 50	4 08	5 07	9 42
33	15 54	11 36	3 40	4 43	9 32
34	15 50	11 22	3 11	4 19	9 22
35	15 47	11 08	2 43	3 54	9 11
36	15 44	10 53	2 14	3 28	9 01
37	15 41	10 39	1 44	3 02	8 50
38	15 37	10 24	1 14	2 35	8 38
39	15 34	10 08	0 43	2 07	8 26
40	15 31	9 53	0 12	1 38	8 14
41	15 27	9 37	29♏40	1 08	8 01
42	15 23	9 21	29 07	0 37	7 48
43	15 20	9 04	28 34	0 05	7 34
44	15 16	8 47	28 00	29♐32	7 20
45	15 12	8 30	27 26	28 58	7 05
46	15 08	8 13	26 50	28 22	6 49
47	15 04	7 55	26 14	27 45	6 32
48	14 59	7 36	25 37	27 06	6 15
49	14 55	7 17	24 59	26 25	5 57
50	14 50	6 57	24 21	25 43	5 37
51	14 46	6 37	23 41	24 58	5 17
52	14 41	6 17	23 00	24 12	4 55
53	14 36	5 56	22 18	23 23	4 31
54	14 31	5 34	21 35	22 31	4 06
55	14 25	5 11	20 50	21 37	3 40
56	14 20	4 48	20 05	20 39	3 11
57	14 14	4 24	19 18	19 38	2 39
58	14 08	3 59	18 30	18 33	2 05
59	14 01	3 33	17 40	17 24	1 28
60	13♎55	3♏06	16♏48	16♐11	0♒46

11h 8m 0s 167° 0' 0"
15 ♍ 53

LAT.	11	12	ASC	2	3
0	18♎26	19♏27	18♐02	15♑40	14♒32
5	18 12	18 25	16 06	14 22	14 02
10	17 59	17 24	14 09	13 02	13 31
15	17 46	16 23	12 12	11 39	12 58
20	17 32	15 21	10 11	10 10	12 24
21	17 29	15 09	9 46	9 51	12 16
22	17 26	14 56	9 21	9 33	12 09
23	17 23	14 43	8 56	9 13	12 01
24	17 20	14 31	8 31	8 54	11 54
25	17 17	14 18	8 05	8 34	11 46
26	17 15	14 05	7 40	8 14	11 38
27	17 12	13 51	7 13	7 53	11 29
28	17 09	13 38	6 47	7 32	11 21
29	17 05	13 25	6 20	7 11	11 12
30	17 02	13 11	5 53	6 49	11 03
31	16 59	12 57	5 26	6 26	10 54
32	16 56	12 43	4 58	6 03	10 45
33	16 53	12 29	4 30	5 39	10 35
34	16 49	12 15	4 01	5 15	10 25
35	16 46	12 00	3 32	4 50	10 15
36	16 43	11 46	3 03	4 24	10 05
37	16 39	11 31	2 33	3 58	9 54
38	16 36	11 15	2 02	3 31	9 42
39	16 32	11 00	1 31	3 03	9 31
40	16 28	10 44	1 00	2 34	9 19
41	16 25	10 28	0 27	2 04	9 06
42	16 21	10 11	29♏55	1 33	8 53
43	16 17	9 54	29 21	1 01	8 39
44	16 13	9 37	28 47	0 27	8 25
45	16 08	9 20	28 12	29♐53	8 10
46	16 04	9 02	27 36	29 17	7 55
47	16 00	8 43	26 59	28 39	7 38
48	15 55	8 24	26 22	28 00	7 21
49	15 51	8 05	25 43	27 19	7 03
50	15 46	7 45	25 04	26 36	6 44
51	15 41	7 25	24 24	25 52	6 23
52	15 36	7 04	23 42	25 04	6 02
53	15 30	6 42	23 00	24 15	5 39
54	15 25	6 19	22 16	23 23	5 14
55	15 19	5 56	21 31	22 28	4 47
56	15 13	5 33	20 45	21 30	4 19
57	15 07	5 08	19 57	20 28	3 48
58	15 01	4 42	19 08	19 22	3 14
59	14 54	4 16	18 17	18 12	2 37
60	14♎47	3♏48	17♏25	16♐58	1♒56

11h 12m 0s 168° 0' 0" 16 ♍ 57					11h 16m 0s 169° 0' 0" 18 ♍ 02						11h 20m 0s 170° 0' 0" 19 ♍ 07					11h 24m 0s 171° 0' 0" 20 ♍ 12				
11	12	ASC	2	3	11	12	ASC	2	3	LAT.	11	12	ASC	2	3	11	12	ASC	2	3
19♎30	20♏26	18♐58	16♑36	15♒32	20♎34	21♏26	19♐53	17♑32	16♒33	0	21♎38	22♏25	20♐49	18♑28	17♒33	22♎42	23♏23	21♐44	19♑24	18♒34
19 16	19 24	17 01	15 18	15 03	20 19	20 22	17 56	16 15	16 04	5	21 23	21 20	18 51	17 11	17 05	22 26	22 18	19 46	18 07	18 06
19 02	18 22	15 04	13 59	14 32	20 05	19 19	15 58	14 55	15 34	10	21 07	20 17	16 53	15 52	16 35	22 10	21 14	17 48	16 48	17 37
18 48	17 20	13 05	12 35	14 00	19 50	18 16	13 59	13 32	15 02	15	20 51	19 13	14 53	14 29	16 04	21 53	20 09	15 47	15 26	17 06
18 33	16 17	11 04	11 07	13 26	19 34	17 13	11 57	12 03	14 28	20	20 35	18 08	12 50	13 00	15 31	21 36	19 04	13 44	13 57	16 34
18 30	16 04	10 39	10 48	13 19	19 31	17 00	11 32	11 45	14 21	21	20 32	17 55	12 25	12 42	15 24	21 33	18 51	13 18	13 39	16 27
18 27	15 52	10 14	10 29	13 11	19 28	16 47	11 07	11 26	14 14	22	20 29	17 42	12 00	12 23	15 17	21 30	18 37	12 53	13 20	16 20
18 24	15 39	9 49	10 10	13 04	19 25	16 34	10 41	11 07	14 07	23	20 26	17 29	11 34	12 04	15 10	21 26	18 24	12 27	13 01	16 13
18 21	15 26	9 23	9 51	12 56	19 22	16 20	10 16	10 47	13 59	24	20 22	17 15	11 08	11 44	15 02	21 23	18 10	12 01	12 42	16 06
18 18	15 12	8 58	9 31	12 48	19 18	16 07	9 50	10 28	13 51	25	20 19	17 02	10 42	11 25	14 55	21 19	17 56	11 34	12 22	15 58
18 15	14 59	8 32	9 10	12 40	19 15	15 54	9 24	10 07	13 44	26	20 15	16 48	10 16	11 04	14 47	21 15	17 42	11 08	12 02	15 51
18 12	14 46	8 05	8 50	12 32	19 12	15 40	8 57	9 47	13 36	27	20 12	16 34	9 49	10 44	14 39	21 12	17 28	10 41	11 41	15 43
18 09	14 32	7 39	8 29	12 24	19 08	15 26	8 30	9 26	13 27	28	20 08	16 20	9 22	10 23	14 31	21 08	17 14	10 14	11 20	15 35
18 05	14 19	7 12	8 07	12 15	19 05	15 12	8 03	9 04	13 19	29	20 05	16 06	8 54	10 01	14 23	21 04	17 00	9 46	10 58	15 27
18 02	14 05	6 44	7 45	12 07	19 02	14 58	7 35	8 42	13 10	30	20 01	15 52	8 27	9 39	14 14	21 01	16 45	9 18	10 36	15 18
17 59	13 51	6 17	7 23	11 58	18 58	14 44	7 08	8 19	13 01	31	19 57	15 37	7 59	9 16	14 05	20 57	16 31	8 50	10 14	15 10
17 55	13 37	5 49	6 59	11 48	18 55	14 30	6 39	7 56	12 52	32	19 54	15 23	7 30	8 53	13 57	20 53	16 16	8 21	9 50	15 01
17 52	13 22	5 20	6 36	11 39	18 51	14 15	6 11	7 32	12 43	33	19 50	15 08	7 01	8 29	13 47	20 49	16 01	7 51	9 27	14 52
17 48	13 08	4 51	6 11	11 29	18 47	14 00	5 41	7 08	12 33	34	19 46	14 53	6 32	8 05	13 38	20 45	15 45	7 22	9 02	14 43
17 45	12 53	4 22	5 46	11 19	18 44	13 45	5 12	6 43	12 23	35	19 42	14 37	6 02	7 40	13 28	20 41	15 30	6 52	8 37	14 33
17 41	12 38	3 52	5 21	11 09	18 40	13 30	4 42	6 17	12 13	36	19 38	14 22	5 31	7 14	13 18	20 36	15 14	6 21	8 11	14 23
17 38	12 22	3 22	4 54	10 58	18 36	13 14	4 11	5 51	12 03	37	19 34	14 06	5 00	6 47	13 08	20 32	14 58	5 50	7 44	14 13
17 34	12 07	2 51	4 27	10 47	18 32	12 58	3 40	5 23	11 52	38	19 30	13 50	4 29	6 20	12 57	20 28	14 41	5 18	7 17	14 02
17 30	11 51	2 20	3 59	10 35	18 28	12 42	3 08	4 55	11 40	39	19 26	13 33	3 57	5 52	12 46	20 23	14 25	4 45	6 48	13 51
17 26	11 35	1 48	3 30	10 23	18 24	12 26	2 36	4 26	11 29	40	19 21	13 17	3 24	5 22	12 34	20 19	14 08	4 12	6 19	13 40
17 22	11 18	1 15	2 59	10 11	18 20	12 09	2 03	3 56	11 16	41	19 17	13 00	2 51	4 52	12 22	20 14	13 50	3 39	5 49	13 28
17 18	11 02	0 42	2 28	9 58	18 15	11 52	1 29	3 24	11 04	42	19 12	12 42	2 17	4 21	12 09	20 10	13 33	3 04	5 17	13 16
17 14	10 44	0 08	1 56	9 45	18 11	11 35	0 55	2 52	10 50	43	19 08	12 25	1 42	3 48	11 56	20 05	13 15	2 29	4 44	13 03
17 09	10 27	29♏33	1 23	9 31	18 06	11 17	0 20	2 18	10 36	44	19 03	12 06	1 06	3 14	11 43	20 00	12 56	1 53	4 11	12 49
17 05	10 09	28 58	0 48	9 16	18 02	10 58	29♏44	1 43	10 22	45	18 58	11 48	0 30	2 39	11 28	19 55	12 37	1 16	3 35	12 35
17 01	9 51	28 21	0 12	9 01	17 57	10 40	29 07	1 07	10 07	46	18 53	11 29	29♏53	2 02	11 13	19 49	12 18	0 39	2 58	12 21
16 56	9 32	27 44	29♐34	8 44	17 52	10 21	28 30	0 29	9 51	47	18 48	11 09	29 15	1 24	10 58	19 44	11 58	0 00	2 20	12 05
16 51	9 13	27 06	28 54	8 27	17 47	10 01	27 51	29♐49	9 34	48	18 43	10 49	28 36	0 44	10 41	19 38	11 37	29♏21	1 40	11 49
16 46	8 53	26 27	28 13	8 09	17 42	9 41	27 12	29 08	9 16	49	18 37	10 29	27 56	0 03	10 24	19 33	11 16	28 40	0 58	11 32
16 41	8 33	25 48	27 30	7 50	17 36	9 20	26 31	28 24	8 58	50	18 31	10 08	27 15	29♐19	10 05	19 27	10 55	27 59	0 14	11 14
16 36	8 12	25 07	26 45	7 30	17 31	8 59	25 50	27 39	8 38	51	18 26	9 46	26 33	28 33	9 46	19 21	10 33	27 16	29♐28	10 54
16 30	7 50	24 25	25 58	7 09	17 25	8 37	25 07	26 51	8 17	52	18 20	9 23	25 50	27 45	9 25	19 14	10 10	26 32	28 39	10 34
16 25	7 28	23 41	25 08	6 46	17 19	8 14	24 23	26 01	7 55	53	18 13	9 00	25 05	26 54	9 03	19 08	9 47	25 47	27 48	10 12
16 19	7 05	22 57	24 15	6 22	17 13	7 51	23 38	25 08	7 31	54	18 07	8 37	24 20	26 00	8 40	19 01	9 22	25 01	26 54	9 49
16 13	6 42	22 11	23 19	5 56	17 07	7 27	22 52	24 11	7 05	55	18 00	8 12	23 33	25 04	8 14	18 54	8 57	24 13	25 56	9 24
16 07	6 17	21 24	22 21	5 28	17 00	7 02	22 04	23 12	6 37	56	17 53	7 47	22 44	24 04	7 47	18 46	8 31	23 24	24 56	8 57
16 00	5 52	20 36	21 18	4 57	16 53	6 36	21 15	22 09	6 07	57	17 46	7 20	21 54	23 00	7 17	18 39	8 05	22 34	23 51	8 28
15 53	5 26	19 46	20 12	4 24	16 46	6 10	20 25	21 01	5 34	58	17 38	6 53	21 03	21 51	6 45	18 31	7 37	21 41	22 42	7 56
15 46	4 59	18 55	19 01	3 48	16 38	5 42	19 32	19 50	4 58	59	17 31	6 25	20 10	20 39	6 10	18 23	7 08	20 48	21 28	7 22
15♎39	4♏31	18♏02	17♐45	3♒07	16♎30	5♏13	18♏38	18♐33	4♒19	60	17♎22	5♏56	19♏15	19♐21	5♒31	18♎14	6♏38	19♏52	20♐09	6♒43

11h 28m 0s 172° 0' 0" 21 ♍ 17					11h 32m 0s 173° 0' 0" 22 ♍ 23						11h 36m 0s 174° 0' 0" 23 ♍ 28					11h 40m 0s 175° 0' 0" 24 ♍ 33				
11	12	ASC	2	3	11	12	ASC	2	3	LAT.	11	12	ASC	2	3	11	12	ASC	2	3
23♎46	24♏22	22♐39	20♑20	19♒35	24♎50	25♏21	23♐34	21♑17	20♒36	0	25♎53	26♏19	24♐30	22♑13	21♒37	26♎57	27♏17	25♐25	23♑10	22♒39
23 29	23 16	20 41	19 04	19 07	24 32	24 14	21 36	20 01	20 09	5	25 35	25 11	22 31	20 58	21 11	26 37	26 09	23 26	21 55	22 13
23 12	22 11	18 42	17 45	18 39	24 14	23 08	19 37	18 42	19 41	10	25 16	24 05	20 31	19 40	20 44	26 18	25 02	21 26	20 37	21 46
22 55	21 06	16 41	16 23	18 09	23 56	22 02	17 35	17 20	19 12	15	24 58	22 58	18 29	18 18	20 15	25 59	23 54	19 24	19 15	21 18
22 37	19 59	14 37	14 55	17 37	23 38	20 55	15 30	15 52	18 40	20	24 39	21 50	16 24	16 50	19 44	25 39	22 45	17 17	17 48	20 48
22 34	19 46	14 11	14 36	17 30	23 34	20 41	15 05	15 34	18 34	21	24 35	21 36	15 58	16 32	19 37	25 35	22 31	16 51	17 30	20 41
22 30	19 32	13 46	14 18	17 23	23 31	20 27	14 39	15 15	18 27	22	24 31	21 22	15 32	16 13	19 31	25 31	22 17	16 25	17 11	20 35
22 27	19 18	13 20	13 59	17 16	23 27	20 13	14 13	14 56	18 20	23	24 27	21 08	15 05	15 54	19 24	25 27	22 03	15 58	16 52	20 28
22 23	19 05	12 53	13 39	17 09	23 23	19 59	13 46	14 37	18 13	24	24 23	20 54	14 39	15 35	19 17	25 23	21 48	15 32	16 33	20 22
22 19	18 51	12 27	13 19	17 02	23 19	19 45	13 19	14 17	18 06	25	24 19	20 39	14 12	15 15	19 10	25 19	21 34	15 05	16 13	20 15
22 15	18 37	12 00	12 59	16 54	23 15	19 31	12 52	13 57	17 59	26	24 15	20 25	13 45	14 55	19 03	25 15	21 19	14 37	15 53	20 08
22 12	18 22	11 33	12 38	16 47	23 11	19 16	12 25	13 36	17 51	27	24 11	20 10	13 17	14 34	18 56	25 10	21 04	14 09	15 32	20 00
22 08	18 08	11 05	12 17	16 39	23 07	19 02	11 57	13 15	17 43	28	24 07	19 55	12 49	14 13	18 48	25 06	20 49	13 41	15 11	19 53
22 04	17 53	10 38	11 56	16 31	23 03	18 47	11 29	12 53	17 36	29	24 03	19 40	12 21	13 51	18 40	25 02	20 34	13 13	14 50	19 46
22 00	17 39	10 09	11 34	16 23	22 59	18 32	11 01	12 31	17 28	30	23 58	19 25	11 52	13 29	18 33	24 57	20 19	12 44	14 28	19 38
21 56	17 24	9 41	11 11	16 14	22 55	18 17	10 32	12 09	17 19	31	23 54	19 10	11 23	13 07	18 24	24 53	20 03	12 15	14 05	19 30
21 52	17 09	9 12	10 48	16 06	22 51	18 02	10 03	11 46	17 11	32	23 49	18 54	10 54	12 44	18 16	24 48	19 47	11 45	13 42	19 22
21 48	16 53	8 42	10 24	15 57	22 46	17 46	9 33	11 22	17 02	33	23 45	18 39	10 24	12 20	18 08	24 44	19 31	11 14	13 18	19 13
21 43	16 38	8 12	9 59	15 48	22 42	17 30	9 02	10 57	16 53	34	23 40	18 22	9 53	11 55	17 59	24 39	19 15	10 44	12 53	19 05
21 39	16 22	7 42	9 34	15 38	22 37	17 14	8 32	10 32	16 44	35	23 36	18 06	9 22	11 30	17 50	24 34	18 58	10 12	12 28	18 56
21 35	16 06	7 11	9 08	15 28	22 33	16 58	8 00	10 06	16 34	36	23 31	17 50	8 50	11 04	17 40	24 29	18 41	9 40	12 02	18 46
21 30	15 49	6 39	8 42	15 18	22 28	16 41	7 29	9 39	16 24	37	23 26	17 33	8 18	10 37	17 30	24 24	18 24	9 08	11 35	18 37
21 26	15 33	6 07	8 14	15 08	22 24	16 24	6 56	9 12	16 14	38	23 21	17 16	7 45	10 09	17 20	24 19	18 07	8 35	11 08	18 27
21 21	15 16	5 34	7 46	14 57	22 19	16 07	6 23	8 43	16 03	39	23 16	16 58	7 12	9 41	17 10	24 14	17 49	8 01	10 39	18 17
21 16	14 59	5 01	7 16	14 46	22 14	15 49	5 49	8 14	15 52	40	23 11	16 40	6 38	9 11	16 59	24 08	17 31	7 27	10 09	18 06
21 12	14 41	4 27	6 46	14 34	22 09	15 31	5 15	7 43	15 41	41	23 06	16 22	6 03	8 41	16 48	24 03	17 12	6 51	9 39	17 55
21 07	14 23	3 52	6 14	14 22	22 04	15 13	4 39	7 11	15 29	42	23 00	16 03	5 27	8 09	16 36	23 57	16 54	6 15	9 07	17 44
21 01	14 04	3 16	5 41	14 09	21 58	14 54	4 04	6 38	15 16	43	22 55	15 44	4 51	7 36	16 24	23 51	16 34	5 39	8 34	17 32
20 56	13 46	2 40	5 07	13 56	21 53	14 35	3 27	6 04	15 04	44	22 49	15 25	4 14	7 02	16 11	23 46	16 14	5 01	7 59	17 19
20 51	13 26	2 03	4 32	13 42	21 47	14 16	2 49	5 29	14 50	45	22 43	15 05	3 36	6 26	15 58	23 40	15 54	4 22	7 23	17 06
20 45	13 07	1 25	3 55	13 28	21 41	13 56	2 11	4 51	14 36	46	22 37	14 44	2 57	5 48	15 44	23 33	15 33	3 43	6 46	16 52
20 40	12 46	0 46	3 16	13 13	21 36	13 35	1 31	4 13	14 21	47	22 31	14 24	2 17	5 10	15 29	23 27	15 12	3 03	6 07	16 38
20 34	12 26	0 06	2 36	12 57	21 29	13 14	0 51	3 32	14 05	48	22 25	14 02	1 36	4 29	15 14	23 20	14 50	2 21	5 26	16 23
20 28	12 04	29♏25	1 54	12 40	21 23	12 52	0 09	2 50	13 48	49	22 18	13 40	0 54	3 46	14 58	23 14	14 28	1 39	4 43	16 07
20 22	11 42	28 43	1 09	12 22	21 17	12 30	29♏27	2 05	13 31	50	22 12	13 17	0 11	3 01	14 40	23 07	14 05	0 55	3 58	15 50
20 15	11 20	27 59	0 23	12 03	21 10	12 07	28 43	1 18	13 12	51	22 05	12 54	29♏26	2 14	14 22	22 59	13 41	0 10	3 10	15 32
20 09	10 57	27 15	29♐34	11 43	21 03	11 43	27 58	0 29	12 53	52	21 57	12 30	28 41	1 24	14 03	22 52	13 16	29♏24	2 20	15 13
20 02	10 33	26 29	28 42	11 22	20 56	11 19	27 12	29♐37	12 32	53	21 50	12 05	27 54	0 32	13 42	22 44	12 51	28 36	1 27	14 53
19 55	10 08	25 42	27 47	10 59	20 49	10 54	26 24	28 42	12 09	54	21 42	11 39	27 06	29♐36	13 20	22 36	12 25	27 47	0 31	14 31
19 47	9 42	24 54	26 50	10 34	20 41	10 28	25 35	27 43	11 45	55	21 34	11 13	26 16	28 37	12 57	22 28	11 58	26 57	29♐32	14 08
19 40	9 16	24 04	25 48	10 08	20 33	10 01	24 44	26 41	11 19	56	21 26	10 45	25 25	27 35	12 31	22 19	11 30	26 05	28 28	13 43
19 32	8 49	23 13	24 43	9 39	20 25	9 33	23 52	25 35	10 51	57	21 17	10 17	24 32	26 28	12 04	22 10	11 01	25 11	27 21	13 16
19 23	8 20	22 20	23 33	9 08	20 16	9 04	22 59	24 24	10 21	58	21 08	9 47	23 37	25 16	11 34	22 00	10 31	24 16	26 09	12 47
19 15	7 51	21 25	22 18	8 34	20 07	8 34	22 03	23 09	9 47	59	20 59	9 17	22 41	24 00	11 01	21 51	10 00	23 19	24 51	12 15
19♎06	7♏20	20♏29	20♐58	7♒57	19♎57	8♏03	21♏06	21♐47	9♒10	60	20♎49	8♏45	21♏43	22♐37	10♒25	21♎40	9♏27	22♏20	23♐27	11♒40

11h 44m 0s — 176° 0' 0" — 25 ♍ 38

LAT.	11	12	ASC	2	3
0	28♎00	28♏15	26♐20	24♑06	23♒41
5	27 40	27 06	24 21	22 52	23 15
10	27 20	25 58	22 20	21 34	22 49
15	27 00	24 50	20 18	20 13	22 21
20	26 40	23 40	18 11	18 46	21 52
21	26 36	23 26	17 45	18 28	21 46
22	26 32	23 12	17 18	18 09	21 39
23	26 27	22 57	16 52	17 50	21 33
24	26 23	22 43	16 25	17 31	21 26
25	26 19	22 28	15 57	17 11	21 20
26	26 14	22 13	15 30	16 51	21 13
27	26 10	21 58	15 02	16 31	21 06
28	26 05	21 43	14 34	16 10	20 58
29	26 01	21 27	14 05	15 48	20 51
30	25 56	21 12	13 36	15 26	20 43
31	25 52	20 56	13 06	15 04	20 36
32	25 47	20 40	12 36	14 40	20 28
33	25 42	20 24	12 05	14 17	20 19
34	25 37	20 07	11 34	13 52	20 11
35	25 32	19 50	11 03	13 27	20 02
36	25 27	19 33	10 31	13 01	19 53
37	25 22	19 16	9 58	12 34	19 44
38	25 16	18 58	9 24	12 06	19 34
39	25 11	18 40	8 50	11 38	19 24
40	25 05	18 22	8 15	11 08	19 14
41	25 00	18 03	7 40	10 37	19 03
42	24 54	17 44	7 03	10 05	18 52
43	24 48	17 24	6 26	9 32	18 40
44	24 42	17 04	5 48	8 57	18 28
45	24 36	16 43	5 09	8 21	18 15
46	24 29	16 22	4 29	7 44	18 01
47	24 23	16 01	3 49	7 04	17 47
48	24 16	15 38	3 07	6 23	17 32
49	24 09	15 16	2 23	5 40	17 17
50	24 01	14 52	1 39	4 55	17 00
51	23 54	14 28	0 54	4 07	16 43
52	23 46	14 03	0 07	3 17	16 24
53	23 38	13 37	29♏19	2 23	16 04
54	23 30	13 10	28 29	1 27	15 43
55	23 21	12 43	27 38	0 27	15 21
56	23 12	12 15	26 45	29♐23	14 56
57	23 03	11 45	25 51	28 15	14 30
58	22 53	11 14	24 55	27 02	14 01
59	22 42	10 43	23 57	25 43	13 30
60	22♎32	10♏10	22♏57	24♐18	12♒55

11h 48m 0s — 177° 0' 0" — 26 ♍ 44

LAT.	11	12	ASC	2	3
0	29♎03	29♏13	27♐15	25♑03	24♒42
5	28 42	28 03	25 16	23 49	24 18
10	28 22	26 55	23 15	22 32	23 52
15	28 01	25 46	21 12	21 11	23 25
20	27 40	24 35	19 04	19 45	22 56
21	27 36	24 21	18 38	19 26	22 50
22	27 32	24 06	18 12	19 08	22 44
23	27 27	23 52	17 45	18 49	22 38
24	27 23	23 37	17 18	18 30	22 31
25	27 18	23 22	16 50	18 10	22 25
26	27 14	23 07	16 22	17 50	22 18
27	27 09	22 52	15 54	17 30	22 11
28	27 05	22 36	15 26	17 09	22 04
29	27 00	22 21	14 57	16 47	21 57
30	26 55	22 05	14 27	16 25	21 49
31	26 50	21 49	13 58	16 02	21 42
32	26 45	21 33	13 27	15 39	21 34
33	26 40	21 16	12 57	15 15	21 26
34	26 35	20 59	12 25	14 51	21 17
35	26 30	20 42	11 53	14 26	21 09
36	26 25	20 25	11 21	14 00	21 00
37	26 19	20 07	10 48	13 33	20 51
38	26 14	19 49	10 14	13 05	20 41
39	26 08	19 31	9 40	12 36	20 32
40	26 03	19 12	9 04	12 07	20 21
41	25 57	18 53	8 28	11 36	20 11
42	25 51	18 34	7 52	11 04	20 00
43	25 44	18 14	7 14	10 31	19 48
44	25 38	17 53	6 36	9 56	19 36
45	25 32	17 33	5 56	9 20	19 24
46	25 25	17 11	5 16	8 42	19 11
47	25 18	16 49	4 35	8 03	18 57
48	25 11	16 27	3 52	7 21	18 42
49	25 04	16 03	3 08	6 38	18 27
50	24 56	15 39	2 24	5 52	18 11
51	24 48	15 15	1 38	5 04	17 54
52	24 40	14 49	0 50	4 14	17 35
53	24 32	14 23	0 01	3 20	17 16
54	24 23	13 56	29♏11	2 23	16 55
55	24 14	13 28	28 19	1 22	16 33
56	24 05	12 59	27 26	0 18	16 09
57	23 55	12 29	26 31	29♐09	15 44
58	23 45	11 58	25 34	27 55	15 15
59	23 34	11 26	24 35	26 35	14 45
60	23♎23	10♏52	23♏34	25♐09	14♒11

11h 52m 0s — 178° 0' 0" — 27 ♍ 49

LAT.	11	12	ASC	2	3
0	0♏06	0♐11	28♐10	26♑00	25♒44
5	29♎45	29♏01	26 10	24 46	25 20
10	29 24	27 51	24 10	23 30	24 55
15	29 02	26 41	22 06	22 09	24 29
20	28 41	25 30	19 58	20 43	24 01
21	28 36	25 15	19 32	20 25	23 55
22	28 32	25 01	19 05	20 07	23 49
23	28 27	24 46	18 38	19 48	23 43
24	28 23	24 31	18 11	19 29	23 36
25	28 18	24 16	17 43	19 09	23 30
26	28 13	24 01	17 15	18 49	23 23
27	28 08	23 45	16 47	18 29	23 17
28	28 04	23 30	16 18	18 08	23 10
29	27 59	23 14	15 49	17 46	23 03
30	27 54	22 58	15 19	17 24	22 55
31	27 49	22 42	14 49	17 02	22 48
32	27 44	22 25	14 19	16 38	22 40
33	27 39	22 09	13 48	16 15	22 32
34	27 33	21 52	13 16	15 50	22 24
35	27 28	21 34	12 44	15 25	22 16
36	27 22	21 17	12 11	14 59	22 07
37	27 17	20 59	11 38	14 32	21 58
38	27 11	20 41	11 04	14 04	21 49
39	27 05	20 22	10 29	13 36	21 39
40	26 59	20 03	9 54	13 06	21 29
41	26 53	19 44	9 17	12 35	21 19
42	26 47	19 24	8 40	12 03	21 08
43	26 41	19 04	8 02	11 30	20 57
44	26 34	18 43	7 23	10 55	20 45
45	26 28	18 22	6 43	10 19	20 33
46	26 21	18 00	6 03	9 41	20 20
47	26 13	17 38	5 21	9 01	20 07
48	26 06	17 15	4 38	8 20	19 53
49	25 59	16 51	3 54	7 36	19 38
50	25 51	16 27	3 08	6 50	19 22
51	25 43	16 02	2 22	6 02	19 05
52	25 34	15 36	1 34	5 11	18 47
53	25 26	15 09	0 44	4 17	18 28
54	25 17	14 42	29♏53	3 20	18 08
55	25 07	14 13	29 01	2 18	17 46
56	24 58	13 44	28 06	1 13	17 23
57	24 48	13 13	27 10	0 04	16 58
58	24 37	12 41	26 13	28♐49	16 30
59	24 26	12 08	25 13	27 28	16 01
60	24♎14	11♏34	24♏11	26♐01	15♒28

11h 56m 0s — 179° 0' 0" — 28 ♍ 55

LAT.	11	12	ASC	2	3
0	1♏08	1♐08	29♐05	26♑57	26♒47
5	0 47	29♏57	27 05	25 44	26 23
10	0 25	28 47	25 04	24 28	25 59
15	0 03	27 37	23 00	23 08	25 33
20	29♎41	26 25	20 52	21 42	25 06
21	29 36	26 10	20 25	21 24	25 00
22	29 31	25 55	19 58	21 06	24 54
23	29 27	25 40	19 31	20 47	24 48
24	29 22	25 25	19 04	20 28	24 42
25	29 17	25 10	18 36	20 08	24 35
26	29 12	24 55	18 08	19 48	24 29
27	29 08	24 39	17 40	19 28	24 22
28	29 03	24 23	17 11	19 07	24 16
29	28 58	24 07	16 41	18 46	24 09
30	28 53	23 51	16 12	18 24	24 02
31	28 47	23 35	15 41	18 01	23 54
32	28 42	23 18	15 11	17 38	23 47
33	28 37	23 01	14 39	17 14	23 39
34	28 31	22 44	14 07	16 50	23 31
35	28 26	22 26	13 35	16 25	23 23
36	28 20	22 08	13 02	15 59	23 15
37	28 14	21 50	12 28	15 32	23 06
38	28 09	21 32	11 54	15 04	22 57
39	28 03	21 13	11 19	14 35	22 48
40	27 56	20 54	10 43	14 05	22 38
41	27 50	20 34	10 06	13 34	22 28
42	27 44	20 14	9 29	13 02	22 17
43	27 37	19 54	8 50	12 29	22 06
44	27 30	19 33	8 11	11 54	21 55
45	27 23	19 11	7 31	11 18	21 43
46	27 16	18 49	6 49	10 40	21 30
47	27 09	18 26	6 07	10 00	21 17
48	27 01	18 03	5 24	9 19	21 03
49	26 53	17 39	4 39	8 35	20 49
50	26 45	17 14	3 53	7 49	20 33
51	26 37	16 49	3 06	7 00	20 17
52	26 28	16 22	2 17	6 09	19 59
53	26 19	15 55	1 27	5 14	19 41
54	26 10	15 27	0 35	4 17	19 21
55	26 00	14 58	29♏42	3 15	19 00
56	25 50	14 28	28 47	2 09	18 37
57	25 40	13 57	27 50	0 59	18 13
58	25 29	13 25	26 52	29♐43	17 46
59	25 18	12 51	25 51	28 22	17 17
60	25♎06	12♏16	24♏48	26♐54	16♒45

12h 0m 0s — 180° 0' 0" — 0 ♎ 00

LAT.	11	12	ASC	2	3
0	2♏11	2♐05	0♑00	27♑55	27♒49
5	1 49	0 54	28♐00	26 42	27 26
10	1 26	29♏44	25 59	25 26	27 02
15	1 04	28 32	23 55	24 07	26 37
20	0 41	27 20	21 46	22 41	26 11
21	0 36	27 05	21 19	22 23	26 05
22	0 31	26 50	20 52	22 05	25 59
23	0 26	26 35	20 25	21 46	25 53
24	0 22	26 19	19 57	21 27	25 47
25	0 17	26 04	19 29	21 08	25 41
26	0 12	25 48	19 01	20 48	25 35
27	0 07	25 33	18 32	20 27	25 28
28	0 01	25 17	18 03	20 07	25 22
29	29♎56	25 00	17 34	19 45	25 15
30	29 51	24 44	17 04	19 23	25 08
31	29 46	24 27	16 33	19 01	25 01
32	29 40	24 10	16 02	18 38	24 54
33	29 35	23 53	15 31	18 14	24 46
34	29 29	23 36	14 59	17 50	24 39
35	29 23	23 18	14 26	17 24	24 31
36	29 18	23 00	13 53	16 58	24 22
37	29 12	22 42	13 19	16 32	24 14
38	29 06	22 23	12 44	16 04	24 05
39	29 00	22 04	12 08	15 35	23 56
40	28 53	21 45	11 32	15 05	23 47
41	28 47	21 25	10 55	14 34	23 37
42	28 40	21 04	10 17	14 02	23 26
43	28 33	20 43	9 39	13 29	23 16
44	28 26	20 22	8 59	12 54	23 05
45	28 19	20 00	8 18	12 18	22 53
46	28 12	19 38	7 36	11 40	22 41
47	28 04	19 15	6 54	11 00	22 28
48	27 56	18 51	6 10	10 18	22 14
49	27 48	18 27	5 24	9 34	22 00
50	27 40	18 02	4 38	8 48	21 45
51	27 31	17 36	3 50	7 59	21 29
52	27 22	17 09	3 01	7 07	21 12
53	27 13	16 41	2 10	6 13	20 54
54	27 03	16 13	1 18	5 14	20 35
55	26 53	15 43	0 24	4 12	20 14
56	26 43	15 13	29♏28	3 06	19 52
57	26 32	14 41	28 30	1 55	19 28
58	26 21	14 08	27 31	0 39	19 02
59	26 09	13 34	26 29	29♐16	18 34
60	25♎57	12♏59	25♏26	27♐47	18♒02

12h 4m 0s — 181° 0' 0" — 1 ♎ 05

LAT.	11	12	ASC	2	3
0	3♏13	3♐03	0♑55	28♑52	28♒52
5	2 50	1 51	28♐55	27 40	28 29
10	2 27	0 40	26 54	26 25	28 06
15	2 04	29♏28	24 49	25 05	27 42
20	1 41	28 14	22 40	23 40	27 16
21	1 36	27 59	22 13	23 22	27 10
22	1 31	27 44	21 46	23 04	27 05
23	1 26	27 29	21 18	22 46	26 59
24	1 21	27 13	20 51	22 27	26 53
25	1 16	26 58	20 23	22 07	26 47
26	1 11	26 42	19 54	21 47	26 41
27	1 05	26 26	19 25	21 27	26 35
28	1 00	26 10	18 56	21 06	26 28
29	0 55	25 54	18 26	20 45	26 22
30	0 49	25 37	17 56	20 23	26 15
31	0 44	25 20	17 25	20 01	26 08
32	0 38	25 03	16 54	19 38	26 01
33	0 33	24 46	16 22	19 14	25 54
34	0 27	24 28	15 50	18 50	25 46
35	0 21	24 10	15 17	18 25	25 39
36	0 15	23 52	14 43	17 59	25 31
37	0 09	23 33	14 09	17 32	25 22
38	0 03	23 14	13 34	17 04	25 14
39	29♎56	22 55	12 58	16 35	25 05
40	29 50	22 35	12 22	16 06	24 56
41	29 43	22 15	11 44	15 35	24 46
42	29 36	21 54	11 06	15 03	24 36
43	29 29	21 33	10 27	14 29	24 26
44	29 22	21 12	9 47	13 54	24 15
45	29 15	20 49	9 06	13 18	24 03
46	29 07	20 27	8 24	12 40	23 51
47	28 59	20 03	7 40	12 00	23 39
48	28 51	19 39	6 56	11 18	23 26
49	28 43	19 14	6 10	10 34	23 12
50	28 34	18 49	5 23	9 47	22 57
51	28 25	18 23	4 34	8 58	22 42
52	28 16	17 56	3 44	8 06	22 25
53	28 07	17 28	2 53	7 11	22 08
54	27 57	16 59	2 00	6 13	21 49
55	27 46	16 29	1 05	5 10	21 29
56	27 36	15 57	0 09	4 03	21 07
57	27 25	15 25	29♏10	2 52	20 44
58	27 13	14 52	28 10	1 34	20 18
59	27 01	14 17	27 08	0 11	19 51
60	26♎48	13♏41	26♏03	28♐40	19♒21

12h 8m 0s — 182° 0' 0" — 2 ♎ 11

LAT.	11	12	ASC	2	3
0	4♏16	4♐00	1♑50	29♑49	29♒54
5	3 52	2 48	29♐50	28 38	29 33
10	3 28	1 36	27 49	27 23	29 10
15	3 05	0 23	25 44	26 05	28 47
20	2 40	29♏09	23 34	24 40	28 21
21	2 35	28 54	23 07	24 22	28 16
22	2 30	28 38	22 40	24 04	28 10
23	2 25	28 23	22 12	23 45	28 05
24	2 20	28 07	21 44	23 27	27 59
25	2 15	27 52	21 16	23 07	27 53
26	2 10	27 36	20 47	22 48	27 47
27	2 04	27 20	20 18	22 27	27 41
28	1 59	27 03	19 49	22 07	27 35
29	1 53	26 47	19 19	21 45	27 29
30	1 48	26 30	18 49	21 24	27 22
31	1 42	26 13	18 18	21 01	27 16
32	1 36	25 56	17 46	20 38	27 09
33	1 31	25 38	17 14	20 15	27 02
34	1 25	25 20	16 42	19 50	26 54
35	1 19	25 02	16 08	19 25	26 47
36	1 12	24 44	15 35	18 59	26 39
37	1 06	24 25	15 00	18 33	26 31
38	1 00	24 05	14 25	18 05	26 23
39	0 53	23 46	13 49	17 36	26 14
40	0 47	23 26	13 12	17 06	26 05
41	0 40	23 05	12 34	16 35	25 56
42	0 33	22 44	11 55	16 03	25 46
43	0 25	22 23	11 16	15 30	25 36
44	0 18	22 01	10 35	14 55	25 25
45	0 10	21 39	9 54	14 18	25 14
46	0 03	21 15	9 11	13 40	25 02
47	29♎54	20 52	8 27	13 00	24 50
48	29 46	20 27	7 42	12 18	24 37
49	29 38	20 02	6 56	11 34	24 24
50	29 29	19 36	6 08	10 47	24 10
51	29 20	19 10	5 19	9 58	23 55
52	29 10	18 42	4 28	9 06	23 39
53	29 00	18 14	3 36	8 10	23 21
54	28 50	17 44	2 43	7 12	23 03
55	28 39	17 14	1 47	6 09	22 44
56	28 28	16 42	0 50	5 01	22 23
57	28 17	16 09	29♏51	3 49	22 00
58	28 05	15 35	28 49	2 31	21 35
59	27 52	15 00	27 46	1 06	21 09
60	27♎39	14♏23	26♏40	29♐35	20♒39

12h 12m 0s — 183° 0' 0" — 3 ♎ 16

LAT.	11	12	ASC	2	3
0	5♏18	4♐57	2♑45	0♒47	0♓57
5	4 53	3 44	0 45	29♑36	0 36
10	4 29	2 32	28♐44	28 22	0 15
15	4 05	1 18	26 39	27 04	29♒52
20	3 40	0 04	24 28	25 40	29 27
21	3 35	29♏48	24 01	25 22	29 22
22	3 30	29 33	23 34	25 04	29 16
23	3 24	29 17	23 06	24 46	29 11
24	3 19	29 01	22 38	24 27	29 06
25	3 14	28 45	22 10	24 08	29 00
26	3 08	28 29	21 41	23 48	28 54
27	3 03	28 13	21 12	23 28	28 48
28	2 57	27 56	20 42	23 07	28 42
29	2 52	27 40	20 12	22 46	28 36
30	2 46	27 23	19 41	22 24	28 30
31	2 40	27 06	19 10	22 02	28 23
32	2 34	26 48	18 38	21 39	28 16
33	2 28	26 30	18 06	21 16	28 10
34	2 22	26 12	17 33	20 51	28 02
35	2 16	25 54	17 00	20 26	27 55
36	2 10	25 35	16 26	20 00	27 48
37	2 03	25 16	15 51	19 34	27 40
38	1 57	24 57	15 15	19 06	27 32
39	1 50	24 37	14 39	18 37	27 23
40	1 43	24 17	14 02	18 08	27 15
41	1 36	23 56	13 24	17 37	27 05
42	1 29	23 35	12 45	17 05	26 56
43	1 21	23 13	12 05	16 31	26 46
44	1 14	22 51	11 24	15 56	26 36
45	1 06	22 28	10 42	15 19	26 25
46	0 58	22 04	9 58	14 41	26 14
47	0 50	21 40	9 14	14 01	26 02
48	0 41	21 15	8 28	13 19	25 50
49	0 32	20 50	7 42	12 35	25 36
50	0 23	20 24	6 53	11 48	25 23
51	0 14	19 57	6 04	10 58	25 08
52	0 04	19 29	5 13	10 06	24 52
53	29♎54	19 00	4 20	9 10	24 36
54	29 43	18 30	3 25	8 11	24 18
55	29 32	17 59	2 29	7 08	23 59
56	29 21	17 27	1 31	6 00	23 39
57	29 09	16 53	0 31	4 47	23 17
58	28 56	16 19	29♏29	3 28	22 53
59	28 44	15 43	28 24	2 03	22 27
60	28♎30	15♏05	27♏18	0♑30	21♒59

12h 16m 0s 184° 0' 0"
4 ♎ 22

LAT.	11	12	ASC	2	3
0	6♏19	5♐54	3♑40	1♒45	2♓00
5	5 55	4 40	1 41	0 35	1 40
10	5 30	3 27	29♐39	29♑21	1 19
15	5 05	2 14	27 33	28 03	0 57
20	4 39	0 58	25 22	26 40	0 33
21	4 34	0 43	24 55	26 22	0 28
22	4 29	0 27	24 28	26 04	0 23
23	4 23	0 11	24 00	25 46	0 17
24	4 18	29♏55	23 32	25 27	0 12
25	4 13	29 39	23 03	25 08	0 07
26	4 07	29 23	22 34	24 49	0 01
27	4 01	29 06	22 05	24 28	29♒55
28	3 56	28 50	21 35	24 08	29 49
29	3 50	28 33	21 05	23 47	29 43
30	3 44	28 16	20 34	23 25	29 37
31	3 38	27 58	20 03	23 03	29 31
32	3 32	27 41	19 31	22 40	29 25
33	3 26	27 23	18 58	22 17	29 18
34	3 20	27 04	18 25	21 53	29 11
35	3 13	26 46	17 52	21 28	29 04
36	3 07	26 27	17 17	21 02	28 57
37	3 00	26 08	16 42	20 35	28 49
38	2 53	25 48	16 06	20 08	28 41
39	2 47	25 28	15 29	19 39	28 33
40	2 39	25 07	14 52	19 09	28 24
41	2 32	24 46	14 13	18 38	28 16
42	2 25	24 25	13 34	18 06	28 06
43	2 17	24 03	12 54	17 33	27 57
44	2 09	23 40	12 12	16 58	27 47
45	2 01	23 17	11 30	16 21	27 37
46	1 53	22 53	10 46	15 43	27 26
47	1 44	22 29	10 01	15 03	27 14
48	1 36	22 04	9 15	14 20	27 02
49	1 27	21 38	8 28	13 36	26 49
50	1 17	21 11	7 39	12 49	26 36
51	1 08	20 44	6 49	11 59	26 22
52	0 57	20 15	5 57	11 07	26 07
53	0 47	19 46	5 03	10 11	25 51
54	0 36	19 15	4 08	9 11	25 33
55	0 25	18 44	3 11	8 07	25 15
56	0 13	18 11	2 12	6 59	24 55
57	0 01	17 37	1 11	5 45	24 34
58	29♎48	17 02	0 08	4 26	24 11
59	29 35	16 25	29♏03	3 00	23 46
60	29♎21	15♏47	27♏56	1♑26	23♒18

12h 20m 0s 185° 0' 0"
5 ♎ 27

LAT.	11	12	ASC	2	3
0	7♏21	6♐50	4♑35	2♒43	3♓03
5	6 56	5 37	2 36	1 33	2 44
10	6 30	4 23	0 34	0 20	2 23
15	6 05	3 09	28♐28	29♑03	2 02
20	5 39	1 52	26 17	27 40	1 39
21	5 33	1 37	25 49	27 23	1 34
22	5 28	1 21	25 22	27 05	1 29
23	5 22	1 05	24 54	26 47	1 24
24	5 17	0 49	24 26	26 28	1 19
25	5 11	0 33	23 57	26 09	1 14
26	5 06	0 16	23 28	25 49	1 08
27	5 00	0 00	22 58	25 30	1 03
28	4 54	29♏43	22 28	25 09	0 57
29	4 48	29 26	21 58	24 48	0 51
30	4 42	29 09	21 27	24 27	0 45
31	4 36	28 51	20 56	24 05	0 39
32	4 30	28 33	20 23	23 42	0 33
33	4 24	28 15	19 51	23 18	0 26
34	4 17	27 56	19 17	22 54	0 20
35	4 11	27 38	18 43	22 29	0 13
36	4 04	27 18	18 09	22 04	0 06
37	3 57	26 59	17 33	21 37	29♒58
38	3 50	26 39	16 57	21 09	29 51
39	3 43	26 19	16 20	20 41	29 43
40	3 36	25 58	15 42	20 11	29 35
41	3 28	25 37	15 03	19 40	29 26
42	3 21	25 15	14 24	19 08	29 17
43	3 13	24 53	13 43	18 35	29 08
44	3 05	24 30	13 01	18 00	28 58
45	2 57	24 06	12 18	17 23	28 48
46	2 48	23 42	11 34	16 45	28 38
47	2 39	23 17	10 49	16 05	28 27
48	2 30	22 52	10 02	15 22	28 15
49	2 21	22 26	9 14	14 38	28 03
50	2 11	21 59	8 25	13 51	27 50
51	2 01	21 31	7 34	13 01	27 36
52	1 51	21 02	6 41	12 08	27 21
53	1 40	20 32	5 47	11 12	27 06
54	1 29	20 01	4 51	10 12	26 49
55	1 18	19 29	3 53	9 08	26 31
56	1 06	18 56	2 54	7 59	26 12
57	0 53	18 21	1 52	6 45	25 52
58	0 40	17 46	0 48	5 25	25 29
59	0 26	17 08	29♏42	3 57	25 05
60	0♏12	16♏29	28♏33	2♑22	24♒38

12h 24m 0s 186° 0' 0"
6 ♎ 32

LAT.	11	12	ASC	2	3
0	8♏23	7♐47	5♑30	3♒41	4♓07
5	7 57	6 33	3 31	2 32	3 48
10	7 31	5 19	1 29	1 20	3 28
15	7 05	4 04	29♐23	0 03	3 07
20	6 38	2 47	27 11	28♑41	2 45
21	6 32	2 31	26 44	28 23	2 40
22	6 27	2 15	26 16	28 06	2 36
23	6 21	1 59	25 48	27 47	2 31
24	6 16	1 43	25 20	27 29	2 26
25	6 10	1 27	24 51	27 10	2 21
26	6 04	1 10	24 22	26 51	2 16
27	5 58	0 53	23 52	26 31	2 10
28	5 52	0 36	23 22	26 11	2 05
29	5 46	0 19	22 51	25 50	1 59
30	5 40	0 01	22 20	25 28	1 53
31	5 34	29♏44	21 48	25 06	1 47
32	5 27	29 26	21 16	24 44	1 41
33	5 21	29 07	20 43	24 20	1 35
34	5 14	28 48	20 10	23 56	1 29
35	5 08	28 29	19 35	23 31	1 22
36	5 01	28 10	19 00	23 06	1 15
37	4 54	27 50	18 25	22 39	1 08
38	4 47	27 30	17 48	22 12	1 01
39	4 39	27 10	17 11	21 43	0 53
40	4 32	26 49	16 33	21 14	0 45
41	4 24	26 27	15 53	20 43	0 37
42	4 17	26 05	15 13	20 11	0 28
43	4 09	25 42	14 32	19 37	0 19
44	4 00	25 19	13 50	19 02	0 10
45	3 52	24 55	13 07	18 26	0 00
46	3 43	24 31	12 22	17 47	29♒50
47	3 34	24 06	11 36	17 07	29 39
48	3 25	23 40	10 49	16 25	29 28
49	3 15	23 13	10 01	15 40	29 16
50	3 05	22 46	9 11	14 53	29 04
51	2 55	22 18	8 19	14 03	28 50
52	2 45	21 48	7 26	13 10	28 36
53	2 34	21 18	6 31	12 14	28 21
54	2 22	20 47	5 34	11 13	28 05
55	2 10	20 14	4 36	10 09	27 48
56	1 58	19 41	3 35	9 00	27 30
57	1 45	19 05	2 33	7 45	27 10
58	1 31	18 29	1 28	6 24	26 48
59	1 17	17 51	0 21	4 56	26 25
60	1♏02	17♏12	29♏11	3♑20	25♒59

12h 28m 0s 187° 0' 0"
7 ♎ 37

LAT.	11	12	ASC	2	3
0	9♏24	8♐43	6♑26	4♒39	5♓10
5	8 57	7 29	4 26	3 31	4 52
10	8 31	6 14	2 24	2 19	4 33
15	8 04	4 59	0 18	1 04	4 13
20	7 37	3 41	28♐06	29♑42	3 52
21	7 31	3 25	27 38	29 24	3 47
22	7 26	3 09	27 11	29 07	3 43
23	7 20	2 53	26 43	28 49	3 38
24	7 14	2 37	26 14	28 30	3 33
25	7 08	2 20	25 45	28 12	3 28
26	7 02	2 03	25 16	27 52	3 23
27	6 56	1 47	24 46	27 33	3 18
28	6 50	1 29	24 16	27 12	3 13
29	6 44	1 12	23 45	26 52	3 07
30	6 38	0 54	23 14	26 30	3 02
31	6 31	0 36	22 42	26 08	2 56
32	6 25	0 18	22 09	25 46	2 50
33	6 18	29♏59	21 36	25 23	2 44
34	6 12	29 41	21 02	24 59	2 38
35	6 05	29 21	20 28	24 34	2 32
36	5 58	29 02	19 52	24 08	2 25
37	5 51	28 42	19 16	23 42	2 18
38	5 43	28 21	18 40	23 15	2 11
39	5 36	28 00	18 02	22 46	2 04
40	5 28	27 39	17 23	22 17	1 56
41	5 20	27 17	16 44	21 46	1 48
42	5 12	26 55	16 03	21 14	1 40
43	5 04	26 32	15 22	20 40	1 31
44	4 56	26 09	14 39	20 06	1 22
45	4 47	25 45	13 55	19 29	1 13
46	4 38	25 20	13 10	18 51	1 03
47	4 29	24 55	12 24	18 10	0 53
48	4 19	24 28	11 36	17 28	0 42
49	4 10	24 01	10 47	16 43	0 30
50	3 59	23 33	9 57	15 56	0 18
51	3 49	23 05	9 04	15 06	0 05
52	3 38	22 35	8 11	14 13	29♒52
53	3 27	22 04	7 15	13 16	29 37
54	3 15	21 32	6 18	12 16	29 22
55	3 03	20 59	5 18	11 11	29 05
56	2 50	20 25	4 17	10 01	28 47
57	2 37	19 50	3 13	8 46	28 28
58	2 23	19 13	2 08	7 24	28 07
59	2 08	18 34	0 59	5 55	27 45
60	1♏53	17♏54	29♏49	4♑18	27♒20

12h 32m 0s 188° 0' 0"
8 ♎ 43

LAT.	11	12	ASC	2	3
0	10♏25	9♐40	7♑21	5♒38	6♓14
5	9 58	8 25	5 21	4 30	5 56
10	9 31	7 10	3 19	3 19	5 38
15	9 04	5 54	1 13	2 04	5 19
20	8 36	4 36	29♐01	0 43	4 58
21	8 30	4 20	28 33	0 26	4 54
22	8 24	4 03	28 05	0 08	4 50
23	8 18	3 47	27 37	29♑50	4 45
24	8 13	3 31	27 08	29 32	4 40
25	8 07	3 14	26 39	29 13	4 36
26	8 00	2 57	26 10	28 54	4 31
27	7 54	2 40	25 40	28 35	4 26
28	7 48	2 22	25 10	28 15	4 21
29	7 42	2 05	24 39	27 54	4 16
30	7 35	1 47	24 07	27 33	4 10
31	7 29	1 29	23 35	27 11	4 05
32	7 22	1 10	23 02	26 48	3 59
33	7 15	0 52	22 29	26 25	3 53
34	7 09	0 33	21 55	26 02	3 47
35	7 02	0 13	21 20	25 37	3 41
36	6 54	29♏53	20 45	25 11	3 35
37	6 47	29 33	20 08	24 45	3 28
38	6 40	29 13	19 31	24 18	3 21
39	6 32	28 51	18 53	23 49	3 14
40	6 24	28 30	18 14	23 20	3 07
41	6 16	28 08	17 34	22 49	2 59
42	6 08	27 45	16 54	22 17	2 51
43	6 00	27 22	16 12	21 44	2 43
44	5 51	26 58	15 29	21 09	2 35
45	5 42	26 34	14 44	20 33	2 25
46	5 33	26 09	13 59	19 54	2 16
47	5 24	25 43	13 12	19 14	2 06
48	5 14	25 17	12 24	18 32	1 56
49	5 04	24 49	11 34	17 47	1 45
50	4 53	24 21	10 43	17 00	1 33
51	4 43	23 52	9 50	16 09	1 21
52	4 31	23 22	8 56	15 16	1 07
53	4 20	22 50	7 59	14 19	0 53
54	4 08	22 18	7 01	13 19	0 39
55	3 55	21 45	6 01	12 13	0 23
56	3 42	21 10	4 59	11 03	0 06
57	3 29	20 34	3 54	9 48	29♒47
58	3 14	19 56	2 48	8 25	29 27
59	2 59	19 17	1 39	6 56	29 06
60	2♏44	18♏36	0♐27	5♑17	28♒42

12h 36m 0s 189° 0' 0"
9 ♎ 48

LAT.	11	12	ASC	2	3
0	11♏26	10♐36	8♑16	6♒37	7♓18
5	10 59	9 21	6 17	5 29	7 01
10	10 31	8 05	4 15	4 19	6 43
15	10 03	6 49	2 08	3 05	6 25
20	9 35	5 30	29♐55	1 44	6 05
21	9 29	5 14	29 28	1 27	6 01
22	9 23	4 57	29 00	1 10	5 57
23	9 17	4 41	28 32	0 52	5 52
24	9 11	4 24	28 03	0 34	5 48
25	9 05	4 07	27 34	0 15	5 43
26	8 59	3 50	27 04	29♑56	5 39
27	8 52	3 33	26 34	29 37	5 34
28	8 46	3 16	26 04	29 17	5 29
29	8 39	2 58	25 32	28 56	5 24
30	8 33	2 40	25 01	28 35	5 19
31	8 26	2 21	24 28	28 14	5 14
32	8 19	2 03	23 56	27 51	5 08
33	8 13	1 44	23 22	27 28	5 03
34	8 06	1 25	22 48	27 05	4 57
35	7 58	1 05	22 13	26 40	4 51
36	7 51	0 45	21 37	26 15	4 45
37	7 44	0 25	21 00	25 49	4 39
38	7 36	0 04	20 23	25 21	4 32
39	7 28	29♏42	19 45	24 53	4 25
40	7 20	29 21	19 06	24 24	4 18
41	7 12	28 58	18 25	23 53	4 11
42	7 04	28 35	17 44	23 21	4 03
43	6 55	28 12	17 02	22 48	3 55
44	6 46	27 48	16 18	22 13	3 47
45	6 37	27 23	15 33	21 37	3 38
46	6 28	26 58	14 48	20 59	3 29
47	6 18	26 32	14 00	20 18	3 20
48	6 08	26 05	13 11	19 36	3 10
49	5 58	25 37	12 21	18 51	2 59
50	5 47	25 09	11 29	18 04	2 48
51	5 36	24 39	10 36	17 14	2 36
52	5 25	24 08	9 41	16 20	2 24
53	5 13	23 37	8 44	15 23	2 10
54	5 01	23 04	7 45	14 22	1 56
55	4 48	22 30	6 44	13 17	1 41
56	4 34	21 55	5 41	12 06	1 24
57	4 20	21 18	4 35	10 50	1 06
58	4 06	20 40	3 28	9 27	0 47
59	3 50	20 00	2 18	7 57	0 27
60	3♏34	19♏18	1♐05	6♑17	0♓04

12h 40m 0s 190° 0' 0"
10 ♎ 53

LAT.	11	12	ASC	2	3
0	12♏27	11♐32	9♑11	7♒35	8♓22
5	11 59	10 16	7 12	6 29	8 06
10	11 31	9 00	5 10	5 20	7 49
15	11 02	7 43	3 04	4 06	7 31
20	10 33	6 24	0 51	2 46	7 12
21	10 27	6 08	0 23	2 29	7 08
22	10 21	5 51	29♐55	2 12	7 04
23	10 15	5 35	29 27	1 54	7 00
24	10 09	5 18	28 58	1 36	6 56
25	10 03	5 01	28 28	1 18	6 51
26	9 56	4 44	27 59	0 59	6 47
27	9 50	4 26	27 29	0 40	6 42
28	9 44	4 09	26 58	0 20	6 38
29	9 37	3 51	26 27	29♑59	6 33
30	9 30	3 33	25 55	29 39	6 28
31	9 23	3 14	25 22	29 17	6 23
32	9 17	2 55	24 49	28 55	6 18
33	9 10	2 36	24 15	28 32	6 13
34	9 02	2 17	23 41	28 08	6 07
35	8 55	1 57	23 06	27 44	6 01
36	8 48	1 37	22 30	27 19	5 56
37	8 40	1 16	21 53	26 53	5 50
38	8 32	0 55	21 15	26 26	5 43
39	8 24	0 33	20 36	25 57	5 37
40	8 16	0 11	19 57	25 28	5 30
41	8 08	29♏49	19 16	24 58	5 23
42	7 59	29 26	18 35	24 26	5 16
43	7 50	29 02	17 52	23 53	5 08
44	7 41	28 38	17 08	23 18	5 00
45	7 32	28 13	16 23	22 42	4 52
46	7 22	27 47	15 36	22 03	4 43
47	7 13	27 20	14 49	21 23	4 34
48	7 02	26 53	13 59	20 41	4 24
49	6 52	26 25	13 09	19 56	4 14
50	6 41	25 56	12 16	19 09	4 03
51	6 30	25 26	11 22	18 19	3 52
52	6 18	24 55	10 26	17 25	3 40
53	6 06	24 23	9 28	16 28	3 27
54	5 53	23 50	8 29	15 27	3 13
55	5 40	23 15	7 27	14 21	2 59
56	5 26	22 39	6 23	13 10	2 43
57	5 12	22 02	5 17	11 53	2 26
58	4 57	21 23	4 08	10 30	2 08
59	4 41	20 43	2 57	8 59	1 48
60	4♏25	20♏00	1♐43	7♑18	1♓26

12h 44m 0s 191° 0' 0"
11 ♎ 58

LAT.	11	12	ASC	2	3
0	13♏27	12♐28	10♑07	8♒34	9♓26
5	12 59	11 12	8 08	7 29	9 10
10	12 30	9 56	6 06	6 20	8 54
15	12 02	8 38	3 59	5 07	8 38
20	11 32	7 18	1 46	3 48	8 20
21	11 26	7 02	1 18	3 31	8 16
22	11 20	6 45	0 50	3 14	8 12
23	11 13	6 29	0 22	2 57	8 08
24	11 07	6 12	29♐53	2 39	8 04
25	11 01	5 55	29 23	2 21	8 00
26	10 54	5 37	28 53	2 02	7 55
27	10 48	5 20	28 23	1 43	7 51
28	10 41	5 02	27 52	1 23	7 47
29	10 34	4 44	27 21	1 03	7 42
30	10 28	4 25	26 49	0 42	7 37
31	10 21	4 07	26 16	0 21	7 33
32	10 14	3 48	25 43	29♑59	7 28
33	10 06	3 28	25 09	29 36	7 23
34	9 59	3 09	24 34	29 12	7 17
35	9 52	2 49	23 59	28 48	7 12
36	9 44	2 28	23 22	28 23	7 06
37	9 36	2 07	22 45	27 57	7 01
38	9 28	1 46	22 07	27 30	6 55
39	9 20	1 24	21 28	27 02	6 48
40	9 12	1 02	20 49	26 33	6 42
41	9 03	0 39	20 08	26 03	6 35
42	8 55	0 16	19 26	25 31	6 28
43	8 46	29♏52	18 43	24 58	6 21
44	8 36	29 27	17 58	24 23	6 13
45	8 27	29 02	17 13	23 47	6 05
46	8 17	28 36	16 26	23 09	5 57
47	8 07	28 09	15 37	22 29	5 48
48	7 57	27 42	14 48	21 46	5 39
49	7 46	27 13	13 56	21 02	5 29
50	7 35	26 44	13 03	20 14	5 19
51	7 23	26 13	12 08	19 24	5 08
52	7 11	25 42	11 12	18 31	4 57
53	6 59	25 09	10 13	17 33	4 45
54	6 46	24 36	9 13	16 32	4 31
55	6 32	24 00	8 10	15 26	4 18
56	6 18	23 24	7 05	14 15	4 03
57	6 03	22 46	5 58	12 58	3 46
58	5 48	22 07	4 49	11 34	3 29
59	5 32	21 25	3 36	10 02	3 10
60	5♏15	20♏42	2♐21	8♑20	2♓49

12h 48m 0s — 192° 0' 0" — 13 ♎ 03

LAT.	11	12	ASC	2	3
0	14♏28	13♐24	11♑02	9♒34	10♓30
5	13 59	12 08	9 03	8 29	10 15
10	13 30	10 51	7 02	7 21	10 00
15	13 00	9 33	4 55	6 09	9 44
20	12 30	8 12	2 41	4 50	9 27
21	12 24	7 56	2 14	4 34	9 23
22	12 18	7 39	1 45	4 17	9 20
23	12 11	7 22	1 17	3 59	9 16
24	12 05	7 05	0 48	3 42	9 12
25	11 59	6 48	0 18	3 24	9 08
26	11 52	6 31	29♐48	3 05	9 04
27	11 45	6 13	29 18	2 46	9 00
28	11 39	5 55	28 47	2 26	8 56
29	11 32	5 37	28 15	2 06	8 51
30	11 25	5 18	27 43	1 46	8 47
31	11 18	4 59	27 10	1 25	8 42
32	11 10	4 40	26 37	1 03	8 38
33	11 03	4 21	26 03	0 40	8 33
34	10 56	4 01	25 28	0 17	8 28
35	10 48	3 41	24 52	29♑53	8 23
36	10 40	3 20	24 16	29 28	8 17
37	10 32	2 59	23 38	29 02	8 12
38	10 24	2 37	23 00	28 35	8 06
39	10 16	2 15	22 21	28 07	8 00
40	10 08	1 53	21 41	27 38	7 54
41	9 59	1 30	20 59	27 08	7 48
42	9 50	1 06	20 17	26 37	7 41
43	9 41	0 42	19 33	26 04	7 34
44	9 31	0 17	18 49	25 29	7 27
45	9 22	29♏51	18 03	24 53	7 19
46	9 12	29 25	17 15	24 15	7 11
47	9 01	28 58	16 26	23 35	7 03
48	8 51	28 30	15 36	22 53	6 54
49	8 40	28 01	14 44	22 08	6 45
50	8 28	27 31	13 50	21 21	6 35
51	8 16	27 01	12 55	20 30	6 25
52	8 04	26 29	11 58	19 37	6 14
53	7 51	25 56	10 59	18 39	6 02
54	7 38	25 21	9 57	17 38	5 50
55	7 24	24 46	8 54	16 32	5 37
56	7 10	24 09	7 48	15 21	5 22
57	6 55	23 30	6 40	14 03	5 07
58	6 39	22 50	5 29	12 39	4 50
59	6 23	22 08	4 16	11 06	4 32
60	6♏05	21♏25	3♐00	9♑24	4♓13

12h 52m 0s — 193° 0' 0" — 14 ♎ 07

LAT.	11	12	ASC	2	3
0	15♏28	14♐20	11♑58	10♒33	11♓34
5	14 59	13 03	9 59	9 29	11 20
10	14 29	11 46	7 58	8 22	11 06
15	13 59	10 28	5 51	7 10	10 51
20	13 28	9 07	3 37	5 53	10 34
21	13 22	8 50	3 09	5 36	10 31
22	13 16	8 33	2 41	5 20	10 28
23	13 09	8 16	2 12	5 02	10 24
24	13 03	7 59	1 43	4 45	10 20
25	12 56	7 42	1 14	4 27	10 17
26	12 50	7 24	0 43	4 09	10 13
27	12 43	7 06	0 13	3 50	10 09
28	12 36	6 48	29♐42	3 30	10 05
29	12 29	6 30	29 10	3 10	10 01
30	12 22	6 11	28 38	2 50	9 56
31	12 15	5 52	28 05	2 29	9 52
32	12 07	5 33	27 31	2 07	9 48
33	12 00	5 13	26 57	1 45	9 43
34	11 52	4 53	26 22	1 22	9 38
35	11 44	4 33	25 46	0 58	9 33
36	11 37	4 12	25 09	0 33	9 28
37	11 28	3 50	24 31	0 07	9 23
38	11 20	3 29	23 53	29♑41	9 18
39	11 12	3 06	23 13	29 13	9 12
40	11 03	2 44	22 33	28 44	9 06
41	10 54	2 20	21 51	28 14	9 00
42	10 45	1 57	21 08	27 43	8 54
43	10 36	1 32	20 25	27 10	8 47
44	10 26	1 07	19 39	26 36	8 40
45	10 16	0 41	18 53	26 00	8 33
46	10 06	0 14	18 05	25 22	8 26
47	9 55	29♏47	17 16	24 42	8 18
48	9 45	29 18	16 25	24 00	8 09
49	9 33	28 49	15 32	23 15	8 01
50	9 22	28 19	14 38	22 28	7 51
51	9 10	27 48	13 42	21 37	7 42
52	8 57	27 16	12 44	20 44	7 31
53	8 44	26 42	11 44	19 46	7 20
54	8 31	26 07	10 42	18 45	7 08
55	8 17	25 31	9 38	17 39	6 56
56	8 02	24 54	8 31	16 27	6 42
57	7 46	24 15	7 22	15 09	6 28
58	7 30	23 34	6 10	13 44	6 12
59	7 13	22 51	4 56	12 11	5 55
60	6♏56	22♏07	3♐39	10♑28	5♓36

12h 56m 0s — 194° 0' 0" — 15 ♎ 12

LAT.	11	12	ASC	2	3
0	16♏28	15♐16	12♑53	11♒32	12♓39
5	15 58	13 59	10 55	10 29	12 26
10	15 28	12 41	8 53	9 23	12 12
15	14 58	11 22	6 47	8 12	11 58
20	14 27	10 01	4 33	6 56	11 42
21	14 20	9 44	4 05	6 39	11 39
22	14 14	9 27	3 37	6 23	11 36
23	14 07	9 10	3 08	6 06	11 32
24	14 00	8 53	2 39	5 48	11 29
25	13 54	8 35	2 09	5 31	11 25
26	13 47	8 17	1 39	5 12	11 22
27	13 40	7 59	1 08	4 54	11 18
28	13 33	7 41	0 37	4 35	11 14
29	13 26	7 23	0 05	4 15	11 10
30	13 19	7 04	29♐32	3 55	11 06
31	13 11	6 45	28 59	3 34	11 02
32	13 04	6 25	28 26	3 12	10 58
33	12 56	6 05	27 51	2 50	10 54
34	12 49	5 45	27 16	2 27	10 49
35	12 41	5 25	26 40	2 03	10 44
36	12 33	5 03	26 03	1 39	10 40
37	12 24	4 42	25 25	1 13	10 35
38	12 16	4 20	24 46	0 47	10 30
39	12 07	3 58	24 06	0 19	10 24
40	11 59	3 35	23 25	29♑51	10 19
41	11 50	3 11	22 43	29 21	10 13
42	11 40	2 47	22 00	28 49	10 07
43	11 31	2 22	21 16	28 17	10 01
44	11 21	1 57	20 30	27 43	9 54
45	11 11	1 30	19 43	27 07	9 48
46	11 00	1 03	18 55	26 29	9 40
47	10 50	0 36	18 05	25 49	9 33
48	10 39	0 07	17 14	25 07	9 25
49	10 27	29♏37	16 21	24 23	9 17
50	10 15	29 07	15 26	23 35	9 08
51	10 03	28 35	14 29	22 45	8 59
52	9 50	28 02	13 30	21 52	8 49
53	9 37	27 29	12 30	20 54	8 39
54	9 23	26 53	11 27	19 53	8 27
55	9 09	26 17	10 22	18 46	8 16
56	8 54	25 39	9 14	17 35	8 03
57	8 38	24 59	8 04	16 16	7 49
58	8 21	24 18	6 51	14 51	7 34
59	8 04	23 34	5 36	13 17	7 18
60	7♏46	22♏49	4♐17	11♑33	7♓00

13h 0m 0s — 195° 0' 0" — 16 ♎ 17

LAT.	11	12	ASC	2	3
0	17♏28	16♐11	13♑49	12♒32	13♓43
5	16 58	14 54	11 51	11 30	13 31
10	16 27	13 36	9 50	10 24	13 18
15	15 56	12 17	7 43	9 15	13 05
20	15 25	10 55	5 29	7 59	12 50
21	15 18	10 38	5 01	7 43	12 47
22	15 11	10 21	4 32	7 26	12 44
23	15 05	10 04	4 04	7 10	12 41
24	14 58	9 46	3 34	6 52	12 37
25	14 51	9 29	3 05	6 35	12 34
26	14 44	9 11	2 34	6 17	12 31
27	14 37	8 53	2 04	5 58	12 27
28	14 30	8 34	1 32	5 39	12 24
29	14 23	8 16	1 00	5 20	12 20
30	14 16	7 57	0 28	5 00	12 16
31	14 08	7 37	29♐54	4 39	12 12
32	14 01	7 18	29 20	4 18	12 08
33	13 53	6 58	28 45	3 56	12 04
34	13 45	6 37	28 10	3 33	12 00
35	13 37	6 16	27 34	3 09	11 56
36	13 29	5 55	26 56	2 45	11 51
37	13 20	5 34	26 18	2 20	11 47
38	13 12	5 11	25 39	1 53	11 42
39	13 03	4 49	24 59	1 26	11 37
40	12 54	4 26	24 18	0 57	11 32
41	12 45	4 02	23 36	0 28	11 26
42	12 35	3 37	22 52	29♑57	11 21
43	12 26	3 12	22 08	29 24	11 15
44	12 16	2 46	21 22	28 50	11 09
45	12 05	2 20	20 34	28 14	11 02
46	11 55	1 53	19 45	27 37	10 55
47	11 44	1 25	18 55	26 57	10 48
48	11 32	0 56	18 03	26 15	10 41
49	11 21	0 26	17 09	25 31	10 33
50	11 09	29♏55	16 14	24 44	10 25
51	10 56	29 23	15 16	23 54	10 16
52	10 43	28 49	14 17	23 00	10 07
53	10 29	28 15	13 16	22 03	9 57
54	10 15	27 39	12 12	21 01	9 47
55	10 01	27 02	11 06	19 55	9 35
56	9 45	26 24	9 57	18 43	9 23
57	9 29	25 43	8 46	17 25	9 10
58	9 12	25 01	7 32	15 59	8 57
59	8 55	24 17	6 16	14 25	8 41
60	8♏36	23♏31	4♐56	12♑40	8♓25

13h 4m 0s — 196° 0' 0" — 17 ♎ 21

LAT.	11	12	ASC	2	3
0	18♏28	17♐07	14♑44	13♒32	14♓48
5	17 57	15 49	12 47	12 31	14 36
10	17 26	14 31	10 46	11 26	14 24
15	16 55	13 12	8 39	10 17	14 12
20	16 22	11 49	6 25	9 02	13 58
21	16 16	11 32	5 57	8 46	13 55
22	16 09	11 15	5 28	8 30	13 52
23	16 02	10 58	5 00	8 14	13 49
24	15 55	10 40	4 30	7 57	13 46
25	15 48	10 22	4 00	7 39	13 43
26	15 41	10 04	3 30	7 21	13 40
27	15 34	9 46	2 59	7 03	13 37
28	15 27	9 27	2 28	6 44	13 33
29	15 20	9 09	1 56	6 25	13 30
30	15 12	8 50	1 23	6 05	13 26
31	15 05	8 30	0 49	5 45	13 23
32	14 57	8 10	0 15	5 23	13 19
33	14 49	7 50	29♐40	5 02	13 15
34	14 41	7 29	29 05	4 39	13 11
35	14 33	7 09	28 28	4 16	13 07
36	14 25	6 47	27 51	3 51	13 03
37	14 16	6 25	27 12	3 26	12 59
38	14 07	6 03	26 33	3 00	12 54
39	13 58	5 40	25 53	2 33	12 49
40	13 49	5 16	25 11	2 05	12 45
41	13 40	4 52	24 28	1 35	12 39
42	13 30	4 28	23 45	1 05	12 34
43	13 20	4 02	23 00	0 32	12 29
44	13 10	3 36	22 13	29♑58	12 23
45	13 00	3 10	21 25	29 23	12 17
46	12 49	2 42	20 36	28 45	12 11
47	12 38	2 14	19 45	28 06	12 04
48	12 26	1 44	18 53	27 24	11 57
49	12 14	1 14	17 58	26 40	11 50
50	12 02	0 43	17 02	25 53	11 42
51	11 49	0 10	16 04	25 03	11 34
52	11 36	29♏37	15 04	24 10	11 25
53	11 22	29 02	14 02	23 13	11 16
54	11 07	28 25	12 57	22 11	11 06
55	10 52	27 48	11 50	21 05	10 56
56	10 37	27 09	10 41	19 52	10 44
57	10 20	26 28	9 29	18 34	10 32
58	10 03	25 45	8 14	17 08	10 19
59	9 45	25 00	6 56	15 33	10 05
60	9♏26	24♏14	5♐35	13♑48	9♓50

13h 8m 0s — 197° 0' 0" — 18 ♎ 26

LAT.	11	12	ASC	2	3
0	19♏27	18♐02	15♑40	14♒32	15♓53
5	18 56	16 44	13 43	13 32	15 42
10	18 25	15 26	11 42	12 28	15 31
15	17 53	14 06	9 36	11 20	15 19
20	17 20	12 43	7 21	10 06	15 06
21	17 13	12 26	6 53	9 50	15 04
22	17 07	12 09	6 25	9 34	15 01
23	17 00	11 51	5 56	9 18	14 58
24	16 53	11 34	5 26	9 01	14 55
25	16 46	11 16	4 57	8 44	14 52
26	16 39	10 58	4 26	8 26	14 49
27	16 31	10 39	3 55	8 08	14 46
28	16 24	10 21	3 23	7 50	14 43
29	16 16	10 02	2 51	7 30	14 40
30	16 09	9 42	2 18	7 11	14 37
31	16 01	9 23	1 45	6 51	14 33
32	15 53	9 03	1 10	6 30	14 30
33	15 45	8 42	0 35	6 08	14 26
34	15 37	8 22	29♐59	5 46	14 23
35	15 29	8 01	29 23	5 22	14 19
36	15 20	7 39	28 45	4 59	14 15
37	15 12	7 17	28 06	4 34	14 11
38	15 03	6 54	27 27	4 08	14 07
39	14 54	6 31	26 46	3 41	14 02
40	14 44	6 07	26 04	3 13	13 58
41	14 35	5 43	25 22	2 44	13 53
42	14 25	5 18	24 37	2 13	13 48
43	14 15	4 53	23 52	1 41	13 43
44	14 05	4 26	23 05	1 07	13 38
45	13 54	3 59	22 17	0 32	13 32
46	13 43	3 31	21 27	29♑55	13 26
47	13 32	3 03	20 36	29 15	13 20
48	13 20	2 33	19 42	28 34	13 14
49	13 08	2 02	18 48	27 50	13 07
50	12 55	1 31	17 51	27 03	13 00
51	12 42	0 58	16 52	26 13	12 52
52	12 28	0 24	15 51	25 20	12 44
53	12 14	29♏48	14 48	24 23	12 35
54	12 00	29 12	13 43	23 21	12 26
55	11 44	28 33	12 35	22 15	12 16
56	11 28	27 54	11 25	21 03	12 06
57	11 11	27 12	10 11	19 44	11 54
58	10 54	26 29	8 56	18 18	11 42
59	10 35	25 44	7 37	16 43	11 29
60	10♏16	24♏56	6♐15	14♑57	11♓15

13h 12m 0s — 198° 0' 0" — 19 ♎ 30

LAT.	11	12	ASC	2	3
0	20♏26	18♐58	16♑36	15♒32	16♓57
5	19 55	17 40	14 39	14 33	16 47
10	19 23	16 21	12 39	13 30	16 37
15	18 51	15 01	10 32	12 23	16 26
20	18 18	13 37	8 18	11 10	16 14
21	18 11	13 20	7 50	10 55	16 12
22	18 04	13 03	7 21	10 39	16 09
23	17 57	12 45	6 52	10 23	16 07
24	17 50	12 27	6 23	10 06	16 04
25	17 43	12 09	5 53	9 49	16 02
26	17 35	11 51	5 22	9 32	15 59
27	17 28	11 33	4 51	9 14	15 56
28	17 21	11 14	4 20	8 55	15 53
29	17 13	10 55	3 47	8 36	15 50
30	17 05	10 35	3 14	8 17	15 47
31	16 58	10 16	2 40	7 57	15 44
32	16 50	9 55	2 06	7 36	15 41
33	16 41	9 35	1 31	7 15	15 37
34	16 33	9 14	0 55	6 53	15 34
35	16 25	8 53	0 18	6 30	15 31
36	16 16	8 31	29♐40	6 06	15 27
37	16 07	8 09	29 01	5 41	15 23
38	15 58	7 46	28 21	5 16	15 19
39	15 49	7 22	27 40	4 49	15 15
40	15 40	6 59	26 58	4 21	15 11
41	15 30	6 34	26 15	3 52	15 07
42	15 20	6 09	25 30	3 22	15 02
43	15 10	5 43	24 45	2 50	14 57
44	14 59	5 16	23 57	2 17	14 52
45	14 48	4 49	23 09	1 42	14 47
46	14 37	4 21	22 18	1 05	14 42
47	14 25	3 52	21 26	0 26	14 36
48	14 13	3 22	20 33	29♑44	14 30
49	14 01	2 51	19 37	29 01	14 24
50	13 48	2 19	18 40	28 14	14 17
51	13 35	1 45	17 40	27 24	14 10
52	13 21	1 11	16 39	26 31	14 03
53	13 07	0 35	15 35	25 34	13 55
54	12 52	29♏58	14 29	24 33	13 46
55	12 36	29 19	13 20	23 27	13 37
56	12 20	28 39	12 09	22 14	13 27
57	12 03	27 57	10 54	20 56	13 17
58	11 45	27 13	9 37	19 29	13 06
59	11 26	26 27	8 17	17 54	12 53
60	11♏06	25♏39	6♐54	16♑08	12♓40

13h 16m 0s — 199° 0' 0" — 20 ♎ 34

LAT.	11	12	ASC	2	3
0	21♏26	19♐53	17♑32	16♒33	18♓02
5	20 54	18 35	15 36	15 34	17 53
10	20 21	17 16	13 35	14 32	17 44
15	19 49	15 55	11 29	13 26	17 34
20	19 15	14 31	9 15	12 14	17 23
21	19 08	14 14	8 47	11 59	17 21
22	19 01	13 57	8 18	11 44	17 18
23	18 54	13 39	7 49	11 28	17 16
24	18 47	13 21	7 19	11 11	17 13
25	18 40	13 03	6 49	10 54	17 11
26	18 32	12 45	6 19	10 37	17 08
27	18 25	12 26	5 48	10 20	17 06
28	18 17	12 07	5 16	10 01	17 03
29	18 10	11 48	4 43	9 43	17 01
30	18 02	11 28	4 10	9 24	16 58
31	17 54	11 08	3 36	9 04	16 55
32	17 46	10 48	3 02	8 43	16 52
33	17 38	10 27	2 26	8 22	16 49
34	17 29	10 06	1 50	8 00	16 46
35	17 21	9 45	1 13	7 38	16 42
36	17 12	9 23	0 35	7 14	16 39
37	17 03	9 00	29♐56	6 50	16 36
38	16 54	8 37	29 16	6 24	16 32
39	16 44	8 14	28 35	5 58	16 28
40	16 35	7 50	27 52	5 30	16 24
41	16 25	7 25	27 09	5 02	16 20
42	16 15	7 00	26 24	4 31	16 16
43	16 04	6 33	25 37	4 00	16 12
44	15 53	6 07	24 50	3 27	16 07
45	15 42	5 39	24 01	2 52	16 03
46	15 31	5 10	23 10	2 15	15 58
47	15 19	4 41	22 17	1 37	15 52
48	15 07	4 11	21 23	0 55	15 47
49	14 54	3 39	20 27	0 12	15 41
50	14 41	3 07	19 29	29♑26	15 35
51	14 28	2 33	18 29	28 36	15 28
52	14 14	1 58	17 27	27 43	15 22
53	13 59	1 22	16 22	26 47	15 14
54	13 44	0 44	15 15	25 45	15 06
55	13 28	0 05	14 05	24 39	14 58
56	13 11	29♏24	12 53	23 27	14 49
57	12 54	28 41	11 38	22 08	14 40
58	12 35	27 57	10 20	20 42	14 29
59	12 16	27 10	8 58	19 06	14 18
60	11♏56	26♏21	7♐34	17♑20	14♓06

13h 20m 0s 200° 0' 0" 21 ♎ 38					13h 24m 0s 201° 0' 0" 22 ♎ 42						13h 28m 0s 202° 0' 0" 23 ♎ 46					13h 32m 0s 203° 0' 0" 24 ♎ 50				
11	12	ASC	2	3	11	12	ASC	2	3	LAT.	11	12	ASC	2	3	11	12	ASC	2	3
22♏25	20♐49	18♑28	17♒33	19♓07	23♏23	21♐44	19♑24	18♒34	20♓12	0	24♏22	22♐39	20♑20	19♒35	21♓17	25♏21	23♐34	21♑17	20♒36	22♓23
21 52	19 30	16 32	16 36	18 59	22 51	20 25	17 29	17 37	20 05	5	23 49	21 20	18 25	18 39	21 11	24 47	22 15	19 22	19 42	22 17
21 20	18 11	14 32	15 35	18 50	22 18	19 06	15 29	16 38	19 57	10	23 16	20 00	16 26	17 41	21 04	24 13	20 55	17 23	18 44	22 11
20 47	16 50	12 26	14 30	18 41	21 44	17 44	13 23	15 34	19 49	15	22 42	18 39	14 21	16 38	20 57	23 39	19 33	15 18	17 43	22 04
20 12	15 26	10 12	13 19	18 31	21 10	16 20	11 09	14 24	19 40	20	22 07	17 14	12 06	15 29	20 49	23 04	18 08	13 04	16 35	21 57
20 05	15 08	9 44	13 04	18 29	21 02	16 02	10 41	14 09	19 38	21	21 59	16 56	11 38	15 15	20 47	22 56	17 50	12 36	16 21	21 56
19 58	14 51	9 15	12 49	18 27	20 55	15 45	10 12	13 54	19 36	22	21 52	16 39	11 10	15 00	20 45	22 49	17 33	12 07	16 06	21 54
19 51	14 33	8 46	12 33	18 25	20 48	15 27	9 43	13 39	19 34	23	21 45	16 21	10 41	14 45	20 43	22 41	17 15	11 38	15 51	21 53
19 44	14 15	8 16	12 17	18 23	20 41	15 09	9 14	13 23	19 32	24	21 37	16 02	10 11	14 29	20 42	22 34	16 56	11 09	15 36	21 51
19 36	13 57	7 46	12 00	18 21	20 33	14 50	8 43	13 06	19 30	25	21 30	15 44	9 41	14 13	20 40	22 26	16 38	10 38	15 20	21 50
19 29	13 38	7 16	11 43	18 18	20 26	14 32	8 13	12 50	19 28	26	21 22	15 25	9 10	13 56	20 38	22 19	16 19	10 08	15 04	21 48
19 21	13 19	6 44	11 26	18 16	20 18	14 13	7 41	12 33	19 26	27	21 14	15 06	8 39	13 40	20 36	22 11	16 00	9 36	14 47	21 46
19 14	13 00	6 13	11 08	18 13	20 10	13 54	7 09	12 15	19 24	28	21 06	14 47	8 07	13 22	20 34	22 03	15 40	9 04	14 30	21 45
19 06	12 41	5 40	10 50	18 11	20 02	13 34	6 37	11 57	19 22	29	20 58	14 27	7 34	13 04	20 32	21 55	15 21	8 31	14 12	21 43
18 58	12 21	5 07	10 31	18 08	19 54	13 14	6 03	11 38	19 19	30	20 50	14 07	7 00	12 46	20 30	21 46	15 01	7 58	13 54	21 41
18 50	12 01	4 33	10 11	18 06	19 46	12 54	5 29	11 19	19 17	31	20 42	13 47	6 26	12 27	20 28	21 38	14 40	7 23	13 35	21 39
18 42	11 41	3 58	9 51	18 03	19 38	12 34	4 54	10 59	19 14	32	20 34	13 26	5 51	12 07	20 26	21 29	14 19	6 48	13 16	21 37
18 33	11 20	3 22	9 30	18 00	19 29	12 13	4 19	10 38	19 12	33	20 25	13 05	5 15	11 47	20 24	21 21	13 58	6 12	12 56	21 35
18 25	10 59	2 46	9 08	17 57	19 21	11 51	3 42	10 17	19 09	34	20 16	12 44	4 39	11 26	20 21	21 12	13 36	5 35	12 35	21 33
18 16	10 37	2 09	8 46	17 55	19 12	11 29	3 05	9 55	19 07	35	20 07	12 22	4 01	11 04	20 19	21 03	13 14	4 58	12 13	21 31
18 07	10 15	1 30	8 23	17 51	19 03	11 07	2 26	9 32	19 04	36	19 58	11 59	3 22	10 41	20 17	20 53	12 51	4 19	11 51	21 29
17 58	9 52	0 51	7 58	17 48	18 53	10 44	1 47	9 08	19 01	37	19 49	11 36	2 42	10 18	20 14	20 44	12 28	3 39	11 28	21 27
17 49	9 29	0 11	7 33	17 45	18 44	10 21	1 06	8 43	18 58	38	19 39	11 13	2 02	9 53	20 11	20 34	12 04	2 58	11 04	21 25
17 39	9 05	29♐29	7 07	17 42	18 34	9 57	0 24	8 17	18 55	39	19 29	10 48	1 20	9 27	20 09	20 24	11 40	2 15	10 38	21 22
17 30	8 41	28 47	6 40	17 38	18 24	9 32	29♐41	7 50	18 52	40	19 19	10 24	0 36	9 01	20 06	20 14	11 15	1 32	10 12	21 20
17 20	8 16	28 03	6 11	17 34	18 14	9 07	28 57	7 22	18 49	41	19 09	9 58	29♐52	8 33	20 03	20 03	10 49	0 47	9 45	21 17
17 09	7 50	27 17	5 42	17 31	18 04	8 41	28 12	6 52	18 45	42	18 58	9 32	29 06	8 04	20 00	19 53	10 23	0 01	9 16	21 15
16 59	7 24	26 31	5 10	17 27	17 53	8 14	27 25	6 21	18 42	43	18 47	9 05	28 19	7 33	19 57	19 42	9 56	29♐13	8 45	21 12
16 48	6 57	25 43	4 38	17 23	17 42	7 47	26 36	5 49	18 38	44	18 36	8 37	27 30	7 01	19 53	19 30	9 28	28 24	8 14	21 09
16 36	6 29	24 53	4 03	17 18	17 30	7 19	25 46	5 15	18 34	45	18 24	8 09	26 39	6 27	19 50	19 18	8 59	27 33	7 40	21 06
16 25	6 00	24 02	3 27	17 14	17 19	6 50	24 54	4 39	18 30	46	18 12	7 40	25 47	5 51	19 46	19 06	8 29	26 40	7 05	21 03
16 13	5 30	23 09	2 48	17 09	17 07	6 20	24 01	4 00	18 25	47	18 00	7 09	24 53	5 13	19 42	18 54	7 59	25 46	6 27	20 59
16 01	5 00	22 14	2 07	17 04	16 54	5 49	23 06	3 20	18 21	48	17 47	6 38	23 57	4 33	19 38	18 41	7 27	24 49	5 48	20 56
15 48	4 28	21 18	1 24	16 59	16 41	5 16	22 08	2 37	18 16	49	17 34	6 05	22 59	3 51	19 34	18 27	6 54	23 51	5 05	20 52
15 34	3 55	20 19	0 38	16 53	16 27	4 43	21 09	1 51	18 11	50	17 20	5 32	21 59	3 05	19 29	18 13	6 20	22 50	4 20	20 48
15 21	3 21	19 18	29♑49	16 47	16 13	4 09	20 07	1 02	18 06	51	17 06	4 57	20 57	2 17	19 25	17 59	5 45	21 47	3 32	20 44
15 06	2 45	18 15	28 56	16 41	15 59	3 33	19 03	0 10	18 00	52	16 51	4 20	19 52	1 25	19 20	17 43	5 08	20 42	2 41	20 39
14 51	2 09	17 09	28 00	16 34	15 43	2 56	17 57	29♑14	17 54	53	16 36	3 43	18 45	0 29	19 14	17 28	4 30	19 34	1 45	20 35
14 36	1 30	16 02	26 59	16 27	15 28	2 17	16 48	28 13	17 48	54	16 19	3 04	17 36	29♑29	19 09	17 11	3 50	18 23	0 45	20 30
14 19	0 51	14 51	25 53	16 19	15 11	1 37	15 37	27 07	17 41	55	16 03	2 23	16 23	28 23	19 02	16 54	3 09	17 10	29♑40	20 24
14 02	0 09	13 38	24 41	16 11	14 54	0 55	14 22	25 56	17 33	56	15 45	1 40	15 08	27 12	18 56	16 36	2 26	15 53	28 29	20 19
13 45	29♏26	12 21	23 22	16 02	14 36	0 11	13 05	24 37	17 26	57	15 26	0 55	13 49	25 53	18 49	16 17	1 40	14 34	27 11	20 12
13 26	28 41	11 02	21 56	15 53	14 16	29♏25	11 45	23 11	17 17	58	15 07	0 09	12 28	24 27	18 41	15 57	0 53	13 11	25 45	20 06
13 06	27 53	9 39	20 20	15 43	13 56	28 37	10 21	21 35	17 08	59	14 47	29♏20	11 02	22 51	18 33	15 37	0 03	11 44	24 09	19 59
12♏46	27♏04	8♐14	18♑33	15♓32	13♏35	27♏46	8♐54	19♑48	16♓58	60	14♏25	28♏29	9♐34	21♑04	18♓24	15♏15	29♏11	10♐14	22♑22	19♓51

13h 36m 0s 204° 0' 0" 25 ♎ 53					13h 40m 0s 205° 0' 0" 26 ♎ 57						13h 44m 0s 206° 0' 0" 28 ♎ 00					13h 48m 0s 207° 0' 0" 29 ♎ 03				
11	12	ASC	2	3	11	12	ASC	2	3	LAT.	11	12	ASC	2	3	11	12	ASC	2	3
26♏19	24♐30	22♑13	21♒37	23♓28	27♏17	25♐25	23♑10	22♒39	24♓33	0	28♏15	26♐20	24♑06	23♒41	25♓38	29♏13	27♐15	25♑03	24♒42	26♓44
25 45	23 10	20 19	20 44	23 23	26 43	24 05	21 17	21 47	24 29	5	27 40	25 00	22 14	22 50	25 35	28 38	25 55	23 11	23 53	26 41
25 11	21 50	18 21	19 48	23 18	26 08	22 45	19 19	20 52	24 25	10	27 06	23 40	20 16	21 56	25 32	28 03	24 35	21 15	23 00	26 39
24 36	20 28	16 16	18 47	23 12	25 33	21 22	17 14	19 52	24 20	15	26 30	22 17	18 12	20 57	25 28	27 27	23 12	19 11	22 03	26 36
24 00	19 02	14 02	17 41	23 06	24 57	19 56	15 00	18 47	24 15	20	25 54	20 51	15 59	19 54	25 24	26 50	21 45	16 57	21 01	26 33
23 53	18 45	13 34	17 27	23 05	24 50	19 39	14 32	18 33	24 14	21	25 46	20 33	15 31	19 40	25 23	26 43	21 27	16 29	20 47	26 32
23 46	18 27	13 05	17 12	23 04	24 42	19 21	14 04	18 19	24 13	22	25 39	20 15	15 02	19 26	25 22	26 35	21 09	16 01	20 34	26 32
23 38	18 08	12 36	16 58	23 02	24 34	19 02	13 34	18 05	24 12	23	25 31	19 57	14 33	19 12	25 21	26 27	20 51	15 32	20 20	26 31
23 30	17 50	12 07	16 43	23 01	24 27	18 44	13 05	17 50	24 11	24	25 23	19 38	14 03	18 57	25 21	26 19	20 32	15 02	20 05	26 30
23 23	17 31	11 36	16 27	23 00	24 19	18 25	12 35	17 35	24 10	25	25 15	19 19	13 33	18 43	25 20	26 11	20 13	14 32	19 51	26 30
23 15	17 13	11 06	16 11	22 58	24 11	18 06	12 04	17 19	24 08	26	25 07	19 00	13 02	18 27	25 19	26 03	19 54	14 01	19 36	26 29
23 07	16 53	10 34	15 55	22 57	24 03	17 47	11 32	17 03	24 07	27	24 59	18 41	12 31	18 11	25 18	25 55	19 34	13 30	19 20	26 28
22 59	16 34	10 02	15 38	22 55	23 55	17 27	11 00	16 46	24 06	28	24 51	18 21	11 58	17 55	25 17	25 46	19 15	12 57	19 04	26 28
22 50	16 14	9 29	15 20	22 54	23 46	17 07	10 27	16 29	24 05	29	24 42	18 01	11 25	17 38	25 16	25 38	18 54	12 24	18 48	26 27
22 42	15 54	8 55	15 03	22 52	23 38	16 47	9 53	16 12	24 03	30	24 34	17 40	10 52	17 21	25 15	25 29	18 34	11 50	18 31	26 26
22 34	15 33	8 21	14 44	22 51	23 29	16 26	9 19	15 53	24 02	31	24 25	17 20	10 17	17 03	25 14	25 20	18 13	11 16	18 13	26 25
22 25	15 12	7 46	14 25	22 49	23 21	16 05	8 44	15 35	24 01	32	24 16	16 58	9 42	16 45	25 13	25 11	17 51	10 40	17 55	26 24
22 16	14 51	7 10	14 05	22 47	23 12	15 44	8 07	15 15	23 59	33	24 07	16 37	9 05	16 26	25 11	25 02	17 30	10 04	17 37	26 24
22 07	14 29	6 33	13 45	22 46	23 02	15 22	7 30	14 55	23 58	34	23 58	16 14	8 28	16 06	25 10	24 53	17 07	9 26	17 17	26 23
21 58	14 07	5 55	13 24	22 44	22 53	14 59	6 52	14 34	23 56	35	23 48	15 52	7 50	15 45	25 09	24 43	16 45	8 48	16 57	26 22
21 48	13 44	5 16	13 02	22 42	22 44	14 36	6 13	14 13	23 55	36	23 39	15 29	7 10	15 24	25 08	24 33	16 21	8 08	16 36	26 21
21 39	13 20	4 35	12 39	22 40	22 34	14 13	5 32	13 50	23 53	37	23 29	15 05	6 30	15 02	25 07	24 23	15 57	7 28	16 14	26 20
21 29	12 56	3 54	12 15	22 38	22 24	13 48	4 51	13 26	23 52	38	23 19	14 41	5 48	14 39	25 05	24 13	15 33	6 46	15 51	26 19
21 19	12 32	3 12	11 50	22 36	22 14	13 24	4 08	13 02	23 50	39	23 08	14 16	5 05	14 15	25 04	24 03	15 08	6 03	15 28	26 18
21 09	12 07	2 28	11 24	22 34	22 03	12 58	3 24	12 36	23 48	40	22 58	13 50	4 21	13 49	25 02	23 52	14 42	5 18	15 03	26 17
20 58	11 41	1 43	10 57	22 32	21 52	12 32	2 39	12 10	23 46	41	22 47	13 24	3 35	13 23	25 01	23 41	14 15	4 32	14 37	26 16
20 47	11 14	0 56	10 28	22 29	21 41	12 05	1 52	11 41	23 44	42	22 35	12 57	2 48	12 55	24 59	23 29	13 48	3 44	14 10	26 15
20 36	10 47	0 08	9 58	22 27	21 30	11 38	1 03	11 12	23 42	43	22 24	12 29	1 59	12 26	24 58	23 18	13 20	2 55	13 41	26 13
20 24	10 19	29♐18	9 27	22 25	21 18	11 09	0 13	10 41	23 40	44	22 12	12 00	1 09	11 56	24 56	23 06	12 51	2 04	13 11	26 12
20 12	9 49	28 27	8 54	22 22	21 06	10 40	29♐21	10 08	23 38	45	22 00	11 30	0 16	11 23	24 54	22 53	12 21	1 12	12 39	26 11
20 00	9 19	27 34	8 19	22 19	20 53	10 10	28 28	9 34	23 36	46	21 47	11 00	29♐22	10 49	24 53	22 40	11 50	0 17	12 06	26 09
19 47	8 48	26 39	7 42	22 16	20 40	9 38	27 32	8 57	23 33	47	21 34	10 28	28 26	10 13	24 51	22 27	11 18	29♐21	11 30	26 08
19 34	8 16	25 42	7 03	22 13	20 27	9 06	26 35	8 18	23 31	48	21 20	9 55	27 28	9 35	24 49	22 13	10 45	28 22	10 52	26 06
19 20	7 43	24 43	6 21	22 10	20 13	8 32	25 35	7 37	23 28	49	21 06	9 22	26 28	8 54	24 46	21 59	10 11	27 21	10 12	26 05
19 06	7 09	23 41	5 36	22 07	19 59	7 57	24 33	6 53	23 25	50	20 51	8 46	25 25	8 10	24 44	21 44	9 35	26 18	9 29	26 03
18 51	6 33	22 38	4 49	22 03	19 44	7 21	23 29	6 06	23 22	51	20 36	8 10	24 20	7 24	24 42	21 28	8 58	25 12	8 43	26 01
18 36	5 56	21 32	3 57	21 59	19 28	6 44	22 22	5 15	23 19	52	20 20	7 32	23 12	6 34	24 39	21 12	8 20	24 03	7 53	25 59
18 20	5 17	20 23	3 02	21 55	19 12	6 05	21 12	4 20	23 16	53	20 04	6 52	22 02	5 40	24 37	20 55	7 40	22 52	7 00	25 57
18 03	4 37	19 11	2 03	21 51	18 55	5 24	20 00	3 21	23 12	54	19 46	6 11	20 48	4 41	24 34	20 38	6 58	21 38	6 02	25 55
17 46	3 55	17 57	0 58	21 46	18 37	4 41	18 44	2 17	23 08	55	19 28	5 28	19 32	3 37	24 31	20 20	6 15	20 20	4 59	25 53
17 27	3 11	16 39	29♑47	21 41	18 18	3 57	17 26	1 07	23 04	56	19 09	4 43	18 12	2 28	24 27	20 00	5 29	18 59	3 50	25 50
17 08	2 25	15 18	28 30	21 36	17 59	3 11	16 04	29♑50	23 00	57	18 49	3 56	16 49	1 11	24 24	19 40	4 41	17 35	2 34	25 48
16 48	1 37	13 54	27 04	21 30	17 38	2 22	14 38	28 24	22 55	58	18 28	3 06	15 22	29♑46	24 20	19 19	3 51	16 07	1 10	25 45
16 27	0 47	12 27	25 29	21 24	17 16	1 31	13 09	26 49	22 50	59	18 06	2 15	13 52	28 12	24 16	18 56	2 58	14 35	29♑36	25 42
16♏04	29♏54	10♐55	23♑41	21♓17	16♏54	0♐37	11♐36	25♑03	22♓44	60	17♏43	1♐20	12♐18	26♑25	24♓11	18♏32	2♐03	12♐59	27♑50	25♓38

13h 52m 0s — 208° 0' 0" — 0 ♏ 06

LAT.	11	12	ASC	2	3
0	0♐11	28♐10	26♑00	25♒44	27♓49
5	29♏35	26 50	24 09	24 56	27 48
10	29 00	25 29	22 13	24 04	27 46
15	28 24	24 06	20 09	23 09	27 44
20	27 46	22 39	17 56	22 08	27 42
21	27 39	22 21	17 29	21 55	27 42
22	27 31	22 03	17 00	21 41	27 41
23	27 23	21 45	16 31	21 28	27 41
24	27 15	21 26	16 01	21 14	27 40
25	27 07	21 07	15 31	20 59	27 40
26	26 59	20 48	15 00	20 45	27 39
27	26 50	20 28	14 29	20 29	27 39
28	26 42	20 08	13 56	20 14	27 38
29	26 33	19 48	13 23	19 58	27 38
30	26 25	19 27	12 49	19 41	27 37
31	26 16	19 06	12 15	19 24	27 37
32	26 07	18 45	11 39	19 06	27 36
33	25 57	18 23	11 03	18 48	27 36
34	25 48	18 00	10 25	18 29	27 35
35	25 38	17 37	9 46	18 09	27 34
36	25 28	17 14	9 07	17 48	27 34
37	25 18	16 50	8 26	17 27	27 33
38	25 08	16 25	7 44	17 05	27 33
39	24 57	16 00	7 00	16 41	27 32
40	24 46	15 34	6 16	16 17	27 31
41	24 35	15 07	5 29	15 52	27 30
42	24 23	14 40	4 41	15 25	27 30
43	24 12	14 11	3 52	14 57	27 29
44	23 59	13 42	3 01	14 27	27 28
45	23 47	13 12	2 08	13 56	27 27
46	23 34	12 41	1 13	13 23	27 26
47	23 20	12 08	0 16	12 48	27 25
48	23 06	11 35	29♐16	12 10	27 24
49	22 52	11 00	28 15	11 31	27 23
50	22 36	10 24	27 11	10 48	27 22
51	22 21	9 47	26 04	10 03	27 21
52	22 04	9 08	24 55	9 14	27 20
53	21 47	8 28	23 43	8 21	27 18
54	21 29	7 45	22 27	7 24	27 17
55	21 11	7 01	21 09	6 21	27 15
56	20 51	6 15	19 47	5 13	27 14
57	20 31	5 27	18 21	3 58	27 12
58	20 09	4 36	16 52	2 35	27 10
59	19 46	3 42	15 19	1 01	27 08
60	19♏22	2♐46	13♐41	29♑16	27♓06

13h 56m 0s — 209° 0' 0" — 1 ♏ 08

LAT.	11	12	ASC	2	3
0	1♐08	29♐05	26♑57	26♒47	28♓55
5	0 33	27 45	25 07	25 59	28 54
10	29♏57	26 24	23 11	25 09	28 53
15	29 21	25 01	21 08	24 15	28 52
20	28 43	23 34	18 56	23 15	28 51
21	28 35	23 16	18 28	23 02	28 51
22	28 27	22 58	17 59	22 49	28 51
23	28 19	22 39	17 30	22 36	28 50
24	28 11	22 20	17 01	22 22	28 50
25	28 03	22 01	16 31	22 08	28 50
26	27 55	21 42	16 00	21 54	28 50
27	27 46	21 22	15 28	21 39	28 49
28	27 38	21 02	14 56	21 24	28 49
29	27 29	20 42	14 23	21 08	28 49
30	27 20	20 21	13 49	20 52	28 49
31	27 11	20 00	13 14	20 35	28 48
32	27 02	19 38	12 38	20 18	28 48
33	26 52	19 16	12 02	20 00	28 48
34	26 43	18 53	11 24	19 41	28 48
35	26 33	18 30	10 45	19 22	28 47
36	26 23	18 07	10 06	19 01	28 47
37	26 13	17 42	9 25	18 40	28 47
38	26 02	17 18	8 42	18 19	28 46
39	25 52	16 52	7 59	17 56	28 46
40	25 41	16 26	7 14	17 32	28 46
41	25 29	15 59	6 27	17 07	28 45
42	25 17	15 31	5 39	16 41	28 45
43	25 05	15 03	4 49	16 13	28 44
44	24 53	14 33	3 58	15 44	28 44
45	24 40	14 03	3 04	15 13	28 44
46	24 27	13 31	2 09	14 41	28 43
47	24 13	12 59	1 11	14 06	28 43
48	23 59	12 25	0 11	13 29	28 42
49	23 44	11 50	29♐09	12 50	28 42
50	23 29	11 14	28 05	12 09	28 41
51	23 13	10 36	26 57	11 24	28 40
52	22 56	9 57	25 47	10 35	28 40
53	22 39	9 16	24 34	9 43	28 39
54	22 21	8 33	23 18	8 47	28 38
55	22 02	7 48	21 58	7 45	28 38
56	21 42	7 01	20 35	6 38	28 37
57	21 21	6 12	19 08	5 23	28 36
58	20 59	5 21	17 37	4 01	28 35
59	20 36	4 27	16 02	2 29	28 34
60	20♏11	3♐29	14♐23	0♒44	28♓33

14h 0m 0s — 210° 0' 0" — 2 ♏ 11

LAT.	11	12	ASC	2	3
0	2♐05	0♑00	27♑55	27♒49	0♈00
5	1 30	28♐40	26 05	27 03	0 00
10	0 54	27 19	24 10	26 14	0 00
15	0 17	25 56	22 08	25 21	0 00
20	29♏39	24 28	19 55	24 23	0 00
21	29 31	24 10	19 28	24 10	0 00
22	29 23	23 52	18 59	23 58	0 00
23	29 15	23 33	18 30	23 45	0 00
24	29 07	23 14	18 01	23 31	0 00
25	28 59	22 55	17 30	23 18	0 00
26	28 50	22 36	17 00	23 04	0 00
27	28 42	22 16	16 28	22 49	0 00
28	28 33	21 56	15 56	22 34	0 00
29	28 24	21 35	15 23	22 19	0 00
30	28 15	21 15	14 49	22 03	0 00
31	28 06	20 53	14 14	21 46	0 00
32	27 57	20 32	13 38	21 29	0 00
33	27 47	20 09	13 01	21 12	0 00
34	27 38	19 47	12 24	20 54	0 00
35	27 28	19 23	11 45	20 35	0 00
36	27 18	19 00	11 05	20 15	0 00
37	27 07	18 35	10 24	19 54	0 00
38	26 57	18 10	9 41	19 33	0 00
39	26 46	17 45	8 58	19 11	0 00
40	26 35	17 18	8 12	18 47	0 00
41	26 23	16 51	7 25	18 23	0 00
42	26 11	16 23	6 37	17 57	0 00
43	25 59	15 54	5 47	17 30	0 00
44	25 47	15 25	4 55	17 01	0 00
45	25 34	14 54	4 01	16 31	0 00
46	25 20	14 22	3 05	15 59	0 00
47	25 06	13 49	2 07	15 25	0 00
48	24 52	13 15	1 07	14 49	0 00
49	24 37	12 40	0 04	14 11	0 00
50	24 21	12 03	28♐59	13 30	0 00
51	24 05	11 25	27 51	12 46	0 00
52	23 48	10 45	26 40	11 58	0 00
53	23 31	10 04	25 26	11 07	0 00
54	23 12	9 20	24 08	10 11	0 00
55	22 53	8 35	22 48	9 10	0 00
56	22 33	7 48	21 23	8 04	0 00
57	22 12	6 58	19 55	6 50	0 00
58	21 49	6 06	18 23	5 29	0 00
59	21 26	5 11	16 47	3 57	0 00
60	21♏00	4♐13	15♐06	2♒14	0♈00

14h 4m 0s — 211° 0' 0" — 3 ♏ 13

LAT.	11	12	ASC	2	3
0	3♐03	0♑55	28♑52	28♒52	1♈05
5	2 27	29♐35	27 03	28 07	1 06
10	1 50	28 14	25 09	27 19	1 07
15	1 13	26 51	23 07	26 27	1 08
20	0 35	25 23	20 55	25 31	1 09
21	0 27	25 05	20 28	25 19	1 09
22	0 19	24 46	19 59	25 06	1 09
23	0 11	24 28	19 30	24 54	1 10
24	0 03	24 09	19 01	24 41	1 10
25	29♏54	23 50	18 31	24 27	1 10
26	29 46	23 30	18 00	24 14	1 10
27	29 37	23 10	17 28	23 59	1 11
28	29 29	22 50	16 56	23 44	1 11
29	29 20	22 29	16 23	23 30	1 11
30	29 11	22 08	15 49	23 14	1 11
31	29 01	21 47	15 14	22 58	1 12
32	28 52	21 25	14 38	22 42	1 12
33	28 42	21 03	14 02	22 24	1 12
34	28 33	20 40	13 24	22 07	1 12
35	28 23	20 17	12 45	21 48	1 13
36	28 12	19 53	12 05	21 29	1 13
37	28 02	19 28	11 23	21 09	1 13
38	27 51	19 03	10 41	20 48	1 14
39	27 40	18 37	9 57	20 26	1 14
40	27 29	18 11	9 11	20 03	1 14
41	27 17	17 43	8 24	19 39	1 15
42	27 05	17 15	7 36	19 14	1 15
43	26 53	16 46	6 45	18 47	1 16
44	26 40	16 16	5 53	18 19	1 16
45	26 27	15 45	4 59	17 50	1 16
46	26 13	15 13	4 02	17 18	1 17
47	25 59	14 40	3 04	16 45	1 17
48	25 45	14 06	2 03	16 10	1 18
49	25 30	13 30	0 59	15 32	1 18
50	25 14	12 53	29♐53	14 52	1 19
51	24 58	12 14	28 45	14 08	1 20
52	24 40	11 34	27 33	13 22	1 20
53	24 23	10 52	26 18	12 31	1 21
54	24 04	10 08	24 59	11 36	1 22
55	23 44	9 22	23 38	10 37	1 22
56	23 24	8 34	22 12	9 31	1 23
57	23 02	7 44	20 43	8 19	1 24
58	22 39	6 51	19 09	6 58	1 25
59	22 15	5 55	17 31	5 28	1 26
60	21♏50	4♐56	15♐49	3♒46	1♈27

14h 8m 0s — 212° 0' 0" — 4 ♏ 16

LAT.	11	12	ASC	2	3
0	4♐00	1♑50	29♑49	29♒54	2♈11
5	3 23	0 30	28 01	29 11	2 12
10	2 47	29♐09	26 08	28 24	2 14
15	2 10	27 45	24 07	27 34	2 16
20	1 31	26 18	21 56	26 39	2 18
21	1 23	25 59	21 28	26 27	2 18
22	1 15	25 41	21 00	26 15	2 19
23	1 07	25 22	20 31	26 03	2 19
24	0 58	25 03	20 01	25 50	2 20
25	0 50	24 44	19 31	25 37	2 20
26	0 41	24 24	19 00	25 24	2 21
27	0 33	24 04	18 29	25 10	2 21
28	0 24	23 44	17 57	24 56	2 22
29	0 15	23 23	17 23	24 41	2 22
30	0 06	23 02	16 50	24 26	2 23
31	29♏56	22 41	16 15	24 11	2 23
32	29 47	22 19	15 39	23 54	2 24
33	29 37	21 56	15 02	23 38	2 24
34	29 27	21 33	14 24	23 20	2 25
35	29 17	21 10	13 45	23 02	2 26
36	29 07	20 46	13 05	22 43	2 26
37	28 56	20 21	12 24	22 24	2 27
38	28 46	19 56	11 41	22 03	2 27
39	28 34	19 30	10 57	21 42	2 28
40	28 23	19 03	10 11	21 19	2 29
41	28 11	18 36	9 24	20 56	2 30
42	27 59	18 07	8 35	20 31	2 30
43	27 47	17 38	7 44	20 05	2 31
44	27 34	17 08	6 51	19 38	2 32
45	27 20	16 37	5 57	19 09	2 33
46	27 07	16 04	5 00	18 38	2 34
47	26 52	15 31	4 01	18 06	2 35
48	26 38	14 56	2 59	17 31	2 36
49	26 22	14 20	1 55	16 54	2 37
50	26 06	13 43	0 49	16 15	2 38
51	25 50	13 04	29♐39	15 32	2 39
52	25 32	12 23	28 26	14 46	2 40
53	25 14	11 41	27 11	13 57	2 42
54	24 55	10 56	25 51	13 03	2 43
55	24 35	10 10	24 28	12 04	2 45
56	24 15	9 21	23 02	11 00	2 46
57	23 53	8 30	21 31	9 48	2 48
58	23 29	7 36	19 56	8 29	2 50
59	23 05	6 40	18 16	7 00	2 52
60	22♏39	5♐40	16♐32	5♒19	2♈54

14h 12m 0s — 213° 0' 0" — 5 ♏ 18

LAT.	11	12	ASC	2	3
0	4♐57	2♑45	0♒47	0♓57	3♈16
5	4 20	1 25	29♑00	0 15	3 19
10	3 43	0 04	27 07	29♒30	3 21
15	3 06	28♐40	25 07	28 41	3 24
20	2 27	27 12	22 56	27 48	3 27
21	2 19	26 54	22 28	27 36	3 28
22	2 10	26 36	22 00	27 25	3 28
23	2 02	26 17	21 31	27 13	3 29
24	1 54	25 58	21 02	27 00	3 30
25	1 45	25 38	20 32	26 48	3 30
26	1 37	25 19	20 01	26 35	3 31
27	1 28	24 59	19 30	26 21	3 32
28	1 19	24 38	18 58	26 07	3 32
29	1 10	24 18	18 24	25 53	3 33
30	1 01	23 56	17 51	25 38	3 34
31	0 51	23 35	17 16	25 23	3 35
32	0 42	23 13	16 40	25 07	3 36
33	0 32	22 50	16 03	24 51	3 36
34	0 22	22 27	15 25	24 34	3 37
35	0 12	22 03	14 46	24 17	3 38
36	0 01	21 39	14 06	23 58	3 39
37	29♏51	21 14	13 24	23 39	3 40
38	29 40	20 49	12 41	23 19	3 41
39	29 29	20 23	11 57	22 58	3 42
40	29 17	19 56	11 11	22 36	3 43
41	29 05	19 28	10 23	22 14	3 44
42	28 53	18 59	9 34	21 49	3 45
43	28 40	18 30	8 43	21 24	3 47
44	28 27	18 00	7 50	20 57	3 48
45	28 14	17 28	6 55	20 29	3 49
46	28 00	16 56	5 58	19 59	3 51
47	27 45	16 22	4 58	19 27	3 52
48	27 30	15 47	3 56	18 54	3 54
49	27 15	15 10	2 52	18 17	3 55
50	26 59	14 33	1 44	17 39	3 57
51	26 42	13 53	0 34	16 57	3 59
52	26 24	13 12	29♐21	16 12	4 01
53	26 06	12 29	28 04	15 23	4 03
54	25 47	11 44	26 44	14 31	4 05
55	25 27	10 57	25 20	13 33	4 07
56	25 05	10 08	23 52	12 30	4 10
57	24 43	9 16	22 20	11 19	4 12
58	24 19	8 22	20 43	10 01	4 15
59	23 55	7 24	19 02	8 34	4 18
60	23♏28	6♐24	17♐16	6♒55	4♈22

14h 16m 0s — 214° 0' 0" — 6 ♏ 19

LAT.	11	12	ASC	2	3
0	5♐54	3♑40	1♒45	2♓00	4♈22
5	5 17	2 20	29♑59	1 19	4 25
10	4 40	0 59	28 07	0 36	4 28
15	4 02	29♐35	26 07	29♒49	4 32
20	3 22	28 07	23 57	28 57	4 36
21	3 14	27 49	23 29	28 46	4 37
22	3 06	27 30	23 01	28 34	4 38
23	2 58	27 11	22 33	28 23	4 39
24	2 49	26 52	22 03	28 11	4 39
25	2 41	26 33	21 33	27 58	4 40
26	2 32	26 13	21 03	27 46	4 41
27	2 23	25 53	20 31	27 33	4 42
28	2 14	25 33	19 59	27 19	4 43
29	2 05	25 12	19 26	27 05	4 44
30	1 56	24 51	18 52	26 51	4 45
31	1 46	24 29	18 17	26 36	4 46
32	1 37	24 07	17 41	26 21	4 47
33	1 27	23 44	17 04	26 05	4 49
34	1 17	23 21	16 26	25 49	4 50
35	1 06	22 57	15 47	25 31	4 51
36	0 56	22 33	15 07	25 14	4 52
37	0 45	22 08	14 25	24 55	4 53
38	0 34	21 42	13 42	24 36	4 55
39	0 23	21 16	12 58	24 15	4 56
40	0 11	20 49	12 12	23 54	4 58
41	29♏59	20 21	11 24	23 32	4 59
42	29 47	19 52	10 34	23 08	5 01
43	29 34	19 22	9 43	22 44	5 02
44	29 21	18 52	8 50	22 17	5 04
45	29 07	18 20	7 54	21 50	5 06
46	28 53	17 47	6 57	21 21	5 07
47	28 38	17 13	5 57	20 50	5 09
48	28 23	16 38	4 54	20 17	5 11
49	28 07	16 01	3 49	19 41	5 14
50	27 51	15 23	2 41	19 03	5 16
51	27 34	14 43	1 30	18 23	5 18
52	27 16	14 01	0 16	17 39	5 21
53	26 58	13 18	28♐58	16 51	5 23
54	26 38	12 33	27 37	15 59	5 26
55	26 18	11 45	26 11	15 03	5 29
56	25 56	10 55	24 42	14 01	5 33
57	25 33	10 03	23 09	12 52	5 36
58	25 10	9 08	21 31	11 35	5 40
59	24 44	8 09	19 48	10 10	5 44
60	24♏17	7♐08	18♐00	8♒32	5♈49

14h 20m 0s — 215° 0' 0" — 7 ♏ 21

LAT.	11	12	ASC	2	3
0	6♐50	4♑35	2♒43	3♓03	5♈27
5	6 13	3 16	0 58	2 24	5 31
10	5 36	1 54	29♑06	1 42	5 35
15	4 58	0 30	27 07	0 56	5 40
20	4 18	29♐02	24 58	0 06	5 45
21	4 10	28 44	24 31	29♒55	5 46
22	4 02	28 25	24 03	29 44	5 47
23	3 53	28 06	23 34	29 33	5 48
24	3 45	27 47	23 05	29 21	5 49
25	3 36	27 28	22 35	29 09	5 50
26	3 27	27 08	22 04	28 57	5 52
27	3 18	26 48	21 33	28 44	5 53
28	3 09	26 27	21 01	28 31	5 54
29	3 00	26 06	20 28	28 18	5 55
30	2 51	25 45	19 54	28 04	5 57
31	2 41	25 23	19 19	27 50	5 58
32	2 31	25 01	18 43	27 35	5 59
33	2 22	24 38	18 06	27 19	6 01
34	2 11	24 15	17 28	27 03	6 02
35	2 01	23 51	16 49	26 47	6 04
36	1 50	23 26	16 09	26 29	6 05
37	1 39	23 01	15 27	26 11	6 07
38	1 28	22 35	14 44	25 52	6 08
39	1 17	22 09	13 59	25 33	6 10
40	1 05	21 42	13 13	25 12	6 12
41	0 53	21 14	12 25	24 50	6 14
42	0 40	20 45	11 35	24 28	6 16
43	0 27	20 15	10 44	24 04	6 18
44	0 14	19 44	9 50	23 38	6 20
45	0 00	19 12	8 54	23 11	6 22
46	29♏46	18 39	7 56	22 43	6 24
47	29 31	18 04	6 56	22 13	6 27
48	29 16	17 29	5 53	21 40	6 29
49	29 00	16 52	4 47	21 06	6 32
50	28 43	16 13	3 38	20 29	6 35
51	28 26	15 33	2 26	19 49	6 38
52	28 08	14 51	1 11	19 06	6 41
53	27 49	14 07	29♐53	18 20	6 44
54	27 29	13 21	28 30	17 29	6 48
55	27 09	12 33	27 04	16 34	6 52
56	26 47	11 42	25 35	15 33	6 56
57	26 24	10 49	23 58	14 26	7 00
58	26 00	9 53	22 19	13 11	7 05
59	25 34	8 54	20 35	11 47	7 10
60	25♏06	7♐52	18♐45	10♒11	7♈16

14h 24m 0s 216° 0' 0"
8 ♏ 23

LAT.	11	12	ASC	2	3
0	7♐47	5♑30	3♒41	4♓07	6♈32
5	7 10	4 11	1 57	3 29	6 37
10	6 32	2 50	0 06	2 48	6 42
15	5 54	1 25	28♑08	2 04	6 48
20	5 14	29♐57	26 00	1 15	6 54
21	5 05	29 39	25 32	1 05	6 55
22	4 57	29 20	25 04	0 54	6 56
23	4 49	29 01	24 36	0 43	6 58
24	4 40	28 42	24 07	0 32	6 59
25	4 31	28 22	23 37	0 21	7 00
26	4 23	28 02	23 06	0 09	7 02
27	4 14	27 42	22 35	29♒56	7 03
28	4 04	27 22	22 03	29 44	7 05
29	3 55	27 01	21 30	29 31	7 06
30	3 46	26 39	20 56	29 17	7 08
31	3 36	26 17	20 21	29 04	7 09
32	3 26	25 55	19 46	28 49	7 11
33	3 16	25 32	19 09	28 34	7 13
34	3 06	25 09	18 31	28 19	7 14
35	2 55	24 45	17 52	28 03	7 16
36	2 45	24 20	17 11	27 46	7 18
37	2 34	23 55	16 29	27 28	7 20
38	2 22	23 29	15 46	27 10	7 22
39	2 11	23 02	15 01	26 51	7 24
40	1 59	22 35	14 15	26 31	7 26
41	1 47	22 07	13 27	26 10	7 28
42	1 34	21 37	12 37	25 48	7 31
43	1 21	21 07	11 45	25 24	7 33
44	1 07	20 36	10 51	25 00	7 35
45	0 53	20 04	9 55	24 33	7 38
46	0 39	19 31	8 56	24 06	7 41
47	0 24	18 56	7 55	23 36	7 44
48	0 09	18 20	6 52	23 05	7 47
49	29♏52	17 43	5 45	22 32	7 50
50	29 36	17 04	4 36	21 56	7 53
51	29 18	16 23	3 23	21 17	7 57
52	29 00	15 41	2 07	20 35	8 01
53	28 41	14 56	0 48	19 50	8 05
54	28 21	14 10	29♐24	19 01	8 09
55	28 00	13 21	27 57	18 07	8 14
56	27 38	12 30	26 25	17 07	8 19
57	27 14	11 36	24 49	16 01	8 24
58	26 50	10 39	23 08	14 48	8 30
59	26 23	9 39	21 22	13 26	8 36
60	25♏56	8♐36	19♐30	11♒52	8♈43

14h 28m 0s 217° 0' 0"
9 ♏ 24

LAT.	11	12	ASC	2	3
0	8♐43	6♑26	4♒39	5♓10	7♈37
5	8 06	5 06	2 56	4 33	7 43
10	7 28	3 45	1 07	3 54	7 49
15	6 49	2 21	29♑09	3 12	7 56
20	6 09	0 52	27 01	2 25	8 03
21	6 01	0 34	26 34	2 15	8 04
22	5 52	0 15	26 06	2 05	8 06
23	5 44	29♐56	25 38	1 54	8 07
24	5 35	29 37	25 09	1 43	8 09
25	5 27	29 17	24 39	1 32	8 10
26	5 18	28 57	24 09	1 21	8 12
27	5 09	28 37	23 38	1 09	8 14
28	4 59	28 16	23 06	0 57	8 15
29	4 50	27 55	22 33	0 44	8 17
30	4 40	27 34	21 59	0 31	8 19
31	4 31	27 12	21 24	0 18	8 21
32	4 21	26 49	20 48	0 04	8 23
33	4 11	26 26	20 12	29♒49	8 25
34	4 00	26 03	19 34	29 34	8 27
35	3 50	25 39	18 54	29 19	8 29
36	3 39	25 14	18 14	29 03	8 31
37	3 28	24 49	17 32	28 46	8 33
38	3 16	24 23	16 49	28 28	8 35
39	3 05	23 56	16 04	28 09	8 38
40	2 53	23 28	15 17	27 50	8 40
41	2 40	23 00	14 29	27 30	8 43
42	2 27	22 30	13 39	27 08	8 45
43	2 14	22 00	12 47	26 45	8 48
44	2 01	21 29	11 52	26 22	8 51
45	1 47	20 56	10 56	25 56	8 54
46	1 32	20 23	9 57	25 29	8 57
47	1 17	19 48	8 56	25 01	9 01
48	1 01	19 11	7 52	24 31	9 04
49	0 45	18 34	6 45	23 58	9 08
50	0 28	17 54	5 34	23 23	9 12
51	0 10	17 13	4 21	22 45	9 16
52	29♏52	16 31	3 04	22 05	9 21
53	29 32	15 46	1 44	21 21	9 25
54	29 12	14 59	0 19	20 33	9 30
55	28 51	14 10	28♐51	19 40	9 36
56	28 28	13 18	27 18	18 42	9 41
57	28 05	12 23	25 40	17 38	9 48
58	27 40	11 26	23 57	16 27	9 54
59	27 13	10 25	22 09	15 06	10 01
60	26♏45	9♐21	20♐16	13♒35	10♈09

14h 32m 0s 218° 0' 0"
10 ♏ 25

LAT.	11	12	ASC	2	3
0	9♐40	7♑21	5♒38	6♓14	8♈43
5	9 02	6 01	3 55	5 39	8 49
10	8 24	4 40	2 07	5 01	8 56
15	7 45	3 16	0 11	4 20	9 03
20	7 05	1 47	28♑03	3 35	9 11
21	6 56	1 29	27 36	3 25	9 13
22	6 48	1 10	27 09	3 15	9 15
23	6 39	0 51	26 41	3 05	9 17
24	6 30	0 32	26 12	2 55	9 18
25	6 22	0 12	25 42	2 44	9 20
26	6 13	29♐52	25 12	2 33	9 22
27	6 04	29 32	24 41	2 22	9 24
28	5 54	29 11	24 09	2 10	9 26
29	5 45	28 50	23 36	1 58	9 28
30	5 35	28 28	23 02	1 45	9 30
31	5 25	28 06	22 28	1 32	9 32
32	5 15	27 44	21 52	1 19	9 34
33	5 05	27 21	21 15	1 05	9 36
34	4 55	26 57	20 37	0 50	9 39
35	4 44	26 33	19 58	0 35	9 41
36	4 33	26 08	19 17	0 20	9 43
37	4 22	25 43	18 35	0 03	9 46
38	4 10	25 16	17 52	29♒46	9 49
39	3 59	24 50	17 07	29 28	9 51
40	3 46	24 22	16 20	29 10	9 54
41	3 34	23 53	15 32	28 50	9 57
42	3 21	23 24	14 41	28 29	10 00
43	3 08	22 53	13 49	28 07	10 03
44	2 54	22 21	12 55	27 44	10 07
45	2 40	21 49	11 58	27 20	10 10
46	2 25	21 15	10 58	26 54	10 14
47	2 10	20 40	9 57	26 26	10 18
48	1 54	20 03	8 52	25 57	10 22
49	1 37	19 25	7 44	25 25	10 26
50	1 20	18 45	6 34	24 51	10 31
51	1 02	18 04	5 20	24 15	10 35
52	0 44	17 21	4 02	23 35	10 40
53	0 24	16 35	2 41	22 53	10 46
54	0 03	15 48	1 15	22 06	10 51
55	29♏42	14 58	29♐45	21 15	10 58
56	29 19	14 06	28 11	20 19	11 04
57	28 55	13 10	26 31	19 17	11 11
58	28 30	12 12	24 47	18 07	11 19
59	28 03	11 11	22 57	16 49	11 27
60	27♏34	10♐05	21♐02	15♒20	11♈36

14h 36m 0s 219° 0' 0"
11 ♏ 26

LAT.	11	12	ASC	2	3
0	10♐36	8♑16	6♒37	7♓18	9♈48
5	9 58	6 57	4 55	6 44	9 55
10	9 20	5 36	3 08	6 08	10 03
15	8 41	4 11	1 12	5 28	10 11
20	8 00	2 43	29♑06	4 45	10 20
21	7 52	2 24	28 39	4 36	10 22
22	7 43	2 05	28 12	4 26	10 24
23	7 34	1 46	27 44	4 17	10 26
24	7 26	1 27	27 15	4 07	10 28
25	7 17	1 07	26 45	3 56	10 30
26	7 08	0 47	26 15	3 46	10 32
27	6 58	0 27	25 44	3 35	10 34
28	6 49	0 06	25 12	3 23	10 36
29	6 40	29♐45	24 40	3 12	10 38
30	6 30	29 23	24 06	3 00	10 41
31	6 20	29 01	23 31	2 47	10 43
32	6 10	28 39	22 56	2 34	10 46
33	6 00	28 15	22 19	2 21	10 48
34	5 49	27 52	21 41	2 07	10 51
35	5 38	27 27	21 02	1 52	10 53
36	5 27	27 02	20 21	1 37	10 56
37	5 16	26 37	19 39	1 22	10 59
38	5 04	26 11	18 56	1 05	11 02
39	4 53	25 43	18 11	0 48	11 05
40	4 40	25 15	17 24	0 30	11 08
41	4 28	24 47	16 35	0 11	11 11
42	4 15	24 17	15 45	29♒51	11 15
43	4 01	23 46	14 52	29 30	11 18
44	3 47	23 14	13 57	29 07	11 22
45	3 33	22 42	13 00	28 44	11 26
46	3 18	22 07	12 01	28 19	11 30
47	3 03	21 32	10 58	27 52	11 35
48	2 47	20 55	9 53	27 24	11 39
49	2 30	20 17	8 45	26 53	11 44
50	2 13	19 37	7 34	26 20	11 49
51	1 54	18 55	6 19	25 45	11 54
52	1 35	18 11	5 00	25 07	12 00
53	1 16	17 25	3 38	24 26	12 06
54	0 55	16 37	2 11	23 41	12 12
55	0 33	15 47	0 40	22 51	12 19
56	0 10	14 54	29♐05	21 57	12 27
57	29♏45	13 58	27 24	20 56	12 34
58	29 20	12 59	25 38	19 49	12 43
59	28 52	11 56	23 46	18 33	12 52
60	28♏23	10♐50	21♐49	17♒07	13♈02

14h 40m 0s 220° 0' 0"
12 ♏ 27

LAT.	11	12	ASC	2	3
0	11♐32	9♑11	7♒35	8♓22	10♈53
5	10 54	7 52	5 55	7 49	11 01
10	10 16	6 31	4 09	7 15	11 10
15	9 36	5 07	2 14	6 37	11 19
20	8 55	3 38	0 09	5 56	11 29
21	8 47	3 20	29♑42	5 47	11 31
22	8 38	3 01	29 15	5 38	11 33
23	8 29	2 42	28 47	5 28	11 35
24	8 21	2 22	28 18	5 19	11 37
25	8 12	2 03	27 49	5 09	11 39
26	8 03	1 43	27 19	4 59	11 42
27	7 53	1 22	26 48	4 48	11 44
28	7 44	1 01	26 16	4 37	11 47
29	7 34	0 40	25 44	4 26	11 49
30	7 25	0 18	25 10	4 14	11 52
31	7 15	29♐56	24 36	4 03	11 54
32	7 05	29 33	24 00	3 50	11 57
33	6 54	29 10	23 23	3 37	12 00
34	6 44	28 46	22 45	3 24	12 03
35	6 33	28 22	22 06	3 10	12 05
36	6 22	27 57	21 26	2 55	12 09
37	6 10	27 31	20 44	2 40	12 12
38	5 58	27 05	20 00	2 24	12 15
39	5 46	26 38	19 15	2 08	12 18
40	5 34	26 09	18 28	1 51	12 22
41	5 21	25 40	17 39	1 32	12 26
42	5 08	25 11	16 49	1 13	12 29
43	4 55	24 40	15 56	0 53	12 33
44	4 41	24 08	15 01	0 31	12 37
45	4 26	23 34	14 04	0 09	12 42
46	4 11	23 00	13 04	29♒44	12 46
47	3 55	22 24	12 01	29 19	12 51
48	3 39	21 47	10 55	28 51	12 56
49	3 22	21 08	9 47	28 22	13 01
50	3 05	20 28	8 35	27 50	13 07
51	2 47	19 46	7 19	27 16	13 13
52	2 27	19 02	6 00	26 40	13 19
53	2 07	18 16	4 36	26 00	13 26
54	1 46	17 27	3 09	25 16	13 33
55	1 24	16 36	1 36	24 28	13 41
56	1 01	15 42	29♐59	23 36	13 49
57	0 36	14 46	28 17	22 37	13 58
58	0 10	13 46	26 29	21 32	14 07
59	29♏42	12 42	24 36	20 19	14 17
60	29♏12	11♐35	22♐36	18♒55	14♈28

14h 44m 0s 221° 0' 0"
13 ♏ 27

LAT.	11	12	ASC	2	3
0	12♐28	10♑07	8♒34	9♓26	11♈58
5	11 50	8 48	6 55	8 55	12 07
10	11 11	7 27	5 10	8 22	12 16
15	10 32	6 02	3 17	7 46	12 26
20	9 50	4 34	1 12	7 06	12 37
21	9 42	4 15	0 46	6 58	12 39
22	9 33	3 56	0 18	6 49	12 42
23	9 25	3 37	29♑51	6 40	12 44
24	9 16	3 18	29 22	6 31	12 47
25	9 07	2 58	28 53	6 21	12 49
26	8 57	2 38	28 23	6 12	12 52
27	8 48	2 17	27 52	6 02	12 54
28	8 39	1 57	27 21	5 51	12 57
29	8 29	1 35	26 48	5 41	12 59
30	8 19	1 14	26 15	5 30	13 02
31	8 09	0 51	25 41	5 18	13 05
32	7 59	0 29	25 05	5 06	13 08
33	7 49	0 05	24 28	4 54	13 11
34	7 38	29♐41	23 50	4 41	13 14
35	7 27	29 17	23 11	4 28	13 18
36	7 16	28 52	22 31	4 14	13 21
37	7 04	28 26	21 49	3 59	13 24
38	6 52	27 59	21 05	3 44	13 28
39	6 40	27 32	20 20	3 28	13 32
40	6 28	27 04	19 33	3 12	13 36
41	6 15	26 35	18 44	2 54	13 40
42	6 02	26 04	17 53	2 36	13 44
43	5 48	25 33	17 01	2 16	13 48
44	5 34	25 01	16 05	1 56	13 53
45	5 19	24 28	15 08	1 34	13 57
46	5 04	23 53	14 07	1 11	14 02
47	4 48	23 17	13 04	0 46	14 08
48	4 32	22 40	11 58	0 20	14 13
49	4 15	22 01	10 49	29♒52	14 19
50	3 57	21 20	9 36	29 21	14 25
51	3 39	20 37	8 20	28 49	14 32
52	3 19	19 53	7 00	28 13	14 38
53	2 59	19 06	5 35	27 35	14 46
54	2 37	18 17	4 07	26 53	14 54
55	2 15	17 25	2 33	26 07	15 02
56	1 51	16 31	0 55	25 16	15 11
57	1 26	15 34	29♐11	24 20	15 20
58	1 00	14 33	27 21	23 17	15 31
59	0 31	13 29	25 26	22 06	15 42
60	0♐01	12♐20	23♐24	20♒45	15♈54

14h 48m 0s 222° 0' 0"
14 ♏ 28

LAT.	11	12	ASC	2	3
0	13♐24	11♑02	9♒34	10♓30	13♈03
5	12 46	9 43	7 56	10 00	13 13
10	12 07	8 22	6 11	9 29	13 23
15	11 27	6 58	4 19	8 55	13 34
20	10 46	5 29	2 16	8 17	13 46
21	10 37	5 11	1 49	8 09	13 48
22	10 28	4 52	1 22	8 01	13 51
23	10 20	4 33	0 55	7 52	13 53
24	10 11	4 13	0 27	7 43	13 56
25	10 02	3 54	29♑58	7 34	13 58
26	9 52	3 34	29 28	7 25	14 01
27	9 43	3 13	28 57	7 16	14 04
28	9 33	2 52	28 26	7 06	14 07
29	9 24	2 31	27 53	6 56	14 10
30	9 14	2 09	27 20	6 45	14 13
31	9 04	1 47	26 46	6 34	14 16
32	8 53	1 24	26 10	6 23	14 19
33	8 43	1 00	25 34	6 11	14 23
34	8 32	0 36	24 56	5 59	14 26
35	8 21	0 12	24 17	5 46	14 29
36	8 10	29♐47	23 37	5 33	14 33
37	7 58	29 21	22 55	5 19	14 37
38	7 46	28 54	22 11	5 04	14 41
39	7 34	28 26	21 26	4 49	14 45
40	7 22	27 58	20 39	4 33	14 49
41	7 09	27 29	19 50	4 17	14 53
42	6 55	26 58	18 59	3 59	14 58
43	6 41	26 27	18 06	3 40	15 03
44	6 27	25 55	17 10	3 21	15 08
45	6 12	25 21	16 12	3 00	15 13
46	5 57	24 46	15 12	2 38	15 18
47	5 41	24 10	14 08	2 14	15 24
48	5 25	23 32	13 02	1 49	15 30
49	5 07	22 53	11 52	1 22	15 36
50	4 49	22 12	10 39	0 53	15 43
51	4 31	21 29	9 22	0 22	15 50
52	4 11	20 44	8 01	29♒48	15 57
53	3 50	19 57	6 36	29 11	16 05
54	3 29	19 07	5 06	28 31	16 14
55	3 06	18 15	3 31	27 46	16 23
56	2 42	17 20	1 51	26 58	16 33
57	2 17	16 22	0 06	26 04	16 43
58	1 50	15 20	28♐14	25 03	16 54
59	1 21	14 15	26 17	23 55	17 07
60	0♐50	13♐06	24♐13	22♒37	17♈20

14h 52m 0s 223° 0' 0"
15 ♏ 28

LAT.	11	12	ASC	2	3
0	14♐20	11♑58	10♒33	11♓34	14♈07
5	13 41	10 39	8 56	11 06	14 18
10	13 02	9 18	7 13	10 36	14 29
15	12 22	7 54	5 22	10 04	14 41
20	11 41	6 25	3 20	9 28	14 54
21	11 32	6 07	2 53	9 21	14 56
22	11 23	5 48	2 27	9 13	14 59
23	11 14	5 29	1 59	9 05	15 02
24	11 05	5 09	1 31	8 56	15 05
25	10 56	4 49	1 02	8 48	15 08
26	10 47	4 29	0 33	8 39	15 11
27	10 38	4 09	0 03	8 30	15 14
28	10 28	3 48	29♑31	8 20	15 17
29	10 18	3 26	28 59	8 11	15 20
30	10 08	3 04	28 26	8 01	15 23
31	9 58	2 42	27 52	7 50	15 27
32	9 48	2 19	27 16	7 40	15 30
33	9 37	1 56	26 40	7 28	15 34
34	9 26	1 32	26 02	7 17	15 37
35	9 15	1 07	25 23	7 05	15 41
36	9 04	0 42	24 43	6 52	15 45
37	8 52	0 16	24 01	6 39	15 49
38	8 40	29♐49	23 17	6 25	15 53
39	8 28	29 21	22 32	6 11	15 58
40	8 15	28 53	21 45	5 56	16 02
41	8 02	28 23	20 56	5 40	16 07
42	7 49	27 53	20 05	5 23	16 12
43	7 35	27 21	19 12	5 05	16 17
44	7 20	26 49	18 16	4 46	16 22
45	7 05	26 15	17 18	4 26	16 28
46	6 50	25 40	16 17	4 05	16 34
47	6 34	25 03	15 13	3 43	16 40
48	6 17	24 25	14 06	3 19	16 46
49	6 00	23 46	12 56	2 53	16 53
50	5 42	23 04	11 42	2 25	17 00
51	5 23	22 21	10 25	1 55	17 08
52	5 03	21 35	9 03	1 23	17 16
53	4 42	20 48	7 36	0 48	17 25
54	4 20	19 58	6 06	0 09	17 34
55	3 57	19 05	4 30	29♒27	17 44
56	3 33	18 09	2 48	28 40	17 54
57	3 07	17 11	1 01	27 49	18 06
58	2 40	16 08	29♐08	26 51	18 18
59	2 11	15 02	27 09	25 45	18 31
60	1♐39	13♐52	25♐02	24♒31	18♈45

14h 56m 0s — 224° 0' 0" — 16 ♏ 28

LAT.	11	12	ASC	2	3
0	15♐16	12♑53	11♒32	12♓39	15♈12
5	14 37	11 35	9 57	12 12	15 24
10	13 58	10 14	8 15	11 44	15 36
15	13 18	8 50	6 25	11 13	15 48
20	12 36	7 21	4 24	10 40	16 02
21	12 27	7 03	3 58	10 32	16 05
22	12 18	6 44	3 31	10 25	16 08
23	12 09	6 25	3 04	10 17	16 11
24	12 00	6 05	2 36	10 09	16 14
25	11 51	5 45	2 08	10 01	16 17
26	11 42	5 25	1 38	9 53	16 20
27	11 32	5 05	1 08	9 44	16 23
28	11 23	4 44	0 37	9 35	16 27
29	11 13	4 22	0 05	9 26	16 30
30	11 03	4 00	29♑32	9 17	16 34
31	10 53	3 38	28 58	9 07	16 37
32	10 42	3 15	28 23	8 57	16 41
33	10 32	2 51	27 47	8 46	16 45
34	10 21	2 27	27 09	8 35	16 49
35	10 09	2 02	26 30	8 24	16 53
36	9 58	1 37	25 50	8 12	16 57
37	9 46	1 11	25 08	7 59	17 01
38	9 34	0 44	24 25	7 46	17 06
39	9 22	0 16	23 39	7 32	17 11
40	9 09	29♐48	22 52	7 18	17 15
41	8 56	29 18	22 03	7 03	17 21
42	8 42	28 47	21 12	6 47	17 26
43	8 28	28 16	20 19	6 30	17 31
44	8 14	27 43	19 23	6 12	17 37
45	7 59	27 09	18 25	5 54	17 43
46	7 43	26 34	17 23	5 33	17 49
47	7 27	25 57	16 19	5 12	17 56
48	7 10	25 18	15 12	4 49	18 03
49	6 52	24 38	14 01	4 25	18 10
50	6 34	23 57	12 47	3 58	18 18
51	6 15	23 13	11 28	3 30	18 26
52	5 55	22 27	10 06	2 59	18 35
53	5 34	21 39	8 38	2 26	18 44
54	5 12	20 48	7 06	1 49	18 54
55	4 48	19 55	5 29	1 09	19 04
56	4 24	18 59	3 46	0 24	19 16
57	3 58	17 59	1 58	29♒35	19 28
58	3 30	16 56	0 03	28 40	19 41
59	3 00	15 49	28♐01	27 37	19 55
60	2♐29	14♐38	25♐53	26♒26	20♈10

15h 0m 0s — 225° 0' 0" — 17 ♏ 28

LAT.	11	12	ASC	2	3
0	16♐11	13♑49	12♒32	13♓43	16♈17
5	15 33	12 30	10 58	13 18	16 29
10	14 53	11 10	9 17	12 52	16 42
15	14 13	9 46	7 29	12 23	16 55
20	13 31	8 17	5 28	11 51	17 10
21	13 22	7 59	5 03	11 44	17 13
22	13 13	7 40	4 37	11 37	17 16
23	13 04	7 21	4 10	11 30	17 19
24	12 55	7 01	3 42	11 23	17 23
25	12 46	6 41	3 14	11 15	17 26
26	12 37	6 21	2 44	11 07	17 29
27	12 27	6 01	2 14	10 59	17 33
28	12 17	5 40	1 44	10 51	17 36
29	12 07	5 18	1 12	10 42	17 40
30	11 57	4 56	0 39	10 33	17 44
31	11 47	4 34	0 05	10 24	17 48
32	11 37	4 11	29♑30	10 14	17 52
33	11 26	3 47	28 54	10 04	17 56
34	11 15	3 23	28 17	9 54	18 00
35	11 04	2 58	27 38	9 43	18 04
36	10 52	2 33	26 58	9 32	18 09
37	10 40	2 06	26 16	9 20	18 13
38	10 28	1 39	25 32	9 08	18 18
39	10 16	1 11	24 47	8 55	18 23
40	10 03	0 43	24 00	8 41	18 28
41	9 49	0 13	23 11	8 27	18 34
42	9 36	29♐42	22 20	8 12	18 39
43	9 22	29 10	21 26	7 56	18 45
44	9 07	28 37	20 31	7 39	18 51
45	8 52	28 03	19 32	7 21	18 58
46	8 36	27 28	18 30	7 02	19 05
47	8 20	26 51	17 26	6 42	19 12
48	8 03	26 12	16 18	6 20	19 19
49	7 45	25 32	15 07	5 57	19 27
50	7 26	24 50	13 52	5 32	19 35
51	7 07	24 06	12 33	5 05	19 44
52	6 47	23 19	11 09	4 36	19 53
53	6 25	22 31	9 41	4 04	20 03
54	6 03	21 40	8 08	3 30	20 13
55	5 39	20 46	6 30	2 51	20 25
56	5 15	19 49	4 45	2 09	20 37
57	4 48	18 49	2 55	1 22	20 50
58	4 20	17 45	0 58	0 30	21 03
59	3 50	16 37	28♐55	29♒31	21 19
60	3♐18	15♐24	26♐44	28♒24	21♈35

15h 4m 0s — 226° 0' 0" — 18 ♏ 28

LAT.	11	12	ASC	2	3
0	17♐07	14♑44	13♒32	14♓48	17♈21
5	16 28	13 26	11 59	14 25	17 34
10	15 49	12 06	10 20	14 00	17 48
15	15 08	10 42	8 32	13 33	18 02
20	14 26	9 13	6 34	13 03	18 18
21	14 17	8 55	6 08	12 56	18 21
22	14 08	8 36	5 42	12 50	18 24
23	13 59	8 17	5 15	12 43	18 28
24	13 50	7 57	4 48	12 36	18 31
25	13 41	7 38	4 20	12 29	18 35
26	13 31	7 17	3 51	12 22	18 38
27	13 22	6 57	3 21	12 14	18 42
28	13 12	6 36	2 50	12 06	18 46
29	13 02	6 14	2 19	11 58	18 50
30	12 52	5 52	1 46	11 50	18 54
31	12 41	5 30	1 13	11 41	18 58
32	12 31	5 07	0 38	11 32	19 02
33	12 20	4 43	0 02	11 22	19 06
34	12 09	4 19	29♑25	11 13	19 11
35	11 58	3 54	28 46	11 03	19 16
36	11 46	3 28	28 06	10 52	19 20
37	11 34	3 02	27 24	10 41	19 25
38	11 22	2 35	26 41	10 29	19 30
39	11 09	2 07	25 56	10 17	19 36
40	10 56	1 38	25 09	10 04	19 41
41	10 43	1 08	24 20	9 51	19 47
42	10 29	0 37	23 29	9 37	19 53
43	10 15	0 05	22 35	9 22	19 59
44	10 00	29♐32	21 39	9 06	20 06
45	9 45	28 58	20 40	8 49	20 12
46	9 29	28 22	19 39	8 31	20 20
47	9 12	27 45	18 34	8 12	20 27
48	8 55	27 06	17 26	7 52	20 35
49	8 37	26 25	16 14	7 30	20 43
50	8 19	25 43	14 58	7 07	20 52
51	7 59	24 58	13 39	6 41	21 01
52	7 39	24 12	12 14	6 14	21 11
53	7 17	23 23	10 45	5 44	21 21
54	6 55	22 31	9 11	5 11	21 33
55	6 31	21 37	7 31	4 35	21 44
56	6 05	20 39	5 46	3 55	21 57
57	5 39	19 38	3 54	3 11	22 11
58	5 10	18 33	1 55	2 22	22 26
59	4 40	17 24	29♐49	1 26	22 42
60	4♐07	16♐11	27♐36	0♓22	23♈00

15h 8m 0s — 227° 0' 0" — 19 ♏ 27

LAT.	11	12	ASC	2	3
0	18♐02	15♑40	14♒32	15♓53	18♈26
5	17 23	14 22	13 01	15 31	18 40
10	16 44	13 02	11 23	15 08	18 54
15	16 03	11 39	9 36	14 43	19 09
20	15 21	10 10	7 39	14 15	19 26
21	15 12	9 51	7 14	14 09	19 29
22	15 03	9 33	6 48	14 03	19 32
23	14 54	9 13	6 22	13 56	19 36
24	14 45	8 54	5 54	13 50	19 40
25	14 35	8 34	5 27	13 43	19 43
26	14 26	8 14	4 58	13 36	19 47
27	14 16	7 53	4 28	13 29	19 51
28	14 06	7 32	3 58	13 22	19 55
29	13 56	7 11	3 27	13 14	19 59
30	13 46	6 49	2 54	13 06	20 04
31	13 36	6 26	2 21	12 58	20 08
32	13 25	6 03	1 46	12 50	20 12
33	13 14	5 39	1 10	12 41	20 17
34	13 03	5 15	0 33	12 32	20 22
35	12 52	4 50	29♑55	12 23	20 27
36	12 40	4 24	29 15	12 13	20 32
37	12 28	3 58	28 33	12 02	20 37
38	12 16	3 31	27 50	11 51	20 42
39	12 03	3 03	27 05	11 40	20 48
40	11 50	2 34	26 18	11 28	20 54
41	11 37	2 04	25 29	11 16	21 00
42	11 23	1 33	24 38	11 02	21 06
43	11 08	1 01	23 44	10 48	21 13
44	10 53	0 27	22 48	10 34	21 20
45	10 38	29♐53	21 49	10 18	21 27
46	10 22	29 17	20 47	10 01	21 34
47	10 05	28 39	19 42	9 43	21 42
48	9 48	28 00	18 34	9 24	21 51
49	9 30	27 19	17 22	9 04	21 59
50	9 11	26 36	16 06	8 42	22 09
51	8 51	25 52	14 45	8 18	22 18
52	8 31	25 04	13 20	7 52	22 29
53	8 09	24 15	11 50	7 24	22 40
54	7 46	23 23	10 15	6 54	22 52
55	7 22	22 28	8 34	6 20	23 04
56	6 56	21 30	6 47	5 42	23 18
57	6 29	20 28	4 53	5 01	23 32
58	6 00	19 22	2 52	4 15	23 48
59	5 30	18 12	0 44	3 22	24 05
60	4♐57	16♐58	28♐28	2♓22	24♈24

15h 12m 0s — 228° 0' 0" — 20 ♏ 26

LAT.	11	12	ASC	2	3
0	18♐58	16♑36	15♒32	16♓57	19♈30
5	18 19	15 18	14 02	16 37	19 45
10	17 39	13 59	12 26	16 16	20 00
15	16 58	12 35	10 41	15 53	20 16
20	16 16	11 07	8 45	15 27	20 33
21	16 07	10 48	8 20	15 21	20 37
22	15 58	10 29	7 54	15 16	20 40
23	15 49	10 10	7 28	15 10	20 44
24	15 39	9 51	7 01	15 04	20 48
25	15 30	9 31	6 34	14 57	20 52
26	15 21	9 10	6 05	14 51	20 56
27	15 11	8 50	5 36	14 45	21 00
28	15 01	8 29	5 06	14 38	21 04
29	14 51	8 07	4 35	14 31	21 09
30	14 41	7 45	4 03	14 23	21 13
31	14 30	7 23	3 29	14 16	21 18
32	14 20	6 59	2 55	14 08	21 22
33	14 09	6 36	2 19	14 00	21 27
34	13 57	6 11	1 43	13 52	21 32
35	13 46	5 46	1 04	13 43	21 37
36	13 34	5 21	0 25	13 34	21 43
37	13 22	4 54	29♑43	13 24	21 48
38	13 10	4 27	29 00	13 14	21 54
39	12 57	3 59	28 15	13 03	22 00
40	12 44	3 30	27 28	12 52	22 06
41	12 30	2 59	26 39	12 41	22 12
42	12 16	2 28	25 48	12 28	22 19
43	12 02	1 56	24 55	12 15	22 26
44	11 47	1 23	23 58	12 02	22 33
45	11 31	0 48	22 59	11 47	22 41
46	11 15	0 12	21 57	11 31	22 49
47	10 58	29♐34	20 52	11 15	22 57
48	10 41	28 54	19 43	10 57	23 06
49	10 23	28 13	18 31	10 38	23 15
50	10 04	27 30	17 14	10 18	23 25
51	9 44	26 45	15 53	9 56	23 35
52	9 23	25 58	14 27	9 32	23 46
53	9 01	25 08	12 57	9 05	23 58
54	8 38	24 15	11 20	8 37	24 10
55	8 13	23 19	9 38	8 05	24 23
56	7 47	22 21	7 49	7 31	24 38
57	7 20	21 18	5 54	6 52	24 53
58	6 51	20 12	3 51	6 09	25 10
59	6 19	19 01	1 41	5 20	25 28
60	5♐46	17♐45	29♐22	4♓24	25♈47

15h 16m 0s — 229° 0' 0" — 21 ♏ 26

LAT.	11	12	ASC	2	3
0	19♐53	17♑32	16♒33	18♓02	20♈34
5	19 14	16 15	15 04	17 44	20 50
10	18 34	14 55	13 29	17 24	21 06
15	17 53	13 32	11 46	17 03	21 22
20	17 10	12 03	9 51	16 39	21 40
21	17 02	11 45	9 26	16 34	21 44
22	16 53	11 26	9 01	16 29	21 48
23	16 43	11 07	8 35	16 23	21 52
24	16 34	10 47	8 09	16 18	21 56
25	16 25	10 28	7 41	16 12	22 00
26	16 15	10 07	7 13	16 06	22 05
27	16 05	9 47	6 44	16 00	22 09
28	15 56	9 26	6 14	15 54	22 13
29	15 45	9 04	5 43	15 47	22 18
30	15 35	8 42	5 12	15 41	22 23
31	15 25	8 19	4 39	15 34	22 27
32	15 14	7 56	4 05	15 27	22 32
33	15 03	7 32	3 29	15 19	22 37
34	14 52	7 08	2 53	15 11	22 43
35	14 40	6 43	2 14	15 03	22 48
36	14 28	6 17	1 35	14 55	22 54
37	14 16	5 51	0 54	14 46	22 59
38	14 04	5 23	0 11	14 37	23 05
39	13 51	4 55	29♑26	14 27	23 12
40	13 38	4 26	28 39	14 17	23 18
41	13 24	3 56	27 51	14 06	23 25
42	13 10	3 24	26 59	13 55	23 32
43	12 55	2 52	26 06	13 43	23 39
44	12 40	2 18	25 10	13 30	23 47
45	12 24	1 43	24 11	13 17	23 55
46	12 08	1 07	23 08	13 02	24 03
47	11 51	0 29	22 03	12 47	24 12
48	11 34	29♐49	20 54	12 31	24 21
49	11 15	29 08	19 41	12 13	24 31
50	10 56	28 24	18 24	11 54	24 41
51	10 36	27 39	17 02	11 34	24 52
52	10 15	26 51	15 36	11 11	25 03
53	9 53	26 01	14 04	10 47	25 15
54	9 29	25 08	12 27	10 21	25 29
55	9 05	24 11	10 43	9 52	25 42
56	8 38	23 12	8 53	9 20	25 57
57	8 11	22 09	6 56	8 44	26 14
58	7 41	21 01	4 51	8 04	26 31
59	7 09	19 50	2 38	7 18	26 50
60	6♐35	18♐33	0♑17	6♓27	27♈11

15h 20m 0s — 230° 0' 0" — 22 ♏ 25

LAT.	11	12	ASC	2	3
0	20♐49	18♑28	17♒33	19♓07	21♈38
5	20 09	17 11	16 06	18 50	21 54
10	19 29	15 52	14 33	18 33	22 11
15	18 48	14 29	12 51	18 13	22 29
20	18 05	13 00	10 58	17 51	22 48
21	17 56	12 42	10 33	17 47	22 52
22	17 47	12 23	10 08	17 42	22 56
23	17 38	12 04	9 43	17 37	23 00
24	17 29	11 44	9 17	17 32	23 04
25	17 19	11 25	8 49	17 27	23 09
26	17 10	11 04	8 22	17 21	23 13
27	17 00	10 44	7 53	17 16	23 18
28	16 50	10 23	7 23	17 10	23 22
29	16 40	10 01	6 53	17 04	23 27
30	16 30	9 39	6 21	16 58	23 32
31	16 19	9 16	5 48	16 52	23 37
32	16 08	8 53	5 15	16 45	23 42
33	15 57	8 29	4 40	16 38	23 47
34	15 46	8 05	4 03	16 31	23 53
35	15 34	7 40	3 25	16 24	23 59
36	15 22	7 14	2 46	16 16	24 04
37	15 10	6 47	2 05	16 08	24 10
38	14 58	6 20	1 22	16 00	24 17
39	14 45	5 52	0 38	15 51	24 23
40	14 31	5 22	29♑51	15 41	24 30
41	14 18	4 52	29 03	15 32	24 37
42	14 03	4 21	28 12	15 21	24 44
43	13 49	3 48	27 18	15 10	24 52
44	13 33	3 14	26 22	14 59	25 00
45	13 18	2 39	25 23	14 46	25 08
46	13 01	2 02	24 20	14 33	25 17
47	12 44	1 24	23 15	14 19	25 26
48	12 27	0 44	22 06	14 04	25 36
49	12 08	0 03	20 52	13 48	25 46
50	11 49	29♐19	19 35	13 31	25 57
51	11 28	28 33	18 13	13 12	26 08
52	11 07	27 45	16 45	12 52	26 20
53	10 45	26 54	15 13	12 30	26 33
54	10 21	26 00	13 34	12 06	26 47
55	9 56	25 04	11 49	11 39	27 01
56	9 30	24 04	9 58	11 10	27 17
57	9 01	23 00	7 59	10 37	27 34
58	8 31	21 51	5 52	10 00	27 52
59	7 59	20 39	3 37	9 18	28 12
60	7♐25	19♐21	1♑13	8♓31	28♈34

15h 24m 0s — 231° 0' 0" — 23 ♏ 23

LAT.	11	12	ASC	2	3
0	21♐44	19♑24	18♒34	20♓12	22♈42
5	21 04	18 07	17 08	19 57	22 59
10	20 24	16 48	15 36	19 41	23 17
15	19 43	15 26	13 56	19 23	23 35
20	19 00	13 57	12 05	19 04	23 55
21	18 51	13 39	11 41	19 00	23 59
22	18 42	13 20	11 16	18 55	24 03
23	18 33	13 01	10 51	18 51	24 08
24	18 24	12 42	10 25	18 46	24 12
25	18 14	12 22	9 58	18 42	24 17
26	18 04	12 02	9 30	18 37	24 21
27	17 55	11 41	9 02	18 32	24 26
28	17 45	11 20	8 33	18 27	24 31
29	17 34	10 58	8 03	18 21	24 36
30	17 24	10 36	7 31	18 16	24 41
31	17 13	10 14	6 59	18 10	24 46
32	17 03	9 50	6 25	18 04	24 52
33	16 51	9 27	5 51	17 58	24 57
34	16 40	9 02	5 14	17 52	25 03
35	16 28	8 37	4 37	17 45	25 09
36	16 16	8 11	3 58	17 38	25 15
37	16 04	7 44	3 17	17 31	25 21
38	15 51	7 17	2 35	17 23	25 28
39	15 38	6 48	1 50	17 15	25 35
40	15 25	6 19	1 04	17 06	25 42
41	15 11	5 49	0 15	16 58	25 49
42	14 57	5 17	29♑25	16 48	25 57
43	14 42	4 44	28 31	16 38	26 05
44	14 27	4 11	27 35	16 28	26 13
45	14 11	3 35	26 36	16 17	26 22
46	13 54	2 58	25 34	16 05	26 31
47	13 37	2 20	24 28	15 52	26 40
48	13 19	1 40	23 18	15 39	26 50
49	13 01	0 58	22 05	15 24	27 01
50	12 41	0 14	20 47	15 08	27 12
51	12 21	29♐28	19 24	14 51	27 24
52	11 59	28 39	17 56	14 33	27 36
53	11 37	27 48	16 23	14 13	27 50
54	11 13	26 54	14 43	13 51	28 04
55	10 48	25 56	12 57	13 27	28 19
56	10 21	24 56	11 04	13 00	28 36
57	9 52	23 51	9 03	12 30	28 54
58	9 22	22 42	6 54	11 57	29 13
59	8 49	21 28	4 37	11 19	29 33
60	8♐14	20♐09	2♑10	10♓36	29♈56

15h 28m 0s — 232° 0' 0" — 24 ♏ 22

LAT.	11	12	ASC	2	3
0	22♐39	20♑20	19♒35	21♓17	23♈46
5	22 00	19 04	18 11	21 04	24 04
10	21 20	17 45	16 41	20 50	24 22
15	20 38	16 23	15 02	20 34	24 41
20	19 55	14 55	13 12	20 16	25 02
21	19 46	14 36	12 48	20 13	25 06
22	19 37	14 18	12 24	20 09	25 10
23	19 28	13 59	11 59	20 05	25 15
24	19 18	13 39	11 33	20 01	25 20
25	19 09	13 19	11 07	19 57	25 24
26	18 59	12 59	10 40	19 52	25 29
27	18 49	12 38	10 12	19 48	25 34
28	18 39	12 17	9 43	19 43	25 39
29	18 29	11 56	9 13	19 39	25 44
30	18 18	11 34	8 42	19 34	25 50
31	18 08	11 11	8 10	19 29	25 55
32	17 57	10 48	7 37	19 23	26 01
33	17 46	10 24	7 02	19 18	26 07
34	17 34	9 59	6 26	19 12	26 13
35	17 23	9 34	5 49	19 06	26 19
36	17 11	9 08	5 10	19 00	26 25
37	16 58	8 42	4 30	18 53	26 32
38	16 45	8 14	3 48	18 46	26 39
39	16 32	7 46	3 04	18 39	26 46
40	16 19	7 16	2 18	18 32	26 53
41	16 05	6 46	1 29	18 24	27 01
42	15 51	6 14	0 38	18 15	27 09
43	15 36	5 41	29♑45	18 07	27 17
44	15 20	5 07	28 49	17 57	27 25
45	15 04	4 32	27 50	17 47	27 35
46	14 48	3 55	26 48	17 37	27 44
47	14 30	3 16	25 42	17 25	27 54
48	14 12	2 36	24 32	17 13	28 04
49	13 54	1 54	23 18	17 00	28 15
50	13 34	1 09	22 00	16 46	28 27
51	13 13	0 23	20 37	16 31	28 39
52	12 52	29♐34	19 08	16 15	28 53
53	12 29	28 42	17 34	15 57	29 07
54	12 05	27 47	15 54	15 37	29 21
55	11 39	26 50	14 06	15 16	29 37
56	11 12	25 48	12 12	14 52	29 54
57	10 43	24 43	10 09	14 25	0♉13
58	10 13	23 33	7 58	13 55	0 33
59	9 40	22 18	5 38	13 21	0 54
60	9♐04	20♐58	3♑09	12♓43	1♉18

15h 32m 0s — 233° 0' 0" — 25 ♏ 21

LAT.	11	12	ASC	2	3
0	23♐34	21♑17	20♒36	22♓23	24♈50
5	22 55	20 01	19 14	22 11	25 08
10	22 15	18 42	17 45	21 58	25 27
15	21 33	17 20	16 08	21 44	25 47
20	20 50	15 52	14 20	21 29	26 08
21	20 41	15 34	13 56	21 26	26 13
22	20 32	15 15	13 33	21 22	26 17
23	20 22	14 56	13 08	21 19	26 22
24	20 13	14 37	12 43	21 15	26 27
25	20 03	14 17	12 17	21 12	26 32
26	19 54	13 57	11 50	21 08	26 37
27	19 44	13 36	11 22	21 04	26 42
28	19 34	13 15	10 53	21 00	26 47
29	19 23	12 53	10 24	20 56	26 53
30	19 13	12 31	9 53	20 52	26 58
31	19 02	12 09	9 22	20 47	27 04
32	18 51	11 46	8 49	20 42	27 10
33	18 40	11 22	8 15	20 38	27 16
34	18 28	10 57	7 39	20 33	27 22
35	18 17	10 32	7 02	20 27	27 28
36	18 05	10 06	6 24	20 22	27 35
37	17 52	9 39	5 44	20 16	27 42
38	17 39	9 12	5 02	20 10	27 49
39	17 26	8 43	4 18	20 04	27 56
40	17 13	8 14	3 32	19 57	28 04
41	16 59	7 43	2 44	19 50	28 12
42	16 44	7 11	1 53	19 43	28 20
43	16 29	6 38	1 00	19 35	28 29
44	16 14	6 04	0 04	19 27	28 38
45	15 58	5 29	29♑05	19 18	28 47
46	15 41	4 51	28 03	19 09	28 57
47	15 24	4 13	26 57	18 59	29 07
48	15 05	3 32	25 47	18 48	29 18
49	14 46	2 50	24 33	18 37	29 30
50	14 27	2 05	23 15	18 25	29 42
51	14 06	1 18	21 51	18 11	29 55
52	13 44	0 29	20 22	17 57	0♉08
53	13 21	29♐37	18 47	17 41	0 23
54	12 57	28 42	17 06	17 24	0 38
55	12 31	27 43	15 17	17 05	0 55
56	12 03	26 41	13 21	16 44	1 13
57	11 34	25 35	11 17	16 20	1 32
58	11 03	24 24	9 04	15 54	1 53
59	10 30	23 09	6 41	15 24	2 15
60	9♐54	21♐47	4♑08	14♓50	2♉40

15h 36m 0s — 234° 0' 0" — 26 ♏ 19

LAT.	11	12	ASC	2	3
0	24♐30	22♑13	21♒37	23♓28	25♈53
5	23 50	20 58	20 17	23 18	26 12
10	23 10	19 40	18 50	23 07	26 32
15	22 28	18 18	17 14	22 55	26 53
20	21 45	16 50	15 28	22 42	27 15
21	21 35	16 32	15 05	22 39	27 20
22	21 26	16 13	14 41	22 36	27 24
23	21 17	15 54	14 17	22 33	27 29
24	21 08	15 35	13 52	22 30	27 34
25	20 58	15 15	13 27	22 27	27 39
26	20 48	14 55	13 00	22 24	27 44
27	20 38	14 34	12 33	22 20	27 50
28	20 28	14 13	12 05	22 17	27 55
29	20 18	13 51	11 35	22 13	28 01
30	20 07	13 29	11 05	22 10	28 07
31	19 57	13 07	10 34	22 06	28 13
32	19 46	12 44	10 01	22 02	28 19
33	19 34	12 20	9 28	21 58	28 25
34	19 23	11 55	8 52	21 53	28 31
35	19 11	11 30	8 16	21 49	28 38
36	18 59	11 04	7 38	21 44	28 45
37	18 46	10 37	6 58	21 39	28 52
38	18 33	10 09	6 16	21 34	28 59
39	18 20	9 41	5 33	21 29	29 07
40	18 07	9 11	4 47	21 23	29 15
41	17 53	8 41	4 00	21 17	29 23
42	17 38	8 09	3 09	21 11	29 32
43	17 23	7 36	2 16	21 04	29 41
44	17 07	7 02	1 21	20 57	29 50
45	16 51	6 26	0 22	20 49	0♉00
46	16 34	5 48	29♑20	20 41	0 10
47	16 17	5 10	28 14	20 33	0 21
48	15 58	4 29	27 04	20 24	0 32
49	15 39	3 46	25 50	20 14	0 44
50	15 19	3 01	24 31	20 03	0 56
51	14 58	2 14	23 07	19 52	1 10
52	14 36	1 24	21 37	19 39	1 24
53	14 13	0 32	20 01	19 26	1 39
54	13 49	29♐36	18 19	19 11	1 55
55	13 23	28 37	16 29	18 54	2 12
56	12 55	27 35	14 32	18 36	2 30
57	12 25	26 28	12 26	18 16	2 50
58	11 54	25 16	10 10	17 53	3 12
59	11 20	24 00	7 45	17 28	3 35
60	10♐44	22♐37	5♑10	16♓59	4♉01

15h 40m 0s — 235° 0' 0" — 27 ♏ 17

LAT.	11	12	ASC	2	3
0	25♐25	23♑10	22♒39	24♓33	26♈57
5	24 45	21 55	21 20	24 25	27 16
10	24 05	20 37	19 55	24 16	27 37
15	23 23	19 15	18 21	24 06	27 58
20	22 39	17 48	16 36	23 55	28 21
21	22 30	17 30	16 14	23 52	28 26
22	22 21	17 11	15 51	23 50	28 31
23	22 12	16 52	15 27	23 48	28 36
24	22 02	16 33	15 02	23 45	28 41
25	21 53	16 13	14 37	23 42	28 46
26	21 43	15 53	14 11	23 40	28 52
27	21 33	15 32	13 44	23 37	28 57
28	21 23	15 11	13 16	23 34	29 03
29	21 12	14 50	12 47	23 31	29 09
30	21 02	14 28	12 18	23 28	29 15
31	20 51	14 05	11 47	23 25	29 21
32	20 40	13 42	11 15	23 21	29 27
33	20 29	13 18	10 41	23 18	29 34
34	20 17	12 53	10 07	23 14	29 40
35	20 05	12 28	9 30	23 10	29 47
36	19 53	12 02	8 53	23 07	29 54
37	19 40	11 35	8 13	23 02	0♉02
38	19 28	11 08	7 32	22 58	0 09
39	19 14	10 39	6 49	22 54	0 17
40	19 01	10 09	6 04	22 49	0 25
41	18 46	9 39	5 16	22 44	0 34
42	18 32	9 07	4 26	22 39	0 43
43	18 17	8 34	3 34	22 33	0 52
44	18 01	7 59	2 38	22 27	1 02
45	17 45	7 23	1 39	22 21	1 12
46	17 28	6 46	0 37	22 14	1 22
47	17 10	6 07	29♑31	22 07	1 33
48	16 52	5 26	28 22	21 59	1 45
49	16 32	4 43	27 07	21 51	1 57
50	16 12	3 58	25 48	21 42	2 10
51	15 51	3 10	24 24	21 33	2 24
52	15 29	2 20	22 54	21 22	2 39
53	15 05	1 27	21 17	21 11	2 54
54	14 41	0 31	19 34	20 58	3 11
55	14 14	29♐32	17 43	20 45	3 29
56	13 46	28 28	15 44	20 29	3 48
57	13 17	27 21	13 36	20 13	4 08
58	12 45	26 09	11 19	19 54	4 31
59	12 11	24 51	8 51	19 32	4 55
60	11♐34	23♐27	6♑12	19♓08	5♉22

15h 44m 0s — 236° 0' 0" — 28 ♏ 15

LAT.	11	12	ASC	2	3
0	26♐20	24♑06	23♒41	25♓38	28♈00
5	25 40	22 52	22 23	25 32	28 20
10	25 00	21 34	21 00	25 24	28 41
15	24 18	20 13	19 28	25 17	29 03
20	23 34	18 46	17 45	25 08	29 27
21	23 25	18 28	17 23	25 06	29 32
22	23 16	18 09	17 00	25 04	29 37
23	23 06	17 50	16 37	25 02	29 43
24	22 57	17 31	16 13	25 00	29 48
25	22 47	17 11	15 48	24 58	29 53
26	22 38	16 51	15 22	24 56	29 59
27	22 28	16 31	14 56	24 53	0♉05
28	22 17	16 10	14 28	24 51	0 11
29	22 07	15 48	14 00	24 49	0 17
30	21 56	15 26	13 31	24 46	0 23
31	21 45	15 04	13 00	24 44	0 29
32	21 34	14 40	12 29	24 41	0 35
33	21 23	14 17	11 56	24 38	0 42
34	21 11	13 52	11 21	24 35	0 49
35	20 59	13 27	10 46	24 32	0 56
36	20 47	13 01	10 08	24 29	1 03
37	20 35	12 34	9 29	24 26	1 11
38	20 22	12 06	8 48	24 22	1 19
39	20 08	11 38	8 06	24 19	1 27
40	19 55	11 08	7 21	24 15	1 36
41	19 40	10 37	6 34	24 11	1 44
42	19 26	10 05	5 44	24 07	1 54
43	19 10	9 32	4 52	24 02	2 03
44	18 55	8 57	3 57	23 57	2 13
45	18 38	8 21	2 58	23 52	2 23
46	18 21	7 44	1 56	23 47	2 34
47	18 03	7 04	0 51	23 41	2 46
48	17 45	6 23	29♑41	23 35	2 58
49	17 25	5 40	28 26	23 29	3 11
50	17 05	4 55	27 07	23 21	3 24
51	16 44	4 07	25 43	23 14	3 38
52	16 21	3 17	24 12	23 05	3 53
53	15 58	2 23	22 35	22 56	4 09
54	15 33	1 27	20 51	22 46	4 27
55	15 06	0 27	18 59	22 35	4 45
56	14 38	29♐23	16 59	22 23	5 05
57	14 08	28 15	14 49	22 09	5 26
58	13 36	27 02	12 29	21 54	5 49
59	13 01	25 43	9 59	21 37	6 14
60	12♐24	24♐18	7♑17	21♓17	6♉42

15h 48m 0s — 237° 0' 0" — 29 ♏ 13

LAT.	11	12	ASC	2	3
0	27♐15	25♑03	24♒42	26♓44	29♈03
5	26 35	23 49	23 27	26 39	29 24
10	25 55	22 32	22 05	26 33	29 45
15	25 13	21 11	20 35	26 27	0♉08
20	24 29	19 45	18 55	26 21	0 33
21	24 20	19 26	18 33	26 19	0 38
22	24 11	19 08	18 11	26 18	0 44
23	24 01	18 49	17 48	26 16	0 49
24	23 52	18 30	17 24	26 15	0 54
25	23 42	18 10	17 00	26 13	1 00
26	23 32	17 50	16 34	26 12	1 06
27	23 22	17 30	16 08	26 10	1 12
28	23 12	17 09	15 41	26 08	1 18
29	23 02	16 47	15 13	26 06	1 24
30	22 51	16 25	14 44	26 05	1 30
31	22 40	16 02	14 14	26 03	1 37
32	22 29	15 39	13 43	26 01	1 44
33	22 17	15 15	13 11	25 59	1 50
34	22 06	14 51	12 37	25 56	1 58
35	21 54	14 26	12 02	25 54	2 05
36	21 42	14 00	11 25	25 52	2 12
37	21 29	13 33	10 46	25 49	2 20
38	21 16	13 05	10 06	25 47	2 28
39	21 02	12 36	9 23	25 44	2 37
40	20 49	12 07	8 39	25 41	2 45
41	20 34	11 36	7 52	25 38	2 55
42	20 20	11 04	7 03	25 35	3 04
43	20 04	10 31	6 11	25 32	3 14
44	19 48	9 56	5 16	25 28	3 24
45	19 32	9 20	4 18	25 24	3 35
46	19 15	8 42	3 16	25 20	3 46
47	18 57	8 03	2 11	25 16	3 58
48	18 38	7 21	1 01	25 11	4 10
49	18 19	6 38	29♑47	25 06	4 24
50	17 58	5 52	28 28	25 01	4 37
51	17 37	5 04	27 03	24 55	4 52
52	17 14	4 14	25 32	24 49	5 08
53	16 50	3 20	23 54	24 42	5 24
54	16 25	2 23	22 09	24 34	5 42
55	15 58	1 22	20 16	24 26	6 01
56	15 30	0 18	18 15	24 17	6 21
57	15 00	29♐09	16 03	24 07	6 43
58	14 27	27 55	13 41	23 55	7 07
59	13 52	26 35	11 08	23 42	7 33
60	13♐14	25♐09	8♑23	23♓28	8♉01

15h 52m 0s — 238° 0' 0" — 0 ♐ 11

LAT.	11	12	ASC	2	3
0	28♐10	26♑00	25♒44	27♓49	0♉06
5	27 30	24 46	24 31	27 46	0 27
10	26 50	23 30	23 11	27 42	0 50
15	26 08	22 09	21 43	27 38	1 13
20	25 24	20 43	20 04	27 34	1 39
21	25 15	20 25	19 43	27 33	1 44
22	25 05	20 07	19 21	27 32	1 50
23	24 56	19 48	18 59	27 31	1 55
24	24 46	19 29	18 35	27 30	2 01
25	24 37	19 09	18 11	27 29	2 07
26	24 27	18 49	17 47	27 28	2 13
27	24 17	18 29	17 21	27 27	2 19
28	24 07	18 08	16 55	27 25	2 25
29	23 56	17 46	16 27	27 24	2 31
30	23 45	17 24	15 59	27 23	2 38
31	23 35	17 02	15 29	27 22	2 44
32	23 23	16 38	14 58	27 20	2 51
33	23 12	16 15	14 26	27 19	2 58
34	23 00	15 50	13 53	27 18	3 06
35	22 48	15 25	13 18	27 16	3 13
36	22 36	14 59	12 42	27 14	3 21
37	22 23	14 32	12 04	27 13	3 29
38	22 10	14 04	11 24	27 11	3 37
39	21 57	13 36	10 42	27 09	3 46
40	21 43	13 06	9 58	27 07	3 55
41	21 28	12 35	9 12	27 05	4 04
42	21 14	12 03	8 23	27 03	4 14
43	20 58	11 30	7 32	27 01	4 24
44	20 42	10 55	6 37	26 59	4 35
45	20 26	10 19	5 39	26 56	4 46
46	20 08	9 41	4 38	26 53	4 58
47	19 50	9 01	3 33	26 50	5 10
48	19 32	8 20	2 23	26 47	5 23
49	19 12	7 36	1 09	26 44	5 36
50	18 51	6 50	29♑50	26 41	5 50
51	18 30	6 02	28 25	26 37	6 05
52	18 07	5 11	26 54	26 32	6 21
53	17 43	4 17	25 16	26 28	6 39
54	17 18	3 20	23 30	26 23	6 57
55	16 51	2 18	21 36	26 17	7 16
56	16 22	1 13	19 33	26 11	7 37
57	15 51	0 04	17 20	26 04	8 00
58	15 18	28♐49	14 56	25 57	8 25
59	14 43	27 28	12 20	25 48	8 51
60	14♐04	26♐01	9♑31	25♓38	9♉21

15h 56m 0s — 239° 0' 0" — 1 ♐ 08

LAT.	11	12	ASC	2	3
0	29♐05	26♑57	26♒47	28♓55	1♉08
5	28 25	25 44	25 35	28 53	1 31
10	27 45	24 28	24 17	28 51	1 54
15	27 03	23 08	22 51	28 49	2 18
20	26 19	21 42	21 15	28 47	2 44
21	26 10	21 24	20 54	28 46	2 50
22	26 00	21 06	20 32	28 46	2 55
23	25 51	20 47	20 10	28 45	3 01
24	25 41	20 28	19 47	28 45	3 07
25	25 32	20 08	19 24	28 44	3 13
26	25 22	19 48	19 00	28 44	3 19
27	25 12	19 28	18 34	28 43	3 25
28	25 01	19 07	18 08	28 43	3 32
29	24 51	18 46	17 41	28 42	3 38
30	24 40	18 24	17 14	28 41	3 45
31	24 29	18 01	16 44	28 41	3 52
32	24 18	17 38	16 14	28 40	3 59
33	24 07	17 14	15 43	28 39	4 06
34	23 55	16 50	15 10	28 39	4 14
35	23 43	16 25	14 36	28 38	4 21
36	23 30	15 59	14 00	28 37	4 29
37	23 18	15 32	13 22	28 36	4 38
38	23 04	15 04	12 43	28 36	4 46
39	22 51	14 35	12 02	28 35	4 55
40	22 37	14 05	11 18	28 34	5 04
41	22 23	13 34	10 32	28 33	5 14
42	22 08	13 02	9 44	28 32	5 24
43	21 52	12 29	8 53	28 30	5 34
44	21 36	11 54	7 59	28 29	5 45
45	21 19	11 18	7 02	28 28	5 57
46	21 02	10 40	6 01	28 27	6 09
47	20 44	10 00	4 56	28 25	6 21
48	20 25	9 19	3 47	28 24	6 34
49	20 05	8 35	2 33	28 22	6 48
50	19 45	7 49	1 13	28 20	7 03
51	19 23	7 00	29♑48	28 18	7 18
52	19 00	6 09	28 17	28 16	7 35
53	18 36	5 14	26 39	28 14	7 52
54	18 10	4 17	24 52	28 11	8 11
55	17 43	3 15	22 57	28 09	8 31
56	17 14	2 09	20 53	28 06	8 53
57	16 43	0 59	18 38	28 02	9 16
58	16 10	29♐43	16 12	27 58	9 42
59	15 34	28 22	13 34	27 54	10 09
60	14♐55	26♐54	10♑42	27♓49	10♉39

16h 0m 0s — 240° 0' 0" — 2 ♐ 05

LAT.	11	12	ASC	2	3
0	0♑00	27♑55	27♒49	0♈00	2♉11
5	29♐20	26 42	26 39	0 00	2 34
10	28 40	25 26	25 23	0 00	2 58
15	27 58	24 07	23 59	0 00	3 23
20	27 14	22 41	22 25	0 00	3 49
21	27 04	22 23	22 05	0 00	3 55
22	26 55	22 05	21 44	0 00	4 01
23	26 46	21 46	21 22	0 00	4 07
24	26 36	21 27	21 00	0 00	4 13
25	26 26	21 08	20 37	0 00	4 19
26	26 16	20 48	20 13	0 00	4 25
27	26 06	20 27	19 48	0 00	4 32
28	25 56	20 07	19 23	0 00	4 38
29	25 46	19 45	18 56	0 00	4 45
30	25 35	19 23	18 29	0 00	4 52
31	25 24	19 01	18 00	0 00	4 59
32	25 13	18 38	17 31	0 00	5 06
33	25 01	18 14	17 00	0 00	5 14
34	24 49	17 50	16 28	0 00	5 21
35	24 37	17 24	15 54	0 00	5 29
36	24 25	16 58	15 19	0 00	5 38
37	24 12	16 32	14 42	0 00	5 46
38	23 59	16 04	14 03	0 00	5 55
39	23 45	15 35	13 22	0 00	6 04
40	23 31	15 05	12 39	0 00	6 13
41	23 17	14 34	11 54	0 00	6 23
42	23 02	14 02	11 06	0 00	6 34
43	22 46	13 29	10 16	0 00	6 44
44	22 30	12 54	9 22	0 00	6 55
45	22 13	12 18	8 25	0 00	7 07
46	21 56	11 40	7 25	0 00	7 19
47	21 38	11 00	6 21	0 00	7 32
48	21 19	10 18	5 12	0 00	7 46
49	20 59	9 34	3 58	0 00	8 00
50	20 38	8 48	2 39	0 00	8 15
51	20 16	7 59	1 14	0 00	8 31
52	19 53	7 07	29♑42	0 00	8 48
53	19 29	6 13	28 04	0 00	9 06
54	19 03	5 14	26 17	0 00	9 25
55	18 35	4 12	24 21	0 00	9 46
56	18 06	3 06	22 15	0 00	10 08
57	17 35	1 55	19 59	0 00	10 32
58	17 01	0 39	17 31	0 00	10 58
59	16 25	29♐16	14 49	0 00	11 26
60	15♐46	27♐47	11♑54	0♈00	11♉58

16h 4m 0s — 241° 0' 0" — 3 ♐ 03

LAT.	11	12	ASC	2	3
0	0♑55	28♑52	28♒52	1♈05	3♉13
5	0 15	27 40	27 43	1 07	3 37
10	29♐35	26 25	26 30	1 09	4 01
15	28 53	25 05	25 08	1 11	4 27
20	28 08	23 40	23 36	1 13	4 54
21	27 59	23 22	23 16	1 14	5 00
22	27 50	23 04	22 56	1 14	5 06
23	27 41	22 46	22 34	1 15	5 12
24	27 31	22 27	22 13	1 15	5 18
25	27 21	22 07	21 50	1 16	5 25
26	27 11	21 47	21 27	1 16	5 31
27	27 01	21 27	21 03	1 17	5 38
28	26 51	21 06	20 38	1 17	5 44
29	26 40	20 45	20 12	1 18	5 51
30	26 30	20 23	19 45	1 19	5 58
31	26 19	20 01	19 17	1 19	6 06
32	26 07	19 38	18 48	1 20	6 13
33	25 56	19 14	18 18	1 21	6 21
34	25 44	18 50	17 46	1 21	6 29
35	25 32	18 25	17 13	1 22	6 37
36	25 19	17 59	16 38	1 23	6 45
37	25 06	17 32	16 02	1 24	6 54
38	24 53	17 04	15 24	1 24	7 03
39	24 40	16 35	14 44	1 25	7 12
40	24 26	16 06	14 01	1 26	7 22
41	24 11	15 35	13 17	1 27	7 32
42	23 56	15 03	12 30	1 28	7 43
43	23 40	14 29	11 40	1 30	7 54
44	23 24	13 54	10 47	1 31	8 05
45	23 07	13 18	9 51	1 32	8 17
46	22 50	12 40	8 51	1 33	8 30
47	22 32	12 00	7 47	1 35	8 43
48	22 12	11 18	6 38	1 36	8 57
49	21 52	10 34	5 25	1 38	9 11
50	21 32	9 47	4 06	1 40	9 27
51	21 09	8 58	2 41	1 42	9 43
52	20 46	8 06	1 10	1 44	10 01
53	20 22	7 11	29♑31	1 46	10 19
54	19 56	6 13	27 43	1 49	10 39
55	19 28	5 10	25 47	1 51	11 00
56	18 58	4 03	23 40	1 54	11 23
57	18 27	2 52	21 22	1 58	11 47
58	17 53	1 34	18 52	2 02	12 14
59	17 16	0 11	16 08	2 06	12 43
60	16♐37	28♐40	13♑09	2♈11	13♉15

16h 8m 0s — 242° 0' 0" — 4 ♐ 00

LAT.	11	12	ASC	2	3
0	1♑50	29♑49	29♒54	2♈11	4♉16
5	1 10	28 38	28 48	2 14	4 40
10	0 30	27 23	27 36	2 18	5 05
15	29♐48	26 05	26 17	2 22	5 31
20	29 03	24 40	24 47	2 26	5 59
21	28 54	24 22	24 28	2 27	6 05
22	28 45	24 04	24 08	2 28	6 11
23	28 36	23 45	23 47	2 29	6 17
24	28 26	23 27	23 26	2 30	6 24
25	28 16	23 07	23 04	2 31	6 30
26	28 06	22 48	22 41	2 32	6 37
27	27 56	22 27	22 18	2 33	6 43
28	27 46	22 07	21 53	2 35	6 50
29	27 35	21 45	21 28	2 36	6 57
30	27 24	21 24	21 02	2 37	7 05
31	27 13	21 01	20 34	2 38	7 12
32	27 02	20 38	20 06	2 40	7 20
33	26 50	20 15	19 36	2 41	7 28
34	26 39	19 50	19 05	2 42	7 36
35	26 26	19 25	18 33	2 44	7 44
36	26 14	18 59	17 59	2 46	7 53
37	26 01	18 33	17 23	2 47	8 02
38	25 48	18 05	16 45	2 49	8 11
39	25 34	17 36	16 06	2 51	8 21
40	25 20	17 06	15 24	2 53	8 31
41	25 05	16 35	14 40	2 55	8 41
42	24 50	16 03	13 54	2 57	8 52
43	24 35	15 30	13 05	2 59	9 03
44	24 18	14 55	12 13	3 01	9 15
45	24 02	14 18	11 17	3 04	9 27
46	23 44	13 40	10 18	3 07	9 40
47	23 26	13 00	9 14	3 10	9 53
48	23 06	12 18	8 06	3 13	10 07
49	22 46	11 34	6 53	3 16	10 22
50	22 25	10 47	5 35	3 19	10 38
51	22 03	9 58	4 10	3 23	10 55
52	21 40	9 06	2 39	3 28	11 13
53	21 15	8 10	1 00	3 32	11 32
54	20 49	7 12	29♑12	3 37	11 52
55	20 21	6 09	27 15	3 43	12 14
56	19 51	5 01	25 07	3 49	12 37
57	19 19	3 49	22 48	3 56	13 02
58	18 45	2 31	20 16	4 03	13 30
59	18 08	1 06	17 29	4 12	13 59
60	17♐28	29♐35	14♑26	4♈22	14♉32

16h 12m 0s — 243° 0' 0" — 4 ♐ 57

LAT.	11	12	ASC	2	3
0	2♑45	0♒47	0♓57	3♈16	5♉18
5	2 05	29♑36	29♒53	3 21	5 42
10	1 25	28 22	28 43	3 27	6 08
15	0 43	27 04	27 26	3 33	6 35
20	29♐58	25 40	25 59	3 39	7 04
21	29 49	25 22	25 40	3 41	7 10
22	29 40	25 04	25 21	3 42	7 16
23	29 31	24 46	25 00	3 44	7 22
24	29 21	24 27	24 40	3 45	7 29
25	29 11	24 08	24 18	3 47	7 35
26	29 01	23 48	23 56	3 48	7 42
27	28 51	23 28	23 33	3 50	7 49
28	28 41	23 07	23 09	3 52	7 56
29	28 30	22 46	22 45	3 54	8 03
30	28 19	22 24	22 19	3 55	8 11
31	28 08	22 02	21 52	3 57	8 18
32	27 57	21 39	21 24	3 59	8 26
33	27 45	21 16	20 55	4 01	8 34
34	27 33	20 51	20 25	4 04	8 43
35	27 21	20 26	19 53	4 06	8 51
36	27 09	20 00	19 20	4 08	9 00
37	26 56	19 34	18 45	4 11	9 09
38	26 42	19 06	18 08	4 13	9 19
39	26 29	18 37	17 29	4 16	9 28
40	26 15	18 08	16 48	4 19	9 39
41	26 00	17 37	16 05	4 22	9 49
42	25 45	17 05	15 20	4 25	10 00
43	25 29	16 31	14 31	4 28	10 12
44	25 13	15 56	13 40	4 32	10 24
45	24 56	15 19	12 45	4 36	10 36
46	24 38	14 41	11 46	4 40	10 49
47	24 20	14 01	10 43	4 44	11 03
48	24 00	13 19	9 36	4 49	11 18
49	23 40	12 35	8 24	4 54	11 33
50	23 19	11 48	7 06	4 59	11 49
51	22 57	10 58	5 41	5 05	12 06
52	22 33	10 06	4 10	5 11	12 25
53	22 08	9 10	2 31	5 18	12 44
54	21 42	8 11	0 43	5 26	13 05
55	21 14	7 08	28♑46	5 34	13 27
56	20 44	6 00	26 37	5 43	13 51
57	20 11	4 47	24 17	5 53	14 16
58	19 37	3 28	21 42	6 05	14 45
59	18 59	2 03	18 53	6 18	15 15
60	18♐19	0♑30	15♑47	6♈32	15♉49

16h 16m 0s — 244° 0' 0" — 5 ♐ 54

LAT.	11	12	ASC	2	3
0	3♑40	1♒45	2♓00	4♈22	6♉19
5	3 00	0 35	0 58	4 28	6 45
10	2 20	29♑21	29♒50	4 36	7 11
15	1 38	28 03	28 36	4 43	7 39
20	0 54	26 40	27 11	4 52	8 08
21	0 44	26 22	26 53	4 54	8 14
22	0 35	26 04	26 34	4 56	8 21
23	0 26	25 46	26 14	4 58	8 27
24	0 16	25 27	25 54	5 00	8 34
25	0 06	25 08	25 33	5 02	8 40
26	29♐56	24 49	25 11	5 04	8 47
27	29 46	24 28	24 49	5 07	8 54
28	29 36	24 08	24 26	5 09	9 02
29	29 25	23 47	24 02	5 11	9 09
30	29 14	23 25	23 37	5 14	9 17
31	29 03	23 03	23 11	5 16	9 24
32	28 52	22 40	22 43	5 19	9 32
33	28 40	22 17	22 15	5 22	9 41
34	28 28	21 53	21 45	5 25	9 49
35	28 16	21 28	21 14	5 28	9 58
36	28 03	21 02	20 42	5 31	10 07
37	27 50	20 35	20 08	5 34	10 16
38	27 37	20 08	19 32	5 38	10 26
39	27 23	19 39	18 54	5 41	10 36
40	27 09	19 09	18 14	5 45	10 46
41	26 55	18 38	17 31	5 49	10 57
42	26 39	18 06	16 46	5 53	11 08
43	26 24	17 33	15 59	5 58	11 20
44	26 07	16 58	15 08	6 03	11 32
45	25 50	16 21	14 14	6 08	11 45
46	25 32	15 43	13 16	6 13	11 59
47	25 14	15 03	12 14	6 19	12 13
48	24 54	14 20	11 07	6 25	12 28
49	24 34	13 36	9 56	6 31	12 43
50	24 13	12 49	8 38	6 39	13 00
51	23 50	11 59	7 14	6 46	13 17
52	23 27	11 07	5 44	6 55	13 36
53	23 02	10 11	4 05	7 04	13 56
54	22 35	9 11	2 17	7 14	14 17
55	22 07	8 07	0 19	7 25	14 39
56	21 36	6 59	28♑10	7 37	15 04
57	21 04	5 45	25 48	7 51	15 30
58	20 29	4 26	23 12	8 06	15 59
59	19 51	3 00	20 20	8 23	16 30
60	19♐10	1♑26	17♑10	8♈43	17♉05

16h 20m 0s — 245° 0' 0" — 6 ♐ 50

LAT.	11	12	ASC	2	3
0	4♑35	2♒43	3♓03	5♈27	7♉21
5	3 56	1 33	2 03	5 35	7 47
10	3 15	0 20	0 58	5 44	8 14
15	2 33	29♑03	29♒45	5 54	8 42
20	1 49	27 40	28 23	6 05	9 12
21	1 39	27 23	28 06	6 08	9 19
22	1 30	27 05	27 47	6 10	9 25
23	1 21	26 47	27 28	6 12	9 32
24	1 11	26 28	27 09	6 15	9 38
25	1 01	26 09	26 48	6 18	9 45
26	0 51	25 49	26 27	6 20	9 52
27	0 41	25 30	26 06	6 23	10 00
28	0 31	25 09	25 43	6 26	10 07
29	0 20	24 48	25 20	6 29	10 14
30	0 09	24 27	24 55	6 32	10 22
31	29♐58	24 05	24 30	6 35	10 30
32	29 47	23 42	24 03	6 39	10 38
33	29 35	23 18	23 36	6 42	10 47
34	29 23	22 54	23 07	6 46	10 55
35	29 11	22 29	22 36	6 50	11 04
36	28 58	22 04	22 05	6 53	11 14
37	28 45	21 37	21 31	6 58	11 23
38	28 32	21 09	20 56	7 02	11 33
39	28 18	20 41	20 19	7 06	11 43
40	28 04	20 11	19 40	7 11	11 54
41	27 49	19 40	18 58	7 16	12 05
42	27 34	19 08	18 14	7 21	12 16
43	27 18	18 35	17 27	7 27	12 28
44	27 02	18 00	16 37	7 33	12 41
45	26 45	17 23	15 44	7 39	12 54
46	26 27	16 45	14 47	7 46	13 08
47	26 08	16 05	13 46	7 53	13 22
48	25 49	15 22	12 40	8 01	13 37
49	25 28	14 38	11 29	8 09	13 53
50	25 07	13 51	10 13	8 18	14 10
51	24 44	13 01	8 50	8 27	14 28
52	24 20	12 08	7 19	8 38	14 47
53	23 55	11 12	5 41	8 49	15 07
54	23 28	10 12	3 53	9 02	15 29
55	23 00	9 08	1 55	9 15	15 52
56	22 29	7 59	29♑45	9 31	16 17
57	21 57	6 45	27 22	9 47	16 44
58	21 22	5 25	24 44	10 06	17 13
59	20 43	3 57	21 50	10 28	17 45
60	20♐02	2♑22	18♑37	10♈52	18♉20

16h 24m 0s — 246° 0' 0" — 7 ♐ 47

LAT.	11	12	ASC	2	3
0	5♑30	3♒41	4♓07	6♈32	8♉23
5	4 51	2 32	3 09	6 42	8 49
10	4 10	1 20	2 06	6 53	9 16
15	3 28	0 03	0 55	7 05	9 45
20	2 44	28♑41	29♒36	7 18	10 16
21	2 35	28 23	29 19	7 21	10 23
22	2 25	28 06	29 01	7 24	10 29
23	2 16	27 47	28 43	7 27	10 36
24	2 06	27 29	28 24	7 30	10 43
25	1 56	27 10	28 04	7 33	10 50
26	1 46	26 51	27 44	7 36	10 57
27	1 36	26 31	27 23	7 40	11 04
28	1 26	26 11	27 01	7 43	11 12
29	1 15	25 50	26 38	7 47	11 20
30	1 04	25 28	26 14	7 50	11 27
31	0 53	25 06	25 49	7 54	11 36
32	0 42	24 44	25 24	7 58	11 44
33	0 30	24 20	24 57	8 02	11 52
34	0 18	23 56	24 29	8 07	12 01
35	0 06	23 31	23 59	8 11	12 10
36	29♐53	23 06	23 28	8 16	12 20
37	29 40	22 39	22 56	8 21	12 30
38	29 27	22 12	22 21	8 26	12 40
39	29 13	21 43	21 45	8 31	12 50
40	28 59	21 14	21 07	8 37	13 01
41	28 44	20 43	20 26	8 43	13 12
42	28 29	20 11	19 43	8 49	13 24
43	28 13	19 37	18 57	8 56	13 36
44	27 56	19 02	18 08	9 03	13 49
45	27 39	18 26	17 16	9 11	14 02
46	27 21	17 47	16 20	9 19	14 16
47	27 03	17 07	15 20	9 27	14 31
48	26 43	16 25	14 15	9 36	14 46
49	26 23	15 40	13 05	9 46	15 02
50	26 01	14 53	11 49	9 57	15 20
51	25 38	14 03	10 27	10 08	15 38
52	25 14	13 10	8 57	10 21	15 57
53	24 49	12 14	7 19	10 34	16 18
54	24 22	11 13	5 32	10 49	16 40
55	23 53	10 09	3 34	11 06	17 03
56	23 23	9 00	1 24	11 24	17 29
57	22 50	7 45	29♑00	11 44	17 56
58	22 14	6 24	26 20	12 07	18 26
59	21 36	4 56	23 23	12 32	18 59
60	20♐54	3♑20	20♑07	13♈01	19♉35

16h 28m 0s — 247° 0' 0" — 8 ♐ 43

LAT.	11	12	ASC	2	3
0	6♑26	4♒39	5♓10	7♈37	9♉24
5	5 46	3 31	4 14	7 49	9 51
10	5 05	2 19	3 13	8 02	10 19
15	4 23	1 04	2 06	8 16	10 48
20	3 39	29♑42	0 49	8 31	11 20
21	3 30	29 24	0 32	8 34	11 26
22	3 21	29 07	0 15	8 38	11 33
23	3 11	28 49	29♒57	8 41	11 40
24	3 01	28 30	29 39	8 45	11 47
25	2 52	28 12	29 20	8 48	11 54
26	2 42	27 52	29 00	8 52	12 01
27	2 31	27 33	28 40	8 56	12 09
28	2 21	27 12	28 19	9 00	12 17
29	2 10	26 52	27 57	9 04	12 24
30	1 59	26 30	27 34	9 08	12 32
31	1 48	26 08	27 10	9 13	12 41
32	1 37	25 46	26 45	9 18	12 49
33	1 25	25 23	26 19	9 22	12 58
34	1 13	24 59	25 51	9 27	13 07
35	1 01	24 34	25 23	9 33	13 16
36	0 48	24 08	24 52	9 38	13 26
37	0 35	23 42	24 21	9 44	13 36
38	0 22	23 15	23 47	9 50	13 46
39	0 08	22 46	23 12	9 56	13 57
40	29♐54	22 17	22 35	10 03	14 08
41	29 39	21 46	21 55	10 10	14 19
42	29 24	21 14	21 13	10 17	14 31
43	29 08	20 40	20 28	10 25	14 44
44	28 51	20 06	19 40	10 33	14 56
45	28 34	19 29	18 49	10 42	15 10
46	28 16	18 51	17 54	10 51	15 24
47	27 57	18 10	16 55	11 01	15 39
48	27 38	17 28	15 51	11 12	15 55
49	27 17	16 43	14 43	11 23	16 12
50	26 55	15 56	13 28	11 35	16 29
51	26 33	15 06	12 07	11 49	16 48
52	26 08	14 13	10 38	12 03	17 07
53	25 43	13 16	9 00	12 19	17 28
54	25 16	12 16	7 14	12 36	17 51
55	24 47	11 11	5 16	12 55	18 15
56	24 16	10 01	3 05	13 16	18 41
57	23 43	8 46	0 41	13 40	19 09
58	23 07	7 24	28♑00	14 06	19 39
59	22 28	5 55	25 01	14 36	20 13
60	21♐46	4♑18	21♑41	15♈10	20♉50

16h 32m 0s — 248° 0' 0" — 9 ♐ 40

LAT.	11	12	ASC	2	3
0	7♑21	5♒38	6♓14	8♈43	10♉25
5	6 41	4 30	5 20	8 56	10 53
10	6 01	3 19	4 22	9 10	11 21
15	5 19	2 04	3 17	9 26	11 51
20	4 34	0 43	2 03	9 44	12 23
21	4 25	0 26	1 46	9 47	12 30
22	4 16	0 08	1 30	9 51	12 37
23	4 06	29♑50	1 13	9 55	12 44
24	3 57	29 32	0 55	9 59	12 51
25	3 47	29 13	0 37	10 03	12 58
26	3 37	28 54	0 18	10 08	13 06
27	3 27	28 35	29♒58	10 12	13 13
28	3 16	28 15	29 37	10 17	13 21
29	3 06	27 54	29 16	10 21	13 29
30	2 55	27 33	28 54	10 26	13 37
31	2 44	27 11	28 31	10 31	13 46
32	2 32	26 48	28 06	10 37	13 54
33	2 21	26 25	27 41	10 42	14 03
34	2 09	26 02	27 15	10 48	14 12
35	1 56	25 37	26 47	10 54	14 22
36	1 44	25 11	26 18	11 00	14 32
37	1 31	24 45	25 47	11 07	14 42
38	1 17	24 18	25 14	11 14	14 52
39	1 03	23 49	24 40	11 21	15 03
40	0 49	23 20	24 04	11 28	15 14
41	0 34	22 49	23 25	11 36	15 26
42	0 19	22 17	22 44	11 45	15 38
43	0 03	21 44	22 00	11 53	15 51
44	29♐46	21 09	21 14	12 03	16 04
45	29 29	20 33	20 24	12 13	16 18
46	29 11	19 54	19 30	12 23	16 32
47	28 52	19 14	18 32	12 35	16 47
48	28 32	18 32	17 30	12 47	17 03
49	28 12	17 47	16 22	13 00	17 20
50	27 50	17 00	15 08	13 14	17 38
51	27 27	16 09	13 48	13 29	17 57
52	27 03	15 16	12 21	13 45	18 17
53	26 37	14 19	10 44	14 03	18 38
54	26 10	13 19	8 58	14 23	19 01
55	25 41	12 13	7 01	14 44	19 26
56	25 10	11 03	4 50	15 08	19 52
57	24 36	9 48	2 25	15 35	20 21
58	24 00	8 25	29♑44	16 05	20 52
59	23 21	6 56	26 42	16 39	21 26
60	22♐38	5♑17	23♑19	17♈17	22♉03

16h 36m 0s — 249° 0' 0" — 10 ♐ 36

LAT.	11	12	ASC	2	3
0	8♑16	6♒37	7♓18	9♈48	11♉26
5	7 36	5 29	6 26	10 03	11 54
10	6 56	4 19	5 30	10 19	12 23
15	6 14	3 05	4 27	10 37	12 54
20	5 30	1 44	3 16	10 56	13 26
21	5 21	1 27	3 01	11 00	13 33
22	5 11	1 10	2 45	11 05	13 40
23	5 02	0 52	2 28	11 09	13 47
24	4 52	0 34	2 11	11 14	13 54
25	4 42	0 15	1 54	11 18	14 02
26	4 32	29♑56	1 35	11 23	14 09
27	4 22	29 37	1 16	11 28	14 17
28	4 12	29 17	0 56	11 33	14 25
29	4 01	28 56	0 36	11 39	14 33
30	3 50	28 35	0 14	11 44	14 42
31	3 39	28 14	29♒52	11 50	14 50
32	3 28	27 51	29 29	11 56	14 59
33	3 16	27 28	29 04	12 02	15 08
34	3 04	27 05	28 39	12 08	15 17
35	2 52	26 40	28 12	12 15	15 27
36	2 39	26 15	27 43	12 22	15 37
37	2 26	25 49	27 14	12 29	15 47
38	2 12	25 21	26 42	12 37	15 58
39	1 58	24 53	26 09	12 45	16 09
40	1 44	24 24	25 34	12 54	16 20
41	1 29	23 53	24 56	13 02	16 32
42	1 14	23 21	24 16	13 12	16 44
43	0 58	22 48	23 34	13 22	16 57
44	0 41	22 13	22 48	13 32	17 11
45	0 24	21 37	22 00	13 43	17 25
46	0 06	20 59	21 07	13 55	17 39
47	29♐47	20 18	20 11	14 08	17 55
48	29 27	19 36	19 10	14 21	18 11
49	29 06	18 51	18 03	14 36	18 28
50	28 45	18 04	16 51	14 52	18 46
51	28 22	17 14	15 32	15 09	19 06
52	27 57	16 20	14 06	15 27	19 26
53	27 32	15 23	12 31	15 47	19 48
54	27 04	14 22	10 45	16 09	20 11
55	26 35	13 17	8 49	16 33	20 36
56	26 04	12 06	6 39	17 00	21 03
57	25 30	10 50	4 14	17 30	21 32
58	24 54	9 27	1 31	18 03	22 04
59	24 14	7 57	28♑28	18 41	22 38
60	23♐31	6♑17	25♑02	19♈24	23♉17

16h 40m 0s — 250° 0' 0" — 11 ♐ 32

LAT.	11	12	ASC	2	3
0	9♑11	7♒35	8♓22	10♈53	12♉27
5	8 32	6 29	7 32	11 10	12 55
10	7 51	5 20	6 39	11 27	13 25
15	7 10	4 06	5 39	11 47	13 56
20	6 25	2 46	4 30	12 09	14 29
21	6 16	2 29	4 16	12 13	14 36
22	6 07	2 12	4 00	12 18	14 43
23	5 57	1 54	3 44	12 23	14 50
24	5 48	1 36	3 28	12 28	14 58
25	5 38	1 18	3 11	12 33	15 05
26	5 28	0 59	2 53	12 39	15 13
27	5 18	0 40	2 35	12 44	15 21
28	5 07	0 20	2 16	12 50	15 29
29	4 57	29♑59	1 56	12 56	15 37
30	4 46	29 39	1 36	13 02	15 46
31	4 34	29 17	1 14	13 08	15 55
32	4 23	28 55	0 52	13 15	16 03
33	4 11	28 32	0 28	13 22	16 13
34	3 59	28 08	0 03	13 29	16 22
35	3 47	27 44	29♒37	13 36	16 32
36	3 34	27 19	29 10	13 44	16 42
37	3 21	26 53	28 41	13 52	16 52
38	3 08	26 26	28 11	14 00	17 03
39	2 54	25 57	27 39	14 09	17 14
40	2 39	25 28	27 05	14 19	17 26
41	2 25	24 58	26 28	14 28	17 38
42	2 09	24 26	25 50	14 39	17 51
43	1 53	23 53	25 09	14 50	18 04
44	1 36	23 18	24 25	15 01	18 17
45	1 19	22 42	23 37	15 14	18 32
46	1 01	22 03	22 46	15 27	18 47
47	0 42	21 23	21 51	15 41	19 02
48	0 22	20 41	20 51	15 56	19 19
49	0 01	19 56	19 47	16 12	19 36
50	29♐39	19 09	18 36	16 29	19 55
51	29 16	18 19	17 19	16 48	20 14
52	28 52	17 25	15 54	17 08	20 35
53	28 26	16 28	14 20	17 30	20 57
54	27 59	15 27	12 36	17 54	21 20
55	27 29	14 21	10 40	18 21	21 46
56	26 58	13 10	8 31	18 50	22 13
57	26 24	11 53	6 06	19 23	22 43
58	25 47	10 30	3 23	20 00	23 15
59	25 07	8 59	0 18	20 42	23 50
60	24♐24	7♑18	26♑50	21♈29	24♉29

16h 44m 0s — 251° 0' 0" — 12 ♐ 28

LAT.	11	12	ASC	2	3
0	10♑07	8♒34	9♓26	11♈58	13♉27
5	9 27	7 29	8 39	12 16	13 56
10	8 47	6 20	7 47	12 36	14 26
15	8 05	5 07	6 50	12 57	14 58
20	7 21	3 48	5 45	13 21	15 32
21	7 12	3 31	5 31	13 26	15 39
22	7 02	3 14	5 16	13 31	15 46
23	6 53	2 57	5 01	13 37	15 53
24	6 43	2 39	4 45	13 42	16 01
25	6 33	2 21	4 29	13 48	16 09
26	6 23	2 02	4 12	13 54	16 16
27	6 13	1 43	3 54	14 00	16 24
28	6 03	1 23	3 36	14 06	16 33
29	5 52	1 03	3 17	14 13	16 41
30	5 41	0 42	2 57	14 19	16 50
31	5 30	0 21	2 37	14 26	16 59
32	5 19	29♑59	2 15	14 33	17 08
33	5 07	29 36	1 52	14 41	17 17
34	4 55	29 12	1 29	14 49	17 27
35	4 43	28 48	1 04	14 57	17 37
36	4 30	28 23	0 37	15 05	17 47
37	4 17	27 57	0 10	15 14	17 57
38	4 03	27 30	29♒41	15 23	18 08
39	3 49	27 02	29 10	15 33	18 20
40	3 35	26 33	28 37	15 43	18 31
41	3 20	26 03	28 02	15 54	18 44
42	3 05	25 31	27 24	16 05	18 56
43	2 48	24 58	26 45	16 17	19 10
44	2 32	24 23	26 02	16 30	19 24
45	2 14	23 47	25 16	16 43	19 38
46	1 56	23 09	24 26	16 58	19 53
47	1 37	22 29	23 33	17 13	20 09
48	1 17	21 46	22 35	17 29	20 26
49	0 56	21 02	21 32	17 47	20 44
50	0 35	20 14	20 23	18 06	21 02
51	0 11	19 24	19 07	18 26	21 22
52	29♐47	18 31	17 44	18 49	21 43
53	29 21	17 33	16 12	19 13	22 05
54	28 53	16 32	14 29	19 39	22 29
55	28 24	15 26	12 35	20 08	22 55
56	27 52	14 15	10 27	20 40	23 23
57	27 18	12 58	8 03	21 16	23 53
58	26 41	11 34	5 19	21 56	24 26
59	26 01	10 02	2 14	22 42	25 02
60	25♐17	8♑20	28♑42	23♈33	25♉41

16h 48m 0s — 252° 0' 0" — 13 ♐ 24

LAT.	11	12	ASC	2	3
0	11♑02	9♒34	10♓30	13♈03	14♉28
5	10 23	8 29	9 45	13 23	14 57
10	9 42	7 21	8 56	13 44	15 28
15	9 01	6 09	8 02	14 07	16 00
20	8 17	4 50	7 00	14 33	16 34
21	8 07	4 34	6 46	14 39	16 41
22	7 58	4 17	6 32	14 44	16 49
23	7 49	3 59	6 17	14 50	16 56
24	7 39	3 42	6 02	14 56	17 04
25	7 29	3 24	5 47	15 03	17 12
26	7 19	3 05	5 31	15 09	17 20
27	7 09	2 46	5 14	15 15	17 28
28	6 58	2 26	4 57	15 22	17 36
29	6 48	2 06	4 38	15 29	17 45
30	6 37	1 46	4 20	15 37	17 53
31	6 26	1 25	4 00	15 44	18 02
32	6 14	1 03	3 39	15 52	18 12
33	6 03	0 40	3 17	16 00	18 21
34	5 51	0 17	2 55	16 08	18 31
35	5 38	29♑53	2 31	16 17	18 41
36	5 26	29 28	2 06	16 26	18 51
37	5 12	29 02	1 39	16 36	19 02
38	4 59	28 35	1 11	16 46	19 13
39	4 45	28 07	0 41	16 57	19 25
40	4 31	27 38	0 10	17 08	19 37
41	4 16	27 08	29♒36	17 19	19 49
42	4 00	26 37	29 00	17 32	20 02
43	3 44	26 04	28 22	17 45	20 15
44	3 27	25 29	27 40	17 58	20 29
45	3 10	24 53	26 56	18 13	20 44
46	2 52	24 15	26 08	18 29	20 59
47	2 33	23 35	25 16	18 45	21 16
48	2 13	22 53	24 20	19 03	21 33
49	1 52	22 08	23 19	19 22	21 51
50	1 30	21 21	22 12	19 42	22 10
51	1 07	20 30	20 58	20 04	22 30
52	0 42	19 37	19 37	20 28	22 51
53	0 16	18 39	18 07	20 55	23 14
54	29♐48	17 38	16 26	21 23	23 38
55	29 18	16 32	14 34	21 55	24 04
56	28 47	15 21	12 27	22 29	24 32
57	28 12	14 03	10 04	23 08	25 03
58	27 35	12 39	7 21	23 51	25 36
59	26 55	11 06	4 15	24 40	26 12
60	26♐10	9♑24	0♒41	25♈36	26♉53

16h 52m 0s — 253° 0' 0" — 14 ♐ 20

LAT.	11	12	ASC	2	3
0	11♑58	10♒33	11♓34	14♈07	15♉28
5	11 18	9 29	10 52	14 29	15 58
10	10 38	8 22	10 05	14 52	16 29
15	9 56	7 10	9 14	15 17	17 02
20	9 12	5 53	8 15	15 45	17 36
21	9 03	5 36	8 02	15 51	17 44
22	8 54	5 20	7 48	15 57	17 51
23	8 44	5 02	7 34	16 04	17 59
24	8 35	4 45	7 20	16 10	18 06
25	8 25	4 27	7 05	16 17	18 14
26	8 15	4 09	6 50	16 24	18 22
27	8 05	3 50	6 34	16 31	18 31
28	7 54	3 30	6 18	16 38	18 39
29	7 44	3 10	6 00	16 46	18 48
30	7 33	2 50	5 42	16 54	18 57
31	7 22	2 29	5 23	17 02	19 06
32	7 10	2 07	5 04	17 10	19 15
33	6 59	1 45	4 43	17 19	19 25
34	6 47	1 22	4 21	17 28	19 35
35	6 34	0 58	3 58	17 37	19 45
36	6 21	0 33	3 34	17 47	19 55
37	6 08	0 07	3 09	17 58	20 06
38	5 55	29♑41	2 42	18 09	20 18
39	5 41	29 13	2 14	18 20	20 29
40	5 26	28 44	1 43	18 32	20 41
41	5 11	28 14	1 11	18 44	20 54
42	4 56	27 43	0 37	18 58	21 07
43	4 40	27 10	0 00	19 12	21 21
44	4 23	26 36	29♒20	19 26	21 35
45	4 06	26 00	28 38	19 42	21 50
46	3 47	25 22	27 52	19 59	22 05
47	3 28	24 42	27 02	20 17	22 22
48	3 08	24 00	26 07	20 36	22 39
49	2 47	23 15	25 08	20 56	22 57
50	2 25	22 28	24 03	21 18	23 16
51	2 02	21 37	22 52	21 42	23 37
52	1 37	20 44	21 32	22 08	23 58
53	1 11	19 46	20 04	22 36	24 21
54	0 43	18 45	18 26	23 06	24 46
55	0 13	17 39	16 36	23 40	25 13
56	29♐41	16 27	14 31	24 17	25 41
57	29 07	15 09	12 09	24 59	26 12
58	28 30	13 44	9 27	25 45	26 46
59	27 49	12 11	6 21	26 38	27 23
60	27♐04	10♑28	2♒46	27♈38	28♉04

16h 56m 0s — 254° 0' 0" — 15 ♐ 16

LAT.	11	12	ASC	2	3
0	12♑53	11♒32	12♓39	15♈12	16♉28
5	12 14	10 29	11 59	15 35	16 59
10	11 34	9 23	11 15	16 00	17 30
15	10 52	8 12	10 26	16 27	18 03
20	10 08	6 56	9 30	16 57	18 38
21	9 59	6 39	9 18	17 04	18 46
22	9 50	6 23	9 05	17 10	18 53
23	9 40	6 06	8 52	17 17	19 01
24	9 31	5 48	8 38	17 24	19 09
25	9 21	5 31	8 24	17 31	19 17
26	9 11	5 12	8 10	17 38	19 25
27	9 01	4 54	7 55	17 46	19 33
28	8 50	4 35	7 39	17 54	19 42
29	8 40	4 15	7 22	18 02	19 51
30	8 29	3 55	7 05	18 10	20 00
31	8 18	3 34	6 47	18 19	20 09
32	8 06	3 12	6 29	18 28	20 18
33	7 55	2 50	6 09	18 38	20 28
34	7 43	2 27	5 48	18 47	20 38
35	7 30	2 03	5 27	18 57	20 49
36	7 17	1 39	5 04	19 08	20 59
37	7 04	1 13	4 40	19 19	21 10
38	6 51	0 47	4 14	19 31	21 22
39	6 37	0 19	3 47	19 43	21 34
40	6 22	29♑51	3 18	19 56	21 46
41	6 07	29 21	2 47	20 09	21 59
42	5 52	28 49	2 14	20 23	22 12
43	5 36	28 17	1 39	20 38	22 26
44	5 19	27 43	1 01	20 54	22 40
45	5 02	27 07	0 20	21 11	22 55
46	4 43	26 29	29♒36	21 29	23 11
47	4 24	25 49	28 48	21 48	23 28
48	4 04	25 07	27 56	22 08	23 45
49	3 43	24 23	26 59	22 30	24 03
50	3 21	23 35	25 56	22 53	24 23
51	2 58	22 45	24 47	23 19	24 43
52	2 33	21 52	23 31	23 46	25 05
53	2 07	20 54	22 05	24 16	25 29
54	1 39	19 53	20 29	24 49	25 54
55	1 09	18 46	18 42	25 25	26 20
56	0 37	17 35	16 39	26 05	26 49
57	0 02	16 16	14 19	26 49	27 21
58	29♐24	14 51	11 39	27 38	27 55
59	28 43	13 17	8 34	28 34	28 32
60	27♐58	11♑33	4♒58	29♈38	29♉14

17h 0m 0s — 255° 0' 0" — 16 ♐ 11

LAT.	11	12	ASC	2	3
0	13♑49	12♒32	13♓43	16♈17	17♉28
5	13 10	11 30	13 05	16 42	17 59
10	12 30	10 24	12 24	17 08	18 31
15	11 48	9 15	11 38	17 37	19 04
20	11 04	7 59	10 45	18 09	19 40
21	10 55	7 43	10 34	18 16	19 48
22	10 46	7 26	10 22	18 23	19 55
23	10 36	7 10	10 10	18 30	20 03
24	10 27	6 52	9 57	18 37	20 11
25	10 17	6 35	9 44	18 45	20 19
26	10 07	6 17	9 30	18 53	20 27
27	9 57	5 58	9 16	19 01	20 36
28	9 46	5 39	9 01	19 09	20 45
29	9 36	5 20	8 45	19 18	20 53
30	9 25	5 00	8 29	19 27	21 03
31	9 14	4 39	8 12	19 36	21 12
32	9 02	4 18	7 54	19 46	21 21
33	8 51	3 56	7 36	19 56	21 31
34	8 39	3 33	7 16	20 06	21 42
35	8 26	3 09	6 56	20 17	21 52
36	8 14	2 45	6 34	20 28	22 03
37	8 00	2 20	6 11	20 40	22 14
38	7 47	1 53	5 47	20 52	22 26
39	7 33	1 26	5 21	21 05	22 38
40	7 19	0 57	4 54	21 19	22 50
41	7 04	0 28	4 24	21 33	23 03
42	6 48	29♑57	3 53	21 48	23 16
43	6 32	29 24	3 19	22 04	23 30
44	6 15	28 50	2 43	22 21	23 45
45	5 58	28 14	2 04	22 39	24 00
46	5 39	27 37	1 22	22 58	24 16
47	5 20	26 57	0 37	23 18	24 33
48	5 00	26 15	29♒47	23 40	24 51
49	4 39	25 31	28 52	24 03	25 09
50	4 17	24 44	27 52	24 28	25 29
51	3 53	23 54	26 45	24 55	25 50
52	3 29	23 00	25 31	25 24	26 12
53	3 02	22 03	24 09	25 56	26 36
54	2 34	21 01	22 36	26 30	27 01
55	2 04	19 55	20 51	27 09	27 28
56	1 32	18 43	18 52	27 51	27 57
57	0 57	17 25	16 35	28 38	28 29
58	0 19	15 59	13 57	29 30	29 04
59	29♐38	14 25	10 52	0♉29	29 42
60	28♐53	12♑40	7♒17	1♉36	0♊24

17h 4m 0s 256° 0' 0"
17 ♐ 07

LAT.	11	12	ASC	2	3
0	14♑44	13♒32	14♓48	17♈21	18♉28
5	14 05	12 31	14 12	17 48	18 59
10	13 26	11 26	13 34	18 16	19 31
15	12 44	10 17	12 51	18 47	20 05
20	12 00	9 02	12 01	19 20	20 42
21	11 51	8 46	11 50	19 28	20 49
22	11 42	8 30	11 39	19 35	20 57
23	11 33	8 14	11 28	19 43	21 05
24	11 23	7 57	11 16	19 51	21 13
25	11 13	7 39	11 03	19 59	21 21
26	11 03	7 21	10 50	20 07	21 29
27	10 53	7 03	10 37	20 16	21 38
28	10 43	6 44	10 23	20 25	21 47
29	10 32	6 25	10 08	20 34	21 56
30	10 21	6 05	9 53	20 43	22 05
31	10 10	5 45	9 37	20 53	22 15
32	9 59	5 23	9 20	21 03	22 24
33	9 47	5 02	9 03	21 14	22 34
34	9 35	4 39	8 44	21 25	22 45
35	9 23	4 16	8 25	21 36	22 55
36	9 10	3 51	8 05	21 48	23 06
37	8 57	3 26	7 43	22 01	23 17
38	8 43	3 00	7 20	22 14	23 29
39	8 29	2 33	6 56	22 28	23 41
40	8 15	2 05	6 30	22 42	23 54
41	8 00	1 35	6 02	22 57	24 07
42	7 44	1 05	5 33	23 13	24 20
43	7 28	0 32	5 01	23 30	24 35
44	7 11	29♑58	4 27	23 48	24 49
45	6 54	29 23	3 50	24 06	25 05
46	6 36	28 45	3 10	24 27	25 21
47	6 16	28 06	2 26	24 48	25 38
48	5 56	27 24	1 39	25 11	25 56
49	5 35	26 40	0 47	25 35	26 15
50	5 13	25 53	29♒49	26 02	26 35
51	4 50	25 03	28 46	26 30	26 56
52	4 25	24 10	27 35	27 01	27 18
53	3 58	23 13	26 16	27 34	27 42
54	3 30	22 11	24 46	28 11	28 07
55	3 00	21 05	23 05	28 51	28 35
56	2 28	19 52	21 09	29 36	29 05
57	1 53	18 34	18 55	0♉25	29 37
58	1 15	17 08	16 20	1 20	0♊12
59	0 33	15 33	13 18	2 23	0 50
60	29♐47	13♑48	9♒44	3♉34	1♊33

17h 8m 0s 257° 0' 0"
18 ♐ 02

LAT.	11	12	ASC	2	3
0	15♑40	14♒32	15♓53	18♈26	19♉27
5	15 01	13 32	15 20	18 54	19 59
10	14 22	12 28	14 44	19 24	20 32
15	13 40	11 20	14 03	19 56	21 06
20	12 57	10 06	13 17	20 32	21 43
21	12 48	9 50	13 07	20 39	21 50
22	12 38	9 34	12 57	20 47	21 58
23	12 29	9 18	12 46	20 55	22 06
24	12 19	9 01	12 35	21 04	22 14
25	12 09	8 44	12 23	21 12	22 23
26	12 00	8 26	12 11	21 21	22 31
27	11 49	8 08	11 58	21 30	22 40
28	11 39	7 50	11 45	21 40	22 49
29	11 28	7 30	11 32	21 49	22 58
30	11 18	7 11	11 17	21 59	23 07
31	11 06	6 51	11 02	22 10	23 17
32	10 55	6 30	10 47	22 20	23 27
33	10 43	6 08	10 30	22 32	23 37
34	10 31	5 46	10 13	22 43	23 47
35	10 19	5 22	9 55	22 55	23 58
36	10 06	4 59	9 36	23 08	24 09
37	9 53	4 34	9 16	23 21	24 20
38	9 40	4 08	8 54	23 35	24 32
39	9 26	3 41	8 31	23 49	24 45
40	9 11	3 13	8 07	24 04	24 57
41	8 56	2 44	7 41	24 20	25 10
42	8 41	2 13	7 13	24 37	25 24
43	8 25	1 41	6 43	24 55	25 38
44	8 08	1 07	6 11	25 14	25 53
45	7 50	0 32	5 36	25 34	26 09
46	7 32	29♑55	4 59	25 55	26 25
47	7 13	29 15	4 18	26 17	26 43
48	6 53	28 34	3 33	26 41	27 01
49	6 32	27 50	2 43	27 07	27 20
50	6 09	27 03	1 49	27 35	27 40
51	5 46	26 13	0 48	28 05	28 01
52	5 21	25 20	29♒41	28 37	28 24
53	4 54	24 23	28 25	29 12	28 48
54	4 26	23 21	27 00	29 51	29 14
55	3 56	22 15	25 22	0♉33	29 42
56	3 23	21 03	23 30	1 20	0♊11
57	2 48	19 44	21 21	2 11	0 44
58	2 10	18 18	18 49	3 09	1 19
59	1 28	16 43	15 51	4 15	1 58
60	0♑42	14♑57	12♒19	5♉29	2♊42

17h 12m 0s 258° 0' 0"
18 ♐ 58

LAT.	11	12	ASC	2	3
0	16♑36	15♒32	16♓57	19♈30	20♉26
5	15 57	14 33	16 27	20 00	20 59
10	15 18	13 30	15 54	20 31	21 32
15	14 37	12 23	15 16	21 05	22 07
20	13 53	11 10	14 33	21 43	22 44
21	13 44	10 55	14 24	21 51	22 52
22	13 35	10 39	14 14	21 59	23 00
23	13 25	10 23	14 04	22 08	23 08
24	13 16	10 06	13 54	22 17	23 16
25	13 06	9 49	13 43	22 26	23 24
26	12 56	9 32	13 32	22 35	23 33
27	12 46	9 14	13 20	22 44	23 42
28	12 36	8 55	13 08	22 54	23 51
29	12 25	8 36	12 55	23 04	24 00
30	12 14	8 17	12 42	23 15	24 09
31	12 03	7 57	12 28	23 26	24 19
32	11 52	7 36	12 14	23 37	24 29
33	11 40	7 15	11 59	23 49	24 39
34	11 28	6 53	11 43	24 01	24 50
35	11 16	6 30	11 26	24 14	25 00
36	11 03	6 06	11 08	24 27	25 12
37	10 50	5 41	10 49	24 41	25 23
38	10 36	5 16	10 29	24 56	25 35
39	10 22	4 49	10 08	25 11	25 48
40	10 08	4 21	9 45	25 27	26 00
41	9 53	3 52	9 21	25 43	26 14
42	9 38	3 22	8 55	26 01	26 28
43	9 21	2 50	8 27	26 20	26 42
44	9 05	2 17	7 57	26 39	26 57
45	8 47	1 42	7 24	27 00	27 13
46	8 29	1 05	6 49	27 22	27 29
47	8 10	0 26	6 10	27 46	27 47
48	7 49	29♑44	5 28	28 11	28 05
49	7 28	29 01	4 42	28 38	28 24
50	7 06	28 14	3 50	29 07	28 45
51	6 42	27 24	2 53	29 38	29 06
52	6 17	26 31	1 49	0♉12	29 29
53	5 51	25 34	0 38	0 49	29 53
54	5 23	24 33	29♒16	1 29	0♊20
55	4 52	23 27	27 43	2 14	0 48
56	4 20	22 14	25 56	3 02	1 18
57	3 44	20 56	23 52	3 56	1 51
58	3 06	19 29	21 25	4 57	2 27
59	2 24	17 54	18 31	6 05	3 06
60	1♑38	16♑08	15♒03	7♉23	3♊50

17h 16m 0s 259° 0' 0"
19 ♐ 53

LAT.	11	12	ASC	2	3
0	17♑32	16♒33	18♓02	20♈34	21♉26
5	16 53	15 34	17 34	21 05	21 58
10	16 14	14 32	17 04	21 38	22 32
15	15 33	13 26	16 29	22 14	23 07
20	14 49	12 14	15 50	22 54	23 45
21	14 40	11 59	15 41	23 02	23 52
22	14 31	11 44	15 32	23 11	24 01
23	14 22	11 28	15 23	23 20	24 09
24	14 12	11 11	15 13	23 29	24 17
25	14 03	10 54	15 04	23 39	24 26
26	13 53	10 37	14 53	23 48	24 34
27	13 43	10 20	14 42	23 58	24 43
28	13 32	10 01	14 31	24 09	24 52
29	13 22	9 43	14 20	24 19	25 01
30	13 11	9 24	14 07	24 30	25 11
31	13 00	9 04	13 55	24 42	25 21
32	12 48	8 43	13 41	24 54	25 31
33	12 37	8 22	13 27	25 06	25 41
34	12 25	8 00	13 12	25 19	25 52
35	12 12	7 38	12 57	25 32	26 03
36	12 00	7 14	12 40	25 46	26 14
37	11 47	6 50	12 23	26 01	26 26
38	11 33	6 24	12 04	26 16	26 38
39	11 19	5 58	11 45	26 32	26 50
40	11 05	5 30	11 24	26 48	27 03
41	10 50	5 02	11 01	27 06	27 17
42	10 34	4 31	10 37	27 24	27 31
43	10 18	4 00	10 11	27 44	27 45
44	10 01	3 27	9 43	28 04	28 01
45	9 44	2 52	9 13	28 26	28 17
46	9 26	2 15	8 40	28 49	28 33
47	9 06	1 37	8 04	29 14	28 51
48	8 46	0 55	7 25	29 40	29 09
49	8 25	0 12	6 41	0♉08	29 29
50	8 03	29♑26	5 54	0 39	29 49
51	7 39	28 36	5 00	1 11	0♊11
52	7 14	27 43	4 00	1 47	0 34
53	6 48	26 47	2 53	2 25	0 59
54	6 19	25 45	1 36	3 07	1 25
55	5 49	24 39	0 08	3 53	1 53
56	5 16	23 27	28♒27	4 44	2 24
57	4 41	22 08	26 28	5 40	2 57
58	4 02	20 42	24 08	6 43	3 33
59	3 20	19 06	21 20	7 54	4 13
60	2♑34	17♑20	17♒56	9♉15	4♊57

17h 20m 0s 260° 0' 0"
20 ♐ 49

LAT.	11	12	ASC	2	3
0	18♑28	17♒33	19♓07	21♈38	22♉25
5	17 50	16 36	18 42	22 11	22 58
10	17 10	15 35	18 14	22 45	23 32
15	16 29	14 30	17 42	23 23	24 07
20	15 46	13 19	17 06	24 04	24 45
21	15 37	13 04	16 59	24 13	24 53
22	15 28	12 49	16 50	24 22	25 01
23	15 19	12 33	16 42	24 32	25 10
24	15 09	12 17	16 33	24 41	25 18
25	14 59	12 00	16 24	24 51	25 27
26	14 49	11 43	16 15	25 01	25 35
27	14 39	11 26	16 05	25 12	25 44
28	14 29	11 08	15 55	25 23	25 53
29	14 18	10 50	15 44	25 34	26 03
30	14 08	10 31	15 33	25 45	26 12
31	13 57	10 11	15 21	25 57	26 22
32	13 45	9 51	15 09	26 10	26 32
33	13 34	9 30	14 56	26 23	26 43
34	13 22	9 08	14 43	26 36	26 54
35	13 09	8 46	14 28	26 50	27 05
36	12 57	8 23	14 13	27 05	27 16
37	12 44	7 58	13 57	27 20	27 28
38	12 30	7 33	13 40	27 36	27 40
39	12 16	7 07	13 22	27 52	27 53
40	12 02	6 40	13 03	28 09	28 06
41	11 47	6 11	12 42	28 28	28 19
42	11 32	5 42	12 20	28 47	28 34
43	11 15	5 10	11 56	29 07	28 48
44	10 59	4 38	11 31	29 29	29 04
45	10 41	4 03	11 03	29 51	29 20
46	10 23	3 27	10 32	0♉16	29 37
47	10 04	2 48	9 59	0 41	29 54
48	9 43	2 07	9 23	1 09	0♊13
49	9 22	1 24	8 43	1 38	0 32
50	9 00	0 38	7 59	2 10	0 53
51	8 36	29♑49	7 09	2 44	1 15
52	8 11	28 56	6 14	3 20	1 38
53	7 45	28 00	5 11	4 00	2 03
54	7 16	26 59	3 59	4 44	2 30
55	6 46	25 53	2 37	5 32	2 58
56	6 13	24 41	1 02	6 24	3 29
57	5 38	23 22	29♒09	7 23	4 03
58	4 59	21 56	26 56	8 28	4 39
59	4 17	20 20	24 16	9 41	5 19
60	3♑30	18♑33	20♒59	11♉05	6♊04

17h 24m 0s 261° 0' 0"
21 ♐ 44

LAT.	11	12	ASC	2	3
0	19♑24	18♒34	20♓12	22♈42	23♉23
5	18 46	17 37	19 49	23 16	23 57
10	18 07	16 38	19 24	23 52	24 31
15	17 26	15 34	18 56	24 32	25 07
20	16 43	14 24	18 23	25 15	25 46
21	16 34	14 09	18 16	25 24	25 54
22	16 25	13 54	18 09	25 34	26 02
23	16 15	13 39	18 01	25 43	26 10
24	16 06	13 23	17 53	25 53	26 19
25	15 56	13 06	17 45	26 04	26 27
26	15 46	12 50	17 37	26 14	26 36
27	15 36	12 33	17 28	26 25	26 45
28	15 26	12 15	17 18	26 37	26 54
29	15 16	11 57	17 09	26 48	27 04
30	15 05	11 38	16 59	27 00	27 14
31	14 54	11 19	16 48	27 13	27 24
32	14 42	10 59	16 37	27 26	27 34
33	14 31	10 38	16 25	27 39	27 44
34	14 19	10 17	16 13	27 53	27 55
35	14 07	9 55	16 00	28 08	28 06
36	13 54	9 32	15 46	28 23	28 18
37	13 41	9 08	15 32	28 38	28 30
38	13 28	8 43	15 17	28 55	28 42
39	13 14	8 17	15 00	29 12	28 55
40	12 59	7 50	14 43	29 30	29 08
41	12 44	7 22	14 24	29 49	29 22
42	12 29	6 52	14 04	0♉09	29 36
43	12 13	6 21	13 42	0 30	29 51
44	11 56	5 49	13 19	0 53	0♊06
45	11 38	5 15	12 54	1 16	0 23
46	11 20	4 39	12 26	1 41	0 40
47	11 01	4 00	11 56	2 08	0 57
48	10 41	3 20	11 23	2 36	1 16
49	10 20	2 37	10 46	3 07	1 36
50	9 57	1 51	10 06	3 40	1 57
51	9 34	1 02	9 20	4 15	2 19
52	9 09	0 10	8 29	4 53	2 42
53	8 42	29♑14	7 32	5 34	3 07
54	8 14	28 13	6 26	6 19	3 34
55	7 43	27 07	5 09	7 09	4 03
56	7 10	25 56	3 41	8 03	4 34
57	6 35	24 37	1 56	9 04	5 08
58	5 56	23 11	29♒51	10 11	5 45
59	5 14	21 35	27 20	11 27	6 25
60	4♑27	19♑48	24♒13	12♉53	7♊10

17h 28m 0s 262° 0' 0"
22 ♐ 39

LAT.	11	12	ASC	2	3
0	20♑20	19♒35	21♓17	23♈46	24♉22
5	19 42	18 39	20 57	24 21	24 56
10	19 03	17 41	20 34	24 59	25 30
15	18 23	16 38	20 09	25 40	26 07
20	17 40	15 29	19 40	26 25	26 46
21	17 31	15 15	19 34	26 35	26 54
22	17 22	15 00	19 27	26 45	27 02
23	17 12	14 45	19 21	26 55	27 10
24	17 03	14 29	19 14	27 05	27 19
25	16 53	14 13	19 06	27 16	27 28
26	16 43	13 56	18 59	27 27	27 37
27	16 33	13 40	18 51	27 38	27 46
28	16 23	13 22	18 42	27 50	27 55
29	16 13	13 04	18 34	28 02	28 05
30	16 02	12 46	18 25	28 15	28 15
31	15 51	12 27	18 15	28 28	28 25
32	15 40	12 07	18 05	28 41	28 35
33	15 28	11 47	17 55	28 55	28 46
34	15 16	11 26	17 44	29 10	28 57
35	15 04	11 04	17 32	29 25	29 08
36	14 51	10 41	17 20	29 40	29 19
37	14 38	10 18	17 07	29 57	29 31
38	14 25	9 53	16 53	0♉14	29 44
39	14 11	9 27	16 39	0 32	29 57
40	13 57	9 01	16 23	0 50	0♊10
41	13 42	8 33	16 06	1 10	0 24
42	13 26	8 04	15 48	1 31	0 38
43	13 10	7 33	15 29	1 53	0 53
44	12 54	7 01	15 08	2 16	1 09
45	12 36	6 27	14 45	2 40	1 25
46	12 18	5 51	14 20	3 06	1 42
47	11 59	5 13	13 53	3 34	2 00
48	11 38	4 33	13 24	4 03	2 19
49	11 17	3 51	12 51	4 35	2 39
50	10 55	3 05	12 14	5 09	3 00
51	10 31	2 17	11 33	5 45	3 22
52	10 06	1 25	10 47	6 25	3 46
53	9 40	0 29	9 55	7 07	4 11
54	9 11	29♑29	8 55	7 54	4 38
55	8 41	28 23	7 45	8 45	5 07
56	8 08	27 12	6 24	9 41	5 39
57	7 32	25 53	4 48	10 43	6 13
58	6 54	24 27	2 53	11 53	6 50
59	6 11	22 51	0 32	13 11	7 31
60	5♑24	21♑04	27♒36	14♉40	8♊16

17h 32m 0s 263° 0' 0"
23 ♐ 34

LAT.	11	12	ASC	2	3
0	21♑17	20♒36	22♓23	24♈50	25♉21
5	20 39	19 42	22 05	25 27	25 55
10	20 00	18 44	21 45	26 06	26 30
15	19 20	17 43	21 23	26 48	27 06
20	18 37	16 35	20 57	27 35	27 46
21	18 28	16 21	20 52	27 45	27 54
22	18 19	16 06	20 46	27 55	28 02
23	18 10	15 51	20 40	28 06	28 11
24	18 00	15 36	20 34	28 17	28 19
25	17 51	15 20	20 28	28 28	28 28
26	17 41	15 04	20 21	28 39	28 37
27	17 31	14 47	20 14	28 51	28 46
28	17 21	14 30	20 07	29 03	28 56
29	17 10	14 12	19 59	29 16	29 05
30	16 59	13 54	19 51	29 29	29 15
31	16 48	13 35	19 43	29 42	29 25
32	16 37	13 16	19 34	29 56	29 36
33	16 26	12 56	19 25	0♉11	29 47
34	16 14	12 35	19 15	0 26	29 58
35	16 02	12 13	19 05	0 41	0♊09
36	15 49	11 51	18 54	0 57	0 21
37	15 36	11 28	18 43	1 14	0 33
38	15 23	11 04	18 31	1 32	0 45
39	15 09	10 38	18 18	1 51	0 58
40	14 54	10 12	18 04	2 10	1 12
41	14 40	9 45	17 49	2 30	1 26
42	14 24	9 16	17 33	2 52	1 40
43	14 08	8 45	17 16	3 15	1 55
44	13 51	8 14	16 58	3 38	2 11
45	13 34	7 40	16 38	4 04	2 27
46	13 16	7 05	16 16	4 31	2 45
47	12 56	6 27	15 52	4 59	3 03
48	12 36	5 48	15 26	5 29	3 22
49	12 15	5 05	14 56	6 02	3 42
50	11 53	4 20	14 24	6 37	4 03
51	11 29	3 32	13 48	7 15	4 25
52	11 04	2 41	13 07	7 55	4 49
53	10 38	1 45	12 20	8 39	5 15
54	10 09	0 45	11 26	9 27	5 42
55	9 39	29♑40	10 24	10 20	6 11
56	9 06	28 29	9 12	11 18	6 43
57	8 30	27 11	7 45	12 22	7 17
58	7 51	25 45	6 01	13 33	7 54
59	7 09	24 09	3 52	14 54	8 36
60	6♑22	22♑22	1♓10	16♉25	9♊21

17h 36m 0s — 264° 0' 0" — 24 ♐ 30

LAT.	11	12	ASC	2	3
0	22♑13	21♒37	23♓28	25♈53	26♉19
5	21 36	20 44	23 12	26 31	26 53
10	20 57	19 48	22 56	27 12	27 29
15	20 17	18 47	22 37	27 56	28 06
20	19 34	17 41	22 15	28 45	28 45
21	19 25	17 27	22 10	28 55	28 53
22	19 16	17 12	22 05	29 06	29 02
23	19 07	16 58	22 00	29 17	29 10
24	18 57	16 43	21 55	29 28	29 19
25	18 48	16 27	21 49	29 39	29 28
26	18 38	16 11	21 43	29 51	29 37
27	18 28	15 55	21 37	0♉04	29 47
28	18 18	15 38	21 31	0 16	29 56
29	18 08	15 20	21 25	0 29	0♊06
30	17 57	15 03	21 18	0 43	0 16
31	17 46	14 44	21 11	0 56	0 26
32	17 35	14 25	21 03	1 11	0 36
33	17 23	14 05	20 55	1 26	0 47
34	17 11	13 45	20 47	1 41	0 58
35	16 59	13 24	20 38	1 57	1 10
36	16 47	13 02	20 29	2 14	1 22
37	16 34	12 39	20 19	2 32	1 34
38	16 20	12 15	20 09	2 50	1 46
39	16 07	11 50	19 57	3 09	1 59
40	15 52	11 24	19 46	3 29	2 13
41	15 38	10 57	19 33	3 50	2 27
42	15 22	10 28	19 19	4 12	2 42
43	15 06	9 58	19 04	4 36	2 57
44	14 49	9 27	18 48	5 00	3 13
45	14 32	8 54	18 31	5 27	3 29
46	14 14	8 19	18 12	5 54	3 47
47	13 55	7 42	17 51	6 24	4 05
48	13 35	7 03	17 28	6 55	4 24
49	13 13	6 21	17 03	7 28	4 44
50	12 51	5 36	16 35	8 04	5 05
51	12 28	4 49	16 04	8 43	5 28
52	12 03	3 57	15 28	9 25	5 52
53	11 36	3 02	14 47	10 10	6 18
54	11 07	2 03	14 01	10 59	6 45
55	10 37	0 58	13 06	11 53	7 15
56	10 04	29♑47	12 03	12 53	7 46
57	9 28	28 30	10 46	13 59	8 21
58	8 50	27 04	9 14	15 12	8 58
59	8 07	25 29	7 20	16 34	9 40
60	7♑20	23♑41	4♓55	18♉08	10♊26

17h 40m 0s — 265° 0' 0" — 25 ♐ 25

LAT.	11	12	ASC	2	3
0	23♑10	22♒39	24♓33	26♈57	27♉17
5	22 32	21 47	24 20	27 36	27 52
10	21 54	20 52	24 06	28 18	28 27
15	21 14	19 52	23 50	29 04	29 05
20	20 31	18 47	23 32	29 54	29 45
21	20 23	18 33	23 28	0♉05	29 53
22	20 14	18 19	23 24	0 16	0♊02
23	20 04	18 05	23 20	0 27	0 10
24	19 55	17 50	23 15	0 39	0 19
25	19 46	17 35	23 11	0 51	0 28
26	19 36	17 19	23 06	1 03	0 37
27	19 26	17 03	23 01	1 16	0 46
28	19 16	16 46	22 56	1 29	0 56
29	19 05	16 29	22 50	1 42	1 06
30	18 55	16 12	22 44	1 56	1 16
31	18 44	15 53	22 38	2 10	1 26
32	18 33	15 35	22 32	2 25	1 37
33	18 21	15 15	22 26	2 41	1 48
34	18 09	14 55	22 19	2 57	1 59
35	17 57	14 34	22 11	3 13	2 10
36	17 45	14 13	22 04	3 31	2 22
37	17 32	13 50	21 55	3 49	2 35
38	17 19	13 26	21 47	4 08	2 47
39	17 05	13 02	21 37	4 27	3 00
40	16 51	12 36	21 27	4 48	3 14
41	16 36	12 10	21 17	5 10	3 28
42	16 20	11 41	21 05	5 32	3 43
43	16 04	11 12	20 53	5 56	3 58
44	15 48	10 41	20 39	6 22	4 14
45	15 30	10 08	20 25	6 49	4 31
46	15 12	9 34	20 09	7 17	4 48
47	14 53	8 57	19 52	7 47	5 07
48	14 33	8 18	19 32	8 20	5 26
49	14 12	7 37	19 11	8 54	5 46
50	13 50	6 53	18 47	9 31	6 08
51	13 26	6 06	18 21	10 11	6 30
52	13 01	5 15	17 51	10 54	6 55
53	12 34	4 20	17 16	11 40	7 20
54	12 06	3 21	16 37	12 31	7 48
55	11 36	2 17	15 51	13 26	8 17
56	11 03	1 07	14 57	14 27	8 49
57	10 27	29♑50	13 52	15 34	9 24
58	9 48	28 24	12 33	16 49	10 02
59	9 05	26 49	10 54	18 13	10 44
60	8♑18	25♑03	8♓48	19♉49	11♊30

17h 44m 0s — 266° 0' 0" — 26 ♐ 20

LAT.	11	12	ASC	2	3
0	24♑06	23♒41	25♓38	28♈00	28♉15
5	23 29	22 50	25 28	28 41	28 50
10	22 51	21 56	25 17	29 24	29 26
15	22 11	20 57	25 04	0♉11	0♊04
20	21 29	19 54	24 50	1 03	0 44
21	21 20	19 40	24 46	1 14	0 52
22	21 11	19 26	24 43	1 26	1 01
23	21 02	19 12	24 40	1 37	1 10
24	20 53	18 57	24 36	1 49	1 18
25	20 43	18 43	24 32	2 02	1 28
26	20 34	18 27	24 28	2 14	1 37
27	20 24	18 11	24 24	2 27	1 46
28	20 14	17 55	24 20	2 41	1 56
29	20 03	17 38	24 16	2 55	2 06
30	19 53	17 21	24 11	3 09	2 16
31	19 42	17 03	24 07	3 24	2 26
32	19 31	16 45	24 02	3 39	2 37
33	19 19	16 26	23 56	3 55	2 48
34	19 08	16 06	23 51	4 11	2 59
35	18 55	15 45	23 45	4 29	3 11
36	18 43	15 24	23 39	4 46	3 23
37	18 30	15 02	23 32	5 05	3 35
38	18 17	14 39	23 25	5 24	3 48
39	18 03	14 15	23 17	5 45	4 01
40	17 49	13 49	23 09	6 06	4 15
41	17 34	13 23	23 01	6 28	4 29
42	17 19	12 55	22 52	6 52	4 44
43	17 03	12 26	22 42	7 16	4 59
44	16 46	11 56	22 31	7 43	5 15
45	16 29	11 23	22 19	8 10	5 32
46	16 11	10 49	22 06	8 39	5 50
47	15 52	10 13	21 52	9 10	6 08
48	15 32	9 35	21 37	9 43	6 27
49	15 11	8 54	21 20	10 19	6 48
50	14 48	8 10	21 01	10 57	7 09
51	14 25	7 24	20 39	11 37	7 32
52	14 00	6 34	20 15	12 21	7 57
53	13 33	5 40	19 47	13 09	8 23
54	13 05	4 41	19 15	14 01	8 50
55	12 35	3 37	18 38	14 57	9 20
56	12 02	2 28	17 54	15 59	9 52
57	11 26	1 11	17 01	17 08	10 27
58	10 47	29♑46	15 56	18 25	11 05
59	10 04	28 12	14 35	19 50	11 47
60	9♑17	26♑25	12♓51	21♉28	12♊34

17h 48m 0s — 267° 0' 0" — 27 ♐ 15

LAT.	11	12	ASC	2	3
0	25♑03	24♒42	26♓44	29♈03	29♉13
5	24 26	23 53	26 36	29 45	29 48
10	23 48	23 00	26 28	0♉30	0♊24
15	23 09	22 03	26 18	1 19	1 03
20	22 27	21 01	26 07	2 12	1 43
21	22 18	20 47	26 05	2 24	1 51
22	22 09	20 34	26 02	2 35	2 00
23	22 00	20 20	26 00	2 47	2 09
24	21 51	20 05	25 57	3 00	2 18
25	21 41	19 51	25 54	3 12	2 27
26	21 32	19 36	25 51	3 25	2 36
27	21 22	19 20	25 48	3 39	2 46
28	21 12	19 04	25 45	3 53	2 55
29	21 01	18 48	25 42	4 07	3 05
30	20 51	18 31	25 38	4 22	3 16
31	20 40	18 13	25 35	4 37	3 26
32	20 29	17 55	25 31	4 53	3 37
33	20 18	17 37	25 27	5 09	3 48
34	20 06	17 17	25 23	5 26	3 59
35	19 54	16 57	25 18	5 43	4 11
36	19 41	16 36	25 14	6 02	4 23
37	19 29	16 14	25 09	6 21	4 35
38	19 15	15 51	25 04	6 41	4 48
39	19 02	15 28	24 58	7 02	5 01
40	18 48	15 03	24 52	7 24	5 15
41	18 33	14 37	24 45	7 46	5 30
42	18 18	14 10	24 38	8 11	5 44
43	18 02	13 41	24 31	8 36	6 00
44	17 45	13 11	24 23	9 03	6 16
45	17 28	12 39	24 14	9 31	6 33
46	17 10	12 06	24 04	10 01	6 51
47	16 51	11 30	23 54	10 33	7 09
48	16 31	10 52	23 42	11 06	7 29
49	16 10	10 12	23 29	11 43	7 49
50	15 48	9 29	23 15	12 21	8 11
51	15 24	8 43	22 59	13 03	8 34
52	14 59	7 53	22 40	13 48	8 58
53	14 33	7 00	22 19	14 37	9 24
54	14 04	6 02	21 55	15 29	9 52
55	13 34	4 59	21 27	16 27	10 22
56	13 01	3 50	20 53	17 30	10 54
57	12 25	2 34	20 13	18 41	11 29
58	11 47	1 10	19 24	19 59	12 08
59	11 04	29♑36	18 21	21 26	12 50
60	10♑16	27♑50	17♓01	23♉05	13♊37

17h 52m 0s — 268° 0' 0" — 28 ♐ 10

LAT.	11	12	ASC	2	3
0	26♑00	25♒44	27♓49	0♉06	0♊11
5	25 24	24 56	27 44	0 49	0 46
10	24 46	24 04	27 38	1 36	1 23
15	24 06	23 09	27 32	2 26	2 01
20	23 25	22 08	27 25	3 21	2 42
21	23 16	21 55	27 23	3 33	2 50
22	23 07	21 41	27 21	3 45	2 59
23	22 58	21 28	27 20	3 57	3 08
24	22 49	21 14	27 18	4 10	3 17
25	22 39	20 59	27 16	4 23	3 26
26	22 30	20 45	27 14	4 36	3 35
27	22 20	20 29	27 12	4 50	3 45
28	22 10	20 14	27 10	5 04	3 55
29	22 00	19 58	27 08	5 19	4 05
30	21 49	19 41	27 06	5 34	4 15
31	21 39	19 24	27 03	5 49	4 26
32	21 27	19 06	27 01	6 06	4 36
33	21 16	18 48	26 58	6 22	4 47
34	21 04	18 29	26 55	6 40	4 59
35	20 52	18 09	26 52	6 58	5 11
36	20 40	17 48	26 49	7 17	5 23
37	20 27	17 27	26 46	7 36	5 35
38	20 14	17 05	26 42	7 57	5 48
39	20 01	16 41	26 38	8 18	6 02
40	19 46	16 17	26 34	8 41	6 15
41	19 32	15 52	26 30	9 04	6 30
42	19 17	15 25	26 26	9 29	6 45
43	19 01	14 57	26 21	9 55	7 00
44	18 44	14 27	26 15	10 22	7 17
45	18 27	13 56	26 09	10 51	7 34
46	18 09	13 23	26 03	11 22	7 51
47	17 50	12 48	25 56	11 54	8 10
48	17 30	12 10	25 48	12 29	8 30
49	17 09	11 31	25 39	13 06	8 50
50	16 47	10 48	25 30	13 45	9 12
51	16 24	10 03	25 19	14 28	9 35
52	15 59	9 14	25 06	15 14	10 00
53	15 32	8 21	24 52	16 03	10 26
54	15 04	7 24	24 36	16 57	10 54
55	14 34	6 21	24 17	17 56	11 24
56	14 01	5 13	23 54	19 00	11 56
57	13 25	3 58	23 27	20 12	12 31
58	12 46	2 35	22 54	21 31	13 10
59	12 04	1 01	22 12	23 00	13 52
60	11♑16	29♑16	21♓17	24♉41	14♊39

17h 56m 0s — 269° 0' 0" — 29 ♐ 05

LAT.	11	12	ASC	2	3
0	26♑57	26♒47	28♓55	1♉08	1♊08
5	26 21	25 59	28 52	1 53	1 44
10	25 43	25 09	28 49	2 41	2 21
15	25 04	24 15	28 46	3 33	2 59
20	24 23	23 15	28 42	4 29	3 41
21	24 14	23 02	28 42	4 41	3 49
22	24 05	22 49	28 41	4 54	3 58
23	23 56	22 36	28 40	5 06	4 07
24	23 47	22 22	28 39	5 19	4 16
25	23 38	22 08	28 38	5 33	4 25
26	23 28	21 54	28 37	5 46	4 34
27	23 18	21 39	28 36	6 01	4 44
28	23 08	21 24	28 35	6 15	4 54
29	22 58	21 08	28 34	6 30	5 04
30	22 48	20 52	28 33	6 46	5 14
31	22 37	20 35	28 32	7 02	5 25
32	22 26	20 18	28 30	7 18	5 36
33	22 15	20 00	28 29	7 36	5 47
34	22 03	19 41	28 28	7 53	5 58
35	21 51	19 22	28 26	8 12	6 10
36	21 39	19 01	28 25	8 31	6 22
37	21 26	18 40	28 23	8 51	6 35
38	21 13	18 19	28 21	9 12	6 48
39	21 00	17 56	28 19	9 34	7 01
40	20 46	17 32	28 17	9 57	7 15
41	20 31	17 07	28 15	10 21	7 30
42	20 16	16 41	28 13	10 46	7 45
43	20 00	16 13	28 10	11 13	8 01
44	19 44	15 44	28 07	11 41	8 17
45	19 26	15 13	28 05	12 10	8 34
46	19 08	14 41	28 01	12 42	8 52
47	18 49	14 06	27 58	13 15	9 10
48	18 30	13 29	27 54	13 50	9 30
49	18 09	12 50	27 50	14 28	9 51
50	17 47	12 09	27 45	15 08	10 13
51	17 23	11 24	27 39	15 52	10 36
52	16 59	10 35	27 33	16 38	11 01
53	16 32	9 43	27 26	17 29	11 27
54	16 04	8 47	27 18	18 24	11 55
55	15 34	7 45	27 08	19 23	12 25
56	15 01	6 38	26 57	20 29	12 58
57	14 25	5 23	26 43	21 41	13 33
58	13 47	4 01	26 26	23 02	14 11
59	13 04	2 29	26 05	24 32	14 54
60	12♑17	0♒44	25♓38	26♉14	15♊41

18h 0m 0s — 270° 0' 0" — 0 ♑ 00

LAT.	11	12	ASC	2	3
0	27♑55	27♒49	0♈00	2♉11	2♊05
5	27 18	27 03	0 00	2 57	2 42
10	26 41	26 14	0 00	3 46	3 19
15	26 02	25 21	0 00	4 39	3 58
20	25 21	24 23	0 00	5 37	4 39
21	25 12	24 10	0 00	5 50	4 48
22	25 04	23 58	0 00	6 02	4 56
23	24 55	23 45	0 00	6 15	5 05
24	24 46	23 31	0 00	6 29	5 14
25	24 36	23 18	0 00	6 42	5 24
26	24 27	23 04	0 00	6 56	5 33
27	24 17	22 49	0 00	7 11	5 43
28	24 07	22 34	0 00	7 26	5 53
29	23 57	22 19	0 00	7 41	6 03
30	23 47	22 03	0 00	7 57	6 13
31	23 36	21 46	0 00	8 14	6 24
32	23 25	21 29	0 00	8 31	6 35
33	23 14	21 12	0 00	8 48	6 46
34	23 02	20 54	0 00	9 06	6 58
35	22 50	20 35	0 00	9 25	7 10
36	22 38	20 15	0 00	9 45	7 22
37	22 26	19 54	0 00	10 06	7 34
38	22 12	19 33	0 00	10 27	7 48
39	21 59	19 11	0 00	10 49	8 01
40	21 45	18 47	0 00	11 13	8 15
41	21 30	18 23	0 00	11 37	8 30
42	21 15	17 57	0 00	12 03	8 45
43	21 00	17 30	0 00	12 30	9 00
44	20 43	17 01	0 00	12 59	9 17
45	20 26	16 31	0 00	13 29	9 34
46	20 08	15 59	0 00	14 01	9 52
47	19 49	15 25	0 00	14 35	10 11
48	19 30	14 49	0 00	15 11	10 30
49	19 09	14 11	0 00	15 49	10 51
50	18 47	13 30	0 00	16 30	11 13
51	18 24	12 46	0 00	17 14	11 36
52	17 59	11 58	0 00	18 02	12 01
53	17 33	11 07	0 00	18 53	12 27
54	17 04	10 11	0 00	19 49	12 56
55	16 34	9 10	0 00	20 50	13 26
56	16 01	8 04	0 00	21 56	13 59
57	15 26	6 50	0 00	23 10	14 34
58	14 47	5 29	0 00	24 31	15 13
59	14 05	3 57	0 00	26 03	15 55
60	13♑18	2♒14	0♈00	27♉46	16♊42

18h 4m 0s — 271° 0' 0" — 0 ♑ 55

LAT.	11	12	ASC	2	3
0	28♑52	28♒52	1♈05	3♉13	3♊03
5	28 16	28 07	1 08	4 01	3 39
10	27 39	27 19	1 11	4 51	4 17
15	27 01	26 27	1 14	5 45	4 56
20	26 19	25 31	1 18	6 45	5 37
21	26 11	25 19	1 18	6 58	5 46
22	26 02	25 06	1 19	7 11	5 55
23	25 53	24 54	1 20	7 24	6 04
24	25 44	24 41	1 21	7 38	6 13
25	25 35	24 27	1 22	7 52	6 22
26	25 26	24 14	1 23	8 06	6 32
27	25 16	23 59	1 24	8 21	6 42
28	25 06	23 45	1 25	8 36	6 52
29	24 56	23 30	1 26	8 52	7 02
30	24 46	23 14	1 27	9 08	7 12
31	24 35	22 58	1 28	9 25	7 23
32	24 24	22 42	1 30	9 42	7 34
33	24 13	22 24	1 31	10 00	7 45
34	24 02	22 07	1 32	10 19	7 57
35	23 50	21 48	1 34	10 38	8 09
36	23 38	21 29	1 35	10 59	8 21
37	23 25	21 09	1 37	11 20	8 34
38	23 12	20 48	1 39	11 41	8 47
39	22 59	20 26	1 41	12 04	9 00
40	22 45	20 03	1 43	12 28	9 14
41	22 30	19 39	1 45	12 53	9 29
42	22 15	19 14	1 47	13 19	9 44
43	21 59	18 47	1 50	13 47	10 00
44	21 43	18 19	1 53	14 16	10 16
45	21 26	17 50	1 55	14 47	10 34
46	21 08	17 18	1 59	15 19	10 52
47	20 50	16 45	2 02	15 54	11 11
48	20 30	16 10	2 06	16 31	11 30
49	20 09	15 32	2 10	17 10	11 51
50	19 47	14 52	2 15	17 51	12 13
51	19 24	14 08	2 21	18 36	12 37
52	18 59	13 22	2 27	19 25	13 01
53	18 33	12 31	2 34	20 17	13 28
54	18 05	11 36	2 42	21 13	13 56
55	17 35	10 37	2 52	22 15	14 26
56	17 02	9 31	3 03	23 22	14 59
57	16 27	8 19	3 17	24 37	15 35
58	15 49	6 58	3 34	25 59	16 13
59	15 06	5 28	3 55	27 31	16 56
60	14♑19	3♒46	4♈22	29♉16	17♊43

18h 8m 0s	1 ♑ 50		272° 0' 0"		
LAT.	11	12	ASC	2	3
0	29♑49	29♒54	2♈11	4♉16	4♊00
5	29 14	29 11	2 16	5 04	4 36
10	28 37	28 24	2 22	5 56	5 14
15	27 59	27 34	2 28	6 51	5 54
20	27 18	26 39	2 35	7 52	6 35
21	27 10	26 27	2 37	8 05	6 44
22	27 01	26 15	2 39	8 19	6 53
23	26 52	26 03	2 40	8 32	7 02
24	26 43	25 50	2 42	8 46	7 11
25	26 34	25 37	2 44	9 01	7 21
26	26 25	25 24	2 46	9 15	7 30
27	26 15	25 10	2 48	9 31	7 40
28	26 05	24 56	2 50	9 46	7 50
29	25 55	24 41	2 52	10 02	8 00
30	25 45	24 26	2 54	10 19	8 11
31	25 34	24 11	2 57	10 36	8 21
32	25 24	23 54	2 59	10 54	8 33
33	25 13	23 38	3 02	11 12	8 44
34	25 01	23 20	3 05	11 31	8 56
35	24 49	23 02	3 08	11 51	9 08
36	24 37	22 43	3 11	12 12	9 20
37	24 25	22 24	3 14	12 33	9 33
38	24 12	22 03	3 18	12 55	9 46
39	23 58	21 42	3 22	13 19	9 59
40	23 45	21 19	3 26	13 43	10 14
41	23 30	20 56	3 30	14 08	10 28
42	23 15	20 31	3 34	14 35	10 43
43	23 00	20 05	3 39	15 03	10 59
44	22 43	19 38	3 45	15 33	11 16
45	22 26	19 09	3 51	16 04	11 33
46	22 09	18 38	3 57	16 37	11 51
47	21 50	18 06	4 04	17 12	12 10
48	21 30	17 31	4 12	17 50	12 30
49	21 10	16 54	4 21	18 29	12 51
50	20 48	16 15	4 30	19 12	13 13
51	20 25	15 32	4 41	19 57	13 36
52	20 00	14 46	4 54	20 46	14 01
53	19 34	13 57	5 08	21 39	14 28
54	19 06	13 03	5 24	22 36	14 56
55	18 36	12 04	5 43	23 39	15 26
56	18 04	11 00	6 06	24 47	15 59
57	17 29	9 48	6 33	26 02	16 35
58	16 50	8 29	7 06	27 25	17 14
59	16 08	7 00	7 48	28 59	17 56
60	15♑21	5♒19	8♈43	0♊44	18♊44

18h 12m 0s	2 ♑ 45		273° 0' 0"		
LAT.	11	12	ASC	2	3
0	0♒47	0♓57	3♈16	5♉18	4♊57
5	0 12	0 15	3 24	6 07	5 34
10	29♑36	29♒30	3 32	7 00	6 12
15	28 57	28 41	3 42	7 57	6 51
20	28 17	27 48	3 53	8 59	7 33
21	28 09	27 36	3 55	9 13	7 42
22	28 00	27 25	3 58	9 26	7 51
23	27 51	27 13	4 00	9 40	8 00
24	27 42	27 00	4 03	9 55	8 09
25	27 33	26 48	4 06	10 09	8 19
26	27 24	26 35	4 09	10 24	8 28
27	27 14	26 21	4 12	10 40	8 38
28	27 05	26 07	4 15	10 56	8 48
29	26 55	25 53	4 18	11 12	8 59
30	26 44	25 38	4 22	11 29	9 09
31	26 34	25 23	4 25	11 47	9 20
32	26 23	25 07	4 29	12 05	9 31
33	26 12	24 51	4 33	12 23	9 42
34	26 01	24 34	4 37	12 43	9 54
35	25 49	24 17	4 42	13 03	10 06
36	25 37	23 58	4 46	13 24	10 19
37	25 25	23 39	4 51	13 46	10 31
38	25 12	23 19	4 56	14 09	10 45
39	24 59	22 58	5 02	14 32	10 58
40	24 45	22 36	5 08	14 57	11 12
41	24 30	22 14	5 15	15 23	11 27
42	24 16	21 49	5 22	15 50	11 42
43	24 00	21 24	5 29	16 19	11 58
44	23 44	20 57	5 37	16 49	12 15
45	23 27	20 29	5 46	17 21	12 32
46	23 09	19 59	5 56	17 54	12 50
47	22 51	19 27	6 06	18 30	13 09
48	22 31	18 54	6 18	19 08	13 29
49	22 11	18 17	6 31	19 48	13 50
50	21 49	17 39	6 45	20 31	14 12
51	21 26	16 57	7 01	21 17	14 36
52	21 02	16 12	7 20	22 07	15 01
53	20 36	15 23	7 41	23 00	15 27
54	20 08	14 31	8 05	23 58	15 56
55	19 38	13 33	8 33	25 01	16 26
56	19 06	12 30	9 07	26 10	16 59
57	18 31	11 19	9 47	27 26	17 35
58	17 52	10 01	10 36	28 50	18 13
59	17 10	8 34	11 39	0♊24	18 56
60	16♑23	6♒55	12♈59	2♊10	19♊44

18h 16m 0s	3 ♑ 40		274° 0' 0"		
LAT.	11	12	ASC	2	3
0	1♒45	2♓00	4♈22	6♉19	5♊54
5	1 10	1 19	4 32	7 10	6 31
10	0 34	0 36	4 43	8 04	7 09
15	29♑56	29♒49	4 56	9 03	7 49
20	29 16	28 57	5 10	10 06	8 31
21	29 08	28 46	5 14	10 20	8 40
22	28 59	28 34	5 17	10 34	8 49
23	28 50	28 23	5 20	10 48	8 58
24	28 42	28 11	5 24	11 03	9 07
25	28 32	27 58	5 28	11 17	9 17
26	28 23	27 46	5 32	11 33	9 26
27	28 14	27 33	5 36	11 49	9 36
28	28 04	27 19	5 40	12 05	9 46
29	27 54	27 05	5 44	12 22	9 57
30	27 44	26 51	5 49	12 39	10 07
31	27 34	26 36	5 53	12 57	10 18
32	27 23	26 21	5 58	13 15	10 29
33	27 12	26 05	6 04	13 34	10 41
34	27 01	25 49	6 09	13 54	10 52
35	26 49	25 31	6 15	14 15	11 05
36	26 37	25 14	6 21	14 36	11 17
37	26 25	24 55	6 28	14 58	11 30
38	26 12	24 36	6 35	15 21	11 43
39	25 59	24 15	6 43	15 45	11 57
40	25 45	23 54	6 51	16 11	12 11
41	25 31	23 32	6 59	16 37	12 26
42	25 16	23 08	7 08	17 05	12 41
43	25 01	22 44	7 18	17 34	12 57
44	24 45	22 17	7 29	18 04	13 14
45	24 28	21 50	7 41	18 37	13 31
46	24 10	21 21	7 54	19 11	13 49
47	23 52	20 50	8 08	19 47	14 08
48	23 33	20 17	8 23	20 25	14 28
49	23 12	19 41	8 40	21 06	14 49
50	22 51	19 03	8 59	21 50	15 12
51	22 28	18 23	9 21	22 36	15 35
52	22 03	17 39	9 45	23 26	16 00
53	21 37	16 51	10 13	24 20	16 27
54	21 10	15 59	10 45	25 19	16 55
55	20 40	15 03	11 22	26 23	17 25
56	20 08	14 01	12 06	27 32	17 58
57	19 33	12 52	12 59	28 49	18 34
58	18 55	11 35	14 04	0♊14	19 13
59	18 13	10 10	15 25	1 48	19 56
60	17♑26	8♒32	17♈09	3♊35	20♊43

18h 20m 0s	4 ♑ 35		275° 0' 0"		
LAT.	11	12	ASC	2	3
0	2♒43	3♓03	5♈27	7♉21	6♊50
5	2 08	2 24	5 40	8 13	7 28
10	1 33	1 42	5 54	9 08	8 06
15	0 55	0 56	6 10	10 08	8 46
20	0 15	0 06	6 28	11 13	9 29
21	0 07	29♒55	6 32	11 27	9 37
22	29♑58	29 44	6 36	11 41	9 46
23	29 50	29 33	6 40	11 55	9 56
24	29 41	29 21	6 45	12 10	10 05
25	29 32	29 09	6 49	12 25	10 14
26	29 23	28 57	6 54	12 41	10 24
27	29 14	28 44	6 59	12 57	10 34
28	29 04	28 31	7 04	13 14	10 44
29	28 54	28 18	7 10	13 31	10 55
30	28 44	28 04	7 16	13 48	11 05
31	28 34	27 50	7 22	14 07	11 16
32	28 23	27 35	7 28	14 25	11 27
33	28 12	27 19	7 34	14 45	11 39
34	28 01	27 03	7 41	15 05	11 51
35	27 50	26 47	7 49	15 26	12 03
36	27 38	26 29	7 56	15 47	12 15
37	27 25	26 11	8 05	16 10	12 28
38	27 13	25 52	8 13	16 34	12 41
39	27 00	25 33	8 23	16 58	12 55
40	26 46	25 12	8 33	17 24	13 09
41	26 32	24 50	8 43	17 50	13 24
42	26 17	24 28	8 55	18 19	13 40
43	26 02	24 04	9 07	18 48	13 56
44	25 46	23 38	9 21	19 19	14 12
45	25 29	23 11	9 35	19 52	14 30
46	25 12	22 43	9 51	20 26	14 48
47	24 53	22 13	10 08	21 03	15 07
48	24 34	21 40	10 28	21 42	15 27
49	24 14	21 06	10 49	22 23	15 48
50	23 52	20 29	11 13	23 07	16 10
51	23 30	19 49	11 39	23 54	16 34
52	23 05	19 06	12 09	24 45	16 59
53	22 40	18 20	12 44	25 40	17 26
54	22 12	17 29	13 23	26 39	17 54
55	21 43	16 34	14 09	27 43	18 24
56	21 11	15 33	15 03	28 53	18 57
57	20 36	14 26	16 08	0♊10	19 33
58	19 58	13 11	17 27	1 36	20 12
59	19 16	11 47	19 06	3 11	20 55
60	18♑30	10♒11	21♈12	4♊57	21♊42

18h 24m 0s	5 ♑ 30		276° 0' 0"		
LAT.	11	12	ASC	2	3
0	3♒41	4♓07	6♈32	8♉23	7♊47
5	3 07	3 29	6 48	9 16	8 24
10	2 31	2 48	7 04	10 12	9 03
15	1 54	2 .4	7 23	11 13	9 43
20	1 15	1 15	7 45	12 19	10 26
21	1 07	1 05	7 50	12 33	10 35
22	0 58	0 54	7 55	12 48	10 44
23	0 50	0 43	8 00	13 02	10 53
24	0 41	0 32	8 05	13 17	11 03
25	0 32	0 21	8 11	13 33	11 12
26	0 23	0 09	8 17	13 49	11 22
27	0 13	29♒56	8 23	14 05	11 32
28	0 04	29 44	8 29	14 22	11 42
29	29♑54	29 31	8 35	14 40	11 52
30	29 44	29 17	8 42	14 57	12 03
31	29 34	29 04	8 49	15 16	12 14
32	29 24	28 49	8 57	15 35	12 25
33	29 13	28 34	9 05	15 55	12 37
34	29 02	28 19	9 13	16 15	12 49
35	28 50	28 03	9 22	16 36	13 01
36	28 38	27 46	9 31	16 58	13 13
37	28 26	27 28	9 41	17 21	13 26
38	28 14	27 10	9 51	17 45	13 40
39	28 01	26 51	10 03	18 10	13 53
40	27 47	26 31	10 14	18 36	14 08
41	27 33	26 10	10 27	19 03	14 22
42	27 18	25 48	10 41	19 32	14 38
43	27 03	25 24	10 56	20 02	14 54
44	26 47	25 00	11 12	20 33	15 11
45	26 31	24 33	11 29	21 06	15 28
46	26 13	24 06	11 48	21 41	15 46
47	25 55	23 36	12 09	22 18	16 05
48	25 36	23 05	12 32	22 57	16 25
49	25 16	22 32	12 57	23 39	16 47
50	24 55	21 56	13 25	24 24	17 09
51	24 32	21 17	13 56	25 11	17 32
52	24 08	20 35	14 32	26 03	17 57
53	23 42	19 50	15 13	26 58	18 24
54	23 15	19 01	15 59	27 57	18 53
55	22 45	18 07	16 54	29 02	19 23
56	22 14	17 07	17 57	0♊13	19 56
57	21 39	16 01	19 14	1 30	20 32
58	21 02	14 48	20 46	2 56	21 10
59	20 20	13 26	22 40	4 31	21 53
60	19♑34	11♒52	25♈05	6♊19	22♊40

18h 28m 0s	6 ♑ 26		277° 0' 0"		
LAT.	11	12	ASC	2	3
0	4♒39	5♓10	7♈37	9♉24	8♊43
5	4 05	4 33	7 55	10 18	9 21
10	3 30	3 54	8 15	11 16	10 00
15	2 54	3 12	8 37	12 17	10 40
20	2 14	2 25	9 03	13 25	11 23
21	2 06	2 15	9 08	13 39	11 32
22	1 58	2 05	9 14	13 54	11 41
23	1 49	1 54	9 20	14 09	11 50
24	1 41	1 43	9 26	14 24	12 00
25	1 32	1 32	9 32	14 40	12 09
26	1 23	1 21	9 39	14 56	12 19
27	1 14	1 09	9 46	15 13	12 29
28	1 04	0 57	9 53	15 30	12 39
29	0 55	0 44	10 01	15 48	12 50
30	0 45	0 31	10 09	16 06	13 01
31	0 35	0 18	10 17	16 25	13 12
32	0 24	0 04	10 26	16 44	13 23
33	0 13	29♒49	10 35	17 04	13 34
34	0 02	29 34	10 45	17 25	13 46
35	29♑51	29 19	10 55	17 47	13 58
36	29 39	29 03	11 06	18 09	14 11
37	29 27	28 46	11 17	18 32	14 24
38	29 15	28 28	11 29	18 56	14 37
39	29 02	28 09	11 42	19 22	14 51
40	28 48	27 50	11 56	19 48	15 06
41	28 34	27 30	12 11	20 15	15 20
42	28 20	27 08	12 27	20 44	15 36
43	28 05	26 45	12 44	21 15	15 52
44	27 49	26 22	13 02	21 46	16 09
45	27 33	25 56	13 22	22 20	16 26
46	27 15	25 29	13 44	22 55	16 44
47	26 57	25 01	14 08	23 33	17 04
48	26 38	24 31	14 34	24 12	17 24
49	26 18	23 58	15 04	24 55	17 45
50	25 57	23 23	15 36	25 40	18 07
51	25 35	22 45	16 12	26 28	18 31
52	25 11	22 05	16 53	27 19	18 56
53	24 45	21 21	17 40	28 15	19 22
54	24 18	20 33	18 34	29 15	19 51
55	23 49	19 40	19 36	0♊20	20 21
56	23 17	18 42	20 48	1 31	20 54
57	22 43	17 38	22 15	2 49	21 30
58	22 06	16 27	23 59	4 15	22 09
59	21 24	15 06	26 08	5 51	22 51
60	20♑39	13♒35	28♈50	7♊38	23♊38

18h 32m 0s	7 ♑ 21		278° 0' 0"		
LAT.	11	12	ASC	2	3
0	5♒38	6♓14	8♈43	10♉25	9♊40
5	5 04	5 39	9 03	11 21	10 18
10	4 30	5 01	9 26	12 19	10 57
15	3 53	4 20	9 51	13 22	11 37
20	3 14	3 35	10 20	14 31	12 20
21	3 06	3 25	10 26	14 45	12 29
22	2 58	3 15	10 33	15 00	12 38
23	2 50	3 05	10 39	15 15	12 48
24	2 41	2 55	10 46	15 31	12 57
25	2 32	2 44	10 54	15 47	13 07
26	2 23	2 33	11 01	16 04	13 17
27	2 14	2 22	11 09	16 20	13 27
28	2 05	2 10	11 18	16 38	13 37
29	1 55	1 58	11 26	16 56	13 47
30	1 45	1 45	11 35	17 14	13 58
31	1 35	1 32	11 45	17 33	14 09
32	1 25	1 19	11 55	17 53	14 20
33	1 14	1 05	12 05	18 13	14 32
34	1 03	0 50	12 16	18 34	14 44
35	0 52	0 35	12 28	18 56	14 56
36	0 41	0 20	12 40	19 19	15 09
37	0 29	0 03	12 53	19 42	15 22
38	0 16	29♒46	13 07	20 07	15 35
39	0 03	29 28	13 21	20 33	15 49
40	29♑50	29 10	13 37	20 59	16 03
41	29 36	28 50	13 54	21 27	16 18
42	29 22	28 29	14 12	21 56	16 34
43	29 07	28 07	14 31	22 27	16 50
44	28 51	27 44	14 52	22 59	17 06
45	28 35	27 20	15 15	23 33	17 24
46	28 18	26 54	15 40	24 09	17 42
47	28 00	26 26	16 07	24 47	18 01
48	27 41	25 57	16 36	25 27	18 22
49	27 21	25 25	17 09	26 09	18 43
50	27 00	24 51	17 46	26 55	19 05
51	26 38	24 15	18 27	27 43	19 29
52	26 14	23 35	19 13	28 35	19 54
53	25 49	22 53	20 05	29 31	20 20
54	25 22	22 06	21 05	0♊31	20 49
55	24 53	21 15	22 15	1 37	21 19
56	24 21	20 19	23 36	2 48	21 52
57	23 47	19 17	25 12	4 07	22 28
58	23 10	18 07	27 07	5 33	23 06
59	22 29	16 49	29 28	7 09	23 49
60	21♑44	15♒20	2♉24	8♊56	24♊36

18h 36m 0s	8 ♑ 16		279° 0' 0"		
LAT.	11	12	ASC	2	3
0	6♒37	7♓18	9♈48	11♉26	10♊36
5	6 03	6 44	10 11	12 23	11 14
10	5 29	6 08	10 36	13 22	11 53
15	4 53	5 28	11 04	14 26	12 34
20	4 14	4 45	11 37	15 36	13 17
21	4 06	4 36	11 44	15 51	13 26
22	3 58	4 26	11 51	16 06	13 35
23	3 50	4 17	11 59	16 21	13 45
24	3 41	4 07	12 07	16 37	13 54
25	3 33	3 56	12 15	16 54	14 04
26	3 24	3 46	12 23	17 10	14 14
27	3 15	3 35	12 32	17 27	14 24
28	3 06	3 23	12 42	17 45	14 34
29	2 56	3 12	12 51	18 03	14 44
30	2 46	3 00	13 01	18 22	14 55
31	2 36	2 47	13 12	18 41	15 06
32	2 26	2 34	13 23	19 01	15 18
33	2 16	2 21	13 35	19 22	15 29
34	2 05	2 07	13 47	19 43	15 41
35	1 54	1 52	14 00	20 05	15 53
36	1 42	1 37	14 14	20 28	16 06
37	1 30	1 22	14 28	20 52	16 19
38	1 18	1 05	14 43	21 17	16 32
39	1 05	0 48	15 00	21 43	16 46
40	0 52	0 30	15 17	22 10	17 01
41	0 38	0 11	15 36	22 38	17 16
42	0 24	29♒51	15 56	23 08	17 31
43	0 09	29 30	16 18	23 39	17 47
44	29♑54	29 07	16 41	24 11	18 04
45	29 37	28 44	17 06	24 45	18 22
46	29 20	28 19	17 34	25 21	18 40
47	29 03	27 52	18 04	26 00	18 59
48	28 44	27 24	18 37	26 40	19 19
49	28 24	26 53	19 14	27 23	19 40
50	28 03	26 20	19 54	28 09	20 03
51	27 41	25 45	20 40	28 58	20 26
52	27 18	25 07	21 31	29 50	20 51
53	26 53	24 26	22 28	0♊46	21 18
54	26 26	23 41	23 34	1 47	21 46
55	25 57	22 51	24 51	2 53	22 17
56	25 26	21 57	26 19	4 04	22 50
57	24 52	20 56	28 04	5 23	23 25
58	24 15	19 49	0♉09	6 49	24 04
59	23 35	18 33	2 40	8 25	24 46
60	22♑50	17♒07	5♉47	10♊12	25♊33

18h 40m 0s — 280° 0' 0" — 9 ♑ 11

LAT.	11	12	ASC	2	3
0	7♒35	8♓22	10♈53	12♉27	11♊32
5	7 02	7 49	11 18	13 24	12 10
10	6 28	7 15	11 46	14 25	12 50
15	5 53	6 37	12 18	15 30	13 31
20	5 15	5 56	12 54	16 41	14 14
21	5 07	5 47	13 01	16 56	14 23
22	4 59	5 38	13 10	17 11	14 32
23	4 50	5 28	13 18	17 27	14 41
24	4 42	5 19	13 27	17 43	14 51
25	4 33	5 09	13 36	18 00	15 01
26	4 25	4 59	13 45	18 17	15 11
27	4 16	4 48	13 55	18 34	15 21
28	4 07	4 37	14 05	18 52	15 31
29	3 57	4 26	14 16	19 10	15 42
30	3 48	4 15	14 27	19 29	15 52
31	3 38	4 03	14 39	19 49	16 03
32	3 28	3 50	14 51	20 09	16 15
33	3 17	3 37	15 04	20 30	16 26
34	3 06	3 24	15 17	20 52	16 38
35	2 55	3 10	15 32	21 14	16 51
36	2 44	2 55	15 47	21 37	17 03
37	2 32	2 40	16 03	22 02	17 16
38	2 20	2 24	16 20	22 27	17 30
39	2 07	2 08	16 38	22 53	17 44
40	1 54	1 51	16 57	23 20	17 58
41	1 41	1 32	17 18	23 49	18 13
42	1 26	1 13	17 40	24 18	18 28
43	1 12	0 53	18 04	24 50	18 45
44	0 56	0 31	18 29	25 22	19 01
45	0 40	0 09	18 57	25 57	19 19
46	0 23	29♒44	19 28	26 33	19 37
47	0 06	29 19	20 01	27 12	19 56
48	29♑47	28 51	20 37	27 53	20 17
49	29 28	28 22	21 17	28 36	20 38
50	29 07	27 50	22 01	29 22	21 00
51	28 45	27 16	22 51	0♊11	21 24
52	28 22	26 40	23 46	1 04	21 49
53	27 57	26 00	24 49	2 00	22 15
54	27 30	25 16	26 01	3 01	22 44
55	27 02	24 28	27 23	4 07	23 14
56	26 31	23 36	28 58	5 19	23 47
57	25 57	22 37	0♉51	6 38	24 22
58	25 21	21 32	3 04	8 04	25 01
59	24 41	20 19	5 44	9 40	25 43
60	23♑56	18♒55	9♉01	11♊27	26♊30

18h 44m 0s — 281° 0' 0" — 10 ♑ 07

LAT.	11	12	ASC	2	3
0	8♒34	9♓26	11♈58	13♉27	12♊28
5	8 02	8 55	12 26	14 26	13 07
10	7 28	8 22	12 56	15 28	13 46
15	6 53	7 46	13 31	16 34	14 27
20	6 15	7 06	14 10	17 46	15 11
21	6 08	6 58	14 19	18 01	15 20
22	5 59	6 49	14 28	18 16	15 29
23	5 51	6 40	14 37	18 32	15 38
24	5 43	6 31	14 47	18 49	15 48
25	5 34	6 21	14 56	19 06	15 57
26	5 26	6 12	15 07	19 23	16 07
27	5 17	6 02	15 18	19 40	16 17
28	5 08	5 51	15 29	19 59	16 28
29	4 59	5 41	15 40	20 17	16 38
30	4 49	5 30	15 53	20 36	16 49
31	4 39	5 18	16 05	20 56	17 00
32	4 29	5 06	16 19	21 17	17 12
33	4 19	4 54	16 33	21 38	17 23
34	4 08	4 41	16 48	22 00	17 35
35	3 57	4 28	17 03	22 22	17 48
36	3 46	4 14	17 20	22 46	18 00
37	3 34	3 59	17 37	23 10	18 13
38	3 22	3 44	17 56	23 36	18 27
39	3 10	3 28	18 15	24 02	18 41
40	2 57	3 12	18 36	24 30	18 55
41	2 43	2 54	18 59	24 58	19 10
42	2 29	2 36	19 23	25 29	19 26
43	2 15	2 16	19 49	26 00	19 42
44	1 59	1 56	20 17	26 33	19 59
45	1 43	1 34	20 47	27 08	20 16
46	1 27	1 11	21 20	27 45	20 34
47	1 09	0 46	21 56	28 23	20 54
48	0 51	0 20	22 35	29 05	21 14
49	0 31	29♒52	23 19	29 48	21 35
50	0 11	29 21	24 06	0♊34	21 57
51	29♑49	28 49	25 00	1 24	22 21
52	29 26	28 13	26 00	2 17	22 46
53	29 01	27 35	27 07	3 13	23 12
54	28 35	26 53	28 24	4 15	23 41
55	28 07	26 07	29 52	5 21	24 11
56	27 36	25 16	1♉33	6 33	24 44
57	27 03	24 20	3 32	7 52	25 19
58	26 27	23 17	5 52	9 18	25 58
59	25 47	22 06	8 40	10 54	26 40
60	25♑03	20♒45	12♉04	12♊40	27♊26

18h 48m 0s — 282° 0' 0" — 11 ♑ 02

LAT.	11	12	ASC	2	3
0	9♒34	10♓30	13♈03	14♉28	13♊24
5	9 01	10 00	13 33	15 27	14 03
10	8 28	9 29	14 06	16 30	14 42
15	7 53	8 55	14 44	17 37	15 23
20	7 16	8 17	15 27	18 50	16 07
21	7 08	8 09	15 36	19 05	16 16
22	7 00	8 01	15 46	19 21	16 25
23	6 52	7 52	15 56	19 37	16 35
24	6 44	7 43	16 06	19 54	16 44
25	6 36	7 34	16 17	20 11	16 54
26	6 27	7 25	16 28	20 28	17 04
27	6 18	7 16	16 40	20 46	17 14
28	6 09	7 06	16 52	21 05	17 24
29	6 00	6 56	17 05	21 24	17 35
30	5 51	6 45	17 18	21 43	17 46
31	5 41	6 34	17 32	22 03	17 57
32	5 31	6 23	17 46	22 24	18 08
33	5 21	6 11	18 01	22 45	18 20
34	5 10	5 59	18 17	23 07	18 32
35	5 00	5 46	18 34	23 30	18 44
36	4 48	5 33	18 52	23 54	18 57
37	4 37	5 19	19 11	24 19	19 10
38	4 25	5 04	19 31	24 44	19 24
39	4 12	4 49	19 52	25 11	19 38
40	4 00	4 33	20 15	25 39	19 52
41	3 46	4 17	20 39	26 08	20 07
42	3 32	3 59	21 05	26 38	20 22
43	3 18	3 40	21 33	27 10	20 39
44	3 03	3 21	22 03	27 43	20 55
45	2 47	3 00	22 36	28 18	21 13
46	2 31	2 38	23 11	28 55	21 31
47	2 13	2 14	23 50	29 34	21 50
48	1 55	1 49	24 32	0♊16	22 11
49	1 36	1 22	25 18	0 59	22 32
50	1 15	0 53	26 10	1 46	22 54
51	0 54	0 22	27 07	2 36	23 18
52	0 31	29♒48	28 11	3 29	23 43
53	0 07	29 11	29 22	4 26	24 09
54	29♑40	28 31	0♉44	5 27	24 37
55	29 12	27 46	2 17	6 33	25 08
56	28 42	26 58	4 04	7 46	25 40
57	28 09	26 04	6 08	9 04	26 16
58	27 33	25 03	8 35	10 31	26 54
59	26 54	23 55	11 29	12 06	27 36
60	26♑10	22♒37	14♉57	13♊52	28♊22

18h 52m 0s — 283° 0' 0" — 11 ♑ 58

LAT.	11	12	ASC	2	3
0	10♒33	11♓34	14♈07	15♉28	14♊20
5	10 01	11 06	14 40	16 28	14 59
10	9 28	10 36	15 16	17 32	15 38
15	8 54	10 04	15 57	18 40	16 20
20	8 17	9 28	16 43	19 54	17 03
21	8 10	9 21	16 53	20 10	17 12
22	8 02	9 13	17 03	20 26	17 22
23	7 54	9 05	17 14	20 42	17 31
24	7 46	8 56	17 25	20 59	17 41
25	7 37	8 48	17 37	21 16	17 51
26	7 29	8 39	17 49	21 34	18 00
27	7 20	8 30	18 02	21 52	18 11
28	7 11	8 20	18 15	22 10	18 21
29	7 02	8 11	18 28	22 30	18 32
30	6 53	8 01	18 43	22 49	18 42
31	6 43	7 50	18 58	23 09	18 54
32	6 33	7 40	19 13	23 30	19 05
33	6 23	7 28	19 30	23 52	19 17
34	6 13	7 17	19 47	24 14	19 29
35	6 02	7 05	20 05	24 38	19 41
36	5 51	6 52	20 24	25 01	19 54
37	5 40	6 39	20 44	25 26	20 07
38	5 28	6 25	21 06	25 52	20 20
39	5 15	6 11	21 29	26 19	20 34
40	5 03	5 56	21 53	26 47	20 49
41	4 50	5 40	22 19	27 16	21 04
42	4 36	5 23	22 47	27 47	21 19
43	4 22	5 05	23 17	28 19	21 35
44	4 07	4 46	23 49	28 53	21 52
45	3 51	4 26	24 24	29 28	22 10
46	3 35	4 05	25 01	0♊05	22 28
47	3 17	3 43	25 42	0 45	22 47
48	2 59	3 19	26 27	1 26	23 07
49	2 40	2 53	27 17	2 10	23 28
50	2 20	2 25	28 11	2 57	23 51
51	1 59	1 55	29 12	3 47	24 14
52	1 36	1 23	0♉19	4 40	24 39
53	1 12	0 48	1 35	5 37	25 06
54	0 46	0 09	3 00	6 39	25 34
55	0 18	29♒27	4 38	7 45	26 04
56	29♑49	28 40	6 30	8 57	26 37
57	29 16	27 49	8 39	10 16	27 12
58	28 41	26 51	11 11	11 42	27 50
59	28 02	25 45	14 09	13 17	28 32
60	27♑18	24♒31	17♉41	15♊03	29♊18

18h 56m 0s — 284° 0' 0" — 12 ♑ 53

LAT.	11	12	ASC	2	3
0	11♒32	12♓39	15♈12	16♉28	15♊16
5	11 01	12 12	15 48	17 29	15 55
10	10 29	11 44	16 26	18 34	16 34
15	9 55	11 13	17 09	19 43	17 16
20	9 18	10 40	17 59	20 58	18 00
21	9 11	10 32	18 10	21 14	18 09
22	9 03	10 25	18 21	21 30	18 18
23	8 55	10 17	18 32	21 46	18 27
24	8 47	10 09	18 44	22 03	18 37
25	8 39	10 01	18 57	22 21	18 47
26	8 31	9 53	19 10	22 39	18 57
27	8 22	9 44	19 23	22 57	19 07
28	8 13	9 35	19 37	23 16	19 17
29	8 04	9 26	19 52	23 35	19 28
30	7 55	9 17	20 07	23 55	19 39
31	7 45	9 07	20 23	24 15	19 50
32	7 36	8 57	20 40	24 37	20 01
33	7 26	8 46	20 57	24 58	20 13
34	7 15	8 35	21 16	25 21	20 25
35	7 05	8 24	21 35	25 44	20 37
36	6 54	8 12	21 55	26 09	20 50
37	6 43	7 59	22 17	26 34	21 03
38	6 31	7 46	22 40	27 00	21 17
39	6 19	7 32	23 04	27 27	21 31
40	6 06	7 18	23 30	27 55	21 45
41	5 53	7 03	23 58	28 25	22 00
42	5 40	6 47	24 27	28 55	22 16
43	5 25	6 30	24 59	29 28	22 32
44	5 11	6 12	25 33	0♊02	22 49
45	4 55	5 54	26 10	0 37	23 06
46	4 39	5 33	26 50	1 15	23 24
47	4 22	5 12	27 34	1 54	23 44
48	4 04	4 49	28 21	2 36	24 04
49	3 45	4 25	29 13	3 20	24 25
50	3 25	3 58	0♉11	4 07	24 47
51	3 04	3 30	1 14	4 57	25 10
52	2 42	2 59	2 25	5 50	25 35
53	2 18	2 26	3 44	6 47	26 02
54	1 53	1 49	5 14	7 49	26 30
55	1 25	1 09	6 55	8 55	27 00
56	0 55	0 24	8 51	10 08	27 32
57	0 23	29♒35	11 05	11 26	28 07
58	29♑48	28 40	13 40	12 52	28 45
59	29 10	27 37	16 42	14 27	29 27
60	28♑27	26♒26	20♉16	16♊12	0♋13

19h 0m 0s — 285° 0' 0" — 13 ♑ 49

LAT.	11	12	ASC	2	3
0	12♒32	13♓43	16♈17	17♉28	16♊11
5	12 01	13 18	16 55	18 30	16 50
10	11 29	12 52	17 36	19 36	17 30
15	10 56	12 23	18 22	20 45	18 12
20	10 20	11 51	19 15	22 01	18 56
21	10 12	11 44	19 26	22 17	19 05
22	10 05	11 37	19 38	22 34	19 14
23	9 57	11 30	19 50	22 50	19 24
24	9 49	11 23	20 03	23 08	19 33
25	9 41	11 15	20 16	23 25	19 43
26	9 33	11 07	20 30	23 43	19 53
27	9 24	10 59	20 44	24 02	20 03
28	9 15	10 51	20 59	24 21	20 14
29	9 07	10 42	21 15	24 40	20 24
30	8 57	10 33	21 31	25 00	20 35
31	8 48	10 24	21 48	25 21	20 46
32	8 39	10 14	22 06	25 42	20 58
33	8 29	10 04	22 24	26 04	21 09
34	8 18	9 54	22 44	26 27	21 21
35	8 08	9 43	23 04	26 51	21 34
36	7 57	9 32	23 26	27 15	21 46
37	7 46	9 20	23 49	27 40	22 00
38	7 34	9 08	24 13	28 07	22 13
39	7 22	8 55	24 39	28 34	22 27
40	7 10	8 41	25 06	29 03	22 41
41	6 57	8 27	25 36	29 32	22 56
42	6 44	8 12	26 07	0♊03	23 12
43	6 30	7 56	26 41	0 36	23 28
44	6 15	7 39	27 17	1 10	23 45
45	6 00	7 21	27 56	1 46	24 02
46	5 44	7 02	28 38	2 23	24 21
47	5 27	6 42	29 23	3 03	24 40
48	5 09	6 20	0♉13	3 45	25 00
49	4 51	5 57	1 08	4 29	25 21
50	4 31	5 32	2 08	5 16	25 43
51	4 10	5 05	3 15	6 06	26 07
52	3 48	4 36	4 29	7 00	26 31
53	3 24	4 04	5 51	7 57	26 58
54	2 59	3 30	7 24	8 59	27 26
55	2 32	2 51	9 09	10 05	27 56
56	2 03	2 09	11 08	11 17	28 28
57	1 31	1 22	13 25	12 35	29 03
58	0 56	0 30	16 03	14 01	29 41
59	0 18	29♒31	19 08	15 35	0♋22
60	29♑36	28♒24	22♉43	17♊20	1♋07

19h 4m 0s — 286° 0' 0" — 14 ♑ 44

LAT.	11	12	ASC	2	3
0	13♒32	14♓48	17♈21	18♉28	17♊07
5	13 01	14 25	18 01	19 31	17 46
10	12 30	14 00	18 45	20 37	18 26
15	11 57	13 33	19 34	21 48	19 08
20	11 22	13 03	20 30	23 04	19 52
21	11 14	12 56	20 42	23 21	20 01
22	11 07	12 50	20 55	23 37	20 10
23	10 59	12 43	21 08	23 54	20 20
24	10 51	12 36	21 22	24 12	20 29
25	10 43	12 29	21 36	24 29	20 39
26	10 35	12 22	21 50	24 48	20 49
27	10 27	12 14	22 05	25 06	20 59
28	10 18	12 06	22 21	25 25	21 10
29	10 09	11 58	22 38	25 45	21 20
30	10 00	11 50	22 55	26 05	21 31
31	9 51	11 41	23 13	26 26	21 42
32	9 42	11 32	23 31	26 48	21 54
33	9 32	11 22	23 51	27 10	22 05
34	9 22	11 13	24 12	27 33	22 17
35	9 11	11 03	24 33	27 57	22 30
36	9 01	10 52	24 56	28 21	22 43
37	8 50	10 41	25 20	28 47	22 56
38	8 38	10 29	25 46	29 13	23 09
39	8 26	10 17	26 13	29 41	23 23
40	8 14	10 04	26 42	0♊09	23 38
41	8 01	9 51	27 13	0 39	23 53
42	7 48	9 37	27 46	1 11	24 08
43	7 34	9 22	28 21	1 43	24 24
44	7 20	9 06	28 59	2 17	24 41
45	7 05	8 49	29 40	2 53	24 58
46	6 49	8 31	0♉24	3 31	25 17
47	6 32	8 12	1 12	4 11	25 36
48	6 15	7 52	2 04	4 53	25 56
49	5 57	7 30	3 01	5 37	26 17
50	5 37	7 07	4 04	6 25	26 39
51	5 17	6 41	5 13	7 15	27 02
52	4 55	6 14	6 29	8 08	27 27
53	4 31	5 44	7 55	9 06	27 53
54	4 06	5 11	9 31	10 07	28 21
55	3 40	4 35	11 18	11 14	28 51
56	3 11	3 55	13 21	12 25	29 23
57	2 39	3 11	15 41	13 44	29 58
58	2 05	2 22	18 21	15 09	0♋36
59	1 28	1 26	21 26	16 43	1 17
60	0♒46	0♓22	25♉02	18♊27	2♋02

19h 8m 0s — 287° 0' 0" — 15 ♑ 40

LAT.	11	12	ASC	2	3
0	14♒32	15♓53	18♈26	19♉27	18♊02
5	14 02	15 31	19 08	20 31	18 42
10	13 31	15 08	19 55	21 38	19 22
15	12 58	14 43	20 46	22 50	20 04
20	12 24	14 15	21 45	24 07	20 48
21	12 16	14 09	21 58	24 24	20 57
22	12 09	14 03	22 12	24 40	21 06
23	12 01	13 56	22 26	24 58	21 16
24	11 54	13 50	22 40	25 15	21 25
25	11 46	13 43	22 55	25 33	21 35
26	11 38	13 36	23 10	25 51	21 45
27	11 29	13 29	23 26	26 10	21 55
28	11 21	13 22	23 42	26 30	22 06
29	11 12	13 14	24 00	26 50	22 16
30	11 03	13 06	24 18	27 10	22 27
31	10 54	12 58	24 37	27 31	22 38
32	10 45	12 50	24 56	27 53	22 50
33	10 35	12 41	25 17	28 15	23 01
34	10 25	12 32	25 39	28 38	23 13
35	10 15	12 23	26 02	29 02	23 26
36	10 05	12 13	26 26	29 27	23 39
37	9 54	12 02	26 51	29 53	23 52
38	9 42	11 51	27 18	0♊19	24 05
39	9 31	11 40	27 47	0 47	24 19
40	9 19	11 28	28 17	1 16	24 34
41	9 06	11 16	28 49	1 46	24 49
42	8 53	11 02	29 23	2 17	25 04
43	8 39	10 48	0♉00	2 50	25 20
44	8 25	10 34	0 40	3 24	25 37
45	8 10	10 18	1 22	4 00	25 54
46	7 55	10 01	2 08	4 38	26 13
47	7 38	9 43	2 58	5 18	26 32
48	7 21	9 24	3 53	6 00	26 52
49	7 03	9 04	4 52	6 45	27 13
50	6 44	8 42	5 57	7 32	27 35
51	6 23	8 18	7 08	8 23	27 58
52	6 02	7 52	8 28	9 16	28 23
53	5 39	7 24	9 56	10 14	28 49
54	5 14	6 54	11 34	11 15	29 17
55	4 47	6 20	13 24	12 21	29 47
56	4 19	5 43	15 29	13 33	0♋19
57	3 48	5 01	17 51	14 51	0 53
58	3 14	4 15	20 33	16 16	1 30
59	2 37	3 22	23 39	17 49	2 11
60	1♒56	2♓22	27♉14	19♊32	2♋56

19h 12m 0s — 288° 0' 0" — 16 ♑ 36

LAT.	11	12	ASC	2	3
0	15♒32	16♓57	19♈30	20♉26	18♊58
5	15 03	16 37	20 15	21 31	19 37
10	14 32	16 16	21 04	22 39	20 18
15	14 00	15 53	21 58	23 51	20 59
20	13 26	15 27	23 00	25 10	21 43
21	13 19	15 21	23 14	25 26	21 53
22	13 11	15 16	23 28	25 43	22 02
23	13 04	15 10	23 43	26 01	22 11
24	12 56	15 04	23 58	26 18	22 21
25	12 48	14 57	24 13	26 36	22 31
26	12 40	14 51	24 29	26 55	22 41
27	12 32	14 45	24 46	27 14	22 51
28	12 24	14 38	25 03	27 34	23 02
29	12 15	14 31	25 22	27 54	23 12
30	12 07	14 23	25 40	28 14	23 23
31	11 58	14 16	26 00	28 35	23 34
32	11 48	14 08	26 21	28 57	23 46
33	11 39	14 00	26 43	29 20	23 57
34	11 29	13 52	27 05	29 43	24 09
35	11 19	13 43	27 29	0♊07	24 22
36	11 09	13 34	27 54	0 32	24 34
37	10 58	13 24	28 21	0 58	24 48
38	10 47	13 14	28 49	1 25	25 01
39	10 35	13 03	29 19	1 53	25 15
40	10 23	12 52	29 50	2 22	25 29
41	10 11	12 41	0♉24	2 52	25 44
42	9 58	12 28	1 00	3 23	26 00
43	9 45	12 15	1 38	3 56	26 16
44	9 31	12 02	2 20	4 31	26 33
45	9 16	11 47	3 04	5 07	26 50
46	9 01	11 31	3 52	5 45	27 08
47	8 44	11 15	4 44	6 25	27 27
48	8 27	10 57	5 40	7 07	27 47
49	8 09	10 38	6 41	7 52	28 08
50	7 50	10 18	7 48	8 39	28 30
51	7 30	9 56	9 02	9 30	28 53
52	7 09	9 32	10 23	10 23	29 18
53	6 46	9 05	11 53	11 21	29 44
54	6 22	8 37	13 34	12 22	0♋12
55	5 56	8 05	15 26	13 28	0 42
56	5 28	7 31	17 33	14 39	1 13
57	4 57	6 52	19 56	15 57	1 48
58	4 24	6 09	22 39	17 21	2 25
59	3 48	5 20	25 45	18 54	3 05
60	3♒07	4♓24	29♉19	20♊36	3♋50

19h 16m 0s — 289° 0' 0" — 17 ♑ 32

LAT.	11	12	ASC	2	3
0	16♒33	18♓02	20♈34	21♉26	19♊53
5	16 04	17 44	21 21	22 31	20 33
10	15 34	17 24	22 13	23 40	21 13
15	15 02	17 03	23 10	24 53	21 55
20	14 28	16 39	24 15	26 12	22 39
21	14 21	16 34	24 29	26 29	22 48
22	14 14	16 29	24 44	26 46	22 58
23	14 07	16 23	24 59	27 03	23 07
24	13 59	16 18	25 15	27 21	23 17
25	13 51	16 12	25 31	27 39	23 27
26	13 44	16 06	25 48	27 58	23 37
27	13 36	16 00	26 06	28 17	23 47
28	13 27	15 54	26 24	28 37	23 57
29	13 19	15 47	26 43	28 57	24 08
30	13 10	15 41	27 03	29 18	24 19
31	13 01	15 34	27 23	29 39	24 30
32	12 52	15 27	27 45	0♊01	24 41
33	12 43	15 19	28 08	0 24	24 53
34	12 33	15 11	28 31	0 48	25 05
35	12 23	15 03	28 56	1 12	25 17
36	12 13	14 55	29 23	1 37	25 30
37	12 03	14 46	29 50	2 03	25 43
38	11 52	14 37	0♉19	2 30	25 57
39	11 40	14 27	0 50	2 58	26 11
40	11 29	14 17	1 23	3 27	26 25
41	11 16	14 06	1 58	3 57	26 40
42	11 04	13 55	2 36	4 29	26 55
43	10 50	13 43	3 15	5 02	27 12
44	10 36	13 30	3 58	5 37	27 28
45	10 22	13 17	4 44	6 13	27 46
46	10 07	13 02	5 34	6 51	28 04
47	9 51	12 47	6 27	7 31	28 23
48	9 34	12 31	7 25	8 14	28 43
49	9 16	12 13	8 28	8 58	29 04
50	8 58	11 54	9 37	9 46	29 25
51	8 38	11 34	10 53	10 36	29 49
52	8 17	11 11	12 16	11 29	0♋13
53	7 55	10 47	13 48	12 27	0 39
54	7 31	10 21	15 31	13 28	1 07
55	7 05	9 52	17 25	14 34	1 36
56	6 37	9 20	19 33	15 45	2 08
57	6 07	8 44	21 57	17 02	2 42
58	5 34	8 04	24 41	18 26	3 19
59	4 58	7 18	27 46	19 58	3 59
60	4♒19	6♓27	1♊18	21♊40	4♋43

19h 20m 0s — 290° 0' 0" — 18 ♑ 28

LAT.	11	12	ASC	2	3
0	17♒33	19♓07	21♈38	22♉25	20♊49
5	17 05	18 50	22 28	23 31	21 28
10	16 35	18 33	23 21	24 40	22 09
15	16 04	18 13	24 21	25 54	22 50
20	15 31	17 51	25 30	27 14	23 35
21	15 24	17 47	25 44	27 31	23 44
22	15 17	17 42	26 00	27 48	23 53
23	15 10	17 37	26 16	28 06	24 03
24	15 02	17 32	26 32	28 24	24 12
25	14 55	17 27	26 49	28 42	24 22
26	14 47	17 21	27 07	29 01	24 32
27	14 39	17 16	27 25	29 20	24 42
28	14 31	17 10	27 44	29 40	24 53
29	14 23	17 04	28 04	0♊01	25 03
30	14 14	16 58	28 24	0 21	25 14
31	14 05	16 52	28 46	0 43	25 26
32	13 57	16 45	29 08	1 05	25 37
33	13 47	16 38	29 32	1 28	25 49
34	13 38	16 31	29 57	1 52	26 01
35	13 28	16 24	0♉23	2 16	26 13
36	13 18	16 16	0 50	2 41	26 26
37	13 08	16 08	1 19	3 07	26 39
38	12 57	16 00	1 49	3 34	26 52
39	12 46	15 51	2 21	4 03	27 06
40	12 34	15 41	2 55	4 32	27 21
41	12 22	15 32	3 32	5 02	27 35
42	12 09	15 21	4 10	5 34	27 51
43	11 56	15 10	4 51	6 07	28 07
44	11 43	14 59	5 35	6 42	28 24
45	11 28	14 46	6 23	7 18	28 41
46	11 13	14 33	7 14	7 57	28 59
47	10 58	14 19	8 09	8 37	29 18
48	10 41	14 04	9 09	9 19	29 38
49	10 24	13 48	10 13	10 04	29 59
50	10 05	13 31	11 24	10 51	0♋21
51	9 46	13 12	12 41	11 41	0 44
52	9 25	12 52	14 06	12 35	1 08
53	9 03	12 30	15 40	13 32	1 34
54	8 40	12 06	17 24	14 33	2 01
55	8 14	11 39	19 20	15 39	2 31
56	7 47	11 10	21 29	16 50	3 02
57	7 17	10 37	23 54	18 07	3 36
58	6 45	10 00	26 37	19 30	4 13
59	6 10	9 18	29 42	21 01	4 53
60	5♒31	8♓31	3♊10	22♊42	5♋36

19h 24m 0s — 291° 0' 0" — 19 ♑ 24

LAT.	11	12	ASC	2	3
0	18♒34	20♓12	22♈42	23♉23	21♊44
5	18 06	19 57	23 34	24 31	22 24
10	17 37	19 41	24 30	25 41	23 04
15	17 06	19 23	25 33	26 55	23 46
20	16 34	19 04	26 44	28 16	24 30
21	16 27	19 00	26 59	28 33	24 39
22	16 20	18 55	27 15	28 50	24 49
23	16 13	18 51	27 32	29 08	24 58
24	16 06	18 46	27 49	29 26	25 08
25	15 58	18 42	28 06	29 45	25 18
26	15 51	18 37	28 25	0♊04	25 28
27	15 43	18 32	28 44	0 23	25 38
28	15 35	18 27	29 04	0 43	25 48
29	15 27	18 21	29 24	1 04	25 59
30	15 18	18 16	29 46	1 25	26 10
31	15 10	18 10	0♉08	1 46	26 21
32	15 01	18 04	0 31	2 09	26 32
33	14 52	17 58	0 56	2 32	26 44
34	14 43	17 52	1 21	2 55	26 56
35	14 33	17 45	1 48	3 20	27 08
36	14 23	17 38	2 17	3 45	27 21
37	14 13	17 31	2 46	4 11	27 34
38	14 02	17 23	3 18	4 39	27 48
39	13 51	17 15	3 51	5 07	28 02
40	13 40	17 06	4 26	5 36	28 16
41	13 28	16 58	5 04	6 07	28 31
42	13 16	16 48	5 44	6 39	28 46
43	13 03	16 38	6 26	7 12	29 02
44	12 49	16 28	7 12	7 47	29 19
45	12 35	16 17	8 00	8 23	29 36
46	12 21	16 05	8 53	9 01	29 54
47	12 05	15 52	9 49	9 42	0♋13
48	11 49	15 39	10 50	10 24	0 33
49	11 32	15 24	11 57	11 09	0 54
50	11 14	15 08	13 09	11 56	1 15
51	10 54	14 51	14 28	12 46	1 38
52	10 34	14 33	15 54	13 40	2 03
53	10 12	14 13	17 29	14 37	2 28
54	9 49	13 51	19 15	15 38	2 56
55	9 24	13 27	21 11	16 43	3 25
56	8 57	13 00	23 21	17 54	3 56
57	8 28	12 30	25 46	19 10	4 30
58	7 56	11 57	28 29	20 33	5 06
59	7 22	11 19	1♊32	22 03	5 46
60	6♒43	10♓36	4♊58	23♊43	6♋29

19h 28m 0s — 292° 0' 0" — 20 ♑ 20

LAT.	11	12	ASC	2	3
0	19♒35	21♓17	23♈46	24♉22	22♊39
5	19 07	21 04	24 40	25 30	23 19
10	18 39	20 50	25 38	26 41	23 59
15	18 09	20 34	26 43	27 56	24 41
20	17 37	20 16	27 57	29 17	25 26
21	17 30	20 13	28 14	29 34	25 35
22	17 23	20 09	28 30	29 52	25 44
23	17 16	20 05	28 47	0♊10	25 54
24	17 09	20 01	29 05	0 28	26 03
25	17 02	19 57	29 23	0 47	26 13
26	16 54	19 52	29 42	1 06	26 23
27	16 47	19 48	0♉02	1 25	26 33
28	16 39	19 43	0 23	1 45	26 44
29	16 31	19 39	0 44	2 06	26 54
30	16 23	19 34	1 06	2 27	27 05
31	16 14	19 29	1 29	2 49	27 16
32	16 06	19 23	1 54	3 12	27 28
33	15 57	19 18	2 19	3 35	27 39
34	15 48	19 12	2 45	3 58	27 51
35	15 38	19 06	3 13	4 23	28 04
36	15 28	19 00	3 42	4 49	28 16
37	15 18	18 53	4 13	5 15	28 29
38	15 08	18 46	4 46	5 42	28 43
39	14 57	18 39	5 20	6 11	28 57
40	14 46	18 32	5 56	6 40	29 11
41	14 34	18 24	6 35	7 11	29 26
42	14 22	18 15	7 16	7 43	29 41
43	14 09	18 07	8 00	8 16	29 57
44	13 56	17 57	8 46	8 51	0♋14
45	13 42	17 47	9 36	9 27	0 31
46	13 28	17 37	10 30	10 06	0 49
47	13 13	17 25	11 28	10 46	1 08
48	12 57	17 13	12 30	11 28	1 28
49	12 40	17 00	13 38	12 13	1 48
50	12 22	16 46	14 52	13 00	2 10
51	12 03	16 31	16 12	13 51	2 33
52	11 43	16 15	17 39	14 44	2 57
53	11 22	15 57	19 16	15 41	3 23
54	10 59	15 37	21 02	16 41	3 50
55	10 34	15 16	22 59	17 47	4 19
56	10 08	14 52	25 10	18 57	4 50
57	9 39	14 25	27 35	20 12	5 24
58	9 08	13 55	0♊16	21 35	6 00
59	8 34	13 21	3 18	23 04	6 39
60	7♒57	12♓43	6♊41	24♊43	7♋22

19h 32m 0s — 293° 0' 0" — 21 ♑ 17

LAT.	11	12	ASC	2	3
0	20♒36	22♓23	24♈50	25♉21	23♊34
5	20 09	22 11	25 46	26 29	24 14
10	19 41	21 58	26 47	27 41	24 55
15	19 12	21 44	27 54	28 56	25 37
20	18 40	21 29	29 11	0♊18	26 21
21	18 34	21 26	29 28	0 36	26 30
22	18 27	21 22	29 45	0 53	26 39
23	18 20	21 19	0♉03	1 11	26 49
24	18 13	21 15	0 21	1 30	26 59
25	18 06	21 12	0 40	1 48	27 08
26	17 59	21 08	1 00	2 08	27 18
27	17 51	21 04	1 20	2 27	27 29
28	17 43	21 00	1 41	2 48	27 39
29	17 36	20 56	2 03	3 08	27 50
30	17 28	20 52	2 26	3 30	28 01
31	17 19	20 47	2 50	3 52	28 12
32	17 11	20 42	3 15	4 14	28 23
33	17 02	20 38	3 41	4 37	28 35
34	16 53	20 33	4 09	5 01	28 47
35	16 44	20 27	4 37	5 26	28 59
36	16 34	20 22	5 08	5 52	29 12
37	16 24	20 16	5 39	6 18	29 25
38	16 14	20 10	6 13	6 45	29 38
39	16 03	20 04	6 48	7 14	29 52
40	15 52	19 57	7 25	7 43	0♋06
41	15 41	19 50	8 05	8 14	0 21
42	15 29	19 43	8 47	8 46	0 36
43	15 16	19 35	9 32	9 20	0 52
44	15 04	19 27	10 20	9 54	1 09
45	14 50	19 18	11 11	10 31	1 26
46	14 36	19 09	12 06	11 09	1 44
47	14 21	18 59	13 05	11 50	2 03
48	14 05	18 48	14 09	12 32	2 22
49	13 48	18 37	15 17	13 17	2 43
50	13 31	18 25	16 32	14 04	3 05
51	13 12	18 11	17 53	14 54	3 27
52	12 53	17 57	19 22	15 47	3 52
53	12 32	17 41	21 00	16 44	4 17
54	12 09	17 24	22 46	17 44	4 44
55	11 45	17 05	24 44	18 49	5 13
56	11 19	16 44	26 55	19 59	5 44
57	10 51	16 20	29 19	21 14	6 17
58	10 21	15 54	2♊00	22 36	6 53
59	9 47	15 24	4 59	24 05	7 32
60	9♒10	14♓50	8♊19	25♊42	8♋14

19h 36m 0s — 294° 0' 0" — 22 ♑ 13

LAT.	11	12	ASC	2	3
0	21♒37	23♓28	25♈53	26♉19	24♊30
5	21 11	23 18	26 51	27 28	25 09
10	20 44	23 07	27 54	28 40	25 50
15	20 15	22 55	29 05	29 57	26 32
20	19 44	22 42	0♉24	1♊19	27 16
21	19 37	22 39	0 41	1 37	27 25
22	19 31	22 36	0 59	1 54	27 35
23	19 24	22 33	1 17	2 13	27 44
24	19 17	22 30	1 36	2 31	27 54
25	19 10	22 27	1 56	2 50	28 04
26	19 03	22 24	2 16	3 09	28 14
27	18 56	22 20	2 37	3 29	28 24
28	18 48	22 17	2 59	3 49	28 34
29	18 40	22 13	3 22	4 10	28 45
30	18 33	22 10	3 46	4 32	28 56
31	18 24	22 06	4 11	4 54	29 07
32	18 16	22 02	4 36	5 16	29 18
33	18 08	21 58	5 03	5 40	29 30
34	17 59	21 53	5 31	6 04	29 42
35	17 50	21 49	6 01	6 29	29 54
36	17 40	21 44	6 32	6 54	0♋07
37	17 30	21 39	7 04	7 21	0 20
38	17 20	21 34	7 39	7 48	0 33
39	17 10	21 29	8 15	8 17	0 47
40	16 59	21 23	8 53	8 46	1 01
41	16 48	21 17	9 34	9 17	1 16
42	16 36	21 11	10 17	9 49	1 31
43	16 24	21 04	11 03	10 23	1 47
44	16 11	20 57	11 52	10 58	2 04
45	15 58	20 49	12 44	11 34	2 21
46	15 44	20 41	13 40	12 13	2 39
47	15 29	20 33	14 40	12 53	2 57
48	15 14	20 24	15 45	13 35	3 17
49	14 58	20 14	16 55	14 20	3 37
50	14 40	20 03	18 11	15 07	3 59
51	14 22	19 52	19 33	15 57	4 22
52	14 03	19 39	21 03	16 50	4 46
53	13 42	19 26	22 41	17 46	5 11
54	13 20	19 11	24 28	18 47	5 38
55	12 57	18 54	26 26	19 51	6 07
56	12 31	18 36	28 36	21 00	6 37
57	12 04	18 16	1♊00	22 15	7 10
58	11 34	17 53	3 40	23 36	7 46
59	11 01	17 28	6 37	25 04	8 24
60	10♒25	16♓59	9♊53	26♊40	9♋06

19h 40m 0s — 295° 0' 0" — 23 ♑ 10

LAT.	11	12	ASC	2	3
0	22♒39	24♓33	26♈57	27♉17	25♊25
5	22 13	24 25	27 57	28 27	26 04
10	21 46	24 16	29 02	29 40	26 45
15	21 18	24 06	0♉15	0♊57	27 27
20	20 48	23 55	1 37	2 20	28 11
21	20 41	23 52	1 54	2 37	28 21
22	20 35	23 50	2 13	2 55	28 30
23	20 28	23 48	2 32	3 13	28 39
24	20 22	23 45	2 51	3 32	28 49
25	20 15	23 42	3 12	3 51	28 59
26	20 08	23 40	3 33	4 11	29 09
27	20 00	23 37	3 54	4 30	29 19
28	19 53	23 34	4 17	4 51	29 29
29	19 46	23 31	4 40	5 12	29 40
30	19 38	23 28	5 05	5 33	29 51
31	19 30	23 25	5 30	5 55	0♋02
32	19 22	23 21	5 57	6 18	0 13
33	19 13	23 18	6 24	6 42	0 25
34	19 05	23 14	6 53	7 06	0 37
35	18 56	23 10	7 24	7 31	0 49
36	18 46	23 07	7 55	7 56	1 02
37	18 37	23 02	8 29	8 23	1 15
38	18 27	22 58	9 04	8 51	1 28
39	18 17	22 54	9 41	9 19	1 42
40	18 06	22 49	10 20	9 49	1 56
41	17 55	22 44	11 02	10 20	2 11
42	17 44	22 39	11 46	10 52	2 26
43	17 32	22 33	12 33	11 25	2 42
44	17 19	22 27	13 23	12 00	2 58
45	17 06	22 21	14 16	12 37	3 15
46	16 52	22 14	15 13	13 15	3 33
47	16 38	22 07	16 14	13 55	3 52
48	16 23	21 59	17 20	14 38	4 11
49	16 07	21 51	18 31	15 22	4 32
50	15 50	21 42	19 47	16 09	4 53
51	15 32	21 33	21 10	16 59	5 16
52	15 13	21 22	22 41	17 52	5 40
53	14 53	21 11	24 19	18 48	6 05
54	14 31	20 58	26 07	19 48	6 32
55	14 08	20 45	28 05	20 52	7 00
56	13 43	20 29	0♊15	22 01	7 31
57	13 16	20 13	2 38	23 15	8 03
58	12 47	19 54	5 16	24 35	8 38
59	12 15	19 32	8 10	26 03	9 17
60	11♒40	19♓08	11♊23	27♊38	9♋58

19h 44m 0s 296° 0' 0" 24 ♑ 06					
LAT.	11	12	ASC	2	3
0	23♒41	25♓38	28♈00	28♉15	26♊20
5	23 15	25 32	29 02	29 25	27 00
10	22 49	25 24	0♉10	0♊39	27 40
15	22 21	25 17	1 24	1 57	28 22
20	21 52	25 08	2 49	3 20	29 06
21	21 46	25 06	3 07	3 38	29 16
22	21 39	25 04	3 26	3 56	29 25
23	21 33	25 02	3 46	4 14	29 34
24	21 26	25 00	4 06	4 33	29 44
25	21 20	24 58	4 27	4 52	29 54
26	21 13	24 56	4 49	5 11	0♋04
27	21 06	24 53	5 11	5 32	0 14
28	20 58	24 51	5 34	5 52	0 24
29	20 51	24 49	5 58	6 13	0 35
30	20 43	24 46	6 23	6 35	0 46
31	20 36	24 44	6 49	6 57	0 57
32	20 28	24 41	7 17	7 20	1 08
33	20 19	24 38	7 45	7 43	1 20
34	20 11	24 35	8 15	8 07	1 32
35	20 02	24 32	8 46	8 32	1 44
36	19 53	24 29	9 18	8 58	1 57
37	19 44	24 26	9 52	9 25	2 10
38	19 34	24 22	10 28	9 52	2 23
39	19 24	24 19	11 06	10 21	2 37
40	19 14	24 15	11 46	10 51	2 51
41	19 03	24 11	12 29	11 22	3 05
42	18 52	24 07	13 14	11 54	3 21
43	18 40	24 02	14 01	12 27	3 36
44	18 28	23 57	14 52	13 02	3 53
45	18 15	23 52	15 46	13 39	4 10
46	18 01	23 47	16 44	14 17	4 28
47	17 47	23 41	17 46	14 57	4 46
48	17 32	23 35	18 53	15 40	5 06
49	17 17	23 29	20 04	16 24	5 26
50	17 00	23 21	21 22	17 11	5 47
51	16 43	23 14	22 46	18 01	6 10
52	16 24	23 05	24 16	18 53	6 33
53	16 04	22 56	25 55	19 49	6 58
54	15 43	22 46	27 43	20 49	7 25
55	15 21	22 35	29 41	21 53	7 53
56	14 56	22 23	1♊50	23 01	8 24
57	14 30	22 09	4 12	24 15	8 56
58	14 01	21 54	6 48	25 34	9 31
59	13 30	21 37	9 40	27 00	10 09
60	12♒55	21♓17	12♊50	28♊34	10♋50

19h 48m 0s 297° 0' 0" 25 ♑ 03					
LAT.	11	12	ASC	2	3
0	24♒42	26♓44	29♈03	29♉13	27♊15
5	24 18	26 39	0♉07	0♊24	27 55
10	23 52	26 33	1 17	1 38	28 35
15	23 25	26 27	2 34	2 56	29 17
20	22 56	26 21	4 01	4 20	0♋02
21	22 50	26 19	4 20	4 38	0 11
22	22 44	26 18	4 39	4 56	0 20
23	22 38	26 16	5 00	5 14	0 29
24	22 31	26 15	5 20	5 33	0 39
25	22 25	26 13	5 42	5 52	0 49
26	22 18	26 12	6 04	6 12	0 59
27	22 11	26 10	6 27	6 32	1 09
28	22 04	26 08	6 51	6 53	1 19
29	21 57	26 06	7 15	7 14	1 30
30	21 49	26 05	7 41	7 36	1 41
31	21 42	26 03	8 08	7 58	1 52
32	21 34	26 01	8 36	8 21	2 03
33	21 26	25 59	9 05	8 44	2 15
34	21 17	25 56	9 35	9 09	2 27
35	21 09	25 54	10 07	9 34	2 39
36	21 00	25 52	10 40	10 00	2 51
37	20 51	25 49	11 15	10 26	3 04
38	20 41	25 47	11 52	10 54	3 18
39	20 32	25 44	12 31	11 23	3 31
40	20 21	25 41	13 12	11 52	3 45
41	20 11	25 38	13 55	12 23	4 00
42	20 00	25 35	14 40	12 55	4 15
43	19 48	25 32	15 29	13 29	4 31
44	19 36	25 28	16 20	14 04	4 47
45	19 24	25 24	17 15	14 41	5 04
46	19 11	25 20	18 14	15 19	5 22
47	18 57	25 16	19 17	15 59	5 40
48	18 42	25 11	20 24	16 41	6 00
49	18 27	25 06	21 36	17 25	6 20
50	18 11	25 01	22 54	18 12	6 41
51	17 54	24 55	24 19	19 02	7 03
52	17 35	24 49	25 50	19 54	7 27
53	17 16	24 42	27 29	20 50	7 52
54	16 55	24 34	29 17	21 49	8 18
55	16 33	24 26	1♊14	22 52	8 46
56	16 09	24 17	3 23	24 00	9 16
57	15 44	24 07	5 43	25 13	9 49
58	15 15	23 55	8 18	26 32	10 23
59	14 45	23 42	11 07	27 57	11 01
60	14♒11	23♓28	14♊13	29♊30	11♋41

19h 52m 0s 298° 0' 0" 26 ♑ 00					
LAT.	11	12	ASC	2	3
0	25♒44	27♓49	0♉06	0♊11	28♊10
5	25 20	27 46	1 12	1 22	28 50
10	24 55	27 42	2 24	2 37	29 30
15	24 29	27 38	3 43	3 55	0♋12
20	24 01	27 34	5 13	5 20	0 57
21	23 55	27 33	5 32	5 38	1 06
22	23 49	27 32	5 52	5 56	1 15
23	23 43	27 31	6 13	6 15	1 24
24	23 36	27 30	6 34	6 33	1 34
25	23 30	27 29	6 56	6 53	1 44
26	23 23	27 28	7 19	7 12	1 54
27	23 17	27 27	7 42	7 33	2 04
28	23 10	27 25	8 07	7 53	2 14
29	23 03	27 24	8 32	8 15	2 25
30	22 55	27 23	8 58	8 36	2 36
31	22 48	27 22	9 26	8 59	2 47
32	22 40	27 20	9 54	9 22	2 58
33	22 32	27 19	10 24	9 45	3 10
34	22 24	27 18	10 55	10 10	3 21
35	22 16	27 16	11 27	10 35	3 34
36	22 07	27 14	12 01	11 01	3 46
37	21 58	27 13	12 37	11 27	3 59
38	21 49	27 11	13 15	11 55	4 12
39	21 39	27 09	13 54	12 24	4 26
40	21 29	27 07	14 36	12 54	4 40
41	21 19	27 05	15 20	13 25	4 55
42	21 08	27 03	16 06	13 57	5 10
43	20 57	27 01	16 55	14 30	5 25
44	20 45	26 59	17 47	15 05	5 42
45	20 33	26 56	18 43	15 42	5 58
46	20 20	26 53	19 42	16 20	6 16
47	20 07	26 50	20 46	17 00	6 34
48	19 53	26 47	21 54	17 42	6 54
49	19 38	26 44	23 07	18 26	7 14
50	19 22	26 41	24 25	19 13	7 35
51	19 05	26 37	25 50	20 02	7 57
52	18 47	26 32	27 21	20 54	8 20
53	18 28	26 28	29 00	21 50	8 45
54	18 08	26 23	0♊48	22 48	9 11
55	17 46	26 17	2 45	23 51	9 39
56	17 23	26 11	4 53	24 59	10 09
57	16 58	26 04	7 12	26 11	10 41
58	16 30	25 57	9 44	27 29	11 15
59	16 01	25 48	12 31	28 54	11 52
60	15♒28	25♓38	15♊34	0♋25	12♋32

19h 56m 0s 299° 0' 0" 26 ♑ 57					
LAT.	11	12	ASC	2	3
0	26♒47	28♓55	1♉08	1♊08	29♊05
5	26 23	28 53	2 17	2 20	29 45
10	25 59	28 51	3 30	3 35	0♋25
15	25 33	28 49	4 52	4 55	1 07
20	25 06	28 47	6 24	6 20	1 52
21	25 00	28 46	6 44	6 38	2 01
22	24 54	28 46	7 04	6 56	2 10
23	24 48	28 45	7 26	7 14	2 19
24	24 42	28 45	7 47	7 33	2 29
25	24 35	28 44	8 10	7 53	2 39
26	24 29	28 44	8 33	8 13	2 49
27	24 22	28 43	8 57	8 33	2 59
28	24 16	28 43	9 22	8 54	3 09
29	24 09	28 42	9 48	9 15	3 20
30	24 02	28 41	10 15	9 37	3 30
31	23 54	28 41	10 43	9 59	3 41
32	23 47	28 40	11 12	10 22	3 53
33	23 39	28 39	11 42	10 46	4 04
34	23 31	28 39	12 14	11 10	4 16
35	23 23	28 38	12 47	11 35	4 28
36	23 15	28 37	13 22	12 01	4 41
37	23 06	28 36	13 58	12 28	4 54
38	22 57	28 36	14 36	12 56	5 07
39	22 48	28 35	15 16	13 25	5 20
40	22 38	28 34	15 59	13 54	5 34
41	22 28	28 33	16 43	14 25	5 49
42	22 17	28 32	17 30	14 57	6 04
43	22 06	28 30	18 20	15 31	6 20
44	21 55	28 29	19 13	16 06	6 36
45	21 43	28 28	20 09	16 42	6 53
46	21 30	28 27	21 09	17 20	7 10
47	21 17	28 25	22 13	18 00	7 28
48	21 03	28 24	23 22	18 42	7 48
49	20 49	28 22	24 35	19 26	8 08
50	20 33	28 20	25 54	20 13	8 28
51	20 17	28 18	27 19	21 02	8 51
52	19 59	28 16	28 50	21 54	9 14
53	19 41	28 14	0♊29	22 49	9 38
54	19 21	28 11	2 17	23 47	10 04
55	19 00	28 09	4 13	24 50	10 32
56	18 37	28 06	6 20	25 57	11 02
57	18 13	28 02	8 38	27 08	11 33
58	17 46	27 58	11 08	28 26	12 07
59	17 17	27 54	13 52	29 49	12 44
60	16♒45	27♓49	16♊51	1♋20	13♋23

20h 0m 0s 300° 0' 0" 27 ♑ 55					
LAT.	11	12	ASC	2	3
0	27♒49	0♈00	2♉11	2♊05	0♋00
5	27 26	0 00	3 21	3 18	0 40
10	27 02	0 00	4 37	4 34	1 20
15	26 37	0 00	6 01	5 53	2 02
20	26 11	0 00	7 35	7 19	2 46
21	26 05	0 00	7 55	7 37	2 56
22	25 59	0 00	8 16	7 55	3 05
23	25 53	0 00	8 38	8 14	3 14
24	25 47	0 00	9 00	8 33	3 24
25	25 41	0 00	9 23	8 52	3 34
26	25 35	0 00	9 47	9 12	3 44
27	25 28	0 00	10 12	9 33	3 54
28	25 22	0 00	10 37	9 53	4 04
29	25 15	0 00	11 04	10 15	4 14
30	25 08	0 00	11 31	10 37	4 25
31	25 01	0 00	12 00	10 59	4 36
32	24 54	0 00	12 29	11 22	4 47
33	24 46	0 00	13 00	11 46	4 59
34	24 39	0 00	13 32	12 10	5 11
35	24 31	0 00	14 06	12 36	5 23
36	24 22	0 00	14 41	13 02	5 35
37	24 14	0 00	15 18	13 28	5 48
38	24 05	0 00	15 57	13 56	6 01
39	23 56	0 00	16 38	14 25	6 15
40	23 47	0 00	17 21	14 55	6 29
41	23 37	0 00	18 06	15 26	6 43
42	23 26	0 00	18 54	15 58	6 58
43	23 16	0 00	19 44	16 31	7 14
44	23 05	0 00	20 38	17 06	7 30
45	22 53	0 00	21 35	17 42	7 47
46	22 41	0 00	22 35	18 20	8 04
47	22 28	0 00	23 39	19 00	8 22
48	22 14	0 00	24 48	19 42	8 41
49	22 00	0 00	26 02	20 26	9 01
50	21 45	0 00	27 21	21 12	9 22
51	21 29	0 00	28 46	22 01	9 44
52	21 12	0 00	0♊18	22 53	10 07
53	20 54	0 00	1 56	23 47	10 31
54	20 35	0 00	3 43	24 46	10 57
55	20 14	0 00	5 39	25 48	11 25
56	19 52	0 00	7 45	26 54	11 54
57	19 28	0 00	10 01	28 05	12 25
58	19 02	0 00	12 29	29 21	12 59
59	18 34	0 00	15 11	0♋44	13 35
60	18♒02	0♈00	18♊06	2♋13	14♋14

20h 4m 0s 301° 0' 0" 28 ♑ 52					
LAT.	11	12	ASC	2	3
0	28♒52	1♈05	3♉13	3♊03	0♋55
5	28 29	1 07	4 25	4 16	1 35
10	28 06	1 09	5 43	5 32	2 15
15	27 42	1 11	7 09	6 52	2 57
20	27 16	1 13	8 45	8 18	3 41
21	27 10	1 14	9 06	8 36	3 50
22	27 05	1 14	9 28	8 54	4 00
23	26 59	1 15	9 50	9 13	4 09
24	26 53	1 15	10 13	9 32	4 19
25	26 47	1 16	10 36	9 52	4 28
26	26 41	1 16	11 00	10 12	4 38
27	26 35	1 17	11 26	10 32	4 48
28	26 28	1 17	11 52	10 53	4 59
29	26 22	1 18	12 19	11 14	5 09
30	26 15	1 19	12 46	11 36	5 20
31	26 08	1 19	13 16	11 59	5 31
32	26 01	1 20	13 46	12 22	5 42
33	25 54	1 21	14 17	12 46	5 53
34	25 46	1 21	14 50	13 10	6 05
35	25 39	1 22	15 24	13 35	6 17
36	25 31	1 23	16 00	14 01	6 30
37	25 22	1 24	16 38	14 28	6 42
38	25 14	1 24	17 17	14 56	6 56
39	25 05	1 25	17 58	15 25	7 09
40	24 56	1 26	18 42	15 55	7 23
41	24 46	1 27	19 28	16 26	7 37
42	24 36	1 28	20 16	16 58	7 52
43	24 26	1 30	21 07	17 31	8 08
44	24 15	1 31	22 01	18 06	8 24
45	24 03	1 32	22 58	18 42	8 41
46	23 51	1 33	23 59	19 20	8 58
47	23 39	1 35	25 04	20 00	9 16
48	23 26	1 36	26 13	20 41	9 35
49	23 12	1 38	27 27	21 25	9 55
50	22 57	1 40	28 47	22 11	10 15
51	22 42	1 42	0♊12	23 00	10 37
52	22 25	1 44	1 43	23 51	11 00
53	22 08	1 46	3 21	24 46	11 24
54	21 49	1 49	5 08	25 43	11 50
55	21 29	1 51	7 03	26 45	12 17
56	21 07	1 54	9 07	27 51	12 46
57	20 44	1 58	11 22	29 01	13 17
58	20 18	2 02	13 48	0♋17	13 50
59	19 51	2 06	16 26	1 38	14 26
60	19♒21	2♈11	19♊18	3♋06	15♋05

20h 8m 0s 302° 0' 0" 29 ♑ 49					
LAT.	11	12	ASC	2	3
0	29♒54	2♈11	4♉16	4♊00	1♋50
5	29 33	2 14	5 29	5 14	2 30
10	29 10	2 18	6 49	6 30	3 10
15	28 47	2 22	8 17	7 51	3 52
20	28 21	2 26	9 56	9 17	4 36
21	28 16	2 27	10 17	9 35	4 45
22	28 10	2 28	10 39	9 53	4 55
23	28 05	2 29	11 01	10 12	5 04
24	27 59	2 30	11 25	10 31	5 14
25	27 53	2 31	11 49	10 51	5 23
26	27 47	2 32	12 13	11 11	5 33
27	27 41	2 33	12 39	11 31	5 43
28	27 35	2 35	13 05	11 52	5 53
29	27 29	2 36	13 33	12 14	6 04
30	27 22	2 37	14 01	12 36	6 15
31	27 16	2 38	14 31	12 58	6 25
32	27 09	2 40	15 02	13 22	6 37
33	27 02	2 41	15 34	13 45	6 48
34	26 54	2 42	16 07	14 10	7 00
35	26 47	2 44	16 42	14 35	7 12
36	26 39	2 46	17 18	15 01	7 24
37	26 31	2 47	17 56	15 28	7 37
38	26 23	2 49	18 36	15 56	7 50
39	26 14	2 51	19 18	16 24	8 03
40	26 05	2 53	20 02	16 54	8 17
41	25 56	2 55	20 48	17 25	8 32
42	25 46	2 57	21 37	17 57	8 46
43	25 36	2 59	22 28	18 30	9 02
44	25 25	3 01	23 23	19 05	9 18
45	25 14	3 04	24 21	19 41	9 34
46	25 02	3 07	25 22	20 19	9 52
47	24 50	3 10	26 27	20 59	10 10
48	24 37	3 13	27 37	21 40	10 28
49	24 24	3 16	28 51	22 24	10 48
50	24 10	3 19	0♊10	23 10	11 09
51	23 55	3 23	1 35	23 58	11 30
52	23 39	3 28	3 06	24 49	11 53
53	23 21	3 32	4 44	25 43	12 17
54	23 03	3 37	6 30	26 40	12 42
55	22 44	3 43	8 24	27 42	13 09
56	22 23	3 49	10 27	28 47	13 38
57	22 00	3 56	12 40	29 56	14 09
58	21 35	4 03	15 04	1♋11	14 42
59	21 09	4 12	17 40	2 32	15 17
60	20♒39	4♈22	20♊29	3♋59	15♋56

20h 12m 0s 303° 0' 0" 0 ♒ 47					
LAT.	11	12	ASC	2	3
0	0♓57	3♈16	5♉18	4♊57	2♋45
5	0 36	3 21	6 33	6 11	3 25
10	0 15	3 27	7 55	7 28	4 05
15	29♒52	3 33	9 25	8 49	4 47
20	29 27	3 39	11 05	10 15	5 31
21	29 22	3 41	11 27	10 34	5 40
22	29 16	3 42	11 49	10 52	5 49
23	29 11	3 44	12 12	11 11	5 59
24	29 06	3 45	12 36	11 30	6 08
25	29 00	3 47	13 00	11 50	6 18
26	28 54	3 48	13 26	12 10	6 28
27	28 48	3 50	13 52	12 30	6 38
28	28 42	3 52	14 19	12 51	6 48
29	28 36	3 54	14 47	13 13	6 58
30	28 30	3 55	15 16	13 35	7 09
31	28 23	3 57	15 46	13 58	7 20
32	28 16	3 59	16 17	14 21	7 31
33	28 10	4 01	16 49	14 45	7 43
34	28 02	4 04	17 23	15 09	7 54
35	27 55	4 06	17 58	15 34	8 06
36	27 48	4 08	18 35	16 00	8 18
37	27 40	4 11	19 14	16 27	8 31
38	27 32	4 13	19 54	16 55	8 44
39	27 23	4 16	20 37	17 24	8 58
40	27 15	4 19	21 21	17 53	9 11
41	27 05	4 22	22 08	18 24	9 26
42	26 56	4 25	22 57	18 56	9 40
43	26 46	4 28	23 49	19 29	9 56
44	26 36	4 32	24 44	20 04	10 12
45	26 25	4 36	25 42	20 40	10 28
46	26 14	4 40	26 44	21 18	10 45
47	26 02	4 44	27 49	21 57	11 03
48	25 50	4 49	28 59	22 39	11 22
49	25 36	4 54	0♊13	23 22	11 41
50	25 23	4 59	1 32	24 08	12 02
51	25 08	5 05	2 57	24 56	12 23
52	24 52	5 11	4 28	25 46	12 46
53	24 36	5 18	6 06	26 40	13 10
54	24 18	5 26	7 51	27 37	13 35
55	23 59	5 34	9 44	28 38	14 02
56	23 39	5 43	11 45	29 42	14 30
57	23 17	5 53	13 57	0♋51	15 00
58	22 53	6 05	16 19	2 05	15 33
59	22 27	6 18	18 52	3 25	16 08
60	21♒59	6♈32	21♊37	4♋51	16♋46

20h 16m 0s — 304° 0' 0" — 1 ♒ 45

LAT.	11	12	ASC	2	3
0	2♓00	4♈22	6♉19	5♊54	3♋40
5	1 40	4 28	7 37	7 08	4 20
10	1 19	4 36	9 00	8 26	5 00
15	0 57	4 43	10 32	9 47	5 42
20	0 33	4 52	12 15	11 14	6 26
21	0 28	4 54	12 37	11 32	6 35
22	0 23	4 56	13 00	11 51	6 44
23	0 17	4 58	13 23	12 10	6 54
24	0 12	5 00	13 47	12 29	7 03
25	0 07	5 02	14 12	12 49	7 13
26	0 01	5 04	14 38	13 09	7 22
27	29♒55	5 07	15 04	13 29	7 32
28	29 49	5 09	15 32	13 50	7 43
29	29 43	5 11	16 00	14 12	7 53
30	29 37	5 14	16 29	14 34	8 04
31	29 31	5 16	17 00	14 56	8 15
32	29 25	5 19	17 31	15 20	8 26
33	29 18	5 22	18 04	15 43	8 37
34	29 11	5 25	18 39	16 08	8 49
35	29 04	5 28	19 14	16 33	9 01
36	28 57	5 31	19 52	16 59	9 13
37	28 49	5 34	20 31	17 26	9 25
38	28 41	5 38	21 12	17 54	9 38
39	28 33	5 41	21 54	18 22	9 52
40	28 24	5 45	22 39	18 52	10 05
41	28 16	5 49	23 26	19 23	10 20
42	28 06	5 53	24 16	19 55	10 34
43	27 57	5 58	25 08	20 28	10 50
44	27 47	6 03	26 03	21 03	11 05
45	27 37	6 08	27 02	21 39	11 22
46	27 26	6 13	28 04	22 16	11 39
47	27 14	6 19	29 09	22 56	11 57
48	27 02	6 25	0♊19	23 37	12 15
49	26 49	6 31	1 34	24 20	12 35
50	26 36	6 39	2 53	25 05	12 55
51	26 22	6 46	4 17	25 53	13 16
52	26 07	6 55	5 48	26 43	13 39
53	25 51	7 04	7 25	27 37	14 02
54	25 33	7 14	9 09	28 33	14 27
55	25 15	7 25	11 01	29 33	14 54
56	24 55	7 37	13 01	0♋37	15 22
57	24 34	7 51	15 11	1 45	15 52
58	24 11	8 06	17 31	2 58	16 24
59	23 46	8 23	20 01	4 17	16 59
60	23♒18	8♈43	22♊43	5♋42	17♋36

20h 20m 0s — 305° 0' 0" — 2 ♒ 43

LAT.	11	12	ASC	2	3
0	3♓03	5♈27	7♉21	6♊50	4♋35
5	2 44	5 35	8 40	8 05	5 15
10	2 23	5 44	10 05	9 23	5 55
15	2 02	5 54	11 39	10 45	6 37
20	1 39	6 05	13 24	12 12	7 21
21	1 34	6 08	13 46	12 30	7 30
22	1 29	6 10	14 09	12 49	7 39
23	1 24	6 12	14 33	13 08	7 48
24	1 19	6 15	14 58	13 27	7 58
25	1 14	6 18	15 23	13 47	8 07
26	1 08	6 20	15 49	14 07	8 17
27	1 03	6 23	16 16	14 28	8 27
28	0 57	6 26	16 44	14 49	8 37
29	0 51	6 29	17 13	15 10	8 48
30	0 45	6 32	17 42	15 32	8 58
31	0 39	6 35	18 13	15 55	9 09
32	0 33	6 39	18 45	16 18	9 20
33	0 26	6 42	19 19	16 42	9 31
34	0 20	6 46	19 53	17 07	9 43
35	0 13	6 50	20 30	17 32	9 55
36	0 06	6 53	21 07	17 58	10 07
37	29♒58	6 58	21 47	18 25	10 20
38	29 51	7 02	22 28	18 52	10 32
39	29 43	7 06	23 11	19 21	10 46
40	29 35	7 11	23 56	19 51	10 59
41	29 26	7 16	24 44	20 21	11 14
42	29 17	7 21	25 34	20 53	11 28
43	29 08	7 27	26 26	21 26	11 43
44	28 58	7 33	27 22	22 01	11 59
45	28 48	7 39	28 21	22 37	12 15
46	28 38	7 46	29 23	23 14	12 32
47	28 27	7 53	0♊29	23 53	12 50
48	28 15	8 01	1 38	24 34	13 08
49	28 03	8 09	2 53	25 17	13 28
50	27 50	8 18	4 12	26 02	13 48
51	27 36	8 27	5 36	26 50	14 09
52	27 21	8 38	7 06	27 40	14 31
53	27 06	8 49	8 43	28 33	14 55
54	26 49	9 02	10 26	29 29	15 19
55	26 31	9 15	12 17	0♋28	15 46
56	26 12	9 31	14 16	1 32	16 14
57	25 52	9 47	16 24	2 39	16 43
58	25 29	10 06	18 41	3 51	17 15
59	25 05	10 28	21 09	5 09	17 49
60	24♒38	10♈52	23♊48	6♋33	18♋26

20h 24m 0s — 306° 0' 0" — 3 ♒ 41

LAT.	11	12	ASC	2	3
0	4♓07	6♈32	8♉23	7♊47	5♋30
5	3 48	6 42	9 43	9 02	6 10
10	3 28	6 53	11 10	10 20	6 50
15	3 07	7 05	12 46	11 42	7 32
20	2 45	7 18	14 32	13 10	8 15
21	2 40	7 21	14 55	13 28	8 25
22	2 36	7 24	15 19	13 47	8 34
23	2 31	7 27	15 43	14 06	8 43
24	2 26	7 30	16 08	14 25	8 52
25	2 21	7 33	16 33	14 45	9 02
26	2 16	7 36	17 00	15 05	9 12
27	2 10	7 40	17 27	15 26	9 22
28	2 05	7 43	17 55	15 47	9 32
29	1 59	7 47	18 25	16 09	9 42
30	1 53	7 50	18 55	16 31	9 53
31	1 47	7 54	19 26	16 53	10 03
32	1 41	7 58	19 59	17 16	10 14
33	1 35	8 02	20 32	17 40	10 26
34	1 29	8 07	21 08	18 05	10 37
35	1 22	8 11	21 44	18 30	10 49
36	1 15	8 16	22 22	18 56	11 01
37	1 08	8 21	23 02	19 23	11 14
38	1 01	8 26	23 44	19 51	11 27
39	0 53	8 31	24 27	20 19	11 40
40	0 45	8 37	25 13	20 49	11 53
41	0 37	8 43	26 00	21 19	12 07
42	0 28	8 49	26 51	21 51	12 22
43	0 19	8 56	27 44	22 24	12 37
44	0 10	9 03	28 39	22 58	12 53
45	0 00	9 11	29 38	23 34	13 09
46	29♒50	9 19	0♊40	24 12	13 26
47	29 39	9 27	1 46	24 50	13 43
48	29 28	9 36	2 56	25 31	14 02
49	29 16	9 46	4 10	26 14	14 21
50	29 04	9 57	5 29	26 59	14 41
51	28 50	10 08	6 53	27 46	15 02
52	28 36	10 21	8 23	28 36	15 24
53	28 21	10 34	9 59	29 28	15 47
54	28 05	10 49	11 41	0♋24	16 11
55	27 48	11 06	13 31	1 23	16 37
56	27 30	11 24	15 28	2 25	17 05
57	27 10	11 44	17 34	3 32	17 35
58	26 48	12 07	19 50	4 44	18 06
59	26 25	12 32	22 15	6 00	18 40
60	25♒59	13♈01	24♊50	7♋23	19♋16

20h 28m 0s — 307° 0' 0" — 4 ♒ 39

LAT.	11	12	ASC	2	3
0	5♓10	7♈37	9♉24	8♊43	6♋26
5	4 52	7 49	10 46	9 59	7 05
10	4 33	8 02	12 15	11 18	7 45
15	4 13	8 16	13 52	12 40	8 27
20	3 52	8 31	15 40	14 08	9 10
21	3 47	8 34	16 04	14 26	9 19
22	3 43	8 38	16 27	14 45	9 28
23	3 38	8 41	16 52	15 04	9 38
24	3 33	8 45	17 17	15 23	9 47
25	3 28	8 48	17 43	15 43	9 57
26	3 23	8 52	18 10	16 03	10 06
27	3 18	8 56	18 38	16 24	10 16
28	3 13	9 00	19 07	16 45	10 26
29	3 07	9 04	19 36	17 07	10 37
30	3 02	9 08	20 07	17 29	10 47
31	2 56	9 13	20 38	17 51	10 58
32	2 50	9 18	21 11	18 14	11 09
33	2 44	9 22	21 45	18 38	11 20
34	2 38	9 27	22 21	19 03	11 32
35	2 32	9 33	22 58	19 28	11 43
36	2 25	9 38	23 36	19 54	11 55
37	2 18	9 44	24 16	20 21	12 08
38	2 11	9 50	24 58	20 48	12 21
39	2 04	9 56	25 42	21 17	12 34
40	1 56	10 03	26 28	21 46	12 47
41	1 48	10 10	27 16	22 17	13 01
42	1 40	10 17	28 07	22 49	13 16
43	1 31	10 25	29 00	23 22	13 31
44	1 22	10 33	29 56	23 56	13 46
45	1 13	10 42	0♊55	24 31	14 02
46	1 03	10 51	1 57	25 09	14 19
47	0 53	11 01	3 03	25 47	14 36
48	0 42	11 12	4 13	26 28	14 55
49	0 30	11 23	5 27	27 10	15 14
50	0 18	11 35	6 45	27 55	15 33
51	0 05	11 49	8 09	28 42	15 54
52	29♒52	12 03	9 38	29 31	16 16
53	29 37	12 19	11 13	0♋23	16 39
54	29 22	12 36	12 54	1 18	17 03
55	29 05	12 55	14 43	2 17	17 29
56	28 47	13 16	16 39	3 19	17 57
57	28 28	13 40	18 43	4 25	18 26
58	28 07	14 06	20 56	5 36	18 57
59	27 45	14 36	23 19	6 51	19 30
60	27♒20	15♈10	25♊52	8♋13	20♋06

20h 32m 0s — 308° 0' 0" — 5 ♒ 38

LAT.	11	12	ASC	2	3
0	6♓14	8♈43	10♉25	9♊40	7♋21
5	5 56	8 56	11 49	10 56	8 00
10	5 38	9 10	13 19	12 15	8 40
15	5 19	9 26	14 58	13 37	9 22
20	4 58	9 44	16 48	15 05	10 05
21	4 54	9 47	17 12	15 24	10 14
22	4 50	9 51	17 36	15 42	10 23
23	4 45	9 55	18 01	16 01	10 32
24	4 40	9 59	18 27	16 21	10 42
25	4 36	10 03	18 53	16 41	10 51
26	4 31	10 08	19 20	17 01	11 01
27	4 26	10 12	19 48	17 22	11 11
28	4 21	10 17	20 17	17 43	11 21
29	4 16	10 21	20 47	18 04	11 31
30	4 10	10 26	21 18	18 26	11 42
31	4 05	10 31	21 50	18 49	11 52
32	3 59	10 37	22 23	19 12	12 03
33	3 53	10 42	22 58	19 36	12 14
34	3 47	10 48	23 34	20 01	12 26
35	3 41	10 54	24 11	20 26	12 37
36	3 35	11 00	24 50	20 52	12 49
37	3 28	11 07	25 30	21 18	13 02
38	3 21	11 14	26 12	21 46	13 15
39	3 14	11 21	26 56	22 14	13 28
40	3 07	11 28	27 42	22 44	13 41
41	2 59	11 36	28 31	23 14	13 55
42	2 51	11 45	29 22	23 46	14 09
43	2 43	11 53	0♊15	24 19	14 24
44	2 35	12 03	1 11	24 53	14 40
45	2 25	12 13	2 10	25 28	14 56
46	2 16	12 23	3 12	26 05	15 12
47	2 06	12 35	4 18	26 44	15 30
48	1 56	12 47	5 28	27 24	15 48
49	1 45	13 00	6 42	28 06	16 06
50	1 33	13 14	8 00	28 51	16 26
51	1 21	13 29	9 23	29 37	16 47
52	1 07	13 45	10 52	0♋26	17 08
53	0 53	14 03	12 26	1 18	17 31
54	0 39	14 23	14 06	2 13	17 55
55	0 23	14 44	15 54	3 10	18 21
56	0 06	15 08	17 48	4 12	18 48
57	29♒47	15 35	19 51	5 17	19 17
58	29 27	16 05	22 02	6 27	19 47
59	29 06	16 39	24 22	7 42	20 20
60	28♒42	17♈17	26♊51	9♋02	20♋56

20h 36m 0s — 309° 0' 0" — 6 ♒ 37

LAT.	11	12	ASC	2	3
0	7♓18	9♈48	11♉26	10♊36	8♋16
5	7 01	10 03	12 52	11 53	8 56
10	6 43	10 19	14 24	13 12	9 36
15	6 25	10 37	16 04	14 34	10 17
20	6 05	10 56	17 55	16 03	11 00
21	6 01	11 00	18 19	16 21	11 09
22	5 57	11 05	18 44	16 40	11 18
23	5 52	11 09	19 09	16 59	11 27
24	5 48	11 14	19 35	17 18	11 36
25	5 43	11 18	20 02	17 38	11 46
26	5 39	11 23	20 30	17 58	11 56
27	5 34	11 28	20 58	18 19	12 05
28	5 29	11 33	21 27	18 40	12 15
29	5 24	11 39	21 57	19 02	12 26
30	5 19	11 44	22 29	19 24	12 36
31	5 14	11 50	23 01	19 46	12 47
32	5 08	11 56	23 35	20 10	12 57
33	5 03	12 02	24 09	20 33	13 09
34	4 57	12 08	24 46	20 58	13 20
35	4 51	12 15	25 23	21 23	13 32
36	4 45	12 22	26 02	21 49	13 44
37	4 39	12 29	26 43	22 16	13 56
38	4 32	12 37	27 25	22 43	14 09
39	4 25	12 45	28 10	23 12	14 22
40	4 18	12 54	28 56	23 41	14 35
41	4 11	13 02	29 45	24 11	14 49
42	4 03	13 12	0♊35	24 43	15 03
43	3 55	13 22	1 29	25 16	15 18
44	3 47	13 32	2 25	25 49	15 33
45	3 38	13 43	3 24	26 25	15 49
46	3 29	13 55	4 26	27 02	16 06
47	3 20	14 08	5 32	27 40	16 23
48	3 10	14 21	6 42	28 20	16 41
49	2 59	14 36	7 55	29 02	16 59
50	2 48	14 52	9 13	29 46	17 19
51	2 36	15 09	10 36	0♋32	17 39
52	2 24	15 27	12 04	1 21	18 01
53	2 10	15 47	13 37	2 12	18 23
54	1 56	16 09	15 17	3 06	18 47
55	1 41	16 33	17 03	4 04	19 12
56	1 24	17 00	18 56	5 04	19 39
57	1 06	17 30	20 57	6 09	20 08
58	0 47	18 03	23 06	7 18	20 38
59	0 27	18 41	25 23	8 32	21 11
60	0♓04	19♈24	27♊50	9♋51	21♋46

20h 40m 0s — 310° 0' 0" — 7 ♒ 35

LAT.	11	12	ASC	2	3
0	8♓22	10♈53	12♉27	11♊32	9♋11
5	8 06	11 10	13 54	12 49	9 51
10	7 49	11 27	15 27	14 08	10 31
15	7 31	11 47	17 09	15 31	11 12
20	7 12	12 09	19 02	17 00	11 55
21	7 08	12 13	19 27	17 18	12 04
22	7 04	12 18	19 52	17 37	12 13
23	7 00	12 23	20 17	17 56	12 22
24	6 56	12 28	20 43	18 16	12 31
25	6 51	12 33	21 11	18 35	12 41
26	6 47	12 39	21 38	18 56	12 50
27	6 42	12 44	22 07	19 16	13 00
28	6 38	12 50	22 37	19 37	13 10
29	6 33	12 56	23 07	19 59	13 20
30	6 28	13 02	23 39	20 21	13 30
31	6 23	13 08	24 12	20 44	13 41
32	6 18	13 15	24 45	21 07	13 52
33	6 13	13 22	25 20	21 31	14 03
34	6 07	13 29	25 57	21 55	14 14
35	6 01	13 36	26 35	22 20	14 26
36	5 56	13 44	27 14	22 46	14 38
37	5 50	13 52	27 55	23 13	14 50
38	5 43	14 00	28 38	23 40	15 02
39	5 37	14 09	29 22	24 08	15 15
40	5 30	14 19	0♊09	24 38	15 29
41	5 23	14 28	0 57	25 08	15 42
42	5 16	14 39	1 48	25 39	15 57
43	5 08	14 50	2 42	26 12	16 11
44	5 00	15 01	3 38	26 46	16 27
45	4 52	15 14	4 37	27 21	16 42
46	4 43	15 27	5 40	27 58	16 59
47	4 34	15 41	6 45	28 36	17 16
48	4 24	15 56	7 54	29 16	17 33
49	4 14	16 12	9 08	29 57	17 52
50	4 03	16 29	10 25	0♋41	18 11
51	3 52	16 48	11 47	1 27	18 32
52	3 40	17 08	13 15	2 15	18 53
53	3 27	17 30	14 47	3 06	19 15
54	3 13	17 54	16 26	4 00	19 39
55	2 59	18 21	18 11	4 56	20 04
56	2 43	18 50	20 02	5 56	20 30
57	2 26	19 23	22 01	7 00	20 59
58	2 08	20 00	24 08	8 09	21 29
59	1 48	20 42	26 23	9 21	22 01
60	1♓26	21♈29	28♊47	10♋39	22♋35

20h 44m 0s — 311° 0' 0" — 8 ♒ 34

LAT.	11	12	ASC	2	3
0	9♓26	11♈58	13♉27	12♊28	10♋07
5	9 10	12 16	14 56	13 45	10 46
10	8 54	12 36	16 31	15 05	11 26
15	8 38	12 57	18 14	16 28	12 07
20	8 20	13 21	20 09	17 57	12 50
21	8 16	13 26	20 34	18 15	12 58
22	8 12	13 31	20 59	18 34	13 07
23	8 08	13 37	21 25	18 53	13 17
24	8 04	13 42	21 51	19 13	13 26
25	8 00	13 48	22 19	19 32	13 35
26	7 55	13 54	22 47	19 53	13 45
27	7 51	14 00	23 16	20 13	13 55
28	7 47	14 06	23 46	20 34	14 04
29	7 42	14 13	24 17	20 56	14 15
30	7 37	14 19	24 48	21 18	14 25
31	7 33	14 26	25 21	21 41	14 35
32	7 28	14 33	25 55	22 04	14 46
33	7 23	14 41	26 31	22 28	14 57
34	7 17	14 49	27 07	22 52	15 08
35	7 12	14 57	27 46	23 17	15 20
36	7 06	15 05	28 25	23 43	15 32
37	7 01	15 14	29 06	24 09	15 44
38	6 55	15 23	29 49	24 37	15 56
39	6 48	15 33	0♊34	25 05	16 09
40	6 42	15 43	1 21	25 34	16 22
41	6 35	15 54	2 09	26 04	16 36
42	6 28	16 05	3 01	26 36	16 50
43	6 21	16 17	3 54	27 08	17 05
44	6 13	16 30	4 50	27 42	17 20
45	6 05	16 43	5 49	28 17	17 36
46	5 57	16 58	6 52	28 53	17 52
47	5 48	17 13	7 57	29 31	18 09
48	5 39	17 29	9 06	0♋11	18 26
49	5 29	17 47	10 19	0 52	18 45
50	5 19	18 06	11 36	1 36	19 04
51	5 08	18 26	12 58	2 21	19 24
52	4 57	18 49	14 24	3 09	19 45
53	4 45	19 13	15 56	3 59	20 07
54	4 31	19 39	17 33	4 52	20 31
55	4 18	20 08	19 17	5 49	20 55
56	4 03	20 40	21 07	6 48	21 22
57	3 46	21 16	23 04	7 51	21 49
58	3 29	21 56	25 09	8 59	22 19
59	3 10	22 42	27 22	10 10	22 51
60	2♓49	23♈33	29♊43	11♋27	23♋25

20h 48m 0s 312° 0' 0" 9 ♒ 34

LAT.	11	12	ASC	2	3
0	10♓30	13♈03	14♉28	13♊24	11♋02
5	10 15	13 23	15 58	14 42	11 41
10	10 00	13 44	17 34	16 01	12 21
15	9 44	14 07	19 19	17 25	13 02
20	9 27	14 33	21 15	18 53	13 44
21	9 23	14 39	21 40	19 12	13 53
22	9 20	14 44	22 06	19 31	14 02
23	9 16	14 50	22 32	19 50	14 11
24	9 12	14 56	22 59	20 09	14 21
25	9 08	15 03	23 26	20 29	14 30
26	9 04	15 09	23 55	20 50	14 39
27	9 00	15 15	24 24	21 10	14 49
28	8 56	15 22	24 54	21 31	14 59
29	8 51	15 29	25 25	21 53	15 09
30	8 47	15 37	25 57	22 15	15 19
31	8 42	15 44	26 31	22 37	15 30
32	8 38	15 52	27 05	23 01	15 40
33	8 33	16 00	27 41	23 24	15 51
34	8 28	16 08	28 17	23 49	16 03
35	8 23	16 17	28 56	24 14	16 14
36	8 17	16 26	29 35	24 39	16 26
37	8 12	16 36	0♊17	25 06	16 38
38	8 06	16 46	1 00	25 33	16 50
39	8 00	16 57	1 45	26 01	17 03
40	7 54	17 08	2 32	26 30	17 16
41	7 48	17 19	3 21	27 01	17 30
42	7 41	17 32	4 12	27 32	17 44
43	7 34	17 45	5 05	28 04	17 58
44	7 27	17 58	6 02	28 37	18 13
45	7 19	18 13	7 01	29 12	18 29
46	7 11	18 29	8 03	29 48	18 45
47	7 03	18 45	9 08	0♋26	19 02
48	6 54	19 03	10 17	1 06	19 19
49	6 45	19 22	11 29	1 47	19 37
50	6 35	19 42	12 46	2 30	19 56
51	6 25	20 04	14 07	3 15	20 16
52	6 14	20 28	15 33	4 02	20 37
53	6 02	20 55	17 03	4 52	20 59
54	5 50	21 23	18 40	5 45	21 22
55	5 37	21 55	20 22	6 41	21 47
56	5 22	22 29	22 11	7 39	22 13
57	5 07	23 08	24 06	8 42	22 40
58	4 50	23 51	26 09	9 48	23 09
59	4 32	24 40	28 19	10 59	23 41
60	4♓13	25♈36	0♋38	12♋15	24♋14

20h 52m 0s 313° 0' 0" 10 ♒ 33

LAT.	11	12	ASC	2	3
0	11♓34	14♈07	15♉28	14♊20	11♋58
5	11 20	14 29	16 59	15 38	12 37
10	11 06	14 52	18 37	16 58	13 16
15	10 51	15 17	20 24	18 21	13 57
20	10 34	15 45	22 21	19 50	14 39
21	10 31	15 51	22 46	20 09	14 48
22	10 28	15 57	23 12	20 27	14 57
23	10 24	16 04	23 38	20 47	15 06
24	10 20	16 10	24 06	21 06	15 15
25	10 17	16 17	24 33	21 26	15 25
26	10 13	16 24	25 02	21 46	15 34
27	10 09	16 31	25 32	22 07	15 44
28	10 05	16 38	26 02	22 28	15 54
29	10 01	16 46	26 33	22 49	16 04
30	9 56	16 54	27 06	23 11	16 14
31	9 52	17 02	27 39	23 34	16 24
32	9 48	17 10	28 14	23 57	16 35
33	9 43	17 19	28 50	24 21	16 46
34	9 38	17 28	29 27	24 45	16 57
35	9 33	17 37	0♊05	25 10	17 08
36	9 28	17 47	0 45	25 36	17 20
37	9 23	17 58	1 27	26 02	17 32
38	9 18	18 09	2 10	26 29	17 44
39	9 12	18 20	2 55	26 57	17 57
40	9 06	18 32	3 42	27 26	18 10
41	9 00	18 44	4 31	27 56	18 23
42	8 54	18 58	5 22	28 27	18 37
43	8 47	19 12	6 16	28 59	18 52
44	8 40	19 26	7 12	29 33	19 07
45	8 33	19 42	8 11	0♋07	19 22
46	8 26	19 59	9 13	0 43	19 38
47	8 18	20 17	10 18	1 21	19 55
48	8 09	20 36	11 26	2 00	20 12
49	8 01	20 56	12 38	2 41	20 30
50	7 51	21 18	13 54	3 24	20 49
51	7 42	21 42	15 15	4 08	21 09
52	7 31	22 08	16 40	4 56	21 29
53	7 20	22 36	18 10	5 45	21 51
54	7 08	23 06	19 45	6 37	22 14
55	6 56	23 40	21 26	7 32	22 38
56	6 42	24 17	23 13	8 30	23 04
57	6 28	24 59	25 07	9 32	23 31
58	6 12	25 45	27 08	10 38	24 00
59	5 55	26 38	29 16	11 48	24 30
60	5♓36	27♈38	1♋32	13♋02	25♋03

20h 56m 0s 314° 0' 0" 11 ♒ 32

LAT.	11	12	ASC	2	3
0	12♓39	15♈12	16♉28	15♊16	12♋53
5	12 26	15 35	18 01	16 34	13 32
10	12 12	16 00	19 40	17 54	14 11
15	11 58	16 27	21 28	19 18	14 52
20	11 42	16 57	23 26	20 47	15 34
21	11 39	17 04	23 52	21 05	15 43
22	11 36	17 10	24 18	21 24	15 52
23	11 32	17 17	24 45	21 43	16 01
24	11 29	17 24	25 12	22 03	16 10
25	11 25	17 31	25 40	22 22	16 19
26	11 22	17 38	26 09	22 43	16 29
27	11 18	17 46	26 39	23 03	16 38
28	11 14	17 54	27 10	23 24	16 48
29	11 10	18 02	27 41	23 46	16 58
30	11 06	18 10	28 14	24 08	17 08
31	11 02	18 19	28 47	24 30	17 19
32	10 58	18 28	29 22	24 53	17 29
33	10 54	18 38	29 58	25 17	17 40
34	10 49	18 47	0♊35	25 41	17 51
35	10 44	18 57	1 14	26 06	18 02
36	10 40	19 08	1 54	26 32	18 14
37	10 35	19 19	2 36	26 58	18 26
38	10 30	19 31	3 19	27 25	18 38
39	10 24	19 43	4 04	27 53	18 51
40	10 19	19 56	4 51	28 22	19 04
41	10 13	20 09	5 40	28 52	19 17
42	10 07	20 23	6 31	29 23	19 31
43	10 01	20 38	7 25	29 55	19 45
44	9 54	20 54	8 21	0♋28	20 00
45	9 48	21 11	9 20	1 02	20 15
46	9 40	21 29	10 21	1 38	20 31
47	9 33	21 48	11 26	2 15	20 48
48	9 25	22 08	12 34	2 54	21 05
49	9 17	22 30	13 46	3 35	21 23
50	9 08	22 53	15 02	4 17	21 41
51	8 59	23 19	16 21	5 02	22 01
52	8 49	23 46	17 46	5 48	22 21
53	8 39	24 16	19 15	6 37	22 43
54	8 27	24 49	20 49	7 29	23 05
55	8 16	25 25	22 29	8 23	23 29
56	8 03	26 05	24 14	9 21	23 55
57	7 49	26 49	26 06	10 22	24 21
58	7 34	27 38	28 05	11 27	24 50
59	7 18	28 34	0♋11	12 36	25 20
60	7♓00	29♈38	2♋24	13♋49	25♋53

21h 0m 0s 315° 0' 0" 12 ♒ 32

LAT.	11	12	ASC	2	3
0	13♓43	16♈17	17♉28	16♊11	13♋49
5	13 31	16 42	19 02	17 30	14 27
10	13 18	17 08	20 43	18 50	15 07
15	13 05	17 37	22 31	20 14	15 47
20	12 50	18 09	24 32	21 43	16 29
21	12 47	18 16	24 57	22 01	16 38
22	12 44	18 23	25 23	22 20	16 47
23	12 41	18 30	25 50	22 39	16 56
24	12 37	18 37	26 18	22 59	17 05
25	12 34	18 45	26 46	23 19	17 14
26	12 31	10 53	27 16	23 39	17 23
27	12 27	19 01	27 46	23 59	17 33
28	12 24	19 09	28 16	24 20	17 43
29	12 20	19 18	28 48	24 42	17 53
30	12 16	19 27	29 21	25 04	18 03
31	12 12	19 36	29 55	25 26	18 13
32	12 08	19 46	0♊30	25 49	18 23
33	12 04	19 56	1 06	26 13	18 34
34	12 00	20 06	1 43	26 37	18 45
35	11 56	20 17	2 22	27 02	18 56
36	11 51	20 28	3 02	27 27	19 08
37	11 47	20 40	3 44	27 54	19 20
38	11 42	20 52	4 28	28 21	19 32
39	11 37	21 05	5 13	28 49	19 44
40	11 32	21 19	6 00	29 17	19 57
41	11 26	21 33	6 49	29 47	20 11
42	11 21	21 48	7 40	0♋18	20 24
43	11 15	22 04	8 34	0 50	20 38
44	11 09	22 21	9 29	1 23	20 53
45	11 02	22 39	10 28	1 57	21 08
46	10 55	22 58	11 30	2 32	21 24
47	10 48	23 18	12 34	3 09	21 40
48	10 41	23 40	13 42	3 48	21 57
49	10 33	24 03	14 53	4 28	22 15
50	10 25	24 28	16 08	5 10	22 34
51	10 16	24 55	17 27	5 54	22 53
52	10 07	25 24	18 51	6 41	23 13
53	9 57	25 56	20 19	7 29	23 35
54	9 47	26 30	21 52	8 20	23 57
55	9 35	27 09	23 30	9 14	24 21
56	9 23	27 51	25 15	10 11	24 45
57	9 10	28 38	27 05	11 11	25 12
58	8 57	29 30	29 02	12 15	25 40
59	8 41	0♉29	1♋05	13 23	26 10
60	8♓25	1♉36	3♋16	14♋36	26♋42

21h 4m 0s 316° 0' 0" 13 ♒ 32

LAT.	11	12	ASC	2	3
0	14♓48	17♈21	18♉28	17♊07	14♋44
5	14 36	17 48	20 03	18 25	15 23
10	14 24	18 16	21 45	19 46	16 02
15	14 12	18 47	23 35	21 10	16 42
20	13 58	19 20	25 36	22 39	17 24
21	13 55	19 28	26 02	22 57	17 33
22	13 52	19 35	26 29	23 16	17 42
23	13 49	19 43	26 56	23 35	17 51
24	13 46	19 51	27 24	23 55	18 00
25	13 43	19 59	27 52	24 15	18 09
26	13 40	20 07	28 22	24 35	18 18
27	13 37	20 16	28 52	24 55	18 28
28	13 33	20 25	29 23	25 16	18 37
29	13 30	20 34	29 55	25 38	18 47
30	13 26	20 43	0♊28	26 00	18 57
31	13 23	20 53	1 02	26 22	19 07
32	13 19	21 03	1 37	26 45	19 18
33	13 15	21 14	2 13	27 09	19 28
34	13 11	21 25	2 51	27 33	19 39
35	13 07	21 36	3 30	27 58	19 51
36	13 03	21 48	4 10	28 23	20 02
37	12 59	22 01	4 52	28 49	20 14
38	12 54	22 14	5 35	29 16	20 26
39	12 49	22 28	6 21	29 44	20 38
40	12 45	22 42	7 08	0♋12	20 51
41	12 39	22 57	7 57	0 42	21 04
42	12 34	23 13	8 48	1 13	21 18
43	12 29	23 30	9 41	1 44	21 32
44	12 23	23 48	10 37	2 17	21 46
45	12 17	24 06	11 35	2 51	22 01
46	12 11	24 27	12 37	3 26	22 17
47	12 04	24 48	13 41	4 03	22 33
48	11 57	25 11	14 48	4 42	22 50
49	11 50	25 35	15 59	5 22	23 08
50	11 42	26 02	17 13	6 03	23 26
51	11 34	26 30	18 32	6 47	23 45
52	11 25	27 01	19 54	7 33	24 05
53	11 16	27 34	21 22	8 21	24 26
54	11 06	28 11	22 54	9 12	24 48
55	10 56	28 51	24 31	10 05	25 12
56	10 44	29 36	26 14	11 01	25 36
57	10 32	0♉25	28 02	12 01	26 02
58	10 19	1 20	29 57	13 04	26 30
59	10 05	2 23	1♋59	14 11	27 00
60	9♓50	3♉34	4♋07	15♋22	27♋31

21h 8m 0s 317° 0' 0" 14 ♒ 32

LAT.	11	12	ASC	2	3
0	15♓53	18♈26	19♉27	18♊02	15♋40
5	15 42	18 54	21 04	19 21	16 19
10	15 31	19 24	22 47	20 42	16 58
15	15 19	19 56	24 38	22 06	17 38
20	15 06	20 32	26 40	23 35	18 19
21	15 04	20 39	27 07	23 53	18 28
22	15 01	20 47	27 33	24 12	18 37
23	14 58	20 55	28 01	24 31	18 46
24	14 55	21 04	28 29	24 51	18 55
25	14 52	21 12	28 58	25 11	19 04
26	14 49	21 21	29 27	25 31	19 13
27	14 46	21 30	29 57	25 51	19 22
28	14 43	21 40	0♊29	26 12	19 32
29	14 40	21 49	1 01	26 34	19 42
30	14 37	21 59	1 34	26 56	19 52
31	14 33	22 10	2 08	27 18	20 02
32	14 30	22 20	2 44	27 41	20 12
33	14 26	22 32	3 20	28 04	20 23
34	14 23	22 43	3 58	28 28	20 34
35	14 19	22 55	4 37	28 53	20 45
36	14 15	23 08	5 17	29 18	20 56
37	14 11	23 21	5 59	29 44	21 08
38	14 07	23 35	6 43	0♋11	21 20
39	14 02	23 49	7 28	0 39	21 32
40	13 58	24 04	8 15	1 07	21 45
41	13 53	24 20	9 04	1 37	21 58
42	13 48	24 37	9 55	2 07	22 11
43	13 43	24 55	10 48	2 39	22 25
44	13 38	25 14	11 44	3 11	22 40
45	13 32	25 34	12 42	3 45	22 55
46	13 26	25 55	13 43	4 20	23 10
47	13 20	26 17	14 47	4 57	23 26
48	13 14	26 41	15 54	5 35	23 43
49	13 07	27 07	17 04	6 14	24 00
50	13 00	27 35	18 18	6 56	24 18
51	12 52	28 05	19 35	7 39	24 37
52	12 44	28 37	20 57	8 25	24 57
53	12 35	29 12	22 24	9 12	25 18
54	12 26	29 51	23 54	10 02	25 40
55	12 16	0♉33	25 30	10 55	26 03
56	12 06	1 20	27 12	11 51	26 27
57	11 54	2 11	28 59	12 49	26 53
58	11 42	3 09	0♋52	13 52	27 20
59	11 29	4 15	2 51	14 58	27 49
60	11♓15	5♉29	4♋58	16♋08	28♋21

21h 12m 0s 318° 0' 0" 15 ♒ 32

LAT.	11	12	ASC	2	3
0	16♓57	19♈30	20♉26	18♊58	16♋36
5	16 47	20 00	22 04	20 17	17 14
10	16 37	20 31	23 49	21 38	17 53
15	16 26	21 05	25 41	23 02	18 33
20	16 14	21 43	27 44	24 31	19 14
21	16 12	21 51	28 11	24 49	19 23
22	16 09	21 59	28 38	25 08	19 32
23	16 07	22 08	29 05	25 27	19 40
24	16 04	22 17	29 33	25 47	19 49
25	16 02	22 26	0♊02	26 06	19 58
26	15 59	22 35	0 32	26 26	20 08
27	15 56	22 44	1 03	26 47	20 17
28	15 53	22 54	1 34	27 08	20 27
29	15 50	23 04	2 07	27 29	20 36
30	15 47	23 15	2 40	27 51	20 46
31	15 44	23 26	3 14	28 13	20 56
32	15 41	23 37	3 50	28 36	21 07
33	15 37	23 49	4 26	29 00	21 17
34	15 34	24 01	5 04	29 24	21 28
35	15 31	24 14	5 43	29 48	21 39
36	15 27	24 27	6 23	0♋13	21 50
37	15 23	24 41	7 05	0 39	22 02
38	15 19	24 56	7 49	1 06	22 14
39	15 15	25 11	8 34	1 34	22 26
40	15 11	25 27	9 21	2 02	22 38
41	15 07	25 43	10 10	2 31	22 51
42	15 02	26 01	11 01	3 02	23 05
43	14 57	26 20	11 54	3 33	23 19
44	14 52	26 39	12 50	4 05	23 33
45	14 47	27 00	13 48	4 39	23 48
46	14 42	27 22	14 48	5 14	24 03
47	14 36	27 46	15 52	5 50	24 19
48	14 30	28 11	16 58	6 28	24 35
49	14 24	28 38	18 08	7 07	24 53
50	14 17	29 07	19 21	7 48	25 11
51	14 10	29 38	20 38	8 31	25 29
52	14 03	0♉12	21 59	9 16	25 49
53	13 55	0 49	23 24	10 03	26 10
54	13 46	1 29	24 54	10 53	26 31
55	13 37	2 14	26 29	11 45	26 54
56	13 27	3 02	28 09	12 40	27 18
57	13 17	3 56	29 54	13 38	27 43
58	13 06	4 57	1♋46	14 40	28 10
59	12 53	6 05	3 43	15 45	28 39
60	12♓40	7♉23	5♋47	16♋54	29♋10

21h 16m 0s 319° 0' 0" 16 ♒ 33

LAT.	11	12	ASC	2	3
0	18♓02	20♈34	21♉26	19♊53	17♋32
5	17 53	21 05	23 05	21 12	18 10
10	17 44	21 38	24 50	22 33	18 49
15	17 34	22 14	26 43	23 58	19 28
20	17 23	22 54	28 48	25 26	20 10
21	17 21	23 02	29 14	25 45	20 18
22	17 18	23 11	29 42	26 04	20 27
23	17 16	23 20	0♊09	26 23	20 35
24	17 13	23 29	0 38	26 42	20 44
25	17 11	23 39	1 07	27 02	20 53
26	17 08	23 48	1 37	27 22	21 03
27	17 06	23 58	2 08	27 43	21 12
28	17 03	24 09	2 39	28 03	21 21
29	17 01	24 19	3 12	28 25	21 31
30	16 58	24 30	3 45	28 46	21 41
31	16 55	24 42	4 19	29 09	21 51
32	16 52	24 54	4 55	29 31	22 01
33	16 49	25 06	5 32	29 55	22 11
34	16 46	25 19	6 10	0♋19	22 22
35	16 42	25 32	6 49	0 43	22 33
36	16 39	25 46	7 29	1 08	22 44
37	16 36	26 01	8 11	1 34	22 56
38	16 32	26 16	8 55	2 01	23 08
39	16 28	26 32	9 40	2 28	23 20
40	16 24	26 48	10 27	2 56	23 32
41	16 20	27 06	11 16	3 25	23 45
42	16 16	27 24	12 07	3 56	23 58
43	16 12	27 44	12 59	4 27	24 12
44	16 07	28 04	13 55	4 59	24 26
45	16 03	28 26	14 52	5 32	24 41
46	15 58	28 49	15 53	6 07	24 56
47	15 52	29 14	16 56	6 43	25 12
48	15 47	29 40	18 02	7 20	25 28
49	15 41	0♉08	19 11	7 59	25 45
50	15 35	0 39	20 24	8 40	26 03
51	15 28	1 11	21 40	9 23	26 21
52	15 22	1 47	23 00	10 07	26 41
53	15 14	2 25	24 25	10 54	27 01
54	15 06	3 07	25 53	11 43	27 23
55	14 58	3 53	27 27	12 35	27 45
56	14 49	4 44	29 05	13 29	28 09
57	14 40	5 40	0♋49	14 26	28 34
58	14 29	6 43	2 39	15 27	29 00
59	14 18	7 54	4 34	16 31	29 29
60	14♓06	9♉15	6♋36	17♋40	29♋59

21h 20m 0s — 320° 0' 0" — 17 ♒ 33

LAT.	11	12	ASC	2	3
0	19♓07	21♈38	22♉25	20♊49	18♋28
5	18 59	22 11	24 05	22 08	19 06
10	18 50	22 45	25 51	23 29	19 44
15	18 41	23 23	27 46	24 53	20 24
20	18 31	24 04	29 51	26 22	21 05
21	18 29	24 13	0♊18	26 40	21 13
22	18 27	24 22	0 45	26 59	21 22
23	18 25	24 32	1 13	27 18	21 31
24	18 23	24 41	1 42	27 38	21 39
25	18 21	24 51	2 11	27 57	21 48
26	18 18	25 01	2 41	28 17	21 57
27	18 16	25 12	3 12	28 38	22 07
28	18 13	25 23	3 44	28 59	22 16
29	18 11	25 34	4 16	29 20	22 26
30	18 08	25 45	4 50	29 42	22 35
31	18 06	25 57	5 24	0♋04	22 45
32	18 03	26 10	6 00	0 27	22 55
33	18 00	26 23	6 37	0 50	23 06
34	17 57	26 36	7 15	1 14	23 16
35	17 55	26 50	7 54	1 38	23 27
36	17 51	27 05	8 34	2 03	23 38
37	17 48	27 20	9 16	2 29	23 50
38	17 45	27 36	10 00	2 55	24 02
39	17 42	27 52	10 45	3 22	24 14
40	17 38	28 09	11 32	3 51	24 26
41	17 34	28 28	12 21	4 20	24 39
42	17 31	28 47	13 11	4 49	24 52
43	17 27	29 07	14 04	5 20	25 05
44	17 23	29 29	14 59	5 52	25 19
45	17 18	29 51	15 56	6 26	25 34
46	17 14	0♉16	16 56	7 00	25 49
47	17 09	0 41	17 59	7 36	26 05
48	17 04	1 09	19 05	8 13	26 21
49	16 59	1 38	20 13	8 52	26 38
50	16 53	2 10	21 25	9 32	26 55
51	16 47	2 44	22 41	10 14	27 13
52	16 41	3 20	24 00	10 58	27 33
53	16 34	4 00	25 24	11 44	27 53
54	16 27	4 44	26 51	12 33	28 14
55	16 19	5 32	28 24	13 24	28 36
56	16 11	6 24	0♋01	14 18	28 59
57	16 02	7 23	1 43	15 14	29 24
58	15 53	8 28	3 31	16 14	29 50
59	15 43	9 41	5 24	17 18	0♌18
60	15♓32	11♉05	7♋24	18♋25	0♌48

21h 24m 0s — 321° 0' 0" — 18 ♒ 34

LAT.	11	12	ASC	2	3
0	20♓12	22♈42	23♉23	21♊44	19♋24
5	20 05	23 16	25 05	23 03	20 02
10	19 57	23 52	26 52	24 24	20 40
15	19 49	24 32	28 48	25 49	21 19
20	19 40	25 15	0♊54	27 17	22 00
21	19 38	25 24	1 21	27 36	22 08
22	19 36	25 34	1 48	27 55	22 17
23	19 34	25 43	2 16	28 14	22 26
24	19 32	25 53	2 45	28 33	22 34
25	19 30	26 04	3 15	28 53	22 43
26	19 28	26 14	3 45	29 13	22 52
27	19 26	26 25	4 16	29 33	23 02
28	19 24	26 37	4 48	29 54	23 11
29	19 22	26 48	5 20	0♋15	23 20
30	19 19	27 00	5 54	0 37	23 30
31	19 17	27 13	6 29	0 59	23 40
32	19 14	27 26	7 04	1 21	23 50
33	19 12	27 39	7 41	1 45	24 00
34	19 09	27 53	8 19	2 08	24 11
35	19 07	28 08	8 58	2 33	24 22
36	19 04	28 23	9 39	2 58	24 33
37	19 01	28 38	10 21	3 23	24 44
38	18 58	28 55	11 04	3 49	24 56
39	18 55	29 12	11 49	4 17	25 07
40	18 52	29 30	12 36	4 45	25 20
41	18 49	29 49	13 25	5 13	25 32
42	18 45	0♉09	14 15	5 43	25 45
43	18 42	0 30	15 08	6 14	25 59
44	18 38	0 53	16 03	6 46	26 13
45	18 34	1 16	17 00	7 18	26 27
46	18 30	1 41	17 59	7 53	26 42
47	18 25	2 08	19 02	8 28	26 57
48	18 21	2 36	20 07	9 05	27 13
49	18 16	3 07	21 15	9 43	27 30
50	18 11	3 40	22 26	10 23	27 47
51	18 06	4 15	23 41	11 05	28 06
52	18 00	4 53	25 00	11 49	28 25
53	17 54	5 34	26 22	12 35	28 44
54	17 48	6 19	27 49	13 23	29 05
55	17 41	7 09	29 20	14 13	29 27
56	17 33	8 03	0♋55	15 06	29 50
57	17 26	9 04	2 36	16 02	0♌15
58	17 17	10 11	4 22	17 01	0 40
59	17 08	11 27	6 14	18 04	1 08
60	16♓58	12♉53	8♋11	19♋10	1♌37

21h 28m 0s — 322° 0' 0" — 19 ♒ 35

LAT.	11	12	ASC	2	3
0	21♓17	23♈46	24♉22	22♊39	20♋20
5	21 11	24 21	26 05	23 59	20 58
10	21 04	24 59	27 53	25 20	21 36
15	20 57	25 40	29 49	26 44	22 15
20	20 49	26 25	1♊57	28 13	22 55
21	20 47	26 35	2 24	28 31	23 04
22	20 45	26 45	2 51	28 50	23 12
23	20 43	26 55	3 19	29 09	23 21
24	20 42	27 05	3 48	29 28	23 30
25	20 40	27 16	4 18	29 48	23 38
26	20 38	27 27	4 48	0♋08	23 47
27	20 36	27 38	5 19	0 28	23 56
28	20 34	27 50	5 51	0 49	24 06
29	20 32	28 02	6 24	1 10	24 15
30	20 30	28 15	6 58	1 32	24 25
31	20 28	28 28	7 32	1 54	24 35
32	20 26	28 41	8 08	2 16	24 45
33	20 24	28 55	8 45	2 39	24 55
34	20 21	29 10	9 23	3 03	25 05
35	20 19	29 25	10 02	3 27	25 16
36	20 17	29 40	10 43	3 52	25 27
37	20 14	29 57	11 25	4 17	25 38
38	20 11	0♉14	12 08	4 44	25 50
39	20 09	0 32	12 53	5 10	26 01
40	20 06	0 50	13 40	5 38	26 14
41	20 03	1 10	14 28	6 07	26 26
42	20 00	1 31	15 19	6 36	26 39
43	19 57	1 53	16 11	7 07	26 52
44	19 53	2 16	17 05	7 39	27 06
45	19 50	2 40	18 02	8 11	27 20
46	19 46	3 06	19 02	8 45	27 35
47	19 42	3 34	20 03	9 20	27 50
48	19 38	4 03	21 08	9 57	28 06
49	19 34	4 35	22 16	10 35	28 23
50	19 29	5 09	23 26	11 15	28 40
51	19 25	5 45	24 40	11 56	28 58
52	19 20	6 25	25 58	12 39	29 16
53	19 14	7 07	27 19	13 25	29 36
54	19 09	7 54	28 45	14 12	29 57
55	19 02	8 45	0♋15	15 02	0♌18
56	18 56	9 41	1 49	15 54	0 41
57	18 49	10 43	3 29	16 50	1 05
58	18 41	11 53	5 13	17 48	1 30
59	18 33	13 11	7 03	18 49	1 57
60	18♓24	14♉40	8♋58	19♋55	2♌26

21h 32m 0s — 323° 0' 0" — 20 ♒ 36

LAT.	11	12	ASC	2	3
0	22♓23	24♈50	25♉21	23♊34	21♋17
5	22 17	25 27	27 04	24 54	21 54
10	22 11	26 06	28 53	26 15	22 32
15	22 04	26 48	0♊51	27 39	23 11
20	21 57	27 35	2 59	29 08	23 51
21	21 56	27 45	3 26	29 26	23 59
22	21 54	27 55	3 54	29 45	24 08
23	21 53	28 06	4 22	0♋04	24 16
24	21 51	28 17	4 51	0 23	24 25
25	21 50	28 28	5 21	0 43	24 33
26	21 48	28 39	5 51	1 03	24 42
27	21 46	28 51	6 22	1 23	24 51
28	21 45	29 03	6 54	1 44	25 01
29	21 43	29 16	7 27	2 05	25 10
30	21 41	29 29	8 01	2 26	25 20
31	21 39	29 42	8 36	2 48	25 29
32	21 37	29 56	9 12	3 11	25 39
33	21 35	0♉11	9 48	3 34	25 49
34	21 33	0 26	10 26	3 57	26 00
35	21 31	0 41	11 06	4 21	26 10
36	21 29	0 57	11 46	4 46	26 21
37	21 27	1 14	12 28	5 11	26 32
38	21 25	1 32	13 11	5 37	26 44
39	21 22	1 51	13 56	6 04	26 55
40	21 20	2 10	14 43	6 32	27 07
41	21 17	2 30	15 31	7 00	27 20
42	21 15	2 52	16 21	7 30	27 33
43	21 12	3 15	17 13	8 00	27 46
44	21 09	3 38	18 08	8 31	27 59
45	21 06	4 04	19 04	9 04	28 13
46	21 03	4 31	20 03	9 37	28 28
47	20 59	4 59	21 04	10 12	28 43
48	20 56	5 29	22 08	10 49	28 59
49	20 52	6 02	23 15	11 26	29 15
50	20 48	6 37	24 26	12 06	29 32
51	20 44	7 15	25 39	12 47	29 50
52	20 39	7 55	26 56	13 29	0♌08
53	20 35	8 39	28 16	14 14	0 28
54	20 30	9 27	29 41	15 01	0 48
55	20 24	10 20	1♋09	15 50	1 09
56	20 19	11 18	2 42	16 42	1 32
57	20 12	12 22	4 20	17 37	1 55
58	20 06	13 33	6 03	18 34	2 20
59	19 59	14 54	7 51	19 35	2 47
60	19♓51	16♉25	9♋44	20♋39	3♌15

21h 36m 0s — 324° 0' 0" — 21 ♒ 37

LAT.	11	12	ASC	2	3
0	23♓28	25♈53	26♉19	24♊30	22♋13
5	23 23	26 31	28 03	25 49	22 50
10	23 18	27 12	29 54	27 10	23 28
15	23 12	27 56	1♊52	28 35	24 06
20	23 06	28 45	4 00	0♋03	24 46
21	23 05	28 55	4 28	0 21	24 55
22	23 04	29 06	4 56	0 40	25 03
23	23 02	29 17	5 24	0 59	25 11
24	23 01	29 28	5 53	1 18	25 20
25	23 00	29 39	6 23	1 38	25 29
26	22 58	29 51	6 54	1 58	25 37
27	22 57	0♉04	7 25	2 18	25 46
28	22 55	0 16	7 57	2 38	25 56
29	22 54	0 29	8 30	2 59	26 05
30	22 52	0 43	9 04	3 21	26 14
31	22 51	0 56	9 39	3 43	26 24
32	22 49	1 11	10 14	4 05	26 34
33	22 47	1 26	10 51	4 28	26 44
34	22 46	1 41	11 29	4 51	26 54
35	22 44	1 57	12 08	5 15	27 05
36	22 42	2 14	12 49	5 40	27 15
37	22 40	2 32	13 31	6 05	27 26
38	22 38	2 50	14 14	6 31	27 38
39	22 36	3 09	14 59	6 58	27 49
40	22 34	3 29	15 45	7 25	28 01
41	22 32	3 50	16 33	7 53	28 13
42	22 29	4 12	17 23	8 23	28 26
43	22 27	4 36	18 15	8 53	28 39
44	22 25	5 00	19 09	9 24	28 53
45	22 22	5 27	20 05	9 56	29 07
46	22 19	5 54	21 04	10 29	29 21
47	22 16	6 24	22 05	11 04	29 36
48	22 13	6 55	23 08	11 40	29 51
49	22 10	7 28	24 15	12 17	0♌08
50	22 07	8 04	25 24	12 56	0 24
51	22 03	8 43	26 37	13 37	0 42
52	21 59	9 25	27 53	14 19	1 00
53	21 55	10 10	29 12	15 04	1 19
54	21 51	10 59	0♋36	15 50	1 39
55	21 46	11 53	2 03	16 39	2 00
56	21 41	12 53	3 35	17 30	2 22
57	21 36	13 59	5 11	18 24	2 46
58	21 30	15 12	6 52	19 21	3 10
59	21 24	16 34	8 38	20 21	3 37
60	21♓17	18♉08	10♋30	21♋24	4♌04

21h 40m 0s — 325° 0' 0" — 22 ♒ 39

LAT.	11	12	ASC	2	3
0	24♓33	26♈57	27♉17	25♊25	23♋10
5	24 29	27 36	29 02	26 44	23 47
10	24 25	28 18	0♊54	28 06	24 24
15	24 20	29 04	2 53	29 30	25 02
20	24 15	29 54	5 02	0♋58	25 42
21	24 14	0♉05	5 29	1 16	25 50
22	24 13	0 16	5 57	1 35	25 58
23	24 12	0 27	6 26	1 54	26 07
24	24 11	0 39	6 55	2 13	26 15
25	24 10	0 51	7 25	2 32	26 24
26	24 08	1 03	7 56	2 52	26 33
27	24 07	1 16	8 27	3 12	26 42
28	24 06	1 29	8 59	3 33	26 51
29	24 05	1 42	9 32	3 54	27 00
30	24 03	1 56	10 06	4 15	27 09
31	24 02	2 10	10 41	4 37	27 19
32	24 01	2 25	11 17	4 59	27 29
33	23 59	2 41	11 54	5 22	27 38
34	23 58	2 57	12 32	5 45	27 49
35	23 56	3 13	13 11	6 09	27 59
36	23 55	3 31	13 51	6 34	28 10
37	23 53	3 49	14 33	6 59	28 21
38	23 52	4 08	15 16	7 25	28 32
39	23 50	4 27	16 01	7 51	28 43
40	23 48	4 48	16 47	8 18	28 55
41	23 46	5 10	17 35	8 46	29 07
42	23 44	5 32	18 25	9 15	29 20
43	23 42	5 56	19 16	9 45	29 33
44	23 40	6 22	20 10	10 16	29 46
45	23 38	6 49	21 06	10 48	0♌00
46	23 36	7 17	22 04	11 21	0 14
47	23 33	7 47	23 04	11 56	0 29
48	23 31	8 20	24 07	12 31	0 44
49	23 28	8 54	25 13	13 08	1 00
50	23 25	9 31	26 22	13 47	1 17
51	23 22	10 11	27 34	14 27	1 34
52	23 19	10 54	28 49	15 09	1 52
53	23 16	11 40	0♋07	15 53	2 11
54	23 12	12 31	1 30	16 39	2 31
55	23 08	13 26	2 56	17 27	2 51
56	23 04	14 27	4 27	18 18	3 13
57	23 00	15 34	6 02	19 11	3 36
58	22 55	16 49	7 41	20 07	4 00
59	22 50	18 13	9 25	21 06	4 26
60	22♓44	19♉49	11♋15	22♋08	4♌54

21h 44m 0s — 326° 0' 0" — 23 ♒ 41

LAT.	11	12	ASC	2	3
0	25♓38	28♈00	28♉15	26♊20	24♋06
5	25 35	28 41	0♊01	27 40	24 43
10	25 32	29 24	1 53	29 01	25 20
15	25 28	0♉11	3 53	0♋25	25 58
20	25 24	1 03	6 03	1 53	26 38
21	25 23	1 14	6 31	2 11	26 46
22	25 22	1 26	6 59	2 30	26 54
23	25 21	1 37	7 27	2 49	27 02
24	25 21	1 49	7 57	3 08	27 11
25	25 20	2 02	8 27	3 27	27 19
26	25 19	2 14	8 57	3 47	27 28
27	25 18	2 27	9 29	4 07	27 37
28	25 17	2 41	10 01	4 27	27 46
29	25 16	2 55	10 34	4 48	27 55
30	25 15	3 09	11 08	5 09	28 04
31	25 14	3 24	11 43	5 31	28 14
32	25 13	3 39	12 19	5 53	28 23
33	25 11	3 55	12 56	6 16	28 33
34	25 10	4 11	13 34	6 39	28 43
35	25 09	4 29	14 13	7 03	28 54
36	25 08	4 46	14 53	7 27	29 04
37	25 07	5 05	15 35	7 52	29 15
38	25 05	5 24	16 18	8 18	29 26
39	25 04	5 45	17 02	8 44	29 37
40	25 02	6 06	17 48	9 11	29 49
41	25 01	6 28	18 36	9 39	0♌01
42	24 59	6 52	19 26	10 08	0 13
43	24 58	7 16	20 17	10 38	0 26
44	24 56	7 43	21 10	11 08	0 39
45	24 54	8 10	22 06	11 40	0 53
46	24 53	8 39	23 03	12 13	1 07
47	24 51	9 10	24 03	12 47	1 22
48	24 49	9 43	25 06	13 22	1 37
49	24 46	10 19	26 11	13 59	1 53
50	24 44	10 57	27 19	14 37	2 09
51	24 42	11 37	28 30	15 17	2 26
52	24 39	12 21	29 44	15 59	2 44
53	24 37	13 09	1♋02	16 42	3 02
54	24 34	14 01	2 23	17 27	3 22
55	24 31	14 57	3 49	18 15	3 42
56	24 27	15 59	5 18	19 05	4 04
57	24 24	17 08	6 51	19 57	4 27
58	24 20	18 25	8 29	20 52	4 50
59	24 16	19 50	10 12	21 51	5 16
60	24♓11	21♉28	12♋00	22♋52	5♌43

21h 48m 0s — 327° 0' 0" — 24 ♒ 42

LAT.	11	12	ASC	2	3
0	26♓44	29♈03	29♉13	27♊15	25♋03
5	26 41	29 45	1♊00	28 35	25 40
10	26 39	0♉30	2 53	29 56	26 17
15	26 36	1 19	4 53	1♋20	26 54
20	26 33	2 12	7 04	2 48	27 33
21	26 32	2 24	7 32	3 06	27 41
22	26 32	2 35	8 00	3 24	27 50
23	26 31	2 47	8 29	3 43	27 58
24	26 30	3 00	8 58	4 02	28 06
25	26 30	3 12	9 28	4 22	28 15
26	26 29	3 25	9 59	4 41	28 23
27	26 28	3 39	10 30	5 01	28 32
28	26 28	3 53	11 02	5 22	28 41
29	26 27	4 07	11 36	5 42	28 50
30	26 26	4 22	12 09	6 04	28 59
31	26 25	4 37	12 44	6 25	29 09
32	26 24	4 53	13 20	6 47	29 18
33	26 24	5 09	13 57	7 10	29 28
34	26 23	5 26	14 35	7 33	29 38
35	26 22	5 43	15 14	7 57	29 48
36	26 21	6 02	15 54	8 21	29 59
37	26 20	6 21	16 36	8 46	0♌09
38	26 19	6 41	17 19	9 11	0 20
39	26 18	7 02	18 03	9 37	0 31
40	26 17	7 24	18 49	10 04	0 43
41	26 16	7 46	19 37	10 32	0 55
42	26 15	8 11	20 26	11 01	1 07
43	26 13	8 36	21 17	11 30	1 20
44	26 12	9 03	22 10	12 00	1 33
45	26 11	9 31	23 05	12 32	1 46
46	26 09	10 01	24 02	13 04	2 00
47	26 08	10 33	25 02	13 38	2 15
48	26 06	11 06	26 04	14 13	2 30
49	26 05	11 43	27 08	14 50	2 45
50	26 03	12 21	28 16	15 27	3 01
51	26 01	13 03	29 26	16 07	3 18
52	25 59	13 48	0♋39	16 48	3 36
53	25 57	14 37	1 56	17 31	3 54
54	25 55	15 29	3 16	18 16	4 13
55	25 53	16 27	4 40	19 03	4 33
56	25 50	17 30	6 08	19 52	4 55
57	25 48	18 41	7 40	20 44	5 17
58	25 45	19 59	9 17	21 38	5 41
59	25 42	21 26	10 58	22 36	6 05
60	25♓38	23♉05	12♋44	23♋36	6♌32

21h 52m 0s — 25 ♒ 44 — 328° 0' 0"

LAT.	11	12	ASC	2	3
0	27♓49	0♉06	0♊11	28♊10	26♋00
5	27 48	0 49	1 59	29 30	26 37
10	27 46	1 36	3 52	0♋51	27 13
15	27 44	2 26	5 53	2 15	27 50
20	27 42	3 21	8 04	3 42	28 29
21	27 42	3 33	8 32	4 01	28 37
22	27 41	3 45	9 00	4 19	28 45
23	27 41	3 57	9 29	4 38	28 53
24	27 40	4 10	9 59	4 57	29 02
25	27 40	4 23	10 29	5 16	29 10
26	27 39	4 36	11 00	5 36	29 19
27	27 39	4 50	11 31	5 56	29 27
28	27 38	5 04	12 03	6 16	29 36
29	27 38	5 19	12 37	6 37	29 45
30	27 37	5 34	13 10	6 58	29 54
31	27 37	5 49	13 45	7 19	0♌04
32	27 36	6 06	14 21	7 41	0 13
33	27 36	6 22	14 58	8 04	0 23
34	27 35	6 40	15 36	8 27	0 33
35	27 34	6 58	16 15	8 50	0 43
36	27 34	7 17	16 55	9 14	0 53
37	27 33	7 36	17 36	9 39	1 04
38	27 33	7 57	18 19	10 04	1 14
39	27 32	8 18	19 03	10 30	1 26
40	27 31	8 41	19 49	10 57	1 37
41	27 30	9 04	20 36	11 24	1 49
42	27 30	9 29	21 25	11 53	2 01
43	27 29	9 55	22 16	12 22	2 13
44	27 28	10 22	23 09	12 52	2 26
45	27 27	10 51	24 03	13 23	2 40
46	27 26	11 22	25 00	13 56	2 53
47	27 25	11 54	25 59	14 29	3 08
48	27 24	12 29	27 01	15 04	3 22
49	27 23	13 06	28 05	15 40	3 38
50	27 22	13 45	29 11	16 17	3 54
51	27 21	14 28	0♋21	16 56	4 10
52	27 20	15 14	1 34	17 37	4 28
53	27 18	16 03	2 49	18 19	4 46
54	27 17	16 57	4 09	19 04	5 05
55	27 15	17 56	5 32	19 50	5 25
56	27 14	19 00	6 58	20 39	5 45
57	27 12	20 12	8 29	21 30	6 07
58	27 10	21 31	10 04	22 24	6 31
59	27 08	23 00	11 44	23 20	6 55
60	27♓06	24♉41	13♋28	24♋20	7♌21

21h 56m 0s — 26 ♒ 47 — 329° 0' 0"

LAT.	11	12	ASC	2	3
0	28♓55	1♉08	1♊08	29♊05	26♋57
5	28 54	1 53	2 57	0♋25	27 33
10	28 53	2 41	4 51	1 46	28 10
15	28 52	3 33	6 53	3 09	28 47
20	28 51	4 29	9 05	4 37	29 25
21	28 51	4 41	9 32	4 55	29 33
22	28 51	4 54	10 01	5 14	29 41
23	28 50	5 06	10 30	5 32	29 49
24	28 50	5 19	10 59	5 51	29 57
25	28 50	5 33	11 29	6 10	0♌06
26	28 50	5 46	12 00	6 30	0 14
27	28 49	6 01	12 32	6 50	0 23
28	28 49	6 15	13 04	7 10	0 31
29	28 49	6 30	13 37	7 31	0 40
30	28 49	6 46	14 11	7 52	0 49
31	28 48	7 02	14 46	8 13	0 59
32	28 48	7 18	15 22	8 35	1 08
33	28 48	7 36	15 58	8 57	1 18
34	28 48	7 53	16 36	9 20	1 27
35	28 47	8 12	17 15	9 43	1 37
36	28 47	8 31	17 55	10 07	1 48
37	28 47	8 51	18 37	10 32	1 58
38	28 46	9 12	19 19	10 57	2 09
39	28 46	9 34	20 03	11 23	2 20
40	28 46	9 57	20 49	11 49	2 31
41	28 45	10 21	21 36	12 17	2 43
42	28 45	10 46	22 24	12 45	2 55
43	28 44	11 13	23 15	13 14	3 07
44	28 44	11 41	24 07	13 44	3 20
45	28 44	12 10	25 01	14 15	3 33
46	28 43	12 42	25 58	14 47	3 47
47	28 43	13 15	26 56	15 20	4 01
48	28 42	13 50	27 57	15 54	4 15
49	28 42	14 28	29 01	16 30	4 30
50	28 41	15 08	0♋07	17 07	4 46
51	28 40	15 52	1 15	17 46	5 02
52	28 40	16 38	2 27	18 26	5 20
53	28 39	17 29	3 42	19 08	5 37
54	28 38	18 24	5 01	19 52	5 56
55	28 38	19 23	6 22	20 38	6 16
56	28 37	20 29	7 48	21 26	6 36
57	28 36	21 41	9 17	22 16	6 58
58	28 35	23 02	10 51	23 09	7 21
59	28 34	24 32	12 29	24 05	7 45
60	28♓33	26♉14	14♋11	25♋04	8♌10

22h 0m 0s — 27 ♒ 49 — 330° 0' 0"

LAT.	11	12	ASC	2	3
0	0♈00	2♉11	2♊05	0♋00	27♋55
5	0 00	2 57	3 55	1 20	28 30
10	0 00	3 46	5 50	2 41	29 06
15	0 00	4 39	7 52	4 04	29 43
20	0 00	5 37	10 05	5 32	0♌21
21	0 00	5 50	10 32	5 50	0 29
22	0 00	6 02	11 01	6 08	0 37
23	0 00	6 15	11 30	6 27	0 45
24	0 00	6 29	11 59	6 46	0 53
25	0 00	6 42	12 30	7 05	1 01
26	0 00	6 56	13 00	7 24	1 10
27	0 00	7 11	13 32	7 44	1 18
28	0 00	7 26	14 04	8 04	1 27
29	0 00	7 41	14 37	8 25	1 36
30	0 00	7 57	15 11	8 45	1 45
31	0 00	8 14	15 46	9 07	1 54
32	0 00	8 31	16 22	9 28	2 03
33	0 00	8 48	16 59	9 51	2 13
34	0 00	9 06	17 36	10 13	2 22
35	0 00	9 25	18 15	10 37	2 32
36	0 00	9 45	18 55	11 00	2 42
37	0 00	10 06	19 36	11 25	2 53
38	0 00	10 27	20 19	11 50	3 03
39	0 00	10 49	21 02	12 15	3 14
40	0 00	11 13	21 48	12 42	3 25
41	0 00	11 37	22 35	13 09	3 37
42	0 00	12 03	23 23	13 37	3 49
43	0 00	12 30	24 13	14 06	4 01
44	0 00	12 59	25 05	14 35	4 13
45	0 00	13 29	25 59	15 06	4 26
46	0 00	14 01	26 55	15 38	4 40
47	0 00	14 35	27 53	16 11	4 54
48	0 00	15 11	28 53	16 45	5 08
49	0 00	15 49	29 56	17 20	5 23
50	0 00	16 30	1♋01	17 57	5 39
51	0 00	17 14	2 09	18 35	5 55
52	0 00	18 02	3 20	19 15	6 12
53	0 00	18 53	4 34	19 56	6 29
54	0 00	19 49	5 52	20 40	6 48
55	0 00	20 50	7 12	21 25	7 07
56	0 00	21 56	8 37	22 12	7 27
57	0 00	23 10	10 05	23 02	7 48
58	0 00	24 31	11 37	23 54	8 11
59	0 00	26 03	13 13	24 49	8 34
60	0♈00	27♉46	14♋54	25♋47	9♌00

22h 4m 0s — 28 ♒ 52 — 331° 0' 0"

LAT.	11	12	ASC	2	3
0	1♈05	3♉13	3♊03	0♋55	28♋52
5	1 06	4 01	4 53	2 15	29 27
10	1 07	4 51	6 49	3 36	0♌03
15	1 08	5 45	8 52	4 59	0 39
20	1 09	6 45	11 04	6 26	1 17
21	1 09	6 58	11 32	6 44	1 25
22	1 09	7 11	12 01	7 02	1 33
23	1 10	7 24	12 30	7 21	1 41
24	1 10	7 38	12 59	7 40	1 49
25	1 10	7 52	13 29	7 59	1 57
26	1 10	8 06	14 00	8 18	2 05
27	1 11	8 21	14 32	8 38	2 14
28	1 11	8 36	15 04	8 58	2 22
29	1 11	8 52	15 37	9 18	2 31
30	1 11	9 08	16 11	9 39	2 40
31	1 12	9 25	16 46	10 00	2 49
32	1 12	9 42	17 22	10 22	2 58
33	1 12	10 00	17 58	10 44	3 08
34	1 12	10 19	18 36	11 07	3 17
35	1 13	10 38	19 15	11 30	3 27
36	1 13	10 59	19 54	11 53	3 37
37	1 13	11 20	20 35	12 18	3 47
38	1 14	11 41	21 18	12 42	3 58
39	1 14	12 04	22 01	13 08	4 08
40	1 14	12 28	22 46	13 34	4 19
41	1 15	12 53	23 33	14 01	4 31
42	1 15	13 19	24 21	14 29	4 43
43	1 16	13 47	25 11	14 57	4 55
44	1 16	14 16	26 02	15 27	5 07
45	1 16	14 47	26 56	15 57	5 20
46	1 17	15 19	27 51	16 29	5 33
47	1 17	15 54	28 49	17 01	5 47
48	1 18	16 31	29 49	17 35	6 01
49	1 18	17 10	0♋51	18 10	6 16
50	1 19	17 51	1 55	18 46	6 31
51	1 20	18 36	3 03	19 24	6 47
52	1 20	19 25	4 13	20 03	7 04
53	1 21	20 17	5 26	20 44	7 21
54	1 22	21 13	6 42	21 27	7 39
55	1 22	22 15	8 02	22 12	7 58
56	1 23	23 22	9 25	22 59	8 18
57	1 24	24 37	10 52	23 48	8 39
58	1 25	25 59	12 23	24 39	9 01
59	1 26	27 31	13 58	25 33	9 24
60	1♈27	29♉16	15♋37	26♋31	9♌49

22h 8m 0s — 29 ♒ 54 — 332° 0' 0"

LAT.	11	12	ASC	2	3
0	2♈11	4♉16	4♊00	1♋50	29♋49
5	2 12	5 04	5 51	3 10	0♌25
10	2 14	5 56	7 47	4 31	1 00
15	2 16	6 51	9 51	5 54	1 36
20	2 18	7 52	12 04	7 21	2 14
21	2 18	8 05	12 31	7 39	2 21
22	2 19	8 19	13 00	7 57	2 29
23	2 19	8 32	13 29	8 15	2 37
24	2 20	8 46	13 59	8 34	2 45
25	2 20	9 01	14 29	8 53	2 53
26	2 21	9 15	15 00	9 12	3 01
27	2 21	9 31	15 31	9 32	3 10
28	2 22	9 46	16 04	9 52	3 18
29	2 22	10 02	16 37	10 12	3 27
30	2 23	10 19	17 11	10 33	3 35
31	2 23	10 36	17 45	10 54	3 44
32	2 24	10 54	18 21	11 15	3 53
33	2 24	11 12	18 57	11 37	4 03
34	2 25	11 31	19 35	12 00	4 12
35	2 26	11 51	20 14	12 23	4 22
36	2 26	12 12	20 53	12 46	4 32
37	2 27	12 33	21 34	13 10	4 42
38	2 27	12 55	22 16	13 35	4 52
39	2 28	13 19	23 00	14 00	5 03
40	2 29	13 43	23 44	14 26	5 14
41	2 30	14 08	24 31	14 53	5 25
42	2 30	14 35	25 19	15 20	5 37
43	2 31	15 03	26 08	15 49	5 48
44	2 32	15 33	26 59	16 18	6 01
45	2 33	16 04	27 52	16 48	6 13
46	2 34	16 37	28 47	17 19	6 26
47	2 35	17 12	29 44	17 52	6 40
48	2 36	17 50	0♋44	18 25	6 54
49	2 37	18 29	1 45	19 00	7 08
50	2 38	19 12	2 49	19 36	7 24
51	2 39	19 57	3 56	20 13	7 39
52	2 40	20 46	5 05	20 52	7 56
53	2 42	21 39	6 17	21 32	8 13
54	2 43	22 36	7 33	22 15	8 31
55	2 45	23 39	8 51	22 59	8 49
56	2 46	24 47	10 13	23 45	9 09
57	2 48	26 02	11 39	24 33	9 29
58	2 50	27 25	13 08	25 24	9 51
59	2 52	28 59	14 41	26 18	10 14
60	2♈54	0♊44	16♋19	27♋14	10♌38

22h 12m 0s — 0 ♓ 57 — 333° 0' 0"

LAT.	11	12	ASC	2	3
0	3♈16	5♉18	4♊57	2♋45	0♌47
5	3 19	6 07	6 49	4 05	1 22
10	3 21	7 00	8 45	5 25	1 57
15	3 24	7 57	10 49	6 48	2 33
20	3 27	8 59	13 03	8 15	3 10
21	3 28	9 13	13 31	8 33	3 17
22	3 28	9 26	13 59	8 51	3 25
23	3 29	9 40	14 28	9 09	3 33
24	3 30	9 55	14 58	9 28	3 41
25	3 30	10 09	15 28	9 47	3 49
26	3 31	10 24	15 59	10 06	3 57
27	3 32	10 40	16 30	10 26	4 05
28	3 32	10 56	17 03	10 45	4 14
29	3 33	11 12	17 36	11 06	4 22
30	3 34	11 29	18 10	11 26	4 31
31	3 35	11 47	18 44	11 47	4 40
32	3 36	12 05	19 20	12 09	4 49
33	3 36	12 23	19 56	12 30	4 58
34	3 37	12 43	20 34	12 53	5 07
35	3 38	13 03	21 12	13 15	5 17
36	3 39	13 24	21 52	13 39	5 27
37	3 40	13 46	22 32	14 03	5 37
38	3 41	14 09	23 14	14 27	5 47
39	3 42	14 32	23 57	14 52	5 57
40	3 43	14 57	24 42	15 18	6 08
41	3 44	15 23	25 28	15 45	6 19
42	3 45	15 50	26 16	16 12	6 31
43	3 47	16 19	27 05	16 40	6 42
44	3 48	16 49	27 56	17 09	6 54
45	3 49	17 21	28 48	17 39	7 07
46	3 51	17 54	29 43	18 10	7 20
47	3 52	18 30	0♋39	18 42	7 33
48	3 54	19 08	1 38	19 15	7 47
49	3 55	19 48	2 39	19 49	8 01
50	3 57	20 31	3 42	20 25	8 16
51	3 59	21 17	4 48	21 02	8 32
52	4 01	22 07	5 57	21 40	8 48
53	4 03	23 00	7 08	22 20	9 05
54	4 05	23 58	8 22	23 02	9 22
55	4 07	25 01	9 40	23 45	9 40
56	4 10	26 10	11 01	24 31	10 00
57	4 12	27 26	12 25	25 19	10 20
58	4 15	28 50	13 53	26 09	10 41
59	4 18	0♊24	15 25	27 02	11 04
60	4♈22	2♊10	17♋01	27♋57	11♌28

22h 16m 0s — 2 ♓ 00 — 334° 0' 0"

LAT.	11	12	ASC	2	3
0	4♈22	6♉19	5♊54	3♋40	1♌45
5	4 25	7 10	7 46	5 00	2 20
10	4 28	8 04	9 44	6 20	2 54
15	4 32	9 03	11 48	7 43	3 30
20	4 36	10 06	14 01	9 09	4 06
21	4 37	10 20	14 29	9 27	4 14
22	4 38	10 34	14 58	9 45	4 21
23	4 39	10 48	15 27	10 03	4 29
24	4 39	11 03	15 57	10 22	4 37
25	4 40	11 17	16 27	10 41	4 45
26	4 41	11 33	16 58	11 00	4 53
27	4 42	11 49	17 29	11 19	5 01
28	4 43	12 05	18 02	11 39	5 09
29	4 44	12 22	18 35	11 59	5 18
30	4 45	12 39	19 08	12 20	5 26
31	4 46	12 57	19 43	12 40	5 35
32	4 47	13 15	20 18	13 02	5 44
33	4 49	13 34	20 55	13 23	5 53
34	4 50	13 54	21 32	13 46	6 02
35	4 51	14 15	22 10	14 08	6 12
36	4 52	14 36	22 50	14 31	6 21
37	4 53	14 58	23 30	14 55	6 31
38	4 55	15 21	24 12	15 19	6 41
39	4 56	15 45	24 55	15 44	6 52
40	4 58	16 11	25 39	16 10	7 02
41	4 59	16 37	26 25	16 36	7 13
42	5 01	17 05	27 12	17 03	7 25
43	5 02	17 34	28 01	17 31	7 36
44	5 04	18 04	28 51	18 00	7 48
45	5 06	18 37	29 44	18 30	8 00
46	5 07	19 11	0♋38	19 00	8 13
47	5 09	19 47	1 34	19 32	8 26
48	5 11	20 25	2 32	20 05	8 40
49	5 14	21 06	3 32	20 38	8 54
50	5 16	21 50	4 35	21 14	9 09
51	5 18	22 36	5 40	21 50	9 24
52	5 21	23 26	6 48	22 28	9 40
53	5 23	24 20	7 58	23 08	9 56
54	5 26	25 19	9 12	23 49	10 14
55	5 29	26 23	10 28	24 32	10 32
56	5 33	27 32	11 48	25 17	10 51
57	5 36	28 49	13 11	26 04	11 11
58	5 40	0♊14	14 38	26 54	11 32
59	5 44	1 48	16 08	27 45	11 54
60	5♈49	3♊35	17♋42	28♋40	12♌17

22h 20m 0s — 3 ♓ 03 — 335° 0' 0"

LAT.	11	12	ASC	2	3
0	5♈27	7♉21	6♊50	4♋35	2♌43
5	5 31	8 13	8 43	5 55	3 17
10	5 35	9 08	10 41	7 15	3 52
15	5 40	10 08	12 46	8 38	4 27
20	5 45	11 13	15 00	10 04	5 03
21	5 46	11 27	15 28	10 21	5 10
22	5 47	11 41	15 56	10 39	5 18
23	5 48	11 55	16 26	10 58	5 26
24	5 49	12 10	16 55	11 16	5 33
25	5 50	12 25	17 25	11 35	5 41
26	5 52	12 41	17 56	11 54	5 49
27	5 53	12 57	18 28	12 13	5 57
28	5 54	13 14	19 00	12 33	6 05
29	5 55	13 31	19 33	12 53	6 14
30	5 57	13 48	20 07	13 13	6 22
31	5 58	14 07	20 41	13 34	6 31
32	5 59	14 25	21 16	13 55	6 39
33	6 01	14 45	21 53	14 16	6 48
34	6 02	15 05	22 30	14 38	6 58
35	6 04	15 26	23 08	15 01	7 07
36	6 05	15 47	23 47	15 24	7 16
37	6 07	16 10	24 28	15 47	7 26
38	6 08	16 34	25 09	16 12	7 36
39	6 10	16 58	25 52	16 36	7 46
40	6 12	17 24	26 36	17 02	7 57
41	6 14	17 50	27 21	17 28	8 08
42	6 16	18 19	28 08	17 55	8 19
43	6 18	18 48	28 57	18 22	8 30
44	6 20	19 19	29 47	18 51	8 42
45	6 22	19 52	0♋39	19 20	8 54
46	6 24	20 26	1 32	19 50	9 07
47	6 27	21 03	2 28	20 22	9 20
48	6 29	21 42	3 25	20 54	9 33
49	6 32	22 23	4 25	21 28	9 47
50	6 35	23 07	5 27	22 03	10 01
51	6 38	23 54	6 31	22 39	10 16
52	6 41	24 45	7 38	23 16	10 32
53	6 44	25 40	8 48	23 55	10 48
54	6 48	26 39	10 00	24 36	11 05
55	6 52	27 43	11 16	25 19	11 23
56	6 56	28 53	12 34	26 03	11 42
57	7 00	0♊10	13 56	26 49	12 01
58	7 05	1 36	15 22	27 38	12 22
59	7 10	3 11	16 51	28 29	12 44
60	7♈16	4♊57	18♋24	29♋23	13♌06

22h 24m 0s	336° 0' 0"	4 ♓ 07		
11	12	ASC	2	3
6♈32	8♉23	7♊47	5♋30	3♌41
6 37	9 16	9 41	6 50	4 15
6 42	10 12	11 39	8 10	4 49
6 48	11 13	13 44	9 32	5 24
6 54	12 19	15 58	10 58	6 00
6 55	12 33	16 26	11 15	6 07
6 56	12 48	16 55	11 33	6 14
6 58	13 02	17 24	11 52	6 22
6 59	13 17	17 53	12 10	6 30
7 00	13 33	18 24	12 29	6 37
7 02	13 49	18 54	12 47	6 45
7 03	14 05	19 26	13 07	6 53
7 05	14 22	19 58	13 26	7 01
7 06	14 40	20 31	13 46	7 10
7 08	14 57	21 05	14 06	7 18
7 09	15 16	21 39	14 27	7 26
7 11	15 35	22 14	14 48	7 35
7 13	15 55	22 50	15 09	7 44
7 14	16 15	23 27	15 31	7 53
7 16	16 36	24 05	15 53	8 02
7 18	16 58	24 44	16 16	8 12
7 20	17 21	25 25	16 40	8 21
7 22	17 45	26 06	17 04	8 31
7 24	18 10	26 48	17 28	8 41
7 26	18 36	27 32	17 53	8 51
7 28	19 03	28 17	18 19	9 02
7 31	19 32	29 04	18 46	9 13
7 33	20 02	29 52	19 13	9 24
7 35	20 33	0♋42	19 41	9 36
7 38	21 06	1 33	20 11	9 48
7 41	21 41	2 26	20 41	10 00
7 44	22 18	3 21	21 12	10 13
7 47	22 57	4 18	21 44	10 26
7 50	23 39	5 17	22 17	10 40
7 53	24 24	6 19	22 51	10 54
7 57	25 11	7 22	23 27	11 09
8 01	26 03	8 28	24 04	11 24
8 05	26 58	9 37	24 43	11 40
8 09	27 57	10 49	25 23	11 57
8 14	29 02	12 03	26 05	12 14
8 19	0♊13	13 21	26 49	12 33
8 24	1 30	14 42	27 35	12 52
8 30	2 56	16 06	28 23	13 12
8 36	4 31	17 33	29 13	13 33
8♈43	6♊19	19♋05	0♌06	13♌56

22h 28m 0s	337° 0' 0"	5 ♓ 10			
11	12	ASC	2	3	LAT.
7♈37	9♉24	8♊43	6♋26	4♌39	0
7 43	10 18	10 38	7 45	5 13	5
7 49	11 16	12 37	9 05	5 47	10
7 56	12 17	14 42	10 27	6 21	15
8 03	13 25	16 56	11 52	6 56	20
8 04	13 39	17 24	12 10	7 04	21
8 06	13 54	17 53	12 27	7 11	22
8 07	14 09	18 22	12 45	7 19	23
8 09	14 24	18 51	13 04	7 26	24
8 10	14 40	19 22	13 22	7 34	25
8 12	14 56	19 52	13 41	7 41	26
8 14	15 13	20 24	14 00	7 49	27
8 15	15 30	20 56	14 20	7 57	28
8 17	15 48	21 29	14 39	8 05	29
8 19	16 06	22 02	14 59	8 14	30
8 21	16 25	22 37	15 20	8 22	31
8 23	16 44	23 12	15 41	8 31	32
8 25	17 04	23 48	16 02	8 39	33
8 27	17 25	24 25	16 24	8 48	34
8 29	17 47	25 02	16 46	8 57	35
8 31	18 09	25 41	17 09	9 07	36
8 33	18 32	26 21	17 32	9 16	37
8 35	18 56	27 02	17 56	9 26	38
8 38	19 22	27 45	18 20	9 36	39
8 40	19 48	28 28	18 45	9 46	40
8 43	20 15	29 13	19 11	9 57	41
8 45	20 44	29 59	19 37	10 07	42
8 48	21 15	0♋47	20 04	10 18	43
8 51	21 46	1 36	20 32	10 30	44
8 54	22 20	2 27	21 01	10 42	45
8 57	22 55	3 20	21 31	10 54	46
9 01	23 33	4 14	22 01	11 06	47
9 04	24 12	5 11	22 33	11 19	48
9 08	24 55	6 09	23 06	11 33	49
9 12	25 40	7 10	23 40	11 47	50
9 16	26 28	8 13	24 15	12 01	51
9 21	27 19	9 18	24 52	12 17	52
9 25	28 15	10 26	25 30	12 32	53
9 30	29 15	11 37	26 10	12 49	54
9 36	0♊20	12 50	26 51	13 06	55
9 41	1 31	14 07	27 34	13 24	56
9 48	2 49	15 26	28 20	13 43	57
9 54	4 15	16 49	29 07	14 03	58
10 01	5 51	18 16	29 57	14 23	59
10♈09	7♊38	19♋46	0♌49	14♌45	60

22h 32m 0s	338° 0' 0"	6 ♓ 14		
11	12	ASC	2	3
8♈43	10♉25	9♊40	7♋21	5♌38
8 49	11 21	11 35	8 40	6 11
8 56	12 19	13 34	10 00	6 44
9 03	13 22	15 39	11 21	7 18
9 11	14 31	17 54	12 46	7 53
9 13	14 45	18 22	13 04	8 01
9 15	15 00	18 50	13 21	8 08
9 17	15 15	19 19	13 39	8 15
9 18	15 31	19 49	13 58	8 23
9 20	15 47	20 19	14 16	8 30
9 22	16 04	20 50	14 35	8 38
9 24	16 20	21 21	14 54	8 46
9 26	16 38	21 53	15 13	8 54
9 28	16 56	22 26	15 33	9 02
9 30	17 14	23 00	15 53	9 10
9 32	17 33	23 34	16 13	9 18
9 34	17 53	24 09	16 34	9 26
9 36	18 13	24 45	16 55	9 35
9 39	18 34	25 21	17 16	9 44
9 41	18 56	25 59	17 38	9 53
9 43	19 19	26 38	18 01	10 02
9 46	19 42	27 18	18 24	10 11
9 49	20 07	27 58	18 47	10 21
9 51	20 33	28 40	19 12	10 31
9 54	20 59	29 24	19 36	10 41
9 57	21 27	0♋08	20 02	10 51
10 00	21 56	0 54	20 28	11 02
10 03	22 27	1 41	20 55	11 13
10 07	22 59	2 30	21 23	11 24
10 10	23 33	3 21	21 51	11 36
10 14	24 09	4 13	22 20	11 48
10 18	24 47	5 07	22 51	12 00
10 22	25 27	6 03	23 22	12 13
10 26	26 09	7 01	23 55	12 26
10 31	26 55	8 01	24 28	12 40
10 35	27 43	9 03	25 03	12 54
10 40	28 35	10 08	25 40	13 09
10 46	29 31	11 15	26 17	13 24
10 51	0♊31	12 24	26 56	13 41
10 58	1 37	13 37	27 37	13 57
11 04	2 48	14 52	28 20	14 15
11 11	4 07	16 11	29 05	14 34
11 19	5 33	17 32	29 51	14 53
11 27	7 09	18 58	0♌40	15 14
11♈36	8♊56	20♋26	1♌31	15♌35

22h 36m 0s	339° 0' 0"	7 ♓ 18		
11	12	ASC	2	3
9♈48	11♉26	10♊36	8♋16	6♌37
9 55	12 23	12 31	9 35	7 09
10 03	13 22	14 31	10 54	7 42
10 11	14 26	16 37	12 16	8 16
10 20	15 36	18 51	13 40	8 50
10 22	15 51	19 19	13 58	8 58
10 24	16 06	19 48	14 15	9 05
10 26	16 21	20 17	14 33	9 12
10 28	16 37	20 46	14 51	9 19
10 30	16 54	21 17	15 10	9 27
10 32	17 10	21 47	15 28	9 34
10 34	17 27	22 19	15 47	9 42
10 36	17 45	22 51	16 06	9 50
10 38	18 03	23 23	16 26	9 58
10 41	18 22	23 57	16 46	10 06
10 43	18 41	24 31	17 06	10 14
10 46	19 01	25 06	17 26	10 22
10 48	19 22	25 41	17 47	10 31
10 51	19 43	26 18	18 09	10 39
10 53	20 05	26 55	18 31	10 48
10 56	20 28	27 34	18 53	10 57
10 59	20 52	28 13	19 16	11 07
11 02	21 17	28 54	19 39	11 16
11 05	21 43	29 36	20 03	11 26
11 08	22 10	0♋19	20 28	11 36
11 11	22 38	1 03	20 53	11 46
11 15	23 08	1 48	21 19	11 56
11 18	23 39	2 35	21 46	12 07
11 22	24 11	3 24	22 13	12 18
11 26	24 45	4 14	22 41	12 30
11 30	25 21	5 06	23 10	12 41
11 35	26 00	5 59	23 40	12 53
11 39	26 40	6 54	24 11	13 06
11 44	27 23	7 52	24 44	13 19
11 49	28 09	8 51	25 17	13 33
11 54	28 58	9 53	25 51	13 47
12 00	29 50	10 57	26 27	14 01
12 06	0♊46	12 03	27 04	14 17
12 12	1 47	13 12	27 43	14 32
12 19	2 53	14 23	28 23	14 49
12 27	4 04	15 38	29 05	15 06
12 34	5 23	16 55	29 49	15 24
12 43	6 49	18 15	0♌35	15 44
12 52	8 25	19 39	1 23	16 04
13♈02	10♊12	21♋06	2♌14	16♌25

22h 40m 0s	340° 0' 0"	8 ♓ 22		
11	12	ASC	2	3
10♈53	12♉27	11♊32	9♋11	7♌35
11 01	13 24	13 28	10 30	8 08
11 10	14 25	15 28	11 49	8 40
11 19	15 30	17 34	13 10	9 13
11 29	16 41	19 48	14 34	9 48
11 31	16 56	20 16	14 52	9 55
11 33	17 11	20 45	15 09	10 02
11 35	17 27	21 14	15 27	10 09
11 37	17 43	21 44	15 45	10 16
11 39	18 00	22 14	16 03	10 24
11 42	18 17	22 44	16 22	10 31
11 44	18 34	23 16	16 41	10 39
11 47	18 52	23 47	17 00	10 46
11 49	19 10	24 20	17 19	10 54
11 52	19 29	24 53	17 39	11 02
11 54	19 49	25 27	17 59	11 10
11 57	20 09	26 02	18 19	11 18
12 00	20 30	26 38	18 40	11 27
12 03	20 52	27 14	19 01	11 35
12 05	21 14	27 51	19 23	11 44
12 09	21 37	28 30	19 45	11 53
12 12	22 02	29 09	20 08	12 02
12 15	22 27	29 49	20 31	12 11
12 18	22 53	0♋31	20 55	12 21
12 22	23 20	1 13	21 19	12 30
12 26	23 49	1 57	21 44	12 40
12 29	24 18	2 43	22 10	12 51
12 33	24 50	3 29	22 36	13 01
12 37	25 22	4 17	23 03	13 12
12 42	25 57	5 07	23 31	13 24
12 46	26 33	5 58	24 00	13 35
12 51	27 12	6 51	24 30	13 47
12 56	27 53	7 46	25 00	13 59
13 01	28 36	8 42	25 32	14 12
13 07	29 22	9 41	26 05	14 26
13 13	0♊11	10 42	26 39	14 39
13 19	1 04	11 45	27 15	14 54
13 26	2 00	12 51	27 51	15 09
13 33	3 01	13 58	28 30	15 24
13 41	4 07	15 09	29 09	15 41
13 49	5 19	16 22	29 51	15 58
13 58	6 38	17 39	0♌34	16 15
14 07	8 04	18 58	1 19	16 34
14 17	9 40	20 21	2 07	16 54
14♈28	11♊27	21♋46	2♌56	17♌14

22h 44m 0s	341° 0' 0"	9 ♓ 26			
11	12	ASC	2	3	LAT.
11♈58	13♉27	12♊28	10♋07	8♌34	0
12 07	14 26	14 24	11 25	9 06	5
12 16	15 28	16 25	12 44	9 39	10
12 26	16 34	18 31	14 05	10 11	15
12 37	17 46	20 45	15 29	10 45	20
12 39	18 01	21 13	15 46	10 52	21
12 42	18 16	21 42	16 03	10 59	22
12 44	18 32	22 11	16 21	11 06	23
12 47	18 49	22 41	16 39	11 13	24
12 49	19 06	23 11	16 57	11 20	25
12 52	19 23	23 41	17 15	11 28	26
12 54	19 40	24 12	17 34	11 35	27
12 57	19 59	24 44	17 53	11 43	28
12 59	20 17	25 17	18 12	11 50	29
13 02	20 36	25 50	18 32	11 58	30
13 05	20 56	26 24	18 52	12 06	31
13 08	21 17	26 58	19 12	12 14	32
13 11	21 38	27 34	19 33	12 22	33
13 14	22 00	28 10	19 54	12 31	34
13 18	22 22	28 47	20 15	12 39	35
13 21	22 46	29 25	20 37	12 48	36
13 24	23 10	0♋04	21 00	12 57	37
13 28	23 36	0 44	21 23	13 06	38
13 32	24 02	1 25	21 46	13 16	39
13 36	24 30	2 08	22 10	13 25	40
13 40	24 58	2 51	22 35	13 35	41
13 44	25 29	3 36	23 00	13 45	42
13 48	26 00	4 23	23 27	13 56	43
13 53	26 33	5 10	23 53	14 07	44
13 57	27 08	5 59	24 21	14 18	45
14 02	27 45	6 50	24 50	14 29	46
14 08	28 23	7 43	25 19	14 41	47
14 13	29 05	8 37	25 49	14 53	48
14 19	29 48	9 33	26 21	15 06	49
14 25	0♊34	10 31	26 53	15 19	50
14 32	1 24	11 31	27 27	15 32	51
14 38	2 17	12 33	28 02	15 46	52
14 46	3 13	13 38	28 38	16 01	53
14 54	4 15	14 45	29 16	16 16	54
15 02	5 21	15 55	29 55	16 32	55
15 11	6 33	17 07	0♌36	16 49	56
15 20	7 52	18 22	1 19	17 06	57
15 31	9 18	19 40	2 03	17 25	58
15 42	10 54	21 02	2 50	17 44	59
15♈54	12♊40	22♋26	3♌39	18♌04	60

22h 48m 0s	342° 0' 0"	10 ♓ 30		
11	12	ASC	2	3
13♈03	14♉28	13♊24	11♋02	9♌34
13 13	15 27	15 21	12 20	10 05
13 23	16 30	17 21	13 39	10 37
13 34	17 37	19 28	14 59	11 09
13 46	18 50	21 42	16 23	11 42
13 48	19 05	22 10	16 40	11 49
13 51	19 21	22 39	16 57	11 56
13 53	19 37	23 08	17 15	12 03
13 56	19 54	23 37	17 33	12 10
13 58	20 11	24 07	17 51	12 17
14 01	20 28	24 38	18 09	12 25
14 04	20 46	25 09	18 27	12 32
14 07	21 05	25 40	18 46	12 39
14 10	21 24	26 13	19 05	12 47
14 13	21 43	26 46	19 25	12 55
14 16	22 03	27 20	19 44	13 02
14 19	22 24	27 54	20 05	13 10
14 23	22 45	28 29	20 25	13 19
14 26	23 07	29 05	20 46	13 27
14 29	23 30	29 42	21 07	13 35
14 33	23 54	0♋20	21 29	13 44
14 37	24 19	0 59	21 51	13 53
14 41	24 44	1 39	22 14	14 02
14 45	25 11	2 20	22 38	14 11
14 49	25 39	3 02	23 01	14 20
14 53	26 08	3 45	23 26	14 30
14 58	26 38	4 30	23 51	14 40
15 03	27 10	5 15	24 17	14 50
15 08	27 43	6 03	24 44	15 01
15 13	28 18	6 51	25 11	15 12
15 18	28 55	7 42	25 39	15 23
15 24	29 34	8 34	26 08	15 35
15 30	0♊16	9 27	26 38	15 47
15 36	0 59	10 23	27 09	15 59
15 43	1 46	11 20	27 41	16 12
15 50	2 36	12 20	28 15	16 25
15 57	3 29	13 21	28 49	16 39
16 05	4 26	14 25	29 25	16 53
16 14	5 27	15 31	0♌02	17 08
16 23	6 33	16 40	0 41	17 24
16 33	7 46	17 51	1 21	17 40
16 43	9 04	19 06	2 03	17 57
16 54	10 31	20 23	2 47	18 15
17 07	12 06	21 43	3 33	18 34
17♈20	13♊52	23♋06	4♌21	18♌54

22h 52m 0s	343° 0' 0"	11 ♓ 34		
11	12	ASC	2	3
14♈07	15♉28	14♊20	11♋58	10♌33
14 18	16 28	16 17	13 16	11 04
14 29	17 32	18 18	14 34	11 35
14 41	18 40	20 24	15 54	12 07
14 54	19 54	22 39	17 17	12 40
14 56	20 10	23 07	17 34	12 47
14 59	20 26	23 35	17 51	12 53
15 02	20 42	24 04	18 09	13 00
15 05	20 59	24 34	18 26	13 07
15 08	21 16	25 03	18 44	13 14
15 11	21 34	25 34	19 02	13 21
15 14	21 52	26 05	19 21	13 29
15 17	22 10	26 37	19 39	13 36
15 20	22 30	27 09	19 58	13 44
15 23	22 49	27 42	20 18	13 51
15 27	23 09	28 15	20 37	13 59
15 30	23 30	28 50	20 57	14 07
15 34	23 52	29 25	21 18	14 15
15 37	24 14	0♋01	21 38	14 23
15 41	24 38	0 37	21 59	14 31
15 45	25 01	1 15	22 21	14 40
15 49	25 26	1 54	22 43	14 48
15 53	25 52	2 33	23 06	14 57
15 58	26 19	3 14	23 29	15 06
16 02	26 47	3 56	23 53	15 16
16 07	27 16	4 38	24 17	15 25
16 12	27 47	5 23	24 42	15 35
16 17	28 19	6 08	25 07	15 45
16 22	28 53	6 55	25 34	15 55
16 28	29 28	7 43	26 01	16 06
16 34	0♊05	8 33	26 29	16 17
16 40	0 45	9 24	26 57	16 28
16 46	1 26	10 18	27 27	16 40
16 53	2 10	11 12	27 58	16 52
17 00	2 57	12 09	28 29	17 05
17 08	3 47	13 08	29 02	17 18
17 16	4 40	14 09	29 36	17 32
17 25	5 37	15 12	0♌12	17 46
17 34	6 39	16 17	0 48	18 00
17 44	7 45	17 25	1 27	18 16
17 54	8 57	18 35	2 06	18 32
18 06	10 16	19 49	2 48	18 49
18 18	11 42	21 04	3 31	19 06
18 31	13 17	22 23	4 16	19 25
18♈45	15♊03	23♋45	5♌04	19♌44

22h 56m 0s — 12 ♓ 39 — 344° 0' 0"

LAT.	11	12	ASC	2	3
0	15♈12	16♉28	15♊16	12♋53	11♌32
5	15 24	17 29	17 13	14 11	12 03
10	15 36	18 34	19 14	15 29	12 34
15	15 48	19 43	21 21	16 48	13 05
20	16 02	20 58	23 35	18 11	13 38
21	16 05	21 14	24 03	18 28	13 44
22	16 08	21 30	24 32	18 45	13 51
23	16 11	21 46	25 00	19 02	13 58
24	16 14	22 03	25 30	19 20	14 05
25	16 17	22 21	26 00	19 38	14 12
26	16 20	22 39	26 30	19 56	14 19
27	16 23	22 57	27 01	20 14	14 26
28	16 27	23 16	27 32	20 33	14 33
29	16 30	23 35	28 04	20 51	14 40
30	16 34	23 55	28 37	21 10	14 48
31	16 37	24 15	29 11	21 30	14 55
32	16 41	24 37	29 45	21 50	15 03
33	16 45	24 58	0♋20	22 10	15 11
34	16 49	25 21	0 55	22 31	15 19
35	16 53	25 44	1 32	22 51	15 27
36	16 57	26 09	2 09	23 13	15 35
37	17 01	26 34	2 48	23 35	15 44
38	17 06	27 00	3 27	23 57	15 53
39	17 11	27 27	4 07	24 20	16 02
40	17 15	27 55	4 49	24 44	16 11
41	17 21	28 25	5 32	25 08	16 20
42	17 26	28 55	6 15	25 32	16 30
43	17 31	29 28	7 00	25 58	16 40
44	17 37	0♊02	7 47	26 24	16 50
45	17 43	0 37	8 35	26 50	17 00
46	17 49	1 15	9 24	27 18	17 11
47	17 56	1 54	10 15	27 46	17 22
48	18 03	2 36	11 07	28 16	17 34
49	18 10	3 20	12 02	28 46	17 46
50	18 18	4 07	12 58	29 17	17 58
51	18 26	4 57	13 56	29 50	18 11
52	18 35	5 50	14 56	0♌23	18 24
53	18 44	6 47	15 58	0 58	18 38
54	18 54	7 49	17 03	1 35	18 53
55	19 04	8 55	18 10	2 12	19 08
56	19 16	10 08	19 19	2 51	19 23
57	19 28	11 26	20 31	3 32	19 40
58	19 41	12 52	21 46	4 15	19 57
59	19 55	14 27	23 04	5 00	20 15
60	20♈10	16♊12	24♋25	5♌46	20♌34

23h 0m 0s — 13 ♓ 43 — 345° 0' 0"

LAT.	11	12	ASC	2	3
0	16♈17	17♉28	16♊11	13♋49	12♌32
5	16 29	18 30	18 09	15 06	13 02
10	16 42	19 36	20 10	16 24	13 33
15	16 55	20 45	22 17	17 43	14 04
20	17 10	22 01	24 31	19 05	14 35
21	17 13	22 17	24 59	19 22	14 42
22	17 16	22 34	25 28	19 39	14 49
23	17 19	22 50	25 56	19 56	14 55
24	17 23	23 08	26 26	20 14	15 02
25	17 26	23 25	26 55	20 31	15 09
26	17 29	23 43	27 26	20 49	15 16
27	17 33	24 02	27 56	21 07	15 23
28	17 36	24 21	28 28	21 26	15 30
29	17 40	24 40	29 00	21 44	15 37
30	17 44	25 00	29 32	22 03	15 44
31	17 48	25 21	0♋06	22 23	15 52
32	17 52	25 42	0 40	22 42	15 59
33	17 56	26 04	1 15	23 02	16 07
34	18 00	26 27	1 50	23 23	16 15
35	18 04	26 51	2 26	23 44	16 23
36	18 09	27 15	3 04	24 05	16 31
37	18 13	27 40	3 42	24 26	16 40
38	18 18	28 07	4 21	24 49	16 48
39	18 23	28 34	5 01	25 11	16 57
40	18 28	29 03	5 42	25 34	17 06
41	18 34	29 32	6 24	25 58	17 15
42	18 39	0♊03	7 08	26 23	17 25
43	18 45	0 36	7 52	26 48	17 34
44	18 51	1 10	8 38	27 14	17 44
45	18 58	1 46	9 26	27 40	17 55
46	19 05	2 23	10 15	28 07	18 05
47	19 12	3 03	11 05	28 35	18 16
48	19 19	3 45	11 57	29 04	18 28
49	19 27	4 29	12 51	29 34	18 39
50	19 35	5 16	13 46	0♌05	18 51
51	19 44	6 06	14 44	0 37	19 04
52	19 53	7 00	15 43	1 11	19 17
53	20 03	7 57	16 44	1 45	19 31
54	20 13	8 59	17 48	2 21	19 45
55	20 25	10 05	18 54	2 58	19 59
56	20 37	11 17	20 03	3 36	20 15
57	20 50	12 35	21 14	4 17	20 31
58	21 03	14 01	22 28	4 59	20 48
59	21 19	15 35	23 44	5 43	21 05
60	21♈35	17♊20	25♋04	6♌29	21♌24

23h 4m 0s — 14 ♓ 48 — 346° 0' 0"

LAT.	11	12	ASC	2	3
0	17♈21	18♉28	17♊07	14♋44	13♌32
5	17 34	19 31	19 05	16 01	14 02
10	17 48	20 37	21 07	17 19	14 32
15	18 02	21 48	23 13	18 38	15 02
20	18 18	23 04	25 27	19 59	15 33
21	18 21	23 21	25 55	20 16	15 40
22	18 24	23 37	26 23	20 33	15 46
23	18 28	23 54	26 52	20 50	15 53
24	18 31	24 12	27 21	21 07	16 00
25	18 35	24 29	27 51	21 25	16 06
26	18 38	24 48	28 21	21 43	16 13
27	18 42	25 06	28 52	22 01	16 20
28	18 46	25 25	29 23	22 19	16 27
29	18 50	25 45	29 55	22 37	16 34
30	18 54	26 05	0♋28	22 56	16 41
31	18 58	26 26	1 01	23 15	16 49
32	19 02	26 48	1 34	23 35	16 56
33	19 06	27 10	2 09	23 55	17 04
34	19 11	27 33	2 44	24 15	17 11
35	19 16	27 57	3 20	24 35	17 19
36	19 20	28 21	3 57	24 57	17 27
37	19 25	28 47	4 35	25 18	17 36
38	19 30	29 13	5 14	25 40	17 44
39	19 36	29 41	5 54	26 02	17 53
40	19 41	0♊09	6 35	26 25	18 01
41	19 47	0 39	7 17	26 49	18 10
42	19 53	1 11	8 00	27 13	18 20
43	19 59	1 43	8 44	27 38	18 29
44	20 06	2 17	9 30	28 03	18 39
45	20 12	2 53	10 17	28 30	18 49
46	20 20	3 31	11 05	28 57	19 00
47	20 27	4 11	11 55	29 24	19 10
48	20 35	4 53	12 46	29 53	19 21
49	20 43	5 37	13 39	0♌23	19 33
50	20 52	6 25	14 34	0 53	19 45
51	21 01	7 15	15 31	1 25	19 57
52	21 11	8 08	16 30	1 58	20 10
53	21 21	9 06	17 30	2 31	20 23
54	21 33	10 07	18 33	3 07	20 37
55	21 44	11 14	19 38	3 43	20 51
56	21 57	12 25	20 46	4 21	21 06
57	22 11	13 44	21 56	5 01	21 22
58	22 26	15 09	23 09	5 42	21 39
59	22 42	16 43	24 24	6 26	21 56
60	23♈00	18♊27	25♋43	7♌11	22♌14

23h 8m 0s — 15 ♓ 53 — 347° 0' 0"

LAT.	11	12	ASC	2	3
0	18♈26	19♉27	18♊02	15♋40	14♌32
5	18 40	20 31	20 01	16 57	15 01
10	18 54	21 38	22 02	18 14	15 31
15	19 09	22 50	24 09	19 32	16 01
20	19 26	24 07	26 23	20 53	16 32
21	19 29	24 24	26 51	21 10	16 38
22	19 32	24 40	27 19	21 27	16 44
23	19 36	24 58	27 48	21 44	16 51
24	19 40	25 15	28 17	22 01	16 57
25	19 43	25 33	28 46	22 18	17 04
26	19 47	25 51	29 17	22 36	17 10
27	19 51	26 10	29 47	22 54	17 17
28	19 55	26 30	0♋18	23 12	17 24
29	19 59	26 50	0 50	23 30	17 31
30	20 04	27 10	1 22	23 49	17 38
31	20 08	27 31	1 55	24 08	17 45
32	20 12	27 53	2 29	24 27	17 53
33	20 17	28 15	3 03	24 47	18 00
34	20 22	28 38	3 38	25 07	18 08
35	20 27	29 02	4 14	25 27	18 16
36	20 32	29 27	4 51	25 48	18 23
37	20 37	29 53	5 29	26 10	18 32
38	20 42	0♊19	6 07	26 31	18 40
39	20 48	0 47	6 47	26 54	18 48
40	20 54	1 16	7 27	27 16	18 57
41	21 00	1 46	8 09	27 40	19 06
42	21 06	2 17	8 52	28 03	19 15
43	21 13	2 50	9 35	28 28	19 24
44	21 20	3 24	10 21	28 53	19 34
45	21 27	4 00	11 07	29 19	19 44
46	21 34	4 38	11 55	29 46	19 54
47	21 42	5 18	12 44	0♌13	20 05
48	21 51	6 00	13 35	0 42	20 15
49	21 59	6 45	14 28	1 11	20 27
50	22 09	7 32	15 22	1 41	20 38
51	22 18	8 23	16 18	2 12	20 50
52	22 29	9 16	17 16	2 44	21 03
53	22 40	10 14	18 16	3 18	21 16
54	22 52	11 15	19 18	3 53	21 29
55	23 04	12 21	20 22	4 29	21 43
56	23 18	13 33	21 29	5 06	21 58
57	23 32	14 51	22 38	5 45	22 14
58	23 48	16 16	23 50	6 26	22 30
59	24 05	17 49	25 04	7 09	22 47
60	24♈24	19♊32	26♋21	7♌53	23♌04

23h 12m 0s — 16 ♓ 57 — 348° 0' 0"

LAT.	11	12	ASC	2	3
0	19♈30	20♉26	18♊58	16♋36	15♌32
5	19 45	21 31	20 57	17 52	16 01
10	20 00	22 39	22 58	19 09	16 30
15	20 16	23 51	25 05	20 27	17 00
20	20 33	25 10	27 19	21 48	17 30
21	20 37	25 26	27 46	22 04	17 36
22	20 40	25 43	28 15	22 21	17 42
23	20 44	26 01	28 43	22 38	17 49
24	20 48	26 18	29 12	22 55	17 55
25	20 52	26 36	29 42	23 12	18 01
26	20 56	26 55	0♋12	23 29	18 08
27	21 00	27 14	0 42	23 47	18 15
28	21 04	27 34	1 13	24 05	18 21
29	21 09	27 54	1 45	24 23	18 28
30	21 13	28 14	2 17	24 42	18 35
31	21 18	28 35	2 50	25 01	18 42
32	21 22	28 57	3 23	25 20	18 50
33	21 27	29 20	3 57	25 39	18 57
34	21 32	29 43	4 32	25 59	19 04
35	21 37	0♊07	5 08	26 19	19 12
36	21 43	0 32	5 44	26 40	19 20
37	21 48	0 58	6 22	27 01	19 28
38	21 54	1 25	7 00	27 23	19 36
39	22 00	1 53	7 39	27 45	19 44
40	22 06	2 22	8 19	28 07	19 52
41	22 12	2 52	9 01	28 30	20 01
42	22 19	3 23	9 43	28 54	20 10
43	22 26	3 56	10 27	29 18	20 19
44	22 33	4 31	11 11	29 43	20 29
45	22 41	5 07	11 57	0♌09	20 38
46	22 49	5 45	12 45	0 35	20 48
47	22 57	6 25	13 34	1 02	20 59
48	23 06	7 07	14 24	1 30	21 09
49	23 15	7 52	15 16	1 59	21 20
50	23 25	8 39	16 10	2 29	21 32
51	23 35	9 30	17 05	2 59	21 44
52	23 46	10 23	18 02	3 31	21 56
53	23 58	11 21	19 01	4 04	22 09
54	24 10	12 22	20 03	4 39	22 22
55	24 23	13 28	21 06	5 14	22 36
56	24 38	14 39	22 12	5 51	22 50
57	24 53	15 57	23 20	6 30	23 05
58	25 10	17 21	24 31	7 10	23 21
59	25 28	18 54	25 44	7 52	23 37
60	25♈47	20♊36	27♋00	8♌35	23♌55

23h 16m 0s — 18 ♓ 02 — 349° 0' 0"

LAT.	11	12	ASC	2	3
0	20♈34	21♉26	19♊53	17♋32	16♌33
5	20 50	22 31	21 52	18 48	17 01
10	21 06	23 40	23 54	20 04	17 30
15	21 22	24 53	26 01	21 22	17 58
20	21 40	26 12	28 14	22 42	18 28
21	21 44	26 29	28 42	22 58	18 34
22	21 48	26 46	29 10	23 15	18 40
23	21 52	27 03	29 38	23 31	18 47
24	21 56	27 21	0♋07	23 48	18 53
25	22 00	27 39	0 37	24 05	18 59
26	22 05	27 58	1 07	24 23	19 06
27	22 09	28 17	1 37	24 40	19 12
28	22 13	28 37	2 08	24 58	19 19
29	22 18	28 57	2 39	25 16	19 26
30	22 23	29 18	3 11	25 35	19 32
31	22 27	29 39	3 44	25 53	19 39
32	22 32	0♊01	4 17	26 12	19 46
33	22 37	0 24	4 51	26 32	19 54
34	22 43	0 48	5 26	26 51	20 01
35	22 48	1 12	6 01	27 11	20 08
36	22 54	1 37	6 38	27 32	20 16
37	22 59	2 03	7 15	27 53	20 24
38	23 05	2 30	7 53	28 14	20 32
39	23 12	2 58	8 32	28 36	20 40
40	23 18	3 27	9 11	28 58	20 48
41	23 25	3 57	9 52	29 21	20 57
42	23 32	4 29	10 34	29 44	21 05
43	23 39	5 02	11 17	0♌08	21 14
44	23 47	5 37	12 02	0 33	21 24
45	23 55	6 13	12 47	0 58	21 33
46	24 03	6 51	13 34	1 24	21 43
47	24 12	7 31	14 23	1 51	21 53
48	24 21	8 14	15 12	2 18	22 03
49	24 31	8 58	16 04	2 47	22 14
50	24 41	9 46	16 57	3 16	22 25
51	24 52	10 36	17 52	3 47	22 37
52	25 03	11 29	18 48	4 18	22 49
53	25 15	12 27	19 47	4 51	23 01
54	25 29	13 28	20 47	5 24	23 14
55	25 42	14 34	21 50	6 00	23 28
56	25 57	15 45	22 55	6 36	23 42
57	26 14	17 02	24 02	7 14	23 57
58	26 31	18 26	25 11	7 53	24 12
59	26 50	19 58	26 24	8 35	24 28
60	27♈11	21♊40	27♋39	9♌18	24♌45

23h 20m 0s — 19 ♓ 07 — 350° 0' 0"

LAT.	11	12	ASC	2	3
0	21♈38	22♉25	20♊49	18♋28	17♌33
5	21 54	23 31	22 48	19 44	18 01
10	22 11	24 40	24 50	21 00	18 29
15	22 29	25 54	26 56	22 17	18 58
20	22 48	27 14	29 09	23 36	19 27
21	22 52	27 31	29 37	23 52	19 33
22	22 56	27 48	0♋05	24 09	19 39
23	23 00	28 06	0 33	24 25	19 45
24	23 04	28 24	1 02	24 42	19 51
25	23 09	28 42	1 32	24 59	19 57
26	23 13	29 01	2 01	25 16	20 04
27	23 18	29 20	2 31	25 34	20 10
28	23 22	29 40	3 02	25 51	20 16
29	23 27	0♊01	3 33	26 09	20 23
30	23 32	0 21	4 05	26 27	20 30
31	23 37	0 43	4 38	26 46	20 37
32	23 42	1 05	5 11	27 05	20 43
33	23 47	1 28	5 45	27 24	20 50
34	23 53	1 52	6 19	27 43	20 58
35	23 59	2 16	6 54	28 03	21 05
36	24 04	2 41	7 30	28 23	21 12
37	24 10	3 07	8 07	28 44	21 20
38	24 17	3 34	8 45	29 05	21 28
39	24 23	4 03	9 24	29 27	21 36
40	24 30	4 32	10 03	29 49	21 44
41	24 37	5 02	10 44	0♌11	21 52
42	24 44	5 34	11 25	0 34	22 01
43	24 52	6 07	12 08	0 58	22 10
44	25 00	6 42	12 52	1 22	22 19
45	25 08	7 18	13 37	1 47	22 28
46	25 17	7 57	14 24	2 13	22 38
47	25 26	8 37	15 11	2 40	22 47
48	25 36	9 19	16 01	3 07	22 58
49	25 46	10 04	16 51	3 35	23 08
50	25 57	10 51	17 44	4 04	23 19
51	26 08	11 41	18 38	4 34	23 30
52	26 20	12 35	19 34	5 05	23 42
53	26 33	13 32	20 32	5 37	23 54
54	26 47	14 33	21 31	6 10	24 07
55	27 01	15 39	22 33	6 45	24 20
56	27 17	16 50	23 37	7 21	24 34
57	27 34	18 07	24 43	7 58	24 48
58	27 52	19 30	25 52	8 37	25 03
59	28 12	21 01	27 03	9 17	25 19
60	28♈34	22♊42	28♋17	10♌00	25♌35

23h 24m 0s — 20 ♓ 12 — 351° 0' 0"

LAT.	11	12	ASC	2	3
0	22♈42	23♉23	21♊44	19♋24	18♌34
5	22 59	24 31	23 43	20 39	19 01
10	23 17	25 41	25 45	21 55	19 29
15	23 35	26 55	27 52	23 11	19 57
20	23 55	28 16	0♋05	24 30	20 25
21	23 59	28 33	0 32	24 46	20 31
22	24 03	28 50	1 00	25 03	20 37
23	24 08	29 08	1 28	25 19	20 43
24	24 12	29 26	1 57	25 36	20 49
25	24 17	29 45	2 26	25 53	20 55
26	24 21	0♊04	2 56	26 10	21 01
27	24 26	0 23	3 26	26 27	21 08
28	24 31	0 43	3 56	26 44	21 14
29	24 36	1 04	4 28	27 02	21 21
30	24 41	1 25	4 59	27 20	21 27
31	24 46	1 46	5 32	27 39	21 34
32	24 52	2 09	6 04	27 57	21 41
33	24 57	2 32	6 38	28 16	21 47
34	25 03	2 55	7 12	28 35	21 54
35	25 09	3 20	7 47	28 55	22 02
36	25 15	3 45	8 23	29 15	22 09
37	25 21	4 11	9 00	29 35	22 16
38	25 28	4 39	9 37	29 56	22 24
39	25 35	5 07	10 15	0♌18	22 32
40	25 42	5 36	10 54	0 39	22 40
41	25 49	6 07	11 35	1 02	22 48
42	25 57	6 39	12 16	1 25	22 56
43	26 05	7 12	12 58	1 48	23 05
44	26 13	7 47	13 42	2 12	23 14
45	26 22	8 23	14 27	2 37	23 23
46	26 31	9 01	15 12	3 02	23 32
47	26 40	9 42	16 00	3 28	23 42
48	26 50	10 24	16 49	3 55	23 52
49	27 01	11 09	17 39	4 23	24 02
50	27 12	11 56	18 31	4 51	24 13
51	27 24	12 46	19 24	5 21	24 24
52	27 36	13 40	20 19	5 52	24 35
53	27 50	14 37	21 16	6 23	24 47
54	28 04	15 38	22 15	6 56	24 59
55	28 19	16 43	23 16	7 30	25 12
56	28 36	17 54	24 19	8 05	25 26
57	28 54	19 10	25 25	8 42	25 40
58	29 13	20 33	26 32	9 20	25 54
59	29 33	22 03	27 42	10 00	26 10
60	29♈56	23♊43	28♋55	10♌42	26♌26

23h 28m 0s — 352° 0' 0" — 21 ♓ 17

11	12	ASC	2	3
23♈46	24♉22	22♊39	20♋20	19♌35
24 04	25 30	24 39	21 35	20 02
24 22	26 41	26 41	22 50	20 29
24 41	27 56	28 47	24 06	20 56
25 02	29 17	0♋59	25 24	21 24
25 06	29 34	1 27	25 40	21 30
25 10	29 52	1 55	25 57	21 36
25 15	0♊10	2 23	26 13	21 42
25 20	0 28	2 52	26 29	21 47
25 24	0 47	3 21	26 46	21 53
25 29	1 06	3 50	27 03	22 00
25 34	1 25	4 20	27 20	22 06
25 39	1 45	4 50	27 38	22 12
25 44	2 06	5 21	27 55	22 18
25 50	2 27	5 53	28 13	22 25
25 55	2 49	6 25	28 31	22 31
26 01	3 12	6 58	28 50	22 38
26 07	3 35	7 31	29 08	22 45
26 13	3 58	8 05	29 27	22 51
26 19	4 23	8 40	29 47	22 58
26 25	4 49	9 15	0♌07	23 06
26 32	5 15	9 52	0 27	23 13
26 39	5 42	10 29	0 47	23 20
26 46	6 11	11 07	1 09	23 28
26 53	6 40	11 46	1 30	23 36
27 01	7 11	12 26	1 52	23 44
27 09	7 43	13 06	2 15	23 52
27 17	8 16	13 48	2 38	24 00
27 25	8 51	14 31	3 02	24 09
27 35	9 27	15 16	3 26	24 18
27 44	10 06	16 01	3 51	24 27
27 54	10 46	16 48	4 17	24 36
28 04	11 28	17 36	4 43	24 46
28 15	12 13	18 26	5 11	24 56
28 27	13 00	19 17	5 39	25 07
28 39	13 51	20 10	6 08	25 17
28 53	14 44	21 04	6 38	25 29
29 07	15 41	22 01	7 10	25 40
29 21	16 41	22 59	7 42	25 52
29 37	17 47	23 59	8 15	26 05
29 54	18 57	25 01	8 50	26 18
0♉13	20 12	26 06	9 26	26 31
0 33	21 35	27 12	10 04	26 46
0 54	23 04	28 21	10 43	27 01
1♉18	24♊43	29♋33	11♌24	27♌16

23h 32m 0s — 353° 0' 0" — 22 ♓ 23

11	12	ASC	2	3	LAT.
24♈50	25♉21	23♊34	21♋17	20♌36	0
25 08	26 29	25 34	22 31	21 03	5
25 27	27 41	27 36	23 46	21 29	10
25 47	28 56	29 42	25 01	21 56	15
26 08	0♊18	1♋54	26 19	22 23	20
26 13	0 36	2 22	26 35	22 29	21
26 17	0 53	2 49	26 51	22 34	22
26 22	1 11	3 17	27 07	22 40	23
26 27	1 30	3 46	27 23	22 46	24
26 32	1 48	4 15	27 40	22 52	25
26 37	2 08	4 44	27 57	22 58	26
26 42	2 27	5 14	28 13	23 04	27
26 47	2 48	5 44	28 31	23 10	28
26 53	3 08	6 15	28 48	23 16	29
26 58	3 30	6 46	29 06	23 22	30
27 04	3 52	7 18	29 24	23 29	31
27 10	4 14	7 51	29 42	23 35	32
27 16	4 37	8 24	0♌01	23 42	33
27 22	5 01	8 58	0 19	23 48	34
27 28	5 26	9 32	0 39	23 55	35
27 35	5 52	10 08	0 58	24 02	36
27 42	6 18	10 44	1 18	24 09	37
27 49	6 45	11 20	1 39	24 17	38
27 56	7 14	11 58	2 00	24 24	39
28 04	7 43	12 37	2 21	24 32	40
28 12	8 14	13 16	2 43	24 40	41
28 20	8 46	13 57	3 05	24 48	42
28 29	9 20	14 38	3 28	24 56	43
28 38	9 54	15 21	3 51	25 04	44
28 47	10 31	16 05	4 15	25 13	45
28 57	11 09	16 50	4 40	25 22	46
29 07	11 50	17 36	5 05	25 31	47
29 18	12 32	18 24	5 32	25 41	48
29 30	13 17	19 13	5 59	25 50	49
29 42	14 04	20 03	6 27	26 01	50
29 55	14 54	20 56	6 55	26 11	51
0♉08	15 47	21 49	7 25	26 22	52
0 23	16 44	22 45	7 56	26 33	53
0 38	17 44	23 42	8 28	26 45	54
0 55	18 49	24 42	9 01	26 57	55
1 13	19 59	25 43	9 35	27 10	56
1 32	21 14	26 47	10 10	27 23	57
1 53	22 36	27 52	10 47	27 37	58
2 15	24 05	29 01	11 26	27 52	59
2♉40	25♊42	0♌11	12♌06	28♌07	60

23h 36m 0s — 354° 0' 0" — 23 ♓ 28

11	12	ASC	2	3
25♈53	26♉19	24♊30	22♋13	21♌37
26 12	27 28	26 29	23 27	22 03
26 32	28 40	28 31	24 41	22 29
26 53	29 57	0♋37	25 56	22 55
27 15	1♊19	2 49	27 13	23 22
27 20	1 37	3 16	27 29	23 28
27 24	1 54	3 44	27 45	23 33
27 29	2 13	4 12	28 01	23 39
27 34	2 31	4 40	28 17	23 44
27 39	2 50	5 09	28 33	23 50
27 44	3 09	5 38	28 50	23 56
27 50	3 29	6 08	29 07	24 02
27 55	3 49	6 38	29 24	24 08
28 01	4 10	7 09	29 41	24 14
28 07	4 32	7 40	29 59	24 20
28 13	4 54	8 12	0♌16	24 26
28 19	5 16	8 44	0 34	24 33
28 25	5 40	9 17	0 53	24 39
28 31	6 04	9 50	1 12	24 46
28 38	6 29	10 25	1 31	24 52
28 45	6 54	11 00	1 50	24 59
28 52	7 21	11 35	2 10	25 06
28 59	7 48	12 12	2 30	25 13
29 07	8 17	12 49	2 50	25 21
29 15	8 46	13 27	3 11	25 28
29 23	9 17	14 07	3 33	25 36
29 32	9 49	14 47	3 55	25 43
29 41	10 23	15 28	4 18	25 51
29 50	10 58	16 10	4 41	26 00
0♉00	11 34	16 53	5 05	26 08
0 10	12 13	17 38	5 29	26 17
0 21	12 53	18 24	5 54	26 26
0 32	13 35	19 11	6 20	26 35
0 44	14 20	19 59	6 47	26 45
0 56	15 07	20 49	7 14	26 55
1 10	15 57	21 41	7 42	27 05
1 24	16 50	22 34	8 12	27 15
1 39	17 46	23 29	8 42	27 26
1 55	18 47	24 26	9 13	27 38
2 12	19 51	25 24	9 46	27 50
2 30	21 00	26 25	10 19	28 02
2 50	22 15	27 27	10 55	28 15
3 12	23 36	28 32	11 31	28 29
3 35	25 04	29 39	12 09	28 43
4♉01	26♊40	0♌49	12♌48	28♌58

23h 40m 0s — 355° 0' 0" — 24 ♓ 33

11	12	ASC	2	3
26♈57	27♉17	25♊25	23♋10	22♌39
27 16	28 27	27 24	24 23	23 04
27 37	29 40	29 26	25 37	23 30
27 58	0♊57	1♋32	26 51	23 55
28 21	2 20	3 43	28 08	24 21
28 26	2 37	4 11	28 23	24 27
28 31	2 55	4 38	28 39	24 32
28 36	3 13	5 06	28 55	24 38
28 41	3 32	5 34	29 11	24 43
28 46	3 51	6 03	29 27	24 49
28 52	4 11	6 32	29 44	24 54
28 57	4 30	7 02	0♌00	25 00
29 03	4 51	7 32	0 17	25 06
29 09	5 12	8 02	0 34	25 12
29 15	5 33	8 33	0 51	25 18
29 21	5 55	9 04	1 09	25 24
29 27	6 18	9 37	1 27	25 30
29 34	6 42	10 09	1 45	25 36
29 40	7 06	10 43	2 04	25 43
29 47	7 31	11 17	2 22	25 49
29 54	7 56	11 51	2 42	25 56
0♉02	8 23	12 27	3 01	26 03
0 09	8 51	13 03	3 21	26 10
0 17	9 19	13 40	3 41	26 17
0 25	9 49	14 18	4 02	26 24
0 34	10 20	14 57	4 23	26 32
0 43	10 52	15 36	4 45	26 39
0 52	11 25	16 17	5 07	26 47
1 02	12 00	16 59	5 30	26 55
1 12	12 37	17 42	5 54	27 03
1 22	13 15	18 26	6 18	27 12
1 33	13 55	19 11	6 43	27 21
1 45	14 38	19 58	7 08	27 30
1 57	15 22	20 46	7 34	27 39
2 10	16 09	21 35	8 01	27 49
2 24	16 59	22 26	8 29	27 59
2 39	17 52	23 19	8 58	28 09
2 54	18 48	24 13	9 28	28 20
3 11	19 48	25 09	9 59	28 31
3 29	20 52	26 07	10 31	28 42
3 48	22 01	27 06	11 04	28 54
4 08	23 15	28 08	11 39	29 07
4 31	24 35	29 12	12 14	29 20
4 55	26 03	0♌18	12 52	29 34
5♉22	27♊38	1♌27	13♌31	29♌48

23h 44m 0s — 356° 0' 0" — 25 ♓ 38

11	12	ASC	2	3
28♈00	28♉15	26♊20	24♋06	23♌41
28 20	29 25	28 19	25 20	24 05
28 41	0♊39	0♋21	26 33	24 30
29 03	1 57	2 27	27 46	24 55
29 27	3 20	4 38	29 02	25 21
29 32	3 38	5 05	29 17	25 26
29 37	3 56	5 32	29 33	25 31
29 43	4 14	6 00	29 49	25 37
29 48	4 33	6 28	0♌05	25 42
29 53	4 52	6 57	0 21	25 47
29 59	5 11	7 26	0 37	25 53
0♉05	5 32	7 55	0 54	25 59
0 11	5 52	8 25	1 10	26 04
0 17	6 13	8 55	1 27	26 10
0 23	6 35	9 26	1 44	26 16
0 29	6 57	9 57	2 02	26 22
0 35	7 20	10 29	2 19	26 28
0 42	7 43	11 02	2 37	26 34
0 49	8 07	11 35	2 56	26 40
0 56	8 32	12 08	3 14	26 47
1 03	8 58	12 43	3 33	26 53
1 11	9 25	13 18	3 52	27 00
1 19	9 52	13 54	4 12	27 07
1 27	10 21	14 31	4 32	27 13
1 36	10 51	15 08	4 53	27 21
1 44	11 22	15 47	5 14	27 28
1 54	11 54	16 26	5 35	27 35
2 03	12 27	17 06	5 57	27 43
2 13	13 02	17 48	6 20	27 51
2 23	13 39	18 30	6 43	27 59
2 34	14 17	19 14	7 07	28 07
2 46	14 57	19 59	7 31	28 16
2 58	15 40	20 45	7 56	28 24
3 11	16 24	21 32	8 22	28 33
3 24	17 11	22 21	8 49	28 43
3 38	18 01	23 11	9 16	28 52
3 53	18 53	24 03	9 45	29 03
4 09	19 49	24 57	10 14	29 13
4 27	20 49	25 52	10 45	29 24
4 45	21 53	26 49	11 16	29 35
5 05	23 01	27 48	11 49	29 47
5 26	24 15	28 49	12 23	29 59
5 49	25 34	29 52	12 58	0♍12
6 14	27 00	0♌57	13 35	0 25
6♉42	28♊34	2♌04	14♌13	0♍39

23h 48m 0s — 357° 0' 0" — 26 ♓ 44

11	12	ASC	2	3	LAT.
29♈03	29♉13	27♊15	25♋03	24♌42	0
29 24	0♊24	29 15	26 16	25 07	5
29 45	1 38	1♋16	27 28	25 31	10
0♉08	2 56	3 21	28 42	25 55	15
0 33	4 20	5 32	29 56	26 20	20
0 38	4 38	5 59	0♌12	26 25	21
0 44	4 56	6 26	0 27	26 30	22
0 49	5 14	6 54	0 43	26 36	23
0 54	5 33	7 22	0 59	26 41	24
1 00	5 52	7 50	1 15	26 46	25
1 06	6 12	8 19	1 31	26 52	26
1 12	6 32	8 48	1 47	26 57	27
1 18	6 53	9 18	2 04	27 03	28
1 24	7 14	9 48	2 20	27 08	29
1 30	7 36	10 19	2 37	27 14	30
1 37	7 58	10 50	2 54	27 20	31
1 44	8 21	11 22	3 12	27 26	32
1 50	8 44	11 54	3 30	27 32	33
1 58	9 09	12 27	3 48	27 38	34
2 05	9 34	13 00	4 06	27 44	35
2 12	10 00	13 34	4 25	27 50	36
2 20	10 26	14 09	4 44	27 57	37
2 28	10 54	14 45	5 03	28 03	38
2 37	11 23	15 21	5 23	28 10	39
2 45	11 52	15 58	5 43	28 17	40
2 55	12 23	16 36	6 04	28 24	41
3 04	12 55	17 15	6 25	28 31	42
3 14	13 29	17 55	6 47	28 39	43
3 24	14 04	18 36	7 09	28 46	44
3 35	14 41	19 18	7 32	28 54	45
3 46	15 19	20 02	7 56	29 02	46
3 58	15 59	20 46	8 20	29 10	47
4 10	16 41	21 32	8 45	29 19	48
4 24	17 25	22 18	9 10	29 28	49
4 37	18 12	23 07	9 36	29 37	50
4 52	19 02	23 56	10 03	29 46	51
5 08	19 54	24 47	10 31	29 56	52
5 24	20 50	25 40	11 00	0♍06	53
5 42	21 49	26 35	11 30	0 17	54
6 01	22 52	27 31	12 01	0 28	55
6 21	24 00	28 29	12 33	0 39	56
6 43	25 13	29 29	13 07	0 51	57
7 07	26 32	0♌31	13 41	1 04	58
7 33	27 57	1 36	14 17	1 16	59
8♉01	29♊30	2♌42	14♌55	1♍30	60

23h 52m 0s — 358° 0' 0" — 27 ♓ 49

11	12	ASC	2	3
0♉06	0♊11	28♊10	26♋00	25♌44
0 27	1 22	0♋10	27 12	26 08
0 50	2 37	2 11	28 24	26 32
1 13	3 55	4 16	29 37	26 55
1 39	5 20	6 26	0♌51	27 20
1 44	5 38	6 53	1 06	27 25
1 50	5 56	7 20	1 22	27 30
1 55	6 15	7 48	1 37	27 35
2 01	6 33	8 16	1 53	27 40
2 07	6 53	8 44	2 08	27 45
2 13	7 12	9 13	2 24	27 50
2 19	7 33	9 42	2 40	27 56
2 25	7 53	10 11	2 57	28 01
2 31	8 15	10 41	3 13	28 07
2 38	8 36	11 11	3 30	28 12
2 44	8 59	11 42	3 47	28 18
2 51	9 22	12 14	4 04	28 24
2 58	9 45	12 46	4 22	28 29
3 06	10 10	13 18	4 40	28 35
3 13	10 35	13 52	4 58	28 41
3 21	11 01	14 25	5 16	28 48
3 29	11 27	15 00	5 35	28 54
3 37	11 55	15 35	5 55	29 00
3 46	12 24	16 11	6 14	29 07
3 55	12 54	16 48	6 34	29 13
4 04	13 25	17 26	6 55	29 20
4 14	13 57	18 05	7 16	29 27
4 24	14 30	18 44	7 37	29 35
4 35	15 05	19 25	7 59	29 42
4 46	15 42	20 06	8 21	29 50
4 58	16 20	20 49	8 45	29 57
5 10	17 00	21 33	9 08	0♍06
5 23	17 42	22 18	9 33	0 14
5 36	18 26	23 04	9 58	0 22
5 50	19 13	23 52	10 24	0 31
6 05	20 02	24 41	10 50	0 40
6 21	20 54	25 32	11 18	0 50
6 39	21 50	26 24	11 46	1 00
6 57	22 48	27 17	12 16	1 10
7 16	23 51	28 13	12 46	1 21
7 37	24 59	29 10	13 18	1 32
8 00	26 11	0♌09	13 51	1 43
8 25	27 29	1 11	14 25	1 55
8 51	28 54	2 14	15 00	2 08
9♉21	0♋25	3♌20	15♌37	2♍21

23h 56m 0s — 359° 0' 0" — 28 ♓ 55

11	12	ASC	2	3
1♉08	1♊08	29♊05	26♋57	26♌47
1 31	2 20	1♋05	28 09	27 10
1 54	3 35	3 06	29 20	27 33
2 18	4 55	5 11	0♌32	27 56
2 44	6 20	7 20	1 46	28 19
2 50	6 38	7 47	2 01	28 24
2 55	6 56	8 14	2 16	28 29
3 01	7 14	8 42	2 31	28 34
3 07	7 33	9 09	2 47	28 39
3 13	7 53	9 37	3 02	28 44
3 19	8 13	10 06	3 18	28 49
3 25	8 33	10 35	3 34	28 55
3 32	8 54	11 04	3 50	29 00
3 38	9 15	11 34	4 06	29 05
3 45	9 37	12 04	4 23	29 11
3 52	9 59	12 35	4 40	29 16
3 59	10 22	13 06	4 57	29 22
4 06	10 46	13 38	5 14	29 27
4 14	11 10	14 10	5 32	29 33
4 21	11 35	14 43	5 50	29 39
4 29	12 01	15 17	6 08	29 45
4 38	12 28	15 51	6 27	29 51
4 46	12 56	16 26	6 46	29 57
4 55	13 25	17 02	7 05	0♍04
5 04	13 54	17 38	7 25	0 10
5 14	14 25	18 16	7 45	0 17
5 24	14 57	18 54	8 06	0 24
5 34	15 31	19 33	8 27	0 31
5 45	16 06	20 13	8 48	0 38
5 57	16 42	20 54	9 11	0 45
6 09	17 20	21 36	9 33	0 53
6 21	18 00	22 20	9 57	1 01
6 34	18 42	23 04	10 21	1 09
6 48	19 26	23 50	10 46	1 17
7 03	20 13	24 37	11 11	1 26
7 18	21 02	25 26	11 37	1 35
7 35	21 54	26 16	12 04	1 44
7 52	22 49	27 07	12 32	1 53
8 11	23 47	28 00	13 01	2 03
8 31	24 50	28 55	13 31	2 14
8 53	25 57	29 51	14 03	2 24
9 16	27 08	0♌50	14 35	2 35
9 42	28 26	1 50	15 08	2 47
10 09	29 49	2 52	15 43	2 59
10♉39	1♋20	3♌57	16♌19	3♍12